OXFORD PAPERBACK REFERENCE

The Concise Oxford Dictionary of
English Etymology

T. F. Hoad is Fellow and Tutor in English Language and Medieval Literature at St Peter's College, Oxford, and Lecturer in English at the University of Oxford. The work of compiling this dictionary was initially undertaken by the late G. W. S. Friedrichsen and the book has the benefit of his many years' experience of etymological work for the Oxford dictionaries.

The most authoritative and up-to-date reference books for both students and the general reader.

Abbreviations
Accounting
Art and Artists
Ballet
Biology
Botany
Business
Card Games
Chemistry
Christian Church
Classical Literature
Computing
Dates
Earth Sciences
Ecology
English Christian Names
English Etymology
English Language
English Literature
English Place-Names
Finance
Food and Nutrition
Fowler's Modern English Usage
Geography
Irish Mythology
King's English
Law
Literary Terms
Mathematics
Medical Dictionary
Modern Quotations
Modern Slang
Music
Nursing
Opera
Philosophy
Physics
Politics
Popes
Popular Music
Proverbs
Quotations
Sailing Terms
Saints
Science
Ships and the Sea
Sociology
Superstitions
Theatre
Twentieth-Century History
Twentieth-Century Poetry
Weather Facts
Women Writers
Word Games
World Mythology
Zoology

The Concise Oxford Dictionary of English Etymology

Edited by
T. F. HOAD

Oxford New York
OXFORD UNIVERSITY PRESS

Oxford University Press, Great Clarendon Street, Oxford OX2 6DP

Oxford New York
Athens Auckland Bangkok Bogota Bombay Buenos Aires
Calcutta Cape Town Dar es Salaam Delhi Florence Hong Kong
Istanbul Karachi Kuala Lumpur Madras Madrid Melbourne
Mexico City Nairobi Paris Singapore Taipei Tokyo Toronto Warsaw

and associated companies
in Berlin Ibadan

Oxford is a trade mark of Oxford University Press

First published 1986
First issued as an Oxford University Press paperback 1993
Reissued in new covers 1996

British Library Cataloguing in Publication Data

Data available

Library of Congress Cataloguing in Publication Data

The concise Oxford dictionary of English etymology / edited by T. F. Hoad. p. cm.
1. English language—Etymology—Dictionaries. I. Hoad, T.F.
422'.03—dc20 PE1580.C66 1993 92-41178

ISBN 0-19-861182-X
ISBN 0-19-283098-8 (pbk.)

20 19 18 17 16 15 14

Printed in Great Britain
by Cox & Wyman Ltd,
Reading, Berkshire

F. C. H.

AND

D. M. H.

Introduction

This dictionary is based upon the *Oxford Dictionary of English Etymology* (1966), compiled by C. T. Onions with the assistance of G. W. S. Friedrichsen and R. W. Burchfield. It was the late Dr Friedrichsen who first produced a draft for a concise version of that dictionary, and the present editor took over the work in 1977. In general, the book remains faithful to Dr Friedrichsen's plan, although a good many changes of detail and of a broader kind have been made, for which the present editor is alone accountable.

The intention is that each entry should give a concise statement of the route by which its headword entered the English language, together with, where appropriate, a brief account of its development in English.

In each case, the headword is followed by a figure in Roman numerals indicating the century in which the word is first recorded in English, or if definitions are provided these are followed by figures in Roman numerals indicating the centuries in which the various senses are first evidenced. In the case of words or senses recorded from the Old English period (*c*.700–*c*.1100), however, these are labelled simply 'OE.' (or at most 'late OE.'), since the nature of the surviving materials usually makes any closer dating impracticable.

Definitions have not been provided for words whose senses have undergone no major change in English, and whose meanings are likely to be readily ascertainable by most readers. The same practice has been adopted in the case of many technical and scientific words, whose senses may be quickly discovered by recourse to a small English dictionary. No attempt has been made to record all the modern senses of words for which definitions are provided, since these are frequently of secondary importance in tracing the etymology and history of the words in question.

A good many early spellings of words have been included, usually after the relevant Roman numeral denoting the century of first occurrence. Such spellings have in particular been included where they help to elucidate the origin and development of particular words.

This dictionary distinguishes three principal kinds of process in the evolution of words:

(1) The normal development of a word within a given language, according to the regular processes of change in that language. Thus, English *goose* is explained as the normal development of the word **ʒans-* in the pre-literary Germanic language from which English is

descended, and Gmc. **ʒans-* is in turn the normal development of an earlier Indo-European **ĝhans-*.

(2) The adoption of a word from one language into some other language. Thus, Eng. *brave* is explained as an adoption ('borrowing') of French *brave*, which in turn is an adoption of Italian *bravo*.

(3) The formation of a word on some existing word or element by means of a derivational device, or by compounding. Thus, Eng. *alleviate* is explained as having been formed on the past participial stem (*alleviāt-*) of the late Latin verb *alleviāre*, by means of the derivational suffix *-ate*, while *alleviāre* is in turn formed on the Latin adjective *levis* by means of the derivational prefix *al-*. The Eng. compound *nightmare* was formed by the combining of *night* and Middle English *mare* 'incubus'.

The symbols used, for brevity, to denote these three processes are listed below. It is, of course, not always possible to reduce the account of the origins and development of words to a simple formula, and where necessary further explanation has been given.

A large number of related and derivative forms has been included, at the ends of the various main entries, although it would be impossible in a dictionary of this size to offer anything like a comprehensive treatment of such forms. In the explanation of derivatives, etc., 'So . . .' normally implies that the source-language(s) of the derivative and of the headword of the entry are the same; the language(s) are not usually named again, nor are the specific forms from which the related or derivative words in English descend usually cited. 'Hence . . .' implies that the derivative is formed on the English headword, or a previously cited English derivative.

No one could compile an adequate etymological dictionary of English on the basis of his or her individual knowledge alone, and the present dictionary is heavily dependent on the work of the editors of many other dictionaries in a wide range of languages, and on that of the authors of a large number of scholarly books and articles. A number of individuals have, furthermore, been generous in answering questions and giving advice. Grateful acknowledgement is here made to the following, for assistance of various kinds: Professor L. V. Berman, the late Professor A. J. Bliss, Professor T. Burrow, Dr D. H. Evans, Professor T. Light, Professor W. B. Lockwood, and the late Professor Sir Ralph Turner. Apology is offered to anyone who should have appeared in the list but is not named here.

Particular thanks are due to three people. Dr R. W. Burchfield, CBE, and Professor E. G. Stanley have been constant sources of advice and support. And Sir Edward Playfair has been of exceptional assistance in supplying information and answering enquiries, principally (but by

no means exclusively) on Arabic matters. To these persons, as to all who have contributed to the completion of this dictionary, warmest thanks are extended.

St Peter's College, Oxford
November 1985

T. F. H.

Abbreviations

In the following list, 'etc.' means that the abbreviation in question may be used to represent, in addition to the word cited, some related form. Thus 'alt.' may represent both 'alteration' and 'altered', and 'sb.' may represent 'substantival' and 'substantivally', as well as 'substantive'. Abbreviations such as '(O)F.' indicate that a word so labelled occurs in the same form in both the 'Old' and the 'Modern' period of the language in question.

a.	ante
abbr., abbrev.	abbreviation, etc.
abl.	ablative
absol.	absolute
abstr.	abstract
acc.	according; accusative
accus.	accusative
act.	active
add.	addition
adj.	adjective, etc.
adv., advb.	adverb, etc.
Aeol.	Aeolic
Afr.	Africa, etc.
agric.	agriculture, etc.
AL.	Anglo-Latin
Alb.	Albanian
alch.	alchemy, etc.
alt.	alteration, etc.
Amer.	America, etc.
AN.	Anglo-Norman
anal.	analogy, etc.
anat.	anatomy, etc.
Angl.	Anglian
Anglo-Ind.	Anglo-Indian
Anglo-Ir.	Anglo-Irish
anthrop.	anthropology, etc.
antiq.	antiquities, etc.
aor.	aorist
Apocr.	Apocrypha
app.	apparently, etc.
Arab.	Arabic
Aram.	Aramaic
arch.	archaic, etc.
archaeol.	archaeology, etc.
archit.	architecture, etc.
arith.	arithmetic, etc.
Arm.	Armenian
art.	article
A.-S.	Anglo-Saxon
assim.	assimilated, etc.
assoc.	associated, etc.
astrol.	astrology, etc.
astr., astron.	astronomy, etc.
attrib.	attributive, etc.
augm.	augmentative, etc.
Austral.	Australia, etc.
Av.	Avestan
A.V.	Authorized Version
Balto-Slav.	Balto-Slavonic
biochem.	biochemistry, etc.
biol.	biology, etc.
bot.	botany, etc.
Bret.	Breton
Bulg.	Bulgarian
B.V.M.	Blessed Virgin Mary
c.	*circa*
Cat.	Catalan
Celt.	Celtic
cent.	century
cf.	*confer*, 'compare'
CGmc.	Common Germanic
Ch.	Chaucer
chem.	chemistry, etc.
ChrGr.	Christian Greek
ChrL.	Christian Latin
classL.	classical Latin
cogn.	cognate
coll.	collective, etc.

colloq.	colloquial, etc.
comb.	combining, etc.
comm.	commerce, etc.
comp.	compound
compar.	comparative
concr.	concrete
conj.	conjugation, etc.; conjunction
cons.	consonant, etc.
contemp.	contemporary, etc.
contr.	contracted, etc.
Corn.	Cornish
corr.	corresponding, etc.
correl.	correlative
Cotgr.	Cotgrave
cryst.	crystallography, etc.
CSl.	Common Slavonic
d.	dative; died
Da.	Danish
dat.	dative
decl.	declension, etc.
def.	definite
dem., demonstr.	demonstrative
deriv.	derivative, etc.
dial.	dialectal, etc.
dim.	diminutive
dissim.	dissimilated, etc.
dist.	distinct
disyll.	disyllabic, etc.
Du.	Dutch
E.	East, etc.
E. Angl.	East Anglian
eccl.	ecclesiastical
ecclGr.	ecclesiastical Greek
ecclL.	ecclesiastical Latin
EFris.	East Frisian
e.g.	*exempli gratia*, 'for example'
el.	element
electr.	electricity, etc.
ellipt.	elliptical, etc.
emph.	emphatic
Eng.	English
ent., entom.	entomology, etc.
equiv.	equivalent
erron.	erroneous, etc.
esp.	especially
etym., etymol.	etymology, etc.
euph., euphem.	euphemistic, etc.
Eur.	European
ex. (exx.)	example (examples)
exc.	except
excl., exclam.	exclamation
expl.	explained
ext.	extended
F.	French
f.	formed on
fem.	feminine
fig.	figurative, etc.
Finn.	Finnish
fl.	*floruit*, 'lived'
Flem.	Flemish
foll.	following, etc.
fortif.	fortification
Frank.	Frankish
freq.	frequent, etc.
frequent.	frequentative
Fris.	Frisian
fut.	future
G.	German
g.	genitive
Gael.	Gaelic
Gallo-Rom.	Gallo-Roman
Gaul.	Gaulish
gen.	general, etc.; genitive
geog.	geography, etc.
geol.	geology, etc.
geom.	geometry, etc.
Gmc.	Germanic
Goth.	Gothic
Gr.	Greek
gram.	grammar, etc.
Heb.	Hebrew
her.	heraldry, etc.
HG.	High German
Hind.	Hindustani
hist.	history, etc.
Hung.	Hungarian
ib., ibid.	*ibidem*, 'in the same book or passage'

Icel. Icelandic
id. *idem*, 'the same'
i.e. *id est*, 'that is'
IE. Indo-European
imit. imitative
immed. immediate, etc.
imper. imperative
imperf. imperfect
impers. impersonal, etc.
ind., indic. indicative
indecl. indeclinable, etc.
Indo-Iran. Indo-Iranian
inf., infin. infinitive
infl. inflected; influenced, etc.
instr. instrumental
int. interjection
interrog. interrogative, etc.
intr. intransitive, etc.
Ir. Irish
iron. ironic, etc.
irreg. irregular, etc.
It. Italian
Jap. Japanese
joc. jocular, etc.
L. Latin
lang. language
Lapp. Lappish
Latv. Latvian
law-L. law-Latin
leg. legal, etc.
LG. Low German
lit. literal, etc.; literary
Lith. Lithuanian
liturg. liturgy, etc.
loc. locative
LXX Septuagint
M Middle (*preceding the abbr. for any language name*)
magn. magnetism
m., masc. masculine
math. mathematics, etc.
MDu. Middle Dutch
ME. Middle English
mech. mechanics, etc.
med. medicine, etc.; medieval (*also preceding the abbr. for any language name*)
medGr. medieval Greek
medL. medieval Latin
metaph. metaphysics, etc.
metath. metathetic
meteor. meteorology, etc.
Mex. Mexican
MHG. Middle High German
midl. midland
mil. military, etc.
min. mineralogy, etc.
MIr. Middle Irish
mistr. mistranslation, etc.
MLG. Middle Low German
mod. modern (*also preceding the abbr. for any language name*)
monosyll. monosyllable, etc.
MS. (MSS.) manuscript (manuscripts)
MSc. Middle Scots
MSw. Middle Swedish
mus. music., etc.
myth. mythology, etc.
N. North, etc.
n. neuter
nat. hist. natural history
naut. nautical
N.E. north-eastern
NEF. north-eastern French
neg. negative, etc.
Nhb. Northumbrian
nom. nominative
north. northern
Norw. Norwegian
N.T. New Testament
N.Z. New Zealand
O Old (*preceding the abbr. for any language name*)
obj. object, etc.
obl. oblique
OBret. Old Breton
OBrit. Old British
obs. obsolete
occas. occasional, etc.
ODa. Old Danish

OE.	Old English	pp.	past participle, etc.
OF.	Old French	ppl.	participle, etc.
OFris.	Old Frisian	Pr.	Provençal
OHG.	Old High German	prec.	preceding
OIr.	Old Irish	pref.	prefix
OL.	Old Latin	prep.	preposition
OLF.	Old Low Franconian	pres.	present
ON.	Old Norse	prim.	primary
ONF.	Old Northern French	prob.	probably, etc.
ONhb.	Old Northumbrian	pron.	pronoun, etc.
OPers.	Old Persian	pronunc.	pronunciation, etc.
OPg.	Old Portuguese	prop.	proper, etc.
OPol.	Old Polish	pros.	prosody, etc.
opp.	opposed to; opposite	prp.	present participle
OPruss.	Old Prussian	Ps.	Psalm
orig.	origin; original, etc.	psych., psychol.	psychology, etc.
ornith.	ornithology, etc.		
OS.	Old Saxon	pt.	past (tense)
OSl.	Old Slavonic	q.v.	*quod vide*, 'which see'
OSp.	Old Spanish	R.C.Ch.	Roman Catholic Church
OSw.	Old Swedish		
O.T.	Old Testament	redupl.	reduplication, etc.
OW.	Old Welsh	ref.	reference, etc.
P.	proprietary term (*see note below*)	refash.	refashioned, etc.
		refl.	reflexive, etc.
palaeogr.	palaeography, etc.	rel.	related (to); relative
pass.	passive	repl.	replacing, etc.
path.	pathology, etc.	repr.	representing, etc.
perf.	perfect	rhet.	rhetoric, etc.
perh.	perhaps	Rom.	Roman; Romance
pers.	person; personal	Rum.	Rumanian
Pers.	Persian	Russ.	Russian
pert.	pertaining	S.	south, etc.
Pg.	Portuguese	S.Afr.	South Africa, etc.
pharm.	pharmacy, etc.	S.Amer.	South America, etc.
philol.	philology, etc.	sb.	substantive, etc.
philos.	philosophy, etc.	sc.	*scilicet*, 'understand' or 'supply'
phon.	phonetics, etc.		
photogr.	photography, etc.	Sc.	Scots, Scottish
phr.	phrase	Scand.	Scandinavian
phys.	physics, etc.	scholL.	scholastic Latin
physiol.	physiology, etc.	S.E.	South East
pl.	plural	Sem.	Semitic
poet.	poetic, etc.	Serb.	Serbian
Pol.	Polish	sg.	singular
pop.	popular	Sh.	Shakespeare
popL.	popular Latin	sing.	singular
poss.	possessive; possibly, etc.	Sinh.	Sinhalese

Skr.	Sanskrit	trans.	transitive, etc.
Sl., Slav.	Slavonic	transf.	transferred, etc.
sl.	slang	trisyll.	trisyllabic, etc.
south.	southern	Turk.	Turkish
Sp.	Spanish	typogr.	typography, etc.
sp.	spelling, etc.	ult.	ultimate, etc.
spec.	specific, etc.	uncert.	uncertain
str.	stress, etc.; strong	unexpl.	unexplained
subj.	subject; subjunctive	Univ.	University
subseq.	subsequently, etc.	unkn.	unknown
superl.	superlative	unstr.	unstressed
surg.	surgery, etc.	U.S.	United States
s.v.	*sub voce*, 'under the word'	usu.	usually, etc.
		var. (varr.)	variant (variants)
Sw.	Swedish	vb.	verb
s.w.	south-western	vbl.	verbal
syll.	syllable	viz.	*videlicet*, 'namely'
syn., synon.	synonym, etc.	voc.	vocative
		Vulg.	Vulgate
Syr.	Syrian	W.	Welsh; west, etc.
techn.	technical, etc.	w.	with
theatr.	theatre, etc.	WGmc.	West Germanic
theol.	theology, etc.	wk.	weak
Toch.	Tocharian	WS.	West Saxon
tr.	transitive, etc.; translation, etc.	zool.	zoology, etc.

NOTE ON PROPRIETARY TERMS

This dictionary includes some words which are or are asserted to be proprietary names or trade marks. Their inclusion does not imply that they have acquired for legal purposes a non-proprietary or general significance, nor is any other judgement implied concerning their legal status. In cases where the editor has some evidence that a word is used as a proprietary name or trade mark this is indicated by the letter **P**, but no judgement concerning the legal status of such words is made or implied thereby.

SPECIAL SYMBOLS

* = indicates a hypothetical form
† = obsolete
= = corresponding to
f. = formed on, as 'L. *discipulus* learner, f. *discere* learn'
\- = adoption of, as 'OE. *discipul* - L. *discipulus*'
:- = normal development of, as 'ME. *mesel* leper (- OF. *mesel* :- L. *misellus*, f. *miser* wretched)'

The printing of a word in SMALL CAPITALS indicates that further information will be found under the word so referred to.

A

A used in the symbol *A1*, applied in Lloyd's Register to ships in first-class condition in respect of hull (A) and stores (1). Hence **A1** adj. first-class.

a[1] reduced form of AN[1] used since XII immed. before a word beginning with a cons. For the loss of *n* cf. MY, THY, NO[2], and *i'*, *o'* for IN, ON.

a[2] ME. *o*, *a* in a distributive sense, e.g. *twice a day*, reduced form of ON; surviving in comps. of A-[1], and NOWADAYS; linked with a gerund, as in *go a-begging*, etc.

a-[1] reduced form of ON prep. (in late OE., but not gen. before XII); the first el. of many predicative adjs. and advs. consisting of the prep. and a sb., e.g. *aback*, *alive*, *asleep*, *away*; early ME. are *afire*, *afoot*; later *aflame*, *ashore*. Some depend upon French, as *aboard*, *across*, *around*, in which the preps. *à*, *en* have been assim. to or replaced by the Eng. prefix. From XVI combined with a vb.- stem as in *adrift*, *astride*.

a-[2] reduced form of OF prep., as in *afresh*, *akin*, *anew*. Cf. †*a clock* (XV-XVIII), now O'CLOCK. Not in living use since ME. In comps. with vbs. the pref. *of-* is repr. in e.g. *athirst*.

a-[3] pref. of vbs., OE. *ā-*, orig. *ar-*, *or-* = OHG. *ar-*, *ir-*, *ur-* (G. *er-*), Goth. *us-*, *ur-*, meaning 'away, out', and hence used as an intensive, as in *abide*, *ago*, *arise*, *ashamed*.

a-[4] pref. of negation and privation, repr. Gr. *a-* (before a vowel AN-[2]) = UN-[1]. Occurs in (i) words repr. Gr. comps., mostly via F. or L., and in which the significance of the pref. is wholly or partially obscured, as *abyss*, *adamant*, *amethyst*, *atom*; (ii) terms of the arts and sciences, having Gr. bases, but coming mainly through late, med., or modL., as *aseptic*, *athematic*; (iii) such terms derived from other bases, as *asexual*; (iv) gen. terms modelled on these, as *amoral*, *asocial*.

ab- L. pref., being the adv.-prep. *ab* (*ā*) away, off (see OF), used in composition with vb.-stems, as in *abdicāre* ABDICATE, etc. Var. ABS-.

aback late OE. *on bæc*, i.e. ON, A-[1] and BACK[1]. From XVII of the sails of a ship laid back against the mast, esp. 'be taken aback' XVIII; hence fig. (of persons) be discomfited (XIX). Aphetic BACK[2].

abacus XVI. - L. *abacus*, f. Gr. *ábax*, *abak-* table.

abaft (esp. naut.) in or to the rear (of). XIII. ME. *o(n) baft*, i.e. ON, A-[1] and *baft*, OE. *beæftan* behind.

abandon[1] †subjugate; give up, orig. to the control of another XIV; †banish XVI. - OF. *abandoner* (mod. *-nn-*), f. phr. *a bandon*, i.e. *a* to (AD-), *bandon* jurisdiction, control, ult. f. **bandum*, var. of medL. *bannum* BAN[1].

abandon[2] freedom from restraint. XIX. - F., f. *abandonner* (see prec.).

abase XIV. ME. *abessen*, *abassen* - OF. *abaissier* (mod. *-sser*), f. *a-*, AD- + *baissier* lower :- Rom. **bassiare*, f. late L. *bassus* BASE[2], whence the present form *abase* (XVI). Hence, or - F., **abasement** XV.

abash XIV. ME. *abaissen* - AN. *abaiss-*, for OF. *e(s)baïss-*, lengthened stem of *e(s)baïr* (mod. *ébahir*) astound, dumbfound.

abate XIII. - OF. *abatre* (mod. *-tt-*) :- Rom. **abbatt(u)ere*, f. AD- + L. *batt(u)ere* beat; cf. BATE. So **abatement** XV.

abattoir XIX. - F., f. *abattre* fell (see prec., -ORY[1]).

abbacy XV. - ecclL. *abbācia*, var. of *abbātia*, f. *abbāt-* ABBOT; see -ACY. **abbé** XVI. - F., see ABBOT. **abbess** XIII. - OF. *ab(b)esse* :- ecclL. *abbatissa*, f. *abbāt-*. **abbey** XIII. - OF. *ab(b)eie* (mod. *abbaye*) :- ecclL. *abbātia*; see next, -Y[3]. **abbot** OE. *abbod*, *-ad* (cf. OHG. *abbat*, Du., G. *abt*) - ecclL. *abbatem*, for *abbātem* (whence F. *abbé*), nom. *abba(s)* - ecclGr. *abbâ* - Aram. *abbā* father; the word was formerly applied in the East gen. to monks. The var. sp. *abbat* (XII) was esp. freq. XV-XVII.

abbreviate XV. f. pp. stem of late L. (Vulg.) *abbreviāre*, f. AB- or AD- + *brevis* BRIEF[2]; see -ATE[3] and cf. ABRIDGE. So **abbreviation** XV. - F. or late L.

abdicate XVI. f. pp. stem of L. *abdicāre*, f. AB- + *dicāre* proclaim; see -ATE[3].

abdomen XVI. - L. *abdōmen*. So **abdominal** XVIII.

abduct XIX. f. *abduct-*, pp. stem of L. *abdūcere*, f. AB- + *dūcere* lead, carry. So **abduction** XVII.

abed XIII. ME. *abedde*, OE. *on bedde*, i.e. ON, A-[1] and BED.

aberration XVI. - L. *aberrātiō*, *-ōn-*, f. *aberrāre*, f. AB- + ERR. So **aberrant** XVI.

abet incite (now, to wrongdoing). XIV. - OF. *abeter*, f. *a-* AD- + *beter* BAIT. So **abetment** XIV.

abeyance (leg.) state of expectancy XVI; suspension XVII. - AN. *abeiance*, OF. *abeance*, f. *abaer* aspire after, f. *a-* AD- + *beer*, *baer* gape.

abhor XV. - L. *abhorrēre*, f. AB- + *horrēre* shudder. So **abhorrence, -ent** XVII.

abide OE. *ābīdan* = Goth. *usbeidan*, f. A-[3] + BIDE.

ability †fitness; sufficient power XIV; faculty of mind XVI. ME. *ablete*, *abilite* - OF. *ableté*, *(h)abilité*, the first form being :- L. *habilitās*, *-tāt-* (f. *habilis* ABLE), the second a later latinization of it (modF. *habileté*).

abject †pp. rejected XV; adj. downcast, degraded XV; sb. outcast XVI. - L. *abjectus*, pp. of *abicere*, f. AB- + *jacere* throw.

abjure XV. - (O)F. *abjurer* or L. *abjūrāre* deny on oath, f. AB- + *jūrāre* swear.

ablative (gram.) of a case expressing removal, source, agent, etc. XV. - (O)F. *ablatif*, *-ive* or L. *ablātīvus*, f. *ablāt-*, used as pp. stem of *auferre* take away; see -IVE.

ablaut (philol.) vowel gradation, as in *sing*, *sang*, *sung*. XIX. - G., f. *ab* OFF + *laut* sound.

ablaze XIX. f. A-[1] + BLAZE[1], after *afire, aflame.*
able having sufficient power; †apt, fit. XIV. - OF. :- L. *habilis*, f. *habēre* have, hold (see -ILE); cf. ABILITY. Hence **ably** XIV.
-able - (O)F. *-able* - L. *-ābilis*, produced orig. by the addition of *-bilis* -BLE to vbs. with *ā*-stems, as *amāre, amābilis*, but extended to vbs. with other stems, e.g. *capere, capābilis* CAPABLE, and to sbs., as *amīcābilis* AMICABLE, *favōrābilis* FAVOURABLE. Eng. formations on sbs. are *actionable, pleasurable, saleable* (XVI). The meaning in new formations is now always passive, but the active meaning, always formerly possible, is seen in *agreeable, comfortable, durable, suitable*. The wide application of the suffix in Eng. is largely due to assoc. with ABLE, *eatable* (e.g.) being analysed as *eat* + *able* 'able to be eaten'; hence its use in *come-at-able* (XVII), *get-at-able* (XVIII). Notable formations are *knowledgeable* and *reliable*. The corr. advs. end in **-ably**.
ablution XIV. - (O)F. *ablution* or ecclL. *ablūtiō, -ōn-*, f. L. *abluere, f.* AB- + *luere* wash; see -TION.
abnegate XVII. f. pp. stem of L. *abnegāre*, f. AB- + *negāre* say no, deny; see -ATE[3]. So **abnegation** XIV. - F. or late L.
abnormal XIX. refash., after †*abnormous* (XVIII-XIX) or its source L. *abnormis*, of earlier †*anormal* - (O)F. *anormal* - medL. *anormālis, -us*, resulting from blending of late L. *anōmalus* ANOMALOUS and *abnormis*; see AB-, NORM, -AL[1].
aboard alongside (a ship) XIV; on or onto (a ship) XV. var. of *on board*, partly after (O)F. *à bord*; see A-[1], BOARD.
abode †delay, stay XIII; dwelling-place XVII. ME. *abād, abōd*, f. *abīden* ABIDE, after OE. *bād* waiting, f. BIDE.
abolish XV. - F. *aboliss-*, lengthened stem of *abolir* - L. *abolēre* destroy; see -ISH[2]. So **abolition** XVI. - F. or L.
abominable XIV. - (O)F. - ecclL. *abōminābilis*, f. *abōminārī* deprecate as an ill omen, f. AB- + *ōmen, ōmin-* OMEN; see -ABLE. In medL., OF., and Eng. (XIV-XVII) commonly spelt *abhom-*, being regarded as f. *ab* and *homō, homin-* man, quasi 'inhuman'. So **abominate**[3] XVII. f. pp. stem of L. *abōminārī*. **abomination** XIV. - (O)F.
aborigines XVI (sg. *aborigine* XIX). - L. *aborīginēs* pl. the first inhabitants of Latium and Italy; usu. expl. as f. *ab orīgine* from the beginning (see OF, ORIGIN); but perh. a proper name alt. by pop. etym. Hence **aboriginal** XVII.
abortion XVI. - L. *abortiō, -ōn-*, f. *abort-*, pp. stem of *aborīrī* miscarry. So **abortive** (first as sb.) XIII. - (O)F.
abound XIV. - (O)F. *abonder* - L. *abundāre*, f. *unda* wave. Cf. ABUNDANCE.
about adv. round, round the outside OE.; afoot, astir; †(with inf.) busy or engaged in XIII; going *to* XVI; prep. in corr. senses; (also) near, approximating to XII; concerning XIII. OE. *onbūtan, abūtan*, ME. *abuten* (XII-XIII), *aboute*; f. ON, A-[1] + *būtan* outside (of); see BUT.
above ME. *abufan* XII, *abuve(n)* XIII, *above(n)* XIII-XV, f. A-[1] + OE. *bufan*, ME. *buven*, f. *be* BY + *ufan* (= OHG. *obana*, G. *oben*) from above, above.
abrade XVII. - L. *abrādere*, f. AB- + *rādere* scrape. Cf. ERASE. So **abrasion** XVII. - L., f. *abrās-*, pp. stem of *abrādere*.
abreast XVI. f. A-[1] + BREAST; cf. F. *de front*.
abridge XIV. ME. *abreg(g)en* - OF. *abregier* (mod. *abréger*) :- late L. *abbreviāre* ABBREVIATE. So **abridg(e)ment** XV.
abroad †widely, at large XIII; out of doors XIV; in or into foreign lands XV. f. A-[1] + BROAD; prob. suggested by ME. **a brēde, on brēde* (OE. *brǣdu* BREADTH).
abrogate XVI. f. pp. stem of L. *abrogāre*, f. AB- + *rogāre* propose (a law); after earlier pp. †*abrogate* (XV). See ROGATION, -ATE[3].
abrupt †broken away or off; sudden XVI; steep XVII. - L. *abruptus*, pp. of *abrumpere*, f. AB- + *rumpere* break; see RUPTURE.
abs- var. of AB- before *c, t*.
abscess XVI. - F. *abcès* - L. *abscessus* (Celsus, rendering Gr. *apóstēma* IMPOST(H)UME), f. *abscess-*, pp. stem of *abscēdere* depart, f. ABS- + *cēdere* go.
abscond XVI. - L. *abscondere*, f. ABS- + *condere* put together, stow.
absence XIV. - (O)F. - L. *absentia*, f. *absent-*, used as prp. stem of *abesse* be away. Cf. ESSENCE, PRESENCE. So **absent** adj. and vb. XIV. Hence **absentee** XVI (earlier also †*absentie*, of obscure orig.).
absinthe wormwood XVII; liqueur orig. flavoured with this XIX. - F. - L. *absinthium* - Gr. *apsínthion* wormwood, of alien orig.
absolute free from imperfection or qualification XIV. - L. *absolūtus* freed, pp. of *absolvere* ABSOLVE; infl. partly by F. †*absolut* (mod. *absolu*). Gram. use based ult. on Gr. *apoleluménos*.
absolution XII. - (O)F. - L. *absolūtiō, -ōn-*, f. *absolūt-*, pp. stem of *absolvere* free, acquit (whence **absolve** XV), f. AB- + *solvere* SOLVE, rendering Gr. *apolúein*.
absorb XV. - (O)F. *absorber* - L. *absorbēre*, f. AB- + *sorbēre* swallow. So **absorbent** XVIII. **absorption** XVI. - L. **absorptive** XVII.
absquatulate XIX. joc. formation with reminiscence of *abscond, squat, perambulate*.
abstain XIV. ME. *abste(i)nen*, repr. tonic stem of (O)F. *abstenir* - L. *abstinēre*, f. ABS- + *tenēre* hold, keep. So **abstention** XVI.
abstemious XVII. f. L. *abstēmius*, f. ABS- + base of *tēmētum* intoxicating drink; see -IOUS.
abstinence XIII. - (O)F. *abstinence* - L. *abstinentia*, f. *abstinēre* ABSTAIN; see -ENCE.
abstract adj. XIV, sb. XV. - (O)F. †*abstract* or L. *abstractus*, pp. of *abstrahere*, f. ABS- + *trahere* draw. So **abstract** vb. XV. Partly f. pp. †*abstract*, partly f. L. *abstract-*, pp. stem of *abstrahere*. **abstraction** XV.
abstruse XVI. - F. *abstrus, -use* or L. *abstrūsus, -a*, pp. of *abstrūdere*, f. ABS- + *trūdere* thrust.
absurd XVI. - F. *absurde* or L. *absurdus*. So **absurdity** XV.
abundance XIV. - (O)F. *abondance* - L. *abundantia*, f. *abundant-* (whence **abundant** XIV), prp. stem of *abundāre* ABOUND; see -ANCE.

abuse sb. XV. - (O)F. *abus* or L. *abūsus*, f. *abūs-*, pp. stem of *abūtī*, f. AB- + *ūtī* USE. So **abuse** vb. XV. **abusive** XVI.

abut A. border *upon* XV; B. end *on* or *against* XVI. In A, - AL. *abuttāre*, f. *a-* AD- + *butta* strip of land; in B, - (O)F. *abouter*, †*abuter*, f. *a-* AD- + *bouter* BUTT[1]. Hence **abutment** XVII.

abysm XIII. ME. *abime*, later *abisme* - OF. *abi(s)me* (mod. *abîme*) - medL. *abysmus*, alt. of *abyssus* ABYSS by assim. to Gr. suffix *-ismós* -ISM. Hence **abysmal** XIX.

abyss XVI. - late L. *abyssus* - Gr. *ábussos* unfathomable (sb. use).

ac- assim. form of AD- before *c*, *q*. In OF., L. *acc-* was reduced to *ac-*, which appears in ME adoptions. In later F., and hence in Eng., *acc-* was restored by latinization, e.g. OF. *acorder*, ME. *acorden*, ACCORD.

-ac suffix primarily of adjs. denoting 'pertaining to', formerly *-aque*, *-ack(e)*, *-ak(e)*, repr. ult. (through L. *-acus*) Gr. *-akós*, as in *kardiakós* CARDIAC, on the model of which others were formed at various periods. Cf. -ACAL.

acacia XIV. - L. - Gr. *akakiā*.

academy XVI. - F. *académie* or L. *acadēmīa* - Gr. *akadēmiā* and *akadḗmeiā* name of a gymnasium (called after the hero Academus) in the suburbs of Athens, where Plato taught, and hence applied to the Platonic school of philosophy; see -Y[3]. So **academic, -ical** XVI. **academician** XVIII. - F.

-acal suffix compounded of -AC and -AL[1], forming adjs., some merely alternative to those in -AC, some with differentiated use, some serving as adjs. to sbs. in *-ac*; e.g. *ammoniacal*, *demoniacal*, *zodiacal*.

acanthus XVII. - L. - Gr. *ákanthos*, f. *ákantha* thorn.

accede XV. - L. *accēdere*, f. AC- + *cēdere* go (CEDE); cf. (O)F. *accéder*. So **accession** XVI. - L. *accessiō*, *-ōn-*, f. *access-*, pp. stem of *accēdere*

accelerate XVI. f. pp. stem of L. *accelerāre*, f. AC- + *celer* swift; see CELERITY, -ATE[3]. So **acceleration** XVI. - (O)F. or L.

accent XIV (rare before XVI). - (O)F. *accent* or L. *accentus* (f. AC- + *cantus* song, CHANT), lit. rendering of Gr. *prosōidiā* PROSODY. So **accent** vb. XVI. - OF. *accenter*. **accentual** XVII. f. L. *accentus*. **accentuate** XVIII. f. medL. *accentuāre*; cf. (O)F. *accentuer*.

accept XIV. - (O)F. *accepter* or L. *acceptāre*, f. *accept-*, pp. stem of *accipere*, f. AC- + *capere* take. So **acceptable** XIV. - (O)F. - late L. **acceptance** XVI. - OF. **acceptation** XV. - (O)F. - late L.

access XIV. - OF. *ac(c)és* (mod. *accès*) :- L. *accessus*, f. *access-*, pp. stem of *accēdere* ACCEDE. So **accessible** XV. - (O)F. or late L. **accession** XVI. - (O)F. or L.

accessary XV. - medL. *accessārius*, f. *access-*; see prec. and -ARY. So **accessory** XV. - medL. *accessōrius*.

accidence part of grammar dealing with inflexions. XIV. - L. *accidentia* (tr. Gr. *parepómena* 'accompanying things'), n. pl. of *accidēns* ACCIDENT, taken as fem. sing.; see -ENCE.

accident something that happens; (philos.) attribute of a subject. XIV. - (O)F. - late L. *accidēns*, *-ent-*, f. prp. stem of *accidere* happen, f. AC- + *cadere* fall; see CASE, -ENT. So **accidental** XIV.

acclaim XVII. - L. *acclāmāre*, f. AC- + *clāmāre*, with sp. assim. to CLAIM. So **acclamation** XVI.

acclimatize XIX. f. F. *acclimater*, f. *climat* CLIMATE + -IZE; has superseded older **acclimate** (now chiefly U.S.) - F.

acclivity ascending slope. XVII. - L. *acclīvitās*, f. *acclīvis*, f. AC- + *clīvus* slope; see LEAN[2], -ITY.

accolade salutation on the bestowal of knighthood. XVII. - F. *accolade* - Pr. *acolada*, f. Rom. **accollāre* embrace about the neck, f. AC- + L. *collum* neck; see COLLAR, -ADE.

accommodate XVI. f. pp. stem of L. *accommodāre*, f. AC- + *commodus*; see COMMODIOUS, -ATE[3]. So **accommodation** XVII. - F. or L.

accompany XV. (Earlier also *accompa(i)gne*) - (O)F. *acompagnier*, f. *compaing* COMPANION; assim. to COMPANY. Hence **accompaniment** XVIII, after F. *accompagnement*.

accomplice XVI. prob. alt., by assoc. with prec., of *complice* (XV) - (O)F. *complice* - late L. *complex*, *-ic-* confederate.

accomplish XIV. - OF. *acompliss-*, lengthened stem (see -ISH[2]) of *acomplir* (mod. *acc-*), f. AC- + *complir* (L. *complēre* fill, COMPLETE). Hence **accomplishment** XV, after F. *accomplissement*.

accord vb. XII. - OF. *acorder* (mod. *acc-*) :- Rom. **accordāre*, f. AC-, after *concordāre* agree (see CONCORD). So **accord** sb. XIII. **accordance** XIV. The use of **according** as adv. dates from XV.

accordion XIX. - G. *akkordion*, f. It. *accordare* tune (an instrument).

accost †lie or go alongside; approach; make up to and address. XVI. - F. *accoster* - It. *accostare* :- Rom. **accostāre*, f. L. AC- + *costa* rib, side; see COAST.

account reckoning XIII; estimation XIV; report XVII. - AN. *ac(o)unte*, OF. *aconte*, f. *acunter*, *aconter* (f. AC- + *conter* COUNT[2]), whence **account** vb. XIV. Hence **accountable** XIV. So **accountant** XV. - Law F. use of prp. of OF. *aconter*.

accoutre furnish with proper equipment. XVI. - (O)F. *accoutrer*, earlier *acoustrer*, f. AC- + *cousture* (mod. *couture*) sewing. So **accoutrement** XVI.

accredit XVII. - F. *accréditer*, after phr. *mettre à crédit* lit. 'put to CREDIT'.

accretion XVII. - L. *accrētiō*, *-ōn-*, f. *accrēt-*, pp. stem of *accrēscere*, f. AC- + *crēscere* grow. See CRESCENT, -TION.

accrue XV. - OF. *acreue*, *ac(c)rue* increase (sb.), f. pp. of *acroistre* :- L. *accrēscere* (see prec.).

accumulate XVI. f. pp. stem of L. *accumulāre*, f. AC- + CUMULUS; see -ATE[3]. So **accumulation** XV. Cf. (O)F. *accumuler*, *-ation*.

accurate XVII. - L. *accūrātus*, f. *accūrāre*, f. AC- + *cūra* care; see CURE, -ATE[2]. Hence **accuracy** XVII.

accurse XII. Now only in pp.; f. A-[3] + CURSE vb.

accusative (gram.) case expressing chiefly destination or the goal of motion. XV. - (O)F. *accusatif* or L. *accūsātīvus* (sc. *cāsus* case), f. pp. stem of *accūsāre* ACCUSE. L. *cāsus accūsātīvus* renders Gr. *ptôsis aitiātikḗ* case of accusing.

accuse XIII. - OF. *acuser*, (also mod.) *accuser* :- L. *accūsāre*, f. AC- + *causa* CAUSE. So **accusation** XIV.

accustom XV. - AN. *acustumer*, OF. *acostumer* (mod. *accoutumer*), f. AC- + *costume* CUSTOM.

ace throw of one at dice XIII; playing-card bearing one pip (reckoned as of the highest value) XVI; the highest or best XVIII. ME. *a(a)s* - (O)F. *as* :- L. *as*, *ass-* unit(y).

-acean f. L. *-āceus* -ACEOUS + -AN. In sb. use supplying an Eng. form for names of groups in **-acea** (n. pl.; sc. *animalia* animals), e.g. *Crustacea*, *crustaceans*.

-aceous f. L. *-āceus* (f. *-āc-* -AC) + -OUS (cf. -EOUS); in nat. hist. it supplies adjs. for names of groups in **-acea**, **-aceae**, e.g. *crustaceous* pert. to the Crustacea, *rosaceous* pert. to the Rosaceae.

acerbity XVI. - F. *acerbité* or L. *acerbitās*, f. *acerbus* bitter; see -ITY.

acetic name of the acid of vinegar. XIX. - F. *acétique*, f. L. *acētum* vinegar, f. *acēre* be sour; see ACID, -IC.

ache OE. *æce*, also *ece*, early ME. *eche* (:- **akiz*), f. base of *acan* str. vb., repl. by weak forms (*akede*, *aked*) in XIV; mod. *ached*. The normal repr. of the OE. sb. was *ache*, and the pronunc. with *-ch* was prevalent until *c*.1820. Infl. of the vb. (earlier repr. of the vb. was *ake*, but now with the sp. proper to the sb.) appears in XV.

achieve XIV. - (O)F. *achever*, f. Rom. **capum*; see AD-, CHIEF. Hence, or - (O)F. *achèvement*, **achievement** XV.

acid XVII. - F. *acide* or L. *acidus*, f. IE. **ak-* be pointed or sharp, as in L. *acēre* be sharp, *acus* needle, etc.; see -ID[1]. So **acidity** XVII. - F. - late L. **acidulated** XVIII. f. L. *acidulus* sourish (whence **acidulous** XVIII); see -ATE[3].

-acious suffix repr. F. *-acieux*, as in *astucieux*, *audacieux*, based on L. sbs. *astūtia*, *audācia* + *-eux* -OUS; *capacious*, *fugacious*, *loquacious*, *rapacious* are immed. f. L. adjs. in *-āx*, *-āc-*. The earliest Eng. exx. are *audacious* and *contumacious*.

acknowledge XV. prob. f. †KNOWLEDGE, on the analogy of the relation of †*aknow* (OE. *oncnāwan*) and KNOW. Hence **acknowledgement** XVI.

acme highest point, culmination. XVII. - Gr. *akmḗ* point, etc., f. IE. **ak-* (see ACID).

acne XIX. - modL. *acnē*, deduced from a misreading *aknás* for *akmás*, acc. pl. of Gr. *akmḗ* eruption on the face (ACME).

acolyte (eccl.) member of one of the minor orders of the Church XIV; minor attendant XVI. - OF. *acolite* (mod. *-yte*) or ecclL. *acolytus*, *-it(h)us* - Gr. *akólouthos* follower.

aconite poisonous plant *Aconitum napellus*. XVI. - F. *aconit* or L. *aconītum* - Gr. *akóniton*.

acorn OE. *æcern* = ON. *akarn*, Goth. *akran* fruit; rel. ACRE. OE. *æcern* is also repr. by ME. and mod. dial. *achern*, but forms with *k* are found XIV, and assoc. with *corn* (and *oak*) had established the present standard form by XVI.

acoustic XVII. - Gr. *akoustikós*, f. *akoúein* HEAR; cf. F. *acoustique* (XVIII); see -IC.

acquaint XIII. ME. *aqueynten*, *aquointen*, *acointen* - OF. *acointier* :- medL. *accognitāre* make known, f. L. *accognitus*, f. AC- + *cognitus*, pp. of *cognōscere* know (see COGNITION). So **acquaintance** XIV.

acquiesce †remain quiet; †submit; agree tacitly. XVII. - L. *acquiēscere*, f. AC- + *quiēscere* rest; see QUIET. So **acquiescence**, **-ent** XVII. Cf. F. *acquiescer*, etc.

acquire XV. ME. *acqueren* - OF. *aquerre* :- Rom. **acquærere*, for L. *acquīrere*, f. AC- + *quærere* seek; superseded *c*.1600 by the latinized form *acquire*. So **acquisition** XIV. - L. *acquīsītiō*, *-ōn-*, f. *acquīsīt-*, pp. stem of *acquīrere*.

acquit XIII. ME. *acwiten*, *aquiten* - OF. *aquiter* - Rom. **acquitāre*, f. AC- + **quitāre* QUIT[2]. Hence **acquittal** XV.

acre †field; unit of square measure of land. OE. *æcer* = OS. *akkar* (Du. *akker*), OHG. *ackar* (G. *acker*), ON. *akr*, Goth. *akrs* :- Gmc. **akraz* :- IE. **agros*, repr. by L. *ager*, Gr. *agrós*, Skr. *ájra-* field.

acrid XVIII. irreg. f. L. *ācer*, *ācr-* sharp + -ID[1], prob. after *acid*.

acrimony XVI. - F. *acrimonie* or L. *ācrimōnia*, f. *ācer*, *ācr-* sharp. So **acrimonious** XVII. - medL. *ācrimōniōsus*.

acro- repr. Gr. *akro-*, comb. form of *ákros* terminal, etc.; in mod. techn. terms XIX.

acrobat XIX. - F. *acrobate* - Gr. *akrobátēs*, f. *akróbatos* walking on tiptoe.

across adv. in the form of a cross, crosswise XIII; transversely, from side to side XVI; prep. XVI. ME. *a cr(e)oiz*, *o cros* (XIII), later *acros*, *acrosse* (XIV), also *in* or *on crosse* (XV-XVI) - OF. *en croiz*; later assim. to native formations in A-[1] and the sb. CROSS.

acrostic XVI. - L. *acrostichis* - Gr. *akrostikhís*, f. *ákros* endmost, ACRO- + *stíkhos* row, line of verse. The etym. sp. *acrostich* has been superseded through assoc. with -IC. Cf. F. *acrostiche*.

act deed XIV; legislative decree XV; section of a drama XVII. Mainly - L. *āctus* doing, *āctum* public transaction, f. *āct-*, pp. stem of *agere* do; partly through F. *acte*. So **act** vb. XV.

action XIV. - (O)F. - L. *actiō*, *-ōn-*, f. *āct-*; see ACT, -TION. Hence **actionable** XVI. So **active** XIV. - L. *āctīvus*, partly through (O)F. *actif*, *-ive*. **activity** XV. - F. or late L. **activate** XVII. f. pp. stem of medL. *āctivāre*; later infl. by F. *activer*, G. *aktivieren*.

actor †steward XIV (in Wycl. Bible Gal. 4: 2 a literalism; later Sc. XV-XVII); †pleader XV; doer XV; stage-player XVI. - L. *āctor*, f. *āct-* (see ACT). Cf. (O)F. *acteur*, and see -OR[1]. Hence **actress** XVI.

actual exhibited in acts, spec. *actual* (opp. *original*) sin; existing in fact XIV. orig. *actuel* - (O)F. *actuel*; later assim. to the source, late L. *āctuālis*, f. *āctus* ACT; see -AL[1]. So **actuality** XIV. - (O)F. or medL. **actually** XV. partly after F. *actuellement*, L. *āctuāliter*.

actuary †registrar XVI; official who compiles statistics of mortality, etc. XIX. - L. *āctuārius* shorthand writer, keeper of accounts, f. *āctus* ACT, see -ARY.

actuate XVI. f. pp. stem of medL. *āctuāre*, f. *āctus* ACT; see ATE[3].

acuity XV. - F. *acuité* or medL. *acuitās*, f. *acuere*; see ACUTE, -ITY.

acumen XVI. - L. *acūmen*, f. *acuere* (see next).
acute XIV. - L. *acūtus*, pp. of *acuere* sharpen (cf. ACID); as applied to accent tr. Gr. *oxeîa*, fem. (sc. *prosōidiā* accent) of *oxús* sharp.
-acy suffix repr. (i) L. *-ācia*, forming nouns of quality on adjs. in *-āx*, *-āc-*, as *fallācia* fallacy (the corr. Eng. adjs. ending in -ACIOUS); (ii) L. *-ātia*, in medL. often *-ācia*, as *abbātia* abbacy; (iii) medL. *-ātia*, forming nouns of state on sbs. in *-ātus*, as *advocātia* advocacy, on the anal. of which the suffix was extended to Eng. sbs. in *-ate*, as *confederacy*, and to adjs. in *-ate*, as *accuracy*, *privacy*.
ad- pref. repr. L. *ad* (see AT) to express motion to, direction towards, etc., as *advenīre* arrive, *adversus* ADVERSE; the *d* was assim. to following *c*, *f*, *g*, *l*, *n*, *q*, *r*, *s*, *t*, producing AC-, AF-, etc.; *ad-* was reduced to *a-* before *sc*, *sp*, *st* (e.g. ASCEND, ASPIRE, ASTRINGENT) and *gn* (as in AGNATE). In OF. the double cons. of *acc-*, *add-*, *agg-*, etc. were reduced to single ones, and *adv-* became *av-*, and OF. words were adopted with such forms in Eng.; but in XIV these began to be latinized (as some had been in French) by the resumption of the second cons., as in *address*, *allow*, *arrest*.
-ad suffix (= F. *-ade*) repr. L. - Gr. *-ad-* (nom. *-as*, pl. *-ades*) in (i) coll. numerals, as TRIAD, MYRIAD, and similarly OLYMPIAD; (ii) fem. patronymics, as DRYAD, NAIAD; (iii) the name of Homer's *Iliad*, imitated in *Dunciad*, etc. (In *decade* the F. form is retained.)
adage XVI. - F. - L. *adagium*, f. AD- + **agjō* (*aiō*) I say.
adagio (mus.) slowly. XVIII. - It., i.e. *ad agio* at ease.
adamant hard rock or mineral, now only as a symbol of extreme hardness (cf. Ezek. 3: 9); †diamond; †loadstone. XIV. - OF. - L. *adamant-* - Gr. *adámās*, *adamant-*, orig. adj. 'invincible', f. A-[4] + *damân* TAME. The sense 'magnet, loadstone' arose from assoc. of medL. *adamās* with L. *adamāre* have a strong liking for. Cf. DIAMOND. So **adamantine** XIII. - L.
adapt XVII (pp. once XV). - (O)F. *adapter* - L. *adaptāre*, f. AD- + *aptāre*, f. *aptus* APT. So **adaptation** XVII.
add unite, say in addition, perform the arithmetical process of addition. XIV. - L. *addere*, f. AD- + base of *facere* DO[1]. So **addendum**, pl. *-a* XVIII. sb. use of gerundive of L. *addere*. **additament** XIV. - L. *additāmentum*, f. *addere*, *addit-*. **addition** XIV. - F. or L. Hence **additional** XVII; cf. F. *additionel*. **additive** XVII. - late L. *additīvus*.
adder †serpent; viper. OE. *nǣd(d)re*, corr. to OS. *nādra*, OHG. *nātara* (G. *natter*) and (with a different vowel-grade) ON. *naðr(a)*, Goth. *nadrs*; rel. to L. *natrix* water-snake. As in *apron*, *auger*, *umpire*, orig. *n-* has been lost by coalescence with a preceding indef. art., *a nadder* becoming *an adder* (XIV). For the reverse process see NEWT, etc.
addict devote or apply habitually. XVI. At first and still mainly in pp. *addicted*, which superseded †*addict* (XVI) - L. *addictus*, pp. of *addīcere*, f. AD- + *dīcere* appoint, allot (see DICTION). Hence **addict** sb. XX.
addle (of an egg) rotten, putrid. XIII. ME. *adel* (in *adel eye* 'addle egg'), adj. use of OE. *adela* stinking urine, etc. Used fig. in *addle-head(ed)* XVII. Hence **addled** XVII (cf. -ED[1]), whence **addle** vb. XVIII.
address †make straight or right; †accoutre, dress; †direct; refl. apply oneself *to* XIV; direct (words or speech) *to* XV; speak directly to XVIII. - OF. *adrecier* (mod. *adresser*) :- Rom. **addīrectiāre*, f. AD- + L. *dīrectus* DIRECT. Cf. DRESS. Hence, or partly - (O)F., **address** sb. XVI.
adduce XV. - L. *addūcere*, f. AD- + *dūcere* lead, bring (cf. DUKE).
-ade repr. F. *-ade* in adoptions of (i) Pr., Sp., Pg. words in *-ada* or It. words in *-ata*, as *ambuscade*, *barricade*, *cavalcade*, *crusade*; (ii) new F. formations, as *balustrade*, *cannonade*, *fusillade*, *lemonade*. (In *ballad* and *salad* reduced to *ad*.) Of limited use in Eng. as a living suffix, e.g. *blockade*, *gingerade*; but several words formerly current with -ADO survive only with *-ade*.
adenoid glandular; sb. pl. glandular growths. XIX. - Gr. *adenoeidḗs*, f. *adḗn*, *aden-* gland; see -OID.
adept XVII. - L. *adeptus*, f. *adept-*, pp. stem of *adipīscī* attain, acquire, f. *apere* fasten (cf. APT).
adequate XVII. - L. *adæquātus*, pp. of *adæquāre* equalize, f. *æquus* equal; see -ATE[2].
adhere XVI. - (O)F. *adhérer* or L. *adhærēre*, f. AD- + *hærēre* stick. So **adherent** adj. XIV; sb. XV. - (O)F. *adhérent* - L. *adhærent-*. **adhesion** XVII. - F. *adhésion* or L. *adhæsiō*, *-ōn-*, f. *adhæs-*, pp. stem of *adhærēre*.
adieu XIV (late ME. also *adew(e)*). - AN. *adeu*, (O)F. *adieu*, f. *à* to (AD-) + *Dieu* God :- L. *deus*.
adipose XVIII. - modL. *adipōsus*, f. L. *adeps*, *adip-* fat; see -OSE.
adjacent XV. - L. *adjacēns*, *-ent-*, prp. of *adjacēre*, f. AD- + *jacēre* lie down; see -ENT.
adjective (gram.) designating an attribute. XIV. - (O)F. *adjectif*, *ive* - late L. *adjectīvus*, *-īva*, f. *adject-*, pp. stem of *adicere* add, f. AD- + *jacere* throw; see -IVE.
adjoin XIV. - OF. *ajoi(g)n-*, stem of *ajoindre* (mod. *adjoindre*) :- L. *adjungere*, f. AD- + *jungere* JOIN.
adjourn †appoint a day for XIV; defer XV. - OF. *ajorner* (mod. *ajourner*), f. phr. *a jorn* (*nomé*) to an (appointed) day, *jorn* :- L. *diurnum* day (whence F. *jour*, etc.), n. of *diurnus* daily (cf. DIURNAL).
adjudicate XVIII. f. pp. stem (see -ATE[3]) of L. *adjūdicāre* (f. AD- + *jūdex*, *jūdic-* JUDGE), whence OF. *ajugier* (mod. *adjuger*), the source of **adjudge** XIV. So **adjudication** XVII. - F. or L.
adjunct adj. and sb. XVI (earlier Sc.). - L. *adjunctus*, *-um*, pp. of *adjungere* ADJOIN.
adjure †put (one) to his oath XIV; charge solemnly XV. - L. *adjūrāre*, f. AD- + *jūs*, *jūr-* oath (cf. JURY). So **adjuration** XIV (rare before XVII). - F. or L.
adjust XVII. - F. †*adjuster* (mod. *ajuster*), f. *juste* JUST. So **adjustment** XVII.
adjutant XVII. - L. *adjūtāns*, *-ant-*, prp. of *adjūtāre*, frequent. of *adjuvāre* help; see -ANT.
ad libitum XVII; abbrev. **ad lib.** XIX. - L. phr., i.e. *ad* according to, *libitum* pleasure.

administer XIV. ME. *a(d)ministren* - OF. *amenistrer* - L. *administrāre*, f. AD- + *ministrāre* MINISTER. So **administration** XIV. - F. or L. **administrative** XVIII. - L. **administrator** XVI. - F. or L.

admiral †Saracen ruler or prince XIII-XV; naval commander-in-chief XV. ME. *a(d)mira(i)l* - (O)F. *amiral* - medL. *a(d)mirālis*, etc., f. Arab. *amīr* commander. See EMIR. So **admiralty** XV.

admire †wonder (at); regard with pleased surprise. XVI (late). - F. *admirer* (OF. *amirer*) or L. *admīrārī*, f. AD- + *mīrārī* wonder (see MIRACLE). So **admirable, admiration** XV.

admit let in XIV; allow the truth of XV. - L. *admittere*, f. AD- + *mittere* send (see MISSION). Hence **admittance** XVI. So **admission** XV. - L. *admissiō, -ōn-*, f. *admiss-*, pp. stem of *admittere*. So **admissible** XVII. - F. - medL.

admixture XVII. f. *admixt-*, pp. stem of L. *admiscēre*, f. AD- + *miscēre* MIX (cf. MIXTURE).

admonish XIV. ME. *amonesten* - OF. *amonester* - Rom. **admonestāre*, unexpl. deriv. of L. *admonēre*, f. AD- + *monēre* advise (cf. MONITION). The initial syll. was latinized to *ad-*, and the final syll. became *-ish* by assoc. with -ISH². So **admonishment** XIII (first *a(d)monestement*). **admonition** XIV (first *amonicio(u)n*).

ado (arch., dial., first in northern and eastern areas) dealings, trouble, fuss. XIV. f. phr. *at do*, f. adoption of ON. *at* (see AT) + DO¹; corr. to the native formation TO-DO.

-ado repr. Sp., Pg. *-ado* (:- L. *-ātus* -ATE²), m. pp. ending of vbs. in *-ar*, as in DESPERADO, TORNADO. This suffix was also freq. used irreg. in late-XVI and XVII adoptions of words in F. -ADE, Sp. *-ada*, It. *-ata*; e.g. *bravado, crusado, palisado*, some of which have survived as the regular form, while in others *-ado* has been superseded by -ADE.

adobe unburnt brick dried in the sun. XVIII. - Sp., f. Arab. *aṭ-ṭūb*, i.e. AL-², *ṭūb* brick.

adolescent sb. XV; adj. XVIII. - (O)F. *adolescent* - L. *adolēscēns, -ent-*, prp. of *adolēscere* grow up; see AD-, ALIMENT, -ESCENT. So **adolescence** XV.

adopt XV. - (O)F. *adopter* or L. *adoptāre* choose for oneself; see AD-, OPT. So **adoption** XIV, **adoptive** XV.

adore XIV. - (O)F. *adorer*, refash., after L., of OF. *ao(u)rer* (whence ME. *aouren* XIV) :- L. *adōrāre* reverence, worship, f. AD- + *ōrāre*; cf. ORATE. So **adorable** XVII. - F. or L. **adoration** XVI.

adorn XIV. - OF. *adorner*, refash., after L., of OF. *ao(u)rner* (whence ME. *aournen*) :- L. *adornāre*, f. AD- + *ornāre* furnish, deck; cf. ORNAMENT. So **adornment** XV.

adown (dial., poet.) down(ward). OE. *adūn(e)*, reduced form of *ofdūne*, i.e. *of* from (A-²) + dat. of *dūn* hill, DOWN¹. Aphetic DOWN².

adrift XVII. f. A-¹ + DRIFT.

adroit XVII. - (O)F. *adroit*, f. adv. phr. *à droit* rightly, i.e. *à* to (AD-) + *droit* right :- L. *dīrectus* DIRECT (cf. DRESS).

adulation XV. - (O)F. *adulation* or L. *adūlātiō, -ōn-*, f. *adūlāt-*, pp. stem of *adūlārī* fawn upon, whence **adulate** XVIII; see -ATION.

adult adj. XVI, sb. XVII. - L. *adultus*, pp. of *adolēscere* (see ADOLESCENT); cf. F. *adulte*.

adulterate †commit adultery; †debauch; falsify, debase. XVI. f. pp. stem of L. *adulterāre*; see -ATE³. So **adulteration** XVI. - F. or L.

adulterer XVI. Used XVI-XVIII beside synon. †*adulter*, but finally established as the more congruent form in the series *adulterate* †commit adultery, *-erer, -eress, -erous, adultery*, which repl. the ME. forms (XIV) *avoutren, -rer, -resse, -rous* (XV), *-rie*, all of which were from derivs. in OF. of L. *adulterāre* (see prec.).

adumbrate shadow forth, prefigure XVI; overshadow XVII. f. pp. stem of L. *adumbrāre*, f. AD- + *umbra* shade, shadow; see -ATE³. So **adumbration** XVI (earlier than the vb.). - L.

advance XIII (first in the sense 'promote, forward'). ME. *ava(u)ncen* - OF. *avancier* (mod. *-cer*), f. Rom. **abantiāre*, f. late L. *abante* (whence F. *avant*), f. L. *ab* OFF, away + *ante* before (see ANTE-). Hence **advance** sb. XVII. So **advancement** XIII.

advantage XIV. ME. *ava(u)ntage* - (O)F. *avantage*, f. *avant* before; see prec. and -AGE. Aphetic VANTAGE. Hence, or - (O)F., **advantage** vb. XV. **advantageous** XVI. - (O)F.

advent Church season preceding Christmas XII; the Coming of Christ XV; arrival XVIII. - OF. *advent*, refash. after L. of *avent* (also mod.) - L. *adventus*, f. *advent-*, pp. stem of *advenīre* arrive, f. AD- + *venīre* COME.

adventitious coming from without, accidental, casual. XVII. f. *adventitius*, medL. sp. of L. *adventīcius*, f. *advent-*; see prec. and -ITIOUS¹.

adventure †chance, hazard, risk XIII; hazardous enterprise XIV. ME. *aventure* - (O)F. :- Rom. **adventūra*, sb. use of fut. part. of L. *advenīre*; see ADVENT, -URE. So **adventure** vb. XIV. **adventurer** XV. **adventurous** XIV. Aphetic VENTURE.

adverb word that qualifies an adjective, a verb, or another adverb. XV. - F. *adverbe* or L. *adverbium*, f. AD- + *verbum* word, VERB; lit. rendering of Gr. *epírrēma* (f. EPI- + *rhêma* word). So **adverbial** XVII, **adverbially** XV.

adverse XIV. - later OF. *advers, -se*, refash. after L. of *avers* :- L. *adversus*, pp. of *advertere* turn towards; see AD-, VERSE. So **adversary** XIV. - (O)F. or L. **adversity** XIII.

advert (obs. or arch.) turn one's attention (cf. ANIMADVERT). XV. (Earlier also *avert*) - (O)F. *avertir* (now only) warn :- Rom. **advertīre*; see next. The rel. **advertence** (XIV), **-ency** (XVII), **-ent** (XVII) are now mainly repr. in the neg. INADVERTENCE, etc.

advertise †take note of; †direct the attention of; give notice of. XV. f. *advertiss-*, lengthened stem (see -ISH²) of F. †*advertir*, refash. of *avertir* warn :- Rom. **advertīre*, for L. *advertere* (see ADVERSE). The current form has been infl. by **advertisement** XV (earlier also *avert-*) - F. *avertissement*, †*ad-*.

advice †opinion XIII; †deliberation; counsel XIV; information given XV. ME. *avis* - (O)F. :- Rom. **advīsum*, f. L. AD- + *vīsum*, n. pp. of *vidēre* see (*vidērī* seem); cf. WIT². So **advise** XIII. ME. *avisen* - (O)F. *aviser* (refash. after L. as †*adviser*) :- Rom. **advīsāre*, f. *-vīsāre*, for L. *vīsere*, f. *vidēre*.

advocate ME. *a(d)vocat* - (O)F. *avocat* - L. *advocātus*, sb. use of pp. of *advocāre* call in as witness or counsellor, f. AD- + *vocāre* call. The form with *ad-* is due to latinization. So **advocate** vb. XVII.

advowson patronage of an ecclesiastical office, etc.; right of presentation to a benefice. XIII. - AN. *a(d)voweson*, OF. *avoeson* :- L. *advocātiō*, *-ōn-*, f. *advocāre*; see prec., -ATION.

adze tool for cutting away the surface of wood. OE. *adesa*, ME. *adese*, later *adys*, etc.; *adz(e)* dates from XVIII; peculiarly Eng.; of unkn. orig.

aegis defence, protection. XVIII. - L. - Gr. *aigis* shield of Zeus (in L. of Jupiter or Minerva).

aegrotat (in Eng. universities) certificate of illness. XIX. 3rd pers. sing. pres. indic. of L. *ægrōtāre* be sick, f. *æger*, *ægr-* sick.

aeon, eon an age of the universe. XVII. - eccl.L. *æon* - Gr. *aiṓn* age, rel. to L. *ævum* (cf. AGE, AY).

aerate XVIII. f. L. *āēr* AIR + -ATE[3], after F. *aérer*, a learned formation on the L.

aerial pert. to or resembling air or the atmosphere. XVII. f. L. *āerius* (f. Gr. *āérios*, f. *āḗr*, *āer-* AIR) + -AL[1].

aerie see EYRIE.

aero- comb. form of Gr. *āḗr* AIR, in many techn. terms, some of which are - F. terms in *aéro-*. **aerodrome** †(i) aeroplane XIX; (ii) airfield XX; in (i) - Gr. *aerodrómos* traversing the air; in (ii) f. Gr. *drómos* course (cf. HIPPODROME). **aerodynamic, -ics** XIX. cf. F. *aérodynamique*. **aeronaut** XVIII. - F., f. Gr. *naútēs* sailor; hence **aeronautical, -ics** XIX. **aeroplane** †(i) plane of a flying-machine; (ii) heavier-than-air flying-machine XIX; in (i) f. PLANE[2]; in (ii) - F. *aéroplane*, f. Gr. *-planos* wandering (see PLANET).

aery aerial; etherial. XVI (in later use poet.). - L. *āerius*, f. *āēr* AIR; suffix assoc. with -Y[1] (cf. AIRY).

aesthetic XIX (but used occas. before 1800 in the Kantian sense 'pert. to the philosophy of sensuous perception'). The current sense 'pert. to the criticism of the beautiful or to the theory of taste' is derived ult. from the title of A. T. Baumgarten's 'Aesthetica' (1750). - Gr. *aisthētikós*, f. *aisthētá* things perceptible by the senses, f. *aísthesthai* perceive; see -IC. Also **aesthetics** XIX. Hence **aesthete** XIX, prob. after *athlete*.

aestival pert. to the summer. XIV. Also, as in early use, *estival* - (O)F. *estival* - L. *æstīvālis*, f. *æstīvus*, f. *æstus* heat; see -IVE, -AL[1].

aetiology, U.S. **etiology** doctrine of cause or causation. XVI. - L. *ætiologia* - Gr. *aitiologiā*, f. *aitiā* cause; see -LOGY.

af- assim. form of AD- before *f*.

afar (†from or) at a distance. ME. *of feor* XII, *on ferr* XIV, later *a fer*, *a far*, i.e. OF from (A-[3]), ON (A-[1]), FAR.

afeard (dial., arch.) afraid. OE. *āfǣred*, pp. of *āfǣran*; see A-[3] and FEAR vb. Superseded by AFRAID.

affable XVI. - (O)F. *affable* - L. *affābilis* easy to be spoken to, f. *fārī* speak; see AF-, FABLE, -ABLE. So **affability** XV.

affair XIII. ME. *afer(e)*, *affer(e)* - OF. *afaire*, *afere* (mod. *affaire*), f. phr. *à faire* to do. Cf. ADO, TO-DO.

affect[1] †aspire to XV; †have a liking for XVI; display or assume openly; assume or pretend falsely XVII. - F. *affecter* or L. *affectāre*, f. *affect-*, pp. stem of *afficere* put to, (refl.) apply oneself to; see next. So **affectation** XVI.

affect[2] attack, influence, move. XVII. - F. *affecter* or f. L. *affect-*, pp. stem of *afficere* act upon, influence, f. AD- + *facere* do.

affected (i) †sought after, cherished; assumed; full of affectation XVI; pp. of AFFECT[1]. (ii) having (a certain) disposition or affection XVI; f. L. *affectus* disposed, pp. of *afficere* (see prec.) + -ED[1]. (iii) infected XVII; pp. of AFFECT[2].

affection emotion, disposition, fondness XIII; bodily state, spec. abnormal XVI. - (O)F. - L. *affectiō*, *-ōn-*, f. *afficere* AFFECT[2]. So **affectionate** XVI. - medL. *affectionātus* or F. *affectionné*. **affective** XV.

affidavit statement confirmed by oath. XVII. 3rd pers. sing. pt. of medL. *affidāre* declare on oath, f. L. AF- + *fīdāre*, f. *fīdus* trusty (see FAITH).

affiliate XVIII. f. pp. stem of medL. *affīliāre*, f. AF- + *fīlius* son (see FILIAL); prob. after F. *affilier*; see -ATE[3]. So **affiliation** XVIII. - F. - medL.

affinity relationship (esp. by marriage) XIV; (nat. hist., chem.) structural likeness XVIII. - OF. *afinité* (mod. *aff-*) - L. *affīnitās*, f. *affīnis* related, lit. bordering on, f. AF- + *fīnis* border; see -ITY.

affirm XIV. ME. *affermen* - OF. *afermer* (mod. *affirmer*) :- L. *affirmāre-*, f. AF- + *firmus* FIRM[1]. So **affirmation** XV. - F. or L.

affix vb. XV. - OF. *affixer* or medL. *affixāre*, f. AF- + *fixāre* FIX. So **affix** sb. (cf. PREFIX, SUFFIX). XVII.

afflict XIV. - L. *afflictāre* or f. *afflict-*, pp. stem of *afflīgere* f. AF- + *flīgere* strike; partly after pp. †*afflict*. So **affliction** XIV. - (O)F. - L. (esp. eccl.).

affluent flowing in abundance XV; wealthy XVIII; sb. feeder of a river XIX. - (O)F. - L. *affluēns*, *-ent-*, prp. of *affluere*, f. AF- + *fluere* flow (see FLUENT). So **affluence** XIV.

afford †further, carry out OE.; be able, have the means XIV; grant, yield XVI. Late OE. *ġeforðian*, f. *ġe-* Y- + *forðian* to further, f. FORTH. After the reduction of the prefix to *a-*, the sp. was assim. to words of L. origin in *aff-*; for the change of *th* to *d* cf. *burden*, *murder*.

afforest convert into forest. XVI. - medL. *afforestāre*, f. AF- + *foresta* FOREST. So **afforestation** XVII.

affray vb. (arch.) startle, frighten. XIV. - AN. *affraier*, OF. *esfrëer*, *effrëer* (mod. *effrayer*) :- Rom. **exfridāre*, f. L. EX-[1] + Rom. **fridus* - Gmc. **friþuz* peace; see AFRAID. So **affray** sb. XIV. - AN. *affrai*, for OF. *esfrei*, *effrei*, f. the vb. Aphetic FRAY[1].

affright (arch.) frighten. XVI. f. †*affright* frightened, OE. *āfyrhted*, pp. of **āfyrhtan* (cf. FRIGHT). Hence **affright** sb. XVI.

affront vb. XIV. - OF. *afronter* strike in the face (mod. *aff-*) :- Rom. **affrontāre*, f. L. phr. *ad frontem*; see AF-, FRONT. Hence **affront** sb. XVI; cf. F. *affront*.

afield on or to the field OE.; abroad XV. OE. *on felda*, ME. *o felde*, *a felde*, i.e. ON, A-[1], and dat. of FIELD.

afire XIII. ME. *afire*, *o(n) fire*, i.e. ON, A-[1], and dat. of FIRE.

aflame XVI. f. A-[1] + FLAME, after AFIRE.

afloat on the water or the sea. XII. - ME. *o(n) flote* on the sea, at sea, i.e. ON, A-[1], and dat. of OE. *flot* sea (see FLOAT); in ME. partly after ON. *á flot* and OF. *a flote*; from XVI prob. a new formation.

afoot on foot (lit. and fig.). XIII. ME. *afote*, *o(n) fote*, i.e. ON, A-[1], and dat. of FOOT; partly after ON. *á fótum*.

afore (arch.) in front, in advance. OE. *onforan*, ME. *on-*, *aforen*, reinforced by *afore* (XIV), f. †*fore* adv. and prep. Hence †**aforehand** (XIV), **aforetime(s)** (XV), **aforesaid** (XIV), modelled on BEFOREHAND, -TIME, †*beforesaid* (XIV). **aforethought** XVI, after †*prepensed*.

afraid XIV. ME. *af(f)raied*, pp. of AFFRAY used as adj. after AN. *afrayé*; superseded AFEARD.

afresh XV. After ANEW (earlier *of (a) fresh* (XV-XVI)); see A-[3], FRESH.

African OE. (sb.), XVI (adj.). - L. *Āfricānus*, f. *Āfrica*, f. *Āfrī* (sg. *Āfer*) ancient people of N. Africa; see -AN.

Afrikaner (earlier also **Afrikander**) white native of S. Africa. XIX. - Afrikaans, earlier (Cape) Du. *Afrikaander*, f. *Afrikaan* (sb.) African + *-der*, pers. suff. after *Hollander* Dutchman. So **Afrikaans** XX. var. of *Afrikaansch*.

aft (prop. naut.) in or near the hinder part. XVII (*fore and aft*). prob. alt. of earlier ABAFT, *baft*, after LG., Du. *achter* (see next).

after OE. *æfter* adv. and prep. = OS., OHG. *aftar* (Du. *achter*), ON. *aptr*, Goth. *aftra*; Gmc. adv., prob. compar. deriv. of **af-* in OE. *æftan* from behind. Hence **after** adj., OE.; later the adv. in attrib. use (cf. next).

after- the adv.-prep. AFTER in comb., in senses 'hinder', 'subsequent(ly)', etc. OE. had, e.g., *æfterboren* posthumous, *æfterfolgere* successor.

after-birth placenta. XVI (also †*after-burthen*). perh. directly - G. *afterbürde* (Luther, Deut. 28: 57), also *aftergeburt*; see prec., BIRTH.

aftermath second crop of grass XVI; esp. fig. XVII. f. AFTER- + †*math* a mowing, OE. *mǣð*, f. Gmc. **mǣ-* MOW[2].

aftermost XVIII. f. AFTER + -MOST.

afternoon XIII. f. AFTER- + NOON; cf. late L. *postmeridiem* adv., F. *après-midi*.

afterward †behind OE.; subsequently XIII. OE. *æfterweard* (also adj.); see AFTER-, -WARD(S).

ag- assim. form of AD- before *g*.

aga, agha Ottoman title. XVI. - Turk. *ağa* master, lord.

again †in the opposite direction, back OE.; †in return XIII; once more, anew XIV; †prep. towards, opposite, against OE. OE. (WS.) *onġēan*, *onġēn*, later *aġēn*, (Angl.) *onġæġn*, *onġeġn*, whence typical ME. forms *aʒen* and *aʒain*, *aʒein*, corr. to OS. *angegin*, OHG. *ingagan* (G. *entgegen*). The native forms in *aʒ-*, *ay-* did not survive beyond XVI, being superseded universally by forms in *ag-* from Scand., and appearing first in northern and eastern texts XIII.

against opposite (now only in *over against*); in resistance to XII; contrary to; in return for XIII. ME. *aʒeines*, *aʒaines*, *aʒens*, f. *aʒein*, etc. + *-es*, see prec., -s. For the parasitic *-t* cf. AMIDST, AMONGST.

agape[1] gaping. XVII. f. A-[1] + GAPE.

agape[2] early Christian love-feast XVII; Christian love XIX. - Gr. *agápē* brotherly love, f. *agapân* vb. love.

agaric kind of fungus. XV. - L. *agaricum* - Gr. *agarikón*, said by Dioscorides to be named from *Agaria* in Sarmatia; see -IC.

agate variety of chalcedony. XVI. - (O)F. - L. *achātēs* - Gr. *akhátēs*.

age sb. XIII. - OF. *ëage*, *äage*, *age* (mod. *âge*) :- Gallo-Rom. **ætāticum*, f. L. *ætās*, *ætāt-*, earlier *ævitās*, f. *ævum* age of time (cf. AEON). Hence **age** vb. XIV. **aged** XV; after F. *âgé*.

-age suffix repr. (O)F. *-age* :- L. *-āticus* -ATIC. For the Rom. extended use of *-āticum* see prec., COURAGE.

agenda items of business to be considered. XIX. - L., pl. of *agendum*, sb. use of n. gerundive of *agere* (see next).

agent XV. - L. *agēns*, *agent-*, sb. use of prp. of *agere* do; see -ENT. So **agency** XVII.

agglomerate gather into a mass. XVII. f. pp. stem of L. *agglomerāre*, f. AG- + *glomus* ball, mass, partly through F. *agglomérer*; see -ATE[3]. So **agglomeration** XVIII. - F. or L.

agglutinate unite as with glue. XVI. f. pp. stem of L. *agglutināre*, f. AG- + *glūten* GLUE; see -ATE[3]. So **agglutination** XVI, **agglutinative** XVII.

aggrandize make or make to appear greater. XVII. f. *agrandiss-*, lengthened stem (see -ISH[2]) of (O)F. *agrandir*, prob. - It. *aggrandire*, f. AG- + *grandire* - L. *grandīre*, f. *grandis* GRAND; the ending was assim. to verbs in -IZE. So **aggrandizement** XVII.

aggravate †burden; add weight or gravity to XVI; incense, provoke XVII. f. pp. stem of L. *aggravāre*, f. AG- + *gravis* heavy, GRAVE[2]; prob. through F. *aggraver*; see -ATE[3]. So **aggravation** XV. - F. - medL.

aggregate collected into one body; sb. sum total, entire mass. XV. - L. *aggregātus*, pp. of *aggregāre*, f. AG- + *grex*, *greg-* flock (cf. GREGARIOUS). Hence **aggregate** vb., **aggregation** XV.

aggression XVII. - F. *agression* or L. *aggressiō*, *-ōn-*, f. *aggress-*, pp. stem of *aggredī* attack, f. AG- + *gradī* walk (see -GRADE). So **aggressive** XIX; perh. after F.

aggrieve XIV. ME. *agreven* - OF. *agrever* make heavier :- L. *aggravāre* AGGRAVATE.

aghast XIII. ME. *agast*, pp. of †*agasten* frighten, f. A-[3] + †*gasten*, app. :- OE. *gǣstan*. The sp. with *gh* (XVIII) is due to assoc. with GHASTLY.

agile XV. - (O)F. *agile* - L. *agilis*, f. *agere* do; see AGENT, -ILE. So **agility** XV.

agitate XVI. f. pp. stem of L. *agitāre* move to and fro, frequent. of *agere* do (see AGENT, -ATE[3]); cf. (O)F. *agiter*. So **agitation** XVI. - F. or L. **agitator** XVII.

agley, aglee (Sc.) crooked, awry. XVIII. f. A-[1] + †*gley*, *gly* (XIII) squint.

agnate kinsman by the father's side XVI (adj. XVIII). f. L. *agnātus*, f. AD- + *(g)nātus* born; see COGNATE.

agnostic XIX. f. A-[4] + GNOSTIC; invented by T. H. Huxley.

ago, (arch. and dial.) **agone** XIV. pp. of ME. *agon*, OE. *āgān* pass away, corr. to OS. *āgangan*, OHG. *irgangan*, *irgān* (G. *ergehen*), Goth. *usgaggan*; see A-[3], GO.

agog XV. prob. modelled (with assim. to formations with A-[1]) on late OF. *en gogues*, i.e. *en* IN, pl. of *gogue* merriment, pleasantry, of unkn. orig.

agony anguish of mind XIV; death struggle XV; extreme bodily suffering XVII. - (O)F. *agonie* or late L. *agōnia* - Gr. *agōniā*, f. *agṓn* contest, struggle; see -Y[3]. So **agonize** XVI.

agoraphobia morbid dread of public places. XIX. - modL., irreg. f. Gr. *agorá* (place of) assembly, market-place; see -PHOBIA.

agrarian XVII. f. L. *agrarius*, f. *ager*, *agr-* land; see ACRE, -ARIAN.

agree †please; become favourable, accede XIV; be in harmony or accord XVI. - (O)F. *agréer* :- Rom. **aggrātāre*, f. L. AG- + *grātus* pleasing (cf. GRACE). So **agreeable** (hence **agreeably**), **agreement** XIV.

agriculture XV. - (O)F. *agriculture* or L. *agricultūra*; see ACRE, CULTURE. Hence **agricultural** XVIII, **-alist** XIX, **agriculturist** XVIII.

agrimony plant of the genus *Eupatorium* or *Agrimonia*. Earlier *egre-*, *egrimoine* (XIV) - (O)F. *aigremoine*; the later *agrimony* (XV) is based directly on L. *agrimōnia*, misreading for L. *argemōnia* - Gr. *argemṓnē* poppy, f. *árgemon* white spot on the eye, which the plant was reputed to cure.

agro- comb. form of Gr. *agrós* field, ACRE.

aground †on or to the ground XIII; on or to the bottom of shallow water XVI. f. A-[1] + GROUND; cf. ON. *á grunn* into the shallows.

ague †acute fever XIII; malarial fever XIV. - OF. :- medL. *acūta*, sb. use (sc. *febris* fever) of fem. of L. *acūtus* ACUTE.

ah int. XIII. Earliest form *a* - OF. *a* (later and mod. *ah*); cf. It., Sp. *ah*, and similar forms in various languages. Comb. with HA produced **aha** XIII.

ahead (orig. naut.) XVII. Earlier †*on head* (XVI); f. A-[1] + HEAD.

ahoy XVIII. f. *a* AH + HOY[1].

aid vb. XV. - OF. *aidier* (mod. *aider*) - L. *adjūtāre*, frequent. of *adjuvāre*, f. AD- + *juvāre* help. So **aid** sb. XV.

aide-de-camp XVII. - F., lit. 'camp assistant'.

ail (arch.) trouble, afflict OE.; be ill (now in prp. *ailing*) XV. OE. *eġlan*, *eġlian*, f. *eġle* troublesome, rel. to Goth. *agls* disgraceful, *aglō* oppression, *usagljan* oppress. Hence **ailment** XVIII.

aileron XX. - F. *aileron*, dim. of *aile* wing.

aim †estimate; direct (a missile, blow). XIV. ME. *a(i)men*; partly - OF. *e(s)mer*, *a(s)mer* :- L. *æstimāre* (see ESTEEM); partly - OF. *ae(s)mer* :- L. **adæstimāre* (see AD-). Hence (or - OF. *ae(s)me*, *e(s)me*) **aim** sb. XIV.

air A. atmosphere XIII; B. appearance, manner XVI; C. melody, tune XVI. prop. three words, but, as in F., the earliest has absorbed the others. In A, ME. *eir*, *air* - (O)F. *air* - L. *āēr*, *āer-* - Gr. *āḗr*. In B, - F. *air* (XVI), prob. repr. OF. *aire* place, race, quality (cf. DEBONAIR); see EYRIE. In C, like later F. *air* (XVII), repr. It. *aria*, orig. :- L. (Gr.) *āera*, acc. of *āēr*, but later infl. by OF. *aire*. Hence **air** vb. XVI. **airy** XIV (cf. AERY).

air-tight XVIII. f. AIR + TIGHT, after *water-*, *wind-tight*; cf. G. *luftdicht*.

airwood see HAREWOOD.

aisle lateral section of a church XIV; passageway in a church XVIII. ME. *ele*, *ile*; later *isle* (XVI-XVIII), *aile*, *aisle* (from XVIII) - OF. *ele* (mod. *aile*) :- L. *āla* wing of bird, army, or building. The forms show confusion with ISLE.

aitch-bone the bone of the buttock. XIX (also *H-bone*), orig. *nache-*BONE (XV), f. earlier *nage* (XIV) - OF. *nache*, *nage*, pl. *naches* :- late L. *naticas*, acc. pl. of *naticæ*, f. L. *natis* (usu. pl. *-es*) buttock.

ajar slightly open. XVIII. alt. of Sc. and north. dial. *achar*, *on char(e)* (XVI), i.e. ON, A-[1], and *char* :- OE. *ċerr* (WS. *ċierr*) turn (see CHARE). The earliest records of the *j*-form (XVII) are in the analytical var. *at jar*, *(up)on the jar*, etc.

akimbo with hands on hips and elbows turned outwards XV. Late ME. *in kenebowe*, later (by assim. to A-[1], ON) *a* or *on kenbow*, etc., *akimbo* (XVIII); prob. - ON. phr. **í keng boginn* 'bent in a curve'; see IN, BOW[2].

akin XVI (earlier *of kin*). f. A-[3], KIN.

al-[1] assim. form of AD- before *l*.

al-[2] Arab. def. art. *al* the, forming an essential element of many words of Rom. (esp. Sp. and Pg.) orig. adopted in Eng., as *alcohol*, *algebra*, *alkali*.

-al[1] suffix repr. L. *-ālis* forming adjs. from sbs. with the sense 'of the kind of, pertaining to'. It became *-el* in OF., with which many F. words were adopted, e.g. *actuel*, *mortel*; this form, to some extent in F. and gen. in Eng., was refash. after L. as *-al*, whence L. adjs. in *-ālis* and F. adjs. in *-el* have been adopted with *-al* unrestrictedly.

The L. adjs. were primarily f. sbs., as *ōrālis* ORAL, f. *ōs*, *ōr-* mouth. This type was greatly increased in medL. and modL. and consequently in the Rom. languages by formations not only on L. but on Gr. stems (after L. *boreālis*, *hebdomadālis*). In L. itself *-ālis* was added to existing adjs., as *annuālis* (f. *annuus*), *infernālis* (f. *infernus*); hence the suffix is added freely in the mod. langs. to many classes of formations, including those with suffixes of Gr. origin, *-ac*, *-ic*, *-oid* (see -ACAL, -ICAL, -OIDAL).

-al[2] earlier *-aile*, repr. F. *-aille*, which was generalized from such words as *bataille* BATTLE, *(e)spousaille(s)* (E)SPOUSAL, *funeraille* FUNERAL, where the orig. L. was a sb. use of the n. pl. of an adj. in -AL[1]. Among the earliest exx. are *acquittal* (XV), *arrival* (XIV); from XVI many derivs. of L. or F. vbs. came into use, e.g. *trial*; a few have been made on native end-stressed vbs., as *bestowal*, *betrothal*, *withdrawal*. *Bridal* and *burial* simulate this ending, though their orig. is different.

alabaster XIV. - OF. *alabastre* (mod. *albâtre*) - L. *alabaster*, *-trum* container for perfume - Gr. *alábast(r)os*.

alack (arch.) excl. of dissatisfaction, (hence) of surprise or regret. XV. prob. f. *a* AH + LACK (sb.), after ALAS. Hence **alack-a-day**; cf. LACKADAISICAL.

alacrity XV. - L. *alacritās*, f. *alacer*, *alacr-* brisk; see AMBLE, -ITY.

alarm †(excl.) to arms! XIV; call to arms, †surprise attack; state of surprise with fear XVI. ME. *alarme*, *alarom*, later *alarum* (XVI) - (O)F. *alarme* - It. *allarme*, i.e. *all'arme* 'to the arms' (see ARM²), orig. a call. Hence **alarm** vb. XVI.

alas XIII. - OF. *a las(se)* (also *helas*, mod. *hélas*) 'ah! weary (that I am)!', i.e. *a* AH + *las(se)* :- L. *lassus*, fem. *lassa* weary (cf. LASSITUDE).

alb (eccl.) long tunic with sleeves. OE. *albe* - ecclL. *alba*, sb. use (sc. *tunica* tunic, *vestis* garment) of L. *albus* white.

albatross XVII. usu. taken to be alt., by assoc. with L. *albus* white, of †*alcatras* pelican, etc. (XVI) - Sp., Pg. *alcatraz*, var. of Pg. *alcatruz* orig. bucket of an irrigating water-wheel, corr. to Sp. *alcaduz* - Arab. *al-ḳādūs*, i.e. AL-², *ḳādūs* pitcher. The changes of sense and form are a serious difficulty.

albeit XIV. Conjunctive phr. *al be it*, fuller form of *albe*, i.e. ALL adv., *be* 3rd sing. pres. subj. of BE, with a clause following (introduced or not by *that*), the orig. meaning being 'let it entirely be (that)'; formerly with corr. pt., †*al were it*. Cf. HOWBEIT.

albino XVIII. - Sp., Pg. *albino*, f. *albo* white + *-ino* (see -INE¹).

Albion Britain. OE. *Albion* - L. *Albiōn*, Gr. *Alouiōn* - Celtic **Albio*, *-on-*; usu. referred to **albho-* (L. *albus*) white, the allusion being to the white cliffs of Britain (cf. ALPS).

album blank book for the insertion of collected items. XVII. - L. *album* (white tablet on which records, etc., were inscribed, list), sb. use of n. of *albus* white; first in G. use as *album amicorum* 'album of friends', in which the owner collected the signatures of fellow scholars.

albumen white of egg. XVI. - late L. *albūmen*, f. *albus* white.

alchemy XIV. ME. *alkamye*, etc. - OF. *alkemie*, *alkamie* (mod. *alchimie*) - medL. *alchimia*, *-chemia* = Arab. *al-kīmiyā'*, i.e. AL-², *kīmiyā'* - Gr. *khēm(e)íā* art of transmuting metals. By assoc. with Gr. *khūmeíā* infusion arose the modL. *alchymia*, whence the frequent XVI-XVIII Eng. sp. *alchymy* (cf. *chymistry*, var. of CHEMISTRY). Hence **alchemical** XVI. So **alchemist** XV (cf. †*alchemister*, etc. XIV). - OF. *alkemiste* or medL. *alchemista*.

alcohol †fine metallic powder, esp. as produced by sublimation XVI; distilled or rectified spirit of wine XVIII; (chem.) compound of the type of this XIX. - F. (now *alcool*) or medL. - Arab. *al-kuḥl*, i.e. AL-², *kuḥl* antimony (used as powder to stain the eyelids). Hence **alcoholic** XVIII, **-ism** XIX.

alcove XVII. - F. *alcôve* - Sp. *alcoba* - Arab. *al-ḳubba*, i.e. AL-², *ḳubba* vault.

aldehyde (chem.) fluid obtained by oxidization of alcohol; compound of this type. XIX. f. *al. dehyd.*, abbr. of *alcohol dehydrogenatum* dehydrogenated alcohol.

alder the tree *Alnus glutinosa*. OE. *alor*, *aler*, rel. OHG. *elira*, *erila* (G. *erle*), ON. *ǫlr*, also to L. *alnus*.

alderman †man of high rank OE.; †warden of a guild XII; (hence) magistrate of a borough. OE. *aldormann*, f. *aldor* (*ealdor*) chief, prince (f. OLD) + MAN. Hence **aldermanic** XVIII.

Aldine XIX. Designation of editions of Gr. and L. classics printed or published by Aldo Manuzio and his family (1450-1597). - modL. *Aldīnus*, f. *Aldus*, latinized form of *Aldo*; see -INE¹.

ale OE. *alu* (*ealu*) = OS. *alo-* (rare), ON. *ǫl*. Only Eng. retains both *ale* and *beer*, the Scand. langs. only *ale*, and the other Gmc. langs. only *beer*.

aleatory depending on chance. XVII. - L. *āleātōrius*. f. *āleātor* gambler, f. *ālea* game of chance; see -ORY².

alecost the plant *Chrysanthemum balsamita*, formerly used for giving a flavour to ale. XVI. f. ALE + *cost* - L. *costum* - Gr. *kóstos* plant used as a spice.

alee (naut.) on or to the lee side. XIV. f. A-¹ + LEE¹, partly after ON. *á hlé*.

alegar malt vinegar. XIV. f. ALE + *-egar* (see EAGER) of *vinegar*. Cf. †*beeregar* (XV) vinegar made from beer.

alembic former distilling apparatus. XIV. ME. *alambic*, *alembike* - (O)F. *alambic* - medL. *alembicus* - Arab. *al-'anbīḳ* i.e. AL-², *'anbīḳ* still - Gr. *ámbix*, *ambīk-* cup, cap of still. Almost superseded by the aphetic *limbeck* (earlier *lembik*) from XV to XVII, when the full form again came into vogue.

alert adj. XVII. - F. *alerte*, earlier *allerte*, *à l'airte* - It. *all'erta* on the watch, f. *erta* look-out (tower).

alexandrine pert. to verse of twelve syllables. XVI. - F. *alexandrin*, f. *Alexandre*, title of a famous OF. romance (XII-XIII), concerning Alexander the Great, in which the metre is used; see -INE¹.

alexin (biochem.) substance having the property of destroying bacteria. XIX. - G. *alexin*, f. Gr. *aléxein* ward off; see -IN.

alfalfa XIX. - Sp. *alfalfa*, formerly *alfalfez* - Arab. *al-faṣfaṣa* 'the best sort of fodder'.

al fresco in the open air. XVIII. - It. phr. *al fresco* 'in the FRESH (air)'. Cf. FRESCO.

alga pl. **algae** XVI. - L. *alga* seaweed.

algebra †bone-setting XIV; branch of mathematics XVI. - medL. *algebra* - Arab. *al-jabr*, i.e. AL-², *jabr* reunion of broken parts, f. *jabara* reunite. Hence **algebraic** XVII, **-ical** XVI, **-ist** XVII.

algid cold, chill. XVII. - L. *algidus*, f. *algēre* be cold; see -ID¹.

algorism Arabic (decimal) system of numeration. XIII. Earliest form *augrim*, later *algorisme* - OF. *augori(s)me*, *algorisme* - medL. *algorismus*, f. Arab. - Pers. *al-Ḵ(w)ārizmī*, surname of 9th-cent. Arab mathematician through the European translation of whose work on algebra Arabic numerals became generally known.

alias otherwise named XVI; another name XVII. - L. *aliās* at another time, otherwise, f. *alius* (see ELSE).

alibi (leg.) †elsewhere; plea of having been elsewhere. XVIII. - L. *alibī* elsewhere, f. *alius* (see ELSE).

alien adj. and sb. XIV. - OF. - L. *aliēnus*, f. *alius* (see ELSE). So **alien** vb. XIV - (O)F. *aliéner*; earlier synon. of **alienate** (XVI), which was preceded by the pp. †*alienate* (XV) - L. *aliēnātus*, pp. of *aliēnāre*. **alienable** XVII. **alienation** XIV. - (O)F. or L.

alight[1] get down, dismount OE.; settle *on* XIII. OE *ālīhtan*, f. A-[3] + *līhtan* (rel. LIGHT[3]).

alight[2] lighted, on fire. XVIII. prob. evolved from phr. †*on* (also *of*, *in*) *a light fire* (XVI-XVIII) ablaze, where *light* appears to be pp. of LIGHT[1] vb. kindle, ignite.

align XVII. - (O)F. *aligner*, f. phr. *à ligne*, repr. L. *ad līneam* in a straight line (see AD-, LINE[2]). So **alignment** XVIII.

alike adj. (now almost always used predic.). OE. *ġelīċ* (ME. *ilich(e)*, *ilik(e)*; *a*-forms from XIV) :- Gmc. **ʒa*- Y- + **līkam* form (see LIKE[2]); for the development of OE. *ġe*- to *a*- cf. AFFORD, AWARE. Cf. LIKE[1]. So **alike** adv. OE. *ġelīċe*. In ME. both words were prob. infl. by ON. adj. *álikr*, adv. *álika* and corr. OE. *onlīċe*, ME. *anlich(e)*, in which the pref. is Gmc. **ana*- (see ON).

aliment XV (rare before XVII). - F. *aliment* or L. *alimentum*, f. *alere* nourish; see -MENT. So **alimentary** XVII. - L.

alimony XVII. - L. *alimōnia*, f. *alere*; see prec. and -MONY.

aliquot XVI. - F. *aliquote*, medL. *aliquota* sb. use of fem. adj. (sc. *pars* part), f. L. *aliquot* some, several.

-ality comp. suffix - (O)F. *-alité* - L. *-ālitās*, *-tāt*-; see -AL[1], -ITY.

alive OE. *on līfe*, ME. *o(n) live*, *alive*, i.e. ON, A-[1], and dat. of LIFE.

alkali †soda ash XIV; saltwort, *Salsola kali* XVI; any substance having the properties of soda XVII; (mod. chem.) hydroxide of sodium, potassium, etc. XIX. - medL. - Arab. *al-ḳily* calcined ashes, f. *ḳalā* fry, roast; see AL-[2], KALI. Cf. F. *alcali*. So **alkaline** XVII; cf. F. *alcalin*. **alkaloid** XIX. - G.

all OE. *all* (*eall*) = OS., OHG. *al* (Du. *al*, G. *all*), ON. *allr*, Goth. *alls*.

Allah XVI. - Arab. *allāh*, for *al-'ilāh*, i.e. AL-[2], *'ilāh* god = Aram. *elāh*, Heb. *elōah*.

allay †lay aside OE.; put down, repress; appease, assuage XIV; dilute, temper XV; mitigate XVII. OE. *āleċġan*, ME. *aleggen*, superseded by *aleien*, *alay* (see A-[3], LAY[1]). The sense-development has been infl. by formal assoc. with OF. *alegier* lighten (see ALLEVIATE) and *aleier*, *aloier* temper, qualify (see ALLOY).

allegation XV. - (O)F. *allégation* or L. *allēgātiō*, *-ōn*-, f. *allēgāre* bring forward, f. AL-[1] + *lēgāre* dispatch, commission (cf. LEGATE); see -ATION.

allege †declare before a tribunal; cite; advance as a reason; assert without proof. XIV. - AN. *alegier*, for OF. *esligier* :- Rom. **exlītigāre* clear at law (f. L. EX-[1] + *līs*, *līt*- lawsuit), used in the senses of L. *allēgāre* (see prec.), whence F. *alléguer* (which cannot be the source of *allege*).

allegiance XIV. - AN. **alligeance* (AL. *alligantia*), f. OF. *ligeance* (AL. *ligantia*), f. *lige* LIEGE; see -ANCE.

allegory XIV. - (O)F. *allégorie* - L. *allēgoria* - Gr. *allēgoriā* 'speaking otherwise', f. *állos* other + *agor*- in *agoreúein* speak; see -Y[3]. So **allegoric** XIV, **-ical** XVI; see -IC, -ICAL. **allegorize** XV. - F. *allégoriser* - late L. *allēgorizāre*.

allegro XVII. - It., repr. L. *alacer* brisk (see ALACRITY).

alleluia XIII. - ecclL. *allēluia* - Gr. *allēloúïa*, the LXX repr. of Heb. HALLELUJAH.

allergy XX. - G. *allergie*, f. Gr. *állos* other, ALLO- + *érgon* work + -Y[3] (cf. ENERGY). Hence **allergic** XX.

alleviate XV. f. pp. stem of late L. *alleviāre*, f. AL-[1] + *levis* light (see LEVITY); see -ATE[3].

alley[1] walk, passage. XIV. - OF. *alee* (mod. *allée*), f. *aller* walk, go :- L. *ambulāre* walk.

alley[2], **ally** toy marble. XVIII. Familiar dim. (see -Y[6]) of ALABASTER. Cf. the similar use of LG., Du. *albast*.

All Hallows (feast of) All Saints, 1 November. OE. *ealra hālgena* (day) of all saints; hence, with retention of the g. pl. inflexion, ME. *alle halewene* (XIII), *all halowen* (XV), *allhollon* (XVI), etc.; with loss of this, *al halow*, *al hal* (XIV), etc.; with substitution of *-s* from XV. See HALLOW[1].

alliance XIII. - OF. *aliance* (mod. *alliance*), f. *alier* ALLY[2]; see -ANCE.

alligator XVII (earlier *lagarto*, *aligarto*, *ala*- XVI). - Sp. *el lagarto* the LIZARD, which was applied spec. to the large saurians of the New World. *Alligator pear* (XVIII) is a corruption of AVOCADO *pear*.

alliteration XVII. - modL. *allitterātiō*, *-ōn*-, f. AL-[1] + *littera* LETTER, after L. *agnōminātiō* paronomasia; see -ATION. Hence **alliterate** XIX, **alliterative** XVIII.

allo- comb. form of Gr. *állos* other.

allocate XVII. f. pp. stem of medL. *allocāre*, f. AL-[1] + *locāre* place, LOCATE; see -ATE[3]. So **allocation** XV.

allocution address, exhortation. XVII. - L. *allocūtiō*, *-ōn*-, f. *allocūt*-, pp. stem of *alloquī* address, f. AL-[1] + *loquī* speak. Cf. LOCUTION.

allodium estate held in absolute ownership. XVII. - medL. *al(l)ōdium*, f. Frankish **alōd*- 'entire property', f. ALL + *ōd* (OHG. *ōt*, OE. *ēad*, ON. *auðr*) property. So **allodial** XVII.

allot assign, orig. by lot. XV. - OF. *aloter* (repl. by mod. *allotir*), f. *a* AL-[1] + *lot* LOT. Hence **allotment** XVI.

allow A. †commend; admit, permit; B. assign, allot. XIV. - OF. *alouer*, later *all*- :- (i) L. *allaudāre*, f. AL-[1] + *laudāre* praise, LAUD, (ii) medL. *allocāre* place, ALLOCATE. The phonetic identification in OF. of the orig. distinct forms involved semantic conflation in which the two main senses were blended, e.g. assign with approval, grant, concede, permit. So **allowable**, **allowance** XIV.

alloy sb. XVI. - (O)F. *aloi*, f. OF. *aloier*, earlier *aleier* :- L. *alligāre*, f. AL-[1] + *ligāre* bind (cf. ALLY[2], LIEN). So **alloy** vb. XVII; superseded †*allay* sb. and vb. (XIV) - OF. *alei(er)*.

allspice pimento. XVII. f. ALL + SPICE, so called because supposed to combine the flavour of cinnamon, nutmeg, and cloves.

allude †'play' upon; refer (*to*). XVI. - L. *allūdere*, f. AL-[1] + *lūdere* play, f. *lūdus* game. So **allusion** XVI.

allure vb. XV. - OF. *alurer*, f. *a* AL-[1] + *luere* LURE. Hence **allure** sb. XVI.

alluvion wash of sea against shore; flood; alluvium. XVI. - F. *alluvion* - L. *alluviō, -ōn-*, f. *alluō*, f. AL-[1] + *luere* wash.

alluvium deposit left by water flowing over land. XVII. - L., n. of *alluvius* washed against, f. AL-[1] + *luv-* of *luere* (cf. prec.). Hence **alluvial** XIX.

ally[1] A. †kindred, kinsman XIV; B. allied person or people XV. In A, - OF. *alié*, sb. use of pp. of *alier* (see next). For the loss of *-é* cf. ASSIGN[2], etc. In B, f. next.

ally[2] join as associate. XIII. - OF. *alier*, analogical alt. of *aleier* (see ALLOY).

almacantar see ALMUCANTAR.

Alma Mater XIX. - L., 'bounteous mother', title given by the Romans to Ceres, Cybele, and other goddesses, transf. to universities and schools as the fostering mothers of their alumni.

almanac XIV. - medL. *almanac(h)* (Roger Bacon, 1267). Its origin remains unknown.

almandine variety of garnet. XVII. - F. †*almandine*, alt. of †*alabandine* - late L. *alabandīna* (sc. *gemma* gem), f. *Alabanda* city of Caria; see -INE[1].

almighty OE. *ælmihtiġ* = OS. *alomahtig*, OHG. *alamahtīg*, ON. *almáttigr*; f. pref. form of ALL + MIGHTY, rendering L. *omnipotēns*.

almond XIII. - OF. *alemande, a(l)mande* (mod. *amande*), for **almandle* - medL. *amandula*, alt. of L. *amygdala* - Gr. *amugdálē*; initial *al-* app. due to assoc. with Rom. words having AL-[2] prefixed.

almoner (orig.) official distributor of alms. XIII. - AN. *aumoner*, OF. *aumo(s)nier*, earlier *almosnier* (mod. *aumônier*) :- Rom. **almosinārius*, for medL. *eleēmosynārius* ELEEMOSINARY, used as sb.; see -ER[2] and cf. ALMS.

almost OE. phr. *eall(e) mǣst* nearly all; see ALL, MOST; substitution of *-most* for regular *-mest* was established XIV.

alms OE. *ælmesse, -mysse*, whence *almes* (XIII-XVII; so in A.V.); reduced to *alms* XVII; corr. to OS. *alamōsna*, OHG. *alamuosan* (G. *almosen*), ON. *ǫlmusa* :- Gmc. **alemos(i)na* - popL., Rom. **alemosina*, alt., prob. through L. *alimōnia* ALIMONY, of ChrL. *eleēmosyna* - Gr. *eleēmosúnē*, f. *eleḗmōn* compassionate, f. *éleos* mercy. Treated as a pl. like *eaves, riches*, which are orig. sings.

almucantar, almac- (pl.) parallels of altitude, XIV. - OF. *almicantarat* or medL. *-arath* - Arab. *al-muḳanṭarāt* pl., f. *ḳanṭara* to arch; see AL-[2].

aloe †(resin or wood of) lign-aloes OE.; liliaceous genus of plants with bitter juice, whence is made a drug XIV. OE. *al(e)we* - L. *aloē* - Gr. *alóē* plant and drug. In late ME. reinforced by OF. *aloes* (mod. *aloès*) or its source *aloēs*, g. sg. of L. *aloē*, as in LIGN-ALOES, whence the frequent use of the word in pl. form.

aloft XII. ME. *o loft(e)* - ON. *á lopt(i)*, i.e. *á* in, on, to, A-[1], *lopt* air, sky (see LOFT).

alone XII. ME. *al ane, al one*, i.e. ALL, OE. *āna* by oneself (f. *ān* ONE). In ME. sometimes written *a lone* (whence LONE).

along OE. *andlang* (cf. ANTI-, LONG[1]). For the development of *ndl* to *l* cf. ELEVEN.

aloof (naut.) †order to the steersman to go to windward; to or at a distance. XVI. Early forms are *a luf, aloufe, on luffe*, i.e. *a*, ON, A-[1], LUFF, prob. after Du. *te loef*.

alopecia XIV. - L. *alōpecia* - Gr. *alōpekiā*, f. *alṓpēx, alōpek-* fox; so named from the resemblance to mange in foxes.

aloud XIV. f. A-[1] + LOUD.

alpaca Peruvian llama, its wool, fabric made from this. XVIII. - Sp. *alpaca* (also *paco*) - Quechua *alpako* (also *pako*), f. *pako* reddish-brown.

alphabet XV. - late L. *alphabētum*, f. Gr. *álpha* + *bêta*, first two letters of the Gr. alphabet taken to repr. the whole; cf. F. *alphabet*, etc. Hence **alphabetic** XVII, **-ical** XVI, **alphabetize** XIX.

Alps (pl.) XIV. - F. *Alpes* - L. *Alpēs* = Gr. *Álpeis*, variously expl. as (i) 'white' (cf. ALBION), and (ii) 'high' (cf. the Italic names of towns in high positions). So **alpine** XV. - L.

already XIV. orig. two words, ALL adv. and READY, used predic. 'fully prepared', passing into adv.

Alsatian German shepherd dog. XX. f. *Alsatia* Alsace.

also OE. *alswā* (*ealswā*) = OHG. *alsō* (G. *also* therefore); see ALL, SO (cf. AS).

altar OE. *altar, alter* = OS., OHG., ON. *altari*; Gmc. adoption of late L. *altar, altāre, altārium* for L. *altāria* n. pl. burnt offerings, altar, prob. rel. to *adolēre* burn in sacrifice. The native OE. word was *wī(ġ)bed, wēofod* 'idol table'; the alien word was applied spec. to the Christian altar.

altazimuth (astron.) instrument for determining the altitude and azimuth. XIX. f. ALT(ITUDE) + AZIMUTH.

alter XIV. - (O)F. *altérer* - late L. *alterāre*, f. *alter* other. So **alteration** XIV. - (O)F. or late L.

altercation XIV. - (O)F. *altercation* - L. *altercātiō, -ōn-*, f. *altercāre* wrangle, f. *alter* other; see -ATION.

alternate adj. XVI. - L. *alternātus*, pp. of *alternāre* do things by turns, f. *alternus*, f. *alter* one or other of two, second. So **alternate** vb. XVI; cf. F. *alterner*; see -ATE[2,3]. **alternation** XV. - F. or L. **alternative** adj. XVI, sb. XVII. - medL.; see -ATIVE.

although XIV. ME. *al þah, þa(u)ȝ, þo(u)ȝ*, i.e. ALL adv., THOUGH. For the use of *al* cf. ALBEIT.

altitude XIV. - L. *altitūdō*, f. *altus*, high; see OLD, -TUDE.

alto highest male voice, counter-tenor. XVIII. - It. *alto* high - L. *altus*.

altogether XII. ME. *al togeder(e)*, i.e. ALL, TOGETHER.

altruism devotion to the welfare of others. XIX. - F. *altruisme*, f. *autrui* somebody else (infl. by L. *alter* other). Hence **altruist, -istic** XIX.

alum XIV. - OF. *alum* (mod. *alun*) :- L. *alūmen*.

aluminium XIX. alt. (after *potassium, sodium*, etc.) of *aluminum*, H. Davy's modification (1812) of the form first suggested by him, viz. *alumium* (1808). *Aluminum* (now U.S.) is parallel to *alumina* (XVIII), modL. formation on the type of *magnesia, potassa, soda* for the 'earth of alum', aluminium oxide. f. L. *alūmen, alūmin-* ALUM. So **aluminous** (F. *alumineux*) XVI.

alumnus XVII. - L., f. *alere* nourish, bring up (cf. ALIMENT).

alveolus small cavity, tooth-socket, etc. XVIII. - L., dim. of *alveus* trough. Hence **alveolar** XVIII.

alway †all the time, every time. OE. *alne weġ*, acc. of ALL and WAY; orig. denoting extent of space or distance, but at its first appearance already transf. to extent of time. Superseded in ordinary use by **always** XIII.

am see BE.

amadou tinder prepared from fungus. XIX. - F. - modPr. *amadou* lit. 'lover' :- L. *amātor*, *-ōr-*.

amalgam mixture of a metal with mercury XV; mixture or combination XVII. - (O)F. *amalgame* or medL. *amalgama*, prob. ult. f. Gr. *málagma* emollient, f. *malássein* soften, through some Arab. form with prefixed AL-[2]. So **amalgamate** XVII, **amalgamation** XVII.

amanuensis XVII. - L. *āmanuēnsis*, f. *ā manū* in *servus ā manū* 'slave at hand', secretary + *-ēnsis* belonging to (see -ESE).

amaranth mythical fadeless flower; genus of ornamental plants. XVII (XVI in L. form). - F. *amarante* or modL. *amaranthus*, alt. after names in *-anthus* (Gr. *ánthos* flower) of L. *amarantus* - Gr. *amáranton*, f. A-[4] + *maran-*, stem of *maraínein* to wither. So **amaranthine** XVII. - modL.

amaryllis genus of bulbous plants. XVIII. modL. (Linnaeus) use of L. *Amaryllis*, Gr. *Amarullís* typical name for a pretty country girl in Theocritus, Virgil, and Ovid.

amass XV. - (O)F. *amasser* :- Rom. **admassāre*, f. AD- + L. *massa* MASS[2].

amateur XVIII. - F. - It. *amatore* - L. *amātor* (see next).

amatory XVI. L. *amātōrius*, f. *amātor* lover, f. pp. stem of *amāre* love; see -ORY[2].

amaze †stun, bewilder OE.; overwhelm with wonder XVI. OE. *āmasian*, pp. *āmasod*, whence ME. *amased*; not frequent till XVI. See (aphetic) MAZE.

Amazon one of a race of female warriors. XIV. - L. *Amazōn* - Gr. *Amazṓn*, *-ónos*, expl. by the Greeks as meaning 'breastless' (as if f. A-[4] + *mazós* breast), but prob. of foreign origin. So **Amazonian** XVI. f. L. *amazonius*.

ambassador XIV. ME. *ambassatour*, *-dour*, *em-*, later with many vars. of sp.; the present sp. *ambassador* dates from XVI. orig. - various Rom. forms, (O)F. *ambassadeur*, etc.; all ult. resting on medL. *ambactia* mission, f. Gmc. **ambaχtija-* (Goth. *andbahti*, OE. *ambeht*, OHG. *ambaht(i)*, G. *amt*), f. **ambaχta-* servant - L. *ambactus*, a Gaulish word **ambactos*, prob. f. **amb-* around + **ag-* drive; see AMBI-, ACT, -OR[1]. Cf. EMBASSY. Hence **ambassadress** XVI.

amber †ambergris; yellow fossil resin. XIV. ME. *aumbre* - (O)F. *ambre* (medL. *ambar(e)*, *ambrum*) - Arab. *'anbar* ambergris, amber.

ambergris wax-like substance found floating in tropical seas, and in the intestines of the sperm whale. XV. - (O)F. *ambre gris* 'grey amber'; this is the orig. sense of *amber* (cf. prec.), the word *gris* being added to distinguish the cetaceous secretion.

ambi- repr. L. *amb(i)-* (Gr. *amphí*, see AMPHI-; rel. OE. *ymb(e)*, OHG. *umbi*, etc.) around.

ambidexter XVI. - late L. *ambidexter*, f. *ambi-*, comb. form of *ambō* both + *dexter* right-handed (see DEXTER). So **ambidextrous** XVII; see -OUS.

ambient XVI. - F. *ambiant* or L. *ambient-*, prp. stem of *ambīre* go round, f. *amb-* AMBI- + *īre* go; see -ENT.

ambiguous XVI. f. L. *ambiguus*, f. *ambigere* go round, f. *amb-* AMBI- + *agere* drive; see ACT, -UOUS. So **ambiguity** XV. - (O)F. or L.

ambit XVI. - L. *ambitus* circuit, etc., f. *ambīre* (see AMBIENT).

ambition XIV. - (O)F. - L. *ambitiō*, *-ōn-* going round to solicit votes, etc., f. *ambīre*, *ambit-* (see AMBIENT, -ITION). So **ambitious** XIV. - (O)F. or L.

amble sb. and vb. (orig. denoting distinctive pace of a horse). XIV. - (O)F. *amble* sb. and its source *ambler* vb. - Pr. *amblar* :- L. *ambulāre* walk.

ambrosia (Gr. myth.) fabled food of the gods. XVI. - L. *ambrosia* - Gr. *ambrosíā* immortality, elixir of life, f. *ámbrotos* immortal. Hence **ambrosial** XVI.

ambulance moving hospital accompanying an army; vehicle to convey injured. XIX. - F. *ambulance*, repl. *hôpital ambulant* 'walking hospital', earlier *hôpital ambulatoire*; F. *ambulant* - prp. of L. *ambulāre* walk; see -ANCE, -ANT.

ambulatory XVII. - L. *ambulātōrius* (in medL. *ambulātōrium* as sb.), f. pp. stem of *ambulāre* walk; see -ORY[1, 2].

ambuscade XVI. - F. *embuscade* - It. *imboscata* or Sp. *emboscada*, Pg. *embuscada*, pp. deriv. of *imboscare*, etc.; in XVI-XVIII also †*ambuscado*; see next, -ADE, -ADO.

ambush vb. XIV. ME. *embushen* - OF. *embuschier* :- Rom. **imboscāre* lit. 'put in a wood', f. *in* IM-[1] + **boscus* wood, BUSH[1]. So **ambush** sb. XV.

ameliorate XVIII. alt. of earlier MELIORATE after F. *améliorer*.

amen XII. - ecclL. *āmēn* - Gr. *āmḗn* - Heb. *āmēn* certainty, truth.

amenable liable to be brought before any jurisdiction; answerable or responsive (*to*). XVI. - legal AN. **ame(s)nable*, f. (O)F. *amener* bring to, f. *a-* AD- + *mener* bring, lead; see -ABLE.

amend XIII. - (O)F. *amender* :- Rom. **admendāre*, alt. of *ēmendāre* EMEND. Aphetic MEND. So **amendment** XIII. **amends** XIII. - (O)F. *amendes*, pl. of *amende* reparation, f. *amender*.

amenity pleasantness. XIV. - (O)F. *aménité* or L. *amœnitās*, f. *amœnus* pleasant. See -ITY.

amerce impose a fine on. XIV. - AN. *amercier*, f. phr. *à merci* at (the) MERCY. So **amercement** XIV.

American XVI. - modL. *Americānus*, f. *America* (1507), f. L. form, *Americus* Vesputius, of the name of the It. navigator *Amerigo* Vespucci (XV); see -AN. Hence **Americanism, -ize** XVIII.

amethyst XIII. ME. *amatist(e)*, *ametist* - OF. *ama-*, *ametiste* - L. *amethystus* - Gr. *améthustos*, sb. use (sc. *líthos* stone) of adj. f. A-[4] + **méthustos*, f. *méthu* wine, MEAD[1]; the stone was supposed to prevent intoxication. In XVI remodelled with *-th-* after later F. and L.

amiable friendly (now only of temper, etc.), †lovable XIV; likeable XVIII. - (O)F. :- late L. *amīcābilis* AMICABLE. Later infl. in sense by F. *aimable* lovable :- L. *amābilis*; see -BLE. Hence **amiability** XIX.

amianthus variety of asbestos. XVII. - L. *amiantus* - Gr. *amíantos*, f. A-[4] + *miaínein* defile; so called because freed from all stains by being thrown into fire. For the sp. with *-th-* cf. AMARANTH.

amicable XV. - late L. *amīcābilis*, f. L. *amīcus* friend (rel. to *amāre* love); see -ABLE, AMIABLE.

amice (eccl.) linen vestment covering neck and shoulders. XIII. - medL. *amicia*, *amisia*, of obscure formation; superseding the var. †*amit* (XIV) - OF. *amit* (mod. *amict*) :- L. *amictus* outer garment, cloak.

amid OE. *on middum*, *on middan*, *on midre*, i.e. ON (in) with obl. case of MID in concord with a sb. ME. *amidde* (XIII) was later extended with -s to *amiddes*, whence **amidst** (XVI), by addition of parasitic *t*; cf. AGAINST, AMONGST.

amide XIX. f. AM(MONIA) + -IDE. So **amine** XIX. Cf. VITAMIN.

amidships XVII. alt., by assoc. with AMID, of *midships* (XVII), prob. of LG. orig. (Du. *midscheeps*; cf. G. *mittschiffs*).

amiss XIII. ME. *a mis*, *on mis*, prob. - ON. *á mis* so as to miss or not to meet, i.e. *á* ON, A-[1], *mis*, rel. to MISS[1].

amity XV. - (O)F. *amitié* :- Rom. **amīcitās*, *-tāt-*, f. L. *amīcus* friend; see -ITY.

ammonia XVIII. - modL. *ammōnia*, so named as being obtained from sal ammoniac. **ammoniac** XIV, earliest form *armoniak* - medL. *armōniacus*, *-um*, alt. of *ammōniacus*, *-um* - Gr. *ammōniakós*, *-kón*, applied to a salt and a gum obtained from a region in Libya near the temple of Jupiter *Ammon*. So **ammoniacal** XVIII. **ammonium** XIX. - modL. *ammōnium*.

ammonite XVIII. - modL. *ammōnītēs*, f. L. name *cornu Ammōnis* 'horn of Ammon' given to these fossils from their resemblance to the involuted horn of Jupiter *Ammon*; see prec. and -ITE.

ammunition military supplies, formerly gen., now only of offensive missiles. XVII. - F. †*am(m)unition*, resulting from a wrong analysis of *la munition* the supplies (see MUNITION) as *l'amunition*.

amnesia XIX. - modL. - Gr. *amnēsiā*, f. A-[4] + **mnē-*; see MIND.

amnesty XVI. - F. *amnestie* or L. *amnēstia* - Gr. *amnēstiā* oblivion; see prec. and -Y[3].

amnion (anat.) caul. XVII. - modL. - Gr. *amníon*, dim. of *amnós* lamb.

amoeba (zool.) microscopic animalcule of the class Protozoa, the shape of which is perpetually changing. XIX. - modL. - Gr. *amoibḗ* change.

among OE. *onġemang*, *-mong*, i.e. ON, *ġemang* (cf. *(ġe)mengan* MINGLE), prop. a phr. used as a prep. with dative; later *onmang*, *-mong*, whence *amang*, *among* (cf. A-[1]). Extended with adv. -s to *amonges* (XIII), whence *amongest*, **amongst** (XVI); cf. AMIDST, AGAINST.

amoral XIX. f. A-[4] + MORAL.

amorous XIV. - OF. *amorous* (mod. *amoureux*) - medL. *amōrōsus*, f. *amor* love; see -OUS.

amorphous XVIII. f. modL. *amorphus* - Gr. *ámorphos*, f. A-[4] + *morphḗ* shape; see -OUS.

amortize (leg.) alienate in mortmain XIV; extinguish (a debt) XIX. f. *amortiss-*, lengthened stem of (O)F. *amortir* :- Rom. **admortīre*, f. AD- + L. *mors*, *mort-* death. Hence **amortization** XVII; in medL. *admortizātiō*.

amount †go up, ascend; rise *to* a certain level. XIII. - AN. *am(o)unter*, OF. *amonter*, f. *amont* upward, i.e. *à mont* :- L. *ad montem* to the hill; see MOUNT[1]. Hence **amount** sb. XVIII.

ampère unit of electric current. XIX. f. name of A. M. *Ampère* (d. 1836); adopted by the Congrès Électrique at Paris, 1881. abbrev. **amp.**

ampersand XIX. For '*and* per se—*and*', i.e. '& by itself = and' (in a primer, etc.).

amphi- repr. Gr. *amphi-*, being the adv.-prep. *amphí* around, on both sides (of) (see AMBI-).

amphibian creature that lives both on land and in water. XVII. f. modL. *amphibium* (sc. *animal*) - Gr. *amphíbion* (sc. *zôion*), sb. use of n. of adj. *amphíbios* (see prec., BIO-). So **amphibious** XVII.

amphitheatre oval or circular building round an arena. XIV. - L. *amphitheātrum* - Gr. *amphithéātron*; see AMPHI-, THEATRE.

amphora two-handed vessel; liquid measure. XIV. - L. - Gr. *amphoreús* lit. 'borne on both sides', f. AMPHI- + **phor-* **pher-* BEAR[2].

ample spacious, copious, quite enough. XV. - (O)F. - L. *amplus*. So **amplify** XV, **amplification** XVI, **amplitude** XVI, **amply** XV.

ampulla vessel for holy oil, etc. OE. - L., dim. of *ampora*, var. of AMPHORA; for Eng. *ampoule*, †*ampul(le)* cf. also (O)F. *ampoule*.

amputate XVII. f. pp. stem of L. *amputāre*, f. *am-* for *amb-*, AMBI- + *putāre* prune, lop; see -ATE[3]. So **amputation** XVII. - F. or L.

amuck, amok in frenzied thirst for blood; also fig. XVII. - Malay *amok* in homicidal frenzy. Appears first in XVI in forms repr. Pg. *amouco*, *amuco* in the sense of 'frenzied Malay'; otherwise chiefly in phr. *run amuck*.

amulet XVII. - F. *amulette* - L. *amulētum*.

amuse †beguile, delude XV; †distract, bewilder XVII; divert with entertaining matter. - (O)F. *amuser* †deceive; entertain, f. *à* AD- + *muser* MUSE[1]. So **amusement** XVII. - F.

an[1] reduced form of OE. *ān* ONE, due to loss of stress; now a var. of A[1] retained before vowel sounds and sometimes before unstressed syllables having initial *h* (e.g. *an historical*).

an[2] reduced form of AND, recorded from XII and in colloq. use since then. For the sense 'if' see AND.

an-[1] assim. form of AD- before *n*.

an-[2] repr. Gr. privative *an-* not, without, lacking, orig. form of A-[4] retained before vowels, as in words taken from Gr., e.g. *anarchy*, *anonymous*, and hence in mod. technical terms, e.g. *analgesic*, *anhydrous*.

-an repr. L. *-ānus*, *-āna*, *-ānum* of or belonging to, as in *silvānus* SILVAN, *urbānus* URBAN. The F. form *-ain*, *-aine* was at first retained in some adoptions, but was later superseded by *-an*. In *german, germane, human, humane, urban, urbane*, there is differentiation of meaning by the use of different forms of the suffix. See also -EAN, -IAN.

ana-, before a vowel **an-** repr. Gr. *aná* up (in place or time), back, again, anew (see ON), as in *Anabaptist, analysis, anatomy*.

Anabaptist one who rebaptizes (German sect). XVI. - F. *anabaptiste* or modL. *anabaptista*, f. ecclL. *anabaptismus*, ecclGr. *anabáptisma*; see ANA-, BAPTIZE, -IST.

anabasis military advance (spec. that of Cyrus the Younger into Asia, related by Xenophon). XVIII. - Gr. *anábasis* ascent, f. *anabaínein* walk up; see ANA-, BASIS.

anachronism XVII. - F. *anachronisme* or Gr. *anakhronismós*, f. *aná* back + *khrónos* time; see CHRONIC, -ISM.

anacoluthon lack of grammatical sequence. XVIII. - lateL. - Gr. *anakólouthon*, n. sg. of adj. 'lacking sequence', f. AN-[2] + *akólouthos* following (cf. ACOLYTE).

anaconda large S. American boa. XVIII. unexpl. alt. of *anacandaia* (XVII) for Sinh. *henakandayā* whipsnake, f. *hena* lightning + *kanda* stem.

anacrusis (pros.) unstressed syllable(s) at the beginning of a line. XIX. - modL. - Gr. *anákrousis* prelude, f. *aná* up, ANA- + *kroúein* strike.

anadromous (zool.) ascending rivers to spawn. XVIII. f. Gr. *anádromos*, f. *aná* up, ANA- + *drom-*, as in *drómos* course; see -OUS.

anaemia morbid lack of blood. XIX. - modL. - Gr. *anaimiā*, f. AN-[2] + *haîma* blood. Hence **anaemic** XIX.

anaesthesia loss of feeling or sensation. XIX. - modL. - Gr. *anaisthēsiā*, f. AN-[2] + *aísthēsis* sensation. So **anaesthetic** XIX. f. Gr. *anaisthētós*. Hence **anaesthetist, -ize** XIX.

anagogic mystical. XIV (rare before XVII). - medL. *anagōgicus* - Gr. *anagōgikós*, f. *anagōgḗ* (religious or ecstatic) elevation, mystical sense, f. *anágein* lift up, elevate. So **anagogical** XVI.

anagram XVI. - F. *anagramme* - modL. *anagramma*, f. Gr. *aná* ANA- + *grámma* letter, after *anagrammatízein* transpose letters.

analects literary gleanings. XVII. - L. *analecta* - Gr. *análekta* (n. pl.) things gathered up, f. *aná* up, ANA- + *légein* gather.

analogue XIX. - Fr. - Gr. *análogon*, sb. use of n. sg. of *análogos* (f. *aná* ANA- + *lógos* ratio) whence, through L. *analogus*, **analogous** XVII.

analogy proportion XV; similarity, parallelism XVII. - (O)F. *analogie* or L. *analogia* - Gr. *analogiā* equality of ratios, f. *análogos* (see prec.). So **analogic** XVII, **analogical** XVI.

analyse XVII. perh. orig. f. †*analyse* (XVII-XVIII), anglicized form of ANALYSIS, and later infl. by F. *analyser*. **analysis** XVI. - medL. - Gr. *análusis*, f. *analúein* unloose, undo. So **analyst** XVII. - F. *analyste*. **analytic** XVI. - late L. - Gr. Also **analytical** XVI.

anapaest (pros.) the foot ⏑⏑—. XVII (XVI in L. form). - L. *anapæstus* - Gr. *anápaistos* reversed. So **anapaestic** XVII.

anaphora (rhet.) repetition XVI; (liturg.) Eucharistic canon XVIII. - L. - Gr. *anaphorā́* carrying back, f. *anaphérein* carry up or back, f. *aná* ANA- + *phérein* BEAR[2].

anarchy XVI. - medL. *anarchia* - Gr. *anarkhiā*, f. AN-[2] + *arkhós* leader (cf. ARCH-); so (O)F. *anarchie*. Hence **anarchic** XVIII, **-ical** XVI; cf. F. *anarchique*. **anarchism, -ist** XVII; in more recent use dependent on F. *anarchisme, -iste*.

anathema curse; accursed thing. XVI. - ecclL. *anathema* - Gr. *anáthema* accursed thing (Rom. 9: 3). So **anathematize** XVI. - F. - ecclL. - Gr.

anatomy (science of) bodily structure XIV; †skeleton XVI; dissection. - F. *anatomie* - late L. *anatomia* - Gr. *anatomiā*, f. *aná* up, ANA- + **tom-* cut (cf. -TOMY). Also aphetic ATOMY[1], etc. XVI. So **anatomist** XVI. - F. *-iste* or medL. **-ista*, f. *anatomizāre*, whence **anatomize** XV.

-ance repr. F. *-ance* :- L. *-antia*, f. *-ant-* -ANT + *-ia* -Y[3]. Through such pairs as *appear, appearance*, it became to some extent a living suffix and was appended to vbs. of non-Rom. origin, e.g. *forbearance, hindrance, riddance, utterance*. Cf. -ANCY.

ancestor XIII. Early forms are of three types: (i) *auncetre*, surviving XVII in latinized sp. *auncitor*; (ii) *ancestre*, antecedent of the present form through *ancestour*, by assim. to *-tour*, -TOR; (iii) *ancessour* (rare). - OF. *ancestre* (mod. *ancêtre*) orig. nom. :- L. *antecēssor*, and OF. *ances(s)our* acc. :- L. *antecēssōrem* predecessor, f. *antecēdere* precede, f. *ante* before + *cēdere* go (cf. CEDE). So **ancestry** XIV. Modification, after *ancestre*, of OF. *ancesserie*, f. *ancessour*.

anchor appliance for mooring a vessel to the bottom. OE. *ancor, -er, ancra* - L. *anc(h)ora* - Gr. *ágkūra*; cf. late OHG., G. *anker*, ON. *akkeri*. Reinforced in ME. by (O)F. *ancre*. So **anchor** vb. XIII. - (O)F. *ancrer* or medL. *anc(h)orāre*. Hence **anchorage** XVI, after F. *ancrage*.

anchorite, -ret religious recluse occupying a cell. XV. - medL. *an(a)chorīta, -rēta* - ecclGr. *anakhōrētḗs*, f. *anakhōrein* retire, retreat, f. *aná* back, ANA- + *khṓrā, khôros* space, place. Superseded earlier †*anchor* (OE. - OIr. *anchara*, shortened - medL. *anachorēta*), whence **anchoress, ancress** XIV. **anchor-hold** (see HOLD[2]) anchorite's cell XVII.

anchovy XVI. - Sp., Pg. *anchova, anchoa*. Further connections disputed.

anchylosis formation of a stiff joint. XVIII. - modL. - Gr. *agkúlōsis*, f. *agkúlos* crooked; see -OSIS. Hence **anchylose** vb. XVIII.

ancient[1] XIV. ME. *auncien, -ian* - AN. *auncien*, (O)F. *ancien*, repr. Rom. **anti-*, **anteānus*, f. *ante* before, ANTE- + *-ānus* -AN. The addition of homorganic *t* to final *n* (XV) is paralleled in *pageant, pheasant*, and *tyrant*.

ancient[2] XVI. (arch.) corruption of ENSIGN by assoc. of such forms as *ensyne* with *ancien*, ANCIENT[1]; in senses (i) standard and (ii) standard-bearer, for †*ancient-bearer*.

ancillary XVII. - L. *ancillāris*, f. *ancilla* handmaid; see -ARY.

-ancy repr. L. *-antia* -ANCE.

and OE. *and, ond*, corr. to OS. *endi*, OHG. *anti, inti*, etc. (G. *und*). A special development of meaning is that of 'if' (OE.). Now usu. sp. *an, an'* in this sense (cf. AN[2]); formerly often coupled with *if*.

andante (mus.) moderately slow. XVIII. - It., prp. of *andare* go.

andiron fire-dog. XIV. ME. *aundire(n)*, etc. - OF. *andier* (mod. *landier* for *l'andier*), with assim. of the second syll. to IRON.

androgynous hermaphrodite; spec. in bot. XVII. f. L. *androgynus* - Gr. *andrógunos*, f. *anḗr, andro-* man + *gunḗ* woman; see -OUS. Also **androgyne** XVI. - (O)F. - L.

-ane[1] see -AN.

-ane[2] (chem.) in the systematic nomenclature of Hofmann (1866), the termination for names of the hydrocarbons called paraffins, e.g. *ethane*; devised to introduce with *a* the vowel series already in vogue, *-ene, -ine, -one* in the nomenclature of other classes of hydrocarbons.

anecdote †(pl.) secret history XVII; story of a detached incident XVIII. orig. pl. - modL. *anecdota* (or its deriv. F. *anecdotes*) - Gr. *anékdota* things unpublished, n. pl. pp. f. AN-[2] + *ek* out + *didónai* give. Derived primarily from the title *Anékdota* of Procopius' unpublished memoirs (VII) of the private life of the Emperor Justinian and Theodora. Hence **anecdotage** XIX.

anele (arch.) anoint, give extreme unction to. XIV. f. *an-* (OE. *on-*) + ME. *elien*, f. OE. *ele* - L. *oleum* OIL. Cf. UNANELED.

anemo- repr. *anemo-*, comb. form of Gr. *ánemos* wind (see ANIMATE); e.g. **anemometer** XVIII.

anemone genus of plants XVI; (*sea anemone*) large polyp with petal-like tentacles XVIII. - L. *anemṓnē* - Gr. *anemṓnē*, perh. f. *ánemos* wind.

anent †beside OE.; †opposite, towards, in respect of XIII; (arch.) concerning. OE. phr. *on ef(e)n, emn*, ME. *onevent, anont, anentes, anenst*, from XIV *anent*; i.e. ON, A-[1], and EVEN[2] side by side (with), etc. (cf. G. *neben*). Parasitic *t* and the suffix *-es, -s* appear *c.*1200; cf. AGAINST, AMIDST.

aneroid kind of barometer not using a column of fluid. XIX. - F. *anéroïde*, f. Gr. A-[4] + *nērós* wet + F. *-oïde* -OID.

anew †recently; afresh. XIV. ME. *of newe, o newe*, i.e. OF, A-[2], NEW, prob. after OF. *de neuf, de nouveau*, L. *dē novō*. The form *anew* was established XVI.

anfractuosity circuitousness, intricacy. XVI. - F. *anfractuosité*, f. late L. *anfractuōsus* winding, f. L. *anfractus* bending. So **anfractuous** circuitous XVII; cf. F. *anfractueux*.

angel XII. - OF. *angele* - ecclL. *angelus* - Gr. *ággelos* messenger. Superseded OE. *enġel* (which survived till XIII) = OS., OHG. *engil* (Du., G. *engel*), ON. *engill*, Goth. *aggilus*; one of the earliest Gmc. adoptions from L. (Goth. poss. immed. - Gr.). So **angelic** XV. Hence **angelical** XV.

angelica XVI. - medL., short for *herba angelica* 'angelic plant'.

angelus devotional exercise commemorating the Incarnation. XVIII. Named from its opening words 'Angelus Domini nuntiavit Mariæ'.

anger †distress, vex XII; excite to wrath XIV. - ON. *angra*, f. *angr* grief, f. base **aŋg-* narrow, repr. also by ON. *ǫngr*, Goth. *aggwus*, and OE. *enġe*, OS., OHG. *engi* (Du., G. *eng*) narrow; rel. to L. *angere* (see ANGUISH). Hence **anger** sb. XIII; whence **angry** XIV.

angina †quinsy XVI; short for *angina pectoris* XVIII. - L. *angina* quinsy - Gr. *agkhónē* strangling, with assim. to *angere* (see ANGUISH).

angio-, first el. in many scientific terms, repr. Gr. *aggeîon* vessel, dim. of *ággos*.

angle[1] (arch.) fishing-hook. OE. *angel* = OS., OHG. *angul* (Du., G. *angel*), ON. *ǫngull*; f. Gmc. **aŋg-* (cf. next). Hence **angle** vb. XV. **angler** XIV.

angle[2] space between two meeting lines or planes. XIV. - (O)F. *angle* or L. *angulus* corner (cf. Gr. *agkúlos* bent, arched, *ágkūra* ANCHOR) see ANKLE.

Angle one of a Gmc. tribe that settled in Britain. XVIII. - L. *Anglus*, pl. *Anglī*, in Tacitus *Angliī* - Gmc. **Aŋgli-* (whence OE. *Engle*; cf. ENGLISH) the people of *Angul* district of Schleswig so called from its shape (mod. *Angeln*), the same word as ANGLE[1]. Hence **Anglian** XVIII.

Anglican XVII. - medL. *Anglicānus* (as *Anglicana ecclesia*), f. *Anglicus*, f. *Anglus* ANGLE; see -IC, -AN.

anglicism English feature or idiom. XVII. f. medL. *Anglicus*; see prec. and -ISM. So **anglicize** XVIII.

Anglo- comb. form of L. *Anglus* ENGLISH, as in modL. *Anglo-Americanus* XVIII, *Anglo-puritanus* XVI; so **Anglomania** mania for what is English XVIII, after F. *anglomanie*; **Anglophobia** XVIII; *Anglo-American, -Catholic, -Irish*; *Anglo-Norman* or *-French*, variety of French current in England in the Middle Ages. See next.

Anglo-Saxon XVII (P. Holland, tr. Camden's 'Britannia'). - medL. *Anglo-Saxones* pl. (see prec.), earlier *Angli Saxones* (Paulus Diaconus, VIII) designation of Continental origin for the 'English Saxons' in distinction from the 'Old Saxons' of the Continent; cf. hybrid form *Angulsaxones*, after OE. *Angelseaxe, -seaxan*.

Angostura (formerly also *Angustura*). Name of a town (now Ciudad Bolivar) in Venezuela; applied to (i) *Angostura bark* (XVIII), exported from Angostura and formerly used as a febrifuge and tonic, (ii) *Angostura bitters* (XIX; P.), a tonic first made in Angostura.

angry see ANGER.

anguish XIII. - AN. *anguisse*, (O)F. *angoisse* :- L. *angustia* narrowness, f. *angustus* narrow, f. IE. **anĝh-* in L. *angere*, Gr. *ágkhein* strangle (cf. ANGER). See -ISH[2].

angular XV. - L. *angulāris*, f. *angulus* ANGLE[2]; see -AR and cf. (O)F. *angulaire*.

anhydrous (chem.) having no water in its composition. XIX. f. Gr. *ánudros*, f. AN-[2] + *hudr-* (cf. *húdōr* WATER); see -OUS.

anile old-womanish. XVII. - L. *anīlis*, f. *anus* old woman, see -ILE.

aniline chemical base, the source of many dyes. XIX. - G. *anilin*, f. *anil* indigo (whence orig. obtained) - F. or Pg. - Arab. *an-nīl*, i.e. AL-[2], Arab.-Pers. *nīl* (cf. LILAC); see -INE[5].

animadvert observe XVI; pass criticism *on* XVII. - L. *animadvertere*, i.e. *animum advertere* turn the mind to. So **animadversion** XVI. - L. or F.

animal XIV. (i) - (O)F. *animal* or L. *animālis* (in medL. bestial), f. *anima* breath, life; see -AL[1]. (ii) sb. ult. - L. *animal*, for *animāle*, sb. use of n. of the adj. Hence **animalism** XIX.

animalcule †tiny animal XVI; (biol.) microscopic animal XVII. - modL. *animalculum*, dim. of *animal*; see prec. and -CULE.

animate vb. XVI. f. pp. stem of L. *animāre* give life to, f. *anima* air, breath, life, soul, rel. to *animus* spirit, Gr. *ánemos* wind; see -ATE[3]. So **animate** adj. XIV. **animation** XVI. - L.

animosity †spiritedness XV; active enmity XVII. - F. *animosité* or late L. *animōsitās*, f. *animus*; see prec. and -OSITY.

animus hostile spirit. XIX. - L.; see ANIMATE.

anion (electr.) ion with negative charge which moves towards the anode during electrolysis. XIX. - Gr. *anión*, f. ANA- + ION; cf. ANODE.

anise umbelliferous plant with aromatic seeds. XIV. - (O)F. *anis* :- L. *anīsum* - Gr. *ánīson*. Hence **aniseed** XIV (*anece seed*).

ankle XIV. - ON. **ankul-* (OIcel. *ǫkla*; cf. MLG. *enkel*, OHG. *ank(a)la*, *enkil*, G. *enkel*), f. Gmc. **aŋk-*, IE. **ang-*, as in L. *angulus* ANGLE[2].

annals pl. XVI. - F. *annales* or L. *annālēs*, m. pl. (sc. *librī* books) of *annālis* yearly, f. *annus* (see ANNUAL). Hence **annalist** XVII; after F. *annaliste*.

anneal †kindle OE.; fuse, fire XIV; burn in colours, temper, etc. with fire XV. OE. *onǣlan*, f. *on-* + *ǣlan* kindle, burn, bake, f. *āl* fire, rel. to *ǣl(e)d* fire = OS. *ēld*, ON. *eldr*.

annelid (zool.) red-blooded worm. XIX. - F. *annélide* or modL. *annelida*, n. pl. f. F. *annelés* 'ringed animals', pp. of *anneler*, f. OF. *annel* (mod. *anneau*) ring. See ANNULAR, -ID[3].

annex[1] something annexed XVI; supplementary building (usu. **annexe**) XIX. - F. *annexe* - L. *annexum*, sb. use of pp. of *annectere* (see next).

annex[2] add, attach. XIV. - (O)F. *annexer*, f. *annex-*, pp. stem of L. *annectere*, f. AN-[1] + *nectere* bind (cf. NEXUS). So **annexation** XV (first in Sc.). - medL.

annihilate XVI. Superseded †*annihil* (XV) - (O)F. *annihiler* - late L. *annihilāre* (f. AN-[1] + *nihil* nothing, NIL), from the pp. of which was derived the pp. *annihilate* (XIV), whence the inf. form; see -ATE[3]. So **annihilation** XVII.

anniversary XIII. - L. *anniversārius* adj., f. *annus* year + *versus* turning + *-ārius*; used sb. in medL. *anniversāria* (sc. *diēs* day) and *-ārium* (sc. *festum* feast); cf. (O)F. *anniversaire* and see ANNUAL, VERSE, -ARY.

Anno Domini XVI. - L., abl. of *annus* year, and gen. of *dominus* lord; see ANNUAL, DOM.

annotate XVIII. f. pp. stem of L. *annotāre*, f. AN-[1] + *nota* mark, NOTE. So **annotation** XV. - F. or L.

announce XV (rare before XVIII). - AN. *an(o)uncer*, OF. *anoncier* (mod. *annoncer*) :- L. *annuntiāre*, f. AN-[1] + *nuntius* (cf. ANNUNCIATION, NUNCIO). Hence **announcement** XVIII.

annoy XIII. - OF. *enoier*, *anoier* (mod. *ennuyer*) :- late L. *inodiāre*, from the L. phr. *mihī in odiō est* it is hateful to me (cf. ODIUM). So **annoyance** XIV.

annual XIV. ME. *annuel* - (O)F. - late L. *annuālis*, for L. *annuus* and *annālis*, f. *annus* year; see -AL[1].

annuity yearly grant XV; investment securing annual payment XVII. - F. *annuité* - medL. *annuitās*, f. *annuus* (see prec.); see -ITY. Hence **annuitant** XVIII.

annul XIV. - OF. *anuller* (mod. *-nn-*) :- late L. (Vulg.) *annullāre*, f. AN-[1] + *nullus* NULL.

annular ring-shaped, ringed. XVI. - F. *annulaire* or L. *annulāris*, f. *annulus*, late form of *ānulus*, dim. of *ānus* ring; see -ULAR.

annunciation announcement (spec. of the Incarnation). XIV. - (O)F. *annonciation* - late L. *annuntiātiō*, *-ōn-*, f. *annuntiāre* ANNOUNCE; see -ATION.

anode (electr.) positive electrode. XIX. - Gr. *ánodos*, f. ANA- + *hodós* way. Cf. CATHODE, ELECTRODE.

anodyne (med.) assuaging pain. XVI. - L. *anōdynus* - Gr. *anṓdynos* free from pain, f. AN-[2] + *odúnē* pain. Cf. F. *anodin*, *-ine*, perh. the immed. source.

anoint XIV. f. †*anoint* anointed - OF. *anoint*, *enoint*, pp. of *enoindre* :- L. *inungere*, f. IN-[1] + *ungere* anoint (cf. OINTMENT). **The (Lord's) Anointed**, the CHRIST. XVI.

anomalous XVII. f. late L. *anōmalus* - Gr. *anṓmalos* uneven, f. AN-[2] + *homós* SAME; see -OUS. So **anomaly** XVI.

anon †in one, at once OE.; soon, now again XVI. OE. *on ān*, *on āne* in(to) one, i.e. ON, and acc. and dat. of *ān* ONE.

anonymous XVII. f. late L. *anōnymus* - Gr. *anṓnumos*, f. AN-[2] + *ónoma* NAME. Hence **anonymity** XIX.

another XIII. ME. *an other* (in two words as late as XVI), i.e. AN[1], OTHER.

anserine goose-like. XIX. - L. *anserīnus*, f. *anser* GOOSE; see -INE[1].

answer sb. OE. *andswaru* (cf. OS. *antswōr*, ON. *andsvar*) :- Gmc. **andswarō*, f. **and-* against (see ANTI-) + **swar-*, base of OE. *swerian* SWEAR; orig. a solemn affirmation in rebutting a charge. Hence **answer** vb. OE. *andswarian* = ON. *andsvara*. **answerable** XVI.

ant OE. *ǣmet(t)e* = MLG. *āmete*, *ēmete*, OHG. *āmeiza* (G. *ameise*) :- WGmc. **āmaitjōn*, f. **ā-* off, away + **mait-* cut, hew. The OE. forms gave two ME. types, (i) *am(e)te*, whence *ant*, and (ii) *emete* (arch. and dial. *emmet*).

ant- var. of ANTI- used before vowels, as *antacid*, formerly also *antiacid* (XVIII).

-ant repr. (O)F. *-ant* :- L. *-āns*, *-ant-*, under which all prps. were levelled in French. See -ENT.

antagonist opponent XVI. - F. *antagoniste* or late L. *antagōnista* - Gr. *antagōnistḗs*, f. *antagōnízesthai* struggle against, vie with; see ANTI-, AGONY. So **antagonism** XIX; prob. after F. **antagonize** oppose XVII; make hostile XIX. - Gr.

Antarctic XIV. ME. *antartik* - OF. *antartique* (mod. *-arctique*) or its source L. *antarcticus* - Gr. *antarktikós* opposite to the north; see ANTI-, ARCTIC.

ante (in poker) stake put up by the player before drawing new cards. XIX. - L. *ante* before (see next).

ante- repr. L. adv.-prep. *ante* in comps. (corr. to Gr. *ánta* over against, and *antí* ANTI-), with the sense 'before' in place or time, as in ANTECEDENT, etc.; also *ante-chapel* XVIII, *antedate* XVI, *antenatal* XIX, *antepenultimate* XVIII, *ante-room* XVIII.

antecedent XIV. - (O)F. *antécédent* or L. *antecēdēns, -ent-*, prp. of *antecēdere*, f. ANTE- + *cēdere* go, CEDE.

antechamber XVII (before XIX usu. *anti-*). - F. *antichambre* - It. *anticamera*; see ANTE-, CHAMBER.

antediluvian before the Flood. XVII. f. ANTE- + L. *dīluvium* DELUGE + -AN.

antelope XV. - OF. *antelop* (once) or medL. *ant(h)alopus* - medGr. *anthólops*.

antenna horn or feeler of insects. XVII. - L. *antenna*, prop. *antemna* sail-yard, used in pl. (XV) to tr. Aristotle's *keraioi* 'horns' of insects.

anterior XVII. - F. *antérieur* or L. *anterior*, f. ANTE- (after *posterior*); see -IOR.

anthem OE. *antef(e)n* - late L. *anti·phona*, for *antiphō·na* ANTIPHON. The pronunc. developed: ante·vne, ante·m(ne), a·ntem, a·nthem, the last from XV; the sp. with *th* finally affected the pronunc., as in *author*.

anther (bot.) part of a stamen containing the pollen. XVIII. - F. *anthère* or modL. *anthēra*, in classL. medicine extracted from flowers - Gr. *anthērá*, fem. of *anthērós*, f. *ánthos* flower.

anthology collection of literary 'flowers'. XVII. - F. *anthologie* or medL. *anthologia* - Gr. *anthologíā*, f. *ánthos* flower.

anthracite XIX. - Gr. *anthrakîtis* kind of coal, f. *ánthrax, anthrak-*; see next and -ITE b.

anthrax †carbuncle XIV; disease of sheep and cattle XIX. - late L. - Gr. *ánthrax* coal, carbuncle.

anthropo- comb. form of Gr. *ánthrōpos* man; e.g. *anthrōpológos* treating of man, whence modL. *anthrōpologia*, Eng. **anthropology** (XVI); ecclGr. *anthrōpomorphitai* sect ascribing human form to God, whence Eng. **anthropomorphite** (XVI); so **anthropomorphism** (XVIII), **-ist** (XVII), **-ic** (XIX).

anti-, before a vowel **ant-**, before *h* **anth-**, repr. Gr. *antí, anti-* opposite, against, instead of, rel. to OE. *and-* (as in ALONG, ANSWER), OS. *and-, ant-*, OHG. *ant-, int-, ent-*, ON. *and-*, Goth. *and* along, above, L. *ante* (ANTE-), Skr. *ánti* before, in the presence of, near. Used in many words adopted from Gr. comps. and in words modelled on these and, as a gen. living formative, very freely prefixed to (i) sbs., on the pattern of ANTICHRIST, *antipope* (XVI; medL. *antipāpa*), (ii) adjs., the prefix governing the sb. implied, as *anti-national, anti-Semitic*; (iii) sbs. in attrib. phr., as *anti-aircraft* (defences), *anti-church* (politics), *anti-slavery* (committee).

antic (arch.) grotesque, fantastic; sb. †fantastic or grotesque figure, clown; ludicrous gesture or posture XVI. - It. *antico* ANTIQUE, used as synon. with *grottesco* GROTESQUE.

Antichrist XII. ME. *ante-, anticrist* - OF. *antecrist* (mod. *antéchrist*) - ecclL. *antichrīstus* - Gr. *antikhrīstos* (1 John 2: 18), f. ANTI- + *Khrīstós* CHRIST.

anticipate XVI. f. (partly after F. *anticiper*) pp. stem of L. *anticipāre*, f. ANTE- + *capere* take; see -ATE[3]. So **anticipation** XIV.

antidote XV. - (O)F. *antidote* or L. *antidotum* - Gr. *antídoton*, sb. use of n. of *antídotos*, f. ANTI- + *do-*, stem of *didónai* give.

antimacassar covering for chair-backs, etc., orig. to protect them from grease in the hair. XIX. f. ANTI- + MACASSAR.

antimony XV. - medL. *antimōnium*.

antinomy contradiction. XVI. - L. *antinomia* - Gr. *antinomíā*, f. ANTI- + *nómos* law; see -Y[3].

antipathy XVII. - F. *antipathie* or L. *antipathīa* - Gr. *antipátheia*, f. *antipathḗs* opposed in feeling, f. ANTI- + *páthos*; see PATHOS, -Y[3]. So **antipathetic** XVII.

antiphon XV. - ecclL. *antiphōna* - Gr. *antiphōna*, n. pl. of *antíphōnos* responsive, f. ANTI- + *phōnḗ* sound; cf. ANTHEM.

antipodes †people inhabiting the opposite side of the globe XIV; places on the earth exactly opposite to each other XVI. - (O)F. or late L. - Gr. *antípodes*, pl. of *antípous* having the feet opposite, f. ANTI- + *poús* FOOT.

antiquary XVI. - L. *antīquārius*, f. *antīquus*; see next and -ARY. So **antiquarian** XVII.

antique XVI. - F. *antique* or L. *antīquus, antīcus*, f. ANTE- + suff. *-īcus*; orig. identical in form and pronunc. with ANTIC, but finally differentiated after 1700. So **antiquity** XIV. - OF. - L. **antiquated** XVII, orig. pp. of *antiquate* (XVI).

antirrhinum XVI. - L. - Gr. *antírrhīnon*, f. *antí* counterfeiting, ANTI- + *rhī́s, rhīn-* nose (cf. RHINOCEROS).

antiseptic XVIII. - modL. *antisēpticus*, f. ANTI- + Gr. *sēptikós* SEPTIC.

antithesis XV. - late L. - Gr. *antíthesis*, f. ANTI- + *tithénai* set, place (cf. THESIS). So **antithetic** XVII, **-ical** XVI. ult. - Gr. *antithetikós*.

antler XIV. ME. *aunteler* - AN. var. of OF. *antoillier*, etc. (mod. *andouiller*).

antonym XIX. - F. *antonyme*, f. Gr. ANTI-, after *synonyme* SYNONYM.

anus XV. - L. *ānus* orig. ring. So **anal** XVIII. - modL.

anvil OE. *anfilt(e), anfealt*, corr. to MDu. *aenvilte*, OHG. *anafalz*, to which are parallel MLG. *anebelte*, MDu. *aen-, anebelt*, and OHG. *anabōz* (G. *amboss*); all based on Gmc. **ana* ON + vb.-stem meaning 'beat' (cf. FELT) and perh. all modelled on L. *incūs* anvil, f. *in* IN-[1] + *cūd-*, stem of *cūdere* beat.

anxious XVII. f. L. *anxius*, f. pp. stem *anx-* of *angere* choke, oppress; see ANGUISH, -IOUS. So **anxiety** XVI. - F., or L. *anxietās*.

any OE. *ǣniġ* = OS. *ēnig* (Du. *eenig*), OHG. *einag* (G. *einig*), ON. *einigr*, Goth. *ainah-* :- Gmc. **ainizaz, -azaz*, f. **ain-* ONE + **-iz-* -Y[1]; cf. L. *ūnicus* UNIQUE. In ME. two types were current, *ani* and *eni*; the present sp. continues the first, the pronunc. the second. **anybody** XIII, **anyhow** XVIII, **anything** OE., **anywhere** XIV.

Anzac XX. Made up of the initials of *A*ustralian and *N*ew *Z*ealand *A*rmy *C*orps.

aorist (gram.) tense denoting past time (simply, without limitation). XVI. - Gr. *aóristos* undefined (sc. *khrónos* time), f. A-[4] + *horistós*, f. *horízein* define (cf. HORIZON).

aorta XVI. - modL. - Gr. *aortḗ*, f. *aeírein* raise; cf. ARTERY.
ap- assim. form of AD- before *p*.
apace XIV. - OF. *a pas* at (a considerable) pace, i.e. *a* AD-, *pas* PACE[1].
apanage, app- provision made for younger children of kings, etc.; natural accompaniment. XVII. - (O)F. *apanage*, f. *apaner* dower (a daughter) - medL. *appānāre*, f. AP- + *pānis* bread; see -AGE.
apart XIV. - (O)F. *à part*, i.e. *à* AD-, PART.
apartheid XX. - Afrikaans, f. Du. *apart* (- F. *à part*, see prec.) + *-heid* -HOOD.
apartment XVII. - F. *appartement* - It. *appartamento*, f. *appartare* separate; see -MENT.
apathy XVII. - F. *apathie* - L. *apathīa* - Gr. *apátheia*, f. *apathḗs* without feeling; see A-[4], PATHOS, -Y[3]. So **apathetic** XVIII, after PATHETIC.
ape OE. *apa* m., *ape* fem. = OS. *apo* (Du. *aap*), OHG. *affo* (G. *affe*), ON. *api* :- Gmc. **apan-*. Hence **apery** XVII, **apish** XV.
apeak (naut.) vertical(ly). XVI. orig. *a pike* - F. *à pic*, i.e. *à* AD-, *pic* PEAK[1] (to which the second syll. was assim.).
aperient XVII. f. L. *aperiēns, -ent-*, prp. of *aperīre* open; see -ENT.
aperture XV. - L. *apertūra*, f. *apert-*, pp. stem of *aperīre*; see prec., -URE.
apex (pl. *apices*). XVII. - L. *apex, apic-*. Hence **apical** XIX.
aphasia (med.) loss of speech. XIX. - modL. - Gr. *aphasiā*, f. A-[4] + *phánai* speak; see -IA[1].
aphelion (astron.) point of a planet's or comet's orbit at which it is farthest from the sun. XVII. Graecized form (Kepler) of modL. *aphēlium*, f. APO- + Gr. *hḗlios* SUN, after L. *apogæum* APOGEE.
aphesis (philol.) loss of a short initial unaccented syllable as in *(a)lone*, *(e)squire*. XIX. - Gr. *áphesis* letting go, f. *aphiénai*, f. APO- + *hiénai* let go, send. So **aphetic** XIX. f. Gr. *áphetos* vbl. adj.
aphis (pl. *aphides*, whence new sg. *aphid* (XIX)) XVIII. - modL. *aphis* (Linnaeus) - late Gr. *áphis* (first in 1523, with gloss *cimex*; prob. an error for *kóris* bug).
aphorism XVI. - F. *aphorisme*, or late L. *aphorismus* - Gr. *aphorismós*, f. *aphorízein* define, f. APO- + *horízein* (see HORIZON).
aphrodisiac XVIII. - Gr. *aphrodīsiakós*, f. *Aphrodítē* goddess of love ('foam-born'; *aphrós* foam).
apiary XVII. - L. *apiārium*, f. *apis* bee; see -ARY. **apiculture** XIX.
apiece XIV. orig. two words, A[1], PIECE sb.
aplomb †perpendicularity, steadiness; self-possession. XIX. - F., f. phr. *à plomb* according to the plummet (see PLUMB).
apo-, before a vowel **ap-**, before *h* **aph-**, prefix repr. Gr. *apo-*, comb. form of prep. *apó* away, OFF, in many words adopted ult. from Gr. and denoting removal, departure, completion, cessation, return, or reversion.
Apocalypse Revelation of St. John the Divine. XIII. - (O)F. *apocalypse* - ecclL. *apocalypsis* - Gr. *apokálupsis*, f. *apokalúptein* uncover, disclose. So **apocalyptic, -ical** XVII.
apocope (gram.) cutting off the end of a word. XVI. - late L. - Gr. *apokopḗ*, f. *apokóptein* cut off. So **apocopate** XIX, **apocopation** XVIII.
Apocrypha †adj. of unknown authorship, uncanonical; sb. writings of doubtful authorship, (spec.) uncanonical books of the O.T. XIV. - n. pl. (sc. *scripta* writings) of ecclL. *apocryphus*, Gr. *apókruphos* hidden, f. *apokrúptein* hide away; see APO- and CRYPT. Hence **apocryphal** XVI.
apodosis (gram.) consequent clause answering to the protasis. XVII. - late L. - Gr. *apódosis* 'a giving back', f. *apodidónai*.
apogee (astron.) point of a planet's orbit at which it is farthest from the earth. XVII (XVI in L. form). - F. *apogée* or modL. *apogæum, -eum* - Gr. *apógeion*, sb. use (sc. *diástēma* distance) of n. of adj. *apógeios* far from the earth, f. APO- + *gê* earth.
apologue moral fable. XVII. - F. *apologue* or L. *apologus* - Gr. *apólogos*, f. APO- + *lógos* discourse (see LOGOS).
apology †defence, justification; acknowledgement of offence given. XVI. - F. *apologie* or late L. *apologia* - Gr. *apologiā* speech in defence, f. *apologeîsthai*, f. APO- + **log-* **leg-* speak (see LOGOS). So **apologetic** XVII; sb. XV. **apologist** XVII. - F. *-iste*, f. Gr. *apologizesthai* render an account (f. *apólogos*; see prec.), whence **apologize** XVI; now assoc. with *apology*.
apo(ph)thegm XVI. - F. *apophthegme* or modL. *apothegma* - Gr. *apóphthegma*, f. *apophthéggesthai* speak one's opinion plainly.
apoplexy sudden loss of powers of sensation and motion. XIV. - (O)F. *apoplexie* - late L. *apoplēxia* - Gr. *apoplēxiā*, f. *apoplḗssein* disable by a stroke. So **apoplectic(al)** XVII.
aport (naut.) on or to the port side. XVII. f. A-[1] + PORT[4], after ALEE.
aposiopesis (gram.) sudden breaking-off in the middle of speech. XVI. - L. - Gr. *aposiṓpēsis*, f. *aposiōpân* be silent, f. APO- + *siōpḗ* silence.
apostate XIV. - (O)F. *apostate* or ecclL. *apostata* - late Gr. *apostátēs*, f. *apostênai*, f. *apó* APO- + *stênai* STAND. So **apostasy** XIV. - ecclL. - late Gr. *apostasiā*, for *apóstasis* defection. **apostatize** XVI. - medL.
apostle OE. *apostol*, ME. *apostel* - ecclL. *apostolus* - Gr. *apóstolos* one sent forth, f. *apostéllein*, f. APO- + *stéllein* place, make ready; the early forms were reinforced or superseded by adoption of OF. *apostle* (mod. *apôtre*). So **apostolic** XII, **-ical** XV.
apostrophe[1] (rhet.) exclamatory address. XVI. - L. - Gr. *apostrophḗ* turning away (to one in particular), f. *apostréphein*. Hence **apostrophize** XVIII.
apostrophe[2] †omission of a sound or letter; the sign ' denoting this. XVII. - F. *apostrophe* or late L. *apostrophus* - late Gr. *apóstrophos* (see prec.); assim. to prec.
apothecary XIV. ME. *apotecarie* - OF. *apotecaire* - late L. *apothēcārius* store-keeper, f. *apothēca* - Gr. *apothḗkē* store-house, f. *apotithénai* put away. Cf. BODEGA, and see -ARY.
apotheosis deification. XVII. - ecclL. *apotheōsis* - Gr. *apothéōsis*, f. *apotheoûn* deify, f. *theós* god (cf. THEO-). Hence **apotheosize** XVIII.

appal XIV. - OF. *apal(l)ir* grow pale (also trans.), f. *a-* AD- + *pale* PALE[1].

appanage see APANAGE.

apparatus XVII. - L. *apparātus*, f. *apparāre* make ready, f. AP- + *parāre* PREPARE.

apparel †prepare, equip XIII; array, attire XIV. ME. *aparailen* - OF. *apareillier* (mod. *appareiller*) :- Rom. **appariculāre* make equal or fit, f. AP- + **pariculum* (F. *pareil* like), dim. of L. *pār* equal. So **apparel** sb. XIV. - OF. *apareil* (mod. *app-*).

apparent manifest XIV; seeming XVII. - OF. *aparant, -ent* (mod. *apparent*) - L. *appārēns, -ent-*, prp. of *appārēre* APPEAR; see -ENT.

apparition action of appearing, something appearing XV; ghost XVII. - (O)F. *apparition* or L. *apparitiō, -ōn-*, f. *appārēre*; see prec. and -ITION.

appeal XIV. - OF. *apeler* (mod. *appeler*) call :- L. *appellāre*, f. AP- + *pell-* of *pellere* drive. So **appeal** sb. XIII.

appear become or be visible or manifest XIII; seem *to be* XIV. ME. *aperen* - tonic stem of OF. *apareir* :- L. *appārēre*, f. AP- + *pārēre* come into view. So **appearance** XIV. ME. *aparaunce* - OF. *aparance, -ence* (mod. *apparence*) :- late L. *appārentia*; see -ANCE.

appease XIV. - AN. *apeser*, OF. *apaisier* (mod. *-er*), f. *a-* AD- + *pais* PEACE. So **appeasement** XV.

appellant XV. - (O)F. *appelant*, prp. of *appeler* APPEAL. So **appellation** XV. **appellative** adj. XV; sb. XVI. - late L.

append XV (Sc.; in Eng. XVII). - L. *appendere*, f. AP- + *pendēre* hang (see PENDENT). Hence **appendage** XVII.

appendix (pl. **-ices, -ixes**) XVI. - L. *appendix, -ic-*, f. *appendere* (see prec.). Hence **appendicitis** XIX.

appertain XIV. ME. *apertenen* - OF. *apartenir* (mod. *app-*) :- Rom. **appartenēre*, alt. of late L. *appertinēre*, f. AP- + *pertinēre* PERTAIN. Cf. APPURTENANCE.

appetite desire, spec. for food. XIV. - OF *apetit* (mod. *appétit*) - L. *appetītus*, f. *appetere*, f. AP- + *petere* seek (see PETITION). So **appetizing** XVII. - (O)F. *appétissant*, with ending assim. to -IZE, -ING[2].

applaud XV. - L. *applaudere*, f. AP- + *plaudere* clap (see PLAUDIT), partly after F. *applaudir*. So **applause** XV. - L. *applausus*, f. *applaus-*, pp. stem of *applaudere*.

apple OE. *æppel*, corr. to OS., (M)Du. *appel*, OHG. *apful* (G. *apfel*), Crimean Goth. *apel* :- Gmc. **aplu-*; cf. ON. *epli*. Rel. to OIr. *ubull*, W. *afal*, OSl. *ablŭko*, Lith. *obuolỹs*.

applicable †compliant XVI; capable of being applied XVII; pertinent XIX. f. L. *applicāre* APPLY + -ABLE; cf. F. *applicable*. Superseded †*appliable* (XIV) in all senses. So **application** XIV. - (O)F. - L.

appliqué XVIII. - F., pp. of *appliquer* - L. *applicāre* (see next).

apply XIV. - OF. *apl(o)ier* :- L. *applicāre*, f. AP- + *plicāre* fold. Hence **appliance** XVI.

appoggiatura XVIII. - It., f. *appoggiare* cause to lean.

appoint XIV. - OF. *apointier*, f. POINT (see AD-). So **appointment** XV.

apportion XVI. - (O)F. *apportionner*; see AP-, PORTION.

apposite XVII. - L. *appositus*, pp. of *appōnere* apply, f. AP- + *pōnere* place (cf. POSIT). So **apposition** XV. - F., or late L. *appositiō, -ōn-*, f. *apposit-*, pp. stem of *appōnere*.

appraise XV. alt., by assim. to PRAISE, of arch. *apprize*, †*apprise* - OF. *aprisier*, f. *a-* AD- + *pris* PRICE. Hence **appraisal** XIX, **appraisement** XVII.

appreciate estimate duly; esteem highly XVII; raise or rise in value (orig. U.S.) XVIII. f. pp. stem of late L. *appretiāre* set a price on, f. AP- + *pretium* PRICE; see -ATE[3]. Cf. (O)F. *apprécier* and APPRAISE. So **appreciation** XVII. - (O)F. - late L. **appreciable** (once XV), **-ative** XIX; after F.

apprehend XIV. - F. *appréhender* or L. *apprehendere*, f. AP- + *prehendere* seize (cf. GET). So **apprehension, -sive** XIV. - (partly through F.) late L. *apprehensiō, -ōn-*, medL. *apprehensīvus*.

apprentice XIV. - OF. *aprentis* (mod. *apprenti*), f. *aprendre* learn. Aphetic PRENTICE.

apprise inform. XVII. f. F. *appris*, fem. *-ise*, pp. of *apprendre* teach (causative of the sense 'learn') :- L. *apprendere*, contr. form of *apprehendere* APPREHEND.

apprize see APPRAISE.

appro abbrev. of APPROBATION or APPROVAL.

approach XIV. - OF. *aproch(i)er* (mod. *approcher*) :- late L. (Vulg.) *appropiāre*, f. AP- + *propius*, compar. of *prope* near. Hence **approach** sb. XV.

approbation XIV. - (O)F. - L. *approbātiō, -ōn-*, f. *approbāre* APPROVE; see -ATION.

appropriate make one's own, take to oneself. XV. f. **appropriate** pp. and adj. (XV), or pp. stem of late L. *appropriāre*, f. AP- + *proprius* own, PROPER, see -ATE[2,3]. So **appropriation** XIV. - (O)F. - late L.

approve †prove, demonstrate; sanction, commend. XIV. - OF. *aprover* (mod. *approuver*) :- L. *approbāre*, f. AP- + *probus* just, good. The tonic stem *appreuv-* of the OF. vb. gave ME. *appreven*. Cf. PROVE. Hence **approval** XVII (rare before XIX).

approximate very near in position or nature XV; nearly exact XIX. - late L. *approximātus*, pp. of *approximāre*, f. AP- + *proximus* PROXIMATE. Hence, or directly f. pp. stem *approximāt-*, **approximate** vb., **approximation** XV.

appurtenance XIV. - AN. *apurtenaunce*, OF. *apartenance* :- Rom. **appertinentia*, f. late L. *appertinēre* APPERTAIN; see -ANCE. So **appurtenant** XIV.

apricot XVI. Earliest forms *abrecock, apricock* - Pg. *albricoque* or Sp. *albaricoque* - Arab. *al-barḳūḳ, -birḳūḳ*, i.e. AL-[2], *birḳūḳ* - late Gr. *praikókion*, Byzantine Gr. *berikokkon* - L. *præcoquum* (sc. *mālum*), f. var. of *præcox* early-ripe (see PRECOCIOUS). Assim. to F. *abricot*.

April XIV. - L. *Aprīlis*, prop. adj. (sc. *mēnsis* month).

apron XV. Evolved by misdivision of *a napron* as *an apron* (cf. ADDER); ME. *napron, -(o)un* (XIV) - OF. *naperon* (mod. *napperon*), f. *nape, nappe* table-cloth (see NAPKIN).

apropos XVII. - F. *à propos*, i.e. *à* to (AD-), *propos* plan, purpose.

apse arched or domed recess in a church. XIX (in L.-Gr. form *apsis* XVIII). - L. *apsis, apsid-* - Gr. *hapsis* vault, etc. Hence **apsidal** XIX.

apt XIV. - L. *aptus*, pp. of *apere* fasten (cf. ADAPT, ADEPT, INEPT). So **aptitude** XV. - (O)F. - late L.; see ATTITUDE.

apteryx kiwi. XIX. - modL., f. A-[4] + Gr. *ptérux* wing.

aquamarine XIX. - L. *aqua marīna* sea-water, i.e. *aqua* water and fem. of *marīnus* MARINE.

aquarelle XIX. - F. - It. *acquerella* water-colour, f. *acqua* :- L. *aqua* water.

aquarium XIX. sb. use of n. sg. of L. *aquārius* of water, f. *aqua* water (see -ARY); after VIVARIUM.

aquatic XV. - (O)F. *aquatique* or L. *aquāticus*, f. *aqua* water; see -ATIC.

aquatint method of etching on copper. XVIII. - F. *aquatinte*, It. *acqua tinta*, repr. L. *aqua* water, *tincta* dyed (see TINT).

aqueduct XVI. - L. *aquæductus*, i.e. *aquæ*, g. of *aqua* water, *ductus* conveyance (see DUCT). Cf. F. *aqueduc*, †*aqueduct* (XVI), perh. the immed. source.

aqueous XVII. f. L. *aqua* water + -EOUS; perh. suggested by F. *aqueux* (- L. *aquōsus*).

aquiline eagle-like, (of nose) hooked. XVII. - L. *aquilīnus*, f. *aquila* EAGLE, prob. after F. *aquilin*; see -INE[1].

ar- assim. form of AD- before *r*.

-ar repr. L. *-āris* belonging to, of the kind or form of, as in *globulāris* GLOBULAR, *lunāris* LUNAR, *stellāris* STELLAR; synon. with -AL[1], but replacing it where *l* preceded. The regular F. descendant of L. *-āri-* is *-ier* (AN. *-er*), whence *-er* in Eng. adoptions, which was often assim. to L. with *-ar*; e.g. L. *scholāris*, AN. *escoler*, ME. *scoler*, later *scholar*. Learned F. formations have *-aire* (cf. -ARY). In *beggar, liar, pedlar*, -ER[1] has been assim. to this suffix.

Arab XIV. - L. *Arab(u)s* - Gr. *Áraps, Arab-* - Arab. *'arab*. So **arabesque** XVII. - F. - It. *arabesco*, f. *arabo* :- L. *Arabus*. **Arabian** XIV. f. OF. *arabi* or L. *Arab(i)us* - Gr. *Arábios*. **Arabic**, -y (-Y[3]) XIV. - (O)F. - L. - Gr.

arable XV. - (O)F. *arable* or L. *arābilis*, f. *arāre* plough; see -ABLE.

arachnid XIX. - F. *arachnide* or modL. *arachnida* (n. pl.), f. Gr. *arákhnē* spider; see -ID[3].

arbalest XI. - OF. *arbaleste* (mod. *arbalète*) :- late L. *arcuballista*, f. *arcus* bow + BALLISTA.

arbiter XV. - L. So **arbitrage** XV. - (O)F. **arbitrament, -ement** XIV. - (O)F. - medL. **arbitrary** XV. - L., perh. after (O)F. *arbitraire*. **arbitrate** XVI. f. pp. stem of L. *arbitrārī*. **arbitration** XIV. - (O)F. - L. **arbitrator** XIV. - late L.

arboreal XVII. f. L. *arboreus*, f. *arbor* tree; see -AL[1]. Hence **arbor(e)ous, -escent** XVII. **arboriculture** XIX.

arbour †plot of grass, flower-garden; bower. XIV. orig. *erber* - AN. *erber*, OF. *erbier* (mod. *herbier*), f. *erbe* HERB + *-ier* -ARIUM. Normal phonetic change gave *(h)arber, (h)arbour*, *-our* being after L. *arbor* tree.

arc XIV. - (O)F. :- L. *arcus* bow, arch.

arcade arched passage. XVIII. - F. - Pr. *arcada* or It. *arcata*, f. Rom. **arca* ARCH[1]; see -ADE.

Arcadian XVI. f. L. *Arcadius*, f. Gr. *Arkadiā*, district in the Peloponnese; see -IAN.

arcana mysterious secrets. XVI. - L., n. pl. of *arcānus* hidden, secret (whence **arcane**), f. *arca* chest; see ARK, -AN.

arch[1] curved structure. XIV. - (O)F. *arche* :- Rom. **arca* n. pl. taken as fem. sg., f. L. *arcus* ARC. Hence **arch** vb. XIV.

arch[2] chief, pre-eminent XVI; (through *arch rogue*, etc.) cunning, waggish XVII. The prefix ARCH- used as an adj.

arch- repr. ult. Gr. *arkh(i)-* chief, comb. form f. base of *arkhós* chief, *arkhḗ* rule, as in *arkhággelos* archangel, *arkhidiákonos* archdeacon, *arkhiepískopos* archbishop, whence L. *archangelus, archidiāconus, archiepiscopus*, OF. *arc(h)angele, arc(h)ediacre, arc(h)evesque*. In OE. at first tr. by *hēah* HIGH, as in *hēahenġel*, but later adopted from L. as *ærċe-, arċe-, erċe-*, as in *ærċebisċop*, etc. The OE. forms gave ME. *erche-, arche-*, the latter coinciding with OF. *arche-*. From such comps. the prefix was generalized, and freely used in the senses 'chief', 'principal', 'pre-eminent', 'extreme'. Cf. ARCHI-.

-arch repr. Gr. *-arkhos* ruling, rel. to *arkhḗ* (see prec.), as in *mónarkhos* MONARCH, *tétrarkhos* TETRARCH. Cf. -ARCHY.

archaeology XVII. - modL. *archæologia* - Gr. *arkhaiologiā*, f. *arkhaîos* ancient; see -LOGY.

archaic XIX. - F. *archaïque* - Gr. *arkhaïkós*, f. *arkhaîos* ancient; see -IC. So **archaism** XVII. - modL. - Gr.

archangel (repl. OE. *hēahenġel*) XII. - OF. *archangele* - ecclL. *archangelus* - ecclGr. (LXX) *arkhággelos*; see ARCH-, ANGEL.

archer XIII. - AN. *archer*, OF. *archier* (mod. *archer*) :- Rom. **arcārius*, f. L. *arcus* bow, ARC; see -ER[2]. So **archery** XIV. - OF.

archetype XVII. - L. *archetypum* - Gr. *arkhétupon*, sb. use of n. of adj. 'first moulded as a model', f. *arkhe-* (var. of *arkhi-*) + *túpos* model, TYPE. Cf. F. *archétype*.

archi- repr. ult. Gr. *arkhi-* (see ARCH-); some adjs. with this prefix have corr. sbs. with *arch-*, e.g. *archidiaconal* (XV), *archdeacon* (OE.).

archimandrite (Gr. Ch.) superior of a monastery. XVII. - F., or ecclL. *archimandrīta* - ecclGr. *arkhimandrítēs*, f. ARCHI- + *mándrā* monastery; see -ITE.

archipelago Aegean Sea; sea with numerous islands; group of many islands. XVI. - It. *arcipelago*, f. ARCHI- + Gr. *pélagos* sea.

architect XVI. - F. *architecte* - It. *architetto*, or their source, L. *architectus* - Gr. *arkhitéktōn*, f. ARCHI- + *téktōn* builder. So **architectonic** XVII. - L. - Gr. **architecture** XVI. - F. or L.

architrave XVI. - F. - It., f. ARCHI- + *trave* beam :- L. *trabs, trabe-*.

archives XVII. - F. - L. *archī(v)a*, Gr. *arkheîa* n. pl., f. *arkhḗ* government. So **archivist** XVIII. - F.

-archy terminal el. of abstract nouns corr. to words in -ARCH, repr. Gr. *-arkhiā* rule, rel. to ARCH-, ARCHI-; e.g. *monarchy, tetrarchy*.

Arctic XIV. ME. *artik* - OF. *artique* (mod. *arctique*) - L. *arcticus* - Gr. *arktikós*, f. *árktos* bear, the Great Bear, north; see -IC.

-ard repr. (O)F. *-ard*, †*-art* - OHG. *-hart*, being the adj. *hart* bold, hardy, HARD, often forming part of personal names, as OHG. *Reginhart* REYNARD; in MHG. and Du. a formative of common nouns, gen. pejorative; in Eng. orig. in adoptions of F. sbs., as *bastard*, *coward*, *mallard*; the depreciatory sense of some of these led to its being used to form similar words on various stems, as *dastard*, *drunkard*, *laggard*, *niggard*, *sluggard*, *wizard*. In several words it conceals endings of a different origin, as *bustard*, *custard*, *hazard*, *leopard*, *steward*, *tankard*.

ardent XIV. - OF. *ardant* (mod. *-ent*) :- L. *ardēns*, *-ent-*, prp. of *ardēre* burn; see -ANT, -ENT. So **ardour** XIV. - OF. *ardour* (mod. *-eur*) :- L. *ardor*, *-ōr-*.

arduous f. L. *arduus* high, steep, difficult; see -UOUS.

are[1] unit of square measure (100 sq. metres). XIX. - F. - L. *ārea* AREA.

are[2] see BE.

area clear open space; superficial extent XVI; enclosed court XVII. - L. *ārea* vacant piece of ground.

arena XVII. - L. *arēna*, prop. *harēna* sand, (sand-covered) centre of an amphitheatre. So **arenaceous** XVII.

argent XV. - (O)F. - L. *argentum* silver.

argon (chem.) inert gas of the atmosphere. XIX. - Gr. *argón*, n. of *argós* idle, inactive, for *aergós*, f. A-[4] + *érgon* work.

argot XIX. - F., of unkn. orig.

argue XIV. - (O)F. *arguer* :- L. *argūtāre* babble, f. *arguere* make clear, prove. So **argument** XIV, **argumentation** XV.

argy-bargy XIX. var. of *argle-bargle* sb. and vb. (XIX), f. dial. *argle* to dispute, bandy words (XVI), prob. alt. of prec. with *-le* as in *haggle*.

aria XVIII. - It.; see AIR.

-arian f. L. *-ārius* -ARY + -AN, first appearing in late XVI in *disciplinarian*, *quinquagenarian*, later (XVII) becoming common in designations of religious bodies and their tenets, e.g. *millenarian*, *predestinarian*, *sectarian*, *Trinitarian*, *Unitarian*, on the analogy of which were formed *humanitarian*, *parliamentarian*, *utilitarian*.

arid XVII. - F. *aride* or L. *āridus*, f. *ārēre* be dry or parched; see -ID[1]. So **aridity** XVI.

aright OE. *on riht*, *ariht*, i.e. ON, A-[1], and RIGHT.

-arious adj. suffix, f. L. *-āris* -AR or *-ārius* -ARY, + -OUS.

arise OE. *ārīsan* = OS. *ārīsan*, OHG. *arrīsan*, Goth. *urreisan*; f. A-[3] + RISE.

aristocracy government by 'the best' citizens; political supremacy of a privileged order XVI; patrician order, nobles XVII. - (O)F. *aristocratie* - Gr. *aristokratiā*, f. *áristos* best; see -CRACY. So **aristocrat** XVIII. - F. *aristocrate* (a word of the French Revolution). **aristocratic** XVII. - (O)F. - Gr. **-ical** XVI.

arithmetic XIII. Earliest forms *arsmetrik(e)*, *-metike* - OF. *arismetique* - Rom. **arismetica*, for L. *arithmētica* - Gr. *arithmētikḗ* (sc. *tékhnē* art) 'art of counting', f. *arithmein*, f. *arithmós* number; assoc. with L. *ars metrica* 'measuring art' led to forms of the type *arsmetrik(e)* which were later (XV) conformed to the orig. L. and Gr. So **arithme·tic** XVI. - L. and Gr. **arithmetical** XVI. **arithmetician** XVI. - F.

-arium - L., n. sg. of *-ārius* -ARY, in sb. use of adjs., e.g. *honorarium*, *sacrarium*, and the group *aquarium*, *herbarium*, *vivarium*.

ark †chest, coffer; floating vessel built by Noah (Gen. 6: 14-16). OE. *arc* (*earc*), corr. to OHG. *archa* (G. *arche*), ON. *ǫrk*, Goth. *arka*; Gmc. - L. *arca*.

arm[1] upper limb of the body. OE. *arm* (*earm*) = OS., OHG. (Du., G.) *arm*, ON. *armr*, Goth. *arms* :- Gmc. **armaz*; cf. L. *armus* shoulder (of animal), Skr. *īrmá-* arm, etc.

arm[2] (pl.) weapons for fighting. XIII. - (O)F. *armes* :- L. *arma* n. pl. (no sg.). So **arm** vb. XIII. - (O)F. *armer* :- L. *armāre*.

armada XVI. Early forms *armado* (see -ADO), *armada*, and *-ade*, *-ata* - Sp. *armada* :- Rom. *armāta* ARMY.

armadillo XVI. - Sp., dim. of *armado* armed man :- L. *armātus*, pp. of *armāre* (see ARM[2]).

Armageddon place of the last decisive battle at the Day of Judgement (see Rev. 16: 16 A.V.; R.V. *Harmagedon*); any 'final' conflict on a large scale XIX. Taken to be the Gr. equivalent of Heb. *har megiddōn* mountain region of Megiddo.

armament XVII. - L. *armāmentum*, f. *armāre*; see ARM[2], -MENT, and cf. F. *armement*.

armature †arms, armour XV; piece of iron placed in contact with the poles of a magnet to preserve its power XVIII; wire-wound core of dynamo, etc. XIX. - F. - L. *armātūra*, f. pp. stem of *armāre*; see ARM[2], -URE.

armiger person entitled to heraldic arms. XVIII. - L. *armiger* bearing arms, f. *arma* ARM[2] + *-ger*, *gerere* bear, carry.

armistice XVIII. - F. *armistice* or modL. *armistitium*, f. *arma* arms (ARM[2]) + *-stitium* stoppage. Cf. SOLSTICE.

armory heraldry. XV. - (O)F. *armoirie*, f. *armoier* blazon, f. *arme* ARM[2]; see -Y[3]. Hence **armorial** XVI.

armour XIII. - OF. *armure*, earlier *armeüre* :- L. *armātūra* ARMATURE.

armoury †armour XIV; place for keeping arms XV. prob. orig. - (O)F. *armoirie* ARMORY, with assim. to ARMOUR.

army †armed expedition XIV; armed force XV. - (O)F. *armée* :- Rom. *armāta*, sb. use of pp. fem. of L. *armāre* ARM; see -Y[5].

aroma XVIII. - L. *arōma* - Gr. *árōma*, *-at-*. So **aromatic** XIV. - F. - late L. - Gr.

around XIV (not frequent before XVI). In earliest use perh. after OF. *a la reonde* roundabout; later f. A-[1] + ROUND[1].

arouse XVI. f. A-[3] + ROUSE, after *rise*, *arise*, *wake*, *awake*.

arpeggio XVIII. - It., f. *arpeggiare* play on the harp, f. *arpa* HARP.

arquebus see HARQUEBUS.

arrack Eastern name for a kind of alcoholic spirit. XVII. ult. - Arab. *'araḳ*. Aphetic RACK[6].

arraign XIV. - AN. *araigner*, *areiner*, OF.

araisnier - Rom. **arratiōnāre*, f. AR- + *ratiō, -ōn-* account, REASON.

arrange XIV. - OF. *arangier, arengier* (mod. *arranger*), f. *a-* AD- + *rangier* RANGE. So **arrangement** XVIII.

arrant notorious, downright. XVI. First in *knight arrant, arrant thief*, in which *arrant* is a later form of ERRANT vagabond; in *arrant thief* it acquired the sense 'public, common', and hence, when transf. to other nouns, 'manifest, undisguised, notorious'.

arras XV. - *arras* in AN. *draps d'arras* 'cloths of *Arras*', name of a town in Artois, France.

array XIV. - AN. *arai*, OF. *arei* (mod. *arroi*), f. AN. *araier*, OF. *areer* :- Rom. **arrēdāre* put in order, f. AR- + Gmc. **rǣð-* prepare (see CURRY[1]). So **array** vb. XIII.

arrear †adv. backward, behind XIV; sb (chiefly pl.) liability overdue, debts unpaid XVII. - OF. *ariere* (mod. *arrière*), AN. *arere* :- medL. *adretrō*, f. *ad* to (AT) + *retrō* backward. As sb. *arrear(s)* took the place of *arrearage(s)* XIV (now U.S.) - OF. *arierages* (mod. *arrérages*), f. *ariere*; cf. AN. sb. *areres* XIV.

arrest vb. XIV. - OF. *arester* :- Rom. **arrestāre*, f. AR- + L. *restāre* stop behind, REST[2]. So **arrest** sb. XIV.

arrival †coming to land XIV; act of arriving XVI. - AN. *ar(r)ivaille*, f. *ariver*; see next and -AL[2].

arrive †come to shore, land XIII; come to the end of a journey, etc. XIV. - OF. *ariver* (mod. *arriver*) :- Rom. **arrīpāre* come to land, f. AR- + L. *rīpa* shore.

arrogance XIV. - (O)F. - L. *arrogantia*, f. *arrogāns, -ant-*, prp. of L. *arrogāre* lay claim to; see -ANCE, ROGATION. So **arrogant** XIV. **arrogate** XVI. f. pp. stem of L. *arrogāre*. **arrogation** XVI.

arrow Late OE. *ar(e)we* - ON. **arw-*, nom. *ǫr* (g. sg., pl. *ǫrvar*), rel. to Goth. *arhwazna* arrow, - Gmc. base **arχw-* :- IE. **arkw-*, whence also L. *arcus* bow, ARC.

arrowroot herb of the W. Indies, the tubers of which were used to absorb poison from wounds, esp. those made by poisoned arrows XVII; starch made from this XIX. Perversion of Aruak *aru-aru* 'meal of meals', by assim. to ARROW and ROOT.

arse OE. *ærs (ears)* = MLG. *ars*, MDu. *aers* (Du. *aars*), OHG. *ars* (G. *arsch*), ON. *ars* :- Gmc. **arsaz* :- IE. **orsos*, whence also Gr. *órrhos*; cf. *ourá* tail (:- **orsā*).

arsenal †naval dock (in early use, of Venice); establishment for storage of weapons and ammunition. XVI. Early forms *arsen-, arzen-, archynale* - F. *arsenal*, †*archenal* or its source It. †*arzanale*, (mod.) *arsenale*, f. Venetian It. *arzanà*, ult. (with unexpl. loss of *d-*) - Arab. *dār aṣ-ṣinā'a*, i.e. *dār* house, AL-[2], *ṣinā'a* industry.

arsenic XIV. - (O)F. - L. *arsenicum* (*arrhen-*) - Gr. *arsenikón* (*arrhen-*), ult. - Iranian (cf. Pers. *zirnīḳ*, f. *zar* gold), but assoc. with *arsenikós* (*arrhen-*) male, f. *ársēn, árrhēn* male. Also **arse·nic** (cf. -IC) XIX, **arsenical** XVII, adjs.

arsis (pros.) unemphatic syllable XVIII; strong syllable XIX. - late L. - Gr. *ársis* lifting, raising, f. *airein* raise; opposed to THESIS. By Gr. writers applied to the raising of the foot in beating time, which marked the unaccented syllable, by later L. writers referred to the raising of the voice, which marked the accented syllable; there is consequently the same opposition of meaning in *thesis*.

arson XVII. - OF. :- med L. *arsiō, -ōn-*, f. *ars-*, pp. stem of *ardēre* burn.

arsy-versy back-foremost, upside-down. XVI. f. ARSE + L. *versus* turned, with -Y[1] added to both elements to make a jingle.

art[1] XIII. - (O)F. :- L. *ars, art-*, f. base **ar-* put together, join, fit (cf. HARMONY). Hence **artful** XVII.

art[2] see BE.

artefact, arti- XIX. f. L. *arte*, abl. sg. of *ars* ART[1] + *factum*, n. pp. of *facere* make, DO[1]; cf. It. *artefatto*.

artery XIV. - L. *artēria* - Gr. *artēriā*, prob. f. base **ar-* raise, repr. in AORTA, ARSIS. So **arterial** XV. - F. †*artérial* (mod. *-el*).

artesian XIX. - F. *artésien* of Artois (name of an old French province), applied orig. to wells made there; see -IAN.

arthritis inflammation of a joint. XVI. - L. *arthritis* - Gr. *arthritis*, f. *árthron* joint (cf. L. *artus* limb, ARTICLE); see -ITIS. So **arthritic** XV. The comb. form **arthro-** of Gr. *árthron* is repr. in various scientific terms, as *arthropod*.

artichoke plant allied to the thistle, having edible parts XVI; *Jerusalem a.* species of sunflower with edible tuberous roots XVII. Earliest forms *archicokk, -choke, artechock*, etc. - northern It. *arti-, arciciocco* - OSp. *alcarchofa* (mod. *alcachofa*) - Arab. *al-ḵaršūfa*, i.e. AL-[2]. *ḵaršūf* artichoke.

article clause of the Creed, of a contract, etc. XIII; †item of business, etc. XV; detail, particular, material thing XVIII. - (O)F. - L. *articulus*, dim. of *artus* joint, f. base **ar-* join (cf. ARM[1], ART[1]). In gram. sense (XVI) repr. the use of L. *articulus* tr. Gr. *árthron* joint.

articulate adj. XVI. - L. *articulātus* jointed, pp. of *articulāre*, f. *articulus* ARTICLE; see -ATE[2]. So **articulate** vb. XVI. **articulation** XV. - F. - L.

artifice XVI. - (O)F. - L. *artificium*, f. *ars, art-* ART[1] + *fic-*, var. of *fac-* of *facere* make, DO[1]. So **artificial** XIV. - (O)F. or L. **artificer** XIV. - AN. *artificer* (cf. medL. *artificiārius*), prob. after OF. *artificien*.

artillery XIV. - (O)F. *artillerie*, f. OF. *artillier*, alt. (after *art*) of *atillier* equip, arm, prob. a by-form of *atirier*, f. *tire* order; see TIER, -ERY.

artisan XVI. - F. - It. *artigiano*, f. *arte* ART[1].

artist XVI. - (O)F. *artiste* - It. *artista*, f. *arte* ART[1]; see -IST. Hence **artistic** XVIII, **artistry** XIX.

artiste XIX. - F. (see prec.).

arum cuckoo-pint, *Arum maculatum*. XV (in form *aron* XV-XVIII). - L. *arum* - Gr. *áron*.

-ary suffix repr. L. *-ārius* 'pertaining to, connected with': formed on sbs., as *honōrārius* HONORARY; on adjs., as *prīmārius* PRIMARY; on advs., as *contrārius* CONTRARY. Many of these adjs. were used as sbs.: in the masc., as *adversārius* ADVERSARY; in the n., as *salārium* SALARY; and occas. in the fem., as *Calvāria*, see

CALVARY. Since L. *-ārius* and *-āris* were repr. in French by *-aire*, it came about that, when F. words in *-aire* were adopted in mod. Eng., they received the ending *-ary*, as *militaire* MILITARY; cf. -AR.

Aryan (arch.) Indo-European; Indo-Iranian. XIX. f. Skr. *ārya-* national name, subsequently 'noble'. See -AN.

as ME. reduced form (XII) of *ase* or *als*, which are divergent developments of *alse* :- OE. *alswā* (*ealswā*) ALSO.

as- assim. form of AD- before *s*.

asafoetida resinous gum with a strong smell. XIV. - medL., lit. 'stinking asa', i.e. *asa* (usu. derived from a Persian *azā* mastic, but this word is of doubtful authenticity), *fœtida*, fem. of *fœtidus* FETID.

asbestos †fabulous unquenchable stone XIV; fibrous mineral made into an incombustible fabric XVII. ME. *albeston* - OF. - medL. - Gr. *ásbeston*, acc. of *ásbestos*, f. A-[4] + *sbestós*, f. *sbennúnai* quench. The present form dates from XVII.

ascend XIV. - L. *ascendere*, f. AD- + *scandere* climb. So **ascendant** XIV. - (O)F. - prp. of L. *ascendere*. **ascendancy** XVIII.

ascension XIV. - (O)F. - L. *ascensiō*, *-ōn-*, f. *ascens-*, pp. stem of *ascendere*. Also **ascent** XVII. f. ASCEND, after the pair *descend*, *descent*.

ascertain make certain XV; learn, find out XVIII. - OF. *acertain-*, tonic stem of *acertener* (later *ass-*, *asc-*, and so in Eng.), f. *a-* AD- + *certain* CERTAIN.

ascetic XVII. - medL. *ascēticus* or Gr. *askētikós*, f. *askētḗs* monk, hermit, f. *askein* exercise; see -IC.

ascribe XV. - L. *ascrībere*, f. AD- + *scrībere* write. Preceded by †*ascrive* (XIV-XVII) - OF. *ascriv-*, stem of *ascrire* - L. *ascrībere*. So **ascription** XVI. - L.

aseptic XIX. f. A-[4] + SEPTIC.

ash[1] forest-tree of genus *Fraxinus*. OE. *æsć* = OS. *ask* (Du. *esch*), OHG. *ask* (G. *esche* is infl. by the adj. *eschen*), ON. *askr* :- Gmc. **askiz*. Rel. L. *ornus*, R. *yásen'*, W. *onnen*; Gr. *oxúē* beech.

ash[2] powdery residue of combustion. OE. *æsće*, *æxe* = MLG. *asche*, Du. *as*, OHG. *asca* (G. *asche*), ON. *aska*; cf. Goth. *azgō*. *Ash Wednesday* first day of Lent XIII; after ecclL. *dies cinerum* 'day of ashes'; cf. F. *jour* or *mercredi des cendres*, G. *aschermittwoch*.

ashamed OE. *āsćamod*, pp. of *āsćamian*, f. *ā-* A-[3] + *sćamian*, f. *sćamu* SHAME.

ashlar squared stone for building. XIV. ME. *as(s)heler* - OF. *aisselier*, f. L. *axis*, *assis* board, plank (whence F. *ais*).

ashore XVI. f. A-[1] + SHORE[1], on the model of the earlier *aland* (XII).

Asian XIV. - L. *Asiānus* - Gr. *Asiānós*; see -IAN. So **Asiatic** XVII.

aside XIV. ME. *on side*, *a side*, i.e. ON, A-[1], SIDE.

asinine XVII. - L. *asinīnus*, f. *asinus* ASS; see -INE[1].

-asis repr. L., Gr. *-āsis*, forming names of diseases, prop. nouns of state or process derived from verbs in Gr. *-áein*, *-ân*; as *elephantiasis*, *psoriasis*.

ask OE. *āscian*, *āxian* = OS. *ēscōn*, OHG. *eiscōn* (G. *heischen*) :- WGmc. **aiskōjan*. Rel. Skr. *iccháti*, OSl. *iskati*, Lith. *ieškóti* seek.

askance sideways, obliquely. XVI. Early forms *a scanche*, *a sconce* suggest a F. origin (but cf. It. *a*, *di*, and *per scancio* obliquely). Source remains unknown.

askari native soldier of E. Africa. XX. - Arab. *'askarī* soldier, f. *'askar* army.

askew XVI. f. A-[1] + SKEW.

aslant XIII. ME. *o slant(e)*, i.e. A-[1], SLANT (var. *on slent*, Sc. *asklent*, *esk-*; relations obscure).

asleep OE. *on slǣpe*, ME. *o slepe*, *aslepe*; see A[1], SLEEP.

asp[1] tree of the poplar family. OE. *æspe* = OHG. *aspa* (G. *espe* is from the adj. *espen*) :- Gmc. **aspōn*. Rel. Russ. *osina*, OPruss. *abse*, Lith. *ēpušė*. Superseded by ASPEN.

asp[2] small viper of N. Africa. XVI. - OF. *aspe* or its source L. *aspis* - Gr. *aspís*, *aspid-*. The L. form was formerly (XIV) current in Eng., as well as *aspic* (XVI) - F.; also †*aspide* - OF.

asparagus XVI. - L. - Gr. *aspáragos*. Various alt. or deriv. forms have been current: (i) *sparagus* (XVII); (ii) *(a)sperage*, *sparage* (XV); (iii) *sparrow-grass*, *sparagrass* (XVII).

aspect XIV. - L. *aspectus*, f. *aspect-*, pp. stem of *aspicere* look at, f. AD- + *specere* look.

aspen adj. of an asp-tree XIV; sb. aspen tree XVI. f. ASP[1] + -EN[1]. The sb. arose in such collocations as *aspen leaf*.

asperity XV. - L. *asperitās*, *-tāt-*, f. *asper* rough; see -ITY.

asperse besprinkle XV; calumniate XVII. f. *aspers-*, pp. stem of L. *aspergere*, f. AD- + *spargere* sprinkle (cf. SPARSE). So **aspersion** XVI.

asphalt XIV. Early forms *aspalt(oun)*, ult. - late L. *asphalton*, *-um* - Gr. *ásphalton*, *-os*; later *asphalt(e)* reproduces the F. *asphalte*.

asphodel liliaceous plant. XVI. - L. *asphodelus* - Gr. *asphódelos*. See DAFFODIL.

asphyxia stoppage of the pulse, (hence) suffocation. XVIII. - modL. - Gr. *asphuxíā*, f. A-[4] + *sphúxis* pulse, f. *sphúzein* beat, throb. Hence **asphyxiate** (-ATE[3]), **-ation** XIX.

aspic[1] savoury meat jelly. XVIII. - F., a use of *aspic* serpent (see ASP[2]), due to comparison of the various colours of the jelly with those of the serpent (F. *sauce* or *ragoût à l'aspic*).

aspic[2] see ASP[2].

aspidistra XIX. - modL., f. Gr. *aspís*, *aspid-* shield (with ref. to the shape of the leaves).

aspire have a desire for something above one XV; rise up, mount XVI. - (O)F. *aspirer* or L. *aspīrāre* have an ambition, etc., f. AD- + *spīrāre* breathe. So **aspirant** XVIII. - F. or L. **aspirate** adj. XVII; sb. XVIII. - pp. of L. *aspīrāre*. **aspirate** vb. XVIII. **aspiration** XIV. - (O)F. - L.

aspirin acetylsalicylic acid, an analgesic and febrifuge. XIX. - G., shortened from *Acetylirte Spirsäure* 'acetylated spiraeic acid' + -IN.

asquint (arch.) *to look* to one side XIII; obliquely through a defect in the eyes, cross-eyed XIV; with a sidelong or furtive glance XV. perh. f. A-[1] + a LG. or Du. form now repr. by Du. *schuinte* obliquity, slant, f. *schuin* oblique = LG. *schüns*. Aphetic SQUINT.

ass donkey OE.; stupid person XV. OE. *assa* - OCelt. **as(s)in* (W. *asyn*) - L. *asinus*. Gmc. **asiluz* (- L. *asinus* or *asellus*) is repr. by OE. *e(o)sol*, OS., OHG. *esil* (Du. *ezel* EASEL, G. *esel*), Goth. *asilus*.

assail XIII. - OF. *asalir* (mod. *assaillir*) :- popL. *assalīre* f. AS- + *salīre* leap. Hence **assailant** XVI, after F. *assaillant*.

assassin (hist., in pl.) Muslim fanatic engaged to murder Christians; one who kills treacherously. XVII. - F. *assassin* or medL. *assassīnus* - Arab. *ḥaššīšī* HASHISH-eater. Hence **assassinate** (see -ATE[3]), **-ation** XVII.

assault sb. XIII. ME. *as(s)aut* (later with *l* as in *fault*) - OF. *asaut* (mod. *assaut*) :- Rom. **assaltus*, f. popL. *assalīre* ASSAIL. So **assault** vb. XV. - OF. *assauter* :- Rom. **assaltare*, f. AS- + *saltāre*, frequent. of *salīre* leap.

assay trial (gen. and spec., now only of metals). XIV. - OF. *assai*, var. of *essai* ESSAY. So **assay** vb. XIV. - OF. *assaier*.

assegai, assagai spear used by African (now esp. S. African) tribes. XVII. - Pg. *azagaia* - Arab. *az-zaġāya*, i.e. AL-[2], *zaġāya* Berber word for 'spear'.

assemble XIII. - (O)F. *assembler* :- Rom. **assimulāre*, f. AS- + L. *simul* together (cf. SIMILAR). So **assembly** XIV. - OF. *assemblée*, sb. use of fem. pp., with ending assim. to -Y[5].

assent vb. XIII. - OF. *assentir* (AN. *assenter*) :- L. *assentīre*, f. AS- + *sentīre* feel, think. So **assent** sb. XIII.

assert XVII. f. *assert-*, pp. stem of L. *asserere*, f. AS- + *serere* join. So **assertion** XV. - F. or L. **assertive** XVII (the corr. adv. is XV). - F. *assertif*.

assess settle the amount of; rate for taxation. XV. - OF. *assesser* - *assess-*, pp. stem of L. *assidēre* sit by, etc. (cf. ASSIDUOUS), in medL. levy, tax, f. AS- + *sedēre* SIT. Hence **assessment** XVI. So **assessor** XIV. - OF. *assessour* (mod. *-eur*) - L. *assessor*.

assets XVI. - legal AN. *assets*, (O)F. *assez* :- Rom. **assatis*, f. AD- + L. *satis* enough (cf. SATISFACTION); orig. in legal phr. *aver asetz* have sufficient (sc. to meet claims).

asseveration XVI. - L. *asseverātiō*, *-ōn-*, f. *asseverāre*, f. AS- + *sevērus* grave, SEVERE; see -ATION. So **asseverate** (see -ATE[3]) XVIII.

assibilate make SIBILANT. XIX. f. pp. of L. *assībilāre*; see AS-, -ATE[3].

assiduous XVI. f. L. *assiduus*, f. *assidēre*, attend or apply oneself to; see ASSESS, -OUS. So **assiduity** XV.

assign[1] vb. XIV. - OF. *as(s)ignier* (mod. *assigner*) :- L. *assignāre*, f. AS- + *signāre* SIGN. So **assignation** XV. **assignee** ASSIGN[2] XIV. - (O)F. *assigné*, pp. of *assigner*, used sb. **assignment** XIX. - OF. *assignement* - medL. *assignāmentum*.

assign[2] one to whom a property or right is assigned. XIV. - AN., (O)F. *assigné*; see ASSIGNEE, from which it is differentiated by the muted final syll. (cf. ALLY[1], ASTRAY, COSTIVE, DEFILE[2], TAIL[2], TROVE).

assimilate make like; absorb and incorporate. XV. f. pp. stem of L. *assimilāre*, f. AS- + *similis* SIMILAR; see -ATE[3]. So **assimilation** XV. **assimilative** XIV. - F. or L.

assist †give help to XV; help; †stand near XVI; be present *at* XVII. - F. *assister* - L. *assistere*, f. AS- + *sistere* take one's stand. So **assistance** XIV. - F. - medL. *assistentia*. **assistant** XV. - F. - medL. *assistēns*, *-ent-*, prp. of *assistere*.

assize XIII. - OF. *assise*, sb. use of fem. of *assis*, pp. of *asseoir* sit, settle, assess :- popL. **assedēre* for *assidēre* (see ASSESS). Cf. SIZE[1].

associate pp. joined in function or status XIV; sb. companion, colleague XVI. - L. *associātus*, pp. of *associāre*, f. AS- + *socius* sharing, allied (cf. SOCIAL); see -ATE[2]. So **associate** vb. XV (see -ATE[3]). **association** XVI. - F. or medL.

assoil (arch.) absolve XIII; acquit XIV. - AN. *as(s)oilier*, *-ir*, f. OF. *as(s)oil-* tonic stem of *asoldre* (mod. *absoudre*) :- L. *absolvere* ABSOLVE.

assonance XVIII. - F., f. L. *assonāre* (of Echo) answer to, f. AS- + *sonāre* SOUND[3].

assort arrange in sorts. XV (rare before late XVIII, when it was prob. readopted). - OF. *assorter*, mod. *assortir*, f. *a-* AD- + *sorte* SORT. So **assortment** XVII; after F. *assortiment*.

assuage XIV. - OF. *asso(u)agier* :- Rom. **assuāviāre*, f. AS- + L. *suāvis* SWEET.

assume take to or upon oneself XV; claim, take for granted XVI. - L. *assūmere*, f. AS- + *sūmere* take.

assumption (feast of) the reception of the Virgin Mary into Heaven XIII; taking to or for oneself, taking for granted, postulate XVII. - OF. *asompsion* (mod. *assomption*) or L. *assumptiō*, *-ōn-*, f. *assūmere*; see prec., -TION. So **assumptive** XVII.

assure XIV. - OF. *asseürer* (mod. *assurer*) :- Rom. **assēcūrāre*, f. AS- + *sēcūrus* SECURE. So **assurance** XIV.

aster genus of plants with radiated flowers. XVIII. - modL. use of L. *astēr* - Gr. *astḗr* STAR.

-aster repr. L. *-āster* (whence F. *-âtre*), suffix of sbs. and adjs. expressing incomplete resemblance, and hence gen. of pejorative force; e.g. *philosophaster* petty philosopher, *oleaster* wild olive. The best-known comp. in Eng. is POETASTER, on which was modelled *criticaster*.

asterisk XVII. - late L. *asteriscus* - Gr. *asterískos*, dim. of *astḗr* STAR.

astern in, at, or towards the stern. XVII. f. A-[1] + STERN[2], after AHEAD.

asteroid XIX. - Gr. *asteroeidḗs* star-like, f. *astḗr* STAR; see -OID.

asthma XIV. - Gr. *ásthma*, *-mat-*. So **asthmatic** XVI.

astigmatism defect in the eye preventing exact focusing. XIX. f. A-[4] + Gr. *stigmat-* point (see STIGMA) + -ISM. So **astigmatic** XIX.

astir stirring, up and about. XIX. Anglicization of Sc. *asteer*, f. ON, A-[1] + Sc. form of STIR.

astonish †dumbfound, stun XV; amaze XVII. First in (Sc.) pp. *astonist*, prob. extension, with -ISH[2], of pp. of †*astonie*, †*astony* (XIV-XVII), obscure var. of †*astone*, the pp. of which is the source of ASTOUND.

astound †shock, stun; amaze. XVII. prob. f. pp. †*astound*, †*astouned*, earlier †*astoned*, †*astuned* (XIII), f. AN. **astoné*, **astuné*, for OF. *estoné*, pp. of *estoner* STUN.

astrakhan XVIII. f. name of a Russian province north of the Caspian Sea.

astral XVII. - late L. *astrālis*, f. *astrum* - Gr. *ástron* STAR; see -AL[1].

astray XIII. ME. *o strai, astrai(e)* - AN. **astraié*, OF. *estraié*, pp. of *estraier*, f. *estree* road :- late L. *strāta* STREET. Aphetic STRAY. For the loss of *-é* cf. ASSIGN[2].

astride XVII. f. A-[1] + STRIDE.

astringent causing contraction of bodily tissues XVI; severe, austere XIX. - F. *astringent* or L. *astringēns, -ent-*, f. *astringere*, f. AD- + *stringere* bind, draw tight (see STRICTURE).

astro- repr. comb. form of Gr. *ástron* STAR.

astrolabe instrument used for taking altitudes and solving astronomical problems. XIV. - OF. *astrelabe* - medL. *astrolabium* - Gr. *astrólabon*, sb. use of n. of adj. *astrólabos* 'star-taking', f. *ástron* STAR + **lab-*, base of *lambánein* take.

astrology XIV. - (O)F. *astrologie* - L. *astrologia* - Gr. *astrologiā*, f. *astrológos* astronomer, f. *ástron* STAR; see -LOGY. So **astrologer** XIV. f. (O)F. *astrologue*, based on L. *astrologus* - Gr. *astrológos*; see -LOGUE (-LOGER). **astrological** XVI. f. F. *-ique* or late L. *-icus* - Gr. *-ikós*.

astronomy XIII. - (O)F. *astronomie* - L. *astronomia* - Gr. *astronomiā*, f. *astronómos*, f. *astronomeîn* observe the stars, f. *ástron* STAR; see -NOMY. So **astronomer** XIV. ME. *astronom(i)er*, f. *astronomy*; earlier *-ien* - OF. **astronomical** XVI. f. F. *-ique* or L. *-icus* - Gr. *-ikós*.

astute XVII. - F. †*astut* or L. *astūtus*, f. *astus* craft, cunning.

asunder ME. *asunder, o sunder*, OE. *on sundran, -um*, i.e. ON, A-[1] + *sundor*; see SUNDER.

aswoon (arch.) in a swoon. XIV. ME. *aswoune*, alt. of *iswouen*, OE. *ġeswōgen*; see SWOON.

asylum sanctuary, place of refuge. XV. - L. *asȳlum* - Gr. *ásūlon*, sb. use of n. of *ásūlos* inviolable, f. A-[4] + *sûlē, sûlon* right of seizure.

asymptote (geom.) line which approaches nearer and nearer to a curve without meeting it. XVII. - modL. *asymptōta* (sc. *līnea* line) - Gr. *asúmptōtos*, sb. use (sc. *grammḗ* line) of adj. 'not falling together', f. A-[4] + *sun-* SYN- + *ptōtós* apt to fall.

asyndeton (gram.) construction in which a conjunctive element is omitted. XVI. - modL. - Gr. *asúndeton*, n. of *asúndetos* unconnected, f. A-[4] + *súndetos*, f. *sun-* SYN- + *dein* bind.

at OE. *æt* = OS. *at*, OHG. *az*, ON., Goth. *at*; CGmc. prep. and verbal prefix denoting position and motion towards, further rel. to L. (and Osco-Umbrian) *ad* to, at, AD-, OIr. *ad-*. Lost in s.w. Eng. dial., as in modDu. and G., and repl. by *to*; in Scand., on the other hand, *to* was lost and repl by *at* (e.g. with the infin.; cf. ADO).

at- assim. form of AD- before *t*.

atavism resemblance to remote ancestors rather than parents. XIX. - F. *atavisme*, f. L. *atavus* great-grandfather's grandfather, f. *avus* grandfather; see -ISM. Hence **atavistic** XIX.

ataxy †disorderliness; (path.) functional irregularity. XVII. - modL. *ataxia* (also used) - Gr. *ataxiā*, f. A-[4] + *táxis* order; see -Y[3].

-ate[1] repr. F. *-at* = Sp. -ADO, It. *-ato* - L. *-ātus*, comp. suffix orig. f. stems of verbs in *-āre* + *-tus* (cf. *juventus* YOUTH), but later added directly to sbs. to form abstract sbs. (i) denoting action or state, as *plōrātus* weeping, *consulātus* consulship; (ii) in coll. sense, as *equitātus* cavalry, *senātus* SENATE; (iii) in concr. sense, as *magistrātus* MAGISTRATE; corr. to OE. *-oð, -að* (as in *fiscoð* fishing), OHG. *-ōd*, Goth. *-ōþu-*.

-ate[2] suffix of pps., ppl. adjs., and sbs., repr. (partly through F. *-at, -ate*) L. *-ātus, -āta, -ātum*, ending of the pps. of verbs in *-āre*, f. *-ā-* + *-tus*, gen. ppl. suffix, as in *doctus, rēctus, audītus*, pps. of *docēre, regere, audīre*. There are many adjs. of this origin, as *desperate, separate* **a.** Added to sbs. with the sense 'provided with', it produced many adjs., as *dentātus* toothed, *foliātus* leaved, *litterātus* LITERATE; on this model were made numerous adjs. in nat. hist., etc., as *angustifoliate* narrow-leaved, *lunulate* crescent-shaped. **b.** L. pps. were used as sbs., in all three genders, as (i) *legātus* LEGATE, (medL.) *prælātus* PRELATE, *curātus* CURATE; (ii) medL. *carucāta* CARUCATE, *virgāta* VIRGATE, and numerous sbs. in the Rom. langs. (repr. by F. *-ée*, Sp. *-ada*, It. *-ata*; cf. -ADE); (iii) L. *mandātum* MANDATE, modL. *præcipitātum* PRECIPITATE. In chem. extended to the nomenclature of salts of acids denominated by adjs. in -IC, as NITRATE, SULPHATE.

-ate[3] suffix of verbs formed on pp. stems (*-āt-*) of L. verbs in *-āre*, orig. on the basis of existing pp. forms in -ATE[2], which were at first often used concurrently with the infs. as their pps., e.g. inf. CONSECRATE, pp. †*consecrate* (later *consecrated*); it consequently became possible to form an Eng. verb in *-ate* on any L. verb in *-āre*. Many F. verbs in *-er* (:- L. *-āre*) have been anglicized by the addition of this suffix to their stems, e.g. FELICITATE.

atheism XVI. - Fr. *athéisme*, f. Gr. *átheos*, f. A-[4] + *theós* god; see -ISM. So **atheist** XVI. - F. *athéiste* or It. *ateista*; hence **atheistic** XVII, **-istical** XVI.

athirst (arch.) thirsting. OE. *ofðyrst*, short form of *ofðyrsted*, pp. of **ofðyrstan* suffer thirst, f. *of-* A-[2] + *þyrstan* THIRST.

athlete XVIII (once XV). - L. *āthlēta* - Gr. *athlētḗs*, f. *athleîn* contend for a prize. So **athletic** XVII. - F. *athlétique* or L. *āthlēticus* - Gr. *athlētikós*; hence **athletics** XVIII, **athletical** XVI.

athwart across. XV (first in Sc.). f. A-[1] + THWART[1], prob. after ON. *um þvert* 'over in a transverse direction'.

-atic repr. F. *-atique* - L. *-āticus*, orig. f. pp. stems in *-āt-* (see -ATE[3]) + *-icus* -IC, as *errāticus* ERRATIC, later extended to sbs., e.g. *aquāticus* AQUATIC. The neuter of such adjs. was used as sb., e.g. VIATICUM, whence the extended use of the suffix in Rom. repr. by -AGE. In AROMATIC, AXIOMATIC, PROBLEMATIC, and the like, *-atic* repr. Gr. *-atikós*, f. n. stems in *-at-*.

-atile repr. F. *-atile* - L. *-ātilis*, in formation (see -ILE) and sense similar to -ATIC, e.g. *volātilis* VOLATILE, (with sb.) *fluviātilis*, f. *fluvius*.

atilt tilted; at the tilt (in jousting). XVI. f. A-[1] + TILT[1].

-ation ME. *-acio(u)n* - OF. (mod. *-ation*) - L. *-ātiō, -ātiōn-*, the form resulting from the addition of *-tiōn-* -TION to verb-stems in *-ā-*. The great majority of Eng. words in *-ation* have corr. vbs. in -ATE[3], as *creation, moderation, saturation*, beside *create, moderate, saturate*; some have no such corr. vb., as *capitation, constellation, duration*; others are formed directly on vbs. in -IZE, as *civilization, organization*. A large number have corr. vbs. of other forms, as *apply* and *application, publish* and *publication, prove* and *probation*. Others have the appearance of being formed on Eng. vbs., as *alteration, causation, formation*; hence the practice (from XVI) of adding the suffix to miscellaneous vbs., as *botheration, flirtation, starvation*.

-ative - F. *-atif, -ative* - L. *-ātīvus, -ātīva*, formed by the addition of *-īvus* -IVE to pp. stems in *-āt-*, as *dēmonstrātīvus* DEMONSTRATIVE; the number of such adjs. was increased in late and medL., and they were the models for many more in the Rom. langs. Cases like *represent, representative* afforded a formal analogy for *talk, talkative* (XV). In medL. *quālitātīvus, quantitātīvus* were formed on the sbs. *quālitās, quantitās*; hence *authoritative*, f. *authority*.

Atlantic XV. - L. *Atlanticus* - Gr. *Atlantikós*, f. *Átlās, Atlant-* name of (i) the Titan who was supposed to hold up the pillars of the universe, and (ii) the mountain in Libya which was held to support the heavens, whence the application of the adj. to the ocean west of Africa.

atlas supporter, mainstay XVI; volume of maps XVII. The Titan Atlas (prec.) was often figured with the terrestrial globe on his shoulders, whence the application of the name to a collection of maps (XVII).

atmosphere XVII. - modL. *atmosphæra*, f. Gr. *atmós* vapour + *sphaîra* SPHERE. Hence **atmospheric** XVIII, **-ical** XVII

atoll ring-shaped coral reef enclosing a lagoon. XIX (in XVII as *atollon*). - Maldive *atoḷu*.

atom †body so small as to be incapable of division XVI; supposed ultimate particle of matter XVII; hence in mod. physics and chem. XIX. - (O)F. *atome* - L. *atomus* - Gr. *átomos*, sb. use of adj. 'indivisible', f. A-[4] + **tom-* (cf. -TOMY). Hence **atomic** XVII. - modL.

atomy[1] (arch.) skeleton (lit. and fig.). XVI. Aphetic of ANATOMY.

atomy[2] (arch.) atom, tiny being. XVI. prob. f. *atomī*, pl. of L. *atomus* ATOM, but assoc. with prec.

atone †reconcile, appease XVI (once XIV be reconciled); make reconcilement, amends XVII. Back-formation from **atonement** (XVI), f. phr. *at one* in harmony (XIII) + -MENT, after medL. *adūnāmentum* (VIII), f. *adūnāre* unite, and earlier *onement*, as used in *make an onement* be reconciled, *set at onement* reconcile.

-ator repr. L. *-ātor*, suffix combining -TOR with vb.-stems in *-ā-* and forming agent-nouns, e.g. *creātor, dictātor, spectātor*. The earliest of such sbs. were first adopted in OF. form with *-atour*. From XVI modL. formations such as *denominator* and *numerator* appear. From XVII the suffix began to be used for names of instruments, e.g. *perambulator*, and in anat., e.g. *levator*; but such formations were not common till early XIX, since when they have become fairly numerous as names of implements and machines, e.g. *detonator, elevator, escalator, generator, refrigerator, ventilator*.

atrabilious melancholy, ill-tempered. XVII. f. L. *ātra bīlis* black BILE, tr. Gr. *melagkholíā* MELANCHOLY; see -IOUS.

atrium central court of Roman house XVII; (anat.) chamber of an organ of the body XIX. - L. *ātrium*.

atrocious XVII. f. L. *atrōx, atrōc-* terrible, fierce, etc., f. *āter* black + *oc-*, stem of *oculus* EYE; see -IOUS and cf. F. *atroce*. So **atrocity** XVI. - (O)F. or L.

atrophy wasting away of the body. XVII. - late L. *atrophia* - Gr. *atrophíā*, f. *átrophos* ill-nourished, f. A-[4] + *tréphein* nourish. So **atrophied** XVI. - F. *atrophié*.

atropine alkaloid poison from deadly nightshade. XIX. f. modL. *atropa* deadly nightshade, fem. f. Gr. *Átropos* ('Inflexible') name of one of the Fates, f. A-[4] + *trópos* turn; see TROPE, -INE[5].

attach seize, arrest XIV; fasten, join XV. - OF. *atachier* (mod. *attacher*), alt., by prefix-substitution, of *estachier* fasten, fix, f. Gmc. **stak-* STAKE[1]. So **attachment** XIV.

attaché one attached to the suite of an ambassador. XIX. - F., pp. of *attacher* ATTACH.

attack vb. XVI. - F. *attaquer* - It. *attaccare* as in *attaccare battaglia* join battle f. Gmc. **stak-* (see ATTACH). Hence, or - F. *attaque* (- It. *attacco*) **attack** sb. XVII.

attain †strike; reach (*to*). XIV. - OF. *atain-, atein-*, stem of *ataindre, -eindre* (mod. *atteindre*) :- L. *attingere* touch on, reach, f. AT- + *tangere* touch. Hence **attainment** XIV.

attainder consequences of sentence of death or outlawry. XV. - AN. *attainder, atteinder*, sb. use of infin., OF. *ataindre* ATTAIN; see -ER[6].

attaint †convict; subject to attainder XIV; (arch.) affect, infect XVI. f. †*attaint* pp. - OF. *ataint, ateint*, pp. of *ataindre* ATTAIN; infl. later in meaning by TAINT. Hence **attaint** sb. XIV.

attar fragrant essence (of roses). XVIII. - Pers. *'iṭr-* Arab., f. *'aṭira* be fragrant.

attempt vb. XIV. - OF. *attempter*, latinized form of *attenter* (also mod.) - L. *attemptāre*, f. AT- + *temptāre* TEMPT. Hence **attempt** sb. XVI.

attend direct the mental or physical faculties, apply oneself to XIII; take care of, wait upon XV; †wait for, expect; be present at XVII. - OF. *atendre* (mod. *attendre* wait for) :- L. *attendere*, f. AT- + *tendere* stretch, TEND[2]. So **attendance** XIV. - OF. *atendance*. **attendant** adj. XIV; sb. XVI. - OF. *atendant*. **attention** XIV (rare before XVI). - L. *attentiō, -ōn-*; cf. F. *attention* (XVI). **attentive** XIV (Sc.). - OF. *atentif*.

attenuate XVI. f. pp. stem of L. *attenuāre*, f AT- + *tenuāre* f. *tenuis* THIN; see -ATE[3].

attest XVI. - F. *attester* - L. *attestārī*, f. AT- + *testārī* witness (cf. TESTAMENT). So **attestation** XV.

attic (archit.) small order placed above a taller one XVII; (room in) the top storey of a building XVIII. spec. use of next.

Attic of Attica, Athenian. XVI. - L. *Atticus* - Gr. *Attikós*.

attire †put in order, equip XIII; dress XIV. - OF. *atir(i)er* arrange, etc., f. phr. OF. *a tire* in order. Aphetic TIRE². Hence **attire** sb. XIII.

attitude †disposition of a figure in statuary or painting XVII; posture XVIII. - F. - It. *attitudine* :- late L. *aptitūdō, -tūdin-* APTITUDE; see -TUDE.

attorney¹ legal agent. XIV. - OF. *atorné*, sb. use of pp. of *atorner* assign, appoint, f. *a-* AD- + *torner* TURN.

attorney² legal agency (in *letter, power of attorney*). XV. - OF. *atornée*, sb. use of fem. pp. of *atorner* (see prec.).

attract XV. f. L. *attract-*, pp. stem of *attrahere*, f. AT- + *trahere* draw (cf. TRACT¹). So **attraction** XV. - F. or L. **attractive** XIV. - F. - late L.

attribute sb. XV. - (O)F. *attribut* or L. *attribūtum*, sb. use of n. pp. of *attribuere*, f. AT- + *tribuere* allot (cf. TRIBUTE). So **attribute** vb. XVI. f. the pp. stem. **attribution** XV. - (O)F. - L. **attributive** XVII. - F.

attrition (theol.) imperfect contrition XIV; rubbing away XV. - late L. *attrītiō, -ōn-*, f. *attrīt-*, pp. stem of *atterere*, f. AT- + *terere* rub; see TRITE, -ITION.

aubergine XVIII. - F. - Cat. *alberginia* - Arab. *al-bāḏinjān*, i.e. AL-², Pers. *bādingān*.

auburn (orig.) yellowish-white, (now) golden-brown. XV. - OF. *alborne, auborne* :- medL. *alburnus*, f. L. *albus* white.

auction sb. XVI. - L. *auctiō, -ōn-*, f. *auct-*, pp. stem of *augēre* increase (cf. AUGMENT); see -TION. Hence **auction** vb. XIX. **auctioneer** XVIII; see -EER.

audacious XVI. f. L. *audāx, audāc-*, f. *audēre* dare; see -IOUS. So **audacity** XV. f. medL. *audācitās;* see -ITY.

audible XVI. - late L. *audībilis*, f. *audīre* hear; see -IBLE. So **audience** XIV. - (O)F. **audit** sb. XV. - L. *audītus* hearing, f. *audīt-*, pp. stem of *audīre*. Hence **audit** vb. XV. **audition** XVI. - L. **auditor** XIV. - AN. *auditour*, (O)F. *auditeur* - L. *audītor, -ōr-*. **auditorium** XVIII, earlier **auditory** XIV. - L.

auger carpenter's boring-tool. OE. *nafogār*, f. *nafu* NAVE¹ + *gār* borer, etc. (cf. GORE²); corr. to OS. *nabugēr*, ON. *nafarr*. Forms showing loss of initial *n* (cf. ADDER) occur XV.

aught (arch.) anything. OE. *āwiht, āuht, āht*, corr. to OS. *ēowiht*, OHG. *eo-, iewiht*; WGmc. comp. of AY and WIGHT. Cf. NAUGHT.

augment sb. XV. - (O)F. *augment* or late L. *augmentum*, f. *augēre* increase; see -MENT. So **augment** vb. XIV. - (O)F. *augmenter* or late L. *augmentāre*. **augmentation** XIV. **augmentative** XVI.

augur Roman religious official with duty of foretelling future events. XIV. - L., f. base of *augēre* (see prec.). Hence **augur** vb. XVI (Sc.), after L. *augurārī*. So **augury** XIV. - OF. *augurie* or L. *augurium*; see -Y⁴.

august of stately dignity. XVII. - (O)F. *auguste* or L. *augustus*, f. base of *augēre* (see AUGMENT).

August eighth month of the year. OE. - L. *Augustus* (see prec.); so named after the first Roman emperor, *Augustus* Cæsar.

auk XVII. - ON. *álka*.

aunt XIII. - AN. *aunte*, OF. *ante* (mod. *tante*) :- L. *amita*. Hence **auntie, -y** XVIII; see -Y⁶.

aura subtle emanation. XVIII. - L. - Gr. *aúrā* breath, breeze.

aural XIX. f. L. *auris* EAR¹ + -AL¹.

aureate golden (lit. and fig.). XV. - late L. *aureātus*, f. *aureus*, f. *aurum* gold; see -ATE².

aureola, -ole saint's crown of glory XIII; halo XVIII. - (O)F. *auréole* or L. *aureola*, sb. use (sc. *corōna* crown) of adj. *aureolus* golden, f. *aurum* gold.

auricle cavity of the heart XV; external ear, lobe-shaped process XVII. - L. *auricula*, dim. of *auris* EAR. So **auricular** XV (see -AR).

aurochs extinct wild ox XVIII; European bison XIX. - G., early var. of *auerochs* (OHG. *ūrohso*, f. *ūr* = OE. *ūr*, of unkn. orig. + *ohso* OX).

aurora dawn XIV; luminous atmospheric phenomenon near the poles, 'northern lights' XVIII; also **aurora borealis** (see BOREAL), so named by Pierre Gassendi in 1621. - L. *aurōra* (see EAST).

auscultation listening (spec. med.) XVII. - L. *auscultātiō, -ōn-*, f. *auscultāre* listen to; see -ATION.

auspice usu. pl. divination by birds XVI; propitious token, favourable influence XVII. - F. *auspice* or L. *auspicium*, f. *avis* bird + **spek-* look (cf. SPY). Hence **auspicious** XVII.

austere XIV. - (O)F. *austère* - L. *austērus* - Gr. *austērós* harsh, severe. So **austerity** XIV.

autarchy absolute sovereignty. XVII. - Gr. *autarkhíā*, f. *aútarkhos*, f. *autós* AUTO- + *árkhein* rule; see -Y³.

autarky self-sufficiency. XVII. - Gr. *autárkeia*, f. *autárkēs*, f. *autós* AUTO- + *arkeîn* suffice; see -Y³.

authentic †authoritative XIV; entitled to acceptance or belief as being reliable; actual, not imaginary XV; genuine, not counterfeit XVIII. ME. *au(c)tentik* - OF. *autentique* - late L. *authenticus* - Gr. *authentikós*; see -IC.

author originator, inventor; composer of a book, etc. XIV. ME. *au(c)tour* - AN. *au(c)tour*, OF. *autor* (mod. *auteur*) - L. *auctor, -ōr-*, f. *auct-*, *augēre* increase (cf. AUGMENT). Hence **authoress** XV. So **authority** XIII. ME. *autorite* (hence **authoritative** XVII). **authorize** XIV.

auto- repr. comb. form of Gr. *autós* self.

autobiography XIX. f. prec. + BIOGRAPHY.

autochthon one sprung from the soil XVII; (pl.) original inhabitants XVIII. - Gr. *autókhthōn*, f. AUTO- + *khthṓn* earth. Hence **autochthonous** XIX.

autocrat XIX. - F. *autocrate* (a word of the French Revolution) - Gr. *autokratḗs*, f. *autós* AUTO- + *krátos* power. So **autocracy** XVII. - Gr. *autokráteia*. **autocratic** XIX.

auto-da-fé sentence of the Inquisition, and (esp.) its execution. XVIII. - Pg., 'act (i.e. judicial sentence) of the faith'.

autograph author's own manuscript XVII; signature XVIII. - F. *autographe* or L. *autographum* - Gr. *autógraphon*; see AUTO-, -GRAPH. Hence vb. XIX.

automaton XVII. - L. *automaton, -um* - Gr.

autómaton, f. *autós* AUTO- + **men-* (see MIND). So **automatic** XVIII, **automation** XX.

automobile adj.; self-propelling; sb. (chiefly U.S.) motor-car. XIX. - F.; see AUTO-, MOBILE.

autonomy XVII. - Gr. *autonomíā*, f. *autós* AUTO- + *nómos* (see -NOMY). Hence **autonomous** XIX.

autopsy XVII. - F. *autopsie* or modL. *autopsia* - Gr. *autopsíā* seeing with one's own eyes; see AUTO-, OPTIC, -Y[3].

autumn XIV (rare before XVI). - OF. *autompne* (mod. *automne*), later directly - L. *autumnus*. So **autumnal** XVI. - L. *autumnālis*.

auxiliary XVII. - L. *auxiliārius*, f. *auxilium* help; see -ARY.

avail be of use or advantage. XIII. Native formation on †*vail* vb. (of equal date). - OF. *valoir* :- L. *valēre* be strong or worth; prob. after pairs like *amount*, *mount*. So **avail** sb. XV; cf. AN. *avail*. Hence **available** XV.

avalanche XVIII. - F., alt., by blending with *avaler* descend, of Alpine F. dial. *lavanche*, of unkn. orig.

avarice XIII. - (O)F. - L. *avāritia*, f. *avārus* greedy. So **avaricious** XIV. - (O)F. *avaricieux*.

avast (naut.) stop! XVII. - Du. *hou' vast*, *houd vast* hold fast; first syll. assim. to A-[1].

avenge XIV. f. A-[1] + OF. *vengier* :- L. *vindicāre* VINDICATE.

avenue XVII. - F. *avenue*, sb. use of fem. pp. of *avenir* :- L. *advenīre* approach, f. AD- + *venīre* COME.

aver †assert the truth of XIV; state positively XVI. - (O)F. *avérer* - medL. *adverāre*, f. L. AD- + *vērus* true (cf. VERY). So **averment** XV.

average †charge over and above the shipment freight XV; loss arising from damage at sea, equitable distribution of such loss XVI; arithmetical mean XVIII. Earlier forms *averays*, *averi(d)ge* - F. *avarie* (pl. *-ies*) damage to ship or cargo - It. *avaria* - Arab. *'awārīya* damaged goods.

averse opposed, disinclined. XVI. - L. *āversus*, pp. of *āvertere*, f. *ā-* AB- + *vertere* turn. So **aversion** XVI. - F. or L. **avert** turn away XV. (Partly through F.) - L. *āvertere*.

aviary XVI. - L. *aviārium*, f. *avis* bird; see -ARY.

aviation XIX. - F., irreg. f. L. *avis* bird + -ATION. So **aviator** XIX. - F. *aviateur*.

avid XVIII. - F. *avide* or L. *avidus*, f. *avēre* long for; see -ID[1]. So **avidity** XV. - F. or L.

avocado XVII (*avogato*). - Sp. *avocado* advocate substituted for Aztec *ahuacatl*, more closely repr. by Sp. *aguacate*; further corrupted, through *avigato*, to *alligator* (*pear*) XVIII.

avocation †distraction from an occupation; task to which one is called away, minor occupation XVII; transf. to ordinary occupation XVIII. - L. *āvocātiō*, *-ōn-*, f. *āvocāre*, f. *ā-* AB- + *vocāre* call.

avocet XVIII. - F. *avocette* - It. *avosetta*, of unkn. orig.

avoid †empty; †withdraw, retire; make void; leave alone, evade. XIV. - AN. *avoider* = (with prefix-substitution) OF. *esvuidier* (mod. *évider* hollow out, cut away), f. *es-* (:- EX-[1]) + *vuide* empty, VOID. Hence **avoidance** XIV.

avoirdupois †merchandise sold by weight XIV; system of weights based on the 16 oz. pound XV. ME. *aver-*, *avoirdepeis* - OF. *aveir de peis* 'goods of weight', i.e. *aveir*, *avoir* (whence ME. *aver*) possession (:- L. *habēre* have), *de* of, *peis* weight (see POISE). *du* for *de* XVII.

avow XIII. - (O)F. *avouer* acknowledge as one's own - L. *advocāre* (see ADVOCATE). Hence **avowal** XVIII; see -AL[2].

avulsion forcible separation or removal. XVII. - L. *āvulsiō*, *-ōn-*, f. *āvuls-* pp. stem of *āvellere*, f. *ā-* AB- + *vellere* pluck; see -SION.

avuncular XIX. f. L. *avunculus* UNCLE; see -AR.

await †watch for XIII; wait for XIV. - AN. *awaitier* (= OF. *ag(u)aitier*), f. *a-* AD- + *waitier* WAIT.

awake be roused from sleep OE.; rouse from sleep XIII. OE. str. pt. *onwōc*, *āwōc*; wk. pt. *āwacode*; see A-[3], WAKE[2]. Hence **awake** adj. XIII; clipped form of str. pp. *awaken*. So **awaken** cease to sleep OE.; rouse from sleep XVI. OE. *onwæcnan*, *āwæcnan*, *āwæcnian*; see WAKEN.

award †decide, determine XIV; determine upon, assign judicially XVI. - AN. *awarder*, var. of ONF. *eswarder*, OF. *esg(u)arder* consider, ordain :- Rom. **exwardāre*, f. EX-[1] + **wardāre* GUARD. So **award** sb. XIV. - AN. *award*, f. the verb.

aware †on one's guard; cognizant *of* XIV. ME. *awar*, for earlier *iwar*, OE. *ġewær* = OS., OHG. *giwar* (G. *gewahr*); WGmc. formation f. **ȝa-* Y- + **war-* WARE[2].

awash XIX. f. A-[1] + WASH.

away Late OE. *aweġ*, for earlier *onweġ*, i.e. ON, A-[1] + WAY.

awe XIII. ME. *aȝe* - ON. *agi* :- **aȝan-*, f. Gmc. **aȝ-*, repr. by Goth. *agis* fear. The Scand. word displaced the native *eie*, *eȝe*, OE. *eġe* (:- **aȝiz*). Hence **awe** vb. XIV. **awestruck** XVII. **awful** XIII, **awfully** XIV.

awhile OE. *āne hwīle*, ME. *ōne hwīle*, acc. of ONE and WHILE, reduced to *a while* and written as one word XIV.

awkward †adv. in the wrong direction XIV; adj. †perverse, untoward XVI; clumsy or ungainly XVI; embarrassing, difficult XVIII. orig. north. and Sc.; f. †*awk* backhanded, perverse (- ON. *ǫfugr* turned the wrong way) + -WARD.

awl OE. *æl* = OHG. *ala* (G. *ahle*), ON. *alr*, of unkn. orig.

awning XVII (prop. naut.). of unkn. orig.

awry XIV. ME. *on wry*, *awri(e)*, i.e. ON, A-[1] + WRY.

axe, U.S. **ax,** OE. *æx* (*eax*), *æces* = OS. *akus* (Du. *aaks*), OHG. *ackus* (G. *axt*), ON. *øx* (obl. *ex-*), Goth. *aqizi* :- Gmc. **akwisjō*, **akusjō*.

axiom XV. - F. *axiome* or L. *axiōma* - Gr. *axíōma* self-evident principle, f. *axioûn* hold worthy, f. *áxios* worthy. Hence **axiomatic** XVIII.

axis XIV. - L. *axis* axle, etc., rel. to Skr. *ákṣa-*, Gr. *áxōn*, and OE. *eax*, *æx*, OHG. *ahsa* (G. *achse*) :- Gmc. **aχsō*; cf. next.

axle XVII. Earlier in **axletree** (XIII) - ON. *ǫxultré*, f. *ǫxull* :- **aχsulaz*, f. **aχsō*, ult. repl. the native *ax-tree*; see prec.

ay ever XII. ME. *ai*, *ei* - ON. *ei*, *ey* = OE. *ā* (ME. *ā*, *ō*), OS. *eo*, OHG. *eo*, *io* (G. *je*), Goth. *aiws* age :- Gmc. **aiwaz*, rel. to L. *ævum* age, Gr. *aei* ever.

aye yes. XVI. In earliest use spelt *I* (XVI–XVIII), later *ai, ay,* and *ey; aye* not common before XIX; of uncert. orig. Cf. OFris. *ay*.

azalea XVIII. - modL. - Gr. *azaléa*, sb. use of fem. of *azaléos* dry, so called because it flourishes in dry soil.

azimuth arc extending from zenith to horizon. XIV. - medL. - Arab. *as-sumūt*, i.e. AL-[2], *sumūt*, pl. of *samt* point of the compass (see ZENITH).

azure †lapis lazuli; bright or clear blue (colour). XIV. ME. *asur(e)* - OF. *asur*, (also mod.) *azur* - medL. *azur(i)um* - Arab. *al-lāzaward*, i.e. AL-[2], Pers. *lāzhward, lājward* LAPIS LAZULI, blue.

B

baa bleat. XVI. imit. Cf. G. *bäh*, L. *bē*, Gr. *bê*.

baba rich cake soaked in rum syrup. XIX. - F.

babble XIII. prob. - MLG. (Du.) *babbelen*, if not a native imit. formation; cf. (O)F. *babiller*; see -LE².

babe see BABY.

babel XIV (see Gen. 11:9). - Heb. *bābhel* Babylon.

baboon †grotesque figure XIV; one of a subdivision of monkeys XV. ME. *baboyne*, *babewyn(e)* - OF. *baboïn* (mod. *babouin*) or medL. *babewynus*. Ult. orig. uncert.

babouche oriental slipper. XVII. - Fr. - Arab. *bābūj* - Pers. *pāpūš*, f. *pā* foot + *pūš* covering.

baby, babe XIV. prob. f. redupl. form **baba* (cf. ME. *baban*) similar to MAMA, PAPA.

baccalaureate bachelor's degree in a university. XVII. - F. *baccalauréat* or modL. *baccalaureatus*, f. medL. *baccalarius* BACHELOR; see -ATE¹.

baccara(t) gambling card game. XIX. - F., of unkn. orig.

bacchanal pert. to Bacchus XVI; riotously drunken XVIII. - late L. *bacchānālis*, f. *Bacchus* - Gr. *Bákkhos* god of wine.

bachelor young man, aspirant to knighthood XIII; knight, university graduate XIV. ME. *bacheler* - OF. *bacheler*, of uncert. orig. For the sp., see -OR¹.

bacillus XIX. mod. use of late L. dim. of *baculum* rod, stick. Cf. BACTERIUM.

back¹ hinder surface. OE. *bæc*, OS., ON. *bak* :- Gmc. **bakam*. Hence **back** vb. XIV; adj. XVI, with superl. **backmost** XVIII. So **backside** XV (prob. Scand., cf. Norw. *bakside*).

back² adv. to the back XIV. Aphetic of ABACK.

back-bite detract from the character of. XIII. - MSw. *bakbīta*, f. *bak* BACK¹ + *bīta* BITE vb.

back-formation formation of a word from a longer word which has the appearance of being derived from it, e.g. *edit* from *editor*. XIX (J. A. H. Murray). Hence G. *rückbildung*.

backgammon XVII. f. BACK² + an earlier form of GAME¹.

backward towards the back or rear. XIV. Aphetic of †*abackward*, f. ABACK + -WARD.

bacon XIV. - OF. *bacon*, AN. *-un* - Frankish **bako* ham, flitch, f. Gmc. **bakam* BACK¹.

bacterium XIX. - modL. - Gr. *baktḗrion*, dim. of *baktēriā* staff, cane. Cf. *bacillus*.

bad XIII (first applied to worthless or contemptible persons). ME. *badde*, perh. repr. OE. *bæddel* hermaphrodite (cf. *bædling* sodomite) with loss of *l* as in MUCH, WENCH.

badge XIV. ME. *bage*, of unkn. orig.

badger XVI (also †*bageard* XVI, †*badgerd* XVI-XVII). perh. f. prec. + -ARD, with allusion to the white mark on the animal's forehead (but *badge* is not recorded in this sense).

badinage banter. XVII. - F., f. *badin* joker, buffoon.

badminton XIX. Name of the Duke of Beaufort's country seat (Avon).

baffle A. †disgrace XVI; B. †hoodwink XVI; foil the plans of XVII. A. perh. f. Sc. *bauchle* (XV) disgrace, of unkn. orig. In B we have perh. a word of different orig. rel. to F. *bafouer* ridicule (XVI).

baffy kind of golf-club. XIX. f. Sc. *baff* sb. stroke or vb. strike (of imit. orig.; cf. G. *baff*, Du. *baffen*) + -Y¹.

bag XIII. poss. Scand., cf. ON. *baggi*; but similar forms are found in Rom., cf. OF. *bague*, Pr. *baga* baggage. Hence **bagpipe** XIV, prob. tr. MLG. *sackpīpe*, Du. †*zakpijp*.

bagatelle A. trifle XVII; B. table ball-game XIX. - Fr. - It. *bagatella*, of uncert. orig. Sense B is purely Eng.

baggage portable property XV; worthless person XVI; young woman XVII. - OF. *bagage*, f. *baguer* tie up, or f. *bagues* (pl.) bundles; see BAG and -AGE.

bagnio oriental prison; Turkish bath, brothel. XVI. - It. *bagno* :- L. *balneum* bath.

bah int. XIX. After F. *bah*.

bail¹ †charge, custody XIV; †(security for) temporary release from custody; person(s) providing such security XVI. - OF. *bail* control, etc., f. *baillier* bear, rule, give :- L. *bājulāre* bear a burden, (later) care for, support, f. *bājulus* carrier. Hence **bail** vb. release on bail, be bail for. XVI.

bail² (cricket, orig. single) XVIII. perh. - F. dial. *bail* cross-bar, prob. rel. to OF. *bail(l)e* BAILEY.

bail³ see BALE³.

bailey (court within) wall surrounding castle XIII. ME. *bail(l)y*, var. *baile*, prob. - OF. *bail(l)e* enclosed court. The Old Bailey in London stood in the ancient 'bailey' of the city wall between Ludgate and Newgate.

Bailey bridge 1944. f. name of the designer, D. C. *Bailey* (1901-).

bailie (now only) municipal magistrate in Scotland. XIV. ME. *bail(l)i* - OF. *bailli*, later form of *baillif* (see next). Hence **bailiwick** XV, with suffix *-wick* :- OE. *wice* office, duty (see WEEK).

bailiff sheriff's officer, landholder's steward. XIV. ME. *baillif* - OF. *baillif*, prob. f. *bail* BAIL¹.

bain-marie XIX. - F. (chem.) waterbath etc., tr. medL. *balneum Mariæ* bath of Maria (alleged Jewish alchemist).

bairn child. XVI. Sc. form of ME. *barn* (as *airm* of *arm*), OE. *bearn* = OS., OHG., ON., Goth. *barn* :- Gmc. **barnam*, f. **bar-*, var. of **ber-*; see BEAR². In ME. reinforced by ON. *barn*.

bait A. set dogs on XII; B. provide provender for XIV; C. furnish with bait XIV. A and B - ON. *beita* pasture, hunt or chase with dogs or hawks, causal of *bíta* BITE. Sense C prob. f. **bait**, sb. food (partly - ON. *beit* and partly f. the vb. (B)).

baize XVI (*baies*). - F. *baies*, fem. pl. sb. use of

bai reddish-brown, BAY[2]. The pl. form was early taken as a sg.; the sp. with *z* was not established before XIX.

bake OE. *bacan* str. vb., f. Gmc. **bak*-. Weak inflexions (*baked*) began to appear before 1400, and were established by XVI.

Bakelite P. name of synthetic resin used as plastic. XX. f. name of L. H. *Baekeland*, Belgian-Amer. inventor (1863-1944); see -ITE.

baksheesh gratuity. XVII. ult. - Pers. *bakšīš*, f. *bakšīdan* give, chiefly through Arab., Turk., or Hind. Cf. BUCKSHEE.

balalaika guitar-like instrument. XVIII. - Russ.

balance weighing-scales, uncertainty XIII; adjustment of accounts XVI; sum remaining over XVIII. - (O)F. :- Rom. **bilancia*, f. late L. *bilanx*, *bilanc*-, f. BI- + *lanx* scale. So **balance** vb. XVI. - (O)F. *balancer*.

balas variety of spinel ruby. XV. - (O)F. - Arab. *balakš*, alt. of *badakš*, f. *Badakšān* province where balas is found.

balcony balustraded platform on the outside of a house. XVII. - It. *balcone*, prob. f. Gmc. **balkan*- beam, BALK. Regularly str. *balco·ny* till early XIX.

bald XIV. ME. *balled(e)*, MSc. *bellit* hairless, having a white blaze, prob. an OE. formation (**bællede*, **beallede*) with suffix -*ede* on a base **ball*- meaning orig. 'white patch'. Cf. PIEBALD, SKEWBALD, and *Ballard* (XIV) bald-headed person, which survives as a surname.

baldachin, baldac(c)hino (hist.) rich embroidered stuff XVI; canopy XVII. - It. *baldacchino* rich stuff, f. (with suffix -*ino* -INE[1]) *Baldacco*, It. form of *Baghdad*, where stuff was orig. made.

balderdash †froth XVI; †mixture of drinks XVII; nonsense XVII. of unkn. orig.

baldric belt worn pendent from one shoulder under the opposite arm. XIV (*baudry*, *bauderyk*; forms with *l* from XVI). The earliest ex. is - OF. *baldrei*; later forms corr. to early MHG. *balderich*, of unkn. orig.

bale[1] evil, harm. OE. *balu* (*bealu*) = OHG. *balo*, ON. *bǫl* :- Gmc. **balwam*, n. of adj. **balwaz*. Cf. Goth. *balwawesei* wickedness. The OE. word was reinforced in ME. by ON. *bǫl*, *bal*-.

bale[2] bundle, package. XIV. prob. - MDu. *bale* (Du. *baal*) - OF. *bale* (mod. *balle*); ult. identical with BALL[1].

bale[3] lade out. XVII. Later sp. of *bail* (XVII), f. †*bail* sb. vessel for lading water (XV) - OF. *baille* bucket, prob. :- Rom. **bajula*, fem. of L. *bājulus* carrier.

baleen whalebone. XIV. - OF. *baleine* whale :- L. *balæna*.

balk A. ridge, esp. between furrows OE.; hindrance XV; B. †wooden fetter OE.; beam of timber XIV. A. Late OE. *balc* - ON. *bálkr* partition (see BULKHEAD) :- Gmc. **balkuz*, rel. to **balkan*- beam; cf. BALCONY. B. OE. *balca* :- WGmc. **balkan*-.

ball[1] globular body. XIII. perh. - ON. *bǫllr*, *ball*- :- Gmc. **balluz*.

ball[2] assembly for dancing. XVII. - (O)F. *bal* dance, f. †*baler* to dance - late L. *ballāre* - Gr. *ballízein*.

ballad XV. - (O)F. *ballade* - Pr. *balada* dancing-song; see BALL[2], -ADE.

ballade specific verse-form. XIV. Early (and modF.) form of BALLAD differentiated in application.

ballast XVI. prob. f. LG., of uncert. orig. (perh. f. (i) *bar* BARE, mere or (ii) *barm* bosom, hull (of a ship) + *last* burden).

ballet XVII. - F. *ballet* - It. *balletto*, dim. of *ballo* BALL[2].

ballista ancient missile engine. XVI (earlier *ballist* XIV). - L., f. (ult.) Gr. *bállein* throw. Hence **ballistic** pert. to projectiles XVIII (sb. **-ics** XIX).

ballock (vulgar) testicle. OE. **balluc* (*bealluc*), dim. of Gmc. **ball*- BALL[1]; see -OCK.

balloon XVI. - Fr. *ballon* or It. *ballone*, augm. of *balla* ball (of Gmc. orig.); see -OON.

ballot (hist.) ball, ticket, etc. used in secret voting; method of such voting, orig. by dropping a ball into a box. XVI (the earliest exx. refer to Venice). - It. *ballotta*, dim. of *balla* ball (see prec.). So vb. XVI (cf. It. *ballottare*).

bally (sl.) XIX. euphem. alt. of BLOODY.

ballyhoo showman's touting speech, noisy publicity, bombastic nonsense. XX. of unkn. orig.

ballyrag see BULLYRAG.

balm aromatic resin; aromatic oil or ointment XIII. ME. *ba(s)me*, *baume* - OF. *basme*, *bau(s)me* :- L. *balsamum* BALSAM. Hence **balmy** XV (see -Y[1]); also in fig. sense, var. of BARMY.

baloney, boloney (orig. U.S.) humbug, nonsense. XX. Commonly regarded as from *Bologna* (*sausage*), but the connection remains conjectural.

balsam XV. - L. *balsamum* - Gr. *bálsamon*, perh. of Sem. orig. Cf. BALM.

baluster one of a series of short moulded shafts supporting a coping or rail. XVII. - F. *balustre* - It. *balaustro*, ult. f. L. *balaustrum* blossom of the wild pomegranate (which the moulded pillar resembled) - Gr. *balaústion*. See BANISTER. So **balustrade** XVII. - F. - It. *balaustrata*.

bambino image of the Infant Jesus. XVIII. - It., dim. of †*bambo* silly.

bamboo XVI (*bambus*, -*os*). - Du. *bamboes* - (with unexpl. -*s*) Pg. *bambu*, of Dravidian orig. *Bamboo* was deduced from *bambus*, etc., taken as pl.

bamboozle trick, cheat, mystify. XVIII. prob. of cant orig.; cf. Sc. *bumbaze*, *bom*- (XVII).

ban[1] in earliest use 'proclamation, summons to arms' (XIII); partly aphetic of ME. *iban*, OE. *ġebann*, partly - OF. *ban* - Gmc. **bannan* BAN[2]. The later senses 'curse' (XV), 'prohibition' (XVII) are prob. partly a separate word, f. BAN[2]. Cf. BANNS.

ban[2] †proclaim, summon OE.; †curse XII; prohibit XIX. OE. *bannan* (str. vb.) = OHG. *bannan* :- Gmc. **bannan*. Weak inflexions from XIII.

banal (hist.) obligatory for all the tenants of a feudal jurisdiction XVIII; commonplace XIX. - (O)F. *banal*, f. *ban* BAN[1]; see -AL[1].

banana XVI. - Pg. - a lang. of W. Africa (Guinea).

band[1] that which binds. XII. - ON. *band* = OHG.

bant (G., Du. *band*) :- Gmc. **bandam*, f. base **band-* of **bindan*, BIND; superseded OE. *bend* BEND[1] in the sense 'fetter' and repl. mainly by BOND[1] in the fig. sense 'restraint, binding agreement'. Now assoc. with BAND[2].

band[2] strip, stripe. XV. - (O)F. *bande*, earlier *bende* (cf. BEND[1]), - Gmc. **bindōn* (OHG. *binda*), f. **bindan* BIND.

band[3] company XV; body of musicians XVII. - (O)F. *bande*, prob. of Gmc. orig. The var. *bende* (- OF. *bende*) was in regular use from late XV to early XVII. Hence **band** vb. XVI; cf. DISBAND.

bandage XVI. - F. *bandage*, f. *bande* BAND[2]; see -AGE.

bandanna coloured handkerchief with spots left white or yellow. XVIII. prob. through Pg. *bandana* from Hind. (cf. *bāndhnū*, mode of dyeing).

bandeau head- or hair-band. XVIII. - F., dim. of *bande* BAND[2].

banderol(e) narrow flag, streamer. XVI. - F. *banderole* - It. *banderuola*, dim. of *bandiera* BANNER.

bandit XVI. Earliest forms *bandetto*, *bandito*; *bandit* from XVII. ult. - It. *bandito*, sb. use of pp. of *bandire* proclaim, proscribe.

bandoleer, -ier XVI. - F. *bandoulière*.

bandy[1] throw, toss; exchange (blows, etc.). XVI. perh. - F. *bander* 'to bandie at Tennis' (Cotgr.).

bandy[2] (of legs) curved inwards. XVII. of uncert. orig.

bane †murderer OE.; †death, destruction XIII; poison XIV; cause of ruin or trouble XVI. OE. *bana* = ON. *bani*, OHG. *bano* :- Gmc. **banan-*.

bang sb., vb., int. XIV. imit.; perh. immed. - Scand. (cf. ON. *bang* hammering, *banga* to hammer, knock).

bangle XVIII. - Hind. *bangrī*, (dial.) *banglī*, orig. coloured glass bracelet.

banian, banyan Indian fig-tree, XVII. An Eng., not native name for the tree; so called because used as a market-place for merchants or 'banyans', - Pg. *banian* or Arab. *banyān*, ult. :- Skr. *vāṇijá-* merchant.

banish XIV. - OF. *baniss-*, lengthened stem (see -ISH[2]) of *banir* (mod. *-nn-*) - Gmc. **bannjan*, f. **bann-* BAN[1].

ban(n)ister XVII. alt. of BALUSTER; var. †*barrister* in XVII by assoc. with BAR[1].

banjo XVIII (†*banjer*, †*-jore*). of uncert. orig.; perh. Negro slave pronunc. *banjo·*, *banjo·re* of *bandore* lute-like instrument.

bank[1] raised ridge XII; bordering slope XIV. - ON. **banki* (OIcel. *bakki*) :- Gmc. **baŋkan-*, rel. to BENCH.

bank[2] †bench XIII; tier of oars XVII; row of keys etc. XIX. - (O)F. *banc* bench, f. Gmc. **baŋk-* (see BENCH).

bank[3] †money-changer's table XV; establishment for the custody of money XVII. - F. *banque* or its source It. *banca* - Gmc. **baŋk-* (see prec.). So **banker** †money-changer, usurer XVI; proprietor of a bank XVII. - F. *banquier* (see -ER[2]).

bankrupt XVI (*banka rota*, *banqueroute*). The orig. sense 'bankruptcy' is found esp. in phr. †*make bankeroute* = F. *faire banqueroute* - It. *banca rotta*, f. *banca* BANK[3], *rotta* broken, insolvent. The forms in Eng. were infl. by F. *banqueroute*, and by L. *ruptus* broken, in medL. ruined or insolvent man. Hence as vb. XVI. **bankruptcy** (-CY) XVI.

banner XIII. - AN. *banere*, OF. *baniere* (mod. *bannière*), prob. f. *ban* BAN[1].

bannock flat round loaf. OE. *bannuc* (once); XV in north. Eng., XVI in Sc.; perh. orig. - OBrit. word repr. by Bret. *bannac'h* drop, bit.

banns proclamation of marriage. XIV. pl. of BAN[1], after medL. pl. *banna*.

banquet XV. - (O)F. *banquet*, dim. of *banc* bench (BANK[2]), corr. to It. *banchetto*, dim. of *banco*; the orig. application seems to have been to a slight meal taken on the domestic bench.

banshee female spirit whose wail portends death. XVIII. - Ir. *bean sídhe*, OIr. *ben síde*, i.e. *ben* woman, *síd* fairy hill.

bantam small variety of domestic fowl. XVIII. app. f. name of westernmost district of Java (Javanese *Bantèn*); the fowl is not native there.

banter ridicule good-humouredly; also sb. XVII. of unkn. orig.

banyan see BANIAN.

baptize, -ise XIII. - OF. *baptisier* (mod. *baptiser*) - ecclL. *baptizāre* - Gr. *baptízein*, f. *báptein* dip; see -IZE. So **baptism** XIV. ME. *bapte(s)m(e)* - OF. *ba(p)tesme* (mod. *baptême*) - ecclL. *baptismus* - ecclGr. *baptismós*. **Baptist** name of John, forerunner of Jesus Christ. XII. - (O)F. *baptiste* - ecclL. *baptista* - ecclGr. *baptistḗs*. **baptistery** XIV. - OF. *baptister(i)e* - ecclL. *baptistērium* - ecclGr. *baptistḗrion*.

bar[1] barrier XIII; rod XIV. - (O)F. *barre* :- Rom. **barra*, of unkn. orig. So **bar** vb. XIII.

bar[2] unit of barometric pressure. XX. - Gr. *báros* weight. So **millibar** a thousandth of a bar.

barb recurved process (of arrow). XIV. - (O)F. *barbe* :- L. *barba* BEARD.

barbaresque pert. to Barbary; barbarous. XIX. - F. - It. *barbaresco* f. *Barberia* (ult. f. Arab. *barbar* BERBER), which was identified with L. *barbaria*, *-iēs* land of barbarians, medGr. *barbaría* (cf. next); see -ESQUE.

barbaric uncivilized XV; not Greek or Roman, foreign XIX. - F. *barbarique* or L. *barbaricus* - Gr. *barbarikós*, f. *bárbaros* foreign, rude. So **barbarian** adj. and sb. XV; see -IAN. **barbarism** XV; see -ISM. **barbarous** XV; f. L. *barbarus* (see -OUS).

barbecue XVII (earliest sense †'wooden framework on which to sleep or to smoke a carcass'). - Sp. *barbacoa* - an indigenous word of the Caribbean area.

barbel freshwater fish with fleshy filaments hanging from mouth XV; such a filament in any fish XVII. - OF. *barbel* (mod. *barbeau*) :- late L. *barbellus*, dim. of *barbus* barbel, f. *barba* BEARD.

barber XIV. - AN. *barber*, *barbour*, (OF. *barbier*, *barbëor*), f. *barbe* (:- L. *barba*) BEARD; see -ER[2], -OR[1].

barbette platform or mound for guns within a fortification. XVIII. - F., dim. of *barbe* (:- L. *barba*) BEARD; see -ETTE.

barbican outer fortification. XIII. - (O)F. *barbacane*, medL. *barbacana*, of unkn. orig.

barbituric XIX. - F. *barbiturique*, f. G.

barbitur(säure), f. *Barbara*, a woman's name. So **barbitone** (-ONE) XX, **barbiturate** (-ATE[2]) XX.

barcarol(l)e Venetian boat-song. XVIII. - F. *barcarolle* - It. *barcarola*, f. *barcarolo* (Venetian dial.) gondolier, f. *barca* BARQUE.

bard Celtic minstrel-poet, etc. XIV. - Gael., Ir. *bárd*, W. *bardd* :- OCelt. **bardos*.

bare OE. *bær* (G. *bar*, Du. *baar*) :- Gmc. **bazaz*.

bargain XIV. - OF. *bargaignier* trade, dispute - Gmc. **borȝanjan*, f. **borȝ-* BORROW. So **bargain** sb. XIV. - OF. *bargaine*.

barge long heavy boat XII. - (O)F. *barge*, poss. :- medL. **barica*, f. Gr. *bâris* Egyptian boat. Cf. BARQUE.

baritone XVII. - It. *baritono* - Gr. *barútonos*, f. *barús* heavy.

barium (chem.) metallic element. 1808 (H. Davy). f. *barytes* native sulphate of barium; see -IUM.

bark[1] yelp as a dog. OE. *beorcan* :- **berkan*, perh. var. of Gmc. **brekan* BREAK[1]. Hence **bark** sb. XVI.

bark[2] outer rind of tree. XIII. - ON. *bark-*, obl. stem of *bǫrkr* (Sw., Da. *bark*).

bark[3] see BARQUE.

barley OE. *bærlic* adj.; as sb. XII; app. f. OE. *bære*, *bere* barley + *-lic* -LY[1]. Cf. ON. *barr*, Goth. *barizeins*.

barm yeast. OE. *beorma* (prob. a Common LG. word; cf. Fris. *berme*, *barm*, LG. *barm(e)*); rel. to L. *fervēre* boil.

barmy frothy XVI; empty-headed, daft XVII. f. prec. + -Y[1]. In the fig. sense also BALMY.

barn OE. *ber(e)n*, earlier *berern*, f. *bere* BARLEY + *ern*, *ærn* (ON. *rann*, Goth. *razn*) house.

barnacle wild goose *Anas leucopsis* XIII; marine crustacean XVI. ME. *bernak*, *-ek(ke)*, corr. to medL. *bernaca*, *-eca*, whence app. F. *barnache*; *barnacle* (XV) corr. to F. *barnacle*, but may be of independent orig.; ult. source unkn. The two meanings depend on an early belief that the goose was generated from a shellfish.

barometer XVII. f. Gr. *báros* weight + *métron* -METER. Hence **barometric** XIX, **-ical** XVII. So **barograph** XIX.

baron XII. - AN. *barun*, (O)F. *baron* :- medL. *barō*, *barōnem* man, male, warrior, of Gmc. orig. For 'baron of beef' cf. SIRLOIN. So **baronage** XIII. ME. *barnage* - OF. *barnage*, medL. *baronagium*. **baroness** XV. - OF. *baronesse* (AL. *-issa*). **baronet** XIV (mod. title instituted 1611). - AL. *barōnettus*. **barony** XIII. - OF. *baronie* (AL. *-ia*).

baroque XIX. - F., orig. of irregular pearl, - Pg. *barroco*, of unkn. orig.

barque, bark boat XV; three-masted vessel XVII. - (O)F. *barque*, prob. - Pr. *barca* :- late L. *barca*, of which a var. **barica* may be repr. by BARGE. Hence **barquentine** XVII, after BRIGANTINE.

barrack[1] (usu. in pl.) soldiers' quarters. XVII. - F. *baraque* - Sp. *barraca* soldiers' tent, of unkn. orig.

barrack[2] shout or jeer at. XIX. alt. of (Austral.) *borak* sb. banter (Aboriginal word).

barrage bar in a watercourse XIX; curtain of artillery fire XX. - F., f. *barrer* BAR[1] vb.

barrel XIV. - (O)F. *baril*, of uncert. orig.

barren incapable of offspring. XIII (*barain*). - OF. (fem.) *barai(g)ne* (mod. *bréhaigne*), of unkn. orig.

barricade sb. XVII. Earlier *barricado* (XVI). - F. *barricade*, f. *barrique* cask. See -ADE, -ADO. Hence **barricade** vb. XVI, after F. *barricader*.

barrier XIV (*bar(r)ere*). - AN. *barrere*, (O)F. *barrière*, f. **barra* BAR[1].

barrister XVI (*barrester*). Obscurely f. BAR[1], perh. after †*legister* lawyer, or *minister*.

barrow[1] †mountain; grave-mound. OE. *beorg*, OHG. (G., Du.) *berg* :- Gmc. **berȝaz*.

barrow[2] ME. *bar(e)we* handbarrow XIV, wheelbarrow XV. - OE. *bearwe* :- **barwōn*, f. **bar-*, **ber-* BEAR[2].

barter XV. poss. f. OF. *barater* cheat, exchange; but connecting links are wanting.

basalt XVII. - L. *basaltēs*, var. of *basanītēs* - Gr. *basanítēs*, f. *básanos* touchstone.

bascule apparatus on the lever principle. XVII. - F. *bascule*, earlier *bacule* see-saw, f. stem of *battre* beat + *cul* posteriors.

base[1] bottom, foundation. XIV. - (O)F. *base* or L. BASIS. Hence **basal**, **basic** XIX; cf. F. *basal*, *basique*.

base[2] of low quality or status. XIV. - (O)F. *bas*, fem. *basse* :- medL. *bassus*, *bassa*, found in classical times as a cognomen.

basement XVIII. prob. - Du. †*basement* foundation, in WFlem. *bazement*, perh. - It. *basamento* base of a column, etc.; see -MENT and cf. (O)F. *soubassement*.

bash strike heavily. XVII. ult. imit., perh. a blend of *bang* and *dash*, *smash*, etc.

bashful XVI. f. †*bash* aphetic of ABASH + -FUL[1]. Cf. *mournful*.

basil aromatic plant. XV. - OF. *basilic* - medL. *basilicum* - Gr. *basilikón*, n. of adj. 'royal' (see next).

basilica XVI. - L. - Gr. *basilikḗ*, sb. use of fem. of *basilikós* royal, f. *basileús* king.

basilisk fabulous reptile XIV; large cannon XVI. - L. *basiliscus* - Gr. *basilískos*, dim. of *basileús* king.

basin XIII. - OF. *bacin* (mod. *bassin*) :- medL. *bacinus*, perh. of Celt. orig.

basis XIV. - L. - Gr. *básis* step, pedestal, rel. to COME.

bask XIV. usu. referred to ON. *baðask*, refl. of *baða* BATHE. Cf. BUSK[1].

basket XIII. AL. *baskettum* (XIII-XV), AN., OF. *basket*, of unkn. orig.

bas-relief XVII. - It. *basso rilievo* (alt. after F. *bas-relief*).

bass[1] fish of the perch family. XV (*bace*). alt. of dial. *barse*, OE. *bærs*, *bears* = MDu., MHG. *bars* (Du. *baars*, G. *barsch*), rel. to OE. *byrst* BRISTLE. For the loss of *r* cf. DACE.

bass[2] XVII. alt. of BAST.

bass[3] deep-sounding; (mus.) of the lowest part. XV. orig. identical in form and still in pronunc. with BASE[2]; from XVI assim. in form to It. BASSO.

basset short-legged hound. XVII. - F. *basset*, f. *bas* low; see -ET.

basset-horn tenor clarinet. XIX. partial tr. of F. *cor de bassette* - It. *corno di bassetto*.

bassinet baby's cradle with hood at one end. XIX. - F., dim. of *bassin* BASIN.
basso (mus.) bass. XIX. - It.; see BASE[2].
bassoon XVIII. - F. *basson*, augm. f. *bas* BASS[2]; see -OON.
bast inner bark of the lime. OE. *bæst*, corr. to (M)Du., (O)HG., ON. *bast* :- Gmc. **bastaz, -am*, of unkn. orig.
bastard XIII. - OF. *bastard* (mod. *bâtard*) :- medL. *bastardus*, of uncert. orig. Hence **bastardize** XVI, **bastardy** XV (cf. AN. *bastardie* XIII); see -IZE, -Y[3].
baste[1] sew loosely. XIV. - OF. *bastir* (mod. *bâtir*) - Gmc. **bastjan* (cf. OHG. *besten* lace, sew), f. **bastaz* BAST.
baste[2] pour fat over (roasting meat). XV. of unkn. orig.
bastinado beating with a stick (esp. on the soles of the feet). XVI. - Sp. *bastonada*, f. *baston* BATON; see -ADO.
bastion projecting part of a fortification. XVI. - F. *bastion* - It. *bastione*, ult. f. Gmc. **bastjan* BASTE[1].
bat[1] club, stout stick OE.; implement for striking ball in games XVIII. Late OE. *batt* 'clava'; some uses poss. from (O)F. *batte* (f. *battre* beat). Hence, or directly - (O)F. *battre*, **bat** vb. XV; in the sense 'wink (the eyelids)' perh. a var. of BATE.
bat[2] mouse-like winged quadruped. XVI. alt. of ME. *bakke* (till XVII in gen. use) - Scand. word repr. in OSw. *aptan-*, *nattbacka* evening or night bat.
batch †process of baking; loaves produced at one baking XV; quantity or number coming at one time, set XVI. ME. *bac(c)he* :- OE. **bæċċe*, f. *bacan* BAKE.
bate reduce, restrain. (now chiefly in *with bated breath*). XIV. Aphetic of ABATE.
bath OE. *bæð* = OS. *bað*, (O)HG. *bad*, ON. *bað* :- Gmc. **baþam*. Hence **bath** vb. XV, a new formation distinct from BATHE, now restricted to the sense 'wash (another or oneself) in a bath'.
bathe OE. *baðian* = OHG. *badōn* (G. *baden*), ON. *baða* :- Gmc. **baþōn*, f. **baþam* BATH.
bathos XVIII. - Gr. *báthos* depth, f. *bathús* deep. Hence **bathetic** XIX; after *pathos, pathetic*.
batiste XVII (*baptist cloth*, tr. F. *toile de Batiste*). - F. *batiste*, of uncert. orig.
batman army officer's servant. XIX. f. *bat* pack-saddle (- OF. *bat*, mod. *bât*) in *bat horse, bat mule*, etc. + MAN.
baton XVI. - F. *bâton* :- Rom. **bastō, -ōn-*, f. **bastāre* drive with a stick (cf. L. *burdubasta* donkey-driver), f. late L. *bastum* stick.
battalion XVI. - F. *bataillon* - It. *battaglione*, augm. of *battaglia* BATTLE.
battels (pl.) college account at Oxford for board etc. XVIII (from XVI in L. *batillī* etc.). of unkn. orig. So **battel** vb. XVI.
batten[1] strip of wood. XV. Earliest forms *bata(u)nt, -ent*. - OF. *batant*, sb. use of prp. of *batre* beat (see BATTERY).
batten[2] †improve in condition XVI; grow fat, thrive (*on*) XVII. - ON. *batna* improve, f. Gmc. **bat-*; see BETTER, -EN[5].
batter[1] beat with repeated blows. XIV. - AN. *baterer*, f. OF. *batre* (mod. *battre*) :- L. *battuere*, later *battere*; cf. BAT[1] and -ER[4].
batter[2] paste used in cooking. XV. prob. f. BATTER[1], but cf. OF. *bat(e)ure* beating.
battery beating (as in *assault and battery*); †battering (as of fortifications by guns); unit of artillery XVI; combination of pieces of equipment etc. (first used with ref. to apparatus for discharge of electricity) XVIII. - (O)F. *batterie*, f. *batre* BATTER[1]; see -ERY.
battle sb. XIII. ME. *bataile* - (O)F. *bataille* (= It. *battaglia*, etc.) :- Rom. **battālia*, for late L. *battuālia* (n. pl.), military or gladiatorial exercises, f. *battuere* beat. So **battle** vb. XIV.
battledore wooden implement for washing, etc. XV; bat used with a shuttlecock XVI. perh. - Pr. *batedor* beater, f. *batre* beat, infl. by †*battle* vb. (XVI), f. BAT[1] vb.; but the history is obscure.
battlement XIV. contemp. with †*battled* - pp. of OF. *batailler* fortify with *batailles* fixed or movable turrets of defence. See -MENT.
battleship XIX. Short for *line-of-battle ship* (XVIII) ship designed to fight in line of battle.
batty (sl.) crazy. XX. f. phr. 'to have bats in the belfry' to be crazy; see BAT[2], -Y[1].
bauble trinket; jester's baton XIV; trifling matter XVI. ME. *babel, babulle* - OF. *babel, baubel* child's toy, plaything, of unkn. orig. (cf. AL. *baubellum* XII-XIII).
bauxite XIX. - Fr., f. Les *Baux*, near Arles, France; see -ITE.
bawbee (Sc.) halfpenny. XVI. Named after the laird of Sille*bawby*, mint-master under James V.
bawd pander, procuress XIV. The fuller form *bawdstrot*, Sc. *bald(e)strod* (XIV-XV) suggests ult. deriv. from OF. *baudetrot, baudestroyt*, app. f. *baud* lively, gay (- Gmc. **bald-* BOLD) + the word repr. by AN. *trote* old woman. Hence **bawdry** XIV. **bawdy** XVI, sb. XVII; see -Y[1].
bawl †bark; cry vociferously. XV. cf. medL. *baulāre* bark; also Icel. *baula* (Sw. *böla*) low, as an ox.
bay[1] †berry XIV; bay tree, *Laurus nobilis*; pl. leaves of this made into a garland XVI. - (O)F. *baie* :- L. *bāca* berry.
bay[2] indentation of the sea. XIV. - (O)F. *baie*, of uncert. orig.
bay[3] opening between columns, etc. XIV; recess XVI. - (O)F. *baie*, f. *bayer*, earlier *baer, beer* gape, stand open. So *bay window* XV.
bay[4] barking of dogs in company XIII; chiefly (now only) in phr. (*keep* etc.) *at bay*, (*bring*, etc.) *to bay* XIV. - OF. *bai*, or aphetic of ME. *abay* - OF. *abai* (mod. *aboi* in phr. *être, mettre aux abois*). See BAY[6].
bay[5] reddish-brown. XIV. - (O)F. *bai* :- L. *badius* chestnut-coloured (of horses).
bay[6] bark with a deep voice. XIV. Aphetic of †*abaye* - OF. *abaiier* (mod. *aboyer*), f. imit. base **bai-*; infl. by BAY[4].
bayonet †short dagger XVII; stabbing blade for fixing to the muzzle of a musket or rifle XVIII. - F. *baïonnette*, said to be f. *Bayonne*, France, the orig. place of manufacture. The early vars. †*bag(o)net* (XVII-XVIII) are not accounted for.
bayou XVIII. - Amer. F. - a Choctaw word.

bazaar oriental market-place XVI; fancy fair XIX. ult. - Pers. *bāzār* market, which has passed directly or indirectly into many Eur. langs.

be Forms: pres. ind. **am**; (arch. and dial.) **art**; **is**; pl. **are**, (arch. and dial.) **be**; past ind. **was**, pl. **were**; pres. subj. **be**; past subj. **were**; pp. **been**. The forms are derived from four bases as follows.

A. IE. **es-*, **s-*. 1st pers. sg. OE. *(e)am*, *eom*, corr. to ON. *em*, Goth. *im*, Gr. *eimí*, Skr. *ásmi* :- IE. **ésmi*.

3rd pers. sg. OE. *is* = OS., (O)HG., Goth. *ist*, ON. *er*, L. *est*, Gr. *estí*, Skr. *ásti* :- IE. **ésti*.

pl. OE. *sind(on)* = OS. *sind(an)*, OHG. *sint* (G. *sind*), Goth. *sind*, L. *sunt*, Gr. *eisí*, Skr. *sánti* :- IE. **sénti*.

pres. subj. OE. *sīe*, pl. *sīen* = OS., OHG. *sī*, *sīn* (G. *sei*, *seien*), L. *siēm*, *sim*, Gr. *eiēn*, Skr. *syā́t* :- IE. **s(i)jḗm*, **s(i)jénti*.

B. Gmc. **ar-* (:- **or-*), of unkn. orig. 2nd pers. sg. OE. *eart*, pl. *(e)aron*.

C. IE. **bheu-*, **bhū-*. 1st pers. sg. OE. *bēo(m)* = OS. *bium*, OHG. *bim* (G. *bin*), corr. to L. *fīo* I become, rel. to *fuī* I was, Gr. *phúein* bring forth, cause to grow, Skr. *bhávati* becomes, is. The orig. meaning of this base is 'grow'; the derived sense 'become' led to its adoption as an element in the paradigm of the verb 'be', esp. for expressing the future.

D. IE. **wes-*. inf. OE. *wesan* = OS., OHG. *wesan*, ON. *vera*, Goth. *wisan*, rel. to Skr. *vásati* dwells, remains. The orig. meaning is 'dwell, remain', and the use of this base is therefore appropriate to the imper. (OE. *wes*, pl. *wesað*) and the past (OE. 1st and 3rd sg. *wæs*, 2nd sg. *wære*, pl. *wæron*), in which latter alone it remains.

be- pref. OE. *be-*, weak var. of BY, varying in cognate comps. with *bī-*, e.g. *begān* surround, *begang* and *bīgeng* circuit; = OS. *be-*, *bī*, OHG. *bī-* (G. *be-*, *bei-*). The main uses are: A. with verbs, meaning (1) 'around, on all sides', 'to and fro, in all ways', as *beset*, *besmear*, *bestrew* (mod. Eng. are *bedaub*, *besmirch*); (2) 'thoroughly, extremely', as *beseech* (early ME.); (3) 'off, away', as *behead*; (4) 'about, over' (lit. and fig.), as OE. *begēotan* sprinkle, *bethink*; B. with sbs. and adjs. 'so as to make what is expressed by them', as *becalm* (XVI), *befoul* (XIV); C. with sbs. 'surround or envelop with', 'affect with', as *befog* (XVII), *benight* (XVI); D. with ppl. adjs., often combining uses A (2) and C, as *bedabbled*, *bemused* (both mod. Eng.).

beach (dial.) shingle, pebbles of the seashore; seashore. XVI. Early forms also *bache*, *baich(e)*. The first sense remained in the local usage of Sussex and Kent; it is difficult to determine the date of the emergence of the present sense; perh. identical with OE. *bæċe*, *beċe* (BECK¹).

beacon †sign, standard OE.; signal-fire, lighthouse XIV. OE. *bēacn* = OS. *bōkan*, OHG. *bouhhan* :- WGmc. **baukna* (cf. BECKON), of unkn. orig.

bead †prayer OE.; (pl.) rosary; ornamental perforated object XIV. OE. *bedu* (ME. *bede* partly aphetic from *ibede*, OE. *ġebed*) = OS. *beda*, OHG. *beta* (and *gibet*, G. *gebet*), Goth. *bida*; f. Gmc. **beð-* BID.

beadle †herald, messenger; parish constable, ceremonial officer, etc. XIII. - OF. *bedel* (mod. *bedeau*), of Gmc. origin. The adopted F. word ousted the native OE. *bydel*, f. Gmc. **buð-*, base of OE. *bēodan* (see BID).

beagle small hound used for hare-hunting. XV. perh. - OF. *beegueule* 'having the mouth open', f. *beer* gape + *gueule* throat (cf. GULLET).

beak XIII. ME. *bec*, *bek* (*beck* continuing till XVIII; the form with the lengthened vowel arose from the obl. form *beke*) - (O)Fr. *bec* :- L. *beccus*.

beaker XIV. - ON. *bikan* = OS. *bikeri*, OHG. *behhāri* (G. *becher*) - popL. **bicārium*, perh. f. Gr. *bîkos* drinking-bowl.

beam †tree; plank; ray of light. OE. *bēam*, OS. *bōm*, OHG. *boum* (G. *baum*) :- WGmc. **bauma*; rel. obscurely to Goth. *bagms*, ON. *baðmr* tree.

bean OE. *bēan* = OHG. *bōna* (G. *bohne*), ON. *baun* :- Gmc. **baunō*, of unkn. orig. Hence **beanfeast** XIX, whence **beano** orig. printers' colloq.; see -O.

bear¹ mammal of the family Ursidae. OE. *bera*, OHG. *bero* (G. *bär*) :- WGmc. **beran-*.

bear² carry; give birth to. OE. str. vb. *beran* = OS., OHG. *beran*, ON. *bera*, Goth. *bairan*, f. Gmc. **ber-* :- IE. **bher-*, as in Skr. *bhárati*, Gr. *phérein*, L. *ferre*. The mod. pt. **bore** dates from *c.*1400, but did not gen. supersede **bare** till after 1600; for the pp. see BORN, BORNE.

beard OE. *beard* = OHG., G. *bart* :- WGmc. **barða*, rel. to OSl. *brada* beard (Russ. *borodá*), L. *barba*.

beast XIII. - OF. *beste* (mod. *bête*) - L. *bestia*. *Beast* displaced *deer* and was itself largely displaced by *animal*.

beat¹ strike repeatedly. OE. *bēatan* = OHG. *bozan*, ON. *bauta* :- Gmc. **bautan*.

beat² strive against a contrary wind or current at sea. XVII. of uncert. orig.

beatific making blessed. XVII (earlier *-ical*). - F. *béatifique* or L. *beātificus*, f. *beātus* blessed, pp. of *beāre* make happy. So **beatify** XVI, **beatitude** XV.

beau dandy XVII; lady's suitor XVIII. - F. :- L. *bellus* pretty, fine. Cf. BELLE.

beau ideal perfect type of beauty. XIX. - F.; *beau* sb., *idéal* adj.; see BEAU, IDEAL; often apprehended as meaning 'beautiful ideal'.

beauty XIII. ME. *bealte*, *beaute* - OF. *be(a)lte*, *biaute* (mod. *beauté*) :- Rom. **bellitāt-*, f. L. *bellus*; see BEAU, -TY. Hence **beautiful** XV, **beautify** XVI.

beaver amphibious rodent. OE. *be(o)for* = (M)LG., (M)Du. *bever*, OHG. *bibar* (G. *biber*), ON. *bjórr* :- Gmc. **bebruz*, rel. to Skr. *babhrús* brown, L. *fiber* beaver, ult. f. IE. **bhru-* brown.

because XIV. ME. *bi cause*, i.e. BY, CAUSE, after OF. *par cause de* by reason of.

béchamel white cream sauce. XVIII. - F., name of Louis de *Béchamel*, steward of Louis XIV.

beck¹ (arch. and dial.) brook. XIV (in place-names XI). - ON. *bekkr* :- Gmc. **bakkiz*, rel. to **bakiz*, whence OE. *beċe*, OS. *beki*, OHG. *bak* (G. *bach*).

beck² (arch. exc. in phr. *at one's beck and call*) significant gesture, as a nod. XIV. f. (now arch.) *beck* vb. (XIV), shortening of ME. *bekene* BECKON, the *-(e)n-* of the stem being taken for the inf. ending.

beckon make a mute signal (to). OE. *bēcnan*, **bīecnan* = OS. *bōknian*, OHG. *bouhnen* :- WGmc. **bauknjan*, f. **baukna* BEACON.

become †come, arrive; come to be; befit. OE. *becuman* = MLG., (M)Du. *becomen*, OHG. *biqueman* (G. *bekommen*) obtain, receive, Goth. *biqiman* come upon; f. BE- + COME.

bed OE. *bed(d)* = OS. *bed, beddi*, OHG. *betti* (G. *bett*), Goth. *badi* :- Gmc. **baðjam* (cf. **baðjaz*, whence ON. *beðr*), ult. orig. uncert.

bedad Anglo-Ir. int. XVIII. For *by dad*, substituted for *by Gad*; see BEGAD.

bedel(l) old forms of BEADLE retained in the universities of Oxford and Cambridge. XVI.

bedevil treat diabolically; play the devil with. XVIII. f. BE- + DEVIL.

bedew cover with dew. XIV. f. BE- + DEW; cf. MHG. *betouwen*, MLG. *bedauwen*.

bedim make dim. XVI. f. BE- + DIM.

bedizen dress up. XVII. f. BE- + †*dizen* (XVI) deck out (f. base repr. by the first syll. of DISTAFF; cf. MDu. *disen*, perh. the immed. source; see -EN[5]).

Bedlam, bedlam Hospital of St. Mary of Bethlehem, orig. for the entertainment of the bishop and canons of the Church of St. Mary at *Bethlehem* XV; †inmate of this XVI; lunatic asylum XVII; scene of uproar XVII. (Early forms of the town name are OE. *Betleem, Bedlem*.)

Bedlington Name of a town in Northumberland applied to a breed of short-haired terrier. XIX.

Bedouin Arab of the desert. XIV (*Bedoyn*). - OF. *beduin* (mod. *bédouin*) - Arab. *badawī*, f. *badw* desert.

bee OE. *bēo* = OHG. *bīa* (G. dial. *beie*), ON. *bý* :- Gmc. **bīōn-*.

beech forest tree of the genus *Fagus*. OE. *bēce* = MLG. *bōke* :- Gmc. **bōkjōn* (wk. fem.), rel. to **bōkō* (str. fem.), whence OE. *bōc*, OHG. *buohha* (G. *buche*), ON. *bók* (cf. BUCKWHEAT); all cogn. w. IE. **bhāgos*, whence Gr. *phāgós* edible oak, L. *fāgus* beech. Cf. BOOK.

beef flesh of the ox. XIII. ME. *boef, beef* - AN., OF. *boef, buef* (mod. *bœuf*) :- L. *bovem*, nom. *bōs* ox (see COW[1]). Hence **beefeater** eater of beef; Yeoman of the Guard. XVII.

Beelzebub the Devil. OE. *Belzebub*, ME. *Beelzebub* - L. *Beelzebub*, rendering (i) Heb. *ba'al zᵉbūb* 'lord of flies' (2 Kings 1: 2) and (ii) Gr. *Beelzeboúb* of the N.T. (Matt. 12: 24).

been see BE.

beer OE. *bēor* = MLG., MDu. *bēr*, OHG. *bior* (Du., G. *bier*), a WGmc. word, perh. - monastic L. *biber* drink, f. L. *bibere* (see IMBIBE). Until XV rarely found exc. in verse; prob. reinforced from LG. on the introduction of hopped liquor.

beestings first milk from a cow after calving. OE. **bēsting* (late WS. *bȳsting*), f. synon. *bēost* = (M)Du. *biest*, OHG. *biost* (G. *biest*, as in *biestmilch*); of unkn. orig.

beet OE. *bēte* = MLG., MDu. *bēte*, OHG. *bieza*; early WGmc. - L. *bēta*, perh. of Celtic orig. Unrecorded between OE. and late ME., when its currency was prob. due to LG. Hence **beetroot** XVI.

beetle[1] beating instrument. OE. *bētel* (WS. *bietel*) :- Gmc. **bautilaz*, f. **bautan* BEAT[1] + *-il-* -LE[1]. Cf. OHG. *bōzil* cudgel.

beetle[2] coleopterous insect. OE. *bitula, -ela*, f. **bit-*, short base of *bītan* BITE; see -LE[1].

beetle-browed XIV. of unkn. orig.

beetroot see BEET.

befall fall (chiefly fig.) OE.; pertain, belong XII; fall out, happen XIII. OE. *befeallan* = OS. *bifallan*, OHG. *bifallen*, f. BE- + FALL[2].

befit XV. f. BE- + FIT[3].

before OE. *beforan* = OS. *biforan*, OHG. *bifora* (G. *bevor*), f. BE- + Gmc. **forana* from the front (f. *fora* FOR). Hence **beforehand** XIII.

beg XIII. ME. *begge*, prob. :- OE. *bedecian* (cf. Goth. *bidagwa* beggar), f. Gmc. **beð-*, base of BID. So **beggar** sb. XIII, vb. XVI; cf. -AR.

begad XVIII. f. BY + GAD[3], cf. BEDAD.

beget pt. *begot*, arch. *begat*, pp. *begotten* †acquire XII; procreate XIII. First in north. texts with *g* repl. *ġ, ȝ* of the native forms OE. *beġietan*, ME. *biȝete*, corr. to OS. *bigetan* seize, OHG. *pigezzan* receive, Goth. *bigitan* find; see BE-, GET (XIII in the sense 'procreate', after ON. *geta*).

begin pt. *began*, pp. *begun*. OE. *beġinnan* = OS., OHG. *biginnan* (Du., G. *beginnen*), WGmc. f. BE- + **ginnan*, of unkn. orig.

begone[1] depart! XIV. imper. *be gone* treated as one word, like BEWARE.

begone[2] see WOE-BEGONE.

begonia XVIII. modL., named by Charles Plumier (d. 1706), French botanist, after Michel *Begon* (d. 1710), French patron of botany; see -IA[1].

beguile delude XIII; charm (away) XVI. f. BE- + †*guile* vb. (cf. GUILE sb.); cf. MDu. *begīlen*, AN. *degiler*.

begum Indian Muslim lady of high rank. XVIII. - Urdu *begam* - E. Turk. *begim*, f. *beg* prince, princess (cf. BEY) + 1st pers. sg. poss. suffix *-im*, i.e. 'my lady'.

behalf XIV. orig. and mainly in phr. with genitive, as *on God's, my*, etc. *behalf*, replacing earlier *on goddes, min, halve*, etc. (in late OE. *on mīnre healfe* for my part); see BY, HALF.

behave XV. orig. refl., lit. hold oneself in a certain respect; f. BE- + HAVE. Hence **behaviour** XV.

behead OE. *behēafdian*, f. BE- + *hēafod* HEAD.

behest †promise; (arch.) command. OE. *behǣs* (f. BE- + Gmc. **χaitan* bid, call) + parasitic *t*.

behind OE. *behindan* = OS. *bihindan*, f. BE- + *hindan* (see HIND[3]). Hence **behindhand** XVI; after BEFOREHAND.

behold OE. *beh(e)aldan* = OS. *bihaldan*, OHG. *bihaltan* (G. *behalten* keep); see BE- and HOLD. Eng. alone has the sense 'watch, look'; the cogn. languages only 'keep, maintain'.

beholden (arch.) obliged. XIV. repr. OE. *behealden* cautious, assiduous, pp. of *behealdan*, in the senses 'guard', 'keep', 'observe' (see prec.).

behoof (arch.) use, advantage. OE. *behōf*, in phr. *tō* . . *behōfe* for (one's) use or needs = (M)Du. *behoef*, MHG. *behuof* (G. *behuf*), WGmc. f. BE- + **χōf-*, var. of the base of **χabjan* HEAVE.

behove (arch.) †need OE.; be needful or fitting XII. OE. *behōfian* = MLG. *behōven*, (M)Du. *behoeven*; f. prec.

beige woollen fabric orig. left in its natural colours; yellowish-grey. XIX. - F. *beige* (OF. *bege*), of unkn. orig.

belabour †labour at; thrash. f. BE- + LABOUR vb.

belated XVII. f. BE- + †*lated* (XVI), f. LATE + -ED[1].

belay †beset, surround OE.; (naut.) fasten a running rope round a pin, etc. XVI. OE. *beleċġan* = OHG. *bileggen* (G. *belegen*), f. BE- + *leċġan* LAY. From XVI a new formation; the current (naut.) sense seems to be after Du. *beleggen*.

belch XV. of uncert. orig.; perh. shortening of OE. *be(a)lċettan*.

beldam †grandmother XV; old woman; hag XVI. f. *bel* (OF. *belle* fair, fem. of *bel* BEAU) as in †*belsire* grandfather + DAME.

beleaguer besiege, invest. XVI. - Du. *belegeren*, f. *be-* BE- + *leger* LEAGUER[2].

belfry †movable siege-tower XIII; bell-tower or -chamber XV. ME. *berfrey*, *belfrey* - OF. *berfrei*, *belfrei* (mod. *beffroi*) - Frankish **berȝfriđ*, prob. f. **berȝan* protect + **friđuz* peace, shelter; the etymol. meaning being 'defensive place of shelter'.

Belial spirit of evil personified; the Devil. XIII. - Heb. *beliya'al* worthlessness, destruction, f. *beli* not, without + *ya'al* use, profit.

belie OE. *belēogan* = OHG. *biliugan*, f. BE- + LIE[2].

believe late OE. *belȳfan*, *belēfan*, replacing, by prefix-substitution, earlier *ġelēfan* = OS. *gilōbian*, OHG. *gilouben* (G. *glauben*), Goth. *galaubjan* :- Gmc. **ȝalaubjan* hold dear, trust in, f. **ȝa-* Y- + **laub-* dear (see LOVE). So **belief** XII, repl. OE. *ġelēafa*.

belike (arch.) probably. XVI. orig. *by like* i.e. BY, LIKE[1] used as sb. 'probability, likelihood'.

belittle XVIII (orig. U.S.) f. BE- + LITTLE.

bell[1] hollow cup-shaped metal body producing a resonant musical sound when struck. OE. *belle* = MLG., MDu. *belle* (Du. *bel*); perh. rel. to BELL[2].

bell[2] bellow, roar. OE. *bellan*, corr. to OHG. *bellan* (G. *bellen*) bark, bray; cf. ON. *belja* and BELLOW.

belladonna deadly nightshade, drug prepared from this. XVIII. - It., lit. 'fair lady'; said to be so named because in Italy a face cosmetic was made from it.

belle handsome woman. XVII. - F., fem. of *bel*, BEAU.

belles-lettres XVIII. - F., lit. 'fine letters or literature', parallel to *beaux arts* fine arts; see BELLE, LETTER. Hence **belletrist**, **belletristic** XIX.

bellicose warlike. XV. - L. *bellicōsus*, f. *bellicus*, f. *bellum* war; see -OSE[1].

belligerent waging war. XVI. Earlier *belligerant* - L. *belligerant-*, prp. stem of *belligerāre*, f. *bellum* war + *gerere* (see GESTATION).

bellow roar as a bull. XIV. ME. *belwen*, of uncert. orig.

bellows instrument used to blow a fire. ME. *belwes*, *belows*, pl. of *belu*, *below*, prob. repr. OE. pl. *belga*, *belgum*, of *bel(i)ġ*, *bæl(i)ġ* BELLY, which in late OE. occurs as abbrev. of earlier *blæstbel(i)ġ* 'blowing-bag' = ON. *blástrbelgr*; see BLAST, BELLY.

belly †bag, pod, bellows OE.; †body XIII; abdomen, stomach XIV. OE. *beliġ* = OHG. *balg*, ON. *belgr*, Goth. *balgs* :- Gmc. **balȝiz* bag, sack, f. **balȝ-* **belȝ-* be inflated, swell; cf. BILLOW, BELLOWS.

belong XIV. f. ME. *longen* (cf. *long*, OE. *ġelang* at hand, dependent on); see BE-. Hence **belongings** circumstances connected with a person or thing XVII; possessions XIX; see -ING[1].

beloved XIV. pp. of (arch.) *belove* (XIII), f. BE- + LOVE.

below XIV (rare before XVI). f. BE- + LOW[1].

belt OE., corr. to OHG. *balz*, ON. *belti*, ult. - L. *balteus*, *-um*.

beluga great sturgeon; white whale. XVIII (in XVI *bellougina*). - Russ. *belúga* (in the latter sense also *belúkha*), f. *bélyĭ* white.

belvedere turret on a building commanding a view. XVI. (partly through F. *belvédère*) - It. *belvedere* lit. 'fair sight', f. *bel*, *bello* beautiful + *vedere* sight.

bemoan XVI. repl. ME. *bemene*, OE. *bemǣnan*; see BE-, MOAN.

bemuse XVIII. f. BE- + MUSE[1].

bench OE. *benċ* = OS., Du., (O)HG. *bank*, ON. *bekkr* :- Gmc. **baŋkiz*; cf. BANK[1].

bend[1] †ribbon, band OE.; (her.) ordinary formed by two parallel lines XV. OE. *bend* :- Gmc. **bandjō*, f. **band-* **bind-* BIND; later coinciding with *bende* - OF. *bende* (mod. *bande*) BAND[2]. Cf. BAND[1].

bend[2] bow, curve. OE. *bendan* (also 'bind, fetter') = MHG. *benden*, ON. *benda* :- Gmc. **bandjan*, f. **band-* BAND[1].

beneath OE. *beniđan*, *beneođan*, f. BE- + *niđan*, *neođan* below, down (f. Gmc. **niþ-*, see NETHER).

Benedictine (monk or nun) of the order of St. Benedict, founded by him *c*.529. XVII. - F. *bénédictin* or modL. *benedictīnus*, f. *Benedictus*; see -INE[1]. So **benedictine** liqueur made by these monks. XIX. - F. *bénédictine* (sc. *liqueur*), fem. of above adj.

benediction XV. - (O)F. *bénédiction* - L. *benedictiō*, *-ōn-*, f. *benedīcere*, *benedict-* bless, f. *bene* well + *dīcere* speak (see DICTION). Cf. BENISON.

benefaction doing good; gift for a charitable purpose. XVII. - late L. *benefactiō*, *-ōn-*, f. *benefícere*, *benefact-*; see next and -TION. So **benefactor** XV.

benefice †favour, benefit; ecclesiastical living. XIV. - OF. *benefice* (mod. *bénéfice* profit, perquisite) - L. *beneficium*, f. *bene* well + *fic-* var. of stem of *facere* DO[1], make. So **beneficence** XVI, **beneficent** XVII. - F. - L. **beneficial** XV. - F. or late L. **beneficiary** XVII. - L. (cf. F. *bénéficiaire*).

benefit †good or kind deed XIV; advantage XV. ME. *ben(e)fet* - AN. *benfet*, OF. *bienfet*, *-fait* :- L. *benefactum* good deed, f. *bene facere* do well. Hence **benefit** vb. XVI.

benevolence XV. - OF. *benivolence* - L. *benevolentia* well-wishing, f. *benevolēns*, *-ent-*, prp. of *bene velle* wish well. So **benevolent** XV.

benighted overtaken by the darkness of night XVI; in intellectual or moral darkness XVII. pp. of †*benight* vb., f. BE- + NIGHT.

benign XIV. - (O)F. *bénigne* fem., *bénin* masc. :-

L. *benigna*, *-us*, f. roots of *bonus* good and *gignere* beget (see KIN). Cf. MALIGN. So **benignant** XVIII. **benignity** XIV. - OF. or L.

bent[1] (arch.) reedy or rush-like grass; grassy plain, field XIV. repr. OE. *beonet-*, found as an element of place-names, e.g. *Bēonetlēah* (Bentley); corr. to OS. *binet*, OHG. *binuz* (G. *binse*) :- WGmc. **binut-*, of unkn. orig.

bent[2] †curved position; inclination; †extent to which a bow may be bent (fig. 'to the top of my bent', Sh.). XV. prob. f. BEND[2] on the analogy of pairs like *descend*, *descent*, *extend*, *extent*.

benthos flora and fauna of the sea-bottom. XIX. - Gr. *bénthos* depth of the sea.

benumb XV. f. †*benome(n)*, pp. of †*benim*, OE. *beniman* take away, f. BE- + *niman* take; see NUMB.

benzene aromatic liquid hydrocarbon XIX. f. BENZOIC acid, whence it is derived; earlier *benzine* (now used for a mixture of petroleum hydrocarbons). So **benzol** (esp. unrefined) benzene.

benzoin resin obtained from tree of genus *Styrax* XVI; a constituent of this; genus of trees (including Benjamin tree) XIX. ult. (through F., etc.) - Arab. *lubān-jāwī* 'frankincense of Java'. Hence **benzoic acid**. XVIII.

bequeath †utter, declare; assign (property), esp. by will. OE. *becweđan*, f. BE- + *cweđan* say; see QUOTH.

bequest XIV. f. (after BEQUEATH) BE- + †*quiste*, repr. OE. *-cwiss* (only in comps.), f. Gmc. **kweþ-* say (see QUOTH); for the parasitic *t* cf. BEHEST.

berate scold XVI. f. BE- + RATE[2].

Berber XIX. - Arab. *barbar*.

bereave OE. *berēafian* = OS. *birōbon*, OHG. *biroubōn*, Goth. *biraubōn* :- Gmc. **biraubōjan*, f. **bi-* BE- + **raubōjan* REAVE.

beret XIX. - F. *béret* Basque cap - s.w. F. dial. *berret*, Pr. *berret* (see BIRETTA).

bergamot kind of pear. XVII. - F. *bergamotte* - It. *bergamotta* - Turk. *begarmūdi*, f. *beg* prince + *armūdi* pear.

beriberi mainly tropical disease marked by paralytic weakness. XIX. - Sinhalese.

berry OE. *beri(ġ)e* = OS., OHG. *beri*, ON. *ber* :- Gmc. **bazja-* (cf. Goth. *-basi*).

berserk(er) Norse warrior who fought with frenzied fury. XIX. repr. ON. *berserkr*, acc. *berserk*, prob. f. **ber-* BEAR[1] + *serkr* coat.

berth (naut.) adequate sea-room XVII; appointment (esp. on board ship); sleeping-place on a ship XVIII. Early vars. *birth*, *byrth*; prob. f. BEAR[2] + -TH[1], with ref. to the nautical sense of the verb 'sail in a certain direction'.

beryl precious stone. XIII. - (O)F. *beril* (mod. *béryl*) - L. *bēryllus* - Gr. *bḗrullos*.

beseech XII. f. BE- + *seche* SEEK. The type *beseek* was current XII-XVII.

beseem †seem; (arch.) suit, befit. XIII. f. BE- + SEEM.

beset surround, besiege OE.; †bestow XII. OE. *besettan* = OS. *bisettian*, OHG. *bisezzan* (G. *besetzen*), Goth. *bisatjan*, f. BE- + Gmc. **satjan* SET[1].

beside(s) by the side (of); apart (from); in addition (to). XIII. ME. *biside(s)*, repr. OE. *be sīdan*, i.e. *be* BY + dat. sg. of *sīde* SIDE; see -S.

besiege XIII. f. (by substitution of prefix BE-) ME. *assiege* (XIII) - OF. *assegier* (mod. *assiéger*) :- Rom. **assedicāre*, f. AS- + **sedicum* SIEGE.

besmirch soil, discolour, (fig.) sully. XVI. f. BE- + SMIRCH.

besom broom. OE. *bes(e)ma*, OS. *besmo*, OHG. *besamo* (G. *besen*) :- WGmc. **besman-*, of unkn. orig.

bespeak †speak or call out OE.; speak for, order, speak to, address XVI; tell of, indicate XVII. OE. *besprecan* = OS. *besprekan*, OHG. *bisprehhan* (G. *besprechen*); WGmc., f. **bi-* BE- + **sprekan* SPEAK. Hence **bespoke** (of work commissioned), earlier †**bespoken** (XVII).

best (adj. and adv.) OE. *bet(e)st*, *best* = (as adj.) OS. (Du.) *best*, OHG. *bezzisto* (wk.; G. *best*), ON. *beztr*, Goth. *batists* :- Gmc. **batistaz*, superl. of **bat-*; see BETTER, -EST. Hence **best** vb. XIX; cf. *worst* (XVII).

bestial of beasts, like a beast. XIV. - (O)F. *bestial* - late L. *bēstiālis*, f. *bēstia* BEAST; see -IAL. So **bestiality** XIV. - (O)F.

bestir rouse to activity. XIV. f. BE- + STIR.

bestow place, deposit, apply. XIV. f. BE- + OE. *stōw* a place. Hence **bestowal** XVIII; see -AL[2].

bestrew OE. *bestrēowian*, f. BE- + STREW.

bestride OE. *bestrīdan*, f. BE- + STRIDE.

bet (lay) a wager. XVI. The sb. and vb. appear in the last decade of XVI, and it is uncertain which is prior; perh. aphetic of ABET (†sb.) 'instigation, support (of a cause)', the vb. being then derived from the sb.

betake †hand over, commit XIII; refl. commit oneself XVI; refl. resort, go XVII. f. BE- + TAKE; in ME. functioning as a var. of †*beteach*, OE. *betǣċan* (f. *tǣċan* TEACH).

betel leaf of the plant *Piper betle*, chewed in the East with areca nut. XIV. - Pg., of Dravidian orig. (Malayalam *verrila*, etc.). Hence **betel-nut** areca nut XVII.

bête noire object of aversion. XIX. - F., lit. 'black beast'.

bethink †think about OE.; (refl.) †collect one's thoughts OE.; reflect, recollect XIII. OE. *beđenċan*, OS. *bithenkian*, OHG. *bidenken*, Goth. *biþagkjan*; Gmc., f. **bi-* BE- + **þaŋkjan* THINK.

betide happen. XIII. f. BE- + TIDE[2]. Surviving mainly in *woe betide...!*

betimes at an early time, in good time. XIV. f. *betime* (XIII), f. *be* BY + TIME; see -S.

betoken XII. OE. **betācnian* = OHG. *bizeihhanōn* (G. *bezeichnen*); see BE-, TOKEN.

betony purple-flowered plant. XIV. - (O)F. *bétoine* - popL. **betonia* for *betonica*.

betray give up treacherously XIII; reveal involuntarily XVI. f. BE- + †*tray* (XIII) - OF. *traïr* (mod. *trahir*) - L. *trādere* deliver up (see TRADITION). Hence **betrayal** XIX; see -AL[2].

betroth engage with promise to marry. XIV. ME. *betrouthen*, f. BE- + *trouthe* TRUTH, later assim. to TROTH. Hence **betrothal** XIX; see -AL[2].

better adj. (OE.); adv. (XIII). OE. *bet(e)ra* (adj.) = OS. *betiro*, OHG. *bezziro* (G. *besser*), ON. *betri*, Goth. *batiza* :- Gmc. **batizan-*, f. **bat-*, rel. to OE. *bōt* BOOT[1], *bētan* improve. Hence **better** vb. XIV. **betterment** XVI.

between OE. *betwēon(um)*, f. Gmc. **bi* BY + **twēon*, rel. to TWO.

bevel †adj.: (her.) having two equal acute alternate angles XVI; oblique XVII; sb.: joiner's tool for setting off angles; slope, sloping surface XVII. - OF. **bevel*, F. *bi-*, *béveau* etc. (XVI), f. OF. *baif* open-mouthed, f. *baer* gape; cf. OF. *bever* give bias to.

beverage XIII. - OF. *bevrage* (mod. *breuvage*), f. L. *bibere* drink; see -AGE.

bevy company of ladies, birds, etc. XV. of unkn. orig.

bewail XIV. f. BE- + WAIL.

beware XIII. orig. *be war*, i.e. BE, WARE[2].

bewilder XVII. f. BE- + †*wilder* (cause to) lose one's way, perh. back-formation from WILDERNESS.

bewitch XIII. f. BE- + WITCH (vb.; OE. *wiccian*).

bewray (arch.) betray. XIII. f. BE- + ME. *wreien*, OE. *wrēġan* accuse = OS. *wrōgian*, OHG. *ruogen* (G. *rügen*), ON. *rœgja* :- Gmc. **wrōʒjan* (in Goth. *wrōhjan*), of unkn. orig.

bey Ottoman title. XVI. - Turk.

beyond OE. *beġeondan*, f. *be* BY + *ġeondan* from the farther side, f. Gmc. **jand-* YOND.

bezel sloping edge or side. XVII. - F. **besel* (mod. *béseau*, *bizeau*); of unkn. orig.

bezique card-game. XIX. - F. *bésigue*, of unkn. orig.

bhang Indian hemp. XVI. ult. (via Pg. *bangue*, Pers. *bang*, Urdu *bhāng*) - Skr. *bhaṅgā*.

bi- repr. L. *bi-* (earlier *dui-* = Gr. *di-*, Skr. *dvi-*) twice, doubly, two-, in L. chiefly in adj. formations on sb. stems, as BICEPS, *bicolor* of two colours, also with pp. ending, as *biformātus* of two forms; in a few, e.g. BIFID, the formation is on a vb.-stem. The prefix appears in Eng. first in adoptions from F., as *bigam* XIII (cf. BIGAMOUS), later from L. words, as *biformed* XVI (L. *biformis*), *bipartite* XVI (L. *bipartītus*). From XVII the L. analogy was widely extended and the prefix used with any adj. to express that a quality or property is doubled or repeated; in mod. scientific terminology forms in *-ate*, *-ated* are most frequently employed.

bias oblique; sb. oblique line, inclination; adv. XVI. - (O)F. *biais*, of unkn. orig. Hence **bias** vb. XVII.

bib sb. cloth to protect the front of a child's dress XVI. perh. f. (arch.) **bib** vb. drink, tipple (XIV), which is poss. - L. *bibere* but may be independently imit.

Bible the Holy Scriptures XIII. - (O)F. - ecclL. *biblia*, n. pl. taken as fem. sg. - Gr. (*tà*) *biblía* '(the) books', pl. of *biblíon*, orig. dim. of *bíblos*, *búblos* papyrus, scroll.

biblio- repr. Gr. *biblio-*, stem of *biblíon* (see prec.), as in **bibliography** (XIX) - F. or modL. - Gr. *bibliographíā* writing of books.

bibulous given to much drinking. XVII. f. L. *bibulus*, f. *bibere* drink; see -ULOUS.

bicameral having two legislative chambers. XIX. f. BI- + L. *camera* CHAMBER + -AL[1].

biceps muscle with double head or attachment. XVII. - L. *biceps* two-headed, f. BI- + *-ceps*, rel. to *caput* HEAD.

bicker †skirmish XIII; altercation XIV. ME. *biker*, *beker*, of unkn. orig. So **bicker** vb. XIII.

bicycle XIX. - F. f. BI- + Gr. *kúklos* CYCLE.

bid pt. (in D) *bade*, (in B) *bid*; pp. (in D) *bidden*, (in B and C) *bid*. A. ask, pray; B. offer; C. announce; D. command. The present forms repr. OE. str. vb. *biddan*, pt. *bæd*, *bǣdon*, pp. *beden* ask, entreat, demand = OS. *biddian*, OHG. (G.) *bitten*, ON. *biðja*, Goth. *bidjan* :- Gmc. **biðjan*.

The present meanings combine those of this vb. with those of OE. *bēodan*, pt. *bēad*, *budon*, pp. *boden* offer, announce, command = OS. *biodan*, OHG. *biotan* (G. *bieten*), ON. *bjóða*, Goth. *biudan*.

OE. *biddan* had already acquired the sense 'command', and the similarity of several of the ME. forms of the two vbs. furthered the unification of the two words.

bide (arch.) remain; wait for OE.; †endure, suffer XIII. OE. *bīdan* = OS. *bīdan*, OHG. *bītan* (G. dial. *beiten*), ON. *bíða*, Goth. *beidan* :- Gmc. **bīðan*; formally identical with Gr. *peíthein* persuade, etc., but the connection of sense is not clear.

biennial lasting two years; recurring every two years. XVII. f. L. *biennis* of two years, *biennium* space of two years; see BI- and ANNUAL.

bier stand for a corpse. OE. *bēr* (WS. *bǣr*) = OS., OHG. *bāra* (G. *bahre*) :- WGmc. **bǣro*, f. **beran* BEAR[2]; the sp. with *ie* dates from *c.*1600.

biffin variety of apple XVIII; baked apple XIX. dial. pronunc. of *beefing*, f. BEEF, in ref. to the deep-red colour of the apple; see -ING[3].

bifid cleft in two. XVII. - L. *bifidus*, f. BI- + **fid-*, base of *findere* cleave.

bifurcate XVII. f. medL. *bifurcāre*, f. L. *bifurcus* two-forked, f. BI- + *furca* FORK; see -ATE[3]. Hence **bifurcation** XVII.

big †strong, stout XIII; of great bulk XVI. The earliest exx. are from northerly texts; of unkn. orig., possibly Scand.

bigamy XIII. - (O)F. *bigamie*, f. *bigame* (whence ME. *bigam*) - late L. *bigamus*, f. BI- + Gr. *-gamos* married. Hence **bigamist** XVII, **-ous** XIX.

bight bend, angle OE.; (loop of a rope XVII); bay XVI. OE. *byht* :- **buχtiz*; cf. (M)LG. (whence G.) *bucht* :- **buʒ-*, short stem of **beuʒ-*, see BOW[2].

bigot †hypocritical or superstitious adherent of religion XVI; obstinate adherent of a creed or opinion XVII. - F., of unkn. orig. Hence **bigoted**, **bigotry** XVII.

bigwig man of note or importance. XVIII. f. BIG + WIG, with ref. to the large wigs worn by men of distinction.

bilberry XVI. prob. of Norse orig.; cf. Da. *bøllebær*, f. *bølle* bilberry + *bær* BERRY.

bile XVII. - F. - L. *bilis*. So **bilious** XVI (see -OUS).

bilge bottom of a ship's hull XV; filth collecting there XIX (cf. *bilge water* XVIII). prob. var. of BULGE, used in the same senses.

bilk spoil an adversary's score at cribbage; defraud; elude. XVII. perh. alt. of BALK vb.

bill[1] (hist.) weapon of war (sword or halberd); pruning-hook. OE. *bil* = OS. *bill*, OHG. *billi* :- WGmc. **bilja*.

bill[2] beak. OE. *bile*, not elsewhere in Gmc.; perh.

from same base as prec. Hence **bill** vb.[1] peck XIII; stroke or caress with the bill XVI.

bill[2] †written document; †legal statement of a case; †list, catalogue XIV; note of charges, account; poster XV; draft of an act of parliament XVI. - AN. *bille* or AL. *billa*, of uncert. orig. Hence **bill** vb.[2] enter in a bill XIV; announce by bill XVII.

billet[1] †short document XV; (f. the vb.) military order to provide board and lodging XVII; place of such lodging; situation, job XIX. - AN. *billete* or AL. *billeta*, dim. of *billa* BILL[2]; see -ET. Hence **billet** vb. assign quarters to. XVI.

billet[2] thick piece of wood. XV. - (O)F. *billette*, *billot*, dims. of *bille* tree-trunk, length of round timber - medL. *billa*, *billus*, prob. of Celtic orig. (cf. Ir. *bile* sacred tree, large tree); see -ET.

billet-doux love-letter. XVII. - F., 'sweet note'; see BILLET[1], DULCET.

billiards XVI. - F. *billard* name of the game and the cue, f. *bille*; see BILLET[2] and -ARD. Made pl. like *bowls*, etc.

billion XVII. - F. *billion*, arbitrarily f. *million* MILLION, by substitution of BI- for the initial *mi-*.

billow XVI. - ON. *bylgja* billow (Sw. *bölja*, Da. *bølge*), f. Gmc. **bulȝ-* **belȝ-* swell; cf. (M)HG. *bulge* †billow, leather bag, and BELLY.

bin †manger OE.; receptacle for corn, etc. XIV. OE. *bin(n)*, *binne* - OBrit. **benna* (W. *ben* cart) :- **bhendhnā*, f. IE. **bhendh-* weave, BIND; or - medL. *benna*, which is the source of F. *banne*, It. dial. *benna* hamper, Du. *ben*, G. *benne* body of a cart.

binary XV. - late L. *bīnārius* two together (cf. BI-); see -ARY.

bind OE. *bindan*, pt. *band*, *bundon*, pp. *bunden* = OS. *bindan*, OHG. *bintan* (G. *binden*), ON. *binda*, Goth. *bindan* :- Gmc. **bendan*, f. IE. base **bhendh-* (Skr. *bandh* bind). Hence **binder** OE. (of books XVI); whence **bindery** XIX (orig. U.S.), after Du. *binderij*.

bindweed XVI. f. BIND + WEED[1].

bine flexible (climbing) stem. XIX. See WOODBINE.

binge XIX. prob. sl. use of dial. *binge* vb. soak (a wooden vessel).

binnacle box containing ship's compass. XV. Earlier forms *biticle*, *bittacle* - Sp. *bitácula*, *bitácora* or Pg. *bitácola* (corr. to It. *abitacolo*, F. *habitacle*) - L. *habitāculum* habitation, f. *habitāre* inhabit; the change from *tt* to *nn* may have been bridged by such a form as *biddikil* (XVII).

binocular adapted to both eyes XVIII; sb. pl. field or opera glasses XIX. f. L. *bīnī* two together (cf. BI-) + *oculus* EYE, after OCULAR.

binomial (math.) having two terms. XVI. f. F. *binôme* or modL. *binōmius*, of uncert. orig. (see BI-, -IAL).

bio- comb. form of Gr. *bíos* life (cf. QUICK), as in **biography** XVII. - F. *biographie* or modL. *biographia*, medGr. *biographía*; so **biographer** XVIII. **biology** XIX. - F. *biologie* - G.

biped XVII. - L. *bipēs*, *biped-*, f. BI- + *pēs* FOOT.

biplane XX. f. BI- + PLANE[4].

birch OE. *bi(e)rce* = MLG. *berke*, OHG. *birka* (G. *birke*) :- Gmc. **berkjōn*; rel. to synon. OE. *be(o)rc* = Du. *berk*, ON. *bjǫrk* :- Gmc. **berkō*; cf. Skr. *bhūrja-*, L. *farnus*, *fraxinus* ash-tree.

bird (obs. or dial.) young bird OE., feathered animal (in this sense superseding *fowl*); maiden, girl XIII. OE. *brid*, of unkn. orig. In the sense 'maiden' there may have been blending with ME. *burde* young woman, lady.

bireme (galley) having two banks of oars. XVII. - L. *birēmis*, f. BI- + *rēmus* oar (cf. ROW[2]).

biretta clerical square cap. XVI. - It. *berretta* or Sp. *birreta*, fem. dims. corr. to Pr. *berret* BERET, based on late L. *birrus*, *-um* hooded cape or cloak, perh. of Celtic orig.

birth XII. - ON. *byrð* birth, descent, corr. to Goth. *(ga)baurþs*, f. Gmc. **bur-* **ber-* BEAR[2]; see -TH[1]. Hence **birthday** XIV; cf. OE. *gebyrddæg*.

biscuit XIV. - OF. *bescuit* (mod. *biscuit*) :- medL. **biscoctus* twice-baked (sc. *panis* bread), f. L. *bis* twice + *coctus*, pp. of *coquere* COOK.

bisect XVII. f. BI- + *sect-*, pp. stem of L. *secāre* cut. So **bisection** XVII.

bishop OE. *biscop*, corr. to OS. *biskop*, OHG. *biscof* (G. *bischof*), ON. *biskup* - popL. **biscopus*, for ecclL. *episcopus* - Gr. *episkopos* overseer (whence Goth. *aipiskaupus*), f. *epí* EPI- + *-skopos* looking (cf. -SCOPE).

bismuth XVII (*bismute*). - modL. *bisemutum*, latinization of G. *wismut*, of unkn. orig.

bison in the present form first recorded from A.V. (Deut. 14: 5 margin), earlier in L. pl. *bisontes* of *bison* (whence F. *bison*) - Gmc. **wisand-*, **wisund-* (OE. *wesend*, OHG. *wisant*, *-unt*, ON. *visundr*); familiar in recent times in connection with the American bison.

bisque rich (esp. crayfish) soup. XVII. - F. *bisque*, of unkn. orig.

bissextile leap(-year). XVI. - late L. *bis(s)extilis* (sc. *annus* year) year of the *bissextus* intercalary day inserted in the Julian calendar every fourth year after the *sixth* day before the calends of March (24 Feb.), f. *bis* twice + *sextus* SIXTH.

bistoury scalpel. XVIII. - F. *bistouri*, of unkn. orig.

bit[1] A. †biting, bite OE.; †cutting edge XIV; boring-piece, borer XVI; B. mouth-piece of a bridle XIV. OE. *bite* = OS. *biti*, OHG. *biz* (G. *biss*), ON. *bit* :- Gmc. **bitiz*, f. **bītan* BITE. The origin of sense B is not clear; cf. OE. *bitol* bridle, ON. *bitull*, G. *gebiss*.

bit[2] portion bitten off; morsel of food OE.; small piece XVI. OE. *bita* = OHG. *bizzo* (G. *bissen*), ON. *biti* (see BITT) :- Gmc. **bitan-*, f. **bītan* BITE.

bitch female dog OE.; bad woman XV. OE. *bicce*, rel. obscurely to ON. *bikkja*, of unkn. orig.

bite pt. *bit*, pp. *bitten*, *bit*. OE. *bītan*, pt. *bāt*, *biton*, pp. *biten* = OS. *bītan*, OHG. *bīzan* (G. *beissen*), ON. *bíta*, Goth. *beitan* :- Gmc. **bītan*; the corr. short base is repr. by Skr. *bhidyáte* is split, L. *fid-*, *findere* cleave. Hence **bite** sb. XV.

bitt (naut.) usu. pl. pair of posts on deck for fastening cables. XIV. prob. orig. a LG. sea term; cf. synon. LG., Du. *beting*, f. Gmc. **bit-*, repr. also by MHG. *bizze* wooden peg, ON. *biti* cross-beam.

bitter[1] contrary of sweet. OE. *biter*, corr. to OS., OHG. *bittar* (Du., G. *bitter*), ON. *bitr*, Goth. *baitrs*; prob. f. Gmc. **bit-*, base of **bītan* BITE. Hence **bitter-sweet** sb. XIV, adj. XVII. Cf. F.

aigre-doux, *amer-doux*, L. *dulcamārum*. So **bitterly** OE. *biterlīce*; see -LY[2]. **bitterness** OE. *biternes*.

bitter[2] 'a Bitter is but the turn of a Cable about the Bitts . . And the Bitters end is that part of the Cable doth stay within boord' (1627, Capt. Smith). f. BITT + -ER[1]. Hence prob. phr. *to the bitter end* to the last extremity (now assoc. with BITTER[1]).

bittern marsh bird with booming note. XIV. Earliest forms *botor*, *butor*, etc. - OF. *butor* - Rom. **būtitaurus*, f. L. *būtiō* bittern + *taurus* bull. Forms with final *n* (XVI) are perh. due to assoc. with *hern* HERON.

bitumen XV. - L. So **bituminous** XVII. - F. *bitumineux* - L. *bitūminōsus*.

bivalve XVII. f. BI- + VALVE.

bivouac (orig.) night-watch under arms; (hence) temporary encampment without tents. XVIII. - F. *bivouac* - MLG. *biwacht* or Du. *bijwacht* lit. 'extra watch'. Hence as vb. XIX.

bizarre XVII. - F. - It. *bizzarro*, of uncert. orig.

blab tell-tale, tatler; loose chatter. XIV. contemp. with †*blabber* vb. babble, chatter and synon. †*lab* sb. and vb. Perh. f. an imit. Gmc. base **blab-*; cf. OHG. *blabbizōn*, MHG. *blepzen*, G. *plappern*. Hence **blab** vb. XV.

black OE. *blæc*, *blac-*, corr. to OS. *blac* ink, OHG. *bla(c)h-*; cf. ON. *blakkr* dusky, dun; of unkn. orig. (In ME. confused with *blac* pale, wan; cf. BLEAK[2].) Superseded SWART in gen. use as a colour-name. Hence vbs. **black** XIII, **blacken** XIII (see -EN[5]). **Blackamoor** Ethiopian, Negro. XVI (orig. *black More*; see MOOR. Forms with inserted *-a-*, unexpl., appear XVI). **black-ball** black ball recording an adverse vote; hence vb. XVIII. **blackberry** OE. pl. *blaceberian*. **blackguard** A. †(coll.) menials, camp-followers, etc. XVI; †vagrants, criminals XVII; B. †man in black, †boot-black, etc. XVI; low worthless character XVIII; orig. meaning and application unknown. **blackleg** turf swindler XVIII; workman taking the place of one on strike XIX; of unkn. orig. **blackmail** (hist., orig. Sc.) tribute (see MAIL[2]) exacted by freebooting chiefs in return for protection XVI; (gen.) payment extorted by intimidation or pressure XIX. **blacksmith** one who works in 'black metal' (i.e. iron). XV.

bladder OE. *blǣdre*, later *blæddre* = OS. *blādara*, OHG. *blātara* (G. *blatter*), ON. *blaðra* :- Gmc. **blǣ-* BLOW[1] + **-dro-*, instr. suffix corr. to L. *-trum*, Gr. *-trā*, *-tron*, Skr. *-tram*.

blade A. leaf OE.; spathe of grass XIV. B. broad flattened part of an implement OE.; thin cutting edge, sword XIV. OE. *blæd*, pl. *bladu* = OS. *blad*, OHG. *blat* (G. *blatt*), ON. *blað* leaf, etc. :- Gmc. **blaðam*, perh. pp. formation (IE. **-tos*) on the base **blō-* BLOW[2]. The present form derives from OE. obl. cases.

blame vb. XII. - OF. *bla(s)mer* (mod. *blâmer*) = Pr. *blasmar*, Sp. *lastimar* :- popL. *blastēmāre* for ecclL. *blasphēmāre* revile, reproach (see BLASPHEME). So **blame** sb. XIII. - (O)F. *blâme*, f. the vb.

blanch XIV. - (O)F. *blanchir*, f. *blanc*, fem. *blanche* white, BLANK.

blancmange †dish of white meat with dressing XIV; jelly made with milk XVI. Earliest form *blancmanger* - (O)F., f. *blanc* white + *manger* food, sb. use of *manger* eat (cf. MANGER). The second el. was shortened to *mange* in XVIII.

bland XV (only Sc.), XVII. - L. *blandus*.

blandish flatter gently. XIV. - OF. *blandiss-*, lengthened stem (see -ISH[2]) of *blandir* :- L. *blandīrī*, f. *blandus* BLAND. Hence **blandishment** XVI.

blank XIV (orig. †'white'). - (O)F. *blanc* white :- Rom. **blancus* - Gmc. **blaŋkaz*.

blanket †white woollen stuff XIII; sheet of soft woollen cloth XIV. - OF. *blanket* (AL. *blanchettum*), var. of *blanchet*, f. *blanc* white; see BLANK, -ET.

blare roar, bellow XIV; trumpet XVIII. ME. *blere* - (M)Du. *bleren* and MLG., MDu. *blaren*; of imit. orig.

blarney cajoling talk. XIX. f. *Blarney*, name of a village near Cork, Ireland.

blasé XIX. - F., pp. of *blaser* exhaust by enjoyment or indulgence.

blaspheme XIV. - OF. *blasfemer* (F. *-ph-*) - ecclL. *blasphēmāre* revile, blaspheme - Gr. *blasphēmein*, f. *blásphēmos* evil-speaking (**pha-* speak; *phēmí* I say). Cf. BLAME. So **blasphemous** XV. **blasphemy** XIII (see -Y[3]).

blast gust of wind or air. OE. *blǣst* = OHG. *blāst*, ON. *blástr* (perh. the immed. source in ME.) :- Gmc. **blǣstaz*, f. **blǣs-* (see BLAZE[3]). Hence **blast** vb. XIV.

blatant first used by Spenser in *the blat(t)ant beast* (F.Q. v. xii. 37, etc.) to describe the thousand-tongued monster produced by Cerberus and Chimæra and symbolizing calumny 1596; offensively noisy or clamorous XVII. perh. alt., after adjs. in -ANT, of Sc. *blatand*, prp. of *blate* BLEAT.

blather, blether talk nonsense. XV. orig. Sc. - ON. *blaðra*, f. *blaðr* nonsense. For the var. *blether* cf. Sc. *gether* for *gather*. Hence as sb. XVIII.

blaze[1] †torch; bright flame or fire. OE. *blæse*, *blase* :- Gmc. *blasōn*; rel., through the gen. sense 'shining', to BLAZE[2]. Hence **blaze** vb. XIII. **blazer** thing that blazes or shines bright XVII; bright-coloured jacket for sports wear XIX; see -ER[1].

blaze[2] white spot. XVII. of uncert. orig., but identical in meaning with ON. *blesi*, MDu. *blesse* (Du. *bles*), G. *blässe*, *blesse*. Hence **blaze** vb. mark a tree with white by stripping the bark, indicate (a trail) in this way. XIX.

blaze[3] †blow (a trumpet, etc.) XIV; proclaim, publish XV. - MLG., MDu. *blāzen* blow = OHG. *blāsan* (G. *blasen*), ON. *blása*, Goth. *-blēsan* :- Gmc. **blǣsan* (cf. BLAST), extension of **blǣ-*; see BLOW[1].

blazon (her.) shield XIII; heraldic description XVI. - (O)F. *blason* orig. shield; of unkn. orig. Hence as vb. XVI.

-ble - (O)F. - L. *-bilis*, adj. suffix denoting tendency, fitness, ability, or capability of doing or being something; added to vb.-stems, as *flēbilis* lamentable, tearful, f. *flēre* weep; *mōbilis* easily moved, MOBILE; *stabilis* steadfast, STABLE[2]; with vb.-stems in *a*, *i*, and *u* it combined to form the compound suffixes repr. in Eng. by -ABLE, -IBLE, and *-uble*, of which the first (the only one in living use) is by far the most common, and capable of being compounded with any verb; the last is repr. only in *soluble, voluble*. The corr. abstract nouns end in *-bility* and advs. in *-bly*.

bleach vb. OE. *blǣcan* = ON. *bleikja* :- Gmc. **blaikjan*, f. **blaik-* shining, white, BLEAK².

bleak¹ small river-fish. XV. prob. - ON. *bleikja* = OHG. *bleicha* :- Gmc. **blaikjōn*, f. **blaik-* white (see next).

bleak² †pale, wan; bare of vegetation, exposed; cold from bareness. XVI. Obscurely rel. to †*blake* pale, yellow, †*bleach* pale, bare, †*bleike, blayke* pale, yellow - ON. *bleikr* shining, white = OE. *blāc* (ME. *blāke, blōke*), OS. *blēk*, OHG. *bleih* :- Gmc. **blaika-*.

blear (of the eyes) dim. XIV (vb. XIII). of uncert. orig. Hence **bleary** XIV; see -Y¹.

bleat OE. *blǣtan* = OHG. *blāzen*, Du. *blaten*; of imit. orig.

bleed OE. *blēdan* = MLG. *blōden*, ON. *blœða* :- Gmc. **blōðjan*, f. **blōðam* BLOOD.

blemish XIV. - OF. *blemiss-*, extended stem (see -ISH²) of *ble(s)mir* render pale, injure, prob. of Gmc. orig. Hence **blemish** sb. XVI.

blench †deceive OE.; start aside XIII. OE. *blenċan* = ON. *blekkja* impose upon :- Gmc. *blaŋkjan*; cf. BLINK.

blend vb. XIII. At first mainly north.; prob. of Scand. orig. and due to *blend-* pres. stem, *blēnd-* pt. stem, of ON. *blanda* mix = OE., OS., Goth. *blandan*, OHG. *blantan*. Cf. BLIND vb.

blende native sulphide of zinc. XVII. - G. *blende*, f. *blenden* deceive (see BLIND); so called because, while often resembling galena, it yielded no lead.

blenny genus of spiny fishes. XVIII. - L. *blennius*, var. of *blendius* - Gr. *blénnos* slime, in ref. to the mucous coating of its scales.

blesbok S. African antelope. XIX. - Afrikaans, f. Du. *bles* BLAZE² + *bok* goat (BUCK).

bless A purely English formation. OE. *blētsian, blēdsian*, perh. f. *blōðam* BLOOD, the etymological meaning being 'mark so as to hallow with blood'; the sense-development was influenced by its being used to translate L. *benedīcere* and Gr. *eulogeîn* in Christian use, and by its formal assoc. with *bliss*.

blight disease in plants, as mildew; baleful influence, orig. on plants. XVII (also *blite*). perh. for earlier **blēht*, repr. formally OE. *blæċðu, blæċð(rust)*, rel. to *blæċe* (all applied to skin diseases), and further to BLEACH.

blighter contemptible fellow. XIX. f. *blighted* euphem. substitute for *blasted* (see BLAST) as an epithet of reprobation; see -ER¹.

Blighty (army sl.) England, home. XX. contr. form, originating in the Indian army, of Hind. *bilāyatī* foreign, (esp.) European, f. Arab. *wilāyat* inhabited country, district.

blimp small non-rigid dirigible airship. XX. of uncert. orig. (said to be based on the adj. LIMP).

blind adj. OE. *blind* = OS. *blind*, OHG. *blint* (G. *blind*), ON. *blindr*, Goth. *blinds* :- Gmc. **blindaz* :- IE. **bhlendhos*; cf. Latv. *blendu* see dimly, and BLUNDER. Hence **blind** vb. XIII; repl. †*blend*, OE. *blendan* = OHG. *blentan* (G. *blenden*) :- WGmc. **blandjan*. **blind** sb. screen; misleading pretext XVII. **blind-man's-buff** (see BUFF¹). XVI. **blind-worm** slow-worm XV; cf. Du. *blindworm*.

blindfold cover the eyes of, with a bandage. XVI. Superseded †*blindfelle* (XII-XVI); OE. *ġeblindfellian* strike blind, f. BLIND + FELL⁴.

blink †A. deceive; start aside XIV; B. twinkle with the eyes or eyelids; †glance XVI; cast a momentary gleam XVIII. prob. of mixed origin; partly later form of synon. †*blenk* XIV, var. of BLENCH; partly - (M)Du. *blinken* shine, glitter, which may be based on a nasalized var. of **blik-* shine (see BLEAK²).

bliss OE. *bliss, blīðs* = OS. *blīdsea*, f. Gmc. **blīþiz* BLITHE.

blister sb. XIII. ME. *blister, blester*, of unkn. orig.; poss. OF. *blestre, blostre* swelling, pimple. Hence **blister** vb. XV.

blithe joyous. OE. *blīðe* = OS. *blīði*, OHG. *blīdi* cheerful, friendly, ON. *blíðr*, Goth. *bleiþs* :- Gmc. **blīþiz*; of unkn. orig. Cf. BLISS.

blithering (colloq.) senselessly talkative; contemptible. XIX. f. *blither*, var. of *blether* (see BLATHER).

blitz shortening of G. *blitzkrieg* 'lightning-war'. XX.

blizzard XIX. of unkn. orig. (first (U.S.) senses 'sharp blow', 'shot').

bloat †*bloat herring*, herring smoked and half-dried. XVI. Hence †**bloated** in the same sense XVII; whence **bloater** XIX; see -ED¹, -ER¹. Of uncert. orig. Identical in form are *bloat* adj. and vb. and *bloated* ppl. adj., which are used of a puffed, swollen, or inflated condition, but it is doubtful whether the two groups have the same ult. orig.

blob XV. In early use north.; imit. Cf. BLUBBER, BUBBLE.

block solid piece or mass (orig. of wood) XIV; mould for a hat, etc. XVI; group of buildings XVIII. - (O)Fr. *bloc* - (M)Du. *blok*, (M)LG. *block*, of unkn. orig. Hence (or - F. *bloquer*) **block** vb. XV; whence **blockade** XVII.

blond XV. - (O)F. *blond*, fem. *blonde* :- medL. *blundus, blondus* yellow, perh. of Gmc. orig.

blood OE. *blōd* = OS. *blōd*, OHG. *bluot* (G. *blut*), ON. *blóð*, Goth. *blōþ* :- Gmc. **blōðam*, of unkn. orig. Hence **bloodhound** XIV, **bloodthirsty** XVI (Coverdale, after Luther's *blutdürstig*). **bloody** OE. *blōdig*; see -Y¹.

bloom¹ blossom, flower XIII; powdery deposit on fruits XVII. ME. *blom(e)* - ON. *blóm* flower, blossom, and *blómi* prosperity, pl. flowers, corr. to OS. *blōmo*, OHG. *bluomo, -ma* (G. *blume*), Goth. *blōma* :- Gmc. **blōma-, *blōman-, -ōn-*, f. **blō-* BLOW². For the OE. syn. see BLOSSOM. Hence **bloom** vb. XIII.

bloom² mass of iron brought into the form of a thick bar. OE. *blōma* identical in form with BLOOM¹, but prob. a different word.

bloomer (chiefly pl.) women's trouser costume. XIX. f. name of Mrs. Amelia *Bloomer*, who advocated the use of the dress.

blossom flower OE.; mass of flowers on a tree XIII. OE. *blōstm, blōs(t)ma* corr. to (M)Du. *bloesem*, MLG. *blōs(s)em*; cf. ON. *blómstr*; gen.

referred to the same base as BLOOM[1], viz. **blō̆*-, of which **blō̆s*- appears to be an extended form. Hence **blossom** vb. OE. *blōstmian*. **blossomy** XIV; see -Y[1].

blot spot, stain. XIV. The distribution of the earliest exx. is consistent with a Scand. orig., but no suitable form is known; cf., however, Icel. *blettr* blot, stain, Da. dial. *blat* spot, blot. Hence **blot** vb. spot, stain. XV (*blotting-paper* XVI).

blotch inflamed patch on the skin XVII; blot (as of ink) XVIII. Partly alt. of synon. †*plotch* (XVI), by assoc. with BLOT and †*botch* pimple, etc. (XIV), partly blending of these. Cf. contemp. SPLOTCH.

blouse XIX. - F., of unkn. orig.

blow[1] produce a current of air; puff air (into). OE. str. vb. *blāwan*, pt. *blēow*, pp. *blāwen*, OHG. *blā(h)an*, also (wk.) *blāen* (G. *blähen* blow up, swell); IE. base **bhlē*-, repr. also by L. *flāre*.

blow[2] (arch.) bloom, flourish. OE. str. vb. *blōwan*, corr. to wk. verbs OS. *blōjan*, OHG. *bluoen* (G. *blühen*); all f. Gmc. **blō̆*- (cf. BLADE, BLOOM[1], BLOSSOM).

blow[3] hard stroke with fist or weapon. XV (first in northern texts as *blaw*). of unkn. orig.

blowzy bloated or red-faced; dishevelled. XVIII. f. †*blowze* wench XVI, of unkn. orig.; see-Y[1].

blub (colloq.) weep effusively. XIX. Shortening of next vb.

blubber vb. †bubble; weep copiously XIV; sb. †foam, bubble XIV; jelly-fish, fat of whales XVII. ME. *blob-*, *bluber* sb., *blob-*, *bluberen* vb., perh. of imit. orig.; cf. G. dial. *blubbern* bubble, gabble.

bludgeon heavy-headed stick. XVIII. of unkn. orig. Hence as vb. XIX.

blue XIII. ME. *bleu* - (O)F. :- Rom. **blāvus* - Gmc. **blǣwaz* (whence OE. *blǣwen*, OHG. *blāw*, G. *blau*, ON. *blár*), prob. rel. to L. *flāvus* yellow. In *blue blood* tr. Sp. *sangre azul*, applied to Spaniards claiming freedom from Moorish, Jewish, or other admixture.

blue-stocking attrib. wearing blue stockings XVII; applied from *c*.1780 to the intellectuals who met in London at the houses of Mrs. Montague and others, where blue worsted stockings were worn by some instead of black silk.

bluff[1] nearly vertical or perpendicular XVII; rough, blunt XVIII; good-naturedly curt or abrupt XIX. orig. naut., perh. of LG. orig. As sb. broad precipitous headland XVII (first in N. America).

bluff[2] (orig. U.S. in poker) give a false impression of strength, etc.; also sb. XIX. - Du. *bluffen* brag, boast, and *bluff* bragging, boasting.

blunder move blindly or stupidly XIV; make a stupid mistake XVIII. prob. of Scand. orig.; cf. MSw., Norw. *blundra* shut the eyes, frequent. of the base found in ON. *blunda*, rel. to BLIND; but the sense-development is not clear.

blunderbuss short gun with large bore. XVII. alt., by assoc. with BLUNDER, of Du. *donderbus*, f. *donder* THUNDER + *bus* gun (orig. box, tube).

blunt †dull, stupid XII; not physically sharp XIV; †rude, unrefined XV; abrupt of speech XVI. of uncert. orig.

blur sb. and vb. smear, stain. XVI. of unkn. orig.

blurb (orig. U.S.) publisher's commendatory advertisement. XX. of unkn. orig.

blurt †puff in scorn; utter abruptly. XVI. prob. imit.

blush vb. OE. *blyscan*, corr. to MLG. *bloschen*, LG. *blüsken*; cf. (M)Du. *blōzen*, OE. *āblysian*.

bluster XV. ult. imit.; cf. LG. *blustern*, *blistern* flutter.

boa large S. American snake. XIX. - modL. use of L. *boa*, of unkn. orig.

boar OE. *bār* = OS. *bēr(swīn)*, OHG. *bēr* :- WGmc. **bairaz*.

board flat piece of wood; table (now only as used for meals); border, edge (now only in *seaboard*); ship's side. OE. *bord* combines two orig. distinct Gmc. words: (i) a str. n. = OS. *bord*, MHG., G. *bort* board, ON. *borð*, Goth. (*fōtu*)*baurd* :- Gmc. **borðam*; (ii) a str. m. = OS. *bord*, ON. *borð* :- Gmc. **borðaz*. The OE. words were reinforced in ME. by the uses of F. *bord* (of Gmc. orig.). Hence **board** vb. XV.

boast sb. XIII; vb. XIV (in early use both sb. and vb. often denote or imply clamorous or threatening utterance). - AN. *bost* and **boster*, of unkn. orig.

boat OE. *bāt*, corr. to ON. *beit* (:- **bait*-, of uncert. orig.). Hence **boatswain** (now commonly *bosun*); late OE. *bātsweġen*.

bob[1] bunch, knob, knot (of hair). XIV. of unkn. orig. Hence **bob** vb. fish with a bob or bunch of worms XVII; make into a bob, cut short, dock XIX.

bob[2] A. †pummel, buffet, rap XIV; B. move with a jerk up or down or to and fro XIV; curtsy XVIII. prob. of imit. orig. Hence **bob** sb. †blow, rap XVI; method of change-ringing XVII; curtsy XIX.

bobbin XVI. - F. *bobine*, †*bobin*, of unkn. orig.

bobby dim. (see -Y[6]) of *Bob*, pet-form of *Robert*, used as a sl. nickname for a policeman, in allusion to *Robert* Peel, Home Secretary when the Metropolitan Police Act was passed in 1828.

bobtail (animal) having the tail cut short. XVII. f. BOB[1] or *bobbed* adj.

Boche (army sl.) German. XX. - F. (sl.) 'rascal', 'German', held to be shortening of *tête (de) boche*, in which *boche* is perh. for *caboche* hard skull (see CABBAGE[1]).

bode †announce, proclaim OE.; betoken, portend XIV. OE. *bodian*, f. *boda* messenger = OS. *bodo*, OHG. *boto* (G. *bote*), ON. *boði* :- Gmc. **buðan*-, f. **buð*-, weak grade of **beuðan* (OE. *bēodan*) BID.

bodega wine-shop. XIX. - Sp. :- L. *apothēca* - Gr. *apothḗkē* store (see APOTHECARY).

bodge see BOTCH.

bodice XVI. orig. *bodies*, pl. of BODY in the sense 'part of a woman's dress above the waist', formerly often in *a pair of bodies*, i.e. stays, corsets. For the retention of the unvoiced pronunc. of the pl. ending cf. *dice*, *pence*.

bodkin †dagger XIV; small pointed instrument XIV; long pin for hair XVI; blunt needle for drawing tape, etc. XVIII. ME. *boidekin*, of unkn. orig.

body OE. *bodiġ*, corr. to OHG. *botah* (MHG. *botich*, mod. Bavarian dial. *bottech* body of a chemise); of unkn. orig.

Boer Dutch-descended S. African. XIX (earliest form *boor*). - Du. (see BOOR).

bog XIV. - Gael. and Ir. *bogach*, f. *bog* soft. Hence **bog** vb. XVII. **boggy** XVI.

bog(e)y person or thing much dreaded. XIX. orig. as proper name (*Bogey* and *Old Bogey* the Devil), presumably rel. to synon. †*bog*, north. dial. *boggard*, *-art*, Sc. *bogle*, north. Eng. *boggle* (all from XVI), and further to BUG[1], but the connections of the group are uncertain.

Bogey (golf) the number of strokes a good player should need for each hole. XIX. Said to be from an imaginary partner 'Bogey' (same as prec.).

boggle start with fright (formerly often of horses) XVI; demur, hesitate XVII. prob. f. dial. *boggle* (see BOGEY) as if orig. 'to see a boggle or spectre'.

bogie (north. dial.) low truck on four wheels; (hence gen.) pivoted undercarriage. XIX. of unkn. orig.

bogle see BOGEY. XVI; its use by Burns, Scott, and Hogg brought it into Eng. literature.

bogus XIX (orig. U.S.). Appears first in 1827 applied to an apparatus for coining false money; of unkn. orig.

bohea black tea of lowest (orig. finest) quality. XVIII. - Fuhkien Chinese *Bui*, local var. of *Wui*, name of hills in northern Fuhkien, whence black tea was first brought to England.

Bohemian gipsy XVII; socially unconventional person XIX. f. *Bohemia* a region of Central Europe + -(I)AN; after F. *bohémien* gipsy, (transf.) vagabond, adventurer.

boil[1] hard inflamed tumour. OE. *bȳl*, *bȳle* = OS. *būla*, OHG. *būlla* bladder (G. *beule*), f. **bûl-* (cf. Goth. *ufbauljan* puff up). The form *boil* dates from XV.

boil[2] bubble up with heat. XIII. - AN. *boiller*, OF. *boillir* (mod. *bouillir*) :- L. *bullire*, f. *bulla* bubble. Hence **boil** sb. XV.

boisterous †stout, stiff, bulky; violent and rough in manner. XVI. var. of †*boisteous*, earlier †*boist(u)ous* (XIII), of unkn. orig.

bolas S. Amer. missile consisting of balls connected by cord. XIX. - Sp., Pg., pl. of *bola* ball.

bold OE. *b(e)ald* = OS., OHG. *bald* (G. adv. *bald* soon), ON. *ballr* dangerous, fatal :- Gmc. **balþaz*. Hence **boldly** OE.

bole tree-trunk. XIV. - ON. *bolr*; cf. MHG. *bole* (G. *bohle*) plank.

bolero lively dance XVIII; short jacket XIX. - Sp., presumably f. *bola* ball.

boll †vesicle, bubble XIII; rounded seed-vessel XV. - MDu. *bolle* (Du. *bol*) round object, introduced in connection with the medicinal use of poppy-heads and flax-cultivation.

bollard (naut.) post in a ship, etc. XIV. of uncert. orig.

Bolshevik XX. - Russ. *bol'shevik*, f. *ból'shiĭ*, compar. of *bol'shóĭ* big. Orig., group favouring a maximum socialist programme. Cf. MENSHEVIK.

bolster OE. *bolster* pillow, cushion = (M)Du. *bolster*, OHG. *bolstar* (G. *polster*), ON. *bolstr* :- Gmc. **bolstraz*, perh. for **bolχstraz*, f. **belʒ-* swell (cf. BELLY). Hence **bolster** vb. (chiefly fig.) prop up XVI.

bolt[1] stout arrow OE.; stout pin for fastening XII; (from LG.) roll of fabric, etc. XV. OE., = MLG. *bolte(n)*, bolt, fetter, piece of rolled-up linen, (M)Du. *bout* bolt, OHG. *bolz* (G. *bolzen*) arrow, bolt for a door; of unkn. orig. Hence **bolt** vb. dart off XIII; fasten with a bolt XVI.

bolt[2], **boult** sift. XIII. - OF. *bul(e)ter* (mod. *bluter*), prob. of Gmc. orig.

bolus large pill. XVII. - medL. *bōlus* - Gr. *bôlos* clod, lump of earth. Cf. HOLUS BOLUS.

bomb sb. XVII. - F. *bombe* - It. *bomba*, prob. f. L. *bombus* - Gr. *bómbos* booming, humming, of imit. orig. Hence (or - F.) **bomb** vb. XVII. So **bombard** early kind of cannon XVI. - F. *bombarde*, medL. *bombarda* **bombard** vb. XV. - F. *bombarder*; hence **bombardment** XVIII. **bombardier** †artilleryman XVI; N.C.O. of artillery XIX. - F.

bombast †cotton-wool, esp. as used for padding; turgid language. XVI. var., with parasitic *t*, of †*bombace* - OF. *bombace* - medL. *bombax*, *-āc-*, alt. of *bombyx* silk. Hence **bombastic** XVIII, **-ical** XVII.

bombinate make a buzzing noise. XIX. f. pp. stem of late L. *bombināre*, also medL. *bombilāre*. So **bombination** XIX (cf. Sir T. Browne's *bombilation*, 1646).

bona fide XVI (as adj. XVIII). - L., 'with good faith', abl. of *bona* (fem. of *bonus* good) *fidēs* (FAITH).

bonanza (U.S.) good luck, prosperity. XIX. - Sp. *bonanza* fair weather, prosperity :- Rom. **bonacia*, f. L. *bonus* good, after L. *malacia* (analysed as if containing *malus* bad) - Gr. *malakíā* softness, f. *malakós* soft.

bonbon XIX. - F., lit. 'good-good', f. *bon* good :- L. *bonus*.

bond[1] fetter; binding force XIII; covenant XIV; deed binding a person to pay money XVI; debenture XVII. var. of BAND[1], and at first interchangeable with it.

bond[2] in bondage or servitude. XIV. adj. use of ME. *bonde* serf, late OE. *bonda* householder - ON. *bóndi* (see HUSBAND). Forming permanent comps. in *bondmaid* (XVI), *bondman* (XIII), *bondservant* (XVI), *bondwoman* (XIV), which are assoc. in sense with BOND[1].

bone OE. *bān* = OS. *bēn*, OHG. (G.) *bein*, ON. *bein* :- Gmc. **bainam*. Hence **bone** vb. XV. **bony** XVI.

bonfire †fire of bones XIV; open-air fire in celebration, etc. XV. f. BONE + FIRE.

bonhomie XVIII. - F., f. *bonhomme* 'good man' (L. *bonus*, *homo*), good-natured fellow.

bonnet XIV. - OF. *bonet* (mod. *bonnet*), short for *chapel de bonet* hat made of a material 'bonet', medL. *bonetus*, *-um*, of unkn. orig.

bonny XV (chiefly Sc. and north. Eng.). of doubtful orig., perh. to be referred to F. *bon* good.

bonus addition to normal pay. XVIII. prob. joc. or ignorant application of L. *bonus* m. for *bonum* n. good thing.

bonze Buddhist priest in Japan, etc. XVI. - F. *bonze* or Pg. *bonzo* (modL. *bonz(i)us*), prob. - Jap. *bonzo* or *bonzi* - Chinese *fan seng* religious person, or Jap. *bo-zi* - Chinese *fa-sze* teacher of the law.

booby silly fellow; gannet. XVII. prob. (with -Y[6]) - Sp. *bobo* (used in both senses) :- L. *balbus* stammering, stuttering (ult. imit.).

book OE. *bōc*, pl. *bēc*, corr. to OS. *bōk*, OHG. *buoh*, pl. *buoh* (G. *buch*), ON. *bók*, pl. *bœkr* :- Gmc. **bōks*, pl. **bōkiz* (cf. Goth. *bōka*, pl. *bōkōs*); usu. taken to be a deriv. of **bōkō* BEECH.

boom[1] give out a deep humming note XV; sail with great speed XVII. ult. imit. (cf. BOMB); cf. Du. *bommen*. Hence **boom** sb. XVI.

boom[2] (naut.) long spar; floating timber barrier. XVI (Sc. *boume*). - Du. *boom* tree, pole, BEAM.

boom[3] (orig. U.S.) sudden activity in commerce. XIX. prob. application of BOOM[1]. Also as vb. XIX.

boomerang XIX. Austral. aboriginal name.

boon[1] †prayer, request; thing prayed for; favour XII; benefit, blessing XVIII. - ON. *bón*, var. of *bœn* = OE. *bēn*; of uncert. orig.

boon[2] good, gracious XIV; surviving in *boon companion* (XVI) in the sense 'jolly', 'convivial'. - (O)F. *bon* good :- L. *bonus*.

boor husbandman XV; Dutch or German peasant XVI (Dutch colonist, BOER XIX); rustic ill-mannered fellow XVI. - LG. *būr* or Du. *boer* (f. Gmc. stem **bū-* dwell, see BOWER[1]).

boost (orig. U.S.) hoist up, give a lift to, increase. XIX. of unkn. orig.

boot[1] (arch.) advantage (in phr. *to boot* †to advantage, in addition); †making good, remedy. OE. *bōt* = OS. *bōta*, OHG. *buoʒa* (G. *busse*), ON. *bót*, Goth. *bōta* :- Gmc. **bōtō*, f. **bōt- *bat-* (see BETTER, BEST). Hence **boot** vb. profit, avail. XIV. **bootless** irremediable (OE. *bōtlēas*); useless XVI.

boot[2] A. covering for the foot and (lower part of) the leg XIV; B. †space for attendants on the outside of a coach XVII; receptacle for luggage on a coach XVIII. ME. *bote* - ON. *boti* or its source, OF. *bote* (mod. *botte*); in AL. *bota* (XII), *botta*; of unkn. orig. The senses under B appear to derive from modF.

booth temporary dwelling; covered stall. XII. - OEast Norse **bóð* (Sw., Da. *bod* stall, shop) = OIcel. *búð* dwelling, f. East Norse *bóa* = OIcel. *búa* dwell (see BOWER[1]).

booty plunder. XV. of uncert. orig.; cf. (O)F. *butin* (whence Eng. †*butin* XV-XVII) - MLG. *būte* exchange, distribution.

booze (sl. or colloq.) drink. XIII. ME. *bous* sb., *bouse* vb.; these normally gave *bouse*, but this pronunc. appears to have been gen. arrested by re-adoption in XVI of the orig. etymon, MDu. *būsen* (Du. *buizen*) drink to excess.

borage genus of plants. XIII. - (O)F. *bourrache* - medL. *bor(r)āgo, -āgin-*, perh. - Arab. *'abū 'araq* 'father of sweat', the Arabian physicians using the plant as a diaphoretic.

borax biborate of sodium. XIV (*boras*; *borax*, after medL., from XVI). - OF. *boras* - medL. *borax, borac-* - Arab. *būraq* - Pers. So **boracic** XIX.

border XIV - OF. *bord(ë)ure* - CRom. deriv. of **bordāre* (F. *border*, etc.), f. **bordus*; see BOARD, -URE. Hence **border** vb. XIV.

bore[1] pierce. OE. *borian* = MLG., MDu. *boren*, OHG. *borōn* (G. *bohren*), ON. *bora* :- Gmc. **borōn*. The IE. base **bhor- *bhr̥* is repr. by L. *forāre* pierce.

bore[2] tidal wave. XVII. of doubtful orig.; cf. ON. *bára* wave, billow.

bore[3] †ennui; †annoyance, nuisance; tiresome thing XVIII; tiresome person XIX. of unkn. orig. (references in XVIII to *French bore* are unexplained). Also as vb. XVIII.

boreal northern. XV. - (O)F. *boréal* or late L. *boreālis*, f. L. *boreās* - Gr. *boréās* north wind; see -AL[1].

born, borne var. forms of the pp. (OE. *boren*) of BEAR[2], differentiated since *c.*1600; *born* is now no longer assoc. with *bear*, the phr. *to be born* being an independent intr. verb equiv. to F. *naître*, L. *nāsci*; *borne* is retained in lit. use for 'carried', 'endured'.

boron (chem.) non-metallic element, extracted from borax and resembling carbon in some of its properties. XIX. f. BOR(AX) + (CARB)ON.

borough †fortress; town (orig. fortified) OE.; town of a certain (political) status XVI. OE. *burg*, *burh* = OS. *burg*, OHG. *burug* (G. *burg*), ON. *borg*, Goth. *baurgs* :- Gmc. **burʒs*, rel. to **berʒan* protect, shelter (cf. BORROW, BURY).

borrow take on pledge or credit. OE. *borgian* = OHG. *borgēn* (G. *borgen*), f. Gmc. **borʒ-*, whence OE., OS. *borg* pledge, rel. to OE. *beorgan* = OS., OHG. *bergan* (Du., G. *bergen*), ON. *bjarga*, Goth. *bairgan* :- Gmc. **berʒan* (see prec.).

borzoi Russian wolf-hound. XIX. - Russ., f. *bórzȳĭ* swift.

bosh nonsense. XIX. - Turk. *boş* empty, worthless; gained currency from its frequent use in J. J. Morier's novel *Ayesha* (1834).

bosom OE. *bōsm* = OS. *bōsom*, OHG. *buosam* (G. *busen*) :- WGmc. **bōsm-*, of uncert. orig.

boss[1] protuberance. XIII. - OF. *boce* (mod. *bosse*) :- Rom. **bokja* or **bottia*, of unkn. orig.

boss[2] (orig. U.S.) master, employer. XIX. - Du. *baas* master, of unkn. orig.

bosun see BOATSWAIN.

botanic XVII. - F. *botanique*, or its source, late L. *botanicus* - Gr. *botanikós*, f. *botánē* plant; see -IC. So **botanical, botanist** XVII. Hence **botany** XVII; on the analogy of *astronomic, astronomy*; see -Y[3].

botargo relish of mullet or tunny roe. XVI. - It. *bottarga*, ult. of Gr. orig. (f. *ōiá* eggs, *tárikhos* salted fish).

botch put a patch on, repair clumsily XIV. of unkn. orig.

both XII. ME. *bāþe*, *bōþe* - ON. *báðir* = OS. *bēðia*, OHG. *bēde*, *beide* (G. *beide*); extended form of the base found in OE. *bēġen*, Goth. *bai*, and as the second element of L. *ambō*, OSl. (Russ.) *oba*, Skr. *ubháu*, Av. *uva* both.

bother (dial.) bewilder with noise, confuse; pester, worry. XVIII. - Ir. *bodhraim* deafen. Hence **bother** sb. XIX.

bottle XIV. - OF. *botele*, *botaille* (mod. *bouteille*) :- medL. *butticula*, dim. of late L. *buttis* BUTT[4].

bottom A. lowest surface or part OE.; valley, dell (surviving in place-names); foundation XV; B. keel of ship, hull XVI. OE. *botm* = OS. *bodom* (Du. *bodem*), corr. with variation of suffix to ON. *botn*, and parallel to OE. *bodan*, corr. to OHG.

bodam (G. *boden* ground, earth) :- Gmc. **bubm- *buþn-* :- IE. **bhudhm(e)n-*, f. **bhudh-*, whence also L. *fundus*, Skr. *budhná-*. Sense B is from Du.

bottomry borrowing on the security of a ship. XVI. - Du. *bodemerij*, f. *bodem* BOTTOM; see -RY.

botulism poisoning by a bacillus found in infected sausages, etc. XIX. f. L. *botulus* sausage + -ISM, after G. *botulismus*.

boudoir lady's private room. XVIII. - F. *boudoir* prop. 'place to sulk in', f. *bouder* pout, sulk, of imit. origin; see -OIR.

bougainvillaea XIX. f. name of Louis Antoine de *Bougainville*, French navigator (1729-1811).

bough †shoulder; †(Sc.) limb; limb of a tree. OE. *bōg*, *bōh* = MLG. *bōch*, *būch* (LG. *boog*), MDu. *boech* (Du. *boeg*), shoulders, bows of a ship, OHG. *buog* (G. *bug*), ON. *bógr* shoulder :- Gmc. **bōȝuz* :- IE. **bhāghús*, repr. also by Gr. *pâkhus*, *pêkhus* fore-arm, Skr. *bāhú-* arm, etc.

bouillon broth. XVIII. - F., f. *bouillir* BOIL[2].

boulder XIII. First as *bulder ston*, of Scand. orig.; cf. Sw. dial. *bullersten*, *buldurstajn*; perh. orig. a stone that causes a rumbling noise in water (cf. Sw. *buller* sb., *bullra* vb. rumble).

boulevard broad tree-lined walk. XVIII. - F. - G. *bollwerk* BULWARK; orig. applied to a promenade laid out on the horizontal portion of a rampart in a demolished fortification.

bounce First in the vb. (*bunsen* †beat, thump XIII); the application to loud explosive noise, blustering, and bounding like a ball appears in vb., sb., and int. in early XVI; poss. from LG., but perh. of independent imit. orig.

bound[1] †landmark XIII; boundary; pl. territory; limit of action XIV. - AN. *bounde*, OF. *bun(n)e*, *bunde*, *bonde*, earlier *bodne* :- medL. *bodina*, earlier *butina*, of unkn. orig. Cf. BOURN[1]. Hence **bound** vb. †limit XIV; form the boundary of XVII. **boundless** XVI.

bound[2] †ready XIII; prepared to go, destined XIV. ME. *būn*, *boun* - ON. *búinn*, pp. of *búa* prepare (cf. BOWER[1]); the final *d* of bound (XVI) may be purely phonetic, as in SOUND[3], but is prob. in part due to assoc. with BOUND[3].

bound[3] obliged, fated, destined. XIV. Shortened form of BOUNDEN.

bound[4] †rebound; spring upwards. XVI. - (O)F. *bondir* resound, (later) rebound :- Rom. **bombitīre*, for late L. *bombitāre*, var. of *bombilāre*. So **bound** sb. XVI. - F. *bond*.

boundary XVII. alt. of (dial.) *bounder* (XVI), f. BOUND[1] vb. + -ER[1].

bounden pp. (OE. *bunden*) of BIND, formerly used in various senses of the vb., in modern times mainly in the sense 'beholden, indebted' (XVI), and in echoes of the phr. *bounden duty* (XVI).

bounder (sl.) A. †four-wheeled dog-cart or trap; B. ill-bred fellow. XIX. f. BOUND[4] + -ER[1].

bounteous XIV. ME. *bounte(v)ous*, f. OF. *bontif*, *-ive* benevolent (f. *bonté* BOUNTY); see -EOUS.

bounty †goodness, excellence; gracious liberality XIII; gift, gratuity XVIII. - (O)F. *bonté* :- L. *bonitās*, *-āt-*, f. *bonus* good; see -TY[2]. Hence **bountiful** XVI.

bouquet XVIII. - F. *bouquet* (earlier, clump of trees), f. dial. var. of OF. *bo(i)s* wood (cf. BUSH[1]); see -ET.

bourdon †undersong XIV; (f. modF.) bass stop in an organ XIX. - (O)F. *bourdon* drone :- Rom. **burdō*, *-ōn-*, of imit. orig. Cf. BURDEN[2].

bourgeois XVI (orig., French citizen of the trading middle class). - (O)F. *bourgeois*, earlier *burgeis* (see BURGESS); adj. XVIII.

bourn[1] (arch.) boundary, limit. XVI. - (O)F. *borne*, earlier *bodne* BOUND[1].

bourn[2] var. of BURN[1].

bourse money exchange, spec. (*B-*) French stock exchange. XIX. - F. *bourse* purse.

boustrophedon alternately from right to left and from left to right. XVII. - Gr., f. *boûs* ox (see COW[1]) + *stroph-* (cf. STROPHE).

bout †circuit; (dial.) length of a furrow and back again; round of exercise, fighting. XVI. var. of †*bought* (XV) bend, fold, turn, prob. - LG. *bucht* (see BIGHT); assoc. with *bout*, aphetic form of ABOUT.

bovine XIX. - late L. *bovīnus*, f. L. *bōs*, *bov-*; see COW[1], -INE[1].

bow[1] weapon for shooting arrows OE.; transf. to various bent objects XIV. OE. *boga* bow, rainbow, arch = OS. *bogo*, OHG. *bogo* (G. *bogen*), ON. *bogi* :- Gmc. **boȝan-*, f. **buȝ-*, short stem of **beuȝan* (cf. BOW[2]).

bow[2] bend (esp. the body) OE.; cause to bend XIII; incline the head in salute XVII. OE. *būgan* = MLG. *būgen*, MDu. *būghen* (Du. *buigen*), corr. to OHG. *biogan* (G. *biegen*), Goth. *biugan* :- Gmc. **beuȝan* (cf. BOW[1]). The obvious connections outside Gmc. have *-g-* (to which Gmc. *-k-* should corr.), viz. L. *fugere*, Gr. *pheúgein* flee, Skr. *bhuj* bow, bend. Hence **bow** sb. XVII.

bow[3] fore-end of a boat. XV. - LG. *boog*, Du. *boeg*; see BOUGH and cf. BOWLINE, BOWSPRIT, which are earlier.

bowdlerize XIX. f. the name of Dr. T. *Bowdler*, who in 1818 published an edition of Shakespeare's works 'in which those words and expressions are omitted which cannot with propriety be read aloud in a family'; see -IZE.

bowel intestine, gut. XIII. ME. *b(o)uel* - OF. *b(o)uel*, *boiel* (mod. *boyau*) :- L. *botellus* pudding, sausage, small intestine, dim. of *botulus* sausage.

bower[1] †dwelling; inner apartment, lady's apartment OE.; arbour XVI. OE. *būr* = OS., OHG. *būr* (G. *bauer* birdcage), ON. *búr* :- Gmc. **būraz*, *-am*, f. **bū-* dwell :- IE. **bhū-* (see BE).

bower[2] either of two anchors carried at the bows. XVII. In full *bower anchor*; f. BOW[3] + -ER[1].

bowie(-knife) large slightly-curved knife. XIX. f. name of Colonel James *Bowie* (d. 1836).

bowl[1] basin. OE. *bolla*, *bolle*, corr. to OS. *bollo* cup, OHG. *bolla* bud, globular vessel.

bowl[2] †ball; globular body used in games; (pl.) game with bowls. XV. - (O)F. *boule* :- L. *bulla* (see BULL[2]). Hence as vb. XV.

bowler low-crowned stiff felt hat. XIX. f. name of John *Bowler*, London hatter.

bowline (naut.) rope connecting the weather side of a sail with the bow. XIII (in ONF. and AN. *boeline* XII-XIII). - MLG. *bōlīne*, MDu. *boechlijne*, f. *boeg* BOW[3] + *lijne* LINE[1]. So **bowsprit** spar running out from the stem of a vessel. XIII. - (M)LG. *bōgsprēt*, MDu. *boechspriet* (see SPRIT).

box[1] evergreen tree *Buxus*. OE. *box* - L. *buxus* - Gr. *púxos*.

box[2] receptacle of wood, etc. Late OE. *box*, prob. - **buxem*, for late L. *buxidem*, acc. of *buxis*, var. of L. *pyxis* (see PYX).

box[3] blow, slap (now usu. on the ear). XIV. of unkn. orig. Hence **box** vb. XVI; whence **boxer** pugilist XVIII.

box[4] phr. *box the compass* repeat the points of the compass in order and backwards; (fig.) make a complete revolution; (in full *box-haul*) veer a ship round on her keel. XVIII. prob. f. Sp. *bojar* (*boxar*) sail round - MLG. *bōgen* to bend, bow, f. base of BOW[1,2].

box-calf XIX. f. name of Joseph *Box*, London bootmaker.

boy †male servant; youth or man of low estate; 'fellow', 'knave' XIII; young male child XIV; native servant, negro slave XVII. ME. *boi(e)*, prob. aphetic - AN. **abuié*, **embuié*, pp. of OF. *embuier* fetter :- L. **imboiāre*, f. IM-[1] + *boia* fetter - Gr. *boeîai* (*doraí*) ox-hides, f. *boûs* ox, COW[1]. The primary meaning would be 'man in fetters', hence 'slave', 'serf'.

boycott XIX (first used of the action of the Irish Land League against those who incurred its hostility). f. name of Captain C. C. *Boycott* (1832-97), who was a victim of such treatment as agent for the estates of the earl of Erne, Co. Mayo, Ireland, at the hands of the tenants.

brace[1] †guard for the arm XIV; pair, couple XV; clasp, strap XIV; (archit.) strengthening band; carpenter's tool to hold a bit XVI; (typogr.) bracket XVII. - OF. *brace* two arms or their extent (mod. *brasse* fathom) :- L. *bracchia*, pl. of *bracchium* arm (whence F. *bras*) - Gr. *brakhíōn*. Some senses depend upon BRACE[2].

brace[2] †embrace, gird XIV; make tense or firm XV. - OF. *bracier* embrace, f. *brace* (see prec.); the later sense is direct from the sb.

bracelet XV. - (O)F. *bracelet*, dim. of *bracel* :- L. *bracchiāle*, f. *bracchium* arm; see BRACE[1], -IAL.

brachy- comb. form of Gr. *brakhús* short, as in **brachycephalic** having a short or broad head XIX; **brachylogy** conciseness of speech XVII. - late L. - Gr.

bracken XIV. ME. *braken* - ON. **brakni* (cf. Sw. *bräken*, Da. *bregne*).

bracket projection serving as a support XVI; (typogr.) one of the marks ( ) [ ] { } XVIII (earlier *brace*). Earliest forms *brag(g)et* - F. *braguette* codpiece, or Sp. *bragueta* codpiece, bracket, dim. of F. *bragues* (pl.) breeches - Pr. *braga*, It. (arch.) *braga* (mod. *braca*, pl. *brache* breeches). The source is L. *brāca*, pl. *brācæ* breeches, long hose, of Gaulish origin (see BREECH). It has been suggested that the bracket of architecture and ship-building was so called from its resemblance to a codpiece or a pair of breeches. See -ET.

brackish saltish. XVI. f. †*brack* salty, brine (XVI) - MLG., MDu. *brac* (LG., Du. *brak*), of unkn. orig.; see -ISH[1].

bract (bot.) small leaf below calyx. XVIII. - L. *bractea* thin plate of metal, gold leaf. So **bracteate** XIX; see -ATE[2].

brad thin flat small-headed nail. XV. var. of (dial.) *brod* shoot, spike, prick (XII) - ON. *broddr* = OE. *brord* point, spike, blade of grass, OHG. *brort* edge, margin :- Gmc. **brozdaz*. Hence **bradawl** XIX.

brae steep bank. XIII. Sc. and north. ME. *brā* - ON. *brá* eyelash = OE. *brǣw* eyelid, OS., OHG. *brāwa* (G. *braue*) eyebrow; the sense-development is parallel to that of BROW.

brag First as †adj. (XIII-XVII), which means (i) 'spirited, brisk, mettlesome', and (ii) 'boastful'; sb. and vb. (XIV) denote arrogant, boastful, or pompous behaviour. of unkn. orig. So **braggart** XVI. - F. *bragard*, f. *braguer* vaunt, brag; see -ARD.

braggadocio idle boaster or swaggerer XVI; boasting XVIII. Spenser's name for his personification of vainglory (F.Q. II. iii. Argt.); f. *r*-less form of BRAGGART + *-occio*, It. augm. suffix.

Brahmin member of the priestly or learned caste of Hindus. XIV (*bragman*; cf. AL. *Bragmannus* XIII). Early forms reflect mainly late L. pl. *Brachmānæ*, *-māni*, *-mānes*, corr. to Gr. *Brakhmânes* - Skr. *brāhmaṇá-* one of the caste, f. *brahmán-* priest.

braid †move with a sudden movement; interweave, plait OE.; (from the sb.) bind or ornament with braid XVIII. OE. str. vb. *breġdan* = OS. *bregdan*, OHG. *brettan*, ON. *bregða* :- Gmc. **breʒðan*, of unkn. orig. Hence **braid** sb. †sudden movement XIII; plait XVI; plaited fabric XVIII.

brail (naut.) pl. small ropes for trussing up sails. XV. - OF. *brail*, *braiel* :- medL. *brācāle* waist-belt, f. *brāca* (see BRACKET). Hence **brail** vb. XVII.

braille embossed printing for the blind, named after the inventor, Louis *Braille* (1809-52).

brain OE. *brægen* = MLG. *bragen*, *bregen*, (M)Du. *brein* :- Gmc. **braʒnam*, a word of the LG. area, prob. ult. rel. to Gr. *brekhmós*, *bregmós* forehead. Hence **brain** vb. XIV.

braise XVIII. - F. *braiser*, f. *braise* hot charcoal (cf. BRAZIER[2]).

brake[1] thicket. OE. *bracu*, corr. to MLG. *brake* branch, etc.; prob. f. **brak-* **brek-* BREAK[1], the orig. sense being 'broken wood'; perh. reinforced in ME. from LG.

brake[2] fern, bracken. XIV. perh. shortening of BRACKEN, through the apprehension of this as a pl. form.

brake[3] apparatus for retarding the motion of a wheel. XVIII. prob. spec. use of †*brake* bridle, curb (XV-XVIII) - MDu. *braeke*, rel. to *breken* BREAK[1].

brake[4] see BREAK[2].

bramble OE. *bræmbel*, later form of *brǣmel*, *brēmel*, f. the base repr. in OE. *brōm* BROOM; see -LE[1].

bran XIII. ME. *bran*, *bren* - (O)F. *bran*, †*bren* bran, (now) excrement, filth; of unkn. orig.

branch XIII. - (O)F. *branche* :- late L. *branca*, of unkn. orig.

brand[1] piece of burning wood OE.; mark made with a hot iron; stigma XVI; trade-mark XIX. OE. *brand* = OHG. *brant* (G. *brand*), ON. *brandr* :-

Gmc. *brandaz, f. *bran- *bren- BURN². Hence **brand** vb. XIV.

brand² (poet.) sword. OE. *brand* = MHG. *brant*, ON. *brandr*; perh. a use of prec.

brandish XIV. - (O)F. *brandiss-*, lengthened stem of *brandir* :- Rom. **brandīre*, f. Gmc. **brandaz* BRAND²; see -ISH².

brand-new, bran- XVI. perh. f. BRAND¹ + NEW, as if meaning 'fresh from the furnace'.

brandy XVII. Earlier *brand(e)wine*, alt. later to *brandy wine*, whence ellipt. *brandy* - Du. *brandewijn*, f. *branden* burn, roast, distil (f. *brand* fire, BRAND¹) + *wijn* WINE.

brant-goose see BRENT.

brash brittle XVI; rash, impetuous XIX; 'raw', showy XX; of unkn. orig.

brass OE. *bræs* = OFris. *bres*, MLG. *bras*; of unkn. orig.

brassie, brassy wooden golf-club shod with brass. XIX. f. BRASS + -Y¹.

brassiere XX. - F. *brassière* camisole, etc., f. *bras* arm (see BRACE¹).

brat XVI. of unkn. orig.

bravado XVI. - Sp. *bravata* (- It., f. *bravo* BRAVO), with alt. of suffix (see -ADO).

brave XV. - F. *brave* - It. *bravo* bold, accomplished, or Sp. *bravo* courageous, fine :- Rom. **brabus*, for L. *barbarus* BARBAROUS, through **brabarus*. So **brave** vb. XVI. - F. *braver*, f. *brave* (after It. *bravare*). **bravery** XVI. - F. *braverie* or It. *braveria*.

bravo cry of approval. XVIII. - F. - It. (see prec.).

bravura XVIII. - It., f. *bravo* BRAVE; see -URE.

braw (Sc.) fine, excellent. XVI. var. of *brawf*, BRAVE.

brawl vb. XIV, sb. XV. of unkn. orig., perh. imit.

brawn fleshy part, muscle; flesh of the boar or swine, now esp. as collared, boiled, etc. XIV. - AN. *braun*, OF. *braon* fleshy part, esp. of the hind leg - Gmc. **brādon* (OHG. *brāto*, G. *braten* roast flesh; cf. synon. OE. *brǣde*, and *brǣdan* roast); prob. ult. rel. to BREATH, BROOD.

bray¹ †cry out XIII; of animals, now esp. of the ass XIV. - (O)F. *braire* :- Rom. **bragere*, perh. of Celtic orig.

bray² crush small. XIV. - AN. *braier*, OF. *breier* (mod. *broyer*) - Gmc. **brekan* BREAK¹.

brazen made of brass. OE. *bræsen*, f. *bræs* BRASS; see -EN³. Hence **brazen** vb. face impudently. XVI.

brazier¹ worker in brass. XIV. prob. f. BRASS on the model of *glass, glazier*.

brazier² pan for holding burning charcoal, etc. XVII. - F. *brasier*, f. *braise* hot coals (see BRAISE).

breach breaking XIV; gap in a fortification XV. - (O)F. *brèche* :- Gallo-Rom. **brecca* - Frankish **breka*, f. **brek-* BREAK¹; cf. OHG. *brecha*.

bread OE. *brēad* = OS., (M)LG. *brōd*, OHG. *brōt* (G. *brot*), ON. *brauð* :- Gmc. **brauðam*, of unkn. orig.

breadth XVI. f. †*brēde* breadth (OE. *brǣdu*, OHG. *breiti* (G. *breite*), ON. *breidd*, Goth. *braidei* :- Gmc. **braidjōn*, abstr. sb. f. **braid-* BROAD) + -TH¹; cf. LENGTH, WIDTH.

break¹ sever into parts. OE. *brecan* = OS. *brekan*, OHG. *brehhan* (G. *brechen*), Goth. *brikan* :- Gmc. **brekan*; IE. base **bhreg- *bhrg-*, whence also L. *frangere* break. The pt. *brake* began to be displaced in XV by **broke** (after the pp. **broken**).

break², brake carriage-frame; large waggonette. XIX. perh. identical with †*brake* cage, rack (XVI), frame (XVII), of unkn. orig.

breaker¹ one who or that which breaks XII; heavy ocean-wave breaking on the shore XVII. f. BREAK¹ + -ER¹.

breaker² (naut.) small keg. XIX. - Sp. *bareca*, var. of *barrica*, f. stem repr. in BARREL.

breakfast XV. f. phr. *break one's fast* (XIV); see BREAK¹, FAST².

bream fresh-water fish of genus *Abramis*. XIV. - OF. *bre(s)me* (mod. *brème*) - WGmc. **breχsman-* beside **braχsman-* (OS. *bressemo*, OHG. *brahsema* (G. *brachsen, brassen*)).

breast OE. *brēost* (freq. in pl.) = OS. *briost*, ON. *brjóst* :- Gmc. **breustam*, parallel to a fem. cons.-stem **brusts* repr. by OHG., G. *brust*, Goth. *brusts*.

breath †odour OE.; †vapour, respiration XIII; air from the lungs XIV. OE. *brǣð* odour, exhalation :- Gmc. **brǣþaz* :- IE. **bhrētos*, f. **bhrē-* burn, heat, as in OE. *brǣdan* roast, and BROOD. Hence **breathe** XIII.

breech usu. pl. **breeches** OE. *brēc̆* (pl. only) = OS. *brōk*, OHG. *bruoh*, ON. *brók* :- Gmc. **brōks*, of uncert. orig.

breed vb. OE. *brēdan* = OHG. *bruotan* (G. *brüten*) :- WGmc. **brōdjan*, f. **brōd-* BROOD. Hence **breed** sb. XVI.

breeze¹ †north(-east) wind XVI; cool wind from the sea (or land) on tropical coasts; light wind XVII. prob. - OSp., Pg. *briza* (Sp. *brisa*) north-east wind.

breeze² small cinders. XVIII. - F. *braise*, earlier *brese* hot charcoal, half-burnt coal.

brent(-goose), also *brant-goose*, kind of wild goose, *Bernicla brenta*. XVI. perh. rel. (with ref. to variegation of colour) to *branded, brended, brinded* (all XVI), for which see BRINDLED.

brethren pl. of BROTHER.

breve ME. *breve* (XIII), var. of BRIEF in various senses; (mus.) orig. the shortest note of the series *large, long, breve* (XV), after medL. *brevis*; in mod. usage (XVII), after It. *breve*, note equal to two semibreves, the longest now used.

brevet official document granting privileges XIV; (in the army) XVII. - (O)F. *brevet*, f. *br(i)ef* BRIEF¹; see -ET.

breviary †epitome XVI; (eccl.) book containing the Divine Office for the year XV. - L. *breviārium* summary, abridgement, f. *breviāre* abridge, ABBREVIATE.

brevity XVI. - AN. *breveté*, (O)F. *brièveté*, f. *bref*, fem. *briève* BRIEF²; see -ITY.

brew make ale, beer, etc. OE. *brēowan* = OS. *breuwan*, OHG. *briuwan*, *brūwan* (G. *brauen*, *bräuen*), ON. *brugga* :- Gmc. **breu(w)an*, f. IE. **bhreu- *bhru-*. Hence **brewery** XVIII. prob. - Du. *brouwerij*; earlier **brewhouse** XIV. **brewster** brewer (see -STER).

briar¹,² see BRIER¹,².

bribe †purloin, steal XIV; corrupt by means of gifts XVI. - OF. *bri(m)ber* beg, be a mendicant = Sp. *bribar* beg; of unkn. orig. So

briber †thief, vagabond, scoundrel XIV; †one who levies blackmail or accepts bribes; one who gives bribes XVI. orig. - AN. *bribour*, OF. *bribeur* beggar, vagabond; later f. the vb.; see -ER¹. **bribery** †theft XIV; †exaction of money; offer or acceptance of bribes XVI. - OF. *briberie*. Hence **bribe** sb. XV.

bric-à-brac XIX. - F., f. phr. †*à bric et à brac* at random, of unkn. orig.

brick XV. prob. introduced by Flemish workmen and so - MLG., MDu. *bri(c)ke* (whence also (O)F. *brique*, which prob. reinforced the adoption from LG.); of unkn. orig.

brickbat piece of brick XVI; (fig.) uncomplimentary remark, etc. XVII. f. BRICK + BAT¹ (in sense †lump XIV, †piece of brick XVI).

bridal (arch., except in attrib. use, which from late XVI has been furthered by assoc. with adjs. in -AL¹) wedding feast, (later) wedding. Late OE. *brȳdealu*, f. *brȳd* BRIDE (in attrib. use equivalent to 'marriage') + *ealu* ALE, i.e. ale-drinking.

bride OE. *brȳd* = OS. *brūd*, OHG. *brūt* (G. *braut*), ON. *brúðr*, Goth. *brūþs* :- Gmc. **brūðiz*, of unkn. orig. Hence **bridegroom** OE. *brȳdguma* = OS. *brūdigomo*, OHG. *brūtigomo* (G. *bräutigam*), ON. *brúðgumi*; alt. by assim. to GROOM. **bridesmaid** XVIII, earlier *bridemaid* XVI.

bridge¹ elevated structure (often arched over water) forming a passageway between two points. OE. *bryċġ* = OS. *bruggia*, OHG. *brucca* (G. *brücke*), ON. *bryggja* :- Gmc. **bruȝjō*. Hence vb. OE. *bryċġian*.

bridge² card game based on whist. XIX. of unkn. orig.

bridle OE. *brīdel* = OFris. *brīdel*, (M)Du. *breidel*, OHG. *brittil*; WGmc. deriv. of **breȝd*-; see BRAID, -LE¹. Hence **bridle** vb. OE. *brīdlian*.

brief¹ letter of authority XIV; letter patent from the sovereign as head of the Church XVI; (leg.) summary of the facts of a case for the instruction of counsel XVII. - AN. *bref*, OF. *brief* :- L. *breve* (in late L., summary), n. of *brevis* (see next).

brief² of short duration. XIV. ME. *bref* - (O)F. *bref* :- L. *brevis*. Cf. BREVITY.

brier¹, **briar**¹ prickly bush OE.; species of wild rose XVI. OE. (Angl.) *brēr*, (WS.) *brǣr*, of unkn. orig.

brier², **briar**² white heath, *Erica arborea*, the root of which is used for tobacco pipes. XIX (*bruyer*). - (O)F. *bruyère* heath :- Gallo-Rom. **brūcāria*, f. **brūcus* - Gaulish **brūko*; assim. in form to prec.

brig XVIII. Shortening of BRIGANTINE², but applied to a ship of a different rig.

brigade XVII. - (O)F. *brigade* - It. *brigata* troop, company, f. *brigare* be busy with, f. *briga* strife, contention, which has been referred to Gmc. **brekan* BREAK; see -ADE. So **brigadier** XVII. - F.

brigand †light-armed irregular foot-soldier XIV; bandit XV. - (O)F. - It. *brigante*, sb. use of prp. of *brigare* (see prec.). Hence **brigandage** XVI; after F.

brigandine, -tine¹ chain or body armour. XV. - (O)F. *brigandine*, f. *brigand* BRIGAND (in the earlier sense); see -INE³.

brigantine² †small vessel attending on larger ships XVI; two-masted vessel XVII. - F. *brigantin* - It. *brigantino*, f. *brigante*; see BRIGAND, -INE³.

bright OE. *beorht*, Anglian *berht*, late Nhb. *breht* = OS. *ber(a)ht*, OHG. *beraht*, *-eht*, ON. *bjartr*, Goth. *bairhts* :- Gmc. **berχtaz*, f. IE. **bhereg*-, repr. also by Skt. *bhrājate* shine, Lith. *brėkšta* dawns, W. *berth* beautiful.

brill flat-fish, *Scophthalmus rhombus*, having brilliant spots. XV. Also *brell*, *prylle* XV, *prill* XVII, *pearl* XVII-XIX, of obscure connections and unkn. orig.

brilliant XVII (not frequent before XVIII). - F. *brillant*, prp. of *briller* shine - It. *brillare*, of unkn. orig. See BERYL.

brim †border, margin, brink XIII; edge of a cup, etc.; projecting rim of a hat XVI. of obscure history, but corr. in sense to MHG. *brem* (G. *brä(h)me*), ON. *barmr* edge.

brimstone sulphur. XII. The earliest forms are *brynstan* etc., continued as *brinston* etc. till XVI; prob. f. OE. *bryne* (= ON. *bruni*) burning + STONE; a common ME. var. *brenston* is due to ON. *brennisteinn*; forms in *brim*- appear *c.* 1300.

brindled brown with streaks of other colour. XVII. alt. (prob. by assoc. with *grizzled*, *speckled*) of (arch.) *brinded* (XVI), earlier †*brended* (XV), f. †*brende*, prob. of Scand. orig. (cf. ON. *bröndóttr* brindled, f. *brandr* burning).

brine OE. *brīne* = MDu. *brīne* (Du. *brijn*), of unkn. orig.

bring OE. *bringan* = OS., OHG. *bringan* (G. *bringen*), Goth. *briggan* :- Gmc. **breŋȝan*.

brink XIII. ME. also *brenk* - ON. **brenkōn*, corr. to MLG. *brink* edge of a field, (brow of) a hill (whence G. *brink* hill), MDu. *brinc* (Du. *brink* grassland), of unkn. orig.

briony see BRYONY.

briquette block of compressed coal-dust. XIX. - F., dim. of *brique* BRICK; see -ETTE.

brisk †smart, spruce XVI; quick and active; sharp (in various senses) XVI. prob. - F. *brusque* BRUSQUE, but the connection of sense is not clear.

brisket breast of a beast. XIV (*brusket*). prob. - AN. **brusket*, **brisket*, vars. of OF. *bruschet*, etc. (mod. *bréchet*), poss. f. ON. *brjósk* cartilage, gristle; see -ET.

bristle sb. XIII. ME. *brüstel*, *bristel*, *brestel*, pointing to OE. **brystel*, **byrstel*, corr. to OS. **brustil*, (M)Du. *borstel*, f. the base repr. by OE. *byrst* bristle, OHG. *burst* (G. *borste*), ON. *burst*, *bursti*.

Britain XIII. ME. *Bretayne* - OF. *Bretaigne* (mod. *-agne*) :- L. *Brittania*, *-annia*, f. *Brit(t)annī* Britons = Gr. *Bret(t)anoí*, *Pret(t)anoí*. (OE. *Breoten*, *Breten*, *Bryten* - L. *Brittones*; cf. BRITISH.)

British pert. to ancient Britons OE.; pert. to Great Britain XIV. OE. *Brettisċ*, *Brit*-, *Bryt*-, f. *Bret*, pl. *Brettas*, etc., based on L. *Brittō* (pl. *Brittones*), or OCelt. **Britto* or **Brittos*; see -ISH¹.

Briton XIII. - (O)F. *Breton* - L. *Brittō*, *-ōn*- (see prec.).

brittle ME. *britil*, *bretil*, *brütil* point to deriv. from *bryt*-, f. mutated form of Gmc. **brut*-, weak grade of **breutan* (OE. *brēotan* = ON. *brjōta*) break up, of unkn. orig. See -LE².

broach A. †pointed rod or pin; roasting-spit XIV; church spire XVI; tapered boring-bit XVIII. B. (f. the vb.) †perforation with a tap XV. - (O)F. *broche* spit (see BROOCH). So **broach** vb. pierce XIV; give vent to XVI. - (O)F. *brocher*.

broad OE. *brād* = OS. *brēd*, (O)HG. *breit*, ON. *breiðr*, Goth. *braiþs* :- Gmc. **braiþaz*, of unkn. orig.

brocade textile fabric with raised figures. XVII. Earlier *broca(r)do* (XVI) - Sp., Pg. *brocado*, with blending of F. *brocart* - It. *broccato*, lit. 'embossed stuff', f. *broco* twisted thread; see -ADE.

broccoli kind of cauliflower. XVII. - It. *broccoli*, pl. of *broccolo* cabbage sprout or head, dim. of *brocco* shoot.

broch (archaeol.) prehistoric tower-like structure in north. Scotland. XVII (*brugh*, *brogh*, *burgh*). var. of BURGH.

brochure XVIII. - F., lit. 'stitching', f. *brocher* stitch; see -URE.

brock (dial.) badger. OE. *broc(c)* - OBrit. **brokkos* (W., Corn., Bret. *broch*, Ir., Gael. *broc*, OIr. *brocc*).

brogue[1] rough shoe of Ireland and the Scottish Highlands XVI; pl. †hose, trousers XVII; strong outdoor shoe XIX. - Ir., Gael. *brōg* (OIr. *bróc*) - ON. *brók* (see BREECH).

brogue[2] strongly marked provincial (esp. Irish) accent. XVII. perh. the same word as prec. used in playful allusion to the foot-gear of Ir. or Sc. speakers.

broil[1] turmoil, quarrel. XVI. f. †*broil* vb. confuse, disturb (cf. EMBROIL) - AN. *broiller*, (O)F. *brouiller*, earlier *brooillier* :- Rom. **brodiculāre*. Cf. IMBROGLIO.

broil[2] †burn XIV; grill XIV. Earliest forms (Sc.) *brulʒe*, *broille*, *bru(y)le* - OF. *bru(s)ler* (mod. *brûler*) burn :- Rom. **brustulāre*, perh. f. Gmc. **brun*- **bren*- BURN[2] + L. *ūstulāre* burn up.

broker †pedlar, small trader; second hand dealer; middleman XIV; appraiser or seller of distrained goods XIX. Late ME. *broco(u)r* - AN. *brocour*, beside *abrocour*, corr. to Pr. *abrocador* broker, *abrocatge* brokerage, beside *brocatge* charge on wine; of unkn. orig. Hence **brokerage** XV; repl. †*brokage* (XIV) - AN. *brocage*.

brolly (colloq.) unexpl. alt. of UMBRELLA. XIX.

bromine (chem.) non-metallic element. XIX. f. F. *brome* (formerly also used in Eng.), f. Gr. *brômos* stink + -INE[5]; so named from its strong irritating smell.

bronchia branches of the bronchi. XVII. - late L. - Gr. n. pl. *brógkhia*, f. *brógkhos* windpipe, whence late L. **bronchus**, pl. **-i** the branches of the windpipe. So **bronchial** XVIII, **bronchitis** XIX. - modL.

bronco (U.S.) half-tamed horse. XIX. - Sp. *bronco* rough, rel. to OF. *bronche*, It. *bronco* block, lump.

brontosaurus XIX. f. Gr. *brontḗ* thunder + *saûros* lizard.

bronze XVIII. - F. - It. *bronzo*, of uncert. orig.

brooch XIII. - (O)F. *broche* spit, long needle :- Rom. **brocca* spike, sb. use of fem. of L. *brocc(h)us* projecting.

brood progeny, offspring. OE. *brōd*, corr. to OHG. *bruot* (G. *brut*), f. Gmc. **brōd*-, f. **brō*- warm, heat. Hence **brood** vb. sit on eggs XV; hover *over* XVI; meditate intensely XVIII. **broody** (*a broody hen*) inclined to sit OE.; †prolific. OE. *brōdig*; see -Y[1].

brook[1] small stream. OE. *brōc*, corr. to LG. and HG. words meaning 'marsh, bog', MLG. *brōk*, (M)Du. *broek*, OHG. *bruoh* (G. *bruch*); of unkn. orig.

brook[2] †enjoy, use OE.; (lit.) put up with, endure XVI. OE. *brūcan* str. vb. = OS. *brūkan*, OHG. *brūhhan* (G. *brauchen* use, want, need) (cf. Goth. *brūkjan*), f. Gmc. **brūk*- make use of :- IE. **bhrug*-, whence L. *fruī* enjoy (see FRUIT). Weak inflexions occur XIV.

broom yellow-flowered shrub OE.; sweeping implement, orig. one of broom twigs XV. OE. *brōm*, corr. to MLG. *brām*, OHG. *brāmo*, *brāma* (cf. G. *brombeere* blackberry), also MLG. *brēme*, *brumme*. Cf. BRAMBLE.

broth OE. *broð* = OHG. *brod*, ON. *broð* :- Gmc. **broþam*, f. **bru*-, base of BREW.

brothel †worthless fellow XIV; †prostitute XV; bawdy-house XVI. ME. *broþel*, f. OE. *abroðen* gone to ruin, pp. of *brēoðan* deteriorate, degenerate, of unkn. orig. In the present sense, short for †*brothel-house*, etc., by assoc. with earlier †*bordel* (- (O)F.), which it superseded.

brother OE. *brōðor*, OS. *brōðar*, OHG. *bruodar* (G. *bruder*), ON. *bróðir*, Goth. *brōþar* :- Gmc. **brōþar* :- IE. **bhrāter*, whence Skr. *bhrātṛ*, Gr. *phrā́tēr*, L. *frāter*, OSl. *bratrŭ*, OCelt. **brāter* (Ir., Gael. *brathair*, W. *brawd*, Breton *breur*).

brougham one-horse closed carriage. XIX. f. name of Henry Peter, Lord *Brougham* (1778-1868).

brow †eyelash, eyelid; arch of hair above the eye OE.; projecting edge of a hill, etc. XV; forehead XVI. OE. *brū* :- Gmc. **brus* :- IE. **bhrūs*, whence also Gr. *ophrûs*, Lith. *bruvìs*, Skr. *bhrūs*.

brown OE. *brūn* = OS., OHG. *brūn* (Du. *bruin*, G. *braun*), ON. *brúnn* :- Gmc. **brūnaz*. Reinforced in ME. from (O)F. *brun* - Gmc. OE. *brūn*, ME. *broun*, ON. *brúnn*, OHG. *brūn* were applied to burnished or glistening surfaces; see BURNISH.

brownie benevolent sprite. XVI. f. BROWN + *-ie*, -Y[6].

browse sb. young shoots and twigs, cattle-fodder; vb. crop and eat, feed *on* leaves, etc. XVI. ult. - early mod. F. *broust* (now *brout*) bud, young shoot, *brouster* (now *brouter*) crop, prob. of Gmc. orig.; but the loss of *t* in Eng. is difficult to account for.

Bruin, bruin common or brown bear. XVII. - Du. *bruin* BROWN, used as a proper name in 'Reynard the Fox' (whence its isolated early occurrence in Caxton's transl.).

bruise (orig.) crush, mangle, (now) injure by a blow or pressure without breaking skin. OE. *brȳsan* (whence ME. *brüse*, *brise*), rel. to OE. *brosnian* crumble, decay. With this coalesced *brüse*, *bro(y)se*, later *bruise* - AN. *bruser*, OF. *bruisier* (mod. *briser*) break, smash, of unkn. orig. Hence **bruise** sb. †breach XV; contusion XVI.

bruit (arch.) noise, rumour. XV. - (O)F. *bruit*,

sb. use of pp. of *bruire* roar :- Rom. **brūgere*, alt. of L. *rugīre* roar by assoc. with **bragere* BRAY[1]. Hence as vb. XV.

brumby (Austral.) wild or unbroken horse. XIX. of unkn. orig.

Brummagem counterfeit, sham. XVII. dial. form of the name of *Birmingham*, England, used allusively, orig. with ref. to the counterfeit groats made there *c.*1680, more recently to the cheap plated and lacquer ware manufactured there.

brunette XVII. - (O)F. *brunette*, fem. of *brunet*, dim. of *brun* BROWN; see -ETTE.

brunt †blow, attack XIV; shock; (chief) stress XVI. of unkn. orig.

brush[1] (dial.) loppings of trees XIV; (U.S., etc.) thicket XVI. ME. *brusche* - AN. *brousse*, OF. *broce*, *brosse* (whence F. *broussaille*) :- Rom. **bruscia*, perh. f. L. *bruscum* excrescence on the maple.

brush[2] utensil for sweeping, etc. XIV. - OF. *broisse*, (also mod.) *brosse*, perh. to be identified with prec.; cf. BROOM. Hence vb. XV.

brush[3] †rush XIV; move briskly *by*, *past*, etc. XVII. poss. - OF. *brosser* go through brushwood, f. *brosse* BRUSH[1]. Hence sb. forcible rush or encounter. XIV.

brusque XVII. - F. *brusque* lively, fierce, harsh - It. *brusco* sour(-looking), tart, a use of the sb. = Sp., Pg. *brusco* butcher's broom :- Rom. **bruscum*, perh. blend of L. *rūscum* butcher's broom with **brūcus* heather (see BRIER[2]). Cf. BRISK.

brutal †animal XV; inhuman, brutish XVI. - (O)F. *brutal* or medL. *brutālis*, f. L. *brūtus* BRUTE + -AL[1]. Hence **brutality** XVI. **brutalize** XVIII. - F. So **brute** adj. (esp. in *brute beast*) of the lower animals XV; brutish; irrational XVI; sb. lower animal XVII. - F. *brut(e)* - L. *brūtus* heavy, stupid, dull. Hence **brutish** XV; see -ISH[1].

bryology science of mosses. XIX. f. Gr. *brúon* mossy seaweed + -LOGY.

bryony climbing plant of genus *Bryonia*. XVI. - L. *bryōnia* - Gr. *bruōniā*. Earlier †*brione* (XIV) - OF. *brione*.

Brythonic pert. to the Celts of South Britain. XIX. f. W. *Brython* Britons (:- Celtic **Brittones*, pl. of **Britto* BRITON) + -IC.

bubble sb. and vb. XIV. prob. imit., like the parallel Du. *bobbel(en)*, G. dial. *bobbel*, *bubbel*, *-en*, Sw. *bubla*, Da. *boble*; perh. in part a modification of the earlier BURBLE.

bubo inflamed swelling in groin or armpits. XIV. - medL. *bubō*, *-ōn-* swelling - Gr. *boubṓn* groin, swelling in groin. Hence **bubonic** XIX.

buccal pert. to the cheek(s). XIX. f. L. *bucca* cheek, mouth; see -AL[1].

buccaneer †curer of flesh on a barbecue; searover. XVII. - F. *boucanier*, f. *boucaner* cure flesh on a *boucan* or barbecue (Tupi *mokaém*). The sb. and vb. *boucan*, *buccan* (from the F. sb. and vb.) appear earlier in XVII. The orig. application was to French and English hunters of oxen and swine in San Domingo and Tortugas.

buck A. male of deer; †he-goat OE.; B. †fellow XIV; gay, dashing man XVIII. (i) OE. *buc* male deer = OHG. *boc* (G. *bock*), ON. *bukkr*, *bokkr* :- Gmc. **bukkaz*; (ii) OE. *bucca* he-goat = ON. *bokki* my good fellow, old buck :- **bukkan-*; prob. of IE. orig. (cf. OIr. *bocc* he-goat, Arm. *buc* lamb, Av. *būza-*, Skr. *bukka-* he-goat). Hence **buck** vb. (dial.) dress *up* (i.e. like a 'buck' or smart fellow); (sl.) cheer *up*; hurry *up* XIX.

bucket XIII. - AN. *buket*, *buquet* tub, pail (cf. AL. *bo-*, *bukettum* XIII), perh. f. OE. *būc* belly, pitcher = MLG. *būk*, OHG. *būh* (G. *bauch*), ON. *búkr* body; see -ET.

buckle sb. XIV. - (O)F. *boucle* metal ring, boss of a shield :- L. *buccula* cheek-strap of a helmet, boss of a shield, dim. of *bucca* cheek. Hence **buckle** vb. fasten with a buckle XIV; (after F. *boucler*) bend under stress XVI. See -CLE.

buckler small round shield. XIII. ME. *boc(e)ler* - OF. *bocler*, *b(o)ucler* (mod. *bouclier*), orig. adj. in *escu boucler* shield having a boss, f. *boucle* boss (see prec.) + *-er* -ER[2].

buckram †fine linen or cotton fabric XIV; coarse linen or cloth stiffened XV. ME. *boker(h)am* - AN. *bukeram*, OF. *boquerant* (mod. *bougran*), obscurely f. *Bukhara*, name of a town in Turkistan.

buckshee (sl.) extra rations; adj., adv. gratuitous(ly). XIX. alt. of BAKSHEESH.

buckthorn shrub *Rhamnus catharticus*. XVI. f. BUCK + THORN; transl. modL. *cervi spina* 'stag's horn'.

buckwheat ceral of genus *Fagopyrum*. XVI. - MDu. *boecweite*, MLG. *bōkwēte* (LG. *bookweten*), f. *boek*, *bōk* (see BEECH) + *weite* WHEAT.

bucolic pastoral, rustic; sb. pl. pastoral poems. XVI. - L. *būcolicus* - Gr. *boukolikós*, f. *boukólos* herdsman, f. *boûs* ox (see COW[1]); see -IC.

bud[1] flower or leaf not opened. XIV. ME. *bodde*, *budde*, of unkn. orig. Hence **bud** vb. XIV.

bud[2] (U.S.) infantile or negro alt. of BROTHER. Also **buddy** (-Y[6]). XIX.

budge stir. XVI. - (O)F. *bouger*, prob. = Pr. *bolegar* disturb oneself, It. *bulicare* bubble up :- Rom. **bullicāre* bubble, f. L. *bulla* bubble.

budgerigar XIX. Austral. aboriginal name, f. *budgeri* good + *gar* cockatoo.

budget †pouch, wallet XV; bundle, stock XVI; annual estimate made by the Chancellor of the Exchequer (who was formerly said to 'open his budget') XVIII. - OF. *bougette*, dim. of *bouge* leather bag :- L. *bulga*; see -ET.

buff[1] blow, buffet (surviving only in BLINDMAN'S-BUFF). XV. - OF. *buffe* BUFFET[1].

buff[2] A. †buffalo, wild ox XVI; B. (earlier *buff leather*) leather of buffalo hide, hence of ox hide; military attire (orig. of this leather) XVI; the bare skin XVII; C. light brownish-yellow (hence as adj.) XVIII. prob. - F. *buffle* BUFFALO.

buffalo XVI. prob. immed. - Pg. *bufalo* (mod. *bufaro*), corr. to It. *bufalo* (whence F. *buffle*) :- late L. *bufalus*, L. *būbalus* - Gr. *boúbalos* antelope, wild ox.

buffer[1] fellow. XVIII. prob. ult. from an imit. base **buff-* blow, puff, make the sound of a soft blow, whence the meanings 'stammerer' XIV, 'soft fellow' (dial.); see next.

buffer[2] device for deadening the force of concussion. XIX. prob. f. *buff* vb., sound as a soft body when struck.

buffet[1] blow. XIII. - OF. (now dial.) *buffet*, dim. of *buffe*, of imit. orig. So **buffet** vb. XIII.

buffet[2] sideboard, cupboard in a recess XVIII; refreshment bar XIX. - F., of unkn. orig.

buffoon clown. XVI. - F. *bouffon* - It. *buffone*, f. *buffare* puff (prob. with allusion to puffing out the cheeks as a comic gesture), of imit. orig.; see -OON.

bug[1] †object of dread. XIV. The earliest of several words of similar form and meaning, the connections of which are obscure; viz. †*bog*, †*boggard*, (dial.) *bogle*, *bogle-bo*, BUGABOO, BUGBEAR, and the more recent BOGEY. Comparison with W. *bwg*, *bwgan* ghost, hobgoblin, *bwgwl* fear, threat, is inevitable, but it is uncertain how these forms are related.

bug[2] insect, beetle; bed-bug, *Cimex lectularius*. XVI. of unkn. orig.

bugaboo bogey, bugbear. XVIII. prob. of dial. orig.; cf. W. *bwcibo* the Devil (*bwci* hobgoblin, *bo* scarecrow), Corn. *buccaboo*. See BUG[1].

bugbear †hobgoblin; object of dread. XVI. app. f. BUG[1] + BEAR[1].

bugger sodomite XVI (*bouguer*, *bowgard*); (vulgar) coarse term of abuse; also fellow, chap XVIII. - MDu. - (O)F. *bougre* †heretic, (arch.) sodomite, (colloq.) 'chap' :- medL. *Bulgarus* Bulgarian, heretic (the Bulgarians being so regarded as belonging to the Greek Church). So **buggery** XIV. - MDu. *buggerie* (OF. *bouguerie*).

buggy light horse-vehicle. XVIII. of unkn. orig.

bugle[1] †buffalo, bull; kind of horn (short for *bugle horn* horn of a wild ox used as a drinking vessel and as a musical instrument). XIV. - OF. *bugle* :- L. *būculus*, dim. of *bōs* ox (see COW[1])

bugle[2] plant of the genus *Ajuga*. XIII. - late L. *bugula*.

bugle[3] tubular glass bead. XVI. of unkn. orig.

bugloss boraginaceous plant. XV. - F. *buglosse* or L. *būglōssus* - Gr. *boúglōssos* lit. 'ox-tongued', f. *boûs* ox (see COW[1]) + *glôssa* tongue (cf. GLOSS).

build OE. *byldan* (cf. *bylda* builder), f. *bold* dwelling, house, var. of *botl* = OS. *bodl*, ON. *ból* :- Gmc. **buþlam*, f. **bū-* dwell (see BOWER[1]).

bulb †onion XVI; 'root' of onion, etc. XVII; roundish dilatation, spec. of a glass tube XVIII. - L. *bulbus* = Gr. *bólbos* onion, bulbous root. Hence **bulbous** XVI; cf. F. *bulbe* (XVI), *bulbeux*.

bulge †wallet, pouch XIII; bottom of a ship's hull XVII; (f. the vb.) protuberance XVIII. - (O)F. *bouge* - L. *bulga* leathern sack, bag, of Gaulish orig.; the second sense is of obscure orig. (cf. BILGE). Hence **bulge** vb. stave in the bottom of a ship; also intr. XVI; protrude XVII.

bulk A. cargo (*in bulk*, in large unbroken quantities) XIV; †heap XV; B. †belly, trunk, body XIV; large body, huge frame XVI; C. magnitude, volume, mass XV. In A - ON. (cf. OIcel. *búlki* cargo); in B perh. at first an alt. of †*bouk*, OE. *būc* belly = OS. *būk*, OHG. *būh* (G. *bauch*), ON. *búkr* :- Gmc. **búkaz*; in C prob. transf. use of either A or B. Hence **bulk** vb. (in several unconnected uses) XVI. **bulky** XV.

bulkhead upright partition in a ship XV; roof of a stall XVIII. f. †*bulk* stall (- ON. *bálkr* partition, etc.) + HEAD.

bull[1] male of the ox, etc. Late OE. *bula* (in place-names), ME. *bole* - ON. *boli*, corr. to MLG. *bulle*, MDu. *bulle*, *bolle* (Du. *bul*), f. a base whence the OE. dim. *bulluc* BULLOCK.

bull[2] papal edict XIII; official seal XIV. - (O)F. *bulle* - L. *bulla* bubble, round object, in medL. seal, sealed document; cf. BOIL[2].

bull[3] †jest; expression containing contradiction in terms or implying ludicrous inconsistency. XVII. of unkn. orig.

bullace species of wild plum. XIV. - OF. *buloce*, (also mod.) *beloce* sloe :- Rom. **bullucea*, f. **bulluca*, perh. of Gaul. orig.

bulldose, -doze (U.S.) intimidate (orig. Negroes) by violence. XIX. f. BULL[1], the second element being uncertain. Hence **bulldozer** XIX (person), XX (machine).

bullet †cannon-ball; ball for small-arms. XVI. - F. *boulette*, dim. of *boule* ball (BOWL[2]).

bulletin †note, warrant, etc. XVII; short account or report XVIII. - F. - It. *bulletino*, *boll-* safe-conduct, pass, f. *bulletta* passport, lottery ticket, dim. of *bulla* BULL[2].

bullfinch[1] finch of the genus *Pyrrhula*. XIV. f. BULL[1] + FINCH; so called from its large head and squat form.

bullfinch[2] high quickset hedge with a ditch. XIX. The first el. is presumably BULL[1]; the second el. may be a corruption of *fence*.

bullion XIV. - AN. *bullion*, which appears to mean 'mint', var. of (O)F. *bouillon* :- Rom. **bullio*, *-ōn-* boiling, f. L. *bullīre* BOIL[2].

bullock Late OE. *bulluc*, dim. of BULL[1]; see -OCK.

bully[1] †sweetheart; fine fellow XVI; bravo, swashbuckler, (hence) tyrannical coward XVII; †hired ruffian; †protector of prostitutes XVIII. prob. - (M)Du. *boel(e)* (MHG. *buole*, G. *buhle*) used as a term of endearment or reproach.

bully[2] (now esp. U.S.) capital, first rate. XVII. perh. arising from attrib. use of prec.

bully[3] (also *bully beef*) corned beef. XVIII. - F. *bouilli* boiled beef, sb. use of pp. of *bouillir* BOIL[2].

bullyrag, ballyrag (orig. U.S.) †bully; use abusive language of. XVIII. of unkn. orig.

bulrush XV. perh. f. BULL[1] (as later used in BULLFINCH[1], *bull-frog*, in the sense 'large' or 'coarse') + RUSH[1].

bulwark rampart, fortification XV; raised side of a ship XIX. immed. source doubtful, but prob. ult. a comp. of the words repr. by BOLE and WORK; cf. late MHG. *bolwerk* ballista, fortification.

bum fundament, buttocks. XIV. ME. *bom*, of unkn. orig. Hence **bum-bailiff** XVII.

bumble-bee XVI. f. †*bumble* frequent. of ME. *bumme*, *bumbe*, *bombe* boom, buzz (see -LE[3]) + BEE. Cf. HUMBLE-BEE.

Bumbledom official pomposity and stupidity. XIX. f. *Bumble* (prob. to be assoc. with prec.) name of the domineering beadle in Dickens's 'Oliver Twist'; see -DOM.

bumboat †scavenger's boat on the Thames XVII; boat for the carriage of small merchandise XVIII. prob. f. Du. *bom* bluff-bowed fishing-boat.

bummalo small fish, *Harpodon nehereus*, of S. Asia. XVII. perh. - Marathi *bombīl(a)*.

bummaree middleman in the fish trade at Billingsgate. XVIII. of unkn. orig.
bump imit. of a heavy dull blow; its result, swelling, protuberance. XVI. The sb. and vb. appear about the same time; perh. of Scand. orig.; cf. MDa. *bumpe* strike with fist. Hence **bump** vb. †swell, bulge XVI; strike heavily XVII. **bumper** full glass of drink XVII; anything unusually large XIX; f. †*bumping* (XVI) prp. adj. huge, 'thumping'.
bumpkin XVI. The earliest ex., with the gloss *Batavus* Batavian, suggests that it was orig. applied joc. to Dutchmen; perh. - Du. *boomken* little tree, or MDu. *bommekijn* little barrel, used fig. for 'squat figure'.
bumptious XIX. joc. f. BUMP, after FRACTIOUS; cf. the fig. uses of *bounce* and *bounder*.
bun[1] kind of cake. XIV. ME. *bunne*, of unkn. orig.
bun[2] (now U.S.) squirrel XVI; (dial.) rabbit XIX. Cf. BUNNY. Of unkn. orig.
bunch †hump, swelling XIV; †bundle XIV; collection of similar things XVI. of unkn. orig.
buncombe early var. of BUNKUM.
bundle †A. bandage XIV; B. collection of things bound together XIV. orig. perh. repr. OE. *byndele* binding, taken in concrete sense = OS. *bundilin*, OHG. *gi-buntili* (G. *bündel*), but reinforced later by (if not wholly due to) LG., Du. *bundel*; f. Gmc. **bund-* (**bend-* **band-*) BIND.
bung stopper. XV. - MDu. *bonghe*, varying with *bomme* and *bonde* (whence MDu. *bonne*, beside Du. *bom*); of doubtful orig.
bungalow XVII (*bungale*). - Gujarati *bangalo* - Hind. *banglā* belonging to Bengal.
bungle XVI. prob. of symbolic formation, like synon. and contemp. †*bumble*.
bunion XVIII. Formerly also *bunnian*, *-on*, *bunyan*, *-on*; rel. to dial. (E. Anglian) *bunny* swelling, earlier *bony* (XV), and obs. dial. (Essex) *boine* - OF. *buigne* (mod. *bigne*) bump on the head.
bunk[1] sleeping-berth in a ship, etc. XIX. of unkn. orig.; perh. rel. to BUNKER.
bunk[2] (sl.) be off, make off. XIX. of unkn. orig.
bunk[3] (sl.) short for BUNKUM. XX.
bunker chest or box often serving as a seat XVI (Sc. *boncure*, etc.; *bunker* XVII); sandy hollow on a golf-course XIX; storage room for coal or oil fuel XIX. Not Eng. before XIX; of unkn. orig.
bunkum political chicanery or clap-trap; humbug. XIX. Said to be f. *Buncombe* name of a county in North Carolina, U.S.A., the member for which, it is reported, in a debate in Congress persisted in speaking, declaring that he was bound to 'make a speech for Buncombe'.
bunny †term of endearment for a woman or a child; rabbit. XVII. f. BUN[2] + -Y[6].
bunsen XIX. f. name of R. W. von *Bunsen* (1811-99), German chemist, applied to a gas-burner, lamp, etc., invented by him.
bunt[1] baggy part of a sail, net, etc. XVI. of unkn. orig.
bunt[2] push, butt. XIX. of unkn. orig.
bunting[1] bird of the sub-family Emberizinae. XIII. of unkn. orig.; perh. f. a base meaning 'short and thick', *buntin(g)* being used in this sense from *c.*1600.
bunting[2] open-made woollen stuff for flags; flags collectively. XVIII (also *-ine*). of unkn. orig.; perh. connected with (dial.) *bunt* sift, boult, as if orig. 'boulting-cloth'.
buoy XIII. Earlier forms *boy(e)*, *buy*, *buie*, *bwoy*; prob. - MDu. *bo(e)ye* (Du. *boei*), perh. - OF. *boie*, *buie* chain, fetter :- L. *boia*, esp. pl. *boiæ* - Gr. *boeiai* (sc. *doraí*) straps of ox-leather, f. *boûs* (see COW[1]).
buoyant XVI. - OF. *bouyant* or Sp. *boyante* light-sailing, prp. of *boyar* float, f. *boya* buoy; see -ANT. Hence **buoyancy** XVIII.
bur, burr[3] rough or prickly seed-vessel or flower-head XIV. perh. of Scand. orig.; cf. Da. *burre* bur, burdock, Sw. *kardborre* burdock, perh. rel. to BRISTLE.
burble †form bubbles, flow with bubbling sound XIV; (revived or formed afresh by Kipling) talk with a continuous murmur XIX. of imit. orig.; there are similar and synon. forms in Rom., e.g. Sp. *borbollar* bubble, gush, *barbullar* talk loud and fast, It. *borbugliare*.
burbot freshwater fish, *Lota lota*. XIV. - F. *bourbotte*, earlier *bourbet(t)e*, prob. f. *bourbe* slime, mud; see -ET.
burden[1], (arch.) **burthen** load. OE. *byrðen* = OS. *burthinna* :- WGmc. **burþinjō*, f. **burþi-* (see BIRTH) + -EN[2]; cf., with different suffix, OHG. *burdi* (G. *bürde*), Goth. *baurþei*. Forms with *d* appear XII, cf. MURDER; for *u* repr. OE. *y* cf. BLUSH. Hence **burden** vb., **†burdenous, burdensome.** XVI.
burden[2] †bass, 'undersong'; refrain XVI; chief theme XVII. Later form of BOURDON, assim. to prec. as if with the notion that the bass or the refrain was 'carried' by the melody or the song.
burdock XVI. f. BUR + DOCK[1].
bureau writing-desk with drawers; office. XVII. - F. *bureau* orig. woollen stuff, baize, used for covering writing-desks. So **bureaucracy** XIX.
burgee (naut.) small three-cornered flag, yacht flag. XVIII. perh. for **burgee's flag*, i.e. owner's flag; - F. *bourgeois* (see BURGESS) in the sense of 'master', 'owner'.
burgeon sb. (arch.) bud. XIII. - OF. *bor-*, *burjon* (mod. *bourgeon*) :- Rom. **burriōn-*, f. late L. *burra* wool (whence F. *bourre* tag-wool, flock-wool, etc.). So **burgeon** vb. XIV. - (O)F. *bourgeonner*.
burgess inhabitant of a borough XIII; parliamentary representative XV. ME. *burge(i)s*, *borges* - OF. *burgeis* :- Rom. **burgensis*, f. late L. *burgus* BOROUGH + *-ensis* (cf. -ESE).
burg(g)rave hereditary ruler of a town in Germany. XVI. - G. *burggraf*, f. *burg* BOROUGH + *graf* count.
burgh Sc. form of BOROUGH since XIV.
burgher citizen. XVI. - G. or Du. *burger*, f. *burg* BOROUGH.
burglar XV. - AN. *burgler* = AL. *burg(u)lātor*, varying with AN. *burge(y)sour*, *-issour*, and AL. *burgātor*, *-isor*, with corr. vb. AL. *burg(u)lāre* and noun of action AN. *burglarie* (whence **burglary** XVI; see -Y[3]); all apparently f. a base **burg-*, repr. by OF. *burgier* pillage, plunder, agent-noun *burgur*, AL. *burgāria*, *-eria*, *-ātio*

burglary. Hence **burglarious** XVIII. **burgle** vb. XIX; joc. back-formation.

burgomaster chief magistrate of a Dutch or Flemish town. XVI. - Du. *burgemeester*, f. *burg* BOROUGH, with assim. to MASTER.

burial †grave XIII; interment XV. ME. *buriel*, *biriel*, spurious sg. of *buriels*, OE. *byrġels* = OS. *burgisli* :- Gmc. **burȝisli-*, f. **burȝ-* (see BURY) + **-isli-*; see -AL².

burin engraving-tool. XVII. - F., rel. to It. *burino* (*bulino*), which has been referred to OHG. *boro* auger (see BORE¹).

burke suffocate, stifle; 'smother', hush up. XIX. f. name of William *Burke*, executed at Edinburgh in 1829 for smothering people in order to sell their bodies for dissection.

burlesque †droll; derisively imitative; sb. burlesque composition. XVII. - F. - It. *burlesco*, f. *burla* ridicule, fun; of unkn. orig.; see -ESQUE.

burly †comely, imposing, stately XIII; hence as a conventional epithet in ME. 'noble'; massively built, corpulent XIV. ME. *borli*, *burli*, *-lich*, prob. :- OE. **būrlić* 'fit for the bower' = OHG. *būrlīh* exalted, excellent, stately; see BOWER¹, -LY¹.

burn¹ stream, brook. OE. *burna* wk. m., *burne* wk. fem., *burn* str. fem., corr. to MLG. *born(e)*, MDu. *borne*, Du., G. *born*, repr. a metathetic form of Gmc. **brunnan-*, *-az*, in OS., OHG. *brunno* (Du. *bron*, G. *brunnen*), ON. *brunnr*, Goth. *brunna*; ult. orig. unkn.

burn² A. be on fire. B. consume with fire. In meaning repr. two OE. verbs: (i) an intr. str. vb. *birnan*, *beornan*; (ii) a trans. wk. vb. *bærnan*. Both verbs contain metathesized forms of Gmc. **bren-* **bran-*; OE. *birnan*, var. of *brinnan* = OS., OHG., Goth. *brinnan*; OE. *bærnan* = OS., OHG. *brennan* (G. *brennen*), ON. *brenna*, Goth. *brannjan*. Hence **burn** sb. XVI.

burnet plant of the genus *Sanguisorba* or *Poterium*. XIV. sb. use of ME. *burnet* (XII) dark-brown - OF. *burnete* BRUNETTE.

burnish XIV. f. *burniss-*, lengthened stem (see -ISH²) of OF. *burnir*, var. of *brunir*, f. *brun* BROWN.

burnous hooded mantle worn by Arabs. XVII. - F. - Arab. *burnus* - Gr. *bírros* kind of cloak.

burr¹ rough edge on cut metal, etc. XVII. prob. same word as BUR. Hence as vb. XIX.

burr² uvular pronunciation of *r*, characteristic of Northumberland XVIII; rough whirring sound XIX. prob. imit., but perh. transf. application of BUR to a 'rough' sound.

burrow sb. XIII. ME. *borwȝ*, *borow*, prob. var. of BOROUGH in the sense of 'fortified or inhabited place'. Hence **burrow** vb. make a burrow XVIII; fig. XIX.

bursar A. treasurer XIII; B. (Sc.) endowed student, exhibitioner XVI. In A - medL. *bursārius*, f. *bursa* PURSE; in B - F. *boursier*, f. *bourse* PURSE; see -AR. So **bursary** treasury, bursar's office XVI; student's endowment XVIII. - medL. *bursāria*.

burst (tr. and intr.) OE. str. vb. *berstan* = OS., OHG. *brestan*, ON. *bresta* :- Gmc. **brestan*; IE. **bhrest-* is repr. also in OIr. *brissim* I break, Gael. *bris*. The form **burst** for all parts prevailed by the end of XVI. Hence **burst** sb. XVII.

burthen var. of BURDEN¹.

burton (naut.) tackle-block used to tighten rigging. XV. orig. in *Breton* or *Brytton takles*; presumably a use of *Breton* of Brittany.

bury OE. *byrġan* :- WGmc. **burȝjan* (cf. BURIAL), f. **burȝ-* **berȝ-*, base of OE. *beorgan* shelter, protect (see BOROUGH).

bus XIX. Short for OMNIBUS.

busby †large bushy wig XVIII; tall fur cap of hussars, etc. XIX. of unkn. orig.; cf., however, *buzz wig* (XVIII-XIX), and the local use of *buzz* for various hairy or downy objects.

bush¹ shrub XIII. Early forms are *buss(ch)e*, *boisshe*, *buysche*, pointing to an OE. **bysć*; beside this, in northern and eastern areas there was a form *busk* (XIII) - ON. *buski*. There were also ME. forms with *-o-*, viz. *bosk* (XIII), surviving dial., beside *bosh*, *bossche* (XIV-XV); these were perh. - OF. *bos(c)*, vars. of *bois* wood.

bush² metal lining of a hole, etc. XV. - MDu. *busse* (Du. *bus*) bush of a wheel (see BOX²). Hence **bush** vb. XVI.

bushel dry measure of capacity. XIV. - OF. *boissel* (mod. *boisseau*); perh. of Gaul. orig.

business †solicitude OE.; †industry, diligence XIII; occupation, pursuit XIV; affair XVI. OE. *bisiġnis*, f. *bisiġ* BUSY + -NESS.

buskin half-boot; high thick-soled boot worn in Attic tragedy. XVI. prob. - late OF. *bouzequin*, var. of *bro(u)sequin* (mod. *brodequin*), corr. to Cat., Sp. *borceguí*, Pg. *borzeguim*, It. *borzacchino*; of unkn. orig.

buss (arch.) sb. and vb. kiss. XVI. of uncert. orig.; cf. earlier †*bass* (XV).

bust¹ sculpture representing head, shoulders, and breast XVII; female bosom XVIII. - F. *buste* - It. *busto*; the Rom. word is of unkn. orig.

bust² vulgar and dial. pronunc. of BURST. XVIII.

bustard bird of the genus *Otis*. XV (earlier as a surname). perh. - AN. **bustarde*, blending of OF. *bistarde* and *oustarde* (mod. *outarde*) :- L. *avis tarda* 'slow bird'; but the bustard is a swift bird, and the L. term may be a perversion of a foreign word.

bustle¹ bestir oneself busily. XVI. perh. alt. of †*buskle*, frequent. of *busk* prepare, hurry (- ON. *búask*); see -LE. Not certainly identical with ME. *bustele* (XIV).

bustle² frame or pad thrusting out a woman's skirt behind. XVIII. of unkn. orig.

busy constantly or fully occupied OE.; officiously active XIV; marked by activity XVI. OE. *bisiġ*, later *bysiġ* (ME. *büsi*, *besy*, *bisy*) = MLG., MDu. *besich* (Du. *bezig*), of unkn. orig. Hence **busybody** XVI.

but †adv. outside; prep. †outside; except; unless, if . . not OE.; adversative conj. XIII. OE. *b(e)ūtan* = OS. *b(i)ūtan*, OHG. *biūzan*; WGmc. comp. of **be*, **bi* BY and **ūtana* from without (see OUT).

butcher XIII. ME. *bo(u)cher* - AN. var. of OF. *bo(u)chier* (mod. *boucher*); f. OF., Pr. *boc* (F. *bouc*) he-goat, prob. - OCelt. **bukkos*; see BUCK, -ER². Hence **butcher** vb. XVI. So **butchery**

slaughter-house, butcher's shop XIV; butcher's trade XV; (brutal) slaughter XVI. - (O)F. *boucherie*.

butler servant having charge of the wine-cellar. XIII. - AN. *buteler*, OF. *bouteillier*, f. *bouteille* BOTTLE; see -ER[4].

butt[1] strike, thrust (now with the head), intr. XII; trans. XVI. - AN. *buter*, OF. *boter* (mod. dial. *bouter* put), of Gmc. orig.

butt[2] (locally) applied to various flat-fish. XIII. - MLG. *but*, MDu. *but(te)*, *bot(te)*, whence also G. *butt(e)*, Sw. *butta* turbot, Da. *bot* flounder; prob. rel. to LG. *but*, MDu. *bot* stumpy. Cf. HALIBUT.

butt[3] mark for archery practice (orig. embankment holding targets) XIV; †goal, object XVI; target for ridicule, etc. XVII. prob. - (O)F. *but*, of unkn. orig.; perh. infl. by F. *butte* (cf. BUTTE) rising ground, knoll, (also) target.

butt[4] cask for wine, etc. XIV. In AL. *butta* (XIII), *bota* (XIV) - AN. *but*, var. of OF. *bo(u)t* :- late L. *buttis*, perh. based on Gr. *būtī́nē*, var. of *pūtī́nē* osier-covered flask. (Cf. BOTTLE.)

butt[5] thicker end of a thing; (dial.) buttock XV; base of a tree-trunk XVII. rel. to the base of which BUTTOCK seems to be a deriv. and which is repr. by words meaning 'short and stumpy', as Du. *bot* (BUTT[2]).

butte (U.S.) isolated hill or peak. XIX. - F. (cf. BUTT[3]).

butter OE. *butere*, corr. to OHG. *butera* (G. *butter*), Du. *boter*; WGmc. - L. *būtȳrum* - Gr. *boútūron*. The L. word is repr. in Rom. by OF. *burre* (mod. *beurre*), Pr. *buire*, It. *butirro*.

buttercup XVII. prob. blending of †*butterflower* (XVI, after Du. *boterbloeme*) with *goldcup* or *kingcup*.

butterfly Late OE. *buttorflēoge*, f. BUTTER + FLY[1]; cf. Du. *botervlieg*, G. *butterfliege* and *buttervogel* (-bird).

butterscotch XIX. perh. orig. of *Scotch* manufacture.

buttery (orig.) store-room for liquor, (hence) for provisions in general. XIV (*boteri*). - AN. *boterie*, **buterie*, prob. f. *but* BUTT[4]; see -ERY. An earlier term was †*botelery* (XIII) - OF. *butelerie*, *bouteillerie*, f. *bouteille* BOTTLE.

buttock (chiefly pl.) rump. XIII. Formally identical with OE. *buttuc* (once) prob. end ridge of land, rounded slope, cf. *butt* (XIII) ridge, strip of land; see -OCK.

button XIV. - (O)F. *bouton*, f. *boter* (see BUTT[1]).

buttress XIII. ME. *butras*, *-es*, *boterace*, *-as* - OF. *bouterez* (*ars bouterez* 'thrusting arch'), inflexional form of *bouteret*, f. *bouter* BUTT[1]; the ending was assim. first to *-ace*, and thence in XVI to *-ess*.

butty (dial.) partner, mate; middleman in mining. XIX. prob. evolved from the phr. *play* BOOTY (XVI) join with confederates to share 'plunder' with them.

butyric (*butyric acid*, found in rancid butter) XIX. f. L. *būtȳrum* BUTTER + -IC.

buxom †obedient, compliant XII; †flexible; †blithe, gay; plump and comely XVI. ME. *buhsum*, etc., repr. OE *(*ġe*)*būhsum*, f. (*ġe*)*būgan* bend, BOW[2] + -SOME[1].

buy pt., pp. *bought* OE. *byċġan* = OS. *buggian*, ON. *byggja*, Goth. *bugjan*; Gmc. wk. vb. of unkn. orig.

buzz[1] make a sibilant humming sound. XVI. Earlier *busse* (XIV); hence as sb. XVII; of imit. orig.

buzz[2] epithet of a large bushy wig. XVIII. abbrev. of BUSBY.

buzzard XIII. - (O)F. *busard*, based like OF. *buson* (whence F. *buse*) on L. *būteō*, *-ōn-*, of unkn. orig.; see -ARD.

by alongside; in the course of; according to; in relation to; marking the means or instrument (ult. superseding *from*, *through*, *of*) OE.; marking the agent (ult. superseding *of*, *from*) XIV. OE. *bī*, unstressed *bi*, *be* = OS., OHG. *bī* (Du. *bij*, G. *bei*), Goth. *bi* :- Gmc. **bi*, prob. identical with the second syll. of Gr. *amphi*, L. *ambi-* (see AMBI-, AMPHI-), OE. *ymb(e)-* around. Cf. BE-, BEFORE, BEHIND, BESIDE, BETIMES, BY-, BY-AND-BY.

by- the adv. BY used attrib. and entering into composition with a sb. in the senses 'lying or situated at one side', 'out of the way', 'running alongside and apart', 'devious', as *by-path*, *byway* (XIV), 'collateral', 'side-', as *by-play*, *by-product* (XIX), 'additional', 'subsidiary', as *by-name* (XIV), *by-election* (XIX).

by-and-by (adv. phr.) †one by one, in succession, on and on XIV; †straightway XV; shortly, before long XVI. prob. originating in the use of BY to denote succession, as in *by two and two*, *by little and little*, ME. *bi sixti and bi sixti*.

bye †second or subsidiary object or course XVI; phr. *by the bye* (i) as a subsidiary matter XVII, (ii) 'by the way' XVIII. The usual sp. of *by* when used sb., but varying with *by*; ellipt. use of BY- meaning 'secondary', 'subsidiary', e.g. as opp. to *main* in dicing, referring to stake, throw, or chance, and in various sports.

bye-bye[1] sounds to lull a child to sleep XV; (nursery colloq., also *bye-byes*) sleep XIX.

bye-bye[2] XVIII. colloq. and child's var. of GOOD-BYE.

bygone past XV; sb. pl. things past; arrears XVI (orig. Sc., and hardly naturalized in England before XVIII). f. BY adv. 'past' + pp. of GO.

by-law, bye-law A. local law or custom established by common consent XIII; B. ordinance regulating internal matters made by a local authority or corporation XIV. In A orig. var. with *birlaw* (XIII) - ON. **bȳjarlagu*, f. gen. sg. of *bȳr* habitation, village, town (f. **bū-*; cf. BOWER[1]) + **lagu* LAW; in B alt. of this by substitution of *by* sb. town and by assoc. with BY-.

byre cow-house. OE. *bȳre*, prob. :- **būrjam*, rel. to **būram* BOWER[1].

byssus fine textile fabric. XVII. - L. - Gr. *bússos*, of Sem. orig. Earlier repr. by ME. *biis*, *bys* - OF. *bysse*.

byword proverb XII; person etc. taken as typical XVI. Early ME. *biword*, preceded by late OE. *bīwyrde* = OHG. *piwurti*, rendering L. *proverbium*; see BY- and WORD.

C

cab XIX. Shortening of CABRIOLET. Hence **cabby** cab-driver; see -Y[4].

cabal †cabbala; private intrigue; clique. XVII. - F. *cabale* - medL. *cab(b)ala*; see CABBALA. Hence **cabal** vb. conduct an intrigue XVII; cf. F. *cabaler*.

caballero Spanish gentleman. XIX. - Sp., = F. *chevalier*, It. *cavaliere* CAVALIER.

cabaret French tavern XVII; restaurant, etc., offering entertainment XX. - (O)F., prob. of Walloon orig.

cabbage[1] green vegetable with a round heart. XIV. Earliest forms *cabache*, *-oche* - (O)F. *caboche* head, Picard var. of OF. *caboce*, of unkn. orig.

cabbage[2] shreds of cloth cut off by tailors and kept as a perquisite. XVII (also *garbage*, *carbage*). of unkn. orig. Hence **cabbage** vb. pilfer, crib. XVIII.

cabbala oral tradition handed down from Moses to the Rabbis; tradition of mystical interpretation of the O.T. XVI. - medL. - Rabbinical Heb. *ḳabbālāh* tradition, f. *ḳibbēl* receive, accept, admit. Hence **cabbalist** XVI, **-istic** XVII, **-istical** XVI.

caber (Sc.) pole, spar. XVI. - Gael. *cabar* = Ir. *cabar*, W. *ceibr* beam, rafter.

cabin †hut, tent; †cell; †cave, den; compartment in a ship XIV; rude habitation XV; †political cabinet (only XVII). ME. *cabane*, ult. (perh. via (O)F. *cabane* - Pr. *cabana*) - late L. *capanna*, *cavanna*; spellings with *-in* appear XVI.

cabinet †hut, tent; †small chamber; †room for exhibiting works of art, etc.; case for keeping valuables XVI; †council room; body of councillors (orig. *cabinet council*) XVII. Early vars. are *cabanet*, *cab(b)onet*; perh. f. *cabane*, *cabon* CABIN, after F. *cabinet* (XVI), if the Eng. word is not to be considered as directly - F.; see -ET.

cable XIII. - AN., ONF. **cable*, var. of OF. *chable* (mod. *câble* - Pr.) - late L. *cap(u)lum* halter - Arab. *ḥabl*, assoc. with L. *capere* seize, hold (cf. HEAVE); perh., however, immed. - Pr. *cable*, and in any case reinforced by (M)LG., (M)Du. *kabel*. Applied *c.*1850 to a rope-like line used for submarine telegraphy; hence **cable** vb. send a message by cable; **cablegram** message so sent. XIX.

cabochon gem polished but not faceted. XVI. - (O)F. *cabochon*, dim. of *caboche* head (see CABBAGE[1]).

caboodle (orig. U.S.) often *whole caboodle* whole lot; varying with *whole kit and boodle* (- Du. *boedel* whole of one's possessions), of which it may be a contraction. XIX.

caboose cook-house (galley) of a ship XVIII; (U.S.) guard's van, etc., on a train XIX. - early modDu. *cabūse*, var. *combūse* (now *kabuis*, *kombuis*) = (M)LG. *kabūse*, of unkn. orig.

cabotage coasting trade. XIX. - F., f. *caboter* coast along, perh. f. †*cabo* (XVI) - Sp. *cabo* CAPE[2].

cabriole curved leg in Queen Anne and Chippendale furniture, its form suggesting a leaping animal's front leg. XVIII. - F., f. *cabrioler*; see next.

cabriolet (hist.) light two-wheeled one-horse vehicle. XVIII. - F., f. *cabrioler*, later form of *caprioler* - It. *capriolare* leap into the air, f. *capriola* CAPRIOLE; see -ET; so named from its springiness.

ca'canny 'going slow' at work. XIX. f. Sc. and north. Eng. phr. *ca' canny* (i.e. CALL vb., in Sc. from XIV 'drive', CANNY used adv. 'warily') drive cautiously, go warily or carefully.

cacao seed from which cocoa is prepared. XVI. - Sp. - Nahuatl *cacauatl* (*uatl* tree). See also COCOA[2].

cachalot sperm-whale. XVIII. - F. - Sp., Pg. *cachalote*, of unkn. orig.

cache XIX. - F., f. *cacher* hide (see next).

cachet (Sc.) seal XVII; stamp, mark XIX. - F., f. *cacher* (in the sense of 'press' repr. now in *écacher* crush) :- Rom. **coacticāre*, for L. *coactāre* constrain, f. *coact-*, pp. stem of *cōgere* compel, f. *co-* CON- + *agere* drive (see ACT).

cachexy depraved condition or habit. XVI. - F. *cachexie* or late L. *cachexia* - Gr. *kakhexíā*, f. *kakós* bad + *héxis* habit, state, f. *ékhein* have, be (in a certain state). So **cachetic** XVII.

cachinnation immoderate laughter. XVII. - L. *cachinnātiō*, *-ōn-*, f. *cachinnāre*, of imit. orig., whence **cachinnate** vb. XIX. See -ATE[3], -ATION.

cachou †CATECHU XVIII; sweetmeat for sweetening the breath XIX. - F. - Pg. †*cacho*, *cachu* - Malay *kachu*.

cackle make a noise as a hen. XIII. perh. - (M)LG., (M)Du. *kākelen*, of imit. orig. (but partly f. *kāke* jaw (CHEEK)). See -LE[2].

caco- repr. Gr. *kako-* stem of *kakós* bad, as in **cacod(a)emon** XVI (Gr. *kakodaímōn*) evil spirit, **cacography** XVI (F. *cacographie*, medGr. *kakographía*) bad writing or spelling, **cacophony** XVI (F. *cacophonie*, Gr. *kakophōníā*) discordant sound.

cactus †cardoon XVII; prickly plant with thick fleshy stems XVIII. - L. - Gr. *káktos* cardoon or Spanish artichoke (of Sicily); the name was adopted by Linnaeus for a genus of entirely different prickly plants.

cad XVIII. Shortening of CADDIE.

cadaver XVI. - L. *cadāver*, prop. 'fallen thing', f. *cadere* fall. So **cadaverous** XV. - L. *cadāverōsus* (see -OUS).

caddie †army cadet XVII; †errand boy, porter, commissionaire XVIII; golfer's attendant XIX. orig. Sc. (earliest form *caudie*) - F. CADET.

caddis(-worm, -fly) XVII. contemp. with synon. (dial.) *cadbait*, *codbait*, *cadew*; of unkn. orig.

caddy small box for holding tea. XVIII. alt. of *catty* (XVI) weight of 1⅓ lb. - Malay *kati*.
cadence rhythm XIV; fall of the voice; close of a musical phrase, etc. XVI. - OF. - It. *cadenza* - popL. **cadentia*, f. *cadent-*, prp. stem of *cadere* fall. So **cadency** †cadence XVII; (her.) descent of a younger branch from the main line XVIII; see -Y[3]. **cadenza** (mus.) flourish at a cadence. XIX. - It.
cadet younger son, etc.; gentleman in the army without a commission XVII; junior officer XVIII. - F. *cadet*, earlier *capdet* - Gascon dial. *capdet* :- Rom. **capitellus*, dim. of *caput* head, CHIEF; orig. applied to Gascon officers (younger sons of noble families) at the French court.
cadge †carry (a pack) XVII; go about begging XIX. of obscure orig.; perh. back-formation from **cadger** orig. carrier, itinerant dealer XV (first in Sc.), of unkn. orig.
cadmium XX. f. †*cadmia* CALAMINE (XVII).
cadre frame(work); permanent establishment of a regiment XIX. - F. - It. *quadro* :- L. *quadrus* square.
caecum (anat.) blind end of the first part of the large intestine. XVIII. - L. (*intestinum*) *cæcum* blind (gut), n. sg. of *cæcus* blind; tr. Gr. *tuphlòn énteron*.
Caesarean, -ian pert. to the delivery of a child by cutting through the walls of the abdomen, as was done, according to legend, at the birth of Julius *Caesar*. XVII. - L. *Cæsariānus* or f. *Cæsareus*; see -EAN, -IAN.
caesium (chem.) metallic element. XIX. - modL., n. of L. *cæsius* bluish-grey; after names in -IUM.
c(a)esura (pros.) division of a foot between two words. XVI. - L. *cæsūra* lit. cutting, f. *cæs-*, pp. stem of *cædere* cut; see -URE. (Early forms †*cesure*, †*ce(a)sure* may be - F. *césure*.)
café coffee-house. XIX. - F. - It. *caffè* COFFEE.
cafeteria (orig. U.S.) restaurant in which customers serve themselves. XX. - Amer. Sp *cafeteria* coffee shop, f. Sp. *cafetero* maker or seller of coffee, f. *café* COFFEE.
caffeine (chem.) alkaloid found in the coffee and tea plants. XIX. - F. *caféine*, f. *café* COFFEE; see -INE[5].
caftan oriental under-tunic. XVI. - Turk. *kaftan*, partly through F. *cafetan*.
cage XIII. - (O)F. :- L. *cavea* stall, cage, coop, etc.
caiman see CAYMAN.
cainozoic (geol.) Tertiary. XIX. f. Gr. *kainós* recent + *zôion* animal; see ZOO, -IC.
caique light boat used in the Mediterranean. XVII. - F. *caïque* - It. *caicco* - Turk. *kayık*.
cairn pile of stones. XV. Earlier *carn* (cf. *barn* BAIRN) - Gael., OIr., W. *carn* heap of stones. So **cairngorm** precious stone, named from a mountain (Gael. *Carngorm* 'blue cairn') where it is found.
caisson chest for ammunition, etc.; watertight vessel used in deep water. XVIII. - F. *caisson*, †*casson* - It. *cassone*; assim. to *caisse* CASE[2]; see -OON.
caitiff †prisoner; †poor wretch; base fellow, villain. XIII. ME. *caitif*, occas. *chaitif* - OF. *caitif* captive, var. of *chaitif* (mod. *chétif* wretched) :- Rom. **cactivus*, alt. of L. *captīvus* CAPTIVE by assoc. with OCelt. **cactos* (= L. *captus*).
cajole delude by flattery, etc. XVII. - F. *cajoler*, perh. a blend of two or more words (cf. *cageoller*, *cajoller* XVI chatter like a jay, prate, babble, and *enjôler* put in GAOL, inveigle, allure). So **cajolery** XVII.
cake (arch.) flat sort of loaf XIII; confectionery made with flour XV; (Sc.) thin hard-baked oaten bread XVI. prob - ON. *kaka* (Icel., Sw. *kaka*, Da. *kage*), f. **kak-*, rel. to **kōk-*, repr. by G. *kuchen*, etc., COOKIE. Hence **cake** vb. form into a cake. XVII.
calabash gourd(-shell). XVII (*calibasse*, *-bash*). - F. *calebasse*, †*cala-* - Sp. *calabaza*.
calamary squid, pen-fish. XVI. - medL. *calamārium* pen-case, n. of L. *calamārius*, f. *calamus* pen - Gr. *kálamos*; see -ARY.
calamine ore of zinc. XVII. - (O)F. - medL. *calamīna*, alt. of L. *cadmīa* - Gr. *kadm(e)iā* (sc. *gê* earth), fem. of the adj. of Cadmus.
calamint aromatic herb. XIV. - (O)F. *calament* - medL. *calamentum*, for late L. *calaminthe* - Gr. *kalaminthē*.
calamity grievous affliction or distress XV; grievous disaster XVI. - (O)F. *calamité* - L. *calamitās*; see -ITY. So **calamitous** XVI. - F. *calamiteux* or L. *calamitōsus*.
calash light carriage with folding hood XVII; woman's hood XVIII. Early forms *caleche*, *galeche*, *calleche* - F. *calèche*, †*galèche* - G. *kalesche* - Pol. *kolaska* or Czech *kolesa*, f. *kolo* WHEEL.
calcareous of the nature of lime. XVII. f. L. *calcārius*, f. *calc-* CALX + *-ārius* -ARY.
calceolaria genus of plants having slipper-shaped flowers. XVIII. - modL., f. L. *calceolus*, dim. of *calceus* shoe (f. *calx* heel) + *-āria*, fem. of *-ārius* -ARY.
calcine reduce to quicklime. XIV. - (O)F. *calciner* or medL. *calcināre* (a term of alchemy), f. late L. *calcīna* lime, quicklime, f. L. CALX, *calc-*. So **calcination** XIV.
calcium XIX. f. L. *calc-* CALX; see -IUM.
calculate XVI. f. pp. stem of late L. *calculāre*, f. *calculus* stone (see next); superseded †**calcule** (XVI-XVI) - (O)F. *calculer*; see -ATE[3]. So **calculation** XIV. - (O)F. - late L.
calculus stone in an animal body; †gen. (system of) calculation XVII; spec. in *differential*, *integral* (etc.) *calculus* XVIII. - L. *calculus* pebble, etc.
Caledonian XVII. f. *Calēdonia*, Roman name of part of northern Britain, now assoc. with the Scottish Highlands or Scotland in general.
calefaction heating. XVI. - (O)F. *caléfaction* or late L. *calefactiō*, *-ōn-*, f. *calefacere*, f. *calēre* be warm + *facere* make, DO[1]; see -TION.
calendar system of divisions of the civil year XIII; table showing these XIV. ME. *kalender* - AN. *calender*, OF. *calendier* (mod. *calendrier*) - L. *kalendārium* account-book, f. *kalendæ* CALENDS, the day on which accounts were due.
calender pass material between rollers for glazing, etc. XV. - (O)F. *calendrer*, of unkn. orig. So **calender** sb. machine for calendering. XVII.
calends XIV. - (O)F. *calendes* - L. *kalendæ*, acc.

-as, first day of the month, when the order of days was proclaimed, f. **kal-* call, proclaim, as in L. *calāre*, Gr. *kaleîn*.

calf[1] young of the cow. OE. *cælf* (*ċealf*), pl. *calfru* = OS. *calf*, OHG. *chalb* (G. *kalb*) n., beside ON. *kálfr* m. and Goth. *kalbō*, OHG. *chalba* fem.

calf[2] fleshy hinder part of the shank of the leg. XIV. - ON. *kálfi*, of unkn. orig.

calibre †diameter of a projectile; bore of a gun; (fig.) weight of character, ability. XVI. - F. - It. *calibro* or Sp. *calibre* - Arab. *ḳālib* mould for casting metal, f. *ḳalaba* turn, convert.

calico XVI. Earliest exx. have *Callicut*, *kalyko*, *Calocowe cloth*; f. name of a city and port on the coast of Malabar, India; relevant forms are Arab. *Kālīkūt*, etc.

calipash, calipee correl. words denoting (i) †the upper/lower shell of the turtle, (ii) gelatinous substance next to these. XVII. Earliest forms of the first are *galley patch*, *calapatch*; perh. of native W. Indian orig., unless a native alt. of Sp. *carapacho* CARAPACE.

caliph Muslim chief ruler (successor of Muhammad). XIV. - (O)F. *caliphe* (medL. *calīpha*, *-es*) - Arab. *ḳalīfa*, f. *ḳalofa* succeed. So **caliphate** XVIII. - F. *caliphat* (medL. *caliphātus*); see -ATE[1].

calix, calyx (pl. *calices*) cup-like cavity. XVIII. - L. *calix* cup.

call cry out OE.; summon with a shout, name XIII. Late OE. *ceallian* (once) - (or perh. only reinforced by) ON. *kalla* cry, summon loudly, name, claim = MLG., (M)Du. *kallen*, OHG. *challōn* talk, chatter :- Gmc. **kallōjan*, f. **kal-* :- IE. **gol-*, repr. also by W. *galw* call, OSl. *glasŭ* voice, *glagolŭ* word.

caller (Sc. and north. dial.) fresh. XIV (*caloure*). var. of ME. *calver*, *calwar*, presumably adj. use of OE. *calwer* curds.

cal(l)i- repr. Gr. *kalli-*, used as comb. form of *kalós* beautiful (cf. *kállos* beauty), as in **calligraphy** (elegant) penmanship. XVII. - modL. *calligraphia* - Gr. *kalligraphíā*. **callisthenics** exercises for developing strength with beauty. XIX. f. Gr. *sthénos* strength.

calliper (usu. pl.) XVI. orig. *calliper compasses* compasses used for measuring the calibre of a bullet, etc., presumably var. of CALIBRE.

callous hardened. XVI. - (partly through F. *calleux*) L. *callōsus*, f. **callus** hardened skin, which has been used in Eng. since XVI.

callow †bald OE.; unfledged XVI. OE. *calu* (*calw-*) = MLG. *kale*, MDu. *kale* (Du. *kaal*), OHG. *kalo* (G. *kahl*) :- WGmc. **kalwa*, perh. - L. *calvus* bald.

calm XIV. The sb., adj., and vb. appear about the same time, and earlier than the corresp. F. words (XV), which are presumed to be - It. *calma*, *calmo*, *calmare*; these are referred to popL. **calma*, alt. of late L. *cauma* - Gr. *kaûma* heat (of the day or sun), by assoc. with L. *calēre* be hot.

calomel mercurous chloride. XVII. - modL. *calomel(es)* (so in F. XVIII), said to be f. Gr. *kalós* beautiful + *mélas* black.

calorie unit of heat. XIX. - F., arbitrarily f. L. *calor* heat; cf. -Y[3]. **calor-**, stem of L. *calor*, as in **calorific** XVII (F. and L.), **calorimeter** XVIII (F. *-mètre*).

calotte skull-cap. XVII. - F. - Pr. *calota* or It. *callotta*, of disputed orig.

caltrop[1] (usu. pl.) name of various plants that entangle the feet; (later) star-thistle, *Trapa natans*. OE. *calcatrippe*, ME. *calketrappe* - medL. *calcatrippa*.

caltrop[2] †trap, snare XIII; (mil.) iron ball with sharp spikes XVI. ME. *calketrap* - OF. *kauketrape*, dial. var. of *c(h)auchetrape*, later (mod.) *chaussetrape*, f. *chauchier* (mod. *côcher*) tread + *trappe* trap; ult. identical with prec.

calumet Amer.-Indian pipe of peace. XVIII. - F., dial. var. (with suffix-substitution) of *chalumeau* - late L. *calamellus*, dim. of *calamus* reed - Gr. *kálamos* HAULM.

calumny XV. - L. *calumnia* false accusation; cf. CHALLENGE and CAVIL. So **calumniate** XVI. f. pp. stem of L. *calumniārī*; see -ATE[3]. **calumniation** XVI. **calumniator** XVI. **calumnious** XV. - (O)F. *calomnieux* or L. *calumniōsus*.

calvary outdoor (life-size) representation of the Crucified Christ. XVIII. - L. *calvāria* skull (f. *calva* scalp, *calvus* bald, rel. to Skr. *kulva-*), tr. in Matt. 27: 33, etc. of Aram. *gogulthō*, *gogolthā* skull (= Heb. *gulgōleth*), rendered in Gr. by *golgothá*; see -ARY.

calve give birth to a calf. OE. *calfian* (*ċealfian*), f. *cælf* CALF; cf. Du. *kalven*, (M)HG. *kalben*.

calvered applied to salmon that is cut up alive. XVII. f. *calver* (see CALLER) + -ED.

calx (alch. and early chem.) powder resulting from calcination of a mineral. XV. - L., 'lime(stone)', prob. - Gr. *khálix* pebble, limestone. Cf. CALCINE, CALCULATE, CALCULUS, and CHALK.

calyx outer envelope of a flower. XVII. - L. - Gr. *kálux* shell, pod, f. base of *kalúptein* hide. Confused with CALIX.

cam projection on a wheel. XVIII. - Du. *cam* COMB, as in *kamrad* toothed wheel, cog-wheel.

camaraderie XIX. - F., f. *camarade* COMRADE; see -ERY.

camber XVII. - OF. *cambre*, dial. var. of OF. *chambre* arched :- L. *camurus* curved inwards. So as vb. XVII.

cambist one skilled in monetary exchange. XIX. - F. *cambiste* - It. *cambista*, f. *cambio* CHANGE.

Cambrian Welsh. XVII (preceded by *Camber* XVI). f. *Cambria*, var. of *Cumbria*, latinization of W. *Cymru* Wales :- OCelt. **Kombroges*, f. **kom-* together, COM- + **brog-* border, region; see -IAN.

cambric XVI (*cameryk*). f. *Kamerijk*, Flemish form of *Cambrai* a town of northern France, famous for fabrics :- medL. *Camaracum*.

camel OE. *camel*, reinforced in ME. by OF. *cameil*, etc. (mod. *chameau*) :- L. *camēlus* (also **camellus*) - Gr. *kámēlos*, of Sem. orig. (Heb. *gāmāl*).

camellia genus of shrubs. XVIII. - modL., f. name of Josef *Kamel* (latinized *Camellus*), a Moravian Jesuit who described the botany of Luzon; see -IA[1].

Camembert soft rich cheese originating from *Camembert*, village of Normandy, France. XIX.

cameo precious stone having two layers of different colours. XV (*cameu*). - OF. *came(h)u*, *camahieu* (mod. *camaïeu*), corr. to Sp., Pg. *camafeo*, pointing to a type **camahæus* (cf. medL. *camahutus*, etc.); later - It. *cam(m)eo*; prob. ult. of Oriental orig.

camera CHAMBER, in several spec. uses. XVIII. - L. *camera* vault, arched chamber - Gr. *kamárā* object with arched cover. In photography, short for *camera obscura*, darkened chamber or box, orig. an optical instrument.

camisole (formerly) woman's jacket, (now) underbodice. XIX. - F. - It. *camiciola* or Sp. *camisola*, dim. of *camicia*, *camisa* shirt (see CHEMISE).

camomile plant of the genus *Anthemis*. XIV. - (O)F. *camomille* - late L. *c(h)amomilla*, alt. of *chamæmēlon* - Gr. *khamaimēlon* 'earth-apple' (*khamaí* on the ground, *mêlon* apple), so called from the apple-like smell of the blossoms.

camouflage XX. - F., f. *camoufler* (thieves' sl.) - It. *camuffare* disguise, deceive, perh. assoc. with *camouflet* whiff of smoke in the face; see -AGE.

camp place where troops are lodged in tents, etc.; temporary quarters. XVI. - (O)F. - It. *campo* :- L. *campus* level field, place for games and military exercises, field of battle, whence Gmc. **kampaz*, repr. by OE., MDu. *camp*, OHG. *champf* (G. *kampf*), ON. *kapp*. So **camp** vb. XVI. - F. *camper*; cf. ENCAMP.

campaign army's operations in the field. XVII. - F. *campagne* - It. *campagna* (used in the mil. sense XVI) = (O)F. *champagne* CHAMPAIGN.

campanile bell-tower. XVII. - It., f. *campana* - late L. *campāna* bell.

campanology bell-ringing. XIX. - modL. *campānologia*, f. late L. *campāna* bell; see prec. and -LOGY.

campanula genus of plants with bell-shaped flowers. XVII. - modL., dim. of *campāna*; see prec. and -ULE. So **campanulate** bell-shaped XVII; see -ATE[2].

Campeachy epithet of a red dye-wood, also called *log-wood*. XVII (*Cam-*, *Compeche wood*, *tree*). Name of a southern state of Mexico, *Campeche*, whence the wood was orig. exported.

camphor XV. Early forms are various, both disyll. and trisyll., *camphire* prevailing from XV to *c*.1800. - OF. *camphore* (later and mod. *camphre*) or medL. *camphora* - (prob. through Sp. *alcanfor*) Arab. *kāfūr*, ult. - Skr. *karpūra-*.

campus (orig. U.S.) college or university grounds. XVIII (first at Princeton, New Jersey). - L. *campus* field.

can[1] vessel for liquid. OE. *canne*, corr. to MDu. *kanne* (Du. *kan*), OHG. *channa* (G. *kanne*), ON. *kanna*; it is uncertain whether the word is orig. Gmc. or - late L. *canna* (VI), whence OF. *channe*, Pr. *cana*. OE. *canne* is recorded only once, after which there is no Eng. evidence till XIV, when the word was prob. introduced from the Continent.

can[2] †know; (with inf.) know how, (passing into) have power, be able. One of the group of preterite-present verbs (see DARE, MAY, SHALL, WIT[2]); the primary meaning was 'have learned', come to know'. OE. *cunnan*, OS. *cunnan*, OHG. *kunnan* (G. *können*), ON. *kunna*, Goth. *kunnan*. For the IE. base **ĝn- *ĝnē- *ĝnō-* see KNOW. See also CON[1], CUNNING, UNCOUTH.

canaille rabble, mob. XVII. - F. - It. *canaglia*, f. *cane* dog :- L. *canis* (see HOUND).

canal †pipe to convey liquid XV; tubular cavity in the body, duct, artificial watercourse XVII. - (O)F., refash. of earlier *chanel* CHANNEL after L. *canālis* or It. *canale*. So **canalize**, **-ation** XIX.

canard cock-and-bull story. XIX. - F., lit. 'duck'; the sense of 'hoax' is said to have arisen from the phr. *vendre un canard à moitié* 'half-sell a duck'.

canary name of a dance, a wine, and a singing-bird from the Canary Islands. XVI. - F. *canarie* - Sp. *canaria*, in L. *Canāria insula* 'Isle of Dogs', so named from its large dogs (L. *canārius* pert. to dogs, f. *canis* dog, HOUND). As the name of the bird modelled on F. *canari*, †*-ie* - Sp. *canario*.

canaster kind of tobacco, so called from the rush basket in which it was imported. XIX. - Sp. *canastro* - medL. **canastrum* - Gr. *kánastron* CANISTER.

cancan XIX. - F., of uncert. orig.

cancel XIV. - (O)F. *canceller* - L. *cancellāre* make lattice-wise, cross out (a writing), f. *cancellus*, pl. *cancellī* cross-bars (see CHANCEL).

cancer zodiacal constellation of the Crab XIV; malignant tumour XVII. - L. *cancer* crab, creeping ulcer, after Gr. *karkínos* crab, *karkinōma* CARCINOMA.

candelabrum, (prop. pl.) **-bra** XIX. - L., f. *candēla* CANDLE.

candid †white; free from bias or malice; frank XVII. - F. *candide* or L. *candidus*, f. *candēre* be white, glisten; see -ID[1].

candidate XVII. - (O)F. *candidat* or L. *candidātus* clothed in white, candidate for office (who appeared in a white toga), f. *candidus*; see prec. and -ATE[1].

candle OE. *candel* - L. *candēla*, later *-della*, f. *candēre* glisten; reinforced in ME. by AN. *candele*, OF. *candeile* (var. of *chandeile*, *-oile*), and OF. *candelle* (mod. *chandelle*). Hence **Candlemas** 2 February; OE. *candelmæssedæġ*; see MASS[1]. **candlestick** OE. *candelsticca*.

candour †purity; freedom from bias or malice XVII; outspokenness XVIII. - F. *candeur* or L. *candor*, f. *cand-* of *candēre* and *candidus* CANDID; see -OUR[2].

candy XVIII. - F. (*sucre*) *candi* SUGAR-CANDY.

candytuft plant of the genus *Iberis*. XVII. f. †*Candy*, the island Candia (Crete), whence orig. brought + TUFT.

cane XIV. ME. *can(n)e* - OF. *cane*, (also mod.) *canne* :- L. *canna* reed, etc. - Gr. *kánna*, *kánnē* - Assyrian *ḳanū* (Heb. *ḳaneh*) - Sumerian *gin*. Hence **cane** vb. XVII.

canine XVII. - F. *canin*, *-ine*, or L. *canīnus*, *-īna*, f. *canis* dog, HOUND; see -INE[1].

canister †basket XVII; small box XVIII. - L. *canistrum* basket for bread, fruit, etc. - Gr. *kánastron* wicker basket, f. *kánna* CANE.

canker OE. *cancer*, reinforced or superseded by ONF. *cancre*, var. of (O)F. *chancre* :- L. *cancer* CANCER.

cannel bituminous coal burning with a bright flame. XVI (*canel*). of uncert. orig.

cannelure grooving. XVIII. - F., f. *canneler*, f. OF. *cannel* CHANNEL.

cannibal XVI. First in pl. *Canibales* - Sp. *Canibales*, a form of the ethnic name *Caribes* (see CARIB).

cannon[1] piece of ordnance. XVI. - (O)F. *canon* - It. *cannone*, augm. of *canna* tube, CANE; see -OON. So **cannonade** XVII; see -ADE.

cannon[2] stroke at billiards. XIX. alt., by assoc. with prec., of *car(r)om* (XVIII), shortening of *carambole* - Sp. *carambola*, f. *bola* ball. Also as vb. XIX.

canny (Sc.) sagacious, cautious XVI; clever, cunning XVIII; (north. Eng.) agreeable, comely XIX. Presumably f. CAN[2] + -Y[1]; corr. to *cunning* in its primary sense.

canoe XVI. - Haitian (whence Sp.) *canoa*.

canon[1] rule, law (of the Church) OE.; central portion of the Mass XIII; books of the Bible accepted as authentic XIV; (mus.) XVI. OE. *canon* - L. *canōn* - Gr. *kanṓn* rule; reinforced or superseded by ME. *cano(u)n* - AN. *canun*, (O)F. *canon*. So **canonic(al)** XV. f. F. *canonique* or L. *canonicus* - Gr. *kanonikós*. **canonize** place in the canon of saints, **-ization** XIV. - medL.

canon[2] clergyman living according to the 'vita canonica', i.e. religious life based on rule. XIII. ME. *can(o)un*, *chan(o)un* - OF. *canonie*, *chanoine* (with ending assim. to *cano(u)n* CANON[1]) - ecclL. *canonicus*.

canopy XIV. Late ME. *canope*, *canape* - medL. *canopeum*, for L. *cōnōpēum* net over a bed - Gr. *kōnōpeîon* Egyptian bed with mosquito curtains, f. *kṓnōps* gnat, mosquito.

canorous melodious. XVII. f. L. *canōrus*, f. *canor* song, f. *canere* sing; see CHANT, -OUS.

cant[1] †edge, border (?) XIV; nook, corner XVII; oblique line or face XIX. prob. - MLG. *kant* point, *kante* side, edge, (M)Du. *cant* border, side, corner - Rom. **canto*, for L. *cant(h)us* iron tire. Hence **cant** vb. bevel, slant, toss, tilt XVI; whence a new sb. **cant** toss, slope, tilt XVIII.

cant[2] (sl.) speak, talk, esp. in the whining fashion of beggars XVI; use the particular jargon of a class or set, affect religious or pietistic phraseology XVII. prob. - L. *cantāre* sing (see CHANT), which was applied contemptuously as early as XII to the singing in church services and perh. later to the speech of religious mendicants. Hence **cant** sb. XVII.

cantaloup XVIII. - F. - It. *Cantaluppi*, name of a former summer residence of the popes near Rome, where it was cultivated.

cantankerous XVIII. perh. blending of Irish *cant* auction, outbidding, with *rancorous*.

cantata XVIII. - It. (sc. *aria* AIR), fem. pp. of *cantare* sing; see CHANT, -ADE.

canteen sutler's shop in a camp, etc.; outfit of cooking and table vessels and utensils. XVIII. - F. *cantine* - It. *cantina* cellar, perh. f. *canto* corner.

canter XVIII. Short for *Canterbury gallop, pace, trot* (XVII), a pace such as mounted pilgrims to Canterbury were supposed to have ridden. Hence as vb. XVIII.

cantharides XV. - L., pl. of *cantharis* - Gr. *kantharís* blister fly.

canticle XIII. - OF., var. of *cantique* - L. *canticum*, f. *cantus* CHANT; prob. reinforced by L. dim. *canticulum* (cf. -CLE).

cantilever bracket of stone, etc. XVII; projecting support in bridge-building XIX. Earliest forms *cantlapper*, *candilever*; of unkn. orig.

canto XVI. - It., lit. 'song' :- L. *cantus* CHANT.

canton †corner; (her.) ordinary of a shield XVI; subdivision of a country XVII. - (O)F. - Pr. :- Rom. **canto*, *-ōn-*, f. L. *cantus* CANT[1]. So **canton** vb. quarter (in various senses). XVI. **cantonment** quarters. XVIII.

cantor XVI. - L., 'singer', f. *canere*, *cant-* (see CHANT, -OR[1]).

canvas strong hemp or flax cloth. XIV. ME. *canevas* - ONF. (and mod.) *canevas*, var. of OF. *chanevaz* :- Rom. **cannapāceum*, f. **cannapum*, for L. *cannabis* HEMP.

canvass A. †toss in a canvas sheet, (hence) criticize destructively, discuss. B. solicit votes, etc. XVI. f. CANVAS; the emergence of sense B is difficult to account for.

canyon deep gorge. XIX. - Sp. *cañon* pipe, conduit, augm. of *caña* CANE.

caoutchouc indiarubber. XVIII. - F. - Carib *cahuchu*.

cap OE. *cæppe* - late L. *cappa*, poss. f. L. *caput* head; cf. CAPE[1]. Hence as vb. XV.

capable XVI. - F. - late L. *capābilis*, f. *capere* take (see HEAVE); see -ABLE. Hence **capability** XVI.

capacious XVII. f. L. *capāx*, *capāc-*, f. *capere* take; see prec., -ACIOUS. So **capacity** XV. - F. - L.

caparison trappings of a horse. XVI. - F. †*caparasson* (mod. *-açon*) - Sp. *caparazón* saddlecloth, f. *capa* CAPE[1]. So as vb. XVI.

cape[1] tippet of a cloak XVI; sleeveless cloak XVIII. - F. - Pr. *capa* :- late L. *cappa*; see CAP.

cape[2] promontory. XIV. - (O)F. *cap* - Pr. :- Rom. **capo*, f. L. *caput* head (cf. CHIEF).

capelin small smelt-like fish. XVII. - F. *capelan* - Pr. *capelan* CHAPLAIN.

caper[1] the shrub *Capperis spinosa* XIV; its flower-buds XV. ME. *capres* - F. *câpres* - L. *capparis* - Gr. *kápparis*. The final *s*, being apprehended as a pl. sign, was dropped to form a new sing. (XVI).

caper[2] frisky leap. XVI. Shortening of CAPRIOLE. Also as vb. XVI.

capercaillie, -lzie wood-grouse. XVI. - Gael. *capull coille* great cock (lit. horse) of the wood. The sp. *lz* (in MSc. *lȝ*) has influenced the Eng. pron., as in *Menzies*.

capillary of hair, hair-like. XVII. - L. *capillāris*, f. *capillus* hair; after F. *capillaire*; see -ARY.

capital[1] †pert. to the head XIII; affecting the head or life (*capital crime, punishment*); (of letters) standing at the head, of the largest size XIV; chief XV; first-rate XVIII. - (O)F. - L. *capitālis*, f. *caput*, *capit-* HEAD; see -AL[1]. So **capitalist** XVIII. - F. *capitaliste*; hence **capitalism** XIX. **capitalize** XIX.

capital[2] head of a column. XIV. - OF. *capitel* (mod. *chapiteau*) - L. *capitellum*, secondary dim. of *caput* HEAD.

capitation XVII. - F. *capitation* or late L. *capitātiō, -ōn-*, f. *caput, capit-* HEAD; see -ATION.
capitular (eccl.) pert. to a chapter. XVII. - late L. *capitulāris*, f. *capitulum* CHAPTER; see -AR.
capitulate †specify as under heads; †propose terms, make terms about XVI; make terms of surrender XVII. f. pp. of medL. *capitulāre* draw up under distinct heads, f. *capitulum* head of a discourse, CHAPTER; see -ATE[3]. So **capitulation** XVI. - late L.
capon castrated cock. Late OE. *capun* - AN. *capun*, var. of (O)F. *chapon* :- Rom. **cappone* for L. *capō, -ōn-*, prob. to be referred to a base meaning 'cut' (cf. Gr. *kóptein*).
caprice sudden unaccountable turn of mind XVII; work of art of lively or sportive character XVIII. - F. - It. *capriccio* orig. horror (the mod. sense being due to assoc. with *capra* goat), f. *capo* head (:- L. *caput*) + *riccio* hedgehog (:- L. *ericeus* URCHIN), lit. 'head with the hair standing on end'. So **capricious** XVI.
Capricorn zodiacal constellation. XIV. - (O)F. *Capricorne* - L. *capricornus*, f. *caper, capr-* goat + *cornu* HORN, 'goat-horn', after Gr. *aigókerōs*.
capriole leap. XVI. - F. (now *cabriole*) - It. *capriola*, f. *capriolare* leap, f. *capriolo* roebuck :- L. *capreolus*, dim. of *caper* goat.
capsicum seed-pod of Guinea pepper. XVIII. - modL., perh. f. *capsa* CASE[2].
capsize XVIII. f. *cap-* as in Pr. *capvirar* = F. *chavirer* capsize; 2nd el. unexpl.
capstan XIV. - Pr. *cabestan*, earlier *cabestran*, of unkn. orig.
capsule XVII. - F. - L. *capsula*, dim. of *capsa* box, CASE[2]; see -ULE.
captain XIV. ME. *capitain* - late OF. (mod. *-aine*), superseding earlier *chevetaigne* CHIEFTAIN and *chataigne, catanie* - late L. *capitāneus* chief, f. *caput, capit-* HEAD. Hence **captaincy** XIX.
caption (arch.) seizure, arrest XIV; †cavilling objection XVII; (orig. U.S.) heading, title XVIII. - L. *captiō, -ōn-*, f. *capere, capt-* take, seize; see HEAVE, -TION.
captious XIV. - (O)F. *captieux* or L. *captiōsus*, f. *captiō* deception, fallacious argument; see prec., -IOUS.
captivate †make captive, capture; enthral. XVI. f. pp. stem of late L. *captivāre* (after *captivate* pp. XIV), f. *captīvus*; see next and -ATE[3]. So **captive** (taken) prisoner. XIV. - L. *captīvus*, f. *capt-*, pp. stem of *capere* take. **captivity** XIV, **captor** XVII. **capture** sb. XVI; hence as vb. XVIII.
capuchin (*C-*) Franciscan friar of the new order of 1528 XVI; woman's hooded cloak XVIII. - F. (now *capucin*) - It. *cappuccino*, f. *cappuccio* hood, augm. of *cappa* CAPE[1]; so named from the pointed hood adopted by the order.
car XIV. ME. *carre* - AN., ONF. - Rom. **carra*, pl. or parallel fem. form of L. *carrum* n., *carrus* m. (whence F. *char*, It. *carro*, etc.; cf. CHARIOT) - OCelt. **karrom* (**karros*), repr. by (O)Ir. *carr*, OW. *carr* (W. *car*), rel. to L. *currus* chariot.
carabineer soldier armed with a carbine. XVII. - F. *carabinier*, f. *carabine* CARBINE; see -EER[1].
carafe XVIII. - F. - It. *caraffa*, prob. (through Sp. *garrafa*) - Arab. *ġarrāfa*, f. *ġarafa* draw water.
caramel XVIII. - F. - Sp. *caramelo*, of unkn. orig.
carapace body-shell of tortoises, etc. XIX. - F. - Sp. *carapacho*, of unkn. orig.
carat measure of weight for precious stones; measure of $\frac{1}{24}$ used in stating the fineness of gold. XVI. - F. - It. *carato* - Arab. *ḳīrāṭ* weight of 4 grains - Gr. *kerátion* fruit of the carob, f. *kéras* horn.
caravan company travelling through the desert; fleet of ships XVI; covered carriage or cart XVII. Mainly - F. *caravane* - Pers. *kārwān*, but some early forms (e.g. *carouan*) repr. the Pers. directly. So **caravanserai** Eastern inn. XVI. ult. - Pers. *kārwānsarāī* (*sarā(ī)* palace, inn), but the various early forms repr. more or less closely F. *caravansérai*, etc.
caraway 'seed' of the umbelliferous plant *Carum carvi*. XIV. The form corr. most closely to OSp. *alcarahueya* (mod. *alcaravea*) = Pg. *alcaravia* - Arab. *al-kar(a)wiyā* (see AL-[2]); the ult. source may be Gr. *káron* cummin.
carbine XVII. Earlier *carabine* - F.; orig. the weapon of the †*carabin* (- F.) mounted musketeer.
carbolic XIX. f. CARB(ON) + -OL + -IC.
carbon XVIII. - F. *carbone*, f. L. *carbō, -ōn-* (char)coal. So **carbonate** XVIII; see -ATE[1]. Hence **carbonaceous** XVIII, **carbonic** XVIII.
carboy large wicker-covered bottle for chemicals. XVIII. ult. - Pers. *ḳar(r)ābah* large flagon.
carbuncle fiery-coloured precious stone XIII; inflammatory tumour XVI. The early forms present several types - OF. *c(h)arbu(n)cle* (mod. *escarboucle*) :- L. *carbunculus* small coal, carbuncle stone, red tumour, dim. of *carbō* coal (cf. CARBON); later assim. to L.
carburet (chem.) compound of carbon with another element. XVIII. Superseded earlier †*carbure* - F., f. L. *carbō* CARBON; see -URET; in turn superseded by **carbide** XIX. Survives in **carburetted** adj., whence **carburettor** XIX.
carcase, carcass XIV. - F. *carcasse*. Earlier forms *carcays, carkeis*, etc. (XIV), prob. repr. a distinct word - AN. *carcois* = OF. *charcois*; ult. orig. unkn.
carcinoma XVIII. - L. - Gr. *karkínōma*, f. *karkínos* crab; cf. CANCER.
card[1] implement orig. consisting of teasel heads set in a frame, for raising the nap on cloth; toothed instrument for combing out fibre. XV. - (O)F. *carde* - Pr. *carda*, f. *cardar* tease, comb :- popL. **caritāre*, f. *cārere* card. So **card** vb. XIV.
card[2] piece of pasteboard XV; †map, chart XVI. - (with unexpl. *d*) (O)F. *carte* - L. *charta* papyrus leaf, paper (whence F. *charte* CHART) - Gr. *khártēs* leaf of papyrus, written work; supposed to be of Egyptian orig.
cardamom, -mum XV. - (O)F. *cardamome* or L. *cardamōmum* - Gr. *kardámōmon*, f. *kárdamon* cress + *ámōmon* Indian spice.
cardiac XVII. - F. *cardiaque* or L. *cardiacus* - Gr. *kardiakós*, f. *kardíā* HEART; see -AC.
cardigan XIX. Named after James Thomas Brudenell, seventh earl of Cardigan (d. 1868).

cardinal chief, principal. XIII. - (O)F. *cardinal* or L. *cardinālis*, f. *cardō*, *cardin-* hinge; in Eng. first applied to the four virtues of justice, fortitude, temperance, prudence, on which conduct 'hinges'; see -AL[1]. So **cardinal** sb. any of the seventy princes (cardinal bishops, priests, and deacons) of the Roman Church that constitute the Pope's council or the Sacred College. XII. - (O)F. - medL.

cardio- comb. form of Gr. *kardiā* HEART, as in *cardiograph* (XIX).

cardoon plant allied to the artichoke. XVII. - F. *cardon*, f. *carde* edible part of the artichoke - Pr. *cardo* :- Rom. **carda*, for L. *cardu(u)s* thistle, artichoke (rel. to *cārere*; see CARD[1]); see -OON.

care †grief; burdened state of mind; serious attention OE.; charge, oversight XIV; object of concern XVI. OE. *caru* = OS., OHG., Goth. *kara*, ON. *kǫr* (gen. *karar*) :- Gmc. **karō*. So **care** vb. OE. *carian* = OS. *karōn*, OHG. *charōn*, *-ēn*, Goth. *karōn* :- Gmc. **karōjan*, *-ǣjan*; in later uses reformed on the sb. Hence **careful** OE. *carful*; see -FUL[1]. See CHARY.

careen position of a ship heeled over. XVI. - F. *carène*, †*carine* - It. *carena*, repr. L. *carīna* keel. Hence **careen** vb. XVI.

career †racecourse; †gallop at full speed; course (of action) XVI; (a re-adoption from F.) course of life or employment XIX. - F. *carrière* - It. *carriera* - Pr. *carreira* :- Rom. **carrāria* (sc. *via*) (carriage-)road, f. *carrus* CAR. Hence **career** vb. XVI.

caress sb. XVII. - F. *caresse* - It. *carezza* :- Rom. **cāritia*, f. *cārus* dear; see CHARITY, -ESS[2]. Hence, or - F. - It., **caress** vb. XVII.

caret mark indicating omission. XVII. - L., 3rd sing. pres. ind. of *carēre* be without, taken to mean 'is lacking'.

cargo XVII. - Sp. *cargo* (also *carga*), corr. to (O)F. *charge* load (etc.) :- Rom. **carricāre* CHARGE.

Carib name of (i) a race of the West Indies, (ii) a group of West Indian languages. XVI. - Sp. *caribe*; formerly often synon. with CANNIBAL.

caribou XVIII. - Canadian F. *caribou*, from a N. Amer. Indian dialect.

caricature XVIII. - F. - It. *caricatura*, f. *caricare* load, exaggerate (see CHARGE). So as vb. XVIII.

caries (med.) decay of bones, etc. XVII. - L., 'rottenness, decay'. So **carious** decayed. XVI. - L. *cariōsus*.

carillon (tune played on) a set of bells. XVIII. - F., alt. of OF. *car(e)ignon*, *quarregnon* - Rom. **quatriniō*, *-ōn-*, peal of four bells, alt. of *quaterniō* (see QUATERNION) after late L. *trīniō* number three, f. *trīnus* threefold.

carl churl XIII; (later, Sc.) fellow. - ON. *karl* man = OHG. *karl* :- Gmc. **karlaz*; see also CHURL.

carline genus of plants allied to thistles. XVI. - F. *carline* = Sp., It. *carlina*, medL. *carlina*, perh. alt. of *cardina* (f. L. *cardō* thistle) by assoc. with *Carolus* Charles, it being said that Charlemagne received a revelation of the plant's efficacy (it was used as a sudorific).

Carlovingian pert. to the French dynasty founded by Charlemagne (Carolus Magnus). XVIII. - F. *carlovingien*, f. *Karl* Charles after *mérovingien* MEROVINGIAN; largely superseded by **Carolingian** (XIX), a re-formation on *Carolus* Charles.

Carmelite one of an order of mendicant friars originating from Mount Carmel, a White Friar. XV. - F. *carmélite* or medL. *carmēlīta*.

carminative expelling flatulence. XV. - (O)F. *carminatif*, *-ive*, or medL. *carminātīvus*, f. *carmināre* CHARM, (hence) heal, or card wool, (hence) purify; see -ATE[3], -IVE.

carmine crimson pigment obtained from cochineal. XVIII. - (O)F. *carmin* or medL. *carminium*, perh. conflation of *carmesīnum* (see CRIMSON) and *minium* cinnabar.

carnage XVI. - F. - It. *carnaggio* :- medL. *carnāticum*, f. *carō*, *carn-* flesh; see -AGE.

carnal XV. - ChrL. *carnālis*, f. *carō*, *carn-* flesh, rel. to Umbrian *karu*, Oscan *carneis* (g.) part, Gr. *keírein* cut; see -AL[1]. So **carnality** XIV.

carnation[1] rosy pink colour. XVI. - F. - It. *carnagione* - late L. *carnātiō*, *-ōn-* fleshiness, corpulence, f. *carō*, *carn-* flesh; see prec. and -ATION.

carnation[2] clove-pink, *Dianthus caryophyllus*. XVI. In early use varying with *coronation*; of uncert. orig.

carnival (orig.) season of revelry immediately preceding Lent. XVI. - It. *carne-*, *carnovale*, f. L. *carō*, *carn-* flesh (see CARNAL) + *levāre* lighten, raise; lit. 'cessation of flesh-eating'.

carnivorous XVII. f. L. *carnivorus*, f. *carō*, *carn-* flesh; see CARNAL, -VOROUS.

carob (fruit of) the leguminous tree *Ceratonia siliqua*. XVI. - F. †*car(r)obe* (mod. *caroube*), superseding OF. *carouge* :- medL. *carrūbia*, *-ium* - Arab. *ḳarrūba*.

carol †ring-dance accompanied by song XIII; †the song itself XIV; hymn of joy for Christmas, etc. XVI. - OF. *carole* = Pr. *carola*, *corola*, of doubtful orig. So **carol** vb. †dance in a ring XIII; sing XIV.

Caroline pert. to Charles. XVII. - med. or modL. *Carolīnus*, f. *Carolus* Charles; see -INE[1].

Carolingian see CARLOVINGIAN.

carotid (anat.) name of the two great arteries supplying blood to the head. XVII. - F. *carotide* or modL. *carōtides* - Gr. *karōtídes*, pl. of *karōtís*, f. *karoûn* stupefy; so named because compression of these arteries was said to produce stupor.

carouse full draught XVI; drinking-bout XVII. From the phr. *drink* or *quaff carouse* (XVI), repr. G. *gar aus trinken* drink completely. So **carouse** vb. XVI.

carp[1] †talk, speak XIII; †sing, recite XV; talk censoriously XVI. - ON. *karpa* brag, with generalization of sense; in the mod. sense infl. by, or a new formation on, L. *carpere* pluck (see HARVEST), (fig.) slander.

carp[2] freshwater fish of genus *Cyprinus*. XIV. - (O)F. *carpe* - Pr. *carpa* or the source late L. *carpa*; perh. of Gmc. origin (cf. (M)LG. *karpe*, (M)Du. *karper*, OHG. *karpfo*, G. *karpfen*, ON. *karfi*).

carpal (anat.) pert. to the wrist. XVIII. - modL. *carpālis*, f. *carpus* (used in Eng. from XVII) - Gr. *karpós* wrist; see -AL[1].

carpel (bot.) division of a compound pistil or

fruit. XIX. - F. *carpelle* or modL. *carpellum*, f. Gr. *karpós* fruit (cf. HARVEST); see -EL[2].

carpenter XIV. - AN. *carpenter*, OF. *carpentier*, (also mod.) *charpentier* :- late L. *carpentārius* (sc. *artifex*) carriage-maker, f. *carpentum* two-wheeled carriage, like *carrus* CAR, of Gaulish origin; see -ER[2]. So **carpentry** XIV; see -RY.

carpet †thick fabric for covering tables, etc. XIV; (piece of) fabric for covering a floor or stairs XV. - OF. *carpite* or medL. *carpīta* - It. †*carpita* woollen counterpane, corr. to (O)F. *charpie* lint, sb. use of pp. of *charpir* :- Rom. **carpīre*, for L. *carpere* pluck, pull to pieces (see HARVEST).

carrel study in a monastic cloister. XV (used hist. XVIII-XIX and more recently revived for a study in a library). - OF. *carole*, medL. *carola*, of unkn. orig.

carriage conveyance, transport XIV; means of conveyance, vehicle XV; manner of carrying oneself, bearing XVI. - ONF. *cariage*, f. *carier* CARRY; see -AGE.

carriole small carriage; Canadian sledge. XIX. - F. - It. *carriuola*, f. *carro* CAR.

carrion †corpse; dead putrefying flesh. XIII. ME. *caroine*, etc. - AN., ONF. *caroi(g)ne*, OF. *charoigne* (mod. *charogne*) :- Rom. **carōnia*, f. L. *carō* flesh (cf. CARNAGE).

carrot XVI. - (O)F. *carotte* - L. *carōta* - Gr. *karōtón*.

carry XIV. - AN., ONF. *carier*, var. of *charier* (mod. *charrier* cart, drag), f. *c(h)ar* CAR. Hence **carrier** XIV; see -ER[1].

cart †carriage; strong two-wheeled vehicle XIII; light sprung two-wheeled vehicle XIX. ME. *carte*; (i) partly metathetic repr. of OE. *cræt*; (ii) partly - cogn. ON. *kartr*; prob. infl. by AN., ONF. *carete* (mod. *charrette* cart), dim. of *c(h)ar* CAR.

carte blanche XVIII. - F. 'blank paper'.

cartel written challenge XVI; written agreement as to exchange of prisoners XVII; (after G. *kartell*), combination for business or political purposes XX. - F. - It. *cartello* placard, challenge, dim. of *carta* paper, letter (cf. CHART); see -EL[2].

Cartesian XVII. - modL. *Cartesiānus*, f. *Cartesius*, latinized form of the surname of René *Descartes*, French philosopher and mathematician (1596-1650); see -IAN.

Carthusian one of an order of monks founded by St. Bruno in 1084. XVI. - medL. *Carthusiānus*, f. *Chart(h)ūsia* Chartreuse, near Grenoble, France. The earlier form of the place-name was *Charteuse*; the altered form *Chartreuse*, AN. *Chartrous*, was adopted in later ME. and, by assim. to HOUSE, became *Charterhouse* (i) Carthusian monastery XVI, (ii) hospital founded 1611 on the site of the C. monastery in London, later a public school.

cartilage XVI. - F. - L. *cartilāgō* (*-āgin-*). So **cartilaginous** XVI. - (O)F. or L. (*-ōsus*).

cartography XIX. - F. *cartographie*, f. *carte* map - L. *charta* CHART; see -O-, -GRAPHY.

carton white disk within the bull's-eye of a target XIX; pasteboard container XX. - F. *carton* pasteboard, cardboard (see next).

cartoon drawing made as a design for a painting XVII; illustration in a periodical as a comment on current events XIX. - F. *carton* - It. *cartone*, augm. of *carta* paper, CARD[2]; see -OON.

cartouche †cartridge; (archit.) corbel, tablet, etc. XVII. - F. *cartouche* cornet of paper, cartridge - It. *cartoccio*, f. *carta* paper (cf. CARD[2]).

cartridge XVI. alt. of prec., but recorded earlier.

c(h)artulary (hist.) place where records are kept; collection or register of records. XVI. - medL. *c(h)artulārium*, f. *c(h)artula*, dim. of *c(h)arta* paper; see CHART, CHARTER, and -ARY.

carucate (hist.) as much land as can be tilled with one plough in one year. XV. - medL. *car(r)ūcāta*, f. *car(r)ūca* orig. coach, chariot, in Gaul early applied to the wheel-plough, rel. to *carrus* CAR; see -ATE[1].

carve †cut; cut artistically or ornamentally OE; cut up meat at table XIII. OE. *ċeorfan* str. vb. = (M)Du. *kerven*, MHG. *kerben* :- WGmc. **kerfan*. The weak conj. is found as early as XV. The normal repr. of OE. *ċeorfan* would be **charve*, but initial *k* had established itself by *c*.1200 in the pres. stem through the infl. of other parts of the vb. or of the Scand. forms.

caryatid (archit.; orig. and usu. pl.) female figure used as a column. XVI. - F. *cariatide* - It. *cariatide*, or their source, L. *caryatides* - Gr. *karuátides* (pl.) priestesses of Artemis at *Karuai* (Caryae) in Laconia.

cascade waterfall. XVII. - F. - It. *cascata*, f. *cascare* fall :- Rom. **cāsicare*, f. L. *cāsus* fall; see CASE[1], -ADE. Hence as vb. XVIII.

cascara (*sagrada*) a laxative drug. XIX. - Sp. '(sacred) bark', f. *cascar* crack, burst.

case[1] †event, chance; instance, example XIII; state, condition XIV; (gram.) inflexional form of noun, etc. XIV; (leg.) state of the facts, cause, suit XIV. ME. *ca(a)s* - (O)F. *cas* - L. *cāsus* fall, chance, grammatical case (tr. Gr. *ptôsis* lit. fall), f. base of *cadere* fall.

case[2] receptacle XIII; protective covering XIV; chest; frame XVI, as in *staircase* (XVII). - OF. *casse*, dial. var. of *chasse* (mod. *châsse* reliquary, frame) :- L. *capsa* box, bookcase, f. base of *capere* hold (see HEAVE).

casein protein constituent of milk. XIX. f. L. *caseus* CHEESE; see -IN.

casement (archit.) hollow moulding XV; window frame opening on hinges XVI (*caze-*, *-mund*). Cf. medL. *cassa*, etc., and *cassa fenestre* casement or moulding; *cassimentum* casement (of window); app. f. CASE[2] + -MENT. For the application of -MENT in Eng. cf. BATTLEMENT.

caseous of cheese. XVII. f. L. *caseus* CHEESE + -OUS.

cash †money-box; money. XVI. - F. †*casse*, or its source, It. *cassa* :- L. *capsa* CASE[2].

cashew large W. Indian tree, *Anacardium occidentale*. XVIII. - Pg. *(a)caju* - Tupi.

cashier[1] one who pays out and receives money. XVI. - Du. *kassier*, or its source, F. *caissier*, f. *caisse* CASH; see -IER.

cashier[2] disband (troops); dismiss from office. XVI (*casseer*, *casseir*). - early Flem. *kasseren* disband (soldiers), revoke (a will) - F. *casser* break, dismiss, rescind = It. *cassare* cancel :- L. *quassāre* QUASH.

cashmere (in full *Cashmere shawl*), shawl made of fine wool obtained from the Kashmir goat; the material itself. XIX. *Kashmir*, name of a province in the W. Himalayas, India.

casino XVIII. - It., dim. of *casa* house :- L. *casa* cottage.

cask hooped wooden vessel; †casket; †helmet. XV. - F. *casque* or Sp. *casco* helmet, CASQUE. The earliest and prevailing sense was prob. imported with the wine trade and depended on provincial uses of the S. French or Sp. region, where, however, the only recorded sense is 'helmet'.

casket XV. of obscure orig.; poss. - AN. alt. of synon. (O)F. *cassette* - It. *cassetta*, dim. of *cassa* :- L. *capsa* box (see CASE²); see -ET.

casque helmet. XVII. - F. - Sp. *casco*; cf. CASK.

cassation annulment. XV. - (O)F. *cassation*, f. *casser* QUASH; see -ATION.

cassava tropical plant of genus *Manihot*; starch obtained from this (tapioca). XVI. The earliest forms *cazibi*, *cas(s)avi*, etc. repr. original Taino *casavi*; the pres. is an alt. of these after F. *cassave*.

casserole XVIII. - F., extension of *cassole*, dim. of *casse* - Pr. *casa* :- Rom. (late L.) *cattia* pan - Gr. *kuáth(e)ion*, dim. of *kúathos* cup.

cassia kind of cinnamon. OE. and ME., but not naturalized till XVI. - L. *cas(s)ia* - Gr. *kasiā* - Heb. *ḳᵉṣī'āh* bark resembling cinnamon, f. *ḳāṣa'* strip off.

cassock soldier's or rider's cloak; long loose coat or gown XVI; long (esp. black) tunic worn by ecclesiastics XVII. - F. *casaque* - It. *casacca*, prob. - Turk. *kazak* tribal name.

cassowary bird related to the ostrich. XVII. - Malay *kĕsuari*.

cast superseded OE. *weorpan* WARP in the sense of THROW, but is now largely itself superseded by the latter in the ordinary physical sense, though used extensively in many transf. and techn. applications. XIII. - ON. *kasta*. Hence **cast** sb. throw XIII; in many derived uses, e.g. †design, device XIII; assignment of parts in a play; twist, turn XVI; tinge, hue XVII; style, sort XVII.

castanet XVII. - Sp. *castañeta* (with later assim. to F. *castagnette*), dim. of *castaña* :- L. *castanea* CHESTNUT; see -ET.

castaway rejected, reprobate; and as sb. XVI. f. pp. of CAST + AWAY.

caste race, stock XVI; hereditary class in Indian society XVII. - Sp., and (particularly in its Indian application) Pg. *casta*, sb. use (sc. *raza*, *raça* race) of fem. of *casto* pure, unmixed (see CHASTE).

castellated built like a castle, as with battlements XVII; furnished with castles XIX. f. medL. *castellātus*, f. L. *castellum* CASTLE; see -ATE², -ED. So **castellation** XIX.

castigate correct by punishment or discipline. XVII. f. pp. stem of L. *castīgāre* correct, reprove, CHASTISE, f. *castus* pure, CHASTE; see -ATE³. So **castigation** XIV. - L.

castle XI. - AN., ONF. *castel*, var. of *chastel* (mod. *château*) :- L. *castellum*, dim. of *castrum* entrenchment, fortified place, fort.

castor¹ beaver, unctuous substance obtained from the beaver (used as a drug). XIV. - (O)F. or L. *castor* - Gr. *kástōr*. The history of the use of *castor oil* (XVIII) for the pale-yellow oil obtained from the seeds of the plant *Ricinus communis* is obscure.

castor² perforated vessel for sprinkling pepper, sugar, etc. XVII; swivel wheel on legs of furniture XVIII. var. of *caster*, agent-noun f. CAST + -ER¹. The sp. *-or* for *-er* (still current) may have been favoured as being more appropriate to an instrument; cf. *razor*, *mirror*, and words in -ATOR.

castrate XVII. f. pp. stem of L. *castrāre*, f. **castrum* knife; see -ATE³. So **castration** XV. - F. or L.

casual accidental XIV; occurring uncertainly XV; occurring without design XVII. - (O)F. *casuel* and L. *cāsuālis* (in its late and med. uses), f. *cāsus* CASE¹; see -AL¹. Hence **casually** XIV; after medL. *cāsuāliter*. **casualty** casual occurrence, loss, etc. XV; casual charge XV; after medL. *cāsuālitās*.

casuist student of cases of conscience. XVII. - F. *casuiste* - Sp. (modL.) *casuista*, f. L. *cāsus* CASE¹; see -IST. Hence **casuistry** XVIII; prob. after *sophistry*, and so at first derogatory.

cat OE. *catt* m. (= ON. *kǫttr*), *catte* fem. (= MDu. *katte*, Du. *kat*, OHG. *kazza*, G. *katze*); reinforced in ME. by AN., ONF. *cat*, var. of (O)F. *chat* :- late L. *cattus*, of unkn. orig.

cata-, before a vowel **cat-**, combining with *h* **cath-**, repr. Gr. adv.-prep. *katá* down, down from, according to, used with the senses (1) down, in position, (2) down, in quantity or degree, (3) amiss, mis-, (4) against, alongside, (5) thoroughly, entirely.

catachresis improper use (of word). XVI. - L. *catachrēsis* - Gr. *katákhrēsis*, f. *katakhrêsthai* use amiss, f. CATA- 3 + *khrêsthai* use. So **catachrestic(al)** adjs. XVII.

cataclysm deluge; great upheaval. XVII. - F. *cataclysme* - L. *cataclysmos* - Gr. *kataklusmós*, f. *kataklúzein*, f. CATA- 1 + *klúzein* wash.

catacombs subterranean cemeteries in Rome, and hence gen. XVII. - F. *catacombes* - late L. *catacumbas*, specific name from c.400 of the cemetery of St. Sebastian on the Appian Way; the word seems to be orig. invariable, but later was treated as acc. pl., from which a sing. *catacumba* was formed, whence the occas. use of the sg. in modern langs.; the ult. orig. is unkn.

catafalque erection in a church to receive the coffin of a deceased person. XVII. - F. - It. *catafalco* (= OF. *escafaut*, mod. *échafaud*). See SCAFFOLD.

catalepsy disease characterized by a seizure or trance. XVI. - F. *catalepsie* or late L. *catalēpsia*, f. Gr. *katálēpsis*, f. *katalambánein* seize upon, f. CATA- 5 + *lambánein* take. See -Y³. So **cataleptic** XVII.

catalogue XV. - (O)F. - late L. *catalogus* - Gr. *katálogos*, f. *katalégein* pick out, enlist, enrol, f. CATA- 5 + *légein* collect, choose, enumerate.

catalysis †dissolution XVII; (chem.) chemical action brought about by a substance that remains unchanged XIX. - modL. - Gr. *katálusis*, f. *katalúein* dissolve, f. CATA- 2 + *lúein* loosen.

Hence **catalyse, catalytic** XIX, **catalyst** XX; after *analyse*, etc.

catamaran XVII. - Tamil *kaṭṭumaram* 'tied wood', f. *kaṭṭu* tie, bond + *maram* wood.

catamite sodomite's subject. XVI. - L. *catamītus* - (through Etruscan *catmite*) Gr. *Ganumḗdēs* Ganymede, cup-bearer of Zeus.

catamountain leopard, panther, etc. XVI (also **catamount** XVII); earlier *cat of the mountain* (XV-XVI), which was first used to render L. *pardus*, Gr. *párdos* PARD.

catapult (mil.) missile engine XVI; shooting instrument consisting of a forked stick with elastic band XIX. - (O)F. *catapulte* or L. *catapulta* - Gr. *katapéltēs*, f. CATA- 1 + **pel-*, var. base of *pállein* hurl.

cataract †(pl.) floodgates of heaven (cf. Gen. 7: 11, 8: 2) XV; †waterspouts; (sg.) waterfall; opacity of the lens of the eye (prob. fig. use of the sense 'portcullis') XVI. - L. *cataracta* - Gr. *katar(r)hákt̄es* down-rush, waterfall, portcullis.

catarrh XVI. - F. *catarrhe* - late L. *catarrhus* - Gr. *katárrhous* rheum, f. *katarrheîn* run down, f. CATA- 1 + *rheîn* flow.

catarrhine (zool.) monkey having the nostrils close together and pointed downwards. XIX. f. Gr. CATA- 4 + *rhī́s*, *rhin-* nostril.

catastrophe dénouement of a drama; disastrous end XVII; event subversive of order XVII; sudden disaster XVIII. - L. *catastropha* - Gr. *katastrophḗ* overturning, sudden turn, f. *katastréphein* overturn. Hence **catastrophic** XIX.

catch †chase; capture, grasp, seize; take, get, receive. XIII. ME. *cac(c)hen* - AN., ONF. *cachier*, var. of OF. *chacier* (mod. *chasser*) :- Rom. **captiāre*, repl. L. *captāre* try to catch, lie in wait for, (hence) hunt, CHASE[1] (the sense in all the Rom. langs.). *Catch* took over the sense 'seize' and its conjugational forms from the native *latch* (OE. *læċċan*), e.g. *ca(u)hte, caught* and *cachte, catched* beside *la(u)hte, laught* and *lachte, latched*. Hence **catch** sb. act of catching, something caught XV; contrivance for checking a mechanism XIV; (mus.) round XVII.

catchup, catsup see KETCHUP.

catechize give systematic oral instruction XV; question systematically (from the question-and-answer form of the Church Catechism) XVII. - ChrL. *catēchīzāre* - ecclGr. *katēkhízein*, f. *katēkhein* sound through, instruct orally, f. CATA- 5 + *ēkhein* sound; see -IZE. So **catechism** catechetical instruction; manual of religious instruction in the form of question and answer. XVI. **catechetic(al)** XVII.

catechu astringent substance obtained from various Eastern barks, etc. XVII. - modL. *catechu*, defined as 'terra japonica' (Japanese earth) on account of its appearance, unexpl. deriv. of Malay *kachu*; see CACHOU.

catechumen convert under instruction. XV. - (O)F. *catéchumène* or ecclL. *catēchūmenus* - Gr. *katēkhoúmenos* being instructed, prp. pass. of *katēkhein* (see CATECHIZE).

category XV. - F. *catégorie* or its source, late L. *catēgoria* - Gr. *katēgoriā* accusation, etc., f. *katḗgoros* accuser, etc., f. CATA- 4 + *agorā́* assembly; see -Y[3]. So **categoric** XVII, **categorical** XVI. - F. *catégorique* or late L. *catēgoricus*.

catena series of quotations in support of a thesis, etc. XVII. Short for ecclL. *catēna patrum* 'chain of the Fathers' (viz. of the Church); see CHAIN. So **catenary** (math.) curve formed by a chain hanging from two points. XVIII. **catenation** linking into or as with a chain. XVII.

cater XVII. f. †*cater* (XIV) buyer of provisions, caterer, aphetic form of †*acater* purchaser - AN. *acatour*, var. of OF. *achatour*, f. *achater* buy (mod. *acheter*) :- Rom. **accaptāre*, f. AC- + *captāre* catch. Hence **caterer** XVI; see -ER[1].

caterpillar XV. The earliest recorded form, *catyrpel*, is prob. - AN. var. of OF. *chatepelose* 'hairy cat'; assoc. in XVI with †*piller* ravager, plunderer (see PILLAGE), prob. brought about the extended form in *-piller, -pillar*.

caterwaul XIV. One of a group of cogn. formations of which the earliest is *caterwawed* caterwauling, a noun of action with *-ed*, repr. OE. *-að*. The first el. is to be identified with CAT, but it is doubtful whether it is rel. to or - LG., Du. *kater* male cat, or whether the *-er-* is merely an arbitrary connective syll.; the second el. appears variously as *-w(r)awe, -wall* (XVI), etc.

catgut dried intestines of sheep, etc. used for the strings of musical instruments. XVI. f. CAT + GUT; the reason for the use of *cat* is unkn.

cathartic cleansing, purgative. XVII. - late L. *catharticus* - Gr. *kathartikós*, f. *kathaírein* cleanse, f. *katharós* clean. So **catharsis** purgation. XIX. - modL. - Gr. *kátharsis*.

cathedral pert. to an episcopal see. XIII. - (O)F. *cathédral* - late L. *cathedrālis*, f. L. *cathedra* - Gr. *kathédrā* seat, f. CATA- 1 + **hed-* :- **sed-* SIT; as sb., short for *cathedral church* XVI.

catheter XVII. f. late L. - Gr. *kathetḗr*, f. *kathe-*, *kathiénai* send or let down, f. CATA- 1 + *hiénai* send + agent-suffix *-tēr*.

cathode (electr.) negative electrode. XIX. - Gr. *káthodos* going down, f. CATA- 1 + *hodós* way. Cf. ANODE, ELECTRODE.

catholic universal (spec. of the Christian Church) XIV; sb. member of the Catholic Church XV. - (O)F. *catholique* or its source ChrL. *catholicus* - Gr. *katholikós* general, universal, f. *katá* in respect of (cf. CATA-) + *hólos* whole. Hence **catholicism, -ize** XVII; **catholicity** XIX.

cation (electr.) a positive ion moving towards the cathode during electrolysis. XIX. - Gr. *katión*, f. CATA- 1 + ION; cf. CATHODE.

catkin XVI. - Du. †*katteken* lit. kitten, dim. of *katte* CAT.

catmint the plant *Nepeta cataria*, which attracts cats. XIII (*kattesminte*). f. CAT + MINT[2], after medL. *herba catti, h. cataria*.

catsup var. of CATCHUP.

cattle †property; livestock. XIII. ME. *catel(l)* - AN., ONF. *catel*, var. of *chatel* (see CHATTEL).

caucus (U.S.) private meeting of the chiefs of a political party XVIII; in Eng. use applied from 1878 to organizations for managing political elections, etc. Perh. repr. an Algonquian word meaning 'elder, adviser'.

caudal pert. to a tail. XVII. - modL. *caudālis*, f. L. *cauda* tail; see -AL[1]. So **caudate** tailed. XVII. - medL.; see -ATE[2].

caudle thin gruel sweetened and spiced. XIII. - ONF. *caudel*, var. of *chaudel* (mod. *chaudeau*) :- medL. **caldellum*, dim. of L. *caldum* hot drink, sb. use of n. of *cal(i)dus* hot.

caul (hist.) woman's close-fitting cap, hairnet; investing membrane, e.g. omentum, amnion. XIII. ME. *calle*, of doubtful orig.; perh. - (O)F. *cale* head-covering, f. *calotte* (see CALOTTE) by back-formation; but the Eng. word is recorded earlier.

cauldron XIII. ME. *caudroun* - AN., ONF. *caudron* (mod. *chaudron*), augm. of Rom. **caldario*, L. *caldārium* hot bath, f. *cal(i)dus* hot. The etymologizing sp. with *l* appeared XV and subseq. infl. the pronunc.

cauliflower XVI. Earlier *cole flory*, *colliflory* alt. (by assim. to COLE) of F. †*chou fleuri* (*flori*), prob. - It. *cavolfiore* or modL. *cauliflōra* 'flowered cabbage'. The second element was assim. to *flower* XVII, as in F. *chou-fleur*.

caulk XV. - OF. *cauquer*, *caukier*, north. var. of OF. *cauchier* tread, press with force :- L. *calcāre* tread, press, f. *calx*, *calc-* heel.

cause ground or reason for action XIII; legal case or suit XIII; that which produces an effect XIV. - (O)F. - L. *causa* reason, motive, law-suit. So **causal** XVI. - late L. *causālis*. **causality, causation** XVII, **causative** XV, all - late L. or F. **cause** vb. be the cause of. XIV. - (O)F. *causer* or medL. *causāre*.

causeway raised road XV; (paved) highway XVII. Early forms are *cawce*, *cawcy*, and *causey way*, reduced to *caus(e)way* XVI. *Causey* (dial.) is - AN. **caucé(e)* = ONF. *cauciée* (mod. *chaussée*) :- Rom. **calciāta* (sc. *via* way, road), fem. pp. f. L. *calx*, *calc-* lime, CHALK.

caustic corrosive XIV; fig. bitter XVIII. - F. *caustique* or L. *causticus* - Gr. *kaustikós* capable of burning, f. *kaustós* combustible, f. **kaϝ-*, base of *kaíein* burn; see -IC.

cauterize XIV. - (O)F. *cautériser* - late L. *cautērizāre*, alt. - Gr. *kautēriázein*, f. *kautḗrion*, whence (through L. *cauterium*) **cautery** XIV cauterizing instrument, drug, or operation; ult. f. Gr. *kaíein*; see CAUSTIC, -IZE.

caution security, bail XIII; taking heed, word of warning XVII. orig. - (O)F. - L. *cautiō*, *-ōn-*, f. pp. stem of *cavēre* take heed; a re-adoption from L. took place *c.*1600; see -TION. Hence **caution** vb. warn. XVII. So **cautious** XVII; see -TIOUS.

cavalcade †ride XVI; procession on horseback XVII. - F. *cavalcade*, earlier †*-cate* - It. *cavalcata*, f. *cavalcare* :- Rom. **caballicāre* ride, f. L. *caballus* pack-horse, nag, in Rom. (VI) soldier's word for 'horse' (F. *cheval*, etc.), which, like Gr. *kabállēs*, is an alien word; see -ADE.

cavalier horseman; courtly gentleman, gallant XVI; Royalist XVII. - F. *cavalier* or its source It. *cavaliere*, deriv. of L. (Rom.) *caballus* horse (see prec.); see -IER.

cavalry XVI (*cavallerie*). - F. *cavallerie* - It. *cavalleria* (corr. to F. *chevalerie* CHIVALRY), f. *cavallo* :- L. *caballus*; see CAVALCADE and -ERY, -RY.

cave[1] underground hollow. XIII. - (O)F. (now 'cellar') - L. *cava*, sb. use of fem. sg. or n. pl. of *cavus* hollow.

cave[2] fall *in* over a hollow. XVIII. prob. var. of dial. (esp. eastern) *calve* (XVIII), *cauve*, which may be of LG. orig.; cf. WFlem. *inkalven* fall in, Du. *afkalven* fall away, *uitkalven* fall out.

caveat XVI. - L., 3rd sing. pres. subj. of *cavēre* beware.

cavern XIV. - (O)F. *caverne* or L. *caverna*, f. *cavus* hollow; cf. CAVE[1] and, for the suffix, CISTERN, TAVERN. So **cavernous** XV. - (O)F. *caverneux*, L. *cavernōsus*.

caviare XVI. Various early forms, repr. It. *caviale* (whence F. †*cavial*), F. *caviar*, etc.; the source appears to be Gr. *khaviári*, of uncert. orig.

cavil XV. - (O)F. *caviller* - L. *cavillārī*, f. *cavilla* scoffing, mockery. So **cavillation** XIV.

cavity XVI. - F. *cavité* or late L. *cavitās*, f. *cavus* hollow; see CAVE[1], -ITY.

cavort (orig. U.S.) prance or caper about, orig. of a horse or rider. XIX. perh. alt. of CURVET.

cavy rodent of the family Caviidae, including the guinea-pig. XVIII. - modL. *cavia*, f. Galibi (French Guiana) *cabiai*.

caw imit. of the cry of rooks and the like. XVI.

cayenne (pepper) XVIII. Early forms *kayan*, *kian*; orig. - Tupi *kyynha*, *quiynha*, later assim. to *Cayenne*, chief town of French Guiana.

cayman, caiman American alligator. XVI. - Sp., Pg. *caiman* - Carib *acayuman*, *cay(e)man*.

cease XIV. ME. *ces(s)en* - (O)F. *cesser* :- L. *cessāre* stop, f. *cess-*, pp. stem of *cēdere* yield, CEDE.

cecity blindness. XVI. - L. *cæcitās*, f. *cæcus* blind; see -ITY.

cedar XIII (*cedre*). - OF. *cedre* (mod. *cèdre*) - L. *cedrus* - Gr. *kédros* juniper, cedar. OE. had *ceder* from L. The sp. with *-ar* dates from XVI.

cede †give way XVII; give up, yield XVIII. - F. *céder* or L. *cēdere* go (away), retire, yield.

cedilla the mark ¸ written under *c*. XVI. - Sp. *cedilla*, now *zedilla*, dim. of *zeda* letter *z*.

ceiling †lining of the inside of roof or walls XIV; †screen of tapestry, curtain XV; (naut.) inside planking of a ship's bottom XVII; plaster covering the top of a room XVI. Late ME. *celynge*, *silling*, early modEng. *syll-*, *seel-*, *ciel-*, *seyl-*, appearing contemp. with *celure*, *selure*, *sil(l)our*, later *seller* canopy, hangings, tapestry (XIV-XVI); these corresp. in use to medL. *cēlum* (XII), *cēlātūra* (XIII), *cēlūra* (XIV), but the meaning is freq. uncert.; possible OF. connections are rare, and it remains doubtful whether L. *cælum* heaven is the ult. base and how far L. *cælāre* engrave, *cælātūra* engraving, carving are concerned.

celadon pale shade of green. XVIII. - F., a use of the name of a languorous gallant in the 'Astrée' of d'Urfé (1610), who took it from Ovid's 'Metamorphoses'.

celandine name of two (distinct) plants bearing yellow flowers. XIII. Earliest form *celidoine*, the intrusive *-n-* being recorded XV. - OF. *celidoine* - medL. *celidonia*, for L. *chelidonia* (sc. *herba* plant), *-onium* - Gr. *khelidónion*, f. *khelidṓn* swallow.

celebrate XV. f. †*celebrate*, pp. (XV) - L. *celebrātus*, pp. of *celebrāre*, f. *celeber*, *celebr-* frequented, frequent, renowned; see -ATE[3]. Hence **celebrated** famous XVII. So **celebration** XVI.

celeriac XVIII. f. CELERY, with arbitrary use of the suffix -AC.

celerity XV. - (O)F. *célérité* - L. *celeritās*, f. *celer* swift; see -ITY.

celery XVII. - F. *céleri* - It. dial. *selleri* - L. *selīnon*, *selīnum* - Gr. *sélinon*.

celestial XIV. - OF. - medL. *celestiālis*, f. L. *cælestis*, f. *cælum* heaven; see -IAL.

celibacy XVII. f. L. *cælibātus*, f. *cælebs*, *cælib-* unmarried; see -ACY.

cell dependent religious house XII; small dwelling or apartment; cavity in an organism XIV; various subsequent uses. - OF. *celle*, or its source L. *cella* store-room, chamber, small apartment, in medL. in the first two senses above, rel. to L. *cēlāre* CONCEAL.

cellar †store-room XIII; underground room XIV. ME. *celer* - AN. *celer* = OF. *celier* (mod. *cellier*) :- late L. *cellārium* set of cells, storehouse for food, f. *cella* CELL.

cello shortening of VIOLONCELLO. XIX.

cellular XVIII. - F. *cellulaire* - modL. *cellulāris*, f. *cellula*, dim. of *cella* CELL; see -AR.

cellulose adj. consisting of cells XVIII; sb. a carbohydrate, main constituent of plant-cell walls XIX. As adj. - modL. *cellulōsus*; as sb. - F. *cellulose*; see prec. and -OSE. Hence **celluloid** XIX; the use of -OID is arbitrary.

Celt, Kelt †a Gaul XVII; one who speaks a Celtic language XVIII. In the earliest use - L. *Celtæ* pl. - Gr. *Keltoi*; in the mod. use - F. *Celte*. So **Celtic** XVII. - L. *Celticus* and F. *celtique*.

celt prehistoric instrument with chisel edge. XVIII. - modL. *celtes*, based on *celte*, which occurs in the Clementine text of Vulg., Job 19: 24 ('stylo ferreo et plumbi lamina vel *celte* sculpantur in silice'), where some MSS. read *certe* 'surely' (corr. to 'for ever' of A.V.); the adoption of the word as a techn. term of archaeology was prob. assisted by a supposed connection with *Celt*.

cement sb. XIII. ME. *siment* - (O)F. *ciment* :- L. *cæmentum* quarry stone, pl. chips of stone, f. **cædmentum*, f. *cædere* hew; see -MENT. So as vb. XIV. - (O)F. *cimenter*.

cemetery XIV. - late L. *cœmētērium* - Gr. *koimētḗrion* dormitory, (in Christian writers) burial-ground, f. *koimân* put to sleep.

cenobite var. of COENOBITE.

cenotaph sepulchral monument to a person buried elsewhere. XVII. - F. *cénotaphe* - late L. *cenotaphium* - Gr. *kenós* empty + *táphos* tomb.

censer vessel in which incense is burnt ceremonially. XIII (*senser*). - AN. *censer*, *senser*, OF. *censier*, aphetic of *ensensier*, f. *ensens* INCENSE[1]. So **cense** vb. burn incense to, fumigate with incense. XIV.

censor supervisor of morals, etc. XVI. - L. *cēnsor*, f. *cēnsēre* pronounce as an opinion, assess, judge. Hence **censor** vb. XIX. So **censure** †judgement XIV; adverse judgement XVII. - (O)F. - L. *cēnsūra*; see -URE. **censure** vb. XVI. - F. *censurer*.

census registration of citizens in ancient Rome XVII; enumeration of population XVIII. - L. *cēnsus*, rel. to prec.

cent (U.S., etc.) $\frac{1}{100}$ of a dollar. XVIII. - F., or It. *cento*, L. *centum* HUNDRED. See also PER CENT.

centaur fabulous creature, half man, half horse. XIV. - L. *centaurus* - Gr. *kéntauros*, of unkn. orig.

centaury plant the medicinal properties of which were said to have been discovered by Chiron the centaur. XIV. - late L. *centauria*, *-ea*, f. L. *centaurion*, *-ēum* - Gr. *kentaúr(e)ion*, f. *kéntauros* CENTAUR.

centenary adj. of a hundred years XVII; sb. †100 pounds XVI; century XVII; centennial anniversary XVIII. - L. *centēnārius*, containing a hundred, f. *centēnī* hundred each, f. *centum* HUNDRED; see -ARY. So **centenarian** 100 years old. XIX. **centennial** of 100 years. XVIII. f. L. *centum*, after *biennial*. **centesimal** hundredth (part). XVII. f. L. *centēsimus* hundredth.

centi- comb. form of L. *centum* hundred, used in the F. metric system to denote the 100th part of a unit, as **centigramme, -litre, -metre**; also in **centigrade** pert. to Celsius's thermometer XIX. - F. *centigrade*, f. L. *gradus* step, GRADE.

centipede XVII. - F. *centipède* or L. *centipeda* (*pēs*, *ped-* FOOT).

centime $\frac{1}{100}$ of a franc. XIX. - F., f. L. *centum* HUNDRED.

cento †patchwork; composition made up of scraps. XVII. - L. *centō* patchwork garment, poem made up of verses from other sources; rel. to Gr. *kenteîn* stitch, *kéntrōn* patchwork garment.

centre, U.S. **center** sb. XIV. - (O)F. *centre* or its source L. *centrum* - Gr. *kéntron* goad, peg, stationary point of a pair of compasses, f. base of *kentein* prick. From XVI to XVIII the prevalent sp. was *center*; *centre* appeared in Bailey's dict. 1727 and was adopted by Johnson. Hence **centre** vb. XVII. So **central** XVI, **-ize** XIX.

centri- comb. form of L. *centrum* CENTRE in *centrifugal*, *centripetal* XVIII, f. modL. *centrifugus*, *-petus*, f. stems of L. *fugere* flee, *petere* seek. In some other techn. terms *centro-*, repr. Gr. *kéntron*, has been used.

centuple hundredfold. XVII. - F. *centuple* or ecclL. *centuplus*, var. of *centuplex*, f. *centum* HUNDRED; cf. -FOLD.

century group of 100 XVI; 100 years XVII. - L. *centuria* assemblage of 100 things, division of the Roman army (orig. 100 horsemen), f. *centum* HUNDRED; see -Y[3]. So **centurion** commander of a century. XIV.

cephalic of the head. XVI. - (O)F. *céphalique* - L. *cephalicus* - Gr. *kephalikós*, f. *kephalḗ* head; see -IC.

ceramic adj. XIX. - Gr. *keramikós*, f. *kéramos* potter's earth, pottery; see -IC.

cere wax-like membrane at the base of a bird's beak. XV. - medL. use of L. *cēra* wax.

cereal adj. and sb. XIX. - L. *cereālis* pert. to the cultivation of grain, f. *Cerēs* goddess of agriculture; see -AL[1].

cerebral XIX. f. L. *cerebrum*, rel. to Skr. *śíra-* head, point, Gr. *kéras* horn, ON. *hiarni* (whence

ME. *hernes*, mod. dial. *harns* brains); see -AL[1]. So **cerebration** action of the brain. XIX.

cerecloth waxed cloth used as a winding-sheet, etc. XV (*sirecloth*). Also *cered cloth*, with pp. of *cire, cere* vb. (XIV) - (O)F. *cirer* assim. to L. *cērāre*, f. *cēra* wax. So **cerements** waxed wrappings for the dead XVII; see -MENT.

ceremony XIV. - (perh. through (O)F. *cérémonie*) L. *cærimōnia* religious worship, (pl.) ritual observances; see -MONY. So **ceremonial** XIV. - late L. **ceremonious** XVI. - F. or late L.

cerise light clear bright red. XIX. adj. use of F. *cerise* :- Rom. **ceresea* CHERRY.

cerium (chem.) metallic element. XIX. - modL., named after the asteroid *Ceres*; see -IUM.

certain fixed; sure XIII; some (particular or definite) XIII; established as truth; fully confident XIV; *a certain* XVIII; *a certain age* (after F. *d'un certain âge* rather elderly) XIX. - (O)F. :- Rom. **certānus*, extension of L. *certus* settled, sure, pp. formation on *cernere* sift, separate, decide, rel. to Gr. *krī́nein* (see CRISIS). So **certainty** XIV. - AN. *certainté*, OF. *certaineté*.

certify XIV. - (O)F. *certifier* - late or medL. *certificāre*, f. *certus* CERTAIN; see -FY. So **certification** XV. **certificate** XV. - F. *certificat* or medL. *certificātum*, sb. use of pp. of *certificāre*; see -ATE[2].

certiorari (leg.) writ from a higher court for the production of records from a lower. XV. pass. of late legal L. *certiōrāre* inform (*certiorem facere*), f. *certior*, compar. of *certus* CERTAIN.

certitude XV. - late L. *certitūdō*, f. *certus* CERTAIN; see -TUDE.

cerulean of a deep blue. XVII. - L. *cæruleus* sky-blue, prob. :- **cælolos*, f. *cælum* sky, heaven; see -EAN.

ceruse white lead. XIV. - (O)F. *céruse* - L. *cērussa*.

cervical XVII. - F. *cervical* or modL. *cervīcālis* (cf. L. *cervīcal* pillow), f. *cervīx, cervīc-* neck; see -AL[1].

cess local rate (in Ireland still the official term). XVI. var. of *sess*, aphetic form of ASSESS.

cessation XIV. - L. *cessātiō, -ōn-*, f. pp. stem of *cessāre* CEASE.

cesser (leg.) cessation. XVI. sb. use of (O)F. *cesser* CEASE; see -ER[5].

cession action of ceding or surrendering. XIV. - (O)F. *cession* or its source L. *cessiō, -ōn-*, f. *cēdere, cess-* CEDE; see -ION.

cesspool excavation in the bottom of a drain to retain solid matter XVII; well to receive soil from privies, etc. XVIII. perh. alt., with assim. to POOL[1], of *cesperalle, susprall, suspirel* settling tank, cesspool (XVI), vars. of †*suspiral* vent, esp. of a conduit, water-pipe - OF. *souspirail* (mod. *soupirail*) air-hole, f. *sou(s)pirer* (L. *suspīrāre*) SUSPIRE + L. *spiraculum* air-hole. Hence **cesspit** XIX.

cetaceous of the whale kind. XVII. f. modL. *cētacea* (used zool. as the name of an order), f. L. *cētus* - Gr. *kêtos* whale; see -ACEOUS.

Chablis French white wine. XVII. - F., f. name of a town in E. France.

chafe †heat, inflame; ruffle, vex XIV; rub so as to warm XV; rage, fret XVI. ME. *chaufe* - OF. *chaufer* (mod. *chauffer*) :- Rom. **calefāre*, for *calefacere* make warm (see CALEFACTION).

chafer beetle (now chiefly in COCKCHAFER). OE. *ċeafor* :- Gmc. **kabraz, -uz*, parallel to *ċefer* = OS., (M)Du. *kever*, OHG. *chefar(o)* (G. *käfer*) :- Gmc. **kebraz*; prob. lit. 'the gnawer', and rel. to next and OE. *ċeafl*, JOWL[1].

chaff[1] husks of grain OE.; refuse XIII; cut hay and straw XVIII. OE. *ċeaf* = MLG., (M)Du., MHG. *kaf* (G. dial. *kaff*), corr. to OHG. *cheva* husk; prob. f. Gmc. base **kaf- *kef-* gnaw, chew.

chaff[2] banter lightly; also as sb. XIX. of slang orig.; perh. a var. of CHAFE, for which sps. with *-ff-* occur from XVI in the sense of 'scolding'.

chaffer traffic, trade; merchandise. XIII. ME. *chaf-, cheffare, ch(e)apfare* :- OE. **ċēapfaru*, f. *ċēap* bargain, sale + *faru* going, journey, proceedings (prob. after ON. *kaupfǫr* trading journey); see CHEAP, FARE. The orig. word became obs. in XVII; a new sb. meaning 'bargaining', f. the vb., appeared XIX. Hence **chaffer** vb. †trade; bargain, haggle XIV.

chaffinch OE. *ċeaffinċ*, f. CHAFF[1] + FINCH.

chagrin †anxious care, melancholy XVII; vexation XVIII; also †adj. grieved, mortified XVII. - F. *chagrin* sb. and adj., of unkn. orig.

chain sb. XIII. - OF. *chaine* (mod. *chaîne*) :- L. *catēna*. Hence, or - (O)F., **chain** vb. XIV.

chair XIII (*chaere, chaier*). - AN. *chaere*, OF. *chaiere* (mod. *chaire* bishop's throne, pulpit, etc.) :- L. *cathedra* - Gr. *kathédrā* (see CATHEDRAL). Hence **chairman** XVII.

chaise pleasure or travelling carriage. XVIII. - F. *chaise*, var. of *chaire* CHAIR.

c(h)alcedony precious stone (now a subspecies of quartz). The present forms, dating from XV-XVI, are - L. *c(h)alcēdonius* - Gr. *khalkēdṓn* (Rev. 21: 19), assumed to mean 'stone of Chalcedon' in Asia Minor, but var. L. forms *carc(h)edonia, -ius* led to the assoc. with Carthage (Gr. *Karkhēdṓn*). Earlier forms, *cassidoine, calcidoine*, etc. (from XIII) were - OF.

chaldron dry measure (32 bushels). XVII. - OF. *chauderon* (mod. *chaudron*) CAULDRON.

chalet XIX. - (Swiss) F., dim. of OF. *chasel* farmstead, dairy :- Rom. **casāle*, f. L. *casa* hut, cottage.

chalice XIII. - (O)F. - L. *calix, calic-* cup, rel. to Gr. *kálux* CALYX.

chalk OE. *ċealc* = OS. *calc*, OHG. *chalch* (G. *kalk*), WGmc. - L. *calx, calc-* lime, which sense has remained in the Gmc. langs. except Eng., where it has taken over that of L. *crēta* (whence F. *craie*; cf. CRAYON). Hence **chalk** vb. XVI. **chalky** XIV.

challenge †accusation XIII; †claim; invitation to a contest XIV; legal exception taken XVI. ME. *c(h)alenge* - OF. :- L. *calumnia* false accusation, malicious action at law (see CALUMNY). So **challenge** vb. XIII. ME. *c(h)alange* - OF. *c(h)alengier* :- L. *calumniārī* CALUMNIATE.

Cham XVI. Earlier form of KHAN.

chamber XIII. - (O)F. *chambre* :- L. *camera* - Gr. *kamárā* vault (cf. CAMERA).

chamberlain attendant on a royal or noble chamber XIII; steward of a king, etc. XV. ME. *cha(u)mberleyn, -laine* - OF. *chamberlain, -lenc* (mod. *chambellan*) - Frank. **kamarling*, f. *kamara* CHAMBER; see -LING[1].

chameleon XIV. - L. *chamæleōn* - Gr. *khamailéōn*, f. *khamaí* on the ground (rel. to HUMUS) + *léōn* LION.

chamfer make a groove in XVI; bevel off a square edge XVII. Back-formation from *chamfering* - (with assim. to -ING[1]) F. *chamfrain*, f. *chant* edge (CANT[1]) + *fraint*, pp. of OF. *fraindre* :- L. *frangere* BREAK.

chamois European antelope; soft pliable leather orig. from this. XVI. First recorded from the Geneva Bible (1560), Deut. 14: 5, where the Vulgate has *camēlopardus*, LXX *kamēlopárdalis*. - (O)F., prob. ult. from a pre-Rom. name current in the Alpine areas.

champ chew noisily, etc. XVI. prob. imit.

champagne wine of *Champagne*, a province of E. France XVII; see next.

champaign level open country. XIV. ME. *champayne* - OF. *champagne* :- late L. *campānia* fem. sg. and n. pl., sb. uses of adj. f. *campus* level field (cf. CAMP), particularized as proper names of regions in France (*Champagne*) and Italy (*Campagna*).

champion fighting man; one who fights on behalf of another. XIII. - (O)F. :- medL. *campio*, f. *campus* field, CAMP. Hence **champion** vb. †challenge XVII; fight on behalf of XIX.

chance sb. XIII. - AN. *ch(e)aunce*, OF. *cheance* (mod. *chance*), f. *cheoir* fall, befall :- Rom. **cadēre*, for L. *cadere* fall. Hence **chance** vb. XIV. **chancy** †Sc. lucky XVI; risky XIX; see -Y[1].

chancel part of a church reserved for clergy and choir. XIV. - OF. *chancel* (now in latinized form *cancel*) :- L. *cancellī* lattice, grating, dim. of *cancer* lattice, perh. dissimilated form of *carcer* barrier, prison.

chancellor *Chancellor of England*, the highest officer of the crown XI; *Chancellor of the Exchequer*, the highest finance minister XIV; head of a university XIV; diocesan vicar-general XVI; (Sc.) foreman of a jury XVIII. The earliest forms *canc(h)eler* were succeeded by *chanceler*, later (XVI) by forms with the substituted suffix *-o(u)r*. - AN. *c(h)anceler*, OF. *cancelier*, (also mod.) *chancelier*, semi-learned - late L. *cancellārius* porter, secretary, f. *cancellī* (see CHANCEL) + *-arius* -ER[2]; the L. word was orig. applied to an officer whose position was *ad cancellos* at the bars (e.g. of a court).

chancery court of the Lord Chancellor; since 1873, a division of the High Court of Justice. XIV. Reduced form of ME. *cha(u)ncel(e)rie* - (O)F. *chancellerie*, f. *chancelier* CHANCELLOR.

chancre venereal ulcer. XVI. - F. - L. *cancer*, *cancr-*; see CANCER.

chandelier (mil.) wooden framework to protect sappers in trenches XVII; branched support to hold lights XVIII. - F., f. *chandelle* CANDLE; see -IER.

chandler maker or seller of candles XIV; retail dealer (now in *corn-chandler*, *ship-chandler*) XVI. - AN. *chaundeler*, OF. *chandelier*, f. *chandelle* CANDLE; see -ER[2].

change alteration, substitution, †exchange XIII; place of meeting for merchants XIV; money given in exchange XVIII. - AN. *chaunge*, OF. *change*, f. *changer* (whence **change** vb. XIII) :- late L. (Rom.) *cambiāre*, f. L. *cambīre* exchange, barter, prob. of Celt. orig. Hence **changeling** †waverer, turncoat; person, esp. an infant, substituted for another XVI; see -LING[1].

channel[1] bed of running water XIII; tubular passage XIV; course, direction XVI; groove XVII. - OF. *chanel*, partly latinized var. of *chenel* :- L. *canālis*, *canāl-* pipe, channel, f. *canna* pipe, CANE; see -EL[2]. Cf. CANAL.

channel[2] (naut.) plank, etc. projecting horizontally from a ship's side. XVIII. alt. of *chainwale* (XVII), f. CHAIN (in the sense 'contrivance used to carry the lower shrouds of a mast outside the ship's side') + WALE.

chant sing XIV; sing as to a chant XV. - (O)F. *chanter* :- L. *cantāre*, frequent. of *canere* sing. Hence **chant** sb. song XVII; tune to which the psalms, etc. are sung XVIII; cf. (O)F. *chant* (:- L. *cantus*).

chanticleer cock, orig. as a proper name. XIII. - OF. *chantecler* (mod. *-clair*), proper name of the Cock in the fabliau of Reynard the Fox, f. *chanter* CHANT + *cler* CLEAR.

chantry endowment for a priest to pray for the departed XIV; chapel, etc., so endowed XV. - OF. *chanterie*, f. *chanter* sing, CHANT; see -ERY, -RY.

chanty var. of SHANTY[2].

chaos †chasm, abyss (as in Luke 16: 26) XV; primordial formless void XVI; utter confusion XVII. - F. or L. - Gr. *kháos* vast chasm, void, f. IE. base **ghəw-* hollow. Hence **chaotic** XVIII.

chap[1] open fissure, spec. in the skin. XIV. rel. to *chap* vb. (north. dial. and Sc.) strike XIV; crack in fissures XV; similar in meaning to (M)LG., (M)Du. *kappen* and to CHOP[1], but initial *ch* is unexpl.

chap[2] jaw, chiefly pl. XVI. Somewhat later in appearance than the synon. CHOP[3]; of unkn. orig.

chap[3] (dial.) purchaser, customer XVI; fellow, (young) man XVIII. abbrev. of CHAPMAN. Hence **chappie** XIX (orig. Sc.); see -IE.

chap-book pamphlet of popular literature formerly hawked by itinerant dealers. XIX. f. *chap* in CHAPMAN + BOOK.

chape metal plate covering an object. XIV. - (O)F. *chape* cope, hood, in techn. uses; see CAPE[1].

chapel oratory in a large house, etc. XIII; compartment (with an altar) of a church XIV; parochial place of worship dependent upon a church XV; nonconformist place of worship XVII; printing office, association of journeyman printers XVII. - OF. *chapele* (mod. *-elle*) :- medL. *cappella* (dim. of *cappa* CAPE[1]), orig. the sanctuary devoted to the preservation of the cloak (*cappella*) of St. Martin of Tours, later (*c.*800) extended to oratories attached to palaces or the like, and to parochial places of worship other than churches; cf. CHAPLAIN. Hence **chapelry** XVI.

chaperon A. †hood, cap XIV; B. woman who accompanies a young unmarried woman as protector (often spelt *-one*, as if a fem. ending were required) XVIII. - (O)F., f. *chape* cope, CAPE[1].

Sense B appears to have arisen from the application of the sb. and of the vb. *chaperonner* (whence **chaperon** vb. XVIII) to protection of various kinds.

chaplain XII. Early ME. *capelein*, superseding OE. *capellān* and superseded by *chapelein* - AN., OF. *c(h)apelain* :- medL. *cappellānus* orig. custodian of the cloak of St. Martin, f. *cappella* CHAPEL; see -AN.

chaplet wreath for the head XIV; string of beads in the rosary XVII. - (O)F. *chapelet* orig. a crown of roses, dim. of *chapel* (mod. *chapeau* hat) :- Rom. **cappellus*, dim. of *cappa* hood, CAPE[1]; see -ET. The application to the rosary arises from the orig. rose form of the beads.

chapman (arch.) trader, dealer OE.; †purchaser, customer (CHAP[3]) XIII. OE. *ċēapman* — (M)Du. *koopman*, OHG. *koufman* (G. *kaufmann*); WGmc. comp. of **kaup-* (see CHEAP) and MAN.

chapter main section of a book XIII; assembly of a religious community or collegiate church (orig. with ref. to the reading of a chapter of Scripture or of the Rule) XIV; members of this XV. - (O)F. *chapitre*, earlier *chapitle* - L. *capitulum*, dim. of *caput* HEAD.

char[1] small trout. XVII. of unkn. orig.

char[2] reduce to charcoal, scorch. XVII. Presumably a back-formation f. CHARCOAL.

char[3] (i) var. of CHARE sb. XIII; (ii) short for CHARWOMAN XIX. Hence as vb.

char-a-banc XIX. - F. *char-à-bancs* lit. 'carriage with seats' (see CAR, BANK[2]), in its earlier form a long light carriage open or only curtained at the sides.

character distinctive mark XIV; graphic symbol XV; sum of mental and moral qualities XVII; personage, personality XVIII. ME. *caracter* - (O)F. *caractère* - (mostly late) L. *charactēr* - Gr. *kharaktḗr* instrument for marking, impress, distinctive nature, f. *kharássein* scratch, engrave. So **characteristic** XVII. - F. - late Gr. **characterize** XVI. - F. or medL. - late Gr.

charade XVIII. - F. - modPr. *charrado* conversation, f. *charra*, perh. of imit. orig.

charcoal XIV. The second el., COAL, orig. meant 'charcoal'; the first el. is obscure, but has been referred to CHARE, as if the comp. meant 'turn-coal'. Cf. CHAR[2].

chard central leaf-stalk of artichoke, midrib of white beet. XVII. - F. *carde*, alt. by assoc. with *chardon* thistle :- late L. *cardō*, *-ōn-*, for L. *carduus*.

chare, char †turn (in various senses) OE.; turn of work, odd job, esp. of household work (cf. CHORE) XIV. OE. *ċerr*, WS. *ċierr*, rel. to *ċierran* turn away or aside, whence **chare, char** vb. †turn OE.; †do or accomplish (a job) XVI; (from the sb.) do odd turns of work XVIII.

charge †load, burden (material or immaterial) XIII; task or duty laid upon one, official instruction XIV; burden of expense; accusation XV; (from F.) impetuous onset XVI; (f. the vb.) quantity loaded (cf. CARGO) XVII. - (O)F. :- Rom. **carrica*, f. late L. *car(ri)cāre*, f. L. *carrus* wagon, CAR; cf. CARRY. So **charge** vb. †load, burden XIII; lay a duty or command upon; put to expense; lay blame or accusation upon XIV; (from F.) put (a weapon) in position for offence; make a powerful onset (upon) XVI.

chargé d'affaires XVIII. - F. 'one charged with affairs'.

chariot †cart, wagon; stately vehicle for the conveyance of persons. XIV. - (O)F. *chariot* wagon, augm. of *char* CAR. Hence **charioteer** XVII.

charisma (theol.) free gift of God's grace. XVII. - Gr. *khárisma*, f. *kharízesthai* show favour, f. *kháris* favour, grace. So **charismatic** XIX.

charity Christian love; benevolence, charitableness, alms. The earliest forms were *carited*, *kariteth* (XI), repr. AN. vars.; these were succeeded by the immed. antecedent of the present form, ME. *charite* (XIII) - (O)F. *charité* - L. *cāritās*, *cāritāt-*, f. *cārus* dear; see -ITY.

charivari serenade of 'rough music', in derision of unpopular persons, babel of noise. XVII. - F. (earlier *chalivali*, *-vari*); many vars. in F. and medL.; of unkn. orig., perh. echoic.

charlatan †mountebank; quack XVII; pretentious impostor XIX. - F. - It. *ciarlatano*, f. *ciarlare* babble.

charlock field mustard. OE. *ċerlic*, *ċyrlic*, synon. with *ċedelc* (cf. dial. *kedlock*, †*cadlock*); the var. *carlock* is found as early as XV; of unkn. orig. Cf. HEMLOCK.

charlotte (usu. *apple charlotte*) dish consisting of apple marmalade baked in bread XIX; also *charlotte russe* (i.e. Russian), custard in a mould of sponge cake. - F.; an unexpl. use of the female proper name.

charm incantation, enchantment XIII; amulet XVI; attractive quality XVII. - (O)F. *charme* :- L. *carmen*, *carmin-* song, oracular response, incantation. So **charm** vb. enchant XIV; fascinate XV.

charnel mortuary XIV; now only *charnel house* (XVI). - OF. :- medL. *carnāle*, sb. use of n. of late L. *carnālis* CARNAL.

chart sb. XVI. - L. *charta* - Gr. *khártēs*, perh. of Egyptian orig. Hence as vb. XIX.

charter document conveying a privilege or right. XIII. - OF. *chartre* :- L. *chartula*, dim. of *charta* CHART.

charter-party deed between owners and merchants for hire of a ship and delivery of the cargo. XV. - F. *charte partie* - medL. *charta partīta* 'divided charter', i.e. deed written out in duplicate and then divided like an indenture; first part assim. to CHARTER.

Chartist (hist.) one of the Eng. political reformers who upheld 'the People's *Charter*' of 1837. f. L. *charta* (used in the sense of 'charter') + -IST.

chartreuse liqueur made at La Grande *Chartreuse*, near Grenoble. XIX. - F., fem. of *Chartreux* CARTHUSIAN.

chartulary see CARTULARY.

charwoman XVI. f. CHARE, CHAR + WOMAN.

chary †sorrowful OE.; †dear, precious XIV; careful, frugal XVI. OE. *ċeariġ*, = OS. *carag*, OHG. *charag* :- WGmc. **karaga*, f. **karō* CARE; see -Y[1].

chase[1] hunting, pursuit. XIII. - OF. *chace* (mod. *chasse*) :- Rom. **captia*, f. **captiāre*. So **chase**

vb. pursue, drive away XIII; hunt XIV. - OF. *chacier* (mod. *chasser*) :- Rom. **captiāre*, for L. *captāre*, frequent. of *capere* take (cf. HEAVE). See CATCH.

chase[2] adorn (metal) with engraving. XIV. contemp. with synon. *enchase*, of which it may be an aphetic deriv.; perh. - (O)F. *enchâsser* enclose in a reliquary, put a gem in a setting, f. EN-[1] + *châsse* casket, reliquary :- L. *capsa* CASE[2].

chase[3] A. (typogr.) frame in which composed type is locked up; B. cavity of a gun-barrel. XVII. perh. f. F. *chas* enclosure, *châsse* setting, case :- L. *capsus* enclosed receptacle and *capsa* repository, CASE[2]; but it is doubtful whether A and B should be coupled.

chasm XVII. - L. *chasma* - Gr. *khásma* yawning hollow, rel. to *khaínein* gape.

chassé perform the gliding step called *chassé*. XIX. - imper. of F. *chasser* CHASE[1], or some other part of the verb similarly pronounced.

chassis †window-frame, SASH XVII; base-frame of a carriage XIX. - F. *châssis* :- Rom. **capsīcium*, f. L. *capsa* CASE[2].

chaste XIII. - (O)F. - L. *castus*. So **chastity** XIII.

chasten discipline, chastise XVI; restrain, subdue XIX. Extension (with -EN[5]) of †*chaste* vb. XIII (- OF. *chastier* :- L. *castigāre* CASTIGATE).

chastise †correct the faults of; inflict punishment on. XIV. of doubtful orig.; prob. (like CHASTEN) a new formation on †*chaste* vb., or its var. †*chasty* (both XIII), after vbs. in *-iser* or *-iss-* (*-ir*); see -IZE, -ISH[2]. Hence **chastisement** XIV.

chasuble (eccl.) sleeveless vestment. XIII. ME. *chesible* - OF. (cf. AL. *cassibula* XIII); vars. of this were in use till XVI; from XVII superseded by *chasuble* - (O)F. :- late L. *casubla*, obscure alt. of L. *casula* little cottage, hut, hooded cloak, dim. of *casa* house.

chat[1] †chatter XIV-XV; converse easily and familiarly XVI. Shortening of CHATTER. So **chat** sb. XVI. Hence **chatty** XVIII; see -Y[1].

chat[2] small bird. XVII. prob. imit.

chatelaine mistress of a castle, etc.; chains on girdle bearing articles of domestic use. XIX. - F. *châtelaine*, fem. of *châtelain* lord of a castle :- L. *castellānus*, f. *castellum* CASTLE. See -AN.

chattel †property XIII; movable possession; property other than real estate XVI. - OF. *chatel* (cf. CATTLE) :- medL. *capitāle*; see CAPITAL[1].

chatter vb. XIII. imit.; see -ER[4]. Hence as sb. XIII. **chatterbox** XIX.

chauffeur XX. - F. 'stoker', 'fireman', f. *chauffer* heat up, CHAFE.

chauvinism bellicose patriotism. XIX. - F. *chauvinisme*, f. name of Nicolas *Chauvin*, a veteran of the First Republic and Empire, noted for demonstrative patriotism, and popularized as the name of a character in 'La Cocarde tricolore' (1831) by the brothers Cogniard; see -ISM.

cheap adj. and adv. XVI. ellipt. for †(*at*) *good cheape* (XIV) 'as a great or good bargain', phr. formed, after (O)F. *à bon marché* 'at good market', on ME. *chēp*, OE. *ċēap* bargain, price = OS. *kōp*, OHG. *kouf* (G. *kauf*) :- WGmc. **kaupa* m. (cf. ON. *kaup* n.); based on an early Gmc. adoption of L. *caupō* small trader, innkeeper.

cheat †escheat XIV; †booty, spoil; †(thieves' cant) stolen thing, (gen.) thing, article XVI; fraud; deceiver, impostor XVII. Aphetic for ESCHEAT. The two last senses are from the vb. (escheat XV; defraud, deceive XVI); but **cheater** is earlier (XIV) - AN. *chetour*, for *eschetour*.

check[1] threat to the king at chess XIV; †attack, reprimand XIV; (f. the vb.) arrest, restriction XVI; counterfoil, identifying token (cf. CHEQUE) XVIII. Aphetic - OF. *eschec* (mod. *échec*), alt. of **eschac* :- Rom. (medL.) *scaccus* - (via Arab.) Pers. *šāh* king, SHAH; cf. CHECKMATE, CHESS, EXCHEQUER. So **check** vb. put in check, arrest, stop. XIV.

check[2] pattern of cross lines forming squares XIV; also vb. XV. prob. short for CHEQUER.

checkmate (chess) the move which puts the king into inextricable check. XIV. Aphetic - OF. *eschec mat* - Pers. *šāh māt* the king is dead; see CHECK[1]. Hence as vb. XIV.

Cheddar epithet of a cheese named after a Somerset village. XVII.

cheek †jaw, jawbone; fleshy side of the face OE.; side, side-piece (in techn. uses) XIV; insolence XIX. OE. *ċēoce* = OFris. *ziāke* :- WGmc. **keukōn*; varying with OE. *ċē(a)ce* = (M)LG. *kāke*, *kēke*, MDu. *kāke* (Du. *kaak*) :- WGmc. **kǣkōn*. Hence **cheeky** XIX.

cheep vb. XVI. In early use only Sc.; of imit. orig.

cheer †face, visage; disposition, mood (arch. or dial. in *What cheer?*, *be of good cheer*, etc.); kindly reception XIII; fare, provisions XIV; (from the verb) shout of encouragement or welcome XVIII. ME. *chere* - AN. *chere*, OF. *chiere* face :- late L. *cara* face - Gr. *kárā* head. Hence **cheer** vb. make cheerful XIV; encourage by word or deed XV. **cheerful** XIV.

cheese[1] food made of pressed curds. OE. *ċēse*, **ċīese*, *ċȳse* = OS. *kāsi* (Du. *kaas*), OHG. *chāsi* (G. *käse*) :- WGmc. **kāsjō* - L. *cāseus*.

cheese[2] (slang) *cheese it*, stop, have done. XIX. of unkn. orig.

cheetah XVIII. - Hind. *cītā* - Skr. *citraka-*, f. *citrá-* bright, variegated.

chef head cook. XIX. - F., for *chef de cuisine* 'head of cooking or kitchen'; see CHIEF.

chef d'œuvre masterpiece. XVII. - F., orig. work qualifying for mastery in a craft (lit. 'principal piece of work').

cheir(o)- see CHIRO-.

chela (zool.) prehensile claw. XVII (*chely*). - modL., alt. of L. *chēlē* or its source Gr. *khēlḗ*.

chemic †alchemical XVI; †pert. to Paracelsian medicine (based on chemical doctrines); pert. to chemistry XVII. Earlier form *chymick* - F. *chimique* or modL. *chimicus*, for *alchimicus* ALCHEMICAL. So **chemical** XVI (earlier than *chemic* in the last sense). The sp. *che-* (XVII) is based on Gr. *khēm(e)íā* (cf. ALCHEMY).

chemise XIX. - (O)F. :- late L. *camīsia* shirt, nightgown.

chemist †alchemist XVI; one versed in chemistry XVII; dealer in medicinal drugs XVII. Earlier form *chymist* - F. *chimiste*, †*chymiste* - modL. *chimista*, for *alchimista* ALCHEMIST. Cf. CHEMIC. Hence **chemistry** †alchemy; branch of science dealing with natural elementary substances.

xvii (*chymistry*). The sp. has been assim. to *chemical*.

chenille kind of velvety cord. xviii. - F. *chenille* hairy caterpillar :- L. *canīcula* small dog, dim. of *canis* dog.

cheque, U.S. **check** (banking) †counterfoil; written order to a banker to pay out money. xviii. Spec. use of CHECK¹ in the sense 'device for checking the amount of an item', with Eng. sp. perh. after EXCHEQUER.

chequer †chess(-board) xiii; †exchequer xiv; chequered pattern xvii. Aphetic of EXCHEQUER. Hence **chequer** vb. diversify as with a chess-board pattern. xiv.

cherish xiv. - (O)F. *chériss-*, extended stem of *chérir*, f. *cher* dear :- L. *cārus*; see -ISH².

cheroot xvii. - Tamil *churuṭṭu* roll of tobacco. Cf. F. *cheroute*.

cherry xiv. ME. *cheri(e)*, *chiri(e)* - ONF. *cherise* (apprehended as pl.), mod. *cerise* :- medL. *ceresia*, for **cerasia*, perh. orig. n. pl. of adj. *ceraseus*, f. L. *cerasus* cherry-tree - Gr. *kérasos*.

chert flint-like variety of quartz. xvii. Local (N. midl.) name of unkn. orig., taken up by geologists.

cherub, (as †sg. and pl.) **cherubim** †(*cherubim*) seat or dwelling of the Deity (after biblical use) OE.; (*cherub*, *-im*, *-in*) angel(s) of the second order xiii; †(*cherubin*) beautiful or beloved woman xvi; (*cherub*) beautiful innocent child xviii. OE. and ME. *cherubin*, *-im*, ult. (through L. and F.) from Heb. *kᵉrûbhīm*, pl. of *kᵉrûbh* - Accadian *karūbu* gracious, *kirūbu* propitious, f. *karābu* incline graciously.

chervil garden herb. OE. *ċerfille*, *-felle*, corr. to (M)LG., (M)Du. *kervel*, OHG. *kervola* (G. *kerbel*) - L. *chærephylla*, *-um* - Gr. *khairéphullon*.

chess xiii. Aphetic - OF. *esches* (mod. *échecs*), pl. of *eschec* CHECK¹. Hence **chessmen** the pieces with which the game is played. xv.

chest box, coffer OE.; thorax xvi. OE. *ċest*, *ċist*, corr. to MDu. *kiste* (Du. *kist*), OHG. *kista* (G. *kiste*), ON. *kista* :- Gmc. **kistō* - L. *cista* - Gr. *kístē* box, chest.

chestnut xvi. The first element is ME. *chesteine*, *chasteine* (xiv) - OF. *chastaine* (mod. *châtaigne*) :- L. *castanea* - Gr. *kastanéā*.

chevalier horseman, knight xiv; cavalier, gallant xvii. ME. *chevaler* - AN. *chevaler*, (O)F. *chevalier* :- medL. *caballārius*, f. L. *caballus* horse; refash. after modF. in xvi. Cf. CAVALIER.

chevaux-de-frise spiked contrivance for obstructing enemy troops. xvii. - F., lit. 'horses of Friesland', so called because they were first used by the Frisians to compensate for their lack of cavalry.

chevron (her.) charge of this shape ∧ xiv; mark of rank xix. - (O)F. :- Rom. **capriōne*, f. *caper* goat, corr. to ON. *hafr* he-goat.

chevrotain, -tin small musk deer. xviii. - F. *chevrotain*, *-tin*, dim. of F. *chevrot*, dim. of *chèvre* goat :- L. *capra*, fem. of *caper* (see prec.).

chew grind to pulp with the teeth. OE. *ċēowan* str. vb. = MLG. *keuwen* (Du. *kauwen*), OHG. *kiuwan* (G. *kauen*) :- WGmc. **kewwan*; rel. to OSl. *žīvati*. Conjugated weak from xiv.

chianti Italian wine. xix. Named from the *Chianti* Mountains, Tuscany, the place of its production.

chiaroscuro †painting in light and shade; disposition of light and shade. xvii. - It., f. *chiaro* CLEAR + *oscuro* dark, OBSCURE.

chiasmus figure of speech in which the order of parallel words in phrases is inverted. xix. - modL. - Gr. *khiasmós* crossing, diagonal arrangement, f. *khiázein* mark with the letter X (*khī*).

chic good style; stylish. xix. - F. (in artists' slang xix), perh. identical with *chic* (xvi) trickery in legal matters, (in Walloon) skill in conducting legal cases (- MLG. *schick* order, skill), or joc. shortening of *chicane* (see next).

chicanery legal trickery, quibbling. xvii. - F. *chicanerie*, f. *chicaner* pursue at law (xv), quibble, wrangle, of unkn. orig.; see -ERY. So **chicane** sb. and vb. xvii.

chick xiv. Shortening of CHICKEN, which prob. lost the final *n*, like pps. and such words as *seven*, in southern dialects (in some of which *chick* is now sg., with pl. *chicken*). Hence **chickabiddy** (†*biddy* fowl) child's name for a fowl xviii.

chicken OE. *ċīcen*, *ċȳcen* (late WS.) :- Gmc. **kiukīnam*, f. **keuk-*, of imit. orig. (cf. COCK), with dim. suffix characteristic of animal names; corr. synon. forms are (M)Du. *kieken*, Du. *kuiken*, (M)LG. *küken*, MHG. *küchelīn* (G. *küchlein*), ON. *kjúklingr*.

chick-pea dwarf species of pea. xvi. Earlier †*ciche pease(n)*, *chick peas* - F. (*pois*) *chiche* (earlier †*ciche*) - L. *cicer* chick-pea.

chickweed xvi. Earlier (and still Sc.) *chickenweed* (xv).

chicory the plant *Cichorium intybus* xv; ground root of this used with or instead of coffee xix. Late ME. *cicoree* - F. †*cicorée*, mod. *chicorée* endive - medL. *cic(h)orēa*, for L. *cichorēum*, *-ium* - Gr. *kikhóreia*, *kíkhora* n. pl., *kikhórion*.

chide †wrangle; dispute angrily with OE.; scold, reprove xiii. OE. *ċīdan* (str. vb.), of unkn. orig.

chief head man; (feudal law) *in chief* (OF. *en chief*, medL. *in capite*) holding or held immediately from the lord paramount xiii; †head, top xiv; (her.) *in chief* on the upper part of the shield xv. - (O)F. *chef*, †*chief* :- Rom. **capum*, for L. *caput* HEAD. As adj. xiii, as in OF.; hence **chiefly** xiv.

chieftain xiv. Late ME. *cheftain*, alt., by assim. to prec., of earlier †*chevetaine* - OF. *chevetaine*, semi-pop. - late L. *capitāneus* (see CAPTAIN).

chiff-chaff one of the warblers, *Phylloscopus collybita*. xviii. imit. of the bird's note.

chiffon (pl.) fallals, finery xviii; diaphanous silky muslin xix. - F., f. *chiffe* scrap of paper, rag, of unkn. orig.

chignon coil of hair worn at the nape of the neck. xviii. - F., orig. nape of the neck, earlier *chaaignon* :- Rom. **catēniōne*, f. L. *catēna* CHAIN; cf. -OON.

chigoe tropical flea. xvii. Earliest in F. form *chique*; later *chego(e)*, *chig(g)er*, *jigger*; native (Carib) name.

chilblain xvi. f. CHILL + *blain* blister, pustule

(OE. *blēġen* = MDu. *bleine*, Du. *blein*, LG. *bleien*; a WGmc. word), or reduction of **chilled blain* (*child-blain* is recorded XVII).

child A word peculiar to English. OE. *ċild* :- **kilþam*, rel. to Goth. *kilþei* womb, *inkilþō* pregnant; OSw. *kulder*, *kolder* (Sw. *kull*), ODa. *kol(l)*, Da. *kuld*, young of a litter, child, have been compared. The nom. pl. of OE. *ċild* appears as *ċild* and *ċildru* (ME. *childre*, mod. dial. *childer*); the addition of the weak pl. ending *-(e)n* produced the surviving standard pl. *children* (XII).

chiliad 1,000, esp. 1,000 years. XVI. - late L. *chīliās*, *-ād-* - Gr. *khīliás*, *-ad-*, f. *khī́lioi* 1,000; see -AD.

chill sb., adj., and vb. The earliest member of this group is the vb. ('grow cold'), which appears in late XIV. Its orig. is obscure; in the pp. †*child* it may repr. an OE. **ċieldan*, **ċildan* (:- Gmc. **kalþjan*, f. **kalþaz* COLD). The adj. *chill* (XVI) may be an alt. of †*child* on the analogy of *cool*, *cold*; the sb. *chill* (XVII) is f. the vb. Hence **chilly** XVI; see -Y[1].

chil(l)i dried pod of capsicum. XVII. - Sp. *chile*, *chili* - Nahuatl *chilli*.

chim(a)era (Gr. myth.) fire-breathing monster; horrible phantasm; wild fancy. XVI. - L. *chimæra* - Gr. *khímaira* she-goat, monster, f. *khímaros* he-goat. So **chimerical** XVII.

chime[1] †cymbal XIII; †apparatus for striking bells XV; set of bells or of sounds produced by them XVI; (musical) concord, harmony XVII. ME. *chim(b)e* prob. arose from *chym(b)e bell* (XIII-XV), which may have been an analysis of a ME. **chimbel* :- OE. *ċimbal* - L. *cymbalum* CYMBAL. So **chime** vb. †make a musical sound XIV; accord or join in harmoniously XVII.

chime[2], **chimb** projecting rim of a cask. XIV. prob. identical with the sb. occurring in OE. *ċimstān* base, pedestal, *ċimīren* clamp-iron, *ċimbing* joint, corr. to MDu. *kimme* (Du. *kim*) edge of a cask, MLG. *kimme*, *kimm* (whence G. *kimme*).

chimney †fireplace; †stove; smoke-flue. XIV. - (O)F. *cheminée* fireplace, chimney - late L. *camīnāta*, perh. orig. for *camera camīnāta* (whence OHG. *kamināta*, (M)HG. *kemenāte*) room with a fireplace, f. *camīnus* - Gr. *kámīnos* oven, furnace, rel. to *kamárā* CHAMBER.

chimpanzee XVIII. - F. *chimpanzé* - native name in Angola, W. Africa.

chin OE. *ċin(n)*, corr. (with variation of gender and decl.) to OFris. *kin*, OS. *kinni* (Du. *kin*), OHG. *kinni* (G. *kinn*), ON. *kinn* chin, lower jaw, Goth. *kinnus* cheek; Gmc. **kinn-* :- **kenw-* :- IE. **genw-*, whence Gr. *génus*, Skr. *hánu-*, L. *gena* cheek, OIr. *gin*, W. *gen* jaw, chin.

china XVII. Short for *china ware*, i.e. ware from China.

chinch bed-bug. XVII. - Sp. *chinche* :- L. *cimex*, *-ic-*.

chinchilla small S. Amer. rodent. - Sp. *chinchilla*, dim. of *chinche* (see prec.).

chine[1] †cleft, chink OE.; (generalized from place-names in Hampshire and the Isle of Wight) deep narrow ravine cut by a stream. XIX. OE. *ċinu* = MDu. *kēne* (Du. *keen*), f. Gmc. base **kī-* burst open, repr. also by OE. *ċīnan* = OS., OHG. *kīnan*, Goth. *keinan* sprout, shoot forth, CHIT[1].

chine[2] spine, backbone. XIV. Aphetic - OF. *eschine* (mod. *échine*) :- Rom. **skīna*, blending of Gmc. **skin-* (in OHG. *skina*, G. *schiene*) and L. *spīna* SPINE.

chine[3] projecting rim. XV. unexpl. var. of CHIME[2].

chink[1] fissure; slit. XVI. rel. in some way, as yet undetermined, to CHINE[1].

chink[2] make a sharp ringing sound. XVI. imit. Hence as sb. XVI.

chintz varicoloured cotton cloth with floral designs. XVII. Earlier *chints*, orig. pl. of *chint* - Hindi *chīṭ*.

chip small thin piece of wood, stone, etc. XIV. repr. OE. *ċipp*, *ċyp* beam, corr. to OS. *kip* post, *kipa* stave, OHG. *kipfa* (G. dial. *kipf(e)*) axle, stave, ON. *keppr* stick, staff. The basic sense seems to be 'piece hewn or cut'. So **chip** vb. †chap XIV; pare the crust from (bread) XV; crack and break open XVI; cut with an axe or adze; cf. OE. **ċippian* = (M)LG., (M)Du. *kippen* hatch out by chipping the shell.

chipmunk, -muck N. Amer. ground-squirrel. XIX. of Algonquian orig.

chippendale f. name of Thomas *Chippendale*, which belonged to three English cabinet-makers of XVIII.

chir(o)- comb. form of Gr. *kheír* hand, more usual var. of CHEIRO-, as in **chirograph** †obligation, bond XV; papal expression of will in writing XVI; indenture XVII. - F. *chirographe* - L. *chirographum* - Gr. *kheirógraphon*. **chiromancy** divination by the hand. XV. - F. or L. - Gr. **chiropodist** one who treats the (hands and) feet. XVIII. f. Gr. *poús*, *pod-* FOOT + -IST.

chirp utter a short sound as a bird, etc. XV. alt. of earlier *chirk* (XIV; cf. OE *ċearcian*) or *chirt* (XIV). Hence **chirrup** XVI.

chisel XIV. - ONF. *chisel* (mod. *ciseau*, in pl. scissors) :- Rom. **cīsellum*, for **cæsellum* after late L. *cīsōrium* (see SCISSORS), f. *cīs-*, var. of *cæs-*, stem of *cædere* cut.

chit[1] young of a beast XIV; very young person; (potato) shoot XVII. perh. repr. obscurely OE. *ċīð*, ME. *chithe* shoot, sprout, corr. to MDu. *kijt*, OHG. *-kīdi* (MHG. *kīde*, *kīt*) sprout; f. Gmc. **kī-* split (cf. CHINE[1]).

chit[2] letter, certificate, pass. XVIII. Shortening of †**chitty** (XVII) - Hindi, Marathi *ciṭṭhī*.

chitterlings smaller intestines of beasts used as food. XIII (*cheterlingis*). orig. form uncert.; perh. OE. **ċieter-*, f. Gmc. **keut-* **kut-*, whence synon. MHG. *kutel* (G. *kutteln*); see -LING[1].

chivalrous †knightly, valorous XIV; (in mod. revived use) pert. to the Age of Chivalry XVIII; having the virtues of the ideal knight XIX. - OF. *chevalerous*, f. *chevalier*; see CHEVALIER, -OUS. So **chivalry** XIII. - (O)F. *chevalerie* - Rom. deriv. of medL. *caballerius*, for medL. *caballārius* CAVALIER.

chive XIV (*c(h)ive*). - dial. var. **chive* of (O)F. *cive* :- L. *cēpa* onion.

chivy chase, harass. XIX. var. of *chevy*; formerly used as a hunting cry, prob. arising out of *Chevy Chase*, name of a ballad celebrating a Border skirmish at *Chevy* or *Chevyat Chase*.

chlorine XIX. f. Gr. *khlōrós* pale green + -INE[5].

chloro-[1] comb. form of Gr. *khlōrós* pale green, as in **chlorophyll** (XIX) - F. *chlorophylle* (Gr. *phúllon* leaf).

chloro-[2] comb. form of CHLORINE.

chloroform XIX. - F. *chloroforme*, f. *chloro-* (see prec.) + *formyl*, as being a chloride of formyl (in its obs. sense of methenyl, CH).

chock (dial.) block, log XVII; piece of wood, etc. for holding an object in position, etc. XIV. prob. - ONF. **cho(u)que* (mod. Picard *choque*, Norman *chouque*), var. of OF. *ço(u)che* (mod. *souche*) log, block of wood = Pr. *soca* stump, trunk, of unkn. orig.

chock-full (colloq.) full to the utmost. The rare ME. (XIV) forms *chokkefulle, chekefull* are of doubtful status because of the uncertainty of the tradition; but, if genuine, they may repr. differentiated forms of OE. *ċēoce* or *ċēace* CHEEK, according as the diphthong was rising or falling. The modern *chokefull* dates from XVII, *chockfull* from XVIII, with a var. *chuckfull*, which may be due to the gen. variation between CHOCK and CHUCK. Hence prob. **chock** adv. (XVIII) close (*up*) *to*, and in *chock-a-block* (i) naut., said of a tackle with the two blocks run close together, (ii) gen., crammed close together.

chocolate beverage made from seeds of the cacao tree; paste made from these ground. XVII. - F. *chocolat*, or its source Sp. *chocolate* - Nahuatl *chocolatl* article of food made from cacao seeds; this seems to have been confounded by Europeans with *cacaua-atl*, which was actually a drink made from cacao.

choice XIII. ME. *chois* - OF. (mod. *choix*), f. *choisir* choose :- Gallo-Rom. **causīre* - Gmc. **kausjan* CHOOSE. Superseded ME. *kire, cüre*, OE. *cyre* :- Gmc. **kusiz*, f. wk. grade **kus-*. Hence as adj. chosen, selected. XIV.

choir †cathedral or collegiate church clergy; body of singers in a church; part of a church appropriated to them XIII; (gen.) organized body of singers XVI. ME. *quer(e)* - OF. *quer* (mod. *chœur*) - L. *chorus* (see CHORUS). The sp. *choir*, with assim. to F. and L., was established XVII.

choke ME. *cheke, choke*, aphetic of *acheke, achoke* :- late OE. *āċēocian* (once), f. *ā-* A-[1] + *ċē(o)ce* jaw, CHEEK.

chok(e)y toll station in India; (sl.) police station. XVII (*chukey, chowkie*). - Hindi *caukī* shed, station, lock-up.

choler bile XIV; anger XVI. ME. *coler(e)* - (O)F. *colère* - L. *cholera*; see next. In late L. *cholera* took over the meanings of Gr. *kholḗ* bile, anger, and became the techn. name for one of the four 'humours' of the old physiologists (cf. MELANCHOLY). So **choleric** †bilious XIV; irascible, angry XVI. - (O)F. *colérique* - L. *cholericus* - Gr. *kholerikós*.

cholera †bile XIV; disorder attended with bilious diarrhoea, etc. XVII; disease endemic in India XIX. - L. - Gr. *kholérā*.

choose OE. *ċēosan* (str. vb.) = OS., OHG. *kiosan*, ON. *kjósa*, Goth. *kiusan* :- Gmc. **kiusan*, **kaus*, **kusum*, **kusanaz*. The IE. base **ĝeus-* **ĝus-* is repr. also by L. *gustāre* taste, *gustus*, Gr. *geúein* give a taste of.

chop[1] cut, hew. XVI. var. of *chap* vb. (see CHAP[1]). Hence **chop** sb. cutting blow XIV; slice of meat with bone XV.

chop[2] barter, exchange XIV; phr. *chop and change* bargain (XV), make frequent changes (XVI); hence, change as the wind, veer XVII. perh. var. of ME. *chappe*, which appears to have been evolved from OE. *ċēapian* with infl. from CHAPMAN.

chop[3] (usu. pl.) jaws XV; opening, entrance (as in *Chops of the Channel* the entrance into the English Channel from the Atlantic) XVII. var. of CHAP[2].

chopsticks XVII. f. Pidgin English *chop* quick + STICK[1]; tr. Chinese *k'wai-tse* nimble boys, nimble ones.

chop suey XIX. - Chinese (Cantonese) *tsap sui*, lit. 'mixed bits'.

choral[1] pert. to a choir XVI; pert. to a chorus XVII. - medL. *chorālis*; see CHORUS and -AL[1].

choral[2] (often *chora le*) German choral song on a devotional theme. XIX. - G. *choral*, f. *choralgesang*, tr. medL. *cantus choralis* (cf. prec.).

chord[1] †harmony XV; (mus.) concord, note of a chord XVI; combination in harmony of simultaneous notes XVIII. orig. *cord*, aphetic of ACCORD.

chord[2] †tendon; line joining extremities of an arc XVI; string of musical instrument. refash. of CORD, after L. *chorda*.

chore XIX. unexpl. var. of CHARE.

chorea convulsive disorder of the body. XIX. Short for earlier *chorea sancti Viti* St. Vitus's dance; L. *chorēa* - Gr. *khoreíā*, f. *khorós* CHORUS.

choreography XVIII. f. Gr. *khoreíā* dancing + -GRAPHY. So **choreographer** XIX.

choric pert. to a chorus. XIX. - late L. *choricus* - Gr. *khorikós*, f. *khorós* CHORUS. See -IC.

chorister member of a choir. XIV. ME. *queristre* - AN. **cueristre*, var. of OF. *cueriste*, f. *quer* CHOIR; refash. (XVI) after †*chorist* or its source (O)F. *choriste*, medL. *chorista* (see CHORUS, -IST).

chorography description or delineation of particular regions. XVI. - F. *chorographie* or L. *chōrographia* - Gr. *khōrographiā*, f. *khṓrā* country; see -GRAPHY.

chortle Invented by 'Lewis Carroll' (C. L. Dodgson) in 'Through the Looking-glass', 1871; a 'portmanteau' word combining *chuckle* and *snort*. Cf. GALUMPH.

chorus in Greek drama and dramatic pieces modelled thereon XVI; band of singers XVII; musical composition to be sung by this; refrain or burden XVIII. - L. - Gr. *khorós* dance, band of dancers, choir.

chough bird of the crow family, *Pyrrhocorax*. XIV. ME. *choghe, chow(e)*, not repr. directly synon. OE. *ċēo, ċīo*. Some ME. forms, e.g. *co, c(h)owe* may be - OF. *cauwe, choue* - Frank. *cava*; but the type *chough* remains unexpl.; no doubt orig. imit.

chow dog of Chinese breed. XIX. Short for next.

chow-chow A. mixture; mixed. B. Chinese dog, CHOW. XIX. perh. Pidgin English.

chowder stew of fish, bacon, etc. XVIII. perh. - F. *chaudière* pot, CAULDRON.

chrestomathy collection of choice passages.

XIX. - F. *chrestomathie*, or its source Gr. *khrēstomátheia*, f. *khrēstós* useful + *-matheia* learning.

chrism consecrated oil OE.; Holy Unction; chrisom cloth XIII. OE. *crisma* - medL. *c(h)risma* - Gr. *khrîsma*, f. *khrîein* anoint (cf. CHRIST); refash. after L. (XVI).

chrisom (orig. *chrisom cloth*) white cloth put on a child at baptism, perh. orig. to protect the chrism. Differentiated form of prec. first appearing in XIII.

Christ the Lord's Anointed, title of Jesus of Nazareth. OE. (= OS., OHG.) *Crīst* - L. *Chrīstus* - Gr. *Khrīstós*, sb. use of *khrīstós* anointed, pp. of *khrîein* anoint; tr. Heb. *māšīaḥ* MESSIAH. So **christen** †make Christian OE.; baptize XII. OE. *crīstnian*, f. *crīsten* Christian (see -EN[5]), whence **Christendom** †Christianity OE.; Christians collectively XII; †baptism XIII. OE. *crīstendōm*. So **Christian** adj. and sb. XVI. - L. *Chrīstiānus*; superseding †*christen*, OE. *crīsten*. **Christianity** †Christendom; the Christian religion. XIV.

Christmas Late OE. *Crīstes mæsse*, ME. *cristes masse, cristmasse*, i.e. MASS[1] 'festival' of CHRIST.

chromatic (mus.) including notes not contained in the diatonic scale XVII; pert. to colour XIX. - F. *chromatique* or L. *chrōmaticus* - Gr. *khrōmatikós*, f. *khrôma*, *khrōmat-* colour, fig. modification; see -IC.

chrome †chromium; hence applied to pigments obtained from chromate of lead. XIX. - F. - Gr. *khrôma* colour (see prec.). Hence **chromium** (metallic element) XIX. See -IUM.

chromo- used as comb. form of Gr. *khrôma* colour, as in *chromo(litho)graph*, *chromosome* (Gr. *sôma* body).

chronic long-continued, inveterate XV; continuous, constant XIX. - F. *chronique* - L. *chronicus* - Gr. *khronikós*, f. *khrónos* time; see -IC.

chronicle register of events in order of time. XIV. ME. *cronikle* - AN. *cronicle*, var. of OF. *cronique* (mod. *chronique*) - L. *chronica* - Gr. *khroniká* annals, sb. use of *khronikós* pert. to time (see prec.).

chrono- comb. form of Gr. *khrónos* time, as in *chronology*, *chronometer*.

chrysalis XVII (occas. with *-ll-*). - L. *chrȳsal(l)is* - Gr. *khrūsallís* gold-coloured sheath of butterflies, f. *khrūsós* gold.

chrysanthemum - L. *chrȳsanthemum* - Gr. *khrūsánthemon*, f. *khrūsós* gold + *ánthemon*, rel. to *ánthos* flower.

chrysolite (in early use) applied to various green gems. XIII. ME. *crisolite* - OF. - medL. *crisolitus*, for L. *chrȳsolithus* - Gr. *khrūsólithos* perh. topaz, f. *khrūsós* gold + *líthos* (see -LITE).

chrysoprase (in early use) golden-green gem, perh. beryl, (in mod. min.) apple-green chalcedony. XIII. ME. *crisopace* - OF. - L. *chrȳsopassus*, var. of *chrȳsoprasus* - Gr. *khrūsóprasos*, f. *khrūsós* gold + *práson* leek.

chub river fish of the carp family, *Leuciscus cephalus*. XV. of unkn. orig.

chubby †thickset XVII; round-faced XVIII. f. CHUB + -Y[1], presumably from the shape of the fish.

chuck[1] (dial.) lump XVII; contrivance for holding work in a lathe XIX. var. of CHOCK. Cf. CHUNK.

chuck[2] give a playful touch under the chin; throw with the hand XVI. Also (dial.) *chock* XVI. perh. - OF. *chuquer*, earlier form of *choquer* knock, bump, of unkn. orig.

chuckle †laugh vehemently XVI; cluck, cackle XVII; laugh in a suppressed manner XIX. perh. *chokelyng* (*c*.1400) repr. an early form; f. *chuck* cluck + -LE[3].

chum one who shares rooms with another, (hence) intimate associate. XVII. prob. short for *chamber-fellow* (XVI), orig. a word of Oxford univ. sl., corr. to the Cambridge *crony*. Hence **chum** vb. share rooms. XVIII.

chump short thick lump of wood XVIII; blockhead XIX. perh. blending of CHUNK and LUMP[1] or STUMP[1].

chunk XVII. prob. alt. of CHUCK[1].

chupatty, chapat(t)i small cake of unleavened bread. XIX. - Hindi *capātī*.

church OE. *ċir(i)ċe*, *ċyr(i)ċe* = OS. *kirika* (Du. *kerk*), OHG. *kirihha* (G. *kirche*) :- WGmc. **kirika* - medGr. *kūrikón*, for *kūriakón*, sb. use (sc. *dôma* house) of n. of *kūriakós* pert. to the Lord, f. *kū́rios* master, lord. Hence **church** vb. present or receive in church. XIV. **churchman** ecclesiastic XVI (earlier XIV *kirkman*); male member of the church (of England) XVII. **churchwarden** XV. **churchyard** XII.

churl †man, husband; free man without rank OE.; †serf; (arch.) peasant, rustic; low base fellow XIII; niggard, miser XVI. OE. *ċeorl* = MLG. *kerle*, (M)Du. *kerel* :- WGmc. **kerla*, rel. to Gmc. **karlaz* CARL. So **churlish** OE. *ċeorlisċ*, *ċierlisċ*; see -ISH[1].

churn butter-making machine. Late OE. *ċyrin*, var. of **ċi(e)rn*, corr. to MLG. *kerne*, *kirne*, MDu. *kerne*, ON. *kirna* :- Gmc. **kernjōn*, of unkn. orig. Hence **churn** vb. XV (also transf. and fig. XVII).

chute rapid fall in a river; steep slope or channel down which stuff is shot. XIX. - F. *chute* fall, refash. of OF. *cheoite*, fem. sb. f. pp. of *cheoir* :- popL. **cadēre*, for L. *cadere* fall; often extended to senses which originated with SHOOT or are still commonly so spelt.

chutney XIX. - Hindi *caṭnī*.

cicada insect, the male of which makes a shrill chirping sound. XIX. - L. *cicāda*, also *cicāla*.

cicatrice scar remaining from a wound. XIV. - (O)F. *cicatrice* or L. *cicātrīx*, *cicātrīc-* (also used in Eng. from XVII).

cicerone guide who shows antiquities, etc. XVIII. - It. *cicerone* :- L. *Cicerō*, *-ōn-* cognomen of the Roman orator Marcus Tullius *Cicero*; orig. applied to learned It. antiquaries.

-cide[1] repr. F. *-cide*, L. *-cīda* -killer, f. *cædere* (*-cīdere*) cut down, kill, as in *homicīda* HOMICIDE[1], *parricīda* PARRICIDE[1].

-cide[2] repr. F. *-cide*, L. *-cīdium* -killing (cf. prec.), as in *homicīdium* HOMICIDE[2], *parricīdium* PARRICIDE[2].

cider †(in biblical use) strong drink (esp. in forms *ciser*, *sicer*); beverage made from apples. XIV. ME. *sither(e)*, *cidre* - OF. *sidre*, earlier *cisdre* (mod. *cidre*) :- ecclL. *sīcera* - ecclGr. *sīkéra* -

Heb. *šēkhār* intoxicating liquor, f. *šākhar* drink heavily.

cigar XVIII (often *segar* till early XIX). - F. *cigare* or its source Sp. *cigarro*, of uncert. orig. So **cigarette** XIX. - F.

cilia (anat.) eyelids, eyelashes. XVIII. - L., pl. of *cilium* (cf. SUPERCILIOUS). So **ciliary** XVII.

cinch saddle-girth (U.S., from Mexican use); (fig.) sure hold, dead certainty. XIX. - Sp. *cincha* :- L. *cingula* girdle, f. *cingere* gird.

cincture †girding XVI; girdle XVII. - L. *cinctūra*, f. *cinct-*, pp. stem of *cingere* gird; see -URE.

cinder scoria, slag OE.; residue of burnt substance XIV. OE. *sinder* = MLG. *sinder*, OHG. *sintar* (G. *sinter*), ON. *sindr*, rel. to OSl. *sędra* stalactite; respelt with *c* from XVI after unrelated F. *cendre* (L. *cinis, ciner-* ashes).

cinematograph XIX. - F. *cinématographe*, f. Gr. *kī́nēma, -mat-* movement, f. *kīneîn* move; see -GRAPH. Abbrev. **cinema** XX (after F. *cinéma*). Comb. form **cine-** XIX; cf. F. *ciné*.

cineraria genus of composite plants. XVI. modL., fem. (sc. *herba* plant) of L. *cinerārius* (see next); so called from the ash-coloured down on the leaves.

cinerary pert. to ashes. XVIII. - L. *cinerārius*, f. *cinis, ciner-* ashes; see -ARY.

cinnabar vermilion XV; red sulphide of mercury XVI. - L. *cinnabaris* - Gr. *kinnábari*.

cinnamon XV. ME. *sinamome* - (O)F. *cinnamome* - L. *cinnamōmum* - Gr. *kinnámōmon*; later refash. after L. *cinnamon, -um* - Gr. *kínnamon*, of Sem. orig. (cf. Heb. *ḳinnāmōn*).

cinquefoil plant *Potentilla reptans*, with leaves of five leaflets. XIII. repr. L. *quinquefolium*, f. *quinque* FIVE + *folium* leaf, FOIL[2].

cipher, cypher A. (arith.) symbol by itself denoting 'nothing' XIV; nonentity; Arabic numeral XVI; B. secret manner of writing; †hieroglyph XVI; literal device, monogram XVII, C. continuous sounding of a note on an organ due to mechanical defect XVIII. ME. *siphre, sipher* - OF. *sif(f)re* (mod. *chiffre*) - medL. *cif(e)ra*, partly through It. *cifra*, †*cifera* f. Arab. *ṣifr* ZERO, sb. use of adj. 'empty', f. *ṣafira* be empty. Hence as vb. work sums; write in cipher. XVI. Cf. DECIPHER.

cipolin an Italian marble. XVIII. - F. *cipolin* or its source It. *cipollino*, f. *cipolla* onion (L. *cēpa*); so called from the resemblance of its foliated structure to the coats of an onion.

circle sb. XIV. ME. *cercle* - (O)F. :- L. *circulus*, dim. of *circus* ring (see CIRCUS); later respelt after L. OE. *circul* was an adoption directly from the Latin, but did not survive. So **circle** vb. XIV. - L. *circulāre*, or from the sb.

circuit distance round XIV; journey through an area, as of judges XV; area of this XVI. - (O)F. - L. *circuitus*, f. *circumīre*, f. CIRCUM- + *īre* go. So **circuitous** XVII.

circular of the form of a circle XV; affecting a 'circle' of persons XVII (circular letter); sb. for 'circular note' XVIII. - AN. *circuler*, OF. *circulier* (mod. *-aire*), learned alt. of *cerclier* :- late L. *circulāris*, f. *circulus* CIRCLE; further latinized in Eng. (XVI). See -AR. So **circulate** †subject to repeated distillation XV; †encircle XVI; move or turn round; pass continuously from place to place XVII. f. pp. stem of L. *circulāre*, f. *circulus*; see -ATE[3]. **circulation** XVI. - F. or L.

circum- repr. L. *circum-*, being the adv. and prep. *circum* round (about), around (orig. acc. of *circus* circle, CIRCUS), used as the first el. of many comp. verbs and sbs.

circumcise XIII. - OF. *circonciser* or f. F. *circoncis-*, stem of *circoncire* - L. *circumcīdere*, f. CIRCUM- + *cædere* cut. So **circumcision** XII.

circumference XIV. - (O)F. *circonférence* - L. *circumferentia*; see CIRCUM-, -FEROUS.

circumflex XVI. - L. *circumflexus* (pp. of *circumflectere* bend round; cf. FLEX[1]), tr. Gr. *perispṓmenos* drawn round, f. *perí* PERI- + *spân* draw (cf. SPASM).

circumjacent lying around. XV. - L. *circumjacent-*, prp. stem of *circumjacēre*; see CIRCUM-, ADJACENT.

circumlocution XV. - F. *circonlocution* or L. *circumlocutiō, -ōn-*, lit. rendering of Gr. *períphrasis* PERIPHRASIS; see CIRCUM-, LOCUTION. Hence **circumlocutory** XVII.

circumscribe draw a line round; describe (a figure) about another; delimit. XV. - L. *circumscrībere*, f. *circum* around + *scrībere* write (see CIRCUM-, SCRIBE). So **circumscription** XV.

circumspect XV. - L. *circumspectus* (of things) well considered, (of persons) considerate, cautious, pp. of *circumspicere* look round, f. CIRCUM- + *specere* look. So **circumspection** circumspect action. XIV (rare before XVI).

circumstance (pl.) adjuncts of an action XIII; condition of affairs XIV; formality, ceremony; accessory matter, detail. - (O)F. *circonstance*, †*circun-* or L. *circumstantia*, f. prp. of *circumstāre* stand around, surround; see CIRCUM-, STAND. Hence **circumstantial** XVI.

circumvallation (construction of) a rampart or entrenchment round a place. XVII. - late L. *circumvallātiō, -ōn-*, f. *circumvallāre*, f. CIRCUM- + *vallum* rampart, WALL; see -ATION.

circumvent encompass with evil or hostility; overreach, outwit. XV. f. *circumvent-*, pp. stem of L. *circumvenīre* surround, beset, deceive, f. CIRCUM- + *venīre* COME. So **circumvention** XV.

circumvolution revolution, rotation XV; winding or rolling round XVI. f. L. *circumvolvere* wind round, after *revolution*.

circus building surrounded with rising tiers of seats XVI; circular area for equestrian and acrobatic feats; circular range for houses XVIII. - L. *circus* circle, circus = Gr. *kírkos, kríkos* ring, circle, prob. rel. to L. *curvus* CURVE.

cirque circus XVII; (poet.) circle, ring XVII; natural amphitheatre XIX. - F. - L. *circus*.

cirrhosis (path.) disease of the liver occurring in spirit-drinkers, orig. so called from the presence of yellow granules. XIX. - modL., f. Gr. *kirrhós* orange-tawny; see -OSIS.

cirrus (bot.) tendril; (zool.) filamentary appendage XVIII; form of cloud having the appearance of wisps XIX. - L., 'curl'; comb. form **cirro-** (see -O-), as in *cirro-cumulus, -stratus* XIX.

Cistercian pert. to (a monk of) the Benedictine order of Cîteaux, founded 1098. XVII. - F.

Cistercien, f. L. *Cistercium* Cîteaux, near Dijon, France (cf. medL. *Cisterciensis*); see -IAN.

cistern XIII. - OF. *cisterne* (mod. *citerne*) :- L. *cisterna*, f. *cista* CHEST; perh. of Etruscan orig., with suffix as in *caverna* CAVERN, *taberna* TAVERN.

citadel XVI. - F. *citadelle* or It. *citadella*, dim. of *cittade*, obs. var. of *città* :- L. *cīvitās*, *-āt-* CITY.

cite summon officially XV; quote, adduce as an authority XVI. - (O)F. *citer* - L. *citāre*, frequent. of *ciēre*, *cīre* set in motion, call, rel. to Gr. *kíō* I go, *kīneîn* move, OE. *hātan* call. So **citation** summons XIII; quotation XVII.

cither (var. of foll.) XVIII. - (O)F. *cithare* or G. *zither* (cf. ZITHER) - L. *cithara* - Gr. *kithárā*.

cithern, cittern instrument of the guitar kind. XVI. - L. *cithara* (see above), crossed with GITTERN.

citizen XIV. - AN. *citezein*, alt. of OF. *citeain* (mod. *citoyen*) :- Rom. **cīvitātānus*, f. L. *cīvitās*, *-āt-* CITY.

citric derived from the citron. XVIII. - F. *citrique*, f. L. *citrus*; see next and -IC. So **citrate** XVIII; see -ATE[2].

citron (tree bearing) fruit like a lemon but larger and less acid. XVI. - (O)F. *citron*, f. (after *limon* LEMON) L. *citrus*.

city †town XIII; town of ecclesiastical or political importance XIV. ME. *cite* - (O)F. *cité* :- L. *cīvitās*, *-āt-* state, city, f. *cīvis* citizen (see CIVIC).

civet (quadruped yielding) the musky secretion called by the same name. XVI. - F. *civette* - It. *zibetto* - medL. *zibethum* - Arab. *zabād* (the secretion). Also *civet-cat* XVII.

civic pert. to a citizen or citizens XVI; of a city XVII; of citizenship, civil XVIII. - F. *civique* or L. *cīvicus*, f. *cīvis* citizen; see HIDE[2], and -IC. As sb. pl. (after *politics*) XIX (orig. U.S.).

civil A. of citizens XIV; befitting a citizen, refined XVI; courteous XVII; B. non-ecclesiastical XVI; non-military XVII. - (O)F. - L. *cīvīlis*, f. *cīvis* citizen; see CIVIC and -ILE. So **civility** XIV. - (O)F. *civilité* - L. *cīvīlitās*. **civilize** XVII. - F. *civiliser*; hence **civilization** XVIII.

civilian student or professor of civil law XIV; †follower of civil (i.e. natural, unregenerate) righteousness XVII; non-military man XVIII. - OF. *civilien*, f. *civil*; see CIVIL, -IAN.

clack chatter XIII; make a clattering noise XVI. prob. - ON. *klaka* twitter, (of birds) chatter; of imit. orig.; cf. Du. *klakken* crack, F. *claquer*. Hence **clack** sb. clatter of talk XV; clapping or clacking noise XVI.

clad see CLOTHE.

claim vb. XIII. - OF. *claim-*, tonic stem of *clamer* cry, call, appeal :- L. *clāmāre* cry, call, proclaim, rel. to *clārus* CLEAR. So **claim** sb. XIII. Hence **claimant** XVIII; primarily a legal term, after *appellant*, *defendant*.

clairvoyance XIX. - F., f. *clairvoyant* (in Eng. also XIX), f. *clair* CLEAR + *voyant*, prp. of *voir* see (see VISION).

clam clamp XIV; bivalve shell-fish XVI (*clam-shell*). OE. *clam* bond, fetter, corr. to OHG. *klamma* (G. dial. *klamm*), and MHG., G. *klemme*, Du. *klemme*, *klem*, f. Gmc. **klam-* press or squeeze together.

clamber XV. Of frequent. form, prob. f. *clamb*, obs. pt. of CLIMB; see -ER[4].

clammy XIV. f. (with -Y[1]) *clam* (XIV) smear, daub, a new formation on *clammed*, pt. and pp. of OE. *clǣman* smear, anoint, daub = MDu. *klēmen*, OHG. *kleimen*, ON. *kleima* daub, plaster :- Gmc. **klaimjan*, f. **klaimaz* clay, f. base repr. by CLAY.

clamour sb. XIV. - AN. *clamur*, OF. *clamour* - L. *clāmor*, *-ōr-*, rel. to *clāmāre*; see CLAIM and -OUR. Hence **clamour** vb. XIV.

clamp[1] brace or band of metal. XIV. prob. of LG. orig.; cf. Du., LG. *klamp*, †*klampe*, f. **klamp-*, by-form of **klamb-* (cf. CLIMB), **klam-* (cf. CLAM). Hence **clamp** vb. XVII.

clamp[2] stack of bricks XVI; (agric.) stack of earth, turf, etc. XVIII. prob. - MDu. *klamp* heap, rel. to CLUMP.

clan group of associated families in Scotland bearing the same name. XIV (Sc. *clen*). - Gaelic *clann* offspring, family, race, corr. to OIr. *cland*, (mod.) *clann* - L. *planta* sprout, scion, PLANT.

clandestine XVI. - F. *clandestin* or L. *clandestīnus*, f. *clam* secretly.

clang sb. XVI. imit. formation parallel to (O)HG. *klang*. Also as vb. XVI; perh. partly - L. *clangere* resound (as a trumpet).

clango(u)r XVI. - L. *clangor*, f. *clangere*, rel. to Gr. *klaggḗ* loud cry. Hence **clangorous** XVIII.

clank sb. XVII. imit. formation parallel to MLG., (M)Du. *klank*, OHG. *klang*. Cf. prec. and CLINK[1]. Also as vb. XVII.

clap[1] make a sharp, forcible, or resounding noise. OE. *clappian* throb, beat = MLG. *klappen*, OHG. *klapfōn*, ON. *klappa* beside OE. *clæppan* = MLG. *kleppen*, OHG. *klepfen*; also OE. *clæpp-*, *cleppet(t)an*; of imit. orig.

clap[2] (sl.) gonorrhoea. XVI. of uncert. orig.; cf. OF. *clapoir* venereal bubo.

clarence four-wheeled four-seated carriage. XIX. Named after the Duke of *Clarence*, afterwards William IV.

clarendon (typogr.) thick-faced type. XIX. Named after the *Clarendon* Press, which was first housed in the *Clarendon* Building at Oxford, erected with funds partly provided by the profits of the sale of the Earl of *Clarendon*'s history of 'the Rebellion and Civil Wars in England' (1647).

claret XIV. orig. qualifying *wine*, after OF. *vin claret* (mod. *clairet*), which superseded OF. *claré* :- medL. *clārātum* (sc. *vinum*) 'clarified wine', n. pp. of *clārāre*, f. L. *clārus* CLEAR.

clarify †illumine, make illustrious XIV; make clear XV. - (O)F. *clarifier* - late L. *clārificāre*, f. *clārus* CLEAR; see -FY.

clarion kind of trumpet. XIV. - medL. *clāriō*, *-ōn-*, f. L. *clārus* CLEAR; cf. OF. *claron* (mod. *clairon*). Hence **clarionet** XVIII; partly alt. of **clarinet** - F. *clarinette*, f. *clarine*, sb. use of fem. of †*clarin*, f. *clair* CLEAR.

clarity †lustre, splendour XVI; clearness XVII. - L. *clāritās*, f. *clārus* CLEAR; see -ITY.

clash sb. XVI. imit. Also as vb. XVI.

clasp sb. fastening consisting of interlocking parts; vb. secure with this. XIV. of unkn. orig.

class division of persons or things. XVII. Prob.

first in gen. use in the sense 'division of pupils in a school', and immed. - L. *classis* each of the six ancient divisions of the Roman people, body of citizens under arms, spec. fleet. Cf. (O)F. *classe*. Hence **class** vb. XVIII. So **classification** XVIII (- F.), whence **classify** XVIII.

classic of the first rank; of the standard authors of ancient Greece or Rome XVII; sb. (esp. pl.) ancient Gr. or L. writer XVIII. - F. *classique* or L. *classicus*, f. *classis* CLASS; see -IC. So **classical** XVI.

clatter XIV. OE. **clatrian*, implied in *clatrung*, corr. to (M)Du. *klateren* rattle, chatter, frequent. formation (see -ER[4]) on imit. base **klat-*.

clause short sentence XIII; article or proviso XIV. - (O)F. *clause* = Gallo-Rom. **clausa*, for L. *clausula* close of a rhetorical period, (later) conclusion of a legal formula, section of a law, fem. dim. of *claus-*, pp. stem of *claudere* CLOSE.

claustral of a cloister. XV. - late L. *claustrālis*, f. *claustrum* CLOISTER; see -AL[1].

claustrophobia XIX. f. *claustro-*, taken as comb. form (see -O-) of L. *claustrum* CLOISTER + -PHOBIA.

clavichord string-and-key instrument. XV. - medL. *clāvichordium*, f. L. *clāvis* key + *chorda* string, CHORD.

clavicle collar-bone. XVII. - L. *clāvicula* key, dim. of *clāvis* key.

clavier keyboard XVIII; keyboard instrument XIX. - F. *clavier* (or its deriv. G. *klavier*) - medL. **clāviārius* (see -ARY), f. *clāvis* key.

claw sb. OE. *clawu* (new formation on the obl. cases, the orig. nom. being **clēa*, whence ME. and dial. *clee*) = OS. *clāuua*, OHG. *klāwa* (G. *klaue*) :- WGmc. **klǣwō*. Hence **claw** vb. OE. *clawian* = MLG. *klāwen*, OHG. *klāwēn*.

clay OE. *clǣġ* = (M)LG., (M)Du. *klei* :- WGmc. **klaijo-*, f. **klai-* **klei-* **kli-*, repr. also by OE. *clām*, mod. dial. *cloam* mud, clay, OE. *clǣman* (see CLAMMY); IE. **gloi-* **glei-* **gli-* as in Gr *glía*, *glínē*, L. *glūs*, *glūten* (see GLUE).

claymore Highlander's two-edged broad-sword. XVIII. f. Gaelic *claidheamh* sword + *mór* great.

-cle terminal el. repr. F. *-cle* - L. *-culus*, *-a*, *-um* -CULE, as in *article*, *follicle*, *versicle*.

clean OE. *clǣne* = OS. *klēni*, OHG. *kleini* clear, delicate, small (G. *klein* small) :- WGmc. **klaini*. The historically orig. sense 'clear, pure' is most nearly preserved by Eng. among the mod. langs. Hence **cleanly** adj. and adv. OE. *clǣnlīċ*, *-līċe*; see -LY[1], -LY[2]. **cleanse** OE. *clǣnsian*.

clear XIII. ME. *clēr* - OF. *cler* (mod. *clair*) :- L. *clārus* bright, clear, manifest. Hence **clear** vb. XIV, **clearance** XVI.

cleat wedge XV; (naut.) block round which a rope is secured XVIII. Formally repr. OE. **clēat* = MLG. **klōt* (Du. *kloot* ball), OHG. *klōz* clod, lump, etc. (G. *kloss* dumpling) :- WGmc. **klauta* (cf. CLOT); but the naut. sense in Eng. is unexpl.

cleave[1] cut asunder, split. OE. *clēofan* str. vb. = OS. *kliođan*, OHG. *kliuban* (G. *klieben*), ON. *kljúfa* :- Gmc. **kleuban*, f. IE. base **gleubh-* (cf. Gr. *glúphein* hollow out, L. *glūbere* peel). Hence **cleaver** XVI.

cleave[2] stick fast, adhere. The present form repr. OE. *cleofian*, *clifian* = OS. *kliđon*, OHG. *klebēn* (G. *kleben*) :- WGmc. wk. vb. **kliđōjan*, *-ǣjan*, f. **kliđ-*, the strong form of which is repr. by OE. *clīfan* = OS. *biklīđan* (Du. *beklijven*), OHG. *klīban*, ON. *klífa*; f. Gmc. **klī-* stick, adhere (cf. CLAY, CLIMB). *Cleft* dates from XVII.

clef (mus.) symbol marking the pitch of notes on a given line of a stave. XVI. - F. :- L. *clāvis* key.

cleft fissure, split. XIII. Earliest form *clift* (cf. OE. *-clyft*, OHG. *kluft*; f. base of CLEAVE[1]); the present form, due to assim. to *cleft*, pp. of CLEAVE[1], dates from XVI.

clematis XVI. - L. *clēmatis* - Gr. *klēmatís*, f. *klêma* vine-branch.

clement XV. - L. *clēmēns*, *-ent-*, of unkn. orig. So **clemency** XV. - L. *clēmentia*.

clench fix or grasp firmly XIII; close tightly (the fist, etc.) XVIII. OE. *-clenċan* = OHG. *klenken* :- Gmc. **klaŋkjan*, f. **klaŋk-* **kleŋk-* **kluŋk-*, parallel to **klaŋg-*, etc. (see CLING). Cf. CLINCH.

clerestory row of lights above the arches or triforium of a church. XV. f. CLEAR + STOREY.

clergy A. body of ordained men in the Church; B. learning (survived in legal phr. *benefit of clergy*). XIII. repr. two F. words, (O)F. *clergé* :- ecclL. *clēricātus*, f. *clēricus* (see CLERK, -ATE[1]), and (O)F. *clergie*, f. *clerc* CLERK + *-ie* -Y[3].

cleric adj. clerical; sb. clergyman. XVII. - ecclL. *clēricus* - Gr. *klērikós* (eccl.) belonging to the Christian ministerial order, f. *klêros* lot, heritage, as used (e.g.) in Acts 1: 17 'the lot (*klêros*) of this ministry'. So **clerical** of the clergy XVI; of a clerk or penman XVIII. - ecclL. *clēricālis*, f. *clēricus*.

clerk ordained minister of the Church XI; learned man, scholar XIII; lay officer of a church (e.g. *singing c.*, *parish c.*); one having charge of records, correspondence, or accounts XVI. Late OE. *cler(i)c* - ecclL. *clēricus* CLERIC; this merged with ME. *clerc* - (O)F. *clerc*, of the same orig. The sp. *clark* appears XV. Hence **clerkly** adj. XVI; modelled on **clerkly** adv. XV, which is after late L. *clēricāliter*; see -LY[1], -LY[2].

clever adroit, dexterous (XIII?) XVI; (dial.) nimble, active; lithe, handsome XVII; (dial.) convenient, agreeable, nice XVIII. The context of the earliest ex. (in the form *cliuer*) suggests etym. connection with †*cliver* claw, as if 'sharp to seize'; rare Sc. *cleverous* apt to seize, similarly assoc. with *cluik* claw, precedes the earliest ex. of *clever* in the mod. period. Cf. LG. *klöver*, *klever*, MDu. *klever* sprightly, smart.

clew (arch.) ball, esp. of thread OE.; (naut.) corner of a sail to which tacks and sheets are made fast XVI. OE. *cliwen*, *cleowen* = MLG., Du. *kluwen*, f. base of OHG. *kliuwi*, *kliuwa*, MHG. *kliuwel(īn)*; prob. ult. rel. to CLAW. See CLUE.

cliché stereotype block; stereotyped phrase, literary tag. XIX. - F., sb. use of pp. of *clicher* stereotype.

click sb. and vb. XVII. ult. imit.; cf. OF. *clique* tick of a clock, *cliquer* vb.

client one under the protection of a patron XIV; one for whom an advocate pleads XV; customer XVII. - L. *cliēns*, *client-*, earlier *cluēns*, sb. use of prp. of *cluere, cluēre* hear, listen; see LISTEN. So **clientele**, orig. (XVI) - L. *clientēla*, but obs. in XVII and readopted from F. XIX.

cliff XII. OE. *clif* = OS. (Du.) *klif*, OHG. *klep*, ON. *klif* :- Gmc. *klibam*; of unkn. orig.

climacteric pert. to a critical period (in human life); also sb. XVI (formerly often *climateric*). - F. *climatérique* or L. *clīmactēricus* - Gr. *klīmaktērikós*, f. *klîmax, klīmak-* ladder + *-tēr* agent-suffix. Also **climacterical** XVI.

climate belt of the earth's surface between two parallels of latitude XIV; (region having certain) atmospheric conditions XVII. - (O)F. *climat* or late L. *clīma, clīmat-* - Gr. *klíma, klímat-*, f. **klī-* as in *klīnein* slope, LEAN[2]. Hence **climatic** XIX.

climax (rhet.) ascending series of expressions XVI; culmination, highest point XVIII. - late L. *clīmax* - Gr. *klīmax* ladder, f. **klī-* (see prec.).

climb OE. *climban* (str. vb.) = (M)LG., (M)Du. *klimmen*, OHG. *klimban* (G. *klimmen*) :- WGmc. **klimban*, nasalized var. of **kliban* (see CLEAVE[2]).

clime XVI (now arch.). - late L. *clīma* CLIMATE.

clinch var. of CLENCH, now differentiated for certain meanings. XVI.

cling †coagulate, congeal; †shrink, wither OE.; adhere, stick, cleave XIII. OE. *clingan* (str. vb.), corr. to MDu. *klingen* stick, adhere, beside OE. *clengan*, ME. *clenge* adhere, cling; f. Gmc. **klaŋg- *kliŋg- *kluŋg-*; see CLENCH.

clinic adj. pert. to the sick-bed XVII; sb. bed-ridden person XVII; private or specialized hospital XIX. - L. *clīnicus* - Gr. *klīnikós*, f. *klīnē* bed; see -IC. So **clinical** XVIII.

clink[1] make a sharp metallic sound. XIV. prob. - (M)Du. *klinken* sound, ring, rel. to MLG., (M)Du. *klank* sound (cf. CLANK), and parallel to OHG. *klank* (G. *klang*); cf. CLANG. Hence **clink** sb. XIV.

clink[2] name of a prison in Southwark; (gen.) prison. XVI. of unkn. orig.

clinker[1] very hard kind of brick XVII; mass of slag or lava XVIII. Earlier *klincard, clincart* - early modDu. *klinckaerd* (now *klinker*), f. *klinken* CLINK[1]; so called because the brick rings when struck.

clinker[2] applied to boats of which the planks are overlapped and secured with clinched nails. XVI. f. *klink*, var. of CLINCH + -ER[1]; prob. infl. by LG., Du. *klinken* rivet. *Clincher-built* has varied with *clinker-built* from XVIII.

clinometer instrument for measuring slopes. XIX. f. *clino-*, used as comb. form of stem of Gr. *klīnein* slope (see LEAN[2]) + -METER.

clip[1] embrace, grip, clutch. OE. *clyppan* = OFris. *kleppa* :- WGmc. **kluppjan*, rel. to Lith. *glóbti* embrace. Hence **clip** sb. instrument that clips or grips. XV.

clip[2] cut, shear XII; mutilate (coin) XIV; cut short (words) XVI; move rapidly XVII. - ON. *klippa*, prob. imit. of the sound produced.

clipper fast-sailing vessel. XIX. f. CLIP[2] in the sense 'move quickly'; prob. infl. by CUTTER.

clique small exclusive set. XVIII. - (O)F., f. OF. *cliquer* make a noise - (M)Du. *klikken* (see CLICK).

cloaca sewer XVIII; (anat.) excretory canal XIX. - L. *cloāca, cluāca*. earlier *clovāca*, rel. to *cluere* cleanse, f. IE. **klu- *kleu- *klou-*, repr. also by OE. *hlūt(t)or* pure, Gr. *klúzein* wash, bathe. So **cloacal** XVII.

cloak sb. XIII. - OF. *cloke, cloque*, dial. var. of *cloche* bell, cloak :- medL. *clocca* (VII), perh. of Ir. origin (cf. CLOCK). Hence **cloak** vb. XVI.

clock XIV. Introduced by Flemish clockmakers imported by Edward I. - MLG., MDu. *klocke* (LG., Du. *klok*), corr. to OE. *clucge*, OFris. *klokke*, OHG. *glocka* (G. *glocke* bell), ON. *klokka, klukka*; Gmc. - medL. *clocca* bell (cf. CLOAK).

clod †clot of blood XIV; lump of earth, etc. XV. In OE. in *clodhamer* fieldfare, *Clodhangra* (place-name); corr. to (M)HG. *klotz*. Hence **clod-hopper** †ploughman, country lout XVII; (pl.) heavy shoes XIX.

clog (dial.) block of wood XIV; wooden-soled shoe XV. of unkn. orig. Hence **clog** vb. fetter, hamper, encumber. XIV.

cloisonné (of enamels) divided into compartments. XIX. pp. of F. *cloisonner*, f. *cloison* partition :- Rom. **clausiō, -ōn-*, f. L. *claus-* (see CLOSE).

cloister enclosure, close XIII; convent, covered walk (esp. round a court) XIV. - OF. *clo(i)stre* (mod. *cloitre*) :- L. *claustrum, clōstrum* bolt, place, f. *claud-*, stem of *claudere* CLOSE, + *-trum*, instr. suffix.

close sb. enclosed space, enclosure XIII; adj. closed, shut up XIV. - (O)F. *clos* :- L. *clausus*, pp. of *claudere* shut, close. So **close** vb. stop an opening. XIII. f. *clos-*, ppl. stem of (O)F. *clore* :- L. *claudere*.

closet private room XIV; cabinet, cupboard, privy XVII. - OF., dim. of *clos*; see prec. and -ET.

closure †barrier, fence XIV; †ENCLOSURE XV; conclusion, close XVI. - OF. :- late L. *clausūra*, f. *claus-*; see CLOSE, -URE. In the last sense a new formation on CLOSE.

clot lump, esp. one formed by coagulation. OE. *clot(t)* = MHG. *kloz* (G. *klotz*) :- WGmc. **klutt-*, f. **klut- *kleut- *klaut-*; cf. CLEAT, CLOUT.

cloth A. piece of woven or felted stuff OE.; the stuff or material itself (in these two uses with mod. pl. *cloths*) XIV; B. †(coll.) clothing, raiment XII, equivalent to **clothes**, OE. *clāðas*, ME. *clāþes, clōþes*. OE. *clāð* = MDu. *kleet* (Du. *kleed*), MHG. *kleit* (G. *kleid*); cf. ON. *klæði*; of unkn. orig. So **clothe** vb., pt., pp. **clothed** and (arch.) **clad** provide with clothes. XII. ME. *clāþen*, pointing to OE. **clāðian*, f. *clāð*.

cloud †hill, rock OE.; visible mass of watery vapour in the air XIII. OE. *clūd*, prob. rel. to CLOD. Hence **cloud** vb. XVI.

clough ravine. OE. *clōh* (in place-names) :- Gmc. **klaŋχ-*, rel. to OHG. *klinga* (G. dial. *klinge*) ravine.

clout †patch, metal plate OE.; piece of cloth XIII; (from the vb.) blow with the hand XIV. OE. *clūt*, corr. to (M)LG., MDu. *klūt(e)* (Du. *kluit* lump, clod), ON. *klútr* kerchief; rel. to CLEAT, CLOT. Hence **clout** vb. patch OE. (*clūtian*, in pp. *ġeclūtod*) cuff heavily XIV.

clove[1] one of the divisions of the bulb of garlic, etc. OE. *clufu*, corr. to the first element of OS. *cluflōk* 'clove-leek', garlic, OHG. *klobolouch* (G.

knoblauch), f. weak grade of Gmc. **kleub-* (see CLEAVE[1]).

clove[2] dried flower-bud of tropical myrtle. XIV. orig. *clow (of) gilofer* - (O)F. *clou de girofle (gilofre)* 'nail of clove-tree', so called from its shape; see GILLYFLOWER. The change from *clow* to *clove* is difficult to account for.

cloven str. pp. of CLEAVE[1], now mainly restricted to adj. use (e.g. *cloven hoof*).

clover OE. *clāfre* = (M)LG., Du. *klāver* :- Gmc. **klaibrōn*, the first syll. of which corr. to OS. *klē*, OHG. *klēo* (G. *klee*) :- WGmc. **klaiwa* clover. The common XV-XVII var. *claver* may repr. OE. *clǣfre*, or may be of LG. or Du. orig.

clown rustic, ill-bred man; fool or buffoon, esp. on the stage. XVI. perh. of LG. orig.; cf. NFris. *klönne*, *klünne* clumsy fellow, *klünj* clod, lump, and the like.

cloy †nail XIV; †clog, obstruct XVI; surfeit, satiate XVI. Aphetic of †*acloy* - AN. *acloyer*, var. of OF. *encloyer* (mod. *enclouer*) :- Rom. **inclāvāre*, f. L. *in* EN-[1] + *clāvus* nail, rel. to *clāvis* key, *claudere* CLOSE.

club heavy stick XIII; stick used in ball-games XV; (tr. It. *bastone*, Sp. *baston* BATON) suit at cards XVI; combination or association of persons XVII. - ON. *klubba* (*klumba*) club, rel. to CLUMP.

cluck vb. XVII. corr. to MHG. *klucken*, Da. *klukke*, Sw. *klucka*, imit. formation to which there are parallel forms with the vowel *o*, OE. *cloccian*, MDu. *clocken* (Du. *klokken*), Sw. dial. *klokka*.

clue later form (XV) of CLEW, now restricted mainly to the sense 'fact, etc., leading (through a difficulty) to a solution or discovery'.

clumber breed of spaniel. XIX. f. *Clumber*, name of a seat of the duke of Newcastle, in Nottinghamshire.

clump compact mass of trees XVI; transf. of other things XVII. - MLG. *klumpe* (LG. *klump*), rel. to MDu. *klompe* (Du. *klomp*) lump, mass, and OE. *clympre* (mod. dial. *clumper*) lump of metal, and further to CLAMP[2]; cf. CLUB.

clumsy †benumbed; moving as if benumbed, awkward in action. XVI. f. (dial.) *clumse* benumb (XIII), prob. of Scand. orig.

Cluniac pert. to (a monk of) the monastery of Cluny. XVII. - medL. *Cluniacus*, f. *Clun(i)æum* Cluny, France; see -AC.

cluster sb. OE. *clyster*, (rare) *cluster* bunch of grapes, prob. f. Gmc. **klut-* (see CLOT).

clutch[1] †crook, bend; seize with claws, seize eagerly. XIV. ME. *clucche*, repr. OE. *clyċċan* crook, clench. Hence **clutch** sb. claw; grasp. XVI.

clutch[2] laying or sitting of eggs, brood of young birds. XVIII. prob. southern dial. var. of synon. north. *cletch* (XVII), rel. obscurely to *cleck* hatch (XV; chiefly Sc.) - ON. *klekja*; assoc. with CLUTCH[1].

clutter †clotted mass XVI; confused mass or crowd, noisy turmoil, confused noise XVII. var. of †*clotter* (XIV), †*clodder* (XV), f. CLOT, CLOD; see -ER[4]; assoc. to some extent with *cluster* and *clatter*. So as vb. XVI.

clypeus (ent.) shield-shaped part of the head of insects. XIX. var. of L. *clipeus*, *clupeus* shield.

co- var. of COM- used before vowels, *h*, and *gn*, as in L. *coalescere* COALESCE, *cognātus* COGNATE, *cohērēs* CO-HEIR; in extensive use from XVII as a living formative in the senses 'together', 'in common', 'joint(ly)', 'reciprocally'. In math. repr. *complement*, in the sense '... of the complement', 'complement of ...', as in COSINE, etc.

coacervation heaping together. XIV. - L. *coacervātiō*, *-ōn-*, f. *coacervāre*, f. CO- + *acervus* heap; see -ATION.

coach large carriage XVI; private tutor (orig. university sl.), instructor in sport and athletics XIX. - F. *coche*. A common European word since XVI, e.g. G. *kutsche*, Du. *koets*, Sp., Pg. *coche*, It. *cocchio*, Pol. *kocz*; ult. - Hungarian *kocsi*, adj. f. *Kocs* name of a town near Raab in Hungary.

coadjutor XV. - (O)F. *coadjuteur*, †*-tor* - late L. *coadjūtor*, f. CO- + *adjūtor* helper (see ADJUTANT).

coagulate XVII. f. pp. stem of L. *coāgulāre*, f. *coāgulum* rennet, f. **coagere* drive together; see COGENT, -ATE[3]. So **coagulation** XV.

coal †glowing piece of wood OE.; †charcoal XIII; black mineral used for fuel XIII (orig. *seacoal*). OE. *col*, corr. to OFris., MLG. *kole*, MDu. *cole* (Du. *kool*), OHG. *kol(o)* (G. *kohle*), ON. *kol*, of uncert. orig.

coalesce XVI. - L. *coalēscere*, f. CO- + *alēscere* grow up, f. *alere* nourish. So **coalition** XVII. - medL.

coalmouse, colemouse the bird *Parus ater*. OE. *colmāse*, corr. to MDu. *koolmēze* (Du. *koolmees*), MHG. *kolemeise* (G. *kohlmeise*), f. *col* COAL (with allusion to its black cap) + *māse* (see TITMOUSE).

coaming (naut.) raised edges of hatches, etc. XVII. of unkn. orig.

coarse †ordinary, common XIV; wanting in fineness or delicacy XVI. Earliest forms *cors(e)*, *course*; the present form appears XVII, but is anticipated by †*cowarce* (XVI); the earliest application is to cloth or clothes; of unkn. orig.

coast †tract, region XIII; †quarter, direction; †side; sea-shore XIV; (N. Amer.) toboggan slide XVIII. ME. *cost(e)* - OF. *coste* (mod. *côte*) :- L. *costa* rib, flank, side. So **coast** vb. †keep or move by the side or coast of; †border *upon* XIV; †traverse, scour XV; (U.S.) slide down a slope on a sled (also in transf. use) XIX.

coat man's outer garment XIII; natural covering XIV. ME. *cote* - OF. *cote* (mod. *cotte*) :- Rom. **cotta* - Frankish **kotta* (cf. OHG. *kozzo* (G. *kotze*) coarse woollen garment or stuff, OS. *cot* woollen coat or cloak), of unkn. orig.

coati Amer. mammal resembling civet and racoon. XVII. - Tupi *coati*, *coatim*, f. *cua* cincture + *tim* nose.

coax †fool, take in; pet, fondle XVI; wheedle XVII. orig. 'make a *cokes* (i.e. fool) of'; of unkn. orig.

cob in many applications which can be mostly grouped under the headings 'head' and 'roundish object, round clump', among the earliest being 'great man, leader' (XV), 'male swan' (XVI), *cob-nut* (XVI); loaf with a round head (XVII); the application to a stout short-legged horse (XIX) has been referred to dial. *cobs* testicles. of obscure orig.; in AL. *cobus* cob-loaf (XIII); cf.

WFlem. *kobbe* tuft of feathers, head of hair, dome of the head, WFris. *kobbe* drop.

cobalt XVII (*cobolt*). - G. *kobalt*, *-old*, disparaging application of MHG. *kobolt* (mod. *kobold*) fairy or demon of the mine, from the miners' belief that cobalt ore was deleterious to the silver ores in which it occurred.

cobble[1] rounded stone XV (in earliest exx. *c.-stone*, also †*cobled stone*); pl. small coal XIX. f. COB + -LE[1].

cobbler XIII. of unkn. orig. Hence **cobble**[2] vb. mend roughly, patch up XV.

coble (Sc.) boat used esp. for salmon-fishing XIII; (north. Eng.) sea fishing-boat XIII. In AL. *cobellum* (XIII), *cobla* (XIV); poss. of Celt. orig. (cf. W. *ceubal* ferry-boat, skiff, Bret. *caubal*).

cobra XIX. Short for *cobra* (*de*) *capello* (XVII) hooded snake - Pg. *cobra* (:- L. *colubra*) snake, *de* with, *capello* hood (:- medL. *cappellus*, dim. of *cappa* CAPE[1]).

cobweb spider's web. XIV. ME. *cop(pe)web*, f. *coppe* :- OE. (*āt(t)ōr*)*coppe* (*āt(t)ōr* poison) = MDu. *koppe*; see WEB.

coca shrub, *Erythroxylon coca*, of which the dried leaves are used as a masticatory, etc. XVI. - Sp. - Quechua *cuca*. Hence **cocaine** alkaloid occurring in the leaves of the coca; see -INE[5].

coccus pl. **cocci** insect of the genus so named XVIII; (bot.) carpel of a dried fruit XIX (earlier *coccum*); (med.) rounded form of bacterium XIX. - modL. - Gr. *kókkos* berry, seed.

coccyx (anat.) terminal bone of the spinal column. XVII. - L. - Gr. *kókkux* CUCKOO (the bone being supposed to resemble a cuckoo's bill).

cochineal dye-stuff consisting of the dried bodies of a S. American insect, which was at first supposed to be a berry. XVI. - F. *cochenille* or Sp. *cochinilla*, which is gen. referred to L. *coccinus* scarlet (Gr. *kókkos* kermes).

cochlea spiral cavity of the internal ear. XVII. - L. *coc(h)lea* snail-shell, screw - Gr. *kokhlías*, prob. rel. to *kógkhē* CONCH.

cock[1] male domestic fowl OE.; male bird XIV; in various transf. applications, the earliest (XV) being 'spout, tap' paralleled by G. *hahn* cock; the latter, like Du. *haan*, is also used, as *cock* is (XVI), for the discharging mechanism of firearms. OE. *cocc*, *kok* = ON. *kokkr*, prob. f. medL. *coccus*, of imit. orig.; reinforced in ME. by (O)F. *coq*. The native Gmc. word is repr. by OE. *hana* (see HEN). Hence **cock** vb. set or stick up (assertively) XVII; prob. from the attitude of fighting-cocks; whence a new sb. upward turn. XVIII.

cock[2] heap of hay. XIV. immed. source uncertain; perh. Scand. (cf. Norw. *kok* heap, lump, Da. dial. *kok* haycock, Sw. *koka* clod), but an OE. **cocc* hill has been assumed for the place-names *Cookham* (*Coccham* VIII), *Coughton* (*Cocton* XIII). Hence as vb. XIV.

cockade rosette, etc., worn in the hat as a badge. XVII (in *cockared cap*), XVIII (*cockard*, *cockade*). - F. *cocarde*, orig. in phr. *bonnet à la coquarde* cap worn assertively on one side; fem. of †*coquard* proud, saucy, as sb. coxcomb, f. *coq* COCK[1]; see -ARD. The ending was assim. to -ADE.

cock-a-hoop orig. in phr. *set cock a hoop* denoting some action preliminary to hard drinking. XVI. of unkn. orig.

cockalorum self-important little man XVIII; *hey cockalorum* cry in certain games XIX. f. COCK[1] in the sense 'leader' (XVI), with fanciful termination simulating L. g. pl. ending *-orum*.

cock-and-bull applied to an idle story. XVIII. orig. in phr. *talk of* (*a story of*) *a cock and a bull* (XVII), said of rambling and misleading talk; parallel to F. *coq-à-l'âne* (anglicized as †*cockalane* XVII), orig. in phr. *saillir du coq en l'âne* 'jump from the cock to the ass'.

cockatoo XVII (*cacatoe*). - Du. *kaketoe* - Malay *kakatua*; infl. by COCK[1].

cockatrice basilisk XIV; (her.) hybrid of cock and serpent XVI. - OF. *cocatris* - medL. *calcātrix*, *cau-* (fem. agent-noun f. *calcāre* tread, (later) track, f. *calx* heel) used to render Gr. *ikhneúmōn*, ICHNEUMON, lit. 'tracker'. OF. *cocatris* came to denote the crocodile; by a further (obscure) transference *cockatrice* was applied in English translations of the Bible to the basilisk; assoc. with COCK[1] produced the her. sense.

cockboat small ship's boat. XV. Formerly also simply *cock* - OF. *coque*, dial. var. of *coche* :- medL. *caudica* (cf. *caudiceus*, *cōdicārius* applied to boats as being carved out of trunks, f. *caudex*, *cōdex* block of wood).

cockchafer XVIII. The second el. is (dial.) *chaf(f)er* :- OE. *ċeafor*, prob. f. Gmc. **kab-* gnaw, parallel to **keb-*, repr. by OE. *ċefer* = OS. *kevera* (Du. *kever*), OHG. *kevar* (G. *käfer* beetle); if the first el. is COCK[1], the reference is obscure.

cocker[1] pamper, indulge, humour. XV. of uncert. orig. (cf. synon. †*cock* and †*cockle* (both XVI)).

cocker[2] spaniel of a breed trained to start woodcock, etc. XIX. f. *cocking* (XVII) shooting of woodcock, f. COCK[1] + -ING[1]; see -ER[1].

cockerel young cock. XV. f. COCK[1] + -EREL.

cockle[1] plant growing among corn. OE. *coccul*, *-el*, perh. - medL. **cocculus*, f. late L. *coccus*, earlier *coccum* kermes - Gr. *kókkos*.

cockle[2] edible bivalve mollusc. XIV. - (O)F. *coquille* shell :- medL. **cochilia* - medGr. *kokhúlia*. pl. of *kokhúlion*, f. *kógkhē* CONCH.

cockle[3] go into rucks, pucker. XVI. - F. *coquiller* blister (bread) in cooking, f. *coquille* shell, etc. (see prec.).

cockloft small upper loft. XVI. prob. f. COCK[1] + LOFT, as being orig. a place where fowls roosted.

cockney †hen's egg (perh. small or mis-shapen, 'cock's egg'); †pampered child XIV; †townsman, as a type of effeminacy; one born in the city of London XVI. ME. *cokeney*, *-ay*, prob. f. *cokene*, g. pl. of *cok* COCK[1] + *ey*, *ay* (OE. *ǣġ*) egg.

cockpit pit or enclosure to be used for cock-fighting XVI; (naut.) after part of the orlop deck of a man of war XVIII. f. COCK[1] + PIT.

cockroach XVII (*cacarootch*, *cockroche*). - Sp. *cucaracha*; unaccountably assim. to *cock* and *roach*.

cocksure †(objectively) quite secure or certain XVI; (subjectively) feeling quite sure or certain XVII. of uncert. orig.

cocktail A. 'cock-tailed' horse, i.e. one with the

tail docked and so sticking up like a cock's tail; beetle that cocks up its 'tail'; B. (orig. U.S.) mixed drink with a spirit as basis. XIX. A. f. COCK[1] vb. + TAIL[1]; B. of unkn orig.

cocky (sl.) arrogantly pert. XVIII. f. COCK[1] + -Y[1].

coco, cocoa[1] †nut of the coco-palm, *Cocos nucifera*, and the tree itself XVI; now only in *coco(a)-*, *coker-nut* XVII. - Sp., Pg. *coco*, orig. playful use of *coco* grinning face, grimace, with allusion to the monkey-like appearance of the base of the nut. Appears first in latinized form †*cocus*, later †*cocos*. The sp. *cocoa* is due to an error in Johnson's dictionary, in which this word and COCOA[2] were combined under one heading; *coker* dates from XVII.

cocoa[2] †seed of a tropical American tree; powder produced by grinding the seed, and beverage made from this. XVIII. Alteration of CACAO (also †*cacoa*). Cf. CHOCOLATE.

cocoon XVII. - F. *cocon* - modPr. *coucoun* egg-shell, cocoon, dim. of *coca* shell.

cocotte XIX. - F., (also) child's word for a fowl, ult. f. *coq* COCK[1].

cod[1] husk OE. (surviving dial., as in *peascod* pea-shell); scrotum; (pl.) testicles XIV; hence **codpiece** XV. OE. *cod(d)* bag, husk, corr. to ON. *koddi*, ODa. *kodde*, Sw. *kudde* cushion, pillow, Norw. *kodd* testicle, scrotum; f. Gmc. **kud-* **keud-* (whence OE. *ċēod* pouch).

cod[2] sea-fish, *Gadus morrhua*. XIII. of unkn. orig.; possibly a use of COD[1], as if 'bag-fish', from its appearance. *Cod's head* was sl. for 'blockhead' (XVI); hence prob. (sl.) *cod* fool, simpleton (XVII), whence **cod** vb. (sl.) hoax, humbug. XIX.

coda (mus.) concluding passage. XVIII. - It. :- L. *cauda* tail.

coddle XIX. prob. a var. of *caudle* (XVII) administer a CAUDLE to; but perh. a fig. use of *coddle* (XVI) parboil, stew. Cf. MOLLYCODDLE.

code systematic collection of laws XIV; system of signals, esp. for secrecy XIX. - (O)F. - L. *cōdex*, *codic-* block of wood, block split into leaves or tablets, book. The L. word **codex** was formerly (XVI-XVIII) in Eng. use in the sense 'law-code', but is now used only for 'manuscript volume'.

codger stingy (old) fellow; familiar appellation for an elderly man; (hence) fellow, chap. XVIII. perh. var. of CADGER.

codicil supplement to a will. XV. - L. *cōdicillus*, dim. of *cōdex* (see CODE).

codlin(g) variety of apple. XV. Earliest form *querd(e)lynge*, later *quodling*, *quadlin*; but *codlyng* occurs XVI, when it appears to be already assoc. with *coddle* vb. cook. The forms correspond to those of the surname *Codling*, earlier *Querdelioun*, *Querdlyng* - AN. *Quer de lion* (F. *Cœur-de-lion*) 'lion-heart'.

coefficient XVII. - modL. *coefficiens*; see CO- and EFFICIENT.

coeliac pert. to the abdomen. XVII. - L. *cœliacus* - Gr. *koiliakós*, f. *koiliā* belly, bowels, f. *koîlos* hollow, rel. to L. *cavus* (see CAVE[1]); see -AC.

coenobite member of a religious order living in a community. XVII. - (O)F. *cénobite* or ecclL. *cœnobīta*, f. *cœnobium* - Gr. *koinóbion* community life, (eccl.) convent, f. *koinós* common + *bíos* life (cf. QUICK); see -ITE.

coerce XVII. - L. *coercēre* shut up, restrain, f. CO- + *arcēre* restrain, ward off. So **coercion** XVIII.

coeval contemporary. XVII. f. late L. *coævus*, f. CO- + *ævum* AGE; see -AL[1].

coffee XVI (*Chaoua*). The present form is first recorded in XVII, with vars. *cahve*, *coffe*, *cauphe*, *cophee*; - Du. *koffie* - Turk. *kahve* - Arab. *ḳahwa*.

coffer XIII. - (O)F. *coffre* :- L. *cophinus* basket; see next.

coffin †chest, box, basket XIV; box for a corpse XVI. - OF. *cof(f)in* little basket, case - L. *cophinus* - Gr. *kóphinos* basket.

cog projecting tooth on a wheel. XIII. ME. *cogge*, of unkn. orig. but prob. Scand. (cf. synon. Sw. *kugge*, *kughjul* cog-wheel, Norw. *kug*).

cogent XVII. - L. *cōgēns*, *-ent-*, prp. of *cōgere* drive together, compel. f. CO- + *agere* drive; see ACT, -ENT.

cogitation XIII. - OF. *cogitacioun* - L. *cōgitātiō*, *-ōn-*, f. *cōgitāre* think, f. CO- + *agitāre* put in motion, spec. turn over in the mind; see AGITATE, -ATION. So **cogitate** XVI; see -ATE[3].

cognac prop. French brandy distilled from Cognac wine. XVI (*Coniacke wine*). - F., f. name of a town in the department of Charente, France.

cognate akin, descended from a common ancestor; also sb. XVII. - L. *cognātus*, f. CO- + *-gnātus* born, f. IE. **gn-* **gen-* produce; see KIN, -ATE[2].

cognition action or faculty of knowing. XV. - L. *cognitiō*, *-ōn-*, f. *cognit-*, pp. stem of *cognōscere* get to know, investigate, f. CO- + *gnōscere*, inchoative of **gnō-*; see KNOW, -TION.

cognizance knowledge (now *take c. of*); device by which one is known XIV; taking legal notice, jurisdiction; acknowledgement, admission XVI. - OF. *conis(s)aunce*, *conus(s)aunce*, vars. of *conois(s)ance* (mod. *connaissance*) - Rom **connōscentia*, f. *cognōscent-*, prp. stem of L. *cognoscere* (see prec.). Latinization of the sp. has infl. the pronunc. Hence **cognizant** XIX.

cognomen third name of a Roman citizen; distinguishing epithet; (sur)name. XIX. - L., f. CO- + **gnōmen* NAME.

cognoscente connoisseur. XVIII. - It., latinized form of *conoscente* :- L. *cognōscent-* (see COGNITION and -ENT).

cognovit (leg.) acknowledgement by defendant that plaintiff's cause is just. XVIII. Short for L. formula *cognovit actionem* he has acknowledged the charge; 3rd sg. pt. of *cognōscere* (see KNOW).

cohabit XVI. - late L. *cohabitāre*. So **cohabitation** XV. Cf. (O)F. *cohabiter*, *-ation*, and see CO-, HABITATION.

co-heir XVI. - L. *cohērēs*; see CO-, HEIR.

cohere XVI. - L. *cohærēre*, f. CO- + *hærēre* stick. So **coherent** XVI, **cohesion** XVII.

cohort body of infantry in the ancient Roman army; also transf. XV. - (O)F. *cohorte* or L. *cohors*, *cohort-* enclosure, company, crowd, f. CO- + **hort-*, as in *hortus* garden.

coif close-fitting cap. XIV. - OF. *coife* (mod. *coiffe*) head-dress :- late L. *cofia* helmet.

coil[1] (arch.) disturbance, confusion, fuss. XVI. of

unkn. orig.; now familiar mainly in *mortal c.* (from Sh. *Hamlet* III. i. 67).

coil[2] lay up (a rope or cable) in concentric rings XVI; twist or twine *up* XVII (also †*quoil*). - OF. *coillir* (mod. *cueillir* gather) :- L. *colligere* COLLECT. Hence **coil** sb. length of rope coiled up XVI (*quille*); series of concentric rings XVII.

coin A. †corner-stone; †corner, angle, wedge; B. †die for stamping money; piece of money; coined money. XIV. - (O)F. *coin*, †*coing*, wedge, corner, †stamping-die :- L. *cuneus* wedge. So **coin** vb. make (money) from metal, make (metal) into money. XIV. - OF. *coignier* mint, f. *coin*. **coinage** coining money XIV; money coined XV. - OF. *coigniage*, f. *coignier*.

coincide XVIII. - medL. *coincidere*, f. CO- + *incidere* fall upon or into, f. IN-[1] + *cadere* fall. So **coincidence** XVII, after **coincident** XVI.

coition †conjunction XVI; copulation XVII. - L. *coitiō*, *-ōn-*, f. *coit-*, pp. stem of *coīre*, f. CO- + *īre* go; see -TION. So **coitus** XVIII.

coke solid residue of the dry distillation of coal. XVII (formerly often pl.). prob. identical with north. dial. *colk* (XIV) core, of unkn. orig.

coker-nut see COCO.

col depression in a mountain chain. XIX. - Fr. *col* :- L. *collum* neck.

col- assim. form of COM-, CON- before *l*. In Rom., L. *coll-*, earlier *conl-*, was reduced to *col-*, and this form was preserved in early adoptions of F. words; the later *coll-* was due to assoc. with L.

colander XIV (*colonur*, *culdor(e)*, etc.). perh. alt. of Pr. **colador* :- Rom. *cōlātōr-*, f. L. *cōlāre* strain.

colchicum genus of plants. XVI. - L. - Gr. *kolkhikón*, sb. use of n. of *Kolkhikós* pert. to Colchis, ancient name of a region east of the Black Sea.

cold OE. (Angl.) *cald* (WS. *ċeald*) = OS. *cald*, (O)HG. *kalt*, ON. *kaldr*, Goth. *kalds* :- Gmc. **kaldaz* prop. chilled, frozen; formation with ppl. suffix (= L. *-tus*, Gr. *-tós*) on **kal-* :- IE. **gol-*, var. of **gel-*, as in L. *gelu* frost, *gelidus* GELID, Lith. *gelumà* severe cold, OSl. *golotī* ice; see CHILL, COOL, and CONGEAL.

cole kind of cabbage. XIV. - ON. *kál*, corr. to OE. *cāwel*, *cāul*, MDu. *cōle* (Du. *kool*), OHG. *chōlo*, *kōl(i)* (G. *kohl*), and Ir., Gael. *cál*, W. *cawl*, all - L. *caulis* (later *caulus*, *-a*) stem, stalk, cabbage. Surviving mainly as in **coleseed** (prob. - Du. *koolzaad*; cf. OE. *cāwelsǣd*), **colewort** XIV. Cf. KALE.

colemouse see COALMOUSE.

coleoptera (zool.) the beetles. XVIII. modL. n. pl., f. Gr. *koleópteros* sheath-winged, f. *koleón* sheath + *pterón* wing (see FEATHER).

colic sb. griping pains in the belly XV; adj. affecting the colon XVI. - (O)F. *colique* - late L. *cōlicus*, *collicus*, f. *cōlon* COLON[1]; see -IC.

collaborate XIX. f. pp. stem of late L. *collabōrāre*, f. COL- + *labor* LABOUR. So **collaboration**, **collaborator** XIX.

collapse vb. XVIII. Back-formation f. pp. *collapsed* (XVII), f. L. *collāpsus*, pp. of *collābī*, f. COL- + *lābī* fall; see LAPSE, -ED[1]. So **collapse** sb. XIX.

collar XIII (various techn. uses from XVII). ME. *coler* - AN. *coler*, OF. *colier* (mod. *collier*) :- L. *collāre*, f. *collum* neck; see -AR. The sp. was early assim. to the L. Hence as vb. lay hold on (first in wrestling) XVI.

collate A. †confer XVI; appoint to a benefice XVII; B. compare critically XVII. f. *collāt-*, stem of the form used as pp. of L. *conferre* CONFER; see -ATE[3].

collateral situated or existing side by side. XIV. - medL. *collaterālis*; see COL- and LATERAL.

collation A. in renderings of Johannes Cassianus' 'Collationes Patrum in Scetico eremo commorantium' (Conferences of hermits in the Egyptian desert); reading of this at monastic meals XIII; light meal after such reading XIV; light meal (gen.) XVI; B. bringing together, esp. for comparison XIV; C. bestowal, spec. of a benefice XIV. Occurs first in sense A in AN. form *collatiun*, and later (XIV) in the form *collacion*, *-tion* - L. *collātiō*, *-ōn-* contribution, collection, comparison, in medL. conference, repast, noun of action to *conferre* CONFER; see COLLATE, -ATION.

colleague XVI. - F. *collègue* - L. *collēga* partner in office, f. COL- + *lēg-* as in *lēx* law, *lēgāre* depute.

collect[1] (liturg.) short prayer, varying with the day or season. XIII. - (O)F. *collecte* - L. *collēcta* collection, (late) assembly, sb. use of fem. pp. of *colligere* COLLECT[2].

collect[2] gather together. XVI. - OF. *collecter* or medL. *collēctāre*, f. *collēct-*, pp. stem of *colligere*, f. COL- + *legere* collect, assemble, choose, read. So **collection** action of collecting XIV; things collected XV. - (O)F. - L. **collective** XV. - F. or L. Hence **collectivism**, **-ist** XIX. **collector** XIV. - AN. *collectour* - medL. *collector*; see -OR[1].

colleen girl. XIX. - Ir. *cailín*, dim. of *caile* countrywoman, girl.

college society or corporation of persons having common functions and rights; building occupied by this. XIV. - (O)F. *collège* or its source L. *collēgium* association, partnership, corporation, f. *collēga* COLLEAGUE. So **collegial** XIV, **collegian** XV, **collegiate** (-ATE[2]) XV.

collide XVII. - L. *collīdere* clash together, f. COL- + *lædere* hurt by striking. So **collision** XV. - late L. *collīsiō*, *-ōn-*, f. *collīs-*, pp. stem of *collīdere*.

collie shepherd's dog. XVII. orig. Sc., perh. f. *coll* COAL (from its black colour) + -IE.

collier †charcoal-burner XIV; coal-miner XVI. ME. *colyer*, f. *col* COAL; see -IER. Hence **colliery** XVII.

colligate bind together. XVI. f. pp. stem of L. *colligāre*, f. COL- + *ligāre* bind; see -ATE[3].

collimation adjustment of the line of sight of a telescope. XVII. - modL. *collimātiō*, *-ōn-*, f. *collimāre*, erron. reading in some editions of Cicero for *collīneāre* aim, f. COL- + *līnea* LINE[2].

collocate place side by side. XVI. f. L. *collocāre*, *-āt-*, f. COL- + *locāre* place, LOCATE. So **collocation** XVII.

collop †fried bacon and egg XIV; fried slice of meat XV; thick fold of flesh XVI. ME. *col(h)oppe* - Scand. word repr. by OSw. *kolhuppadher* roasted on coals (f. *kol* COAL + *huppa* leap), Sw. *kalops*, dial. *kollops* dish of stewed meat.

colloquy conversation. XVI. - L. *colloquium* (also used in Eng. XVII), f. COL- + *loquī* speak.

collotype process or print in which a thin sheet of gelatine is used. XIX. f. Gr. *kólla* glue + TYPE.

collusion XIV. - (O)F. *collusion* or L. *collūsiō, -ōn-*, f. *collūdere, collūs-* have a secret agreement (whence **collude** XVI), f. COL- + *lūdere* play, f. *lūdus* play, sport.

collywobbles (sl.) belly-ache. XIX. Fancifully f. COLIC and WOBBLE.

colon[1] greater portion of the large intestine. XVI. - (O)F. *côlon* or L. *cōlon* - Gr. *kólon*.

colon[2] member of a sentence; the punctuation mark (:). XVI. - L. *cōlon* - Gr. *kôlon* limb, clause.

colonel XVI. In earliest use both *coronel* and *colonel*, but the first prevailed before mid-XVII. - F. †*coronel* (so also Sp.), later and mod. *colonnel* - (orig. with dissimilation of *l* .. *l* to *r* .. *l*) It. *colonnello*, f. *colonna* COLUMN, the officer being so named as leader of the first company of a regiment.

colonnade XVIII. - F., f. *colonne* COLUMN; see -ADE.

colony XVI. - L. *colōnia* farm, landed estate, settlement, f. *colōnus* cultivator, settler, f. *colere* cultivate; see -Y[3]. Hence **colonial** XVIII, **colonize** XVII (whence **colonist** XVIII).

colophon inscription containing title, date, etc., at the end of a book. XVIII. - late L. *colophōn* - Gr. *kolophṓn* summit, finishing touch.

colophony dark or amber-coloured resin. XIV. - L. (*rēsīna*) *colophōnia* resin of Colophon, a town in Lydia.

coloration XVII. - F. *coloration* or late L. *colōrātiō, -ōn-*, f. *colōrāre* COLOUR; see -ATION. So **coloratura** (mus.) XIX. - It.; see -URE. **colorific** XVII. - F. or modL.

colossus gigantic statue, e.g. that at Rhodes. XIV. - L. *colossus* - Gr. *kolossós*. So **colossal** XVIII. - F.

colour, U.S. **color** XIII. - OF. *col(o)ur* (mod. *couleur*) :- L. *color, colōr-*, rel. to *cēlare* hide, CONCEAL; see -OUR[2]. So **colour** vb. XIII. - OF. *coulourer* (mod. *colorer*) - L. *colōrāre*.

colt OE. *colt*, applied to the young of the ass and the camel; of obscure orig.

colubrine snake-like. XVI. - L. *colubrīnus*, f. *coluber* snake; see -INE[1].

columbarium dove-cot; underground sepulchre with niches. XVIII. - L., f. *columba* dove, pigeon; see -ARIUM.

columbine dove-like. XIV. - (O)F. *colombin, -ine* - L. *columbīnus*, f. *columba* dove. As sb., name of plants. XIII. - OF. *colombine* - medL. *columbīna* (sc. *herba*) 'dove's plant', so called from the resemblance of the inverted flower to five pigeons clustered together.

Columbine (orig. in It. comedy) the mistress of Harlequin. XVIII. - F. *Colombine* - It. *Colombina*, sb. use of fem. of *colombino* dove-like in gentleness (cf. prec.).

column pillar XV; vertical division of a page, etc. XV. Partly - OF. *columpne* (mod. *colonne*), partly - its source L. *columna* pillar, f. **col-*, var. of **cel-*, as in **cellere* (see EXCEL), *celsus* high. So **columnar** XVIII, **columniated** XVIII, **columniation** XVII.

colure each of the great circles intersecting at right angles at the poles. XVI. - late L. *colūrī* pl. - Gr. *kólourai* (sc. *grammaí* lines), pl. of *kólouros* truncated, f. *kólos* docked + *ourá* tail; so called because their lower part is permanently cut off from view.

colza (oil expressed from) coleseed. XVIII. - F. (Walloon) *kolza*, earlier *kolzat* - LG. *kōlsāt*, Du. *koolzaad*; see COLE, SEED.

com- repr. L. *com-*, arch. form of the prep. *cum* with, used in comps. with the meanings 'together, in combination or union', 'altogether, completely'. *Com-* was retained before *b, p, m,* and some vowels (as in *comes* COUNT[1]), assim. before *r, l* (as in *corruptus* CORRUPT, *collātiō* COLLATION), and reduced to co- before most vowels; elsewhere it became CON- (but before *f*, as in COMFIT, COMFORT, *com-* has replaced *con-* in Eng.).

coma[1] unnatural deep and prolonged sleep XVII. - medical L. - Gr. *kôma, kōmat-*, rel. to *koítē* bed, *keîsthai* lie down. Hence **comatose** XVIII.

coma[2] (bot.) tuft XVII; (astron.) nebulous envelope of a comet XVIII. - L. *coma* - Gr. *kómē* hair of the head; cf. COMET.

comb toothed implement for straightening the hair; cock's crest, which is indented or serrated OE.; flat cake of cells of wax made by bees (an exclusively Eng. use, the orig. of which is doubtful), late OE. in *hunigcamb* honeycomb. OE. *camb, comb* = OS. *camb*, OHG. *kamb* (G. *kamm*), ON. *kambr* :- Gmc. **kambaz* :- IE. **gombhos*, whence also Gr. *gómphos*, Skr. *jámbha-*, OSl. *zǫbŭ* tooth. Hence **comb** vb. XIV; repl. *kemb*, OE. *cemban* (:- Gmc. **kambjan*), which survives in UNKEMPT.

combat sb. XVI. - F., f. *combattre* vb. (whence **combat** vb. XVI), OF. *cumbatre* - late L. *combattere*, f. COM- + **battere*, for *batuere* fight. So **combatant** XV. - OF. *combatant*, prp. of *combattre*.

combe see COOMB.

combine vb. XV. - (O)F. *combiner* or late L. *combīnāre* join two and two, f. COM- + *bīnī* two together. So **combination** XIV. Hence **combine** sb. †plot XVII (rare); commercial (etc.) combination XIX (orig. U.S.).

combustion XV. - (O)F. *combustion* or late L. *combustiō, -ōn-*, f. *combust-*, pp. stem of L. *combūrere* burn up, f. COM- + **būrere*, see -TION.

come OE. str. vb. *cuman* = OS. *cuman*, OHG. *queman, koman* (G. *kommen*), ON. *koma*, Goth. *qiman* :- Gmc. **kweman*, **kuman*. The IE. base **g^wem-* **g^wm-* is repr. also by Skr. *gámati* goes, Gr. *baínein* go, L. *venīre* come (cf. ADVENT, CONVENE, etc.).

comedy †narrative poem with a pleasant ending XIV; †miracle play or interlude with a happy ending XVI; light and amusing play XVII. - (O)F. *comédie* - L. *cōmœdia* - Gr. *kōmōidiā*, f. *kōmōidós* comic actor, comic poet, f. *kômos* revel. So **comedian** comic writer XVI; comic actor, †stage-player XVII.

comely †decent, proper; pleasant to look at, fair XIII. ME. *cumelich, cumli*, prob. aphetic of †*becumelich* (XII), f. BECOME + -LY[1].

comestible eatable. XV (†adj.), XIX (sb.). - (O)F. - medL. *comestibilis*, f. *comest-*, pp. stem of L. *comedere* eat up, f. COM- + *edere* EAT; see -IBLE.

comet XIII (XII in L. form). - (O)F. *comète* - L. *comēta* - Gr. *komḗtēs* long-haired, sb. comet (for *astḗr komḗtēs* 'long-haired star'), f. *komân* wear the hair long, f. *kómē* hair of the head, tail of a comet.

comfit sweetmeat. XV. ME. *confyt* - OF. *confit(e)* :- L. *confectum, confecta*, sb. uses of n. and fem. of *confectus*, pp. of *conficere* prepare (see CONFECTION).

comfort †encouragement, support; relief in distress XIII; cause of satisfaction or content XVI; material well-being XIX. - OF. *confort*, Rom. sb. f. late L. *confortāre*, f. CON- + *fortis* strong. So **comfort** vb. XIII. **comfortable** †encouraging, reassuring, pleasant XIV; affording content; at ease XVIII. - AN. *confortable*.

comfrey the plant *Symphytum officinale*, formerly esteemed as a vulnerary. XV. - AN. *cumfirie*, OF. *confi(e)re* :- medL. **confervia*, for L. *conferva*, f. *confervēre* intr. heal, prop. boil together (see CON-, FERVENT).

comic pert. to comedy XVI; ludicrous, funny XVIII. - L. *cōmicus* - Gr. *kōmikós*, f. *kômos* revel; see COMEDY, -IC. So **comical** XV.

comitadji Balkan (esp. Bulgarian and Macedonian) rebel against the Ottoman Empire before World War I. XX. - Turk. *komitacı*, f. *komita* (- F. *comité* COMMITTEE) + occupational suffix *-cı*; lit. 'member of a (revolutionary) committee'.

comity courtesy XVI; friendly understanding XIX. - L. *cōmitās*, f. *cōmis* courteous; see -ITY.

comma phrase smaller than a colon; the punctuation mark (,); (mus.) minute interval. XVI. - L. - Gr. *kómma* piece cut off, short clause, f. **kop-*, stem of *kóptein* strike, cut.

command vb. XIII. ME. *com(m)a(u)nde* - AN. *comaunder*, OF. *comander* (mod. *comm-*) :- late L. *commandāre*, f. COM- (intensive) + *mandāre* enjoin; see MANDATE. Hence **command** sb. XVI. So **commandant** XVII. - F., or It., etc. **commander, commandment** XIII. - OF. **commando** (orig. S. Africa) military party, raid. XIX. - Pg.

commandeer (orig. S. Africa) seize for military use. XIX. - Afrikaans *kommanderen* - F. *commander* (see prec.).

commemorate XVI. f. pp. stem of L. *commemorāre*, f. COM- (intensive) + *memorāre* relate, f. *memor* mindful (see MEMORY). So **commemoration** XIV. - (O)F. or L.

commence XIV (reduced form *comse, cumse* XIII). - OF. *com(m)encier* :- Rom. **cominitiāre*, f. COM- (intensive) + *initiāre* INITIATE. So **commencement** XIII.

commend A. give in trust or charge; B. approve conduct or character of. XIV. - L. *commendāre*, f. COM- (intensive) + *mandāre* commit, entrust (see MANDATE). In earlier ME. *command*, like OF. *comander*, was used in this sense. So **commendable** XIV. - (O)F. - L. **commendation** XIII. - (O)F. - L. **commendatory** XVI. - late L.

commensal (one) who eats at the same table. XIV. - medL. *commensālis*, f. COM- + *mensa* table; see -AL[1].

commensurable XVI. - late L. *commensurābilis*, f. COM- + *mensurābilis* MEASURABLE. So **commensurate** XVII. - late L. *commensurātus*; see -ATE[2].

comment †commentary; explanatory note. XV. - L. *commentum* invention, interpretation, comment, f. *comment-*, pp. stem of *comminiscī* devise, contrive, f. COM- + **men-*, base of *mēns* MIND. Hence (or - F. *commenter*) **comment** vb. XVI. So **commentary** XV. **commentator** †chronicler XIV; writer of a commentary XVII.

commerce XVI. - F. *commerce* or L. *commercium* trading, merchandise, intercourse, f. COM- + *merx, merc-* merchandise (cf. MERCHANT). Hence **commercial** XVII.

commination threatening of punishment or vengeance. XV. - L. *comminatiō, -ōn-*, f. *comminārī* MENACE; see COM-, -ATION.

comminute reduce to small particles. XVII. f. L. *comminuere, comminūt-*, f. COM- (intensive) + *minuere* lessen (see MINUTE[2]). So **comminution** XVI. - late L.

commiserate XVII. f. L. *commiserārī, -āre, -āt-*, f. COM- (intensive) + *miserārī* lament, pity, f. *miser* wretched; see MISERY, -ATE[3]. So **commiseration** XVI.

commissar head of a government department in the U.S.S.R. XX. - Russ. *komissár* - F. *commissaire* - medL. *commissārius* COMMISSARY.

commissary (eccl.) officer representing another XIV; official having charge (esp.) of supplies XV. - medL. *commissārius* officer in charge, f. *commiss-*, pp. stem of L. *committere* COMMIT; see -ARY. So **commissariat** (Sc. law) commissary's court XVII; military department charged with providing supplies XVIII; partly - medL. *commissāriātus*, partly - F. *commissariat*; see -ATE[1].

commission authoritative charge; warrant of authority XIV; body charged with special authority XV. - (O)F. - L. *commissiō, -ōn-*, f. *commiss-*, pp. stem of *committere* COMMIT; see -ION. So **commissioner** XV. - medL. *commissionārius*; cf. -ER[2]. **commissionaire** XVIII. - F. - medL. (as above).

commissure juncture, seam XV; (physiol.) bundles of nerve-substance XIX. - L. *commissūra*, f. *commiss-*, pp. stem of *committere* put together; see next and -URE.

commit A. entrust XIV; B. perpetrate XV; C. engage, involve XVII. - L. *committere* join, join (battle), practise, perpetrate, place with another for safety, etc., entrust, f. COM- + *mittere* put, send (see MISSION). Hence **commitment** XVII, **committal** XIX.

committee A. (surviving leg.) one to whom a charge is committed XV; B. body of persons appointed for a special business XVII. f. COMMIT + -EE[1].

commode †woman's tall head-dress XVII; chest of drawers XVIII; close-stool XIX. - F. *commode* (in first two senses), sb. use of *commode* convenient - L. *commodus* (see next).

commodious †advantageous, serviceable XV; conveniently roomy XVI. - F. *commodieux* or medL. *commodiōsus*, f. L. *commodus* of due measure, convenient, f. COM- + *modus* measure (see MODE). So **commodity** XIV. - (O)F. - L.

commodore XVII. orig. *commandore*, later

commadore, prob. - Du. *komandeur* - F. *commandeur* COMMANDER; but the form suggests Sp. or Pg. influence.

common adj. XIII. - OF. *comun* (mod. *commun*) :- L. *commūnis*, OL. *comoinis*, cogn. with OE. *ġemǣne*, OHG. *gimeini* (G. *gemein*), Goth. *gamains*. So **commonalty** †people of a nation, etc. XIII; general body of the community, common people XIV; †the commons XVI. - OF. *comunalté* (mod. *communauté*) - medL. *commūnālitās*; see -AL[1], -ITY. **commoner** †burgess, citizen XIV; member of the House of Commons; student or undergraduate not on the foundation of a college XVII. - medL. *commūnārius*.

commonplace †passage of general application, leading text, theme; notable passage stored up for use in a *book of common places* or *commonplace book*; ordinary topic, stock theme or subject. XVI. As adj. XVII. tr. L. *locus commūnis*, tr. Gr. *koinòs tópos* (cf. TOPIC).

common weal, commonweal the body politic, state, community XIV; the general good, public welfare XV. orig. and properly two words, rendering L. *rēs commūnis*, F. *le bien commun*. See WEAL[1].

commonwealth †public welfare XV; the body politic, state, community XVI; republic, or democratic state; spec. (hist.) the republican government established under Oliver Cromwell XVII. See WEALTH. Both *common weal* and *common wealth* were at first used indiscriminately in the senses 'public welfare' and 'body politic', but in XVI *commonwealth* became the ordinary Eng. term for the latter sense, whence the later sense 'republic' was developed.

commotion public disturbance XV; (gen.) agitation, perturbation XIV. - (O)F. *commotion* or L. *commōtiō, -ōn-*; see COM-, MOTION.

commune[1] communicate, esp. orally, *with* XIII; hold spiritual intercourse *with* XVII. - OF. *comuner* share, f. *comun* COMMON.

commune[2] in France, territorial division XVIII; (hist.) commonalty, corporation XIX. - F. *commune*, earlier †*comugne* - medL. *commūnia*, n. pl. of *commūnis* COMMON, taken as fem. sing. in sense 'group of people having a common life'. So **communal** XIX.

communicate give a share of, share in; receive, administer Holy Communion; hold intercourse *with* XVI; have a common channel of passage XVIII. f. pp. stem of L. *commūnicāre*, f. *commūnis* COMMON; see -ATE[3]. So **communication, communicative** XIV.

communion sharing, participation; spiritual fellowship XIV; sacrament of the Lord's Supper, participation in this XV (in religious uses earlier †*communing*). - (O)F. *communion* or L. *commūniō, -ōn-*, f. *commūnis* COMMON; see -ION.

communism XIX. - F. *communisme*, f. *commun* COMMON; see -ISM. So **communist** XIX. - F. *communiste*.

community A. a body of people associated by common status, pursuits, etc. XIV; B. common character XV. Late ME. *comunete* - OF. *comuneté* (mod. *communité*) - L. *commūnitās, -tāt-*, f. *commūnis* COMMON; see -ITY; later assim. to modF. and L.

commute †exchange; change *for* something else. XVII. - L. *commūtāre* change altogether, exchange, f. COM- + *mūtāre* change (see MUTATION). So **commutation** XV. - (O)F. or L. **commuter** XIX.

compact[1] covenant, contract. XVI. - L. *compactum*, sb. use of n. of pp. of *compacīscī* make an agreement; see COM-, PACT.

compact[2] closely packed or knit together. XIV. - L. *compactus*, pp. of *compingere* put closely together, f. COM- + *pangere* fasten. Hence **compact** sb. compact make-up powder, etc. XX. So **compact** vb. join firmly together. XVI. f. pp. stem of L. *compingere*.

compages compacted whole, framework of conjoined parts. XVII (earlier anglicized †*compage*). - L. *compāges*, f. *com* COM- + *pāg-* as in *pangere* (see prec.).

companion[1] associate, mate. XIII. ME. *compainoun* - OF. *compaignon* :- Rom. **compāniōn-*, stem of **compāniō* (whence OF. *compain*, mod. *copain*), f. L. COM- + *pānis* bread, after Gmc. *ʒaχlaibaz* (Goth. *gahlaiba*, OHG. *galeipo* messmate) 'one who eats bread with another', f. **ʒa-* Y- + **χlaib-* LOAF. Hence **companionable** XVII. So **company** XIII. ME. *compainie, -paig-* - AN. *compainie*, OF. *compa(i)gnie* :- Rom. **compānia*, f. **compāniō*; see -Y[3].

companion[2] (naut.) framed windows over a hatchway, hooded staircase to the captain's cabin. XVIII. alt., by assoc. with prec., of Du. †*kompanje* (now *kam-*) - OF. *compagne* - It. *compagna* (for *camera della compagna* store-room for provisions, caboose) :- Rom. **compānia* 'what is eaten with bread', f. L. COM- + *pānis* bread.

compare represent as similar. XV (earlier *comper* XIV). - (O)F. *comparer* (earlier *comperer*) :- L. *comparāre* pair, match, f. *compar* like, equal, f. COM- + *pār* equal (see PEER[1]). So **comparative** XV. - L. *comparātīvus*, f. *comparāre, -āt-*. **comparison** XIV. - OF. *comparesoun* (mod. *-aison*) :- L. *comparatiō, -ōn-* (see -ATION).

compartment XVI (*-iment, -ement*). - F. *compartiment* - It. *compartimento*, f. *compartire* share - late L. *compartīrī*, f. COM- (intensive) + *partīrī*, f. *pars, part-* PART; see -MENT.

compass †designing, ingenuity; †area, space XIII; †circle, circuitous course; (pl.) two-legged measuring instrument XIV; instrument showing magnetic or true north XVI. - (O)F. *compas* †measure, rule, pair of compasses, etc. The transference of sense to the mariner's instrument is held to have arisen in It. *compasso*, from the circular shape of the compass-box. So **compass** vb. contrive, devise XIII; go round, encircle XIV; attain to XVI. - (O)F. *compasser* (now only) measure as with compasses, repr. Rom. **compassare* measure, f. L. COM- + *passus* step, PACE.

compassion XIV. - (O)F. - ecclL. *compassiō, -ōn-*, f. *compass-*, pp. stem of *compatī* suffer with, feel pity; see COM- and PASSION. So **compassionate** characterized by compassion. XVI.

compatible †sympathetic XV; mutually tolerant, congruous XV. - F. - medL. *compatibilis* (as in *beneficium compatibile* benefice tenable with another), f. *compatī*; see prec. and -IBLE.

compatriot XVII. - (O)F. *compatriote* - late L. *compatriōta*; see COM-, PATRIOT.

compeer companion, fellow XIII; peer, equal XV. ME. *comper* - OF.; see COM-, PEER[1].

compel constrain XIV; drive or force together XV. - L. *compellere* (lit. and fig.), f. COM- + *pellere* drive.

compendious XIV. - (O)F. *compendieux* - L. *compendiōsus* abridged, brief, f. **compendium** (XVI; lit. 'that which is weighed together', saving, abbreviation), f. *compendere*, f. COM- + *pendere* weigh.

compensate XVII. f. pp. stem of L. *compensāre* weigh (one) against another, counterbalance, f. COM- + *pensāre*, frequent. of *pendere* weigh; see prec. and -ATE[3]. So **compensation** XIV. - (O)F. - L.

compère organizer of an entertainment. XX. - F. 'godfather', 'accomplice', 'announcer' - Rom. **compater*, f. L. COM- + *pater* FATHER. Also vb.

compete XVII (not frequent before XIX). - L. *competere*, in its late sense of 'strive for (something) together with another', f. COM- + *petere* aim at, seek. So **competition** XVII. - late L. (cf. PETITION). **competitive** XIX. **competitor** fellow candidate, rival. XVI. - F. (*-eur*) or L.; see -OR[1].

competent suitable, proper, adequate XIV; legally qualified or sufficient XV. - (O)F. *compétent* or L. *competēns, -ent-*, prp. of *competere* in the sense 'be fit, proper, or qualified'; see prec. and -ENT. Hence **competence, -ency** sufficiency (of qualification). XVI.

compile XIV. - (O)F. *compiler* put together, collect, or its presumed source L. *compīlāre* plunder, (contextually) plagiarize, f. COM- + *pīla* PILE[2]. So **compilation** XV, **compiler** XIV.

complacent †pleasing XVII; satisfied, esp. with oneself XVIII. - L. *complacēns, -ent-*, prp. of *complacēre*, f. COM- (intensive) + *placēre* PLEASE; see -ENT. So **complacence** XV. **complacency** XVII. - medL. *complacentia*. Cf. COMPLAISANT.

complain XIV. ME. *compleigne* - (O)F. *complaign-*, pres. stem of *complaindre* (orig. refl.) :- Rom. (medL.) *complangere*, f. COM- (intensive) + *plangere* lament (cf. PLAINT). So **complaint** XIV.

complaisant politely agreeable. XVII. - F. *complaisant* obliging, prp. of *complaire* acquiesce in order to please, repr. L. *complacēre* (see COMPLACENT). So **complaisance** XVII.

complement accomplishment, consummation XIV; something which completes a whole XVI; †adjunct, personal accomplishment; †observance of ceremony, tribute of courtesy XVI. - L. *complēmentum*, f. *complēre*; see next and -MENT, and cf. COMPLIMENT. Hence **complemental, -mentary** †accessory; †ceremonious, complimentary XVII; forming a complement XIX.

complete entire, finished, perfect. XIV. - (O)F. *complet* or L. *complētus*, pp. of *complēre* fill up, finish, fulfil, f. COM- (intensive) + **plē-*, base of *plēnus* FULL. Hence **complete** vb. XVI. So **completion, completive** XVII. - late L.

complex XVII. - F. *complexe* or its source L. *complexus*, pp. of *complectere, complectī* encompass, embrace, comprise; but sometimes analysed as COM- + *plexus* woven. Hence **complexity** XVIII.

complexion combination of the four humours of the body, (hence) bodily constitution and (further) habit of mind XIV; natural texture of the skin XV. - (O)F. - L. *complexiō, -ōn-* combination, association, (late) bodily habit, f. *complex-*; see prec. and -ION.

compliant XVII. f. COMPLY + -ANT, prob. after PLIANT. Hence **compliance** XVII.

complicate †intertwine; mix up *with* XVII; make complex XIX. f. pp. stem of L. *complicāre*, f. COM- + *plicāre* fold. So **complication** XVII.

complicity partnership in wrong. XVII (rare before XIX). f. †*complice* (XV) - (O)F. (see ACCOMPLICE), perh. partly after F. *complicité*; see -ITY.

compliment ceremonious tribute of courtesy, esp. polite phrase of commendation XVII; pl. formal greetings XVIII. - F. - It. *complimento*, repr. Rom. **complimentum*, for L. *complementum* COMPLEMENT.

compline last of the canonical hours. XIII (*comp(e)lin*). alt., prob. after *matin(e)s*, of (O)F. *complie* (now pl. *complies*), sb. use of fem. pp. pl. of *complir* complete :- Rom. **complīre* (cf. ACCOMPLISH) for L. *complēre* COMPLETE.

comply A. †fulfil; B. †use compliments, observe formalities; †be complaisant *with*; act in accordance *with* circumstances, others' desires, etc. XVII. - It. *complire* - Cat. *complir*, Sp. *cumplir* - L. *complēre* COMPLETE.

component composing, constituent; also sb. XVII. - L. *compōnēns, -ent-*, prp. of *compōnere* COMPOUND; see -ENT.

comport †bear, endure; agree *with* XVI; behave *oneself* XVII. - L. *comportāre*, f. COM- + *portāre* carry, bear (see PORT[3]).

compose A. put together, make up XV; set up (type); B. arrange, adjust; pacify, tranquillize XVII. - (O)F. *composer*, based on L. *compōnere*; see COMPOUND[2], POSE[1]. Hence **composure** †composition, in various senses XVI; composed state XVII; see -URE. So **composite** (archit.) fifth of the classical orders XVI; of compound structure XVII. - F. *composite* or L. *compositus*, pp. of *compōnere*. **composition** XIV. - (O)F. - L. **compositor** †(Sc.) arbiter XIV; type-setter XVI. - AN. - L.

compost (cookery) compote XIV; prepared manure XVI; (arch.) composition XVII. - OF. *composte* and *compost* :- L. *composta, -tum*, sb. uses of fem. and n. of *compōnere* COMPOUND[2].

compote fruit preserved in syrup, (later) fruit salad. XVII. - F., later form of OF. *composte* stew, dish consisting of fruit :- L. *composita*, sb. use of fem. of *compositus*, pp. of *compōnere* COMPOUND[2].

compound[1] compounded, composite. XIV. pp. of *compoune*; see next. Also sb. compound word XVI; compound substance XVII.

compound[2] put together, combine, compose XIV; trans. and intr. settle differences, etc. XV. ME. *compoune* - OF. *compo(u)n-*, pres. stem of *compondre* :- L. *compōnere* put or bring together, arrange, devise; see COM-, POSITION.

The orig. ME. form was superseded by the present form in XVI.

compound[2] in the East, enclosure within which a (European) residence or factory stands. XVII. - Pg. *campon* or Du. *kampoeng* - Malay *kampong* enclosure, fenced-in space, quarter occupied by a particular nationality.

comprehend XIV. - OF. *comprehender* or L. *comprehendere*, f. COM- + *prehendere* seize (cf. GET). So **comprehensible** XVI, **comprehension** XV, **comprehensive** XV.

compress press together XIV; condense XVIII. - OF. *compresser* or late L. *compressāre*, or f. pp. stem *compress-* of *comprimere*; see COM-, PRESS. So **compress** sb. (surg.) mass of material formed into a pad. XVI. - F. *compresse*, f. *compresser*. **compression** XIV.

comprise †lay hold of; comprehend, include. XV. f. F. *compris, -ise*, pp. of *comprendre* COMPREHEND, on the analogy of comps. of *prendre*, of which a sb. and vb. in *-prise* existed, as *enterprise* (†*emprise*), *surprise* (†*supprise*).

compromise †joint agreement to abide by a decision XV; coming to terms by concessions on both sides XVI. - (O)F. *compromis* - juridical L. *comprōmissum*, sb. use of n. of pp. of *comprōmittere* consent to arbitration, f. COM- + *prōmittere* PROMISE. Hence **compromise** vb. XV.

comptometer calculating-machine. XIX. f. F. *compte* COUNT[1] + -O- + -METER.

comptroller sp. of CONTROLLER, due to assoc. of *cont-* with COUNT[1] (L. *computus*), used in certain official designations. XVI.

compulsion XV. - (O)F. - late L. *compulsiō, -ōn-*, f. *compuls-*, pp. stem of *compellere* COMPEL; see -SION. So **compulsive** XVII, **compulsory** XVI.

compunction pricking of the conscience XIV; in weakened sense XVIII. - (O)F. *componction* - ChrL. *compunctiō, -ōn-*, f. *compungere*, f. COM- + *pungere* prick (see PUNCTURE and -TION).

compurgator witness who swears to the credibility of an accused person when he purges himself by oath. XVI. - medL. *compurgātor*, f. COM- + *purgātor* purger (see PURGE). So **compurgation** XVII.

compute XVII. - F. *computer* or L. *computāre*, f. COM- + *putāre* clear or settle (an account), reckon, think. So **computation** XV, **computer** XVII.

comrade XVI. Earlier *came-, camarade*, etc. - F. *camerade, camarade* (orig. fem.) - Sp. *camarada* room-mate, f. *camara* CHAMBER; see -ADE.

con[1] 'get to know, learn', hence 'get by heart, commit to memory', 'peruse, scan'; differentiated var. of ME. *cunne*, OE. *cunnan* know (see CAN[1]); not clearly evidenced (with pt. and pp. *conned*) before XV, earlier instances of *conne, konne* being normal graphic vars. of *cunne*.

con[2] direct the steering of (a ship) from a commanding position. XVII (*cun, con*). Reduced form of †*cond*, †*cund* (XVII), shortening of †*condie*, †*condue* (XIV) - (O)F. *conduire* :- L. *condūcere* CONDUCT. Survives mainly in *conning-tower* pilot house of a warship or submarine. XIX.

con[3] see PRO[1].

con[4] (U.S.) short for CONFIDENCE (man, trick). XIX.

con- comb. form of L. prep. *com* (later *cum*) with, used regularly before all consonants except *b, p, m, h, r*, and *l*; see COL-, COM-. In OF. *conv-* was reduced to *cov-*, e.g. COVENANT, COVET; many Eng. adoptions preserve this, but in some words *con-* was restored, e.g. CONVENT (q.v.). For the meaning see COM-.

conation (philos.) faculty of volition. XIX. - L. *cōnātiō, -ōn-*, f. *cōnārī, -āt-* endeavour; see -ATION. So **conative** XIX.

concatenate link together. XVI. f. pp. stem of late L. *concatēnāre*, f. CON- + *catēna* CHAIN; see -ATE[3]. So **concatenation** XVII. - F. or L.

concave XV. - L. *concavus* (perh. through F. *concave*), f. CON- + *cavus* hollow. So **concavity** XIV. - F. or late L.; see -ITY.

conceal XIV. - OF. *conceler* - L. *concēlāre*, f. CON- + *cēlāre* hide, f. IE. base **kel-*. So **concealment** XIV.

concede XVII. - F. *concéder* or its source L. *concēdere* withdraw, yield; see CON- and CEDE. So **concession** XVI.

conceit †conception, thought; personal opinion XIV; fanciful opinion, etc., fancy XV; for *self-conceit* XVII. f. CONCEIVE on the analogy of the pairs *deceive, deceit, receive, receipt*, which have French originals. The sense-development was infl. by It. *concetto* (cf. CONCEPT), which the Eng. word was prob. designed to represent. Hence **conceit** vb. XVI. **conceited** XVI. f. vb. or sb.; see -ED[2].

conceive become pregnant (with) XIII; take into the mind XIV; formulate in words XVI. - OF. *conceiv-*, tonic stem of *concevoir*, for **conceivre* :- L. *concipere* take to oneself, etc. f. CON- + *capere* take. So **conceivable** XVI.

concentrate bring to a common centre. XVII. f. †*concentre* (XVI) - F. *concentrer*; see CON-, CENTRE vb., -ATE[3]. So **concentration** XVII. **concentric** having a common centre XIV (rare before XVII; *concentrical* from XVI). - (O)F. *concentrique* or medL. *-icus*; see -IC.

conception action of conceiving in the womb XIII; apprehension, imagination XIV; notion XVII. - (O)F. - L. *conceptiō, -ōn-*, f. *concipere, concept-* CONCEIVE. So **concept** †thought, opinion, etc. XVI; (philos.) XVII. - late L. *conceptus*, f. pp. stem of *concipere*. **conceptual** XVII. - medL. *conceptuālis*, f. *conceptus*; hence **conceptualist** (scholastic philos.) XVIII, **-ism** XIX.

concern †discern; relate to XV; engage the attention of XVI; pass. be interested, involved XVII. - (O)F. *concerner* or late L. *concernere* sift, distinguish, in medL. have respect or reference to, f. CON- + *cernere* sift (cf. CERTAIN). Somewhat earlier in prp. **concerning** (XV) in uses leading to its use as prep., prob. modelled on a similar use of F. *concernant*. Hence **concern** sb. XVI.

concert[1] harmony; musical performance. XVII. - F. - It. CONCERTO.

concert[2] †unite XVI; arrange by agreement XVII. - F. *concerter* - It. *concertare* bring into agreement or harmony, of obscure orig.

concertina XIX (invented by Sir Charles Wheatstone, 1829). f. CONCERT[1].

concerto XVIII. - It., f. *concertare* (see CONCERT[2]).
concession XVI. - (O)F. *concession* or L. *concessiō, -ōn-*, f. *concess-*, pp. stem of *concēdere* CONCEDE; see -ION. So **concessive** (chiefly gram.) XVIII. - late L.
conch shell(-fish). XVI. - L. *concha* bivalve, mussel, pearl oyster, etc. - Gr. *kógkhē*.
concierge janitor, caretaker. XVII. - F. (OF. *cumcerges*) :- Rom. **conservius*, alt. of L. *conservus* fellow slave (see CON-, SERF).
conciliar pert. to a council. XVII. - medL. *conciliarius*, f. L. *concilium* COUNCIL.
conciliate gain the goodwill of, win over; reconcile. XVI. f. pp. stem of L. *conciliāre* unite, procure, win, f. *concilium* COUNCIL; see -ATE[3]. So **conciliation, conciliator, conciliatory** XVI.
concinnity congruity; elegance of literary style. XVI. - L. *concinnitās*, f. *concinnus* skilfully put together, elegant, neat; see -ITY.
concise XVI. - F. *concis, -ise* or L. *concīsus* divided, broken up, brief, pp. of *concīdere* cut or divide up, f. CON- (intensive) + *cædere* cut.
conclave †private chamber; private place of assembly of cardinals XIV; private assembly XVI. - F. - L. *conclāve*, f. CON- + *clāvis* key.
conclude †enclose, include; bring or come to a close, settlement, decision; infer, prove. XIV. - L. *conclūdere*, f. CON- + *claudere* shut (cf. CLOSE). So **conclusion** XIV. - (O)F. *conclusion* or L. *conclūsiō, -ōn-*, f. *conclūdere, conclūs-*. **conclusive** XVI. - late L.
concoct †digest (food) XVI; compose, devise XVII. - L. *concoct-*, pp. stem of *concoquere* digest, etc., f. CON- + *coquere* cook, f. *coquus* COOK. So **concoction** XVI.
concomitant XVII. - prp. of late L. *concomitārī* accompany, f. CON- + *comitārī*, f. *comes, comit-* companion; see COUNT[2], -ANT. So **concomitance** XVI.
concord XIII. - (O)F. *concorde* - L. *concordia*, f. CON- + *cor, cord-* HEART. So **concordance** A. alphabetical register with citations of words contained in a work (orig. and esp. the Bible) XIV; B. agreement XV. **concordant** agreeing. XV. **concordat** agreement, compact. XVII. - F. *concordat* or L. *concordātum*, sb. use of n. pp. of *concordāre* agree.
concourse running or flowing together, meeting XIV; concurrence; assemblage XVII. - (O)F. *concours* - L. *concursus*, f. *concurrere, concurs-* run together, CONCUR.
concrete †united, composite; opp. to *abstract* XIV; sb. concreted mass XVII; composition of sand or gravel and cement XIX. - F. *concret* or L. *concrētus*, pp. of *concrēscere* grow together, f. CON- + *crēscere* grow. So **concretion** XVI.
concubine XIII. - (O)F. - L. *concubīna*, f. CON- + *cub-* lie down (cf. CUBICLE). So **concubinage** XIV. **concubinary** (one) living in concubinage. XVI. - medL. *concubīnārius*.
concupiscence XIV. - (O)F. - late L. *concupiscentia*, f. prp. stem of *concupiscere*, inceptive of *concupere*, f. CON- + *cupere* desire; see -ENCE.
concur †collide, converge XV; fall together, coincide; agree in action or opinion XV. - L. *concurrere*, f. CON- + *currere* run. So **concurrent** XIV, **concurrence** XV.
concussion violent agitation XV; injury due to the shock of a blow, etc. XVI. - L. *concussiō, -ōn-*, f. *concuss-*, pp. stem of *concutere* dash together, shake violently, f. CON- + *quatere* shake (cf. QUASH); see -ION.
condemn XIII. - OF. *condem(p)ner* (mod. *condamner*) - L. *condem(p)nāre*, f. CON- + *damnāre* DAMN. So **condemnation** XIV. - late L.
condense increase the density of XV; reduce from vapour to liquid XVII. - (O)F. *condenser* or L. *condensāre*, f. *condensus* very dense; see CON-, DENSE. So **condensation** XVII. - late L.
condescend †settle down *to* XIV; bend down *to*, be complaisant, agree XV. - (O)F. *condescendre* - ecclL. *condēscendere* stoop (fig.), in medL. accede, agree to, f. CON- + *dēscendere* DESCEND. So **condescension** XVII. - ecclL.
condign †of equal worth; †worthy, deserving; deserved, fitting, esp. in *condign punishment*. XV. - (O)F. *condigne* - L. *condignus* wholly worthy, f. CON- (intensive) + *dignus* worthy (cf. DIGNITY).
condiment XV. - L. *condīmentum*, f. *condīre* preserve, pickle, by-form of *condere* preserve, prop. put together.
condition convention, stipulation; mode of being. XIV. - OF. *condicion* (mod. *-tion*) - L. *condiciō, -ōn-* agreement, etc., rel. to *condīcere* agree upon, etc., f. CON- + *dīcere* declare, say (cf. DICTION). So **conditional** XIV. - OF. *condicionel* (mod. *-tionnel*) or late L. *condiciōnālis*.
condole †sorrow greatly; †trans. grieve with or over XVI; express sympathy *with* XVII. - ChrL. *condolēre*, f. CON- + *dolēre* suffer pain, grieve. So **condolence** †sympathetic grief; outward expression of sympathy. XVII. f. the vb.; but in the second sense orig. in the form †*condoleance* - F. *condoléance*.
condominium joint rule. XVIII. - modL., f. CON- + L. *dominium* DOMINION.
condone XIX. - L. *condōnāre* refrain from punishment as a favour, f. CON- + *dōnāre* give (cf. PARDON), a term of canon law with spec. reference to violation of the marriage vow. So **condonation** XVII.
condor large S. American vulture. XVII. - Sp. *cóndor* - Quechua *cuntur*.
condottiere leader of mercenary troops. XVIII. - It., f. *condotta* contract, troop of mercenaries under contract.
conduce †lead XV; †engage, hire; contribute, lead, or tend *to* XVI. - L. *condūcere* bring together (and all the above senses), f. CON- + *dūcere* lead. Hence **conducive** XVII (earlier *conductive* XVI).
conduct guiding, leading (surviving in *safe conduct*); management XV; manner of conducting oneself XVII. - L. *conductus*, f. *condūcere, conduct-* (see prec.). Preceded by *condu(i)t(e)* (XIII-XVI) - OF. *conduit*, (also mod.) *conduite* - medL. *conductus*, Rom. **conducta*. Cf. CONDUIT. So **conduct** vb. lead, guide XV; command XVI; direct, manage XVII. Preceded by *conduite* (XV), f. (O)F. *conduite*, pp. of *conduire*; later assim. to the L. pp. *conductus*. **conduction** †leading, leadership; †management; †hiring XVI;

conducting (of liquid) XVII; transmission of heat, electricity, etc. XIX. - (O)F. or L. **conductor** A. leader, commander XVI; manager XVII; director of singers and musicians XVIII; B. substance or object that conducts heat, etc. XVIII. - (O)F. *conducteur* - L.; see -OR[1].

conduit channel or pipe for the conveyance of liquid. XIV. ME. *condut, condit* - (O)F. *conduit* :- medL. *conductus*, f. *conduct-*, pp. stem of *condūcere* CONDUCE.

condyle rounded process at the end of a bone. XVII. - F. - L. *condylus* - Gr. *kóndulos* knuckle.

cone figure of which the base is a circle and the summit a point XVI (in earlier use her. †angular division of a shield XV). - F. *cône* or L. *cōnus* - Gr. *kônos* pine-cone, geometrical cone, etc., rel. to HONE. So **conic, -ical** XVI. - modL. *cōnicus* - Gr. *kōnikós*.

confab XVIII. colloq. shortening of **confabulation** talk, chat. XV. - late L. *confabulātiō, -ōn-*, f. *confabulārī* converse (see CON-, FABLE), whence **confabulate** XVII, also abbrev. *confab*.

confection compounded medicinal preparation; prepared dish, preparation of fruit, etc., conserve, sweetmeat. XIV. - (O)F. - L. *confectiō, -ōn-* preparation (abstr. and concr.), f. *confect-*, pp. stem of *conficere* prepare, f. CON- + *facere* put, make. Hence, through the vb. *confection* (XVI), **confectioner** maker of sweetmeats, cakes, etc. XVI; see -ER[1]; whence **confectionery** XVIII.

confederate leagued, allied XIV; sb. accomplice XV; ally XVI. - late (eccl.) L. *confœderātus*; see CON-, FEDERATE. So **confederation** league, alliance, †conspiracy XV; body of states leagued together XVII. - (O)F. or late L. **confederacy** (in same senses) XIV. - AN. *confederacie*.

confer †bring together, collect; compare, collate; converse, take counsel; bestow. XVI. - L. *conferre*, f. CON- + *ferre* bring, BEAR[2]. So **conference** †collation, collection; taking counsel, discourse; meeting for consultation. XVI. - F. *conférence* or medL. *conferentia*.

confess own to, acknowledge, esp. guiltily, hear the confession of, shrive. XIV. - (O)F. *confesser* :- Rom. **confessāre*, f. L. *confessus*, pp. of *confitērī* acknowledge, f. CON- + *fatērī* declare, avow, rel. to *fārī* speak, *fābula* FABLE. So **confession** acknowledgement (of guilt) XIV; matter confessed XV; formulary of belief XVI. **confessional** place for hearing confessions. XVIII. - F. *confessional* - It. *confessionale* - medL., sb. use of n. sg. of adj. **confessor** (eccl.) one who avows his religion in the face of danger but does not suffer martyrdom XII; (gen.) one who makes confession (of belief, guilt, etc.) XIII; (eccl.) one who hears confessions XIV. - AN. *confessur*, OF. *confessour* (mod. *-eur*) - eccL. *confessor*; see -OR[1].

confetti small sweets used as missiles at a carnival, small disks of paper so used at weddings. XIX. - It., pl. of *confetto* = OF. *confit(e)* COMFIT.

confide put faith *in*. XV. - L. *confīdere*, f. CON- (intensive) + *fīdere* trust (see FAITH). So **confident** trusting, self-assured XVI; †trusted, trusty XVII; sb. confidential friend or adviser XVII; in the earlier sense - L. *confīdēns, -ent-*; in the later, and as sb. - F. - It. *confidente*; in sb. use superseded by **confidant**, fem. **-ante** (XVIII), which are not regular F. forms, but were presumably adopted orig. to represent the pronunc. of F. *confidente*. **confidential** †confident XVII; done in confidence, betokening intimacy XVIII.

configuration (astron.) relative position XVI; conformation, outline XVII. - late L. *configūrātiō, -ōn-*, f. L. *configūrāre* fashion after a pattern; see CON-, FIGURE, -ATION.

confine have a common boundary *with*, border; keep within bounds, imprison. XVI. - F. *confiner*, f. *confins* CONFINES. Hence (or - F. *confinement*) **confinement** imprisonment XVII; childbed XVIII.

confines (pl.) †region XIV; boundaries, borders XVI. - F. *confins*, †*confines* - L. *confīnia*, pl. of *confīne* and *confīnium*, f. *confīnis* bordering, f. CON- + *fīnis* end, limit (pl. *fīnes* territory).

confirm settle, establish XIII; administer confirmation to; strengthen, fortify XIV. - OF. *confermer* (later *confirmer*) - L. *confirmāre*, f. CON- (intensive) + *firmāre* strengthen, f. *firmus* FIRM. So **confirmation** eccl. rite conveying special grace for the strengthening of the baptized; corroboration, ratification. XIV.

confiscate appropriate to the public treasury XVI; seize summarily XIX. f. L. *confiscāre, -āt-*, f. CON- + *fiscus* chest, treasury; see FISCAL, -ATE[3]. So **confiscation** XVI. - L.

conflagration †consumption by fire; great fire. XVI. - L. *conflagrātiō, -ōn-*, f. *conflagrāre* burn up; see CON-, FLAGRANT, -ATION.

conflation blowing or fusing together XVII; fusion of textual readings XIX. - late L. *conflātiō, -ōn-*, fanning (of fire), fusion (of metals), f. *conflāre* kindle, effect, fuse; see CON-, BLOW[1], -ATION. So **conflate** XVII. f. ppl. stem of L. *conflāre*; see -ATE[3].

conflict sb. XV. - L. *conflīctus*, f. *conflīct-*, pp. stem of *conflīgere*, f. CON- + *flīgere* strike. So **conflict** vb. XV.

confluence flowing together, junction of streams. XVI. - late L. *confluentia*, f. *confluēns, -ent-*, prp. of *confluere*; see CON-, FLUENT. So **confluent** XVII.

conform XIV. - (O)F. *conformer* - L. *conformāre*; see CON-, FORM vb. So **conformable** XVI. - medL. **conformist** XVII. **conformation** XVI. - L. **conformity** XV. - (O)F. or late L.

confound †overthrow XIII; bring to perdition; throw into confusion XIV. - AN. *conf(o)undre*, (O)F. *confondre* :- L. *confundere* pour together, mix up, f. CON- + *fundere* pour (see FOUND[3]).

confraternity organized (religious) brotherhood. XV. - (O)F. *confraternité* - medL. *confrāternitās*, f. *confrāter* CONFRÈRE; see -ITY.

confrère †fellow member of a fraternity, etc. XV; fellow member of a learned body XVII. - (O)F. - medL. *confrāter*; see CON- and FRIAR.

confront stand in front of, face with hostility XVI; bring face to face XVII. - F. *confronter* - medL. *confrontāre*, f. L. CON- + *frōns, front-* forehead, face, FRONT.

confused †discomfited, confounded XIV; thrown into disorder, mixed XVI. f. (O)F. *confus* or its source L. *confūsus*, pp. of *confundere* CONFOUND + -ED. Hence **confuse** vb. in corr. active senses, and in the sense 'mix up in the mind'. XVIII. So **confusion** discomfiture XIII; throwing into disorder, result of this XIV.

confute prove to be wrong or false. XVI. - L. *confūtāre* check, restrain, answer conclusively, f. CON- + **fūt-*, as in *refūtāre* REFUTE. So **confutation** XVI.

congeal make or become solid as by freezing. XIV. - (O)F. *congeler* - L. *congelāre*, f. CON- + *gelāre* freeze (see GELID).

congener member of the same class or group. XVIII. - L., f. CON- + *gener-* GENUS.

congenial of the same disposition or temperament XVII; suited to one's taste XVIII. f. CON- + GENIUS + -AL[1].

congenital dating from one's birth. XVIII. f. L. *congenitus* born along with, connate, f. CON- + *genitus*, pp. of *gignere* produce (see GENITAL).

conger large species of eel. XIV. - (O)F. *congre* :- L. *congrus*, also *conger*, - Gr. *góggros*.

congeries XVII. - L. *congeriēs* heap, pile, f. *congerere* (see next).

congestion †accumulation XVI; (med.) of blood XV; overcrowded state XIX. - (O)F. - L. *congestiō*, *-ōn-*, f. *congest-*, pp. stem of *congerere* heap together (whence **congest** XVI), f. CON- + *gerere* carry; see -TION.

conglomerate †massed together XVI; (physiol.) of complex glands XVII; (geol.) formed of fragments cemented together (also sb.) XIX. - L. *conglomerātus*, pp. of *conglomerāre*, f. CON- + *glomus*, *glomer-* ball, rel. to *globus* GLOBE; see -ATE[2]. So **conglomeration** XVII.

congratulate XVI. f. pp. stem of L. *congrātulārī*, f. CON- (intensive) + *grātulārī* manifest one's joy, f. *grātus* pleasing; see GRATEFUL, -ATE[3]. So **congratulation** XV.

congregation A. meeting, assembly XIV; B. orig. in biblical language, in O.T. assembly of Israelites XIV; in N.T. body of Christians; body assembled for worship XVI. - (O)F. *congrégation* or L. *congregātiō*, *-ōn-*, f. *congregāre*, whence **congregate** collect together XV; see CON-, GREGARIOUS, -ATE[3], -ATION. Hence **congregational** XVII.

congress meeting, union XVI; formal assembly of delegates, etc. XVII; legislative body of U.S.A. XVIII. - L. *congressus*, f. *congress-*, pp. stem of *congredī* go together, meet, f. CON- + *gradī* step, walk.

congressional XVIII. f. CONGRESS with insertion of *-ion-* from L. *congressiōn-*; see -ION, -AL[1].

congruent conforming, accordant, agreeable. XV. - L. *congruēns*, *-ent-*, prp. of *congruere* meet together, agree, correspond, f. CON- + **gruere*, *ruere* fall, rush; see RUIN, -ENT. So **congruity** XV. - F. or late L. **congruous** XVI.

conic see CONE.

conifer XIX. - L. *cōnifer*, f. *cōnus* CONE. So **coniferous** cone-bearing. XVII.

conjecture †interpretation of signs, etc. XIV; (formation of) an opinion on grounds insufficient for proof XVI. - (O)F. *conjecture* or L. *conjectūra* conclusion, inference, f. *conject-*, pp. stem of *conicere* throw together, put together in speech or thought, conclude; see CON-, ABJECT, -URE. So **conjecture** vb. XIV. - (O)F. *conjecturer* - late L. *conjecturāre*. **conjectural** XVI. - F. - L.

conjoin XIV. Late ME. *conjoigne*, *-oyne* - (O)F. *conjoign-*, pres. stem of *conjoindre* :- L. *conjungere* (see CONJUNCT). So **conjoint** XVIII (earlier in adv. *conjointly*). - (O)F. *conjoint*, pp. of *conjoindre*.

conjugal XVI. - L. *conjugālis*, f. *conju(n)x*, *conjug-* spouse, f. CON- + **jug-*, base of *jungere* JOIN; see -AL[1]. So **conjugate** joined. XV. - L. *conjugātus*, pp. of *conjugāre*, whence **conjugate** †couple, yoke; inflect (a verb) in its various forms XVI. See -ATE[2,3]. **conjugation** earliest in gram. sense XV.

conjunct XV. - L. *conjunctus*, pp. of *conjungere*, f. CON- + *jungere* JOIN. So **conjunction** union, connection (gen. and astron.), (gram.) connecting particle. XIV. - (O)F. *conjonction* - L. *conjunctiō*, *-ōn-*, f. *conjungere*. **conjunctive** XV. - late L. **conjunctivitis** (see -ITIS) inflammation of the *membrana conjunctiva* 'conjunctive membrane' connecting the inner eyelid and the eyeball.

conjure A. constrain by oath or by a sacred invocation XIII; B. affect or effect by jugglery XVI. - (O)F. *conjurer* to plot, exorcise, adjure :- L. *conjūrāre* band together by an oath, conspire, in medL. invoke, f. CON- + *jūrāre* swear, f. *jūs*, *jūr-* right, law. Hence **conjurer** one who conjures spirits XIV; one who practises legerdemain XVIII. Partly - AN. *conjurour*, OF. *conjurere*, *-eor* - medL. *conjūrātor*, *-ōr-*; see -ER[1].

conkers children's game played orig. with snail-shells, later with chestnuts on a string. XIX. f. dial. *conker* snail-shell, presumably f. CONCH.

connate existing from birth, congenital XVII; congenitally united XVIII. - late L. *connātus*, pp. of *connascī*, f. CON- + *nascī* be born (see NATAL).

connect XVII. - L. *connectere* (*cōnectere*), f. CON- + *nectere* bind, fasten. Hence **connective** XVII. So **connection, connexion** XIV. - L. *connexiō*, *-ōn-*, f. *connectere*, *connex-*.

conning-tower see CON[2].

connive shut one's eyes to, wink *at*. XVII. - F. *conniver* - L. *connivēre* (*cōnivēre*) shut the eyes, f. CON- + **nivēre*, rel. to *nictāre* blink. So **connivance** XVI. orig. *connivence* - F. *connivence* or L. *connīventia*.

connoisseur XVIII. - F., earlier sp. of *connaisseur*, f. ppl. stem of *connaître* know.

connote XVII. - scholastic L. *connōtāre* mark in addition, f. CON- + *notāre* NOTE. So **connotation** XVI.

connubial XVII. - L. *connūbiālis*, f. *connūbium* marriage, wedlock, f. CON- + *nūbere* marry; see NUPTIAL and -IAL.

conquer XIII. - OF. *conquerre* :- Rom. **conquerere*, for L. *conquīrere* seek for, procure, gain, win, f. CON- + *quærere* seek. So **conqueror** XIII. - AN. *conquerour*, OF. *-eor*, f. *conquerre*; see -OR[1].

conquest XIII. - OF. *conquest*, *conqueste* (mod. *conquête*), repr. sb. uses of n. and fem. of Rom. **conquestus*, pp. of **conquerere*.

consanguinity XIV. - L. *consanguinitās*, f. *consanguineus* of the same blood, f. CON- + *sanguis*, *sanguin-* blood; see -ITY.

conscience XIII. - (O)F. - L. *conscientia* privity of knowledge, consciousness, f. *conscīre* know or be privy with (another or oneself); see CON- and SCIENCE. So **conscientious** XVII. **conscionable** conscientious, scrupulous. XVI. f. †*conscions*, var. of *conscience*, + -ABLE; now familiar in *unconscionable*. **conscious** †privy *to* a thing with another or within oneself; aware *of*. XVII. f. L. *conscius*, f. CON- + **sci*-, base of *scīre* know.

conscript enrolled or elected as a senator XV; enrolled by compulsory enlistment XIX (also as sb. after F. *conscrit*). - L. *conscriptus*, pp. of *conscrībere* enrol, f. CON- + *scrībere* write. So **conscription** †enrolment XIV; compulsory enlistment XIX (after F. *conscription*). - late L. Hence **conscript** vb. XIX.

consecrate devote to a sacred purpose XV; dedicate XVI; make sacred XVII. f. (after †*consecrate* pp. XIV) L. *consecrāre*, *-āt-*, f. CON- (intensive) + *sacrāre* dedicate, f. *sacer*, *sacr-* SACRED; see -ATE[3]. So **consecration** XIV. - (O)F. or L.

consecution logical sequence XVI; succession XVII. - L. *consecūtiō*, *-ōn-*, f. *consequī*, *consecūt-* follow closely; see CONSEQUENCE and -TION. So **consecutive** XVII. - F. *consécutif* - medL. *consecūtīvus*.

consensus general agreement. XIX. - L., f. *consēns-*, pp. stem of *consentīre* CONSENT.

consent sb. XIII. - OF. *consente*, f. *consentir* (whence **consent** vb. XIII) - L. *consentīre* agree, accord, f. CON- + *sentīre* feel (see SENSE).

consequence thing resulting, logical result XIV; importance, moment (orig. in phr. *of consequence* prop. having issues or results) XVI. - (O)F. *conséquence* - L. *consequentia*, f. *consequī*, *consequent-* follow closely; see CON-, SEQUENCE. So **consequent** resulting XV (earlier in **consequently**), **consequential** XVII.

conservancy control of, (hence) commission controlling, a port, river, etc. XVIII. alt., by assim. to -ANCY, of †*conservacy* (XV-XVIII) - AN. *conservacie* - AL. *conservātia* (see -ACY), by-form of L. *conservātiō* CONSERVATION.

conservatoire academy for instruction in music, etc. XVIII. - F. - It. *conservatorio* - modL. *conservātōrium*, sb. use of n. of late L. *conservātorius*, f. *conservāre*, *-āt-* to preserve, CONSERVE. So **conservatory** †preservative XVI; †storehouse; greenhouse for tender plants XVII; (U.S.) conservatoire XIX. - late L.

conserve vb. XIV. - (O)F. *conserver* - L. *conservāre*; see CON- (intensive) and SERVE. So as sb. †preservative XIV; medicinal or confectionary preparation XVI. - (O)F., f. the vb. **conservation** XIV. - (O)F. or L. **conservative** preservative XIV; (in politics) XIX; hence **conservatism** XIX.

consider XIV. - (O)F. *considérer* - L. *consīderāre*, f. COM- (intensive) + base **sīder-*, found also in *dēsīderāre* DESIRE. Hence **considerable** †that can be considered XV; worthy of consideration, large in amount, etc. XVII. - medL. *considerābilis*. So **consideration** XIV.

consign †attest, confirm XV; †mark with the cross; hand or make over XVI. - F. *consigner* - L. *consignāre* attest with a seal, f. CON- (intensive) + *signāre* SIGN.

consist XVI. - L. *consistere* stand still, remain firm, exist, f. CON- (intensive) + *sistere* place, stand firm or still, stop. So **consistence, -ency** XVI. - F. *consistance*, †*-ence* or late L. *consistentia*. **consistent** †remaining still XVI; agreeing, esp. self-consistent XVII.

consistory †council chamber; council; (eccl.) bishop's court, papal 'senate' XIV; court of presbyters XVI. - AN. *consistorie* = (O)F. *consistoire* - late L. *consistōrium*, f. *consistere* (see CONSIST); see -ORY[1]. Hence **consistorial** XV.

consolation XIV. - (O)F. - L. *consōlātiō*, *-ōn-*, f. *consōlārī*, *-āt-*, whence, or through F. *consoler*, **console**[1] vb. XVII; see CON- (intensive), SOLACE, -ATION.

console[2] (archit.) kind of bracket XVIII; ensemble of keyboards and stops in an organ XIX. - F., obscure deriv. of *consolider* CONSOLIDATE.

consolidate XVI. f. pp. stem of L. *consolidāre*, f. CON- (intensive) + *solidāre*, f. *solidus* SOLID; see -ATE[3]. So **consolidation** XV. - late L.

consols XVIII. Short for *consolidated annuities*, the government securities of Great Britain, consisting orig. of a great variety of public securities, which were *consolidated* in 1751 into a single stock.

consommé XIX. - F., sb. use of pp. of *consommer* - L. *consummāre* CONSUMMATE; the nutriment of the meat is completely used up.

consonant sb. XIV. - (O)F. - L. *consonāns*, *-ant-*, sb. use of prp. of *consonāre* sound together (see CON-, SOUND[3]); so named because it can only be 'sounded with' a vowel. So **consonant** adj. in harmony, concordant. XV. **consonance** XV, **-ancy** XIV. - (O)F. or L.

consort[1] †partner, mate XV; ship sailing with another; partner in marriage, spouse. XVII. - F. *consort*, fem. *-sorte* - L. *consors*, *-sort* sharing in common, partner, colleague, f. CON- + *sors* portion, lot (see SORT).

consort[2] †accompany, escort; associate or accord *with*. XVI. In the first sense f. CONSORT[1]; in the second prob. a reinforcement of SORT vb.

conspectus XIX. - L., f. *conspect-*, pp. stem of *conspicere* look attentively, f. CON- (intensive) + *specere* (see ASPECT).

conspicuous XVI. f. L. *conspicuus*, f. *conspicere*; see prec. and -UOUS.

conspire XIV. - (O)F. *conspirer* - L. *conspīrāre* agree, combine, f. CON- + *spīrāre* breathe (see SPIRIT). So **conspiracy** XIV. - AN. *conspiracie*, alt. of (O)F. *conspiration* (- L.), whence earlier ME. *conspiration* (XIII). **conspirator** XV.

constable chief officer of the household, etc. of a sovereign; governor of a royal castle XIII; officer of the peace XIV. - OF. *cune-*, *conestable* (mod. *connétable*), repr. late L. *comes stabulī* lit. COUNT (i.e. head officer) of the STABLE; cf. the development of the senses of *marshal*. So **constabulary** †constable's office or district XVI; body of constables XIX. - medL.

constant steadfast XIV; invariable XVI. - (O)F. - L. *constāns*, *-ant-*, prp. of *constāre* stand firm; cf. COST, STAND, and see -ANT. So **constancy** XVI. - L. *constantia*.

constellation †(astrol.) relative position of the stars; (astron.) number of fixed stars artificially grouped together. XIV. - (O)F. - late L. *constellātiō, -ōn-*, f. CON- + *stella* STAR; see -ATION.

consternation XVII. - F. *consternation* or L. *consternātiō, -ōn-*, f. *consternāre* lay prostrate, terrify, f. CON- + *sternere* lay low; see -ATION.

constipate †pack or bind close together; confine the bowels. XVI. f. pp. stem of L. *constīpāre*, f. CON- + *stīpāre* press, cram; see -ATE[3]. So **constipation** XV. - (O)F. or late L.

constituent A. adj. jointly constituting XVII; constituting or appointing a representative XVIII; having the power to frame a constitution XIX; B. sb. one who appoints a representative XVII; elector; constituent element XVIII. - (partly through F. *constituant*) L. *constituēns, -ent-*, prp. of *constituere*; see next and -ENT. Hence **constituency** body of constituents. XIX.

constitute set up, establish XV; make up, form XVI. f. L. *constitūt-*, pp. of *constituere* establish, appoint, f. CON- (intensive) + *statuere* set up (see STATUTE). So **constitution** decree, ordinance XIV; nature, disposition XVI; mode or principles of state organization XVII. - (O)F. - L. Hence **constitutional** XVII. **constitutive** constructive XVI; formative, component XVII.

constrain force, compel, confine forcibly. XIV. - OF. *constraindre*, pres. stem *constraign-* (mod. *contraindre*) :- L. *constringere* bind tightly together; see CON- and STRINGENT. So **constraint** †affliction XIV; compulsion, confinement XVI; restraint of natural feelings XVIII. - OF. *constrainte*, fem. pp. sb. f. *constraindre*.

constriction compression XV; constricted part XIX. - late L. *constrictiō, -ōn-*, f. *constrict-* (whence **constrict** vb. XVIII), pp. stem of *constringere* (whence **constringe** vb. XVII); see prec. and -TION. So **constrictor** (anat.) constricting muscle XVIII; large snake that crushes its prey XIX. - modL.; see -OR[1].

construct XVII. f. *construct-*, pp. stem of L. *construere* pile up, build, f. CON- + *struere* (see STRUCTURE). So **construction** A. †construing XIV; interpretation XV; (gram.) syntactical arrangement XVI; B. building XV; mode of building, etc. XVI. - (O)F. - L. **constructive** inferential XVII; pert. to construction XIX.

construe (gram.) analyse the construction of; expound, interpret. XIV. - L. *construere* CONSTRUCT.

consubstantiation see TRANSUBSTANTIATION.

consul supreme magistrate in the ancient Roman republic XIV; applied to various magistrates or chief officials, spec. head of a merchant company resident in a foreign country XV; representative agent of a state in commercial relations with a foreign country XVI. - L., rel. to *consultāre* (see next). So **consulate** XIV; see -ATE[1].

consult XVII. - (O)F. *consulter* - L. *consultāre*, frequent. f. *consult-*, pp. stem of *consulere* take COUNSEL. So **consultation** XV. - (O)F. or L.

consume XIV. - (partly through F. *consumer*) L. *consūmere*, f. CON- + *sūmere* take. So **consumption** using up, wasting away, spec. by disease. XIV. - (O)F. *consomption* - L. *consumptiō, -ōn-*, f. *consumere, consumpt-*. **consumptive** XV. - medL. *consumptīvus*.

consummate pp. †completed XV; adj. complete, perfect XV. - L. *consummātus*. So **consummate** vb. bring to completion. XVI. f. L. *consummāre, -āt-*, f. CON- + *summa* SUM, *summus* highest, utmost, supreme; see -ATE[2,3]. **consummation** completion, perfection XIV; crowning end XVII. - (O)F. *consommation* or L. *consummātiō*.

contact sb. XVII. - L. *contāctus*, f. *contāct-*, pp. stem of *contingere* touch closely, border on, be CONTIGUOUS to, f. CON- + *tangere* touch.

contagion contagious disease, infecting influence. XIV. - L. *contāgiō, -ōn-*, f. CON- + base of *tangere* touch. So **contagious** XIV.

contain keep within certain limits XIII; have in it, comprise XIV. ME. *conte(i)ne* repr. tonic stem of (O)F. *contenir* :- L. *continēre*, f. CON- + *tenēre* hold.

contaminate XV. f. pp. stem of L. *contamināre*, f. *contāmen-, -min-* contact, pollution, for **contagmen*, f. CON- + **tag-*, base of *tangere* touch; see -ATE[3]. So **contamination** XV. - late L.

contango percentage which a buyer of stock pays to the seller to postpone transfer. XIX. perh. arbitrary formation on the anal. of L. 1st pres. sing. in *-ō*, poss. with the notion '(I) make contingent'.

contemn XV. - OF. *contemner* or L. *contemnere*, f. CON- (intensive) + *temnere* despise.

contemplate XVI. f. L. *contemplārī, -āt-*, f. CON- + *templum* open space for observation, TEMPLE[1]; see -ATE[3]. So **contemplation** XIII. - (O)F. - L. **contemplative** XIV.

contemporary XVII. - medL. *contemporārius*, f. CON- + *tempus, tempor-* time, after L. *contemporāneus* (whence **contemporaneous** XVII) and late L. *contemporālis*. See -ARY.

contempt XIV. - L. *contemptus*, f. *contempt-*, pp. stem of *contemnere* CONTEMN. So **contemptible** XIV. - (O)F. or late L. **contemptuous** †contemptible; full of contempt. XVI. - medL. *contemptuōsus*.

contend XV. - OF. *contendre* or L. *contendere*, f. CON- + *tendere* stretch; see TEND[2]. So **contention** XIV. - (O)F. *contention* or L. *contentiō, -ōn-*, f. *content-*, pp. stem of *contendere*. **contentious** XV. - (O)F. *contentieux* - L. *contentiōsus*.

content[1] (usu. pl.) what is contained; containing capacity or extent. XV. - medL. **contentum*, pl. *-ta* things contained, sb. use of n. of L. *contentus*, pp. of *continēre* CONTAIN.

content[2] satisfied, gratified. XIV. - (O)F. :- L. *contentus* that is satisfied, pp. of *continēre* fig. repress, restrain (see CONTAIN). So **content** vb., **contentment** XV.

content[3] satisfaction. XVI. immed. source obscure; perh. f. prec. as a shorter form equiv. to the earlier †*contentation* (XV) or *contentment* (XV), and corr. to Sp., Pg., It. *contento*.

conterminous having a boundary in common. XVII. f. L. *conterminus*, f. CON- + *terminus* boundary, TERM; see -OUS.

contest †bear witness to XVI; contend for, dispute XVII. - L. *contestārī* call to witness, introduce (a suit) by calling witnesses, set on foot (an action), f. CON- + *testārī* bear witness. Hence, or - F. *conteste* (f. the corr. vb.), **contest** sb. wordy strife, (gen.) conflict. XVII.

context †construction, composition XV; connected structure of a composition or passage, parts immediately before and after a given passage XVI. - L. *contextus*, f. *context-*, pp. stem of *contexere* weave together, f. CON- + *texere* weave. Hence **contextual** XIX.

contiguous XVII. f. L. *contiguus*, f. *contingere*; see CONTACT and -UOUS. So **contiguity** XVII.

continence (sexual) self-restraint. XIV. - (O)F. *continence* or L. *continentia*, f. *continēns, -ent-*, prp. of *continēre* restrain, CONTAIN, whence **continent** self-restraining XIV: †cohering, continuous XV (†*continent land*); sb. †container; †summary; continuous land, mainland XVI (spec. of Europe, Asia, etc. XVII). Hence **continental** XVIII.

contingent liable to happen XIV; dependent upon or subject to conditions XVI; sb. †accident, possibility XVI; †proportion falling to one; spec. of troops contributed to a force XVIII. - L. *contingēns, -ent-*, prp. of *contingere* be CONTIGUOUS, in connection or in contact, befall. So **contingency** XVI.

continual XIV. - (O)F. *continuel*, f. *continuer*; see below and -AL[1]. So **continuous** uninterrupted in space or time. XVII. f. L. *continuus*. **continuity** XV. **continue** carry on, persist, last. XIV. - (O)F. *continuer* - L. *continuāre*, f. *continuus* uninterrupted, f. *continēre* in its intr. sense of 'hang together' (cf. CONTINENT). **continuance** XIV. **continuation** †persistency XIV; prolongation XV. **continuum** XVII. - L., n. sg. of *continuus*.

contort XV. f. *contort-*, pp. stem of L. *contorquēre*, f. CON- (intensive) + *torquēre* twist. So **contortion** XVII.

contour outline. XVII. - F. - It. *contorno*, f. *contornare* draw in outline, f. CON- + *tornare* TURN.

contra against; adv. on or to the contrary XIV; prep., esp. in absol. use in *pro and contra* (abbrev. CON[2]) for a motion (etc.) and against it XV; sb. the contrary or opposite; now only in *per contra* on the opposite side of the account, as a set-off XVI; orig. an It. banking term. - L. *contrā* against (adv. and prep.).

contra- repr. L. prefix *contrā-* (cf. prec.), denoting opposition or the opposite side or direction, which, somewhat rare in classical L., became common in later L. and Rom. (in Sp., Pg., It. *contra-*, in F. *contre-* COUNTER-).

contraband sb. and adj. XVI. The present form was not current before XVII, the earlier forms being †*counterbande* (after F. *contrebande*) and †*contrabanda* - Sp. *-banda* - It. *-bando* (now *contrabb-*), f. *contra-* (see prec.) and *bando* BAN[1].

contraceptive XIX. irreg. f. CONTRA- + (CON)-CEPT(ION) + -IVE. So **contraception** XIX.

contract[1] sb. XIV. - OF. (mod. *contrat*) - L. *contractus*, f. pp. stem of *contrahere*; see next.

contract[2] A. agree upon, make a contract; B. incur, be involved in; C. reduce in compass or in limits. XVI. Based partly on earlier *contract* pp. (now used only of contracted grammatical forms) - OF. - L. *contractus*, pp. of *contrahere*, f. CON- + *trahere* draw. So **contraction** XIV. **contractor** †contracting party XVI; undertaker of a work XVIII. - late L.; see -OR[1].

contradict XVI. f. *contrādict-*, pp. stem of L. *contrādīcere*, orig. *contrā dīcere* speak against. So **contradiction** XIV. - (O)F. - L. **contradictory** adj. and sb. XIV. - late L. *contrādictōrius*. See CONTRA-, DICTION.

contralto XVIII (earlier *contrealt*). - It., f. CONTRA- and ALTO.

contraption XIX. perh. f. *contrive* (cf. *deceive/deception*), by assoc. with TRAP[1].

contrapuntal (mus.) pert. to counterpoint. XIX. f. It. *contrappunto* COUNTERPOINT + -AL[1].

contrary XIV. - AN. *contrarie*, (O)F. *contraire* - L. *contrārius*, f. CONTRA; see -ARY. Regularly stressed *contra·ry* till XVIII, and still so in the sense of 'perverse, obstinate'.

contrast A. †contention XVI; B. (in art) juxtaposition of varied forms, etc., to heighten effect; hence gen. XVIII. - F. *contraste* - It. *contrasto* strife, opposition, f. *contrastare* withstand, strive :- medL. *contrāstāre*, i.e. *contrā* against, *stāre* STAND. So as vb. XVII.

contravene XVI. In earliest use Sc. - late L. *contrāvenīre*, i.e. *contrā* against, *venīre* COME. So **contravention** XVI. - (O)F. - medL.

contretemps †(fencing) inopportune thrust XVII; inopportune occurrence XIX. - F., orig. motion out of time, f. *contre* against, CONTRA- + *temps* (:- L. *tempus*) time.

contribute XVI. f. L. *contribūt-*, pp. stem of *contribuere* bring together, f. CON- + *tribuere* bestow (see TRIBUTE). So **contribution** XIV. - (O)F. or late L. **contributory** XV. - medL.

contrite broken in spirit. XIV. - (O)F. *contrit, -te* - L. *contrītus, -ta*, pp. of *conterere*, f. CON- + *terere* rub, grind. So **contrition** XIII.

contrive XIV. ME. *controve, contreve* - OF. *controver* (mod. *controuver*) †imagine - medL. *contropāre* compare, prob. f. L. CON- + *tropus* TROPE. The transition to *contrive* (XV) is unexpl. Hence **contrivance** XVII.

control check (accounts) by comparison with a duplicate register; exercise restraint or sway over. XV. - AN. *contreroller*, F. †*conteroller* (now *contrôler*) - medL. *contrārotulāre*, f. *contrārotulus*, f. *contrā* opposite + *rotulus* ROLL[1]. Hence, or - F. *contrôle*, **control** sb. restraint, check, sway. XVI. So **controller**, COMPTROLLER.

controvert XVII. First in pp. and ppl. adj. *controverted*, replacing †*controversed* disputed, called in question - F. *controversé*, for earlier †*controvers* - L. *contrōversus* disputed, questionable, f. *contrō-*, var. of CONTRA- + *versus*, pp. of *vertere* turn. So **controversy** XIV. - L. *contrōversia* (see -Y[3]). **controversial** XVI. - late L. **controversialist** XVIII.

contumacy rebellious stubbornness. XIV. - L. *contumācia*, f. *contumāx, -āc-*, perh. f. CON- (intensive) + *tumēre* swell; see -ACY. Hence **contumacious** XVI.

contumely insulting or offensively contemptuous treatment. XIV. - OF. *contumelie* - L. *contumēlia*, f. CON- + *tumēre*, as in prec. So **contumelious** XV.

contuse bruise. xv. f. *contūs-*, pp. stem of L. *contundere*, f. CON- + *tundere* beat. So **contusion** xiv. - F. or L.

conundrum †whim, crotchet xvi; †pun xvii; riddle involving a pun, puzzling statement or question xviii. In early use also *conimbrum, quinombrum, quonundrum, quadundrum*; of obscure orig., but prob. based on some L. formula (involving *quoniam* or *quin*) current in the schools.

conurbation xx. f. CON- + L. *urbs, urb-* city (cf. URBAN) + -ATION.

convalesce xv (not in regular use till xix). - L. *convalēscere*, f. CON- (intensive) + *valēscere* grow strong, f. *valēre* be strong or well. So **convalescence** xv. - F. or late L.; hence **convalescent** (see -ESCENT).

convection xix (a casual instance of *conuexion* occurs xvii). - late L. *convectiō, -ōn-*, f. *convect-*, pp. stem of *convehere*, f. CON- + *vehere* carry (see WAY).

convene come together xv; call together xvi. - L. *convenīre* assemble, f. CON- + *venīre* COME. So **convenient** †accordant, suitable xiv; personally fitting, commodious xv. - L. *conveniēns, -ent-*, pp. of *convenīre*. **convenience** xv.

convention A. assembly xv; B. agreement, covenant xv; general agreement or consent; conventional usage xviii. - (O)F. - L. *conventiō, -ōn-*, meeting, covenant. **conventional** xv. - F. *conventionnel* or late L. *conventiōnālis*.

convent company of religious persons living together xiii (since xviii often restricted to nunneries); building housing this xvi. ME. *covent* - OF. *covent* (varying with *convent* with latinized sp., which finally prevailed in Eng.), mod. *couvent* :- L. *conventus* assembly, company, f. *convent-*, pp. stem of *convenīre* CONVENE. So **conventual** xv. - medL. *conventuālis*.

conventicle †meeting, assembly, esp. of a clandestine or illegal kind, at first political, later religious xiv; meeting or meeting-place of Protestant Dissenters xvi. - L. *conventiculum* (place of) assembly, in form dim. of *conventus* meeting (see CONVENT), but not used with derogatory reference till medieval times.

converge xvii. - late L. *convergere*; see CON- and VERGE[2]. Hence **convergent** xviii.

conversation †(mode of) living xiv; familiar discourse xvi; †acquaintance, company xvii. - (O)F. - L. *conversātiō, -ōn-*, frequent use or abode, intercourse, f. *conversārī* CONVERSE[1]; see -ATION. Hence **conversational** xviii. So **conversant** †dwelling habitually; associating familiarly *with* xiv; versed *in*, familiar *with* xvi. - prp. of (O)F. *converser* CONVERSE[1].

conversazione assembly for conversation and social or intellectual recreation, orig. in Italy. xviii. - It.

converse[1] †dwell xiv; †associate familiarly *with* xvi; talk *with* xvii. - (O)F. *converser* †pass one's life, exchange words :- L. *conversārī* live, have intercourse, middle use of *conversāre* turn round, f. CON- + *versāre*, frequent. of *vertere* turn. Hence as sb. †intercourse; conversation; communion. xvii.

converse[2] proposition or relation turned round or upside down. xvi. - L. *conversus*, pp. of *convertere* CONVERT.

convert turn or change *into*. xiii. - (O)F. *convertir* :- Rom. **convertīre*, f. L. *convertere* turn about, transform, f. CON- + *vertere* turn. Hence **convert** converted person xvi. So **convertible, conversion** xiv. - (O)F. - L.

convex xvi. - L. *convexus* vaulted, arched.

convey †escort xiii; †guide, conduct; transport; communicate xiv; transfer; steal xv. - OF. *conveier* (mod. *convoyer* CONVOY) :- medL. *conviāre*, f. CON- + *via* way. Hence **conveyance** xvi.

convict prove guilty xiv; bring error home to; †convince xviii. f. *convict-*, pp. stem of L. *convincere* CONVINCE; the pp. was adopted earlier as *convi·ct* (also in AN.) pronounced or proved guilty, whence, with shift of stress, **convict** sb. †convicted person xvi; condemned criminal xviii.

convince †overcome in argument; †convict; †prove xvi; bring to a belief xvii. - L. *convincere* convict of error, prove clearly (guilt, etc.), f. CON- (intensive) + *vincere* overcome.

convivial xvii. - L. *convīviālis*, f. *convīvium* feast, f. CON- + stem of *vīvere* live; see VIVID, -IAL.

convocation xiv. - L. *convocātiō, -ōn-*, f. *convocāre*, whence **convoke** xvi; see CON-, VOCATION.

convolution xvi. - medL. *convolūtiō, -ōn-*, f. pp. stem of *convolvere*, f. CON- + *volvere* roll; see -TION. So **convolvulus** xvi.

convoy accompany, escort xiv; †convey, conduct xv. - (O)F. *convoyer* CONVEY. So as sb. xvi.

convulse xvii. f. *convuls-*, pp. stem of L. *convellere* pull violently, wrench, f. CON- + *vellere* pluck, pull. So **convulsion** xvi. - F. or L.

con(e)y rabbit (fur). xiii. Earliest forms *cunin(g), conyng* - AN. *coning*, OF. *conin*, parallel form to OF. *conil* - L. *cunīculus*, prob. of Iberian orig. The form *cony* (xiv) is a back-formation from pl. *conyes* - AN. *con(i)ys*, pl. of *conil*. In the cant sense of 'dupe' familiar xvi-xvii in *cony-catcher* cheat, swindler, *cony-catching*.

cook preparer of food. OE. *cōc* - popL. *cōcus*, for L. *coquus*. The base of L. *coquus* is **qeqo* :- IE. **peqo-* (as in Gr. *péssein* ripen, boil, cook; cf. OSl. *pekǫ* I bake, roast, Skr. *pácati* cook, bake). Hence **cook** vb., **cookery** xiv.

cookie xviii. - Du. *koekje*, dim. of *koek* cake.

cool adj. OE. *cōl* = MLG., MDu. *kōl* (Du. *koel*) :- Gmc. **kōluz*, f. **kōl-* **kal-* (see COLD); as sb. from xiv. Hence **cool** vb. OE. *cōlian* = OS. *cōlon* :- Gmc. **kōlōjan*, f. **kōluz*.

coolie, cooly hired native labourer (prop.) in India and China. xvii. - Urdu *ḳulī*, Bengali, etc., *kūlī*, of Dravidian orig. (cf. Tamil *kūli* wages, etc.).

coomb, combe deep hollow, valley. OE. *cumb*, not found in OE. or ME. literature, but occurring from early times in south. place-names. In gen. use from xvi.

coon (U.S.) raccoon xviii; fellow; negro xix. Aphetic of RACCOON.

coop †basket xiii; cage for poultry xv; place of confinement xvi. - MLG., MDu. *kūpe* (Du. *kuip* tub, vat), parallel with OS. *kōpa*, OHG. *kuofa* (G.

kufe) cask - L. *cūpa*, also medL. *cōpa* tun, barrel. Hence as vb. XVI.

cooper one who makes and repairs casks, etc. XIV (earlier as a personal designation passing into a surname XIII). - MDu., MLG. *kūper*, f. *kūpe* COOP; see -ER[1].

co-operate XVII. f. pp. stem of ecclL. *cooperārī*, f. co- + *operārī* work, OPERATE. So **co-operation** XIV. - L., partly, in later use, through F. *coopération*. **co-operative** XVII, **co-operator** XV.

co-opt XVII. - L. *cooptāre*, f. co- + *optāre* choose (see OPT).

co-ordinate of equal rank XVII; sb. (math.) each of two or more magnitudes used to define a position XIX. f. co- + L. *ordinātus*, pp. of *ordināre* arrange, ORDAIN, after the earlier SUBORDINATE. So **co-ordinate** vb. XVII. **co-ordination** XVII. - F. or late L.

coot XIV (first in *balled cote* 'bald coot'). prob. of LG. orig. (cf. Du. *koet*).

cop (sl.) catch, capture. XVIII. prob. var. of *cap* arrest, seize (XVI) - OF. *caper* seize - L. *capere* take. Hence **cop, copper**[2] (-ER[1]) policeman. XIX.

copal resin yielding varnish. XVI. - Sp. - Nahuatl *copalli* incense.

coparcener co-heir(ess). XV. f. CO- + PARCENER.

cope[1] long cloak or cape (esp. eccl.) XIII; 'canopy' of night, heaven XIV; outer mould in founding XIX. ME. *cāpe*, repr. OE. *-cāp*, **cāpe* = ON. *kápa* - medL. *cāpa*, var. of *cappa* (whence F. *chape*; cf. CAP, CHAPEL). Hence **cope-stone** top stone of a building XVI; whence prob. **cope** vb. cover (a wall) with a head stone XVII; **coping** uppermost course of masonry or brickwork XVII; see -ING[1].

cope[2] †come to blows (*with*) XIV; meet or contend *with* XVI. - OF. *coper*, var. of *colper* (mod. *couper*) strike, (now) cut, f. *co(l)p* (mod. *coup*) blow :- Rom. **colpus* :- L. *colaphus* - Gr. *kólaphos*.

copious XIV. - (O)F. *copieux* or L. *cōpiōsus*, f. *cōpia* abundance, f. co- + **ops* wealth, OPULENCE, opp. of *inopia* want, see -IOUS.

copper[1] metal of reddish colour OE.; vessel made of this XVII; copper money XVIII. OE. *copor, coper*, corr. to MDu. *coper* (Du. *koper*), ON. *koparr* (cf. MLG. *kopper*, OHG. *kupfar* (G. *kupfer*)) - late L. *cuprum*, for L. *cyprium* (*æs*) '(metal) of Cyprus', so named from its most noted ancient source.

copper[2] see COP.

coppice XIV (*cop(e)ys*). - OF. *copeïz* :- Rom. **colpātīcium*, f. **colpāt-*, pp. stem of **colpāre* cut (F. *couper*; see COPE[2]).

copra dried kernel of the coconut. XVI. - Pg. (and Sp.) - Malayalam *koppara*.

copse, contr. of *coppis*, COPPICE. XVI.

copula (gram.) part of a proposition connecting subject and predicate, spec. the verb 'to be'; connection XVII. - L. *cōpula* connection, linking of words, f. co- + *apere* fasten; see APT, -ULE, and cf. COUPLE. So **copulate** †couple; unite sexually. XVII. f. pp. stem of L. *cōpulāre*, f. *cōpula*; see -ATE[3]. **copulation** XIV. - (O)F. - L.

copy transcript of an original XIV; individual specimen of a work XV. (The etymol. sense of 'abundance' occurs XIV-XVII.) - (O)F. *copie* - L. *cōpia* abundance, plenty, pl. ability, opportunity (see COPIOUS). The sense 'transcript', which is medL. and Rom., arose from such phr. as *copiam describendi facere* give permission to transcribe, whence the sense 'right of reproduction' and simply 'reproduction'. Hence **copyhold** holding of lands by copy of the manorial court roll XV. **copyright** right to print, publish, and sell copies of a work of literature or of art. XVIII.

coquette XVII. - F., fem. of *coquet* gallant, amorously forward, f. *coqueter* flirt, prop. strut like a cock before hens, f. *coq* COCK[1].

cor- assim. form of *com* CON- before *r*.

coracle small wickerwork boat. XVI (*corougle*). - W. *corwgl, cwrwgl*, f. *corwg* coracle, †carcass (= Ir., Gael. *curach* CURRACH).

coral XIV. - OF. *coral* (mod. *corail*) :- L. *corallum, -alium* - Gr. *korállion, kourálion*, prob. of Sem. orig.

corbel (archit.) projection jutting from a wall to support a weight. XV. - OF. *corbel* (mod. *corbeau*) raven, also archit., dim. of †*corp, corb* : L. *corvus* raven.

corbie (Sc.) raven. XV. - OF. *corb* (see prec.) + -IE.

cord string XIII; cord-like structure XV; measure of cut wood XVII. - (O)F. *corde* :- L. *chorda* - Gr. *khordḗ* gut, string of musical instrument. Hence **cordage** XVI.

cordial pert. to the heart XIV; stimulating to the heart; hearty XV; sb. XIV. - medL. *cordiālis*, f. *cor, cord-* HEART; see -IAL. Hence **cordiality** XVII.

cordite smokeless explosive so called from its cord-like appearance. XIX. f. CORD + -ITE.

cordon projecting course of stones XVI; line of military posts or police XVIII. - It. *cordone*, augm. of *corda* CORD; superseded by F. *cordon*.

cordovan Cordova leather. XVI. - Sp. *cordován* (now *-bán*); cf. CORDWAINER.

corduroy XVIII. prob. f. CORD + †*duroy*, †*deroy* (XVII) coarse West-of-England woollen stuff, of unkn. orig.

cordwainer shoemaker, orig. maker of Cordovan leather. XI. - AN. *cordewaner*, OF. *cordoanier* (mod. *cordonnier*), f. *cordewan, cordoan*, f. *Cordoue* - Sp. *Córdoba*, †*Cordova* :- L. *Corduba* town in Spain where a goatskin (later, horsehide) leather was made. The Sp. adj. †*cordovano* and sb. †*cordován* were adopted in Eng. as CORDOVAN.

core horny seed-capsule of apple, etc. XIV; unburnt centre of coal XV; hard centre of a boil XVI; central or innermost part XVII. of unkn. orig.

corf basket, (later) spec. in mining. XIV. - (M)LG., (M)Du. *korf* - L. *corbis*; reintroduced in XVII by continental miners.

coriaceous leathery. XVII. f. late L. *coriaceus*, f. *corium* hide, leather; see -ACEOUS.

coriander the plant *Coriandrum sativum*. XIV. - (O)F. *coriandre* - L. *coriandrum* - Gr. *koríannon, -dron*.

cork bark of the cork-oak XIV; †cork sole or sandal XIV; stopper, prop. of cork XVI. prob. - Du., LG. *kork* - Sp. *alcorque* cork sole or shoe, of Arab. orig. (see AL-[2]). Hence as vb. †furnish with a cork sole XVI; stop with a cork XVII.

cormorant XIII. - OF. *cormaran* (mod. *cormoran*), earlier *cormareng*, for **corp mareng*, repr. (with assim. of adj. suffix to Gmc. *-ing*) medL. *corvus marīnus* 'sea raven'. For the final parasitic *t* cf. *pageant*, *pheasant*.

corn[1] grain, seed, fruit of a cereal. OE. *corn* = OFris., OS., OHG., ON. *korn*, Goth. *kaurn* :- Gmc. **kurnam* :- IE. **gr̥nóm* 'worn down particle', n. pp. of base **gr̥-* **ger-* wear away, grow old, whence also L. *grānum* GRAIN, OIr. *grān*, OSl. *zrŭno* seed, Gr. *graûs* old woman, *gérōn* old man, Skr. *jīryati* wastes away, *jīrṇá-* wasted, old. Hence **corn** vb. †make or become granular; sprinkle with salt in grains, preserve with salt (as corned beef). XVI. **corncrake** XV; see CRAKE.

corn[2] horny hardening of the skin. XV. - AN. *corn* = (O)F. *cor* :- L. *cornū* HORN.

cornea (anat.) horny covering of the eyeball. XIV. - modL., short for medL. *cornea tēla* or *tunica* horny tissue or coating; fem. of *corneus* (whence **corneous** XVII), f. L. *cornū* HORN.

cornel tree of the genus *Cornus*. XVI. orig. in *cornel berry*, *cornel tree*, semi-tr. of G. *kornelbeere*, *-baum* (OHG. *kornulberi*, *-boum*, the source of which is some medL. deriv. of L. *cornus* cornel tree).

cornelian red or reddish variety of chalcedony. XIV (*corneline*). - OF. *corneline* (mod. *cornaline*); refash. after medL. *cornelius*.

corner sb. XIII. - AN. *corner*, OF. *cornier* :- Rom. **cornārium*, f. L. *cornū* HORN, point, end; see -ER[2]. Hence **corner** vb. furnish with, place in, a corner XIV; (orig. U.S.) drive into a corner XIX. **cornerstone** XIII.

cornet wind-instrument XIV; conical twisted paper, and other transf. uses XVI. - (O)F., dim. of Rom. **corno*, L. *cornū* HORN; see -ET.

cornice XVI (*cornish*). - F. *corniche*, †*-ice*, †*-isse* - It. *cornice*, perh. - L. *cornix*, *cornic-* crow (cf. CORBEL), but with blending of a deriv. of Gr. *korōnís* coping-stone.

Cornish XV. f. first el. of *Cornwall*, OE. *Cornwēalas*, f. OCelt. **Kornovjos*, *-ja*, whence medL. *Cornubia* Cornwall; see WELSH, -ISH[1]. The native name was *Kernūak*, *Kernewec*, f. *Kernóu* (cf. W. *Cernyw* Cornwall, Breton *Kernéō* Cornouailles in Brittany).

cornucopia XVI. - late L. *cornūcōpia*, earlier *cornū cōpiæ* 'horn of plenty', the horn of the goat Amalthea placed in heaven, emblem of fruitfulness and abundance.

corolla †little crown, garland XVII; (bot.) whorl of petals XVIII. - L., dim. of *corōna* CROWN.

corollary (geom.) proposition appended to another as a self-evident inference XIV; immediate deduction or consequence XVII. - L. *corollārium* money paid for a garland, present, gratuity, f. *corolla*; see prec. and -ARY.

corona member of a cornice XVI; circle or halo of light XVII. - L., CROWN.

coronation XIV. - (O)F. - medL. *corōnātiō*, *-ōn-*, f. L. *corōnāre* CROWN vb.; see -ATION.

coroner (hist.) officer orig. charged with maintaining the rights of crown property XIV; officer who holds inquests on persons who have died by violence or accident XV. - AN. *coro(u)ner*, f. *coro(u)ne* CROWN, after the L. title *custos placitorum coronæ* guardian of the pleas of the crown; latinized as *corōnārius*, *corōnātor* (XIII). From XV freq. in contr. form *crowner*.

coronet XV. - OF. *coronet(t)e*, dim. of *corone* CROWN; see -ET.

corporal[1] linen cloth on which the host and chalice are placed at the Eucharist. XIV. - (O)F. *corporal* or medL. *corporāle*, sb. use of *corporālis* CORPORAL[2].

corporal[2] bodily; †corporeal, material. XIV. - OF. (mod. *corporel*) - L. *corporālis*, f. *corpus* body; see -AL[1]. So **corporality** XIV. - late L.

corporal[3] non-commissioned officer below a sergeant. XVI. - F. †*corporal*, var. of *caporal* - It. *caporale*, of which there appears to have been a Venetian form †*corporale*, f. *corpus*, *corpor-* body (of troops), the standard form being assim. to *capo* head. Cf. prec.

corporate forming a corporation XV; corporeal, belonging to the body politic XVII. - L. *corporātus*, pp. of *corporāre* fashion into or with a body, collect, f. *corpor-*; see CORPUS, -ATE[2]. So **corporation** †incorporation XV; body of persons, esp. one formally incorporated XV; (large) abdomen XVIII (cf. the obs. use of *corporate* for 'corpulent').

corposant ball of light observed on the masts and yards of a ship on stormy nights. XVII (earlier in foreign forms). - OSp., It., Pg. *corpo santo* 'holy body', i.e. of a saint.

corps XVIII. - F. *corps*, used as short for *corps d'armée* army corps; see next.

corpse †body, person; lifeless body. XIV. orig. graphic var. of *cors* (XIII), later *corse* (XIV; still arch.) - OF. *cors* (mod. *corps*) :- L. *corpus* body (see CORPUS). The inserted *p* had infl. the pronunc. before 1500; the sp. *corpse* (with final *e*), though appearing as early as XVI, did not become general before XIX.

corpulent †material, gross; bulky of body. XIV. - L. *corpulentus*, f. *corpus*; see next and -ULENT.

corpus pl. *corpora* body XIV; body of writings XVIII. - L. 'body'. In XIV-XVI perh. a var. of *corpes*, CORPSE.

corpuscle minute particle of matter. XVII. - L. *corpusculum*, dim. of CORPUS. See -CLE.

corral XVI. - Sp., OPg. *corral*, Pg. *curral*, whence KRAAL.

correct[1] vb. XIV. f. *correct-*, pp. stem of L. *corrigere*, f. COR- + *regere* lead straight, direct (see REGENT). So **correction** XIV. - (O)F. - L. **corrective** adj. XVI; sb. XVII. - F.

correct[2] that is in accordance with a standard XVII; with truth XVIII. - F. - L. *correctus* amended, correct, pp. of *corrigere* (see prec.). Hence **correctitude** correctness of conduct. XIX.

correlate XVIII. Back-formation from **correlation, correlative** XVI. - scholL. *correlātiō*, *-ātīvus* (XIII); see COR-, RELATION.

correspond be agreeable *to* or congruous *with* XVI; communicate by interchange of letters XVII. - (O)F. *correspondre* - medL. *correspondēre*; see COR-, RESPOND. So **correspondence** congruity XV; †(gen.) relation XVI; intercourse spec. by letters XVII. **correspondent** adj. XV; sb. XVII.

corridor covered way XVI; outside gallery round a court, etc. XVII; passage through a building, etc. XIX. - F. - It. *corridore*, alt., by assim. to *corridore* runner, of *corridoio* :- Rom. **curritōrium*, f. **currit-*, for *curs-*, pp. stem of L. *currere* run (see CURRENT, -ORY[1]).

corrie (Sc.) circular hollow on a mountainside. XVIII. - Gael. *coire* cauldron, hollow.

corrigendum, pl. **corrigenda** XIX. - L., sb. use of n. of gerundive of *corrigere* CORRECT[1].

corroborate strengthen, confirm XVI; support (an opinion, etc.) by concurrent evidence XVIII. f. pp. stem of L. *corrōborāre*, f. COR- + *rōborāre* strengthen, f. *rōbur* strength; see ROBUST, -ATE[3]. So **corroboration** XV. - F. or late L.

corroboree native Australian dance. XIX. Aboriginal word.

corrode XIV. - L. *corrōdere*, f. COR- + *rōdere* gnaw (see RODENT). So **corrosion** XIV. - OF. or late L. **corrosive** adj. and sb. XIV. - OF. *corosif* - medL. *corrōsīvus*.

corrugated wrinkled XVII; of iron, etc. XIX. f. pp. of L. *corrūgāre*, f. COR- (intensive) + *rūgāre*, f. *rūga* wrinkle; see -ATE[3], -ED[1].

corrupt †as pp. corrupted; unsound, rotten, debased, venal. XIV. - OF. *corrupt* or L. *corruptus*, pp. of *corrumpere* destroy, ruin, falsify, seduce, f. COR- + *rumpere* break (see RUPTURE). Hence **corrupt** vb. XIV. So **corruption** XIV. - (O)F. - L.

corsage †body XV; bodice XIX. - (O)F., f. *cors* body; see CORPSE, -AGE.

corsair privateer XV. Not in gen. use in this form before XVII, current early forms being *corsale, cursarie, corsar(i)o*. - F. *corsaire*, †*c(o)ursaire*, Sp. *corsario*, It. *corsale, -are*, †*-ar(i)o* :- Rom. (medL.) *cursārius*, f. *cursa* and *cursus* hostile inroad, plunder, COURSE.

corse arch. form of CORPSE.

corset close-fitting body garment XIV; laced inner bodice, stays XVIII. - (O)F., dim. of *cors* body; see CORPSE, -ET.

corslet garment, spec. defensive armour, covering the body. XV. - (O)F., dim. of *cors* body; see CORPSE, -LET.

cortège XVII. - F. - It. *corteggio*, f. *corteggiare* attend court, keep a retinue, f. *corte* COURT.

cortical XVII. - modL. *corticālis*, f. L. *cortex, cortic-* bark (whence Eng. **cortex** XVII), rel. to *corium* leather; see -AL[1].

corundum mineral allied to sapphire and ruby. XVIII. - Tamil *kurundam* = Telugu *kuruvindam* - Skr. *kuruvinda-* ruby.

coruscate sparkle, glitter. XVIII. f. pp. of L. *coruscāre* vibrate, glitter; see -ATE[3]. So **coruscation** XV. - L.

corvette XVII. - F., dim. f. MDu. *korf* kind of ship; see -ETTE.

corvine of the crow kind. XVII. - L. *corvīnus*, f. *corvus* raven; see -INE[1].

corymb (bot.) species of raceme. XVIII. - F. *corymbe* or L. *corymbus* - Gr. *kórumbos* summit, cluster of fruit or flowers, close head of a composite flower.

cos variety of lettuce introduced from the island of *Cos* (Gr. *Kôs*) in the Aegean Sea. XVII.

cosh stout stick, truncheon. XIX. of unkn. orig.

cosine (math.) sine of the complement of an angle. XVII. f. CO-, SINE. So **cosecant, cotangent** XVII.

cosmetic adj. and sb. XVII. - F. *cosmétique* - Gr. *kosmētikós*, f. *kosmein* adorn, f. *kósmos*; see next and -IC.

cosmos XVII (isolated ex. XII). - Gr. *kósmos* order, ornament, order of the universe, (with the Pythagoreans) the world. Hence **cosmic** XIX. So **cosmogony** XVII, **cosmography** XV, **cosmology** XVII; all ult. from Gr. forms through F. or (mod)L. **cosmopolitan, cosmopolite** citizen of the world XVII; as adjs. XIX.

cosset XVII. f. dial. *cosset* pet lamb, prob. a transf. use of AN. *coscet, cozet* cottager - OE. *cotsǣta*, f. COT[1] + **sǣt-* var. of **set-*, base of SIT.

cost sb. XIII. - AN. *cost*, OF. *coust* (mod. *coût*) :- Rom. **costo*, f. **costāre* stand firm, be fixed, stand at a price, f. CON- (intensive) + *stāre* STAND. So **cost** vb. XIV. - OF. *co(u)ster* (mod. *coûter*) :- Rom. **costāre*. Hence **costly** XIV; see -LY[1].

costal pert. to the ribs. XVII. - F. - modL. *costālis*, f. *costa* rib; see -AL[1].

costard large prominently ribbed variety of apple. XIV. - AN., f. *coste* rib :- L. *costa*; see -ARD. Hence †*costardmonger*, **costermonger** (XVI) fruiterer, in mod. use a seller of fruit, vegetables, fish, etc., from a barrow in the street.

costive constipated. XIV. - AN. **costif*, for OF. *costivé* :- L. *constipātus* (see CONSTIPATE). For the loss of *-é* cf. ASSIGN[2].

costmary aromatic plant. XV. f. *cost* (OE. *cost* - L. *costum, -os* - Gr. *kóstos* - Arab. *ḳust* - Skr. *kúṣṭha-*) + the name of the Virgin Mary.

costume †manners and customs proper to a time and place XVIII; mode of personal attire; set of outer garments, etc. XIX. - F. - It. *costume* custom, fashion, habit :- L. *consuetūdō, -din-* CUSTOM. So **costumier** maker of costumes. XIX.

cosy, cozy adj. XVIII; sb. cover to keep tea-pot etc. warm XIX. orig. Sc., earliest form *colsie*; of unkn. orig.

cot[1] cottage. OE. *cot* = MLG., MDu., ON. *kot* :- Gmc. **kutam*, rel. to COTE.

cot[2] light bedstead XVII; swinging bed for officers, the sick, etc., XVIII; small child's bed XIX. - Hindi *khāṭ* bedstead, couch, hammock :- Prakrit *khaṭṭā*, Skr. *kháṭvā*.

cote †cottage XI; small building for sheltering small animals, as *dovecot(e), sheepcote* XIV. OE. *cote*, corr. to LG. *kote* (whence G. *kote*) :- Gmc. **kutōn*, rel. to COT[1].

coterie †society, club; exclusive set or clique. XVIII. - F. (in OF. feudal tenure, tenants holding land together), f. **cote* hut (cf. †*cotin*) - MLG. *kote* COTE; see -ERY.

cothurnus buskin of ancient tragic actors. XVIII. - L. - Gr. *kóthornos*.

cotillion one of several kinds of dance. XVIII. - F. *cotillon* petticoat, dance, dim. of *cotte* COAT.

cotoneaster genus of rosaceous trees. XVIII. f. L. *cotōneum* QUINCE; see -ASTER.

cottage XIV. - AN. **cotage*, AL. *cotāgium* (XII), f. COT[1], COTE; see -AGE. Hence **cottager** XVI; see -ER[1].

cotter[1], **cottar** (Sc.) cottager paying rent-service. XIV. f. COT[1] + -ER[1].

cotter[2] pin, etc. for fastening a thing into its place. XVII. Earlier (dial.) *cotterel* XVI; perh. transf. uses of COTTER[1] and **cotterel* (cf. AL. *coterellus* cottager).

cottier cottager XIV; (in Ireland) peasant cultivating a smallholding XIX. - (O)F. *cotier*, f. **cote*; see COTERIE, -IER.

cotton XIV. - (O)F. *coton* - Arab. *ḳutn*, in Sp. Arab. *ḳoton*. Hence **cotton** vb. furnish with or take on a nap XV; (prob. transf. from the production of a nap in the finishing of cloth) †prosper, get on XVI (orig. in *This gear* or *matter cottons*); get on *with* XVII; take *to* XIX.

cotyledon seed-leaf. XVIII. - L. *cotylēdon* navelwort, pennywort - Gr. *kotulēdṓn* applied to various cup-shaped cavities, f. *kotúlē* hollow, cup.

couch XIV. - (O)F. *couche*, f. *coucher* (whence **couch** vb. lay down, lie down XIV) :- L. *collocāre* lay in its place, COLLOCATE.

couch-grass var. of QUITCH. XVI.

cougar XVIII. - F. *couguar*, ult. repr. Guarani *guaçu ara*.

cough vb. XIV. ME. *coȝe*, *cowhe*, *co(u)we*, f. imit. base **koχ-* repr. by OE. *cohhetan* shout, (M)LG., (M)Du. *kuchen* cough, MHG. *kūchen* breathe, exhale. Hence as sb. XIV.

could pt. of CAN[2].

coulisse groove in which a partition slides; side-scene or wings of a stage. XIX. - F., sb. use of fem. of *coulis*, orig. adj. sliding, f. *couler* flow, glide, slide.

coulomb unit of electric quantity. XIX. f. name of C. A. de *Coulomb* (1736-1806), French physicist.

coulter OE. *culter* - L. *culter* knife, ploughshare.

council XII. - AN. *cuncile*, *concilie* - L. *concilium* convocation, assembly, f. CON- + *calāre* call, summon, rel. to Gr. *kalein* call. In form and meaning blended at an early date with *counsel*, but differentiation began XVI. So **councillor** XIV; alt. of COUNSELLOR by assim. to *council*.

counsel consultation, advice XIII; body of legal advisers XIV; legal advocate XVIII. - OF. *c(o)unseil* (mod *conseil*) :- L. *consilium* consultation, advice, judgement, deliberating body, f. CON- + **sal-*; cf. CONSUL, CONSULT. Now restricted to the above senses; for the sense 'deliberating body' see COUNCIL. So **counsel** vb. advise. XIII. **counsellor** adviser. XIII.

count[1] reckoning, ACCOUNT XIV; consideration, notice XV; particular of a legal charge XVI. - OF. *co(u)nte* (mod. *compte* reckoning, *conte* tale) :- late L. *computus* calculation, f. *computāre* COUNT[3].

count[2] used to repr. foreign titles of nobility (F. *comte*, G. *graf*, etc.). XVI. - OF. *conte* (mod. *comte*) :- L. *comes*, *comit-* companion, associate, one of the imperial retinue, (late L.) occupant of a state office; for **comis* :- **comits* lit. 'one who goes with', f. COM- + ppl. stem *it-* of *īre* go. So **countess** XII.

count[3] tell over; reckon. XIV. - OF. *c(o)unter* reckon, relate (mod. *compter* count, *conter* relate) :- L. *compūtāre* calculate, COMPUTE. Cf. RECOUNT.

countenance †demeanour, conduct; composure XIII; †aspect, appearance; facial look or expression; face, visage XIV; moral support XVI. - AN. *c(o)untenaunce*, (O)F. *contenance* bearing, behaviour, mien, contents, f. *contenir* maintain (oneself), CONTAIN; see -ANCE. Hence **countenance** vb. †make a show (of), pretend XV; †face *out*; †set off; give support to XVI.

counter[1] object used in counting; desk for counting money, etc., (hence) money-changer's table, tradesman's table in his shop. XIV. - AN. *count(e)our*, OF. *conteo(i)r* (mod. *comptoir*) :- medL. *computātōrium*, f. L. *computāre* COMPUTE.

counter[2] A. †opposite direction to that taken by the game XVI; B. part of a horse's breast lying between the shoulders; curved part of a ship's stern XVII. f. COUNTER[3] or [5].

counter[3] opposed, opposite. XVI. adj. use of the prefix COUNTER-.

counter[4] go counter to, oppose XIV; give a counterblow XIX. orig. aphetic of †*acounter*, var. of ENCOUNTER; in later use a fresh formation on COUNTER- or COUNTER[5].

counter[5] in the opposite direction. XV. - OF. *countre* :- L. *contrā* adv. and prep. against, in return; cf. CONTRA.

counter- prefix, ME. *countre-* - AN. *countre-*, (O)F. *contre-* :- L. *contrā-* CONTRA-; denoting (i) against, opposite, in opposition to, (ii) in reversal of or parallelism with a former action, as *counter-reformation*, *-revolution*, (iii) in reciprocation or reply, as *countersign*, (iv) as the opposite member or constituent, as *counterfoil*, *-part*, (v) with a contrary action or movement, etc., in mutual opposition, as *counterchange*. **counterblast** XVI. **counterfeit** made in imitation; also sb. XIV. - OF. *countrefet*, *-fait* (mod. *contrefait*). So **counterfeit** vb. XIII. - AN. *countrefeter*, f. *countrefet* pp. **counterfoil** XVIII; see FOIL[2]. **countermand** XV. - OF. *contremander*; see MANDATE. **counterpane** XVII. alt., by assim. to PANE in the same sense (XIV), of †*counterpoint* (XV) - OF. *contrepointe*, alt. of **coutrepointe*, *cou(l)tepointe* :- medL. *culcit(r)a puncta* 'quilted mattress'; see POINT. **counterpart** XV. **counterpoint** XV. - (O)F. *contrepoint* - medL. *contrāpunctum*, *cantus contrāpunctus* 'song pointed-against', the accompaniment being orig. noted by points or pricks set against those of the plainsong melody. **counterpoise** weight balancing another weight XV; equilibrium XVI. - OF. *contrepeis*, *-pois*. **countersign** sign used in response to another sign. XVI. - F. *contresigne* - It. *contrasegno*. **countertenor** XIV. - OF. *contreteneur* - It. †*contratenore*.

countervail match, counterbalance, compensate. XIV. - OF. *contrevaloir* (pres. stem *-vail-*) - L. phr. *contrā valēre* be effective or avail against (cf. VALID).

country tract of land; *one's* native land XIII; territory of a nation; nation, people XIV; rural districts XVI. ME. *cuntre(e)*, *contre(e)* - OF. *cuntrée*, (mod.) *contrée* :- medL., Rom. *contrāta*, sb. use (sc. *terra* land) of fem. of adj. meaning 'lying opposite or facing one', hence 'the landscape spread out before one'. Hence **countryman**

native XIV; compatriot XV; husbandman XVI. So **countrywoman** XV. **countryside** particular region of a country; orig. Sc.

county XIV. - AN. *counté*, OF. *cunté*, *conté* (mod. *comté*) :- L. *comitātus*, f. *comes*, *-it-* COUNT[2].

coup XVIII. - F. (see COPE[3]).

coupé short four-wheeled closed carriage for two. XIX. - F., short for *carosse coupé* 'cut carriage', the body having the form of a berline from which the hind seat has been cut away; sb. use of pp. of *couper* cut, f. *coup* (see COPE[3]).

couple sb. XIII. - (O)F. :- L. *cōpula* tie, connection (see COPULA). So **couple** vb. XIII. - OF. *copler*, *cupler* (mod. *coupler*) :- L. *cōpulāre*. **couplet** XVI. - (O)F., dim. of *couple*.

coupon XIX. - F. *coupon* piece cut off, slice, f. *couper* cut; see COPE[3].

courage †heart as the seat of feeling, spirit XIII; †intention, purpose; bravery, valour XIV. - OF. *corage*, *curage* (mod. *courage*) :- Rom. **corāticum*, f. *cor* HEART; see -AGE. So **courageous** XIII.

courier running messenger XVI; servant employed to make travelling arrangements XVIII. - F. †*courier*, (also mod.) *courrier* - It. *corriere*, f. *corre* :- L. *currere* run (see CURRENT).

course running, onward movement; path, direction; progress, order XIII; set of dishes for a meal, one of the successive parts of a meal XIV; series, serial succession; sail attached to lower masts or yards XV. - (O)F. *cours* :- L. *cursus*, f. *curs-*, pp. stem of *currere* run (cf. CURRENT); reinforced XV by (O)F. *course* :- Rom. **cursa*, sb. use of corr. fem. form of ppl. Hence **course** vb. chase, hunt; cause to run; run about. XVI.

courser XIII. - OF. *corsier* (mod. *coursier*) :- Rom. **cursārius*, f. *cursus* COURSE; see -ER[2].

court (residence of) royal household and retinue; assembly held by a sovereign XII; (place of) assembly of judges, etc.; enclosed area, yard XIII; homage, courtly attention XVI. - AN. *curt*, OF. *cort* (mod. *cour*) :- late L. (Rom.) *curt-*, earlier *co(ho)rt-* yard, enclosure, crowd, retinue, COHORT. **court-card** picture card of a suit. XVII. alt. of †*coat card* card bearing a 'coated' or habited figure (XVI-XVII). **court-martial** XVII; earlier †*martial court*. **court-plaster** sticking-plaster for wounds XVIII; so called from being used for the black silk patches worn on the face by ladies at court. **court** vb. †frequent the court; pay court to, woo. XVI; after OIt. *corteare* (later *corteggiare*), OF. *courtoyer* (later *courtiser*), f. *corte*, *court*. **courtier** attendant at the court of a sovereign. XIII. ME. *courteour* - AN. *courte(i)our*, f. OF. **cortoyeur*, f. *cortoyer*; suffix assim. to -IER. **courtly** XV; see -LY[1]. **courtship** XVI.

courteous XIII. - OF. *corteis*, *curteis* (mod. *courtois*) :- Rom. **cortensis*, f. **corte* COURT; see -ESE. The suffix -EOUS replaced *-eis* XVI.

courtesan XVI. - F. *courtisane* - It. †*cortigiana*, fem. of *cortigiano* COURTIER, f. *corte* COURT.

courtesy XIII. - OF. *cur-*, *co(u)rtesie* (mod. *courtoisie*); f. *courteis*, etc., COURTEOUS; see -Y[3].

cousin †relative; son or daughter of one's uncle or aunt XIII; term of address from one sovereign to another, or to a peer XV. - OF. *cosin*, *cusin* (mod. *cousin*) :- L. *consobrīnus* mother's sister's child :- **consuesrīnos*, f. CON- + **swesōr* SISTER + *-*īnos* -INE[1].

cove[1] †bedchamber, storechamber; (Sc. and north.) hollow in a rock, etc. OE.; sheltered recess on a coast XVI. OE. *cofa* chamber = MLG. *cove*, MHG. *kobe* (G. *koben*) stable, pigsty, ON. *kofi* hut, shed :- Gmc. **kuban-*.

cove[2] (colloq.) fellow, chap. XVI. orig. thieves' cant, perh. identical with Sc. *cofe* chapman, pedlar.

covenant mutual agreement; divine contract with mankind XIII; legal agreement or contract XIV. - OF. *covenant* (later and mod. *convenant*), sb. use of prp. of *co(n)venir* agree (see CONVENE). Hence as vb. XIV.

cover vb. XIII. - OF. *cuvrir*, *covrir* (mod. *couvrir*) :- L. *cooperīre*, f. CON- (intensive) + *operīre* cover. Hence **cover** sb. XIV; or partly variant of COVERT.

coverlet XIII. - AN. *covrelet*, *-lit*, f. *covre-* pres. stem of OF. *covrir* COVER + *lit* bed (cf. LITTER).

covert covering XIV; woody shelter for game XIV; feathers covering the bases of larger feathers XVIII. - OF. *covert* (mod. *couvert*), pp. of *co(u)vrir* COVER. So **covert** adj. covered, hidden. XIV. **coverture** cover, covering XIII; position of a woman during her married life XVI.

covet XIII. ME. *cuveite*, *coveite* - OF. *cu-*, *coveitier* (mod. *convoiter*) :- Rom. **cupiditāre*, f. *cupiditās* CUPIDITY. So **covetous** XIII.

covey brood of partridges, etc. XIV. - OF. *covee* (mod. *couvée*) :- Rom. **cubāta* hatching, f. L. *cubāre* lie.

covin †company; private agreement; collusion, fraud. XIV. - OF. *covin*, *covine* :- medL. *convenium*, pl. or fem. sg. *-ia*, f. *convenīre* come together, agree (see CONVENE).

cow[1] female bovine animal. OE. *cū* = OS. *kō* (Du. *koe*), OHG. *kuo* (G. *kuh*), ON. *kýr* :- Gmc. **kō(u)z* :- IE. **gʷōus*, whence also Skr. *gáu-*, Arm. *kov*, Gr. *boûs*, L. *bōs*, OIr. *bó*, Latv. *gùovs*. The normal descendant of the mutated OE. pl. *cȳ* is north. *kye*; the form *kine* (now arch.) descends from a ME. (XIII) extension of this with *-n* from the weak decl.

cow[2] depress with fear. XVII. prob. - ON. *kúga* oppress, tyrannize over.

coward XIII. ME. *cu(e)ard* - OF. *cuard*, later *couard*, f. Rom. **cōda*, L. *cauda*, tail; see -ARD. In the OF. 'Roman de Renart', *coart* is the name of the hare. So **cowardice** XIII. - OF. *couardise*.

cower XIII (*koure*). - MLG. *kūren* lie in wait.

cowl hooded garment worn by religious OE.; hood of the habit or of a cloak XVI; hood-shaped top of a chimney XIX. OE. *cug(e)le*, *cūle*, corr. to MLG., MDu. *cōghel*, OHG. *cucula*, *cugula* (G. *kugel*, *kogel*) - ecclL. *cuculla*, f. L. *cucullus* hood of a cloak. In ME. reinforced by *kuuele* :- OE. *cufle* = MLG., MDu. *cōvele* (Du. *keuvel*), ON. *kofl*, *kufl*, and prob. by (O)F. *coule* :- ecclL. *cuculla*.

cowrie shell of a small gastropod, *Cypraea moneta*. XVII. - Urdu, Hindi *kauṛī* :- Skr. *kaparda-*, *kapardikā-*.

cowslip OE. *cūslyppe*, f. *cū* COW[1] + *slyppe* viscous or slimy substance, i.e. 'cow-slobber' or 'cow-dung'.

cox shortening of COXSWAIN; hence as vb. XIX.

coxcomb cap worn by a professional fool (in shape and colour like a *cock's comb*); (arch.) †head; †fool; fop. XVI.

coxswain helmsman of a boat. XV. f. *cock* (see COCKBOAT) + SWAIN.

coy †quiet, still; shyly reserved. XIV. - (O)F. *coi*, earlier *quei* :- Rom. **quētus*, for L. *quiētus* QUIET. Cf. QUIT[1].

coyote prairie wolf of N. America. XIX. - Mex. Sp. - Nahuatl *coyotl*.

coz abbrev. of †*cozen*, COUSIN. XVI.

cozen cheat, defraud. XVI. prob. orig. vagrants' cant, and perh. to be assoc. with COUSIN, through OF. *cousin* dupe, or *cousiner* 'to clayme kindred for aduantage, or particular ends' (Cotgr.); but the frequent sp. with *-on* has suggested deriv. from It. *cozzonare* 'to play the horse-breaker, to play the craftie knaue' (Florio). Hence **cozenage, cozener** XVI.

crab[1] crustacean of the tribe Brachyura. OE. *crabba* = (M)LG., (M)Du. *krabbe*, ON. *krabbi*, rel. to OS. *krēbit*, MLG. *krēvet*, (M)Du. *kreeft*, OHG. *krebiz*, *krebaz* (G. *krebs*), and to MLG. *krabben*, ON. *krafla* scratch, claw.

crab[2] wild apple. XIV. contemp. with north. *scrab* (prob. of Scand. orig.; cf. Sw. dial. *skrabba* wild apple), of which it may be an alteration by assoc. with prec. or CRABBED.

crab[3] (of hawks) scratch, claw XVI; (sl.) find fault with, 'pull to pieces' XIX. - (M)LG. *krabben* (see CRAB[1]).

crabbed †froward, wayward XIII; out of humour; †harsh, rugged XIV; difficult to deal with or make sense of; cross-tempered XVI. f. CRAB[1] + -ED[2], with orig. ref. to the gait and habits of the crab, which suggest cross-grained or fractious disposition. There has been later assoc. with CRAB[2] with connotation of sourness.

crack A. make a sharp short noise OE.; break with a sudden sharp report XIII; B. utter loudly or sharply XIV; (dial.) boast XVI (whence *crack up* eulogize XIX). OE. *cracian* sound, resound = (M)Du. *krāken*, OHG. *krahhōn* (G. *krachen*). The normal repr. of the OE. word, i.e. *crake* (now dial.), has been superseded by the short form by assoc. with (i) **crack** sb. XIV, or with (ii) F. *craquer* (XVI), of Gmc. orig. Hence **crack** adj. pre-eminent, first-class. XVIII. **cracked** crazy. XVII. **cracker** †boaster, liar; kind of fire-work XVI; instrument for cracking or crushing XVII. **crackle** XVI; see -LE[3]; whence **crackling** crisp skin of roast pork XVIII.

cracknel light crisp biscuit. XV. alt. of F. *craquelin* - MDu. *krākelinc*, f. *krāken* CRACK.

-cracy repr. F. *-cratie*, medL. *-cratia*, Gr. *-kratíā* power, rule (f. *krátos* strength, might, authority) in Gr. originals of ARISTOCRACY, DEMOCRACY, PLUTOCRACY. The suffix has in modern times acquired the sense of 'ruling body or class' of the kind denoted by the first element.

cradle child's light bed or cot OE.; framework of bars, cords, etc. XIV. OE. *cradol*; perh. f. the same base as OHG. *kratto*, (MH)G. *kratte* basket.

craft A. †strength, power OE.; B. skill, deceit OE.; C. art, trade OE.; D. structure, work XII; E. vessels, boats XVII. OE. *cræft* = OS., (O)HG. *kraft*, ON. *kraptr*, with no cogns. outside Gmc. As a second el. of comps. in the sense 'art', in *handicraft*, *statecraft*, *witchcraft*. Hence **craftsman** XIV. **crafty** †strong; †skilful OE.; cunning, wily XIII. OE. *cræftiġ* = OS. *kraftag*, *-ig*, OHG. *kreftig* (G. *kräftig*), ON. *krǫptugr*; see -Y[1].

crag XIII. of Celt. orig.; not, however, from a form repr. by Ir., Gael. *creag*, W. *craig* rock (:- **krakjo-*) but prob. from an OBrit. **crag* (:- **krako-*). Hence **craggy** XV; see -Y[1].

crake (dial.) crow, raven XIV; CORNCRAKE XV. - ON. *kráka*, *krákr*, of imit. orig. (cf. CROAK).

cram OE. (*ġe*)*crammian*, corr. to MLG. *kremmen*, ON. *kremja* squeeze, pinch, Du. *krammen* cramp, clamp, MHG. *krammen* claw; f. Gmc. **kram-* **krem-*; cf. OE. (*ġe*)*crimman* cram, stuff, and further L. *gremium* bosom, OSl. *gramada*, Lith. *grāmatas* heap, Skr. *grā́ma-* group of men.

crambo rhyming game; (contemptuously) rhyme, rhyming. XVII. alt. of †*crambe* (two sylls.) used XVI-XVIII in phr. echoing Juvenal's *crambe repetita* (VII. 154) cabbage served up again.

cramp[1] violent contraction of the muscles. XIV. - (O)F. *crampe* - MLG., MDu. *krampe* = OHG. *krampho*, rel. to OS. *kramp*, (O)HG. *krampf*, sb. uses of an adj. meaning 'bent'; cf. CRIMP. Hence **cramp** vb. affect with cramp; (in applications infl. by CRAMP[2]) compress, confine narrowly. XVI.

cramp[2] metal bar with bent end(s). XV. - MDu. *krampe* = OHG. *krampho*, MHG. *kramphe*, of the same ult. orig. as prec.

cranberry fruit of the shrub *Vaccinium oxycoccos*. XVII. First used in England for the imported American species, *Vaccinium macrocarpon*, and thence transf. to the native European kind. Adopted by the colonists of N. America from G. *kranbeere* or LG. *kranebere* 'CRANE-berry'.

crane large wading bird OE.; machine for raising and lowering weights (so Gr. *géranos*, L. *grūs* battering-ram, F. *grue*, G. *kran*, etc.). XIV. OE. *cran*, corr. to MLG. *krān*, *krōn*, and MDu. *crāne* (Du. *kraan*), OHG. *krano* (G. *kran* machine), also (with *k*-suffix; cf. *hawk*, *lark*), OE. *cranoc*, *cornuc*, MLG. *krānek*, OHG. *kranuh*, *-ih* (G. *kranich* bird); IE. bird-name f. imit. base **ger-*, repr. also by L. *grūs*, Gr. *géranos*, Arm. *kŕunk*, Lith. *garnỹs* heron, stork, *gérvė* crane, OSl. *žeravĭ*, W. *garan*. Hence **crane** vb. hoist or lower with a crane XVI; stretch one's neck XVIII.

cranium XVI. - medL. *crānium* - Gr. *krānion*, rel. to *kárā* head, and hence to the group of *kéras*, L. *cornū* HORN. The comb. form is **cranio-** (see -O-), as in **craniology** XIX. Hence **cranial** XVIII.

crank[1] portion of an axle bent at right angles. OE. *cranc* in *crancstæf* weaver's implement, rel. to *crinċan* (rare), parallel to *crinġan* fall in battle, of which the primary meaning appears to have been 'bend up, crook, curl up', hence 'shrink, give way, become weak'; cf. (M)HG., Du. *krank* sick, ill. Cf. CRINGE, CRINKLE.

crank[2] †bend, crook; fanciful turn of speech XVI; crotchet, whim; (orig. U.S., back-formation from CRANKY) eccentric or crotchety person XIX. prob. ult. identical with prec.

crank² (naut.) liable to capsize. XVII (also *cranke sided*). perh. to be connected with *crank* adj. crabbed, awkward (XVIII), infirm, shaky (XIX), and CRANK¹.

cranky (dial.) sickly XVIII; out of order; wayward, cross-tempered; (colloq.) crotchety XIX. perh. orig. f. cant †*crank* (XVI) rogue who feigned sickness (see CRANK¹), but infl. later by assoc. with CRANK²; see -Y¹.

crannog ancient lake-dwelling. XIX. - Ir. *crannog*, Gael. *crannag* timber structure, f. *crann* tree, beam.

cranny XV. Earliest form *cranye*; poss. based on (O)F. *cran, cren(ne)* :- late popL. *crēna* notch.

crape thin gauze-like fabric. XVII (earliest exx. have *crispe, crespe*). - F. †*crespe, crêpe*, sb. use of OF. *crespe* curled, frizzed (see CRISP).

crapulous grossly excessive in drink or food XVI; suffering from such excess XVIII. - late L. *crāpulōsus*, f. *crāpula* intoxication - Gr. *kraipálē* result of a drunken debauch; see -OUS.

crash¹ dash to pieces XIV; make the noise of this XVI. imit. formation, perh. partly suggested by *craze* and *dash*. Hence as sb. XVI.

crash² coarse linen. XIX. - Russ. *krashenína* dyed and glossed linen.

crasis blending of elements XVII; combination of two vowels in one XIX. - Gr. *krâsis* mixture, combination, f. base of *keránnūnai* mix.

crass coarse, gross XVI; grossly stupid XVII. - L. *crassus* solid, thick, fat. So **crassitude** †thickness XV; gross ignorance XVII.

-crat repr. F. *-crate*, Gr. *-kratēs* in *aristocrate, démocrate* partisan of an aristocracy or democracy (at the time of the French Revolution, passing into) member of the aristocracy, etc. The corr. abstr. sbs. end in -CRACY, the adjs. in *-cratic(al)*.

cratch (dial.) crib, manger XIII; wooden grating, hurdle XIV. ME. *crecche* (mod. dial. *cretch*) - OF. CRÈCHE.

crate XVII. Earliest forms *creat* (XVII), *crade* (XVIII); poss. introduced with imports from Holland; cf. Du. *krat* tailboard of a wagon, †basket, †box of a coach, of unkn. orig.

crater mouth of a volcano XVII; hole made in the ground by an explosion XIX. - L. *crātēr* bowl, basin, aperture of a volcano - Gr. *krātḗr* bowl, lit. mixing-vessel.

cravat XVII. - F. *cravate*, appellative use of *Cravate* - G. *Krawat*, dial. var. of *Kroat*; see CROAT. The early form of the cravat was copied from the linen scarf worn round the neck by Croatian mercenaries in France.

crave †demand OE.; beg for XII; yearn for XIV. OE. *crafian*, rel. to ON. *krǫf* request; the base is perh. that of CRAFT, with the radical sense of 'force, exact'.

craven defeated XIII; poor-spirited, pusillanimous XIV; sb. XVI. ME. *crauaunt*, later *crauaunde, cravand*, perh. - clipped AN. form (cf. ASSIGN²) of OF. *cravanté* overcome, vanquished, pp. of *cravanter* crush, overwhelm - Rom. **crepantāre*, f. *crepant-*, prp. stem of L. *crepāre* rattle, burst; later assim. to pps. in -EN⁶.

craw pouch-like enlargement of the gullet in birds. XIV. - or orig. cogn. with MLG. *krage*, MDu. *crāghe* (Du. *kraag*) neck, throat, gullet, of unkn. orig.

crawfish see CRAYFISH.

crawl XIV. ME. *crawle*, superseding earlier *creule, croule*, of unkn. orig.

crayfish †crustacean XIV; fresh-water crustacean XV; spiny lobster XVIII. ME. *crevis(se), -es(se)* - OF. *crevis* (mod. *écrevisse*) - OHG. *krebiz* (G. *krebs*) CRAB. Stressed orig. on the final syll., the word developed two types, (i) *crevis*, whence *crevish*, which became *crayfish* (XVI), and (ii) *cravis* which, through *cravish, crafish* (XVI), became **crawfish** (XVII), which survives as the U.S. form.

crayon XVII. - F., f. *craie* chalk :- L. *crēta* chalk, clay; see -OON.

craze †shatter, crack XIV; †break down in health; impair in intellect (cf. *cracked*) XV. perh. - ON. **krasa* (cf. Sw. *krasa* crunch). Hence **craze** sb. †crack, flaw XVI; †crack-brain XVII; insane fancy, mania XIX. **crazy** unsound, liable to fall to pieces; †failing in health XVI; of unsound mind XVII; see -Y¹.

creak †croak XIV; †speak stridently or querulously XV; make a shrill grating noise XVI. orig. synon. with †*crake* (XIV) and CROAK, and of similar imit. orig.

cream oily part of milk XIV; best or choice part XVI; applied to purified preparations XVII. ME. *creme* (*creym, craym*) - OF. *creme, craime, cresme* (mod. *crème*), repr. blending of late L. *crāmum, crāma* (perh. of Gaulish orig.) with late L. *chrisma* CHRISM.

crease sb. and vb. XV. In XVI-XVII also *creast*, which was a frequent var. of CREST; orig. *crēst*, which was reduced to *crease* by assim. to the var. *cress* (XVI-XVII) of the vb., the mark of a fold being looked on as a ridge in the material.

create XV. first as pp. *created*, extension (see -ED¹) of †*creat* (XIV) - L. *creātus*, pp. of *creāre* bring forth, produce, cause to grow, prob. rel. to *crēscere* grow. So **creation** XIV. - (O)F. - L. **creative** XVII. **creator** XIII. - OF. *creat(o)ur* (mod. *créateur*) :- L. *creātor, -ōr-*. **creature** XIII. - (O)F. *créature* - late L. *creātūra*.

crèche public nursery for infants. XIX. - F., 'manger, crib', 'day nursery' :- Rom. **creppia* - Frank. **krippja* CRIB.

credence A. †trust, confidence, credit; belief XIV. B. †assaying of food XV; †sideboard for dishes, etc. XVI; (eccl.) in full *credence table*, side table near an altar for holding vessels XIX. - (O)F. *crédence* - medL. *crēdentia* (whence It. *credenza*, the source of F. *crédence* in the senses under B above), f. *crēdēns, crēdent-*, prp. of L. *crēdere* believe; see -ENCE. So **credential** recommending or entitling to credit, esp. in *letters credential, c. letters* XVI; sb. pl. XVII. - medL. *crēdentiālis*; see -IAL. **credible** believable, reliable. XIV. - L. *crēdibilis*; see -IBLE. So **credibility** XVI. - medL. **credit** faith, trust; (favourable) repute; power based on confidence; confidence in or reputation of solvency XVI; sum at one's disposal in a bank XVII; acknowledgement of payment (hence fig. phr. *give* a person *credit for*) XVIII. - F. *crédit* - It. *credito* or L. *crēditum* thing entrusted to one, loan, n. pp. of *crēdere*. Hence, or f. pp. *crēdit-* of *crēdere*, **credit** vb. put trust in; †do credit to XVI; enter on the credit side of an account XVII; ascribe to XIX. So **creditor** XV. - AN. *creditour*, (O)F. *créditeur* - L. *crēditor*; see -OR[1].

credo creed. XII. 1st pers. pres. sg. ind. of L. *crēdere* believe. So **credulous** ready (now over-ready) to believe. XVI. f. L. *crēdulus*; see -ULOUS. **credulity** †belief, credence XV; over-readiness to believe. - (O)F. - L.

creed OE. *crēda* - L. *crēdō* I believe (with cogns. in Indo-Iranian and Celtic), the first word of the Apostles' and the Nicene Creeds in the Latin versions.

creek A. narrow inlet in a coast XIII; arm or branch of a river (esp. in non-British use) XVI; B. chink, corner, nook XIII. (i) ME. *crike* - ON. *kriki* chink, nook (in *handarkriki* armpit), whence also (O)F. *crique*, which may be partly a source of the Eng. word; (ii) ME. *crēke*, either - MDu. *crēke* (Du. *kreek* creek, bay), or by lengthening of *ĭ* in *crike*; ult. orig. unkn. (a stem with *ī* occurs in ON. *kríkar* m. pl. groin).

creel large wicker basket. XV. orig. Sc., of unkn. orig.

creep move forward with the body prone and close to the ground OE.; move forward cautiously or slowly XII; grow along the ground, a wall, etc. XVI. OE. *crēopan* str. vb. = OS. *criopan*, ON. *krjúpa* :- Gmc. **kreupan*; cogn. forms have *ū* in the pres. stem, as OS. *krūpan* (Du. *kruipen*, MLG. *krūpen*); rel. to CRIPPLE. Weak forms of the pt. are found as early as *c*.1300 and of the pp. in XV.

creese see KRIS.

cremate XIX. f. pp. stem of L. *cremāre*, or back-formation from **cremation** XVII. So **crematorium** XIX.

crenate (nat. hist.) notched, finely scalloped. XVIII. - modL. *crēnātus*, f. L. *crēna* notch; cf. next and see -ATE[2].

crenellate provide with embattlements or embrasures. XIX (first in pp.). f. (O)F. *créneler*, f. *crenel* embrasure :- popL. **crenellus* (medL. *kernellus*), dim. of late L. *crēna* (see prec.). So **crenellation** XIX.

Creole (descendant of) European or Negro settler in the W. Indies, etc. XVII (*criole*). - F. *créole*, earlier *criole* - Sp. *criollo*, prob. - Pg. *crioulo* Negro born in Brazil, home-born slave, formerly of animals reared at home, f. *criar* nurse, breed :- L. *creāre* CREATE.

creosote XIX. - G. *kreosote*, f. Gr. *kreo-*, *kreō-*, comb. form of *kréas* flesh + *sōtḗr* saviour, *sōtēriā* safety, with ref. to the antiseptic properties.

crêpe transparent dress material, esp. in *crêpe de chine* 'China crape'. XIX. - F., see CRAPE.

crepitation crackling noise XVII; (path.) sound accompanying breathing in lung disease, etc. XIX. - F. *crépitation* - late L. *crepitātiō*, *-ōn-*, f. *crepitāre*, frequent. of *crepāre* crack, creak, of imit. orig. So **crepitate** XVII; see -ATE[3]. **crepitus** (path.) crepitation. XIX. - L.

crepuscular pert. to twilight. XVII. f. L. *crepusculum* (evening) twilight, f. **crepus*, *creper* dark, obscure; see -AR.

crescendo (mus.) direction for increase in loudness. XVIII. - It., prp. of *crescere* INCREASE.

crescent figure as of the waxing moon XIV; row of buildings in an arc XVIII. ME. *cressa(u)nt* - AN. *cressaunt*, OF. *creissant* (mod. *croissant*) :- L. *crēscēns*, *-ent-*, prp. of *crēscere* grow, INCREASE. In XVII assim. to the L. form, which was already current in **crescent** adj. XVI. See -ENT.

cress cruciferous plant with pungent edible leaves. OE. *cressa*, *cresse*, *cærse*, *cerse* = MLG. *kerse*, MDu. *kersse*, *korsse* (Du. *kers*), OHG. *kresso*, *kressa* (G. *kresse*) :- WGmc. **krasjōn*, *-jan-*.

crest tuft or plume of feathers; top, ridge XIV; ridge of an animal's neck XVI. - OF. *creste* (mod. *crête*) :- L. *crista* tuft, plume.

cretaceous chalky. XVII. f. L. *crētāceus*, f. *crēta* chalk; see -ACEOUS.

cretin deformed idiot of the Alpine valleys. XVIII. - F. *crétin* - Swiss F. *creitin*, *crestin* :- L. *Chrīstiānus* CHRISTIAN, the reprs. of which in Rom. langs. also mean 'human being' as dist. from the brutes.

cretonne figured cotton cloth. XIX. - F., f. *Creton* village in Normandy famous for linen manufacture.

crevasse XIX. - F.; see next.

crevice XIV. ME. *crevace*, *crevisse*, later *creves(se)*, *-ice* - OF. *crevace* (mod. *crevasse*), f. *crever* burst, split :- L. *crepāre* crack, break with a crash.

crew †military reinforcement XV; (armed) company XVI; ship's company XVII. Late ME. *crue* - OF. *creue* increase, reinforcement, sb. use of fem. pp. of *croistre* (mod. *croître*) :- L. *crēscere* grow, INCREASE.

crewel thin worsted yarn. XV. orig. *crule*, *crewle*, *croole*; of unkn. orig.

crib rack for fodder, manger OE.; ox-stall; †wicker basket XIV; cabin, hovel XVI; child's bed XVII. OE. *crib(b)* = OS. *kribbia*, OHG. *krippa* (G. *krippe*); beside OE. *crybb* (also repr. by *crib* in standard Eng.) = MLG. *krübbe*, Du. *krub*. Hence **crib** vb. †feed as at a manger XV; confine narrowly XVII; pilfer, thieve XVIII (prob. orig. thieves' cant from the sense 'basket' of the sb.).

cribbage card-game, a characteristic feature of which is the *crib*, which consists of cards thrown out from each player's hand and belonging to the dealer. XVII. of unkn. orig.

crick painful stiffness in the neck. XV. of unkn. orig.

cricket[1] chirping house-insect. XIV. - (O)F. *criquet* †grasshopper, cricket, f. *criquer* crackle, of imit. orig.

cricket[2] game played with ball, bat, and wicket. XVI. of uncert. orig.; perh. - OF. *criquet* stick used as aiming-mark in a ball-game, with which cf. Flem. *krick(e)* stick.

crikey dial. and sl. excl. of astonishment. XIX. euphem. alt. of CHRIST.

crime XIV. - (O)F. :- L. *crīmen* judgement, accusation, offence, f. reduced form of base of *cernere* decide, give judgement; cf. DISCERN. So **criminal** XV. - late L. *crīminālis*.

crimp crumple, wrinkle. Sparsely evidenced

before XVII; prob. - (M)LG., (M)Du. *krimpen* shrink, wrinkle, shrivel = OHG. *krimphan* (MHG. *krimpfen*), rel. distantly to OE. (*ġe*)*crympan* curl, with which, though it would now be repr. by *crimp*, there appears to be no continuity. Cf. CRAMP[1].

crimson XIV. ME. *crem-, crimesin* - medL. *cremesīnus*, var. of *kermesīnus*, or corr. Rom. forms, - Arab. (Pers.) *ḳirmizī*, f. *ḳirmiz* KERMES.

cringe XIII. ME. *crenge*, varying with *crenche*, corr. to OE. *crinġan, crinċan* fall in battle, Du. *krengen* heel over, and rel. to ON. *krangr* weak, frail, *kranga* creep along, and MLG., Du., MHG. *krenken* weaken, injure, (M)LG., (M)HG. *krank* sick, ill, slight (see CRANK[1]).

cringle ring or eye of rope. XVII. - LG. *kringel*, dim. of *kring* circle, ring.

crinkle XIV (in pp. *krynkeled, crenkled*). frequent. f. base of OE. *crinċan* yield, orig. weaken, CRINGE; see -LE[3].

crinoid lily-shaped. XIX. - Gr. *krinoeidḗs*, f. *krínon* lily; see -OID.

crinoline stiff fabric of horse-hair, etc.; stiff petticoat. XIX. - F., irreg. f. L. *crīnis* hair + *līnum* thread, with ref. to the warp of horsehair and the weft of thread.

cripple sb. OE. *crypel*, ME. *crüpel*, corr. to OLG. *krupil*; also OE. *crēopel*, ME. *crēpel*, corr. to MLG., MDu. *krēpel*, rel. to CREEP. Hence as vb. XIII.

crisis turning-point of a disease XV; vital or decisive stage in events XVII. - L. - Gr. *krísis* decision, event, turning-point of a disease, f. *krínein* decide.

crisp curly OE.; wrinkled, rippled XIV; brittle but hard or firm XVI. OE. *crisp, crips* - L. *crispus* curled.

criss-cross A. †figure of a cross; †alphabet XVI; B. transverse crossing (also adj., adv., and vb.) XIX. Early modEng. *c(h)ris(se)-crosse*, for *Christscrosse* figure of a cross, esp. as used in front of the alphabet in hornbooks and primers; in later sense usu. regarded as a redupl. formation on CROSS[1] with variation of vowel.

criterion XVII. - Gr. *kritḗrion* means of judging, test, f. *kritḗs* judge.

critic XVI. - L. *criticus* - Gr. *kritikós*, sb. use of adj. f. *kritḗs* judge, rel. to CRISIS; see -IC. So **critical** XVI. f. L. *criticus*. **criticism** XVII. **criticize** XVII. **critique** criticism, esp. a critical review XVII. Later form of †*critic(k)* XVII, alt. after F. *critique*, the orig. source, which is based on Gr. (*hē*) *kritikḗ* the critical art.

croak vb. XVI. Preceded by synon. †*crok* (XIII), with similar imit. formations, viz. OE. *crǣccettan*, ME. †*crake* (XIV), †*creke* (see CREAK), †*crouk* (XIV), †*craik* (XV).

crochet knitting with a hooked needle. XIX. - F., dim. of *croc* hook (see CROTCH).

crock[1] earthen pot, etc. OE. *croc* and *crocca*, rel. to synon. Icel. *krukka*, and prob. further to OE. *crōg* (= OHG. *kruog*, G. *krug*), OE. *crūce* (= OS. *krūka*, Du. *kruik*, MHG. *krūche*), Ir. *crogán*, Gael. *crog(an)*, W. *crochan*, Gr. *krōssós* (:- **krōkjos*).

crock[2] old ewe XV; old broken-down horse; decrepit person or thing XIX. In earliest use Sc.; perh. of Flem. orig., cf. MDu. *kraeke* (Du. *krak*), Flem. *krake*; presumably rel. to CRACK.

crocket †curl; (archit.) small ornament on the inclined side of a pinnacle, etc. XVII; bud of a stag's horn XIX. - var. of (O)F. *crochet* CROTCHET.

crocodile XIII. ME. *coko-, cokadrille* - OF. *cocodrille* (mod. *crocodile*) :- medL. *cocodrillus*, for *crocodīlus* - Gr. *krokódīlos*, for **krokódrīlos* 'worm of the stones', f. *krókē* pebble + *drīlos* worm. The present form, assim. to L., appears XVI.

crocus XVII. - L. - Gr. *krókos*, of Sem. orig.

croft enclosed piece of land OE.; small agricultural holding XVIII. of unkn. orig.

cromlech prehistoric erection of large unhewn stones. XVII. - W., f. *crom*, fem. of *crwm* bowed, arched + *llech* flat stone.

crone withered old woman XIV; old ewe XVI. prob. - MDu. *c(a)roonje* carcass, old ewe - ONF. *carogne* CARRION (also, cantankerous woman), which may be the source of the first sense.

crony XVII. Earliest form *chrony* - Gr. *khrónios* long-lasting, f. *khrónos* time; orig. university sl.

crook trick, wile XII; hooked instrument; †claw XIII; shepherd's staff, bishop's staff XIV; bend, curve XV. ME. *crōk* - ON. *krókr* hook, bend. Hence **crook** vb. bend, curve XII.

crooked not straight (lit. and fig.). XIII. f. CROOK sb. + -ED[2], prob. after ON. *krókóttr* crooked, winding, cunning.

croon (dial.) bellow, roar, rumble XIV; utter a low murmuring sound XVIII. north. Eng. and Sc. *croyne, crune* - MLG., MDu. *krōnen* lament, mourn, groan (Du. *kreunen* groan, whimper), of imit. orig.

crop A. bird's craw OE.; B. †head of a plant OE.; top of an object XV; upper part of a whip XVI (hence, whipstock with a handle and loop XIX); C. produce of plants used for food XIII. OE. *crop(p)*, corr. to MLG., MDu. *kropp*, (O)HG. *kropf*, ON. *kroppr*; further relations uncert. Hence **crop** vb. lop, poll XIII; pluck, pull XIV; raise a crop on, bear a crop XVI; come *up* to the surface XVII; whence a new sb. **crop** cropping (in various uses) XVII.

croquet XIX. Supposed to be - var. of F. *crochet* hook; see CROCHET, CROTCHET.

croquette fried ball of potato, etc. XVIII (occas. *croquet*). - F., f. *croquer* crunch, of imit. orig.; see -ETTE.

crosier, crozier †cross-bearer to an archbishop XIV; bearer of a bishop's pastoral staff, hence (through the phr. *crosier('s) staff*) the staff itself XIV. Two words have blended here, (i) - F. *croisier* cross-bearer, f. *crois* CROSS, (ii) - OF. *crocier, crossier* bearer of a bishop's *crosse* or crook (OF. *croce* :- Rom. **croccia*, f. **croccus* CROOK).

cross[1] gibbet consisting of a vertical post with transverse bar; sign or symbol representing this, esp. in Christian use. Late OE. *cros* - ON. *kross* - OIr. *cros* - L. CRUX, *cruc-*, whence also OF. *croiz* (mod. *croix*), Sp. *cruz*, etc. The L. word is also repr. by OE. *crūċ*, ME. *crouch* (whence *crouched* adj. wearing a cross, esp. in *Crouched*, later *Crutched*, *Friars*, earlier †*crossed freres*). Hence **cross** vb. †crucify; set or lie in a cross-position XIV (draw a line across XVIII); mark with a cross; put or pass across XV; thwart, oppose XVI.

cross[2] adj. lying or passing athwart; contrary, opposite; †contentious XVI; out of humour, peevish XVII. Partly attrib. use of CROSS[1], partly ellipt. use of CROSS[3] adv.

cross[3] †adv. crosswise, and prep. across. XVI. Aphetic of ACROSS; the prep. survives in *cross-country* adj. (XVIII).

crotch fork or fork-shaped stake, branch, etc. XVI. perh. identical with ME. *croche* crook, *crozier* - OF. *croche* hook, etc., f. *crocher*, f. *croc* hook - ON. *krókr* CROOK.

crotchet A. †crocket XIV; hook (latterly techn.) XV; B. (mus.) note in the form of a stem with a black head XV; C. whimsical fancy XVI. - (O)F. *crochet*, dim. of *croc* hook (see prec.); see -ET.

croton XVIII. - modL. - Gr. *krótōn* sheep-tick, castor-oil plant.

crouch XIV. poss. - OF. *crochir* be bent, f. *croc* hook (see CROTCH).

croup[1] hindquarters. XIII. - (O)F. *croupe* :- Rom. **croppa* - Gmc. **kruppō*, rel. to CROP.

croup[2] throat-disease with a sharp cough. XVIII. f. *croup* vb. XVI, of imit. orig.

croupier †second standing behind a gamester; raker-in of money at a gaming-table; assistant chairman at a dinner. XVIII. - F., orig. one who rides behind on the croup, f. *croupe* CROUP[1].

crow[1] black carrion-feeding bird OE.; bar of iron with beak-like end XIV. OE. *crāwe*, corr. to OS. *krāia* (Du *kraai*), OHG. *krāwa*, *krā(ha)* (G. *krähe*); f. next.

crow[2] utter the cry of a cock. OE. *crāwan*, corr. to Du. *kraaien*, OHG. *krā(w)en* (G. *krähen*). WGmc. word of imit. orig. The str. pt. is still prevalent in the proper sense, but *crowed* is used in the sense 'utter joyful cries'. Hence **crow** sb. act of crowing XIII.

crowd press on OE.; †push; press in a throng XIV; fill up with compression XVI. OE. *crūdan* intr. push forward, orig. str. vb. corr. to MLG., MDu. *krūden*; cf. OE. *croda* crowd. Hence **crowd** sb. dense multitude. XVI.

crown circlet, wreath, etc., worn on the head XII; †tonsure; vertex of the skull XIII; various coins, orig. bearing the figure of a crown XV; top, summit XVI. ME. *c(o)rune* (superseding OE. *corona*) - AN. *corune*, OF. *corone* (mod. *couronne*) :- L. *corōna* wreath, chaplet - Gr. *korṓnē* anything bent (*korōnís* crown), rel. to *curvus* bent (see CURVE). So **crown** vb. XII. - AN. *coruner*, OF. *coroner* (mod. *couronner*) :- L. *corōnāre*; cf. CORONATION.

crowner see CORONER.

crozier see CROSIER.

crucial cross-shaped XVIII; that decides between rival hypotheses, decisive XIX. - F., f. L. *crux, cruc-* CROSS[1]; see -IAL.

crucible vessel for fusing metals. XV (early forms *corusible, kressibulle*). - medL. *crucibulum* night-lamp, crucible, f. L. *crux, cruc-* CROSS[1]; perh. orig. lamp hanging before a crucifix.

crucifer cross-bearer XVI; cruciferous plant XIX. - ChrL., f. L. *crux, cruc-* CROSS[1]; see -FEROUS. So **cruciferous** bearing or wearing a cross XVII; (bot.) belonging to the Cruciferae (having petals crosswise) XIX. **cruciform** cross-shaped. XVII. - modL.

crucifix figure of Christ on the cross. XIII. - (O)F. - late L. *crucifixus*, i.e. *crucī fixus* fixed to a cross. So **crucifixion** XVII. - late L. **crucify** put to death on a cross. XIII. - (O)F. *crucifier* :- Rom. **crucificāre*, repl. ChrL. *crucifigere*, i.e. *crucī figere* FIX to a CROSS.

crude in a raw state XIV; ill-digested, not matured XVI. - L. *crūdus* raw, rough, cruel; see RAW. So **crudity** XV.

cruel XIII. - (O)F. :- L. *crūdēlis*, rel. to *crūdus* CRUDE. So **cruelty** XIII. - OF. *crualté* (mod. *cruauté*) :- Rom. **crūdālitās*, for L. *crūdēlitās*.

cruet small bottle or vial. XIII. - AN. **cruet(e)*, dim. of OF. *crue* - OS. *krūka* (see CROCK[1]).

cruise vb. XVII. prob. - Du. *kruisen* cross, f. *kruis* sb. (cf. CROSS[1]). So **cruiser** XVII.

crumb sb. OE. *cruma*, corr. with variation of vowel to MDu. *crūme* (Du. *kruim*), MLG., MDu. *crōme*, (M)HG. *krūme*, Icel. *kr(a)umr*; rel. to L. *grūmus* mound, Gr. *grūméā* crumb. The parasitic *b* appears XVI. Hence **crumb** vb. superseding †*crim* (XV) - OE. *ġecrymman* :- **krumjan*. **crumble** vb. break into crumbs or little bits. XVI.

crumpet XVII. of doubtful orig.

crumple XVI. f. *crump* curve, curl up (XIV), rel. to CRAMP[1]; see -LE[3].

crunch crush with the teeth. XIX. var. of *craunch* (XVII), assim. to *munch*.

crupper leather strap passing under a horse's tail XIII; horse's hindquarters XVI. - AN. *cropere*, OF. *cropiere* (mod. *croupière*) :- Rom. **croppāria, -ēria*, f. **croppa* - Gmc. **krupp-* CROP; see -ER[2].

crural pert. to the leg. XVI. - L. *crūrālis*, f. *crūs, crūr-* leg; see -AL[1].

crusade military expedition for the recovery of the Holy Land from the Muslims XVI; gen. XVII. The earlier forms were (i) *croisade* (XVI) - F., alt. of earlier *croisée* by assim. to the Sp. form (see -ADE); (ii) *crusado, -ada* (XVI) - Sp. *cruzada*; (iii) *croisado, -ada* (XVII), blends of (i) and (ii). Cf. CROSS[1]. The current form is first recorded XVIII.

crush †crash, clash; compress with violence XIV; break down the power of XVI. - AN. *crussir*, *corussier*, OF. *croissir, cruissir* gnash (the teeth), crash, crack :- Rom. **cruscīre*, of unkn. orig.

crust XIV. ME. *crouste* - OF. *crouste* (mod. *croûte*) :- L. *crusta* rind, shell, incrustation, rel. to Gr. *krúos* frost, *krústallos* CRYSTAL, L. *crūdus* CRUDE, OHG. *hrosa* crust, ice, OE. *hruse* earth, ON. *hrúðr* crust, scab. Hence **crusted, crusty** XIV.

crustaceous that is or having a hard integument; of the crustacea. XVII. f. modL. *crustāceus*, f. L. *crusta* CRUST; see -ACEOUS. So **crustacea** XIX. - modL., n. pl. of the adj.

crutch staff with crosspiece for an infirm person. OE. *cryċ(ċ)* = OS. *krukka*, OHG. *krucka* (G. *krücke*), ON. *krykkja*; cf. CROOK.

Crutched Friars see CROSS[1].

crux pl. **cruxes, cruces** †conundrum, riddle XVIII; difficulty the solution of which perplexes XIX. - L., 'CROSS[1]'; short for *crux interpretum*, *crux philosophorum* torment of interpreters, of philosophers.

cry call out (for); announce publicly; shout in lamentation XIII; weep XVI. - (O)F. *crier* :- L. *quirītāre* cry aloud, wail. So **cry** sb. loud utterance. XIII. - (O)F. *cri*.

cryo- comb. form of Gr. *krúos* frost, icy cold.

crypt XVIII. - L. *crypta* - Gr. *krúptē* vault, sb. use of fem. of *kruptós* hidden. Cf. GROT.

cryptic hidden, secret. XVII. - late L. *crypticus* - Gr. *kruptikós*, f. *kruptós*; see prec. and -IC. So **crypto-** used as comb. form of Gr. *kruptós* hidden, as in **cryptography** secret manner of writing. XVII. - modL. *cryptographia*. So **cryptographer** XVII.

crystal †ice; pure quartz (resembling ice) OE.; piece of rock crystal, etc., XIV; highly transparent glass XVI; mineralogical form XVII. - (O)F. *cristal* - L. *crystallum* - Gr. *krustallos* ice, f. *krustaínein* freeze, *krúos* frost. So **crystalline** XIV. - (O)F. *cristallin* - L. - Gr.; see -INE[1]. **crystallize** XVI.

cub young of the fox, bear, etc. XVI. of unkn. orig.

cubby-hole XIX. f. dial. *cub* cattle-pen, coop, crib, prob. of LG. orig. (cf. COVE[1]).

cube XVI. - (O)F. *cube* or L. *cubus* - Gr. *kúbos*. So **cubic, cubical** XV. **cubism** form of pictorial art in which the design is based on cubes. XX. - F. *cubisme*.

cubeb berry of the shrub *Piper cubeba*. XIV (*quibibe*). - (O)F. *cubèbe*, †*quibibe* :- Rom. **cubēba* - Arab. *kabāba*.

cubicle †bedchamber XV; one of a series of sleeping-rooms XIX. - L. *cubiculum*, f. *cubāre* recline, lie in bed; see -CLE.

cubit †forearm; measure of length derived from this. XIV. - L. *cubitum* elbow, distance from the elbow to the finger-tips.

cucking-stool instrument of punishment consisting of a chair (sometimes in the form of a close-stool) in which the offender was exposed or ducked. XIII. orig. varying with †*cuckstool* (XIII); presumably f. †*cuck* void excrement - ON. **kúka*, rel. to *kúkr* excrement.

cuckold husband of an unfaithful wife. XIII (*cukeweld*, later *cokewold*, *cokwald*, *cocold*). - AN. **cucuald*, var. of OF. *cucuault*, f. *cucu* CUCKOO + pejorative suffix *-ald*, *-aud*, *-ault*.

cuckoo XIII. - OF. *cucu* (mod. *coucou*); of imit. orig.

cucumber Late ME. *cucumer* (XIV-XVII) was superseded by *cucumber* (XV), †*cocomber*, by assim. to OF. *co(u)combre* (mod. *concombre*) - L. *cucumer*.

cud half-digested food of a ruminant. OE. *cudu*, earlier *cwudu*, *cwidu* what is chewed, mastic, corr. to OHG. *quiti*, *kuti* glue (G. *kitt* cement, putty) and rel. ult. to L. *bitūmen* BITUMEN, pitch, Skr. *játu* resin, gum and further to ON. *kváða* resin.

cudbear dyeing powder prepared from lichen. XVIII. f. var. *Cudber(t)* of the name of Dr. *Cuthbert* Gordon, who patented the powder.

cuddle XVIII. perh. f. dial. *couth* comfortable, snug + -LE[3]. But cf. †*cull* (XVI) fondle, var. of †*coll* (XIV) aphetic - OF. *acoler* embrace.

cudgel OE. *cyċġel*, of unkn. orig.

cue[1] actor's word(s) serving as a signal for another to enter or speak; (hence) hint. XVI (*q*, *qu*, *quew*, *kew*, *cue*). of unkn. orig.

cue[2] pigtail; billiard-player's stick. XVIII. var. of QUEUE.

cuff[1] †glove, mitten XIV; band at the bottom of a sleeve XVI; fetter for the wrist XVII. of unkn. orig.

cuff[2] strike with the fist or open hand. perh. imit. of the sound. Hence **cuff** sb. XVI.

cuirass armour for the body (orig. of leather). XV. - F. *cuirasse*, †*curas*, †*-ace*, perh. - It. *corazza* :- Rom. **coriācia*, sb. use of fem. of L. *coriāceus*, f. *corium* leather (see -ACEOUS). So **cuirassier** XVII.

cuisine cookery. XVIII. - F. *cuisine* kitchen, cookery :- L. *coquīna* (cf. KITCHEN).

cuisse, cuish thigh-piece of armour. XV. pl. *cus(c)hes*, *cushies*, *cuisses*, later forms of ME. *cussues*, *quyssues* (XIV) - OF. *cuisseaux*, pl. of *cuissel* :- late L. *coxāle*, f. *coxa* hip.

cul-de-sac (anat.) vessel, etc., open at only one end XVIII; blind alley XIX. - F., lit. 'bottom of the sack'.

-cule terminal element (var. with -CLE) repr. F. *-cule*, L. *-culus*, *-a*, *-um*, dim. suffix of all three genders.

culinary XVII. - L. *culīnārius*, f. *culīna* kitchen; see KILN, -ARY.

cull select, pick XV; gather XVII. Earlier *co(i)le* and (rare) *cuyl* (XIV). - OF. *coilli(e)r*, *cuiller*, (also mod.) *cueillir*, repr. L. *colligere* (see COLLECT[2]), Rom. **colgere*.

cullet refuse glass with which crucibles are replenished. XVII. Earlier *collet* neck of glass left on the end of a blowing-iron - OF. *collet*, dim. of *col*, *cou* neck :- L. *collum* (cf. COLLAR); but cf. F. *cueillette* rags collected for making paper.

cully (sl.) dupe, simpleton; man, mate. XVII. prob. orig. rogues' cant; of unkn. orig.

culm[1] (dial.) coal dust XIV; soot XV; anthracite XVIII (hence geol. series of shales containing anthracite XIX). repr. earlier in *colmie* (XIII), *culmy* (XIV) sooty; of unkn. orig., but presumably based on *col* COAL.

culm[2] (bot.) stalk of a plant. XVII. - L. *culmus*; cf. HAULM.

culminate XVII. f. pp. stem of late L. *culmināre* exalt, extol, f. *culmen*, *culmin-* summit, acme; see -ATE[3]. So **culmination** XVII.

culpable guilty XIV; blameworthy XVII. ME. *coupable* - (O)F. :- L. *culpābilis*, f. *culpāre* blame, censure, f. *culpa* blame; see -ABLE. The sp. and pronunc. were later assim. to L. Hence **culpability** XVII.

culprit in the formula 'Culprit, how will you be tried?', formerly said by the Clerk of the Crown to a prisoner who pleaded Not Guilty; the accused XVII; (by assoc. with L. *culpa* guilt) offender XVIII. According to legal tradition, compounded of *cul*, short for AN. *culpable* guilty (cf. prec.), and *pri(s)t* (= OF. *prest*, F. *prêt*) ready; it is supposed that, when the prisoner had pleaded Not Guilty, the Clerk replied with *Culpable: prest daverrer notre bille*, i.e. 'Guilty: ready to aver our indictment', and that this was noted in the form *cul. prist*.

cult XVII. - F. *culte* or L. *cultus*, sb. of action f. *colere* inhabit, cultivate, protect, honour with worship (see COLONY).

cultivate XVII. f. medL. *cultivāre*, *-āt-*, f. medL. *cultīvus*, in *cultīva terra* arable land, f. *cult-*, pp. stem of *colere*; see prec., -IVE, -ATE[3]. So **cultivation** XVIII, **cultivator** XVII.

culture piece of tilled land; cultivation XV; cultivating *of* the mind, etc., XVI; intellectual training and refinement XIX. - F. *culture* (repl. earlier †*couture*) or its source L. *cultūra*, f. *cult-*; see prec. and -URE. Hence **cultural** XIX.

culverin gun and cannon formerly in use. XV. - (O)F. *coulevrine*, f. *couleuvre* snake :- Rom. **colobra*, for L. *colubra*, beside *coluber* snake; see -INE[1].

culvert tunnel drain for water crossing a road, etc. XVIII. of unkn. orig.

cumber †harass, overwhelm XIII; burden, load XIV. prob. aphetic of †*acumber*, ENCUMBER, but there are difficulties of chronology. Hence **cumbersome** †obstructive, harassing XIV; inconveniently bulky or heavy XVI; see -SOME. **cumbrous** XIV.

Cumbrian pert. to Cumberland or to the ancient British kingdom of Cumbria. XVIII. f. medL. *Cumbria*, f. W. *Cymry* (cf. CYMRIC) :- OW. **kombrogī*, pl. of **kombrogos* fellow countryman, f. **kom-* COM- + **mrog-* (W. *bro*) region (cf. MARK[1]); see -IAN.

cummerbund XVII. - Hind. - Pers. *kamarband* 'waist-band'.

cum(m)in XII. - OF. *cumin*, *comin* :- L. *cumīnum* - Gr. *kúmīnon*, prob. of Sem. orig.

cumquat small variety of orange. XVII. Cantonese var. of Chinese *kin kü* 'gold orange'.

cumulate XVI. f. pp. stem of L. *cumulāre*, f. *cumulus* heap; see -ATE[3]. So **cumulative** XVII.

cumulus heap, accumulation XVII; (meteor.) cloud of rounded masses heaped one on the other XIX.

cuneiform wedge-shaped, spec. of the elements of Assyrian and other inscriptions. XVII (*cune(o)form*). - F. *cunéiforme* or modL. *cuneiformis*, f. *cuneus* wedge (cf. COIN); see -FORM.

cunning learning, wisdom XIV; (arch.) ability, skill XIV; skilful deceit, craftiness XVI. perh. - ON. *kunnandi*, f. *kunna* know (see CAN[2]). So *cunning* adj. †learned XIII; able, skilful XIV; crafty, artful XVI. - ON. *kunnandi*. In both words the ON. suffix has been assim. to the native -ING[1,2]; the sb. was perh. modelled on the adj. rather than derived immed. from ON.

cup OE. *cuppe* - medL. *cuppa*, presumably differentiated var. of L. *cūpa* tub, vat. ME. byforms *c(o)upe*, *cop(p)e* repr. partly OF. *cupe*, etc. (mod. *coupe*), but there was some blending with the descendant of OE. (late Nhb.) *copp* = MLG., Du. *kop*, (O)HG. *kopf* head. Hence **cupboard** †sideboard (to hold cups, etc.) XIV; cabinet XVI.

cupel vessel for assaying gold and silver. XVII. - F. *coupelle* - late L. *cūpella*, dim. of *cūpa* (see CUP); assim. to the L. form.

Cupid XIV. - L. *Cupīdō*, personification of *cupīdō* desire, f. *cupere* desire, long for. So **cupidity** XV. - F. *cupidité* or L. *cupiditās*, f. *cupidus*, eagerly desirous, f. *cupere*; see -ID[1], -ITY.

cupola rounded dome XVI; furnace for melting metals, orig. with a dome leading to the chimney XVIII. - It. - late L. *cūpula* little cask, small burying-vault, dim. of *cūpa* (see CUP).

cupreous of copper. XVII. f. late L. *cupreus*, f. *cuprum* COPPER[1]; see -EOUS.

cupro- used as comb. form (see -O-) of late L. *cuprum* COPPER[1].

cur watch-dog, shepherd's dog; now always, low-bred dog. XIII. prob. orig. in *cur-dog*, perh. f. ON. *kurr* grumbling, *kurra* murmur, grumble, as if 'growling dog'.

curaçao liqueur flavoured with rind of bitter oranges. XIX. - F. name of one of the Antilles that produces the oranges.

curare substance obtained from plants, used by S. Amer. Indians to poison arrows. XVIII. Also *woorara* (XVIII), *urari*, *(w)oorali*, *(wo)urali* (all XIX). - Carib.

curate (arch.) one having the cure of souls XIV; assistant to a parish priest XVI. - medL. *cūrātus*, f. *cūra* CURE; see -ATE[1]. Hence **curacy** XVII.

curative XV. - F. *curatif*, *-ive* - medL.; see -ATIVE.

curator †one having a cure of souls XIV; guardian of a minor, lunatic, etc., XV; manager, governor, spec. as member of an academic body XVII. - AN. *curatour*, (O)F. *curateur*, or the source L. *cūrātōr*, *-ōr-*, agent-noun f. *cūrāre*; see CURE, -ATOR.

curb[1] chain or strap passing under a horse's lower jaw and fastened to the bit. XV. Early forms *co(u)rbe*, prob. f. †*co(u)rbe* vb. bend, curve (XIV) - (O)F. *courber* :- L. *curvāre* CURVE. Hence **curb** vb. put a curb on (a horse); restrain, check. XVI.

curb[2] enclosing framework or border. XVI. f. CURB[1]. See also KERB.

curd coagulated substance formed from milk. XIV. ME. *crud(de)*, *crod(de)*; the present form dates from XV; of unkn. orig., but Gael., (M)Ir. *gruth* curds have been plausibly compared. Hence **curd** vb. curdle XIV. **curdle** form into curd(s). XVI; see -LE[3].

cure A. †care, charge, office XIII; spiritual charge, as of a parish XIV; B. (successful) medical treatment XIV. - (O)F. :- L. *cūra*. So **cure** vb. A. †take care or charge of XIV; B. †treat medically; heal XIV; preserve for keeping XVII. - (O)F. *curer* take care of, clean :- L. *cūrāre* care for, cure, f. *cūra*. **curable** XIV. - (O)F. or L.

curette surgeon's small scraping instrument. XVIII. - F. *curette*, f. *curer* (see CURE) in the sense 'clear, cleanse' + -ETTE.

curfew ringing of an evening bell for the covering or extinction of domestic fires; also transf. and gen. XIII. - AN. *coeverfu* (mod. *couvrefeu*), f. tonic stem of *couvrir* COVER + *feu* fire :- L. *focus* hearth.

curia (Rom. antiq.) XVI; Papal Court XIX. - L. *cūria* division of the Roman people, its place of assembly, (hence) senate; of unkn. orig. So **curial** XV. - F. - L.

curio XIX. Shortening of *curiosity*, prob. suggested by the form of It. words.

curious A. †careful, studious; †ingenious, skilled; eager to know or learn; B. †carefully or skilfully wrought XIV; †interesting XVII; exciting attention by being strange or odd XVII. - OF. *curios* (mod. *curieux*) :- L. *cūriōsus* (only in subjective sense) careful, inquisitive, f. *cūra* care; see CURE, -IOUS. So **curiosity** †carefulness, attention XIV; eager desire to know, inquisitiveness XVI.

curl twist or form into ringlets. First recorded (XIV) in pp. *crolled*, *crulled*, extended form with -ED[1] of ME. *crolle*, *crulle* - MDu. *krul* (= MHG. *krol*) curly, prob. rel. to MLG. *krūs* crisp, curly (G. *kraus* curled). Hence **curl** sb. XVII; whence **curly** (see -Y[1]) XVIII.

curlew †quail; wading bird with musical cry. XIV. ME. *cor-*, *curlu(e)* - (O)F. *courlieu*, var. of *courlis*, orig. imit. of the bird's cry, but prob. assim. to OF. *courliu* courier, messenger, f. *courre* run (cf. CURRENT), *lieu* place :- L. *locus* (cf. LOCAL).

curling Sc. game played on the ice with large rounded stones. XVII. perh. f. CURL with ref. to the motion given to the stone; see -ING[1]. Also **curler**; whence prob. **curl** vb. XVIII.

curmudgeon miser, churl. XVI. Early vars. are *cormogeon*, *curmuggion*, *curre-megient*; of unkn. orig.

currach (Sc. and Anglo-Ir.) small wicker boat. XV. - Ir., Gael. *curach* boat; cf. CORACLE.

currant dried fruit prepared from a dwarf seedless grape of the Levant; transf. (XVI) to species of *Ribes*, popularly supposed to be the source of the Levantine currant. orig. (XIV) in pl. phr. *raysons of coraunce* (see RAISIN) - AN. *raisins de corauntz*, for OF. *raisins de Corinthe* grapes of Corinth (their orig. place of export).

current flowing XIII; in circulation or vogue XV; in progress XVII. ME. *cora(u)nt* - OF. *corant*, prp. of *courre* :- L. *currere* run; see -ENT. Also sb. stream XIV; course, progress (of time, etc.) XVI; (electr.) XVIII. Hence **currency** circulation, vogue XVII; medium of exchange XVIII.

curricle two-wheeled carriage. XVIII. - L. *curriculum* racing-chariot, dim. f. *currere* (see prec.). In the orig. sense of 'course' the L. word *curriculum* has been adopted (XIX) for 'course of study or training'.

currier leather-dresser. XIV. ME. *corier* - OF. :- L. *coriārius*, f. *corium* leather.

curry[1] rub down with a comb and brush XIII; dress (tanned leather) XV. - OF. *correier* arrange, equip, curry (a horse) :- Rom. **conrēdāre*, modelled on Gmc. **ȝarǣðjan*, f. **ȝa-* Y- + **raið-* READY. Hence **currycomb** XVI.

curry[2] dish (esp. of rice) cooked with a preparation of turmeric. XVI (*carriel*), XVII (*carree*). - Tamil *kari* relish with rice, Kannada *kaṟi*.

curse utterance consigning an object to evil; formal ecclesiastical censure OE.; evil inflicted by supernatural power XVI. Late OE. *curs*, of unkn. orig.; it has been referred to OIr. *cūrsagim* I censure, chastise. Hence **curse** vb.; late OE. *cursian*.

cursive written in a 'running' hand. XVIII. - medL. *cursīvus* (in *scriptura cursiva*), f. *curs-*, pp. stem of L. *currere* run; see -IVE.

cursory XVII. - L. *cursōrius*, f. *cursor* runner; see prec. and -ORY[2]. So **cursorily** adv. XVI; see -LY[2].

curt short, terse XVII; so brief as to be lacking in courtesy XIX. - L. *curtus* cut short.

curtail †dock; cut short. XVI. orig. *curtal(l)*, f. †*curtal* horse with docked tail (XV) - F. *courtault*, *-auld* (mod. *courtaud*), f. *court* short; assoc. at an early date with TAIL[1].

curtain sb. XIII. ME. *cortine*, *curtine*, later *curtain(e)*, *-ein(e)* - OF. *cortine* (mod. *courtine*) :- late L. *cortīna*, used in the Vulgate (Exodus 26: 1) to render Gr. *aulaía* curtain (f. *aulḗ* court), as if it was regarded as a deriv. of L. *co(ho)rt-* COURT, whereas in classical L. it meant 'cauldron' and was hence applied to circular or arched objects. Hence **curtain** vb. XIII.

curtana pointless sword used at English coronations. XIII. - AL. *curtāna* fem. (sc. *spatha* sword) - AN. *curtain*, OF. *cortain* name of Roland's sword, so called because it had broken at the point when thrust into a block of steel, f. *cort*, *curt* short.

curtilage area attached to and enclosing a dwelling-house. XIV. - AN. *curtilage*, OF. *co(u)rtillage*, f. *co(u)rtil* small court, f. *cort* COURT; see -AGE.

curts(e)y XVI. var. of COURTESY, formerly used in various senses of this, but restricted since *c*.1700. Hence as vb. XVI.

curve †curved XV; sb. short for *curve line* XVII. - L. *curvus*, app. rel. to Gr. *kurtós* curved, and further to *circus* CIRCLE, *corōna* CROWN. So **curve** vb. XVII. - L. *curvāre*. **curvature** XV. - OF. or L.

curvet special leap of a horse in the manège. XVI. - It. *corvetta*, dim. of *corva*, early form of *curva* curve :- L. *curva*, fem. of *curvus*; see prec. and -ET. Hence as vb. XVI.

cushion XIV. Two types are repr. in ME. by (i) *quisshon*, (ii) *cushin* - OF. (i) *coissin*, *cuissin*, (ii) *cossin*, *cussin*, (also mod.) *coussin* :- a Gallo-Rom. form based on L. *culcita* mattress, cushion.

cushy (sl.) easy, comfortable. XX (orig. used in the British army in India). f. Hind. (- Pers.) *ḵuš* excellent, charming, healthy, happy + -Y[1].

cusp (astrol.) entrance of a house XVI; point, apex XVII. - L. *cuspis*, *-id-* point, pointed weapon. So **cuspidate(d)** sharp-pointed. XVII. - pp. of L. *cuspidāre*; see -ATE[2].

cuspidor (U.S.) spittoon. XVIII. - Pg. *cuspidor* spitter, f. *cuspir* spit :- **conspuīre*, for L. *conspuere*, f. CON- (intensive) + *spuere* spit.

cuss[1] (orig. U.S.) colloq. var. of CURSE. So **cussed** pp. used as adj.

cuss[2] (sl.) person or thing regarded as an affliction or a nuisance; (humorously) fellow, chap. XVIII. prob. orig. identical with CUSS[1], but later regarded as short for *customer*.

custard †open meat or fruit pie, thickened with eggs, etc. XV; dish or sweet made from eggs beaten up with milk XVII. In early recipes varying with †*custade*, also †*crustarde* - AN. **crustade*, f. *cruste*, OF. *crouste* CRUST; see -ADE.

custody safe-keeping XV; the keeping of an officer of justice; imprisonment XVI. - L. *custōdia*, f. *custōs*, *custōd-* guardian, keeper; see -Y[3]. Hence **custodian** XVIII.

custom habitual practice XII; established usage; tribute, impost XIV; business, patronage XVI. - OF. *custome*, *co(u)stume* (mod. *coutume*) :- **costumne*, for **costudne* :- L. *consuetūdō*, *-din-*, f. *consuēscere* accustom, accustom oneself, f. CON- + *suēscere* become accustomed, f. *suī* g. sg. of refl. pron. 'oneself'. So **customary** liable to customs or dues, holding by custom XVI; accustomed XVII. - medL. *custumārius*, f. *custuma*, f. AN. *custume*. **customer** †customary tenant; †collector of customs XIV; customary purchaser XV; (colloq.) person (to have to do with) XVI. orig. - AN. *custumer*, medL. *custumārius*; in some senses newly f. *custom*; see -ER[1].

cut[1] lot, in phr. *draw cuts* formerly *cut*. XIII. of unkn. orig.

cut[2] make a way with an edged instrument into (an object). XIII. The earlier dial. vars. *cutte*, *kitte*, *kette* point to an OE. **cyttan*, f. **kut-* (cf. Norw. *kutte*, Icel. *kuta* cut with a little knife, *kuti* sb. little blunt knife). Hence **cut** sb. XVI.

cutaneous XVI. - modL. *cutāneus*, f. L. *cutis* skin; see HIDE[1], -AN, -EOUS.

cute clever XVIII; (U.S.) attractive XIX. Aphetic of ACUTE.

cuticle epidermis. XVII. - L. *cutīcula*, dim. of *cutis*; see CUTANEOUS.

cutlass XVI. - F. *coutelas*, corr. to It. *coltellaccio*, repr. Rom. **cultellāceum*, f. L. *cultellus*, dim. of *culter* COULTER.

cutler XIV. - AN. *cotillere*, (O)F. *coutelier*, f. *coutel* (mod. *couteau*) knife :- L. *cultellus*, dim. of *culter* COULTER; see -ER[2]. So **cutlery** XIV.

cutlet XVIII. - F. *côtelette*, OF. *costelette*, dim. of *coste* (mod. *côte*) rib :- L. *costa*; assim. to CUT[2] sb. and -LET.

cutter ship's rowing and sailing boat; small one-masted vessel. XVIII. perh. f. CUT[2] + -ER[1].

cuttle *cuttle-fish* (XVI). Later OE. *cudele*, ME. *codel*, f. base of COD[1], with allusion to its ink-bag. The unexpl. change of *-d-* to *-t-* appears XV (*cotul*).

-cy suffix corr. to F. *-tie*, †*-cie*, originating in L. *-cia*, *-tia*, Gr. *-k(e)íā*, *-t(e)íā*, f. *-k-*, *-t-* + *-íā*, etc. -Y[3]; occurs chiefly in -ACY, -ANCY, -CRACY, -ENCY, -MANCY. On the model of *prophet/prophecy* was formed *idiocy* from *idiot*, and thence *secrecy* from *secret*. The correspondence of *agent* and *agency* and consequently of *lieutenant* and *lieutenancy* gave rise to *captaincy*, *chaplaincy*, from *captain*, *chaplain*. The suffix is added to some words ending in *t*, as *bankruptcy*, *baronetcy*, *paramountcy*.

cyan(o)- comb. form of Gr. *kúanos* dark-blue mineral, *kuáneos* dark-blue, in designation of certain bluish salts and minerals, as **cyanogen** (XIX) - F. *cyanogène*, so named from its entering into the composition of Prussian blue. So *cyanic*, *cyanide*, etc.

cybernetics theory of control and communication in animals and machines. XX. f. Gr. *kubernḗtēs* steersman, f. *kubernân* steer, GOVERN; see -ICS.

cyclamen XVI. - medL. *cyclamen*, for L. *cyclamīnos*, *-on* - Gr. *kukláminos*, perh. f. *kúklos* circle, CYCLE, with ref. to its bulbous roots.

cycle recurrent period of years XIV (only occas. before XVII); recurrent succession of things XVII; series of poems, etc., relating to a central event or epoch XIX. - F. *cycle* or late L. *cyclus* - Gr. *kúklos* circle (see WHEEL). So **cyclic** XVIII. - F. *cyclique* or L. *cyclicus* or Gr. *kuklikós*.

cyclo- comb. form of Gr. *kúklos* CYCLE, in: (i) scientific terms denoting circular or coiled forms or parts, e.g. *cyclostomatous*, *cyclostomous* having a round sucking mouth, as the lamprey, (ii) names of inventions having circular parts or concerned with circles, e.g. *cyclometer* instrument for measuring arcs, apparatus for registering distance travelled by a vehicle. XIX.

cyclone orig. storm in which the wind takes a circular course XIX; (hence) tornado; system of rotating winds. prob. intended to repr. Gr. *kúklōma* wheel, coil of a snake, f. *kúklos* CYCLE; *cyclome* occurs as an early var.

cyclopaedia XVII. Clipped form of ENCYCLOPAEDIA (in Gr. form in the title of 'Lucubrationes vel potius absolutissime κυκλοπαιδεία' by Joachim Fortius Ringelbergius, 1541). As the title of an English work it appears first in Ephraim Chambers's 'Cyclopædia, or General Dictionary of Arts and Sciences' (1728).

Cyclops (Gr. myth.) one of a race of one-eyed giants. XV. - L. *Cyclōps* - Gr. *Kúklōps* 'round-eyed', f. *kúklos* (see CYCLE) + *ṓps* EYE.

cyder var. of CIDER.

cygnet XV (*signett*). prob. - AN. **cignet*, f. OF. *cigne* (mod. *cygne*) swan, latinized form of earlier †*ci(s)ne* :- medL. (Rom.) *cīcinus*, for L. *cycnus* (in late MSS. *cygnus*) - Gr. *kúknos*; see -ET.

cylinder XVI. - L. *cylindrus* - Gr. *kúlindros* roller, f. *kulindein* roll. So **cylindrical** XVII. f. modL. *cylindricus* - Gr. *kulindrikós*.

Cymric pert. to the Welsh or their language. XIX. f. W. *Cymru* Wales, *Cymry* the Welsh, CUMBRIAN; see -IC.

cynic sect of ascetic philosophers in ancient Greece; sneering critic. XVI. - L. *cynicus* - Gr. *kunikós* dog-like, churlish, Cynic (the application being derived from the gymnasium (*Kunósarges*) where they taught or from certain dog-like qualities), f. *kúōn*, *kun-* dog (HOUND); see -IC. So **cynical** XVI, **cynicism** XVII.

cynosure constellation Ursa Minor; 'guiding star' XVI; centre of interest XVII. - F. *cynosure* or L. *cynosūra* - Gr. *kunósoura*, f. *kunós*, g. of *kúōn* dog + *ourā́* tail.

cypher see CIPHER.

cypress dark-foliaged coniferous tree. XIII. ME. *cipres* (assim. later to L.) - OF. *cipres* (mod. *cyprès*) - late L. *cypressus* - Gr. *kupárissos*.

Cyrillic of the alphabet used by Slavonic peoples in the Eastern Church, the invention of which is traditionally attributed to the Greek missionary *Cyril* (IX). XIX; see -IC.

cyst sac, esp. of morbid matter. XVIII. - modL. *cystis* - Gr. *kústis* bladder.

czar, tzar, tsar emperor of Russia. XVI. Russ. *tsar'*, ult. repr. L. *Caesar* through the medium of Gmc., in which the word meant 'emperor' (cf. MLG. *ke(y)ser*, OHG. *keisar*, ON. *keisari*, Goth. *kaisar*).

D

dab[1] (dial.) strike with a sharp blow XIV; strike with soft pressure XVI. Rare before XVI, when there may have been a fresh formation, but perh. in continuous use from early times; of imit. orig., but cf. DABBLE.
dab[2] small flatfish. XV. of unkn. orig.
dab[3] adept, expert. XVII. of unkn. orig. Hence synon. **dabster** XVIII.
dabble make or become wet by splashing or dipping. XVI. - Du.†*dabbelen*, or f. DAB[1] + -LE[3].
dabchick XVI. The early forms *dap-*, *dop-chick*, and (later) *dipchick* suggest connection with OE. *dufe doppa* 'pelicanus', ME. *doue|doppe*, *dyve dap* (later *divedopper*, *-dapper*), OE. *dop ened*, *dop|fugol* moorhen, and hence with the base **deup-* **dup-* (see DEEP, DIP).
dabster see DAB[3].
da capo (mus.) direction to repeat from a certain point. XVIII. - It., *da* from, *capo* beginning (:- Rom. **capum*, for L. *caput* head; see CHIEF).
dace XV (*da(r)ce*, *darse*). - OF. *dars*, nom. of *dart* dace (identical with DART).
dachshund XIX. - G., lit. 'badger-dog.'
dacoit class of robber in India and Burma. XIX. - Hindi *ḍakait*, f. *ḍākā* gang-robbery.
dactyl †date (fruit); (pros.) the foot —◡◡. XIV. - L. *dactylus* - Gr. *dáktulos* finger, date, dactyl. So **dactylic** XVI.
dad (colloq.) father; also **daddy** (see -Y[6]) XVI; **dad(d)a** XVII. Cf. the series *bab(by)*, *baby*, *baba* and *mam(my)*, *mam(m)a*, and synon. Gr. *táta*, Skr. *tatá-*, W. *tad*, etc.; perh. of infantile orig.
dado cubical block of a pedestal XVII; lining along the lower part of a wall XVIII. - It. *dado* die, cube (= F. *dé* DIE[2]).
daemon(ic) see DEMON, DEMONIC.
daffodil †asphodel; plant of the genus *Narcissus*. XIV. Alt. (with unexpl. *d-*) of †*affodil* (XV-XVII) - med L. *affodillus*, prob. a book-perversion of **asfodillus*, var. of L. *asphodilus*, *-elus* ASPHODEL.
daft †mild, meek XIII; stupid XIV; crazy XVI. ME. *daffte*, repr. OE. *ġedæfte* mild, gentle, meek :- Gmc. **ʒaðaftjaz*, *f.* **ʒaðafti*, f. stem **dab-* of Goth. *gadaban* become, be fit (cf. OE. *ġedæftlīċe* fitly, suitably, *ġedæftan* make fit, prepare). The transition to the sense 'stupid' may have been assisted by ME. †*daff* (of unkn. orig.) simpleton, fool. See DEFT.
dagger XIV. Has the form of an agent-noun in -ER[1], and perh. f. ME. *dagge* (XIV) pierce, stab; but infl. by (O)F. *dague* (XIII) - Pr. or It. *daga*, which has been referred to Rom. **daca* 'Dacian knife', sb. use of fem. of *Dacus* Dacian.
dago American Spaniard. XIX (*dego*). alt. of *Diego*, Sp. equivalent of the name JAMES.
daguerreotype early photographic process. XIX. - F. *daguerréotype*, f. name of Louis-Jacques-Mandé *Daguerre* (1789-1851) the inventor; see -O- and TYPE.
dahlia XIX. f. the name of Andreas *Dahl*, Swedish botanist; see -IA[1].
daily see DAY.
dainty †honour, esteem; †liking, pleasure; choice or delightful thing, delicacy. XIII. - AN. *dainté*, OF. *daintié*, *deintié* :- L. *dignitās*, *-āt-* worthiness, worth, beauty, DIGNITY. Hence **dainty** adj. †choice, excellent; pleasing to the taste, of delicate beauty XIV; fastidious XVI.
dairy XIII. ME. *deierie*, *dayerie*, f. *deie*, *daye* female servant, dairy-woman :- OE. *dǣġe* kneader of bread = ON. *deigja* :- Gmc. **daiʒjōn*, f. base of Goth. *deigan* knead; cf. DOUGH. See -RY.
dais †high table in a hall; raised platform for this. XIII. ME. *deis* - OF. :- L. *discus* quoit, DISH, in medL. table. Obsolete in Eng. use before 1600; the present use is due to revival since 1800.
daisy OE. *dæġes ēaġe* 'day's eye'; so named from its covering the yellow disc in the evening and disclosing it in the morning.
dale OE. *dæl* n. corr. to OS. (Du.) *dal*, OHG. *tal*, m. and n., ON. *dalr* m., Goth. *dals* m. or *dal* n. :- Gmc. **dalam* n., **dalaz* m., the relations of which are doubtful. Reinforced in ME. from ON.
dally talk lightly XIV; sport, esp. amorously XV; trifle, spend time idly XVI. - OF. *dalier* converse, chat, of unkn. orig. Hence **dalliance** talk; sport, amorous play XIV; frivolous action XVI.
dalmatic (eccl.) wide-sleeved tunic slit up the sides. XV. - (O)F. *dalmatique* or late L. *dalmatica*, sb. use (sc. *vestis* robe, prop. made of Dalmatian wool) of *Dalmaticus* pert. to Dalmatia; see -IC.
dam[1] barrier checking the downward flow of water. XII (in *mulnedam* 'mill-dam'). - (M)LG., (M)Du. *dam*, f. a base repr. also by OE. *fordemman* (ME. *demme*), OFris. *demmen*, Goth. *faurdamnjan* dam up, close up; of doubtful orig. Hence **dam** vb. XVI.
dam[2] †dame, lady XIII; female parent XIV. var. of DAME.
damage (arch.) loss, detriment; injury, harm XIV; money value of something lost XV. - OF. *damage* (mod. *dommage*), f. *dam(me)* loss, damage, prejudice - L. *damnum* loss, hurt; see DAMN and -AGE. So **damage** vb. XIV.
damascene pert. to the city of Damascus, famous for its steel and its silk fabrics; also sb. XIV. - L. *Damascēnus* - Gr. *Damaskēnós*, f. *Damaskós* - Sem. name. Hence **damascene** vb. ornament (steel) by inlaying XIX; earlier (XVI) in the form *damaskene*, later *-keen* - F. *damasquiner*, f. *damasquin* - It. *damaschino*. Cf. next and DAMSON.
damask in various names of natural and artificial products reputed to derive from *Damascus* (cf. prec.); orig. attrib. uses of the name (in ME. *Damaske*), in some uses absol. as sb., e.g. *damask (cloth)* XIV; *damask plum*, *damask rose* XVI;

†*damask water*; *damask* (*steel*) XVII; the colour of the damask rose XVI.

dame †female head or superior; as a form of address or title; †mother, dam XIII; (arch.) lady of the house XIV. - (O)F. :- L. *domina* fem. corr. to *dominus* lord.

damn †condemn XIII; doom to eternal perdition XIV; (in imprecations) XVI. - (O)F. *damner* - L. *damnāre* orig. inflict loss upon, f. *damnum* loss, damage. Cf. CONDEMN. Hence **damn** sb. the imprecation 'damn!' XVII. So **damnable** XIV (rare before XVI), **damnation** XIII. **damnatory** XVII. - L.

damp vapour, (noxious) gas XIV; fog, mist; humidity; depression, discouragement, †stupor XVI. - (M)LG. *damp* vapour, steam, smoke = (O)HG. *dampf* steam; rel. to OHG. *dempfen* (G. *dämpfen*) = OS. *bithempian*; f. Gmc. **þamp-* (rel. to **þump-*, (O)HG. *duft*). Hence **damp** adj. †dazed XVI; †noxious; slightly wet XVIII. **damp** vb. XIV. **dampen** XVII; see -EN[5].

damsel young unmarried lady XIII; young unmarried woman (without implication of rank or respect) XIV; female attendant. ME. *dameisele*, *damisel* - OF. *dam(e)isele* (mod. *demoiselle*), alt. (after *dame*) of *danzele*, *donsele* :- Gallo-Rom. **dominicella*, dim. of *domina* lady, DAME.

damson XIV. ME. *dama(s)cene*, *damesene* - L. *damascēnum* (sc. *prunum*) plum of Damascus (see DAMASCENE).

dance vb. XIII. - OF. *dancer*, (also mod.) *danser* :- Rom. **dansāre*, of unkn. orig. So **dance** sb. XIII.

dandelion XV (*dent de lyon*). - F. *dent-de-lion*, rendering medL. *dēns leōnis* 'lion's tooth'; so called from the toothed leaves.

dander temper. XIX. of uncert. orig.

Dandie Dinmont terrier from the Scottish border. XIX. Name of a character in Walter Scott's 'Guy Mannering' (ch. xxii 'Dandy Dinmont's Pepper and Mustard Terriers').

dandle XVI. of unkn. orig.; presumably f. a symbolic base **dand-* **dond-* denoting from-side-to-side motion (cf. F. *se dandiner* waddle, It. *dondolare* waggle).

dandruff XVI. The first el. is obscure; the second el., *-ruff*, may be identical with late ME. *rove*, later *ro(u)fe* scurviness, scab - ON. *hrufa* or MLG., MDu. *rōve* (Du. *roof*) rel. to OE. *hrēof*, OHG. *riob*, ON. *hrjúfr* scabby, leprous.

dandy beau, fop; *the dandy* the correct thing XVIII; applied to various trim or handy objects XIX. First recorded from the Scottish Border; perh. a shortening of *jack-a-dandy* pert fellow (XVII); the source of *dandy* remains unkn., but it may be ult. identical with *Dandy*, pet-form of *Andrew*.

Dane native of Denmark XIII; breed of dog XVIII. - ON. *Danir* pl. (late L. *Danī*); superseding OE. *Dene*, which is repr. in *Denmark* (OE. *Denemearc*). So **danegeld** tax imposed *c.*1000. XI. - ON. **Danagjald* (ODa. *Danegjeld*), f. g. pl. of *Danir* Danes + *gjald* payment, tribute (cf. YIELD). **Danelaw** the Danish laws anciently in force over the part of England occupied by the Danes, (hence) the region itself. Late OE. *Dena lagu* 'Danes' law', ME. *Denelawe*, was modernized by Lambarde (1576) as *Dane lawe*, and taken up by historians of XIX in the forms *Danelage*, *-lagh*, *-law*.

dang XVIII. euphem. alt. of DAMN suggested by *hang!*

danger †power of a master, dominion XIII; †liability to punishment, etc.; †hesitation, reluctance XIII; liability to injury XIV. - AN. *da(u)nger*, OF. *dangier* :- Rom. **domniāri-um*, f. *dom(i)nus* lord, master. So **dangerous** †difficult to deal with or please XIII; †reluctant to comply XIV; fraught with danger XV.

dangle XVI. of symbolic formation; cf. NFris. *dangeln*, Sw. *dangla*, Da. *dangle*, parallel to Icel., Sw. *dingla*, Da. *dingle*, of similar meaning; see -LE[3].

dank †wet, watery XIV; (injuriously) damp XVI. Implied earlier in the deriv. *dank* vb. (XIII); prob. of Scand. orig. (cf. Sw. *dank* marshy spot, Icel. *dökk* pit, pool).

dapper XV. - MLG., MDu. *dapper* heavy, powerful, strong, stout (Du. *dapper* bold, valiant) = OHG. *tapfar* heavy, weighty, firm (G. *tapfer* brave), ON. *dapr* sad, dreary.

dappled XIV. contemp. with *dapple-grey*, whence **dapple** sb., adj., and vb. (all XVI). of unkn. orig.; *dappled* varies XIV with *pomelee* (- OF. *pommelé* 'appled'), and the notion 'apple-grey' is expressed in ON. *apalgrár*, OHG. *aphulgrā* (G. *apfelgrau*).

dare pt. *durst*, pt. and pp. *dared* have boldness or courage (*to dare*) OE; trans. senses with a plain object appear XVI. A preterite-present verb (cf. CAN[2]), OE. *durran*, corr. to OS. *gidurran*, OHG. *giturran*, Goth. *gadaursan*; f. the Gmc. series **ders-* **dars-* **durs-* :- IE. **dhers-* **dhors-* **dhṛs-*, whence Skr. *dhṛṣ*, perf. *dadhárṣa* be bold, Gr. *tharseîn* be bold, *thrasús* bold, OSl. *drŭzati* be bold.

dark OE. *deorc*, prob. f. Gmc. base **derk-* **dark-*, whence also OHG. *tarkenen* conceal, hide (:- **darknjan*). Hence **darken** XIII (rare in ME.); see -EN[5]. **darkling** in the dark XV; being, lying, etc., in darkness XVIII; see -LING[2]. Whence as a back-formation **darkle** XV.

darling OE. *dēorling*; see DEAR and -LING[1].

darn[1] mend (clothes) with yarn or thread. XVI. poss. a use of *darn*, later form of †*dern* conceal, hide (OE. *diernan*); cf. MDu. *dernen* stop holes in (a dike).

darn[2], **darned, darnation.** Earliest in *darn* adv. (late XVIII), used as an intensive, which Noah Webster identified with †*dern* (OE. *d(i)erne*) 'concealed', later 'dark, drear, dim', as in the phr. *dern and dismal*, which presumably became *darn(ed) dismal*; cf. var. *durn*. When *darn(ed)* had become a mild substitute for *damn*, *darnation* would readily follow. Cf. U.S. *tarnation* sb., adj., adv. (XVIII), which is prob. to be assoc. with the similarly used and somewhat earlier *tarnal*, aphetic form of *etarnal*, *eternal*.

darnel the grass *Lolium temulentum*. XIV. prob. of NEF. orig., e.g. Walloon *darnelle* (var. *-ette*), which has been connected with words denoting giddiness and the like, the plant being so named from its stupefying properties.

dart pointed missile to be hurled through the

air. XIV. - OF. *dart* (mod. *dard*) :- Gmc. **daroðaz* spear, lance, repr. by OE. *daroð*, OHG. *tart*, ON. *darraðr*. Hence **dart** vb. cast as a dart XIV; move swiftly XVII.

dartre herpes, etc.; tetter, scab. XIX. - (O)F. :- medL. *derbita*, of Gaulish orig.

dash strike with violence (with many transf. and fig. uses) XIII; move violently XIV; euph. for 'damn' (partly from the use of a dash — in place of this word) XIX. ME. *dasche*, *dasse*, prob. of imit. orig.; an appropriate base **dask*- is repr. by Sw. *daska*, Da. *daske* beat, but no older Scand. forms are recorded. Hence **dash** sb. act of dashing XIV; stroke made with a pen, etc. XVI.

dastard †dullard, sot; despicable coward. XV. of obscure orig.; prob. to be referred ult. to ME. *dase*, DAZE, but perh. immed. based on ME. †*dasart* (XIV) dullard and †*dasiberd* (XIV), f. †*dasi* inert, dull + *berd* BEARD, with infl. from DOTARD.

data pl. of DATUM.

date[1] fruit of the palm *Phoenix dactylifera*. XIII. - OF. *date* (mod. *datte*) :- L. *dactylus* (see DACTYL). The application to the date-palm has reference to the finger-like shape of its leaves.

date[2] time or period of an event. XIV. - (O)F. - medL. *data*, sb. use of fem. of *datus*, pp. of *dare* give. Derived from the L. formula used in dating letters, e.g. *Data* (sc. *epistola* letter) *Romæ*, given or delivered at Rome, i.e. by the writer to the bearer. So **date** vb. XV.

dative (Sc.) appointed by the king or the commissary; (gram.) case denoting 'to' or 'for'. XV. - L. *datīvus* pert. to giving, f. *dat*-, pp. stem of *dare* give; see -IVE.

datum thing given or granted; chiefly pl. *data*. XVII. - L., n. pp. of *dare* give.

daub coat with a layer of mortar, etc. XIV; lay on colours crudely XVII. - OF. *dauber* :- L. *dēalbāre* whiten, whitewash, plaster, f. DE- 3 + *albus* white. Hence **daub** sb. mortar, plaster XV; coarsely executed painting XVIII.

daughter OE. *dohtor* = OS. *dohtar* (Du. *dochter*), OHG. *tohter* (G. *tochter*), ON. *dóttir*, Goth. *dauhtar* :- Gmc. **doχtēr*, earlier **dhuktēr* :- IE. **dhughətēr*, whence also Skr. *duhitár*-, Av. *duγðar*, Gr. *thugátēr*, Arm. *duštr*, OSl. *dŭšti*; of unkn. orig.

daunt †overcome, tame XIII; dispirit, abash XV. - AN. *daunter*, OF. *danter*, var. of *donter* (mod. *dompter*) :- L. *domitāre*, frequent. of *domāre* TAME.

dauphin title of the King of France's eldest son. XV (*daulphyn*, *dolphyn*). - F. *dauphin*, earlier †*daulphyn* - Pr. *dalfin* - medL. *dalphīnus* (VIII), for L. *delphīnus* DOLPHIN; orig. a title attached to certain seigneuries. Hence **dauphiness** XVI; see -ESS[1].

davenport writing-table with drawers. XIX. Supposed to be f. the maker's name.

davit crane for hoisting an anchor, ship's boat, etc. XVII. Formerly also *David*, and an application of that Christian name. Cf. F. *davier*, the name of several tools, etc., alt. f. *daviet*.

davy in full *Davy lamp*, *Davy's lamp*, miner's safety lamp invented by Sir Humphrey *Davy* (1778-1829), natural philosopher. XIX.

Davy Jones (naut. sl.) spirit of the sea, sailor's devil; *Davy Jones's locker*, grave of those who perish at sea. XVIII. The allusion is unkn.

daw jackdaw; †simpleton; (Sc.) sluggard. slut. XV. prob. to be referred to an OE. **dāwe*, rel. to OHG. *tāha* (G. dial. *tach*), beside MHG. *dāhele* (G. *dahle*, *dohle*).

dawdle XVII. prob. of dial. orig. (there are vars. *daddle*, *daidle*, *doddle*); see -LE[2].

dawn vb. XV. Back-formation from *dawning*, ME. *dai(ʒ)ening*, *da(i)ning* (XIII), *dawenyng* (XIV), alt. of *daiing*, *dawyng* (OE. *dagung*, f. *dagian* grow light) after Scand. (OSw. *daghning*, Sw., Da. *dagning*); see DAY, -ING[1]. Hence **dawn** sb. XVI.

day OE. *dæġ* = OS. (Du.) *dag*, OHG. *tac* (G. *tag*), ON. *dagr*, Goth. *dags* :- Gmc. **daʒaz*, beside which a gradation-var. **dōʒ*- is repr. by OE. *dōgor* (*s*-stem), Nhb. *dœg* day, ON. *dœgr* 12 hours, Goth. *fldurdōgs* of four days. Hence **daily** adj. and adv. XV; see -LY[1,2].

daze benumb the senses of. XIV. First in pp. *dased* - ON. pp. *dasaðr* weary or exhausted from cold or exertion (cf. Icel. *dasask* refl. become exhausted, *dasi* lazy fellow, Sw. *dasa* lie idle).

dazzle †lose distinctness of vision XV; confuse the vision of XVI. Late ME. *dasele*, f. *dase* DAZE + -LE[3].

de- repr. (often through F. *dé*-) L. *dē*-, which is the prep. *dē* down from, away from, off, aside, used in vbl. comps., as *dēcrēscere* DECREASE, *dēfendere* DEFEND. The earliest adoptions of such vbs. in Eng. were through F., as OF. *decreistre*, *defendre*; later adoptions were direct from L. infins. or pps. The meanings denoted are (1) down (from or to a place or state), as in DEPEND, DEPRESS; (2) off, away, aside, as in DECLINE, DETER; (3) down to the bottom or dregs, (hence) completely, thoroughly, as in L. *dēcoquere* (see DECOCTION); sometimes merely strengthening vbs., as in DECLARE, DENUDE; (4) with pejorative sense, as in DECEIVE, DERIDE; (5) by late L. grammarians used uniquely in *dēcompositus* derived from a compound word, further compounded, whence *decomposite*, *decompound* in chem., bot., etc.; (6) with the sense of undoing or reversing what is expressed by a vb., as in L. *dēarmāre* disarm, *dēvelāre* unveil, whence the formation of similar vbs. from sbs. to denote removal, as in DEFLOWER, DESPOIL; a similar notion was expressed by L. *dis*-, as in DISJOIN, and the use of this prefix, repr. in Rom. by *des*-, was widely extended, and through F. *dé*- (OF. *des*-) it became in Eng. adoptions identical with *de*- (cf. DEBATE, DEVELOP). Hence (7) as a living formative *de*- forms vbs., with corr. sbs., (*a*) denoting removal or riddance, as †*debowel* (XIV) disembowel, *defrost* (XX), DEHYDRATE; (*b*) with privative or reversive force mainly from late XVIII, as *decentralize*, *decontrol*, *demagnetize*.

deacon OE. *diacon* - ecclL. *diāconus* - Gr. *diā́konos* servant, messenger, (eccl.) Christian minister (cf. *diākonein* serve). Hence **deaconess** XVI.

dead OE. *dēad* = OS. *dōd* (Du. *dood*), (O)HG. *tōt*, ON. *dauðr*, Goth. *dauþs* :- Gmc. **dauðaz* :- **dhautós*, pp. of base **dhau*-, repr. also in OS. *dōian*, OHG. *touwen*, ON. *deyja* DIE[1]. Hence

deaden XVII; see -EN[5]. **deadly** adj. and adv. OE. *dēadlić*, *-līće*; see -LY[1,2].

deaf OE. *dēaf* = OS. *dōf* (Du. *doof*), OHG. *toup* (G. *taub*), ON. *daufr*, Goth. *daufs* :- Gmc. **daubaz*. The IE. base **dhoubh- *dheubh- *dhubh-* is repr. also by Gr. *tuphlós* blind. The pronunc. with a long vowel was still gen. current in XVIII, and remains widely diffused dial. and in U.S. Hence **deafen** XVI; see -EN[5].

deal[1] †part, portion; quantity, amount. OE. *dǣl* = OS. *dēl* (Du. *deel*), (O)HG. *teil*, Goth. *dails* :- Gmc. **dailiz*, f. **dail-*; see DOLE[1]. So **deal** vb. A. †divide; distribute, bestow among a number OE.; deliver (blows) XIII; B. †take part in XII; have to do *with* XIII. OE. *dǣlan* = OS. *dēlian*, (O)HG. *teilen*, ON. *deila*, Goth. *dailjan*. Hence **deal** sb. distribution of cards XVII; transaction (orig. U.S.) XIX.

deal[2] plank, board of fir or pine XIV; wood of these XVII. Introduced through the Baltic trade in timber. - MLG., MDu. *dele* plank, floor, corr. to OHG. *dil*, *dil(l)o*, *dilla* (G. *diele*), ON. *þilja*, OE. *þille* :- Gmc. **þelaz*, **þeliz*, **þeljōn*.

dean[1], **dene** valley. OE. *denu*, rel. to DEN.

dean[2] head of cathedral or collegiate chapter XIV; supervisor of conduct and studies in a college; president of a university faculty XVI. ME. *deen*, *den(e)* - AN. *de(e)n*, OF. *d(e)ien* (mod. *doyen*) :- late L. *decānus* - Gr. *dekānós* one set over ten, f. *déka* TEN. Hence **deanery** XV.

dear †glorious, noble; regarded with esteem and affection; †precious OE.; high-priced, costly XI. OE. *dēore*, WS. *dīere* = OS. *diuri* (Du. *dier* beloved, *duur* high-priced), OHG. *tiuri* (G. *teuer*), ON. *dýrr* :- Gmc. **deurjaz*, of unkn. orig.

dearth XIII. ME. *derþ*, f. *dēr* DEAR + -TH[1]; cf. OS. *diuriða* (Du. *duurte*), MHG. *tiurde* honour, value, ON. *dýrð* glory.

death OE. *dēað* = OS. *dōð*, OHG. *tōd* (G. *tod*), ON. *dauðr*, Goth. *dauþus* :- Gmc. **dauþuz*, f. **dau-* (cf. ON. *deyja* DIE[1]) + -TH[1].

débâcle breaking up of ice, sudden deluge; sudden downfall or rout. XIX. - F., f. *débâcler* unbar, remove a bar, f. *dé-* DE- 6 + *bâcler* bar.

debar bar out, exclude XV; prohibit, prevent XVI. - F. *débarrer*, OF. *desbarer*, f. *des-* DE- 6 + *barrer* BAR.

debark disembark. XVII. - F. *débarquer*, f. *dé-*, *des-* DE- 6 + *barque* BARQUE.

debase †abase; †decry, vilify; lower in quality or character. XVI. f. DE- 1, 3 + BASE[2].

debate contention XIII; dispute, discussion XIV. - (O)F. *débat*. repr. a Rom. deriv. of the vb. So **debate** vb. XIV. - (O)F. *débattre* :- Rom. **desbattere* (see DE- 6, BATTERY).

debauch †seduce from allegiance XVI; seduce from virtue or chastity XVII. - F. *débaucher*, OF. *des-*, f. *des-* DE- 6 + an el. of unkn. orig. So **debauch** sb., **debauchee, debauchery** XVII.

debenture voucher for a sum due XV; †certificate of a loan made to a government XVIII; bond issued by a corporation acknowledging indebtedness for interest XIX. mod. use of L. *dēbentur* are owing or due, 3rd pl. pres. ind. pass. of *dēbēre* owe (see DEBT), occurring as the first word of a certificate of indebtedness (XIV); there has been assim. of the final syll. to -URE.

debility XV. - (O)F. *débilité* - L. *dēbilitās*, *-tāt-*, f. *dēbilis* weak. See -ITY. So **debilitate** XVI. f. pp. stem of L. *dēbilitāre*, f. *dēbilitās*; see -ATE[3]. **debilitation** XV. - (O)F. - L.

debit †debt XV; entry of a sum owing XVIII. - L. *dēbitum* DEBT; in the later sense - F. *débit*.

debonair †gracious, courteous; genial. XIII. - OF. *debonaire* (mod. *débonnaire*), prop. phr. *de bon aire* of good disposition.

debouch emerge from a narrow into a wider space. XVIII. - F. *déboucher*, f. DE- 6 + *bouche* mouth (:- L. *bucca*).

debris XVIII. - F. *débris*, f. *débriser* break down or up, f. DE- 1 + *briser* break.

debt XIII. ME. *det(te)* - (O)F. *dette* :- Rom. **dēbita*, feminized pl. of L. *dēbitum*, pp. n. of *dēbēre*, f. DE- 6 + *habēre* have. From XIII to XVI spelt *debte* in F., whence *debt* in Eng. from XVI onwards. So **debtor** XIII. - OF. *det(t)or*, *-our* :- L. *dēbitor*, *-ōr-*; see -OR[1].

debunk (orig. U.S. sl.) remove the humbug and pretence from. XX. f. DE- 7 + BUNK[3].

début entry into society. XVIII. - F., f. *débuter* make the first stroke in a game, f. DE- + *but* goal.

deca- repr. Gr. *déka* TEN, as in **decagon** ten-sided figure (XVII) - modL. *decagōnum* - Gr. *dekágōnon* (*gōniā* angle); **decasyllable** XIX.

decade group of ten, esp. of ten years. XV. - (O)F. *décade* - late L. *decas*, *decad-* - Gr. *dekás*, f. *déka* TEN. See -AD.

decadence XVI. - F. *décadence* - medL. *dēcadentia*, f. *dēcadēre* DECAY. So **decadent** XIX.

decalogue the Ten Commandments. XIV. - F. *décalogue* or ecclL. *decalogus* - Gr. *dekálogos*, orig. fem. adj. (sc. *bíblos* book), f. DECA- + *lógos* saying.

decamp break up a camp XVII; make off XVIII. - F. *décamper*, earlier †*descamper*, f. DE- 6 + *camp* CAMP.

decanal pert. to a dean; of the decani side. XVIII. f. late L. *dēcanus* DEAN[2] + -AL[1]. So **decani** dean's side of the choir (opp. *cantoris*). XVIII. g. sg. of. L. *decānus*.

decant pour off (liquid) so as not to disturb the sediment. XVII. - medL. *dēcanthāre*, f. L. *dē-* DE- 1 + *canthus* angular lip of a jug - Gr. *kánthos* corner of the eye. Hence *decanter* XVIII; see -ER[1].

decapitate XVII. f. pp. stem of late L. *dēcapitāre*, f. DE- 6 + *caput*, *capit-*; see -ATE[3].

decay XV. - OF. *decair*, by-form of *decaoir*, var. of *dechaoir*, *decheoir* (mod. *déchoir*) :- Rom. **dēcadere*, **dēcadēre*, for L. *dēcidere*, f. DE- 1 + *cadere* fall. Hence **decay** sb. XV.

decease death. XIV. - (O)F. *décès* - L. *dēcessus* departure, death, f. pp. stem of *dēcēdere* go away, depart, f. DE- 2 + *cēdere* go. Hence vb. XV.

deceit XIII. - OF. *deceite*, f. pp. *deceit* of *decevoir* DECEIVE. So **deceive** †ensnare, betray XIII; lead into error XIV. - OF. *deceivre*, *deçoivre* :- L. *dēcipere*, f. DE- 4 + *capere* take, seize; or - *deceiv-*, tonic stem of OF. *deceveir* (mod. *décevoir*) :- Rom. **dēcipēre*. So **deception** XIV. - (O)F. or late L.

decelerate XIX. f. DE- 7, after ACCELERATE.

December XIII. - (O)F. *décembre* - L. *December*, f. *decem* TEN, this being the tenth month of the ancient Roman year.

decennial pert. to a period of 10 years. XVII. f. L. *decennium* decade, f. *decennis*, f. *decem* TEN + *annus* year; see -IAL.

decent †becoming, fitting; modest, in good taste XVI; respectable; fair, tolerable XVIII. - F. *décent* or L. *decēns*, *decent-*, pp. of *decēre* be fitting, rel. to DECOROUS, DIGNITY. So **decency** XVI. - L. *decentia*; see -Y[3].

deci- in the metric system, short for L. *decimus* tenth, f. *decem* TEN, designating weights and measures that are one tenth of the standard unit.

decide determine XIV; settle a question XVIII. - F. *décider* or L. *dēcīdere* cut off, cut the knot, determine, f. DE- 2 + *cædere* cut. So **decision** XV. - (O)F. *décision* or L. *dēcīsiō*, f. *dēcīs-*, pp. stem of *dēcīdere*. **decisive** XVII. - F. - medL.

deciduous falling off at a particular season. XVII. f. L. *dēciduus*, f. *dēcidere* fall down or off, f. DE- 2 + *cadere* fall.

decimal proceeding by powers of 10; also sb. XVII. - modL. *decimālis*, f. *decimus* tenth, f. *decem* TEN; see -AL[1].

decimate exact tithe from; put to death one in ten of a number. XVII. f. pp. stem of L. *decimāre*, f. *decimus* tenth; see prec. and -ATE[3]. So **decimation** exaction of tithe XV; destruction of one in ten. XVI. - late L.

decipher reduce to ordinary writing, make out (a writing in cipher, etc.). XVI. f. DE- 7 + CIPHER.

deck[1] †covering; platform extending from side to side of a ship XV; pack of cards XVI. - MDu. *dek* roof, covering, cloak (cf. THATCH); the nautical sense appears to be an Eng. development, since it does not appear for the Du. word till late XVII.

deck[2] †cover; clothe richly, array. XVI. - (M)Du. *dekken* cover = OE. *þeċċan* cover, roof over, THATCH.

deckle in paper-making, contrivance to limit the size of the sheet. XIX. - G. *deckel* cover, lid, dim. of *decke* covering (f. base of *decken* DECK[2]); cf. -LE[2].

declaim XIV. - F. *déclamer* or L. *dēclāmāre*; see DE- 3 and CLAIM. So **declamation** XV. **declamatory** XVI. - L.

declare †manifest; state publicly or explicitly. XIV. - L. *dēclārāre* make clear, f. DE- 3 + *clārāre*, f. *clārus* CLEAR. So **declaration** XIV, **declaratory** XV.

declension XV. repr. (O)F. *déclinaison*, f. *décliner* DECLINE, after L. *dēclīnātiō* DECLINATION.

decline turn aside, deviate (trans. and intr.); bend or go down; (gram.) inflect XIV; turn aside or away from XV. - (O)F. *décliner* - L. *dēclīnāre*, f. DE- 2 + *clīnāre* bend, cogn. with Gr. *klínein* bend; cf. LEAN[2]. Hence **decline** sb. XIV. So **declination** (astron.) XIV; †(gram.) declension XV; turning aside or down XVI. -L.

declivity downward slope. XVII. - L. *dēclīvitās*, f. *dēclīvis* sloping downwards, f. DE- 1 + *clīvus* slope; see -ITY.

decoction liquor in which a substance has been boiled. XIV. - (O)F. *décoction* or late L. *dēcoctiō*, *-ōn-*, f. pp. stem of *dēcoquere* boil down, f. DE- 3 + *coquere* COOK; see -TION. Hence **decoct** †pp. adj. and vb. XV.

decode XIX. f. DE- 7 + CODE.

décolleté cut low at the neck. XIX. - F., pp. of *décolleter*, f. DE- 6 + *collet*, dim. of *col* collar :- L. *collum* neck.

decompose separate into its parts; decay. XVIII. - F. *décomposer*, f. DE- 6 + *composer* COMPOSE. So **decomposition** XVII.

décor theatre scenery. XIX. - F., f. *décorer* DECORATE.

decorate †adorn XVI; deck with ornamental accessories XVIII; invest with an honour XIX. f. *decorate* pp. (XV) or its source L. *decorātus*, *-āre* beautify, f. *decus*, *decor-*; see DECOROUS and -ATE[3]. So **decoration** XV. - (O)F. or late L. **decorative** XV. - F. **decorous** f. L. *decōrus*, rel. to *decēns* DECENT. **decorum** XVI. - L.

decorticate strip the bark from. XVII. f. pp. stem of L. *dēcorticāre*, f. DE- 6 + *cortic-*, CORTEX; see -ATE[3].

decoy pool with netted approaches for the capture of wildfowl. XVII. Evidence for the corr. vb. is earlier in Sc. (XVI) and in the gen. sense 'entice, allure'; but the sb. was no doubt prior, and perh. - Du. *de kooi* 'the decoy', with assim. to †*decoy* gambling card-game (XVI), of unkn. orig. Du. *kooi*, †*koye* is a parallel development to MDu. *kouwe*, MLG. *kaue* - L. *cavea* CAGE.

decrease grow less. XIV. - OF. *de(s)creiss-*, pres. stem of *de(s)creistre* (mod. *décroître*) :- Rom. **discrēscere*, for L. *dēcrēscere*, f. DE- 6 + *crēscere* grow. So **decrease** sb. XIV.

decree ordinance, edict. XIV. OF. *decré*, var. of *decret* - L. *dēcrētum*, sb. use of n. of *dēcrētus*, pp. of *dēcernere*, f. DE- 2 + *cernere* separate, distinguish, decide. So **decree** vb. XIV.

decrement decrease, lessening. XVII. - L. *dēcrēmentum*, f. *dēcrē-*, stem of *dēcrēscere* DECREASE; see -MENT.

decrepit XV. - (partly through F. *décrépit* XVI) L. *dēcrepitus*, f. DE- 3 + *crepitus*, pp. of *crepāre* rattle, creak, of imit. orig. Hence **decrepitude** XVII.

decretal adj. of a decree or decretal XV; sb. papal decree XIV. - (O)F. *décrétal* - late L. *dēcrētālis* (medL. *dēcrētālēs*, sc. *epistolæ*, papal letters containing decrees, *dēcrētāle* decree), f. *dēcrēt-*, pp. stem of *dēcernere* DECREE.

decry denounce by proclamation; disparage openly. XVII. f. DE- 4 + CRY vb.

decuman (of a wave) very large. XVII. - L. *decumānus*, var. of *decimānus* of the tenth part, f. *decimus* tenth (cf. DECIMAL); see -AN. The application to waves rests on the belief that every tenth wave is greater than the others.

dedicate devote to the service of a deity XV; assign to an end or purpose XVI. f. pp. stem of L. *dēdicāre* proclaim, devote, consecrate, f. DE- 2 + *dic-*, weak var. of *dīc-* say (cf. DICTION); see -ATE[3]. So **dedication** XIV. - (O)F. or L.

deduce †bring, convey; †derive; trace the course of; draw as a conclusion XV; †deduct XVI. - L. *dēdūcere*, f. DE- 2 + *dūcere* lead. So **deduct** take away, subtract XV; †derive; †trace out; deduce by reasoning XVI. f. *dēduct-*, pp. stem of L. *dēdūcere*. **deduction** subtraction, abatement XV; †detailed account; deducing a conclusion, inference by reasoning XVI. - (O)F. - L.

deed that which is done OE.; legal instrument in writing XIV. OE. (Angl.) *dēd*, (WS.) *dǣd* = OS. *dād*, OHG. *tāt* (G. *tat*), ON. *dáð*, Goth. *-dēþs* :- Gmc. **dǣdiz* :- IE. **dhētis*, f. **dhē-* **dhō-* (see DO[1]). **deed poll** deed made by one party only, so called because it is 'polled' or cut even, not indented. XVI.

deem †give judgement, judge; think, consider. OE. *dēman* = OS. *dōmian* (Du. *doemen*), OHG. *tuomen*, ON. *dœma*, Goth. (= Gmc.) *dōmjan*, f. **dōmaz* DOOM. Hence **deemster** either of the two judges of the Isle of Man. XVII; see -STER.

deep having great extension downwards; fig. profound OE.; penetrating XIII; (of colour) intense; subtle, crafty XVI. OE. *dēop* = OS. *diop*, *diap* (Du. *diep*), OHG. *tiuf* (G. *tief*), ON. *djúpr*, Goth. *diups* :- Gmc. **deupaz*, f. **deup-* **dup-* (see DIP). As sb. deep water OE.; *the deep* the ocean (XIV). Hence **deepen** XVI, **deeply** XV; see -EN[5], -LY[2].

deer †animal OE.; antlered ruminant XII. OE. *dēor* = OS. *dior* (Du. *dier*), OHG. *tior* (G. *tier*), ON. *dýr*, Goth. **dius* (in d. pl. *diuzam*) :- Gmc. **deuzam* :- IE. **dheusóm* orig. 'breathing creature' (cf. the sense-development in ANIMAL), if rel. to OSl. *duchŭ*, *duša* breath, Lith. *dùsti* sigh.

deface XIV. - F. †*defacer*, earlier *deffacer*, for *desfacer*, f. DE- 6 + *face* FACE.

defalcate †lop off, retrench, deduct XV; commit defalcation XIX. f. pp. stem of medL. *dēfalcāre*, f. DE- 2 + L. *falx*, *falc-* sickle, scythe; see -ATE[3]. So **defalcation** †diminution, reduction XV; fraudulent monetary deficiency XVIII. - medL.

defame †render infamous; attack the good name of. XIV. ME. *diffame*, *defame* - OF. *diffamer* (also *desf-*, *def(f)-*) - L. *diffāmāre* spread about as an evil report, f. *dis-* DIF-, DE- 6 + *fāma* FAME. So **defamation** XIV. **defamatory** XVI. - medL.

default sb. XIII. ME. *defaut(e)* - (1) OF. *defaute*, f. *defaillir*, on the model of *faute* FAULT, *faillir* FAIL; (2) (O)F. *défaut*, back-formation on *defaute*. Hence **default** vb. XIV.

defeasance (Sc.) discharge (of debt, etc.) XIV; (leg.) condition upon the performance of which an instrument is made void XV; annulment XVI. - OF. *defesance*, f. *defesant*, prp. of *de(s)faire* (mod. *défaire*) undo, f. DE- 6 + *faire* make; see -ANCE.

defeat †undo, ruin, destroy XIV; frustrate, nullify XV; †disappoint, defraud; discomfit, vanquish XVI. ME. *def(f)ete* - AN. *defeter*, f. *defet*, OF. *deffait*, *desfait*, pp. of *desfaire* (mod. *défaire*) :- medL. *disfacere* undo, mar, f. L. *dis-* DE- 6 + *facere* make, DO[1]. Hence **defeat** sb. XVI. So **defeatism, defeatist** sb. and adj. XX. - F.

defecate clear from impurities XVI; void the faeces XIX. f. †*defecate* pp. (XV) - L. *dēfæcātus*, *-āre*, f. DE- 6 + *fæx*, *fæces* dregs; see -ATE[3]. So **defecation** XVII. - late L.

defect shortcoming, deficiency. XV. - L. *dēfectus*, f. *dēfect-*, pp. stem of *dēficere* leave, desert, fail, f. DE- 2 + *facere* make, DO[1]. So **defection** failing, falling away. XVI. **defective** XV. - (O)F. or late L.

defend guard from attack; †ward off, prevent, prohibit XIII; vindicate (a cause, person) XV. - (O)F. *défendre* :- L. *dēfendere* ward off, protect, f. DE- 2 + *-fendere* (only in comps.). So **defendant** XIV. - (O)F. *défendant*, sb. use of prp. of *défendre*. **defender** XIII. - AN. *defendour*; see -ER[2]. **defence,** U.S. **defense** XIII. ME. *defens* and *defense*, *-ence* - OF. *defens* and (also mod.) *défense* - L. (Rom.) *dēfēnsum*, *dēfēnsa*, sb. uses of n. and fem. pp. of *dēfendere*. **defensible** †defensive; defendable, justifiable. XV. late L. *dēfēnsibilis*, f. *dēfēns-*, pp. stem of *dēfendere*.

defenestration action of throwing out of a window. XVII. - modL. *dēfenestrātiō*, *-ōn-*, f. DE- 1 + *fenestra* window; see -ATION.

defer[1] put off, postpone. XIV. ME. *differre*, *deferre* - (O)F. *différer* defer, differ - L. *differre* carry apart, delay, bear in different directions, differ. Often spelt with *diff-* until XVII, but finally differentiated from the ult. identical DIFFER, perh. partly by assoc. with *delay*.

defer[2] †submit oneself, submit or refer (a matter) XV; †offer, proffer XVI; submit in opinion *to* XVII. - (O)F. *déférer* - L. *dēferre* carry away, grant, report, refer (a matter), f. DE- 2 + *ferre* BEAR[2]. So **deference** XVII. Hence **deferential** XIX.

defiance declaration of hostilities XIV; challenge to combat XV; setting at nought XVIII. - (O)F. *défiance* (now only 'distrust'), f. *défier* DEFY; see -ANCE. Hence **defiant** XIX.

deficient wanting in something. XVI. - L. *dēficiēns*, *-ent-*, prp. of *dēficere* undo, take oneself away, fail, f. DE- 2, 6 + *facere* make, DO[1]. Hence **deficiency** XVII.

deficit XVIII. - F. *déficit* - L. *dēficit* there is wanting, 3rd pers. sing. pres. ind. of *dēficere* (see DEFECT); formerly placed against an item in an account.

defile[1] make foul or unclean. XIV. alt. of †*defoul*, †*defoil*, by assoc. with synon. †*befile*, OE. *befȳlan* (f. BE- + *fȳlan*, f. *fūl* FOUL). The earlier *defoul* (XIII), of which there is an unexpl. var. *defoil* (XIV), was - OF. *def(o)uler* trample down, outrage, violate, f. DE- 1 + *fouler* tread, trample :- Rom. **fullāre* stamp, f. L. *fullō* FULLER. Hence **defilement** XVII.

defile[2] narrow pass between mountains. XVII. orig. *defilé*, *defilee* - F. *défilé*, sb. use of pp. of *défiler* march by files, f. DE- 2 + *file* FILE[2]. For the loss of the final syll. cf. ASSIGN[2].

define determine the limits of; state exactly what (a thing) is. XIV. - OF. *definer* - Rom. **dēfīnāre*, for L. *dēfīnīre*, f. DE- 3 + *fīnīre* FINISH. So **definite** having fixed limits. XV. - L. *dēfīnītus*, pp. of *dēfīnīre*. **definition, definitive** XIV. - (O)F. - L.

deflate XIX. f. DE- 6 + *-flate* of INFLATE.

deflect XVII. - L. *dēflectere*, f. DE- 3 + *flectere* bend. So **deflexion, deflection** XVII.

deform XV. - OF. *difformer*, *de(s)former* (mod. *difformer*, *déformer*) - medL. *difformāre*, Rom. **disformāre*, L. *dēformāre*, f. DIS-, DE- 6 + *forma* FORM. So **deformation, deformity** XV.

defraud XIV. - OF. *defrauder* or L. *dēfraudāre*, f. DE- 3 + *fraudāre* cheat, f. *fraus*, *fraud-* FRAUD.

defray †disburse; discharge (expense). XVI. - (O)F. *défrayer* (†*deff-*, †*desf-*), f. DE- 6 + †*frai(t)* (usu. pl. *frais*, †*fres*) expenses, cost :- medL.

fredus, fine for breach of the peace - Frank. **friðu* peace.

deft †gentle, meek XIII; skilful XV; neat, pretty (now dial.) XVI. ME. *defte*, var. of DAFT.

defunct XVI. - L. *dēfunctus* discharged (from an office or obligation), deceased, pp. of *dēfungī* discharge, perform, finish, f. DE- 3 + *fungī* perform (see FUNCTION).

defy †renounce allegiance to; (arch.) challenge to a contest; challenge the power of, set at nought. XIV. - (O)F. *défier* :- Rom. **disfīdāre*, f. L. *dis*-, DE- 6 + *fīdus* trustful, rel. to *fidēs* FAITH. Cf. DEFIANCE.

degenerate that has declined in character or qualities. XV. - L. *dēgenerātus*, pp. of *dēgenerāre* depart from its race or kind, f. *dēgener* debased, ignoble, f. DE- 2 + *genus*, *gener*- KIND[1]. So **degenerate** vb. become degenerate. XVI. f. pp. stem of the L. vb.; see -ATE[2,3]. **degeneration** XVII. - F.

degrade reduce to a lower rank. XIV. - (O)F. *dégrader* :- ecclL. *dēgradāre*, f. DE- 1 + *gradus* rank, DEGREE. So **degradation** XVI. - (O)F. *dégradation* or ecclL. *dēgradātiō*.

degree step (now only her. in lit. sense); relative rank XIII; unit of geometrical measurement XIV; musical interval XVII; unit of temperature XVIII. - (O)F. *degré* :- Rom. **dēgradus*, f. L. DE- 1 + *gradus* step, GRADE.

dehydrate f. DE- 7 + Gr. *húdōr*, *hudr*- WATER + -ATE[3].

deictic pointing, demonstrative. XVII. - Gr. *deiktikós* showing directly, f. *deiktós*, vbl. adj. of *deiknúnai* show, rel. to L. *dīcere* say.

deify XIV. - (O)F. *déifier* - ChrL. *deificāre*, f. *deus* god; see DIVINE, -FY. So **deification** XIV.

deign think fit, vouchsafe XIII; condescend to give XVI. - OF. *degnier*, later *degner*, (also mod.) *daigner* :- L. *dignāre*, *-ārī* deem worthy, f. *dignus* worthy.

deist one who acknowledges the existence of God but rejects revealed religion. XVII. - F. *déiste*, f. L. *deus* god (see DIVINE) + *-iste* -IST. So **deism** XVII.

deity XIV. - (O)F. *déité* - ChrL. *deitās*; see DIVINE, -ITY.

deject †cast down XV; depress in spirits XVI. f. *dēject*-, pp. stem of L. *deicere*, f. DE- 1 + *jacere* throw.

delaine light textile fabric. XIX. Short for *muslin delaine* = F. *mousseline de laine* 'MUSLIN of wool'.

delay put off till later XIII; impede the progress of XIV. - OF. *delayer*, var. of *deslaier*, presumably f. *des*- DIS- + *laier* leave (of unkn. orig.). So **delay** sb. XIII. - (O)F. *délai*, f. the vb.

delectable delightful. XIV. - (O)F. *délectable* - L. *dēlectābilis*, f. *dēlectāre* DELIGHT; see -ABLE. So **delectation** XIV.

delegate person chosen to act for another. XIV. - L. *dēlēgātus*, pp. of *dēlēgāre*, f. DE- 2 + *lēgāre* send on a commission (cf. LEGATE). Hence **delegacy** delegation XV; body of delegates XVII. So **delegate** entrust to another XVI; commission XVII. f. pp. stem of the above vb.; see -ATE[3]. **delegation** XVII. - L.

delete †destroy, abolish; obliterate. XVII. f. *dēlēt*-, pp. stem of L. *dēlēre*. So **deletion** XVI. - L.

deleterious XVII. f. medL. *dēlētērius* - Gr. *dēlētérios*, f. *dēlētēr* destroyer, f. *dēleisthai* injure, destroy; see -IOUS.

delf(t) orig. *Delf(t) ware*, kind of glazed earthenware made at *Delf*, now *Delft*, in Holland. XVIII.

deliberate adj. XV. - L. *dēlīberātus*, pp. of *dēlīberāre*, f. DE- 3 + *lībrāre* weigh, f. *lībra* scales. So **deliberate** vb. †think over; think carefully XVI. See -ATE[2,3]. **deliberation** XIV. - (O)F. - L. **deliberative** XV. - F. or L.

delicate †delightful, elegant, dainty; †indolent, †fastidious XIV; fine, not coarse or robust XVI; finely sensitive or skilful XVI. - (O)F. *délicat* or L. *dēlicātus*; of unkn. orig., but assoc. in sense-development with L. *dēliciæ* (see next); see -ATE[2]. Hence **delicacy** XIV; concr. XV.

delicious XIII. - OF. *delicious* (mod. *délicieux*) - late L. *dēliciōsus*, f. L. *dēlicia*, pl. *-iæ*, f. *dēlicere* allure aside, f. DE- 2 + *lic*-, as in *ēlicere* ELICIT.

delight sb. XIII. ME. *delit* - OF., f. stem of *delitier*, etc. :- L. *dēlectāre* allure, charm, frequent. of *dēlicere* (see prec.). The sp. with *-gh*- on the anal. of native words such as *light* dates from XVI. So **delight** vb. XIII. - OF. *delitier*.

delineate XVI. f. pp. stem of L. *dēlīneāre*, f. DE- 3 + *līnea* LINE[2]; see -ATE[3].

delinquent XVII. - L. *dēlinquēns*, *-ent*-, pp. of *dēlinquere* be at fault, offend, f. DE- 3 + *linquere* leave; see -ENT.

deliquesce dissolve by absorption of moisture. XVIII. - L. *dēliquēscere*, f. DE- 3 + *liquēscere*, f. *liquēre* be fluid; see LIQUID, -ESCENT.

delirium XVI. - L. *dēlīrium*, f. *dēlīrāre* deviate from a straight line, be deranged, f. DE- 2 + *līra* ridge between furrows. Hence **delirious** XVIII.

deliver A. set free XIII; disburden XIV; B. give up, give over, surrender XIII; C. give or send forth, utter XVI. - (O)F. *délivrer* :- Gallo-Rom. **dēlīberāre*, f. DE- 3 + *līberāre* LIBERATE. So **deliverance** XIII. **delivery** handing over, †deliverance XV; being delivered of a child; utterance of words XVI. - AN. *délivrée*, sb. use of fem. pp. of *délivrer*; see -Y[3].

dell deep hollow or valley. OE. *dell* = MLG., MDu. *delle* (Du. *del*), MHG. *telle* :- Gmc. **daljō* (cf. Goth. *ibdalja* slope of a mountain), f. **dal*- (see DALE).

Delphic pert. to *Delphi* on the slope of Mt. Parnassus in Greece and the oracle of Apollo there; obscure and ambiguous. XVI. See -IC.

delphinium XVII. - modL. *delphinium* - Gr. *delphī́nion* larkspur, f. *delphís*, *delphīn*- DOLPHIN; so called from the dolphin-like form of the nectary.

delta triangular tract of alluvial land at the mouth of a river, orig. of the Nile. XVI. Name of the fourth letter of the Greek alphabet, Δ, derived from Phoenician *daleth* (𐤃).

delude XV. - L. *dēlūdere* play false, mock, f. DE- 4 + *lūdere* play, f. *lūdus* play, game. So **delusion** XV. - late L. **delusive** XVII, **delusory** XV. f. *dēlūs*-, pp. stem of the vb.

deluge sb. XIV. - (O)F. *déluge*, alt. of earlier *diluvie* - L. *dīluvium*, rel. to *lavere*, *lavāre* wash. Hence **deluge** vb. XVII.

delve dig, lit. and fig. (dial. and lit.). OE. *delfan*

str. vb. = OS. *bidelban* (Du. *delven*), OHG. *bitelban* :- WGmc. **delb-* **dalb-* **dulb-*. The weak form of the pt. appeared in XIV and of the pp. in XVI.

demagogue leader of the people or of a popular faction. XVII. - Gr. *dēmagōgós*, f. *dêmos* people + *agōgós* leader, f. *ágein* lead. So **demagogic** XIX. **demagogy** XVII. - Gr. *dēmagōgiā*; see -Y[3].

demand sb. XIII. - (O)F. *demande*, f. *demander* (whence **demand** vb. XV) :- L. *dēmandāre* hand over, entrust, f. DE- 3 + *mandāre* enjoin (see MANDATE).

demarcation marking a boundary, orig. applied in the phr. *line of demarcation* to the division of the New World in XV between the Spaniards and the Portuguese. XVIII. - Sp. *demarcación*, f. *demarcar* mark out the bounds of, f. *de-* DE- 3 + *marcar* MARK; see -ATION. Hence **demarcate** vb. XIX.

démarche proceeding. XVII. - F., f. *démarcher* march, take steps, f. DE- 3 + *marcher* MARCH[2].

demean[1] †carry on, manage XIII; conduct *oneself* XIV. - (O)F. *démener* lead, exercise, practise, (refl.) behave :- Rom. **dēmināre*, f. L. DE 3 + *mināre* drive (animals), orig. urge on with threats (L. *minārī* threaten). Hence **demeanour** conduct, behaviour. XV.

demean[2] lower, humble. XVII. f. DE- 4 + MEAN[2].

demented XVI. f. *dēmentātus*, pp. of late L. *dēmentāre*, f. *dēmēns*, *-ent-*, f. DE- 6 + *mēns*, *ment-* MIND; see -ED[1].

Demerara epithet of a kind of brown cane sugar orig. from *Demerara* in Guyana. XIX.

demerit †desert, merit XIV; †sin, offence XV; ill-desert, want of merit XVI. - OF. *de(s)merite* or L. *dēmeritum*, f. pp. stem of *dēmerērī* merit, deserve, f. DE- 3 + *merērī* MERIT; in Rom. the prefix was taken in a pejorative or negative sense.

demesne possession of real estate as one's own; possession, estate XIV. - AN., OF. *demeine*, later AN. *demesne*, sb. use of adj. belonging to a lord, seigneurial, that is private property :- L. *dominicus* pert. to a lord or master (see DOMINICAL).

demi- - F. *demi* :- medL. *dīmedius*, for L. *dīmidius*, used in comb. to denote things that are half the normal or full size, length, etc.

demijohn large bulging bottle usu. in wicker case. XVIII. prob. f. F. *dame-jeanne*, with early assim. to DEMI- and later to the proper name *John*; prop. 'Lady Jane'.

demi-monde class of women of doubtful reputation. XIX. - F., 'half-world' (Alexandre Dumas fils, 1855, who used the term for the kind of society midway between the conventional respectable life and the life of licence and vice).

demise transfer of an estate XVI; transfer of sovereignty XVII; death (as occasioning this) XVIII. - AN. **demise*, sb. use of fem. pp. of OF. *de(s)mettre* (mod. *démettre*) DISMISS, (refl.) resign, abdicate.

demiurge creator of the world (in Platonism). XIX (earlier in L. form). - ecclL. *dēmiūrgus* - Gr. *dēmiourgós* handicraftsman, artisan, etc., f. *dḗmios* public + **erg-* WORK.

demobilize disband (armed forces); also **demobilization.** XIX. - F. *démobiliser*, *-isation*; see DE- 7, MOBILIZE. abbrev. **demob** vb. XX.

democracy XVI. - (O)F. *démocratie* - late L. *dēmocratia* - Gr. *dēmokratiā*, f. *dêmos* people; see -CRACY. So **democrat** XVIII. - F. *démocrate*, f. *démocratie*, after *aristocrate*. **democratic** XVII.

demolish XVI. - *démoliss-*, lengthened stem of (O)F. *démolir* - L. *dēmōlīrī*, f. DE- 1 + *mōlīrī* construct, f. *mōles* mass; see -ISH[2]. So **demolition** XVII.

demon inferior divinity, genius, attendant spirit; evil spirit, devil. XV. - medL. *dēmōn*, L. *dæmōn* - Gr. *daímōn* divinity, genius. In both senses repr. L. *dæmonium*, Gr. dim. *daimónion*. So **demoniac** (one) possessed by an unclean spirit. XIV. - (O)F. - ChrL. **demoniacal** XVII. **demonic** XVII.

demonetize deprive of standard monetary value. XIX. - F. *démonétiser*, f. DE- 7 + L. *monēta* MONEY; see -IZE.

demonstrate †indicate, exhibit; make evident by proof. XVI. f. pp. stem of L. *dēmonstrāre*, f. DE- 3 + *monstrāre* show; see -ATE[3]. So **demonstration** XIV. - (O)F. or L. **demonstrative** XIV. - (O)F. - L.

demoralize corrupt the morals of XVIII; lower the morale of XIX. - F. *démoraliser*; see DE- 7, MORAL, -IZE.

demote reduce in rank or grade. XIX. f. DE- 7 + *-mote* of PROMOTE.

demotic of the people; spec. of the popular form of ancient Egyptian character. XIX. - Gr. *dēmotikós* popular, f. *dēmótēs* one of the people, f. *dêmos* people; see -IC.

demulcent soothing. XVIII. - L. *dēmulcēns*, *-ent-*, prp. of *dēmulcēre* soothe caressingly, f. DE- 3 + *mulcēre* stroke, appease; see -ENT.

demur †linger XIII; †hesitate; put in a demurrer; make difficulties XVII. - OF. *demourer*, (also mod.) *demeurer* :- Rom. **dēmorāre*, for L. *dēmorārī*, f. DE- 3 + *morārī* delay. The present sp. begins in XVI, superseding *demo(u)re*, and appears to be based on *demurrer*. So **demurrage** †delay; detention of a vessel beyond the agreed time; payment for this XVII. **demurrer** (leg.) pleading which stops an action XVI. - AN., sb. use of inf.; see -ER[5].

demure †(of the sea) calm XIV; sober, serious XV; †affectedly or unnaturally grave XVII. perh. (with muting of *é* as in ASSIGN[2], etc.) - AN. *demuré*, OF. *demoré*, pp. of *demorer* (mod. *demeurer*) remain, stay (see prec.), but infl. by OF. *m(ë)ur* grave (mod. *mûr*) :- L. *mātūrus* ripe, MATURE.

demy †(Sc.) half-mark; foundation scholar at Magdalen College, Oxford (L. *semicommunarius* one whose commons were orig. half that of a Fellow) XV; size of paper XVI. ellipt. uses of DEMI-, the sp. with *-y* being appropriate for the final position.

den lair of a wild beast OE.; cave XIII; (Sc.) dingle XVI. OE. *denn*, corr. to MLG., MDu. *denne* low ground, OHG. *tenni* (G. *tenne*) floor, threshing-floor :- Gmc. **danjam*, **danjō*; rel. to DEAN[1].

denarius ancient Roman coin. XVI. - L. (ellipt. for *dēnārius nummus* coin containing ten asses), f. *dēnī* by tens, distributive of TEN.

denationalize deprive of nationality. XIX. - F. *dénationaliser*; see DE- 7, NATIONAL, -IZE.

dendrite tree-like form in stone or mineral. XVIII. - F. - Gr. *dendrítēs* pert. to a tree, f. *déndron* tree; see -ITE.

dene sandy tract by the sea. XIII. The meaning suggests affinity with LG. *düne* and Du. *duin* sand-hill on the coast (see DUNE).

dene-hole ancient excavation in SE. England and northern France traditionally attributed to the activities of the Danes. XVIII. perh. repr. OE. **Denahol*, f. *Dena*, g. pl. of *Dene* Danes + *hol* HOLE; assoc. by later archaeologists with DENE and DEN.

dengue fever epidemic in E. Africa, etc. XIX. - W. Indian Sp. - Swahili *denga*, *dinga*. Identified with Sp. *dengue* fastidiousness, prudery.

denier twelfth of a sou XV; unit of fineness of silk yarn, etc. XIX. - AN. *dener*, (O)F. *denier* :- L. *dēnārius* DENARIUS.

denigrate blacken, lit. and fig. XVI. - pp. stem of L. *dēnigrāre*, f. DE- 3 + *nigrāre*, f. *niger*, *nigr-* black; see -ATE[3]. So **denigration** XV.

denim (formerly) kind of serge, (now) coloured twill cotton. XVII. orig. *serge de Nim* - F. *serge de Nîmes* 'serge of Nîmes', a manufacturing town in S. France.

denizen inhabitant XV; foreigner admitted to residence XVI. ME. *deynseyn* - AN. *deinzein*, f. OF. *deinz* within (:- late L. *dē intus* from within) + *-ein* (:- L. *-āneus*).

denominate XVI. f. pp. stem of L. *dēnōmināre*; see DE- 3, NOMINATE. So **denomination** naming XIV; appellation, designation; (arith.) class of one kind of unit XV; class, sort, sect (of individuals) XVII. - (O)F. or L. **denominative** XVII. - OF. - late L. **denominator** (spec. in math.) XVI. - F. or medL.

denote mark out, distinguish by a sign; indicate, signify XVII. - (O)F. *dénoter* or L. *dēnotāre*; see DE- 3, NOTE. So **denotation** XVI.

denouement XVIII. - F., f. *dénouer* (earlier *des-*), f. *des-* DIS- + *nouer* :- L. *nodāre* knot, f. *nodus* NODE.

denounce declare to be XIII; give formal information of XIV; declare to be evil XVII; (after modF.) announce formally the termination of XIX. - OF. *denoncier* (mod. *dénoncer*) :- L. *dēnuntiāre* give official intimation, f. DE- 3 + *nuntiāre* make known, report.

dense thick, crowded XV; stupid XIX. - F. *dense* or L. *dēnsus*. So **density** XVII.

dent †stroke, blow XIII; hollow made as if by a blow XVI. In the first sense, var. of DINT, in the second, f. **dent** vb. XIV, which is prob. aphetic of INDENT.

dental XVI. - medL. *dentālis*, f. L. *dēns*, *dent-* TOOTH; see -AL[1]. So **dentifrice** toothpaste or -powder. XVI. - F. *dentifrice* - L. *dentifricium*, f. *dēns*, *dent-* + *fricāre* sub. **dentine** XIX; see -INE[4]. **dentist** XVIII. - F.; whence **dentistry** XIX. **dentition** cutting of the teeth XVII; arrangement of the teeth XIX. - L. *dentītiō*, *-ōn-*, f. *dentīre* teethe. **denture** set of (artificial) teeth. XIX.

denude XV. - L. *dēnūdāre*, f. DE- 3 + *nūdāre* bare, f. *nūdus* NUDE. So **denudation** XV.

denunciate denounce. XVI. f. pp. stem of L. *dēnuntiāre* DENOUNCE; see -ATE[3]. So **denunciation** †proclamation XV; warning announcement; public condemnation XVI. - (O)F. or L.

deny XIII. ME. *denie* - tonic stem-form *deni-* of (O)F. *dénier*, earlier *deneier*, *denoier* :- L. *dēnegāre*, f. DE- 3 + *negāre* (see NEGATION). Hence **denial** XVI; see -AL[2].

deodand chattel which has been the instrument of death forfeited to the crown for pious uses. XVI. - law F. *deodande* - AL. *deōdanda*, *-um*, i.e. *Deō danda*, *-um* that is to be given to God (d. of *deus* god, gerundive of *dare* give).

deontology science of duty. XIX. f. Gr. *déon*, *deont-* that which is binding, duty, n. prp. of *deî* it is binding, it behoves + -LOGY.

depart †divide into parts, distribute; †sunder, separate XIII; go away XIII; leave, quit XIV; die XVI. - (O)F. *départir*, †*des-* :- Rom. **dē-*, **dispartīre*, for L. *dispertīre* divide; see DE- 2, DIS- 1, and PART. So **department** separately allotted province, division, or part. XVIII. **departure** †separation; going away, setting out; deviation. XV.

depend be suspended, be resultant or contingent *upon*. XV. - (O)F. *dépendre* - Rom. **dēpendere*, for L. *dēpendēre*; see DE- 1, PENDENT. So **dependant** †dependency; dependent person. XVI. - F. *dépendant*, sb. use of prp. of *dépendre*. **dependent** pendent XV; contingent XVI; subordinate, subject XVII. orig. *dependant* - (O)F. *dépendant*. So **dependence** †dependency XV; dependent condition XVII. - (O)F. *dépendance*. **dependency** dependence XVI; dependent country or province XVII; see -ENCY.

depict represent in colours XVII; portray XVIII. f. *dēpict-*, pp. stem of L. *dēpingere*; cf. pp. *depictyd* (XV, once), †*depict* (XV-XVI) and see DE- 3, PAINT.

depilate remove hair from. XVI. f. pp. stem of L. *dēpilāre*, f. DE- 3 + *pilāre* deprive of hair. So **depilation** XV, **depilatory** adj. and sb. XVII.

deplete empty (orig. as by blood-letting). XIX. f. *dēplēt-*, pp. stem of L. *dēplēre*, f. DE- 6 + *-plēre* FILL. So **depletion** XVII. - late L. *dēplētiō*, *-ōn-*, repl. late L. *dēplētūra* blood-letting.

deplore XVI. - (O)F. *déplorer* or It. *deplorare* - L. *dēplōrāre*, f. DE- 3 + *plōrāre* wail, bewail. Hence **deplorable** XVII. - F. or late L.

deploy XVIII. - F. *déployer* :- L. *displicāre* unfold, DISPLAY.

deponent gram. XV; one who makes a deposition XVI. - L. *dēpōnēns*, *-ent-*, prp. of *dēpōnere* lay aside, put down, deposit, (medL.) testify, f. DE- 1 + *pōnere* place, lay; see -ENT. Deponent verbs in Latin were regarded as having 'laid aside' a passive meaning.

depopulate †lay waste; deprive of population. XVI. f. pp. stem of L. *dēpopulāre*, *-ārī*, ravage, f. DE- 3 + *populāre*, *-ārī* lay waste (f. *populus* PEOPLE), in medL. deprive of inhabitants, by assoc. with Rom. **dispopulāre* (OF. *despeupler*, mod. *dé-*, whence *dispeople* XV). So **depopulation** XV. - L.

deport A. †bear with, forbear, refrain XV; refl. comport oneself XVI; B. carry away or off XVII. In A - OF. *deporter*, f. DE- 3 + *porter* carry :- L.

portāre; in B - F. *déporter* - L. *dēportāre* (see DE- 2). So **deportment** †conduct; personal carriage. XVII.

depose put down from office, dethrone XIII; lay aside, lay down, remove XIV; testify (to), attest XV. - (O)F. *déposer*, based on L. *dēpōnere* lay aside or down, deposit, entrust, f. DE- 2+*pōnere* place; see POSE[1]. So **deposit** sb. (- L. *dēpositum*, sb. use of n. of pp. of *dēpōnere*) and vb. (- F. †*dépositer* or medL. *dēpositāre*, f. L. *dēpositum*) XVII. **depositary** one with whom a thing is deposited XVII; place of deposit XVIII. - late L. *dēpositārius*. **deposition** degradation, dethronement XIV; giving of testimony on oath XV; taking down of Christ from the Cross XVI. - (O)F. - L. **depository** keeper of a deposit XVII; place of deposit XVIII. - medL. *dēpositōrium*. **depot** place for military stores or troops XVIII; depository; (U.S.) railway station XIX. - F. *dépôt*, OF. *depost* - L. *dēpositum* DEPOSIT.

deprave XIV. - (O)F. *dépraver* or L. *dēprāvāre*, f. DE- 3+*prāvus* crooked, perverse, bad. So **depravity** XVII.

deprecate pray against; plead for the avoidance of. XVII. f. pp. stem of L. *dēprecārī*, f. DE- 2+*precārī* PRAY; see -ATE[3]. So **deprecation** XV. - L. **deprecatory** XVI. - late L.

depreciate lower in value or estimation XV; fall in value or estimation (orig. U.S.) XVIII. f. pp. stem of late L. *dēpretiāre* (medL. *-prec-*), f. DE- 1+*pretium* PRICE; see -ATE[3].

depredation XV. - F. *déprédation* - late L. *dēprædātiō, -ōn-*, f. *dēprædārī*, f. DE- 3+*prædārī* prey; see -ATION.

depress †subjugate XIV; press down; bring down in vigour or spirits XV. - OF. *depresser* - late L. *dēpressāre*, frequent. f. *dēpress-*, pp. stem of *dēprimere* press down, f. DE- 1+*premere* PRESS. So **depression** (astron.) angular distance below the horizon, etc., XIV; lowering of condition or powers XV. - (O)F. or L.

deprive XIV. - OF. *depriver* - ecclL. *dēprīvāre*, f. DE- 3+*prīvāre* deprive. So **deprivation** XV. - ecclL.

depth XIV. prob. based on ME. *dēpnes* deepness+-TH[1]; cf. MDu. *diepde*, (also mod.) *-te*, MLG. *dēpede*. OE. had *dīepe*, etc. (:- Gmc. **deupīn-*), *dēopnes*; see DEEP.

depute XV. Partly - (O)F. *députer* - L. *dēputāre* destine, assign, f. DE- 2+*putāre* consider; partly based on *depute* pp. (XIV) - (O)F. *député*, the final syll. of which was dropped as in ASSIGN[2], etc. So **deputation** appointment, delegation XIV; body of deputed persons XVIII. - late L. **deputy** XVI. var. of *depute* (see above) with final syll. retained; see -Y[5]. Hence **deputize** XVIII.

deracinate XVI. f. F. *déraciner* (OF. *des-*), f. DE- 6+*racine* :- late L. *radīcīna*, f. L. *rādix, rādīc-* root; see -ATE[3].

derail XIX. - F. *dérailler*, f. DE- 2+*rail* RAIL[2].

derange XVIII. - F. *déranger*, OF. *desrengier*; see DE- 6, RANGE.

Derby name of an annual horse-race founded in 1780 by the twelfth earl of *Derby*; (U.S.) bowler hat. XIX.

derelict XVII. - L. *dērelictus*, pp. of *dērelinquere*, f. DE- 3+*relinquere* leave. So **dereliction** abandonment XVII; reprehensible neglect (of duty, etc.) XVIII.

deride XVI. - L. *dērīdēre*, f. DE- 3+*rīdēre* laugh (at). So **derision** XV. - (O)F. - late L.

derive pass. and intr. emanate, take its origin XIV; trans. conduct (water) *from* a source *into* a channel XV; †convey, direct; obtain from a source XVI. - (O)F. *dériver* or L. *dērīvāre*, f. DE- 2+*rīvus* brook, stream. So **derivation** origination, spec. of a word; deviation into a channel; (med.) withdrawal of morbid fluid. XV. **derivative** XV. - F. - L.

dermat(o)- comb. form, varying with the shortened form **dermo-**, of Gr. *dérma, -mat-* skin.

derogate †abrogate in part; †detract from, disparage; take away a part *from* XV; fall away *from* a standard XVII. f. pp. stem of L. *dērogāre*, f. DE- 2+*rogāre* ask, question, propose (a law). So **derogation** XV. - (O)F. or L. **derogatory** XVI. - late L.

derrick †hangman; †gallows XVI; hoisting contrivance XVIII. f. surname of a noted hangman at Tyburn *c.* 1600.

derring-do (arch.) feats of daring. XVI. Taken up from sixteenth-century prints of Lydgate's 'Chronicle of Troy', where *derrynge do* is misprinted for orig. *dorryng do* 'daring to do'. Its currency in mod. writers is due to Scott's use of *deeds of such derring-do* ('Ivanhoe' xxix).

derringer (U.S.) small pistol. XIX. f. surname of the inventor.

dervish Muslim ascetic. XVI. - Turk. *derviş* - Pers. *darvēš, darvīš* poor, (sb.) religious mendicant.

descant sb. XIV. orig. *deschaunt* - OF. *deschant* (mod. *déchant*) - medL. *discantus* part-song, refrain, f. L. *dis-* asunder, apart+*cantus* song; see DIS-, CHANT. The present form is due to partial assim. to L. So **descant** vb. XVI. prob. f. the sb.

descend XIII. - (O)F. *descendre* :- L. *dēscendere*, f. DE- 1+*scandere* climb. So **descendant** issue, offspring. XVI. - (O)F., prp. of *descendre*. **descent** XIV.

describe XV. - L. *dēscrībere* write down, copy off, f. DE- 1+*scrībere* write. So **description** XIV. - (O)F. - L.

descry A. †proclaim, declare; †disclose; †cry down, decry XIV; B. catch sight of, discern XIV. - OF. *descrier* cry, publish, DECRY. Sense B appears to have arisen through identification with †*descrie* (- OF. *descrire*) DESCRIBE, which combined the senses of 'write down' and 'mark down, discern'.

desecrate XVII. Formed with DE- 6 as the antithesis of CONSECRATE. So **desecration** XVIII.

desert[1] worthiness, meritoriousness XIII; action or quality deserving appropriate recompense XIV. - OF. *desert, deserte*, sb. derivs. of *deservir* DESERVE (obs. pp. *desert*, repr. Rom. **dēservitus*, for L. *dēservītus*).

desert[2] waste tract of country. XIII. - (O)F. *désert* - ecclL. *dēsertum*, sb. use of n. of *dēsertus* abandoned, left waste, pp. of *dēserere* sever connection with, leave, forsake. The L. pp. is the source of (O)F. *désert* adj., whence **desert** adj.

(XIII), which is now apprehended as an attrib. use of the sb.

desert[3] forsake, abandon. XV. f. †*desert* pp. or - F. *déserter*, in OF. make desert, ult. f. L. *dēsertus* DESERT[2]. So **desertion** XV. - (O)F. - late L.

deserve †become entitled to earn or claim XIII; be worthy to have XIV. - OF. *deservir* (now *dess-*) :- L. *dēservīre* serve zealously or well, f. DE- 3 + *servīre* SERVE. So **deservedly** XVI. f. pp. *deserved* + LY[2].

deshabille see DISHABILLE.

desiccate XVI. f. pp. stem of L. *dēsiccāre*, f. DE- 3 + *siccāre* make dry, f. *siccus* dry; see -ATE[3]. So **desiccation** XV. - late L.

desiderate feel the want or loss of. XVII. f. pp. stem of L. *dēsīderāre*, f. DE- 1, 2 + base **sīder-*, as in *consīderāre* CONSIDER; see -ATE[3] and cf. DESIRE. So **desideratum** something wanting and desired. XVII. sb. use of n. sg. of the pp. of the L. vb. **desiderative** (gram.) expressing desire. XVI. - late L.

design[1] plan, scheme, purpose XVI; plan for a work of art XVII. Earliest forms *des(e)igne, disseigne* - F. †*desseing*, †*des(s)ing* (mod. *dessein*), f. †*desseigner* (see next).

design[2] A. point out, designate; B. plan, purpose, intend XVI; C. delineate, draw XVII. In form - F. *désigner* indicate, designate, and L. *dēsignāre* mark out, point out, delineate, depict, contrive, DESIGNATE. All the meanings derive ult. from the L. word, but sense B has been affected by DESIGN[1] and F. †*desseigner*, sense C by F. *dessiner*, †*dessigner* (an alt. of *desseigner* after It. *disignare*). So **designate** †indicated XV (once), marked out or selected for office, appointed or nominated XVII. - L. *dēsignātus*, pp. of *dēsignāre*, f. DE- 3 + *signāre* mark, SIGN; see -ATE[2]. **designate** vb. appoint or nominate for office XVIII; point out, name XIX. f. pp. stem of L. *dēsignāre*; see -ATE[3]. **designation** XIV. - (O)F. or L.

desire vb. XIII. - (O)F. *désirer* :- L. *dēsīderāre* (see DESIDERATE). So **desire** sb. XIV. - (O)F. *désir*, f. the vb. **desirous** XIV. - AN. *desirous*, OF. *-eus* (mod. *désireux*).

desist XV. - (O)F. *désister* - L. *dēsistere*, f. DE- 2 + *sistere*, redupl. formation on *stāre* STAND.

desk XIV. - medL. *desca*, prob. based on Pr. *desc(a)* basket or It. *desco* table, butcher's block :- L. *discus* quoit, DISH, DISC; cf. DAIS.

desolate left alone; deserted XIV; destitute of life, joy, or comfort XV. - L. *dēsōlātus*, pp. of *dēsōlāre* abandon, f. DE- 3 + *sōlus* alone, SOLE[3]; see -ATE[2]. So **desolation** XIV. - late L. or partly through (O)F.

despair vb. XIV. f. *despeir-*, tonic stem of OF. *desperer* :- L. *dēspērāre* (see DESPERATE). So **despair** sb. XIV. - AN. **despeir*, for OF. *desespeir* (mod. *désespoir*).

despatch see DISPATCH.

desperado †one in despair; desperate adventurer. XVII. refash. of the somewhat earlier †*desperate*, sb. use of next (XVI), after Sp. words in -ADO.

desperate XV. - L. *dēspērātus* despaired of, pp. of *dēspērāre* despair, f. DE- 6 + *spērāre* hope; see -ATE[2]. So **desperation** XIV. - OF. - L.

despise XIII. f. *despis-*, pres. stem of OF. *despire* :- L. *dēspicere*, f. DE- 1 + *specere* look.

despite †scorn; outrage, injury XIII; indignation, vexation, spite XIV. - OF. *despit* (mod. *dépit*) :- L. *dēspectus* looking down (upon), f. *dēspect-*, *dēspicere* (see prec.).

despoil XIII. - OF. *despoill(i)er, despuillier* (mod. *dépouiller*) :- L. *dēspoliāre*, f. DE- 6 + *spoliāre* (see SPOIL).

despond lose heart or confidence. XVII. - L. *dēspondēre* give up, resign, abandon, f. DE- 2 + *spondēre* promise. Hence **despondence, -ency, -ent.** XVII.

despot lord, prince, ruler XVI; absolute ruler, tyrant XVIII. - F. *despote*, earlier †*despot* - medL. *despota* - Gr. *despótēs* master, lord. So **despotic** XVII, **despotism** XVIII.

desquamation scaling, peeling of skin. XVIII. - F. *désquamation* or modL. *dēsquāmātiō, -ōn-*, f. *dēsquāmāre* remove the scales from, f. DE- 6 + *squāma* scale; see -ATION.

dessert course of fruit after dinner. XVII. - F. *dessert* m., *desserte* fem., pp. derivs. of *desservir* remove what has been served at table, f. *des-* DIS- 2 + *servir* SERVE.

destine vb. XIV. - (O)F. *destiner* - L. *dēstināre* make fast or firm, establish. Hence **destination** XV. - (O)F. or L. **destiny** XIV. - (O)F.

destitute †abandoned, forsaken, forlorn XIV; devoid *of* XV; bereft of resources XVIII. - L. *dēstitūtus* forsaken, pp. of *dēstituere*, f. DE- 1, 2 + *statuere* set up, place.

destroy XIII. ME. *destru(i)(e), destr(o)ie* - OF. *destruire* (mod. *détruire*) :- Rom. **dēstrūgere*, for L. *dēstruere*, f. DE- 6 + *struere* pile up. Hence **destroyer** XIV. So **destruction** XIV. - (O)F. - L. **destructive** XV. - (O)F. - late L.

desuetude XV. - F. *désuétude* or its source L. *dēsuētūdo*, f. *dēsuēscere, dēsuēt-* disuse, become unaccustomed, f. DE- 6 + *suēscere* be wont; see -TUDE.

desultory shifting from one place or thing to another XVI; disconnected and irregular XVIII. - L. *dēsultōrius* pert. to a vaulter, superficial, f. *dēsultor*, f. *dēsult-*, pp. stem of *dēsilīre* leap down, f. DE- 1 + *salīre* leap; see -ORY.

detach XVII. - F. *détacher*, earlier †*destacher*, f. *des-* DIS- 1 + stem of *attacher* ATTACH. So **detachment** XVII.

detail *in detail* item by item; minute account XVII; minute part; (mil.) distribution in detail of the daily orders to the officers concerned, body detached for special duty XVIII. - F. *détail*, f. *détailler* (f. *dé-* DE- 3 + *tailler* cut up in pieces), whence **detail** vb. deal with in detail XVII; (mil.) XVIII.

detain XV. repr. tonic stem of (O)F. *détenir* (AN. *detener*) :- Rom. **dētenēre*, for L. *dētinēre*, f. DE- 2 + *tenēre* hold. So **detainer** (leg.) detention XVII. - AN. **detention** XV. - F. or late L.

detect †uncover, expose XV; expose the secrecy of XVI. f. *dētect-*, pp. stem of L. *dētegere*, f. DE- 6 + *tegere* cover; after †*detect* pp. (XIV). So **detection** XV. - late L. **detective** XIX; first in *detective police(man)*; hence ellipt. as sb.

detent in clocks and watches, the catch which regulates the striking. XVII; (gen.) stop or catch in a machine XIX. - F. *détente*, earlier *destente* orig. mechanism in a cross-bow by which the string is released, f. *destendre* slacken, f. *des-* DIS- (privative) + *tendre* stretch (see TEND).

détente easing of strained relations. XX. - F.; see prec.

deter XVI. - L. *dēterrēre*, f. DE- 2 + *terrēre* frighten. So **deterrent** XIX.

deterge wipe or clear away (esp. med.). XVII. - F. *déterger* or L. *dētergēre*, f. DE- 2 + *tergēre* wipe. So **detergent** adj. and sb. XVII.

deteriorate make worse XVI; grow worse XVIII. f. pp. stem of late L. *dēteriōrāre*, f. *dēterior* worse, compar. of **dēter-*, f. *dē* down (see DE-) + compar. suffix; see -ATE[3].

determine XIV. - (O)F. *déterminer* - L. *dēterminąre* bound, limit, fix, f. DE- 3 + *termināre* TERMINATE. So **determinant** XVII, **determination** XIV.

determinism (philos.) doctrine that human action is necessarily determined. XIX. - F. *déterminisme* or its source G. *determinismus* (Kant, 1793), which may have been extracted from *prädeterminismus*, if not directly f. *determinieren* - L. *dēterminąre* (see prec.) + *-ismus* -ISM.

detest †execrate; have abhorrence of. XVI. - L. *dētestārī* denounce, renounce, f. DE- 4 + *testārī* bear witness, call to witness, f. *testis* witness; perh. partly back-formation from **detestation** (XV) - (O)F. - L.

detonate XVIII. f. pp. stem of L. *dētonāre*, f. DE- 3 + *tonāre* THUNDER (see -ATE[3]); partly back-formation from **detonation** (XVII) - F. *détonation*, f. *détoner* - L. *dētonāre*. Hence **detonator** XIX.

detour XVIII. - F. *détour* change of direction, f. *détourner* (OF. *destorner*) turn away; see DE- 2, TURN.

detract XV. f. *dētract-*, pp. stem of L. *dētrahere* draw off, take away, disparage, f. DE- 2 + *trahere* draw. So **detraction** XIV. - (O)F. - L.

detriment XV. - (O)F. *détriment* or L. *dētrīmentum*, f. pt. stem *dētrī-* of *dēterere* wear away, f. DE- 2 + *terere* rub; see -MENT. Hence **detrimental** XVII.

detritus †wearing away by rubbing XVIII; (after F. *détritus*) matter produced by such action XIX. - L. *dētrītus*, f. *dētrī-* (see prec.).

deuce[1] two at dice or cards XV; (at tennis) the point at which each side has scored 40 and the game is *à deux* 'at two', i.e. when two successive points must be gained to win XVI. - OF. *deus* (mod. *deux*) :- L. *duōs* acc. TWO.

deuce[2] in imprecatory phr. †*a deuce on*, the (†*a*) *deuce take*, *what the* (†*a*) *deuce*, plague, mischief, (later) the Devil. XVII. - LG. *duus* = G. *daus*, prob. to be identified ult. with prec. as a dicer's exclamation on making the lowest throw, viz. a two.

deuterium (chem.) an isotope of hydrogen. symbol D. XX. f. Gr. *deúteros* (cf. next) + -IUM.

deutero- comb. form of Gr. *deúteros* second, also in the sense 'secondary'.

deutzia genus of shrubs. XIX. f. name of J. *Deutz* of Amsterdam; see -IA[1].

devastate XVII (rare before XIX). f. pp. stem of L. *dēvāstāre*, f. DE- 3 + *vāstāre* lay waste, f. *vāstus* WASTE; see -ATE[3]. So **devastation** XV.

develop unfold, lay open (more fully). XVII (first as pp. *developed*; preceded by †*disvelop* (XVI-XVIII)). - OF. *desveloper*, mod. *développer* :- Rom. vb. f. L. DIS- 2 + **volup-*, **velup-* (ult. orig. unkn.). So **development** XVIII.

deviate XVII. f. pp. stem of late L. *dēviāre*, f. DE- 2 + *via* way; see -ATE[3]. So **deviation** XVII. - F. - medL.

device plan, planning; pleasure, fancy XIII; †opinion; design, figure XIV; contrivance XIV. ME. *devis*, later *devise*, from XV *device*; the present form is - OF. *devis* m.; *devise* is - OF. *devise* fem.; - Rom. derivs. of L. *dīvīs-*, pp. stem of *dīvīdere* DIVIDE. Cf. DEVISE.

devil the supreme spirit of evil; malignant being OE.; printer's apprentice XVII; (highly seasoned) fried or boiled dish XVIII. OE. *dēofol* = OS. *diubul*, *-al* (Du. *duivel*), OHG. *tiufal* (G. *teufel*), ON. *djǫfull*, Goth. *diab(a)ulus*. The Goth. forms were directly - Gr. *diábolos* prop. accuser, slanderer, f. *diabállein* slander, traduce, f. *diá* across + *bállein* throw. The other Gmc. forms were - ChrL. *diabolus* (whence also (O)F. *diable*, etc.). Hence **devil** vb. †play the devil XVI; grill, broil (with hot condiments) XVIII; act as devil to a lawyer or writer XIX. **devilish** XV; see -ISH[1]. **devilry** XIV; after (O)F. *diablerie*.

devious lying out of the way XVI; deviating from the direct way XVII. f. L. *dēvius*, f. DE- 2 + *via* way; see -OUS.

devise[1] order, appoint XIII; assign by will; plan, contrive XIV. - (O)F. *deviser* divide, dispose (of), design, contrive, discourse :- Rom. **dīvīsāre*, f. *dīvīs-*, pp. stem of L. *dīvīdere* DIVIDE.

devise[2] testamentary disposition. XVI. - OF. *devise* (see DEVICE) - medL. *dīvīsa*, used for *dīvīsiō* DIVISION.

devoid XV. orig. pp. (contr.) of †*devoid* make void or empty (XIV) - OF. *devoidier*, *-vuidier* (mod. *dévider*), f. DE- 3 + *voidier*, *vuidier* VOID.

devolve †roll down XV; pass or cause to pass *to* or fall *upon* another XVI. - L. *dēvolvere*, f. DE- 1 + *volvere* roll (see VOLUME). So **devolution** XVI.

devote XVI. f. *dēvōt-*, pp. stem of L. *dēvovēre*, f. DE- 3 + *vovēre* vow. Hence **devotee** XVII. See -EE. So **devotion** XIII. - (O)F. - L.

devour XIV. f. *devour-*, tonic stem of (O)F. *dévorer* - L. *dēvorāre*, f. DE- 3 + *vorāre* swallow.

devout XIII. - (O)F. *dévot* - L. *dēvōtus*, pp. of *dēvovēre* DEVOTE.

dew OE. *dēaw* = OS. *dau* (Du. *dauw*), OHG. *tou* (G. *tau*), ON. *dǫgg* :- Gmc. **dawwaz*, *-am*, f. the base repr. in Skr. *dhāv* flow, Gr. *theîn* run.

dew-claw rudimentary inner toe in dogs. XVI. prob. f. DEW + CLAW, being so called because it touches only the dewy surface of the ground.

dew-lap fold of loose skin hanging from the throat. XIV. f. DEW + LAP[1], perh. after ON. **dǫggleppr*.

dexter (her.) right-hand. XVI. - L. *dexter*, compar. formation, f. IE. base seen also in Gr. *dexiós* on the right hand (with Indo-Iran., Balto-Slav., Gmc., Celt., and Alb. cogns.); the primary meaning passes sometimes into 'adroit'. So **dexterity** XVI. - F. - L. Hence **dext(e)rous** XVII.

dextrin (chem.) gummy substance into which starch is converted at high temperatures, having the property of turning the plane of polarization to the right, whence its name. XIX. - F. *dextrine*, f. L. *dextrā* on the right hand, abl. fem. of *dexter*; see prec. and -IN.

dextro- used as comb. form of L. *dexter*, *dextr-* right-handed (see DEXTER) or *dextrā* on the right-hand, in physical and chemical terms to denote 'turned or turning to the right' with ref. to the property of causing a ray of polarized light to turn to the right.

dhow native vessel used on the Arabian Sea. XIX. ult. orig. unkn.; in Marathi as *ḍāw*, in Arabic as *dāw*.

di-[1] see DIS-.

di-[2] repr. Gr. *di-*, for *dís* twice (cf. TWO).

dia- before a vowel **di-**[3] repr. Gr. *dia-*, *di-*, the prep. *diá* (app. alt. of IE. **dis* in two, apart; cf. DIS-) in comps. with the senses 'through', 'thoroughly', 'apart', occurring in a few words going back (sometimes through F. and L.) to Gr. originals, as DIALECT, DIATRIBE, and in many mod. scientific and techn. formations.

diabetes disease marked by immoderate discharge of urine containing glucose. XVI. - L. *diabētēs* - Gr. *diabḗtēs*, f. *diabaínein* go through; see DIA- and COME.

diablerie dealings with the devil, devilry XVIII; devil-lore XIX. - F., f. *diable* DEVIL; see -ERY.

diabolic XIV, **diabolical** XVI. - or f. (O)F. *diabolique*, ChrL. *diabolicus*, f. *diabolus* DEVIL; see -IC, -ICAL.

diaconal pert. to a deacon. XVIII. - ChrL. *diāconālis*, f. *diāconus* DEACON; see -AL[1]. So **diaconate** XVII. See -ATE[1].

diacritic serving to distinguish XVII; sb. diacritic sign XIX. - Gr. *diakritikós*, f. *diakrínein* distinguish; see DIA-, CRITIC.

diadem XIII. - (O)F. *diadème* - L. *diadēma* - Gr. *diádema*, f. *diadeîn* bind round, f. DIA- + *deîn* bind.

diaeresis (sign ¨ marking) the separation of a vowel from its neighbour. XVII. - late L. - Gr. *diaíresis*, f. *diaireîn* divide, f. DIA- + *haireîn* take.

diagnosis XVII. - modL. - Gr. *diágnōsis*, f. *diagignṓskein* distinguish, discern, f. DIA- + *gignṓskein* perceive (see KNOW).

diagonal XVI. - L. *diagōnālis*, f. Gr. *diagṓnios*, f. DIA- + *gōniā* angle; see -AL[1].

diagram XVII. - L. *diagramma* - Gr. *diágramma* (-at-), f. *diagráphein* mark out by lines, f. DIA- + *gráphein* write; see -GRAM. So **diagrammatic** XIX.

dial instrument to tell the time of day by the shadow cast by the sun. XV. Obscure deriv. of medL. *diālis*, f. *diēs* day; see -AL[1].

dialect XVI. - F. *dialecte* or L. *dialectus* - Gr. *diálektos*, f. *dialégesthai* hold discourse, f. DIA- + *légein* speak. Hence **dialectal** XIX; *dialectical* was earlier in this sense XVIII. So **dialectic** XVII, **-ical** XVI pert. to logical disputation. **dialectic** sb. investigation of truth by discussion XIV. **dialectician** XVII. - F.

dialogue XIII. - OF. *dialoge* (mod. *dialogue*) - L. *dialogus* - Gr. *diálogos* conversation, discourse, f. *dialégesthai* converse (see DIALECT).

dialysis †statement of disjunctive propositions, asyndeton XVI; (chem.) separation of the soluble crystalloid substances in a mixture from the colloid XIX. - L. - Gr. *diálusis*, f. *dialúein* part asunder, f. DIA- + *lúein* set free.

diamanté material scintillating with powdered crystal, etc. XX. - F., pp. formation on *diamant* DIAMOND.

diameter XIV. - (O)F. *diamètre* - L. *diametrus*, -*os* - Gr. *diámetros*, f. DIA + *métron* measure. So **diametrical** XVI.

diamond XIII. ME. *diama(u)nt* - (O)F. *diamant* - medL. *diamas*, *diamant-*, alt. of L. *adamās* ADAMANT, by assoc. with words in DIA-.

diapason (mus.) †octave XIV; harmonious or melodious succession of notes or parts; foundation stop in an organ XVI; scale, range, pitch XVIII. - L. *diapāsōn* - Gr. *diapāsôn*, i.e. *dià pāsôn* 'through all (the notes)', i.e. of the scale.

diaper linen fabric with a small diamond pattern XIV; pattern of this kind XVII; small towel XVI. - OF. *diapre*, earlier *diaspre* - medL. *diasprum* - medGr. *díaspros*, f. DIA- + *áspros* white. Hence **diaper** vb., **diapered** ppl. adj. XIV.

diaphanous transparent. XVII. f. medL. *diaphanus*, f. Gr. *diaphanḗs*, f. DIA- + *phan-*, *phaínein* show; see -OUS.

diaphoretic sudorific. XV. - late L. *diaphorēticus* - Gr. *diaphorētikós*, f. *diaphórēsis* perspiration, f. *diaphoreîn* throw off by perspiration, f. DIA- + *phoreîn* carry, rel. to *phérein* BEAR[2].

diaphragm partition dividing the thorax from the abdomen. XVII (earlier in L. form). - late L. *diaphragma* - Gr. *diáphragma* f. DIA- + *phrágma* fence.

diarrhoea XVI (also *diaria*, *diarie* XV). - late L. - Gr. *diárrhoia*, f. *diarrheîn* flow through, f. DIA- + *rheîn* flow.

diary XVI. - L. *diārium* daily allowance, (later) journal, in form sb. use of n. of *diārius* daily (which, however, is not pre-medieval), f. *diēs* day; see -ARY. Hence **diarist** XIX.

Diaspora the Jews dispersed among the Gentiles. XIX. - Gr. *diasporá*, f. *diaspeírein* disperse, f. DIA- + *speírein* sow, scatter.

diastole (physiol.) dilatation. XVI. - late L. - Gr. *diastolḗ* separation, expansion, f. *diastéllein*, f. DIA- + *stéllein* place.

diatessaron †(mus.) interval of a fourth XIV; medicine of four ingredients XV; harmony of the four Gospels XIX. - late L. *diatessarōn*, f. Gr. *dià tessárōn* 'through, i.e. composed of, four' (*diá* DIA-, *tessárōn*, g. of *téssares* FOUR).

diatonic XVII (†*diatonical* XVI). - (O)F. *diatonique* or its source, late L. *diatonicus* - Gr. *diatonikós* proceeding through, i.e. at the interval of, a tone, f. DIA- + *tónos* TONE; see -IC.

diatribe disquisition XVI; severely critical discourse XIX. - F. - L. *diatriba* - Gr. *diatribḗ* employment (of time), study, discourse, f. *diatríbein* consume, waste, while away, f. DIA- + *tríbein* rub.

dibble instrument for making holes in the ground. XV. In form a deriv. with -LE of †*dib* vb. (XIV), a syn., and prob. a modified form, of DIP; but the senses of this vb. that are more directly connected with *dibble* are of much later emergence.

dibs pl. children's game played with pebbles or knuckle-bones XVIII; (sl.) money XIX. perh. f. *dib* vb. (see prec.) tap, dip, bob, apprehended as a var. of DAB.

dice XIV. pl. of DIE[2].

dichotomy division into two parts. XVII. - Gr. *dikhotomiā*, f. *dikhótomos* cut in two, equally divided, f. *dikho-*, comb. form of *díkha* in two, rel. to *dís* (see DI-[2]) + -TOMY. So **dichotomize** XVII.

dickens euph. substitute for *devil*. XVI. prob. a fanciful use of the personal name *Dickens*, f. *Dicken*, *Dickon*, dim. of *Dick*, alt. of *Rick*, pet-form of *Rickard*, *Richard*.

dicker ten, esp. of hides. ME. *dyker* (XII) points to an OE. **dicor*, corr. to MLG. *dēker*, MHG. *techer*, (also mod.) *decher* :- WGmc. **decura* - L. *decuria* set of ten. Hence (perh.) **dicker** vb. trade by barter, haggle. XIX. A use supposed to be due to the bartering of skins on the N. Amer. frontier.

dicky[1] he-ass, donkey; †under-petticoat XVIII; driver's or rear seat in a carriage; detached shirt-front; small bird (also *dicky-bird*) XIX. dim. of the proper name *Dick* (cf. DICKENS); see -Y[6].

dicky[2] (colloq.) shaky, insecure, 'queer'; feeling ill. XVIII. perh. orig. f. *Dick* in phr. 'as queer as Dick's hatband'; see -Y[1].

dicotyledon (bot.) flowering plant having two seed-lobes. XVIII. - modL. pl. *dīcotylēdones*; see DI-, COTYLEDON.

dictate utter aloud (something to be written down); lay down authoritatively. XVII. f. *dictāt-*, pp. stem of L. *dictāre* pronounce, prescribe, f. *dīcere* say (see DICTION). So **dictate** sb. XVI. - L. *dictātum*, sb. use of n. pp. of *dictāre*. **dictation** XVII. - late L. **dictator** XIV. - L.

diction †word, phrase XV; choice of phraseology, wording XVII. - (O)F. *diction* or L. *dictiō*, *-ōn-* saying, mode of expression, (later) word, f. *dict-*, pp. stem of *dīcere* say, rel. to Gr. *deiknúnai* show, Goth. *gateihan* announce, OHG. *zīhan* (G. *zeihen*), OE. *tēon* (:- **teohan*) accuse, ON. *tjá* show, tell; see -TION.

dictionary XVI. - medL. *dictiōnārium*, *-us*, f. L. *dictiō* phrase, word; see prec., -ARY.

dictum XVII. - L. 'thing said', sb. use of n. pp. of *dīcere* say.

didactic XVII. - Gr. *didaktikós*, f. stem *didak-* of *didáskein* teach; see -IC.

didapper dabchick. XV. Reduced form of *dive-dapper* (not recorded so early), extension of *dive-dap* (cf. OE. *dufedoppa*; see DABCHICK).

die[1] cease to live. XII. ME. *de(i)ʒen*, *deye*, pt. *de(i)ʒede*, *deide*, of disputed orig.: two hypotheses are admissible: (i) that the ME. forms repr. unrecorded OE. **dīeġan*, **dēġan* = OS. *dōian*, OHG. *touwen* (MHG. *töuwen*), ON. *deyja* :- Gmc. **dawjan*, f. **daw-*, repr. also in DEAD, DEATH, and Goth. *afdauiþs* vexed, rel. by gradation to *diwans* mortal, *undiwanei* immortality; but it is more likely (ii) that the ME. forms were immed. - ON. *deyja*. In OE. the words for 'die' were *steorfan* (see STARVE), *sweltan* (see SWELTER), or *wesan dēad*, pt. *wæs dēad* ('be, was dead').

die[2] pl. DICE cube used in games of chance. XIII. ME. *dē*, *dee*, pl. *dēs*, *dees* - OF. *dé*, pl. *dés* :- L. (Rom.) *datum*, sb. use of n. pp. of *dare* give, spec. play.

diet[1] food XIII; customary or prescribed course of food XIV. - (O)F. *diète* - L. *diæta* - Gr. *díaita* course of life. Hence **diet** vb. XIV. So **dietary** course of diet XV; adj. XVII. - medL. *diætārium*.

diet[2] †day's journey; appointed day or time, meeting, session XV; metal scraped from gold and silver plate assayed day by day at the Mint XVII. - medL. *diēta* day's journey, allowance, work, wages.

dif- assim. form of DIS- before *f*, as in L. *differre* DIFFER. In Rom. it became *def-*, OF. *de-*, as in DEFY.

differ XIV. - (O)F. *différer* (i) put off, DEFER, (ii) be different - L. *differre*, f. DIF- + *ferre*, carry, BEAR[2]. So **different, difference** XIV. - (O)F. - L. **differential** XVII. **differentiate, -ation** XIX. - medL.

difficult XIV. Back-formation from **difficulty** (XIV) - L. *difficultās*, f. DIF- + *facultās* FACULTY.

diffident †distrustful XV; wanting in self-confidence XVIII. - L. *diffīdēns*, *-ent-*, prp. of *diffīdere* mistrust, f. DIF- + *fīdere* trust, rel. to *fides* FAITH; see -ENT. So **diffidence** XV. - F. or L.

diffraction XVII. - F. *diffraction* or modL. *diffractio*, f. *diffract-*, pp. stem of L. *diffringere* break in pieces, f. DIF- + *frangere* BREAK[1].

diffuse †confused, indistinct XV; opp. of *confined* and *condensed* XVIII. - F. *diffus* (fem. *-use*) or L. *diffūsus* extensive, ample, prolix, pp. of *diffundere* pour out, f. DIF- + *fundere* pour. So **diffuse** vb. XVI. f. *diffūs-*, pp. stem of L. *diffundere*. **diffusion** †outpouring XIV; spreading abroad XVI; permeation of a fluid by another XVIII. - L.

dig XIII. ME. *digge*, perh. f. OE. **dīċiġian*, f. *dīc* DITCH. Orig. weak (*digged*); the new *dug* appears XVI.

digamma Gr. letter ϝ. XVII. - L. - Gr. *digamma* (so called from its shape, which suggests two gammas (see DI-[2], GAMMA) set one above the other).

digest methodical or systematic compendium. XIV. - L. *dīgesta* 'matters methodically arranged', n. pl. of *dīgestus*, pp. of *dīgerere* divide, distribute, digest, f. DI-[1] + *gerere* carry. So **digest** arrange methodically; assimilate (food) in the body. XV. f. *dīgest-*, pp. stem of *dīgerere*. **digestion** digesting of food. XIV. - (O)F. - L.

digit any numeral from 0 to 9 XV; $\frac{1}{12}$ of the diameter of sun or moon XVI; finger, toe; finger's breadth XVII. - L. *digitus* finger, toe.

digitalis plant of the foxglove family XVII; drug prepared from this XVIII. - modL., sb. use of L. *digitālis* pert. to the finger, after the G. name of the foxglove, *fingerhut* 'finger-hat', thimble.

dignify XV. - F. *dignifier* - late L. *dignificāre*; see next and -FY.

dignity worth, nobility, honourable estate or office XIII; nobility or gravity of manner XVII. - OF. *digneté* (mod. *dignité*, with latinized sp.) - L. *dignitās*, f. *dignus* worthy; see -ITY. Hence **dignitary** XVII.

digraph group of two letters representing one sound. XVIII. f. Gr. DI-² + *graphḗ* writing.

digress XVI. f. *dīgress-*, pp. stem of L. *dīgredī*, f. DI-¹ + *gradī* step, walk, f. *gradus* step. So **digression** XIV. - (O)F. - L.

dike, dyke A. (dial.) ditch XIII; B. embankment XV. - ON. *dík, díki* or MLG. *dīk* dam, MDu. *dijc* ditch, pool, mound, dam (Du. *dijk* dam); see DITCH. In A prob. of Norse orig.; in B prob. originating from the Low Countries in connection with drainage works. So **dike, dyke** vb. XIV.

dilapidate XVI. f. pp. stem of L. *dīlapidāre*, f. DI-¹ + *lapis, lapid-* stone; see -ATE³. So **dilapidation** XV. - late L.

dilate A. †relate at length XIV; discourse at large *upon* XVI; B. make wider XV; become wider, expand XVII. - (O)F. *dilater* - L. *dīlātāre* spread out, f. DI-¹ + *lātus* wide. So **dilatation** XIV, largely superseded by the shorter **dilation** (XV), formed as if *dilate* contained the suffix -ATE³.

dilatory tending to cause delay XV; given to delaying XVII. - L. *dīlātōrius*, f. *dīlātor* delayer, f. *dīlāt-*, pp. stem of *differre* DEFER¹; see -ORY².

dilemma form of argument involving the opponent in the choice of alternatives; choice between two equally unfavourable alternatives. XVI. - L. - Gr. *dílēmma*, f. DI-² + *lêmma* assumption, premiss (see LEMMA).

dilettante amateur of the fine arts; (later) mere amateur. XVIII. - It. 'lover (of music or painting)', sb. use of prp. of *dilettare* :- L. *dēlectāre* DELIGHT.

diligent XIV. - (O)F. - L. *dīligēns, -ent-* assiduous, attentive, adj. use of prp. of *dīligere* esteem highly, choose, take delight in, f. DI-¹ + *-legere* (as in *neglegere* NEGLECT). So **diligence** XIV.

dill the plant *Anethum graveolens*, having carminative properties. OE. *dile* and *dyle*, corr. to OS. *dilli* (Du. *dille*), OHG. *tilli*, and MDu. *dulle*, MHG. *tülle*, ON. *dylla*; of unkn. orig.

dilly-dally XVII. redupl., with variation of vowel, of DALLY.

dilute XVI. f. *dīlūt-*, pp. stem of L. *dīluere* wash away, dissolve, f. DI-¹ + *-luere*, comb. form of *lavāre* wash, LAVE. Hence **dilution** XVII.

diluvial pert. to the Flood XVII; (geol.) caused by extraordinary action of water on a large scale XIX. - late L. *dīluviālis*, f. *dīluvium* flood, DELUGE.

dim adj. OE. *dim(m)* = OFris. *dim*, ON. *dimmr*, rel. to synon. OHG. *timbar* (MHG., mod. dial. *timmer*), OSw. *dimber*, OIr. *dem* black, dark. Hence *dim* vb. XIII; in OE. comps. *ādimmian, fordimmian*, corr. to ON. *dimma* darken.

dime †tenth part XIV; $\frac{1}{10}$ of a dollar XVIII. - (O)F. *dime*, †*disme* :- L. *decima* tithe, sb. use (sc. *pars* part) of fem. of *decimus* TENTH.

dimension XIV. - F. - L. *dīmēnsiō, -ōn-*, f. *dīmēns-*, pp. stem of *dīmetīrī*; see DI-¹ and MEASURE.

dimidiation halving. XV. - L. *dīmidiātiō, -ōn-*, f. *dīmidiāt-*, pp. stem of *dīmidiāre*, f. *dīmidium* half, f. DI-¹ + *medius* middle, MID; see -ATION.

diminish XV. Resulting from a conflation of †*diminue* XIV (- (O)F. *diminuer* - L. *dīminuere*) and *minish* (- OF. *menu(i)sier* :- Rom. **minūtiāre*, f. *minūtus* MINUTE). So **diminution** XIV. - (O)F. - L. **diminutive** XIV (as sb. in gram.). - (O)F. - late L.

dimissory XIV. - late L. *dīmissōrius*, f. *dīmiss-*, pp. stem of *dīmittere*; see DISMISS.

dimity stout cotton fabric. XV (*demyt*). - It. *dimito* or medL. *dimitum* - Gr. *dímitos*, f. DI-² + *mítos* thread of the warp.

dimorphous XIX. f. Gr. *dímorphos*, f. DI-² + *morphḗ* form; see -MORPH, -OUS. So **dimorphic** XIX.

dimple †hollow in the ground XIII; small hollow in the cheek or chin XIV. prob. repr. OE. **dympel*, corr. to OHG. *tumphilo* (G. *tümpel*) deep place in water, f. Gmc. **dump-*, perh. nasalized form of **dup-* **deup-* DEEP; see -LE¹.

din sb. OE. *dyne* (:- **duniz*) and *dynn*, corr. to OHG. *tuni*, ON. *dynr* (:- **dunjaz, -uz*). So **din** vb. †sing, resound OE.; assail with din, make resound, make a din XVII. OE. *dynian* = OS. *dunian*, MHG. *tünen* roar, rumble, ON. *dynja* come rumbling down, gush, pour :- Gmc. **dunjan*. The IE. base **dhun-* is repr. also by Skr. *dhúni-* roaring, Lith. *dundéti* sound.

dinar name of various Oriental coins. XVII. - Arab., Pers. *dīnār* - late Gr. *dēnárion* - L. *dēnārius* DENARIUS.

dine XIII. - (O)F. *diner*, earlier *disner* :- Rom. **disjūnāre*, for **disjējūnāre* break one's fast, f. DIS- 2 + *jējūnium* fast.

ding-dong redupl. form imit. of the tolling of a bell. XVI.

dinghy native Indian rowing-boat; (gen.) small rowing-boat. XIX. - Hindi *ḍēgī*.

dingle deep hollow. XIII (once; not otherwise recorded in literature till XVII). perh. a dim. form (see -LE¹); ult. orig. unkn.

dingo wild dog of Australia. XVIII. Aboriginal name.

dingy XVIII. perh. to be referred ult. to OE. *dynge* dung, manured land, f. *dung* DUNG; see -Y¹.

dinky (colloq.) neat, spruce. XIX. f. Sc. and north. *dink* decked out, trim (XVI); of unkn. orig.; see -Y¹.

dinner XIII. - (O)F., sb. use of *diner* DINE.

din(o)- comb. form in modL. terms of Gr. *deinós* terrible, denoting certain huge extinct animals, as **dinornis** moa (Gr. *órnis* bird), **dinosaur** (Gr. *saûros* lizard), **dinothere** proboscidean quadruped (Gr. *thērion* wild beast). XIX.

dint †stroke, blow OE.; force of attack or impact XIV; (by assoc. with *dent, indent*) mark made by a blow, dent XVI. OE. *dynt*, reinforced in ME. by the rel. ON. *dyntr* (*dyttr*), *dynta*. Phr. †*by dint of sword* (XIV-XVIII); *by dint* (earlier *dent* XVI) *of*, by means of XVII. So **dint** vb. XIII. - ON. *dynta* (*dytta*).

diocese XIV. - OF. *diocise* (mod. *diocèse*) - late L. *diocēsis*, for L. *diœcēsis* governor's jurisdiction, district, (eccl.) diocese - Gr. *dioíkēsis* administration, government, (Roman) province, (eccl.) diocese, f. *dioikeîn* keep house, administer, f. DI-³ + *oikeîn* inhabit, manage, f. *oîkos* house. So **diocesan** XV.

dioecious (bot.) having the two sexes in separate individuals. XVIII. f. DI-² + Gr. *oîkos* house; see -IOUS.

diorama XIX. f. DI-[3] + Gr. *hórāma* view, f. *horân* see.

dip let down into liquid OE.; go down, sink XIV; have a downward inclination XVII. OE. *dyppan* :- **dupjan*, f. Gmc. **dup- *deup-* (see DEEP). Hence **dip** sb. act of dipping XVI; depression; downward inclination XVIII.

diphtheria infectious disease affecting chiefly the throat. XIX. - modL. - F. *diphthérie* (now *diphtérie*), substituted for earlier *diphthérite*, f. Gr. *diphthérā*, *diphtheris* skin, hide, piece of leather; so named on account of the tough membrane which forms on parts affected by the disease.

diphthong XV. - F. *dipthongue* - L. *diphthongus* - Gr. *díphthoggos*, f. DI-[2] + *phthóggos* voice, sound.

diploma official document of state or church; document conferring an honour, privilege, or license. XVII. - L. *diplōma* - Gr. *díplōma* folded paper, letter of recommendation or conveying a license or privilege, f. *diploûn* double, fold, f. *diploûs* double.

diplomacy XVIII. - F. *diplomatie*, f. *diplomatique*. **diplomatic** pert. to original official documents; concerned with diplomacy. XVIII. In the former sense - modL. *diplōmaticus*, f. L. *diplōmat-* DIPLOMA; in the latter sense - F. *diplomatique*. As sb. **diplomatic** A. †diplomatist; diplomacy XVIII; B. (also *-ics*) study of original documents XIX. A. sb. uses of the adj.; B - F. *diplomatique*. So **diplomat** XIX. - F. *diplomate*, back-formation from *diplomatique*. **diplomatist** XIX. f. F. *diplomate* or L. stem *diplōmat-*.

dipsomania XIX. f. Gr. *dípsa*, *dípsos* thirst + MANIA. So **dipsomaniac** XIX.

diptera two-winged flies. XIX. - Gr. *díptera*, n. pl. of *dípteros* two-winged (f. DI-[2] + *pterón* wing) used sb. So **dipterous** XVIII.

diptych two-leaved hinged tablet for writing. XVII. - late L. *diptycha* - late Gr. *díptukha*, n. pl. of *díptukhos* double-folded, f. DI-[2] + *ptukhḗ* fold.

dire XVI. - L. *dīrus*, rel. to Gr. *deídein* vb. fear, *deinós* terrible.

direct address (a letter or message) XIV; instruct XV. prob. based immed. on pp. *direct* - L. *dīrectus*, pp. of *dīrigere*, *dē-* straighten, direct, guide, f. DI-[1], DE- 3 + *regere* put straight, rule, whence also **direct** adj. straight XIV; straightforward, immediate XVI. So **direction** action of directing XV; course pursued XVII. - F. or L. **directive** adj. XV, sb. XVII. - medL. **director** XV. - AN. **directory** adj. serving to direct XV; sb. book of directions XVI.

dirge office of matins for the dead XIII; song of mourning XVI. ME. *dirige* (later *dyrge*, *derg(i)e*), the first word of the L. antiphon to the first psalm in the office: '*Dirige*, Domine, Deus meus, in conspectu tuo viam meam' Direct, O Lord my God, my way in thy sight; imper. of L. *dīrigere* DIRECT.

dirigible that can be directed or steered. XVI. f. L. *dīrigere* DIRECT + -IBLE.

diriment nullifying. XIX. - L. *dirimēns*, *-ent-*, prp. of *dirimere* separate, interrupt, f. DIS- + *emere* take; see -ENT.

dirk XVII. Earliest in Sc. *durk*, *dowrk*; of unkn. orig.

dirt excrement; unclean matter XIII; soil XVII. ME. *drit* - ON., corr. to MDu. *drēte* (Du *dreet*), rel. to the vb. OE. *ġedrītan*, ON. *dríta*, MDu. *drīten* (Du. *drijten*) void excrement.

dis- prefix repr. L. *dis-*, rel. to Gr. DIA-. It was reduced to *dī-* before some voiced consonants, as in *dīrigere* DIRECT, *dīvidere* DIVIDE, became *dir-* between vowels in *dirimere* (see DIRIMENT), was assim. before *f*, as in *differre* DIFFER, but retained its full form before *p*, *t*, *c*, and *s*.

In Eng. *dis-* appears (i) as repr. *dis-* in words adopted direct from L., (ii) as repr. OF. *des-* (mod. *dé(s)-*) :- L. *dis-*, (iii) as repr. late L. *dis-*, Rom. **des-*, substituted for L. *dē-*, (iv) as a living prefix combined with words of no matter what origin.

As an etymol. el. *dis-* occurs (1) with the meanings 'apart', 'asunder', 'separately', as in *discuss*, *disperse*; hence (2) with privative, negative, or reversive force, as in *disaster*, *dissuade*, or with intensive force, as in *disturb*. As a living prefix from XV with such privative or reversive force it (3) forms comp. vbs., as *disestablish*, *disinter*, *disown*, (4) with sbs. forms vbs. meaning to free or deprive of a quality or character, or reverse a condition, as *dischurch*, *disrobe*, (5) with adjs. forms vbs., as *disable*, (6) with sbs. expresses the reverse or lack of, as *disquiet*, *disservice*, (7) with adjs. expresses the negative or opposite, as *discourteous*, *disreputable*, and (8) is used with intensive force, as *disannul*.

disability XVI. DIS- 6. **disable** XV. DIS- 5. **disabuse** XVII. DIS- 3, 4. **disadvantage** sb. XIV. - (O)F. *désavantage*; DIS- 2. **disaffect** †dislike; (esp. in pp.) alienate the friendship or loyalty of. XVII. DIS- 3. **disagree** XV. - (O)F. *désagréer*; DIS- 2. **disallow** XIV. - OF. *desalouer*; DIS- 2.

disappear XV. f. DIS- 3 + APPEAR, after F. *disparaître*. Hence **disappearance** XVIII.

disappoint †deprive of appointment; frustrate the expectation or fulfilment of. XV. - (O)F. *désappointer*, f. *des-* DIS- 2 + *appointer* APPOINT. Hence **disappointment** XVII.

disarm XIV. - (O)F. *désarmer*; see DIS- 2, ARM[2]. So **disarmament** XVIII.

disarray XIV. - AN. **desarei*, OF. *desaroi*; see DIS- 2, ARRAY.

disaster XVI. - F. *désastre* or its source It. *disastro*, f. *dis-* DIS- 2 + *astro* (:- L. *astrum*) STAR; lit. 'unfavourable aspect of a star'. So **disastrous** †ill-starred, ill-boding XVI; calamitous XVII. - F. *désastreux* - It. *disastroso*.

disband XVI. - F. †*desbander* (mod. *dé-*); see DIS- 1, BAND[3].

disbelief XVII. DIS- 6. So **disbelieve** XVII. DIS- 3. **disburden** XVI. DIS- 4.

disburse XVI. - OF. *desbourser* (mod. *débourser*), f. *des-* DIS- 2 + *bourse* PURSE.

disc, disk XVII. - F. *disque* or its source L. DISCUS.

discard reject (a card) from the hand; cast off, abandon. XVI. f. DIS- 4 + CARD[2].

discern XIV. - (O)F. *discerner* - L. *discernere* separate, distinguish, f. DIS- 1 + *cernere* separate, rel. to Gr. *krī́nein* (see CRISIS).

discharge disburden, relieve XIV; remove (a charge) XV; acquit oneself of XVI. - OF. *descharger* (mod. *décharger*); see DIS- 2, CHARGE. Hence **discharge** sb. XV.

disciple OE. *discipul* - L. *discipulus* learner, f. *discere* learn, rel. to *docēre* teach (see DOCTOR); reinforce in ME. by OF. *deciple*; later conformed to the L. sp.

discipline chastisement, penitential correction XIII; †instruction, schooling; branch of learning XIV; training in action or conduct XV; system of control over conduct XVI. - OF. - L. *disciplīna*, f. *discipulus* (see prec.). So **disciplinary** XVI. - medL. **disciplinarian** XVI.

disclaim XVI. - law AN. *desclaim-*, tonic stem of *desclamer*, f. *des-* DIS- 2 + *clamer* CLAIM. So **disclaimer** XV. See -ER[4].

disclose XIV. f. OF. *desclos-*, pres. stem of *desclore*; see DIS- 2, CLOSE. Hence **disclosure** XVI.

discolour XIV. - OF. *descolorer* or medL. *discolōrāre*; DIS- 2. So **discoloration** XVII.

discomfit defeat utterly; thwart, disconcert. XIV. ME. *disconfite*, based on pp. *disconfit* (XIII) - OF. *desconfit*, pp. of *desconfire* (mod. *déconfire*) :- Rom. **desconficere*, f. *des-* DIS- 2 + L. *conficere* put together, complete. So **discomfiture** XIV.

discomfort †discouragement, distress, desolation XIV; being uncomfortable XIX. - OF. *desconfort* (mod. *dé-*). So vb. XIV. See DIS- 2, 6.

disconcert XVII. - F. †*desconcerter* (mod. *dé-*), f. *des-* DIS- 2 + *concerter* CONCERT[2].

disconsolate XIV. - medL. *disconsōlātus*, f. DIS- 2 + *consōlātus*, pp. of *consōlārī* CONSOLE.

discontinue XV. - (O)F. *discontinuer*; DIS- 2. So **discontinuance** XIV. - AN. **discontinuous** XVII.

discord XIII (mus. XV). - OF. *des-*, *discord*, f. *des-*, *discorder* - L. *discordāre* be at variance, f. *discors*, *discord-* discordant, f. DIS- 2 + *cor*, *cord-* HEART. So **discordant** XIV.

discount XVII. - F. *descompte* (mod. *décompte*), f. *descompter* vb., whence, if not direct f. It. *(di)scontare*, **discount** vb. XVII. See DIS- 2, COUNT[3].

discountenance discourage, disfavour. XVI. DIS- 4.

discourage XV. - OF. *descourager* (mod. *dé-*); see DIS- 2, 4, COURAGE.

discourse †reasoning XIV; conversation, talk; treatment of a subject; †course XVI. - L. *discursus* running to and fro, (late) intercourse, (med.) argument, f. *discurs-*, pp. stem of *discurrere* run to and fro, (late) speak at length, f. DIS- 1 + *currere* run; assim. in form to COURSE. Hence **discourse** vb. XVI.

discover disclose to knowledge XIII; reveal, exhibit; †uncover XIV; find out XVI. - OF. *descovrir* (mod. *découvrir*) :- late L. *discooperīre*, f. DIS- 2 + *cooperīre* COVER. Hence **discovery** XVI.

discredit sb. disrepute XVI; distrust XVII; vb. disbelieve; destroy confidence in; bring into discredit XVI. DIS- 6, 3.

discreet showing good judgement. XIV. - (O)F. *discret*, *-ète* - L. *discrētus* separate, DISCRETE, which in late L. and Rom. took over its new meaning from *discrētiō* DISCRETION.

discrepant XV. - L. *discrepāns*, *-ant-*, prp. of *discrepāre* be discordant, f. DIS- 1 + *crepāre* make a noise, creak; see -ANT. So **discrepancy** XVII.

discrete distinct, separate. XIV (rare before XVI). - L. *discrētus*, pp. of *discernere* separate, DISCERN. Cf. DISCREET. So **discretion** discrimination; liberty or power of deciding; sound judgement. XIV. - OF. - L.

discriminate XVII. f. pp. stem of L. *discrīmināre*, f. *discrīmen*, *-min-*, distinction, f. *discernere* DISCERN; see -ATE[3]. So **discrimination** XVII. - late L.

discursive passing rapidly from one thing to another XVI; ratiocinative XVII. - medL. *discursīvus*, f. *discurs-*; see DISCOURSE, -IVE.

discus XVII. - L. - Gr. *dískos* :- **díkskos*, f. *dikeîn* throw.

discuss A. investigate, decide XIV; examine by argument XV; B. †dispel, disperse XIV. f. *discuss-*, pp. stem of L. *discutere* dash to pieces, disperse, dispel, in Rom. investigate; f. DIS- 1 + *quatere* shake. So **discussion** XIV. - OF. - L.

disdain sb. XIII (*dedeyn*). - OF. *desdeign*, AN. *dedeign* (mod. *dédain*), f. Rom. **disdignāre*, for L. *dēdignārī* reject as unworthy; see DIS- 2, DEIGN. So as vb. XIV.

disease †uneasiness, discomfort; morbid physical condition. XIV. - AN. *des-*, *disease*, OF. *desaise*, f. *des-* DIS- 2, 6 + *aise* EASE.

disembark XVI. - F. *désembarquer*, Sp. *desembarcar*, or It. *disimbarcare*; see DIS- 2, EMBARK.

disembogue †come out of the mouth of a river, etc., into the open sea; (of a river, etc.) discharge itself. XVI (early forms also *disemboque*, *-boke*). - Sp. *desembocar*, f. *des-* DIS- 2 + *embocar* run into a creek or strait, f. *en* IN-[1] + *boca* mouth :- L. *bucca*.

disembowel XVII. Intensive (DIS- 8) of †*embowel* (XVI) eviscerate - OF. *embouler*, alt. of *esbouler*, f. *es-* EX-[1] + *bouel* BOWEL.

disfigure XIV. - OF. *desfigurer* (mod. *dé-*); see DIS- 2, FIGURE.

disgorge eject from the throat XV; transf. and fig. XVI. - OF. *desgorger* (mod. *dé-*), f. *des-* DIS- 1, DE- 6 + *gorge* throat, GORGE.

disgrace sb. XVI. - F. *disgrâce* - It. *disgrazia*, f. *dis-* DIS- 2 + *grazia* GRACE. So as vb. XVI.

disgruntled XVII. f. DIS- 8 + †*gruntle* grunt, complain (XVI), frequent. of GRUNT + -ED[1].

disguise alter the dress of, now only to conceal identity XIV; conceal by a counterfeit appearance XVI. - OF. *desguisier* (mod. *déguiser*), f. Rom. **dis-* DE-, DIS- 2 + **guisa* GUISE. Hence as sb. XIV.

disgust XVI. - F. *desgoust* (mod. *dégoût*) or It. *disgusto*, f. *desgouster* (mod. *dégoûter*), *disgustare*, whence **disgust** vb. XVII (ppl. adj. *disgusting* XVIII); see DIS- 2, 6 and GUSTO.

dish broad shallow vessel OE.; food served ready for eating XV. OE. *disc* plate, bowl, platter, corr. to OS. *disk* (Du. *disch*) table, OHG. *tisc* plate (G. *tisch* table), ON. *diskr* (perh. - OE.) - L. *discus* DISCUS, disc, dish. Hence as vb. XIV.

dishabille XVII. - F. *déshabillé*, sb. use of pp. of *déshabiller* undress, f. *dés-* DIS- 2 + *habiller* dress. For the loss of *-é* cf. ASSIGN[2].

dishearten XVI. DIS- 3.

dishevelled †without head-dress XV; (of the hair) unconfined XVI; fig. disorderly XVII. f. late ME. †*dischevel(ee)*, -*y* - OF. *deschevelé*, f. *des-* DIS-1 + *chevel* hair; see -ED[1].

dishonest †entailing dishonour XIV; †unchaste; fraudulent, not straightforward or honest XVII. - OF. *deshoneste* (mod. *déshonnête*); see DIS- 2.

dishonour, U.S. **-or** sb. XIII. - OF. *deshonor* (mod. *déshonneur*); see DIS- 2, HONOUR. So as vb. XIV.

disincline(d), -inclination. XVII. DIS- 3, 6, 7.

disinherit XV. f. DIS- 3 + INHERIT.

disinter XVII. - F. *désenterrer*; see DIS- 3, INTER.

disinterested XVII. DIS- 7.

disjunctive XV. - L. *disjunctīvus*, f. *disjunct-*, pp. stem of *disjungere*, whence OF. *desjoindre*, *-joign-* (mod. *déjoindre*), the source of **disjoin** XV; see DIS- 1, JOIN, -IVE.

disk var. of DISC.

dislike †displease; not to like. XVI. f. DIS- 3 + LIKE[2]. Hence **dislike** sb. †displeasure; distaste, aversion. XVI.

dislocate XVII. prob. back-formation from **dislocation** (XIV; first in medical sense) - OF. or medL.; see DIS- 1, LOCATE.

dismal †sb. evil days, orig. the unpropitious days, two in each month, of the medieval calendar XIII; adj. †(of days) unlucky XIV; †(of other things) disastrous; causing dismay or gloom; depressingly dreary XVI. - AN. *dis mal* :- medL. *diēs malī* evil days. The (orig. superfluous) addition of *day* to *dismal* led to the apprehension of *dismal* as an adj.

dismantle †uncloak; divest, strip. XVII. - F. *desmanteller* (mod. *démanteler*); see DIS- 2, MANTLE.

dismay vb. XIII. - OF. **de(s)maier* :- Rom. **dismagāre* deprive of power, f. L. DIS- 2 + Gmc. **maʒ-* be able, MAY[1]. Hence sb. XIV.

dismember XIII. - OF. *desmembrer* - Rom. **desmembrāre*, f. *des-* DIS- 2 + L. *membrum* MEMBER.

dismiss XV. First in pp., repr. OF. *desmis* (mod. *démis*) :- medL. *dismissus*, for L. *dīmissus*, pp. of *dīmittere*, f. DIS- 1 + *mittere* send. So **dismission** XVI; after F. †*desmission* (mod. *dé-*); largely repl. by **dismissal** XIX.

dismount remove (a thing) from that on which it has been mounted; come down, esp. alight from a horse, etc. XVI. f. DIS- 3 + MOUNT[2].

disobey XIV. - (O)F. *désobéir* :- Rom. **desobedīre*, for late L. *inobēdīre*; see DIS- 2, OBEY. So **disobedience, -ent** XV.

disorder (arch.) put out of order XV; derange XVI. app. modification after ORDER vb. of earlier †*disordeine* (XIV) - OF. *desordener* (see DIS- 2, ORDAIN). Hence **disorder** sb. XVI; whence **disorderly** XVII.

disorganize XVIII. - F. *désorganiser*, f. *dés-* DIS- 2 + *organiser* ORGANIZE.

disparage †match unequally; bring discredit on XIV; speak of slightingly XVI. - OF. *desparagier*, f. *des-* DIS- 2 + *parage* (high) rank, prop. equality of rank :- Rom. **paraticum*, f. L. *pār* equal; see PEER, -AGE. So **disparagement** XV.

disparity XVI. - F. *disparité* - late L. *disparitās*; see DIS- 2, PARITY.

dispatch, despatch vb. XVI. - It. *dispacciare* or Sp. *despachar*, f. *dis-*, *des-* DIS- 2 + base of It. *impacciare* hinder, stop, Sp. *empachar* impede, embarrass; of uncert. orig. Hence (or f. It. *dispaccio*, Sp. *despacho*) **dis-, despatch** sb. XVI.

dispel XVII. - L. *dispellere*, f. DIS- 1 + *pellere* drive.

dispense A. deal out, distribute, administer XIV; make or put up (medicine) XVI; B. arrange administratively *with*; relax or release administratively XIV. - OF. *despenser* (mod. *dépenser* spend) - L. *dispensāre* weigh out, disburse, administer, dispose, frequent. of *dispendere*, f. DIS- 1 + *pendere* weigh. The phr. *dispense with* (medL. *dispensare cum*) has an extensive development. So **dispensation** distribution; administration, management; act of dispensing with a requirement. XIV. **dispensary** place for dispensing medicines XVII; †collection of drugs; †book containing formulae for making up medicines XVIII. - absol. use of medL. adj. *dispensārius*.

dispeople depopulate. XV. - OF. *despeupler* (mod. *dé-*), Rom. formation on L. DIS- 2 + *populus* PEOPLE.

disperse XIV. - F. *disperser*, f. *dispers* - L. *dispersus*, pp. of *dispergere*, f. DIS- 1 + *spargere* strew. Hence **dispersal** XIX; see -AL[2]. **dispersion** XIV (earliest in spec. meaning of 'Jews dispersed among Gentiles after the Babylonian Captivity' tr. Gr. DIASPORA).

displace XVI. DIS- 3.

display †unfold; expose to view XIV; exhibit, manifest XVI; show off XVII. - OF. *despleier* (mod. *déploier* DEPLOY), earlier *desplier* :- L. *displicāre* scatter, (medL.) unfold, unfurl, f. DIS- 1, 2 + *plicāre* fold (see PLY). Hence sb. XVII.

displease XIV. - *desplais-*, pres. stem of OF. *desplaire* (mod. *dé-*) - Rom. **displacēre*, for L. *displicēre*, f. DIS- 2 + *placēre* PLEASE. So **displeasure** XV.

disport †divert; refl. enjoy oneself, frolic. XIV. - AN. *desporter* (cf. F. *déporter* DEPORT), f. *des-* DIS-1 + *porter* carry. So **disport** sb. (arch.) diversion, pastime. XIV. - OF. *desport*, f. the vb. Aphetic SPORT.

dispose put in a suitable place; prepare the mind of, incline (esp. in pp.); make arrangements, ordain events XIV; with *of* †(i) order, control, (ii) put away, get rid of XVI. - (O)F. *disposer*, f. *dis-* DIS- 1 + *poser* place, set in order, settle (see POSE[1]), after L. *dispōnere*, *-pos-*. Hence **disposal** XVII. So **disposition** arrangement, management, bestowal; inclination, aptitude. XIV. - (O)F. - L. *dispositiō*, *-ōn-*.

dispraise vb. XIII. - OF. *despreisier* - Rom. **despretiāre*, for L. *dēpretiāre* DEPRECIATE; see DIS- 2.

disproof XVI. f. DIS- 6 + PROOF, after **disprove** XIV. - OF. *desprover*; see DIS- 2.

disproportion, disproportionate XVI. DIS- 6, 7 (after F. *disproportion*, *disproportionné*).

dispute debate or discourse argumentatively XIII; debate upon XIV; argue against, contest XVI. - (O)F. *disputer* - L. *disputāre* argue, debate,

f. DIS- 1 + *putāre* reckon, consider. Hence as sb. XVII. So **disputation** XIV, **disputant** XVII.

disquisition investigation; treatise or discourse in which a subject is investigated. XVII. - (O)F. - L. *disquīsītiō*, *-ōn-*, f. *disquīsīt-*, pp. stem of *disquīrere*, f. DIS- 1 + *quærere* seek.

disrobe XVI. DIS- 3 or 4.

disruption XVII. - L. *disruptiō*, *-ōn-*, f. *disrupt-*, pp. stem of *disrumpere*; see DIS- 1, RUPTURE. So **disrupt** intr. XVII; trans. XIX. f. the L. pp.

dissect XVII. f. *dissect-*, pp. stem of L. *dissecāre*; see DIS- 1, SECTION. So **dissection** XVII. - medL.

disseisin (leg.) dispossession of property. XIV. - AN. *disseisine*, OF. *dessaisine*; see DIS- 4, SEISIN. So **disseise, -ze** XIV. - AN. *disseisir*.

dissemble †feign XV; pretend not to see; disguise by feigning XVI; intr. conceal one's intentions. ME. *dissemile*, *-immil*, alt. of †*dissimule* (XIV) - (O)F. *dissimuler* - L. *dissimulāre* (see DIS- 2, SIMULATE), through †*dissimble*, and assoc. with SEMBLANCE, etc.

disseminate XVII. f. pp. stem of L. *dissēmināre*, f. DIS- 1 + *sēmen*, *sēmin-* SEED; see -ATE³. So **dissemination** XVII. - L.

dissension XIII. - (O)F. - L. *dissensiō*, *-ōn-*, f. pp. stem of *dissentīre*, whence (partly through F. *dissentir*) **dissent** withhold assent or consent XV; disagree, differ XVI; whence **dissent** sb. XVI, **dissenter** spec. dissentient from prescribed or established religious creed or practice XVII. So **dissentient** adj. and sb. XVII. See DIS- 1, SENTIENT, -SION.

dissertation †discussion; spoken or (usu.) written discourse containing a discussion at length. XVII. - L. *dissertātiō*, *-ōn-*, f. *dissertāre* discuss, debate, frequent. of *disserere* treat, examine, discourse, f. DIS- 1 + *serere* join, connect, join words in composition.

dissever separate, disjoin XIII; divide into parts XIV. - AN. *des(c)everer*, OF. *desevrer* :- late L. *dissēparāre*; see DIS- 1, SEVER.

dissident at variance XVI; sb. XVIII. - F. *dissident* or L. *dissidēns*, *-ent-*, prp. of *dissidēre* disagree, f. DIS- 1 + *sedēre* sit; see -ENT.

dissimilar XVII. f. DIS- 7 + SIMILAR, after L. *dissimilis*. So **dissimilation** XIX; after *assimilation*. **dissimilitude** XV. - L.

dissimulate dissemble XV; †pretend not to see XVI. f. pp. stem of L. *dissimulāre*; see DIS- 2, SIMULATE. So **dissimulation** XIV. - (O)F. - L.

dissipate scatter, dispel XV; squander; distract XVII. f. pp. stem of L. *dissipāre*, f. DIS- 1 + **supāre*, **sipāre* throw; see -ATE³. So **dissipation** dissolution XV; †dispersion XVI; squandering XVII; distraction of mind XVIII, (hence) frivolous diversion, (passing into) dissolute living XVIII. - (O)F. or L.

dissociate XVII. f. pp. stem of L. *dissociāre*, f. DIS- 1 + *sociāre* join together, f. *socius* companion; see -ATE³. So **dissociation** XVII.

dissoluble XVI. - OF. *dissoluble* or L. *dissolūbilis*, f. *dissolvere* DISSOLVE; see SOLUBLE. So **dissolute** relaxed, remiss XIV; †enfeebled; †unrestrained XV; †disconnected; lax in morals XVI. - L. *dissolūtus* loose, disunited, pp. of *dissolvere*. **dissolution** separation into parts XIV; †relaxation XV; breaking-up, dispersal XVI; death XVI.

dissolve loosen the parts of, spec. †melt, fuse, (now) diffuse in liquid; release from life, esp. pass.; undo (†a knot, bond, union) XIV; intr. XV. - L. *dissolvere*, f. DIS- 1 + *solvere* loosen, SOLVE.

dissonant XV. - (O)F. *dissonant* or L. *dissonāns*, *-ant-*, prp. of *dissonāre* disagree in sound, f. DIS- 1 + *sonāre* sound. So **dissonance** XV.

dissuade advise against XV; seek to divert *from* XVI. - L. *dissuādēre*, f. DIS- 2 + *suādēre* advise, urge. So **dissuasion** XV.

distaff stick to hold material to be spun. OE *distæf*, a peculiarly Eng. word; f. the base of MLG. *dise(ne)* distaff, bunch of flax (LG. *diesse*); the second el. is STAFF.

distal (anat.) situated away from the centre of the body. XIX. irreg. f. next + -AL¹.

distant separate XIV; far apart; remote XV. - (O)F. *distant* or L. *distāns*, *-ant-*, prp. of *distāre*, f. DIS- 1 + *stāre* STAND. So **distance** †discord, dissension XIII; extent of space between objects XV; remoteness XVI. - (O)F. - L. *distantia*.

distaste XVI. f. DIS- 6 + TASTE, after F. *dégoût*, It. *disgusto* DISGUST.

distemper¹ †disturb or derange the condition of; put out of humour; derange the physical or bodily condition of. XIV. - late L. *distemperāre* (whence also OF. *destremper*, mod. *dé-*), f. L. DIS- 2 + *temperāre* proportion or mingle duly, TEMPER. Hence, or f. DIS- 6 + TEMPER sb., **distemper** sb.¹ disturbance of the bodily 'humours' or 'temper', (hence) ill health, disease XVI (spec. of a catarrhal disease of dogs XVIII).

distemper² †mix with liquid, soak XIV; fig. dilute XVI; (f. the sb.) paint in distemper XIX. - OF. *destemprer* or late L. *distemperāre* soak, macerate, f. L. DIS- 1, 2 + *temperāre* mingle, qualify, TEMPER. Hence (after OF. *destrempe*, mod. *dé-*) **distemper** sb.² method of painting on plaster XVII; whiting mixed with size and water used in this XIX.

distend †stretch out or apart XIV; swell out from within XVII. - L. *distendere*; see DIS- 1, TEND². So **distension** XV. - L.

distich pair of verse lines. XVI. - L. *distichon* - Gr. *dístikhon*, sb. use of n. of *dístikhos* of two rows or verses, f. DI-² + *stikhos* STICH.

distil(l) (let) fall in minute drops; vaporize by heat and condense; also intr. XIV. - (partly through (O)F. *distiller*) L. *distillāre*, for *dēstillāre*, f. DE- 1 + *stillāre*, f. *stilla* drop. So **distillation** XIV. **distillery** †distillation XVII; place for distilling XVIII.

distinct XIV. - L. *distinctus*, pp. of *distinguere* DISTINGUISH. So **distinction** †division, class XIII; discrimination XIV; distinguishing excellence XVII. - (O)F. - L. **distinctive** XV. f. *distinct-*, pp. stem of L. *distinguere*.

distinguish divide into classes; make, or mark as, different; perceive plainly; make prominent. XVI. irreg. f. F. *distinguer* or L. *distinguere* + ISH²; cf. *extinguish*.

distort XVI. f. *distort-*, pp. stem of L. *distorquēre*, f. DIS- 1 + *torquēre* twist. So **distortion** XVI. - L.

distract draw away or in different directions.

XIV. f. *distract-*, pp. stem of L. *distrahere*, f. DIS- 1 + *trahere* draw, drag. So **distraction** XV. - L.

distrain (hist.) force to perform an obligation by the seizure of a chattel, etc. XIII; levy a distress XIV; in various casual senses 'press', 'compress', 'oppress', 'strain out' XIV. - OF. *destreign-*, pres. stem of *destreindre* :- L. *distringere* exert opposing strains on (see DIS- 1). Aphetic STRAIN.

distrait XVIII. - F., pp. of *distraire* DISTRACT. In ME. (XIV-XV) 'greatly perplexed' - OF. *destrait*.

distraught mentally distracted XIV; mentally deranged XV. alt. of (pp.) adj. *distract* by assim. to *straught*, obs. pp. of STRETCH.

distress (dial.) strain, stress; strain of adversity; (leg.) act of distraining. XIII. - OF. *destre(s)ce*, *-esse* (mod. *détresse*) :- Gallo-Rom. **districtia*, f. pp. stem of L. *distringere* DISTRAIN. So as vb. XIV. - AN. *destresser*, OF. *-ecier*, f. the sb. Aphetic STRESS.

distribute XV. f. *distribūt-*, pp. stem of L. *distribuere*, f. DIS- 1 + *tribuere* grant, assign (cf. TRIBUTE). So **distribution** XIV. - (O)F. or L.

district †territory under the jurisdiction of a feudal lord; portion of territory marked off for a purpose (various spec. uses) XVII; region, quarter XVIII. - F. *district* - medL. *districtus* (power of) exercising justice, territory involved in this, f. *district-*, pp. stem of L. *distringere* DISTRAIN.

distrust †intr. be suspicious *of* XV; trans. not trust XVI. f. DIS- 3 + TRUST. So sb. XVI (DIS- 6).

disturb †deprive *of*; agitate (lit. and fig.). XIII. - OF. *desto(u)rber* - L. *disturbāre*, f. DIS- 2 + *turbāre* disorder, disturb, f. *turba* tumult, crowd. So **disturbance** XIII. - OF.

disuse †make (a person) unaccustomed; †misuse, abuse XIV; cease to use XV. - OF. *desuser*. Hence as sb. XV. See DIS- 2 and USE.

disyllable, diss- XVI. - F. *dissyllabe* - L. *disyllabus* - Gr. *disúllabos*, f. DI-² + *sullabḗ* SYLLABLE. So **di(s)syllabic** XVII.

ditch long narrow excavation OE.; (dial.) embankment, dike XVI. OE. *dīc*, corr. to OS. *dīk* (Du. *dijk*), MHG. *tīch* (G. *teich* pond, pool), ON. *díki* ditch, DIKE; of unkn. orig. Hence **ditch** vb. surround with a ditch, dig ditches in XIV; (orig. U.S.) throw into a ditch XIX; not repr. OE. *dīcian* dig, make an embankment.

dither quake, quiver. XVII. var. of (dial.) *didder* (XIV), orig. and still north., of symbolic orig.

dithyramb Greek choric hymn in honour of Dionysus (Bacchus) XVII; inflated discourse XIX. - L. *dīthyrambus* - Gr. *dīthúrambos*, of unkn. orig. So **dithyrambic** XVII.

dittany herb of genus *Dictamnus*. XIV. Late ME. *ditane*, *diteyne* - OF. *dita(i)n* :- medL. *dictamus*, for L. *dictamnus*, *-um* - Gr. *diktamnon*, perh. f. *Diktḗ* mountain in Crete, a well-known habitat of the plant. The trisyllabic form appears XV; it depends on medL. *ditaneum*, late L. *dictamnium*.

ditto XVII. - It., Tuscan var. of *detto* said - L. *dictus*, pp. of *dīcere* say.

dittography (palaeogr.) unintentional writing of a letter, etc., twice. XIX. f. Gr. *dittós* double + -GRAPHY.

ditty song, lay XIII; †words of a song, theme XVI. ME. *dite(e)* - OF. *dité* composition, treatise :- L. *dictātum*, sb. use of n. pp. of *dictāre* express in language, compose (see DICTATE).

ditty-bag sailor's bag for small necessaries. XIX. So **ditty-box**, used by American fishermen. of unkn. orig.

diuretic XV. - (O)F. *diurétique* or L. *diūrēticus* - Gr. *diourētikós*, f. *dioureîn* urinate, f. *diá* through + *oûron* urine.

diurnal occupying a day; occurring daily XV; of the day XVII. - late L. *diurnālis*, f. *diurnus*, f. *diēs* day.

diva prima donna. XIX. - It., 'goddess' :- L. *dīva*, sb. use of fem. of *dīvus* DIVINE¹.

divagation XVI. f. L. *dīvagārī*, *-āt-*, f. DI-¹ + *vagārī* wander; see -ATION.

divan Oriental council of state; court of justice, council chamber XVI; long seat against the wall of a room XVIII; smoking-room with lounges XIX. - F. *divan* or It. *divano* - Turk. *divan* - Pers. *dīwān* (orig.) brochure, (hence) account-book, office of accounts, court, council chamber, (cushioned) bench.

divaricate stretch or spread apart. XVII. f. pp. stem of L. *dīvaricāre*, f. DI-¹ + *varicāre* stretch (the legs) asunder, f. *varicus* straddling; see -ATE³. So **divarication** XVI.

dive vb. trans. OE.; intr. XIII. OE. *dȳfan* wk. trans. dip, submerge = ON. *dýfa* :- **dūbjan*, f. Gmc. **dūb-*; OE. *dūfan* intr. did not survive, being replaced by the wk. form; belongs to the Gmc. series **daub-* **deub-* **dub-*, parallel to **daup-* **deup-* **dup-* DEEP, DIP. Hence as sb. XVII; in the U.S. sense of 'low resort for drinking, etc.' from the sense of the vb. 'dart out of sight'.

diverge XVII. - medL. *dīvergere*, f. DI-¹ + *vergere* bend, incline, VERGE². So **divergent, -ence** XVII.

divers †different, diverse; (arch.) sundry, several, many. XIII. ME. *divers(e)*, - (O)F. - L. *dīversus* contrary, separate, different, prop. pp. of *dīvertere* DIVERT. So **diverse** different; †divers, sundry. XIII. Identical in orig. with prec., in later use differentiated from it in form and pronunc. So **diversity** XIV. **diversify** XV. - OF. *diversifier* - medL. *dīversificāre*.

divert turn aside XV; distract XVI; entertain, amuse XVII. - F. *divertir* - L. *dīvertere* turn away, leave one's spouse (cf. DIVORCE), differ (cf. *dēvertere* turn aside), f. DI-¹ + *vertere* turn. So **diversion** XVII. - late L. (med.); the mil. use may be immed. - F. *diversion* or It. *diversione*.

divest XVII. refash. on L. models in DI-¹ of earlier *devest* (XVI) - OF. *devestir*, *des-* (mod. *dévêtir*) - Rom. **disvestīre*; see DIS- 2, VEST².

divide XIV. - L. *dīvidere* cleave, apportion, separate, f. DI-¹ + **videre*, f. IE. **widh-* (see WIDOW). So **dividend** portion of anything divided. XVI. - AN. *dividende* - L. *dīvidendum*, sb. use of n. gerundive of *dīvidere*. **divider** XVI. pl. dividing compasses XVIII. **division** XIV. - OF. *devisiun* (mod. *division*) - L. **divisor** (math.) XV. - F. or L.; see -OR¹.

divine¹ pert. to God or a god; god-like; heavenly XIV; of surpassing excellence XV. - OF. *devin*, fem. *-ine*, later, by assim. to L., *divin(e)* - L. *dīvīnus*, f. *dīvus* god-like, god, rel. to *deus* god :- IE. **deiwos*; see -INE¹. So **divinity** XIV.

divine² †soothsayer, seer; ecclesiastic, theologian. XIV. - OF. *devin* (:- L. *dīvīnus* soothsayer), later *divin* theologian, after medL. *dīvīnus* doctor of divinity, theologian; sb. use of prec.

divine³ make out as by supernatural insight; practice divination. XIV. ME. *devine* - (O)F. *deviner*, f. *devin* DIVINE², after L. *dīvīnāre* foretell, predict. So **divination** XIV.

divorce sb. XIV. - (O)F. - L. *dīvortium* separation, divorce, f. *dīvortere*, var. of *dīvertere* DIVERT. So as vb. XIV. - (O)F. - late L. Hence **divorcee** XIX; also in F. form *divorcé(e)*. **divorcement** XVI.

divot piece of turf. XVI. orig. Sc. *deva(i)t*, *diffat*, etc.; of unkn. orig.

divulge †publish abroad XV; reveal (something secret) XVII. - L. *dīvulgāre* make commonly or publicly known, f. DI-¹ + *vulgāre* publish, propagate, f. *vulgus* common people (cf. VULGAR). So **divulgate, -ation.** XVI.

divvy colloq. deriv. of DIVIDEND + -Y⁶. XIX.

dizzy (dial.) foolish, stupid OE.; giddy XIV. OE. *dysig* = MDu. *dosech*, *dösech*, LG. *dusig*, *dösig* giddy, OHG. *tusic* foolish, weak, f. WGmc. **dus-*, found also in OE. *dys(e)lic* foolish, LG. *dusen* be giddy, and with *l*-suffix in LG. *düsel* giddiness, MDu. *dūselen* (Du. *duizelen*) be giddy or stupid; see -Y¹.

do¹ pt. *did*, pp. *done* trans. †A. put, place (cf. DOFF, DON¹); B. perform, execute; C. cause; D. as auxiliary of tense. OE. intr. A. act (in a specified way) OE.; B. fare, get on XIII; C. (in perf. tenses) make an end XIV; D. be (well or ill) XV; E. serve the purpose, suffice XVI. OE. *dōn*, pt. *dyde*, pp. *ġedōn*, of which the pt. *dyde* is isolated amongst the Gmc. langs., the others having forms corr. to OE. pl. *dǣdon*, Angl. *dēdon* (a type which survived only into ME.), e.g. OS. *dōan*, *deda*, *dādun*, *gidōn* (Du. *doen*, *deed*, *deden*, *gedaan*), OHG. *tuon*, *teta*, *tātum*, *gitān* (G. *tun*, *tat*, *getan*).

This common WGmc. vb., the history of which remains in some points obscure, is based on a widespread IE. **dhō*, **dhē-* **dhə-*, repr. by Skr. *dádhāti* put, lay, Gr. *títhēmi* place, L. *facere* make, do, *-dō*, *-dere* in *addere* ADD, etc. (overlapping with the root (IE. **dō-*) of *dare* give), Lith. *dėti*, OSl. *děti* put, lay. Cf. DEED, DOOM.

do² see DOH.

Dobbin (typical name for) a draught- or farm-horse. XVI. var. of *Robin* (see ROBIN).

docent †adj. teaching XVII; sb. (U.S.) teacher in a college or university (after G.) XIX. - L. *docēns*, *-ent-*, prp. of *docēre* teach; see DOCTOR, -ENT.

docile teachable XV; tractable XVIII. - L. *docilis*, f. *docēre* teach; see DOCTOR, -ILE.

dock¹ coarse weed of genus *Rumex*. OE. *docce*, corr. to MDu. *docke*, of unkn. orig.

dock² solid fleshy part of a horse's tail; crupper XIV; cut end, stump XVI. perh. identical with OE. *-docca* (or *-e*) in *fingerdoccan* finger-muscles, and corr. to Fris. *dok* bunch, ball (of twine, etc.), (M)LG. *docke* bundle of straw, OHG. *tocka* (south G. *docke*) doll; the meanings point to a basic sense 'something round'. Hence as vb. cut short, curtail. XIV.

dock³ †bed or hollow in which a ship rests at low water; artificial basin for the reception of ships. XVI. - MLG., MDu. *docke* (mod. *dok*), of unkn. orig. Hence **dock** vb. XVI. **docker** dweller near docks XVIII; dock labourer XIX.

dock⁴ prisoner's enclosure in a criminal court. XVI. prob. rogues' cant and identical with the word repr. by Flemish *dok* cage, pen, hutch, of unkn. orig.

docket †summary, minute XV; abstract, memorandum, register XVI; endorsement, label XVIII. of unkn. orig., poss. f. DOCK² + -ET. Hence vb. XVII.

doctor teacher; one highly proficient in a branch of learning or holding the highest university degree; spec. doctor of medicine, (hence) medical practitioner. XIV. - OF. *doctour* - L. *doctor*, *-ōr-*, teacher, f. *doct-*, pp. stem of *docēre* teach, causative corr. to *discere* learn (:- **di-dc-sc-*).

doctrine XIV. - (O)F. - L. *doctrīna* teaching, learning, f. *doctor* (see prec.). So **doctrinal** XV. - late L. *doctrīnālis*; earlier sb. 'text-book' (XV) after OF. *doctrinal*, medL. *doctrīnāle* (sb. use of n. adj.). **doctrinaire** XIX (orig. one of a F. political party which aimed at an ideal of reconciliation of extremes).

document †instruction; †evidence XV; something written, etc. furnishing evidence XVIII. - (O)F. - L. *documentum* lesson, instance, specimen, in medL. written instrument, official paper, f. *docēre* teach; see DOCTOR and -MENT. Hence as vb. †instruct XVII; furnish with documents (as evidence) XVIII. Whence **documentation** XVIII.

dodder¹ parasitic genus of plants, *Cuscuta*. XIII. corr. to MLG. *dod(d)er*, MHG. *toter* (G. *dotter*), of unkn. orig.

dodder² (dial.) tremble, shake XVII; totter, potter XIX. var. of or parallel form to †*dadder* (XV). Hence **doddery** XX.

doddered XVII. used, after Dryden, of old oaks that have lost the top or branches; alt. form, simulating a pp., of †*doddard* (Dryden), f. †*dod* poll, lop (XIII), of unkn. orig.; see -ARD.

dodecagon (geom.) 12-sided plane figure. XVII. - Gr. *dōdekágōnon*, f. *dṓdeka* 12; see -GON. So **dodecahedron** XVI. - Gr. **dodecasyllable** XVIII.

dodge haggle, trifle XVI; avoid an encounter with; move to and fro XVII. of unkn. orig. So sb. XVI.

dodo XVII. - Pg. *doudo* simpleton, fool; applied to the bird because of its clumsy appearance.

doe female of the fallow deer OE.; female of hare or rabbit XVII. OE. *dā*, of unkn. orig.

doff XIV. ME. *dof(fe)*, contr. of *do of(fe)*, OE. *dōn of*, *of dōn* take off, remove; see DO¹, OFF.

dog sb. Late OE. *docga* (once in a gloss; also g. pl. in place-names, *doggeneford*, *doggeneberwe*), of unkn. orig.; the gen. term was *hund* HOUND, which *dog* finally displaced in this status. For the formation cf. the animal-names FROG¹, PIG, STAG, **sucga* in *hæġsucga* hedge-sparrow, **wicga* beetle in EARWIG. Hence **dog** vb. follow like a dog. XVI. **dogged** †ill-conditioned XIV, †canine XV; pertinacious XVIII; see -ED².

doge chief magistrate of the republics of Venice

and Genoa. XVI. - F. - It. (Venetian *doze*) :- L. *dux, duc-*; cf. DUKE. So **dogate** office of a doge. XVIII. - F. *dogat* - It. (Venetian) *dogato*, f. *doge*; see -ATE[1].

dogger two-masted fishing vessel XIV. - MDu. *dogger* trawler, fishing-boat (Du. *dogger* cod-fisher), of uncert. orig.

doggerel XIV. In earliest use adj. in *rym dogerel* (Ch.), presumably f. DOG (with contemptuous implication as in *dog Latin*, †*dog rime* XVII) + -EREL.

doggo (sl.) *lie doggo* lie quiet, remain hid. XIX. app. f. DOG + -O.

doggone (U.S.) confound! damn! XIX. app. development of earlier *dog on it* (etc.), of obscure orig., as a euph. substitute for *God damn it*. Cf. Sc. *dagone!* deuce take it!

dogma XVII. - L. *dogma* philosophical tenet - Gr. *dógma, dogmat-* opinion, tenet, f. *dokeîn* seem (good), think, suppose. So **dogmatic, -ical** XVII. - late L. *dogmaticus* - Gr. *dogmatikós*. **dogmatism** XVII, **-ist** XVI. - F. **dogmatize** XVII. - F. or late L.

doh, do[2] (mus.) first note of the scale in solmization. XVIII. - It. *do*.

doily †woollen stuff for summer wear XVII; small ornamental napkin or mat XVIII. f. name of *Doiley, Doyley*, a draper.

doldrums XIX. prob. orig. dial. or sl. f. *dol* DULL.

dole[1] †part, portion OE.; (arch.) share, lot XIII; portion doled out XIV. OE. *dāl* :- **dailaz*; see DEAL[1]. Hence **dole** vb. XV.

dole[2] (arch.) grief, sorrow, lamentation. XIII. ME. *dol*, with vars. *doel, de(o)l, du(i)l* - OF. *dol, doel, duel*, etc. (mod. *deuil* mourning) :- pop. L. *dolus*, f. L. *dolēre* suffer pain or grief. Hence **doleful** XIII.

dolerite mineral allied to basalt. XIX. - F. *dolérite*, f. Gr. *dolerós* deceptive; so named from the difficulty of discriminating its constituents; see -ITE.

dolichocephalic (ethnology) long-headed. XIX. f. Gr. *dolikhós* long + *kephalḗ* head + -IC.

doll †mistress XVI; child's toy-baby XVII; pretty but silly woman XIX. Pet-form of the female name *Dorothy*. Hence **dolly** in same senses XVII; also applied to contrivances having a fancied resemblance to a doll XVIII; see -Y[6].

dollar German thaler; Spanish peso or piece of eight (i.e. eight reales) XVI; standard unit of coinage in U.S.A., Canada, etc. XVIII. - early Flem., LG. *daler* (Du. *daalder*) - G. *taler* (formerly *thaler*) short for *Joachimst(h)aler*, applied to a silver coin made from metal obtained in *Joachimst(h)al* (i.e. 'Joachim's valley') in the Erzgebirge, Czechoslovakia. The forms *dolor, -er* appeared XVI, *dollor, -ar* XVII.

dollop †tuft, clump XVI; shapeless lump XIX. perh. of Scand. orig. (cf. Norw. dial. *dolp* lump).

Dolly Varden name of a character in Dickens's 'Barnaby Rudge', applied (XIX) to (1) a large hat with one side bent downward and abundantly trimmed with flowers, (2) a print frock with large flower pattern, (3) a Californian trout or char.

dolman Turk's robe open in front XVI (*dolyman*); hussar's jacket worn with sleeves hanging loose, woman's mantle with cape-like appendages XIX. In the first sense - F. *doliman*, in the second - F. *dolman* - G. - Hung. *dolmány*; ult. - Turk. *dolama(n)*.

dolmen cromlech. - F., perh. improperly f. Bret. *taol* table, *maen* stone (the Bret. form being *taolvaen*), or repr. the Corn. comp. cited as *tolmēn* 'hole of stone' in 1754.

dolomite (min.) native carbonate of lime and magnesia. XVIII. - F. *dolomite*, also *dolomie*, f. name of D. de *Dolomieu*, French geologist (1750-1801); see -ITE.

dolour, (U.S.) **dolor** †pain; grief, sorrow. XIV. - OF. *dolo(u)r*, (mod. *douleur*) :- L. *dolor, -ōr-*, rel. to *dolēre* suffer pain or grief. So **dolorous** XIV. - OF. *doleros* (mod. *douloureux*) - late L. *dolōrōsus*.

dolphin XIII. Three types of form have been current: (i) *delfyn, delphin* - L. *delphīnus* - Gr. *delphís, -īn-*; (ii) *dalphyn* - OF. *daulphin* (see DAUPHIN); (iii) *dolfyn, dolphin*, app. Eng. alts. of (ii).

dolt XVI. prob. rel. to †*dold* (XV) numb, and *dol(l)*, var. of DULL.

dom A. Pg. title of dignity; B. title prefixed to the name of Benedictines and Carthusians XVIII. In A, - Pg. *dom* :- L. *dominus* master (spec. of a household), f. *domus* house. In B, shortening of L. *dominus*.

-dom suffix denoting condition or state, as in *freedom, wisdom* state of being free, wise, passing to the sense of domain, realm, territory, as in *Christendom, kingdom*, and to that of experience, as in *martyrdom*. OE. *-dōm* = OS. *-dōm*, OHG. *-tuom* (G. *-tum*), suffixal use of OE. *dōm* DOOM.

domain estate, lands, dominions XVII; sphere of thought or action XVIII; lordship XIX. - F. *domaine*, alt-, by assoc. with L. *dominium* (see DOMINION), of OF. *demaine, demeine* DEMESNE.

dome (arch.) house, mansion XVI; †cathedral church; rounded vault, cupola XVII; vaulted roof, canopy, etc. XVIII. In the first sense - L. *domus* house; in the others - F. *dôme* - It. *domo* house, house of God, cathedral, cupola :- L. *domus*.

Domesday survey of the lands of England made in 1086 by order of William the Conqueror. XII (*domesdei*). ME. form of DOOMSDAY, popular appellation given to the book as being a final and inexorable authority.

domestic pert. to the household; pert. to one's country XVI; tame XVII; sb. †inmate XVI; household servant XVIII. - (O)F. *domestique* - L. *domesticus*, f. *domus* house, rel. to Gr. *dómos*, Skr. *dáma-*, OSl. *domŭ*, OIr. *doim* in the house. So **domesticate** XVII. f. pp. stem of medL. *domesticāre*; see -ATE[3]. **domesticity** XVIII.

domicile XV. - (O)F. - L. *domicilium*, f. *domus* house (see prec.). Hence **domiciliary** XVIII.

dominant ruling, commanding XV; (mus.) (pert. to) the fifth note of the scale of any key XIX. - (O)F. - L. *domināns, -ant-*, prp. of *dominārī* (f. *dominus*), on the pp. stem of which was formed **dominate** XVII; see DOM, -ANT, -ATE[3]. So **domination** XIV. - (O)F. - L.

domineer XVI. - Du. †*domineren* - F. *dominer* - L. *dominārī*; see prec.
dominical pert. to the Lord or the Lord's Day (Sunday). XV. - (O)F. *dominical* or late L. *dominicālis*, f. *dominicus*, f. *dominus* lord, master; see DOM, -ICAL.
Dominican pert. to the Order of Friars Preachers (Black Friars). XVII. - medL. *Dominicānus*, f. *Dominicus*, L. form of the name of *Domingo* de Guzman (St. Dominic), *c.* 1170-1221, founder of an order of preaching friars; see -AN.
dominie (now Sc.) schoolmaster, pedagogue. XVII. sp. of L. *domine*, orig. term of respectful address to clerics, voc. case of *dominus* master, lord (see DOM).
dominion lordship, sway XV; domains of a feudal lord or sovereign (hist., designation of some countries of the British Commonwealth) XVI. - OF. - medL. *dominiō*, *-ōn-*, f. *dominium*, f. *dominus* master, lord (see DOM).
domino A. cloak with a half-mask worn at masquerades, person wearing this XVIII; the mask itself XIX; B. rectangular piece used in the game (*dominoes*) having the under side black and the upper blank or marked with pips XIX. - F. *domino*, presumably a deriv. of L. *dominus* (see DOM).
don[1] put on. XIV. contr. of *do on*; DO[1] (in the sense 'put') ON adv.
don[2], **Don** Sp. title prefixed to a man's Christian name; Sp. gentleman, Spaniard; distinguished or important man; (in English universities) head, fellow, or tutor of a college. XVII. - Sp. :- L. *dominus* (see DOM).
donate XIX. Back-formation from **donation** (XV) - (O)F. - L. *dōnātiō*, noun of action f. *dōnāre*, f. *dōnum* gift. So **donative** XV. - L., n. of *dōnātīvus*. **donor** XV. - AN. *donour*, OF. *doneur* :- L. *dōnātor*, *-ōr-*. Hence **donee** XVI.
done pp. of DO[1].
donjon arch. sp. of DUNGEON.
donkey XVIII. In early use pronounced so as to rhyme with *monkey*, whence the proposed derivs. from DUN[1] and from the proper name *Duncan* (cf. *dicky*, *neddy*).
donor see DONATE.
doodle simpleton XVII; larva of tiger-beetle (also **doodle-bug**, applied in 1944 to the 'flying bomb') XIX; aimless scrawl on paper XX. In the first sense - LG. *dudel-* in *dudeltopf*, *-dopp* simple fellow; the connection of the other senses is doubtful; the last is prob. rel. to dial. vb. *doodle* fritter time away.
doom ordinance, decision, trial, judgement OE.; (final) fate XIV. OE. *dōm* = OFris., OS. *dōm*, OHG. *tuom*, ON. *dómr*, Goth. *dōms* :- Gmc. **dōmaz* lit. that which is set or put, f. **dō-* place, set, DO[1]. Hence **doom** vb. XV.
doomsday Day of Judgement. OE. *dōmes dæg*, g. of DOOM, and DAY.
door (i) OE. *duru* (fem. *u*-stem) = OS. *duru*, corr. to other Gmc. (orig. pl.) forms with *i*-stem, ODu. *dori* pl. (Du. *deur* fem. sg.), OHG. *turi* (G. *tür* fem. sg.), ON. *dyrr* fem. pl. and n., Goth. *daurōns* fem. wk. pl. (ii) OE. *dor* n. = OS. *dor*, (O)HG. *tor* gate, Goth. *daur* n. The IE. base **dhur-* **dhwĕr-* is repr. also by Skr. *dvắr-*, Gr. *thúrā*, L. *forēs*, OIr. *dorus*, OSl. *dvĭrĭ* gate, *dvorŭ* court, Lith. *dùrys* gate. The ME. descendants of OE. *duru* and *dor* coalesced.
dope (orig. U.S.) lubricating fluid; opium or other narcotic XIX. - Du. *doop* sauce, f. *doopen* dip, mix, adulterate (rel. to DIP), whence **dope** vb.
dor species of fly or beetle OE.; flying beetle XV. OE. *dora*; prob. imit. of humming noise.
Dorian pert. to Doris, a division of ancient Greece; (mus.) name of one of the ancient Gr. musical modes. XVII. f. L. *Dōrius* - Gr. *Dṓrios*, f. *Dōrís*; see -IAN. So **Doric** Dorian XVI; one of the main dialects of ancient Greek; (hence) rustic; one of the Greek orders of architecture XVII. - L. *Dōricus* - Gr. *Dōrikós*.
dormant (hist.) fixed, stationary XIV; sleeping; inactive, quiescent XVI. - (O)F. *dormant*, prp. of *dormir* : L. *dormīre* sleep, rel. to OSl. *drěmati* (Russ. *dremát'* slumber), and further to Skr. *drắti*, *drắyati* sleeps, Gr. *édrathon* I slept. So **dormer** projecting vertical window in a sloping roof (orig. dormitory window). XVI. - OF. *dormeor*. **dormitory** XV. - L. *dormītōrium*, sb. use of n. of *dormītōrius*, f. *dormīt-*, pp. stem of *dormīre* sleep. **dorter, -our** (hist.) dormitory (e.g. of a monastery). XIII. - OF. *dortour* (mod. *dortoir*) :- L. *dormītōrium*.
dormouse XV. of unkn. orig.
dormy (golf) leading by as many holes as there are holes to play. XIX. of unkn. orig.
dorsal XV. - (O)F. *dorsal* or late L. *dorsālis*, for L. *dorsuālis*, f. *dorsum* back; see -AL[1].
dory yellow fish *Zeus faber* (also *John Dory*). XIV (*darre*). - F. *dorée*, sb. use of fem. pp. of *dorer* gild :- late L. *dēaurāre*, f. DE- + *aurāre* gild, f. *aurum* gold.
dose prescribed quantity of medicine. XV. - F. - late L. *dosis* - Gr. *dósis* giving, gift, portion of medicine, f. *didónai* give. Hence **dose** vb. XVII.
doss (sl.) sb. bed; vb. sleep. XVIII (*dorse*). f. L. *dorsum* (F. *dos*) back. For the loss of *r* cf. BASS[1], DACE.
dossal ornamental cloth on or at the back of a chair, an altar, etc. XVII (*do(r)sel*). - medL. *dossāle*, n. of *dossalis*, for *dorsalis* (see DORSAL).
dossier set of documents relating to a matter. XIX. - F. *dossier* bundle of papers in a wrapper having a label on the back, f. *dos* back; see DOSS, -IER[2].
dost arch. 2nd pers. sg. pres. ind. of DO[1].
dot[1] (dial.) small lump, clot XVI; minute mark XVII. OE. *dott* (once) head of a boil, perh. in continuous colloq. use, but not recorded again till XVI in the gen. sense of 'small knob or lump', when its appearance may be due to Du. *dot* knot, prob. rel. to OHG. *tutto*, *tutta* nipple; for the prob. base **dutt-* cf. OE. *dyttan* (:- **duttjan*), dial. *dit* stop up, plug. Hence **dot** vb. XVIII.
dot[2] dowry. XIX. - (O)F. - L. *dōs*, *dōt-*, f. **dō-* give.
dote A. be silly or weak-minded XIII; B. bestow excessive fondness *upon* XV. perh. OE., corr. to MDu. *doten* be silly. Hence **dotage, dotard** XIV.
doth arch. 3rd pers. sg. pres. ind. of DO[1].
dott(e)rel species of plover; †dotard. XV. f. DOTE + -REL; the bird was presumably so named from its (alleged) stupidity.

dotty covered with dots; (sl.) of unsteady gait (cf. phr. *dot and go one*, said of one who has a wooden leg, XVIII); of feeble mind, daft XIX. f. DOT[1] + -Y[1].

double consisting of two, twofold XIII; twice as many XIV. - OF. *doble*, *duble*, later and mod. *double* :- L. *duplus* DUPLE. So **double** vb. XIII.

double entendre XVII. - F. phr. (rare) 'double understanding'; see DOUBLE, INTEND.

doublet (hist.) close-fitting body garment for men XIV; one of two things exactly alike XVI. - (O)F. *doublet*, f. *double*; see prec. and -ET.

doubloon (hist.) Sp. gold coin, orig. double of the pistole. XVII. - F. *doublon* or its source Sp. *doblón*, augm. of *doble* (= F. *double*) DOUBLE. See -OON.

doubt †fear; be in uncertainty XIII. - OF. *doter*, *duter* (mod. *douter*) :- L. *dubitāre* waver, hesitate, rel. to *dubius* DUBIOUS. The latinized sp. with *b* appears XV. So **doubt** sb. †fear; uncertainty. XIII. - OF. *dote*, *dute* (mod. *doute*), f. *douter*. Hence **doubtful, doubtless** XIV.

douche stream of water applied to the body. XVIII. - F. - It. *doccia* conduit pipe, f. *docciare* pour by drops :- Rom. **ductiare*, f. *ductus* DUCT.

dough OE. *dāg* = MLG. *dēch* (Du. *deg*), OHG. *teic* (G. *teig*), ON. *deig*, Goth. *daigs* :- Gmc. **daiȝaz*, f. IE. base **dhoigh-* **dheigh-* **dhigh-* smear, knead (so Goth. *digan*), whence also Skr. *degdhi* smears, L. *fingere* (see FICTION), Gr. *teîkhos*, *toîkhos* wall, Lith. *dýžti* thrash.

doughty †worthy; valiant, stout. Late OE. *dohtiġ*, new formation prob. after *dohte*, pt. of *dugan* be of use or worthy, repl. *dyhtiġ*, corr. to MLG., MDu. *duchtich* (Du. *duchtig*), MHG. *tühtic* (G. *tüchtig* brave, competent); f. Gmc. base **dauȝ-* **duȝ-* avail, be fit (see -Y[1]).

dour (Sc. and north.) hard, stern XIV; stubborn, sullen XV. prob. - Gael. *dúr* dull, stupid, obstinate, which may be - L. *dūrus* hard.

douse[1], **dowse** †strike XVI; strike (sail) XVII; doff; extinguish XVIII. perh. rel. to MDu., LG. *dossen*, G. dial. *dusen* beat, strike.

douse[2] †plunge in liquid; drench. XVI. prob. imit., but poss. identical with prec.

dove XII. ME. *d(o)uve*, *dofe* - ON. *dúfa* = OS. *dūba* (Du. *duif*), OHG. *tūba* (G. *taube*), Goth. *dūbō* :- Gmc. **dūbōn*.

dowager woman whose husband is dead and enjoys a title or property derived from him. XVI. - OF. *douag(i)ere*, f. *douage* dower, f. *douer* ENDOW; see -ER[2].

dowd †ugly woman XIV; shabbily or drably dressed woman XVIII. of unkn. orig. Hence **dowdy** sb. XVI; adj. XVII; denoting ugliness until XVIII.

dowel headless peg, bolt, etc. XIV. perh. - MLG. *dovel*, corr. to OHG. *tubili* (MHG. *tübel*), f. Gmc. **dub-* :- IE. **dhubh-*, whence Gr. *túphos* wedge.

dower (arch.) dowry; portion of a deceased husband's estate allowed to a widow XIV. - (O)F. *douaire* - medL. *dōtārium*, f. L. *dōs*, *dōt-* dowry, *dōtāre* endow; cf. -ARY. So **dowry** †dower; money that a wife brings her husband XIV. - AN. *dowarie* = (O)F. *douaire*.

dowlas †coarse linen, (now) strong calico. XV. f. name of *D(a)oulas*, a town in Brittany.

down[1] †hill OE.; open expanse of high ground, spec. in pl. XIII. OE. *dūn* = OS. *dūna* (Du. *duin*; cf. DUNE), a word of the LG. area; of uncert. orig.

down[2] first feathering of young birds. XIV. - ON. *dúnn*, rel. to *dýja* shake.

down[3] adv. to or in a low(er) position. OE. *dūne*, aphetic of *adūne* ADOWN. Hence **down** prep. in descending direction along. XIII. **downcast** XVII. **downfall** XIII. **downhearted** XVIII. **downright** vertically downwards XIII; thoroughly, outright XIV; adj. XVI. **downward** XII.

dowse use the divining rod. XVII (*deusing rod*). of unkn. orig.

doxology formal ascription of praise to God. XVII. - medL. *doxologia* - Gr. *doxologiā*, f. *doxológos* giving glory, f. *dóxa* glory; see -LOGY.

doyen senior member of a body. XVII. - F.; see DEAN[2].

doyl(e)y see DOILY.

doze †stupefy, muddle, perplex; sleep drowsily. XVII. perh. of Scand. orig. cf. Da. *døse* drowse, etc. Hence **doze** sb. XVIII.

dozen XIII. ME. *dozein(e)* - OF. *dozeine*, *-aine* (mod. *douzaine*); Rom. deriv. with *-ēna* (as in L. *decēna*, *centēna*, etc. group of 10, 100, etc.), f. **do(t)ze* :- **dōdece* :- L. *duodecim* 12, f. *duo* TWO + *decem* TEN.

drab[1] slattern; harlot. XVI. prob. in orig. a cant or slang word; perh. from Du. or LG., cf. Du. *drab* dregs, LG. *drabbe* thick dirty liquid, mire.

drab[2] †kind of cloth XVI; (adj.) dull yellowish-brown colour XVII. prob. alt. of †*drap* cloth (of which it was an alternative form XVII-XVIII) - (O)F. - late L. *drappus* (see DRAPE).

drabble become or make wet with muddy water. XIV. - LG. *drabbelen* walk or paddle in water or mire; see DRAB[1], -LE[3].

drachm †drachma; unit of weight, DRAM. XIV. Late ME. *dragme* - OF. *dragme* or late L. *dragma*, var. of L. *drachma* - Gr. *drakhmḗ* Attic weight and coin, prob. orig. 'handful of coins', f. base **drakh-* of *drássesthai* seize, grasp. Also **drachma** XVI.

draconic, Draconic A. pert. to a dragon XVII; B. pert. to Draco (archon at Athens 621 B.C.) or his severe code of laws XVIII. f. L. *dracō*, *-ōn-* DRAGON or the proper name *Dracō*, Gr. *Drákōn* + -IC. So **draconian, D-** XIX.

draff dregs, refuse. XIII. perh. repr. OE. **dræf* = MLG., (M)Du. *draf*, OHG. (pl.) *trebir* (G. *treber*, *träber* husks, grains).

draft sb. var. of DRAUGHT, recorded XVI and established since XVIII for certain senses. Hence **draft** vb. XVIII.

drag XV. Obscurely developed from OE. *dragan* DRAW, or - cogn. ON. *draga*. Hence, or partly - MLG. *dragge* grapnel, **drag** sb. XIV.

draggle soil (a garment), etc., by dragging it through wet or mire. XVI. f. DRAG vb. + -LE[3].

dragoman interpreter. XVI. - F. †*dragoman* (now *drogman*) - It. *dragomano* - medGr. *dragómanos* - early Arab. *targumān*, now *tarjumān*, f. *targama*, *tarjama* interpret.

dragon XIII. - (O)F. - L. *dracō*, *-ōn-* - Gr. *drákōn*, rel. to *dérkesthai*, aorist *drakeîn* see clearly.

dragonnade persecution directed by Louis

XIV against French protestants in which dragoons were quartered upon the victims. XVIII. - F., f. *dragon* DRAGOON; see -ADE.

dragoon †carbine, musket, so called from its 'breathing fire' like a dragon; cavalry soldier, orig. applied to mounted infantry armed with this weapon. XVII. - F. *dragon* DRAGON; see -OON. Hence vb. set dragoons upon, force rigorous measures upon. XVII.

drain †strain OE.; draw liquid away in small quantities. XVI. OE. *drēahnian, drēhnian*, prob. f. **drēaʒ-* :- Gmc. **drauʒ-* (see DRY). Hence as sb. XV. Hence **drainage** XVII.

drake[1] †dragon OE.; (f. LG.) kind of cannon; angler's name for species of fly XVII. OE. *draca* = MLG., MDu. *drake* (Du. *draak*), OHG. *trahho* :- WGmc. **drakan-* - L. *dracō* DRAGON.

drake[2] male of the duck. XIII. of obscure orig.; rel. to G. dial. (LG.) *drake, drache* and the second el. of OHG. *antrahho, antrehho*, the first el. of this comp. being OHG. *anut* = OE. *ened*, MLG. *anet* (Du. *eend*), ON. *ǫnd* ; widespread IE. word for 'duck', repr. by L. *anas, anat-*, Gr. *nêssa*, etc.

dram †drachm, drachma XV; $\frac{1}{8}$ fluid ounce, (hence) small draught of spirit, etc. XVI. - OF. *drame* or medL. *drama*, var. of DRACHMA.

drama XVII. - late L. *drāma* - Gr. *drâma, -at-* deed, action, play (esp. tragedy), f. *drân* do, act. So **dramatic** XVI. **dramaturge** playwright. XIX. - F. - Gr. *dramatourgós*, f. *dramat-* + **erg-* WORK. Hence **dramatist** XVII, **dramatize** XVIII.

drape A. †make into cloth XV; B. cover with drapery XIX. In A - OF. *draper*, f. *drap* cloth :- late L. *drappus*, poss. of Celt. orig.; in B back-formation from DRAPERY, suggested by F. *draper*. So **draper** XIV. - AN. *draper*, (O)F. *drapier*. **drapery** cloth, textile fabric XIV; business or shop of a draper XV; artistic arrangement of clothing; stuff with which an object is draped XVII. - (O)F. *draperie*.

drastic XVII. - Gr. *drastikós* active, effective, f. *drastós*, ppl. adj. of *drân* do; see -IC.

drat mild substitute for 'damn!'. XIX. Aphetic for *od rat* (XVIII), i.e. *od* (for GOD) and RAT[2].

draught act of drawing XII; that which is drawn or pulled XIII; †move at chess, etc.; pl. game played on a board XIV; †picture, sketch XV; design, plan XVI; (perh. short for †*withdraught*) †cesspool, privy XVI; current of air XVIII. ME. *draht*, if not in OE., - ON. **drahtr, dráttr*, later reinforced from MDu. *dragt* ; abstr. sb. f. Gmc. **draʒ-* in DRAW; see -T[1]. Cf. DRAFT.

draw pt. *drew*, pp. *drawn* general vb. for the expression of various kinds of traction OE.; delineate on a surface XIII; frame, formulate XVI; intr. make one's way OE. A Common Gmc. str. vb.: OE. *dragan*, pt. *drōh, drōgon*, pp. *dræġen, dragen* = ON. *draga* draw, pull, and (in the sense 'bear, carry', 'wear') OS. *dragan*, OHG. *tragan* (G. *tragen*), Goth. *(ga)dragan*.

drawer receptacle sliding in and out of a table frame, etc. XVI. f. DRAW + -ER[1].

drawers two-legged under-garment suspended from the waist. XVI. f. DRAW + -ER[1] with pl. *-s*.

drawing-room XVII. Shortening of *withdrawing-room* (XVI).

drawl †crawl or drag along; speak with indolent or affected slowness. XVI. prob. orig. vagrants' cant - EFris., LG., Du. *dralen* delay, linger.

dray †sled or cart without wheels XIV; low cart without sides for heavy loads XVI. ME. *dreye, draye* (AL. *dreia*), corr. formally (though evidence of continuity is wanting and the meanings are different) to OE. *dræġe* drag-net, f. base of *dragan* DRAW (cf. MLG. *drage* bier, litter, OHG. *traga*, ON. *draga* trailing load of timber).

dread vb. XII. ME. *drēden*, aphetic of OE. *adrǣdan*, late form of *ondrǣdan* = OS. *antdrādan*, OHG. *intrātan*, f. *ond-, and-*, (as in ANSWER) + a WGmc. base of obscure orig. Hence sb. XII. **dreadnought** thick coat worn in rough weather XIX; specially powerful type of battleship XX.

dream sb. XIII. ME. *drēm*, identical in form with the ME. repr. of OE. *drēam* joy, jubilation, music, minstrelsy (= OS. *drōm* mirth, noise), but corr. in sense to OFris. *drām*, OS. *drōm* (Du. *droom*), OHG. *troum* (G. *traum*), ON. *draumr*, with which it may be identical. Hence vb. XIII.

drear shortening of DREARY. XVII.

dreary †dire, grievous, sad, doleful OE.; dismal, gloomy XVII. OE. *drēoriġ* bloody, gory, grievous, sorrowful, f. *drēor* gore, flowing blood :- Gmc. **dreuzaz*, f. **dreus- *draus-*, whence also OE. *drēosan* drop, fall, OS. *driosan*, Goth. *driusan*, and OS. *drōr*, OHG. *trōr*, ON. *dreyri* gore, blood, MHG. *trūrec* (G. *traurig* sorrowful); see -Y[1].

dredge[1] instrument for dragging the bed of a river, etc. XVI. rel. in some way to early Sc. *dreg* (XV), which may be - MDu. *dregghe*; but the final cons. of the Eng. word suggests a native orig. Hence **dredge** vb.[1], **dredger**[1] XVI.

dredge[2] †sweetmeat containing spice. XVI. alt. of ME. *drag(g)e, dragie* (XIV) - OF. *dragie*, (also mod.) *dragée*, with medL. *drageia, dragētum, dragāta* obscurely rel. to L. *tragēmata*, Gr. *tragḗmata* spices, condiments. Hence **dredge** vb.[2] sprinkle with powder XVI; whence **dredger**[2] box with perforated lid for sprinkling XVII.

dreg (usu. pl.) sediment of liquor; refuse. XIV (also *dragges, dredges* XVI-XVII). prob. of Scand. orig.; cf. ON. pl. *dreggjar*. Hence **dreggy** XV.

drench draught, potion OE.; medicinal dose for an animal XVI. OE. *drenċ* :- Gmc. **draŋkiz*, f. **draŋk-*, var. of **driŋk-* DRINK; corr., with variation of declension, to OS. *dranc*, OHG. *tranc* (G. *trank*), ON. *drekka*, Goth. *dragk*. So **drench** make to drink OE. (now spec. in veterinary lang.); †submerge, drown; soak, saturate XIII; wet through XVI. OE. *drenċan* = OS. *drenkian*, OHG. *trenchen* (G. *tränken*), ON. *drekkja*, Goth. *dragkjan* :- Gmc. **draŋkjan*.

dress †make or put straight or right; prepare, treat (later, in a specific way) XIV; array, equip, attire XIV; line up (troops) XVIII. - (O)F. *dresser* :- Rom. **dīrectiāre*, f. *dīrectus* DIRECT. Hence **dress** sb. †setting right XVI; personal attire XVII.

dresser sideboard. XV. - OF. *dresseur, dreçor* (mod. *dressoir*), f. *dresser* prepare; see -ER[2].

dribble A. let flow or fall in a trickling stream XVI; B. (football) work the ball forward with repeated touches of the feet XIX. f. †*drib* (XVI), modified form of DRIP + -LE[3]. With sense B (perh. a different word) cf. Du. *dribbelen* toddle, trip.

driblet small sum or quantity. XVII. f. †*drib* vb.; see prec. and -LET; assoc. later with *dribble*.

drift driving or driven snow XIII; driving or being driven XIV; (dial.) drove XV; course, direction; meaning, tenor XVI. orig. - ON. *drift* snowdrift, drifting snow; later - (M)Du. *drift* drove, course, current, impulse, impetuous action; f. base of DRIVE; see -T[1].

drill[1] A. bore a hole in XVII; B. train in military evolutions XVI. - MDu. *drillen* bore, turn in a circle, brandish = MLG. *drillen* roll, turn, whence (M)HG. *drillen* turn, bore, drill soldiers; ult. orig. unkn. Hence **drill** sb. A. boring instrument; B. military evolutions. XVII.

drill[2] W. African baboon. XVII. prob. native name. Cf. MANDRILL.

drill[3] small furrow; machine for sowing seed in this. XVIII. perh. a use of †*drill* small stream, rivulet, of unkn. orig.

drill[4] coarse twilled fabric. XVIII. Shortening of *drilling* (XVII), alt. of G. *drillich*, earlier †*drilich* - L. *trilix*, *trilīc-* woven in threefold, f. *tri-* THREE + *līcium* thread.

drink vb. OE. *drincan* = OS. *drinkan*, OHG. *trinkan* (G. *trinken*), ON. *drekka*, Goth. *drigkan* :- Gmc. str. vb. **dreŋkan*, with no ulterior cognates. So sb. OE.

drip let fall in drops XV; intr. XVII. - MDa. *drippe* (Da. *dryppe*), f. Gmc. **drupp-* (see DROP). Hence **drip** sb., **dripping** XV.

drive force to move before one; move or advance rapidly; carry on vigorously. OE. *drīfan* = OS. *drīban* (Du. *drijven*), OHG. *trīban* (G. *treiben*), ON. *drífa*, Goth. *dreiban* :- Gmc. str. vb. **drīƀan*, with no certain cogns. outside Gmc. Hence **drive** sb. act of driving XVII; carriage road XIX.

drivel dribble, slaver; talk foolishly. XIV. ME. *drevele*, *dryuele*, repr. OE. *dreflian* (in prp. glossing medL. *reumaticus* rheumy); perh. rel. to DRAFF; see -LE[3].

drizzle vb. and sb. XVI. prob. f. ME. *drēse*, OE. *drēosan* fall (see DREARY); see -LE[3].

drogue contrivance attached to a harpoon line to check the progress of a whale XVIII; canvas bag towed at a boat's stern to prevent it from broaching to XIX; in aeronautics, canvas cone used as an anchor, etc. XX. of unkn. orig.

droll XVII. - F. *drôle*, earlier †*drolle* (uncertainly rel. to MDu. *drolle* little chap). So **droll** sb. waggish fellow; †farce, puppet-show; †jesting, burlesque. XVII. perh. - MDu. **droll** vb. make fun (of). XVII. - F. †*drôler*. **drollery** †puppet show, comic picture XVI; waggery XVII. - F. *drôlerie*.

-drome repr. Gr. *drómos* running, course, race, as in HIPPODROME; rel. to *dramein* run, Skr. *drámati*.

dromedary light fleet one-humped camel. XIV. - AN. **dromedarie*, OF. *dromedaire* (mod. *dromadaire*), or late L. *dromedārius*, for **dromadārius*, f. *dromas*, *dromad-* dromedary (- Gr. *dromás*, *-ad-* runner; cf. prec.); see -ARY.

drone male of the honey-bee. OE. *drān*, *drǣn*; corr. to OS. *drān*, *dreno*, MLG. *drāne*, *drōne*, (with *e*-grade) OHG. *treno* (MHG. *tren(e)*, G. dial. *träne*), prob. f. **dran- *dren *drun-* boom (cf. MDu. *drōnen*, Du. *dreunen*, LG. *drönen*, Icel. *drynja* roar), with which Gr. *anthrḗnē* wild bee, *tenthrḗnē* kind of wasp, have been connected. The Eng. form *drone* (XV; cf. ME., mod. dial. *drane*) is perh. - (M)LG. *drōne*. Cf. **drone** hum, buzz (sb. and vb.). XVI.

droop XIII. ME. *dr(o)upe* - ON. *drúpa* hover, hang the head for sorrow, rel. to next.

drop small quantity of liquid. OE. *dropa* = OS. *dropo*, ON. *dropi* :- Gmc. **dropan-*; beside OE. **droppa* (whence the present form) = OHG. *tropfo* (G. *tropfen*) :- Gmc. **droppan-*; f. **drup-*, weak grade of the base **dreup-* of OE. *drēopan* fall in drops (= OS. *driopan*, OHG. *triofan*, ON. *drjúpa*). So **drop** vb. fall in drops OE.; let fall XIV. OE. *drop(p)ian*.

dropsy disease marked by accumulation of watery fluid. XIII. Aphetic of *idrop(e)sie* - OF. *idropesie* - medL. *(h)ydrōpisia*, for L. *hydrōpisis*, f. Gr. *húdrōps* dropsy, f. *húdōr*, *hudr-* WATER.

dross scum thrown off from metals in smelting OE.; dreggy matter, refuse XIV. OE. *drōs* = MDu. *droes(e)* dregs; cf. OE. *drōsna* (gen. pl.), MLG. *drōsem*, (M)Du. *droesen(e)* (Du. *droesem*), OHG. *truosana* (G. *drusen*) dregs, lees.

drought Late OE. *drūgaþ*, f. **drūȝ-*, base of *drȳġe* DRY; cf. (M)LG. *drogede*, (M)Du. *droogte*, f. *droog* dry; see -T[2].

drove herd or flock of beasts, crowd. OE. *drāf*, f. gradation-var. **draiƀ-* of base of *drīfan* DRIVE. Hence **drover** driver of cattle. XV (*dravere*); see -ER[1].

drown XIII. ME. (orig. north.) *dr(o)un(e)*, pointing to an OE. **drūnian*, rel. to ON. *drukna* be drowned, f. Gmc. **druŋk-*, gradation-var. of **dreŋk-* DRINK.

drowsy XVI. prob. based on the stem of OE. *drūsian* be languid or sluggish, f. **drūs-*, var. of base *drēosan* fall (cf. DREARY). See -Y[1]. Hence, by back-formation, **drowse** be inactive, or heavy or dull with sleep. XVI.

drub beat as with a stick; in early use esp. to bastinado. XVII. - Arab. *ḍarb* beating, bastinado - *ḍaraba* beat.

drudge work slavishly. XVI. poss. a continuation with extended meaning of ME. *drugge* (XIII–XIV) drag or pull heavily. So **drudge** sb. servile worker. XV. **drudgery** XVI.

drug sb. XIV. ME. pl. *drogges*, *drouges* - (O)F. *drogue(s)*, of unkn. orig. Hence **drug** vb. mix with a drug XVII; administer drugs to XVIII. So **druggist** XVII. - F. *droguiste*.

drugget kind of woollen stuff. XVI. - F. *droguet*, of unkn. orig.

Druid one of an order of priests in ancient Britain and Gaul. XVI. - F. *druide* or its source L. (pl.) *druidæ*, *druides*, Gr. *druīdai* - Gaul. *druides*, of uncert. orig. Hence **druidic**, **-ical** XVII.

drum percussive musical instrument; drummer XVI (*drom(me)*); tympanum of the ear XVII; drum-shaped object XVIII. perh. shortening of †*drom(b)slade*, †*drombyllsclad* (XVI), alt. - LG. *trommelslag* drum-beat, f. *trommel* drum. Hence **drummer** XVI.

drunk inebriated XIV; as sb. XIX. Clipped form of DRUNKEN. So **drunkard** XV. prob. - MLG. *drun-*

kert, f. *drunken*; cf. MDu. *dronker*, Du. *dronkaard*. **drunken** intoxicated, drunk. OE. *druncen*, pp. of DRINK = OS. *drunkan*, OHG. *trunkan*, ON. *trukkinn*, Goth. **drugkans*, all of which have the same active meaning.

drupe (bot.) stone-fruit. XVIII. - L. *drūpa*, *druppa* over-ripe olive - Gr. *drúppā* olive.

druse crystals lining a rock-cavity. XIX. - F. - G. *druse* weathered ore = MLG. *drūse*, *drōse*, Du. *droes*.

dry adj. OE. *drȳġe* :- **drūʒiz*, rel. to (M)LG. *dröge*, *dreuge*, MDu. *drōghe* (Du. *droog*) :- **drauʒiz*, f. Gmc. **drauʒ-* **dreuʒ-* **drûʒ-*; cf. DROUGHT. Hence **dry** vb. OE. *drȳġan*.

dryad wood nymph. XIV. - (O)F. *dryade* - L. *Dryades*, pl. of *Dryas* - Gr. *Druádes*, sg. *Druás*, f. *drûs* TREE; see -AD.

dual XVII. - L. *duālis*, f. *duo* TWO; see -AL[1]. Hence **dualism** XVIII. So **duality** XIV. - late L.

dub invest with a dignity (spec. that of knighthood) XI; dress, trim XIII; spec. in tanning; smear with grease XVII. Late OE. **dubbian*, in phr. *dubbade tō rīdere*, 'dubbed to knight', knighted, modelled on AN. *aduber a chevaler*. - AN. *duber*, aphetic of *aduber*, OF. *adober* (mod. *adouber*) equip with armour, repair, mend; of Gmc. orig. Hence **dubbin, -ing** preparation of grease for softening and waterproofing leather. XVIII; see -ING[1].

dubious XVI. - L. *dubiōsus*, f. *dubium* doubt, sb. use of n. of *dubius* doubtful, obscurely f. *duo* TWO, and meaning 'hesitating between two alternatives'; cf. DOUBT. So **dubiety** XVIII. - late L. *dubietās*.

ducal pert. to a duke. XVI. - F., f. *duc* DUKE; see -AL[1].

ducat Italian coin. XIV. - It. *ducato* or its source medL. *ducātus* DUCHY.

duchess XIV. - (O)F. *duchesse* - medL. *ducissa*, f. L. *dux*, *duc-*; see DUKE and -ESS[1].

duchy XIV. - (i) OF. *duché*, later form of *duchée* fem. :- Rom. **ducitās*, *-tāt-*, f. L. *dux*, *duc-* (see DUKE and -ITY); and (ii) (O)F. *duché* m. :- medL. *ducātus* (see -ATE[1]).

duck[1] swimming bird of the family Anatidae. OE. *dûce*, f. base of *dūcan* dive, DUCK[2]. The ME. vars. *duk(ke)*, *dōke*, *douke*, point to orig. variation in the quantity of the stem-vowel.

duck[2] plunge into liquid, trans. and intr. XIV; stoop quickly XVI. ME. *douke*, *dūke*, repr. OE. **dūcan* = MLG., MDu. *dūken* (Du. *duiken*), OHG. *tūhhan* (G. *tauchen*), corr. to forms with a short vowel in MHG. *tücken* stoop quickly, G. *ducken* (with LG. initial cons.). The short vowel is evidenced XVI.

duck[3] strong untwilled fabric XVII; pl. trousers or a suit of this XIX. - (M)Du. *doek* linen = OS. *dōk*, OHG. *tuoh* (G. *tuch*), of unkn. orig.

duct †course, direction; †stroke drawn; tube or canal in an animal or vegetable body XVII; conduit XVIII. - L. *ductus* leading, conduct, in medL. aqueduct, f. *duct-*, pp. stem of *dūcere* lead (see TEAM).

ductile malleable; flexible, pliable. XIV. - (O)F. - L. *ductilis*, f. *duct-*; see prec. and -ILE.

dud[1] †coarse cloak XIV; pl. (sl.) clothes; (dial.) rags, tatters XVI. of unkn. orig.

dud[2] (dial.) delicate, soft, or contemptible person; worthless object XIX. perh. transf. use of prec.

dude fastidious or exquisite 'swell'. XIX. orig. U.S. sl.; prob. - G. dial. *dude* fool.

dudeen short clay tobacco-pipe. XIX. - Ir. *dúidín*, dim. of *dúd* pipe.

dudgeon feeling of resentful anger. XVI. freq. in phr. *in dudgeon*; of unkn. orig.

due owing XIII; proper, suitable XIV; that is to be ascribed *to* XVII. - OF. *deü* (mod. *dû*, fem. *due*) :- Rom. **dēbūtus*, for L. *dēbitus*, pp. of *dēbēre* (F. *devoir*) owe. Also adv. †duly; directly, straight XVI. So **due** sb. XV. - OF. (see above), sb. use of pp. of *devoir*. Hence **duly** adv. XIV.

duel single combat. XV. - It. *duello* or L. *duellum*, arch. form of *bellum* war, used in medL. for the official single combat. Hence **duellist** XVI.

duenna chief lady-in-waiting; elderly woman acting as family governess XVII; chaperon XVIII. - Sp. *dueña*, formerly *duenna* :- L. *domina* lady, mistress (cf. DAME).

duet XVIII. - G. *duett* or It. *duetto*, dim. of *duo* DUO; see -ET.

duff (dial.) dough; flour-pudding boiled in a bag. XIX. north. var. of DOUGH.

duffer (colloq.) incapable or inefficient person; (sl.) counterfeit article; (Austral. sl.) unproductive mine. XIX. poss. alt. of Sc. *doofart*, *dowfart* stupid or dull person, f. *dowf* (*dolf* XVI) dull, spiritless, perh. - ON. *daufr* DEAF.

duffle, duffel coarse woollen cloth with a thick nap XVII (*duffield*; earlier in N. Amer. use); (U.S.) articles of dress for camping, etc. XIX. f. *Duffel*, name of a town in Brabant.

dug pap, teat. XVI. of unkn. orig.

dugong large aquatic herbivorous animal XVIII. ult. - Malay *duyong* (recorded 1751 as *dugung*).

dug-out (U.S.) canoe made by hollowing out a tree-trunk; dwelling made by an excavation in the ground XIX; roofed shelter in trench warfare XX. sb. use of pp. of DIG *out*.

duke sovereign prince, ruler of a duchy XII; †leader, captain, ruler XIII; hereditary title of nobility XIV. - (O)F. *duc* - L. *dux*, *duc-* leader, rel. to *dūcere* lead (see TEAM).

dulcet sweet. XIV. Early form also †*doucet* - (O)F. *doucet* (dim. of *doux*, fem. *douce*), refash. after L. *dulcis*; see -ET.

dulcimer musical string instrument. XV. orig. *doussemer*, *dowcemere* - OF. *doulcemer*, *-mele*, supposed to repr. L. **dulce melos* sweet song.

dull not sharp of wit XIII; not brisk XIV; not clear or bright; tedious XV. - MLG., MDu. *dul*, corr. to OE. *dol* stupid (:- **dulaz*), OS. (Du.) *dol*, OHG *tol* (G. *toll*). Hence **dull** vb. XIV. **dullard** XV. prob. - MDu. *dull-*, *dollaert*.

dulse edible seaweed. XVII. - Ir., Gael. *duileasg*.

dumb destitute of speech, mute. OE. *dumb* = OS. *dumb* (Du. *dom*) stupid OHG. *tump* stupid, deaf (G. *dumm* stupid), ON. *dumbr*, Goth. *dumbs* mute; of unkn. orig.

dumb-bell (i) hist. apparatus like that for swinging a church bell, but without the bell, used for exercise or ringing practice; (ii) pl. pair of instruments held in the hands and swung for exercise. XVIII. f. prec.

dumbfound XVII. prob. f. DUMB + *-found* of CONFOUND.

dum-dum soft-nosed bullet. XIX. f. *Dum Dum*, name of a military station and arsenal near Calcutta, India.

dummy dumb person XVI; imaginary player at whist, etc. XVIII; dolt XVIII; counterfeit or substituted article XIX. orig. Sc. *dummie*, with var. *dumbie*, f. DUMB + -Y[6].

dump[1] fit of melancholy or depression, freq. and now only pl.; †mournful tune. XVI. prob. of LG. or Du. orig. and a fig. use of MDu. *domp* exhalation, haze, mist, rel. to DAMP.

dump[2] †A. throw down or fall with sudden force XIV; B. throw down in a mass (orig. U.S.) XIX. In north. ME. perh. of Scand. orig. (cf. Da. *dumpe*, Norw. *dumpa* fall suddenly or with a rush, and Sw. *dimpa*, pt. *damp*, pp. *dumpit*); but an independent imit. orig. is poss. Hence sb. matter dumped, place of dumping. XIX.

dumpling XVI. Much earlier than the simplex *dump*, which is applied to various short thick objects (late XVIII) and is app. f. **dumpy** adj. short and stout (mid-XVIII); see -LING[1].

dun[1] dull or dingy brown. OE. *dun(n)* = OS. *dun*, prob. rel. to OS. *dosan*, OHG. *tusin* (cf. DUSK).

dun[2] importunate creditor, agent employed to collect debts. XVII. poss. abbrev. of †*dunkirk* (XVII) privateer, orig. ship from *Dunkirk*, town on the French coast. Hence vb. XVII.

dunce †disciple of Duns Scotus; dull pedant; dullard, blockhead XVI. orig. *Duns*, name of John *Duns* Scotus (d. 1308), scholastic theologian, whose disciples formed a predominant scholastic sect at the universities until they were attacked by the humanists and reformers; occurring first in phr. *Duns men*, *Dunces disciples*.

dunderhead XVII. perh. rel. to dial. *dunner* resounding noise.

dune sandhill on the sea-coast. XVIII. - (O)F. - MDu. *dūne* (Du. *duin*) = OE. *dūn* DOWN[1].

dung OE. *dung* = MDu. *dung(e)*, OHG. *tunga* manuring (G. *dung*, also *dünger* manure); cf. (with mutated vowel) Sw. *dynga* muck, dung, Da. *dynge*, Icel. *dyngja*; of unkn. orig. Hence vb. XIV.

dungaree coarse Indian calico XVII; (pl.) trousers of this XIX. - Hindi *dungrī*.

dungeon castle keep; strong cell. XIV. - (O)F. *donjon* :- Gallo-Rom. **domniō*, *-ōn-*, 'lord's tower', or 'mistress tower', f. L. *dominus* master, lord.

dunlin red-backed sand-piper. XVI. prob. for **dunling*, f. DUN[1] + -LING[1].

dunnage light material, brushwood, etc. stowed among a cargo. XIV (in AL. form *dennagium*), XV (*donage*), XVII (*dynnage*). of unkn. orig.

duo (mus.) duet. XVI. (F. *duo*) - It. - L. *duo* TWO.

duodecimal pert. to 12th parts; based on the number 12. XVIII. f. L. *duodecimus* twelfth, *duodecim* twelve, f. *duo* TWO + *decem* TEN; cf. DECIMAL. So **duodecimo** size of a book in which a page is $\frac{1}{12}$ of a sheet. XVII.

duodenum XIV. - medL. (short for *intestinum duodenum digitorum* 'of twelve digits'; so named from its length), f. *duodēnī*, distributive of *duodecim* twelve (see prec.).

duologue dramatic piece for two actors. XIX. irreg. f. L. *duo* or Gr. *dúo* TWO, after *monologue*.

dupe victim of deception. XVII. - F. *dupe*, earlier †*duppe*, said in a text of XV to be a cant term; joc. application of (dial.) *dupe* hoopoe (of obscure orig.), from the bird's stupid appearance. Hence vb. XVIII; after F. *duper*.

duple XVI. - L. *duplus*, f. *duo* TWO + **pl-* -FOLD. So **duplex** XIX. - L., f. *duo* + *plic-* FOLD[2].

duplicate adj. XV; sb. XVI. - L. *duplicātus* pp. of *duplicāre*, f. *duplus* (see prec., -ATE[2]). So vb. XV. **duplication** XV. - F. or L.

duplicity quality of being double-faced. XV. - (O)F. *duplicité* or late L. *duplicitās*, f. *duplic-* DUPLEX; see -ITY.

durable XIV. - (O)F. - L. *dūrābilis*, f. *dūrāre* last, ENDURE; see -ABLE.

duralumin aluminium alloy. XX. P.; - G., perh. f. *Düren* (in the Rhineland) + *alumin(i)um* ALUMINIUM.

dura mater outermost envelope of brain and spinal cord. XV. - medL., lit. 'hard mother', tr. Arab. *al-'umm al-jalīda* or *al-jāfiya* 'the hard mother'; so called because it was thought to be the source of every other membrane in the body; cf. PIA MATER. Hence **dural** XIX.

durance †duration, lastingness XV; forced confinement or restraint, now esp. in phr. *durance vile*; †stout cloth XVI. - OF., f. *durer* last :- L. *dūrāre*; see next and -ANCE.

duration continuance. XIV. - OF. - medL. *dūrātiō*, *-ōn-*, f. *dūrāre* harden, endure, f. *dūrus* hard; see -ATION.

duress(e) †hardness, harshness XIV; forcible restraint, imprisonment; constraint XV. - OF. *duresse* :- L. *dūritia*, f. *dūrus* hard; see -ESS[2].

during XIV (in Sc. †*durand*, *-ant*). - (O)F. *durant* :- Rom. **dūrante*, abl. of L. *dūrāns*, prp. of *dūrāre* last, continue (cf. DURATION and see -ING[2]).

durmast variety of oak. XVIII. perh. orig. an error for *dunmast*, i.e. DUN[1] (dark-coloured) + MAST[2].

durn see DARN[2].

durst see DARE.

dusk adj. dark-coloured (OE.); sb. darker stage of twilight XVII; vb. grow dark (OE.). The form *dusk* (XIV) is difficult to account for (cf., however, for the vowel OE. *ġeðuxod*, *ġeðuhsod* darkened); it was preceded by ME. *dosk* sb., *doskin* vb. XIII, which are characteristically western forms and repr. OE. *dox* dark, swarthy (:- **duskaz* :- IE. **dhuskos*, whence L. *fuscus* dark, dusky), and its deriv. *doxian* become dark in colour; rel. to OS. *dosan*, OHG. *tusin* darkish (of colour), dull (cf. DUN[1]).

dust sb. OE. *dūst* = MDu. *donst*, *dūst* (LG. *dust*, Du. *duist* meal-dust, bran), ON. *dust*. The primary notion seems to be 'that which rises in a cloud'; cf. OHG. *tun(i)st* wind, breeze, G. *dunst* vapour. Hence **dust** vb. †rise as dust

XIII; †reduce to dust XV; soil with dust; free from dust XVI (whence **duster** XVI). **dusty** OE. *dūstiġ*.

dutch (sl.) wife. XIX. Short for DUCHESS.

Dutch †German XIV; pert. to the people of Holland XVI. - MDu. *dutsch* Dutch, German (Du. *duitsch* German) = OE *þēodisċ* Gentile, also sb. a language, OS. *thiudisc* :- Gmc. **þeudiskaz*, f. **þeudā* (OE. *þēod* people); see -ISH[1]. In Germany the adj. was orig. used to distinguish 'the vulgar tongue' from Latin, hence to denote German vernaculars and consequently the speakers of any of these.

duty conduct due to a superior XIII; obligation, function; †due charge or fee XIV; payment enforced or levied XV. - AN. *deweté*, *dueté*, f. *du(e)* DUE; see -TY[2]. Hence **duteous, dutiful** XVI, **dutiable** XVIII.

dwarf OE. *dweorg*, *dweorh* = MDu. *dwerch* (Du. *dwerg*), OHG. *twerg* (G. *zwerg*), ON. *dvergr* :- Gmc. **dwerʒaz*. Hence vb. render dwarfish. XVII. **dwarfish** XVI.

dwell †lead astray OE.; †tarry, delay; continue in a place or state XII; have one's abode XIII; spend time *on* XVI. OE. *dwellan*, pt. *dwealde* lead astray, corr. to OS. *bidwellian* hinder, MDu. *dwellen* stun, perplex, OHG. *twellen* delay, harass, ON. *dvelja* trans. delay, intr. and refl. tarry, stay; f. Gmc. **dwel-* **dwal-* **dwul-*. The sense 'abide, stay' was adopted from ON.

dwindle XVI. f. (dial.) *dwine*, OE. *dwīnan* waste away = (M)LG., MDu. *dwīnen*, ON. *dvína*; see -LE[3].

dyad number two. XVII. - late L. *dyas*, *dyad-* - Gr. *duás*, *duad-*, f. *dúo* TWO; see -AD.

dye vb. OE. *dēagian*, of unkn. orig. Not recorded again till XIV, though the agent-nouns **dyer, dyester** are recorded from XIII. So **dye** sb. OE. *dēag*, *dēah*, rare ME. *dēh*; the present word is a new formation on the vb. (XVI). The words are peculiarly Eng.

dyke see DIKE.

dynamic pert. to force. XIX. - F. *dynamique* - Gr. *dunamikós*, f. *dúnamis* strength (rel. to *dúnasthai* be able); see -IC. So **dynamical** XIX, **dynamics** XVIII.

dynamite XIX. Named by Alfred Nobel; f. Gr. *dúnamis* force (see prec.) + -ITE.

dynamo XIX. short for *dynamo-(electric-) machine*, f. Gr. *dúnamis* force (see DYNAMIC); for the comb. form see -O-.

dynasty XV. - F. *dynastie* or late L. *dynastīa* - Gr. *dunasteíā* power, domination, f. *dunastḗs* (L. *dynastēs*, whence **dynast** XVII), f. *dúnasthai* be able or powerful.

dyne unit of force in the centimetre-gramme-second system. XIX. - F. *dyne*, f. Gr. *dúnamis* force.

dys- prefix in L. adoptions repr. Gr. *dus-* = Skr. *dus-*, Gmc. **tus-* (OE. *tō-*, OHG. *zur-* (G. *zer-*), ON. *tor-*); denoting the reverse of easy, favourable, or fortunate, used in direct derivs. from Gr. and in new (chiefly scientific) formations.

dysentery inflammation of the large intestine. XIV. - OF. *dissenterie* or L. *dysenteria* - Gr. *dusenteríā*, f. *dusénteros*, f. DYS- + *éntera* bowels; see -Y[3].

dyslogistic having an unfavourable meaning. XIX. f. DYS-, after EULOGISTIC.

dyspepsia XVIII. - L. - Gr. *duspepsíā*, f. *dúspeptos* difficult of digestion, f. DYS- + *peptós* cooked, digested; see -Y[3].

E

e- see EX-[1].

each OE. *ǣlċ* = OFris., (M)LG. *el(li)k*, MDu. *el(li)c*, Du. *elk*, f. Gmc. **ʒalīkaz* (see ALIKE). For the disappearance of *l* cf. WHICH, SUCH, EVERY.

eager †ardent, fierce XIII; keenly desirous or impatient; †pungent, acid (cf. VINEGAR) XIV. - AN. *egre*, (O)F. *aigre* :- Rom. **acrum*, for L. *ācrem*, nom. *ācer* pungent, swift, strenuous, f. IE. **ăk-* be sharp or pointed (cf. ACID).

eagle XIV. - AN. *egle*, (O)F. *aigle*, replacing *†aille*, refash. after Pr. *aigla*, etc. :- L. *aquila*, perh. rel. to *aquilus* dark-brown. So **eaglet** young eagle. XVI. see -ET; after F. *aiglette*, *†eglette*.

eagre tidal bore. XVII. of uncert. orig.

-ean suffix formed by adding -AN to *e* or *ē* of L. *-eus*, *-ēus* (varying with *-æus*), corr. to Gr. *-eos*, *-eios* (*-aios*); formerly often with parallel forms in *-æan*, *-(e)ian*; it has in some words an immed. F. original in *-éen*.

ear[1] organ of hearing. OE. *ēare* = OS., OHG. *ōra* (Du. *oor*, G. *ohr*), ON. *eyra*, Goth. *ausō* :- Gmc. **auzan-*, f. **aus-* :- IE. **ous-*, whence also L. *auris*, Gr. *ôs*, *oûs* (:- **oúsos*), Lith. *ausis*, OSl. *ucho*. Hence **earring.** OE. *ēarhring*.

ear[2] spike of corn. OE. *ēar* (Nhb. *æhher*) = OS. *ahar* (Du. *aar*), OHG. *ahir*, *ehir* (G. *ähre*), ON. *ax*, Goth. *ahs* :- Gmc. **aχuz*, **aχiz*, rel. to L. *acus*, *acer-* husk, chaff, f. IE. **ak-* be sharp or pointed (cf. EDGE).

earing (naut.) small rope fastening the upper corner of a sail to the yard. XVII. perh. f. EAR[1] + -ING[1] or RING[1].

earl †warrior, nobleman, prince, OE.; equiv. of *count* XII. OE. *eorl* = OS., OHG. *erl*, ON. *jarl* (runic *erilaR*), of unkn. orig. Hence **earldom** XII.

early OE. (late Nhb.) *ǣrlīċe*, beside *ārlīċe*, f. *ǣr* ERE + *-līċe* -LY[2], after ON. *árliga*. As adj. XIII (after ON. *árligr*).

earn OE. *earnian* = MLG. *arnen*, OHG. *arnēn*, *-ōn* reap :- WGmc. **aznōjan*, *-ǣjan*, rel. to OE. *esne* labourer, man, OHG. *esni*, Goth. *asneis*, and further to OHG. *aran*, Goth. *asans* harvest.

earnest[1] †ardour in battle; seriousness. OE. *eornust*, *-ost* = MLG. *ernest*, OHG. *ernust* (G. *ernst*); cf. ON. *ern* brisk, vigorous, Goth. *arniba* safely; of unkn. orig. So **earnest** adj. OE. *eornost(e)* = MLG. *ernest*. **earnestly** OE. *eornostlīċe*.

earnest[2] money paid as an instalment. XIII. Earliest forms *(e)ernes*; prob. alt., with assim. to -NESS, of synon. and contemp. *erles* - OF. **erles* :- Rom. **arrulas*, dim. (pl.) of L. *arra* pledge; assim. to prec. appears XV.

earth OE. *eorðe* = OS. *ertha* (Du. *aarde*), OHG. *erda* (G. *erde*), ON. *jǫrð*, Goth. *airþa* :- Gmc. **erþō*, f. base **er-*, appearing also in OHG. *ero* earth, ON. *jǫrfi* gravel, Gr. *éraze* on the ground, W. *erw* field. Hence **earth** vb. †bury XIV; cover *up* with earth XVII. **earthen** XIII (see -EN[3]), whence **earthenware** XVII. **earthly.** OE. *eorðlić*. **earthquake** XIV. **earthy** XVI; see -Y[1].

earwig insect so called because it is supposed to penetrate the ear. OE. *ēarwicga*, f. *ēare* EAR[1] + *wicga* earwig, prob. rel. to WIGGLE. For the form of *wicga* cf. DOG.

ease †opportunity, means; comfort, convenience. XIII. - AN. *ese*, OF. *eise*, (also mod.) *aise* †elbow-room; †favourable occasion, convenience :- Rom. **adjaces* for (sb. use of) *adjacēns* ADJACENT. So **ease** vb. relieve, comfort. XIV.

easel standing frame to support a picture. XVII. - Du. *ezel* ASS.

easement redress XIV; convenience; accommodation in or about a house; privilège of using something not one's own XV. - OF. *aisement*, f. *aisier* EASE vb.; see -MENT.

east adv. OE.; sb. (OE. *ēaste* fem.); adj. (in OE. only compar. *ēast(er)ra*, superl. *ēast(e)mest*). OE. *ēast-* in comps. (e.g. *ēastende* eastern region, *Ēastangle* East-Anglians) = OFris. *āst*, OS., OHG. *ōst* (Du. *oost*, G. *ost*), repr. Gmc. **austa-* (with suffix **-nō-* in OE. *ēastan*, OS., OHG. *ōstana*, ON. *austan* from the east); as adv. prob. shortening of **ēaster* = OS., OHG. *ōstar*, ON. *austr* toward the east :- Gmc. **austra-*, which is found in the proper names *Ēstranglī* (Bede) East-Anglians, OHG. *Ōstarrīhi* (G. *Österreich*) Austria; f. IE. base **aus-*, as in L. *aurōra* (:- **ausōsā*), Gr. (Aeolic) *aúōs*, Lith. *aušrà*, Skr. *uṣā́-* dawn. So **†easter** eastern. XIV-XIX. perh. continuing OE. compar. *ēasterra*. Hence prob. **easterly** XVI. **eastern.** OE. *ēasterne* = OS., OHG. *ōstroni*, ON. *austrœnn* :- Gmc. **austrōnja-*. **eastward** adv. toward the east. OE. *ēastewearde*; hence as adj. XV.

Easter Christian festival commemorating the resurrection of Jesus Christ. OE. *ēastre*, mainly in pl. = OFris. *āsteron*, MHG. *ōsteren*, OHG. *ōstarūn* (G. *Ostern* pl.); derived by Bede from the name of a goddess whose feast was celebrated at the vernal equinox, *Ēostre*, Nhb. var. of *Ēastre* :- Gmc. **Austrōn-* (rel. to prec.). Several OE. comps. of the comb. form *Ēaster-* survive: *Ēasterǣfen* Easter Eve, *Ēasterdæġ* Easter Day, *Ēastersunnandæġ* Easter Sunday, *Ēastertīd* Eastertide, *Ēasterwuce* Easter week.

easy at ease, free from constraint or discomfort XII; causing little or no discomfort or difficulty; not oppressive or painful XIV. - AN. *aisé*, OF. *aisié* (mod. *aisé*), pp. of *aisier* put at ease (see EASE vb.); see -Y[1]. Hence **easy-chair** XVIII. **easy** adv. XIV; comb. in *easy-going* XVII.

eat pt. *ate*, pp. *eaten*. OE. str. vb. *etan* = OS. *etan* (Du. *eten*), OHG. *ezzan* (G. *essen*), ON. *eta*, Goth. *itan* :- Gmc. **etan*; f. IE. base **ed-*, whence L.

edere, Gr. *édein*, Ir., Gael. *ith*, Lith. *édmi*, OSl. *jami*, Skr. *ádmi* I eat.

eau - F. *eau* :- L. *aqua* water, as in **eau-de-Cologne** perfume orig. made at Cologne, Germany XIX; **eau-de-vie** 'water of life', brandy XVIII.

eaves OE. *efes*, corr. to OFris. *ōse*, MLG. *ōvese*, MDu. *ō(ve)se*, OHG. *obasa*, *-isa*, MHG. *ob(e)se* (G. dial. *obsen*) eaves, porch, ON. *ups*, Goth. *ubizwa* portico :- Gmc. **obaswō*, **obiswō*, prob. f. **ob-* of OVER. The final *s* is treated as a pl. ending and the word takes pl. concord. Hence **eaves-dropper** one who listens under walls to hear gossip, secret listener. XV. prob. - ON. *upsar-dropi*, corr. to OE. *yfæsdrypæ*; see DRIP, DROP. Hence by back-formation **eavesdrop** vb. XVII.

ebb sb. OE. *ebba* = (M)LG., MDu. *ebbe* (Du. *eb(be)*) :- WGmc. **abjan*, *ōn*, f. **ab* (see OF), as if 'a running off or away'. So **ebb** vb. OE. *ebbian* = (M)LG., (M)Du. *ebben*.

ebonite vulcanite. XIX. f. next + -ITE.

ebony XVI (*hebeny*). Preceded by †*eban* (XV) - OF. *eban* (also *ebaine*, mod. *ébène*) - medL. *ebanus*, var. of L. *(h)ebenus* - Gr. *ébenos* ebony tree, of Sem. orig.; later *ebon* (XVI), latinized *(h)eben*, which was superseded by forms with *-y*, perh. after *ivory*.

ebullient boiling, bubbling over. XVI. - L. *ēbulliēns*, *-ent-*, prp. of *ēbullīre*, f. E- + *bullīre* BOIL[2]. So **ebullition** XVI (once XIV). - late L.

ec- var. of EX-[2] before consonants.

eccentric not concentric XVI (as sb. XV); not central or referable to a centre; irregular, odd XVII; sb. (person) XIX, after F. - late L. *eccentricus*, f. Gr. *ékkentros*, f. *ek* out, EX-[2] + *kéntron* CENTRE; cf. (O)F. *excentrique*. Hence **eccentricity** XVI.

ecclesiastic adj. XV; sb. XVII. - F. *ecclésiastique* or ChrL. *ecclēsiasticus* - Gr. *ekklēsiastikós*, f. *ekklēsiastḗs* member of the ecclesia or public assembly of citizens (in LXX rendering Heb. *ḳōheleth* one who addresses a public assembly), f. *ekklēsiázein* hold or summon to an assembly, (eccl.) summon to church, f. *ekklēsiā* assembly, (eccl.) church, f. *ekklētós*, pp. adj. of *ekkalein*, f. *ek* out, EX-[2] + *kaleîn* call, summon. So **ecclesiastical** XV.

echelon military formation in parallel divisions but with no two on the same alignment. XVIII. - F. *échelon*, f. *échelle* ladder :- L. *scāla* SCALE[3]; cf. -OON.

echinus (zool.) sea-urchin XIV; (archit.) ovolo moulding next below the abacus XVI. - L. - Gr. *ekhinos* hedgehog, sea-urchin.

echo sb. XIV. - (O)F. *écho* or L. *ēchō* - Gr. *ēkhṓ* (cf. *ēkhḗ*, *êkhos* noise), perh. rel. to OE. *swōg* noise. Hence **echo** vb. XVI. **echoic** of the nature of echo, applied by J. A. H. Murray (1880) to words that are held to imitate sounds denoted by them.

éclair XIX. - F. ('lightning'), f. *éclairer* :- Rom. **exclāriāre*, f. EX-[1] + *clārus* CLEAR.

eclectic epithet of philosophers not attached to a school XVII; collecting or collected from different sources XIX. - Gr. *eklektikós*, f. *eklektós* selective, f. *eklégein*, f. *ek* out, EX-[2] + *légein* choose; see LECTION, -IC.

eclipse interception of the light of a heavenly body. XIII - OF. *e(s)clipse* (mod. *éclipse*) - L. *eclīpsis* - Gr. *ékleipsis*, f. *ekleípein* be eclipsed, etc., f. *ek* out, away, EX-[2] + *leípein* LEAVE[2]. Hence vb. XIV; cf. (O)F. *éclipser*.

ecliptic pert. to an eclipse XIV; sb. great circle of the celestial sphere, the apparent orbit of the sun, so called because eclipses happen only when the moon is on or very near this line XIV. - L. *eclīpticus* - Gr. *ekleiptikós* (also sb.), f. *ekleípein*; see prec. and -IC.

eclogue pastoral dialogue (esp. of Theocritus and Virgil). XV. - L. *ecloga* short poem - Gr. *eklogḗ* selection, esp. of poems, f. *eklégein* (see ECLECTIC).

ecology (biol.) study of the relations of plants and animals with their habitat. XIX. - G. *ökologie*, f. Gr. *oikos* house (used for 'habitat'); see WICK[2], -LOGY.

economy management (of a house) XVI; careful management, thrift; administration of a community or establishment XVII; *political economy*, tr. F. *économie politique* XVIII. - (O)F. *économie* or L. *œconomia* - Gr. *oikonomiā*, f. *oikonómos* manager of a household, steward, f. *oîkos* house (cf. WICK[2]) + *-nómos* managing, *némein* manage; see -Y[3]. So **economic, -ical.**

écru colour of unbleached linen. XIX. - (O)F., f. *é-* (intensive) + *cru* CRUDE.

ecstasy XIV (rare before XVI; earlier forms *ex(s)tasie*, *-acy*, the sp. *ecst-*, accommodated to Gr., appearing XVII). - OF. *extasie* - (with assim. to sbs. in *-sie*, L. *-sia*) late L. *extasis* - Gr. *ékstasis*, f. *eksta-*, stem of *existánai* put out of place (in phr. *existánai phrenôn* drive out of one's wits), f. *ek* out, EX-[2] + *histánai* place (see STAND). So **ecstatic** XVII. - F. *extatique* - Gr. *ekstatikós*.

ecto- repr. Gr. *ektós* outside (f. *ek* EX-[2] after *entós* = L. *intus* within), used as comb. form in scientific terms such as *ectoderm*, *ectoplasm*.

ecumenical pert. to the universal church XVI; world-wide XVII. f. late L. *œcumenicus* - Gr. *oikoumenikós*, f. *hē oikouménē* (sc. *gê* earth) the inhabited world, pp. fem. of *oikein* inhabit, f. *oîkos* house; see WICK[2], -ICAL.

eczema XVIII. - modL. - Gr. *ékzema*, f. *ekzein* boil over, (of disease) break out, f. *ek* out, EX-[2] + *zeîn* boil.

-ed[1] formative of the pp. of weak verbs, in OE. *-ed*, *-ad* (*-od*, *-ud*), the vowels of which repr. the thematic vowels of the class to which the verbs belong, the suffix proper being *-d* :- Gmc. **-ðaz* :- IE. **-tós*, repr. by Skr. *-tás*, Gr. *-tós* (in verbal adjs.), L. *-tus*. In some OE. verbs, the suffix being added immed. to the base appears as *-d*, after unvoiced cons. as *-t*, e.g. *seald*, pp. of *sellan* SELL, *boht*, pp. of *byċgan* BUY. In ME. the several OE. variants were levelled under *-ed*; this *-ed* is usu. retained in writing, although the pronunc. is normally reduced to *d* or *t*, e.g. *robed*, *hoped*. The pronunc. *-id* occurs regularly in ordinary speech only in the endings *-ded*, *-ted*. A few pps., as *beloved*, *blessed*, *cursed*, have escaped the tendency to contraction when used as adjs.; and *learned* as adj. is pronounced with *-id*, but as pp. with *-d* or *-t*.

-ed[2] repr. OE. *-ede* = OS. *-ōdi* :- Gmc. **-ōðja-*, and appended to sbs. to form adjs. denoting the possession or the presence of the thing or attribute expressed by the sb., e.g. OE. *hōcede* hooked (f. *hōc*), *hringede* ringed (f. *hring*). This suffix corresponds in function to the *-tus* of L. formations like *caudātus* tailed (f. *cauda* tail), *aurītus* eared (f. *auris* ear); it is now added without restriction to a sb. to form an adj. with the sense 'provided with, characterized by' (something), as in *booted, cultured, diseased, moneyed, wooded*, and notably in parasynthetic adjs., as *dark-eyed, three-pronged*.

In mod. Eng. and to a large extent in ME. there is no formal distinction between exx. of this suffix and ppl. adjs. in -ED[1] derived ult. from sbs. through unrecorded vbs.

edacious eating, devouring. XIX. f. L. *edāx, edāc-*, f. *edere* EAT; see -IOUS.

edaphic (bot.) pert. to the soil. XX. - G. *edaphisch*, f. Gr. *édaphos* ground, soil (orig. base, bottom, f. **sed-* SIT); see -IC.

eddy small whirlpool. XV (Sc. *ydy*). perh. of Scand. orig. (cf. ON. *iða* eddy, whirlpool); prob. f. base of OE. *ed-* again, back = OHG. *et(a)-*, ON. *ið-*, Goth. *iþ* then, but, rel. to L. *et* and, Gr. *éti* yet; cf. MHG. *itwæge* flood, whirlpool (*-wæge* corr. to OE. *wǣġ* wave).

edelweiss XIX. - G., f. *edel* noble + *weiss* WHITE.

Eden abode of Adam and Eve (Gen. 2: 15) XIV; delightful abode, paradise XVI. - L. (Vulg.) *Ēden*, Gr. (LXX) *Edén* - Heb. *'ēdhen*, orig. 'delight'.

edentate of the order of Edentata, which lack incisor and canine teeth. XIX. - L. *ēdentātus*, f. E- + *dēns, dent-* TOOTH; see -ATE[2].

edge sharp side of a blade OE.; boundary of a surface XIV. OE. *eċġ* = OS. *eggia* (Du. *egge*), OHG. *ekka* (G. *ecke* corner), ON. *egg* :- Gmc. *azjō*, f. IE. **ak-* be sharp or pointed (see ACID). Hence **edge** vb. give an edge to XIII; incite XVI (cf. EGG[2]).

edible XVII. - late L. *edibilis*, f. *edere* EAT; see -IBLE.

edict XV. - L. *ēdictum*, sb. use of n. pp. of *ēdīcere* proclaim, f. E- + *dīcere* say, tell (cf. DICTION).

edification building up of the church, of the soul in holiness, etc.; mental or moral improvement XIV; †building XV. - L. *ædificātiō, -ōn-*, f. *ædificāre* build; see -FICATION. So **edifice** building. XIV. - (O)F. *édifice* - L. *ædificium*, f. *ædis* dwelling, orig. hearth, + *fic-*, wk. stem of *facere* make. **edify** build up, lit. and fig. XIV. - (O)F. *édifier* - L. *ædificāre*.

edit †publish (rare); prepare an edition of XVIII; be the editor of XIX. partly - F. *éditer* (based on *édition*); partly back-formation from EDITOR. So **edition** †publication; †production, creation; one of the forms in which a literary work is produced. XVI. - (O)F. *édition* - L. *ēditiō, -ōn-*, f. *ēdit-*, pp. stem of *ēdere* put forth, f. E- + *dare* put. **editor** †publisher XVII (rare); one who prepares an edition XVIII; conductor of a periodical XIX. - L. *ēditor* producer, exhibitor, f. *ēdit-*. Hence **editorial** XVIII.

educate XV. f. pp. stem of L. *ēducāre*, rel. to *ēdūcere* EDUCE; see -ATE[3]. So **education** XVI. - (O)F. or L. Hence **educationist** XIX, which is earlier than **educationalist**, f. **educational** (XVII). **educative** XIX.

educe †lead or draw forth XV; bring out, develop from a latent condition XVII. - L. *ēdūcere*, f. E- + *dūcere* lead (cf. DUCT).

edulcorate soften. XVII. f. pp. stem of medL. *ēdulcorāre*, f. E- + late L. *dulcor* sweetness, f. L. *dulcis* sweet; see -ATE[3].

-ee[1] suffix repr. AN. *-e(e)*, (O)F. *-é* :- L. *-ātus, -ātum*, endings (m. and n.) of pps. of vbs. in *-are*, as in *dēputātus* deputy, *mandātum* command (cf. MAUNDY). It occurs earliest (XV) in legal terms of AN. orig. denoting the recipient of a grant or the like, e.g. *feoffee, grantee, lessee, patentee*, on the model of which many others were made denoting the indirect obj. of vbs. The common correspondence of agent-nouns in *-or* or *-er* with nouns in *-ee*, e.g. *lessor* and *lessee, obligor* and *obligee*, led to the general application of the suffix, as in *addressee*. By mid-XVII *-ee* had become the regular repr. of F. *-é* in adopted words, e.g. *debauchee*. Later exx. are *examinee, employee, escapee*, in XX *internee, evacuee*.

-ee[2] suffix used in a few names of garments, primarily with dim. force, as *bootee, coatee* (XVIII); also *goatee* (orig. U.S.), var. *goaty*; perh. a variation on *-ie*, -Y[6].

eel OE. *ǣl* = OS., OHG. *āl* (Du., G. *aal*), ON. *áll* :- Gmc. **ǣlaz*, of unkn. orig.

e'en see EVEN[1,2].

e'er see EVER.

-eer suffix repr. mostly F. *-ier* :- L. *-ārius* -ARY, and denoting 'one who is concerned with, handles, or deals with'. In several words there were earlier vars. in *-er* and *-ier* (which was gen. replaced by *-eer* in XVII); *charioteer* and *engineer* go back to ME. antecedents adopted from OF. forms in *-eor* (mod. *-eur*).

Most of the sbs. have deriv. vbs., which are used particularly in the gerund and prp., e.g. *electioneering, mountaineering*.

eerie †fearful, timid XIII; uncanny, weird XVIII. Orig. north. Eng. and Sc. *eri*; of obscure orig. (cf. OE. *earg* cowardly).

ef- form of EX-[1] used before *f*.

efface wipe out, obliterate. XV. - (O)F. *effacer*, f. EF- + *face* FACE.

effect result XIV; accomplishment XV; operative influence, impression XVII; pl. goods and chattels XVIII. - OF. *effect* (mod. *effet*) or L. *effectus*, f. *effect-*, pp. stem of *efficere* work out, f. EF- + *fic-, facere* make, DO[1]. Hence **effect** vb. XVI. Also **effective** XIV. - L. **effectual** XIV. - medL. **effectuate** XVI. f. medL. *effectuāre, -āt-*.

effeminate XIV. - L. *effēminātus*, pp. of *effēmināre* make feminine, f. EF- + *fēmina* woman; see FEMININE, -ATE[2]. Hence **effeminacy** XVII.

efferent conducting outwards. XIX. - L. *efferēns, -ent-*, prp. of *efferre*, f. EF- + *ferre* BEAR[2]; see -ENT.

effervesce give off bubbles of gas. XVIII. - L. *effervēscere*, f. EF- + *fervēscere*, inceptive of *fervēre*; see FERVENT, -ESCENT. So **effervescent, -ence** XVII.

effete †that has ceased to bring forth; worn out. XVII. - L. *effētus* that has brought forth young, exhausted as by bearing young, f. EF- + *fētus* FOETUS.

efficacious XVI. f. L. *efficāx*, *-āc-*, f. *efficere*; see EFFECT, -ACIOUS. So **efficacity** XV. - F. - L.

efficient making a thing what it is XIV; adequately operative or skilled XVIII. - prp. of L. *efficere*. **efficiency** XVI.

effigy XVIII (*effigies* sg. XVI-XIX). - L. *effigiēs*, f. *effig-*, stem of *effingere*, f. EF- + *fingere* fashion.

effloresce burst forth as in flower; change to fine powder. XVIII. - L. *efflōrēscere*, f. EF- + *flōrēscere* (see FLORESCENCE). So **efflorescence** XVII, **efflorescent** XIX.

effluent flowing out XVIII (once XV); sb. XIX. - L. *effluēns*, *-ent-*, prp. of *effluere*, f. EF- + *fluere* flow. So **effluence** XVII (once XIV). **effluvium** outflow of (electric, etc.) particles; (noxious) odour. XVII. **efflux, effluxion** XVII. - (O)F. or late L.

effort XV. - (O)F. *effort*, earlier *esforz* nom., f. *esforcier* (mod. *efforcer*) :- Rom. **exfortiāre*, f. L. EF- + *fortis* strong (see FORCE).

effrontery XVIII. - F. *effronterie*, f. *effronté* shameless, impudent, OF. *esfronté* :- Rom. **exfrontātus*, f. **exfrōns*, for late L. *effrōns* barefaced, f. EF- + *frōns* forehead; see FRONT, -ERY.

effulgent gleaming forth. XVIII. - L. *effulgēns*, *-ent-*, prp. of *effulgēre*; see EF-, FULGENT. So **effulgence** XVII. - late L.

effusion pouring out or forth, shedding (of blood). XV. - (O)F. - L. *effūsiō*, *-ōn-*, f. *effundere*, *effūs-*; see EF-, FUSION. So **effuse** XVI, **effusive** XVII.

eftsoons (arch.) again; †(soon) afterwards. OE. *eft sōna* 'afterwards immediately', ME. *eftsōne*, to which advb. -s was added XIV; OE. *eft* (= OS. *eft*, MLG., MDu. *echt*, ON. *ept*; cf. AFTER) + *sōna* SOON.

egad (arch.) euph. excl., veiling *by God*. XVII. See GAD[2].

egg[1] 'ovum'. XIV. - ON.; superseding cognate ME. *ey* :- OE. *ǣġ* = OS., (O)HG., Du. *ei* :- Gmc. **ajjaz-* n., rel. to L. *ōvum*, Gr. *ōión*, Ir. *og*, W. *wy*, and poss. further to words for 'bird' in Skr. *ví-*, L. *avis*.

egg[2] incite. OE. (late Nhb.) *ġeeggedon*, pt. pl. of *ġeeggia* - (with *ġe-* Y- prefixed) ON. *eggja*, rel. to *egg* EDGE.

eglantine sweet-briar. XV. - OF. *églantine*, ult. f. *aculeus* prickle, sting.

ego (philos.) conscious thinking subject; (colloq.) self. XIX. - L., the pron. I. So **egoism** belief that nothing exists but one's own mind; theory which regards self-interest as the basis of morals XVIII; egotism XIX. - F. *égoïsme* - modL. *egōismus*. **egotism** practice of talking about oneself; self-conceit, selfishness XVIII; the *t* is of uncert. orig. So **egoist, egotist** XVIII.

egregious eminent; gross, flagrant. XVI. f. L. *ēgregius* surpassing, illustrious, f. E- + *grex*, *greg-* flock; see -IOUS.

egress going out. XVI. - L. *ēgressus*, f. *ēgress-*, pp. stem of *ēgredī*, f. E- + *gradī* step.

egret white heron. XV. - AN. *egrette*, (O)F. *aigrette* - Pr. *aigreta*, f. stem of *aigron*, corr. to (O)F. *héron* HERON; see -ET.

eider-down down of the **eider-duck** XVIII; quilt XIX. ult. - Icel. *æðr* eider-duck + DOWN[2]; cf. Icel. *æðardūn*.

eidolon unsubstantial image. XIX. - Gr. *eídōlon* IDOL.

eight OE. *ehta* (*eahta*) = OS., OHG. *ahto* (Du., G. *acht*), ON. *átta*, Goth. *ahtau*, corr. to L. *octō*, Gr. *oktṓ*, (O)Ir. *ocht*, W. *wyth*, Lith. *aštuonì*, Skr. *aṣṭáu*, Av. *ašta*. So **eighteen** OE. *e(a)htatēne* = OS. *ahtotian* (Du. *achttien*), OHG. *ahtozehan* (G. *achtzehn*), ON. *áttján*; see -TEEN. **eighteenth** ME. *eȝtetenthe*, repl. OE. *e(a)htotēaða*; see -TH[2]. **eighth** OE. *e(a)htoða* = OHG. *ahtodo* (G. *achte*); see -TH[2]. **eightieth** (-ETH[1]). **eighty** ME. *eȝteti*, repl. OE. *hunde(a)htatiġ*; see HUNDRED and -TY[1].

eisteddfod congress of Welsh bards. XIX. - W., 'session', f. *eistedd* sit, for **eitsedd*, f. IE. **sed-* SIT.

either each of the two OE.; one or other of the two XIII; adv. introducing alternatives XIV. OE. *ǣġðer*, contr. form of *ǣġ(e)hwæðer* = MLG., MDu. *ed(d)er* (as adv.), OHG. *eogihwedar* :- Gmc. phr. **aiwo ȝiχwaþaraz*, i.e. 'ever each of two'; see AY, WHETHER.

ejaculate eject (fluid) XVI; utter suddenly XVII. f. pp. stem of L. *ējaculārī*, f. E- + *jaculārī* dart, f. *jaculum* dart, javelin, f. *jacere* throw; see -ATE[3]. So **ejaculation** XVII.

eject XV. f. *ēject-*, pp. stem of L. *ē(j)icere*, f. E- + *jacere* throw. So **ejection** XV; - L.

eke[1] (arch.) also OE. *ē(a)c* = OS. *ōk* (Du. *ook*), OHG. *ouh* (G. *auch*), ON., Goth. *auk*; of uncert. orig.

eke[2] †augment XII; (with *out*) supplement, prolong XVI. OE **ēacan* (implied in *ēacen*, pp. increased, strong, pregnant; cf. *ēacian* intr. increase) = OS. *ōkian*, ON. *auka*, Goth. *aukan*, rel. to L. *augēre* increase, Gr. *aúkhein*, f. base **aug-* (cf. WAX[2]). The OE. sb. *ēaca* increase (ME. *eke*) may have been partly the source of the ME. vb.

-el[1] repr. OE. *-el*, *-ela*, *-ele* :- Gmc. **-ilaz*, **-ilan-*, **-ilōn*, usu. retained as -LE[1], but cf. *kernel*.

-el[2] repr. OF. *-el* (mod. *-eau*) :- L. *-ellus*, *-ella*.

elaborate †produced by labour XVI; highly or minutely finished XVII. - L. *ēlabōrātus*, pp. of *ēlabōrāre*; f. E- + *labor* LABOUR. So **elaborate** produce by labour; give finish to. XVII. See -ATE[2,3]. So **elaboration** XV.

élan vivacity, impetuosity. XIX. - F., f. *élancer* cast or launch forth, f. *é-* EX-[1] + *lancer* LAUNCH[1]; see also LANCE.

eland S. Afr. antelope. XVIII. - Afrikaans (Du.) *eland* elk - G. *elend* - Lith. *élnis* = OSl. *jelenĭ* stag, rel. to Gr. *ellós* fawn.

elapse XVII. f. *ēlaps-*, pp. stem of L. *ēlābī* slip away; see E-, LAPSE.

elastic adj. (orig. applied to the 'impulsive force' of the atmosphere) XVII. - modL. *elasticus* - Gr. *elastikós* propulsive, impulsive, f. **elaϝ-*, stem of *elaúnein* drive. Hence **elasticity** XVII.

elate †elevate XVI; (chiefly in pp.) †encourage; puff up XVII. f. *ēlāt-*, pp. stem of L. *efferre*, f. EF- + *ferre* BEAR[2]; see -ATE[3]. So **elation** XIV. - OF. *elacion* and L. *ēlātiō*.

elater †elasticity XVII; skipjack beetle; (bot.) elastic spiral filament XIX. modL. - Gr. *elatḗr* driver, f. **elaϝ-*, *elaúnein* drive.

elbow OE. *el(n)boga* = MDu. *elleboghe* (Du. *elleboog*), OHG. *elinbogo* (G. *ellenbogen*), ON. *ǫlnbogi* :- Gmc. **alinobozan-*, f. **alinō* arm (cf. ELL) + **bozān-* BOW¹.

elder¹ tree of genus *Sambucus*. OE. *ellærn*, ME. *eller*, *eldre*, corr. to MLG. *ellern*, *elderne*, *elhorn*, *alhorn*, prob. orig. an adj. formation.

elder², **eldest** compar. and superl. of OLD. OE. *eldra* (WS. *ieldra*) = OS. *aldira*, OHG. *altiro*, *eltiro* (G. *älter*), ON. *ellri*, Goth. *alþiza* :- Gmc. **alþizan-*, f. **alþaz* OLD; see -ER³. OE. *eldest* (WS. *ieldest*) = OHG. *altist* (G. *ältest*), ON. *ellztr*, Goth. *alþista* :- Gmc. **alþistaz*; see -EST. Superseded, except in special uses, by *older* and *oldest* (*alder*, *-este* XIII). As sb. *elder* was used in OE. and later for 'parent, ancestor', from *c.*1200 for 'one's senior' or 'superior in age', from XIV rendering L. *senior* and *senatus*, by Tindale used to tr. N.T. Gr. *presbúteros* PRESBYTER; in the Presbyterian and other bodies, title of an office believed to corr. to that of elder in the apostolic church.

eldorado *El Dorado* name of a fictitious place in S. America abounding in gold XVI; fig. source of boundless wealth XIX. - Sp., *el* the, *dorado*, pp. of *dorar* gild :- Rom. **dēaurāre*, f. DE- (3) + *aurum* gold.

eldritch (Sc.) pert. to elves or fairies; weird, unnatural. XVI. poss. from attrib. use of OE. **ælf-*, **elfrīce* 'fairy realm' (see ELF, RICH).

elecampane composite plant, *Inula helenium*. XIV. ult. - medL. *enula campāna*, i.e. *enula* for L. *inula* - Gr. *helénion*, and *campāna* prob. of the fields (cf. CHAMPAIGN).

elect chosen, select XV; (theol.) XVI; chosen for an office (but not yet installed) XVII. - L. *ēlectus*, pp. of *ēligere*, f. E- + *legere* choose. So **elect** vb. choose, esp. by vote. XV. f. corr. pp. stem. **election** choice. XIII (with ref. to representative bodies XVII). - (O)F.; hence **electioneer** (first in vbl. sb.) XVIII. **elective** XVI (once XV). - (O)F. **elector** one who has the right to vote XV (prince of the Holy Roman Empire, *Kurfürst*, entitled to elect the Emperor XVI). - (O)F. or L.; hence **electoral** XVII (of a German Elector), **electorate** XVII.

electric, -ical XVII. - modL. *ēlectricus*, f. L. *ēlectrum* - Gr. *ḗlektron* amber; see -IC, -ICAL. Hence **electrician** XVIII, **electricity** XVII, **electrify**, **electrification** XVIII.

electro- comb. form of Gr. *ḗlektron* amber, used in the sense 'electricity', 'electric', as in **electrometer** (XVIII); *electro-dynamic*, *electrolysis*, *electromagnet(ical)*, *-plate* (vb.), *-type* XIX.

electrocution execution by electricity. XIX. alt., after prec., of †*electricution* (XIX), f. *electri(cal)* (*exe*)*cution*; hence by back-formation †*electricute*, **electrocute** XIX.

electrode XIX. f. ELECTRIC + Gr. *hodós* way. Cf. ANODE, CATHODE.

electron (phys.) elementary particle with a negative charge of electricity. XIX (applied to the unit of electric charge). f. ELECTRIC + *-on* of ION. Hence **electronic, -ics** XX.

electuary medicinal conserve or paste. XIV. - late L. *ēlectuārium*, prob. alt. deriv. of synon. Gr. *ekleiktón*, f. *ekleíkhein* LICK up (see EX-²).

eleemosynary pert. to alms. XVII. - medL. *eleēmosynārius*, f. ChrL. *eleēmosyna* ALMS; see -ARY.

elegant XVI. - (O)F. *élégant* or L. *ēlegāns*, *-ant-*, rel. to *ēligere* select, ELECT. The etymol. sense is 'choosing carefully'. So **elegance** XVI. - F. - L.

elegy song of lamentation; poem in elegiac metre. XVI. - F. *élégie* - L. *elegīa* - Gr. *elegeíā* (sb. use of adj., sc. *ōidḗ* ode), f. *élegos* (flute-) song, lament, of unkn. orig.; see -Y³. So **elegiac** pert. to elegy, written or writing in a metre consisting of alternate hexameters and pentameters. XVI. - late L. - Gr.

element one of the four constituents of the universe (earth, water, air, fire) XIII (whence ult. the use in mod. chem. XIX); constituent portion; pl. rudiments XIV. - (O)F. *élément* - L. *elementum* esp. pl. principles, rudiments, letters of the alphabet (used to tr. Gr. *stoikheîon* step, base, element, etc.), of unkn. orig. Hence **elemental** XV. So **elementary** XVII (earlier *elementare* XIV, *-air* XVI). - L. *elementārius*.

elenchus form of syllogism in refutation. XVII (earlier anglicized †*elynch* XV, †*elench* XVI). - L. - Gr. *élegkhos* argument of refutation, of uncert. orig.

elephant XIII. ME. *olif(a)unt*, *-ont*, later (XIV) with assim. to L., *elifant*, etc. - OF. *olifant*, *elefant* (mod. *éléphant*) - Rom. **olifantus* (cf. OE. *olfend*, Goth. *ulbandus* camel), alt. of L. *elephantus* (whence OE. *elpend*) - Gr. *eléphās*, *elephant-* ivory, elephant, of unkn. orig. So **elephantiasis** skin disease resembling an elephant's hide. XVI. **elephantine** XVII. - L. - Gr.

elevate XV. f. pp. stem of L. *ēlevāre*, f. E- + *levāre* lighten, raise, rel. to *levis* light; see -ATE³. So **elevation** XIV. - (O)F. or L. **elevator** muscle that raises XVII; machine for raising objects XIX.

eleven OE. *endleofon*, *-lufon*, *ellefne*, ME. *endleven(e)*, *elleven(e)* = OS. *elleƀan*, OHG. *einlif* (Du., G. *elf*), ON. *ellifu*, Goth. *ainlif* :- Gmc. **ainlif-*, f. **ainaz* ONE + **lif-* (cf. TWELVE), app. repr. IE. **liq-* leave (see LOAN), i.e. 'one left (over ten)', and rel. to Lith. *-lika* in *vienúolika* eleven. Hence **eleventh** (XIV), superseding OE. *endleofeða*, itself a new formation superseding previous *endlyfta* = OS. *ellifto*, OHG. *einlifto* (Du. *elfde*, G. *elfte*), ON. *ellifti* :- Gmc. **ainliftan-*; see -TH².

elf dwarf supernatural being OE.; mischievous creature XVI. OE. *elf*, WS. **ielf*, *ylf* = MDu. *elf*, beside MHG. *elbe* fem. :- **albiz*, parallel to **albaz*, whence OE. *ælf* (ME. pl. *alven*) = OS., MLG. *alf*, MHG. *alp* (G. *alp* nightmare), ON. *álfr*. Hence **elfin** adj. XVI (poss. suggested by ME. *elevene*, g. pl. of *elf*), **elfish** XVI, **elvish** XIV.

elicit XVII. f. *ēlicit-*, pp. stem of L. *ēlicere* draw forth, f. E- + *lacere* entice, inveigle, rel. to *lax* deceit.

elide †annihilate; (leg.) annul XVI; omit in pronunciation XVIII. - L. *ēlīdere*, f. E- + *lædere* injure, harm. So **elision** XVI. - late L., f. *ēlīs-*, pp. stem of *ēlīdere*.

eligible XV. - F. *éligible* - late L. *ēligibilis*, f. *ēligere* choose; see ELECT, -IBLE. Hence **eligibility** XVII.

eliminate XVI. f. pp. stem of L. *ēlīmināre* thrust

out of doors, expel, f. E- + *līmen, līmin-* threshold; see -ATE[3]. Hence **elimination** XVII.

élite *the* pick (*of*). XVIII. - F., sb. use of fem. of †*e(s)lit*, pp. of *élire*, †*eslire* :- Rom. **exlegere*, for L. *ēligere* ELECT.

elixir alchemist's preparation for changing metals to gold or prolonging life. XIV. - medL. - Arab. *al-'iksīr*, perh. f. AL-[2] + Gr. *xērion* desiccative powder for wounds, f. *xērós* dry.

elk XV. prob. repr. OE. *e(o)lh*. OE. had also *ēola* (:- **eolha*), cogn. with OHG. *elaho* (G. *elch*), repr. IE. **elk-*, beside **olkis*, whence Gmc. **alȝiz* (ON. *elgr*) and CSlav. **olsĭ* (Russ. *los'*, OPol. *łoś* elk); cf. L. *alcēs* pl. and Gr. *álkē* - Gmc.

ell measure of length (in England 45 inches). OE. *eln* = MDu. *elne, elle* (Du. *el*), OHG. *elina* (G. *elle*), ON. *ǫln* (*aln-*) cubit, ell, forearm, Goth. *aleina* cubit :- Gmc. **alīnō*, orig. '(fore)arm'; cogn. with L. ULNA, Gr. *ōlénē, ōlḗn* ELBOW, OIr. *u(i)len*, W. *elin*, Skr. *aratní-*, etc.

ellipse XVIII. - F. - L. *ellīpsis* (see next). Hence **ellipsoid** XVIII.

ellipsis †ellipse XVI; (gram.) omission of words supposed to be essential to the complete form of a sentence XVII. - L. *ellīpsis* - Gr. *élleipsis* defect, ellipse (conic section), grammatical ellipsis, f. *elleípein* leave out, fall short, f. *en* IN + *leípein* leave. So **elliptic** XVIII. **elliptical** pert. to an ellipse XVII; (gram.) XVIII. - Gr. *elleiptikós* (chiefly gram.) defective.

elm OE. *elm*, corr. to OHG. *elm(o)* (MHG. *elme, ilme*, G. dial. *ilm*), and, with vowel variation, ON. *álmr*, L. *ulmus*, MIr. *lem*.

elocution †literary or oratorical style XV; oral utterance or delivery XVII. - L. *ēlocūtiō, -ōn-*, f. *ēlocūt-*, pp. stem of *ēloquī*; see ELOQUENCE, -TION.

elongate A. †remove XVI (as pp. XV); †depart XVII; B. lengthen XVI. f. pp. stem of late L. *ēlongāre* remove, prolong, orig. f. E- + *longē* far off, but later taken as if f. E + *longus* LONG, i.e. 'lengthen out'. So **elongation** XIV.

elope orig. of a wife running away with a paramour. XVII. - AN. *aloper*, perh. f. ME. **alope(n)*, pp. of **alepe* run away, f. A-[3] + LEAP; cf. MDu. *ontlōpen*, G. *entlaufen* run away. Hence **elopement** XVII.

eloquent XIV. - (O)F. *éloquent* - L. *ēloquēns, -ent-*, prp. of *ēloquī* speak out, f. E- + *loquī* speak; see -ENT. So **eloquence** XIV.

else (with pron.) other; otherwise, if not. OE. *elles* = MDu. *els*, OHG. *elles, alles*, g. sg. (corr. to Goth. *aljis*) of Gmc. **aljaz*, cogn. with Gr. *állos*, L. *alius* other. Hence **elsewhere.** OE. *elles hwǣr* = MDu. *elswaer*.

elucidate XVI. f. pp. stem of late L. *ēlūcidāre*, f. E- + *lūcidus* LUCID; see -ATE[3]. So **elucidation** XVI.

elude †delude, baffle XVI; slip away from XVII. - L. *ēlūdere*, f. E- + *ludere* play. So **elusion** †deception XVI; evasion XVII. f. *ēlūs-*, pp. stem of L. *ēlūdere*. **elusive** XVIII.

elver young eel. XVII. var. of *eelvare* (XVI), south. form of *eelfare* brood of young eels, f. EEL + FARE[1], i.e. passage of (young) eels up a river.

Elysium state or abode of the blessed dead. XVI. - L. - Gr. *Elýsion* (sc. *pedíon* plain), of uncert. orig. Hence **Elysian** XVI.

elytron pl. *elytra* (zool.) outer wing-case. XVIII. - Gr. *élytron* sheath, rel. to *eilúein* envelop, L. *volvere* roll.

em (typogr.) square of the body of a type, orig. of the type m, used as a unit of measuring the amount of printed matter. XVIII. from the name of the letter M. Cf. EN.

'em orig. unstressed var. of *hem* (OE. *heom*), d. and acc. pl. of the 3rd pers. pron. HE[1]; later felt as a clipped form of THEM. XII.

em-[1] see EN-[1].

em-[2] see EN-[2].

emaciate XVII. f. pp. stem of L. *ēmaciāre*, f. E- + *maciēs* leanness; see -ATE[3].

emanate XVIII. f. pp. stem of L. *ēmānāre*, f. E- + *mānāre* flow. So **emanation** XVI. - late L.

emancipate set free. XVII. f. pp. stem of L. *ēmancipāre*, f. E- + *mancipium*; see MANCIPLE, -ATE[3]. So **emancipation** XVII.

emasculate XVII. f. pp. stem of L. *ēmasculāre* castrate, f. E- + *masculus* MALE; see -ATE[3].

embalm impregnate (a corpse) with spices. XIII. ME. *embaume* - (O)F. *embaumer*, f. EM-[1] + *baume* BALM.

embank enclose with banks. XVII. f. EM-[1] + earlier synon. *bank* vb., f. BANK[1]. Hence **embankment** bank for confining a watercourse XVIII; raised bank for carrying a road XIX.

embargo prohibitory order on the passage of ships; suspension of commerce, etc. XVI (*in-bargo*). - Sp., f. *embargar* arrest, impede :- Rom. **imbarricāre*, f. IM-[1], EM-[1] + *barra* BAR[1].

embark put or go on board ship. XVI. - F. *embarquer*, f. EM-[1] + *barque* BARQUE.

embarrass hamper, perplex. XVII. - F. *embarrasser* - Sp. *embarazar*, prob. - Pg. *embaraçar*, f. *baraça* cord, halter.

embassy function or office of an ambassador; †message of an ambassador XVI; body of persons sent as ambassadors XVII. In early use also *ambassy*. - OF. *ambas(s)ée*, corr. to Pr. *ambaissada*, OSp. *ambaxada*, It. *ambasciata*, medL. *ambasc(i)ata* (f. Rom. **ambactiāre*; see AMBASSADOR).

embattle[1] set in battle array. XIV. - OF. *embataillier*, f. EM-[1] + *bataille* BATTLE.

embattle[2] furnish with battlements. XIV. f. EM-[1] + OF. *bataillier* (see BATTLEMENT).

embay enclose (as) in a bay. XVI. f. EM-[1] + BAY[2].

embed, imbed XVIII. f. EM-[1], IM-[1] + BED.

embellish XIV. f. lengthened stem of (O)F. *embellir*, f. EM-[1] + *bel* beautiful; see -ISH[2]. Hence **embellishment** XVII. - (O)F.

ember OE. *ǣmyrġe, ǣmerġe* = MLG. *ēmere*, OHG. *eimuria* pyre (MHG. *eimere*) ON. *eimyrja* embers :- Gmc **aimuzjōn*, rel. to ON. *eimi, eimr* steam, vapour, *ím* dust, ashes.

Ember Day (eccl.) any of the days of fasting and prayer (Wednesday, Friday, Saturday of the same week) occurring at the four seasons (ecclL. *quatuor tempora*) in the year at which ordinations take place. Late OE. *ymbrendagas* pl., beside *ymbrenwice* (-week), *-fæsten* (-fast); the first el. (OE. *ymbren* sg. and pl.) may be an alt. of *ymbryne* period, revolution of time, f. *ymb* about, around + *ryne* course (f. **run-* RUN); but the possibility that it is based partly on *quatuor* *tempora* is suggested by the form of G. *quatember*.

ember-goose northern diver or loon. XVIII. - Norw. *emmergaas*; cf. Icel. *himbrimi*, earlier *himbrin*, and Faroese *imbrim*.

embezzle †make away with XV; †impair; divert wrongfully to one's own use XVI. - AN. *embesiler*, f. EN-[1] + *besiler* in same sense = OF. *besillier*, Pr. *besillar* maltreat, ravage, destroy, of unkn. orig.

embitter XVII. f. EM-[1] + BITTER.

emblem †allegorical picture XV; symbolical representation, figured object with symbolic meaning XVII. - L. *emblēma* inlaid work, raised ornament - Gr. *émblēma*, *-at-*, insertion, f. *emblē-*, *embállein* throw in, insert, f. EM-[2] + *bállein* throw. Hence **emblematic(al)** XVII.

embody put into a body XVI; incorporate XVII. f. EM-[1] + BODY, after L. *incorporāre* INCORPORATE.

embolism intercalation of a day or days in a calendar XIV; (path.) plugging of a blood-vessel XIX. - late L. *embolismus* - Gr. *embolismós*, f. *embállein* throw in (see EMBLEM).

embonpoint plumpness. XVIII. - F., f. phr. *en bon point* in good condition.

emboss mould in relief XIV; cover with protuberances XV. - OF. **embocer*, f. EM-[1] + *boce*, *bosse* BOSS[1].

embouchure mouth of a river or creek. XVIII. - F., f. *emboucher* refl. discharge itself by a mouth, f. EM-[1] + *bouche* mouth; see -URE.

embrace clasp in the arms, receive gladly XIV; comprise XVII. - OF. *embracer* (mod. *embrasser*) :- Rom. **imbracchiāre*, f. IM-[1] + L. *bracchium* arm (see BRACE[1,2]). Hence **embrace** sb. XVI.

embrasure opening widening from within. XVIII. - F., f. *embraser*, varying with *ébraser* bevel off, etc.; of unkn. orig.; see -URE.

embrocation †fomentation; liniment. XV. f. medL. *embrocāre*, f late L. *embroc(h)a* - Gr. *embrokhḗ* lotion, f. *embrékhein* steep, foment, f. EM-[2] + *brékhein* wet; see -ATION.

embroider XV. Earlier also *-bro(u)d-*; extension of *embroude* - AN. *enbrouder*, f. EM-[1] + *brouder*, *broisder* (mod. *broder*), of Gmc. orig.; the form *broid-* is partly due to blending with ME. *broiden*, pp. of BRAID. So **embroidery** XIV. - AN. *enbrouderie*.

embroil bring into confusion or discord. XVII. - F. *embrouiller*; see EM-[1], BROIL[1].

embryo XVI (also †*embryon*, *-ion* XVI-XVIII). - late L. *embryō*, alt. of *embryon* - Gr. *émbruon* new-born animal, foetus, f. EM-[2] + *brúein* swell, grow.

emend correct XV; remove errors from (a text) XVIII. - L. *ēmendāre*, f. E- + *menda* fault. So **emendation** improvement XVI; correction of a text XVII.

emerald XIII. ME. *emeraude* - OF. *e(s)meraude* (mod. *émeraude*) = It. *smeraldo*, Sp. *esmeralda* :- Rom. **smaralda*, *-o*, alteration of L. *smaragdus* - Gr. *smáragdos*. The sp. with *-ld* is prob. due to It. or Sp. influence in XVI.

emerge come to light, arise XVI; rise out of a liquid XVII. - L. *ēmergere*, f. E- + *mergere* dip, MERGE. So **emergence, emergency** XVII. - medL. **emergent** XV, **emersion** XVII. - late L.

emeritus honourably discharged from service. XIX. - L., pp. of *ēmerērī* earn (one's discharge) by service, f. E- + *merērī* deserve (see MERIT).

emery coarse corundum for polishing. XV. - F. *émeri(l)*, var. of †*esmeril* - It. *smeriglio* :- Rom. **smericulum*, f. medGr. *smḗri*, Gr. *smúris* polishing powder (see SMEAR).

emetic XVII. - Gr. *emetikós*, f. *émetos* vomiting, f. *emeîn* VOMIT; see -IC.

emigrate XVIII. f. pp. stem of L. *ēmigrāre*, f. E- + *migrāre* MIGRATE. So **emigration** XVII. - late L.

eminent conspicuous, signal XV; lofty, prominent XVI; exalted, distinguished XVII. f. prp. stem of L. *ēminēre*, poss. rel to *mōns* MOUNT[1]; see -ENT. So **eminence, -ency.** XVII. - L.

emir Arab prince or governor; descendant of Muhammad. XVII. - F. *émir* - Arab. *'amīr*, f. *'amara* command.

emissary XVII. - L. *ēmissārius* scout, spy, f. *ēmiss-*, pp. stem of *ēmittere* EMIT; see -ARY.

emit XVII. - L. *ēmittere*, f. E- + *mittere* let go, send. So **emission** XVII.

emollient softening. XVII. f. prp. stem of L. *ēmollīre*, f. E- + *mollis* soft; see MOLLIFY, -ENT.

emolument profit or salary arising from an office, etc. XV. - (O)F. *émolument* or L. *ēmolumentum*, *ēmoli-* gain, orig. prob. 'payment to a miller for the grinding of corn', f. *ēmolere* grind up, f. E- + *molere* grind; see MEAL[1], -MENT.

emotion †agitation, tumult XVI; †physical disturbance; disturbance of mind or feeling; affection of the mind, feeling XIX (rare before second half of XVII). - F. *émotion*, f. *émouvoir* excite, move the feelings of (:- Rom. **exmovēre*; see EX-[1], MOVE), after *mouvoir*, *motion*. Hence **emotional** XIX. So **emotive** †causing movement XVIII (rare); pert. to or expressing emotion XIX. f. pp. stem *ēmōt-* of L. *ēmovēre*.

empanel, im- enrol on a panel. XV. - AN. *empaneller*; see EM-[1], PANEL.

empathy XX. Rendering, after Gr. *empátheia*, of G. *einfühlung*, f. *ein* IN[1] + *fühlung* FEELING; see EM-[2], -PATHY.

emperor XIII. ME. *emperere*, *emperour* - respectively OF. *emperere*, nom. and *emperour*, *-ëor*, obl. (mod. *empereur*), semi-pop. - L. *imperātor*, *imperātōrem*, f. *imperāre* command, f. IM-[1] + *parāre* PREPARE, contrive; see -OR[1].

emphasis intensity of statement XVI; intensity of feeling, etc. XVII; prominence XIX. - L. *emphasis* use of language to imply more than is said - Gr. *émphasis* orig. (mere) appearance, f. EM-[2] + base of *phaínein* show. So **emphatic** XVIII. - late L. - Gr. **emphatical** †allusive, suggestive; strongly expressed or expressive. XVI.

empire XIII. - (O)F. *empire*, earlier *emperie* - L. *imperium*, rel. to EMPEROR.

empiric sb. member of the sect of ancient physicians called *Empirici*; untrained practitioner, quack XVI; adj. XVII. - L. *empīricus* - Gr. *empeirikós*, f. *empeiriā* experience, f. *émpeiros* skilled, f. EM-[2] + *peîra* trial, experiment. So **empirical** adj. XVI.

emplacement XIX. - F., f. EM-[1] + *place* PLACE; see -MENT.

employ apply to a purpose XV; use the services of XVI. - (O)F. *employer* :- Rom. **implicāre*, for L. *implicārī* be involved (in) or attached (to), pass. of *implicāre* enfold, involve (see IMPLICATE). Hence **employ** sb. XVII, **employer, employment** XVI, **employee** XIX (orig. U.S.).

emporium XVI. - L. - Gr. *empórion*, f. *émporos* merchant, f. EM-[2] + IE. **por-* (see FARE[2]).

empress XII. ME. *emperice, emperesse* - OF. *emperesse*, f. *emperere* EMPEROR; see -ESS[1].

empty adj. OE. *ǣmtiġ, ǣmet(t)iġ*, f. *ǣmetta* leisure. Hence **empty** vb. XVI.

empyrean (of) the highest heaven. XVII. In ancient cosmology, the sphere of the element of fire, in Christian use the abode of God and the angels. f. medL. *empyreus*, as n. sb. *eum* - Gr. *empúrios*, as n. sb. *-ion*, f. EM-[2] + *pûr* FIRE; see -EAN. So **empyreal** adj. XV.

emu †cassowary XVII; †American ostrich (?) XVIII; flightless Australian bird XIX. Earliest forms *emia, eme*, later *emeu, emew*, orig. - Pg. *ema*.

emulate strive to equal or rival. XVI. f. pp. of L. *æmulārī*, f. *æmulus* rival, prop. adj. striving, rel. to *imitārī* IMITATE, *imāgō* IMAGE; see -ATE[3]. So **emulation** XVI. - L. **emulous** †imitative (of) XIV; †zealous XVI; emulating, rival XVII. f. L. *æmulus*.

emulsion milky fluid. XVII. - F. *émulsion* or modL. *ēmulsiō, -ōn-*, f. *ēmuls-*, pp. stem of *ēmulgēre* milk out, f. E- + *mulgēre* MILK.

emunctory cleaning by excretion; cleansing organ or canal. XVI. - medL. *ēmunctōrius* (sb. *-ium*), f. *ēmunct-*, pp. stem of L. *ēmungere* wipe or blow the nose, f. E- + base rel. to MUCUS; see -ORY[1,2].

en (typogr.) unit of measurement in composition equivalent to the average width of a letter. XVIII. from the name of the letter N. Cf. EM.

en-[1] pref. repr. (O)F. *en-*, the form assumed by the L. prefix IN-[1]; before *b* and *p* and occas. before *m* it takes the form EM-[1], but this was not established in Eng. sp. before XVII, *enb-, enp-* being more frequent than *emb-, emp-* in ME., as in OF. From an early date IN-[1], IM-[1] have been substituted for *en-, em-*, and vice versa, the former being gen. preferred in XVII; in some words (e.g. *em-, imbed, en-, inclose*) both are still current; in others (e.g. *impair, inquest*) *im-, in-* have replaced *em-, en-*, where these are historically appropriate; in *ensure* and *insure* the variants have been allocated to different meanings. As a living formative (from XIV) *en-* has been used in senses mainly identical with those of L. IN-[1]: viz. put in, into, or on (something), as *encase, enthrone*; bring or come into a certain state, as *enable, endear*; with emphatic or neutral force, as *enlighten, enliven*.

en-[2] repr. Gr. *en-*, the prep. *en* IN used as prefix, as in *endemic, energy*; before *b, m, p, ph* it takes the form EM-[2]; before *l* it becomes *el-* (as in *ellipse*).

-en[1] suffix forming (chiefly) dims., as from names of animals; OE. *-en* = OHG. *-īn*, Goth. *-ein* :- Gmc. **-īnam*, formally the neuter of **-īnaz* -EN[3], as in *ċyċen* CHICKEN, *filmen* FILM, *mæġden* MAIDEN, *tiċċen*, ME. *ticchen* kid.

-en[2] suffix chiefly forming fem. sbs. from mascs., and fem. abstr. and concr. sbs.; OE. *-en* = (O)HG. *-in* :- Gmc. **-inī*, **-injō-*; e.g. OE. *biren* she-bear (f. *bera* BEAR[1]), *gyden* goddess (f. *god* GOD); VIXEN is the only surviving example of this type (but OE. *fyxen* is found only as adj.); *hæften* custody, *byrðen* BURDEN, *rǣden* arrangement, rule, condition (see -RED).

-en[3] adj. suffix denoting 'pert. to', 'of the nature of', 'made or consisting of'; OE. *-en* = OS. *-in*, OHG. *-īn* (G. *-en*), ON. *-in*, Goth. *-eins* :- Gmc. **-īnaz*, corr. to Gr. *-īnos*, L. *-īnus* -INE[1]. OE. adjs. formed with this suffix have normally mutation of the stem-vowel, as *stǣnen* of stone, f. *stān* stone, *gylden* golden, f. *gold*; these have not survived, but from ME. onwards new adjs. have been extensively formed direct from the sbs., as *earthen, golden*.

-en[4] inflexion of the weak declension, ME. reduction of OE. *-an*, as in *oxan* oxen, which was extended to other declensions, esp. in the south and west; exx. of this in Standard Eng. are seen in *children* (pl. of CHILD), *brethren* (pl. of BROTHER).

-en[5] suffix forming verbs based on sbs. and adjs., OE. *-nian* = ON. *-na*, OHG. *-inōn*, Goth. *-nan*, e.g. OE. *fæstnian* FASTEN, *war(e)nian* WARN, *wilnian* desire. The relation *fast* adj. / *fasten* gave a model for such vbs. as *darken, deepen, madden, moisten, widen*; the extension to sbs. began in late ME., e.g. *heighten, lengthen, strengthen*. Some verbs in *-en* are extensions of earlier forms, e.g. CHASTEN of †*chaste*, HASTEN of *haste*, HEARTEN of †*heart*.

-en[6] suffix forming the regular ending of pps. of strong verbs; OE. *-en* = OS., OHG. *-an* (Du., G. *-en*), ON. *-inn*, Goth. *-ans*, repr. Gmc. **-anaz*, **-enaz*, **-iniz* :- IE. **-ónos*, **-énos*, **-énis* (OE. and ON. generalized **-en*-forms, and OS., OHG., and Goth. **-on*-forms).

enable †invest with legal status XV; give (legal) power to, supply with means *to do* XVI. f. EN-[1] + ABLE adj.

enact A. †enter among the acts or public records; make into an act, decree XV; B. perform (a play, etc.), act (a part) XVI. f. EN-[1] + ACT sb. and vb. Hence **enactment** XIX.

enamel glass-like composition laid on a surface. XV. f. **enamel** vb. XIV. - AN. *enameler, enamailler*, f. EN-[1] + *amail* = OF. *esmail* (mod. *émail*), new formation on the nom. *esmauz* - Gmc. **smalt-* (OHG. *smalz*, G. *schmalz* melted fat), rel. to SMELT[2].

enamour XIV. - (O)F. *enamourer*, f. EN-[1] + *amour* love.

enarthrosis (anat.) ball-and-socket joint. XVII. - Gr. *enárthrōsis*, f. *énarthros* jointed; see EN-[2], ARTHRITIS, -OSIS.

encaenia †dedication (of a temple, etc.) XIV; annual commemoration of founders and benefactors at the university of Oxford XVII. - L. - Gr. (*tà*) *egkainia* n. pl. 'festival of renewal', f. EN-[2] + *kainós* new. See -IA[2].

encase, incase XVII. f. EN-[1], IN-[1] + CASE[2].

encaustic produced by burning in pigments.

XVII. - L. *encausticus* - Gr. *egkaustikós*, f. *egkaiein* burn in; see EN-², CAUSTIC.

-ence suffix - (O)F. - L. *-entia*, f. *-ent-* -ENT with abstr. suffix. In popL. *-entia* was superseded by *-antia*, repr. in OF. by *-ance*, e.g. *aparance* APPEARANCE, *contenance* COUNTENANCE. Later, L. sbs. in *-ntia* were adopted in F. with the L. vowels, e.g. *absence*, *élégance*, *présence*, and both classes were adopted in ME. with their F. forms and meanings; but in early mod. Eng. some sbs. in *-ance* have been altered back to *-ence*, and all sbs. adopted since have followed the L. forms. The result is that mod. spelling shows many variations, e.g. *assistance*, *existence*, *resistance*, *subsistence*.

enchant lay under a spell XIV; charm, delight XVI. - (O)F. *enchanter* :- L. *incantāre*, f. EN-¹ + *cantāre* sing (see CHANT). So **enchanter** XIII, **enchantment, enchantress** XIV.

enchase adorn with figures in relief; set (a jewel) XV; enshrine as a relic XVII. - (O)F. *enchâsser* enshrine, set (gems), encase, f. EN-¹ + *châsse* shrine, casket, CASE².

enchiridion manual. XVI. - late L. - Gr. *egkheirídion*, f. EN-² + *kheír* hand + *-idion* dim. suffix.

enclave portion of territory entirely surrounded by alien dominions. XIX (†*enclaved* pp. once XV). - F., f. (O)F. *enclaver* :- popL. **inclāvāre*, f. EN-¹ + *clāvis* key.

enclitic (gram.) 'leaning' its accent on the preceding word. XVII. - late L. *encliticus* - Gr. *egklitikós*, f. *egklínein* lean on, f. EN-² + *klínein* LEAN²; see -IC.

enclose, inclose XIV. f. (O)F. *enclos(e)*, pp. of *enclore* :- popL. **inclaudere*, for L. *inclūdere* INCLUDE. So **enclosure** XV. - legal AN., OF.

encomium XVI. - L. *encōmium* - Gr. *egkṓmion*, sb. use of n. of adj., f. EN-² + *kômos* revel (in which a conqueror was led in procession). So **encomiast** XVII, **encomiastic** XVI. - Gr. *egkōmiastḗs*, *-astikós*.

encore int. and sb. XVIII. - F. *encore* again, of uncert. orig. Hence as vb. XVIII. Not so used in F.

encounter sb. XIII. - (O)F. *encontre*, f. *encontrer* (whence **encounter** vb. XIII) :- Rom. **incontrāre*, f. EN-¹ + *contrā* against.

encourage XV. - (O)F. *encourager*; see EN-¹, COURAGE.

encrinite (geol.) fossil crinoid. XIX. f. modL. *encrinus*, f. EN-² + Gr. *krínon* lily; see -ITE.

encroach †seize wrongfully XIV; intrude usurpingly upon XVI. - OF. *encrochier* seize, fasten upon, f. EN-¹ + *crochier* crook, f. *croc* hook (of Gmc. orig.; cf. CROOK).

encumber obstruct, hamper. XIV. - (O)F. *encombrer* block up, f. the base seen in later *combre* barrage in a river; see EN-¹. So **encumbrance** XIV.

-ency suffix - L. *-entia* (see -ENCE, -Y³), used in the formation of sbs. denoting qualities or states, from which concr. or semi-concr. senses have been developed in Eng. adoptions, as distinct from the derivs. in -ENCE, which have freq. the sense of action or process in addition to or to the exclusion of that of quality or state. Examples of the difference now gen. established between the suffixes are *recurrence* and *currency*, *emergence* and *emergency*, *dependence* and *dependency*; several forms in *-ency* have become established to the exclusion of parallel forms in *-ence*, as *decency*, *efficiency*, *inconsistency*.

encyclical intended for universal circulation. XVII (sb. XIX). f. late L. *encyclicus*, f. Gr. *egkúklios* circular, general, f. EN-² + *kúklos* circle; see -ICAL.

encyclop(a)edia †general course of instruction XVI; repertory of information on all branches of knowledge XVII. - modL. - spurious Gr. *egkuklopaideiā*, for *egkúklios paideiā* 'general education'; cf. prec.

end extremity, final limit OE.; †termination, completion XIII; death; event, issue; intended result, purpose XIV. OE. *ende* = OS. *endi* (Du. *einde*), OHG. *enti* (G. *ende*), ON. *endi(r)*, Goth. *andeis*, f. Gmc. **andja-*; cf. Skr. *ánta-* end, boundary, death, and OHG. *endi*, ON. *enni* forehead, L. *antiæ* forelock, *ante* before, OIr. *ētan* forehead, *ēt* end, point, Gr. *antí(os)* opposite. So **end** vb. OE. *endian* = OS. *endion* (Du. *einden*), OHG. *entōn* (G. *enden*), ON. *enda*. Hence **endways, -wise** XVI.

endear †raise the value of XVI; make dear or beloved XVII. f. EN-¹ + DEAR.

endeavour make an effort, strive. XIV. orig. refl.; f. phr. *put oneself in dever* (*devoir*), after F. *se mettre en devoir* do one's utmost (*devoir* :- L. *dēbēre* owe, used as sb.). Hence **endeavour** sb. XV.

endemic regularly found among a people or in a country. XVIII (as sb. pl. XVII). - F. *endémique* or modL. *endēmicus*, f. Gr. *éndēmos*, *endḗmios* pert. to a people, native, f. EN-² + *dêmos* people; see -IC.

endive XV. - (O)F. - late L. *endivia* - medGr. *éntubi(o)n*, f. *éntubon* - L. *intibum*, *intubus*.

endo- comb. form of Gr. *éndon* within, f. *en* IN + **dom-* house (see DOMESTIC), used in many comps. of mod. formation, as *endocarp*, *-derm*, *-gamy*. **endogen** (bot.) plant that develops wood in the interior of the stem. XIX. - F. *endogène*.

endorse write, put one's signature, etc., on the back of XVI; (after **endorsement** ratification XVII) confirm, countenance XIX. - medL. *indorsāre*, f. IN-¹ + L. *dorsum* back.

endow enrich, as with property XIV; provide a dower for XVI. - legal AN. *endouer*, f. EN-¹ + (O)F. *douer* :- L. *dōtāre*, f. *dōs*, *dōt-* dowry, rel. to *dare* give. Hence **endowment** XV.

endue The earliest appearance is of *c*.1400 in the rare sense 'induct'; established in XV in various senses, viz. †(of a hawk) pass food into the stomach, digest; †assume (a form), put on (clothes); invest with property, endow with power, etc. orig. - (O)F. *enduire* (i) :- L. *indūcere* lead in (INDUCE); (ii) a new formation, f. EN-¹ + *duire* :- L. *dūcere* lead; by crossing with L. *induere* put on (a garment), clothe, the word became partly synon. with *endow* and *invest*.

endure †harden; continue; undergo, bear XIV;

tolerate XV. - (O)F. *endurer* :- L. *indūrāre* harden, f. EN-[1] + *dūrus* hard. So **endurance** XV.

-ene (chem.) terminal el. of the names of certain hydrocarbons (e.g. *benzene, naphthalene, toluene*), the vowel *e* being used to complete the sequence *a, e, i, o*. Cf. -ANE[2], -INE[5], -ONE.

enema XV. - late L. - Gr. *énema*, f. *eniénai* send or put in, inject, f. EN-[2] + *hiénai* send.

enemy XIII. - OF. *enemi* (mod. *ennemi*) :- L. *inimīcus*, f. IN-[2] + *amīcus* friend.

energumen possessed person, demoniac. XVIII. - late L. *energūmenus* - Gr. *energoúmenos*, pass. ppl. of *energeîn* work in or upon, f. EN-[2] + *érgon* WORK.

energy vigour of expression XVI; working, operation; power displayed XVII; vigour or intensity of action XIX. - F. *énergie* or late L. *energīa* - Gr. *enérgeia*, f. *energḗs* active, effective, f. EN-[2] + *érgon* WORK; see -Y[3]. So **energetic(al)** †powerfully operative; full of energy. XVII. - Gr. *energētikós* active. **energize** XVIII.

enervate weaken. XVII. f. pp. stem of L. *ēnervāre*, f. E- + *nervus* sinew, NERVE. So **enervation** XV. - late L.

enfeoff invest with a fief. XIV. - AN. *enfeoffer*, OF. *enfeffer*, f. EN-[1] + *fief* FIEF. Hence **enfeoffment** XV.

enfilade †suite of apartments, the doors of which are placed opposite to each other; fire sweeping a line of works or troops from one end to the other. XVIII. - F., f. *enfiler* thread on a string, f. EN-[1] + *fil* FILE[2]; see -ADE.

enforce †strengthen physically or morally; †drive by force, use force upon; †refl. and intr. strive XIV; press home, emphasize XV; compel. - OF. *enforcier*, (also mod.) *enforcir* :- Rom. **infortiāre, *infortīre*, f. IN-[1] + *fortis* strong.

enfranchise set free; make a person or town municipally 'free' XV; admit to political status XVII. f. *enfranchiss-*, lengthened stem of OF. *enfranchir*, f. EN-[1] + *franc, -che* free, FRANK. Hence **enfranchisement** XVI.

engage pledge or secure by a pledge XV; persuade, win over XVII; employ, occupy; bring or come into conflict; hire for employment XVIII; attract, charm. - (O)F. *engager*; see EN-[1], GAGE[1]. So **engagement** XVII.

engender XIV. - (O)F. *engendrer* :- L. *ingenerāre*, f. IN-[1] + *generāre* GENERATE.

engine A. †contrivance, artifice XIII; †ingenuity, genius XIV; B. machine of war XIII; mechanical contrivance XIV; complex machine (later spec. as source of power) XVII. - OF. *engin* :- L. *ingenium* natural quality or disposition, talents, genius, clever device.

engineer designer or constructor of engines or works, orig. of military engines. XIV. ME. *engineor, -our* - OF. *engigneor, -our* (mod. *ingénieur*) :- medL. *ingeniātor, -ōr-*, f. *ingeniāre*, f. *ingenium* ENGINE. The ending was later assim. to *-ier*, -EER[1]. Hence **engineer** vb. intr. XVII; tr. XIX.

England OE. *Engla land* (orig.) country of the Angles (see ANGLE), (later) of the Germanic inhabitants of Great Britain; hence OFris. *Angelond*, OS. (Du.) *Engeland*, (O)HG., Icel., etc. *England*. So **English** OE. *englisċ* pert. to the group of Germanic peoples known coll. as *Angelcynn*, lit. 'race of Angles'; also adj. and sb., of their language. Hence **Englishman** OE. *Engliscmon*.

engraft graft or implant in. XVI. f. EN-[1] + GRAFT vb.

engrain, ingrain A. †dye with cochineal XIV; B. work into the texture or structure of XVII. In sense A - OF. *engrainer* dye, f. phr. *en graine* (whence Eng. *in* GRAIN); in sense B f. EN-[1] + GRAIN. Now mainly in pp. (chiefly *ingrained*) in senses (i) thoroughgoing, incorrigible, (ii) deep-rooted, inveterate.

engrave carve, †sculpture XVI; represent by lines incised on a metal plate or wood block XVII. f. EN-[1] + GRAVE[3], after F. †*engraver*; pp. *engraven, in-* was in use XVI-XIX (latterly poet. or arch.).

engross A. †buy up wholesale XIV; †get together XVI; gain or keep exclusive possession of, occupy exclusively XVII; B. write in large letters, as in legal documents XV. - AN. *engrosser* and AL. *ingrossāre*, in sense A f. phrs. *en gros* and *in grossō* in the lump, by wholesale, in sense B f. *en* in + OF. *grosse*, medL. *grossa* large writing; see GROSS[2].

enhance †raise, exalt XIV; heighten, intensify XV; raise in price. - AN. *enhauncer*, prob. alt. of OF. *enhaucer* :- Rom. **inaltiāre*, f. EN-[1] + *altus* high.

enharmonic XVII. - late L. *en(h)armonicus* - Gr. *enarmonikós*, f. EN-[2] + *harmoniā* HARMONY; see -IC.

enigma riddle in verse XVI; puzzling problem XVII. - L *ænigma, -mat-* - Gr. *aínigma*, f. base of *ainissesthai* speak allusively or obscurely, f. *aînos* fable. So **enigmatic** XVII. - F. *énigmatique* or late L. *ænigmaticus*. **enigmatical** XVI.

enjamb(e)ment continuation of sentence beyond end of line, couplet, or stanza. XIX. - F., f. *enjamber* stride, f. EN-[1] + *jambe* leg; see -MENT.

enjoin A. impose (a penalty, task, etc.) XIII; prohibit by an injunction XVI; B. †join together XIV. f. *enjoi(g)n-*, stem of (O)F. *enjoindre* :- L. *injungere* join, attach, impose, f. EN-[1] + *jungere* JOIN.

enjoy †be joyful XIV; possess or experience with joy XV; refl. XVII. - OF. *enjoier* give joy to, refl. enjoy, f. EN-[1] + *joie* JOY, or - OF. *enjoïr* enjoy, rejoice, f. EN-[1] + *joïr* :- L. *gaudēre*. Hence **enjoyment** XVI.

enkindle cause to blaze up, set on fire. XVI. See EN-[1].

enlarge make larger or more extensive XIV; †set at large XV; †refl. expand in words; intr. speak at large XVII. - OF. *enlarger, -ir*, f. EN-[1] + *large* LARGE; some of the uses are due to (O)F. *eslargir*, mod. *élargir* set free.

enlighten XIV (rare before XVI). f. EN-[1] + LIGHTEN[1] or f. EN-[1] + LIGHT[1] + -EN[5]. Hence **enlightenment** XVII (in XIX used as tr. of G. *Aufklärung*).

enlist tr. enrol on the 'list' as a soldier XVII; intr. XVIII. f. EN-[1] + LIST[4] sb. or vb. Hence **enlistment** XVIII.

enliven †give life to; animate, inspirit; cheer.

XVII. Extended form of †*enlive* (XVI), f. EN-[1] + LIFE, after LIVE[1].

enmity XIII. - OF. *enemi(s)tié* (mod. *inimitié*) :- Rom. **inimīcitās*, *-tāt-*, f. L. *inimīcus*; see ENEMY, -ITY.

ennoble XVI (pp. XV). - (O)F. *ennoblir*; see EN-[1], NOBLE.

ennui XVIII. - F. (cf. ANNOY).

enormous †abnormal, monstrous; †irregular, outrageous; of excessive size. XVI. f. L. *ēnormis*, f. E- + *norma* pattern; see NORM, -OUS. So **enormity** XV. - (O)F. - L.

enough OE. *ġenōg*, *ġenōh* (used in acc. as adv.) = OS. *ginōg* (Du. *genoeg*), OHG. *ginuog* (G. *genug*), ON *gnógr*, Goth. *ganōhs* :- Gmc. **ʒanōʒaz*, rel. to impers. preterite-present vb. OE. *ġeneah*, OHG. *ginah*, Goth. *ganah* it suffices, f. Gmc. **ʒa-* Y- + **naχ-*, which is repr. also in OE. *beneah* (he) enjoys, requires, Goth. *binah* it is right or needful, and is rel. to L. *nancīscī* (pp. *nactus*) obtain, Skr. *aśnóti* reaches. The infl. forms of *ġenōg* gave ENOW, in literary use at least till XVIII (later with Sc. writers and dial.).

enounce enunciate. XIX. - F. *énoncer* - L. *ēnuntiāre* ENUNCIATE, after *announce*, *pronounce*.

enow see ENOUGH.

enrage †be distracted; †pp. maddened; put in a rage or fury. XVI. - (O)F. *enrager*; see EN-[1], RAGE. The tr. use arose in Eng. through the apprehension of pp. *enraged* as a passive.

enrapture XVIII. f. EN-[1] + RAPTURE.

enrich XIV. - (O)F. *enrichir*, f. EN-[1] + *riche* RICH.

enrol(l) inscribe on a roll or list. XIV. - OF. *enroller* (mod. *enrôler*), f. EN-[1] + *rolle* ROLL[1].

ens pl. *entia* being, entity. XVI. - late L., sb. use of n. of prp. f. *esse* be, on the supposed analogy of *absēns* ABSENT.

ensconce †fortify, shelter behind a fortification; establish †secretly or securely. XVI. f. EN-[1] + SCONCE[3].

ensemble all the parts together. XV. - (O)F., sb. use of adv. 'together' :- Rom. **insemul*, for L. *insimul*, f. IN[2] + *simul* at the same time.

ensign †battle-cry, watchword; sign, badge; banner XIV (naval flag XVIII); ensign-bearer (hence, various military and naval officers) XVI. - (O)F. *enseigne* :- L. *insignia*; see INSIGNIA.

ensilage preservation of green fodder in a pit. XIX (first in U.S.). - F., f. *ensiler* - Sp. *ensilar*, f. *en* EN-[1] + *silo*; see SILO, -AGE. So **ensile** XIX.

enslave XVII. f. EN-[1] + SLAVE.

ensue †follow, in various gen. senses, tr. and intr. XIV; follow in the course of events or as a result XV. - OF. *ensiw-*, *ensu-*, stem of *ensivre* (mod. *ensuivre*) :- Rom. **insequere*, f. IN-[1] + L. *sequī* follow.

ensure †make (a person) sure or safe XIV; secure, make certain XVIII. - AN. *enseurer*, alt. (see EN-[1]) of OF. *asseurer* ASSURE. Cf. INSURE.

-ent suffix repr. F. *-ent* - L. *-ēns*, *-ent-*, prp. ending belonging to the IE. series **-ont-*, **-ent-*, **-nt-*, repr. by Skr. *-ant-*, Gr. *-ont-*, Goth. *-and-*, OE. *-end-*. Examples are *confident*, *latent*, *salient*; many such ppl. adjs. had become sbs. in L. or in F.; whence e.g. *agent*, *parent*, *president*, *student*; some are names of inanimate objects or abstractions, as *continent*, *deterrent*, *solvent*, *torrent*.

entablature (archit.) part of an order above the column XVII. - (partly through F. *entablement*) It. *intavolatura* boarding, f. *intavolare* board up, f. *in* EN-[1] + *tavola* TABLE.

entail (leg.) settle (an estate) on a number of persons in succession XIV; †attach as an inseparable appendage XVI; impose (trouble) *upon* XVII; involve as a consequence XIX. f. EN-[1] + AN. *taile* or *tailé* TAIL[2]. Hence **entail** sb. XIV.

entangle XV. f. EN-[1] + TANGLE.

entelechy (philos.) realization of a function. XVII. - late L. - Gr. *entelékheia*, f. EN-[2] + *télei* d. of *télos* end, perfection + *ékhein* be in a (certain) state; see -Y[3].

entente understanding. XIX. - F., f. *entendre* INTEND; earliest in *entente cordiale*.

enter go or come in XIII; go or come into, cause to go in, put in or into XIV. - (O)F. *entrer* :- L. *intrāre*, f. *intrā* within (see INTRA-).

enteric pert. to the intestines; typhoid. XIX. - Gr *enterikós*, f. *énteron* intestine, rel. to L. *inter* between, among (see INTERIOR). So **enteritis** XIX. **entero-**, comb. form of Gr. *énteron*.

enterprise work taken in hand, bold undertaking; daring spirit. XV. - (O)F. *entreprise*, sb. use of fem. pp. of *entreprendre* undertake, later var. of *emprendre* :- Rom. **imprendere*, f. IM-[1] + L. *pre(he)ndere* take.

entertain †keep in a certain state; keep up, maintain; treat; receive, e.g. as a guest XV; †retain in service; engage the attention of XVI; amuse XVII. - (O)F. *entretenir* :- Rom. **intertenēre*, f. INTER- + *tenēre* hold. Hence **entertainment** †maintenance, provision XVI; reception (of a guest); meal, amusement XVII; public performance XVIII.

enthral(l) enslave (fig. hold spellbound). XVI. f. EN-[1] + THRALL.

enthrone XVII. repl. †*enthronize* (XIV) - OF. *introniser* - late L. *inthronizāre* - Gr. *enthronízein*, f. EN-[2] + *thrónos* THRONE.

enthusiasm †prophetic or poetic frenzy; vain confidence in divine inspiration, misguided religious emotion XVII; rapturous or passionate eagerness XVIII. - F. *enthousiasme* or late L. *enthūsiasmus* - Gr. *enthousiasmós*, f. *enthousiázein* be inspired or possessed by the god, f. *énthous*, *éntheos* inspired, possessed, f. *en* IN + *theós* god. So **enthusiast** XVII. - F. or ecclL. **enthusiastic** XVII. - Gr. Hence **enthuse** vb. XIX.

enthymeme syllogism in which one premiss is suppressed. XVI. - L. *enthȳmēma* - Gr. *enthū́mēma*, f. *enthūmeisthai* consider, infer, f. EN-[2] + *thūmós* passion, mind.

entice †incite XIII; allure XIV. - OF. *enticier*, prob. :- Rom. **intītiāre*, f. L. *in* EN-[1] + **tītius*, for L. *tītiō* firebrand, as if 'set on fire'. So **enticement** XIV.

entire XIV. ME. *ent(i)er* - AN. *enter*, (O)F. *entier* :- Rom. **integro*, for L. *integrum* (nom. *integer*), f. IN-[2] + **tag-*, base of *tangere* touch. So **entirety** XVI.

entitle XIV. - AN. *entitler*, OF. *entiteler* (mod. *intituler*) - late L. *intitulāre*, f. IN-[1] + *titulus* TITLE.

entity XVI. - F. *entité* or medL. *entitās*, f. L. ENS, *ent-*; see -ITY.

ento- before a vowel **ent-**, comb. form of Gr. *entós* within.

entomology science of insects. XVIII. - F. or modL., f. Gr. *éntomon*; see INSECT, -LOGY.

entourage environment; persons in attendance. XIX. - F., f. *entourer* surround.

entr'acte interval, or performance of music, etc., between acts of a play. XIX. - F., f. *entre* between + *acte*; see INTER-, ACT.

entrails XIII. - (O)F. *entrailles* - medL. *intrālia*, alt. of L. *interānea*, sb. use of n. pl. of *interāneus* internal, f. *inter* amid (cf. INTERIOR).

entrain draw as an accompaniment or consequence. XVI (now rare). - (O)F. *entraîner*, f. EN-[1] + *traîner* drag (see TRAIN).

entrance[1] coming or going in; place of entry. XVI. - OF., f. *entrer* ENTER; see -ANCE. So **entrant** sb. and †adj. XVII. - prp. of F. *entrer*.

entrance[2] put into a trance, carry away as in a trance. XVI. f. EN-[1] + TRANCE vb.

entrap XVI. - OF. *entrap(p)er*, f. EN-[1] + *trappe* TRAP[1].

entreat †treat XIV; beseech, implore XV. - OF. *entraiter*, f. EN-[1] + *traiter* TREAT. The sense 'implore' was carried over from *treat*, which was used intr. and tr. in that sense. Hence **entreaty** †treatment; earnest request XVI; after TREATY.

entrechat leap in dancing with crossings of the legs. XVIII. - F., alt. (perh. after It. *capriola intrecchiata* intricate caper) of earlier †*entrechas(se)*, f. *entrechasser* chase in and out, f. *entre* between, INTER- + *chasser* CHASE.

entrée entrance, leave of entry XVIII; dish served before the joint XIX. - F.; see ENTRY.

entrench, in- place within a trench XVI; encroach (upon) XVII. f. EN-[1], IN-[1] + TRENCH. Hence **entrenchment** XVI.

entrepôt storehouse; mart. XVIII. - F., f. *entreposer* store, f. *entre* among + *poser* place; see INTER-, POSE.

entrepreneur XIX. - F., f. *entreprendre* undertake (see ENTERPRISE).

entresol storey between ground and first floor. XVIII. - F., f. *entre* between, INTER- + *sol* ground.

entropy XIX. - G. *entropie*, f. Gr. *en* EN-[2] + *tropḗ* transformation (see TROPE), after *energy*; see -Y[3].

entrust, in- XVII. f. EN-[1] + TRUST.

entry entering, passage affording entrance XIII; entering in a book, item entered XV. - (O)F. *entrée* :- Rom. **intrāta*, sb. use of fem. pp. of L. *intrāre* ENTER; see -Y[5].

enumerate XVII. f. pp. stem of L. *ēnumerāre*, f. E- + *numerus* NUMBER; see -ATE[3]. So **enumeration** XVI. - F. or L.

enunciate give expression to XVII; pronounce XVIII. f. pp. stem of L. *ēnuntiāre*, E- + *nuntiāre* ANNOUNCE. So **enunciation** XVI. - F. or L.

envelop XIV. ME. *envolupe* - OF. *envoluper*, *-oper* (mod. *envelopper*), f. EN-[1] + **volup-*, **velup-*, of unkn. orig.; cf. DEVELOP. So **envelope** XVIII.

envious XIII. - AN. *envious*, OF. *envieus* (mod. *-eux*), f. *envie* ENVY.

environ surround, encompass. XIV. - OF. *environer* (mod. *-onner*), f. *environ* surroundings, around, f. *en* in + *viron* circuit, f. *virer* turn, VEER. Hence **environment** XVII (rare before XIX). So **environs** neighbourhood. XVII.

envisage look straight at; view, contemplate. XIX. - F. *envisager*, f. EN-[1] + *visage* face, VISAGE.

envoy[1] conclusion of a poem, etc. XIV. - (O)F. *envoi*, f. *envoyer* send, f. phr. *en voie* on the way. Cf. VIA[1].

envoy[2] minister sent on a diplomatic mission. XVII. alt. of F. *envoyé*, sb. use of pp. of *envoyer* (see prec.). For the loss of F. *-é* cf. ASSIGN[2].

envy †malice; feeling of ill will at another's well-being. XIII. - (O)F. *envie*, semi-pop. - L. *invidia* malice, ill will, f. *invidēre* look maliciously upon, grudge, envy, f. *in* upon, against + *vidēre* see; see EN-[1], VISION. So **envy** vb. XIV.

enzyme XIX. - G. *enzym*, f. modGr. *énzumos* leavened, f. Gr. *en* IN + *zúmē* leaven.

eocene (geol.) second lowest division of the tertiary. XIX. f. Gr. *ēṓs* dawn + *kainós* new, recent. So **miocene** following the oligocene. f. Gr. *meíōn* less. **oligocene** following the eocene. f. Gr. *olígos* OLIGO-. **palaeocene** lowest division of the tertiary. See PALAEO-. **pleistocene** following the pliocene. f. Gr. *pleîstos* most. **pliocene** highest division of the tertiary, following the miocene. f. Gr. *pleíōn* more.

eon see AEON.

-eous suffix of adjs. the majority of which are formed on L. adjs. in *-eus* (= Gr. *-eos*); these are based on sbs. denoting material things and usu. have the sense 'composed of', as well as that of 'of the nature of, resembling', while the Eng. derivs. have the latter meaning only; exx. are *erroneous*, *igneous*, *ligneous*, *vitreous*, and (from scholL.) *heterogeneous*, *homogeneous*. In adoptions of F. adjs. in *-eux* based on sbs. in *-age* the suffix took this form, as in *advantageous*, *courageous*, *outrageous*; in *hideous* and *piteous*, *-eous* has replaced *-ous*; *aqueous* is isolated; in *bounteous*, *courteous*, *gorgeous*, *plenteous*, *righteous* other endings have been assim. to *-eous*; in *beauteous* and *duteous* the ending has arisen from the addition of -OUS to *-te*, early form of -TY[2]. See also -ACEOUS.

epact number of days by which the solar exceeds the lunar year; number of days in the age of the moon at the new year. XVI. - (O)F. *épacte* - late L. *epactæ* pl. - Gr. *epaktaí* (sc. *hēmérai* days), fem. pl. of *epaktós*, pp. adj. of *epágein* intercalate, f. EPI- + *ágein* lead, bring (cf. ACT).

eparch governor of a province; (eccl.) metropolitan. XVII. - Gr. *éparkhos*, f. EPI- + *arkhós* chief, ruler (cf. -ARCH). So **eparchy** XVIII. See -Y[3].

epaulet(te) XVIII. - F. *épaulette*, f. *épaule* shoulder; see -ETTE.

epenthesis (philol.) insertion of a sound between two others. XVII. - late L. - Gr. *epénthesis*, f. *epenthe-*, stem of *epentithénai* insert, f. EPI- + *en* IN + *tithénai* place. So **epenthetic** XIX.

epergne ornamental centre dish for the dinner table to hold dessert, etc. XVIII. of unkn. orig.

ephemeral existing only for a day or a very short time. XVI. f. Gr. *ephḗmeros* (whence fem. and n. in **-a**, **-on** as sbs.), f. EPI- + *hēmérā* day; see -AL[1]. So **ephemeris** table showing the places of heavenly bodies for every day of a period XVI;

astronomical almanac XVII. - L. - Gr. *ephēmeris* diary.

ephod Jewish priestly vestment. XIV (*ephoth*). - Heb. *'ēphōdh*, f. *'āphadh* put on.

ephor Spartan magistrate. XVI. - L. *ephorus* - Gr. *éphoros*, f. EPI- + **ϝor-*, base of *horân* see.

epi- prefix repr. Gr. *epi-*, before an unaspirated vowel *ep-*, before an aspirated vowel *eph-*, a use of the adv.-prep. *epí* on, upon, over, close up in time or space, in addition (to) = Skr. *ápi* moreover, also, at, in (rel. to L. *ob* towards, against, in OL. around, near).

epic adj. XVI; sb. XVIII. - L. *epicus* - late Gr. *epikós*, f. *épos* word, song; see -IC.

epicene (gram.) of common gender. XV. - late L. *epicœnus* - Gr. *epíkoinos*, f. EPI- + *koinós* common.

epicentre XIX. f. EPI- + CENTRE.

epiclesis XIX. - Gr. *epíklēsis*, f. *epikaleîn* call upon, f. EPI- + *kaleîn* call.

epicure †Epicurean; †glutton, sybarite; one who is choice in eating and drinking. XVI. - medL. *epicūrus* one whose chief happiness is in carnal pleasure; appellative use of L. *Epicūrus*, Gr. *Epíkouros* name of an Athenian philosopher, *c.*300 B.C. So **Epicurean** XIV. - F. *épicurien*, f. L. *epicūrēus* - Gr. *epikoúreios*; see -EAN. Hence **Epicureanism** XVIII. So **epicurism** XVI; partly f. *Epicūrus*, after F. *épicurisme*; partly f. EPICURE.

epicycle XIV. - (O)F. *épicycle* or late L. *epicyclus* - Gr. *epíkuklos*; see EPI-, CYCLE.

epidemic of diseases prevalent among a people at a particular time. XVII; sb. XVIII. - F. *épidémique*, f. *épidémie* - late L. *epidēmia* - Gr. *epidēmíā* prevalence of a disease, f. *epidḗmios* adj., f. EPI- + *dêmos* people; see -IC.

epidermis XVII. - late L. - Gr. *epidermís*, f. EPI- + *dérma* skin.

epigram XV. - F. *épigramme* or L. *epigramma* - Gr. *epígramma*, f. EPI- + *gráphein* write. So **epigraph** inscription XVII; short quotation at the beginning of a work, etc. XIX. - Gr. *epigraphḗ*. Hence **epigraphy** (science of) inscriptions. XIX.

epilepsy XVI. - F. *épilepsie* or late L. *epilēpsia* - Gr. *epilēpsíā*, f. *epilab-*, stem of *epilambánein* seize upon, attack, f. EPI- + *lambánein* take hold of; see -Y[3]. So **epileptic** XVII.

epilogue XV. - (O)F. *épilogue* - L. *epilogus* - Gr. *epílogos*, f. EPI- + *lógos* speech.

Epiphany (feast of) the manifestation of Jesus Christ to the Gentiles. XIII. - (O)F. *épiphanie*, - ecclL. *epiphania* - ecclGr. *epipháneia* n. pl. of **epiphánios*, f. *epiphaínein* manifest, f. EPI- + *phaínein* show; see -Y[3].

epiphany manifestation of a supernatural being. XVII. - Gr. *epipháneia* manifestation, appearance of a divinity, f. *epiphanḗs* manifest, *epiphaínein* (see prec.).

epiphyte (bot.) vegetable parasite. XIX. f. Gr. EPI- + *phutón* plant.

episcopal XV. - (O)F. *épiscopal* or ecclL. *episcopālis*, f. *episcopus* BISHOP; see -AL[1]. Hence **episcopalian** XVIII, **episcopally** XVI. So **episcopacy, episcopate** XVII.

episode dialogue between choric songs; incidental narrative XVII; incidental event XVIII. - Gr. *epeisódion*, sb. use of n. of *epeisódios* coming in besides, f. EPI- + *eísodos* entrance, f. *eis* into + *hodós* way, passage.

epistemology XIX. f. *epistemo-*, comb. form of Gr. *epistḗmē* knowledge, f. *epístasthai* know (how to do), f. EPI- + *stánai* STAND; see -LOGY.

epistle apostolic letter of the N.T. XIII; (gen.) letter XIV. OE. *epistol*, beside *pistol*, ME. *pistle* - L. *epistola*; ME. *epistle* - OF. *epistle* (mod. *épître*) - L. *epistola* - Gr. *epistolḗ*, f. *epistéllein* send, esp. as a message, f. EPI- + *stéllein* send. So **epistolary** XV. f. F. *épistolaire* or L. *epistolāris*.

epistyle (archit.) architrave. XVII. - F. *épistyle* or L. *epistȳlium* - Gr. *epistū́lion*, f. EPI- + *stûlos* pillar.

epitaph XIV. - (O)F. *épitaphe* - L. *epitaphium* funeral oration - Gr. *epitáphion*, f. EPI- + *táphos* obsequies, tomb.

epithalamium nuptial song. XVII. - L. - Gr. *epithalámion*, f. EPI- + *thálamos* bridal chamber.

epithet XVI. - F. *épithète* or L. *epitheton*, sb. use of n. of Gr. *epíthetos* attributed, pp. adj. of *epitithénai* put on or to, f. EPI- + *tithénai* place.

epitome abridgement, summary. XVI. - L. *epitomē* - Gr. *epitomḗ*, f. *epitémnein* cut into, cut short, f. EPI- + *témnein* cut. Hence **epitomize** XVI.

epoch XVII. - modL. *epocha* - Gr. *epokhḗ* stoppage, station, fixed point of time, f. *epékhein* stop, take up a position, f. EPI- + *ékhein* hold, intr. be in a certain state.

epode lyric poem in which a long line is followed by a shorter one XVI; part of a lyric ode following the strophe and the antistrophe XVII. - F. *épode* or L. *epōdos* - Gr. *epōidós*; see EPI-, ODE.

eponymous XIX. f. Gr. *epṓnumos* given as a name, f. EPI- + *-ōnum-*, var. stem of *ónoma* NAME; see -OUS.

epopee epic poem or poetry. XVII. - F. *épopée* - Gr. *epopoiíā*, f. *épos* word, song + *poieîn* make. So **epos** XIX. - L. - Gr.

Epsom salt(s) XVIII. orig. the salt obtained from *Epsom water*, the water of a mineral spring at *Epsom* in Surrey.

equable XVII. - L. *æquābilis*, f. *æquāre* make level or equal, f. *æquus*; see next and -ABLE. So **equability** XVI.

equal XIV. - L. *æquālis*, f. *æquus* level, even. So **equality** XIV. - OF. - L. Hence **equalize** XVI.

equanimity †fairness; evenness of temper. XVII. - L. *æquanimitās*, f. *æquanimis*, f. *æquus*; see prec., ANIMATE, -ITY.

equate average XV; make or treat as equal XVII. f. pp. stem of L. *æquāre*, f. *æquus* even; see EQUAL and -ATE[3]. So **equation** equal partition XIV; (math.) statement of equality, formula affirming the equivalence of two quantities XVI. - (O)F. or L.

equator great circle of the celestial sphere XIV; great circle of the earth XVII. - (O)F. *équateur* or medL. *æquātor*, in full *circulus æquator diei et noctis* circle equalizing day and night, f. *æquāre* (see prec.).

equerry †royal or princely stables, officer in charge of these; (now) officer of the royal household. XVI (*esquiry*, *equirrie*, *quirry*). - (O)F. *esquierie* company of squires, prince's stables (mod. *écurie* stable), f. OF. *esquier* ESQUIRE. Perh. assoc. with L. *equus* horse.

equestrian XVII. f. L. *equestris*, f. *eques* horseman, knight, f. *equus* horse; see EQUINE, -IAN. Hence **equestrienne** horsewoman. XIX. pseudo-F.; fem. of a supposed **équestrien*.

equi- repr. *æqui-*, comb. form of L. *æquus* EQUAL, used in parasynthetic adjs. for 'equal(ly)', as in *equidistant*, *equilateral* XVI, *equipollent* of equal power XV, EQUIVALENT, EQUIVOCAL.

equilibrium XVII. - L. *æquilībrium*, f. *æqui-* EQUI- + *lībra* balance.

equine XVIII. - L. *equīnus*, f. *equus* horse, rel. to OE. *eoh*, ON. *jór*, Goth. *aihwa-*, OIr. *ech*, Gr. *híppos*, Skr. *áśva-*; see -INE[1].

equinox XIV. - (partly through (O)F. *équinoxe*) L. *æquinoctium*, in medL. *-noxium*, f. *æqui-* EQUI- + *nox*, *noct-* NIGHT. So **equinoctial** XIV. - (O)F. *équinoxial* L. *æquinoctiālis*.

equip XVI. - F. *équiper*, prob. - ON. *skipa* man (a vessel), fit up, arrange, f. *skip* SHIP; prob. a different word from OF. *eschiper*, *esquiper* put to sea. So **equipage** †equipment, apparatus; †train of attendants XVI; carriage and horses, orig. with attendant servants XVIII. **equipment** XVIII.

equitation XVI. - F. *équitation* or L. *equitātiō*, *-ōn-*, f. *equitāre* ride on horseback, f. *eques*, *equit-* horseman, f. *equus* horse; see EQUINE, -ATION.

equity fair dealing XIV; (leg.) natural justice XVI. - (O)F. *équité* - L. *æquitās*, *-tāt-*, f. *æquus* fair; see EQUI-, -ITY. So **equitable** fair, just XVII; valid in equity XVIII.

equivalent adj. XV; sb. XVI. - (O)F. *équivalent* - prp. of late L. *æquivalēre*, f. *æqui-* EQUI- + *valēre* be worth. So **equivalence, -ency** XVI.

equivocal †nominal only; capable of twofold interpretation XVII; of doubtful genuineness, questionable XVIII. f. late L. *æquivocus*, f. *æqui-* EQUI- + *vocāre* call, name; see -AL[1]. So **equivocally** XVI. after late L. *æquivocē*. **equivocation** XIV. - late L. *æquivocātiō*, *-ōn-*, f. *æquivocāre* (whence **equivocate** XV).

-er[1] suffix denoting one who or a thing which has to do with something and so the regular formative for agent-nouns; OE. *-ere*, corr. to OS. *-ari* (Du. *-er*), OHG. *-āri* (MHG. *-ære*, G. *-er*), ON. *-ari*, Goth. *-areis* :- Gmc. **-arjaz*, prob. - L. *-ārius* -ARY, of which an accentual var. with *ă* was perh. evolved.

In the early Gmc. stage, such a deriv. as Goth. *laisareis* teacher, from **laisō* LORE, became assoc. with *laisjan* teach, and was apprehended as its agent-noun; thus the model was provided for the universal application of the suffix to vb.-stems, as OE. *bæcere* baker, f. *bacan*, *leornere* learner, f. *leornian*, etc. Some Gmc. sbs. seem to be directly based on or suggested by L. agent-nouns formed on sbs.: e.g. OE. *bōcere* scribe = OHG. *buochari*, Goth. *bokareis*, f. **bōk-* BOOK, after L. *librārius* copyist, scribe, f. *liber* book; direct formations on sbs. occur in OE., e.g. *sangere* singer, f. *sang* SONG, and continued to be made in ME. and later, e.g. *docker*, *hatter*, *slater*. OE. *-ere*, ME. *-er(e)* eventually became established as the universal suffix for new agent-nouns.

In ME. and later, *-er* was substituted for other suffixes or added superfluously to sbs. of which the endings did not obviously suggest their function; e.g. *astrologer*, *astronomer* superseded †*astrologien*, †*astronomien*; †*cater*, †*fruiter*, †*sorcer* were extended to *caterer*, *fruiterer*, *sorcerer*; prob. on the model of *philosopher*, derivs. of Gr.-L. words in *-graphus*, *-logus* assumed the forms -GRAPHER, -LOGER; an isolated instance is *widower*, in which *-er* provides a masculine counterpart to *widow*. A var. *-ier* is established in some occupational names, e.g. *clothier*, *glazier*, *hosier*; see -IER[1].

The suffix occurs also in designations of natives or inhabitants, as *Londoner*, *Britisher*, *New Zealander*; so *foreigner*, *islander*, *northerner*, *villager*.

Some personal designations occur esp. as the fixed second el. of comps.; e.g. new*comer*, on*looker*, iron*monger*, care*taker*.

Many formations are applied almost exclusively to inanimate objects, as *boiler*, *cracker*, *duster*, *poker*, *runner*, *stopper*; (in pl. form mainly) *clippers*, *dividers*; articles of clothing are *blazer*, *jumper*, *slipper*; pl. *drawers*, *trousers*. There are many colloq. and sl. formations in which *-er* expresses 'one', as *backhander*, *goner*, *header*, *sixfooter*, *ten-tonner*. Akin to these are derogatory terms like *blighter*.

-er[2] repr., in adoptions from French, (i) OF. *-er* :- L. *-āris* -AR, or (ii) AN. *-er*, OF. *-ier* :- L. *-ārius*, *-ārium* -ARY. Some ME. exx. in *-er* have been refash. with *-ar* after Latin, as *coler* COLLAR, *scoler* SCHOLAR. See also -IER, -OR[2].

-er[3] suffix of compar. adjs. and advs. A. In adjs., ME. *-er(e)*, *-re*, OE. *-ra* m., *-re* fem., n. repr. two Gmc. suffixes, (i) **-izan-* (OS., OHG. *-iro*, ON. *-ri*, Goth. *-iza*, accompanied by mutation) and (ii) **-ōzan-* (OHG. *-ōro*, ON. *-ari*, Goth. *-ōza*), which were formed on the adv. suffixes **-iz*, **-ōz* (see below). A few OE. compars. show mutation, as *strengra* (f. *strang* strong); traces have remained in *better* :- **batizan-* and *elder* :- **alðizan-*; *worse* and *less* contain the suffix **-izan-* in a disguised form. B. In advs., OE. *-or* = OS., OHG. *-ōr*, Goth. *-ōz* :- Gmc. **-ōz*, beside which there was **-iz* (corr. to L. *-is*, as in *magis* more, *nimis* too much), repr. by ON. *-r* (with mutation) and Goth. *-is* (e.g. *hauhis* higher), and by the mutation in OE. compars. like *leng* longer :- **laŋgiz*, *bet* better :- **batiz*, which were superseded in ME. by regular forms in *-er*. Cf. -EST.

-er[4] suffix forming iterative and frequent. vbs.; OE. *-(e)rian* = OS. *-arōn*, MLG., MDu. *-eren*, OHG. *-arōn*, *-irōn* (G. *-ern*), ON. *-ra* :- Gmc. **-rōjan*. There are a few exx. in OE., e.g. *claterian* CLATTER, *flicerian* FLICKER, *floterian* float, *hwæstrian* whisper, *stam(e)rian* STAMMER; to some there are corr. adjs., as *gliddrian* slip, beside *gliddor*, *slidrian* SLITHER, beside *sliddor*. The number of such words was greatly increased in ME. and later, partly by analogous formations of an echoic or symbolic kind (sometimes from native bases), partly by direct adoption or assimilation of ON. or LG. verbs; e.g.

blunder, clamber, glimmer, mutter, quiver[2], *stagger*.

-er[5] ending (*-er* :- L. *-āre*) of a number of AN. infins. (= OF. *-er, -ir, -eir*, or *-re*), used orig. as sbs. in leg. language, mostly of XV or XVI: e.g. *cesser, demurrer, retainer, waiver; attainder, remainder; tender*; the same ending is in *dinner* and *supper*.

-er[6] suffix (prob. an extended application of -ER[1]) used in sl. formations by adding it to the (sometimes alt.) first syll. or early sylls. of a word; e.g. *bedsitter* bed-sitting room, *footer* football, *fresher* freshman, *rugger* / *soccer* Rugby / Association football.

era system of chronology reckoned from a point of time; date from which a period is reckoned XVII; period or epoch XVIII. - late L. *æra*, orig. pl. of *æs, æris* copper, in the sense 'counters (for calculation)', used as fem. sg. for 'number used as a basis of reckoning', 'epoch from which time is reckoned'.

eradicate pull up by the roots. XVI. f. pp. stem of L. *ērādicāre*, f. E- + *rādix, rādic-* ROOT; see -ATE[3].

erase XVII. f. *ērās-*, pp. stem of L. *ērādere*, f. E- + *rādere* scrape. Hence **eraser** XIX, **erasure** XVIII.

ere (arch.) before (of time). OE. *ǣr* = OS., OHG. *ēr* (Du. *eer*, G. *eher*), Goth. *airis* :- Gmc. **airiz*, compar. of **air* (ON. *ár*, Goth. *air*) early, rel. to Gr. *êri-* early (adv.), Av. *ayarə* day; cf. ERST. Hence **erelong** before the lapse of much time. XVI. **erewhile** (arch.) some time ago. OE. *ǣrhwīlum*.

erect upright. XIV (rare before XVI). - L. *ērectus*, pp. of *ērigere* set up, f. E- + *regere* direct. So **erect** set up or upright. XV. f. *ērect-*, pp. stem of *ērigere*. So **erection** XV. - F. or L. **erector** XVI.

-erel see -REL.

eremite (arch.) hermit. XIII. - OF. *eremite*, var. of *(h)ermite* HERMIT. So **eremitic** XV, **eremitical** XVI. - F. *érémitique*, medL. *erēmiticus*.

erg unit of work. XIX. - Gr. *érgon* WORK.

ergo therefore. XIV. - L., as prep. in consequence of, absol. consequently.

ergot disease of rye. XVII. - F. *ergot*, OF. *ar(i)got, argor* cock's spur, of unkn. orig.

eristic XVII. - Gr. *eristikós*, f. *erízein* wrangle, f. *éris, erid-* strife; see -IC.

erl-king XVIII. partial tr. of G. *erlkönig* 'alder-king', misunderstanding of Da. *elle(r)konge* (for *elve(r)konge*) king of elves.

ermine stoat XII; fur of this, often having the black tails arrayed upon it XIII. - OF. *(h)ermine* (mod. *hermine*), :- medL. *(mūs) Armenius* 'Armenian mouse', equiv. to L. *mūs Ponticus* 'mouse of Pontus' (Armenia and Pontus were conterminous). But contact with similar Gmc. words is possible, viz. OHG. *harmīn* adj., f. *harmo* stoat, weasel (G. *harme*) = OE. *hearma* (etc.).

-ern suffix in *eastern, western, northern, southern*; OE. *-erne* = OS., OHG. *-rōni*, ON. *-rœnn* :- Gmc. **-rōnjaz*, f. **-ro-* (as in **austro-*; see EAST) + **-ōnjaz* = L. *-āneus* -ANEOUS.

erode eat or wear away. XVII. - F. *éroder* or L. *ērōdere*, f. E- + *rōdere* gnaw. So **erosion** XVI. - F. *érosion* - L. *ērōsiō, -ōn-*, f. *ērōs-*, pp. stem of *ērōdere*.

erotic pert. to the passion of love. XVII. - F. *érotique* - Gr. *erōtikós*, f. *érōs, erōt-* sexual love; see -IC. So **erotism, eroticism, erotomania** XIX.

err go astray; †roam. XIV. - (O)F. *errer* :- L. *errāre* :- **ersāre*, rel. to Goth. *airzei* error, *airzjan* lead astray, OS., OHG. *irri* (G. *irre*), OE. *ierre* astray, angry.

errand †message, mission OE.; business on which one is sent XIII; journey taken to convey a message, etc. XVII. OE. *ǣrende* = OS. *ārundi*, OHG. *ārunti*. Obscurely rel. to synon. ON. *e(y)rindi, ørindi*, and to OE. *ār*, OS. *ēru*, ON. *árr*, Goth. *airus* messenger.

errant A. travelling in quest of adventure, as in *knight errant* XIV; B. †thorough (see ARRANT); C. wandering, straying XV. - (O)F. *errant*, in which two distinct words have coalesced: (i) prp. of OF. *errer*, earlier †*edrer* travel as in quest of adventure :- Rom. **iterāre*, for L. *itinerāre* (see ITINERANT), f. *iter* journey; (ii) prp. of (O)F. *errer* wander, ERR. In C - L. *errāns, -ant-*, prp. of *errāre*. So **error** false belief XIII; mistake, wrongdoing XIV; wandering XVI. - OF. *err(o)ur* (mod. *erreur*) :- L. *error, errōr-* :- **ersor* (cf. ERR).

erratic †wandering, vagrant XIV; eccentric or irregular in conduct XIX. - (O)F. *erratique* - L. *errāticus*, f. *errāt-*, pp. stem of *errāre* ERR; see -IC. So **erratum** XVI. sb. use of n. pp. of *errāre*. **erroneous** wrong, faulty. XIV. - OF. or L.; see -EOUS.

ersatz XX. - G. 'compensation', 'replacement', f. *ersetzen* replace, f. *er-* A-[3] + *setzen* SET[1].

Erse Irish, esp. applied to Irish and Scots Gaelic. XIV (*ersche*). early Sc. var. of IRISH.

erst †earliest, first, (arch.) formerly, before. OE. *ǣrest*, superl. corr. to *ǣr* ERE = OS. *ērist* (Du. *eerst*), OHG. *ērist* (G. *erst*) :- WGmc. **airista* (see -EST). Hence **erstwhile** XVI.

erubescent XVIII. - L. *ērubēscēns, -ent-*, prp. of *ērubēscere*, f. E- + *rubēscere*, f. *rubēre* be RED; see -ESCENT.

eructate XVII. f. pp. stem of L. *ēructāre*, f. E- + *ructāre* belch; see -ATE[3]. So **eructation** XV. - L.

erudite XV. - L. *ēruditus*, pp. of *ērudīre* instruct, f. E- + *rudis* RUDE; see -ITE. So **erudition** XV. - (O)F. or L.

eruption XV. - (O)F. *éruption* or L. *ēruptio, -ōn-*, f. *ērumpere, ērupt-* burst forth, f. E- + *rumpere* break; see -TION. So **erupt, eruptive** XVII.

-ery suffix first occurring (ME. *-erie*) in adoptions from F. and subsequently used on the analogy of these in formations on various kinds of base. Repr. (O)F. *-erie*, which arose from the addition of *-ie* -Y[3] to personal designations in *-(i)er, -eur*, to denote quality, action, or occupation; e.g. *archerie* ARCHERY (f. *archer*), *chevalerie* CHIVALRY (f. *chevalier*). Such comps. came to be apprehended as directly rel. to the ult. base, as *chevalerie* to *cheval* horse; consequently, formations on various kinds of sb. were made; this was extended to adjs. and to vbs.; and the practice was followed in Eng. formations, as *drudgery, gunnery, slavery*.

The suffix came to be esp. assoc. with -ER[1] and -ER[2], so that all agent-nouns in *-er* have actually or potentially a deriv. in *-ery*, e.g. *bookbindery, grocery, joinery, millinery*; hence, by extension, in designations of premises, fittings, etc., as *bakery, crockery, nursery, scenery, surgery*; the pl. *-eries* is used also beside the sg. in names of wares, as *groceries* (XVII). Cf. -RY.

eryngo sea holly. XVI. irreg. - It. or Sp. *eringio* - L. *ēryngium* - Gr. *ērúggion*, dim. of *ḗruggos*.

erysipelas disease with red inflammation. XVI (XIV-XV *erisipila*). - L. - Gr. *erusípelas*, perh. f. base of *eruthrós* RED + **pel-* skin, FELL[1].

erythema inflammation of the skin. XVIII. - Gr. *erúthēma*, f. *eruthaínein* be red, f. *eruthrós* RED.

escalade scaling the walls of a fortified place. XVI. - F. - It. *scalata*, f. medL. *scalāre* SCALE vb.; see -ADE.

escalator XX. (orig. U.S.). f. stem of prec. + -ATOR.

escallop later form (XVII) of SCALLOP.

escape vb. XIV. The earliest recorded forms are *ascape* and (aphetic) *scape* (- AN., ONF. *ascaper*); the present form is - AN., ONF. *escaper* (mod. *échapper*) :- Rom. **excappāre*, f. EX-[1] + late L. *cappa* cloak. So sb. XIV. In earliest use - OF. *eschap*, later f. the vb. **escapade** escape, runaway flight XVII; flighty piece of conduct XIX. **escapee** XIX. **escapement** in a clock or watch. XVIII. - F. *échappement*; the ref. is to the 'escape' of the toothed wheel from its detention by the pallet.

escarpment (fortif.) ground cut to form a steep slope; (geol.) abrupt face of a ridge or hill range. XIX. - F. *escarpement*, f. *escarper* vb.; see -MENT.

-escent suffix repr. F. *-escent* and its source L. *-ēscēns, -ēscent-*, prp. ending of vbs. in *-ēscere*, chiefly inceptives f. vbs. of state in *-ēre*, e.g. *liquēscere*, f. *liquēre* be LIQUID; primarily occurring in adjs. - L. prps. (orig. through F.), as *deliquescent, effervescent, obsolescent*, the gen. sense being 'beginning to assume a certain state'; also used in several words describing the play of light and colour, as *fluorescent, iridescent, opalescent, phosphorescent*. The corr. sb. suffix is **-escence,** less freq. **-escency.**

eschatology XIX. f. Gr. *éskhatos* last + -LOGY.

escheat lapsing of an estate to the overlord, estate so lapsed. XIV. - OF. *eschete* :- Rom. **excadecta*, sb. use of pp. of **excadēre*, for L. *excidere* fall away, pass away, escape the memory, f. EX-[1] + *cadere* fall. Hence vb. XIV.

eschew XIV. - OF. *eschiver* :- Rom. **skivāre* - Gmc. **skeuχ(w)an* (OHG. *sciuhen*, G. *scheuen*), f. **skeuχ(w)az* SHY[1].

escort armed guard or convoy XVI; accompanying person or persons XVIII. - F. *escorte* - It. *scorta*, sb. use of fem. pp. of *scorgere* guide, conduct :- Rom. **excorrigere*, f. EX-[1] + L. *corrigere* set in order, CORRECT[1]. So vb. XVIII.

escritoire XVIII. - OF. *escritoire* (mod. *écritoire*) orig. 'study' :- L. SCRIPTORIUM.

escrow (leg.) species of deed. XVI. - AN. *escrowe*, OF. *escroe* :- medL. *scrōda* - WGmc. **skraud-* SHRED.

esculent XVII. - L. *ēsculentus*, f. *ēsca* food (:- **ēdskā*), f. **ed-* of *edere* EAT; see -ULENT.

escutcheon XV. - AN., ONF. *escuchon* (OF. *escusson*, mod. *écusson*) :- Rom. **scūtiō, -ōn-*, f. L. *scūtum* shield.

-ese suffix repr. OF. *-eis* (mod. *-ois, -ais*) - L. *-ēnsis, -ēns-*, which meant 'belonging to, originating in (a place)', as *hortēnsis*, f. *hortus* garden, *prātēnsis*, f. *prātum* meadow, and in many adjs. of local names, as *Athēniēnsis* Athenian, f. *Athēnæ* Athens. As a living suffix it forms derivs. of names of countries, as *Chinese, Japanese, Portuguese* (F. *chinois, japonais, portugais*) and from some names of foreign towns, as *Cantonese, Viennese*. Such adjs. are used sb. as names of languages or as designations of peoples.

Eskimo XVI (formerly *Esquimaux*). - Da. *Eskimo* - F. *Esquimaux* pl. - N. Amer. Indian word meaning 'eaters of raw flesh'.

esoteric XVII. - Gr. *esōterikós*, f. *esōtérō* inner, compar. of *ésō* within, f. *es* (*eis*) into; see -IC.

espalier XVII. - F. - It. *spalliera* applied to supports for the shoulders, hence to stakes of that height, f. *spalla* shoulder.

esparto Spanish grass, *Stipa tenacissima*. XVIII. - Sp. :- L. *spartum* - Gk. *spárton*.

especial XIV. - OF. - L. *speciālis*, f. *speciēs* SPECIES. Hence **especially** XVI.

Esperanto XIX. Pen-name Dr. *Esperanto* (i.e. 'hoping one') of the inventor, L. L. Zamenhof.

espionage XVIII. - F. *espionnage*, f. *espionner*, f. *espion* SPY.

esplanade open level space. XVII. - F. - Sp. *esplanada*, f. *esplanar* :- L. *explānāre* flatten out, level; see EXPLAIN, -ADE.

espousal XIV. - OF. *espousaille*, chiefly *espousailles* fem. pl. (mod. *épousailles*) :- L. *spōnsālia*, sb. use of n. pl. of *spōnsālis*, f. *spōnsus* SPOUSE; see -AL[2]. So **espouse** marry XV; embrace opinions XVII.

espy †spy upon; descry. XIV. - OF. *espier* (mod. *épier*); see SPY.

-esque suffix forming adjs., repr. F. *-esque* - It. *-esco* :- Rom. **-iscus* - Gmc. **-iskaz* -ISH[1]; first in adoptions from It. through F. in the basic sense of 'resembling the style of', 'partaking of the characteristics of', as in *arabesque, burlesque, Dantesque, grotesque, picturesque*.

esquire young man attending on a knight; man ranking immediately below a knight XV; as a title XVI. Early forms *escuyer, -ier* - OF. *esquier* (mod. *écuyer*) :- L. *scūtārius* shield-bearer, f. *scūtum* shield. Aphetic SQUIRE is earlier.

-ess[1] suffix forming sbs. denoting female persons and animals - (O)F. *-esse* :- Rom. **-essa*, for late L. *-issa* - Gr. *-issa*.

The suffix became generalized for the formation of fem. derivs. of masc. sbs., e.g. F. *comtesse* (f. *comte*), whence Eng. *countess*, and similarly *duchess, hostess, lioness, mistress, princess*. In OF. *-esse* was added to mascs. in *-ere, -eor*, e.g. *enchanteresse* enchantress; so in ME. *-ess* was added to agent-nouns in *-er* and *-ster*, as *huntress, seamstress, songstress*, contraction taking place where possible; the older †*governeresse* was reduced to *governess*; there are several cases of sbs. in *-tor* with fems. in *-tress* (e.g. *actress, benefactress, traitress*), with the result that this ending corr. to F. *-trice*, L. *-trix*. There was gen. extension to other kinds of sb., as *authoress, goddess, mayoress, poetess, prioress*, for some of which, however, there are F. models.

-ess[2] ME. *-esse* - (O)F. *-esse*, :- L. *-itia*, forming sbs. of quality or condition, as *trīstitia* sadness, f. *trīstis* sad; examples are DURESS, LARGESS, PROWESS, †*richesse* RICHES, all adopted from F.

essay †try, test XV; try *to do* XVI; attempt, try to accomplish XVII. alt. of ASSAY by assim. to F. *essayer* :- Rom. **exagiāre* weigh, f. late L. *exagium* weighing, balance, f. *exag-*, base of L. *exigere* weigh. So **essay** sb. trial, attempt, result of this; form of literary composition. XVI. - (O)F. *essai*. Hence **essayist** XVII.

essence (theol.) substance XIV; †existence, being XVI; that by which a thing is what it is; chemical (etc.) extract of a substance; perfume XVII. - (O)F. - L. *essentia*, f. **essent-*, assumed prp. stem of *esse* be, on the model of Gr. *ousíā*, f. *ont-*, prp. stem of *einai* be. So **essential** XIV - late L. *essentiālis*.

Essene member of a Jewish ascetic sect. XVI. - L. pl. *Essēnī* - Gr. *Essēnoí*, presumably of Heb. or Aram. orig.

-est suffix of superl. adjs. and advs., repr. two OE. suffixes, (i) *-ost* :- Gmc. **-ōstaz* (OS., OHG., Goth. *-ōst*, ON. *-ast*) and (ii) *-(e)st* (accompanied by mutation) :- Gmc. **-istaz* (OS., OHG., Goth. *-ist-*); there are parallels in Gr. *-isto-*, *Skr. -iṣṭha-*. Cf. -ER[3].

establish settle XIV; set up and settle XV; install XVI; prove valid XVIII. - *establiss-*, lengthened stem of OF. *establir* (mod. *établir*) - L. *stabilīre*, f. *stabilis* STABLE[2]; see -ISH[2]. Hence **establishment** XV. Aphetic *stablish* is earlier.

estate (arch.) condition, status XIII; outward pomp XIV; class of the body politic; interest in property XV; property, possessions XVI; landed property XVIII. Early forms *(a)estat, astat(e)* - OF. *estat* (mod. *état*) - L. *status*, f. *stat-*, pp. stem of *stāre* STAND. Cf. STATE.

esteem A. †value, assess XV; hold in (such-and-such) estimation XVI; B. †judge of XV; account, consider XVI. - (O)F. *estimer* - L. *æstimāre* (orig.) fix the price of, estimate (cf. AIM). So **esteem** sb. XIV, **estimable** XVI. **estimate** †judge, esteem XVI; †value, assess; form an approximate notion of XVII. f. pp. stem of L. *æstimāre*. Hence, or - L. *æstimātus*, **estimate** sb. XVI. So **estimation** XIV.

estrange XV. - AN. *estraunger*, OF. *estranger* (mod. *étranger*) :- L. *extrāneāre*, f. *extrāneus* STRANGE.

estuary XVI. - L. *æstuārium* tidal part of a shore, tidal channel, f. *æstus* swell, surge, tide; see -ARY.

esurient hungry. XVII. - L. *esuriēns, -ent-*, prp. of *ēsurīre* be hungry, desiderative vb. f. *ēs-*, pp. stem of *edere* EAT; see -ENT.

-et suffix forming dims. from sbs., repr. (O)F. *-et* m., *-ette* fem., :- Rom. **-itto*, **-itta*, **-ētto*, *-a* of unkn. (perh. non-L.) orig.; it occurs in many adoptions from French, as *budget, gibbet, hatchet, mallet, turret*, in most of which there is no longer any consciousness of a dim. force. For its use in adjs. see *dulcet, russet*. The combination in OF. of *-et* with *-el* produced *-elet*, for which see -LET.

et cetera late OE. - L., *et* and, *cētera* the rest, n. pl. of *cēterus* remaining over.

etch XVII. - Du. *etsen* - G. *ätzen* (OHG. *azzen, ezzen*) :- Gmc. **atjan*, causative of **etan* EAT.

eternal XIV. - OF. *eternal, -el* (mod. *éternel*) - late L. *æternālis*, f. *æternus*, for **æviternus*, f. *ævum* age; see -AL[1]. So **eternity** XIV.

etesian name of certain winds in the Mediterranean area blowing for a certain period annually. XVII. f. L. *etēsius* - Gr. *etḗsios* annual, f. *etes-*, (ϝ)*étos* year; see -IAN.

eth- first part of ETHER used in the formation of names of members of the bicarbon series of hydrocarbons, *ethane, ethene, ethyl*; see -ANE[2], -ENE, -YL.

-eth in *twentieth* to *ninetieth*: see -TH[2].

ether clear sky; (phys.) substance permeating space XVII; (chem.) liquid obtained by the action of acid on alcohol XVIII. - (O)F. *éther* or L. *æthēr* - Gr. *aithḗr* upper air, f. base of *aíthein* kindle, burn, shine, *aíthrā* fine weather, L. *æstās* summer, OIr. *aed* fire. So **etherial** of the ether; heavenly; airy XVI; impalpable XVII; pert. to ether XVIII. f. L. *ætherius* - Gr. *aithérios*. Hence **etherialize** XIX.

ethic adj. XV (now mostly repl. by **ethical** XVII). - F. *éthique* or L. *ēthicus* - Gr. *ēthikós*, f. *êthos* usage, character, personal disposition; sb. sg. moral science XIV, after (O)F. *éthique*, L. *ēthicē*, Gr. (*hē*) *ēthikḗ* (sc. *tékhnē*); **ethics** pl. XV; after OF. *ethiques*, medL. *ethica* n. pl. - Gr. *tà ēthiká*. See -IC, -ICAL, -ICS. So **ethos** XIX. - late L. - Gr. *êthos*.

ethnic †Gentile, pagan XIV; pert. to race XIX. - ecclL. *ethnicus* heathen - Gr. *ethnikós*, f. *éthnos* nation. Hence **ethnography, -ology** XIX.

ethyl see ETH-.

etiolate blanch. XVIII. - F. *étioler* (see -ATE[3]) - Norman F. (*s'*)*étieuler* grow into haulm, f. *ét(i)eule*, (OF. *esteule*) :- pop L. **stupila*, for L. *stipula* straw. So **etiolation** XVIII.

etiology var. (now U.S.) of AETIOLOGY.

etiquette prescribed or conventional code of behaviour XVIII. - F. *étiquette*, the primary sense of which is repr. by TICKET.

etna vessel for heating liquid. XIX. f. the name of the volcano *Etna* in Sicily.

-ette suffix repr. F. *-ette* (OF. *-ete*), and forming dim. sbs., being the fem. corr. to masc. (O)F. *-et* (see -ET). In ME. the F. *-et* and *-ette* were not clearly distinguished, and old adoptions in *-et(t)e* usu. survive with *-et*, e.g. *egret, hatchet*. The sp. *-ette* is preserved in adoptions dating from XVII onwards, as *cigarette, coquette, etiquette, gazette, rosette*. In XIX it began to be extended to Eng. sbs., as *waggonnette*, and esp. in names of materials intended as imitations, as *flannelette, leatherette*.

étui small case for small articles. XVII. - F. *étui*, OF. *estui* prison, f. *estuier* shut up, keep.

etymology origin, formation, and development (of a word), account of this XIV; †branch of grammar dealing with forms (formerly equiv. to *accidence*) XV. - OF. *ethimologie* (mod. *étymologie*) - L. *etymologia* - Gr. *etumologiā*, f. *etumológos* student of etymology, f. *étumon* literal sense of a word, original form, primary or basic word, sb. use of n. of *étumos* true, whence in L. form **etymon** XVI; see -LOGY. So **etymological** XVI, **etymologist** XVII, **-ize** XVI.

eu- prefix repr. Gr. *eu-*, comb. form of Gr. (Epic) *eús* good, brave, used in n. form *eû* as adv. 'well'. Gr. words with *eu-* are predominantly adjs. of the form *eúphōnos* of good sound, well-sounding, EUPHONIOUS. For mod. formations see EUGENIC, etc.; **eurhythmics** harmony of bodily movement as an object of education.

eucalyptus XIX. modL., intended to denote 'well-covered' (f. EU- + Gr. *kaluptós* covered, f. *kalúptein* cover, conceal), the flower before it opens being protected by a cap.

eucharis S. Amer. plant with bell-shaped flowers used for bouquets, etc. XIX. modL. - Gr. *eúkharis* pleasing, f. EU- + *kháris* grace (cf. next).

Eucharist XIV. - OF. *eucariste* (mod., with latinized ending, *eucharistie*) - ecclL. *eucharistia* - ecclGr. *eukharistíā* giving of thanks, f. *eukháristos* grateful, f. EU- + *kharízesthai* show favour, give freely, f. *kháris*, *kharit-* favour, grace. So **eucharistic** XVII, **-ical** XVI.

euchre card-game originating in U.S.A. XIX (early sp. *(e)uker*, *yuker*). of unkn. orig.

eud(a)emonism system of ethics having happiness for its end. XIX. - Gr. *eudaimonismós*, f. *eudaimonízein* call or account happy, f. EU- + *daímōn* guardian genius; see DEMON, -ISM. So **eud(a)emonist** XIX.

eudiometer (orig.) instrument for testing the amount of oxygen in the air. XVIII. f. Gr. *eúdios* (of weather) clear, f. EU + stem of *Diós*, gen. of *Zeús* god of the sky and the atmosphere; see -METER.

eugenic concerned with the production of fine offspring; (pl. *-ics*) science of this. XIX. f. EU- + Gr. *gen-* produce (see KIN).

eulogy XVI. (once †*euloge* XV). - medL. *eulogium*, app. blending of L. *ēlogium* (of obscure orig.) inscription on a tomb, etc., and medL. *eulogia* - Gr. *eulogiā* praise, f. phr. *eû légein* speak well of; cf. EU-, -LOGY. Hence **eulogist** XVIII, **eulogistic** XIX.

eunuch XV. - L. *eunūchus* - Gr. *eunoûkhos*, f. *eunḗ* bed; lit. 'bedchamber guard'.

euonymus (bot.) genus of shrubs. XVIII. mod. use of L. *euōnymus* - Gr. *euṓnumos* lucky, f. EU- + *ónuma*, var. of *ónoma* NAME.

eupeptic pert. to good digestion. XVII. f. Gr. *eúpeptos* easy of digestion, having a good digestion, f. EU- + *péptein* digest; see -IC.

euphemism XVII. - Gr. *euphēmismós*, f. *euphēmízein* speak fair, f. *eúphēmos* fair of speech, f. EU- + *phḗmē* speaking; see FAME, -ISM. So **euphemistic** XIX.

euphonium XIX. f. Gr. *eúphōnos*; see next.

euphony XVII (once XV). - F. *euphonie* - late L. *euphōnia* - Gr. *euphōníā*, f. *eúphōnos* well-sounding, f. EU- + *phōnḗ* sound, voice; see -Y[3]. Hence **euphonious** XVIII.

euphorbia the spurge genus. XVII. alt. (by assim. to -IA[1]) of L. *euphorbea*, f. *Euphorbus*, name of a physician of Juba II, king of Mauretania, who is said to have named the plant after him.

euphrasy the plant eye-bright. XV. - medL. *euphrasia* - Gr. *euphrasiā* cheerfulness, f. *euphraínein* be cheerful, f. EU- + *phrḗn* mind; see -Y[3].

euphuism precious style of diction characteristic of John Lyly's '*Euphues*, the anatomy of wyt' (1579) and '*Euphues* and his England' (1580). XVI. f. Gr. *euphuḗs* well endowed by nature, f. EU- + *phu-* (BE); see -ISM. Hence **euphuist, euphuistic** XIX.

Eurasian pert. to the continental area comprising Europe and Asia; of mixed European and Asiatic parentage. XIX. f. *Eur(ope)* + *Asia*; see -AN.

eureka exclamation (Gr. *heúrēka* I have found, perf. of *heurískein* find) uttered by Archimedes when he discovered the means of determining by specific gravity the proportion of base metal in Hiero's golden crown. XVII.

European XVII. - F. *européen*, f. L. *eurōpæus*, f. *Eurōpa* - Gr. *Eurṓpē* (of unkn. orig.), first applied to central Greece; see -EAN.

Eustachian (anat.) epithet of organs or structures discovered by Bartolomeo *Eustachi*, Italian anatomist (*c.*1500-74); see -IAN. XVIII.

euthanasia easy death XVII; means of bringing this about XVIII. - Gr. *euthanasiā*, f. EU- + *thánatos* death.

evacuate XV. f. pp. stem of L. *ēvacuāre*, f. E- + *vacuus* empty; see -ATE[3]. So **evacuation** XIV. - late L. Hence **evacuee** XX.

evade XVI. - F. *évader* - L. *ēvādere*, f. E- + *vādere* go (cf. WADE). So **evasion** XV, **evasive** XVIII.

evaluate XIX. Back-formation, after (O)F. *évaluer*, from **evaluation** (XVIII; - (O)F.; see E-, VALUATION).

evanescent XVIII. - F. *évanescent* - prp. of L. *ēvānēscere*, whence **evanesce** XIX; see E-, VANISH, -ENT.

evangel (arch.) gospel. XIV. ME. *evangile* (later assim. to L.) - (O)F. *évangile* - ecclL. *ēvangelium* - Gr. *euaggélion* (in eccl. use) good news, (in classical Gr.) reward for bringing good news, pl. sacrifice on receiving good news, f. *euággelos* bringing good news, f. EU- + *aggéllein* announce. So **evangelic** XV, now more usu. **evangelical** XVI. - ecclL. *ēvangelicus* - ecclGr. *euaggelikós*. **evangelism** XVII. **evangelist** writer of one of the four gospels XII; preacher of the gospel XIV. - (O)F. - ecclL. - ecclGr. **evangelize** †intr. XIV, trans. XVII. - ecclL. - ecclGr.

evaporate XVI (pa. pple. XIV). f. pp. stem of L. *ēvaporāre*; see E-, VAPOUR, -ATE[3]. So **evaporation** XIV. - L.

eve (poet.) evening; day before a festival. XIII. var. of EVEN[1], orig. southern. For loss of *-n*, cf. *clew*, *game*, *maid*.

even[1] (poet., dial.) close of the day OE.; eve of a holy day XIV. OE. *ǣfen*, rel. to synon. OS. *āband*,

MLG., MDu. *āvont* (Du. *avond*), OHG. *āband* (G. *abend*), perh. rel. to Gr. *epí* (see EPI-). Synon. ON. *aptann* may be another formation on the same base, or (more prob.) a deriv. of the base of AFTER. In contr. form *e'en* arch. and dial. Cf. EVE, EVENING. Hence **evensong, eventide,** OE. *ǣfensang, -tīd*.

even² flat, level (obs. in gen. use; naut. in *an even keel*); uniform, equal, equally balanced OE.; exactly adjusted, precise XIII; of number, opp. to *odd* XIV. OE. *efen* = OS. *eƀan* (Du. *even, effen*), OHG. *eban* (G. *eben*), ON. *jafn*, Goth. *ibns* :- Gmc. **eƀnaz*, of unkn. orig. So **even** adv. (poet. **e'en**) †evenly, equally; (arch.) exactly, fully OE.; in the extreme case XVI. OE. *efne* = OS. *efno* (Du. *even*), OHG. *ebano* (G. *eben*) :- WGmc. **eƀnō*. **even** vb. OE. *efnan* and *(ġe)efnian*.

evening †closing of the day OE.; latter part of the day. XV. OE. *ǣfnung*, f. *ǣfnian* grow towards night, f. *ǣfen* EVEN¹; see -ING¹.

event outcome, issue; anything that happens. XVI. - L. *ēventus*, f. *ēvent-*, pp. stem of *ēvenīre* come out, result, happen, f. E- + *venīre* COME. Hence, or direct from L. *ēventus*, **eventual** †pert. to an event or events; that will take effect in certain contingencies XVII. **eventuate** XVIII. orig. U.S.

ever OE. *ǣfre*, a purely Eng. formation, of unkn. orig. The first syll. is prob. the mutation of *ā* ever, AY. Hence **evergreen** XVII, **everlasting** XIV, **evermore** XIII.

everglade (US.) marshy tract under water, (esp. pl.) the vast swampy region of Florida. XIX. Presumably f. EVER + GLADE.

every Late OE. *ǣfriċ*, ME. *efri(ch), eauer euch, euere(l)ch*, repr. OE. *ǣfre ǣlċ*, **ǣfre ylċ*; see EVER, EACH. Comp. **everybody** XIV, **every one** XIII, **everything** XIV. In **everywhere** (XII) two formations have coalesced: (i) *ever* + *iwhere* (OE. *ġehwǣr* anywhere, everywhere), and (ii) *every* + *where*.

evict recover (property) XV; expel (a person) by judicial process; †conquer, overcome; †prove XVI. f. *ēvict-*, pp. stem of L. *ēvincere* conquer, obtain by conquering, recover, overcome and expel, eject judicially, prove; see EVINCE. So **eviction** XVI. - L.

evident XIV. - (O)F. *évident* or L. *ēvidēns, -ent-*, f. E- + prp. of *vidēre* see, used in a middle sense ('making itself seen'). So **evidence** significant appearance, token XIII; ground for belief XIV; information (given in a legal inquiry) tending to establish fact XVI; clarity XVII. - (O)F. - L.; whence **evidential** XVII. **evidently** XIV.

evil adj. and sb. OE. *yfel* = OS. *uƀil*, MDu. *evel* (Du. *euvel*), OHG. *ubil* (G. *übel*), Goth. *ubils* :- Gmc. **ubilaz*, prob. f. IE. base **up-* (see OVER), the primary sense being 'exceeding due limits'. So **evil** adv., OE. *yfle*; survives in literary use in *speak evil* (of), *evil-disposed*, and the like.

evince †overcome; †convince; †prove; make evident. XVII. f. L. *ēvincere*, f. E- + *vincere* conquer. Cf. EVICT.

eviscerate XVII. f. pp. stem of L. *ēviscerāre*; see E-, VISCERA, -ATE³.

evoke call forth. XVII. - L. *ēvocāre*, f. E- + *vocāre* call. So **evocation** XVII (once XV). **evocative** XVII. - late L.

evolution XVII. - L. *ēvolūtiō, -ōn-* unrolling of a book, f. *ēvolūt-*, pp. stem of *ēvolvere* (f. E- + *volvere* roll), whence **evolve** XVII.

evulsion forcible extraction. XVII. - L. *ēvulsiō, -ōn-*, f. *ēvuls-*, pp. stem of *ēvellere*, f. E- + *vellere* pluck; see -SION.

ewe OE. *ēowu*, corr. to OS. *ewwi* (MDu. *oie*, Du. *ooi*), OHG. *ou(wi)* (G. *aue*), ON. *ær* :- Gmc. **awi-* (repr. in Goth. by *awistr* sheepfold, *aweþi* flock) :- IE. **owi-*, repr. also by L. *ovis*, Gr. *ó(ϝ)is*, OIr. *ói*, OSl. *ovĭca*, Lith. *avìs*, Skr. *ávi-* sheep.

ewer XIV. - AN. **ewere*, ONF. *eviere*, (O)F. *aiguière* :- Rom. **aquāria*, fem. of L. *aquārius* pert. to water, f. *aqua* water; see -ARY.

ex L. *ex* out of, prep. and prefix (see EX-¹, E-) = Gr. *ex* (see EX-²), OIr. *ess-*. In Eng. in certain L. phrs., as **ex cathedra** from the CHAIR (i.e. of authority) XIX; **ex libris** 'out of the books' (of somebody), from the LIBRARY (of) XIX; **ex officio** by virtue of one's OFFICE XVI; **ex(-)parte** with respect to a PART, (leg.) on one side only XVII; **ex voto** (short for *ex voto suscepto* from a vow undertaken) offering made in pursuance of a vow XVIII.

b. Prefixed to titles of rank after late L. usage in *excōnsul*, nom. evolved from *ex cōnsule* 'from (being) consul', (hence) lately consul; whence gen. with the sense 'former', as in *ex-professor*, and by further extension prefixed to adjs. (after *ex-consular* XVII) or to sbs. used attrib., as *ex-service*.

c. In commercial use, with ref. to goods, 'out of', 'landed from' (a ship); similarly *ex-warehouse*; 'without', 'exclusive of', as in *ex dividend*.

ex-¹ prefix repr. L. *ex-*, the prep. (see prec.) used in combination. After *ex-*, *s* (as in *exsequī, exserere, exstare*) was later dropped; hence the spelling of EXECRATE, EXECUTE, EXERT, EXTANT, EXTIRPATE. *Ex-* was reduced to *ē-* before *b, d, g, i* (*j*), *l, m, n, r*, and *u* (cf. EBULLIENT, EDICT, EGRESS, EJECT, ELECT, EMIT, ENUNCIATE, ERECT, EVADE), and to *ef-* before *f* (cf. EFFECT).

ex-² prefix repr. Gr. *ex-*, the prep. (see EX) used in combination; before consonants *ek-*, EC-.

exacerbate increase the bitterness of. XVII. f. pp. stem of L. *exacerbāre*, f. EX-¹ + *acerbus* bitter; see -ATE³. So **exacerbation** XVI. - late L.

exact XVI. - L. *exactus*, pp. of *exigere* complete, bring to perfection, examine, ascertain, f. EX-¹ + *agere* perform. So **exact** vb. demand esp. by force and with authority. XV. f. *exact-*, pp. stem of L. *exigere* drive out, enforce payment of, demand, etc. (as above). **exaction** XIV. **exactitude** XVIII. - F.

exaggerate †accumulate, pile up XVI; make (a thing) out greater than it is XVII. f. pp. stem of L. *exaggerāre*, f. EX-¹ + *aggerāre* heap up, f. *agger* heap, prob. f. AG- + *gerere* carry; see -ATE³. So **exaggeration** XVI. - L.

exalt XV. - L. *exaltāre*, f. EX-¹ + *altus* high. So **exaltation** lifting up XIV; elation XV. - (O)F. or late L.

exam short for EXAMINATION. XIX.

examine XIV. - (O)F. *examiner* - L. *exāmināre* weigh accurately, f. *exāmen*, *-in-* tongue of a balance, weighing, for **exagmen*, f. **exag-*, base of *exigere* examine, weigh (see EXACT). So **examination** XIV.

example object or action to copy or imitate; instance to warn or deter XIV; typical instance XV. - OF. *example* (mod. *exemple*), refash. after L. of *essample* - L. *exemplum*, f. **exem-*, *eximere* take out (see EXEMPT).

exarch governor of a province under the Byzantine emperors; metropolitan in the Eastern Church. XVI. - ecclL. *exarchus* - Gr. *éxarkhos* leader, chief, f. *exárkhein* take the lead, f. EX-[2] + *árkhein* rule.

exasperate XVI. f. pp. stem of L. *exasperāre*, f. EX-[1] + *asper* rough; see -ATE[3]. So **exasperation** XVI. - L.

excavate XVI. f. pp. stem of L. *excavāre*, f. EX-[1] + *cavāre*, f. *cavus* hollow; see -ATE[3]. So **excavation** XVII. - F. or L.

exceed †pass the limits of; be greater than XIV; be superior to XV. - (O)F. *excéder* - L. *excēdere* depart, go beyond, surpass, f. EX-[1] + *cēdere* go.

excel XV. - L. *excellere* be eminent, (rarely in physical sense) rise, raise, f. EX-[1] + *-cellere*, rel. to *celsus* high, *columna* COLUMN. So **excellent** †exalted, supreme XIV; extremely good XVII. - (O)F. - L. **excellence, -ency** XIV.

except[1] leave out of account. XV. f. *except-*, pp. stem of L. *excipere*, f. EX-[1] + *capere* take. So **exception** action of excepting, case excepted XIV; defendant's plea in bar of plaintiff's action XV; objection, demur XVI. - (O)F. - L. Hence **exceptionable** XVIII, **exceptional** XIX. **excepting** prp. passing into prep., if one excepts, except. XV.

except[2] †pp. excepted; prep. if one leaves out of account XIV; †conj. unless XV; otherwise than XVI. - L. *exceptus*, pp. of *excipere* (see prec.). The prep. arose (i) partly from the use of the pp. in concord with a following sb. or pronoun, e.g. *except women*, i.e. women excepted, (ii) partly in imitation of (O)F. *excepté* excepted, and late L. abl. *exceptō*, which was used as a prep. by extension of the classical L. usage with a clause, *exceptō quod* . . . except that . . . (whence the conjunctional use of *except*).

excerpt sb. XVII. - L. *excerptum*, sb. use of n. pp. of *excerpere*, f. EX-[1] + *carpere* pluck. So vb. XVI (pp. once XV). f. L. *excerpt-*, pp. stem.

excess †extravagant feeling or conduct; overstepping limits of moderation XIV; fact of exceeding in amount XVI. - (O)F. *excès* - L. *excessus*, f. *excess-*, pp. stem of *excēdere* EXCEED. So **excessive** XIV.

exchange sb. XIV. ME. *eschaunge*, later (by assim. to L.) *exchaunge* - AN. *eschaunge*, OF. *eschange* (F. *échange*), f. *eschanger* (mod. *é-*), whence **exchange** vb. XV; f. *es-* :- EX-[1], CHANGE.

exchequer †chess-board XIII; department of state concerned with the royal revenues, so called orig. with ref. to the table covered with a cloth divided into squares on which the accounts were kept by means of counters XIV; court of law theoretically concerned with revenue; office charged with the receipt and custody of public revenue XV; pecuniary possessions XVII. ME. *escheker* - AN. *escheker*, OF. *eschequier* - medL. *scaccārium* chess-board, f. *scaccus* CHECK[1]; see -ER[2]. The form with *ex-* (from XV) is due to assoc. of OF. *es-* with EX-[1], as in *exchange*.

excise[1] †toll, tax XV; duty on commodities XVII. - MDu. *excijs* - OF. *acceis* :- Rom. **accēnsum*, f. L. AC- + *cēnsus* tax (see CENSUS).

excise[2] cut out. XVI. f. *excīs-*, pp. stem of L. *excīdere*, f. EX-[1] + *cædere* cut. So **excision** XV. - (O)F. - L.

excite XIV. - (O)F. *exciter* or L. *excitāre*, frequent. of *exciēre* (pp. *excitus*) call out or forth; see EX-[1], CITE. So **excitation** XIV. - (O)F. - late L. **excitement** †instigation, incentive XVII; (path.) abnormal activity XVIII; mental stimulation XIX.

exclaim XVI. - F. *exclamer* or L. *exclamāre*; see EX-[1], CLAIM. So **exclamation** XIV. **exclamatory** XVI. - L.

exclude XIV. - L. *exclūdere*, f. EX-[1] + *claudere* shut (see CLOSE). So **exclusion, exclusive** XV.

excommunicate XV. f. pp. stem of ecclL. *excommūnicāre*, f. EX-[1] + *commūnis* COMMON, after *commūnicāre* COMMUNICATE. So **excommunication** XV. - late L.

excoriate remove the skin from, flay. XV. f. pp. stem of L. *excoriāre*, f. EX- + *corium* hide; see -ATE[3]. So **excoriation** XV.

excrement †dregs; faeces. XVI. - F. *excrément* or L. *excrēmentum*, f. *excrē-*, pp. base of *excernere*, f. EX-[1] + *cernere* sift; see -MENT. So **excreta** XIX. sb. use of n. pl. of *excrētus*, pp. of *excernere*. **excretion** XVII.

excrescence XV. - L. *excrēscentia*, f. prp. of *excrēscere* grow out; see EX-[1], INCREASE, -ENCE. So **excrescent** XVII.

excruciate torture. XVI. f. pp. stem of L. *excruciāre*, f. EX-[1] + *cruciāre* torment, f. *crux* CROSS; see -ATE[3].

exculpate XVII. f. pp. stem of medL. **exculpāre*, f. EX-[1] + *culpa* blame; see -ATE[3].

excursion †escape; sally, sortie XVI; journey from home XVII. - L. *excursiō*, *-ōn-*, f. *excurs-*, pp. stem of *excurrere* run out, issue forth, f. EX-[1] + *currere*; see COURSE, -ION. Hence **excursionist** XIX. So **excursus** XIX.

excuse offer an apology for XIII; obtain exemption or release for; accept as an excuse for or from XIV; serve as an excuse for XVI. ME *escuse*, *excuse* - OF. *escuser*, (also mod.) *excuser* - L. *excusāre* free from blame, plead in excuse, absolve, dispense with, f. EX-[1] + *causa* accusation (see CAUSE). So sb. XIV. - (O)F., f. *excuser*. The pronunc. with *s* instead of *z* in the sb. is due to the analogy of pairs like *use*, *abuse* vbs. and sbs., *advise* and *advice*, where the F. sbs. are masculines ending in *s*.

exeat †stage direction repl. by *exit* XVI; permission to go out or leave XVIII. - L., 'let him go out', 3rd pers. sg. pres. subj. of *exīre* go out.

execrate express or feel abhorrence of. XVI. f. pp. stem of L. *ex(s)ecrārī* curse, f. EX-[1] + *sacrāre* devote religiously, f. *sacer*, *sacr-* religiously set apart; see SACRED, -ATE[3]. So **execration** XIV. - (O)F. or L. **execrable** †involving a curse XIV;

abominable XV. - (O)F. *exécrable* - L. (in act. and pass. senses).

execute A. carry into effect, carry out XIV; fulfil, discharge XIV; make valid by signing, etc.; carry out the design of, perform XVIII; B. inflict capital punishment on XV. - (O)F. *exécuter* - medL. *executāre*, f. *ex(s)ecūt-*, pp. stem of L. *ex(s)equī* follow up, carry out, pursue judicially, punish, f. EX-[1] + *sequī* follow. So **execution** carrying into effect XIV; infliction of capital punishment XV; enforcement of a judgement, effective action XVI; hence **executioner** XVI. **executive** XVII; sb. XVIII (first U.S.). **executor** XIII (of an estate). - AN. *executo(u)r* - L. *execūtor*.

exegesis XVII. - Gr. *exḗgēsis*, f. *exēgeîsthai* interpret, f. EX-[2] + *hēgeîsthai* guide. So **exegete** XVIII. - Gr. *exēgētḗs*. **exegetic, -ical** XVII. - Gr. *exēgētikós*.

exemplar pattern, example XIV; typical specimen XVII. - (O)F. *exemplaire* - late L. *exemplārium*, f. L. *exemplum* EXAMPLE. So **exemplary** XVI. - late L. *exemplāris*. **exemplify** XV. - medL. *exemplificāre*.

exempt †removed, excluded *from* XIV; *exempt from* not subject to XV. - (O)F. - L. *exemptus*, pp. of *eximere* take out, deliver, free, f. EX-[1] + *emere* take. So **exempt** vb. XV, **exemption** XIV.

exequatur (leg.) official authorization. XVIII. - L., 'let him perform', 3rd pers. sg. pres. subj. of *exequī* EXECUTE.

exequies funeral rites. XIV. - OF. - L. acc. *exsequiās*, nom. *-iæ* funeral procession or ceremonies, f. *exsequī* follow after, accompany (see EXECUTE).

exercise employment, practice XIV; task prescribed for training or testing; religious observance XVI. - (O)F. *exercice* - L. *exercitium*, f. *exercēre* keep busy or at work, practise, train, vex, f. EX-[1] + *arcēre* shut up, keep off, restrain, prevent. Hence vb. XIV.

exert †discharge, emit; exercise, bring to bear. XVII. f. *exert-*, pp. stem of L. *ex(s)erere* put forth, f. EX-[1] + *serere* bind, entwine, join. So **exertion** XVII.

exeunt stage direction for certain actors to leave the stage. XV. - L., 'they go out', 3rd pers. pl. pres. ind. of *exīre* go out.

exhale give off as vapour XIV; breathe or blow out XVI. - (O)F. *exhaler* - L. *exhalāre*, f. EX-[1] + *halāre* breathe. So **exhalation** XIV.

exhaust draw off or out, drain. XVI. f. *exhaust-*, pp. stem of L. *exhaurīre*, f. EX-[1] + *haurīre*, draw (water), drain. Hence as sb. XIX. So **exhaustion** XVII.

exhibit †offer, furnish, administer XV; submit to view, display XVI. f. *exhibit-*, pp. stem of L. *exhibēre*, f. EX-[1] + *habēre* hold. So **exhibition** visible display XIV; †maintenance, allowance XV (surviving in spec. sense of school or college bursary XVII); public display of objects, etc. XVIII. - (O)F. - late L. (delivery, maintenance).

exhilarate XVI. f. pp. stem of L. *exhilarāre*, f. EX-[1] + *hilaris* cheerful, gay; see -ATE[3].

exhort XIV. - (O)F. *exhorter* or L. *exhortārī*, f. EX-[1] + *hortārī* encourage. So **exhortation** XIV.

exhume XVIII (once XV). - F. *exhumer* - medL. *exhumāre*, f. EX-[1] + *humus* ground. So **exhumation** XVIII (once XV).

exigent †sb. exigency, extremity XV; adj. urgent XVII; exacting XIX. As sb. - OF. *exigent* sb.; as adj. - L. *exigēns, -ent-*, prp. of *exigere* EXACT; see -ENT. So **exigence, -ency** XVI. - (O)F. and late L.

exiguous XVII. f. L. *exiguus* scanty in measure or number, f. *exigere* weigh exactly; see EXACT, -UOUS.

exile[1] enforced removal or absence from one's country. XIII. - (O)F. *exil*, latinized refash. of earlier *essil* - L. *exilium*, f. *exul* exiled person, f. EX-[1] + **-ul-*, as in *ambulāre* walk (see AMBLE). So **exile**[2] exiled person. XIV. prob. - (O)F. *exilé*, pp. of *exiler*, with muting of the final syll. as in ASSIGN[2], etc., infl. by L. *exul*. **exile**[3] vb. make an exile of. XIV. - (O)F. *exil(i)er*, refash. of *essilier* - late L. *exiliāre*, f. *exilium*.

exist XVII. ult. - L. *ex(s)istere* appear, come forward, come into being, f. EX-[1] + *sistere* take up a position, redupl. formation on **sta-* STAND; prob. immed. back-formation on **existence** XIV - (O)F. or late L. **existent** XVI. - L.

exit A. (theatr.) direction to a player to leave the stage (repl. EXEAT), (hence) departure from the stage XVI. B. departure from life, death; egress, outlet XVII. In A 3rd pers. sg. pres. ind. of L. *exīre* go out, f. EX-[1] + *īre* go; in B mainly - L. *exitus*, f. pp. stem of *exīre*.

exo- prefix repr. Gr. *éxō* outside, f. EX-[2]; used in e.g. **exogamy** (Gr. *gámos* marriage) custom of a man's taking a wife from outside his clan. XIX. **exogen** (bot.) plant of which the stem grows by deposit on the outside (- F. *exogène*). XIX.

exodus departure, spec. of the Israelites out of Egypt (hence, title of the second book of the Pentateuch, which relates this). XVII. - ecclL. *Exodus* - Gr. *éxodos*, f. EX-[2] + *hodós* way.

exonerate †unload, relieve of a burden; relieve or free *from* an obligation, reproach, etc. XVI (pp. once XV). f. pp. stem of L. *exonerāre*, f. EX-[1] + *onus, oner-* burden; see -ATE[3].

exorbitant deviating from the right or normal path XV; (grossly) exceeding proper bounds XVII. prp. of ChrL. *exorbitāre*, f. EX-[1] + *orbita* ORBIT; see -ANT.

exorcism expulsion of an evil spirit by adjuration, etc. XIV. - ecclL. *exorcismus* - ecclGr. *exorkismós*, f. *exorkízein*, f. EX-[2] + *hórkos* oath; see -ISM. So **exorcist** XIV. **exorcize** XV. - F. or ecclL.

exordium beginning of a discourse. XVI. - L., f. *exordīrī*, f. EX-[1] + *ordīrī* begin, rel. to *ordō* ORDER.

exoteric XVII. - L. *exōtericus* - Gr. *exōterikós*, f. *exōtérō*, compar. of *éxō* outside; see EXO-, -IC.

exotic foreign, not indigenous. XVI. - L. *exōticus* - Gr. *exōtikós*, f. *éxō* outside (see EXO-).

expand XV. - L. *expandere*, f. EX-[1] + *pandere* spread. So **expanse** wide extent. XVII. - L. *expansum* (n. of *expansus*, pp. of *expandere*). **expansion** XVII.

expatiate (arch.) walk about at large XVI; discourse at length XVII. - L. *ex(s)patiārī, -āt-*, f. EX-[1] + *spatiārī* walk, f. *spatium* SPACE; see -ATE[3].

expatriate withdraw from one's native country. XVIII. f. medL. *expatriāre, -āt-*, f.

EX-[1] + *patria* native land. Hence **expatriate** sb., **expatriation** XIX.

expect †wait, wait for; look for in anticipation. XVI. - L. *ex(s)pectāre*, f. EX-[1] + *spectāre* look (see SPECTACLE). So **expectant** XIV. - L. *expectāns* prp. **expectancy, -ation** XVI.

expectorate eject (phlegm) XVII; spit XIX. f. pp. stem of L. *expectorāre*, f. EX-[1] + *pectus, pector-* breast; see -ATE[3].

expedite †clear of difficulties; help forward, dispatch. XVII. f. *expedīt-*, pp. stem of L. *expedīre* extricate (orig. free the feet), make ready, put in order, f. EX-[1] + *pēs, ped-* FOOT; see -ITE. So **expedient** XIV. f. prp. of the L. vb. **expedition** †prompt action, dispatch; warlike enterprise XV; journey made for a purpose; prompt movement XVI. - (O)F. - L. Hence **expeditious** XV.

expel XIV. - L. *expellere*, f. EX-[1] + *pellere* drive, thrust. So **expulsion, expulsive** XIV.

expend XV. - L. *expendere*, f. EX-[1] + *pendere* weigh, pay, rel. to *pendēre* hang. Hence **expenditure** XVIII; after †*expenditor* officer having charge of expenditure XV-XIX (- medL., f. *expenditus*, irreg. pp. of *expendere*). So **expense** XIV. - AN. *expense*, alt. of OF. *espense* - late L. *expensa*, fem. of pp. **expensive** XVII. f. *expens-*, pp. stem; assoc. early with *expense*.

experience †trial; observation of facts; condition or event by which one is affected XIV; knowledge resulting from observation; state of having been occupied in some way XV. - (O)F. *expérience* - L. *experientia*, f. *experīrī* try; see EX-[1], PERIL, -ENCE. Hence vb. XVI. So **experiment** †test, trial; action undertaken to discover or test something. XIV. Hence vb. †experience, ascertain, test XV; make an experiment XVIII. **experimental** XV. - (O)F. or medL. **expert** trained by experience XIV. - (O)F. *expert*, refash. of †*espert* after L. *expertus*, pp. of *experīrī*. **expert** one who is expert, specialist. XIX. - F., sb. use of the adj. **expertise** XIX. - F.

expiate †bring to an end XVI; avert evil from; do away the guilt of, make amends for XVII. f. pp. stem of L. *expiāre*, f. EX-[1] + *piāre* seek to appease (by sacrifice), f. *pius* devout, PIOUS; see -ATE[3]. So **expiation** XV. - L.

expire breathe one's last, come to an end XV; breathe out XVI. - (O)F *expirer* - *ex(s)pīrāre*, f. EX-[1] + *spīrāre* breathe. So **expiration** coming to an end, †death XVI; breathing out XVII (once XV). - L. Hence **expiry** dying, death XVIII; termination XIX. **expiratory** XIX.

explain unfold (a matter), give details of XV; †open out, smoothe; assign a meaning to XVII; account for XVIII. - L. *explānāre*, f. EX-[1] + *plānus* PLAIN. So **explanation** XIV, **explanatory** XVII.

expletive serving to fill out; sb. expletive word. XVII (used of a profane oath, etc. XIX). - late L. *explētīvus*, f. *explēre*, f. EX-[1] + *plēre* fill; see FULL, -IVE.

explicate unfold, †lit. and fig. XVI. f. pp. stem of L. *explicāre*, f. EX-[1] + *plicāre* fold; see PLY[1], -ATE[3]. So **explicable** XVI. **explication** XVI. - F. or L. **explicit**[1] XVII. - F. *explicite* or L. *explicitus*, pp. of *explicāre*.

explicit[2] late L. formula used by scribes to indicate the end of a book or piece, prob. orig. short (on the analogy of INCIPIT) for *explicitus est liber* the book is unfolded or exhibited (see prec.), but regarded as a verb in 3rd pers. sing. ('here ends').

explode †reject XVI; bring into discredit XVII (now chiefly in pp.); 'go off' or cause to do so with a loud noise XVIII. - L. *explōdere* drive out by clapping, hiss off the stage, f. EX-[1] + *plaudere* clap the hands. So **explosion** XVII. - F. or L. **explosive** XVII; sb. XIX. f. *explōs-*, pp. stem.

exploit †progress, success XIV; †attempt to control or capture XVI; deed, feat XVI. ME. *es-*, *exploit, -pleit* - OF. *esploit* m., *esploite* fem. (mod. *exploit*, with latinized prefix) :- Gallo-Rom. **explictum*, *-*ta*, L. *explicitum, -ta* n. and fem. pps of *explicāre* EXPLICATE; orig. 'something unfolded or put forth'. So vb. †achieve XIV; †prosper XV; (after mod. F.) turn to account, make capital out of, esp. in unfavourable sense XIX. - OF. *espleiter* accomplish, enjoy (mod. *exploiter*) :- Gallo-Rom. **explicitare*, f. *explicāre*. **exploitation** XIX.

explore seek to ascertain, examine into XVI; search into (a country, etc.) XVII. - F. *explorer* - L. *explōrāre* search out. So **exploration** XVI. - F. or L.

exponent interpreting XVI; sb. (math.) index of a power XVIII; expounder, interpreter XIX. - L. *expōnēns, -ent-*, prp. of *expōnere* EXPOUND. So **exponential** (math.) XVIII. - F. *exponentiel*.

export †carry away XV; send from one country to another XVII. - L. *exportāre*, f. EX-[1] + *portāre* carry (cf. PORT[4]). Hence sb. XVII. So **exportation** XVII.

expose deprive of shelter; lay open; disclose XV; exhibit or offer publicly XVII. - (O)F. *exposer*, based on L. *expōnere*; see EXPOUND, POSE[1]. So **exposition** explanation, interpretation XIV; setting forth in description; displaying to view XVII. - (O)F. or L. **expositor** XIV. - (O)F. or late L. **expository** XVII. - late L. *expositōrius*. **exposure** XVII.

ex post facto erron. division of medL. *ex postfacto* from what is done afterwards, i.e. *ex* from, out of, with abl. of *postfactum*, i.e. *post* after + pp. of *facere* DO[1]. XVII (attrib. XVIII).

expostulate †demand, urge, complain of; make friendly objections. XVI. f. pp. stem of L. *expostulāre*; see EX-[1], POSTULATE. So **expostulation** XVI. - L.

expound XIII. ME. *expoun(d)e* - OF. *espondre* (pres. stem *espon-*) :- L. *expōnere* put out, publish, explain, f. EX-[1] + *pōnere* put, place. Cf. EXPOSITION (which serves as noun of action to the vbs. *expose* and *expound*).

express portray, represent; press out XIV. - OF. *expresser* - Rom. **expressāre*, f. EX-[1] + *pressāre* PRESS; repr. in use L. *exprimere*. So adj. explicitly stated; specially designed for a purpose XIV (*express train* orig. special train, XIX). - (O)F. *exprès* - L. *expressus* distinctly or manifestly presented, pp. of *exprimere*. **expression** representation, manifestation XV; pressing out XVI. **expressive** †tending to expel XIV; full of expression XVII; serving to express XVIII. - F. or medL.

expropriate XVII. f. pp. stem of medL. *ex-*

propriāre, f. EX-[1] + *proprium* PROPERTY; see -ATE[2]. So **expropriation** XV (rare before XIX).

expulsion see EXPEL.

expunge XVII. - L. *expungere* mark for deletion by points set above or below, f. EX-[1] + *pungere* prick; see POINT.

expurgate XVII. f. pp. stem of L. *expurgāre*; see EX-[1], PURGE, -ATE[3]. So **expurgation** XV (rare before XVII). **expurgatorial** XIX, **expurgatory** XVII. - modL. *expurgātōrius*.

exquisite †ingenious, abstruse, choice XV; †accurate, exact; carefully elaborated; highly cultivated; consummate XVI; intense, keenly sensitive XVII. - L. *exquīsītus*, pp. adj. of *exquīrere* search out, f. EX-[1] + *quærere* search, seek; see -ITE.

exsert (biol.) thrust out or forth. XIX. f. *exsert-*, pp. stem of L. *exserere* (see EXERT).

exsiccate make dry, dry up. XV. f. pp. stem of L. *exsiccāre*, f. EX-[1] + *siccāre*, f. *siccus* dry; see -ATE[3].

extant †standing out or forth; (still) existing. XVI. - L. *ex(s)tāns*, *-ant-*, prp. of *exstāre* be prominent or visible, exist, f. EX-[1] + *stāre* STAND; see -ANT.

extempore adv. XVI; adj. XVII. f. L. phr. *ex tempore* on the spur of the moment, i.e. *ex* out of, *tempore*, abl. of *tempus* time. So **extemporaneous** XVII. - L. *extemporālis*, late L. *-āneus*. **extemporary** XVII. Hence **extemporize** XVIII.

extend stretch out XIV; enlarge the scope of; stretch forth, hold out XVI. - L. *extendere*, f. EX-[1] + *tendere* stretch, TEND[2]. So **extension** stretching, distension XIV; enlargement XVI; state of being extended, range XVII. - late L. *extensiō*, *-ōn-*. **extensive** distended XV; of large extent XVII. - F. or late L. **extent** (hist.) valuation of property XIV; (leg.) seizure of lands, etc.; breadth or width of application, etc. XVI; length and breadth XVII. - AN. *extente* - medL. *extenta*, sb. use of fem. pp. of *extendere*.

extenuate †make thin, diminish, †disparage the magnitude of; underrate, seek to lessen the importance of. XVI. f. pp. stem of L. *extenuāre*, f. EX-[1] + *tenuis* THIN. So **extenuation** XVI. - L.

exterior XVI. - L., compar. formation on *exterus* that is outside (itself a compar.), f. EX; cf. EXTREME.

exterminate †expel, banish XVI; destroy utterly XVII. f. pp. stem of L. *extermināre*, f. EX-[1] + *terminus* boundary; see -ATE[3]. So **extermination** XV. - late L.

external exterior. XV. f. L. *externus*, f. *exterus* that is outside (cf. EXTERIOR); see -AL[1].

extinct that has burned out XV; that has died out XVI. - L. *ex(s)tinctus*, pp. of *extinguere*, f. EX-[1] + *stinguere* quench. So **extinction** XVI. **extinguish** XVI. irreg. f. L. *ex(s)tinguere*; see -ISH[2].

extirpate root out. XVI. f. pp. stem of L. *ex(s)tirpāre*, f. EX-[1] + *stirps* stem or stock of a tree; see -ATE[3].

extol †lift up; praise highly, boast of. XV. - L. *extollere*, f. EX-[1] + *tollere* raise.

extort XVI. f. *extort-*, pp. stem of L. *extorquēre*, f. EX-[1] + *torquēre* twist. So **extortion** XIII. - late L. **extortionate** XVIII. **extortioner** XIV.

extra that is beyond the usual XVIII; adv., sb. XIX. prob. short for EXTRAORDINARY.

extra- L. adv.-prep. *extrā* outside (contr. of *exterā*, abl. fem. of *exterus* EXTERIOR) used to form adjs. on the model of L. *extrāordinārius* EXTRAORDINARY, *extrāmūrānus* extramural (f. *extrā mūrōs* outside the walls), in which an adj. termination is added to a phr. consisting of *extrā* governing an acc.

extract †pp. derived, descended XV; draw out or forth XVI; take *out of*, copy out XVII. f. *extract-*, pp. stem of L. *extrahere*, f. EX-[1] + *trahere* draw. So sb. substance extracted XVI; passage excerpted XV. - L. *extractum*, sb. use of n. pp. **extraction** lineage, origin XV; drawing out XVI. - (O)F. - late L.

extradition XIX. - F., f. L. EX-[1] + *trāditiō* TRADITION. Hence by back-formation **extradite** XIX.

extraneous XVII. f. L. *extrāneus*; see EXTRA-, -EOUS.

extraordinary that is out of the usual course XV; exceptional XVI. - L. *extrāordinārius*, f. phr. *extrā ordinem* out of course, in an unusual manner; see EXTRA-, ORDINARY.

extrapolate find by calculation based on known terms of a series other terms outside them. XIX. f. INTERPOLATE by substitution of EXTRA- for *inter-*. So **extrapolation** XIX.

extravagant epithet of certain papal decrees not contained in particular collections. XIV; exceeding due bounds XVI. - prp. of medL. *extrāvagārī*, f. EXTRA- + *vagārī* wander; see -ANT. So **extravagance** †digression XVII; unrestrained excess XVII; excessive prodigality XVIII. - F. **extravaganza** (mus., etc.) extravagant composition. XVIII. - It. *(e)stravaganza*; refash. after EXTRA-.

extreme last, final; utmost, exceedingly great; outermost, farthest. XV. - OF. *extreme* (mod. *-ême*) - L. *extrēmus*, superl. corr. to *exterus* EXTERIOR. So **extremity** XIV. - (O)F. or L.

extricate unravel, disentangle. XVII. f. pp. stem of L. *extricāre*, f. EX-[1] + *trīcæ* perplexities; see -ATE[3]. So **extrication** XVII.

extrinsic †exterior, external XVI; pert. to external aspects or conditions XVII. - late L. *extrinsecus* adj. outer, f. L. *extrinsecus* adv. outwardly, f. EXTRA- + *-im* (as in *interim*) + *secus* alongside of. The ending was assim. to -IC.

extro- alt. of L. *extrā* outside, on the analogy of *intrō-/intrā-* inside; e.g. *extroversion*, *-vert* vb. XVII.

extrude XVI. - L. *extrūdere*, f. EX-[1] + *trūdere* thrust. Hence **extrusion** XVI.

exuberant growing luxuriantly, abundantly fertile; abounding in health and spirits. XV. - F. *exubérant* - L. *exūberāns*, *-ant-*, prp. of *exūberāre*, f. EX-[1] + *ūberāre* be fruitful, f. *ūber* fertile, rel. to UDDER; see -ANT. So **exuberance** XVII.

exude XVI. - L. *ex(s)ūdāre*, f. EX-[1] + *sudāre* SWEAT.

exult †leap up; rejoice exceedingly. XVI. - L. *ex(s)ultāre*, frequent. of *exsilīre*, f. EX-[1] + *salīre* leap. So **exultant** XVII, **exultation** XV.

eye OE. *ēaġe*, Angl. *ēġe* = OFris. *āge*, OS. *ōga* (Du. *oog*), OHG. *ouga* (G. *auge*), ON. *auga*, Goth. *augō* :- Gmc. **auʒan-*, rel. ult. to IE. **oq-* on which are based many synon. forms, e.g. Skr.

(Vedic) *ákṣi*, Lith. *akis*, OSl. (Russ.) *óko*, Gr. *ósse* (:- **ókje*) the two eyes, *ómma* (:- **opma*), *ophthalmós* eye, *óps* face, L. *oculus* eye, *-ōx* in *atrōx*, ATROCIOUS, *ferōx* FEROCIOUS.

Comps. **eye-ball** XVI. **eyebrow** XVI. repl. (dial.) *eyebree* (OE. *ēagbrǣw*). **eyelash** XVIII. **eyelid, eyesight, eyesore** XII. **eyetooth, eye-witness** XVI.

eyelet XIV. ME. *oilet, oylette* - OF. *oillet* (mod. *œillet*), dim. of †*oil, œil* :- L. *oculus* EYE; see -ET. The present sp. (*eylet* XVI) and pronunc. are due to assoc. with EYE and -LET.

eyrie, aerie nest of a bird of prey. XVI. - medL. *airea, eyria*, etc., prob. f. (O)F. *aire* :- L. *area* (see AREA).

F

fa see FAH.

fable XIII. - (O)F. - L. *fābula* discourse, story, f. *fārī* speak (cf. FAME). So vb. tell tales XIV; relate as fiction XVI.

fabliau medieval French humorous tale in verse. XIX. - F., evolved from OF. (Picard) *fablia(u)x*, pl. of *fablel*, dim. of *fable*; see prec. and -EL².

fabric edifice XV; construction or structure of a building XVII; textile stuff XVIII. - (O)F. *fabrique* - L. *fabrica*, f. *faber* worker in metal, etc. So **fabricate** construct XV; invent, forge XVIII. f. pp. stem of L. *fabricāre*, f. *fabrica*. **fabrication** XV. - L.

fabulist XVI. - F. *fabuliste*, f. L. *fābula* FABLE; see -IST.

fabulous pert. to, of the nature of fables. XV. - F. *fabuleux* or L. *fābulōsus*, f. *fābula* FABLE; see -OUS.

façade XVII. - F., f. *face*, after It. *facciata*; see next and -ADE.

face XIII. - (O)F. :- Rom. **facia*, alt. of L. *faciēs* form, appearance, visage. Hence vb. XV. **facial** †(in *f. sight, vision*) face-to-face XVII; pert. to the face XIX. - medL. *faciālis*.

facet XVII. - F. *facette*, dim. of *face*; see prec. and -ET.

facetiae pleasantries. XVII. - L., pl. of *facētia* jest. So **facetious** XVI. - F. *facétieux*.

facia var. of FASCIA.

-facient terminal el. repr. L. *-faciēns, -facient-*, prp. of *facere* DO¹.

facile easy XV; easily led XVI; moving freely XVII. - F. *facile* or L. *facilis*, f. *facere* DO¹; see -ILE. So **facility** XV. **facilitate** XVII. - F. *faciliter*.

facsimile exact copy. XVII (orig. two words). f. L. *fac*, imper. of *facere* make, DO¹ + *simile*, n. of *similis* like, SIMILAR.

fact deed (now only in leg. use *after, before the fact*, etc.); something that has occurred, what has happened; truth, reality XVI; (pl.) circumstances and incidents of a case XVIII. - L. *factum*, sb. use of n. pp. of *facere* DO¹. Hence (after ACTUAL) **factual** XIX.

faction XVI. - (O)F. - L. *factiō, -ōn-*, f. *facere* DO¹; see -TION, and cf. FASHION, in some senses of which this word was formerly used. So **factious** XVI. - F. *factieux* or L. *factiōsus*.

-faction repr. L. *-factiō, -ōn-*, terminal el. of sbs. rel. to vbs. in *-facere* -FY, e.g. *satisfaction*; extended to cases like *petrifaction*, where the corr. L. vb. would be in *-ficāre*.

factitious †made by art; made up for the occasion. XVII. f. L. *factīcius*, f. *fact-*; see FACT, -ITIOUS¹.

factitive - modL. *factitīvus*, irreg. f. *fact-*, pp. stem of *facere* DO¹; see -IVE.

factor agent XV; (math.) any of the quantities which multiplied together produce a given quantity XVII. - F. *facteur* or L. *factor*, f. *fact-*; see FACT, -OR¹.

factory A. factorship, agency (Sc.) XVI; B. merchant company's trading station XVI; C. manufactory, works XVII. prob. of mixed orig.; in A repr. medL. *factōria* (see FACTOR, -Y³); in B repr. Pg. *feitoria* (= It. *fattoria*, Sp. *factoria*, F. †*factorie*); in C, ult. - late L. *factōrium* (recorded in the sense 'oil-press').

factotum XVI. - medL. *factōtum*, f. L. *fac*, imper. of *facere* DO¹ + *tōtum* the whole (cf. TOTAL).

faculty ability, capacity; †branch of knowledge (from medL. *facultas*); department of learning XIV; power, licence XVI. - (O)F. *faculté* - L. *facultās*, f. *facilis* FACILE; see -TY².

fad XIX. prob. the second el. of earlier *fidfad* (XVIII), shortening of FIDDLE-FADDLE.

fade lose freshness or brightness. XIV. - OF. *fader*, f. *fade* vapid, dull, faded :- Rom. **fatidus*, prob. resulting from a blending of L. *fatuus* silly, insipid, FATUOUS with *vapidus* lifeless, spiritless, VAPID.

f(a)eces dregs XV; excrement XVII. - L., pl. of *fæx* dregs.

faerie, faery fairyland. var. of FAIRY, perh. based on OF. *faerie*, adopted by Spenser in 'The Faerie Queene' (1590-6).

fag¹ †something hanging loose; last remnant XV; extreme end XVI (more fully **fag-end** XVII). of unkn. orig.

fag² †flag, decline XVI; work hard, toil; tire, weary XVIII. of unkn. orig.; cf. FLAG⁴. Hence *fag* sb. drudgery, fatique; in Eng. public schools, junior who performs duties for a senior XVIII (whence as vb., act as a fag XIX).

fag³ (sl.) cigarette XIX. abbrev. of *fag-end*.

faggot bundle of sticks, etc., tied together. XIII. - (O)F. *fagot*, of uncert. orig.

fa(h) (mus.) fourth note of the scale in solmization. XIV. See UT.

Fahrenheit mercurial thermometer named after its inventor, G. *Fahrenheit* (1686-1736), German physicist. XVIII.

faience porcelain. XVIII. - F. *faïence* short for *poterie* or *vaisselle de Faïence*, i.e. pottery or ware of the Italian town Faenza.

fail¹ (sb.) default (now only in *without fail*). XIII. - OF. *fail(l)e*, f. *faillir* (see next).

fail² be wanting or insufficient; lose power; fall or come short, be in default. XIII. - (O)F. *faillir* be wanting :- Rom. **fallīre*, for L. *fallere* deceive, used in the sense 'disappoint expectation, be wanting or defective'. So **failure** XVII. orig. *failer* - AN. (leg.) *failer*, for OF. *faillir*, inf. used as sb. (see -ER⁵); assim. to the suffix -URE.

fain (arch.) glad, happy; used advb. gladly, willingly. XII. OE. *fæġ(e)n*, corr. to OS. *fagan, -in*, ON. *feginn* :- Gmc. **faȝin-, -an-*, f. **faχ-*, repr. by OE. *ġefēon*, OHG. *gifehan* rejoice, and OE. *ġefēa*, OHG. *gifeho*, Goth. *fahēþs* joy; ult. orig. unkn.

fainéant idler. xvii. - F. do-nothing, etymologizing sp. (*fait* does, *néant* nothing) of OF. *faignant* sluggard, prp. of *faindre* skulk (see FEIGN).

fain(s) (sl.) used in formulae, e.g. *fains I, fainit*, deprecating further actions. xix. var. of *fen*, clipped form of FEND, in the sense 'forbid' or 'ward off'.

faint †feigned; †sluggish xiii; †weak; inclined to swoon xiv; feeble, indistinct xvi. - OF. *faint, feint* feigned, sluggish, cowardly, pp. of *faindre, feindre* FEIGN. Hence vb. xiv.

fair[1] beautiful, pleasing OE.; free from blemish xii; favourable xiii; light-coloured (opp. *dark*) xvi. OE. *fæġer* = OS., OHG. *fagar*, ON. *fagr*, Goth. *fagrs* :- Gmc. **faȝraz*.

fair[2] periodical gathering of buyers and sellers. xiii. - OF. *feire* (mod. *foire*) :- late L. *fēria*, sg. of classL. *fēriæ* holiday, rel. to *festum* FEAST.

fairy †fairy-land; †fairy-folk; †magic; diminutive supernatural being. xiv. - OF. *fa(i)erie* (mod. *féerie*), f. *fay* FAY; see -ERY. Cf. FAERIE. The application to a single being is peculiar to Eng. Hence **fairyland** xvi, **fairy-tale** xviii.

faith trust; belief; faithfulness; loyalty. xii. ME. *fe(i)þ* - AN. *fed*, OF. *feid, feit* (pronounced *feiþ*) :- L. *fidēs, fide-* f. **fid-* var. of **fīd-* in *fīdus* trustworthy, *fīdere* trust, rel. to Gr. *peíthein* persuade, *pístis* faith, f. IE. **bhidh-* **bheidh-* **bhoidh-*. Hence **faithful** xiii.

fake 'do', do for; do up, make so as to deceive. xix (orig. thieves' sl.). Later form of †*feak*, †*feague* beat, thrash - G. *fegen* polish, furbish, sweep, (sl.) thrash, scold, rate. Hence as sb.

fakir Muslim religious mendicant or ascetic. xvii. - Arab. *faḳīr* poor, poor man.

Falangist adherent of the *Falange* (spec. use of *falange* PHALANX), Sp. Fascist party founded 1933; see -IST.

falbala xviii; see FURBELOW.

falcate (nat. hist.) sickle-shaped. xix - L. *falcātus*, f. *falx, falc-* sickle; see -ATE[2]. So **falcated** xviii.

falchion broad curved convex-edged sword. xiv. ME. *fauchoun* - OF. *fauchon* :- Rom. **falciō, -ōn-*, f. L. *falx, falc-* sickle. Latinized sp. with *l* appears xvi.

falcon xiii. ME. *faucon* - (O)F., obl. case of *fauc* :- late L. *falcō, -ōn-*, of uncert. orig.; sp. (*l*) xv after Latin. So **falconer** xiv.

falderal trifle, gewgaw. xix (xviii as a meaningless refrain). Obscurely rel. to FAL-LAL.

faldstool movable prayer-desk xvii; armless chair used by prelates, etc. xix. - medL. *faldistolium* - WGmc. **faldistōl* = late OE. *fældestōl, fyld(e)stōl*, f. Gmc. **falþan* FOLD[2] + **stōlaz* STOOL.

fall[1] descent xii; lapse into sin; falling from an erect posture xiii; autumn (orig. †*fall of the leaf*) xvi. ME. *fal(l)*, superseding OE. *(ġe)feall* and *fæll, f(i)ell, fyll* (:- **falliz*); partly - ON. *fall*, partly a new formation on FALL[2].

fall[2] pt. *fell*, pp. *fallen* descend, sink. OE. str. vb. *f(e)allan* = OS., OHG. *fallan* (Du. *vallen*, G. *fallen*) :- Gmc. redupl. str. vb. **fallan*, perh. rel. to Lith. *pùlti* fall, Arm. *p'ul* downfall.

fallacy deception xv; logical flaw, delusive notion xvi; delusive nature xviii. - L. *fallācia*, f. *fallāx, fallāc-*, f. *fallere* deceive. So **fallacious** xvi. - (O)F. *fallacieux*. See -ACY, -ACIOUS.

fal-lal piece of finery. xviii. One of various redupl. formations expressing the notion of something trivial; cf. FALBALA.

fallible xv. - medL. *fallibilis*, f. *fallere* deceive; see -IBLE.

Fallopian (anat.) applied to parts described by Gabriello *Fallopio* (1523-62), It. anatomist. xviii; see -IAN.

fallow[1] ploughed or arable land OE.; ground ploughed and harrowed but left uncropped xvi. OE. *fealh, fealg-* = MLG. *valge* (G. *felge*); used as adj. xiv. Hence **fallow** vb. break up (land) as for sowing. OE. *fealgian* = MHG. *valgen, velgen*.

fallow[2] reddish-yellow (now only in *fallow deer*). OE. *f(e)alu*, obl. *fealwe*, etc. = OS. *falu* (Du. *vaal*), OHG. *falo* (G. *fahl, falb*), ON. *fǫlr* :- Gmc. **falwaz*, f. IE. **pol-* **pel-* **pl-*, as repr. by Skr. *palitás* grey, Gr. *poliós, pelitnós* grey, *pellós* dark-coloured, L. *pallēre* be pale, *pullus* grey, blackish, (O)Ir., Gael. *liath*, W. *llwyd* grey, OSl. *plavŭ* white.

false wrong; untrue, deceitful; spurious. OE. *fals* adj. in *false ġewihta* wrong weights, *falspening* counterfeit penny (cf. ON. *falspeningr*) and sb. (= ON. *fals*) 'fraud, deceit, falsehood' - L. *falsus* adj. and *falsum* n. sb., prop. pp. of *fallere* deceive. In ME. reinforced by or newly - OF. *fals, faus*, fem. *false* (mod. *faux, fausse*) :- L. *falsus, -a*. Hence **falsehood** xiv. **falsify** xv. - F. or late L. **falsity** xvi. - L. *falsitās*; cf. ME. *fals(e)te* treachery, fraud - OF. *falseté* (mod. *fausseté*).

falsetto (mus.) voice of a register above the natural. xviii. - It., dim. of *falso* FALSE.

falter stumble in step or speech xiv; give way, waver xvi. of obscure orig.

fame reputation; †rumour. xiii. - OF. *fame* (now *fâme* in comps. only) - L. *fāma* = Gr. *phḗmē* speaking, f. IE. **bhā-* in L. *fārī*, Gr. *phánai* speak. So **famous** xiv. - AN. *famous*, OF. *fameus* (mod. *fameux*) - L. *fāmōsus*.

family xv. - L. *familia* household, f. *famulus* servant; see -Y[3]. So **familiar** xiv. Early forms *familier, famuler* are - (O)F. *familier*, †*famulier*, but forms in *-iar(e)* are also early and reflect the orig. L. *familiāris*. **familiarize** xvii. - F. **familiarity**. xiii. - (O)F. - L.

famine xiv. - (O)F., f. *faim* hunger :- L. *famēs*.

famish xiv. Extended form (after vbs. in -ISH[2]) of ME. *fame* (xiv), aphetic - OF. *afamer* (mod. *affamer*) :- Rom. **affamāre*, f. L. AF- + *famēs* hunger.

fan[1] instrument for winnowing grain OE.; instrument for agitating the air xiv. OE. *fann* - L. *vannus*. Hence **fan** vb. OE. *fannian*. **fanlight** fan-shaped window over a door. xix.

fan[2] abbr. of FANATIC. An early isolated use (*phan, fann*) is recorded from late xvii; the present use dates from late xix and is orig. U.S.

fanatic †frenzied, as through divine or demonic possession xvi; marked by excessive enthusiasm xviii; sb. †(religious) maniac; unreasoning enthusiast xvii. - F. *fanatique* or L. *fānāticus* pert. to a temple, inspired by a deity, frenzied, f. *fānum* temple, FANE; see -ATIC. Also **fanatical** XVI. Hence **fanaticism** XVII.

fancy arbitrary or capricious preference, individual taste XV; imagination XVI; invention XVII. Early forms *fantsy*, *fansey*; contr. of FANTASY. Hence vb. XVI.

fandangle trinket, tomfoolery. XIX. perh. alt. (after *newfangle*) of FANDANGO, which was occas. used earlier in this sense.

fandango lively Sp. dance. XVIII. - Sp., of unkn. orig.

fane (poet.) temple. XIV. - L. *fānum*, prob. :- **fasnom* and rel. to *fēriæ* (see FERIAL).

fanfare XVII. - F., of imit. orig.

fang †A. capture, catch XI; B. canine tooth, tusk XVI. Late OE. - ON. *fang* capture, grasp = OS., OHG. *fang* (Du. *vang*, G. *fang*), f. Gmc. **faŋg-*, **faŋχ-*, repr. by OE. *fōn* capture, OS., OHG. *fāhan*, ON. *fá*, Goth. *fāhan*, rel. to L. *pangere* fix; the development of sense B is obscure.

fan-tan Chinese gambling game depending on divisions by four. XIX. Chinese *fan t'an* repeated divisions.

fantasia musical composition in which form is subordinated to fancy. XVIII. - It.; see FANTASY.

fantastic †imaginary XIV; †imaginative XV; extravagantly fanciful XVI. - (O)F. *fantastique* - medL. *fantasticus*, lateL. *phantasticus* - Gr. *phantastikós*, f. *phantázein* make visible, *phantázesthai* have visions, imagine; cf. next and see -IC. So **fantastical** XV. The sp. with *ph-* was frequent XVII-XVIII.

fantasy, phantasy †mental apprehension; †phantom; †delusive imagination; baseless supposition XIV; changeful mood XV; imagination XVI. - OF. *fantasie* (mod. *fantaisie*; = It. *fantasia*) - L. *phantasia* - Gr. *-siā* appearance (later, phantom), mental process, sensuous perception, faculty of imagination, f. *phantázein*; see prec. and -Y[3].

faquir var. of FAKIR.

far OE. *feor(r)* = OS., OHG. *fer(ro)* (Du. *ver*), ON. *fjarri*, Goth. *fairra* :- Gmc. **ferrō*, compar. formation on **fer-* :- IE. **per-*, repr. by Skr. *pára*, Gr. *pérā* further, OIr. *ire* beyond.

farad (electr.) unit of capacity. XIX. f. name of Michael *Faraday*, English electrician (1791-1867), with assim. to the suffix -AD.

farce short dramatic work the sole object of which is to excite laughter. XVI. - (O)F. *farce*, orig. 'stuffing', f. *farcir* stuff :- L. *farcīre* (in medL. pad out, interlard). The latinized form *farsa*, *farcia*, was applied in XIII to phrases interpolated in liturgical texts, hence to impromptu amplifications of the text of religious plays, whence the transition to the present sense was easy. Hence **farcical** XVIII.

farcy disease of horses allied to glanders. XV. Earlier *farcin* - F. :- late L. *farcīminum*, beside *farcīmen*, f. *farcīre* stuff; so named from the purulent eruptions with which the affected animal is 'stuffed'.

fardel (arch.) bundle, parcel. XIII. - OF. *fardel* (mod. *fardeau*) burden, load :- dim. of Rom. **fardum*; see -EL[2].

fare[1] †journey OE.; (supply of) food XIII; passage money XV; passenger XVI. orig. two words, (i) OE. *fær* str. n. = OHG. *far* transit, landing-place, harbour, ON. *far* :- Gmc. **faram*; (ii) OE. *faru* str. fem. = MLG. *vare*, MHG. *var*, ON. *fǫr* :- Gmc. **farō*; f. base of next.

fare[2] †go on a journey; get on (well or ill) OE.; †behave, act; happen. XIII. Now only literary. OE. str. vb. *faran* = ON. *fara*, OS., OHG., Goth. *faran* (Du. *varen*, G. *fahren*) :- Gmc. **faran*, f. **far-* :- IE. **por-* (cf. Gr. *poreúesthai* proceed; also FORD). Hence **farewell** int. ('proceed happily'; see WELL[1]), orig. imper. phr.; also as sb. XIV.

farinaceous XVII. f. late L. *farīnāceus*, f. *farīna* flour, f. *far* corn; see -ACEOUS.

farm fixed annual payment as rent, etc. XIII (orig. in *to farm*, *at* or *in farm*); tract of land leased; farm-house XVI. ME. *ferme* - (O)F. :- medL. *firma* fixed payment, f. L. *firmāre* fix, settle, in medL. contract for, f. *firmus* FIRM[1]. Hence vb. †rent XV; let or lease out XVI. So **farmer** collector of revenue; bailiff, steward XIV; cultivator of a farm XVI. ME. *fermour* - AN. *fermer*, (O)F. *fermier*, which combined the uses of medL. *firmārius* and *firmātor*; in the more mod. uses apprehended as f. *farm* vb. + -ER[1].

faro gambling card-game. XVIII. sp. of †*Pharaoh*, var. of †*Pharaon* - F. *pharaon*, title of the kings of ancient Egypt, which is said to have been applied orig. to the king of hearts in the game.

farouche shy and repellent. XVIII. - F., alt. of OF. *faroche*, beside *forache* :- medL. *forasticus*, f. L. *foras* out-of-doors.

farrago medley. XVII. - L. *farrāgo* orig. mixed fodder for cattle, f. *far*, *farr-* corn, spelt.

farrier shoeing-smith, veterinary surgeon. XVI. - OF. *ferrier* :- L. *ferrārius*, f. *ferrum* horseshoe, prop. iron. Hence **farriery** veterinary surgery. XVIII.

farrow †young pig OE.; litter of pigs XVI. OE. *færh* (*fearh*) = OHG. *farah* :- WGmc. **farχa* :- IE. **porkos*, whence L. *porcus*, Gr. *pórkos* pig, Lith. *paršas* gelded pig, OIr. *orc*. Hence vb. XIII.

fart break wind. OE. **feortan* (in *feorting* vbl. sb.), ME. *uerten* (XIII), corr. to MLG. *verten*, OHG. *ferzan* (G. *farzen*, *furzen*), ON. *freta* :- Gmc. **fertan*, **fartan*, **furtan* :- IE. base **perd-* **pord-* **pr̥d-*, as repr. by Skr. *pard-*, *pr̥d-*, Av. *pərədən* (3rd pl.), Gr. *pérdein*, Russ. *perdét'*.

farther adv. XIII; adj. XIV. ME. *ferþer*, var. of FURTHER, which came to be used as a compar. of FAR instead of †*farrer*, earlier †*ferrer*, a new formation with -ER[3] on the orig. compar. (OE. *fierr* :- **ferriz*). So **farthest** adj. XIV (*ferþest*), adv. XVI.

farthing OE. *fēorðing*, *-ung*, f. *fēorða* FOURTH; see -ING[3].

farthingale hooped petticoat. XVI. (Early forms *vard-*, *verd-*, *fard-*) - OF. *verdugale*, *vertugalle*, alt. - Sp. *verdugado*, f. *verdugo* rod, stick, f. *verde* green.

fascia (archit.) long flat surface or band XVI; (anat.) sheath investing an organ. XVIII. - L. *fascia* band, fillet, casing of a door, etc., rel. to *fascis* bundle.

fascicle bundle, cluster XV; part or number of a written work XVII. - L. *fasciculus*, dim. of *fascis* bundle. Also **fascicule** XVII; after F.

fascinate cast a spell over, bewitch. XVI. f. pp.

stem of L. *fascināre*, f. *fascinum* spell, witchcraft. So **fascination** XVII. - L.

fascine (fortif.) long faggot. - F. - L. *fascina*, f. *fascis* bundle.

Fascist orig. member of the *Fascio nazionale di combattimento* 'national fighting force', formed by Benito Mussolini in March 1919 to combat communism. - It. *fascista*, f. *fascio* association (of forces) :- L. *fascis* bundle; see -IST. So **Fascism.**

fash (chiefly Sc.) annoy, trouble. XVI. - F. *fâcher* :- Rom. **fastidicāre*, f. L. *fastus* disdain (cf. FASTIDIOUS).

fashion make, shape XIII; mode, manner XIV; established custom, conventional usage XV. ME. *faciun*, *fas(s)oun* - AN. *fasun*, (O)F. *façon* :- L. *factiō*, *-ōn-*, f. *fact-*, *facere* make, DO[1]; cf. FACTION. Hence as vb. XV. **fashionable** XVII.

fast[1] firm OE.; rapid (after the adv.) XVI; dissipated XVIII. OE. *fæst* = OS. *fast* (Du. *vast*), OHG. *festi* (G. *fest*), ON. *fastr*; prob. orig. :- Gmc. **fastuz* (but transf. to other declensions in some langs.). So adv. firmly OE.; closely; quickly; rapidly XIII; dissipatedly XVII. OE. *fæste* = OS. *fasto* (Du. *vast*), OHG. *fasto* (G. *fast* almost), ON. *fast* :- Gmc. **fastō*.

fast[2] abstain from food. OE. *fæstan* = (M)Du. *vasten*, OHG. *fastēn* (G. *fasten*), ON. *fasta*, Goth. *fastan* :- Gmc. **fastējan*, f. **fastuz*; see prec. The gen. sense was 'hold fast', hence 'keep, observe' (as in Gothic), of which 'observe abstinence' was a spec. application. So sb. act or season of fasting. XII. - ON. *fasta* = OS., OHG. *fasta*.

fasten †establish, settle OE.; make fast, secure XII; become fixed or attached XIII. OE. *fæstnian* = OS. *fastnon*, OHG. *fastinōn*, *fest-* :- WGmc. **fastinōjan*, f. Gmc. **fastuz* FAST[1]; see -EN[5].

fastidious †disdainful, scornful XV; easily offended XVII. - L. *fastīdiōsus*, f. *fastīdium* loathing; see -IOUS.

fastness quality of being fast; stronghold. OE. *fæstnes*; see FAST[1], -NESS.

fat adj. and sb. OE. *fǣt(t)* = MDu., MLG. *vett* (Du. *vet*), OHG. *feizzit* (G. *feist*) :- WGmc. **faitiða*, pp. formation on Gmc. **faitjan* fatten (OHG. *veizzen*, ON. *feita*), f. **faitaz* adj. fat, repr. by OS. *feit*, OHG. *feiz*, ON. *feitr*. So vb. surviving in arch. *fatted calf*; OE. *fǣttian*. **fatling** XVI. **fatten.** OE. *(ġe)fættnian* (see -EN[5]). **fatty** XIV.

fatal †fated; fateful XIV; of fate or destiny XV; deadly XVI; disastrous XVII. - (O)F. *fatal* or L. *fātālis*, f. *fātum* FATE; see -AL[1]. So **fatality** XV. **fatalism, -ist** XVII. cf. F. *fatalisme*, *-iste*, perh. the immed. source, and It. *fatalismo*.

fata morgana mirage seen on the Calabrian coast, once attributed to fairy agency. XIX. - It. *fata Morgana* Morgan le FAY (i.e. M. the fairy or witch), sister of King Arthur.

fate predetermination of events; predestined lot XIV; destiny (spec. fatal end), goddess of destiny XV. Not common before XVI. Orig. - It. *fato*, later - its source L. *fātum*, sb. use of n. pp. of *fārī* speak (cf. FAME). Hence **fateful** XVIII.

father OE. *fæder* = OS. *fadar* (Du. *vader*) OHG. *fater* (G. *vater*), ON. *faðir*, Goth. *fadar* (once) :- Gmc. **faðēr* :- IE. *pətḗr*, repr. also by L. *pater*, Gr. *patḗr*, Skr. *pitár-*, OIr. *athir*. For the change of *d* to *ð* cf. *mother*, *gather*, *hither*, *together*, *whether*.

fathom †embrace; †cubit; length made by the outstretched arms, 6 feet. OE. *fæðm*, corr. to OS. *faðmos* pl. two arms outstretched (Du. *vadem*, *vaam* 6 feet), OHG. *fadum* cubit (G. *faden* 6 feet), ON. *faðmr* embrace, bosom :- Gmc. **faþmaz*, f. base **faþ-* :- IE. **pot-* **pet-* **pt-*, whence also L. *patēre* be open, Gr. *pétalos* spreading, broad. So vb. †encircle, embrace OE.; take soundings (of), get to the bottom of XVII. OE. *fæðmian*.

fatidic(al) prophetic. XVII. - L. *fātidicus*, f. *fātum* FATE + *-dicus*, f. weak var. of base of *dīcere* say; see DICTION, -AL[1].

fatigue weariness; fatiguing duty or labour XVII (mil. sense XVIII). - F., f. (O)F. *fatiguer* vb. (whence **fatigue** vb. XVII) - L. *fatīgāre* exhaust, weary, f. **fatis* in *ad fatim*, *affatim* abundantly, enough, prop. 'to bursting' (cf. *fatiscāre*, *-ārī* burst open, gape open).

fatuous XVII. f. L. *fatuus* + -OUS. So **fatuity** XVII. - F. or L.

faucet (now U.S.) tap for drawing off liquid. XIV. - (O)F. *fausset* - Pr. *falset*, f. *falsar* bore.

fault †lack, default XIII; defect in character, etc.; error; culpability XIV; (geol.) break XVIII. ME. *faut(e)* - (O)F. *faut(e)* :- Rom. **fallita*, *-tum*, sb. use of fem. and n. of **fallitus*, pp. of L. *fallere* FAIL[2]. Hence **faulty** XIV.

faun ancient rural deity. XIV. - (O)F. *faune* or L. *Faunus* god or demi-god worshipped by shepherds and farmers and identified with Pan; perh. rel. to *favēre* be FAVOURABLE.

fauna animals of a region or epoch. XVIII. modL. application of the proper name *Fauna* of a rural goddess, sister of Faunus (see prec.).

fauvism style of painting with vivid use of colour. XX. - F. *fauvisme*, f. *fauve* wild (beast); see -ISM.

faux pas XVII. - F.; see FALSE, PACE[1].

favour friendly regard; partiality; †attraction, charm XIV; (arch.) appearance, countenance XV (hence *ill-*, *well-favoured*); gift as a mark of regard XVI. - OF. *favo(u)r* (mod. *faveur*; = It. *favore*) - L. *favor*, *-ōr-*, f. *favēre* regard with goodwill, rel. to *fovēre* cherish (see FOMENT). So **favour** vb., **favourable** XIV.

favourite sb. XVI; adj. XVIII. - F. †*favorit* (mod. *favori*, *-ite*) - It. *favorito*, pp. of *favorire*, f. *favore* FAVOUR. Hence **favouritism** XVIII.

fawn[1] young fallow deer. XIV. - (O)F. *faon* :- Rom. **fētō*, *-ōn-*, f. *fētus* offspring.

fawn[2] (of a dog) show delight XIII; be servile XIV. ME. *faunen* repr. OE. *fagnian*, var. of *fæġnian* rejoice (= OS., OHG. *faganōn*, ON. *fagna*, Goth. *faginōn*), f. *fæġen* FAIN.

fay (arch.) fairy. XIV. - OF. *fa(i)e* (mod. *fée*; = It. *fata*) :- L. *fāta* the Fates (pl. of *fātum* FATE) taken as fem. sg. in Rom.

fealty obligation of fidelity. XIV. ME. *fe(a)ute*, *fealtie* - OF. *feau(l)te*, *fealte* (mod. *féauté*) :- L. *fidēlitās*, *-āt-*, f. *fidēlis* faithful, f. *fidēs* FAITH; see -TY[2].

fear sb. XIII. ME. *fēre*, repr. OE. *fǣr* sudden calamity, danger, corr. to OS. *vār* ambush, MDu. *vāre* fear (cf. Du. *gevaar* danger), OHG. *fāra* ambush, danger, deceit (G. *gefahr* danger), ON. *fár* misfortune :- Gmc. *fǣraz, -am, -ō. Hence **fearful** XIV. So **fear** vb. †frighten OE.; intr. and †refl. feel fear; regard with fear. XIV. OE. *fǣran* (more freq. in comp. *āfǣran*) = OS. *fāron* lie in wait, OHG. *fārēn* plot against, lie in wait, ON. *færa* taunt, slight. Ult. connections unkn.

feasible XV. - (O)F. *faisable*, †*faisible*, f. *fais-*, pres. stem of *faire* (:- L. *facere* DO[1]); see -BLE.

feast religious festival; sumptuous meal or entertainment. XIII. - OF. *feste* (mod. *fête*) :- L. *festa* n. pl. (taken as fem. sg. in Rom.) of *festus* festal, joyous, rel. to *fēriæ* (see FERIAL). So vb. XIV.

feat (notable) deed. XIV. ME. *fete*, later *fayte* - OF. *fet*, (also mod.) *fait* :- L. *factum*, sb. use of n. sg. of *factus*, pp. of *facere* DO[1].

feather OE. *feðer* = OS. *fethara* (Du. *veer*), OHG. *fedara* (G. *feder*), ON. *fjǫðr* :- Gmc. *feþrō :- IE. *petrā, f. *pet- *pt-, repr. also by Skr. *pátram* wing, *pátati* fly, Gr. *pterón*, *ptérux* wing, L. *penna* (:- *pet(s)nā) PEN[2]. Hence vb. furnish with feathers OE.; move like a feather; present a feather edge (of an oar) to the air. XVIII. OE. *ġefiðrian*; from XIII (in pp.) a new formation on the sb.

feature †form, shape; †pl. elements constituting bodily form; lineaments of the face XIV; characteristic part XVII. - OF. *feture*, *faiture* form :- L. *factūra* formation, creature, f. *fact-* pp. stem of *facere* DO[1]; see -URE. Hence vb. resemble in features; portray the features of. XVIII.

febrifuge XVII. - F. *fébrifuge* - modL. *febrifugus*, f. the same elements as late L. *febrifuga* FEVERFEW.

febrile XVII. - F. *fébrile* or medL. *febrīlis*, f. *febris* FEVER; see -ILE.

February XIII. The earliest recorded forms are *feouereles* (repr. as late as XVI by *feverell*) and *feouerreres moneð*; - OF. *feverier* (mod. *février*) :- late L. (Rom.) *febrārius*, for L. *februārius*, f. *februa* n. pl. Roman festival of purification held on 15 February. The ME. type *feverer* is repr. as late as XVIII by (partially latinized) *februeer*; the present fully latinized form (*februari*) is found XIV.

feckless ineffective, futile; weak, helpless. XVI. f. Sc. *feck* effect, purport, efficiency, aphetic form of *effeck* (as in *the feck* for *th'effeck*), Sc. var. of EFFECT; see -LESS.

feculent turbid, as with dregs. XV. - F. *féculent* or L. *fæculentus*, f. *fæc-*; see FAECES and -ULENT.

fecund XIV. - F. *fécond* or L. *fēcundus*, rel. to *fēlix* happy, FOETUS. So **fecundity** XV.

federal XVII. f. L. *fœdus*, *fœder-* covenant; see -AL[1]. Hence **federalism, -ist** XVIII, **-ize** XIX. So **federation** XVIII.

fee estate in land (orig. on feudal tenure); payment for services or privileges. XIV. - AN. *fee* = OF. *feu*, *fi(e)u*, (also mod.) *fief*, pl. *fiez* :- Rom. *feudum, medL. *feodum*, *feudum*, perh. - Frankish *fehuōd 'cattle-property', i.e. OHG. *fehu* (G. *vieh*) = OE. *feoh*, cogn. with L. *pecu*, *pecus* (cf. PECULIAR), and *ōd*, as in **allodium.** Cf. FIEF.

feeble XII. - AN., OF. *feble*, var. of *fieble* (mod. *faible*), later forms of *fleible* :- L. *flēbilis* that is to be wept over, (hence in Rom.) weak, f. *flēre* weep; see -BLE. Hence **feebly** XIII.

feed vb. OE. *fēdan* = OS. *fōdian* (Du. *voeden*), OHG. *fuoten*, ON. *fœða*, Goth. *fōdjan* :- Gmc. *fōðjan, f. *fōðan- FOOD. Hence sb. XVI.

feel vb. OE. (*ġe*)*fēlan* (see Y-) = OS. *gifōlian* (Du. *voelen*), OHG. *fuolen* (G. *fühlen*) :- WGmc. *fōljan, f. *fōl- :- IE. *pōl- *pal- *pl-, repr. also by OE., OS. *folm*, OHG. *folma* hand, L. *palma* PALM[2], Gr. *palámē*. Hence sb. XIII. **feeler** XVII, **feeling** XII.

feign XIII. - (O)F. *feign-*, pres. stem of *feindre* :- L. *fingere* form, conceive, contrive.

feint[1] feigned attack. XVII. - (O)F. *feinte*, sb. use of fem. pp. of *feindre* FEIGN.

feint[2] commercial sp. of FAINT, in *feint lines*. XIX.

fel(d)spar any of a group of crystalline white or flesh-red minerals. XVIII. alt. of G. *feldspat(h)*, f. *feld* field + *spat(h)* spar. Cf. SPAR[3]. Hence **feldspathic** adj. XIX.

felicity XIV. - (O)F. *félicité* - L. *fēlicitās*, *-āt-*, f. *fēlīx*, *fēlīc-* happy, orig. fertile, rel. to *fēcundus* FECUND, *fētus* FOETUS; see -ITY. Hence **felicitous** XVIII. So **felicitate** †make happy; congratulate. XVII. f. F. - L.; see -ATE[3].

feline XVII. - L. *fēlīnus*, f. *fēlēs* cat; see -INE[1].

fell[1] skin, hide. OE. *fel(l)* = OS., OHG. *fel* (Du. *vel*, G. *fell*), ON. *berfjall* bearskin, Goth. *þrūtsfill* 'swelling-skin', leprosy (= OE. *þrūstfell*) :- Gmc. *fellam :- IE. *pello-, the base being repr. also by L. *pellis* skin.

fell[2] hill; wild stretch of land. XIII. - ON. *fjall* and *fell* hill, mountain, presumably rel. to OS. *felis*, OHG. *felis(a)* (G. *fels*) rock, Skr. *pāṣyá-* stone, (O)Ir. *all* rock (IE. *pels-).

fell[3] (arch.) fierce, cruel, dire. XIII. - OF. *fel* :- Rom. *fellō; cf. FELON.

fell[4] strike down. OE. (Anglian) *fellan*, (WS.) *fyllan*, *fiellan = OS. *fellian* (Du. *vellen*), OHG. *fellen* (G. *fällen*), ON. *fella* :- Gmc. *falljan, causative of *fallan FALL[2].

fellah pl. *fellahin* Arab (esp. Egyptian) peasant. XVIII. - Arab. *fellāḥ* (pl. *fellāḥīn*), f. *falaḥa* till the soil.

felloe, felly outer rim of a wheel; pl. the sections forming this. OE. *felg*, pl. *felga*, corr. to MLG., MDu. *velge* (Du. *velg*), OHG. *felga* (G. *felge*), of unkn. orig.

fellow †partner, associate XI; mate, peer XIII; one of a company or corporation XIV; man XV. Late OE. *fēolaga* - ON. *félagi*, f. *fé* (= OE. *feoh* FEE) + *laȝ-, base of LAY[1]; primarily, one who lays down money in a joint undertaking. Hence **fellowship** XII.

felly var. of FELLOE.

felo de se one who deliberately puts an end to his life. XVII. AL. *felo* FELON, *dē sē* of himself.

felon adj. (poet.) cruel, wicked; sb. †wicked person; one who has committed felony. XIII. - (O)F. *felon* (OF. nom. *fel*) :- medL. *fellō*, *-ōn-*, of unkn. orig. So **felony** †villainy, perfidy, crime XIII; (leg.) crime of greater gravity than a misdemeanour XIV. - (O)F. *felonie*; see -Y[3]. Hence **felonious** XVI.

felt stuff of rolled and pressed wool, etc. OE. *felt*, corr. to OS. *filt* (Du. *vilt*), (O)HG. *filz* :- WGmc. *felta, *felti, app. f. IE. *pel- strike, drive (cf. L. *pulsus* PULSE[1]).

felucca small Mediterranean vessel. XVII. - It. *feluc(c)a* - Sp. †*faluca*, var. of *falúa*; of uncert. (prob. Arab.) orig.

female (adj. and sb.). XIV (*femele, female*). - (O)F. *femelle* :- L. *fēmella*, dim. of *fēmina* woman (see FEMININE). The present form is due to assoc. with *male*.

feminine †female XIV; (gram.); relating to a woman, womanly XV; (pros.) of rhyme XVIII. - (O)F. *féminin, -ine* or L. *fēminīnus, -īna*, f. *fēmina* woman, f. IE. **dhē(i)- *dhəi *dhī* suck, suckle, as in L. *fēlāre*, Gr. *thêsai* suckle, Skr. *dháyati* sucks, etc. Hence **femininism**, and directly from L. *fēmina* **feminism**, both *c.* 1850. **femininity** XIV, **feminity** XV. †**feminie** womankind. XIV. - OF.

femoral (anat.) pert. to the femur. XVIII. f. L. *femur, -or-* thigh, whence **femur** XVIII; see -AL[1].

fen OE. *fen(n)* = OS. *fen(n)i* (Du. *veen*), OHG. *fenna, fenni* (G. *fenn*), ON. *fen*, Goth. *fani* :- Gmc. **fanjam *-jaz *-jō* :- IE. **pano-*, rel. to Skr. *páṅka-* mud, OPruss. *pannean* marsh.

fence †defence XIV; art of fencing XVI; enclosing hedge, wall, etc. XVI; receiver of stolen goods XVII. ME. *fens*, aphetic of *defens*, DEFENCE. Hence vb. enclose, screen, protect (lit. and fig.) XV; practise the 'science' of 'defence' with the sword XVI; (sl.) deal in stolen goods XVII.

fend (obs. or arch.) defend XIII; ward off; make an effort XVI (now in *fend for oneself* XVII). Aphetic of DEFEND. Hence **fender** †defender XV; protective device XVII; see -ER[1].

fennel OE. *finugl, finule* fem., *fenol, finul* m. - pop. forms **fēnuclum, -oclum* of L. *fæniculum*, dim. of *fænum* hay; coincided in ME. with the adoption of OF. *fenoil* (mod. *fenouil*), from the same L. source.

fenugreek OE. *fenogrecum*, superseded in ME. by the adoption of (O)F. *fenugrec* - L. *fænugræcum*, for *fænum græcum* 'Greek hay'.

feoff †(leg.) put in possession of, ENFEOFF. XIII. - AN. *feoffer*, OF. *fieuffer, fieffer*, f. *fief* FIEF. Now repr. by derivs. **feoffee** XV, **feoffment** XIV.

feral[1] deadly; funereal. XVII. - L. *fērālis*, perh. rel. to *fēriæ* (see FERIAL).

feral[2] wild, savage. XVII. f. L. *ferus*, rel. to Gr. *thḗr* wild beast, Lith. *žvėris*, OSl. *zvěrĭ*; see -AL[1].

feretory portable shrine XIV; chapel for shrines XV. ME. *fertre* - OF. *fiertre* :- L. *feretrum* - Gr. *phéretron* bier, f. *phérein* BEAR[2].

ferial pert. to a weekday XIV; †pert. to a holy day XV. - (O)F. *férial*, or its source medL. *fēriālis*, f. *fēriæ* holiday (cf. FAIR[2]). In ecclL. *fēria* (whence **feria**, in vernacular use from XIX) is used with an ordinal numeral, to designate a particular weekday (e.g. *secunda fēria* Monday, etc.), and hence in liturgical use for a weekday as dist. from a Sunday or other feast day. The use appears to have arisen from the naming of the days of the octave of Easter *feria prima, secunda* (etc.), 'first, second (etc.) holy or festival day'; the designation was transferred thence to the days of ordinary weeks.

ferment leaven; fermentation (lit. and fig.). XV. - (O)F. *ferment* or L. *fermentum*, f. *fervēre* boil. So vb. XIV. **fermentation** XIV. - late L.

fern OE. *fearn* = MDu. *væren* (Du. *varen*), OHG. (G.) *farn* :- WGmc. **farna* :- IE. **porno-*, whence Skr. *parṇá-* wing, feather, leaf; rel. further to Lith. *papártis*, Russ. *páporotnik*, (O)Ir. *raith* (:- **pratis*). The prim. meaning is doubtless 'feathery leaf'; cf. also Gr. *pterón* feather, *pteris* fern.

ferocious XVII. f. L. *ferōx, ferōc-*, rel. to *ferus* FERAL[2]; for the second el. see EYE. So **ferocity** XVII. - F. or L.

-ferous see -IFEROUS.

ferreous pert. to iron. XVII. f. L. *ferreus*, f. *ferrum* iron; see -EOUS. So **ferric** XVIII, **ferrous** XIX.

ferri-, formerly *ferrid-*, comb. form of L. *ferrum*.

ferro- used as comb. form (see -O-) of *ferrum*.

ferret[1] half-tamed variety of pole-cat. XIV. - OF. *fuiret*, (also mod.) *furet*, by suffix-substitution from OF. *fuiron* (:- Rom. **fūriōn-*), beside *furon* :- late L. *fūrō, fūrōn-* thief, hence vb. XV.

ferret[2] †floss-silk XVI; stout tape XVII. prob. - It. *fioretti* floss-silk, pl. of *fioretto*, dim. of *fiore* flower.

ferruginous of the nature or colour of iron rust. XVII. f. L. *ferrūgō, -gin-* iron rust, dark red, f. *ferrum* iron; see -OUS.

ferrule band or cap of metal, etc., strengthening the end of a stick or tube. XVII (*ferrel, -il*). alt. (prob. by assim. to L. *ferrum* iron, and -ULE) of *verrel, -il* (XVII), later form of *vyrelle, -ille, -ol* (XV) - OF. *virelle*, (also mod.) *virole* - L. *viriola*, f. *viriæ* bracelet.

ferry place where boats pass over to transport passengers, etc. XII (in personal names), XIV. - ON. *ferja* ferry-boat or *ferju-*, as in *ferjukarl, -maðr* ferryman, *-skip* ferryboat = MDu. **vēre* (Du. *veer*), MHG. *vër(e)* (G. *fähre*) :- Gmc. **farjōn*, f. **far-* go (see FARE[2]). So vb. - ON. *ferja* = OS., OE. *ferian* carry, transport, OHG. *ferren* (MHG. *vern*), Goth. *farjan* :- Gmc. **farjan*.

fertile XV. - F. - L. *fertilis*, based on pp. formation **fertus* = Gr. *phertós* borne, f. *phérein* BEAR[2]; see -ILE. So **fertility** XV. Hence **fertilize** XVII.

ferule †giant fennel (providing rods) XV; rod used for punishment XVI. - L. *ferula*.

fervent XIV. - (O)F. - L. *fervēns, -ent-*, prp. of *fervēre* boil, glow; see -ENT. So **fervid** XVI. - L. *fervidus*. **fervour** XIV. - OF. *fervo(u)r* (mod. *-eur*) - L. *fervor*; see -OUR[2].

fescue †straw XIV; small stick for pointing XVI; genus of grasses XVIII. Late ME. *festu(e)* - (O)F. *festu* (mod. *fétu*) :- Rom. **festūcum*, for L. *festūca*. The dissimilative change from *festue* to *fescue* appears XVI.

festal XV. - OF. - late L. *fēstālis*, f. *fēstum* FEAST; see -AL[1]. So **festival** adj. XIV; sb. XVI. - OF. - medL. *fēstivālis*, f. L. *fēstīvus*, whence **festive** XVII. **festivity** XIV. - (O)F. or L.

fester †fistula; ulcer, suppuration. XIII. - OF. *festre* :- L. *fistula*. So vb. XIV. f. the sb. or OF. *festrir*.

festoon curved chain of flowers, etc. XVII. - F. *feston* - It. *festone* prop. 'festal ornament', f. *festa* FEAST; see -OON. Hence as vb. XVIII.

fetch go in quest of and bring back. Late OE. *feċċ(e)an*, alt. of *fetian*; prob. rel. to OE. *fatian*, OFris. *fatia*, OHG. *fazzōn* (G. *fassen*) grasp, perh. orig. 'put in a vessel' (cf. VAT).

fête sb. XVIII. - F., mod. form of *feste* FEAST. Hence as vb. XIX.

fetid, foetid stinking XVI. - L. *fētidus, fœt-*, f. *fētēre, fœt-* stink. Hence **fetidness** XVIII.

fetish inanimate object worshipped by savages. XVII (*fateish*; earlier in form direct - Pg., *fetisso*). - F. *fétiche* - Pg. *feitiço* charm, sorcery, sb. use of the adj. meaning 'made by art' :- L. *factīcius* FACTITIOUS.

fetlock XIV. ME. *fete-*, *feetlak*, *fitlok*, corr. to MHG. *vizzeloch*, *vizloch*, *-lach* (G. *fissloch*), rel. to G. *fessel* fetlock, deriv. of Gmc. **fet-* (:- IE. **ped-*), var. of the base of FOOT.

fetter sb. OE. *feter*, corr. to OS. pl. *feteros* (Du. *veter* lace), OHG. *fezzera* (early mod. G. *fesser*), ON. *fjǫturr* :- Gmc. **feterō*, **feteraz*, f. **fet-* (see prec.), as in synon. L. *pedica*, Gr. *pédē*. Hence (or orig. - ON.) vb. XIII.

fettle make ready, put in order. XIV. f. †*fettle* sb., OE. *fetel* girdle = OHG. *fezzil* (G. *fessel*) chain, band, ON. *fetill* bandage, strap :- Gmc. **fatilaz*, f. **fat-* hold (cf. FETCH). Hence sb. condition, trim. XVIII.

fetus var. of FOETUS.

feu (Sc. law) tenure or lease for a fixed return. XV. - OF. *feu*; see FEE.

feud[1] †active hostility XIII; state of mutual hostility XV. of obscure history. Northern ME. *fede*, later mainly Sc. (XIII-XVIII) - OF. *fe(i)de*, f. Gmc.; cf. OE. *fæhð(u)* enmity, OFris. *fāithe*, *fēithe* :- Gmc. **faixiþō* (whence OHG. *fēhida*, G. *fehde*), f. **faix-*; see FOE and -TH[1].

feud[2] (hist.) fief. XVII. - medL. *feudum*, *feodum* (IX), usu. taken to be of Gmc. origin. So **feudal** XVII, **feudatory** XVI.

fever OE. *fēfor* m., corr. to MLG. *feber*, OHG. *fiebar* m. (G. *fieber*) - L. *febris* fem., of obscure orig. Reinforced in ME. from AN. *fevre*, (O)F. *fièvre* :- L. *febris*. Hence **feverish** XIV.

feverfew OE. *feferfuge* - late L. *febrifuga*, *-fugia*, f. L. *febris* FEVER + *fugāre* drive away; the mod. form is - AN. **fevrefue*, *fewerfue*.

few OE. *fēawe*, *fēawa*, contr. *fēa*, corr. to OS. *fa(o)*, OHG. *fao*, *fō*, ON. *fár*, Goth. pl. *fawai*; repr. Gmc. **faw-* :- IE. **pau-*, as in L. *paucus*, Gr. *paûros* small.

fez crimson cap formerly worn in Turkey. XIX. - Turk. (perh. through F.); named after the town *Fez* in Morocco, once chief place of its manufacture.

fiacre French hackney coach. XVII. Named after the Hôtel de St. *Fiacre*, Paris, where these carriages were stationed.

fiancé, fiancée XIX. - F., pp. of *fiancer* betroth :- Rom. **fidantiāre*, f. **fidantia*, f. L. *fīdāre* trust.

fiasco failure, breakdown, orig. in a dramatic or musical performance. XIX. - It., in phr. *far fiasco* lit. 'to make a bottle' (see FLASK), with unexpl. allusion.

fiat authoritative sanction or command. XVII. - L. 'let it be done', 3rd sg. pres. subj. of *fierī* (see BE), used as passive of *facere* to do.

fib XVII. prob. short for *fible-fable* (*fybble-fable* XVI), redupl. formation on FABLE. So as vb. XVII.

fibre †lobe of the liver XIV; thread-like body in animal or vegetable tissue XVII. - (O)F. - L. *fibra*. Hence **fibrous** XVII; see -OUS.

fibula clasp, brooch; long bone on the outer side of the leg. XVII. L. *fībula*.

-fic repr. L. *-ficus* making, doing, causing to be (what is denoted by the first element of the comp.), f. weak var. of the stem of *facere* DO[1], forming adjs. (i) from sbs., as *pācificus* PACIFIC; (ii) from adjs., as *beātificus* BEATIFIC; (iii) from vbs., as *terrificus* TERRIFIC; (iv) from advs., only in *beneficus* BENEFICENT, *maleficus* MALEFIC.

-fication repr., through F. *-fication*, L. *-ficātiō*, *-ōn-*, formative of nouns of action (see -ATION) from vbs. in *-ficāre* -FY. Many L. words with this suffix were adopted in OF. with their corr. vbs. in *-fier*, and from XIV such sbs. have been freely adopted in Eng., e.g. *edification*, *mortification*, *purification*, *sanctification*; and *-fication* is established as the gen. ending for nouns of action related to verbs in *-fy*, except such as repr. L. vbs. in *-facere* (cf. -FACTION). Formations not based on L. types are exemplified by *beautification* (XVII), *Frenchification*, *jollification* (XVIII), *transmogrification* (XVII).

fichu triangular piece of stuff worn on the neck, etc. XIX. - F., of uncert. orig.

fickle †false, treacherous OE.; changeful, inconstant XIII. OE. *ficol*, rel. to *ġefic* deceit, *befician* deceive (Gmc. **fik-*), and further to *fǣcne* deceitful, *fācen* deceit, deceitful (Gmc. **faik-*), corr. to OS. *fēkan*, OHG. *feihhan*, ON. *feikn* portent.

fictile XVII. - L. *fictilis*, f. *fict-*, pp. stem of *fingere* fashion; see -ILE.

fiction something feigned, invention XIV; composition dealing with imaginary events XVI. - (O)F. - L. *fictiō*, *-ōn-*, f. *fict-*; see prec. and -TION. So **fictitious** XVII. f. L. *fictīcius*.

fid (naut.) conical pin, square bar; plug of oakum or tobacco. XVII. of unkn. orig.

-fid repr. L. *-fidus* cleft, divided, f. base of *findere* cleave, as in *bifid*.

fiddle stringed musical instrument played with a bow. OE. *fiðele* = (M)Du. *vedel* (*veel*), OHG. *fidula* (G. *fiedel*), ON. *fiðla* :- Gmc. **fiþula* of obscure orig.; cf. VIOL, VIOLA[2], VIOLIN, and medL. *vidula*, *fidula*, *vitula*, etc. Hence vb. XIV. **fiddler** OE. *fiðlere*.

fiddle-faddle trifling talk or action. XVI. redupl. formation on FIDDLE.

fideism doctrine that knowledge depends upon faith. XIX. f. L. *fidēs* FAITH + -ISM.

fidelity XV. - F. *fidélité* or L. *fidēlitās*; see FEALTY.

fidget physical uneasiness with spasmodic movements. XVII. prob. f. (dial.) *fidge* (XVI) to move restlessly; the relation with similar synon. forms is undetermined, viz. †*fig* (XVI), (north. dial.) *fitch* (XVII) and *fike* (XIII) - ON. *fikja*. Hence vb. XVIII.

fiducial XVII. - late L. *fīdūciālis*, f. L. *fīdūcia* trust, f. *fīdere* to trust, rel. to *fidēs* FAITH; see -IAL. So **fiduciary** XVII. - L. *fīdūciārius*.

fie excl. of disgust or reproach. XIII. - (O)F. *fi* :- L. *fī*.

fief feudal estate. XVII. - (O)F. *fief* FEE.

field open land, piece of land used for pasture or tillage OE.; ground on which a battle is fought XIII. OE. *feld*, corr. to OS. *feld* (Du. *veld*), (OH)G. *feld* :- WGmc. **felþu*; ult. rel. to OE. *folde* earth, ground, OS. *folda*, ON. *fold* and further to Gr. *platús*, Skr. *pṛthú-* broad.

fieldfare XIV (cf. once OE. *feldeware* 'scorellus'). perh. f. *feld* FIELD + stem of FARE[2].

fiend †enemy; the Devil. OE. *fēond* = OS. *fīond* (Du. *vijand*), OHG. *fīant* (G. *feind*), ON. *fjándi*, Goth. *fijands* :- Gmc. prp. of **fijējan* hate (OE. *fēogan*, ON. *fía*, Goth. *fijan*), rel. to Skr. *pī́yati* blames, reviles. Cf. FRIEND.

fierce †brave, valiant; †proud; violent and intractable. XIII. - AN. *fers*, OF. *fiers*, nom. of *fer*, *fier* (mod. *fier* proud) :- L. *ferus* wild, untamed, see FERAL[2].

fiery XIII. f. FIRE + -Y[1].

fife flute-like instrument. XVI. - G. *pfeife* PIPE[1] or F. *fifre* - Swiss G. *pfifre* (G. *pfeifer*) piper.

fifteen, etc., see FIVE.

fig (fruit of) the fig-tree. XIII. - (O)F. *figue* - Pr. *figa* :- Rom. **fīca*, for L. *fīcus*.

fight pt., pp. *fought* do battle, contend. OE. str. vb. *feohtan* = OS., OHG. *fehtan* (Du. *vechten*, G. *fechten*) :- WGmc. **feχtan*, formally identical with L. *pectere* comb. So **fight** sb. OE. *feohte* wk. fem., (*ġe*)*feoht* str. n., corr. to OS., OHG. *fehta*, OHG. *gifeht* (Du. *gevecht*, G. *gefecht*).

figment XV (rare before late XVI). - L. *figmentum*, f. **fig-*, base of *fingere* fashion.

figure A. numerical symbol XIII; B. (bodily) shape or form XIII. - (O)F. - L. *figūra*, f. **fig-*; see prec., -URE. So vb. XIV. So **figurative** XIV. - late L. *figūrātīvus*, f. *figūrāt-*, pp. stem of L. *figūrāre*; see -ATIVE.

figurine XIX. - F. - It. *figurina*, dim. of *figura* FIGURE; see -INE[1].

figwort name of plants reputed to cure 'the fig', i.e. piles. XVI. see FIG, WORT.

filament XVI. - F. *filament* or modL. *filamentum*, f. late L. *fīlāre*, f. *fīlum* thread.

filbert (nut of) the cultivated hazel. XIV. - AN. *philbert*, short for **noix de Philibert* (cf. Norman dial. *noix de filbert*) St. Philibert's nut, so named from its ripening about his day, 20 Aug.

filch XVI. of unkn. orig.

file[1] metal instrument for abrading surfaces. OE. *fīl* = OS. *fīla* (Du. *vijl*), OHG. *fī(ha)la* (G. *feile*) :- WGmc. **fīχala*, f. IE. **peik-* cut, repr. also by OSl. *pĭsati* write, Gr. *pikrós* sharp, bitter. Hence **file** vb.[1] smooth with a file. XIII.

file[2] A. string or wire on which papers are strung XVI; collection of papers so preserved or arranged in order XVII. B. line of men, etc., one behind another XVI. - (O)F. *fil* :- L. *fīlum* thread. Hence **file** vb.[2] place on or in a file XV; †place (men) in a file XVI; move in file XVII.

filial XV. - (O)F. *filial* or ChrL. *fīliālis*, f. L. *fīlius* son, *fīlia* daughter. So **filiation** (theol.) becoming or being a son XV; relationship or descent as of a son XVII. - (O)F. - ChrL.

filibuster piratical adventurer. XVI (*flibutor*, *fleebuter*). The ult. source is Du. *vrijbuiter* FREEBOOTER; later (XVIII) - F. *flibustier*, succeeded (XIX) by the present form - Sp. *filibustero*. Hence as vb. XIX.

filigree jewel work made with threads and beads. XVII. alt. of *filigreen*, var. of *filigrane* (XVII-XIX) - F. - It. *filigrana*, f. L. *fīlum* thread + *grānum* seed, GRAIN.

fill[1] A. full supply of food OE.; B. quantity that fills XVI. OE. *fyllu* = OHG. *fullī* (G. *fülle*), ON. *fyllr*, Goth. (*ufar*)*fullei* :- Gmc. **fullīn*, f. **fullaz* FULL. In B. f. FILL[2], with which this sb. has always been associated.

fill[2] make full. OE. *fyllan* = OS. *fullian* (Du. *vullen*), OHG. *fullen* (G. *füllen*), ON. *fylla*, Goth. (= Gmc.) *fulljan*; f. Gmc. **fullaz* FULL.

fillet narrow flat band XIV; slice of meat or fish XV. ME. *filet* - (O)F. - Rom. dim. of L. *fīlum* thread; see -ET.

fillip movement made with a finger suddenly released from contact with the thumb XV; (fig.) stimulus XVII. imit. Also as vb. (XVI).

fillister rabbeting-plane. XIX. perh. based on synon. F. *feuilleret*.

filly young mare. XV. prob. much older if - ON. *fylja*, parallel to OHG. *fulihha*, *fulī(n)* (G. *füllen*), f. Gmc. **ful-*, Cf. FOAL.

film †membrane OE.; thin pellicle, fine thread XVI. OE. *filmen* membrane, caul, prepuce = OFris. *filmene* skin :- Gmc. **filminjam*, f. **fellam* FELL[1]. Hence **filmy** XVII.

filoselle floss silk. XVII. - F. *filoselle*, superseding OF. *filloisel* - It. dial. *filosello*, for **folisello* :- Rom. **follicellus* cocoon, for L. *folliculus* FOLLICLE.

filter †felt XIV; piece of felt, etc., for freeing liquids of impure matter XVI; any apparatus for this XVII. - OF. *filtre*, var. of *feltre* (mod. *feutre* felt) - medL. *filtrum* - WGmc. **filtir* FELT. Hence as vb. XVI. So **filtrate** vb. XVII (hence sb. XIX). f. pp. stem of modL. *filtrāre*.

filth †putrid matter OE.; unclean matter XIII. OE. *fȳlð* = OS. *fūlitha* (Du. *vuilte*), OHG. *fūlida*; f. Gmc. **fūlaz* FOUL; see -TH[1]. Hence **filthy** XIV.

fimbria (techn.) fringe. XVIII. - late L. (earlier pl. *fimbriæ*). So **fimbriate** (her. and nat. hist.) fringed. XIX. - L. *fimbriātus*; see -ATE[2]. **fimbriated** XV.

fin OE. *fin(n)* = MLG. *finne*, MDu. *vinne* (Du. *vin*); prob. ult. rel. to L. *pinna* feather, wing.

final XIV. - (O)F. *final* or L. *fīnālis*, f. *fīnis* end, see -AL[1]. So **finality** XVI (once; not current till early XIX). - F. - late L. **finally** XIV, **finalize** XX.

finance †end; †settlement, payment XIV; supply, stock; †tax, taxation XV; (pl.) pecuniary resources; management of (public) money XVIII. - (O)F. *finance* †end, †payment, money, f. *finer* make an end, settle, procure, f. *fin* end, FINE[1]. Hence **financial** XVIII. So **financier** XVII. - F.

finch OE. *finċ* = MDu. *vinke* (Du. *vink*), OHG. *finc(h)o* (G. *fink*) :- WGmc. **fiŋk-*.

find pt., pp. *found*. OE. str. vb. *findan* = OS., OHG. *findan* (Du. *vinden*, G. *finden*), ON. *finna*, Goth. (= Gmc.) *finþan*, f. IE. base **pent-* (whence OIr. *ētain* I find). Hence sb. XIX.

fine[1] †end, conclusion XII; final agreement, settlement of a suit; composition paid XIII. - (O)F. *fin* :- L. *fīnis*, *fīn-* end, in medL. sum to be paid on concluding a lawsuit. So, or - OF. *finer*, **fine** vb.[1] †pay a fine XIII; impose a fine on XVI.

fine[2] consummate in quality XIII; delicate, subtle; handsome, excellent, admirable XIV; elegant XVI; (of the weather) XVIII. - (O)F. *fin* :- Rom. **fīnus*, f. *fīnīre* FINISH. Hence **fine** vb.[2] refine XIV; make fine, small, etc., XVI.

finesse †fineness, purity; delicacy, refinement; artfulness, artifice. XV. Many of the earliest exx. of *fynes(se)*, *fines* are spellings of *fineness*, and it is difficult to determine the date of the adoption of F. *finesse*. See FINE[2], -ESS[2].

finger OE. *finger* = OS., OHG. *fingar* (Du. *vinger*, G. *finger*), ON. *fingr*, Goth. *figgrs* :- Gmc. **fiŋʒraz*, perh. :- IE. **peŋqrós*, f. **peŋqe* FIVE. Cf. FIST.

fingering kind of knitting wool. XVII. Earliest forms *fingram*, *-rum*, *-rine*; poss. alt. of OF. *fin grain* 'fine grain'.

finial †adj. final; sb. (archit.) terminal ornament of an apex or corner. XIV. - AN. **finial* or AL. **finiālis*, f. *fin*, *fīnis* end; see -IAL.

finical over nice or particular. XVI. prob. academic sl. in orig. f. FINE[2] + -ICAL. Hence **finicking** XVII, **finicky** XIX.

finish bring or come to an end XIV; bring to completion XV. - (O)F. *finiss-*, lengthened stem (see -ISH[2]) of *finir*, alt. from *fenir* :- L. *fīnīre*, f. *fīnis* boundary, limit, end. So **finite** XV. - L. *fīnītus*, pp. of *fīnīre*.

finnan haddock cured with the smoke of green wood, etc. XVIII. Earlier forms *findon*, *findram*, *fintrum*, *findhorn*; name of the river *Findhorn*, confused with *Findon*, a village in Kincardineshire.

fiord, fjord XVII. - Norw. *fjord* :- ON. *fjǫrðr* :- Gmc. **ferþuz* (see FORD).

fir XIV. prob. - ON. *fyri-* (in *fyriskógr* fir-wood, etc.) :- Gmc. **furχjōn*, f. **furχō*, whence OE. *furh(wudu)* fir-wood, OHG. *forha* (G. *föhre*), ON. *fura*; cf. L. *quercus* (:- **perkus*) oak.

fire principle of combustion; burning material OE.; conflagration XII; heat of fever, passion, etc. XIV; firing of guns XVI. OE. *fȳr* = OS. *fiur* (Du. *vuur*), OHG. *fiur*, *fuir* (G. *feuer*) (cf. ON. poet. *fúrr*, *fýrr*), corr. to Gr. *pûr*, Umbrian *pir*, Czech *pýř*, Arm. *hur*, Toch. *por*, *pwār*. Hence **fire** vb. OE. *fȳrian* supply with firing; set on fire, lit. and fig. XIII; discharge, explode XVI.

firkin †cask; quarter of a 'barrel' XV (*ferdekyn*, *ferken*). prob. - MDu. **vierdekijn*, dim. of *vierde* FOURTH; see -KIN.

firm[1] fixed, immovable XIV; stable, not yielding XV. ME. *ferm(e)* - (O)F. *ferme* :- L. *firmus*. Conformed XVI to L. sp.

firm[2] †signature XVI; (style of) a commercial house XVIII. In the earliest use - Sp. *firma*, later - It. *firma*, of the same orig., medL. *firma* (cf. FARM), f. L. *firmāre* strengthen, in late L. confirm by one's signature, f. *firmus* FIRM[1].

firmament XIII. - (O)F. - L. *firmāmentum*, f. *firmāre* strengthen, f. *firmus* FIRM[1]; see -MENT. The L. word, meaning orig. 'support, foundation', was adopted in the Vulg., in imitation of LXX Gr. *steréōma* (f. *stereoûn* make firm), as the rendering of Heb. *rāḳī'a* vault of the sky, prob. lit. expanse, f. *rāḳīa'* spread out, beat or tread out, (in Syriac) make firm or solid.

first OE. *fyr(e)st* = OHG. *furist* (*furisto* prince, whence G. *fürst*), ON. *fyrstr* :- Gmc. **furistaz*, superl. formation on **fur-*, **for-* (see FOR, -EST, and cf. FOREMOST) :- IE. **pr̥*, whence the various formations with superl. suffixes meaning 'first', e.g. Gr. *prôtos*, *prṓtistos*, L. *prīmus*, Skr. *prathamá-*. Hence **firstling** first product or offspring XVI. See -LING[1].

firth XV. orig. Sc. - ON. *fjǫrðr* FIORD.

fiscal XVI. - F. *fiscal* or L. *fiscālis*, f. *fiscus* treasury, orig. rush-basket, purse.

fish[1] vertebrate water animal with gills. OE. *fisc* = OS., OHG. *fisc* (Du. *visch*, G. *fisch*), ON. *fiskr*, Goth. *fisks* :- Gmc. **fiskaz* :- IE. **piskos*, rel. to L. *piscis*, Ir. *iasc*, Gael. *iasg*. So **fish** vb. OE. *fiscian*, **fisher** OE. *fiscere*.

fish[2] mend (a broken spar, etc.) with a piece of wood (fish or fish-plate). XVII. - (O)F. *ficher* :- Rom. **fīgicāre*, intensive of L. *fīgere* FIX. Hence (after F. *fiche*) sb. (naut.) piece of wood used to strengthen another XVII; plate of iron, etc., to protect or strengthen a beam, rail, etc. XIX.

fish[3] flat piece of bone, etc., used as a counter in games. XVIII. - F. *fiche*, f. *ficher* (see prec.), assoc. with FISH[1].

fissile XVII. - L. *fissilis*, f. *fiss-*, pp. stem of *findere* cleave; see -ILE. So **fission** XIX. **fissure** XIV. - (O)F. *fissure* or L. *fissūra*.

fist clenched hand. OE. *fȳst* = MLG. *fūst* (Du. *vuist*), OHG. *fūst* (G. *faust*) :- WGmc. **fūsti*, perh. :- **fūŋχstiz* :- **fuŋχstiz* :- IE. **pn̥qstis* (whence OSl. *pęstĭ*), f. **peŋqe* FIVE; cf. FINGER. Hence **fistic** XIX, **fistical** XVIII. **fisticuffs** XVII; prob. f. *fisty* adj. (XVII) + pl. of CUFF[2].

fit[1] †dangerous position or experience XIV; paroxysm, sudden state of activity XVI. OE. *fitt* (once) prob. 'conflict', of unkn. orig. Hence **fitful** XVII.

fit[2] well suited, proper XIV; qualified, prepared XVI. perh. pp. of next.

fit[3] be or make proper or suitable; supply, equip. XVI. In these senses not recorded before late XVI, but a verb *fitte* marshal forces (XIV) may point to a ME. vb. with the gen. sense 'arrange, adjust, match'; cf. (rare) ME. *fitte* person's match (XIII). Hence sb. XVII.

fitchew polecat and its fur. XIV. - OF. *ficheau*, dial. var. of *fissel*, later *fissau*, dim. of a word appearing in early Du. as *fisse*, *visse*, *vitsche*, whence ult. also synon. **fitch** XVI.

five repr. inflected form *fīfe* (*fīfa*, *fīfum*) of OE. *fīf* = OS. *fīf* (Du. *vijf*), OHG. *fimf*, *finf* (G. *fünf*), ON. *fimm*, Goth. *fimf* :- Gmc. **fimfi* :- IE. **pempe*, alt. by assim. from **peŋqe*, whence Skr. *páñca*, Gr. *pénte*, L. *quīnque*, OIr. *cóic*, OW. *pimp* (mod. *pump*), Lith. *penki*. So **fifteen.** OE. *fīftēne* (*-tīene*) = OS. *fīftein* (Du. *vijftien*), OHG. *fimfzehan* (G. *fünfzehn*), ON. *fimtán*, Goth. *fimftaihun*. Hence **fifteenth.** Late OE. *fīftēnða* (XI); see -TEEN. **fifth.** OE. *fīfta* = OS. *fīfto* (Du. *vijfde*), OHG. *fimfto* (G. *fünfte*), ON. *fimti*; the standard form has -TH[2] after *fourth*. **fifty.** OE. *fīftiġ* = OS. *fīftich* (Du. *vijftig*), OHG. *fimfzug* (G. *fünfzig*), ON. *fimmtigr*, Goth. *fimftigjus*; see -TY[1]. Hence **fiftieth.** OE. *fīftiġeoða*.

fives ball-game. XVII. pl. of FIVE; of uncert. orig., but perh. so called because orig. played by two teams of five persons.

fix make firm or stable XV; place in a definite position or state XVI. Partly f. pp. †*fix* (XIV) - OF. *fix* (mod. *fixe*) or its source L. *fīxus*, pp. of *fīgere* fix, fasten; partly - medL. *fīxāre*, f. L. *fīxus*. Hence sb. (orig. U.S.) XIX. So **fixation** XIV. -

medL. **fixity** XVII. **fixture** XVII. alt. of †*fixure* (XVII) - late L. *fixūra*.

fizz make a hissing sound, as of effervescence. XVII. imit.; cf. next. Hence as sb. †disturbance XVIII; effervescing sound, (sl.) champagne XIX.

fizzle †break wind silently XVI; (orig. U.S.) come to a lame conclusion, fail XIX. app. f. FIZZ (but this is recorded later) + -LE[3].

flabbergast XVIII. perh. fanciful formation on FLABBY and AGHAST.

flabby XVII. Expressive alt. of synon. *flappy* (XVI), f. FLAP + -Y[1].

flaccid XVII. - F. *flaccide* or L. *flaccidus*, f. *flaccus* flabby; see -ID[1].

flag[1] plant of the genus *Iris*; (formerly) reed, rush. XIV. of unkn. orig.; cf. Du. *flag*, Da. *flæg* yellow iris.

flag[2] turf, sod XV; flat slab of stone XVII. prob. of Scand. orig.; cf. Icel. *flag* spot where a turf has been cut out, ON. *flaga* slab of stone (cf. FLAW[1]).

flag[3] piece of stuff used as a standard or signal. XVI. perh. orig. an application of †*flag* adj. (see next).

flag[4] †hang down; become limp or feeble. XVI. rel. to †*flag* adj. hanging loose (XVI), of unkn. orig. Cf. FAG[1,2].

flagellant XVI. - L. *flagellāns*, *-ant-*, prp. of *flagellāre* whip (whence **flagellate** XVII, **flagellation** XV), f. *flagellum*, dim. of *flagrum* scourge; see -ANT.

flageolet XVII. - F., dim. of OF. *flag(e)ol* (whence ME. *flagel* XIV) - Pr. *flaujol*, of unkn. orig.; see -ET.

flagitious XIV. - L. *flāgitiōsus*, f. *flāgitium* noisy protest against a person's conduct, scandal, (hence) shameful act, crime, f. *flāgitāre* demand earnestly or vociferously; see -IOUS.

flagon XV. ME. *flakon*, *flagan* - AN. **flagon*, (O)F. *flacon*, earlier **flascon* :- late L. *flascō*, *-ōn-* FLASK.

flagrant (arch. or obs.) blazing, burning, ardent XV; glaring, notorious XVIII. - F. *flagrant* or L. *flagrāus*, *-ant-*, prp. of *flagrāre* burn, blaze, f. **flag-*, repr. a var. of IE. **bhleg-* (cf. FULGENT); see -ANT.

flail sb. OE. **flegil* (once late *fligel*), ME. *fleȝʒl*, *fleil*, *fleyl* = OS. *flegil*, (M)Du. *vlegel*, (O)HG. *flegel* :- WGmc. **flagil*, prob. - L. *flagellum* scourge, (in Vulgate) flail (whence OF. *flaiel*, *fleel*). Examples of the Eng. word are rare before XV, and the late ME. currency was prob. due to adoption from OF. or MDu.

flair sagacious perceptiveness. XIX. - F., f. *flairer* smell :- Rom. **flāgrāre*, for L. *frāgrāre*.

flak anti-aircraft fire. XX. - G., f. initials of *fliegerabwehrkanone* 'aircraft-defence-gun'.

flake one of the small pieces in which snow falls XIV; piece of ignited matter thrown off XIV; flat or scaly fragment XV. immed. source(s) unkn.; cf. Norw. *flak*, *flāk* patch, flake, *flake* form into flakes, Sw. *isflak* ice-floe, ON. *flakna* flake off, split. Cf. FLAW[1]. Hence vb. XV.

flambeau torch. XVII. - (O)F., dim. of *flambe*, †*flamble* :- L. *flammula*, dim. of *flamma* FLAME.

flamboyant (orig. archit.) characterized by waved flame-like forms; flamingly coloured. XIX. - F., prp. of *flamboyer*, f. *flambe*; see prec.

flame sb. XIV. ME. *flaume*, *flam(m)e* - AN. **flaume*, OF. *flame*, (also mod.) *flamme* :- L. *flamma*, f. base repr. by FLAGRANT. So as vb. XIV. - OF. *flam(m)er*.

flamen †supposed grade of priest in heathen Britain XIV; priest of a particular deity in ancient Rome XVI. - L. *flāmen*.

flamingo XVI. - Pg. *flamengo* - Pr. *flamenc*, f. *flama* FLAME + Gmc. suffix **-iŋg-* -ING[3]; so named because of its bright plumage.

flan disc of metal before stamping; open tart. XIX. - F. *flan*, OF. *flaon* :- late L. *fladō* - Frankish **flado* (G. *fladen*), prob. rel. to Gr. *platús* broad.

flange widening part XVII; projecting flat rim XVIII. of uncert. orig.

flank side of the body of an animal XII; side of an army XVI. - (O)F. *flanc* - Frank. **hlanca* side; cf. FLINCH, LINK[1].

flannel woollen stuff. XIV. Early forms *flanell*, beside *flan(n)en*, *flan(n)ing*; the latter are perh. the orig. forms and - W. *gwlanen* woolen article, f. *gwlân* WOOL.

flap †blow XIV; fly-flapper XV; loose pendent part XVI. **flap** vb. strike with something flexible and broad XIV; (of birds) beat the wings XVI. prob. imit.; cf. Du. *flap* blow, fly-flapper, lid of a can, *flappen* strike, clap. Hence **flapper** one who or that which flaps XVI; young partridge XIX (hence sl., young woman XX).

flare spread out, as hair, etc. XVI; burn with a spreading flame XVII. of unkn. orig. Hence sb. XIX.

flash sudden burst of flame or light XVI; sudden rush of water; superficial brilliance; brilliant or showy person; †(sl.) wig XVII; ornament sewn to the collar of a tunic XIX. f. **flash** vb., first with ref. to the rushing or dashing of water (XIV), its application to light or flame being doubtful before XVI. Hence **flashy** XVI, of which *flash* adj. (XVII) is a partial syn. App. of echoic orig.

flask †container for wine, clothing XIV; case for gunpowder XVI; (wine) bottle with long, narrow neck XVII. In the second sense - F. *flasque*, in the third prob. - It. *fiasco*; the F. form (OF. *flasche*, *flaske*) repr. medL. *flasca*, the It. form late L. *flascō* (see FLAGON); ult. orig. dubious. Cf. OE. *flasce*, *flaxe*.

flat[1] level, prostrate XIV; not curved or undulating XV; unqualified, plain, dull, below true pitch XVI; of drink XVII; in many sb. uses from XIV. - ON. *flatr* = OHG. *flaz* :- Gmc. **flataz*, of uncert. orig. Hence **flatten** vb. XVII; see -EN[5].

flat[2] storey of a house; suite of rooms on one floor. XIX. alt. by assoc. with prec. of Sc. *flet* inner part of a house (OE. *flet* floor, dwelling :- Gmc. **flatjam*, f. **flataz* FLAT[1]).

flatter XIII. of unkn. orig.; perh. back-formation from **flattery** (XIV) - (O)F. *flatterie*, f. *flatter* vb. flatter, prob. f. Gmc. **flat-* FLAT[1], and orig. meaning 'pat, smooth, caress'.

flatulent XVI. - F. - modL. *flātulentus*, f. L. *flātus* blowing, blast, f. *flāre* BLOW[1]; see -ULENT. So **flatulence** XIX, **-ency** XVII.

flaunt (intr.) wave gaily or proudly; display (oneself) ostentatiously. XVI. of unkn. orig.

flautist XIX. - It. *flautista*, f. *flauto* FLUTE; see -IST.

flavine (chem.) yellow dye-stuff. XIX. f. L. *flāvus* yellow + -INE[5]. So **flavo-** comb. form.

flavour smell, aroma XIV; element in the taste of a substance depending on the sense of smell XVII. - OF. *flaor*, infl. by *savour*.

flaw[1] †flake XIV; fissure, rift; blemish XVII. perh. from ON. *flaga* slab of stone, prob. :- Gmc. **flaχ-*, **flaʒ-*, parallel and synon. with **flak-* (cf. FLAKE).

flaw[2] sudden squall, etc. XVI. prob. - MLG. *vlāge*, MDu. *vlaghe* (Du. *vlaag*), the primary sense of which may be 'stroke' (cf. FLAY).

flax blue-flowered plant producing textile fibre and linseed. OE. *flæx* (*fleax*) = (M)Du. *vlas*, OHG. *flahs* (G. *flachs*) :- WGmc. **flaχsa*, prob. to be referred to Gmc. **flaχ-* **fleχ-* :- IE. **plok-* **plek-* in Gr. *plékein*, L. *plectere*, G. *flechten* plait. Hence **flaxen** XVI. See -EN[3].

flay strip off the skin of OE.; with skin as obj. XIII. OE. str. vb. *flēan* = MDu. *vlae(gh)en* (Du. *vlaen*), ON. *flá* :- Gmc. **flaχan*, of unkn. orig.; str. forms lasted till XV in pt. *flogh*, till XVII in pp. *flain*, *flean*; but wk. forms were current in XVI.

flea OE. *flēa(h)*, corr. to MLG., MDu. *vlō* (Du. *vlo*), OHG. *flōh* (G. *floh*), ON. *fló*; perh. rel. to FLEE.

fleam lancet. XVI. - OF. *flieme* (mod. *flamme*) :- Rom. **fleutomum*, for late L. *phlebotomus* - Gr. *phlebotómon*, sb. use of n. of adj. (see PHLEBOTOMY).

fleck spot, speck. XVI. The earliest recorded words of the group are **flecked** ppl. adj. dappled XIV and **fleck** vb. XV; the proximate source may be synon. ON. *flekkr* sb., *flekka* vb., or MLG., MDu. *vlecke* (Du. *vlek*) = OHG. *flec*, *fleccho* (G. *fleck*, *flecken*), of unkn. orig.

fledge acquire or provide with feathers. XVI. f. †*fledge* adj. (XIV) having feathers (for flight), repr. var. **fleċġe* of OE. **flyċġe* recorded only in *unfligge* (X) glossing L. *implumes*; corr. to MDu. *vlugghe* (Du. *vlug*), OHG. *flucchi* :- WGmc. **fluʒʒja*, f. **fluʒ-*, weak base of Gmc. **fleuʒan* FLY[2]. Hence **fledgeling** XIX; see -LING[1].

flee pt. and pp. *fled*. OE. str. vb. *flēon* = OS. *fliohan* (MDu. *vlīen*, Du. *vlieden*), OHG. *fliohan* (G. *fliehen*), ON. *flý(j)a*, Goth. *þliuhan*. The str. forms continued till XV; but wk. forms occur as early as XIII. *Flee* and *fly* in OE. had identical pt. and pp., and in later usage became interchangeable in sense.

fleece sb. OE. *flēos* = Du., (M)HG. *vlies* :- WGmc. **fleusa*, and OE. *flēs* (WS. *flīes*) = MLG. *vlūs*, MDu. *vluus*, MHG. *vlius* :- WGmc. **fleusi*, rel. to MLG., MHG. *vlūs* sheepskin (G. *flaus* woollen coat) :- **flūsa-*; prob. ult. rel. to the base of L. *plūma* PLUME. Hence vb. lit. and fig. XVI.

fleer †grin, grimace XIV; laugh mockingly, gibe XV. prob. of Scand. orig.; cf. Norw. and Sw. dial. *flira*, Da. dial. *flire* grin, laugh unbecomingly.

fleet[1] naval force. OE. *flēot* (once) ship or ships coll., f. *flēotan* float, swim, FLEET[3].

fleet[2] (dial.) run of water OE.; (hist.) *The Fleet* that flowing into the Thames between Ludgate Hill and *Fleet* Street; (hence) the prison near it XIII. OE. *flēot* (also *flēote* or *-a*), corr. to OFris. *flēt*, (M)Du. *vliet*, MHG. *vliez*, ON. *fljót*, f. Gmc. **fleut-* FLEET[3].

fleet[3] †float OE.; (arch.) flow or glide away XII. OE. str.vb. *flēotan* float, swim = OS. *fliotan* (Du. *vlieten*), OHG. *fliozan* (G. *fliessen*), ON. *fljóta* float, flow :- Gmc. **fleutan*; f. IE. **pleud-* **plud-*, extension of **pleu-* **plou-* *plu-* (repr. by Gr. *plein* :- **pleϝfein* sail, OSl. *pluti*, Skr. *plávate* swim, float, L. *pluere* rain); cf. FLY[2]. Surviving mainly in **fleeting** ppl. adj. †floating, swimming OE.; †shifting, inconstant XIII; passing quickly away XVI.

fleet[4] swift. XVI. prob. much older if - ON. *fljótr*, f. Gmc. **fleut-* (see prec.).

Flemish pert. to Flanders or its inhabitants XIV; sb. the form of Dutch spoken in Flanders XVIII. - MDu. *Vlāmisch* (Du. *Vlaamsch*). So **Fleming** native of Flanders. XV. - MDu. *Vlāming*, f. *Vlam-*, whence *Vlaanderen* Flanders; see -ISH[1], -ING[3].

flense cut up the fat of a whale, skin a seal. XIX. - Da. *flense*. Also *flench*, *flinch*.

flesh sb. OE. *flǣsc* = OS. *flēsk* (Du. *vlees*), OHG. *fleisc* (G. *fleisch*), ON. *flesk* pork, bacon :- Gmc. **flaiskaz*, *-iz*; rel. to FLITCH, the orig. meaning being 'slice, slit, split' (cf. Lith. *pléišėti* crack). Hence vb. reward (a hawk, etc.) with a portion of the quarry; inure to bloodshed, gen. initiate; inflame, incite; plunge into flesh. XVI. **fleshly** OE. *flǣsclić*. **fleshpot** XVI, **fleshy** XIV.

fletcher (hist.) arrow-maker. XIV. - OF. *flech(i)er*, f. *fleche* arrow, of unkn. orig. see -ER[2].

fleur-de-lis iris flower; heraldic lily. XIX. ME. *flour de lys* - OF., i.e. *flour* FLOWER, *de* of, *lis* (L. *līlium* LILY).

fleury, flory (her.) decorated with fleurs-de-lis. XV. - OF. *flo(u)ré* (mod. *fleuré*), f. *fleur* FLOWER; see -Y[5].

flew see FLY[2].

flews chaps of a hound. XVI. of unkn. orig.

flex[1] bend. XVI. f. *flex-*, pp. stem of L. *flectere* bend. So **flexible** XV. - (O)F. or L. **flexion** XVII, **flexure** XVI. - L.

flex[2] flexible insulated electric wire. XX. Shortening of FLEXIBLE.

flibbertigibbet (dial.) chattering person XV; flighty woman XVI; †name of a fiend XVII; character so nicknamed in Scott's 'Kenilworth' (1821); hence, impish urchin. The earliest forms, *flibbergib*, *flebergebet*, are perh. imit. of senseless chatter.

flick slight blow as with the end or tip of something. XV. imit. Hence vb. XIX.

flicker †flutter, hover OE.; †fondle, dally XIII; flutter, vibrate XV; burn fitfully, flash up and die away XVII. OE. *flicorian*, *flicerian* (cf. LG. *flickern*, Du. *flikkeren*), synon. in its earliest use with ME. *flakere*, prob. repr. an OE. **flacorian*, f. *flacor* (of arrows) flying, f. imit. base **flak-*, repr. also in MHG. *vlackern* flicker (G. *flackern*), ON. *flǫkra* flutter. Hence sb. XIX.

flight[1] act of flying OE.; collection of beings or things flying together XIII; volley (of missiles) XVI; set of steps XVIII. OE. *flyht*, corr. to OS. *fluht*,

(M)Du. *vlucht* :- WGmc. **fluχti*, f. weak grade of Gmc. **fleuʒan* FLY[2]. Hence **flighty** †swift, rapid XVI; given to flights of fancy, etc.; inconstant XVIII.

flight[2] act of fleeing. OE. **flyht* = OS., OHG. *fluht* (Du. *vlucht*, G. *flucht*), ON. *flótti*, f. the base of FLEE.

flimsy XVII. orig. dial. or sl.; prob. based on **flim-flam** nonsense, humbug, adj. frivolous, vain (XVI), symbolic redupl. formation. See -SY.

flinch give way, draw back XVI; shrink or wince from pain XVII. - OF. *flenchir*, *flainchir* turn aside - WGmc. **χlaŋkjan*, whence (M)HG. *lenken* bend, turn; rel. to FLANK.

flinders (dial.) shivers, splinters. XV. prob. of Scand. orig. (cf. Norw. *flindra* thin chip or splinter).

fling pt. and pp. *flung* (intr.) move with violence XIII; (trans.) cast, hurl XIV. perh. of Scand. orig. (cf. ON. *flengja* flog).

flint OE. *flint* = MDu. *vlint*, rel. to OHG. (G. dial.) *flins*; perh. rel. to Gr. *plínthos* tile (see PLINTH).

flip[1] give a smart blow or jerk to; strike (something) in this way. XVI. prob. contr. of FILLIP; but cf. **flip-flap** (XVI), redupl. form. on FLAP. Hence as sb. XVII.

flip[2] mixture of beer and spirit sweetened and heated with a hot iron. XVII. perh. f. prec. vb. with the notion of 'whipping up' into froth.

flippant †nimble, pliant; †voluble, glib XVII; showing unbecoming levity XVIII. f. FLIP[1] + -ANT. Hence **flippancy** XVIII.

flirt A. †smart stroke; sudden jerk XVI; B. †flighty woman XVI; one who plays at courtship XVIII. This, with the corr. vb. of similar date and parallel meanings, seems to be an imit. formation. Hence **flirtation** XVIII; whence **flirtatious** XIX.

flit remove to another place, trans. and intr. XII. - ON. *flytja*, f. **flut-*, weak grade of the base of *fljóta* (see FLEET[3]).

flitch side of a hog. OE. *flicce*, corr. to MLG. *vli(c)ke*, ON. *flikki* :- Gmc. **flikkjam*; rel. to FLESH.

flitter XV. f. FLIT + -ER[4].

float vb. Late OE. *flotian* = OS. *flotōn* (MDu. *vlōten*), ON. *flota* :- Gmc. **flotōjan*, f. **flot-*, weak grade of base of FLEET[3]. Reinforced in ME. by, if not entirely due to, OF. *floter* (mod. *flotter*) :- Rom. **flottāre*, prob. - Gmc. **flot-*. **floatation** see FLOTATION. So **float** sb. OE. *flot* sea. = ON. *flot* and OE. *flota* ship, fleet = ON. *floti*; various mod. uses are f. the vb.

flocculent like tufts of wool. XIX. f. L. *floccus* FLOCK[2] + -ULENT.

flock[1] band or company, esp. of (domestic) animals. OE. *flocc* = MLG. *vlocke*, ON. *flokkr* (in OE. and ON. used only of persons); of unkn. orig. Hence vb. †trans. and intr. XIII.

flock[2] tuft of wool, etc. XIII. - (O)F. *floc* :- L. *floccus*.

floe XIX. prob. - Norw. *flo* layer, level piece :- ON. *fló* layer, stratum.

flog XVII. prob. imit.; perh. suggested by L. *flagellāre* FLAGELLATE.

flood sb. OE. *flōd*, corr. to OS. *flōd* (Du. *vloed*), OHG. *fluot* (G. *flut*), ON. *flóð*, Goth. *flōdus* :- Gmc. **flōðuz*, *-am*, f. **flō-* :- IE. **plō-* (as in Gr. *plṓein* swim).

floor sb. OE. *flōr*, corr. to (M)Du. *vloer*, MHG. *vluor* (G. *flur*), ON. *flór* :- Gmc. **flōruz*; rel. to OIr. *lár*, W. *llawr* :- Celt. **plār-*. Hence vb. cover with a floor XV; bring to the ground XVII.

flop vb. XVII. var. of FLAP.

flora (*F-*) goddess of flowering plants XVI; plant life of a region, period, etc. XVIII (as a book-title XVII). - L., f. *flōs*, *flōr-* FLOWER. So **floral** XVII. L. *flōrālis* or directly f. L. *flōr-*.

florescence (state or period of) flowering. XVIII. - modL. *flōrescentia*, f. prp. stem of L. *flōrēscere*, inceptive of *flōrēre*; see FLOURISH, -ESCENCE.

floret XVII. f. L. *flōs*, *flōr-* FLOWER + -ET.

florid †flourishing, blooming; (of style) flowery; ruddy. XVII. - F. †*floride* or L. *flōridus*, f. *flōs*, *flōr-*; see FLOURISH, -ID[1].

florilegium collection of literary 'flowers'. XVII. modL. (L. *flōs* FLOWER, *legere* gather), tr. Gr. *anthológion* ANTHOLOGY.

florin gold coin first issued at Florence in 1252 XIV; two-shilling piece XIX. - (O)Fr. - It. *fiorino*, f. *fiore* FLOWER; the coin orig. so named bore the figure of a lily on the obverse.

florist XVII. f. L. *flōs*, *flōr-* FLOWER + -IST.

floruit period of 'flourishing'. XIX. - L., 3rd sg. pt. indic. of *flōrēre* FLOURISH.

flory see FLEURY.

floss rough silk. XVIII (also *floss-silk*). Early forms also *flosh*, *flox* - F. *floche*, as in *soie floche* floss-silk, OF. *flosche* down, pile of velvet; of unkn. orig.

flotation, floatation XIX. f. FLOAT vb. + -ATION.

flotilla XVIII. - Sp., dim. of *flota* fleet, rel. to FLOAT.

flotsam floating wreckage. XVI. Early forms also *flotsen*, *-son*; - AN. *floteson*, f. *floter* FLOAT.

flounce[1] dash or plunge with violent or jerky motion. XVI. of obscure orig.

flounce[2] ornamental appendage to a skirt. XVIII. alt., prob. by assim. to FLOUNCE[1], of earlier †*frounce* wrinkle, fold, pleat - (O)F. *fronce*, f. *froncir* wrinkle - Gmc. **χruŋkjan* (cf. ON. *hrukka*, MHG. *runke* wrinkle). So vb. XVIII; cf. †*frounce* vb. wrinkle (XIII), curl, pleat (XVI).

flounder[1] flat-fish. XIV. - AN. *floundre*, OF. *flondre*, prob. of Scand. orig. (cf. OSw. *flundra*, Da. *flynder*, ON. *flyðra*).

flounder[2] †stumble; plunge or tumble about clumsily. XVI. of uncert. (perh. imit.) orig.

flour 'flower' or finer portion of meal, (now) wheat meal XIII; fine powder resulting from pulverizing XIV. Differentiated sp. of FLOWER; the sp. *flower* continued till early XIX.

flourish A. †blossom, flower XIII; thrive XIV; be in the prime XIV; B. †adorn, embellish XIII; C. †display, parade; brandish XIV; brag, swagger XVI. - (O)F. *floriss-*, lengthened stem (see -ISH[2]) of *florir* (mod. *fleurir*) :- Rom. **flōrīre*, for L. *flōrēre*, f. *flōr-* FLOWER. Hence sb. A. (dial.) mass of bloom; †vigour, prime XVI; B. embellishment XVII; C. brandishing of a weapon; fanfare XVI.

flout treat mockingly. XVI. perh. - Du. *fluiten* whistle, play the FLUTE, hiss.

flow vb. OE. str. vb. *flōwan*, f. Gmc. **flō-*, whence

also ON. *flóa* flood, Du. *vloeien* flow and FLOOD. The orig. str. conj. began to be superseded by wk. forms in the pt. in early ME. Hence sb. xv.

flower reproductive organ in plants; blossom; choicest individual xiii. ME. *fl(o)ur* - AN. *flur*, OF. *flo(u)r* (mod. *fleur*) :- L. *flōs, flōr-*, f. IE. **bhlō-* as in BLOOM[1], etc. Hence **flower** vb. xiii, **flowery** xiv. Cf. FLOUR.

flu colloq. shortening of INFLUENZA xix.

fluctuate xvii. f. pp. stem of L. *fluctuāre*, f. *fluctus* current, wave, f. *fluct-*, pp. stem of *fluere* flow; see -ATE[3]. So **fluctuation** xv. - (O)F. or L.

flue chimney, smoke duct in this, etc. xvi (*flew*). of unkn. orig.

fluent flowing freely or easily (lit. and fig.); ready in speech. xvi. - L. *fluēns, fluent-*, prp. of *fluere* flow; see -ENT.

fluff light feathery stuff. xviii. prob. alt. of *flue* †down (xvi).

fluid adj. xv; sb. xvii. - (O)F. *fluide* or L. *fluidus*, f. *fluere* flow; see -ID[1]. Hence **fluidity** xvii.

fluke[1] flat fish, esp. flounder OE.; parasitic worm resembling this xvii. OE. *flōc*, corr. to ON. *flóki*, rel. to MLG., MDu. *flac*, OHG. *flah* (G. *flach*) flat; ult. IE. **plaq-*, further repr. by Gr. *plakoûs*, L. *placenta* flat cake.

fluke[2] triangular plate on either arm of an anchor xvi; triangular extremity of a whale's tail. perh. transf. use of FLUKE[1], from its shape.

fluke[3] (orig. billiards) successful stroke made by chance. xix. perh. of dial. orig. (cf. dial. *fluke* guess, miss in fishing).

flummery (dial.) kind of porridge xvii; transf. mere flattery, humbug xviii. - W. *llymru*, of unkn. orig.

flummox (sl.) confound, bewilder. xix. prob. of dial. orig.; cf. dial. *flummock* confuse, *flummox* maul, mangle, *flummocky* slovenly; imit. or symbolic formations.

flump (colloq.) fall or throw *down* heavily. xix. imit.

flunkey man in livery xviii; obsequious person xix. orig. Sc.; poss. f. *flanker* one who stands at a person's FLANK + -Y[6].

fluor †flux, fluid state; one of a class of minerals used as fluxes xvii; mineral of this kind containing fluorine (esp. *fluorspar*) xviii. - L. *fluor* flow, flux, f. *fluere* flow. Hence **fluorescence, -escent** xix. So **fluorine** xix. - F.; see -INE[5].

flurry sudden gust xvii; sudden agitation or commotion xviii. f. †*flurr* scatter, ruffle, fly up with a whirr, prob. after *hurry*. Hence vb. xviii.

flush[1] fly up suddenly. xiii. first in pt. forms *fliste, fluste*; of imit. orig.

flush[2] hand containing cards all of one suit. xvi. - F. †*flus, flux* - L. *fluxus* FLUX.

flush[3] A. (of liquids) rush out suddenly or copiously xvi; B. emit light or glow suddenly; produce or show heightened colour xvii. orig. identical with FLUSH[1].

flush[4] abundantly full, plentifully supplied xvii; even, level with xviii. prob. f. prec.

fluster excite, esp. with drink xvii (xv in vbl. sb. *flostrynge*); intr. for pass. xvii; flurry xviii. of unkn. orig.; cf. Icel. *flaustr* hurry, *flaustra* bustle.

flute cylindrical musical wind-instrument with holes along its length xiv; channel, furrow, groove xvii. The earliest forms are *flowte, floite* (xiv), in xvi-xvii often *fluit* - OF. *flahute, fleüte, flaüte* (mod. *flûte*), prob. - Pr. *flaüt*, perh. blending of *flaujol* (cf. FLAGEOLET) with *laüt* LUTE[1]. So vb. xiv; channel, groove xvi.

flutter †float to and fro; flap the wings rapidly OE.; quiver, tremble excitedly. xvi. OE. *floterian, -orian*, frequent. of Gmc. **flut-*; see FLEET[3], -ER[4].

fluvial xiv. - L. *fluviālis*, f. *fluvius* river, prop. adj. formation on base of *fluere* flow; see -AL[1]. So **fluviatile** xvi. - F. - L.; see -ATILE.

flux copious flowing of blood, etc. xiv; (gen.) flowing; continuous succession xvi; incoming tide, opp. of reflux xvii; substance facilitating fusion (earlier †*fluss* - G.) xviii. In early use (xiv-xvii) also †*flix* - (O)F. *flux* or L. *fluxus*, f. *fluere* flow. So **fluxion** †flow, flowing xvi; (math.) rate of change of a continuously varying quantity xviii.

fly[1] winged insect. OE. *flȳġe, flēoġe* = OS., OHG. *flioga* (Du. *vlieg*, G. *fliege*) :- WGmc. **fleuʒ(j)ō*, f. **fleuʒan* (see next); cf. ON. *fluga*.

fly[2] move with wings; (now in pres. stem only) flee. OE. str. vb. *flēogan* = OS. **fliogan* (Du. *vliegen*), OHG. *fliogan* (G. *fliegen*), ON. *fljúga* :- Gmc. **fleuʒan* :- IE. **pleuk-*, extension of **pleu-* (cf. **pleud-* FLEET[3]). The normal ME. pt. *flegh* was at first replaced by the type *flough, flow*, which was transferred from the pl. to the sing.; this was superseded by *flew*, an unexpl. form perh. due to assoc. with the pt. of FLOW, the pp. of which had become identical with that of *fly*.

fly[3] flight xv; speed-regulating device, compass-card, etc. xvi; †stage-coach xviii; light carriage xix. f. FLY[2].

fly[4] (sl.) sharp, wide-awake. xix. Has been doubtfully referred to FLY[2].

foal OE. *fola* = OS. *folo*, MDu. *volen*, (also mod.) *veulen*, OHG. *folo* (G. *fohlen* n.), ON. *foli*, Goth. *fula* :- Gmc. **folan-*, rel. to synon. L. *pullus*, Gr. *pôlos*, Arm. *ul*. Cf. FILLY.

foam sb. OE. *fām* = (O)HG. *feim* :- WGmc. *faima* :- IE. **poimo-*, rel. to L. *pūmex* PUMICE, OSl. *pěna*, Skr. *phéna-* foam. Hence vb. xiv.

fob[1] cheat, trick, put *off* deceitfully. xv. Parallel to †*fop* vb. and G. *foppen* quiz, banter. Hence sb. trick. xvii. ME. *fobbe* impostor (once, xiv) is isolated.

fob[2] small pocket. xvii. orig. cant term; prob. of G. orig. (cf. G. dial. *fuppe* pocket).

fo'c'sle see FORECASTLE.

focus point toward which lines, rays, etc. converge xvii; point at which an object must be situated so that a well-defined image of it may be produced by the lens; centre of activity xviii. - L. *focus* fire-place, domestic hearth. So **focal** xviii.

fodder (now sl.) food; spec. cattle food. OE. *fōdor* = MLG. *vōder*, (M)Du. *voeder*, OHG. *fuotar* (G. *futter*), ON. *fóðr* :- Gmc. **fōðram*, f. **fōð-* (see FOOD).

foe Early ME. *fā, fō*, pl. *fān, fōn*, aphetic reduction of *ifā(n), ifō(n)*, OE. *ġefā(n)*, sb. use of *ġefāh* at feud (with) = OHG. *gafēh*, (MHG. *gevēch, gevē*) :- WGmc. **ʒafaiχa*, f. **ʒa-* Y- + **faiχ-* (OE. *fāh* at feud, hostile), whence also OE.

fǣhð (see FEUD[1]); ult. orig. unkn. Hence **foeman** OE.

foetus XIV. - L. *fētus* giving birth, young offspring, abstr. sb. parallel to adj. *fētus* pregnant, productive, prob. rel. to *fēcundus* FECUND, *fēmina* woman (see FEMININE).

fog[1] (dial.) aftermath grass, long or rank grass XIV; moss XV. prob. of Scand. orig.; cf. Norw. *fogg* long-strawed, weak, scattered grass in a moist meadow. Hence **foggy**[1] XVI. An earlier occurrence of *fog* is implied in AL. *fogagium* (*c.* 1200) (privilege of) pasturing cattle on *fog*.

fog[2] thick mist. XVI. of unkn. orig. Hence **foggy**[2] XVI.

fog(e)y (colloq.) old-fashioned fellow. XVIII. rel. to sl. *fogram* (XVIII) antiquated, old-fashioned (person), of unkn. orig.

foible XVII. - F., obs. var. of *faible* FEEBLE.

foil[1] tread under foot XIII; overthrow, discomfit, frustrate XVI. irreg. repr. (O)F. *fouler* :- Rom. **fullāre*, f. L. *fullō* FULLER.

foil[2] †leaf; thin sheet of metal XIV; thin leaf of metal placed under a precious stone to increase its brilliance, etc.; a thing that serves by contrast to set off another thing XVI. (i) - OF. *foil* :- L. *folium* leaf; (ii) - OF. *foille* (mod. *feuille*) :- L. *folia*, pl. of *folium* (n. pl. taken as fem. sg.).

foil[3] small sword with blunt edge and blunted point. XVI. of unkn. orig.

foison (dial.) power, capacity; (arch.) plenty, abundance. XIII. - (O)F. :- Rom. **fusiō*, for L. *fūsiō, -ōn-* outpouring (see FUSION).

foist †palm (a die) so as to be able to introduce it when required; introduce surreptitiously or unwarrantably. XVI. prob. - Du. *vuisten*, f. *vuist* FIST.

fold[1] enclosure for domestic animals. OE. *fald*, contr. of *falæd, -od, -ud*, corr. to OS. *faled*, MLG. *valt*, Du. *vaalt*. Hence vb. shut up in a fold. OE. *faldian*.

fold[2] double or bend over upon itself; lay (the arms) together. OE. str. vb. *f(e)aldan* = MDu. *vouden* (Du. *vouwen*), OHG. *faltan* (G. *falten*), ON. *falda*, Goth. *falþan* :- Gmc. **falþan*, f. IE. **pel- *pl-* (cf. Gr. *dípaltos, diplásios* twofold, *haplóos* simple); rel. to L. *plicāre* fold. Hence sb. XIII.

-fold OE. *-f(e)ald* = OS. *-fald* (Du. *-voud*), (O)HG. *-falt*, ON. *-faldr*, Goth. *-falþs*, Gmc. terminal el. rel. to FOLD[2] and equiv. to Gr. *-paltos, -plasios*, and more remotely with *-plo-* in Gr. *haplóos* single, *diplóos* double (L. *duplus*); appended to cardinal numerals and adjs. meaning 'many', orig. with the sense 'folded in two, etc., folds', 'plaited in so many strands'. In OE. the adjs. were already used as sbs. and advs.

foliage XV. Early forms *foillage, fuellage* (assim. later to L. *folium*) - (O)F. *feuillage*, †*foillage*, f. *feuille*; see FOIL[2], -AGE.

foliation A. being in leaf, arrangement in leaves XVII; B. consecutive numbering of folios XIX. In A. f. L. *folium*; see FOIL[2], -ATION. In B. f. FOLIO.

folic (chem.) name of an acid abundant in green leaf. XX. irreg. f. L. *folium* leaf, FOIL[2] + -IC.

folio A. leaf of paper, parchment, etc.; B. *in folio* in the form of a full-sized sheet folded once (hence simply *folio* adj. and sb.). XVI. In A. a generalization of the medL. use of the abl. of L. *folium* leaf, FOIL[2], in references 'at leaf so-and-so', or a latinization of It. *foglio*; in B. - It. *in foglio*.

folk people, race; men, people. OE. *folc* = OS., OHG. *folc* (Du., G. *volk*), ON. *folk* people, army :- Gmc. **folkam*, the orig. meaning of which is perh. best preserved in ON. Hence **folk-lore, folk-song** XIX. From XIV the pl. *folks* has been used, and since XVII is the ordinary form, the sing. being *arch.* or *dial.*

follicle (anat., etc.) small sac. XVII. - L. *folliculus* little bag, dim. of *follis* bellows; see -CLE.

follow OE. *folgian*, corr. to OS. *folgon* (Du. *volgen*), OHG. *folgēn* (G. *folgen*), f. Gmc. **fulʒ-*; of unkn. orig.

folly quality or state of being foolish XIII; costly structure considered to have shown folly in the builder XVI. - (O)F. *folie*, f. *fol* foolish, FOOL[1]; see -Y[3]. In the second sense derived from a similar use of OF. *folie*.

foment bathe with warm lotion; promote the growth of; foster, stimulate. XV. - (O)F. *fomenter* - late L. *fōmentāre*, f. *fōmentum* lotion, poultice, lenitive :- **fovementum*, f. *fovēre* heat, cherish, rel. to Skr. *dáhati*, Lith. *degù* burn, Gr. *téphrā* ash, ember; cf. DAY.

fond (dial.) foolish, silly XIV; (dial.) foolishly affectionate, doting; †eager, desirous; having a strong liking (for) XVI. ME. *fonned, -yd*, having the form of a pp. of *fon* vb. (recorded later in XIV) be foolish, which is obscurely rel. to †*fon* sb. fool (XIII). The occurrence in ME. and in E. Angl. dial. (XVII-XIX) of the sense 'insipid', 'of sickly flavour', has suggested that the vb. *fon* orig. meant 'lose savour'; but this sense is later than that of 'foolish', and is of obscure orig.; moreover, the chronology of the words as known suggests that ME. *fonned* was directly f. *fon* sb. + -ED[2] (cf. the etym. of *wicked, wretched*).

fondant kind of sweetmeat that melts quickly in the mouth. XIX. - F., sb. use of the prp. of *fondre* melt; see FOUND[3], -ANT.

fondle †pamper XVII; treat with fondness, caress XVIII. app. frequent. of FOND; see -LE[3].

font[1] receptacle for the water used in baptism. Late OE. *font*, var. of *fant* - OIr. *fant, font* - L. *fōns, font-* spring, FOUNTAIN, in spec. eccl. use *fons* or *fontes baptismi* water(s) of baptism.

font[2] var. of FOUNT[2].

fontanelle (anat.) †hollow between muscles XVI; outlet for a discharge XVII; membranous space in the skull of an infant XVIII. - F. - modL. *fontanella*, latinization of OF. *fontenelle*, dim. of *fontaine* FOUNTAIN; see -EL[2].

food what is taken to support life. Late OE. *fōda* :- **fōðan-*, a unique formation, the synon. words in other Gmc. langs. being f. **fōðjan* FEED, viz. ON. *fœði, fœða*, Goth. *fōdeins*; f. Gmc. **fōð- *fað-* :- IE. **pat-*, as in Gr. *patéesthai* eat.

fool[1] A. one deficient in judgement or sense XIII; professional jester, clown XIV; B. adj. foolish XIII; now only (exc. dial.) as attrib. use of the sb. ME. *fōl* sb. and adj. - OF. *fol* (mod. *fou* mad) :- L. *follis* bellows, inflated ball, (later fig.) 'windbag', empty-headed person. Hence **fool** vb. play the fool, make a fool of. XVI. **foolery** XVI. **foolhardy** XIII. - OF. *folhardi* 'foolish-bold'. **foolscap** (*fool's cap*) cap of a professional fool; folio paper of a kind that orig. bore a watermark representing a fool's cap. XVII.

fool[2] †clotted cream XVI; dish composed of crushed fruit with cream, etc. XVIII. perh. transf. use of prec. suggested by *trifle*.

foot pl. *feet* part of the leg beyond the ankle joint; unit of measurement 12 in.; metrical unit OE.; lowest part XII; what is at the foot or bottom (pl. *foots*) XV. OE. *fōt*, pl. *fēt* = OS. *fōt*, *fuot* (Du. *voet*), OHG. *fuoz* (G. *fuss*), ON. *fótr*, Goth. *fōtus*; the Gmc. cons.-stem **fōt-* :- IE. **pōd-*, which with its vars. **pod-* **ped-* is repr. by Skr. *pát*, L. *pēs*, *ped-*, Gr. *poús*, *pod-* Arm. *otn* foot. Hence **foot** vb. dance XIV; †add *up* XV; walk; strike, etc. with the foot XVI. **footing** (dial.) foothold XIV; (fig.) XVI; settled condition XVII. **football** XV, **footfall** XVII, **foothold** XVII. **footman** foot-soldier XIII; (dial.) pedestrian XIV; attendant on foot XV. **footnote** XIX. **footpace** walking-pace; raised floor (for an altar). XVI. **footpad** highwayman who robs on foot. XVII; *pad*, canting use of var. of PATH. **footpath** XVI. **footstep** XIV (once XIII as pl. *fet steppes*). **footstool** XVI.

footle (colloq.) fool about, trifle, potter. XIX (esp. in prp. **footling** trifling, paltry). perh. alt., by assoc. with -LE[3], of (dial.) *footer* bungle, idle or potter about, presumably rel. to *footer* contemptible fellow, transf. use of *foutre* - (O)F. *foutre* have sexual relations with :- L. *futuere*.

fop †fool XV; one who is vain of his appearance, etc. XVII. corr. in form to G. *foppen* hoax. Cf. FOB[1]. Hence **foppery** XVI, **foppish** XVII.

for prep. †before; representing, instead of; in defence of; with a view to; in the character of; by reason of, in spite of OE.; to obtain, in order *to* XIII; with the object of; in relation to XIV; during XV; conj. (for OE. *for þon þe*, *for þǣm þe*, *for þȳ þe* on account of the fact that) because, since XII. OE. *for* = OFris., OS. *for*, Goth. *faur*, prob. reduction of Gmc. **fora* before (of place and time), repr. by OE. *fore* = OFris., OS., OHG. *fora*, Goth. *faura*, beside OS., OHG. forms with *-i*, viz. *furi* (G. *für*) and ON. *fyrir*; see FORE-. Hence **forasmuch** (arch.) seeing that. XIII. tr. OF. *por tant que* for so much as.

for-[1] OE. *for-*, *fær-* = OS. *for-*, OHG. *fir-*, *far-* (Du., G. *ver-*), Goth. *fair-*, *faur-*, corr. to Gr. PERI-, PARA-[1], L. PER-, Skr. *pári*, *purá*, OIr. *ar-*, *air-*; IE. prefix with variation of form and wide extent of meaning, but esp. implying (1) rejection, exclusion, prohibition, (2) destruction, (3) exhaustion.

for-[2] var. of FORE-. Cf. also FORECLOSE, FORFEIT.

forage food for cattle. XIV. - (O)F. *fourrage*, f. *feurre* - Gmc. **fōðram* FODDER; see -AGE. So vb. XV.

foramen (anat.) opening for the passage of something. XVII. - L., f. *forāre* BORE[1].

foray hostile incursion. XIV (in early use Sc.). prob. f. *foray* vb. (XIV), back-formation from ME. *forayer* forager, raider, var. of *forrier* - OF. :- Rom. **fodrārius*, f. **fodro* FODDER (cf. FORAGE).

forbear[1] †bear, bear with; endure the loss of; abstain from OE. (intr. XIV). OE. *forberan* = OHG. *firberan* abstain, Goth. *frabairan* endure; f. FOR-[1] + BEAR[2]. Hence **forbearance** XVI.

forbear[2], **forebear** (usu. pl.) ancestor. XV (orig. Sc.). f. FORE- + †*beer*, agent-noun of BE.

forbid OE. *forbēodan* = Du. *verbieden*, OHG. *farbiotan* (G. *verbieten*), Goth. *faurbiudan*; f. FOR-[1] + BID.

forby prep. †close by XIII; adv. (dial.) aside, along, past XIV; (Sc.) besides XVI. f. FOR adv. + BY.

force strength, power XIII; body of armed men XIV. - (O)F. :- Rom. **fortia*, f. L. *fortis* strong. So vb. XIII. **forcible** done by force XV; †strong; producing a powerful effect XVI.

force-meat XVII. f. *force* (XIV), var. of *farce* stuff (XIV; - OF. *farsir*, mod. *farcir* :- L. *farcīre*) + MEAT.

forceps XVII. - L.

ford sb. OE. *ford* = OFris. *forda*, OS. *-ford* in place-names (Du. *voorde*), (O)HG. *furt* :- WGmc. **furdu* (cf. ON. *fjǫrðr* FIORD :- **ferþuz*) :- IE. **pr̥tús*, repr. also by OW. *rit* (W. *rhyd*) ford, L. *portus* harbour, PORT[1], f. **por-* **per-* **pr̥-* (see FARE[2]).

fordo pp. *fordone* (arch.) put an end to, destroy, spoil. OE. *fordōn* = OS. *fardōn* (Du. *verdoen*), OHG. *fartuon* (G. *vertun*); see FOR-[1], DO[1]. In pp. (poet.) exhausted, wearied out XVI.

fore[1] adj. †earlier; that is in front XV; sb. in (orig.) Sc. and Anglo-Ir. phr. *to the fore* present, surviving; ready, available XVII; conspicuous XIX. Evolved from analysis of comps. of prefix FORE-, e.g. *forehead*, *foreland*, *forepart*.

fore[2] adv., now only in *fore and aft* from stem to stern, all over the ship. XVII. Not continuous with OE. and ME. *fore*; perh. of LG. orig.

fore[3] int. (in golf) warning cry to people in front of the intended stroke. XIX. prob. aphetic form of BEFORE or AFORE.

fore- prefix meaning 'before', identical with the adv. *fore* in front, before, OE. *fore* = OS., OHG. *fora* (Du. *voor*, G. *vor*), Goth. *faura*, perh. :- Gmc. **forai*, corr. to Gr. *paraí*, a dative formation, the base of which is repr. also in L. *prō*, *prǣ*, *per* (see PER-, PRE-, PRO-[1]), Gr. *pró*, *pará*, *perí* (see PARA-[1], PERI-), Skr. *purá* before.

A few of the foll. comps. had orig. the prefix FOR-[2].

forearm[1] arm beforehand. XVI. **forearm**[2] part of the arm below the elbow. XVIII. **forecast** †contrive beforehand XIV; estimate beforehand XVI. Hence as sb. XV. **forecastle** (whence the sp. *fo'c'sle*) †short raised deck in the bow, orig. a castle-like structure to command the enemy's decks XIV; fore part of a ship XV. **forefather** XIII. - ON. *forfaðir*. **forefinger** XV. **forefoot** XIV. **forefront** principal face, foremost part (now dial. exc. fig.). XV (orig. Sc.). **foregoing** XV. **foregone** that has gone before. XVI. **foreground** XVII. **forehead** OE. *forhēafod* = MLG. *vorhōved*, Du. *voorhoofd*, G. *vor(der)haupt*. **forejudge** XVI. **foreknowledge** XVI. Cf. **foreknow** XIV. **foreland** cape, promontory. XIV. **forelock** OE. *forelοccas* pl.; but a new formation in XVI. **foreman** †leader XV; principal juror; principal of workmen XVI; perh. after ON. *formaðr* captain, leader, or - Du. *voorman*. **forename** XVI. **forenoon** XV. **forepart** XIV. **forerunner** one who goes before to prepare the way (first of John the Baptist) XIII; one whom another follows XVI; tr. L. *præcursor* PRECURSOR. **foresail** XV. **foresee** OE. *forsēon*; but prob. a new formation in ME. **foreshore** XVIII. **foreshorten** XVII. **foreshow** XVI. **foresight** †(divine) providence XIII; provision for the future XIV; action of foreseeing or looking forward XV; prob. after ON. *forsjá*, and later felt as etym. rendering of (O)F. *providence*, L. *prōvidentia*. **foreskin** XVI. **forestall** †obstruct XIV; buy up (goods) before they reach public markets XIV; hinder by anticipation, anticipate in action XVI. Implied earlier in AL. *forstallatio* obstruction, *forstallator* (XII), AN. *forstallour* forestaller of markets (XIII), f. OE. *for(e)steall* interception, ambush. **foretaste** sb. and vb. XV. **foretell** XIII. **forethought** †premeditation; previous thought. XIII. parallel to †*forethink*, OE. *foreðenċan* consider beforehand, and repl. OE. *foreðanc* consideration, forethought, providence. **foretop** †lock of hair at the front XIII; †forepart of the crown XIV; top of a foremast XV. **forewarn** warn beforehand. OE. *forewarnian* (trans. and intr.). **foreword** XIX.

foreclose exclude, preclude XV; deprive of the equity of redemption, bar (a right of redemption) XVIII. f. *foreclos-*, pp. stem of (O)F. *forclore*, f. *for-* (:- L. *forīs* outside) + *clore* CLOSE; there has been assoc. with FOR-[1], or with FOR-[2], FORE-. Hence **foreclosure** XVIII.

foreign †out of doors (rare); pert. to another, alien; pert. to another region, not in one's own land XIV; not domestic or native XV. - OF. *forain*, *forein*, *-e* :- Rom. **forānus*, f. L. *forās* acc. pl., *forīs* loc. pl. of **fora*, var. of *forēs* DOOR. Hence **foreigner** XV.

foremost The present form, dating from XVI, is an alt., by assoc. with FORE-, of *formost*, itself an alt., by assoc. with -MOST, of *formest* (XII), f. *forme*, OE. *forma* first (= OFris. *forma*, OS. *formo*), with superl. *-m-* suffix as in L. *prīmus* PRIME, + -EST, *formest* having repl. *fürmest*, *firmest* :- OE. *fyrmest* (= Goth. *frumists*), f. *forma*, the result being a double superl. Cf. FORMER.

forensic pert. to courts of law. XVII. f. L. *forēnsis*, f. *forum*; see FORUM, -IC.

forest XIII. - OF. *forest* (mod. *forêt*) - late L. *forestis* (*silva*) 'outside wood', royal forest reserved for hunting, obscurely f. *forīs* out of doors, outside (see FOREIGN); prob. meaning orig. woodland lying outside the park and unfenced; in AL. *foresta*, *forestum* (XI). So **forester** XIII.

forfeit †misdeed, misdemeanour XIII; fine, penalty XV; trivial fine for breach of rule XVII. ME. *forfet* - OF. *forfet*, (also mod.) *-fait* crime, f. *for(s)faire* commit crime (medL. *forisfacere*), f. *for(s)-* beyond, outside, sc. what is right (:- L. *forīs* outside) + *faire* do. Hence vb. †sin, transgress XIV; lose the right to XV. **forfeiture** †crime, sin; loss or liability to deprivation. XIV.

for(e)fend †forbid; avert XIV; (now U.S.) protect by precautionary measures XVI. f. FOR-[1](1) + FEND.

for(e)gather (chiefly Sc.) gather together XVI; meet *with* XVI. - Du. *vergaderen*, with accommodation to FOR-, GATHER.

forge[1] smithy XIV; furnace for melting metal XVII. - (O)F. :- Rom. **faurga* :- L. *fabrica* trade, manufactured object, workshop, forge (see FABRIC). So vb. shape, fashion (now only in a forge) XIII; fabricate, make a fraudulent imitation of XIV. Hence **forger** XIV, **forgery** XVI.

forge[2] (orig. naut.) make way *ahead*. XVII. perh. aberrant pronunc. of FORCE vb., similarly used from XVII.

forget pt. *forgot*, pp. *forgotten*, arch. and dial. *forgot*. OE. str. vb. *forġietan* = OS. *fargetan* (Du. *vergeten*), OHG. *firgezzan* (G. *vergessen*), f. FOR-[1](1) + Gmc. **ʒetan* take hold of, GET. Hence **forgetful** XIV. alt. of *forʒetel*, *forgetel*, OE. *forġietel* by substitution of -FUL[1] for the final syll. **forget-me-not** XVI. tr. OF. *ne m'oubliez mie* do-not-forget-me.

forgive pt. *forgave*, pp. *forgiven* †give, grant; remit, pardon. OE. str. vb. *forġiefan*; see FOR-[1] (1) and GIVE; corr. to Du. *vergeven*, OHG. *fargeban* (G. *vergeben*), ON. *fyrirgefa* forgive, Goth. *fragiban* grant. So **forgiveness** OE. *forġief(e)nes*, rarely *-ġiefennes*.

forgo, forego pt. *forewent*, pp. *for(e)gone* †intr. pass away, trans. pass over, neglect; abstain from. OE. *forgān*, pt. *forēode*; see FOR-[1], GO.

fork pronged instrument for digging OE., for eating XV; divergence into branches, bifurcation XIV. OE. *forca*, *force*, corr. to OS. *furka*, OHG. *furcha* (Du. *vork*, G. *furke*), ON. *forkr*; Gmc. - L. *furca* pitchfork, forked stake, whence (O)F. *fourche*, ONF. *fourque* (which reinforced the word in ME.).

forlorn †morally lost, abandoned XII; †ruined, doomed XIV; forsaken, desolate; pitiable, wretched XVI. pp. of ME. *forlēse*, OE. *forlēosan* = OS. *far-*, *forliosan* (Du. *verliezen*), OHG. *firliosan* (G. *verlieren*), Goth. *fraliusan*; Gmc., f. **fer-* **fra-* FOR-[1] (1) + **leusan* lose.

forlorn hope picked force detailed for an attack, (hence) desperate adventurers, players, etc. XVI; (by misapprehension) hopeless enterprise XVII. - Du. *verloren hoop* 'lost troop', i.e. *verloren*, pp. of *verliezen* (see prec.), *hoop* company (HEAP).

form A. visible aspect of a thing XIII; (scholastic philos.) that which makes matter a determinate kind of thing XIV. B. character, nature, †degree XIII (class in school XVI); due observance or procedure XIV. C. lair of a hare XIII; long seat without a back XIV; (typogr.) see FORME XV. ME. *forme*, *f(o)urme* - (O)F. *forme*, †*f(o)urme* :- L. *fōrma* mould, shape, beauty, of uncert. orig. So vb. give a form to XIII; be the components of XIV; draw up or dispose in order XVIII. - OF. *fourmer*, (also mod.) *former* - L. *fōrmāre*. **formal** XIV. - L. **formalism** XIX, **-ist** XVII, **formality** XVI. **formation** XV. - (O)F. or L. **formative** XV.

-form repr. F. *-forme*, L. *-fōrmis*, f. *fōrma* FORM, termination to form adjs. meaning (i) 'having the form of', (ii) 'of (so many) forms'.

format XIX. - F. - L. *fōrmātus*, pp. of *fōrmāre* FORM.

forme, form (typogr.) body of type locked up in a chase for printing. XV. spec. use of FORM.

former earlier in time XII; †first, primeval XIII; †more forward XIV; first of two XVI. f. ME. *forme* (OE. *forma*; see FOREMOST) + -ER[3]. Hence **for-**

merly †just now; †beforehand; in former days XVI.

formic (chem.) of an acid contained in a fluid emitted by ants. XVIII. f. L. *formīca* ant; see -IC.

formidable XV. - F. *formidable* or L. *formīdābilis*, f. *formīdāre* fear, f. *formīdō* dread; see -ABLE.

formula set form of words XVII; recipe; rule, etc., expressed by symbols XVIII. - L. *fōrmula*, dim. of *fōrma* FORM; see -ULE. So **formulary** collection or system of formulas. XVI. **formulate** XIX.

fornication XIII. - (O)F. - late L. *fornicātiō, -ōn-*, f. *fornicārī* (whence **fornicate** XVI), f. *fornix, fornic-* arch, vault, vaulted room such as was tenanted by the lower orders and prostitutes; see -ATION. So **fornicator** XIV. - late L.

forsake pt. *forsook*, pp. *forsaken* †decline, refuse; give up, renounce. OE. str. vb. *forsacan* = OS. *forsakan* (Du. *verzaken*), OHG. *firsahhan*; WGmc. f. FOR-[1] + **sakan* quarrel, accuse (see SAKE[1]).

forsooth OE. *forsōð*, i.e. FOR, SOOTH.

forswear OE. *forswerian*; see FOR-[1], SWEAR.

forsythia XIX. f. name of William *Forsyth* (1737–1804), Eng. botanist; see -IA[1].

fort XV. - (O)F. *fort* or It. *forte*, sb. uses of *fort*, *forte* strong :- L. *fortis*.

fortalice fortress, (now) small outwork. XV. - medL. *fortalitia, -itium*, f. L. *fortis* strong.

forte[1] strong point or feature. XVII (*fort*). - F. *fort*, sb. use of adj. (see FORT); the F. fem. form was substituted in Eng. use.

forte[2] (mus.) loud. XVIII. - It. :- L. *fortis* strong. So **fortissimo** XVIII. - It., superl. of *forte*.

forth forwards (now only in *back and forth*); onwards (surviving in gen. use in *and so forth*); forward into view; away. OE. *forð* = OS. *forth* (Du. *voort*), MHG. *vort* (G. *fort*) :- Gmc. **furþa* (cf. Goth. *faurþis* further) :- IE. **pr̥to-*, f. base repr. in FORE-. **forthcoming** about or ready to appear XVI; ready to make advances XIX. **forthright** OE. *forðriht* adj., *-rihte* adv. **forthwith** †at the same time; immediately XIV; partly short for earlier *forthwithal* (XI), partly repl. ME. *forth mid* along with, at the same time as, used absol.

fortify XV. - (O)F. *fortifier* - late L. *fortificāre*, f. *fortis* strong; see -FY. So **fortification** XV.

fortitude XV. - OF. - L. *fortitūdō*, f. *fortis* strong; see -TUDE.

fortnight OE. *fēowertīene niht*, ME. *fourten(n)iht* fourteen nights.

fortress XIII. - (O)F. *forteresse* strong place :- Rom. **fortaritia*, f. L. *fortis* strong.

fortuitous XVII. - L. *fortuītus*, f. *forte* by chance, abl. of *fors* chance :- IE. **bhr̥tis* 'that which is brought', f. base of L. *ferre* BEAR[2].

fortune chance, luck XIII; (good or bad) luck; position depending on wealth, wealth XVI. - (O)F. - L. *fortūna* chance as a divinity, luck, esp. good luck, (pl.) gifts of fortune, (also sg.) riches, orig. sb. use (sc. *dea* goddess) of adj. *fortūnus*, f. *fors* (see prec.). So **fortunate** XIV. - L. *fortūnātus*.

forty OE. *fēowertiġ* = OS. *fiwartig* (Du. *veertig*), OHG. *viorzug* (G. *vierzig*), ON. *fjórir tigir*, Goth. *fidwōr tigjus*; see FOUR, -TY[1]. So **fortieth**. OE. *fēowertiġoða* = ON. *fertugandi*; see -TH[2].

forum (Rom. antiq.) market-place, spec. in ancient Rome a place of assembly for judicial and other business XV; court, tribunal XVII. - L. *forum*, rel. to *forēs* (outside) DOOR; orig. enclosure surrounding a house.

forward towards the future OE.; towards or to the front, onward XIV. OE. *forweard*, var. of *forðweard* onwards, continually, f. FORTH + -WARD. Hence adj. in an advanced state or position; eagerly ready; pert XVI. Hence vb. help forward, advance XVI; send forward XVIII. So **forwards** XIV; cf. OE. *forðweardes*. See -WARDS.

forweary (arch.) tire out XIII; see FOR-[1]. So **forworn** (arch.) worn out XVI.

fosse ditch, trench. XIV. - (O)F. :- L. *fossa*, f. pp. stem *foss-* of *fodere* dig.

fossick (Austral. mining) search for gold by digging out crevices, etc.; (sl.) rummage. XIX. of unkn. orig.; cf. dial. *fossick* troublesome person, *fossicking* troublesome, *fossick* make a fuss, bustle about.

fossil (rock, etc.) dug out of the earth, esp. of remains of the prehistoric past. XVII. - F. *fossile* - L. *fossilis*, f. *foss-*, pp. stem of *fodere* dig; see -ILE.

foster †nourish, feed OE.; †bring up (a child); promote the growth of XIII; cherish, 'nurse' XIV. OE. *fōstrian*, f. *fōster* food, f. Gmc. **fōð-* FOOD. The stem was used as comb. form in OE. *fōsterbearn, -ċild* child as related to those who have reared it as their own, *fōsterbrōðor*/*-sweostor* male/female child reared with another of different parentage, *fōsterfæder*/*-mōdor* one who acts as father/mother to another's child; so *fōsterling* (-LING[1]) foster-child.

foul grossly offensive to the senses; opp. of *clean* OE.; opp. of *fair* ME. OE. *fūl* = OS., OHG. *fūl* (Du. *vuil* dirty, G. *faul* rotten, unsound, lazy), ON. *fúll*, Goth. *fūls* stinking :- Gmc. **fūlaz*, f. **fū-* :- IE. **pū-*, as in L. *pūs* PUS, *putridus* PUTRID, etc.

foulard (handkerchief of) silk material. XIX. - F., of unkn. orig.

foumart polecat. XIV. Early forms *folmarde*, *fulmert*, *fullimart*, f. *fūl* FOUL (i.e. stinking) + *mart* (see MARTEN).

found[1] set up, establish. XIII. - (O)F. *fonder* :- L. *fundāre*, f. *fundus* BOTTOM. So **foundation** XIV. Hence **founder** XIV, whence **foundress** XV; see -ESS[1].

found[2] mix XIV; melt (esp. metal or glass for casting) XVI. - (O)F. *fondre* :- L. *fundere* pour, melt, f. IE. **ghud-* **gheud-* (repr. by OE. *ġēotan* pour), extension of **ghu-* **gheu-*, whence Gr. *khéein, kheúein* pour, Skr. *juhóti* pour libations, sacrifice. Hence **founder** XV, **foundry** XVII.

founder †smash in XIII; †send to the bottom XIV; (of a horse) stumble and fall, go lame XIV; fill with water and sink XVI. Partly - OF. *fondrer* send to the bottom, submerge, but mainly aphetic of †*afounder* (XIV), †*enfounder* (XV) - OF. **a-, es-, enfondrer*, mod. *effondrer* :- Rom. **ex-, infundorāre*, f. EX-[1], IN-[1] + **fundor-*, taken as stem of L. *fundus* BOTTOM.

foundling deserted infant whose parents are

not known. XIII. ME. *fundeling, foundling*, f. *funden*, pp. of FIND + -LING[1]. ME. had also *findling* and *funding*.

fount[1] spring, fountain. XVI. prob. back-formation from FOUNTAIN, suggested by F. *fonts* (L. *fōns*).

fount[2] (typogr.) set of type of a particular size. XVII. alt. of FONT[2] †founding, casting (XVI) - F. *fonte*, f. *fondre* FOUND[3].

fountain (arch.) spring of water XV; artificially formed jet of water XVI. - (O)F. *fontaine* :- late L. *fontāna*, sb. use of fem. of *fontānus*, f. *fōns, font-* spring, fountain.

four OE. *fēower* = OS. *fi(u)war, fiori*, OHG. *fior, fier* (Du., G. *vier*), ON. *fjórir*, Goth. *fidwōr*, ult. :- IE. **qetwōr-*, whence (with vowel-variation) OW. *petguar* (W. *pedwar*), OIr. *cethir*, L. *quattuor*, Gr. *téssares*, OSl. *četyre*, Lith. *keturi*, Skr. *catvā́ra-*; hence **fourteen** OE. *fēowertīene* = OS. *fiertein* (Du. *veertien*), OHG. *fiorzehan* (G. *vierzehn*), ON. *fjórtán*, Goth. *fidwōrtaihun*; see -TEEN. **fourteenth** ME. *fourtenþe*, repl. OE. *fēowertēoða*; see -TH[2]. **fourth**. OE. *fēo(we)rða* = OS. *fiorðo* (Du. *vierde*), OHG. *fiordo* (G. *vierte*), ON. *fjórði*; see -TH[2]. Cf. FORTY.

fowl (arch., exc. in *wild-fowl*) bird OE.; domestic cock or hen XVI. OE. *fugol* = OS. *fugal*, OHG. *fogal* (Du., G. *vogel*), ON. *fugl*, Goth. *fugls* :- Gmc. **foʒlaz*, **fuʒlaz*, perh. dissim. form of **fluʒlaz*, f. **fluz-*, **fleuʒ-* FLY[2]. Hence **fowler** OE. *fug(e)lere*, f. *fug(e)lian* catch wild-fowl.

fox OE. *fox* = OS. *vuhs* (Du. *vos*), OHG. *fuhs* (G. *fuchs*) :- WGmc. **fuχs*; rel. to Skr. *púccha-* tail, Russ. *pukh* fine woolly hair, down; the name may mean orig. 'the tailed one'. Cf. VIXEN. Hence **fox-glove** OE. *foxesglōfa*, f. g. sg. of *fox* (with unexpl. assoc.); the flower resembles a finger-stall in shape.

foyer XIX. - F. hearth, home :- Gallo-Rom. **focarium*, f. L. *focus* fire (see FOCUS).

fracas XVIII. - F., f. *fracasser* - It. *fracassare* make an uproar, of unkn. orig.

fraction numerical quantity that is not an integer XIV; breaking or its result XV. - (O)F. - ChrL. *fractiō, -ōn-*, breaking (as of bread), f. *fract-*, pp. stem of *frangere* BREAK[1]; see -TION. Hence **fractional** XVII. **fractious** refractory, (now) cross, peevish XVIII; f. FRACTION (in obs. sense 'discord, dissention'). So **fracture** sb. XV. - (O)F. *fracture* or L. *fractūra*. Hence **fractured** XVII, whence **fracture** vb. XIX.

fragile XVII. - (O)F. *fragile* or L. *fragilis*, f. **frag-*, base of *frangere* BREAK[1]. So **fragility** XIV, **fragment** XV. Hence **fragmentary** XVII (rare before XIX).

fragrant XV. - F. *fragrant* or L. *fragrāns, -ant-*, prp. of *fragrāre* smell sweet; see -ANT. So **fragrance** XVII.

frail[1] rush basket for figs, raisins, etc. XIII. ME. *fraiel* - OF., of unkn. orig.

frail[2] morally or physically weak (XIII in *frelnes*); liable to break XIV. - OF. *fraile, frele* (mod. *frêle*) :- L. *fragilis* FRAGILE. So **frailty** XIV.

framboesia yaws, characterized by raspberry-like excrescences. XIX. modL., f. (O)F. *framboise* raspberry. See -IA[1].

frame A. †be profitable; †progress OE.; B. †prepare timber for building XIV; (gen.) shape, construct, contrive XIV. OE. *framian* be of service, make progress, f. *fram* forward (see FROM). The rel. ON. *fremja* (= OE. *fremman, fremian*) further, advance, perform, prob. infl. the sense-development. Hence **frame** sb. framed work, structure XIV; order, plan XVI; whence *framework* XVII.

franc monetary unit of France etc. XIV. - (O)F. *franc*, from the legend *Francorum rex* king of the Franks, on gold coins first struck in the reign of Jean le Bon (1350–64).

franchise †freedom XIII; legal immunity or privilege XIV; (hist.) district over which a privilege extends XV; right of voting at a public election XVIII. - (O)F., f. *franc*, fem. *franche* free, FRANK + *-ise*, repr. L. *-itia* -ESS[2].

Franciscan friar of the order founded by St. Francis of Assisi in 1209. XVI. - F. *franciscain* - modL. *Franciscanus*, f. *Franciscus* Francis; see -AN.

Franco- comb. form of medL. *Francus* FRANK, meaning 'Frankish' or 'French and . . .'; see -O-. XVIII.

francolin bird of the partridge family. XVII. - F. - It. *francolino*, of unkn. orig.

franc-tireur one of a corps of light infantry. XIX. - F., i.e. *franc* free + *tireur* shooter, f. *tirer* shoot.

frangible XV. - OF. *frangible* or medL. *frangibilis*, f. L. *frangere* BREAK[1]; see -IBLE.

frangipane perfume obtained from red jasmine XVII; cream for pastry XIX. - F., f. *Frangipani*, name of an Italian marquis who invented a perfume for scenting gloves.

frank †free XIII; bounteous, generous; †of superior quality XV; ingenuous, candid XVI. - (O)F. *franc* :- medL. *francus* free, identical with the ethnic name (see FRANK), which acquired the sense 'free' because in Frankish Gaul full freedom was possessed only by those belonging to or adopted by the dominant people. Hence (from the sense †'free of charge' of the adj.) vb. superscribe (a letter, etc.) with one's signature to ensure free conveyance, (hence) stamp XVIII; facilitate the passage of XIX.

Frank A. of the Germanic nation (or nations) that conquered Gaul and from which the country received the name of France (*Francia*) OE.; B. (in the Levant) individual of Western nationality XVI. OE. *Franca* = OHG. *Franko*; supposed to be named from their national weapon, OE. *franca* javelin.

frankincense XIV. - OF. *franc encens*; see FRANK ('of superior quality'), INCENSE.

franklin landholder of free but not noble birth. XIII. - AL. *francālānus*, f. *francālis*, f. *francus* free, FRANK; see -AL[1], -AN.

frankpledge system by which each member of a tithing was responsible for every other. XV. - law L. *franciplegium*, latinization of AN. *frauncplege*, f. *franc* FRANK + *plege* PLEDGE, mistranslation of OE. *friðborh* peace-pledge (*frið*, f. **frī-* love, as in FRIEND), through the corrupt forms *freo-, friborh*, in which the first element was identified with *free*.

frantic †insane XIV; frenzied XVI. ME. *frentik, frantik* - (O)F. *frénétique* PHRENETIC.

frap (naut.) bind tightly XVI. - OF. *fraper* (mod. *frapper*), of unkn. orig.

frass excrement from larvae. XIX. - G., f. *fressen* devour (see FRET[1]).

frater (hist.) refectory in a religious house. XIII. ME. *freitore, freit(o)ur* - OF. *fraitur*, aphetic of *refreitor* - medL. *refectōrium* REFECTORY.

fraternal XV. - medL. *frāternālis*, f. L. *frāternus*, f. *frāter* BROTHER; see -AL[1]. So **fraternity** XIV. - (O)F. - L. **fraternize** XVII, **fraternization** XVIII. - F.

fratricide[1] one who kills his (or her) brother XV. - F. *fratricide* or L. *frātricīda*, f. *frāter*; see prec. and -CIDE[1]. So **fratricide**[2] killing of one's brother. XVI. - (O)F. *fratricide* or late L. *frātricīdium*; see -CIDE[2].

fraud XIV. - (O)F. *fraude* - L. *fraus, fraud-*. So **fraudulent** XV. - OF. or L.

fraught (arch.) laden XIV; stored, supplied XV; attended *with* XVI. pp. of †*fraught* load (a ship) XIV - MDu. *vrachten*, f. *vracht* = MLG. *vracht* beside *vrecht* FREIGHT, prob. corr. to OHG. *frēht* earnings :- Gmc. **fraaiχtiz*, f. **fra-* FOR- + **aiχtiz* acquisition, property (rel. to OWE).

fraxinella species of dittany. XVII. modL., dim. of L. *fraxinus* ash (cf. BIRCH).

fray[1] (arch.) frighten. XIII. Aphetic of AFFRAY. Hence sb. alarm; disturbance, conflict. XIV.

fray[2] †rub XIV (in vbl. sb. *fraying* noise of friction); †bruise; †clash, collide XV; spec. (of deer) rub their horns XVI; rub away XVIII. - F. *frayer*, earlier *freiier* :- L. *fricāre* rub.

freak sudden change (as of fortune), capricious notion XVI; capricious prank XVII; product of sportive fancy XVIII; monstrous individual of its kind XIX. prob. of dial. orig. Hence as vb. variegate XVII (esp. pp. *freaked*); practise freaks XVII; gambol, frolic XIX.

freckle XIV. Early forms *fracel, frakel*; alt. of (dial.) *freken, fraken* - ON. *freknur* pl. Hence **freckled** XIV.

free not in bondage or subject to control from outside. OE. *frēo* = OFris., OS., OHG. *frī* (Du. *vrij*, G. *frei*), ON. **frīr* as in *frjáls* free :- **frīhals* 'free-necked'), Goth. *freis* :- Gmc. **frijaz* :- IE. **prijos*, the stem of which is repr. also by Skr. *priyá-* dear, W. *rhydd* free, OSl. *prijatelĭ* friend, OE. *frēoġan* love, set free, Goth. *frijōn* love; cf. FRIEND. The primary sense is 'dear'. **freebooter** piratical adventurer. XVI. - Du. *vrijbuiter*. **freedom** OE. *frēodōm*. **freeholder** XV. tr. AN. *fraunc tenaunt* 'free tenant', one who possesses a **freehold** estate, AN. *fraunc tenement* 'free holding'. **free-lance** military adventurer. XIX; later esp. fig. **freely** OE. *frēolīċe*. **freeman** OE. *frēoman*. **freemason** †skilled worker in stone (perh. orig. one emancipated from the control of guilds) XIV; member of a fraternity which grew out of a practice of admitting to societies of stonemasons other persons not of that craft (first called *accepted masons*) XVII. **freestone** fine-grained sandstone or limestone. XIV. tr. OF. *franche piere*, AL. *lapis liber*, the adj. meaning 'of superior quality'. **free thinker** one who refuses to submit his reason to the control of authority. XVII. **free thought** XVIII. **freewill** unrestrained choice, (theol.) power of directing one's actions without constraint by necessity. XIII.

freesia XIX. modL., f. the name of Friedrich H. T. *Freese*, German physician; see -IA[1].

freeze pt. *froze*, pp. *frozen* (impers.) be so cold that ice forms OE.; be converted into ice XIII; convert into ice XV. OE. str. vb. *frēosan* = MLG., MDu. *vrēsen* (Du. *vriezen*), OHG. *frīosan* (G. *frieren*), ON. *frjósa* :- Gmc. **freusan*, f. **freus-* **fraus-* **frus-* :- IE. **preus-* **prous-* **prus-*, repr. by L. *pruīna* hoarfrost, Skr. *pruṣvā́*.

freight hire of a transport vessel XV; cargo, lading XVI. - MLG., MDu. *vrecht*, var. of *vracht* (see FRAUGHT).

French pert. to France. Late OE. *frenċisċ* :- Gmc. **fraŋkiskaz*, f. **Fraŋkan-* FRANK; see -ISH[1]. Hence **Frenchify** XVI.

frenzy mental derangement, (passing into) wild agitation of mind. XIV. - (O)F. *frénésie* - medL. *phrenēsia*, for L. *phrenēsis* - Gr. *phrénēsis*, f. *phrḗn, phren-* mind; see -Y[3].

frequent †crowded; †commonly practised; addicted *to* XVI; recurring often, constant, habitual XVII. - (O)F. *fréquent* or L. *frequēns, -ent-* crowded, frequent, of unkn. orig.; see -ENT. So **frequence** XVI. - (O)F. - L. *frequentia*, whence also **frequency** XVI. **frequent** visit, associate with, resort to; †practise. XV. - (O)F. *fréquenter* or L. *frequentāre*. **frequentative** (gram.) XVI. - L.

fresco painting in water-colour on a wall, etc., before the plaster is dry. XVI. orig. *in fresco*, †*al fresco*, †*a fresco*, repr. It. *affresco*, i.e. *al fresco* 'on the fresh (plaster)'; see FRESH.

fresh †eager, ardent XII; brisk, vigorous; not salty XIII; new, novel, recent; having the signs of newness, not tainted, sullied, or worn XIV; of wind XVI. - OF. *freis*, fem. *fresche* (mod. *frais, fraîche*) = It. *fresco* :- Rom. **friscus* - Gmc. **friskaz*, repr. by OE. *fersċ* in senses 'not salted, not salt' = OFris., MDu. *fersc* (Du. *vers*), OHG. *frisc* (G. *frisch*), ON. *ferskr*. Hence **freshen** XVII; see -EN[5].

freshet stream of fresh water XVI; flood XVII. prob. - OF. *freschet*, f. *frais* FRESH; see -ET.

fret[1] †devour OE.; gnaw; also fig. XII; chafe, irritate, vex XIII. OE. str. vb. *fretan* = MLG., MDu. *vrēten* (Du. *vreten*), OHG. *frezzan*, (G. *fressen*), Goth. *fraïtan*; f. Gmc. **fra-* FOR-[1] + **etan* EAT. Hence as sb. XV.

fret[2] (chiefly in pp. *fretted*) †adorned with interlaced work XIV; adorned with carved or embossed work XVII. prob. f. OF. *freter*, rel. to *frete* trellis, interlaced work (mod. *frette*), of unkn. orig. So sb. XIV. prob. - OF. *frete*. Comp. **fretwork** XVIII.

fret[3] (mus.) bar of wood, etc., to regulate the pitch in some stringed instruments. XVI. of unkn. orig.

friable easily reducible to powder. XVI. F. *friable* or L. *friābilis*, f. *friāre* crumble, rel. to *fricāre* rub; see -ABLE.

friar XIII. ME. *frere* - (O)F. *frère* brother, friar :- L. *frāter, frātr-* BROTHER.

fricandeau fricassee of veal. XVIII. - F.; of unkn. orig.

fricassee ragout of sliced meat. XVI. - F. *fricassée*, sb. use of fem. pp. of *fricasser* mince and cook in gravy; of unkn. orig.

fricative XIX. - modL. *fricātīvus*, f. L. *fricāre*; see next and -ATIVE.

friction XVI. - F. - L. *frictiō*, *-ōn-*, f. *fricāre* rub; see -TION.

Friday OE. *frīġedæġ*, corr. to MLG., MDu. *vrīdach* (Du. *vrijdag*), OHG. *frīatag* (G. *freitag*); i.e. DAY of *Frīġ* = ON. *Frigg* name of the wife of Odin, prop. sb. use of fem. of Gmc. **frījaz* noble, FREE; WGmc. tr. of late L. *Veneris dies* day of the planet Venus.

friend OE. *frēond*, pl. *frīend* = OS. *friund* (Du. *vriend*), OHG. *friunt* (G. *freund*), ON. (with change of decl. in the sg.) *frændi*, Goth. *frijōnds*; Gmc. prp. formation on **frijōjan* (whence OE. *frēoġan*, Goth. *frijōn* love), f. **frijaz* beloved, FREE.

frieze[1] coarse woollen cloth with a nap. XV. - F. *frise* - medL. *(*lāna) frīsia* Frisian wool.

frieze[2] (archit.) member of entablature between architrave and cornice. XVI. - F. *frise* - medL. *frisium*, var. of *frigium*, for L. *Phrygium* (sc. *opus*) Phrygian work.

frigate (orig.) light swift vessel (later variously applied). XVI. - F. *frégate* - It. *fregata*, of unkn. orig.

fright sb. OE. *fryhto*, var. of *fyrhto* = Goth. *faurhtei* :- Gmc. **furχtīn*, f. **furχtaz* afraid, repr. by OE. *forht*, etc. No known cogns. outside Gmc. So vb. terrify. OE. *fryhta*, var. of *fyrhtan* = OS. *forahtian*, OHG. *for(a)htan*, *furihten* (G. *fürchten*), Goth. *faurhtjan*. Superseded by **frighten** XVII. See -EN[5].

frigid XVII (once XV). - L. *frīgidus*, f. *frīgēre* be cold, f. *frīgus* cold; see -ID[1]. So **frigidity** XV. - F. - late L.

frill wavy ornamental edging. XVI. contemp. with the corr. vb.; of unkn. orig.

fringe ornamental border of stuff with dependent threads XIV; edging, border XVII. Late ME. *frenge* - OF. *frenge*, *fringe* (mod. *frange*) :- Rom. **frimbria*, alt. of late L. *fimbria*, earlier only pl. fibres, shreds, fringe. Hence as vb. XV.

frippery †old clothes XVI (*freprie*); finery in dress XVII; empty display XVIII. - F. *friperie*, OF. *freperie*, f. *frepe*, *ferpe*, etc. rag, old clothes, of unkn. orig.; see -ERY.

frisk move briskly and sportively. XVI. f. *frisk* adj. brisk, lively - OF. *frisque* vigorous, lively, of unkn. orig.

frit calcined mixture of sand, etc., to be melted to form glass. XVII. - It. *fritta* (perh. through F. *fritte*), sb. use of fem. pp. of *friggere* FRY[2].

fritillary plant of the genus *Fritillaria* XVII; spotted butterfly XIX. - modL. *fritillāria*, f. L. *fritillus* dice-box, presumably applied to the chessboard; so named in ref. to the markings of the corolla. Cf. -ARY.

fritter[1] portion of batter fried in oil, etc. XIV. - (O)F. *friture* :- Rom. **frīctūra*, f. *frict-*, pp. stem of L. *frīgere* FRY[2]; see -URE.

fritter[2] †break into fragments; do away with piecemeal, waste in trifling. XVIII. f. *fritters* fragments (XVII), expressive alt. of (dial.) *fitters* (XVI), f. †*fitter* break into small fragments; see -ER[4].

frivolous XV. f. L. (mainly late) *frīvolus* silly, trifling + -OUS. Hence, by back-formation, colloq. **frivol** vb. XIX. **frivolity** XVIII. - F., f. (O)F. *frivole* adj. - L. *frīvolus*.

friz(z) curl (the hair) in crisp curls. XVII. earliest forms *freeze*, *frize* - F. *friser*, of unkn. orig.

frizzle frizz (the hair). XVI. first in pp. *frisled*, and earlier than *friz(z)*, of which it might be supposed to be a deriv.; of symbolic orig.

fro prep. (now dial.) from XII; adv. in *to and fro* XIII. - ON. *frá* FROM.

frock long eccl. open-sleeved habit; long coat or tunic; skirted outer garment, gown. XIV. - (O)F. *froc* - Frankish **hroc* (= OHG. *hroc*).

frog[1] tailless amphibious animal. OE. *frogga*, similar in form to *docga* DOG, etc.; rel. to OE. *forsċ*, *frosċ*, *frox* = MLG., Du. *vorsch*, OHG. *frosc* (G. *frosch*), ON. *froskr* :- Gmc. **froskaz*, prob. :- **frudskaz*, f. **frud-* **fraud-* **frūd-*, whence also ME. *frūde*, *froude* (XII-XV) frog or toad, ON. *frauðr*.

frog[2] substance in the sole of a horse's hoof. prob. a transf. use of FROG[1] partly induced by the formal similarity of synon. It. *forchetta* and Fr. *fourchette*, dim. of *forca*, *fourche* FORK.

frog[3] attachment to the waist-belt to carry a sword, etc.; ornamental fastening for a military coat. XVIII. of unkn. orig.

frolic †joyous; sportive. XVI (*frowlyke*). - Du. *vrolijk*, f. (M)Du. *vro* glad, joyous (= OS., OHG. *frao*, *frō*, G. *froh*, ON. *frár* swift) + *-lijk* -LY[1]. Hence as vb. XVI, whence as sb. XVII.

from prep. OE. *fram*, *from* = OS., OHG., Goth. *fram*, ON. *frá* FRO; f. *fra-* = PRO-[1] + *-m* suffix (cf. Gr. *prómos* foremost). The primary sense was 'forward'; cf. ON. *fram(m)* = Goth. *framis* (compar.) forward (adv.), OE. *fram*, *from*, ON. *framr* forward, valiant; see also FRAME.

frond (bot.) leaf-like organ formed by the union of stem and foliage. XVIII. - L. *frōns*, *frond-* leaf.

front (arch.) forehead, face XIII; foremost part XIV. - (O)F. *front* forehead :- L. *frōns*, *front-*. Hence **frontage** (rare before XIX), **frontal** adj. XVII. So **frontal** †ornament for the forehead; covering for the front of an altar. XIV. - OF. *frontel* - L. *frontāle*. **frontier** †front part XIV; boundary of a country XV. - (O)F. *frontière*.

frontispiece principal face of a building XVI; pediment; †front page of a book; illustration facing the title-page XVII. - F. *frontispice* or late L. *frontispicium* examination of the forehead, countenance, façade, f. L. *frōns*, *front-* FRONT + *-spicium* (cf. AUSPICE); early assim. in sp. to *piece*.

frore (dial.) frozen XIII; (arch.) very cold, frosty XV. obs. pp. of FREEZE (OE. *froren*).

frost OE. *frost*, usu. *forst* = OS., (O)HG., ON. *frost* (Du. *vorst*) :- Gmc. **frustaz*, *-am*, f. wk. grade of **freusan* FREEZE + abstr. suffix *-t-*. The form *frost* was doubtless established by ON. influence. Hence **frosty** XIV.

froth sb. XIV. - ON. *froða* or *frauð*, f. Gmc. **freuþ-* **frauþ-* **fruþ-*. Hence vb. XIV.

frou-frou rustling, as of silk. XIX. - F., of imit. orig.

froward perverse, refractory. XIII. f. FRO + -WARD.

frown vb. XIV. - OF. *fro(i)gnier* (surviving in

renfrogner), f. *froigne* surly look, of Celt. orig. (cf. W. *ffroen* nose).

frowzy fusty, musty XVII; dirty and unkempt XVIII. prob. rel. to earlier synon. (dial.) *frowy* (XVI), †*frowish* (XVII), and later *frowsty* (XIX). of unkn. orig.

fructify bear fruit XIV; make fruitful XVI. - (O)F. *fructifier* - L. *frūctificāre*, f. *frūctus* FRUIT; see -FY. So **fructuous** XIV. - OF. or L.; see -OUS.

frugal sparing in the use of things XVI; sparingly supplied XVII. - L. *frūgālis*, back-formation from *frūgālior*, *-issimus*, compar. and superl. of *frūgī* indeclinable adj. (evolved from phr. *frūgī bonæ* 'to good advantage', serviceable, useful), d. of *frux*, chiefly pl. *frūgēs* produce of the soil (cf. FRUIT); see -AL[1]. So **frugality** XVI. - (O)F. or L.

fruit (esp. pl.) vegetable products gen. XII; edible products of a tree; (arch.) offspring; produce, product XIII. - (O)F. :- L. *frūctus* (enjoyment of) the produce of the soil, fruit, revenue, f. **frūg-*, base of *fruī* enjoy, perh. orig. feed on, *frūgēs* 'fruits' of the earth; cf. BROOK[2]. So **fruit** vb. bear fruit. XIV. **fruiterer** XV. Extension with -ER[1] of *fruiter* (XV) - (O)F. *fruitier* (see -ER[2]). **fruitful** XIII. **fruitless** ineffectual XIV; unproductive XV; unavailing XIX.

fruition enjoyment, peaceable possession. XV. - (O)F. - late L. *fruitiō*, *-ōn-*, f. *fruī* enjoy; see FRUIT, -TION.

frumenty, furmety dish made of hulled wheat boiled in milk. XIV. - OF. *fru-*, *fourmentee*, f. *fru-*, *fourment* (mod. *froment*) wheat :- L. *frūmentum*; see -Y[5].

frump †sneer, jeer, hoax XVI; (pl., dial.) ill humour, sulks XVII; dowdy woman XIX. prob. shortening of (dial.) *frumple* wrinkle (XIV), as vb. - MDu. *verrompelen*, f. *ver-* FOR- + *rompelen* RUMPLE.

frustrate vb. XV. f. *frustrate* pp. (XV) - L. *frustrātus*, pp. of *frustrāre*, f. *frustrā* in vain, rel. to *fraus* FRAUD; see -ATE[3]. So **frustration** XVI. - L.

frustum XVII. - L., 'piece cut off'.

frutescent (bot.) becoming shrubby. XVIII. irreg. f. L. *frutex* bush + -ESCENT. So **fruticose** shrub-like. XVII. - L. *fruticōsus*. **frutex** (bot.) shrub. XVII.

fry[1] †offspring; young of fish XIV; young or insignificant creatures XV. Implied in AL. *frium* XIII-XIV. - ON. **frío*, **frjó* seed = Goth. *fraiw*; of unkn. orig.

fry[2] cook in boiling fat. XIII. - (O)F. *frire* = It. *friggere* :- L. *frīgere* (cf. Gr. *phrûgein*, Skr. *bhṛjjáti* grill).

fuchsia XVIII. modL., named after Leonhard *Fuchs*, G. botanist (d. 1566); see -IA[1].

fucus †cosmetic XVI; genus of seaweeds XVIII. - L. *fūcus* rock-lichen, red dye or cosmetic - Gr. *phûkos*.

fuddle tipple; intoxicate. XVI. of unkn. orig.

fudge[1] patch up, fake. XVII. perh. alt. of earlier *fadge*, occas. *fodge* fit, adjust and ult. identical with ME. *fage*, dial. *fadge* deceive, beguile, of unkn. orig. Hence sb. made-up story, deceit; int. stuff and nonsense! XVIII.

fudge[2] soft sweetmeat. XIX. perh. f. prec.

fuel sb. XIV. - AN. *fuaille*, *fewaille*, OF. *fouaille* :- Rom. **focālia* (in medL., obligation to furnish or right to demand fuel), f. *focus* fire (see FOCUS). Hence as vb. XVI.

fug stuffy atmosphere. XIX. of symbolic orig.

fugacious fleeting XVII; failing or fading early XVIII. f. L. *fugāx*, *fugāc-*, f. *fugere* flee; see -ACIOUS.

fugitive adj. and sb. XIV. - (O)F. *fugitif*, *-ive* - L. *fugitīvus*, *-īva*, f. *fugit-*, pp. stem of *fugere* flee; see -IVE.

fugue (mus.) XVI. - F. *fugue* or its source It. *fuga* - L. *fuga* flight, rel. to *fugere* flee. Hence **fugal** XIX.

-ful[1] suffix appended to sbs., forming adjs. orig. with meaning 'full of', which has in many instances weakened to 'characterized by', 'having', 'possessing the qualities or attributes of' what is denoted by the sb. OE. formations are repr. by *careful*, *harmful*, *rightful*, *shameful*, *sorrowful*, *wilful*; many comps. of OE. orig. did not survive, but new ones arose in abundance in ME. and later, as *beautiful*, *delightful*, *gainful*, *hateful*, *lawful*, *tearful*; many have both subjective and objective meanings. Based on vb.-stems are *mournful*, *resentful*. Special cases are BASHFUL, FORGETFUL, GRATEFUL, THANKFUL.

-ful[2] suffix repr. the adj. FULL and forming sbs. denoting a receptacle filled with a substance, and hence the quantity that fills or would fill it. There are a few exx. in OE., the chief of which is HANDFUL. The suffix soon became of universal application.

fulcrum prop, support, spec. in mechanics. XVII. L. *fulcrum* post or foot of a couch, f. base of *fulcīre* support.

fulfil †fill up OE.; †furnish fully; satisfy, carry out XIII. Late OE. *fullfyllan* (once), f. FULL + FILL[2].

fulgent (arch.) glittering. XV. - L. *fulgēns*, *-ent-*, prp. of *fulgēre* shine; see -ENT.

fuliginous sooty. XVI. - late L. *fūlīginōsus*, f. *fūlīgō*, *fūlīgin-* soot, prob. rel. to *fūmus* smoke, FUME; see -OUS and cf. F. *fuligineux*, perh. the immed. source.

full adj. OE. *full* = OS. *ful* (Du. *vol*), OHG. *foll* (G. *voll*), ON. *fullr*, Goth. *fulls* :- Gmc. **fullaz* :- **fulnaz* :- IE. *pḷnós*, whence also OIr. *lān*, Lith. *pìlnas*, OSl. *plŭnŭ*, Skr. *pūrṇá-*, f. IE. **pol-* **pel-* **pl-* with the vars. **plē-* **plō-*, repr. by OE. *fela*, OHG. *filu* (G. *viel*), Gr. *polús*, Skr. *purú-* many, abundant, L. *plēnus*, Gr. *plḗrēs* full.

fuller one who cleanses and thickens cloth by treading or beating. OE. *fullere* - L. *fullō*, with native suffix -ER[1]. So **full** vb. XIV. prob. back-formation infl. by (O)F. *fouler* or medL. *fullāre*.

fulmar sea-bird. XVII. orig. a word of the Hebrides dial.; perh. f. ON. *fúll* FOUL (with ref. to the bird's offensive smell) + *már* gull, MEW[1].

fulminate thunder forth; orig. a rendering of medL. *fulmināre*, used spec. of formal censure by eccl. authority. XV. f. pp. stem of L. *fulmināre*, f. *fulmen*, *-min-* lightning; see -ATE[3]. So **fulmination** XVI. - L.

fulsome †abundant, plentiful XIII; †well-grown; †satiating, cloying; offensive XIV. f. FULL + -SOME[1]; perh. infl. by ME. *fūl* FOUL.

fumble speak haltingly; use the hands clumsily. XVI. - LG. *fummeln*, Du. *fommelen*.

fume sb. XIV. - (i) OF. *fum* :- L. *fūmus*; (ii) OF.

fume, f. *fumer* :- L. *fumāre* smoke, whence **fume** vb. XIV. So **fumigate** XVI. f. pp. stem of L. *fūmigāre*; see -ATE[3]. **fumigation** XIV. - (O)F. or medL.

fumitory plant of the genus *Fumaria*. XIV (*fumeterre*). - (O)F. *fumeterre* - medL. *fūmus terræ* 'smoke of the earth'; so named because its growth was supposed to resemble the spread of smoke over the ground; assim. to words in -ARY, -ORY[1].

fun †hoax, practical joke XVII; diversion, sport XVIII. f. †*fun* vb. hoax (XVII), prob. dial. var. of †*fon* make a fool of (see FOND). Hence **funny** comical XVIII; queer, odd XIX.

funambulist rope-walker. XVIII. f. F. *funambule*, It., Sp. *funambulo*, or their source L. *fūnambulus*, f. *fūnis* rope + *ambulāre* walk; see -IST.

function action or activity proper to anything XVI; religious or other public ceremony XVII; (math.) variable quantity in relation to other variables XVIII. - (O)F. *fonction* - L. *functiō, -ōn-*, f. *fungī, funct-* perform; see -TION. Hence vb. XIX. **functional** XVII, **functionary** XVIII.

fund A. †bottom, foundation, basis; B. source of supply; stock of money. XVII. refash. of †*fond* after L. *fundus* BOTTOM, piece of land, farm, estate, which is the ult. source of F. *fond* bottom, basis, and *fonds* stock; Eng. *fond* and *fund* were used XVII indifferently in both these senses. Hence vb. XVIII.

fundament foundation; buttocks, anus. XIII. ME. *funde-, fondement*, later *fund-, fondment* - (O)F. *fondement* :- L. *fundāmentum*, f. *fundāre* FOUND[1] (see -MENT); latinized forms (*fonda-*) appear XIV. So **fundamental** XV. - F. or late L., whence **fundamentalism, -ist** XX.

funebrial XVII. f. L. *fūnebris*, f. *fūnus* FUNERAL; see -IAL.

funeral adj. XIV; sb. XVI. The adj. is - OF. *funeral* - late L. *fūnerālis*, f. *fūnus, fūner-* obsequies, death, corpse; the sb. is - (O)F. *funéraille(s)* - medL. *fūnerālia*; see -AL[1]. So **funereal** XVIII. f. L. *fūnereus*.

fungible (leg.) that can serve for another (thing). XVIII. - medL. *fungibilis*, f. *fungī* perform; see -IBLE.

fungus mushroom or the like XVI; spongy excrescence XVII. - L. *fungus*, perh. connected with Gr. *sp(h)óggos*, SPONGE. So **fungous** XV. - L. *fungōsus*.

funicular pert. to a hypothetical filament of rarefied matter XVII; depending on a rope or its tension XIX. f. L. *fūniculus*, dim. of *fūnis* rope + -AR.

funk cowering fear, panic. XVIII (first recorded as Oxford Univ. sl.). perh. identical with sl. *funk* tobacco smoke. So vb. show fear. XVIII.

funnel XV. ME. *fonel* (prob. orig. a term of the wine trade with the S. of France) - Pr. (*en*)*fonilh* :- L. *infundibulum*, (late) *fundibulum*, f. (*in*)*fundere* pour (in); see FOUND[2].

funny see FUN.

fur sb. XIV. f. **fur** vb. line or trim with fur XIII; cover, become covered, with a coating (whence a new sb. XIX) XVII. - AN. **furrer*, OF. *forrer* (mod. *fourrer*) line, sheathe f. OF. *forre, fuerre* - Gmc. **fōðram* sheath (OE. *fōddor*, OHG. *fuotar*, G. *futter*, ON. *fóðr*, Goth. *fōdr*), f. IE. **pō-* protect. Hence **furry** XVII; see -Y[1].

furbelow pleated border; pl. showy trimming XVIII. alt. of synon. and contemp. *falbala* - F., of unkn. orig.

furbish remove rust from, brighten *up*. XIV. - OF. *forbiss-*, lengthened stem (see -ISH[2]) of *forbir* (mod. *fourbir*) - Gmc. **furbjan* (OHG. *furben*).

furcate forked. XIX. - late L. *furcātus*, f. *furca* FORK; see -ATE[2]. So **furcation** XVII.

furious see FURY.

furl XVI. - (O)F. *ferler*, earlier *fer(m)lier*, f. *fer(m)* FIRM + *lier* bind.

furlong OE. *furlang*, f. *furh* FURROW + *lang* LONG[1]; orig. the length of the furrow in the common field.

furlough XVII (*vorloffe, fore-loofe, furlogh*). - Du. *verlof*, modelled on G. *verlaub*, f. *ver-* FOR-[1] + **laub-* LEAVE[1].

furmety see FRUMENTY.

furnace XIII. - OF. *fornais* m., fem. (mod. *fournaise*) :- L. *fornāx, -āc-*, and popL. **fornātia*, f. L. *fornus, furnus* oven, rel. to *formus* WARM.

furnish †accomplish; supply, provide XV. - OF. *furniss-*, lengthened stem (see -ISH[2]) of *furnir* (mod. *fournir*) :- Rom. **fornīre*, alt. of **formīre*, **fromīre* - Gmc. **frumjan* (OS. *frummian*, OHG. *frummen*) promote, accomplish, supply. So **furniture** †action of furnishing; provision, equipment (with various applications); the sense 'movable articles in a room, etc.' is peculiarly Eng. XVI. - F. *fourniture* (OF. *forneture*).

furore XIX. - It. :- L. *furor, -ōr-*, f. *furere* rage.

furrier XVI. alt., after *clothier*, etc., of ME. *furour* - OF. *forreor* (mod. *fourreur*), f. *forrer* trim with FUR. Hence **furriery** XVIII. See -Y[3].

furrow OE. *furh* = OFris. *furch*, MLG., MDu. *vore* (Du. *voor*), OHG. *furuh* (G. *furche*), ON. *for* trench, drain, f. Gmc. base **furχ-*, rel. to L. *porca* ridge between furrows, W. *rhych* furrow.

further to or at a more advanced point OE.; in addition XII (amplified to *furthermore* XIII); at a greater distance XIV. OE. *furðor, -ur*, corr. to OFris. *further*, OS. *furðor* (early mod. Du. *voorder*), OHG. *furdar, -ir*, f. Gmc. **furþ-* FORTH + compar. suffix (see -ER[3]).

furtive XV (rare before XVII). - (O)F. *furtif, -ive* or L. *furtīvus, -īva*, f. *furt-* in *furtum* theft, rel. to *fūr* thief; see -IVE.

furuncle boil, inflamed tumour. XVII. - L. *fūrunculus* petty thief, knob on a vine ('stealing' the sap), boil, dim. of *fūr* (see prec.).

fury XIV. - (O)F. *furie* - L. *furia*, f. *furiōsus* mad, f. *furere* rage. So **furious** XIV.

furze OE. *fyrs*, of uncert. orig. (Gr. *práson*, L. *porrum* leek corr. formally, but have no connection of meaning).

fuscous dusky. XVII. f. L. *fuscus* (see DUSK) + -OUS.

fuse[1], fuze cord, casing, etc., filled with combustible material for igniting explosive. XVII. - It. *fuso* :- L. *fūsus* spindle.

fuse[2] melt with intense heat. XVII. f. *fūs-*, pp. stem of L. *fundere* pour, melt, FOUND[2]. So **fusible** capable of fusion. XIV (readopted XVII). - medL. **fusile** XIV. - L.

fuselage XX. - F., f. *fuseler* shape like a spindle, f. *fuseau* spindle; see -AGE.

fusil †steel for a tinder-box XVI; light musket XVII. - (O)F. :- popL. *focīle, f. *focus* (in popL.) fire; see FOCUS. So **fusilier** orig. soldier armed with a fusil. XVII. See -IER[2]. **fusillade** XIX.

fusion melting XVI; union as if by melting XVIII. - F. *fusion* or L. *fūsiō, -ōn-*, f. *fūs-*, pp. stem of *fundere* pour; see FOUND[3], -SION.

fuss sb. and vb. XVIII. of unkn. orig.

fustanella white kilt worn by men in Albania and Greece. XIX. - It., f. modGr. *phoústani*, Alb. *fustan*, prob. - It. *fustagno* FUSTIAN.

fustian †coarse cloth; thick twilled cotton cloth XII; as adj. fig. bombastic, pretentious XVI. - OF. *fustaigne* (mod. *futaine*), repr. medL. (*tēla*) *fustānea*, (*pannus*) *fustāneus*, i.e. cloth of *Fostat*, suburb of Cairo, from which such cloth was exported.

fustigate (joc.) cudgel. XVII. f. pp. stem of late L. *fūstigāre*, f. *fūstis* cudgel; see -ATE[3]. So **fustigation** XVI. - L.

fusty stale-smelling XIV; also fig. XVII. - OF. *fusté*, f. *fust* trunk of a tree, barrel :- L. *fūstis* club.

futile XVI. - L. *fūtilis*, better *futtilis*, lit. 'that pours out', f. *fud-, base of *fundere* pour; see FOUND[3], -ILE. So **futility** XVII. - F. or L.

futtock (naut.) one of the middle timbers of the frame of a ship. XIII. ME. (pl.) *votekes, futtokes, foteken*; perh. repr. MDu. *voetkijn*, dim. of *voet* FOOT (see -KIN), with assim. to -OCK.

future adj. and sb. XIV. - (O)F. *futur* - L. *futūrus*, fut. ppl. of *esse*, f. *fu-; see BE. Hence **futurism** belief that biblical prophecies are still to be fulfilled XIX; in art use (XX) - F. - It. So **futurity** XVII.

fuze see FUSE[1].

fuzzy spongy XVII; fluffy XVIII. cf. Du. *voos* spongy, LG. *fussig* spongy (cf. synon. Sc. *fozy* XIX); see -Y[1]. So or hence **fuzz** loose, volatile matter XVII, **fuzz-ball** fungus, puff-ball XVI.

-fy suffix forming vbs., the oldest of which were adoptions of F. vbs. in *-fier*, derived from L. vbs. in *-ficāre, -ārī* (orig. f. adjs. in *-ficus* -FIC) or modelled on these. The L. words fall into three classes according to the force of the suffix, viz. (i) 'make', 'convert into something', as *ædificāre* EDIFY, *pācificāre* PACIFY; (ii) 'bring into a certain state', as *modificāre* MODIFY, *sanctificāre* SANCTIFY; (iii) with causative sense, as *horrificāre* HORRIFY. In medL. *-ficāre* was substituted for *-facere*, so that F. and Eng. words in *-fier, -fy* often corr. to L. words in *-facere*, e.g. *satisfier* SATISFY, *stupéfier* STUPEFY. The suffix normally takes the form -IFY, which has been consequently generalized for new formations (e.g. *codify* XVIII, *indemnify* XVII) and has been freely used (esp. for trivial and joc. coinages), with the senses: 'make a specified thing', as *speechify*; 'assimilate to the character of something', as *countrify* (chiefly in pp.); 'invest with certain attributes', as *Frenchify*. An early ex. is *beautify*; *crucify* is a special case.

Nouns of action corr. to vbs. in *-ify* end in *-ification*; those corr. to vbs. in *-efy* end in *-faction*.

G

gab (colloq.) talking, talk. XVIII. var. of dial. *gob* (XVII, *gift of the gob*), prob. a use of north. dial. and sl. *gob* mouth (XVI; var. *gab* XVIII), poss. - Gael., Ir. *gob* beak, mouth.

gabardine see GABERDINE.

gabble talk volubly XVI; (of geese) gaggle XVII. - MDu. *gabbelen*, of imit. orig. Cf. GAB.

gabbro (min.) rock composed of feldspar and diallage. XIX. - It. (Tuscan) :- L. *glaber*, *glabr-* smooth.

gaberdine loose upper garment. XVI. Earliest form *gawbardine* - OF. *gauvardine*, *gallevardine*, perh. f. MHG. *wallevart* pilgrimage; Sp. *gabardina* is closest to the present form. In the form **gabardine** adopted as the name of a dress material XX.

gabion (fortif.) wicker basket filled with earth. XVI. - F. - It. *gabbione*, augm. of *gabbia* cage.

gable XIV (*gavel*, *gable*). of twofold orig., - (i) ON. *gafl* and (ii) OF. *gable*, itself prob. - the ON. word; the corr. words in the other Gmc. langs. mean 'fork' (OE. *ġeafol*, OHG. *gabala*, G. *gabel*, etc.), the words for 'gable' showing another vowel-grade, e.g. MDu. *ghevel*, OHG. *gibil* (G. *giebel*), Goth. *gibla*.

gaby (colloq.) simpleton. XVIII. dial. and sl. in orig.; see -Y[6].

gad[1] go idly from place to place. XV. prob. back-formation from †*gadling* companion, (low) fellow, (later) wanderer, vagabond, OE. *gædeling* (rel. to GATHER).

gad[2] euphem. pronunc. of GOD in oaths, esp. (*by*) *gad!*. XVII. Cf. BEGAD, EGAD, GADZOOKS.

gadfly cattle-biting fly. XVI. f. †*gad* spike (- ON. *gaddr*; rel. YARD[2]) + FLY[1].

gadget XIX. orig. a seaman's term; of unkn. orig.

gadoid pert. to the Gadidae (cod-fishes). XIX. f. modL. *gadus* - Gr. *gádos* kind of fish + -OID.

gadroon one of a set of curved lines used in decoration. XVIII. - F. *godron*, prob. rel. to *goder* pucker, crease; see -OON.

gadzooks (arch.) mild expletive. XVII. perh. for *God's hooks*, i.e. God's nails, sc. of Christ crucified; see GAD[2].

Gael Celtic native of the Scottish Highlands. XIX. - Sc. Gaelic *Gaidheal*, corr. to Ir. *Goidel*. Hence **Gaelic** XVIII.

gaff[1] hook XIII; fishing-spear XVII; steel spur XVIII. - Pr. *gaf* hook, of uncert. orig.

gaff[2] (sl.) secret, in phr. *blow the gaff*. XIX. of unkn. orig.

gaffe (sl.) indiscreet act, faux pas. XIX. - F. *gaffe*, f. *gaffer* - Pr. *gafar* seize, f. *gaf* GAFF[1].

gaffer XVI. prob. contr. of GODFATHER; cf. GAMMER.

gag †suffocate, choke XV; stop the mouth of XVI. perh. imit. Hence sb. XVI.

gaga (sl.) daft. XX. - F., of imit. orig.

gage[1] pledge, security XIV. - (O)F., ult. - Gmc. **waðjam* (see WED). Cf. WAGE. So vb. †pledge, pawn; †stake, wager. XVI. - (O)F. *gager* or aphetic of ENGAGE.

gage[2] see GREENGAGE.

gage[3] var. of GAUGE.

gaggle (of geese) cackle. XIV. imit.; cf. MHG. *gāgen*, *gāgern* cry like a goose, Du. *gaggelen* gabble, ON. *gagl* gosling. Cf. -LE[3]. Hence as sb. flock (of geese). XV.

gaiety, gaily see GAY.

gain sb. XV. - (O)F. *gain* m., *gaigne* fem. (mod. *gagne*), f. *gaigner* (mod. *gagner*; hence **gain** vb. XVI) - OF. *gaaigner*, of Gmc. orig.; cf. OHG. *weidenen* graze, pasture, forage, etc., f. Gmc. **waiþō* (OHG. *weida* fodder, pasture, hunting, OE. *wāð*, ON. *veiðr* hunting). Hence **gainful** XVI.

gainsay pt. *gainsaid* XIII. f. *gain-*, formerly a common prefix meaning 'against', 'in opposition' (see AGAIN) + SAY[1].

gait XVI. A particular use of GATE[2], which is otherwise obs. in gen. use; the sp. was established XVIII.

gaiter XVIII. - F. *guêtre*, perh. repr. **wistr-*, var. of Gmc. **wirst-*, **wrist-* (G. *rist* instep, withers); see WRIST.

gala festive attire XVII; †festivity, gaiety XVIII; festive occasion XIX. - F. *gala* or its source It. *gala* - Sp. - OF. *gale* rejoicing, f. *galer* rejoice (of Gmc. orig.).

galacto- comb. form of Gr. *gála*, *galakt-* milk. XVII.

galantine †sauce for fish and fowl XIV; jellied meat XVIII. - F., alt. of *galatine* - medL. *galatina*.

galanty show pantomime of shadows thrown on a screen. XIX. perh. - It. *galanti*, pl. of *galante* GALLANT.

galaxy the Milky Way XIV; brilliant assemblage XVII. - (O)F. *galaxie* - medL. *galaxia*, late L. *galaxias* - Gr. *galaxías*, f. *gála*, *galakt-* milk; see -Y[3].

galbanum gum resin from species of ferula. XIV. - L. - Gr. *khalbánē*, of Sem. orig.

gale[1] bog myrtle. OE. *gagel(le)* = MDu. *gaghel*, Du., G. *gagel*.

gale[2] strong wind. XVI. of unkn. orig.

galeated helmet-shaped; helmeted. XVII. f. L. *galeātus*, f. *galea* helmet + -ED[1]. Also **galeate** XVIII. See -ATE[2].

galena lead ore. XVII. - L.

galilee porch or chapel at the entrance of a church. XV. - OF. *galilée* - medL. *galilæa*; the name of a province of Palestine. First recorded of Durham cathedral, and taken up thence by antiquarian writers of XIX.

galimatias meaningless language. XVII. - F., of unkn. orig.

galingale E. Indian aromatic root XIII; kind of sedge XVI. - OF. *galingal* - Arab. *ḵalanjān* - Pers.

gall[1] bile; bitterness. XII. - ON. *gall*, corr. to OE. *ġealla*, OS., OHG. *galla* (Du. *gal*, G. *galle*) :-

Gmc. *ʒallam, *ʒallan-, -ōn, f. IE. *ghol- *ghel- (repr. by Gr. *kholḗ*, L. *fel* bile); cf. YELLOW.

gall[2] swelling, pustule XIV; bare spot XVI. - MLG., MDu. *galle* (Du. *gal*), corr. to OE. *ġealla* sore on a horse, (M)HG. *galle*, ON. *galli* fault, flaw, perh. identical with prec. Hence **galled** sore from chafing XIV (cf. OE. *ġeallede*); whence **gall** vb. chafe, fret XIV.

gall[3] excrescence growing on the oak, etc. XIV. - (O)F. *galie* :- L. *galla*.

gallant A. †adj. splendid XV; †fine, stately XVI; chivalrously brave XVI; B. attentive to women; amatory XVII; sb. (fine) gentleman XIV; lady's man XV. - (O)F. *galant*, prp. of *galer* make merry, make a show (cf. GALA). Hence **gallantry** XVII.

galleon XVI (*gailʒeown*). - MDu. *galjoen*, - (O)F. *galion*, augm. of *galie* GALLEY or - Sp. *galeon*.

gallery †covered walk, colonnade XV; long balcony; apartment for the exhibition of works of art XVI. - (O)F. *galerie* - It. *galleria* gallery, †church porch - medL. *galeria*, perh. alt. of *galilæa* GALILEE.

galley low flat-built sea-going vessel XIII; large open rowing-boat XV; ship's kitchen XVIII. - OF. *galie* (mod. *galée*) - medL. *galea*, medGr. *galaía*.

galliambic kind of lyric metre. XIX. f. L. *galliambus* song of the *Gallī* or priests of Cybele, + -IC; see IAMBIC.

galliard †valiant; (arch.) lively, gay XIV. - (O)F. *gaillard*, perh. f. Rom. **gallia* strength, power, of Celt. orig.; see -ARD. As the name of a lively dance (XVI) - F. *galliarde*, sb. use of fem. adj.

gallic (chem.) name of a crystalline acid occurring in gall-nuts. XVIII. - F. *gallique*, f. *galle* GALL[3]; see -IC.

Gallic Gaulish, French. XVII. - L. *Gallicus*, f. *Gallus*, *Gallia* Gaul (see GAULISH). So **Gallican** XVI. - F. *gallican* or L. *Gallicānus*. **Gallicism** XVII. - F. See -IC, -AN.

galligaskins (arch.) wide hose or breeches XVI; (dial.) leggings XIX. Early forms *gallogascaine*, *galeygascoyne*, *galigascon*; preceded by or contemp. with *gally slopes*, *breeches*, *hose*, and *gaskin*, *gascoigne hose*; perh. ult. f. F. †*garguesque*, var. of †*greguesque* - It. *grechesca*, sb. use of fem. of *grechesco* Greek; there has been blending with *Gascon*, but the origin of *galli-* remains unkn.

gallimaufry hodge-podge, jumble. XVI. - F. *galimafrée*, of unkn. orig.

gallinaceous pert. to the Gallinae (domestic poultry, etc.). XVIII. f. L. *gallīnāceus*, f. *gallīna* hen, f. *gallus* cock; see -ACEOUS.

gal(l)iot small galley. XIV. - (O)F. *galiote* - It. *galeotta*, dim. of medL. *galea* GALLEY.

gallipot small earthen pot. XV (*gal(e)y pott*). prob. f. GALLEY + POT, as orig. denoting pottery brought in galleys, i.e. from the Mediterranean.

gallium (chem.) metallic element. XIX. modL., said to be f. L. *gallus* cock, tr. the name of its discoverer, *Lecoq* de Boisbaudran; see -IUM.

gallivant XIX. of unkn. orig.

Gallo- used as comb. form (see -O-) of L. *Gallus* inhabitant of Gaul.

gallon XIII. - ONF. *galon*, var. of *jalon* :- Rom. **gallone*, f. base of medL. *gallēta*, *gallētum*; perh. of Celt. orig.

galloon ribbon or braid for trimming. XVII. - F. *galon*, f. *galonner* trim with braid, of unkn. orig.; see -OON.

gallop vb. XV.; sb. XVI. - (O)F. *galoper*, *galop*, for which see WALLOP.

gallows apparatus for hanging a person XIII (*galu treo*, *galwe tree*, *galwes*). - ON. *gálgi* = OE. *ġealga*, *galga*, OS., OHG. *galgo* (Du. *galg*, G. *galgen*), Goth. *galga* :- Gmc. *ʒalʒan-.

galoot (sl.) raw soldier or marine; U.S. (uncouth) fellow. XIX. of unkn. orig.

galop lively dance. XIX. - F. (see GALLOP).

galore XVII. - Ir. *go l(e)ór*, i.e. *go* to, *leór* sufficiency.

galosh, golosh †wooden shoe, patten; (now) over-shoe. XIV. - (O)F. *galoche*, irreg. repr. late L. *gallicula*, dim. of L. *gallica*, sb. use of *gallicus* GALLIC, prob. 'Gaulish sandal'.

galumph invented by 'Lewis Carroll' (C. L. Dodgson) in 'Through the Looking-glass', 1871; a 'portmanteau' word combining *gallop* and *triumphant*. Cf. CHORTLE.

galvanism electricity developed by chemical action. XVIII. - F. *galvanisme*, f. the name of Luigi *Galvani*, who first described the phenomenon; see -ISM. So **galvanic** XVIII, **galvanize** XIX.

gambado sb. bound, spring. XIX. - Sp. *gambada*, f. *gamba* leg; see -ADO.

gambier astringent extract from the plant *Uncaria gambier*. XIX. - Malay *gambir* name of the plant.

gambit opening at chess. XVII (*gambett*). - It *gambetto* tripping up, f. *gamba* leg (cf. JAMB); the form in *-it* is via F.

gamble XVIII. prob. continuing †*gamel* (XVI) play games, sport, alt. (with assim. to -LE[3]) of †*gamene*, early form of GAME vb.

gamboge gum-resin from E. Asian trees, used as a pigment. XVIII. - modL. *gambaugium*, var. of *cambugium*, *-bugia*, *-bogia*, f. *Cambodia*, former name of the Khmer Republic.

gambol sb. XVI (*gambad(e)*). - F. *gambade* - It. *gambata* trip-up, f. *gamba* leg; the forms show the development *gambade*, *gambaude*, *gambauld*, *gambold*, *gambol* (XVII). Also as vb. XVI.

gambrel (dial.) stick for stretching XVI; horse's hock XVII; kind of roof XIX. - ONF. *gamberel*, f. *gambier* forked stick, f. *gambe*, var. of *jambe* leg; see -EREL.

game[1] amusement OE.; organized amusement XIII; †sport derived from the chase, (hence) wild animals pursued for sport XIII. OE. *gamen*, *gomen* = OS., OHG., ON. *gaman*; of unkn. orig. For loss of *-n* cf. *clue*, *eve*, *maid*. Hence vb.; a new formation of XIII, distinct from OE. *gam(e)nian*. Hence **gamester** XVI.

game[2] full of spirit. XVIII. adj. use of GAME[1] sporting sense of 'spirit for fighting, pluck'.

game[3] (colloq.) lame. XVIII. of unkn. orig.; cf. synon. GAMMY.

gamete XIX. - modL. *gameta* - Gr. *gametḗ* wife, *gamétēs* husband, f. *gámos* marriage.

gamin (street) urchin. XIX. - F., of unkn. orig.

gammadion swastika (which involves the form of Γ). XIX. - late Gr. *gammádion*, f. *gamma* (Γ) third letter of the Gr. alphabet.
gammer XVI. prob. contr. of GODMOTHER; cf. GAFFER. *Gandmer* (XVI) shows assoc. with GRANDMOTHER.
gammon[1] †ham XV; joint of bacon XVI. - ONF. *gambon* (modF. *jambon*) ham, f. *gambe* leg.
gammon[2] lashing of the bowsprit. XVII. perh. identical with prec., the allusion being to the tying up of a gammon or ham.
gammy XIX. dial. var. of GAME[2].
gamp (colloq.) umbrella. XIX. f. name of Mrs. Sarah *Gamp*, monthly nurse in Dickens's 'Martin Chuzzlewit', who carried a large cotton umbrella.
gamut (hist.) lowest note of the medieval musical scale XV; Guido d'Arezzo's 'great scale' comprising the seven hexachords and so all the notes used in medieval music XVI; (gen.) compass, range XVII. Earliest forms *gammuthe*, *-othe*, *-outh(e)*, contr. of medL. *gamma ut*, i.e. *gamma* note one tone lower than A + UT.
gander male of the goose. Late OE. *gan(d)ra*, corr. to MLG. *ganre* (LG., Du. *gander*); f. the same base as GANNET.
gang A. †going, journey XII; (dial.) way, road XV; B. (dial.) set of articles of one kind XIV; band of persons XVII. - ON. *gangr* m. and *ganga* fem., walking, motion, course = OE., OS., OHG. (Du., G.) *gang*, Goth. *gaggs*; Gmc. noun of action to **ʒaŋʒan* go (cf. GO). Hence **gangster** member of a criminal gang. XIX (orig. U.S.).
ganglion (path.) †tumour in a tendon; (physiol.) complex nerve centre XVIII. - Gr. *gágglion*.
gangrene XVI. - F. *gangrène* - L. *gangræna* - Gr. *gággraina*. Hence **gangrenous** XVII.
gangue matrix of an ore. XIX. - F. - G. *gang* vein or lode of metal, techn. use of *gang* course (see GANG).
gangway XVII. prob. of continental orig.; see GANG, WAY; not continuous with OE. *gangweġ*.
gannet OE. *ganot*, corr. to MLG. *gante*, Du. *gent*, MHG. *ganiz*, *genz*, OHG. *ganazzo*, MHG. *ganze* gander :- Gmc. **ʒanitaz*, **ʒanatan-*, f. same base as GANDER; cf. GOOSE.
ganoid having a smooth shiny surface. XIX. - F. *ganoïde*, f. Gr. *gános* brightness; see -OID.
gantry, gauntry four-footed wooden stand for barrels XIV; platform for a travelling crane, etc. XIX. prob. f. *gawn*, dial. form of GALLON + TREE.
gaol, jail sb. XIII. ME. (i) *gay(h)ole*, *gail(l)e* - ONF. *ga(i)ole*; (ii) *iai(o)le* - OF. *jaiole*, *jeole* (mod. *geôle*) :- Rom. **gaviola*, for **caveola*, dim. of L. *cavea* CAGE. The form *gaol* repr. a pronunc. with hard *g* which was current till XVII; the pronunc. repr. by *jail* was equally early (XIII). Hence vb. XVII. Comp. **gaol-bird** prisoner in gaol, habitual criminal XVII. So **gaoler, jailer, -or** XIII. ME. *gayholere*, *gailer* and *iailere*, *geilere* - OF. *gaiolere* and *jaioleur*, *jeolier* (mod. *geôlier*).
gap breach in a defence XIV; opening in a mountain range; unfilled space XVI. - ON. *gap* chasm, rel. to *gapa* GAPE.
gape XIII. - ON *gapa* = (M)Du. *gapen*, (M)HG. *gaffen*; in OE. repr. only by *ofergapian* neglect; further relations uncert. Hence sb. XVI.
garage XX. - F., f. *garer* take care. Cf. WARE[2], -AGE.
garb †grace, elegance; †style, fashion XVI; (fashion of) dress XVII. - F. †*garbe* (now *galbe*) - It. *garbo* - Gmc. **ʒarwī* (OHG. *garawī* adornment), f. **ʒarwu-* ready.
garbage offal of an animal XV; refuse, filth XVI. of unkn. (prob. AN.) orig.
garble †sift, take the pick of XV; make selection from (unfairly or with a bias) XVII. - It. *garbellare* sift, f. *garbello* sieve - Arab. *ġirbāl*, perh. - late L. *crībellum*, dim. of *crībrum*.
garboard first range of planks or plates laid on the keel. XVII. - Du. †*gaarboord*, perh. f. *garen*, contr. form of *gaderen* GATHER + *boord* BOARD.
garden XIV. - ONF. *gardin*, var. of (O)F. *jardin* :- Rom. **gardīno*, f. **gardo-* - Gmc. **ʒardan-*; see YARD[1]. Hence vb. XVI. So **gardener** XIII.
gardenia XVIII. modL., f. name of Alexander *Garden*, Sc. naturalist (d. 1791); see -IA[1].
gare-fowl, gairfowl great auk. XVI (*gare*), XVII (*gair-fowl*). - Gael. *gearbhul* - ON. *geirfugl*; of uncert. orig.
garfish fish having a spear-like snout. XV. app. f. OE. *gār* spear (see GOAD) + FISH[1].
Gargantuan XVI. f. *Gargantua*, name of the large-mouthed voracious giant in Rabelais's work of that name; see -AN.
gargle XVI. - F. *gargouiller* gurgle, †gargle, f. *gargouille* (see next).
gargoyle XV. - OF. *gargouille* throat, gargoyle; of imit. orig.
garibaldi (orig. red) blouse imitating the red shirt worn by the Italian Giuseppe *Garibaldi* (1807-82) and his followers. XIX.
garish XVI. Also *gaurish*, and perh. f. ME. †*gaure* stare; cf. -ISH[1].
garland wreath of flowers, etc. XIV. ME. *gerland*, *garland* - OF. *gerlande*, *garlande* (mod. *guirlande*); of unkn. orig.
garlic OE. *gārlēac*, f. *gār* spear + *lēac* LEEK.
garment XIV. (*gar(ne)ment*). - (O)F. *garnement* equipment, f. *garnir* GARNISH; see -MENT.
garner (now lit.) granary. XII (*gerner*). - AN. *gerner*, OF. *gernier* (mod. *grenier*) :- L. *grānārium* GRANARY; see -ER[2]. Hence vb. XIV.
garnet vitreous mineral, a precious kind of which is used as a gem. XIII. ME. *gernet*, *grenat*, prob. - MDu. *gernate*, *garnate* - OF. *grenat* - medL. *grānātus*, perh. transf. use of L. *grānātum* POMEGRANATE, the stone being compared in colour to the pulp of the fruit.
garnish A. furnish, fit out, embellish XIV (now obs. or rhet., exc. for embellishing a dish of food XVIII); B. (leg.) warn, as with a notice XVI. - (O)F. *garniss-*, lengthened stem (see -ISH[2]) of *g(u)arnir* :- Gmc. **warnjan*, prob. rel. to *warnējan*, *-*ōjan* become aware, (hence) guard, defend, provide for (see WARN). Hence **garnishee** (leg.) XVII. So **garniture** furniture, outfit XVI; ornament XVII; (of a dish) XVIII.
garret †turret, watch-tower XIV; attic room XV. - OF. *garite* (mod. *guérite*), f. *garir* defend (see next).
garrison †treasure, gift XIII; †defence XIV; †for-

tress; defensive force in a fortress XV. - OF. *garison* defence, safety, provision, store, f. *garir* defend, furnish - Gmc. **warjan* defend (OE., OS., OHG. *werian*, ON. *verja*, Goth. *warjan*). Infl. by †*garnison* XIV - OF., f. *garnir* fit out, GARNISH. Hence vb. furnish with, station as, a garrison XVI; occupy as a garrison XVII.

gar(r)otte †packing-stick; Sp. method of capital punishment by strangulation XVII; highway robbery by throttling the victim XIX. - Sp. *garrote* orig. cudgel. So vb. XIX. - F. *garrotter* or Sp. *garrotear*.

garrulous XVII. f. L. *garrulus*, f. *garrīre* chatter; see -ULOUS. So **garrulity** XVI. - F. †*garrulité* - L.

garter XIV. - OF. *gartier*, var. of *jartier* (also *jartiere*, mod. *jarretière*), f. *garet*, *jaret* bend of the knee, calf of the leg (whence Sp. *jarrete*, It. *garretto*), prob. of Celt. orig.

gas[1] (hist.) occult principle supposed to be present in all bodies XVII; any completely elastic fluid XVIII. - Du. *gas* (J. B. van Helmont, 1577-1644), based on Gr. *kháos* CHAOS. Hence **gas** vb. treat, poison, etc., with gas; (colloq.) talk aimlessly. XIX.

gas[2] (U.S.) colloq. abbrev. of GASOLINE.

gash sb. XVI. Later form of †*garsh*, var. of †*garse* (XIII-XVII). - OF. **garse*, f. *garcer*, *jarcer* scarify (mod. *gercer* chap, crack), perh. abnormally repr. late L. *charaxāre* - Gr. *kharássein* (cf. CHARACTER). So vb. XVI. For loss of *r* cf. BASS[1], DACE.

gasket (naut.) small rope securing a furled sail. XVI. of unkn. orig.

gasoline, -olene XIX. f. GAS[1] + -OL + -INE[5], -ENE.

gasometer vessel for holding gas XVII; reservoir for storing gas XIX. - F. *gazomètre*, f. *gaz* GAS[1] + *-mètre* -METER.

gasp vb. XIV. Early var. *gayspe* - ON. *geispa*, alt. of **geipsa*, f. base of *geipa* talk idly; cf., with weak grade of the base, OE. *ġipian* yawn (only in prp. *ġipiende*), *ġipung* open mouth. Hence sb. XVI.

gast(e)ropod mollusc, so called from the ventral position of the locomotive organs. XIX. - F. *gastéropode* - modL. *gasteropoda* n. pl., f. Gr. *gastḗr*, *gaster-* belly + *poús*, *pod-* FOOT. So **gastric** XVII. **gastronomy** XIX. - F.

gate[1] opening in a wall capable of being closed by a barrier; barrier itself. OE. *ġæt*, *ġeat*, pl. *gatu*, corr. to OFris. *gat* hole, opening, OS. *gat* eye of a needle (LG., Du. gap, hole, breach), ON. *gat* opening, passage :- Gmc. **ʒatam*. Forms with initial *y*, repr. OE. forms *ġeat*, etc., remain in northerly dial.; the standard form has been *gate* since XVI.

gate[2] A. (north. dial.) way XIII; street (surviving in place-names) XV; B. †going, journey XIII; manner of going (see GAIT). - ON. *gata* = OHG *gazza* (G. *gasse* lane), Goth. *gatwō* :- Gmc. **ʒatwōn*, of unkn. orig.

gather bring or come together OE.; infer, conclude XVI. OE. *gaderian* = MLG. *gadern*, (M)Du. *gaderen*, MHG. *gatern* :- WGmc. **ʒadurōjan*, f. **ʒadurī* TOGETHER. For the change of OE. *d* to *th* cf. FATHER.

gatling machine-gun named after the inventor, R. J. *Gatling* (d. 1903); first used in the American civil war. XIX.

gauche XVIII - F. *gauche* left-handed.

Gaucho one of mixed European and Indian people in S. America. XIX. - Sp., of native orig.

gaud †trick, sport, jest XIV; (arch.) plaything XV; (pl.) showy things XVII. perh. - AN. deriv. of (O)F. *gaudir* rejoice - L. *gaudēre*.

gaudy[1] rejoicing; annual college feast. XVI (*gaudye dayes*). - L. *gaudium* joy (f. *gaudēre* rejoice) or L. *gaudē*, imper. of *gaudēre*.

gaudy[2] brilliantly gay, glaringly showy. XVI. prob. the first word of †*gaudy green* (XIV-XVI) yellowish green, prop. green dyed with weld, f. (O)F. *gaude* WELD[1] + -Y[1].

gauge, U.S. **gage** fixed measure XV; graduated instrument XVII. - ONF. *gauge*, var. of F. *jauge*. So vb. XV. - OF. *gauger* (mod. *jauger*).

Gaulish XVII. f. *Gaul* Gallia (France and Upper Italy) - F. *Gaule*, ult. - Gmc. **walχaz* foreign (cf. WELSH); see -ISH[1].

gault (geol.) applied to beds of clay and marl. XVI. of unkn. orig.

gaunt †slim; tall and lean. XV. of unkn. orig.

gauntlet[1] metal-plated glove of medieval armour. XV. - (O)F. *gantelet*, dim. of *gant* glove :- Gmc. **want-*, extant only in ON. *vǫttr* (:- **wantuz*) glove; see -LET.

gauntlet[2] in phr. *run the gauntlet*. XVII. alt., by assim. to prec., of †*gantlope* (XVII-XIX) - Sw. *gatlopp*, f. *gata* lane, GATE[2] + *lopp* course (see LEAP); a term introduced through the Thirty Years War.

gauze XVI. - F. *gaze*, prob. f. *Gaza* name of a town in Palestine.

gavel mallet. XIX. of unkn. orig.

gavelkind Kentish form of land-tenure XIII; in Kent and elsewhere, division of a deceased man's property equally among his sons. XVI. ME. *gavel(i)kinde*, *-kende*; repr. OE. **gafolġecynd*, f. *gafol* tribute + *ġecynd* KIND[1]; presumably orig. tenure by the payment of a fixed service.

gavial long-snouted Asian crocodile. XIX. - F. - Hind. *ghaṛiyāl* (whence the var. *gharial*).

gavotte XVII. - F. - Pr. *gavoto*, f. *Gavot* name in Provence for inhabitants of the Alps.

gawk awkward lout, simpleton. XIX. rel. to *gawk* vb. stare vacantly XVIII, *gawky* adj. XVIII; perh. based on †*gaw(e)* XII (cf. ON. *gá* heed).

gay mirthful, merry XIII; bright-coloured, showy XIV; 'fast', dissipated XVII. - (O)F. *gai*, of unkn. orig. So **gaiety** XVII. Hence **gaily** XIV.

gaze vb. XIV. of unkn. orig.; poss. rel. to the base of ME. *gawe* stare (see GAWK).

gazebo turret, look-out. XVIII. perh. joc. f. GAZE, in imitation of L. futures in *-ēbō*.

gazelle XVII. - (O)F. - Arab. *ġazāl*.

gazette XVII (*gazet(ta)*). - F. *gazette* or its source It. *gazzetta*, so called because sold for a *gazeta*, Venetian coin of small value; see -ETTE. So **gazetteer** †journalist XVII; geographical dictionary XVIII. - F. *gazettier* - It. *gazzetiere*.

gear equipment, apparatus, etc. XIII. - ON. *gervi*, *gǫrvi*, corr. to OS. *gerwi*, *garewi*, OHG. *garawī*, *gar(e)wī* :- Gmc. **ʒarwīn-*, f. **ʒarwu-* ready.

gecko XVIII. - Malay *chěchak*, *chichak*, etc.

gee int. word of command to a horse. XVII. Hence as sb. esp. redupl. **gee-gee** (XIX) child's name for a horse.

geezer (sl.) elderly person. XIX. dial. pronunc. of *guiser* masquerader, mummer, f. *guise* †attire fantastically, dial. go about in disguise, masquerade, f. GUISE in the sense 'attire'; see -ER[1].

geisha XIX. - Jap., 'person of pleasing accomplishments'.

gel (chem.) semi-solid colloidal solution. XIX. abbr. of next.

gelatin(e) XIX. - F. *gélatine* - It. *gelatina*, f. *gelata* JELLY; see -INE[5]. So **gelatinous** XVIII. - F. *gélatineux*.

geld castrate. XIII. - ON. *gelda*, f. *geldr* barren. So **gelding** (see -ING[3]) †eunuch; castrated animal. XIV.

gelid extremely cold. XVII. - L. *gelidus*, f. *gelu* frost, intense cold (cf. COLD); see -ID[1].

gelignite variety of gelatin dynamite. XIX. perh. f. GEL(ATIN) + L. *ignis* fire + -ITE.

gem XIII. - (O)F. *gemme* :- L. *gemma* bud, jewel; superseded the OE. adoption of the L. word, viz. *ġim(m)*, ME *ʒimme*. So **gemma** (bot.) leaf-bud. XVIII. - L. **gemmation** (bot.) budding. XVIII. - F.

gemination XVI. - L. *geminātiō, -ōn-*, f. *gemināre* vb. double (whence **geminate** XVII), f. *geminus* twin; see GEMINI, -ATE[3], -ATION.

Gemini the twins Castor and Pollux. XIV. - L., pl. of *geminus* double, twin.

-gen repr. Gr. *-genḗs* (rel. to *génos* KIN), through F. *-gène*, which, by ref. to Gr. *gennân* beget, produce, was used first in *oxygène* OXYGEN, *nitrogène* NITROGEN, and later in *endogène* ENDOGEN, *exogène* EXOGEN, in the sense 'producing', whereas the orig. Gr. formative was used in the senses (i) 'born, produced', as in *eggenḗs* native, and (ii) 'of a (certain or specified) condition', as in *heterogenḗs* HETEROGENEOUS, *homogenḗs* HOMOGENEOUS.

gendarme †mounted armed man XVI; soldier employed in police duties XVIII. - F., sg. formed on pl. *gens d'armes* 'men of arms'. Hence **gendarmery** XVI; after F.

gender †kind, sort; (gram.) any of the three 'kinds', masculine, feminine, and neuter, of nouns, adjectives, and pronouns. XIV. - OF. *gendre* (mod. *genre*) - Rom. **genero*, f. L. *gener-* GENUS.

genealogy XIII. - (O)F. *généalogie* - late L. *geneālogia* - Gr. *geneālogiā*, f. *geneā́* race, generation; see -LOGY. So **genealogical** XVI, **genealogist** XVII.

general applicable to all XIII; (mil.) of an officer having superior rank and extended command XVI; sb. †(esp. pl.) general idea, principle, etc.; head of a religious order; (mil.) orig. †*general captain* XVI. - (O)F. *général* - L. *generālis* pert. to the whole kind, f. *gener-*, GENUS; see -AL[1]. So **generality** XV (†*generalty* XIV). **generalize** XVIII. - F. **generalissimo** supreme commander. XVII. - It., superl. adj. Hence **generally** XIII.

generate produce (orig. offspring). XVI. f. pp. stem of L. *generāre*, f. GENUS, *gener-*; see -ATE[3]. So **generation** offspring of the same parent(s), etc. XIII; act of generating XIV. - (O)F. - L. **generative** XIV. - late L. **generator** begetter XVII; apparatus for producing power, etc. XVIII. - L.

generic XVII. - F. *générique*, f. L. GENUS, *gener-*. See -IC.

generous †nobly born; magnanimous XVI; free in giving; ample; of rich quality XVII. - (O)F. *généreux* - L. *generōsus* noble, magnanimous, f. GENUS, *gener-*; see -OUS. So **generosity** XV (rare before XVI). - F. or L.

genesis first book of the Old Testament OE.; (mode of) origin VII. - L. - Gr. *génesis* generation, creation, nativity, f. **gen-*, base of *gígnesthai* be born or produced (see KIN). Hence **genetic** XIX.

genet civet-cat of genus *Genetta*. XV. - OF. *genete* (mod. *genette*), of uncert. orig.; cf. Afr. Arab. *jarnaiṭ*.

Geneva spirit otherwise called hollands (flavoured with the juice of juniper berries). XVIII. - Du. *genever* (assim. to the name of *Geneva* in Switzerland) - OF. *genevre* (mod. *genièvre*) :- **jeniperus*, for L. *jūniperus* JUNIPER. Cf. GIN[2].

genial (arch.) nuptial, generative XVI; conducive to growth XVII; kindly XVIII. - L. *geniālis* nuptial, productive, joyous, pleasant, f. *genius* GENIUS; see -AL[1].

genie sprite of Arabian tales. XVIII. - F. *génie* GENIUS, used by translators of 'The Arabian Nights' to render the Arab. word (see JINN) which it resembled in sound and sense.

genista (bot.) broom. XVII. - L.

genital adj. and sb. pl. XIV. - (O)F. *génital* or L. *genitālis* (n. sg. and pl. as sb.), f. *genitus*, pp. of *gignere* beget; see KIN, -AL[1].

genitive XIV. - (O)F. *génitif, -ive*, or L. *genitīvus, -īva* (*gene-*), f. *genit-*, pp. stem of *gignere* beget, produce; see KIN, -IVE.

genius tutelary deity or spirit; demon; characteristic or prevalent disposition or spirit XVI; innate capacity, person as possessing this XVII, extraordinary native intellectual power XVIII. - L. *genius* attendant spirit, inclination, appetite, (rarely) intellectual capacity, prob. :- **gn̥jos*, corr. to Gmc. **kunjam* KIN. (In XVII–XVIII forms repr. F. *génie* and It. *genio* were used in various senses of *genius*).

genocide XX. irreg. f. Gr. *génos* race (see KIN) + -CIDE[2].

-genous terminal el. (i) f. L. *-genus* (f. IE. **gen-*; see KIN) + -OUS, as in *indigenous*; (ii) f. -GEN, as in (chem.) *hydrogenous*, *nitrogenous*; (iii) f. F. *-gène* (see -GEN), as in (bot.) *endogenous*, *exogenous*.

genre XIX. - F. (see GENDER).

gent shortening of GENTLEMAN, in designations (like *esq.* for *esquire*) XVI; hence taken up as an independent word.

genteel suited or appropriate to the gentry or persons of quality XVI; †polished, refined; elegant XVII. - F. *gentil*, fem. *-ille*, an earlier adoption of which is repr. by GENTLE. First recorded in the form *gentile*, which was distinguished from GENTILE by retention of the F. pronunc. with final stress, and prob. the nasal sound of the first syll.

gentian XIV. - L. *gentiāna*, so called, acc. to Pliny, after *Gentius*, a king of Illyria; see -IAN.

gentile non-Jewish, †pagan XIV; pert. to a tribe or nation XVI. - L. *gentīlis* of the same family or nation, (in eccl. use) heathen, pagan, f. *gēns, gent-* race, people, f. IE. **gen-* (see KIN).

gentility gentle birth XIV; gentle or genteel state or manner XVI. - (O)F. *gentilité*, f. *gentil*; see next and -ITY.

gentle well-born; noble, generous XIII; †domesticated, tame XV; †pliant, soft; mild. XVI. - (O)F. *gentil* high-born, noble (in modF. pleasant, kind, agreeable) :- L. *gentīlis* belonging to the same gens or stock, (Rom.) belonging to a good family; see also GENTEEL, GENTILE. As sb. (arch.) one of gentle birth XIV; larva of the bluebottle, used for bait by anglers (spec. use of the sense 'soft') XVI. Hence **gentleman** XIII, whence **gentlemanly** XV. So **gentlewoman** XIII.

gentry gentle birth XIV; people of gentle birth XVI. prob. alt. of †*gentrice* (XIII) - OF. *genterise*, var. of *gentelise*, f. *gentil* GENTLE, by assoc. with †*gentlery* (XIII).

genuflexion, -flection XV. - late L. *genuflexiō, -ōn-*, f. *genuflectere* (f. *genu* KNEE + *flectere* bend), whence (back-formation) **genuflect** XVII.

genuine †natural, native XVI; not spurious or counterfeit XVII. - L. *genuīnus*, f. *genu* KNEE; the orig. ref. was to the recognition of a new-born child by the father placing it on his knees; later assoc. with *genus* race, KIN; see -INE[1].

genus (techn.) kind, class. XVI. - L. *genus* birth, race, stock, KIN.

-geny terminal el. = F. *-génie*, modL. *-genia*, based on Gr. adjs. in *-genēs* or on the first syll. of GENESIS, meaning 'mode of production', as in *cosmogeny, ontogeny, physiogeny*, with corr. sbs. in *-genesis* and adjs. in *-genetic*.

geo- repr. *geō-*, comb. form of Gr. *gê* earth, as in many scientific terms of XIX.

geode XVII. - L. *geōdēs* - Gr. *geṓdēs* earthy, f. *gê* earth.

geodesy †land-surveying XVI; (math.) study which determines areas of the earth's surface XIX. - F. *géodésie* or modL. *geōdæsia* - Gr. *geōdaisiā* (*daiein* divide). Hence **geodetic** XVII.

geography XVI. - (partly through F.) L. *geōgraphia* - Gr. *geōgraphiā*; see GEO-, -GRAPHY. So **geographer** XVI, **geographic** XVII, **-ical** XVI.

geology XVIII. - modL. *geōlogia*; see GEO-, -LOGY. So **geological, geologist** XVIII.

geomancy divination from signs derived from the earth. XIV. - medL. *geōmantīa*; see GEO-, -MANCY.

geometry XIV. - (O)F. *géométrie* - L. *geōmetria* - Gr. *geōmetriā*; see GEO-, -METRY. So **geometric** XVII, **geometrical** XVI.

geranium genus of plants with fruit shaped like a crane's bill XVI; genus *Pelargonium* XVIII. - L. - Gr. *geránion*, f. *géranos* CRANE.

gerfalcon XIV. - OF. *gerfaucon* (mod. *gerfaut*) - OFrankish **gērfalco* (G. *ger-, gierfalke*) - ON. *geirfálki*, the first el. of which is obscure; see FALCON.

germ rudimentary form. XVII. - (O)F. *germe* :- L. *germen* sprout. Preceded by **germen** XVII, which remains in botanical use.

german closely related; now only in *brother-, sister-, cousin-german*. XIV. - (O)F. *germain* :- L. *germānus* genuine, real (as sb. *germānus* brother, *germāna* sister).

German pert. to Germania or Germany. XVI. - L. *Germānus*, perh. of Celt. orig. (cf. OIr. *gair* neighbour). So **Germanic** XVII.

germander XV. - medL. *germandr(e)a*, alt. of *gama(n)drea*, for *chamedreos* - late Gr. *khamaidruon, -drûs* 'ground-oak', f. *khamai* on the ground + *drûs* oak.

germane XIX. var. of GERMAN.

germinate XVII. f. pp. stem of L. *germināre*, f. *germen, germin-* sprout; see -ATE[3]. So **germination** XVI. - L.

-gerous see -IGEROUS.

gerrymander (orig. U.S.) manipulate election districts unfairly so as to secure disproportionate representation. XIX. f. name of Elbridge *Gerry*, governor of Massachusetts, who is related to have constructed a district map of the U.S.A. in which the shape of one district suggested to an artist the addition of head, wings, and claws; he exclaimed 'That will do for a salamander!', to which another retorted 'Gerrymander!'

gerund XVI - late L. *gerundium*, f. *gerundum*, var. of *gerendum*, gerund of *gerere* carry on. So **gerundial** XIX. **gerundive** adj. pert. to a gerund XVII; sb. gerund XV; passive verbal adjective expressing 'to be —ed' XVIII.

gestalt (psych.) XX. - G., 'form, aspect'.

gestation †carrying, being carried XVI; process of carrying young XVII. - L. *gestātiō, -ōn-*, f. *gestāre*, frequent. f. *gest-*, pp. stem of *gerere* carry.

gesticulate XVII. f. pp. stem of L. *gesticulārī*, f. *gesticulus*, dim. of *gestus* action, GESTURE; see -ATE[3]. So **-ation** XVII. - L.

gesture †bearing, carriage XV; †attitude, posture; movement of the body XVI. - medL. *gestūra*, f. *gest-*, pp. stem of *gerere* carry.

get pt. *got*, pp. *got*, U.S. *gotten* obtain, procure; beget; succeed in coming or going *to*, etc. XIII; make oneself, become XVI. - ON. str. vb. *geta* obtain, beget, guess = OE. **ġietan* (only in comps.) :- Gmc. **ʒetan*, f. IE. base **ghed-* seize, found in L. *præda* booty, PREY, and with inserted nasal in L. *prehendere* lay hold of (cf. APPREHEND, etc.), Gr. *khandánein* hold.

The orig. conjugation was repr. in literary use by *get, gat, getten* as late as XVI; but pp. *gotten* (which survives dial. and U.S.) is found before 1400; the clipped form *got* of the pp., and the pt. *got* (based on the pp.), date from XVI.

gewgaw paltry thing, plaything, trifle. XIII (*gwgaw*; later *guygaw, guegay*, etc.). of unkn. orig.

gey (Sc.) considerable, -ly. XVIII. var. of GAY.

geyser gushing hot spring XVIII; water-heating apparatus XIX. - Icel. *Geysir* proper name of a certain hot spring in Iceland, rel. to *geysa* gush.

gharial see GAVIAL.

ghastly †terrible, (now) suggesting the horror of death or carnage XIV; spectre-like, death-like XVI; as adv. XVI. ME. *gastlich*, f. *gaste* terrify (perh. repr. OE. *gæstan* torment; cf. AGHAST) +

-lich -LY[1]; the sp. with *gh-* (after GHOST) became current through Spenser.

gha(u)t mountain pass XVII; descent to a riverside, landing-place XVIII. - Hindi *ghāṭ*; applied pl. (the *Ghauts*) by Europeans to two mountain-ranges of India.

ghee butter made from buffalo's milk. XVII. - Hindi *ghī* :- Skr. *ghṛtá-*.

gherkin XVII (*girkin*). - early mod. Du. *(a)gurkkijn (now *gurkje*, *augurkje*), dim. of *(a(u))gurk*; ult. - Slav. word repr. by Pol. *ogórek*, Russ. *ogurets*, deriv. with dim. suffix of late Gr. *aggoúrion*.

ghetto Jewish quarter of a town, etc. XVII. - It. *Ghetto*, name of Venetian island where Jews were confined in 1516.

ghost soul, spirit OE.; disembodied spirit XIV. OE. *gāst* = OS. *gēst* (Du. *geest*), (O)HG. *geist* :- WGmc. **ȝaista*, which has been connected with Skr. *héḍa-* anger. The sp. with *gh-* is first recorded in Caxton's works and is there prob. due to Flem. *gheest*; it became established late in XVI. Hence **ghostly** OE. *gāstliċ*.

ghoul demon preying on corpses. XVIII. - Arab. *ġūl*.

ghyll var. of GILL[2].

giant XIII. ME. *geant* (later infl. by the L. form) - (O)F. *géant*, †*jaiant* :- Rom. **gagante*, for L. *gigant-*, nom. *gigās* - Gr. *gigās*, *gigant-*.

gibber XVII. imit.

gibberish XVI. Earlier than *gibber*, but presumably to be connected, the ending being based on language-names in -ISH[1].

gibbet XIII - (O)F. *gibet* staff, cudgel, gallows, dim. of *gibe* staff, club; of uncert. orig.; see -ET.

gibbon long-armed S.E. Asian ape. XVIII. - F. - native name.

gibbous convex; hump-backed. XIV. - late L. *gibbōsus*, f. *gibbus* hump. So **gibbosity** XIV.

gibe, jibe speak sneeringly. XVI. perh. - OF. *giber* handle roughly, mod. dial. kick (cf. JIB[3]), of unkn. orig. Hence sb. XVI.

giblets †appendage XIV; †entrails XV; pl. eatable portions of a bird removed before cooking XVI. - OF. *gibelet* game stew, perh. for **giberet*, f. *gibier* game.

giddy †mad, foolish OE.; dizzy XVI; easily distracted, flighty. Peculiar to Eng. OE. *gidiġ*, **gydiġ* :- Gmc. **ȝuđiȝaz*, f. **ȝuđ-* GOD, the primary sense being 'possessed by a god'; see -Y[1].

gift XIII. - ON. *gipt*, corr. to OE. *ġift* payment for a wife, pl. wedding, OS. *sundargift* privilege, MDu. *gift(e)* (Du. *gift* fem. gift, n. usu. *gif* poison), OHG. *gift* fem. gift, poison (G. *gift* fem. gift, n. poison), Goth. *fragifts* espousal :- Gmc. **ȝeftiz*, f. **ȝeb-*, base of GIVE; see -T[1].

gig A. †flighty girl XIII; †whipping-top XV; †fancy, whim XVI; (dial.) fun, glee; (dial.) odd person, fool XVIII; B. (in full, *gig-mill*) machine for raising a nap on cloth XVI; light two-wheeled one-horse carriage; light ship's boat XVIII. All these uses may be referred to the gen. notion of light or quick movement, which is also that of the later JIG; but the history of both words is obscure.

gigantic XVII. f. L. *gigās*, *gigant-* GIANT + -IC.

giggle vb. XVI. imit. Hence as sb. XVII.

giglet †wanton woman; giggling girl. XIV. perh. f. GIG + -LET.

gigot (now Sc.) leg of mutton, etc. XVI. - F., dim. of dial. *gigue* leg.

gild[1] cover with gold. OE. *-gyldan* (in pp. *ġegyld* GILT[1] and comps.) = ON. *gylla* :- Gmc. **ȝulþjan*, f. **ȝulþam* GOLD.

gild[2] see GUILD.

gill[1] organ of respiration in fishes. XIV. - ON. **gil* :- Gmc. **ȝeliz* rel. to Gr. *khelū́nē* lip, jaw, *kheîlos* lip.

gill[2] rocky cleft, ravine XI (in place-names), XIV (in literature); narrow stream XVII. - ON. *gil* deep glen. The fanciful sp. *ghyll* was introduced by Wordsworth.

gill[3] ¼ pint. XIV. - OF. *gille*, *gelle*, in medL. *gillo*, *gellus*, late L. *gello*, *gillo* waterpot.

gill[4] lass, wench. XV. Short for *Gillian*.

gillie attendant on a Highland chief XVII; one who attends on a sportsman XIX. - Gael. *gille* lad, servant.

gillyflower †clove XIV; clove-scented pink, wallflower, etc. XV. ME. *gilofre*, *gerofle* - OF. *gilofre*, *girofle* - medL. *caryophyllum* - Gr. *karuóphullon* clove-tree, f. *káruon* nut + *phúllon* leaf. Alt. in Eng. (XV) by assim. to *flower*.

gilt[1] gilded. XIV. OE. *ġegyld*; see GILD[1]. Hence sb. †gilt plate XV; gilding XVI.

gilt[2] young sow XIV. - ON. *gylte*.

gimbals (pl.) †joints, links XVI; (naut.) self-adjusting bearings to keep articles horizontal XVIII. var. of *gimmal* (XVI) joints, etc., alt. of *gemel* (XIV) pl. twins, etc. - OF. *gemel* (mod. *jumeau*) :- L. *gemellus*, dim. of *geminus* twin.

gimcrack †fanciful notion, dodge; mechanical contrivance; knick-knack; †fop XVII; adj. trivial, trumpery XVIII. alt. of ME. *gibecrake* (XIV) kind of ornament; of unkn. orig.

gimlet XIV. - OF. *guimbelet*, of Gmc. orig.

gimp silk, worsted, or cotton twist with a cord running through it. XVII. - Du., of unkn. orig.

gin[1] †ingenuity, craft, trick; (arch.) contrivance, esp. for snaring game. XIII. Aphetic - OF. *engin* ENGINE.

gin[2] ardent spirit distilled from grain and malt. XVIII. abbrev. of GENEVA.

ginger hot spicy root. XIII. ME. *gingivere*, repr. a conflation of OE. *ġinġifer(e)*, *ġinġiber* (directly - medL.) with OF. *gingi(m)bre* (mod. *gingembre*) - medL. *gingiber*, *zingeber*, L. *zingiber(i)* - Gr. *ziggiberis* - Prakrit *siṃgabera* - Skr. *śṛṅgavera-*. Hence vb. flavour with ginger; treat (a horse) with ginger, (hence gen.) spirit *up*. XIX.

gingerbread †A. preserved ginger XIII; B. cake flavoured with ginger XV; adj. tawdry, gimcrack XVIII. Earliest forms *gingebras*, *-brat*, *-bred* - OF. *gingembras*, *-brat* - medL. *gingibrātum*, *-etum*, f. *gingiber* GINGER + *-ātum* -ATE[1]. The final syll. assumed a form resembling or suggesting *bread*, and for sense B the insertion of *r* in the second syll. completed the semblance of a comp.

gingerly †elegantly, daintily, mincingly XVI; very cautiously or reluctantly XVII; also adj. perh. f. OF. *gensor*, *genzor*, prop. compar. of *gent* noble, but used also as a positive, 'pretty, delicate'. See -LY[1,2].

gingham XVII. - (prob. through Du. *gingang*) Malay *genggang* striped fabric.

gingival of the gums. XVII. - modL. *gingīvālis*, f. L. *gingīva* gum; see -AL[1].

ginglymus (anat.) joint of which the motion is in only one plane. XVII. modL. - Gr. *gígglumos* hinge.

gipsy, gypsy member of a nomadic race, called by themselves Romany, of Hindu origin, in XVI supposed to have come from Egypt. XVI. Earlier forms †*gipcyan*, †*gipsen*, *-son*, aphetic of *Egyptian* (in the same use).

giraffe XVII. There are early forms depending on It. *giraffa* and OF. *girafle*, and occas. on Arab. *zarāfa* (ult. source of the word in the Eur. langs.); the present form, hardly established before XVIII, is - F. *girafe*.

girandole revolving firework XVII; branched support for candles XVIII. - F. - It. *girandola*, f. *girare* - late L. *gyrāre* GYRATE.

girasol variety of opal having a red glow. XVI. - F. *girasol* or its source It. *girasole*, f. *girare* (see prec.) + *sole* sun.

gird[1] pt., pp. *girt* encircle; invest, endue; fasten (on) as with a belt. OE. *gyrdan* = OS. *gurdian* (Du. *gorden*), OHG. *gurten* (G. *gürten*), ON. *gyrða* :- Gmc. **ʒurðjan*. Hence **girder** main beam supporting joists. XVII. See -ER[1].

gird[2] †strike XIII; †thrust, impel XIII; intr. rush (dial.) XIV; gibe *at* XVI. of unkn. orig.

girdle[1] belt worn round the waist. OE. *gyrdel* (earlier *gyrdels*) = MDu. *gurdel* (Du. *gordel*), OHG. *gurtil(a)*, (C. *gürtel*), ON. *gyrðill*, f. **ʒurðjan* GIRD[1]; see -LE[1]. Hence as vb. XVI.

girdle[2] (Sc.) iron plate for baking cakes. XV. Metathetic form of GRIDDLE.

girl †youth or maiden XIII; female child XVI. of uncert. orig.; the ME. vars. *gurle*, *girle*, *gerle* suggest an orig. *ü*.

girt surround, gird XVI; take the girth of XVII. f. *girt* sb. (XVI), var. of GIRTH surviving in techn. uses; infl. by pp. *girt* of GIRD[1].

girth band fastened round the body of a beast of burden XIV; measurement round a circumference XVII. - ON. *gjǫrð* girdle, girth, hoop (:- **ʒerðu*) = Goth. *gairda* girdle :- Gmc. **ʒerðō*.

gist (leg.) ground of an action, etc. XVIII; substance or essence of a matter XIX. - OF. *gist* (mod. *gît*), 3rd sg. pres. ind. of F. *gésir* lie (:- L. *jacēre*).

gittern (arch.) XIV. - OF. *guiterne* (perh. through MDu. *giterne*), obscurely rel. to CITHERN and GUITAR.

give pt. *gave*, pp. *given* hand over OE.; intr. yield XVI. OE. str. vb. *ġ(i)efan* = OS. *geban* (Du. *geven*), OHG. *geban* (G. *geben*), ON. *gefa*, Goth. *giban* :- Gmc. **ʒeban*, with no certain IE. cognates. OE. *ġ(i)efan* was repr. by ME. *yive*; the present form with initial g appears XII and is due to Scand., the vowel reflecting OSw. *giva*, ODa. *give*.

gizzard XIV. ME. *giser* - OF. *giser*, *gezier*, *juisier*, also *guisier* (mod. *gésier*) :- Rom. **gicerium*, for L. *gigeria* pl. The final *d* appears XVI. The pronunc. with hard *g* seems to be due to OF. *guisier*.

glabrous smooth. XVII. f. L. *glaber* hairless, bald (see GLAD) + -OUS.

glacé smooth and highly polished; iced, sugared. XIX. - F., pp. of *glacer* ice, give a gloss to, f. *glace* ice.

glacial XVII. - F. *glacial* or L. *glaciālis* icy, f. *glaciēs* ice; see -AL[1].

glacier XVIII. - F. *glacier*, earlier *glacière* (an Alpine word), f. *glace* ice :- Rom. **glacia*, for L. *glaciēs*.

glacis sloping bank, (fortif.) sloping parapet. XVII. - F., f. OF. *glacier* slide, f. *glace* ice.

glad †shining, bright; †cheerful, merry; full of joy OE.; suggestive of joy XVII. OE. *glæd* = OS. *glad* (in comp. *gladmōd*), ON. *glaðr* bright, joyous. The orig. sense survives in OHG. *glat* (G. *glatt*) smooth; Gmc. **ʒlaðaz* is rel. to OSl. *gladŭkŭ*, L. *glaber* smooth, GLABROUS. Hence **gladsome** XIV.

glade XVI. of unkn. orig.; cf. synon. †*glode* (XIV).

gladiator XV. - L. *gladiātor*, f. *gladius* sword; see -ATOR. So **gladiatorial** XVIII. f. L. *gladiātōrius*.

gladiolus XVI. - L., dim. of *gladius* sword.

Gladstone name of William Ewart *Gladstone* (1808-98), Eng. statesman, used attrib. or ellipt. to designate (i) French wine of which the importation was increased as a result of his reduction of customs duty, (ii) a kind of portmanteau. XIX.

Glagolitic early Slavonic alphabet XIX. - modL. *glagoliticus*, f. Serbo-Croatian *glagolica*, f. *glagol* word; see -IC.

glair white of egg. XIV. - (O)F. *glaire* :- medL. *glarea*, var. of **clarea* (sb. use of fem. of L. adj. *clārus* CLEAR). Hence **glairy** viscid, slimy. XVII.

glaive †lance, spear XIII; †halbert; (arch.) sword, broadsword XV. - (O)F. *glaive*, †*glavie* †lance, (now) sword, presumed to be - L. *gladius* sword.

glamour magic, spell XVIII; magic beauty XIX. orig. Sc.; alteration of GRAMMAR with the sense of GRAMARYE. For the form with *gl-* cf. medL. *glomeria*, prob. - AN. **glomerie*, for *gramarie* GRAMMAR.

glance glide *off* an object struck; †move rapidly XV; make a flash of light; flash a look XVI. The earliest forms *glench*, *glence*, *glanch* suggest an alt. of †*glace* (XIV) glance, glide (- OF. *glacier*; see GLACIS) by crossing with synon. †*glent* (XIII) and *lanch*, LAUNCH[1]. Hence **glance** sb. swift oblique movement; flash, gleam; hurried look. XVI.

gland XVII. - F. *glande*, later form of OF. *glandre* (see next).

glander †glandular swelling XV; (pl.) disease of horses XVI. - OF. *glandre* :- L. *glandulæ* pl. throat glands, swollen glands in the neck.

glare shine with dazzling light XIII; look fixedly and fiercely XVII. - MLG., MDu. *glaren* gleam, glare, prob. ult. rel. to GLASS.

glass OE. *glæs* = OS., (O)HG. *glas* :- WGmc. **ʒla·sam*, of which a var. **ʒlaza·m* is repr. by ON. *gler* glass; prob. rel. to OE. *glǣr*, MLG. *glār* amber.

Glauber's salt(s) sulphate of sodium. XVIII. named after Johann Rudolf *Glauber* (1604-68),

German chemist, by whom it was first artificially made.

glaucoma XVII. - L. - Gr. *glaúkōma*, f. *glaukós*; see next and -OMA.

glaucous dull-green. XVII. f. L. *glaucus* - Gr. *glaukós* bluish-green or grey; see -OUS.

glaze fill with glass XIV; cover with a vitreous substance XV. ME. *glase*, f. GLASS. Hence **glazier** XIV.

gleam (orig.) brilliant light; (now) subdued or transient light. OE. *glǣm* (:- **ʒlaimiz*), corr. to LG. *glēm*, OHG. *gleimo* glow-worm, and rel. to OS. *glīmo* brightness, OHG. *glīmo* glow-worm, MHG. *glīmen* shine, glow, and further to GLIMMER. Hence vb. XIII.

glean gather reaped corn. XIV. - OF. *glener* :- late L. (Gallo-Roman) *glennare* (VI), prob. of Celt. orig.

glebe soil, earth; field; portion of land attached to a benefice. XIV. - L. *glēba*, *glǣba* clod, land, soil; cf. Pol. *gleba*, Russ. *glýba* clod, and see GLOBE.

glee †play, sport; †minstrelsy, music OE. (unaccompanied part-song XVII); mirth, rejoicing XII. OE. *glēo*, *glīo* = ON. (rare) *glý* :- **ʒliujam* (not repr. in other Gmc. langs.).

glen XV. In early use Sc. *glen*; taken up by Spenser in the forms *glenne*, *glinne*; in gen. Eng. use the form *glen* dates from mid-XVIII. - Gael., Ir. *gleann*, earlier *glenn* = W. *glyn*.

glengarry XIX. f. name of a town in Inverness, Scotland.

glenoid (anat.) pert. to a shallow cavity on certain bones. XVIII. - F. *glénoïde* - Gr. *glēnoeidḗs*, f. *glḗnē* ball or pupil of the eye, shallow joint-socket; see -OID.

glib (dial.) smooth and slippery XVI; ready and fluent XVII. rel. to synon. †*glibbery*, corr. formally to Du. *glibberig*, MLG. *glibberich* (LG. *glibbrig*), f. base **ʒlīb-* (cf. OHG. *gleif* sloping).

glide pass easily or smoothly. OE. str. vb. *glīdan* = OS. *glīdan* (Du. *glijden*), OHG. *glītan* (G. *gleiten*) :- WGmc. **ʒlīðan*, of which no cogns. are known.

glim light, candle, lantern. XVII. perh. abbr. of GLIMMER or GLIMPSE.

glimmer †shine brightly XIV; shine faintly XV. prob. of Scand. orig. (cf. Sw. *glimra*, Da. *glimre*, to which corr. (M)HG., Du. *glimmern*); f. Gmc. **ʒlim-* **ʒlaim-*; see GLEAM, -ER[4]. Hence **glimmer** sb. XVI.

glimpse †have faint vision XIV; (arch.) shine faintly or intermittently XV; (from the sb.) see momentarily or partially XVIII. deriv. of the base of GLIMMER, perh. repr. an OE. **glimsian* = MHG. *glimsen* :- WGmc. **ʒlimisōjan*. Hence **glimpse** sb. XVI.

glint move quickly, esp. obliquely; shine with flashing light. XIV (not common till XVIII). alt. of earlier (dial.) *glent* (XIII), prob. of Scand. orig.

glissade sb. XIX. - F. *glissade*, f. *glisser* slip, slide; see -ADE.

glisten OE. *glisnian*, f. base of *glisian* (= OFris. *glisa*, MLG. *glisen*), f. Gmc. **ʒlis-*, extension of **ʒli-*, repr. by ON. *gljá* shine.

glister (poet., dial.) glitter. XIV. prob. - MLG. *glistern*, (M)Du. *glisteren*, f. Gmc. **ʒlis-*; see prec.

glitter vb. XIV. - ON. *glitra* = (MH)G. *glitzern*, sparkle, frequent. (see -ER[4]) f. Gmc. **ʒlīt-*, in OS. *glītan*, OHG. *glīzan* (G. *gleissen*) shine, ON. *glit* brightness, *glita* shine, Goth. *glitmunjan* (of clothes) shine bright.

gloaming evening twilight. XV. In the literary language an early-XIX adoption from Sc. writers. Cf. OE. *glōmung*.

gloat †look askance or furtively XVI; †cast amorous glances XVII; gaze with intense satisfaction (*over*, *upon*) XVIII. of unkn. orig. Cf. ON. *glotta* grin, (M)HG. *glotzen* stare.

globe XVI. - (O)F. *globe* or L. *globus*, rel. to *glēba* GLEBE and referred by some to a base **gel-* roll together, stick. Hence **global** XX. So **globose** XV. - L. **globous** XVII. - F. or L. **globular** XVII. f. L. *globulus*, dim. of *globus*. **globule** XVII. - F. or L.

glomerate (bot.) compactly clustered. XVIII. - L. *glomerātus*; cf. CONGLOMERATE.

gloom look sullen; (of the sky, etc.) lower XIV; make dark XVI; look dark XVIII. ME. *gloum(b)e*; the earliest evidence is predominantly north.; of unkn. orig. Hence **gloom** sb. (Sc.) sullen look XVI; darkness, obscurity XVII (prob. back-formation from *gloomy*); melancholy state XVIII. **gloomy** dark, obscure XVI; sullen, depressed XVI; depressing, dismal XVIII.

Gloria short for the liturgical *Gloria Patri* (*et Filio et Spiritui Sancto*) Glory be to the Father (and to the Son and to the Holy Ghost), *Gloria in excelsis Deo* Glory to God in the highest, and *Gloria tibi Domine* Glory be to thee, O Lord. XIII.

glory †boastful spirit; resplendent beauty; splendour (in religious lang., of God, etc.) XIII; exalted praise or honour XIV; halo, nimbus XVII. - OF. (AN.) *glorie* (mod. *gloire*) - L. *glōria*. So **glory** vb. exult, †boast. XIV. - L. *gloriārī*, f. *glōria*. **glorify** XIV. - (O)F. - ecclL. **glorious** XIII. - AN. *glori(o)us*, OF. *glorieux* - L. *glōriōsus*.

gloss[1] superficial lustre. XVI. of unkn. orig. Hence as vb. (infl. by GLOSS[2]) give a specious appearance to, smoothe *over*. XVII. **glossy** XVI.

gloss[2] interlinear or marginal explanation; (sophistical) interpretation. XVI. refash. of GLOZE after L. *glōssa*.

glossary XIV. - L. *glossārium*, f. *glōssa* GLOSS[2]; see -ARY. Hence **glossarist** XVIII.

glosso- rarely *glotto-*, comb. form of Gr. *glôssa*, *glôtta* tongue, language, as in *glossographer* (Gr. *glōssográphos*), *-graphy* XVII, *glossology* science of language XVIII, *glottology* XIX.

glottis XVI. - modL. - Gr. *glōttís*, f. *glôtta*, var. of *glôssa* tongue. Hence **glottal** XIX.

glove OE. *glōf* corr. to ON. *glófi*, by some taken to be :- Gmc. **ʒalōfō*, *-an-* f. **ʒa-* Y- + base of ON. *lófi*, Goth. *lōfa* hand.

glow emit (bright) light. OE. str. vb. *glōwan*, corr. to the wk. vbs. OS. *glōjan* (Du. *gloeien*), OHG. *gluoen* (G. *glühen*), ON. *glóa*; f. Gmc. **ʒlō-* :- IE. **ghlō-*, **ghlē-*, whence W. *glo* coal, Lith. *žlėjà* twilight. Hence **glow-worm** XIV.

glower (Sc.) stare with wide-open eyes XVI; scowl XVIII. perh. Sc. var. of synon. (dial.) *glore* (XIV), the earlier sense of which seems to be 'shine, gleam', perh. - LG. *glōren* or Scand. (cf. Icel. *glóra* gleam, stare), rel. to GLOW.

gloxinia XIX. modL., named after B. P. *Gloxin*, German botanist, who described the plant in 1785.

gloze flattery, deceit XIII; comment, gloss XIV. - (O)F. *glose* - medL. *glōsa*, for L. *glōssa* word needing explanation, the explanation itself - Gr. *glôssa* tongue, (foreign) language, foreign or obscure word. So as vb. talk speciously XIII; †gloss, explain XIV; explain away. - (O)F. *gloser*.

glucose XIX. - F., irreg. - Gr. *gleûkos* must, sweet wine, rel. to *glukús* sweet; see -OSE[2].

glue sb. XIV. - (O)F. *glu* :- late L. *glūs*, *glūt-*, for L. *glūten*, rel. to Gr. *gloiā*, *gloiá*, *gliā*, *gloiós* glue, Lith. *glitùs* slippery; f. IE. **gloi-* **glei-* **gli-* stick. So **glue** vb. XIII. - (O)F. *gluer*. Hence **gluey** XIV; see -Y[1].

glum XVI. rel. to (dial.) *glum* vb. frown, scowl (XV), var. of †*glom(e)*, †*gloumbe*, GLOOM.

glume (bot.) husk. XVIII. - L. *glūma* :- **glūbmā*, f. **glūb-* (as in *glūbere* shell).

glut feed to repletion. XIV. Earliest forms *gloute*, *glotte*, *glotye*, prob. - (O)F. *gloutir* swallow :- L. *gluttīre* (see GLUTTON). Hence sb. XVI.

gluteus (anat.) any of the three muscles of the buttock. XVII. modL., f. Gr. *gloutós* rump.

gluten †albuminous element of animal tissues XVI; sticky or viscid substance XVII; (chem.) nitrogenous part of flour XIX. - F. - L. *glūten* GLUE. So **glutinous** XVI. - (O)F. or L.

glutton A. gormandizer XIII; B. voracious animal, wolverine XVII. - OF. *gluton*, *gloton* (mod. *glouton*) :- L. *gluttō*, *-ōn-*, rel. to *gluttīre* swallow, *gluttus* greedy, and further to *gula* throat. Hence **gluttonous** XIV.

glycerin(e) XIX. - F. *glycerin*, f. Gr. *glukerós* sweet, rel. to synon. *glukús*, of which the comb. form in gen. use is **glyco-** instead of *glycy-*.

glyph (archit.) vertical channel in a frieze XVIII; sculptured mark XIX. - F. *glyphe* - Gr. *gluphḗ* carving, rel. to *glúphein* carve.

glyptic pert. to carving. XIX. - F. *glyptique* or Gr. *gluptikós*, f. *glúptēs* carver, f. *glúphein* carve; see -IC.

gnarled XVII. Once in Sh. ('Measure for Measure' II ii 116), and taken up thence by early-XIX writers; var. of **knarled*, **knurled*, f. *knarl*, *knurl*, extensions of *knar* (XIII) rugged rock, knot in wood, *knur*, *knor* (XV) hard excrescence, corr. to MLG., MDu., MHG. *knorre* (Du. *knor*, G. *knorren*) knobby protuberance.

gnash XV. alt. of †*gnacche* (XIV) or †*gnast* (XIII), which had an early var. †*gnaist* - ON. base of echoic orig., repr. by *gnast(r)an* gnashing of teeth, *gnesta* crash, clatter.

gnat OE. *gnætt*, corr. to LG. *gnatte*, G. dial. *gnatze*, rel. to MLG. *gnitte*, G. *gnitze*.

gnathic pert. to the jaws. XIX. f. Gr. *gnáthos* jaw + -IC.

gnaw pt. *gnawed*, pp. *gnawed* (from XVIII). *gnawn*. OE. str. vb. *gnagan* = OS. *gnagan*, OHG. *(g)nagan* (G. *nagen*), ON. *gnaga*; ult. imit.

gneiss (geol.) kind of metamorphic rock. XVIII. - G. *gneiss*, perh. rel. to OHG. *gneisto* (=OE. *gnāst*, etc.) spark, the rock being named from its sheen.

gnomic pert. to general maxims. XIX. - Gr. *gnōmikós* (perh. through F. *gnomique*), f. *gnṓmē* opinion, judgement, f. IE. **gnō-*; see KNOW, -IC.

gnomon indicator, esp. of a sundial; †nose; part of a parallelogram remaining after a similar one is taken from one corner (from the resemblance to a carpenter's square ⅂). XVI. - F. *gnomon* or L. *gnōmōn* - Gr. *gnṓmōn* inspector, indicator, carpenter's square, f. IE. **gnō-*; see KNOW.

gnosis knowledge of spiritual mysteries. XVIII. - Gr. *gnôsis* investigation, knowledge, f. IE. **gnō-* KNOW. So **gnostic** adj. cognitive, intellectual XVII; sb. one of a sect of early Christians claiming *gnosis* XVI. - ecclL. *gnōsticus* - Gr. *gnōstikós*, f. *gnōstós*; see -IC.

gnu XVIII. ult. - Bushman *nqu*, prob. through Du. *gnoe*.

go pt. *went* (see WEND), pp. *gone* †walk; move along, proceed. OE. *gān* = OS. *-gān* (Du. *gaan*), OHG. *gān* and *gēn* (G. *gehen*), f. Gmc. **ʒai-*, **ʒǣ-* :- IE. **ghē(i)-*, prob. repr. in Gr. *kíkhēmi* I reach, Skr. *jáhāti* leaves, forsakes.

goad pointed rod for driving cattle. OE. *gād* :- Gmc. **ʒaiðō*, f. IE. **ghai-* (as in Gr. *khaîos*, *khaîon* shepherd's staff); rel. to OE. *gār* spear.

goal terminal point of a race; (in football), posts through which the ball is driven. XVI. of unkn. orig.

goat OE. *gāt* she-goat (the male being called *bucca* BUCK and *gātbucca*), pl. *gǣt* = OS. *gēt* (Du. *geit*), OHG. *geiz* (G. *geiss*), ON. *geit*, Goth. *gaits* :- Gmc. **ʒaitaz*, rel. to L. *hædus* kid :- IE. **ghaidos*. Hence **goatee** (U.S.) beard resembling the tufted beard of a he-goat. XIX.

gob lump. XIV. - OF. *go(u)be* mouthful, lump (mod. *gobbe* food-ball, pill), f. *gober* swallow, gulp, perh. of Celt. orig. (cf. Gael. *gob* beak, bill, Ir. *gob* bill, mouth, whence prob. Sc. and north. Eng. *gob* mouth XVI).

gobbet portion, fragment; lump of food, etc. XIV. - OF. *gobet*, dim. of *gobe* GOB; see -ET.

gobble[1] swallow hurriedly. XVII. prob. f. GOB + -LE[3].

gobble[2] make the characteristic noise of a turkey. XVII. imit., but perh. suggested by prec.

goblet XIV. - (O)F. *gobelet*, dim. of *gobel*, of unkn. orig.; see -ET.

goblin XIV. prob. - AN. **gobelin* (recorded in F. XV and surviving in Norman dial.), medL. *gobelīnus*; prob. appellative use of a proper name, dim. of *Gobel* (now *Gobeau*), app. rel. to *kobold* (see COBALT).

goby XVIII. - L. *gōbius*, var. of *cōbius* - Gr. *kōbiós* some small fish.

god, God OE. *god* (pl. *godu* n., *godas* m.) = OS. (Du.) *god* m., OHG. *got* (G. *gott*) m., ON. *god* n., heathen god, *guð* m. and n., God, Goth. *guþ* (pl. *guda* n.); Gmc. **ʒuð-*, of uncert. orig. Hence **goddess** XIV; **godfather, -mother, -daughter, -son** late OE. *godfæder*, *-mōdor*, *-dohtor*, *-sunu*; cf. GOSSIP; **godchild** XIII. **godhead** XIII. **God's acre** churchyard XVII. - G. *Gottesacker* 'God's seed-field', in which the bodies of the dead are 'sown' in hope of the Resurrection. **godsend** XIX. for †*God's send* (XVII) alteration of ME. *goddes sand* God's message, dispensation, or ordinance. **Godspeed** XV. f. phr. *God speed* 'May God prosper (one)'. See also GOOD-BYE.

godetia genus of hardy annuals. XIX. f. name of C. H. *Godet*, Swiss botanist (d. 1879); see -IA[1].

godwit marsh-bird resembling the curlew. XVI. of unkn. orig.

goffer make wavy, crimp. XVIII. - F. *gaufrer* impress with a pattern-tool, f. *gaufre* honeycomb, pastry made on a mould, impressed pattern, AN. *walfre* - MLG. *wāfel*; see WAFFLE, WAFER.

goggle (dial.) squint, roll the eyes or the head. XIV. prob. frequent. of a base **gog*, expressive of oscillating movement; cf. *jog*, *joggle*, and see -LE[3]. So **goggle-eyed** XIV. Hence **goggle** sb. †squint, stare XVII; (pl.) the eyes; spectacles XVIII.

Goidel Celt of the branch represented by the Irish and the Highlanders of Scotland. XIX. - OIr. *Goidel*; see GAEL. Hence **Goidelic** XIX.

goitre XVII. - F., either (i) - Pr. *goitron* (also in OF.) :- Rom. **gutturiōnem*, f. L. *guttur* throat, or (ii) back-formation from F. *goitreux* :- L. **gutturiōsus* adj.

gold sb. OE. = OS., OHG. *gold* (Du. *goud*, G. *gold*), ON. *gull*, Goth. *gulþ* :- Gmc. **ʒulþam* :- IE. *ĝhḷtom* (cf. OSl. *zlato*), f. **ĝhel-* YELLOW. Hence **golden** XIII; superseding †*gilden*, OE. *gylden*; see -EN[3]. **goldfinch.** OE. *goldfinc*. **goldsmith.** OE.

golf XV. of unkn. orig.

golliwog fanciful invented name for a black-faced doll. XIX.

golly (orig. U.S.) substitute for GOD in excls. XIX.

golosh see GALOSH.

goluptious luscious. XIX. perh. perversion of *voluptuous*.

-gon, repr. Gr. *-gōnos* -angled (cf. KNEE), in *heptagon*, *hexagon*, *pentagon*.

gondola XVI. - (Venetian) It. So **gondolier** XVII. - F. - It.

gonfalon banner. XVI. - It. *gonfalone* = F. *gonfalon*, later form of *gonfanon* - Gmc. **gundfano* (= OE. *gūðfana*, ON. *gunnfani*), f. **ʒund-* :- Gmc. **ʒunþiō* war + *fano* banner.

gong XVII. - Malay.

goniometer instrument for measuring angles. XVIII. - F. *goniomètre*, f. Gr. *gōniā* angle + *métron* measure; see -METER.

gonorrhoea XVI. - late L. - Gr. *gonórrhoia*, f. *gónos* semen (cf. KIN) + *rhoía* flux, rel. to *rhein* flow.

good OE. *gōd* = OS. *gōd* (Du. *goed*), OHG. *guot* (G. *gut*), ON. *góðr*, Goth. *gōþs* :- Gmc. **ʒōðaz*, f. var. of the base **ʒað-* bring together, unite, as in *gaderian* GATHER, the primary sense being 'fitting, suitable' (cf. OSl. *goditi* be pleasing). Compared BETTER, BEST; adv. WELL. See also GOODS. Hence **goodly** comely, fair OE.; notable in size XIII; excellent, proper XIV; kindly XIV. **goodman** (i) male head of a house XIV (householder, husband XVI); (ii) †prefixed to designations, names of yeomen, etc., (hence) yeoman, Scottish laird XVI. Similarly (dial.) **goodwife** XIV; cf. GOODY[1]. **goodwill** †virtuous disposition; favourable regard, benevolence OE.; cheerful acquiescence XIII; privilege granted by the seller of a business to the purchaser of trading as his successor XVI.

good-bye XVI. Early forms *God be wy you*, *God buy'ye*, *God b'uy*, *Godbuy*, contr. of phr. *God be with you* or *ye*, with later substitution of *good* for *God*, after *good day* (XIII), *good night* (XIV).

goods (pl.) property, possessions XIII; merchandise, wares XV. Superseded synon. use of sg. *good* (XII); partly after ON. *góðs*, g. sg. of *góð* (n. of *góðr*) used as an indecl. sb. in the sense 'property', partly after L. *bona*, sb. use of n. pl. of *bonus* good.

goody[1] lowly form of address to a (married) woman. XVI. Hypocoristic f. GOODWIFE.

goody[2] sweetmeat. XVIII. f. GOOD; see -Y[6].

goody[3] weakly or sentimentally good. XIX. f. GOOD + -Y[6]. Also redupl. **goody-goody** XIX.

googly (orig. Austral.) in cricket, a ball that breaks from the off. XX. of unkn. orig.

goosander XVII. prob. f. GOOSE + second el. of *bergander* sheldrake (XVI), which prob. repr. ON. *ǫnd* duck, pl. *andir*.

goose pl. **geese.** OE. *gōs*, pl. *gēs* = MLG. *gōs*, (M)Du., (O)HG. *gans*, ON. *gás* :- Gmc. **ʒans-* :- IE. **ĝhans-*, whence also L. *anser* (:- **hanser*), Gr. *khḗn*, Skr. *haṁsá-*, Lith. *žąsis* goose, OIr. *géis* swan.

gooseberry XVI. app. f. GOOSE + BERRY.

gopher[1] the wood of which Noah's Ark was built. XVII. - Heb. *gōpher*.

gopher[2] (orig. U.S.) land tortoise XVIII (also †*magofer*); pouched rat; ground squirrel XIX. of uncert. orig.

gore[1] †dung, filth OE.; blood shed (and clotted) XVI. OE. *gor* = (M)Du. *goor*, OHG. *gor* mud, filth, ON. *gor* cud, slimy matter, rel. to OIr. *gor*, W. *gôr* matter, pus.

gore[2] triangular piece of land OE.; skirt front, petticoat XIII; triangular piece, spec. of cloth XIV. OE. *gāra* = MDu. *ghere* (Du. *geer*), OHG. *gēro* (G. *gehre*), ON. *geiri*, rel. to *gār* spear (a spear-head being triangular).

gore[3] †stab XIV; pierce with the horns XVI. of unkn. orig.

gorge throat XIV; crop of a hawk XV; contents of the stomach (phr. *one's gorge rises*) XVI; neck of a bastion XVII; ravine XVIII. - (O)F., 'throat' :- Rom. **gurga*, for L. *gurges* whirlpool. Hence vb. fill the gorge (of). XIV.

gorgeous XV. Early forms *gorgayse*, *gorges*, *gorgyas* - OF. *gorgias* fine, stylish, elegant, of unkn. orig.; assim. in ending to words in -EOUS.

gorget throat armour XV; wimple, necklace XVI. - OF. *gorgete*, f. *gorge* throat, GORGE; see -ET.

gorgio gipsies' name for one who is not a gipsy. XIX. - Romany.

gorgon terrible- or repulsive-looking person. XVI. Generalized use of the proper name *Gorgon* - L. *Gorgō*, *-ōn-* - Gr. *Gorgṓ*, f. *gorgós* terrible.

gorgonzola cheese named from a village near Milan, Italy. XIX.

gorilla XIX. Adopted by Thomas Savage in 1847 as the specific name; - Gr. *gorilla* (only in acc. pl.), an alleged African name of a wild or hairy man (prop. the female).

gormandize XVI. f. †*gormandize* sb. gluttonous feeding (XV) - (O)F. *gourmandise*, f. *gourmand* glutton.

gorse OE. *gors(t)*, app. rel. to L. *hordeum*, Gr. *krīthḗ*, OHG. *gersta* (G. *gerste*) barley.

gorsedd meeting of Welsh bards and druids. XVIII. - W., 'throne, tribunal', lit. 'high seat'.

gosh Deformation of GOD used in oaths. XVIII (earlier †*gosse* XVI).

goshawk OE. *gōshafoc*, f. *gōs* GOOSE + *hafoc* HAWK.

gosling XV. orig. *gesling* - ON. *gæslingr*, f. *gás* GOOSE; assim. (XV) to Eng. *goose*; see -LING[1].

gospel the 'good tidings' proclaimed by Jesus Christ; any of the four books written by the Evangelists; portion of any of these read at the Eucharist OE.; something 'as true as the gospel' XIII; something 'to swear by' as doctrine to be believed XVII. OE. *gōdspel*, i.e. *gōd* GOOD, *spel* news, tidings (SPELL[1]), rendering of ecclL. *bona annuntiatio*, *bonus nuntius*, used as literal renderings of ecclL. *evangelium*, Gr. *euaggélion* EVANGEL. Identification of the first syll. with GOD in Eng. is reflected in forms adopted in the Gmc. langs. of peoples evangelized from England, viz. OS. *godspell*, OHG. *gotspell*, ON. *guð-*, *goðspjall*. Hence **gospeller** (which illustrates various uses of -ER[1]), OE. *gōdspellere*, f. *gōdspel* or the corr. vb. *gōdspellian*, †one of the four evangelists (OE.-XVII); †gospel-book XV; one who recites the Gospel at the Eucharist; one who professes the faith of the gospel, esp. fanatically (*hot-gospeller*) XVI.

gossamer fine film spun by spiders. XIV (*gosesomer*, *gossomer*). The earliest forms suggest deriv. from GOOSE + SUMMER[1], but the allusion is obscure.

gossip †sponsor at baptism OE.; †familiar acquaintance XIV; idle talker, tattler XVI; (from the vb.) tittle-tattle, easy talk XIX. Late OE. *godsibb*, corr. to ON. *guðsefi* godfather, *guðsifja* godmother, comp. of GOD and SIB denoting the spiritual affinity of the baptized and their sponsors. Hence **gossip** vb. be or act as gossip XVI; talk idly XVII.

got, gotten see GET.

Goth name of a Germanic tribe prominent in Europe A.D. III-V. OE. *Gota*, usu. in pl. *Gotan*, was superseded in ME. (XIV) by the adoption of late and medL. *Gothī* pl. = Gr. *Gót(t)hoi* pl. - Goth. **Gutōs* or **Gutans* pl. So **Gothic** pert. to the Goths; †Germanic, Teutonic; †medieval, romantic, of the Dark Ages; spec. of the style of architecture characterized particularly by the pointed arch; †barbarous, savage; black-letter (type). XVII. - F. *gothique* or late L. *Gothicus*.

gouache water-colour painting with opaque colours. XIX. - F. - It. *guazzo*.

gouge chisel with concave blade. XV. - (O)F. :- late L. *gu(l)bia*, perh. of Celt. orig. Hence vb. XVI.

goulash stew of steak and vegetables XIX; redeal in contract bridge XX. - Hung. *gulyáshús*, f. *gulyás* herdsman + *hús* meat.

gourd XIV. - AN. *gurde*, OF. *gourde*, repr. ult. L. *cucurbita*.

gourmand †glutton XV; judge of good feeding XVIII. - (O)F., of unkn. orig.

gourmet connoisseur in the delicacies of the table. XIX. - F. *gourmet*, orig. (wine-merchant's) assistant, wine-taster, infl. in sense by GOURMAND.

gout disease orig. so named from the notion of the dropping of morbid matter from the blood into the joints. XIII. - OF. *goute* (mod. *goutte*) drop, gout :- L. *gutta* drop. Hence **gouty** XV.

govern rule with authority XIII; direct, regulate, sway XIV; (of grammatical regimen) XVI. - OF. *governer* (mod. *gouverner*) :- L. *gubernāre* steer, direct, rule - Gr. *kubernân* steer. So **governance** XIV. - OF. **governess** XV. Shortening of †*governeress* (XIV); see -ESS[1]. **government** XVI. - (O)F. **governor** XIII. - OF. *governeor* (mod. *gouverneur*) - L. *gubernātor*.

gowan (Sc. and north.) applied to various yellow and white field flowers. XVI. prob. alteration of (dial.) *gollan* (XIV) ranunculus, caltha, chrysanthemum, which is prob. rel. to *gold* in MARIGOLD.

gowk (dial.) cuckoo XIV; fool, half-wit XVII. - ON. *gaukr* = OE. *ġēac*, OS. *gāk*, OHG. *gouh* (in MHG. fool, G. *gauch*) :- Gmc. (exc. Gothic) **ʒaukaz*, of imit. orig.

gown XIV. - OF. *goune*, *gon(n)e* :- late L. *gunna* fur garment. Hence **gownsman** (earlier †*gownman*) †adult Roman XVI (tr. L. *togātus* 'gowned man'); civilian, opp. soldier; lawyer, clergyman; university man XVII.

grab XVI. prob. - MLG., MDu. *grabben*, to which there is a frequent. formation, Du., LG. *grabbeln* scramble for a thing, whence prob. (dial.) **grabble** (XVI) grope, scramble, etc.

grace favour XII; prayer of blessing or thanksgiving XIII; pleasing quality XIV. - (O)F. *grâce*, semi-pop. - L. *grātia*, f. *grātus* pleasing (see GRATEFUL). So **gracious** XIII. Hence **graceful** in casual use from XV till late XVI, when the present senses begin. **graceless** XIV.

grackle bird of any genus orig. included in *Gracula*. XVIII. - modL. *grācula*, fem. formed to corr. to L. *grāculus* jackdaw.

gradation †(rhet.) climax; †gradual progress; series of stages XVI; scale of degrees XVII; ablaut XIX. - L. *gradātiō*, *-ōn-*, f. *gradus* step; see -ATION. So **grade** †angular degree XVI; step, stage, DEGREE XVIII. - L. *gradus* or F. *grade*. Hence as vb. †in pp. admitted to a degree XVI; arrange in grades XVII. **-grade** adj. suffix repr. L. *-gradus* stepping, as in RETROGRADE, TARDIGRADE. **gradient** amount of inclination (of a road) to the horizontal. XIX. prob. f. *grade* with ending suggested by *salient*. **gradine** set of low steps or seats one above another; shelf at the back of an altar. XIX. - It. *gradino*, dim. of *grado* step. **gradual** †graded, in steps XV; proceeding by degrees XVII. - medL. *graduālis*, f. L. *gradus*. Also sb. (eccl.) portion of the Eucharistic office between the epistle and the gospel, orig. recited on the steps of the ambo. XVI. - medL. *graduāle*, n. of *graduālis* used sb. **graduate** (i) adj. and sb. (ii) vb. XV. (i) -, (ii) f. medL. *graduātus*, pp. (used sb.) of *graduārī* take a degree; see -ATE[2,3]. **gradus** short for *Gradus ad Parnassum* (steps to Parnassus), L. title of a dictionary of L. prosody used as an aid to versification. XVIII.

Gr(a)ecism Greek idiom or style. XVI. - F. *grécisme* or medL. *Græcismus*, f. *Græcus* GREEK;

see -ISM. So **Gr(a)ecize** XVII. - L. *Græcizāre*. **Gr(a)eco-** mod. comb. form of L. *Græcus*. XVII.

graffito pl. *-i* drawing or writing scratched on a wall. XIX. - It., irreg. f. *graffiare* scratch, f. *graffio* scratching, hook, of Gmc. orig.

graft[1] shoot inserted in another stock. XV. alt. of †*graff* (XIV) - OF. *grafe*, *grefe*, (also mod.) *greffe* - L. *graphium* - Gr. *graphion*, *grapheion* stylus, f. *gráphein* write; the transf. of meaning was suggested by the similarity of shape. Hence **graft** vb. XV. alt. of †*graff* (XIV).

graft[2] (orig. U.S.) means of making illicit profit; dishonest gains; (political) bribery. XIX. of unkn. orig.

grail[1] (eccl.) gradual. XIV. ME. *grael* - OF. :- ecclL. *gradāle*, for *graduāle* GRADUAL.

grail[2] cup used by Jesus Christ at the Last Supper, in which Joseph of Arimathea is said to have received his blood at the Crucifixion. XIV. ME. *greal*, *graal* - OF. *graal*, *grael*, *greel*, *greil* :- medL. *gradālis* dish, of unkn. orig.

grain A. small hard particle XIII; granular texture; †berry, grape; seed, spec. of corn or cereal XIV; smallest Eng. unit of weight XVI. B. kermes, which was thought to consist of seeds or berries (phr. *in grain*; cf. INGRAINED); (fast) dye XIV. In A - (O)F. *grain* :- L. *grānum* CORN[1]; in B - (O)F. *graine* :- Rom. **grāna* fem., orig. pl. of *grānum* n.

grallatorial (ornithology) wading. XIX. f. modL. *grallātōrius*, f. L. *grallātor* walker on stilts, f. *grallæ* stilts; see -ATOR, -IAL.

gralloch disembowel. XIX. - Gael. *grealach* entrails.

gram[1] chick-pea. XVIII. - Pg. †*gram*, *grão* :- L. *grānum* GRAIN.

gram[2] var. of GRAMME.

-gram repr. Gr. *grámma* something written, letter of the alphabet, rel. to *gráphein* write in (i) words directly derived from Gr., as *anagram*, *diagram*, *program(me)*, or modelled on Gr. types, as *chronogram*, *logogram*, (ii) words compounded with a numeral with *grámma* (or *grammḗ* line), as *monogram*, *pentagram*. Also, in the denominations of weight in the metric system, repr. GRAMME.

gramarye †grammar, learning XIV; (arch.) occult learning, magic XV. - AN. *gramarie* = OF. *gramaire* GRAMMAR; cf. GLAMOUR.

gramineous grassy. XVII. f. L. *grāmineus*, f. *grāmen*, *grāmin-* grass; see -EOUS.

grammalogue word represented by a single shorthand sign. XIX. irreg. f. Gr. *grámma* letter + *lógos* word.

grammar XIV. - AN. *gramere*, OF. *gramaire* (mod. *grammaire*) - L. *grammatica* - Gr. *grammatikḗ*, sb. use of fem. of *grammatikós* pertaining to letters (whence, through L. and F., **grammatical** XVI), f. *grámma*, *grammat-* (see -GRAM). So **grammarian** XIV. - OF. *gramarien* (mod. *grammairien*), f. *gramaire*.

gramme XVIII. - F. - Gr. (late L.) *grámma* small weight.

gramophone XIX. Formed by inverting the first and last sylls. of PHONOGRAM. Preceded by *graphophone* (XIX), from *phonograph*.

grampus name for several delphinoid cetaceans. XVI. Earliest forms *graundepose*, *grampoys*, alt. (by assim. to GRAND) of †*gra(s)peys* (XIV) - OF. *grapois*, *graspeis*, also *craspois* :- medL. *craspiscis*, f. L. *crassus* fat, CRASS, *piscis* FISH.

granadilla passion-fruit. XVIII. - Sp. *granadilla*, dim. of *granada* POMEGRANATE.

granary XVI. - L. *grānārium* (usu. pl. *-ia*), f. *grānum* GRAIN; see -ARY.

grand great, pre-eminent, principal XV; imposing, sublime XVIII. - F. *grand* large, tall, sublime, or its source L. *grandis* full-grown, abundant, tall, powerful, sublime. The use of F. *grand* to denote the second degree removed in ascent of relationship was adopted, *grand-père*, *grand'mère* being repr. by **grandfather, -mother** XVI, earlier †*graunt-* XV; it was extended (XVI) to the corr. degree of descent in **grandchild, -son, -daughter,** where F. has *petit* little.

grandee XVI. - Sp., Pg. *grande*, sb. use of *grande* adj. grand; the ending was illogically assim. to -EE[1].

grandeur †height XV; †eminence; transcendent or sublime greatness, lofty dignity. XVII. - (O)F. *grandeur*, f. *grand* great, GRAND.

grandiloquent XVI. f. L. *grandiloquus*, f. *grandis* great, GRAND + *-loquus* speaking, f. *loquī* to speak; see -ENT.

grandiose XIX. - F. - It. *grandioso*, f. *grande* grand; see -OSE[1].

grange (arch.) granary; farming establishment XIII; outlying farmhouse of an estate XIV. - (O)F. :- medL. *grānica*, sb. use of fem. of **grānicus* pert. to grain, f. *grānum* GRAIN.

granite XVII. - It. *granito* lit. grained, granular, pp. formation on *grano* grain. Hence **granitic** XVIII.

granny XVII (*-ee*). f. *grannam*, var. of *grandam* (- AN. *graund dame*; see GRAND, DAME) + -Y[6].

grant agree to, allow, concede XIII; bestow formally XIV. - OF. *gra(a)nter*, *greanter*, alteration of *creanter* guarantee, assure :- Rom. **crēdentāre*, f. *credent-*, prp. stem of L. *crēdere* believe, trust (see CREDIT). Hence **grant** sb. XIII.

granule XVII. - late L. *grānulum*, dim. of *grānum* GRAIN; see -ULE. So **granular** XVIII, **granulate, -ation** XVII, **granulose** XIX, **granulous** XVI.

grape berry of the vine XIII; morbid growth on the pastern of a horse XVI; more fully *grape-shot* (XVIII) cannon shot consisting of cast-iron balls connected together XVII. Earlier in *wingrape* 'wine-cluster', cluster of grapes (XIII). - OF. *grape* (mod. *grappe*) bunch of grapes; later in XIII used first in coll. pl., subsequently in sg. OF. *grape* was prob. a verbal sb. f. *graper* gather (grapes), f. *grap(p)e* hook, of Gmc. orig. Hence **grape-fruit** (orig. U.S.) XIX.

graph XIX. orig. (chem.) short for GRAPHIC *formula*, in which lines are used to indicate the connections of elements; hence in math.

-graph repr. F. *-graphe*, L. *-graphus* - Gr. *-graphos*, which was used (i) in the sense 'written', as *autógraphos* autograph, *kheirógraphos* chirograph, (ii) in the sense 'writing', 'describing', as *bibliográphos* writer of books, *geōgráphos* geographer. Several of the Gr. passive formations have been anglicized, and analogous formations have been made on Gr. models such as *lithograph*, *photograph*, which have been imitated in hybrid formations such as *pictograph*. Most of the current words in *-graph* are of the technical order and usu. denote a thing that records or expresses (as if in writing), e.g. *heliograph*, *ideograph*, *phonograph*, *seismograph*, *telegraph*. The Gr. active formations are usu. repr. by forms in **-grapher**, which furnish agent-nouns for formations in **-graphy**. Some words in *-graphy* denote processes or styles of writing or graphic representation, as *calligraphy*, *orthography*, *photography*, *typography*; but mostly they are names of sciences, as *bibliography*, *geography*, *lexicography*, *topography*. Hybrid formations like *stratigraphy* are few. The corr. adjs. end in **-graphic(al)**, with advs. in *-graphically*.

graphic †drawn with pencil or pen (rare); vividly descriptive XVII; pert. to drawing or painting XVIII; characterized by diagrams XIX. - L. *graphicus* - Gr. *graphikós*, f. *graphḗ* drawing, writing. So **graphical** XVII, **graphically** XVI.

graphite XVIII. - G. *graphit*, f. Gr. *gráphein* write (the stuff being used for pencils); see -ITE.

grapnel XIV. - AN. **grapenel*, f. synon. OF. *grapon* (mod. *grappin*), of Gmc. orig.; see -EL².

grapple grapnel. XVI. - OF. *grapil* - Pr., f. *grapa* hook, of Gmc. orig. Hence **grapple** vb. XVI.

grasp †clutch (intr.) XIV; seize with the hand XVI; fig. XVII. ME. *graspe*, *grapse*, perh. :- OE. **grǣpsan* :- Gmc. **ȝraipisōn*, parallel to **ȝraipōjan* GROPE; but perh. of LG. orig.

grass herbage for fodder OE.; grassy earth XIII; pasture XV; non-cereal gramineous plant XVI. OE. *græs*, *gærs* = OS. (Du.), (O)HG., ON., Goth. *gras* :- Gmc. **ȝrasam*, f. **ȝra-* **ȝrō-* (see GROW). So **grasshopper** XV. Extended form of †*grasshop*, OE. *gærshoppa* (f. *gærs* + *hoppa*, agent-noun of *hoppian* HOP¹). **grass widow** †unmarried woman who has cohabited XVI; married woman away from her husband XIX (first in India). The first el. may have alluded orig. to a bed of grass or hay. **grassy** XVI.

grate¹ †grating, grille XIV; †cage, prison XVI; barred frame for holding fuel XVII. - OF. :- Rom. **crāta*, **grāta*, for L. *crātis* hurdle.

grate² †scrape, scarify; rasp small XV; rub harshly *upon* XVI. - OF. *grater* (mod. *gratter*) :- Rom. **grattāre* - Frankish **krattōn* (G. *kratzen* scratch). So **grater** grating or rasping instrument. XIV. Partly - OF. *grateor*, *-our*, partly f. the above vb.; see -ER¹,².

grateful pleasing; thankful. XVI. f. †*grate* (XVI) - L. *grātus* (in the same senses), pp. formation corr. to Skr. *gūrtá-* welcome, agreeable, rel. to words of the Indo-Iran. and Baltic groups denoting 'praise'; the unusual formation with -FUL¹ may have been suggested by It. *gradevole* pleasing.

gratify †reward, recompense; give pleasure to XVI. - F. *gratifier*, or its source L. *grātificārī* do a favour to, make a present of, f. *grātus*; see GRATEFUL and -FY. So **gratification** XVI.

gratin (cookery) garnishing of grated or rasped material. XIX. - F., f. OF. *grater* GRATE².

gratis for nothing, freely. XV. - L. *grātīs*, reduction of *grātiīs*, abl. pl. of *grātia* favour, GRACE.

gratitude †favour, free gift; gratefulness. XVI. - F. *gratitude* or medL. *grātitūdō*, f. *grātus*; see GRATEFUL, -TUDE.

gratuity †graciousness, favour; gift, present. XVI. - (O)F. *gratuité* or medL. *grātuitās* gift, f. L. *grātus*; see GRATEFUL, -ITY. So **gratuitous** XVII. f. L. *grātuītus* freely given, spontaneous.

gravamen grievance or its presentation XVII; part of an accusation that bears most heavily XIX. - late L. *grāvāmen* physical inconvenience, in medL. grievance, f. L. *gravāre* weigh upon, oppress, f. *gravis* heavy, GRAVE³.

grave¹ place dug out for a burial. OE. *græf* = OS. *graf*, OHG. *grap* (G. *grab*) :- WGmc. **ȝraƀa* (cf. ON. *grǫf*, Goth. *graba* :- **ȝraƀō*); f. **ȝraƀ-* GRAVE².

grave² (dial.) dig OE.; (dial., orig. from ON.) bury XIII; (arch.) engrave OE. OE. str. vb. *grafan* = OS. *bigraƀan* (Du. *graven*), OHG. *graban* (G. *graben*), ON. *grafa*, Goth. *graban* dig :- Gmc. **ȝraƀan*; IE. cogns. are OSl. *-grebǫ* I dig, Latv. *grebju* I scrape. The strong pt. died out in XV; pp. *graven* survives as a literary arch.; wk. forms appeared in XIV in pt. and pp.

grave³ weighty, important; serious XVI; plain, sombre XVII; (gram.) opp. *acute* XVII. - (O)F. *grave* or L. *gravis* heavy, important, corr. to Skr. *gurú-*, Gr. *barús*, Goth. *kaurus* heavy.

grave⁴ clean (a ship's bottom) by burning and tarring; esp. in *graving dock*. XV. prob. f. dial. F. *grave*, var. of *grève* shore.

gravel XIII. - (O)F. *gravelle*, dim. of *grave* gravel, coarse sand; see GRAVE⁴, -EL². Hence **gravel-blind**, joc. intensive in Sh. 'Merchant of Venice' II ii 38 of SAND-BLIND.

graven see GRAVE².

gravid pregnant. XVI. - L. *gravidus* laden, pregnant, f. *gravis* heavy; see GRAVE³, -ID¹.

gravitate †exert weight or pressure; be affected by the force of gravity. XVII. f. pp. stem of modL. *gravitāre*, f. L. *gravitās* GRAVITY; see -ATE³. So **gravitation** XVII.

gravity †influence, authority; seriousness; weighty dignity XVI; physical weight, later only spec. XVII. - (O)F. *gravité* or L. *gravitās*, f. *gravis* heavy; see GRAVE³, -ITY.

gravure abbrev. of PHOTOGRAVURE. XIX.

gravy †dressing for white meats, etc. consisting of broth spiced XIV; fat and juices exuding from flesh during and after cooking XVI. ME. *graue(y)*, perh. originating in a misreading of *grane* - OF. *grané* (in printed texts often *gravé*), prob. f. *grain* spice; see GRAIN¹, -Y⁵.

gray see GREY. Hence **grayling** fish of silver-grey colour. XV.

graze¹ feed on herbage OE.; put to pasture XVI. OE. *grasian*, f. *græs* GRASS.

graze² touch lightly so as to abrade. XVII. The earliest application is to a shot or shaft glancing off a surface; perh. a spec. use of prec., as if 'take off the grass close to the ground'.

grazier one who grazes cattle for market. XVI. f. GRASS + -IER[1].

grease melted fat XIII; fat of a beast of the chase XIV. - AN. *grece, gresse*, (O)F. *graisse* :- Rom. **crassia*, f. L. *crassus* fat. Hence **grease** vb. XV. **greasy** XVI.

great (dial.) thick, coarse, bulky; large, of considerable size OE.; pregnant XII; important, eminent XIII. OE. *grēat* = OS. *grōt* (Du. *groot*), OHG. *grōz* (G. *gross*) :- WGmc. **ʒrautaz*, of unkn. orig. The use of the adj. to designate persons one degree further removed in ascending or descending relationship is after the use of F. *grand*. Hence **greatly** XII, **greatness** late OE.

greave (usu. pl.) armour for the leg below the knee. XIV. - OF. *greve* calf of the leg, shin, armour, of unkn. orig.

greaves fibrous refuse of tallow. XVII. - LG. *greven* pl., corr. to OHG. *griubo, griobo* (G. *griebe* refuse of lard or tallow), of unkn. orig.

grebe XVIII. - F. *grèbe*, of unkn. orig.

Grecian XVI. - OF. *grecien* or medL. **græciānus*, f. L. *Græcia* Greece; see -IAN.

greedy OE. *grēdiġ, grǣdiġ* = OS. *grādag*, OHG. *grātag*, ON. *gráðugr*, Goth. *grēdags* :- Gmc. **grǣðagaz, -ugaz*, f. **grǣðuz* hunger, greed (in OE. *grǣdum* d. pl. eagerly, ON. *gráðr*, Goth. *grēdus*), of unkn. orig. Hence **greed** sb., by backformation. XVII.

Greek native of Greece OE.; language of Greece XIV; cheat, sharper XVI; adj. XIV. OE. *Grēcas* (pl.; and so for the most part till XVI), corr. to MLG. *Grēke*, MDu. *Grieke*, G. *Grieche*, ON. *Grikkir* (pl.), of which the earlier forms are OE. *Crēcas*, OHG. *Chrēch*, Goth. *Krēks* :- Gmc. **Krēkaz* - L. *Græcus* (applied by the Romans to the people who called themselves *Hellēnes*; see HELLENE) - Gr. *Graikós*; cf. L. *Graius*, used (esp. pl.) as a poet. syn. of *Græcus*.

green of the colour of growing herbage, verdant OE.; fresh, young, unripe, immature XVII. OE. *grēne* = OS. *grōni* (Du. *groen*), OHG. *gruoni* (G. *grün*), ON. *grœnn* :- Gmc. **ʒrōnjaz*, f. **ʒrō-* (see GROW). Hence **greenery** XVIII. **greengage** XVIII. f. name of Sir William *Gage*. **greenhorn** perh. orig. ox with green (i.e. young) horns XV; inexperienced person XVII. **greening** †variety of pear; apple which is green when ripe. XVII. prob. - MDu. *groeninc* (Du. *groening*) kind of apple. **greenness** OE.

greet[1] address, salute, esp. with expressions of goodwill OE.; receive with welcome XVII. OE. *grētan*, **grœ̄tan* handle, touch, visit, attack, treat, salute = OS. *grōtian* call upon (Du. *groeten* salute), OHG. *gruozzen* address, attack (G. *grüssen* salute) :- WGmc. **ʒrōtjan* cry out, call upon, (hence) provoke to action, assail, address; perh. based on IE. **ghrōd- *ghrēd-* resound, repr. by Skr. *hrād-*. Some take this vb. and the next to have a common basis.

greet[2] (Sc.) weep. (i) OE. (Anglian) *grētan*, **grǣtan* (prob. str., but once wk. pt. *begrette*) = OS. *grātan* str., MHG. *grazen* (wk.) cry out, rage, storm, ON. *gráta* (str.), Goth. *grētan* (str.) :- Gmc. **ʒrǣtan*; cf. prec.; (ii) OE. *grēotan* (= OS. *griotan*), of uncert. orig.

gregarious f. L. *gregārius*, f. *grex, greg-* flock, herd (cf. OIr. *graig* herd of horses, Gr. *agorá* (place of) assembly); see -ARIOUS.

gremial pert. to the bosom or lap XVII; (hist.) 'internal', resident (member) XVI; sb. (eccl.) apron for a bishop's lap XIX. - medL. *gremiālis, -āle*, f. L. *gremium* lap, bosom; see -IAL.

grenade †pomegranate; small explosive shell. XVI. - F., alt. of OF. (*pume*) *grenate* POMEGRANATE after Sp. *granada*. So **grenadier** †soldier armed with grenades, (now) soldier of a regiment of guards. XVII. see -IER[2].

grenadine dress fabric. XIX. - F. *grenadine*, formerly *grenade* silk of a grained texture, f. *grain* GRAIN; see -INE[4].

grey, gray OE. *grǣġ* = MDu. *gra(u)* (Du. *grauw*), OHG. *grāo* (G. *grau*), ON. *grár* :- Gmc. **ʒrǣwaz*.

grid grating. XIX. Back formation from GRIDIRON.

griddle †gridiron XIII; circular plate for baking cakes on XIV. - OF. *gredil, gridil* gridiron (mod. *gril*) :- Rom. **crāticulum*, dim. of *crātis* hurdle, etc. See GRILL.

gridiron frame of parallel metal bars used for broiling. XIII (*gredire*). app. alt. of *gredile* GRIDDLE by assoc. with *ire(n)* IRON.

grief †hardship, suffering; †displeasure, grievance XIII; †hurt, mischief, injury; mental distress XIV. - AN. *gref*, OF. *grief* (mod. *grief* grievance, injury, complaint), f. *grever* cause injury or grief, harass :- Rom. **grevāre*, alt. of L. *gravāre*, f. *gravis* GRAVE[3]. So **grieve** †harass, trouble, hurt; affect with deep sorrow; provoke to anger XIII; feel or show grief XIV. - OF. *grever*. **grievance** †injury, distress XIII; †hurt, disease XIV; ground of complaint XV. - OF. *grevance*.

griffin, griffon[1], **gryphon** fabulous animal combining eagle and lion; vulture. XIV. - OF. *grifoun* (mod. *griffon*) :- Rom. **grȳphō, -ōn-*, augm. of late L. *grȳphus*, f. *grȳps, grȳph-* - Gr. *grúps*.

griffon[2] breed of dog. XIX. - F. *griffon* (applied to an Eng. dog) GRIFFIN.

grig †dwarf XIV; short legged hen XVI; young eel XVII. of unkn. orig. The phr. *merry grig* extravagantly lively person, synon. and contemp. with *merry Greek* (XVI), was perh. orig. an alteration of the latter.

grill gridiron. XVII. - (O)F. *gril*, earlier *grail*, *greil*, m. form based on fem. *grille* (see next). So **grill** vb. broil on a gridiron. XVII. - F. *griller*. Hence a new sb. *grill* broiled meat, etc. XVIII.

grille grating, lattice-screen. XVII. - (O)F. *grille*, earlier *graïlle* :- Rom. **grātīcula*, for L. *crātīcula*, dim. of *crātis* hurdle, etc.

grilse (Sc. and north.) young salmon for the year following its first return from the sea. XV. Of obscure orig.; the Sc. vars. †*girsil* (XV), †*grissil* (XVI) may be closer to the orig. form (cf. OF. *grisel* grey).

grim fierce, cruel OE.; stern or harsh of aspect or demeanour XIV; (of laughter, etc.) unrelenting XVII. OE. = OS. (Du.), OHG. *grim* (G. *grimm*), ON. *grimmr* :- Gmc. **ʒrimmaz*, f. **ʒrem-* **ʒram-* (whence OE. *gram* angry, *gremian* make angry) :- IE. **ghrem- *ghrom-* (whence Gr. *khremízein* neigh, OSl. *gromŭ* thunder).

grimace sb. XVII. - F. *grimace*, earlier †*grimache* - Sp. *grimazo* caricature, f. *grima* fright (- Gmc. stem of GRIM) with pejorative suffix *-azo* :- L. *-āceum* (cf. -ACEOUS). Hence, or - F. *grimacer*, **grimace** vb. XVIII.

grime soil with soot, etc. XV. - MLG., MDu. **grīmen*. Hence **grime** sb. XVI. **grimy** XVII.

grin draw back the lips and show the teeth, in pain or †anger OE., in a smile XV. OE. *grennian*, rel. to OHG. *grennan* mutter (MHG. *grennen* wail, grin) and OHG. *granōn* grunt (MHG. *grannen*), ON. *grenja* howl; f. Gmc. **ʒran-*. Cf. GROAN. Hence **grin** sb. XVII.

grind reduce to small particles; make a scraping or grating noise OE. (spec. gnash; also trans. XIV); sharpen the edge of XIII; work laboriously (at) XVIII. OE. str. vb. *grindan*, of which there are no Gmc. cogns. An IE. base **ghrendh-* is repr. by L. *frendere* rub away, gnash, Lith. *gréndžiu* I rub. Hence **grind** sb. hard task XIX. **grindstone** XIII.

gringo (among Spanish Americans) Anglo-American. XIX. transf. use of Sp. *gringo* gibberish.

grip sb. (i) OE. *gripe* grasp, clutch, corr. to OHG. *grif-* in comb., MHG. *grif* (G. *griff*) grasp, handle, claw, ON. *grip* grasp, clutch, *gripr* possession, property; (ii) OE. *gripa* handful, sheaf; both f. wk. base of *grīpan* GRIPE. So **grip** vb. OE. (late Nhb.) *grippa*.

gripe †grasp OE.; seize firmly XIII; †afflict XVI; pinch with pain XVII. OE. str. vb. *grīpan* = OS. *grīpan* (Du. *grijpen*), OHG. *grīfan* (G. *greifen*), ON. *grípa*, Goth. *greipan*; cogn. with Lith. *griebiù*. Cf. GROPE. Weak inflexions were established in XV. Hence **gripe** sb. XIV; in pl. griping pains, colic XVII.

grippe influenza. XVIII. - F., f. *gripper* seize - Gmc. **ʒripjan* GRIP.

grisaille painting in grey monochrome. XIX. - F., f. *gris* grey.

grisette French working-class woman. XVIII. - F., orig. inferior grey dress fabric, formerly the garb of women of the poorer classes, f. *gris* grey + -ETTE.

griskin lean part of pig's loin. XVII. Obscurely f. (dial.) *gris* pig, †occas. pork (- ON. *gríss*).

grisly causing horror (later in weaker sense). Late OE. *grislić*, f. wk. base of **grīsan* (in *āgrīsan* terrify) = MLG., MDu. *grīsen*; perh. partly aphetic of OE. *angrislić*.

grist †grinding OE.; corn to be ground XV. OE. *grist* :- Gmc. **ʒrinst-*, f. **ʒrindan* GRIND.

gristle cartilage. OE. *gristle* = MLG. *gristel*, *gerstel*, MHG. *gruschel*; similar synon. forms are OE. *grost*, OHG. *chrustila* (MHG. *krostel*, *krustel*); ult. orig. unkn.

grit sand, gravel, (now) minute stony particles OE.; coarse sandstone XIII; texture of stone XVI; (orig. U.S.) pluck, stamina XIX. OE. *grēot* = OS. *griot*, OHG. *grioz* (G. *griess*), ON. *grjót* :- Gmc. **ʒreutam* (cf. GROATS, GROUT[1]).

grizzle[1] grey. XV (earlier as sb. grey-haired old man XIV). - OF. *grisel*, f. *gris* grey - Gmc. **ʒrīsiaz* (OS., MLG. *grīs*), of unkn. orig. Hence **grizzled, grizzly** XVI. *Grizzly bear* XVIII.

grizzle[2] (dial.) grin XVIII; cry in a fretful or whining fashion XIX. of unkn. orig.

groan vb. OE. *grānian* :- **ʒrainōjan*, f. Gmc. **ʒrain- *ʒrīn-*. whence also OHG. *grīnan* grin with laughing or weeping (G. *greinen*), MHG. *grinnen* gnash the teeth. Cf. GRIN.

groat small coin. XIV. - MDu. *groot*, MLG. *grōte*, sb. uses of the adj. (= GREAT) in the sense 'thick'.

groats hulled grain. Late OE. *grotan* pl., rel. to *grot* fragment, particle, *grēot* GRIT, *grytt* bran, chaff, coarse oatmeal, and *grūt* GROUT[1].

grocer †dealer in gross; trader in spices, sugar, dried fruits, etc. XV. - AN. *grosser*, OF. *grossier* :- medL. *grossārius*, f. *grossus* GROSS[2]. The Grocers' Company consisted of wholesale dealers in foreign produce, whence the second sense. Hence **grocery** XV, **greengrocer** XVIII.

grog spirits (orig. rum) and water as served out to the Royal Navy. XVIII. Said to be from 'Old *Grog*' ', reputed nickname of the Admiral Vernon who gave the order in 1740 for the mixture to be used instead of neat spirit, derived from his wearing a *grogram* cloak. Hence **groggy** intoxicated XVIII; (of a horse) diseased or weak in the forelegs; shaky, tottering XIX.

grogram coarse mixed fabric. XVI (*grow graine*, *grograyn*, *grogerane*). - F. *gros grain* 'coarse grain' (see GROSS[2], GRAIN).

groin depression between abdomen and thigh XV; (archit.) intersection of two vaults XVIII. ME. *grynde*, early modE. *gryne*, in late XVI *groin*; perh. transf. use of OE. *grynde* ?orig. depression (recorded only in the sense 'abyss'), f. Gmc. **ʒrundu-* GROUND.

grommet var. of GRUMMET.

gromwell - plant of the genus *Lithospermum*. XIII. ME. *gromil* - OF. *gromil*, *grumil* (mod. *grémil*), repr. L. *milium* MILLET and a first el. of uncert. orig.

groom A. †boy XIII; †man XIV; B. †man-servant XIII (surviving in the spec. sense of horse attendant XVII); officer of the royal household XV; C. BRIDEGROOM XVII. of unkn. orig.

groove (dial.) mining shaft, mine XV; channel, hollow XVII. - Du. †*groeve* furrow, ditch (mod. *groef*) = OHG. *gruoba* (G. *grube* pit, ditch), ON. *gróf*, Goth. *grōba*; f. Gmc. **ʒrōb-*, rel. to **ʒrab-* GRAVE[1,2].

grope OE. *grāpian* = OHG. *greifōn* :- WGmc. **ʒraipōjan*, f. Gmc. **ʒraip- *ʒrīp-* (see GRIP[1], GRIPE).

grosbeak hawfinch, etc. XVII. - F. *grosbec*, f. *gros* large, GROSS[2] + *bec* BEAK.

groschen small German coin. XVII - G., alteration of late MHG. *gros(se)*, in medL. *denarius grossus* 'thick penny'; see GROSS[2].

gross[1] twelve dozen. XV. - F. *grosse*, sb. use (sc. *douzaine* dozen) of fem. of *gros* great; see next.

gross[2] Late ME. *groos* (XIV) became common first in XV in senses 'large, bulky' (now obs. or dial.), †'palpable, obvious', †'dense, thick', 'coarse', 'concerned with large masses'. - (O)F. *gros*, fem. *grosse* :- late L. *grossus*.

grot (poet.) grotto. XVI. - F. *grotte* - It. *grotta* = OF. *cro(u)te* :- Rom. **crupta*, **grupta* (L.

crypta) - Gr. *krúptē* vault. CRYPT. So **grotto** (rocky) cavern, imitation of this. XVII (earlier *grotta*).

grotesque sb. decorative painting or sculpture with fantastic interweaving of forms XVI; adj. pert. to work of such a character, fantastically extravagant XVII; ludicrously incongruous XVIII. Earliest forms *crotescque, -esco, grot(t)esco*; - F. *crotesque* - (with assim. to OF. *crote* GROT) It. *grottesca*, fem. of *grottesco*, f. *grotta*; finally assim. to F. *grotesque*; see GROT, -ESQUE. The special sense is said to be due to the Rom. application of *grotta* to chambers of old buildings revealed by excavation and containing mural paintings of a certain type.

grouch (U.S.) grumble, complain. XX. var. of *grutch* (XIII) - OF. *gruchier, grouch(i)er*, of unkn. orig.

ground A. bottom, now only of the sea OE.; pl. dregs, lees XIV; B. base, foundation, now mainly techn. or fig. (reason, motive XIII) OE.; C. surface of the earth OE.; specific portion of this XIV (pl. enclosed land attached to a building XV). OE *grund* = OS. *grund* (Du. *grond*), OHG. *grunt* (G. *grund*), Goth. **grundus* :- Gmc. **ʒrunduz*, rel. to ON. *grund* grassy plain, *grunnr* bottom. Hence **ground** vb. †lay the foundation of XIII; give a basis to XIV; put on the ground or ashore, strand XV.

groundling small fish such as gudgeon and loach XVII. cf. MDu. *grundelinck* (Du. *grondeling*), MHG. *grundelinc* (G. *gründling*) gudgeon; see GROUND, -LING[1]. The origin of the application to the frequenters of the pit of a theatre (Sh. 'Hamlet' III ii 12) is obscure.

groundsel plant of the genus *Senecio*. OE. *grundeswylige*, earlier *gundæswelg(i)æ*, perh. f. *gund* pus + **swulʒ-* **swelʒ-* SWALLOW[2], the etymol. meaning being 'pus-absorber', with ref. to its use in poultices to reduce abscesses; on this view, the later OE. form in *grund-* is due to assoc. with GROUND.

group assemblage of figures or objects in an artistic design XVII; assemblage of persons or things (gen.) forming a unity XVIII. - F. *groupe* - It. *gruppo*, of Gmc. orig. Hence, or - F., **group** vb. XVIII.

grouper marine food-fish XVII (*gro(o)per*). - Pg. *garupa*, prob. native S. Amer. name.

grouse[1] gallinaceous bird with feathered feet. XVI. The pronunc. points to an orig. *ū*, which is preserved (perh. locally) in such early forms as *grewes, groose*; of unkn. orig.

grouse[2] grumble. XIX. orig. a soldier's word; its resemblance in form to Norman dial. *groucer*, OF. *groucier*, var. of *grouchier* (see GRUDGE) is remarkable, but immediate connection with it seems impossible.

grout[1] (now obs. or dial.) coarse meal; infusion of malt OE.; coarse porridge XVI; sediment XVII. OE. *grūt*, corr. to MDu. *grūte, gruut* coarse meal, peeled grain, malt, yeast (Du. *gruit* dregs), MHG. *grūz* (G. *grauss*) grain, small beer; f. **ʒrūt-*, var. of **ʒraut-* **ʒreut-* **ʒrut-* (see GRIT, GROATS). The later meanings are prob. due to Scand. (cf. ON. *grautr* porridge) and Du.

grout[2] thin mortar. XVII. perh. a use of prec.; but cf. F. dial. *grouter* grout a wall.

grove small wood. OE. *grāf*, rel. to *grǣfa* brushwood, thicket.

grovel XVI. Back-formation from **grovelling** adj. prone (XVI), attrib. use of the †adv. face downward, in a prone position (XIV), earlier †*grovellings* (XIII), f. *gruf* on the face, on the belly (for phr. *on grufe, ogrufe* - ON. *á grúfu*) + -LING[2].

grow pt. *grew* pp. *grown* (orig.) show the development characteristic of living things. OE. str. vb. *grōwan* = MDu. *groeyen* (Du. *groeien*), OHG. *gruoan*, ON. *gróa*; CGmc., f. **ʒrō-*. Hence **growth** XVI.

growl make a guttural sound. XVIII. Cf. late ME. *grolle, groule*, and *gurle* rumble, AN. *growler* make the cry of the crane, OF. *grouller* grumble, scold; but the modern word is prob. an independent imit. formation.

groyne timberwork or masonry run out into the sea. XVI. transf. use of (dial.) *groin* (XIV) snout - (O)F. *groin* (also †cape, promontory) :- Rom. **grunnium*, f. L. *grunnīre* grunt.

grub[1] †dwarfish fellow XIV; insect larva XV; (sl.) food (as grubs are for birds) XVII. Occurs as a surname (*Grubbe*) XIII, prob. orig. as a nickname, and presumably f. next, but the sense-development is not clear.

grub[2] dig (on the surface) XIII; labour ploddingly XVIII. perh. to be referred to an OE. **grybban* :- **grubbjan*, f. Gmc. **ʒrub-*, rel. to **ʒrab-* GRAVE[1,2] (cf. OHG. *grubilōn* dig, search closely, MDu. *grobben* scrape together, Du. *grobbelen* root out). Hence **grubber** XIV; survives esp. in *money-grubber*.

Grub Street name of a street near Moorfields, London (now Milton Street), once inhabited by inferior and needy writers, transf. tribe of poor authors and literary hacks. XVII.

grudge †murmur, grumble; be unwilling to grant. XV. Alteration of †*grutch* (XIII) - OF. *grouchier* (of unkn. orig.).

gruel †fine meal; liquid food made from oatmeal. XIV. - OF. *gruel* (mod. *gruau*) :- Rom. **grūtellum*, dim. f. Gmc. **ʒrūt-* GROUT[1].

gruesome inspiring awe or horror. XVI (*growsome*). orig. north. and Sc.; f. *grue* XIII, now Sc. and north., feel horror - Scand. word repr. by OSw. *grua*, ODa. *grue* (= OHG. *ingrūēn* shudder, G. *grauen* be awed, shudder, Du. *gruwen* abhor); see -SOME[1].

gruff (Sc. and techn.) coarse-grained XVI; rough and surly XVII. First in Sc. and prob. orig. in commercial use - Du. *grof* = MLG. *grof* coarse, (O)HG. *grob* :- WGmc. **ʒaχruba*, f. **ʒa-* Y- + **χrub-* **χreub-* (OE. *hrēof* rough, scabby, etc.).

grumble XVI. frequent. f. †*grumme* (XV-XVI) + -LE[3]; cf. (M)Du. *grommen*, MLG. *grommelen*, G. *grummeln*; f. imit. Gmc. **ʒrum-* (cf. GRIM).

grume clot of blood. XVII. - L. *grūmus* little heap, rel. to OE. *crūma* CRUMB. So **grumous** XVII. - modL.

grummet, grommet (naut.) ring of rope, etc. XV. - F. †*grom(m)ette, gourmette* chain joining the ends of a bit, f. *gourmer* curb, bridle, of unkn. orig.

grumpy XVIII. prob. of dial. orig.; f. *grump*, as

in †*humps and grumps* surly or ill-tempered remarks (of imit. orig.); see -Y[1].

Grundy surname of an imaginary *Mrs Grundy* who is proverbially referred to as a personification of the tyranny of social opinion; derived from T. Morton's play 'Speed the Plough' (1798), in which Dame Ashfield, constantly fearing the sneers of her neighbour Mrs Grundy, freq. asks 'What will (would) Mrs Grundy say?'

grunt make the characteristic sound of a pig. OE. *grunnettan* = OHG. *grunnizōn* (G. *grunzen*), intensive formation on the imit. base **ʒrun-* (OE. *grunian* grunt, OHG. *grun* wailing, MHG. *grunnen*); cf. DISGRUNTLED.

Gruyère cheese orig. made in the district of *Gruyère*, in Switzerland. XIX.

gryphon see GRIFFIN.

grysbok S. Afr. antelope. XVIII. - Afrikaans, f. Du. *grijs* GREY + *bok* BUCK.

guaiacum tree, wood, and resin of the West Indies. XVI. modL., f. Sp. *guayaco, guayacán*, of Haitian orig. Also anglicized **guaiac** (XVI).

guana see IGUANA.

guanaco kind of llama. XVII. - Quechua *huanaco, -acu*.

guano natural manure found on islands about Peru XVII; artificial (fish-)manure XIX. - Sp. *guano* - Quechua *huanu* dung.

guarantee party giving security XVII; act of giving security, security given XVIII; something providing security XIX. The earliest forms, *garanté, garante*, are perh. - Sp. *garante* = F. *garant* WARRANT; in its later use the word was identified with F. *garantie* GUARANTY. Hence as vb. be a guarantee for XVIII; secure (a person or thing) in possession XIX.

guaranty security, warranty, undertaking by a guarantor XVI; something that guarantees XVII. - AN. *guarantie*, (O)F. *garantie*, var. of *warantie* WARRANTY.

guard †custody; protector, defender XV; body of persons as defenders; protection, defence XVI. - (O)F. *garde*, f. *garder* :- Rom. **wardāre* - Frankish **wardōn* (cf. WARD[2]). So **guard** vb. XVI. f. the sb. or - (O)F. *garder*, †*guarder*. **guardian** XV. ME. *gardein* - AN. *gardein*, OF. *garden* (mod. *gardien* from XIII, with assim. of suffix to *-ien* -IAN, which was followed in Eng.).

guava tropical Amer. tree. XVI (*guayava, -avo*). - Sp. *guayaba, -abo*, of S. Amer. orig.

gubernatorial (chiefly U.S.). XVIII. f. L. *gubernātor* GOVERNOR + -IAL.

gudgeon[1] small freshwater fish XV; bait; gullible person XVI. Late ME. *gogen, gojo(u)n* - (O)F. *goujon* :- L. *gōbiō, -ōn-*, f. *gōbius* GOBY.

gudgeon[2] pivot of metal, etc. XIV. - (O)F. *goujon* pin, dowel, tenon, dim. of *gouge* GOUGE.

Guelder rose XVI (*Gelders Rose*). - Du. *geldersche roos*, f. *Gelderland* or *Gelders*, province of Holland.

guerdon sb. (arch.) reward. XIV. - OF. *guer(e)don* :- Rom. (medL.) *widerdōnum* - WGmc. **widarlōn* (= OHG. *widarlōn*, OE. *wiðerlēan*, f. *wiðer* again + *lēan* payment) with assim. of the second el. to L. *dōnum* gift. So as vb. XIV.

guer(r)illa irregular war carried on by small bodies; (transf.) one engaged in such warfare. XIX. - Sp. *guerrilla*, dim. of *guerra* WAR.

guess[1] †take aim XIII; form an approximate judgement or estimate of XIV. ME. *gesse*, with early var. *agesse*; perh. orig. naut. and - vars. with *-e-* of MLG., MDu. (Du., Fris.) *gissen*, or OSw. *gissa*, ODa. *gitse*; ult. f. base of GET. So **guess** sb. XIV.

guess[2] (with var. *guest*) in **guess-rope** XVII (*guestrope*), **guess-warp** XV (*gyes warpe*), rope for steadying a boat in tow, etc.; of uncert. orig.

guest XIII. - ON. *gestr*; superseding OE. *ġ(i)est* = OS., OHG. (Du., G.) *gast*, Goth. *gasts* :- Gmc. **ʒastiz* :- IE. **ghostis*, repr. also by L. *hostis* enemy, orig. stranger, OSl. *gostĭ* guest, friend, and perh. by Gr. *xénos* stranger.

guffaw sb. and vb. XVIII. orig. Sc., of imit. orig.; cf. the earlier Sc. synon. *gawf* (XVI).

guide direct the course of. XIV. - (O)F. *guider*, alteration of †*guier* :- Rom. **wīdāre* - Gmc. **wītan*, f. **wīt-*, gradation-var. of **wit-* (see WIT[2]), repr. by OE., OS. *wītan* blame, Goth. *fraweitan* avenge, *fairweitjan* gaze upon (cf. the meanings of other derivs. of this base, OE. *wīse* direction, WISE[1], *wissian* direct, guide, G. *weisen* indicate, direct). So **guide** sb. XIV. - (O)F. *guide* - It. *guida*.

guidon pennant broad next the staff and pointed at the other end. XVI. - F. - It. *guidone*, f. *guida* GUIDE.

guild, gild[2] confraternity for mutual aid. XIV. The present form is prob. - MLG., MDu. *gilde* (Du. *gild*) :- **ʒelðjōn*, rel. to OE. *ġi(e)ld* payment, offering, sacrifice, idol, (also) guild, OS. *geld* payment, sacrifice, reward, OHG. *gelt* payment, tribute (Du., G. *geld* money), ON. *gjald* payment, Goth. *gild* tribute :- Gmc. **ʒelðam*. The base **ʒelð-* is prob. to be taken in the sense 'pay, offer' (cf. YIELD), so that the sb. would primarily mean an association of persons contributing to a common object.

guilder coin of the Netherlands. XV (*guldren*; later *gildren, gilder*). alt. of Du. *gulden* (see GULDEN).

guile XIII. - OF. *guile*, prob. of Gmc. orig.

guillemot auk of the genus *Uria* or *Cepphus*. XVII. - F. *guillemot*, deriv. (perh. alt. of an orig. imit. word) of *Guillaume* William.

guillotine machine with knife blade for beheading. XVIII. - F., f. name of Joseph-Ignace *Guillotin*, French doctor who recommended its use.

guilt †offence, crime OE.; †responsibility for something XII; †desert XIII; fact of having committed an offence XIV; state of having wilfully offended XVI. OE. *gylt*, of unkn. orig. Hence **guilty** OE. *gyltiġ*.

guimp var. of GIMP.

guinea name of a portion of the west coast of Africa, applied to things derived thence (or, with vague reference, from some other distant country) as *Guinea fowl* (XVIII), *Guinea hen* (XVI), *Guinea pig* (XVII), *Guinea worm* (XVII). The gold coin named *guinea* was first struck in 1663 'in the name and for the use of the Company of Royal Adventurers trading with Africa', being intended for the Guinea trade and made of gold from Guinea.

guipure kind of lace and of gimp. XIX. - (O)F. *guipure*, f. *guiper* cover with silk, wool, etc. - Gmc. **wīpan* wind round.

guise style, fashion. XIII. - (O)F. :- Rom. **wīsa* - Gmc. **wīsōn* WISE[1]. Cf. DISGUISE.

guitar XVII (*guittara, guitarra, g(h)ittar*). - (partly through F. *guitare*) Sp. *guitarra* - Gr. *kithárā*; cf. CITHER, ZITHER.

gulch (U.S.) deep ravine. XIX. perh. f. dial. vb. *gulch* swallow, sink in.

gulden coin of Netherlands and Germany, orig. of gold, later of silver. XVI. - Du., G. *gulden*, sb. use of adj. GOLDEN = OE. *gylden* (Gmc. **ʒulþinaz*).

gules (her.) red. XIV. - OF. *go(u)les* (mod. *gueules*), pl. of *gole, gueule* throat (cf. GULLET), used, like medL. pl. *gulæ*, for pieces of fur used as a neck-ornament and dyed red.

gulf kind of bay; chasm, abyss. XIV. - (O)F. *golfe* - It. *golfo* :- Rom. **colp(h)us* - Gr. *kólpos*, (late) *kólphos* bosom, fold, gulf.

gull[1] (dial.) unfledged bird; gosling. XIV. prob. sb. use of †*gull* yellow (- ON. *gulr*). Hence, perh. partly the use of *gull* for 'credulous person, dupe' (late XVI), but cf. the somewhat earlier *gull* vb. dupe, cheat, surviving in **gullible** XIX, which itself may be a transf. use of †*gull* vb. swallow (XVI), rel. to †*gull* sb. throat, gullet (XV) - OF. *go(u)le* (see GULLET).

gull[2] long-winged web-footed sea-bird. XV. prob. - W. *gwylan*, Cornish *guilan* :- Celt. **voilenno-*.

gullet oesophagus XIV (*golet*); †water-channel XVI. - OF. **golet, goulet*, dim. of *go(u)le* (mod. *gueule*) :- L. *gula* throat, rel. to OIr. *gelim* I swallow, OE. *ċeole*, OS., OHG. *kela* (G. *kehle*) throat; see -ET.

gully †gullet XVI; channel or ravine worn by water XVII; deep gutter XVIII. - F. *goulet* neck of a bottle, outlet, narrow passage of water; see prec.

gulp swallow hastily or greedily XV; gasp, choke XVI. prob. - MDu. *gulpen* swallow, guzzle, of imit. orig.

gum[1] †inside of mouth or throat OE.; firm flesh in which the teeth are fixed. XIV. OE. *gōma*, corr. to OHG. *guomo* (MHG. *guome*) gum, ON. *gómr* roof or floor of the mouth, finger-tip, rel. to OHG. *goumo* (G. *gaumen*).

gum[2] viscid secretion from trees. XIV. - (O)F. *gomme* :- Rom. **gumma*, for L. *gummi*, var. of *cummi* - Gr. *kómmi*, of Egyptian orig. Hence **gummy** XIV. **gum** vb. †treat with aromatic gums XV; fasten or stiffen with gum XVI.

gum[3] XIX. (sl.) alt. of GOD, in *by* or *my gum*.

gumbo (U.S.) okra plant or pods; soup thickened with the pods; (geol.) local clay or mud. XIX. Of Negro (Afr.) orig.

gumption common sense XVIII; in painting, a vehicle for colour XIX. orig. Sc.; also *rum(ble)-gumption*; of unkn. orig.

gun heavy piece of ordnance, cannon XIV; †large engine of war; portable fire-arm XV. ME. *gunne, gonne*; perh. repr. pet-form (**Gunna*) of the Scand. female name *Gunnhildr* (f. *gunnr* + *hildr*, both meaning 'war'). Hence **gunner** XIV. Whence **gunnery** XVII, **gunpowder, -shot** XV, **-smith** XVI, **-stock** XV. So **gun** vb. XVII.

gunwale, gunnel upper edge of a ship's side, formerly serving to support the guns. XV (*gonne walles*). f. GUN + WALE.

gunyah Australian hut. XIX. - Austral. aboriginal name.

gup (sl., orig. Anglo-Indian) gossip; (hence) vapid talk, blather. XIX. - Hind.

gurgitation †swallowing XVI (rare); surging up and down, ebullient motion. XIX. - modL. **gurgitātiō, -ōn-*, f. late L. *gurgitāre* engulf, f. *gurges, gurgit-* gulf, abyss.

gurgle †gargle (rare); make the sound of bubbling liquid. XVI. prob. imit., if not directly - similarly formed vbs., e.g. MLG., Du. *gorgelen*, G. *gurgeln*, and It. *gorgogliare* :- Rom. **gurguliāre*, f. L. *gurguliō* gullet.

gurnard, gurnet fish of the family Triglidae. XIV. - OF. *gornart*, for **gronart*, f. *gronir*, var. of *grondir* :- L. *grundīre, grunnīre* GRUNT; see -ARD. The fish is so named because it makes a grunting sound when caught.

guru Hindu spiritual teacher. XVII. - Hind. *guru*, sb. use of Skr. *gurú-* weighty, grave, dignified.

gush flow or rush out violently. XIV. prob. imit.

gusset flexible piece between two pieces of mail XV; triangular piece let into a garment XVI. - (O)F. *gousset* crescent-shaped piece of armour under the armpit, piece of cloth let in, formally dim. of *gousse* pod, shell (though this is much later), of unkn. orig.

gust XVI. - ON. *gustr*, f. **ʒus-*, weak grade of the base of ON. *gjósa* gush.

gustation tasting, taste. XVI. - L. *gustātiō, -ōn-*, f. *gustāre*, f. *gustus*; see next and -ATION. So **gustative, gustatory** XVII.

gusto taste, liking; keen relish; style of a work of art XVII. - It. :- L. *gustus* taste, rel. to CHOOSE.

gut (pl.) bowels OE.; (sg.) intestine XIV; narrow passage or channel XVI. OE. pl. *guttas*, prob. f. base **ʒut-* of OE. *ġēotan* pour (see FOUND[3]). Hence as vb. XIV.

gutter †watercourse XIII; shallow trough to carry away water XIV. - AN. *gotere*, OF. *gotiere* (mod. *gouttière*) :- Rom. **guttāria* (cf. -ARY), f. L. *gutta* drop. Hence **gutter** vb. channel XIV; stream XVI; (of a candle) melt rapidly by being channelled on one side XVIII. **gutter-snipe** common snipe, also called *mire snipe*; gatherer of refuse, street urchin. XIX. f. *gutter* in dial. sense of 'mud, filth'.

guttle eat greedily. XVII. f. GUT, after *guzzle*.

guttural pert. to the throat. XVI. - F. *guttural* or modL. *gutturālis*, f. *guttur* throat; see -AL[1].

guy[1] (naut.) rope, chain, etc., used to steady a thing. First in *guy-rope* (*girap* XIV, *gyerope* XV), prob. of LG. orig.; cf. Du. *gei* brail.

guy[2] effigy of *Guy* Fawkes; grotesque person, 'fright'; (U.S.) man. XIX. Hence **guy** vb. (U.S.) ridicule. XIX.

guzzle XVI. poss. - OF. *gosiller*, a deriv. of *gosier* throat, but found only in the senses 'chatter' and 'vomit'.

gwyniad fish of the salmon kind with white flesh. XVII. - W., f. *gwyn* white.

gybe, jibe (naut.) swing from one side of the vessel to the other, as a sail; put (a boat) about. XVII. - Du. †*gijben* (mod. *gijpen*).

gymkhana in India, public resort for games; in Europe, athletic sports display, meeting for horse-riding competition. XIX. alt., by assim. to *gymnastic*, of Hind. *gendkhāna* 'ball-house', racket court.

gymnasium XVI. - L. - Gr. *gumnásion*, f. *gumnázein* train, f. *gumnós* naked. So **gymnast** XVI. - F. *gymnaste* or Gr. *gumnastḗs* trainer of athletes. **gymnastic** adj. and sb. XVI (sb. pl. XVII).

gymno- comb. form of Gr. *gumnós* naked, in many nat. hist. terms, the earliest of which is *gymnospermous* naked-seeded (XVIII).

gymnosophist ascetic Hindu philosopher who wore little or no clothing. XIV. (later - F. *gymnosophiste*) - L. (pl.) *gymnosophistæ* - Gr. (pl.) *gumnosophistai*, f. *gumnós* GYMNO- + *sophistḗs* SOPHIST.

gynaeceum (antiq.) women's apartments XVIII; (bot.) female organs (usu. sp. *gynoecium*, by assim. to Gr. *oikíon* house) XIX. - L. - Gr. *gunaikeîon*, f. *gunḗ*, *gunaik-* woman (see QUEAN).

gynaeco-, U.S. **-eco-** repr. Gr. *gunaiko-*, comb. form of *gunḗ* woman, female (see QUEAN), as in **gynaecocracy** female rule (XVII). - F. *gynécocratie* or modL. *gynæcocratia* - Gr. **gynaecology** XIX.

gyno- before a vowel **gyn-,** shortened form of GYNAECO-; used in bot. terms to denote 'pistil', 'ovary'. So **-gynous** repr. Gr. *-gunos*, used for 'having such-and-such pistils or female organs', e.g. *androgynous*, *monogynous*.

gyp (at Cambridge and Durham Univ.) college servant. XVIII. perh. short for †*gippo* scullion (XVII), transf. use of †*gippo* tunic - (O)F. *jupeau*.

gypsum hydrated calcium sulphate, from which plaster of Paris is made. XVII. - L. - Gr. *gúpsos*, of Sem. orig. So **gypseous** XVII. f. late L. *gypseus*.

gypsy see GIPSY.

gyrate move in a circle or spiral. XIX. f. pp. stem of late L. *gȳrāre*, f. *gȳrus* - Gr. *gûros* ring, circle; see -ATE[3]. So **gyration** XVII. - late L. **gyre** revolution, whirl, circle. XVI. - L. *gȳrus*. **gyro-** comb. form of Gr. *gûros*.

gyrfalcon var. of GERFALCON.

gyve (arch.) fetter. XIII. of unkn. orig. Hence vb. XIII.

H

ha excl. denoting surprise, joy, scorn, suspicion, etc. XIII; †eh? XVI; in hesitating speech XVII. So in many other langs., but not found in OE. in its simple form (cf. HA-HA[1]).

habeas corpus (leg.) writ requiring a person to be brought before the court. XV. First words of the writ beginning *Habeas corpus ad subjiciendum* (etc.) you shall produce the body (of the person concerned, in court) to undergo (what the court may award); L. *habeās*, 2nd pers. sg. pres. subj. of *habēre* have, *corpus* body.

haberdasher XIV. perh. - AN. **haberdasser*, **hapertasser* (cf. *haberdasshrie* XV), presumably f. *hapertas* (XV), of unkn. orig. and uncert. meaning (Eng. †*haberdash* was used for 'small wares' XV-XVII); see -ER[2]. So **haberdashery** XVI.

habergeon sleeveless coat of armour. XIV. - (O)F. *haubergeon*, f. OF. *hauberc* HAUBERK; cf. -OON.

habiliment equipment; †pl. munitions of war; pl. apparel. XV. - OF. *abillement* (later and mod. *habillement*), f. *habiller* render fit, fit out, (hence, by assoc. with *habit*) clothe, dress, f. *habile* ABLE; see -MENT.

habilitate qualify. XVII. f. pp. stem of medL. *habilitāre*, f. *habilitās* ABILITY; see -ATE[3].

habit A. apparel, dress XIII; B. mental constitution XIV; settled disposition, custom XVI. ME. (*h*)*abit* - OF. *abit* (later and mod. *habit*) :- L. *habitus*, f. *habit-*, pp. stem of *habēre* have, hold, refl. be constituted, be. The range of meaning (in modF. distributed between *habit* dress and *habitude* custom) was fully developed in L. So **habit** vb. A. †dwell (cf. INHABIT) XIV; B. dress XVI. - (O)F. *habiter* - L. *habitāre*. **habitation** XIV. **habitat** XVIII. - L. 'dwells', 3rd pers. sg. pres. ind. of *habitāre* dwell, inhabit; from its use in floras and faunas to introduce the place of occurrence of a species (e.g. 'Common Primrose. Habitat in sylvis'). **habitual** †pert. to the inward disposition XVI; pert. to habit, customary XVII. - medL. *habituālis*. So **habituate** XVI. f. pp. stem of late L. *habituāre*. **habitué** habitual visitor. XIX. - F., pp. of *habituer*. **habitude** constitution, temperament XIV; disposition, habit XVII.

hachure (pl.) lines used in hill-shading in physical geography. XIX. - F. *hachure*, f. *hacher* HATCH[3]; see -URE.

hacienda XVIII. - Sp., 'domestic work, landed property' :- L. *facienda*, n. pl. of gerundive of *facere* DO[1].

hack[1] cut with heavy blows XII; break up (ground), etc. XVII. OE. (*tō*)*haccian* cut in pieces = MLG., MDu., (M)HG. *hacken* (Du. *hakken*); WGmc. deriv. of imit. base **χak-*; cf. synon. OE. *hæċċan*, OHG. *hecken*. So **hack** sb. tool for breaking or chopping up XIII; gash, cut, notch XVI. Partly - MLG. *hakke* mattock; partly f. the vb.

hack[2] board for a hawk's meat XVI; rack XVII. var. of HATCH[1].

hack[3] from XVII in various senses of HACKNEY (esp. 'riding-horse' and 'drudge'), of which it is a shortening. Hence vb. make a hack of, etc. XVIII.

hackle flax-comb; long feathers on the neck of a domestic cock, etc. XV. var. of *hatchel* (XVII), *hechel* (XIII) :- OE. **hæċel*, corr. to (M)LG., (M)Du. *hekel*, (M)HG. *hechel* :- WGmc. **χakila*, f. **χak-* HOOK.

hackney riding-horse, esp. for hire XIV; †common drudge, prostitute XVI; short for *hackney-coach* XVII. In AN. *hakenei* (XIV), AL. *hakeneius* (XIII); perh. f. ME. *Hakenei* Hackney in Middlesex.

had see HAVE.

haddock XIV. In AL. *haddocus* (XIII); prob. - AN. *hadoc*, var. of OF. (*h*)*adot*, pl. *hadoz*, *haddos*, of unkn. orig.

Hades XVI. - Gr. *Háidēs*, of unkn. orig.

hadji pilgrim to the tomb of Mohammed. XVII.- (partly through Turk. *hacı*) Pers. *hājī*, f. Arab. *ḥājj*.

h(a)ematite ferric oxide as ore. XVII. - L. *hæmatītēs* - Gr. *haimatī́tēs* blood-like, f. *haima*, *haimat-* blood; see -ITE.

h(a)emat(o)-, h(a)em(o)-, comb. forms of Gr. (*h*)*aîma* blood, as in *ha*(*e*)*moglobin*, *ha*(*e*)*maturia* XIX. **h(a)emorrhage** XVII (earlier *emorogie*, *hemoragie*). - F. *hémorr*(*h*)*agie*, †*emorogie* - L. *hæmorrhagia* - Gr. *haimorrhagíā*, f. *haimo-* + **rhag-*, base of *rhēgnúnai* break, burst. **h(a)emorrhoid** XIV. ME. *emeroudis*, whence *emerods* (XVI-XVII) - OF. *emeroyde*, later *hémorrhoïdes* (XVI) - L. *hæmorrhoida* - Gr. *haimorrhoís* discharging blood, pl. (as sb.) *-oídes* bleeding piles, f. *haimo-* + **rhoϝ-* flow.

hafnium modL., f. *Hafnia*, L. name of Copenhagen (Køben*havn*), Denmark; see -IUM.

haft handle. OE. *hæft*(*e*), corr. to MLG. *hechte* (Du. *hecht*, *heft*), OHG. *hefti* (G. *heft*), ON. *hepti* :- Gmc. **χaftjam*, f. **χaf-* HEAVE; see -T[1].

hag[1] female evil spirit XIII; repulsive old woman XIV(?). ME. *hegge*, *hagge*; rare before XVI. perh. shortening of OE. *hægtesse*, *hegtes* fury, witch = MDu. *haghetisse* (Du. *hecse*), OHG. *hagazissa* (G. *hexe*), of unkn. orig.

hag[2] (Sc. and north.) †gap, chasm XIII; piece of soft bog XVII; spot of firmer ground in a peat bog XIX. - ON. **haggw-*, *hǫgg* gap, breach, orig. cutting blow (whence the Sc. and north. Eng. senses 'cutting, hewing', 'cut wood'), f. **haggwa*, *hǫggva* HEW.

haggard (of a hawk) untamed, wild XVI; †gaunt, lean; wild-looking XVII. - (O)F. *hagard*, of uncert. orig.; see -ARD. Later infl. in sense by HAG[1] (for which *haggard* occurs XVII-XVIII).

haggis XV (*hagese*, *hagas*). of unkn. orig.

haggle mangle with cuts XVI; wrangle in

bargaining XVII. f. dial. *hag* cut (XIV - ON. **haggw- hǫggva* HEW) + -LE[3].

hagio- repr. Gr. *hágios* holy, used for 'saint' in **hagiography, hagiology** (XIX) and derivs. **hagiographa** books of the O.T. not included in the Law and the Prophets. XVI - late L. - Gr., 'sacred writings'. **hagioscope** opening in the wall of an aisle, etc., supposed to provide a view of the high altar (also called *squint*). XIX.

ha-ha[1] excl. OE. *ha ha* (see HA).

ha-ha[2] sunk fence. XVIII. - F. *haha* (XVII), perh. so named from the expression of surprise at meeting the obstacle; redupl. of HA.

hail[1] frozen vapour falling in pellets. OE. *hæ̆gl*, corr. to OS., OHG. *hagal* (Du., G. *hagel*), ON. *hagl* :- Gmc. **haʒ(a)laz, -am*, rel. to Gr. *kákhlēx* pebble. Hence **hail** vb. XV.

hail[2] excl. of salutation. XII. ellipt. use of †*hail* adj. (cf. WASSAIL) - ON. *heill* WHOLE. Hence **hail** vb. XII.

hair OE. *hǣr, hēr* = OS., OHG. *hār* (Du., G. *haar*), ON. *hár* :- Gmc. **χǣram*, of unkn. orig. The present sp. and pronunc. are abnormal (for **here* or **hear*) and are supposed to be due to assim. to †*haire* hair shirt - (O)F., of Gmc. orig. Hence **hair(s)breadth** XVI (earlier *hairbrede* XV). **hairy** XIII.

hake cod-like fish. XV. perh. for **hakefish*, f. (dial.) *hake* hook (- ON. *haki*; see HOOK).

halberd, halbert combined spear and battle-axe. XV. - F. *hallebarde*, †*alabarde* - It. *alabarda* - MHG. *helmbarde* (G. *hellebarde*), f. *helm* handle, HELM[2] + *barde, barte* hatchet (rel. to *bart* BEARD).

halcyon bird fabled to breed on the sea. XIV (*alceon*). - L. *(h)alcyon* - Gr. *alkuṓn* kingfisher (*halkuṓn* by assoc. with *háls* sea and *kúōn* conceiving), rel. to L. *alcēdō*. *Halcyon days* 14 days during which the kingfisher broods and the sea is calm. XVI.

hale[1] (dial.) sound, whole XIII; in robust health XVIII: ME. *hāl*, north. var. of WHOLE.

hale[2] draw, pull. XIII. - (O)F. *haler* - OS. *halōn* (= OFris. *halia*, OHG. *halōn, holōn*; Du. *halen*, G. *holen* fetch; cf. OE. *ġeholian* acquire), poss. rel. to L. *calāre*, Gr. *kaleîn* call.

half adj. OE. *h(e)alf* = OS. (Du.) *half*, (O)HG. *halb*, ON. *hálfr*, Goth. *halbs* :- Gmc. **χalƀaz*; ult. connections doubtful. Applied to relatives that are such on one side only, as *half-brother* (XIV), *half-sister* (XIII), prob. - ON. Comp. **halfpenny** (XIV), in OE. *healfpeniġwurð* (see WORTH), whence †*halpeny, ha'penny*, †*halp(w)orth, ha'p'orth*. Also sb. †side; one of two equal parts. OE. *h(e)alf* = OS. *halƀa*, OHG. *halba*, ON. *hálfa* region, part, lineage, Goth. *halba* side, half. So **half** adv. OE. in comb., e.g. *healfcwicu* 'half-alive', half-dead, *healfrēad* reddish, and in correl. use, e.g. *healf man healf assa* half man half ass (onocentaur). Hence **halve** divide into two. XIII.

halibut large flatfish. XV (also *holibut*, from XVII). f. *hāly*, HOLY + BUTT[3].

halitosis XIX. f. L. *halitus* breath, exhalation + -OSIS, used irreg.

hall †spacious roofed place OE.; large public room XI; building for residence of students, business of a guild, etc. XIV; large dining-room in a college, etc., XVI; vestibule, lobby XVII. OE. *h(e)all* = OS., OHG. *halla* (Du. *hal*, G. *halle*), ON. *hǫll* :- Gmc. **χallō*, f. **χal- *χel-* cover, conceal.

hallelujah XVI. - Heb. *hallᵉlûyāh* praise Jah (i.e. Jehovah), f. imper. pl. of *hallēl* praise.

halliard see HALYARD.

hallo(a) excl. calling attention and used in greeting. XIX. Later form of HOLLO. Also (with other vowels in the unstressed syll.) **hello(a)** XIX, **hillo(a)** XVIII (*illo* XVII), **hullo(a)** XIX.

halloo shout 'halloo' to incite hounds to the chase. XVI. perh. var. of HALLOW[3]. Survives in *view-halloo* (XVIII). Also *holloo* (XVII-XVIII).

hallow[1] saint. OE. *hālga*, sb. use of definite form of *hāliġ* HOLY; obs. exc. as in ALL HALLOWS, (Sc.) **Hallowe'en** (XVIII), (hist.) **Hallowmas** (XIV; see MASS[1]).

hallow[2] make or regard as holy, consecrate, bless. OE. *hālgian* = OS. *hēlagōn*, OHG. *heilagōn* (G. *heiligen*), ON. *helga*; Gmc. vb. f. **χailaʒ-* HOLY.

hallow[3] shout so as to incite hounds. XIV. prob. - OF. *halloer*, imit. of shouting.

hallucination XVII. - L. *hallūcinātiō, -ōn-*, late form of *ālūcinātiō*, f. *ālūcinārī* wander in thought or speech - Gr. *alússein* be distraught or ill at ease, with ending as in *vāticinārī* VATICINATE.

halma board game with leaping moves. XIX. - Gr. *hálma* leap (sb.).

halo circle of light round the sun, etc., XVI; nimbus of a saint XVII; fig. XIX. - medL. *halō*, for L. *halōs, -ōn-*, - Gr. *hálōs* threshing-floor, disk of the sun, moon, or a shield.

halt[1] (arch.) lame. OE. *h(e)alt* = OS. *halt*, OHG. *halz*, ON. *haltr*, Goth. *halts* :- Gmc. **χaltaz*, of unkn. orig. So **halt** vb. be lame OE.; waver XIV; proceed lamely XV. OE. *healtian*, corr. to OS. *halton*, OHG. *halzēn*, f. the adj.

halt[2] temporary stoppage on a march or journey. XVII (earlier †*alto* XVI, †*alt* XVII). orig. in phr. *make halt* - G. *halt machen* (whence also F. *faire halte*, It. *far alto*); in the G. phr. *halt* is prob. orig. based on the imper. ('stop', 'stand still') of *halten* HOLD[1]. Hence vb. XVII.

halter rope or strap with a noose OE.; rope for hanging XV. OE. *hælfter, hælftre*, corr. to OLF. *heliftra*, MLG. *helchter*, MDu. *hal(f)ter* :- WGmc. **χal(i)ftra*, f. **χalƀ-*; see HELVE.

halyard, halliard XIV. orig. *halier, hallyer*, f. HALE[2] + -IER; altered XVII by assoc. with YARD[2].

ham hollow or bend of the knee OE.; thigh of a hog used for food XVII. OE. *ham, hom* = MLG. *hamme*, OHG. *hamma* (G. dial. *hamm*), rel. to synon. MLG. *hame*, OHG. *hama*, ON. *hǫm*, f. Gmc. **þam-* be crooked. Hence **hamstring** one of the tendons at the back of the knee. XVI; hence as vb. disable (as if) by cutting these XVII.

hamadryad wood-nymph. XIV (*ama-*). - L. *Hamādryas, -ad-*, Gr. *Hamādruas, -ad-*, f. *háma* together + *drûs* TREE.

hame each of the curved pieces forming the collar of a draught-horse. XIV. - MDu. *hame* (Du. *haam*), of unkn. orig.

Hamitic pert. to a group of African languages

comprising ancient Egyptian, Berber, Galla, etc. XIX. f. *Hamite* descendant of Ham (Hebrew *Kham*), second son of Noah (Gen. 6: 10), whose descendants were supposed to have peopled northern Africa; see -ITE, -IC.

hamlet XIV. - AN. *hamelet(t)e*, OF. *hamelet*, f. *hamel* (mod. *hameau*), dim. f. *ham* - MLG., MDu. see -LET.

hammer sb. OE. *hamor*, *hamer*, *homer* = OS. *hamur* (Du. *hamer*), OHG. *hamar* (G. *hammer*), ON. *hamarr* hammer, back of an axe, crag; poss. rel. to OSl. *kamy*, Russ. *kámen'* stone. Hence vb. XIV.

hammer-cloth cloth covering the seat in a coach. XV (first as the name of an unidentified material). of unkn. orig.

hammock XVI (*hamaca*, *hammaker*; *hamack*, -OCK XVII). - Sp. *hamaca*, of Carib orig.; the ending has been assim. to -OCK.

hamper[1] large wicker-work receptacle. XIV. Reduced form of AN. *hanaper*, OF. *hanapier*, f. (O)F. *hanap* drinking-vessel, cup (of Gmc. orig.); see -ER[2].

hamper[2] obstruct the movement of. XIV. of unkn. orig.

hamster XVII. - G. :- OHG. *hamustro* = OS. *hamustra*, corn-weevil, rel. to OSl. *khoměstorŭ*.

hand extremity of the arm comprising palm and fingers; side OE.; handwriting XIV; source of information, etc. XVI; manual worker XVII (employed person, orig. with reference to skill XVIII). OE. *hand*, *hond* = OS. *hand*, OHG. *hant* (Du., G. *hand*), ON. *hǫnd*, Goth. *handus*; of uncert. orig. Hence **hand** vb. handle, furl; lead by the hand; deliver with the hand XVII. Comps.: **handbook** OE. *handbōc*, tr. medL. *manuālis liber*, late L. *manuāle* MANUAL. **handcuff** XVIII, **-ful** OE., **-kerchief** XVI, **-maid** XIV, **-maiden** XIII, **-writing** XVI.

handicap †lottery in which one person challenged an article belonging to another and offered something in exchange, an umpire decreeing the respective values XVII; †*handicap match* match between two horses, in which the umpire decided the extra weight to be carried by the superior horse; so *handicap (race)* XVIII; hence gen., and later applied to the extra weight itself, and so to any disability in a contest XIX. Presumably f. phr. *hand i'* (i.e. *in*) *cap*, the two parties and the umpire in the orig. game all depositing forfeit money in a cap or hat. Hence vb. †draw as in a lottery XVII; engage in a handicap; weight race-horses; penalize (a superior competitor) XIX.

handicraft manual skill XV; manual art XVI. alt. of earlier †*handcraft* (OE. *handcræft*) after next; see CRAFT.

handiwork OE. *handġeweorc*, f. *hand* HAND + *ġeweorc*, coll. formation (see Y-) on *weorc* WORK; analysed in XVI as HANDY *work*.

handkerchief see KERCHIEF.

handle sb. OE. *handle*, *-la* = MLG. *hantel*, f. *hand* HAND; see -LE[1]. So **handle** vb. Late OE. *handlian* feel with the hands, treat of, corr. to OS. *handlon*, OHG. *hantalōn* (G. *handeln*), ON. *hǫndla* seize, treat; see -LE[3].

han(d)sel †omen XII; New Year's gift XIV; earnest money; first use, first-fruits XVI. corr. formally to late OE. *handselen* delivery into the hand, and ON. *handsal* giving of the hand, esp. in a promise or bargain; f. HAND + base of SELL. Hence as vb. XV.

handsome †easy to handle XV; †handy; †(exc. U.S. dial.) apt, happy; moderately large, considerable; of fine appearance; graciously generous XVI. f. HAND + -SOME[1].

handspike wooden bar used as lever. XVII. - Du. †*handspaeke* (now *-spaak*), f. *hand* HAND + MDu. *spāke* pole, rod; assim. to SPIKE[1].

handy †manual XVI (*handy laboure*); ready to hand; dexterous XVI. In the first sense evolved from HANDIWORK; in the later (for which ME. had *hend(e)* :- OE. *ġehende* at hand) a new formation on HAND + -Y[1].

hang pt. and pp. *hung*, *hanged* intr. be attached above without support beneath OE.; trans. attach in this way XIII. The present stem derives from (i) intr. OE. *hangian*, pt. *hangode* (pp. *hanged* from XIV) = OS. *hangon*, OHG. *hangēn* (Du., G. *hangen*) :- WGmc. wk. vb. **χaŋʒōjan*, *-*ǣjan*, (ii) trans. ON. *hanga*, pt. *hekk*, pp. *hanginn* = OE. *hōn* (which continued till XIII), pt. *heng* (till XVI), pp. *hangen* (till XV), OS., OHG. *hāhan*, MLG., MDu. *hān*, MHG. *hāhen*, Goth. *hāhan* (pt. *haihāh*) :- Gmc. redupl. vb. **χaŋχan* (prob. rel. to L. *cunctārī* delay, Skr. *śáṅkate* hesitate); pt. and pp. *hung* were established in literary Eng. in late XVI, with *hanged* largely restricted to the sense 'kill by hanging'. Hence **hangman** XIV.

hangar shed, now spec. for aircraft. XIX. - F., of unkn. orig.

hanger[1] wood on a steep bank. OE. *hangra*, f. *hangian* HANG.

hanger[2] one who hangs; pendent or suspending object. XV. f. HANG + -ER[1].

hanger[3] short sword. XV. prob. identical with prec.; cf. early modDu. *hangher* rapier, which may be the immed. source.

hank XIII. - ON. **hanku* (later *hǫnk*; cf. *hanki* hasp, clasp). So **hank** vb. XIII. - ON. *hanka*.

hanker (dial.) linger, loiter *about*; have a longing *after*, *for*. XVII. f. dial. *hank* (XVI) + -ER[4]; prob. f. **haŋk-*, parallel to **haŋg-* HANG.

hanky XIX. colloq. for HANDKERCHIEF; see -Y[6].

hanky-panky XIX. Rhyming jingle based on *hokey pokey*, *hocus pocus*, with possible suggestion of 'sleight of *hand*'.

Hansard official record of Parliamentary Debates, which began to be printed in 1805 by T. L. *Hansard*.

Hanse merchant guild; entrance fee of such a guild XII; commercial league of German towns XV. First in *hanshus* 'hanse-house', guildhall - MLG. *hanshūs*, and in medL. form *hansa* - OHG. *hansa*, (M)HG. *hanse* = OE. *hōs* troop, company, Goth. *hansa* company, crowd :- Gmc. **χansō*; of unkn. orig. So **Hanseatic** XVII. - medL.

hansel see HAN(D)SEL.

hansom short for *hansom cab*. XIX. f. name of Joseph Aloysius *Hansom* (1803-82), architect, who registered a Patent Safety Cab in 1834.

hap sb. XIII. - ON. *happ* chance, good luck, rel.

to OE. *ġehæp(lic)* fitting, convenient, orderly (cf. OSl. *kobŭ* fate). Hence **hap** vb. XIV; superseded by **happen** XIV. **haply** by chance XIV. **happy** prosperous XIV; having a feeling of content XVI. **happy-go-lucky** XVII.

haplo- comb. form of Gr. *haploûs* single, simple, as in *haplography*, *haplology* writing/speaking once instead of twice. XIX.

hara-kiri suicide by disembowelment. XIX. - Jap., f. *hara* belly + *kiri* cutting.

harangue XV (*arang;* first in Sc.; in Eng. after 1600). - F. *harangue*, earlier †*arenge* - medL. *harenga*, - Frankish **χariχriŋg-* assembly, f. Gmc. **χarja-* host, crowd (see HARRY) + **χriŋg-* RING[1]. So vb. XVII.

harass †tire *out*; trouble, worry. XVII. - F. *harasser*, pejorative deriv. of *harer* set a dog on, f. *hare* cry used for this purpose.

harbinger †one who provides lodging, host XII; purveyor of lodging, e.g. for an army XIV; forerunner XVI. ME. *herbergere*, *-geour* - OF. *herbergere*, obl. case *-geour*, f. *herbergier* provide lodging for, f. *herberge* lodging - Frankish (= OHG.) *heriberga* 'shelter for an army', lodging, f. Gmc. **χarja-* host, army (see HARRY) + **berʒ-* protect (see BOROUGH). The intrusive *n* occurs XV.

harbour (arch.) shelter, lodging OE.; place of shelter XIII; spec. for ships, port XVI. Late OE. *herebeorg* (perh. - ON.), corr. to OS., OHG. *heriberga* (Du. *herberg*, G. *herberge*), ON. *herbergi*; see prec. So as vb. shelter, lodge, entertain OE.; fig. XIV. Late OE. *herebeorgian*. Hence **harbourage** XVI.

hard resisting pressure; difficult to endure, severe; intense, violent OE.; sb. beach or jetty for landing XIX. OE. *h(e)ard* = OS. (Du.) *hard*, (O)HG. *hart*, ON. *harðr*, Goth. *hardus* :- Gmc. **χarðuz* :- IE. **kratús*, whence Gr. *kratús* strong, powerful. Hence **harden** make hard XIII; become hard XV. Hence **hardly** †forcibly; †boldly XIII; severely; not easily, (hence) barely, not quite XVI. **hardship** †severity; oppressive condition. XIII. **hardware** ironmongery. XVI.

hardy courageous, daring XIII; capable of physical endurance XVI. - (O)F. *hardi*, pp. of *hardir* become bold - Gmc. **χarðjan*, f. **χarðuz* HARD. Hence **hardihood** XVII.

hare OE. *hara* = MDu. *haese* (Du. *haas*), OHG. *haso* (G. *hase*), ON. *heri* :- Gmc. **χasan-*; rel. to W. *ceinach*, OPruss. *sasins*, Skr. *śaśas*; prob. sb. use of a colour-adj. (cf. OE. *hasu*, ON. *hǫss* grey, L. *cascus* old, beside OHG. *hasan* grey, L. *cānus* hoary). Hence **harebell** XIV, **hare-brain**, **hare-lip** XVI.

harem XVII. - Arab. *ḥaram* and *ḥarīm* (that which is) prohibited, (hence) sacred place, sanctuary, women's apartments, wives, women, f. *ḥarama* prohibit, make unlawful.

haricot[1] kidney bean, French bean. XVII. - F. *haricot*, of uncert. orig.

haricot[2] ragout (orig. of mutton). XVIII. - F. *haricot*, earlier *hericoq* (*de mouton*), *hericot*, perh. orig. rel. to OF. *harigoter* cut up, and later assim. to prec.

hark give ear to XII; listen XIII. ME. *herkien* :- OE. **he(o)rcian*, rel. to MLG., MDu. *horken*, OHG. *hōrechen*, (G. *horchen*). *Hark back* is a hunting phr. arising from the use of 'hark!' as a call to retrace one's course.

harlequin character (associated with Columbine) in It. comedy and Eng. pantomime (clothed in variegated costume, whence the application of the word to animals with variegated coat, plumage, etc.). XVI. - F. †*harlequin* (mod. *arlequin*, after It. *arlecchino*), later var. of *Herlequin* leader of the Wild Host or troop of demon horsemen riding by night, which has been plausibly referred (as if for **Herlechingi*) to OE. *Herla cyning* king Herla, whose characteristics have been identified with those of Woden.

harlot †vagabond, rascal, low fellow XIII; †itinerant jester; †male servant; †'fellow' XIV; prostitute XV. - OF. *(h)arlot*, *herlot* young fellow, knave, vagabond. Hence **harlotry** XIV.

harm sb. OE. *hearm* = OS., (O)HG. *harm*, ON. *harmr* (chiefly) grief, sorrow :- Gmc. **χarmaz*, rel. to OSl. *sramŭ* shame, injury, Pers. *šarm*. So **harm** vb. OE. *hearmian*.

harmony †melody, music XIV; (mus.) combination of notes to make chords; agreement, accord XVI. - (O)F. *harmonie* - L. *harmonia* - Gr. *harmoniā* joint, agreement, concord, f. **harmo-* of *harmós* joint, *harmózein* fit together. So **harmonic** XVI. - L. - Gr. *harmonikós*. **harmonica** first applied (1762) by B. Franklin to a developed form of musical glasses; fem. sg. or n. pl. (used sb.) of L. *harmonicus*. **harmonious** XVI. - (O)F. **harmonium** XIX. - F. **harmonize** XV (rare before XVII).

harness †baggage, equipment XIII; trappings of a horse; (arch.) body armour; tackle, gear (now techn.) XIV. ME. *harnais*, *herneis* - OF. *harneis* military equipment (mod. *harnais*) - ON. **hernest* 'provisions for an army', with assim. of the termination to **-isk-* (cf. OF. *harneschier* equip), f. *herr* army (see HARRY) + *nest* = OE., OHG. *nest* provisions, Goth. *ganists* safety. So vb. XIV.

harp sb. OE. *hearpe* = OS. *harpa* (Du. *harp*), OHG. *harfa* (G. *harfe*), ON. *harpa* :- Gmc. **χarpōn*. So vb. OE. *hearpian*.

harpoon sb. XVII. - F. *harpon*, f. *harpe* dog's claw, cramp-iron, clamp - L. *harpē*, *harpa* - Gr. *hárpē* sickle. Hence vb. XVIII.

harpsichord XVII. - F. †*harpechorde*, f. late L. *harpa* HARP + *chorda* CHORD; the intrusive *s* is of obscure orig.

harpy fabulous monster half woman half bird; also transf. XVI. - (O)F. *harpie* or its source L. *harpȳia*, pl. *-iæ* - Gr. *hárpūiai* 'snatchers', rel. to *harpázein* seize.

(h)arquebus early portable gun. XVI. - F. *(h)arquebuse*, ult. - MLG. *hakebusse* (mod. *haakbus*) or MHG. *hake(n)bühse* (mod. *hakenbüchse*); f. *hake(n)* hook + *bus(se)* fire-arm (a hook being orig. cast on the gun). So **(h)arquebusier** XVI.

harridan XVII. presumed to be alt. of F. *haridelle* old jade of a horse, of unkn. orig.

harrier[1] hound for hunting the hare XVI; member of a hare-and-hounds team XIX. Early forms *hayrere*, *heirere*, f. *hayre* HARE + -ER[1]; assim. to next.

harrier[2] one who harries; falcon of the genus *Circus*. XVI. (In the second sense, early forms *har(r)oer, harrower*.) f. HARROW[1], HARRY + -ER[1].

harrow[1] (arch.) rob, despoil (esp. *harrow hell*). XIII. ME. *harwe, herwe*, var. of *herie* HARRY.

harrow[2] toothed timber-frame dragged over ploughed land to clean it. XIII. - ON. **harwjan-*, prehistoric form of *herfi*, rel. obscurely to MLG., MDu. *harke* (Du. *hark*) rake. Hence **harrow** vb. XIII; fig. lacerate the feelings of XVII.

harry make raids OE.; overrun or despoil with an army; harass XIII. OE. *her(ġ)ian*, corr. to OS. *herion*, OHG. *heriōn*, ON. *herja* :- Gmc. **χarjō(ja)n*, f. **χarjaz* host, army (OE. *here*, ON. *herr* etc.); rel. to MIr. *cuire*, Lith. *kãrias* army, Gr. *koíranos* 'military commander', lord, king. Conflation with synon. OF. *harier, her(r)ier* is probable.

harsh rough to the touch, taste, or hearing; repugnant to feeling or aesthetic taste. XVI. - MLG. *harsch* rough, lit. 'hairy', f. *haer* HAIR; see -ISH[1].

hart OE. *heor(o)t*, = OS. *hirot* (Du. *hert*), OHG. *hir(u)z* (G. *hirsch*), ON. *hjǫrtr* :- Gmc. **χerutaz*; prob. lit. 'horned beast', and based on IE. **k̂erw-* (as in L. *cervus* stag, W. *carw* hart, OSl. *srŭna* roe), rel. ult. to HORN.

hartebeest XVIII. - Afrikaans (now *hartbees*), f. Du. *hert* HART + *beest* BEAST.

harum-scarum adv. XVII; adj., sb. XVIII. rhyming jingle perh. f. HARE and SCARE; sometimes taken as *hare 'em, scare 'em*.

harvest autumn, spec. as the season for gathering the ripened grain OE.; the gathering itself, corn-crop XVI. OE. *hærfest* = (M)Du. *herfst*, OHG. *herbist* (G. *herbst* autumn), ON. *haust* :- Gmc. **χarƀistaz, *-ustaz*, f. **χarƀ-* :- IE. **karp-*, as in L. *carpere* pluck, Gr. *karpós* fruit. Hence vb. XIV. **harvest-home** XVI.

has see HAVE.

hash cut up (meat) small for cooking; fig. mangle. XVII. - (O)F. *hacher*, f. *hache* HATCHET. Hence **hash** sb.

hashish XVI. - Arab. *ḥašīš* dry herb, hay, hashish.

haslet pig's fry, pluck of sheep, etc. XIV. - OF. *hastelet* (mod. *hâtelet(te)*), dim. of *haste* (*hâte*) spit, roast meat - Frankish (= OHG.) *harst* piece of roast meat; see -LET.

hasp hinged fastening. OE. *hæpse* (:- **hæspe*), corr. to MLG. *haspe, hespe*, OHG. *haspa* (G. *haspe*), ON. *hespa*.

hassock clump of matted vegetation OE.; cushion for kneeling or resting the feet on XVI. OE. *hassuc*, of unkn. orig.; see -OCK.

hastate spear-shaped. XVIII. - L. *hastātus*, f. *hasta* spear; see -ATE[2].

haste swiftness of movement; hurry XIII; obligation or eagerness to act quickly XIV. - OF. *haste* (mod. *hâte*) - WGmc. **χaisti* (OE. *hǣst* violence, fury, ON. *heifst, heipt* hate, revenge, Goth. *haifsts* strife; OE. *hǣste* violent, OHG. *heisti* powerful); of unkn. orig. So **haste** vb. XIII. - OF. *haster* (mod. *hâter*); superseded by **hasten** XVI. Hence **hasty** †speedy; †hurried XIV; precipitate, rash XV. - OF. *hasti(f)* (mod. *hâtif*).

hat OE. *hætt*, corr. to ON. *hǫttr* hood, cowl :- Gmc. **χattuz*; rel. to HOOD. Hence **hatter** XIV.

hatch[1] half door, wicket OE.; †movable planking forming a deck, (now) framework covering openings in a deck XIII; flood-gate XVI. OE. *hæċċ, heċċ*, corr. to MLG. *heck*, MDu. *hecke* (Du. *hek*); f. Gmc. **χak-*, of unkn. orig.

hatch[2] bring forth from the egg. XIII. ME. *hacche*, pt. *haȝte*, pp. *yhaht, iheyȝt* and *hacchid, hetchid*, points to an OE. **hæċċan*, rel. to MHG. *hecken*, Sw. *häcka*, Da. *hække*; of unkn. orig.

hatch[3] inlay XV; engrave lines on XVI. - (O)F. *hacher*, f. *hache* HATCHET.

hatchet XIV. - (O)F. *hachette*, dim. of *hache* axe - Gmc **χapja* (OHG. *happa, heppa* sickle-shaped knife); see -ET.

hatchment escutcheon. XVI. Early forms *(h)achement, achivment*, shortening of ACHIEVEMENT stressed on the first syll.

hate vb. OE. *hatian* – OS. *haton* (Du. *haten*), OHG. *hazzōn, -ēn* (G. *hassen*), ON. *hata*, Goth. *hatan* :- Gmc. **χatōjan, *-ǣjan*, f. base of **χatis-* (see below). So **hate** sb. XIII; partly - ON. *hatr*, partly f. *hate* vb. under the infl. of **hatred** XIII (ME. *haterede(n)*, f. the vb.-stem + -RED). Both sbs. superseded OE. synon. *hete* (to XIII) = OS. *heti*, OHG. *haz* (G. *hass*), ON. *hatr*, Goth. *hatis* :- Gmc. **χatis-* :- IE. **k̂ədes-* (cf. Av. *sādra-*, Gr. *kêdos* suffering, W. *cawdd* anger, insult, trouble).

hauberk defensive armour for neck and shoulders. XIII. - OF. *hauberc* :- Frankish **halsberg* (= OHG. *halsberc*, OE. *healsbeorg*), f. *hals* neck + **berg-* protect.

haugh (Sc. and north.) flat land by a river side. ME. *hawch, hawgh*, prob. :- OE. *healh* corner, nook, rel. to *holh* HOLLOW.

haughty lofty and disdainful; †eminent, exalted; †high. XVI. Extension with -Y[1] of †*haught*, earlier *haut* (XV) - (O)F. *haut* high :- L. *altus* high.

haul pull, drag; trim (sails) XVI; (of the wind) veer XVIII. Earliest form *hall*; var. of HALE[2]. So **haulier** XV (*hallier*). - OF. *hallier*.

ha(u)lm stems or stalks. OE. *h(e)alm* = OS. (Du.), (O)HG. *halm*, ON. *hálmr* :- Gmc. **χalmaz* :- IE. **k̂olmos*; cf. L. *culmus* haulm, Gr. *kálamos* reed, OSl. *slama* straw.

haunch XIII. - (O)F. *hanche*, of Gmc. origin (cf. LG. *hanke* hind leg of a horse).

haunt †practise habitually; resort (to) habitually XIII; frequent the company of XV; visit frequently XVI (spec. of ghosts). - (O)F. *hanter*, of Gmc. orig.

hautboy wooden wind instrument. XVI. - F. *hautbois*, f. *haut* high + *bois* wood; so named from its high pitch. Superseded by OBOE.

have pt., pp. *had*. OE. *habban*, pt. *hæfde*, pp. *(ġe)hæfd* = OS. *hebbian* (Du. *hebben*), OHG. *habēn* (G. *haben*), ON. *hafa*, Goth. *haban*, prob. rel. to **χabjan* (IE. **kap-*) HEAVE (connection with L. *habēre* 'have' is doubtful).

haven harbour (now rhet. or fig.). Late OE. *hæfen, hæfne* (XI) - ON. *hafn-, hǫfn* = MLG., MDu. *havene*, Du. *haven*, rel. to (O)Ir. *cuan* curve, bend, recess, bay.

haversack XVIII. - F. *havresac* - G. *habersack* orig. bag in which cavalry carried the oats for their horses, f. *haber* oats + *sack* SACK.

havoc in phr. *cry havoc* sound the signal for spoliation; hence *make havoc (of)* plunder, devastate. XV. - AN. *havok*, alt. of OF. *havo(t)*, of unkn. orig.

haw[1] fruit of the hawthorn. OE. *haga*, identical in form with *haga* hedge, fence (see HEDGE), connection with which appears to be shown by the forms of **hawthorn**, OE. *haga-*, *haguðorn* = MDu. *hagedorn* (Du. *haagdoorn*), MHG. *hagendorn* (G. *hagedorn*), ON. *hagþorn*; cf. OE. *hæġðorn* 'hedge-thorn'.

haw[2] nictitating membrane in a horse's (dog's, etc.) eye; inflamed state of this. XVI. of unkn. orig.

haw[3] utterance marking hesitation; also as vb. XVII.

hawk[1] bird of prey. OE. *h(e)afoc* = OS. *haƀuk* (Du. *havik*), OHG. *habuh* (G. *habicht*), ON. *haukr* :- Gmc. **χaƀukaz*, rel. to Pol. *kobuz*, Russ. *kóbets* species of hawk or kite. Hence **hawk** vb. XIV.

hawk[2] plasterer's hod. XIV. of unkn. orig.

hawk[3] clear the throat noisily. XVI. prob. imit.

hawker itinerant seller. XVI. prob. - LG. (cf. MLG. *hoker*, Du. *heuker*); see HUCKSTER. Hence, by back-formation, **hawk**[4] vb. XVI.

hawse (naut.) part of the bows of a ship XIV; space about the stem of a vessel, situation of cables there XVI. Early form *halse*, prob. - ON. *háls* neck, ship's bow, etc. (= OE. *heals* neck, prow).

hawser (naut.) large rope. XIV. - AN. *hauce(ou)r*. f. OF. *haucier* (mod. *hausser*) hoist :- Rom. **altiāre*, f. L. *altus* high; see -ER[2].

hawthorn see HAW[1].

hay grass cut and dried. OE. *hēġ*, *hī(e)ġ* = OS. *hōi*, OHG. *hewi*, *houwi* (Du. *hooi*, G. *heu*), ON. *hey* (whence the native word was reinforced), Goth. *hawi* :- Gmc. **χaujam*, f. **χauwan* cut down, HEW.

hayward officer having charge of fences and enclosures. XIII. f. ME. *heie*, *haie*, OE. *heġe* hedge + WARD[1].

hazard game at dice XIII; chance, venture XIV; risk, peril XVI. - (O)F. *hasard*, perh. - Sp. *azar* - Arab. *az-zahr*, *az-zār* gaming die. So **hazard** vb., **hazardous** XVI.

haze[1] †thick fog; thin mist. XVIII. prob., along with *haze* vb. drizzle (XVII), back-formation from earlier **hazy** adj. (orig. naut.) †foggy, (now) misty (XVII), of unkn. orig. (earliest forms *hawsey*, *heysey*, *haizy*, besides *hasie*, *hazy*).

haze[2] (dial.) scare, scold, beat XVII; (naut.) harass with excessive work; (U.S.) subject to brutal horseplay XIX. In the first sense preceded by (dial.) *hazen* (early XVII); of uncert. orig. (cf. OF. *haser* tease, anger, insult).

hazel small nut-tree, *Corylus* OE.; reddish-brown colour of the ripe hazel-nut XVI. OE. *hæsel*, corr. to MDu. *hasel* (Du. *hazelaar* hazel tree), OHG. *hasal(a)* (G. *hasel*), ON. *hasl* :- Gmc. **χasalaz* :- IE. **kosolos*, **koselos*, whence also L. *corylus*, *-ulus*.

he[1] 3rd sg. m. pers. pron. OE. *hē* = OS. *he*, *hi(e)*; f. Gmc. dem. stem **χi-*, repr. also in OHG. (Franconian) *her*, *hē* he; also OHG. *hiutu* (:- **hiu tagu* this day), G. *heute* today, ON. dem. *hinn*, Goth. *himma daga* today. See also HIM, HIS, HITHER, HENCE, IT. IE. **k̑(e)i*, **k̑e* are repr. also in L. *cis* on this side, dem. particle *-ce*, OIr. *cē* this, Lith. *šis*, OSl. *sĭ* this, Gr. *ekeî* there.

he[2] excl. of laughter, usually repeated *he he (he)*. OE. *he he*.

head anterior (in man, upper) part of the body, containing the mouth, sense organs, and brain; various transf. uses. OE. *hēafod* = OS. *hōƀid* (Du. *hoofd*), OHG. *houbit* (G. *haupt*), Goth. *haubiþ* (cf. ON. *hǫfuð*) :- Gmc. **χauƀuðam*, *-iðam*, the relation of which with L. *caput*, head, Skr. *kapā́la-* skull, is not clear. Hence **headland** strip of land left at the head of furrows OE. (*hēafodland*); promontory XVI. **headman** chief. OE. *hēafodmann*. **headquarters** XVII. **headsman** †chief XIV; executioner XVII. **headstrong** XIV. **headway** motion ahead or forward XVIII; for **aheadway* (f. AHEAD). **heady** headlong (†lit. and fig.) XIV.

-head *-hēd(e)*, repr. OE. **-hǣdu*, mutated form corr. to *-hād* -HOOD, and used alongside it from XIII, but surviving in present Eng. only in *godhead* and (arch.) *maidenhead*; orig. attached to adjs., as *boldhede*, *fairhede*, but extended later to sbs.

headlong headforemost, precipitately. XV. alt., by assoc. with ALONG, of †*headling* (XIII), f. HEAD + -LING[2].

heal OE. *hǣlan* = OS. *hēlian* (Du. *heelen*), OHG. *heilan* (G. *heilen*), ON. *heila*, Goth. *hailjan* :- Gmc. **χailjan*, f. **χailaz* WHOLE.

health soundness of body, mind, or spirit OE.; toast drunk to a person's welfare XVI. OE. *hǣlð* = OHG. *heilida* :- WGmc. **χailiþa*, f. Gmc. **χailaz* WHOLE; see -TH[1]. Hence **healthful** salubrious XIV; having good health XVI (superseded in this sense by **healthy** XVI).

heap collection of things lying one upon another; †great company OE.; (colloq.) a great deal XVII (earlier pl. XVI). OE. *hēap* = OS. *hōp* (Du. *hoop*), OHG. *houg* :- WGmc. **χaupa*, rel. to MLG. *hūpe*, OHG. *hūfo* (G. *haufen*) :- Gmc. **χūpan-*. Hence as vb. OE. *hēapian*.

hear pt., pp. *heard*. OE. (Angl.) *hēran*, (WS.) *hīeran* = OS. *hōrian* (Du. *hooren*), OHG. *hōren* (G. *hören*), ON. *heyra*, Goth. *hausjan* :- Gmc. **χauzjan*, perh. rel. to Gr. *akoúein* hear. Hence **hearsay** XVI. orig. in phr. *by hear say*.

hearken OE. *he(o)rcnian*, f. **he(o)rcian*; see HARK, -EN[5].

hearse structure placed over a bier at a funeral XIV; †bier, coffin, grave XVII; funeral carriage XVII. - (O)F. *herse* harrow, triangular frame for candles :- medL. *erpica*, Rom. **herpica*, for L. *(h)irpex*, *(h)irpic-* kind of harrow.

heart bodily organ, regarded as the centre of vital functions, the seat of affections, etc. OE.; dear person; innermost part XIII; vital part; †stomach XVI. OE. *heorte* = OS. *herta* (Du. *hart*), OHG. *herza* (G. *herz*), ON. *hjarta*, Goth. *hairtō* :- Gmc. **χertan-*, *-ōn*. The IE. base **k̑ērd-* **k̑ṛd-* is repr. also by Gr. *kêr*, *kardiā*, L. *cor*, *cord-*, Lith. *širdis*, OIr. *cride*, etc. Hence **hearten** XVI.

hearth OE. *heorð* = OS. *herth* (Du. *haard*), OHG. *hert* (G. *herd*) :- WGmc. **χerþa*.

heat sb. OE. *hǣtu* = MDu. *hēte*, OHG. *heizi* :-

WGmc. *χaitīn, f. Gmc. *χaitaz HOT; also OE. hǣte (:- *χaitja). So **heat** vb. OE hǣtan.

heath[1] open waste land. OE. hǣð, corr. to OS. hētha, MLG., MDu. hēde, MHG. heide (Du., G. heide), ON. heiðe, Goth. haiþi :- Gmc. *χaiþiz :- IE. *kait-, repr. also by Gaul. cēto- in place-names, OW. coit (W. coed) wood, forest.

heath[2] plant of the genus *Erica*. OE. hǣð = OS. hēth(i)a, (M)LG., (M)Du. heide, OHG. heida (G. heide) :- WGmc. *χaiþjō; f. prec.

heathen OE. hǣðen = OS. hēthin (Du. heiden), OHG. heidan (G. heide), ON. heiðinn, in Goth. repr. by haiþnō Gentile woman; gen. regarded as a spec. Christian use (perh. originating in Gothic) of Gmc. adj. *χaiþanaz, -inaz inhabiting open country, savage, f. *χaiþiz HEATH[1]; see -EN[1]. Hence **heathendom** OE. hǣðendōm. **heathenish** OE. hǣðenisċ.

heather XIV (Sc. and north. *hathir*, etc.). The form *hadder* or *hather* prevailed in Eng. use from XVI to XVIII, when *heather* is first recorded; of unkn. orig., perh. repr. OE. *hǣddre; app. assim. to HEATH[1] or [2].

heave (obs. dial. or techn.) lift, raise OE.; throw, cast, haul up XVI; rise XIV. OE. str. vb. hebban = OS. hebbian (Du. heffen), OHG. heffen (G. heben), ON. hefja, Goth. hafjan :- Gmc. *χaƀjan, rel. to L. *capere* take. Pt. *hove* survives in some uses, but for the most part weak forms (already found in late OE.) prevailed.

heaven sky, firmament; region beyond the sky; habitation of God and his angels OE.; state of bliss XIV. OE. heofon, corr. to OS. heƀan, ON. himinn (inflected stem hifn- :- *hiƀn-), Goth. himins; parallel formations with *l*-suffix are OS., OHG. himil (Du. hemel, G. himmel); ult. orig. uncert.

Heaviside name of Oliver *Heaviside* (1850-1925), Engl. physicist, applied to a *layer* of the ionosphere able to reflect long radio waves.

heavy OE. hefiġ = OS. heƀig (Du. hevig), OHG. hebig, ON. hǫfugr :- Gmc *χaƀuʒa-, *χaƀiʒa-, f. *χaƀiz (OE. hefe) weight, f. *χaƀjan HEAVE; see -Y[1].

hebdomadal †lasting seven days XVII; weekly XVIII. - late L. *hebdomadālis*, f. *hebdomas, -ad-* group of seven, etc. (whence **hebdomad** XVI) - Gr. *hebdomás*, f. *heptá* SEVEN.

hebetate make blunt. XVI. f. pp. stem of L. *hebetāre*, f. *hebes, hebet-* blunt; see -ATE[3].

Hebrew adj. and sb. XIII. ME. *ebreu* - OF. *ebr(i)eu* (mod. *hébreu*) - medL. *Ebrēus*, for L. *Hebræus* - late Gr. *Hebraios* - Aram. *'ebrāyā*, for Heb. *'ibrī* lit. 'one from the other side' (sc. of the river). So **Hebraic** XIV. - ChrL. *Hebraicus* - late Gr. *Hebraïkós*. **Hebraism** XVI. - F. or modL. **Hebraist** XVIII.

hecatomb sacrifice of many victims. XVI. - L. *hecatombē* - Gr. *hekatómbē*, f. *hekatón* HUNDRED + *boûs* OX.

heckle var. of HACKLE. XV. Hence vb. dress (flax or hemp) with a heckle XV; examine searchingly; harass (a speaker) with questions XIX (orig. Sc.).

hectic of a wasting fever XIV; consumptive, feverish XVII; feverishly active, exciting XX. ME. *etik* - OF. *etique* - late L. *hecticus* - Gr. *hektikós* habitual, hectic, consumptive, f. *héxis* habit, state of body or mind, f. *ékhein* intr. (with adv.) be (in such-and-such a state); superseded XVI by the mod. form - F. *hectique* or late L.

hect(o)- - F., contr. of Gr. *hekatón* HUNDRED, esp. in terms of the metric system, as *hectare, hectolitre, hectometre* (XIX).

hector play the bully, (tr.) bully. XVII. f. *Hector* name of 'the prop or stay of Troy', son of Priam and Hecuba, sb. use of Gr. adj. *héktōr* holding fast, f. *ékhein* hold; f. the use of the sb. (common in late XVII) for 'swaggering fellow'.

hedge OE. heċġ(e) = MDu. hegghe (Du. heg), OHG. hegga, hecka (G. hecke) :- WGmc. *χaʒjō, rel. to HAW[1], HAY. Hence **hedgehog** XV, **hedgerow** XVI.

hedonism XIX. f. Gr. *hēdonḗ* pleasure + -ISM. So **hedonist** XIX.

-hedron repr. n. sg. (used as sb.) of Gr. adjs. ending in *-edros*, f. *hédrā* seat, base, in comps. with numerals, as *hexahedron*.

heed vb. OE. hēdan = OS. hōdian (Du. hoeden), OHG. huoten (G. hüten) :- WGmc. *χōdjan, f. *χōda care, keeping (MLG. hōde, OHG. huota, G. hut). Hence as sb. XIII.

heel[1] hinder part of the foot OE. hēla, hǣla, corr. to MDu. hiele (Du. hiel), ON. hæll :- Gmc. *χāχil- :- *χaŋχil-, f. *χaŋχ- (whence OE. hōh heel), rel. to Lith. *kìnka* hough.

heel[2] incline to one side. XVI. prob. evolved from †*heeld*, †*hield* through apprehending final *d* as a pt.-pp. suffix. OE. hieldan = OS. ofheldian, MDu. helden (Du. hellen) :- WGmc. *χalþjan, f. Gmc. *χalþaz (OE. heald, OHG. hald, ON. hallr inclined).

hefty XIX. of U.S. and dial. origin; f. (dial.) **heft** weight, prob. f. *heave*; see -Y[1].

hegemony XVI (*aegemonie*; rare before XIX) - Gr. *hēgemoníā*, f. *hēgemṓn* leader, f. *hēgeîsthai* lead, rel. to L. *sāgīre* track, and SEEK; see -MONY.

hegira, hejira Muslim era. XVI. - medL. *hegira* - Arab. *hijra* departure (spec. *al-hijra* the flight of Muhammad from Mecca to Medina in A.D. 622, from which the Muslim era is reckoned), f. *hajara* separate, go away.

heifer OE. heahfore, heahfru, -fre, of unkn. orig.

height OE. hēhðu (WS. hīehðu) = MDu. hogede, hoochte (Du. hoogte), OHG. hōhida, Goth. hauhiþa :- Gmc. *χauχiþō; see HIGH, -TH[1]. Dissimilation of *-hþ* (*-ʒþ*) to *-ht* (*-ʒt*), orig. northern, appears before 1300. Hence **heighten** XVI.

heinous hateful. XIV. - OF. *haïneus*, f. *haïne* hatred, f. *haïr* - Frankish *hatjan, rel. to HATE; see -OUS.

heir XIII. ME. *eir* - OF. *(h)eir* :- late L. *hērem*, for earlier *hērēdem*, nom. *hērēs*. Hence **heiress** XVII, **heirloom** XV.

hejira see HEGIRA.

hele †hide, keep secret OE.; (local) cover (with earth or tiles) XIII. OE. hellan, helian = OS. hellian, OHG. -hellen :- WGmc. *haljan f. *χel- *χal- *χul- :- IE. *k̂el-, repr. in L. *celāre*, Gr. *kalúptein* hide.

helianthus sunflower genus. XVIII. modL., f. Gr. *hḗlios* SUN + *ánthos* flower.

helicopter XIX. - F. *hélicoptère*, f. Gr. *heliko-* (see HELIX) + *pterón* wing.

helio- repr. comb. form of Gr. *hḗlios* SUN, as in *heliocentric* (xvii), *-graph* (xix), *-graphic*, *-graphy*, *-meter*, *-stat* (xviii), *-tropic*, *-tropism* (xix).

heliotrope plant of which the flowers turn towards the sun, e.g. formerly, sunflower, marigold, now the genus *Heliotropium*. xvii. - L. *hēliotropium* - Gr. *hēliotrópion*, f. *hḗlios* SUN + *-tropos* turning.

helium xix. f. Gr. *hḗlios* SUN (see -IUM); so named from the discovery of its existence in the solar spectrum.

helix xvi. - L. *helix*, *helic-* - Gr. *hélix*, *-ik-*, f. IE. **wel-* roll. Hence **helical** xvii. **helicoid** xviii. - modL. - Gr.

hell OE. *hel(l)* = OS. *hellia* (Du. *hel*), OHG. *hella* (G. *hölle*), ON. *hel*, Goth. *halja* :- Gmc. **χaljō*, f. **χal-* **χel-* **χul-* cover, conceal (OE. *helian*, *helan*, OS., OHG. *helan*, etc.; OE. *hyllan*, Goth. *huljan*, etc.).

hellebore xiv (preceded by *eleboryne* xiii). ME. *el(l)ebre*, *eleure* - OF. *ellebre*, *elebore* or medL. *eleborus*, L. *elleborus* - Gr. *(h)elléboros*.

Hellene Greek. xvii. - Gr. *Héllēn*. So **Hellenic**, **Hellenism** xvii, **Hellenistic** xviii.

hello see HALLO(A).

helm[1] (arch.), helmet. OE. *helm* = OS., OHG. (Du., G.) *helm*, ON. *hjálmr*, Goth. *hilms* :- Gmc. **χelmaz*, f. IE. base **ḱel-* cover, conceal; cf. Skr. *śárman-* covering, protection. So **helmet** xv. - OF., dim. of *helme* (mod. *heaume*), - Gmc.; see -ET.

helm[2] tiller. OE. *helma*, corr. to MLG. *helm* handle, OHG. *helmo*, *halmo*, ON. *hjalmvǫlr* 'rudder-stick'; of uncert. orig.

helminthology xix. f. Gr. *hélmins*, *helminth-* worm; see -LOGY.

helot serf in ancient Sparta. xvi. - L. *(H)īlōtæ*, *Hēlōtes* pl. - Gr. *Heilōtes*, *Heilōtai*; of unkn. orig.

help sb. OE. *help* = OS. *helpa*, OHG. *helfa*, ON. *hjálp* :- Gmc. **χelpō*, f. base seen also in **help** vb. OE. str. vb. *helpan* = OS. *helpan* (Du. *helpen*), OHG. *helfan* (G. *helfen*), ON. *hjálpa*, Goth. *hilpan*; cf. Lith. *šel̃pti* help. The orig. pt. survived till xv in the form †*halp*, which was succeeded by †*holp* (xvi), modelled on the pp. †*holpen*; the weak form *helped* appears xiii, orig. northern. Hence **helpmate** xviii. f. MATE[1], doubtless by assoc. with *helpmeet*, which arose from the use of *help-meet for man* (xvii), based on *an helpe meet for him* 'a help suitable for him' Gen. 2: 18, 20.

helter-skelter in disorderly haste. xvi. rhyming jingle, perh. based ult. on ME. *skelte* hasten.

helve handle of a weapon or tool. OE. *h(i)elfe*, corr. to OS. *helfi* (MDu. *helf*, *helve*), OHG. *halp*; f. WGmc. **χalƀ-* (cf. HALTER) :- IE. **kalp-*, as in OPruss. *kalpus* waggon-rail, Lith. *kálpa* cross piece of a sledge.

hem[1] edging of cloth or garment OE. (transf. and techn., from xiii); border on a cloth made by doubling in the edge xvii. OE. *hem*, corr. to OFris. *hemme* enclosed land, presumably rel. to OE. *hamm* meadow, etc. Hence **hem** vb. edge, border (cloth) xiii; shut *in* xvi.

hem[2], h'm repr. the sound made in clearing the throat. xvi. So **hem** vb. xv (in vbl. sb. *hemynge*).

hemi- repr. Gr. *hēmi-*, comb. el. = SEMI-.

hemisphere In the form †*(h)emisperie*, *-sphery* (xiv) - L. *hēmisphærium* - Gr. *hēmisphaírion* (see *hēmi-* HEMI-, SPHERE); in the form *hemisphere* (xvi), †*-spere* (xv) - OF. *emisp(h)ere* (mod. *hémisphère*).

hemistich (pros.) half-line. xvi. - late L. *hēmistichium* - Gr. *hēmistíkhion*, f. *stíkhos*; see HEMI-.

hemlock OE. *hymlic(e)*, *hemlic*, of unkn. orig.; forms in *hum-*, *hom-* continued till xvi; the alt. of the final syll. to *-lock* (xv) is paralleled in CHARLOCK.

hemorrhoid see H(A)EMORRHOID.

hemp herbaceous plant *Cannabis sativa* OE.; fibre of this xiii. OE. *henep*, *hænep* = OS. *hanap* (Du. *hennep*), OHG. *hanaf* (G. *hanf*), ON. *hampr* :- Gmc. **χanipiz*, **χanapiz*, rel. to Gr. *kánnabis*, Lith. *kanãpės*, Russ. *konoplyá*.

hen female of the domestic fowl OE.; female of other birds xiv. OE. *henn* = MLG. *henne*, OHG. *henna* (G. *henne*) :- WGmc. **χannja*, f. Gmc. **χanan-* cock (OE. *hana*, OS., OHG. *hano*, Du. *haan*, G. *hahn*, ON. *hani*, Goth. *hanō*, rel. to L. *canere* sing.

hence xiii. ME. *hen(ne)s*, f. *hen(ne)* :- OE. *hio-*, *heonan(e)* = OS., OHG. *hinan(a)*, (G. *hinnen*), also OE. *hina*, *heona* = MLG., MDu. *hēne* (Du. *heen*), OHG. *hina* (G. *hin*); WGmc. formations on the pronominal base **χi-* HE[1]. Cf. THENCE, WHENCE.

henchman squire, page of honour xiv; personal attendant of a Highland chief xviii; trusty follower, (esp. U.S.) stout political partisan xix. ME. *hengest-*, *henx(st)-*, *hensman*, perh. orig. horse attendant, f. OE. *heng(e)st* (= MLG. *hengest*, OHG. *hengist*, Du., G. *hengst*, ON. *hestr*) stallion, gelding + MAN.

hendeca- comb. form of Gr. *héndeka* eleven, f. *hén*, n. of *heîs* one + *déka* TEN. **hendecagon** xviii. **hendecasyllable** xviii. f. L. - Gr.

henna (dye obtained from) Egyptian privet, *Lawsonia inermis*. xvi. - Arab. *ḥinnā'*.

henry (electr.) unit of inductance. xix. f. name of Joseph *Henry* (1797-1878), Amer. physicist.

hepatic pert. to the liver, liver-coloured. xv. - L. *hēpaticus* - Gr. *hēpatikós*, f. *hêpar*, *hēpat-* liver; see -IC.

hepta- before a vowel **hept-**, comb. form of Gr. *heptá* SEVEN, e.g. **heptachord** xviii, **heptagon** xvi, **heptarchy** xvi, **Heptateuch** xvii.

heptad group of seven. xvii. - Gr. *heptás*, *heptad-*, f. *heptá* SEVEN; see -AD.

her[1] g. of the fem. 3rd pers. sg. pron. OE. *hire* = MDu. *hare* (Du. *haar*), f. pronominal base **χi-* HE[1]; cf. parallel forms on the base **i-*, viz. OS., OHG. *ira*, *iro* (G. *ihr*), Goth. *izōs*. Hence **hers** absol. pron. xiv; see -S.

her[2] orig. dat., later acc. of the fem. 3rd pers. sg. pron. OE. *hire* = MDu. *hare* (Du. *haar*), f. pronominal base **χi-* HE[1]; cf. the parallel forms on the base **i-*, viz. OS. *iru*, OHG. *iru*, *iro* (G. *ihr*), Goth. *izai*. Hence **herself** xii, in OE. *hire sylfre* (dat.).

herald officer who delivers proclamations, etc.; envoy xiv; forerunner xvi; one skilled in heraldry XIX. ME. *herau(l)d* - OF. *herau(l)t* (mod. *héraut*) - Gmc. *χ*ariwald*-, f. *χ*arjaz* army + **wald*- rule, WIELD. So vb. XIV. Hence **heraldic** XVIII, **heraldry** XVI.

herb XIII. ME. *(h)erbe* - OF. *erbe* (mod. *herbe*) :- L. *herba* grass, green crops, herb. The pronunc. without initial aspirate was regular till early XIX. So **herbaceous** XVII. f. L. **herbage** XIV. - OF. **herbal** book treating of plants. XVI. - medL.; whence **herbalist** XVI. **herbarium** collection of dried plants. XVIII. - late L.; see -ARY.

herd[1] company of animals. OE. *heord* = MLG. *herde*, OHG. *herta* (G. *herde*), ON. *hjǫrð*, Goth. *hairda* :- Gmc. *χ*erðō*; cf. Skr. *śárdha*-, W. *cordd* tribe, family, OSl. *črěda*.

herd[2] keeper of a herd. OE. *hi(e)rde* = OS. *hirdi*, *herdi*, OHG. *hirti* (G. *hirte*), ON. *hirðir*, Goth. *hairdeis* :- Gmc. *χ*erðjaz*, f. *χ*erðō* (see prec.). Hence **herd** vb. intr. XIV; trans. XVI. **herdsman** XVII. alt. of *herdman* (OE. *hierdemann*).

here OE. *hēr* = OS. *hēr*, OHG. *hiar* (Du., G. *hier*), ON. *hér*, Goth. *hēr*; obscurely f. Gmc. pronominal base *χ*i*- this (see HE[1]).

hereditament XV. - medL. *hērēditāmentum*, f. late L. *hērēditāre*, f. *hērēs*, *hērēd*- HEIR; see -MENT. So **hereditable** XV. - obs. F. or medL. **hereditary** XVI. - L. **heredity** inheritance (rare) XVI; heritable character XVIII; (biol.) XIX. - (O)F. or L.

heresy XIII. ME. *(h)eresie* - OF. *(h)eresie* (mod. *hérésie*) - L. *hæresis* - Gr. *hairesis* choice, (hence) school of thought, etc., f. *haireisthai* choose. So **heretic** XIV. **heretical** XVI. - medL.

heriot (orig.) feudal service consisting of military equipment restored to the lord on the death of a tenant. OE. *heregeatwa*, *-we*, f. *here* army + *geatwa* trappings.

heritage XIII. - OF. *(h)eritage* (mod. *hé*-), f. *(h)eriter*, etc. - ecclL. *hērēditāre*, f. *hērēs*, *hērēd*- HEIR. So **heritable** XIV. **heritor** XV (*-er*). - AN. *heriter* = (O)F. *héritier* :- L. *hērēditārius*; conformed to -OR[1] in XVI.

hermaphrodite XV. - L. *hermaphrodītus* - Gr. *hermaphródītos*, orig. proper name of a son of *Hermes* and *Aphrodite*, who grew together with the nymph Salmacis while bathing in her fountain and so combined male and female characters.

hermeneutics science of interpretation. XVIII. - modL. *hermēneutica* - Gr. *hermēneutikḗ*, sb. use of fem. sg. of adj. (see -IC, -ICS), f. *hermēneutḗs*, agent-noun f. *hermēneúein* interpret, f. *hermēneús* interpreter.

hermetic pert. to (the supposed writings of) *Hermes* Trismegistus; (hence) pert. to occult science, esp. alchemy; *h. seal* airtight closure (as used by alchemists). XVII. - modL. *hermēticus*, f. *Hermēs Trismegistus* (Gr. *Hermês trìs mégistos*) 'thrice-greatest Hermes', name given by Neoplatonists, mystics, and alchemists to the Egyptian god Thoth, who was identified with the Grecian Hermes (god of science, etc.) as the author of occult science and esp. alchemy; see -IC. So **hermetically** XVII.

hermit XIII. ME. *armite*, *(h)er(e)mite* - OF. *(h)ermite* (mod. *ermite*) or ChrL. *erēmīta* (medL. *her*-) - Gr. *erēmī́tēs*, f. *erēmíā* desert, f. *érēmos* solitary, deserted. So **hermitage** XIII.

hernia XIV. - L.

hero man of superhuman qualities, demigod XIV (rare before XVI); illustrious warrior XVI; man admired for his great deeds and noble qualities XVII; chief man in a poem, play, etc. In earliest use chiefly pl. *heroes*, with sg. *heroe* (both of 3 sylls.) and *heros* - L. *hērōs*, pl. *hērōēs* - Gr. *hḗrōs*, pl. *hērōes*. The common *heroe* (XVI-XVIII) was superseded by *hero* (XVII), with pl. *heroes* (2 sylls.). So **heroic** XVI. - F. or L. - Gr. *hērōïkós*. **heroi-comic(al)** XVIII. **heroine** XVII. - F. or L. - Gr. *hērōínē*. **heroism** XVIII. - F.

heroin XIX. - G., of uncert. orig.; see -IN.

heron poet. **hern** XIV. ME. *he(i)roun*, *herne* - OF. *hairon* (mod. *héron*) - Gmc. *χ*aiȝaran*- (whence OHG. *heigaro*; cf. ON. *hegri*), dissimilated form of *χ*raiȝran*- (cf. OE. *hrāgra*, MLG. *rēger*, MDu. *reiger*, OHG. *reigaro*, G. *reiher*), of imit. orig. Hence **heronry** XVII.

herpes XVII. - L. *herpēs* - Gr. *hérpēs* shingles, lit. 'creeping', f. *hérpein* creep.

herring OE. *hǣring*, *hēring* = MLG. *hērink*, *hārink* (Du. *haring*), OHG. *hāring* (G. *häring*, *hering*) :- WGmc. *χ*ēringa*, beside which a var. with *χ*ar*- is repr. by medL. *haringus*; perh. orig. 'greyish-white fish', f. HOAR; see -ING[3].

hertz (electr.) frequency of one cycle per second. f. name of H. R. *Hertz* (1857-94), G. physicist.

hesitate XVII. f. pp. stem of L. *hæsitāre* stick fast, stammer, be undecided, f. *hæs*-, pp. stem of *hærēre* stick, ADHERE; see -ATE[3]. So **hesitation** XVII. - L.

Hesperian western. XVI. f. L. *hesperius*, Gr. *hespérios*, f. *Hesperia*, Gr. *Hespería* (poet.) land of the West, f. *Hesperus*, *Hésperos*, adj. western, sb. evening star; see -IAN.

Hessian pert. to *Hesse* in Germany; *H. boot* top-boot with tassels first worn by Hessian troops XIX; *H. fly*, so named because it was erron. supposed to have been carried into America by Hessian troops during the War of Independence XVIII; see -IAN.

hest (arch.) bidding, BEHEST. XII. f. (on the model of abstr. sbs. in *-te*) ME. *hes*, OE. *hǣs* :- Gmc. *χ*aittiz*, f. *χ*aitan* call (see HIGHT).

hetero-, heter- comb. form of Gr. *héteros* other. **heterodox** XVII. - Gr. *heteródoxos* (*dóxā* opinion); **heterodyne** XX; **heterogeneous** XVII. - medL. *heterogeneus*, f. Gr. *heterogenḗs* (*génos* KIND[1]).

hetman military commander in Poland, etc. XVIII. - Pol., prob. - G. *hauptmann* 'head man', captain.

heuristic serving to find out. XIX. irreg. f. Gr. *heurískein* find; see -ISTIC.

hew pp. *hewn*. OE. str. vb. *hēawan* = OS. *hauwan* (Du. *houwen*), OHG. *houwan* (G. *hauen*), ON. *hǫggva* :- Gmc. *χ*auwan*, f. IE. **kou*- **kow*-, found also in OSl. *kovǫ* forge, Lith. *káuju* strike, forge.

hexa- before a vowel **hex-**, comb. form of Gr. *héx* SIX, e.g. **hexagon, -agonal**[1] XVI, **-hedron** XVI, **hexameter,** XVI.

hexad group of six. XVII. - Gr. *hexás, hexad-*, f. *héx* SIX; see -AD.

heyday (arch.) excl. denoting gaiety, surprise, wonder. XVI (*heyda*). The earliest form agrees with LG. *heida*, also *heidi* hurrah! Hence sb. state of exaltation or excitement XVI; prime, bloom XVIII.

hiatus gap, chasm XVI; interruption of continuity XVII; break between two vowels XVIII. - L. *hiātus* gaping, opening, f. *hiāre* gape.

hibernate spend the winter. XIX. f. pp. stem of L. *hībernāre*, f. *hīberna* winter quarters, n. pl. of *hībernus* pert. to winter, f. *hiems* winter. So **hibernation** XVII (nat. hist. XIX).

Hibernian Irish. XVII. f. L. *Hibernia* Ireland, alt. of *I(u)verna, Iuberna*, - Gr. *I(ϝ)érnē*, of Celt. orig. (cf. Ir. *Ériu*); see -IAN.

hibiscus XVIII. - L., of unkn. orig.

hiccough sb. and vb. XVI. imit.; early forms *hickop, hi(c)kup*, which superseded earlier †*hicket*, †*hickock*. The form *hiccough* (XVII) is due to assim. to *cough*, but the pronunc. has not been affected.

hickory XVII. of N. Amer. Indian orig.

hidalgo Spanish gentleman. XVI. - Sp., formerly *hijo dalgo*, i.e. *hijo de algo* 'son of something'.

hide[1] skin. OE. *hȳd* = OS. *hūd* (Du. *huid*), OHG. *hūt* (G. *haut*), ON. *húð* :- Gmc. **χūðiz* :- IE. **kūtis* (cf. Gr. *kútos*, L. *cutis* CUTICLE). Hence as vb. thrash, whence (colloq.) **hiding** thrashing. XIX.

hide[2] measure of land reckoned sufficient to support a free family with dependants. OE. *hīd*, earlier *hīġid*, f. *hīġ-, hīw-* (in comb.) = OHG. *hī-*, ON. *hý-*, Goth. *heiwa-*, rel. to L. *cīvis* citizen and to OE. *hīwan* (pl.) members of a household, OHG. *hī(w)un*, ON. *hjún* man and wife.

hide[3] pt. *hid* pp. *hidden* put or keep out of sight. OE. *hȳdan* = MDu., MLG. *hūden* :- WGmc. **χūdjan*, prob. based on IE. **keudh-*, repr. also by Gr. *keúthein*, W. *cuddio* hide.

hideous frightful, (hence) frightfully ugly. XIII. ME. *hidous* - AN. *hidous*, OF. *hidos, -eus* (mod. *hideux*), earlier *hisdos*, f. *hi(s)de* fear, of unkn. orig. The ending was assim. to -EOUS XVI.

hie †strive, exert oneself OE.; (arch.) hasten XII. OE. *hīġian*, of unkn. orig.

hierarchy division of angels, etc. XIV; priestly or ecclesiastical rule XVI; body of ecclesiastical rulers XVII. ME. *ierarchie, gerarchie* (superseded by latinized forms in XVI) - OF. *ierarchie, gerarchie* (mod. *hiérarchie*) - medL. *(h)ierarchia* - Gr. *hierarkhiā*, f. *hierárkhēs* steward of sacred rites, high priest, f. *hierós* sacred, holy + *-arkhēs, -arkhos* ruling, ruler; see ARCH-, -Y[3]. So **hierarch** ecclesiastical ruler XVI; archangel XVII. - medL. - Gr. **hierarchical** XV.

hieratic pert. to a priestly class, (hence) of a style of ancient Egyptian writing. XVII. - L. *hierāticus* - Gr. *hierātikós* priestly, sacerdotal, f. *hierâsthai* be a priest, f. *hiereús* priest, f. *hierós* sacred.

hieroglyphic pertaining to ancient Egyptian writing; sb. character in such picture-writing; symbolic or enigmatic figure. XVI. - F. *hiéroglyphique* or late L. *hieroglyphicus* - Gr. *hierogluphikós*, f. *hierós* sacred + *gluphḗ* carving. Hence, as back-formation or after F. *hiéroglyphe*, **hieroglyph** XVII.

hierophant expounder of mysteries. XVII. - late L. *hierophanta, -ēs* - Gr. *hierophántēs*, f. *hierós* sacred + *-phan-*, base of *phaínein* reveal.

higgle cavil as to terms. XVII. var. of HAGGLE.

higgledy-piggledy XVI. Rhyming jingle prob. based on PIG, with ref. to swine herding together.

high OE. *hēah* = OS., OHG. *hōh* (Du. *hoog*, G. *hoch*), ON. *hár*, Goth. *hauhs* :- Gmc. **χauχaz* :- IE. **koukos* (cf. Lith. *kaũkas* swelling, boil, *kaũkarus* height, hill, ON. *haugr* hill, Goth. *hiuhma* heap, Russ. *kúcha* heap). Cf. HEIGHT. Combs. **high-brow,** back-formation from **high-browed** (orig. U.S.) XX; **high-churchman** (whence **high church**) XVII; **highland** OE. *hēahlond*; **high street** highway, main road; main street of a town. OE. *hēahstrǣt* often used of the Roman roads; **highway** public road. OE. *hēiweġ*; hence **highwayman** XVII.

high-falutin' (orig. U.S. sl.) sb. bombastic speech; adj. absurdly pompous. XIX. f. HIGH + an el. of unkn. orig.

high-flown †elevated, elated, intoxicated; hyperbolical, bombastic; †extreme in opinion. XVII. orig. f. *high* adv. + old strong pp. of FLOW, from the sense 'in flood', 'swollen'; later assoc. with pp. of FLY[2].

hight in lit. arch. use now only in pt. 'is called', 'was called', and pp. 'called, named'. The only surviving form of a Gmc. str. vb. meaning 'call by name, name, call to do something, bid, command, promise', repr. by OE. *hātan* (pt. *heht, hēt*, pp. *hāten*), OS. *hētan*, OHG. *heizzan* (G. *heissen* call, bid, be called), ON. *heita*, Goth. *haitan* (pt. *haihait*, pp. *haitans*); f. a base which has been related to L. *ciēre* summon, CITE.

hike jerk, pull, drag XVIII; move away or off; (latterly) tramp, esp. for pleasure XIX. of unkn. orig. Hence sb. XIX.

hilarity cheerfulness XVI; boisterous joy XIX. - F. *hilarité* - L. *hilaritās*, f. *hilaris* = Gr. *hilarós* cheerful, gay; see -ITY. Hence **hilarious** XIX.

Hilary name of a saint and doctor of the Church, bishop of Poitiers (d. 367), whose feast, falling on 13 January, gives his name to the first of the law and university terms of the calendar year. XVI. - medL. *Hilarius*.

hill OE. *hyll* = LG. *hull*, MDu. *hil(le)*, *hul* :- WGmc. **χulni*, rel. to L. *collis*, Gr. *kolōnós, kolṓnē*, Lith. *kálnas* hill. Hence **hillock, hilly** XIV.

hillo(a) var. of HALLO(A). XVII.

hilt OE. *hilt* m. and n. and *hilte* fem., corr. to OS. *hilte, helta*, MLG. *hilte*, MDu. *helte*, OHG. *helza*, ON. *hjalt* :- Gmc. **χeltaz, -iz, -jōn*, of unkn. orig.

him orig. dat. of HE[1], it; later also as direct object. OE. *him* = MDu. *hem(e)*, *him* (Du. *hem*), f. pronominal base **χi-* HE[1]; cf. parallel forms on the base **i-*, viz. OS., OHG. *imu, imo* (G. *ihm*), Goth. *imma*.

hind[1] female of the deer. OE. *hind*, corr. to OS. *hind-*, (M)Du. *hinde*, OHG. *hinta* (G. *hinde*), ON. *hind* :- Gmc. **χinþjō*, f. IE. **k̂em-* hornless, repr. by Gr. *kemás* young deer, Skr. *śáma-*, Lith. *šmùlas* hornless.

hind² farm servant; farm bailiff. XVI. Later form of late OE., ME. *hine* pl. household servants, (hence) sg. (esp. farm) servant, lad; presumably developed from OE. *hīġna*, g. pl. of *hīgan*, *hīwan* (cf. HIDE²).

hind³ situated at the back, posterior. XIII. This and synon. **hinder¹** (XIV) appear to be abstracted from OE. *hinde(r)weard* backward, back-, *bihindan* BEHIND. Cf. OE. *hindan* from behind, *hinder* below, corr. to OHG. *hintana* (G. *hinten*) adv. behind, Goth. *hindana* prep. beyond, and OS. *hindiro*, MLG. *hinder*, OHG. *hintar* (G. *hinter*), ON. compar. *hindri*, Goth. *hindar* prep. beyond, the further relations of which are doubtful. Hence **hindermore, hindermost, hindmost** XIV.

hinder² †injure OE.; keep back, delay XIV. OE. *hindrian* = MLG., MDu. *hinderen*, OHG. *hintarōn* (G. *hindern*), ON. *hindra* :- Gmc. **χindarōjan*, f. **χindar*; see prec. Hence **hindrance** XV.

Hindi XVIII. - Urdu *hindī*, f. *hind* India. So **Hindu, Hindoo** XVII. - Urdu - Pers. *hindū*, f. *hind* India = Skr. *síndhu-* river, the Indus, (hence) region of the Indus, Sindh. **Hindustani** XVIII.

hinge sb. XIII. of obscure orig.; ME. *he(e)ng*, *hing*, with deriv. (see -LE¹) *he(e)ngle*, *hingle*, corr. to MLG., MHG. *hengel* (G. *hängel*), f. the base of HANG; cf. (M)LG. *henge* hinge, Du. *hengel* handle, *hengsel* hinge, handle. Hence vb. XVII.

hinny offspring of a she-ass and a stallion. XVII. f. L. *hinnus* - Gr. *(g)ínnos*.

hint †opportunity; slight indication or suggestion. XVII. of obscure orig.; presumably var. of rare †*hent* grasp, intention, f. *hent* vb., OE. *hentan* seize. Hence vb. XVII.

hinterland XIX. - G., f. *hinter* behind (see HIND³) + *land* LAND.

hip¹ projection of pelvis and top of thigh. OE. *hype* = MDu. *höpe*, *hüpe* (Du. *heup*), OHG. *huf*, pl. *huffi*, Goth. *hups* :- Gmc. **χupiz*, rel. to HOP¹.

hip² fruit of the (wild) rose. OE. *hēope*, *hīope*, corr. to OS. *hiopo* (Du. *joop*), OHG. *hiufo* thornbush, bramble :- WGmc. **χeup-*.

hip³ †excl. of calling XVIII; as a cheer, in *hip hip hooray* XIX.

hippo short for HIPPOPOTAMUS. XIX.

hippo- comb. form of Gr. *híppos* HORSE. **hippocampus** sea-horse. XVI - L. - Gr. (*kámpos* sea-monster); **hippogriff** fabulous griffin-like creature. XVII. - F. *hippogriffe* - It. *ippogrifo* (*grifo* :- L. *grȳphus* GRIFFIN).

hippocras wine flavoured with spices. XIV. ME. *ypocras* - OF. *ipo-*, *ypocras*, forms of the name *Hippocrates* (ancient Gr. physician V B.C.), the wine being so called because it was strained through 'Hippocrates' bag', a conical bag used as a filter.

Hippocrene name of a fountain on Helicon, sacred to the Muses, (hence) poetic inspiration. XVII. - L. *Hippocrēnē* - Gr. *Hippokrḗnē*, f. *híppos* horse + *krḗnē* fountain; so named because fabled to have been produced by a stroke of Pegasus' hoof.

hippodrome circus (prop.) for horse and chariot races. XVI. - (O)F. *hippodrome* or L. *hippodromus* - Gr. *hippódromos*, f. *híppos* horse + *drómos* race.

hippopotamus XVI. - L. - late Gr. *hippopótamos*, for earlier *híppos ho potámios* the horse of the river (*potamós* river).

hircine goatish. XVII. - L. *hircīnus*, f. *hircus* he-goat; see -INE¹.

hire payment for the temporary use of a thing; wages, reward. OE. *hȳr* = OS. *hūria*, MLG., MDu. *hūre* (Du. *huur*) :- WGmc. **χūrja*. Hence **hire** vb. OE. *hȳrian*. **hireling** OE. (rare) *hȳrling*; formed afresh in XVI.

hirsute XVII. - L. *hirsūtus*, rel. to synon. *hirtus*.

his possessive adj. and pron. OE. *his*, gen. of HE¹ and IT; cf. parallel forms on the base **i-*, viz. OS., Goth. *is*, OHG. *is*, *es*.

hispid bristly, shaggy. XVII. - L. *hispidus*; see -ID¹

hiss vb. XIV. imit. Hence sb. XVI.

hist excl. enjoining silence. XVII (cf. †*ist* XVI).

histo- repr. comb. form of Gr. *histós* web, tissue, rel. to *histánai* set up (cf. STAND), as in **histology** science of organic tissues. XIX. - F. *histologie*.

history †story, tale; methodical narrative of events, branch of knowledge dealing with these XV; methodical account of natural phenomena XVI. - L. *historia* - Gr. *historíā* learning or knowing by inquiry, narrative, history, f. *hístōr* knowing, learned, wise man :- **ϝídtōr*, f. **ϝid-* know (see WIT²). So **historian** XV. - (O)F. **historic** XVII; **historical** XVI. f. L. *historicus* - Gr. *historikós*.

histrionic XVII. - late L. *histriōnicus*, f. L. *histriō*, *-ōn-* actor in stage plays. See -IC.

hit pt., pp. *hit* light upon XI; strike XIII. Late OE. *(ġe)hittan* - ON. *hitta* light upon, meet with, of unkn. orig. Hence sb. XVI.

hitch A. move jerkily XV; B. catch with a hoop, loop, etc. XVII. of uncert. orig. Hence as sb. XVII.

hither OE. *hider*, corr. to ON. *heðra* here, hither, Goth. *hidrē* hither, f. demonstr. base **χi-* (see HE¹, HENCE, HERE) + suffix appearing in L. *citrā* on this side.

hive OE. *hȳf*, f. **χūf-*, whence also ON. *húfr* ship's hull; cf. L. *cūpa* barrel, Gr. *kúpē*, Skr. *kū́pa-* hole.

ho excl. of surprise, triumph, to attract attention, etc., and (repeated) of laughter. XIII. Partly - ON. *hó* or OF. *ho* halt!

hoar (arch.) grey-haired, greyish-white. OE. *hār* = OS., OHG. *hēr* old, venerable (G. *hehr* august, stately), ON. *hárr* hoary, old :- Gmc. **χairaz* :- IE. **k̂oira-* (cf. OSl. *sěrŭ* grey). Survives in **hoarfrost** (XIII) and **hoarhound,** HOREHOUND. Hence **hoary** XVI.

hoard sb. OE. *hord* = OS. *hord*, *horth* treasure, secret place, OHG. *hort*, ON. *hodd*, Goth. *huzd* :- Gmc. **χuzdam* (rel. to HIDE¹). So vb. OE. *hordian*.

hoarding temporary fence made of boards. XIX. f. *hoard*, earlier *ho(u)rd* (XVIII), which seems to be based ult. on AN. *h(o)urdis*, f. OF. *hourd*, *hort* (- Frankish **hurð* = OHG. *hurd* HURDLE) + *-is* :- L. *-ītiu-s*; see -ING¹.

hoarhound see HOREHOUND.

hoarse XIV. - ON. **hārs* (:- **hairsaR*), *háss*; this

superseded ME. *ho(o)s*, OE. *hās* = MLG. *hēs(ch)* (Du. *heesch*), OHG. *heis(i)*, (M)HG. *heiser* :- Gmc. **χais(r)az*, **χairsaz*, of unkn. orig.

hoax deceive by a fiction; earlier, poke fun at. XVIII. perh. contr. of HOCUS. Hence sb. XIX.

hob[1] rustic, clown XIV; sprite, elf XV. By-form of *Rob*, short for *Robin*, *Robert*. Hence **hobgoblin** (cf. *Robin Goodfellow*) XVI.

hob[2] side of a grate, perh. orig. back of a grate formed of a mass of clay XVI (*hubbe*); peg or pin as a target XVI. of unkn. orig.; cf. HUB. Hence **hobnail** XVI.

hobble[1] †move unsteadily up and down; walk with unsteady rising and falling gait. XIV. prob. of LG. orig. (cf. early Du. *hobbelen* toss, rock from side to side, halt, stammer, frequent. of *hobben*).

hobble[2] fasten together the legs of a horse, etc. XIX. var. of earlier *hopple* (XVI), prob. of LG. orig. (cf. early Flem. *hoppelen*), infl. by prec.

hobbledehoy, hobbadehoy clumsy or awkward youth. XVI (*hobledehoye*, *hobbard de hoy*). of unkn. orig.

hobby[1] (arch.) small horse XIV; (*h.-horse*) in the morris dance, etc., figure of a horse manipulated by a performer; stick with a horse's head used as a toy XVI; favourite pastime XVII. Earliest forms *hobyn*, *hoby*, i.e. *Hobin*, *Hobby* by-forms of the name *Robin*.

hobby[2] small species of falcon. XV (*hoby*). - OF. *hobé*, *hobet*, dim. of *hobe* small bird of prey; of unkn. orig.

hobgoblin see HOB[1]. **hobnail** see HOB[2].

hob-nob drink together XVIII; be on familiar terms XIX. orig. *hob or nob*, *hob-a-nob*, *hob and nob*, f. phr. (*drink*) *hob or nob*, etc., drink to one another alternately; continuing earlier *hab* (*or*) *nab* (XVI) get or lose, hit or miss, repr. some part of HAVE and its negative (OE. *habban* and *nabban*).

hobo (U.S.) migrant labourer; tramp. XIX. of unkn. orig.

hock[1] joint of the hind leg XVI; knuckle end of a gammon XVIII. Short for *hockshin* (*hokschyne* XIV), OE. *hōhsinu*; see HOUGH.

hock[2] German white wine. XVII. Short for †*hockamore* - G. *Hochheimer* (*wein*) wine of *Hochheim* on the Main, Germany.

hockey XVI (?). of unkn. orig.

hocus pocus †conjurer, juggler; conjuring formula; jugglery, trickery. XVII (*hocas pocas*, *hokos pokos*). Based ult. on *hax pax max Deus adimax* (XVI), pseudo-L. magical formula coined by vagrant students. Hence as vb. juggle, hoax. XVII. Also, by shortening, **hocus** †sb. juggler; jugglery. XVII; vb. play a trick upon XVII; drug XIX. Cf. HOAX.

hod open receptacle for carrying bricks, etc. XIV; receptacle for holding coal XIX. synon. with, and perh. alt. of, *hot* (XIII) - (O)F. *hotte* pannier, creel (prob. of Gmc. orig.).

hodden (Sc.) coarse woollen cloth. XVIII. of unkn. orig.

Hodge typical name for an English yokel. XVI. pet-form of the Christian name *Roger* (ME. *Hogge*).

hodge-podge see HOTCHPOT.

hodometer, odometer by a wheeled vehicle. XVIII. - F. *odomètre*, f. Gr. *hodós* way + *métron* measure.

hoe sb. XIV. ME. *howe* - (O)F. *houe* - Frankish **hauwa* = OHG. *houwa* (G. *haue*), rel. to *houwan* HEW. Hence vb. XV.

hog (esp. castrated) swine OE.; young sheep XIV; coarse or filthy person XV. Late OE. *hogg*, *hocg*, of unkn. orig.

hogmanay (Sc. and north.) last day of the year. XVII. Corr. in meaning and use to OF. *aguillanneuf* last day of the year, new-year's gift, of which the Norman form *hoguinané* may be the immed. source of the Eng. word.

hogshead large cask for liquids XIV; 52½ imperial gallons XV. f. HOG'*s* + HEAD, but the reason for the name is unkn.

hoist vb. XVI. alt. of *hoise* (XVI), earlier *hys(s)e* (XV), Sc. *heis* (XVI); prob. - Du. *hijschen* or LG. *hissen*, *hiesen*, but the Eng. forms are earlier than any cited from elsewhere. The word appears early as an int. used in hauling: Eng. *hissa*, *heisau*, etc.

hoity-toity sb. riotous behaviour, romping; adj. frolicsome, flighty; int. expressing surprise at flighty conduct. XVII. Rhyming jingle f. †*hoit* indulge in riotous mirth, romp (XVI).

hokey-pokey A. (dial.) hocus pocus; B. cheap sort of ice-cream. XIX. In A alteration of HOCUS POCUS; in B of unkn. orig.

hold[1] pt., pp. *held* †guard; keep from getting away, falling, etc.; keep in a certain condition. OE. str. vb. *h(e)aldan* = OS. *haldan* (Du. *houden*), OHG. *haltan* (G. *halten*), ON. *halda*, Goth. *haldan*. Hence, and partly - ON. *hald* hold, fastening, support, custody, **hold**[2] sb. XII.

hold[2] cavity in a ship for the stowage of cargo. XVI. alt., by assim. to prec., of *hole*, *holl* (XV), prob. - (M)Du. *hol* HOLE.

hole OE. *hol* etc. = ON. *hol*, orig. n. sg. of *hol* hollow = OS., (M)Du., OHG. *hol* (G. *hohl*), ON. *holr* :- Gmc. **χulaz*; ult. f. var. of IE. **k̂el-* cover, conceal. So **hole** vb. make a hole (in). OE. *holian* = OHG. *holōn*, Goth. *-hulōn*.

holiday religious festival; day of cessation from work. OE. *hāliġdæġ*, late *hālidæiġ*; also as two words inflected, HOLY DAY.

holla int. XVI. - F. *holà*, i.e. *ho* (see HO), *là* there. Cf. HALLO(A), HOLLO.

holland linen fabric orig. named *holland cloth* from *Holland*, a province of the Netherlands, its place of manufacture. XV.

hollands kind of gin. XVIII. Formerly *Hollands genever* and *gin*. - Du. *hollandsch*, *hollandsche genever* Dutch gin.

hollo cry out loud. XVI. var. of HOLLA; cf. U.S. *holler*.

hollow adj. XII. ME. *holȝ*, *holu*, inflected *hol(e)we*, attrib. use of OE. *holh* hole, cave, obscurely rel. to *hol* HOLE. Hence vb. XV, sb.

holly XII. Reduced form of OE. *hole(ġ)n*, ME. *holin*, later *hollen*, rel. to OS., OHG. *hulis* (MHG. *huls*, G. *hulst*).

hollyhock †marsh mallow XIII; *Althaea rosea* XVI. f. HOLY + *hock*, OE. *hoc* mallow, with ref. to some sacred assoc.

holm(e) islet, esp. in a river XI; low-lying land

by a river XIII. - ON. *holmr* islet, meadow on the shore, corr. to OE. (poet.) *holm* billow, wave, sea, OS. *holm* hill.

holm-oak evergreen oak, *Quercus ilex*. XVI. f. *holm* holly (XIV), holm-oak (XVI), alt. of †*holin* HOLLY + OAK.

holo-, before a vowel **hol-,** comb. form of Gr. *hólos* whole, entire.

holocaust whole burnt offering XIII; complete sacrifice XV; complete destruction XVII. - (O)F. *holocauste* - late L. *holocaustum* - Gr. *holókauston*, f. *hólos* whole + *kaustós*, var. of *kautós* burnt, f. *kaíein* burn.

holograph (letter, etc.) written wholly by the person in whose name it appears. XVII. - F. *holographe* or late L. *holographus* - Gr. *hológraphos*; see HOLO-, -GRAPH.

holster XVII. corr. to and contemp. with Du. *holster*, but the earlier history of neither word is apparent.

holt (dial.) wood, copse. OE. *holt* = OS., ON. *holt*, (M)Du. *hout*, (O)HG. *holz* :- Gmc. **χultam* :- IE. **kḷdo-*; cf. Gr. *kládos* twig, OIr. *caill*, (mod.) *coill*, Gael. *coill(e)*, W. *celli*.

holus-bolus all in a lump, all at once. XIX. Presumably burlesque latinization of *whole bolus* or repr. assumed Gr. **hólos bôlos* 'whole lump' (see BOLUS).

holy OE. *hāliġ* = OS. *hēlag*, OHG. *heilag* (Du., G. *heilig*), ON. *heilagr*, Goth. *hailag* :- Gmc. **χailaʒaz*, f. **χailaz* WHOLE; the primary meaning may have been either 'of good augury' or 'inviolate'. Hence **holy day** OE. *hāliġ dæġ*; revived in XIX; **Holy Ghost** OE. *se hālga gāst* 'the holy spirit', *hāliġ gāst*, *hāligāst* (often as one word in ME.), tr. ecclL. *sanctus spiritus* (**Holy Spirit** XIII); **holystone** piece of sandstone for scouring decks XIX; said to be so named because the work is done kneeling.

homage XIII. ME. *(h)omage* - OF. *(h)omage* (mod. *hommage*) :- medL. *homināticum*, f. *homō*, *homin-* man; see -AGE.

home house, abode OE.; native place XIV; one's own place or country XVI. OE. *hām* n. collection of dwellings, village, estate, house, corr. to OS. *hēm* (Du. *heem*), (O)HG. *heim* n., ON. *heimr* m., Goth. *haims* fem. village; ult. relations disputed. Hence vb. go home XVIII; whence (of birds) **homer, homing** XIX. **homely** †domestic, familiar; plain, simple XIV; uncomely XVI.

homicide[1] killer of another human being. XIV. - (O)F. - L. *homicīda*, f. shortened stem of *homō*, *homin-* man + *-cīda* -CIDE[1]. So **homicide**[2] killing of another human being. XIV. - (O)F. - L. *homicīdium*. Hence **homicidal** XVIII.

homily XIV. ME. *omelie* - OF. *omelie* (mod. *homélie*) - ecclL. *homīlia* - Gr. *homīliā* intercourse, discourse, (eccl.) sermon, f. *hómīlos* crowd, f. *homoû* together + *ilē* crowd, troop; see -Y[3]. Finally assim. to the L. form in XVI. So **homiletic** XVII. - late L. - Gr. *homīlētikós*, f. *homīlētós*, vbl. adj. of *homīlein* consort or hold converse with.

hominy maize boiled with water or milk. XVII. of N. Amer. Indian orig.

homo-, before a vowel **hom-,** comb. form of Gr. *homós* SAME. **homogeneous** XVII. f. scholL. *homogeneus*, f. Gr. *homogenḗs*, *-gene-*, f. *génos*, *gene-* KIN. So **homogeneity** XVII, **homologous** XVII. **homonym** XVII. - L. *homōnymum* - Gr. *homṓnumon*, n. of *homṓnumos* (see NAME). **homophone** XVII (only in dictionaries before XIX). - Gr. *homóphōnos* (*phōnḗ* sound).

homoeopathy system of medical practice in which 'likes are cured by likes'. XIX. - modL. *homœopathia*, G. *homöopathie*, f. Gr. *hómoios* like + *-pátheia* -PATHY. So **homoeopath, homoeopathic** XIX.

hom(o)ousian (theol.) consubstantial. XVI. - late L. *homoūsiānus*, f. *homoūsius* - Gr. *hom(o)oúsios*, f. *homós* SAME + *ousiā* ESSENCE; see -IAN. **homoiousian** of like substance. XVIII. - late L., f. Gr. *homoioúsios*, f. *hómoios* like.

homunculus XVII. - L., dim. of *homō* man; see -CLE.

hone whetstone. XIV. spec. use of OE. *hān* stone (often one serving as a landmark) = ON. *hein* :- Gmc. **χainō*. Hence vb. XIX.

honest marked by uprightness or probity; †comely, decent XIII; †honourable, respectable; †chaste XIV. ME. *onest(e)* - OF. *(h)oneste* (mod. *honnête*) - L. *honestus*, f. *honōs*, *hones-* HONOUR. So **honesty** XIV. - OF. *(h)onesté* - L. *honestās*, for **honestitās* (-TY).

honey sweet fluid collected from flowers by bees OE.; sweetheart XIV; sweetness XVI. OE. *huniġ* = OS. *honeg*, *-ig*, OHG. *hona(n)g* (Du., G. *honig*), ON. *hunang* :- Gmc. **χuna(ŋ)gam*. Hence **honeycomb** OE. *huniġcamb*. **honeymoon** XVI; expl. by early writers with ref. to affection of married people changing with the moon. **honeysuckle** clover XIII; woodbine, *Lonicera* XVI. ME. *hunisuccle*, *-soukel*, extension of *hunisuce*, *-souke*, OE. *huniġsūce*, *-sūge* (f. *sūcan*, *sūgan* SUCK). **honeyed, honied** sweetened as with honey. XIV.

honk cry of the wild goose XIX; noise made by a motor-horn XX. imit.

honorarium XVII. - L., gift made on being admitted to a post of honour, sb. use of n. of *honōrārius*, whence **honorary** XVII. So **honorific** conferring honour. XVII.

honour, U.S. **honor** renown, reputation XII; high rank or dignity XIII; high respect or esteem; chastity XIV; upright character XVI. ME. *(h)on(o)ur*, *an(o)ur* - AN. *an(o)ur*, OF. *(h)onor*, *(h)onur* (mod. *honneur*) :- L. *honor* (earlier *honōs*), *honōr-*. So **honour** vb. XIII. - OF. *onorer*, *onurer* (F. *honorer*) :- L. *honōrāre*. **honourable** XV. - (O)F. - L.

hooch (U.S) (esp. poor or illicit) liquor. XX. abbrev. of *Hoochinoo*, name of an Indian tribe of Alaska that made such liquor.

hood OE. *hōd* = MDu. *hoet* (Du. *hoed*), OHG. *huot* (G. *hut* hat) :- WGmc. **χōda*, rel. to HAT. Hence **hoodwink** cover the eyes to prevent vision XVI; fig. XVII.

-hood OE. *-hād* = OS. *-hēd*, (O)HG. *-heit*, orig. a Gmc. independent sb. meaning 'person', 'sex', 'condition, rank', 'quality', OE. *hād*, OS. *hēd*, OHG. *heit*, ON. *heiðr* (honour, worth), Goth. *haidus* (kind, manner), rel. to ON. *heið* bright sky, Skr. *ketú-* brightness, *keta-* form, shape, sign. This suffix may be added freely to most sbs. denoting a person or a concrete thing to express its condition or state, as OE. *ċildhād* childhood, *prēosthād* priesthood; it lends itself readily to nonce-formations, e.g. *doghood, soulhood*. It has been added to a few adjs., e.g. *falsehood, hardihood, likelihood*, which superseded formations with the parallel -HEAD. Where comps. in *-head* and *-hood* survive side by side, as in *godhead* and *-hood, maidenhead* and *-hood*, there is differentiation of meaning. A few comps. have developed particularized or semi-concrete meanings, as *brotherhood, knighthood, neighbourhood*.

hoodlum (U.S. sl.) XIX. of unkn. orig.

hoodoo (U.S.) XIX. unexpl. alt. of VOODOO.

hoof OE. *hōf* = OS. *hōf* (Du. *hoef*), OHG. *huof* (G. *huf*), ON. *hófr* :- Gmc. **χōfaz*, rel. to synon. Skr. *śaphá-*, Av. *safa-*.

hook sb. OE. *hōc* = MLG., MDu. *hōk* (Du. *hoek*) corner, angle, point of land, rel. to OE. *haca* bolt, OS. *haco* (MDu. *hake*, Du. *haak*), OHG. *hāko* (G. *haken*) hook, ON. *haki*, and Russ. *kógot'* claw, iron hook. Hence **hook** vb. †bend, curve XIII; attach (as) with a hook XVI.

hookah Eastern tobacco-pipe. XVIII. - Urdu *ḥuḳḳa* - Arab. *ḥuḳḳa* casket.

hooligan XIX. of unkn. orig.

hoop[1] circle of metal, etc. XII. Late OE. *hōp* = MDu. *hoop* (Du. *hoep*) :- WGmc. **χōpa*, rel. to ON. *hōp* small land-locked bay.

hoop[2] utter a cry of 'hoop'. XIV. ME. *houpe, howpe* - (O)F. *houper*, f. *houp* (imit.). Hence *hooping* (later *whooping*)*-cough* XVIII. Cf. WHOOP.

hooray var. of HURRAH. XIX.

hop[1] spring on one foot. OE. *hoppian*, corr. to (M)HG. *hopfen*, ON. *hoppa*, f. a base repr. also in OE. *hoppetan*, G. *hopsen*. Hence **hopper** creature that hops XIII; part of a grinding-mill having orig. a hopping movement XIV.

hop[2] (pl. ripened cones of the female) hop-plant, *Humulus lupulus*. XV (*hoppe*). - MLG., MDu. *hoppe* (Du. *hop*), in OS. *feldhoppo* = late OHG. *hopfo* (G. *hopfen*).

hope sb. Late OE. (*tō*)*hopa*, corr. to OLF. *tōhopa*, MLG., MDu. *hope* (Du. *hoop*). Also **hope** vb. Late OE. *hopian* = (M)Du. *hopen*. of unkn. orig.

hoplite XVIII. - F. - Gr. *hoplī́tēs*, f. *hóplon* weapon; see -ITE.

hopscotch XIX. f. HOP[1] + SCOTCH[1] scored line or mark; earlier †*scotch-hoppers* (XVII), †*hop-scot* (XVIII).

horary relating to the hours. XVII. - medL. *hōrārius*, f. *hōra* HOUR; see -ARY.

horde band of Mongol nomads XVI (*hord*(*a*)); great troop XVII. Directly or indirectly - Pol. *horda* - Mongol *ordo* - OTurk. *ordō* royal encampment.

horehound, hoarhound the plant *Marrubium vulgare*, characterized by a white downy pubescence. OE. *hāre hūne*, f. *hār* HOAR + *hūne* 'marrubium', of unkn. orig.

horizon XIV. Late ME. *orizon*(*te*), - OF. *orizon*(*te*) (mod. *horizon*) - late L. *horīzōn, -ont-* - Gr. *horī́zōn*, sb. use of prp. of *horī́zein* bound, limit, f. *hóros* boundary, limit. In later OF. and Eng. conformed to the L. nom. So **horizontal** pert. to the horizon XVI; parallel to the plane of the horizon XVII. - F. or modL.

horn bony excrescence (often curved and pointed) on the head of cattle, etc.; instrument made from or in imitation of this OE.; pointed projection XIII; substance of it XV. OE. *horn* m., corr. to OS. *horn* m., OHG., ON. *horn* n. (Du. *hoorn*, G. *horn*), Goth. *haurn* n. :- Gmc. **χurnaz, -am*, rel. to L. *cornū*, Skr. *śṛ́nga-*, and further to Gr. *kéras*; cf. HART. Hence **hornblende** XVIII. - G. **hornbook** ABC tablet covered with horn. XVI.

hornet The present form appears XV, succeeding to earlier *hernet, harnet*, prob. all - MLG. *hornte*, MDu. *horn*(*e*)*te*, corr. to OE. *hyrnet*(*u*), earlier *hurnitu, hirnitu*, OS. *hornut*, OHG. *hornuz* (G. *hornisse*), which have the appearance of derivs. of HORN; see -ET.

horologe timepiece, clock. XIV. - OF. *or*(*i*)*loge* (mod. *horloge*) :- L. *hōrologium* - Gr. *hōrólogion*, f. *hōrológos*, f. *hṓrā* time, HOUR + *-logos* telling (see -LOGUE).

horoscope plan showing the disposition of the heavens at a particular moment. XVI (earlier in L. form). - (O)F. - L. *hōroscopus* - Gr. *hōroskópos* sign in the ascendant at a birth, horoscope, f. *hṓrā* time, HOUR + *skopós* observer (cf. SCOPE).

horrible exciting horror. XIV. - OF. (*h*)*orrible* - L. *horribilis*, f. *horrēre* (of hair) stand on end, tremble, shudder; see -IBLE. So **horrid** bristling, shaggy, rough XVI; horrible XVII. **horrific** XVII. - F. or L. **horrify** XVIII. - L. *horrificāre*. **horror** XIV. - OF. (*h*)*orrour* (mod. *-eur*) - L. *horror, -ōr-*; see -OR[2].

horripilation 'goose-flesh'. XVII. - late L. *horripilātiō, -ōn-*, f. *horripilāre*, f. *horrēre* (see prec.) + *pilus* hair; see -ATION.

hors d'œuvre dish served as a relish at a meal. XVIII. - F., something out of the ordinary course, prop. 'outside of (the) work'.

horse the quadruped *Equus caballus* OE.; contrivance whose use suggests the service of a horse XIV. OE. *hors* n. = OS. *hros, hers* (MLG. *ros, ors*, MDu. *ors*, Du. *ros*), OHG. (*h*)*ros* (MHG. *ros, ors*, G. *ross*) n., ON. *hross* m. :- Gmc. **χursam, -az*, of unkn. orig. In attrib. use often denoting coarseness, roughness, or large size, as *horse chestnut* (XVI), *laugh* (XVIII), *leech* (XV), *mackerel* (XVII), *play* (XVI), *radish* (XVII). Hence **horse** vb. OE. *horsian*.

hortatory - late L. *hortātōrius*, f. *hortāt-*, pp. stem of *hortārī* EXHORT; see -ORY.

horticulture XVII. f. L. *hortus* garden.

hosanna Jewish liturgical formula, adopted in Christian worship. In OE. and ME. *osanna*, later *hosanna* - late L. (*h*)*ōsanna* - Gr. (*h*)*ōsanná* - Heb. *hôšaʿ-nā*, abbrev. of *hôšīʿāh-nnā* save, pray!

hose A. article of clothing for the leg OE.; B. flexible pipe for conveying liquid XV. Late OE. *hosa, -e* = OS., OHG., ON. *hosa* (Du. *hoos* stocking, water-hose, G. *hose*) :- Gmc. **χusan-, -ōn*. Sense B is prob. from Du. Hence **hosier** XV.

hospice XIX. - (O)F. - L. *hospitium* hospitality, lodging, f. *hospes, hospit-* HOST[2].

hospital (hist.) hostel, hospice XIII; asylum for the destitute or infirm XV; institution for the care of the sick XVI. - OF. *hospital* (mod. *hôpital*) - medL. *hospitāle*, sb. use of n. of *hospitālis*, f. *hospit-*; see prec. and -AL¹. So **hospitality** XIV. **hospitable** XVI. f. medL. *hospitāre* receive as a guest. **hospitaller** member of certain charitable religious orders XIV; spiritual officer of a hospital XVI. - OF. *hospitalier* - medL. *hospitālārius*.

host¹ (arch.) army XVIII; great company, large number XVII. - OF. *(h)o(o)st* :- L. *hostis* stranger, enemy, (in medL.) army; see GUEST.

host² man who lodges and entertains XIII. - (O)F. *(h)oste* (mod. *hôte*) :- L. *hospes, hospit-*, of unkn. orig. So **hostess** XIII. - OF. *ostesse* (mod. *hôtesse*).

host³ †victim, sacrifice; Eucharistic wafer. XIV. - OF. *(h)oiste* :- L. *hostia* victim, sacrifice.

hostage †handing over of a person as a pledge; person thus held in pledge. XIII. - (O)F. *(h)ostage* (mod. *otage*) :- Rom. **obsidāticum*, f. late L. *obsidātus* hostageship, f. *obses, obsid-* hostage, f. OB + **sed-* SIT; see -AGE. The initial *h* is by assim. to HOST².

hostel †place of sojourn, lodging XIII; public place of lodging XIV; students' house of residence XVI. - OF. *(h)ostel* (mod. *hôtel* HÔTEL) :- medL. *hospitāle* HOSPITAL. So **hostelry** XIV. - (O)F. *(h)ostelerie* (mod. *hôtellerie*), f. *(h)ostelier*; see OSTLER.

hostile pert. to an enemy, engaged in warfare XVI; unfriendly, inimical XVIII. - F. *hostile* or L. *hostīlis*, f. *hostis* enemy; see HOST¹, -ILE. So **hostility** XVI.

hostler see OSTLER.

hot OE. *hāt* = OS. *hēt* (Du. *heet*), OHG. *heiz* (G. *heiss*), ON. *heitr* :- Gmc. **χaitaz*.

hotch-pot mixture, medley XIV (spec. in cookery XV); (leg.) collation of properties to secure equality of division XVI. - AN., (O)F. *hochepot*, f. *hocher* shake + *pot* POT. Altered by rhyming assim. to **hotchpotch** XV, **hodge-podge** XVII.

hotel large †private or public residence XVII; house for entertainment of strangers and travellers XVIII. - F. *hôtel*, later form of *hostel* HOSTEL.

hough quadruped's hock XIV; leg of beef, etc. XV. ME. *ho(u)ȝ*, prob. f. first el. of OE. *hōhsinu* hamstring, f. *hōh* heel + *sinu* sinew. Cf. HOCK¹.

hound dog (also fig.) OE.; dog kept for the chase XIII. OE. *hund* = OS. *hund* (Du. *hond*), OHG. *hunt* (G. *hund*), ON. *hundr*, Goth. *hunds* :- Gmc. **χundaz*, f. IE. *k̑un-*, repr. by (O)Ir. *cú*, Gr. *kúōn*, Lith. *šuõ*, Skr. *śvá*, and (obscurely) rel. to L. *canis*.

hour XIII. ME. *ure, our(e)*, later *hour(e)* - AN. *ure*, OF. *ore, eure* (mod. *heure*) :- L. *hōra* - Gr. *hṓrā* season, time of day, hour (cf. YEAR).

houri nymph of the Muslim paradise. XVIII. - F. - Pers. *ḥūrī*, f. Arab. *ḥūr*, pl. of *ḥaurā'* black-eyed.

house OE. *hūs* = OS., OHG. *hūs* (Du. *huis*, G. *haus*), ON. *hús*, Goth. *hūs* (only in *gudhūs* temple) :- Gmc. **χūsam*, of unkn. orig. Hence **house** vb. OE. *hūsian* = MLG., MDu. *hūsen*, OHG. *hūsōn* (Du. *huizen*, G. *hausen*), ON. *húsa*. **household** †contents, etc., of a house XIV; inmates of a house coll. XIV; †housekeeping XV. cf. MDu. *huushoud*. **housewife** XIII.

housings cloth covering, esp. for a horse. XIV. f. synon. ME. *house* XIV - OF. *houce* (mod. *housse*) - medL. *hultia* for **hulftia* - Frankish **χulftī* (MDu. *hulfte* pocket for bow and arrow, MHG. *hulft* covering); see -ING¹.

hovel shed XV; rude dwelling-place XVII. perh. of LG. orig., but no corr. form is known.

hover XIV. frequent. f. synon. ME. *hove* hover, tarry, linger (from XIII), of unkn. orig.; see -ER⁴.

how OE. *hū* = OS. *(h)wō, hwuo* (MLG. *woe*, Du. *hoe*), OHG. *wuo* :- WGmc. **χwō*, adv. formation on **χwa-* WHO, WHAT. Hence **howbeit** (arch.) however IT may BE, †conj. although. XIV; cf. ALBEIT. **however** XIV, **howsoever** XV.

howdah seat erected on an elephant's back. XVIII. - Urdu, Pers. *haudah* - Arab. *haudaj* litter carried by a camel or elephant.

howitzer XVI. - Du. *houwitser* - G. *haubitze*, †*hau(f)enitz* - Czech *houfnice* stone-sling, catapult.

howl vb. XIV. corr. to MLG., MDu. *hūlen* (Du. *huilen*), MHG. *hiulen, hiuweln*, rel. to OHG. *hūwila* (MHG. *hiuwel*) owl; perh. immed. f. ME. *hūle* OWL. Hence **howl** sb. XVI.

hoy¹ cry to excite attention (naut. in hailing or calling aloft). XIV. Cf. AHOY.

hoy² small sailing-vessel. XV. - MDu. *hoei*, var. of *hoede, heude* (mod. *heu*), of unkn. orig.

hoya genus of climbing plants. XIX. modL., f. name of Thomas *Hoy*, Eng. gardener (d. 1821).

hoyden †rude fellow, boor XVI; boisterous girl XVII. of uncert. orig.

hub nave of a wheel. XVII. of unkn. orig. Cf. HOB².

hubble-bubble kind of hookah XVII; bubbling sound XVIII. Rhyming jingle on BUBBLE.

hubbub confused noise XVI; noisy disturbance XVII. perh. of Ir. orig.; cf. Ir. *abu* used in battle-cries, and Gael. *ub! ubub!* int. of aversion or contempt.

hubby colloq. abbr. of HUSBAND. XVII. See -Y⁶.

hubris wanton insolence. XIX. - Gr. So **hubristic** XIX.

huckaback stout linen fabric with a rough surface. XVII. of unkn. orig.

huckleberry XVII. prob. alt. of *hurtleberry*, WHORTLEBERRY.

hucklebone hip-bone, haunch-bone. XVI. f. *huckle* (XVI), dim. (see -LE¹) of *huck* hip, haunch; perh. to be referred ult. to **hūk-*, as repr. in MLG., MDu. *hūken, hukken* sit bent, crouch.

huckster petty tradesman. XII. The earliest representative of a group based on **huk-*, prob. of LG. orig. (cf. MDu. *hoek(st)er*), other members being *huckstery* (XIV), *huck* vb. (XV), †*hukker* sb. (XIII), *hucker* vb. (XVI); see -STER.

huddle †conceal; pile or push together in disorderly fashion; crowd together confusedly. XVI (contemp. with †*huddle* adv. confusedly and *huddling* prp.). perh. of LG. orig. and ult. f. **hūd-* HIDE¹; see -LE³.

hue †form, aspect; colour. OE. *hē(o)w* form, appearance, colour, beauty = ON. *hý* down on plants, Goth. *hiwi* form, appearance :- Gmc. **χiujam*, of unkn. orig.

hue and cry outcry calling for the pursuit of a

felon. XVI. - legal AN. *hu e cri*, i.e. *hu* outcry (f. *huer* shout, of imit. orig.), *e* and, *cri* CRY.

huff blow, puff XVI; †bully; (at draughts) remove (an opponent's man) as a penalty (the removal being marked by blowing on the piece) XVII. imit. Hence **huff** sb. †puff of wind; †gust of anger; fit of petulance. XVIII.

hug vb. XVI. of unkn. orig. Hence as sb. XVII.

huge XIII. ME. *huge, ho(w)ge*, aphetic - OF. *ahuge, aho(e)ge*, of unkn. orig.

hugger-mugger secrecy XVI; disorder, confusion XVII. Preceded by similar rhyming jingles, *hucker mucker* or *moker* (XVI), and *hoder moder* (XV); perh. based on ME. *mokere* hoard, and ME. *hoder* huddle, wrap up; ult. orig. unkn.

Huguenot French Protestant. XVI. - F., alt., by assim. to the name of a Geneva burgomaster, Besançon *Hugues*, of †*eiguinot* - Du. *eedgenoot* - Swiss G. *eidgenoss* confederate, f. *eid* OATH + *genoss* associate.

hulk A. ship, esp. large ship of burden OE.; body of a dismantled ship XVII; B. big unwieldy person XVI. Late OE. *hulc*, prob. reinforced in ME. from MLG. *hulk, holk(e)*, MDu. *hulc, -ke* (Du. *hulk*).

hull[1] (dial.) shell of peas and beans. Late OE. *hulu*, f. base of *helan* cover. Hence vb. XIV.

hull[2] body or frame of a ship. XV (*ho(o)le, holle*). perh. sb. use of *hol* HOLLOW.

hullaballoo XVIII (*hollo-ballo*). jingle with various forms of the first el., viz. *hollo-, hallo(o)-, holli-, hulla-*, corr. to HALLO(A), etc.

hullo(a) var. of HALLO(A). XIX.

hum vb. XIV. imit. Also sb. XV, int. XVI.

human pert. to man. XIV. In earliest use *humain(e)* - (O)F. *humain*, fem. *-aine* - L. *hūmānus*, rel. to *homō* man; see -AN. The sp. *humane* persisted in gen. use till early XVIII, but the form *human* (based directly on L.) occurs in late XVII. The variant **humane** became restricted during XVIII for the senses (i) characterized by disposition or behaviour befitting a man (formerly spec. †gentle, courteous XV-XVI), and (ii) pert. to studies that tend to humanize or refine (XVII). So **humanism** †belief in the mere human nature of Christ; devotion to human interests or the humanities XIX; after **humanist** one devoted to the humanities. XVI. - F. *humaniste* - It. *umanista*. **humanity** humane disposition or conduct XIV; human quality or attributes XV; polite learning, spec. (and from XVIII pl.) the ancient Greek and Latin classics; mankind XVI. - (O)F. - L. Hence **humanitarian** one who affirms the humanity of Christ; one devoted to humane action. XIX. **humanize** XVII. - F.

humble having a low estimate of oneself XIII; of lowly condition XIV. ME. *(h)umble* - OF. *umble*, (also mod.) *humble* - L. *humilis* low, lowly, mean, f. *humus* ground, earth, rel. to *homō* man. Hence vb. XIV.

humble-bee large wild bee, bumble-bee. XV. cf. MLG. *hummelbē, homelbē*, and BUMBLE-BEE.

humble-pie †pie made of the umbles of an animal XVII (rare); phr. *to eat humble-pie* (by assoc. with HUMBLE) to submit to humiliation XIX. f. unexpl. var. of UMBLES + PIE[2].

humbug †hoax, imposture, fraud XVIII; pretence, sham; impostor XIX. of unkn. orig.

humdrum XVI (not common before XVIII). of unkn. orig.

humeral pert. to the humerus or the shoulder(s). XVII. f. L. *humerus* shoulder (used in anat. for 'upper arm'); see -AL[1].

humid XVI. - F. *humide* or L. *hūmidus*, var. of *ūmidus*, f. *ūmēre* be moist; see HUMOUR, -ID[1]. So **humidity** XIV.

humiliate †humble XVI; reduce the dignity of XVIII. f. pp. stem of late L. *humiliāre*, f. *humilis* HUMBLE; see -ATE[3]. So **humiliation, humility** XIV. - (O)F. - late L.

hummock protuberance of earth, etc. XVI (*ham-, hom-*). of unkn. orig.

humour, U.S. **humor** fluid, spec. any of the four chief fluids of the body (blood, phlegm, choler, melancholy) XIV; mental disposition, orig. as determined by the proportion of these XV; mood, temper, inclination XVI; quality of action or speech which excites amusement; faculty of perceiving this XVII. - AN. *(h)umour*, OF. *(h)umor, -ur* (mod. *humeur*) - L. *(h)ūmor, -ōr-*, f. *(h)ūm-*, as in HUMID. Hence **humour** comply with the humour of. XVI. So **humo(u)rist** †person subject to 'humours'; humorous or facetious person. XVI. - F. **humorous** †moist, humid; pert. or subject to 'humours' XVI; showing humour XVIII.

hump protuberance on the back, etc. XVIII; (sl.) fit of ill humour XIX (perh. from 'humping the back' in sulkiness). Earlier in *humpback(ed)* (XVII), repl. earlier synon. *crump-backed*, and perh. a blending of this with synon. *hunch-backed*; cf. LG. *humpe*, Du. *homp* lump, hunk. Hence vb. XIX.

humph †excl. used as a signal XVII; excl. of doubt or dissatisfaction XIX.

humus XVIII. - L., 'mould, ground, soil'.

Hun OE. (pl.) *Hūne, Hūnas*, corr. to MHG. *Hûnen, Hiunen* (G. *Hunnen*), ON. *Húnar*, also *Hýnar* - late L. *Hunnī, Hūnī*, Gr. *Hoûnnoi* - Sogdian *χwn*. Hence **Hunnish** XIX.

hunch (dial.) thrust, shove XVI; compress into a hump XVII. So **hunch** sb. †push, thrust XVII; (dial.) lump, hunk XVIII. To be grouped with **hunchbacked** humpbacked XVI (whence **hunchback** XVIII), which are synon. with †*bunch-backed*, †*hulch-backed* (XVI); of unkn. orig.

hundred A. ten times ten. B. division of a shire, reckoned as 100 hides of land. OE *hundred* = OS. *hunderod* (Du. *honderd*), (M)HG. *hundert*, ON. *hundrað*; Gmc., f. **χundam* hundred, whence OE., OS. *hund*, OHG. *hunt*, Goth. (pl. only) *hunda* = L. *centum*, Gr. *hekatón*, Lith. *šim̃tas*, OIr. *cēt*, Skr. *śatá-* Av. *satəm* :- IE. *k̑m̥tóm*; the ending is Gmc. **raþ-* number (rel. RATIO).

Hungarian XVI. f. *Hungary*, medL. *Hungaria*, f. *(H)ungarī, U(n)grī*, medGr. *Oúggroi*, foreign name of the people called by themselves *Magyar*.

hunger OE. *hungor, -ur* = OS., OHG. *hungar* (Du. *hónger*, G. *hunger*), ON. *hungr* :- Gmc. **χuŋȝruz* (Goth. *hūhrus* :- **χuŋχruz*); further relations are doubtful. So **hunger** vb. OE. *hyngr(i)an* (= OS. *gihungrian*, Goth. *huggrjan*) was superseded in ME. by *hungeren*, through assim. to the sb. **hungry** OE. *hungriġ* = OHG. *hung(a)rag* (G. *hungrig*).

hunk large piece cut off. XIX. cf. WFlem. *hunke* chunk of bread or meat, of which there are no obvious cogns.

hunks (arch., dial.) surly old person, miser. XVII. of unkn. orig.

hunt go in pursuit of (wild animals). OE. *huntian*, f. wk. grade of base of *hentan* seize, rel. *hūð* booty, OHG. *herihundu* spoils of war, Goth. *frahinþan* take prisoner, *hunþs* booty. Hence **hunter** XII, **huntress** XIV, **huntsman** XVI.

hurdle rectangular wattled framework. OE. *hyrdel*, f. Gmc. **χurðiz*, repr. by OS. *hurth*, MLG. *hurt*, *hort*, (M)Du. *horde*, OHG. *hurt* (G. *hürde*) hurdle, ON. *hurð*, Goth. *haurds* door; see -LE¹.

hurdy-gurdy (orig.) rustic instrument having strings producing a drone, with keys to produce the notes of the melody, (later) barrel-organ. XVIII. of imit. orig.

hurl †be carried along with violence XIII; impel or throw with violence XIV. prob. imit.; cf. LG. *hurreln* toss, throw, push, dash.

hurly-burly XVI. Preceded by †*hurling and burling*, a jingling collocation based on †*hurling* (XIV), †*hurl* (XV) strife, commotion (f. prec.).

hurrah, hurray, hooray excl. of exultation. XVII. modification of HUZZA.

hurricane XVI. Earliest forms *furacan(e)*, *-ana*, *-ano*, *haurachana*, *hurricano*, *uracan* - Sp. *huracan* and Pg. *furacão*, of Carib orig.

hurry (tr. and intr.) XVI. of uncert. orig. Hence sb. †commotion, agitation XVI; excessive haste XVII. In its earliest use synon. with *hurly* (XVI). **hurry-scurry** adv., adj., sb., vb. XVIII. Jingling extension.

hurst (sandy) eminence; grove, copse. OE. *hyrst*, f. base repr. by OS., OHG. *hurst*, (also mod.) *horst*.

hurt pt., pp. *hurt* †knock, strike; do harm to. XII (*hirrtenn*). - OF. *hurter* (mod. *heurter*) :- Gallo-Rom. **hūrtare*, perh. of Gmc. orig. So sb. †knock, blow; (bodily or material) injury, damage. XIII.

hurtle (lit. or arch.) dash or knock (one thing against another) XIII; come into collision XIV; dash, rush XVI. f. HURT + -LE³.

hurtleberry XV. Earlier than synon. *hurt* (XVI) and *whort*, *whortleberry*; of unkn. orig.

husband †master of a household OE.; man joined to a woman in marriage; †tiller of the soil, husbandman XIII; housekeeper, steward XV (*ship's husband* XVIII); †one who manages affairs XVI. Late OE. *hūsbonda* - ON. *húsbóndi* master of a house, husband, f. *hús* HOUSE + *bóndi*, contr. of **bóandi*, **búandi*, sb. use of prp. of *bóa*, *búa* dwell, have a household = OE., OS., OHG. *būan*, Goth. *bauan* (cf. BOWER¹). Hence vb. XV, **husbandman** XIV, **husbandry** XIII.

hush repr. an excl. enjoining silence. First recorded as vb. 'make or become silent' (XVI), which is followed by adj., int., and sb. in XVII; preceded by †*hust*, int. and adj. XIV. Hence **hushaby** word used in lulling a child. XVIII. **hush-money** money paid for hushing something up. XVIII.

husk XIV. of uncert. orig.; cf. LG. *hūske* little house, core of fruit, sheath = MDu. *hūskijn* (Du. *huisken*), dim. of *hūs* HOUSE. Hence **husky** full of husks, dry as a husk XVI; dry in the throat XVIII; (N. Amer.) tough, hefty XIX.

Husky Eskimo; (*h-*) Eskimo dog. XIX. abbr. of a form of ESKIMO.

hussar one of a body of light horsemen raised in Hungary in XV; hence applied to other light cavalry regiments. XVI. - Hung. *huszar* †freebooter, (later) light horseman - OSerb. *hu(r)sar*, *gusar* - It. *corsaro* CORSAIR.

hussy, huzzy †housewife XVI; bold, shameless, or †light woman or girl XVII. Reduction of *hūswif*, HOUSEWIFE.

husting(s) sg. (hist.) deliberative assembly XI; court held in Guildhall, London XII (sg.; from XV pl.); †platform in Guildhall on which the members sat XVII; platform from which nomination of candidates for election to parliament was made, (hence) the election itself XVIII. Late OE. *hūsting* - ON. *húsþing* 'house assembly', one held by a king, etc., with his immediate followers, opp. to the ordinary *þing* (see THING) or general assembly.

hustle †shake to and fro XVII; push about roughly XVIII. - (M)Du. *husselen*, *hutselen* shake, frequent. of *hutsen* = MHG. *hutzen* (cf. *hussen* run, *hutschen* push). Hence sb. XVIII.

hut wooden structure for housing troops XVII; mean dwelling of rude construction XVII. - F. *hutte* (MH)G. *hütte*, OHG. *hutt(e)a*, perh. f. base of HIDE³.

hutch †chest, coffer XIV; box-like pen XVII. - (O)F. *huche* :- medL. *hūtica*, of unkn. orig.

huzza hurrah. XVI. Said by writers of XVII–XVIII to have been orig. a sailor's cheer or salute. Cf. HURRAH.

hyacinth precious stone (cf. JACINTH); plant-name. XVI. - F. *hyacinthe* - L. *hyacinthus* - Gr. *huákinthos* purple or dark-red flower, precious stone. So **hyacinthine** XVII. - L. - Gr.

Hyades group of stars near the Pleiades. XVI. - Gr. *húades* fem. pl., prob. f. *hûs* SOW¹.

hyaline glass-like, vitreous. XVII. - late L. *hyalinus* - Gr. *húalinos*, f. *húalos* transparent stone, amber, etc., glass; see -INE². So **hyaloid** XIX; - F.

hybrid sb. and adj. half-breed, mongrel; also fig. XVII (rare before XIX). - L. *hybrida*, *(h)ibrida* offspring of a tame sow and a wild boar, one born of a Roman father and a foreign mother or of a freeman and a slave.

hydatid (path.) watery cyst. XVII (in L. pl. form *hydatides*). - modL. *hydatis*, *-id-* - Gr. *hudatis*, *-id-*, f. *húdōr*, *hudat-* WATER; see -ID².

hydra fabulous many-headed snake whose heads grew again as fast as they were cut off XVI (earlier *(h)ydre*, *idre*); genus of freshwater polyps, so named from the fact that cutting it into pieces multiplies its numbers XVIII. - L. - Gr. *húdrā* water-serpent (cf. OTTER).

hydrangea XVIII. - modL. *hydrangea*, f. Gr. *hudōr*, *hudr-* WATER + *ággos* vessel; so called with ref. to the cup-like form of the seed-capsule.

hydrant XIX (orig. U.S.). irreg. f. Gr. *húdōr, hudr-* WATER + -ANT.

hydrate (chem.) compound of water with another compound or an element. XIX. - F., f. Gr. *húdōr, hudr-* WATER; see -ATE². So **hydride** †hydrate; compound of hydrogen with an element or radical. XIX.

hydraulic XVII. - L. *hydraulicus* - Gr. *hudraulikós*, f. *húdōr, hudr-* WATER + *aulós* pipe; see -IC.

hydro-, before a vowel **hydr-** comb. form of Gr. *húdōr* WATER in many terms, of which some came from L. adoptions of Gr. words either direct or through F. but many are of mod. orig.; (in gen. terms) **hydrographer, -graphy, hydrophobia** XVI, **hydroponics** (Gr. *pónos* labour) XX; (path.) denoting accumulation of fluid, as **hydrocele** XVI, **hydrocephalus** (Gr. *hudroképhalon*; *kephalḗ* head) XVII; (chem.) denoting combination with water, and (hence) with HYDROGEN (of which it functions as comb. form), as **hydrobromic, -carbon, -chloric, hydroxide** XIX; (physics) concerned with liquids, as **hydrodynamics** XVIII, **-mechanics** XIX, **-statics** XVII.

hydrogen XVIII. - F. *hydrogène*, f. Gr. *húdōr, hudr-* WATER; see -GEN.

hy(a)ena XVI (earlier *hyene* XIV). - L. *hyæna* - Gr. *húaina*, f. *hûs* swine, sow¹.

hygiene XIX. - F. *hygiène* - modL. *hygieina* - Gr. *hugieinḗ*, sb. use of fem. of *hugieinós* healthful, f. *hugiḗs* healthy, f. IE. **su-* well + **gʷi-* living. Hence **hygienic** XIX.

hygro- comb. form of Gr. *hugrós* wet, moist, fluid, as in **hygrometer, hygroscope** (XVII).

hylic pert. to matter. XIX. - late L. *hȳlicus* - Gr. *hūlikós* material, f. *hū́lē* wood, matter; see -IC. So **hylo-** comb. form of Gr. *hū́lē*.

hymen XVII. - late L. *hymēn* - Gr. *humḗn* :- **sjumen-*, f. IE. **sjū-* SEW.

hymn XIII. ME. *imne, ymme* - OF. *ymne* - L. *hymnus* - Gr. *húmnos* song in praise of a god or hero. The later form was refash. after L. Hence vb. XVII. So **hymnal** XV. - medL. *hymnāle* (*imnale*). **hymnody** singing or composing of hymns XVIII; body of hymns XIX. - medL. - Gr. *humnōidíā* (cf. ODE). **hymnographer, hymnology** XVII. - Gr.

hyoid *h. bone*, horseshoe-shaped bone in the root of the tongue. XIX. - F. *hyoïde* - modL. *hyoïdēs* - Gr. *huoeidḗs*, f. *hû* name of the letter *υ*; see -OID.

hyoscyamus genus of plants, henbane. XVIII. modL. - Gr. *huoskúamos*, f. *húos*, g. of *hûs* swine, sow¹ + *kúamos* bean. Hence **hyoscyamine** (chem.) alkaloid obtained from this. XIX.

hypaethral open to the sky. XVIII. f. L. *hypæthrus* - Gr. *húpaithros*, f. *hupó* under, HYPO- + *aithḗr* air, ETHER; see -AL¹.

hypallage (rhet.) figure of speech in which two elements are interchanged. XVI. - late L. *hypallagē* - Gr. *hupallagḗ*, f. *hupó* HYPO- + *allag-*, stem of *allássein* exchange, f. *állos* other.

hyper- repr. comb. form of Gr. *hupér* prep. and adv. 'over', 'above', 'overmuch', 'above measure'. Among the older comps. are: **hyperbaton** (rhet.) inversion of logical or natural order. XVI. - L. - Gr. *hupérbaton*, n. of *hupérbatos* 'overstepping'. **hyperbola** (geom.) conic section having two equal and similar infinite branches, so called because it has an eccentricity greater than unity. XVII. modL. - Gr. *huperbolḗ*, f. *huperbállein* exceed, f. *bállein* throw. **hyperbole** (rhet.) exaggerated statement. XVI. - L. - Gr. (see prec.). So **hyperbolic** XVI, **hyperbolical** XV. **hyperborean** pert. to the extreme north. XVI. - late L. *hyperboreānus*, f. L. *hyperboreus* - Gr. *huperbóreos*. **hypercritical** XVII. **hyperdulia** (theol.) superior veneration as paid to the Virgin Mary. XVI. - medL. **hypertrophy** (path.) excessive enlargement. XIX. modL., f. Gr. *-trophíā, trophḗ* nourishment.

hypericum XVI. - L. *hyperīcum* - Gr. *hupéreikon*, f. *hupér* HYPER- + *ereíkē* heath.

hyphen sb. XVII. - late L. - late Gr. *huphén* the sign ◡, sb. use of *huphén* together, f. *huph-, hupó* under, HYPO- + *hén*, n. of *heîs* one. Hence **hyphen** vb., **hyphenate** XIX.

hypnotic A. soporific XVII; B. pert. to hypnotism XIX. - F. *hypnotique* - late L. *hypnōticus* - Gr. *hupnōtikós* narcotic, f. *hupnoûn* put to sleep, f. *húpnos* sleep; see -IC. Hence **hypnotism, hypnotist, hypnotize** XIX.

hypo-, before a vowel **hyp-**, repr. Gr. *hup(o)-*, prefix-form of *hupó* under (adv. and prep.) = L. *sub* (see SUB-), in words derived immed. or ult. from Gr. (see below) with meanings 'under', 'beneath', 'below', 'slight(ly)', and in numerous mod. formations. **hypocaust** under-chamber for heating a house or bath. XVII. - L. *hypocaustum* - Gr. *hupókauston* (*kaíein* burn). **hypochondria** A. (anat.) region of the abdomen under the ribs, formerly held to be the seat of melancholy XVI; B. morbidity of mind, marked by depression and regarded as due to 'vapours' XVIII. - late L.; in A pl. of *hypochondrium* - Gr. *hupokhóndrion* (*khóndros* cartilage); in B taken as fem. in transf. sense. **hypocoristic** of the nature of a pet-name. XVIII. - Gr. *hupokoristikós* (*kóros* child). **hypocrisy** XIII. - OF. *ypocrisie* (mod. *hypo-*) - ecclL. *hypocrisis* - Gr. *hupókrisis* acting, feigning (*krínein* decide, judge). So **hypocrite** XIII. - (O)F. - ecclL. - Gr. *hupokritḗs* actor, pretender. **hypocritical** XVI. **hypostasis** †sediment; (theol.) person of Christ, of the Godhead XVI; substance, essence XVII. - ecclL. - Gr. *hupóstasis* (**sta-* STAND). **hypotenuse** side of a right-angled triangle subtending the right angle. XVI. - L. *hypotēnūsa* - Gr. *hupoteínousa*, pp. fem. of *hupoteínein* stretch under. **hypothec** legal security. XVI. - F. *hypothèque* - late L. *hypothēca* - Gr. *hupothḗkē* deposit, pledge (*thē-* place, DO¹). So **hypothecate** mortgage. XVII. f. pp. stem of medL. *hypothēcāre*. **hypothesis** †particular case of a general proposition XVI; proposition set as a basis for reasoning; supposition to account for known facts XVII. - late L. - Gr. *hupóthesis* foundation (*thē-* place, DO¹). So **hypothetic** XVII, **-thetical** XVI. - L. - Gr. *hupothetikós*.

hyrax genus of rabbit-like quadrupeds. XIX. modL. - Gr. *húrax* shrew-mouse.

hyssop bushy aromatic shrub; bunch of this used in ceremonial purification. OE. *(h)ysope*, reinforced in ME. by OF. *ysope, isope*, later assim. to the source, L. *hyssōpus, -um* - Gr. *hússōpos, -on*, of Sem. orig.

hysteria functional disturbance of the nervous system, which was thought to be due to disturbance of the uterine functions. XIX. modL., f. L. *hystericus* - Gr. *husterikós*, f. *hustérā* womb; see -IA¹. So **hysteric** XVII, **-ics** XVIII, **hysterical** XVII.

hysteron proteron figure of speech reversing the proper order of words. XVI. – late L. - Gr. *hústeron próteron* 'latter (put as) former'.

I

I 1st sg. pers. pron. OE. *iċ* = OS. (Du.) *ik*, OHG. *ih* (G. *ich*), ON. *ek*, Goth. *ik* (:- Gmc. **eka*), corr., but with variation of vowel, cons., and ending, to L. *egṓ*, Gr. *egṓ(n)*, Skr. *ahám*, Av. *azəm*, OSl. *(j)azŭ*. The reduced form *i* of OE. *iċ* appears XII; in stressed position this became *ī*, which was finally generalized for all positions. The inflexional system of the pronoun is made up of four distinct bases; see ME, MY (MINE), WE, US, OUR.

-i pl. inflexion of L. masc. sbs. in *-us* and *-er*, and of It. sbs. in *-o* and *-e*, retained in Eng. in learned and techn. use, e.g. *foci*, *radii*; *banditti*, *dilettanti*; *illuminati*, *literati*.

-i- L. stem- or connective vowel as in OMNI-, *pacificus* PACIFIC, *uniformis* UNIFORM.

-ia[1] repr. the termination of L. and Gr. fem. sbs. denoting conditions, qualities, and entities. Exx.: *hydrophobia*, *mania*; *dahlia*, *lobelia*; *ammonia*, *morphia*.

-ia[2] repr. the termination of L. and Gr. pls. of sbs. in *-ium* or *-e*, and *-ion*. Exx.: *paraphernalia*, *regalia*; *Mammalia*.

-ial repr. L. *-iālis*, n. *-iāle*, comp. suffix f. -I- and -AL[1].

iambus XVI. - L. - Gr. *íambos*. Anglicized **iamb** XIX. So **iambic** XVI. - F. - late L. - Gr.

-ian earlier also *-yan*, repr. ult. (sometimes through F. *-ien*), L. *-iānus* (see -I-, -AN), as in CHRISTIAN, *Vergiliānus* Virgilian, subsequently by modification of L. forms, as BARBARIAN, EQUESTRIAN, HISTORIAN, PATRICIAN; freely used in mod. formations on proper names, as in *Devonian*, *Johnsonian*, *Pickwickian*. See also -ARIAN, -ICIAN.

ib., ibid., abbrevs. of **ibidem** in the same place, passage, book, etc. XVII. - L., f. *ibī* there + -*dem*, as in IDEM, TANDEM.

Iberian XVII. f. L. *Ibēria*, f. *Ibēres* - Gr. *I'bēres* Spaniards, also a people of the Caucasus; see -IAN.

ibex XVII. - L. *ibex*, prob. Alpine word like CHAMOIS.

ibis XIV. - L. - Gr. *íbis*, of Egyptian orig.

-ible suffix repr. F. *-ible*, L. *-ibilis*, *-ībilis*, f. *-i-*, *-ī-* connective or stem-vowel of vbs. in *-ēre*, *-ere*, *-īre* + *-bilis* -BLE.

-ic repr. (often through (O)F. *-ique*) L. *-icus*, as in *cīvicus*, *civique* CIVIC, *domesticus* DOMESTIC, *publicus* PUBLIC, or in adoptions from Gr., as in *cōmicus*, *kōmikós* COMIC, *poēticus*, *poiētikós* POETIC. The L. suffix became more widely used in late L. and Rom. in the comp. suffix *-āticus* (see -ATIC, -AGE).

Derivative abstract sbs. end in **-icity**, as *domesticity*, *publicity*.

Gr. words in *-ikós* were used absol. as sbs. (i) in the m. sg., e.g. *kritikós* CRITIC; (ii) in the fem. sg., in names of arts, systems of thought, etc., e.g. *hē mousikḗ* MUSIC; (iii) in the n. pl., e.g. *tà oikonomiká* ECONOMICS. The distinction between fem. sg. and n. pl. tended to become obliterated, so that *hē physikḗ* and *tà physiká* were synonymous. Moreover, in pairs like *physikḗ*, *physiká*, both forms gave L. *physica*, which might be repr. by *physic* or *physics*. Early adoptions in Eng. were in the sg. form, which has survived in *arithmetic*, *logic*, *magic*, *music*, *rhetoric*. Later, forms in **-ics** occur as names of treatises, e.g. *etiques*, i.e. Aristotle's *tà ēthiká*, the Ethics; this form was then applied to the subject-matter of such treatises, as *mathematics*, *physics*, *tactics*, and finally became the accepted form with names of sciences, as *acoustics*, *linguistics*, *optics*, or matters of practice, as *athletics*, *gymnastics*, *politics*. There are also many sbs. formed from adjs. in *-ic* taken absol., as *cosmetic*, *epic*, *lyric*, *rustic*.

-ical comp. suffix consisting of -IC and -AL[1], repr. (O)F. *-ical(e)*, late L. *-icālis*, as in *clérical*, *clēricālis*, *grammaticālis*; the number of these was increased in medL. While F. adjs. in *-ical* are not numerous, Eng. formations are abundant, and are very freq. earlier than corr. words in -IC. A distinction of application is often made where there are parallel forms, e.g. *economic* in 'economic theory', *economical* in 'economical housekeeper', *optic* in 'optic nerve', *optical* in 'optical illusion'. In many cases the main distinction is that one form is more usual than the other, as *authentic*, *idiotic*, *linguistic*, but *farcical*, *syntactical*, *theatrical*. Derivative sbs. end in **-icality** and advs. in **-ically**, which serves also for adjs. in *-ic*, e.g. *drastic/drastically*, *specific/specifically*.

ice OE. *īs* = OS., OHG. *īs* (Du. *ijs*, G. *eis*), ON. *íss* :- Gmc. **īsam*, **īsaz*, rel. to Av. *isu-* icy. *Ice cream* (XVIII) is for earlier *iced cream* (XVII). Hence **icy** XVI (not continuous with OE. *īsiġ*). So **iceberg** †Arctic glacier; detached portion of this in the sea. XVIII. prob. - (M)Du. *ijsberg* (see BARROW[1]).

-ice suffix repr. OF. *-ice* - L. *-itia*, or *-itius*, *-itium*, as in *avarice*, *notice*, *novice*, *police*, *service*. F. formations are *cowardice*, *jaundice*. *-ice* may be of other orig., as in *bodice*, *caprice*, *poultice*, *practice*.

ichneumon N. Afr. mongoose which destroys crocodiles' eggs XVI; insect of a family parasitic on the larvae of others XVII. - L. *ichneumōn* - Gr. *ikhneúmōn* lit. tracker, f. *ikhneúein* track, f. *íkhnos* track, footstep.

ichnography ground plan. XVI. - F. *ichnographie* or L. *ichnographia* - Gr. *ikhnographíā*, f. *íkhnos* track, trace; see -GRAPHY.

ichor blood; (Gr. myth.) ethereal fluid flowing in the veins of the gods; (med.) watery discharge. XVII. - Gr. *īkhṓr*.

ichthy(o)- repr. comb. form of Gr. *ikhthús* fish, as in **ichthyology** XVII, **ichthyosaurus** XIX.

-ician as in *logician, musician, physician, statistician, tactician*, repr. F. *-icien*, L. *-iciānus*, f. names of sciences in *-ica* -IC(S) + *-iānus* -IAN.
icicle XIV. ME. *iisse ikkle, ysekele, iseyokel*, f. ICE + *i(c)kel, ȝokyl*, after MSw. *isikil*; repl. OE. **īsġiċel*, for which *īses ġiċel* 'icicle of ice' is attested; OE. *ġiċel(a)*, cogn. with ON. *jǫkull* icicle, glacier.
-icity see -IC.
icon, ikon †image, picture XVI; (Eastern Church) representation in the flat of a sacred personage XIX. - L. *īcōn* - Gr. *eikṓn* likeness, image, f. **ϝeik-* be like. comb. form **icono-** in **iconoclast** XVII. - modL. *īconoclastēs* - Gr. *eikonoklástēs* (*klân* break); so **iconoclastic** XVII. **iconography** †drawing, plan; illustration by means of drawings. XVII. - medL. - Gr. **iconostasis** screen bearing icons. XIX. - ecclL. - ecclGr. *eikonóstasis* (*stásis* position, station, f. **sta-* STAND).
icosahedron solid contained by 20 faces. XVI. - Gr. *eikosáedron*, n. of adj. used sb., f. *eíkosi* :- **eϝikosi* (rel. to L. *vīgintī* twenty) + *hédrā* seat, base (see SIT).
-ics see -IC.
icteric pert. to jaundice. XVI. - L. *ictericus* - Gr. *ikterikós*, f. *íkteros* jaundice; see -IC.
ictus metrical stress. XVIII. - L. 'blow, stroke', f. *ict-*, pp. stem of *īcere* strike.
id., abbr. of **idem** the same name, title, author, etc. XVII. - L. *īdem* m. (for **isdem*), *idem* n. (for **iddem*), f. *is, id* that one + *-dem*, as in IBIDEM.
-id[1] suffix repr. F. *-ide* - L. *-idus, -ida, -idum*, used to form adjs. chiefly from vbs. with *ē*-stems, as *acidus* ACID, f. *acēre, torridus* TORRID, f. *torrēre*, less freq. from others, as *fluidus* FLUID, f. *fluere*, and from sbs., as *morbidus* MORBID, f. *morbus*.
-id[2] suffix of sbs., repr. F. *-ide* - L. *-is, -id-*, Gr. *-is, -id-*, as in *chrysalid, pyramid*; bot. denoting a member of a family, e.g. *orchid*.
-id[3] (zool.) in sbs. and adjs. from L. names of families in *-idæ* and of classes in *-ida*, m. and n. pl. respectively of L. - Gr. *-idēs*.
-id[4] early var. of -IDE still retained in U.S.
ide fish allied to the carp. XIX. - modL. *idus* - Sw. *id*.
-ide formerly also -ID[4], repr. F. *-ide*, first used in OXIDE - F. *oxyde*, on the analogy of which it is regularly affixed to a shortened form of the name of the element which combines with another element or a radical to form the compound so designated.
idea archetype (as in Platonic philosophy), conception, design; †form, figure; mental image, notion. XVI. - L. *idea* (in Platonic sense) - Gr. *idéā* look, form, nature, ideal form, f. **ϝid-* see (see WIT[2]). So **ideal** adj. XVII, sb. XVIII. - F. *idéal* - late L. *ideālis*. Comb. form **ideo-**, as in **ideologue** XIX. - F.
idem see ID.
identity quality of being the same. XVI. - late L. *identitās*, f. L. *idem* same. So **identic(al)**, **identify** XVII. - medL.
ideology science of ideas XVIII; ideal or visionary speculation XIX; system of ideas XX. - F. *idéologie*, f. Gr. *idéā* IDEA + *-logiā* -LOGY.
Ides in the ancient Roman Calendar, the 8th day after the Nones. XV. - (O)F. - L. *īdūs* (pl.), perh. of Etruscan orig.
idio- repr. Gr. *idio-*, comb. form of *ídios* personal, peculiar, separate.
idiom proper language of a people or country, dialect; specific character of a language XVI; expression peculiar to a language XVII. - F. *idiome* or late L. *idiōma* - Gr. *idíōma* property, peculiar phraseology, f. *idioûsthai* make one's own, f. *ídios* own, private. So **idiomatic** XVIII.
idiosyncrasy XVII. - Gr. *idiosugkrāsiā, -krāsis*, f. IDIO- + *súgkrāsis* commixture, tempering, f. *sún* SYN- + *krāsis* mixture.
idiot XIII. - (O)F. - L. *idiōta* ignorant person - Gr. *idiṓtēs* private person, plebeian, ignorant, lay(man), f. *ídios* private, peculiar. Hence **idiocy** XVI, **idiotic** XVIII, **-ical** XVII.
idle †empty; worthless, useless; doing nothing, inactive OE.; lazy, indolent XIII. OE. *īdel* = OS. *īdal* empty, worthless (Du. *ijdel*), OHG. *ītal* (G. *eitel*), ult. orig. unkn. Primary meaning prob. 'empty'.
idol image of a deity XIII; object of devotion; phantom, fiction XVI. ME. *ydel, ydol* - OF. *id(e)le*, (also mod.) *idole* - L. *īdōlum* image, form, apparition, (eccl.) idol - Gr. *eídōlon* (same meanings), f. *eîdos* form, shape (cf. IDEA). So **idolater** XVI. Earlier †*idolatrer*, †*-trour* (XIV), either f. (O)F. *idolâtre* + -ER[1], *-our*, -OR[1], or f. *idolatry*; the present form was either a phonetic reduction of *idolatrer* or - F. *idolâtre*, ult. - Gr. *eidōlolátrēs* (*latreúein* worship). **idolatry** XIII, **idolize** XVI, **idolatrous** XVI.
idyll short poem descriptive of a picturesque (rustic) scene or incident. XVII (earlier *idyllium, -ion* XVI). - L. *īdyllium* - Gr. *eidúllion*, dim. of *eîdos* form, picture. Hence **idyllic** XIX.
-ie var. of Y[6], e.g. *birdie, dearie, doggie, Jeanie, Willie*.
-ier[1] var. *-yer*, in agent-nouns based on native words and functioning as -ER[1]. Among the earliest exx. (XIII) are *tiliere*, extension with *-ere* of OE. *tilia* tiller, cultivator, *bowiare* bowyer, maker of bows; these may have served as models for other formations of various and sometimes obscure orig., e.g. *brazier, clothier, collier, drovier, glazier, grazier, haulier, hosier, lawyer, sawyer*.
-ier[2] repr. F. *-ier* (:- L. *-ārius* -ARY), appears first in XVI, as in *bombardier, cashier, cavalier*; later exx. are *brigadier, fusilier, grenadier*. Cf. -EER[1].
-ies pl. ending of certain ellipt. words, as *civvies, movies, undies*.
-iety suffix repr. F. *-iété* - L. *-ietās* expressing the quality or condition of what is denoted by adjs. in *-ius* -IOUS, as in *anxiety, (im)propriety, notoriety, society, variety*.
if OE. *ġif, ġyf*, corr. to OS. *ef, of* (Du. *of*), OHG. *ibu, oba* (G. *ob* whether, if), ON. *ef* if, Goth. *ibai, iba* whether, lest, *jabai* if, although; ult. orig. unkn.
-iferous f. L. *-ifer*, f. -I- + *-fer* bearing, furnishing, f. base of *ferre* BEAR[2]; see -OUS.
-ify see -FY.

-igerous f. L. *-iger*, f. -I- + base of *gerere* carry; see -OUS.

igloo XIX. of Eskimo orig.

igneous XVII. f. L. *igneus*, f. *ignis* fire (rel. to OSl. *ogni*, Lith. *ugnis*, Skr. *agni-*); see -EOUS. **ignite** make intensely hot, spec. to the point of combustion or chemical change XVII; trans. set on fire XVIII; intr. take fire XIX. f. *ignīt-*, pp. stem of L. *ignīre* set on fire. So **ignition** XVII.

ignis fatuus will-o'-the-wisp. XVI. modL., 'foolish fire', so named from its erratic flitting from place to place.

ignoble XVI. - F. *ignoble* or L. *ignōbilis*, f. *i-* IN-[2] + *gnōbilis* NOBLE. So **ignobility** XV. - L.

ignominy XVI. - F. *ignominie* or L. *ignōminia*, f. *i-* IN-[2] + **gnōmen*, *nōmen* NAME, reputation; see -Y[3]. So **ignominious** XVI.

ignoramus †endorsement made formerly by a grand jury on a bill returned as not a true bill XVI; ignorant person XVII. - L. 'we do not know', in legal use 'we take no notice (of it)', 1st pers. pl. pres. ind. of *ignorāre* IGNORE.

ignorance XIII. - (O)F. - L. *ignōrantia*, f. prp. of *ignōrāre* not to know, misunderstand, disregard, rel. to *ignārus* unaware; see -ANCE. So **ignorant** XIV. **ignore** †not to know XVII; (of a grand jury) reject (a bill); refuse to take notice of XIX. - (O)F. *ignorer* or L. *ignōrāre*.

iguana large arboreal lizard. XVI. - Sp., of Carib orig. Hence **iguanodon** large fossil lizard. XIX.

il-[1] assim. form of L. *in-* IN-[1] before *l*.

il-[2] assim. form of negative *in-* IN-[2] before *l*.

-il former regular var. of -ILE surviving in e.g. *civil*, *fossil*, *utensil*.

-ile adj. suffix repr. F. *-il*, chiefly *-ile*, and its sources L. *-ilis*, *-īlis*, which was added to vb.-stems with the senses of capacity or suitability, e.g. *agilis* agile, *fragilis* fragile, and with wider meaning to noun-stems, e.g. *juvenīlis* juvenile, *humilis* humble.

ilex XIV. - L.

ilk †same OE.; surviving only in phr. *of that ilk* of the same place or name (e.g. *Guthrie of that ilk* for Guthrie of Guthrie). XVI (erron. *that ilk* that family or set XIX). OE. *ilca* m., *ilce* fem. and n., f. **ī-* that, the same (as in Goth. *is* he, L. *is* that, *īdem*, *idem* same) + **līk-* form (see LIKE[2]).

ill A. (dial.) morally evil XII; causing harm, pain, or disaster XIII; of bad quality; of evil intent XIV. B. out of health, sick XV; sb. evil XII; adv. evilly, badly XII. - ON. *illr* adj.; *illa* adv., *ilt* n. of adj. as sb.; ult. orig. unkn.

illative (gram.) inferential. XVI. - L. *illātīvus*, f. *illātus*, used as pp. of *inferre* INFER; see -IVE. So **illation** XVI.

illegal XVII. - (O)F. *illégal* or medL. *illegālis*; see IL-[2], LEGAL.

illegitimate not born in lawful wedlock XVI; unauthorized XVII. f. late L. *illegitimus*, after LEGITIMATE; see IL-[2].

illicit XVII. - L.; see IL-[2], LICIT.

illiterate XVI. - L.; see IL-[2], LITERATE.

illuminate light up, give light to XVI; decorate with colour XVIII. f. pp. stem of late L. *illumināre*, f. IL-[1] + *lūmen*, *lūmin-* LIGHT[1]; see -ATE[3]. So **illumination** spiritual enlightenment XIV; lighting up XVI; embellishment with colour XVII. - (O)F. - late L. **illumine** enlighten (first in spiritual sense). XIV. - (O)F. - L.

illuminati applied to several sects claiming special enlightenment: (i) the Sp. heretics *Alumbrados* XVI; (ii) G. *Illuminaten*, secret society founded by Adam Weishaupt XVIII; (hence gen.) persons claiming special knowledge XIX. - L., pl. of *illūminātus*, pp. of *illūmināre* (see prec.), or - It., pl. of *illuminato*.

illusion †deception XIV; deceptive appearance, etc. XIV; perception of an external object involving a false belief XVIII. - (O)F. - L. *illūsiō*, *-ōn-*, f. *illūdere* mock, jest at (whence rare **illude** XV), f. IL-[1] + *lūdere* play, sport. So **illusory** XVI. - late L.

illustrate throw light or lustre on; elucidate XVI; exemplify; elucidate with pictures XVII. f. pp. stem of L. *illustrāre*, f. IL-[1] + *lustrāre* illuminate, rel. to *lūmen* LIGHT[1]. So **illustration** †illumination XIV; exemplification, example XVI; pictorial elucidation XIX. - (O)F. - L. **illustrative** XVII. **illustrious** distinguished by rank, etc. XVI. f. L. *illustris*.

im-[1] assim. form of IN-[1] before *p*, *b*, *m*.

im-[2] assim. form of IN-[2] before *p*, *b*, *m*.

image artificial representation of an object, likeness, statue; (optical) counterpart XIII; mental representation XIV. - (O)F. - L. *imāgō*, *imāgin-*, rel. to IMITATE. So **imagery** XIV. - OF. *imagerie*, f. *imageur* maker of images. **imagine** XIV. - (O)F. *imaginer* - L. *imāgināre* form an image of, represent, fashion, *imāginārī* picture to oneself, fancy. **imagination** XIV. - (O)F. - L. **imaginable** XIV. - late L. **imaginary** XIV. - L. **imaginative** XIV. - (O)F.

imago (entom.) final stage of an insect. XVIII. mod. use of L. *imāgō* IMAGE.

imam XVII. - Arab. *'imām* leader, f. *'amma* lead.

imbecile weak XVI; mentally weak, idiotic (also sb.) XIX. Earliest form *imbecille* - F. †*imbécille* (now *-ile*) - L. *imbēcillus*, *-is*, of uncert. orig. So **imbecility** XVI. - (O)F. - L.

imbibe †A. soak, saturate XIV; B. drink in, absorb XVI. In A - F. *imbiber* soak (not recorded before XVI), in B - its source L. *imbibere*, f. IM-[1] + *bibere* drink.

imbricate (nat. hist.) covered with scales overlapping like roof tiles. XVII. - pp. of L. *imbricāre*, f. *imbrex*, *imbric-* roof tile, f. *imber* rain; see -ATE[2].

imbroglio confused heap XVIII; confusion and entanglement XIX. - It., f. *imbrogliare* confuse, corr. to F. *embrouiller* EMBROIL.

imbrue †sully XV; stain *with* blood XVI. - OF. *embr(o)uer* bedaub, bedabble, f. EM-[1] + OF. *breu*, *bro* (cf. mod. *brouet* broth) - Rom. **brodum* - Gmc. **broþ-* BROTH.

imbue saturate, impregnate. XVI. First in pp. f. F. *imbu*, †*imbu(i)t*, or its source L. *imbūtus*, pp. of *imbuere* moisten, stain, imbue.

imide (chem.) XIX. arbitrary alteration of AMIDE.

imitate XVI. f. pp. stem of L. *imitārī* copy, rel. to *imāgō* IMAGE and *æmulārī* EMULATE; see -ATE[3]. So **imitation** XVI. - (O)F. or L. **imitative** XVI. - late L. **imitator** XVI. - L.

immaculate xv. - L. *immaculātus*; see IM-², MACULATE.
immanent xvi. - prp. of late L. *immanēre*, f. IM-¹ + *manēre* remain, dwell; see -ENT. So **immanence** xix, **-ency** xvii.
immaterial incorporeal xiv (not freq. before xvi); unimportant xvii. - late L.; see IM-², MATERIAL.
immediate xvi. - (O)F. *immédiat* or late L. *immediātus*, f. IM-² + *mediātus* MEDIATE. Hence **immediacy** xvii, **immediately** xv.
immemorial xvii. - medL. *immemōriālis*; see IM-², MEMORIAL.
immense extremely great xv; †boundless, infinite xvi. - (O)F. - L. *immēnsus* immeasurable, f. IM-² + *mēnsus*, pp. of *mētīrī* MEASURE. So **immensity** xv.
immerse xvii. f. *immers-*, pp. stem of L. *immergere*, f. IM-¹ + *mergere* dip, MERGE. So **immersion** xvii. - late L.
immigrate xvii. f. pp. stem of L. *immigrāre*; see IM-¹, MIGRATE. So **immigrant** xviii, **immigration** xvii.
imminent xvi. - L. *imminēns*, *-ent-*, prp. of *imminēre* project, be impending, f. IM-¹ (cf. EMINENT, PROMINENT).
immolate sacrifice. xvi. f. pp. stem of L. *immolāre* (orig.) sprinkle with sacrificial meal, f. IM-¹ + *mola* MEAL¹; see ATE². So **immolation** xvi.
immortal xiv. - L. *immortālis*, f. IM-² + *mortālis* MORTAL. So sb. xvii. **immortality** xiv. - (O)F. - L. **immortelle** everlasting flower. xix. - F.
immune †free, exempt xv; secure from contagion, etc. xix. - L. *immūnis* exempt from a service or charge, f. IM-² + *mūnis* ready for service (cf. COMMON). So **immunity** exemption from service or liability xiv; non-susceptibility to contagion, etc. xix.
immure †wall in; shut within walls xvi; build into a wall xvii. - medL. *immurare*, f. IM-¹ + *mūrus* wall.
imp †young shoot, sapling OE.; offspring, child xiv; 'child' of the Devil, evil spirit xvi; mischievous child xvii. OE. *impa* or *impe*. So **imp** vb. †graft, engraft OE.; engraft feathers in a bird's wing so as to improve or restore its flight xv; enlarge, eke *out* xvi. OE. *impian*, corr. to OHG. *impfōn* (G. *impfen*), shortened analogues of OHG. *impitōn* (MHG. *impfeten*) - Rom. **impotare*, f. medL. *impotus* graft - Gr. *émphutos* implanted, engrafted, vbl. adj. of *emphúein* implant, f. EM-² + *phúein* (see BE C).
impact sb. xviii. f. *impact-*, pp. stem of L. *impingere* IMPINGE.
impair xiv (*em-*). - OF. *empeirier* (mod. *empirer*) :- Rom. **impējōrāre* make worse, f. IM-¹ + late L. *pējōrāre* (cf. PEJORATIVE); the pref. was latinized to *im-* xv.
impale surround with a palisade, fence in xvi; (her.) combine (coats of arms) palewise; fix upon a stake or point xvii. - F. *empaler* or medL. *impālāre*, f. IM-¹ + *pālus* PALE¹.
imparisyllabic of Gr. and L. nouns that have different numbers of syllables in different cases. xviii. f. L. *impar* unequal, f. IM-² + *par* equal, PEER¹; see SYLLABIC.
impart make partaker of xv; make known xvi. - OF. *impartir* - L. *impartīre*, f. IM-¹ + *pars*, *part-* share, PART.
impasse cul-de-sac; insoluble difficulty. xix. - F., f. IM-² + stem of *passer* PASS².
impassible incapable of suffering xiv; incapable of suffering injury xv; incapable of feeling xvi. - (O)F. - ecclL. *impassibilis*; see IM-², PASSIBLE. So **impassive** xvii.
impassion xvi. - It. *impassionare*, f. IM-¹ + *passione* PASSION; chiefly in pp.
impasto laying on of colour thickly. xviii. - It., f. *impastare*, f. IM-¹ + *pasta* PASTE.
impatience xiii. - (O)F. - L.; see IM-², PATIENCE. So **impatient** xiv.
impeach †impede; accuse, charge xiv; charge with a high misdemeanour; call in question, disparage xvi. ME. *empe(s)che* - OF. *empe(s)cher* (mod. *empècher* prevent) :- late L. *impedicāre* catch, entangle, f. IM-¹ + *pedica* FETTER. So **impeachment** xiv.
impeccable not liable to sin xvi; faultless xvii. - L. *impeccābilis*, f. IM-² + *peccāre* sin; see -ABLE.
impecunious xvi. f. L. IM-² + *pecunia* money (cf. PECUNIARY).
impede xvii. - L. *impedīre*, f. IM-¹ + *pēs*, *ped-*. Hence **impedance** (electr.) xix. So **impediment** hindrance xiv; †pl. baggage (of an army) xvi. - L. *impedīmentum*, the pl. of which, **impedimenta**, is used in the second sense (xvi).
impel xv. - L. *impellere*, f. IM-¹ + *pellere* drive.
impend hang threateningly xvi; be imminent xvii; hang *over* xviii. - L. *impendēre*, f. IM-¹ + *pendēre* hang.
imperative (gram.) expressing command; commanding, peremptory xvi; urgent xix. - late L. *imperātīvus*, f. *imperāt-*, pp. stem of *imperāre* command (cf. EMPEROR); see -IVE.
imperfect not perfect xiv; (gram.) of a tense xvi. ME. *inperfit* - (O)F. *imparfait*; see IM-², PERFECT. So **imperfection**.
imperial xiv. - (O)F. *impérial* - L. *imperiālis*, f. *imperium* rule, EMPIRE; see -IAL. Hence **imperialism** xix, **imperialist** xvii.
imperil xvi (*em-*). f. *em-*, IM-¹ + PERIL.
imperious †imperial; †sovereign, majestic; overbearing. xvi. - L. *imperiōsus*, f. *imperium* command, EMPIRE; see -IOUS.
impersonal (gram.) xvi; not personal xvii. - late L. *impersōnālis*; see IM-², PERSONAL.
impersonate invest with a personality xvii; assume the person of xviii. f. L. IM-¹ + *persōna* PERSON.
impertinent †unrelated xiv; irrelevant xiv; inappropriate, not consonant with reason xvi; presumptuously intrusive, insolent xvii. - (O)F. *impertinent* or late L. *impertinens* not pertinent; see IM-², PERTINENT. Hence (or - F.) **impertinence** xvii.
imperturbable xv (rare before xviii). - late L.; see IM-², PERTURB, -ABLE.
impervious xvii. - L.; see IM-², PERVIOUS.
impetigo xvi. - L., f. *impetere* assail, f. IM-¹ + *petere* seek.
impetrate obtain by entreaty. xvi. f. pp. stem

of L. *impetrāre*, f. IM-[1] + *patrāre* bring to an end; see -ATE[3] and cf. PERPETRATE. So **impetration** XV. - AN. *impetracioun* and L. *-ātiō*.

impetuous XIV. - (O)F. *impétueux* - L. *impetuōsus*, f. *impetus* onset, violent impulse, f. *impetere*; see IMPETIGO, -UOUS. So **impetus** XVII. - L.

impinge †thrust *upon* XVI; strike, dash XVII. - L. *impingere*, f. IM-[1] + *pangere* fix, drive in.

impious XVI. f. L. *impius*; see IM-[2], PIOUS. So **impiety** XIV. - (O)F. or L.

implacable XVI. - F. or L.; see IM-[2], PLACABLE.

implant vb. XVI. - F. *implanter* or late L.; see IM-[1], PLANT.

implement[1] (pl.) equipment, outfit XV; (orig. pl.) apparatus, set of utensils, tools XVI. - medL. *implēmenta* (pl.) noun of instrument corr. to medL. *implēre* employ, spend, extended use (by assoc. with *implicāre* EMPLOY) of L. *implēre* fill up, fulfil, f. IM-[1] + *plēre* FILL.

implement[2] †essential constituent XVII; (Sc.) fulfilment XVIII. - late L. *implēmentum* filling up, noun of action of L. *implēre* (see prec.). Hence vb. (orig. Sc.) carry into effect. XIX.

implicate (arch.) intertwine, entangle; involve (as in guilt). XVI. f. pp. stem of L. *implicāre*, f. IM-[1] + *plicāre* fold (see PLY[1], -ATE[3]). So **implication** XV. - L.

implicit implied but not plainly expressed XVI; †entangled, entwined XVII. - F. *implicite* or L. *implicitus*, later form of *implicātus*, pp. of *implicāre* (see prec.).

implore beg or pray (for) XVI; beseech (one) XVII. - F. *implorer* or L. *implōrāre* invoke with tears, f. IM-[1] + *plōrāre* weep.

implosion XIX. f. IM-[1] + *-plosion*, of EXPLOSION. So **implosive** adj. and sb. XIX.

imply †enfold, involve XIV; involve the truth or existence of; express indirectly XVI. - OF. *emplier* :- L. *implicāre* IMPLICATE. The OF. var. *empleier*, *emploier* is the source of EMPLOY, with which *imply* to some extent overlapped XVI-XVII.

impolite XVII. See IM-[2], POLITE.

import A. carry as its purport, signify, imply XV; be of significance or importance (to) XVI; B. bring in from outside XVI. - L. *importāre*; in A in its med. sense of 'imply, mean'; in B in the orig. sense 'carry in', f. IM-[1] + *portāre* bring, carry, rel. to *portus* PORT[1]. Hence sb. A. purport, significance XVI; B. commodity imported XVII. So **importance** XVI. - (O)F. - medL. *importantia*. **important** XVI. - F. - medL. *importāns*, *-ant-*.

importunate persistent in asking. XV. f. L. *importūnus* + -ATE[2]. So **importunity** XV. - (O)F. - L. **importune** vb. XVI. - F. *importuner* or medL. *importūnārī*.

impose †impute XV; lay on (in various uses) XVI; exert influence *upon*, as with fraudulent intent or effect XVII. - (O)F. *imposer*, †*emposer*, f. *em-*, *im-* IM-[1] + *poser*, to repr. L. *impōnere* place on or into, lay as a burden, deceive, trick; see POSE[1]. Hence **imposing** exacting XVII; impressive XVIII. So **imposition** laying-on of hands XIV; impost XV; exercise imposed as punishment XVIII. - (O)F. or L.

impossible XIII. - (O)F. - L.; see IM-[2].

impost[1] tax, duty. XVI. - F. †*impost* (now *impôt*) - medL. *impostus*, *-um*, sb. use of *impos(i)tus*, pp. of L. *impōnere* IMPOSE.

impost[2] (archit.) upper course of a pillar XVII; horizontal block supported by upright stones XVIII. - F. *imposte* or its source It. *imposta*, sb. use of fem. pp. of *imporre* :- L. *impōnere* IMPOSE.

impostor one who imposes on others. XVI. - F. *imposteur* - late L. *impostor*, contr. of *impositor*, f. pp. stem of L. *impōnere* IMPOSE; see -OR[1]. So **imposture** XVI.

impost(h)ume (arch.) purulent swelling, abscess. XIV. - OF. *empostume*, alt. of *apostume*, later form of *aposteme* - L. *apostēma* - Gr. *apóstēma* lit. separation (cf. ABSCESS), f. *apostênai*, f. *apó* APO- + *stênai* STAND; assim. in pref. and ending to L. IM-[1] and *post(h)umus*.

impotent physically weak. XIV. - (O)F. - L.; see IM-[2], POTENT. So **impotence, -ency** XV.

impound enclose in a pound XVI; take (an object) into formal custody XVII. f. IM-[1] + POUND[2].

impoverish XV (*emporisshe*). f. *empoveriss-*, lengthened stem of OF. *empov(e)rir* (mod. *empauvrir*), f. EM-[1] + *povre* POOR; see -ISH[2].

imprecation invocation of evil. XVI. - L. *imprecātiō*, *-ōn-*, f. *imprecārī* (whence **imprecate** XVII), f. IM-[1] + *precārī* PRAY; see -ATE[3], -ATION. So **imprecatory** XVI. - medL.

impregnable XV (*imprenable*). - (O)F. *imprenable*, f. IM-[2] + *prenable* takeable, f. *pren-*, stem of *prendre* take :- L. *prehendere*; see -ABLE. The later forms *impre(i)gnable*, which depend upon OF. vars., induced the pronunc. with *g*.

impregnate make pregnant; imbue, saturate. XVII. f. *impregnate* pp. (XVI) or its source late L. *imprægnātus*, f. IM-[1] + *prægnāre* be PREGNANT; see -ATE[3].

impresario XVIII. - It., undertaker, contractor, f. *impresa* undertaking.

impress[1] stamp, imprint (a mark, etc.), lit. and fig. XIV (also *en-*); mark *with* a stamp XVI; affect strongly XVIII. - OF. *em-*, *impresser*, f. EM-[1], IM-[1] + *presser* PRESS[1] (cf. L. *imprimere*). Hence sb. stamp, mark. XVI. So **impression** effective action, effect XIV; mark produced by pressure XIV; printing XVI; notion impressed on the mind XVII. - (O)F. - L. *impressiō*, *-ōn-* onset, attack, emphasis, mental impression, f. *impress-*, pp. stem of *imprimere*, f. IM-[1] + *premere* PRESS[1]. **impressionable** XIX. - F. **impressionist** XIX. - F. *impressionniste*, used in an unfavourable sense with ref. to a picture by Claude Monet entitled *Impression*. **impressive** †susceptible XVI; making a deep impression XVIII.

impress[2] levy, enlist, esp. by force. XVI. f. IM-[1] + PRESS[2]. Hence sb. XVII.

imprimatur licence to print given by the L. formula *imprimātur* let it be printed, 3rd sg. pres. subj. pass. of *imprimere*; see IMPRINT. XVII.

imprint impressed mark or stamp XV (*em-*); publisher's name, etc., on a title-page XVIII. - (O)F. *empreinte*, sb. use of pp. fem. of *empreindre* :- L. *imprimere* impress, f. IM-[1] + *premere* PRESS[1]. So vb. mark by pressure, impress. XIV (*em-*). - OF.

imprison put in prison. XIII. - OF. *emprisoner*

(mod. *-onner*); see IM-[1], PRISON. So **imprisonment** XIV.

impromptu adv. and sb. XVII. - F. - L. phr. *in promptū* at hand, in readiness (*prōmere*; see PROMPT).

improper XVI. - (O)F. or L.; see IM-[2], PROPER.

impropriate annex *to* a person or corporation. XVI. f. pp. stem of medL. *impropriāre*, f. IM-[1] + *proprius* PROPER; see -ATE[3].

improve (†refl.) make one's profit; turn (an event, etc.) to good account, turn to profit or advantage; now (U.S.) make use of, occupy; enhance, augment XVI; raise to a better quality or condition XVII. Early forms *em-*, *improwe* - AN. *emprower*, *emprouer*, f. OF. EM-[1] + *prou* profit (:- late L. *prōde*, evolved from L. *prōdest* is of advantage), later infl. by PROVE. So **improvement** XV (*emprowement* profitable use, profit).

improvise compose without preparation. XIX. - F. *improviser* or its source, It. *improvvisare*, f. *improvviso* extempore - L. *imprōvīsus* unforeseen, f. IM-[2] + *prōvīsus*, pp. of *prōvīdere* PROVIDE. So **improvisation** XVIII.

impudent †immodest XIV; unblushingly presumptuous XVI. - L. *impudēns*, *-ent-* f. IM-[2] + *pudēns* ashamed, modest, orig. prp. of *pudēre* feel ashamed, shame. So **impudence** XIV.

impugn assail. XIV. - L. *impugnāre*, f. IM-[1] + *pugnāre* fight.

impulse act of impelling; stimulation of the mind. XVII. - L. *impulsus*, f. pp. stem of *impellere* IMPEL; cf. PULSE[1]. So **impulsive** impelling to action XVI; actuated by impulse XIX. - (O)F. *impulsif*, *-ive* or late L. *impulsīvus*.

impunity exemption from punishment XVI; security XVIII. - L. *impūnitās*, f. *impūnis* unpunished, f. IM-[2] + *pœna* penalty; see PAIN, -ITY.

impure XVI. - L.; see IM-[2], PURE. So **impurity** XV.

impute lay the fault of (a thing) *to* XIV; (theol.) attribute by vicarious substitution XVI. - (O)F. *imputer* - L. *imputāre* bring into the reckoning or charge, f. IM-[1] + *putāre* reckon.

in[1] prep. marking bounds or limits within which. OE. *in* = OS., OHG. (Du., G.), Goth. *in*, ON. *í*, rel. to L. *in* (older *en*), Gr. *en(i)*, OIr. *i n-*, *in*, W. *yn*, Lith. *į*, OSl. *vŭ(n-)* :- IE. **en*, **n̥*. Distinct in origin from **in** adv., which repr. (i) OE. *in(n)*, used with vbs. of motion = OS., Du. *in*, OHG. *īn* (with secondary lengthening), G. *ein*, ON., Goth. *inn*, (ii) OE. *inne*, used with vbs. of position = OS. *inna*, OHG. *inne*, ON. *inni*, Goth. *inna*, orig. loc.

Arising orig. from syntactical juncture of adv. *in* with a vb. are stable comps. such as *inbred*, *income*, *incoming*, *ingrowing*, *inlay*, *inroad*, many of the sbs. depending on phrasal units, as *inlet*, f. *let in*. In attrib. or adj. use *in* is or has been variously used, as in *in-land*, *inshore*, *inside*, *in-patient*. Cf. INNER, INMOST.

in[2] L. *in* (see prec.) with the abl. 'in', with the acc. 'into', 'against', 'towards, for the purpose of', in many phrases frequent in Eng. contexts from XVI onwards, as *in extenso*, *in extremis*, *in flagrante delicto*, *in medias res*, *in memoriam*, *in situ*, *in toto*, *in vacuo*. For designations of sizes of books, e.g. *in-folio*, see the sbs. FOLIO, etc.

in-[1] repr. L. *in-* (cf. prec.), used in combination mainly with vbs. and their derivs. with the senses 'in, into, within, on, towards, against'; in earlier L. the prefix retained its *n*, but later this was assim. to *l*, *m*, *r* (see IL-[1], IM-[1], IR-[1]). In OF. *in-*, *im-* became *en-*, *em-* (see EN-[1], EM-[1]) in inherited words, but in learned words *in-*, *im-* were regularly retained.

in-[2] repr. L. *in-*, cogn. and synon. with Gr. *a(n)-* A-[4] and Gmc. **un-* UN-[1], as in *fēlix* happy/*infēlix* unhappy, *nocēns* hurtful/*innocēns* innocent; in earlier L. the pref. retained its *n*, but later this was assim. to *l*, *m*, *r* (see IL-[2], IM-[2], IR-[2]); before *g* it was reduced to *i-*, as in *ignōrāre* ignore. In a few OF. words this *in-* became *en-*, e.g. L. *inimīcus*, OF. *enemi* enemy, L. *invidia*, OF. *envie* envy; but most F. words containing this pref. are of learned orig. and retain *in-* (*il-*, etc.).

-in (chem.) modification of -INE[5].

-ina[1] L. fem. suffix as in *rēgīna* queen (f. *rēg-*, *rēx* king), in It. and Sp. and thence in Eng. forming female titles, as *czarina*, and in proper names, as *Clementina*; it is used for some names of musical instruments, as *concertina*, *ocarina*.

-ina[2] n. pl. of L. *-īnus* -INE[1] used in names of groups of animals.

inadvertence lack of attention. XVI. - medL. *inadvertentia*; see IN-[2], ADVERT.

inamorato male lover. XVI. - It. †*inamorato* (now *innam-*), pp. of *in(n)amorare* = OF. *enamourer* ENAMOUR. So **inamorata** female lover. XVII.

inane †empty XVII; empty-headed XIX. - L. *inānis* empty, vain. So **inanity** †emptiness; vanity, hollowness XVII; vacuity XVIII.

inanimate XVI. - late L. (see IN-[2]).

inanition †emptying of a body XIV; exhausted condition XVIII. - late L. *inānītiō*, *-ōn-*, f. *inānīre*, f. *inānis*; see INANE and -ITION.

inasmuch in so far *as*, (hence) seeing that, considering that. XIV. tr. OF. *en tant* (*que*), repr. L. *in tantum* (ut), IN[2], *tantum* so much (n. of *tantus* so great).

inaugural XVII. - F., f. *inaugurer* inaugurate; see -AL[1]. So **inaugurate** admit formally to an office XVII; initiate formally XVIII; initiate the public use of XIX. f. pp. stem of L. *inaugurāre* take omens, f. IN-[1] + *augurāre* AUGUR. **inauguration** XVI. - (O)F. or late L.

inborn †native OE. (newly formed XVII); implanted by nature XVI. OE. *inboren*, after late L. *innātus* INNATE; see IN-[1], BORN.

incandescent XVIII. - F. - prp. of L. *incandēscere* glow, f. IN-[1] + *candēscere* become white, f. *candidus*; see CANDID, -ENT.

incantation XIV. - (O)F. - late L. *incantātiō*, *-ōn-*, f. *incantāre* chant, charm, f. IN-[1] + *cantāre* sing, CHANT; see -ATION.

incapable XVI. - F. or late L.; see IN-[2].

incarcerate XVI (preceded by pp. *incarcerate* XV). f. pp. stem of medL. *incarcerāre*, f. IN-[1] + *carcer* prison; see -ATE[3]. So **incarceration** XVI. - (O)F. or late L.

incarnadine flesh-coloured, blood-red. XVI. - F. *incarnadin*, *-ine* - It. *incarnadino*, north. var.

of *incarnatino* carnation, flesh-colour, f. *incarnato* INCARNATE; see next and -INE[1]. Hence vb. XVII.

incarnate embodied in flesh XIV; flesh-coloured XVI. - ecclL. *incarnātus*, pp. of *incarnārī* be made flesh, f. IN-[1] + *carō, carn-* flesh; see CARNAL, -ATE[2]. So **incarnation** embodiment in flesh XIII (concr. XVIII); †flesh-colour XV. - (O)F. - ecclL.

incendiary adj. and sb. XVII. - L. *incendiārius*, f. *incendium* burning, fire; see next and -ARY.

incense[1] aromatic gum burnt to produce a sweet smell XIII; smoke of this XIV. ME. *ansens, encens* - (O)F. *encens* - ecclL. *incensum*, sb. use of n. of *incensus*, pp. of *incendere* set fire to, f. IN-[1] + **candere* cause to glow (*candēre* glow). Hence vb. XIV.

incense[2] †set on fire; inflame with wrath. XV. - OF. *incenser*, f. L. *incens-*, pp. stem of *incendere* (see prec.).

incentive (something) that incites to action. XV. - L. *incentīvus* that sets the tune, that provokes or incites (sb. *-īvum*), f. *incent-*, var. of *incant-*; see INCANTATION, -IVE.

inception XV. - (O)F. *inception* or L. *inceptiō, -ōn-*, f. *incept-*, pp. stem of *incipere*; see INCIPIENT, -TION. So **inceptive** XVII.

incessant XVI. - F. *incessant* or late L. *incessāns, -ant-*, f. IN-[2] + *cessāns*, prp. of *cessāre* CEASE; see -ANT. So **incessantly** XV.

incest XIII. - L. *incestus*, or *incestum*, sb. use of n. of *incestus* impure, unchaste, f. IN-[2] + *castus* CHASTE. So **incestuous** XVI. - late L.

inch[1] twelfth part of a foot. Late OE. *ynće*, corr. to OHG. *unza*, Goth. *unkja* - L. *uncia* twelfth part (see OUNCE[1]).

inch[2] (Sc.) small island. XV. - Gael. *innis* = (O)Ir. *inis*, W. *ynys*.

inchoate XVI. - L. *inchoātus*, pp. of *inchoāre, incohāre* begin; see -ATE[2]. So **inchoative** XVI. - late L.

incident liable to befall or occur; attaching itself as a privilege, etc. XV. - F. *incident* or L. *incidēns, -ent-*, prp. of *incidere* fall upon, happen to, f. IN-[1] + *cadere* fall; see -ENT. So sb. XV. Hence **incidental, incidentally** XVII.

incinerate XVI. f. pp. stem of medL. *incinerāre*, f. IN-[1] + *cinis, ciner-* ashes; see -ATE[3]. So **incineration** XVI. - medL.

incipient XVII. - L. *incipiēns, -ent-*, prp. of *incipere* undertake, begin, f. IN-[1] + *capere* take.

incipit beginning or first words of a literary work. XIX. - L., 3rd pers. sg. pres. ind. of *incipere* begin (see prec.).

incise XVI. - F. *inciser*, f. *incīs-*, pp. stem of L. *incīdere*, f. IN-[1] + *cædere* cut. So **incision** XV. - (O)F. or late L. **incisive** XVI. - medL. **incisor** front (cutting) tooth. XVII. - medL.

incite XV. - (O)F. *inciter* - L. *incitāre*, f. IN-[1] + *citāre* set in rapid motion, rouse; see CITE.

inclement †unmerciful; (of weather) not mild XVII. - F. or L.; see IN-[2], CLEMENT.

incline bend towards a thing, forward or downward. XIII. ME. *encline* - OF. *encliner*; these Eng. and F. forms survived till XVII, but forms assim. to the L. source *inclīnāre* finally prevailed; see IN-[1], LEAN[2]. Hence sb. XVII. So **inclination** XIV (not common till XVI). - (O)F. or L. **inclinometer** XIX.

inclose, inclosure see ENCLOSE.

include shut in; comprise. XV. - L. *inclūdere*, f. IN-[1] + *claudere* shut, CLOSE. So **inclusion, inclusive** XVI.

incognito XVII. - It. - L. *incognitus* unknown; see IN-[2], QUAINT. Abbreviated **incog** XVII.

income A. †entrance, arrival XIII; †fee paid on entering XVI; B. receipts from work, etc., revenue XVII. In ME. use prob. - ON. *innkoma* arrival; later, a new formation on phr. *come in*.

incommensurable (math.) having no common measure. XVI. f. IN-[2] + late L. *commensurābilis* COMMENSURABLE.

incommode XVI. - F. *incommoder* or L. *incommodāre*, f. *incommodus* inconvenient; see IN-[2], COMMODIOUS.

incomprehensible not to be circumscribed; not to be grasped by the understanding XIV; (hence) that cannot be understood XVII. - L.; see IN-[2].

incom(m)unicado XIX. - Sp. *incomunicado*, f. *in-* IN-[2] + pp. of *comunicar* COMMUNICATE.

incongruous XVII. - L. *incongruus*; see IN-[2]. So **incongruity** XVI.

incontinence, -ent XIV. - (O)F. or L.; see IN-[2], CONTINENCE.

incorporate put into the body of something XIV; combine or form into one body, adopt into a body XVI. f. pp. stem of late L. *incorporāre*; see IN-[1], CORPORATE. So **incorporation** XIV. - late L.

incorrect XV. - F. or L. So **incorrigible** XIV. See IN-[2], CORRECT.

increase become or make greater. XIV. ME. *encres* - AN. *encres(s)-*, OF. *encreis(s)-*, stem of *encreistre* :- L. *incrēscere*, f. IN-[1] + *crēscere* grow; the prefix was assim. to L. XV. Hence sb. XIV.

increment increase XV; amount of increase, profit XVII. - L. *incrēmentum*, f. stem of *incrēscere*; see prec., -MENT.

incriminate charge with a crime XVIII; involve in an accusation, inculpate XIX. f. pp. stem of late L. *incrīmināre* accuse, f. IN-[1] + *crīmen* charge; see CRIME, -ATE[3]. So **incrimination** XVII.

incubate XVIII. f. pp. stem of L. *incubāre*, f. IN-[1] + *cubāre* lie; see CUBICLE, -ATE[3]. So **incubation** XVII. - L. **incubator** XIX.

incubus demon descending upon persons in their sleep XIV; nightmare XVI; oppressive person or thing XVII. - late L. *incubus*, earlier *incubo*, f. *incubāre*; see prec.

inculcate impress (a thing) upon a person. XVI. f. pp. stem of L. *inculcāre* stamp in with the heel, press in, f. IN-[1] + *calcāre* tread; see CAULK, -ATE[3].

inculpate accuse, blame XVIII; incriminate XIX. f. pp. stem of late L. *inculpāre*; see IN-[1], CULPABLE.

incumbent falling as a duty or obligation XVI; leaning or resting with its weight XVII. - prp. of L. *incumbere* lie or lean upon, apply oneself to, f. IN-[1] + **cumbere*, f. nasalized stem corr. to *cubāre* (cf. CUBICLE); see -ENT. The sb. use of 'holder of an ecclesiastical benefice' (XV) is peculiarly Eng.

incunabula earliest stages or first beginnings; books produced in the 'infancy' of printing, i.e.

before 1501 A.D. XIX - L. n. pl., swaddling-clothes, cradle, birthplace, infancy, origin, f. IN-[1] + *cūnabula*, f. *cūnæ* cradle.

incur †intr. run, fall (*into*); tr. run or fall into, become liable to. XVI. - L. *incurrere*, f. IN-[1] + *currere* run. So **incursion** hostile inroad XV; running in or against XVII.

incus (anat.) anvil bone of the ear. XVII. - L., 'anvil'.

indebted under obligation. XIII. ME. *an-, endetted*, f. OF. *endetté*, pp. of *endetter* involve in debt; see -ED[1]; assim. to L. (medL. *indebitāre*; see DEBT).

indeed in reality XIV; as a matter of fact; it is true, truly; (interrog.) Is it so? XVI; as int. of contempt or incredulity XIX. ME. adv. phr. *in dede*, i.e. IN[1] prep., d. of DEED.

indefatigable XVI. - F. †*indéfatigable* or L. *indēfatigābilis*; see IN-[2], DE- 3, FATIGUE, -ABLE.

indefinite XVI (first in gram.). - L.; see IN-[2].

indelible XVI (*indeleble*). - F. *indélébile* or L. *indēlēbilis*, f. IN-[2] + *dēlēbilis*, f. *dēlēre* DELETE; the ending was assim. to -IBLE.

indemnity security against contingent injury XV; compensation for loss XVI; legal exemption from liabilities incurred XVII. - (O)F. *indemnité* - late L. *indemnitās*, f. *indemnis* free from loss or hurt, f. IN-[2] + *damnum*; see DAMAGE, -ITY. So **indemnify** XVII.

indent make tooth-like incision in, spec. for the purpose of an INDENTURE XIV; make a covenant XV; †contract for XVI; engage (a servant) by contract, orig. in U.S. and Anglo-Indian use XVIII; make a requisition *for*, draw *upon* XIX; (typogr.) set back from the margin XVII. - AN. *endenter*, AL. *indentāre*, f. IN[1] + *dēns, dent-* TOOTH. So **indenture** deed with mutual covenants executed in two or more copies, all having their edges correspondingly indented XIV; indentation XVII. Earliest in MSc. *en-, indenture* - AN. *endenture* (OF. *-eure*), medL. *indentūra* (also *indentātūra*), f. *indentātus*, pp. of *indentāre*. Hence as vb. XVII.

independent XVII. f. IN-[1] + DEPENDENT. So **independence** XVII.

index pl. *indexes, indices* forefinger; pointer; guiding principle; †table of contents; alphabetical list of subjects appended to a book XVI; (math.) XVII. - L. *index*, pl. *indicēs*, forefinger, informer, sign, inscription, f. IN-[1] + *-dex, -dic-*, f. IE. **deiḱ-, dik-* point out.

India In OE. *India, Indea*, but the present use dates from XVI (prob. immed. after Sp. or Pg.). - L. - Gr. *India*, f. *Indós* the river Indus - Pers. *hind* (cf. HINDU). Hence **Indian** adj. and sb. XV; pert. to America and the West Indies XVII (*Indian rubber* XVIII, the earlier form for *India rubber* XIX). **Indies** orig. India with the adjacent islands. XVI. pl. of †*Indie, Indy* (XVI-XVII) - L. *India*.

indicate XVII. f. pp. stem of L. *indicāre* declare, mention, f. IN-[1] + *dicāre* proclaim; cf. INDEX and see -ATE[3]. So **indication** XVI. - F. - L. **indicative** (gram.) XVI; suggestive *of* XVII. - (O)F. - late L.

indict XIV. ME. *endite*, later with latinized pref. *indite, indict* (XVI). - legal AN. *enditer*, corr. in form but not in sense to OF. *enditier* declare, dictate, compose, INDITE :- Rom. **indictāre*, f. *indict-*, pp. stem of L. *indīcere* proclaim, impose, f. IN-[1] + *dīcere* pronounce, utter. So **indictment** XIV.

indiction declaration or proclamation, spec. of the Roman emperors fixing the valuation for property tax at the beginning of each fiscal period of 15 years; the period from 1 Sept. 312 instituted by the emperor Constantine by which dates were reckoned, (also) specified year in such a period. XIV. - L. *indictiō, -ōn-*, f. *indīcere*; see prec. and -TION.

indifferent A. (arch.) impartial, neutral XIV; without interest; neither good nor bad XVI (euphem. not very good XIX); B. †not different; unimportant, immaterial XVI. - F. *indifférent* or L. *indifferēns* making no difference, of no consequence; see IN-[2], DIFFERENT. Hence **indifference** XVI, **indifferently** XIV.

indigenous XVII. f. L. *indigena* native (adj. and sb.), f. *indi-*, strengthened form of IN-[1] + *-gena*, f. **gen-*, base of *gignere* beget.

indigent needy XIV; †wanting, deficient XV. - (O)F. - L. *indigēns, -ent-*, prp. of *indigēre* lack, f. *indi-* (cf. prec.) + *egēre* be in want, need; see -ENT. So **indigence** XIV. - (O)F. or L.

indign (arch.) unworthy. XV. - (O)F. *indigne* or L. *indignus*, f. IN-[2] + *dignus* worthy. So **indignity** †unworthiness; unworthy treatment. XVI.

indignant XVI. - L. *indignāns, -ant-*, prp. of *indignārī* regard as unworthy, f. *indignus*; see prec., -ANT. So **indignation** †disdain; anger at what is considered unworthy XIV. - (O)F. or L.

indigo blue dye obtained from plants of the genus *Indigofera*. XVI. The usual form in XVI-XVII was *indico* - Sp. - L. *indicum* - Gr. *indikón*, sb. use of n. of *Indikós* Indian. The form *indigo* (XVI), occas. †*endego*, is - Pg.

indirect XV. - (O)F. or late L.; see IN-[2], DIRECT. Hence **indirection** XVI.

indiscreet †without discernment XV; injudicious, unwary XVI. - L. *indiscrētus*. So **indiscretion** XIV. - (O)F. or late L.

indispensable (eccl.) that cannot be allowed or condoned XVI; that cannot be remitted; that cannot be done without XVII. - medL.; see IN-[2], DISPENSE.

indisposed †not in order; unfitted; †ill-disposed XV; out of health XVI; not disposed or inclined XVII. Partly - F. *indisposé* or L. *indispositus* disordered, unprepared; partly directly f. IN-[2] + pp. of DISPOSE. So **indisposition** †unfitness XV; disordered physical state XVI. - F. or f. IN-[2] + DISPOSITION.

indite †dictate; put into words, compose. XIV. - OF. *endit(i)er* :- Rom. **indictāre*, f. IN-[1] + *dictāre* declare, DICTATE. Cf. INDICT.

individual †indivisible XV (rare before XVII); existing as a separate entity; pert. to a single person or thing XVII; sb. XVII. - medL. *indīviduālis*, f. L. *indīviduus* indivisible, inseparable, f. IN-[2] + *dīviduus* divisible, f. *dīvidere* DIVIDE; see -AL[1]. So **individualism** XIX, **individuality** XVII.

indivisible XIV (rare before XVI). - late L. *indīvisībilis*; see IN-[2], DIVIDE.

indolent (path.) painless XVII; averse to exertion XVIII. - late L. *indolēns, -ent-*, f. IN-[2] + prp. of *dolēre* suffer pain, give pain; see -ENT. So **indolence** XVI. - F. or L.

indomitable †untameable XVII; not to be overcome XIX. - late L. *indomitābilis*, f. IN-[2] + *domitāre*; see DAUNT, -ABLE.

indoor(s) inside a house, etc.; adj. pert. to the interior. XVIII. See IN[1], DOOR. For earlier *withindoor(s)* XVI.

indubitable XVIII. - F. *indubitable* or L. *indubitābilis*; see IN-[2], DOUBT.

induce lead to some action, etc. XIV; †introduce; give rise to, lead to XV; infer XVI. - L. *indūcere*, f. IN-[1] + *dūcere* lead; from XIV to XVIII often with *en-* after F. *enduire* (cf. ENDUE). Hence **inducement** XVI. So **induct** (eccl.) introduce formally to a benefice XIV; conduct, introduce XVI. f. *induct-*, pp. stem of L. *indūcere*. **induction** (eccl.) XIV; gen. †introduction, initiation XVI; (logic) opp. to *deduction* XV; (electr. and magn.) XIX. **inductive** inducing XVII; (logic) XVII; (electr.) XIX.

indulge treat with undeserved favour, gratify by compliance XVII; give free course *to* XVII; take one's pleasure freely *in* XVIII. - L. *indulgēre*, of uncert. orig. So **indulgence** XIV. - (O)F. - L. **indulgent** XVI. - F. or L. **indult** special licence or privilege. XVI (first in Sc.). - F. - late L. *indultum*, sb. use of n. pp. of *indulgēre*.

indurate harden. XVI. f. pp. stem of L. *indūrāre*; see ENDURE, -ATE[3]; preceded by pp. †*indurate* XV. So **induration** XIV. - F. or late L.

indusium (anat.) amnion XVIII; (bot.) membranous shield of the sorus of a fern XIX. - L., 'tunic', f. *induere* put on.

industry †skill, dexterity XV; diligence, assiduity; systematic labour, form or kind of this XVI. - (O)F. *industrie* or L. *industria*; see -Y[3]. So **industrious** †skilful, ingenious; painstaking, hardworking. XVI. **industrial** XVI (isolated exx. before XIX); hence **industrialism** XIX.

indwell dwell in, inhabit. XIV. f. IN[1] + DWELL.

-ine[1] suffix repr. F. *-in*, fem. *-ine* and its source L. *-īnus, -īna* (corr. to Gr. *-īnos, -ī́nē*), affixed to nominal and some other stems with the sense 'of or pert. to', 'of the nature of', as *canīnus* CANINE, *dīvīnus* DIVINE[1], *genuīnus* GENUINE, sometimes in comb. with another suffix, as in *clandestīnus* CLANDESTINE. In the terminology of nat. hist. *-ine* is used freely in adjs. formed on generic names, as *accipitrine, passerine*, after *bovine, equine*.

-ine[2] suffix forming adjs., repr. F. *-in*, fem. *-ine*, or its source L. *-inus, -ina* (corr. to Gr. *-inos, -inē*), having in the Rom. langs. and in Eng. the same form and sense as -INE[1].

-ine[3] suffix of fem. sbs., repr. F. *-ine*, L. *īna*, Gr. *-īnē*, as in Gr. *hērōī́nē*, L. *hērōīna*, F. *héroïne* HEROINE (the only survival in Eng.).

-ine[4] suffix repr. F. *-ine* (*-in*) or L. *-īna* (*-īnus*), in orig. identical with -INE[1], used in abstr. formations on vbs. and agent-nouns, as *doctrīna* DOCTRINE, *ruīna* RUIN, and concr. sbs. on other stems, as *fascīna* FASCINE. The adjs. in *-īnus, -īna* were used also sb., as in *concubīna* CONCUBINE, *consobrīnus* COUSIN. Some are anglicized with *-in*, as *ruin*.

In techn. and commercial use this suffix has a vague application and forms names of textile materials, natural and artificial substances, etc., as *brilliantine, dentine, grenadine, nectarine*.

-ine[5] suffix of chem. terms, in origin a variation of -INE[4], in such names as *gelatine* (now superseded by *gelatin* exc. in pop. use), and those of the four elements *bromine, chlorine, fluorine, iodine*.

inebriate XV. f. *inebriate* ppl. adj. (XV) or pp. of L. *inēbriāre*, f. IN-[1] + *ēbriāre* intoxicate, f. *ēbrius* drunk; see -ATE[3].

ineffable XV. - F. *ineffable* or L. *ineffābilis*, f. IN-[2] + *effābilis*, f. *effārī* speak out, f. EF- + *fārī*; cf. FAME, -ABLE.

ineluctable inescapable. XVII. - L., f. IN-[2] + *ēluctārī* struggle out.

inept †(leg.) void XVI; (arch.) unsuited, inappropriate; foolish XVII. - L. *ineptus*, f. IN-[2] + *aptus* APT.

inequality XV. - OF. or L.; see IN-[2], EQUALITY.

inequity XVI. f. IN-[2] + EQUITY.

inert inactive, inanimate XVII; sluggish XVIII. - L. *iners, inert-* unskilled, inactive, f. IN-[1] + *ars* skill, ART. So **inertia** XVIII. - L.; see -IA[1].

inestimable too great to be estimated XIV; priceless XVI. - (O)F. - L.; see IN-[2].

inevitable XV. - L., f. IN-[2] + *ēvitābilis*, f. *ēvītāre*, f. E- + *vītāre* avoid; see -ABLE.

inexorable XVI. - F. *inexorable* or L. *inexōrābilis*, f. IN-[2] + *exōrābilis*, f. *exōrāre*, f. EX-[1] + *ōrāre* pray; see -ABLE.

infallible XV. - F. *infaillible* or medL. *infallibilis*; see IN-[2], FALLIBLE. So **infallibility** XVII.

infamous XIV. - medL. *infamōsus*, for L. *infāmis*; see IN-[2], FAMOUS. So **infamy** XV. - (O)F.

infant XIV. ME. *enfaunt* (with early assim. to L.) - (O)F. *enfant* :- L. *infāns, -ant-*, sb. use of *infāns* unable to speak, f. IN-[2] + prp. of *fārī* speak; see FAME, -ANT. So **infancy** XV. - L. *infantia*. **infantile** XVII. - F. or L. **infantry** XVI. - F. *infanterie* - It. *infanteria*, f. *infante* youth, foot-soldier.

infatuate †turn (a thing) to folly; make foolish, possess with an extravagant passion. XVI. f. pp. stem of L. *infatuāre*, f. IN-[1] + *fatuus* FATUOUS; see -ATE[3].

infect affect with disease; taint, deprave XIV; imbue, esp. injuriously XV; †dye, stain XV. f. *infect-*, pp. stem of L. *inficere* dip in, stain, taint, spoil, f. IN-[1] + *facere* put, DO[1]. So **infection** XIV. - (O)F. or late L. Hence **infectious** XVI. **infective** XIV. - medL.

infer †bring about, induce; †bring in, introduce; draw as a conclusion; imply. XVI. - L. *inferre* bear or bring in, in medL. infer, f. IN-[1] + *ferre* BEAR[2]. So **inference** XVI. - medL. *inferentia*.

inferior lower XV (in physical sense now chiefly techn.); of lower or low degree XVI; sb. XVI - L., compar. of *inferus* low; see UNDER, -IOR.

infernal pert. to hell XIV. - (O)F. - ChrL. *infernālis*, f. *infernus*, parallel to *inferus*: see -AL[1].

infest †attack, assail XV; trouble with hostile attacks, swarm in XVII. - (O)F. *infester* or L. *infestāre*, f. *infestus* hostile, unsafe.

infidel non-Christian XV; professed unbeliever XVI. - F. *infidèle* or L. *infidēlis* unfaithful, (eccl.)

unbelieving, f. IN-[2] + *fidēlis* faithful, f. *fidēs* FAITH. So **infidelity** XVI.

infiltrate XVIII. f. IN-[1] + FILTRATE. So **infiltration** XVIII.

infinite (arch.) unlimited in number XIV; having no limit or end XV. - L. *infīnītus*; see IN-[3], FINITE. So **infinitesimal** reciprocal of an infinite quantity; indefinitely small. XVIII. f. modL. *infīnītēsimus*, f. L. *infīnītus*, after *centēsimus* hundredth. **infinitive** (gram.). XVI. - L. *infīnītīvus*, f. IN-[3] + *fīnītīvus* definite. **infinitude** XVII. f. L. *infīnītus*. **infinity** XIV. - (O)F. - L.

infirm †weak, unsound XIV; not firm, irresolute XVI; weak through age or illness XVII. - L. *infirmus*; see IN-[3], FIRM[1]. So **infirmary** XVII. - medL. *infirmāria*. **infirmity** XIV. - L.; cf. F. *infirmité*.

infix (philol.) element inserted in the body of a word. XIX. After *prefix*, *suffix*; see IN-[1], FIX.

inflame (lit. and fig.) XIV. ME. *inflaume*, *-flamme* - (O)F. *enflammer* :- L. *inflammāre*, f. IN-[1] + *flamma* FLAME. So **inflammation** XVI. - L.

inflate XVI. f. pp. †*inflate* (XV) - L. *inflātus*, pp. of *inflāre*, f. IN-[1] + *flāre* BLOW[1]. So **inflation** XIV. - L.

inflect bend XV; (gram.) vary the termination of XVII; modulate the tone of XIX. - L. *inflectere*, f. IN-[1] + *flectere* bend. **inflection, inflexion** bending, curvature XVI; modulation of voice XVI; (gram.) modification of form in declension, etc. XVII. - (O)F. or L. (see FLEXION).

inflexible XIV. - L.; see IN-[3], FLEXIBLE.

inflict XVI. f. *inflict-*, pp. stem of L. *inflīgere*, f. IN-[1] + *flīgere* strike. So **infliction** XVI. - late L.

inflorescence XVI. - modL. *inflōrēscentia*, f. late L. *inflōrēscere* come into flower; see IN-[1], FLORESCENCE.

influence (astrol.) emanation of ethereal fluid from the heavens affecting mankind XIV; †infusion of power; †influx XV; insensible action of one *on* another XVI; power of ascendancy *over*. - (O)F. *influence* or medL. *influentia* (whence also It. *influenza*), f. prp. of L. *influere* flow in, f. IN-[1] + *fluere* flow; see -ENCE. Hence vb. XVII. So **influential** XVI. f. medL. *influentia*.

influenza XVIII. - It. *influenza* INFLUENCE, used spec. for visitation or outbreak of an epidemic (e.g. *influenza di catarro*, *influenza di febbre scarlattina*), hence absol. epidemic.

influx XVII. - F. *influx* or late L. *influxus*, f. *influere* flow in; see IN-[1].

inform †give form to; give a character to, imbue, inspire; furnish with knowledge XIV. ME. *enfo(u)rme* - OF. *enfo(u)rmer* (mod. *informer*) - L. *informāre* shape, form an idea of, describe; see IN-[1], FORM. So **informant** XVII, **information** XIV.

infra- pref. repr. L. *infrā* adv. and prep. below, underneath, found occas. in comps. in late and medL., e.g. *infrāforeānus* situated beneath the forum, *infrāmūrānus* lying within the walls, on the model of which are made formations such as *infra-axillary* below the axilla, *inframammary* below the breasts; it is extended to denotation of a condition, as in *infrabestial* below (that of) the beasts; it is attrib. or adverbial in *infraposition*, etc.; **infralapsarian** (theol.) pert. to the view that God's election of some was consequent to his prescience of the Fall of Man. XVIII. f. L. *lapsus* fall, LAPSE. **infra-red,** applied to the rays that lie beyond the red end of the spectrum. XIX.

infraction XVII. - L. *infractiō*, *-ōn-*, f. *infract-*, pp. stem of *infringere* INFRINGE.

infra dig. XIX. abbrev. of L. *infrā dignitātem* beneath (one's) dignity.

infringe XVI. - L. *infringere*, f. IN-[1] + *frangere* break.

infuse pour in XV; instil; steep XVI. f. *infūs-*, pp. stem of L. *infundere*, f. IN-[1] + *fundere* pour. So **infusion** XV; concr. XVI. - (O)F. or L.

infusoria (zool.) class of protozoa, so called because found in infusions of decaying matter. XVIII. sb. use of n. pl. of modL. **infūsōrius*, f. *infūs-*; see prec. and -IA[2], -ORIOUS.

-ing[1] suffix forming derivs. orig. of vbs., primarily nouns of action, but subsequently developed in application and meaning in various ways: OE. *-ung* and *-ing* (which superseded the more frequent *-ung* in early ME.) = OS. *-unga*, MLG., MDu. *-inge*, Du. *-ing*, OHG. *-unga* (G. *-ung*), ON. *-ung*, *-ing*. In OE. the earliest and commonest use of the suffix is in formations from weak vbs., e.g. *ācsung* asking (f. *ācsian* ask), *fēding* (f. *fēdan* feed), *macung* (f. *macian* do, make). Extension to str. vbs. began in OE., e.g. *brecung* breaking, *eting* eating, *hlēapung* leaping; and before 1200 the suffix was used with verbs of any class, whether native or adopted. Formation on advs. is typified by *inning*, *offing*, *outing*.

In OE. itself was developed the notion of a completed action or process or the result of this, (whence) habit, art, e.g. *blētsung*, *-ing* blessing, benediction, *gaderung* collection, assembly, *leornung* learning, study; transference to concrete or material accompaniment or product of a process followed, as in *bedding* bed-clothes, *eardung* dwelling, *offrung* sacrifice. The existence of a parallel sb. of the same form as the vb. (as in *clothes/clothing*) has led to the creation of *-ing*-forms without a corresponding verb, as *coping*, *scaffolding*, *tubing*. Individualized use, with consequent pluralization, began early and became prominent in later periods, e.g. *a* long *sitting*, three *sittings*; *a* bad *beginning* but *a* happy *ending*; *an outing*, frequent *outings*. In some plurals the concr. use appears almost exclusively, e.g. *earnings*, *leavings*, *trappings*. EVENING and MORNING are special formations.

b. The outstanding development of the verbal sb. in *-ing* is its use as a gerund, so that it may be qualified by adjs. and advs. and may take an object and a predicative noun or adj., e.g. the habit of *rising early*, engaged in *building a house*; (with an object and predicated pp.) after *having* written *a letter*. The germ of such constructions may be seen in such OE. comps. as *āðswerung* swearing of oaths, *feaxfallung* falling-out of hair, *mynsterclǣnsung* purification of a church, where the first el. is a sb. in subjective, objective, or adverbial relation, or an adverb, and in such constructions as *oftrǣd-*

liċe rǣdinga hāligra bōca frequent readings of holy books (objective genitive). The attrib. use of the gerund, as in *breeding place, dancing lesson, living room, thanksgiving day, winning post*, has its antecedent models in the earliest periods; e.g. OE. *cenningstōw* birthplace, *huntingspere* hunting-spear, ME. *gretinng word* salutation.

-ing² suffix of the prp., ME. alt. of OE. *-ende*, later *-inde*, in late Nhb. *-ande* (after ON.) = OS. *-and* (Du. *-end*), OHG. *-anti, -enti, -onti* (G. *-end*), ON. *-andi*, Goth. *-ands*, corr. to L. *-ant-* -ANT, *-ent-* -ENT, Gr. *-ont-*, Skr. *-ant-*. The forms *-inde, -ende* continued in the Kentish area till XIV, but from the end of XII there was a general tendency to assim. *-inde* to -ING¹. Several words of ppl. orig. or nature are used only or mainly as adjs., e.g. *strapping, unavailing, willing*; others (mostly of F. orig.) are preps., viz. *concerning, during, pending*.

As a morphological feature the prp. enters into the formation of the tenses with the verb *be*, variously known as progressive, continuous, indefinite: e.g. I *am coming*, They *were fighting*; the use is found in the earliest OE.

-ing³ suffix forming masc. sbs. based on sbs. or adjs. with the sense 'one belonging to or of the kind of . . ', 'possessing the qualities of . . ', as a patronymic 'one descended from . . '; OE. *-ing* (corr. to OHG. *-ing*, ON. *-ingr, -ungr*) as in: *cyning* KING, *flȳming* fugitive, *lytling* little one; patronymics, as *Æðelwulfing*/*Wodening* son of Æthelwulf/Woden; names of coins, *pending, penning* PENNY, *sċilling* SHILLING; fractional parts, *feorðing* FARTHING, *thriding* RIDING (of ON. orig.). Other words, of various ages from OE. onwards, are chiefly names of animals and fruits, as *bunting, gelding* (of ON. orig.), *herring* (OE.), *sweeting, whiting* (OE.).

ingeminate utter twice, reiterate. XVI. f. pp. stem of L. *ingemināre* redouble, repeat, f. IN-¹ + *gemināre* GEMINATE.

ingenious †of high intellectual capacity XV; skilful in invention XVI; †used for INGENUOUS XVI. - F. *ingénieux* or L. *ingeniōsus*, f. *ingenium* natural quality, genius; see -IOUS.

ingénue artless (young) woman. XIX. - F., fem. of *ingénu* - L. *ingenuus* (see next).

ingenuous †noble-minded; honourably straightforward XVI; free-born XVII. f. L. *ingenuus* native, free-born, noble, frank, f. IN-¹ + **gen-*, base of *gignere* beget; see KIN, -UOUS. So **ingenuity** A. †free-born condition; †nobility of character; ingenuousness (now rare); B. †intellectual capacity XVI; skill in contriving XVII. - L. *ingenuitās*. The uses of branch B are peculiarly Eng. and depend on confusion with INGENIOUS in XVI-XVII.

ingle (Sc., etc.) fire, flame, hearth. XVI. of obscure orig.; perh. - Gael. *aingeal* fire, light.

ingot †mould in which metal is cast XIV; mass of cast metal XV. orig. obscure; form and meaning suggest deriv. from IN¹ and OE. *goten*, pp. of *ġēotan* pour, cast in metal (see FOUND²).

ingrained XVI. var. of *engrained*; see ENGRAIN.

ingratiate †bring into favour; refl., get oneself into favour. XVII. f. L. phr. *in grātiam* into favour (see GRACE) + -ATE³.

ingredient XV. - prp. of L. *ingredī* enter, f. IN-¹ + *gradī* step, go; see GRADE, -ENT.

ingress XV. - L. *ingressus*, f. pp. stem of *ingredī*; see prec.

inguinal pert. to the groin. XVII. - L. *inguinālis*, f. *inguen, inguin-* (swelling in the) groin; see -AL¹.

ingurgitate swallow greedily. XVI. f. pp. stem of L. *ingurgitāre*, f. IN-¹ + *gurges, gurgit-* whirlpool, gulf. So **ingurgitation** XVI.

inhabit XIV. ME. *en-, inhabite* - OF. *enhabiter* or L. *inhabitāre*, f. IN-¹ + *habitāre* (see HABIT).

inhale XVIII. - L. *inhālāre*, f. IN-¹ + *hālāre* breathe. So **inhalation** XVII. - medL.

inhere exist as an attribute *in* XVI; †remain fixed *in* XVII. - L. *inhærēre*, f. IN-¹ + *hærēre* stick. So **inherent** XVI.

inherit †make heir; take or receive as heir. XIV. ME. *en(h)erite* - OF. *enheriter*, f. EN-¹ + *hériter* :- late L. *hērēdītāre*, f. *hērēs, hērēd-* HEIR. So **inheritance** XIV. - AN. **inheritor** XV, **inheritrix** XVI.

inhibit (eccl. law) forbid, interdict XV; restrain XVI. f. *inhibit-*, pp. stem of L. *inhibēre* hold in, hinder, f. IN-¹ + *habēre* have, hold. So **inhibition** XIV. - OF. or L.

inhuman, inhumane XV. - F. or L.; see IN-², HUMAN, HUMANE. So **inhumanity** XV.

inhume bury. XVII. - L. *inhumāre*, f. IN-¹ + *humus* ground. So **inhumation** XVII. - F.

inimical XVII. - late L. *inimīcālis*, f. *inimīcus*; see ENEMY, -AL¹.

iniquity XIV. - OF. *iniquité* - L. *inīquitās*, f. *inīquus*, f. IN-² + *æquus* just, righteous (see EQUITY).

initial pert. to a or the beginning. XVI. - L. *initiālis*, f. *initium* beginning, f. *init-*, pp. stem of *inīre* enter upon, begin, f. IN-¹ + *īre* go, rel. to Skr. *éti*, Gr. *eîmi*; see -AL¹. So **initiate** XVII. **initiation** XVI. - L. **initiative** sb. XVIII. - F. **initiatory** XVII.

inject XVII. f. *inject-*, pp. stem of L. *inicere* throw in, f. IN-¹ + *jacere* throw, rel. to Gr. *hiénai*. So **injection** XVI. - F. or L.

Injun colloq. and dial. U.S. form of INDIAN. XVII (*Ingin, Engiane*, later *Indjon*).

injunction XVI. - late L. *injunctiō, -ōn-*, f. *injunct-*, pp. stem of *injungere* ENJOIN; see -TION. So **injunctive** XVII.

injury wrongful action XIV; loss, damage XV; †insult, affront XVI. - AN. *injurie* (mod. *injure* insult) - L. *injūria*, sb. use of fem. of *injūrius* unjust, wrongful, f. IN-² + *jūs, jūr-* right; see -Y³. Hence **injure** XVI. So **injurious** XV. - F. or L.

ink XIII. ME. *enke*, later *inc(k), inke* - OF. *enque* (mod. *encre*) :- late L. *encau(s)tum* - Gr. *égkauston* purple ink used by Gr. and Rom. emperors for their signatures, f. *egkaíein* burn in. Comp. **inkhorn** vessel (orig. a horn) for holding ink XIV; *i. term*, learned or literary word XVI. Hence **ink** vb., **inky** XVI.

inkling faint mention or report XIV; hint XVI. f. ME. *inkle* utter in an undertone (of unkn. orig.) + -ING¹.

in-law XIX. sb. use of phr. denoting connection

by marriage, e.g. *brother-in-law* (XIII), *father-in-law* (XIV); after AN. *en ley*, OF. *en loi* (*de mariage*) 'in law (of marriage)'; also used of step-relationship.

inlet small arm of the sea, creek XVI; (arch.) admission XVII. f. phr. *let in* (LET[1]).

inly (arch.) inwardly; closely, fully. OE. *in(n)līce*, f. *inn* IN[1] (adv.) + -LY[2].

inmate †lodger, subtenant; (fellow) occupier or occupant. XVI. prob. orig. f. INN dwelling (later assoc. with IN[1]) + MATE[1].

inmost XIV. Earlier ME. *inmest*, *in(ne)mast* :- OE. *innemest*, f. *in*, *inne* IN[1]; see -MOST.

inn †dwelling-place OE.; hostelry, hotel; lodging-house for (university or law) students XIV. OE. *inn*, f. base of *inne* IN[1]; cf. ON. *inni*.

innards see INWARD.

innate XV. - L. *innātus*, pp. of *innascī* (see IN-[1], NATIVE).

inner OE. *inner(r)a*, *in(n)ra* = OHG. *innaro*, *-ero* (G. *innere*), ON. *innri*, *iðri*; compar. f. IN[1] (adv.); see -ER[3]. Hence **innermost** XV.

innings XVIII. f. IN[1] adv. + pl. of -ING[1]; invariable for sg. and pl. in Eng. use; in U.S. a sg. *inning* is current.

innocent free from wrong, sin, or guilt XIV; not injurious XVII. Also sb. XIV. - (O)F. *innocent* or L. *innocēns*, *-ent-*, f. IN-[2] + *nocēns*, prp. of *nocēre* hurt, injure; see -ENT. So **innocence** XIV. - (O)F. - L. **innocuous** XVI. f. L. *innocuus*.

innovate †renew, †introduce as new; bring in something new. XVI. f. pp. stem of L. *innovāre* renew, alter, f. IN-[1] + *novāre* make new, f. *novus* NEW; see -ATE[3]. So **innovation** XVI. - L.

innuendo †parenthetical explanation or specification; oblique hint or suggestion. XVII. - L., 'by nodding, pointing to, intimating', abl. gerund of *innuere* nod to, signify, f. IN-[1] + *nuere* nod.

inoculate set in (a bud or scion), bud (a plant) XV; implant (a disease); impregnate with the virus of a disease XVIII. f. pp. stem of L. *inoculāre* engraft, implant, f. IN-[1] + *oculus* EYE, bud; see -ATE[3].

inordinate irregular; immoderate. XIV. - L. *inordinātus*, f. IN-[2] + *ordinātus*, pp. of *ordināre* ORDAIN; see -ATE[2].

inquest legal inquiry XIII; jury, esp. coroner's jury XIV. ME. *enqueste* - OF. :- Rom. **inquesta*, sb. use of fem. of pp. of **inquærere*; see next.

inquire, enquire ask about XIII; seek information XIV. ME. *enquere* - OF. *enquerre* (mod. new formation *enquérir*) :- Rom. **inquærere*, for L. *inquīrere*, f. IN-[1] + *quærere* ask. Assim. to L. in XV. Hence **inquiry** investigation XV; interrogation XVI.

inquisition inquiry, investigation; judicial inquiry XIV; (R.C.Ch.) ecclesiastical tribunal (the Holy Office) XVI. - (O)F. - L. *inquīsītiō*, *-ōn-* (legal) examination, f. *inquīsīt-*, pp. stem of *inquīrere* INQUIRE; see -ITION. So **inquisitive** XIV. - OF. - late L. **inquisitor** XVI.

inroad hostile incursion, raid. XVI. f. IN[1] + ROAD in the etym. sense of 'riding'.

insane XVI. - L. *insānus*, f. IN-[2] + *sānus* SANE. So **insanity** XVI.

inscribe write in or on; (geom.) delineate within a figure XVI; enrol; mark with characters XVII. - L. *inscrībere*, f. IN-[1] + *scrībere* write. So **inscription** XIV.

inscrutable XV. - late L. *inscrūtābilis*, f. IN-[2] + *scrūtārī*; see SCRUTINY, -ABLE.

insect XVII. - L. *insectum*, sb. use of n. of pp. of *insecāre* cut into or up, f. IN-[1] + *secāre* cut.

insert set or put in. XVI. f. *insert-*, pp. stem of L. *inserere*, f. IN-[1] + *serere* plant, join, put into (see SOW[2]). So **insertion** XVI. - late L.

inset leaf or sheet inserted. XIX. f. pp. *inset*, i.e. set in; see IN[1], SET[1].

inside inner side or surface XVI; adj. XVII; adv. XIX; prep. XVIII. f. IN[1] + SIDE.

insidious XVI. - L. *insidiōsus*, f. *insidiæ* ambush, trick, rel. to *insidēre* sit in or upon, be settled, f. IN-[1] + *sedēre* SIT; see -IOUS.

insight †mental vision or perception XII; penetration by the understanding *into* XVI. prob. of Scand. and LG. orig.; comp. of IN[1] and SIGHT.

insignia XVII. - L., pl. of *insigne* sign, badge of office, sb. use of n. of *insignis* distinguished (as by a mark), f. IN-[1] + *signum* SIGN; see -IA[2].

insinuate XVI. f. pp. stem of L. *insinuāre*, f. IN-[1] + *sinuāre* curve, f. *sinus* curve; see -ATE[3]. So **insinuation** XVI. - L.

insipid tasteless. XVII. - F. *insipide* or late L. *insipidus*, f. IN-[2] + *sapidus* SAPID. Hence or - F. **insipidity** XVII.

insist †continue steadfastly *in*; dwell emphatically *on*. XVI. - L. *insistere* stand upon, persist, f. IN-[1] + *sistere* stand.

insolation exposure to the sun. XVII. - L. *insōlātiō*, *-ōn-*, f. *insōlāre*, f. IN-[1] + *sōl* SUN; see -ATION.

insolent †haughty, arrogant XIV; contemptuous of dignity or authority XVII. - L. *insolēns*, *-ent-* unusual, excessive, arrogant, f. IN-[2] + prp. of *solēre* be accustomed; see -ENT. So **insolence** XIV.

insoluble †indissoluble XIV; that cannot be solved XIV; that cannot be dissolved in liquid XVIII. - (O)F. or L.; see IN-[2], SOLUBLE.

insomnia XVIII. - L., f. *insomnis* sleepless (f. IN-[2] + *somnus* sleep) + -IA[1].

insomuch XIV. tr. OF. *en tant* (*que*); at first alternative to INASMUCH, but later differentiated.

insouciant XIX. - F., f. IN-[2] + *souciant*, prp. of *soucier* care :- L. *sollicitāre* disturb, agitate.

inspect XVII. f. *inspect-*, pp. stem of L. *inspicere*, f. IN-[1] + *specere* look; or - L. frequent. *inspectāre*. So **inspection** XIV. - (O)F. - L. **inspector** XVII. - L.

inspire infuse into the mind; impart or suggest by divine agency; †breathe XIV; breathe in XVI. - (O)F. *inspirer* - L. *inspīrāre*, f. IN-[1] + *spīrāre* breathe. So **inspiration** XIV. - (O)F. - late L.

inspissate thicken. XVII. f. pp. stem of late L. *inspissāre*, f. *in* IN-[1] + *spissus* thick, dense; see -ATE[3]. So **inspissation** XVII.

install invest with or place in an office, orig. by placing in an official stall XVI; (after F.) to place in position XIX. - medL. *installāre*, f. IN-[1] + *stallum* STALL[1]; cf. (O)F. *installer*. So **installation** XVII. - medL. Hence **instalment**[1] U.S. **install-** installation. XVI.

instalment[2], U.S. **install-** †arrangement for payment; agreed part of a sum to be paid XVIII;

part supplied at a certain time XIX. alt. (prob. by assoc. with prec.) of earlier †*(e)stallment* - AN. *estalement*, f. *estaler* fix; see STALL², -MENT.

instance urgency, urgent action (now in phr. *at the instance of*) XIV; †case adduced in objection; example in support of a general proposition XVI; process, suit (*court of first i.*); hence *in the first i.* as the first step XVII. - (O)F. *instance* eagerness, solicitation, judicial process, new argument - L. *instantia* presence, urgency, pleading or process, in scholL. objection, example to the contrary, f. *instāns, -ant-* INSTANT. Hence vb. †urge XV; cite as an instance XVII.

instant urgent XV; present (of time); of the current month; imminent, immediate XVI. - (O)F. *instant* assiduous, at hand - L. *instāns, -ant-*, prp. of *instāre* be present or at hand, urge, f. IN-¹ + *stāre* STAND. As sb. point of time, moment XV; after medL. Hence **instantly** †urgently; †just now XV; forthwith XVI. So **instantaneous** XVII. f. medL. *instantāneus*.

instate establish in a position. XVII. f. IN¹ + STATE sb.

instead in the place or room (*of* another), as deputy or successor XIII; in its stead, as a substitute XVII. phr. *in (the) stead of* (see STEAD), after OF. *en* (now *au*) *lieu de*.

instep XVI. app. f. IN¹ and STEP.

instigate spur or urge on. XVI. f. pp. stem of L. *instīgāre*, f. IN-¹ + *stīgāre* prick, incite; see -ATE³. So **instigation** XV. - F. or L.

instil put in by drops; infuse gradually. XVI. - L. *instillāre*, f. IN-¹ + *stillāre*, f. *stilla* drop.

instinct †impulse XV; innate impulse or propensity, intuition XVI. - L. *instinctus* instigation, impulse, f. *instinct-*, pp. stem of *instinguere* incite, impel, f. IN-¹ + *stinguere* prick. So **instinct** pp. †innate XVI; †impelled XVII; imbued *with* XVIII. - L. *instinctus* pp. **instinctive, instinctively** XVII.

institute †purpose; established usage; principle(s) or element(s) of instruction XVI; (after F.) society to promote an object; building used for this XIX. - L. *institūtum* design, ordinance, precept, sb. use of n. of pp. of *instituere* establish, ordain, teach, f. IN-¹ + *statuere* set up. So vb. set up, found XV; establish in an office, esp. eccl. XVI. f. pp. stem of *instituere*. **institution** establishment, esp. eccl. in a benefice XIV; established law, etc. XVI; establishment or organization for the promotion of an object XVIII. - (O)F. - L. **institutional** XVII.

instruct impart knowledge to XV; direct, command XVI; †put in order XVII. f. *instruct-*, pp. stem of L. *instruere* set up, fit out, teach, f. IN-¹ + *struere* pile up, build. So **instruction** XV. - (O)F. - late L. **instructive** XVII. **instructor** XV. - F. *-eur*.

instrument tool, implement XIII (earliest of a musical instrument); something used by an agent; means XIV; legal document XV. - (O)F. - L. *instrūmentum*, f. *instruere*; see prec. and -MENT. So **instrumental** serving as instrument or means XIV; of music composed for instruments XVI (whence **instrumentalist** XIX); (gram.) XIX. **instrumentation** composition of music for instruments XIX. **instrumentality** XVII.

insular pert. to an island XVII; characteristic of islanders, as being narrow or prejudiced XVIII. - late L. *insulāris*, f. *insula* island; see -AR. So **insulate** convert into an island XVI; detach, ISOLATE (also electr.) XVIII. **insulator** XIX.

insulin hormone extracted from the islets of Langerhans in the pancreas of animals. XX. f. L. *insula* island; see -IN¹.

insult †glory or triumph *over* XVI; treat with scornful abuse or disrespect XVII. - L. *insultāre*, f. IN-¹ + *saltāre*, iterative-intensive f. *salīre* leap, jump. So **insult** (arch.) attack; affront. XVII. - F. *insulte* or - ecclL. *insultus*.

insuperable †unconquerable XIV; unsurmountable XVII. - OF. or L.; see IN-², SUPERABLE.

insure XV. var. of ENSURE, with substitution of IN-¹ for EN-¹, established in the sense of securing payment on death or damage (XVII). So **insurance** XVII.

insurgent one who rises in active revolt. XVIII. - F. †*insurgent* - L. *insurgēns, -ent-*, prp. of *insurgere* rise up; see IN-¹, SURGE, -ENT. So **insurrection** XV. - (O)F. - late L., f. *insurrect-*, pp. stem of *insurgere*.

intact untouched, unblemished. XV. - L. *intactus*, f. IN-² + *tāctus*, pp. of *tangere* touch.

intaglio figure incised or engraved; incised gem. XVII. - It., f. *intagliare* engrave, f. IN-¹ + *tagliare* cut.

intake f. phr. *take in*; see TAKE, IN¹.

integer XVI. - L. *integer* intact, ENTIRE. So **integral** making up a whole, made up of parts XVI; (math.) XVIII. - late L. *integrālis*. **integrate** XVII. f. pp. stem of L. *integrāre*. **integration** XVII. - L. **integrity** XV. - F. or L.

integument covering, coating. XVII. - L. *integumentum*, f. *integere* cover; see IN-¹, TEGUMENT.

intellect XIV. - (O)F. *intellect* or L. *intellectus* perception, discernment, sense, f. pp. stem of *intellegere*; see below. So **intellection** understanding. XVII. - L. **intellectual** XIV (whence **-ism** XIX, **-ist** XVII). - L. **intellectuality** XVII. - late L. **intelligent** XVI. - prp. of L. *intellegere*, *-ligere* lit. choose among, f. INTER- + *legere* gather, choose. (So **intelligence** XIV. - (O)F. - L.; hence **intelligencer** XVI). **intelligentsia** XX. - Russ. *intelligéntsiya* - Pol. *inteligiencja* - L. *intellegentia*. **intelligible** XIV.

intemperate XV. - L. *intemperātus*; see IN-², TEMPERATE. So **intemperance** XV. - (O)F. or L.

intend direct the mind or attention XIV; design for a purpose XVI. ME. *entende, in-* - (O)F. *entendre*, †*intendre* - L. *intendere* extend, direct, intend, f. IN-¹ + *tendere* stretch, TEND². So **intended** purposed, designed XVI; sb. intended spouse XVIII. **intendment** †understanding, meaning XIV; (leg.) XVI.- (O)F. *entendement*. **intense** XIV. - (O)F. *intens(e)* or L. *intēnsus* stretched, tight, violent, pp. of *intendere*; hence **intensify** XIX. **intension** tension, intentness, intensity XVII; internal content of a concept XIX. **intensive** †intense XVI; relating of or pert. to intensity; intensifying XVII. **intent**[1] intention XIII; end proposed XIV (obs. exc. in phr. *to all intents* XVI). ME. *entent* - OF. *entent* :- L. *intentus*, and *entente* - (O)F. *entente* :- Rom. **intenta*, f. pp. of L. *intendere*. **intent**[2] earnestly attentive or bent *upon*. XVII. - L. *intentus*, pp. of *intendere*. **intention** †understanding; †meaning, import; purpose XIV; (logic) direction of the mind to an object, conception XVI; (theol.) XVII. ME. *entencion* - OF. *entencion* (mod. *intention*) - L. **intentional** XVI. - F. or medL.

inter bury. XIV. ME. *enter(re)* - (O)F. *enterrer* - Rom. **interrāre*, f. IN-[1] + *terra* earth. Hence **interment** XIV.

inter- L. prep. 'between', 'among', repr. in F. by *entre-* (see ENTER-), used as a prefix with the senses: (1) between, in between, in the midst, as in INTERCALARY, INTERPOSE, INTERVENE; (2) at intervals, as in INTERMIT; (3) with preventive or destructive effect, as in INTERCEPT. The earliest adoptions of such words in Eng. came through F. forms with *entre-*, but in XVI remodelling of these forms on the L. *inter-* began, and at the same time the use of the prefix was widely extended. Meanwhile the prefix had acquired a mutual or reciprocal sense, as in *interdependence, intermarriage, interplay*. The other large group of comps. in which *inter-* has become a living formative is that in which it governs prepositionally (with the senses 'between', 'among', and 'forming a link between') the sb. implied in the radical part of the comp., as in *interalveolar, intercollegiate, interdenominational, international, intervocalic*. The prefix enters freely into combination with sbs. to form attrib. phrases, as in *inter-county* match.

intercalary inserted at intervals (in the calendar) XVII, intervening XVIII. - L. *intercalāri(u)s*, f. *intercalāre* proclaim the insertion of a day, etc., in the calendar, from pp. stem of which is **intercalate** XVII; so **intercalation** XVI (- F. or L.).

intercede †come between XVI; intervene on behalf of another XVII. - (O)F., or L. *intercēdere*, f. INTER- + *cēdere* go. So **intercession** XVI. **intercessor** XV. - L.; hence **intercessory** XVI.

intercept XVI. f. *intercept-*, pp. stem of L. *intercipere*, f. INTER- + *capere* take, seize. So **interception** XVI. - F. or L.

interchange vb. XIV. ME. *enterchaunge* - OF. *entrechangier*; see INTER-, CHANGE. Hence as sb. XVI. So **interchangeable** (whence **-ably**) XIV. - OF.

intercommunicate XVI. - AL.; see INTER-, COMMUNICATE.

intercourse mutual dealings XV; social or spiritual communication XVI. Earlier *entercourse* - (O)F. *entrecours* - L. *intercursus*, f. *intercurrere* run between or among, intervene; see INTER-, COURSE.

interdict (eccl.) sentence debarring the faithful from church functions and privileges XIII; authoritative prohibition or decree XVII. ME. *entredit* - OF. - L. *interdictum* (to which the Eng. word was assim. XVI), sb. use of n. of pp. of *interdīcere* interpose by speech, forbid by decree, f. INTER- + *dīcere* say. Hence vb. XIII.

interest A. (legal) concern or right *in* XV; advantageous or detrimental relation XVI; matter in which persons are concerned XVII; feeling of one concerned XVIII; B. †injury, damages; money paid for use of money lent XVI. Late ME. alt. of †*interesse*, †*ent(e)resse*, partly by addition of parasitic *t*, partly by assoc. with OF. *interest* damage, loss (mod. *intérêt*), app. sb. use of L. *interest* it makes a difference, concerns, 3rd pers. sg. pres. ind. of *interesse* differ, be of importance, f. INTER- + *esse* BE (the history is, however, obscure). So **interest** vb. invest with a title or share; cause to have or take an interest XVII; affect with a feeling of concern XVIII. Alt. of †*interess* vb. XVI. - F. *intéresser* †damage, concern. **interesting** †important; apt to excite interest. XVIII.

interfere (of horse) knock one leg against another XVI; collide, come into opposition, intermeddle *with* XVII; intervene XVIII. - OF. (refl.) *s'entreferir* strike each other, f. *entre-* INTER- + *férir* :- L. *ferīre* strike. Hence **interference** XVIII, **interferometer** XIX.

interim (arch.) meanwhile; intervening time, interval of time. XVI. - L., 'in the meantime', f. INTER- + advb. suffix *-im*.

interior situated (more) within. XV. - L., compar. adj. f. *inter* within.

interjection ejaculation XV; (gram.) XVI. - (O)F. - L. *interjectiō, -ōn-*, f. *interject-*, pp. stem of *intericere* interpose, f. INTER- + *jacere* throw. So **interject** XVI.

interlace XIV. - OF. *entrelacier*; see INTER-, LACE vb.

interlard †pass. have alternate layers of fat and lean; diversify by intermixture. XVI. Earlier *enter-* - (O)F. *entrelarder*, f. *entre-* INTER- + *larder* LARD vb.

interleave vb. XVII. f. INTER- + LEAF, pl. *leaves*. Hence **interleaf** sb. XVIII.

interline XV. - medL. *interlīneāre*; see INTER-, LINE[2]. So **interlinear** XV.

interlocutor XVI. - modL., f. L. *interloquī*, *-locūtiō*; see INTER-, LOCUTION.

interloper †unauthorized trader XVI; one who thrusts himself into an affair XVII. f. INTER- + *loper* (as in LANDLOPER). Hence **interlope** vb. XVII.

interlude light or humorous dramatic representation, (later XVII-XVIII) comedy, farce XIV; interval in the performance of a play XVII; intervening time or space XVIII. - medL. *interlūdium*, f. INTER- + *lūdus* play.

intermeddle XIV. ME. *entremedle* - AN. *entremedler* = OF. *entremesler*; see INTER-, MEDDLE.

intermediate XVII. - medL. *intermediātus*, f. L. *intermedius*, f. INTER- + *medius* MID; see -ATE[2]. So **intermediary** XVIII.

intermezzo (mus.) piece intervening between two main parts of a composition. XIX. - It. - L. *intermedius* (see prec.).

interminable XIV. - (O)F. or late L. (see IN-[3]).

intermit leave off, discontinue. XVI. - L. *intermittere*, f. INTER- + *mittere* let go. So **inter-**

mission XVI, **intermittent** XVII (see -ENT). - F. or L.

intern confine within prescribed limits of residence. XIX. - F. *interner*, f. *interne* - L. *internus* inward, internal.

internal XVI. f. contemp. †*intern* or its source, L. *internus*; see prec., -AL[1].

international XVIII. f. INTER- + NATION + -AL[1].

internecine attended with great slaughter XVII; (misinterpreted by Johnson as) mutually destructive XVIII. - L. *internecīnus*, f. *interneciō* general slaughter, massacre, extermination, f. *internecāre* slaughter, exterminate, f. INTER- + *necāre* kill; see -INE[1].

internuncio XVII. - It. *internunzio*; see INTER-, NUNCIO.

interpellation †pleading, intercession XVI; †interruption XVII; (after F.) interruption of the order of the day in the French Chamber XIX. - L. *interpellātiō*, *-ōn-*, f. *interpellāre* interrupt by speaking, f. INTER- + *-pellāre* thrust or direct oneself.

interpolate XVII. f. pp. stem of L. *interpolāre*, f. INTER- + *-polāre*, rel. to *polīre* POLISH. So **interpolation** XVII.

interpose XVI. - (O)F. *interposer*, based on L. *interpōnere*; see INTER-, POSE[1]. So **interposition** XV. - (O)F. or L.

interpret XIV. - (O)F. *interpréter* or its source L. *interpretārī* explain, translate, f. *interpres*, *-pret-* agent, broker, translator, interpreter, f. INTER- + unkn. el. Hence **interpreter** XIV. So **interpretation** XIV.

interregnum †temporary authority exercised during a vacancy; period intervening between a ruler and his successor. XVI. - L., f. INTER- + *regnum* REIGN.

interrogate XV. f. pp. stem of L. *interrogāre*, f. INTER- + *rogāre* ask; see ROGATION, -ATE[3]. So **interrogation** XIV. - (O)F. or L. **interrogative, interrogatory** XVI. - late L.

interrupt XV. f. *interrupt-*, pp. stem of L. *interrumpere*, f. INTER- + *rumpere* break (see RUPTURE). So **interruption** XIV. - (O)F. or L.

intersect XVII. see INTER-, BISECT. So **intersection** XVI.

intersperse XVI. f. *interspers-*, pp. stem of L. *interspergere*; see INTER- and DISPERSE.

interstice XVII. - late L. *interstitium*, f. INTER- + base of *stāre* STAND.

interval period between two events XIII; space between two things XV. ult. - L. *intervallum* orig. space between ramparts, f. INTER- + *vallum* (see WALL), but the earliest forms, *entrewal*, *entervale*, *intervalle*, are - OF. *entreval(e)*, later *-valle* (mod. *intervalle*).

intervene XVI. - L. *intervenīre*, f. INTER- + *venīre* COME. So **intervention** XV. - F. or L.

interview meeting of persons face to face. XVI. Earlier form *enterview(e)* - F. †*entrev(e)ue*, f. *entrevoir* have a glimpse of, *s'entrevoir* see each other (f. *entre* INTER- + *voir* see), after *vue* VIEW.

intestate XIV. - L. *intestātus*, f. IN-[2] + *testātus*, pp. of. *testārī* bear witness, make a will, f. *testis* witness; see -ATE[2]. Hence **intestacy** XVIII.

intestine internal. XVI. - L. *intestīnus*, f. *intus* within (corr. to Gr. *entós*); sb. (esp. pl.) lower part of the alimentary canal. XVI. - L. *intestīnum*, sb. use of n. of adj.

intimate inward, essential, intrinsic; pert. to the inmost thoughts; closely associated (also sb.). XVII. - late L. *intimātus*, pp. of *intimāre*, f. *intimus* inmost, f. *int-* of INTER- + superl. suffix; see -ATE[2]. Hence **intimacy** XVII. So **intimate** make known formally; indicate indirectly. XVI. f. pp. of late L. *intimāre*. **intimation** formal announcement XV; expression by sign XVI. - (O)F. or late L.

intimidate XVII. f. pp. stem of medL. *intimidāre*, f. IN-[1] + *timidus* TIMID; see -ATE[3].

intinction †dipping, infusion XVI; (eccl.) dipping of the bread in the wine at the Eucharist XIX. - late L. *intinctiō*, *-ōn-*, f. *intingere*; see IN-[1], TINCTURE.

intitule ENTITLE (now leg. in ref. to acts of parliament). XV. - (O)F. *intituler* - late L. *intitulāre*.

into OE. *in(n) tō*, i.e. IN[1] adv., TO prep.

intolerable XV. - F. or L.; see IN-[2].

intone XV (rare before XIX). - medL. *intonāre*, f. IN-[1] + *tonus* TONE; in XV-XVI *entone* - OF. *entoner* (mod. *-onner*). So **intonation** XVII. - medL. *intonātiō*, *-ōn-*.

intoxicate †poison; stupefy with a drug or strong drink. XVI. f. pp. stem of medL. *intoxicāre*, f. IN-[1] + L. *toxicum* poison; see TOXIC, -ATE[3]. So **intoxication** XV. - F. or medL.

intra- repr. L. prep. *intrā* 'on the inside', 'within', used occas. in late L. as prefix, as in *intrāmūrānus* lying within the walls. Cf. EXTRA-.

intractable XVI. - F. or L.; see IN-[2].

intrados (archit.) lower curve of an arch. XVIII. - F., f. L. *intrā* INTRA- + F. *dos* back.

intransigent XIX. - F. *intransigeant*, based on Sp. *los intransigentes* party of the extreme left in the Spanish Cortes, extreme republicans; ult. f. IN-[2] + prp. of L. *transigere* come to an understanding; see TRANSACT, -ENT.

intransitive XVII. - late L.; see IN-[2].

intrepid XVII. - F. *intrépide* or L. *intrepidus*, f. IN-[2] + *trepidus* agitated, alarmed.

intricate XV. - L. *intrīcātus*, pp. of *intrīcāre* entangle, perplex, f. IN-[1] + *trīcæ* trifles, tricks, perplexities; see -ATE[2].

intrigue †intricacy, maze; underhand plotting. XVII. - F. - It. *intrigo*, f. *intrigare*, *-icare* :- L. *intrīcāre*; see prec. So vb. XVII.

intrinsic †inward, inner XV-XVII (later anat. XIX); of its own, proper XVII. - (O)F. *intrinsèque* - late L. *intrinsecus*, f. L. adv. *intrinsecus* inwardly, inwards; from the first the ending was assim. to -IC. So **intrinsically** XVI.

intro- L. adv. *intrō* to the inside (parallel to INTRA-) used as a prefix in *intrōducere* INTRODUCE, *introitus* INTROIT, *intrōmittere* INTROMIT.

introduce XVI. - L. *intrōdūcere*, f. *intrō* INTRO- + *dūcere* lead, bring. So **introduction** XIV. - (O)F. or L.

introit †entrance; (eccl.) antiphon and psalm recited as the celebrant approaches the altar. XV. - (O)F. *introït* - L. *introitus* entrance, f. *introīre* enter, f. *intrō* INTRO- + *īre* go.

intromit XV. - L. *intrōmittere* introduce, f. *intrō*

INTRO- + *mittere* send. So **intromission** XVI. - F. or L.

introspection XVII. Hence **introspective** XIX. Cf. INSPECTION and see INTRO-.

introvert turn (the mind) upon itself. XVII. f. modL. *intrōvertere*, f. *intrō* INTRO- + *vertere* turn. Hence sb. part turned within XIX; (psych.) XX.

intrude XVI. - L. *intrūdere*, f. IN-[1] + *trūdere* thrust. So **intrusion** (leg.) thrusting oneself into an estate or benefice XIV; uninvited entrance or appearance XVI. - (O)F. or medL.

intuition †contemplation, view XV (rare before XVII); †regard, reference; (philos.) immediate knowledge or apprehension XVI; (gen.) immediate insight XVIII. - late L. *intuitiō*, *-ōn-*; see IN-[1], TUITION. So **intuitive** XVI. - medL.

inundate XVII. f. pp. stem of L. *inundāre*, f. IN-[1] + *undāre* flow, f. *unda* wave; see -ATE[3]. So **inundation** XV. - (O)F. or L.

inure accustom, habituate XV; †put into operation; (leg.) come into operation XVI. - AN. **eneurer*, f. phr. **en eure* in use or practice, i.e. *en* IN[1], **eure* work (:- L. *opera*; see OPERA).

invade make a hostile attack (upon). XV. - L. *invādere*, f. IN-[1] + *vādere* go (see WADE). So **invasion** XVI. - (O)F. or late L.

invalid[1] not valid. XVI. - L. *invalidus*; see IN-[1], VALID. So **invalidate** XVI, **invalidity** XVI.

invalid[2] infirm or disabled from sickness or injury XVII; sb. XVIII. spec. use of prec. with modified pronunc. after F. *invalide*.

invaluable XVI. See IN-[2].

invar alloy of nickel and steel with a negligible coefficient of expansion. XX. **P.** abbrev. of **invariable** (XVII); see IN-[2].

inveigh †bring in, introduce XV; give vent to denunciation XVI. - L. *invehere* carry in, *invehī* be borne into, attack, assail with words, f. IN-[1] + *vehere* carry (cf. VEHICLE). So **invective** adj. (arch.) marked by denunciatory or vituperative language XV; sb. speech of this kind XVI. - (O)F. *invectif*, *-ive* adj., *invective* sb. - late L. *invectīvus*, *invectīva* as sb., f. *invect-*, pp. stem of *invehere*.

inveigle †beguile, deceive XV; gain over by enticement XVI. Earlier *enve(u)gle* - AN. *envegler*, alt. of (O)F. *aveugler* blind, f. *aveugle* adj. blind, prob. :- Rom. **ab oculīs* 'without eyes'.

invent †come upon, find XV; devise, esp. by way of original contrivance XVI. f. *invent-*, pp. stem of L. *invenīre*, f. IN-[1] + *venīre* COME. So **invention** finding (surviving in *Invention of the Cross* church festival of 3rd May) XV; contrivance XVI. - L. **inventive** XV. - OF. **inventory** detailed list of articles. XVI. - medL. *inventōrium*, for late L. *inventārium*.

inverse adj. and sb. XVII. - L. *inversus*, pp. of *invertere*, f. IN-[1] + *vertere* turn. So **inversion** XVI. **invert** vb. XVI. - L. *invertere* 'turn in, turn outside in', reverse.

invertebrata (sb. pl.) animals having no backbone. XIX. modL., after F. *invertébrés*, f. *in-* IN-[2] + *vertèbre*, L. VERTEBRA. Anglicized **invertebrate** XIX.

invest A. clothe, spec. with the insignia of office; establish in possession, endow with power; B. enclose with a hostile force XVI; C. put out (money) at interest XVII. - (O)F. *investir* or L. (rare) *investīre* clothe, surround (extended in meaning in medL.), f. IN-[1] + *vestis* clothing; in C after It. *investire*, the notion being that of giving the capital another 'form'. So **investiture** XIV (rare before XVI). - medL. *investītūra*. Hence **investment** †clothing XVI; investiture, investing of capital XVII.

investigate XVI. f. pp. stem of L. *investīgāre*, f. IN-[1] + *vestīgāre* track, trace out; see VESTIGE, -ATE[3]. So **investigation** XV. - (O)F. or L.

inveterate established by age or long standing; obstinately embittered. XVI. - L. *inveterātus*, ppl. adj. of *inveterāre* make old, f. IN-[1] + *vetus*, *veter-* old; see -ATE[2]. Hence **inveteracy** XVII.

invidious tending to or entailing odium. XVII. - L. *invidiōsus*, f. *invidia* ill will, ENVY; see -IOUS.

invigilate keep watch. XVI. f. pp. stem of L. *invigilāre*, f. IN-[1] + *vigilāre* watch, f. *vigil* watchful; see -ATE[3].

invigorate XVII. f. L. IN-[1] + *vigor* VIGOUR; see -ATE[3].

invincible XV. - (O)F. - L. *invincibilis*, f. IN-[2] + *vincibilis*, f. *vincere* conquer; see -IBLE.

inviolate XV. - L. *inviolātus*, f. IN-[2] + pp. of *violāre* VIOLATE.

invisible XIV. - OF. or L.; see IN-[2].

invite XVI. - F. *inviter* or L. *invitāre*. So **invitation** XVI. - F. or L.

invoice XVI. app. orig. pl. of †*invoy* (recorded only later) - F. †*envoy*, *envoi*; see ENVOY[1].

invoke XV. - (O)F. *invoquer* - L. *invocāre*, f. IN-[1] + *vocāre* call. So **invocation** XIV.

involucre envelope XVI; (bot.) whorl of bracts XVIII. - F. *involucre* or L. *involūcrum*, f. *involvere* INVOLVE.

involuntary XVI. - late L.; see IN-[2].

involve wrap round, lit. and fig.; implicate in trouble, etc. XIV; implicate in a charge; include XVII. - L. *involvere*, f. IN-[1] + *volvere* roll (see VOLUME). So **involute** rolled or curled up XVII; sb. (math.) XVIII. f. *involut-*, pp. stem of L. *involvere*. **involution** involved condition XVII; (math.) XVIII. - late L.

inward adj. that is within; adv. towards the inside. OE. *innanweard*, *in(ne)weard*, f. *innan*, *inne*, *in(n)* IN[1] + *-weard* -WARD; cf. MDu. *in(ne)wert*, OHG. *inwart* adj., *-wert* adv., ON. *innanverðr* adj. Also **inwards** XIII; sb. sg. †entrails OE.; inward part XIV, XIX; pl. internal parts, entrails XIII; vulgarly *innards*. See -WARDS.

iodine (chem.) non-metallic element which volatilizes into a violet-coloured vapour. XIX. f. F. *iode* - Gr. *iṓdēs* violet-coloured. f. *íon* violet + *-eidēs* -like; see -INE[5]. Hence **iodoform** XIX. After CHLOROFORM.

ion XIX. - Gr. *ión*, prp. n. of *iénai* go. Hence **ionize** XIX.

-ion suffix repr. (O)F. *-ion* - L. *-iō*, *-iōn-*, which forms nouns of condition and action from (i) adjs. or sbs., as in COMMUNION, DOMINION; (ii) verb-stems, as in LEGION; but chiefly from (iii) pp. or supine stems in *t*, *s*, *x* (see -TION, -SION).

ionosphere XX. f. ION + -O- + SPHERE.

-ior formerly also *-iour* - F. *-ieur*, †*-iour* - L. *iōrem*, nom. *-ior*, suffix of compar. of adj., as in *anterior*, *exterior*, *inferior*, *interior*, *junior*, *pos-*

terior, senior, ulterior. In *warrior* the ending has another orig.

iota the Gr. letter ι; least particle. XVII. - Gr. *iôta*. See JOT.

I O U (XVII) XVIII. repr. of *I owe you*.

-ious comp. suffix meaning 'characterized by', 'full of', (i) repr. F. *-ieux*, L. *-iōsus*, f. -I- + *ōsus* -OUS, or (ii) directly f. a L. suffix consisting of *i* and another suffix (viz. *-ia*, *-ius*, *-iō*, *-iēs*, *-ium*) + -OUS. See also -ACIOUS, -ITIOUS.

ipecacuanha root of a S. Amer. plant, used medicinally. XVII. - Pg. *ipecacuanha* - Tupi-Guarani *ipe-kaa-guéne*. abbr. colloq. **ipecac** XVIII.

ipomoea genus of convolvulaceous plants. XVIII. modL., f. Gr. *íps*, *ip-* worm + *hómoios* like.

ir-[1] assim. form of IN-[1] before *r*.

ir-[2] assim. form of IN-[2] before *r*.

irascible XVI. - (O)F. - late L. *īrāscibilis*, f. *īrāscī* grow angry, f. *īra* IRE; see -IBLE. So **irate** XIX. - L. *īrātus*; see -ATE[2].

ire (poet.) anger. XIII. - (O)F. :- L. *īra*. Hence **ireful** XIII.

iridescent displaying colours like those of the rainbow. XVIII. f. L. *īris*, *īrid-* IRIS + -ESCENT. So **iridium** (chem.) white metal of the platinum group. XIX. See -IUM; named 'from the striking variety of colours which it gives, while dissolving in marine acid' (Tennant).

iris species of crystal XIV; rainbow XV; flat circular coloured membrane in the aqueous humour of the eye; genus of tuberous or bulbous plants XVI. - L. *īris* - Gr. *îris* rainbow, coloured circle, etc., iris (plant), (*I-*) female messenger of the gods, whose sign was a rainbow.

Irish pert. to Ireland. XIII. OE. *Īras* inhabitants of *Īrland* Ireland (obscurely based on OIr. *Ériu*; cf. HIBERNIAN) + -ISH[1].

irk †grow weary, be loath XIII (*forhirked* wearied); weary, annoy XV. contemp. with †*irk* adj. weary, loath; of obscure orig. Hence **irksome** †tired, disgusted XV; wearisome, burdensome XVI.

iron sb. OE. *īren*, perh. for **īrern*, alt. of *īsern* (by assoc. with the var. *īsen*) = OS., OHG. *īsarn* (Du. *ijzer*, G. *eisen*), ON. *ísarn*, Goth. *eisarn* :- Gmc. **īsarnam*, prob. - Celt. **īsarno-* (W. *haearn*, Ir. *iarann*). Hence **ironclad** cased with iron or steel plates, spec. of ships, XIX. **ironmonger** XIV.

irony figure of speech in which the intended meaning is the opposite of that expressed XVI; condition of affairs opposite to that expected XVII. - L. *īrōnia* - Gr. *eirōneiā*, f. *eírōn* dissembler; see -Y[3]. So **ironic** XVII. - F. *ironique* or late L. *īrōnicus* - Gr. *eirōnikós*; preceded by **ironical, -ically** XVI.

irrational XV (math. XVI). - L.; see IR-[2].

irredentist advocate of the return to Italy of all Italian-speaking regions. XIX. - It. *irredentista*, f. (*Italia*) *irredenta* unredeemed or unrecovered (Italy); see IR-[2], REDEEM, -IST.

irrefragable incontrovertible, undeniable. XVI. - late L. *irrefrāgābilis*, f. IR-[2] + L. *refrāgārī* oppose, contest; see -ABLE.

irrelevant XVI. see IR-[2]. Hence **irrelevancy** XVI.

irrigate XVII. f. pp. of L. *irrigāre*, f. IR-[1] + *rigāre* wet, water; see -ATE[3]. So **irrigation** XVII. - L.

irritate †incite; excite to anger, fret XVI; excite to morbid action XVII. f. pp. stem of L. *irrītāre*; see -ATE[3]. So **irritable** XVII, **irritation** XVI. - L.

irruption bursting in. XVI. - L. *irruptiō*, *-ōn-*, f. *irrupt-*, pp. stem of *irrumpere*, f. IN-[1] + *rumpere* break; see RUPTURE, -TION.

is see BE.

isabella greyish yellow, light buff. XVI. In early use always *I. colour*; f. the female name (immediate ref. unkn.). Also **isabel** XIX.

isagogic introductory. XIX. - L. *īsagōgicus* - Gr. *eisagōgikós*, f. *eisagōgḗ* introduction, f. *eiságein* introduce, f. *eis* into + *ágein* lead; see -IC.

isatin (chem.) crystalline substance obtained from indigo. XIX. f. L. *isatis* woad + -IN.

ischiatic sciatic. XVII. - medL. *ischiaticus*, for L. *ischiadicus*, f. *iskhiás*, *-ad-* pain in the hip, f. Gr. *iskhíon* hip-joint (L. **ischium** XVII); see -IC.

-ise see -IZE.

-ish[1] suffix forming adjs.: OE. *-isć* = OS., OHG. *-isc* (Du., G. *-isch*), ON. *-iskr*, Goth. *-isks* :- Gmc. **-iskaz* = Gr. dim. suffix *-iskos*; in some words reduced to *-sh*, with a var. *-ch*; in Sc. usu. *-is*, with reduced vars. *-s*, *-ce*. Words of old formation are ENGLISH, SCOTS (see SCOTTISH, SCOTCH), WELSH, FRENCH. Formations in OE. on common nouns are *ċeorlisċ* churlish, *ċildisċ* childish, *hǣðenisċ* heathenish, *ūtlendisċ* foreign; their number was greatly increased in ME., at first with the uncoloured meaning of 'pert. to or of the nature of', but later chiefly on dyslogistic words, as *boorish*, *foolish*, *shrewish*, or with the derogatory force 'having the bad or unpleasant qualities of', as *babyish*, *selfish*, *womanish*.

From XIV onwards *-ish* was added to adjs. with the sense 'approaching the quality of, somewhat, rather', first to adjs. of colour, as *blueish*, *greenish*, *reddish*, but later to any (esp. monosyllabic) adjs., as *softish*. This use has been extended in XX to the qualification of hours of the day or numbers of years, as *four-ish*, *1940-ish*. Endings of other origin have been assim. to *-ish* in, e.g., *lavish*, *squeamish*.

-ish[2] repr. F. *-iss-*, extension of the stem of vbs. in *-ir*, e.g. *abolir* ABOLISH, *périr* PERISH, prp. *abolissant*, *périssant*, 3rd pers. pl. pres. ind. *abolissent*, *périssent*; originating in the *-isc-* of L. inceptive vbs., the use of which in F., Pr., and It. was extended to form a class corr. to L. vbs. in *-īre* and *-ēre*, together with some others that were assim. to these. The earliest forms in Eng. were *-is*(*e*), *-iss*(*e*), which were superseded by *-ische*, *-ish*(*e*); in Sc. *is*(*se*) remained to a later date and appeared in XVI as *-eis*(*e*). (In a few words F. *-iss-* is repr. by *-ise* or *-ize*, viz. *advertise*, *aggrandize*, *amortize*; *réjouir*, *réjouiss-* has given *rejoice*.) Other endings have been assim. to this suffix in, e.g., *admonish*, *astonish*, *distinguish*, *publish*, *relish*.

isinglass gelatin obtained from air-bladder of sturgeon, etc., fish-glue. XVI (*isomglas*, *ison-*). With assim. to *glass* - early Du. †*huysenblas*, f. †*huys*(*en*) sturgeon + †*blas* (mod. *blaas*) bladder.

Islam XIX. - Arab. *'islām*, f. *'aslama* resign oneself (to God).

island OE. (Angl.) *ēġland*, (WS.) *ī(e)ġland*, later *īland* = MDu., MLG. *eilant* (Du. *eiland*), ON. *eyland*; f. OE. *ī(e)ġ* island, in comp. water, sea, OHG. *ouwa* stream, watery meadow, island (G. *au(e)* brook, meadow, pasture), ON. *ey* island :- Gmc. **aujō* for **aʒwjō*, adj. formation on **aʒwō*- stream, water (whence OE. *ēa*, OS., OHG. *aha*, ON. *á*, Goth. *ahwa*), rel. to L. *aqua* water (cf. AQUATIC). The present sp. (from XVI) is due to assim. to next.

isle (arch. exc. as in place names) island. XIII. ME. *ile*, later *isle* - OF. *ile* (mod. *île*), (latinized) †*isle* :- L. *insula*, of uncert. orig. So **islet** XVI. - OF. *islette* (mod. *îlette*).

-ism repr. F. *-isme*, L. *-ismus* - Gr. *-ismós*, forming nouns of action for vbs. in *-ízein* -IZE, e.g. *baptismós* dipping, BAPTISM. A freq. use of *-ismós* was to express the sense of acting like or adopting the habits of a body of people, as *Attikismós* siding with Athenians, Attic fashion or idiom; so *Ioudaïsmós* Judaism, *Khristianismós* Christianity; on this model was formed medL. *pāgānismus* PAGANISM. In Eng. *Judaism* is recorded in XV, and from XVI formations with the suffix become numerous. The chief uses are: (1) to form a noun of action naming the process, the completed action, or its result, e.g. *baptism*, *criticism*, *nepotism*; (2) with emphasis on conduct or character, e.g. *barbarism*, *heroism*, *patriotism*; (3) forming the name of a system of theory or practice, e.g. *Arianism*, *Catholicism*, *positivism*, and (by extension) to designations of doctrines or principles, e.g. *agnosticism*, *altruism*, *egotism*, *romanticism*, *universalism*; (4) forming a term denoting a trait or peculiarity, as of language, e.g. *Americanism*, *Gallicism*, *colloquialism*; for (3) and (4) there is an extensive record of nonce-words. Adjectives of sbs. in *-ism* end in -ISTIC. Hence **ism** form of theory, etc., such as may be designated by a word in *-ism*. XVII.

iso-, before a vowel sometimes **is-** comb. form of Gr. *ísos* equal, in many techn. terms, as **isobar** XIX (Gr. *báros* weight; cf. BAROMETER); **isochronal** XVII, **-chronous** XVIII (Gr. *khrónos* time); **isomeric** XIX (- G. *isomerisch*, f. Gr. *méros* part).

isolated XVIII. f. F. *isolé* - It. *isolato* :- late L. *insulātus* made into an island, f. *insula* ISLE; see -ATE[2], -ED[1]. Hence **isolate** vb. (of which *isolated* is now regarded as the pp.), **isolation** XIX.

isosceles XVI. - late L. *isoscelēs* - Gr. *isoskelḗs*, f. ISO- + *skélos* leg.

isotope XX. f. ISO- + Gr. *tópos* place (i.e. in the periodic table of elements).

Israel In OE. in g. pl. *Israela folc*, ME. *israel folk*; - ecclL. (Gr.) *Isrāēl* - Heb. *yisrā'ēl* 'he that striveth with God', name conferred on the patriarch Jacob (Gen. 32: 28). So **Israelite** XIV. - late L. *Isrāēlīta* - Gr. *Isrāēlítēs* - Heb. *yisrā'ēlī*.

issue exit, outflow XIII; offspring, progeny; proceeds; outcome XIV; (leg.) point in question XVI (earlier in *join i.* submit jointly for decision XV); (from the vb.) public giving out XIX. - (O)F. :- Rom. **exūta*, sb. use of fem. of pp. **exūtus*, for L. *exitus*, pp. of *exīre* go out or forth (see EXIT). Hence as vb. XIV. prob. f. (O)F. pp. *issu*, of *issir* :- L. *exīre*.

-ist repr. F. *-iste*, L. *-ista*, *-tēs* - Gr. *-istḗs*, forming agent-nouns from vbs. in *-ízein* -IZE, consisting of the agential suffix *-tēs* added to the vb.-stem, as in *baptistḗs* BAPTIST. Several Gr. words were adopted into classical L. (e.g. *citharista* player on the cithara, *grammatista* grammarian), and many more by Christian writers (e.g. *baptista*, *psalmista*); later the suffix came into regular use for the designations of observers of particular tenets or rites or the followers of religious leaders (e.g. *Catharista*, *Platonista*, *nōminālista*). In Eng. and the mod. langs. the suffix forms not only agent-nouns having corr. verbs in *-ize*, but analogues of sbs. in *-ism* (e.g. *altruism*, *-ist*), and names of followers of a leader or a school, of adherents of a party, and of devotees of a profession or art, e.g. *Bonapartist*, *Chartist*, *cyclist*, *nonconformist*, *philologist*, *royalist*. Cf. -ISM.

isthmus narrow neck of land. XVI. - L. - Gr. *isthmós* narrow passage, isthmus, of uncert. orig.

-istic repr. F. *-istique*, L. *-isticus* - Gr. *-istikós*, comp. suffix f. *-istḗs* -IST + *-ikós* -IC, as in *sophistikós* SOPHISTIC(AL); but used also where there is a corr. vb. in *-izein* -IZE, and sb. in *-ismós* -ISM but not a sb. in *-istḗs* -IST, as in *kharaktēristikós* CHARACTERISTIC. The use of this suffix was much extended in medL. and mod. langs. An alternative secondary form is **-istical**, whence the gen. adv. **-istically**; there is also a parallel **-isticate** for related vbs.; e.g. *sophistic*, *-ical*, *-ically*, *-icate(d)*.

it 3rd sg. n. pers. pron. OE. *hit* = (M)Du. *het* it, Goth. *hita* this, f. Gmc. dem. stem **χi*- (cf. HE[1]). The parallel stem **i*- is the base of OS. *it*, OHG *iz* (G. *es*). Loss of initial *h* took place at first in unstressed positions, but as early as 1200 *it* is found in stressed positions. Reduction to *t* in enclitic position (e.g. *is't* for *is it*) is equally early; in proclitic position (e.g. *'tis*) it is common from XVI. The orig. g. and d. were HIS, HIM; the present g. is ITS. Hence **itself** OE. *hit self*; in XVII-XVIII sometimes written *its self*.

Italian XV. - It. *italiano*, f. *Italia* Italy; see -IAN. So **Italianate** XVI. - It. *italianato*. **Italic** pert. to a school of philosophy founded in Magna Graecia XVI; pert. to ancient Italy or its tribes; (*i*-) of printing type introduced by Aldo Manuzio of Venice XVII. - L. *Italicus* - Gr. *Italikós*: hence **italicize** print in italics XVIII. **Italiot(e)** pert. to Gr. colonies or colonists in ancient Italy. XVII. - Gr. *Italiṓtēs*. **Italo-**, used as comb. form of *Italian*. XVIII.

itch feel irritation of the skin OE.; have a restless desire XIII. OE *ġiċċan*, *ġyċċan*, corr. to OS. *jukkian*, (M)Du. *jeuken*, OHG. *jucchen* (G. *jucken*), f. Gmc. **juk*- (whence also OHG. *jucchido*, MLG. *jeucte*, OE. *ġyċða* itch). So sb. OE. *ġyċċe*.

-ite suffix corr. to F. *-ite* and Sp., It. *-ito*, G. *-it* - L. *-īta*, *-ītēs* - Gr. *-ítēs*, forming adjs. and sbs. with the sense 'pert. to or connected with', 'member of', as in *hoplítēs* HOPLITE, *polítēs* citizen (see POLITIC). There were many formations in Gr. on proper names; in LXX and N.T. and later Christian use this type was widely extended for the names of sects, heresies, etc., and in late L. and the mod. langs. the suffix has been used without limit for 'follower, devotee, or admirer', as in *Jacobite, Shelleyite, Wycliffite*.

b. In scientific terminology, *-ite* is used after the type of Gr.-L. words in *-ītēs* or *-ītis* in names of fossils and minerals. In chem., it is used in the names of certain organic compounds, and in inorganic chem. is the termination of salts of acids denominated by adjs. in *-ous*, e.g. *nitrite/ nitrous*. It forms also certain names of explosives, e.g. *cordite, dynamite*, and of commercial products such as *ebonite, vulcanite, xylonite*.

item adv. likewise, moreover XIV; sb. †maxim, hint; article in an enumeration XVI; detail of news XIX. - L. adv., 'just so', 'in like manner', 'moreover', f. *ita* so, based on the pronominal stem **i-* (see IT). Hence **item** vb. XVII, **itemize** (esp. U.S.) XIX.

iterate do or say again. XVI. f. pp. stem of L. *iterāre* repeat, f. *iterum* again, compar. formation on the pronominal base **i-*; see prec. and ATE³. So **iteration** XV. - L. **iterative** XV. - F. or late L.

-itic terminal el. of adjs. based on forms in (i) -ITE, (ii) -ITIS.

itinerant XVI. - prp. of late L. *itinerārī*, medL. *-āre*, f. L. *iter, itiner-* journey, f. IE. **i-* go (L. *īre*, Gr. *iénai*); see -ANT. So **itinerary** XV. - late L. *itinerārium*.

-ition suffix repr. F. *-ition*, L. *-ĭtiō, -ōn-*, forming nouns of action (see -ION) on verbs with pps. in *-it-* and *-īt-*, as *positiō* POSITION, *audītiō* AUDITION.

-itious¹ comp. suffix f. L. *-icius, -īcius* + -OUS; these L. endings were commonly written with *t* in medL. manuscripts and this form was perpetuated in ADVENTITIOUS, FACTITIOUS, FICTITIOUS, SUPPOSITITIOUS, etc.

-itious² repr. L. *-ĭtiōsus*, f. *-ĭtiō* -ITION + *-ōsus* -OUS, as in AMBITIOUS, SUPERSTITIOUS; similarly NUTRITIOUS, SEDITIOUS.

-itis suffix repr. Gr. *-ītis*, prop. forming fems. of adjs. in *-ítēs*, used to qualify *nósos* disease, as *arthrîtis* (disease) of the joints (*árthron*), *pleurîtis* pleurisy (*pleurá* side, rib). On the analogy of these *-itis* came into use in mod. medical L. esp. for names of inflammatory diseases, as APPENDICITIS, BRONCHITIS, MENINGITIS, TONSILLITIS. The deriv. adjs. end in **-itic**.

-itous comp. suffix f. *-it-* of -ITY + -OUS; corr to F. *-iteux*, L. *-itōsus*, as L. *calamitōsus*, F. *calamiteux* CALAMITOUS.

its poss. adj. of *it*. XVI. f. IT + g. -S; superseded *it* (XIV-XVII in literature, later dial.), which was adopted as an unambiguous substitute for HIS (OE. to XVII).

-ity in ME. *-it(i)e*, repr. (O)F. *-ité*, L. *-itās, -itāt-*, the form in which *-tās, -tāt-* -TY usu. appears (cf. -I-), as in *suāvitās* suavity, f. *suāvis*, *pūritās* purity, f. *pūrus*, *auctōritās* authority, f. *auctor*; after *i* the suffix became *-etās*, as in *pietās*, *varietās*, f. *pius, varius*; it was added to many adj. suffixes, whence the Eng. forms *-acity, -ality, -anity, -arity, -bility, -idity, -ility, -ivity, -ocity, -osity, -uity*.

-ium terminal el. of the names of many metallic elements, used first by Davy (1807). CADMIUM was based on †*cadmia*; hence *sodium* on *soda*, etc.

-ive in ME. *-if(e), -yf(e)* - (O)F. *-if*, fem. *-ive* :- L. *-īvus, -īvum*, fem. *-īva*, suffix added mainly to pp. stems, e.g. *actīvus, -īva* ACTIVE, *nātīvus* inborn, NATIVE, but also to pres. stems, e.g. *cadīvus* falling, f. *cadere*, and to sbs., e.g. *tempestīvus* seasonable, f. *tempestās* TEMPEST. Eng. formations on vb.-stems often assume the appearance of being of the pp. type, as *adoptive, selective*; see also -ATIVE. Some L. adjs. were used sb., as *captīvus, fugitīvus*; of this usage there is a wide extension in mod. langs. and Eng. (*adjective, explosive, missive, sedative*).

ivory XIII. ME. *ivor, yvor(e), yvory* - OF. *yvoire*, AN. **ivorie* (mod. *ivoire*) - Rom. **eboreum*, f. L. *ebur, ebor-* ivory.

ivy OE. *īfiġ*, obscurely rel. to OHG. *ebah* and the first el. of MLG. *iflōf, iwlōf*, LG., Du. *eilof* (enlarged with the word LEAF), and OHG. *ebahewi*, MHG. *ebehöu, ephöu*, G. *efeu* (enlarged with the word HAY); of unkn. orig.

ixia (bot.) genus of iridaceous plants. XVIII. mod. use of L. *ixia* - Gr. *ixíā* kind of thistle.

-ize, -ise suffix of verbs, repr. F. *-iser* - late L. *-īzāre* - Gr. *-ízein*, which was used to form both intr. and trans. vbs., as *barbarízein* play the barbarian, side with barbarians (f. *bárbaros* BARBARIAN), *thesaurízein* treasure up (f. *thēsaurós* TREASURE). Many verbs have come into Eng. through F., in which they are spelt with *s*, with the result that *-ise* has been generalized, and is retained, as against *-ize*, in the practice of some printing houses; exx. are *civiliser* CIVILIZE, *humaniser* HUMANIZE. The corr. nouns of action end in **-ization**, and agent-nouns in **-izer**.

J

jab vb. XIX. var., orig. Sc., of JOB[1].
jabber vb. XV. imit. Hence as sb. XVIII.
jabot frill on the bosom of a shirt, etc. XIX. - F., 'bird's crop', 'shirt-frill'.
jacinth XIII. ME. *iacin(c)t* - OF. *iacinte* (mod. *jacinthe*), or medL. *iacintus*, L. *hyacinthus* HYACINTH.
jack[1] in numerous transf. applications of the name JACK to implements and machines, or their parts, the male of animals (cf. JACKASS), fishes (esp. pike, orig. young or small pike), etc., from XVI. Hence vb. (with *up*) hoist with a jack (lifting machine); (sl.) ruin; give up, abandon. XIX.
jack[2] A. †jacket; (arch.) leather or iron-plated tunic XIV; B. (leathern) vessel for liquor XVI. - (O)F. *jaque*, of unkn. orig.
jack[3] ship's flag smaller than the ensign. XVII. prob. spec. application of JACK[1] to an object of small size. XVII.
Jack pet form of the name *John* XIII; figure of a man on a clock XV; †fellow, chap XVI (cf. *every man jack* XIX); sailor XVII (cf. *Jack* TAR XVIII); knave of a card suit XVII; (also *j*-) male worker XVII (*jack-of-all-trades*; *cheap-jack*, *steeple-jack* XIX). ME. *Iacke*, *Iakke*, used from the first as familiar by-form of *John*, perh. through dim. *Jankin*; the resemblance to F. *Jacques* James (:- Rom. **Jacobus*, for L. *Jacōbus*) is a difficulty.
jackal XVII. - Turk. *çakal* - Pers. *šaġāl*, rel. to Skr. *śṛgālá-*
jackanapes †ape; pert fellow, coxcomb. XVI. First recorded (XV) as a nickname (*Jac(k) Napes*); of unkn. orig.
jackass he-ass XVIII (fig. dolt, blockhead XIX); *laughing j.*, giant kingfisher of Australia (from its loud discordant cry) XVIII. f. JACK[1] + ASS.
jackboot XVII. f. JACK[1] + BOOT[2].
jackdaw XVI. f. JACK[1] + DAW.
jacket XV. - OF. *ja(c)quet*, dim. of *jaque* JACK[2]; see -ET.
jack-knife XVIII. orig. Amer.; presumably f. JACK[1].
Jacobin[1] A. Dominican (friar), orig. from the convent near the church of Saint-Jacques (L. *Jacōbus*) in Paris XIV; B. member of a political club established at Paris 1789 near the old Jacobin convent XVIII. - (O)F. *Jacobin* - medL. *Jacōbīnus*.
Jacobin[2] breed of domestic pigeon with reversed feathers on the back of the neck suggesting a monk's cowl. XVII. - F. *jacobine*, fem. of *Jacobin* (see prec.).
Jacobite member of a monophysite sect taking its name from *Jacobus* Baradaeus, of Edessa (VI) XIV; adherent of James II of England after his abdication, or of his family XVII. f. L. *Jacōbus* James; see -ITE.
jaconet cotton fabric. XVIII. alt. of Urdu *jagannāthī*, f. *Jagannāth* 'Juggernaut-town' (now Puri), in India, the place of origin.
jactation boasting XVI; (path.) tossing of the body to and fro XVII. - L. *jactātiō*, *-ōn-*, f. *jactāre* toss about, discuss, boast, frequent. of *jacere*, *jact-* throw; see -ATION. So **jactitation** tossing of the body, twitching. XVII. - medL. *jactitatiō*, *-ōn-*, f. *jactitāre*, frequent. of *jactāre*.
jade[1] poor or worn-out horse XIV; reprehensible woman or girl XVI. of unkn. orig.
jade[2] hard mineral. XVIII. - F.; *le jade* was for earlier *l'ejade* - Sp. *ijada* (in *piedra de ijada* 'colic stone') :- Rom. **iliata*, f. L. *ilia* flanks.
jag (dial.) stab, prick; slash, pink XIV; make ragged XVI. prob. symbolic formation. Hence **jag** sb. XV, **jagged** XV.
jaguar XVII. - Tupi-Guarani *jaguara*.
jail see GAOL.
jalap purgative drug from *Exogonium purga*; the plant itself XVII. - F. - Sp. *jalapa*, f. *Jalapa* (†*Xalapa*) city in Mexico.
jalousie XIX. - F. *jalousie* JEALOUSY, applied to a blind or shutter which allows of seeing without being seen - It. *gelosia* in this sense.
jam[1] press or squeeze tightly. XVIII. of symbolic orig. Hence sb. XIX.
jam[2] conserve of fruit. XVIII. perh. identical with prec. sb.
jamb XIV. - (O)F. *jambe* leg, vertical supporting piece :- late L. *gamba* hoof, veterinary breeder's term - Gr. (cf. *kampḗ* flexure, joint).
jamboree XIX. of unkn. orig.
jangle †chatter, babble XIII; talk angrily or harshly; also trans. XIV; cause (a bell) to give out a discordant sound XVII. - OF. *jangler*, *gengler*, perh. of Gmc. orig.
janissary one of the Sultan of Turkey's bodyguard; Turkish soldier; henchman. XVI. Early forms repr. various Rom. forms, all ult. - Turk. *yeniçeri*, f. *yeni* new + *çeri* militia.
janitor XVII. - L. *jānitor*, f. *jānua* door, f. *jānus* arched passage (cf. JANUARY); see -TOR.
January XIV. - L. *Jānuārius*, sb. use of adj. of *Jānus*, name of an ancient Italian deity figured with faces looking forwards and backwards; see -ARY. The earliest Eng. forms are *Ien-*, *Ianeuer* (XIII) - AN., OF. *Jeneuer*, *Genever* (mod. *janvier*).
japan exceptionally hard varnish, orig. from Japan. XVII. f. the name. Hence vb. XVII. Hence **Japanese** XVII.
jape vb. †A. trick; †B. have carnal knowledge (of); C. jest. XIV. Appears to combine the form of OF. *japer* (mod. *japper*) yelp, yap, with the sense of OF. *gaber* mock, deride. Hence sb. XIV.
japonica XIX. fem. of modL. *Japonicus* JAPANESE.
jar[1] harsh sound; discord, strife XVI; (from the vb.) act of jarring XIX. So **jar** vb. sound harshly, make a discord; cause to vibrate; be at discord

or strife. XVI. Early vars. are *gerre, ier, charre*; prob. imit.

jar² (orig. large) cylindrical vessel. XVI. - F. *jarre* = Pr. *jarro*, Sp., Pg. *jarra*, It. *giarra* - Arab. *jarra*.

jar³ in phr. †*at jar*, (*up*)*on the jar*; see AJAR.

jardinière XIX. - F., fem. of *jardinier* GARDENER.

jargon †twittering or chattering of birds XIV; meaningless talk XIV; debased or hybrid language; speech peculiar to a trade or profession XVII. - OF. *jargoun, gergon, gargon*; ult. orig. unkn.

jargonelle early variety of pear (orig. an inferior gritty kind). XVII. - F. *jargonelle*, dim. of *jargon* JARGOON (cf. -EL²).

jargoon variety of zircon. XVIII. - F. *jargon* - It. *giargone*; prob. to be identified ult. with ZIRCON.

jarrah mahogany gum-tree of W. Australia. XIX. - Austral. aboriginal *djarryl, jerryhl*.

jasmine, jessamine XVI. The two forms repr. F. *jasmin* and †*jessemin* - Arab. *yāsamīn* - Pers. *yāsmin, yāsaman*.

jasper XIV. - OF. *jaspre*, var. of *jaspe* - L. *iaspis*, *-id-* - Gr. *iaspis, -id-*, of Oriental orig.

jaundice XIV. - OF. *jaunice* (mod. *-isse*) 'yellowness', f. *jaune* yellow (:- L. *galbinus*, f. *galbus*).

jaunt †ride (a horse) up and down; †trudge about XVI; make a short trip XVII. Also contemp. sb; of unkn. orig.

jaunty †well-bred; †elegant; sprightly. XVII. In early use *jentee, juntee, ja(u)ntee* - F. *gentil* (see GENTLE); assim. later to adjs. in -Y¹.

javelin XVI. - (O)F. *javeline*, alt. of *javelot*, prob. of Celt. orig. (OIr. *gabul*, W. *gafl, gaflach*).

jaw one of the bones forming the framework of the mouth XIV; (sl.) offensive or tedious talk XVIII. ME. *jow(e)* - OF. *joe* cheek, jaw; of uncert. orig.

jay XIII. - OF. *jay* (mod. *geai*) :- late L. *gaius*, beside *gaia*; perh. f. the L. proper name *Gaius* (cf. the use of other personal names, as *jackdaw, robin*).

jazz XX. orig. U.S.; of unkn. orig.

jealous suspicious of rivalry XIII; zealous (for) XIV; (dial.) suspicious XVI; suspiciously vigilant XVII. ME. *gelus, ielus* - OF. *gelos* (mod. *jaloux*) :- medL. *zēlōsus*, f. ChrL. *zēlus* - Gr. *zêlos* ZEAL; see -OUS. So **jealousy** XIII.

jean twilled cotton cloth XVI; (pl.) garments of this XIX. orig. *ie(a)ne, ge(a)ne fustian*; attrib. use of *Jene, Gene* - OF. *Janne* (mod. *Gênes*) :- medL. *Janua* Genoa.

jeep small utility motor truck. XX (orig. U.S.). f. initials *G.P.* '*g*eneral *p*urposes', prob. infl. by Eugene the Jeep, name of animal in U.S. comic strip by E. C. Segar.

jeer XVI. Earliest forms are *gy(e)re, geere*; of unkn. orig.

Jehovah the Lord God. XVI. alt. of Heb. JHVH, the ineffable name of the Almighty, produced by the insertion of the vowel-points repr. the vowels of *Adonai* as a direction to substitute this. It is held that the orig. name was *Jahve(h), Jahwe(h)*.

jejune unsatisfying, meagre. XVII. - L. *jējūnus* fasting, barren, meagre; cf. DINE.

jelly article of food consisting chiefly of gelatin. XIV. ME. *geli, -y(e)* - (O)F. *gelée* frost, jelly = It. *gelata* frost :- Rom. *gelāta*, sb. use of fem. pp. of *gelāre* freeze, f. *gelu* frost (cf. CONGEAL). Hence **jellied** XVI; (back-formation) **jell** vb. orig. U.S. XIX.

jemmy burglar's crowbar. XIX. dim. of name *James*; see -Y⁶.

jennet small Spanish horse. XV. - F. *genet* - Sp. *jinete* short-stirruped light horseman - Arab. *Zanāta* Berber tribe famed for horsemanship.

jenny pet-form (see -Y⁶) of *Janet* (or *Jane*), used as a prefix to denote a female animal, as *j. ass, j. wren* (XVII), and in the names of machines, as *spinning-j.* (XVIII).

jeopardy †chess problem; †(even) chance; risk of injury or death. XIV. - OF. *iu* (*ieu, giu*) *parti* 'divided play', even game, (hence) uncertain chance, uncertainty (= medL. *jocus partītus*, i.e. *jocus* game, JOKE, *partītus*, pp. of *partīrī* divide, PART). Hence **jeopardize** XVII.

jerboa small rodent remarkable for its jumping powers. XVII. - Arab. *yarbū'*.

jeremiad XVIII. - F. *jérémiade*, f. *Jérémie* - ecclL. *Jeremias* Jeremiah, in allusion to the Lamentations of Jeremiah in O.T.; see -AD.

jerk¹ †stroke with a whip; sharp sudden pull or thrust. XVI. gen. synon. with †*jert* and †*yerk* (XVI); all three forms may be phonetically symbolical in origin.

jerk² cure (beef) by cutting it into strips and drying it. XVIII. An earlier form is found in †*jerkin beef* (XVII); repr. Amer. Sp. *charquear*, f. *charqui* - Quechua *echarqui* dried flesh in long strips.

jerkin close-fitting jacket. XVI. of unkn. orig.

jeroboam large bowl or wine-bottle. XIX. So called in allusion to *Jeroboam*, 'a mighty man of valour' (1 Kings 11: 28), 'who made Israel to sin' (ibid. 14: 16).

jerry¹ (sl.) chamber-pot. XIX. Supposed to be short for prec.; cf. -Y⁶.

jerry² (colloq.) unsubstantial(ly), as in *jerry-built, -builder, -building*. XIX. of unkn. orig.

jerrymander var. of GERRYMANDER.

jersey (Jersey) worsted XVI; knitted close-fitting tunic XIX. Name of the largest of the Channel Islands, in which the knitting of worsted articles was a staple industry.

jess (chiefly pl.) straps for a hawk's legs. XIV (*ges*). - OF. *ges* nom. sg. and acc. pl. (mod. *jet* cast) :- Rom. **jectus*, for L. *jactus* throw, f. *jacere* (cf. EJECT).

jessamine see JASMINE.

jest †deed, exploit XIII; †idle tale XV; mocking speech; witticism, joke XVI. ME. *geste* - OF. :- L. *gesta* doings, exploits, n. pl. of pp. of *gerere* do, perform.

Jesuit XVI. - F. *Jésuite* or modL. *Jēsuīta*, f. *Jēsūs* + *-īta* -ITE. Hence **Jesuitical** XVI.

Jesus, Jesu the Founder of Christianity. Not used in OE., in which it was rendered by *Hǣlend* Saviour; in ME. (XII) not usu. written in full, but almost always in the abbreviated Gr. forms *ihu(s), ihs*, etc.; repr. ChrL. *Iēsūs*, obl. cases

Iēsū - Gr. *Iēsoûs, Iēsoû* - late Heb. or Aramaic *yēšūa'*, for earlier *yʰhōšua'* Joshua, which is explained as 'Jah (or Jahveh) is salvation'.

jet[1] hard black form of lignite. XIV. ME. *geet, jeet,* later *jeat, jeit* - AN. *geet, *jeet,* OF. *jaiet, jayet* (mod. *jais*) :- L. *gagātēs* - Gr. *gagátēs*, f. *Gágas* town in Lycia, Asia Minor.

jet[2] †project, protrude XVI; spout forth XVII. - (O)F. *jeter* throw :- Rom. **jectāre*, for L. *jactāre* (see JACTATION). Hence (partly - F. *jet*) **jet** sb. †projection; †swagger; stream of water, etc., shot out. XVII.

jetsam goods thrown overboard to lighten a vessel and afterwards washed ashore. XVI. Early forms *jetson, -sen,* later *-sam* (cf. FLOTSAM), contr. form of JETTISON.

jettison action of throwing goods overboard. XV. - AN. *getteson*, OF. *getaison* :- L. *jactātiō, -ōn-*, f. *jact-, jactāre*; see JET[2], -ATION. Hence vb. (often fig.) XIX.

jetty pier running out into the sea, etc.; †overhanging upper storey. XV. - OF. *jetee, getee* projecting part of a building, structure to protect a harbour, sb. use of fem. pp. of *jeter* throw; see JET[2].

Jew XII (*Giw, Gyu, Iu(w), Ieu*). - OF. *giu*, earlier *juiu* (mod. *juif*) :- L. *jūdæus* - Gr. *ioudaîos*, f. Aram. *yʰhûdhāi*, Heb. *yʰhûdhī*, f. *yʰhûdhah* Judah, name of a Jewish patriarch and the tribe descended from him. OE. had pl. *Iudeas*. *Jew's* EAR fungus growing on trees, esp. the elder (on which Judas Iscariot, acc. to legend, hanged himself) XVI; mistr. of medL. *auricula Judæ* Judas's ear. *Jews'* HARP, earlier *Jews'* TRUMP (XVI), rudimentary musical instrument, the ascription of which to Jews is unexpl. Hence **Jewish** XVI; OE. had *Iudeisc*. **Jewry** Jews' quarter, ghetto XIII; Jews; †Judea, Palestine XIV. - AN. *juerie*, OF. *juierie* (mod. *juiverie*).

jewel †costly ornament of gold, silver, or precious stone XIII (fig. 'treasure', 'gem' XIV); precious stone, esp. as an ornament XVI. ME. *iuel, iowel, gewel* - AN. *j(e)uel*, OF. *joel* (nom. sg. *joiaus*; mod. *joyau*); of doubtful formation, but ult. based on L. *jocus* jest, in Rom. game, sport. So **jeweller** XIV. - AN. *jueler*, OF. *juelier* (mod. *joaillier*). **jewellery, jewelry** in ME. (XIV) - OF. *juelerie* (mod. *joaillerie*); in mod. use (XVIII) a new formation.

Jezebel shameless woman. XVI. Name of the infamous wife of Ahab, king of Israel (1 Kings 16: 31; 19: 1, 2; 21; and 2 Kings 9: 30-7).

jib[1] (naut.) triangular stay-sail XVII (*gibb*). of unkn. orig. Also **jib** vb. (naut.) pull a sail round XVII; synon. with Da. *gibbe*, Du. *gijpen*, G. *geipen*, but the initial cons. is against any immed. connection; cf. GYBE.

jib[2] projecting arm of a crane. XVIII. of unkn. orig.

jib[3] (of a horse, etc.) stop and refuse to go on. XIX (*gib, jibb*). of unkn. orig.; remarkably like OF. *giber* kick, *regiber* (mod. *regimber*), whence ME. (once) *regibben*, but no historical connection may be supposed.

jibe see GIBE, GYBE.

jiffy (colloq.) moment, minute. XVIII. of unkn. orig. Also **jiff** XVIII.

jig lively springy dance, music for this; †lively ballad, light dramatic performance; (dial., sl.) joke, sport. XVI. of unkn. orig. The mod. (XIX) applications to various mechanical devices are from **jig** vb. in the sense 'move rapidly or jerkily up and down or to and fro' (XVII), which most prob. derives from the sb.

jigger[1] †dancer of a jig XVII; (naut.) small tackle; and in various names of mechanical contrivances similar to those called *jig* XVIII. f. prec. + -ER[1].

jigger[2] XVIII. Later var. of CHIGOE.

jiggered in (colloq.) *I'm jiggered*, euphem. substitute for a profane or indecent word. XIX.

jiggery-pokery (colloq.) underhand or tricky dealing. XIX. synon. with and perh. alt. of Sc. and north. dial. *jookery pawkery*, earlier *juwkry-pawkry*, jingling formation on (dial.) *jouk* dart, dodge, duck (XVI), of unkn. orig.; see -ERY.

jiggle move restlessly with slight jerks. XIX. partly f. JIG vb. + -LE[3]; partly modification of JOGGLE, to express smaller movements.

jig-saw machine fretsaw XIX (orig. U.S.); (*jig-saw puzzle*) XX. f. JIG + SAW[1].

jill var. of GILL[4]. XVII.

jilt †loose woman; woman who casts off a lover. XVII. 'A new canting word' in Blount's 'Glossographia' of 1674, of unkn. orig.; hence as vb., the earliest recorded ex. of which (1660) shows a wider sense of 'deceive, cheat'.

jim-jam †A. fanciful or trivial article XVI; B. pl. (orig. U.S.) delirium tremens XIX. fanciful redupl. formation.

jimmy var. of JEMMY.

jingle vb. XIV (*gynglen*); sb. XVI. imit.; cf. JANGLE; sp. with *g-* continued till XIX.

jingo Recorded first (XVII) in conjuror's patter, usu. *hey* or *high jingo*, then (Motteux's Rabelais, 1694, tr. F. *par Dieu*) in *by jingo!*, a vigorous asseveration; of unkn. orig. The use of this excl. in the refrain of a music-hall song (1878) by G. W. Hunt gave rise to the use of *jingo* as a nickname for supporters of Disraeli's resistance to the Russian advance on Turkey, whence it became a gen. term for advocates of a bellicose policy in dealing with foreign powers. Hence **jingoism** XIX.

jink quick turn so as to elude XVIII; *high jinks* †frolic at a drinking-party XVII, lively or boisterous sport XIX. So as vb. move with sudden quick motion, make a quick elusive turn. XVIII. orig. Sc., of unkn. orig.

jinn (one of) an order of spirits in Muslim demonology. XVII (*dgen*). - Arab. *jinn*, coll. of *jinnī* GENIE (also **jinnee** XIX).

jinricksha light two-wheeled man-drawn vehicle. XIX. - Jap. *jin-riki-sha*, f. *jin* man + *riki* strength, power + *sha* vehicle. Cf. RICKSHAW.

jinx (U.S.) person or thing that brings bad luck. XX. of unkn. orig.

jitter (U.S.) act in a nervous way. XX. So **jitters** sb. pl., **jittery** XX. of unkn. orig.

jiu-jitsu var. of JU-JITSU.

job[1] pierce to a slight depth as with a pointed object. XV. of symbolic orig.; cf. BOB[2], STAB (†*stob*), JAB, DAB[1].

job[2] piece of work XVI; transaction, operation XVII; position of employment XIX (orig. U.S. colloq.). poss. transf. use of †*job* piece, lump (XIV), cart-load (XVI), of unkn. orig.

Job patriarch of the O.T. taken as a type of destitution and of patience. XVI.

jobation f. †*jobe* rebuke, reprimand (XVII), f. JOB, in allusion to the lengthy reproofs addressed to him by his friends; see -ATION.

Jock Sc. var. of JACK; rustic (cf. HODGE). XVI.

jockey pet-form of JOCK; man of the people; lad XVI; †horse-dealer; professional rider in horse-races XVII. f. JOCK + *-ey*, -Y[6]. Hence as vb. play the 'jockey' with, outwit, trick XVIII; ride as a jockey XIX.

jocose XVII. - L. *jocōsus*, f. *jocus*; see JOKE, -OSE. So **jocular** XVII.

jocund XIV. - OF. *jocond, jocund* - L. *jōcundus*, late form of *jūcundus* pleasant, agreeable (:-**juvicundus*), f. *juvāre* help, delight.

jodhpurs riding breeches tight from knee to ankle. XIX. f. *Jodhpur*, name of a town in Rajasthan (Rajputana), India.

joey young kangaroo. XIX. - Austral. aboriginal *joè*.

jog †stab, prod; give a slight push to, nudge; intr. move as with a jolting pace. XIV. of symbolic orig.; not common in literature before XVI. Hence **joggle** shake to and fro. XVI.

Johannine pert. to the apostle and evangelist John. XIX. f. ecclL. *Jōhannēs* JOHN + -INE[1].

johannisberger white wine produced at *Johannisberg* in the Rheingau, Germany. XIX.

John one of the commonest Jewish and Christian names (the name of two saints of the N.T., John Baptist and John Apostle and Evangelist). ME. *Io(ha)n*, later *Ihon, Iohn, John* (sp. being based partly on abbrevs. of the L. form, *Ihes, Ihōēs, Iohs*, etc.) - late L. *Iōannēs* (medL. *Iōhannēs*) - N.T. Gr. *Iōánnēs* - Heb. *yôḥānān*, for *yᵉhôḥānān*, expl. as 'God (Jah) is gracious'. Cf. JACK. *John Bull* typical or individual Englishman; from the name of a character repr. the Eng. nation in Arbuthnot's satire 'Law is a Bottomless Pit', 1712. *John* DORY XVIII. Hence **johnny, -ie** (*J-*) pet-form of *John*; transf. fellow, chap. XVII.

join put or bring together; come or be put together. XIII. - *joign-*, pres. stem of (O)F. *joindre* :- L. *jungere*, f. IE. **jug-* (see YOKE). So **joinder** joining. XVII. - legal AN. *joinder*, sb. use of OF. *joindre*. **joint** articulation, as of bones XIII; part so joined XIV; (U.S.) place of resort (orig. of meeting), esp. for illicit purposes XIX. - OF. *joint* and *jointe*, sb. uses of m. and fem. pp. of *joindre*. **joint** adj. joined, combined (now only attrib.) XIV; holding or held in conjunction XV. - (O)F. *joint*, pp. of *joindre*. **jointure** †junction, joint XIV; holding of property jointly, sole estate limited to the wife XV. - (O)F. :- L. *junctūra* JUNCTURE.

joist XIV. ME. *giste*, early mod. *iust* - OF. *giste* beam supporting a bridge (mod. *gîte*) :- sb. use of L. *jacitum*, n. pp. of *jacēre* lie down.

joke sb. XVII (*joque*). orig. sl.; poss. - L. *jocus* word-play, jest. So **joke** vb. XVII. Hence **joker** jester, merry fellow XVIII; something used in playing a trick; odd card in a pack (orig. U.S.) XIX.

jolly (arch.) of gay disposition, festive, jovial; †gallant, brave; †confident; †amorous XIV; splendid, fine; delightful XVI. ME. *jolif* - OF. *jolif*, (later and mod.) *joli* †gay, †pleasant, pretty, perh. f. ON. *jól* midwinter festival, feast, YULE.

jolly-boat ship's boat. XVIII. of unkn. orig.; cf. app. synon. †*jolywat, gellywatte* (XV-XVII), and YAWL.

jolt move with jerks from one's seat XVI; †butt, nudge XVII. synon. with somewhat earlier †*jot*, but the origin of both words is unkn., as also of the formally corr. first el. of *jolthead* large clumsy head, blockhead (XVI).

jongleur itinerant minstrel in medieval France. XVIII. - F., alt. of *jougleur* (OF. *jogleor*) (see JUGGLER).

jonquil species of narcissus. XVII. In early use *junquilia* - It. *giunchiglia*; the present form is - modL. *jonquilla* or F. *jonquille* - Sp. *junquillo*, dim. of *junco* :- L. *juncus* rush, reed.

jorum large drinking-bowl. XVIII. perh. f. name of *Joram*, who 'brought with him vessels of silver, and vessels of gold, and vessels of brass' (2 Sam. 8: 10).

joss Chinese idol. XVIII. perh. ult. - Pg. †*deos, deus* :- L. *deus* god.

jostle †meet *with* in an encounter XIV; (trans. and intr.) knock or push (*against*) XVI. f. *just*, JOUST + -LE[3].

jot least part or point. XVI. Formerly also *io(a)te* - L. *iōta* - Gr. *iôta* IOTA. Hence (presumably) **jot** vb. set *down* in the briefest form. XVIII.

joule electrical unit, named 1882 after James Prescott *Joule*, English physicist.

jounce jolt, bump. XV. of unkn. orig.; cf. *bounce, flounce, pounce, trounce*, all applied to kinds of abrupt or forcible movement.

journal A. †diurnal (service-book) XIV; †itinerary; daily record of transactions; record of events XVI; daily newspaper XVIII. B. part of a shaft or axle that rests on the bearings XIX. - OF. *jurnal, jornal* (mod. *journal*), sb. use of *journal* adj., for earlier *jornel* :- late L. *diurnālis* DIURNAL. The development of sense B is unexpl. Hence **journalist** XVII (whence **journalistic** XIX); **journalism** XIX. **journalize** enter in a journal XVIII; practise journalism XIX.

journey †day's travel; spell of travel XIII; (dial.) day's work (hence in *journeyman*, orig. one qualified to work for day wages) XIV; amount produced in a day's work (e.g. at the British Mint) XVI. - OF. *jornee* (mod. *journée* day, day's work or travel) :- Rom. **diurnāta*, f. L. *diurnum* daily portion, in Rom. langs. day, sb. use of n. of *diurnus* DIURNAL. So vb. travel. XIV. - AN. *journeyer*.

joust sb. XIII. - OF. *j(o)uste*, f. *juster* (mod. *jouter*) bring together, engage on horseback (whence **joust** vb. XIII) :- Rom. **juxtāre* come together, encounter, f. L. *juxtā* near together, rel. to *jugum* YOKE, *jungere* JOIN.

Jove Jupiter. XIV. *By Jove* XVI. See next.

jovial †under the influence of the planet Jupiter, regarded astrol. as the source of happiness;

characterized by mirth. XVI. - F. - It. *gioviale*, f. *Giove* Jove, Jupiter :- L. *Jov-*, stem of OL. *Jovis* (for which classical L. had the comp. with *pater* father, *Juppiter*, JUPITER, corr. to Skr. *dyaúṣ pitā́* 'heaven father'; cf. DEITY, DIVINE); see -IAL.

jowl[1] jaw, jawbone; as in phr. *cheek by jowl*, which repl. *cheek by cheek*. XVI. Later form of *chawle*, reduction of ME. *chauel*, OE. *ċeafl*, corr. to OS. **kabal* (in d. pl. *kaflun*), rel. to MHG. *kivel*, Du. *kevel*.

jowl[2] dewlap, crop, wattle. XVI. Later form of ME. *cholle* (XIV), OE. *ċeole*, *-u* = OS., OHG. *kela* (G. *kehle*), throat, gullet.

jowl[3] head. XIV (*jolrap* head-rope). Later form of *cholle* (XIV), of unkn. orig.

joy XIII. - (O)F. *joie* :- Rom. **gaudia*, fem. for L. *gaudia*, pl. of *gaudium* joy, f. *gaudēre*. So **joy** vb. †rejoice XIII; †ENJOY XIV. - OF. *joïr* (mod. *jouir*) :- Rom. **gaudīre*, for L. *gaudēre* rejoice. So **joyance** XVI. **joyous** XIV. - AN. *joyous*, OF. *joios* (mod. *joyeux*).

jubilation XIV. - L. *jūbilātiō*, *-ōn-*, f. *jūbilāre* (rustic word) call, halloo, (in Chr. writers) shout for joy; see -ATION. So **jubilant** XVII. Not orig. rel. to next.

jubilee year of emancipation and restoration of the Jews, kept every 50 years (see Lev. 25); fiftieth anniversary. XIV. - (O)F. *jubilé* - ChrL. *jūbilæus* adj. - (with assim. to *jūbilāre*; see prec.) ChrGr. *iōbēlaîos*, f. *iṓbēlos* - Heb. *yōbhēl* jubilee, orig. ram, (hence) ram's horn, with which the jubilee year was proclaimed.

Judaic XVII; earlier **Judaical** XV. - L. *Jūdaicus* - Gr. *Ioudaïkós*, f. *Ioudaîos* JEW. So **Judaism** XVI. - ChrL. *Jūdaismus* - Gr. *Ioudaïsmós*. So **Judaize** XVI. - ChrL. *jūdaizāre* - Gr. *ioudaḯzein*.

judas opening through which one can look without being seen. XIX. - F. *judas*, transf. use of the name of the disciple who betrayed Jesus Christ (Matt. 26: 48).

judge officer appointed to administer the law; arbiter, umpire. XIV. - OF. *juge* :- L. *jūdex*, *jūdic-*, f. *jūs* right, law + *-dicus* speaking (see DICTION). So vb. XIII. - (O)F. *juger* :- L. *jūdicāre*. **judg(e)ment** XIII. - (O)F. *jugement*, f. *juger*. Hence **judgmatic(al)** judicious. XIX.

judicature action or office of a judge; body of judges. XVI. - medL. *jūdicātūra*, f. pp. stem of *jūdicāre* JUDGE; see -URE.

judicial pert. to judgement or a judge XIV; giving judgement XVI. - L. *jūdiciālis*, f. *jūdicium* judgement, f. *jūdex*, *jūdic-* JUDGE; see -IAL. So **judicious** XVI. - F. *judicieux*.

Judy wife of Punch. XIX. pet-form of the female name *Judith*.

jug[1] deep vessel with a handle for holding liquid XVI; (sl.) prison XIX. prob. a use of the proper name *Jug*, pet-form of *Joan*, *Joanna*, and *Jenny*.

jug[2] imit. of the notes of the nightingale. XVI.

juggernaut (*J-*) title of Krishna, avatar of Vishnu; idol of this carried in an enormous car, under which (it was once said) devotees threw themselves. XVII; also fig. - Hindi *Jagannath* - Skr. *Jagannātha-*, f. *jágat-* world + *nāthá-* lord, protector.

juggins (sl.) simpleton. XIX. perh. a use of the surname *Juggins*, f. *Jug* (see JUG[1]).

juggler †jester, buffoon; †magician, wizard; conjurer. XII. ME. *iugelere*, *-lour*, *iogeler* - OF. *jog-*, *j(o)uglere*, acc. *jogleor*, etc. :- L. *joculātor*, *-ōr-*, f. *joculārī* jest; also OF. *jogler* :- medL. *joculāris* buffoon, sb. use of the adj. So **jugglery** XIII. Hence (or - OF. *jugler*) **juggle** XIV.

jugular pert. to the neck or throat. XVI. - late L. *jugulāris*, f. L. *jugulum* collar-bone, dim. of *jugum* YOKE; see -AR.

juice XIII (*iuys*). - (O)F. *jus* - L. *jūs* broth, sauce, vegetable juice (cf. Skr. *yūṣ-*, OSl. *jucha* soup, broth, Gr. *zū́mē* leaven), f. IE. **jeu-* mix.

ju-jitsu, -jutsu XIX. - Jap. *jūjutsu*, f. *jū* gentle + *jutsu* science.

jujube edible fruit of plant of genus *Zizyphus* XIV; lozenge of the shape of or flavoured with this XIX. - (O)F. *jujube* or medL. *jujuba*, ult. - L. *zizyphum* - Gr. *zízuphon*.

julep sweet or syrupy liquor XIV; (U.S.) iced and flavoured spirit and water (esp. *mint julep*) XIX. - (O)F. *julep* (ult.) - Arab. *julāb* rose-water - Pers. *gulāb*, f. *gul* rose + *āb* water.

julienne vegetable soup. XIX. - F., for *potage à la julienne*, f. proper name *Jules* or *Julien* (the reason is unkn.).

July XIII. - AN. *julie* - L. *Jūlius*, so named after Caius *Julius* Caesar, who was born in this month, the orig. name *Quin(c)tilis* being changed to *Julius* after his death and apotheosis.

jumble †intr. move about in disorder; †make a confused or discordant noise; mingle in confusion. XVI. partly synon. with late ME. †*jumpere*, †*jombre*, both app. being formed on a symbolic base with iterative or frequent. suffix. So sb. medley, disorder. XVII.

jumbo big clumsy person, animal, etc. XIX. prob. the second element of MUMBO-JUMBO.

jump move or be moved up and down as with a leap or spring XVI; leap over XVII; (U.S. and Colonial) take summary possession of (a claim) XIX. prob. imit.; cf. *bump*, *thump*. Hence **jump** sb. XVI.

jumper loose garment for the torso. XIX. of uncert. orig.

junction XVIII. - L. *junctiō*, *-ōn-*, f. *junct-*, pp. stem of *jungere* JOIN; see YOKE, -TION. So **juncture** place of joining XIV; convergence of events XVII. - L. *junctūra* joint.

June XII. - (O)F. *juin* :- L. *Jūnius*, var. of *Jūnōnius* sacred to the goddess Juno.

jungle (orig.) waste land; (hence) land overgrown with underwood. XVIII. - Hindi *jaṅgal* :- Skr. *jaṅgala-* arid region.

junior younger XVII; of lower standing XVIII; sb. XVI. - L. *jūnior* (:- **juvenior*), compar. of *juvenis* YOUNG.

juniper XIV. - L. *jūniperus*.

junk[1] old rope XV (hence, worthless stuff, rubbish XX); salt meat used on long voyages (compared to pieces of rope) XVIII. of unkn. orig.

junk[2] native sailing vessel, esp. of the China seas. XVII. - F. †*juncque* (mod. *jonque*), Pg. *junco*, or Du. *jonk* - Javanese *djong*, Malay *jong*.

junker young German noble; spec. reactionary

member of Prussian aristocracy. XVI (not common till XIX). - G., for earlier *junkher(r)*, f. MHG. *junc* YOUNG + *herre* (mod. *herr*) lord.

junket (rush) basket for fish XIV; dish prepared with cream, orig. laid in or on rushes XV; †dainty dish or confection; feast, banquet XVI. - (O)F. *jonquette*, f. *jonc* rush :- L. *juncus*.

junta (in Spain and Italy) deliberative or administrative council XVII; body of men combined for a common (political) purpose XVIII. - Sp., Pg. *junta* :- Rom. sb. use of fem. pp. *juncta* of L. *jungere* JOIN. In the latter sense often also **junto** (XVII), with ending assim. to Sp. sbs. in *-o*.

Jupiter supreme deity of the ancient Romans XIII (in earliest use *Iubiter*); largest of the planets XIII; (alch.) †tin XIV; †(her., in blazoning by the names of heavenly bodies) azure XVI. - L.; see JOVIAL.

jurassic (geol.) pert. to oolitic formations of which the Jura mountains chiefly consist. XIX. - F. *jurassique*, f. *Jura*.

jurat[1] municipal official or magistrate in the Cinque Ports, the Channel Islands, and some French towns, etc. XV. - L. *jūrātus* (cf. foll.).

jurat[2] (leg.) memorandum of the swearing of an affidavit. XVIII. - L. *jūrātum*, n. pp. of *jūrāre*; see JURY.

juridical XVI. f. L. *jūridicus*, f. *jūs*, *jūr-* law (with Indo-Iranian cogns.) + *-dicus* saying, f. *dīcere* say. So **jurisconsult** one learned in the law. XVII. - L. *jūrisconsultus*, f. *jūris*, g. of *jūs* + *consultus*. **jurisdiction** XIII. Earliest forms *iure-*, *iuridiccioun* - OF. *jure-*, (also mod.) *juridiction*, later conformed to the orig. L. *jūrisdictiō*, *-ōn-*; f. *jūris* + *dictiō* declaration (see DICTION). **jurisprudence** †skill in law; system of law XVII; science of law XVIII. - late L. **jurist** †lawyer XV; legal writer XVII. - F. *juriste* or medL. *jūrista*. **juror** XIV. - AN. *jurour* :- L. *jūrātor*, *-ōr-*. **jury** company of men sworn to give a verdict. XIV. ME. *iuree* - AN. *juree* - OF. *jurée* oath, juridical inquiry, inquest - (AL. *jūrāta*) sb. use of fem. pp. of L. *jūrāre* swear; see -Y[5].

jury-mast (naut.) temporary mast. XVI. of uncert. orig.

jussive (gram.) expressing command. XIX. f. *juss-*, pp. stem of L. *jubēre* command; see -IVE.

just righteous, fair; well-founded; proper, correct, †exact. XIV. - (O)F. *juste* - L. *jūstus*, f. *jūs* (cf. JURY). Hence **just** adv. exactly, precisely XIV; precisely (now or then); not more than, barely XVII; not less than, quite XVIII.

just var. of JOUST.

justice exercise of judicial authority; judicial officer, judge XII; quality of being just XIV; rightfulness XVI. - (O)F. - L. *jūstitia* righteousness, equity, f. *jūstus* JUST; see -ICE. So **justiciar** (hist.) XV, **justiciary** XVI. - medL. *justitiārius*; see -AR, -ARY.

justify †judge, condemn, punish; show to be just; make good, verify XIV; maintain the justice of; make exact, adjust (esp. printing type) XVI. - (O)F. *justifier* - ChrL. *jūstificāre* do justice to, vindicate, f. *justus* JUST: see -FY. So **justification** XIV (theol. XVI). - (O)F. or ChrL. **justifiable** XVI. - F.

jut project, stick *out*. XVI. var. of JET[2], by assim. to †*jutty* (XV) project, also †*jetty* (XVI), and †*jutty* (XV) pier, JETTY.

jute fibre from the bark of Indian trees (genus *Corchorus*) used for sacking, etc. XVIII. - Bengali *jhōṭo*, *jhuṭo*.

juvenile adj. XVII; sb. XVIII. - L. *juvenīlis*, f. *juvenis* YOUNG; see -ILE. So **juvenilia** works produced in one's youth. XVII. - L. n. pl.

juxtaposition placing close together. XVII. - F., f. L. *juxtā* (cf. JOUST). So **juxtapose** XIX. See POSE, POSITION.

K

Kabyle Berber of Algeria or Tunis. XIX. - Arab. *ḳabā'il*, pl. of *ḳabīla* tribe.

kaddish portion of the daily ritual of the synagogue. XVII. - Aram. *ḳaddīš* holy.

Kaffir †infidel; member of a S. Afr. people of the Bantu family. XIX. - Arab. *kāfir*, prp. active of *kafara* be unbelieving.

kailyard see KALE.

kainite (min.) hydrous chlorosulphate of magnesium and potassium. XIX. - G. *kainit*, f. Gr. *kainós* new + -ITE; named by C. F. Zincken in 1865 with ref. to its recent formation.

kaiser emperor. XVI. - G. *kaiser* and Du. *keizer*, †*ke(i)ser*, a Gmc. adoption of L. *Cæsar* through Gr. *kaisar*, repr. by OE. *cāsere*, OS. *kēsur*, OHG. *keisar*, ON. *keisari*, Goth. *kaisar*.

kale, kail cabbage XIII (*cale*); cabbage broth XV. north. var. of COLE. Hence **kailyard** cabbage-garden (YARD¹), familiar since 1895 as an epithet of fiction and its authors (*literature of the k., k. school*) describing, with much use of the vernacular, common life in Scotland.

kaleidoscope XIX. f. Gr. *kalós* beautiful + *eîdos* shape + -SCOPE.

kalends see CALENDS.

kali prickly saltwort, *Salsola kali* XVI; †soda ash XVIII; (*lemon k.*) mixture of tartaric acid and bicarbonate of soda XIX. - Arab. *ḳily*; see ALKALI.

kalmia genus of Amer. evergreen shrubs. XVIII. modL., f. name of Peter *Kalm*, a pupil of Linnaeus; see -IA¹.

kampong Malay village. XIX. See COMPOUND².

kangaroo XVIII. Said by Capt. James Cook (1770) and Joseph Banks (1770) to have been a native Australian name (*kangooroo*), which is supported by some later writers, but denied by others.

Kantian pert. to Immanuel *Kant* (1724-1804), G. philosopher; see -IAN. XIX (*Kantianism*).

kaolin fine white porcelain clay. XVIII. - F. - Chinese *kao-ling* name of a mountain (*kao* high, *ling* hill) in N. China, whence the stuff was orig. obtained.

kapok fine cotton wool from the seeds of a tree. XVIII (*capoc*). ult. - Malay *kapok*.

kaput finished, done for. - G. *kaputt* broken, done for - F. *capot* (*faire c.* 'capsize' or 'beat at cards by taking all the tricks'), of uncert. orig.

Karaite member of a Jewish sect which bases its tenets on literal interpretation of the scriptures. XVIII. f. Heb. *ḳ^erā'īm* scripturalists, f. *ḳārâ* read; see -ITE.

karma fate, destiny (as determined by one's actions in a former state of existence). XIX. Skr. *karma-* action, effect, fate, f. IE. **qer-* make.

kar(r)oo barren tract of land in S. Africa. XVIII. of Hottentot orig.

karyo- comb. form of Gr. *káruon* nut, kernel, in biol. terms referring to the nucleus of a cell. XIX.

katabolism (biol.) destructive metabolism. XIX. f. Gr. *katabolḗ*, f. *katabállein* throw down; see CATA-, -ISM.

katydid (U.S.) insect of the locust family, producing a noise which the name is taken to echo. XVIII.

kava intoxicating beverage. XIX. of S.W. Polynesian orig.

kayak XVIII. - Eskimo.

kebab XVII (*cabob*). - Urdu (Pers.) - Arab. *kabāb*; also through Turk.

kedgeree Indian dish of rice with condiments; dish made from cold fish, etc., served hot. XVII (*kits-*, *ketch-*, *kichery*). - Hindi *khicṛī*, f. Skr. *khiccā-* dish of rice and peas.

keel¹ lowest longitudinal timber (or iron plating) of a ship XIV; (nat. hist.) central ridge XVI. ME. *kele* - ON. *kjǫlr* :- Gmc **keluz*. So **keel-haul, -hale** XVII. - Du. *kielhalen*. See HALE².

keel² flat-bottomed vessel, lighter. XIV. ME. *kele* - MLG. *kēl*, MDu. *kiel* ship, boat = OE. *ċēol*, OS., OHG. *kiol* (Du., G. *kiel*), ON. *kjóll* :- Gmc. **keulaz*.

keelson see KELSON.

keen¹ †wise; †brave, fierce OE.; having a sharp edge or point; pungent, biting XIII; ardent, intense XIV; penetrating, acute XVIII. OE. *cēne* = OS. **kōni*, MLG. *kōne* (Du. *koen*), OHG. *kuoni* (G. *kühn*) bold, brave, ON. *kœnn* skilful, expert :- Gmc. **kōnjaz*, which has no certain cogns.

keen² lament. XIX. - Ir. *caoinim* I wail.

keep pt., pp. *kept* A. †seize, hold, watch (for); pay regard to, observe OE.; B. take care of, guard XII; preserve, maintain; withhold, restrain XIV; C. reside, dwell (in) XIV. Late OE. *cēpan*, pt. *cēpte*, of which no cogns. are known. Its sense-development has been infl. by its being used to render L. *servare*, with its comps. *con-*, *ob-*, *præ-*, *reservare*. Hence sb. A. †care, heed; B. donjon of a castle XIII; C. act of keeping, being kept XVIII; sustenance XIX. (The origin of B is not certain.) **keepsake** thing kept for the SAKE of the giver XVIII; literary annual containing collections of tales, poems, etc., intended as a gift, common in early XIX.

keg XVII. dial. var. of north. *cag* (XV) - Icel. *kaggi*.

kelp large seaweed XIV; calcined ashes of seaweed XVII. ME. *culp(e)*, of unkn. orig.

kelpie water-sprite of the Scottish Lowlands. XVIII. of unkn. orig.

kelson, keelson line of timber inside a ship parallel to the keel. XVII. ME. *kelswayn*, *-sweyn*, *-syng*, mod. *kelsine*, perh. points to an original **kelswin*, the nearest parallel to which, and the prob. source, is LG. *kielswīn* (whence also G. *kielschwein*, Da. *kølsvin*, Sw. *kölsvin*), f. *kiel* KEEL¹ + (prob.) *swīn* SWINE, used, like *cat*, *dog*, *horse*, for a timber. The form *keelson* is due to assim. to KEEL¹.

kempt see UNKEMPT.

ken †make known OE.; (arch., dial.) know XIII. OE. *cennan* = OS. *kennian* (Du. *kennen*), (O)HG. *kennen*, ON. *kenna*, Goth. *kannjan*, f. Gmc. **kann-* know, CAN². Prop. causative, 'make known', which was the only use in OE. and Gothic, but in Gmc. langs. gen. it acquired the sense 'know' at an early period; in Eng. this use may be immed. due to Norse; in Sc. it has displaced *knaw*, KNOW. Hence **ken** sb. †measure of distance at sea; range of vision or perception. XVI.

kennel¹ house for the shelter of a house-dog or hounds. XIV. - AN. **kenil* = OF. *chenil*, It. *canile* :- medL. *canīle*, f. *canis* dog (cf. HOUND). Hence vb. be in, put into, a kennel. XVI.

kennel² street gutter. XVI. Later form of *can(n)el* watercourse (XIII), gutter (XIV) - ONF. *canel* = OF. *chanel* CHANNEL¹.

kenosis (theol.) renunciation by Jesus Christ of attributes of the divine nature in the Incarnation. XIX. - Gr. *kénōsis* emptying, f. *kenoûn* (f. *kénos*) empty, with ref. to *heautòn ekénōse* 'he emptied himself' (Phil. 2: 7). So **kenotic** XIX.

Kentish OE. *Centisċ*, f. *Cent* - L. *Cantium*, Gr. *Kántion* (*ákron*), f. OCelt. **kanto-* (i) rim, border, or (ii) white; see -ISH¹.

kepi French military cap. XIX. F. *képi* - Swiss G. *käppi*, dim. of *kappe* cap.

kerb edging of stone for a raised path, etc. XVIII (*kerb-stone*). var. of CURB with quasi-phonetic sp.

kerchief (arch.) cloth head-covering. XIII. ME. *c(o)urchef*, *kerchif* - AN. *courchef* = (O)F. *couvre-*, *cuevre-chef*, f. *couvrir* COVER + *chief* head (see CHIEF). The form *kerchief* is from the var. *cuevrechef* (cf. ME. *kever* cover, from *cuevr-*, stressed stem of *couvrir*). Hence **handkerchief** XVI, **neckerchief** XIV (*necke couerchef*, *neckerchef*).

kerf cut, spec. of a saw. OE. *cyrf* (ME. *kirf*, *kerf*) :- Gmc. **kurƀiz*, f. **kurƀ-* **kerƀ-* CARVE; cf. ON. *kurfr* chip and ME., mod. dial. *carf* (continuing ME. *kerf*).

kermes female of the insect *Kermes ilicis*, formerly supposed to be a berry; red dye-stuff obtained therefrom; (*k. oak*) evergreen oak on which it lives XVI; (*k. mineral*) red sulphide of antimony XVIII. - F. *kermès* - Arab. (Pers.) *ḳirmiz* (cf. CRIMSON).

kermis fair, carnival. XVI. - Du. *kermis*, †*-misse*, f. *kerk* CHURCH + *misse* MASS¹; orig. feast of dedication of a church accompanied by a fair.

kern¹ light-armed Irish foot-soldier; peasant. XIV. - Ir. *ceithern* :- OIr. *ceitern* band of foot-soldiers.

kern² part of a metal type extending beyond the body or shank. XVII. perh. for **carn* - F. *carne* corner, salient angle, Norman-Picard var. of OF. *charne* - L. *cardō*, *cardin-* hinge.

kernel †seed, pip; inner edible part of a nut; (dial.) enlarged gland OE.; nucleus, core XVI. OE. *cyrnel*, dim. of *corn* seed, CORN¹; see -EL¹. Present sp. appears XIV as a var. of north. and midl. *kirnel*.

kerosene XIX. irreg. f. Gr. *kērós* wax + -ENE.

kersey kind of coarse cloth. XIV. prob. f. name of *Kersey* in Suffolk (cf. AL. *panni cersegi* XIII, *carsea* XV, AN. *drap de kersy* XIV).

kerseymere twilled woollen cloth. XVIII. alt. of *cassimere*, early var. of CASHMERE, by assoc. with prec.

kestrel XV. Earliest form *castrell*, perh. for **casserell* - dial. var. *casserelle* of F. *crécerelle*, †*cresserelle*, f. synon. *crécelle* rattle, kestrel, perh. ult. of imit. orig.

ketch XVII. Earlier *cache* (XV), perh. f. CATCH.

ketchup XVIII (earlier *catchup* XVII, *catsup* XVIII). - Chinese (Amoy) *kōe-chiap*, *kē-tsiap* brine of fish; cf. Malay *kechap*.

kettle XIII. - ON. *ketill* = OE. *ċetel*, WS. *ċietel* (ME., dial. *chetel*), OS. (Du.) *ketel*, OHG. *kezzil* (G. *kessel*), Goth. **katils* :- Gmc. **katilaz* - L. *catillus*, dim. of *catīnus* deep vessel for serving or cooking food. Hence **kettledrum** XVI.

key instrument to lock and unlock. OE. *cǣġ(e)* = OFris. *kei*, *kay*; of unkn. orig.

Keys pl. of KEY in spec. application to the 24 members forming the elective branch of the legislature of the Isle of Man, more fully *House of Keys*. XV.

khaki dull-brownish yellow; fabric of this colour. XIX. - Urdu *ḵākī* dusty, f. *ḵāk* (- Pers.) dust.

khan title of rulers (later of officials, etc.) in countries of the East. XIV. Early forms *caan*, *c(h)an(e)* - OF. *chan* or medL. *ca(a)nus*, *canis* - E. Turkish (hence Arab., Pers.) *khān* lord, prince, alt. of *khāḳān*.

khedive title of viceroy of Egypt. XIX. - F. *khédive*, ult. - Pers. *ḵedīv* prince.

kibble large bucket used in mining. XVII. - G. *kübel* (cf. OHG. *miluh-chubilī* milk-pail) = OE. *cyfel* - medL. *cupellus*, *-a* corn-measure, drinking-vessel, f. *cuppa* CUP.

kibe chilblain. XIV. of uncert. orig.; cf. W. *cibi*, *cibwst*.

kibosh in phr. *put the k. on* dispose of finally; sb. (app. assoc. with *bosh*) nonsense. XIX. of unkn. orig.

kick strike with the foot. XIV. ME. *kike*, of unkn. orig. Hence sb. XVI.

kickshaw(s) fancy dish in cookery; trifle, gewgaw. XVI. - F. *quelque chose* something.

kid¹ young of a goat XII; skin of a kid; (young) child XVI. - ON. *kið* :- **kiðjam*, rel. to OHG. *chizzī*, *kizzīn* (G. *kitze*), f. Gmc. **kið-*, of which no cogns. are known. Hence **kiddy** young goat XVI; (sl., colloq.) little child XIX.

kid² small tub. XVIII. perh. var. of KIT¹.

kid³ (sl.) hoax, humbug. XIX. perh. 'make a kid of', f. KID¹; *kiddy* has been similarly used. Hence **kid** sb. humbug.

kidnapper, U.S. **-naper** one who steals children (and others), orig. to provide servants and labourers for the American plantations. XVII. f. KID¹ + *napper*, cant word (XVII) for 'thief' (f. *nap*, var. of NAB + -ER¹). Hence vb. XVII.

kidney organ that secretes urine XIV; transf. temperament, nature XVI. of obscure orig. ME. sg. *kidnei* and pl. *kidneiren* suggest that the word was a comp. of *ei*, pl. *eiren* (OE. *ǣġ*, pl. *ǣġru*) EGG¹, the pl. *kidneires* being partly analogical, partly due to assoc. with ME. and dial. *nere(s)* kidney(s) :- OE. **nēore*, corr. to OHG.

nioro m. (G. *niere* fem.), ON. *nýra*, rel. to Gr. *nephrós* kidney, scrotum, L. *nefrōnes* loins. On the other hand, if the first el. is (dial.) *kid* pod (:- OE. **cydda* :- **kuddja-*; see COD[1]), the word may have been OE. **cyd(e)nēora*, the ME. repr. of which was assoc. with *ei*, *eiren*, the shape of the kidney assisting the comparison.

kier vat. XVI (earlier in combs. *boiling-*, *brewing-*, *gyle-*, *gyling-*). - ON. *ker* vessel, tub = OHG. *char*, Goth. *kas*; of unkn. orig.

kilderkin cask for liquids, fish, etc.; measure of capacity. XIV. ME. *kilderkyn*, alt. of *kyn(d)erkyn* - MDu. *kindekijn*, *kinne-* (Du. *kinnetje*), f. medL. *quintāle* (see QUINTAL).

kill †strike, beat XIII; put to death XIV. ME. *kulle*, *kille*, *kelle*; these vars. point to an OE. **cyllan* :- Gmc. **kuljan*, rel. by gradation to **kwaljan* kill, QUELL.

kiln OE. *cylene* - L. *culīna* kitchen, cooking-stove.

kilo- - F. (1795), arbitrarily f. Gr. *khílioi* thousand, in weights and measures, as *kilogramme* (abbrev. *kilo*), *kilometre*; hence in *kilowatt*.

kilt skirt of Highland dress. XVIII. f. north. dial. *kilt* vb. gird or tuck up, of Scand. orig. (cf. Sw. dial. *kilta* swathe, Da. *kilte (op)* tuck up, OIcel. *kilting*, *kjalta* skirt, lap).

kimono long Jap. robe with sleeves; in Eur. use, form of dressing-gown. XIX. - Jap., f. *ki-* wear + *mono* thing.

kin family, race; class, kind. OE. *cyn(n)* = OFris. *kin*, *ken*, *kon*, OS. *kunni* (Du. *kunne*), OHG. *kunni*, ON. *kyn*, Goth. *kuni* :- Gmc. **kunjam*, f. weak grade of **kin-* **kan-* **kun-* :- IE. **ĝen-* **ĝon-* **ĝn-* produce (whence Gr. *génos*, L. *genus* race, kind, sex, GENUS, Gr. *gígnesthai* become, L. *gignere* beget). Hence **kinsfolk** XV, **kinship** XIX, **kinsman** XII, **kinswoman** XIV.

-kin suffix forming dims. - MDu. *-kijn*, *-ken*, MLG. *-kīn* = OHG., OS. *-kīn* (G. *-chen*); of WGmc. extent, but not in OE.; first found (XIII) in personal names; formations on common nouns appeared in XIV, but they are not frequent till XVI (*boykin*, *ladykin*, *lambkin*); some are - Du. (*catkin*, *manikin*); others are of obscure orig. (*jerkin*). See also -KINS.

kind[1] †birth, descent; nature; manner; race, kin; class, genus, species. OE. *cynd(e)*, earlier *ġecynd(e)* :- Gmc. **ʒakundiz*, *-jam*, f. **ʒa-* Y- + **kunjam* KIN + **-diz* :- IE. **-tis* (abstr. suffix). Hence **kindly** adj. †natural; †lawful OE.; goodnatured XIV; adv. †naturally OE.; goodnaturedly XIII. OE. *ġecyndeliċ*, *-līċe*.

kind[2] †natural, native OE.; †well-born, well-bred; naturally well-disposed XIII; showing benevolence XIV. OE. *ġecynde* :- Gmc. **ʒakundjaz*, f. **ʒakundiz* KIND[1]; the pref. was dropped in early ME.

kindergarten XIX. - G., 'children's garden', f. g. pl. of *kind* child + *garten* GARDEN.

kindle set fire to. XII. f. ON. *kynda* + -LE[3].

kindred relationship by blood; body of persons so related, kin. XII. ME. *cun-*, *kinrede(n)*, f. KIN + *-rēd(e)*, -RED condition. ME. has also *kindreden* (perh. f. KIND[1]), but the present form appears to have arisen from intercalation of *d* between *n* and *r*, as in *thunder*.

kine (arch., dial.) cattle. XIII. ME. *cun*, *kyne*, *ke(e)n*, based on OE. *cȳna*, g. pl. of *cū* COW[1].

kinetic pert. to motion. XIX. - Gr. *kīnētikós*, f. *kīnein* move; see -IC.

king OE. *cyning*, later *cyng*, *cing* = OFris. *kin-*, *kon-*, *kening*, OS., OHG. *kuning* (Du. *koning*, G. *könig*), :- Gmc. **kuniŋgaz* (ON. *konungr* has a var. form of the suffix), prob. f. **kunjam* KIN + **-iŋgaz* -ING[3], as if 'scion of the (noble) race'. Hence **kingdom** †kingship OE.; realm XIII. OE. *cyningdōm*. **kingfisher** XVI (†*king's-* XV). In comb. applied to large or principal features, as *king-bolt* (XIX), *-post* (XVIII). **king's evil** scrofula, for which the sovereign 'touched'. XIV.

kink twist or curl in rope, etc., XVII; mental twist (orig. U.S.) XIX. orig. naut. - (M)LG. *kinke* (Du. *kink*).

-kins dim. suffix, var. of -KIN (from XVI) in certain oath-words, as *bodikins*, *lakins*, *maskins*, *pittikins*, and in words like *babykins*, *boykins*, *lambkins*.

kiosk open pavilion or summer-house XVII; light structure for sale of newspapers, etc., XIX. - F. *kiosque* - Turk. *köşk* pavilion - Pers. *kūšk* palace.

kipper A. (?) male salmon in the spawning season OE.; B. salmon, herring, etc., cured by rubbing with salt and drying XVIII. Of obscure history; identical in form with OE. *cypera* (*-e*?) (once, in collocation with *leax* salmon), ME. *kypre*, *kiper* (XIV), *kepper* (XVI), used app. in sense B. Hence vb. cure (fish) in the above manner. XVIII.

kirk (north. and Sc.) church. XII. - ON. *kirkja* - OE. *ċir(i)ċe* CHURCH.

kirsch(wasser) liqueur made from wild cherries crushed. XIX. - G. *kirsch(en)wasser*, f. *kirsche* cherry + *wasser* WATER.

kirtle (obs. or dial.) man's tunic or coat; (arch. or dial.) woman's gown or skirt. OE. *cyrtel* :- Gmc. **kurtilaz*, f. **kurt-*, usu. taken to be - L. *curtus* short; see CURT, -LE[1].

kismet fate. XIX. - Turk. - Arab. (Pers.) *ḳismat* portion, fate, f. *ḳasama* divide, apportion.

kiss vb. OE. *cyssan* (pt. *cyste*, pp. *cyssed*) = OS. *kussian* (Du. *kussen*), OHG. *kussen* (G. *küssen*), ON. *kyssa* :- Gmc. **kussjan*, f. **kussaz* a kiss, whence OE. *coss* (to XVI), OS. *kos*, *kus* (Du. *kus*), (O)HG. *kuss*, ON. *koss*. Hence sb. XIV, superseding *coss*.

kit[1] circular wooden hooped vessel XIV; soldier's necessaries packed in a knapsack; outfit; set, lot XVIII. - MDu. *kitte* (Du. *kit* tankard), of unkn. orig.

kit[2] (arch.) small fiddle. XVI. perh. deduced from the first syll. of L. *cithara*, Gr. *kithárā* CITHER.

kitchen OE. *cyċene* = OS. **kukina* (MLG. *kökene*, MDu. *cokene*, Du. *keuken*), OHG. *chuhhina* (MHG. *küchen*, G. *küche*) - **cocīna* pop. var. of late L. *coquīna*, f. *coquere* COOK.

kite bird of prey OE.; toy to be flown XVII. OE. *cȳta*, prob. of imit. orig.

kith †knowledge; †native place; †one's friends, fellow-countrymen, neighbours OE.; *kith and kin* country and kinsfolk, (in mod. use) relatives generally XIV. OE. *cȳð(ð)*, earlier *cȳððu* = OHG. *chundida* :- Gmc. **kunþiþō*, f. **kunþ-* known; see UNCOUTH.

kitten XIV. ME. *kitoun, ketoun* - AN. **kitoun*, **ketoun*, var. of OF. *chitoun, chetoun* (mod. *chaton*), dim. of *chat* CAT; the ending was assim. to -EN[1]. Hence **kit**[2] XVI.

kittiwake XVII. imit.

kittle (orig. Sc. and north. dial.) ticklish, risky, delicate. XVI. f. *kittle* vb. tickle, prob. of ON. origin, corr. to late OE. *kitelung* 'titillatio', noun of action from a vb. repr. by OS. *kitilōn* (Du. *kittelen*), MLG. *ketelen*, OHG. *kizzilōn, kuzzilōn* (G. *kitzeln*), ON. *kitla*.

kiwi XIX. - Maori.

klepht one of the Greeks who refused to submit to the Turks after the conquest of Greece in XV; brigand. XIX. - modGr. *kléphtēs* = Gr. *kléptēs* thief; cf. next.

kleptomania XIX. f. *klepto-*, comb. form of Gr. *kléptēs* thief, rel. to *kléptein* = L. *clepere*, Goth. *hlifan* steal; see MANIA.

klipspringer S. Afr. antelope. XVIII. - Afrikaans, f. Du. *klip* rock + *springer*, agent-noun (see -ER[1]) of *springen* SPRING[2].

kloof (in S. Africa) ravine. XVIII. - Du. *kloof*, MDu. *clove* = OHG. *klobo* (G. *kloben*), etc. :- Gmc. **kluƀan-* (cf. CLEAVE[1]).

knack trick, dodge XIV; dexterous faculty; †toy, knick-knack XVI. prob. identical with *knack* sharp blow or sound (XIV); ult. of imit. orig., but perh. immed. - Du., LG. *knak*.

knacker A. (dial.) saddler XVI; B. dealer in old horses, horse-slaughterer, etc.; C. (dial. and sl.) old worn-out horse XIX. In A perh. orig. maker of small articles belonging to harness (f. KNACK + -ER[1]); the relation of the senses is obscure.

knapsack XVII. - MLG. *knapsack*, Du. *knapzak*; the first el. is held to be identical with G. *knappen* bite, eat, and the second is SACK[1].

knapweed XV (*knopweed*). f. KNOP + WEED[1]; alt. to *knap-* XVI.

knave †boy; †male servant OE.; base fellow XIII; lowest court card of a suit XVI. OE. *cnafa* = OHG. *knabo* (G. *knabe* boy) :- WGmc. **knaƀan-*, rel. obscurely to synon. OE. *cnapa* = OS. *cnapo*, and OHG. *knappo* (G. *knappe* page, squire). Hence **knavery** XVI, **knavish** XIV.

knead OE. str. vb. *cnedan* = OS. *knedan* (Du. *kneden*), OHG. *knetan* (G. *kneten*); WGmc., f. **kned-* **knad-*, of which another grade appears in ON. *knoða*. Weak inflexions appear XIV.

knee OE. *cnēo(w)* = OS. *knio* (Du. *knie*), OHG. *kniu, kneo* (G. *knie*), ON. *kné*, Goth. *kniu* :- Gmc. **knewam* :- IE. **ĝnewom*, f. base **ĝneu-* **ĝenu-* **ĝonu-* (cf. L. *genu*, Gr. *gónu* knee). So **kneel** (pt., pp. *kneeled, knelt*). OE. *cnēowlian*, corr. to (M)LG. *knēlen*, Du. *knielen*. The form *knelt* is of recent orig.

knell sound of a bell struck or rung. OE. *cnyll*, rel. to *cnyllan* **knell** vb. †bang, knock, ring a bell; the present form appears to date from *c.*1500 and may be due to assoc. with *bell*. Cf. MHG. *erknellen* resound, G. *knall, knallen*, Du. *knal, knallen*, applied to banging or cracking noises.

knickerbockers loose-fitting breeches. XIX. f. name of Diedrich *Knickerbocker*, the pretended author of Washington Irving's 'History of New York' (1809). The name is said to have been given to the garment from its resemblance to the knee-breeches of the Dutchman in Cruikshank's illustrations to the History. abbrev. **knickers** XIX.

knick-knack †pretty trick or artifice; light dainty article, trinket. XVII. redupl. of KNACK, with alternation of vowel as in *dilly-dally, riff-raff*, etc.

knife sb. XI. Late OE. *cnīf* - ON. *knífr* = OFris., MLG. *knīf*, MDu. *cnijf* (Du. *knijf*) :- Gmc. **knīƀaz*, of uncert. orig. Hence vb. XIX.

knight †boy, youth OE.; military follower; name of a rank, orig. in military service XI; *knight of the shire* XIV. OE. *cniht* boy, youth, man of arms, hero = OS. *knecht*, OHG. *kneht* (Du., G. *knecht*) :- WGmc. **kneχta*, of unkn. orig. Hence **knight-errant** XIV. **knighthood** XIII (OE. *cnihthād* boyhood). **knightly** XIV (OE. *cnihtlić* boyish).

knit †tie in or with a knot OE.; draw close together XIV; form a close texture of yarn or thread XVI. OE. *cnyttan* = MLG., MDu. *knutten* (G. dial. *knütten*) :- WGmc. **knuttjan*, f. **knuttan-* KNOT[1].

knob small rounded lump or mass XIV; knoll; small lump of coal, etc. XVII; the head (see NOB[1]) XVIII. - MLG. *knobbe* knot, knob, bud; cf. Flem. *knobbe(n)* lump of bread, etc., Du. *knobbel* bump, knob, knot.

knobkerry stick with a knobbed head in S. Africa. XIX. f. KNOB + *kerrie* (- Hottentot *kirri, keeri* stick), after Afrikaans *knopkierie*.

knock strike with a sounding blow. OE. *cnocian* = MHG. *knochen*, ON. *knoka*; f. imit. base (cf. the similar and synon. OE. *cnucian*, MLG. *knaken*, Sw. *knaka*).

knoll[1] †summit of a hill; hillock, mound. OE. *cnoll*, corr. to MDu., MHG. *knolle* clod (Du. *knol* turnip, tuber, G. *knolle(n)* clod, lump, tumour), ON. *knollr* mountain summit, perh. :- Gmc. **knuðlō*, f. base of KNOT[1].

knoll[2] toll, ring a knell. XV. f. late ME. *knoll* church bell, tolling, perh. imit. alt. of KNELL.

knop small round protuberance; bud of a flower. XIV. prob. - MLG., MDu. *knoppe* (Du. *knop*) = (O)HG. *knopf* knob, knot, button; of unkn. orig.

knot[1] intertwining of parts of rope, etc. (fig. something intricate) OE.; hard lump XIII; thickened tissue of a plant; cluster or small group XIV. OE. *cnotta* = Du. *knot*, MLG. *knotte*, MHG. *knotze* knob, knot :- WGmc. **knuttan-*; cf. OHG. *knodo, knoto* (G. *knoten*), ON. *knútr* knot, *knǫttr* ball. Hence **knot** vb. XVI, **knotted** XII.

knot[2] red-breasted sandpiper. XVI. of unkn. orig.; later vars. were *knat, gnat*.

knout whip, scourge. XVIII. - F. - Russ. *knut* - Icel. *knútr* (see KNOT[1]).

know pt. *knew*, pp. *known* perceive, recognize, distinguish XI; be acquainted or familiar with; be aware of or conversant with, apprehend as fact or truth XII. Late OE. (rare) str. vb. *cnāwan*, earlier *ġecnāwan*, corr. to OHG. *-cnāen*, ON. pres. ind. sg. *kná*. In the earliest OE. and in

OHG. this vb. appears only in comps.; it is absent from LG. and Du. areas and from Gothic; in ON. it had lost the pres. inf. and meant 'can', (as an aux.) 'do', and in OHG. it had lost the orig. str. pt. and pp. An orig. redupl. vb. based on IE. **ĝn- *ĝnē- *ĝnō-*, repr. also by CAN², KEN, and L. *nōscere, cognōscere*, Gr. *gignṓskein*, OSl. *znati*, Skr. *jānā́ti* know.

knowledge †confession; fact of knowing, acquaintance. XIII. In earliest use north. (*knaulage*), later in gen. use *knowleche, -lache*; prob. f. **knowledge** vb. acknowledge, recognize (XIII), early ME. *cnaw-, cnouleche* :- OE. **cnāwlǣċan* (*cnāwelāċing* is recorded), f. (*ġe*)*cnāwan* know + *-lǣċan*, f. *lāc* (see -LOCK). Hence **knowledg(e)able** †(f. the vb.) recognizable XVII; (f. the sb.; orig. dial.) well informed XIX.

knub small lump or swelling. XVI. - MLG. *knubbe*, var. of *knobbe* KNOB.

knuckle †end of a bone at a joint XIV; spec. bone at a finger-joint XV. ME. *knokel* - MLG. *knökel*, corr. to MDu. *knokel, knökel* (Du. *kneukel*), MHG. *knuchel, knüchel* (G. *knöchel*), dim. of the base of MLG. *knoke* (Du. *knok*), MHG. *knoche* (G. *knochen*) bone.

koala XIX. - Austral. aboriginal *kūlla, kūlā*. The current form *koala* arose perh. as a misreading of *koola*, which was formerly current.

kobold (in G. folk-lore) familiar spirit, goblin. XIX. - G. *kobold*, MHG. *kobolt* = MDu. *cobout* (Du. *kabouter*), perh. for **kobwalt*, f. *kobe* house, COVE¹ + stem of *walten* rule (see WIELD); cf. OE. *cofgodas, -godu* 'house-gods', lares and penates.

kodak camera. XIX. **P.**; arbitrary word invented by George Eastman as a trade-mark, patented 1888.

kohl powder used to darken the eyelids. XVIII. - Arab. *kuḥl*; cf. ALCOHOL.

kohlrabi cabbage with turnip-like stem. XIX. - G. - (with assim. to *kohl* COLE) It. *cauli* or *cavoli rape*, pl. of *cavolo rapa*, repr. medL. *caulorapa*; see COLE, RAPE².

kopje, koppie small hill in S. Africa. XIX. - Du. *kopje*, Afrikaans *koppie*, dim. of *kop* head = OE. *copp*, (O)HG. *kopf*.

koran sacred book of Islam. XVIII (*currawn*). - Arab. *ḳur'ān* recitation, f. *ḳara'a* read.

kosher adj. and sb. of meat prepared according to Jewish law. XIX. - Heb. *kāshēr* right.

kotow, kowtow Chinese gesture of respect by touching the ground with the forehead. XIX. - Chinese *k'o-t'ou*, f. *k'o* knock + *t'ou* head. Hence vb. act obsequiously. XIX.

koumiss fermented liquor made from mare's milk. XVII (*chumis*; earlier in corrupt forms *cosmos, cosmus*). - F. *koumis*, G. *kumyss*, Pol. *kumys*, Russ. *kumýs*, of Turkic orig.

kraal Central or S. Afr. village; cattle enclosure XVIII. - Afrikaans - Pg. *curral* CORRAL.

Kremlin citadel in a Russian town. XVII. - F., ult. f. Russ. *kreml'*; of uncert. orig.

kriegspiel game simulating movements in warfare. XIX. - G., 'war-game'.

kris, creese Malay dagger. XVI. ult. - Malay *kĕris* (through such forms as Du. *kris*, Sp., Pg. *cris*, F. *criss*).

krummhorn obs. wind-instrument. XVII. - G., 'crooked horn'.

krypton (chem.) rare gas. - Gr. *kruptón*, n. of *kruptós* hidden.

kudos XVIII. - Gr. *kûdos*.

Ku-Klux-Klan XIX. Fanciful invention said to be based on Gr. *kúklos* circle, CYCLE, and CLAN.

kukri curved knife used by Gurkhas. XIX. - Hindi *kukrī*.

kummel prop. **kümmel.** German liqueur flavoured with cummin. XIX. - G. *kümmel* :- OHG. *kumil* CUMMIN, var. of *kumīn* - L. (Rom.) *cumīnum*.

kursaal public building for the use of visitors at a health resort. XIX. - G., f. *kur* - L. *cūra* CURE + *saal* hall, room.

kvass fermented beverage of Russia. XVI (*quass*). Russ. *kvas*, rel. L. *cāseus* CHEESE.

kyanize treat (wood) so as to prevent decay. XIX. f. name of the inventor J. H. *Kyan* + -IZE.

kyloe One of a small long horned breed of Highland cattle. XIX. Also locally *kyley*, etc., repr. old vars. of the Northumberland place-name *Kyloe* (OE. *cȳ-lēah* cow pasture).

kyrie XVI; short for **kyrie eleison** XIV. - medL., repr. of Gr. *Kúrie eléēson* Lord, have mercy.

L

la see LAH.

laager encampment. XIX. - Afrikaans *lager* (now *laer*) = G. *lager*, Du. *leger*; see LAIR, LEAGUER.

labarum Roman standard of the late Empire. XVII. - late L., of unkn. orig.

labdanum XVI. med. form of L. *lādanum* (see LADANUM).

labefaction overthrow, downfall. XVII. f. *labefact-*, pp. stem of L. *labefacere* weaken, f. *lābī* fall + *facere* make, DO[1]; see -TION.

label †narrow band or strip XIV; narrow strip carrying the seal of a document XVI; slip containing name or description of an object XVII; dripstone XIX. - OF. *label* ribbon, fillet (now *lambeau* rag), perh. - Gmc. form rel. to LAP[1], with dim. suffix. Hence vb. XVI.

labial XVI. - medL. *labiālis*, f. *labia* lips; see LIP, -AL[1]. So **labiate** XVIII. - modL.

labile XV. - late L. *lābilis*, f. *lābī* fall; see -ILE.

laboratory XVII. - medL. *labōrātōrium*, f. *labōrāre*, *-āt-*; see next and -ORY[1]. Abbrev. **lab** XIX.

labour, U.S. **labor** toil, work XIII; travail of childbirth XVI. - OF. *labo(u)r* (mod. *labeur* ploughing) - L. *labor*, *-ōr-* exertion, trouble, suffering, perh. orig. burden under which one staggers, rel. to *labāre* slip. So **labour** vb. XIV. - (O)F. *labourer* (now chiefly, plough). **labourer** XIV. - (O)F. *laboureur*; see -ER[1], -ER[2]. **laborious** XIV. - (O)F. *laborieux*.

laburnum XVI. - L., prob. of foreign orig.

labyrinth XVI. - F. *labyrinthe* or L. *labyrinthus* - Gr. *labúrinthos*, of non-Hellenic orig.

lac dark-red resin, red dye. XVI (*lack(e)*, *lacca*). - (through Du. *lak*, F. *laque*, or Sp., Pg. *laca*, It. *lacca*) Hind. *lākh* :- Prakrit *lakkhā-* :- Skr. *lākṣá*. Cf. LAKE[2], SHELLAC.

lace †noose, snare; string or cord for tying XIII; ornamental braid; openwork of cotton, silk, etc. XVI. ME. *la(a)s*, (later) *lace* - OF. *laz*, *las* (mod. *lacs* noose) :- Rom. **lacium*, for L. *laqueus* noose, rel. to *lax* deception, *lacere*, *-licere* entice. So **lace** vb. XIII. - OF. *lacier* (mod. *lacer*).

lacerate XVI. f. pp. stem of L. *lacerāre*, f. *lacer* mangled, torn; see -ATE[3].

lacertian pert. to the lizards. XIX. f. L. *lacerta* LIZARD + -IAN. So **lacertine**.

laches remissness, neglect XIV; (leg.) negligence in the performance of a legal duty XVI. - AN. *laches(se)* = OF. *laschesse* (mod. *lâchesse* cowardice), f. *lasche* (mod. *lâche*) :- Rom. **lascus*, for L. *laxus* LAX; see -ESS[2].

lachrymal pert. to tears. XVI. - medL. *lachrymālis*, *lacrimālis*, f. *lacrima*, earlier *lacruma* tear, rel. to Gr. *dákru*; see -AL[1]. So **lachrymatory** tear-vase. XVII. **lachrymose** tearful. XVII. - L.

laciniate (nat. hist.) jagged, slashed. XVIII. f. L. *lacīnia* tuft, fringe, skirt of a garment + -ATE[2].

lack vb. †be wanting XII; †blame, disparage XIII; be without XIV; sb. †defect, fault XII; want, need XIV. perh. f. a Gmc. base **lak-* orig. expressing 'deficiency', 'defect', which may have been repr. in OE.; cf. MLG., MDu. *lak* deficiency, fault (Du. *lak* calumny), *laken* be wanting, blame, ON. *lakr* defective; but some uses may be of Scand. or LG. orig.

lackadaisical marked by vapid sentiment. XVIII. f. *lackadaisy* (XVIII), extended form of *lack-a-day* (XVII), aphetic of *alack-a-day*, earlier ALACK *the day* + -ICAL.

lackey, lacquey XVI. Formerly also *alakay* (XVI, Sc.) - F. *laquais*, †*alaquais*, of uncert orig. Hence vb. XVI.

laconic (*L-*) Lacedaemonian, Spartan; brief of speech. XVI. - L. *Lacōnicus* - Gr. *Lakōnikós*, f. *Lákōn* member of the Spartan race, renowned for brevity of speech; see -IC.

lacquer, U.S. **lacker** †lac (the dye) XVI; varnish made from a solution of shellac in alcohol XVII. - F. †*lacre* kind of sealing-wax, Sp., Pg. *lacre*; app. unexpl. var. or extension of Sp., Pg. *laca* LAC.

lacrim-, lacrym- see LACHRYMAL, etc.

lacrosse XVII. f. F. (*le jeu de*) *la crosse* '(the game of) the hooked stick' ((O)F. *crosse* prob. of Gmc. orig.; cf. CRUTCH).

lact- stem of L. *lac*, *lact-* milk (cf. Gr. *gála*, *galakt-*; see GALAXY) in derivs.: **lactation** XVII (f. L. *lactāre*), **lacteal** XVII (f. L. *lacteus*), **lacteous** XVII, **lactescent** XVII (f. L. *lactēscere*), **lactic** (chem.) XVIII (whence **lactate** XVIII), **lactiferous** XVII, irreg. comb. form **lacto-** XIX, **lactose** XIX.

lacuna XVII. - L. *lacūna* pool, cavity, f. *lacus* LAKE[1].

lacustrine pert. to a lake. XIX. f. L. *lacus* LAKE[1]; see -INE[1].

lad †serving-man, varlet XIII; youth, young fellow XVI. ME. *ladde*, of unkn. orig. Hence **laddie** XVI.

ladanum XVI. - L. *lādanum* - Gr. *lḗdanon*, *lēdanon*, f. *lêdon* mastic.

ladder OE. *hlǣd(d)er* = MDu. *lēdere* (Du. *leer*), OHG. *leitara* (G. *leiter*) :- WGmc. **χlaidr-*, f. **χlai-* **χli-* (see LEAN[2]).

lade A. load (a ship, etc.); B. draw (water, etc.), bale. OE. str. vb. *hladan*, corr. to OS., OHG. *hladan* (Du., G. *laden*), ON. *hlaða*, Goth. *-hlaþan*; rel. to OSl. *klasti* lay, place. Hence **lading** XV.

ladle sb. OE. *hlædel*, f. *hladan* LADE; see -LE[1].

lady †mistress of a household; (arch.) female ruler; (*Our L.*) the Virgin Mary OE.; woman of superior position (hence as a title); wife XIII; woman of refinement XIX. OE. *hlǣfdiġe*, f. *hlāf* LOAF + **-dīg-* knead (cf. OE. *dǣġe* kneader of bread, female (farm) servant, dairy-woman; also DOUGH); like LORD, peculiar to Eng. The OE. g. *hlǣfdiġan* (ME. *ladie*) is repr. in *Lady Day* (ME. *ure lefdi day* XIII, i.e. 'Our Lady's day'); so *Lady* *chapel* XV; also in plant-names, as *lady smock* XVI, and *ladybird*.

lag[1] fail to keep pace, fall behind. XVI. contemp. with **lag** sb.[1] last or hindmost person, and adj. hindmost, falling behind, which may be a perversion of LAST[3] in *fog, seg, lag*, used dial. in children's games for 'first, second, last'.

lag[2] †carry off, steal XVI; (sl.) transport, apprehend XIX. of unkn. orig. Hence **lag** sb.[2] (sl.) convict; term of penal servitude. XIX.

lag[3] stave of a barrel XVII; lath or strip of material in a covering or casing (whence vb.) XIX. prob. of Scand. orig., cf. ON. *lǫgg* rim of a barrel, f. Gmc. **laȝ*- LAY[1].

lagan goods or wreckage on the sea bottom. XVI. - OF., perh. f. ON. *lagn*-, as in *lǫgn*, g. *lagnar* drag-net, f. Gmc. **laȝ*- LAY[1].

lager (beer) XIX. - G. *lagerbier* 'beer for keeping', f. *lager* store (cf. LAIR) + *bier* BEER.

lagoon area of salt water separated from the sea. XVII. - It., Sp. *laguna* (partly through F. *lagune*) :- L. *lacūna* pool (see LACUNA).

la(h) sixth note of the scale in solmization. XIV. See UT.

laic XVI. - late L. *lāicus* LAY[3]. So **laical** XVI, **laicize** XIX.

lair †lying down; grave, tomb; bed, couch OE.; animal's place of rest XV. OE. *leġer* = OS. *legar* bed (Du. *leger* bed, camp), OHG. *leger* bed, camp (G. *lager*, infl. by *lage* situation), Goth. *ligrs*; f. Gmc. **leȝ*- (see LIE[1]).

laird (Sc.) landed proprietor. XV. Sc. form of LORD.

laity XVI. f. LAY[3] + -ITY.

lake[1] body of water surrounded by land; †pond, pool XIII; †pit, grave XIV. ME. *lac* - (O)F. - L. *lacus* basin, tank, lake, pool, rel. to Gr. *lákkos* hole, ditch, Gael., Ir. *loch* LOCH, OE. *lagu*, ON. *lǫgr* sea, water, OSl. *loky* pool, reservoir.

lake[2] reddish pigment. XVII. unexpl. var. of LAC.

Lallan(s) Scottish dialect. XVIII. Sc. var. of LOWLAND(S).

lallation †childish utterance; pronunciation of *r* as *l*. XVII. f. L. *lallāre* make lulling sounds, such as *lalla*.

lam beat soundly. XVI. perh. of Scand. orig. (cf. ON. *lemja* beat so as to cripple, LAME). Hence synon. **lambaste** XVII.

lama Buddhist priest of Mongolia and Tibet. XVII. - Tibetan *blama* (with silent *b*). So **lamasery** monastery of lamas. XIX. - F. *lamaserie*, irreg. f. *lama*.

lamb OE. *lamb*, pl. *lambru* = OS., OHG., ON., Goth. *lamb* (Du. *lam*, G. *lamm*; in Goth. 'sheep') :- Gmc. **lambaz* (n. of a class corr. to Gr. n. nouns in *-os*, L. in *-us*, as *génos, genus*); no certain cogns. are known outside Gmc. Hence **lamb** vb. XVII, **lambkin** XVI.

lambent (of flame) playing lightly upon a surface, shining with soft clear heat. XVII. - L. *lambēns, -ent-*, prp. of *lambere* lick, rel. to LAP[2].

lame adj. OE. *lama* = OS. *lamo* (Du. *lam*), OHG. *lam* (G. *lahm*), ON. *lami*, f. Gmc. **lam*-, rel. to OHG. *luomi* dull, slack, gentle, OSl. *lomiti* break. Hence vb. XIII; first in pp. after ON. *lamiðr*.

lamella thin plate. XVII. - L., dim. of LAMINA.

lament sb. XVI. - L. *lāmentum*; or f. **lament** vb. (XVI) - F. *lamenter* or L. *lāmentārī*. So **lamentable** XV, **lamentation** XIV.

lamina thin plate or scale. XVII. - L. *lāmina, lammina*. Hence **laminate, -ated** XVII; see -ATE[2], -ED[1].

Lammas 1st August, the feast of St. Peter in Chains, observed in A.-S. England by the consecration of bread made from the first ripe corn. OE. *hlāfmæsse*, f. *hlāf* LOAF + *mæsse* festival, MASS[1].

lammergeyer bearded vulture. XIX. - G. *lämmergeier*, f. *lämmer*, g. pl. of *lamm* LAMB + *geier* vulture.

lamp XII. - (O)F. *lampe* :- late L. *lampada* - Gr. *lampás, lampad-* torch, rel. to *lámpein* shine. comp. **lampblack** XVI.

lampoon virulent or scurrilous satire. XVII. - F. *lampon*, said to be f. *lampons* let us drink (used as a refrain), 1st pl. imper. of *lamper* gulp down, booze, nasalized form of *laper* LAP[2]; see -OON. Hence vb. XVII.

lamprey XIII. - OF. *lampreie* (mod. *lamproie*) :- medL. *lamprēda* (whence also OE. *lamprede*); poss. alt. of *lampetra*, expl. as f. *lambere* lick + *petra* stone (with allusion to the lamprey attaching itself to stones). Cf. LIMPET.

lance sb. XIII. - (O)F. :- L. *lancea*, of alien orig. *Lance corporal* (XVIII) was based on synon. †*lancepesade* - F. †*lancespessade* - It. *lancia spezzata* lit. 'broken lance'; *lance sergeant* (XIX) was analogical. So **lance** vb. fling, hurl; (dial.) spring, bound; pierce, make incision in XIV. - (O)F. *lancer*, †*-ier*. **lancer** soldier armed with a lance. XVI. - F. *lancier*.

lanceolate shaped like a spearhead. XVIII. - late L. *lanceolātus*, f. *lanceola*, dim. of L. *lancea* LANCE; see -ATE[2].

lancet surgical instrument for making incisions XV; (archit.) applied attrib. to pointed windows XVIII. - (O)F. *lancette*, dim. of *lance*; see LANCE, -ET.

lancinate pierce. XVII. f. pp. stem of L. *lancināre* tear, rel. to *lacer*; see LACERATE and -ATE[3].

land solid portion of the earth's surface; ground, soil; country, territory; †country (opposed to *town*); ridge in a ploughed field OE.; strip division of a field XIV; (Sc.) building divided into tenements XV. OE. *land* = OS., ON., Goth. *land*, OHG. *lant* (Du., G. *land*) :- Gmc. **landam*, rel. to OCeltic **landā* (Ir. *land, lann* enclosure, W. *llan* enclosure, church, Cornish *lan* open space, plain, Breton *lann* heath). The IE. base **londh*- is not evidenced in other langs., but the var. **lendh*- is repr. by OSl. *lędina* heath, desert, (O)Sw. *linda* fallow land. comps. **landlady** XVI, after **landlord**, OE. *landhlāford*; **landmark**, OE. *landmearc*; **landslide** U.S. (XIX) equiv. of **landslip** XVII. Hence **land** vb. bring to land XIII; come to land XIV. Whence **landing** disembarkation XV; platform in a flight of stairs XVIII.

landau four-wheeled carriage. XVIII. Name of a town in Germany where the vehicle was first made. (The G. name is *landauer*, short for *landauer wagen*). Hence **landaulet** XVIII.

landloper (hist.) vagabond. XVI. - MDu. *landlooper*, f. *land* LAND + *loopen* run, LEAP.

landrail corn-crake. XVIII. f. LAND + RAIL[3].

landscape picture representing natural inland scenery XVI (*landskip*); view of such scenery XVII (*lantskip*). - MDu. *lantscap*, (mod.) *landschap* landscape, province (cf. OE. *landsċipe* region, tract, OS. *landskipi*, OHG. *lantscaf*, ON. *landskapr*); see LAND, -SHIP.

lane OE. *lane* = MDu. *lāne* (Du. *laan*), of unkn. orig.

lang syne (Sc.) long ago. XVI. Sc. *lang* LONG + *syne*, contr. form of *sithen* SINCE. Familiar in *auld lang syne* (from Burns).

language XIII. ME. *langage*, later *language* - (O)F. *langage* (AN. also *language*, after *langue* tongue, speech) :- Gallo-Rom. **linguāticum*, f. *lingua* TONGUE, language; see -AGE.

languish XIII. - (O)F. *languiss-*, lengthened stem of *languir* :- Rom. **languīre*, for L. *languēre* languish, rel. to *laxus* slack, LAX[2]; see -ISH[2]. So **languid** XVI. - F. or L. **languor** †disease, woeful plight, mental distress XIII; faintness, weariness XVIII. - OF. *languor* (mod. *langueur*) - L. *languor*, *-ōr-*; reinforced later from L.

laniary (of teeth) adapted for tearing. XIX. - L. *laniārius*, f. *laniāre* tear with the nails, etc.; see -ARY.

laniferous wool-bearing. XVII. f. L. *lānifer*, f. *lāna* WOOL; see -IFEROUS. So **lanigerous** wool-bearing. XVII. f. L.

lank loose, flabby, hollow OE.; straight and flat XVII. OE. *hlanc*, f. Gmc. **χlaŋk-*, which appears in (M)HG. *lenken* bend, turn aside, OHG. *lancha* loin, side; cf. LINK[1]. Hence **lanky** XVII.

lanner species of falcon. XIV. - (O)F. *lanier*, perh. sb. use of *lanier* cowardly, a derogatory application of *lanier* weaver :- L. *lānārius* wool-merchant, f. *lāna* WOOL; see -ER[2].

lanolin fatty matter from sheep's wool. XIX. - G., f. L. *lāna* WOOL + *oleum* OIL + -IN.

lansquenet (hist.) mercenary soldier in Germany; German card-game. XVII. - F. - G. *landsknecht*, f. g. of *land* LAND + *knecht* soldier, KNIGHT.

lantern case of glass, etc., containing and protecting a light XIII; glazed turret-like erection XV. - (O)F. *lanterne* :- L. *lanterna*, f. Gr. *lamptḗr* torch, lamp (f. *lámpein* shine; cf. LAMP). The frequent form *lanthorn* is due to assoc. with *horn*, lanterns having been formerly made with horn windows.

lanthanum (chem.) rare metallic element. XIX. modL., f. Gr. *lanthánein* escape the notice of (from its having remained undetected in cerium oxide).

lanyard †whip-lash XV; (naut.) short piece of rope XVII. - (O)F. *lanière*, earlier *lasniere*, f. *lasne*, perh. due to crossing of *laz* LACE and *nasle* - Frankish **nastila-* (G. *nestel* string, lace); the final syll. was assoc. with YARD[2].

Laodicean 'lukewarm, neither cold nor hot', like the church of Laodicea (Rev. 3: 15, 16). XVII. f. L. *Lāodicēa*, Gr. *Lāodikeia*, name of a city in Asia Minor (now Latakia); see -EAN.

lap[1] †skirt of a garment; †lobe OE.; †fold of a robe; front part of a skirt and of the body from waist to knees XIII. OE. *læppa*, corr. to OS. *lappo*, OHG. *lappa*; cf. ON. *leppr* rag, lock of hair; Gr. *lobós* LOBE has been compared. comp. **lapdog** XVII.

lap[2] take up with the tongue. OE. *lapian*, corr. to MLG., MDu. *lapen*, OHG. *laffan*, f. Gmc. **lap-*, repr. also by OHG. *gilepphen* swallow, MHG. *leffen*, Icel. *lepja* lick, OS. *lepil*, MLG. *lepel*, OHG. *leffil* (G. *löffel*) spoon, and rel. to L. *lambere*, Gr. *láptein* lick, lap. OE. *lapian* is repr. directly by ME., dial. *lape*, Sc. *laip*, the present *lap* being prob. due to (O)F. *laper* (of Gmc. orig., if not independently imit.).

lap[3] wrap, enfold XIII; lay over, so as to cover; project beyond (cf. OVERLAP) XVII. Earlier in †*bilappe*, f. *bi-* BE- + *lappe* LAP[1]. Hence sb. amount by which something overlaps XVIII; act of encircling, turn round a track XIX.

laparo- comb. form of Gr. *lapárā* flank, f. *laparós* soft; in medical terms, as *laparotomy* (XIX).

lapel XVIII. f. LAP[1] + -EL[1]. Hence **lapelled** XVIII.

lapidary sb. one who cuts stones XIV; adj. suitable for monumental inscriptions XVIII. - L. *lapidārius*, f. *lapis*, *lapid-* stone; see -ARY.

lapilli fragments of stone from a volcano. XVIII. - pl. of It. *lapillo* - L. *lapillus*, dim. of *lapis* stone.

lapis lazuli silicate producing ultramarine pigment. XIV. f. L. *lapis* stone + *lazulī*, g. of medL. *lazulum*, varying with *lazur*, *lazurius*, f. Pers. *lāzhward* AZURE.

Lapp XIX. - Sw. *Lapp*, perh. orig. a term of contempt (cf. MHG. *lappe* simpleton).

lappet fold, flap XVI; lobe of ear, etc., XVII. f. LAP[1] + -ET.

lapse slip of the memory, etc.; fall from rectitude, grace, etc.; termination of a right XVI; gliding, flow XVII; passing (of time) XVIII. - L. *lapsus*, f. *laps-*, pp. stem of *lābī* glide, slip, fall; cf. *labāre* slip, *labor* LABOUR. So **lapse** vb. fall, pass away XVII; fall in, become void; glide, sink XVIII. Partly - L. *lapsāre* (f. *laps-*), partly f. the sb.

Laputan pert. to Laputa, visionary, chimerical. XIX (Swift's form is *Laputian*). f. *Laputa*, the flying island in 'Gulliver's Travels' III ii (1726); see -AN.

lapwing OE. *hlēapewince*, the first el. of which is formally identical with LEAP, and appears in Fris. names of the bird, the second el. contains the base (meaning 'move sideways or from side to side') of OE. *wincian* WINK; the present form is due to assoc. with LAP[3] and WING.

lar pl. **lares** household god(s); hearth, home XVI. - L. *lār*, pl. *lārēs*; prob. orig. 'infernal divinities' and hence rel. to *lārva* spectre, ghost (LARVA).

larboard side of a ship to the left of a person looking from stern to bows. XIV. orig. *lad(d)borde*, *lathebord*, the second el. of which is BOARD (OE. *bord*, ON. *borði* ship's side), the first is of uncert. orig., but may be from LADE, the orig. sense being 'the side on which cargo was taken in'.

larceny XV. - AN. **larcenie* = (O)F. *larcin* :- L. *latrōcinium*, f. *latrō*, *-ōn-* brigand, robber, (earlier) mercenary soldier, rel. to Gr. *látron* pay.

larch XVI. - early mod. G. *larche, lerche* (G. *lärche*) :- OHG. **larihha, lerihha* - L. *larix, laric-*, prob. of alien orig.

lard †(fat) bacon or pork; internal fat of swine's abdomen. XV. - (O)F. *lard* bacon :- L. *lār(i)dum*; cf. Gr. *lārinós* fat. So **lard** vb. XIV. **larder** XIV. - AN. *larder*, OF. *-ier*, medL. *lardārium*.

lares see LAR.

large †liberal, generous XII; †ample; wide in range or capacity XIII; †broad XIV; great, big XV. - (O)F. *large* (now 'broad, wide') :- L. *larga*, fem. of *largus* abundant, bountiful. So **largess** †liberality XIII; liberal bestowal of gifts XIV. **largo** (mus.) slow and dignified; movement so marked. XVII. - It., 'broad'.

lariat XIX. - Sp. *la reata* the rope used to tie mules together, f. *reatar* tie up again, f. *re-* RE- + *atar* tie :- L. *aptāre* fit, f. *aptus* APT.

lark[1] bird known for its morning song. OE. *lāwerce, lǣwerce*, corr. to MLG., MDu. *lēwer(i)ke* (Du. *leeuwerik*), OHG. *lērahha* (G. *lerche*), ON. *lævirki* (perh. from Eng.); of unkn. orig. The Sc. var. **laverock** descends from ME. *laverok*. comp. **larkspur** XVI (*larkes spur*); so called from the spur-shaped calyx.

lark[2] (colloq.) play tricks, frolic. XIX. poss. repr. dial. *lake* play, sport - ON. *leika* = OE. *lācan*. Hence sb. XIX.

larrup (colloq.) thrash. XIX. of unkn. orig.

larum (arch.) XVI. Aphetic of *alarum*; see ALARM.

larva A. †spectre, ghost XVII; B. insect in the grub state XVIII. - L., disembodied spirit, ghost, mask; sense B is an application of the sense 'mask' (the perfect insect not being recognizable in the larva).

larynx XVI. - modL. - Gr. *lárugx*; comb. form *laryngo-*. Hence **laryngeal** XVIII. f. modL. *laryngeus*.

lascivious XV. - late L. *lascīviōsus*, f. L. *lascīvia* licentiousness, f. *lascivus* sportive, lustful, wanton.

lash[1] A. make a sudden movement; dash XIV; B. †lavish XVI; C. (from the sb.) flog XIV. prob. echoic or symbolic. Hence sb. blow, esp. with a whip; flexible part of a whip. XIV.

lash[2] †lace XV; (naut.) make fast with a cord XVII. perh. of LG. orig.; cf. MDu. *lasche* rag, patch, Du. *laschen* patch, sew together.

lashings pl. (Anglo-Ir.) 'floods', abundance. XIX. f. LASH[1] in sense 'lavish'; see -ING[1].

lass XIII. ME. *lasce, las(se)*. perh. north. development (cf. *ass* for **ask* ashes and *ask* vb., *buss* for *busk* vb.) of **lask* :- ON. **laskw-* unmarried, repr. by OSw. *løsk kona* unmarried woman (spec. use of the sense 'unoccupied' or 'having no fixed abode'; cf. OIcel. *lǫskr* 'weak, good for nothing').

lassitude XVI. - F. *lassitude* or L. *lassitūdō*, f. *lassus* weary; see -TUDE.

lasso rope with a noose to catch cattle. XIX. - Sp. *lazo* = OF. *laz*, etc., LACE.

last[1] †footprint; shoemaker's wooden or iron model of a foot. OE. *lāst* footprint, *lǣst* boot, *lǣste* shoemaker's last = MLG. *lēst(e)*, Du. *leest*, OHG. *leist* (G. *leisten*) last, ON. *leistr* foot, sock, Goth. *laists* footprint, track; f. Gmc. **lais-* follow a track; cf. Goth. *lais* I know, L. *līra* furrow, and LEARN.

last[2] measure of weight, capacity, or quantity. XIV. OE. *hlæst* load, burden = (M)LG., (M)Du. *last*, OHG. *hlast* (G. *last*) :- WGmc. **hlatsta-, -sti-*; rel. to LADE.

last[3] following all the others, coming at the end. OE. *latost*, Nhb. *lætest*, corr. to OS. *la(t)st, letist* (Du. *laatst, lest*), OHG. *lazzōst, lezzist* (G. *letzt*), ON. *latastr* :- Gmc. **latast-*, **latist-*, superl. of *læt* adj., *late* adv. LATE; see -EST.

last[4] †follow; †carry out, perform; go on, continue. OE. *lǣstan*, corr. to OS. *lēstian* execute, (O)HG. *leisten* afford, yield, Goth. *laistjan* follow :- Gmc. **laistjan*, f. **laist-* LAST[1].

latakia kind of Turkish tobacco produced near *Latakia*, the ancient Laodicea, seaport of Syria. XIX.

latch A. (dial.) loop, noose; B. fastening for door or gate. XIV. In sense A prob. var. of LACE (OF. var. *lache* of *laz*); in sense B prob. f. (dial.) **latch** vb. OE. *læććan* seize, grasp, perh. rel. to Gr. *lázesthai*.

latchet (arch., after Mark 1: 7) thong, esp. to fasten a shoe. XIV. - OF. *lachet*, var. of *lacet*, f. *laz* LACE; see -ET.

late slow, tardy; delayed in time OE.; belonging to an advanced stage XIV; recently dead XV. OE. *læt* = OS. *lat*, OHG. *laz* (G. *lass*), ON. *latr*, Goth. *lats* :- Gmc. **lataz* slow, sluggish, f. **lat-* :- IE. **lad-* (repr. by L. *lassus* weary :- **ladtos*); see LET[1]. Also **late** adv. OE. *late* slowly, at an advanced period = OHG. *laz, lazzo* slowly, lazily. The mod. form *late* repr. infl. forms of OE. *læt*, and OE. adv. *late*. The regular compar. from OE. *lætra* is **latter** (now restricted, except for phr. like *latter days, latter end*, to uses in contrast with *former*); hence **latterly** XVIII; **later, latest** (XVI) are new formations, cf. LAST[3].

lateen triangular sail. XVIII. - F. *latine*, in *voile latine* 'Latin sail', so called from its use in the Mediterranean; fem. of *latin* LATIN.

latent XVII. - L. *latēns, -ent-*, prp. of *latēre* lie hid; see -ENT.

lateral pert. to or at the side. XVI. - L. *laterālis*, f. *latus, later-* side; see -AL[1].

laterite (min.) red porous ferruginous rock. XIX. f. L. *later* brick + -ITE[1].

lath OE. *lætt* (corr. to MDu. *latte*, Du. *lat*, G. dial. *latz*) survives in mod. dial. *lat*, but began to be replaced XIV in general use by *lat(h)the*, which appears to repr. an OE. **læðð-*, corr. to OHG. *latta* (G. *latte*); ult. relations obscure.

lathe[1] administrative district of Kent. XII. irreg. repr. OE. *lǣð*, corr. to ON. *láð* landed possession, land, rel. to **lǣð-* in Goth. *unlēds* 'unlanded', poor, OE. *unlǣd(e)* wretched.

lathe[2] supporting structure, stand XV; machine for turning wood, etc. XVII. Varies XVII with †*lare*; the two forms may repr. parallel adoptions of ODa. *lad* stand, supporting framework, perh. a special use of *lad* pile, heap :- ON. *hlað*, rel. to *hlaða* LADE.

lather sb. XVI. OE. *lēaðor* washing soda = ON. *lauðr* :- Gmc. **lauþram* :- IE. **loutrom*, whence Gr. *loetrón, loutrón* bath, OIr. *loathar* 'pelvis', 'canalis', Gaul. *lautra* 'balneo', f. IE. **lou-* wash,

LAVE. In its mod. sense f. **lather** vb. cover with lather OE.; become covered with foam XIII.

Latin pert. to Latium or the ancient Romans; sb. the Latin language. XIII. - (O)F. *latin* or L. *Latīnus*, f. *Latium* designation of the portion of Italy which included Rome. In OE. the learned form *latin* occurs occas.; the pop. repr. was *lǣden* Latin, language, ME. *leden* speech, utterance. So **Latinist** XVI. - medL. *Latinista*. **Latinity** XVII. - L.

latitude †breadth; angular distance on a meridian, etc. XIV; (arch.) extent, scope XVI; freedom from restriction XVII. - L. *lātitūdō*, f. *lātus* broad; see -TUDE. The geographical applications of L. *latitudo* and *longitudo* orig. referred to the 'breadth' and 'length' of the oblong map of the known world. Hence **latitudinal, latitudinarian** XVII.

latria worship that may be paid only to God. XVI. - late L. - Gr. *latreíā* service, worship, rel. to *latreúein* serve (as with prayer).

latrine XVII. - F. - L. *latrīna* bath, privy, contr. of *lavātrīna*, f. *lavāre* wash, LAVE.

-latry repr. Gr. *-latreíā* worship, as in *eidōlolatreíā* IDOLATRY. On this model have been formed, e.g., *bibliolatry*, *Mariolatry*; cf. -o-. The corr. personal designations end in **-later** (Gr. *-latrēs*), the adjs. in **-latrous.**

latten XIV. ME. *lato(u)n* - OF. *laton*, *leiton* (mod. *laiton*); of unkn. orig.

latter see LATE.

lattice XIV. - OF. *lattis*, f. *latte* LATH (- Gmc.).

laud praise; pl. first of the day hours of the Western Church, the psalms of which end with psalms 148-50 (called collectively *laudes*). XIV. - OF. *laude*, pl. *laudes* - L. *laudēs*, pl. of *laus* praise. So **laud** vb. XIV. - L. *laudāre*. **laudable, laudation** XV. - L. **laudatory** XVI. - late L.

laudanum XVI. - modL. *laudanum*, Paracelsus's name for a medicament for which he gives a pretended prescription of costly ingredients but which was early suspected to contain opium, whence the gen. application to opiate preparations; perh. alt. of LADANUM.

laugh vb. OE. str. vb. (Angl.) *hlæhhan* (WS. *hliehhan*) = OS. **hlahhian*, OHG. *hlahhan* (beside wk. *hlahhēn*; Du., G. *lachen*), ON. *hlǽja*, Goth. *hlahjan*; f. Gmc. **χlaχ- *χlōχ- *χlaʒ-* :- IE. imit. base **klak- *klōk-* (cf. Gr. *klṓssein* cluck :- **klōkj-*). So **laughter** OE. *hleahtor* = OHG. *hlahtar*, ON. *hlátr* :- Gmc. **χlaχtraz*.

launce sand-eel. XVII. perh. an application of LANCE.

launch[1] †pierce, lance; hurl, shoot; be set in motion; cause (a vessel) to move from land XIV; put out from land XVI. - AN. *launcher*, ONF. *lancher*, var. of *lancier* LANCE.

launch[2] largest boat of a man-of-war XVII; large boat propelled by steam, etc. XIX. - Sp. *lancha* pinnace, perh. of Malay origin; cf. Malay *lanchar* quick, nimble.

laundress XVI. f. †*launder* (XIV) or the extended form (see -ER[2]) *launderer* (XV) person whose occupation is washing clothes; see -ESS[1]. So **launder** wash and get up (linen). XVI. f. †*launder* sb. **laundry** †washing of clothes; establishment for this. XVI. *Launder* sb. and *laundry* are contr. forms of (i) †*lavender* (XIII) - OF. *lavandier* - Rom. **lavandārius*, f. *lavanda* things to be washed, n. pl. of gerundive of L. *lavāre* wash, LAVE; (ii) †*lavendry* (XIV) - OF. *lavanderie* (cf. L. *lavandāria* things to be washed); see -RY.

laureate worthy of the laurel crown, as an eminent poet XIV; (in sense of L. *laureus*) of laurel XV; crowned with laurel XVII. - L. *laureātus*, f. *laurea* laurel tree, laurel crown, sb. use of fem. of adj. *laureus*, f. *laurus*; see next and -ATE[2].

laurel ME. *lorer* (XIII), *lorel* (XIV) - OF. *lorier* (mod. *laurier*) - Pr. *laurier*, f. *laur* :- L. *laurus*, prob. of Mediterranean orig. The later form shows disim. of *r..r* to *r..l*.

laurustinus evergreen shrub. XVII. - modL. *laurus tīnus*, i.e. *laurus* LAUREL, *tīnus* wild laurel.

lava †stream of molten rock; substance resulting from the cooling of this; fluid matter from a volcano. XVIII. - It. *lava* (Neapolitan dial.) †stream suddenly caused by rain, the lava stream from Vesuvius, f. *lavare* LAVE.

lavabo (eccl.) ritual washing of the celebrant's hands. XIX. - L., 1st pers. sg. fut. ind. of *lavāre* wash, LAVE; first word of Ps. 26: 6 '*Lavabo* inter innocentes manus meas' (I will wash my hands among the innocents), the recital of which accompanies the ceremony.

lavatory vessel for washing XIV; lavabo XVI; apartment for washing the hands and face XVII. - late L. *lavātorium*, f. *lavāt-*, pp. stem of *lavāre*; see LAVE, -ORY.

lave (arch.) wash, bathe; pour out. XIII. - (O)F. *laver* :- L. *lavāre*, corr. obscurely to Gr. *loúein* wash, Arm. *loganam* I bathe. Coalesced in ME. with OE. *lafian* wash by affusion, pour (water), if this vb. survived (= (M)Du. *laven*, OHG. *labōn*, G. *laben* refresh - L. *lavāre*).

lavender fragrant labiate plant. XV. - AN. *lavendre*, for **lavendle* - medL. *lavendula*, also *livendula*, *lavindula*, etc.; of uncert. orig.

laver[1] (arch. or rhet.) vessel for washing; baptismal font. XIV. ME. *lavo(u)r* - OF. *laveo(i)r* (mod. *lavoir*) - L. *lavātōrium* LAVATORY.

laver[2] (edible) seaweed. XVI. - L. *laver* a water-plant; of unkn. orig.

laverock see LARK[1].

lavish adj. XV. adj. use of †*lavish* sb., earlier †*lavas* profusion, prodigality - OF. *lavasse* deluge of rain (cf. OF. *lavis* 'torrent' of words), f. *laver* wash, pour, LAVE; cf. -ISH[1]. Hence vb. XVI.

law body or code of rules; an individual rule. Late OE. *lagu*, pl. *laga* (ME. *laʒe*, *lawe*) - ON. **lagu* (OIcel. *lǫg*), pl. of *lag* layer, share or partnership, price, tune, f. Gmc. **laʒ-* place (see LIE[1]). Hence **lawful** XIII, **lawless** XII; after ON. *lǫgfullr*, *lǫglauss*. **lawyer** XIV (*lawier*, beside *lawer*); see -IER[1].

lawk(s) int. Lord! XVIII. var. of *lack!* (XVII), alt. of LORD, perh. suggested by ALACK.

lawn[1] kind of fine linen. XV. prob. f. *Laon*, name of a town in France, an important place of linen manufacture.

lawn[2] (arch.) open space between woods XVI; portion of level grass-covered ground kept mown XVIII. Later form of *laund* glade - OF. *launde* (mod. *lande*), of Celt. orig. (see LAND).

lawyer see LAW.

lax[1] salmon. OE. *læx* (WS. *leax*) = LG. *las*, OHG. *lahs* (G. *lachs*), ON. *lax* :- Gmc. **laχs-*, rel. to Lith. *lašišà*, Russ. *losós'*; cf. Toch. *laks* fish. The OE. word appears to have died out, and the Scand. word, adopted in XIII, continued in local use till XVII.

lax[2] (of the bowels) loose XIV; slack, not strict XV. - L. *laxus* loose; see SLACK[1]. So **laxative** relaxing. XIV. (O)F. or late (medical) L. **laxity** XVI. - F. or L.

lay[1] pt., pp. *laid* cause to lie. OE. *leċġan*, pt. *leġde*, pp. *ġeleġd* = OS. *leggian* (Du. *leggen*), (OH)G. *legen*, ON. *legja*, Goth. *lagjan*, f. Gmc. **laʒ-*, var. of **leʒ-* LIE[1]. The normal repr. of OE. *leċġan* is seen in ME. *legge* and mod. dial. *ledge* lay (eggs); the form *lay* derives from 2nd and 3rd pers. sg. (OE.) *leġest*, *leġeþ*.

lay[2] short poem of a kind intended to be sung. XIII. - (O)F. *lai*, corr. to Pr. *lais*, of unkn. orig.

lay[3] not in clerical orders. XIV. - OF. *lai* (now repl. by *laïque*) :- ecclL. *lāicus* - Gr. *lāikós*, f. *lāós* the people. Hence **layfolk, layman** XV.

lay[4] †wager, stake; †layer, stratum; (dial.) impost, tax XVI; line of business, plan of work XVIII. f. LAY[1].

layer A. one who lays XIV; B. thickness of matter spread over a surface; C. shoot or twig pegged down to take root XVII. Several words appeared to have coalesced under one form, all ostensibly f. LAY[1] + -ER[1]; in sense B the earliest form is *lear*, which may be a var. of LAIR; sense C may be after synon. Du. *(af)legger*.

layette clothes, etc. for a new-born child. XIX. - F., dim. of OF. *laie* drawer, box - MDu. *laege*; see -ETTE.

lay figure jointed wooden model of the human figure used by artists. XVIII. f. *lay* as in synon. †**layman** (XVII) - Du. *leeman* for **ledenman*, f. *led* (now *lid*) limb, joint (cf. LIMB[1]).

laystall †burial-place; place where refuse and dung are laid. XVI. f. LAY[1] + STALL[1].

lazar (arch.) poor or diseased person, esp. leper. XIV (*lazre*, *laser*). - (partly through OF. *lasdre*, mod. *ladre*) medL. *lazarus*, use of *Lazarus* name of the beggar in the parable (Luke 16: 20), 'full of sores' - Heb. *Elʿāzār* 'God (my) help'. So **lazaret** (XVII) and **lazaretto** house to receive 'lazars' XVI (slightly earlier *lazar house*); building set apart for quarantine XVII. - F. *lazaret*, It. *lazaretto*.

lazy XVI. Early forms *la(y)sie*, *laesy*; perh. of LG. or Du. orig. (cf. LG. *lasich* languid, idle). Hence, by back-formation, **laze** vb. XVI.

-le[1] suffix of sbs., repr. OE. *-el* (cf. BRIDLE, LADLE), *-la*, *-le* (cf. HANDLE), *-ol* (cf. CRADLE, SADDLE), and *-l* (cf. NEEDLE, SETTLE), and corr. to OS., OHG. *-il*, *-al*, *-la* (LG., Du., G. *-el*), ON. *-al*, *-ill*, *-ull*, Goth. *-ils*, and rel. further to IE. **-(i)lo-*, **-(u)lo-*, **-(e)lā*, as in L. *cingulus*, *-ula*, *-ulum* girdle, *sella* (:- **sedlā*) saddle, Gr. *hellá* seat, denoting appliances or instruments; there are also a few names of animals and plants, as *beetle*, *bramble*, *cuttlefish*, *thistle*; cf. *cripple*. This suffix was not gen. productive, but some adoptions of words containing it were made from ON. and LG., as *axle*, *kettle*, *pickle*, *scuttle*. In *fowl*, *snail*, *stile*, the suffix has ceased to be syllabic. Cf. -EL[1]. In *angle*, *battle*, *candle*, *muzzle*, *syllable*, *uncle*, etc., the ending is of other orig.

-le[2] suffix of adjs., repr. OE. *-el*, *-ol*, *-ul*, corr. to OS., OHG. *-al*, *-il*, Goth. *-ils*, *-uls*, and rel. further to IE. **-ulo-*, **-ilo-*, as in L. (esp. with pejorative force) *bibulus*, *crēdulus*, *pendulus*, *querulus* (cf. Goth. *sakuls* quarrelsome, OHG. *ezzal* greedy, OE. *slāpol* sleepy, *wacol* vigilant), L. *agilis*, *facilis*, *similis*, *humilis*, Gr. *homalós* smooth. Surviving words of OE. date are *fickle*, *idle*, *little* (cf. *evil*).

-le[3] suffix of verbs with frequent. or dim. force, repr. OE. *-lian*, corr. to OS., OHG. *-lōn* (Du., G. *-len*), ON. *-la* :- Gmc. **-lōjan*; surviving words of OE. date are *handle*, *nestle*, *startle*, *twinkle*. There were many new formations in ME. and modEng., chiefly expressive of repeated action or movement, some being adopted from foreign sources, some being of native echoic or symbolic creation, e.g. *bubble*, *chuckle*, *dabble*, *drizzle*, *giggle*, *hobble*, *mumble*, *niggle*, *paddle*, *scribble*, *topple*, *wriggle*. *Darkle*, *sidle*, *suckle* are back-formations; cf. *grovel*.

lea tract of open ground, (hence) grassland. OE. *lēa(h)*, corr. to OHG. *lōh* (MHG. low brushwood, scrub-land) :- Gmc. **lauχ-* :- IE. **louq-*, repr. also by L. *lūcus* grove, Lith. *laũkas* field, Skr. *loká-* open space; the basic meaning was prob. 'clearing', and developed from that of LIGHT[1].

lead[1] the heaviest of the base metals. OE. *lēad* = MLG. *lōd* (Du. *lood*) lead, MHG. *lōt* (G. *lot*) plummet, solder :- WGmc. **lauda*; rel. to Ir. *luaidhe*, Gael. *luaidh*. Hence **leaden** (-EN[3]) adj. OE.

lead[2] take with one, conduct; carry on (now mainly with *life* as obj.) OE.; precede, be foremost (in) XIV (first in *lead the dance*). OE. *lǣdan* = OS. *lēdian* (Du. *leiden*), (O)HG. *leiten*, ON. *leiða* :- Gmc. **laiðjan*, f. **laiðō* LOAD. Hence **lead** sb. XIII. **leader** late OE. *lǣdere*.

leaf part of a plant; fold of paper. OE. *lēaf*, corr. to OS. *lōf* (Du. *loof*), OHG. *loup* (G. *laub*), ON. *lauf*, Goth. *laufs* :- Gmc. **laubaz*, *-am*, of which there are no certain cognates.

league[1] distance of three miles. XIV. The earliest forms show two types, *leuge* and *leghe*, the first - late L. *leuca*, *leuga*, late Gr. *leúgē* (of Gaul. orig.), the second - Pr. *lega*, whence (O)F. *lieue*; the second type has survived.

league[2] covenant for mutual assistance. XV. Early forms (*ligg*, *ligue*, *leag(u)e*, *lege*) show deriv. (i) partly from F. *ligue* - It. *liga*, latinized form of *lega*, f. *legare* bind :- L. *ligāre*; (ii) partly immed. from It. *lega*. Hence vb. XVII. **leaguer**[1] member of a league. XVI; see -ER[1].

leaguer[2] (arch.) military camp; siege. XVI. - Du. *leger* camp, corr. to OE. *leġer* LAIR.

leak hole in a vessel containing or immersed in fluid. XV. So vb. pass away by a leak XV; allow the passage of fluid through a leak XVI. †adj. leaky. XVI. prob. all of LG. or Du. orig.; cf. MDu. *lek*, *lēk-* sb. and adj., *lēken* vb. let water through, corr. to OE. *(h)lec* adj., OHG. *lechen* wk. vb., ON. *leki* sb.; f. Gmc. **lek-*, var. of **lak-* LACK.

leal (now Sc.) loyal, faithful, true. XIII. - AN. *leal*,

OF. *leel*, of which the var. *leial* became *loial* LOYAL.

lean[1] wanting in flesh. OE. *hlǣne*, of uncert. orig.

lean[2] recline; incline. OE. *hleonian, hlinian*, corr. to OS. *hlinon* (Du. *leunen*), OHG. *(h)linēn* (G. *lehnen*), f. Gmc. **χlī-* :- IE. **k̂lī-* (cf. Gr. *klîmax* ladder, CLIMAX, L. *clīvus* declivity, Skr. *śri-* lean), with *-n-* formative as in Gr. *klī́nein* bend, L. *inclīnāre* INCLINE.

leap †run, rush; jump. OE. str. vb. *hlēapan* = OS. *-hlōpan* (Du. *lopen*), OHG. *loufan* (G. *laufen* run), ON. *hlaupa*, Goth. *-hlaupan* :- Gmc. **χlaupan*, without cogns. elsewhere. So **leap** sb. OE. **hlīep, hlȳp* :- **χlaupiz*; cf. Du. *loop*, OHG. *hlouf* (G. *lauf*), ON. *hlaup*, comp. **leap-frog** XVI. **leap-year** year having one day (29 February) more than the common year. XIV (but prob. much earlier than it is recorded). The term prob. refers to the fact that in the bissextile year any fixed festival falls on the next weekday but one to that on which it fell in the preceding year.

learn pt., pp. *learnt* A. acquire knowledge OE.; B. impart knowledge to, teach (now dial. or vulgar) XIII. OE. *leornian*=OS. *līnon* (:- **liznōn*), OHG. *lernēn, lirnēn* (G. *lernen*) :- WGmc. **liznōjan*, **liznējan*, f. **lis-*, weak grade of **lais-* (see LAST[1]). Hence **learned** deeply read, erudite. XVI; in absol. use, after L. *doctus* (pp. of *docēre* teach); succeeding to the sense '(well) instructed', const. *in*, †*of*; preceded by ME., late OE. *lēred*, pp. of *lēran* teach.

lease conveyance of property by contract, etc. XV. - AN. *les* = OF. *lais, leis*, f. spec. use of *lesser, laissier* (mod. *laisser*) let, leave (:- L. *laxāre*), whence **lease** vb. XVI.

leash XIII. - OF. *lesse*, (also mod.) *laisse*, f. spec. use of *laisser* let (a dog) run on a slack lead; see prec.

least OE. *lǣst*, contr. of *lǣsest* :- Gmc. **laisistaz*, f. **laisiz* LESS; see -EST. Hence **leastways, -wise.**

leat open watercourse. OE., in *wæterġelǣt* water channel; f. base of *lǣtan* LET[1].

leather OE. *leðer* (only in comps.)=OS. *leðar* (Du. *leer*), OHG. *ledar* (G. *leder*), ON. *leðr* :- Gmc. **leþram* :- IE. **letrom*, whence also OIr. *lethar*, W. *lledr*, Breton *ler*. Hence **leathern** OE. *leðeren* (see -EN[3]).

leave[1] permission. OE. *lēaf*=OHG. **louba* (MHG. *loube*, G. †*laube*) :- WGmc. **laubā*, whence **laubjan* permit (OE. *līefan*, etc.). The form *leave* repr. OE. obl. forms. The etymol. meaning is prob. 'pleasure, approval', and the base that of LOVE.

leave[2] A. have as remainder, cause or allow to remain; B. depart (from). OE. *lǣfan* = OS. *-lēbian*, OHG. *leiban* (cf. OHG. *bilīban*, G. *bleiben* remain), ON. *leifa*, Goth. *-laibjan* :- Gmc. **laibjan* remain, continue, f. **laibō* remainder (OE. *lāf* remainder, ON. *leif* heritage, etc., of which the vars. **līb-* appear in LIFE, LIVE[1]. Referred to an IE. base **loip-* **leip-* **lip-* stick, adhere, repr. by Gr. *līparḗs* persevering, importunate, *lipos* grease, Lith. *lipti*, OSl. *lĭpěti* adhere, Skr. *lip-, rip-* smear, adhere to.

leaven substance added to dough to produce fermentation. XIV. ME. *levain* - (O)F. :- Gallo-Rom. use of L. *levāmen* lit. 'means of raising', only in sense 'alleviation, relief', f. *levāre* lighten, relieve, raise (cf. LEVITY). Hence vb. XV.

lecher XII. - OF. *lichiere* (nom.), *lecheor, -ur* (acc.), f. *lechier* live in debauchery or gluttony (mod. *lécher* lick) - Frankish **likkōn* :- Gmc. **likkōjan* LICK. So **lecherous** XIV, **lechery** XIII.

lectern XIV. ME. *lettorne, let(t)ron* - OF. *lettrun, leitrun* - medL. *lectrīnum, lectrum*, f. L. *legere* read (see next). The present form shows assim. to medL.

lection reading; liturgical lesson. XVI. - L. *lectiō, -ōn-*, f. *lect-*, pp. stem of *legere* read, orig. gather, choose, rel. to Gr. *légein* collect, say; see -TION. So **lecture** †reading XIV; discourse XVI. - (O)F. *lecture* or medL. *lectūra*. Hence **lecturer** XVI, **lectureship** XVII.

ledge transverse bar or strip XIV; narrow projecting shelf XVI. poss. f. ME. *legge* LAY[1]; cf. MHG. *legge* layer, edge.

ledger A. sb. †book lying permanently in one place XV; principal one of a set of commercial books; horizontal timber, flat slab XVI. B. resident ambassador XVI; adj. †resident, stationary; (mus.) *ledger line* separate short line above or below the stave XVII. Early forms *legger, lidger, ligger*, corr. in sense to Du. *legger, ligger* (f. *leggen* LAY[1], *liggen* LIE[1]) on which the Eng. forms were prob. modelled; see -ER[1].

lee[1] protection, shelter OE.; sheltered side XIV. OE. *hlēo, hlēow-*=OS. *hleo* m., *hlea* fem., ON. *hlé* :- Gmc. **χlēw-*, not known outside Gmc. The naut. sense was mainly from ON. Hence **leeward** (on) the side turned away from the wind. XVI.

lee[2] usu. coll. pl. *lees* sediment, dregs. XIV. - OF. *lie*=medL. pl. *liæ* - Gaul. **liga* or **ligja* (cf. OIr. *lige*).

leech[1] (arch.) physician. OE. *lǣce* = OS. *lāki*, OHG. *lāhhi*, Goth. *lēkeis* :- Gmc. **lǣkjaz*.

leech[2] blood-sucking worm, OE. *lǣce* (Kentish *lȳce*), MDu. *lake, l(i)eke*; orig. a distinct word from prec. but assim. to it.

leech[3] (naut.) vertical or sloping side of a sail. XIV (*lich(e)*). Obscurely connected with ON. (naut.) *lík* (cf. Sw. *lik*, Da. *lig* bolt rope).

leek OE. *lēac*, corr. to MDu. *looc* (Du. *look*), OHG. *louh* (G. *lauch*), ON. *laukr* :- Gmc. **laukaz*, **-am*, of which no cogns. are known outside Gmc.

leer look askance (now only with a sly or malign expression). XVI. Early *leare, le(e)re*, poss. f. *leer* sb. cheek (OE. *hlēor*), as if 'to look over the cheek'. Hence sb. XVI.

leet[1] court of record held by lords of certain manors. XV. - AN. *lete*, AL. *leta*, of unkn. orig.

leet[2] (mainly Sc.) list of persons eligible or selected for an office. XV (*lite, lytte, lythe*). of obscure orig., but prob. - AN., OF. *lit(t)e*, var. of *liste* LIST[4].

left side opposite to the right. XIII. ME. *luft, lift, left* :- OE. **lyft* (as in *lyftādl* 'left-disease', paralysis), Kentish *left* 'inanis'; the primary sense of 'weak, worthless' is found in EFris. *luf*, Du. dial. *loof*, and the derived sense in MDu., LG. *luchter, lucht, luft*, NFris. *leeft, leefter*; the ult. orig. is unkn.

leg XIII. - ON. *leggr* (also in comps. limb, viz. *armleggr, handleggr* arm, *lærleggr, fótleggr* leg) :- **laʒjaz* (cf. Lombardic *lagi* thigh), of which there are no certain cogns. elsewhere.

legacy †legateship XIV; bequest XV. - OF. *legacie* - medL. *lēgātia* legateship, f. *lēgātus* LEGATE. In the second and current sense repr. AL. *lēgantia*, f. *lēgāre* (see LEGATE).

legal XVI. - (O)F. *légal* or L. *lēgālis*, f. *lēx, lēg-* law; see AL[1]. So **legality** XV.

legate ecclesiastic deputed to represent the Pope XII; ambassador, delegate XIV. - (O)F. *légat* - L. *lēgātus*, sb. use of pp. of *lēgāre* depute, delegate; see -ATE[1]. So **legation** XV. - (O)F. or L.

legatee person to whom a legacy is bequeathed. XVII. f. *legate* bequeath (XVI), f. pp. of L. *lēgāre*; see prec., -ATE[3], -EE.

legato (mus.) smooth and connected. XIX. - It., pp. of *legare* :- L. *ligāre* bind.

legend A. story of a saint's life or collection of these XIV; book of liturgical lessons XV; non-historical story; B. inscription, motto XVII. - (O)F. *légende* - medL. *legenda*, prop. 'things to be read', n. pl. of gerundive of *legere* read (see LECTION), taken as fem. sg. So **legendary** XVI. - medL. *legendārius* (sb. *-ium*).

legerdemain sleight of hand XV; trickery XVI. - F. *léger de main*, i.e. *léger* light, *de* of, *main* hand.

leghorn kind of straw plaiting; breed of fowls. XIX. f. place-name *Leghorn* (Italy) - It. †*Legorno*, now *Livorno*, repr. L. *Liburnus*.

legible XIV. - late L. *legibilis*, f. *legere* read; see LECTION, -IBLE. Hence **legibility** XVII.

legion body of infantry in the ancient Roman army; vast host. XIII. - OF. *legiun, -ion* (mod. *légion*) - L. *legiō, -ōn-*, f. *legere* choose, levy (see LECTION).

legislator XVII. - L. *lēgis lātor*, i.e. *lēgis* g. of *lēx* law, *lātor* proposer, mover, agent-noun f. *lātus*, pp. of *tollere* raise. So **legislation** XVII. Hence **legislative, legislature** XVII.

legitimate lawfully begotten XV; lawful, regular XVII. - medL. *lēgitimātūs*, pp. of *lēgitimāre* declare to be lawful, legitimize, f. L. *lēgitimus*, f. *lēx, lēg-* law. So **legitimate** vb. XVI, **legitimation** XV. See -ATE[2], -ATE[3]. **legitimist** XIX. - F. (political party). **legitimize** XIX. f. L.

leguminous pert. to pulse; of the pea and bean family. XVII. - modL. *legūminōsus*, f. L. *legūmen, -min-* pulse, bean (whence, through F., **legume** beans, peas, etc. XVII; pod of leguminous plant XVIII); see -OUS.

leisure †freedom or opportunity; freedom from occupation, free time. XIV. ME. *leisour, -er* - AN. *leisour*, OF *leisir* (mod. *loisir*) :- Rom. sb. use of L. *licēre* be permitted.

leman (arch.) lover, sweetheart; illicit lover, paramour. XIII. ME. *le(o)fman, lemman*, f. LIEF + MAN.

lemma pl. **lemmata, lemmas** (math.) subsidiary proposition XVI; heading, title, theme XVII. - L. - Gr. *lêmma*, pl. *lḗmmata* something taken for granted or assumed, theme, argument, title, f. **lab-*, base of *lambánein* take.

lemming XVII. - Norw.

lemon[1] pale-yellow acid fruit. XIV. ME. *lymon* - (O)F. *limon* (now restricted to the lime), corr. to Sp. *limón*, Pg. *limão*, It. *limone*, medL. *limō, -ōn-* - Arab. *laimūn* - Pers. *līmū(n)*. So **lemonade** XVII. - F. *limonade*.

lemon[2] in *lemon sole* species of plaice. XIX. - F. *limande* (XIII; beside *lime*; cf. It. *lima, limanda*), of unkn. orig.

lemur XVIII. - modL. *lemur*, f. L. pl. *lemurēs* shades of the departed; so named because of its spectre-like face.

lend XV. Late ME. *lende*, superseding *lēne(n)* :- OE. *lǣnan*, corr. (with difference of conjugation) to Du. *leenen*, OHG. *lēhanōn* (G. *lehnen* enfeoff); f. *lǣn* LOAN. From the pt. *lende* and pp. *lent* of *lēne*, by assoc. with the conjugation of *bend, send, wend*, arose an inf. *lende*.

length OE. *lengðu* (rare; usu. *lengu, lenge*) = Du. *lengte*, ON. *lengd* : Gmc. **laŋgiþō*, f. **laŋgaz* LONG[1]; see -TH[1]. Hence **lengthen** XVI (see -EN[5]). **lengthy** XVII.

lenient softening, relaxing XVII; indisposed to severity XVIII. - L. *lēniēns, -ent-* prp. of *lēnīre* soothe, f. *lēnis* soft, mild; see -ENT. Hence **leniency** XVIII. So **lenity** XVI. - OF. - L.

lens XVII. - L. *lens* LENTIL; so called on account of its shape.

Lent †spring; period from Ash Wednesday to Easter Eve. XIII. Shortened form of ME. *lenten*, OE. *lencten* = MDu. *lentin*, OHG. *len(gi)zin* :- WGmc. **laŋgitīna*, either f. **laŋgita-, -tan-* (whence MDu. *lenta*, Du. *lente*, OHG. *langiz, -uz, lenzo*, G. *lenz*) with suffix *-īna-*, or f. Gmc. **laŋgaz* long[1] + **tīna-* of Goth. *sinteins* daily, rel. to Skr. *dina-*, OSl. *dĭnĭ*, Lith. *dienà* day; the ult. deriv. from LONG[1] is undoubted and may have ref. to the lengthening of the day in spring; the eccl. sense is peculiar to Eng. *Lenten* survives in attrib. use, apprehended as an adj. in -EN[3].

lenticular lens- or lentil-shaped. XVII. - L. *lenticulāris*, f. *lenticula*; see next and -AR.

lentil XIII. - (O)F. *lentille* :- Rom. **lentīcula*, for L. *lenticula*, dim. of *lēns, lent-* lentil.

lentisk mastic tree. XV. - L. *lentiscus*, prob. of alien orig.

leonid (astron.) one of a group of meteors which appear to radiate from Leo. XIX. f. L. *leō, -ōn-* LION + -ID[2].

leonine[1] lion-like, pert. to a lion. XIV. - (O)F. *léonin, -ine* or L. *leōnīnus, -īna*, f. *leō, -ōn-* LION; see -INE[1]. Identical in form and ult. in orig. is **leonine**[2] in *leonine verse*, Latin verse with internal rhyme, from the name *Leo* or *Leonius* (w. uncert. ref.).

leopard XIII. ME. *leo-, leupard, lub-, lebard* - OF. *leop-, leupard, lebard* (mod. *léopard*) - late L. *leopardus* - late Gr. *leópardos*, also *leontópardos*, f. *léōn, leont-* LION + *párdos* PARD.

leper XIV. prob. arising from attrib. use of †*leper* (XIII) leprosy - (O)F. *lèpre* - L. *lepra* - Gr. *léprā*, sb. use of fem. of *leprós* scaly, f. *lépos, lepis* scale. So **leprous** XIII. - OF. - late L. Hence **leprosy** XVI.

lepidoptera order of insects with scale-covered wings. XVIII. modL., f. Gr. *lepís, lepido-* scale + *pterón* wing (cf. FEATHER).

leporine hare-like. XVII. - L. *leporīnus*, f. *lepus, lepor-* hare; see -INE[1].

leprechaun in Ir. folk-lore, a pygmy sprite. XVII (*lubrican*). - Ir. *lupracán, leipracán, liopracháan*, in MIr. *luchrupán*, OIr. *luchorpán*, f. *lu* small + *corp* body (- L. *corpus*).

lepto- comb. form of Gr. *leptós* fine, small, delicate (prop. ppl. adj. of *lépein* scale, peel, rel. to *lepis* shell, scale), in many bot. and zool. terms.

Lesbian pert. to homosexuality in women; also sb. XIX. f. L. *Lesbius*, f. *Lesbos* birthplace of the poetess Sappho (*c.*600 B.C.; poss. homosexual) + -IAN.

lese-majesty treason. XV. - F. *lèse-majesté* - L. *læsa mājestās* hurt or violated majesty, i.e. of the sovereign people; *læsa*, pp. of *lædere* injure, *mājestās* MAJESTY.

lesion XV. - (O)F. *lésion* - L. *læsiō, -ōn-*, f. *lædere, læs-* injure, hurt; see -SION.

less OE. *lǣssa* = OFris. *lēssa* :- Gmc. **laisizō*, f. **laisiz* (whence OE. *lǣs* adv.), compar. formation on **laisa-* :- IE. **loiso-* (cf. Gr. *loisthos* last, and LEAST). Hence **lessen** vb. XIV (-EN[5]). **lesser** XIII (-ER[3]); double compar.

-less orig. an adj. rel. to LOOSE, LOSE, LOSS, OE. *lēas* devoid (of), free (from), governing the g., e.g. *firena lēas* free from crimes, but more freq. the second el. of adj. compounds, the first el. being a sb., e.g. *wīflēas* without a wife. The sb. may be a noun of action with the same form as the related vb., and some adjs. so formed have the sense 'not to be --ed', 'un—able', e.g. *countless, numberless*. On the supposed analogy of these *-less* has been added (from late XVI) to many verbs, e.g. *dauntless, fadeless, tireless*.

lessee tenant under a lease. XV. - AN. *lessee*, OF. *lessé*, pp. of *lesser* (mod. *laisser* leave, let); see LEASE. So **lessor** XV. - AN. *lesso(u)r*.

lesson portion of sacred scripture read in divine service; portion of a book to be studied; portion or period of teaching XIII; †lecture XIV. - (O)F. *leçon* :- L. *lectiō, -ōn-* LECTION.

lest OE. *þȳ lǣs þe* 'whereby less that' (*þȳ* instr. case of the dem. and rel. pron., *lǣs* LESS, *þe* rel. particle; see THE[2]), late OE. *þe lǣste*, whence ME. *lest(e)*, by aphesis of the first word of the phr.

let[1] †leave behind or undone, omit; put out to hire or rent; allow, cause. OE. str. vb. *lǣtan* = OS. *lātan* (Du. *laten*), OHG. *lāzan* (G. *lassen*), ON. *láta*, Goth. *lētan*; Gmc. (orig. redupl.) vb., f. **lǣt-* (:- **lēd-*), rel. to **lat-* LATE :- **lad-*, repr. by L. *lassus* weary (:- **ladtós*). The primary sense was prob. 'let go through weariness'.

let[2] (arch.) hinder, prevent. OE. *lettan* = OS. *lettian* (Du. *letten*), OHG. *lezzen*, ON. *letja*, Goth. (Gmc.) *latjan*, f. **lata-* slow, LATE. Hence sb. hindrance. XII.

-let suffix used since XVI, but not freq. till XVIII, to form diminutives; presumably deduced from *bracelet, crosslet*, etc., which appear to be f. *brace, cross*, but which are actually - F. words formed by the addition of *-ette* (-ET) to sbs. ending in *-el*, or from *tartlet*, which is - F. *tartelette*, dim. of *tarte* TART, through the by-form *tartre*, whence **tarterette*, and by dissim. *tartelette*.

Armlet, necklet, wristlet, denoting ornaments for parts of the body, were perh. first suggested by a false analysis of *frontlet*, and furthered by the common *bracelet*.

lethal XVII. - L. *lethālis*, f. *lēthum*, var. of *lētum* death, by assoc. with Gr. *lḗthē* oblivion, used as a proper name in L. (whence **Lethe** XVI) for a river in Hades, the water of which, when drunk, produced oblivion of the past; see -AL[1].

lethargy morbid drowsiness; torpor, apathy. XIV. Earliest form *litargie* - OF. *litargie* (mod. *léth-*) - late L. *lēthargia* (medL. *litargia*) - Gr. *lēthargiā*, f. *lḗthargos* forgetful, f. **lēth-* (cf. prec.), var. of **lath-* in *lanthánein* escape notice, *lanthánesthai* forget, prob. rel. to L. *latēre* be hid. So **lethargic** XIV (rare before XVI). - L. - Gr.

letter alphabetic character; epistle; pl. literature, learning. XIII. - (O)F. *lettre* :- L. *littera* letter of the alphabet, pl. epistle, written document, literature, culture. So **lettered** learned, educated. XIV.

lettuce XIII. ME. *letus(e)*, obscurely rel. to (O)F. *laitue* :- L. *lactūca*, f. *lac, lact-* milk; so called with ref. to the milky juice of the plant.

leuco- before a vowel **leuc-**, comb. form of Gr. *leukós* white (see LIGHT[1]). XVII.

levant abscond, bolt; esp. of a debtor. XVIII. perh. f. *levant* in sl. phr. *come the l., run or throw a l.*, make a bet with the intention of absconding if it is lost, ult. based on *Levant*, as in the F. phr. *faire voile en Levant* 'to be stolne, filched, or purloyned away' (Cotgr.). But cf. Sp. *levantarse con algo* seize something.

Levant †the East; eastern part of the Mediterranean. XV. - F. *levant*, sb. use ('point where the sun rises') of prp. of *lever* rise (see LEVY). So **Levantine** XVII.

levator (anat.) muscle that raises. XVII. - late L., agent-noun of L. *levāre* raise (see LEVY, -ATOR).

levee reception of visitors on rising from bed XVII; assembly held by a sovereign, etc., esp. in the early afternoon XVIII. - F. *levé*, sb. use of pp. of *lever* raise, (refl.) rise; see LEVY, -EE[1].

level instrument to indicate a line parallel to the horizon XIV; †level condition XV; position marked by a horizontal line XVI; social, etc., plane; level surface XVII. ME. *level, livel* - OF. *livel*, later *nivel* (mod. *niveau*) :- Rom. **libellum*, for L. *lībella*, dim. of *lībra* balance, scales. Hence adj. XVI, vb. XV.

lever bar used to prize up a heavy object. XIII. - AN. *lever*, (O)F. *levier*, alt. of OF. *leveor*, f. *lever* raise (see LEVY).

leveret XV. - AN., dim. of *levre*, (O)F. *lièvre* :- L. *lepus, lepor-* hare (of alien orig.); see -ET.

leviathan large aquatic animal in the Bible; †Satan XIV; used by Hobbes for the commonwealth 1651. - L. - Heb. *liwyāthān*.

levigate make smooth. XVII. f. pp. stem of L. *lēvigāre*, f. *lēvis* smooth (cf. Gr. *leîos*) + *-ig-*, var. of base of *agere* do, make; see ACT and -ATE[3]. So **levigation** XV. - L.

levin lightning. XIII. ME. *leuen(e)*, prob. of ON. orig.

levirate custom by which a brother of a deceased man marries his widow. XVIII. f. L. *lēuir* brother-in-law + -ATE[1].

levitate XVII. f. L. *levis* light (see LEVITY). So **levitation** XVII.

levity XVI. - L. *levitās*, f. *levis* light, rel. to Gr. *elakhús* short, OSl. *līgŭkŭ* light; see -ITY.

levy action of raising money, an army, etc. XV. - (O)F. *levée*, sb. use of fem. pp. of *lever* :- L. *levāre* raise, f. *levis* light (see prec. and -Y[5]). Hence vb. raise (money, taxes, etc.) XIV; raise (an army); make, start (war) XV.

lewd †lay, not clerical OE.; unlearned XIII; †low, vulgar; lascivious, unchaste XIV. OE. *lǣwede*, of unkn. orig.

lewis iron contrivance for raising blocks of stone. XVIII. perh. f. the name *Lewis*.

lewisite vesicant oily fluid. XX. f. name of the inventor, W. J. *Lewis* + -ITE.

lexical XIX. f. Gr. *lexikós* and *lexikón*; see next and -AL[1].

lexicon XVII. - modL. - Gr. *lexikón*, n. sg. of *lexikós* pert. to words, f. *léxis* phrase, word, f. *légein* speak; see LECTION. So **lexicographer, -graphy** XVII.

liable obliged by law XV; exposed or subject *to* XVI. poss. - AN. **liable*, f. (O)F. *lier* :- L. *ligāre* bind; but the late appearance of the word and its absence from AN. and AL. records would be inexplicable. Hence **liability** XVIII. See -BLE.

liaison †thickening for sauces XVII; illicit intimacy XIX; (mil.) co-operation of forces XX. - F., f. *lier* bind (cf. prec.).

liane tropical climbing and twining plant. XVIII. - F. *liane*, †*liene*, of uncert. orig. Also **liana** XIX.

liar OE. *lēogere* (= OHG. *liugari*, ON. *ljúgari*), f. *lēogan* LIE[2]; see -AR.

lias blue limestone rock XVII (*lyas*); (geol.) strata forming the lowest division of the Jurassic XIX. - F. *liais*, of unkn. orig.

libation XIV. - L. *lībatiō*, *-ōn-*, f. *lībāre* taste, pour as an offering, rel. to Gr. *leíbein* pour drop by drop; see -ATION.

libel †formal statement or writing XIII; plaintiff's declaration or plea XIV; †published bill or pamphlet XVI; damaging or defamatory statement XVII. - OF. *libel*, (mod.) *libelle* - L. *libellus*, dim. of *liber* book. Hence **libel** vb. XVI, **libellous** XVII.

liberal pert. to the arts considered 'worthy of a free man'; free in bestowing XIV; †unrestrained XV; free from prejudice XVIII; (of political opinion) XIX. - (O)F. *libéral* - L. *līberālis*, f. *līber* free, rel. to Gr. *eleútheros*; see -AL[1]. So **liberality** XIV. **liberate** XVII. - f. L. *līberāt-*, *-āre*. **liberation** XV. - (O)F. or L.

libertine †freedman XIV; antinomian, freethinker; licentious man XVI. - L. *lībertīnus*, f. *lībertus* made free, f. *līber* free (see prec.); partly through F. *libertin*.

liberty XIV. - (O)F. *liberté* - L. *lībertās*, *-tāt-*, f. *līber* free, see LIBERAL, -TY[2]. Hence **libertarian** XVIII.

libidinous XV. - L. *libīdinōsus*, f. *libīdō*, *-din-* lust (cf. *libet* it is pleasing); see -OUS. So **libido** (psych.) XX.

library XIV. - (O)F. *librairie* (now only 'bookshop') - Rom. **librāria*, alt. of L. *librāria* bookseller's shop, sb. use of *librārius* pert. to books, f. *liber*, *libr-* book; see -ARY, -Y[3]. So **librarian** †scribe XVII; keeper of a library XVIII. f. L. *librārius* + -AN.

libration oscillation, balancing. XVII. - L. *lībrātiō*, *-ōn-*, f. *lībrāre* balance, f. *lībra* pound weight, scales; see -ATION.

libretto XVIII. - It., dim. of *libro* book.

licence, U.S. **license** leave, permission; liberty of action XIV; formal permission from authority; excessive liberty XV; deviation from normal form XVI; licentiousness XVIII. - (O)F. *licence* - L. *licentia*, f. *licent-*, prp. stem of *licēre* be lawful; see -ENCE. Hence **license** vb. XV. So **licentious** XVI. - L.

lichen XVIII. - L. *līchēn* - Gr. *leikhḗn*.

lich-, lych-gate roofed gateway to a churchyard under which the bier is set down at a funeral. XV (*lycheyate*). f. †*lich* body (OE. *līċ* :- Gmc. **līkam*) + GATE[1].

lichi see LITCHI.

licit XV. - L. *licitus*, pp. of *licēre* be lawful.

lick vb. OE. *liccian* = OS. *likkōn*, *lekkōn* (Du. *likken*), OHG. *leckōn* (G. *lecken*) :- WGmc. **likkōjan*; based ult. on IE. **liĝh- *leiĝh- *loiĝh-*, found in Skr. *reḍhi*, *leḍhi*, Gr. *leikhein*, L. *lingere*, OIr. *ligim*, OSl. *lizati*. Hence sb. XVII.

lickerish (arch.) dainty; greedy; lecherous. XVI. Alt. by substitution of -ISH[1], of †*lickerous* (XIII) - AN. **likerous*, var. of *lecheros* LECHEROUS. Also *liquorish* (XVIII), to suggest fondness for liquor.

lictor officer in ancient Rome. XVI (earlier †*littour* XIV). - L., of unkn. orig.

lid cover of a vessel OE.; eyelid XIII. OE. *hlid* = MLG. *lit* (*-d-*), Du. *lid*, OHG. (*h*)*lit* (now in G. (*augen*)*lid* eyelid), ON. *hlið* gate(way), gap :- Gmc. **χliðam*, f. **χlīð-* cover, as in OE. *behlīdan* cover.

lido name of a bathing-place near Venice; transf. public open-air swimming-pool. XX. - Venetian It. *lido* :- L. *lītus* shore.

lie[1] pt. *lay*, pp. *lain* be in a prostrate or recumbent position. OE. str. vb. *liċġan* = OS. *liggian* (Du. *liggen*), OHG. *liggen*, ON. *liggja* :- Gmc. **liʒjan*, f. base **leʒ- *laʒ- *lǣʒ-* :- IE. **legh- *logh- *lēgh-*, repr. also by Gr. *léktron*, *lékhos* bed, L. *lectus* bed, OSl. *ležati* lie. The form *lie* is from the stem of the 2nd and 3rd pers. sg. pres. ind. OE. *liġ(e)st*, *līst*, *liġ(e)ð*, *līð*; cf. LAY[1]. Hence **lie** sb. XVII.

lie[2] pt., pp. *lied* tell an untruth. OE. str. vb. *lēogan* = OS. *liogan* (Du. *liegen*), OHG. *liogan* (G. *lügen*), ON. *ljúga*, Goth. *liugan*; Gmc. vb. f. **leuʒ- *louʒ- *luʒ-* (whence OE. *lyġe* sb.); cf. OSl. *lŭža* lie. Hence **lie** sb. untruth. XIII.

lief †adj. beloved, dear. OE. *lēof* = OS. *liob* (Du. *lief*), OHG. *liub* (G. *lieb*), ON. *ljúfr*, Goth. *liufs* (*liub-*) :- Gmc. **leubaz* :- IE. **leubhos* (whence OSl. *ljubŭ*); see also LOVE. As adv. (compared *liever*, *lievest*) dearly, gladly. XIII.

liege entitled to feudal service (as *liege lord*, OF. *lige segnur*) XIII; bound to render this (as *liege man*, OF. *home lige*). - OF. *li(e)ge* - medL. *lēticus*, *lǣticus*, prob. of Gmc. orig.

lien (leg.) right to retain possession of property. XVI. - F. *lien*, OF. *loien* :- L. *ligāmen* bond, f. *ligāre* bind.

lieu place, stead. XIII. - (O)F. :- L. *locus* place.

lieutenant (arch.) vicegerent XIV; military and naval rank (orig. of one 'holding the place' of a captain) XVI. - (O)F., f. *lieu* place + *tenant* holder (see LIEU, TENANT). Forms with *f*, to which the traditional Eng. pronunc. corresponds, appear in XIV; infl. of LEAVE[1] is possible. Hence **lieutenancy** XV. Also **lieutenant-general** †vicegerent XV; rank next below a general XVI. - F. *lieutenant général*, in which the second word is orig. adj. In **lord-lieutenant** *lieutenant* is adj.

life OE. *līf*, corr. to OS. *līf* life, person (Du. *lijf* body), OHG. *līb* life (G. *leib* body), ON. *líf* life, body :- Gmc *lībam (-az), f. *līb-, the weak grade of which appears in LIVE[1]. Hence **lifeguard** bodyguard of soldiers. XVII. prob. after Du. †*lijfgarde*, G. *leibgarde* (in which the first el. means 'body'), later assoc. with *life*.

lift vb. XIII. - ON. *lypta* = (M)HG. *lüften* :- Gmc. *luftjan, f. *luftuz air, sky. Hence sb. XVI.

ligament short band of animal tissue XIV; ligature XVI. - L. *ligāmentum*, f. *ligāre* bind, tie; see -MENT. So **ligature** XIV.

light[1] emanation from the sun, etc.; illumination; lighted body. OE. *lēoht* (Angl. *līht*) = OS., OHG. *lioht* (Du., G. *licht*) :- WGmc. *leuχta :- IE. *leuktom, f. *leuk- *louk- *lŭk-, repr. in Gr. *leukós* white, L. *lūx*, *lūmen* (:- *leuksmen) light, *lūna* (:- *leuksnā) moon, OIr. *luach* shining, ON. *logi* flame, OSl. *luča* beam, Skr. *ruc* shine. So **light** adj. OE. *lēoht*, *līht* = OS. (Du.), (O)HG. *licht*. **light** vb. OE. *līhtan* = OS. *liuhtian*, etc., Goth. *liuhtjan*, largely superseded by **lighten[1]** XIII. comp. **lighthouse** XVII.

light[2] of little weight. OE. *lēoht*, *līht* = OS. *-līht* (Du. *licht*), OHG. *līht(i)* (G. *leicht* easy), ON. *léttr*, Goth. *leihts* :- Gmc. *liŋχt(j)az, f. *liŋgw- :- IE. *lengʷh, as in Lith. *leñgvas* light. Hence **lighten[2]** XV.

lightning XIV. Special use of *lightening*, vbl. sb. of LIGHTEN[1], with differentiated sp.

lights lungs (now of slaughtered beasts). XII. ME. *lihte*, pl. of LIGHT[2] used sb.; cf. LUNG.

lign-aloes aloes, aloes wood XIV; aromatic wood of a Mexican tree XIX. - late L. *lignum aloēs* 'wood of the ALOE'.

ligneous woody in texture. XVII. - L. *ligneus*, f. *lignum* wood (:- *legnom, f. *legere* COLLECT, fallen branches being collected for burning); see -EOUS.

like[1] having the same character or quality. XII. - ON. *líkr*, aphetic of *glíkr* = OE. *ġelīċ* ALIKE. Hence **liken** compare. XIV. See -EN[5]. **likewise** XV.

like[2] please, be pleasing OE.; find agreeable, be pleased with XII. OE. *līcian* = OS. *likon* (Du. *lijken*), OHG. *līhhēn*, ON. *líka*, Goth. *leikan* :- Gmc. *līkǣjan, -ōjan, f. *līkam appearance, form. Hence **lik(e)able** XVIII. So **liking** OE. *līcung*.

likely probable XIII; suitable, fit XIV; capable-looking; handsome XV. - ON. *líkligr*, f. *líkr* LIKE[1] + *-ligr* -LY[1]. Also adv. probably. XIV. So **likeness** OE. *(ġe)līcnes*.

lilac shrub *Syringa vulgaris*. XVII. - F. †*lilac* (now *lilas*) - Sp. *lilac* - Arab. *līlak* - Pers. *līlak*, var. of *nīlak* bluish, f. *nīl* blue, indigo. So named from the bluish tinge of the flowers of some varieties.

liliaceous XVIII. - late L. *līliāceus*, f. *līlium* LILY; see -ACEOUS.

Lilliputian diminutive. XVIII. f. *Lilliput* name of an imaginary country in Swift's 'Gulliver's Travels' (1726), peopled by pygmies six inches high; see -IAN.

lilt sound (a note), lift up (the voice), sing XIV; sing with a swing XVIII. ME. *lilte*, *lulte*, of obscure orig. Hence **lilt** sb. (Sc.) song, tune XVIII; swing of a tune or verse XIX.

lily OE. *lilie* (weak fem.) - L. *līlium*; of alien orig. (cf. Gr. *leírion*).

limb[1] part of the body, spec. a member such as the arm, leg, wing; branch (*l. of Satan*, etc., imp, mischievous person; in OE. *dēofles limu* 'devil's limbs'; whence simply *limb* XVII). OE. *lim* n., pl. *limu*, corr. to ON. *limr* m.; prob. rel. to OE. *liđ* limb (= Du. *lid*; see LAY-FIGURE). Parasitic *b* prob. arose in obl. forms, and has now disappeared in pronunc.

limb[2] A. †limbo of Hell XV; B. edge or boundary of a surface or instrument XVI. - F. *limbe* or its source L. *limbus* (see LIMBO).

limber[1] shaft; forepart of a gun-carriage. XV (*lymo(u)r*). of obscure orig. Hence **limber** vb.[1] XIX.

limber[2] pl. holes in timbers for the passage of water. XVII. perh. - (O)F. *lumière* light, hole (used in the same techn. sense) :- Rom. *lūmināria, fem. sg. use of pl. of L. *lūmināre* light, lamp, f. *lūmen*, *lūmin-* (see LIGHT[1]).

limber[3] flexible, pliant. XVI. perh. from LIMBER[1] in allusion to the motion of shafts. Hence **limber** (*up*) vb.[2] XVIII.

limbo region on the border of Hell XIV; prison, confinement XVI; neglect, oblivion XVII. orig. in phr. *in, out of limbo*, repr. medL. *in, ē limbō*; abl. of L. *limbus* hem, selvage, fringe.

lime[1] birdlime; mortar, cement; calcium oxide. OE. *līm*, corr. to MDu., OHG. *līm* (Du. *lijm*, G. *leim*), ON. *lím*; f. Gmc. *līm-, var. of *laim- LOAM, ult. rel. to L. *līmus*. Hence vb. XIII.

lime[2] kind of citrus fruit. XVII. - F. - modPr. *limo*, Sp. *lima* - Arab. *līma*, coll. *līm* fruits of the citron kind.

lime[3] linden. XVII. unexpl. alt. of *line*, var. of *lind* (see LINDEN).

limen (psych.) limit below which a stimulus ceases to be perceptible. XIX. - L. *līmen*, *līmin-* threshold. So **liminal** XIX. Cf. SUBLIMINAL.

limerick XIX. Said to be derived from a custom of singing 'Will you come up to Limerick?' at parties at which verses were extemporized.

limit sb. XIV. - L. *līmes*, *līmit-* frontier. So **limit** vb. XIV. - (O)F. *limiter* or L. *līmitāre*. **limitation** XIV.

limitrophe adj. on the frontier XIX; †sb. borderland XVI. - F. - late L. *limitrophus*, f. *līmit-* LIMIT + Gr. *-trophos* supporting (*tréphein* nourish).

limn illuminate XV; paint, portray XVI. contr. of †*lumine* (XIV) - OF. *luminer* - L. *lūmināre*, f. *lūmen*, *lūmin-* LIGHT[1]. So **limner** illuminator XIV; painter XVI. contr. of †*luminer* (XIV).

limnology XIX. f. Gr. *límnē* lake, marsh + -OLOGY.

limousine motor-car with closed body. XX. - F., f. *Limousin* name of a province of France; orig. caped cloak worn by natives of the province.

limp[1] walk lame. XVI. cogn. w. †*limphalt* lame, OE. *lemphealt, læmpihalt* (second el. *healt* HALT[1]); cf. MHG. *limpfen* limp.

limp[2] not stiff. XVIII. of unkn. orig.

limpet ME. *lempet* :- OE. *lempedu* - medL. *lamprēda* limpet, LAMPREY.

limpid pellucid, clear. XVII. - F. *limpide* or L. *limpidus*.

linchpin pin in an axle to keep the wheel in place. XIV (*lynspin*). f. ME. *lins* :- OE. *lynis* = OS. *lunisa* (Du. *luns, lens*), MHG. *luns, lunse* (G. *lünse*).

Lincoln green bright green stuff made at *Lincoln*, county town of Lincolnshire, England, a seat of cloth manufacture. XVI.

linden lime-tree. XVI. In *linden tree* - Du. *linde-*, †*lindenboom*, G. *lindenbaum*, f. *linde* (with wk. inflexion) + *boom, baum* tree (BEAM). The first el. corr. to OE. *lind(e)* lime-tree, shield, ON. *lind*.

line[1] flax; flax thread or cloth. OE. *līn* = OS., OHG. *līn* (Du. *lijn-*, G. *lein-*), ON. *lín*, Goth. *lein* :- Gmc. **līnam* = or - L. *līnum* flax, rel. to Gr. *línon*, Ir. *lín*, Lith. *linaĩ* pl. Now dial. exc. as surviving in LINSEED. Hence **line** vb.[1] apply a layer of material to the inside of (a garment). XIV. w. ref. to linen being used for the purpose.

line[2] cord, string; string, row, series OE.; thread-like mark, stroke XIII; serial succession XIV; track, course XV. Two words of ult. identical etym. have coalesced: (1) OE. *līne* rope, line, series, rule = MDu. *līne* (Du. *lijn*), OHG. *līna* (G. *leine* cord), ON. *lína*, prob. Gmc. - L. *līnea*; (2) ME. *li(g)ne* - (O)F. *ligne* :- Rom. **linja*, for L. *līnea*, orig. sb. use of fem. of *līneus* pert. to flax, f. *līnum*; see prec. Hence **line** vb.[2] tie with a line, etc. XIV; trace with a line XVI; bring into line XVII.

line[3] cover (the bitch). XIV. - (O)F. *ligner*, also *aligner*; identical with LINE vb.[2], but the sense-development is obscure.

lineage XIV. - (O)F. *lignage*, †*linage* :- Rom. **līneāticum*, f. L. *līnea* LINE[2]; see -AGE. The sp. *lineage* (XVII) is due to assoc. with *line*; the pronunc. has followed it.

lineal pert. to a line or lines XIV; in the direct line of descent XV. - (O)F. *linéal* - late L. *līneālis*; see LINE[2], -AL[1]. So **linear** XVII. - L. *līneāris*.

lineament distinctive feature XV; †line, outline XVI. - L. *līneāmentum*, f. *līneāre* make straight, f. *līnea* LINE[2]; see -MENT. So **lineation** XIV.

linen adj. made of flax OE.; now, as attrib. use of the sb., made of linen; sb. cloth woven from flax; garments, etc., of this. XIV. OE. *līnen*, *linnen* = OS., OHG. *līnin* (Du. *linnen*, G. *leinen*) :- WGmc. **līnīn*, f. **līnam* LINE[1]; see -EN[3].

liner ship or aircraft belonging to a line (LINE[2]), i.e. a regular succession of vessels plying between certain places. XIX. See -ER[1].

ling[1] long slender cod-like fish. XIII. ME. *leng(e)*, prob. of Du. or LG. orig.; cf. Du. *leng*, earlier *lenghe, linghe*; rel. to LONG[1].

ling[2] plant of the heather family. XIV. - ON. *lyng*, of unkn. orig.

-ling[1] suffix, of Gmc. orig., forming sbs. OE., OS., OHG. *-ling*, ON. *-lingr*, Goth. *-liggs*, comp. of **-ila-* -EL[1], -LE[1], and **-inga-* -ING[3], but treated as a simple suffix. In OE., added to sbs. to denote a person concerned with . . ., e.g. *hȳrling* HIRELING; added to adjs. (occas. an adv.) to denote a person having the quality implied, e.g. *dēorling* DARLING. In ON. the suffix was dim. in force, esp. in names of the young of animals, e.g. *gæslingr* GOSLING. ME. and later formations on the same lines are *grayling, nestling, sapling*; with unfavourable sense (since *c.*1600), e.g. *groundling*, *worldling*. Formations on verb-stems are *changeling, starveling, suckling*. Many new dim. formations appear from XVI, e.g. *lordling*, *princeling*.

-ling[2] also †*-lings*. adv. suffix, repr. a var. of Gmc. **-liŋg-* **-laŋg-* **-luŋg-*, all of which appear in OE., as *bæcling* on or towards the back, *nihtlanges* for a night, *grundlunga, -linga* to the ground; so MLG., MDu. *-ling(e)*, Fris. *-lings*, etc. The orig. use to form advs. of direction is continued in ME. *grufelyng* (see GROVELLING), *sideling(s)*; more numerous formations denote condition or situation, as *darkling(s)*, *flatling(s)*.

linger †dwell XIII; stay behind, tarry, be tardy XVI. north. ME. *lenger*, frequent. (see -ER[4]) of †*leng* linger - ON. *lengja* = OE. *lengan* :- Gmc. **laŋgjan* prop. make or be long, f. **laŋg-* LONG[1].

lingerie XIX. - F., f. *linge* linen :- L. *līneus* of linen (f. *līnum* LINE[1]), used sb.; see -ERY.

lingo foreign, strange or unintelligible language. XVII. prob. - Pg. *lingoa* :- L. *lingua* TONGUE.

lingua franca orig. mixed jargon based on Italian, used in the Levant. XVII. - It., 'Frankish tongue'; see FRANK.

linguist XVI. f. L. *lingua* LANGUAGE + -IST. Hence **linguistic** XIX (earlier *-ical*).

liniment †grease XV; embrocation XVI. - late L. *linimentum*, f. L. *linere* smear, anoint; see -MENT.

link[1] loop of a chain, etc. XIV (implied in AL. *linkum*). - ON. **hlenkr* (OIcel. *hlekkr*) :- Gmc. **χlaŋkjaz*, rel. to OE. *hlencan* pl. armour, MHG. *gelenke* (coll.) flexible parts of the body, *gelenk* joint, link; cf. LANK. Hence vb. XIV.

link[2] torch. XVI. of obscure orig.

links (pl.) undulating sandy ground on the seashore XV; golf-course XVIII. repr. OE. *hlincas*, pl. of *hlinc* ridge, bank, perh. f. the base of OE. *hlinian* LEAN[2].

linn (Sc.) cascade, pool XVI; precipice XVIII. - Gael. *linne*, Ir. *linn*.

Linn(a)ean XVIII. f. *Linnæus*, latinized form of the surname of Carl von *Linné*, Sw. naturalist (1707-78); see -AN.

linnet XVI. - OF. *linette*, earlier *linot* (mod. *linot(te)*), f. *lin* flax (see LINEN); the bird feeds on the seed of flax and hemp.

linoleum floor-cloth in which a coating of linseed oil is used. XIX. f. L. *līnum* flax, LINE[1] + *-oleum* OIL. Abbr. **lino** XX.

linotype (typogr.) machine for producing lines or bars of words. XIX. **P.**; for *line o'* (i.e. *of*) *type*.

linseed seed of flax. OE. *līnsǣd*, i.e. LINE[1] + SEED.

linsey fabric, (now) of coarse wool on a cotton warp. XV. prob. f. name of *Lindsey* in Suffolk, where the manufacture is said to have originated. Hence **linsey-woolsey** XV; + WOOL, with jingling ending.

linstock staff to hold a lighted match. XVI. Early *lintstocke* - Du. *lontstok*, f. *lont* match + *stok* stick; assim. to LINT from use of refuse of flax as tinder.

lint flax; dressing for wounds prepared by scraping linen. XIV. ME. *lyn(n)et*, perh. - (O)F. *linette* (known only in the sense 'linseed'), f. *lin* flax, LINE[1] + -ETTE.

lintel XIV. - OF. *lintel* (mod. *linteau*), alt. of **linter*, *lintier* :- Rom. **līmitāris*, alt. of *līmināris* pert. to the threshold (used sb.), by crossing of *līmes*, *līmit-* LIMIT with *līmen*, *līmin-* threshold.

lion ME. *li(o)un*, *leoun* - AN. *liun* (F. *lion*) - L. *leō*, *leōn-* - Gr. *léōn*. So **lioness** XIII. - OF.

lip OE. *lippa* = MLG., MDu. *lippe*, OSw. *lippe*, *lippa* :- Gmc. **lipjan-*, rel. to synon. OS. *lepor*, OHG. *leffur*, *lefs* :- Gmc. **lepaz-*, **leps*; rel. to L. *labia*, *labra* n. pl. lips.

liquefy reduce to or become a liquid. XVI. - F. *liquéfier* - L. *liquefacere*, pass. *liquefierī*, f. *liquēre*; see LIQUOR, -FY. So **liquefaction** XV. - F. or late L. **liquescent** XVIII.

liquid adj. neither solid nor gaseous XIV; (of air, sound, light) pure, clear XVI. - L. *liquidus*, f. *liquēre* (cf. LIQUOR). Hence sb. (in phon.) XVI; liquid substance XVIII. So **liquidate** †make clear, set out clearly XVI; clear off (a debt) XVIII; set out the liabilities of XIX; (after Russ. *likvidirovat'*) wipe out XX. f. pp. stem of medL. *liquidāre*. **liquidation** XVI. **liquor** liquid substance. XIII. ME. *lic(o)ur* - OF. *lic(o)ur* (mod. *liqueur*) - L. *liquor*, *-ōr-*, rel. to *liquāre* liquefy, *liquēre* be fluid. **liqueur** in its specific sense was adopted from F. in XVIII.

liquorice, licorice rhizome of *Glycyrrhiza glabra*, preparation from this. XIII. - AN. *lycorys*, OF. *licoresse* - (with assim. to *licor* LIQUOR) late L. *liquiritia* - Gr. *glukúrrhiza*, f. *glukús* sweet + *rhíza* root.

lira unit of It. currency. XVII. - It. - Pr. *liura* = F. *livre*, It. *libbra* :- L. *lībra* pound.

Lisle name of a French town, now *Lille*, used attrib. as in *L. thread*, *lace*. XIX.

lisp speak with defective (sibilant) utterance. OE. **wlispian* (only in *āwlyspian*), f. *wlisp*, *wlips* adj. lisping; cf. MLG. *wlispen*, *wilspen* (Du. *lispen*), OHG. *lisp* stammering, *lispen* lisp (G. *lispeln*); imit.

lissom XVIII. for **lithsom*, f. LITHE + -SOME[1].

list[1] A. border, edging, strip OE.; B. †boundary; pl. barrier enclosing space for tilting XIV. OE. *līste* = MDu. *lijste* (Du. *lijst*), OHG. *līsta* (G. *leiste*) :- Gmc. **līstōn* (whence F. *liste*). In its application to tilting used to repr. OF. *lisse* (mod. *lice*).

list[2] †be pleasing OE.; (arch.) desire. XIV. OE. *lystan* = OS. *lustian* (Du. *lusten*), OHG. *lusten* (G. *lüsten*), ON. *lysta* :- Gmc. **lustjan*, f. **lust-* pleasure, LUST. Hence sb. †pleasure, desire XIII; whence **listless** without zest or spirit XV.

list[3] (arch.) listen. OE. *hlystan*, f. *hlyst* hearing = OS., ON. *hlust* :- Gmc. **χlustiz* :- IE. **k̂lustis* (cf. Skr. *śruṣṭí-* obedience), f. **k̂lus-*, extension of **k̂lu-* hear (see LOUD). So **listen** OE. *hlysnan*, corr. to MHG. *lüsenen* :- WGmc. **χlusinōjan*.

list[4] catalogue of names, etc. XVII. - F. *liste*, presumably identical with LIST[1], the special application being developed from 'strip' (of paper). Hence vb. XVII.

list[5] inclination of a ship to one side. XVII. of unkn. orig. So vb. XVII.

litany liturgical form of supplication. XIII. ME. *letanie* (later assim. to L.) - OF. *letanie* (mod. *litanie*) - ecclL. *litanīa* - Gr. *litaneíā* prayer, entreaty, f. *litanós* suppliant, f. *litḗ* supplication, *litésthai* entreat.

litchi, lichi, lychee Chinese fruit. XVI (*lechia*, *lichea*). - Chinese, *li-tchi*.

-lite final el. in many names of minerals, repr. F. *-lite* (in G. *-lit(h)*), Gr. *líthos* stone.

literal pert. to a letter or letters. XIV. - (O)F. *littéral* or late L. *lit(t)erālis*, f. *lit(t)era* LETTER; see -AL[1]. So **literary** XVII. - L. **literate** educated, learned XV; literary. XVII. - L. **literature** polite learning XIV; literary work XVIII. - (partly through F. *littérature*) L. *lit(t)erātūra* (coll.) alphabetic letters, grammar, learning. **literatim** letter by letter. XVII. - medL.

litharge monoxide of lead. XIV. ME. *litarge* - OF. *litarge* (mod. *litharge*) - L. *lithargyrus* - Gr. *lithárguros*, f. *líthos* stone + *árguros* silver.

lithe †gentle, mild OE.; pliant, supple XV. OE. *līðe* = OS. *līthi*, OHG. *lindi* (G. *lind*) soft, gentle :- WGmc. **linþja-*, rel. to ON. *linr* soft, yielding, OE. *linnan*, OHG., Goth. *-linnan*, ON. *linna* cease (cf. L. *lentus* pliant, slow).

lithia lithium oxide. XIX. modL., alt. of *lithion* (as if - Gr. *lítheion*, n. of *lítheios* stony, f. *líthos* stone). Hence **lithium** metallic element. XIX. See -IUM.

litho- comb. form of Gr. *líthos* stone. **lithography** making designs on stone to be printed from. XIX. **lithotomy** XVIII. - late L. - Gr.

litigation †disputation XVI; legal proceedings XVII. - late L. *lītigātiō*, *-ōn-*, f. *lītigāre*, *-āt-* (whence **litigant**, **-ate**), f. *līs*, *līt-* strife, lawsuit + *agere* do. So **litigious** XIV. - (O)F. or L.

litmus blue colouring matter from lichens. XVI. - ONorw. *litmosi*, f. ON. *litr* dye + *mosi* MOSS.

litotes (rhet.) affirmative expressed by the negative of the contrary, as 'a citizen of *no mean* city'. XVII. - late L. - Gr. *lītótēs*, f. *lītós* single, simple, meagre.

litre XIX. - F., suggested by †*litron* old measure of capacity, f. medL. *lītra* - Gr. *lítrā* Sicilian monetary unit (of same alien orig. as L. *lībra* pound).

litter †bed XIII; portable couch XIV; straw, etc., for bedding; number of young brought forth at a birth XV; disorderly accumulation of things XVIII. - AN. *litere*, (O)F. *litière* :- medL. *lectāria*, f. *lectus* bed; see LIE[1]. Hence vb. furnish (horse, etc.) with litter XIV; bring forth (young) XV; strew with or as litter XVIII.

little OE. *lȳtel*, corr. to OS. *luttil* (Du. *luttel*), OHG. *luzzil* (MHG., G. dial. *lützel*); WGmc. **lûttila*, f. **lût-*, repr. also by OE. *lȳt* adv. little. Compared LESS, LEAST.

littoral adj. pert. to the shore XVII. sb. region along the shore XIX. - L. *littorālis*, var. of *lītorālis*, f. *lītus*, *lītor-* shore; see -AL[1].

liturgy service of the Eucharist; form of (Christian) public worship. XVI. - F. *liturgie* or late L. *līturgia* - Gr. *leitourgiā* public service, worship of the gods, f. *leitourgós* public servant, minister. So **liturgic(al)** XVII. - medL. - Gr.

live[1] have life; subsist. OE. (i) *libban*, pt. *lifde*, (ii) *lifian*, pt. *lifode*, corr. to OS. *libbian*, *lebon*, OHG. *lebēn* (G. *leben*), ON. *lifa* live, remain, Goth. *liban*; f. Gmc. base **lib-* remain, continue; see LIFE, LEAVE[2].

live[2] living. XVI. Aphetic of ALIVE.

livelihood XVI. Alt., by assim. to LIVELY and -HOOD, of *livelode* course of life, sustenance, OE. *līflād*, f. *līf* LIFE + *lād* course, way (see LOAD).

livelong emotional intensive of the adj. *long*. XIV. ME. *lefe longe*, *leve longe*, i.e. LIEF, LONG[1]. In XVI apprehended as f. LIVE[1] or LIVE[2], and so alt. in form.

lively †living; †vital OE.; vigorous, active XIII; life-like, animated XIV; gay XVI. OE. *līflić*, f. *līf* LIFE + *-lić* -LY[1]; cf. OHG. *līblīch*, ON. *lífligr*. So **lively** adv. OE. *līflīce* (-LY[2]); but newly formed in XIV.

liver bile-secreting organ. OE. *lifer* = MDu. *lever* (Du. *lever*), OHG. *libara* (G. *leber*), ON. *lifr* :- Gmc. **librō*, having no certain cogns.

Liverpudlian belonging to (a native of) *Liverpool*, of which the final syll. was joc. altered to *puddle*; see -IAN. XIX.

livery dispensing of provisions to retainers XIII; allowance of provender for horses; suit of clothes for retainers XIV; legal delivery of property XV. - AN. *liveré*, (O)F. *livrée*, sb. use of fem. pp. of *livrer* DELIVER, dispense :- L. *līberāre*; see -Y[5].

livid of bluish leaden colour. XVII. - F. *livide* or L. *līvidus*, f. *līvēre* be bluish; see -ID[1].

lixivium lye. XVII. - late L., sb. use of n. of *lixīvius*, f. *lix* ashes, lye. So **lixiviate**, **lixiviation** XVII. - modL.

lizard XIV. ME. *lesard(e)* - OF. *lesard*, *-arde* (mod. *léz-*), repr. L. *lacertus*, *lacerta*, which appears to be identical with *lacertus* muscle.

llama S. Amer. ruminant allied to the camel. XVI. - Sp. - Quechua.

llano treeless plain or steppe in S. Amer. XVII. - Sp. :- L. *plānum* PLAIN.

lo int. repr. (i) ME. *lō* :- OE. *lā*, excl.; (ii) ME. *lō*, prob. short for *lōke* :- OE. *lōca*, imper. of *lōcian* LOOK.

loach small freshwater fish. XIV. - (O)F. *loche*, of unkn. orig.

load †carriage OE.; burden XIII; transf. and fig. XVI. OE. *lād* way, journey, conveyance = OHG. *leita* course, leading, procession (G. *leite*), ON. *leið* way, course :- Gmc. **laiðō*, whence **laiðjan* LEAD[2]. The development of meaning has been infl. by assoc. with LADE. Hence vb. XV.

loadstone, lodestone magnetic oxide of iron; this used as a magnet. XVI. f. *load*, LODE + STONE; lit. 'way-stone', so named from the use of the magnet in guiding mariners.

loaf[1] pl. *loaves* †bread; portion of bread baked in one mass OE.; moulded conical mass of sugar XIV. OE. *hlāf* = OHG. *leip* (G. *laib*), ON. *hleifr* loaf, Goth. *hlaifs* bread :- Gmc. **χlaibaz*.

loaf[2] (orig. U.S.) spend time idly. XIX. prob. back-formation from contemp. *loafer*, of obscure orig.

loam †clay, earth OE.; clay moistened to form a paste XV; fertile soil mixture XVII. OE. *lām* = (M)Du. *leem*, MLG. *lēm*, rel. to OHG. *leimo* (G. dial. *leimen*) :- WGmc. **laimaz*, **laiman-*, f. **lai-*, **lī-* be sticky (see LIME[1]).

loan †gift, grant OE.; thing lent, act of lending XIII. - ON. *lán*, corr. to OE. *lǣn* (see LEND), MDu. *lēne* (Du. *leen*), OHG. *lēhan* (G. *lehen*) :- Gmc. **laiχwniz*, *-az* :- IE. **loiqnes-*, *-os-* (cf. Skr. *réknạ-* inheritance, wealth), f. **loiq-* **leiq-* **līq-*, repr. also by Gr. *leípein* leave, L. *linquere*, Goth. *leihwan*, OHG. *līhan* (G. *leihen*), OE. *lēon* lend. Hence vb. XVI (latterly esp. U.S.). comp. **loanword** XIX. after G. *lehnwort*.

loath, loth †hostile; †hateful, loathsome OE.; (f. the vb.) disinclined, unwilling XIV. OE. *lāð* = OS. *lēð* (Du. *leed*), OHG. *leid* (cf. G. *leid* sorrow, pain), ON. *leiðr* :- Gmc. **laiþaz*. So **loathe** be hateful OE.; be averse to, (later) dislike intensely XII. OE. *lāðian* = OS. *lēthon*, ON. *leiða* :- Gmc. **laiþōjan*. Hence **loathly** OE. *lāðlić*. **loathsome** XIII.

lob †pollack XIV; (dial.) bumpkin XVI; pendulous object XVII; lump XIX. prob. of LG. or Du. orig.; cf. EFris. *lob(be)* hanging lump of flesh, MLG., †Du. *lobbe*, *lubbe* hanging lip, Du. *lobbes* bumpkin, gawk. Hence **lob** vb. droop XVI; move or throw heavily XIX.

lobby †(perh.) monastic cloister XVI; passage or corridor attached to a building XVI (spec. in the House of Commons XVII). - medL. *lobium*, *lobia* (see LODGE).

lobe roundish projecting part of an organ. XVI. - late L. *lobus* - Gr. *lobós* lobe of ear or liver, pod. So **lobate** XVIII, **lobule** XVII. - modL.

lobelia XVIII. modL., f. name of Matthias de *Lobel* (1538-1616), botanist to James I; see -IA[1].

lobscouse dish of meat stewed with vegetables and ship's biscuit. XVIII. of unkn. orig.; cf. Da. *lapskaus*, Du., G. *lapskous*.

lobster OE. *loppestre*, *lopystre*, *lopustre* - L. *lōcusta* crustacean, LOCUST, with unexpl. *p* for *c*, and *-stre* after agent-nouns in *-stre* -STER.

local XV. - (O)F. - late L. *locālis*, f. *locus* place; see -AL[1]. So **locale** XIX, later form of **local** sb. XVIII. - F. *local*, sb. use of the adj. **locality** XVII. - F. or late L. **locate** appoint the place of. XVIII. f. L. *locāre*, *locāt-*. **location** hiring; placing. XVI. - L. **locative** (gram.). XIX.

loch (Sc.) lake. XIV. - Gael.

lochia XVII. - medL. - Gr. *lókhia*, sb. use of n. pl. of *lókhios* pert. to childbirth, f. *lókhos* lying-in.

lock[1] division of a head of hair. OE. *loc*, corr. to OS. *lok*, OHG. *loc* (MDu., G. *locke*, Du. *lok*), ON. *lokkr* :- Gmc. **lokkaz*, **lukkaz*, f. IE. **lug-*, whence Gr. *lugoûn*, *lugízein* bend.

lock[2] A. contrivance for fastening a door, etc. OE.; mechanism of discharge in fire-arms XVI; B. barrier on a river XIII; C. (? f. the vb.) interlocking grip XVI. OE. *loc* = OS. *lok*, OHG. *loh* (G. *loch*) hole, ON. *lok* lid, end, conclusion (Goth. has *usluk* opening) :- Gmc. **lokam*, **lukam*, f. **luk-* **lūk-* close, enclose, whence str. vb. **lūkan*, OE. *lūcan*, which was repl. (XIII) by **lock** vb., a new deriv. of the native sb. or an adoption of ON. *loka*. Hence **locker** XV.

lock[3] as in *lock hospital* (for venereal diseases). XVII (*The Lock*). The 'Lock lazar-house' in

Southwark (mentioned 1452) became such a hospital, whence the name was generalized; perh. orig. so called because specially isolated (LOCK[2]).

-lock, suffix surviving only in WEDLOCK, repr. OE. *-lāc*, which may be rendered 'actions or proceedings, practice', as *beado-*, *feoht-*, *heaðolāc* fighting, warfare, *brȳdlāc* nuptials, *rēaflāc* robbery, *wedlāc* pledge-giving, nuptials; = ON. *-leikr*, identical with OE. *lāc* play, sport, ON. *leikr*, Goth. *laiks* dance.

locket †iron cross-bar of a window XIV; metal plate on a scabbard XVI; †group of jewels in a pattern; †catch or spring to fasten an ornament; small case hung as an ornament from the neck XVII. - OF. *locquet* (mod. *loquet* latch), dim. of (chiefly AN.) *loc* latch, lock - the Gmc. source of LOCK[2].

locomotive pert. to locomotion; moving by its own powers XVII; of mechanism (e.g. *locomotive engine*, whence *locomotive* sb.) XIX. - modL. *locōmōtīvus*, f. L. *locō*, abl. of *locus* place + *mōtīvus* MOTIVE, after scholL. *in locō movērī = movērī locāliter* move by change of position in space. So **locomotion** XVII. **locomotor** sb. and adj. XIX.

locum tenens XVII. - medL., 'one holding the place (of another)'; L. *locum*, acc. of *locus* place, and *tenēns*, prp. of *tenēre* hold.

locus XVIII. - L., 'place'.

locust A. destructive insect migrating in swarms XIII; B. fruit of the carob (supposed to have been the food of John the Baptist); carob-tree, etc. XVII. - (O)F. *locuste* - L. *locusta* locust, lobster, of unkn. orig.

locution †utterance; form of expression XV. - (O)F. *locution* or L. *locūtiō, -ōn-*, f. *locūt-*, pp. stem of *loquī* talk, speak; see -TION.

lode †way, journey OE.; watercourse; loadstone XVI; vein of ore XVII. OE. *lād* LOAD, of which *lode* is a sp.-var. **lodestar** pole star, guiding star. XIV. **lodestone** see LOADSTONE.

lodge small house, tent, arbour XIII; small lodging, cottage, etc. XV. ME. *log(g)e* - (O)F. *loge* arbour, summer-house, hut = It. *loggia*, etc. :- medL. *lobia* LOBBY, of Gmc. orig. So vb. XIII.

loess (geol.) deposit of loam. XIX. - G. *löss*, f. Swiss G. *lösch* 'loose'.

loft †air, sky OE.; upper chamber, attic XIII; gallery, etc. XVI. Late OE. *loft* - ON. *lopt* air, upper room, balcony, rel. to LIFT. Hence **lofty** XVI.

log[1] bulky mass of wood XIV; (naut.) apparatus for calculating a ship's speed consisting of a thin wooden float attached to a line XVI. prob. earlier; cf. AL. *loggiare* cut into logs XIII; of unkn. orig.

log[2] abbr. of LOGARITHM. XVII.

loganberry XIX. Named after J. H. *Logan*, of U.S.A., by whom it was first grown in 1881.

logaoedic (pros.) composed of dactyls combined with trochees or of anapaests with iambs. XIX. - late L. *logaœdicus* - Gr. *logaoidikós*, f. *lógos* speech + *aoidḗ* song.

logarithm XVII. - modL. *logarithmus*, f. Gr. *lógos* ratio + *arithmós* number (cf. LOGOS, ARITHMETIC).

logger-head †blockhead XVI; large head XVI (applied to large-headed animals XVII); instrument with a long handle and bulbous head; *at loggerheads* quarrelling XVII. prob. f. *logger* hobble for horses (f. LOG) + HEAD.

loggia open gallery or arcade. XVII. - It.; see LODGE.

logic science that treats of forms of thinking XIV; logical argumentation XVII. - (O)F. *logique* - late L. *logica* - Gr. *logikḗ*, for *hē logikḗ tékhnē* the art of reasoning; *logikḗ*, fem. of *logikós*, f. *lógos* reasoning, discourse (see LOGOS). So **logical** XVI. - medL. **logician** XIV. - (O)F.

logistics art of moving and quartering troops, etc. XIX. - F. *logistique*, f. *loger* quarter, LODGE; see -ISTIC, -ICS.

logo- comb. form of Gr. *lógos* mainly in the sense of 'word' (see next). The earliest recorded Eng. words are: **logogriph** kind of enigma involving words (XVI), - F. *logogriphe*, f. Gr. *lógos* + *grîphos* fishing-basket, riddle; **logomachy** contention about words (XVI), - Gr. *logomakhiā*. A mod. formation is **logotype** type of several letters cast in one piece (XIX).

logos 'the Word' of John 1: 1. XVI. - Gr. *lógos* account, ratio, reason, argument, discourse, saying, (rarely) word, rel. to *légein* gather, choose, recount, say.

-logue, U.S. **-log,** repr. Gr. *-logos*, *-logon* speaking or treating of, chiefly through F., as *analogue*, *catalogue*, *dialogue*. Now rare or obsolescent in designations of persons (except *ideologue*, *Sinologue*), derivs. in *-loger*, *-logist*, *-logian* being gen. preferred; cf. †*astrologue*, †*philologue*, †*theologue* and *astrologer*, *philologist*, *theologian*. The living formative is **-logist** (f. -LOGY + -IST, sometimes after F., e.g. *etymologist*); **-loger** survives in ASTROLOGER, **-logian** in THEOLOGIAN, which are the earliest formations of their kind.

-logy repr. F. *-logie*, medL. *-logia*, Gr. *-logiā*, which is partly f. *lógos* discourse, speech, partly f. *log-*, var. of *leg-*, *légein* speak; hence derivs. in *-logia* mean either (1) saying or speaking in such-and-such a way, as *eulogy*, *tautology*, or (2) the science or study with which a person (designated by *-logos* -LOGIST, -LOGER, etc.) is concerned, or that deals with a certain subject. Of the latter class, the first el. is a sb. and in combination ends in *o*, so that the regular form of such words is in *-ology*; an exception is MINERALOGY. Mod. formations in *-logy* imply correl. formations in **-logical,** formerly also, now rarely, **-logic** (F. *-logique*, L. *-logicus*, Gr. *-logikós*), and **-logist** (see prec.).

loin part of the body between short ribs and hip-bone. XIV. - OF. *loigne*, eastern var. of *longe* (in modF. loin of veal) :- Rom. **lumbia*, fem. of **lumbeus*, f. *lumbus* loin; rel. to OE. *lendenu* pl. loins, OS. *lendin*, OHG. pl. *lentīn* (G. *lende*), ON. *lend*.

loiter idle, (later) linger indolently. XV. perh. introduced by vagrants from the Low Countries and - MDu. *loteren* wag about, Du. *leuteren* shake, totter, dawdle.

loll droop, dangle (intr. and trans.); lean idly XIV; hang out (the tongue) XVII. perh. f. a base ult. identical with that of †*lill* (XVI) hang out the tongue; the orig. meaning may have been 'allow to hang loose'.

Lollard contemptuous name for certain heretics. XIV. - MDu. *lollaerd* lit. mumbler, mutterer, f. *lollen* mumble; see -ARD.

lollipop XVIII. perh. f. dial. *lolly* tongue (cf. LOLL) + POP.

lollop lounge, walk with lounging gait XVIII; bob up and down awkwardly XIX. of unkn. orig.; cf. LOLL.

Lombard one of the Langobardi who conquered Italy in VI and from whom Lombardy took its name; native of Lombardy; money-changer or banker of this nationality XIV (whence *Lombard* Street in London); †bank, pawnshop XVII. - MDu., MLG. *lombaerd* or F. *lombard* - It. *lombardo*, repr. medL. *Lango-, Longobardus* - Gmc. **Laŋgobarðaz, -an-* (OE. pl. *Langbeardas, -an*), f. **laŋga-* LONG¹ + ethnic name *Bardi*.

lone XIV. Aphetic of ALONE. Hence **lonely** XVI, **lonesome** XVII.

long¹ great from end to end. OE. *lang, long* = OS. (Du.), (O)HG. *lang*, ON. *langr*, Goth. *laggs* :- Gmc. **laŋgaz*. The nature of the relation with L. *longus*, Ir. *long* long, and Gaulish *longo-* (in a proper name) is disputed.

long² †A. grow long OE.; B. (impers.) arouse desire in OE.; have a yearning desire XIII. OE. *langian* = OS. *langon* (MDu. *langen* seem long, desire, extend, offer, Du. *langen* offer, present), OHG. *langēn* impers. (G. *langen* reach, extend, suffice), ON. *langa* impers. and pers. desire, long :- Gmc. **laŋgōjan, *-ǣjan*, f. **laŋgaz* LONG¹.

-long suffix forming advs.; first appears in *endlong* (XIII), in which it is orig. the adj. LONG, but in analogical formations like *headlong, sidelong*, it has, by assoc. with -LING², assumed its meaning.

longanimity long-suffering. XV. - late L. *longanimitās*, f. *longanimis* (f. *longus* long, *animus* mind); see -ITY.

longevity XVII. - late L. *longævitās*, f. *longævus*, f. *longus* long + *ævum* age; see -ITY.

longitude length (spec. east or west in geog. and astron.; see LATITUDE). XIV. - L. *longitūdō*, f. *longus* LONG¹; see -TUDE.

long-shore frequenting the shore. XIX. Aphetic of *alongshore* (XVIII), i.e. ALONG, SHORE¹. Hence **longshoreman** XIX.

loo round card game. XVII. Shortening of *lanterloo* (XVII) - F. *lantur(e)lu*, orig. refrain of a song popular in XVII. Hence vb. subject to a forfeit at loo. XVII.

looby lazy fellow, lout. XIV. of unkn. orig.

loofah fibrous substance of a plant used as sponge. XIX. - Arab. *lūfa*.

look direct one's sight OE.; have a certain appearance XIII. OE. *lōcian* = OS. *lōkon*, MDu. *loeken* :- WGmc. **lōkōjan*, parallel to **lōʒǣjan*, whence OHG. *luogēn* (G. dial. *lugen*) see, look, spy; no further cogns. are known. Hence sb. XII.

loom¹ tool; bucket, tub XIII; weaving machine XV (for earlier *weblome* 'weaving implement' XIV). ME. *lōme*, aphetic of OE. *ġelōma* utensil, implement.

loom² (orig. naut.) move slowly up and down; appear indistinctly. XVI. perh. of LG. orig.; cf. EFris. *lōmen* move slowly, rel. to MHG. *lüemen* be weary, f. *lüeme* slack, soft.

loon¹ (chiefly north. and Sc.) rogue, scamp XV; man of low birth or condition; fellow, lad XVI. of unkn. orig.

loon² name of various aquatic birds. XVII. prob. alt. of *loom* guillemot, etc. (XVII) - ON. *lómr*.

loony (sl.) lunatic. XIX. f. LUNATIC, assoc. with LOON¹; see -Y¹.

loop A. opening in a wall to look or shoot through XIV (hence *loop-hole* XVI); B. doubling upon itself of a string, etc. XIV; curved piece or part XVII. In sense A identical with AL. *loupa* (XIV) loop-hole, of unkn. orig. The identity of later senses is not certain.

loose unbound, unattached XIII; not close XIV; not careful, inexact XVII. - ON. *lauss* = OE. *lēas* lying, untrue, OS., OHG. *lōs*, Goth. *laus* :- Gmc. **lausaz*, f. **laus- *leus- *lus-*; see LOSS. Hence **loose** vb. XIII. **loosen** (-EN⁵) XIV.

loosestrife XVI. tr. L. *lysimachia* (- Gr. *lusimákheion*), erron. taken to be directly f. Gr. *lusi-*, comb. form of *lúein* LOOSE + *mákhē* strife, whereas it is f. *Lusímakhos*, the name of its discoverer, an application of the adj. *lusímakhos* loosing (i.e. ending) strife.

loot war booty. XIX. - Hindi *lūṭ*. Hence vb. XIX.

lop¹ cut off branches, etc. of. OE. **loppian*, implied in pp. *lopped*; cf. Lith. *lùpti* strip, peel. Hence **lop** sb. smaller branches or twigs. XV.

lop² hang loosely. XVI. rel. to LOB. Hence **lop-ear(ed)** XVII, **lop-sided** XIX (earlier *lap-* XVIII).

lope (dial.) leap XV; run with long bounding strides XVI. var. of dial. *loup* (XIV) - ON. *hlaupa* LEAP.

loquacious XVII. f. L. *loquāx, loquāc-*, f. *loquī* talk, speak; see -IOUS. So **loquacity** XVII. - F. - L.

loquat fruit of *Eriobotrya japonica*. XIX. - Chinese *luh kwat* 'rush orange'.

lord master, ruler, †husband OE.; designation of rank XIV; peer of the realm XV. OE. *hlāford*, once *hlāfweard*, f. Gmc. **χlaib-* LOAF + **ward-* keeper, WARD¹. The etymol. sense expresses the relation of the head of a household to his dependants who 'eat his bread'. The word is, like LADY, a peculiarly Eng. formation. It was reduced to one syll. (XIV) by the fall of *v* in *lōverd* and contr. of the vowels. Hence vb. XIII. **lordly** OE. *hlāfordliċ*. **lordship** OE. *hlāfordsċipe*.

lore¹ teaching; doctrine; learning. OE. *lār* = OS., OHG. *lēra* (Du. *leer*, G. *lehre*) :- WGmc. **laizō*, f. **lais-* LEARN.

lore² (nat. hist.) strap-like part. XIX. - L. *lōrum* strap.

lorgnette XIX. - F., f. *lorgner* squint, f. *lorgne* squinting. So **lorgnon** XIX.

loricate having armour of plates or scales. XIX. - L. *lōrīcātus*, f. *lōrīca* breastplate, f. *lōrum* strap; see -ATE².

lorimer, -iner (hist.) maker of horses' bits, spurrier, etc. XIII. - OF. *loremier, lorenier*, f. *lorain* strap of harness :- Rom. **lōrānum*, f. L. *lōrum* strap, thong; see -ER².

lorn †lost; (arch.) FORLORN. XIII. contr. form of *loren*, pp. of OE. *lēosan* LOSE.

lorry, lurry long waggon without sides. XIX. of unkn. orig.

lose pt., pp. *lost* orig. intr. †perish, pass. *be lost* be brought to destruction; in late Nhb. OE. appears in trans. senses †(i) destroy, (ii) become unable to find, in the latter meaning finally repl. †*leese* (OE. *lēosan*). OE. *losian*, f. *los* LOSS; corr. to OS. *lōsian*, *-on* (MLG. *lösen*) become free, ON. *losa* loosen, refl. get loose.

losel (arch.) profligate, scoundrel. XIV. prob. f. *los-*, stem of LOSE; see -EL[1].

loss XIV. prob. back-formation from *lost*, pp. of LOSE; cf. the synon. contemp. †*lost*. Not continuing OE. *los* (only in phr. *tō lose* to destruction), corr. to OHG. *(far)lor*, ON. *los*, f. Gmc. **lus-* **laus-* (see LOOSE), **leus-* (OE. *lēosan*, whence ME. *leese* lose, and LORN), extension of IE. **lou-* **leu-* **lu-* (Gr. *lúein* set free, L. *luere*, *solvere* pay, SOLVE).

lot object used in deciding a matter by appeal to chance; what falls to a person thus OE.; prize in a lottery XVI; plot of land XVII; set of articles XVIII; party or set XVI; large number XIX. OE. *hlot* portion, choice, decision, corr. to MLG. *lot*, (M)Du. *lot*, ON. *hlutr*, *hluti*; f. Gmc. **χlut-* (also in OE. *hlȳt* lot), rel. to **χleut-*, in OE. *hlēotan*, OS. *hliotan*, OHG. *liozan*, ON. *hljóta* cast lots, obtain by lot, and to **χlaut-*, in OE. *hlīet* (:- **χlautiz*), OS. *hlōt*, OHG. *(h)lōz* (G. *loos*, *los*), Goth. *hlauts* lot. The Gmc. word appears in F. *lot*, It. *lotto*.

lotion liquid preparation for external use XIV; †washing XVI. - (O)F. *lotion* or L. *lōtiō*, *-ōn-* washing, f. *lōt-*, *laut-*, pp. stem of *lavāre* LAVE; see -TION.

lottery XVI. prob. - Du. *loterij*; see LOT, -ERY.

lotto XVIII. - It. *lotto* or its deriv. F. *loto*; see LOT.

lotus plant yielding a soporific fruit; water-lily of Asia, etc. XVI. - L. *lōtus* - Gr. *lōtós*, of unkn. orig.

loud OE. *hlūd* = OS. *hlūd* (Du. *luid*), OHG. *hlūt* (G. *laut*) :- WGmc. **χluðaz* :- IE. **k̑lūtós*, pp. of **k̑leu-* **k̑lu-* hear, whence also Gr. *klúein* hear, *klutós* famous, L. *cluēre* be famed, W. *clywed* hear, OIr. *rochluiniur* I hear, OSl. *slava* glory, *slovo* word, Skr. *śru* hear, *śráva-* glory.

lough in Ireland = Sc. LOCH. XIV. ME. *lowe*, *loȝe*, *lou(g)h*, repr. OE. (Nhb.) *luh* pool, strait, gulf - Ir. *loch*.

louis French gold coin. XVII. In full *louis d'or* (of gold); application of the name of many French kings :- *Ludovīcus*, latinization of G. *Ludwig*.

lounge move lazily XVI; recline lazily XVII. of unkn. orig. Hence sb. XVIII.

lour, lower[2] look sullen XIII; be dark and threatening XV. of unkn. orig.

louse, pl. *lice* OE. *lūs*, pl. *lȳs* = MLG., MDu., OHG. *lūs* (Du. *luis*, G. *laus*), ON. *lús*; cf. W. *lleuen*, pl. *llau*. Hence **lousy** XIV.

lout awkward ill-mannered fellow. XVI. perh. f. †*lout* vb. bend or bow low (OE. *lūtan* = ON. *lúta*).

louver dome on a roof XIV; series of sloping boards to admit air and exclude rain XVI. - OF. *lover*, *-ier* skylight, of unkn. orig.

lovage XIV. ME. *lov(e)ache*, alt., as if *love-ache* 'love parsley' (ME. - (O)F. *ache* parsley), of OF. *levesche*, *luv-* (mod. *livèche*) :- late L. *levisticum*, for earlier *ligusticum*, n. of *ligusticus* Ligurian.

love sb. OE. *lufu* = OHG. *luba* (cf. Goth. *brōþrulubō* brotherly love), f. wk. grade of WGmc. **leub-* **laub-* **lub-*, repr. also by OS. *lubig* loving, OHG. *gilob* precious, and OE., OS., ON. *lof*, OHG. *lob* praise; cf. LIEF, LEAVE[1], BELIEVE. Outside Gmc. the base appears in L. *lubet* it is pleasing, *lubīdō* (see LIBIDINOUS), OSl. *ljubŭ* dear, *ljubiti* love, Skr. *lúbhyati* desires. So **love** vb. OE. *lufian*. The sense of 'no score' in games (XVIII) derives from the phr. *for love* without stakes, for nothing (XVII). comps.: **lovelock** XVI. **lovely** †loving, amorous; †lovable OE.; attractive on account of beauty XIII. OE. *luflīċ*. **lovesome** (arch.) lovable, lovely. OE. *lufsum*.

low[1] not high or tall. XII. ME. *lāh*, inflected *lāȝe* - ON. *lágr* = MDu. *lage* (Du. *laag*), MHG. *læge* (G. dial. *läg*) flat :- Gmc. **lǣȝjaz*, f. **lǣȝ-*, see LIE[1]. Hence adv. XIII. ME. *lahe*, *laȝe*. **lowland** less hilly region of a country (spec. Scotland). XVI. **lowly** adj. XIV. see -LY[1].

low[2] utter characteristic sound of cattle. OE. *hlōwan* = OLF. *luogin*, *luon* (Du. *loeien*), OHG. *(h)luoen*, ON. *hlóa* roar, f. Gmc. **χlō-* :- IE. **klā-*, as in L. *clāmare* shout.

lower[1] more low, inferior. XII. ME. *lahre*, compar. of LOW[1] (see -ER[3]). Hence vb. XVII. So superl. **lowest** XII.

lower[2] see LOUR.

loxodromic pert. to oblique sailing or sailing by the rhumb. XVII. - F. *loxodromique*, f. Gr. *loxós* oblique + *drómos* course; see -IC.

loyal XVI. - F. *loyal*, OF. *loial*, *leial* - L. *lēgālis* LEGAL. So **loyalty** XIV. - OF. *loialté* (mod. *loyauté*); see -TY[2].

lozenge rhomb, diamond XIV; medicated tablet, orig. diamond-shaped XVI. - OF. *losenge* (mod. *losange*); of uncert. orig.

£. s. d. XIX. abbr. of L. *libræ* pounds, *solidī* shillings, *denariī* pence.

lubber clumsy fellow, lout XIV; clumsy seaman (cf. *land-lubber*) XVI. ME. *lobre*, *lobur*, poss. - OF. *lobeor* swindler, parasite, f. *lober* deceive, sponge upon, mock.

lubricate make slippery or smooth XVII; treat with oil XVIII. f. pp. stem of L. *lūbricāre*, f. *lūbricus* slippery; see -ATE[3]. So **lubricity** wantonness XIV; slipperiness XVII. - F. - late L.

luce pike. XIV. - OF. *lu(i)s* :- late L. *lūcius*.

lucerne plant resembling clover. XVII. - F. *luzerne* - modPr. *luzerno*, transf. use of *luzerno* glow-worm, with ref. to the shiny seeds.

lucid shining XVI; unclouded, clear XVII. - F. *lucide* or It. *lucido* - L. *lūcidus*, f. *lūcēre* shine; see LIGHT[1], -ID[1].

Lucifer morning star; Satan. OE. - L. *lūcifer*, f. *lūx*, *lūc-* LIGHT[1] + *-fer* bearing. As the name of a friction match *Lucifer* succeeded to *Promethean* (both XIX).

luck XV. prob. orig. as a gambling term - LG. *luk*, aphetic of *geluk*, in MDu. *ghelucke* (Du. *geluk*) = MHG. *gelücke* (G. *glück* good fortune, happiness), f. *ge-* Y- + a base of unkn. orig. Hence **lucky** XV.

lucre gain, profit (now rare except in *filthy lucre*). XIV. - F. *lucre* or L. *lucrum* gain, rel. to

Gr. *apolaúein* enjoy, Goth. *laun*, OS., OHG. *lōn* (Du. *loon*, G. *lohn*), OE. *lēan* wages, reward.

lucubration (nocturnal) study or its product. XVI. - L. *lūcubrātiō, -ōn-*, f. *lūcubrāre* work by lamplight, f. *lūx, lūc-* LIGHT[1]; see -ATION.

ludicrous †sportive, jocular; †frivolous, witty XVII; ridiculous XVIII. f. L. *lūdicrus*, f. *lūdicrum* stage play, f. *lūdere* play; see -OUS.

lues plague. XVII. - L.

luff †contrivance for altering a ship's course XIII (often in phr. *wend* or *turn the luff*); †weather side of a ship XIV; side of a sail next to the mast XVI; broadest part of a ship's bow XVII. - OF. *lof*, prob. of LG. or Du. orig. Hence **luff** vb. bring nearer to the wind. XIV (*love*). perh. immed. - Du. *loeven*.

lug[1] pull, drag along. XIV. prob. of Scand. orig. (cf. Sw. *lugga* pull a person's hair, *lugg* forelock, nap of cloth); perh. rel. to Sc. and north. *lug* (i) flap, lappet XV, (i) ear XVI, prob. orig. 'something that can be pulled or laid hold of'.

lug[2] large marine worm. XVII. of unkn. orig.

luggage XVI. f. LUG[1] + -AGE, after *baggage*.

lugger vessel with four-cornered sails fore and aft. XVIII. f. *lugsail* (XVII) four-cornered sail hanging obliquely, prob. f. *lug* flap, lappet; see LUG[1].

lugubrious doleful, mournful. XVII. f. L. *lūgubris*, f. *lūgēre* mourn; see -IOUS.

lukewarm XIV. f. ME. *luke* (XIII), app. rel. to *lew* (cf. *lew-warm* XV), OE. **hlēow* (in *ġehlēow* warm, *unhlēow* cold, *hlēowe* warmly) = ON. *hlýr* warm, mild, rel. obscurely to OHG. *lāo* (G. *lau*). See WARM.

lull soothe to sleep or quiescence. XIV. imit. of the repetition of *lu lu* or similar sounds (cf. *lully, lulla, lullay* XV) to sing a child to sleep. Hence **lullaby** XVI; cf. BYE-BYE[1], HUSHABY.

lumbago XVII. - L. *lumbāgo*, f. *lumbus* LOIN, whence also **lumbar** (- modL. *lumbāris*) XVII.

lumber[1] move clumsily or heavily. XIV (*lomere*). perh. of symbolic orig.

lumber[2] useless odds and ends XVI; roughly prepared timber XVII. poss. f. LUMBER[1], but later assoc. with *lumber(house), Lumber Street* var. of *lombard* (XVII) pawnshop (considered as a storehouse of odds and ends); see LOMBARD.

luminary light-giving (celestial) body; source of intellectual, etc., light. XV. - OF. *luminarie* (mod. *-aire*) or late L. *lūminārium*, f. *lūmen, lūmin-* LIGHT[1]; see -ARY. So **luminous** XV.

lump[1] compact shapeless mass. XIII. of unkn. orig.; cf. Da. *lump(e)* lump, Norw., Sw. dial. *lump* block, stump, log, Du. *lomp*, †*lompe* rag, LG. *lump* coarse, rude.

lump[2] ugly spiny-finned fish. XVI. - MLG. *lumpen*, MDu. *lumpe*, perh. identical with LUMP[1].

lump[3] look sulky XVI; (coupled with *like*) be displeased at XIX. of symbolic orig.

lunar XVII. - L. *lūnāris*, f. *lūna* moon; see LIGHT[1], -AR. In *lunar caustic* the meaning is 'of silver', *luna* being used by alchemists for silver. So **lunation** time from one full moon to the next. XIV. -medL.

lunatic orig. affected with the kind of insanity that was supposed to depend on changes of the moon XIII; sb. XIV. - (O)F. *lunatique* - L. *lūnāticus*, f. *lūna* moon; see prec., -ATIC. Hence **lunacy** XVI.

lunch and **luncheon** appear first towards the end of XVI in the sense 'thick piece, hunch, hunk'; of uncert. orig. (perh. - Sp. *lonja* slice). The sense 'slight repast between morning meals' appears XVII, for *luncheon*, and first in the forms *lunchin(g)*; the present use of *lunch* (XIX) is a shortening of this, whence **lunch** vb.

lunette XVI. - F. *lunette*, dim. of *lune* moon; see -ETTE.

lung OE. *lungen* = MLG. *lunge*, MDu. *longe* (Du. *long*), OHG. *lungun* (G. *lunge*), corr. to ON. *lunga*; f. Gmc. **luŋg-* :- IE. **lṇgʷh-*; see LIGHT[2]. The lungs were so named because of their lightness; cf. LIGHTS.

lunge[1] sword-thrust. XVIII. Aphetic of *allonge, elonge* (XVII), f. vbs. of the same form - F. *allonger* lengthen (in phr. *allonger un coup d'épée* give a sword-thrust), f. *à* AD- + *long* LONG[1]. So vb. XVIII.

lunge[2] †thong XVII; long rope used in training horses XVIII. - F. *longe*, shortening of *allonge* (as in *allonge d'un courroie* piece to lengthen a leather), f. *allonger* (see prec.).

lupin XIV. - L. *lupīnus, -um*, prob. rel. to *lupus* WOLF.

lupus (path.) ulcerous disease of the skin. XVI. - L., 'WOLF'.

lurch[1] vb. beat at a game in a particular manner XIV; sb. †game resembling backgammon, †final score in a game, †discomfiture, †cheat, and in phr. †*have in the lurch* have at a disadvantage, *leave in the lurch* leave in unexpected difficulty (perh. partly alt. of *leave in the lash*, of obscure orig.) XVI. The immed. source appears to be F. †*lourche* game resembling backgammon, also in phr. *demeurer lourche* be discomfited (orig. in the game), prob. - MHG. *lurz* wrong, in modG. *lurz werden* fail in a game.

lurch[2] sudden leaning over to one side. XIX. app. orig. in *lee-lurch*, perh. alt. of *lee-larch* (XVIII), for *lee-latch* drifting to leeward, f. LEE + †*latch* (XVII) ?leeway, ?lurch. Hence vb. XIX.

lure falconer's apparatus to recall a hawk; tempting thing XIV; angler's device for alluring fish XVII. - OF. *luere* (mod. *leurre*) - Gmc. **lōþr-* (cf. MHG. *luoder*, G. *luder* bait), prob. rel. to **laþōn* invite (OE. *laðian*, etc.). Hence vb. XIV.

lurid wan and sallow, sickly pale XVII; shining with a red glare; yellow-brown XVIII; ominous, 'ghastly' XIX. - L. *lūridus*, f. *lūror* wan or yellowish colour; see -ID[1].

lurk lie hid or in ambush. XIII. perh. f. *lūr-* LOUR + frequent. suffix *-k* as in *talk*.

luscious sweet and highly pleasant. XVI. of uncert. orig.

lush[1] flaccid, soft XV; succulent and luxuriant. XVII. poss. var. (assoc. with prec.) of *lash* (XV) soft and watery (of plants).

lush[2] liquor, drink. XVIII. perh. joc. application of LUSH[1].

lust pleasure, desire; sexual desire OE.; passionate desire XVII. OE. *lust*, corr. to (O)HG. *lust*, ON. *losti*, Goth. *lustus*, f. Gmc. **lust-* (cf. LIST[2]). Hence **lust** vb. XIII. **lustful** OE. **lusty** †joyful; †pleasing XIII; †lustful; powerful, strong XIV.

lustre[1] period of five years. XIV. - L. *lūstrum*, prop. quinquennial purification, of uncert. orig. So more usual **lustrum** XVI. **lustration** expiatory sacrifice, etc., purification. XVII.

lustre[2] sheen, gloss; luminosity, brilliance. XVI. - F. - It. *lustro*, f. *lustrare* :- L. *lūstrāre* light up :- **lūcstrāre*, f. *lūx*, *lūc-* LIGHT[1]. Hence **lustrous** XVII.

lute[1] stringed musical instrument. XIV. - F. †*lut* (mod. *luth*), prob. - Pr. *laüt* - Arab. *al-'ūd* (see AL-[2]).

lute[2] clay or cement to stop holes, etc. XIV. - (O)F. *lut* or medL. *lutum*, spec. use of L. *lutum* mud, potter's clay.

luteous of deep-yellow colour. XVII. f. L. *lūteus*, f. *lūtum* yellow weed; see -EOUS.

luxation dislocation. XVI. - F. - late L. *luxātiō*, *-ōn-*, f. *luxāre*, f. *luxus* dislocated; see -ATION.

luxury †lasciviousness XIV; use of and indulgence in choice or costly things XVII; means of such indulgence XVIII. - OF. *luxurie*, var. of *luxure* - L. *luxuria*, f. *luxus* abundance, sumptuous enjoyment, perh. the noun corr. to *luxus* (see prec.) and meaning orig. 'excess'. So **luxuriant** prolific XVI; profusely growing, etc. XVII. - prp. of L. *luxuriāre* grow rank (whence **luxuriate** XVII). **luxurious** †lascivious, †excessive XIV; self-indulgent XVII.

-ly[1] suffix appended to sbs. and adjs. to form adjs. OE. *-lic*, ME. *-lich*, *-lik*, *-li*, corr. to OS., OHG. *-līk* (Du. *-lijk*, G. *-lich*), ON. *-ligr*, *-legr*, Goth. *-leiks*. The Eng. forms in *-li*, *-ly* are due to ON. The orig. Gmc. adjs. were comps. of **līkam* appearance, form, body (cf. SUCH, WHICH), e.g. **frijōndlika-* friendly, having the appearance of a friend, **ʒōðalīka-* goodly, having the appearance or form of what is good, of good appearance. The most general senses in all Gmc. langs. are 'having the qualities appropriate to', 'characteristic of', 'befitting'; *-ly* was added to sbs. of alien orig., as *courtly*, *princely*, *scholarly*; formations on designations of things are infrequent, as *earthly*, *heavenly*, *leisurely*; exx. of *-ly* appended to adjs. are *kindly*, *lowly*, *poorly*, *sickly*. *Deadly*, *likely*, *lively*, *lovely*, *only* are exceptional in form. A further use is to denote periodic occurrence, e.g. *daily*, *yearly*.

-ly[2] suffix forming advs. of manner. OE. *-līce*, ME. *-liche*, *-līke*, *-liʒe*, *-li(e)* = OS., OHG. *-līko* (Du. *-lijk*, G. *-lich*), ON. *-liga*, Goth. *-leikō*: f. -LY[1] with Gmc. adv. suffix **-ō*. The Eng. forms in *-li(e)*, *-ly* are due to ON. In Gmc. an adv. with this suffix no doubt orig. implied the existence of a corr. adj. in -LY[1]; in OE. some advs. are formed on simple adjs., as *bealdlīce* BOLDLY, *swētlīce* SWEETLY, and this type increased greatly in ME. The general sense is 'in a manner characteristic of one who or a thing that is so-and-so', hence, 'in a so-and-so fashion', 'to a so-and-so degree'. Advs. referring to moments or periods of time, such as *formerly*, *instantly*, *lately*, *quarterly*, *yearly*, were prob. based at first on *early*; *firstly*, *secondly*, etc., were modelled on F. *premièrement*, L. *primo*, etc.; formations on sbs. such as *namely*, *partly* are prob. based on L. *nominatim*, *partim*; formations on pps., such as *admittedly*, *allegedly* have become frequent.

lycanthropy XVI. - modL. *lycanthrōpia* - Gr. *lukanthrōpiā*, f. *lukánthrōpos*, f. *lúkos* WOLF + *ánthrōpos* man; see -Y[3].

lyceum the garden in Athens where Aristotle taught XVI; place of study or instruction XVIII. - L. *Lycēum* - Gr. *Lúkeion*, n. of *Lúkeios* epithet of Apollo, to whose temple the Lyceum was adjacent.

lychee see LITCHI.

lych-gate see LICH-GATE.

lychnis XVII. - L. - Gr. *lukhnís* some red flower, f. *lúkhnos* lamp.

lycopodium XVIII. modL. - Gr. *lúkos* WOLF + *poús*, *pod-* FOOT; so named from the claw-like shape of the root.

lyddite kind of high explosive. XIX. f. *Lydd*, name of the town in Kent where it was first tested; see -ITE.

lye alkalized water or alkaline solution used for washing. OE. *lēag* = MDu. *lōghe* (Du. *loog*), OHG. *louga* (G. *lauge*) lye, ON. *laug* hot bath :- Gmc. **lauʒō*, f. **lau-* :- IE. **lou-* wash, LAVE.

lymph (rhet.) water; †sap XVII; colourless alkaline fluid in the body XVIII. - F. *lymphe* or L. *lympha*, of uncert. orig. So **lymphatic** A. †frenzied; B. pert. to lymph. XVII. - L. *lymphāticus* mad.

lynch law earlier †*Lynch's law* (XVIII) infliction of punishment by a self-constituted court. XIX. prob. named after Captain William *Lynch* of Virginia, who first set up this self-created judicial tribunal. Hence **lynch** vb. XIX.

lynx feline animal credited with very keen sight. XIV. - L. - Gr. *lúgx*, rel. to OE. *lox*, OHG. *luhs* (G. *luchs*), Lith. *lúšis*, MIr. *lug*; prob. f. IE. **leuk-*, as in Gr. *leússein* see (see LIGHT[1]).

lyre XIII. - OF. *lire* (mod. *lyre*) - L. *lyra* - Gr. *lúrā*. So **lyric** XVI. - F. *lyrique* or L. *lyricus* - Gr. *lurikós*. **lyrical** XVI.

M

ma see MAMMA[1].

ma'am XVII. contr. of MADAM. Also repr. by **marm** in the joc. (orig. U.S.) *school-marm* schoolmistress XIX.

macabre in *Dance Macabre*, the Dance of Death XV (*daunce of machabree*); (from modF.) gruesome XIX. The form now usual repr. F. *macabre* (XIX), error for OF. *macabré*, perh. alt. of OF. *Macabé* Maccabee; the orig. ref. may have been to a miracle play containing the slaughter of the Maccabees.

macadam applied to a kind of roadway (or the material used for it) invented by John Loudon *McAdam* (1756-1836). Hence **macadamize**, etc. XIX.

macaroni pasta in tubes XVI; exquisite, fop XVIII. - It. *maccaroni*, later *maccheroni*, pl. of *macca-*, *maccherone*. The sl. application to dandies perh. orig. indicated a preference for foreign food.

macaronic applied to burlesque verse in which vernacular words are mingled with Latin in a latinized form. XVII. - modL. *macarōnicus* - It. †*macaronico* (*maccheronico*), joc. f. *macaroni* (see prec.). The form was popularized by Teofilo Folengo (XVI), who described his verses as a literary analogue of macaroni ('a gross, rude, and rustic mixture of flour, cheese, and butter').

macaroon XVII. - F. *macaron* - It. *maccarone* MACARONI.

macassar name of an unguent for the hair made in early XIX by Rowland & Son and represented to contain ingredients from *Macassar*, district in Celebes. XIX.

macaw bird of the parrot kind. XVII. - Pg. *macao*, of unkn. orig.

mace[1] heavy club XIII; sceptre, staff of office XV; old form of billiard cue XVIII. - (O)F. *masse* :- Rom. **mattea* club. So **macer** macebearer; (Sc.) official in a court of law. XIV. - OF. *massier*.

mace[2] outer covering of the nutmeg. XIV (*macis*). - AL. or (O)F. *macis* - L. *macir* red spicy bark from India; the form *macis* being apprehended as a pl., a new sg. *mace* was formed from it.

macedoine medley of fruits in syrup or jelly. XIX. - F. *macédoine*, presumably a sb. use of OF. adj. - L. *macedonicus* Macedonian.

macerate soften by steeping; cause to waste away. XVI. f. pp. stem of L. *mācerāre* steep, soften, weaken; see -ATE[3]. So **maceration** XV. - F. or L.

machete see MATCHET.

machicolation (archit.) opening between corbels supporting a parapet, through which missiles were dropped on assailants. XVIII. f. *machicolate* (XVIII), f. OF. *machicoler*, AL. *machicollāre*, of uncert. orig.; see -ATION.

machination plotting, plot. XV. - (O)F. *machination* or L. *māchinātiō*, *-ōn-*, f. *māchinārī* contrive, f. *māchina* MACHINE; see -ATION.

machine †structure, fabric XVI; military engine; wheeled vehicle; apparatus for applying mechanical power, etc. XVII. - (O)F. - L. *māchina* device, contrivance, engine - Gr. *mākhanā́* (Doric), *mēkhanḗ*, f. *mēkhos* contrivance, rel. to Gmc. **maȝan* have power; see MAY[1]. Hence **machinery** XVII.

-machy always with connective -o-, repr. Gr. *-makhiā* fighting, in sbs. derived from adjs. in *-makhos* that fights, rel. to *mákhē* battle; e.g. *logomachy* (see LOGO-).

mackerel XIII. - AN. *makerel*, OF. *maquerel* (mod. *maquereau*), medL. *macarellus*; of unkn. orig. See -REL.

mac(k)intosh applied to a kind of waterproof material invented by Charles *Macintosh* (1766-1843). XIX.

macle twin crystal; dark spot in a mineral. XIX. - F. - L. *macula* spot, mesh (cf. MAIL[1]). A var. *macule* of the F. word is repr. by **mackle** blur in printing, blurred sheet XVIII, with a corr. vb. XVI. - F. *maculer*.

macro- comb. form of Gr. *makrós* long, large, rel. to L. *macer* thin, MEAGRE. The chief and oldest comp. is **macrocosm** the universe (XVI) - medL. *macrocosmus*, repr. Gr. **makròs kósmos* 'great world' (see COSMIC).

macron horizontal mark ¯ placed over a vowel sign to denote length. XIX. - Gr. *makrón*, n. of *makrós* MACRO-.

maculate spotted. XV. - L. *maculātus*, pp. of *maculāre*, f. *macula* spot (cf. MAIL[1]); see -ATE[2]. Now only in contrast with IMMACULATE.

mad out of one's mind, foolish, (now) insanely foolish; wildly excited, furious. XIII (*mad, med*). Aphetic of ME. †*amad*, repr. OE. *ġemǣd(d)*, *ġemǣded*, pp. of **ġemǣdan* render insane, f. *ġemād* insane = OS. *gimēd* foolish, OHG. *gameit*, *kimeit* foolish, vain, boastful, Goth. *gamaiþs* crippled :- Gmc. **ʒamaiðaz*, f. **ʒa-* Y- + **maiða-* :- IE. **moitó-*, pp. formation on **moi-* **mei-* change (cf. L. *mūtāre*); cf. Goth. *maidjan* adulterate, *inmaideins* exchange. Hence **madden** XVIII (-EN[5]); superseded **mad** vb. (XIV) in gen. use.

madam polite title of address to a woman XIII; †lady of rank, fine lady XVI; kept mistress XVIII; hussy XIX. - OF. *ma dame* (mod. *madame*), i.e. *ma* my, *dame* lady; see DAME. The form **madame** (XVII) is now mainly confined to use with the surname of a French married woman. See also MA'AM.

madder herbaceous climbing plant cultivated for a dye-stuff; formerly in wider use. OE. *mædere*, corr. to OHG. *matara*, ON. *maðra*, rel. to MLG., MDu. *mēde*; of uncert. orig.

madeira white wine of *Madeira*, island off N.W. Africa. XVI.

mademoiselle title applied to an unmarried Frenchwoman, miss. XVII. - F.; *ma* my, *demoiselle* young woman (see DAMSEL).

madonna †my lady, madam XVI; the Virgin Mary, picture or statue of her XVII. - It. *madonna*, i.e. *ma*, old unstr. form of *mia* my (:- L. *mea*), *donna* lady (:- L. *domina*).

madrepore perforate coral. XVIII. - F. *madrépore* or modL. *madrepora*, - It. *madrepora*, app. taken by Ferrante Imperato (XVI) to be f. *madre* MOTHER + *poro*, L. *porus* PORE, but the second el. may be L. *pōrus* - Gr. *pôros* calcareous stone, stalactite.

madrigal amatory lyrical poem, esp. to be set to music; kind of part song, XVI. - It. *madrigale* (whence F., Sp. *madrigal*), of uncert. orig.

maelstrom whirlpool in the Arctic Ocean off Norway; also gen. XVII. - early modDu. *maelstrom* (now *maalstroom*), f. *maalen* grind, whirl round + *stroom* STREAM.

Maenad Bacchante. XVI. - L. *Mænas, -ad-* - Gr. *Mainás, -ad-*, f. *maínesthai* rave.

maffick back-formation from *mafficking*, orig. applied to the uproarious rejoicings in London, etc., on the relief of the siege of *Mafeking* (1900) in the Boer War, the place-name being treated as a gerund or prp. in -ING.

mafia violent hostility to law and order; body of people manifesting this. XIX. - Sicilian It.

magazine storehouse, spec. for arms; stores, munitions XVI; †storehouse of information XVII; periodical publication XVIII. - F. *magasin* - It. *magazzino* - Arab. *maḵāzin*, pl. of *maḵzan* store-house, f. *ḵazana* store up.

magdalen reformed prostitute XVII; home for the reformation of prostitutes XVIII. From *the Magdalen* (XIV), after (O)F. *la Madeleine* - ecclL. (*Maria*) *Magdalēna, -lēnē* - Gr. (*María*) *Magdalḗnē* (Mary) of *Magdala* in Palestine, identified with the 'sinner' of Luke 7: 37.

mage see MAGUS.

magenta brilliant crimson aniline dye discovered soon after the battle (1859) at *Magenta* in N. Italy. XIX.

maggot worm, grub XIV; whimsy, crotchet XVII. perh. AN. alt. of ME. *maddo(c)k*, earlier *maðek* - ON. *maðkr*, f. the base of OE. *maða, -u* = OS. *matho*, OHG. *mado* (Du., G. *made*), Goth. *maþa* :- Gmc. **maþan-, -ō*, of unkn. orig.

magic sb. XIV. - OF. *magique* (superseded by *magie*) - late L. *magica* - Gr. *magikḗ*, f. *magikós* adj., f. *mágos* MAGUS. So **magic** adj. XIV, **magical** XVI, **magician** XIV.

magilp see MEGILP.

magisterial pert. to a master or magistrate. XVII. - medL. *magisteriālis*, f. late L. *magisterius*, f. L. *magister* MASTER; see -IAL.

magistral †authoritative; devised by a physician for a particular case, †sovereign XVI; (fortif.) principal XIX. - F. *magistral* or L. *magistrālis*; see MASTER, -AL.

magistrate officer concerned with the administration of laws XIV; justice of the peace XVII. - L. *magistrātus* magistracy, magistrate, f. *magistr-* MASTER; see -ATE[1]. Hence **magistracy** XVI. So **magistrature** office of a magistrate. XVII. - F.

magma †dregs of a semi-liquid substance XV; thin pasty mixture of substances XVII; (geol.) stratum of fluid matter XIX. - L. - Gr. *mágma* thick unguent, f. base **mag-* of *mássein* knead.

magnanimous XVI. f. L. *magnanimus*, f. *magnus* great + *animus* mind. See MAGNITUDE, ANIMAL, -OUS. So **magnanimity** XIV. - (O)F. - L.

magnate XV (*magnates*, prob. the L. pl., and so until XVIII or XIX). - late L. pl. *magnātēs* (sg. *magnās, -āt-*), f. *magnus* great; see MAGNITUDE.

magnesia A. †(alch.) mineral ingredient of the philosopher's stone XIV; B. †(spec. *black m.*) manganese XVII; C. (spec. †*white m.*) hydrated magnesium carbonate, used medicinally; (chem.) magnesium oxide XVIII. - medL. *magnēsia* - Gr. (*hē*) *Magnēsía* (*líthos*) 'the Magnesian stone', (1) loadstone, (2) stone with silvery sheen; the development of senses B and C is obscure. Hence **magnesium** XIX.

magnet †magnetic oxide of iron XV; †piece of loadstone; piece of iron or steel having the same attractive properties XVII. - L. *magnēta* (whence OF. *magnete*, perh. in part the source), acc. of *magnēs* - Gr. *mágnēs*, for *ho Mágnēs líthos* the Magnesian stone. So **magnetic** XVII, **-etical** XVI. - late L. *magnēticus*. **magnetism** XVII. - modL. Hence **magnetize** XVIII, **magneto-** (see -O-) XIX.

magni- comb. form of L. *magnus* great (see MAGNITUDE), as in **magniloquent** grandiloquent XVII, f. L. *magniloquus* (*loquī* speak); see -ENT.

magnific †renowned; †sumptuous XV; (arch.) grand XVI; also **magnifical** XVI. - F. *magnifique* or L. *magnificus*; see prec., -FIC. So **magnificent** great in achievement; †royally munificent; grand, splendid. XVI. - F. *magnificent* or L. *magnificent-*, alt. stem of *magnificus*. **magnificence** XIV. - F. or L. **magnifico** Venetian magnate XVI. - It., sb. use of adj. - L. *magnificus*.

magnify A. (arch.) act for the honour of; B. (arch.) augment XIV; C. increase the apparent size of XVII. - (O)F. or L.

magnificat the canticle beginning '*Magnificat* anima mea Dominum' My soul doth magnify the Lord (Luke 1: 46); 3rd pers. sg. pres. ind. of L. *magnificāre* MAGNIFY.

magnitude greatness XIV; (relative) size XVI. - L. *magnitūdō*, f. *magnus* great, large, rel. to Gr. *mégas* (cf. MEGA-), Skr. *mahā́nt-* great, Gmc. **mikil-* MUCH; see -TUDE.

magnolia XVIII. modL., f. name of Pierre *Magnol* (1638-1715) professor of botany at Montpellier; see -IA[1].

magnum bottle containing two quarts. XVIII. - n. sg. of L. *magnus* large (see MAGNITUDE).

magpie XVII. f. *Mag*, pet-form of *Margaret* + PIE[1].

magus (in pl. *magi*) the 'wise men' who came 'from the East' to worship the child Jesus (Matt. 2: 1) XIV; member of an ancient Persian priestly caste XVI. - L. - Gr. *mágos* - OPers. *maguš*. Also anglicized **mage** wise man, magician. XIV. Hence **magian** XVI.

maharajah title of some Indian princes. XVII (*mau raja*). - Hind. *mahārājā*, f. *mahā* great + *rājā* RAJAH. So **maharanee** XIX. - Hind. *mahārānī* (*rānī* queen).

mahatma in Buddhism, one possessing preternatural powers. XIX. - Skr. *mahātman-*, f. *mahā-* great + *ātmán-* soul.

mahdi spiritual and temporal leader expected by Muslims. XVIII. - Arab. *mahdīy* 'he who is guided right', pp. of *hadā* lead in the right way.

mah-jong XX. - Chinese, 'house sparrow'.

mahlstick see MAULSTICK.

mahogany XVII (*mohogoney*). of unkn. orig.

Mahomet XIV. ME. *Mac(h)amete, Mako-* - (O)F. *Mahomet*, †*Mach-*, medL. *Ma(c)hometus* - Arab. *Muḥammad* ('highly praised', f. *ḥamida* praise), now repr. by **Mohammed, Muhammad** founder of the religion of Islam. So **Mahometan** XVI. - medL. *Mahometānus*, etc. **Mahound,** later form (XVI) of †*Mah(o)un* (XIII). - OF. *Mahun, -um*, shortening of *Mahomet*.

mahout elephant-driver. XVII. - Hindi *mahāut, mahāwat* :- Skr. *mahāmātra* high official, lit. 'great in measure'.

maid XII. Shortening of MAIDEN; in sense 'female servant' XIV. For loss of *-n* cf. *clue, eve, game*.

maiden girl, young woman; virgin; female servant. OE. *mæġden* = OHG. *magatīn* :- Gmc. **maȝadīnam*, dim. (see -EN[1]), f. **magaþiz* maid, virgin, which is repr. by OE. *mæġ(e)ð*, OS. *magath*, OHG. *magad* (G. *magd*), Goth. *magaþs*, and is rel. to Gmc. **maȝuz* (OE., OS. *magu*, ON. *mǫgr*, Goth. *magus* son, young man), f. IE. **magh-*, whence OIr. *mug* slave, Av. *magu* young man.

maieutic pert. to the Socratic method of bringing out latent conceptions. XVII. - Gr. *maieutikós* obstetric (used fig. of Socratic methods), f. *maieúesthai* act as midwife, f. *maîa* midwife; see -IC.

maigre involving abstinence from flesh meat. XVII. - F.; see MEAGRE.

mail[1] ring or plate of armour; armour composed of rings XIV; breast feathers of a hawk XV. - (O)F. *maille* mesh :- L. *macula* spot, mesh.

mail[2] (now Sc.) payment, tax, tribute. north. repr. of late OE. *māl* - ON. *mál* speech, agreement = OE. *mǣl* speech; in sense the Eng. word corr. rather to ON. *máli* stipulation, stipulated pay.

mail[3] (now Sc. and U.S.) pack, bag XIII; bag of letters for conveyance by post; person or vehicle conveying this XVII. ME. *male* - OF. *male* (mod. *malle* bag, trunk), of Gmc. orig. Hence vb. (orig. U.S.). send by post. XIX.

maim XIII. - OF. *mahaignier, mayner* :- Rom. **mahagnāre*, of unkn. orig.

main[1] physical strength (surviving only in *with might and m.*). OE. *mæġen* = OS. *megin*, OHG. *magan, megin*, ON. *magn, meg(i)n*, f. Gmc. base **maȝ-* have power; see MAY[1].

main[2] (dial.) of great size XIII; strong, mighty (surviving only in sense 'sheer' in phr. *by m. force*); (dial.) great in number or degree XIV; chief in size, extent, or order XV. Partly repr. OE. *mæġen* MAIN[1] in comps., as *mæġenfolc* great company of people, *mæġenstrengo* great strength; partly - rel. ON. *megenn, megn* strong, powerful, or *megin* (in combination). There are many special collocations: e.g. *m. chance* XVI, *mainland* XIV, †*m. sea* XVI, *m. drain* XVIII; from these, by ellipsis, arose sb. uses of *main*: e.g. (1) prob. from *the m. chance*, a throw in the game of hazard, the most important part, etc. (now chiefly in phr. *in the m.*) XVI; (2) from *the m. sea*, the high sea XVI; (3) from *m. drain*, chief sewer XVIII. Hence **mainly** †vigorously XIII; †greatly XIV; for the most part XVII.

maintain support the person or cause of XIII; †practise habitually; carry on, continue; support, provide for XIV. ME. *mainte(i)ne*, repr. tonic stem of (O)F. *maintenir* (AN. *maintener*) :- Rom. **manūtenēre*, f. L. *manū*, abl. of *manus* hand + *tenēre* hold. So **maintenance** †demeanour; support of a party or cause; provision of livelihood. XIV. - OF.

maiolica var. of MAJOLICA.

maison(n)ette small house XIX; part of a house let separately XX. - F., dim. of *maison*; see MANSION, -ETTE.

maize XVI (*mais, mahiz, mayis*, etc.). - F. *maïs*, †*mahiz*, or its source Sp. *maiz*, †*mahiz, -is*, †*mayz*, of Carib orig.

majesty sovereign power (first of the glory of God) XIII; kingly dignity XVI. - (O)F. *majesté* L. *mājestās, -tāt-*, rel. to *mājor*; see MAJOR, -TY. Hence **majestic** XVII, **-ical** XVI.

majolica fine kind of Italian pottery. XVI. - It., f. name of the island Majorca, formerly †*Majolica*, where the best ware of this kind was said to be made.

major[1] officer below the rank of lieutenant-colonel. XVII. - F. (short for *sergent-major* sergeant-major, orig. a much higher rank than now) - L. *mājor*; see next. Also in *m.-general* (XVII), earlier *sergeant-m.-general* (XVII). - F. *major-général*, where *major* is sb. and *général* adj. So **major-domo** chief official of a household. XVI. Earliest forms *maior-, mayordome* - (partly through F. *majordome*) Sp. *mayordomo*, It. *maggiordomo* - medL. *mājor domūs* (*domūs*, g. of *domus* house) highest official of the royal household under the Merovingians.

major[2] greater. XVI. - L. *mājor* (:- **māgjōs*) compar. of *magnus* great (see MAGNITUDE). So **majority** †superiority; state of being of full age XVI; greater number or part XVII. - F. *majorité* - medL. *mājōritās*.

majuscule †capital (letter); (palaeogr.) large (also sb.). XIX. - F. - L. *mājusculus* somewhat larger, dim. of *mājor* MAJOR[2].

make pt., pp. *made* bring into existence, subject to an operation, cause to be, cause (something to happen). OE. *macian* (not freq.) = OS. *makon* (Du. *maken*), OHG. *mahhōn* (G. *machen*) :- WGmc. **makōjan*, f. **mak-* MATCH[1]; plausibly referred to IE. **maĝ-* repr. by Gr. *mássein* knead, OSl. *mazati* anoint, grease. The sense-history is uncert. Hence sb. manner, style, form. XIV. **maker** manufacturer, creator XIII; (arch.) poet (ult. tr. Gr. *poētḗs*) XIV.

mal- formerly often †*male-* (one syll.), repr. F.

mal-, L. *male* badly, ill (cf. MALE-), first in words adopted from F., later generalized, as in *malcontent* XVI, *malodorous* XIX, *malpractice* XVII.

malachite XVI (*melo-*). - OF. *melochite* (now *malachite*) - L. *molochītēs* - Gr. *molokhîtis*, f. *molókhē*, var. of *malákhē* MALLOW; see -ITE.

malaco- comb. form of Gr. *malakós* soft, as in *malacology* (- F. *malocologie*) science of molluscs.

malady XIII. - (O)F. *maladie*, f. *malade* sick, ill :- Rom. **male habitus* 'in bad condition', i.e. L. *male* badly + *habitus*, pp. of *habēre* have, hold; see HABIT, -Y[3].

Malaga white wine exported from *Malaga*, a seaport in the south of Spain. XVII (*Mallego*, *Maligo*).

Malagasy pert. to (a native of) Madagascar; sb. its language. XIX. f. *Malegass*, *-gash*, varr. of *Madegass*, *-cass*, after or parallel with F. *malgache*, *madécasse*, adj. f. the name of the island.

malaise bodily discomfort. XVIII. - (O)F. *malaise*, f. OF. *mal* bad (L. *malus*) + *aise* EASE.

malanders var. of MALLENDERS.

malapert (arch.) impudent. XV. - OF., f. *mal-* (indicating the opposite) + *apert*, var. of *espert* EXPERT, but apprehended as if f. MAL- improperly + *apert* bold, PERT.

malapropism XIX. f. name of Mrs. *Malaprop*, character in Sheridan's 'The Rivals' (1775), remarkable for her misuse of words, f. *malapropos* inopportune(ly) (XVII) - F. *mal à propos* not to the purpose; see MAL-, APROPOS, -ISM. *Malaprop* was formerly so used, and as adj.

malaria fever formerly supposed to be caused by exhalations from marshy places. XVIII. - It. *mal'aria* for *mala aria* 'bad AIR'; cf. MAL-.

male XIV. - OF. *male*, earlier *masle* (mod. *mâle*) :- L. *masculus* (cf. MASCULINE).

male-, repr. L. *male-*, comb. form of adv. *male* (see MAL-) in **malediction** XV. - L. *maledictiō*, *-ōn-*; see DICTION. **malefactor** XV. - (partly through OF. *malfaicteur*) L. *malefactor* (*facere* DO[1]). **malefic** productive of evil XVII. - L. *maleficus*. **maleficent** XVII. **malevolent** XVI. - OF. *malivolent* or L. *malevolēns*, *-ent-* (*volēns*, prp. of *velle* WILL). **malevolence** XV. - OF. or L.

malfeasance (leg.) official misconduct. XVII. - AN. *malfaisance*, f. MAL- + OF. *faisance* act, action (f. *faire* do); cf. MISFEASANCE.

malice XIII. - (O)F. - L. *malitia*, f. *malus* bad; see MAL-. So **malicious** XIII. - OF. *malicius* (mod. *-ieux*) - L. *malitiōsus*.

malign evil in nature and effects XIV; (arch.) malevolent XV. - OF. *maligne*, fem. of *malin*, or its source L. *malignus*, f. *malus* evil; cf. BENIGN. So vb. †speak evil, plot XV; †dislike, envy XVI; speak ill of XVII. - OF. *malignier* or late L. *malignāre* contrive maliciously. **malignity** XIV. - OF. or L. **malignant** †disposed to rebel; of evil effect or disposition. XVI. - prp. of L. *malignāre*.

malinger feign illness XIX. Back-formation from **malingerer** (XVIII), app. f. (O)F. *malingre*, perh. f. MAL- + *haingre* weak, thin, prob. of Gmc. orig. (cf. MHG. *hager* thin, lean).

malison (arch.) curse. XIII. - OF. *mal(e)ison* - L. *maledictiō*, *-ōn-* MALEDICTION.

mall see PALL-MALL.

mallard wild drake or duck. XIV. - OF. *mallart*, (now) *malart*, prob. for **maslart*, f. *masle* MALE; see -ARD.

malleable that may be hammered without breaking. XIV. - OF. - medL. *malleābilis*, f. L. *malleāre* hammer, f. *malleus*; see MAUL, -ABLE.

mallenders pl. scabby eruption in horses. XV (†sg.; pl. from XVII). - (O)F. *malandre* :- L. *malandria* (pl.) pustules on the neck.

mallet XV (*mail(ȝ)et*). - (O)F. *maillet*, f. *mailler* vb. hammer, f. *mail* sb. hammer, MAUL.

mallow plant of genus *Malva*. OE. *mealuwe*, *-(e)we* - L. *malva*, rel. to Gr. *malákhē*, *molókhē*, and prob. of Mediterranean orig.

malm soft friable rock, light loamy soil. OE. **mealm* (in *mealmstān* friable stone, and *mealmiht* sandy) = ON. *malmr* ore, metal, Goth. *malma* sand, f. Gmc. **mal-* **mel-* grind (see MEAL[1]); cf. OS., MHG. *melm* dust.

malmaison variety of carnation. XIX. Short for *souvenirs de Malmaison* 'memories of Malmaison' (the château at which the empress Josephine held her court), orig. the name of a blush rose.

malmsey XV (*malmesey*). - MDu., MLG. *malmesie*, *-eye* (in medL. *malmasia*), f. Gr. placename *Monemvasia* in the Morea, of which the var. *Malvasia* gave MALVOISIE.

malt barley, etc., for brewing. OE. *m(e)alt* = OS. *malt* (Du. *mout*), (O)HG. *malz*, ON. *malt* :- Gmc. **maltaz*, rel. to OHG. *malt* (G. *malz*) soft, weak, ON. *maltr* rotten; f. base of MELT. Hence **maltster** XIV; see -STER.

maltha kind of cement XV; bitumen, mineral pitch or tar. XVII. - L. - Gr. *máltha*, *málthē* mixture of wax and pitch.

Malthusian pert. to Thomas Robert *Malthus* (1766-1834), who advocated checks on the growth of population; see -IAN.

malvaceous pert. to the mallows. XVII. f. L. *malvāceus*, f. *malva* MALLOW; see -ACEOUS.

malversation corrupt administration. XVI. - F., f. *malverser* - L. *male versārī* (*male* ill, MAL- + *versārī* behave, conduct oneself, f. *vers-*, pp. stem of *vertere* turn).

malvoisie (arch.) malmsey. XIV. ME. *malvesin*, *malvesie* - OF. *malvesie*, from the F. form of the place-name *Monemvasia*; see MALMSEY. The present form is that of modF.

mam (dial.) mother. XVI. prob. imit.; cf. MAMMA[1]. Hence **mammy** (-Y[6]) XVI.

mama see MAMMA[1].

Mameluke one of the military body, orig. Caucasian slaves, that ruled Egypt 1254-1811. XVI. - F. *mameluk* (OF. *mamelus*), It. *mammalucco*, Sp., Pg. *mameluco*, medL. *mameluc*, *-uchus* - Arab. *mamlūk* slave, sb. use of pp. of *malaka* possess.

mamilla nipple. XVII. - L., dim. of *mamma* breast, teat; see next. Hence **mamillary** XVII.

mamma[1], mama mother. XVI. repr. redupl. of a syllable instinctively uttered by young children; cf. Gr. *mámmē*, L. *mamma* (mother, teat, breast; see next), OSl., Russ., Lith. *mama*, Ir., W. *mam*. Shortened to **ma** (dial. and U.S.) XIX.

mamma[2] (anat.) breast in mammals. XVII. - L. (see prec.). Hence **mammary** XVII.

mammal XIX; animal of the class **mammalia** (XVIII), who suckle their young. modL., n. pl. of L. *mammālis*, f. *mamma*; see prec., -AL[1].

Mammon (personification of) riches. XVI. Earlier *Mammona* as a proper name for 'the devil of covetousness' - late L. *mam(m)ōna*, *mam(m)on* - N.T. Gr. *mam(m)ōnâs* (Matt. 6: 24, Luke 16: 9-13) - Aram. *māmônā*, *māmôn* riches, gain.

mammoth large extinct elephant. XVIII. - Russ. *mámo(n)t*, of uncert. orig.

man pl. **men** human being; adult male OE.; vassal, manservant XII; (dial.) husband XIII. OE. *man(n)*, *mon(n)*, pl. *menn* (:- **manniz*), also *manna*, *monna*, corr. to OS., OHG. *man* (Du. *man*, G. *mann*), ON. *maðr* (g. *manns*, pl. *menn*), Goth. *manna* (g. *mans*, pl. *mans*, *mannans*); the various forms belong to two Gmc. stems **mann-*, **mannan-*, rel. to Skr. *mánu-* man, mankind, OSl. *mǫžĭ*.

The prominent sense in OE. was 'human being', the words distinctive of sex being *wer* and *wīf*, *wǣp(n)man* and *wīfman* WOMAN. The sense 'ship' (as in *Frenchman*) appears in XV. Among spec. phr. is *man-at-arms* (XVI; formerly †*man of arms*), tr. OF. *homme d'armes* and *à armes*. The sense of 'piece' used in chess appears c.1400. Hence **man** vb. Late OE. *(ġe)mannian*. **manhood, †-head** XIII. **mannish** †human; masculine XIV; pert. to a grown man XVI; characteristic of a male XVIII. repl. OE. *menniśċ*. **manslaughter** XVII. Superseded †*manslaught*, OE. (Angl.) *mannslæht*, the second el. being :- Gmc. **slaχtiz*, f. **slaχ-* SLAY[1].

manacle fetter for the hand. XIV. ME. *manicle* - (O)F. *manicle* handcuff, also (as in modF.) gauntlet - L. *manicula* little hand, handle, in medL. gauntlet, dim. of *manus* hand (see MANUAL); assim. later to words in *-acle*. Hence vb. XIV.

manage (arch.) training of a horse; action and paces of a horse XVI; riding-school XVII. - It. *maneggio* (whence F. *manège*), f. *maneggiare* :- Rom. **manidiare*, f. *manus* hand (see MANUAL), whence **manage** vb. train (a horse); handle, wield; conduct (an affair), control (a person) XVI; do successfully XVIII. First in the form **manege**; the ending was early assim. to -AGE, but in the techn. uses the F. form finally prevailed. In XVII-XVIII the vb. was often identified with F. *ménager* use sparingly (cf. MÉNAGE). Hence **management** XVI.

manatee large aquatic cetacean. XVI. - Sp. *manati*, of Carib orig.

manciple official who purchases provisions. XIII. - AN., OF. *manciple*, var. of *mancipe* :- L. *mancipium* purchase, slave (orig. one obtained by legal purchase), f. *manus* hand + *capere*, **cip-* take; see MANUAL, CAPTURE.

-mancy repr. (O)F. *-mancie* - late L. *-mantīa* - Gr. *manteíā* divination, f. *manteúesthai* prophesy, f. *mántis* prophet, diviner. Some of the comps. with this ending repr. Gr. words, as *chiromancy*, *necromancy*, others late L. or medL. words, as *geomancy*, *hydromancy*; and others have been formed on Gr. models, as *crystallomancy*, *lithomancy*.

mandamus (leg.) writ directing the performance of a certain act. XVI. - L. 'we command', 1st pers. pl. pres. ind. of *mandāre* (see MANDATE).

mandarin[1] Chinese official. XVI. - Pg. *mandarin* (after *mandar* command) - Malay *mantĕri* - Hindi *mantrī* :- Skr. *mantrin-* counsellor, f. *mántra-* counsel (rel. to MIND).

mandarin[2] small kind of orange. XIX. - F. *mandarine*, fem. of *mandarin* (see prec.); prob. so named from the yellow of mandarins' costume.

mandate command, spec. legal or judicial XVI; commission or contract by which one acts for another XVII. - L. *mandātum*, sb. use of n. pp. of *mandāre* enjoin, commit, f. *manus* hand + *dare* give; see MANUAL, -ATE[1]. So **mandatary** XVII, **mandatory** XVI. - late L.

mandible XVI. - OF. *mandible*, later *mandibule*, or its source late L. *mandibula*, *-ulum*, f. *mandere* chew.

mandolin(e) XVIII. - F. *mandoline* - It. *mandolino*, dim. of *mandola*, var. of *mandora*.

mandragora plant of S. Europe and the East having emetic and narcotic properties. In OE. in L. form; in ME. anglicized or - (O)F. *mandragore* - medL. *mandragora*, L. *-as* - Gr. *mandragóras*.

mandrake mandragora. XIV. ME. also *-ag(g)e*, prob. - MDu. *mandrage*, *mandragre* - medL. MANDRAGORA; alt. to *mandrake* was prob. in allusion to the man-like form of the root of the plant, and assoc. with DRAKE[1] dragon because of the plant's supposed magical properties.

mandrel A. miner's pick XVI; B. arbor of a lathe XVII; C. core of cast or moulded metal XVIII. of unkn. orig.

mandrill large baboon. XVIII. app. f. MAN + DRILL[2].

manducation eating XVI; chewing XVII. - late L. *mandūcātiō*, *-ōn-*, f. L. *mandūcāre*, f. *mandūcō* guzzler, f. *mandere* chew.

mane OE. *manu* = (M)Du. *mane*, OHG. *mana* (G. *mähne*), ON. *mǫn* :- Gmc. **manō*.

manege see MANAGE.

manes souls of the departed, esp. as beneficent spirits (XIV) XVII. - L. *mānēs* pl., perh. f. *mānis*, *mānus* good.

manganese black mineral XVII; element of which this is the oxide XVIII. - F. *manganèse* - It. *manganese*, unexpl. alt. of medL. *magnēsia* MAGNESIA.

mange XIV. ME. *maniewe*, later *mangie*, shortened to *mange* (XVI) - OF. *manjue*, *mangeue* itch, f. *manju-*, pres. ind. sg. stem of *mangier* (mod. *manger*) eat :- L. *mandūcāre* (see MANDUCATION). Hence **mangy** XVI.

mangel-, mangold-wurzel XVIII. - G. *mangoldwurzel*, f. *mangold* beet + *wurzel* root (cf. WORT[1]).

manger XIV (*manyour*). - (O)F. *mangeoire* :-

Rom. **mandūcātōria*, f. *mandūcāt-*; see MANDUCATION.

mangle[1] hack or cut about. XIV. - AN. *mangler*, **mahangler* (cf. medL. *mangulare*), prob. frequent. of *mahaignier* MAIM; see -LE[3].

mangle[2] machine for rolling and pressing laundered clothing, etc. XVIII. - Du. *mangel*, short for synon. *mangelstok*, f. *mangelen* mangle + *stok* staff, roller, STOCK.

mango XVI (*manga, -as*). first - Pg. *manga* (whence modL. *mangas*), later - Du. *mango* - Malay *mangga* - Tamil *māṅkāy*.

mangonel military engine for casting stones. XIII. - OF. *mangonel, -elle* (mod. *mangonneau*) - medL. *manganellus, -gon-*, dim. f. late L. *manganum* - Gr. *mágganon* engine of war, axis of a pulley.

mangosteen fruit of the E. Indian tree *Garcinia mangostana*. XVI. - Malay *manggustan* (now *manggis*).

mangrove tree of the genus *Rhizophora*. XVII. Early forms *mangrowe, mangrave*, later assim. to GROVE; obscurely connected with Pg. *mangue*, Sp. *mangle*.

manhandle †wield (a tool) XV; move by force of men alone XIX; handle roughly. f. MAN + HANDLE.

mania highly excited form of madness XIV; great enthusiasm, craze XVII. - late L. *mania* - Gr. *maniā*, rel. to *maínesthai* be mad, f. IE. **mn-* **men-*; see MIND, -IA[1]. As a terminal el. it was used in later Gr., e.g. in *gunaikomaniā* mad passion for women, *hippomaniā* passionate love of horses, on the model of which a number of comps. were formed in mod. medical L., e.g. *nymphomania*; later imitations of these are *kleptomania, megalomania*. The sbs. in *-mania* have corr. adj. forms in *-maniac* (one) affected with the particular mania. So **maniac, maniacal** XVII. - late L. *maniacus* - late Gr. *maniakós*.

Manichee heretic holding dualistic belief in God and Satan. XIV. - late L. *Manichæus*, f. name of the founder of the sect, *Manes* or *Manichæus*. Also **Manichaean** XVI.

manicure one who treats (or treatment of) the hands and finger-nails. - F., f. L. *manus* hand + *cūra* care; see MANUAL, CURE.

manifest adj. XIV. - (O)F. *manifeste* or L. *manifestus*, earlier *manufestus*, f. *manus* hand (see MANUAL) + **festus* struck, f. base of *dēfendere* DEFEND. So vb. XIV. **manifestation** XV. - late L. **manifesto** †proof; public declaration. XVII. - It., whence also **manifest** sb. †manifestation XVI; †manifesto XVII; list of ship's cargo XVIII.

manifold adj. OE. *manigf(e)ald* = OHG. *manacfalt* (G. *mannig falt*), Goth. *managfalþs*, etc.; see MANY, -FOLD. As sb. pl. XIII; see MANYPLIES.

manikin little man, dwarf XVII; artist's lay figure XVIII. - Du. *manneken*, dim. of *man* MAN; see -KIN. Cf. MANNEQUIN.

manilla short for *Manilla hemp*. XIX; the correct form is *Manila*, name of the capital of the Philippine Islands.

manille second best trump or honour at quadrille and ombre. XVII (*mallilio*). The current form is - F. *manille* - Sp. *malilla*, dim. of *mala*, fem. of *malo* bad.

manioc cassava. XVI (*manihot*, - F.). - Tupi *mandioca*.

maniple (eccl.) vestment worn suspended from the left arm; subdivision of the Roman legion XVI; †handful XVII. - OF. *maniple* (mod. *manipule*) or L. *manipulus* handful, troop of soldiers, f. *manus* hand (see MANUAL) + an unkn. el.

manipulation method of handling chemical apparatus XVIII; manual management or examination XIX. - F. - modL. **manipulātiō, -ōn-*, f. **manipulāre*, f. L. *manipulus* handful; see prec. and -ATION. So **manipulate** XIX.

mankind XIII. repl. †*mankin*, OE. *mancynn* (MAN, KIN), by substitution of KIND[1].

manna miraculous food of Exodus 16 OE.; juice from the bark of *Fraxinus ornus* (manna ash) XVI. - late L. - Hellenistic Gr. *mánna* - Aram. *mannā* - Heb. *mān*.

mannequin later (F.) form of MANIKIN, in sense 'lay figure', 'dressmaker's model'. XVIII.

manner kind, sort XII; way or mode of action; customary practice; (pl.) moral character; outward bearing XIII; (pl., †sg.) external behaviour XIV; method or style XVII. ME. *manere* - AN. *manere*, (O)F. *manière* :- Rom. **manuāria* sb. use of fem. of L. *manuārius* pert. to the hand, f. *manus* hand (see MANUAL, -ARY). Hence **mannered, mannerism** XIX, **-ist** XVII. **mannerly** (see -LY[1,2]) XIV.

manœuvre, U.S. **maneuver** evolution of naval or military forces. XVIII. - F. *manœuvre* (OF. *manuevre*), f. *manœuvrer* (whence **manœuvre** vb. XVIII) :- medL. *manuoperāre*, for L. *manū operārī* (*-āre*) work with the hand; see MANUAL, OPERATE.

manometer XVIII. - F. *manomètre*, f. Gr. *manós* thin, rare; see -METER.

manor †mansion, country residence XIII; †mansion of a lord with the land appertaining XIV; territorial unit, orig. a feudal lordship XVI. ME. *maner(e)* - AN. *maner*, OF. *maneir*, (now) *manoir* dwelling, habitation, sb. use of *maneir* dwell :- L. *manēre* remain. Hence **manorial** XVIII.

mansard broken roof. XVIII. - F. *mansarde*, f. name of the F. architect François *Mansard* (1598-1666).

manse †mansion house XV; (hist.) measure of land sufficient to support a family; ecclesiastical residence XVI. - medL. *mansus, -a, -um* dwelling, house, measure of land, f. *māns-* (see next).

mansion †dwelling, abiding; †abiding-place XIV; †manor-house XVI; stately residence XIX. - (O)F. - L. *mānsiō, -ōn-* stay, dwelling-place (whence (O)F. *maison* house), f. *māns-*, pp. stem of *manēre* remain, stay.

mansuetude (arch.) gentleness. XIV. - (O)F., or L. *mānsuētūdō*, f. *mānsuētus* gentle, f. *manus* hand + *suētus* accustomed; see MANUAL, DESUETUDE.

mantel †movable shelter for besiegers; piece of timber supporting the masonry above a fireplace (hence *mantelpiece, -shelf*). XV. var. of MANTLE, with senses derived from F. *manteau*, †*mantel*.

mantis insect which holds its forelegs in a position suggesting hands folded in prayer. XVII. - modL. - Gr. *mántis* prophet, diviner, rel. to MANIA.

mantissa †unimportant addition XVII; (math.) decimal part of a logarithm XIX. - L. *mantissa*, *-īsa* makeweight.

mantle loose sleeveless cloak XIII; applied to various coverings from XIV. ME. *mantel* - OF. *mantel* (mod. *manteau*) :- L. *mantellum*, rel. to late L. *mantus*, medL. *mantum*, **manta* short cloak, whence Sp., It. *manto* (F. *mante*) cloak, Sp. *manta* blanket, tapestry; perh. ult. of Celt. orig. So **mant(e)let** cape, cloak XIV; movable shelter for men-at-arms XVI; screen for men working a gun XIX. - OF., dim. of *mantel*. **mantilla** woman's veil. XVIII. - Sp., dim. of *manta*. **mantua** loose gown for women. XVII. alt. of *manteau* by assoc. with the It. place-name *Mantua*. Hence **mantle** vb. XIV.

manu- repr. abl. sg. of L. *manus* hand (see next) as in MANUFACTURE, MANUSCRIPT; e.g. **manuduction** guidance XVI, **manumission** XV, after L.

manual pert. to the hands. XV. Earliest form *manuel* (later assim. to L.) - (O)F. *manuel* - L. *manuālis*, f. *manus* hand, rel. to OE., ON. *mund*, OHG. *munt*; see -AL[1]. As sb. small book for handy use (XV) based ult. on late L. *manuāle*, sb. use of n. of adj.; as a term for the keyboard of an organ (XIX) distinguished from *pedal*.

manufacture †product of manual labour XVI; †manual work; making things by physical labour or mechanical power, thing so made XVII. - F. - It. *manifattura* (XIV), with refash. after L. *manū factum* made by hand (see MANUAL, FACT, -URE). So **manufactory** XVII; after FACTORY.

manure †occupy, administer; †till, cultivate XIV; (from the sb.) apply manure to XVI. Earliest forms *maynoyre*, *-oure*, *manour* - AN. *mainoverer*, OF. *mano(u)vrer* MANŒUVRE; assim. in ending to -URE. Hence sb. dung or compost used for fertilizing XVI.

manuscript adj. written by hand; sb. writing; codex. XVI. - medL. *manūscrīptus*, i.e. *manū* with the hand and *scrīptus*, pp. of *scrībere* write; see MANU-, SCRIBE.

Manx XVI. Earlier *Manks* - (with metathesis) ON. **Manskr*, f. *Man-* (nom. *Mǫn* :- **Manu* - OIr. *Manu*) + *-skr* -ISH[1].

many a great number of (with *a*, *an* XIII). OE. *maniġ*, *moniġ*, later *mæniġ*, corr. to OS. *manag*, MDu. *menech*, Du. *menig*, OHG. *manag*, *menig* (G. *manch*), OSw. *mangher*, Goth. *manags* :- Gmc. **manaʒaz*, **maniʒaz* :- IE. **monogho-* **menogho-*, whence also OSl. *mŭnogŭ* much, OIr. *menice* abundant, W. *mynych* often. As sb. in *a* (*great*) *many* (*of*), etc. XVI; orig. modelled on *a few*, but also assoc. with MEINIE. Cf. MANIFOLD.

manyplies (dial.) omasum. XVIII (*monyple*, *manyplus*). f. MANY + pl. of PLY[1]; modelled on synon. *manifolds* (XIII).

Maori (member of) aboriginal race of New Zealand. XIX. - native name.

map sb. XVI. - medL. *mappa*, short for *mappa mundī* 'sheet of the world', i.e. *mappa* (in classL. table-cloth, NAPKIN), *mundī* g. of *mundus* world. Hence vb. XVI.

maple In OE. *mapeltrēow*, *mapulder* maple-TREE. The simplex is first recorded XIV.

maquis underground patriotic movement in France in the war of 1939-45. - F., 'scrub' - It. *macchia* spot, thicket :- L. *macula* spot.

mar †hinder; †spoil, impair OE.; harm, injure, ruin (now in lighter sense) XIII. OE. *merran* (WS. *mierran*) = OS. *merrian* hinder (Du. *marren* fasten, loiter), OHG. *marren*, *merren* hinder, ON. *merja* bruise, crush, Goth. (Gmc.) *marzjan* cause to stumble.

maraschino liqueur made from the marasca cherry. XVIII. - It., f. *marasca*, aphetic of *amarasca*, f. *amaro* bitter - L. *amārus*.

marasmus (path.) wasting disease. XVII. modL. - Gr. *marasmós*, f. *maraínein* wither, waste.

Marathon name of the place at which the Athenians defeated the Persians in 490 B.C., applied to a long-distance foot-race introduced at the revived Olympic Games at Athens (1896) in allusion to the feat of the Gr. runner who brought the news of the battle to Athens.

marauder XVII (*maroder*). - F. *maraudeur*, f. *marauder* (whence, or as back-formation, **maraud** XVIII), f. *maraud* rogue, vagabond, of unkn. orig.

marble XII (*marbelston*). ME. *marbel*, *marbre* - OF. *marble*, by dissim. from (O)F. *marbre* :- L. *marmor* - Gr. *mármaros* shining stone, orig. stone, block of rock, but later assoc. with *marmaírein* shine.

marc refuse after grapes are pressed. XVII. - F. *marc*, f. *marcher* tread, MARCH[3].

marcasite XV. - medL. *marcasīta* - Arab. *marḳašīṭā* - Pers. *marḳašīšā*; assoc. with -ITE.

March[1] XII. - OF. *march(e)*, north-eastern var. of *marz*, (also mod.) *mars* :- L. *Martius* lit. '(month) of Mars'.

march[2] boundary. XIII. - (O)F. *marche* - Rom. (medL.) *marca* - Frankish **marka* :- Gmc. **markō* MARK[1]. So vb. border *upon*. XIV. - OF. *marchir*.

march[3] walk in a military manner. XVI. - (O)F. *marcher* walk, orig. tread, trample :- Gallo-Rom. **marcāre*, f. late L. *marcus* hammer. Hence (or - F. *marche*) **march** sb. XVI.

marchioness wife or widow of a marquess. XVI. - medL. *marchionissa*, f. *marchiō*, *-ōn-*, prop. captain of the marches, f. *marca* MARCH[2]; see -ESS[1].

marchpane marzipan. XVI. The various forms, *march-*, *marts-*, *maza-*, *-pain(e)*, *-pan(e)*, repr. diverse Continental forms, as F. †*marcepain* (mod. *massepain*), It. *marzapane*, Sp. *mazapan*, G. *marzipan* MARZIPAN (the present current form).

mare Early ME. *māre* (XII), with stem-vowel from obl. cases of OE. *mearh* horse, finally superseding *mēre*, *mūre*, OE. **mēre*, **mīere*, *mȳre* :- Gmc. **marχjōn* (MLG., MDu. *mer(r)ie*, OHG. *mar(i)ha*, Du. *merrie*, G. *mähre*, ON. *merr*), f. **marχaz* horse (OHG. *marah*, ON.

marr), corr. to Gaulish (acc. sg.) *márkan*, (O)Ir., Gaelic *marc*, W. *march*.

maremma low marshy land by the sea-shore. XIX. - It. :- L. *maritima* (fem.) MARITIME.

margarine XIX (repl. *oleomargarine* XIX). - F. (orig. supposed glyceride of 'margaric acid'), f. *margarique*, f. Gr. *márgaron*, *margarītēs* pearl, with ref. to the pearly lustre of the crystals or scales of the acid.

margin XIV. - L. *margō*, *margin-*, rel. to MARK[1]. So **marginal** XVI. - medL. **marginalia** XIX. - n. pl. of medL. *margināIis*.

margrave German title orig. of the governor of a border province. XVI. - MDu. *markgrave* = OHG. *marcgrāvo* (G. *markgraf*); see MARK[1]; the second el. is of obscure orig.

marguerite XIX. - F. form of the female name *Margaret*, ult. - L. *margarīta* - Gr. *margarītēs*, f. *márgaron* pearl.

marigold XIV. In early use often pl. *marygoulden*, *marygoldes*; f. proper name *Mary* (presumably with ref. to the Virgin Mary) + (dial.) *gold*, OE. *golde* marigold, prob. rel. to GOLD.

marijuana, marihuana XIX. - Amer. Sp.

marinade pickle, pickled meat or fish. XVII. - F. - Sp. *marinada*, f. *marinar* pickle in brine, f. *marino* MARINE; see -ADE. Hence vb. XVII.

marine pert. to the sea. XV. - (O)F. *marin*, fem. *marine* :- L. *marīnus*, f. *mare* sea, rel. to Goth. *marei*, Ir. *muir*, W. *môr*, OSl. *more*; see -INE[1]. So **mariner** XIII. - AN. *mariner*, (O)F. *marinier* :- medL. *marīnārius*.

Mariolatry see -LATRY.

marionette XVII. - F. *marionnette*, f. *Marion*, dim. of *Marie* MARY; see -ETTE.

marish see MARSH.

marital XVII. - L. *marītālis*, f. *marītus* husband; see MARRY[1], -AL[1].

maritime XVI. - (partly through F. *maritime*) L. *maritimus*, f. *mare* sea (see MARINE) + *-timus*, as in *fīnitimus* neighbouring, *lēgitimus* LEGITIMATE.

marjoram XIV. ME. *majorane*, *mageram* - OF. *majorane* (mod. *marjolaine*) - medL. *majorana*.

mark[1] A. (hist.) boundary (*landmark*); trace, orig. as a sign OE.; B. target XIII; C. (f. MARK[3]) remark, note XVI. OE. (Angl.) *merc*, (WS.) *mearc* = OS. *marka* (Du. *mark*), OHG. *marcha* (G. *mark*), ON. *mǫrk* (recorded only in sense 'forest'), Goth. *marka* :- Gmc. **markō*; rel. to L. *margō* MARGIN, OIr. *mruig* (Ir. *bruig*) boundary, territory, W. *bro* district, Av. *marəzu* boundary, Pers. *marz* landmark. Hence **marksman** XVII (earlier †*markman* XVI); see B above.

mark[2] weight of gold or silver; money of account. OE. *marc*, corr. to MDu. *marc* (Du. *mark*), MHG. *marke*, ON. *mǫrk*; the Gmc. forms, which vary in gender, are prob. all - medL. *marcus*, *marca*; perh. ult. identical with MARK[1].

mark[3] A. put a mark upon OE.; B. notice, observe, REMARK XIV. OE. *mearcian* = OS. (*gi*)-*markōn* appoint, observe (Du. *marken*), OHG. *marchōn* plan, ON. *marka* mark, observe :- Gmc. **markōjan*, f. **markō* MARK[1].

market gathering of people for buying and selling XII; public place for this XIII; (opportunity for, rate of) purchase and sale XVI; seat of trade XVII. Early ME. *market*, recorded earlier in the late OE. comp. *ġēarmarkett* (XI; see YEAR); both simplex and comp. appear to be - OS. *iārmarket* = OHG. *iārmarchāt* (of which the second el. - L. *mercātus*, f. *mercārī* buy, f. *merx*, *merc-* merchandise. Hence vb. XVII (*marketing* XVI).

marl kind of clayey soil. XIV. - OF. *marle* :- medL. *margila*, f. L. *marga*. Hence vb. XIV.

marline (naut.) small line. XV (also *marling* XVII). - Du. *marlijn*, f. *marren* bind + *lijn* LINE[1], and Du. *marling*, f. *marlen*, frequent. of *marren* + *-ing* -ING[1]. Hence **marlin(g)spike** XVII.

marm see MA'AM.

marmalade XVI. - F. *marmelade* - Pg. *marmelada*, f. *marmelo* quince :- L. *melimēlum* - Gr. *melímēlon* kind of apple grafted on a quince, f. *méli* honey + *mêlon* apple; see -ADE.

marmoset small monkey XIV; †grotesque figure XV; †term of playful reproach XVI. - (O)F. *marmouset* (latinized *marmosetus*) grotesque image, little man or boy, (dial.) ape, of unkn. orig.

marmot XVII. - F. *marmotte*, of uncert. orig.

maroon[1] †sweet chestnut of S. Europe XVI; brownish crimson (as of the nutshell); firework XVIII. - F. *marron* - It. *marrone* - medGr. *máraon*.

maroon[2] negro of Surinam and W. Indies XVII; (in full *maroon party*), pleasure party, picnic XVIII. - F. *marron*, †*maron* - Sp. *cimarron* wild, untamed, runaway slave, f. *cimarra* furred coat; see -OON. Hence vb. †pass. and intr. be lost in the wilds XVII, put ashore on a desolate coast XVIII.

marque †reprisals; *letters of marque*, orig. royal licence authorizing reprisals on a hostile state. XV. - F. - Pr. *marca*, f. *marcar* seize as a pledge.

marquee large tent. XVII (also †*markee*). Spurious sg. form deduced from MARQUISE (formerly so used in Eng.) apprehended as pl. and assim. in ending to -EE[2].

marquess see MARQUIS.

marquetry, -terie XVI. - F. *marqueterie*, f. *marqueter* variegate, f. *marque* mark; see -RY.

marquis, marquess ruler (orig.) of a 'march' or frontier district; peer between the ranks of duke and earl XIV; †marchioness XVI-XVII. ME. *marchis*, *markis* - OF. *marchis*, alt. later to *marquis* after the corr. Pr. *marques*, Sp. *marqués*; f. Rom. **marca* MARCH[2] + **-ese* :- L. *-ēnsem* -ESE; prop. adj. The sp. with *-ess* (XVI) is now used for the British title. Hence **marquisate** XVI. So **marquise** kind of pear; †marquee. XVIII. - F., fem. of *marquis*.

marram bent-grass. XVII. - ON. *marálmr*, f. *marr* sea, MERE[1] + *hálmr* HAULM.

marrow soft substance in the cavity of bones OE.; central or vital part XV; (*vegetable*) *m.*, fruit of *Cucurbita pepo* XIX. OE. *mærh*, *mærg* (WS. *mearh*, *mearg*), corr. to OS. *marg* (Du. *merg*), OHG. *mar(a)g* (G. *mark*), ON. *mergr* :- Gmc. **mazgam*, *-az*.

marry[1] join in or enter into wedlock. XIII. - (O)F. *marier* :- L. *marītāre*, f. *marītus* married, husband, of uncert. orig. So **marriage** XIII. - (O)F. *mariage*.

marry[2] int. XIV (*Marie*). The name of the Virgin MARY used as an oath, etc.; in XVI the oath *by Mary Gipcy* (the Egyptian) appears to have suggested the add. of *gip, gup* to *Mary*, and, as these were used in driving horses, *come up* was later substituted for them, *Marry come up*.

Marsala XIX. f. name of a town on the west coast of Sicily.

Marseillaise XIX. - F., fem. of *Marseillais* of Marseilles; so named from having been first sung in Paris by Marseilles patriots.

marsh OE. *mer(i)sċ* = MLG. *mersch, marsch*, MDu. *mersch(e)* (whence G. *marsch*, Du. *marsk*) :- WGmc. **marisk-*, whence medL. *mariscus*, the source of (O)F. *marais*, †*mareis*, adopted in ME. as *mar(r)eis, mar(r)ais* (XIV), alt. later to **marish** (XVI). Hence **marshy** (see -Y[1]) XIV.

marshal high officer of state, of the army, †of a court, in charge of ceremonies XIII; †farrier XIV. - OF. *mareschal* (mod. *maréchal*) :- Frankish L. *mariscalcus* - Gmc. **marχaskalkaz* (OHG. *marahscalh*), f. **marχaz* horse (see MARE[1]) + **skalkaz* (OE. *sċealc*) servant. For the sense-development cf. *constable*. Hence vb. XV.

marsupial of or resembling a pouch XVII; epithet of mammals having a pouch for their young XIX. - modL. *marsūpiālis*, f. L. *marsūpium* pouch - Gr. *marsúpion, marsípion*, dim. of *mársipos* purse, bag; see -AL[1].

mart †market, fair XV; market-place XVI; centre of commerce, emporium XVII. - Du. †*mart*, var. of *markt* MARKET.

Martello designation of a small circular fort. XVIII (*Mortella*). alt., perh. by assoc. with It. *martello* hammer, of the name of Cape *Mortella* in Corsica, where there was a tower of this kind which the Eng. fleet captured in 1794.

marten fur-bearing animal, †orig. the fur itself. XV. Early forms *martren, martro(u)n* - MDu. *martren* - OF. *martrine* marten fur, sb. use of *martrin*, f. *martre* - WGmc. **marþr-* (OHG. *mardar*, G. *marder*), ext. form of Gmc. **marþuz* (OE. *mearð*, ON. *mǫrðr*).

martial pert. to war or battle XIV; pert. to the army, military (*court martial, martial law*); warlike XV; of the planet Mars XVII. - (O)F. *martial* or L. *mārtiālis*, f. *Mārs* (for *Māvors*), *Mārti-*, Roman god of war, planet fourth in order of distance from the sun; see -IAL. So **Martian** pert. to the planet Mars XIV; to the month of March XVII. - OF. *martien* or L. *Mārtiānus*.

martin bird of the swallow family. XV (Sc. *martoune*). prob. a use of the name *Martin*, after St. Martin of Tours.

martinet †system of drill devised by General Martinet XVII; officer who is a stickler for discipline; also gen. XVIII. f. name of a F. general, drill-master of the reign of Louis XIV.

martingale A. strap for restraining the movements of a horse's head XVI; B. (naut.) rope for guying down the jib-boom XVIII; C. doubling the stake when losing at cards XIX. - F. *martingale* in *chausse à la m.* kind of hose fastening at the back, which has been derived from modPr. *martegalo*, fem. of *martegal* inhabitant of *Martigue* in Provence.

martini gin-and-vermouth cocktail. XIX. f. name *Martini* and Rossi, It. wine-makers.

Martinmas feast of the translation of St. Martin of Tours, 11 Nov. XIII. f. *Martin* + MASS[1].

martlet swift; (her.) imaginary bird without feet. XVI. - F. *martelet*, alt. of *martinet*, dim. of *Martin* MARTIN.

martyr (prop.) one who voluntarily undergoes death for the Christian faith. OE. *martir*, corr. to OS., OHG. *martir* - ecclL. *martyr* - Gr. *mártur*, var. of *mártus, martur-* witness, (in Christian use) martyr; reinforced in ME. by OF. *martir, martre* (mod. *martyr*); the sp. was finally assim. to the L. form. Hence **martyr** vb. OE. *(ġe)martyrian, martrian*. **martyrdom** OE. So **martyrology** XVI. - medL. - ecclGr.; see -LOGY.

marvel †miracle XIII; wonderful thing XIV. - (O)F. *merveille* :- Rom. use as fem. sg. of *mirabilia*, n. pl. of L. *mirābilis* wonderful, f. *mirārī* wonder; see MIRACLE, -ABLE. So **marvel** vb., **marvellous** XIII.

Mary OE. *Maria, Marie*, reinforced in ME. by (O)F. *Marie* - ecclL. *Marīa* - Gr. *Mariá* and *Mariám* - Heb. *Miryām* Miriam; in asseverations from XIV (cf. MARRY[2]).

marzipan XIX. - G. *marzipan*, earlier *marcipan*, etymol. alt. (as if *Marci panis* 'Mark's bread') of *marczapan* - It. *marzapane*, of uncert. orig.; cf. MARCHPANE.

mascot thing supposed to bring good luck. XIX. - F. *mascotte* - modPr. *mascotto*, fem. of *mascot*, dim. of *masco* witch.

masculine †male XIV; (gram.); (pros.) of rhyme XVI; pert. to or characteristic of the male sex XVII. - (O)F. *masculin*, fem. *-ine* - L. *masculīnus, -īna*, f. *masculus* MALE; see -INE[1].

mash malt mixed with hot water to form wort OE.; warm food of meal for cattle, etc., pulpy mass XVI. OE. *māsċ* = MLG. *mēsch, māsch*, MHG. *meisch* crushed grapes (G. *maisch*) :- WGmc. **maisk-*, of unkn. orig., but perh. rel. to MIX. Hence vb. infuse (malt) XIV; beat into a pulp XVII.

mashie iron golf club with a short head. XIX. of unkn. orig.

mask covering to conceal the face. XVI. - F. *masque* - It. *maschera*, perh. - Arab. *maskara* buffoon. Hence vb. XVI.

masochism XIX. f. name of Leopold von Sacher-*Masoch*, Austrian novelist (d. 1895), who described the condition; see -ISM. Hence **masochistic** XX.

mason builder and worker in stone XIII; FREEMASON XV. Earliest forms *mach(o)un*, - ONF. *machun*; later *mascun, masoun* - OF. *masson* (mod. *maçon*) :- Rom. **matiōn-* or **maciōn-*, prob. of Gmc. orig. So **masonry** XIV. Hence **masonic** XVIII.

Mas(s)orah body of tradition relating to the text of the Hebrew Bible. XVII (earlier *masoreth*). repr. Heb. *māsōreth*, in Exod. 20: 37 interpreted 'bond (of the covenant)', f. *'āsar* bind, in post-biblical Heb. in the sense 'tradition', as if f. *māsar* hand down. So **Mas(s)orete** one who contributed to this. XVI. - F. *Massoret* and modL. *Massōrēta*; orig. misapplication of *masoreth*, with subseq. assim. of the ending to L. *-ēta*, Gr. *-ētēs*.

masque masked ball; histrionic entertainment consisting of dancing and dumb show XVI; dramatic composition for an entertainment of this kind XVII. var. of MASK, the F. sp. being now restricted to these senses.

masquerade masked ball. XVI. First in quasi-Sp. forms *mascarado, masquerada* (see -ADO), later superseded by *mascarade*, and (with assim. to MASQUE) *masquerade*; - F. *mascarade* - It. *mascherata* or Sp. *mascarada*, f. *maschera, máscara* MASK; see -ADE.

mass[1] Eucharistic service. OE. *mæsse, messe*, corr. to OS. *missa* (Du. *mis*), OHG. *messa, missa* (G. *messe*), ON. *messa* - ecclL. *missa* (Rom. **messa*). L. *missa* (IV) is a verbal sb. from pp. stem *miss-* of *mittere* send, send away (cf. MISSION); its application to a service perh. results from a transference of meaning in phr. such as *Ite, missa est* Depart, it is the dismissal (i.e. the service is at an end), *Et missæ fiant* And let the dismissals be made (at the end of an office).

mass[2] coherent body of raw material XIV; relatively large body of matter XV; dense aggregation, large amount XVI; solid bulk XVII; (in physics) XVIII. - (O)F. *masse* - L. *massa* - Gr. *mâza* barley-cake, perh. rel. to *mássein* knead. So vb. XIV.

massacre indiscriminate killing. XVI. - (O)F., of unkn. orig. So vb. XVI.

massage sb. XIX. - F., f. *masser* apply massage to, perh. - Pg. *amassar* knead, f. *massa* dough (MASS[2]); see -AGE. Hence vb. XIX. So **masseur, -euse** XIX.

massicot yellow oxide of lead. XV. Earlier *masticot* - F. *massicot*, †*masticot*, obscurely rel. to It. *marzacotto* unguent, cosmetic, Sp. *mazacote* kali, mortar.

massif †block, mass XVI; large mountain mass XIX. - F., sb. use of *massif* MASSIVE.

massive XV. - F. *massif*, fem. *-ive*, alt. of OF. *massiz* :- pop. L. **massīceus*, f. *massa* MASS[2]; see -IVE. Finally repl. (arch.) **massy** XIV, perh. orig. - OF. *massiz*, with later assim. to -Y[1].

mast[1] long pole set up on the keel of a ship to support the sails. OE. *mæst* = (M)LG., (M)Du., (O)HG. *mast* :- WGmc. **masta* :- IE. **mazdos*, whence poss. L. *mālus* mast, OIr. *matan* club.

mast[2] fruit of forest-trees, esp. as food for swine. OE. *mæst* = MDu., MLG., OHG. *mast* :- WGmc. **masta*.

master A. man having control or authority; B. teacher OE. (one who has received an academic degree orig. conveying authority to teach XIV); C. title of rank or compliment XIII; title of presiding officer, etc. XIV. OE. *mæġister, maġister* (corr. to OS. *mēster*, (O)HG. *meister*, ON. *meistari*), a Gmc. adoption from L.; reinforced by OF. *maistre* (mod. *maître*) - L. *magistrum*, nom. *magister*, usu. referred to *magis* adv. more. Cf. MISTER[1]. Hence **masterful** XIV. **masterpiece** XVII; after Du. *meesterstuk* or G. *meisterstück* piece of work qualifying a craftsman. **mastery** XIII. ME. *meistrie* - OF. *maistrie*.

mastic gum or resin from *Pistacia lentiscus* XIV; the tree XV. - (O)F. *mastic* - late L. *mastichum, -a*, vars. of L. *mastichē* - Gr. *mastikhē*, presumed to be f. *mastikhân* (see next).

masticate chew. XVII. f. pp. stem of late L. *masticāre* - Gr. *mastikhân* grind the teeth, rel. to *masâsthai* chew, and perh. to synon. L. *mandere*; see -ATE[3]. So **mastication** XVI. - (O)F. or late L. Hence **masticatory** XVII.

mastiff XIV. repr. obscurely OF. *mastin* (mod. *mâtin*) :- Rom. **mānsuētīnus*, f. L. *mānsuētus* tamed, tame, earlier *mānsuēs*, f. *manus* hand (see MANUAL) + base of *suēscere* (pp. *suētus*) accustom.

mastodon extinct elephantine mammal having nipple-shaped tubercles on the molars. XIX. f. Gr. *mastós* breast + *odṓn, odont-* TOOTH.

mastoid (anat., of bones, etc.) nipple-shaped. XVIII. - F. *mastoïde* or modL. *mastoīdēs* - Gr. *mastoeidḗs*, f. *mastós* breast; see -OID.

masturbate XIX (earlier †*mastuprate* XVII). f. pp. stem of L. *masturbārī*, perh. alt. of **man(ū)-stuprāre* 'defile with the hand'.

mat[1] piece of coarse fabric of plaited fibre OE.; piece of material laid on a surface for protection XV (naut.). OE. *m(e)atte*, corr. to MDu. *matte*, OHG. *matta* (Du. *mat*, G. *matte*); WGmc. - late L. *matta*.

mat[2], **matt** lustreless, dull. XVII. - F. *mat*, identical with *mat* MATE[2]. So vb. XVII.

matador in Sp. bull-fights, man appointed to kill the bull; principal card. XVII. - Sp. *matador*, f. *matar* kill.

match[1] A. †mate, fellow OE.; person equal or corresponding XIII; B. †matching of adversaries XIV; contest; matrimonial alliance XVI. OE. *ġemæċċa* :- Gmc. **ʒamakjan-*, rel. to **ʒamakan-* (OE. *ġemaca*, dial. *make* match, mate; corr. to OS. *gimaco*, OHG. *gimahho* fellow, equal), sb. use of **ʒamakaz* (OE. *ġemæċ*, OHG. *gimah* well-matched, G. *gemach* easy, comfortable), f. **ʒa-* Y- + **mak-* fitting; see MAKE. Hence **match** vb. join as a pair or one of a pair in marriage, combat, etc. XIV.

match[2] †wick XIV; piece of inflammable cord, wood, etc., to be ignited XVI. - OF. *meiche, mesche* (mod. *mèche*), corr. to Sp., Pg. *mecha*, It. *miccia*, etc., which have been referred to L. *myxa* (- Gr. *múxā*) nozzle of lamp (in medL. lamp-wick), with crossing of Rom. **muccare* blow the nose, snuff a wick.

matchet XVI (*-eto*). - Sp. *machete*, prob. f. *macho* hammer. Also MACHETE XIX.

mate[1] habitual companion (also in comps.) XIV; (naut.) officer assistant to another XV; one of a wedded pair XVI. - MLG. *(ge)mate* = OHG. *gimazzo* :- WGmc. **ʒamatan-*, f. **ʒa-* Y- + **mat-*, base of MEAT, the lit. sense being 'messmate'.

mate[2] at chess, state of the king when he is in check and cannot move out of it; (fig.) total defeat. XIV. ME. *mat* - (O)F. *mat*, in *eschec mat* CHECKMATE. So vb. XIII.

maté calabash in which leaves of a S. Amer. shrub are infused, (also) the infusion and the shrub. XVIII. - Sp. *mate* - Quechua *mati*.

material consisting of matter XIV; pert. to matter; of substantial import XVI; sb. pl. XVI. ME. *materiel* (rare), *-ial* - (O)F. *matériel*, †*-ial* - late L. *māteriālis*, f. *māteria* matter; see -AL[1]. Hence **materialism** XVIII, **-ist** XVII, **-ize** XVIII.

materia medica remedies used in medicine. XVII. modL., tr. Gr. *húlē iatrikḗ* healing material; see MATTER, MEDICAL.

matériel material equipment or resources. XIX. - F., sb. use of adj. *matériel* MATERIAL.

maternal XV. - (O)F. *maternel* or f. L. *māternus*, f. *māter* MOTHER[1]; see -AL[1]. So **maternity** XVII. - F. - medL.

mathematic, -ical XVI. - or f. (O)F. *mathématique* or its source L. *mathēmaticus* - Gr. *mathēmatikós*, f. *máthēma*, *-mat-* something learnt, science, f. **math-* (rel. to MIND), *manthánein* learn; see -IC, -ICAL. As sb. (XIV) ME. *matematik*, *math-*, *-ique*, - (O)F. *mathématique* - L. *mathēmatica* - Gr. *mathēmatikḗ*, fem. of *mathēmatikós*; now **mathematics** XVI; colloq. abbrev. **maths** XX.

matico (leaves of) tropical Amer. wild pepper. XIX. - Sp. *yerba Matico*, i.e. *yerba* HERB, *Matico* dim. of *Mateo* Matthew; said to have been named after a soldier who discovered its styptic properties.

matins, mattins XIII. ME. *matines* - (O)F. :- ecclL. *mātūtīnās*, nom. *-īnæ*; see MATUTINAL.

matrass glass distilling vessel. - F. *matras*, of uncert. orig.

matriarch XVII. f. L. *māter*, *mātri-* MOTHER[1], after PATRIARCH, apprehended as being f. L. *pater* FATHER.

matriculate insert (a name) in a register, admit into a university, etc. XVI. f. pp. stem of medL. **mātrīculāre*, f. late L. *mātrīcula*, dim. of *mātrīc-* MATRIX; see -ATE[3]. So **matriculation** XVI.

matrimony XIV. - AN. *matrimonie* = OF. *matremoi(g)ne* - L. *mātrimōnium*, f. *māter*, *mātri-* MOTHER[1]; see -MONY. So **matrimonial** XVI. - (O)F. or L.

matrix uterus; place or medium of production XVI; enclosing mass; mould XVII. - L. *mātrix*, *-īc-* pregnant animal, female used for breeding, parent stem, (later) womb, register, f. *māter*, *mātr-* MOTHER[1].

matron married woman XIV; married woman having expert knowledge of pregnancy, etc. XV; woman in charge of domestic arrangements XVII. - (O)F. *matrone* - L. *mātrōna*, f. *māter*, *mātr-* MOTHER[1].

matt see MAT[2].

matter thing, affair, concern; material of thought, speech, or action XIII; substance serving as material XIV; physical or corporeal substance XVII; things written or printed XVII. ME. *materie*, *mat(i)ere* - AN. *mater(i)e*, (O)F. *matière* - L. *māteria* (also *-iēs*) hard part of a tree, timber, stuff of which a thing is made, cause, occasion, subject of discourse, matter, orig. substance of which consists the *māter* (MOTHER[1]). Hence **matter** vb. XVI.

mattock OE *mattuc*, of unkn. orig.

mattress XIII. ME. *materas* - OF. - It. *materasso* - Arab. *maṭraḥ* place where something is thrown, mat, cushion, f. *ṭaraḥa* throw.

mature fully developed or ripened (lit. and fig.). XV. - L. *mātūrus* timely, early, f. **mātu-* (as in next), rel. to *māne* early, in the morning. So **maturate** ripen, spec. bring to a head. XVI. f. pp. stem of L. *mātūrāre*, whence **mature** vb. XVI. **maturation** XVI, **maturative, maturity** XIV. - F. or L.

matutinal of the (early) morning. XVII. - late L. *mātūtīnālis*, f. L. *mātūtīnus*, f. *Mātūta* goddess of the dawn, rel. to *māturus* early, MATURE; see -AL[1].

maudlin †weeping, tearful; weakly sentimental XVII; but the earliest recorded use is as adv. in *maudlin* (†*maudlayne*, †*mawdlen*) drunk XVI. attrib. use of *Maudlin*, ME. *Maudele(y)n* (XIV) - (O)F. *Madelaine* - ecclL. *Magdalēna* MAGDALEN. The reference to tears comes from pictures in which the Magdalen is shown weeping.

maugre sb. †ill-will; (arch.) prep. in spite of (orig. to the displeasure of). XIII. - (O)F. *maugré* (mod. *malgré* prep.), i.e. *mal* bad, evil :- L. *malum* (see MAL-), *gré* pleasure :- L. *grātum*, sb. use of n. of *grātus* pleasing (cf. GRATEFUL).

maul †club XIII; hammer, beetle XIV. ME. *meall*, *mal(e)* - (O)F. *mail* :- L. *malleus* hammer. Cf. MALLET, PALL-MALL. Hence **maul** vb. †beat down, hammer, batter XIII; damage XVI; handle roughly XVII.

maulstick light stick used by painters to support the right hand. XVII (*mol-*). - Du. *maalstok*, f. *maalen* paint + *stok* stick; see MOLE[1], STOCK.

maunder †grumble XVII; act or talk in a dreamy or inconsequent manner XVIII. of uncert. orig.

maundy ceremonial washing of the feet of poor persons on the Thursday next before Easter. XIII (*Maundy Thursday* XVI). - OF. *mandé* :- med. use of L. *mandātum* command (see MANDATE), first word of the first antiphon sung at the ceremony, viz. '*Mandatum* novum do vobis' (A new commandment give I unto you), taken from the discourse which follows the washing by Christ of the Apostles' feet, John 13. See -Y[5].

mausoleum XVI. - L. *mausōlēum* - Gr. *mausōleion* the magnificent tomb of *Mausōlus*, king of Caria, erected 353 B.C. at Halicarnassus by his queen Artemisia and accounted one of the seven wonders of the world.

mauve bright but delicate purple dye. XIX. - F. *mauve* mallow, mallow-colour :- L. *malva* MALLOW.

maverick (U.S.) unbranded calf, etc. XIX. f. name of Samuel A. *Maverick*, a Texas cattle-owner who left the calves of his herd unbranded.

mavis song-thrush. XIV. - (O)F. *mauvis*, of uncert. orig.

mavourneen (Anglo-Ir.) my darling. XVIII. - Ir. *mo mhuirnín* (*mo* my, *muirnín*, dim. of *muirn* affection, love).

maw stomach. OE. *maga*, corr. to MDu. *maghe*

(Du. *maag*), OHG. *mago* (G. *magen*), ON. *magi* :- Gmc.**maȝan-*,-*ōn*.

mawkish †nauseated, without appetite, nauseating XVII; feebly sentimental XVIII. f. *mawk* maggot + -ISH[1].

maxilla jaw, jawbone. XVII. - L. *maxilla*, corr. to *māla* cheek, as *axilla* shoulder-blade to *āla* wing. Hence **maxillary** XVII.

maxim †axiom XV; aphoristic proposition; rule of conduct XVI. - F. *maxime* or its source modL. *maxima*, sb. use of fem. of *maximus*, superl. of *magnus* great (see MAGNITUDE).

Maxim *M.*(*-gun*), machine-gun invented by Hiram S. *Maxim* (1840-1916). XIX.

maximum XVIII. - (through F.) modL. *māximum*, sb. use of n. of *māximus* (see MAXIM).

may[1] pt. *might* †be strong; †be able; be allowed; as an aux. of the subjunctive. Gmc. preterite-present vb. (cf. CAN[2]). OE. *mæġ*, corr. to OS. (Du.), (O)HG. *mag*, ON. *má*, Goth. *mag*. The primary sense was 'have power' (cf. the cogn. sbs. MAIN[1], MIGHT); the IE. base **mogh-* **mēgh-*, is repr. also by Gr. *mēkhanḗ* MACHINE, OSl. *mogǫ* I can. Hence **maybe** XV.

may[2] blossoms of the hawthorn. XVI. - (O)F. *mai* flowers and branches collected to celebrate 1 May, from the name of the month (see next), dial. hawthorn. So vb. celebrate May-day, chiefly in gerund *(a)maying*. XIV.

May - (O)F. *mai* :- L. *Maius* prop. pert. to *Māia*, Italic goddess, daughter of Faunus and wife of Vulcan (later identified with Gr. *Maîa*). Hence **May-day** XV.

mayhem (leg.) crime of violently inflicting bodily injury. XV. - AN. *ma(i)hem*, *mahaym* MAIM.

mayonnaise XIX. - F. *mayonnaise*, also *magnonaise*, *mahonnaise*, the latter being app. fem. of *mahonnais* pert. to Port *Mahon*, capital of Minorca.

mayor chief officer of a municipal corporation. XIII. ME. *mer*, *mair* - (O)F. *maire* :- L. *mājor* greater, compar. of *magnus* great (see MAGNITUDE). So **mayoralty** XIV. - OF.

mayweed stinking camomile. XVI. alt. of †*maid-*, *mayde(n)wede* (XV), for **maithe(n)wede*, f. synon. †*maithe(n)*, OE. *maġoðe*, *mæġða* (obl. cases *-an*) + WEED.

maz(z)ard †mazer; (sl.) head XVII; face XVIII. alt. of MAZER by assoc. with -ARD.

mazarine deep rich blue. XVII. perh. f. name of Cardinal Jules *Mazarin* (1602-61) or the Duchesse de *Mazarin* (died 1699).

maze (dial., arch.) stupefy, daze XIII; bewilder XV. First in pps. *mased*, *amased*, and *bimased*, in OE. *āmasod* (see AMAZE). Hence **maze** sb. †delusion, deception XIII; complex network of paths XIV.

mazer (hist.) hard (? maple) wood XII; bowl or goblet, orig. of mazer wood XIV. - OF. *masere* (of Gmc. orig.; in modF. *madré* veined, variegated, like maple-wood), perh. reinforced from MDu. *maeser* maple = OHG. *masar* (G. *maser*) excrescence on a tree, †maple, ON. *mǫsurr* maple.

mazurka lively Polish dance. XIX. - F. *mazurka*, G. *masurka* - Pol. *mazurek* 'Masurian dance'.

me[1] obj. form of *I*. OE. *mē̆* (i) acc., corr. to OS. *mī*, *mē* (Du. *mij*) and further to L. *mē*, Gr. *me*, *emé*, OIr. *mē*, W. *mi*, Skr. *mā*; OE. had also *mec*, corr. to OS. *mik*, OHG. *mih* (G. *mich*), ON., Goth. *mik* :- IE. **mege* (Gr. *emége*), in which a limiting particle **ge* (Gr. *ge* at least) is added; (ii) dative, corr. to OS. *mī* (Du. *mij*), (O)HG. *mir*, ON. *mér*, Goth. *mis*. See MINE[1], MY.

me[2] see MI.

mead[1] drink made by fermenting a mixture of honey and water. OE. *me(o)du* = MLG. (Du.) *mede*, OHG. *metu*, *mitu* (G. *met*), ON. *mjǫðr* :- Gmc. **meduz* :- IE. **medhu-*, whence Gr. *méthu* wine (cf. METHYLATE), OIr. *mid*, W. *medd*, OSl. *medŭ* honey, wine, Lith. *midùs* mead, Skr. *mádhu* honey, sweet drink.

mead[2] (arch.) MEADOW. OE. *mǣd*.

meadow XIII. repr. OE. *mǣdwe*, etc., obl. cases of *mǣd* MEAD[2] :- Gmc. **mǣdwō*, rel. to MOW[1].

meagre lean, thin XIV; poor, scanty XVI. ME. *megre* - AN. *megre*, (O)F. *maigre* :- L. *macrum*, nom. *macer*, rel. to Gr. *makrós* long.

meal[1] powder of ground grain or pulse. OE. *melu* (*melw-*) = OS. *melo* (Du. *meel*), OHG. *melo* (G. *mehl*), ON. *mjǫl* :- Gmc. **melwam*, f. **mel-* **mal-* **mul-* :- IE. **mel-* **mol-* **ml̥-*, whence OHG., Goth. *malan*, ON. *mala*, L. *molere*, OSl. *mlěti*, Lith. *málti*, OIr. *melim* grind, W. *malu*, L. *mola* millstone, sacrificial meal, *molīna* MILL, Gr. *múlē*, *múlos* mill(stone).

meal[2] †measure; habitual or customary occasion of taking food OE.; repast XII. OE. *mǣl* mark, sign, measure, fixed time, etc., corr. to OS. *-māl* sign, measure (Du. *maal* n. meal, m. time), OHG. *māl* time (G. *mal* time, *mahl* meal), ON. *mál* mark, measure, point or portion of time, mealtime, Goth. *mēl* time :- Gmc. **mǣlaz*, *-am*, f. IE. base **mē-* MEASURE. The OE. dat. pl. *mǣlum*, in the sense 'measure', 'quantity taken at a time', was used in comb. with sbs., e.g. *dropmǣlum* drop by drop; the only surviving comp. in gen. use is PIECEMEAL.

mealie S.Afr. maize. XIX. - Afrikaans *mielie* - Pg. *milho* MILLET.

mealy-mouthed XVI. var. of contemp. †*meal-mouthed*, f. †*mealmouth* sb. and adj., f. MEAL[1] + MOUTH + -ED[2].

mean[1] have in mind, intend; import. OE. *mǣnan* = OS. *mēnian* intend, make known (Du. *menen*), (O)HG. *meinen* (now chiefly, have an opinion) :- WGmc. **mainjan*, rel. to OSl. *mĭniti*; f. IE. **men-* (see MIND). Hence **meaning** intention, signification. XIV.

mean[2] (dial.) common to two or more XII; inferior XIII; undignified, low XIV; ignoble XVII. OE. *mǣne* (rare), ME. *mene*, for OE. *ġemǣne* (ME. *-mene*) = OS. *gimēni* (Du. *gemeen*), OHG. *gimeini* (G. *gemein*), Goth. *gamains* :- Gmc. **ȝamainiz*, f. **ȝa-* Y- + **mainiz* :- IE. **moinis* (repr. in **com-moinis*, antecedent form of L. *commūnis* COMMON), f. **moi-* **mei-* change, exchange; see MUTATION, MUTUAL, MUNICIPAL. The development of meaning from 'possessed by all' to 'ordinary', 'inferior', was assisted by the coincidence of the native Eng. form with MEAN[3].

mean[3] †middle; †intermediary; intermediate in

time (now only in *mean time, mean while*); intermediate in kind or degree; mediocre, middling. XIV. - AN. *me(e)n*, OF. *meien, moien* (mod. *moyen*) :- L. *mediānus* MEDIAN. Hence **meantime** adv. XVI; **meanwhile** adv. XV; reduction of adv. phr. *in the m. time* and *m. while* (XIV).

meander (pl.) windings (of a river, a maze), †intricacies (of affairs) XVI; circuitous course XVII. - (partly through F. *méandre*) L. *mæander* - Gr. *maiandros*, appellative use of the name of a river in Phrygia famous for its notoriously winding course. Hence vb. XVII.

measles infectious disease marked by an eruption. XIV. ME. *maseles* (pl.), prob. - MLG. *masele*, MDu. *masel* pustule, spot on the skin (Du. *mazelen* measles) = OHG. *masala* blood-blister, f. Gmc. **mas*- spot, excrescence (cf. MAZER). The change of form from *masel* to *mesel* (whence the present form) appears to be due to assim. to ME. *mesel* leper (- OF. *mesel* :- L. *misellus*, f. *miser* wretched, MISERABLE).

measure prescribed or limited extent; action, result, or means of measuring XIII; 'measured' or rhythmic sound or movement XIV. - (O)F. *mesure* :- L. *mēnsūra*, f. *mēns*-, pp. stem of *mētīrī* measure, f. IE. **mēt*- (cf. Skr. *mā́trā* measure, Gr. *mêtis* prudence, OE. *mǣð* measure, proportion, power, rank, respect), extension of **mē*- measure (cf. MEAL[2], METRE). So **measure** vb. XIII. **measurable** †moderate XIII; that can be measured XVI. - (O)F. *mesurable* - late L. *mēnsūrābilis* MENSURABLE. **measurement** XVIII.

meat food (arch. and dial. exc. as in *meat and drink, flesh meat*) OE.; flesh food XIV. OE. *mete* = OS. *meti*, ON. *matr*, Goth. *mats* :- Gmc. **matiz*, f. **mat*- **met*- measure, METE.

meatus passage, spec. in anat. XVII. - L., 'passage, course', f. *meāre* go, pass.

Mecca name of Muhammad's birthplace, a place of Muslim pilgrimage; (hence) sacred spot of resort. XIX. - Arab. *Makka*.

mechanic pert. to manual work XIV; pert. to machines XVII; sb. handicraftsman, artisan XVI; skilled workman, esp. having to do with machinery XVII. - (partly through (O)F. *mécanique*) L. *mēchanicus* - Gr. *mēkhanikós*, f. *mēkhanḗ* MACHINE; see -IC. So **mechanical** XV, **mechanics, mechanism, mechanize** XVII.

Mechlin name of lace made at *Mechlin* in Belgium. XVII.

meconic (chem.) epithet of an acid obtained from opium. XIX. f. Gr. *mḗkōn* poppy + -IC. So **meconium** †opium XVII; first faeces of a newborn infant (from its dark colour likened to opium juice) XVIII. - L. - Gr. *mēkṓneion*, f. *mḗkōn*.

medal †metal disk used as a charm, etc. XVI; coin-shaped piece of metal with an inscription, effigy, etc. XVII. - F. *médaille* - It. *medaglia* :- Rom. **medallia* :- popL. **metallea* (n. pl.), f. L. *metallum* METAL. So **medallion** XVII. - F. *médaillon* - It. *medaglione*, augm. of *medaglia*.

meddle †mix, mingle; intr. mix or mingle in company or conflict XIV; busy oneself *with* XV. - OF. *me(s)dler*, var. of *mesler* (mod. *mêler*) :- Rom. **misculāre*, f. L. *miscēre* MIX.

mediaeval see MEDIEVAL.

medial †(math.) mean XVI; that is in the middle; ordinary. XVIII. - late L. *mediālis*, f. *medius* MID; see -AL[1]. So **median** (first in anat.) *m. vein* XVI; (gen.) middle XVII. - F. *médian* or L. *mediānus*; cf. MEAN[3].

mediastinum (anat.) membranous septum between cavities. XVI. modL., sb. n. of medL. *mediastīnus* medial, f. *medius* MID.

mediate †halve; effect by intercession XVI; be an intermediary XVII. f. pp. stem of L. *mediāre*, f. *medius* MID; in part prob. back-formation from **mediation** XIV (- late L. *mediātiō, -ōn-*) or **mediator** XIII (- (O)F. *médiateur*, †*-our* - ChrL. *mediātor*). So **mediatrix** XV. - late L.

medical XVII. - F. *médical* or medL. *medicālis*, f. L. *medicus* physician, f. base of *medērī* heal; see -ICAL. So **medicament** XIV. - F. *médicament* or L. *medicāmentum*, f. *medicārī* administer remedies to, whence **medicate, medication** XVII. So **medicine** medicament XIII; art of preserving and restoring health XIV. - OF. *medecine, medicine* (mod. *médecine*) - L. *medicīna* physician's art or laboratory, medicament. **medicinal** XIV. - (O)F. - L. **medico** medical practitioner or student. XVII. - It. - L. *medicus*. Also **medic** XVII.

medick plant of the genus *Medicago*. XV. - L. *mēdica* - Gr. *mēdikḗ* Median.

medieval XIX. f. L. *medius* MID + *ævum* AGE; see -AL[1]. So **medievalist** XVIII.

mediocre XVI. - (partly through F. *médiocre*) L. *mediocris* lit. 'of middle height', f. *medius* MID + *ocris* rugged mountain. So **mediocrity** XVI. - (O)F. - L.

meditate XVI. f. pp. stem of L. *meditārī*, frequent. f. IE. **med*- **mēd*- **mod*- measure (see METE). So **meditation** meditative discourse XIII; action of meditating XIV. - (O)F. - L.

mediterranean (of water) land-locked XVI; (of land) midland, inland XVII. f. L. *mediterrāneus* inland, in late L. applied to the Mediterranean Sea, *Mare Mediterraneum*, in which the orig. notion may have been 'in the middle of the earth' rather than 'enclosed by land'; f. *medius* MID + *terra* land, earth.

medium middle degree or condition; †middle term, mean; intervening substance XVI (whence, pervading or enveloping substance XIX); intermediate agency, means XVII; (in painting) liquid vehicle XIX. - L. *medium* middle, midst, medL. means, sb. use of n. of *medius* MID.

medlar (fruit of) the tree so named, *Mespilus germanica*. XIV. - OF. *medler*, f. **medle*, for **mesdle, mesle* :- L. *mespila, -us, -um* - Gr. *mespílē, méspilon*.

medley †combat, conflict XIV; †combination, mixture XV; (in disparaging sense) XVII. - OF. *medlee*, var. of *meslee* (mod. *mêlée*) :- Rom. **misculāta*, sb. use of fem. pp. of **misculāre* MEDDLE.

medoc wine produced in *Médoc*, a district of S.W. France. XIX.

medulla marrow, pith. XVII. - L. *medulla*, perh. f. *medius* MID. Hence **medullary** XVII.

medusa (*M*-) one of the three Gorgons, having snakes for the hair of the head XVI (XIV *Meduse*); (*m*-) jellyfish, sea-nettle XVIII. - L. *Medūsa* - Gr. *Médousa*.

meed †wages, hire OE.; reward, guerdon XIV. OE. *mēd* = OS. *mēda, mieda*, OHG. *mēta, mieta* (G. *miete*) :- WGmc. **mēda*, rel. to OE. *meord*, Goth. *mizdō* reward; the IE. base **mizdh-* is repr. also by Gr. *misthós*, OSl. *mizda*, Skr. *mīḍhá-* reward.

meek †gentle, kind; free from pride and self-will XII; submissive XIV. Early ME. *me(o)c* - ON. **miúkr, mjúkr* soft, pliant, gentle, rel. to Goth. **mūks* in *mūkamōdei* meekness.

meerschaum hydrated magnesium silicate found in soft white masses; tobacco-pipe having a bowl made of this. XVIII. - G. *meerschaum*, f. *meer* MERE[1] + *schaum* foam (see SCUM).

meet[1] †made to fit XIII; (rhet.) suitable, fit XIV. Aphetic of earlier ME. *imete* :- OE. (Angl.) **ġemēte*, (WS.) *ġemǣte* = OHG. *gamāzi* (G. *gemäss*), f. **ʒa-* Y- + **mǣtō* measure, f. **mǣt-* **met-* measure, METE; the etymol. sense is 'commensurate'.

meet[2] pt., pp. *met* come or light upon OE.; come face to face or into contact *with* XIII. OE. *mētan*, also *ġemētan* (see Y-) = OS. *mōtian* (Du. *moeten*), ON. *mǿta*, Goth. *gamōtjan* :- Gmc. *(*ʒa*)*mōtjan*, f. **mōtam* meeting, MOOT. Hence **meeting** XIII.

mega-, before a vowel **meg-**, comb. form of Gr. *mégas* great (see MAGNITUDE), as in **megalithic, megaphone, megatherium** XIX; similarly **megal(o-)**, the Gr. stem, as in **megalomania** XIX.

megilp vehicle for oil colours. XVIII. of unkn. orig.

megrim severe headache. XIV. Early forms *mygrame, -ane* - (O)F. *migraine*, semi-pop. - late L. *hēmicrānia* - Gr. *hēmikrāniā*, f. *hēmi-* half, HEMI- + *krānion* skull, CRANIUM.

meinie (arch.) household, retinue XIII; multitude XIV. - (O)F. *meiné, mesné* :- Rom. **mansiōnāta*, f. L. *mansiō, -ōn-* MANSION; see -Y[5].

meiosis (rhet.) †diminishing figure of speech XVI; litotes XVII. - Gr. *meíōsis*, f. *meioûn* lessen, f. *meíōn* less (see MINOR).

melancholy †morbid condition of having too much 'black bile'; †ill-temper; sadness and depression. XIV. - (O)F. *mélancolie* - late L. *melancholia* - Gr. *melagkholiā*, f. *mélās, melan-* black + *kholḗ* bile; see GALL[1], -Y[3]. So **melancholic, melancholious** XIV. Both adjs. were gen. superseded by an adj. use of the sb. (XVI), the termination of which suggests an adj. formation.

meld (U.S.) declare at pinocle. XIX. - G. *melden* announce.

mêlée irregular or confused fighting. XVII. - F. *mêlée*, earlier *mellée* MEDLEY.

melic pert. to poetry intended to be sung. XVII. - L. *melicus* - Gr. *melikós*, f. *mélos* song; see MELODY, -IC.

meliorate XVI. f. pp. stem of late L. *meliorāre*, f. L. *melior* better. Cf. AMELIORATE.

mellifluous sweet as if flowing with honey. XV. f. OF. *melliflue* or its source late L. *mellifluus*, f. L. *mel* honey + *flu-*; see FLUENT, -OUS.

mellow soft with ripeness XV; ripe, mature XVI; (of sound, etc.) rich and soft; genial with liquor XVII. perh. from attrib. use of OE. *melu* (*melw-*), ME. *melow* MEAL[1].

melodeon wind instrument with keyboard; kind of accordion. XIX. alt. of *melodium* (f. MELODY, after *harmonium*), or f. MELODY after *accordion*.

melodrama (orig.) stage play with appropriate music; (later) sensational play with a happy ending. XIX. alt. (after *drama*) of earlier *melodrame* - F. *mélodrame*, f. Gr. *mélos* song; see next and DRAMA. Hence **melodramatic** XIX.

melody sweet music XIII; tune, air XVII; element of musical form XVIII. - (O)F. *mélodie* - late L. *melōdia* - Gr. *melōidiā* singing, f. *melōidós* singing songs, musical, f. *mélos* song, rhythmical chant, orig. limb, member; see ODE, -Y[3]. So **melodic** XIX, **melodious** XIV.

melon XIV. - (O)F. :- late L. *mēlō, -ōn-*, shortening of *mēlopepō* - Gr. *mēlopépōn*, f. *mêlon* apple + *pépōn*, sb. use of *pépōn* ripe.

melt liquefy or be liquefied by heat. OE. (1) str. vb. *me(a)ltan* :- Gmc. **meltan*, (2) wk. vb. (Angl.) *meltan*, (WS.) *mieltan* = ON. *melta* digest, malt (grain) :- Gmc. **maltjan* (cf. ON. *maltr* rotten, OHG. *malz* melting, Goth. *gamalteins* dissolution). The base **melt-* **malt-* **mult-* repr. IE. **meld-* **mold-* **mḷd-*, whence Gr. *méldein* melt, L. *mollis*, Skr. *mṛdú-* soft. The str. pp. *molten* survives as adj.

melton epithet of a hunting jacket formerly worn and of a stout cloth. XIX. f. name of *Melton* Mowbray, town in Leicestershire, a famous hunting centre.

member organ, limb XIII; constituent portion or individual XIV; one elected to a parliament, etc. XV; division of a sentence XVI. - (O)F. *membre* :- L. *membrum*, app. rel. to OIr. *mīr* piece of meat, Skr. *māṃsá-*, OSl. *męso*, Goth. *mimz* meat, Gr. *mērós* thigh.

membrane XVI (first in sense 'parchment'). - L. *membrāna* (partly through F.) 'skin covering a part of the body' (prop. sb. use of fem. of adj. in *-ānus* -AN), f. *membrum* MEMBER. So **membranaceous** XVII. f. late L. **membranous** XVI. - F.

memento either of two prayers beginning with *memento* ('remember') in the canon of the Mass XV; reminder, warning XVI; object serving as a memorial XVIII. - L. *mementō*, imper. of *meminisse* remember, rel. to MIND.

memoir †note, memorandum XVI; (pl.) record of events, esp. from a personal or particular source; dissertation on a learned subject XVII. - F. *mémoire* (m.) specialized use of *mémoire* (fem.) MEMORY, arising from the appositional use as in *écrit mémoire*. So **memorable** worth remembering. XV. - F. or L. **memorandum** XVI. Derived from the heading of a note, '(It is) to be remembered *that* . . .'; n. sg. of L. *memorandus*, gerundive of *memorāre* bring to mind, f. *memor* (below). **memorial** preserving a memory XIV; sb. commemorative act, record, etc. XV. - (O)F. or L. **memoria technica** system of mnemonics. XVIII. modL., 'artificial memory' (see TECHNICAL). **memorize** cause to be remembered XVI; commit to memory XIX; f. next. **memory** faculty by which one remembers; recollection, remembrance. XIV. ME. *memorie, memoire* - OF.

memorie, (also mod.) *mémoire* - L. *memoria*, f. *memor* mindful, remembering; see -Y[3].

mem-sahib (in India) European married lady. XIX. f. *mem*, repr. native pronunc. of MA'AM + SAHIB.

menace threat. XIII. ME. *manas*, *manace* - OF. *manace* (later and mod. *menace*) :- L. *mināciа* (only pl. in classL.), f. *mināx*, *mināc-* threatening, f. base of *minārī* threaten, *minæ* overhanging or projecting parts, threats, rel. to *mōns* MOUNT. So vb. XIV. - AN. *manasser*, OF. *manacier* (mod. *menacer*) :- Rom. **mināciāre*.

ménage housekeeping, domestic establishment. XVII. - F. *ménage*, earlier *menaige*, *manaige* :- Rom. **mansiōnāticum*, f. L. *mansiō*, *-ōn-* MANSION.

menagerie collection of wild animals, esp. for exhibition; †aviary. XVIII. - F. *ménagerie* orig. domestic management of cattle, etc., f. *ménage*; see prec. and -ERY.

mend (arch.) free from fault or defect XII; †make amends for XIII; restore to wholeness, repair XIV. - AN. *mender*, aphetic of *amender* AMEND.

mendacious XVII. f. L. *mendāx*, *mendāc-*, prob. orig. speaking incorrectly or falsely, f. *mendum* defect, fault. So **mendacity** XVII.

Mendelian XX. pert. to the doctrine of heredity of Gregor Johann *Mendel* (1822-84); see -IAN.

mendicant adj. begging XVI; sb. beggar XV. - pp. of L. *mendīcāre* beg, f. *mendīcus* beggar, f. *mendum* fault, blemish; see -ANT.

menhaden fish of the herring family. XVII. of N. Amer. Indian orig.

menhir tall monumental stone. XIX. - Breton *men hir* (*maen* stone, *hir* long) = W. *maen hir*, Corn. *medn hir*.

menial domestic XIV; proper to a domestic servant, servile XVII, sb. XIV. - AN. *menial*, *meignial*, f. *meinie*; see MEINIE, -IAL.

meningitis inflammation of the meninges (enveloping brain and spinal cord). XIX. - modL., f. *mēninx*, *mēning-*, Gr. *mēnigx*, pl. *mḗnigges*; see -ITIS.

meno- comb. form of Gr. *mḗn* MONTH, used in path. terms for 'menses', as in **menopause** (Gr. *paûsis*); **menorrhagia** (Gr. *rhag-*, *rhēgnúnai* break, burst forth); **menorrhoea** (Gr. *-rhoiā* flow, flux).

menology calendar, esp. of the Orthodox Church. XVII. - modL. *mēnologium* - late Gr. *mēnológion*, f. *mḗn*, *mēno-* MONTH + *lógos* account; see -LOGY.

Menshevik XX. - Russ. *Men'shevik*, f. *mén'she*, compar. of *málȳĭ* little. Cf. BOLSHEVIK.

menses monthly discharge from the womb. XVI. - L. *mēnsēs*, pl. of *mēnsis* MONTH.

menstruum uterine secretion XVI; solvent XVII. - L. *mēnstruum*, in classL. only pl. menstrual blood, sb. use of n. of *mēnstruus*, f. *mēnsis* MONTH; cf. prec. The sense 'solvent' in medL. arose from the alchemists' view of the transmutation of base metal into gold by a solvent liquid, which they compared to the action on sperm in the womb of the menstrual blood. So **menstrual** XIV. **menstruous** XVI. - F. or late L.

mensuration measuring. XVI. - late L. *mēnsūrātiō*, *-ōn-*, f. *mēnsūrāre* MEASURE; see -ATION. So **mensurable** measurable, (hence) having assigned limits XVII; (mus.) having fixed rhythm and length of notes XVIII. - F. *mensurable* or late L. *mēnsūrābilis*.

-ment suffix forming sbs., repr. (O)F. *-ment* :- L. *-mentum*, which was added to vb.-stems to form sbs. expressing the result or product of an action or the means or instrument of it, e.g. *fragmentum* broken piece (f. *frag-*, *frangere*), *ōrnāmentum* that with which a thing is arranged (f. *ōrnāre*), *pavimentum* floor of stones beaten down (f. *pavīre*). In popL. it was extended to the formation of nouns of action (repl. *-tiō* -TION); this was continued in Rom. and is thus widely exemplified in Eng. adoptions from French, e.g. *abridgement*, *government*, *management*. This set the fashion for the treatment of *-ment* as if it were native, as in *amazement*, *fulfilment*, *wonderment*. Formations on adjs. are uncommon, as *merriment*, *oddments*. The corr. adjs. end in **-mental**.

mental[1] pert. to the mind. XV. - (O)F. *mental* or late L. *mentālis*, f. *mēns*, *ment-* MIND; see -AL[1]. Hence **mentality** XVII.

mental[2] pert. to the chin. XVIII. - F. *mental*, f. L. *mentum* chin; see -AL[1].

menthol XIX. - G. *menthol*, f. *mentha* MINT[2]; see -OL.

mention act of commemorating by speech or writing. XIV. - (O)F. - L. *mentiō*, *-ōn-*, f. base **men-* of *meminisse* remember; cf. COMMENT. So vb. XVI. - F. *mentionner*, medL. *mentiōnāre*.

mentor experienced and trusted counsellor. XVIII. - F. *mentor*, appellative use of L. *Mentor* - Gr. *Méntōr*, name of the Ithacan noble whose disguise Athene assumed to act as guide to the young Telemachus in the 'Odyssey'; the name was prob. chosen for its etymol. significance (f. **men-* **mon-* remember, think, counsel).

menu XIX. - F., sb. use of *menu* small, MINUTE[2], for *menu de repas* 'list of items of a meal'.

Mephistophelian XIX. of the character of *Mephistopheles*, an evil spirit to whom Faust, the hero of dramas by Marlowe and Goethe, sells his soul.

mephitic offensive to the smell, pestilential. XVII. - late L. *mephīticus*, f. L. *mephītis* noxious vapour; see -IC.

mercantile XVII. - F. - It. *mercantile*, f. *mercante* MERCHANT; see -ILE.

mercenary adj. XVI; sb. XIV. - L. *mercēnārius*, earlier *mercennārius*, f. *mercēs*, *mercēd-* reward, wages; see -ARY.

mercer dealer in silks and other textiles. XIII. - AN. *mercer*, (O)F. *mercier* :- Rom. **merciārius*, f. L. *merx*, *merc-* MERCHANDISE; see -ER[2]. So **mercery** XIII. - (O)F. *mercerie*.

mercerize prepare (goods) with chemicals for dyeing. XIX. f. name of John *Mercer*, dyer of Accrington; see -IZE.

merchandise †exchange of commodities; commodities of commerce. XIII. ME. *marchaundise*, *mercandise* - (O)F. *marchandise*, dial. †*marcandise*, f. *marchand* + *-ise*, repr. L. *-ītia*. So **merchant** XIII. ME. *marchand*, *-aunt* -

(O)F. *marchand*, †*march(e)ant* :- Rom. **mercātante*, sb. use of prp. of **mercātāre*, f. *mercārī*, *mercāt-*, f. *merx*, *merc-* merchandise, whence also *Mercurius* (see MERCURY).

Mercian pert. to, native of, the Anglo-Saxon kingdom of Mercia XVI; the dialect of Old English spoken there XIX. f. medL. *Mercia*, f. OE. *M(i)erċe* (pl.) lit. people of 'the march', 'borderers'; see MARCH², -IAN.

mercury (*M-*) Roman divinity identified with the Gr. Hermes, god of eloquence, messenger of the gods, patron of traders and roads, guide of departed souls (hence messenger, guide XVI); planet nearest the sun; quicksilver; (after L. *herba mercurialis*) plant-name. XIV. - L. *Mercurius*, orig. god of commerce, f. *merx*, *merc-* MERCHANDISE; the application to the planet appears in classL., and like other names of planets, *Mercurius* became in medL. the name of a metal. So **mercurial** XIV. - (O)F. or L.

mercy XII. - (O)F. *merci*, now chiefly in sense 'thanks' and in phr. *à la merci de* in the absolute power of :- L. *mercēs*, *mercēd-* pay, reward, wages, revenue, in ChrL. used for *misericordia* pity and *gratiæ* thanks. Hence **merciful** XIII, **merciless** XIV.

mere¹ †sea; lake. OE. *mere*, corr. to OS. *meri* sea (Du. *meer* sea, pool), OHG. *mari*, *meri* (G. *meer*), ON. *marr* sea, Goth. *mari-*, *marei* :- Gmc. **mari* :- IE. **mori-*; see MARINE.

mere² done without another's help XV; †unmixed, pure; †absolute, entire; that is only what it is said to be XVI. - AN. *meer*, OF. *mier* or its source L. *merus* not mixed, pure. Hence **merely** XVI.

meretricious characteristic of a harlot, showily attractive. XVII. f. L. *meretrīcius*, f. *meretrīx*, *-trīc-* harlot, f. *merēre* earn money, serve for hire; see -TRIX, -ICIOUS.

merganser XVIII. - modL. *merganser*, f. *mergus* diver (water-fowl), f. L. *mergere* dive (see next) + *anser* goose.

merge †plunge, immerse XVII; (leg.) extinguish or be extinguished by absorption XVIII. - L. *mergere* dip, plunge; f. IE. **mezg-*, whence also Lith. *masgóti* wash, Skr. *majj-* dive, sink; in leg. use through AN. *merger*. Hence **merger** extinguishment of a right, etc. XVIII; combination of one trading company with another XIX. - sb. use of the AN. vb.

meridian A. †midday XIV; point of sun's or star's highest altitude XV; B. great circle of the earth or a celestial sphere XIV; individual locality XVI; adj. XIV. - (O)F. *méridien* or L. *merīdiānus*, f. *mērīdiēs*, nom. f. loc. *merīdiē*, by dissim. from **mediei diē* at midday. So **meridional** XIV. - F. - late L.

meringue XVIII. - F., of unkn. orig.

merino variety of sheep prized for its fine wool XVIII; stuff made from the wool XIX. - Sp. *merino*, of disputed orig.

merit fact or condition of deserving XIII; †what is deserved; something that entitles one to recompense XIV. - (O)F. *mérite* - L. *meritum* price, value, service rendered, sb. use of n. pp. of *merēre*, *-ērī* earn, deserve, rel. to Gr. *meíresthai* obtain as a share, *moîa* share, fate, *méros* part. So **merit** vb. †reward XV; deserve XVI. - F. *mériter*. **meritorious** XV. f. L. *meritōrius*.

merle (poet.) blackbird. XV. - (O)F. *merle* :- L. *merula*, (late) *merulus*.

mermaid XIV. f. MERE¹ + MAID. Hence **merman** XVII.

mero-, before a vowel **mer-**, comb. form of Gr. *méros* part; in many techn. terms. XIX.

-merous ending of bot. terms denoting (see MERO-, -OUS) 'having (a specified number of) parts', as *pentamerous*.

Merovingian pert. to the line of Frankish kings founded by Clovis (*c.*500). XVII. - F. *mérovingien*, f. medL. *Merovingī* pl., f. L. form (*Meroveus*) of the name of their reputed founder; see -ING³, -IAN.

merry †pleasing, agreeable OE.; full of lively enjoyment XIV (hilarious from drink XVI); (arch., of a saying) amusing XV; (arch.) pleasantly amused XVII. OE. *myri(ġ)e* :- Gmc. **murȝjaz* (cf. MIRTH). Outside Eng. the only cognate corr. in sense is MDu. **merch*, whence *merchte* mirth, *merchtocht* rejoicing, *mergelijc* joyful, *mergen* be merry. Hence **merriment** XVI. **merry-make** XVI, **-making** XVIII; f. phr. *make m.* **merry-thought** wish-bone. XVII.

mésalliance marriage with one of inferior social status. XVIII. - F.; see MIS-², ALLIANCE. The anglicized form **misalliance** (used in a gen. sense) is somewhat earlier.

meseems (arch.) it seems to me. XIV. f. ME¹ (dative) + 3rd pers. sg. pres. ind. of SEEM.

mesembryanthemum (bot.) genus of plants of which several species open their flowers only about midday. XIX. modL., for **mesembri-*, f. Gr. *mesēmbriā* noon (f. *mésos* MID, *hēmérā* day) + *ánthemon*, f. *ánthos* flower.

mesentery (anat.) fold of peritoneum. XVI. - medL. *mesenterium* - Gr. *mesentérion*, f. *mésos* MID + *énteron* intestine.

mesh open space or interstice of a network. XVI. Early forms also *meish*, *meash*, *mash*; prob. - MDu. *maesche* (Du. *maas*), and *masche*, repr. Gmc. **mǣsk-* (whence OHG. *māsca*) and **mask-* (whence OE. *max*, **mæsċ* net, *mæscre* mesh, OHG. *masca*, G. *masche*).

mesmerism (production of) a hypnotic state in a person by exercise of another's will-power. XIX. f. name of Friedrich Anton *Mesmer* (1733-1815), Austrian physician + -ISM. Hence **mesmerize** XIX.

mesne (leg.) intermediate, mean. XV. - law F. *mesne*, var. of AN. *meen* MEAN³.

meso-, before a vowel **mes-**, comb. form of Gr. *mésos* middle, MID, used in scientific terms of modern formation (XIX), many of which have correls. in PRO-, PROTO-, META-; those of **mesozoic** (geol.) secondary are CAINOZOIC tertiary, PALAEOZOIC primary (all XIX).

mess A. portion or serving of food, dish of food XIII; made dish XV; mixed food for an animal XVIII; medley, confused or shapeless mass XIX; B. company of persons eating together XV. - OF. *mes* (in sense A), mod. *mets* (infl. by *metre* place) :- late L. *missus* course of food, f. *miss-*, pp. stem of *mittere* send (out), put forth, (in Rom.) put, place. Hence **mess** vb. (dial.)

serve up (food) XIV; take one's meals XVIII; make a mess (of) XIX. **messmate** (sense B) XVIII. **messy** XIX.

message XIII - (O)F. :- Rom. **missāticum*, f. *miss-*; see prec. and -AGE. So **messenger** XIII. ME. *messager* (later *messanger*) - (O)F. *messager*, f. *message*.

Messiah XVI. Earlier forms *Messie* XIV (- (O)F. *Messie*), *Messias* XIII - late L. *Messīās* - Gr. *Messíās* - Aram. *mᵉšīḥā*, Heb. *māšīªḥ* anointed, f. *māšaḥ* anoint. So **Messianic** XIX. - modL. *Messiānicus*.

messieurs XVII. - F., pl. of MONSIEUR.

messuage orig. portion of land for a dwelling-house, (now) dwelling-house with appurtenances and land assigned thereto. XIV. - AN. *mes(s)uage* house, household, AL. *mes(s)uāgium*, supposed to be misreadings of *mesnage*, *mesnagium* MÉNAGE.

mestizo Sp. or Pg. half-caste; offspring of a Spaniard and an American Indian. XVI. - Sp. :- Rom. **mixtīcius*, f. L. *mixtus*, pp. of *miscēre* MIX.

meta-, before a vowel usu. **met-**, before *h* **meth-**, repr. Gr. *meta-*, *met-*, *meth-*, comb. form of Gr. *metá* with, after denoting chiefly sharing, joint action, pursuit, quest, (and esp.) change, corr. to L. TRANS-; used freely (and not always in accordance with Gr. analogy) in scientific terms since *c.*1850.

metabolism process of chemical change in an organism. XIX. f. Gr. *metabolḗ* change, f. *metabállein*, f. *metá* META- + *bállein* throw; see -ISM.

metal XIII. - (O)F. *métal*, †*metail* or its source L. *metallum* mine, quarry, metal - synon. Gr. *métallon*. So **metallic** XVI. **metalline** XV. - F. Hence **metallize** XVI. See METTLE.

metamorphosis - L. (in pl. as the title of a work by Ovid) - Gr. *metamórphōsis*; see META-, -MORPH, -OSIS. So **metamorphose** XVI. - F. *métamorphoser*.

metaphor XVI. - (O)F. *métaphore* or L. *metaphora* - Gr. *metaphorā́*, f. *metaphérein* transfer; see META-, BEAR². So **metaphorical**, **-phorically** XVI.

metaphysic sb. XIV. - (O)F. *metaphysique* - medL. *metaphysica* fem. sg., for earlier n. pl. (repr. by **metaphysics** XVI) - medGr. *(tà) metaphusikà*, for *tà metà tà phusiká* 'the things (works) after the Physics'; see META-, PHYSIC(S). So **metaphysic** adj. XVI, **-ical** XV, **-ician** XVI. Aristotle's *Metaphysics* followed in the received arrangement the treatises on natural science known as *tà phusiká* 'the physics'.

metatarsus XVII. - modL.; see META-, TARSUS.

metathesis XVII. - late L. - Gr. *metáthesis*, f. *metatithénai* transpose; see META-, THESIS. So **metathetic** XIX.

mete (arch.) measure *out*. OE. *metan* = OS. *metan*, OHG. *mezzan* (Du. *meten*, G. *messen*), ON. *meta*, Goth. *mitan* :- Gmc. **metan*; the IE. base **med-* is repr. also by L. *meditārī* MEDITATE, Gr. *médesthai* care for, OIr. *midiur* I judge, beside **mod-*, of L. *modus* MODE.

metempsychosis transmigration of the soul. XVI. - late L. - Gr. *metempsū́khōsis*, f. *metá* META- + *en* IN¹ + *psūkhḗ* soul (see PSYCHIC).

meteor †atmospheric phenomenon XV; fireball, shooting star XVI. - modL. *meteōrum* or Gr. *meteōron*, sb. use of n. of *meteōros* raised up, lofty, f. *metá* META- + **eōr-*, var. of base of *aeirein* raise. Hence, or partly - medL. *meteōricus*, **meteoric** †elevated, lofty XVII; †pert. to the atmosphere XVIII; pert. to meteors XIX. **meteorite** XIX. **meteorology** XVII. - F. or modL. - Gr. *meteōrologiā*. **meteorological** XVI.

meter¹ measurer. XIV. f. METE + -ER¹.

meter² apparatus for measuring quantities. XIX. First in *gas m.*; perh. a use of METER¹ suggested by *gasometer* (see next).

-meter terminal el. in names of instruments for scientific measuring, the earliest of which (XVII) were adopted, partly through F., from modL. terms in *-metrum* (intended to repr. Gr. *métron* METRE¹), e.g. *barometer*, *thermometer*, which are not, however, formed according to Gr. analogies. In XVIII and XIX hybrid formations came in, such as *calorimeter*, *galvanometer*, *gasometer*, *taximeter*. The corr. nouns of action end in **-metry**.

methane XIX. f. METH(YL) + -ANE.

metheglin spiced or medicated mead. XVI. - W. *meddyglyn*, f. *meddyg* medicinal (- L. *medicus* MEDICAL) + *llyn* liquor.

methinks (arch.) it seems to me. OE. *mē þyncð*, ME., early mod. Eng. *me thinketh*, repl. by *methinks* (XVI); see ME and THINK; pt. *methought* (XIII), repl. OE. *mē þūhte*.

method †systematic treatment of a disease; special form of procedure; orderly arrangement. XVI. - F. *méthode* or L. *methodus* - Gr. *méthodos* pursuit of knowledge, mode of investigation, f. *metá* META- + *hodós* way. So **methodical** (hist.) belonging to a school of physicians (between 'dogmatists' and 'empirics'); pert. to method XVI. f. late L. *methodicus* - Gr. **methodist** physician of the methodical school; one who follows a certain method XVI; member of the Holy Club established at Oxford in 1729; member of religious bodies originating in this. - modL. *methodista*; hence **methodism** XVIII.

methyl XIX. - F. *méthyle*, G. *methyl*, back-formations from F. *méthylène*, G. *methylen* (whence **methylene** XIX), f. Gr. *méthu* wine, MEAD¹ + *húlē* wood. Hence **methylated** pp. (see -ATE³).

meticulous †timid XVI; over-careful about details XIX. f. L. *metīculōsus*, f. *metus* fear, after *perīculōsus* PERILOUS.

métier one's trade, business, or line. XVIII. - F. :- Rom. **misterium* MYSTERY².

metonymy (rhet.) substitution for the name of a thing the name of an attribute of it, etc. XVI. First in late L. form *metōnymia* - Gr. *metōnumiā*, f. *metá* META- + *ónoma*, *ónuma* NAME; see -Y³.

metope (archit.) square space between triglyphs of the Doric frieze. XVI (*methopa*). - L. *metopa* - Gr. *metópē*, f. *metá* between, META- + *opai* holes in a frieze to receive the beam ends.

metre¹, U.S. **meter** form of poetic rhythm, metrical form, verse. XIV. - (O)F. *mètre* - L. *metrum* - Gr. *métron*, f. IE. **mē-* MEASURE + instr. suffix. Also in comps. *hexameter*, *pentameter*, etc. So **metrical** pert. to metre XV; relating to measurement XVII. - L. *metricus* - Gr. **metrist** XVI. - medL. *metrista*.

metre[2], U.S. **meter** unit of length of the metric system. XVIII. - F. *mètre* - Gr. *métron* (see prec.). So **metric** XIX.

metro short for Metropolitan Railway. XX.

metro- comb. form of Gr. *métron* measure (see METRE[1]), as in **metronome** (XIX).

metropolis (hist.) see of the bishop of a province; chief city. XVI. - late L. *mētropolis* - Gr. *mētrópolis*, f. *mḗtēr* MOTHER + *pólis* city (cf. POLITIC). So **metropolitan** XVI. - late L. *metropolītānus*, f. Gr. *mētropolítēs* citizen of a metropolis, metropolitan bishop.

mettle quality of temperament XVI; (of a horse) vigour, spirit; (of persons) XVI. In earliest use (late XVI) *mettal(l)*, *-ell*, vars. of METAL, which began to be established as *mettle* in early XVII to distinguish the fig. uses.

mew[1] sea-gull. OE. *mǣw*, corr. to OS. *mēu* (MLG., MDu. *mēwe*, Du. *meeuw*) :- Gmc. **mai(ȝ)wiz*.

mew[2] cage for hawks while moulting; coop, breeding-cage. XIV. - (O)F. *mue*, f. *muer* moult, in OF. also change :- L. *mūtāre* (see MUTATION). So **mew** vb. cast (feathers), esp. of a hawk. XIV. - (O)F. *muer*. A second vb. **mew** put a hawk 'in mew', cage, (transf.) shut *up*, confine XV, is f. the sb.

mew[3] utter the characteristic cry of the cat. XIV. echoic; cf. MIAOW.

mewl whimper, whine, mew. XVII. Echoic; cf. *miaul*, MIAOW.

mews royal stables at Charing Cross, London XIV; stabling built round an open space XVII. pl. of MEW[2].

mezzanine low storey between two higher ones. XVIII. - F. - It. *mezzanino*, dim. of *mezzano* middle.

mezzotint †half-tint; method of engraving a metal plate for printing. XVIII. Earlier in It. form **mezzotinto** (XVII); f. *mezzo* half + *tinto* TINT.

mho (electr.) unit of conductivity. XIX. reversal of OHM.

mi, me[2] (mus.) third note of the scale in solmization. XVI. See UT.

miaow XVII. echoic; cf. F. *miaou*, and Eng. *miaul* (XVII) - F. *miauler*; also MEW[3].

miasma noxious exhalation. XVII. - Gr. *míasma* defilement, pollution, rel. to *miaínein* pollute.

mica †small plate of talc, etc.; mineral consisting essentially of silicate of aluminium occurring in glittering scales or in crystals. XVIII. - L. *mīca* grain, crumb; the use in min. was prob. orig. contextual ('a particle' of . . .); perh. assoc. with L. *micāre* shine. Hence **micaceous** XVIII.

Michaelmas feast of St. Michael the archangel, 29 September (a quarter-day). OE. *sancte Micheles mæsse* Saint Michael's mass (see MASS[1]), ME. *Mi(ȝh)elmasse* (XIII), *Mykylmes* (XV).

mickle, muckle (dial.) great, much. north. and eastern ME. *mikel* (XIII), later north. *mekil* - ON. *mikell* = OE. *miċel* MUCH. The var. ME. *mukel* (XIV) arose from assoc. with *muchel*, MUCH. Also adv. XIII, sb. XIV.

micro-, before a vowel **micr-**, comb. form of Gr. *mīkrós*, var. of *smīkrós* small, poss. rel to SMALL; used in many scientific terms. **microcosm** man viewed as an epitome of the universe. XV. - F. *microcosme* or medL. *mīcro(s)cosmus* - Gr. *mīkròs kósmos* little world. **micrometer** XVII. - F. *micromètre*. **microphone** XVII. **microscope** XVII.

microbe minute living being, esp. bacterium. XIX. - F., f. Gr. *mikrós* MICRO- + *bios* life (see BIO-).

micturition desire to make water, making water. XVIII. - L. *micturītiō*, *-ōn-*, f. pp. stem of *micturīre*, desiderative formation on *mict-*, *minct-*, pp. stem of *mingere* make water.

mid the middle or midst of. OE. **midd*, only in obl. forms *midde*, *middes*, *midne*, *midre*, *middum* (cf. AMID), corr. to OS. *middi*, OHG. *mitti*, ON. *miðr*, Goth. *midjis* :- Gmc. **miðja-*, **meðja-* :- IE. **medhjo-*, whence also L. *medius*, Gr. *méssos*, *mésos*, OIr. *mide*, OSl. *meždu* between, Skr. *mádhya-*. **midday, midnight, midsummer, midwinter** occur in OE. both as two words (with *mid* inflected) and as comps. **midland** (XVI), contr. of ME. *middel land* (XIII). **midmost** (XVII), alt. (by assoc. with -MOST) of OE., ME. *midmest*; for formation and development cf. FOREMOST. **midway** adv. in the middle of the distance XIII. ME. *midwei*, for *o midweie*, OE. *on midweġe*.

midden dunghill, manure heap. XIV. ME. *mydding*, of Scand. orig.; cf. Da. *mødding*, earlier *møgdyng(e)*, f. *møg* MUCK + *dynge* heap (cf. DUNG).

middle OE. *middel* adj. and (by ellipsis) m. sb. = OS. *middil-*, in comps. (Du. *middel* adj. and sb.), OHG. *mittil* (G. *mittel* adj. and sb.) :- WGmc. **middila*, f. **middi* :- Gmc. **miðja-* MID + *-il* -LE[2].

middling †intermediate XV; of medium size or quality. XVI (first in Sc. use). prob. f. MID + -LING[2]. Cf. OE. *mydlinga* moderately.

midge OE. *myċġ(e)*, corr. to OS. *muggia* (Du. *mug*), OHG. *mucca* (G. *mücke*), ON. *mý* :- Gmc. **muȝjaz*, **muȝjōn*, rel. to L. *musca* fly, Gr. *muîa*. Hence **midget** sand-fly (in Canada); extremely small person. XIX.

midrash Jewish commentary on the Hebrew scriptures. XVII. - Heb. *midhrāš*, f. *dāraš* investigate, search.

midriff diaphragm. OE. *midhrif*, f. **midd* MID + *hrif* belly (= OHG. *href*; of unkn. orig.).

midshipman XVII. Earlier †*midshipsman*, f. †*midships* (see AMIDSHIPS) + MAN.

midst middle point or position. XIV. ME. *middest*, alt. of †*middes* (XIV), which was evolved from advb. phr. *in middes*, *on middes*; see MID.

midwife XIV. prob. f. *mid* (prep. and adv.) with, together + WIFE in the sense 'woman', the notion being 'a woman who is *with* the mother at the birth'. Hence **midwifery** XV.

mien person's bearing or look. XVI. Earlier *men(e)*, *meane*, *mine*; prob. aphetic of †*demean* sb. (XV; f. the vb.), later assim. to F. *mine* look, aspect.

might[1] quality of being able, power, strength. OE. *mi(e)ht*, non-WS. *mæht* = OS., OHG. *maht* (Du., G. *macht*), Goth. *mahts* :- Gmc. **maχt-*, f.

maʒ-* be able; see MAY¹, -T¹. Hence **mighty OE. *mihtiġ*.

might² see MAY¹.

mignonette XVIII. - F. *mignonnette*, fem. dim. of *mignon* delicately small, of unkn. orig.; see -ETTE.

migraine XVIII. - F. (see MEGRIM).

migration XVII. - F. *migration* or L. *migrātiō, -ōn-*, f. *migrāre*, prob. based on **mei-* change (cf. MUTABLE); see -ATION. So or hence **migrate** (-ATE³) XVII.

mikado XVIII. - Jap., orig. the gate (of the imperial palace), f. *mi* (honorific prefix) + *kado* gate.

milch giving milk, in milk. XIII. ME. *mielch, melche, milche*, repr. OE. **mielċe* :- Gmc. **melukjaz*, f. **meluk-* MILK.

mild †gracious, kind; gentle, not rough OE.; †tame XIII; operating gently XIV; not rough, strong, or severe XV. OE. *milde* = OS. *mildi*, OHG. *milti* (Du., G. *mild*), ON. *mildr*, Goth. *-mildeis, -milds* :- Gmc. **milðjaz, *milðiz*, f. IE. **meldh- *moldh- *mḷdh-*, whence Gr. *malthakós* soft, Skr. *márdh* neglect, despise, OIr. *meldach* pleasing, OSl. *mladŭ* young, tender, L. *mollis* soft.

mildew †honey-dew OE., morbid growth on plants, etc. XIV. OE. *mildēaw, meledēaw* = OS. *milidou* (Du. *meeldauw*), OHG. *militou* (G., with assim. to *mehl* MEAL¹, *mehltau*), Sw. *mjöldagg*; f. Gmc. **meliþ* honey + **dawwaz* DEW.

mile Roman measure of 1,000 paces (*mille passus* or *passuum*) estimated at 1,618 yards; unit of measure derived from this, viz. 1,760 yards in English-speaking countries. OE. *mīl* fem. = MDu. *mīle* (Du. *mijl*), OHG. *mīl(l)a* (G. *meile*) :- WGmc. **mīlja* - L. *mīl(l)ia*, pl. of *mīl(l)e* thousand.

milfoil yarrow. XIII. - OF. *milfoil* (now *millefeuille*, after *feuille* leaf) :- L. *mīl(l)efolium*, f. *mīl(l)e* thousand + *folium* leaf (see FOIL²), after Gr. *murióphullon* (*múrios* myriad, *phúllon* leaf); the ref. is to the finely-divided leaves.

miliary resembling millet seed. XVII. - L. *miliārius*, f. *milium* MILLET; see -ARY.

milieu XIX. - F., f. *mi* (:- L. *medius*) MID + *lieu* (:- L. *locus*) place.

militant engaged in warfare XV; combative XVII. - F. *militant* or L. *mīlitāns, -ant-*, prp. of *mīlitāre* serve as a soldier, f. *mīles, milit-* soldier; see -ANT. So **militarism** XIX. - F. *militarisme*, f. *militaire*. **militarist** †soldier XVII; (now) one dominated by military ideas. **military** XVI. f. F. *militaire* or L. *mīlitāris*. **militate** (-ATE³) †serve as a soldier; †conflict *with*, be evidence *against* XVII. **militia** †military discipline or service; military force, esp. citizen army. XVI. - L.; see -IA¹.

milk sb. OE. (Angl.) *milc*, (WS.) *meol(o)c* = OS. *miluk* (Du. *melk*), OHG. *miluh* (G. *milch*), ON. *mjólk*, Goth. *miluks* :- Gmc. **meluks*, f. **melk-* (repr. by the vbs. OE. *melcan*, OHG. *melchan*) :- IE. **melĝ- *mlĝ-*, whence OIr. *melg* sb. and the vbs. L. *mulgēre*, Gr. *amélgein*, OIr. *bligim*. Hence vb. OE. *milcian*. **milksop** orig. SOP dipped in milk, (hence) one who is fed on such food, †young infant, (transf.) effeminate fellow XIV.

milky XIV (*M. Way* (XIV) tr. L. *via lactea*; cf. GALAXY).

mill building fitted with apparatus for grinding corn OE.; the apparatus itself XVI; building in which an industry or manufacture is carried on XVI. OE. *mylen* m. and fem. :- **mulino, -ina*, for late L. *molīnus, -īna, -īnum*, f. and repl. L. *mola* grindstone, mill (see MEAL¹). Hence **millstone** late OE. **mill** vb. XVI.

millboard stout pasteboard. XVIII. alt. of *milled board*, i.e. board flattened by rolling or beating.

millennium period of 1000 years, spec. that during which Christ will reign on earth (Rev. 20: 1-5). XVII. - modL., f. L. *mille* thousand, after *biennium* (see BIENNIAL). So **millenarian** pert. to (sb. one who believes in) the millennium. XVII. f. late L. *millenarius*, f. *millēnī*, distributive of *mille*; see -ARIAN; whence also **millenary** XVI.

millepede XVII. - L. *millepeda* woodlouse, f. *mille* thousand + *pēs, ped-* FOOT.

miller XIV. ME. *mulnere, mylnere, millere*, prob. (with assim. to MILL) - MLG., MDu. *molner, mulner* (Du. *molenaar, mulder*), in OS. *mulineri*, corr. to OHG. *mulināri* (G. *müller*), ON. *mylnari* - late L. *molīnārius*, f. *molīna* MILL; see -ER¹.

millesimal thousandth (part). XVIII. f. L. *millesimus*, f. *mille* thousand; see -AL¹.

millet XIV. - (O)F. *millet*, dim. of (dial.) *mil* :- L. *milium*, rel. to Gr. *melínē*, Lith. *málnos* pl.

milli- comb. form of L. *mille* thousand, used esp. in the metric system to denote the thousandth part of a unit, e.g. *milligramme, millimetre* (XIX).

milliner †vendor of fancy ware such as was orig. made at Milan; maker-up of articles of female apparel (now esp. hats). XVI. f. *Milan* in Italy, famous for textile fabrics + -ER¹. Hence **millinery** XVII.

million a thousand thousands XIV; *the* multitude XVII. - (O)F. *million*, prob. - It. †*millione*, now *milione*, f. *mille* thousand + augm. suffix *-one*. So **millionaire** XIX. - F. *millionnaire*.

milt A. spleen in mammals OE.; B. (perh. from Du.) soft roe. XV. OE. *milt(e)*, corr. to MDu. *milte* (Du. *milt*) spleen, milt of fish, OHG. *milzi* n. (G. *milz* fem.), ON. *milti* :- Gmc. **miltjaz, *miltjōn*, perh. rel. to *meltan* MELT.

mime jester, buffoon; farcical drama of the Greeks and Romans. XVII. - L. *mīmus* - Gr. *mîmos* imitator, actor. Hence vb. XVII. So **mimeograph** stencil device. XIX. irreg. f. Gr. *mīméomai* I imitate. **mimetic** pert. to imitation or mimicry. XVII. - Gr. *mīmētikós*. **mimic** pert. to a mime or buffoon; imitative; sb. burlesque performer; imitator XVI. - L. *mīmicus* - Gr. *mīmikós*. Hence **mimic** vb., **mimicry** XVII.

mimosa sensitive plant, *Mimosa pudica*, and its allies. XVIII. - modL. *mīmōsa*, app. f. L. *mīmus* MIME + *-ōsa*, fem. of *-ōsus* -OSE¹, and so named from its imitation of animal sensitiveness.

mina, myna(h) Indian starling. XVIII. - Hindi *mainā*.

minaret XVII. - F. *minaret* or Sp. *minarete*, It. *minaretto* - Turk. *minare* - Arab. *manāra* minaret, lighthouse, f. base of *nūr* light.

minatory XVI. - late L. *minātōrius*, f. *mināt-*, pp. stem of *minārī* MENACE; see -ORY².

mince cut up small XIV; †minimize, disparage; extenuate, moderate; talk, walk, etc., affectedly XVI. - OF. *mincier* :- Rom. **minūtiāre*, f. L. *minūtia* see MINUTIA. Hence sb. minced meat. XIX. *Mincemeat, mince-pie* (both XVII) are for *minced meat, minced pie*.

mind memory (surviving in phr. *in m., to m., time out of m.*); thought, purpose, intention; mental faculty. XII. ME. *mind(e), münd(e), mend(e)*; aphetic of *imünd*, etc. :- OE. *gemynd*, corr. to OHG. *gimunt*, Goth. *gamunds* memory :- Gmc. **ʒamunðiz*, f. **ʒa-* Y- + **mun-*, weak grade of the series **men- *man- *mun-* :- IE. **men- *mon- *mn-* revolve in the mind, think (repr. also by e.g. L. *mēns, ment-* mind). Hence **mind** vb. REMIND; remember, give heed to XIV; (dial.) perceive, notice XV; contemplate XVI; be careful about XVIII.

mine[1] poss. pron. OE. *mīn* = OS., OHG. *mīn* (Du. *mijn*, G. *mein*), ON. *minn*, Goth. *meins* :- Gmc. **mīnaz*, f. IE. locative **mei* of *me* ME[1] + adj. suffix **-nó-*. In XIII the final *n* of the adj. was already dropped before a cons. in southern and midland Eng.; but it was retained in the north, and survived till XV in Sc. See MY.

mine[2] dig in the earth for ore, coal, etc. XIII. - (O)F. *miner*, perh. orig. Gallo-Rom. deriv. of a Celt. word repr. by Ir., Gael. *mein* ore, mine, W. *mwyn* ore, †mine. So (or hence) **mine** sb. excavation for mining; †mineral, ore XIV. **miner** (-ER[2]) maker of underground mines XIII; excavator for mineral XIV.

mineral XV. - OF. *mineral* or medL. *minerāle*, sb. use of n. sg. of *minerālis*, f. *minera* ore, Rom. **mināria*, f. **mina, *mināre* MINE[2]; see -AL[1]. So adj. XVI. - F. or medL. Hence **mineralogy, mineralogist** XVII.

mingle XV. ME. *menglen*, f. *mengen, mingen* mix - ON. *menga* = OE. *mengan*, (O)HG. *mengen* :- Gmc. **maŋgjan* + -LE[3], perh. suggested by (M)Du. *mengelen*.

miniature reduced image, small representation XVI; †illumination in manuscripts XVII; portrait on a small scale XVIII; adj. XVIII. - It. *miniatura* - medL. *miniātūra*, f. *miniāre* rubricate, illuminate, f. L. *minium* native cinnabar, red lead. So **miniaturize, miniaturization** XX.

minify diminish in estimated size, etc. XVII. irreg. f. L. *minor* less, *minimus* least, after MAGNIFY.

minikin (dial.) playful term for a female XVI; diminutive thing XVIII; adj. dainty, mincing, diminutive XVI. - Du. *minneken*, f. *minne* love (rel. to MIND) + *-ken, -kijn*.

minim A. (mus.) note half the value of a semibreve XV; B. friar of the Ordo Minimorum Eremitarum; C. thing of the least size or importance XVI; single down stroke of the pen XVII. - medL. ellipt. or absol. uses of L. *minimus, -a, -um* least; see MINOR. So **minimize** XIX. **minimum** †atom; least amount attainable, etc. XVII; lowest or least value, etc. XVIII. - L., n. of *minimus* used sb. **minimal** (-AL[1]) XVII.

minion †lover, lady-love XVI; favourite; printing type. XVII. - F. *mignon*, of unkn. orig.

minister †servant, subordinate officer XIII; one engaged in the celebration of worship or charged with spiritual functions XIV; officer of state XVII. - (O)F. *ministre* - L. *minister* servant, f. **minis-*, var. of *minus* less, adv. of *minor* MINOR, in formation parallel to the correl. *magister* MASTER. So vb. (arch.) serve, supply, ADMINISTER. XIV. **ministerial** XVI. - F. *ministériel* or late L. *ministeriālis*. **ministration** XIV. - OF. or L. **ministry** rendering of service; function of a minister of religion XIV; body of ministers XVI (in politics XVIII). - L. *ministerium*.

miniver fur used for lining and trimming. XIII. ME. *meniver, menuver* (the forms with *min-* date from XV) - AN. *menuver*, (O)F. *menu vair*, i.e. *menu* little (:- L. *minūtus* MINUTE[2]), *vair* variegated fur (:- L. *varius* VARIOUS).

mink skin or fur of stoat-like animal XV; the animal itself XVII. of uncert. orig.; cf. Sw. *menk, mänk* mink, LG. *mink* otter.

minnow XV. Early form *menow*, later *minew*, perh. orig. repr. OE. **mynwe* (beside recorded OE. *myne*) = OHG. *muniwa*, but infl. by ME. *menuse, menise* - OF. *menuise* :- Rom. **minūtia* n. pl. small objects (cf. MINUTIAE).

minor less, smaller; applied first to Franciscan friars (*friars minor*, †*minors*). XIII. - OF. *menour* (:- L. *minōrem*) in *freres menours* (medL. *fratres minores*); in other uses - L. *minor*, which functions as compar. of *parvus* small, and is rel. to *minuere* lessen, Gr. *minúthein*, and *méiōn* less. So **minoress** nun of the second order of St. Francis. XIV. **minority** XVI. - F. or medL.

Minorca black variety of domestic fowl named after *Minorca*, one of the Balearic islands. XIX.

Minotaur fabulous monster confined in the Cretan labyrinth. XIV. - OF. *Minotaur* (now *-taure*) - L. *Minotaurus* - Gr. *Minṓtauros*, f. *Mínōs* Minos, king of Crete, whose wife Pasiphae was the mother of the Minotaur + *taûros* bull.

minster †monastery; church originating in a monastic establishment; large church. OE. *mynster* = OHG. *munistri* (G. *münster*), MDu. *monster*, ON. *mustari* - popL. **monisterium* for ecclL. *monastērium* MONASTERY.

minstrel XIII. ME. *men(e)stral, min(i)stral, -el*, - OF. *menestral, -(e)rel, mini-*, entertainer, handicraftsman, servant - Pr. *menest(ai)ral* officer, employed person, musician - late L. *ministeriālis* official, officer, f. *ministerium* MINISTRY; see -AL[1]. So **minstrelsy** art of a minstrel; body of minstrels XIV; minstrel poetry XIX (Scott). - OF. *menestralsie*.

mint[1] †coin OE.; place where money is coined XV. OE. *mynet*, corr. (with variation of gender) to OS. *munita* (Du. *munt*), OHG. *muniz(za)* (G. *münze*) - WGmc. **munita* - L. *monēta*; see MONEY. Hence **mint** vb. coin XVI; not continuous with OE. *mynetian*. **mintage** XVI.

mint[2] aromatic plant. OE. *minte* = OHG. *minza* (G. *minze*) :- WGmc. **minta* - L. *ment(h)a* - Gr. *mínthē* (also *mínthos*).

minuet XVII. - F., sb. use of adj. *menuet* small, fine, delicate, dim. of *menu* MINUTE[2], but infl. in form and pronunc. by It. *minuetto* (- F.); see -ET.

minus with the deduction of XV; verbal rendering of the sign – XVI; (electr.) negative(ly)

XVIII. - L. 'less', n. of *minor* (see MINOR) used as adv.

minuscule (of a letter) small, not capital XVIII; (gen.) extremely small XIX. - F. *minuscule* - L. *minuscula*, fem. of *minusculus* rather less, dim. of MINOR.

minute[1] A. 60th part of an hour or a degree XIV; B. rough draft, memorandum XVI. - (O)F. - late L. sb. use of L. *minūta*, fem. of *minūtus* MINUTE[2]. Sense A rests ult. on medL. *pars minuta prima* 'first minute part', the $\frac{1}{60}$ of a unit in the (Babylonian) system of sexagesimal fractions (cf. SECOND[1] sb.). Sense B depends (perh. through F.) on the medieval use of L. *minūta*, which may be for *minuta scriptura* draft in small writing as dist. from the engrossed copy. Hence **minute** vb. XVII.

minute[2] †chopped small XV; †lesser XVI; very small; very precise XVII. - L. *minūtus* (whence F. *menu*), pp. of *minuere* lessen, diminish (see MINOR).

minutia, usu. pl. **minutiae** very small matters. XVIII. - late L. *minūtia*, pl. *iæ*, f. *minūtus* MINUTE[2]; see -Y[3].

minx †pet dog; pert young woman. XVI. of unkn. orig.

miocene see EOCENE.

miracle marvellous event to be ascribed to supernatural intervention XII; wonderful thing; medieval play based on the life of Christ or the saints XIV. - (O)F. - L. *mīrāculum* object of wonder, f. *mīrārī*, *-āre* wonder, look at, f. *mīrus* wonderful. So **miraculous** XVI. - (O)F. or medL.

mirage XIX. - F. *mirage*, f. *mirer* refl. look at oneself in a mirror - L. *mīrāre*; see prec., -AGE.

mire †swamp, bog; mud. XIV. ME. *müre*, *myre* - ON. *mýrr*, rel. to MOSS.

mirk see MURK.

mirror XIII. ME. *mirour* - OF. *mirour* (mod. *miroir*) :- Rom. **mīrātōrium*, f. *mīrāre*, *mīrāt-* look at, (in pre-classical L.) wonder (see MIRACLE); from XVI the sp. was modelled on words in -OR[2].

mirth joy, happiness OE.; rejoicing, gaiety XIII; gaiety of mind; diversion, sport XIV. OE. *myr(i)ġð* (cf. MDu. *merchte*) :- Gmc. **murʒiþō*, f. **murʒjaz* MERRY; see -TH[1].

mis-[1] OE. *mis-* (ME. *mis(se)-*, *mes-*) = OS. *mis-*, OHG. *missi-* (Du. *mis-*, G. *miss-*), ON. *mis-*, Goth. *missa-* :- Gmc. **missa-* (whence **missjan* MISS[1] vb.), meaning predominantly 'amiss', 'wrong(ly)', 'improper(ly)', which is the only sense recognized in new formations, but in OE. there are also exx. of a negative and of a pejorative intensive use. Cf. next.

mis-[2] in a few comps. adopted from French, repr. OF. *mes-* (mod. *mé(s)-*, *mes-*) :- Rom. **minus-*, a use of L. *minus* (see MINUS) in the senses 'bad(ly)', 'wrong(ly)', 'amiss', 'ill-', and with negative force; at first *mes-*, later assim. to MIS-[1].

misadventure ill-luck XIII; (leg.) homicide committed accidentally in the course of a lawful act XVI. ME. *misaventure* - OF. *mesaventure*, f. *mesavenir* turn out badly (f. *mes-* MIS-[2] + *avenir* :- L. *advenīre*; cf. ADVENT), after *aventure* ADVENTURE.

misalliance see MÉSALLIANCE.

misanthrope XVII. - F. *misanthrope* or Gr. *mīsánthrōpos*, f. *mīs(o)-*, comb. form of base of *mīsein* hate + *ánthrōpos* man. So **misanthropy** XVII. - F. or Gr.

miscall misname XIV; (dial.) revile XV. MIS-[1].

miscarry †go astray; †come to harm XIV; be prematurely delivered XVI; go wrong, fail XVII. - OF. *mescarier*; see MIS-[2], CARRY. Hence **miscarriage** †misconduct; mismanagement; untimely delivery; failure to arrive. XVII.

miscegenation mixture of races. XIX (orig. U.S.). irreg. f. L. *miscēre* MIX + GENUS race + -ATION.

miscellaneous XVII. f. L. *miscellāneus*, f. *miscellus* mixed, f. *miscēre* MIX; see -ANEOUS. So **miscellany** XVI. - (with assim. to -Y[3]) F. *miscellanées* fem. pl., or L. *miscellānea* n. pl.

mischance XIII. - OF. *mesch(e)ance*, f. *mescheoir*; see MIS-[2], CHANCE.

mischief †misfortune, distress XIII; harm, injury XIV; cause of harm XVI; conduct causing petty trouble, playful maliciousness XVIII. - OF. *mesch(i)ef*, (mod. *méchef*), f. *meschever* meet with misfortune, f. *mes-* MIS-[2] + *chever* 'come to a head', happen :- Rom. **capāre*, f. **capum*, L. *caput* head. So **mischievous** †unfortunate XIV, harmful XV; disposed to acts of playful malice XVII. - AN. *meschevous*, f. OE. *meschever*. See -OUS.

miscreant †heretic(al), infidel XIV; villain(ous) XVI. - OF. *mescreant* (mod. *mécréant*) misbelieving, unbelieving, prp. of *mescroire* (mod. *mécroire*) disbelieve, f. *mes-* MIS-[2] + *croire* :- L. *crēdere* believe.

misdeed OE. *misdǣd* = OHG. *missitāt*, Goth. *missadēþs*; see MIS-[1], DEED.

misdemeanour XV. MIS-[2]. Hence **misdemeanant** XIX.

misdoubt (dial., arch.) have doubts about, be suspicious of. XVI. MIS-[1].

miser A. †wretch; B. avaricious person. XVI. - L. *miser* wretched, unfortunate. So **miserable** A. wretched XVI; B. †miserly XV. - OF. *misérable* - L. *miserābilis* pitiable, f. *miserārī* be pitiful. Hence **miserly** XVI. **miserere** fifty-first (fiftieth) psalm, beginning Miserere mei Deus 'Have mercy upon me, O God' XIII; prayer for mercy XVII; misericord (seat) XVIII. imper. sg. of L. *miserērī* have pity, f. *miser*; the last sense is a misuse. **misericord** †pity, mercy XIV; dagger for giving the coup de grâce XV; choir seat giving support to one standing XVI. - OF. *miséricorde* - L. *misericordia*, f. *misericors* pitiful, f. *miseri-*, stem of *miserērī* + *cors*, *cord-* HEART. **misery** wretchedness of external conditions XIV; extreme unhappiness XVI; †miserliness XVI. - AN. **miserie*, for (O)F. *misère*, or - L. *miseria*, f. *miser*; see -Y[3].

misfeasance (leg.) transgression, trespass. XVI. - OF. *mesfaisance*, f. prp. of *mesfaire* (mod. *méfaire*), f. *mes-* MIS-[2] + *faire* :- L. *facere* DO[1]; see -ANCE. Cf. MALFEASANCE.

misfortune XV. MIS-[2].

misgive A. (of the heart, mind) suggest doubt or foreboding; B. (dial.) fail, miscarry. XVI. f. MIS-[1] + GIVE (in A with the ME. sense of 'suggest', in B with meaning as in *give out*, *give over*).

mishap †ill luck; unlucky accident. XIV. f. MIS-[1] + HAP, prob. after OF. *mescheance* MISCHANCE.

mish-mash medley, hodge-podge. XV. redupl. of MASH, with variation of vowel.

mishna(h) collection of precepts forming the basis of the Talmud. XVII. - post-biblical Heb. *mišnāh* repetition, instruction, f. *šānah* repeat, teach or learn (oral tradition).

mislike (chiefly lit. or dial.) not to like. OE. MIS-[1].

misnomer (leg.) mistake in naming XV; use of a wrong name XVII. - AN., sb. use of OF. *mesnom(m)er*, f. *mes-* MIS-[2] + *nommer* :- L. *nōmināre*; see NOMINATE, -ER[5].

misogynist woman-hater. XVII. f. Gr. *mīsogúnēs*, f. *mīso-*, comb. form of *mīsein* hate + *gúnē* woman; see -IST.

misprision[1] (leg.) wrongful action or omission XV (*m. of treason* or *felony* XVI; often taken to mean 'failure to denounce'); (arch.) misunderstanding, mistake XVI. - AN. *mesprisioun* = OF. *mesprison* error, wrong action or speech, f. *mesprendre* (mod. *méprendre*), f. *mes-* MIS-[2] + *prendre* take.

misprize (arch.) despise. XV. - OF. *mesprisier* (mod. *mépriser*), f. *mes-* MIS-[2] + *priser* PRIZE[2]. Hence **misprision**[2] contempt. XVI.

misrule †disorderly conduct; bad government. XIV (*Lord of M.* XV). f. MIS-[1] + RULE.

miss[1] A. fail to hit or reach OE.; fail to attain XIII; B. discover the absence of XII; C. omit XVI. OE. *missan* = (M)LG., (M)Du. *missen*, (O)HG. *missen*, ON. *missa* :- Gmc. **missjan*, f. **missa-* (cf. MIS-[1]), ppl. formation with **-to-* on an IE. base **mith-*, repr. by Skr. *mithá-*, OSl. *mitě* alternating, cogn. with Skr. *méthati* alternates, L. *mūtāre* (see MUTATION), Goth. *maidjan* falsify. So **miss** sb. OE. *miss* loss, corr. to MLG., MHG. *misse* (Du. *mis*), ON. *missa*, *-ir*.

miss[2] (dial.) kept mistress; title prefixed to the name of an unmarried woman. XVII. Clipped form of MISTRESS. Hence **missy** (-Y[6]) XVII.

missal XIV (*messel*). - (partly through OF. *messel*, mod. *missel*) medL. *missāle*, use of n. sg. of *missālis* pert. to the Mass, f. *missa* MASS[1]; see -AL[1].

missel-thrush thrush (*Turdus viscivorus*) that feeds on mistletoe berries. XVIII. Earlier *missel-bird* (XVII); f. †*missel* (OE. *mistel*) MISTLETOE.

missile adapted for throwing; sb. missile weapon. XVII. - L. *missilis* (n. sg. *missile* as sb.), f. *miss-*; see next and -ILE.

mission †sending, esp. abroad XVI; sending forth on a service (spec. Mission of the Holy Ghost) or with authority; body of persons sent; commission, errand XVII; establishment of missionaries XVIII; personal duty or vocation XIX; operational sortie XX. - F. *mission* or L. *missiō*, *-ōn-*, f. *miss-*, pp. stem of *mittere* let go, send; see -ION. So **missionary** XVII.

missis, missus (colloq.) *the m.*, one's wife; servant's mistress. XIX. Slurred pronunc. of MISTRESS; now the oral equiv. of MRS.

missive *letter m.*, (orig. techn.) letter sent by a superior authority XV; †missile XVI; sb. letter (esp. and orig. official), in early use mainly Sc. XVI. - medL. *missīvus*, f. *miss-* (see MISSION) + *-īvus* -IVE.

mist vapour of water; dimness, obscurity. OE. *mist* = (M)LG., (M)Du. *mist*, OIcel. *-mistr* :- Gmc. **miχstaz*, f. **mīʒ-* (cf. Du. *miggelen* drizzle) :- IE. **migh-* **meigh-*, as in Gr. *omíkhlē*, OSl. *mĭgla* mist, Skr. *meghá-* cloud. Hence **misty** (-Y[1]) OE.

mistake †err, transgress XIII; †take wrongly XIV; misunderstand XV; make a mistake XVI. In earliest use north. - ON. *mistaka* take in error, refl. miscarry, f. *mis-* MIS-[1] + *taka* TAKE. Cf. OF. *mesprendre* (mod. *se méprendre*), which has prob. infl. the meaning. Hence sb. XVII. **mistaken** †wrongly supposed XVI; of wrong opinion XVII.

mister[1] (obs. exc. arch. and dial.) handicraft, employment; (*this*, *what*) kind of; office, duty; need, necessity. XIII. - AN. *mester*, OF. *mestier* (mod. MÉTIER) :- Rom. **misterium*, for L. *ministerium*; see MYSTERY[2].

mister[2] title of courtesy for a man, MR. XVI. Weakened form of MASTER originating from reduced stress in proclitic use.

mistletoe OE. *misteltān* (= ON. *mistilteinn*), f. *mistel* mistletoe (= OHG. *mistil* (G. *mistel*), Du. *mistel*, ON. *mistil*) + *tān* twig (= Du. *teen* withe, OHG. *zein* rod, ON. *teinn* twig, spit, Goth. *tains* twig).

mistral cold north-west wind of the Mediterranean. XVII. - F. - Pr. :- L. *magistrālis* MAGISTRAL.

mistress female correlative of 'master' XIV; feminine title of courtesy; female paramour XV. ME. *maistresse* - OF. *maistresse* (mod. *maîtresse*), f. *maistre* MASTER + *-esse* -ESS[1]. Forms in *mis-* (due to light stress) are recorded from XV; cf. MISTER[2]. See also MISS[2], MISSIS.

misunderstand XII. MIS-[1]. So **misunderstanding** XV.

mite[1] minute insect; now spec. an acarid, and chiefly the cheese-mite. OE. *mīte* = MLG., MDu. *mīte* (Du. *mijt*), OHG. *mīza* gnat :- Gmc. **mītōn*, perh. to be referred to **mait-* (OHG. *meizan*, ON. *meita*, Goth. *maitan*) cut.

mite[2] Flemish coin of very small value; (hence) any small monetary unit; jot, whit XIV; very small object XVI. - MLG., MDu. *mīte* (Du. *mijt*) :- Gmc. **mītōn*, prob. identical with prec.

mithridatism immunity against the effects of poison, produced by the administration of gradually increasing doses of the poison itself. XIX. f. *Mithridates*, king of Pontus (d. 63 B.C.), who was said to have made himself immune against poisons by constant use of antidotes. So **mithridatize** XIX.

mitigate appease; alleviate, lessen the violence or burden of. XV. f. pp. stem of L. *mītigāre*, f. *mītis* mild, gentle; see -ATE[3]. So **mitigation** XIV. - (O)F. or L.

mitrailleuse machine-gun. XIX. - F., fem. of *mitrailleur*, agent-noun f. *mitrailler*, f. *mitraille* small shot or projectile (in OF. small money, pieces of metal), alt. of *mitaille*, coll. dim. of *mite* MITE[2].

mitral pert. to a mitre XVII; of the left auriculo-ventricular valve of the heart, so called from its shape XVIII. - F. *mitral*, f. *mitre* MITRE; see -AL[1].

mitre ceremonial episcopal head-dress XIV; joint between boards meeting at right angles XVII. - (O)F. - L. *mitra* - Gr. *mítrā* girdle, head-band, turban.

mitten XIV. ME. *mytayne* - (O)F. *mitaine* :- Rom. **medietāna*, f. L. *medietās* half, MOIETY. Shortened to **mitt** XVIII.

mittimus (leg.) warrant to the keeper of a prison to hold the person sent. XV. - L., 'we send', the first word of the writ; 1st pers. pl. pres. ind. of *mittere* (see MISSION).

mix put together in union or combination XVI; intr. be mixed, associate *with* XVII. As infin. not earlier than the second quarter of XVI; back-formation from pp. *mixed*, var. of †*mixt* (XV in legal use) - (O)F. *mixte* - L. *mixtus*, pp. of *miscēre* mingle, mix, rel. to Gr. *misgein*, Ir. *meascaim* mix, Lith. *mišras*, Skr. *miśrá-* mixed.

mixen (dial., arch.) dunghill. OE. *mixen*, f. Gmc. **mīʒ* - make water (OE. *micge*, *migga* urine, OE. *mīgan*, LG. *mīgen*, ON. *míga* urinate).

mixture XV. - F. *mixture* or L. *mixtūra*, f. *mixt-*, pp. stem of *miscēre*; see MIX and -TURE.

miz(z)en (naut.) fore-and-aft sail set on the **mizen mast** (the aftermost mast of a three-masted ship). XV (*mesan*, *-eyn*, *-on*). - F. *misaine* (now, foresail, foremast) - It. *mezzana*, sb. use of fem. of *mezzano* middle; forms with *mi-* appear in XVI.

mizzle[1] drizzle. XV. prob. - LG. *miseln* = Du. dial. *miezelen*, frequent. formation (see -LE[3]) on the base found in Du. dial. *miesregen* drizzle, *miezig*, LG. *misig* drizzling.

mizzle[2] (sl.) decamp, be off. XVIII. of unkn. orig.

mnemonic adj. and sb. XVIII. - medL. *mnēmonicus* - Gr. *mnēmonikós*, f. *mnḗmōn*, *mnēmon-* mindful; rel. to MIND. So **mnemonical** XVII.

moan complaint XIII; (with imit. suggestion) long murmur expressing pain XVII ME. *mone*, repr. unrecorded OE. **mān* :- Gmc. **main-*, whence vb. **mainjan*, OE. *mǣnan*, ME. *mę̄ne*, which was repl. by **moan** vb. XVI, from the sb.

moat ditch surrounding a town, castle, etc. XIV; (dial.) pond, lake XV. ME. *mot(e)*, identical with †*mote* mound, embankment, - OF. *mot(t)e* clod, mound, castle hill, castle (mod. *motte* clod, mound).

mob[1] †strumpet; †négligé attire XVII; in full *mob-cap* women's indoor headgear XVIII. var. of *mab* slattern, loose woman (XVI), short for the female name *Mabel*.

mob[2] disorderly or promiscuous crowd; *the* common mass of people XVII; gang of thieves XIX. Shortening of earlier synon. †*mobile* (XVII), itself for L. *mobile vulgus* the excitable or fickle crowd; see next. Hence vb. throng, gather in a mob. XVIII.

mobile movable XV; easily moved XIX. - (O)F. - L. *mōbilis*, f. *movēre*, *mō-* MOVE; see -ILE. So **mobility** XV. - (O)F. - L. **mobilize** render movable; prepare for active service. XIX. - F. **mobilization** XIX. - F.

mocassin XVII. of Algonquian orig.

mocha, Mocha[1] variety of chalcedony. XVII (*mocus*, *moc(h)o*). poss. the same word as next.

Mocha[2] applied to fine coffee, orig. that produced in Yemen, in which *Mocha* (the port of shipment, at the entrance of the Red Sea) is situated. XVIII.

mock hold up to ridicule; act or speak in derision XV. - OF. *mocquer* deride, jeer (mod. *se moquer de* laugh at); cf. Sp. *mueca* grimace, Pg. *moca* derision. Hence sb. XV, adj. XVI, **mock-up** XX. So **mockery** XV. - F.

mode A. †tune, melody XIV; †mood in grammar and logic XVI; (mus.) form of scale; manner (spec. in philos.) XVII; B. fashion XVII. In A - L. *modus* measure, size, manner, method, tune, f. IE. **mod-* **med-*; see METE. In B - F. *mode* fem. (with change of gender) - L. *modus*. Hence **modish** (-ISH[1]) XVII. So **modiste** dressmaker. XIX. - F.

model †architect's plans; design, make XVI; representation or figure in three dimensions; exemplar, pattern XVII. - F. †*modelle*, now *modèle* - It. *modello* :- Rom. **modellus*, for L. *modulus*, dim. of *modus* (see prec.). Hence vb. XVII.

moderate avoiding extremes, of medium quantity or quality. XIV. - L. *moderātus*, pp. of *moderārī*, *-āre* reduce, abate, control, f. **moder-* :- **modes-*, parallel with **modos*, *modus* MODE; cf. MODEST. So vb. render less violent or intense XV; control, preside over XVI. f. pp. stem of L. *moderāre*, *-ārī*. See -ATE[2,3]. So **moderation** XV. - F. - L. **moderator** †ruler XIV; title of various presiding officials XVI. - L.

modern †now existing; pert. to or characteristic of present or recent times; †ordinary XVI. - (O)F. *moderne* or late L. *modernus*, f. L. *modo* just now. Hence **modernist** †person of modern times XVI, supporter of modern ways XVIII; (theol.) XX. **modernism** XVIII. So **modernity** XVII. - medL. **modernize** XVIII. - F.

modest †well-conducted; having a moderate estimate of oneself; chastely decorous XVI; not excessive XVII; unpretentious XVIII. - (O)F. *modeste* - L. *modestus* keeping due measure, f. **modes-* (see MODERATE) + **-tos*, ppl. suffix. So **modesty** (-Y[3]) XVI. - (O)F. or L.

modicum moderate amount. XV. - L. *modicum* little way, short time, n. sg. of *modicus* moderate, f. *modus* (due or proper) measure, MODE.

modify †limit, repress; moderate XIV; (Sc. law) assess award XV; †determine, differentiate XVII; change partially XVIII. - (O)F. *modifier* - L. *modificāre*, *-ārī*, f. *modus* MODE; see -FY. So **modification** XVI.

modillion (archit.) projecting bracket in certain orders. XVI. - F. *modillon*, †*modiglion* - It. *modiglione* :- Rom. **mutellione*, f. **mutellus*, for L. *mutulus* MUTULE.

modulate †make melody XVI; regulate, adjust; attune XVII; pass from one key *to* another XVIII. f. pp. stem of L. *modulārī* measure, adjust to rhythm, make melody, f. *modulus* (dim. of *modus* MODE); see -ATE[3]. So **modulation** XIV. - L. **module** XVI. - F. or L.

Mogul Mongolian; *The* (*Great* or *Grand*) *M*., the Emperor of Delhi. XVI. - Arab., Pers. *muġal*, *-ul*, pronunc. of *Mongol*.
mohair fine camlet made from Angora goat's hair, (later) fabric imitating this. XVI (*mocayare*, *moochary*, *mockaire*). ult. - Arab. *muḵayyar* cloth of goat's hair (lit. 'select, choice', pp. of *ḵayyara* choose), but coming into Eng. through various channels and later assim. to HAIR.
Mohammed(an) see MAHOMET.
moidore Portuguese gold coin. XVIII (*moyodore*). - Pg. *moeda d'ouro* 'coin of gold' (*moeda* :- L. *monēta* MONEY, *ouro* :- L. *aurum* gold).
moiety half. XV (*moit(i)e*). - OF. *moité*, (also mod.) *moitié* :- L. *medietās*, *-tāt-*, f. *medius* middle, MID.
moil (dial., arch.) moisten, soil, bedaub XIV; toil, drudge (as in wet and mire) XVI. - OF. *moillier* wet, moisten, paddle in mud (mod. *mouiller*) :- Rom. **molliāre*, f. L. *mollis* soft.
moire watered mohair, (later) watered silk. XVII. - F. *moire* - Eng. MOHAIR. Also **moiré** watered. XIX. - F. *moiré*, pp. of *moirer* give a watered appearance to.
moist †new, fresh; †liquid, watery; slightly wet. XIV. - OF. *moiste* (mod. *moite*), perh. :- Rom. **muscidus* mouldy, (hence) wet, alt. of L. *mūcidus* (cf. MUCUS) by assoc. with *musteus* new, fresh, f. *mustum* MUST[1]. Hence **moisten** (-EN[5]); preceded by (dial.) **moist** XIV. **moisty** †new (of ale); damp. XIV. So **moisture** XIV. alt. of OF. *moi(s)tour* (mod. *moiteur*).
moither worry, perplex XVII; be incoherent or wandering XIX. of unkn. orig.
moke (sl.) donkey. XIX. of unkn. orig.
molar grinding (tooth). XVI. - L. *molāris* of a mill, sb. millstone, grinder tooth, f. *mola* millstone; see MILL, -AR.
molasses syrup obtained from sugar. XVI (*melasus*, *molassos*, *malassos*). - Pg. *melaço* :- late L. *mellāceum* must, n. sg. of **mellāceus* (cf. -ACEOUS), f. *mel*, *mell-* honey.
mole[1] †discoloured spot OE.; spot or blemish on the human skin XIV. OE. *māl*, corr. to MLG. *mēl*, OHG. *meil*, *meila*, Goth. **mail* (in g. pl. *maile*) :- Gmc. **mailam*, *-ōn*, whence also OE. *mǣlan*, OHG. *meilen* stain.
mole[2] small burrowing mammal. XIV. ME. *mol(l)e*, *mulle*, prob. - MDu. *mol*, *moll(e)*, (M)LG. *mol*, *mul*.
mole[3] A. (stone) pier or breakwater, (hence) harbour; B. †large mass XVI. - F. *môle* - It. *molo* - medGr. *môlos*, *mólos* - L. *mōlēs* shapeless mass, huge bulk (whence sense B), dam, pier.
molecule XVIII. - F. *molécule*, dim. f. L. *mōlēs* MOLE[3]. Hence **molecular** XIX.
molest †vex, annoy XIV; meddle with injuriously XV. - OF. *molester* or L. *molestāre* trouble, annoy, f. *molestus* troublesome. So **molestation** XIV. - (O)F. - medL.
moll (sl.) prostitute, female paramour. XVII. appellative use of *Moll*, var. of †*Mall*, pet-form of MARY.
mollify XV. - F. *mollifier* or L. *mollificāre*, f. *mollis* soft, rel. to *molere* grind; see MILL, -FY. So **mollification** XIV. - (O)F. - medL.
mollusc XVIII. - F. *mollusque*, f. modL. *mollusca*, n. pl. of L. *molluscus* soft, f. *mollis* soft (see prec.).
molly (dial.) lass, wench; (sl.) milksop. XVIII. f. MOLL + -Y[6]. Hence **molly-coddle** sb. and vb. XIX.
molten see MELT.
moly fabulous herb XVI; a wild garlic XVII. - L. *mōly* - Gr. *môlu*.
molybdenum (min.) metallic element. XIX. f. †*molybdena* (XVII), former name of salts of molybdenum, use of L. - Gr. *molúbdaina* angler's plummet, f. *mólubdos* lead.
moment very brief portion of time XIV; †small particle XIV; importance, weight XVI; †motive of action XVII. - (O)F. - L. *mōmentum* (i) movement, moving power, (ii) importance, consequence, (iii) moment of time, particle :- **movimentum*, f. *movēre* MOVE; see -MENT. So **momentary** XVI, **momentum** XVII. - L. Hence **momentous** of moment XVII.
Momus captious critic. XVI. - L. - Gr. *Mômos* god of ridicule (*mômos*).
monachal monastic, monkish. XVI. - (O)F. *monacal* or ecclL. *monachālis*, f. *monachus* MONK; see -AL[1]. So **monachism** XVI.
monad the number one XVII; ultimate unit of being XVIII; simple organism, element, etc. XIX. - F. *monade* or its source late L. *monas*, *-ad-* - Gr. *monás* unit, f. *mónos* alone; see -AD[1].
monarch XV. - (O)F. *monarque* or late L. *monarcha* - Gr. *monárkhēs*, more freq. *mónarkhos*, f. *mónos* alone; see -ARCH. So or hence **monarchal** XVI, **-ic** XVII, **-ical** XVI, **monarchist** XVII. **monarchy** (-ARCHY) XIV. - (O)F. - late L. - Gr.
monastery XV. - ecclL. *monastērium* - ecclGr. *monastḗrion*, f. *monázein* live alone, f. *mónos* alone. So **monastic** XVI. - (O)F. *monastique* or late L. *monasticus* - Gr. *monastikós*.
Monday OE. *mōnandæġ*, corr. to MLG., MDu. *mān(en)dach* (Du. *maandag*), OHG. *mānatag* (G. *Montag*), ON. *mánadagr*; f. MOON + DAY, tr. late L. *lūnæ diēs* 'day of the moon' (after Gr. *hēmérā Selḗnēs*).
monde *the* fashionable world. XVIII. - F., 'world' :- L. *mundus*.
monetary XIX. - F. *monétaire* or late L. *monētārius*, f. L. *monēta* MINT[1]; see -ARY.
money coin, cash, esp. in ref. to its purchasing power XIII; particular coin or coinage XV. ME. *monei(e)*, *mone* - OF. *moneie* (mod. *monnaie* change) :- L. *monēta* mint (in Rome), money, orig. epithet of Juno, in whose temple the mint was housed. So **moneyer** †money-changer XIII; coiner, minter XV; †banker, capitalist XVIII. - OF. *mon(n)ier*, *-oier* (mod. *monnayeur*) :- late L. *monētārius* minter.
mong in ME. XII *mang*, *mong*, aphetic of *amang*, AMONG or †*imong*; from XVI poet. clipping of AMONG, and so written *'mong*. So **mongst** XVI.
monger dealer, trader; now used only in conscious analysis of words like *cheesemonger*, *fishmonger*, *ironmonger*, which, with *costermonger*, *scandal-monger*, *whore-monger*, are the commonest exx. OE. *mangere* (= OHG., ON. *mangari*), agent-noun of *mangian* (= OS. *mangon*, ON. *manga*) :- Gmc. **maŋgōjan*, f. L. *mangō* dealer, trader; see -ER[1].
mongoose XVII. - Marathi *māgūs*.

mongrel dog of mixed breed XV; in various transf. uses XVI. Early forms *meng-*, *mang-*, *m(o)(u)ngrel(l)*, the variety of which suggests derivation, with pejorative -REL, from vars. of Gmc. **maŋg-* mix, MINGLE.

monial (archit.) mullion. XIV (*moinel*). - OF. *moinel* (mod. *meneau*), sb. use of *moi(e)nel* adj. middle, f. *moien* MEAN[3] + *-el* -AL[1].

moniliform necklace-shaped. XIX. - F. *moniliforme*, f. L. *monīle* necklace.

monism doctrine of one (supreme) being; theory which denies the duality of matter and mind. XIX. f. Gr. *mónos* single; see -ISM.

monition XIV. - (O)F. - L. *monitiō*, *-ōn-*, f. *monit-*, pp. stem of *monēre* advise, warn (rel. to MIND); see -ITION. So **monitor** (-TOR) one who warns or advises; senior pupil in a school, etc. XVI; †backboard XVIII; species of lizard supposed to give warning of crocodiles XIX. - L. **monitor** (poet.) to guide XIX; (var. techn. uses) control, regulate XX. f. the sb. **monitory** (-ORY[2]) warning, admonishing. XV. - L. *monitōrius*.

monk OE. *munuc* = OS. *munik* (Du. *monnik*), OHG. *munih* (G. *mönch*), ON. *múnkr*; Gmc. - popL. **monicus*, for late L. *monachus* - late Gr. *mónakhos*, sb. use of adj. 'single, solitary' (early transf. to coenobites), f. *mónos* alone. Hence **monkery**, **-ish** XVI. **monkshood** *Aconitum napellus*, etc., having hood-shaped flowers. XVI.

monkey XVI. of unkn. orig.

mono- comb. form of Gr. *mónos* alone, only, single, occurring in numerous words adopted from Gr. (many through late L. or medL.), but in recent times combined with words or stems of any origin, as *monocycle*, *monodrama*, *monoplane*, *monotint*, *monoxide*. The following early: **monochord** one-stringed musical instrument, etc. XV. - (O)F. *monocorde* - late L. *monochordon* - Gr. *monókhordon*, sb. use of n. of *monókhordos* having a single string. **monochrome** painting in different tints of one colour XVII; representation in one colour XIX; the earlier use - medL. *monochrōma*, evolved from Gr. (-L.) *monokhrṓmatos* of one colour; later - F. *monochrome* - Gr. *monókhrōmos*. **monogamy** XVII. - F. - ecclL. - Gr. (*gámos* marriage). **monogram** A. †sketch without shading or colour; B. character composed of two or more letters interwoven XVII; in sense A - L. *monogrammus*; in sense B - F. *monogramme* - late L. *monogramma*, f. Gr. **monógrammos*. **monograph** (nat. hist.) separate treatise on a species, genus, etc.; (more widely) one on a single object or topic. XIX. repl. earlier **monography** (XVIII) - modL. *monographia*. **monolith** single block, mass, pillar of stone. XIX. - F. *monolithe* - Gr. *monólithos* (*líthos* stone). **monologue** XVII. - F. **monophysite** XVII. - ecclL. *monophysīta* - ecclGr. *monophusī́tēs* (Gr. *phúsis* nature). **monothelite** XVI. - modL. *monothelīta* - (with assim. to *-īta*, -ITE) late Gr. *monothelḗtēs*, f. *thélein* will. **monotheism**, **-theist** XVII. **monotone** having but one tone or note XVIII; sb. utterance on one tone XVII. - modL. *monotonus* - Gr. *monótonos*. **monotonous** XVIII. **monotony** XVIII. - F. - Gr. *monotoniā*. **monotype** XIX.

monocle XIX. - F., sb. use of adj. 'one-eyed' - late L. *monoculus*, f. Gr. *mónos* MONO- + *oculus* EYE.

monody ode sung by a single voice in Greek tragedy; mournful song, dirge. XVII. - late L. *monōdia* - Gr. *monōidiā*, f. *mónos* MONO- + *ōid-* sing; see ODE, -Y[3].

monopoly exclusive possession of the trade in some article XVI (also fig.); commodity subject to this XIX. - L. *monopōlium* - Gr. *monopṓlion*, *-pōliā*, f. *mónos* MONO- + *pōlein* sell. Hence **monopolist**, **monopolize** XVII.

monsieur F. equiv. of MR. XV. - F., f. *mon* my, *sieur* lord :- Rom. **seiōre*, for L. *seniōrem*, SENIOR. So **monseigneur** XVI, **monsignor** XVII.

monsoon seasonal wind esp. in the Indian Ocean XVI; rainy season (time of the south-west monsoon) XVIII. - early modDu. †*monssoen* (mod. *moesson*) - Pg. *monção*, †*moução* - Arab. *mausim* season, f. *wasama* vb. mark.

monster misshapen creature XIII; †prodigy; horribly cruel or savage person; huge object XVI. - (O)F. *monstre* - L. *mōnstrum* something marvellous or prodigious, orig. divine portent, f. *monēre* warn. So **monstrous** XV. - OF. or L. **monstrosity** XVI. - late L.

monstrance (eccl.) vessel in which the Host is exposed. XVI. - medL. *mōnstrantia*, f. prp. stem of L. *mōnstrāre* show, f. *mōnstrum*; see prec. and -ANCE.

montbretia iridaceous plant of genus *Crocosmia*. XIX. modL., f. name of A. F. E. Coquebert de *Montbret*, French botanist (1780-1801); see -IA[1].

monte Spanish card game. XIX. - Sp. *monte* mountain (MOUNT[1]), applied to the stock of cards left after each player has received his share.

month OE. *mōnað* = OS. *mānoth* (Du. *maand*), OHG. *mānōd* (G. *monat*), ON. *mánuðr*, Goth. *mēnōþs* :- Gmc. **mǣnōþ(āz)*; cf. MOON. Hence **monthly** adj. and adv. XVI; see -LY[1,2].

monument †place of burial XIII; †written document, piece of evidence XV; commemorative object or structure XVI. Early forms also †*mony-*, †*moniment* - (O)F. *monument*, †*moniment* - L. *monumentum*, *monimentum*, f. *monēre* remind; see MONITION, -MENT. Hence **monumental** XVII.

-mony repr. (1) L. *-mōnia*, as in *acrimony*, *ceremony*, (2) *-mōnium*, as in *matrimony*, *testimony*, and both in *alimony*, *ceremony*; rel. by gradation to *-men* (as in *forāmen* opening), of which *-mentum* -MENT is an extended form.

moo XVI. imit. of the characteristic voice of the cow.

mooch, **mouch** (dial.) play truant XVII; loaf, skulk; steal XIX. of uncert. orig.; cf. late ME. *mowche* (of doubtful meaning).

mood[1] †mind, thought, feeling OE.; †pride OE.; †anger XII; frame of mind, disposition. OE. *mōd*, corr. (with variety of gender) to OS. *mōd* (Du. *moed*), OHG. *muot* (G. *mut*), ON. *móðr* anger, grief, Goth. *mōþs*, *mōd-* anger, emotion :- Gmc. **mōðaz*, **mōðam*, of unkn. orig. Hence **moody** †brave, †proud OE.; †angry XII; subject to fits of ill humour, etc. XVI.

mood[2] (logic) class of syllogism; (gram.) form in the conjugation of a verb indicating function;

†(mus.) mode. XVI. alt. of MODE by assoc. with MOOD[1].

moon the satellite of the earth OE.; (lunar) month XIV. OE. *mōna* = OS. *māno* (Du. *maan* fem.), OHG. *māno* (G. *mond*), ON. *máni*, Goth. *mēna* :- Gmc. **mǣnan-*, prob. rel. to **mǣnōþ-* MONTH; cogn. words for 'moon' and 'month' based on **mēn(e)s-* are L. *mēnsis* month, Gr. *meís*, *mḗn* month, *mḗnē* moon, Skr. *mā́s-* moon, month, Ir. *mí* month, OSl. *mēsęcĭ* moon, month; referred ult. to the IE. base **mē-*, as in L. *mētīrī* MEASURE, the moon being the star by which time is measured.

The foll. comps. are of special interest: **mooncalf** †false conception XVI; born fool XVII; perh. after G. *mondkalb*; cf. G. *mondkind*, MLG. *maanenkind* 'moon-child'. **moonlight** XIV; hence **moonlighting** operation (esp. illicit) by night. XIX. **moonlit** XIX. **moonshine** moonlight; appearance without substance, empty talk, etc. XV. **moonstone** XVII; after L. *selēnītēs* SELENITE. **moonstruck** deranged, as if by the influence of the moon (cf. *lunatic*). XVII.

moor[1] tract of unenclosed waste ground. OE. *mōr* waste land, marsh, mountain, corr. to OS. *mōr* marsh, (M)Du. *moer*, (M)LG. *mōr*, OHG. *muor* :- Gmc. **mōraz*, **mōram*, rel. to MERE[1]. comp. **moorland** OE. *mōrland*.

moor[2] secure a floating boat, etc., to a fixed place. XV. prob. - (M)LG. *mōren*; cf. OE. *mǣrels*, *mārels* mooring-rope, MDu. vbs. *māren*, *mēren* (Du. *meren*), *moeren*.

Moor (in ancient times) native of Mauretania, (later) of north-west Africa XIV. ME. *More* - (O)F. *More*, (mod.) *Maure* - L. *Maurus*, medL. *Mōrus* - Gr. *Maûros*. Hence **Moorish** XV (*morys*).

moose XVII. of Algonquian orig.

moot assembly of people, esp. for a judicial purpose XII; †argument, discussion XIII; discussion of a hypothetical case in the Inns of Court XVI. ME. *(i)mōt* :- OE. *mōt* (in comps. only; later reinforced from ON.), and *ġemōt* :- Gmc. **(ʒa)mōtam*; cf. MDu. *moet*, (also mod.) *gemoet*, MHG. *muoze* meeting, attack, ON. *mót*, and MEET[2]; of unkn. orig. Hence **moot** adj. debatable, arguable XVI; developed from attrib. uses of the sb. (*m. case*, *m. point*).

mop[1] bundle of yarn, etc., fixed to a stick for use in cleaning. XV. First in naut. use and in the form †*mapp(e)*, which survived till XVIII, the form *mop* appearing XVII (but †*moppe* is recorded for 'doll' XV); obscurely rel. to somewhat earlier †*mappel*, †*mapolt*, *-old* (XV); of unkn. orig.

mop[2] (arch.) grimace. (sb. and vb.) XVI. Chiefly in phr. *mop(s) and mow(s)*; perh. imit. of the pouting of the lips; cf. Du. *moppen* be surly, pout.

mope (dial.) wander; be listless and dejected. XVI. prob. rel. to †*mope* (XVI), earlier †*mopp(e)* fool (XIV); and †*mop(p)ish* bewildered (XIV); of uncert. orig.

moquette material used for carpeting. XVIII. - F. *moquette*; of unkn. orig.

mora (leg.) delay XVI; (pros.) unit of metrical time XIX. - L. *mora*.

moraine mountain debris carried down by a glacier. XVIII. - F.

moral pert. to character or conduct. XIV. - L. *mōrālis*, f. *mōs*, *mōr-* custom, pl. *mōres* manners, character (whence **mores** XX). As sb. pl. rendering the L. title *Moralia* of certain works XIV; sg. moral lesson XV; pl. moral habits XVII. So **morale** (- F., fem. of *moral* used sb.) †morals XVIII; disposition and spirit as of troops XIX. **morality** XIV. - (O)F. or late L. **moralize, -ation** XV. - (O)F. or medL.

morass wet swampy tract. XVII. - Du. *moeras*, †*-asch*, alt. (by assim. to *moer* MOOR[1]) of MDu. *maras(ch)* - (O)F. *marais* MARSH.

moratorium legal authorization to postpone payment. XIX. modL., sb. use of n. sg. of late L. (legal) *morātōrius*, f. pp. stem of *morārī* delay; see -ORY.

morbid pert. to disease XVII; unwholesome, sickly XIX. - L. *morbidus*, f. *morbus* disease; see -ID[1]. So **morbific** XVII. - F.

mordant biting. XV. - (O)F., prp. of *mordre* bite :- Rom. **mordere*, for L. *mordēre*.

mordent (mus.) kind of grace. XIX. - G. - It. *mordente*, sb. use of prp. of *mordere* bite (L. *mordēre*).

more A. greater (surviving in *(the) m.'s the pity*, *the m. fool you*, etc.) OE. B. existing in greater quantity or degree XIV. C. a greater number of, more numerous XVI. D. additional XIII. OE. *māra*, fem., n. *māre* = OS. *mēro*, OHG. *mēro* (G. *mehr-*), ON. *meiri*, Goth. *maiza* :- Gmc. **maizan-* f. **maiz* :- IE. **məis*, with compar. suffix *-is* (cf. -ER[3]). Hence as sb. late OE., as adv. XII. Hence **moreover** in phr. *and yet more over* 'and still more beyond', whence, introducing an additional statement, 'besides'. XIV.

-more use of prec. in advs. denoting place in the compar. degree, many of which have given rise to adjs. of the same form; added chiefly to advs. ending in -ER[3]; the majority of such words have parallel forms in -MOST. The earliest, *furthermore* (XII), *farthermore*, and *innermore* (XIII), are based on Scand. forms (ON. *-meir*).

moreen stout stuff for curtains, etc. XVII (*-ine*). perh. fancifully f. MOIRE.

morello dark-coloured bitter cherry. XVII. app. a use of It. *morello* blackish :- medL. *mo-*, *maurellus*, f. *Maurus* MOOR.

mores see MORAL.

moresque Moorish. XVII. - F. - It. *moresco*; see MOOR, -ESQUE.

morganatic applied to a marriage of a man with a woman of inferior station in which wife and children do not share in his rights. XVIII. - F. *morganatique*, G. *morganatisch*, or their source medL. *morganaticus*, prob. based on Gmc. **murʒanʒeba* (OE. *morgenġifu*, G. *morgengabe*; f. **murʒan-* MORN + **ʒeƀ-* GIVE) gift made by husband to wife on the morning after consummation of the marriage and relieving him of further liability.

morgue[1] haughty demeanour. XVI. - F., of unkn. orig.

morgue[2] building in Paris where people found dead are exposed for identification; (gen.) mortuary. XIX. Presumed to be identical with prec.

moribund about to die. XVIII. - L. *moribundus*, f. *morī* die (see MORTAL).

morion soldier's helmet without beaver or visor. XVI. - F. - Sp. *morrion*, f. *morra* top of the head.

Mormon member of the Church of Jesus Christ of Latter-Day Saints. XIX. Name of the alleged author of 'The Book of Mormon', which Joseph Smith (Manchester, New York, 1830) professed to have translated from the original miraculously discovered by him.

morn OE. *morgen*, inflected *mor(g)n-* = OS., OHG. *morgan* (Du., G. *morgen*) :- WGmc. **murȝanaz*; cf., with variation of suffix, ON. *morgunn*, also OE. *myrgen-*, ON. *myrginn*, Goth. *maurgins* (:- Gmc. **murȝinaz*), and, with different vowel grade of the base, OE. *merġen*, MDu. *margen*, *mergen*, ON. *merginn* :- Gmc. **marȝanaz*, **marȝinaz*. The typical ME. developments of OE. *morġen* were: *morȝen*, *morwen*; *morun*, *moren*, *morn*; *morwe*, *moru*, MORROW. Hence (after EVENING) **morning** XIII.

Morocco applied to things originating in the country of north-west Africa so named, esp. to leather of goatskin. XVII. - It. *Marocco*, f. the name of the chief city *Marrakesh*.

moron XX. - n. of Gr. *mōrós* stupid.

morose XVI. - L. *mōrōsus* peevish, wayward, fastidious, f. *mōs*, *mōr-* manner (in the special sense of 'humour', 'fancy'); see MORAL, -OSE[1].

-morph terminal element repr. Gr. *-morphos*, f. *morphḗ* shape. The corr. adjs. and abst. nouns end in *-morphic(al)*, *-morphous*, *-morphism*, *-morphy*.

morpheme XX. - F. *morphème*, f. Gr. *morphḗ* form, after PHONEME.

morphia narcotic principle of opium. XIX. - modL. *morphia*, alt. of *morphium*, f. *Morpheus* (f. Gr. *morphḗ* shape), Ovid's name for the god of dreams, son of the god of sleep. Also **morphine** (-INE[5]) XIX.

morpho- comb. form of Gr. *morphḗ* shape, form, as in **morphology** (XIX).

morris dance by persons in fancy costume representing characters esp. from the Robin Hood story. XV. orig. in *mor(e)ys* DANCE; var. of MOORISH.

morrow XIII. ME. *morwe*, *-ewe*, *-owe*, *moru*; see MORN.

morse[1] fastening of a cope. XV. - OF. *mors* - L. *morsus* bite, catch, f. *mors-*, pp. stem of *mordēre* bite.

morse[2] walrus. XV. ult. - Lappish *moršša*, whence Finnish *morsu*, Russ. *morzh*.

morse[3] signalling code invented by S. F. B. *Morse* (1791-1872). XIX.

morsel bite, mouthful, small piece. XIII. - OF. *morsel* (mod. *morceau*), dim. of *mors* :- L. *morsus*; see MORSE[1], -EL[2].

mort[1] (antiq.) note sounded at the death of the deer. XVI. - (O)F. :- L. *mors*, *mort-* death (cf. MORTAL).

mort[2] (dial.) great quantity or number. XVII. of uncert. orig.

mortal subject to death, human; deadly, fatal XIV; (of sin) XV; of or pert. to death XVI. - OF. *mortal*, latinized var. of OF. (also mod.) *mortel*, whence ME. *mortel*; or directly - L. *mortālis*, f. *mors*, *mort-* death, f. IE. **mor-* **mer-* **mr̥-* die, as in L. *morī* die, *mortuus* dead, Gr. *brotoí* mortals, *émorten* died, OSl. *mĭrǫ*, Lith. *mìrštu* I die, Skr. *mriyáte* dies; see -AL[1]. So **mortality** XIV. - (O)F. - L.

mortar[1] A. cup-shaped vessel in which drugs, etc., are pounded with a pestle XIII; B. short piece of ordnance (so named from its squat shape) XVII (orig. *mortar piece* XVI). partly AN. *morter*, (O)F. *mortier* :- L. *mortārium* (to which the Eng. sp. was finally assim.); partly - MLG. *mortēr* (Du. *mortier*) - L.

mortar[2] mixture of lime and sand with water, used for building. XIII. - AN. *morter* (see prec.), with transference of meaning from the vessel to the substance produced in it.

mortgage conveyance of property by a debtor to a creditor as security for a debt. XIV (*morgage*; the sp. *mortgage* was established by leg. usage XVI). - OF. *mortgage* 'dead pledge', f. *mort* dead :- popL. var. **mortus* of L. *mortuus* (see MORTAL) + *gage* GAGE[1]. Hence **mortgage** vb. XVI; **mortgagee, mortgagor** (-EE[1], -OR[1]) XVI.

mortify †kill XIV; bring (the body, etc.) into subjection; (Sc. law) dispose of in mortmain XV; (cookery) make tender by hanging XVI; become gangrenous; humiliate or vex deeply XVII. - (O)F. *mortifier* - ecclL. *mortificāre* kill, subdue (the flesh), f. *mors*, *mort-* death; see MORTAL, -FY. So **mortification** subjection of the flesh XIV; (Sc. law) disposal in mortmain XV; gangrene, necrosis XVI; humiliation, vexation XVII.

mortise, -ice hole made in a piece of wood to receive the end of another piece. XIV. ME. *mortais*, *-eis* - OF. *mortoise* (mod. *mortaise*), of uncert. orig.

mortmain condition of lands inalienably held by a corporation. XV. - AN., OF. *mortemain* - medL. *mortua manus* 'dead hand', i.e. *mortua*, fem. of *mortuus* dead, *manus* hand (cf. MORTAL, MANUAL); perh. a metaphor for 'impersonal ownership'.

mortuary sb. gift claimed by the parson from the estate of a deceased parishioner XIV; †obsequies XV; dead-house XIX; adj. pert. to burial or death XVI. As sb. orig. - AN. *mortuarie* - ecclL. *mortuārium*, n. sg. of *mortuārius* (whence the Eng. adj.), f. *mortuus* dead; see MORTAL, -ARY.

mosaic XVI. - F. *mosaïque* - It. †*mosaico*, *musaico* - medL. *mōsaicus*, *mūsaicus*, obscurely f. late Gr. *mouseion*, *mousion* mosaic work (cf. MUSEUM).

Mosaic pert. to Moses. XVII. - F. *mosaïque* or modL. *Mōsāicus*, f. *Mōsēs*; see -IC.

moselle dry white wine. XVII. - F. name (- G. *Mosel*, in L. *Mosella*) of a river which joins the Rhine at Koblenz and in the neighbourhood of which the wine is produced.

Moslem see MUSLIM.

mosque XIV (*moseak*, *musketh*), XVI (*muskay*, *mosquee*). The earliest forms are of obscure orig.; the present form is a shortening (XVII) of *mosquee* - F. *mosquée* - It. *moschea* - Arab. *masgid*, Egyptian var. of *masjid*, †*sajada* worship.

mosquito XVI. - Sp., Pg. *mosquito*, dim. of *mosca* :- L. *musca* fly (see MIDGE).

moss A. (dial.) bog, swamp OE.; B. small plant of the class Musci. XIV. OE. *mos* = MLG., (M)Du., OHG. *mos* (G. *moos*) bog, moss :- Gmc. **musam*, rel. to ON. *mosi* wk. m. bog, moss, and further to OE. *mēos*, OHG. *mios* (G. *mies*) moss (:- Gmc. **meus-*), ON. *mýrr* MIRE, and outside Gmc. to L. *muscus*, OSl. *mŭchŭ* moss :- IE. **mus-*). The application in Eng. to the plant may be due to ON. *mosi*.

mossbunker (U.S.) menhaden. XVII (*marsbancker*), XVIII (*mos-*). - Du. *marsbanker*, of unkn. orig.

most greatest OE.; greatest amount of XIV; adv. in the greatest degree OE. The present form repr. partly OE. *māst*, which is recorded only from late Nhb., partly a modification of ME. *mēst*, OE. *mǣst*, by assim. to MORE; OE. *māst* = OS. *mēst* (Du. *meest*), (O)HG. *meist*, ON. *mestr*, Goth. *maists* :- Gmc. **maistaz*, f. base of **maiz* (see MORE) + *-*ista*- -EST. Hence **mostly** XVI.

-most suffix forming superl. adjs. and advs.; alt. form of OE. *-mest* = Goth. *-umists*, which is a combination of two Gmc. (and IE.) superl. suffixes, viz. *-*mo*-, as in OE. *forma* first, L. *prīmus* first (PRIME), and *-*isto*- -EST. Cf. -MORE.

mot saying. - F. 'word' :- Gallo-Rom. **mottum*, alt. of L. *muttum* (not) a word or syllable, rel. to *muttīre* MUTTER, murmur.

mote particle of dust. OE. *mot*, corr. to Du. *mot* sawdust, dust of turf (in MDu. *steenmot*, *turfmot*), of unkn. orig. The present form (ME. *moot* XIV) descends from OE. obl. case-forms (*mott*, repr. the uninflected form, survived till XVIII).

motet part-song; later spec. harmonized vocal composition, esp. for church use. XIV. - (O)F. *motet*, dim. of *mot* word, saying (see MOT); see -ET.

moth insect of the genus *Tinea* or (earlier) its larva OE.; nocturnal lepidopterous insect XVIII. OE. *moððe*, *mohðe*; obscurely rel. to synon. MLG., MDu., (M)HG. *motte* (Du. *mot*), ON. *motti*.

mother[1] A. female parent OE.; term of address to an elderly woman; applied to the B.V.M. XIV; head of community of nuns XVII. B. †womb XIV; †hysteria XV. OE. *mōdor* = OS. *mōdar* (Du. *moeder*), OHG. *muotar* (G. *mutter*), ON. *móðir* (wanting in Gothic) :- Gmc. **mōðar*- :- IE. **māter*-, whence also L. *māter*, Gr. *mḗtēr*, *mḗtēr*, OSl. *mati*, OIr. *māthir*, Skr. *mātā́*. Important collocations are: *m. country* (XVI), after F. *terre mère*; *m. earth* (XVI), cf. L. *Terra Mater*, taken as a goddess; *m. land* (XVIII); *m. tongue* (XIV), in which *mother* is orig. uninflected g. Hence vb. be a mother to. XVI. *Mothering Sunday*, Midlent Sunday, so called from the custom of going a-mothering (XVII), i.e. visiting parents, on that day. **motherly** OE. *mōdorlić*.

mother[2] †dregs, scum XVI; (in full *m. of vinegar*) mucilaginous substance produced in vinegar by fermentation XVII. corr. in form and sense to MDu. *moeder* (mod. *moer*), G. *mutter*; perh. identical with prec.; the orig. notion may have been that the substance was a portion of the 'mother' or original crude substance. So also in **mother-of-pearl** iridescent inner layer of shells. XVI.

motif XIX. - F., 'MOTIVE'.

motion action or process of moving XV; formal proposition XVI. - (O)F. - L. *mōtiō*, *-ōn-*, f. *mō-* of *movēre* (*mōtum*) MOVE; see -TION. Hence **motion** vb. †propose, move XVI; make a gesture XVIII. **motive** †motion, proposition XIV; that which moves a person to act XV; motif XIX. ME. *motyf*, *-yve* - (O) F. *motif*, sb. use of adj. - late L. *mōtīvus*, whence **motive** adj. XVI. So **motivate** XIX.

motley diversified in colour XIV; sb. †varicoloured fabric XIV; particoloured dress of a jester XVI. Late ME. *mottelay*, *-ley*, perh. - AN. **motelé*, f. MOTE (but the formation remains obscure).

motor agent or force producing motion XVI; machine supplying motive power XIX. - L. *mōtor* (rare) mover, later in philos. use, f. *mōt-*, *movēre* MOVE; see -OR[1]. Hence vb. (XIX) drive an automobile, whence **motorist** XIX, **motorway** XX.

mottle surface variegated with spots; so vb. and ppl. adj. *mottled*. XVII. prob. back-formation from MOTLEY.

motto XVI. - It. - F. MOT.

motu proprio papal rescript the terms of which are decided by the pope himself. XIX. - L., 'by one's own motion', abl. of *mōtus* motion, *proprius* PROPER.

moufflon wild sheep *Ovis musimon*. XVIII. - F. *mouflon*.

mouillé (phonetics) palatalized. XIX. - F., pp. of *mouiller* moisten, make 'liquid'.

moujik, muzhik Russian peasant. XVI (*mousick*, *musick*). - Russ. *muzhik*.

mould[1], U.S. **mold** (dial.) friable earth, surface soil; (poet.) earth of the grave; the earth's surface OE.; garden soil XIV. OE. *molde* = (M)Du. *moude*, OHG. *molta*, ON. *mold*, Goth. *mulda* :- Gmc. **muldō*, f. **mul*- (**mel*-, **mal*-) pulverize, grind (cf. OE. *myl*, MDu. *mul*, *mol* dust, and MEAL[1]).

mould[2], U.S. **mold** A. native character XIII; (bodily) form XVI; B. pattern or matrix by which a thing is shaped XIV. Presumably metathetic alt. of OF. *modle* (mod. *moule*) - L. *modulus* (see MODULATE). Hence **mould** vb. XV.

mould[3], U.S. **mold** woolly or furry growth consisting of minute fungi. XV. prob. developed from †*moul(e)d*, pp. of †*moule*, earlier †*muwle* grow mouldy - ON. **mugla*, rel. to synon. ON. *mygla*. Hence **mouldy** (-Y[1]) XIV.

moulder, U.S. **molder** crumble to dust. XVI. poss. f. MOULD[1] + -ER[4]; but adoption from Scand. is more likely (cf. Norw. dial. *muldra* crumble).

moult, U.S. **molt** (of feathers) be shed in the change of plumage XIV; shed (feathers) XV. ME. *moute*, *mowte*, later *molt* (XVI), *moult* (XVII); repr. OE. **mūtian* (as in *mūtung*, *bimūtian* exchange) = MLG., MDu. *mūten* change, moult, OHG. *mūzzōn* (G. *mause(r)n*); WGmc. - L. *mūtāre* change (see MUTATION). Cf. MEW[2].

mound[1] †world XIII; orb intended to represent the globe XVI. - (O)F. *monde* :- L. *mundus* world (see MUNDANE).

mound[2] (dial.) hedge, fence; embankment XVI; artificial elevation of earth or stones, tumulus XVIII. perh. f. the somewhat earlier *mound* vb. enclose with a fence, of unkn. orig.

mount[1] mountain, hill OE.; †earthwork; †mound. XVI. OE. *munt* - (reinforced in ME. from (O)F. *mont* :-) L. *mōns, mont-*.

mount[2] go upwards, ascend, rise XIV; cause to ascend, etc., set in position XVI. - OF. *munter*, (also mod.) *monter* :- Rom. **montāre*, f. *mont-* MOUNT[1]. Hence **mount** sb. †amount XIV; mounting XV; fitting, setting; ridden animal XIX.

mountain XIII. - OF. *montaigne* (mod. *-agne*) :- Rom. **montānia* or *-ea*, fem. sg. or n. pl. of adj. **montānius, -eus*, f. L. *mōns, mont-* MOUNT[1]; see -AN. Hence **mountaineer** XVII, **mountainous** XV (rare before XVII).

mountebank itinerant quack, juggler, etc., appearing on a platform; charlatan. XVI. - It. *montambanco, montimbanco*, for *monta in banco* 'mount (imper.) on bench'.

mourn feel sorrow (for) OE.; lament (a death, someone dead) XIII. OE. str. vb. *murnan* (also wk. pt. *murnde*), corr. to wk. vbs. OS. *mornon, mornian*, OHG. *mornēn* be anxious, ON. *morna* pine away, Goth. *maurnan* be anxious; prob. to be referred to IE. **(s)mer-*, repr. by Skr. *smárati* remember, Gr. *mérimna* care, sorrow, L. *memor* mindful. Hence **mournful** XVI.

mouse pl. *mice* OE. *mūs*, pl. *mȳs* = OS., OHG. *mūs* (Du. *muis*, G. *maus*), ON. *mús*; Gmc. and IE. **mūs-* is repr. also by L. *mūs*, Gr. *mûs*, OSl. *myšĭ*, Skr. *mūṣ-*; f. a base identical with one meaning 'steal, rob'. Hence vb. XIII. **mouser** OE. *mūsere* mouse-hawk.

mousse XIX. - F., 'moss'.

moustache XVI. - F. - It. *mostaccio* MUSTACHIO.

mouth sb. OE. *mūð* = OS. *mūth, mund* (Du. *mond*), (O)HG. *mund*, ON. *munnr, muðr*, Goth. *munþs* :- Gmc. **munþaz* :- IE. **mn̥tos*, corr. to L. *mentum* chin. Hence vb. XIII.

move vb. XIII. - AN. *mover* - OF. *moveir* (mod. *mouvoir*) :- L. *movēre*, pt. *mōvī*, pp. *mōtus*, f. IE. base **mou-* **meu-* **mu-*. Hence sb. XVII. So **mov(e)able** XIV. - OF. *movable*. **movement** XIV. - (O)F. *mouvement* - medL. *movimentum*.

mow[1] stack of hay, corn, etc. OE. *mūga, mūha, mūwa*, corr. to ON. *múgi* swath, crowd; of unkn. orig.

mow[2] cut down (grass, etc.) with scythe or machine. OE. str. vb. *māwan*; WGmc. vb., in other langs. wk., repr. by MDu. *maeien* (Du. *maaien*), OHG. *māen* (G. *mähen*); cf. MEADOW.

mow[3] (arch., dial.) grimace. XIV (sb.). prob. - OF. *moe*, (also mod.) *moue* †mouth, †lip, pouting; otherwise - MDu. *mouwe*, which may be the source of the OF. word. Hence vb. XV.

Mozarabic epithet of the ancient ritual of the church in Spain, prob. so called from being used by the Mozarabs after being disused by others. XVIII. f. Sp. *Mozarabe* - Arab. *musta'rib* one who adopts Arab customs, f. base of *'arab* ARAB; see -IC.

Mr as a title orig. abbrev. of *Master* XV; †in 16th and 17th cent. used gen. for MASTER, as in *Mr of Arts, Mr Gunner*; its present oral equiv. is MISTER[2].

Mrs abbrev. of MISTRESS. XVII. Cf. MISSIS.

much †great (surviving in place-names, as *M. Wenlock*); great amount of XIII; adv. greatly; sb. great deal XIV. ME. *muche, moche*, shortening of *muchel, mochel*, repr. late OE. *myćel*, var. of *mićel* = OS. *mikil*, OHG. *michil*, ON. *mikill*, Goth. *mikils*; Gmc. deriv. of IE. **meg-*, repr. by L. *magnus*, Gr. *mégas*, Skr. *mahā-* great. Hence **muchly** XVII (in XIX a new joc. formation). **muchness** XIV (*m. of a muchness* XVIII).

mucilage viscous fluid XIV; gummy secretion XVII; (U.S.) adhesive gum XIX. - (O)F. - late L. *mūcilāgō, -āgin-* musty juice, f. *mūcus* MUCUS. Hence **mucilaginous** XVII.

muck dung XIII; dirt, filth XIV. prob. of Scand. orig. and - forms rel. to ON. *myki, mykr* dung, Da. *møg*, Norw. *myk*, f. Gmc. **muk-* **meuk-* soft (rel. to MEEK).

mucus viscid or slimy substance. XVII. - L. *mūcus*, also *muccus* mucus of the nose, rel. to synon. Gr. *múxa, mússesthai* blow the nose, *muktḗr* nose, nostril. So **mucous** XVII. - L. *mūcōsus*.

mud XIV. prob. - MLG. *mudde*, MHG. *mot* (G. dial. *mott*) bog, bog-earth, peat. Hence **muddy** XVI. **mudlark** grubber or worker in dirty places. XVIII. joc. formation after *skylark*.

muddle †wallow in mud; make muddy, (hence) confuse. XVII. perh. - MDu. *moddelen*, frequent. of *modden*, see MUD, -LE[3].

muezzin Muslim crier who proclaims the hours of prayer. XVI. - Pers. and Turk. pronunc. of Arab. *mu'aḏḏin*, active ppl. of *aḏḏana*, frequent. of *'aḏana* proclaim, f. *'uḏn* ear.

muff[1] cylindrical covering for the hands. XVI. - Du. *mof*, shortening of MDu. *moffel, muffel* (corr. to F. *moufle*) - medL. *muff(u)la*, of unkn. orig.

muff[2] awkward person at sport, (gen.) duffer. XIX. of unkn. orig. Hence vb. make a muddle of. XIX.

muffin (dial.) wheat or oat cake; flat spongy cake eaten toasted and buttered. XVIII. of unkn. orig. Hence **muffineer** (-EER[1]) XIX.

muffle[1] wrap up, as in a cloth XV; †blindfold, stifle XVI; deaden the sound of XVIII. perh. aphetic of OF. **amoufler, enmoufler*, f. EN-[1] + *moufle* thick glove (cf. MUFF[1]). Hence **muffler** scarf. XVI.

muffle[2] thick part of upper lip and nose (of beasts). XVII. - F. *mufle*, of unkn. orig.

mufti Muslim priest or expounder of the law. XVI. - Arab. *muftī*, active pple. of *'aftā* give a *fatwā* or decision on law. The sense 'plain clothes' (XIX) may be a joc. allusion to the costume of a mufti on the stage.

mug[1] (dial.) pot, jug XVI; cylindrical drinking-vessel XVII. prob. of Scand. orig. (cf. Norw. *mugge*, Sw. *mugg* pitcher with handle).

mug[2] (sl.) face. XVIII. prob. transf. use of prec., drinking-mugs being freq. made to represent a grotesque face.

mug[3] (sl.) simpleton, duffer. XIX. perh. transf. use of MUG[1] with ref. to stupid looks. Hence synon. **muggins**, prob. by assoc. with the surname *Muggins*.

muggy (dial.) moist, damp; (of weather) damp and close. XVIII. f. dial. *mug* sb. mist, drizzle, dull weather (XVIII) or *mug* vb. drizzle (XIV) + -Y[1]; ult. of Scand. orig. (cf. ON. *mugga* mist, drizzle, Norw., Sw. dial. *mugg* mould, mildew).

mugwort plant *Artemisia vulgaris*. OE. *mucgwyrt*, f. base of MIDGE + WORT¹.

mugwump (U.S.) great man, boss; one who holds aloof from party politics. XIX. of Algonquian orig.

Muhammad(an) see MAHOMET.

mulatto offspring of a European and a Negro. XVI (*mulatow*). - Sp., Pg. *mulato* young mule, (hence) one of mixed race, obscurely f. *mulo* = F. *mule* MULE.

mulberry XIV. OE. *mōrberie*, **mūrberie* (cf. *mūrbēam* mulberry tree), ME. *murberie* (XIII), corr. to Du. *moerbezie*, OHG. *mōr-*, *mūrberi* (MHG. *mūlber*, G. *maulbeere*); f. **mōr* - L. *mōrum* mulberry, *mōrus* mulberry-tree + BERRY.

mulch half-rotten straw. XVII. sb. use of *mulsh* adj. (XV) soft, (dial.) of 'soft' weather, rel. to (dial.) *melsh* mellow, soft, mild (XIV) :- OE. *mel(i)sċ*, *mil(i)sċ*, *mylsċ*, f. **mel-* **mul-* (whence also MHG. *molwic*, G. *mollig*, etc. soft, OHG. *molawēn* be soft, cogn. with L. *mollis* tender); see -ISH¹.

mulct inflict a fine on. XV (*multe*). - F. †*multer*, *mulcter* - L. *mul(c)tāre*, f. *mul(c)ta* sb. fine (whence **mulct** sb. XVI).

mule offspring of he-ass and mare XIII; transf. of various hybrids, e.g. a kind of spinning machine XVIII. - OF. *mul* m., (also mod.) *mule* fem. :- L. *mūlus* m., *mūla* fem. So **muleteer** mule-driver. XVI. - F. *muletier*, f. *mulet*, dim. f. OF. *mul*; see -ET, -EER¹.

mull¹ promontory. XIV. cf. Gael. *maol*, Icel. *múli* (perh. identical with *múli* snout).

mull² make (wine, beer, etc.) into a hot drink with sugar, spices, etc. XVII (*mulled sack*). of unkn. orig.

mull³ (sl.) muddle, mess. XIX. perh. f. (dial.) *mull* pulverize, crumble (XV), f. *mull* dust, ashes (XIV) - (M)Du. *mul*, *mol* (see MULLOCK).

mullah Muslim theologian. XVII. - Pers., Turk., Urdu *mullā* - Arab. *maulā*.

mullein plant of the genus *Verbascum*. XV. - OF. *moleine* (mod. *molène*), of uncert. orig.

mullet XV (*molet*). - OF. *mulet*, dim. f. L. *mullus* red mullet - Gr. *múllos*, rel. to *mélās* black.

mulligatawny Indian highly-seasoned soup. XVIII. - Tamil *miḷagu-taṇṇīr* 'pepper-water'.

mulligrubs state or fit of depression; (later) colic. XVI (*mulliegrums*). fanciful formation.

mullion (archit.) vertical bar dividing the lights of a window. XVI. metathetic alt. of ME. *munial*, MONIAL, as the contemp. **munnion** is an assim. form (*n* . . *l* to *n* . . *n*).

mullock (dial.) rubbish, refuse XIV; (Austral.) rock not containing gold XIX. f. dial. *mull* (XIV) dust, ashes, rubbish, rel. to OE. *myl* dust, cogn. with (M)Du. *mul*, *mol*, ON. *moli* crumb, *mylja* crush, f. Gmc. **mul-*; see MEAL¹, -OCK.

multi- comb. form of L. *multus* much, many; the earliest comps. in Eng. are **multiformity**, **multiloquy** (XVI) talkativeness, **multifarious** (XVII) many and various (L. *-fāriam* adv.), and the el. becomes prolific later, esp. in techn. use, e.g. **multilateral, multinomial** (after BINOMIAL) XVII; an ex. of the gen. use is **multimillionaire** (XIX).

multiple consisting of many elements XVII. - F. - late L. *multiplus*, f. *multus* (see prec.); cf. *duplus* DUPLE. So **multiplex** XVI. - L. (cf. -FOLD). **multiplicity** XVI. - late L. **multiply** XIII. - (O)F. *multiplier* - L. *multiplicāre*. **multiplication** XIV. - (O)F. or L. **multitude** XIV. - (O)F. - L.; hence **multitudinous** XVII.

multure toll of grain carried or flour made. XIII. - OF. *mo(u)lture* (mod. *mouture*) :- medL. *molitūra*, f. *molit-*, pp. stem of *molere* grind; see MILL, -URE.

mum¹ †inarticulate sound made with closed lips; command to be silent or secret. XIV. imit.; cf. MLG. *mummen*, Du. *mommen*.

mum² (hist.) beer orig. brewed in Brunswick, Germany. XVII. - G. *mumme*; of uncert. orig.

mum³ see MUMMY².

mumble eat as with toothless gums; speak indistinctly. XIV. ME. *momele*, frequent. formation on MUM¹; see -LE³; cf. LG. *mummelen*, Du. *mommelen*, *mummelen*, G. *mummeln*, Sw. *mumla*, Da. *mumle*, and ME. *mamele* mutter, chatter (corr. formally to OHG. *mammalōn* stammer).

mumbo-jumbo grotesque idol said to have been worshipped by African negroes; (transf.) object of unintelligent veneration. XVIII. of unkn. orig.

mumchance †dicing game; †masquerade XVI; (dial.) one who acts in dumb show, dummy XVII; adj. silent XVII. - MLG. *mummensc(h)anze* game of dice, masked serenade (= MDu. *mommecanse*), f. *mummen* (see MUMMER) + *schanz* - (O)F. *chance* CHANCE.

mummer †mutterer XV; actor (†in dumb show) in a Christmas play XVI. - OF. *momeur*, f. *momer* act in dumb show, rel. to *momon* mask, Sp. *momo* grimace; perh. of Gmc. orig. (cf. MDu. *momme*, Du. *mom* mask, MLG. *mummen* mask, disguise); see -ER². So **mummery** mummer's performance; play-acting. XVI. - OF. *mommerie* (mod. *momerie*). Hence **mumming** XV.

mummy¹ †medicinal preparation of the substance of mummies, unctuous liquid XIV; †sovereign remedy, etc. XVI; body embalmed for burial XVII. - (O)F. *momie*, †*mumie* - medL. *mumia* - Arab. *mūmiya* embalmed body, f. *mūm* wax (used in embalming). Hence **mummify** XVII.

mummy² nursery var. of MAMMY (S.V. MAM). XIX. Also **mum.**

mump †grimace (sb.); (pl.) swelling of the parotid and salivary glands in the neck (with ref. to the appearance produced). XVI. So **mump** vb. mumble, grimace, munch, sulk. XVI. symbolic repr. of the movement of the lips in mumbling or chewing. Cf. Du. *momp(el)en* mumble in speech, G. *mumpf(el)en* mumble in eating.

munch XIV. imit.; cf. *crunch*, *scrunch*.

mundane worldly, earthly XV; cosmic XVII. orig. *mondaine* - (O)F. *mondain* - late L. *mundānus*, f. *mundus* world, (earlier) universe of celestial bodies, spec. use of *mundus* personal adornment, after Gr. *kósmos* (see COSMOS). Later assim. to L. (see -ANE¹).

municipal †pert. to the internal affairs of a state; pert. to local self-government, esp. of a town. XVI. - L. *mūnicipālis*, f. *mūnicipium*

Roman city of which the inhabitants had Roman citizenship, f. *mūniceps*, *-cip-*, f. *mūnia* civic offices + *capere* take. So **municipality** XVIII. - F.

munificent XVI. f. L. *mūnificent-*, used as stem of *mūnificus*, f. *mūnus* office, duty (cf. prec.), gift. So **munificence** XVI.

muniment document preserved as evidence of rights or privileges. XV. - (O)F. - L. *mūnīmentum* (in medL.) title-deed, f. *munīre* fortify, secure, earlier *mœnīre*, f. *mœnia* walls, ramparts, rel. to *mūrus* wall; see -MENT.

munition †fortification; ammunition. XVI. - (O)F. - L. *mūnītiō*, *-ōn-*, f. *mūnīre*, *mūnīt-*; see prec. and -ITION.

munnion see MULLION.

mural adj. XVI. - (O)F. - L. *mūrālis*, f. *mūrus* wall; see -AL[1]. So sb. †wall XV, wall-painting XX.

murder sb. OE. *morðor* = Goth. *maurþr* :- Gmc. **murþram*, f. IE. **mṛt-* (see MORTAL), repr. also by Gmc. **mortam* (whence OE., OS., ON. *morð*, (O)HG. *mord*, Du. *moord*); reinforced in ME. by OF. *murdre* (mod. *meurtre*) - Gmc., whence the establishment of the forms with *u* and *d*. So **murder** vb. XIII. prob. f. the sb. **murderer** XIII. partly f. the vb., partly - AN. *murdreour*.

murex shell-fish yielding a purple dye. XVI. - L. *mūrex*.

muriatic †pert. to brine; 'marine' (acid), hydrochloric. XVII. - L. *muriāticus*, f. *muria* brine (the acid being obtained by heating salt with sulphuric acid); see -ATIC.

murk, mirk sb. darkness; adj. dark. XIII. The ME. evidence points to Scand. orig. (ON. *myrkr* sb. and adj. = OS. *mirki* adj.) rather than to OE. *mirce*. Hence **murky** XIV.

murmur subdued continuous sound; inarticulate complaining XIV; softly spoken word(s) XVII. - (O)F. *murmure* or L. *murmur* rumbling noise, murmur, rel. to vb. *murmurāre* (whence (O)F. *murmurer*, Eng. vb. XIV), corr. to Gr. *mormúrein* and with variation OHG. *murmurōn*, *-ulōn* (G. *murmeln*), Du. *murmelen* burble; redupl. f. imit. base.

murrain †plague XIV; infectious disease of cattle XV. - AN. *moryn*, (O)F. *morine*, †*moraine*, f. stem of *mourir*, †*morir* :- Rom. **morīre*, for L. *morī* die (see MORTAL).

murrey (arch.) purple-red. - OF. *moré* adj. and sb., *morée* sb. - medL. *morātum*, *-āta*, f. L. *mōrum* MULBERRY; see -Y[5].

murrhine (Rom. antiq.) pert. to **murra** fine earth of which precious vases, etc., were made. XVI. - L. *murr(h)inus*, f. *murra*; see -INE[1].

muscat strong sweet wine (XVI) from the grape so called (XVII). - (O)F. - Pr. *muscat*, f. *musc* MUSK; see -ATE[1]. So **muscatel, -del** in the same senses (XIV and XVI; - OF.); and **muscadine** (XVI and XVII; of doubtful orig.).

muscle contractile fibrous bundle producing movement in an animal body. XVI. - (O)F. - L. *mūsculus*, dim. of *mūs* MOUSE, the form and movements of some muscles suggesting those of a mouse. Hence **muscular** XVII. **musculo-**, comb. form of L. *mūsculus*.

muscology study of mosses. XIX. - modL. *muscologia*, f. L. *muscus* MOSS; see -LOGY.

muscovado unrefined sugar. XVII. - Sp. *mascabado*.

Muscovy (arch.) Russia. XVI. - F. *Muscovie*, †*Moscovie* - modL. *Moscovia* (see -IA[1]), f. Russ. *Moskvá* Moscow. So **Muscovite** Russian. XVI.

muse[1] be absorbed in thought. XIV. - (O)F. *muser* †meditate, waste time, trifle :- Rom. **musāre*, presumably rel. to medL. *mūsum* (see MUZZLE), but the sense-development is not obvious.

Muse, muse[2] goddess inspiring learning and the arts; a poet's inspiring goddess. XIV. - (O)F. *muse* or L. *mūsa* - Gr. *moûsa*.

museum †building devoted to learning and the arts (regarded as 'a home of the Muses'); building for exhibition of objects of art or science (first applied to 'Mr. Ashmole's Museum at Oxford'). XVII. - L. *mūsēum* library, study - Gr. *mouseîon* seat of the Muses, sb. use of n. of *mouseîos*, f. *moûsa* MUSE[2].

mush (N.Amer.) porridge made with meal XVII; (f. the vb.) pulpy mess or substance XIX. prob. symbolic alt. of MASH. So vb. XVIII. Hence **mushy** XIX.

mushroom XV. Late ME. *musseroun*, *musheron*, by assim. *musherom* (XVI) - (O)F. *mousseron* - late L. *mussiriō*, *-ōn-*. Hence vb. XVIII (once, trans.), XIX (intr.).

music art of combining sounds in a certain order for aesthetic effect XIII; sounds in melodic or harmonic combination XIV; company of musicians, band XVI; musical score XVII. - (O)F. *musique* - L. *mūsica* - Gr. *mousikḗ*, sb. use of fem. of *mousikós* pert. to a Muse or the Muses, concerning the arts, f. *moûsa* MUSE[2]. So **musical** XV. - (O)F. - medL. **musician** XIV (*-ien*). - (O)F., f. *musique*.

musk odoriferous substance secreted by the musk-deer. XIV. - late L. *muscus* - Pers. *mušk*, perh. - Skr. *muṣká-* scrotum (the shape of the musk-deer's musk-bag being similar).

musket XVI. - F. *mousquet*, †*-ette* - It. *moschetto*, *-etta* (formerly) bolt from a crossbow, f. *mosca* fly :- L. *musca*, rel. to Gr. *muîa* (cf. MIDGE). Hence **musketeer** XVI; after F. *mousquetaire*. So **musketry** XVII. - F. *mousqueterie*.

Muslim, Moslem Muhammadan. XVII. - Arab. *muslim*, act. ppl. of *'aslama* (see ISLAM).

muslin XVII. - F. *mousseline* - It. *mussolina*, *-ino*, f. *Mussolo* Mosul (Arab. *(al-)Mauṣil*), where muslin was formerly made; cf. -INE[1].

musquash large aquatic rodent, musk-rat. XVII (*mussascus*, *musquassus*). of Algonquian orig.

mussel bivalve mollusc. OE. *mus(c)le*, *muxle* (- L.), and - MLG. *mussel*, MDu. *mosscele* (Du. *mossel*) - Rom. **muscula*, alt. f. L. *musculus*, dim. (see -CLE) of L. *mūs* MOUSE.

Mussulman Muslim. XVI. - Pers. *musalmān*, f. *muslim* MUSLIM.

must[1] unfermented juice of the grape. OE. *must* = (O)HG. *most* - L. *mustum*, sb. use of n. of *mustus* new, new-born.

must[2] is obliged or required to. XIII. OE. *mōste*, pt. of *mōt* am permitted or obliged, may, must = OS. *mōt*, *muot* (Du. *moet*), OHG. *muoz* find room or opportunity, may, must (G. *muss*), Goth. *gamōt* (it) has room, rel. to MLG. *mōte*,

OHG. *muoza* (G. *musse*) leisure :- Gmc. **mōtōn*; of unkn. orig.

must[2] mustiness, mould. XVII. back-formation from MUSTY.

mustachio XVI (*mustaccio*, *-achio*, *mastacho*). - Sp. *mostacho* and its source It. *mostaccio*, based ult. on Gr. *mústax*, *mustak-* upper lip, moustache.

mustang wild horse of the American plains. XIX. app. blending of Sp. *mestengo* (now *mesteño*) and *mostrenco*, both applied to wild or masterless cattle, the former being f. *mesta* (:- L. *mixta*, sb. use of fem. pp. of *miscēre* MIX) association of graziers, who appropriated wild cattle.

mustard seeds of black and white mustard (plant of the genus *Brassica*) powdered and used as a condiment, etc. XIII. - OF. *mo(u)starde* (mod. *moutarde*), f. Rom. **mosto*, L. *mustum* MUST[1]; prop. applied to the condiment as orig. prepared by making the ground seeds into a paste with must.

muster A. †exhibition, display; †pattern, example, sample; B. assembling of soldiers, etc.; assembly, collection. XIV. ME. *mo(u)stre* - OF. *moustre* (later in latinized form *monstre*, mod. *montre*), repr. Rom. sb. f. **mostrare* :- L. *mōnstrāre* show (cf. MONSTER). So **muster** vb. †show, display XIII; collect, assemble XV. - OF. *moustrer* (mod. *montrer*).

musty XVI. perh. alt. of MOISTY by assoc. with MUST[1].

mutable XIV. - L. *mūtābilis*; see -ABLE. So **mutation** XIV. - L. *mūtātiō*, *-ōn-*, f. *mūtāre*, *mūtāt-* change, f. IE. **moit-*, extension of the base **moi-* **mei-*, repr. also in MEAN[2], etc. Hence, by back-formation, **mutate** (-ATE[3]) XIX.

mutch (dial., esp. Sc.) cap, coif. XV. - MDu. *mutse* (Du. *muts*), corr. to (M)HG. *mütze*, shortened by-forms of MDu. *a(l)mutse*, MHG. *armuz*, *almuz*) - medL. *almucia*; of uncert. orig.

mute silent, dumb. XIV. Early forms also *mewet*, *muwet*; - (O)F. *muet*, dim. formation on OF. *mu* :- L. *mūtus*, f. symbolic syll. **mu* as in Gr. *múndos*, *mukós*, Skr. *mū́ka-* dumb, Arm. *munj*, and MUTTER. The form became permanently assim. to L. XVI. Hence vb. XIX.

mutilate deprive of a limb or principal part. XVI. f. pp. stem of L. *mutilāre* cut or lop off, f. *mutilus* maimed; see -ATE[3]. So **mutilation** XVII. - late L.

mutiny open revolt against authority. XVI. f. (after words in -Y[3]) †*mutine* - (O)F. *mutin* rebellious, mutinous, sb. rebel, mutineer, in XVI rebellion, mutiny, f. *muete* (mod. *meute*) :- Rom. **movita* movement, f. **movit-*, for L. *mōt-* (see MOTION). So **mutineer** XVII. Hence **mutiny** vb. XVI, **mutinous** XVI.

mutter speak almost inaudibly with nearly closed lips. XIV. frequent. formation (see -ER[4]) on a base **mu-*, repr. also in MUTE; cf. G. dial. *muttern*, ON. *muskra* murmur, L. *muss(it)āre*, *muttīre*, Gr. *múzein*.

mutton XIII. ME. *moto(u)n* - OF. *moton* (mod. *mouton*) :- medL. *multō*, *-ōn-*, prob. of Gaul. orig. (cf. (O)Ir. *molt* ram, Gael. *mult* wether, W. *mollt* sheep).

mutual felt or done by each to the other XV; respective; pert. to both, common XVI. - (O)F. *mutuel*, f. L. *mūtuus* borrowed, mutual :- **moitwos*, f. IE. **moi-* change, as in *mūtāre*; see MUTABLE, -AL[1].

mutule (archit.) projection of stone or wood, modillion. XVI. - F. *mutule* - L. *mutulus*, prob. of Etruscan orig.

muzhik see MOUJIK.

muzzle A. beast's nose and mouth XV; open end of a gun XVI; B. contrivance confining an animal's mouth XIV. ME. *mosel* - OF. *musel* (mod. *museau*) :- Gallo-Rom. **mūsellum*, dim. of medL. *mūsum*, of unkn. orig. Hence vb. XV.

muzzy †(of places, etc.) dull, gloomy; stupid, fuddled. XVIII. In early use also *mussy*; words similar in form and meaning are †*mossy* (XVI-XVII); dial. *mosey*, *mosy* (XV); *muzz*, *muzzle* vbs. (XVIII); but their relations and orig. are obscure.

my poss. pron. XII. ME. *mī*, reduced form of *mīn* MINE[1], orig. before a cons., as *my son* but *mine eyes*; cf. THY.

mylodon extinct gigantic sloth. XIX. f. Gr. *múlē*, *múlos* molar, prop. MILL, millstone + *odṓn* TOOTH.

myna(h) see MINA.

mynheer Du. equiv. of 'sir', 'Mr'; Dutchman. XVII. - Du. *mijnheer*, f. *mijn* MINE[1] + *heer* lord, master, repr. compar. of Gmc. **χairaz* HOAR (lit.) grey-haired, (hence) honourable, august.

myo- comb. form of Gr. *mûs* MUSCLE, as in **myology** science of muscles (XVII).

myopia short-sightedness. XVIII. - modL. - late Gr. *mūōpiā*, f. *múōps*, f. *múein* shut + *ṓps* EYE. Hence **myopic** XVIII.

myosotis plant of the genus so named. XIX. - L. - Gr. *muosōtis*, f. *muós*, g. of *mûs* MOUSE + *oûs*, *ōt-* EAR[1]; so called from the soft hairy leaves.

myriad ten thousand; countless number. XVI. - late L. *mȳrias*, *mȳriad-* - Gr. *mūriás*, *mūriad-*, f. *mūríos* countless, innumerable, pl. *mūrioi* ten thousand; see -AD.

myrmidon one of a warlike race of Thessaly XIV; †soldier of a bodyguard, faithful follower; unscrupulously faithful attendant XVII. - L. pl. *Myrmidones* - Gr. *Murmidónes*, acc. to legend created orig. from ants (*múrmēkes*).

myrobalan plum-like fruit used now in tanning, etc. XVI. - F. *myrobolan* or its source L. *myrobalanum* - Gr. *murobálanos*, f. *múron* balsam, unguent + *bálanos* acorn, date, ben-nut.

myrrh gum resin from trees of genus *Commiphora*. OE. *myrra*, *myrre*, corr. to OS. *myrra* (Du. *mirre*), OHG. *myrra* (G. *myrrhe*), ON. *mirra*; Gmc. - L. *myrrha* - Gr. *múrrā*, of Sem. orig. (cf. Arab. *murr*, Aram. *mūrā*); reinforced in ME. from OF. *mirre* (mod. *myrrhe*).

myrtle †myrtle-berry XIV; plant of the genus *Myrtus* XVI. - medL. *myrtilla*, *-us*, dim. of L. *myrta*, *-us* - Gr. *múrtos*.

myself OE. *mē self* (accus. *selfne*); see ME[1] and SELF; altered to *mi self* (XIII) partly by loss of stress, partly on the analogy of HERSELF, in which *her* was apprehended as genitive.

mystagogue one who introduces to religious mysteries. XVI. - F. *mystagogue* or L. *mysta-*

gōgus - Gr. *mustagōgós*, f. *mústēs* initiated person + *ágōgos* leading, *ágein* lead (see ACT).

mystery¹ †phr. *in (a) m.*, mystically XIV; religious truth or doctrine; hidden or secret thing XIV; religious rite XVI; (after F. *mystère*) miracle play XVIII. - AN. **misterie* (OF. *mistere*, mod. *mystère*) or its source L. *mystērium* - Gr. *mustḗrion* secret thing or ceremony, f. **mus-* as in *mustikós* MYSTIC. So **mysterious** XVII. - F.

mystery² occupation, handicraft, art XIV; trade guild or company XV. - medL. *misterium*, contr. of L. *ministerium* MINISTRY, by assoc. with *mystērium* (see prec.).

mystic spiritually symbolical XIV; occult, enigmatical; pert. to direct communion with God XVII; sb. exponent of mystic theology; one who practises mystical communion XVII. - (O)F. *mystique* or L. *mysticus* - Gr. *mustikós*, f. *mústēs* initiated one, f. *mûein* close (of eyes, lips), *muein* initiate. Hence **mystical** secret, occult, symbolical XV; pert. to mystics or mysticism XVII. **mysticism** XVIII. So **mystique** XX. - F., sb. use of adj.

mystify XIX. - F. *mystifier*, irreg. f. *mystère* MYSTERY¹ or *mystique* MYSTIC; see -FY. So **mystification** XIX.

myth XIX. Formerly also *mythe* (cf. F. *mythe*); - modL. *mȳthus*, used in Eng. context (XIX), beside *mythos* (from XVIII) - late L. *mythos*, f. Gr. *mûthos*. So **mythic(al)** XVII. - late L. *mȳthicus* - Gr. *mūthikós*. **mythology** †exposition of myths or fables XV; †symbolical story, mythical meaning XVII; body of myths XVIII. - F. *mythologie* or late L. *mȳthologia* - Gr. *mūthologiā*.

N

nab (colloq.) catch, seize. XVII. of unkn. orig.; parallel to synon. and contemp. *nap*, which survives in KIDNAPPER.

nabob Muslim official acting as deputy governor in the Mogul empire XVII; rich person, spec. one who has returned from India XVIII. - Pg. *nababo* - Urdu *nawāb* (whence **nawab** XVIII), prob. - Arab. *nawwāb*, intensive form of *nā'ib* deputy (confused with *nuwwāb*, Arab. pl.).

nabs (colloq.) *his nabs* himself, †*my nabs* myself. XVIII. of unkn. orig.; cf. synon. NIBS.

nacre shell-fish yielding mother-of-pearl XVI; mother-of-pearl XVIII. - (O)F.; see NAKER. Hence **nacr(e)ous** XIX.

nadir (astron.) †point in the heavens diametrically opposite to another XIV; point opposite to the zenith XV; lowest point XVIII. - (O)F. - Arab. *naẓīr* opposite. In the second sense for *naẓīr as-samt* opposite to the ZENITH.

naevus mole on the skin. XIX. - L. ; of uncert. orig.

naffy canteen in charge of N.A.A.F.I. (*N*avy *A*rmy and *A*ir *F*orce *I*nstitutes). XX. f. the initials.

nag[1] small riding-horse. XIV. of unkn. orig.

nag[2] (dial.) gnaw; be persistently worrying or annoying. XIX. Also *gnag*, *knag*; repr. by *naggy* XVII (*knaggie*) adj.; perh. of Scand. or LG. orig. (cf. Norw., Sw. *nagga* gnaw, nibble, irritate, LG. (*g*)*naggen* (XV) irritate, provoke).

naiad water-nymph. XVII. - L. - Gr. *Nāïás*, *Nāïad-*, rel. to *náein* flow. The pl. *Naiades* (XIV) repr. F. *Naiades* or L. *Nāïadēs*.

naïf see NAÏVE.

nail hard terminal covering of finger and toe; small spike of metal OE.; the applications (XV) to measures of weight and length are of uncert. orig. OE. *næġ(e)l* = OS., OHG. *nagal* (Du., G. *nagel*), ON. *nagl* :- Gmc. **naȝlaz*, f. an IE. base **nogh-* repr. also by Lith. *nāgas* nail, claw, OSl. *nogŭtĭ* nail, *noga* foot, Gr. *ónux*, Skr. *nakhá-*, rel. further to L. *unguis*, OIr. *ingen*. Hence **nail** vb. OE. *næġlan*.

nainsook cotton fabric of Indian orig. XIX. - Urdu (Hindi) *nainsukh*, f. *nain* eye + *sukh* pleasure.

naïve, naive XVII. - (O)F. *naïve*, fem. of *naïf* (adopted earlier in Eng. XVI) :- L. *nātīvus* NATIVE. So **naïveté** XVII, anglicized **naivety** XVIII.

naked OE. *nacod* = MLG., MDu. *naket* (Du. *naakt*), OHG. *nackut* (G. *nackt*), ON. *nǫkkviðr*, Goth. *naqaþs* :- Gmc. **nakwaðaz*, *-*iðaz* :- IE. **nogʷodhos*, *-*edhos*, ppl. deriv. of **nogʷ-*, repr. also in L. *nūdus* NUDE, OIr. *nocht*, Skr. *nagná-*, OSl. *nagŭ* (Russ. *nagói*), Lith. *núogas*.

naker (arch.) kettledrum. XIV (not in use later till revived by Scott). - OF. *nacre*, *nacaire* - It. *nacchera* - Arab. *naḳḳāra* drum.

namby-pamby weakly sentimental, childishly simple. XVIII. joc. redupl. formation on the name of *Amb*rose Philips (d. 1749), author of pastorals, which were ridiculed by H. Carey and Pope.

name particular designation OE.; reputation XIII. OE. *nama*, *noma* = OS., OHG. *namo* (Du. *naam*, G. *name*), ON. *nafn*, *namn*, Goth. *namo* :- Gmc. **naman-*, f. an IE. base **onðmen-*, **enðmen-* repr. by L. *nōmen*, Gr. *ónoma*, dial. *ónuma*, *ōnum-*, OSl. *imę* (Russ. *ímya*), OIr. *aińm*, OW. *anu*, W. *enw*, Skr. *nāman-*. So **name** vb. OE. (*ġe*)*namian*; repl. ME. *nemne*, OE. *nemnan* :- **namnjan*. **namely** †especially XII; that is to say XV. ME. *name-*, *nomeliche*, corr. to MDu. *namelīke* (Du. *namelijk*), MHG. *nam(e)-*, *nem(e)līche* (G. *nämlich* especially), ON. *nafnliga* by name. **namesake** XVII. prob. orig. said of persons or things coupled together 'for the *name*('*s*) *sake*'.

nankeen cotton cloth orig. made at *Nankin*(*g*) in China. XVIII.

nanny children's nurse. XVIII. appellative use of pet-form of the female name *Ann*(*e*); see -Y[6].

nap[1] take a short sleep. OE. *hnappian*, rel. to OHG. (*h*)*naffezan* slumber (MHG. *nafzen*), of unkn. orig. Hence sb. XIII.

nap[2] surface of cloth raised and cut smooth. XV (*noppe*). - MLG., MDu. *noppe*, rel. to *noppen* trim by shearing the nap.

nap[3] †napoleon (20-franc piece); card-game in which the player who calls five is said to *go nap*, formerly *go the Napoleon*. XIX. Short for *Napoleon*, Christian name of certain French emperors, esp. Napoleon I (1769-1821), after whom the coin was named.

napalm jellied petrol. XX. f. initial sylls. of NAPHTHA and PALMITIC.

nape (hollow at) the back of the neck. XIII. ME. *naupe*, of unkn. orig.

napery household linen. XIV. - OF. *naperie*, f. *nape* (mod. *nappe*) linen; see NAPKIN, -ERY.

naphtha inflammable oil from coal. XVI. - L. - Gr. *náphtha*, also *náphthas*, of Oriental orig.

Napier's bones slips of bone, etc. used to facilitate multiplication and division according to a method devised by John *Napier* of Merchiston (1550-1617). XVII. So **Napierian** applied to the logarithms invented by him. XIX.

napkin XV. f. (O)F. *nappe* linen cloth :- L. *mappa* MAP + -KIN.

Napoleon see NAP[3].

narcissism morbid self-love. XX. f. *Narcissus*, in Gr. myth. name of a beautiful youth who fell in love with his own reflection and pined away; see -ISM.

narcissus XVI. - L. - Gr. *nárkissos*, the termination of which suggests a Mediterranean orig.

narcotic substance inducing stupor XIV; adj. XVII. - (O)F. *narcotique* or medL. *narcōticus*, sb.

-icum - Gr. *narkōtikós*, sb. *-ikón*, f. *narkoûn* benumb, stupefy, f. *nárkē* numbness, stupor; see -OTIC.

nard aromatic unguent XIV, derived from the plant so named (cf. SPIKENARD) XVI. - L. *nardus* - Gr. *nárdos*, of Sem. orig.

narghile hookah. XIX. - (partly through F. *narghileh*, *narguilé*) Pers. (Turk.) *nārgīleh*, f. Pers. *nārgīl* coconut, of which the receptacle for the tobacco was made.

nark (sl.) police spy or informer. XIX. - Romany *nāk* nose.

narrate XVII. f. pp. stem of L. *narrāre* (f. *gnārus* knowing), or back-formation from **narration** (XV, - (O)F. or L.). So **narrative** sb. XVI; adj. XVII. - F. *narratif*, *-ive* adj. and †sb. - late L. *narrātīvus*.

narrow having little breadth OE.; (dial.) parsimonious, 'close', strict, close XIII; lacking in breadth of view or sympathy XVII. OE. *nearu* (stem *nearw-*) = OS. *naru* (MDu. *nare*, *naer*, Du. *naar*) :- Gmc. **narwaz* (repr. in MHG. *narwe*, G. *narbe*, MLG. *nar(w)e* scar, sb. use of the adj.), of which no certain cogns. are known. So **narrow** vb. OE. *nearwian* confine, †oppress, become narrow; but in ME. (XIII) a new formation on the adj.

narthex (archit.) vestibule extending across the west end of a church. XVII. - L. *narthēx* - Gr. *nárthēx* giant fennel, stick, casket, narthex.

narwhal XVII. - Du. *narwal* - Da. *narhval*; the second el. is WHALE. The relation to synon. ON. *náhvalr* is obscure; the latter appears to be f. *nár* corpse, and the allusion is supposed to be to the colour of the animal's skin.

nary see NEVER.

nasal adj. XVII. - F. *nasal* or medL. *nāsālis*, f. *nāsus* NOSE; see -AL[1]. Also sb. nose-piece of a helmet XIV (*nasel*). - OF. *nasal*, *-el* medL. *nāsāle*, sb. use of n. of adj.

nascent being born or produced. XVII. - L. *nāscēns*, *-ent-*, prp. of *nāscī* be born; see NATAL, -ENT.

naso- used as comb. form of L. *nāsus* NOSE (for the regular *nasi-*). XIX.

nasturtium genus of cruciferous plants (watercress, etc.) having a pungent taste XVII; trailing plant of the genus *Tropaeolum* XVIII. - L.; of uncert. orig.

nasty filthy, dirty XIV; nauseous XVI; (of weather) foul, dirty XVII; offensive XVIII; ill-natured XIX. Early vars. †*naxty*, †*naxte*, which with †*naskie* (XVII) suggest ult. derivation from an obscure base **nask-* (**nax-*), which appears also in Sw. dial. *naskug*, *nasket* dirty, nasty; see -Y[1].

natal pert. to birth or nativity. XIV. - L. *nātālis*, f. *nāt-*, pp. stem of *nāscī* be born, f. **gn-* produce; see KIN, -AL[1].

natation XVI. - L. *natātiō*, *-ōn-*, f. *natāre* swim, frequent. of *nāre*, f. IE. **sna-*, repr. also by Gr. *nḗkhein* swim, Skr. *snā́ti* bathe, Ir. *snám* swimming, W. *nawf*; see -ATION. So **natatorial** XIX, **natatory** XVIII. - late L. *natātōrius*.

nation XIII. - (O)F. *nation*, †*nacioun* - L. *nātiō*, *-ōn-* breed, stock, race, f. *nāt-*, pp. stem of *nāscī* be born; see NATAL, -TION. So **national** XVI, **nationality** XVII. **nationalize, nationalist** XVIII. **native** (hist.) born thrall XV; (astrol.) subject of a horoscope; one born in a particular place XVI; original or usual inhabitant XVII. - medL. *nātīvus*, sb. use of L. *nātīvus* adj. (whence adj. XIV, of one's birth XV), f. *nāt-*, pp. stem of *nāscī*; see -IVE. **nativity** (festival of) the birth of Jesus Christ, the Virgin Mary, or St. John Baptist XII; birth XIV. - (O)F. - late L.

natron native hydrated sodium carbonate. XVII. - F. - Sp. - Arab. *naṭrūn* - Gr. *nítron* NITRE.

natter vb. XIX. of imit. orig. Also sb. XX.

natterjack toad *Bufo calamita*. XVIII. perh. f. prec. (from its loud croak) + JACK[1] (applied dial. to newts and flies).

natty neatly smart XVIII; (dial.) deft, clever XIX. orig. dial. or sl.; rel. obscurely to NEAT[2]; see -Y[1].

nature essential qualities or innate character *of*; vital powers *of* XIII; inherent power dominating one's action; creative and regulative power in the world XIV; material world XVII. - (O)F. - L. *nātūra*, f. pp. stem of *nāscī* (see NATAL). So **natural** XIV. Earlier *naturel* - (O)F. *naturel*, †*natural* - L. *nātūrālis*. **naturalize** XVI. - F. *naturaliser*. **naturalism** system of morality having natural basis XVII; extreme form of realism XIX. - F.

naught nothing. OE. *nāwiht*, *nāwuht*, *nauht*, f. *nā* NO[3] + *wiht* WIGHT. Cf. NOUGHT. Used predicatively, passing into adj. OE.; superseded by deriv. **naughty** †poor, needy XIV; †bad, of inferior quality XIV; morally bad XVI; (of children) wayward, inclined to disobedience XVII.

nausea feeling of sickness XVI; strong disgust XVII. - L. *nausea*, *nausia* - Gr. *nausíā*, *nautíā*, seasickness, nausea, f. *naûs* ship (see NAVAL). So **nauseate** reject with nausea; affect with nausea. XVII. f. pp. stem of L. *nauseāre*. **nauseous** XVII.

nautch E. Indian exhibition of professional dancing. XIX. - Urdu (Hindi) *nāc* Prakrit *nacca-* - Skr. *nṛtya-* dancing, f. *nṛt* dance.

nautical XVI. f. L. *nauticus* - Gr. *nautikós*, f. *naútēs* sailor, f. *naûs* ship; see NAVAL, -ICAL.

nautilus cephalopod which has webbed dorsal arms formerly believed to be used as sails. XVII. - L. - Gr. *nautílos* sailor, nautilus, f. *naútēs* (see prec.).

naval XVI. - L. *nāvālis*, f. *nāvis* ship, rel. to Skr. *naú-*, Gr. *naûs*, Ir. *nau*, ON. *nór*; see -AL[1].

nave[1] central block of a wheel. OE. *nafu* and *nafa*, corr. to MDu. *nave* (Du. *naaf*), OHG. *naba* (G. *nabe*), ON. *nǫf* :- Gmc. **nabō*, rel. to Latv. *naba* navel, Skr. *nā́bhi-* nave, navel; cf. NAVEL.

nave[2] main body of a church. XVII. - medL. spec. use of L. *nāvis* ship (see NAVAL).

navel OE. *nafela* = (M)LG., (M)Du. *navel*, OHG. *nabalo* (G. *nabel*), ON. *nafli* :- Gmc. **nabalan-*, rel. to L. *umbō* boss of shield, *umbilīcus* navel, Gr. *omphalós* navel, boss of shield, Skr. *nā́bhi-*, OIr. *imbliu* navel; cf. NAVE[1].

navicular (anat.) of bones in the hand and the foot. XVI. - F. *naviculaire* or late L. *nāviculāris*, f. *nāvicula*, dim. of *nāvis* ship; see NAVAL, -AR.

navigable XVI. - F. *navigable* or L. *nāvigābilis*, f. *nāvigāre* (whence **navigate** XVI), f. *nāvis* ship (see NAVAL) + *-ig-*, comb. stem of *agere* drive (see

ACT). So **navigation** XVI. - (O)F. or L. **navigator** XVI. - L.

navvy XIX. colloq. abbrev. of NAVIGATOR used in this sense (XVIII), prop. one who constructs a 'navigation' or artificial waterway.

navy †ships, shipping; (arch.) fleet XIV; state's ships of war XVI. - OF. *navie* ship, fleet - popL. *nāvia* ship, boat, coll. formation on L. *nāvis* ship; see NAVAL, -Y[3].

nawab see NABOB.

nay adv. no XII; sb. denial, refusal XIV. - ON. *nei*, f. *né* neg. particle (see NO[3]) + *ei* AY.

Nazi (member) of German National Socialist party. XX. repr. pronunc. of *Nati-* in G. *Nationalsozialist*.

neap applied to tides at which high-water level is at its lowest. OE. *nēp* in *nēpflōd*, then not recorded till XV; of unkn. orig.

near adv. (dial.) almost, nearly XII; to, within, or at a little distance XIII. First in northerly and easterly texts in the form *ner* - ON. *nǽr*, compar. of *ná-* NIGH, corr. to OE. *nēar* (superseded in gen. use by the new formation **nearer** (XVI)), OS. *nāhor* (Du. *naar* to, for, after), OHG. *nāhor*, Goth. *nēhwis* :- Gmc. **nēχwiz*, **nēχwōz*. Hence prep. close to XIII; adj. closely placed or related XIV, niggardly XVII. **nearly** (-LY[2]) closely XVI; almost XVII; superseded *near* adv. in all exc. the purely physical uses.

neat[1] (arch., dial.) animal of the ox kind; cattle. OE. *nēat* = OS. *nōt* (Du. *noot*), OHG. *nōz*, ON. *naut* :- Gmc. **nautam*, f. **naut- *neut- *nut-* make use of, enjoy, whence also OE. *nēotan*, OHG. *niozan* (G. *geniessen*), ON. *njóta*, *neyta*, Goth. *niutan* use, enjoy.

neat[2] †clean, †clear; free from reductions; smart, dainty, tidy. XVI. - (O)F. *net* :- L. *nitidus* shining, clean, f. *nitēre* shine.

neb (dial.) beak, bill; nose; †face OE.; nib; peak, tip. XVI. OE. *nebb* = ON. *nef*, rel. to MLG., MDu. *nebbe* (Du. *nebbe*, *neb*) :- Gmc. **naƀja-*. Cf. NIB.

nebula film over the eye XVII; cloud-like cluster of stars XVIII. - L. *nebula*, rel. to OE. *nifol* dark, OS. *neƀal* (Du. *nevel*), OHG. *nebul* (G. *nebel*) cloud, OIr. *nēl*, Gr. *nephélē* cloud, the simple IE. base being repr. by OSl. *nebo*, Gr. *néphos* cloud, Skr. *nábha-* cloud, mist. So **nebuly** (-Y[5]) (her.) wavy like the edges of clouds. XVI. - F. *nébulé*, medL. *nebulātus*. **nebulous** XVI. - F. *nébuleux* or L. *nebulōsus*.

necessary inevitably determined; not to be done without; also sb. XIV. - AN. **necessarie* (OF. *nécessaire*) or L. *necessārius*, f. *necesse* (*esse*, *habēre*) (be, consider) necessary; see -ARY. So **necessity** XIV. - (O)F. - L. **necessitous** needy. XVII. - F.

neck OE. (in various transf. uses from XIV). OE. *hnecca*, corr. to MDu. *nac*, *necke* (Du. *nek*), OHG. (*h*)*nac* (G. *nacken* nape), ON. *hnakki* nape :- Gmc. **χnak(j)-*; rel. to OIr. *cnocc*, OBret. *cnoch* hill, elevation (cf. OHG. *hnack* summit). Hence **neckerchief** XIV (see KERCHIEF). **necklace** XVI.

necro- comb. form of Gr. *nekrós* corpse, rel. to L. *nex* slaughter.

necromancy XIII. Earliest forms in *nigro-*, *nigra-*, *negro-* - OF. *nigromancie* - Rom. (medL.) *nigromantia*, alt., by assoc. with *niger*, *nigr-* black, of late L. *necromantīa* - Gr. *nekromanteíā*, f. *nekrós* + *manteíā*; see prec., -MANCY; refash. XVI as in F. after L. and Gr. So **necromancer** (-ER[2]) XIV.

necropolis cemetery. XIX. - Gr. *nekrópolis*, f. *nekrós* NECRO- + *pólis* city, -POLIS.

necrosis (path.) mortification of tissue. XVII. - Gr. *nékrōsis* state of death, f. *nekroûn* kill, mortify, f. *nekrós*; see NECRO-, -OSIS.

nectar drink of the gods; delicious drink, sweet fluid. XVI. - L. - Gr. *néktar*, of uncert. orig. So **nectarean** XVII, **-eous** XVIII, **-ian** XVII; after L. *nectareus*, Gr. *nektáreos*, F. *nectaréen*. **nectarine** (-INE[1]) variety of peach. XVII. prob. sb. use of *nectarine* adj. **nectary** (bot.) part of a flower that secretes nectar. XVIII. - modL. *nectārium*.

neddy donkey. XVIII. f. *Ned*, pet form of the Christian name *Edward* + -Y[6].

née XVII. - F., 'born', fem. pp. of *naître* :- Rom. **nascere*, for L. *nāscī* (see NATAL).

need †force, constraint; necessity; lack, want; matter requiring action. OE. (non-WS.) *nēd*, (WS.) *nīed* = OS. *nōd* (Du. *nood*), OHG. *nōt* (G. *not*), ON. *nauð*, Goth. *nauþs* :- Gmc. **nauðiz*, **nauþiz*, rel. to OPruss. *nautin* need. So **need** vb. be necessary OE.; have need, be in need. OE. *nēodian* (rare). Hence **needful** †needy XII; requisite, necessary XIV. **needy** indigent XII.

needle pointed implement for sewing OE.; magnetized steel of a compass; pillar, obelisk; sharp-pointed mass of rock XIV. OE. *nǣdl* = OS. *nādla*, *nāthla*, MLG. *nālde*, OHG. *nādala* (Du. *naald*, G. *nadel*), ON. *nál*, Goth. *nēþla* :- Gmc. **nēþlō*, f. IE. **nē-* sew, repr. also by MDu. *naeyen* (Du. *naaien*), OHG. *nāian* (G. *nähen*), L. *nēre* spin, Gr. *nêma* thread. See -LE[1].

needs of necessity, necessarily. OE. *nēdes*; finally superseding earlier †*need*, OE. *nēde* (*nȳde*, *nīde*), instrumental case of *nēd* NEED; see -S.

nefarious XVI. f. L. *nefārius*, f. *nefās* wrong, wickedness, f. *ne-* (see NO[3]) + *fās* divine permission or law (as opposed to *jūs* human law).

negation negative statement, denial. XVI. - (O)F. *négation* or L. *negātiō*, *-ōn-*, f. *negāre* say no, deny, f. *neg-*; see NO[3], -ATION. Also **negative** adj. and sb. XIV. - (O)F. or late L.; hence vb. XVIII.

neglect vb. XVI. f. *neglēct-*, pp. stem of L. *neglegere* disregard, slight, f. *neg-* + *legere* choose; see NO[3], LECTION. Hence sb. XVI. So **negligence**, **-ent** XIV. - (O)F. or L.

negotiate hold conference (*with*) XVI; manage; convert into money XVII; (orig. in hunting) succeed in getting over, etc., clear XIX. f. pp. stem of L. *negōtiāri* carry on business, f. *negōtium* business, f. *neg-* + *ōtium* leisure; see NO[3], OTIOSE, -ATE[3]. So **negotiation** XVI. - L.

Negro black man, blackamoor. XVI - Sp., Pg. *negro* :- L. *niger*, *nigr-* black. So **Negress** (-ESS[1]) XVIII - F. *négresse*. **negrillo**, **negrito** XIX. - Sp.

Negus ruler of Ethiopia. XVI (*neguz*). - Amharic *n'gus* king.

negus hot spiced drink. XVIII. f. name of the inventor, Colonel Francis *Negus* (d. 1732).

neigh (of a horse) utter its characteristic cry.

OE. *hnǣgan* = MDu. *neyen*, MHG. *nēgen*, of imit. orig. Hence sb. XVI.

neighbour OE. *nēahġebūr*, *nēahhebūr*, f. *nēah* NIGH + *ġebūr* peasant, freeholder (f. Gmc. **bū-* dwell; cf. BOOR); corr. to MDu. *nagebuer*, OHG. *nāhgibūr*; cf. OS. *nābūr*, MLG., MDu. *nabur*, MHG. *nāchbūr* (G. *nachbar*), ON. *nábúi*. Hence **neighbourhood** XV.

neither A. adv. not either XIII; nor, nor yet XV; B. adj. and sb. not the one or the other XIII. ME. *naiðer*, *neiðer*, alt., after EITHER, of *na(u)ther*, *no(u)ther*, OE. *nawðer*, *nāðer*, **nōðer*, contr. of *nāhwæðer*, f. *nā* NO[3] + *hwæðer* WHETHER.

nemato- comb. form of Gr. *nêma*, *nēmat-* thread (see NEEDLE), used in terms of nat. hist. XIX.

nemertean, -ine (one) of a class of flat-worms. XIX. f. modL. *Nemertēs* - Gr. *Nēmertḗs* name of a sea-nymph; see EAN, -INE[1].

nemesis goddess of retribution; retributive justice. XVI. - Gr. *némesis* righteous indignation (also personified), f. *némein* to deal out what is due, rel. to *nómos* custom, law.

nenuphar water-lily. XVI. - medL. - Arab. and Pers. *nīnūfar*, *nīlūfar* - Skr. *nīlōtpala* blue lotus, f. *nī́la-* blue + *utpala-* lotus.

neo- comb. form of Gr. *néos* NEW. **neologism, neology** XVIII. - F.

neophyte XVI. - ecclL. *neophytus* - N.T. Gr. *neóphutos* 'newly planted', f. *néos* NEO- + *phutón* plant (n. of pp. formation on *phúein* cause to be (see BE)).

neoteric recent, modern. XVI. - late L. *neotericus* - Gr. *neōterikós*, f. *neṓteros*, compar. of *néos* NEW; see -IC.

nepenthe drug supposed to banish grief or trouble from the mind XVI; plant yielding the drug XVII. alt., after It. *nepente*, of **nepenthes** (XVI) - L. *nēpenthes* - Gr. *nēpenthés*, n. of *nēpenthḗs* banishing pain, f. *nē-* (see NO[3]) + *pénthos* grief (see PATHOS).

nephelo- comb. form of Gr. *nephélē* cloud (see NEBULA). XIX.

nephew XIII. ME. *neveu* - (O)F. *neveu*, also ONF. *nevu*, *nevo* = It. *nepote* :- L. *nepōs*, *nepōt-* grandson, nephew, descendant; rel. to Skr. *nápāt*, Gr. *anepsiós* nephew, OLith. *nep(u)otis*, Ir. *nia* sister's son, and in Gmc. OE. *nefa*, OS. *nevo* (Du. *neef*), OHG. *nevo* (G. *neffe*), ON. *nefi*. Cf. NIECE.

nephritic affecting the kidneys. XVI. - late L. *nephrīticus* - Gr. *nephrītikós*, f. *nephrītis* (whence, through late L., **nephritis** XVI), f. *nephrós* KIDNEY; -IC. So **nephro-** comb. form of the Gr. sb. XVII.

ne plus ultra command to go no further; utmost limit. XVII. - L. phr., 'not more beyond', said to have been inscribed on the Pillars of Hercules (Strait of Gibraltar).

nepotism XVII. - F. *népotisme* - It. *nepotismo*, f. *nepote* NEPHEW; see -ISM.

Neptunian (geol.) pert. to the action of water. XVIII. f. L. *Neptūnius*, f. *Neptūnus* god of the sea; see -IAN.

nereid sea-nymph. XVII. - L. *Nēreis*, *Nēreid-* - Gr. *Nērēis*, *Nērēid-* f. *Nēreús* ancient sea-god, f. base of L. *nāre* swim; see NATATION, -ID.

neroli XVII. - F. *néroli* - It. *neroli*, said to be from the name of its discoverer, an Italian princess.

nerve sinew, tendon XVI; fibrous connection conveying sensation, etc. between the brain and other parts XVII. - L. *nervus* sinew, bowstring, rel. to Gr. *neûron* sinew, nerve, and further to L. *nēre* spin (see NEEDLE). So **nervous** XIV. - L. *nervōsus*. **nervy** (-Y[1]) XVII.

nescience lack of knowledge. XVII. - late L. *nescientia*, f. *nesciēns*, *-ent-* (whence **nescient** XVII), prp. of *nescīre* be ignorant, f. *ne-* (see NO[3]) + *scīre* know.

ness OE. *næs(s)*, *nes(s)*, *næsse*, corr. to LG. *nesse*, ON. *nes*, rel. to OE. *næs-*, *nasu* NOSE. The generalization of the form *ness*, as opposed to *nass*, is due partly to the prevalence of place-names in *-ness*, partly to ON. *nes*.

-ness suffix expressing state or condition appended to adjs. and pps., in more recent use to prons., advs., and phrs. OE. *-nes(s)*, *-nis(s)* = OS. *-nessi*, *-nissi* (Du. *-nis*), OHG. *-nessi*, *-nissi*, *-nassi* (G. *-nis*), Goth. *-nassus*; f. **-n-* (of str. pps.) + **-assus*, f. **-atjan* verbal suffix (the vowel-variation *a e i* is unexpl.). A concr. sense is developed in FASTNESS, LIKENESS, WILDERNESS, WITNESS.

nest bird's laying- and hatching-place OE.; set of similar objects XVI. OE. *nest* = (M)Du., (O)HG. *nest* :- IE. **nizdo-*, whence also L. *nīdus*, OIr. *net* (mod. *nead*), W. *nyth* nest, Skr. *nīḍá-* resting-place; f. **ni* down (cf. NETHER) + **sed-* SIT. Hence vb. XIII; repl. OE. *nistan* = MDu., (O)HG. *nisten*.

nestle have a nest OE.; refl. and intr. settle oneself comfortably XVI. OE. *nestlian* = MLG., (M)Du. *nestelen* (cf. OE. *nistl(i)an*, MHG. *nistelen*); see prec. and -LE[3]. So **nestling** young bird in the nest XIV; f. NEST or NESTLE, perh. after MDu. *nestelinc* (mod. *-ling*).

Nestor name of a Homeric hero famous for his age and wisdom, used allus. for a wise old man. XVI.

net[1] sb. OE. *net(t)* = OS. *net(ti)*, (M)Du. *net*, MLG., MDu. *nette*, OHG. *nezzi* (G. *netz*), ON. *net*, Goth. *nati*; perh. rel. to L. *nassa* narrow-necked basket for catching fish. Hence vb. XVI.

net[2] †trim, smart, clean, bright XIV; free from deduction XVI. - F. *net*, fem. *nette* NEAT[2].

nether lower (now rare exc. in *nether garments*, *n. regions*). OE. *neoðera*, *niðera* = OS. *nithiri* (Du. *neder*), MLG. *ned(d)er*, OHG. *nidari*, *-eri*, *-iri* (G. *nieder*), ON. *neðri*; f. Gmc. **niþar* (repr. by OE. *niðer*, etc.) down, downwards = Skr. *nitarā́m*, f. **ni-* down, with compar. suffix.

nettle OE. *net(e)le*, *netel* = OS. *netila*, MLG. *net(t)ele*, MDu. *netele* (Du. *netel*), OHG. *nezzila* (G. *nessel*), OSw., Icel. *netla* :- Gmc. **natilōn*; see -LE[1]. Hence **nettle** vb. beat or sting with nettles XV; irritate, vex XVI.

neume (mus., in plainsong) group of notes sung to one syllable XV; sign used in plainsong notation XIX. - (O)F. *neume* - medL. *neu(p)ma* - Gr. *pneûma* breath.

neural pert. to the nerves. XIX. f. Gr. *neûron* NERVE + -AL[1].

neuralgia affection of a nerve causing pain. XIX. f. Gr. *neûron* NERVE + *álgos* pain.

neuro-, before a vowel **neur-**, comb. form of

Gr. *neûron* nerve, as in **neurasthenia, neuritis** XIX. **neurology** XVII. - modL. *neurologia* - mod Gr. *neurologia*. **neurotomy** XVIII.

neuter neither masculine nor feminine XIV; intransitive; neutral XVI; asexual, sterile XVIII. - (O)F. *neutre* or its source L. *neuter*, f. *ne-* (see NO[3]) + *uter* either of two. So **neutral** not taking sides; occupying a middle position XVI; (chem.) XVII. - F. †*neutral* or L. *neutrālis*. **neutrality** XV. - (O)F. or medL.

névé granular snow on a glacier; field of frozen snow. XIX. - Swiss F. *névé* glacier :- Rom. **nivātum*, f. L. *nix, niv-* SNOW.

never OE. *nǣfre*, f. *ne* + *ǣfre*; see NO[3], EVER. The contr. form *ner(e)*, with indef. art. *nere a, ne'er a*, became (dial.) *narrow a, narra*, (esp. U.S.) *nary*. Hence **nevertheless** XIII; repl. earlier *notheless, natheless* OE. *nā þȳ lǣs*, f. *nā, nō* NO[1] + instr. case of THE + LESS.

new OE. *nī(o)we, nēowe* = OS. *niuwi, nigi*, MLG. *ni(g)e*, MDu. *nieuwe, nuwe, nie* (Du. *nieuw*), OHG. *niuwi* (G. *neu*), ON. *nýr*, Goth. *niujis* :- Gmc. **neujaz* :- IE. **newjos*, repr. by Gr. (Ionic) *neîos*, OIr. *nūe*, OSl. *novŭ*, Lith. *naũjas*, modification of **newos*, repr. by L. *novus*, Gr. *néos*, Skr. *náva-*.

newel pillar forming the centre of a winding stair XIV; post supporting the handrail of a staircase XIX. ME. *nowel* - OF. *no(u)el* knob :- medL. *nōdellus*, dim. of *nōdus* knot.

newfangled fond of novelty XV; new-fashioned XVI. alt. (by addition of -ED[1]) of *newefangel* XIV, f. *nēwe* adv. f. NEW + **fangel*, repr. an OE. **fangol* 'inclined to seize', f. Gmc. **faŋg-*; see FANG, -LE[2].

news †novelties XIV; tidings XV. pl. of NEW; after OF. *noveles*, pl. of *novele* (mod. *nouvelle*) NOVEL; or after medL. *nova*, pl. of *novum* new thing, sb. use of n. of *novus* NEW. Hence **newspaper** XVII.

newt XV. f. *-n* of AN + *ewt*, var. of *ewet*, OE. *efeta*; of unkn. orig.

next lying nearest; nearest in kinship; immediately preceding or succeeding OE.; immediately following in time XII. OE. (non-WS.) *nēhsta*, (WS.) *nīehsta* = OS. *nā(h)isto* (Du. *naaste*), OHG. *nāhisto* (G. *nächste*), ON. *næstr, næsti* ; superl. of NIGH (see -EST).

nexus bond, link XVII; connected group XIX. - L., f. *nex-*, pp. stem of *nectere* bind.

nib (dial.) beak, bill XVI; pen-point; (pl.) short handles on the shaft of a scythe XVII; peak, tip XVIII; (pl.) small pieces into which cocoa-beans are crushed XIX. prob. - MDu. *nib* or MLG. *nibbe*, var. of *nebbe* beak, NEB.

nibble take little bites (of); fig. carp. XV. cf. LG. *nibbeln*, also *gnibbeln, knibbeln* gnaw = Du. *knibbelen* gnaw, murmur, squabble.

niblick golf club having a small round heavy head. XIX. of unkn. orig.

nibs XIX. See NABS.

nice †foolish, stupid XIII; †wanton XIV; †coy, shy XV; fastidious, dainty; difficult to manage or decide; minute and subtle; precise, critical; minutely accurate XVI; dainty, appetizing; agreeable, delightful XVIII. - OF. *nice* silly, simple :- L. *nescius* ignorant, f. *ne-* (see NO[3]) + *scīre, sci-* know. So **nicety** XIV. - OF. *niceté*.

Nicene pert. to (councils of the Church held at) Nicaea (Gr. *Nīkaia*) in Bithynia, esp. of the creed adopted at the first of these (A.D. 325). XV. - late L. *Nīcēnus, Nīcænus*.

niche XVII. - (O)F. *niche*, f. *nicher* make a nest, nestle :- Rom. **nīdicare*, f. L. *nīdus* NEST.

nick sb. notch XV; precise moment XVI; vb. make a notch in; hit off; win at the game of hazard; trick, cheat XVI. of unkn. orig.

Nick *Old N.*, the devil. XVII. usu. taken to be abbrev. of the name *Nicholas*, but no reason for such an application is known.

nickel hard silvery-white lustrous mineral. XVIII. shortening of G. *kupfernickel* 'copper nickel' (mining name of the copper-coloured ore from which the metal was first obtained); *-nickel* app. = *nickel* dwarf, mischievous demon, the name being given to the ore because it yielded no copper in spite of its appearance.

nickname XV. ME. *nekename*, f. *-n* of AN + †*ekename* (XIV), f. *eke* addition (see EKE[2]) + NAME, after ON. *aukanafn*.

nicotine XIX. - F., f. modL. *nicotiāna* tobacco-plant, f. name of Jacques *Nicot*, French ambassador at Lisbon, by whom tobacco was first introduced into France in 1560; see -INE[5].

nictitate blink, wink. XVIII. f. pp. stem of medL. *nictitāre*, frequent. of L. *nictāre* blink; see -ATE[3]. So **nictitation** XVIII.

nidification nest-building. XVII. - medL. *nīdificātiō, -ōn-*, f. L. *nīdificāre* (whence **nidificate** XIX, **nidify** XVII), f. *nīdus* NEST.

niece XIII. - (O)F. *nièce* :- popL. **neptia*, for L. *neptis*, corr. to Skr. *naptī-*, Gmc. **niptiz*, whence OE., OHG. *nift*, MDu. *nichte* (Du. *nicht*), ON. *nipt*. Cf. NEPHEW.

niello black composition for filling in engraved designs, etc. XIX. - It. :- L. *nigellus*, dim. of *niger* black.

niggard sb. stingy person; adj. stingy, miserly. XIV. alt., with substitution of suffix -ARD, of earlier †*nigon* (XIV-XVI), f. †*nig* (XIII-XVII); prob. of Scand. orig. (cf. Sw. *njugg*, ON. *hnǫggr*, Norw. *nögg*), and ult. rel. to OE. *hnēaw* niggardly, corr. to MDu. *nauwe* (Du. *nauw* narrow, tight), MHG. *nouwe* careful, exact, *(ge)nouwe* scarcely (G. *genau* exactly). Hence **niggardly** XVI; see -LY[1], -LY[2].

nigger Negro. XVIII. Later form of (dial.) *ne(e)ger* XVI (- F. *nègre* - Sp. *negro*), †*niger* XVI-XVIII (- L. *niger* black).

niggle do anything in a trifling or ineffective way. XVI. app. of Scand. orig. (cf. Norw. *nigla*).

nigh (arch., dial.) near. OE. *nē(a)h*, corr. to OS., OHG. *nāh* (Du. *na*, G. *nah*), ON. *ná-*, Goth. *nēhw*; of unkn. orig. Fully declined as adj. only in OHG.; in OE. chiefly in advb. use or with obj. dative. Cf. NEAR, NEXT.

night OE. *ni(e)ht*, with vowel generalized from case-forms in which mutation was regular, the normal (Angl.) nom. being *næht, neaht* = OS., OHG. *naht* ((M)Du., G. *nacht*), ON. *nátt, nótt*, Goth. *nahts*. The IE. base **noqt-* is repr. also by L. *nox, noct-*, Gr. *núx, nukt-*, OSl. *noštĭ*, Lith. *naktìs*, OIr. *nocht*, W. *nos*, Skr. *nákt-*.

nightingale ME. *nihtingale* (XIII), alt. of *nihtegale*, OE. *nihtegala* (*nehte-, næhte-*, etc.) = OS., OHG. *nahta-, nahtigala* (Du. *nachtegaal*, G.

nachtigall), ON. *nætrgali*; f. Gmc. **naχt(i)*- NIGHT + **ʒalan* sing (see YELL).

nightmare female incubus XIII; bad dream with a feeling of suffocation XVI. f. NIGHT + ME. *mare*, OE. *mære* incubus, corr. to MLG. *mar*, MDu. *mare*, *maer*, OHG., ON. *mara* (G. *mahr*) :- Gmc. **maran*-, **marōn*.

nightshade plant of genera *Solanum* and *Atropa*. OE. *nihtsċada*, corr. to MLG., MDu. *nachtschade*, OHG. *nahtscato* (G. *nachtschatten*); app. f. NIGHT + SHADE, prob. with allusion to the poisonous or narcotic properties of the berries.

nigrescent blackish. XVIII. - prp. stem of L. *nigrēscere* grow black, f. *niger* black; see -ESCE, -ENT.

nihilism negative doctrines in religion or morals; extreme revolutionary principles involving destruction of existing institutions. XIX. Also **nihilist** XIX. f. L. *nihil* (short for *nihilum*, for **nīhīlum*, f. *nī*, var. of *nē* (see NO³) + *hīlum* small thing, trifle) + -ISM, -IST.

nil nothing. XIX. - L., contr. of *nihil* (see prec.).

Nilometer gauge for measuring the height of the river Nile. XVIII. - Gr. *neilométrion*, with assim. to words in -METER.

nimble ME. *nemel* (XIII), later *nemble*, *neam(b)le*, app. repr. OE. *nǣmel* quick at seizing, f. the base of *niman* str. vb. take; superseded by *nymel* (XV), later *nymble*, which may repr. either a phonetic development or an OE. **nimol* (cf. *numol* grasping, biting); see -LE².

nimbus cloud-like splendour investing a god XVII; halo XVIII; rain-cloud XIX. - L. *nimbus* rain, cloud, aureole.

Nimrod †tyrant XVII; great hunter XVIII. - Heb. *Nimrōdh* valiant, strong; name of 'a mighty one in the earth' and a 'mighty hunter before the Lord' (Gen. 10: 8, 9).

nincompoop XVII (*nicom*-, *nickum*-), of unkn. orig.

nine OE. *nigon* = OS. *nigun*, -*on* (Du. *negen*) :- **niʒun*, var. of Gmc. **niwun* (repr. by OHG. *niun*, G. *neun*, ON. *níu*, Goth. *niun*) :- IE. **(e)newn*, repr. by L. *novem*, Gr. *ennéa*, OIr. *nói(n)*, OSl. *devętī*, Lith. *devynì*, Skr. *náva*-. So **nineteen** OE. *nigontȳne* = OS. *nigentein* (Du. *negentien*), OHG. *niunzehan* (G. *neunzehn*), ON. *nítján*. **nineteenth** OE. *nigontēoða*. **ninth** ME. *niʒonþe* (XII), a new formation superseding OE. *nigoða* = OS. *niguðo*, MLG. *negede*. **ninety** OE. *nigontiġ*. **ninepins** XVI.

ninny XVI. Appellative use of *Ninny*, pet-form of *Innocent*, with prefixed *n*- and -Y⁶.

nip¹ pinch XIV; snatch, seize smartly XVI; move nimbly XIX. prob. of LG. or Du. orig.; cf. †Sc. *gnip* (XIV), †*knip* (XVI). Hence sb. XVI. **nipper** †thief XVI; costermonger's boy, (hence) youngster XIX.

nip² †half-pint of ale XVIII; small quantity of spirits XIX. prob. short for †*nipperkin* (XVII) measure of half a pint or less, small quantity of drink, rel. to LG., Du. *nippen*.

nipple XVI. Early forms also *neble*, *nible*, perh. dim. of NEB, NIB point; see -LE¹.

nirvana (in Buddhism) extinction of individual existence. XIX. - Skr. *nirvāṇa*-, sb. use of n. pp. of *nirvā* be extinguished, f. *nis* out + *vā*- blow.

nisi (leg.) attached to *decree*, *order*, *rule*, to indicate that these are not absolute or final, but are to be taken as valid *unless* some cause is shown, etc. XIX. - L. *nisi* unless. So **nisi prius** writ named from the first two words of the proviso '*nisi prius* justiciarii ad assisas capiendas venerint' *unless* the judges come to take the assize *before*.

nit egg of a louse, etc. OE. *hnitu* = MLG., MDu. *nēte* (Du. *neet*), OHG. *(h)niz* (G. *nisse*) :- WGmc. **χnitō*.

nitid shining, glossy. XVII. - L. *nitidus*, f. *nitēre* shine; see -ID¹.

nitre †sodium carbonate, (now) saltpetre XIV; †supposed nitrous element in air or plants XVII. - (O)F. - L. *nitrum* - Gr. *nítron*, of Sem. or Egyptian orig. (cf. Heb. *netr* natron, Egyptian *nṯr*); cf. NATRON. The comb. form is **nitro-**. So **nitric** (-IC) applied to an acid produced by the treatment of nitrates with sulphuric acid. XVIII. - F. *nitrique*. **nitrate** (-ATE²) XVIII. - F. **nitrous** (-OUS) XVII. - L. *nitrōsus*; later - F. *nitreux*.

nitrogen XVIII. - F. *nitrogène*; see NITRO-, -GEN. So named from being a constituent of nitric acid.

nix¹ (sl.) nothing. XVIII. - colloq. G. *nix*, for *nichts*, g. of *niht* nothing (cf. NOUGHT).

nix² water-sprite. XIX. - G. *nix*, MHG. *nickes*, OHG. *nihhus*. So **nixie** water-nymph. XIX. - G. *nixe* :- OHG. *nicchessa*, with assim. of ending to -IE.

no¹ not (in lit. use surviving only in *or no* (XV)). OE. *nō*, f. *ne* + *ō*, var. of *ā* ever. The midl. and south. ME. repr. of OE. *nā* (see NO³) coalesced with this and influenced the pronunc.

no² not any. XIII (*na*, *no*). Clipped form of NONE¹, orig. used (like A¹) before words beginning with a cons. Compo. **nobody** XIV, **nohow** XVIII, NOTHING OE., **noway(s)** XIII, NOWHERE, NOWHITHER OE.

no³ expressing a negative answer. XIII. midl. and south. ME. form of OE. *nā*, f. *ne* neg. particle (= OS., OHG. *ne*, *ni*, ON *né*, Goth. *ni*; corr. to L. *ne* (vars. *nec*-, *neg*-), OSl. *ne*, Skr. *na*, etc., with long vowel L. *nē* lest. Gr. *nē*-, Goth. *nē*, Skr. *nā*; cf. UN-¹ + *ā* ever (cf. AY).

no. (read as *number*). XVI. abbr. of L. *numerō* in number, abl. of *numerus* NUMBER; later, perh. after F. *numéro*.

nob¹ (sl.) head. XVII. perh. var. of KNOB.

nob² (sl.) person of wealth or distinction. XIX. In XVIII Sc. *nab*, *knabb*, of unkn. orig. Hence **nobby** smart, elegant XIX; in XVIII Sc. *knabby*.

nobble (sl.) tamper with (a racing horse); steal, seize. XIX. of obscure orig.

noble illustrious by position, character, or birth; distinguished by splendour or magnificence XIII; of great or lofty character XVI. - (O)F. - L. *nōbilis*, for earlier *gnōbilis*, f. IE. **ĝnō*- KNOW; see -BLE. So **nobility** XIV. - (O)F. or L. **noblesse** XIII. - (O)F.; see -ESS².

nock tip of horn on a bow or arrow XIV; (naut.) end of a yard-arm or sail XVI. - MDu. *nocke* (Du. *nock*).

nocti-, before a vowel **noct-**, comb. form of L. *nox*, *noct*- NIGHT.

noctule largest species of British bat. XVIII. - F. - It. *nottola, -o*, f. *notte* night.

nocturn division of the office of matins. XIII. - (O)F. *nocturne* or ecclL. *nocturnus, -um*, sb. use of L. *nocturnus* pert. to the night, f. *nox, noct-* NIGHT. So **nocturnal** XV. - late L.

nod vb. XIV. of uncert. orig. Hence sb. XVI.

noddy simpleton, noodle; tropical sea-bird. XVI. perh. sb. use of †*noddy* adj. foolish, silly, perh. f. NOD + -Y[1].

node complication, entanglement XVI; hard tumour; point of intersection XVII. - L. *nōdus* knot, etc., perh. rel. to *nectere* bind. So **nodule** XVI. - L. *nōdulus*. **nodose** knotty. XVIII. - L. **nodosity** XVII. - late L.

noel Christmas carol. XIX. - F. *noël* NOWEL.

noetic pert. to the intellect. XVII. - Gr. *noētikós*, f. *noētós* intellectual, f. *noein* think, perceive, f. *noûs, nóos* mind.

noggin mug, cup; small quantity of liquor. XVII. of unkn. orig.

noil short pieces and knots of wool combed out of the long staple. XVII. prob. in earlier use and - OF. *noel* :- medL. *nodellus*, dim. of L. *nōdus* knot (see NODE).

noise loud outcry; †rumour; loud or harsh sound XIII; †agreeable sound XIV; †band of musicians XVI. - (O)F. *noise* outcry, disturbance, noisy dispute :- L. *nausea* sea-sickness, NAUSEA. Hence (or - OF.) vb. XIV. **noisy** XVII.

noisome harmful, injurious XIV; offensive XV. f. †*noy* to trouble, vex, harm, aphetic of ANNOY + -SOME.

nomad XVI. - F. *nomade* - L. *Nomas*, pl. *Nomades* pastoral people wandering about with their flocks - Gr. *nomás, nomad-* roaming about, esp. for pasture, pl. *Nomádes* pastoral people, rel. to *némein* pasture; see -AD. So **nomadic** XIX. - Gr. *nomadikós*.

nomenclature †name; set of names. XVII. - F. - L. *nōmenclātūra*, f. *nōmenclātor* one who names, f. *nōmen* NAME + *calāre* call; see -URE.

nominal pert. to a noun XV; pert. to a name; existing only in name XVII. - F. *nominal* or L. *nōminālis*, f. *nōmen* NAME; see -AL[1]. Hence **nominalism** XIX, **-ist** XVII. **nominally** (-LY[2]) by name XVII; in name XVIII.

nominate XVI. f. pp. stem of L. *nōmināre*, f. *nōmen, nōmin-* NAME; see -ATE[3]. So **nomination** XV. - (O)F. or L. **nominative** (gram.) XIV. - (O)F. *nominatif*, fem. *-ive* or L. *nōminātīvus*, tr. Gr. *onomastikḗ*. Hence **nominee** (-EE[1]) XVII.

-nomy terminal el. of sbs., repr. Gr. *-nomiā* arrangement, management, rel. to *nómos* law, *némein* distribute (see NIM), as in ASTRONOMY, ECONOMY, GASTRONOMY. The corr. adjs. end in *-nomic, -nomical*; see -Y[3].

non- prefix expressing negation, used with sbs., adjs., vbs. (ppl. adjs., gerunds), and advs.; first in the AN. form *noun-* = OF. *non-, nom-, nun-, num-* :- L. *nōn* 'not' used as a prefix. The earliest exx. are *non-power, non-residence, nonsuit* (XIV); similar comps. of a technical kind prevail until XVII, when the application was widened. The prefix is normally unstressed, but cf. *nonage, nonchalance, nondescript, nonsense, nonsuit*.

nonage period of legal infancy. XIV. - AN. *nounage*, OF. *nonage*; see NON-, AGE.

nonagenarian 90 years old. XIX. f. L. *nōnāgēnārius*, f. *nōnāgēnī*, distributive of *nōnāginta* ninety, f. *novem* NINE; see -ARIAN.

nonce phr. *for the nonce* †for the particular purpose, expressly XII; for the occasion, for the time being XVI. ME. *for þe nanes*, alt. (by misdivision) of *for þen anes*, f. (with advb. -s) **for þen ane* 'for the one (purpose)'; cf. ONCE.

nonchalance XVII. - (O)F., f. *nonchalant* (adopted in Eng. XVIII), f. *non-* NON- + prp. of *chaloir* be concerned :- L. *calēre* be hot.

nonconformist one who does not conform to the Church of England (or other established church). XVII. See NON-, CONFORMIST. So †**nonconformitan, -formity** XVII.

nondescript †(nat. hist.) not hitherto described XVII; not easily described, neither one thing nor another XIX. f. NON- + *descript* - L. *dēscriptus*, pp. of *dēscrībere* DESCRIBE.

none[1] no one, nobody; not any. OE. *nān* = OS. *nēn*, (M)Du. *neen*, (O)HG. *nein* no (adv.), ON *neinn*; comp. of *ne* (see NO[3]) and ONE; cf. L. *nōn* not :- **nē oinom* 'not one (thing)'. As adv. XII; now chiefly in *none the . . ., none too . . .*

nonentity non-existent thing XVI; non-existence; person or thing of no importance XVII. See NON-, ENTITY.

nones A. ninth day before the Ides XV; B. the fourth of the day offices of the Church. XVIII. In A - (O)F. - L. *nōnæ*, acc. *nōnās*, fem. pl. of *nōnus* ninth, f. *novem* NINE; in B f. NONE[2] after *mattins, lauds, vespers*. Also **none**[2] third quarter of the day XVII; nones (sense B) XIX. - (O)F. - L. *nōna*. Cf. NOON.

nonesuch XVI, now usu. **nonsuch** XVII unmatched, unrivalled thing; plant-name. Extracted from such phr. as 'There is *none such*', but no doubt suggested partly by NONPAREIL.

nonpareil having no equal XV; unique person or thing XVI; size of printing type XVII. - F., f. NON- + *pareil* like :- Rom. **pariculus*, dim. of *par* equal.

nonplus state in which no more can be said or done, esp. in phr. *be at, put to, a nonplus*. XVI. f. L. phr. *nōn plūs* not more, no further. Hence vb. XVI.

nonsense XVII. f. NON- + SENSE. Hence **nonsensical** XVII.

nonsuit (leg.) cessation or stoppage of a suit. XIV. - AN. *no(u)nsuit* ; see NON-, SUIT.

noodle[1] simpleton. XVIII. of unkn. orig.

noodle[2] strip of dough as an ingredient of soup. XVIII. - G. *nudel* ; of unkn. orig.

nook XIII (first in *feower-noked* four-cornered). of unkn. orig.

noon †ninth hour of the day reckoned from sunrise, 3 p.m.; †office of nones OE.; †midday meal XII; midday XIII. OE. *nōn*, corr. to OS. *nōn(e)*, (M)Du. *noen*, OHG. *nona* (G. *none*), ON. *nón* - L. *nōna*, fem. sg. of *nōnus* ninth (see NINE); cf. NONES. The common phr. *(be)fore noon, after noon* have given rise to the sbs. FORENOON, AFTERNOON. Hence **noonday** XV. **noontide** OE. *nōntīd*.

noose XV (rare before XVII). ME. *nōse*, perh.

- OF. *no(u)s*, nom. sg. and acc. pl. of *no(u)*, later *noud*, mod. *nœud* (:- L. *nōdus* NODE).

nopal Amer. cactus. XVIII. - F. *nopal* or its source Sp. *nopal* - Mex. *nopalli* cactus.

nor XIV. contr. of †*nother* (see NEITHER).

norm XIX. - L. *norma* carpenter's square, pattern, rule. So **normal** (-AL[1]) rectangular, perpendicular XVII; conforming to a standard XIX (*n. school*, after F. *école normale*). - F. *normal* or (of schools) L. *normālis*. Hence **normalcy, normality, normalize** XIX.

Norman pl. **-mans** native of Normandy XIII; adj. XVI. orig. in pl. - (O)F. *Normans, -anz*, pl. of *Normant* (mod. *-mand*) - ON. *Norðmaðr*, pl. *-menn*, which was adopted as OE. *Norðmann*, pl. *-menn*; see NORTH, MAN.

Norn female fate in Scand. myth. XVIII. - ON. *norn*, of unkn. orig.

Norroy third King of Arms, whose jurisdiction lies north of the Trent. XV (*-ey*). - AN. **norroi*, f. (O)F. *nord* NORTH + *roi* king.

Norse (hist.) Norwegian XVI; sb. and adj. the Norwegian tongue XVII (*Old N.*, the language of Norway and its colonies to XIV). - Du. *noorsch*, var. of *noordsch*, f. *noord* NORTH + *-sch* -ISH[1].

north OE. *norð* = OS. *norð* (Du. *noord*), (O)HG. *nord*, ON. *norðr*; Gmc., of unkn. orig. So **northerly** XVI, **northern** OE. (hence **northerner** XIX), **northing** (-ING[1]) XVII, **northward** XII, **northwards** OE.

Northumbrian pert. to Northumbria, that part of England lying north of the Humber. XVII. f. †*Northumber* pl. inhabitants of this, repr. OE. *Norðhymbre*, f. *norð* north + *Humbre* Humber; see -IAN.

Norwegian XVII. f. medL. *Norvegia* - ON. *Norvegr* (whence late OE. *Norweġ*, mod. *Norway*), f. *norðr* NORTH + *vegr* WAY, region.

nose sb. OE. *nosu* – MDu. *nōse*, *nuese* (Du. *neus*). Of IE. extent, but the relation of the several forms is obscure; cf. OE. *nasu*, OHG. *nasa* (G. *nase*), ON. *nasar* pl., L. *nārēs* pl. nostrils, *nās(s)us* nose, OSl. *nosŭ*, Lith. *nósis*, Skr. *nas-*; also early ME. *nese* = MLG., MDu. *nese*. Hence vb. perceive by smell XVI; poke *about*, pry XVII. **nosegay** XV; *gay* sb. in the sense 'ornament', 'toy' (XIV to mod. dial.). **nos(e)y** sb. one having a large nose XVIII; adj. evil-smelling; (colloq.) inquisitive XIX.

nosology classification of diseases. XVIII. f. Gr. *nósos* disease; see -LOGY.

nostalgia home-sickness. XVIII. f. Gr. *nóstos* return home + *álgos* pain; see -IA[1].

nostoc genus of algae. XVII. invented by Paracelsus.

Nostradamus seer. XVII. Latinization of the name of Michel de *Nostredame* ('Our Lady'), F. physician (1503-66), who published a book of prophecies in rhyme.

nostril OE. *nosðyrl*, *nosterl*, f. *nosu* NOSE + *þȳr(e)l* hole (rel. to *þurh* THROUGH).

nostrum medicine the composition of which is not made public; 'patent' remedy. XVII. - L., n. of *noster* our; from the label *nostrum* 'of our own make' formerly attached to such medicines.

not XIV. Reduced form of *noht*, *noȝt*, NOUGHT.

notable worthy of note XIV; †conspicuous, noticeable XVI; †energetic XVII. - (O)F. - L. *notābilis*, f. *notāre* NOTE vb.; see -ABLE. As sb. XV. So **notability** XIV. - (O)F.

notary †clerk, secretary; one authorized to draw up deeds. XIV. - L. *notārius* shorthand-writer, clerk, f. *nota* NOTE; see -ARY.

notch sb. XVI. - AN. *noche* (XIV), of uncert. orig. Also vb. XVI.

note sign denoting a musical sound; musical sound of a certain pitch; †melody, tune, call of a bird XIII; mark, sign, character XIV; abstract, brief record or statement XV; annotation, comment; short letter; distinction; notice, regard XVI; written promise to pay XVII. - (O)F. - L. *nota* mark, etc. So **note** vb. observe, indicate XIII; mark XV. - (O)F. *noter* - L. *notāre*. **notation** †explanation of a term; †annotation XVI; representation by signs XVIII. - L. or (O)F.

nothing OE. *nān þing*, ME. *nā þing*, later *nǭ þing*; see NO[2], THING. Hence **nothingness** XVII.

notice (formal) intimation XV; heed, cognizance XVI; †notion, idea XVII; sign giving information XIX. - (O)F. - L. *nōtitia* being known, acquaintance, knowledge, notion, f. *nōtus* known, pp. of *nōscere* KNOW. Hence **notice** vb. †notify XV; mention, refer to XVII; observe, remark XVIII.

notify †observe; give notice of. XIV. - (O)F. *notifier* - L. *nōtificāre*, f. *nōtus* known; see prec. and -FY. So **notification** XIV.

notion XVI. - L. *nōtiō*, *-ōn-* becoming acquainted, examination, idea, f. *nōt-*, pp. stem of *nōscere* KNOW; see -TION. So **notional** XVI. - F. or medL.

notorious well or generally known; noted *for* some bad quality. XVI. - medL. *nōtōrius*, f. *nōtus* known; see NOTICE, -ORIOUS.

notwithstanding in *this n.*, *n. this*, etc. in spite of this XIV; adv. nevertheless XV; conj. although XV. f. NOT + prp. of WITHSTAND; orig. in absol. phr., hence with a clause as regimen (passing into conj.) or without regimen (passing into adv.).

nougat XIX. - F. - Pr. *nogat*, f. *noga* nut (:- Rom. **nuca*, for L. *nux*, *nuc-* NUT) + *-at* :- L. *-ātum* -ATE[1].

nought nothing OE.; adv. (dial.) in no degree; not OE.; †adj. bad, good for nothing XIV. OE. *nōwiht*, f. *ne* (see NO[3]) + *ōwiht*, var. of *āwiht* AUGHT. Cf. NAUGHT. Parallel formations in Gmc. are OS. *neo-*, *niowiht*, MDu. *niewet* (Du. *niet*), OHG. *niwiht* (G. *nicht*).

noumenon (metaph.) object of purely intellectual intuition. XVIII. - G. - Gr. *nooúmenon*, n. of prp. pass. of *noein* apprehend, conceive.

noun XIV. - AN. *noun* = OF. *nun*, *num* (mod. *nom*) :- L. *nōmen* NAME.

nourish †bring up, nurture; foster (fig.); †suckle, nurse XIII; sustain with proper nutriment XIV. - OF. *noriss-*, lengthened stem (see -ISH[2]) of *norir* (mod. *nourrir*) :- L. *nūtrīre* feed, foster, cherish; see NUTRIMENT. Hence **nourishment** XV.

nous (Gr. philos.) mind, intellect XVII; (colloq.) intelligence, gumption XVIII. - Gr. *noûs*, contr. form of *nóos* mind.

novel A. †novelty; †pl. news XV; B. short story of Boccaccio's 'Decameron', etc. XVI; fictitious prose narrative XVII. In A - OF. *novelle* (mod.

nouvelle) :- L. *novella*, n. pl. (construed as sing.) of *novellus* young, new, f. *novus* NEW; in B - It. *novella*, orig. fem. (sc. *storia* story) of *novello* new = OF. *novel* (mod. *nouveau*), whence **novel** adj. XV. Hence **novelist** †innovator XVI; †newsmonger; writer of novels XVIII. **novelty** XIV. - OF. *novelte* (mod. *nouveauté*).

November eleventh (formerly ninth) month of the year. XIII. - (O)F. *novembre* - L. *November*, f. *novem* NINE.

novena nine days' devotion. XIX. - medL. *novēna*, f. L. *novem* NINE.

novercal stepmotherly. XVII. - L. *novercālis*, f. *noverca* stepmother, f. *novus* NEW; see -AL[1].

novice probationer in a religious community XIV; inexperienced person XV. - (O)F. - L. *novīcius*, f. *novus* NEW; see -ITIOUS[1]. So **noviciate** (-ATE[1]) XVI. - F. or medL.

now adv. at the present time; conj. since, seeing that. OE. *nū* = OS., OHG., ON., Goth. *nū* (Du. *nu*; G. *nun*, with advb. *n*); corr. to L. *num*, *nunc*, Gr. *nu(n)*, *nûn*, OSl. *nyně*, Lith. *nù*, Skr. *nū*. Hence **nowaday(s)** XIV. f. ME. *aday(s)*, from the blending of OE. *on dæġe* and g. *dæġes*; see -S.

nowel cry used in celebrating Christmas, retained in carols. XIV. - OF. *no(u)el* (mod. *noël*), obscure var. of *nael*, *neel* :- L. *nātālis* NATAL.

nowhere OE. *nāhwǣr*, later *nōhwǣr*, f. *nā* NO[2] + *hwǣr* WHERE. So **nowhither** OE. *nā-*, *nōhwider*.

noxious XVII. f. L. *noxius*, f. *noxa* hurt, damage, rel. to *nex* slaughter, *nocēre* injure; see -IOUS.

noyade execution by drowning. XIX. - F., f. *noyer* drown :- L. *necāre* kill; see -ADE.

noyau liqueur made from brandy flavoured with kernels. XVIII. - F., earlier *noiel* kernel :- Rom. **nucāle*, sb. use of n. of late L. *nucālis*, f. *nux*, *nuc-* NUT.

nozzle candle-socket; small spout or mouthpiece. XVII. Early forms *nosle*, *nos(s)el*; if f. NOSE + -LE[1], a much earlier existence must be presumed.

nuance shade of feeling, meaning, etc. XVIII; shade of colour XIX. - F. f. *nuer* show variations of shades of colour like clouds, f. *nue* cloud :- popL. **nūba*, L. *nūbēs*; see -ANCE.

nub †husk of silk XVI; knob, lump XVIII; gist XIX. var. of KNUB.

nubile (of women) marriageable. XVII. - L. *nūbilis*, f. *nūbere* take a husband; see -ILE.

nucleus condensed portion of the head of a comet; central part, kernel. XVIII. - L. *nucleus* nut, kernel, inner part, var. of *nuculeus*, f. *nucula* small nut, dim. (see -ULE) of *nux*, *nuc-* NUT. Hence **nuclear** XIX.

nude (leg.) not formally attested; †bare, mere XVI; naked, unclothed XVII (rare before XIX, except as sb. XVIII, after F. *nu*). - L. *nūdus* :- **now(e)dos*, **nogwedos* NAKED. So **nudity** XVII. - (O)F. or late L. **nudist** XX.

nudge vb. XVII. of unkn. orig.; perh. in much earlier use and rel. ult. to Norw. dial. *nugga*, *nyggja* push, rub. Hence sb. XIX.

nugatory worthless, useless. XVII. - L. *nūgātōrius*, f. pp. stem of *nūgārī* trifle, f. *nūgæ* jests, trifles; see -ORY[2].

nugget lump, orig. of native gold. XIX. perh. dim. of s.w. dial. *nug* lump, block, unshapen mass, of unkn. orig.; see -ET.

nuisance injury, harm XV; injurious or obnoxious thing XV; source of annoyance XIX. - OF. (now arch.) *nuisance* hurt, f. *nuis-*, stem of *nuire* injure :- L. *nocēre*; see -ANCE.

null not valid (*n. and void*) XVI; insignificant; non-existent XVIII. - (O)F. *nul*, fem. *nulle*, or L. *nūllus*, *-a* no, none, f. *ne* (see NO[3]) + *ūllus* any, f. *ūnus* ONE. So **nullify** make null. XVI. - late L. *nullificāre* despise. **nullification** XVIII. **nullity** XVI. - F. or medL.

nullah (in India) river, river-bed, ravine. XVIII. - Hindi *nālā* brook, rivulet, ravine.

numb deprived of feeling or the power of movement. XIV. ME. *nome(n)*, pp. of *nimen*, OE. *niman* take, seize. Hence vb. XVII.

number sum of individuals or units; full tale or count XIII; multitude, aggregate; aspect or property of things as units; symbol of arithmetical value XIV; (pl.) groups of musical notes, melody; metrical periods, verses XVI. ME. *no(u)mbre*, *numbre* - AN. *numbre*, (O)F. *nombre* :- L. *numerus*. So **number** vb. XIII. - (O)F. *nombrer* :- L. *numerāre*.

numbles entrails of an animal as used for food. XIV. - OF. *numbles*, *nombles* pl. :- L. *lumbulus*, dim. of *lumbus* LOIN; cf. HUMBLE-PIE.

numen XVII. - L. *nūmen* divine will, divinity, rel. to *-nuere* nod, Gr. *neúein* nod, incline the head. So **numinous** XVII. f. L. *nūmen*, *nūmin-*.

numeral adj. pert. to number; sb. figure denoting a number. XVI. - late L. *numerālis*, f. *numerus* NUMBER; see -AL[1]. So **numeration** XV. - L. **numerator** XVI. - F. or late L. **numerical** XVII. f. modL. *numericus*. **numerous** plentiful, copious, many; measured, rhythmical. XVI. - L. *numerōsus*.

numismatic XVIII. - F. *numismatique*, f. L. *nūmisma*, *-mat-*, var. (infl. by *nummus* coin) of *nomisma* - Gr. *nómisma* current coin, f. *nomízein* have in use, f. *nómos* use, custom; see -ISM, -ATIC.

nummary pert. to money or coinage. XVII. - L. *nummārius*, f. *nummus* coin; see -ARY.

nummulite (geol.) coin-shaped fossil of a foraminiferous cephalopod. XIX. f. L. *nummulus*, dim. of *nummus* coin; see -ITE.

numskull blockhead, dolt; pate, noddle. XVIII. f. NUMB + SKULL.

nun OE. *nunne* = OHG., ON. *nunna*, beside ME. *nonne* (partly - OF. *nonne*) = MDu., G. *nonne* (Du. *non*) - ecclL. *nonna*, fem. of *nonnus* monk, orig. titles given to elderly persons. So **nunnery** XIII. - AN. **nonnerie*.

Nunc dimittis title of canticle beginning in the Vulg. 'Nunc dimittis servum tuum . .', Now lettest thou thy servant depart . . (Song of Simeon, Luke 2: 29-32) XVI; transf. permission to depart, departure XVII.

nuncio XVI. - It. †*nuncio*, †*nuntio* (mod. *nunzio*) - L. *nuntius* messenger.

nuncupative (leg.) oral, not written (as a will). XVI. - late L. *nūncupātīvus*, f. pp. of L. *nūncupāre* name, declare, f. **nōmiceps* or *-*capos* 'name-taking', f. *nōmen* NAME + *capere* take; see -ATIVE.

nuptial adj. XV; sb., usu. pl. XVI. - F. *nuptial* or

L. *nuptiālis*, f. *nuptiæ* wedding, f. *nupt-*, pp. stem of *nūbere* marry; see -IAL.

nurse sb. XVI. reduced form of †*norice*, †*n(o)urice* (XIII-XVIII) - OF. *nourice* (mod. *-rr-*) :- late L. *nūtrīcia*, sb. use of fem. of L. *nūtrīcius*, f. *nūtrīre* NOURISH. So **nurse** vb. XVI; alt. of †*nurish*, †*norsh* NOURISH, by assim. to the sb. **nursery** †upbringing of children; apartment for nurse and children XIV; ground, etc. for young plants XVI. prob. - AN. **noricerie*.

nurture †upbringing; †nourishment XIV; fostering care XVII. - OF. *nourture*, contr. of *noureture* (mod. *nourriture*), f. *nourrir* NOURISH; see -URE. Hence vb. XV.

nut OE. *hnutu* = MLG. *note*, MDu. *note*, *neute* (Du. *noot*, *neut*), OHG. *(h)nuz* (G. *nuss*), ON. *hnot* :- Gmc. **χnut-*; cf. OIr. *cnū*, W. *cneuen* (pl. *cnau*), further L. *nux*, *nuc-*, in which **kn-* is reduced to *n*, but which has an extension in *-k-*, whereas the Gmc. langs. have *-t-*.

nutation nodding XVII; oscillation of the earth's axis XVIII. - L. *nūtātiō*, *-ōn-*, f. *nūtāre*, *nūtāt-* nod, f. base of *-nuere* nod; see -ATION.

nuthatch XIV. ME. *notehache*, with later vars. in *-hak*, *-hagge*, which suggest deriv. from NUT and HACK[1], †*hag*, HATCH[2], with allusion to the bird's habit of cracking nuts.

nutmeg XIV. ME. *nute-*, *notemug(g)e*, later *notmyg* (XV), *note-*, *nutmeg* (XVI), partial tr. of AN. **nois mugue*, for OF. *nois mug(u)ede* (also *musguete*; now *noix muscade*) :- Rom. **nuce muscāta* 'musk-smelling nut' (L. *nux* NUT, *muscus* MUSK).

nutriment - L. *nūtrīmentum*, f. *nūtrire* nourish, rel. to Skr. *snauti* drips, trickles (said, e.g., of a mother's milk): see -MENT. So **nutrition** XVI. **nutritious** XVII. - L. *nūtrītius*, *-īcius*, f. *nūtrīx*, *nūtrīc-* NURSE. **nutritive** XV. - F. - medL.

nux vomica seed of an E. Indian tree from which strychnine is obtained. XVI. - medL., i.e. *nux* NUT and fem. of *vomicus*, f. L. *vomere* VOMIT.

nuzzle †grovel XV; burrow or push with the nose XVI; nestle XVII. perh. orig. back-formation on †*noseling* with the NOSE to the ground (see -LING[2]), but perh. infl. later by Du. *neuzelen* poke with the nose, f. *neus*; see -LE[3].

nyctalopia night-blindness. XVII. - late L., f. Gr. *nuktálōps*, f. *núx*, *nukt-* NIGHT + *alaós* blind + *ṓps* EYE.

nylon invented name of a strong plastic material used for yarn, bristles, etc. XX.

nymph (myth.) semi-divine female being XIV; young beautiful woman; pupa XVI. - OF. *nimphe* (mod. *nymphe*) - L. *nympha* - Gr. *númphē* bride, nymph, rel. to L. *nūbere* marry. comb. form **nympho-**, as in *nympholepsy*, *nymphomania* XVIII.

O

o, o' (mostly arch. or dial.) reduced form of (i) ON, in ME. varying with *a* (cf. A-[1]) XII; (ii) OF (cf. A-[2]), surviving sparsely in gen. use, e.g. *o'clock, cat-o'-nine-tails, man-o'-war, will-o'-the-wisp, John o' Groats.*

O int. standing before a vocative or introducing a wish or an asseveration. XII. - (O)F. - L. *ō*; cf. Gr. *ô, ṓ*, Goth., OHG. *ō*.

-o an add. to a word, or first part of a word, forming a colloq. or sl. expression or a familiar or joc. equiv., as *like billy-o, lie doggo, ammo* (for *ammunition*), *beano* (for *bean-feast*); sometimes, the last syll. of an abbrev. form. as *compo|sition, hippo|potamus, photo|graph*; in *cheer(i)o, right(y)o, -ho*, perh. the int. O, or after *hallo*.

-o- connective vowel originating in the *-o-* of Gr. comb. forms (often having adv. force), e.g. (from Gr.) *aero-, cyclo-, geo-, hydro-, philo-, pseudo-*, and (on L. bases) *oleo-, radio-*; a special class is that of comp. proper names as *Anglo-Saxon, Finno-Ugrian, Sino-Japanese*. It appears regularly before -CRACY, -GRAPHY, -LOGY, -METER, and so forms stable suffixes with them, e.g. mob*ocracy*, sex*ology*, soci*ology*, fool*ometer*.

oaf XVII (*oph, oaf*). Varying at first with *ouph* and *au(l)fe*, orig. 'elf', 'goblin' - ON. *álfr*; see ELF.

oak OE. *āc* (pl. *ǣc*) = MLG. *ēk* (Du. *eik*), OHG. *eih* (G. *eiche*), ON. *eik* :- Gmc. **aiks*; ulterior connections unkn.

oakum †tow OE.; fibre obtained by picking old rope XV. OE. *ācumbe, ācum(b)a*, var. of *ǣcumbe, ǣcuma*, corr. to OHG. *āchambi* (MHG. *ākambe, ākamp*), f. *ǣ-, ā-* away, off + **camb-*, stem of *camb* and *cemban* COMB; the etym. meaning is 'off-combing'.

oar OE. *ār* = ON. *ár* :- Gmc. **airō*. Hence **oarlock** OE. *ārloc*; see ROWLOCK.

oasis XVII. - late L. - Gr. *óasis*, presumably of Egyptian orig.; cf. Coptic *ouahe* dwelling-place, oasis, f. *ouih* dwell.

oast kiln for drying malt, hops, lime. OE. *āst* = MLG. *eist* (Du. *eest*) :- Gmc. **aistaz*, f. IE. base **aidh-* **idh-* burn, repr. also by OE. *ād*, OHG. *eit* blazing pile, funeral pyre, L. *ædēs* hearth, house, Gr. *aîthos* heat, OIr. *aedh* heat.

oat (pl.) grains of the cereal *Avena sativa*. OE. *āte*, pl. *ātan*, peculiar to Eng. and of unkn. orig. Hence **oaten** (-EN[3]) XV.

oath solemn appeal to God as a witness OE.; trivial use of sacred names XII. OE. *āð* = OS. *ēth* (Du. *eed*), (O)HG. *eid*, ON. *eiðr*, Goth. *aiþs* :- Gmc. **aiþaz*; cf. OIr. *ōeth*.

ob- comb. form of L. *ob* towards, against, in the way (of), with vars. OC-, OF-, OP-, occas. *o-* (as in OMIT); mostly in words already existing in L.; in mod. scientific L. (hence in Eng. adoptions) in the sense 'inversely', 'in the opposite direction', virtually repr. modL. *obversē* obversely, e.g. *obovate* ovate with the wider end presented.

obbligato (mus.) a part essential to the effect of a composition. XVIII. - It., sb. use of pp. of *obbligare* OBLIGE.

obdurate XV. - L. *obdūrātus*, pp. of *obdūrāre*, f. OB- + *dūrāre* harden; see -ATE[2].

obedient XIII. - OF. *obédient* - L. *obœdiēns, -ent-*, prp. of *obœdīre* OBEY; see -ENT. So **obedience** XIII. **obedientiary** †one subject to obedience XVI; member of a religious body having an office under the superior XVIII. - medL.

obeisance †obedience; respectful salutation XIV. - (O)F. *obéissance*, f. *obéissant*, prp. with lengthened stem (see -ISH[2]) of *obéir* OBEY. So **obeisant** XIII.

obelisk tapering column of stone; any of the signs —, ÷, †. XVI. - L. *obeliscus* small spit, obelisk - Gr. *obelískos*, dim. of *obelós* spit, pointed pillar. So **obelus** (in second sense) XIV. - late L. - Gr.

obese XVII. - L. *obēsus* that has eaten himself fat, stout, plump, f. OB- + *ēsus*, pp. of *edere* EAT. So **obesity** XVII. - F. or L.

obey XIII. ME. *obeie* - (O)F. *obéir* - L. *obœdīre*, f. OB- + *audīre* hear.

obfuscate XVI. f. pp. stem of late L. *obfuscāre*, f. OB- + *fuscāre* darken, *fuscus* dark; see DUSK, -ATE[3]. So **obfuscation** XVII (once XV). - late L.

obit †death, decease; †obsequies; commemoration of the dead XIV. - (O)F. - L. *obitus* going down, death, f. *obit-*, pp. stem of *obīre* go down, die, f. OB- + *īre* go.

obiter by the way. XVI. - L., f. phr. *ob iter*, i.e. *ob* (see OB-), *iter* journey, road.

obituary XVIII. - medL. *obituārius*, f. *obitus* OBIT; see -ARY.

object (from classL.) †objection, obstacle XIV; (from medL.) something presented to the sight or observed XIV; (gram.) XVIII. - L. *objectum*, sb. use of the pp. of *obicere* throw towards, place in front of, f. OB- + *jacere* throw. So **object** vb. bring forward in opposition or as a charge XV; †exhibit, expose XVI. f. *object-*, pp. stem of L. *obicere* or - L. *objectāre*. **objection** XIV. - OF. or late L.; hence **objectionable** XVIII. **objective** †material; pert. to an object of consciousness XVII; (gram.) XVIII; dealing with what is external to the mind XIX. - medL. *objectīvus*.

objurgate rebuke severely. XVII. f. pp. stem of L. *objurgāre*, f. OB- + *jurgāre* quarrel, scold, f. *jurgium* quarrel, strife; see -ATE[3]. So **objurgation, objurgatory** (-ORY[2]) XVI. - L.

oblate[1] person devoted to a religious work. XIX. - F. *oblat* - medL. *oblātus*, sb. use of pp. of *offerre* OFFER; see OBLATION, -ATE[1].

oblate[2] (geom.) flattened at the poles. XVIII. - modL. *oblātus*, f. OB- + *lātus*, as in L. *prōlātus* PROLATE.

oblation XV. - (O)F. *oblation* or late and ecclL. *oblātiō, -ōn-*, f. *oblāt-*, used as pp. stem of *offerre* OFFER; see -ATION.

oblige bind by oath XIII; make indebted, confer a favour on; pass. be bound *to* XVI; constrain XVII. - (O)F. *obliger* = It. *obbligare* - L. *obligāre* bind around or up, bind by oath or other tie, restrain, f. OB- + *ligāre* bind. Hence **obligee** (-EE[1]), **obligor** (-OR[1]) XVI. So **obligation** XIII. - (O)F. - L. **obligatory** XV. - late L.

oblique having a slanting or sloping direction XV; (gram.) XVI. - (O)F. - L. *oblīquus*, f. OB- + obscure el. So **obliquity** divergence from moral rectitude XV; oblique direction XVI.

obliterate XVI. f. pp. stem of L. *oblit(t)erāre* strike out, erase, f. OB- + *lit(t)era* LETTER; see -ATE[3].

oblivion forgetfulness XIV; state of being forgotten XV. - (O)F. - L. *oblīviō, -ōn-*, f. stem *oblīv-* of *oblīviscī* forget, f. OB- + **līv-*, of obscure orig. So **oblivious** XV.

oblong XV. - L. *oblongus* somewhat long, oblong, elliptical, f. OB- + *longus* LONG.

obloquy XV. - late L. *obloquium* contradiction, f. OB- + *loquī* speak; see LOCUTION, -Y[3].

obnoxious A. †exposed *to* harm; †subject *to* authority XVI; B. (by assoc. with NOXIOUS) †hurtful, injurious; offensive, highly objectionable XVII. - L. *obnoxiōsus* or f. *obnoxius* exposed to harm, subject, liable, f. OB- + *noxa* hurt, injury; see -IOUS.

oboe XVIII. - It. - F. *hautbois* HAUTBOY.

obol coin of ancient Greece. XVII. - L. *obolus* - Gr. *obolós*, var. of *obelós* OBELISK.

obscene offensive to the senses, etc.; offensive to decency XVI. - F. *obscène* or L. *obscēnus, obscænus* ill-omened, disgusting, indecent. So **obscenity** XVII.

obscure devoid of light XIV; remote from observation; not manifest to the mind, hard to understand XV. - (O)F. *obscur*, latinized form of earlier *oscur, oscur* :- L. *obscūrus*. So **obscurity** XV. - (O)F. - L.

obsecration earnest entreaty XIV. - L. *obsecrātiō, -ōn-*, f. *obsecrāre* entreat, beseech (orig. by the name of the gods), f. OB- + *sacrāre* hold SACRED; see -ATION.

obsequies XIV. Formerly also sg. - AN. *obsequie(s)* = OF. *ob-, osseque(s)* (mod. *obsèques*) - medL. *obsequiæ*, prob. alt. of L. *exsequiæ* EXEQUIES, by assoc. with *obsequium*, dutiful service; see next and -Y[3].

obsequious readily compliant XV; servilely compliant XVII. - L. *obsequiōsus*, f. *obsequium*, f. *obsequī* comply with, f. OB- + *sequī* follow; see SEQUENCE, -IOUS.

observe A. attend to in practice, keep to XIV; celebrate, solemnize XVI; B. give heed to, watch XIV (rare before XVI); C. say by way of remark XVII. - (O)F. *observer* - L. *observāre* watch, attend to, guard, f. OB- + *servāre* watch, keep. So **observance** XIII (in sense 'prescribed act or practice'). **observant** applied to Franciscans of the Strict Observance XV; attentive to rule or law; taking notice XVII. **observation** †observance XIV; action of observing XVI. - L. **observatory** (-ORY[1]) building for making observations. XVII. - F. *observatoire*.

obsess beset, as a besieging force. XVI (rare in XVIII, revived XIX). f. *obsess-*, pp. stem of L. *obsidēre* sit down before, f. OB- + *sedēre* SIT. So **obsession** †siege XVI; being assailed by an evil spirit or a fixed idea XVII. - L.

obsidian volcanic glass. XVII (*o. stone*). - erron. L. *obsidiānus*, in earliest printed editions of Pliny's 'Natural History', for *obsiānus*, so named from its resemblance to a stone found in Ethiopia by one *Obsius*; see -IAN.

obsolete fallen into disuse XVI; worn out, effete, effaced; (biol.) indistinct, imperfectly developed XVIII. - L. *obsolētus* grown old, worn out, pp. of **obsolēre* (repr. by inchoative *obsolēscere* grow old, fall into disuse), f. OB- + *solēre* be accustomed or used. So **obsolescent** XVIII, **-escence** XIX.

obstacle XIV. - (O)F. *obstacle* (earlier *ostacle*) - L. *obstāculum*, f. *obstāre* stand in the way, f. OB- + *stāre* STAND; see -CLE.

obstetric XVIII. f. L. *obstetrix, -trīc-* midwife, lit. 'a woman who is present', f. *obstāre*; see prec., -TRIX.

obstinate XIV. - L. *obstinātus*, pp. of *obstināre* persist, f. OB- + **-stan-* (rel. to STAND); see -ATE[2]. So **obstinacy** XIV.

obstreperous clamorous, noisy XVI; unruly, turbulent XVII. f. L. *obstreperus*, f. *obstrepere* shout at, oppose noisily, f. OB- + *strepere* make a noise.

obstruct XVII. f. *obstruct-*, pp. stem of L. *obstruere* build against, block up, f. OB- + *struere* pile, build. So **obstruction** XVI. - F. or L.

obtain come into possession of XV; be prevalent XVII. ME. *obte(i)ne* repr. tonic stem of (O)F. *obtenir* - L. *obtinēre*, f. OB- + *tenēre* hold.

obtrude XVI. - L. *obtrūdere* (pp. *obtrūsus*), f. OB- + *trūdere* thrust. So **obtrusion** XVI, **obtrusive** XVII.

obtund XIV. - L. *obtundere* beat against, blunt, dull, f. OB- + *tundere* beat. So **obtuse** A. not sensitive or perceptive; B. greater than a right angle; (bot.) of a leaf, etc., rounded at the extremity. XVI. - L. *obtusus*, pp. of *obtundere*.

obturate XVII. f. pp. stem of L. *obturāre*, f. OB- + *turāre* close up; see -ATE[3]. So **obturator** (anat.) membrane closing the thyroid foramen. XVIII. - medL.

obverse adj. opposite, (of a figure) narrower at the base or point of attachment than at the apex or top XIX; sb. face of a coin, etc. XVII (not common till XIX); counterpart XIX. - L. *obversus*, pp. of *obvertere* turn towards, f. OB- + *vertere* turn.

obviate XVI. f. pp. stem of late L. *obviāre* meet in the way, prevent, f. OB- + *via* way; see -ATE[3]. So **obvious** †lying in the way; plainly perceptible. XVII. f. L. *obvius*.

oc- assim. form of OB- before *c*.

ocarina XIX. - It., dim. of *oca* goose (with ref. to its shape).

occasion favourable juncture of circumstances; reason, cause XIV; juncture calling for action, particular case or time of happening XVI. - (O)F. *occasion* or L. *occasiō, -ōn-* juncture, opportunity, motive, reason, (later) cause, f. *occās-*, pp. stem of *occidere* go down, set, f. OB- + *cadere* fall; see -ION. Hence **occasional** †casual XVI; happening on or limited to a particular occasion XVII.

Occident XIV. - (O)F. - L. *occidēns, -ent-* setting,

sunset, west, sb. use of prp. of *occidere* go down, set; see prec., -ENT. So **occidental** (-AL[1]) western. XIV. - (O)F. or L.

occiput back of the head. XVI (once XIV). - L. *occiput*, *-pit-*, f. OC- + *caput* HEAD. Comb. form **occipito-**. So **occipital** XVI. - F. - medL.

occlude XVI. - L. *occlūdere*, f. OC- + *claudere* CLOSE. So **occlusion** XVII, **occlusive** XIX.

occult hidden, secret, recondite XVI; pert. to early sciences held to involve secret and mysterious knowledge XVII. - L. *occultus*, pp. of *occulere*, f. OC- + base of *cēlāre* CONCEAL. So **occultation** XV. - F. or L.

occupy †take possession of; have in one's possession; take up, use up; employ, engage XIV; †lay out, invest XVI. - AN. **occupier*, for (O)F. *occuper* - L. *occupāre* seize, f. OC- + *cap-* of *capere* take, seize. So **occupant** XVI, **occupier, occupation** XIV.

occur †meet *with*; present itself to the mind, in the course of events, etc. XVI. - L. *occurrere* run to meet, present itself, befall, f. OC- + *currere* run. So **occurrence** XVII. - F. or L.

ocean †proper name of the great outer sea surrounding the mass of land of the Eastern Hemisphere XIII; any of the main regions into which the water of the globe is geographically divided XIV. ME. *occean(e)* - OF. *occean(e)* (mod. *océan*) - L. *ōceanus* - Gr. *ōkeanós* orig. the great river encompassing the disc of the earth and personified as a god, son of Uranus (heaven) and Gaia (earth). So **oceanic** XVII. - medL. *ōceanicus*.

ocelot XVIII. - F., shortening of Nahuatl *tlalocelotl*, f. *tlalli* field + *ocelotl* tiger, jaguar, the abbr. form being transf. from the jaguar to another feline beast.

och excl. of surprise, etc., ah! oh! XVI. - Ir., Gael. *och*.

ochlocracy mob-rule. XVI. - F. *ochlocratie* - Gr. *okhlokratiā*, f. *ókhlos* crowd; see -CRACY.

ochre XV. - (O)F. *ocre* - L. *ōchra* - Gr. *ṓkhrā*, f. *ōkhrós* pale yellow. So **ochreous** XVIII, **och(e)ry** (-Y[1]) XVI.

-ock suffix forming dims.; in OE. *-oc*, *-uc*, as in BULLOCK, HASSOCK, MATTOCK. The number was extended in ME. and later, as in HILLOCK, PADDOCK.

-ocracy, -ocrat see -O- and -CRACY.

o'clock see O, O'.

octa- comb. form of Gr. *oktṓ* EIGHT, as in **octagon** (XVII), **octahedron** (XVI).

octad group of eight. XIX. - late L. *octas*, *octad-* - Gr. *oktás*, f. *oktṓ* EIGHT; see -AD.

octant eighth part of a circle; (spec. astron.) point 45° (i.e. $\frac{1}{8}$ of 360°) distant from another. XVII. - L. *octāns*, *-ant-* half quadrant, f. *octō* EIGHT.

octave (eccl.) formerly pl., eighth day after a festival, period of eight days beginning with the festival XIV; (pros.) group of eight lines of verse XVI; (mus.) note eight diatonic degrees above a given note XVII; interval, or series of notes, between a note and its octave; (fencing) XVIII; group of eight XIX. - (O)F. *octave*, superseding semi-pop. *oitieve*, *utave* - L. *octāva*, fem. of *octāvus* eighth, f. *octō* EIGHT. So **octavo** size of the page of a book for which the sheets are so folded that each leaf is one-eighth of a full sheet XVII, earlier *in o.* XVI 'in an eighth'; abl. of L. *octāvus*.

octet(te) (mus.) composition for eight instruments or voices; (pros.) group of eight lines. XIX. - It. *ottetto*, or its deriv. G. *oktett*; f. *otto* eight.

octo- before a vowel **oct-**, comb. form of L. *octō* EIGHT, as in **octogenarian** (L. *octōgēnārius*) XIX, **octosyllable** (late L. *-bus*) XVIII.

October tenth (formerly eighth) month of the year. Late OE. - L. *octōber*, *-bris*, f. *octō* EIGHT; ME. *octobre* - (O)F. was superseded by the L. form.

octopus XVIII. - Gr. *oktṓpous*, (usu.) *oktápous*, f. *oktṓ* EIGHT + *poús* FOOT.

octoroon person having $\frac{1}{8}$ negro blood. XIX. f. L. *octō* EIGHT, after QUADROON.

octroi †concession, grant XVII; duty levied on articles on their admission to a town XVIII. - F., f. *octroyer* grant :- Gallo-Rom. **auctōricāre*, medL. *auctōrizāre* AUTHORIZE.

octuple XVII. - F. *octuple* or L. *octuplus*, f. *octō* EIGHT + *-plus*, as in *duplus* DOUBLE.

ocular XVI. - F. *oculaire* - late L. *oculāris*, f. L. *oculus* EYE; see -AR. So **oculist** XVII.

od (phys.) hypothetical force held by Baron von Reichenbach (1788-1869) to pervade all nature. XIX. of arbitrary formation. Hence **odic** XIX.

Od, 'od XVI. Clipped form of GOD used to avoid the overt profanation of the sacred name, as in *Ods-me*, *Ods my life*, *Odso*, *Odsbodikins* (XVI-XVIII). Cf. DRAT.

odal land held in absolute ownership, as in Scand. countries. XIX. - ON. *óðal* (Norw., Sw. *odal*), corr. to OE. *ǣðel*, *ēðel*, OS. *ōðil*, OHG. *uodal*, f. Gmc. **ōþ-* **aþ-*, whence also OE. *æðele*, OHG. *edili* (G. *edel*) noble, OE. *æðelu*, OS. *aðali*, OHG. *adal* (G. *adel*) noble descent, ON. *aðal* native quality, nature. Cf. UDAL.

odalisque female slave, concubine. XVII. - F. - Turk. *odalık*, f. *oda* room (sc. in a harem) + *-lik* affix expressing function.

odd that remains after a division into pairs; that remains over and above a definite sum or round number XIV; (dial.) single, singular; †unique, distinguished; extraneous, additional XV; not ordinary or normal XVI. ME. *odde* - ON. *odda-*, comb. form of *oddi* point, angle, third or odd number, rel. to OE., OS. *ord*, OHG. *ort* point, etc. (G. *ort* place). Hence **oddity, oddment** XVIII.

odds first in phr. *make o. even* (XVI); perh. unequal things, (hence) difference, esp. in favour, dissension (esp. *at o.*), advantage conceded in wagering; presumably sb. pl. of the adj. Also in phr. *odds and ends* (XVIII), for earlier †*odd ends* (XVI-XVII), in which *end* means 'fragment'.

ode XVI. - F. - late L. *ōda*, *ōdē* - Gr. *ōidḗ*, Attic var. of *aoidḗ* song, lay, f. *aeídein* sing.

-ode repr. Gr. *-ṓdēs*, *-ódes* of the nature of, like, for *-oeidḗs* -OID.

odeum theatre or hall for the performance of music. XVII. - F. *odéum* or L. *ōdēum* - Gr. *ōideîon*, f. *ōidḗ* singing (see ODE).

odious XIV. - OF. *odious*, *odieus* (mod. *odieux*) - L. *odiōsus*, f. *odium* (whence **odium** XVII), rel. to *ōdī* I hate.

odometer see HODOMETER.

odonto- comb. form of Gr. *odoús, odont-* TOOTH. XIX.

odour XIII. - AN. *odour*, OF. *odor, odur* (mod. *odeur*) - L. *odor, odōr-*, rel. to Gr. *odmḗ, osmḗ* smell. So **odoriferous** XV. f. L. *odōrifer*. **odorous** XVI. f. L. *odōrus*.

odyssey long adventurous journey. XIX. transf. use of the name of the Homeric poem describing the ten years' wandering of Odysseus. - L. *Odyssēa* - Gr. *Odússeia*, f. *Odusseús*.

oecology, oecumenical vars. of ECOLOGY, ECUMENICAL.

oedema (path.) swelling produced by serous fluid. XVI. - late L. - Gr. *oidēma, -mat-*, f. *oidein* swell. Hence **oedematous** XVII.

œillade amorous glance. XVI. - F., f. *œil* (:- L. *oculus* EYE); see -ADE.

oeno- comb. form of Gr. *oînos* WINE.

oesophagus XIV. - medL. - Gr. *oisophágos*, of which the first el. is unkn. and the second appears to be *-phagos* eating.

oestrus gadfly XVII; frenzy XIX. - L. - Gr. *oistros*.

of prep. OE. *of*, orig. stressless var. of *æf* (surviving only as prefix), corr. to OS., MLG., (M)Du., ON., Goth. *af*, OHG. *aba* :- Gmc. adv. and prep. **ab(a)* :- IE. **ap(o)*, repr. also by L. *ab*, Gr. *apó*, Lith. *apa-*, Skr. *ápa* away from, down

of- assim. form of OB- before *f*.

off adv. away, so as to be separated, discontinued, etc.; prep. away from, in detachment from. Var. of OF from XV, but not finally differentiated from it until after 1600 in the above uses. **off-hand** without preparation or premeditation XVII; adj. †impromptu; free and easy, unceremonious XVIII.

offal (techn., dial.) shavings, chips, scraps XIV; entrails XV; refuse, garbage XVI. - (M)Du. *afval*, f. *af* OFF + *vallen* FALL, with assim. to the corr. Eng. elements.

offence, U.S. **offense** (arch.) stumbling, stumbling-block; attack; †harm, damage; act of offending; displeasure; breach of law or decorum. XIV. ME. *offens(e)* - (O)F. *offens* - L. *offensus* annoyance, and (O)F. *offense* - L. *offensa* striking against, hurt, wrong, displeasure; both L. forms f. *offens-*, pp. stem of *offendere*, whence (or from the deriv. OF. *ofendre*) **offend** †stumble; †wrong; †attack; wound the feelings of. XIV. See OF-, and cf. DEFEND. So **offensive** pert. to attack; †injurious; repulsive. XVI. - F. *offensif, -ive* or medL.

offer present as an act of worship OE.; tender for acceptance or refusal XIV; propose *to do* XV; propound XVI. OE. *offrian* sacrifice, bring an offering = OS. *offron* (Du. *offeren*), ON. *offra*; an early Gmc. adoption of L. *offerre* present, offer, bestow, f. OF- + *ferre* bring, BEAR[2]. Reinforced in ME. from (O)F. *offrir*, which brought in the primary senses. Hence **offering** (-ING[1]) OE. *offrung*. **offer** sb. XV. So **offertory** passage recited at the offering of bread and wine at the Eucharist XIV; the offering itself XVI. - ecclL. *offertōrium* place of offering, oblation; see -ORY[1].

office duty, (obligatory) service; position to which duties are attached; †introit XIII; form of divine service; place for transacting business XIV. - (O)F. - L. *officium*, orig. performance of a task :- **opificium*, f. *opus* work + *-fic-*, *facere* DO[1]. So **officer** (-ER[2]) one who holds office XIV; (in army, navy, etc.) XVI. - AN. *officer*, (O)F. *officier* - medL. *officiārius*. **official** (-AL[1]) sb. XIV. Partly - (O)F. *official*, partly sb. use of adj. (XVI) - L. *officiālis*. **officiate** XVII. f. pp. stem of medL. *officiāre* perform divine service.

officinal (of a herb) used in medicine and the arts; (of remedies) sold 'in the shops', made up according to the pharmacopoeia. XVIII. - medL. *officīnālis*, f. L. *officīna* workshop, manufactory, laboratory, for *opificīna*, f. *opifex, -fic-* workman, f. *opus* work + *-fic-*, *facere* DO[1]; see -AL[1].

officious †eager to please or serve; †dutiful XVI; importunate in offering service; †official XVII; (in diplomatic use) friendly and informal XIX. - L. *officiōsus* (or F. *officieux*), f. *officium* OFFICE; see -IOUS.

offing part of the sea visible to an observer on shore or ship; position at a distance off shore. XVII. perh. f. OFF + -ING[1].

offspring OE. *ofspring*, f. OF †'from' + *springan* SPRING[2].

oft (arch.) many times. OE. *oft* = OS. *oft(o)*, OHG. *ofto* (G. *oft*), ON. *opt, oft*, Goth. *ufta*; Gmc. adv., of uncert. orig. In ME. extended to *ofte* (XII), whence, by further extension (prob. after *selden* SELDOM), **often** XIV. The comps. *oft-times* (XIV) and *often-times* (XV), repl. †*oft(e)sithe(s)* XIII, repr. OE. *oftsīðum* d. pl., *on oftsīðas* on frequent occasions (partly also the corr. ON. *optsinnis, -sinnum*).

ogdoad the number 8, group of eight. XVII. - late L. *ogdoas, -ad-* - Gr. *ogdoás, -ad-*, f. *ógdoos* eighth, *oktṓ* EIGHT; see -AD.

ogee †ogive XV; S-shaped double curve XVII. prob. reduced form of *ogive*, perh. through the pl. form *ogi(v)es*.

og(h)am alphabet of the ancient British and Irish. XVII. - OIr. *ogam, ogum* (modIr. *ogham*, Gael. *oghum*), traditionally assoc. with the name *Ogma* of the supposed inventor.

ogive (archit.) diagonal rib of a vault. XVII. - F. *ogive*, earlier *augive, orgive*, of unkn. orig. So **ogival** XIX.

ogle XVII. prob. of LG. or Du. orig.; cf. LG. *oegeln*, frequent. of *oegen* look at, also early modDu. *oogheler, oegeler* flatterer, *oogen* cast sheep's eyes at. See -LE[3].

ogre XVIII (*hogre*). - F.; of unkn. orig. Hence **ogress** XVIII.

oh XVI. var. of O, formerly used in positions where *O* is now more usual, now chiefly as an excl. of pain, terror, surprise, or disapproval. - F. *oh*, L. *ōh*.

ohm unit of electrical resistance. XIX. f. name of Georg Simon *Ohm*, German physicist (1787-1854).

oho excl. combining O with HO. XIV.

ohone excl. of lament. XV. - Gael., Ir. *ochòin*.

-oid suffix equiv. to *-form, -like*, repr. F. *-oïde*, L. *-oīdēs*, from Gr. *-oeidḗs*, f. *-o-* + *eîdos* form, shape. So **-oidal** (-AL[1]).

oil in early use, liquid expressed from the olive; later, any similar viscid smooth liquid. XII. ME. *oli(e), oile* - AN., ONF. *olie*, OF. *oile* (mod.

huile) - L. *oleum* (olive) oil, for **oleiuom*, **olaiwom* - Gr. *élai(ϝ)on*; cf. OLIVE. The adoption from F. ousted OE., ME. *ele* = OS., OHG. *oli* (Du. *olie*, G. *öl*) - popL. *olium*, L. *oleum*. Hence **oily** (-Y[1]) XVI.

ointment XIV. alt., after †*oint* vb. (XIV), of earlier †*oi(g)nement* (XIII) - OF. *oignement* :- popL. **unguimentum*, f. L. *unguentum* UNGUENT; see -MENT.

O.K. XIX (orig. U.S.). app. f. the initial letters of *oll korrect*, joc. alt. or dial. pronunc. of *all correct*; also, initials of *Old Kinderhook* (near Albany), name of the birthplace of a Democratic candidate, Martin Van Buren, used as a slogan.

-ol (chem.) terminal syll. of *alcohol*, used to form names of substances which are alcohols in the wider sense, or compounds analogous to alcohol, e.g. *methol*, *naphthol*, *phenol*. From *phenol* the ending has been transferred to the phenol group.

old OE. (as a familiar epithet XIV). OE. (Angl.) *ald* (WS. *eald*) = OS. *ald* (Du. *oud*), (O)HG. *alt* :- WGmc. **alða* (cf. ON. compar. *ellri* ELDER[2], superl. *ellztr* ELDEST, Goth. *alþeis* old); pp. formation on the base of OE. *alan*, ON. *ala* nourish, Goth. *alan* grow up, rel. to L. *alere* nourish, with the parallel formation *altus* high, deep. Hence **olden** (-EN[3]) ancient. XV.

oleaginous XVI. - F. *oléagineux*, f. L. *oleāginus*, f. *oleum* OIL; see -OUS.

oleander XVI. - medL. *oleander*, *oliandrum*; of obscure orig.

oleo- used as comb. form of (i) L. *oleum* OIL (XVIII), as in **oleograph** picture printed in oil-colours, (ii) *oleic*, *olein*, as in **oleomargarine** (XIX).

olfactory pert. to the sense of smell. XVII. - L. **olfactōrius*, f. *olfactāre*, frequent. of *olfacere* smell (trans.), f. *olēre*; see -ORY[2].

olibanum aromatic gum-resin. XIV. - medL., ult. repr. Gr. *libanos* frankincense tree, incense (of Sem. orig.).

oligarchy XVII. - (O)F. *oligarchie* or medL. *oligarchia* - Gr. *oligarkhíā*, f. *oligárkhēs* (whence **oligarch** XVII), f. *oligos* few; see -ARCH.

oligocene see EOCENE.

olio dish consisting of a medley of meats, vegetables, etc.; hotchpotch, miscellany. XVII. alt. of Sp. *olla* (Pg. *olha*) :- Rom. **olla*, for L. *ōlla* pot, jar.

olive (fruit of) the evergreen tree *Olea europaea*. XIII. - (O)F. - L. *olīva* - Gr. *elaí(ϝ)ā*, rel. to *élai(ϝ)on* OIL. Hence **olivaceous** XVII.

olla podrida olio. XVI. - Sp., 'rotten pot'; *olla* (see OLIO), *podrida* putrid.

-ology (see -O-, -LOGY); as sb. any of the sciences or departments thereof. XIX.

Olympiad period of four years between celebrations of the Olympic games (ancient Gr. festival). XVI. - F. *Olympiade* or L. *Olympias*, *-ad-* - Gr. *Olumpiás*, f. *Olúmpios*, adj. of *O'lumpos* lofty mountain in Thessaly, Greece, home of the gods in Gr. myth.; see -AD. So **Olympian, Olympic** XVI.

-oma suffix repr. modL. *-ōma* - Gr. *-ōma*, as in *rhízōma*, *sárkōma*, *tríkhōma*, f. vbs. in *-oûsthai*, as *rhizoûsthai* take root, f. *rhiza* ROOT. (i) Used to denote a formation or member of the nature of that denoted by the radical part; now superseded by **-ome**, as in RHIZOME; (ii) used in names of tumours or other morbid growths, as SARCOMA.

ombre card-game played by three persons with 40 cards. XVII (earlier also *l'hombre*, *l'ombre*). - Sp. *hombre* (:- L. *hominem*, nom. *homō* man); cf. F. *(h)ombre* chief player at ombre, and the game itself.

omega last letter of the Gr. alphabet (Ω, ω); last of a series, end. XVI. - Gr. *ô méga* (cf. MEGA-) 'great o'.

omelet(te) XVII (also *aumelet*, *am(m)ulet*, *amlet*). - F. *omelette*, also †*a(u)melette*, metath. alt. of †*alumette*, by-form of †*alumelle*, †*alemel(l)e*, which arose from *lemele* blade of a sword or knife, by wrong analysis of *la lemel(l)e* (- L. *lamella*, dim. of *lamina* thin plate of metal); the omelette is presumed to have been named from its thin flat shape.

omen XVI. - L. *ōmen*, *ōmin-*, of uncert. orig. So **ominous** XVI. - L. *ōminōsus*.

omentum (anat.) caul. XVI. - L.

-ometer the el. -METER preceded by -O-, as in *gasometer*.

omit XV. - L. *omittere*, f. OB- + *mittere* send, let go. So **omission** XIV. - (O)F. or late L.

omni- comb. form of L. *omnis* all, as in **omnipotent** XIV (- (O)F. -L.), **omnipresent** XVII (- medL.), **omniscience, -scient** XVII (- medL.), **omnivorous** XVII (f. L. *omnivorus*).

omnibus XIX. - F. *omnibus*, also *voiture omnibus* carriage for all (L. *omnibus*, d. pl. of *omnis* all).

omnium gatherum gathering of all sorts, miscellaneous assemblage. XVI. f. L. *omnium* g. pl. of *omnis* all + mock-L. formation on GATHER, for 'a gathering'.

omoplate (anat.) shoulder-blade. XVI. - Gr. *ōmoplátē*, f. *ômos* shoulder + *plátē* broad surface, blade.

omphal(o)- comb. form of Gr. *omphalós* NAVEL. XVII.

on prep. and adv. expressing the relation of contact with or proximity to a surface (hence with implication of support by it) and motion to or toward a position (later often expressed by *on to*, *onto* XVI); in early use covering also some of the uses now expressed by *in* and *at*. OE. *on*, orig. unstressed var. of *an* = OS., OHG. *ana*, *an* (Du. *aan*, G. *an*), ON. *á*, Goth. *ana*, rel. to Gr. *aná*, *ána* on, upon, Skr. *ā* up, Av. *ana*, OSl. *na*. Hence **onward(s)** XVI.

onager wild ass. XIV (afterwards not before XVIII). - L. - Gr. *ónagros* for *ónos ágrios* (*ónos* ass, *ágrios* wild).

onanism XVIII. - F. or modL. *onanismus*, f. *Onan* (Gen. 38: 9); see -ISM.

once one time only XII; at any one time, on any occasion XIV. ME. *ānes*, *ōnes*, g. of *ān*, *ōn* ONE (see -S), finally superseding *ēnes*, OE. *ǣnes*, which repl. adv. instr. *ǣne* (ME. *ene*) of *ān* ONE; cf. MDu. *eenes*, MLG. *ēnes*, MHG. *ein(e)s*, G. *einst*. Hence **at once** XIII.

one OE. *ān* = OS. *ēn* (Du. *een*), (O)HG. *ein*, ON. *einn*, Goth. *ains* :- Gmc. **ainaz* :- IE. **oinos*, whence also OL. *oinos*, L. *ūnus*, OSl. *inŭ* other,

Lith *víenas*, OIr. *óen*, *óin*; in other langs. with other suffixes, as Skr. *éka-* one, Gr. *oî(ϝ)os* alone.

-one (chem.) used in the names of various compounds. - Gr. *-ōnē* fem. patronymic suffix.

oneiro- comb. form of Gr. *óneiros* dream, as in **oneiromancy** (XVII).

onerous XIV. - (O)F. *onéreux* - L. *onerōsus*, f. *oner-*, ONUS; see -OUS.

onion XIV. ME. *unyon*, *oyn(y)on* - AN. *union*, (O)F. *oignon*, L. *uniōnem*, nom. *unio*.

only (dial.) solitary; of which there are no others OE.; single XV. OE. *ānlić*, late var. of *ǣnlić* corr. to MLG. *einlīk*, MDu. *een(e)lijc*. Hence adv. ME. *onliche* (XIII); partly alt. of OE. *ǣnlīce*, after the adj., partly developed from predic. uses of the adj. See ONE, -LY[1,2].

onomatopoeia word-formation based on imitation. XVI. late L. - Gr. *onomatopoiíā* making of words, f. *onomatopoiós*, f. *ónoma*, *-mat-* NAME + *-poios* -making. Hence **onomatopoeic**, **-poetic** XIX.

onslaught XVII. Early forms also *anslaight*, *onslat* - early MDu. *aenslag* (mod. *aan-*), f. *aan* ON + *slag* blow, stroke, rel. to *slagen* strike, SLAY[1]; with assim. (XVII) to †*slaught*, OE. *slæht* SLAUGHTER.

ontology study of being. XVIII. - modL. *ontologia*, f. Gr. *onto-*, comb. form of *ón*, g. *óntos* being, n. of *ṓn*, prp. of *eînai* be; see -LOGY.

onus burden of responsibility. XVII. - L. 'burden'.

onymous bearing a name (as of the author). XVIII. Extracted from ANONYMOUS.

onyx XIII (*oniche*). - OF. *oniche*, *onix* - L. acc. *onycha*, nom. *onyx* - Gr. *ónukha*, *ónux* NAIL, claw, onyx stone.

oo- comb. form of Gr. *ōión* EGG, ovum, in scientific terms, as **oolite** (min. and geol.) XVIII (- F. *oölithe*, modL. *oolitēs*), **oology** XIX (- F. *oölogie*, modL. *oologia*), **oospore** XIX.

oof (sl.) money. XIX. Shortening of *ooftish*, Yiddish for G. *auf tisch*, i.e. *auf dem tisch* on the table, said of money laid on the table in gambling.

-oon repr. F. *-on* in words with stress on the final syll. adopted XVI-XVIII, e.g. *dragoon*, as distinguished from the *-on* of adoptions from AN. (OF.), e.g. *baron*, *felon*, and of more modern adoptions, e.g. *chignon*; hence repr. gen. F. dim. *-on*, and the corr. It. augm. *-one*, Sp. augm. *-on* - L. *-ōnem*, nom. *-ō*, forming sbs. of the nickname or pejorative type, e.g. *balatrō* jester, *nāsō* big-nosed man; exx. of various types of deriv. are *balloon*, *buffoon*, *cartoon*, *harpoon*, *lampoon*, *macaroon*, *platoon*, *quadroon*; rarely used as an Eng. formative, as in *spittoon*.

ooze[1] †juice, sap OE.; liquor of a tan vat, decoction of bark XVI; (from the vb.) exudation XVIII. OE. *wōs*, corr. to MLG. *wōs(e)* scum, ON. *vás*. Cf. next. Hence **ooze** vb. exude, cause to exude XIV; percolate as through pores XVIII. ME. *wōse*. Now assoc. with OOZE[2].

ooze[2] mud, slime. OE. *wāse* = OFris. *wāse*, ON. *veisa* stagnant pool, puddle.

op- assim. form of OB- before *p*.

opal XVI. - F. *opale* or L. *opalus*, prob. ult. (like late Gr. *opállios*) - Skr. *úpala-* stone. Hence **opalescent** XIX.

opaque (arch.) dark, dull XV; not transparent XVII. - L. *opācus*, partly through F. *opaque*. So **opacity** XVII. - F. - L.

ope (arch.) open (adj.). XIII. Clipped form of OPEN, with loss of *n* as in pps. *awake*, *bespoke*. Hence vb. XV.

open not shut, confined, or covered (with many fig. uses). OE. *open* = OS. *opan* (Du. *open*), OHG. *offan* (G. *offen*), ON. *opinn* :- Gmc. **upanaz*, having the form of a strong pp. (see -EN[6]) f. UP, as if meaning 'put or set up'. Hence **open** vb. OE. *openian* = OS. *opanon* (Du. *openen*), OHG. *offanōn* (G. *öffnen*).

opera XVII. - It. :- L. *opera* labour, work produced, fem. coll. corr. to *opus*, *oper-* work (see OPUS). Hence **operatic** XVIII. irreg., after *dramatic*. So (dim.) **operetta** XVIII. - It.

operate †produce an effect; effect, produce, bring about XVII; (orig. U.S.) cause or direct the working of XIX. f. *operāt-*, pp. stem of L. *operārī* work, bestow labour upon, f. *oper-*, OPUS; see -ATE[3]. So **operation** working, performance XIV; surgical act XVI; (mil., math.) XVIII. - (O)F. - L. **operative** XVI; sb. worker XIX. - late L. **operator** XVI. - late L.

operculum (zool., etc.) cover, lid. XVIII. - L., f. *operīre* cover, close, parallel formation to *aperīre* open; see -CULE.

operose laborious (subjectively and objectively). XVII. - L. *operōsus*, f. *oper-*, OPUS; see -OSE[1].

ophicleide musical wind-instrument developed from the ancient 'serpent'. XIX. - F. *ophicléïde*, f. Gr. *óphis* serpent (see next) + *kleís*, *kleid-* key, rel. to L. *clāvis* (see CLEF).

ophidian serpent-like. XIX. f. modL. *Ophidia* order of reptiles, f. Gr. *óphis*, *ophid-* serpent; see -IAN. The comb. form of *óphis* (used in scientific terms) is **ophi(o)-**. So **ophite** XVII. - L. *ophītēs* - Gr. *ophī́tēs* serpentine.

ophthalmia inflammation of the eye. XVI (earlier not naturalized). - late L. - Gr. *ophthalmíā*, f. *ophthalmós* EYE; see -IA[1]. So **ophthalmic** XVII. - L. - Gr.

opiate containing opium, narcotic XVI; sb. XVII. - medL. *opiātus*; see OPIUM, -ATE[2].

opinion what one thinks, belief XIII; estimate, estimation XIV. - (O)F. - L. *opīniō*, *-ōn-*, f. stem of *opīnārī* think, believe (whence **opine** XVI). Hence **opinionated** XVII. f. †*opinionate* (XVI). **opinionative** XVI.

opistho- comb. form of Gr. *ópisthen* behind, as in **opisthograph** manuscript written on the back as well as the front (XVII; - Gr. *opisthógraphos*).

opium XIV (anglicized †*opie*). - L. - Gr. *ópion*, dim. of *opós* vegetable juice.

opodeldoc in the work of Paracelsus (*opodeltoch*) applied to various medical plasters and believed to have been invented by him. XVII.

opopanax fetid gum-resin from the root of *Opopanax chironium*. XIV. - L. - Gr. *opopánax*, f. *opós* juice + *pánax*, n. of *panakḗs* all-healing; see PANACEA.

opossum XVII. of Algonquian orig.

oppidan townsman; spec. of a member of Eton

College who boards in the town. XVI. - L. *oppidānus*, f. *oppidum* (fortified) town; see -AN.

oppilation obstruction. XIV. - late L. *oppīlātiō*, *-ōn-*, f. L. *oppīlāre* stop up, f. OP- + *pīlāre* ram down, stop up; see -ATION.

opponent one who maintains a contrary argument XVI; antagonist XVII. - L. *oppōnēns*, *-ent-*, prp. of *oppōnere* set against, f. OP- + *pōnere* place.

opportune XV. - (O)F. *opportun*, fem. *-une* - L. *opportūnus* (orig. of wind) driving towards the harbour, (hence) seasonable, f. OP- + *portus* harbour, PORT¹. So **opportunity** XIV. **opportunism, opportunist** XIX. - It. *opportunismo*, F. *opportunisme*, etc.

oppose †confront with objections, pose, appose XIV; set against in opposition XVI. - (O)F. *opposer*, based on L. *oppōnere*; see OPPONENT, POSE¹. So **opposite** placed over against XIV; contrary XVI. - (O)F. - L. *oppositus*, pp. of *oppōnere*. **opposition** (astron. and astrol.) XIV; contrary or hostile action XVI; (of a party) XVIII.

oppress †press hard upon, put down, quell; lie heavy on; keep under wrongfully or tyrannously. XIV. - (O)F. *oppresser* - medL. *oppressāre*, f. *oppress-*, pp. stem of *opprimere*, f. OP- + *premere* PRESS¹. So **oppression** XIV. - (O)F. - L. **oppressive** XVII. - F. - medL.

opprobrious XIV. - late L. *opprobriōsus*, f. *opprobrium* (in Eng. use from XVII) infamy, reproach, f. OP- + *probrum* shameful deed, disgrace; see -IOUS.

oppugn †assault, besiege XV; assail in speech or action XVI. - L. *oppugnāre* fight against, f. OP- + *pugnāre* (see PUGNACIOUS).

opsimathy learning acquired late in life. XVII. - Gr. *opsimathíā*, f. *opsimathḗs* (whence **opsimath** XIX), f. *opsi-*, *opsé* late + **math-* (see MATHEMATIC); see -Y³.

opt XIX. - F. *opter* - L. *optāre* choose, desire. So **optative** (gram.) expressing wish. XVI. - F. *optatif*, *-ive* - late L. *optātīvus*. **option** choice. XVII. - F. or L.; whence **optional** XVIII.

optic pert. to sight or the organ of sight. XVI. - (O)F. *optique* or medL. *opticus* - Gr. *optikós*, f. *optós* seen, visible, f. **op-*; see EYE, -IC. So **optical, optics** XVI.

optimism doctrine of Leibniz that the present world is the best of all possible worlds XVIII; view that presumes the predominance of good; disposition to hope for or expect the best XIX. - F. *optimisme*, f. L. *optimum*, sb. use of n. of *optimus* best; see -ISM. So **optimist** XVIII, **optimum** XIX.

opulent abundantly wealthy. XVII. - L. *opulēns*, *-ent-* or *opulentus*, f. **ops*, pl. *opes* resources, wealth; see -ULENT. So **opulence** XVI.

opus work, esp. musical composition. XVIII (first in *magnum o.*, *o. magnum* great work). - L., rel. to Skr. *ápa-*. So **opuscule** XVII. - (O)F. - L. **opusculum** XVII.

or¹ (adv., prep., conj.) before; sooner, ere; rather than. XIII (from XV often in *or ever*, *or e'er*, *or ere*). late Nhb. OE. *ār* early, ME. (in Scandinavianized areas) *ār*, later *ǫr* - ON. *ár* = OE. *ǣr* ERE.

or² particle introducing an alternative. XII. reduced form of †*other* (XII-XV), app. alt. of OE. *oððe* by assim. of the ending to words expressing an alternative, as *either*, *whether* (cf. the alt. of OHG. *odo*, MHG. *ode*, to *odar*, *oder* by assim. to *weder* neither).

or³ (her.) the tincture gold or yellow. XVI. - (O)F. :- L. *aurum*.

-or¹ suffix of agent-nouns repr. ult. (i) L. *-or* chiefly as appended to pp. stems, as in the comp. forms -TOR, -ATOR, *-itor*, and *-(s)sor* (e.g. *censor*, *oppressor*, *sponsor*); (ii) L. *-ātōrem*, *-itōrem* (nom. *-ātor*, *-itor*), whence OF. *-ëo(u)r*, later and mod. *-eur* (see -OUR¹). It has been generalized in legal use for the terms corr. to those in -EE¹. In, e.g., *bachelor*, *chancellor*, *sailor*, *-or* has superseded other endings.

-or² suffix forming (orig.) abstr. sbs., as in *error*, *horror*, *liquor*, *pallor*, *squalor*, *terror*, repr. ult. L. *-or*, earlier *-ōs* (e.g. *colōs* COLOUR, *honōs* HONOUR), corr. to Skr. *-as*, Gr. *-as*, and rel. for the most part to intr. vbs. in *-ēre*. The earliest forms of the above words were in *-our*, which is the current British spelling in others of the same type (see -OUR²).

orach(e) plant of the genus *Atriplex*. XV (*orage*, *arage*). - AN. *arasche*, OF. *arache*, *arrace* (mod. *arroche*) :- L. *atriplex*, *-plic-* - Gr. *atráphaxus*.

oracle mouthpiece of a deity; divine revelation or message XIV; holy of holies in the Jewish temple XV; authoritative or infallible guide XVI. - (O)F. - L. *ōrāculum*, f. *ōrāre* speak, pray, ORATE; see -CLE. So **oracular** XVII.

oral pert. to the mouth or to speech. XVII. - late L. *ōrālis*, f. L. *ōs*, *ōr-* mouth; see -AL¹.

orange (fruit of) an evergreen tree, *Citrus aurantium* XIV (*orenge*). - OF. *orenge* in *pomme d'orenge*, later and mod. *orange*; ult. - Arab. *nāranj* - Pers. *nārang*. So **orangeade** XVIII.

Orange name of a town (*Arausio* in the ancient province of Gallia Narbonensis) on the Rhône in France, which in 1530 passed to the house of Nassau and so to the ancestors of William III of England ('William of O.', i.e. O.-Nassau), after whom were named (late XVIII) the O. lodges, Orangemen, and O. boys of an ultra-Protestant party in Ireland formally constituted into a secret society in 1795. The coincidence of this name with that of the fruit made the wearing of orange-coloured badges a symbol of attachment to William III and of membership of the O. Society.

orang-utan, -outang XVII. - Malay *orang utan* jungle dweller, prob. through Du. *orang oetang*; prop. the Malay name for wild races of men misapplied by Europeans.

orator †advocate XIV; †petitioner; (eloquent) public speaker XV; as a university official XVII. - AN. *oratour* = (O)F. *orateur* - L. *ōrātor*, *-ōr-* speaker, pleader, f. pp. stem of *ōrāre*, whence (or in part back-formation) **orate** †plead XVI; deliver a speech XVIII; see -ATE³, -ATOR. So **oration** †petition XIV; formal speech XVI. - L. *ōrātiō*, *-ōn-* formal language, discourse, advocate's speech, (eccl.) prayer.

oratorio XVIII. - It. - ecclL. *ōrātōrium* ORATORY¹; so named from the musical performances held in the church of the *Oratory* of St. Philip Neri in Rome from the latter part of XVI.

oratory¹ place of prayer, esp. a small chapel XIV; title of certain religious congregations in

R.C.Ch. (orig. of the O. of St. Philip Neri established in 1564) XVII. - AN. *oratorie* = (O)F. *oratoire*, It. *oratorio* - ecclL. *ōrātōrium*, sb. use of n. of *ōrātōrius*, f. *ōrāt-*; see ORATOR, -ORY[1].

oratory[2] art of the orator, eloquent speaking. XVI. - L. *ōrātōria*, sb. use of fem. of *ōrātōrius*, f. *ōrātor*; see ORATOR, -ORY[2]. Hence, or directly f. L. *ōrātorius*, **oratorical** XVII.

orb †(old astron.) hollow sphere surrounding the earth; †circle, ring; heavenly body XVI; eyeball, eye XVII; cross-surmounted globe of the regalia XVIII. - L. *orbis* ring, round surface, disc. Hence **orbed** (-ED[2]) XVI. So **orbicular** circular, spherical. XVI. - late L. *orbiculāris*, f. L. *orbiculus*, dim. of *orbis*; see -CULE, -AR.

orbit eye-socket XVI; path of a heavenly body XVII. - L. *orbita* wheel-track, course, path (of the moon), in medL. eye-cavity, sb. use of fem. of *orbitus* circular, f. *orbis*, *orb-* ORB.

orc †ferocious (sea-)monster; cetacean of the genus *Orca*. XVI. - F. *orque* or L. *orca* kind of whale - Gr. *óruga*, acc. of *órux* ORYX.

orchard OE. *ortġeard*, *orċe(a)rd* garden, orchard = Goth. *aurtigards* garden; the first element is prob. - L. *hortus* garden; the second is YARD[1].

orchestra in the ancient Gr. theatre, semicircular area for the chorus XVII; part of a theatre, etc., assigned to musicians; band of musicians itself XVIII. - L. *orchēstra* - Gr. *orkhḗstrā*, f. *orkheîsthai* dance. Hence **orchestral** XIX.

orchid XIX. f. modL. *Orchideæ* or *Orchidaceæ*, f. *orchid-*, wrongly assumed stem of L. *orchis* - Gr. *órkhis* testicle, applied to the plants from the shape of the tubers in most species.

orchil dye prepared from lichens XV; lichen *Roccella* XVIII. - OF. *orcheil*, *orcele*, *orseil* (mod. *orseille*), of uncert. orig.

ordain confer (holy) orders upon; appoint, decree; †arrange, dispose. XIII. ME. *ordeine* - AN *ordeiner* = OF. *ordener*, later *-oner* (mod. *-onner*) - L. *ōrdināre*, f. *ōrdō*, *ōrdin-* ORDER.

ordeal ancient mode of trial by subjection to a dangerous physical test OE.; trying experience XVII. OE. *ordāl*, *ordēl* (whence AL. *ordālium*, etc.) = OS. *urdēli* (Du. *oordeel*), OHG. *urteili* (G. *urteil*) judgement :- Gmc. **uzdailjam*, corr. to OE. *ādǣlan*, OS. *ādēlian*, OHG. *ar-*, *irteilan* (G. *urteilen*) adjudge as one's share, give judgement :- Gmc. **uzdailjan* share out, f. **uz-* out- + **dailjan* (Goth. *-dailjan*) DEAL[1]. In ME. recorded only in the form *ordal*, prob. from medL. *ordālium*; thereafter in forms also dependent on medL. (*ordale*, *ordele*) until XVII, when the present form *ordeal* became current through etymol. assoc. with DEAL[1].

order A. rank of angels; grade in the Christian ministry; (gen.) rank, grade; monastic society or fraternity XII (*o. of chivalry*, etc. XIV); (archit.) system of parts in established proportions XVI; (math.) degree of complexity of form; higher group of animals, etc. XVIII; B. sequence, disposition; method of procedure or action XIV (*in o. to*, *take o.* XVI); condition of observance of law and usage XV; C. regulation, direction, mandate XVI. ME. *ordre* - (O)F. *ordre*, earlier *ordene* - L. *ōrdinem*, nom. *ōrdō* row, etc., rel. to *ōrdīrī* begin, *ōrnāre* ADORN. Hence **orderly** arranged in or observant of order XVI; charged with the conveyance or execution of orders XVIII (*o. man*, *officer*, †*sergeant*, hence as sb., by ellipsis). So **ordinal** †(rare) regular, orderly XIV; (of numbers) XVI; (nat. hist.) pert. to an order XIX. - late L. *ōrdinālis*. **ordinal** sb. book of the order of divine service XIV; form of ordination XVII. - medL. *ōrdināle*, n. sg. of *ōrdinālis*. **ordinance** A. (arch.) regular arrangement; authoritative direction; prescribed usage XIV; B. †provision, supply; spec. military supplies (now *ordnance*) XIV. - OF. *ordenance* (now *ordonnance*) - medL. *ōrdinantia*, f. *ōrdināre* ORDAIN. **ordinand** one about to be ordained. XIX. **ordinary** A. (eccl. and leg.) one having immediate jurisdiction or authority in juridical matters; B. book of divine service; C. sb. uses of the adj. from XVI. - AN., OF. *ordinarie* (later and mod. *ordinaire*) - medL. *ōrdinārius*, and in n. sg. *ōrdinārium*. So adj. belonging to the regular order or course; having regular jurisdiction XV; of the usual kind XVI. - L. *ōrdinārius* orderly, usual; see -ARY. **ordination** XV. - (O)F. or L., f. *ordināre* ORDAIN. **ordnance** XVII (see ORDINANCE). **ordonnance** systematic arrangement. XVII. - F., alt. of OF. *ordenance*, after F. *ordonner*.

ordure XIV. - (O)F. *ordure*, f. *ord* filthy :- L. *horridus* HORRID; see -URE.

ore OE. *ōra* unwrought metal (corr. to Du. *oer*, LG. *ūr*, of unkn. orig.), repr. by *oor(e)*, *(o)ure* from XIV to XVII; superseded by the descendant of OE. *ār* = OS., OHG. *ēr*, ON. *eir*, Goth. *aiz* :- Gmc. **aiz*, corr. to L. *æs* crude metal, bronze, money.

oread mountain nymph. XVI. - L. *Orēas*, *-ad-* - Gr. *Oreiás*, *-ad-*, f. *óros* mountain; see -AD.

oreography, oreology see OROGRAPHY.

orfray see ORPHREY.

organ in versions of the Bible and allusions thereto, applied to various instruments of music XIII; musical instrument consisting of pipes supplied with wind and sounded by keys XIV; instrument or means of function XV. - OF. *organe*, *orgene* (mod. *orgue*) - L. *organum* instrument, engine, musical instrument - Gr. *órganon*, f. IE. **worĝ-* **werĝ-* WORK. So **organic** †serving as an organ XVI; pert. to organs or an organized body XVIII (chem. XIX). - F. - L. **organism** †organic structure XVII; organized system or body XVIII. - F. **organist** XVI. - F. - medL. **organize** XV. - (O)F. - medL.

organdie XIX. - F., of unkn. orig.

orgasm paroxysm of excitement. XVII. - F. *orgasme* or modL. *orgasmus* - Gr. *orgasmós*, f. *orgân* swell as with moisture, be excited.

orgy (in pl.) secret rites of the worship of Greek and Roman deities, etc. XVI; (sg.) licentious revel XVIII. orig. pl. - F. *orgies* - L. *orgia* - Gr. *órgia* n. pl., f. IE. **worĝ-* **werĝ-* WORK; see -Y[3]. So **orgiastic** XVII. - Gr. *orgiastikós*.

-orial suffix combining L. *-ōrius* -ORY[2] and *-ālis* -AL[1], and usu. identical in sense with *-ory*, e.g. *inquisitorial*, *territorial*, *visitatorial*; it is preferred where there is a sb. in *-ory*, e.g. *purgatory/purgatorial*.

oriel †porch; gallery, balcony, upper storey XIV; windowed recess projecting from a building XV; *o. window* XVIII. ME. *oriole* - OF. *oriol, eurieul* passage, gallery, of unkn. orig.

orient[1] adj. eastern, (hence, of stones) precious, excellent; sb. *the* East, eastern lands. XIV. - (O)F. - L. *oriēns, -ent-* rising, rising sun, east, prp. of *orīrī* rise; see -ENT. So **oriental** XIV - (O)F. or L.

orient[2] place so as to face the east XVIII; determine the bearings of; (refl.) ascertain one's bearings XIX. - F. *orienter*, f. *orient*; see prec. So, by extension with -ATE[3], **orientate** XIX; prob. after **orientation** situation so as to face east (of a church, east and west), bearing or lie of a thing, determination of bearings XIX, which appears to be directly f. *orient* vb.

orifice XVI. - (O)F. - late L. *ōrificium*, f. *ōs, ōri-* mouth (see ORAL) + *fic-*, var. of *facere* make, DO[1].

oriflamme sacred banner of St. Denis, of red or orange-coloured silk. XV (also *-flambe*). - (O)F. *oriflambe, -flamme*, in medL. *auriflamma*, f. *aurum* gold + *flamma* FLAME.

origanum wild marjoram, etc. XVI. - L. - Gr. *orīganon*, of unkn. orig.

origin descent, ancestry XIV; point or place of beginning. XVI. - F. *origine* or L. *orīgō, orīgin-*, f. *orīrī* rise. So **original** pert. to origin (first of *o. sin* XIV); sb. †origin; pattern, exemplar XIV; singular or eccentric person XVII. - (O)F. *original* or L. *orīginālis*. **origination** XVII. - F. - L. *orīginātiō* derivation of words, f. pp. stem of **orīgināre*, whence **originate** (-ATE[3]) XVII.

oriole name of various yellow-plumaged birds. XVIII. - med. and modL. *oriolus* - OF. *oriol* :- L. *aureolus*, f. *aureus* golden, f. *aurum* gold.

-orious comp. suffix forming adjs. by the addition of -OUS to L. *-ōri-* of *-ōrius* -ORY[2], with which and -ORIAL it is mainly synonymous, but not of like currency.

orison (arch.) prayer. ME. *ureisun, oreison, oriso(u)n* - AN. *ur-*, OF. *oreison, orison* (now *oraison*) :- L. *ōrātiō, -ōn-* speech, ORATION.

-orium suffix repr. n. sg. of L. *-ōrius*, used in sbs. denoting 'place of . .', 'thing used or requisite for . .', as in *auditorium, crematorium, sanatorium*, and in such techn. terms as *sensorium* seat of sensation. Cf. -ORY[1].

orle (her.) band round the shield. XVI. - (O)F. *orle* (cf. mod. *ourlet* hem), f. *ourler* hem :- Rom. **ōrulāre*, f. **ōrula*, dim. of L. *ōra* edge, border.

orlop (orig.) floor or deck with which a ship's hold was covered in; (later) lowest deck. XV (*overloppe*). - (M)Du. *overloop*, f. *overloopen* run over; see OVER-, LEAP.

ormer sea-ear (edible mollusc). XVII. - Channel Islands F. *ormer* = F. *ormier* :- L. *auris maris* 'ear of the sea' (so called from its resemblance to the ear).

ormolu gold leaf, gilded bronze, gold-coloured alloy. XVIII. - F. *or moulu* 'ground gold', i.e. *or* gold (:- L. *aurum*), *moulu*, pp. of *moudre* :- L. *molere* grind.

ornament †adjunct; accessory equipment (now only of the furnishings of a church); decoration, embellishment. XIII. ME. *(o)urnement* - AN. *urnement*, OF. *o(u)rnement* - L. *ōrnāmentum*, f. *ōrnāre* ADORN. Later refash. after L. Hence **ornament** vb. XVIII, whence **ornamentation** XIX. **ornamental** XVII. So **ornate** (-ATE[2]) XV. - pp. of L. *ōrnāre*.

ornithology XVII. - modL. *ornithologia*, f. Gr. *ornīthológos* treating of birds, f. *órnis, ornītho-* bird; see -LOGY. So **ornithologist** XVII.

orography, oreography description of mountains. XIX. f. *oro-, ore(i)o-*, comb. forms of Gr. *óros* mountain; see -GRAPHY. So **or(e)ology** XVIII; see -LOGY.

orotund marked by fullness and clarity of tone. XVIII. f. L. phr. *ōre rotundō* lit. 'with round mouth'.

orphan (one) deprived of parents. XV. - late L. *orphanus* - Gr. *orphanós*, rel. to L. *orbus* bereft, Arm. *orb* orphan. Hence vb. XIX.

Orphic pert. to Orpheus or mysteries associated with him. XVII. - L. *Orphicus* - Gr. *Orphikós*, f. *Orpheús*; see -IC.

orphrey, orfray †rich embroidery XIII; ornamental band on a vestment XIV. Falsely inferred sg. from ME. *orphreis* taken as pl. - OF. *orfreis* (mod. *orfroi*) - medL. *aurifrisium*, alt. of *auriphrygium* gold embroidery, i.e. *aurum Phrygium* 'Phrygian gold'.

orpiment yellow arsenic. XIV. - (O)F. - L. *auripigmentum*, f. *aurum* gold + *pigmentum* PIGMENT.

orpin(e) succulent herbaceous plant. XIV. - OF. *orpine* yellow arsenic, presumably shortening of *orpiment*.

Orpington breed of poultry. XIX. f. name of *Orpington*, a town in Kent.

orrery mechanism for representing the motions of the planets. XVIII. Named after Charles Boyle, Earl of *Orrery*, for whom a copy of the machine invented by George Graham *c.*1700 was made.

orris[1] (root of) iris. XVI (*oreys, oris, arras*). unexpl. alt. of IRIS.

orris[2] gold and silver lace pattern. XVIII (*or(r)ice, -ace*). poss. alt. of *orfris* ORPHREY.

ortho- before a vowel **orth-**, comb. form of Gr. *orthós* straight, right, correct. **orthoepy** correct pronunciation. XVII. - Gr. *orthoépeia* (*épos* word). **orthography** correct spelling. XV. - (O)F. - L. - Gr.

orthodox according with accepted opinion XVI; spec. epithet of the Eastern Church XVIII. - ecclL. *orthodoxus* - Gr. *orthódoxos*, f. *orthós* straight, right + *dóxa* opinion, f. base of *dokeîn* seem, rel. to L. *decet* (see DECENT). So **orthodoxy** XVII. - late L. - late Gr.

ortolan species of bunting, *Emberiza hortulana*. XVII. - F. - Pr. *ortolan* gardener - L. *hortulānus*, f. *hortulus*, dim. of *hortus* garden.

-ory[1] earlier *-orie* - AN. *-orie* = (O)F. *-oire*, repr. L. *-ōria, -ōrium*, fem. and n. of *-ōrius* -ORY[2], used sb. to denote a room or an instrument, as *directory, dormitory, lavatory, refectory, repository*, but sometimes with other applications, as in *promontory, territory*; in *priory, rectory* it is formed on a sb. in -OR[1] with -Y[3].

-ory[2] adj. suffix repr. L. *-ōrius*, fem. *-ōria*, n. *-ōrium* (partly through F. *-orie*), primarily f. agent-nouns in *-ōr-* -OR[1] + *-ius* -IOUS, as in *amatory, dilatory, initiatory, satisfactory, supplicatory*; later extended, as in *compulsory, illusory, perfunctory*. Cf. -ORIAL, -ORIOUS.

oryx species of antelope. XIV. - L. - Gr. *órux* stonemason's pickaxe, applied to an antelope or gazelle having pointed horns.

oscillate XVIII. f. pp. stem. (see -ATE[3]) of L. *ōscillāre*, f. *ōscillum* little mask of Bacchus hung from the trees, especially in vineyards, so as to be easily moved by the wind, dim. of *ōs* face; (or back-formation from) **oscillation** XVII. - L.

oscitant gaping from drowsiness. XVII. - prp. of L. *oscitāre* gape, perh. f. *ōs* mouth + *citāre* put in motion; see -ANT. So **oscitation** XVI. - L.

osculate kiss; (techn.) bring or come into close contact. XVII. f. pp. stem of L. *ōsculārī* kiss, f. *ōsculum* little or pretty mouth (cf. -CULE), kiss, hypocoristic dim. of *ōs* mouth; see -ATE[3]. So **osculation** XVII. - L.

-ose[1] suffix repr. L. *-ōsus*, forming adjs. from sbs. with the meaning 'full of', 'abounding in', e.g. *annōsus* full of years (f. *annus* year), *jocōsus* JOCOSE, *mōrōsus* MOROSE, *verbōsus* VERBOSE. The corr. sbs. end in **-osity**, repr. F. *-osité*, L. *-ōsitās*. Cf. -OUS.

-ose[2] (chem.) suffix originating in the final syll. of GLUCOSE and used to form names of related carbohydrates, as *cellulose, dextrose*.

osier XIV. - (O)F. *osier*, m. form corr. to fem. (dial.) *osière* :- medL. *ausēria*, of uncert. orig.

-osis terminal el. of many ancient and modL. terms derived from or modelled on Gr. terms in *-ōsis*, which were primarily based on vbs. in *-óein* (*-oûn*) but were later formed directly on sbs. and adjs., e.g. *cyanosis, metamorphosis, sclerosis, thrombosis*; corr. adjs. end in -OTIC.

-osity see -OSE[1], -OUS, and -ITY.

Osmanli see OTTOMAN.

osmium (chem.) metal of the platinum group, distinguished by a pungent smell. XIX. f. Gr. *osmḗ* ODOUR + -IUM.

osmund flowering fern. XV. - AN. *osmunde*, (O)F. *osmonde*, of unkn. orig.

osprey sea-eagle, fish-hawk XV; egret plume XIX. - OF. *ospres* (mod. *orfraie*), repr. obscurely L. *ossifraga* OSSIFRAGE.

osseous pert. to bone. XVIII. f. L. *osseus*, f. *os, oss-* bone, rel. to Skr. *ásthi*, Gr. *ostéon* OSTEO-; see -EOUS.

ossifrage lammergeyer; osprey. XVII. - sb. uses of L. *ossifragus, -fraga* bone-breaking, f. *os, oss-* bone (see prec.) + **frag-* break (see FRAGMENT).

ossify XVIII. - F. *ossifier*, f. L. *os, oss-* bone; see OSSEOUS, -IFY. So **ossification** XVII.

ossuary charnel-house, bone-urn. XVII. - late L. *ossuārium*, f. *ossua*, var. of *ossa*, pl. of *os* bone; see OSSEOUS, -ARY.

ostensible †that may be shown; †conspicuous; exhibited as actual and genuine. XVIII. - F. - medL. *ostensibilis*, f. *ostens-*, pp. stem of *ostendere*, f. OB- + *tendere* stretch; see -IBLE. So **ostensory** (-ORY[1]) monstrance. XIX (earlier in foreign forms *ostensorio, -orium, -oir*). - medL. *ostensōrium*. **ostentation** XV. - (O)F. - L., f. *ostentāre*, frequent. of *ostendere*.

osteo- comb. form of Gr. *ostéon* bone (see OSSEOUS), as in **osteology** science of bones (XVII; - modL. *osteologia*), **osteopath, osteopathy** XIX (orig. U.S., after *homoeopath, allopath*).

ostler stable-man, groom. XIV. var. sp. of *hostler* (XIII) innkeeper, etc. - AN. *hostiler* = OF. *hostelier*, f. *hostel* HOSTEL (see -ER[2]).

ostracism method of banishment in ancient Greece by voting with potsherds or tiles on which the name of the person proposed to be banished was written. XVI. - F. *ostracisme* or modL. *ostracismus* - Gr. *ostrakismós*, f. *ostrakízein* (whence **ostracize** XVII), f. *óstrakon* shell, tile, potsherd, rel. to *ostakós* crustacean, *ostéon* bone; see OSTEO-, -ISM.

ostrich XIII. ME. *ostric(h)e, -ige* - OF. *ostric(h)e, -usce* (mod. *autruche*) :- Rom. **avistrūthius*, f. L. *avis* bird + late L. *strūthiō* - Gr. *strouthíōn* ostrich, f. *strouthós* sparrow, ostrich.

-ot, -ote repr. F. *-ote*, L. *-ōta*, Gr. *-ṓtēs*, expressing nativity in ancient Gr. names, as *Epirot*, Gr. *Epeirṓtēs*, native of Epirus, in mod. names of inhabitants of certain places in or near Greece, as *Cypriot(e)*. The form *-ot* occurs in the common nouns HELOT, IDIOT, PATRIOT, ZEALOT.

other †one of two; *the* remaining (orig. one of two); existing besides OE.; different (as in ANOTHER) XIII. OE. *ōðer* = OS. *ōðar, andar*, OHG. *andar* (Du., G. *ander*), ON. *annarr*, Goth. *anþar* :- Gmc. **anþeraz* :- IE. **anteros* (compar. formation with **-teros*); parallel to Skr. *ántara-* different, Lith. *añtras*, based on IE. **an-* as in Skr. *anyá-* other. Hence **otherwise** (OE. *on ōðre wīsan*).

-otic repr. ult., through F. *-otique*, L. *-ōticus*, Gr. *-ōtikós*, f. sbs. in *-ōtes* -OT, -OTE, adjs. in *-ōtos*, f. vbs. in *-óein, -oûn*, and so rel. to sbs. in -OSIS, e.g. *hypnotic* and *hypnosis, sclerotic* and *sclerosis*. Of different formation in Gr. are *demotic, erotic, exotic*; a mod. analogical formation is *chaotic* on *chaos*.

otiose of no practical effect XVIII; (arch.) unemployed XIX. - L. *ōtiōsus*, f. *ōtium* leisure; see -OSE.

oto- comb. form of Gr. *oûs, ōt-* EAR[1].

ottava rima (pros.) It. stanza of eight 11-syllable lines rhyming abababcc. XIX. - It., 'eighth rhyme'.

otter OE. *otr, ot(t)or* = MLG., Du. *otter*, OHG. *ottar* (G. *otter*), ON. *otr* :- Gmc. **otraz* :- IE. **udros*, repr. by Skr. *udrá-*, Gr. *húdros* water-snake; rel. to WATER.

otto unexpl. alt. of *ottar, otter*, vars. of ATTAR. XVII.

ottoman cushioned seat of the sofa type. XIX. - F. *ottomane* (XVIII), fem. of *ottoman*, adj. of next.

Ottoman pert. to the Turkish dynasty founded *c.*1300 by Othman (Osman); Turkish, Turk. XVII. - F. *Ottoman*, It. *Ottomano*, medL. *Ottomānus*, f. Arab. *'uṯmān* Othman; *Osman*, the Turk. pronunc. of *Othman* + Turk. adj. suffix *-li* gives *Osmanli* (XIX).

oubliette secret dungeon. XIX. - F., f. *oublier* forget :- Rom. **oblītāre*, f. *oblīt-*, ppl. stem of L. *oblīviscī*; see OBLIVION, -ETTE.

ought[1] am bound, was bound, should be bound or obliged. OE. *āhte*, pt. ind. and subj. of *āgan* OWE; (literally) owed as a duty; (through the subj. use) should owe as a duty, passing into ind. use expressing (present or past) obligation, duty, or propriety.

ought[2] alt. of NOUGHT in the sense 'cipher', 'zero'. arising from misdividing *a nought* as *an ought*. XIX.

ouija (in spiritualism) *o. board*, one lettered with an alphabet for obtaining messages. XX. **P.**; f. F. *oui* yes + G. *ja* yes.

ounce[1] unit of weight. XIV. ME. *unce* - OF. *unce* (mod. *once*) = It. *oncia*, †*onza* :- L. *uncia* twelfth part of a pound or foot (cf. INCH[1]), f. *ūnus* ONE, prob. intended orig. to express a unit.

ounce[2] †lynx XIII; mountain panther XVIII. - AN. **unce*, OF. *once*, beside *lonce* (the *l* of which was taken for the def. art.), repr. Rom. **luncia*, f. *lynx*, *lync-* LYNX.

our poss. pron. A. g. pl. ('of US') of the 1st pers. pron. OE. *ūre* (*ūs(s)er*) = OS. *ūser*, OHG. *unsēr*, ON. *vár*, Goth. *unsara*. B. as pron. adj. OE. *ūre* = OS. *unsa* (Du. *onze*, *ons*), OHG. *unsēr* (G. *unser*), ON. *várr*, Goth. *unsar*. Hence **ours** ME. *ūres* (XIII); repl. †*our* (OE. *ūre* to XVII); *ourn* (XIV to mod. dial.). **ourself** XIV, repl. *usself*; with pl. inflexion *ourselven*, *ourselves* XIV.

-our[1] the older form in many agent-nouns in -OR[1], surviving in SAVIOUR.

-our[2] surviving spelling in British use (as against U.S. *-or*) in several sbs. in -OR[2], e.g. *ardour*, *colour*, *favour*, *honour*, *labour*, *odour*, *rigour*, *savour*, *tumour*, *valour*.

-ous adj. suffix denoting 'characterized by', 'having the quality of', 'full of', 'abounding in', repr. ult. L. *-ōsus*, *-ōsa*, *-ōsum* (cf. -OSE[1]); first appearing as *-os*, *-us* - AN., OF. *-os*, *-us*, mod. *-eux* (e.g. *coveitos*, *coveitus* COVETOUS).

The addition of *-ous* to L. stems of many types became the commonest mode of anglicizing L. adjs. ending in *-eus*, *-ius*, *-uus*, *-āci-*, *-ōci-*, *-endus*, *-ulus*, *-ōrus*, etc., e.g. *aqueous*, *atrocious*, *nefarious*, *stupendous*, *garrulous*, and of forming adjs. directly from sbs. of all origins; see also -EOUS, -IOUS, -UOUS; rel. sbs. have -OSITY.

In chem. *-ous* indicates a larger proportion of the element denoted by the stem than the termination *-ic*, as *cuprous*, *ferrous*.

oust dispossess XVI; turn out, eject XVII. - AN. *ouster* = OF. *oster* (mod. *ôter*) take away, remove :- L. *obstāre* oppose, hinder (see OBSTACLE). So **ouster** (-ER[5]) (leg.) ejection from a possession. XVI. - law F. *ouster*, sb. use of the vb.

out adv. of motion or position beyond certain limits; with many transf. and fig. applications. OE. *ūt* = OS. *ūt* (Du. *uit*), OHG. *ūz* (G. *aus*), ON. *út*, Goth. *ūt*; Gmc. adv. rel. to Skr. prefix *ud-* out (cf. Gr. *hústeros* later :- **udteros*). The comp. prep. *out of* descends from OE. *ūt of* (see OF). OE. *ūtan(e)* is continued in BUT and WITHOUT. As adj., of restricted use (cf. *outhouse*, OUTSIDE, *outsize*, and OUT-). As sb. chiefly in techn. uses XVIII. As vb. OE. *ūtian* = OHG. *uzōn*; newly formed XIV and later. **out-and-out** completely XIV; adj. XIX. Hence **out-and-outer** (-ER[1]) perfect or extreme one of its kind. XIX. The compar. formed with -ER[3] (XIII) superseded UTTER in certain uses (cf. OUTMOST); hence **outermost** XVI.

out- repr. OE. *ūt-*, found in some thirty comps. meaning chiefly 'outward(s)', 'outlying', 'foreign', 'exterior, external'; much increased in number and extended in application, in ME. and later; e.g. on the model of OE. *ūthealf* outward side are *outside*, *outskirts*, *outline*; = 'outside the premises or area', as in *outhouse*, *outland* (OE. *ūtland*); = 'external', as *out-patient*; on intr. verbal phrases such as *break out*, *cry out*, *fit out*, *lay out*, *look out* were formed *outbreak*, *outcry*, *outfit*, *outlay*, *outlook*; on trans. verbal phrases in the sense 'exceed or go beyond a person or thing in something', as *outbid*, *outdo*, *outgrow*, *outlast*, *outline*, *outrun*; *out-Herod* exceed Herod in violence; *outstrip* (XVI) is based on an obs. vb. meaning 'move swiftly'; similarly with sbs., as *outwit*, *out-general*; with prepositional sense, as *outdoor* XVIII.

outing †expedition XIV; †expulsion; (orig. dial.) airing, excursion XIX. partly f. OUT vb., partly f. the adv.

outlaw one put outside the protection of the law. Late OE. *ūtlaga* - ON. *útlagi*, f. *útlagr* outlawed, banished, f. *út* OUT + **lagu*, *lǫg* LAW. So **outlaw** vb. Late OE. *ūtlagian*. **outlawry** XIV; in AN. *utlagerie*, *-larie*, AL. *utlagaria*, *-eria*.

outmost XIV. alt. of *utmest* (see UTMOST).

outrage †intemperance, excess, violent action; violent injury. XIII. - (O)F. :- Rom. **ultrāticum*, f. L. *ultrā* beyond; see ULTRA-, -AGE. So **outrage** vb. XIV. **outrageous** XIV. - OF. *outrageus* (mod. *-eux*).

outré out of the way, eccentric, extravagant. XVIII. - F., pp. of *outrer* †go beyond due limits, f. *outre* :- L. *ultrā* (cf. ULTRA-).

outrigger (naut.) in various senses preceded by, and perh. an alt., by assoc. with RIG, of †*outligger* (XV) 'outlier'.

outright †straight onward, straightway XIII; to the full, completely XIV. f. OUT adv., -RIGHT.

outside sb. XVI; adj. XVII; adv. and prep., for *o. of* XVIII. See OUT, SIDE. Hence **outsider** (-ER[1]) XVIII.

outskirts the outer border. XVII (*outskirt* XVI). See OUT-, SKIRT.

outspoken XIX (orig. Sc.). See SPOKEN.

oval egg-shaped. XVI. - medL. *ōvālis*, f. L. *ōvum* EGG[1]; see -AL[1]. So **ovate** (-ATE[2]) XVIII. - L.

ovary XVII. - modL. *ōvārium*, f. L. *ōvum* EGG[1]; see -ARY.

ovation (in ancient Rome) lesser triumph XVI; †exultation XVII; enthusiastic applause XIX. - L. *ovātiō*, *-ōn-*, f. *ovāre* celebrate a (lesser) triumph, perh. f. Gr. *euoî*, exultant cry at the Bacchanalia; see -ATION.

oven †furnace; receptacle for food to be cooked by radiating heat. OE. *ofen* = (M)LG., (M)Du. *oven*, OHG. *ovan* (G. *ofen*), ON. *ofn*, *ogn*, Goth. **auhns*; obscurely rel. to Skr. *ukhá-* cooking-pot, Gr. *ipnós* oven, furnace.

over adv. (also prep. in corr. senses) above; to or on the other side; above a certain quantity OE.; excessively, too XIII; through the whole extent XIV; gone by, done with XVII. OE. *ofer* = OS. *obar* (Du. *over*), OHG. *ubar* prep., *ubiri* adv. (G. *über*), ON. *yfir*, Goth. *ufar* :- Gmc. **uberi* :- IE. **uperi*, compar. formation (cf. Skr. *upári*, Gr. *hupér*, L. *super*) on **upó* from under towards.

over adj. ME. *ouere* (XIII) began as a graphic var. of *uuere* (with *o* for *u* before *u*) :- OE. *ufer(r)a, yfer(r)a*; superseded in gen. use by the adv. form.

over- repr. OE. *ofer-*, comb. form of prec., of which there are some 300 comps.; the number was increased in ME. and later, with modifications and developments of the primary meanings. The chief senses are 'situated above', 'upper', 'in excess', 'extra', 'lying, extending, or moving across', 'passing over a limit or an obstacle', 'beyond in degree or quality', 'covering a surface', 'with dominating or damaging influence or effect'; 'with disturbance of situation', as *overbalance* (XVI), *overcast* (XIII), *overset* (XVI), *overturn* (XIV), OVERWHELM; special uses are those in *overhear* hear without intention (XVI), *overlook* look over and beyond and so not see or notice (XVI), OVERTAKE; *overcoat* and *overshoe* (XIX) are orig. U.S. and are prob. renderings of the corr. G. or Du. words.

overall outer covering or garment. XVIII. f. OVER prep. + ALL.

overplus XIV. partial tr. of (O)F. *surplus* SURPLUS.

overt †open, uncovered; open to view or knowledge. XIV. - OF. *overt* (mod. *ouvert*), pp. of *ovrir* (*ouvrir*) open :- popL. **operīre* for L. *aperīre*.

overtake come up with, catch up XIII; come upon suddenly XIV. f. OVER- + TAKE.

overtone (acoustics, mus.) harmonic. XIX. - G. *oberton*, for *oberpartialton* 'upper partial tone'.

overture †opening, aperture XIV; opening of negotiations XV; (Sc.) formal motion in an assembly XVI; (mus.) orchestral piece forming the introduction to a work XVII. - OF. *overture* (now *ouverture*) :- popL. **opertūra* for L. *apertūra* APERTURE.

overweening presumption, arrogance. XIV. f. OVER-, WEEN, -ING[1].

overwhelm (dial.) upset XIV; overcome, overpower XVI. f. OVER- + WHELM.

ovi-[1] comb. form of L. *ōvum* EGG[1], as in *oviduct* (XVIII).

ovi-[2] comb. form of L. *ovis* sheep (see EWE), as in (joc.) *ovicide* sheep-slaughter (XIX).

ovine pert. to sheep. XIX. - late L. *ovīnus*, f. *ovis*; see EWE, INE[1].

ovo- used irreg. for OVI-[1]. XIX.

ovoid egg-shaped. XIX. - F. *ovoïde* - modL. *ōvoīdēs*, f. *ōvum* EGG[1]; see -OID. So **ovoidal** XVIII.

ovolo (archit.) convex moulding the section of which is a quarter-circle or ellipse. XVII. - It. *ovolo*, dim. of †*ovo*, *uovo* :- L. *ōvum* EGG[1].

ovule (bot.) rudimentary seed; (zool.) unfertilized ovum. XIX. - F. *ovule* - modL. *ōvulum*, dim. of L. *ōvum* EGG[1]; see -ULE.

ovum egg (female reproductive cell). XVIII. - L., see EGG[1].

owe †A. have, own OE.; B. have to pay XII; C. have as a duty or obligation XII; D. cherish, entertain XIV; have to ascribe or attribute XVI. OE. *āgan* = OS. *ēgan*, OHG. *eigan*, ON. *eiga*, Goth. *aigan*; Gmc. preterite-present vb., rel. to Skr. *īśe* owns. The orig. conjugation has been repl. by a new one (*owed* XIV) based directly on the inf., and the orig. pt. has become a distinct word (OUGHT[1]). A special use of the prp. **owing** is in the sense 'attributable to' (XVII), whence the adv. *owing to* because of (XIX).

owl OE. *ūle* = MLG., MDu. *ūle*, Du. *uil*, ON. *ugla* :- Gmc. **uwwalōn*, parallel with **uwwilōn*, repr. by OHG. *ūwila* (MHG. *iule*, G. *eule*). For the imit. orig. cf. L. *ulula*, perh. f. vb. *ululāre* howl. Hence **owlet** (-ET) XVI.

own pert. to oneself or itself. OE. *āgen* = OS. *ēgan*, OHG. *eigan* (Du., G. *eigen*), ON. *eiginn* :- Gmc. **aiʒanaz*, adj. use of the pp. of OWE, prop. 'possessed', 'owed'. Hence vb. OE. *āgnian* †take possession of; hold as one's own OE. (disused XIV-XVI exc. as repr. in **owner** (XIV), whence revived XVII by back-formation); acknowledge as one's own, as true or valid, etc. XVII.

ox pl. *oxen* bovine animal, esp. castrated male of the domestic species. OE. *oxa* = OS., OHG. *ohso* (Du. *os*, G. *ochse*), ON. *uxi*, *oxi*, Goth. *auhsa* :- Gmc. **oχsan-*, rel. to W. *ych*, pl. *ychen*, OIr. *oss* stag, Skr. *ukṣán-* bull, cattle.

oxalic epithet of a poisonous sour acid found in wood-sorrel, etc. XVIII. - F. *oxalique*, f. L. *oxalis* - Gr. *oxalis* wood-sorrel, f. *oxús* sour, acid; see -IC.

oxide XVIII. - F. *oxide* (now *oxyde*), f. *oxygène* OXYGEN + *-ide*, after *acide* ACID.

oxlip flowering herb, hybrid between cowslip and primrose. OE. *oxanslyppe*, f. *oxan*, g. sg. of *oxa* OX + *slyppe* slimy or viscous dropping (see COWSLIP).

Oxonian pert. to Oxford, esp. to its university. XVI. f. *Oxonia*, latinization of OE. *Ox(e)naford*, ME. *Oxen(e)ford*, f. *oxan*, g. pl. of OX + FORD; see -IAN.

oxy repr. *oxu-*, comb. form of Gr. *oxús* sharp, acid, used in many scientific terms, in chem. repr. *oxygen*.

oxygen XVIII. - F. *oxygène*, intended to mean 'acidifying principle' (acid-producer), f. Gr. *oxús* sharp, acid + *-gène* -GEN.

oxymoron (rhet.) figure in which contradictory terms are conjoined. XVII. - Gr. *oxúmōron*, n. sg. of *oxúmōros* pointedly foolish, f. *oxús* sharp + *mōrós* foolish.

oyer (leg.) in full *o. and terminer* 'hear and determine', commission to hear and judge indictments. XV. - AN. *oyer* = OF. *oïr* (mod. *ouïr*) :- L. *audīre* hear. See -ER[5].

oyez, oyes call to command attention, as by a public crier or a court officer. XV. - AN., OF. *oiez*, *oyez* hear ye!, imper. pl. of *oïr* (see prec.).

oyster XIV. ME. *oistre* - OF. *oistre*, *uistre* (mod. *huitre*) - L. *ostrea* (whence also OE. *ostre*), also *ostreum* - Gr. *óstreon*, rel. to *ostéon* bone.

oz symbol for OUNCE[1]. XVI. - It. *o̅z*, abbrev. of *onza*, pl. *onze*.

ozokerite, ozocerite aromatic waxlike fossil resin. XIX. - G. *ozokerit*, f. Gr. *ózein* smell + *kērós* beeswax; see -ITE.

ozone XIX. - G. *ozon* - Gr. *ózon*, n. prp. of *ózein* smell, rel. to *odmé* ODOUR; so named from its peculiar smell.

P

pa see PAPA.
pabulum food, nutriment. XVII. - L. *pābulum*, f. base **pā-* of *pāscere* feed.
pace[1] step; rate of progression; †step of a stair, floor raised by a step; †mountain pass. XIII. ME. *pa(a)s* - (O)F. *pas* - L. *passus* step, pace, lit. 'stretch (of the leg)', f. *pass-*, pp. stem of *pandere* stretch, extend. Hence **pace** vb. walk with measured pace (along) XVI; set the pace for XIX.
pace[2] by leave of. XIX. - L., abl. of *pāx* PEACE, as in *pāce tuā* by your leave.
pacha see PASHA.
pachisi four-handed game played in India, of which ludo is a simplified form. XVIII. - Hindi *pacīsī*, adj. f. *pacīs* twenty-five (the highest throw), f. *pãc* five.
pachy- comb. form of Gr. *pakhús* thick, as in *pakhúdermos* thick-skinned (*dérma* skin), on which is based modL. *pachydermata*, whence **pachyderm, pachydermatous** XIX.
pacific making or tending to peace XVI; peaceful XVII (*P. Ocean*, modL. *Mare Pacificum*, so called by Magellan because he found it comparatively free from violent storms). - (O)F. *pacifique* or L. *pācificus*, f. *pāx*, *pāc-* PEACE; see -FIC. Hence **pacificism, -ist**, usu. in shortened form **pacifism, -ist** XX. So **pacify** XV. - (O)F. *pacifier* or L. *pācificāre*. **pacification** XV. - F. - L.
pack[1] bundle, bale XIII; company, set of people XIV; set of playing-cards XVI; company of animals kept or herding together XVII. - (M)Du., (M)LG. *pak*; of unkn. orig. So **pack** vb. XIV. - (M)Du., (M)LG. *pakken*. Hence **package** XVII.
pack[2] †make a plot; †bring into a plot; make up (a jury, etc.) for a wrong purpose; shuffle (cards) fraudulently. XVI. perh. f. †*pact* vb. (f. PACT sb.) by apprehending the final *-t* as an inflexion.
packet small pack or package XVI; short for *p.-boat* XVIII. f. PACK[1] + -ET; perh. of AN. formation. Hence **packet-boat** vessel plying between two ports, mail-boat. XVII; orig. boat maintained for the conveyance of 'the packet' of state papers.
pact XV. - (O)F. *pacte*, †*pact* - L. *pactum*, *-us*, sb. uses of pp. of *pacīscī* make a covenant, f. base of *pāx* PEACE.
pad[1] (orig. sl., now dial.) path, road XVI; road-horse, nag; highwayman, FOOTPAD XVII. - LG., Du. *pad* PATH. Hence, or - LG. *padden*, **pad** vb.[1] tread, tramp. XVI.
pad[2] †bundle of straw to lie on; soft stuffed saddle XVI; small cushion XVII; hairy foot or paw XVIII; sheets of paper forming a block XIX. of obscure orig.; cf. Flem. †*pad*, *patte*, LG. *pad* sole of the foot. Hence **pad** vb.[2] stuff, fill out. XIX.
pad[3] dull sound of steps on the ground. XVI. mainly imit., but cf. PAD vb.[1]
paddle[1] spud for cleaning a ploughshare XV; short oar for propelling a canoe, etc.; one of a series of spokes, boards, or floats for propelling a vessel in the water XVII. of unkn. orig.; the suffix is -LE[1]. Hence vb. XVII.
paddle[2] walk or move the feet about in mud or shallow water XVI; toddle XVIII. of obscure orig.; cf. LG. *paddeln* tramp about, frequent. of *padden* PAD vb.[1]; see -LE[3].
paddock small enclosure of grass land. XVII. alt. of (dial.) *parrock*, OE. *pearroc*, *-uc* PARK.
paddy[1] rice in the straw or in the husk. XVII (*batte* XVI, *batty* XVII). - Malay *padi*, corr. to Javanese *pārī*; cf. Kannada *b(h)atta*.
paddy[2] Irishman XVIII; fit of temper XIX. pet-form of Ir. *Padraig* Patrick; see -Y[6].
paddymelon, pademelon small brush kangaroo. XIX. alt. of Austral. aboriginal name.
pad(i)shah title applied to the Shah of Persia, Sultan of Turkey, Great Mogul, etc. XVII. - Pers. *pādšāh*, in poetry *pādišah* :- Pahlavi *pātaχšā(h)*, f. OPers. *pati* (= Skr. *pati*) master, lord, ruler + *šāh* king, SHAH.
padlock XV. first el. of unkn. orig.; see LOCK[1].
padre (title of a) minister of religion. XVI. - It., Sp., Pg. *padre* :- L. *pater*, *patr-* FATHER.
paduasoy silk fabric. XVII. Earliest form *pou-desoy* - F. *pou-de-soie*, earlier *pout de soie* (XIV), of unkn. orig.; altered to the present form by assoc. with earlier †*Padua say* (XVII), kind of serge from Padua in Italy.
paean song of triumph or exultation. XVI. - L. *pæān* - Gr. *paiā́n* hymn to Apollo invoked by the name *Paiā́n*, Doric var. of Ionic *Paiḗōn*, Attic *Paiṓn*, orig. the Homeric name of the physician of the gods, afterwards Apollo.
p(a)ediatrician XX. f. Gr. *paîs*, *paid-* child + *iātrós* physician + -ICIAN. So **p(a)ediatrist** XIX.
p(a)edo- comb. form of Gr. *paîs*, *paid-* boy, child, as in **paedobaptism** infant baptism (XVII).
paeon (pros.) metrical foot of four syllables, one long and three short, named, acc. to the position of the long syllable, first, second, third, and fourth paeon. XVII. - L. *pæōn* - Gr. *paiṓn*; see PAEAN.
pagan XIV. - L. *pāgānus* rustic, peasant, citizen, civilian, (in ChrL.) non-Christian, non-Jewish, f. *pāgus* (rural) district, the country, orig. landmark fixed in the earth, f. IE. **paĝ-* as in L. *pangere* fix; see -AN. The sense 'heathen' of L. *pāgānus* is of uncert. orig. Hence **paganism** XV.
page[1] †boy, lad XIII; †youth in training for knighthood; †male person of low condition; boy (or man) employed as servant or attendant XIV, as in a great household, or (XVIII) a foot-boy or errand-boy at a house, hotel, etc. - (O)F. *page*, perh. - It. *paggio*; of uncert. orig.
page[2] one side of a leaf of a book, etc. XV. - (O)F. *page* (reduction of *pagene*) - L. *pāgina* vine-trellis, column of writing, page or leaf, f.

IE. **paĝ-* fix (cf. PAGAN). Hence vb. XVII. So **paginate** XIX; back-formation from **pagination** XIX. - F.

pageant †scene acted on a stage XIV; †stage on which scenes were acted, esp. in the open-air performances of the miracle plays XV; †tableau or series of tableaux XVI; brilliant spectacle XIX; scenic exhibition of local history XX. Late ME. *pagyn* (in contemp. AL. *pagina*), of unkn. orig. With parasitic *d, t*, from XIV (cf. *ancient, peasant, tyrant*). Hence **pageantry** XVII.

pagoda idol temple; idol; coin of S. India (from the figure thereon). XVII (*pagod(e)* XVI). - Pg. *pagode*, prob. ult. - Pers. *butkada* idol temple, f. *but* idol + *kada* habitation.

pail OE. *pæġel* (glossing medL. *gillo* GILL[3]), corr. to (M)Du. *pegel* gauge, scale, mark, LG *pegel* half a pint, of unkn. orig.

paillasse see PALLIASSE.

pain (arch.) punishment, penalty (now only in phr.); suffering; †trouble, difficulty XIII; (pl.) trouble taken in doing something XVI (earlier sg. *do one's p.*, etc.). ME. *peine, paine* - (O)F. *peine* :- L. *pœna* penalty, punishment, (later) pain, grief - Gr. (Dorian) *poinā́*, (Attic) *poinḗ* expiation, ransom, punishment, rel. to OSl. *cěna* price, Av. *kaēnā-* punishment, Skr. *cáyate* avenge, punish. Hence **painful** hurtful; †laborious. XIV.

paint make (a picture) on a surface in colours XII; depict in words XV. prob. first in pp. (*i*)*peint* - (O)F. *peint(e)*, pp. of *peindre* :- L. *pingere* embroider, paint, embellish, f. nasalized form of IE. **pig-* **peig-*, repr. also by Skr. *piṅkte* paints, and parallel with **peiḱ-* **poiḱ-*, repr. by OE. *fāh*, OHG. *fēh*, Goth. *-faihs* coloured. Hence **paint** sb. pigment, colour. XVII. So **painter**[1] XIV. - OF. *peintour*, nom. *peintre* :- Rom. **pinctōrem*, for L. *pictōrem*, nom. *pictor*, f. *pict-*, pp. stem of *pingere*; see -OR[1], -ER[1].

painter[2] rope to secure an anchor, etc. XV. contemp. with †*paint* vb. make fast with a rope, which is prob. a back-formation; of unkn. orig., but cf. OF. *pentoir, penteur* strong rope.

pair set of two; set of parts forming a whole. XIII (e.g. string *of beads* XIV, flight *of stairs* XVI). - (O)F. *paire* :- L. *paria* equal or like things, n. pl. of *pār, par-* equal. Hence vb. XVII.

Pakistan XX. Earlier *Pakstan*, f. initials of *P*unjab, *A*fghan Province, *K*ashmir, *S*ind, and Baluchi*stan*.

pal XVII. - Eng. Gypsy *pal* brother, mate = Turk. Gypsy *pral, plal* :- Skr. *bhrā́tar-* BROTHER.

palace official residence of a king, pope, bishop XIII; stately mansion XIV; building, often spacious and attractive, for entertainment XIX. ME. *paleis* - OF. *paleis*, (also mod.) *palais* - L. *palātium* orig. name of one of the seven hills of Rome, (later) the house of Augustus there situated, the palace of the Caesars which finally covered the hill.

paladin one of the Twelve Peers of Charlemagne's court, of whom the Count Palatine was the foremost; (hence) knightly champion or hero. XVI. - F. - It. *paladino* - L. *palātīnus* pert. to the palace, PALATINE.

palaeo-, U.S. **paleo-** comb. form of Gr. *palaiós* ancient, in many scientific terms often having correlatives in NEO-; among the earliest are **palaeography** (XVIII; - F. *paléographie*), **palaeontology** (XIX); archaeol., geol. opp. to MESO-, NEO-, as **palaeolithic, -zoic** (for *palaeocene* see EOCENE).

palaestra wrestling-school. XVI. - L. *palæstra* - Gr. *palaístrā*, f. *palaíein* wrestle.

palafitte prehistoric lake dwelling in Switzerland or N. Italy. XIX. - F. - It. *palafitta* fence of piles, f. *palo* PALE[1] + *fitto* fixed.

palanquin, palankeen covered litter used in India and elsewhere. XVI. - Pg. *palanquim* - an E. Indian word repr. by Pali *pallaṅka-*, Hindi *pālkī* :- Skr. *palyaṅka-*, *paryaṅka-* bed, couch, f. *pári* round, about, PERI-.

palate XIV (*palet*). - L. *palātum*; of unkn. orig. Hence vb. taste, relish. XVII. **palatable** XVII. **palatal** XIX. - F. *palatal*. The comb. form of *palate* is **palato-** XVIII.

palatine (of a count or county) possessing royal privileges XV; sb. lord having sovereign power over a province or dependency of an empire or realm XVI. - F. *palatin(e)* - L. *palātīnus* belonging to the *palātium* PALACE, sb. officer of the Roman imperial palace, chamberlain; hence applied in the Middle Ages to great feudatories exercising royal privileges. Hence **palatinate** (-ATE[1]) territory of a count palatine, county palatine. XVI.

palaver parley, conference; profuse or idle talk. XVIII (hence as vb.). - Pg. *palavra* :- L. *parabola* PARABLE.

pale[1] pointed stake used in forming a fence; fence of these; limit, boundary XIV; (her.) ordinary consisting of a vertical band XV; territory within determined bounds XVI. - (O)F. *pal*, var. of *pel* (mod. *pieu*) = It. *palo* :- L. *pālus* stake, f. IE. **paĝ-*, base of *pangere* fix. So vb. enclose with pales. XIV. - (O)F. *paler* ; surviving in **paling** XV. **palisade** XVI. - F. *palissade*.

pale[2] of whitish colour XIII; faint, dim XIV. - OF. *pal(l)e* (mod. *pâle*) - L. *pallidus* PALLID. So vb. XIV. - OF. *palir* (mod. *pâlir*).

paletot loose outer garment. XIX. - F. *paletot*, formerly †*pal(e)toc*, in ME. †*paltok* (XIV); of unkn. orig.

palette XVII. - F.; see PALLET[2].

palfrey saddle-horse. XII. - OF. *palefrei* (mod. *palefroi*) :- medL. *palefrēdus*, for *paraverēdus*, f. Gr. *pará* beside, extra (see PARA-[1]) + late L. *verēdus* light horse, courier's horse (of Gaulish orig.).

palimpsest †material prepared for writing on and wiping out XVII; parchment, etc., in which the original writing has been erased to make place for a second XIX. - L. *palimpsestus* - Gr. *palímpsestos* (as sb. *-on*), f. *pálin* again + *psestós*, pp. formation on *psên* rub smooth.

palindrome XVII. - Gr. *palíndromos* running back again, f. *pálin* again + *drom-*, *dramein* run.

palinode song in which a poet retracts something said before, recantation. XVI. - F. †*palinode* or late L. *palinōdia* - Gr. *palinōidiā*, f. *pálin* again + *ōidḗ* song, ODE.

pall[1] A. (arch.) cloth, esp. (a) rich cloth OE.; cloth spread on a coffin or hearse XV; B. (arch.)

robe, mantle OE.; papal pallium XV; C. 'mantle' of cloud, mist, smoke XV. OE. *pæll* - L. *pallium* Greek mantle, philosopher's cloak, later in various eccl. uses; see PALLIUM.

pall[2] †become dim or faint XIV; become vapid or stale XV; (fig.) become insipid XVIII. Aphetic of †*appall*, APPAL.

Palladian pert. to the school of the It. architect Antonio *Palladio* (1518-80), who imitated ancient Roman architecture. XVIII. See -IAN.

palladium[1] image of Pallas in the citadel of Troy, on which the safety of the city depended XIV; safeguard, protection XVI. - L. - Gr. *palládion*, f. *Pallás*, *-ad-* epithet of the goddess Athene.

palladium[2] metal of the platinum group. XIX. - modL.; so named from the newly discovered asteroid *Pallas*; see prec. and -IUM.

pallet[1] (straw) mattress. XIV. ME. *pail(l)et* - AN. *paillete* straw, f. OF. *paille* straw :- L. *palea* chaff, straw.

pallet[2] flat-bladed wooden instrument XVI; flat board; projection which engages with the tooth of a wheel XVIII. - (O)F. *palette*, dim. of *pale* spade, blade :- L. *pāla* spade, shovel, rel. to *pālus* stake, PALE[1].

palliasse, paillasse straw mattress. XVIII. - F. *paillasse* - It. *pagliaccio* :- Rom. **paleāceum*, f. L. *palea* chaff, straw.

palliate †cloak, conceal; alleviate (disease, etc.) XVI; disguise the enormity or offensiveness of; †mitigate XVII. f. pp. stem of late L. *palliāre* (*palliātus* cloaked, fig. protected, is earlier), f. PALLIUM; see -ATE[3]. So **palliation** XVI. - (O)F. - medL. **palliative** XVI. - (O)F.

pallid XVII. - L. *pallidus*, rel. to *pallēre* be pale; see FALLOW[2] and -ID[1]. So **pallor** (-OR[2]) XVII. - L.

pallium large cloak XVI; vestment worn by the pope and conferred by him on archbishops XVII; (zool.) mantle of a mollusc, etc. XIX. - L. *pallium*, rel. to *palla* long wide outer garment of Roman ladies; of unkn. orig.

pall-mall †mallet used in the game (also so called) in which a ball was driven through an iron ring XVI; †alley in which this was played, (hence) name of an alley in London XVII, now *Pall Mall*. - F. †*pal(le) mail(le)* - It. *pallamaglio*, f. *palla* ball + *maglio* mallet.

palm[1] tree of the (chiefly tropical) family Palmae: leaf or 'branch' of a palm tree OE.; branch or sprig of a tree substituted for the palm in Palm Sunday processions XIV. OE. *palm(a)*, *palme* = OS., OHG. *palma* (Du. *palm*, G. *palme*), ON. *pálmr*; Gmc. - L. *palma* PALM[2] (the palm-leaf was likened to the hand with the fingers extended). In ME. the word coincided with the repr. of AN. (modF.) *palme*, OF. *paume*. **Palm Sunday** Sunday next before Easter, on which processions are held in which palms are carried. OE. *palm-sunnandæġ*, tr. ecclL. *Dominica Palmarum*. Hence **palmy** abounding in palms; flourishing. XVII.

palm[2] part of the hand between the fingers and the wrist; flat part of a deer's horn XIV; measure of length XV. ME. *paume* - (O)F. *paume* = Sp., It. *palma* :- L. *palma* palm of the hand, part of the trunk of a tree from which branches spring, palm-leaf, palm-tree (see prec.), rel. obscurely to Gr. *palámē* palm of the hand, Ir. *lám* hand, OE. *folm*. ME. *paume*, through *paulme* (also OF.), was finally assim. to the L. Hence **palm** vb. XVII.

palmary XVII. - L. *palmārius* that carries off the palm of victory, f. *palma* PALM[1]; see -ARY.

palmate shaped like an open hand. XVIII. - L. *palmātus*, f. *palma* PALM[2]; see -ATE[2].

palmer pilgrim from the Holy Land, carrying a palm-branch as a sign XIII; destructive hairy caterpillar XVI. - AN. *palmer*, *-our*, OF. *palmier* :- medL. *palmārius*, f. *palma* PALM[1]; see -ER[2].

palmette ornament with divisions resembling a palm-leaf. XIX. - F., dim. of *palme* PALM[1]; see -ETTE.

palmetto small species of palm. XVI (*palmito*). - Sp. *palmito* dwarf fan-palm, dim. of *palma* PALM[1]; later assim. to It. dims. in *-etto*.

palmiped having palmate feet. XVII. - L. *palmipēs*, *-ped-*, f. *palma* PALM[2] + *pēs* FOOT.

palmistry XV (*pawmestry*). f. PALM[2] + *-estry*, of obscure formation; alt. to *-istry* XVI, perh. after *sophistry*. Hence by back-formation **palmist** XIX.

palmitic (chem.) acid contained in palm-oil. XIX. - F., arbitrarily f. *palme* PALM[1]; see -IC. Hence **palmitate** (-ATE[3]) XIX.

palmyra palm, *Borassus flabellifer*. XVII. Formerly *palmero*, *palmeira* - Pg. *palmeira*, Sp. *palmera*, It. *palmero*, f. *palma* PALM[1]; the present sp. suggests assim. to *Palmyra*, name of a city in Syria.

palpable tangible, sensible XIV; plainly observable XV; evident, manifest XVII. - late L. *palpābilis*, f. *palpāre* touch soothingly; see -ABLE. So **palpation** handling. XV. - F. or L.

palpebral pert. to the eyelids. XIX. - late L. *palpebrālis*, f. *palpebra* eyelid, rel. to *palpāre*; see prec. and -AL[1].

palpitate XVII. f. pp. stem of L. *palpitāre*, frequent. of *palpāre* stroke; see PALPABLE, -ATE[3]. So **palpitation** XVII. - L.

palsgrave count palatine. XVI. - early Du. *paltsgrave* (mod. *paltsgraaf*), f. *palts* palatinate + †*grave*, *graaf* count.

palstave form of celt fitting into a split handle. XIX. - Da. *paalstav* :- ON. *pálstafr*, f. *páll* hoe, spade (- L. *pālus* PALE[1]) + *stafr* STAVE.

palsy XIII. ME. *pa(r)lesi* - (O)F. *paralisie* (AN. *parlesie*) - Rom. **paralisia*, for L. *paralysis* PARALYSIS. Hence **palsied** XVI.

palter †mumble, babble; †jumble XVI; shuffle in statement or dealing XVII. Of the form of a frequent. or iterative in -ER[4], but the base is unkn.; perh. ult. rel. to next.

paltry XVI. adj. use of (dial.) *paltry* sb. (XVI) rubbish, trash; cf. MLG. *palterlappen* rags, LG. *paltrig* ragged, torn.

paludal pert. to marshes. XIX. f. L. *palūs*, *palūd-* marsh. See -AL[1].

paly (her.) divided by vertical lines (palewise). XV. - (O)F. *palé*, f. *pal* PALE[1]; see -Y[6].

pampa usu. pl. **pampas** vast treeless plain in S. America. XVIII. - Sp. - Quechua *pampa* plain.

pamper †cram with food, feed luxuriously XIV; over-indulge XVI. frequent. (see -ER[4]) of synon. †*pamp* (XIV), dial. *pomp*; prob. of LG. or Du. orig.

pamphlet small treatise of smaller compass than a 'book' XIV; short treatise or booklet on a matter of current or temporary interest XVI. ME. *pamflet, paunflet*, in AL. *panfletus*; generalized use of *Pamphilet, Panflet* (in OF. and MDu. respectively), vernacular name of the L. amatory poem 'Pamphilus seu de Amore'. Hence **pamphleteer** (-EER[1]) XVII (†*pamphleter* XVI).

pan A. broad shallow vessel OE.; †skull (*brain pan*) XIV; B. depression in the ground XVI; C. hard substratum of the soil XVIII. OE. *panne* = OS. *panna*, (M)LG., MDu. *panne* (Du. *pan*), OHG. *pfanna* (G. *pfanne*) :- WGmc. **panna*; perh. - popL. **panna* :- L. *patina* (see PATEN). Hence **pan** vb. wash (gravel, etc.) in a pan, separate the gold; (usu. with *out*) yield gold when so washed; also fig. XIX. **pancake** XV, prob. after MLG. *pannekōke* (Du. *pannekoek*).

pan- comb. form of Gr. *pâs*, n. *pân* all, used freely in Gr. with adjs. in the sense 'wholly, completely, of all, by all', and less freq. with sbs. meaning 'all', 'complete' (cf. PANACEA, PANCREAS, PANDECT, PANOPLY, etc.); extensively used in later XIX to express the notion of universality in political or religious activities, as *Pan-African, Pan-Anglican, Panslavism*.

panacea universal remedy. XVI. - L. *panacēa* - Gr. *panákeia*, f. *panakḗs* all-healing, f. PAN- + base of *ákos* remedy.

panache plume of feathers XVI; swagger XX. - F. - It. *pennacchio* :- late L. *pinnāculum*, dim. of *pinna* feather.

panada dish of pulped bread with flavouring. XVI. - Sp. :- Rom. **panātā*, f. *pānis* bread.

panama name of a town and state in Central America and of the isthmus joining N. and S. America, misapplied to a hat which originated in Ecuador. XIX.

pancratium athletic contest combining wrestling and boxing. XVII. - L. - Gr. *pankrátion*, f. PAN- + *krátos* strength, mastery.

pancreas gland discharging a digestive secretion, sweetbread. XVI. - Gr. *págkreas*, f. PAN- + *kréas* flesh. Hence **pancreatic** XVII.

panda XIX. - Nepali name.

Pandean, -aean pert. to Pan or the pipes reputedly invented by him. XIX. irreg. f. *Pan*, Gr. rural deity + -EAN.

pandect compendium of Roman law made by order of the emperor Justinian; complete treatise or digest. XVI. - F. *pandecte* or L. *pandecta, -tes* - Gr. *pandéktēs* (pl. *pandéktai* as a title), f. PAN- + *dékhesthai* receive.

pandemic (of a disease) prevalent over the whole of an area. XVII. f. Gr. *pándēmos*, f. PAN- + *dêmos* people; see -IC.

pandemonium abode of all devils XVII; haunt of great wickedness, (later) place or gathering of lawless violence XVIII. modL., f. Gr. PAN- + *daímōn* DEMON.

pander go-between in clandestine amours XVI; one who ministers to base passions or designs XVII. Earliest form *pandar*; appellative use of *Pandare* - It. *Pandaro* (- L. *Pandarus*, Gr. *Pándaros*), name used by Boccaccio and thereafter by Chaucer for the man who procured for Troilus the love of Criseyde (Griseida). The sp. *pander* is due to assoc. with -ER[1]. Hence vb. XVII.

pandora, pandore stringed musical instrument of the cither type. XVI. - It. †*pandora, -iera, pandura* - late L. *pandūra* - Gr. *pandoûra, -doúrā* three-stringed lute.

pane A. †piece of cloth XIII (survives in COUNTERPANE); B. section or side (now only in some techn. uses) XIV; C. division of a window XV; panel XVI. ME. *pan*, later *pane* - (O)F. *pan* :- L. *pannus* cloth, piece of cloth.

panegyric XVII. - F. *panégyrique* - L. *panēgyricus* public eulogy, sb. use of adj. - Gr. *panēgurikós* pert. to public assembly, f. *panḗguris* general assembly, f. PAN- + *-ēguris* = *agorá* assembly. So **panegyrical** XVI, **panegyrist** XVII. **panegyrize** XVII. - Gr. *panēgurízein*.

panel piece of cloth placed under the saddle XIII; saddle consisting of a rough pad XVI; piece of parchment (attached to a writ) on which names of jurors were written, (hence) list of jurymen, jury XIV; section of a fence XV; compartment of a door, etc. XVI; thin board used for a painting XVIII; large size of photograph XIX. - OF. *panel* piece of cloth, saddle cushion, piece (mod. *panneau*) :- Rom. **pannellus*, dim. of L. *pannus* PANE; see -EL[2].

pang XVI. In earliest use *pange(s) of deth, panges of child bed*; unexpl. var. of earlier †*pronge*, †*prange* (XV). The forms in *pr-* corr. to MLG. *prange* pinching, Du., LG. *prangen* pinch, Goth. *anapraggan* oppress, Sc. *p(r)ang* pack tight, cram.

pangolin scaly ant-eater. XVIII. - Malay *pĕngguling*, f. *pĕng-* (denominative element) + *guling* roll, with ref. to its habit of rolling itself up.

panic[1] millet. XV. - L. *pānicum*, rel. to *pānus* stalk of a panicle; of uncert. orig.

panic[2] adj. in *p. fear*, etc., such as was attributed to the influence of Pan XVII; sb. †contagious emotion so ascribed XVII; sudden and extreme alarm XVIII. - F. *panique* - modL. *pānicus* (in *p. terror*) - Gr. *pānikós* (also n. *-ón* as sb.), f. *Pán* Pan, name of a deity part man part goat, whose appearance or unseen presence caused terror and to whom woodland noises were attributed; see -IC. Hence **panicky** (-Y[1]) XIX.

panicle compound inflorescence. XVI. - L. *pānicula*, dim. of *pānus*; see PANIC[1], -CLE.

panjandrum nonsense word, simulating comps. of PAN-, occurring in the farrago of nonsense composed by Samuel Foote in 1755 to test the memory of the retired actor Macklin; hence used as a mock title (orig. 'the Grand Panjandrum') for a pretended great personage.

pannage mast on which swine feed XIV (*pownage*); (right of) feeding swine in a forest XV. - OF. *pannage* (mod. *panage*) :- medL. *pāstiōnāticum*, f. L. *pāstiō, -ōn-* feeding, pasturing, f. *pāst-*, pp. stem of *pāscere* feed; see -AGE.

pannier basket, esp. a large one (as carried by a beast of burden, etc.). XIII. - (O)F. *panier*, †*pannier* :- L. *pānārium* bread-basket, f. *pānis* bread.

pannikin small metal drinking-mug. XIX. f. PAN; see -KIN.

panoply complete suit of armour. XVII. - F.

panoplie or modL. *panoplia* - Gr. *panopliā*, f. PAN- + *hópla* arms.

panopticon Bentham's name for a circular prison in which warders could at all times observe their prisoners XVIII; show-room XIX. f. Gr. PAN- + *optikón*, n. of *optikós* OPTIC.

panorama picture of a scene unfolded so as to show the parts in succession XVIII; (fig.) continuous passing scene XIX. Invented *c.*1789 by Robert Barker (who in his patent of 1787 called it 'La nature à coup d'œil', i.e. 'nature at a glance'), f. Gr. PAN- + *hórāma* view, f. *horân* see.

pansy XV (*pensee*, later *pensy*, *paunsie*). - (O)F. *pensée* thought, fancifully applied to the plant, f. *penser* think - L. *pēnsāre* weigh, ponder, consider, in Rom. think.

pant XV. - AN. **panter*, based on OF. *pantaisier* be agitated, gasp, pant :- Rom. **pantasiāre*, for **phantasiāre* be oppressed as with nightmare, gasp with oppression - Gr. *phantasioûn* cause to imagine, make game of, f. *phantasiā* FANTASY. Hence sb. XVI.

pantalet(te)s (pl.) XIX. f. next + -ETTE.

pantaloon Venetian character in It. comedy represented as a lean and foolish old man XVI; †(pl.) breeches in fashion after the Restoration XVII; tight-fitting trousers which superseded knee-breeches XVIII; trousers in general (esp. U.S.) XIX. - F. *pantalon* - It. *pantalone* Venetian character in It. comedy, alleged to be appellative use of the name of *San Pantal(e)one*, formerly a favourite saint in Venice.

pantechnicon name of a bazaar of miscellaneous artistic work, intended to be held in a building in Motcomb Street, Belgrave Square, London, which became a large warehouse for furniture; (hence, short for *p. van*) a furniture-removing van. XIX. f. Gr. PAN- + *tekhnikón*, n. of *tekhnikós* TECHNICAL.

pantheist adherent of the doctrine that God and the universe are identical. XVIII. f. Gr. PAN- + *theós* god; cf. THEIST. Hence **pantheism** XVIII.

pantheon sacred building in ancient Rome dedicated to all the gods XIV; habitation of all the gods, deities collectively XVI; applied to modern buildings resembling the Pantheon in Rome XVIII. ME. *panteon* - medL. *panteon*; adopted afresh XVI - L. *pantheon* - Gr. *pántheion*, f. PAN- + *theios* divine, f. *theós* god.

panther leopard (but in early use with vague reference) XIII; puma, cougar, jaguar XVIII. ME. *panter(e)* - OF. *pantere* (mod. *panthère*) - L. *panthēra* - Gr. *pánthēr*, of Oriental orig.

pantile (prop.) roofing tile curved to an ogee shape. XVII. f. PAN + TILE.

panto-, before a vowel **pant-**, repr. Gr. *pant(o)-*, comb. form of *pâs*, *pant-* all (see PAN-).

pantograph instrument for the mechanical copying of a design. XVIII. - F. *pantographe*, f. Gr. PANTO- + *-graphos* -GRAPH.

pantomime ancient Roman actor who performed in dumb show XVII; dramatic entertainment by gestures to a musical accompaniment; performance of a dramatized tale followed by a transformation scene and clowning XVIII. - F. *pantomime* or L. *pantomīmus* - Gr. *pantómīmos* adj. and sb.; see PANTO-, MIME. Abbrev. **panto** XIX. So **pantomimic** XVII. - L.

pantry XIV. - AN. *panetrie*, OF. *paneterie*, f. *panetier* - Rom. **pānātārius* (in medL. *pāne-*, *pānitārius*), for *pānārius* (in late L.) bread-seller, f. *pānis* bread; see -RY.

pants XIX. Shortening of pl. of PANTALOON.

pap[1] teat, nipple. XII. ME. *pappe*, prob. immed. from Scand. (cf. Sw. and Norw. dial. *pappe*), ult. f. an imit. base **pap-* expressing the noise of sucking; cf. L. *papilla*, late L. *papula* nipple, Lith. *pāpas* teat. Cf. next.

pap[2] soft or semi-liquid food for infants. XV. prob. - (M)LG., MDu. *pappe* (Du. *pap*), prob. - medL. *pappa*, f. L. *pappāre* eat, ult. derived from baby language (cf. L. *pap(p)a*, used by infants in calling for food).

papa father. XVII. - F. - late L. *pāpa* - Gr. *páp(p)as* child's word for father. Shortened to **pa** (dial.) XIX. The var. *pappa* (XVIII) survives in U.S. **poppa**, abbrev. **pop** XIX.

papacy office of pope XIV; papal system XVI. - medL. *pāpātia*, f. *pāpa* POPE[1]; see -ACY. So **papal** XIV. - (O)F. - medL.

papaveraceous of the poppy family. XIX. f. L. *papāver* POPPY; see -ACEOUS.

papaw, pawpaw XVI (*papaio*). - Sp. *papaya*, Pg. *papayo* - Carib; the change to *papaw* (XVII), *pawpaw* (XVIII) is unexplained.

paper substance made of interlaced and compressed fibre for writing, drawing, or printing on, etc.; sheet of this containing a document, etc. XIV; short for *newspaper*; essay, article XVII; set of examination questions XIX. ME. *papir* - AN. *papir*, (O)F. *papier* - L. *papȳrus* - Gr. *pápūros* PAPYRUS. Hence **paper** vb. XVI, **paper-hanging, paper-money** XVII.

papier mâché XVIII. Not of F. orig., though composed of F. words, viz. *papier* PAPER and *mâché*, pp. of *mâcher* chew.

papilionaceous like a butterfly. XVII. f. L. *pāpiliō*, *-ōn-* butterfly + -ACEOUS.

papilla nipple-like protuberance. XVIII. - L. (see PAP[1]). So **papillary** XVII.

papist adherent of the Pope or the papal system, Roman Catholic. XVI. - F. *papiste* or medL. *pāpista*, f. ecclL. *pāpa* POPE[1]; see -IST. Hence **papistic(al), papistry** XVI.

papoose XVII. of Algonquian orig.

pappus (bot.) downy appendage on fruits. XVIII. - Gr. *páppos* (i) grandfather, (ii) down on plants. So **pappose** (-OSE[1]) XVII.

papyrus kind of sedge from which ancient writing material was made XIV; writing material so prepared XVIII. - L. *papȳrus* - Gr. *pápūros* paper-rush, of unkn. orig. The comb. form is **papyro-**, as in **papyrology, papyrologist** (XIX).

par equality of value, equal footing; recognized value of currency, etc. XVII; average amount XVIII. - L. *pār* equal.

para-[1], before a vowel or *h* usu. **par-**, repr. comb. form of Gr. *pará* prep. by the side of, alongside, past, beyond. Also in numerous techn. comps. in which it had cogn. advb. and adj. uses, as 'to one side', 'amiss', 'irregular(ly)', 'wrong(ly)'.

para-[3] repr. F. *para-* - It. *para-*, imper. of *parare* ward off :- L. *parāre* PREPARE.

parabasis in ancient Gr. comedy, choric song addressed to the audience. XIX. - Gr. *parábasis*, f. *parabaínein* go aside, step forward; see PARA-[1].

parable (arch.) similitude, dark saying, proverb; fictitious narrative or allegory for teaching spiritual truth. XIV. ME. *parab(i)le* - (O)F. *parabole* - L. *parabola* comparison, in ChrL. allegory, proverb, speech - Gr. *parabolḗ* comparison, analogy, proverb, f. *parabállein* put alongside, compare, f. PARA-[1] + *bállein* throw.

parabola (geom.) plane curve formed by the intersection of a cone by a plane parallel to a side of the cone. XVI. - modL. - Gr. *parabolḗ* juxtaposition, application; see prec. So **parabolic** pert. to parable, metaphorical XVII. - late L. - late Gr.; pert. to a parabola XVIII. **parabolical** (in both senses) XVI.

parachute sb. XVIII. - F., f. PARA-[2] + *chute* fall. Hence vb. XIX.

Paraclete title of the Holy Ghost. XV. - (O)F. *paraclet* - ChrL. *paraclētus* - Gr. *paráklētos* advocate, intercessor, f. *parakaleîn* call to one's aid, f. PARA-[1] + *kaleîn* call. *Paráklētos* was assoc. by the Gr. Fathers with the Hellenistic sense 'console, comfort' (cf. *paraklḗtōr* comforter).

parade show, display; mustering of troops for inspection, etc.; place of such assembly; public square or promenade; †parry. XVII. - F. - Sp. *parada* :- Rom. **parāta*, sb. use of fem. pp. of L. *parāre* PREPARE, with various specific applications in Rom.; see -ADE. Hence vb. XVII.

paradigm pattern, example XV; (gram.) example of the inflexions of a class of words XVI. - late L. *paradīgma* - Gr. *parádeigma* example, f. *paradeiknúnai* show side by side, f. PARA-[1] + *deiknúnai* show.

paradise garden of Eden; Heaven XII; paradisaical place or state XIII; park, pleasure-ground; (after Luke 23: 43, etc.) the Intermediate State XVII. ME. *paradis*, also *parais* (XII-XV) - (O)F. *paradis*, also in semi-pop. form *parais* - ChrL. *paradīsus* - Gr. *parádeisos*, first used of the parks of Persian kings and nobles, (hence) garden, orchard, in LXX and N.T. Eden, abode of the blessed - Av. *pairidaēza* enclosure, f. *pairi* around, PERI- + *diz* mould, form. Hence **paradisaic** XVIII, **paradisaical** XVII. So **paradisiac, paradisiacal** XVII. - ChrL. *paradīsiacus* - Gr. *paradeisiakós*. Vars. of greater or less currency are *paradisean* XVII, *paradisial* XVIII, *paradisian* XVII, *paradisic* XVIII, *paradisical* XVII.

parados (fortif.) elevation of earth behind a fortified place. XIX. - F., f. PARA-[2] + *dos* back :- L. *dorsum*.

paradox statement or tenet contrary to received opinion; proposition on the face of it (in pop. use, actually) self-contradictory XVI; phenomenon conflicting with preconceived notions XVII. - late L. *paradoxum*, *-doxon*, sb. use of n. of *paradoxus* - Gr. *parádoxos*, f. PARA-[1] + *dóxa* opinion. Hence **paradoxical** XVI.

paraffin orig. colourless or white substance being a mixture of hydrocarbons; spec. a hydrocarbon of the methane series (*p. oil*, kerosene). XIX. - G., f. L. *parum* too little, barely + *affīnis* related; so named with ref. to its neutral quality and the small affinity it possesses for other bodies.

paragoge addition of a letter or syllable to a word. XVIII. - late L. *paragōgē* - Gr. *paragōgḗ* derivation, addition to the end of a syllable, f. PARA-[1] past, beyond + *agōgḗ* leading. Hence **paragogic** XVIII.

paragon pattern of excellence; †match, mate; †comparison; perfect diamond XVI; †double camlet; †black marble XVII; size of printing type XVIII. - F. †*paragon* (now *parangon*) in the above senses - It. *paragone* touchstone, comparison - medGr. *parakónē* whetstone, f. Gr. *parakonân* sharpen against, f. PARA-[1] + *akónē* whetstone.

paragraph character ¶ or ⁋ marking a section of a discourse, etc.; passage or section of a book, etc. XVI; short passage or notice in a journal XVII. - (O)F. *paragraphe* or medL. *paragraphus*, *-um* - Gr. *parágraphos* short horizontal stroke written below the beginning of a line in which a break of sense occurs, passage so marked, f. PARA-[1] by the side + *-graphos* -GRAPH.

parakeet XVI. Three types are repr.: (i) *parroket*, *-quet*, *perroquet* XVI, (ii) *paraquito*, *-quetto* XVI, (iii) *par(r)akeet* XVII, the last being anglicized forms of the former, which are - (O)F. *paroquet* (mod. *perroquet* parrot); perh. ult. based on dims. of the name 'Peter' (F. *Pierrot*, Sp. *Perico*).

parallax XVII. - F. *parallaxe* - Gr. *parállaxis* change, alternation, mutual inclination of two lines meeting in an angle, f. *parallássein*, *-allakt-* alter, alternate, f. PARA-[1] + *allássein* exchange, f. *állos* other. So **parallactic** XVII. - Gr.

parallel lying alongside (one) another and always the same distance apart XVI; precisely similar or corresponding XVII. - F. *parallèle* - L. *parallēlus* - Gr. *parállēlos*, f. PARA-[1] alongside + *allḗlōn* (g. pl.) etc. one another, redupl. of *állos* other. So **parallelepiped** XVII (in Gr. form XVI). - Gr. *parallēlepípedon*, f. *parállēlos* + *epípedon* plane surface, sb. use of n. of *epípedos* plane, f. EPI- + *pédon* ground. **parallelogram** XVI. - F. *parallélogramme* - late L. *parallēlogrammum* - Gr. *parallelógrammon*, sb. use of n. of adj. f. *parállēlos* + *grammḗ* line (cf. -GRAM).

paralogism false reasoning, fallacy. XVI. - F. *paralogisme* or late L. *paralogismus* - Gr. *paralogismós*, f. *paralogízesthai* reason falsely, f. *parálogos* beyond reason; see PARA-[1], LOGOS, -ISM.

paralysis XVI. - L. - Gr. *parálusis*, f. *paralúesthai* be 'loosened' or disabled at the side, pass. of *paralúein*, f. PARA-[1] + *lúein* loosen. So **paralyse**, U.S. **-yze** XIX. - F. *paralyser*. **paralytic** XIV. - (O)F. - L. - Gr.

parameter (math.) third proportional to any given diameter and its conjugate XVII; quantity constant in a given case, but varying in different cases XIX. - modL. *parameter*, *-metrum*, f. Gr. PARA-[1] beside, subsidiary to + *métron* measure.

paramount (of a feudal lord) superior, supreme. XVI (also †*pera-*). - AN. (Law F.) *paramont*, *peramont*, adj. use of adv. *paramont* above, f. (O)F. *par* by + *amont* above; see AMOUNT.

paramour adv. phr. *paramour(s)* by way of (sexual) love, for love's sake, as a lover. XIII. - OF. *par amour(s)* by or through love. Hence sb. †(sexual) love; †lover, sweetheart XIII; illicit lover or mistress XIV. The sb. use may have arisen partly from a mistaken analysis of the ME. phr. *to love paramour(s)*.

paranoia XIX. - Gr. *paránoia*, f. *paránoos* distracted, f. PARA-¹ + *nóos*, *noûs* mind. Hence **paranoi(a)c** adj. and sb. XIX.

parapet XVI. - F. *parapet* or its source It. *parapetto* wall breast-high, f. PARA-² + *petto* :- L. *pectus* breast.

paraph †paragraph XIV; (distinctive) flourish after a signature XVI. - F. *paraphe*, *-afe* - medL. *paraphus*, syncopated form of *paragraphus* PARAGRAPH.

paraphernalia articles of personal property which the law allows a married woman to regard as her own XVII; trappings, accessories, appurtenances XVIII. - medL. *paraphernālia*; sb. use of n. pl. of *paraphernālis*, f. late L. *parapherna* - Gr. *parápherna* n. pl. articles of property held by a wife besides her dowry, f. PARA-¹ + *pherné* dowry, rel. to *phérein* BEAR²; see -AL¹, -IA².

paraphrase sb. XVI. - F. *paraphrase* or L. *paraphrasis* - Gr. *paráphrasis*, f. *paraphrázein* tell in other words; see PARA-¹, PHRASE. Hence vb. XVII.

paraplegia partial paralysis. XVII. - Gr. *paraplēgiā*, f. *paraplḗssein*, f. PARA-¹ + *plḗssein* strike; see -IA¹.

paraselene see PARHELION.

parasite one who obtains hospitality, etc. by obsequiousness XVI; animal or plant supported by another XVIII. - L. *parasītus* - Gr. *parásītos* one who eats at the table of another, toady, f. PARA-¹ + *sitos* food. So **parasitic** XVII. Hence **parasitical** XVI.

parasol XVII. - F. - It. *parasole*, f. PARA-² + *sole* sun.

parasynthetic (gram.) based on a syntactical combination or compound, as *hardhearted* from *hard heart*, *get-at-able* from phr. *get at*. XIX. f. late Gr. *parasúnthetos*, f. PARA-¹ + *súnthetos*, ppl. formation on *suntithénai* combine; see SYNTHESIS.

parataxis (gram.) placing of propositions or clauses side by side without connecting words. XIX. - Gr. *parátaxis*, f. *paratássein* place side by side; see PARA-¹. So **paratactic** XIX.

parboil †A. boil thoroughly; B. boil partially. XV. - OF. *parboillir* - late L. *perbullīre*; see PER-, BOIL². Sense B is due to assoc. with PART.

parbuckle (naut.) sling or looped rope used for raising and lowering. XVII. Early forms *-bunkle*, *-bunkel*, alt. XVIII by assoc. with BUCKLE; of unkn. orig.

parcel part, portion, particle, surviving in *part and parcel*; separate part, unit, or item XIV; portion of land XV; small party or company XVI; quantity of a thing or things put together in a package XVII; quantity of a commodity dealt with XVIII. ME. *parcelle* - (O)F. :- Rom. **particella*, f. L. *particula* PARTICLE. In advb. use 'partly, partially' from XV, e.g. in *parcel-gilt*, becoming obs. XVII, and revived by Scott XIX. Hence **parcel** vb. divide into portions XV; (naut.) cover with canvas strips XVII; the latter sense may have a separate orig.

parcener †partner XIII; (leg.) co-heir XVI. - AN. *parcener* = OF. *parçonier* :- Rom. **partiōnārius* for **partītiōnārius*, f. L. *partītiō* PARTITION; see -ER².

parch dry by exposure to great heat XIV; scorch, shrivel XVI. Also *perch* XIV-XVI, *pearch* XVII; of unkn. orig.

parchment XIII. ME. *parchemin* - (O)F. :- Rom. **particamīnum*, which resulted from a blending of L. *pergamīna* 'writing-material prepared from skins invented at *Pergamum* in Asia Minor' with *Parthica pellis* 'Parthian skin'. Assimilation of the ending of the Eng. word to the suffix -MENT appears XV.

parclose †close, conclusion; partition, screen. XIV. ME. *parclos(e)* - OF. *parclos* m., *parclose* fem., sb. uses of pp. of *parclore*, f. *par-*, L. *per-* thoroughly, PER- 4 + *clore* :- L. *claudere* CLOSE.

pard (arch.) panther, leopard. XIII. OE. *pard*; in ME. - OF. *pard* - L. *pardus*; ult. of oriental orig.

pardon remission of punishment for an offence (spec. papal indulgence) XIII; excusing of a fault XVI. - OF. *pardun*, *perdun* (mod. *pardon*), f. OF. *pardoner*, *perduner* (mod. *pardonner*) (whence **pardon** vb. XV) :- medL. *perdōnāre*, f. L. PER- + *dōnāre* give. So **pardoner** (arch.) ecclesiastic licensed to sell pardons. XIV. - AN.

pare trim by cutting. XIII. - (O)F. *parer* adorn, arrange, peel (fruit) :- L. *parāre* PREPARE, which in Rom. acquired specialized uses.

paregoric assuaging pain XVII; sb. for *p. elixir* camphorated tincture of opium XIX. - late L. *parēgoricus* - Gr. *parēgorikós* encouraging, soothing, f. *parēgorein* console, soothe, f. PARA-¹ beside + *ēgor-*, var. of *agor-* in *agoreúein* speak in the assembly; see -IC.

parenchyma (anat. and zool.) substance of the liver, etc.; (bot.) cellular tissue. XVII. - Gr. *parégkhuma*, *-mat-* 'something poured in besides', f. PARA-¹ + *égkhuma* infusion, f. *egkhein*, f. EN-² + *khein* pour. Hence **parenchymatous** XVII.

parent father or mother; †relative. XV. - (O)F. *parent* (in both senses) :- L. *parēns*, *parent-* father or mother, pl. *parentēs* parents, progenitors, kinsfolk, (prop.) procreators, orig. prp. of *parere* bring forth; see -ENT. So **parentage** XV. - (O)F. **parental** XVII. - L.

parenthesis qualifying matter introduced into a passage XVI; device used to mark this, e.g. ( ) XVIII. - late L. - Gr. *parénthesis*, f. *parentithénai* place in besides; see PARA-¹, EN-², THESIS. So **parenthetic(al)** XVII. - medL.

parergon (in painting) something subordinate to the main theme; subordinate piece of work. XVII. - L., extra ornament in art - Gr. *párergon* subordinate or secondary business; see PARA-¹, WORK.

paresis (path.) partial paralysis. XVII. - Gr. *páresis*, f. *pariénai* relax, f. PARA-¹ + *hīénai* let go.

parget daub with plaster. XIV. - OF. *pargeter*, *parjeter*, f. *par* through, all over + *jeter* cast :- medL. *jectare*, for L. *jactāre* throw.

parhelion (astron.) mock sun. XVII. In early use *par(h)elion*, *par(h)elius* - L. *parēlion* - Gr. *parḗlion*, also *-ios*, f. PARA-¹ + *hḗlios* SUN. So **paraselene** mock moon (Gr. *selḗnē* moon). XVII.

pariah member of a low Hindu caste XVII; social outcast XIX. Earlier *parea*, *parrier*, *par(r)iar* - Tamil *paraiyaṉ*, pl. *paṟaiyar* name of the largest of the lower castes in S. India, lit. 'drummer', f. *paṟai* large drum beaten at certain festivals.

parietal (anat.) pert. to the wall of the body or a bodily organ XVI; (U.S.) pert. to residence within walls of a college XIX. - F. *pariétal* or late L. *parietālis*, f. *pariēs*, *pariet-* wall, partition wall; see -AL¹.

parish district for administrative purposes, orig. township having its own church and priest. XIII. ME. *paro(s)che*, *-osse*, *-isshe* - AN., OF. *paroche* and (O)F. *paroisse* - ecclL. *parochia*, alt. (after *parochus* - Gr. *párokhos* public purveyor) of *parœcia* - Gr. *paroikíā* sojourning, f. *pároikos* dwelling near, sojourner, stranger, f. PARA-¹ + *oîkos* dwelling, house; it is doubtful whether the notion 'neighbour' or 'sojourner' was prevalent in determining the application of *parœcia*, *parochia*. So **parishioner** inhabitant of a parish XV; superseded earlier *parishion*, *-shen* (XIV), alt., after PARISH, of †*paroschian*, *-ien* (XIII) - OF. *parochien*, *-ossien* (mod. *paroissien*); -ER¹ was added to suggest more clearly a personal designation.

parisyllabic XVII. f. L. *pari-*, *pār* equal, PAR + *syllaba* SYLLABLE + -IC.

park enclosed land held by royal grant or prescription for the chase XIII; (north.) field, paddock XVI; enclosed ground for public recreation; space in a camp occupied by artillery, etc. XVII. - (O)F. *parc* :- medL. *parricus* - Gmc. base repr. by OHG. *pfarrih*, *pferrih* (G. *pferch*) pen, fold, corr. to OE. *pearruc* (see PADDOCK), MLG., MDu. *perc* (Du. *perk*). Hence **park** vb. XVI f. the sb.

parkin kind of gingerbread. XIX. perh. f. proper name *Parkin*, *Perkin*, dim. of *Per* Peter.

parky (colloq.) chilly. XIX. of unkn. orig.

parlance (arch.) speech XVI; mode of speech, idiom XVIII. - OF., f. *parler* speak :- Rom. **paraulare*, f. **paraula* word; see PAROLE, -ANCE.

parley speech, talk; (conference for) discussion of terms. XVI. perh. - OF. *parlee*, sb. use of fem. pp. of *parler* speak (see prec.). Hence **parley** vb. XVI. So **parleyvoo** (joc.) sb. French talk XVIII; Frenchman XIX; vb. talk French XVIII. - F. *parlez-vous (français)?* do you speak (French)?

parliament †talk, conference; deliberative assembly XIII; Great Council of the realm XIV. ME. *parlement* - (O)F., f. *parler* speak; see PARLANCE, -MENT. The present form (XV) follows AL. *parliamentum*, which is prob. based on ME. *parliment*, etc. Hence **parliamentarian** sb., **parliamentary** XVII.

parlour, U.S. **parlor** apartment set aside for conversation in a religious house XIII; smaller room in a mansion, dwelling-house, etc. for private talk, (hence) family sitting-room XIV. - AN. *parlur*, OF. *parleor*, *parleur* (mod. *parloir*), f. Rom. **paraulare* speak (see PARLANCE); the ending is assim. to -OUR².

parlous exposed to danger XIV; dangerously cunning XV. ME. *perlous*, *parlous*, syncopated forms of *perelous*, *parelous* PERILOUS.

Parmesan epithet of a cheese made in the province of Parma and elsewhere in N. Italy. - F. - It. *parmigiano*, f. *Parma*.

Parnassian of or belonging to Parnassus, poetic XVII; epithet of school of French poetry (*les Parnassiens*) XIX. f. L. *Parnassus* - Gr. *Parnassós* Parnassus, mountain anciently sacred to the Muses. See -IAN.

parochial pert. to a parish. XIV. - AN. *parochiel*, OF. *parochial* - ecclL. *parochiālis*, f. *parochia* PARISH; see -AL¹.

parody sb. XVI. - medL. *parōdia* or Gr. *parōidíā* burlesque poem or song, f. PARA-¹ + *ōidḗ* song, poem; see ODE, -Y³. Hence **parody** vb., **parodist** XVIII.

parol oral statement XV; (leg.) pleadings filed in an action XVII; adj. oral XVI. - (O)F. *parole*, in law F. *parol*; see next.

parole word of honour XVII; password used by an officer or inspector of the guard XVIII. - (O)F. *parole* word, in the sense 'formal promise, engagement' :- Rom. **paraula* :- L. *parabola* PARABLE.

paronomasia XVI. - L. - Gr. *paronomasíā*, f. PARA-¹ + *onomasíā* naming, after *paronomázein* alter slightly in naming, f. PARA-¹ + *ónoma* NAME; see -IA¹.

paronymous XVII. f. Gr. *parṓnumos*, f. PARA-¹ + *ónuma*, *ónoma* NAME; see -OUS.

parotid (anat.) situated beside or near the ear. XVII. - F. *parotide* - L. *parōtis*, *-id-* - Gr. *parōtis*, *-id-*, f. PARA-¹ + *oûs*, *ōt-* EAR¹; see -ID².

-parous repr. L. *-parus* bearing, producing, rel. to *parere* bring forth; see -OUS.

paroxysm increase of the acuteness of a disease, violent access, fit. XVII. - F. *paroxysme* - medL. *paroxysmus* irritation, exasperation - Gr. *paroxusmós*, f. *paroxúnein*, f. PARA-¹ + *oxúnein* sharpen, f. *oxús* sharp.

parpen binding stone passing through a wall from side to side. XV (*perpend*, *-poynt*, etc.). - OF. *parpain*, etc. (mod. *parpaing*), whence also adj. in *pierre parpaigne*; of uncert. orig.

parquet flooring consisting of pieces of wood set in a pattern; (U.S.) part of the floor near the orchestra in a theatre. XIX. - (O)F. *parquet* small marked-off space, etc., dim. of *parc* PARK; see -ET.

parr young salmon. XVIII. of unkn. orig.

parricide¹ murderer of a father, near relative, or revered person, traitor. XVI. - (O)F. *parricide* or L. *pār(r)icīda*, of uncert. orig.; for the second el. see -CIDE¹. So **parricide**² murder of a father, etc. XVI. - F. *parricide* or L. *pār(r)icīdium*; see -CIDE².

parrot XVI. perh. appellative use of F. †*Perrot* (cf. PIERROT), dim. of *Pierre* Peter; cf. F. *pierrot* sparrow, and PARAKEET.

parry ward off or turn aside a weapon. XVII. prob. repr. F. *parez* (used as a word of command in fencing), imper. of *parer* - It. *parare* ward off, specialized use of the sense 'prepare' (cf. PARADE).

parse XVI. (*pars(e)*, *peirse*, *pearse*, in XVII *p(e)arce*). of uncert. orig.

Parsee, Parsi descendant of Persians who fled to India to escape Mohammedan persecution. XVII. - Pers. *Pārsī* Persian, f. *Pārs* Persia.

parsimony (arch.) care in the use of money XV; stinginess XVI. - L. *parsimōnia*, f. *pars-*, pp. stem of *parcere* refrain, spare; see -MONY. Hence **parsimonious** XVI.

parsley The earliest antecedents of the present form, *percely*, *pers(e)le*, *-ly* (XIV), appear to repr. a blend of (i) OE. *petersilie*, corr. to MDu. *petersilie* (mod. *-selie*), OHG. *petersilia* (G. *-silie*) - Rom. **petrosilium*, for L. *petroselīnum* - Gr. *petrosélīnon*, f. *pétrā* rock, *pétros* stone + *sélīnon* parsley, with (ii) ME. *percil*, *per(e)sil* - OF. *peresil* (mod. *persil*), of the same L. - Gr. orig.

parsnip XIV. The immed. antecedents of the present form, *pars(e)nep* (XVI), are alts. of earlier *pas(se)nep* - (with assim. to ME. *nep*, OE. *nǣp* turnip - L. *nāpus*) OF. *pasnaie* (mod. *panais*) :- L. *pastināca*.

parson parish priest XIII; clergyman, minister XVI. ME. *person*, later *parso(u)n* - OF. *persone*, (law F.) *parsone* :- L. *persōna* PERSON, used in the eccl. sense at the Council of Clermont 1096 ('mortuis . . vel mutatis Clericis quos Personas vocant'). The genesis of the application is much disputed, but in England the parson has been long held to be the legal *persona* who could sue and be sued in respect of the parish. So **parsonage** †benefice XIV; for *p. house* XV. - OF. *personage*.

part A. portion of a whole; portion allotted, share XIII; portion of the body XIV; melody assigned to a voice or instrument XVI; B. region; side XIV. - (O)F. *part* = It. *parte* :- L. *pars*, *part-* share, part of a whole, side, direction. Also adv. and adj. in part, partly, partial XVI. Hence **partly** (-LY²) XVI. So **part** vb. A. divide into parts; B. put or go asunder; C. depart XIII. - (O)F. *partir* :- L. (Rom.) *partīre*, *partīrī* divide, distribute, part.

partaker one who takes a part, participator. XIV. f. PART sb. + *taker*, agent-noun of TAKE, after L. *particeps*; so **partaking** XIV, after late L. *participātiō* PARTICIPATION; see -ER¹, -ING¹. Hence by back-formation **partake** vb. XVI.

parterre level space in a garden with ornamental flower-beds. XVII. - F., sb. use of phr. *par terre* on or along the ground.

parthenogenesis reproduction without sexual union. XIX. f. Gr. *parthénos* virgin + *génesis* birth, GENESIS.

partial A. inclined to favour one party or individual XV; B. pert. to a part XVII. - OF. *parcial* (mod. *partial* in sense A, *partiel* in sense B) - late L. *partiālis*, f. L. *pars*, *part-* PART; see -AL¹. So **partiality** XV. - (O)F. *partialité* - medL. **partially** XV. after late L. *partiāliter* (i) partly, (ii) with partiality, or in sense 'partly' - (O)F. *partiellement*.

partible divisible. XVI. - late L. *partībilis*, f. L. *partīrī* divide, PART; see -IBLE.

participate XVI. f. pp. stem of L. *participāre*, f. *particeps*, *-cip-* taking part, f. *pars*, *part-* PART + *cip-*, weakened form of *cap-* of *capere* take; see -ATE³. So **participant** XVI. **participation** XIV. - (O)F. - late L.

participle (gram.) word that partakes of the nature of a verb and an adjective XIV; †person or thing partaking of two natures XV. - OF., byform of *participe* - L. *participium*, f. *particeps* (see prec.).

particle small or minute part XIV; (gram.) XVI. - L. *particula*, dim. of *pars*, *part-* PART; see -CLE.

particoloured partly of one colour and partly of another. XVI. In early use also *partie* or *party coloured*; f. PARTY² + *coloured*.

particular †partial; pert. to a single individual XIV; †private, personal XV; distinguished as an individual XVI; †bestowing marked attention XVII; attentive to details XIX; sb. †part, section; minute part; particular instance; item, detail XVI. ME. *particuler* - OF. *particuler* (mod. *particulier*) - L. *particulāris*, f. *particula* PARTICLE; see -AR; conformed to L. XVI. Hence **particularism** XIX, **particularist** XVIII, **particularly** XIV. So **particularity** XVI. - (O)F. *particularité* or late L. *particulāritās*. **particularize** XVI. - F. *particulariser*.

partisan zealous supporter XVI; guerrilla soldier or chief XVII. - F. - It. dial. *partisano* = It. *partigiano*, f. *parte* PART.

partition action of dividing, orig. of property; (her.) division of a shield XV; division in general XVI. - (O)F. - L. *partītiō*, *-ōn-* f. *partīrī* divide, share, PART; see -ITION. So **partitive** (gram.) XVI. - F. *partitif* or medL. *partītīvus*.

partner partaker, associate XIV; (comm.) XVI; in games XVII; alt. of PARCENER by assoc. with PART.

partners (naut.) framework fitted around a hole or scuttle. XIII (*pauteneres*). - pl. of OF. *pautonier* servant.

partridge XIII. ME. *partrich*, north. and Sc. *partrick*, also *per-* - OF. *perdriz*, *-triz* (mod. *perdrix*), alt. of *perdiz* - L. *perdīx*, *-īc-*.

parturient about to bring forth. XVI. - L. *parturiēns*, *-ent-*, prp. of *parturīre* be in labour, inceptive, f. *part-*, pp. stem of *parere* bring forth; see -ENT. So **parturition** XVII. - late L.

party¹ A. †part, portion; side in a contest, etc.; company of persons; person considered spec. as litigant, etc. XIII; (now vulgar) individual, person XV; body of adherents XVI; detachment of troops XVII; gathering, assembly XVIII. ME. *parti(e)* - (O)F. *partie* :- Rom. **partīta*, sb. use of fem. pp. of L. *partīrī* PART. Some of the Eng. meanings ('military party', 'political party') are due to later (O)F. *parti* :- Rom. **partītum*, n. pp.

party² †particoloured, variegated XIV; (her.) of a shield divided into parts of different tinctures XV. - (O)F. *parti* :- L. *partītus*, pp. of *partīrī* divide, PART.

parvenu XIX. - F., sb. use of pp. of *parvenir* arrive, reach a position :- L. *pervenīre*, f. PER- + *venīre* COME.

parvis court in front of a church, church portico. XIV. - (O)F. *parvis*, † *parevis* (beside *pareis*) :- Rom. **paravīsus*, for late L. *paradīsus* PARADISE (applied in the Middle Ages to the atrium in front of St. Peter's, Rome).

paschal XV. - (O)F. *pascal* - ecclL. *paschālis*, f.

pascha Passover, Easter - Gr. *páskhā* - Aram. *pashā*, rel. to Heb. *pesah* PASSOVER.

pasha, pacha Ottoman title of officers of high rank. XVII. - Turk. *paşa*, perh. identical with *başa*, f. *baş* head, chief.

pasque-flower species of anemone. XVI. orig. *passeflower* - F. *passe-fleur*, f. *passer* PASS[2] +*fleur* FLOWER; alt. to *pasque-flower* (XVI) after *pasque* Easter (- OF. *pasques* (mod. *Pâques*) :- Rom. **pascua*, alt. of ecclL. *pascha*; see PASCHAL), because flowering about Easter.

pass[1] ME. *pa(a)s* (XIII), var. of PACE[1] which became restricted to the sense 'passage' (as between mountains, across a river); the sp. was infl. by next.

pass[2] intr. (the most general vb. expressing onward motion); also trans. go by, through, or beyond. XIII. - (O)F. *passer* :- Rom. **passāre*, f. L. *passus* step, PACE[1]. Hence **passable** that may be passed; that passes muster. XV. - (O)F.

pass[3] event, issue XV; act of passing; permission to go; lunge, thrust XVI. Partly - F. *passe*, f. *passer* PASS[2]; partly f. PASS[2].

passage action of passing; way by which one passes XIII; event, act (surviving in *p. of arms*); part of a discourse or musical composition XVI. - (O)F. *passage* - Gallo-Rom. **passāticum*, f. **passāre* PASS[2]; see -AGE.

passant †passing, surpassing XIV; (her.) walking XV. - (O)F. *passant*, prp. of *passer* PASS[2]; see -ANT.

passé XVIII. - F., pp. of *passer* PASS[2].

passenger †traveller, wayfarer XIV; one who travels in a vessel or vehicle XVI. ME. *passager* - (O)F., sb. use of adj. 'passing', f. *passage* PASSAGE; see -ER[2].

passe-partout master-key XVII; plate of cardboard, etc. cut out to receive a picture XIX. - F., f. *passer* PASS[2] + *partout* everywhere.

passerine XVIII. f. L. *passer* sparrow + -INE[1].

passible capable of suffering. XIV. - (O)F. *passible* or ChrL. *passibilis*, f. *pass-*, pp. stem of *patī* suffer; see PATIENT, -IBLE.

passim XIX. - L., here and there, everywhere, f. *passus* spread abroad, scattered, f. base of *pandere* spread out.

passion suffering of pain (earliest, of the sufferings of Jesus Christ) XII; †being acted upon; powerful affection of the mind XIV; outburst of anger; amorous feeling XVI; sexual impulse; strong predilection XVII. - (O)F. - ChrL. *passiō*, *-ōn-*, f. *pass-*, pp. stem of *patī* suffer; see -ION. So **passionate** prone to anger XV; marked by strong emotion XVI. - medL. *passionātus*. **passion-flower** genus *Passiflora*. XVII. tr. modL. *flōs passiōnis*; so named from the comparison of the corona to the Crown of Thorns.

passive (gram.) XIV; suffering action from without XV; (Sc. law) under a liability XVI. - (O)F. *passif*, *-ive* or L. *passīvus*, *-īva*, f. *pass-*; see PASSION, -IVE. Hence **passivity** XVII.

Passover Jewish feast, the lamb sacrificed at this, the Paschal Lamb (see Exodus 12: 11, 13; 1 Cor. 5: 7). XVI. f. phr. *pass over*, rendering Heb. *pesah*, f. *pāsah* pass over.

passport XV. - F. *passeport*, f. *passer* PASS[2] +*port* PORT[1].

past that is gone or has passed away, ago XIV; (gram.) XVI; sb. *the p.* XVI; *one's p.* XIX. ME. *passed, past*; arising out of the perfect tense of the vb. PASS[2] formed with the vb. 'to be', e.g. *the daies ben (i)passed/(i)past*. Hence as prep. beyond in time or place XIII; arising from such construction as 'The day is short and *it is passed* pryme'; whence ellipt. as adv. XIX (e.g. *to go past*).

paste flour moistened and kneaded XIV; mixture of flour and water used as a glue XVI; applied to various other mixtures XVII. - OF. *paste* (mod. *pâte*) = Sp., It. *pasta* :- late L. *pasta* small square piece of a medicinal preparation - Gr. *pástē*, pl. *pastá*, *pastaí* barley porridge, sb. uses of *pastós* sprinkled, f. *pássein* sprinkle. Hence **paste** vb. XVI. **pasteboard** material made by pasting sheets of paper together XVI. **pasty**[1] (-Y[1]) like paste. XVII.

pastel dry paste used for crayon XVII; drawing in this XIX. - F. *pastel*, or its source It. *pastello*, dim. of *pasta* PASTE.

pastern †tether or hobble for a horse XIV; part of a horse's foot between fetlock and hoof XVI. ME. *pastron* - OF. *pasturon* (mod. *pâturon*), f. *pasture* hobble, alt. by change of suffix of **pastoire* (corr. to It. *pastoia* shackle for sheep when being sheared) - medL. *pāstōria*, *-ōrium*, sb. uses of fem. and n. of L. *pāstōrius* pert. to a shepherd, f. *pāstor* PASTOR.

pasteurize sterilize by the method devised by the F. scientist Louis *Pasteur* (1822-95); see -IZE. XIX.

pasticcio hotchpotch, pot-pourri; work of art made up of fragments of an original. XVIII. - It. *pasticcio* pie, pasty, etc. :- Rom. **pastīcius*, f. late L. *pasta* PASTE. So **pastiche** XIX. - F. - It. *pasticcio*.

pastille roll of aromatic paste; lozenge. XVII. - F., either - L. *pastillus*, dim. of *pānis* loaf, or - Sp. *pastilla*, dim. of *pasta* PASTE.

pastime XV. f. PASS[2] + TIME, rendering F. *passe-temps*.

past-master A. one who has filled the office of master in a guild, etc. XVIII; B. one who is proficient in a subject XIX. In sense A, f. PAST; in B var. of *passed master* (XVI), f. phr. *pass master* graduate as a master in a faculty.

pastor †shepherd; shepherd of souls. XIV. - AN., OF. *pastour* (mod. *pasteur*), acc. of *pastre* (mod. *pâtre*) :- L. *pāstor*, *-ōr-*, f. **pās-*, extended form of **pā-* in *pāscere* feed, graze; see -TOR. So **pastoral** pert. to shepherds XV; pert. to a spiritual pastor XVI; sb. pastoral play or poem XVI. - L. *pāstōrālis*.

pastry (coll.) articles of food made of flour. XVI. f. PASTE, after OF. *pastaierie*, f. *pastaier* pastry-cook; see -RY.

pasture growing grass for cattle XIII; †feeding, food XIV. - OF. *pasture* (mod. *pâture*) :- late L. *pāstūra*, f. pp. stem of *pāscere* feed, pasture. So vb. XIV. - OF. *pasturer* (mod. *pâturer*). **pasturage** XVI.

pasty[1] see PASTE.

pasty[2] meat pie. XIII. ME. *paste(e)* - OF. *pasté(e)* (mod. *pâté(e)*) :- medL. **pastāta*, *-tātum*, f. late L. *pasta* PASTE; see -Y[5].

pat A. (dial.) stroke, blow XIV; gentle stroke or tap XIX; B. sound made by patting XVII; C. small mass shaped by patting XVIII. imit., like (dial.) *bat*, of similar date; not evidenced XV-XVI and app. re-formed XVII from **pat** vb. strike XVI, tap or beat lightly XVII. Hence **pat** adv. 'with a fitting stroke', aptly, opportunely; first in phr. *hit pat*.

patagium (anat.) fold of skin. XIX. - medL. use of L. *patagium* gold edging of a tunic - Gr. *patageîon*.

patch piece of cloth, etc., used to mend a hole, etc. XIV; various transf. uses XVI. ME. *pacche, patche*, perh. var. of *peche* - AN. **peche*, OF. *pieche*, dial. var. of *piece* PIECE. Hence vb. XV.

pate head. XIV. of unkn. orig.

pâté XVIII. - F.; see PASTY[2].

patella (anat.) knee-cap. XVII. - L. *patella*, dim. of *patina* shallow dish; see next.

paten round shallow dish for the Bread at the Eucharist. XIII. ME. *pateyne, patyn* - AN. **pateine*, (O)F. *patène* or L. *patina* shallow dish or cooking-pan - Gr. *patánē* plate, dish.

patent A. in *letters p.*, formerly also *letters p—s*, open letter from an authority recording, enjoining, or conferring something XIV; conferred by these XVI; protected by letters patent, as an invention XVIII; B. (gen.) open, manifest XVI. In A - (O)F. *patent, -ente* (in *lettres patentes*) - L. *patēns, -ent-*, prp. of *patēre* lie open; in B, directly - L. Hence as sb., by ellipsis of *letters* XIV.

paterfamilias male head of a family or household. XV. - L., f. *pater* FATHER + arch. g. of *familia* FAMILY.

paternal fatherly; derived from one's father. XVII. - late L. *paternālis*, f. L. *paternus*, f. *pater* FATHER; see -AL[1]. So **paternity** XV. - (O)F. or late L.

paternoster the Lord's Prayer OE.; rosary, or a bead of this XIII; form of words used as a charm XIV. - L. *pater noster* our Father, the first words of the Lord's Prayer in Latin.

path OE. *pæð* ≡ LG., Du. *pad*, OHG. *phad* (G. *pfad*) :— WGmc. **paþa*. Hence **pathway** XVI. Cf. PAD[1].

pathetic pert. to (esp. arousing) the emotions. XVI (earlier *-ical*). - F. *pathétique* - late L. *pathēticus* - Gr. *pathētikós* sensitive, f. *pathētós* liable to suffer, f. *pathe-* of *páthos* PATHOS; see -IC.

patho- repr. comb. form of Gr. *páthos* PATHOS, in formations on Gr. types, as **pathology** study of disease XVII (so **pathological, -ologist** XVII).

pathos quality in speech, etc., exciting pity or sadness. XVII. - Gr. *páthos*, rel. to *páskhein* suffer, *pénthos* grief.

-pathy repr. Gr. -*pátheia* 'suffering, feeling', as in HOMOEOPATHY; extended in the sense 'method of cure', e.g. in *hydropathy*.

patience XIII. - (O)F. - L. *patientia*, f. *patiēns, -ent-*, prp. of *patī* suffer. So **patient** suffering or enduring without complaint XIV; capable *of* XVII. - (O)F. - L.; as sb. †sufferer; one under medical treatment XIV.

patina film produced by alteration of the surface of bronze, marble, etc. XVIII. - It. - L. *patina* dish; see PATEN.

patois local dialect, spec. of France or French Switzerland; hence gen. XVII. - (O)F. *patois* 'rough speech', perh. f. OF. *patoier* handle roughly, trample, f. *patte* paw.

patriarch chief of a family or tribe XII; bishop of certain pre-eminent sees XIII; father of an institution XVI; venerable old man XIX. - (O)F. *patriarche* - ecclL. *patriarcha* - Gr. *patriárkhēs* head of a family, f. *patriá* family, clan (f. *patḗr* FATHER) + *-arkhēs* ruler (see -ARCH). So **patriarchal** XVI. - late L. **patriarchate** XVII. - medL. **patriarchy** †patriarchate XVI; patriarchal government XVII. - medL.

patrician noble in ancient Rome or the later Roman Empire XV; nobleman, aristocrat XVII. - (O)F. *patricien*, f. L. *patricius*, sb. use of adj. 'of a noble father', f. *pater, patr-* FATHER; see -IAN.

patrimony XIV (*patrimoyne*). - (O)F. *patrimoine* - L. *patrimōnium*, f. *pater, patr-* FATHER + *-mōnium* -MONY; later conformed to L.

patriot †compatriot XVI; (orig., as in F., with commendatory adj.) one whose ruling passion is the love of his country XVII. - F. *patriote* - late L. *patriōta* - Gr. *patriṓtēs*, f. *pátrios* of one's fathers, *patrís* fatherland, sb. use of adj. 'ancestral', f. *patḗr, patr-* FATHER; see -OT. So **patriotic** XVII. - late L. - Gr. *patriōtikós*. **patriotism** XVIII.

patristic pert. to the Fathers of the Church. XIX. - G. *patristisch*, f. L. *pater, patr-* FATHER; see -ISTIC.

patrol going the rounds of a camp, etc.; person or body that does this. XVII. - G. *patro(ui)lle* - F. *patrouille*, f. *patrouiller* (whence ult. **patrol** vb. XVII), alt. of *patouiller* paddle about in mud, f. *patte* paw, foot.

patron holder of an advowson; tutelary saint; protector, upholder XIV; (in various uses repr. Rom. ones) †captain or master of a galley, etc. XV. - (O)F. - L. *patrōnus* protector of clients, advocate, defender; (colloq.) affectionate term of address, f. *pater, patr-* FATHER. So **patronage** XV. - (O)F. **patronal** XVII. - F. or L. **patroness** XV. **patronize** XVI. - †F. or medL.

patronymic XVII. - late L. *patrōnymicus* - Gr. *patrōnumikós*, f. *patrṓnumos* named from the father, f. *patḗr, patr-* FATHER + *ónuma, ónoma* NAME; see -IC.

pattee, patée (her.) of a cross the arms of which widen out from the centre ✠. XV. - F. *patté(e)*, f. *patte* paw, of unkn. orig.; see -Y[5].

patten wooden shoe, thick-soled shoe. XIV. - (O)F. *patin*, f. *patte* paw, foot; see prec., -INE[1].

patter[1] repeat the paternoster or other prayers, etc., rapidly or glibly XIV; talk rapidly or fluently XV. f. *pater*, short for PATERNOSTER. Hence sb. XVIII.

patter[2] make a rapid succession of taps or light strokes XVII; run with rapid short steps XIX. frequent. f. PAT vb. + -ER[4].

pattern object serving as a model or specimen XIV; decorative design XVI. ME. *patron* - (O)F. *patron* PATRON, model, pattern. The change of form is evidenced in XVI.

patty little pie or pasty. XVIII. var. of PÂTÉ.

paucity XV. - F. *paucité* or L. *paucitās*, f. *paucus*; see FEW, -ITY.

paunch[1] belly, stomach. XIV. - AN. *pa(u)nche*, ONF. *panche*, var. of OF. *pance* (mod. *panse*) :- Rom. **pantice*, L. *pantex*, *-tic-* (esp. pl.) bowels, intestines.

paunch[2] (naut.) thick mat or wooden shield to prevent chafing. XVII. prob. identical with prec. through the use of OF. *pance* (whence Eng. †*paunce*) for belly armour.

pauper XVI. - L. *pauper* POOR.

pause sb. XV. - (O)F. *pause* or L. *pausa* - Gr. *paûsis*, f. *paúein* stop, cease. So **pause** vb. XVI. - F. *pauser* or L. *pausāre*.

pavan stately dance in elaborate costume. XVI. - F. *pavane* - Sp. *pavana* - It. *pavana* of Padua.

pave XIV. - (O)F. *paver*, prob. back-formation from † *pavement* (whence **pavement** XIII) - L. *pavīmentum* beaten or rammed floor, f. *pavīre* beat down, ram. So **paviour** XV. Earlier *pavier*, alt. of *paver* - (O)F. *paveur* ; see -OUR[1], -IER[1].

pavilion (large peaked) tent XIII; projecting subdivision of a building or façade; building of light construction for pleasure or amusement XVII. - (O)F. *pavillon* tent, canopy :- L. *pāpiliō*, *-ōn-* butterfly, tent (as being likened to a butterfly's wings).

pavis large convex shield. XIV. ME. *paveis* - OF. **paveis*, *pavais* (now *pavois*) - It. *pavese* - medL. *pavense*, f. *Pavia* name of a town in Italy where such shields were orig. made.

pavonine pert. to a peacock. XVII. - L. *pāvonīnus*, f. *pavō*, *-ōn-* PEACOCK; see -INE[1].

paw foot of a beast having claws or nails. XIII. ME. *powe*, *pawe* - OF. *po(u)e* :- Rom. **pauta* - Gmc. **pauta*, repr. by MDu. *pōte*, Du. *poot*. Hence vb. XVII.

pawky (Sc.) sly, humorously tricky. XVII. f. *pawk* (XVI) trick, cunning device, of unkn. orig.; see -Y[1].

pawl (naut.) bar to prevent a capstan, etc. from recoiling. XVII. poss. - LG., Du. *pal* rel. to adj. *pal* immobile, fixed, of unkn. orig.

pawn[1] piece of the smallest value in chess. XIV. ME. *poun* - AN. *poun*, OF. *peon* :- medL. *pedō*, *-ōn-* foot-soldier, f. L. *pēs*, *ped-* FOOT. The use goes back to Pers. *piyāda*, f. *pai* foot.

pawn[2] pledge, surety XV; state of being pledged XVI. - OF. *pan*, also *pand*, *pant* pledge, security, plunder :- WGmc. **panda*, repr. by OS., MDu. *pant* (Du. *pand*), OHG. *pfant* (G. *pfand*). Hence vb. XVI.

pawpaw see PAPAW.

pay[1] A. †pacify, please XII; give what is due in discharge of an obligation XIII; render (something due or exacted) XIV. B. (naut.) let out (rope); cause to fall, fall, to leeward XVII. - (O)F. *payer* :- L. *pācāre* appease, pacify (in medL. pay), f. *pāx*, *pāc-* PEACE. So **pay** sb. XIII. - (O)F. *paie*. **payment** XIV. - (O)F. *paiement*.

pay[2] (naut.) smear with pitch, etc. XVII. - OF. *peier* :- L. *picāre*, f. *pix*, *pic-* PITCH.

paynim †pagan countries, heathendom XIII; (arch.) pagan, heathen XIV. ME. *painim(e)* - OF. *pai(e)nime* :- ecclL. *pāgānismus* heathenism, f. *pāgānus* PAGAN; see -ISM.

pea (round seed of) the plant *Pisum sativum*. XVII. Evolved as if a sg. from PEASE apprehended as a pl.

peace freedom from war, disturbance, or dissension XII; quiet, stillness, concord XIII. ME. *pais*, *pes* - AN. *pes*, OF. *pais* (mod. *paix*) :- L. *pāx*, *pāc-*. Hence **peacemaker** XV.

peaceable disposed to peace; †peaceful. XIV. ME. *pe(i)sible* - OF. *peisible* (mod. *paisible*), with var. † *plaisible* :- late L. *placibilis* pleasing, f. *placēre* PLEASE; see -IBLE. In F. assoc. with and conformed to L. *pāx* PEACE, and in Eng. to adjs. in -ABLE.

peach[1] (fruit of) the tree *Prunus persica*. XIV. ME. *peche* - OF. *pe(s)che* (mod. *pêche*) :- medL. *persica*, for L. *persicum* lit. 'Persian'.

peach[2] †impeach XV; †inform against; turn informer XVI. Aphetic of *appeach*, ME. *appeche* - AN. **apecher*, for OF. *empecher* IMPEACH.

peacock XIV. ME. *pecok*, f. OE. *pēa* (- L. *pāvō*) + COCK[1]. So **peahen** XIV.

pea-jacket short stout overcoat. XVIII (first in Amer. sources). prob. (with assim. to JACKET) - Du. *pijjakker*, f. *pij*, MDu. *pīe* coat of coarse stuff + *jekker* jacket.

peak[1] pointed extremity; projecting part of the brim of a cap XVI; pointed top of a mountain XVII. prob. back-formation from *peaked*, var. of (dial.) *picked* pointed, f. PICK[1] + -ED[2]. In the earliest exx. of the last sense, rendering or repr. Sp., Pg. *pico*.

peak[2] †fall, tumble; †shrink, slink, sneak XVI; look sickly or emaciated (*p. and pine*) XVII. of unkn. orig.

peal[1] †appeal, summons XIV; ringing of a bell or bells, esp. as a summons; loud volley of sound XVI; set or ring of bells XVIII. ME. *pele*, aphetic of *apele*, APPEAL sb. Hence vb. XVII.

peal[2] young or small salmon. XVI. of unkn. orig.

pear OE. *pere*, *peru*, corr. to MLG., MDu. *pere* (Du. *peer*) - popL. **pira*, fem. sg. repl. L. *pirum*, of unkn. orig.

pearl XIV. ME. *perle* - (O)F., prob. - It. *perla*, repr. L. *perna* leg, ham, leg-of-mutton shaped bivalve. Hence **pearled** (-ED[2]) XIV, **pearly** (-Y[1]) XV.

pearmain variety of †pear XV, of apple XVI. ME. *par-*, *permayn* - OF. *par-*, *permain* kind of pear, prob. - Rom. **Parmānus* (repl. L. *Parmēnsis*) of *Parma*, It. town and province.

peasant one who lives in the country and works on the land. XV. - AN. *paisant*, OF. *païsant*, *païsent* (mod. *paysan*), refash. of earlier *païsenc*, f. *païs* (mod. *pays*) country (:- Rom. **pāgēnsis*, f. *pāgus* country district) + Gmc. *-*iŋg-*, denoting origin. Hence **peasantry** (-RY) XVI.

pease (arch. or dial.) pea plant or its seed. OE. *pise*, pl. *pisan* - late L. *pisa*, pl. *pisæ*, for earlier *pisum*, pl. *pisa* - Gr. *píson*, pl. *písa*. See PEA.

peat XIV. - AL. *peta* (XII), also in *petamora* 'peat-moor', *petaria*, *-er(i)a* peat-bog, perh. f. the Celt. base **pett-*, which is prob. the ult. source of PIECE.

peavey lumberer's hook. XIX. f. surname of the inventor.

pebble Late OE. (i) *papel*, *popel* (found only in comb. with *stān* STONE); (ii) *pyppel* in *pyppelrīpig* pebble-stream; a var. of the latter with *b*, **pybbel*, is repr. by s.w. † *puble* (XIII-XIV), midl. †*pibbil* (XIV), later †*pible*, *pibble*, of which *pebble* may be a var.

peccable liable to sin. XVII. - F. - medL. *peccābilis*, f. *peccāre* sin; see -ABLE. So **peccadillo** XVI. - Sp. *pecadillo*, dim. of *pecado* - L. *peccātum*, sb. use of n. pp. of *peccāre*. So **peccant** sinning; (med., after (O)F.) morbid. XVII. - L. *peccāns*, *-ant-*, prp. of *peccāre*. **peccavi** XVI. - L., 'I have sinned', 1st sg. pt. of *peccāre*.

peccary Central and S. Amer. quadruped allied to the swine. XVII (*pakeera*, *pec(c)ary*). - Carib *pakira*.

peck[1] ¼ bushel. XIII. - AN. *pek*, of unkn. orig.

peck[2] strike or take food with the beak XIV; strike with pointed tool XVI. of uncert. orig.; cf. PICK[2], and MLG. *pekken* peck with the beak.

pecten comb-like structure. XVIII. - L. *pecten*, *-in-* comb, rel. to *pectere*, Gr. *pékein* comb (vb.), OE. *feax*, OHG. *fahs* hair. So **pectinate** (-ATE[2]) formed like a comb. XVIII. - L.

pectic (chem.) *p. acid*, gelatinous substance forming a constituent of fruit jellies. XIX. - Gr. *pēktikós*, f. *pēktós* congealed; see -IC. Also **pectin, pectose** (-IN, -OSE[2]).

pectoral pert. to the breast or chest XVI; sb. object worn on the breast XV; medicine for affections of the chest XVII. - (O)F. - L. *pectorālis*, f. *pectus*, *-tor-* breast, chest.

peculation wrongful appropriation of property. XVII. f. pp. stem of L. *pecūlārī*, rel. to *pecūlium* property; see next and -ATION.

peculiar that is one's own XV; individual, particular XVI; uncommon, odd XVII; sb. parish or church independent of the jurisdiction of the ordinary XVI. - L. *pecūliāris* not held in common with others, f. *pecūlium* property, f. *pecu* herd, rel. to Vedic *páśu-*, OE *feoh* live stock, property, OS., OHG. *fehu* (G. *vieh*), ON. *fé*, Goth. *faihu*; f. IE. base **peku-*. See -AR. Hence **peculiarity** XVII.

pecuniary XVI. - L. *pecūniārius*, f. *pecūnia* money, orig. 'riches in cattle', f. *pecu* herd; see prec. and -ARY. So **pecunious** moneyed (XIV; rare), now repr. by IMPECUNIOUS. - L. *pecūniōsus*.

pedagogue XIV. - L. *pædagōgus* - Gr. *paidagōgós* slave who took a boy to and from school, f. *pais*, *paid-* boy (cf. PAEDO-) + *agōgós* leading, *ágein* lead (see ACT). So **pedagogic** XVII. - L. **pedagogy** XVI. - F.

pedal sb. XVII. - F. *pédale* - It. *pedale* foot-stalk, tree-trunk (*pedale d'organo* organ pedal) :- L. *pedālis*, f. *pēs*, *ped-* FOOT; see -AL[1].

pedant †schoolmaster; person who overrates book-learning. XVI. - F. *pédant* - It. *pedante*, of obscure orig.; the first el. is presumably that of PEDAGOGUE, to which has been added the prp. ending *-ante*, -ANT. Hence **pedantic** XVII, **-ical** XVI, **pedantry** XVII.

peddle A. follow the occupation of a pedlar XVI; B. busy oneself with trifles XVI. First recorded in *peddling*; in A back-formation from *peddler*, PEDLAR; in B prob. var. of PIDDLE by assoc. in form and sense with A.

pedestal base supporting a column, etc. XVI. - F. *piédestal* - It. *piedestallo*, i.e. *piè* foot, *di* of, *stallo* stall; the first syll. was conformed to L. *pēs*, *ped-* FOOT.

pedestrian going on foot; prosaic, uninspired; also sb. XVIII. f. F. *pédestre* or its source L. *pedester*, *-tr-* going on foot, f. *pēs*, *ped-* FOOT; see -IAN.

pediatrician see P(A)EDIATRICIAN.

pedicel (bot.) small stalk of a plant. XVII. - modL. *pedicellus*, f. L. *pediculus* (whence **pedicle** XV), dim. of *pēs*, *ped-* FOOT.

pedicure one whose business is the surgical treatment of the feet (also **pedicurist**); the treatment. XIX. - F. *pédicure*, f. L. *pēs*, *ped-* FOOT + *curāre* CURE.

pedigree genealogy in tabular form; one's line of ancestors; family descent. XV (*pedegru*, *-gre*, *petegreu*, *-gree*). - AN. **pe de gru* = OF. **pie de grue* crane's foot, i.e. *pie* (mod. *pied* :- L. *pēs*, *ped-* FOOT), *de* of, *gru* crane; so called from the mark / | \ used to denote succession in a genealogical tree; later forms show assim. to *degree*.

pediment A. triangular gable-like part crowning a façade XVII; B. base, foundation XVIII. Earlier *pedament*, *pedement*, refash. of *periment* (XVI), prob. deformation of PYRAMID. Sense B is due to direct assoc. with L. *pēs*, *ped-* FOOT and -MENT, and the present form simulates derivation from these elements.

pedlar travelling vendor of small wares. XIV (*pedlere*). alt. of † *pedder* (XIII), f. (dial.) *ped* wicker pannier (XIV), of unkn. orig. + -ER[1]; for the ending *-ler* cf. (dial.) *tinkler* (XII), beside *tinker*. See -AR. Hence PEDDLE XVI.

pedo- see P(A)EDO-.

pedometer instrument for recording the number of steps taken. XVIII. - F. *pédomètre*, f. *pedo-*, irreg. comb. form of L. *pēs* FOOT; see -OMETER.

peduncle (bot.) stalk of flower or fruit. XVIII. - modL. *pedunculus*, f. L. *pēs*, *ped-* FOOT; see -UNCLE.

pee (dial., colloq.) make water. XVIII. euphem. or nursery substitute for PISS; cf. F. *faire pipi*.

peek peer, peep. XVI. Early mod. *pe(e)ke*, preceded by rare ME. *pike*; parallel to *kike*, *keek* (XIV, now Sc. and dial.), which has LG. cogns. Also *peek-bo!* (XVI), superseded by *peep-bo!*

peel[1] †stake, fence of stakes XIV; (prob. short for † *p. house* XVI) small fortified dwelling or tower on the Scottish Border XVIII. - AN., OF. *pel* (mod. *pieu*) stake :- L. *pālus* PALE[1].

peel[2] A. †plunder, pillage XIII; B. strip outer layer of XV. ME. *peolien*, *pilien*, later *pele*, *pile*, *pill*, repr. OE. **peolian*, **pilian*, recorded only late in *pyleð* peels (intr.) - L. *pilāre*. Hence **peel** sb. rind, skin. XVI.

peel[3] (U.S., dial., and techn.) shovel. XIV (*pele*). - OF. *pele* (mod. *pelle*) :- L. *pāla*.

peeler (hist.) policeman. XIX. orig. nickname for a member of the Irish constabulary founded under the secretaryship (1812-18) of Robert *Peel*; see -ER[1].

peep[1] utter a weak shrill sound. XV. of imit. orig. Hence sb. XV.

peep[2] look through a narrow opening XV; emerge a little into view XVI. For the expressive combination of initial *p* with *ee* cf. PEEK, PEER[2]. Hence sb. XVI.

peer[1] (one's) equal XIII; member of the nobility XIV. - AN., OF. *pe(e)r* (mod. *pair*) :- L. *pār, par-* equal. Hence **peerage** XV, **peeress** XVII.

peer[2] look narrowly; peep *out*, show itself XVI. of uncert. orig.; cf. *pire* (XIV), corr. to LG. *pīren*; perh. partly aphetic of APPEAR.

peevish †silly, foolish XIV; †spiteful, malignant XV; †perverse, obstinate; querulous, fretful XVI. Rare before XVI; of unkn. orig. Hence **peeved** (orig. U.S.) annoyed, vexed. XX. ppl. formation on a supposed verb-stem.

peewit XVI (*puwyt, puet, -it*). of imit. orig.

peg pin or bolt of wood, etc. (cf. *pegtop*) XV; (dial.) tooth; (in stringed instruments) pin with which the tension of the strings is adjusted; step, degree XVI; (orig. Anglo-Ind.) measure of drink XIX. prob. of Du. or LG. origin (cf. MDu. *pegge*, Du. dial. *peg* plug, peg, LG. *pigge* peg; also MLG., MDu. *pegel* peg, pin, bolt). Hence **peg** vb. fix with a peg XVI; mark with pegs; *p. out*, die (sl.) XIX.

pejorative depreciatory in meaning. XIX. - F. *péjoratif, -ive*, f. pp. stem of late L. *pējōrāre* make worse, f. *pējor* worse; see -ATIVE.

pekoe superior black tea. XVIII (*peco, pack-ho*). - Chinese (Amoy) *pek-ho*, i.e. *pek, pak* white, *ho* down, hair; so called because the leaves are picked young while the down is on them.

pelage fur, wool, etc. of a quadruped. XIX. - F. *pelage*, f. *poil*, OF. *peil, pel* hair (:- L. *pilus*); see -AGE.

pelagic pert. to the open sea, oceanic. XVII. - L. *pelagicus*, f. *pelagus* sea - Gr. *pélagos*; see -IC.

pelerine mantle, cape. XVIII. - F. *pèlerine* deep collar on a mantle, fem. of *pèlerin* PILGRIM.

pelf †spoil, booty XIV; †property XV; money, 'filthy lucre'; †trash, (now dial.) refuse XVI. - ONF. **pelfe*, recorded as *peuffe* (mod. Norman F. *peufe*), var. of OF. *pelfre, peufre* spoil, rel. to *pelf(r)er* pillage, rob; of unkn. orig.; cf. PILFER.

pelican large gregarious fish-eating water-fowl OE.; †form of alembic; instrument for extracting teeth XVI. OE. *pellican*, reinforced in ME. by (O)F. *pélican* - late L. *pelicānus* - Gr. *pelekán*, prob. f. *pélekus* axe, with reference to the bird's bill.

pelisse fur or furred garment; long mantle worn by women. XVIII. - (O)F. *pelisse* - medL. *pellicia*; see PILCH.

pellagra deficiency disease marked by cracked skin. XIX. - It., f. *pelle* skin (:- L. *pellis* FELL[1]) + *-agra*, after PODAGRA.

pellet small ball; ball of stone used as a missile, cannon-shot, (now) small shot. XIV. ME. *pelote, pelet* - (O)F. *pelote* :- Rom. **pilotta*, dim. of L. *pila* ball.

pellicle thin skin, cuticle, film. XVI. - F. *pellicule* - L. *pellicula*, dim. of *pellis* skin, FELL[1]; see -CLE.

pellitory A. plant with pungent-flavoured root, 'p. of Spain'; B. low bushy plant, 'p. of the wall'. XVI. In sense A alt. of ME. *peletre* (XIV) - OF. *peletre*, alt. of *peretre* - L. PYRETHRUM. In sense B alt. of †*peritorie*, †*paretorie* - AN. *paritarie*, OF. *paritaire* (mod. *pariétaire*) - late L. *parietāria*, sb. use of fem. of *parietārius*, f. *pariēs, -iet-* wall.

pell-mell in mingled confusion, †indiscriminately, in hurried disorder; also adj. and sb. XVI (earlier †*pelly melly* XV). - F. *pêle-mêle*, OF. *pesle mesle*, jingling redupl. on *mesle*, stem of *mesler* (mod. *mêler*) mix, MEDDLE.

pellucid transmitting light. XVII. - L. *pellūcidus*, f. *pellūcēre, perlūcēre* shine through; see PER-, LUCID.

pelmet valance, as to conceal curtain rods. XIX. prob. alt. - F. *palmette* palm-leaf design on a cornice; see PALMETTE.

pelota Basque game played in a court with a ball. XIX. - Sp. *pelota* ball - OF. *pelote*; see PELLET.

pelt[1] skin with short wool on it XV; raw skin of an animal XVI. Either (1) var. of †*pellet* - OF. *pel(l)ete*, dim. (see -ET) of *pel* (mod. *peau*) :- L. *pellis* skin, FELL[1]; or (2) back-formation from PELTRY.

pelt[2] attack with many and repeated blows (now with something thrown) XV; speed along XIX. of uncert. orig. Hence sb. act of pelting; (dial.) outburst of temper XVI; *full p.* at full speed XIX.

peltate shield-shaped. XVIII. f. L. *pelta* (bot.) applied to shield-like structures; see -ATE[2].

peltry undressed skins, fur-skins coll. XV. - AN. *pelterie*, OF. *peleterie* (mod. *pelleterie*), f. *peletier* furrier, f. *pel* (mod. *peau*) :- L. *pellis* FELL[1]; see -RY. Not exemplified between XVI and XVIII; in mod. use re-adopted through Canadian F.

pelvis XVII. - L. *pelvis* basin; the anat. applications are modern.

pemmican (among N. Amer. Indians) meat prepared by drying, pounding, mixing with fat, etc. XVIII. of Algonquian orig.

pen[1] enclosure for domestic animals. XIV. presumably repr. OE. *penn*, evidenced only in designations of local features of uncertain meaning; implied in OE. *onpennad* 'unpenned', opened. So **pen** vb.[1] enclose, confine. XII.

pen[2] instrument, orig. quill, for writing XIII; (dial.) feather XIV. ME. *penne* - (O)F. - L. *penna* feather, pl. pinions, wings, in late L. pen; see FEATHER. Hence **pen** vb.[2] XV. **penknife** XV. orig. one used for mending quill pens.

penal XV. - (O)F. *pénal* or L. *pœnālis*, f. *pœna* PAIN; see -AL[1]. Hence **penalize** XIX. So **penalty** (-TY[2]) punishment imposed. XVI. - leg. AN. **penalte*, for F. *pénalité* - medL. *pœnālitās*.

penance †repentance, penitence; penitential discipline or observance XIII; ordinance for administering this (one of the sacraments) XIV. - OF. :- L. *pænitentia* PENITENCE; see -ANCE.

penates household gods of the Romans. XVI. - L. *Penātēs* pl., f. *penus* provision of food.

penchant XVII. - F., sb. use of prp. of *pencher* incline :- Gallo-Rom. **pendicāre*, f. L. *pendēre* hang.

pencil artist's paint brush XIV; writing implement of black lead, chalk, etc.; set of convergent rays XVII; set of straight lines meeting in a point XIX. ME. *pensel, -cel* - OF. *pincel* (mod. *pinceau*) :- Gallo-Rom. **pēnicellum*, for L. *pēnicillum* paint brush, dim. of *pēniculus* brush, dim. of *pēnis* tail, PENIS; see -CULE. Hence **pencil** vb. XVI.

pendant hanging part XIV; (archit., etc.) truss,

spandrel; (naut.) hanging rope. PENNANT; tapering flag, pennon XV; that by which a thing is suspended XVI; parallel, match XVIII. - (O)F., sb. use of prp. of *pendre* hang; see next.

pendent hanging, overhanging XV; (gram.) XIX. ME. *penda(u)nt* (later latinized) - (O)F. *pendant*, prp. of *pendre* :- Gallo-Rom. **pendere*, for L. *pendēre* hang, rel. to *pendere* weigh, *pondus* weight; see -ENT.

pendentive (archit.) each of the spherical triangles formed by the intersection of a hemispherical dome by two pairs of opposite arches. XVIII. - F. *pendentif*, f. L. *pendēns, -ent-*, prp. of *pendēre* hang; see -IVE.

pending A. awaiting decision XVIII; B. prep. throughout the continuance of XVII. Anglicization of (O)F. *pendant* (see PENDENT) in suspense, not concluded or settled.

pendulous hanging down XVII; suspended so as to swing XVIII. f. L. *pendulus*, f. *pendēre* hang; see PENDENT, -ULOUS.

pendulum XVII. - modL., sb. use of n. of L. *pendulus* PENDULOUS.

penetralia innermost parts. XVII. - L., pl. of *penetrāle*, f. stem of *penetrāre*; see next.

penetrate XVI. f. pp. stem of L. *penetrāre* place within, enter within, f. *penitus* inner, inmost, into the inmost recesses, rel. to *penes* within, in the power of. So **penetrable** XV. **penetration** XVII. - F. - L.

penguin †great auk (of Newfoundland); bird of the southern hemisphere having scaly paddles. XVI. of unkn. orig.

penicillate tufted, pencilled. XIX. f. L. *pēnicillum* PENCIL + -ATE[2].

penicillin XX. f. modL. *Penicillium* generic name of moulds, so named from their brush-like sporangia, f. L. *pēnicillum* PENCIL; see -IN.

peninsula XVI. - L. *pæninsula*, f. *pæne* almost + *insula* island. Hence **peninsular** XVII.

penis XVII. - L. *pēnis* tail, usu. male copulatory organ, rel. to Gr. *péos*, Skr. *pása-*.

penitence †penance XII; contrition leading to amendment XVI. - (O)F. *pénitence* - L. *pænitentia*, f. *pænitēns, -ent-*, prp. of *pænitet* cause want or discontent to, make sorry, perh. rel. to *pæne* scarcely; see -ENCE and cf. PENANCE. So **penitent** adj. XIV; sb. XV. - (O)F. - L. **penitential** XVI. - late L. *pænitentiālis*. **penitentiary** adj. pert. to penitence XVI; pert. to reformatory treatment of criminals XVIII; sb. official dealing with penitents XV. - medL. *pænitentiārius*.

pennant †pendant; pennon. XVII. blending of PENDANT and PENNON.

pennon long narrow flag or streamer XIV; (poet.) wing, pinion XVII. - (O)F. :- Rom. deriv. of L. *penna* PEN[2].

penny OE. *penig, pænig*, earlier *pen(n)ing, pending* = OS. (Du.) *penning*, OHG. *pfenning* (G. *pfennig*) :- WGmc. **panniŋga*, **pandiŋga*, of uncert. orig. OE. pl. *penegas* gave ME. *peneȝes*, whence *penies, pen(n)is*, contr. *pens* XIV, later sp. *pence* (XVI); *pennies* repr. a new formation.

pennyroyal species of mint. XVI (*pen(n)eryall, peny-*). alt. of *puliol(e) reall* (*ryall*) XV - AN. *puliol real*, i.e. OF. *pouliol* (mod. *pouliot*; :- Rom. **pūlegeōlum*, f. L. *pūle(g)ium* thyme) and *real* ROYAL.

penology scientific study of punishment. XIX. f. L. *pœna* penalty; see PAIN, -OLOGY.

pensile hanging, vaulted. XVII. - L. *pēnsilis*, f. *pēns-*, pp. stem of *pendēre* hang; see PENDENT, -ILE.

pension fixed or regular payment, spec. out of the revenues of a benefice XIV; payment made by members of a society (as an inn of court) for general expenses XV; annuity for past services XVI; †payment for board and lodging or education; boarding-house XVII. - (O)F. - L. *pēnsiō, -ōn-* payment, rent, f. *pēns-*, pp. stem of *pendere* weigh, pay; see PENDENT, -ION. So **pensioner** (-ER[2]) one in receipt of a pension; one who makes a stated periodical payment, spec. commoner at Cambridge Univ. XV. - AN. *pensionner*, OF. *pensionnier* - medL. *pensiōnārius* (whence **pensionary** XVI).

pensive XIV. ME. *pensif, -ive* - (O)F., f. *penser* think - L. *pēnsāre* weigh, balance, consider; see POISE, -IVE.

pent closely confined. XVI. pp. of †*pend* (XV), extended form of PEN vb.[1], due partly to pt. and pp. *penned*.

penta- repr. Gr. *penta-*, comb. form of *pénte* FIVE, used since late XVII in techn. terms from Gr. elements or on Gr. analogies.

pentacle XVI. f. Gr. *penta-* + *-culum*; see PENTA-, -CLE.

pentad number five, group of five XVII; (chem.) XIX. - Gr. *pentás, -ad-*, f. *pénte* FIVE; see -AD.

pentagon XVI. - F. *pentagone* or late L. *pentagōnum* - Gr. *pentágōnon*, sb. use of n. of *pentágōnos*; see PENTA-, -GON. So **pentagonal** XVI. - F. or medL.

pentagram XIX. - Gr. *pentágrammon*, sb. use of n. of *pentágrammos* of five lines; see PENTA-, -GRAM.

pentameter XVI. - L. - Gr. *pentámetros, -on*, sb. uses of m. and n. of adj., f. PENTA- + *métron* METRE[1].

pentangle XIV. perh. - medL. **pentangulum*, alt. of **pentaculum* PENTACLE after L. *angulus* ANGLE[2].

Pentateuch the first five books of the O.T. XVI (in earliest use pl.). - ecclL. *pentateuchus* - ecclGr. *pentáteukhos*, sb. use of adj., f. PENTA- + *teûkhos* implement, vessel, (later) book.

Pentecost the Jewish Feast of Weeks; Christian feast observed on the seventh Sunday ('the fiftieth day') after Easter, Whitsunday (cf. Acts 2: 1 for the transf. application). OE. *pentecosten* - acc. of ecclL. *Pentēcostē* - Gr. *Pentēkostḗ*, sb. use of fem. ordinal adj. of *pentḗkonta* fifty; re-adopted in ME. from OF. *Pentecoste* (mod. *-côte*). So **Pentecostal** XVI. - ecclL.

penthouse subsidiary structure attached to the wall of a main building, esp. one with a sloping roof. XIV. ME. *pentis*, rarely *pendis* - AN. **pentis*, aphetic of OF. *apentis, apendis* - med. use of late L. *appendicium* appendage, f. L. *appendere* hang on, attach in a dependent state, f. AP- + *pendere* hang; refash. (late XIV) by assoc. with HOUSE, as if 'sloping house'.

penultimate XVII. f. L. *pænultimus* (f. *pæne* almost + *ultimus* last), after ULTIMATE.

penumbra (astron.) partly shaded region on the edge of a total shadow. XVII. - modL., f. L. *pæne* almost + *umbra* shadow.

penury indigence, want; dearth. XV. - L. *pēnūria, pænūria*, perh. rel. to *pæne* almost; see -Y³.

peon (in India) foot-soldier, orderly XVII; (in Sp. America) day-labourer XIX. - Pg. *peão* and Sp. *peon* :- medL. *pedo, -ōn-* one who goes on foot (in classL. broad-footed man), f. *pēs, ped-* FOOT.

peony OE. *peonie* - L. *peōnia, pæōnia* - Gr. *paiōniā*, f. *Paiṓn* physician of the gods (the root, flowers, and seeds were formerly used in medicine).

people nation, race, persons coll., e.g. in relation to a place, person in authority, etc. XIII; *the* commonalty XIV. ME. *p(u)eple, people* - AN. *poeple, people*, OF. *pople*, (also mod.) *peuple* :- L. *populus*. So vb. XV. - (O)F. *peupler*.

pep (orig. U.S.) great vigour. XX. abbrev. of next.

pepper OE. *piper, -or* = OS. *pipari, pepar* (Du. *peper*), OHG. *pfeffar* (G. *pfeffer*); WGmc. - L. *piper* - Gr. *péperi*, of oriental orig.; cf. Skr. *pippalī* berry, peppercorn. Hence vb. XVI; cf. OE. *(ġe)pip(o)rian*.

pepsin enzyme contained in the gastric juice. XIX. - G., f. Gr. *pépsis* digestion, f. **pep-* cook, digest; see -IN. So **peptic** digestive. XVII. - Gr. *peptikós*, f. *peptós* cooked, digestive. **peptone** XIX. - G. *pepton* - Gr. *peptón*, n. of *peptós*.

per (1) L. prep. 'through', 'by', 'by means of', rel. to PRE-; in L. expressions from XV; e.g. *per se* by or in himself or itself; (2) OF. *per*, as in phrases repr. by the comp. advs. *peradventure, perforce, perhaps*; (her.) denoting partition in the direction of an ordinary, e.g. *party per pale*; (3) as an Eng. prep.: by, by means of, e.g. *per bearer*; as indicated or shown by, e.g. *per invoice*, joc. (*as*) *per usual*; (in distributive sense) for each or every, e.g. *so much per head*.

per- L. prep. *per* (see prec.) used in comp. with vbs., adjs., and their derivs., partly through F., partly directly from L., with the senses: (1) through in space or time, throughout, all over, as in PERAMBULATE, PERVADE; (2) thoroughly, completely, as in PERFECT, PERPETRATE; (3) away, entirely, to destruction, as in PERDITION, PEREMPTORY; (4) perfectly, extremely, very, as in PERFERVID. **b.** (chem.) denoting the (supposed) maximum of some element in a combination, as in *peroxide*.

peradventure by chance. XIII. phr. *per* or *par auenture* - OF. (see PER, ADVENTURE). Hence sb. uncertainty, doubt, hazard XVI.

perai voracious S. Amer. freshwater fish. XVIII (*peri*). - Tupi *piraya* (in Brazil *piranʸa*, whence **piranha** XIX), lit. 'scissors'.

perambulation travelling through a place, tour; spec. for the purpose of recording boundaries XV; bounds XVII. - AN. *perambulation* or medL. *perambulātiō, -ōn-*, f. L. *perambulāre*, whence **perambulate** XVI, earlier †*peramble*; see PER-, AMBLE, -ATE³, -ATION. So **perambulator** †traveller, pedestrian; †hodometer XVII; hand carriage for young children XIX.

perceive A. apprehend with the mind XIII; apprehend through the senses XIV; B. †receive, collect XIV. - AN. **perceiver*, OF. **perceivre, par-*, var. of *perçoivre* (now repl. by *percevoir*) :- L. *percipere* (i) seize, obtain, collect, (ii) understand, apprehend, f. PER- + *capere* take. So **perception** A. collection of rents, etc.; †partaking of Holy Communion XV; B. taking cognizance or being aware of objects XVII. In. A. - (O)F. *perception*, in B. - L. *perceptiō, -ōn-* (i) collecting, (ii) perceiving. **perceptible** †perceptive XVI; cognizable XVII. - OF. or late L. **perceptive** XVII. **percipient** XVII. - prp. of L. *percipere*.

per cent by the hundred, in every hundred. XVI. In earliest exx. *per cento, per centum*; prob. orig. as a financial term - It. *per cento*, with partial assim. to F. *pour cent*; often written *per cent.*, as if an abbrev. of L. *per centum*; see PER, CENT. Hence **percentage** XVIII.

perch¹ freshwater fish. XIII. - (O)F. *perche* :- L. *perca* - Gr. *pérkē*, rel. to *perknós* blackish, bluish.

perch² †pole, stake XIII; fixed bar, esp. for birds to rest upon; linear measure equal to 5½ yards XIV; superficial measure XV. - (O)F. *perche* :- L. *pertica*. So vb. XV. - (O)F. *percher*.

perchance XIV. orig. phr. - AN. *par chance*, i.e. (O)F. *par* by, *chance* CHANCE; with later assim. to PER-.

percolate pass or cause to pass through a porous substance. XVII. f. pp. stem of L. *percōlāre*, f. PER- 1 + *cōlāre* strain, f. *cōlum* sieve, strainer; see -ATE³.

percussion striking of one body by another. XVI. - (O)F. *percussion* or L. *percussiō, -ōn-*, f. pp. stem of *percutere* strike or thrust through, f. PER- 1 + *quatere* shake, strike, dash.

perdition †utter destruction; final spiritual damnation. XIV. - OF. *perdiciun* (mod. *-tion*) or late L. *perditiō, -ōn-*, f. pp. stem of *perdere* destroy, (hence) lose.

perdu †*sentinel perdue, p. sentinel* post of sentinel, or sentinel himself, in a hazardous position XVI; *be p.* be placed in such a position, (hence) lie in wait XVII, and gen. be concealed XVIII. - (O)F. *perdu* lost, perished, past hope of recovery :- Rom. **perdutus*, for L. *perditus*, pp. of *perdere* destroy, lose.

peregrinate travel (abroad). XVI. f. pp. stem of L. *peregrīnārī* sojourn or travel abroad, f. *peregrīnus* foreign; see next and -ATE³. So **peregrination** XVI. - L.

peregrine species of falcon esteemed for hawking XIV; foreign, outlandish XVI. In the first use repr. (O)F. *faucon pèlerin*, medL. *falcō peregrīnus*, so named because the young were caught in their passage from the breeding-place; in other uses directly - L. *peregrīnus* foreign, f. *pereger* that is abroad or on a journey, f. PER- 1 + *ager* territory, country; see -INE¹.

peremptory (leg.) that precludes all debate, question, or delay; decisive, final. XVI. - AN. *peremptorie* = (O)F. *péremptoire* - L. *peremptōrius* deadly, mortal, decisive, f. *perempt-*, pp. stem of *perimere* take away entirely, destroy, f. *emere* take; see PER- 3, -ORY.

perennial XVII. f. L. *perennis*, f. PER- 1 + *annus* year; see -IAL.

perfect thoroughly versed or trained; in a complete state XIII; in a faultless state, accurate XIV; (arith.) XV; unqualified, unalloyed XVI; (gram.) of a tense. ME. *parfit*, *-fite*, later *parfet*, (by assim. to L.) *perfect* XV - OF. *parfit*, *-fite* (mod. *-fait*) - L. *perfectus*, pp. of *perficere* accomplish, complete, f. PER- 2 + *facere* make, DO[1]. Hence **perfect** vb. XIV. So **perfectible** XVII. - medL. **perfection** †complete state XIII; bringing to completion; condition of being perfect XIV. - (O)F. - L. **perfective** conducing to perfection XVI; (gram.) XIX. - medL.

perfervid XIX. - PER- 4 + FERVID.

perfidy XVI. - L. *perfidia*, f. *perfidus* treacherous, f. PER- 3 + *fidēs* FAITH; see -Y[3]. So **perfidious** XVI. - L.

perforate make a hole through. XVI. f. pp. stem of L. *perforāre*, f. PER- 1 + *forāre* BORE[1], pierce; see -ATE[3]. So **perforation** XV. - (O)F. - medL.

perforce †forcibly XIV; of necessity XVI. - OF. phr. *par force*, i.e. *par* by, *force* FORCE; with assim. as in PERCHANCE.

perform †complete, finish; †bring about, effect; carry out (an order, etc.) XIV; †construct XV; go through formally XVIII. - AN. *par-*, *perfourmer*, alt. of OF. *parfournir* (in medL. *perfurnīre*), f. *par-* PER- 2, 4 + *fournir* FURNISH. Hence **performance** XVI (at first leg.). prob. - AN. **performance*.

perfume odorous vapour, (fragrance of) liquid scent. XVI. In early use also *par-*, but regularly assim. to PER-. - F. *parfum*, f. *par-*, †*perfumer* (whence **perfume** vb. XVI) - It. †*par-*, †*perfumare* (now *pro-*), lit. smoke through; see PER- 1, FUME. Hence **perfumery** XVIII.

perfunctory done or acting merely by way of duty. XVI. - late L. *perfunctōrius* careless, negligent, f. *perfunct-*, pp. stem of *perfungī* perform, discharge, get rid of, f. PER- + *fungī* perform; see -ORY[2].

pergola arbour formed with plants trained over a trellis. XVII. - It. :- L. *pergula* projecting roof, vine arbour, f. *pergere* come or go forward, f. PER- 1 + **reg-* move in a straight line.

perhaps XVI. f. PER 2 + pl. of HAP, repl. ME. phr. *by hap(s)*.

peri- repr. comb. form of Gr. *péri*, *perí* adv. and prep. about, around, roundabout, rel. to L. PER.

perianth (bot.) †calyx, involucre XVIII; outer part of a flower XIX. - F. *périanthe* - modL. *perianthium*, f. Gr. PERI- + *ánthos* flower.

periapt amulet (worn about the person). XVI. - F. *périapte* - Gr. *periapton*, f. PERI- + *háptos* fastened, *háptein* fasten.

pericardium XVI. - modL. - Gr. *perikárdion*, f. PERI- + *kardíā* HEART. Hence **pericardiac** XIX, **pericardial** XVII, **pericarditis** XVIII.

pericarp XVIII. - F. *péricarpe* - Gr. *perikárpion* pod, husk, shell, f. PERI- + *karpós* fruit.

pericope paragraph. XVII. - late L. *pericopē* - Gr. *perikopḗ* section, f. PERI- + **kop-* cut; see COMMA.

pericranium XVI. - modL. *pericranium* - Gr. *perikránion*, sb. use of n. of *perikránios* round the skull; see PERI-, CRANIUM.

peridot †chrysolite XIV; the variety called olivine XVII. ME. *peritot* - OF. *peritot* (mod. *-dot*), of which there are several vars.; of unkn. orig.

perigee (astron.) point in the orbit of a planet that is nearest to the earth. XVI. In early use varying with forms directly repr. L. and Gr.; - F. *périgée* - modL. *perigēum*, *-æum* - late Gr. *perigeion*, sb. use of n. of *perígeios* 'close round the earth', f. PERI- + *gêē*, *gaia*, *gê* earth.

perihelion XVII. Graecized form of modL. *perihēlium*, f. Gr. PERI- + *hḗlios* SUN.

peril XIII. - (O)F. *péril* :- L. *perīc(u)lum* experiment, risk, f. **per-* in *experīrī* try + *-culum* -CLE. So **perilous** XIII. - OF. *perillous*, *-eus* (mod. *périlleux*) :- L. *perīculōsus*.

perimeter XVI. - F. *périmètre* - L. *perimetros* - Gr. *perímetros*, f. PERI- + *métron* METRE[1].

period extent of time; end of a course; complete sentence, esp. one containing several clauses; full pause at end of this, full stop. XVI (*parodie* XIV). - (O)F. *période* - L. *periodus* cycle, sentence - Gr. *períodos* circuit, recurrence, course, rounded sentence, f. PERI- + *hodós* way, course. So **periodic(al)** XVII. - F. or L. - Gr. *periodikós*. **periodicity** XIX. - F.

peripatetic (member) of the school of philosophy founded by Aristotle, who taught in a *perípatos* or walking place in the Lyceum at Athens. XVI. - (O)F. *péripatétique* or L. *peripatēticus* - Gr. *peripatētikós*, f. *peripatein* walk up and down, f. PERI- + *pateîn* tread; see -IC.

periphery †layer of air XIV (once); boundary of a rounded surface XVI. - late L. *peripherīa* - Gr. *periphéreia*, f. *peripherḗs* revolving round, f. PERI- + *phérein* BEAR[2]; see -Y[3]. Hence **peripheral** XIX.

periphrasis XVI. - L. - Gr. *periphrasis*, f. *periphrázein*, f. PERI- + *phrázein* declare; see PHRASE. So **periphrastic** XIX. - Gr. *periphrastikós*.

periscope XIX. f. PERI- + SCOPE.

perish come to a violent or untimely end, cease to exist; pass. be destroyed, lost, injured by exposure, etc. XIII. f. *périss-*, extended stem of (O)F. *périr* :- L. *perīre* pass away, come to nothing, lose one's life, f. PER- 3 + *īre* go. See -ISH[2]. Hence **perishable** XVII.

peristaltic pert. to the automatic muscular movement in the alimentary canal. XVII. - Gr. *peristaltikós* clasping and compressing, f. *peristéllein* wrap up or round, f. PERI- + *stéllein* place; see -IC.

peristyle (archit.) colonnade surrounding a building. XVII. - F. *péristyle* - L. *peristȳlum* - Gr. *peristūlon*, sb. use of n. of *peristūlos* having pillars all round, f. PERI- + *stûlos* column.

peritoneum XVI. - late L. *peritonæum*, *-ēum* - Gr. *peritónaion*, *-eion*, sb. use of n. of *peritónaios*, f. *perítonos* stretched around, f. PERI- + *-tonos* stretched.

periwig XVI. alt., through the stages *perewike*, *-wig*, of *perwike*, *-wick*, vars. of PERUKE.

periwinkle[1] plant of the genus *Vinca*. XIV. ME. *pervenke*, *-vinke* - AN. *pervenke*, var. of (O)F. *pervenche* :- late L. *pervinca*, earlier *vi(n)ca pervi(n)ca*. The mod. form appears XVI as *per(i)wyncle*, prob. by assim. to next.

periwinkle[2] winkle. XVI (*purwinkle*, *pere-*, *periwinkle*). of unkn. orig.; OE. *winewinclan* pl., also read as *pinewinclan*, may perh. be repr. by dial. forms in *penny-*; in any case the second el. is the same.

perjure pass. *be p—d* be forsworn or guilty of false swearing XV (now rare), repr. AN., OF. *estre parjuré(z)*; refl. *p. oneself* XVIII, repr. F. *se parjurer* forswear oneself, for which the intr. *perjure* was formerly used XVII-XVIII (so in AN.). - (O)F. *parjurer*, †*per-* - L. *perjūrāre*, refash. of *pe(r)ierāre* break one's oath, f. PER- 3 + *jūrāre* swear. So **perjury** (-Y[3]) XIV. - AN. *perjurie* (modF. *parjure*) - L. *perjūrium*.

perk (intr., pass.) carry oneself jauntily, be spruce or smart XIV; (trans.) project or raise in a brisk manner XVI. The earliest instances refer to the action of birds and suggest deriv. from *perk* sb., var. of PERCH[2], or a transf. use of *perk* vb. perch (both now obs. or dial.) - dial. F. **perque*, **perquer*, vars. of *perche*, *percher*. Hence **perky** (-Y[1]) XIX.

perk(s) sl. abbr. of PERQUISITE(*s*). XIX.

perlustrate travel through and survey. XVI. f. pp. stem of L. *perlūstrāre*, f. PER- 1 + *lūstrāre* purify, pass in review, f. *lūstrum* LUSTRE[1]; see -ATE[3].

permafrost permanently frozen subsoil. XX. f. next, FROST.

permanent XV. - (O)F. *permanent* or L. *permanēns*, *-ent-*, prp. of *permanēre* remain to the end, f. PER- + *manēre* remain. So **permanence** XV. - (O)F. or medL.

permeable XV. - late L. *permeābilis*, f. *permeāre* (the pp. stem of which gave **permeate** XVII), f. PER- 1, *meāre* pass, go; see -ABLE.

Permian (geol.) pert. to the upper division of palaeozoic strata, characteristic of *Perm*, former province of E. Russia. XIX. See -IAN.

permission XV. - (O)F. *permission* or L. *permissiō*, *-ōn-*, f. pp. stem of *permittere* surrender, allow, f. PER- + *mittere* let go. So **permit** vb. XV (whence sb. XVIII). - L. *permittere*. **permissible** XV, **permissive** XVII.

permute †exchange XIV; †change, transmute XV; transpose XIX. - L. *permūtāre*, f. PER- + *mūtāre* change. So **permutation** †exchange, barter XIV; †alteration, transmutation; transposition (spec. math.) XVI. - (O)F. or L.

pernicious XVI. - L. *perniciōsus*, f. *perniciēs* destruction, f. PER- + *nex*, *nec-* death, destruction; see -IOUS.

pernickety XIX. orig. Sc.; of uncert. orig.

pernoctate pass the night, spec. in prayer. XVII. f. pp. stem of L. *pernoctāre*, f. PER- + *nox*, *noct-* NIGHT; see -ATE[3]. So **pernoctation** XVII. - late L.

peroration XV - F. *péroration* or L. *perōrātiō*, *-ōn-*, f. *perōrāre* (whence **perorate** XVII), f. PER- + *ōrāre* speak.

perpend (arch.) ponder. XVI. - L. *perpendere* weigh exactly, consider; see PER- 2, PENDENT.

perpendicular situated or having a direction at right angles XIV (not gen. current till XVI); applied to the third style of English pointed architecture XIX; sb. XVI. - L. *perpendiculāris*, f. *perpendiculum* plummet, plumb-line, f. PER- 2 + *pendēre* hang; see PENDENT, -CULE, -AR.

perpetrate XVI. f. pp. stem of L. *perpetrāre* perform, f. PER- + *patrāre* bring about, lit. perform or execute as father, f. *pater*, *patr-* FATHER; see -ATE[3]. So **perpetration** XV. - F. or late L.

perpetual XIV (*-el*). - (O)F. *perpetuel* - L. *perpetuālis*, f. *perpetuus*, f. *perpes*, *perpet-* continuous, uninterrupted, f. PER- + *petere* be directed towards; assim. to L. form XVI; see -AL[1]. So **perpetuate** (-ATE[3]) XVI. f. pp. stem of L. *perpetuāre*. **perpetuation** XIV. - medL. **perpetuity** XV. - (O)F. - L.

perplex trouble with doubt or uncertainty XVI; make uncertain or involved through intricacy XVII. back-formation from *perplexed* (XV), extension of †*perplex* adj. (XIV-XVII) - (O)F. *perplexe* or L. *perplexus* involved, intricate, f. PER- + *plexus*, pp. of *plectere* plait, interweave, involve. So **perplexity** XIV. - (O)F. or late L.

perquisite †property acquired otherwise than by inheritance XV; casual profits or emoluments XVI; gratuity XVIII. - medL. *perquīsītum* acquisition, sb. use of n. of pp. of L. *perquīrere* search diligently for, f. PER- + *quærere* seek.

perry beverage made from pears. XIV. ME. *pereye*, *perre(e)*, *perrye* - OF. *peré* :- Rom. **pirātum*, f. L. *pirum* PEAR; see -Y[5].

persecute †pursue, chase; pursue with malignity; †prosecute at law. XV. - (O)F. *persécuter*, f. L. *persecūt-*, pp. stem of *persequī*, f. PER- + *sequī* follow. So **persecution** XIV. - (O)F. - L.

persevere XIV. - (O)F. *persévérer* - L. *persevērāre* abide by strictly, persist, f. *persevērus* very strict; see PER-, SEVERE. So **perseverance** XIV. - (O)F. - L.

Persian XIV. ME. *persien* - OF. - medL. **Persiānus* (repl. L. *Persicus*), f. *Persia*, f. Gr. *Persís* - OPers. *Pārsa* (mod. *Pārs*, Arab. *Fārs*); assim. to -IAN XVI.

persiflage light banter, raillery. XVIII. - F., f. *persifler* banter, f. *per-* for *par-* + *siffler* whistle; see -AGE.

persimmon XVII. of Algonquian orig.

persist continue firmly *in* a state, etc. XVI; remain in existence XVIII. - L. *persistere*, f. PER- + *sistere* stand.

person †character, part played; human being XIII; living body of a human being; individual personality XIV; (theol.) distinction of being in the Godhead XIII; (gram.) XVI. - OF. *persone* (mod. *personne*) :- L. *persōna* mask used by a player, one who plays a part, character acted, etc.; perh. of Etruscan orig. The normally developed var. *parson* (XIV-XVII) has been differentiated with a special meaning; *person* is a reversion to L. form. So **personable** having a well-formed person. XV. - F. †*personnable*. **personage** †image, effigy; body of a person XV; person of note; person in a drama XVI. - OF. *personage* (mod. *personnage*). **personal** XIV. - OF. *personal*, *-el* (mod. *personnel*) - L. *persōnālis*. **personality** XIV. - (O)F. - late L. **personalty** personal estate. XVI. - law F. *personalté*. **personate** act the part of, IMPERSONATE XVI; represent, typify XVII. f. pp. stem of late L. *persōnāre*. **personify** XVIII. - F. *personnifier*; hence **personification** XVIII. **personnel** XIX. - F., sb. use of *personnel* PERSONAL.

perspective †optics; †optical instrument XIV;

(after It. *perspectiva*) art of drawing so as to give the effect of solidity and relative size XVI; drawing in perspective XVII. - medL. *perspectīva*, sb. use of fem. of late L. *perspectīvus*, f. *perspect-*, pp. stem of L. *perspicere* look at closely, f. PER- + *specere* look; see -IVE. So **perspective** adj. †optical XV; pert. to perspective XVII. - late L. **perspicacious** XVII. f. L. *perspicax*, *-āc-* sharp-sighted; see -IOUS. **perspicacity** XVI. - F. or late L. **perspicuous** †transparent XV; lucid, evident XVI. f. L. *perspicuus*. **perspicuity** XV. - L.

perspiration †breathing through; †evaporation, exhalation; excretion of moisture through the pores. XVII. - F., f. *perspirer* - L. *perspirāre* (whence **perspire** vb. XVII); see PER-, SPIRIT, -ATION.

persuade induce to believe or act in a certain way; †induce belief in or practice of, commend XVI. - L. *persuādēre*, f. PER- + *suādēre* advise, recommend. So **persuasion** action of persuading XIV; religious belief or denomination XVII. - L. *persuāsiō*, *-ōn-*; see SUASION.

pert (dial.) expert, intelligent XIII; open, manifest XIV; forward in behaviour XIV; (dial.) brisk, lively XVI. Aphetic of †*apert* (in these senses) XIII; - OF. *apert* - L. *apertus* open, pp. of *aperīre*; partly blended with OF. *aspert*, *espert* :- L. *expertus* expert.

pertain XIV. ME. *parte(i)ne*, repr. tonic stem of (O)F. *partenir* - L. *pertinēre* extend, tend or belong (to), f. PER- + *tenēre* hold. So **pertinent** relevant, apposite XIV; †appurtenant, suitable XV. - (O)F. *pertinent* or L. *pertinēns*, prp. of *pertinēre*.

pertinacious XVII. f. L. *pertinax*, *-āc-*; see PER-, TENACIOUS. So **pertinacity** XVI. - F.

perturb XIV. - OF. *pertourber* - L. *perturbāre*; see PER-, DISTURB. So **perturbation** XIV.

peruke †natural head of hair; wig. XVI. - F. *perruque* (XV, †head of hair) - It. *perrucca*, *parrucca*, of unkn. orig.

peruse †use up; go through so as to examine, revise, etc. XV; read through XVI. prob. based on AL. **perūsāre*, *perūsitāre* use up, f. L. PER- + medL. *ūsāre*, L. *ūsitārī* use often, frequent. f. *ūs-* USE. Hence **perusal** XVI.

pervade (arch.) pass through; diffuse itself throughout. XVII. - L. *pervādere*, f. PER- + *vādere* go; see WADE. So **pervasive** XVIII. f. pp. stem of *pervādere*.

perverse turned from the right way, perverted XIV; froward, wayward XV. - (O)F. *pervers*, *-e* - L. *perversus*, *-a*, pp. of *pervertere* (see below). So **perversion** XIV. - L. *perversiō*, *-ōn-*. **pervert** †overthrow, subvert; turn aside from a right course or opinion XIV. - (O)F. *pervertir* or its source L. *pervertere* turn round, overturn, ruin, corrupt, f. PER- + *vertere* turn. **pervert** perverted or apostate person. XVII. sb. use of †*pervert* adj. (XV-XVI), short for *perverted*, or an analogical formation after *convert* sb.

pervious XVII. f. L. *pervius*, f. PER- + *via* way.

peseta Spanish silver coin and monetary unit. XIX. - Sp., dim. of *pesa* weight :- L. *pēnsa*, pl. of *pēnsum* (see POISE).

pessary †suppository XIV; instrument to remedy uterine displacement XVIII. - late L. *pessārium*, f. late L. *pessum*, *-us* - Gr. *pessós*, *-ón* draught-board, oval stone used in a game, medicated plug; see -ARY.

pessimism †the worst condition possible XVIII; tendency to look at the worst aspect of things XIX. f. L. *pessimus* worst + -ISM, on the model of OPTIMISM.

pest †pestilence, plague XVI; noxious person or thing XVII. - F. *peste* or L. *pestis* plague, contagious disease. So **pestiferous** plague-bringing, pernicious. XVI. - L. *pestifer*, *-ferus*. **pestilence** XIV. - (O)F. - L. *pestilentia*, f. *pestilēns*, *-ent-*, *-entus* (whence **pestilent** XV). **pestilential** XIV. - medL. Hence **pesticide** XX.

pestle XIV. - OF. *pestel* = It. *pestello* - L. *pistillum*, dim. of **pistrum*, f. *pist-*, pp. stem of *pinsāre* pound; cf. -EL[2].

pet[1] animal domesticated and treated as a favourite; indulged child XVI; darling, favourite XVIII. orig. Sc. and north. dial.; of Celt. orig. (cf. Ir., Gael. *peata*).

pet[2] offence at being slighted. XVI. of unkn. orig. Hence **pettish** (-ISH[1]) XVI.

petal XVIII. - modL. *petalum*, in medL. metal plate - Gr. *pétalon* lamina, leaf, sb. use of n. of adj. *pétalos* outspread, f. base *pet-*, as in *petánnusthai* unfold.

petard small bomb for making a breach XVI; firework XVII. - F. *pétard*, f. *péter* break wind, f. *pet* fart :- L. *pēditum*, f. *pēdere* break wind; see -ARD.

peter (orig. U.S.) become exhausted, give *out*. XIX (first in trans. use). of unkn. orig.

petiole leaf-stalk. XVIII. - F. *pétiole* - L. *petiolus* little foot, fruit-stalk, specialized by Linnaeus.

petite XVIII. - F., fem. of *petit* small, PETTY.

petition action of begging or supplicating, orig. in prayer XIV; formally drawn-up request from an inferior to a superior or body in authority XV. - (O)F. *pétition* - L. *petītiō*, *-ōn-*, f. pp. stem of *petere* aim at, ask, seek; see -TION. Hence vb. XVII.

petrel XVII (early vars. *pitteral*, *pittrel*). of uncert. orig.

petrify convert into stone XVI; deprive of movement or feeling XVII. - F. *pétrifier*, f. L. *petra* rock - Gr. *pétrā*; see -FY. Hence **petrifaction** XVII.

petro- comb. form of Gr. *pétrā* rock or *pétros* stone, as in **petrography** XVII, **petrology** XIX.

petrol †petroleum XVI; refined petroleum used in internal combustion engines XIX. - F. *pétrole* - medL. *petroleum*; see next.

petroleum mineral oil, occurring in rocks, etc. XVI. - medL., f. L. *petra* rock (see PETRIFY) + *oleum* OIL.

petronel large pistol or carbine. XVI. - F. *petrinal*, var. of *poitrinal*, sb. use of adj. 'pert. to breast or chest', f. *poitrine* :- Rom. **pectorīna*, f. L. *pectus*, *pector-* breast; so called because in firing it the butt end rested against the chest.

petticoat †small coat worn under the doublet XV; †tunic or chemise XV; skirt dependent from the waist XVI. orig. two words, PETTY and COAT.

pettifogger legal practitioner of inferior status XVI; (gen.) petty practioner XVII. f. PETTY + *fogger* lawyer of low class, of unkn. orig. Hence **pettifogging** (-ING[1,2]) XVI.

pettitoes (orig.) giblets; (later) pig's trotters XVI. In form and sense corr. to F. *petite oie* 'little goose', giblets of a goose; assim. to PETTY and pl. of TOE took place early.

petty †small XIV; minor, secondary, subordinate XVI. ME. *pety*, var. of *petit* - (O)F. :- Rom. **pittittus*, f. **pit-*, repr. in late L. *pitinnus*, *pitulus* very small.

petulant †wanton, lascivious XVI; †pert, saucy XVII; pettishly impatient XVIII. - (O)F. *pétulant* - L. *petulāns*, *-ant-*, prp. of **petulāre*, f. *petere* direct oneself to, attack; see -ANT. So **petulance** XVII.

petunia XIX. - modL., f. F. *petun* tobacco (also in Eng. use XVI-XVII) - Guarani *petȳ*; see -IA[1].

pew raised enclosure or desk in a church, †in a court, etc. XIV; pl. fixed benches with backs XVII. ME. *pywe*, *puwe* - OF. *puye*, *puie* - L. *podia*, pl. of *podium* elevated place, parapet - Gr. *pódion* base, pedestal, dim. of *poús*, *pod-* FOOT.

pewit see PEEWIT.

pewter XIV. - OF. *peutre*, *peaultre* :- Rom. **peltrum*, of unkn. orig. So **pewterer** XIV. - AN. *peautrer*, OF. *peautrier*.

pfennig $\frac{1}{100}$ of the German mark. XVI (*phen(n)ing*). - G.; see PENNY.

phaeton four-wheeled open carriage. XVIII. - F. *phaéton* - L. *Phaethōn* - Gr. *Phaéthōn* (myth.) son of Helios (sun) and Clymene, famous for his unlucky driving of the sun-chariot, sb. use of prp. *phaéthōn* shining, rel. to *phaínein* show (cf. PHENOMENON).

phago- repr. Gr. *phago-* eating, *phageîn* eat, as in *phagocyte*. So **-phagous** -eating, f. L. *-phagus*, Gr. *-phagos*, **-phagy**, f. Gr. *-phagiā*, as in *ichthyophagous*, *-phagy*.

phalanx line of battle XVI; (anat.) joint of a digit XVII; (bot.) bundle of stamens XVIII. - L. - Gr. *phálagx*. So **phalange** XVI. - F. - L.

phallus XVII. - late L. - G. *phallós*. So **phallic** XVIII.

phantasm illusion XIII; apparition, ghost; imagination, fancy XV; mental image XVI. - (O)F. *fantasme*, †*-esme* - L. *phantasma*; see next. So **phantasmagoria** exhibition of optical illusions; shifting succession of imaginary figures XIX. prob. - F. *fantasmagorie*, f. *fantasme* with fanciful termination.

phantasy see FANTASY.

phantom †illusion, deception XIII; apparition XIV; mental image XVI; appearance without substance XVII. ME. *fanto(s)me*, *-um* - OF. *fanto(s)me* (mod. *fantôme*) :- Gr. dial. **phantagma* (Gr. *phántasma*), f. *phantázein* make visible, f. *phaínein*, *phant-* show (see PHENOMENON).

Pharisee OE. *fariseus*, early ME. *farisew* - late L. *pharīsæus*, *-ēus* - Gr. *pharīsaîos* - Aram. *p^erīšaiyā*, emphatic pl. of *p^erīš* = Heb. *pārûš* separated, separatist. The present form is from ME. *f-*, *pharise(e)* - OF. *pharise* - L.

pharmacy administration of medicines XIV; art of preparing drugs XVII; dispensary XIX. - OF. *farmacie* (mod. *pharmacie*) - medL. *pharmacia* - Gr. *pharmakeíā* practice of a *pharmakeús* druggist, f. *phármakon* drug, medicine; see -Y[3]. So **pharmaceutical** XVII. f. late L. *pharmaceuticus* - Gr. *-keutikós*. **pharmacopoeia** XVII. modL. - Gr. *pharmakopoiía* (*-poiós* -making, -maker).

pharos lighthouse. XVI. Appellative use of L. *Pharos* - Gr. *Pháros* name of an island off Alexandria on which stood a famous lighthouse.

pharynx XVII. - modL. - Gr. *phárugx* (cf. *pháragx* cleft, chasm). Hence **pharyng(e)al** XIX.

phase aspect (orig. astron. of a planet). XIX. Partly - F., partly new sg. evolved from *phases*, pl. of **phasis** (XVII) - modL. - Gr. *phásis* appearance, phase, f. **pha-*, as repr. by *phôs*, *pháos* light.

pheasant XIII. - AN. *fesaunt*, for (O)F. *faisan* - Pr. :- L. *phāsiānus* - Gr. *phāsiānós* of Phasis, a river in Colchis, whence the bird is said to have spread westwards. For parasitic *-t* cf. *ancient*, *pageant*, *tyrant*.

phen(o)- repr. Gr. *phaino-*, rel. to *phaínein* shine; orig. applied to coal-tar products arising from the manufacture of 'illuminating' gas, later as in *phenacetin*, *pheno-barbitone*.

phenol (chem.) hydroxyl derivative of benzene, carbolic acid. XIX. - F. *phénole*, f. *phène* benzene; see -OL.

phenomenon, pl. **-mena** thing or fact perceived or observed XVII; notable or exceptional fact or occurrence XVIII. Also, in early use, *phaino-*, *phaeno-*; - late L. *phænomenon* - Gr. *phainómenon*, sb. use of prp. pass. of *phaínein* show, pass. be seen, appear.

phial XIV. ME. *fyole* - (O)F. *fiole* - L. *phiola*, *phiala* saucer, censer - Gr. *phiálē* broad flat vessel.

-phil(e) repr., through med. and modL. *-philus*, F. *-phile*, Gr. terminal el. *-philos* 'dear to', 'beloved by', as in *Theophilus* dear to God; with sense 'loving, devoted or favourable to' in medL. and later, e.g. modL. *botanophilus* amateur botanist, Eng. *bibliophile* (- F.), and many formations like *Anglophil(e)*. The corr. adj. suffix is **-philous**, frequent in bot. and zool., with the sense 'having affinity to or preference for', as *hygrophilous*; with corr. nouns of state or quality in **-phily**, **-philism.**

philander †(passionate) lover. XVII. - Gr. *phílandros*, f. *phil-* PHILO- + *anḗr*, *andr-* man, husband; used as a character-name in poetry and drama. Hence vb. make love, esp. flirtatiously. XVIII.

philanthropy XVII. - late L. *philanthrōpia* - Gr. *philanthrōpiā*, f. *philánthrōpos*, f. *phil-* PHILO- + *ánthrōpos* man; see -Y[3]. So **philanthropic, philanthropist** XVIII.

philately postage-stamp-collecting. XIX. - F. *philatélie*, f. Gr. *phil-* PHILO- + *ateleiā* exemption from payment, f. A-[4] + *télos* charge, tax; see -Y[3]. Hence **philatelic, philatelist** XIX.

philharmonic devoted to music. XVIII. - F. *philharmonique* - It. *filarmonico*; see PHILO-, HARMONIC.

philippic (pl.) name of the orations of Demosthenes against Philip II, king of Macedon (IV B.C.); hence applied to Cicero's orations against Mark Antony, and gen. to any invective or denunciatory speech. XVI. - L. *philippicus* - Gr. *Philippikós*, f. *Phílippos*; see -IC.

Philistine one of a people in ancient Palestine

who harassed the Israelites; an enemy into whose hands one may fall XVI; †in Germany, one who is not a student at the university; person deficient in liberal culture XIX. - F. *Philistin* or late L. *Philistīnus*, also *Palæstīnus*, usu. pl. - late Gr. *Philistînoi*, *Palaistînoi* - Heb. *pᵉlištīm*, rel. to *pᵉlešeth* Philistia, Palestine. Hence **Philistinism** XIX.

philo-, before a vowel or *h* **phil-**, repr., often through F. or L., Gr. *phil(o)-*, comb. form of *phílos* meaning 'lover', 'loving', as in *philósophos* PHILOSOPHER; in many comps. (often nonce-words) from XVII, among which in later use are numerous specimens of the type of Gr. *philéllēn* loving or favourable to the Greeks, **philhellene** (XIX).

philology †study of literature XVII; science of language XVIII. - F. *philologie* - L. *philologia* - Gr. *philologiā* devotion to dialectic, love of learning and literature, love of language, f. *philólogcs* fond of talking, etc.; see PHILO-, LOGOS. Hence **philological, philologist** XVII.

philosopher XIV. - AN. *philo-, filosofre*, var. of (O)F. *philosophe* - L. *philosophus* - Gr. *philósophos* 'lover of wisdom', f. PHILO- + base of *sophós* wise. So **philosophic** XVII, **philosophical** XIV. - late L. *philosophicus*. **philosophize** XVI. corr. in use to F. *philosopher*, L. *philosophārī*, Gr. *philosophein*. **philosophy** (-Y³) XIII.

philtre, U.S. **philter** love-potion. XVI. - F. *philtre* - L. *philtrum* - Gr. *phíltron*, f. **phil-* as in *phileîn* love + *-tron*, suffix of instrument or means.

phiz face. XVII (*phyz, phys*). colloq. shortening of *physnomy*, early var. of PHYSIOGNOMY.

phleb(o)- comb. form of Gr. *phléps, phleb-* vein. **phlebotomy** blood-letting. XIV (*fl-*). - OF. *flebothomie* (mod. *phlébotomie*) - late L. *phlebotomia* - Gr. *phlebotomiā*; see -TOMY. So **phlebotomize** XVI.

phlegm mucus, considered as one of the four humours (cold and moist) XIV; as a secretion of membranes XV; coldness or sluggishness supposed to proceed from the predominance of the humour XVI. The present form appears XVI, as the result of assim. to the Gr.-L. original or earlier *fle(u)me, fleam(e)* - OF. *fleume* (mod. *flegme*) - late L. *phlegma* clammy moisture of the body - Gr. *phlégma* inflammation, morbid humour as the result of heat, f. *phlégein* burn, blaze. So **phlegmatic** XIV (*fleu-*).

phlogiston (old chem.) principle of inflammability. XVIII. - Gr. *phlogistón*, n. of *phlogistós* burnt up, inflammable, f. *phlogízein* set on fire, f. **phlog-* burn; see next.

phlox herbaceous plant. XVIII. - L. - Gr. *phlóx* lit. flame, f. **phlog-* **phleg-* :- IE. **bhleg-* (cf. FLAGRANT).

-phobe terminal el. - F. - L. *-phobus*, Gr. *-phobos* fearing, f. *phóbos* fear, as in *hydrophobe*, and many comps. with national names, as *Anglophobe*; so **-phobia** (- L. - Gr. *-phobiā*) in the sense 'dread', 'horror', as in *hydrophobia*, and *Anglophobia*, etc., some of which are modelled on F. words in *-phobie*.

phoenix mythical bird of gorgeous plumage living for centuries in the Arabian desert, then burning itself to ashes, from which it emerged with renewed youth. OE., ME. *fenix* - L. *phœnix* and OF. *fenix* (mod. *phénix*), the L. being - Gr. *phoînix*, of unkn. orig.

phone¹ abbrev. of TELEPHONE. XX.

phone² (philol.) element of spoken language. XIX. - Gr. *phōnḗ* sound (see PHONETIC).

-phone terminal el., repr. Gr. *phōnḗ* voice, sound, used in the names of instruments for transmitting, reproducing, or amplifying sound, as *gramophone, megaphone, microphone, radiophone, telephone*.

phoneme XIX. - F. *phonème* - Gr. *phṓnēma*, f. *phōneîn* speak.

phonetic pert. to or representing vocal sounds; (sb. pl.) science of speech-sounds. XIX. - modL. *phōnēticus* - Gr. *phōnētikós*, f. *phōnētós*, ppl. formation on *phōneîn* speak, f. *phōnḗ* voice, rel. to L. *fāma* FAME; see -IC. Hence **phonetician** XIX.

phoney (sl.) deceptive, fraudulent. XX. of unkn. orig.

phonogram character representing a spoken sound; †sound-record made by a phonograph. XIX (see GRAMOPHONE). **phonograph** †symbol representing a sound; instrument for recording and reproducing sounds. XIX. f. Gr. *phōnḗ* sound + *-graphos* written, *-gráphos* -writing; see prec. and -GRAPH. So **phonography** †phonetic spelling XVIII; phonetic shorthand invented by Isaac Pitman XIX. **phonology** science of vocal sounds esp. as applied to particular languages. XVIII.

-phore terminal el. repr. F. *-phore*, modL. *-phorus* - Gr. *phóros* bearing, bearer, f. **phor-* **pher-* BEAR², as in *semaphore*. So **-phoric, -phorous.**

phosphate (chem.) salt of phosphoric acid. XVIII. - F. *phosphat*, f. *phosphore* PHOSPHORUS + *-at* -ATE².

phosphorus †morning star; phosphorescent substance; highly inflammable non-metallic element luminous in the dark. XVII. - L. *phōsphorus* - Gr. *phōsphóros* light-bringing, sb. morning star, f. *phôs* light + *-phóros* -PHORE. So **phosphoric** (- F.), **phosphorous** XVIII. Hence **phosphoresce, -escence, -escent** XVIII.

photo- repr. *phōto-*, comb. form of Gr. *phôs, phōt-* light, as in **photometer** XVIII; later esp. in connection with photography, as **photogravure** (F. *gravure* engraving) XIX.

photograph picture produced by the action of light on a sensitized film. First used, together with **photographic** and **photography,** by Sir John Herschel (1792-1871) in a paper read before the Royal Society on 14 March 1839; preceded by G. *photographie*. f. Gr. *phôs, phōto-* light + *-graphos* written; see PHOTO-, -GRAPH. *Photographic* superseded *photogenic* (XIX), which is now used for 'offering a good subject for photography'.

phrase style of expression, diction; small group of words in a sentence; pithy expression. XVI. In earliest use also *phrasis, -ys*, from the pl. of which (*phrases*) a sg. *phrase* appears to have been evolved. - L. *phrasis* - Gr. *phrásis* speech, manner of speaking, f. *phrázein* indicate, declare, tell. So **phraseology** XVII. - modL. *phraseologia*, spurious Gr. *phraseologiā*.

phrenetic frenzied, FRANTIC. XIV. - (O)F. *frénétique* - L. *phrenēticus* - late Gr. *phrenētikós*, for *phrenītikós*, f. *phrenîtis* delirium, f. *phrḗn*, *phren-* heart, mind; see -ITIS, -IC.

phrenology XIX. f. Gr. *phrḗn*, *phren-* mind + -LOGY.

phthisic (having) pulmonary consumption. XIV. ME. *tisik*, later *ptisike*, *phthisick* - OF. *tisike*, *-ique*, later *ptisique*, *thisique* (repl. by mod. *phtisie*) :- Rom. *(*ph*)*thisica*, sb. use of fem. of L. *phthisicus* - Gr. *phthisikós* consumptive, f. *phthísis*, f. **phthi-*, *phthínein* waste away; see -IC. So **phthisis** XVI. - L. - Gr.

phut (sl.) *go ph.*, be a failure. XIX. f. Hindi *phaṭnā* burst.

phylactery small box containing four texts of Scripture worn by Jews as a reminder of the obligation to keep the law. XIV; in various uses from XVII. Early forms *fil-*, *philaterie* - OF. **filaterie*, *-atiere* - late L. *fyl-*, *phylactērium* - Gr. *phulaktḗrion* safeguard, amulet, f. *phulaktḗr* guard.

phyllo- repr. comb. form of Gr. *phúllon* leaf.

phylo- repr. comb. form of Gr. *phūlḗ*, *phûlon* race (whence modL. **phylum** XIX), as in **phylogeny** (Gr. *génos* GENUS) racial or tribal history.

physic healing art, medicine XIII; †natural science XIV; medicinal preparation, medicine XVI. ME. *fisike* - OF. *fisique* medicine (mod. *physique* natural science, now physics) - L. *physica*, *-ē* - Gr. *phusikḗ*, sb. use of fem. of *phusikós*, f. *phúsis* nature; see -IC. So **physic** adj. †medical, medicinal XV; physical, natural XVI. **physical** medical, medicinal XV; natural, material XVI; pert. to physics; bodily, corporeal XVIII. - medL. *physicālis*. **physicist** XIX. **physics** natural science XVI; science that treats of matter and energy XVIII; rendering L. n. pl. *physica* - Gr. *tà phusiká* title of Aristotle's physical treatises.

physician XIII. ME. *fisicien* - OF. (mod. *physicien* physicist), f. *fisique* PHYSIC; see -IAN.

physio- repr. *phusio-*, comb. form of Gr. *phúsis* nature. **physiognomy** judging character from bodily lineaments; face, countenance. XIV. ME. *fisnamye*, *fis-*, *phisonomie*, later *phisnomy* (XV-XVII), *phisognomie* (XVI-XVII), *physiognomy* (XVI) - OF. *phisonomie*, *-anomie* (mod. *physionomie*) - medL. *phiso-*, *physionomia* - late Gr. *phusiognōmiā* for Gr. *phusiognōmoniā*, f. *phúsis* nature + *gnṓmōn*, *gnōmon-* interpreter, f. **gnō-* (see KNOW). **physiography** description of natural phenomena; physical geography. XIX. - F. *physiographie*; so **physiographical** XVIII. **physiology** †natural science, natural philosophy XVI; science of the phenomena of living things XVII. - F. *physiologie* or L. *physiologia* - Gr. *phusiologiā*; hence **physiological** XVII. **physiologist** †natural philosopher XVII; student of animal or vegetable physiology XVIII.

physique XIX. - F., sb. use of *physique* PHYSICAL.

-phyte terminal el. repr. Gr. *phutón* plant, f. *phúein* bring forth (see BE), and denoting a vegetable organism, as in *saprophyte*, *zoophyte*.

phyto- repr. comb. form of Gr. *phutón* (see prec.), used in many bot. terms.

pi (math.) ratio of the circumference of a circle to the diameter. XIX. name of the Gr. letter Π π (P p), initial letter of *periphéreia* periphery and *perímetros* perimeter.

piacular pert. to expiation. XVII. - L. *piāculāris*, f. *piāculum* expiation, f. *piāre* appease, f. *pius* PIOUS; see -AR.

pia mater delicate innermost of the three meninges of the brain and spinal cord. XVI. - medL., tr. Arab. *al-umm ar-raḳīḳa* the thin or tender mother; cf. DURA MATER.

pianoforte XVIII. - It., evolved from the descriptive name *gravecembalo col piano e forte* 'harpsichord with soft and loud' used by the inventor Bartolomeo Cristofori of Padua (*c.*1710). Now usu. abbr. **piano** XIX.

piastre Sp. piece of eight or dollar; small Turk. coin. XVII. - F. - It. *piastra* metal plate, coin, repr. L. *emplastra*, var. of *emplastrum* PLASTER.

piazza public square XVI; (erron.) colonnade, covered ambulatory XVII; (U.S.) veranda XVIII. - It. *piazza* = F. *place* PLACE.

pibroch series of variations for the bagpipe. XVIII. - Gael. *piobaireachd*, f. *piobair* piper (f. *piob* pipe) + *-achd* suffix of function, etc.

pica (typogr.) size of printing type. XVI. transf. use of medL. *pica* almanac for the recitation of divine service (perh. ult. identical with L. *pīca* PIE[1]).

picador in bullfighting, mounted man who provokes the bull with a lance. XVIII. - Sp., 'pricker', f. *picar* prick.

picaresque pert. to rogues, orig. of Sp. literary fiction. XIX. - F. - Sp. *picaresco*, f. *picaro* roguish, sb. rogue; see -ESQUE.

picaroon pirate, pirate ship; rogue. XVII. - Sp. *picaron*, augm. of *picaro* rogue; see prec. and -OON.

picayune (in Louisiana, etc.) Spanish half-real, (U.S.) 5-cent piece; insignificant object; adj. mean, paltry. XIX. - F. *picaillon* old copper coin of Piedmont, cash - modPr. *picaioun*, of unkn. orig.

piccalilli XVIII. prob. fancifully f. PICKLE.

piccaninny little one, child, esp. Black child. XVII. W. Indian Negro formation on Sp. *pequeño* or Pg. *pequeno* little, small (of unkn. orig.); perh. directly based on Pg. dim. *pequenino*.

piccolo XIX. - It. *piccolo* small.

pick[1] pointed tool for breaking up a surface. XIV. ME. *pic*, *pykk*, app. collateral form of *pike* pick, pointed object (surviving dial.), OE. *pīc*, rel. to *pīcung* pricking, vbl. sb. of **pīcian* or **pīcan* (see next).

pick[2] probe with a pointed instrument, etc.; pluck, gather; choose *out*; rob, plunder. XV. Succeeded to *pike* XIV (surviving dial.), prob. through the infl. of F. *piquer* or MLG., MDu. *picken* (Du. *pikken*), in the senses 'pick', 'peck', 'pierce', 'puncture'.

pick-a-back, piggyback on the shoulders or back like a pack. XVI. Earlier (†*a*) *pick-back*, †*on* or *a pick-pack* (still dial.); it is doubtful whether the orig. form referred to the pitching of a pack on the shoulders or the back on which it is pitched.

pickaxe XV. alt., by assim. of the final syll. to AXE, of ME. *pikois, -eis* (XIV) - OF. *picois* (rel. to PICK[1]).

pickerel young pike. XIV. f. PIKE[1] + -EREL.

picket A. pointed stake, etc. XVII; B. small detachment of troops (orig. with horses tied to stakes) XVIII. - F. *piquet*, f. *piquer* prick, pierce; see PICK[2], -ET.

pickle salt liquor in which food is preserved XIV; article of food so preserved XVII. ME. *pekille, pykyl* - MLG., MDu. *pekel*, of unkn. orig. Hence vb. XVI.

picnic (orig.) social entertainment in which each person contributed a share of the food; (now) outdoor pleasure party with a repast. XVIII. - F. *piquenique*, app. f. *piquer* PICK[2] + *nique* (cf. *faire la nique à* mock, show scorn of).

picotee variety of carnation. XVIII. - F. *picoté*, pp. of *picoter* mark with pricks or points, f. *picot*, dim. of *pic* point, prick.

picquet card-game. XVII. - F. *piquet*, †*picquet*, prob. f. *pic* in *faire pic* make sixty, of obscure orig.

picric (chem.) *p. acid*. f. Gr. *pikrós* bitter + -IC.

Pict one of an ancient people of N. Britain. XIV. - late L. *Pictī*, identical in form with *pictī* painted or tattooed people (pp. of L. *pingere* PAINT), adopted in OE. as *Pihtas*, var. *Peohtas*.

picture †pictorial representation XV; individual painting or drawing XV; visual impression, mental image; graphic description XVI. - L. *pictūra* painting, f. *pict-*, pp. stem of *pingere* PAINT, embroider. Hence vb. XV. So **picturesque** XVIII. - (with assim. to prec., to express 'in the style of a picture') F. *pittoresque* - It. *pittoresco* 'in the style of a painter', f. *pittore* :- L. *pictor, -tōr-* painter, f. *pict-*.

piddle A. (dial.) trifle XVI; B. (colloq.) urinate XVIII. In A perh. alt. of PEDDLE; in B. presumably based on PISS or PEE.

pidgin, pigeon[2] in *P. English*, commercial jargon used esp. in the Far East. XIX. Chinese corruption of BUSINESS.

pie[1] magpie. XIII. - (O)F. :- L. *pīca* magpie.

pie[2] dish composed of meat, etc., enclosed in paste and baked. XIV. prob. identical with PIE[1] (*pīca* being the medL. equiv.); it has been conjectured that the reason for the application is that the magpie collects miscellaneous objects.

pie[3] (typogr.) confused mass of type (spec. *printer's p.*). XVII. perh. tr. F. *pâté* pasty, as in *caractères tombés en pâté*.

piebald of two colours mingled, esp. white and black. XVI. f. PIE[1] + BALD (in the sense 'streaked with white').

piece A. separate or detached portion XIII; (dial.) portion of time or space; quantity (of matter or substance) XIV; B. section or armour, etc. XIV; fire-arm; coin XVI; 'man' in a game XVI; C. person XIII. - ME. *pece*, later *piece* - AN. *pece*, OF. *piece* (mod. *pièce*) :- Rom. **pettia* (cf. medL. *petia, pecia, pet(t)ium*), prob. of Gaulish orig. (cf. W. *peth* quantity, part, Breton *pezh* piece :- Brythonic **petti-*). Hence **piece** vb. XIV. **piecemeal** piece by piece XIII.

pied particoloured, orig. of black and white like a magpie. XIV. f. PIE[1] + -ED[2].

pier one of the supports of the spans of a bridge XII; solid structure extending into the sea, etc. XIV; pillar XVII. ME. *per* - AL. *pera* or *pēra*, of unkn. orig.

pierce XIII. ME. *perce* - (O)F. *percer* :- Rom. **pertūsiāre*, f. L. *pertūsus*, pp. of *pertundere* bore through, f. PER- + *tundere* thrust.

pierrot French pantomime character; clown with whitened face in fancy costume. XVIII. - F., appellative use of pet-form of *Pierre* Peter.

pietà representation of the Virgin Mary mourning over the body of the dead Christ. XVII. - It. :- L. *pietās, -tāt-* PIETY.

pietism movement for the revival of piety in the Lutheran communion; hence gen. XVII. - G. *pietismus*. f. L. *pietās* PIETY; see -ISM. So **pietist** XVII.

piety †pity XIII; faithfulness to filial (or similar) duties XVI; devotion to religious duties XVII. - OF. *piete* (mod. *piété*) - L. *pietās, -tāt-* dutifulness; f. *pius* PIOUS; see PITY, from which *piety* was not fully differentiated till late XVI.

piezometer instrument for measuring pressure. XIX. f. Gr. *piézein* press + -OMETER.

piffle trifle (*away*), talk ineffectively. XIX. of symbolic orig. (cf. -LE[3]). Hence sb. XIX.

pig young of swine XIII; swine of any age; oblong piece of metal, ingot XVI. ME. *pigge* :- OE. **picga*, **pigga*, of unkn. orig.; for the formation cf. DOG. Hence **pigtail** twist of tobacco XVII; plait of hair XVIII.

pigeon[1] †young dove; bird of the family Columbidae XIV; †young woman, girl; dupe, gull XVI. ME. *peion, pyion, pegeon* - OF. *pijon* young bird, esp. young dove (mod. *pigeon*) :- Rom. **pībiō, -ōn-*, for late L. *pīpiō, -ōn-*, f. imit. base **pīp-*.

pigeon[2] see PIDGIN.

piggyback var. of PICK-A-BACK.

pigment XIV. - L. *pigmentum*, f. **pig-*, base of *pingere* PAINT; see -MENT.

pike[1] large voracious freshwater fish. XIV. perh. of OE. date (being perh. repr. XI in place-names), and identical with OE. *pīc* point, pick, the fish being so named from its pointed jaw.

pike[2] weapon consisting of a long wooden shaft with pointed head. XVI. - (O)F. *pique*.

pike[3] short for TURNPIKE. XIX.

pikestaff A. staff with metal point XIV; B. wooden shaft of a pike XVI. In sense A prob. - ON. *píkstafr*, f. *pík* (corr. to PICK[1]); see STAFF; in sense B. f. PIKE[2]. In *as plain as a p.* (XVI) an alt. of *packstaff*, i.e. a staff on which a pedlar supports his pack, with poss. ref. to its smoothness.

pilaff, pilau, pilaw XVII. - Turk. *pilav* - Pers. *pilāw*.

pilaster XVI. - F. *pilastre* - It. *pilastro*, medL. *pīlastrum*, f. L. *pīla* pillar, PILE[2]; see -ASTER.

pilch outer garment of skin dressed with the hair or of woollen stuff OE.; saddle pad XVI; baby's wrapper XVII. OE. **pileće*, (late) *pyl(e)će* = OHG. *pelliz* (G. *pelz* fur, furred coat) - medL. *pellicia* cloak, for L. *pellicea*, f. *pellis* skin.

pilchard XVI. of unkn. orig.

pile[1] †dart, shaft, spike OE.; pointed stake or

post, esp. for driving into soft ground for support of a structure XI; (her.) charge of the form ∧ XV. OE. *pīl* = MLG., MDu. *pīl* (Du. *pijl*), OHG. *pfīl* (G. *pfeil*) - L. *pīlum* javelin.

pile² †pillar, pier; heap of things laid one upon the other XV; heap of combustibles XVI; lofty mass of buildings XVII; series of metal plates in a battery XIX. - (O)F. *pile* heap, pyramid, mass of masonry :- L. *pīla* pillar, pier. Hence **pile** vb. heap up. XV.

pile³ fine soft hair XV; nap of cloth XVI. prob. - AN. *pyle*, var. of *peil* kind of cloth, (O)F. *poil* :- L. *pilus* hair.

pile⁴ haemorrhoid. XV. prob. - L. *pila* ball.

pilfer sb. (obs.) plunder. XIV. ME. *pylfre, pelfyr* - AN., OF. *pelfre*, f. *pelfrer*, whence **pilfer** vb. plunder, (later) steal in small quantities XVI; see PELF. The form was early affected by assoc. with †*pill* (see PILLAGE).

pilgrim †wayfarer XII; one who journeys to a sacred place as an act of religious devotion XIII; *P. Fathers* XVIII. ME. *pilegrim* - Pr. *pelegrin* = (O)F. *pèlerin* - L. *peregrīnus* foreign; see PEREGRINE. So **pilgrimage** XIII (*pelrim-, pilegrim-*). - Pr. *pilgrinatge* = (O)F. *pèlerinage*.

pill small ball of medicinal substance to be swallowed XV; transf. pellet, ball XVI. - MLG., MDu. *pille*, Du. *pil*, presumably - reduced form of L. *pilula* PILULE.

pillage spoliation, plunder. XIV. - (O)F., f. *piller* plunder (whence *pill* †plunder, pillage, dial. peel XIII, superseding †*pile*, OE. **pilian, pylian* XII), in OF. only in *espiller*, f. OF. *peille* rag :- L. *pilleum* felt cap; see -AGE. Hence vb. XVI.

pillar XIII. ME. *piler(e)* - AN. *piler*, (O)F. *pilier* :- Rom. **pīlāre*, f. L. *pīla* pillar, PILE²; assim. in sp. to words in -AR from XIV.

pillion saddle, esp. a woman's light saddle; also, cushion or pad behind a saddle. XVI. - Gael. *pillean, pillin*, Ir. *pillín*, dim. of *pell* couch, cushion - L. *pellis* skin, FELL¹.

pillory sb. XIII. ME. *pillori* - AL. *pillorium* (XII) - (O)F. *pilori*, †*pillori*, †*pellori* (XII), prob. - Pr. *espilori*, of obscure orig. Hence vb. XVI.

pillow ME. *pilwe* (XIV) :- OE. **pylw-*, obl. stem of *pyle*, later *pylu* (whence ME. *pile, pule, pele*, dial. *pill, peel*), corr. to MLG. *pöle*, MDu. *po(e)luwe* (Du. *peluw*), OHG. *pfuluwī, pfuluwo* (G. *pfühl*), repr. WGmc. **pulwī(n)* - L. *pulvīnus* cushion, bolster.

pilose hairy. XVIII. - L. *pilōsus*, f. *pilus* hair, PILE³; see -OSE¹. So **pilous** XVII.

pilot steersman, esp. for harbour service. XVI. - F. *pilote* - It. *piloto, -a*, varying with *pedot(t)o, pedotta* - medGr. **pēdṓtēs*, f. Gr. *pēdón* oar, pl. rudder, f. **pēd-*, **ped-* FOOT; cf. -OT. So vb. XVII.

pilule pill. XVI. - F. - L. *pilula*, dim. of *pila* ball; see -ULE.

pimento Jamaica pepper or allspice, tree yielding this. XVII. - Sp. *pimiento* - L. *pigmentum* PIGMENT, in medL. spiced drink, (hence) spice, pepper.

pimp pander, procurer. XVII. of unkn. orig.

pimpernel †great burnet, salad burnet; plant *Anagallis arvensis*. XV. - OF. *pimpernelle* (mod. *pimprenelle*), earlier *piprenelle* - Rom. **piperīnella* f. **piperīnus* pepper-like, f. L. *piper* PEPPER, the fruit of burnet resembling peppercorn.

pimple XIV. Nasalized form corr. to late OE. *piplian* (in prp.) break out into pustules; parallel to obs. and dial. var. *pumple* (XVI); of unkn. orig.

pin peg OE.; pointed length of stiff wire used as a fastener XIV; (pl.) legs; skittles XVI. Late OE. *pinn*, corr. to MLG. *pin*, (M)LG., (M)Du. *pinne* (Du. *pin*), OHG. *pfinn* (MHG. *pfinne*), Icel. *pinni* - L. *pinna* applied to various objects likened to a wing or feather, of uncert. orig.; cf. *penna* feather, PEN². Hence **pin** vb. XIV. **pincushion** XVII. **pin-feather** immature feather. XVII. **pin-money** allowance made to a woman for dress, etc., typified by the pins used for fastening or adorning garments. XVII. **pin-prick** XIX.

pinafore XVIII. f. PIN vb. + AFORE, because orig pinned over the dress in front. Hence **pinny** (-Y⁶) XIX.

pinaster pine tree of south-western Europe. XVI. - L. *pīnaster*, f. *pīnus* PINE¹; see -ASTER.

pince-nez XIX. - F., f. *pincer* PINCH + *nez* NOSE.

pincers XIV. ME. pl. *pinsers, -ours* - AN. **pincers, ours*, f. OF. *pincier*; see PINCH, -ER².

pinch compress between the tips of finger and thumb, the teeth, etc. XIV; nip as with cold; stint, restrict XVI. - AN., ONF. **pinchier*, var. of OF. *pincier* (mod. *pincer*) :- Rom. **pīnctiāre*, alt. of **punctiāre* (see PUNCHEON¹) by assoc. with **pīk-* PICK².

pinchbeck alloy of copper and zinc XVIII; fig. counterfeit, spurious XIX. Named after the inventor, Christopher *Pinchbeck* (d. 1732), watch- and toy-maker of Fleet Street, London.

pine¹ tree of the coniferous genus *Pinus*. OE. *pīn* - L. *pīnus*, coalescing in ME. with adoption of (O)F. *pin*. Hence **pineapple** A. †pine-cone XIV; B. plant *Ananas comosus*, the collective fruit of which develops from a conical spike XVII.

pine² †afflict, torment OE.; †cause to languish or waste away XIII; become wasted XV; be consumed with longing XVI. OE. *pīnian*, corr. to MDu., MLG. *pīnen* (Du. *pijnen*), OHG. *pīnōn*, ON. *pína*, rel. to OE. **pīne* (ME. *pine*) PAIN, = OS., OHG. *pīna* (Du. *pijne, pijn*, G. *pein*), ON. *pína*, Gmc. - medL. *pēna*, L. *pœna*.

pinfold pound (later, fold) for cattle, etc. XIV. Late OE. *pundfald*, f. **pund* POUND² + *fald* FOLD¹; hence in ME. and mod. dial. forms *pun(d)-, po(u)nd-*, but from *c.*1400 assoc. with *pind*, OE. *pyndan* shut up, dam, and PIN vb. enclose, bar up.

ping XIX. imit. Hence **ping-pong** table-tennis. XIX.

pinguin (fruit of) W. Indian plant allied to the pineapple. XVII. of unkn. orig.

pinion¹ terminal segment of a bird's wing, (gen.) wing. XV. - OF. *pignon* pl. wing-feathers, wings, (now only 'gable') :- Rom. **pinniō, -ōn-*, augm. of L. *pinna* PIN. Hence **pinion** vb. cut the pinions of; bind the arms of. XVI.

pinion² small cog-wheel the teeth of which engage with those of a larger one. XVII. - (O)F. *pignon*, alt. of †*pignol* :- Rom. **pīneolus*, f. L. *pīnea* pine-cone, f. *pīnus* PINE¹.

pink[1] (small flatbottomed) sailing vessel. XV. - MDu. *pin(c)ke*, small seagoing vessel, fishing-boat; of unkn. orig.

pink[2] species of *Dianthus*; fig. finest 'flower', embodied excellence *of* XVI; adj. of a pale red colour XVIII; hence sb. pink colour XIX. perh. short for †*pink eye* (see PINK-EYED).

pink[3] intr. and tr. prick, pierce XIV; ornament (cloth, etc.) by cutting holes in it, (later) ornament with scalloped edges, etc. XVI. perh. of LG. or Du. orig. (cf. LG. *pinken* strike, peck).

pink-eyed (dial.) having narrow or half-closed eyes. XVI. f. *pink eyes* - early Du. *pinck oogen*, i.e. *pinck* small (cf. Du. *pink* the little finger, etc.), *ooghen*, pl. of *ooghe* EYE; see -ED[2].

pinnace XVI. - F. *pinace*, †*pinasse* - It. *pinaccia* or Sp. *pinaza*, which have been referred to Rom. **pīnācea*, f. L. *pīnus* PINE[1], poet. ship.

pinnacle pointed turret; mountain-peak XIV; highest pitch or point XV. - OF. *pin(n)acle* (mod. *pinacle*) - late L. *pinnāculum*, dim. of L. *pinna* feather, wing, pinnacle; see PIN, -CLE.

pinnate XVIII. - L. *pinnātus* feathered, winged, f. *pinna;* see PIN, -ATE[2]. Also **pinnated** XVIII.

pinoc(h)le (U.S.) game of cards resembling bezique. XIX. of unkn. orig.

pint XIV. - (O)F. *pinte*, of unkn. orig.

pintado †chintz; species of petrel; guinea-fowl. XVII. - Pg. *pintado* guinea-fowl, sb. use of pp. ('spotted') of *pintar* :- Rom. **pinctāre*, f. **pinctus*, pp. of L. *pingere* PAINT.

pintle (dial.) penis OE.; pin, bolt XV. OE. *pintel*, dim. f. a base repr. by OFris., LG., Du., G. *pint*; see -LE[1].

pioneer soldier going in advance of an army to prepare the way XVI; first or original investigator, etc. XVII. orig. *pion(n)er* - F. *pionnier*, OF. *paonier*, *peon(n)ier*, f. *paon*, *peon* (see PAWN[1]); the suffix later assim. to -EER[1].

pious faithful to the duties owed to God, parents, etc.; practised for the sake of religion or a good object XVII. f. L. *pius*; see -OUS. Cf. F. *pieux*, perh. the immed. source.

pip[1] disease of birds marked by secretion of thick mucus. XV. - MLG. *pip*, MDu. *pippe*, reduced form corr. to OHG. *pfiffiz* :- WGmc. **pipit* - medL. **pip(p)īta*, presumably alt. of *pītuīta* mucus; pip.

pip[2] each of the spots on playing-cards, dice, etc. XVI; single blossom of an inflorescence XVIII. Earlier *peepe*, of unkn. orig.

pip[3] †pippin (apple) XVI; seed of fleshy fruits XVIII. Shortening of PIPPIN.

pipe[1] musical wind instrument: hollow cylinder or tube OE.; tubular passage or canal XIV; narrow tube used for smoking tobacco XVI. OE. *pīpe* = OFris., MLG., MDu. *pīpe* (Du. *pijp*), OHG. *pfīfa* (G. *pfeife*), ON. *pípa* :- Gmc. **pīpa* - Rom. **pīpa*, f. L. *pīpāre* peep, chirp, of imit. orig.; reinforced in ME. by (O)F. *pipe*. So **pipe** vb.[1] OE. *pīpian* play on a pipe. Hence **piper** (-ER[1]). OE. *pīpere*. Also vb.[2] draw through a pipe XVI.

pipe[2] large cask for wine, esp. as a measure of capacity. XIV. - AN. *pipe*, AL. *pipa;* spec. use of PIPE[1] in the tense 'tubular or cylindrical vessel'.

pipe[3] account of a sheriff, etc. as sent in and enrolled at the Exchequer; department of the Exchequer concerned with these. XV. - AN. *pipe*, AL. *pipa*; perh. spec. use of PIPE[1], from the cylindrical shape of a roll (cf. **pipe-roll** XVII) or of a container.

pipette XIX. - F., dim. of *pipe* PIPE[1]; see -ETTE.

pipistrelle small species of bat. XVIII. - F. - It. *pipistrello*, alt. of *vipistrello*, repr. L. *vespertīliō* bat, f. *vesper* evening.

pipit lark-like bird. XVIII. prob. imit. of the bird's short feeble note.

pippin (dial.) seed of certain fruits, pip XIII; variety of apple XV. ME. *pepin*, *pipin* - OF. *pepin* (mod. *pépin*), rel. to synon. Sp. *pepita*, It. *pippolo*, *pipporo*; of obscure orig.

piquant †piercing, trenchant XVI; appetizing; exciting keen interest XVII. - F., prp. of *piquer* prick, sting; see next. Hence **piquancy** XVII.

pique †quarrel or animosity between persons; offence taken. XVI. - F., f. *piquer* prick, sting :- Rom. **piccāre* PICK[2]. Hence vb. XVII.

piqué cotton fabric with a raised pattern. XIX. - F. *piqué*, sb. use ('quilted work, quilting') of pp. of *piquer* prick, pierce, back-stitch; see prec.

piranha see PERAI.

pirate sea-robber XV; marauder XVI; fig. of literary or other plundering XVIII. - L. *pīrāta* - Gr. *peirātḗs*, f. *peirân* attempt, attack, *peira* attempt, trial, f. **per-*, as in PERIL. So **piracy** XVI. - AL. *pirātia* - Gr. *peirāteíā*. **piratical** XVI. f. L. *pīrāticus* - Gr. *peirātikós*.

pirouette spinning round on one foot or on the point of the toe. XVIII. - F., orig. kind of dice; of unkn. orig.

pis-aller last resource. XVII. - F., f. *pis* (:- L. *pējus*) worse + *aller* go; based on phr. *au pis aller* 'at the worst procedure'.

piscary right of fishing XV; fishing-ground XVII. - medL. *piscāria* fishing rights, n. pl. used sb. of L. *piscārius*, f. *piscis* FISH; see -ARY. So **piscatorial** XIX, **piscatory** (-ORY[2]) XVII. f. or - L. *piscātōrius*, f. *piscātor* angler, f. *piscārī* fish.

Pisces twelfth zodiacal constellation and sign of the zodiac. XIV. pl. of L. *piscis*. **piscina** A. fishpond XVI; B. (eccl.) perforated stone basin for carrying away the ablutions at Mass XVIII.

pisé clay or earth kneaded and used for building. XVIII. - F., sb. use of pp. of *piser* :- L. *pīnsāre* beat, pound, stamp.

pismire ant. XIV. ME. *pissemyre*, f. PISS + *mire* ant (prob. of Scand. orig.; cf. Da. *myre*); so called from the urinous smell of an ant-hill.

piss urinate. XIII. - (O)F. *pisser* :- Rom. **pišāre*, of echoic orig. Hence sb. XIV.

pistachio XVI. Earlier *pistachie*, *pistace* - OF. *pistace*, (also mod.) *-ache*; superseded by Sp. *pistacho*; ult. - L. *pistācium* - Gr. *pistákion*, *-ákē*; cf. Pers. *pista*.

pistil (bot.) female organ of a flower. XVIII. - F. *pistile* or L. *pistillum* PESTLE.

pistol XVI. - F. *pistole* - G. - Czech *pišťala* pipe, pistol.

pistole applied to various foreign gold coins. XVI. - F. *pistole*, shortening of *pistolet* (also Eng. XVI).

piston XVIII. - F. - It. *pistone*, var. of *pestone* pestle, rammer, augm. f. *pest-* in *pestello* PESTLE.

pit hole in the ground OE.; hell; hollow in a surface XIII. OE. *pytt* = OFris. *pett*, OS. *putti* (MDu. *putte*, Du. *put*), OHG. *pfuzzi* (G. *pfütze* pool, puddle) :- WGmc. **putti*, *puttja* - L. *puteus* well, pit, shaft. Hence **pit** vb. put in a pit; make pits in XV; set (opponents) together in a (cock)pit; match, oppose XVIII. **pitfall** XIV.

pit-a-pat with palpitations, with light quick steps. XVI. Earlier *pit pat*, also *a-pit-(a-)pat*; imit. of rapidly alternating sounds; cf. PITTER-PATTER.

pitch[1] black or dark brown resinous substance. OE. *piċ*, corr. to OS. *pik* (Du. *pek*), OHG. *peh* (G. *pech*), ON. *bik*, Gmc. - L. *pix*, *pic-*. Hence vb. OE. (*ġe*)*piċian*.

pitch[2] †thrust or fix in; fix and erect XIII; set in order or in a fixed place; cast, throw XIV. The ME. conjugation *pic(c)he*, *pihte*, *(i)piht* suggests the existence of an OE. **piċċ(e)an*, rel. to *picung* 'stigmata', of unkn. orig. Hence **pitch** sb. act of pitching; inclination, slope XV; highest point; position taken up XVI.

pitchblende (min.) native oxide of uranium. XVIII. - G. *pechblende*, f. *pech* PITCH[1]; see BLENDE.

pitcher large usu. earthenware vessel. XIII. - AN. *picher*, OF. *pichier* (mod. *pichet*), var. of *bichier* :- lateL. *becarius*.

piteous †pious; exciting pity XIII; full of pity XIV. ME. *pito(u)s*, *pituo(u)s*, later *pite(o)us* - AN. *pitous*, OF. *pitos*, *piteus* :- Rom. **pietōsus*, f. L. *pietās* PIETY; see -EOUS.

pith medulla of plants; central or vital part OE.; might, mettle XIII; core, marrow XV; gravity XVII. OE. *piða*, corr. to MLG., MDu. *pit(te)*; of unkn. orig.

pithecanthrope ape-man. XIX. - modL. *pithēcanthrōpus*, f. Gr. *píthēkos* ape + *ánthrōpos* man.

pittance (hist.) pious donation XIII; small allowance, orig. of food XIV; sparing allowance XVI. ME. *pita(u)nce* - OF. *pi(e)tance* food - popL. **pietantia*, f. L. *pietās* PIETY; see -ANCE.

pitter-patter †pattering repetition XV; PIT-A-PAT XVII. of imit. orig.

pituitary mucous. XVII. - L. *pītuītārius*, f. *pītuīta* mucus, gum; see -ARY.

pity †clemency, mercy; compassion XIII; †piety XIV. ME. *pite* - OF. *pité* (mod. *pitié*) :- L. *pietās*, *-tāt-* PIETY. In later L. *pietās* acquired the sense of compassion, kindness; OF. *pite* and *piete* had both senses, but were subsequently differentiated, and this was reflected in the corr. Eng. forms as now used. Hence **pity** vb. XVI, **pitiable** XV, **pitiful** XIV, **pitiless** XV.

pivot sb. XVII. - (O)F. *pivot*, of uncert. orig. Hence vb. XIX.

pixie, pixy supernatural being akin to a fairy. XVII. of unkn. orig.; the ending is assoc. with -IE, -Y[6].

pizzicato XIX. - It., pp. of *pizzicare* pinch, twitch, f. *pizzare*, f. (O)It. *pizza* point, edge.

pizzle penis of a bull, etc. XVI (*peezel*, *pysell*). - LG. *pēsel*, Flem. *pēzel*, dim. of MLG. *pēse*, MDu. *pēze* (Du. *pees* sinew, string, penis); cf. -EL[1], -LE[1].

placable †agreeable XV; capable of being appeased, mild XVI. - OF. *placable* or L. *plācābilis*, f. *plācāre*, pp. stem *plācāt-*, whence **placate** XVII; see PLEASE, -ABLE, -ATE[3].

placard †licence, ordinance, etc., orig. with a thin seal attached to its surface XV; †plate of armour, placket, etc.; sheet containing a notice on one side of it, to be posted up XVI. - F. †*placquart*, *-ard* (mod. *placard*), f. OF. *plaquier* (mod. *plaquer*) lay flat, plaster - MDu. *placken*.

place †space, room; portion of space XIII; space where people dwell; residence; particular spot, passage in a book, etc.; position; situation XIV; office, situation XVI. - (O)F. :- Rom. **plattja* (after **plattus* flat), for L. *platea* broad way, open space - Gr. *plateîa* broad way, fem. of *platús* broad. Hence **place** vb. XVI.

placebo (liturg.) vespers for the dead. XIII. First word of the antiphon to the first psalm in the office: '*Placebo* Domino in regione vivorum' (Psalm 114: 9) I shall please the Lord in the land of the living.

placenta (anat.) afterbirth; (bot.) part of carpel to which scales are attached. XVII. - L. - Gr. *plakóenta* (*-oûnta*), accus. of *plakóeis* (*-oûs*) flat cake, sb. use of adj. f. *plak-*, in *pláx* flat surface.

placer (U.S.) deposit of sand, etc. XIX. - Amer. Sp. *placer* deposit, shoal, rel. to *placel* sandbank, f. *plaza* = F. *place* PLACE.

placet vote of assent. XVI. - L. *placet* it pleases, 3rd sg. pres. ind. of *placēre* PLEASE.

placid XVII. - F., or L. *placidus* pleasing, favourable, gentle, f. *placēre* PLEASE; see -ID[1].

placket slit at the top of a skirt. XVII. alt. (by assoc. with -ET) of *plackerd*, PLACARD.

plafond (archit.) ceiling. XVII (*platfond*). - F. †*platfond*, now *plafond*, f. *plat* flat + *fond* bottom.

plagal (mus.) pert. to an ecclesiastical mode having its sounds comprised between the dominant and its octave. XVI. - medL. *plagālis*, f. *plaga* plagal mode, f. L. *plagius* - medGr. *plágios*, in ancient Gr. oblique, f. *plágos* side; see -AL[1].

plagiary †adj. plagiarizing XVI; sb. †kidnapper; plagiarist; plagiarism XVII. - L. *plagiārius* kidnapper, literary thief, f. *plagium* man-stealing, kidnapping - Gr. *plágion*. Hence **plagiarism, -ist** XVII, **-ize** XVIII.

plagio-, before a vowel or *h* **plagi-**, comb. form repr. Gr. *plágios* oblique, f. *plágos* side. XIX.

plague †blow, wound; affliction; malignant epidemic, pestilence. XIV. - L. *plāga* stroke, wound, (Vulg.) pestilence, infection, prob. - Gr. (Doric) *plāgā́*, (Attic) *plēgḗ*, f. **plāg-* strike, rel to L. *plangere*. Hence vb. XV.

plaice XIII. - OF. *plaïz*, *plaïs*, later *plaïse*, *pleisse* - late L. *platessa* - unrecorded deriv. of Gr. *platús* broad.

plaid outer garment of Highland costume XVI; stuff of which this is made XVII. - Gael. *plaide* = Ir. *ploid* blanket, of unkn. orig.

plain clear, manifest XIII; †flat, level, even; unembellished; free from duplicity or ambiguity XIV; ordinary, simple XVI. - OF. *plain*, fem. *-e* :- L. *plānus*, *-a*, f. base **plā-* flat, of obscure orig. Hence **plainly** XIV. So **plain** sb. flat tract of country. XIII. OF. *plain* (superseded by *plaine* :- L. coll. n. pl.) :- L. *plānum*, sb. use of n. of adj. See also PLANE[3,4].

plain-sailing simple or easy course of action.

XIX. pop. use (assoc. with the adj. PLAIN) of *plane* (†*plain*) *sailing* (XVII), i.e. navigation by a *plane chart* (XVII), on which the meridians and parallels are represented by equidistant straight lines (a method approximately correct for short distances).

plainsong music composed in the medieval modes and in free rhythm; simple musical theme. XVI. tr. medL. *cantus plānus*; see PLAIN, SONG. So **plainchant** XVIII. - F.

plaint (arch.) lamentation; complaint XIII; statement of grievance made to a court of law XIV. ME. *pleint(e)* - (O)F. *plainte*, sb. use of pp. fem. of *plaindre* and OF. *plaint, pleint* (on which *plainte* was modelled) :- L. *planctus*, f. *plangere* lament.

plaintiff XIV. - law F. *plaintif*, sb. use of (O)F. *plaintif*, fem. *-ive* (f. *plainte* PLAINT), whence **plaintive** †complaining XIV, expressive of sorrow XVI.

plaister see PLASTER.

plait fold of cloth or similar fabric (now PLEAT) XV; braided band of hair, straw, etc. XVI. - OF. *pleit* fold, manner of folding :- Rom. **plic(i)tum*, sb. use of n. of *plicitus*, pp. of *plicāre* fold (see PLY[1]). Hence vb. XIV.

plan XVIII (earlier *plane* XVII). - F. *plan* ground-plan, alt. (after *plan* adj. PLANE[4]) of †*plant*, f. *planter* (vb.) PLANT, after It. *pianta* plan of an edifice.

plane[1] tree of the genus *Platanus*. XIV. - (O)F. :- L. *platanus* - Gr. *plátanos*, f. stem of *platús* broad.

plane[2] tool for smoothing surfaces. XIV. - (O)F., var. (under the infl. of vb. *planer*) of †*plaine* :- late L. *plāna* planing instrument, f. *plānāre* PLANE[5].

plane[3] plane surface. XVII. - L. *plānum* flat surface, sb. use of n. of *plānus* PLAIN.

plane[4] level, flat. XVII. refash. of PLAIN adj. after F. *plan*, fem. *plane*.

plane[5] †make level or even; smooth with a plane XIV (also *pleyne, plaine, plain* until XVIII). - (O)F. *planer* :- L. *plānāre*, f. *plānus* PLAIN.

planet †(old astron.) heavenly body having an apparent motion among the fixed stars XII; (mod. astron.) heavenly body revolving round the sun XVII. - (O)F. *planète* - late L. *planēta*, *planētēs* (only in pl. *planētæ*, for older L. *stellæ errantes*) - Gr. *planḗtēs* wanderer (pl. *astéres planêtai* wandering stars), f. *planân* lead astray, wander. So **planetary** XVII. - late L.

plangent loud-sounding, orig. of waves breaking on the shore. XIX. - L. *plangēns, -ent-*, prp. of *plangere* beat, strike noisily; see -ENT.

plani- comb. form of L. *plānus* PLAIN, PLANE[4], as in **planimetry** (XIV; - F. *planimétrie*), **planisphere** (XIV; - medL. *plānisphærium*).

planish †level XVI; flatten on an anvil, etc. XVII. f. *planiss-*, lengthened stem of OF. *planir*, f. *plain* PLAIN, PLANE[4]; see -ISH[2].

plank sb. XIII. - ONF. *planke* (mod. dial. *planque*) = (O)F. *planche* :- late L. *planca* plank, slab, sb. use of fem. of *plancus* flat, flat-footed, prob. rel. to Gr. *pláx* flat surface. Hence **plank** vb. cover with planks XV; (orig. U.S.) set down, deposit XIX.

plankton XIX. - G. - Gr. *plagktón*, n. of *plagktós* wandering, drifting, f. base of *plázein* strike, cause to wander.

plant young tree or herb newly planted or intended for planting (OE.), XIV; member of the vegetable kingdom XVI. OE. *plante*, if it survived, coalesced in ME. with - (O)F. *plante* :- Rom. use of L. *planta* shoot for planting (whence the OE. word), prob. f. *plantāre*, perh. orig. thrust in with the sole of the foot (*planta*), whence **plant** vb. OE. *plantian*, reinforced in ME. from (O)F. *planter*. So **plantation** XV. - F. or L.

plantain[1] plant of the genus *Plantago*. XIV. - (O)F. :- L. *plantāgō, -āgin-*, f. *planta* sole of the foot, so called from its broad prostrate leaves.

plantain[2] tropical plant allied to the banana; fruit of this. XVI. In early use also *platan* - Sp. *plátano, plántano*, identical with the forms meaning 'plane-tree'.

plantigrade walking on the soles of the feet. XIX. - F., f. L. *planta* sole; see -GRADE.

plaque ornamental plate or tablet. XIX. - F. - Du. *plak* tablet.

plash PLEACH. XV. - OF. *plassier, plaissier* :- Rom. **plectiāre*, f. L. *plectere* weave, plait.

plasma †form; green variety of quartz XVIII; colourless coagulable liquid of blood XIX; ionized gas XX. - late L. *plasma* mould, image, f. Gr. *plássein* fashion, form.

plaster A. curative application cohesive to the skin OE.; B. plastic composition to be spread on a surface XIV. OE. *plaster*, corr. to OS. *plāstar*, OHG. *phlastar* (G. *pflaster*), ON. *plástr* - medL. *plastrum*, for L. *emplastrum* (prob. through the infl. of *plasticus* PLASTIC) - Gr. *émplastron*, f. *emplastós* daubed, plastered, f. *emplássein*, f. EM-[2] + *plássein* (see prec.); in ME. reinforced in sense B from OF. *plastre* (mod. *plâtre*). The once common (now dial.) form *plaister* (XIV-XIX) is based on occas. OF. *plaistre*, of obscure orig. *P. of Paris* (medL. *plastrum parisiense*) was orig. prepared from the gypsums of Montmartre, Paris.

plastic characterized by moulding or modelling, causing growth or development XVII; capable of being moulded XVIII; of synthetic material XX. As sb., art of modelling figures XVI; plastic substance XX. - F. *plastique* or L. *plasticus* - Gr. *plastikós*, f. *plastós*, ppl. adj. f. *plássein;* see PLASMA, -IC.

plastron breast-shield XVI; ornamental front to a bodice; (nat. hist.) ventral part XIX. - F. - It. *piastrone*, augm. of *piastra* breastplate (spec. application of the sense 'metal plate', 'lamina') - L. *emplastrum* PLASTER.

plat see PLOT.

plate flat sheet of (precious) metal, etc. XIII; utensils of metal for the table or house, orig. of silver or gold XIV; shallow vessel for food XV. - OF. *plate* thin sheet of metal - medL. *platta*, sb. use of fem. of *plattus* flat (F. *plat*, etc.), of unkn. orig. In the last sense a separate word - (O)F. *plat* dish. Hence vb. cover with metal plates. XIV.

plateau XVIII. - F. *plateau*, OF. *platel*, f. *plat*; see prec., -EL[2].

platen †paten XV; flat plate of metal, spec. in a printing-press XVI. - (O)F. *platine*, f. *plat* flat (see PLATE) + *-ine* -INE[4].

platform †plane figure or surface; †plan of action, design; †site of a building, etc.; level place for mounting guns XVI; raised level floor of planks, etc. XVIII (spec. raised flooring in a hall from which speeches are delivered, whence, orig. U.S., basis of political or other policy XIX). - F. *plateforme* plan, f. *plate*, fem. of *plat* flat (see PLATE) + *forme* FORM.

platinum XIX. alt., in conformity with metal-names in *-um*, of †**platina** (XVIII) - Sp., dim. of *plata* silver.

platitude XIX. - F., f. *plat* flat (see PLATE), after *certitude, exactitude*, etc.; see -TUDE.

Platonic pert. to Plato, Greek philosopher (*c*.429-347 B.C.) XVI; *P. love*, tr. medL. *amor platonicus*, used synon. with *amor socraticus* by Marsilio Ficino (XV) to denote the kind of interest in young men with which Socrates was credited XVII. - L. *Platōnicus* - Gr. *Platōnikós*, f. *Plátōn*; see -IC. So **Platonism, Platonist** XVI.

platoon XVII. - F. *peloton* little ball, group of people, dim. of *pelote* PELLET; see -OON.

platter XIV. - AN. *plater*, f. *plat* dish, sb. use of (O)F. *plat* flat (see PLATE).

platy- comb. form of Gr. *platús* broad, as in **platypus** (XVIII) - Gr. *platúpous* flat-footed (see FOOT).

plaudit XVII. Shortening of trisyllabic †*plaudite* (XVI), orig. appeal for applause at the close of a play - L. *plauditē* applaud!, 2nd pers. pl. imper. of *plaudere* clap the hands in approval.

plausible †laudable; †acceptable, agreeable; having an appearance of truth or value. XVI. - L. *plausibilis*, f. *plaus-*, pp. stem of *plaudere;* see prec., -IBLE.

play exercise oneself, spec. by way of diversion, engage in (a game); perform on (a musical instrument) OE.; move swiftly, briskly, freely; act the character of XIV. OE. *pleg(i)an, plægian* = MDu. *pleien* dance, leap for joy, rejoice; doubtfully rel. to OFris. *plega* be wont, OS. *plegan* (Du. *plegen*), OHG. *pflegan* (G. *pflegen*) have charge of, attend to, be in the habit of. So **play** sb. OE. *plega, plæga* rapid movement, exercise, sport OE. (cessation of work, being idle XVII); dramatic performance, drama XIV; action, dealing, as in *fair p., foul p.* XVI; *p. of, on*, or *upon words*, after F. *jeu de mots* XVIII. **playhouse** XVI (not continuous with OE. *pleghūs* 'theatrum').

plea (arch., dial.) action at law, suit XIII; pleading before a court XIV; that which is pleaded XV. ME. *ple*, also *plai(t), plaid* - AN. *ple, plai*, OF. *plait*, earlier *plaid* agreement, lawsuit, discussion - L. *placitum* decision, decree, sb. use of pp. n. of *placēre* PLEASE.

pleach intertwine (branches) to make a fence. XIV. ME. *pleche* - OF. **plechier* (mod. dial. *plècher*), var. of *ple(i)ssier, pla(i)ssier* PLASH.

plead †go to law, argue *with* XIII; address the court as advocate XIV; maintain (a plea), allege formally XV. ME. *plaide, plede* - AN. *pleder*, OF. *plaidier* (mod. *plaider*), f. *plaid* PLEA.

pleasance (arch.) pleasure; pleasantness XIV; pleasure ground XVI. - (O)F. *plaisance*, f. *plaisant* (whence **pleasant** XIV), prp. of †*plaisir* PLEASE.

please A. be agreeable (to), surviving in *if you p.*, where *you* is orig. dat.; B. *be pleased* be gratified, (hence) have the desire, choose, be good enough *to* XIV; intr. in the same sense XVI; C. as imper., for †*p. you* 'may it p. you', equiv. to 'be pleased' XVII. ME. *plaise, plese* - OF. *plaisir* (repr. by *plaire*) :- L. *placēre* be pleasing, f. base of *placāre* PLACATE. So **pleasure** XIV. ME. *plesir* - OF. *plesir*, (also mod.) *plaisir* :- Rom. sb. use of the inf.; the final syll. was assim. (XV) to -URE. Hence **pleasurable** XVI.

pleat vb. fold (cloth), gather (drapery) into pleats XIV; sb. fold of cloth or drapery XVI. Early form *plete*, var. of PLAIT.

plebeian pert. to, a member of, the Roman plebs XVI; of low birth or rank XVII. f. L. *plēbēius*, f. *plēbs, plēb-* commonalty of ancient Rome, perh. rel. to *plēnus* FULL, Gr. *plêthos, plēthús* multitude; see -AN. So **plebiscite** law enacted by the plebs XVI; direct vote of the whole electorate XIX. - (O)F. *plébiscite* - L. *plēbiscītum*, f. *plēbs, plēb-* + *scītum* ordinance, sb. use of n. pp. of *sciscere* approve, vote for, rel. to *scīre* know.

plectrum XVII. - L. *plēctrum* - Gr. *plêktron*, f. *plḗssein* strike.

pledge bail, surety XIV; something handed over as security XV; token of favour or goodwill XVI; solemn promise XIX. ME. *plege* - OF. *plege* (mod. *pleige*) :- Frankish L. *plebium* (VI), corr. to *plebīre* warrant, assure, engage, of unkn. orig. Hence **pledge** vb. XV.

pledget compress of soft material, esp. for application to wounds. XVI. Early forms *plaget, pleggat, pleget*; of obscure orig.

plenary XVI. - late L. *plēnārius*, f. *plēnus* FULL; see -ARY. **plenipotentiary** XVII. - medL. *plēnipotentiārius*, f. L. *potentia* power; see POTENTIAL, -ARY. **plenitude** fullness. XV. - OF. - late L. **plenteous** XIII. ME. *plentivous, -ifous*, later *plentevous, plentuous, plentious, -eois* - OF. *plentivous, -evous*, f. *plentif, -ive*, f. *plente* + *-if, -ive* -IVE. **plenty** XIII. ME. *plenteth*, later *plente, -ee, -ie* - OF. *plentet*, mod. dial. *plenté* :- L. *plēnitās, -tāt-*. Also adj. XIII. Hence **plentiful** XV. **plenum** A. space filled with matter XVII; B. full assembly XVIII. - L. *plēnum*, n. of *plēnus*.

pleistocene see EOCENE.

pleonasm (rhet.) redundancy of expression. XVII (in L. form XVI). - late L. *pleonasmus* - Gr. *pleonasmós*, f. *pleonázein* be superfluous, f. *pléon* more, compar. of *polú* much. So **pleonastic** XVII.

plesiosaurus one of a genus of extinct marine reptiles. XIX. f. Gr. *plēsios* near + *saûros* lizard.

plethora (path.) condition marked by overfullness of blood, etc. XVI; excessive quantity XVII. - late L. *plēthōra* - Gr. *plēthṓrē* fullness, repletion, f. *plḗthein* be full. So **plethoric** XVII. - F. - late L. - Gr.

pleura (anat.) membrane lining the thorax and enveloping the lungs. XVII. - medL. - Gr. *pleurá* side, rib. So **pleurisy** inflammation of the pleura. XIV. - OF. *pleurisie* (mod. *pleurésie*) - late L. *pleurisis*, for earlier *pleurītis* - Gr. *pleurîtis*. **pleuritic** XVI. - (O)F. *pleurétique* - L. *pleurīticus* - Gr. *pleurītikós*. **pleuro-** comb. form of Gr. *pleurá*.

plexus (anat.) network of fibres or vessels.

XVII. - modL. *plexus*, f. *plex-*, pp. stem of *plectere* interweave, PLAIT.

pliable XV. - F., f. *plier* bend; see PLY[1], -ABLE. So **pliant** XIV.

pliers XVI. pl. of *plier*, agent-noun f. *ply* (vb.) bend; see PLY[1], -ER[1].

plight[1] †danger, risk OE.; (arch.) undertaking, engagement XIII. OE. *pliht* = OFris., (M)Du. *plicht*, OHG. *phliht* (G. *pflicht* duty), f. Gmc. **pleχ-*, whence OE. *pleoh* peril, risk. In the second sense in mod. use prob. deduced from *trothplight*, which was orig. *troth plight* 'plighted troth'. Hence **plight** vb. pledge, engage. XIII.

plight[2] A. †fold, plait XIV; B. condition, state XIV. - AN. *plit*, var. of OF. *ploit*, *pleit* fold, PLAIT. In sense B. perh. infl. by prec.

plimsoll *P.('s) line*, *mark* load-line on the hull of a ship XIX; rubber-soled sports shoe XX. Name of Samuel *Plimsoll*, English politician, to whose agitation the Merchant Shipping Act of 1876 was largely due.

plinth XVII. - F. *plinthe* or L. *plinthus* - Gr. *plínthos* tile, brick, stone squared for building.

pliocene see EOCENE.

plod walk heavily; toil laboriously. XVI. of unkn. orig., but prob. symbolic.

plop imit. of the sound made by a smooth object dropping into water. XIX.

plosive (phon.) stop consonant. XX. - F.

plot A. small piece of ground XI; B. †ground-plan, scheme, outline XVI; plan of a literary work XVII; C. secret plan, conspiracy XVI. Properly three words; in A late OE. *plot*, of unkn. orig.; in B alt. of *plat* (early XVI, now U.S.), which was orig. a var. of *plot* in sense A, or (as in *grass plat*, etc.), partly assoc. with late ME. *plat* flat place or space (- (O)F. *plat* PLATE); in C superseding earlier *complot* XVI (- (O)F. *complot* †dense crowd, secret project, of unkn. orig.) by assoc. with sense B. Hence **plot** vb. to make a plan of, contrive. XVI.

plough, U.S. **plow** implement for cutting furrows in soil. Late OE. *plōh* - ON. *plógr* = OS. *plōg* (Du. *ploeg*), OHG. *phluog* (G. *pflug*) :- Gmc. **plōʒaz*. Hence vb. XV. **ploughland** XIII unit of land assessment based on the area tillable by a team of eight oxen in a year. **ploughshare** XIV.

plover XIV. - AN. *plover*, OF. *plo(u)vier* (mod. *pluvier*, alt. after *pluie* rain) :- Rom. **ploviārius*, **pluviārius*, f. L. *pluvia* rain.

pluck A. pull off, draw forcibly XIV; B. reject (a candidate) in an examination XVIII. Late OE. *ploccian*, *pluccian*, corr. to MLG. *plucken*, MDu. *plocken*, ON. *plokka*, *plukka* :- Gmc. **plukkōn*, *-*ōjan*, a parallel form with mutation **plukkjan* being repr. by OE. **plyċċan* (ME. *plicchen*), (M)Du. *plukken*, (M)HG. *pflücken*; prob. all to be referred to Rom. **piluccāre*, whence OF. *peluchier*, etc., obscurely f. L. *pīlus* hair, PILE[3]. The origin of sense B is obscure. Hence **pluck** sb. act of plucking XV; heart, liver, and lungs of a beast, as being 'plucked' out of the carcass XVII; (orig. pugilistic slang) 'heart', courage, 'guts'; cf. *pluck up heart*, etc. XVIII.

plug piece of wood, etc. to stop a hole, etc. XVII; cock of water-pipe; tobacco pressed into a cake XVIII. - MLG., MDu. *plugge* (Du. *plug*); of unkn. orig. Hence **plug** vb. XVII.

plug-ugly (U.S.) city ruffian. XIX. of unkn. orig.

plum (fruit of) tree of the genus *Prunus* OE.; dried grape or raisin (as in *p. pudding*) XVII. OE. *plūme*, corr. to MLG. *plūme*, MHG. *pflūme* (G. *pflaume*; in OHG. *pflūmo* plum-tree), ON. *plóma* (perh. - OE.), with by-forms (M)LG., MDu. *prūme* (Du. *pruim*), OHG. *pfrūma* - medL. *prūna* (see PRUNE), orig. pl. of L. *prūnum* plum (cf. *prūnus* plum-tree), parallel to Gr. *proûmnon* plum. The shortening of the vowel appears XIV in the sp. *plumbe*.

plumage XV. - (O)F., f. *plume* PLUME; see -AGE.

plumb ball of lead attached to a line. XIII (now familiar chiefly in phr. *out of p.* out of the vertical, and *p.-line* XVI). ME. *plumbe*, prob. - OF. **plombe*, repr. by *plomme* sounding-lead :- Rom. **plumba*; later assim. to (O)F. *plomb* lead :- L. *plumbum*, of obscure orig. Hence **plumb** adj. vertical, adv. vertically XIV; **plumb** vb. sound with a plummet XVI.

plumbago †yellow and red oxides of lead XVII; black lead, graphite XVIII: genus of plants, leadwort XVIII. - L. *plumbāgō* (i) lead ore, (ii) leadwort, flea-wort, f. *plumbum* lead (see prec.). Hence **plumbaginous** XVIII.

plumber worker in lead. XIV. - OF. *plommier* (mod. *plombier*) :- L. *plumbārius*, f. *plumbum* lead; see PLUMB, -ER[2].

plume feather (now spec.). XIV. - (O)F. :- L. *plūma*. Hence vb. furnish with plumes XV; refl. of a bird, to dress its feathers XVIII.

plummer-block metal case for supporting a revolving shaft. XIX (also *plumber-*, *plomer-*). perh. f. a proper name.

plummet lead weight attached to a line. XIV. ME. *plomet* - OF. *plommet*, *plombet*, dim. of *plomb* lead; see PLUMB, -ET.

plump[1] fall or come down with heavy and abrupt impact XIV; trans. XV; blurt *out* XVI; vote *for* one candidate only XIX. - (M)LG. *plumpen* = (M)Du. *plompen* fall into water; of imit. orig. In the last sense f. **plump** adv. (XVI), e.g. *refuse plump*, †*vote plump*.

plump[2] †dull, blockish XV; of full and rounded form XVI. ME. *plompe* - (M)Du. *plomp*, MLG. *plomp*, *plump* blunt, obtuse, unshapen, blockish, perh. ult. identical with prec.

plumule (bot.) rudimentary shoot, etc. XVII; (ornith.) down-feather XIX. - F. *plumule* or L. *plūmula*, dim. of *plūma* PLUME; see -ULE.

plunder rob forcibly; appropriate wrongfully, loot. XVII. - (M)HG. *plündern* - (M)LG. *plünderen* pillage, sack, lit. to rob of household effects, f. MHG. *plunder* bedclothes, clothing, household stuff (modG. lumber, trash). Hence sb. XVII.

plunge thrust or cast (*oneself*) *into* liquid; also fig. XIV. - OF. *plungier*, *plongier* (mod. *plonger*) :- Rom. **plumbicāre*, f. L. *plumbum* lead; see PLUMB.

pluperfect XVI. f. L. *plūs quam perfectum* 'more than perfect'.

plural (gram.) denoting more than one (or two); also sb. XIV. ME. *plurel* - OF. *plurel* (mod. *pluriel*) - L. *plūrālis*, f. *plūs*, *plūr-* more; see PLUS, -AL[1]. Hence **plurally** (-LY[2]) XIV. So **plurality**

holding of two or more benefices concurrently by the same person XIV; state of being plural; majority XVI; U.S. excess of votes polled by the leading candidate above those polled by the next XIX. - (O)F. *pluralité* - late L. *plūrālitās*. **pluri-** comb. form of L. *plūs*, *plūr-* more, *plūrēs* several, used in various techn. terms. XIX.

plus verbal rendering of the sign + XVI; with the addition of XVII; (electr.) positive(ly) XVIII. - L. *plūs* more, earlier *plous*.

plus-fours long wide knickerbockers so called because four inches are added to the usual length to produce the overhang. XX. See prec., FOUR.

plush kind of cloth having a longer nap than velvet. XVI. - F. †*pluche*, contr. of *peluche*, f. OF. *peluchier* PLUCK.

plutocracy XVII (thereafter not till XIX). - Gr. *ploutokratíā*, f. *ploûtos* wealth, prob. rel. ult. to FULL; see -CRACY. Hence **plutocrat** XIX.

plutonic (geol.) pert. to the action of internal heat. XVIII. f. Gr. *Ploútōn* (Pluto) god of the infernal regions + -IC.

pluvial (eccl.) cope. XVII. - medL. *pluviāle* 'rain-cloak', sb. use of n. of L. *pluviālis*, f. *pluvia*, *pluere* rain, see -AL[1].

ply[1] (Sc.) plight, condition XV; fold, layer XVI (in earliest use Sc.); bend, turn, twist XVI (fig. from XVII). - (O)F. *pli*, f. *plier*, †*pleier* (whence **ply** vb. bend, lit. and fig. XIV) :- L. *plicāre*; cf. FOLD[2].

ply[2] apply, employ XIV; work away at; solicit earnestly XVI; (naut.) XVI. Aphetic of APPLY.

pneumatic XVII. - F. *pneumatique* or L. *pneumaticus* - Gr. *pneumatikós*, f. *pneûma*, *pneumat-* wind, breath, spirit; see -IC.

pneumonia XVII. - Gr. *pneumoniā*, f. *pneumōn*, *-on-* lung, alt., by assoc. with *pnein*, *pneûsai* breathe, of *pleúmōn*, rel. to L. *pulmō* lung (cf. PULMONARY).

poach[1] cook (an egg) by dropping it without the shell into boiling water. XV. - OF. *pochier* (mod. *pocher*) orig. enclose in a bag, f. *poche* bag, pocket, POKE[1].

poach[2] encroach or trespass *on* land, etc., spec. steal game. XVII. perh. - (O)F. *pocher* in spec. use of 'pocket'; see prec.

pock pustule OE.; pl. XIV (cf. POX). Late OE. *poc*, *pocc-* = MLG., MDu. *pocke* (Du. *pok*, LG. *pocke*).

pocket bag, sack, as a measure of hops, wool, etc.; small pouch attached to a garment. XV. - AN. *poket(e)*, dim. of *poke* POKE[1], var. of OF. *pochet(te)*. See -ET. Hence **pocket** vb. XVI. **pocket handkerchief** XVIII.

pod XVII. prob. back-formation from dial. *podware*, *podder* (XVI), of unkn. orig., which succeeded to †*codware* (XIV; see COD[1], WARE[1]).

podagra gout. XV. - L. - Gr. *podágrā*, f. *poús*, *pod-* FOOT + *ágrā* seizure, trap. Earlier †*podagre* (XIII) - OF.

podestà magistrate in Italian cities. XVI. - It. :- L. *potestās*, *-tāt-* power, authority, magistrate.

podium projecting base XVIII; (zool.) fore or hind foot XIX. - L., elevated place, balcony - Gr. *pódion*, dim. of *poús*, *pod-* FOOT.

poem XVI. - (O)F. *poème* or L. *poēma* - Gr. *póēma*, early var. of *poíēma* work, fiction, poetical work, f. *poein*, *poiein* make, create, rel. to Skr. *cinóti*, *cáyati* assemble, heap up, construct, OSl. *činŭ* arrangement, series. So **poesy** (arch.) poetry, poem XIV; †POSY XV. - (O)F. *poésie* - Rom. **poēsia*, for L. *poēsis* - Gr. *póēsis*, *poíēsis* creation, poetry, poem; see -Y[3]. **poet** XIII. - (O)F. *poète* - L. *poēta* - Gr. *poētḗs*, *poiētḗs* maker, author, poet. **poetaster** XVI - modL. *poētāster*; see -ASTER. **poetic** XVI. - (O)F. *poétique* - L. *poēticus* - Gr. *po(i)ētikós*. **poetical** XIV (rare before XVI). **poetics** treatise on poetry, as that of Aristotle. XVIII. **poetry** XIV. - medL. *poētria*.

pogrom XX. - Russ. *pogróm* devastation, destruction, f. *gromít'* destroy.

poignant XIV. - (O)F. :- L. *pungēns*, *-ent-*, prp. of *pungere* prick; see -ANT.

poinsettia XIX. f. name of J. R. *Poinsett* (d. 1851), Amer. minister to Mexico, discoverer of the plant; see -IA[1].

point A. minute part or particle XIII; small mark, dot; precise position, time, fact, or quality XIV; B. sharp end XIV. In A - (O)F. *point*, in B - (O)F. *pointe*, repr. respectively L. *punctum*, sb. use of n. pp. of *pungere* prick, pierce, and Rom. (medL.) *puncta*, corr. use of the fem pp. So **point** vb. XIV. Partly - (O)F. *pointer*, partly f. the sb.; hence **pointer** in techn. uses from *c.*1500; rod to point with XVII; dog that indicates position of game XVIII. Comp. **point-blank** direct (horizontal) aim or range; also adj. and adv. XVI. of unkn. orig., but presumed to involve the sb. *blank* 'white spot in a target'.

pointillism method of impressionist painters consisting in the use of small dots of colour. XIX. - F., f. *pointiller* mark with small points or dots, f. *pointille* - It. *puntiglio*, f. *punto* = F. *point* POINT; see -ISM.

poise †weight XV; balance, equilibrium XVI. - OF. *pois* (mod. *poids*), earlier *peis* :- Rom. **pēsum*, for L. *pēnsum* weight, sb. use of n. of pp. of *pendere* weigh (cf. PENDENT). So **poise** vb. †weigh XIV; place or hold in equilibrium XVI. f. OF. *poise*, var. of *peise*, stem-str. form of *peser* :- Rom. **pēsāre*, for L. *pēnsāre*, frequent. of *pendere*.

poison †(deadly) potion XIII; substance introduced into an organism that destroys life or injures health XIV. ME. *puison*, *poison* - OF. *puison*, (also mod.) *poison* (in OF. magic potion) :- L. *potiō*, *-ōn-* POTION. So **poison** vb. XIII. - OF. *poisonner*.

poke[1] bag, small sack (now dial. except in 'to buy a pig in a poke'). XIII. - ONF. *poque*, *poke*, var. of (O)F. *poche* (cf. POUCH).

poke[2] thrust with the finger or a pointed instrument. XIV. - (M)LG., (M)Du. *poken*, of unkn. orig. Hence (prob.) **poke** sb. projecting brim of a bonnet. XVIII (so **poke-bonnet** XIX). **poker**[1] (-ER[1]) instrument for poking a fire. XVI.

poker[2] card-game, a variety of brag. XIX. orig. U.S., of doubtful orig., but cf. G. *poch(spiel)* 'bragging game', f. *pochen* brag, perh. cogn. with POKE[2].

polacre, polacca three-masted merchant ship of the Mediterranean. XVII. - F. *polacre*, *polaque*, It. *polacra*, *polacca*; identical with the words meaning 'Polish, Pole', but the reason for the name is unkn.

polder low-lying land reclaimed from the sea. XVII. prob. - MDu. *polre*, (mod.) *polder*.

pole[1] (orig.) stake; (later) long slender piece of wood used as a support OE.; linear measure of 5½ yards XVI; square measure of 30¼ yards XVII. Late OE. *pāl*, corr. to (M)LG. *pāl*, MDu. *pael* (Du. *paal*), OHG. *phāl* (G. *pfahl*), ON. *páll*; Gmc. - L. *pālus* stake, prop.

pole[2] each of the two points in the celestial sphere XIV; each extremity (north and south) of the earth's axis; each of two opposite points on surface of magnet at which magnetic forces are manifested XVI. - L. *polus* end of an axis - Gr. *pólos* pivot, axis (see WHEEL). Cf. F. *pôle*, in part the source. So **polar** XVI. - F. *polaire*, It. *polare*, or medL. *polāris*; whence **polarity** XVII. **polarize** XIX. - F. *polariser*.

Pole †Poland, country of E. Europe XVI; native of this XVII. - G. *Pole*, sg. of *Polen*, in MHG. *Polān*, pl. *-āne* - (O)Pol. *Polanie* 'plain-dwellers', f. *pole* plain. So **Polack** (obs. in England; U.S immigrant from Poland). XVII (earlier †*Polaker*). - F. *Polaque*, G. *Polack* - Pol. *Polak*. Hence **Polish** XVIII.

poleaxe battle-axe XIV; halbert XVI. ME. *pol(l)ax*, *-ex* - MDu. *pol(l)aex*, MLG. *pol(l)exe*, f. *pol(le)* POLL[1] + *aex* AXE; later assoc. with POLE[1].

polecat XIV (*polcat*). The first el. is of unkn. orig. the second is CAT.

polemic disputatious, controversial. XVII. - medL. *polémicus* - Gr. *polemikós* f. *pólemos* war; see -IC. Also **polemical** XVII.

polenta porridge made from barley, chestnut meal, etc. XVI. - It. :- L. *polenta* pearl barley, rel. to POLLEN.

police †policy; †civil organization XVI; civil administration regulating public order; civil force appointed to maintain public order XVIII. - F. - medL. *polītia* for L. *polītīa* POLITY. Hence **policeman, -woman** XIX.

policy[1] †government, administration XIV; prudence in procedure; course of action deemed expedient XV. - OF. *policie* (in first sense) - L. *polītīa* POLITY.

policy[2] in full *p. of assurance* or *insurance* document containing an undertaking to pay certain sums for loss of property. XVI (earliest form *police*). - F. *police* - It. *polizza* prob. :- medL. *apódissa*, *-ixa*, alt. of L. *apodīxis* - Gr. *apódeixis* demonstration, proof.

poliomyelitis (path.) inflammation of the grey matter of the spinal cord. XIX. f. Gr. *poliós* grey + *muelós* marrow; see -ITIS. abbr. **polio** XX.

poliorcetic pert. to siegecraft. XIX. - Gr. *poliorkētikós*, f. *poliorkeîn* besiege a city, f. *pólis* city + *orkeîn* besiege. So **poliorcetics** XVI.

-polis repr. Gr. *pólis* city, as in METROPOLIS, NECROPOLIS.

polish make smooth (and glossy) by friction XIII; refine XIV. ME. *polis(s)* - *poliss-*, lengthened stem of (O)F. *polir* - L. *polīre*; see -ISH[2]. Hence sb. XVI.

Polish see POLE.

polite †polished XV; refined XVI; of refined courteous manners XVII. - L. *polītus*, pp. of *polīre* POLISH.

politic †political; characterized by policy, shrewd, judicious XV; sb. pl. science and art of government XVI; political affairs or life XVII. - (O)F. *politique* - L. *polīticus* - Gr. *polītikós* civic, civil, political, f. *polítēs* citizen, f. *pólis* city, state; see -IC. So **political** XVI. Comb. form **politico-** XVIII. **politician** †schemer, intriguer; one versed in politics. XVI. **polity** civil organization, form of government. XVI. - L. *polītīa* - Gr. *polīteiā*.

polka XIX. - G., F. *polka* - Czech, identical with the word meaning 'Polish woman'. Cf. MAZURKA.

poll[1] A. human head XIII; B. counting by heads, (hence) of votes XVII. perh. of Du. or LG. orig. (cf. obs. Du., LG. *polle*). Hence **poll** vb. cut short, cut off the hair of XIII (pp. *pollid*); cut off the head or top of XVI; count heads, record votes XVII.

poll[2] in *poll deed*, *deed poll*, legal writing polled or cut even at the edge (not indented). XVI. orig. for *pold*, *polled*, pp. of *poll* vb. (see prec.).

Poll var. of and contemp. with POLLY XVII (*Pall*), as proper name of a parrot; alt. of *Moll* (XVI); see MOLL.

pollack sea-fish allied to the cod. XVII. Earlier Sc. *podlok* (XVI), later *podley*; of unkn. orig.

pollard horned animal that has lost its horns XVI; tree that has been polled or cut back XVII. f. POLL[1] + -ARD. Hence vb. XVII.

pollen †fine flour XVI; (bot.) powdery substance produced by the anther XVIII. - L. *pollen* flour, fine powder, rel. *pulvis* POWDER.

pollicitation promising, promise (spec. leg.). XVI. - F. or L. *pollicitātiō*, f. *pollicitārī* bid at auction, f. *pollicērī* promise; see -ATION.

polliwog, polly- (dial. and U.S.) tadpole. XV. ME. *polwygle*, later *porwigle* (XVII), *polwigge* (XVI), *polliwig*, *polliwog* (XIX); f. POLL[1] + WIGGLE and synon. dial. *wig*.

pollute render impure. XIV. f. *pollūt-*, pp. stem of L. *polluere*, f. **por-* PRO-[1] + base of *lutum* mud. So **pollution** XIV. - (O)F. *pollution* or late L. *pollūtiō*, *-ōn-*.

Polly, polly female name used for a parrot. XVII (*Poolye*). dim. of POLL; see -Y[6].

polo XIX. - Balti *polo* ball.

polonaise female dress orig. suggested by that of Polish women; slow dance of Polish origin. XVIII. - F., sb. use of fem. of *polonais* Polish.

polonium (chem.) radioactive metallic element. XIX. - F., f. medL. *Polōnia* Poland (see -IUM); so called from the Polish nationality of Mme Curie, who, with her husband, discovered it in pitchblende.

polony sausage of partly cooked pork. XVIII (*pullony sausage*). prob. for *Bolognian sausage* (XVI), Bologna, a town in Italy, being noted for a kind of sausage.

poltergeist XIX. - G., f. *poltern* make a noise, create a disturbance + *geist* GHOST.

poltroon XVI. - F. *poltron*, †*poultron* - It. *poltrone* sluggard, coward, perh. f. †*poltro* bed (as if 'lie-abed').

poly- repr. Gr. *polu-*, comb. form of *polús*, *polú* much, pl. *polloí* many (cf. FULL); in many techn. terms. **polyanthus** XVIII. modL. (Gr. *ánthos* flower). **polychrome** XIX. - F. - Gr. *polúkhrōmos* (*khrôma* colour). **polygamous** XVII practising **polygamy** XVI. - F. *polygamie* -

eccIGr. *polugamiā* (*gámos* marriage). **polyglot** XVII. - F. *polyglotte* - Gr. *polúglōttos* (*glôtta* tongue). **polygon** XVI. - late L. *polygōnum* - Gr. *polúgōnon* (-GON). So **polygonal** XVIII. **polyhedron** XVI. - Gr. *polúedron* (-HEDRON). **polymath** XVII. - Gr. *polumathḗs* (*manthánein* learn). **polynomial** XVII. after BINOMIAL. **polysyllable** XVI. f. medL. *polysyllaba*. **polytechnic** dealing with various arts. XIX. - F. *polytechnique*, f. Gr. *polútekhnos*. **polytheism** XVII. - F. *polythéisme*, f. Gr. *polútheos*.

polyp (path.) polypus XIV; †octopus, cuttle-fish, or the like XVI; applied gen. to animals of low organization XVIII. - F. *polype* - L. *polypus* (see next).

polypus (path.) tumour usu. having tentacle-like ramifications XIV; †hydra, octopus, etc. XVI. - L. - Gr. (Doric, Aeolic) *pṓlupos*, var. of Attic *polúpous* cuttle-fish, f. *polús* POLY- + *poús* FOOT.

pomace mash of crushed apples in cider-making. XVI (*pomes*, *pomois*). - medL. *pōmācium* cider (f. L. *pōmum* apple), with transference of sense.

pomade scented ointment for the skin and hair (in which apples are said to have been orig. an ingredient). XVI. - F. *pommade* - It. *pomata* :- medL. **pōmāta*, fem. corr. to n. **pomatum** (f. L. *pōmum*, as prec.), also used in Eng. from XVI; see -ADE.

pomander ball of aromatic substances carried as a preservative against infection. XV. The orig. form is repr. by *pom(e)amber* (XVI) - AN. **pome ambre*, for OF. *pome d'ambre* - medL. *pōmum ambræ*, *pōmum de ambra* 'apple of AMBER'.

pomegranate XIV (the earliest forms have *poum-* and metathetic *-garnet*, *-garnade*). - OF. *pome grenate*, *p. garnate*, etc., i.e. *pome* (:- Rom. **pōma* for L. *pōmum*) apple, *grenate* (mod. *grenade*) pomegranate :- Rom. **grānāta* for L. *grānātum* 'having many seeds' (see GRAIN).

pommel †round body or prominence; knob terminating the hilt of a sword XIV; saddle-bow XV. - OF. *pomel* (mod. *pommeau*) :- Rom. **pōmellum*, dim. of L. *pōmum* fruit, apple. Hence vb. beat as with a pommel. XVI.

pomology science of fruit-growing. XIX. - modL. *pōmologia*, f. L. *pōmum* fruit, apple; see -OLOGY.

pomp splendour, magnificence; ostentatious display. XIV. - (O)F. *pompe* - L. *pompa* - Gr. *pompḗ* sending, solemn procession, parade, display, rel. to *pémpein* send. So **pompous** XIV. - (O)F. *pompeux* - late L. *pompōsus*.

pompadour designating dress, hair-style, furniture, colour, etc. named after the Marquise de *Pompadour* (d. 1764), mistress of Louis XV of France. XVIII.

pom-pom automatic quick-firing gun. XIX. imit. of the sound of the discharge.

pompon ornament on a long pin XVIII; globular chrysanthemum XIX. - F., of unkn. orig.

poncho S. Amer. cloak. XVIII. - S. Amer. Sp. - Araucanian.

pond XIII. ME. *po(o)nde*, *pounde*, identical with POUND², which survives dial. in this sense.

ponder †estimate the value of; weigh mentally, meditate upon XIV; intr. XVII. - (O)F. *pondérer* consider (mod. balance, moderate) - L. *ponderāre* weigh, reflect upon, f. *pondus*, *ponder-* weight, rel. to *pendere* weigh; see PENDENT.

ponderous physically weighty XIV; laboured in manner XVIII. - L. *ponderōsus*, f. *pondus*, *ponder-* weight; see prec., -OUS.

pone bread of N. Amer. Indians made of maize flour. XVII. of Algonquian orig.

pongo large anthropoid ape. XVII. - Congolese *mpongo*.

poniard dagger. XVI. - F. *poignard*, repl. OF. *poignal* - medL. *pugnālis*, n. *-āle*, f. L. *pugnus* fist; cf. -ARD.

pontiff member of the principal college of priests in ancient Rome; bishop, spec. pope. XVII. - F. *pontife* - L. *pontifex*, *-fic-*, f. *pōns*, *pont-* (see next) + *facere*, *-fic-* make, DO¹. So **pontifical** adj. XV; sb. pl. bishop's vestments XIV; book of episcopal rites XVI. - L. **pontificate** officiate as bishop. XIX. f. pp. of medL. *pontificāre*.

pontoon¹ boat (or other vessel), of which a number are used to support a temporary bridge. XVII (*ponton*). - (O)F. *ponton* :- L. *pontō*, *-ōn-* punt, bridge of boats, f. *pōns*, *pont-* bridge, rel. to Indo-Iran. and Balto-Slav. words, with Gr. *pátos*, meaning 'road', 'path', but the relevance of the sense in PONTIFF (if this is 'path-maker') is not clear; see -OON.

pontoon² app. alt. of F. *vingt-(et-)un* 'twenty-one' (card game). XX.

pony XVII. orig. Sc. *pown(e)y*, of uncert. orig.; perh. for **poulney* - F. *poulenet*, dim. of *poulain* foal :- late L. *pullāmen*, orig. coll. f. L. *pullus* young animal (cf. FOAL).

poodle XIX. - G. *pudel*, taken to be short for *pudelhund*, f. *pudeln* splash in water, the poodle being a water-dog.

pooh int. XVII. of imit. orig.

Pooh-Bah name of a character in W. S. Gilbert's 'The Mikado' (1885) who holds many offices at the same time; joc. made up from the disdainful excls. POOH and BAH.

pool¹ small body of still water. OE. *pōl* = (M)LG., MDu. *pōl* (Du. *poel*), OHG. *pfuol* (G. *pfuhl*), f. WGmc. **pōl-*, rel. to OE. *pyll* creek; further relations uncert.

pool² collective amount of stakes in a card-game, †game at cards XVII; transf. of other games, (hence) common fund, combine XIX. - F. *poule* stake, prop. hen (see PULLET); assoc. with POOL¹. Hence vb. XIX.

poop stern of a ship. XV. - OF. *pupe*, *pope* (mod. *poupe*) :- Rom. **puppa*, for L. *puppis* stern.

poor having few or no possessions. XIII. ME. *povere*, *pou(e)re*, *pore* - OF. *povre*, (also dial.) *poure* (mod. *pauvre*) :- L. *pauper* (Rom. **pauperus*); rel. to FEW.

pop¹ sb., vb., int., and adv., of imit. orig. The earliest uses (XIV), surviving dial., of sb. and vb. have reference to rapping or knocking; not recorded for abrupt explosive sound before XVI; vb. put, move suddenly XVI; (sl.) pawn XVIII; *pop the question* XVIII; sb. effervescing beverage XIX. comps. **pop-corn** for *popped corn* XIX (U.S.); **pop-eyed, -eyes** (having) prominent eyes XIX; **pop-gun** XVII; **popping-crease** (cricket) XVIII.

pop[2] see PAPA.

pope[1] the Head of the R.C.Ch. OE. *pāpa* - ecclL. *pāpa* bishop - ecclGr. *pápas, papâs* bishop, patriarch, later form of *páppas* father (see PAPA). Hence **popery, popish** XVI.

pope[2] parish priest of the Orthodox Church in Russia, etc. XVII. - Russ. (OSl.) *popŭ* - WGmc. **papo* (cf. OHG. *pfaffo*) - later Gr. *pápas*; see PAPA, POPE[1].

popinjay (arch.) parrot XIII; vain or conceited person XVI. ME. *pape(n)iai, pope(n)iay, -gay* - AN. *papeiaye*, OF. *papegay, papingay* (mod. *papegai*) - Sp. *papagayo* - Arab. *babaġā'*; the final syll. is assim. to JAY.

poplar XIV. ME. *popler(e)* - AN. *popler*, OF. *poplier* (mod. *peuplier*), f. *pople* :- L. *pōpulus*. With the form *poplar* (XVI) cf. contemp. *briar, cedar, medlar*.

poplin XVIII. - F. †*papeline*, dubiously held to be from It. *papalina*, sb. use of fem. of *papalino* PAPAL, and to be so named because orig. manufactured at Avignon, which was a papal town from 1309 to 1791; see -INE[1].

poppa see PAPA.

poppet small person or human figure, (hence) pet XIV; †puppet XVI; (naut.) short piece of wood XIX. of obscure orig.; based ult. on L. *pūpa, puppa* girl, doll; cf. PUPPET, and see -ET.

popple tumble as water, boil or bubble up. XIV. perh. - (M)Du. *popelen* murmur, babble, quiver, throb, of imit. orig. Hence sb. and **popply** XIX.

poppy OE. *popæġ, papæġ*, later *popiġ* :- **papāg*, **popāg*, for **pāpau* - medL. **papāuum*, alt. of L. *papāver*.

popsy-wopsy endearing appellation for a girl. XIX. redupl. formation on dial. *pop* (f. POPPET) + -SY.

populace XVI. - F. - It. *popolaccio, -azzo*, f. *popolo* = F. *peuple* PEOPLE, with pejorative suffix (:- L. *-āceus* -ACEOUS). So **popular** pert. to the people XV; finding favour with the people XVII. - AN. *populer*, OF. *populeir* (later and mod. *populaire*) or L. *populāris*. Hence (or - F.) **popularity** XVII, **popularize** XVIII, **populate** (-ATE[3]) XVI f. pp. stem of medL. *populāre*. **population** †inhabited place XVI; number of people XVII. - late L. *populātiō, -ōn-*. **populous** XV. - late L. *populōsus*.

porcelain XVI. The earliest forms in *-ana, -an* are It. or immed. - It.; superseded by forms - F. *porcelaine*, earlier *pourcelaine* - It. *porcellana* cowrie, polished substance of this, (hence) china ware (from its resemblance to this substance), deriv. in fem. adj. form of *porcella*, dim. of *porca* sow :- L. *porca*, fem. of *porcus* swine; the shells are said to have been so named from their resemblance to the vulva of a sow.

porch covered approach to a building XIII; *the P.*, allusively with ref. to the Stoic school XVII. - (O)F. *porche* :- L. *porticus* colonnade, gallery, porch (cf. STOIC), f. *porta* 'passage', PORT[2].

porcine swine-like. XVII. - F. *porcin, -ine* or L. *porcīnus*, f. *porcus* swine; see -INE[1].

porcupine XIV. ME. *porc despyne*, later *porke-, porcupine* - OF. *porc espin* (also *porc d'espine*), mod. *porc-épic* - Pr. *porc espi(n)* :- Rom. **porcospīnus*, f. L. *porcus* pig + *spīnus* SPINE.

pore[1] minute orifice in a body. XIV. - (O)F. - L. *porus* - Gr. *póros* passage, pore, f. **por-* **per-* **pr̥*; see FORD. So **porous** XIV. - (O)F. *poreux* - medL. *porōsus*. **porosity** XIV. - medL.

pore[2] look intently. XIII. ME. *p(o)ure, powre*, perh. :- OE. **pūrian*, f. **pūr-*, a mutated form of which (OE. **pȳran*) may be the source of synon. ME. *pire* (XIV.). See PEER[2].

porism geometrical proposition in ancient Gr. mathematics. XIV (thereafter not before XVII). - late L. *porisma* - Gr. *pórisma* deduction, corollary, problem, f. *porízein* carry, deduce, f. *póros* way, passage; see PORE[1], -ISM.

pork flesh of the pig used as food XIII; †swine, pig XIV. - (O)F. *porc* - L. *porcus* swine, hog (see FARROW). Hence **porker** (-ER[1]) pig raised for food. XVII.

pornographer XIX. f. F. *pornographe* - Gr. *pornográphos*, f. *pórnē* prostitute; see -GRAPHER. So **pornographic, -ography** XIX.

porphyry XIV. Three types are found: (i) *porfurie, -firie*, (ii) *purfire, porphire*, (iii) *porphyry*; all ult. - medL. *porphyreum*, for L. *porphyrītēs* - Gr. *porphurī́tes*, f. *pórphuros* PURPLE.

porpoise XIV. ME. *porpa(y)s, -poys* - OF. *po(u)rpois, -peis, -pais* :- Rom. **porcopiscis*, f. L. *porcus* swine, *piscis* FISH.

porrect (techn.) stretch out XV; put forward XVIII. f. *porrect-*, pp. stem of L. *porrigere*, f. *por-* = PRO-[1] + *regere* stretch, direct; cf. DIRECT.

porridge †pottage or soup XVI; soft food made with oatmeal XVII. alt. of POTTAGE, intermediate forms being repr. by *podech* (XVI), *podditch, -idge*.

porringer bowl for liquid food. XVI. alt., through the var. †*poddinger* (XV), of (dial.) *pottinger*, †*potinger* (XV), †*poteger* - (O)F. *potager*, f. *potage*; see POTAGE, -ER[2].

port[1] harbour, haven; town having a harbour. OE. - L. *portus* (see FORD), rel. to *porta* (cf. next). In ME. prob. a new word - (O)F.

port[2] gate, gateway, spec. of a city or walled town XIII; opening in the side of a ship XIV. - (O)F. *porte* :- L. *porta* (cf. prec.). Hence **porthole** XVI.

port[3] (arch.) carriage, bearing XIV; †style of living, state XVI. - (O)F. *port*, f. *porter* carry, bear :- L. *portāre* (if orig. transport, bring into port), f. *portus* PORT[1]. Hence **portly** †of dignified bearing, imposing; large and corpulent. XVI.

port[4] left side of a vessel looking forward. XVII (but no doubt earlier, cf. the vb.). prob. orig. the side turned towards the port (PORT[1]) or place of lading (cf. LARBOARD). Hence vb. put (the helm) to port. XVI.

port[5] red (also white) wine of Portugal. XVII. Short for †*Oporto wine*, later †*Oporto*, †*Porto*, prop. wine from Oporto (Pg. *O Porto* 'the port'; see PORT[1]), the chief port of shipment for Portuguese wines.

portable XIV. - (O)F. *portable* or late L. *portābilis*, f. *portāre* carry; see PORT[3], -ABLE. So **portage** transportation, carriage; mariner's venture in cargo. XV. - F.

portal[1] stately doorway or gateway. XIV. - OF. - medL. *portāle*, sb. use of n. of *portālis*, f. *porta* PORT[2]; see -AL[1].

portal² (anat.) pert. to the porta or tranverse fissure of the liver. XIX. - modL. *portālis* (see prec.).

portcullis XIV. ME. *port colice, -coles, -(e)cules, porcules* - OF. *porte coleïce*, i.e. *porte* door (PORT³), *col(e)ïce, coulice*, fem. of *couleïs* gliding, sliding :- Rom. **cōlātīcius*, f. L. *cōlāre, -āt-* filter.

portend XV. - L. *portendere*, f. **por-* = PRO-¹ + *tendere* stretch. So **portent** ominous sign XVI; prodigious thing XVIII. - L. *portentum* strange sign, monster. **portentous** XVI. - L. *portentōsus*.

porter¹ door-keeper. XIII. - AN. *porter*, (O)F. *portier* - late L. *portārius*, f. *porta* PORT²; see -ER².

porter² bearer. XIV. - OF. *port(e)our* (mod. *porteur*) :- medL. *portātor, -ōr-*, f. *portāre* carry; see PORT³, -ER¹, -OR¹.

porter³ kind of dark-brown beer. XVIII. Earlier *porter* or *porter's ale*, presumably so named because drunk chiefly by porters and the like. Comp. **porterhouse** (U.S.) house where porter and other malt liquors are sold; transf. of steaks, etc. supplied there. XIX.

portfolio case for keeping papers XVIII; such a case for state documents, (hence) office of a minister of state XIX. Earlier *porto folio, portefolio* - It. *portafogli*, f. *porta*, imper. of *portare* = F. *porter* carry (see PORT³) + *fogli*, pl. of *foglio* = OF. *foil* leaf, FOIL²; alt. by assim. to F. *portefeuille*.

portico roofed walk supported on columns. XVII. - It. *portico* :- L. *porticus* PORCH.

portière curtain hung over a doorway. XIX. - F., f. *porte* door, PORT² + *-ière* (:- L. *-āria* -ARY).

portion part allotted, share XIII; part of a whole XIV. - OF. *porcion*, (also mod.) *portion* - L. *portiō, -ōn-*, attested first in phr. *prō portiōne* portionally, in PROPORTION. So **portion** vb. APPORTION XIV; dower XVIII. - OF. *portionner* (medL. *portiōnāre*).

portmanteau case for carrying clothing, etc. XVI. - F. *portemanteau* official who carries a prince's mantle, valise, clothes-rack, f. *porter* carry (see PORT³) + *manteau* MANTLE.

portrait XVI. - F., sb. use of pp. of OF. *portraire* picture, depict (whence **portray** XIV), f. *por-* (:- L. PRO-¹) + *traire* draw (:- Rom. **tragere*, for L. *trahere*). So **portraiture** XIV. - OF.

pose¹ A. †suppose or assume XIV; lay down (a claim, etc.) XVI; B. place in or assume an attitude XIX. - (O)F. *poser* :- late L. *pausāre* cease, PAUSE; in Rom. this vb. took over the senses of L. *pōnere*, pt. *posuī*, pp. *positum* place (see POSITION) and became its regular repr. So **pose** sb. attitude. XIX. - F.

pose² †interrogate XVI; perplex, nonplus XVI. Aphetic of †*appose* (XIV) - OF. *aposer*, var. of *opposer* OPPOSE. Hence **poser** examiner XVI; puzzling problem XVIII.

posh (sl.) tiptop, 'swell'. XX. of unkn. orig.

posit (chiefly in pp.) situate, place; assume, lay down as a basis. XVII. f. *posit-*, pp. stem of L. *pōnere* place. So **position** †laying down, affirmation, proposition stated XV; place occupied XVI; posture, attitude XVIII. - (O)F. or L., f. *posit-*, rendering Gr. *thésis* THESIS, *théma* THEME. **positive** formally or explicitly stated XIII; unqualified XV; dealing with fact XVI; affirmative, additive XVII. - (O)F. or L. **positivism** (philos.) XIX. - F. *positivisme*, for earlier *philosophie positive*. **positron** XX. f. POSI(TIVE), (ELEC)TRON.

posse A. potentiality (often in phr. *in p.* potential(ly) XVI; B. body of men that a sheriff may call to arms, (hence) armed force, strong band XVII. - medL. sb. use of L. *posse* be able (see POTENT¹); in A from scholastic terminology, in B for *posse comitātus* 'force (power) of the county'.

possess †occupy, inhabit; hold as property; put in possession. XV. - OF. *possesser*, f. L. *possess-*, pp. stem of *possīdēre*, f. *potis* (see POTENT) + *sīdere*, rel. to *sedēre* SIT. So **possession** XIV. - (O)F. or L. **possessive** (gram.) XVI. - L. *possessīvus*.

posset (hist.) drink of hot milk curdled with ale, etc. XV. of unkn. orig.

possible XIV. - (O)F. *possible* or L. *possibilis*, f. *posse* be; see POTENT, -IBLE. So **possibility** XIV. - (O)F. or late L.

possum Aphetic of OPOSSUM; now esp. in colloq. phr. (orig. U.S.) *play p.* pretend to be disabled, with ref. to the opossum's feigning death when attacked. XVII.

post¹ stout piece of timber set upright. OE. - L. *postis*, perh. f. *por-* PRO-¹ + base of *stāre* STAND; prob. reinforced in ME. from OF. and MLG., MDu. Hence **post** vb.¹ affix to a post. XVII; whence **poster** bill or placard posted or displayed. XIX.

post² †men with horses stationed along a route to carry the king's 'packet' or other letters from stage to stage; †courier, postman; †mail-coach, packet-boat XVI; single dispatch of letters, the mail; short for *post-office*, public department having the conveyance of letters XVII; short for *post-paper*, size of writing-paper, orig. bearing as water-mark a postman's horn XVIII. - F. *poste* - It. *posta* - Rom. **posta*, contr. of L. *posita*, fem. pp. of *pōnere* place (see POSIT). Used adv., with post-horses, with haste XVI; e.g. *ride p.*, orig. in phr. *ride in p.* Hence or - F. *poster*, **post** vb.² XVI. **postage** carriage of letters XVI; charge for this XVII. **postal** (-AL¹) XIX. - F. Comps. **postcard** XIX. **post-haste** †speed in travelling; adv. with all haste. XVI. **postmaster**¹ XVI, **post office** XVII.

post³ soldier's station XVI; position taken up by a body of soldiers; position of employment XVII; (naut.) position as full-grade captain XVIII. - F. *poste* - It. *posto* - Rom. **postum*, contr. of popL. *positum*, pp. of *pōnere* place (cf. prec.).

post⁴ pile of hand-made paper fresh from the mould. XVIII. - G. *posten* parcel, batch, lot - It. *posto* POST³.

post⁵ (esp. in *first, last p.*) bugle-call warning of the hour for retiring for the night. XIX. prob. short for *call to post* or the like (POST³, first sense).

post⁶ L. prep. & adv., earlier *poste*, **posti*, 'after'; current in phrases such as *p. bellum* after the war, *p. meridiem* after midday, *post partum* after childbirth.

post- comb. form of POST⁶ as in **post-communion** (liturg.) part of the Eucharistic service following the communion XV (- medL.);

post-date affix a later date to XVII; **post-obit** taking effect after a person's death XVIII; **postpone** put off, defer XVI; place after XVII (orig. Sc. - L. *postpōnere*; so **postposition** †(Sc.) postponement; placing after XVII); **postprandial** occurring after dinner XIX (L. *prandium*); **postscript** something added after the signature to a letter XVI (- L. *postscriptum*, sb. use of n. pp. of *postscrībere*).

poste restante XVIII. - F., 'post remaining' (see REST).

posterior latter XVI; hinder XVII; sb. †(usu. pl.) descendants XVI; hinder parts, buttocks XVII. - L. *posterior*, compar. of *posterus* following, future, f. *post* after; see POST[6], -IOR. So **posterity** XIV. - F. - L.

postern back or side door. XIII. - OF. *posterne* (mod. *poterne*), alt. of *posterle* :- late L. *posterula*, dim. f. *posterus* that is behind (see prec.).

posthumous born after the father's death; appearing or occurring after death. XVII. f. L. *postumus* last of all, spec. applied as in first sense, used as superl. of *post* after (see POST[6]), later assoc. with *humus* ground, *humāre* bury, whence the sp. with *h*.

postil marginal note or comment, series of these. XV. - OF. *postille* :- medL. *postilla*, of uncert. orig.

postil(l)ion †forerunner XVI; post-boy, swift messenger; one who rides the near horse of a pair XVII. - F. *postillon* - It. *postiglione* post's boy, f. *posta* POST[2].

postmaster[2] scholar of Merton College, Oxford. XVI. of unkn. orig.

postulant XVIII. - F. *postulant* or L. *postulāns*, *-ant-*, prp. of *postulāre* demand; see next.

postulate †demand XVI; proposition claimed to be granted, (geom.) problem of self-evident nature XVII. - L. *postulātum* (also used), sb. use of n. pp. of *postulāre*, prob. f. base of *poscere* (see PRAY). So vb. XVI.

posture †position; disposition of parts, attitude. XVII. - F. - It. *postura* :- L. *positūra* position, situation, f. *posit-*, pp. stem of *pōnere* place; see POSITION, -URE.

posy A. (arch.) motto, orig. line of verse; B. nosegay. XVI. contr. form of POESY.

pot round or cylindrical vessel used as a container. Late OE. *pott*, corr. to OFris., (M)LG., (M)Du. *pot* - popL. **pottus* (whence (O)F. *pot*), of unkn. orig.; prob. reinforced in ME. from OF. The north. word meaning deep hole, pit (XIV) may be identical or may be of Scand. orig.; so prob. **pot-hole** XIX. comb. **pothook** hook to hang over a fireplace XV; hooked character in writing XVII. **pot-hunter** †perh. sycophant, parasite XVI; sportsman who shoots anything he comes across XVIII; (sl.) one who competes in a contest merely for the prize XIX. **pot-luck** one's chance of what may be in the pot ready for a meal. XVI. **potsherd** (arch.) fragment of earthenware. XIV. **pot shot** shot taken at game merely to provide something for the pot, shot aimed directly at something within reach. XIX. **potwaller** householder qualified to vote as having a separate fire-place. XVIII. lit. 'pot-boiler'; alt. to **pot-walloper** (XVIII) by assim. to WALLOP.

potable XVI. - F. *potable* or late L. *potābilis*, f. *pōtāre*; see POTION, -ABLE. So **potation** XV. - OF. - L.

potage soup. XVI. - (O)F. (see POTTAGE).

potash (pl.) lixiviated ashes of vegetables evaporated in pots XVII; potassium carbonate (which these contain in crude form); hydroxide or monoxide of potassium XVIII. - Du. *potasschen* (mod. *potasch*); see POT, ASH[2]. So F. *potasse*, whence **potass** XVIII. **potassa** XIX. modL. form, appropriated to potassium monoxide by Davy, who (1807) coined the name **potassium** to designate the metallic element which is the basis of potash.

potato A. (tuber of) *Ipomoea batatas*, now dist. as sweet or Spanish potato; B. (tuber of) *Solanum tuberosum*, widely cultivated for food. XVI. - Sp. *patata*, alt. of Taino *batata* (sense A); the transference to sense B was due to the likeness of the two plants in producing esculent tubers.

potent[1] powerful. XV. - L. *potēns*, *-ent-*, prp. of **potēre*, *posse* be powerful or able, for *potis esse*; the base **pot-* is repr. also by Skr. *páti-* lord, possessor, husband, Gr. *pósis* spouse, etc.; see -ENT. So **potentate** (-ATE[1]) XIV. - (O)F. *potentat* or L. *potentātus*. **potential** possible, latent XIV (rare before XVI); (gram.) of a mood XVI. - OF. *potencial* (now *-tiel*) or late L. *potentiālis*, f. *potentia*, whence **potency** XVI, earlier **potence** XV (partly - OF. *potence*).

potent[2] (her., of a cross) having the limbs terminating in crutch-heads. XVII. attrib. use of †*potent* crutch (XIV), alt. of (O)F. *potence* supporting piece, crutch - L. *potentia* power (in medL. crutch), f. *potēns*, *-ent-*; see prec.

pot(h)een whisky distilled privately in Ireland. XIX. - Ir. *poitín*, dim. of *pota* pot.

pother choking smoke or dusty atmosphere; commotion. XVI. of uncert. orig.

potion XIII. - (O)F. - L. *pōtiō*, *-ōn-* drink, poisonous draught, f. *pōt-*, stem of *pōtāre* drink, f. IE. **pō(i)-* **pī-*, repr. also by Skr. *píbati* drinks, Gr. *pépōka* I have drunk, etc.; see -TION.

pot-pourri mixture of dried petals kept for perfume XVIII; musical or literary medley XIX. - F., 'rotten pot', i.e. *pot* POT, pp. of *pourrir* rot; tr. Sp. OLLA PODRIDA.

pott var. sp. of POT applied to a size of printing-paper, orig. bearing the watermark of a pot.

pottage dish of vegetables and/or meat boiled to softness XIII; †oatmeal porridge XVII. - (O)F. *potage*, f. *pot* POT; see -AGE.

potter[1] maker of pots. Late OE. *pottere*; see -ER[1]. Hence or - (O)F. *poterie* **pottery** potter's factory XV; potter's art, product of this XVIII.

potter[2] (dial.) poke again and again XVI; meddle XVII; (dial.) perplex, bother; trifle, dabble XVIII; move about idly or aimlessly XIX. frequent. of (dial.) *pote*, OE. *potian* thrust, push, PUT[1]; see -ER[4].

pouch small bag XIV; bag-like cavity in an animal body XV. - ONF. *pouche*, var. of (O)F. *poche* bag, pouch, (now) pocket; cf. POKE[1].

poult young of domestic fowl and game-birds. XV. ME. *pult*, contr. of *poulet* PULLET. So (arch.) **poulter** XIV (- OF. *pouletier*), extended to

poulterer dealer in poultry XVII, prob. after *poultery*, earlier *pulletrie*, vars. of **poultry** XIV (- OF. *pouletrie*); see -ER[1], -RY.

poultice soft mass of bread, etc. applied as an emollient, etc. XVI. orig. pl. *pultes*, later taken as sg. - L. *pultes*, pl. of *puls, pult-* pottage, pap; see PULSE[2].

pounce[1] claw of a bird of prey XV; †stamp or punch, hole pinked in a garment XVI. perh. shortening of PUNCHEON. So **pounce** vb.[1] pink. XIV. Hence **pounce** vb.[2] †seize, as a bird of prey XVII; seize *upon* suddenly XVIII; whence as sb. act of pouncing XIX.

pounce[2] finely powdered sandarac, etc. used to prevent ink from spreading; stamping-powder. XVIII. - (O)F. *ponce* :- popL. **pōmicem* PUMICE. So **pounce** vb.[3] smooth with pumice or pounce; transfer (a design) with pounce; †powder (esp the face). XVI.

pound[1] measure of weight; English money of account (orig. pound weight of silver). OE. *pund* = OS. *pund*, MDu. *pont* (Du. *pond*), OHG. *phunt* (G. *pfund*), ON., Goth. *pund* :- Gmc. **punda* - L. *pondō* (indeclinable) pound weight, orig. abl. of **pondos* (*libra pondō* pound by weight), rel. to *pondus* weight.

pound[2] enclosure, esp. for cattle; place of confinement. XIV. Earlier in the comps. ME. *pundbreche* XII breaking open (see BREACH) of a pound, OE. *pundfeald* PINFOLD; of unkn. orig. Hence vb. shut up, confine (cf. IMPOUND). XV.

pound[3] break down and crush as with a pestle OE.; strike heavily XVII; move with heavy steps, proceed heavily XIX. Late OE. *pūnian*, ME. *poune*, f. **pūn-* (whence also Du. *puin*, LG. *pün* rubbish), of unkn. orig. The final *d* appears XVI.

pour XIII. of unkn. orig.

pout protrude the lips, in displeasure, XIV. of unkn. orig.; perh. repr. OE. **pūtian*, f. **pūt-* be inflated, which appears to be the base of Sw. dial. *puta* be inflated, Sw., Norw. *puta* pad, Da. *pude* cushion, pillow. Hence **pouter** breed of pigeon capable of inflating the crop. XVIII.

poverty XII. ME. *poverte* - (i) OF. *poverte* :- L. *paupertās*; this type survived till XVI as *povert*; (ii) OF. *poverté* (mod. *pauvreté*) :- L. *paupertās, -tāt-*, f. *pauper* POOR; see -TY.

powder solid matter in minute particles XIII; gunpowder XIV. - (O)F. *poudre*, earlier *pol(d)re* :- L. *pulvis, pulver-* dust. So vb. (in earliest use, season, salt) XIII. - (O)F. *poudrer*, or f. the sb.

power A. dominion, rule, authority XIII; ability XIV; B. body of armed men XIII; one possessed of authority XIV; deity, divinity XVI; C. (math., etc.) XVI. ME. *po(u)er* - AN. *poer, po(u)air*, OF. *poeir*, later *po(v)oir*, sb. use of inf. :- Rom. **potēre*, superseding L. *posse* be able, f. **pot-* (see POTENT). Hence **powerful** XIV.

powwow priest or medicine man of N. Amer. Indians; magical rites held by them XVII; conference of Indians, hence gen. congress, palaver XIX. of Algonquian orig. Hence vb. XVII.

pox disease marked by pocks, spec. syphilis. XVI. alt. sp. of *pocks*, pl. of POCK; so *chicken-pox, cow-pox*, SMALLPOX.

pozzolana volcanic ash. XVIII. - It. *pozz(u)olana*, sb. use of fem. adj. 'pert. to *Pozzuoli*', town near Naples (Italy) in the neighbourhood of Mount Vesuvius.

practicable XVII. - F. *praticable*, f. *pratiquer* put into practice, use, f. *pratique*; see below and -ABLE. So **practical** XVII, which superseded **practic** (XIV) - F. †*practique*, var. of *pratique*, or late L. *practicus* - Gr. *praktikós* concerned with action; see -ICAL.

practice scheming, machination; (habitual or continuous) performance; exercise of a profession; (arith.) compendious method of multiplication by aliquot parts. XVI. f. *practise*, after *advice/advise, device/devise*; superseded †**practic** (XIV) - OF. *practique* (mod. *pratique*) - medL. *practica* - Gr. *praktikḗ*, sb. use of fem. of *praktikós*. **practise** perform (now habitually) XV; implied earlier in **practiser** XIV. - OF. *pra(c)tiser* or medL. *practizāre*, alt. of *practicāre*. So **practitioner** XVI. Extension with -ER[1] of **practician** (XV; - F. †*practicien*).

prae- see PRE-.

praecipe (leg.) writ requiring something to be done. XV. First of the opening L. words of the writ, *præcipe quod reddat* enjoin that he render . . .; imper. of *præcipere* (see PRECEPT).

praemunire (leg.) in full *p. facias* name of a writ (Stat. 16 Richard II) derived from a formula in the text of it. XV. - L. *præmunīre* fortify or protect in front, in medL. (by assoc. with *præmonēre*; see PREMONITION) forewarn, admonish.

praenomen name preceding the nomen, personal name. XVIII. - L., f. *præ* PRE- + *nōmen* NAME.

praetor, U.S. **pretor** magistrate of ancient Rome. XV. - F. *préteur* or L. *prætor* (*-ōr-*), perh. :- **præitor* 'one who goes before', f. *præ* PRE- + pp. stem of *īre* go + -OR[1]. So **pr(a)etorian** XV. - L.

pragmatic relating to affairs of a state, etc.; †busy, active, officious XVII (sb. XVI). - late L. *prāgmaticus* - Gr. *prāgmatikós*, f. *prâgma, prāgmat-* act, deed, affair. Also (earlier) **pragmatical** XVI. So **pragmatism** (philos.) XIX; hence **pragmatist** XX (earlier XVII in sense 'pragmatical person').

prairie XVIII. - F. *prairie*, OF. *pra(i)erie* :- Rom. **prātāria*, f. L. *prātum* meadow; see -RY.

praise vb. XIII. - OF. *preisier* price, value, praise :- late L. *pretiāre*, f. L. *pretium* price. Hence sb. XV; whence **praiseworthy** XVI.

praline confection made by browning nuts in boiling sugar. XVIII. - F., f. name of César de Choiseul, comte de Plessis-*Praslin* (1598-1675), by whose cook it was invented.

pram[1], **praam** flat-bottomed boat. XVI. - MDu. *prame, praem* (Du. *praam*), MLG. *prām(e)* - OSl. *pramŭ*.

pram[2] short for PERAMBULATOR. XIX.

prance XIV. of unkn. orig.

prang (Air Force sl.) bomb heavily; crash. XX. of unkn. orig. Also sb.

prank †mischievous trick XVI; mad frolic; also with contemp. †vb. Of unkn. orig.

prate talk idly or aimlessly. XV. - (M)LG., (M)Du. *praten*; prob. of imit. orig.

pratincole bird of the genus *Glareola*, allied to the plover. XVIII. - modL. *pratincola*, f. L. *prātum* meadow + *incola* inhabitant.

pratique licence to a ship to hold intercourse with a port after quarantine, etc. XVII. - (O)F. *pratique* practice, intercourse, corr. to or - It. *pratica* - medL. *practica*, sb. use of *practicus* PRACTICAL.

prattle vb. XVI. - MLG. *pratelen*, f. *praten* PRATE; see -LE[3]. Hence sb. XVI.

prawn XV (*prayne, prane*). of unkn. orig.

praxis practice, exercise. XVI. - medL. - Gr. *prâxis* doing, action, f. **prāk-*, base of *prâssein* do.

pray ask earnestly, make earnest request or petition. XIII. ME. *preie* - OF. *preier* (mod. *prier*) :- late L. (Rom.) *precāre*, for L. *precārī* entreat (rel. to *poscere* demand). So **prayer** XIII. ME. *preiere* - OF. *preiere* (mod. *prière*) :- Gallo-Rom. **precāria*, sb. use of fem. of L. *precārius* obtained by entreaty (see PRECARIOUS).

pre- (e.g. in *predicate, preface, premiss, preposition, presage, presence*), pref. repr. F. *pré-* or its source L. *præ-*, later *prē-*, i.e. the adv.-prep. *præ* (of place, rank, time) before, in front, in advance, OL. *prai* = Oscan *prai, prae-*, Umbrian *pre*, cogn. with (O)Ir. *ar* before, at, in, OSl. *pri* near, and rel. to the groups of PER, *prī-* (repr. by PRIME, PRIOR), and *prŏ* (see PRO-[1], PRO-[2]).

Many L. comps. of various dates are repr. variously in Eng. (see below), chiefly based on vbs. and corr. sbs., with the meanings 'before', 'previously', 'in advance' (in time or order of succession, action, thought, performance, or execution) in adv. relation to the combined el., as in *precede, predestine, prefix, preserve, pretend, previous*, and as in *comprehend, predatory, prehensile*; with implication of 'beyond or over all others' as in *predominate, pre-eminent, prevail*; hence as a living prefix, e.g. in *prejudge* (XII), *prepossess* (XVII); of anterior position, as in (anat.) *precerebellar, -dentate, -hallux*. **b.** In prepositional relation, as in *pre-Cambrian, prehistoric, pre-Shakespearian*.

preach XIII. ME. *preche* - OF. *prechier* (mod. *prêcher*), earlier *preechier* :- L. *prædicāre* proclaim, eccl. preach; see PREDICATE. Hence **preachment** XIV. - OF.; in mod. use a new formation, often with derogatory force.

preamble XIV. - (O)F. *préambule* - medL. *præambulum*, sb. use of n. sg. of *præambulus* going before, in medL. preliminary, f. *præ-* PRE- + stem of *ambulāre* walk; see AMBLE.

prebend portion of cathedral revenue granted as stipend to a member of the chapter; land or tithe as source of this XV; †prebendary XVI. - (O)F. *prébende* - late L. *præbenda* pension, pittance, church living, lit. 'things to be supplied', n. pl. of gerundive of L. *præbēre*, f. *præ-* PRE- + *habēre* hold, have. So **prebendary** holder of a prebend. XV. - medL.

precarious (leg.) held by another's favour; dependent on chance XVII; perilous XVIII. f. L. *precārius*, f. *prex, prec-* entreaty, prayer; see PRAY, -ARIOUS.

precatory of the nature of entreaty. XVII. - late L. *precātōrius*, f. pp. stem of *precārī* PRAY; see -ATE[2], -ORY[2].

precaution XVII. - F. *précaution* - late L. *præcautiō, -ōn-*, f. L. *præcaut-*, pp. stem of *præcavēre* be on one's guard; see PRE-, CAUTION.

precede †surpass, exceed XIV; go before in place or rank XV; go before in time XVI. - (O)F. *précéder* - L. *præcēdere*; see PRE-, CEDE. So **precedent** †thing or person that goes before; previous instance or case XV; †adj. preceding XIV. Hence **precedence** XV.

precentor XVII. - F. *précenteur* or L. *præcentor*, f. *præcent-*, pp. stem of L. *præcinere*, f. *præ* + *canere* sing; see PRE-, CHANT.

precept general command, esp. of divine origin XIV; writ, warrant XV. - L. *præceptum* maxim, order, sb. use of n. pp. of *præcipere* take beforehand, warn, instruct, enjoin, f. *præ* PRE- + *capere* take. So **preceptor** (-OR[1]) XV.

precession (astron.) of the equinoxes. XVI. - late L. *præcessiō, -ōn-*, f. *præcēdere* PRECEDE.

precinct space enclosed by boundaries; district or province of government. XV. - medL. *præcinctum*, also pl. *præcincta*, sb. uses of n. pp. of L. *præcingere* gird about, encircle, f. *præ* PRE- + *cingere* gird.

precious of great worth or price XIII; aiming at choiceness or refinement XIV (in mod. use from XVIII); egregious, arrant, 'fine' XV. - OF. *precios* (mod. *précieux*) - L. *pretiōsus*, f. *pretium* PRICE. So **preciosity** XIV.

precipice †headlong fall XVI; vertical steep face of rock, etc. XVII. - F. *précipice* or L. *præcipitium*, f. *præceps, præcip-* headlong, steep, or *præcipitāre*, f. *præ-* PRE- + *caput, capit-* head. Hence **precipitate** sb. (chem.) XVI; adj. headlong, headforemost XVII; vb. throw headlong XVI; deposit in solid form from a solution XVII; **precipitation** XVII (- F. or L.). So **precipitous** precipitate XVII; of the nature of a precipice. - F. †*précipiteux*.

précis concise account or version. XVIII. - F. *précis*, sb. use of pp. (see next).

precise strictly expressed; strict in observance; exact. XVI. - F. *précis, -ise* - L. *præcīsus, -īsa*, pp. of *præcīdere* cut short, abridge, f. *præ-* PRE- + *cædere* cut. So **precisely** XV. **precision** †cutting short XVII; preciseness XVIII. - F. *précision* or L. *præcīsiō, -ōn-*; orig. vbl. sb. of action, later abstract sb. corr. to *precise*. Hence **precisian** one who is precise, esp. in religious observance, Puritan. XVI.

preclude XVII. - L. *præclūdere*, f. *præ-* PRE- + *claudere* shut.

precocious flowering or fruiting early; prematurely developed. XVII. f. L. *præcox, -coc-*, f. *præcoquere* boil beforehand, ripen fully, f. *præ-* PRE- + *coquere* cook; see -IOUS. So **precosity** XVII. - F. or modL.

preconize proclaim publicly. XV. - medL. *præcōnīzāre*, f. L. *præcō, -ōn-* public crier, herald.

precursor XVI. - L. *præcursor*, f. *præcurrere*, f. *præ-* PRE- + *currere* run; see COURSE, -OR[1].

predatory XVI. - L. *prædātōrius*, f. *prædātor* plunderer, f. *prædārī* plunder, f. *præda* booty, plunder; see PREY, -ORY[2].

predecessor XIV. - (O)F. *prédécesseur* - late L. *prædēcessor*, f. *præ-* PRE- + *dēcessor*, f. *dēcēdere* depart; see DECEASE.

predestination XIV. - ecclL. *prædestinātiō*,

-ōn-, f. *prædestināre* appoint beforehand, f. *præ-* PRE- + *destināre* DESTINE. The L. vb. is also the ult. source of **predestine** vb. XIV and **predestinate** pp. (XIV) and pt. (XV), the latter form being used as present tense from XVI; see -ATE[3].

predial pert. to land or farms. XVI. - medL. *prædiālis*, f. L. *prædium* farm, estate, f. *præs, præd-* surety, bondsman; see AL[1].

predicament category of predication XIV; class, category; situation XVI. - late L. *prædicāmentum*, f. L. *prædicāre*; see next and -MENT.

predicant adj. preaching XVII; sb. preacher XVI (now only in Du. form **predikant** minister of the Du. Reformed Church, esp. in S. Africa XIX). - L. *prædicāns, -ant-*, prp. of *prædicāre* PREACH.

predicate (logic and gram.) that which is asserted of the subject. XVI. - late L. *prædicātum*, n. pp. of *prædicāre* proclaim, declare, in medL. predicate, f. *præ-* PRE- + *dicāre* make known, rel. to *dīcere* say; see DICTION, -ATE[1]. So **predicate** (-ATE[3]) assert, affirm. XVI. **predication** †preaching XIV; assertion, affirmation XVI. - (O)F. or L. **predicative** (gram.) forming the whole or part of the predicate. XIX.

predict XVII. f. *prædict-*, pp. stem of L. *prædīcere*, f. *præ-* PRE- + *dīcere* say (see DICTION). (*Predicted* - L. pp. *prædictus* before-mentioned, aforesaid, occurs XVI.) So **prediction** XVI. - L.

predilection XVIII. - F. *prédilection* - **prædīlēctiō, -ōn-*, f. medL. *prædīligere* prefer, f. *præ-* PRE- + *dīligere*; see DILIGENT, -TION.

pre-emption purchase before an opportunity is offered to others. XVI. - medL. *præemptiō, -ōn-*, f. L. *præemere, -empt-*, f. *præ-* PRE- + *emere* buy. Hence, by back-formation after L. agent-noun *præemptor*, **pre-empt** vb. XIX.

preen trim (the feathers) with the beak; also transf. XIV. ME. *preyne, prayne*, varying with *proyne* (see PRUNE[2]), of which it may be an alt. by assim. to (dial.) *preen* pin, OE. *prēon*, corr. to MLG. *prēme*, (M)Du. *priem(e)* bodkin, dagger, MHG. *pfrieme* (G. *pfriem*) awl, ON. *prjónn* pin, peg, with ref. to the action of the bird's beak.

prefab abbrev. of **prefabricated** (XX); see PRE-, FABRICATE.

preface introduction to a literary work XIV; introduction to the canon of the Mass XV. - (O)F. *préface* - medL. *præfātia*, for L. *præfātiō*, f. *præfārī, -fāt-*, f. *præ-* PRE- + *fārī* speak (see FABLE). Hence vb. XVII. So **prefatory** (-ORY[2]) XVII.

prefect governor, chief administrator. XIV. - OF. *prefect* (mod. *préfet*) - L. *præfectus*, sb. use of pp. of *præficere* set over, f. *præ-* PRE- + *facere* make, constitute. So **prefecture** XVI. - (O)F. or L.

prefer †advance, promote XIV; set before others in esteem XIV; put forward XVI. - (O)F. *préférer* - L. *præferre*, f. *præ-* PRE- + *ferre* BEAR[2]. So **preferable** XVII. - F. *préférable*. **preference** XVII. - (O)F. - medL.; whence **preferential** XIX. Hence **preferment** XV.

prefix verbal element placed before and in combination with another XVII; title prefixed XIX. - modL. *præfixum*, sb. use of n. of *præfixus*, pp. of L. *præfigere* fix in front; see PRE-, FIX. So vb. XV. - (O)F. *préfixer*.

pregnant[1] (arch.) compelling, cogent. XIV. (thereafter not till XVI). - F. *preignant*, prp. of *preindre* :- L. *premere* PRESS[1]; see -ANT.

pregnant[2] with child, with young. XVI. - F. *prégnante* (fem.) or L. *prægnāns, -ant-*, alt., by assim. to *-āns* -ANT, of *prægnās*, prob. f. *præ-* PRE- + base of *(g)nāscī* be born (see NASCENT).

prehensile XVIII. - F. *préhensile*, f. *prehens-*, pp. stem of L. *prehendere* seize; see -ILE.

prehistoric XIX. - F. *préhistorique*; see PRE-, HISTORIC. Hence **prehistory** XIX.

prejudge pass judgement on before trial or inquiry; prejudice. XVI. f. PRE- + JUDGE vb. So **prejudice** sb. injury, detriment XIII; †previous or premature judgement XIV; preconceived opinion XVII. - (O)F. *préjudice* - L. *præjūdicium*, f. *præ-* PRE- + *jūdicium* judgement. **prejudice** vb. affect injuriously XV; †prejudge XVI; fill with prejudice XVII. - (O)F. *préjudicier*. **prejudicial** injurious XV; †prejudiced XVI. - (O)F. or late L.

prelate XIII. - (O)F. *prélat* - L. *prælātus*, (eccl.) sb. use of pp. corr. to *præferre* PREFER; see -ATE[1]. So **prelacy** †office of a prelate; government by prelates. XIV. - AN. *prelacie* - medL. *prælātia*. Hence **prelatic(al)** XVII.

prelection public lecture in a college or university. XVI. - L. *prælectiō, -ōn-*; see PRE-, LECTION. So **pr(a)elector** (-OR[1]) XVI.

preliminary introductory to the main business. XVII. - F. *préliminaire* or modL. *prælīmināris*, f. L. *præ-* PRE- + *līmen, līmin-* threshold.

prelude introductory action, condition, etc. XVI; (mus.) XVII. - F. *prélude* or medL. *prælūdium*, f. *prælūdere* play beforehand, preface, f. *præ-* PRE- + *lūdere* play. So vb. XVII. - L.

premature occurring before the time. XVI. - L. *præmātūrus* very or too early, f. *præ-* PRE- + *mātūrus* MATURE.

premeditate XVI. f. pp. stem of L. *præmeditārī*; see PRE-, MEDITATE. So **premeditation** XV. - (O)F. or L.

premier first in position or rank XV; first in time XVII; sb. prime minister (for *p. minister* XVII - F. *premier ministre* 'first minister') XVIII. - (O)F. :- L. *prīmārius* PRIMARY.

premiss, premise A. (logic) proposition from which another follows; pl. the two propositions of a syllogism (now distinguished as *major* and *minor premiss*) XIV. B. (leg., etc.) pl. matters stated previously; subject of a conveyance or bequest; lands and tenements as before mentioned XV; building with its appurtenances XVIII. - (O)F. *prémisse* - medL. *præmissa*, sb. use of fem. sg. and n. pl. pp. of L. *præmittere* send or set before, f. *præ-* PRE- + *mittere* put, send.

premium reward, prize; sum to be paid in an insurance policy, etc. XVII; fee for instruction in a trade, etc. XVIII. - L. *præmium* booty, reward, f. *præ-* PRE- + *emere* buy, orig. take.

premonition XVI. - F. *premonicion* or late L. *præmonitiō, -ōn-*, f. L. *præmonēre*; see -ITION. So **premonitory** XVII.

prentice aphetic of APPRENTICE. XIII.

preoccupy occupy or engage in advance. XVI. f. PRE- + OCCUPY; after L. *præoccupāre* seize beforehand. F. *préoccuper*. So **preoccupation** XVI. - F. or L.

prep (colloq.) short for *preparation, preparatory*. XIX.

prepare XV. - F. *préparer* or L. *præparāre*, f. *præ-* PRE- + *parāre* make ready. So **preparation** XIV. - (O)F. - L. **preparatory** XV. - late L.

preponderate weigh more or heavier. XVII. f. pp. stem of L. *præponderāre*, f. *præ-* PRE- + *pondus, ponder-* weight; see -ATE[3]. So **preponderance** XVII.

preposition XIV. - L. *præpositiō, -ōn-* putting before, preposition, f. *præpōnere*; see PRE-, POSITION.

prepossess †possess beforehand; cause to be preoccupied; cause to have an opinion beforehand, esp. impress favourably. XVII. f. PRE- + POSSESS. Hence **prepossession** XVII.

preposterous inverted in position; contrary to nature or reason. XVI. f. L. *præposterus* 'before-behind', reversed, out of order or season, f. *præ* + *posterus*; see PRE-, POSTERIOR, -OUS.

prepuce foreskin. XIV. - L. *præpūtium*, f. *præ-* PRE- + an el. of unkn. orig.

prerogative prior or peculiar privilege. XIV. - (O)F. *prérogative* or L. *prærogātīva* tribe or century to which it fell by lot to vote first in the comitia, previous choice, prognostic, privilege, sb. use of fem. of *prærogātīvus*, f. *prærogāre* ask first, f. *præ-* PRE- + *rogāre* ask; see ROGATION, -ATIVE.

presage prognostic, omen XIV (not current till XVI); presentiment, foreboding XVI. chiefly - F. *présage*, but in XIV immed. - its source, L. *præsāgium*, f. *præsāgīre* forebode, f. *præ-* PRE- + *sāgīre* perceive keenly. So vb. XVI. - F. or L.

presbyopia (path.) failure of eyesight characteristic of old age. XVIII. - modL., f. Gr. *présbus* old man + *ṓps* EYE + -IA[1].

presbyter elder in the early Christian church; Christian minister of the second order XVI; †presbyterian XVII. - ecclL. *presbyter* - Gr. *presbúteros* in N.T. 'elder' of the Jewish sanhedrin, 'elder' of the apostolic church, sb. use of compar. of *présbus* old. So **presbyterate** (-ATE[1]) office of presbyter, body of presbyters. XVII. - ecclL. *presbyterātus*. **presbyterian** pert. to government by presbyters or elders; also sb. XVII. f. ecclL. *presbyterium*. **presbytery** part of a church reserved for the clergy, sanctuary XV; body of presbyters or elders; presbyterianism XVI; priest's house XIX. - OF. *presbiterie* - ecclL. *presbyterium* - Gr. *presbutérion*; see -Y[4].

prescience XIV. - (O)F. - ecclL. *præscientia*, f. *præsciēns, -ent-* (whence **prescient** XVII), prp. of *præscīre*, f. *præ-* PRE- + *scīre* know.

prescribe †hold by prescription XV; lay down as an injunction; order the use of (a medicine, etc.) XVI. - L. *præscrībere*, f. *præ-* PRE- + *scrībere* write. So **prescription** (title acquired by) uninterrupted use from time immemorial XIV; limitation of time XV; physician's prescribing of medicine XVI. - (O)F. - L. **prescriptive** XVIII. - late L.

presence fact of being present; †assembly, company XIV; carriage or aspect XVI. - (O)F. *présence* - L. *præsentia*, f. *præsēns, -ent-* (whence, through (O)F., **present** adj. XIII), f. *præ-* PRE- + *-sēns*, prp. of *sum* I am. So **present** sb. †presence; thing presented. XIII. - OF. *présent*; orig. †*in present* in or into the presence (of), hence, as a gift. **present** vb. make present XIII; make an offering of XIV. - (O)F. - L. *præsentāre*, f. *præsent-*; see -ENCE, -ENT. **presentation** XIV. - (O)F. - late L. **presently** †so as to be present XIV; (dial.) at present, now XV; soon XVI.

presentiment XVIII. - F. †*presentiment* (mod. *press-*), f. *pré-* PRE- + *sentiment* feeling, SENTIMENT.

preserve keep safe XIV; keep alive; keep from physical change XVI; keep (game) for private use XVII. - (O)F. *préserver* - late L. *præservāre*, f. *præ-* PRE- + *servāre* keep, protect. Hence **preserve** sb. †preservative; confectionery preparation XVI; wood or water preserved XIX. So **preservation** XV, **preservative** XIV. - (O)F. or medL.

preside XVII. - F. *présider* - L. *præsidēre*, f. *præ-* PRE- + *sedēre* SIT. So **president** XIV. - (O)F. *président* - L. *præsidēns, -ent-*, sb. use of prp. of *præsidēre*. **presidency** XVI. - Sp., Pg. *presidencia*, It. *presidenza* - medL. *præsidentia*.

presidium presiding body; standing committee in communistic bodies. XX. Russ. *prezídium* - L. *præsidium*, f. *præsidēre* (see prec.).

press[1] A. crowd, throng XIII; B. instrument used to compress XIV; machine for imposing the impression of type on paper, etc.; place for printing XVI; matter printed (*letter-p.*) XVIII. C. large cupboard XIV. - (O)F. *presse*, f. *presser* - L. *pressāre*, f. *press-*, pp. stem of *premere* press. So **press** vb. bear down upon or against with force; crowd, push forward XIV; urge XVI. - (O)F. - L. **pressure** weight of pain, grief, etc. XIV; action of moral or mental force; action of pressing XVII. - L. *pressūra*.

press[2] force (a man) into the navy or army, impress. XVI. alt., under the infl. of PRESS[1], of †*prest* (XVI), f. †*prest* sb. loan, impost payment in advance, earnest-money paid to a recruit on enlistment XV, enlistment XVI. - OF. *prest* (mod. *prêt*) loan, advance pay for soldiers, f. *prester* (mod. *prêter*) afford, lend :- L. *præstāre* furnish, medL. lend, rel. to *præstō* at hand, within reach. Hence **press** sb. (hist.) impressing of men for service XVI; whence *p.-gang* XVII.

prestige †illusion, conjuring trick XVII; brilliance or glamour derived from past success, etc. XIX. - F. - L. *præstigium* illusion, more usu. *præstigiæ* fem. pl. juggler's tricks, for **præstrigiæ*, f. *præstringere* bind fast, blind, dazzle (the eyes), f. *præ-* PRE- + *stringere* bind, press.

presto (conjurer's word) quickly, at once. XVI. - It., adv. use of adj. :- Rom., late L. *præstus* ready, quick, for earlier *præstō* at hand. As a musical direction *presto* is an independent adoption (XVII).

presume take upon oneself; take for granted. XIV. - (O)F. *présumer* - L. *præsūmere* anticipate, (later) assume, venture, f. *præ-* PRE- + *sūmere* take. So **presumption** XIII, **presumptive** XVI, **presumptuous** XIV.

pretend †(refl.) put oneself forward XIV; profess falsely, feign XV. - F. *prétendre* or - L. *prætendere* stretch forth, put forward, allege, claim,

f. *præ-* PRE- + *tendere* stretch, TEND[2]. So **pretence,** U.S. **pretense** claim XV; purpose, esp. false or alleged XVI. - AN. *pretense.* **pretension** assertion of claim. XVII. - medL. Hence **pretender** (-ER[1]) XVI.

preter- pref. repr. L. adv.-prep. *præter* past, beyond, more than, besides, compar. formation on *præ* PRE-: e.g. **pretermit** leave out, neglect XVI; leave off XIX. - L. **preternatural** beyond the range of nature. XVI. - medL.

preterite, U.S. **-it** past; spec. (gram.) after L. *præteritum tempus* past tense. XIV (thereafter not before XVI). - (O)F. *prétérit* or L. *præteritus* gone by, pp. of *præterīre,* f. *præter* PRETER- + *īre* go.

pretext XVI. - L. *prætextus* outward display, f. *prætext-,* pp. stem of *prætexere* weave in front, border, disguise, f. *præ-* PRE- + *texere* weave.

pretor, pretorian see PRAETOR.

pretty †crafty, wily OE. (only); †clever; ingenious; fine, 'brave' XIV; beautiful in a slight or dainty manner; considerable in quantity XV. OE. *prættig,* corr. to MLG. *prattich* capricious, overbearing, MDu. *(ghe)pertich* brisk, clever, roguish, Du. †*prettig* sportive, humorous; f. WGmc. **pratt-* trick (whence OE. *præt*), of unkn. orig.; see -Y[1].

prevail †become strong XIV; be superior, gain the ascendant XV; predominate XVII. ME. *prevayle* - L. *prævalēre* have greater power (see PRE-), with assim. to AVAIL. So **prevalent** †having great power XVI; †predominant; in most extended use XVII. - L. *prævalēns, -ent-,* prp. of *prævalēre.*

prevaricate †swerve from the right course XVI; act or speak evasively XVII. f. pp. stem of L. *prævāricārī* go crookedly, deviate from the right path, (of an advocate) practise collusion, (Vulg.) transgress, f. *præ-* PRE- + *vāricāre* spread the legs apart, straddle, f. *vārus* knock-kneed; see -ATE[3]. So **prevarication** †deviation from rectitude XIV; †corrupt action XVI; evasive dealing XVII. - L.

prevenient preceding, spec. theol. of grace. XVII. - L. *præveniēns, -ent-,* prp. of *prævenīre*; see next and -ENT.

prevent †act in anticipation of XV; anticipate with guidance; forestall by previous measures, hinder XVI. f. *prævent-,* pp. stem of L. *prævenīre* precede, anticipate, hinder, f. *præ-* PRE- + *venīre* COME. So **prevention** XVI. - (O)F. or late L. Hence **preventive** †anticipatory; acting as an obstacle XVII; also **preventative** XVII.

previous coming or going before XVII; coming too soon (orig. U.S.) XIX. f. L. *prævius,* f. *præ-* PRE- + *via* way.

prey that which is taken by violence; animal hunted or killed XIII; fig. victim XIV. ME. *praie, preie* - OF. *preie* (mod. *proie*) :- L. *præda* booty, prob. :- **praiheda,* f. *prai, præ* PRE- + **hed-,* base of *præhendere* seize. So **prey** vb. XIII. - OF. *pre(i)er* :- late L. *prædāre,* for earlier *prædārī.*

priapism persistent erection of the penis XVII; licentiousness XVIII. - F. *priapisme* - late L. *priāpismus* - Gr. *priāpismós,* f. *priāpízein* act Priapus, be lewd, f. *Priāpos* (*Priapus*) Greek and Roman god of procreation.

price money, etc. paid for something; †value, worth; †honour, praise; †pre-eminence, superiority; †reward, prize. XIII. ME. *pris* - OF. *pris* (mod. *prix*) :- L. *pretium* price, value, wages, reward. See PRAISE, PRIZE[3], which superseded this word in some of its meanings; but *prize* vb. 'assign a price to' was repl. by **price** XV.

prick puncture, point, dot OE.; pointed object XIII; act of pricking XIV. OE. *prica,* also *pricca, price* = MLG. *pricke* (LG., Du. *prik*), of unkn. orig. So **prick** vb. pierce OE.; urge on XIII; mark with dots XIV; raise, erect XVI. OE. *prician* = (M)LG., (M)Du. *prikken.*

pricket A. spike on which to stick a candle, candle itself XIV; B. buck in its second year, having straight unbranched horns XV. - AL. *prikettus, -um,* dim. f. PRICK; see -ET.

prickle †goad OE.; sharp-pointed excrescence of the epidermis of a plant. XV. OE. *pricel,* later form of *pricels,* f. base of PRICK (see -LE[1]); corr. to MLG., MDu. *prickel, prēkel* (Du. *prikkel*). Hence **prickly** XVI.

pride high opinion of oneself OE.; consciousness of what is fitting to oneself; (arch.) magnificence, pomp XIII; *the* prime or flower XV. Late OE. *prȳde,* secondary form (prob. after *prūd* PROUD or ON. *prýði*) of *prȳte, prȳtu,* abstr. sb. f. *prūd.* Hence **pride** vb. †be proud; show *oneself* proud. XIII.

priedieu prayer-desk. XVIII. - F., f. *prier* PRAY + *Dieu* God.

priest clergyman in the second of the holy orders; (sacrificing) minister of religion. OE. *prēost* (with unexpl. *ēo*), corr. to OHG. *priast, prēst*; shortening of the form repr. by OFris. *prēstere,* OS., OHG. *prēster* (MDu., Du., MHG., G. *priester*) - ecclL. *presbyter* PRESBYTER, through pop. **prēster.* Hence **priestess** XVII. - (O)F. **priesthood** OE.

prig †tinker XVI; (sl.) thief; †dandy, coxcomb; †as vague pejorative; †precisian, puritan, nonconformist minister XVII; one who affects an offensive propriety XVIII. rel. to **prig** vb. steal, haggle XVI; (Sc.) beg XVIII; of unkn. orig.

prim affectedly precise or formal. XVIII. rel. to *prim* sb. and vb., of similar meaning (XVII) and prob. to †*prim* sb. pretty young woman (XVI); perh. ult. - OF. *prin,* fem. *prime* excellent, fine, delicate :- L. *prīmus* PRIME[2].

prima donna XVIII. - It., 'first lady'.

prima facie XV. - L. *prīmā faciē,* i.e. abl. of fem. of *prīmus* first, PRIME[2], and of *faciēs* FACE.

primal primitive XVII; principal XIX. - medL. *prīmālis,* f. *prīmus* PRIME[2]; see -AL[1].

primary earliest, original XV; of the first rank XVI; of the first order or stage XVII. - L. *prīmārius* chief, principal, f. *prīmus* PRIME[2]; see -ARY.

primate[1] chief bishop of a province. XIII. ME. *primat* - (O)F. - late L. *prīmās, -at-,* sb. use of L. *prīmās* of the first rank, chief, f. *prīmus* first, PRIME[2]. So **primatial** XVII. - F., f. medL. *prīmātia* (for earlier *prīmātus*), whence, partly through (O)F. *primatie,* **primacy** XIV.

primates (zool.) highest order of mammalia. XVIII. - modL. use of pl. of *prīmās*; see prec. Hence **primate**[2] member of this order. XIX.

prime[1] earliest of the day hours of the Western

Church OE.; (arch.) first hour of the day XIII; golden number XIV; beginning, earliest time XIV; choicest or finest part, time, etc. XVI. OE. *prīm* - L. *prīma* (fem.; see next), reinforced from (O)F. *prime*, from which or independently from L. the non-eccl. senses were derived.

prime² †first in order of time XIV; (arith.) having no integral factors but itself and one XVI; of first rank, importance, or quality XVII; *p. minister* PREMIER XVII. - (O)F. - L. *prīmus* first, f. **prī-*, rel. to *præ* PRE-, *prō* PRO-¹, PRO-². Hence **prime** sb. prime number XVI.

prime³ fill, charge, load. XVI. of unkn. orig.

prime⁴ cover with a first coat of paint. XVII. of unkn. orig. (perh. identical with prec.).

primer prayer-book for the laity XIV; first reading-book, orig. containing elements of religious instruction; size of type XVI; elementary text-book XIX. - AN. *primer* - medL. *prīmārius, -um*, sb. uses of m. and n. of L. *prīmārius* PRIMARY.

primeval, -aeval XVII. f. L. *prīmævus*, f. *prīmus* first, PRIME² + *ævum* age; see -AL¹.

primitive XIV. - (O)F. *primitif, -ive*, or L. *prīmitīvus* first or earliest of its kind, f. *prīmitus* in the first place, f. *prīmus* first, PRIME²; see -IVE.

primogeniture XVII. - medL. *prīmōgenitūra*, f. L. *prīmō* adv. of *prīmus* first + *genitūra* birth; see PRIME², GENITIVE.

primordial XIV. - late L. *prīmōrdiālis*, f. *prīmōrdium*, sb. use of n. of *prīmōrdius* original, f. *prīmus* first, PRIME² + base of *ōrdīrī* begin; see -IAL.

primrose XV. ME. *primerose*, corr. to OF. *primerose* (now, hollyhock), medL. *prima rosa* 'first' or 'earliest rose'; the reason for the name is unkn.

primula XVIII. - medL. *prīmula*, fem. of dim. (see -ULE) of *prīmus* first, PRIME²; orig. in *prīmula vēris* 'little firstling of spring', applied to the cowslip and the field daisy.

primum mobile supposed outermost sphere added to the Ptolemaic system, carrying with it other spheres in its revolution. XV. - medL., 'first moving thing', n. of L. *prīmus* first, PRIME² and *mōbilis* MOBILE.

primus presiding bishop in the Scottish Episcopal Church. XIX. - L. *prīmus* first, PRIME².

prince sovereign ruler; chief; ruler of a small state XIII; male member of a royal family XIV. - (O)F. - L. *princeps, princip-* chief, leader, sovereign, f. *prīmus* first, PRIME² + *-cip-*, comb. form of stem of *capere* take.

principal chief XIII; constituting the primary or original sum XIV; (gram.) XVI; sb. chief, head, superior; original sum XIV; chief actor XVI. - (O)F. - L. *principālis* first, chief, original, f. *princeps, princip-* first; see PRINCE, -AL¹. So **principality** principalship; territory of a prince. XIV. - OF. *principalite*; varying in ME. with *principalte* - OF. *principalte* (mod. *principauté*) - late L. *principālitās*. **principate** (-ATE¹) XIV. - (O)F. or L.

principle †origin, source; fundamental source, quality, truth, etc. XIV; general law or rule XVI (of nature XIX); (elementary) constituent XVII. - AN. **principle*, var. of (O)F. *principe* - L. *principium* beginning, source, (pl.) foundations, elements, f. *princeps, princip-*, first; see PRINCE.

print impression, impress XIII; (typographical uses) XV. ME. *prient(e), preint(e), pre(e)nt(e)*, later *print(e)* - OF. *priente, preinte*, sb. use of fem. pp. of *preindre* :- L. *premere* PRESS¹. Hence **print** vb. impress, stamp XIV; (in typographical uses) XVI. **printer** XVI.

prior¹ officer of an abbey next below the abbot; head of offshoot of an abbey. XI. Late OE. *prior*, reinforced in ME. by OF. *pri(o)ur* (mod. *prieur*) - L. *prior* (*-ōr-*), sb. use of *prior* former, elder, superior, compar. f. OL. *pri* (*præ* PRE-) before. So **prioress** (-ESS¹) XIII. - OF. *prioresse*. **priory** (-Y³) XIII. - AN. *priorie*, medL. *priōria*.

prior² earlier, anterior; also adv. XVIII. - L.; see prec. So **priority** XIV. - (O)F. - medL.

prism (geom.) solid figure of which the two ends are similar, equal, and parallel rectilinear figures and the sides parallelograms XVI; (optics) transparent body of this form XVII. - medL. *prisma* - Gr. *prísma, -mat-* lit. thing sawn, f. *prízein* (vb.) saw. So **prismatic** XVIII. - F.

prison XII. - OF. *prisun*, (mod.) *prison* :- L. *prēnsiō, -ōn-*, for *præhensiō, -ōn-*, n. of action f. *præhendere* seize. So **prisoner** (-ER²) XIII.

pristine pert. to the earliest period. XV. - L. *pristinus*, f. base of *priscus* early, *prīmus* first, PRIME²; see -INE¹.

prithee XVI. Earlier *pray the, preythe*, clipped form of *I pray thee*.

private †applied by Wyclif to the friars XIV; not open to the public; not holding a public position XV. - L. *prīvātus* withdrawn from public life, peculiar to oneself, sb. man in private life, prop. pp. of *prīvāre* bereave, deprive, f. *prīvus* single, individual, private; see -ATE². So **privation** depriving, being deprived XIV. - L. **privative** XVI. - F. or L. Hence **privacy** XV (rare before XVI). **privateer** vessel owned and officered by private persons holding letters of marque, commander of this. XVII.

privet evergreen shrub *Ligustrum vulgare*. XVI. of unkn. orig.

privilege XII. ME. *privileg(i)e* - AN. **privilegie*, (O)F. *privilège* - L. *prīvilēgium* legal provision affecting an individual, prerogative, f. *prīvus* PRIVATE + *lēx, lēg-* law. So vb. XIV. - (O)F. *privilégier* - medL. *prīvilēgiāre*. So **privy** †private; hidden, secret XIII; participating in knowledge (of) XIV; sb. †intimate XIII; lavatory XIV; (leg.) partaker XV. ME. *prive, priv(e)y* - (O)F. *privé* (as sb. in OF. familiar friend, private place) :- L. *prīvātus* PRIVATE. See -Y⁵. **privity** †secret thing; †privacy XIII; (chiefly pl.) private parts XIV; private knowledge XVI. - OF. *priveté, -ité*.

prize¹ †booty XIV; ship, etc. captured at sea XVI. - (O)F. *prise* capture (of a ship), booty, captured vessel or cargo :- Rom. **prē(n)sa*, sb. use of fem. pp. of **prēndere* :- L. *præhendere* seize; became identified finally with PRIZE³.

prize² †estimate the value of; esteem highly. XIV. - OF. *pris-*, tonic stem of *preisier* PRAISE.

prize³ reward for superiority in a contest. XVI. Differentiated sp. of *pris(e)*, PRICE.

prize⁴ lever up. XVII. f. (dial.) *prize* (XIV) levering instrument - OF. *prise* grasp, seizure, PRIZE¹.

pro[1] argument or person in favour of a proposal XIV; now only in *pro and con* (reasons) for and against XVI. - L. *prō* for, on behalf of, to be grouped with PER, *præ* PRE-, *prī-* as in *prior*, *prīmus* PRIME[2]; see PRO-[1], PRO-[2].

pro[2] short for PROFESSIONAL. XIX.

pro-[1] repr. comb. form of L. adv.-prep. *prō* (see PRO[1]) having a var. *prōd-* as in *prodigal*; as a living prefix chiefly in the senses (1) 'for', 'instead of', 'in place of', as *pro-cathedral*; 'acting as a deputy', in imitation of, as *proconsul*; (2) 'on the side of', 'favouring', as in *pro-German*, *pro-war*.

pro-[2] repr. comb. form of Gr. *pró* before (of time, position, priority), as in *problem*, *programme*, *prologue*, *prophet*, *prostate*; in recent scientific terms denoting (1) 'earlier', 'primitive'; **prochronism**, referring something to a too early date XVII; **propaedeutic** pert. to preliminary instruction (Gr. *propaideúein* teach beforehand) XIX; (2) 'anterior' (of position), 'front', as **procephalic** pert. to the fore-part of the head, **prognathous** having projecting jaws (Gr. *gnáthos* jaw) XIX.

probable †such as to commend itself XIV; †demonstrable XV; having an appearance of truth XVII. - (O)F. - L. *probābilis* provable, credible, f. *probāre* approve, test, PROVE; see -ABLE. So **probabiliorism, -ist** XVIII; **probabilism, -ist** XVII; designating tenets based on a greater or less degree of probability.

probang (surg.) strip of whalebone with sponge, button, etc. for introducing into the throat. XVII. orig. *provang*, so named by the inventor, W. Rumsey; of unkn. orig., alt. prob. after PROBE.

probate official proving of a will. XV. - L. *probatum* thing proved, sb. use of n. pp. of *probāre* PROVE; see -ATE[1]. So **probation** testing; proving. XV. - L.; hence **probationer** (-ER[2]) XVII.

probe blunt instrument for exploring wounds, etc. XVI. - late L. *proba* proof, medL. examination, f. *probāre* test, PROVE; hence **probe** vb. XVII.

probity XVI. - F. *probité* or L. *probitās*, f. *probus* good, honest; see -ITY.

problem †difficult question, enigma XIV; question proposed for discussion; matter of inquiry; (geom.) proposition in which something is required to be done XVI. - (O)F. *problème* or L. *problēma* - Gr. *próblēma*, f. *probállein* put forth, f. PRO-[2] + *bállein* throw. So **problematic** XVII, **-atical** XVI. - F. or late L. - Gr.

proboscis elephant's trunk; elongated (tubular) part of insect's mouth. XVII. - L. - Gr. *proboskis* lit. 'means of providing food', f. PRO-[2] + *bóskein* cause to feed.

proceed XIV. - (O)F. *procéder* - L. *prōcēdere*, f. PRO-[1] + *cēdere* go. So **procedure** XVII. - (O)F.

process fact of going on or being carried on XIV; proceedings at law; outgrowth XVI; continuous operation XVII. - (O)F. *procès* - L. *prōcessus*, f. pp. stem of *prōcēdere* PROCEED. Hence **process** vb.[1] A. (orig. Sc.) institute a process against XVI; B. treat by a special process XIX. In A - OF. *processer*; in B f. the sb. So **procession** formal or ceremonial act of going in orderly succession XII; emanation (chiefly theol.) XIV. - (O)F. - L. *prōcessiō, -ōn-* advance, (later) religious procession; hence **process** vb.[2] go in procession XIX.

proclaim XIV. ME. *proclame* - L. *prōclāmāre* cry out, f. PRO-[1] + *clāmāre* shout; see CLAIM, to the sp. of which this word was assim. So **proclamation** XV. - (O)F. - L.

proclitic (gram.) of a monosyllable closely linked with the following word and having no accent of its own. XIX. - modL. *procliticus*, f. Gr. *proklī́nein* lean forward, after late L. *encliticus* ENCLITIC.

proclivity XVI. - L. *prōclīvitās*, f. *prōclīvis* inclined, f. PRO-[1] + *clīvus* slope; see -ITY.

proconsul governor of an ancient Roman province XIV; governor of a modern colony, etc. XIX. - L. *prōconsul*, for *prō consule* (one acting) for the consul; see PRO-[1], CONSUL. So **proconsular** XVII. - L. *prōconsulāris*. Similarly **propraetor** XVI. - L., for *prō prætōre*.

procrastinate XVI. f. pp. stem of L. *prōcrāstināre*, f. PRO-[1] + *crāstinus* belonging to tomorrow, f. *crās* tomorrow; see -ATE[3].

procreate XVI. f. pp. stem of L. *prōcreāre*, f. PRO-[1] + *creāre* CREATE; see -ATE[3]. So **procreation** XIV. - (O)F. or L.

Procrustean XIX. f. Gr. *Prokroústēs* name of a fabulous robber of Attica who stretched or amputated his victims to conform them to the length of his bed, f. *prokroúein* beat or hammer out, stretch out, f. PRO-[2] + *kroúein* knock; see -EAN.

procto- comb. form of Gr. *prōktós* anus, in (mainly) anat. and surg. terms. XIX.

proctor †agent, deputy, proxy XIV; advocate, attorney XV; university officer representative of the Masters of Arts; representative of clergy in Convocation XVI. ME. *proctour*, syncopated form of *procketour*, *procutour*, reduction of *procuratour* PROCURATOR.

procurator orig. form of PROCTOR, surviving in Sc. *p. fiscal*, public prosecutor of a district. XIII. - OF. *procurateur* or L. *prōcūrātor* manager, agent, deputy, collector in a province, f. *prōcūrāre* PROCURE; see -ATOR.

procure †contrive; bring about by effort; obtain, win. XIII. - (O)F. *procurer* - L. *prōcūrāre* take care of, attend to, manage, f. PRO-[1] + *cūrāre* look after. So **procurer** XIV (in earliest use, advocate, defender, manager). - AN. *procurour*, OF. *procureur* - L. *prōcūrātor*, *-ōr-* PROCURATOR.

prod stab or poke with a pointed instrument, etc. XVI. perh. of purely symbolic orig.

prodigal XVI. - medL. *prōdigālis*, f. *prōdigus* lavish, rel. to *prōdigere* drive forward, cast before one, squander, f. *prōd-*, var. of PRO-[1] + *agere* drive; see -AL[1]. So **prodigality** XIV. - (O)F. - late L.

prodigy †omen, portent XVI; marvel; one of precocious genius XVII. - L. *prōdigium*, f. *prōd-*, var. of PRO-[1] + an el. of uncert. orig.; see -Y[4]. So **prodigious** †ominous, portentous; of the nature of a prodigy. XVI. - L. *prōdigiōsus*.

produce bring forward XV; bring into existence; extend in length XVI. - L. *prōdūcere*, f. PRO-[1] + *dūcere* lead. Hence sb. XVII. So **product** quantity produced by multiplying XV; thing produced by an operation XVII. - L. *prōductum* (math.), sb. use of n. pp. of *prōdūcere*. **production** XV. - (O)F. - L. **productive** XVII. - F. or late L.

proem XIV. ME. *proheme* (also *prohemie*) - OF. *pro(h)eme* (mod. *proème*) or L. *prooemium* (medL. *prohēmium*) - Gr. *prooímion* prelude, f. PRO-² + *oímē* song, lay.

profane secular XV; ritually impure; characterized by disregard of sacred things XVI. - OF. *prophane* (mod. *profane*) or L. *profānus* not sacred, uninitiated, impious, lit. 'before, i.e. outside, the temple', f. PRO-¹ + *fānum* temple, FANE. So **profane** vb. desecrate, violate. XIV - L. *profānāre*. **profanation** XVI. - F. or late L. **profanity** XVII. - late L.

profess *be professed* have taken solemn religious vows XIV; trans. declare openly, affirm allegiance to, lay claim to knowledge of, teach as a professor XVI. In earliest use in pp. repl. †*profess* (- (O)F. *profès* - L. *prōfessus*); later f. *prōfess-*, pp. stem of L. *prōfitērī* declare aloud or publicly, f. PRO-¹ + *fatērī* declare, CONFESS, rel. to *fābula* FABLE. So **profession** taking of vows in a religious order XIII; avowal of belief in or obedience to religion; occupation professed XVI. - (O)F. - L.; hence **professional** (-AL¹) XVIII. **professor** (-OR¹) public teacher of the highest rank in a faculty of learning XIV; one who makes a profession (gen.) XV. - (O)F. *professeur* or L. *professor*. Hence **professorate** XIX. So **professorial** XVIII. f. L. *prōfessōrius*. **professoriate** XIX.

proffer XIII. - AN., OF. *proffrir*, earlier *poroffrir*, *puroffrir*, f. *por* (:- L. PRO-¹) + *offrir* OFFER. So sb. XIV. - AN. *profre*.

proficient †making progress; that has made progress in learning. XVI. - L. *prōficiēns*, *-ent-*, prp. of *prōficere* advance, f. PRO-¹ + *facere* DO¹, make; see -ENT. Hence **proficiency** XVI.

profile XVII. - It. †*profilo*, now *proffilo*, f. †*profilare* draw in outline.

profit advantage, benefit; revenue, proceeds XIV; gain in a transaction XVII. - (O)F. :- L. *prōfectus* progress, profit, f. pp. stem of *prōficere* advance (see PROFICIENT). So **profit** vb. XIV. - (O)F. *profiter*; hence **profiteer** (-EER) XX.

profligate †overthrown XVI; abandoned to vice XVI (sb. XVIII). - L. *prōflīgātus* ruined, dissolute, pp. of *prōflīgāre* cast down, ruin, f. PRO-¹ + base *flīg-* beat; see -ATE². Hence **profligacy** XVIII.

profound showing depth of thought or knowledge XIV; abstruse, recondite; physically deep XV. - AN., OF. *profund*, (also mod.) *profond* :- L. *profundus*, f. PRO-¹ + *fundus* bottom. So **profundity** XV. - OF. or late L.

profuse liberal to excess XV; very abundant XVII. - L. *prōfūsus*, adj. use of pp. of *prōfundere* pour forth, f. PRO-¹ + *fundere* pour. So **profusion** XVI. - F. or L.

progeny XIII. - OF. *progenie* - L. *prōgeniēs* descent, family, f. PRO-¹ + **gen-* (see KIN).

prognosis forecast of the course of a case of disease. XVII. - late L. *prognōsis* - Gr. *prógnōsis*, f. *progignṓskein* know beforehand; see PRO-². So **prognostic** previous indication or token XV; symptom XVI. Earlier form *pron-* - OF. *pronostique* (mod. *-ic*) - L. *prognōsticum*, *-con* - Gr. *prognōstikón*, sb. use of n. of adj. f. *progignṓskein*; see -IC. **prognosticate** (-ATE³) XVI. f. pp. stem of medL. *pro(g)nōsticāre*.

programme, U.S. **program** A. †Sc. public notice XVII; B. descriptive notice or plan of intended proceedings XIX. In sense A - late L. *programma* - Gr. *prógramma* public written notice, f. *prográphein* write publicly, f. PRO-² + *gráphein* write; in sense B - F. *programme*.

progress onward march; visit of state XV; forward movement XVI. - L. *prōgressus*, f. pp. stem of *prōgredī* go forward, f. PRO-¹ + *gradī* step, walk, go, f. *gradus* step. Hence **progress** vb. XVI; became obs. in England in XVII, but retained or formed afresh in America, whence it was re-adopted in England *c.*1800. So **progression** XIV. - F. or L. **progressive** XVII. - F.

prohibit XV. f. *prohibit-*, pp. stem of L. *prōhibēre* hold back, prevent, forbid, f. *prō* in front, PRO-¹ + *habēre* hold. So **prohibition** XIV. - (O)F. or L. **prohibitive** XVII. - F.

project †design, scheme XIV; †conception, notion XVI; proposal for execution XVII. - L. *prōjectum*, n. of pp. of *prōicere* throw forth, expel, f. PRO-¹ + *jacere* throw. So **project** vb. plan XV; throw forward XVI. f. *prōject-*, pp. stem of L. *prōicere*. **projectile** XVII. - modL. *projectilis*. **projection** action of projecting; earliest in techn. sense of representation of a spherical surface on the flat. XVI. - L.

prolate (geom.) lengthened in the direction of the polar axis XVII. - L. *prōlātus*, used as pp. of *prōferre* bring forward, produce.

prolegomena XVII. pl. of L. *prolegomenon* - Gr. *prolegómenon*, n. of prp. pass. of *prolégein* say beforehand, f. PRO-² + *légein* say.

prolepsis anticipation, esp. as techn. device in rhet. and gram. XVI. - late L. *prolēpsis* - Gr. *prólēpsis*, f. *prolambánein* anticipate, f. PRO-² + *lambánein* take. So **proleptic** XVII. - Gr.

proletarian pert. to the lowest class of the people XVII; wage-earning XIX. f. L. *prōlētārius* Roman citizen of the lowest class under the constitution of Servius Tullius, one who served the state not with his property but only with his offspring, (hence) common, low, f. **prōlētus* provided with offspring, f. *prōlēs* offspring; see -ARIAN. So **proletariat(e)** XIX. - F. *prolétariat*.

prolific producing (much) offspring. XVII. - medL. *prōlificus*, f. L. *prōlēs* offspring; see prec. and -FIC.

prolix lengthy XV; lengthy in discourse XVI. - (O)F. *prolixe* or L. *prōlixus* spreading abroad, extended, lit. 'poured forth', f. PRO-¹ + pp. formation on base of *liquēre* be LIQUID. So **prolixity** XIV. - (O)F. - late L.

prolocutor spokesman of an assembly. XV. - L. *prōlocūtor* pleader, advocate, agent-noun of *prōloquī* speak out; see PRO-¹, LOCUTION.

prologue preface to a discourse or drama XIII; speaker of this XVI. - (O)F. - L. *prologus* - Gr. *prólogos*, f. PRO-² + *lógos* speech.

prolong extend in duration XV; lengthen in space XVI. - late L. *prōlongāre*, f. PRO-¹ + *longus* LONG¹. So **prolongation** XV. - (O)F. or late L.

prolusion preliminary attempt, essay, or dissertation. XVII. - L. *prōlūsiō, -ōn-*, f. pp. stem of *prōlūdere* carry out preliminary exercises, f. PRO-[1] + *lūdere* play; see -SION.

promenade walk taken for exercise or amusement XVI (*purmenade, -ado*); place for this XVII. - F. *promenade*, f. *se promener* walk, refl. of *promener* cause to walk, alt. of *pourmener*, f. *pour* (:- L. *prō* PRO-[1]) + *mener* lead; see -ADE. Hence vb. XVI.

prominent projecting XVI; conspicuous XVIII. - L. *prōminēns, -ent-*, prp. of *prōminēre* jut out, f. PRO-[1] + base repr. also by *mōns* MOUNT[1]; see -ENT. So **prominence** XVI.

promiscuous of mixed or disorderly character. XVII. f. L. *prōmiscuus*, f. PRO-[1] + *miscēre* MIX; see -UOUS. Hence **promiscuity** XIX.

promise sb. XIV. - L. *promissum*, sb. use of n. pp. of *prōmittere* send or put forth, promise, f. PRO-[1] + *mittere* send. Hence vb. XV. So **promissory** XVII. - medL. *prōmissōrius*.

promontory XVI. - medL. *prōmontōrium*, alt. (after *mōns, mont-* MOUNT[1]) of L. *prōmunturium*, gen. considered to be f. *prō* PRO-[1] and a deriv. of *mōns*; cf. -ORY[1].

promote advance in position XIV; further in growth XVI. f. *prōmōt-*, pp. stem of L. *prōmovēre* move forward; see PRO-[1], MOVE. So **promotion** XV. - (O)F. - L.

prompt ready or quick to act. XV. - (O)F. *prompt* or L. *promptus* brought forth, manifest, ready, disposed, pp. of *prōmere* bring forth, f. PRO-[1] + *emere* take. So **prompt** vb. incite to action XIV; assist (a speaker) by suggesting what is to be said XV; suggest, inspire XVII. perh. - medL. **promptāre*. Hence **prompter** XV (theatr. XVII).

promulgate XVI. f. pp. stem of L. *prōmulgāre* expose to public view, f. PRO-[1] + base of *mulgēre* (vb.) milk, (hence) cause to issue forth, bring to light; see -ATE[3].

prone naturally inclined, disposed XIV; bending forward and downward XVI; lying flat XVII. - L. *prōnus*, f. *prō* forward (see PRO-[1]). So **pronation** (physiol.) putting a fore limb into a prone position. XVII. - F. or medL. (f. late L. *prōnāre*). **pronator** muscle effecting this. XVIII.

prong forked instrument XV; tine of a fork XVII In early use also *prang* and varying with (dial.) *sprong* (XV); the form suggests connexion with MLG. *prange* pinching, pinching instrument, etc. (see PANG).

pronoun (gram.). XVI. f. PRO-[1] instead of + NOUN, after F. *pronom*, L. *prōnōmen*, tr. Gr. *antōnumíā* f. ANTI- + *ónuma, ónoma* NAME. So **pronominal** XVII. - late L. *prōnōminālis*.

pronounce utter formally; speak in a set way. XIV. - OF. *pronuncier* (mod. *prononcer*), for earlier *purnuncier* - L. *prōnuntiāre* proclaim, narrate, f. PRO-[1] + *nuntiāre* ANNOUNCE. So **pronunciation** XV. - (O)F. or L.

proof that which makes good a statement XIII; action of proving or testing XIV; something produced as a test XVI. Later ME. *prōf* (pl. *prōves*), superseding earlier *prēf, prēve* - OF. *pr(o)eve, prueve* (mod. *preuve*) :- late L. *proba*, f. *probāre* test, PROVE. The substitution of *prōf* for *prēf* was due to assim. to the vb. Hence **proof** adj. of tested strength XVI; prob. from ellipsis of *of* in †*armour of proof*.

prop rod, stake, or beam to support a weight. XV. perh. - MDu. *proppe* vine-prop, support, corr. in form to MLG. *proppe* plug, stopper, bung, OHG. *pfropfo* sucker, shoot, graft, but the diversity of sense makes difficulties. Hence, or - (M)LG., (M)Du. *proppen*, **prop** vb. XV.

propaganda committee of cardinals charged with the foreign missions of the Church XVIII; systematic scheme for the dissemination of a doctrine or practice XIX. - It. (Sp., Pg.) *propaganda*, extracted from the modL. title *congregatio de propaganda fide* congregation for propagating the faith; fem. gerundive of L. *prōpāgāre* PROPAGATE.

propagate multiply specimens of (a plant, etc.); cause to increase or spread. XVI. f. pp. stem of L. *prōpāgāre* (prop.) multiply by means of layers or slips, rel. to *prōpāgō, prōpāgēs* set, layer, offspring, f. PRO-[1] + **pāg-* fix (cf. PAGE[2]); see -ATE[3]. So **propagation** XV. - (O)F. or L.

propel †expel XV; drive forward XVII. - L. *prōpellere*, f. PRO-[1] + *pellere* drive. So **propulsion** XVII. - medL. *prōpulsiō, -ōn-*

propensity XVI. f. *propense* disposed (XVI) - L. *prōpensus* inclining, inclined, pp. of *prōpendēre*, f. PRO-[1] + *pendēre* hang; see -ITY.

proper pert. to oneself or itself or to a person or thing particularly XIII; strictly pertaining; thorough, complete; excellent, fine XIV; specially adapted XV (cf. the adv.). ME. *propre* - (O)F. - L. *prŏprius* one's own, special, peculiar, prob. f. **prō prīuō* as a PRIVATE or peculiar thing. Hence **properly** XIII (appropriately, fittingly). So **property** ownership (esp. private) XIII; thing or things owned XIV; attribute, quality; †propriety; portable article for a dramatic performance XV. ME. *proprete* - AN. **proprete*, (O)F. *propriété* - L. *prŏprietās* PROPRIETY.

prophecy action or function of a prophet, utterance of a prophet, prediction of events. XIII. - OF. *profecie* (mod. *prophétie*) - late L. *prophētīa* - Gr. *prophētiā*, f. *prophḗtēs* prophet; see -CY. So **prophesy** speak as a prophet. XIV. - OF. *prophecier*, f. *prophecie*. **prophet** inspired revealer of God's will XII; one who predicts XIII. - (O)F. *prophète* - L. *prophēta, -tēs* - Gr. *prophḗtēs* interpreter, spokesman, esp. of the will of a deity, as in LXX and N.T., f. PRO-[2] + *-phētēs* speaker, f. *phē-, phánai* speak. **prophetess** (-ESS[1]) XIII. - OF. *prophetesse* - late L. *prophētissa*. **prophetic** XVI, **-ical** XV. - F. or late L.

prophylactic preventive of disease. XVI. - F. *prophylactique* - Gr. *prophulaktikós*, f. *prophulássein* keep guard before; see PRO-[2], PHYLACTERY, -IC.

propinquity nearness, proximity. XIV. - OF. *propinquité* or L. *propinquitās*, f. *propinquus* neighbouring, f. *prope* near; see -ITY.

propitiate render propitious. XVII. f. pp. stem of L. *propitiāre*, f. *propitius* favourable, gracious; see -ATE[3]. So **propitiation** XIV. **propitiatory** (-ORY[2]) XIII. - ecclL. **propitious** XV. - OF. *propicieus* or f. L. *propitius*.

propolis bee-glue, resinous substance with

which bees line their hives. XVII. - L. - Gr. *própolis* (i) suburb, (ii) bee-glue, f. PRO-[2] + *pólis* city.

proportion comparative part, share; comparative relation, relative size. XIV (not fully current before XVI). - (O)F. *proportion* or L. *prōportiō, -ōn-*, derived from phr. *prō portiōne* proportionally, i.e. *prō* PRO-[1] + abl. of *portiō* PORTION. So vb. make proportionate. XIV. - (O)F. or medL. *prōportiōnāre*. **proportionable** XIV. - late L. **proportional** XIV (sb.). - L. **proportionate** XIV. - late L.

propose XIV. - (O)F. *proposer*, repr. L. *prōpōnere* (see PRO-[1], POSE). Hence **proposal** (-AL[2]) XVII. So **proposition** act of propounding or plan propounded XIV; (math.) XVI. - (O)F. or L., f. pp. stem of *prōpōnere*, whence **propound** XVI. alt. of †*propoune* (for earlier *propone* XIV).

propraetor see PROCONSUL.

proprietary grantee of one of certain Amer. colonies; proprietorship XVII; adj. XV. - late L. *proprietārius* (in medL. as sb. holder of property), f. *proprietās* PROPERTY; see -ARY. So **proprietor** XVII. alt. of prec. by irreg. substitution of suffix -TOR.

propriety †property XV; fitness, appropriateness XVII; conformity with good usage XVIII. - (O)F. *propriété* - L. *prŏprietās* peculiarity, ownership, f. *prŏprius* PROPER; see -ITY.

propulsion see PROPEL.

propylaeum entrance to a temple, etc.; introduction. XVIII. - L. - Gr. *propúlaion*, sb. use of n. adj. 'before the gate'. f. PRO-[2] + *púlē* gate.

prorogue †extend in time; discontinue the meeting of (a legislative body, etc.). XV. - (O)F. *proroger*, †*-guer* - L. *prōrogāre*, f. PRO-[1] + *rogāre* ask. So **prorogation** XV. - (O)F. or L.

proscenium in the ancient theatre, space between background and orchestra XVII; in the mod. theatre, space between curtain and orchestra XIX. - L. *proscēnium* - Gr. *proskḗnion*, f. PRO-[2] + *skēnḗ* SCENE.

proscribe post up the name of (a person) as condemned XVI; denounce, interdict XVII. - L. *prōscrībere* publish in writing, f. PRO-[1] + *scrībere* write. So **proscription** XIV.

prose form of language not restricted in measure or rhythm XIV; (eccl.) sequence XV; matter-of-fact expression XVI; prosy discourse XVII. - (O)F. - L. *prōsa*, sb. use of fem. of *prōsus*, for earlier *prorsus* straightforward, direct, contr. of *prōversus*, pp. of *prōvertere* turn forwards, f. PRO-[1] + *vertere* turn. So **prosaic** XVI. - F. or late L. *prōsaicus*. Hence **prosy** XIX.

prosecute follow up, go on with XV; carry on; institute legal proceedings against XVI. f. *prōsecūt-*, pp. stem of L. *prōsequī* pursue, accompany, f. PRO-[1] + *sequī* follow. So **prosecution** XVI. - OF. or late L.

proselyte XIV. - ChrL. *prosēlytus* - Gr. *prosḗluthos* stranger, sojourner (LXX), convert to Judaism (N.T.), f. 2nd aorist stem (*proselūth-*) of *prosérkhesthai* come to, approach. Hence **proselytize** XVII.

prosody XV. - L. *prosōdia* accent of a syllable - Gr. *prosōidiā* song sung to music, tone of a syllable, f. *prós* to + *ōidḗ* song, ODE; see -Y[3].

prosopopoeia (rhet.) figure by which an imaginary or absent person is represented as acting, (hence) personification. XVI. - L. - Gr. *prosōpopoiiā* representation in human form, f. *prósōpon* face, person (f. *pròs* to + *ṓps* face) + *poiein* make.

prospect view afforded by a position XV; spectacle, scene; mental vista XVII. - L. *prōspectus* look-out, view, f. *prōspicere*, f. PRO-[1] + *specere* look. So or hence **prospect** vb. †look forward XVI; explore a region *for* mineral XIX (from the use of the sb. for 'spot giving promise of mineral deposit'). **prospective** XVI. - obs. F. or late L. **prospectus** XVIII. - L.

prosper be fortunate or successful XV; trans. XVI. - (O)F. *prospérer* or L. *prosperāre*, f. *prosper*, *prosperus* doing well or successfully. So **prosperity** XIII. - (O)F. - L. **prosperous** XV. - F. †*prospereus*.

prostate (anat.) gland at junction of neck of the bladder and the urethra. XVII. - F. - Gr. *prostátēs* one that stands before, guardian, f. PRO-[2] + *statós* placed, standing.

prosthesis (philol.) addition of a letter or syllable at the beginning of a word. XVI. - late L. - Gr. *prósthesis*, f. *prostithénai* add, f. *prós* to; see THESIS.

prostitute †adj. offered or exposed to lust XVI; sb. XVII. - L. *prōstitūtus* (fem. *prōstitūta* as sb.), pp. of *prōstituere* expose publicly, offer for sale, prostitute, f. PRO-[1] + *statuere* set up, place. So **prostitute** vb. XVI. f. pp. stem of the L. vb. **prostitution** XVI. - (O)F. or late L.

prostrate XIV. - L. *prōstrātus*, pp. of *prōsternere* throw in front, cast down, f. PRO-[1] + *sternere* lay low; see -ATE[2]. So vb. XV. f. the pp. stem. **prostration** XVI. - (O)F. or late L.

protagonist chief personage in a drama XVII; leading person in a contest or cause XIX. - Gr. *prōtagōnistḗs*, f. *prôtos* first + *agōnistḗs* combatant, actor, f. *agōnízesthai* contest; see -IST.

protasis †first part of a play; (gram.) introductory clause of a sentence. XVII. - L. - Gr. *prótasis* proposition, problem, etc., f. *proteínein* put forward, tender, f. PRO-[2] + *teínein* stretch.

protect XVI. f. *prōtect-*, pp. stem of L. *prōtegere* cover in front, f. PRO-[1] + *tegere* cover. So **protection** XIV. - (O)F. or late L. **protector** XIV. - (O)F. - late L.; hence **protectorate** (-ATE[1]) XVII.

protégé, fem. **-gée** XVIII. - F., pp. of *protéger* - L. *prōtegere* PROTECT.

protein (chem.) one of a class of organic compounds forming essential constituents of living organisms. XIX. - F. *protéine*, G. *proteïn*, f. Gr. *prōteios* primary, f. *prôtos* first; see -IN.

protest protestation XIV; formal written declaration XVII; declaration of dissent XVIII. - F. †*protest* (mod. *protêt*), f. *protester* (whence **protest** vb. XV). - L. *prōtestārī* declare formally, f. PRO-[1] + *testārī* be a witness, assert. So **Protestant** applied to those who joined in the protest at the Diet of Spires in 1529; (hence) non-Roman-Catholic XVI; (*p*-) one who protests (gen.) XVII. - L. *prōtestāns*, prp. of *prōtestārī*. **protestation** XIV. - (O)F. - late L.

proteus (Gr. and Rom. myth.) sea-god fabled to change his shape, transf. and fig. XVI; amoeba;

genus of bacteria; genus of amphibians XIX. - L. - Gr. *Proteús*. Hence **protean** changing, varying. XVI.

proto- comb. form of Gr. *prôtos* first, obscurely rel. to *pró* PRO-[2]; in many techn. terms. **protomartyr** first martyr, e.g. St. Stephen. XV. - medL. **protonotary** principal notary, chief clerk. XV. - medL. **protoplasm** substance constituting the physical basis of life. XIX. - G. *protoplasma* (see PLASMA). **prototype** XVII. - F. or late L. **protozoa** (zool.) division of animals of the most primitive type. XIX. - modL., f. Gr. *zôia* animals; see ZOOLOGY.

protocol original note or minute of a transaction XVI; original draft or record of a diplomatic document XVII; etiquette of precedence, etc. XIX. orig. *prothocoll* (in earliest use Sc.) - OF. *prothocole* (mod. *protocole*) - medL. *prōtocollum* - Gr. *prōtókollon* first leaf of a volume, fly-leaf glued to the case and containing an account of the contents, f. PROTO- + *kólla* glue.

proton (phys.) unit of matter associated with a charge of positive electricity. XX. - n. sg. of Gr. *prôtos* first.

protract A. lengthen out; B. draw to scale. XVI. f. *prōtract-*, pp. stem of L. *prōtrahere* prolong, defer, in medL. also in sense B, f. PRO-[1] + *trahere* draw. So **protraction** XVI. - F. or late L. Hence **protractor** (-OR[1]) one who prolongs time, etc.; instrument used in setting off and measuring angles. XVII.

protrude XVII. - L. *prōtrūdere*, f. PRO-[1] + *trūdere* press, thrust. So **protrusion** XVII. - F.

protuberant XVII. - prp. of late L. *prōtūberāre*, f. PRO-[1] + *tūber* bump, swelling; see -ANT. Hence **protuberance** XVII.

proud having a high opinion of oneself OE.; feeling honoured, stately, grand XIII, †valiant XIV; overgrown, tumid XVI. Late OE. *prūd* (also *prūt*) - OF. *prud*, *prod*, nom. *pruz*, *pro(u)z* (mod. *preux*) valiant, gallant - Rom. **prōdis*, f. L. *prōdesse* be of value, be good, f. *prōd*, var. of *prō* PRO-[1] + *esse* be.

prove try, test XII; make good, establish XIII. OE. *prōfian*, succeeded by - OF. *prover* (mod. *prouver*) :- L. *probāre* test, approve, demonstrate, f. *probus* good.

provenance XIX. - F., f. prp. of *provenir* come forth - L. *prōvenīre*, f. PRO-[1] + *venīre* COME. So **provenience** XIX. derived immed. from the prp. of the L. vb. See -ANCE, -ENCE.

Provençal pert. to Provence, former province in south-east France XVI; the Romance language spoken there XVII. - F. - L. *prōvinciālis* PROVINCIAL; the southern part of ancient Gaul, under Roman rule long before the rest, was familiarly styled (*nostra*) *provincia* the or our province.

provender †prebend; food, provisions. XIV. - OF. *provendre*, var. of *provende* :- Rom. **prōbenda*, alt. of L. *præbenda* PREBEND.

proverb XIV. - (O)F. *proverbe* or L. *prōverbium*, f. PRO-[1] + *verbum* WORD, as if 'a set of words put forth'. So **proverbial** XV. - L.

provide †(intr.) exercise foresight; furnish for use; fit out. XV. - L. *prōvidēre* foresee, attend to, f. PRO-[1] + *vidēre* see. So **providence** foresight, timely care XIV; applied to God XVII. - (O)F. or L. **provident** XV. - L.; hence **providential** XVII.

provision appointment to a see or benefice not yet vacant XIV; †foresight, providing in advance; clause providing for a matter; supply of necessaries, etc. XV; supply of food XVII. - (O)F. - L. *prōvīsiō*, *-ōn-*, f. pp. stem of *prōvidēre* PROVIDE; see -ION. So **proviso** XV. - L. *prōvīsō*, abl. sg. n. of pp. of *prōvidēre*, as used in medL. phr. *prōvīsō quod* (or *ut*) . . it being provided that . . **provisor** holder of a certain grant (now hist. in *Statute of Provisors*); (arch.) one who provides, or purveys XIV. - AN. *provisour* (F. *proviseur*) - L. *prōvīsor*; see -OR[1]. Hence **provisional** (-AL[1]) XVII.

province district, region XIV; territory outside Italy under Roman rule, hence gen.; department of activity XVII. - (O)F. - L. *prōvincia* charge, official duty, administration or region of conquered territory; of unkn. orig. So **provincial** XIV. Hence **provincialism** XVIII.

provoke XV. - (O)F. *provoquer* or L. *prōvocāre*, f. PRO-[1] + *vocāre* call. So **provocation**, **provocative** XV. - (O)F. or (late) L.

provost official set over others (in various spec. uses). Late OE. *profost* (also *prafost*), corr. to MLG., MDu. *provest*, MDu. *proofst* (Du. *proost*), OHG. *probost* (G. *probst*, *propst*), ONorw. *prófastr*; in ME. reinforced from AN. *provost* (also *prevost*, modF. *prévôt*) - medL. *prōpositus*, used alongside *præpositus*, sb. use of pp. of L. *præpōnere* place in front, set in authority, f. *præ* PRE-, PRO-[1] + *pōnere* place.

prow XVI. - (O)F. *proue* - Pr. *proa* or It. dial. *prua* :- L. *prōra* - Gr. *prôira*, f. base repr. by L. *prō* before, in front of (PRO-[1]).

prowess valour, manly courage. XIII. - OF. *proesce* (mod. *prouesse*), f. *prou*, early *prod*, etc. valiant; see PROUD, -ESS[2].

prowl XIV. ME. *prolle*, of unkn. orig.

proximate immediately adjacent XVI; coming next XVII. - L. *proximātus*, pp. of *proximāre* approach, f. *proximus* nearest, superl. of **proqe*, var. of *prope* near; see -ATE[2]. So **proximity** XV. - (O)F. or L.

proxy action of a substitute or deputy XV; document authorizing a person to act for another XVI. Earlier forms *procusie*, *prokecye*, *proccy*, contr. of †*proc(u)racy*, - medL. *prōcūrātia*, repl. L. *prōcūrātiō* procuration; see -ACY.

prude sb. and †adj. XVIII. - F. *prude* adj. and sb., back-formation from *prudefemme*, misunderstood as adj. + sb. but prop. fem. (f. **preu de femme*) corr. to *prud'homme* good man and true, earlier *prodome* (f. **pro de ome* 'fine thing of a man'); cf. PROUD. Hence **prudish** (-ISH[1]) XVIII. So **prudery** XVIII. - F.

prudent XIV. - (O)F. *prudent* or L. *prūdēns* foreseeing, sagacious :- **prōwidēns*, f. PRO-[1] + prp. of *vidēre* see. So **prudence** XIV. - (O)F. - L. **prudential** XVII. - medL. or f. L. *prūdentia*.

prune[1] dried fruit of the plum-tree. XIV. - (O)F. :- Rom. **prūna*, fem. sg. for L. n. *prūna*, pl. of *prūnum* PLUM.

prune[2] trim (feathers) with the beak. XIV. ME. *pru(y)ne*, also *proyne* - pres. stem *poroign-* of OF. *poroindre*, f. *por-* (mod. *pour-*; :- L. PRO-[1]) + *oindre* (:- L. *ungere* anoint).

prune² lop superfluous growth from. XV. Early forms *prouyne, proine, pruine* - OF. *proignier*, earlier *prooignier* :- Rom. **prōrotundiāre*, f. PRO-¹ + **rotundiāre* cut round, f. *rotundus* ROUND.

prunella strong (worsted) stuff used for academic gowns. XVII. of uncert. orig.

prurient itching, having an itching desire XVII; given to lewd thoughts XVIII. - L. *prūriēns, -ent-*, prp. of *prūrīre* itch, long, be wanton; see -ENT. So **prurigo, pruritus** XVII.

prussic pert. to or derived from *Prussian blue*, which was so called from having been discovered (1704) by Diesbach, a Berlin colourmaker; *p. acid* hydrocyanic acid. XVIII. - F. *prussique*, f. *Prusse* Prussia; see -IC.

pry¹ look closely or inquisitively. XIV. of unkn. orig.

pry² (dial. and U.S.) prize *up*. XIX. Evolved from PRIZE⁴ through apprehending the final cons. as the ending of the 3rd sg. pres. ind.

psalm OE. *(p)s(e)alm* (reinforced in ME. from OF.), corr. to OHG. *(p)salmo* (G. *psalm*), ON. *(p)salmr* - late L. *psalmus* - Gr. *psalmós* plucking with the fingers, sounding of the harp, (in LXX and N.T.) song sung to the harp, f. *psállein* pluck, sing to the harp. So **psalmist** XV. - late L. **psalmody** (-Y³) XIV. - late L. *psalmōdia* - Gr. *psalmōidiā* (see ODE). So **psalter** OE. *(p)saltere*, corr. to OHG. *(p)salteri*, ON. *(p)saltari* - late L. *psaltērium* - Gr. *psaltḗrion* stringed instrument, (in ChrL. and ChrGr. writers) the book of Psalms of the O.T.; and ME. *sauter* - AN. *sauter*, OF. *sautier* (mod. *psautier*). **psaltery** ancient stringed instrument. XIII. ME. *sautr(i)e* - OF. *sauter(i)e* - L. *psaltērium*; all finally superseded by latinized forms in *ps-*, which have been exclusively used since 1600.

psephology study of public elections. XX. f. Gr. *psêphos* pebble, vote + -LOGY.

pseudo-, before a vowel **pseud-**, repr. comb. form of Gr. *pseudḗs* false, *pseûdos* falsehood, in comps. adopted (often through L.) from Gr. or modelled on them.

pseudonym XIX. - F. *pseudonyme* - Gr. *pseudṓnumon*, n. of *pseudṓnumos* (*ónuma, ónoma* NAME), whence **pseudonymous** XVIII.

psittacosis contagious disease of birds, esp. parrots. XIX. f. L. *psittacus* - Gr. *psittakós* parrot; see -OSIS.

psoriasis (path.) disease of the skin. XIX. - Gr. *psōríāsis*, f. *psōriân* itch.

psyche soul, spirit, mind. XVII. - L. *psȳchē* - Gr. *psūkhḗ* breath, soul, life, rel. to *psū́khein* breathe, blow. So **psychic** XIX, **-ical** XVII (rare before XIX); first in senses pert. to soul or mind, later pert. to conditions supposed to be outside the physical domain. - Gr. *psūkhikós*. **psycho-**, before a vowel **psych-**, repr. comb. form of Gr. *psūkhḗ* used in techn. terms since XVII, but prolifically only since mid-XIX. **psychiatry** healing of mental disease (Gr. *iātrós* healer). **psychology** science of the human soul or mind. XVII (rare before XIX). - modL. *psȳchologia*. So **psychological** XVIII.

ptarmigan XVI. Early forms (in Sc. use) *termigan(t), termagant, tormichan* - Gael. *tarmachan*, of unkn. orig.; fancifully sp. *ptarmigan* (XVII) after Gr. words with *pt-*, e.g. *pterón* wing.

pterido- repr. comb. form of Gr. *pterís, -id-* fern.

pterodactyl extinct winged reptile. XIX. f. Gr. *pterón* wing + *dáktulos* finger.

ptisan medicinal decoction, orig. barley-water. XIV. Earlier *tizanne, tysan*, later *ptisane* (XVI) - (O)F. *tisane*, later †*ptisane* - medL. *tisana*, L. *ptisana* - Gr. *ptisánē* peeled barley, barley-water.

puberty XIV (not frequent till XVI). - L. *pūbertās* (or the deriv. F. *puberté*), f. *pūbēs, -er-* adult; see -TY. So **pubes** XVI, whence **pubic** XIX. **pubescent** of the age of puberty XVII; downy XVIII. - F. *pubescent* or L. *pūbēscēns, -ent-*, prp. of *pūbēscere* reach the age of puberty. **pubescence** XVII.

public pert. to the people or to a community as a whole XV; sb. *in p.* XV; *the* state or commonwealth; *the* community as a whole XVII; short for *p. house* (XVII), i.e. of entertainment XVIII. - (O)F. *public, -ique* or L. *pūblicus*, based on *pūbēs* 'adult' with crossing from *poplicus*, f. *populus* PEOPLE; see -IC. So **publican** tax-gatherer XII; keeper of a public house XVIII. - (O)F. *publicain* - L. *pūblicānus* orig. farmer general of the revenues, f. *pūblicum* public revenue, sb. use of n. of *pūblicus*. **publicist** one learned in international law XVIII; political journalist XIX; publicity agent XX. - F., f. L. *(jūs) pūblicum* public law. **publicity** being open to public observation XVIII; making things public XX. - F. **publicize** XX.

publish make publicly known XIV; issue copies of (a book, etc.) to the public XVI. ME. *puplise, -ische, publishe*, f. stem of OF. *puplier*, (also mod.) *publier* - L. *pūblicāre* make public, f. *pūblicus* PUBLIC; see -ISH². So **publication** XIV. - (O)F. - L.

puce purplish-brown. XVIII. - (O)F. *puce* flea (*couleur puce* 'flea colour' XVII) :- L. *pūlex, pūlic-*.

puck †evil spirit or demon, spec. the Devil OE.; mischievous sprite XVI. Late OE. *pūca* = ON. *púki* mischievous demon; ult. orig. unkn.

pucka see PUKKA.

pucker contract into wrinkles. XVI. prob. frequent. f. base *pok-* of POKE¹, POCKET, as if 'make pockets', 'form into bag-like gatherings'; see -ER⁴. Hence sb. XVIII.

pudding animal's stomach or intestine stuffed with meat, etc. XIII; (dial.) pl. entrails XV; preparation of food with basis of flour boiled, orig. in a bag XVI. ME. *poding, puddyng*, corr. in meaning to (O)F. *boudin*.

puddle XIV. ME. *podel*, later *puddel*, dim. of OE. *pudd* ditch, furrow; see -LE¹. So vb. dabble in mud, etc. XV; make muddy XVI; stir (molten iron) XVIII.

pudendum pl. **-enda** private parts XVII (once XIV). - late L. *pudenda*, sb. use of n. sg. and pl. of *pudendus*, gerundive of L. *pudet* it is shameful.

puerile XVII. - F. *puéril* or L. *puerīlis*, f. *puer* boy, child; see -ILE. So **puerility** XVI.

puerperal pert. to parturition. XVIII. f. L. *puerperus* parturient, f. *puer* child + *-parus* bringing forth; see prec., PARENT, -AL¹.

puff short emission of air or vapour XIII; swollen or inflated object (light pastry) XV; (exaggerated) commendation XVII. So vb. expel breath with the lips XIII; inflate XVI. perh. repr. OE. **puf* or *pyf(f)* sb., **puffan* or *pyffan* vb., corr. to (M)Du. *puffen*, Du. *pof, poffen*, LG. *pof, puf*; imit. of the sound of the breath.

puffin XIV. ME. *poffo(u)n, pophyn*; prob. f. PUFF.

pug †term of endearment; †courtesan, harlot; bargeman XVI; †imp; monkey XVII; dwarf breed of dog XVIII; genus of moths XIX. of unkn. orig.; it is not certain that all the senses belong to the same word.

pugilist XVIII. f. L. *pugil*, f. base of *pugnus* fist, *pugnāre* fight; see -IST. So **pugnacious** XVII. f. L. *pugnāx, -āc-*, f. *pugnāre*. **pugnacity** XVII. - L.

puisne younger, junior (now only of judges). XVI. leg. sp. of PUNY.

puissant (arch.) powerful. XV. - (O)F. :- Gallo-Rom. **possiantem*, for L. *potēns, potent-* POTENT[1]. So **puissance** XV. See -ANCE, -ANT.

puke vomit. XVI. prob. of imit. orig.

pukka, pucka of full weight; genuine; reliable, permanent. XVII. - Hindi *pakkā* cooked, ripe, mature, real.

pule whine, cry plaintively. XVI. prob. of imit. orig.

pull Late OE. *pullian*, having ostensible similarity in form and sense to LG. *pūlen* shell, strip, pluck, MDu. *polen* strip, and (M)LG. *pūle*, Du. *peul* husk, shell, the meaning 'pluck, snatch' being prob. the original. Hence sb. XIV.

pullet XIV. - (O)F. *poulet*, fem. *-ette*, dim. of *poule* hen :- Rom. **pulla*, fem. of L. *pullus* young animal, chicken.

pulley XIV. ME. *poley* - OF. *polie* (mod. *poulie*) :- Rom. **polidia* (n. pl. used as fem. sg.), pl. of **polidium*, prob. - medGr. **polídion*, dim. of *pólos* POLE[2], also windlass, capstan.

Pullman railway carriage constructed as a saloon. XIX. f. name of the Amer. designer, George M. *Pullman* (1831-97).

pullulate sprout XVII; swarm XIX. f. pp. stem of L. *pullulāre* spring forth, grow, f. *pullulus*, dim. of *pullus* young of an animal, chick; see -ATE[3].

pulmonary XVIII. - L. *pulmōnārius*, f. *pulmō, -ōn-* lung; see -ARY.

pulp fleshy part of fruit, etc. XVI; soft formless mass XVII. - L. *pulpa*.

pulpit XIV. - L. *pulpitum* scaffold, platform, stage, medL. pulpit; of unkn. orig.

pulse[1] rhythmical dilatation of the arteries. XIV. ME. *pous, pouce*, later *puls* - OF. *pous*, later (latinized) *pouls* :- L. *pulsus* beating :- **pelssos* f. base of *pellere* drive, beat. So **pulse** vb. †drive; pulsate. XVI. - L. *pulsāre*, frequent. of *pellere*. **pulsate** XVIII, **pulsation** XVI. - L.

pulse[2] edible seeds of leguminous plants. XIII. ME. *pols* - OF. *pols* (mod. dial. *poul(s), pou*) :- L. *puls* (*pult-*) thick pottage of meal or pulse (cf. Gr. *póltos* porridge), rel. to POLLEN. Latinized in form from XV.

pulverize reduce to powder. XVI. - late L. *pulverizāre*, f. *pulvis, pulver-* dust, POWDER; see -IZE. So **pulverulent** powdery, crumbling. XVII. - L.

puma XVIII. - Sp. - Quechua.

pumice XV. ME. *pomys* - OF. *pomis* - L. dial. *pōmic-*, var. of *pūmex, pūmic-*.

pummel XVI. Earlier *pomell, poumile, pumble*, f. POMMEL, the orig. sense being 'strike with the pommel of a sword (instead of the edge or point)'.

pump[1] mechanical device for raising water, etc. XV. In earliest use naut.; corr. to late MDu. *pompe* wood or metal pipe, stone conduit, Du. *pomp* ship's pump, LG. *pump(e)*; the evidence is inadequate to decide whether the word was prior in Eng. or LG. Hence **pump** vb. XVI.

pump[2] light close-fitting shoe. XVI. of unkn. orig.

pumpernickel German rye bread. XVIII. - G., of unkn. orig.

pumpkin XVII. alt. (by assim. of the ending to -KIN) of *pumpion*, earlier *pompon* - F. †*pompon*, nasalized form of †*popon*, var. of **pepon* - L. *pepō, -ōn-* - Gr. *pépōn* large melon, sb. use of *pépōn* ripe.

pun sb. XVII. perh. short for †*pundigrion*, of uncert. orig. Hence vb. XVII. **punster** XVII.

punch[1] †dagger XV (rare); instrument for pricking or piercing XVI, for impressing a design XVII. Shortening of PUNCHEON[1], which it has mostly superseded, if not f. PUNCH[4].

punch[2] (*Punch*) hump-backed short grotesque male figure; principal character in the puppet-show of Punch and Judy XVIII; short fat man (also adj.) XVII; one of a breed of thick-set horses (e.g. *Suffolk p.*) XIX. Shortening of PUNCHINELLO.

punch[3] beverage from wine, spirits, mixed with hot water or milk, etc. XVII. of unkn. orig.

punch[4] (dial.) poke, prod, †stab XIV; pierce with holes; deliver a sharp blow at esp. with the fist XVI. var. of †*pounce* emboss, pink the edge of (XV), prob. of Rom. orig. (cf. next).

puncheon[1] pointed tool or †weapon. XIV. ME. *pons(y)on, ponchon* - OF. *poinson, po(i)nchon* (mod. *poinçon*) :- Rom. **punctiōne(m)*, f. Rom. **punctiāre* prick, punch.

puncheon[2] (mostly Sc.) large cask (esp. one of specific capacity). XV. Identical in form with prec., but if it is the same word the sense-development is obscure.

Punchinello principal character in an Italian puppet show. XVII. Current from the outset in two main forms *Policinello* and *Punchinello* (with vars. in *Pon-, -elle*). - Neapolitan dial. *Polecenella*, in literary It. *Pulcinella*, perh. based on dim. of *pollecena* young of the turkey-cock (whose hooked beak the nose of Punch resembles).

punctilio †fine or minute point; minute detail of conduct. XVI (*puntilio*). - It. *puntiglio*, Sp. *puntillo*, dim. of *punto* POINT; later assim. to L. So **punctilious** XVII. - F. *pointilleux*. **punctual** pert. to a point or dot XIV; †bearing on the point, precise; †minutely observant of rule, etc.; exactly observant of appointed time XVII. - medL. *punctuālis* (see -AL[1]); hence **punctuality** XVII. **punctuate** point out (rare) XVII; put the stops in (a sentence) XIX. f. pp. stem of medL. *punctuāre* prick, point, etc.; see -ATE[3]. So **punctuation** †pointing of the psalms XVI; insertion of vowel points in Hebrew, etc., of stops in a sentence

XVII. - medL. *punctuātiō*. **puncture** prick, perforation. XIV (rare before XVI). - L. *punctūra* (see -URE); hence vb. XVII.

pundit learned Hindu. XVII. - Hindi *paṇḍit* :- Skr. *paṇḍitá-* learned, skilled, sb. learned man, scholar.

pungent XVI. - L. *pungēns, -ent-*, prp. of *pungere* prick; see -ENT.

punish XIV. ME. *punisse, -ische* - (O)F. *puniss-*, extended stem (see -ISH²) of *punir* :- L. *pūnīre*, earlier *pœnīre*, f. *pœna* PAIN. Hence **punishment** XV. - OF. *punissement*. So **punitive** XVII. - F. *punitif, -ive* or medL. *pūnītīvus*, f. *pūnīt-*, pp. stem of *pūnīre*.

punk¹ (obs. or arch.) prostitute. XVI. of unkn. orig.

punk² rotten wood, touchwood XVIII; something worthless XIX; person of no account XX. of unkn. orig.

punkah portable fan XVII; fan of cloth stretched on a frame XIX. - Hindi *pankhā* fan :- Skr. *pakṣaka-* fan, f. *pakṣá-* wing.

punnet XIX. perh. dim. of *pun*, dial. var. of POUND¹; see -ET.

punt¹ flat-bottomed shallow boat. XV. In earliest use (E. Anglian) *pontebot, punte boot* (BOAT) - MLG. *punte, punto* ferry-boat, mud-boat, corr. to late OE. *punt* (which did not survive), MDu. *ponte* (Du. *pont*) ferry-boat, pontoon - L. *pontō* Gaulish transport vessel, PONTOON. Hence vb. XIX.

punt² at cards, lay a stake against the bank. XVIII. - F. *ponter*, rel. to *ponte* punt in ombre, player against the bank - Sp. *punto* = (O)F. *pointe* POINT (the Sp. word is used in ombre, quadrille, etc. for the ace of certain suits).

punt³ in Rugby football, kick (the ball) after dropping it from the hands before it reaches the ground. XIX. prob. spec. use of dial. *punt* push with force.

puny †junior, PUISNE; †inexperienced; of inferior size or strength. XVI. - OF. *puisne* (mod. *puîné*), f. *puis* (:- L. *postea* or Rom. **postius*) afterwards + *né* (:- L. *nātus*) born; the ending has been assim. to -Y¹.

pup XVIII. back-formation f. PUPPY, as if this were a dim. in -Y⁶.

pupa chrysalis. XIX. - modL. use of L. *pūpa* girl, doll.

pupil¹ orphan who is a minor and hence a ward XIV; one under instruction XVI. - (O)F. *pupille* m. and fem. or its source, L. *pūpillus, -illa* orphan, ward, dim. of *pūpus* boy, *pūpa* girl.

pupil² circular opening in the iris of the eye. XVI. - (O)F. *pupille* or L. *pūpilla*, dim. of *pūpa* girl, doll, pupil of the eye (see prec.). The application of the L. words to the pupil of the eye is based on, or parallel to, that of Gr. *kórē-* maiden, girl, doll, pupil (the allusion being to the tiny images of persons and things that may be seen therein).

puppet †doll; (human) figure jointed and moving on strings or wires XVI; lathe-head XVII. Earlier in deriv. **puppetry**; var. of POPPET.

puppy †lap dog, toy dog XV; young dog XVI; contemptuously of a person XVI. ME. *popi(e)*, corr. in form to OF. *popée*, (also mod.) *poupée* doll :- Rom. **puppāta*, f. **puppa* girl, doll; see POPPET, -Y⁶.

Purana sacred works of Hindu mythology. XVII. - Skr. *purāṇá-* pert. to olden times, sb. tale of the past, f. *purā́* formerly.

purblind †quite blind XIII; †blind in one eye XIV; partially blind, short- or dim-sighted XVI. orig. *pur(e) blind*, i.e. *pur(e)*, ME. adv. use of PURE, and BLIND adj.

purchase †contrive, devise XIII; †procure, acquire; buy XIV; (naut.) haul in or up XVI. - AN. *purchacer*, OF. *pourchacier* seek to obtain, procure, f. intensive *pur-, por-, pour-* (:- L. PRO-¹) + *chacier* (mod. *chasser*) CHASE¹. So sb. XIII.

purdah curtain, esp. to screen women from sight XVIII; system of seclusion of Indian women XIX. - Urdu - Pers. *pardah*.

pure not mixed XIII; guiltless, innocent XIV; chaste XV. - (O)F. *pur*, fem. *pure* :- L. *pūrus*, rel. to Skr. *pūtá-* purified, Ir. *úr* green, fresh. So **purify, purification** XIV. - (O)F. or (late) L. **purist** XVIII. - F. *puriste*. **purity** XIII (*purete*). - (O)F. *pureté*; later assim. to late L.

purée soup made from vegetables, etc. pulped and passed through a sieve. XIX. - (O)F., f. *purer* purify, squeeze (fruits, etc.) to obtain the pulp.

purfle adorn with a border. XIV. - OF. *purfiler* - Rom. **prōfīlāre*, f. PRO-¹ + *fīlum* thread.

purge A. make pure, cleanse, free from guilt XIV; B. empty (the bowels) XV. - (O)F. *purger* :- L. *purgāre* purify, for *pūrigāre*, f. *pūrus* PURE. So **purgation** XIV. - (O)F. or L. **purgative** XV. - (O)F. or late L. **purgatory** condition or place of spiritual purging. XIII. - AN. *purgatorie*, (O)F. *purgatoire* - medL. *purgātōrium*, sb. use of n. of late L. *purgātōrius* cleansing; hence **purgatorial** XV.

Puritan Protestant who aimed at further purification of Reformed doctrine and practice. XVI. f. late L. *pūritās* purity (cf. PURE) + -AN. Hence **puritanic, -ical** XVII.

purl¹ cord made of twisted gold or silver wire; †pleat, frill XVI; loop on the edge of lace, etc. XVII; inversion of stitches in knitting producing a ribbed appearance XIX. So vb. XVI. orig. *pyrle, pirle*, of unkn. orig. The last sense of the sb. may be a different word.

purl² (of water) whirl with a murmuring sound. XVI. So sb. †small rill XVI; purling motion or sound XVII. prob. imit.; cf. Norw. *purla* bubble up, gush out, Sw. dial. *porla* ripple, gurgle.

purl³ revolve, whirl round XVIII; turn head over heels XIX. perh. identical with PURL¹. Hence **purler** headlong fall, swingeing blow. XIX.

purlieu tract of land on the border of a forest XV; (one's) haunt or bounds; outlying district, esp. of a mean sort XVII. orig. *purlew*, presumably alt. (by assim. to LIEU) of AN. *purale(e), -ley* perambulation, tract of land between the wider bounds of a forest and those fixed by a perambulation, OF. *pourallee*, f. *po(u)raler* traverse, f. *por-, pour-* (:- L. *prō* forth, PRO-¹) + *aller* go.

purlin (archit.) horizontal beam running along the length of a roof. XV. of uncert. orig.

purloin †remove, do away with XV; take dishonestly XVI. - AN. *purloigner*, OF. *porloigner*,

f. *por-*, *pour-* (:- L. *prō* forth, PRO-[1]) + *loign* (mod. *loin*) far (:- L. *longē*, adv. of *longus* LONG[1]).

purple (orig.) of crimson or other red colour; (later) of a colour obtained by mixing red and blue OE.; sb. XV. Late OE. *purple*, reduced and dissimilated form of *purpuran*, obl. case of *purpure* 'purple' clothing or garment - L. *purpura* - Gr. *porphúrā* shellfish that yielded the Tyrian purple dye, dye itself, cloth dyed therewith.

purport tenor or substance of a document, etc. XV. - AN., OF. *pur-*, *porport* produce, contents, f. *purporter* :- medL. *prōportāre*, f. L. *prō* PRO-[1] + *portāre* carry, bear. So **purport** vb. state, mean. XVI. - OF. *purporter*.

purpose object in view XIII; intention, aim; matter in hand, now only in phr. *to the p.* XIV; *on p.* by design XVI. - OF. *porpos*, *purpos* (mod. *propos*, after L. *prōpositum*), f. *por-*, *purposer* design, intend (whence **purpose** vb. XIV), f. L. *prōpōnere* PROPOSE, after *poser* (see POSE[1]).

purr sb. and vb. XVII. imit. of the vibratory sound made by a cat.

purse money-bag of leather, etc. OE. *purs* - late L. *bursa* (whence also (O)F. *bourse*), var. of *byrsa* - Gr. *búrsa* leather, bag (cf. BURSAR). Hence **purse** vb. pocket XIV; wrinkle XVII. **purser** †maker of purses; purse-bearer, treasurer, esp. ship's officer who keeps the accounts and provisions. XV.

purslane herb *Portulaca oleracea*. XIV. ME. *purcelan(e)* - OF. *porcelaine*, identical in form with the F. word for PORCELAIN, and prob. assim. to that from L. *porcil(l)āca*, more usu. *portulāca*.

pursue XIII. ME. *pursiwe*, *-sewe* - AN. *pursiwer*, *-suer* = OF. *porsivre* (mod. *poursuivre*) :- Rom. **per-*, **prōsequere*, for L. *prōsequī* PROSECUTE. So **pursuant** consequent and conformable. XVII. **pursuance** XVI. **pursuit** †persecution XIV; †suit, petition; act of pursuing XV; following of an occupation XVI. - (O)F. *poursuite* (see SUIT). **pursuivant** junior officer attendant on heralds. XIV. - OF. *pursivant*, sb. use of prp. of *pursivre*.

pursy †short-winded XV; (arch.) corpulent XVI. Later form of †*pursive*, *-if* - AN. *porsif*, alt. of OF. *polsif* (mod. *poussif*), f. *polser* breathe with difficulty, pant :- L. *pulsāre* drive or agitate violently.

purulent of the nature of pus. XVI. - L. *purulentus*, f. *pūs*, *pūr-* PUS; see -ULENT.

purvey †see to, foresee; provide, supply. XIII. ME. *porvaie*, *-veie* - AN. *por-*, *purveier*, OF. *porveeir* (mod. *pourvoir*) :- L. *prōvidēre* PROVIDE. So **purveyor** (-OR[1]) XIII. - AN. *purveur*, OF. *porveour*, *-eur*.

purview body of a statute, following the preamble XV; scope of a document, etc. XVIII. - AN. *purveu*, OF. *porveu* (mod. *pourvu*), pp. of *porveeir* PURVEY; orig. clause introduced by *purveu est* it is provided, or *purveu que* provided that.

pus XVI. - L. *pūs*, *pūr-*.

push vb. XIII. - AN. **pusser*, (O)F. *pousser*, †*pou(l)ser* :- L. *pulsāre*, frequent. f. *puls-*, pp. stem of *pellere* drive, thrust. Hence sb. XVI.

pusillanimous XVI. f. late L. *pūsillanimis*, f. *pūsillus* very small, weak (f. *pūsus* boy, rel. to *puer* boy) + *animus* mind; see -OUS.

puss cat, esp. as a call name XVI (also **puss-cat**); hare; applied to a girl or woman XVII. prob. - MLG. *pūs* (also *pūskatte*), Du. *poes*; cf. Ir., Gael. *pus*; of unkn. orig. Hence **pussy** (-Y[6]) XVIII.

pustule XIV. - (O)F. *pustule* or L. *pustula* blister, f. imit. base **pu-* **phu-* blow, inflate; see -ULE.

put[1] (obs. or dial.) push, thrust, knock, butt (cf. PUTT); transf. in various applications ranging from forcing or urging to placing or setting in a place or position. Fully evidenced from XII onwards; repr. OE. **putian* (*u* of uncertain quantity), repr. only in noun of action *putung* instigation; parallel forms are OE. *potian*, ME. *pot(t)e*, OE. *pȳtan*, ME. *pitte*; ult. orig. unkn.

put[2] see PUTT.

putative XV. - (O)F. *putatif* or late L. *putātīvus*, f. pp. stem of L. *putāre* reckon, think; see -IVE.

putlog, putlock short horizontal timber in scaffolding. XVII. of uncert. orig.

putrefaction rotting, decomposition. XIV. - (O)F. *putréfaction* or late L. *putrefactiō*, *-ōn-*, f. L. *putrefacere*, f. *puter*, *putr-* rotten + *facere* make, DO[1]. So **putrefy** XV. - L. *putrefacere*. **putrid** (-ID[1]) XVI. - L. *putridus*. **putrescence** XVII, **-escent** XVIII.

putt, put[2] (Sc.) †push, shove XVI; throw, hurl (stone or weight) XVIII; (spec. in golf). Formally identical with PUT[1], with differentiated pronunc.

puttee strip of cloth wound spirally round the leg. XIX. - Hindi *paṭṭī* band, bandage.

putty jeweller's polishing powder; plasterer's fine cement XVII; glazier's cement for fixing panes XVIII. - F. *potée* potter's glaze, jeweller's putty, loam for moulds, orig. potful, f. *pot* POT; see -Y[5].

puzzle vb. XVI. of unkn. orig. Hence sb. XVII.

puzzolana var. of POZZOLANA.

py(a)emia (path.) blood-poisoning marked by the formation of pus foci. XIX. f. Gr. *púon* PUS + *haima* blood; see -IA[1].

pygmy, pigmy XIV. In earliest use pl. *pygmeis* - L. *pygmæī*, pl. of *pygmæus* - Gr. *pugmaîos* dwarf(ish), f. *pugmḗ* measure of length from elbow to knuckles, fist.

pyjamas, U.S. **pajamas** (prop.) loose trousers tied round the waist, (by extension) sleeping suit of these with jacket. XVIII. - Urdu (Pers.) *pāy jāma* 'leg-clothing'.

pylon (archit.) gateway XIX; tower, mast, etc. marking a course, supporting a span of wire, etc. XX. - Gr. *pulṓn*, f. *púlē* gate.

pylorus (anat.) opening from the stomach into the duodenum. XVII. - late L. *pylōrus* - Gr. *pulōrós*, *pulourós* gate-keeper, f. *púlē* gate + *oûros* watcher, warder.

pyo-, before a vowel **py-**, comb. form of Gr. *púon* pus, as in **pyorrhoea** (Gr. *rhoiā* flow) (path.) discharge of pus. XVIII.

pyramid monumental (esp. Egyptian) structure with polygonal base and sloping sides meeting in an apex; pile of this shape. XVI. - (orig. used in L. nom. form) L. *pyramis*, *-id-* - Gr. *puramís*, *-id-*. So **pyramidal** XVI. - medL.

pyre XVII. - L. *pyra* - Gr. *purā́*, f. *pûr*, *pur-* FIRE.

pyrethrum pellitory of Spain XVI; feverfew XIX. - L. - Gr. *púrethron* feverfew.

pyretic pert. to fever. XIX. f. Gr. *puretós* fever, f. *pûr* FIRE; see -IC.

pyrexia (path.) febrile disease. XVIII. modL., f. Gr. *púrexis*, f. *puréssein* be feverish, f. *pûr* FIRE; see -IA[1].

pyrites †fire-stone; sulphide of iron. XVI. - L. *pyrītēs* - Gr. *purítēs* sb. use of adj. pert. to fire, f. *pûr, pur-* FIRE; see -ITE.

pyro- comb. form of Gr. *pûr* FIRE, in many techn. terms; in Eng. use first in **pyrotechny** †manufacture of gunpowder, firearms, etc.; †technical use of fire XVI; making and use of fireworks XVII. - F. *pyrotechnie*. So **pyrotechnic** XVIII, **-ical** XVII.

pyrrhic (pros.) foot consisting of two short syllables. XVII. - L. *pyrrichius* - Gr. *purrhíkhios*, f. *purrhíkhē* war dance; see foll.; -IC.

Pyrrhic[1] war-dance of ancient Greeks. XVI. - L. *pyrricha* or Gr. *purrhíkhē*, said to be named from the inventor, *Púrrhikhos*.

Pyrrhic[2] *P. victory*, one gained at too great cost, like that by Pyrrhus, king of Epirus, over the Romans at Asculum. XIX. f. *Pyrrhus* + -IC.

python (Gr. myth.) huge serpent slain by Apollo near Delphi XVI; (zool.) genus of large snakes XIX. - L. *Pȳthōn* - Gr. *Púthōn*.

pythoness female soothsayer, witch. XIV. ME. *phitones(se)* - OF. *phitonise* (mod. *pythonisse*) - medL. *phītōnissa*, for late L. *pȳthōnissa* (Vulg., 1 Chron. 10: 13), fem. of *pȳthō* (Deut. 18: 11) - late Gr. *púthōn* (Acts 16: 16), identical with *púthōn* PYTHON; assim. to the L. form; see -ESS[1].

pyx vessel for the reservation of the Host XIV; box at the Royal Mint in which gold and silver coins are deposited to be tested XVI. - L. *pyxis* - late Gr. *puxís* BOX[2].

Q

qua in the capacity or status of. XVII. - L. *quā*, abl. sg. fem. of *quī* who.

quack[1] (of a duck) utter its characteristic cry. XVII. of imit. orig.; cf. Du. *kwakken*, G. *quacken* croak. Early vars. are †*quake* XVI, †*queke* XIV, *quackle* XVI.

quack[2] ignorant pretender to (medical or surgical) knowledge or skill. XVII. Short for **quack-salver** XVI (now rare) - early modDu. *quacksalver* (now *kwakzalver*), of which the second el. is f. *salf, zalf* SALVE, and the first is prob. the stem of †*quacken, kwakken* prattle.

quad abbrev. of QUADRANGLE (XIX), (typogr.) QUADRAT (XIX), QUADRUPLET (esp. pl. *quads*) (XIX).

quadragenarian (one) forty years old. XIX. f. late L. *quadrāgēnārius*, f. *quadrāgēnī*, distrib. of *quadrāgintā* forty (see next).

quadragesimal (of a fast) lasting forty days; of Lent, Lenten. XVII. - late L. *quadrāgēsimālis*, f. *Quadrāgēsima* (Eng. **Quadragesima** XIV; then not before XVII), name of the first Sunday in Lent and reckoned the fortieth day before Easter, and hence of the whole season, sb. use of fem. of L. *quadrāgēsimus* fortieth, ordinal of *quadrāgintā* forty, f. *quadrā-*, repr. old n. of *quattuor* FOUR + *-gintā*, corr. to Gr. *-konta*; see -AL[1].

quadrangle figure having four angles (and four sides) XV; square or rectangular space or court XVI. - (O)F. *quadrangle* or late L. *quadrangulum*, sb. use of n. of *quadrangulus*; see QUADRI-, ANGLE[2]. So **quadrangular** XVI. - medL. *quadrangulāris*.

quadrant †fourth part, quarter, now only of a quarter-circle; instrument (of the form of a graduated quarter-circle) used for making angular measurements. XIV. - L. *quadrāns, -ant-* quarter, orig. of the as; see QUADRI-.

quadrat †square XIV; (typogr.) small block of metal used for spacing XVII. - L. *quadrātum* (or the deriv. F. *quadrat*), sb. use of n. of *quadrātus*, pp. of *quadrāre* square (cf. *quadrum* sb., square); see QUADRI-. So **quadrate** adj. XIV, vb. XVI. **quadratic** square; (math.) involving the second and no higher power of an unknown or variable. XVII. - F. *quadratique* or modL. *quadrāticus*. **quadrature** squaring. XVI. - F. or L.

quadrennial occurring every four years; lasting for four years. XVII. f. L. *quadr(i)ennium* + -AL[1].

quadri- comb. form of L. *quattuor* FOUR, as in **quadrilateral** XVII, **quadriliteral** XVIII, **quadripartite** XV (L. *partītus*, pp. of *partīrī* divide).

quadrille[1] card-game played by four persons with forty cards. XVIII. - F., perh. - Sp. *cuartillo* (f. *cuarto* fourth), with assim. to next.

quadrille[2] any of four groups of horsemen taking part in a tournament, etc.; square dance performed by four couples. XVIII. - F. - Sp. *cuadrilla*, It. *quadriglia* troop, company, f. *quadra* square (cf. CADRE).

quadrillion fourth power of a million; (U.S.) fifth power of a thousand. XVII. - F. *quadrillon*, f. QUADRI- + *(m)illion*.

quadrivium see TRIVIUM.

quadroon one who has a quarter of Negro blood. XVIII. Earliest forms *quartero(o)n* (through F. *quarteron*) - Sp. *cuarteron*, f. *cuarto* fourth, quarter; later assim. to words in *quadri-*.

quadru- occas. var. of L. QUADRI- before *p*; also in **quadrumanous** XVIII (modL.).

quadruped XVII. - F. *quadrupède* or L. *quadrupēs, -ped-*, f. *quadru-* + *pēs*; see prec. and FOOT. So **quadrupedal** XVII. - medL.

quadruple fourfold. XVI. - (O)F - L. *quadruplus*; see QUADRU-, DUPLE. So vb. XIV. - F. or late L. **quadruplicate** adj. and vb. XVII. - L. **quadruplication** XVI. - late L. **quadruplet** one of four at a birth. XVIII; after *triplet*.

quaere one may ask, it is a question; question, query. XVI. - L., imper. of *quærere* ask, inquire.

quaestor (Rom. antiq.) official having charge of public finances. XIV. - L. *quæstor*, f. **quæs-*, old form of stem of *quærere* seek, inquire (see prec.) + -TOR.

quaff drink copiously or deeply. XVI. prob. imit.; in earliest use †*quaft*, †*quaught*.

quagga extinct S. Afr. animal allied to the ass and the zebra. XVIII. Said to be orig. Hottentot, but now Xhosa in the form *iqwara*.

quagmire piece of wet boggy ground. XVI. f. (dial.) *quag* (XVI; of uncert. orig.) + MIRE.

quail[1] migratory bird allied to the partridge. XIV. - OF. *quaille* (mod. *caille*) :- medL. *coacula*, prob. of imit. orig.

quail[2] fail, give way XV; lose heart, be cowed XVI; also trans. Of unkn. orig.

quaint †skilled, clever; †skilfully made, fine, elegant; †proud, fastidious XIII; †strange, unfamiliar XIV; uncommon but attractive XVIII. ME. *cointe, queinte* - OF. :- L. *cognitus* known, pp. of *cognōscere* ascertain, f. co- + *gnōscere* KNOW.

quake shake, tremble. OE. *cwacian*, rel. to *cweċċan* (:- **kwakjan*) shake (trans.), in mod. dial. *quetch, quatch*; cf. OS. *quekilīk* waving to and fro. For the symbolic *cw-, qu-* cf. QUAVER, QUIVER[2].

Quaker member of the Society of Friends. XVII. f. QUAKE + -ER[1]. 'Shaking and quaking' was attributed to them.

qualify invest with a quality or condition; modify, moderate. XVI. - F. *qualifier* - medL. *quālificāre*, f. *quālis* of what kind, f. base of *quī, quis* WHO + *-ālis* -AL[1]; see -FY. So **qualification** XVI. - F. or medL. **quality** †character, disposition; †title, description XIII; attribute, property; nature, kind; rank, position XIV; †profession XVI.

ME. *qualite* - (O)F. *qualité* - L. *quālitās*. **qualitative** XVII. - late L.

qualm feeling of faintness or sickness XVI; strong scruple of conscience XVII. of uncert. orig.

quandary XVI. of unkn. orig.

quantic (math.) rational, integral homogeneous function of two or more variables. XIX. f. L. *quantus* how great (see next) + -IC.

quantity XIV. - (O)F. *quantité* - L. *quantitās*, f. *quantus* how great, how much, f. base of *quī*, *quis* WHO; see -ITY. So **quantitative** XVI. - medL.

quantum amount required or allotted. XVII. - n. of L. *quantus*.

quaquaversal turning in every direction. XVIII. f. L. *quāquā versus*, i.e. *quāquā* where-, whithersoever, *versus* turned, towards.

quarantine A. (leg.) period of forty days during which a widow had the right to remain in her husband's chief mansion house; B. period of isolation of persons and animals suspected of contagious disease. XVII. In sense A - medL. *qua(d)rantēna*, f. **quadranta*, for L. *quadrāgintā* forty; in sense B - It. *quarantina*, f. *quaranta* forty; see -INE[1].

quarenden, quarender variety of apple common in Somerset and Devon. XV (*quaryndon*). of unkn. orig.

quarrel[1] short square-headed arrow XIII; square or diamond-shaped pane of glass XV. - OF. *quar(r)el* (mod. *carreau*) :- Rom. **quadrellus*, dim. of late L. *quadrus* square.

quarrel[2] †complaint, accusation; ground of complaint XIV; violent contention XVI. ME. *querele* - OF. *querele* (mod. *querelle*) :- L. *querella*, var. of *querēla* complaint, f. *querī* complain. So vb. XIV (then not before XVI). In ME. - OF. *quereler*; afterwards f. the sb. Hence **quarrelsome** (-SOME[1]) XVI.

quarry[1] parts of a deer placed on the hide and given to the hounds; collection of deer killed XIV; animal hunted or hawked at XV. ME. *quirre*, *querre* - AN. **quire*, **quere*, OF. *cuiree* (mod. *curée*), alt., by crossing with *cuir* leather and *curer* cleanse, spec. disembowel (:- L. *curāre* CURE), of *couree* :- Rom. **corāta* entrails, f. *cor* HEART; see -Y[6].

quarry[2] open-air excavation from which stone is obtained. XV. - medL. *quarreia*, shortened var. of *quareria* = OF. *quarriere* (mod. *carrière*), f. **quarre* :- L. *quadrum* square. Hence vb. XVIII.

quarry[3] square tile, etc. XVI; †square-headed arrow; pane of glass XVII. alt. of QUARREL[1], prob. after †*quarry* square (XIII-XVII) - OF. *quarré* (mod. *carré*) :- L. *quadrātus* QUADRAT.

quart[1] one-fourth of a gallon. XIV. - (O)F. *quarte* :- L. *quarta*, sb. use of fem. of *quartus* fourth, ordinal of *quattuor* FOUR.

quart[2] position in fencing XVII; sequence of four cards XVIII. - F. *quarte* :- L. *quartus* fourth (see prec.).

quartan of a fever in which the paroxysms occur every third (acc. to old reckoning, fourth) day. XIII. ME. *quartain* - (O)F. *quartaine* :- L. *quartāna*, fem. of *quartānus*, f. *quartus* fourth; see QUART[1] and -AN.

quarter one of four parts; measure of 8 bushels XIII; fourth part of a year; region, district XIV; place of residence, pl. soldier's lodgings; assigned position (spec. in *close q-s*); relations with another, terms of treatment XVI; exemption from being immediately put to death XVII. - AN. *quarter*, (O)F. *quartier* :- L. *quartārius* fourth part of a measure, quartern, gill, f. *quartus* fourth; see QUART[1]. Hence vb. divide into quarters XIV; lodge in quarters XVI. **quarterage** quarterly payment XIV. **quarter-deck** orig. smaller deck above the half-deck XVII. **quarterly** adv. XV, adj. XVI. **quartermaster** officer in navy and army (*q*. in the senses of assigned position and lodging) XV. **quarterstaff** stout pole used as a weapon. XVI.

quartern quarter, esp. of certain weights and measures XIII. - AN. *quartrun*, OF. *quart(e)ron*, f. *quart* fourth, QUART[1], or *quartier* QUARTER.

quartet(te) composition for four voices or instruments XVIII; set of four XIX. - F. *quartette* - It. *quartetto* (which was used somewhat earlier in Eng.), f. *quarto* fourth (cf. QUART[1]); see -ET, -ETTE.

quartile (astr.) pert. to an aspect of two heavenly bodies which are 90° (i.e. ¼ of a circle) distant. XVI. - medL. *quartīlis*, f. *quartus* fourth; see QUART[1] and -ILE.

quarto size of paper produced by folding a whole sheet twice so as to form four leaves (8 pages) XVI; book made up of such paper XVII. orig. in L. phr. *in quarto* 'in a fourth' (see QUART[1]).

quartz XVIII. - (M)HG. *quar(t)z*; of uncert. orig.

quash annul, invalidate XIV; bring to nought XVII. - OF. *quasser* (mod. *casser* break) :- L. *quassāre* shake violently, break to pieces, shatter, freq. of *quatere* (pp. stem *quass-*) shake. Senses connected with those of *shake* and *break* were current XIV-XVII.

quasi as it were XV; (a) kind of XVII; seemingly, almost XIX. - L., reduced form of *quansei*, f. **quām*, acc. sg. fem. (denoting extent) of the base of WHO, WHAT + *sei*, *sī* if.

quassia (wood, etc. of) a S. Amer. tree, *Quassia amara*. XVIII. f. the name of a Surinam Negro named Graman (i.e. 'grand man') *Quassi*, the discoverer of the root's medicinal properties in 1730.

quaternary sb. set of four things XV; adj. consisting of four things XVII; (geol.) fourth in order (to match *tertiary*) XIX. - L. *quaternārius*, f. *quaternī* four together, f. *quater* four times, f. base of *quattuor* FOUR; see -ARY.

quaternion group of four XIV; quire of four sheets XVII; (math.) XIX. - late L. *quaterniō*, *-ōn-*, f. *quaternī* four together (see prec.).

quatorzain poem of 14 lines. XVI. - F. *quatorzaine* set of fourteen, f. *quatorze* fourteen (:- Rom. **quattordecem*, for L. *quattuordecim*) + *-aine* (see -AN).

quatrain stanza of four lines. XVI (*quadrain*). - F. *quatrain*, †*quadrain*, f. *quatre* FOUR + *-ain* (see -AN).

quatrefoil compound leaf or flower of four leaflets. XV. - AN. **quatrefoil*, f. (O)F. *quatre* FOUR + *foil* leaf, FOIL[2].

quaver vibrate, tremble XV; trill or shake in singing; also trans. XVI. frequent. (see -ER[4]) of ME. *quave, cwauien* (XIII), perh. repr. OE. **cwafian*, parallel symbolic formation to *cwacian* QUAKE. Hence **quaver** sb. (mus.) note equal to half a crotchet XVI; shake or trill XVII; tremulous cry, etc. XVIII.

quay XIV. ME *key(e)*, later *kay*, and finally *quay* (XVII) by assim. to modF. *quai*; - OF. *kai, cay* - Gaulish *caio* :- OCelt. **kagio-* (cf. OIr. *cae* enclosed place, house, W. *cae* hedge), perh. rel. to Gmc. **χaʒ-* HEDGE.

quean orig. woman; (arch.; from early ME. times) bold impudent woman, jade, hussy; Sc. girl, lass XV. OE. *cwene* = OS. *cwena* (Du. *kween* barren cow), OHG. *quena, quina*, ON. *kona*, Goth. *qinō* woman :- Gmc. *kwenōn* wk. fem., f. IE. base **gʷen-*, **gʷn-*, repr. by Gr. *gunḗ*, Skr. *gnā́*, OSl. *žena*, OIr. *ben* woman; cf. QUEEN.

queasy †unsettled; unsettling the stomach XV; easily upset, inclined to nausea; fastidious, scrupulous XVI. Early forms *coisy, que(y)sy, quasy* suggest AN., OF. **coisi*, **queisi* or *-ié*, rel. to *coisier* hurt, wound, but there is no evidence.

queen OE. *cwēn* = OS. *quān*, ON. *kvæn* (also *kván*), Goth. *qēns* :- Gmc. **kwǣniz*, f. IE. **gʷēn-*, **gʷen-* (see QUEAN). Hence **queenly** XVI.

queer odd, strange XVI (first in Sc.); out of sorts, drunk XVIII. of uncert. orig. Identical in form with sl. *queer* bad (XVI). Hence **queer** vb. quiz, puzzle, ridicule XVIII; spoil XIX.

quell †kill OE.; suppress, extinguish XIV; crush, subdue XVI. OE. *cwellan* = OS. *quellian* (Du. *kwellen*), OHG. *quellen* (G. *quälen*), ON. *kvelja* :- Gmc. **kwaljan*, f. **kwal-* **kwel-*, repr. also by OE. *cwalu* death = ON. *kvǫl* torment, OE. *cwealm* death, torture, plague, OS., OHG. *qualm*, OE. *cwelan* die = OS. *quelan*, OHG. *quelan*; the IE. base **gʷel* is repr. by Lith. *gėlà*, OSl. *žalĭ* sorrow, OIr. *atbalim* I die, Arm. *kelem* I torment.

quench XII. ME. *quenchen* :- OE. **cwenċan* (in *ācwenċan*) :- **kwaŋkjan*, causative of OE. **cwincan* (in *ācwincan*) be extinguished = OFris. *quinka* :- **kweŋkan*. Hence **quenchless** XVI.

quern hand-mill. OE. *cweorn(e)* = OS. *quern* (Du. *kweern*), OHG. *quirn(a)*, ON. *kvern*, Goth. *-qairnus*, f. Gmc. **kwern-* :- IE. **gʷern-*, repr. also by Lith. *gìrna*, OSl. *žrŭny*, OIr. *bró*, Skr. *grāvan-*.

querulous XVI. f. L. *querulus* or - late L. *querulōsus*, f. *querī* complain; partly superseding late ME. *querelous* - OF. *querelous* (mod. *querelleux*), f. *querele* QUARREL[2]; see -OUS.

query anglicization of QUAERE, with ending assim. to *inquiry*. XVII.

quest (obs. or dial.) inquiry, inquest; search, pursuit XIV; collection of alms XVI. - OF. *queste* (mod. *quête*) :- Rom. **quæsita* (for L. *quæsīta*), sb. use of fem. pp. of L. *quærere* seek, inquire. So **quest** vb. go in pursuit of game XIV; search, seek XVII; search for, seek out XVIII. - OF. *quester* (mod. *quêter*).

question XIII. - AN. *questiun*, (O)F. *question* - L. *quæstiō, -ōn-*, f. *quæst-*, pp. stem of *quærere* seek, inquire. So vb. XV. - (O)F. *questionner*. Hence **questionable** XVI. **questionnaire** XIX. - F., f. *questionner* + *-aire* -ARY.

queue (her.) tail of a beast XVI; long plait of hair XVIII; line of persons, etc. XIX. - F. :- L. *cauda* tail.

quibble play on words; equivocating or evasive speech. XVII. f. synon. †*quib* (XVI), app. f. L. *quibus* (d. and abl. pl. of *quī, quæ, quod* WHO, etc.) as a word of frequent occurrence in legal documents and so assoc. with verbal niceties or subtle distinctions; see -LE[1]. Hence **quibble** vb. †pun; evade the point by a quibble. XVII.

quick (arch.) living, alive OE.; lively, mobile, active; rapid, swift XIII; functionally active XIV. OE. *cwic(u)* = OS. *quik* (Du. *kwik*), OHG. *quek* (G. *keck* bold), ON. *kvikr* :- Gmc. **kwikwaz*, rel. to Goth. **qius* (in pl. *qiwai*) :- **kwiwaz*, f. IE. base **gʷi-* repr. also in L. *vīvus*, Lith. *gývas*, OSl. *živŭ*, OIr. *biu, beo*, Skr. *jīvá-* living, Gr. *bíos*. Hence **quick** sb. *the q.*, sensitive flesh in the body. XVI. **quicken** give life to; receive life XIII; make quick or quicker XVII. In earliest use - ON. *kvikna* (intr.). Comps. **quicklime** lime that has been burned but not slaked. XIV. **quicksand** bed of loose wet sand. XV. **quickset** live slips set in the ground as for a hedge XV; also adj. XVI. **quicksilver** mercury. OE. *cwicseolfor* = Du. *kwiksilver*, OHG. *quecsilbar* (G. *quecksilber*), ON. *kviksilfr*; tr. L. *argentum vīvum* 'living silver'.

quid[1] (sl.) sovereign, †guinea. XVII. of unkn. orig.

quid[2] piece of tobacco, etc. to be chewed. XVIII. dial. var. of CUD.

quiddity A. essence of a thing XV; B. subtlety, quibble XVI. - medL. *quidditās*, f. *quid* what; see -ITY.

quid pro quo (in apothecaries' language) one thing in place of another; one thing in return for another, tit for tat. XVI. - L. *quid* something, *pro* for, instead of, *quō* (abl. of *quid*) something.

quiescent XVII. - L. *quiēscēns, -ent-*, prp. of *quiēscere* be still, f. *quiēs* quiet; see -ENT.

quiet freedom from disturbance or noise. XIV. - AN. *quiete*, OF. *quieté*, f. *quiet* (- L. *quiētus*, pp. of *quiēscere* be QUIESCENT), whence **quiet** adj. XIV. Hence **quiet** vb. XV, **quieten** (-EN[2]) XIX. So **quietism** mysticism characterized by passive contemplation. XVII. - It. *quietismo*. **quietude** XVI. - F. *quiétude* or medL. *quiētūdō*.

quietus discharge or acquittance XVI; death XVII. Short for *quiētus est*, medL. formula 'he is QUIT[1]'.

quiff (oiled) lock of hair worn on the forehead. XIX. of unkn. orig.

quill †hollow stem or reed XV; pipe, tube XV; tube or barrel of a feather, esp. as used for writing XVI; spine of the porcupine XVII. of uncert. orig.; cf. synon. (M)LG. *quiele*, MHG. *kil* (G. *kiel*).

quilt (orig.) article of bed furniture to lie on, consisting of two pieces of material with padding between; (later) coverlet similarly made, counterpane. XIII. - OF. *coilte, cuilte* (mod. *couette*), with var. *coute* :- L. *culcita* mattress, cushion. Hence vb. XVI.

quin abbrev. of QUINTUPLET, chiefly pl. *quins*. XX.

quinary of the number five. XVII. - L. *quīnārius*, f. *quīnī*, distributive of *quinque* FIVE; see -ARY.

quince XIV. orig. coll. pl. of *coyn*, *quoyn* - OF. *cooin* (mod. *coing*) :- L. *cotōneum*, varying with *cydōneum* (apple) of Cydonia (now Canea) in Crete.

quincentenary XIX. irreg. f. L. *quinque* FIVE + CENTENARY. Also **quingentenary** XIX. f. L. *quingentī* 500 after *centenary*.

quincunx arrangement of five objects so placed that four occupy the corners and the fifth the centre. XVII. - L. *quincunx* five-twelfths ($\frac{5}{12}$ of an as was denoted by five dashes arranged as above), f. *quinque* FIVE + *uncia* twelfth (see OUNCE[1]).

quinine XIX. f. *quina* bark of cinchona, etc. - Sp. - Quechua *kina* bark; see -INE[5].

Quinquagesima †period beginning on the Sunday immediately preceding Lent and ending on Easter Eve XIV; (*Q. Sunday*) the Sunday itself. XVII. - medL., sb. use of fem. of L. *quinquāgēsimus* fiftieth, f. *quinquāgintā* fifty; cf. QUADRAGESIMA.

quinque- comb. form of L. *quinque* FIVE, as in **quinquereme** having five banks of oars (XVI; L. *rēmus* oar).

quinquennial lasting five years XV; occurring every fifth year XVII. f. L. *quinquennis*, f. QUINQUE- + *annus* year; see -AL[1].

quinsy XIV. ME. *quinaci*, *quinesye* - OF. *quinencie* - medL. *quinancia*, f. Gr. *kunágkhē*, f. *kúōn*, *kun-* dog + *ágkhein* throttle.

quintain post set up to be tilted at; exercise of tilting at this. XIV. - OF. *quintaine*, *-eine* = medL. *quintana*, *-ena*, usu. taken to be identical with L. *quintāna* market of a camp, f. *quintus* fifth (sc. *manipulus* maniple).

quintal 112 lbs. XV. - OF. *quintal*, medL. *-āle* - Arab. *ḳinṭār*.

quintessence substance latent in all things, the extraction of which was one of the objects of alchemy XV; most essential part XVI. - F. *quintessence*, †*quinte essence* - medL. *quinta essentia* 'fifth essence', the fifth primary body besides the elements of earth, fire, air, and water. Hence **quintessential** XVII.

quintet(te) composition for five voices or instruments. XIX. - F. *quintette* - It. *quintetto* (formerly used in Eng. XVIII), f. *quinto* :- L. *quintus* fifth; see -ET, -ETTE.

quintillion fifth power of a million; (U.S.) sixth power of a thousand. XVII. f. L. *quintus* fifth + *(m)illion*; cf. BILLION.

quintuple fivefold. XVI. - F., f. L. *quintus* fifth, after *triple*, etc. Hence vb. XVII. **quintuplet** set of five; one of five at a birth. XIX. Cf. QUADRUPLET.

quip sharp or sarcastic remark. XVI. prob. abbrev. of †*quippy* (XVI), perh. - L. *quippe* indeed, forsooth (with sarcastic force).

quire †small book, short poem, etc.; set of four sheets of parchment or paper doubled so as to make eight leaves; hence, any gathering of sheets. XV. ME. *quaer*, later *quayer*, *quair*, *quere*, *quire* - OF. *qua(i)er* (mod. *cahier* quire, copy-book) :- Rom. **quaternum*, f. L. *quaternī* set of four, f. *quater* four times, f. *quattuor* FOUR.

quirk verbal trick or subtlety XVI; sudden turn or twist XVII. of unkn. orig.

quirt riding-whip used in Southern U.S. and Sp. America. XIX. - Sp. *cuerda* = (O)F. *corde* CORD.

quisling XX. Surname of Major Vidkun *Quisling*, a Norwegian who collaborated with the Germans when they invaded Norway in World War II.

quit[1] adj. free, clear *of*. XIII. (i) ME. *quīt*, *quīte* (surviving in QUITE) - OF. *quite* - L. *quiētus* QUIET. Superseded by (ii) later ME. or early mod. *quit(te)* - (O)F. *quitte* - medL. *quittus*, special development of L. *quiētus*.

quit[2] vb. †A. set free, clear, clear off; B. †repay, requite; C. renounce; leave. XIV. ME. *quitte*, repl. earlier *quite* (XIII), - (O)F. *quitter*, earlier *quiter*; cf. medL. *quittāre*, *quiētāre*, f. L. *quiētus* QUIT[1].

quitch couch grass. OE. *cwiċe* = MLG. *kwēke*; supposed to be rel. to *cwic* QUICK, with ref. to the vitality of the grass.

quitclaim XIV. - AN. *quiteclamer* declare free, f. *quite* QUIT[1] + *clamer* proclaim (see CLAIM). So sb. †release XV; renunciation XVII.

quite completely, entirely XIV; in the fullest sense, absolutely XVI. adv. use of *quite*, earlier form of QUIT[1] free, clear.

quits †clear, discharged XV; even (*with*) by repayment or retaliation XVII. prob. - colloq. use of medL. *quittus* QUIT[1].

quittance release XIII; release from debt, receipt XIV; requital, reprisal XVI. - OF. *quitance* (later *quittance*), f. *quiter* QUIT[2]; see -ANCE.

quiver[1] case for holding arrows. XIII. - AN. **quiver*, *quiveir*, OF. *quivre*, *coivre* - WGmc. word repr. by OE. *cocor*, OS. *kokar(i)* (Du. *koker*), OHG. *kohhar(i)* (G. *köcher*).

quiver[2] shake with small rapid movements. XV. f. ME. *cwiver* nimble, quick, OE. *cwifer* (in adv. *cwiferlīce*).

qui vive phr. *on the qui vive* on the alert. XVIII. - F. *Qui vive?* sentry's challenge, lit. 'Long live who?', orig. expecting an answer in the form *Vive le roi*, *Vive la France*, etc.

Quixote enthusiastic visionary. XVII. f. name of Don *Quixote*, now in Sp. *Quijote*, hero of Miguel de Cervantes' romance. Hence **quixotic** XVIII.

quiz[1] †eccentric person; one who quizzes XVIII; practical joke, hoax XIX. So **quiz** vb. make fun of, turn to ridicule. XVIII. of unkn. orig. Hence **quizzical** XVIII.

quiz[2] question, examine; also sb. examination (spec. oral). XIX. of unkn. orig.

quod (sl.) prison. XVII. of unkn. orig.

quodlibet question proposed in scholastic disputation; scholastic debate or exercise. XIV. - medL. *quodlibetum*, f. L. *quodlibet*, f. *quod* WHAT, *libet* it pleases.

quoin external angle of a wall or building, corner-stone; wedge, wedge-shaped block. XVI. var. of COIN.

quoit flat disc, etc., thrown as an exercise of strength or skill; pl. sport of throwing quoits at a pin. XV (*coyte*). of unkn. orig.

quondam former. XVI. adj. use of L. *quondam* formerly (orig. 'at any given moment'), f. *quom* (later *cum*) when + generalizing particle *-dam*.

quorum justice of the peace whose presence was necessary on the bench, later gen. XV; fixed number of persons whose presence is necessary in the transaction of business XVII. g. pl. of L. *quī* WHO; taken from the wording of commissions designating such persons, *quorum vos . . duos* (etc.) *esse volumus* of whom we will that you be . . two (etc.).

quota part or share of a total. XVII. - medL. *quota*, sb. use of fem. of L. *quotus* of what number, f. *quot* how many.

quote †mark with numbers or (marginal) references XIV; cite or refer to; †note XVI; repeat (a passage) *from* a book, etc. XVII. - medL. *quotāre* number, f. *quot* how many, or *quota* QUOTA. So **quotation** †numbering XV; †marginal reference XVI; (typogr.) large quadrat used for filling up blanks (orig. between marginal references); quoting, passage quoted XVII; price of stocks, etc. XIX. - medL. *quotātiō, -ōn-*.

quoth (arch.) said. OE. *cwæð*, pt. of *cweðan* say = OS. *queðan*, OHG. *quedan*, ON. *kveða*, Goth. *qiþan* :- Gmc. **kweþan*; early ME. *cwað* became *quoth* by rounding of *a* in contiguity with *w* in unstressed positions; a common var. XIV-XVI was *quod*. Hence **quotha** XVI; for *quoth (h)a* said he.

quotidian daily, spec. of a fever recurring every day. XIV. ME. *cotidien, -ian, quot-*, orig. - OF. *cotidien* (mod. *quotidien*); early assim. to L. *quotīdiānus*, earlier *cott-*, *cōtīdīanus*, f. *cott-*, *cōtīdiē* (*quot-*) every day, f. base of *quotus* (see QUOTA) + *diēs* day; see -IAN.

quotient result obtained by dividing one quantity by another. XV. - L. *quotiēns* how many times (f. *quot* how many), taken as a prp. in *-ēns*; cf. -ENT.

R

rabbet channel or groove made in wood, stone, etc.; rectangular recess. XV. - OF. *rab(b)at* act of beating down, recess in a wall, f. *rabattre* beat back or down, REBATE; the ending has been assim. to -ET.

rabbi (title of respect given to) a Jewish doctor of the law. XIV (*raby*). - OF. *rab(b)i* (mod. *rabbin*), ecclL. *rabbi* - Heb. *rabbī* my master, f. *rabh* master, with pronominal suffix. So **rabbin** XVI. - F. *rabbin* or medL. *rabbīnus*. Hence **rabbinic(al)** XVII.

rabbit XIV (orig. applied to the young). ME. *rabet(te)*, perh. - an OF. form repr. by dial. F. *rabotte, rabouillet* young rabbit, poss. of LG. or Du. orig. (cf. Flem. *robbe*, Du. †*robett*).

rabble A. †pack, swarm of animals XIV; disorderly crowd XVI; B. †long string of words XVI; (dial.) rigmarole. of obscure orig.; sense B suggests immed. connection with dial. *rabble* vb. utter in a rapid confused manner (XIV; cf. MDu. *rabbelen*, LG. *rabbeln*).

rabid furious, raging XVII; affected with rabies XIX. - L. *rabidus*, f. *rabere* rave, be mad; see -ID[1]. So **rabies** canine madness. XVII. - L. *rabiēs*.

rac(c)oon XVII. of Algonquian orig.

race[1] †onward movement, rush XIII; (dial.) running, run XIV; strong current of water (channel for water, e.g. *mill-race* XVI); contest of speed XVI. north. ME., MSc. *rās, raas* - ON. *rás* running, race, rush of water, channel; of uncert. origin. Taken into gen. Eng. use from the north in XVI.

race[2] class of persons, animals, plants; group of persons, etc. having a common ancestry or character; class of wine XVI; characteristic style of speech or writing XVII. - F. - It. *razza*; of unkn. orig. Hence **racial** XIX. **racy** (in senses derived from the last two of the sb. above) XVII.

race[3] root *of* ginger. XVI. - OF. *rais, raiz* :- L. *rādīx, rādīc-* root.

raceme XVIII. - L. *racēmus* cluster of grapes. So **racemose** (-OSE[1]) XVII.

rachitis (med.) rickets. XVIII. - modL. - Gr. *rhakhîtis*, f. *rhákhis* spine, ridge; see -ITIS.

rack[1] A. †shock, collision XIII; B. mass of driven cloud XIV. prob. of Scand. orig.; cf. Norw. and Sw. dial. *rak* (Sw. *vrak*, Da. *vrag*) wreck, wreckage, refuse, f. *reka* drive; the identity of A and B is not certain.

rack[2] †bar, or framework of bars, esp. used for support or suspension. XIV. ME. *rakke*, occas. *rekke* - (M)Du., MLG. *rak, rek*, prob. f. *recken* stretch (see next).

rack[3] instrument of torture in the form of a frame with a roller at each end. XV. prob. spec. use of RACK[2]. So vb. stretch the joints of XV; in various transf. and fig. uses XVI. - MLG., MDu. *racken*, also *recken* = OE. *reċċan*, OS. *rekkian*, OHG. *recchan* (G. *recken*), ON. *rekja*, Goth. *-rakjan* stretch; rel. to L. *regere* DIRECT.

rack[4] horse's gait in which the two feet on each side are lifted simultaneously. XVI. contemp. with rel. vb.; of unkn. orig.

rack[5] phr. *to rack* (*and ruin*) to destruction. XVI. var. of WRACK[1].

rack[6] Aphetic of ARRACK. XVII.

racket[1] bat of network used in ball games; pl. game played with ball and rackets XVI; (N. Amer.) snow-shoe XVII. - F. *raquette* †palm of the hand, racket, snow-shoe - It. *racchetta*, f. Arab. *rāḥet* palm of the hand.

racket[2] disturbance, uproar XVI; social excitement XVIII; trying experience XIX; illicit scheme XX (U.S.). perh. imit. of clattering noise. Hence **racket** vb., **rackety** XVIII.

raddle red ochre. XVI. var. of RUDDLE.

radial XVI. - medL. *radiālis*, f. RADIUS (cf. RAY[1]); see -AL[1].

radiant shining brightly XV; pert. to radiation XVIII. - L. *radiāns, -ant-*, prp. of *radiāre* radiate, f. *radius* RAY[1]. Hence **radiance** XVII, **-ancy** XVII. So **radiate** (-ATE[3]) emit rays XVII; spread in all directions from a centre XIX. f. *radiāt-*, pp. stem of L. *radiāre*. **radiation** XVII. - L. **radiator** one or that which radiates XIX (in sense 'apparatus for circulating hot water to warm an apartment' orig. U.S.).

radical pert. to the moisture inherent in animals and plants XIV; (math., philol., etc.) pert. to a root or radix; inherent, fundamental XVI; going to the root or origin, thorough XVII (*r. reform* XVIII); sb. radical element XVII; advocate of 'radical reform' XIX. - late L. *rādīcālis*, f. L. *rādīx, rādīc-* root; see -AL[1]. Hence **radicalism** XIX.

radicle (bot.) part of the embryo which develops into the primary root. XVIII. - L. *rādīcula*, dim. of *rādīx, rādīc-* root; see -CLE.

radio XX. abbrev. of *radiotelegraphy, -telephony*; see next.

radio- used as comb. form of RADIUS (cf. RAY[1]) (i) anat., as *radio-carpal* pert. to radius and carpus, (ii) pert. to X-rays and other forms of radiation, as *radioactive, radiotelegraphy, radiology* XIX.

radish OE. *rædiċ* (ME. *redich, radich*) - L. *rādīx, rādīc-* root; late ME. *radish* (XV), alt. of this perh. by blending with F. *radis* - It. *radice* :- L.

radium XIX. f. L. *radius* RAY[1]; see -IUM.

radius †staff of a cross XVI; thicker and shorter bone of the forearm; straight line drawn from the centre of a circle to the circumference XVII; (techn.) rod, bar, ray XVIII. - L. *radius* staff, spoke, ray, radius of a circle, of the arm, etc.

radix (chiefly techn.) root, basis. XVI. - L. *rādīx* root of a plant.

raffia XIX. var. of *raphia*, var. *rofia* kind of palm (*rofeer* XVIII); of Malagasy orig.

raffle †game of chance played with three dice XIV; (f. the vb.) form of lottery XVIII. - OF. *raffle*, (also mod.) *rafle* throw at dice of all three alike, clean sweep; of unkn. orig. Hence or - F. *rafler* **raffle** vb. XVII.

raft †beam, spar; structure of planks, etc., forming a means of transport over water. XV - ON. *raptr* rafter, rel. to OHG. *rāvo* beam, ON. *ráfr*, *rǽfr* roof; cf. next.

rafter OE. *ræfter* = OS. *rehter*, MLG. *rafter*, *rachter*, rel. to RAFT.

rag[1] small fragment of textile material XIV; remnant, scrap XV; thing (contemptuously) regarded as such XVI. ME. *ragge*, perh. back-formation on **ragged** (-ED[2]) shaggy, rough XIII; of irregular or straggling shape XIV; in rags XIV - ON. *rǫggvaðr* tufted; or on **raggy** (-Y[1]) late OE. *raggiġ* shaggy, f. **ragg* - ON. *rǫgg* tuft or strip of fur; of unkn. orig.

rag[2] (†piece or mass of) coarse or rough stone XIII (*ragghe*); *ragstone* XIV. of unkn. orig., but assoc. later with prec.

rag[3] (sl.) scold, rate XVIII; annoy, esp. in a rough or noisy fashion XIX. of unkn. orig. Cf. BULLYRAG.

ragamuffin XVI (*ragamoffyn* occurs XIV as the name of a demon); perh. based on RAG[1].

rage †madness; violent anger, furious passion XIII; violent feeling or desire XIV; fervour, enthusiasm, excitement XVI. - (O)F. :- Rom. **rabia*, for L. *rabiēs* ferocity, madness, RABIES. So vb. XIII.

raglan overcoat without shoulder seams. XIX. f. name of Fitzroy James Henry Somerset, 1st Baron *Raglan* (d. 1855), British commander in the Crimean war.

ragout meat stewed with vegetables. XVII. - F. *ragoût*, f. *ragoûter* revive the taste of, f. *ra-* (i.e. RE- + *a-*) + *goût* taste.

rag-tag rabble, riff-raff. XIX. For older *tag-rag* (XVII), which replaced *tag and rag* (XVI); see TAG[1].

raguly (her.) having short oblique projections. XVII. f. RAG[1] or RAGGY after NEBULY. See -Y[3].

ragweed XVII, **ragwort** XV. f. RAG[1] + WEED[1], WORT[1]; with ref. to the ragged form of the leaves.

raid military expedition, orig. on horseback, foray. XV. Sc. form of ROAD, with extension of meaning. Hence vb. XIX.

rail[1] †garment, mantle OE.; †neckerchief XV; *night-rail* dressing-gown XVI. OE. *hræġ(e)l* = OFris. *(h)reil*, OHG. *(h)regil*, of unkn. orig.

rail[2] bar of wood, etc. fixed in a horizontal position XIII; hand-rail of a staircase XV; bar or continuous line of bars laid for wheels to run on (so *railroad*, *railway*) XVIII. ME. *reyle*, *raile* - OF. *reille* iron rod :- L. *rēgula* staff, rod, RULE.

rail[3] bird of the family Rallidae. XV. - (O)F. *râle* (Norman-Picard dial. *raille*; AN. *radle*); of uncert. orig.

rail[4] utter abusive language. XV. - F. *railler*, †*ragler* - Pr. *ralhar* jest. Cf. RALLY[2].

raillery XVII. - F. *raillerie*, f. *railler* RALLY[2]; see -ERY.

raiment XV. Aphetic of *arrayment* (XIV) - AN. *araiement*, OF. *areement*; see ARRAY, -MENT.

rain sb. OE. *reġn* = OS., OHG. *regan* (Du., G. *regen*), ON. *regn*, Goth. *rign*; CGmc., but isolated in IE. So **rain** vb. OE. *reġnian*. The comps. *rainbow*, *-drop*, *-shower*, *-water*, and **rainy** are all of OE. age.

raise set up or upright; build up, construct; remove to a higher position XII; levy; end (a siege) XIV; to make higher or greater XV. - ON. *reisa* = OE. *rǣran* REAR[1].

raisin XIII. - (O)F. *raisin* grape :- Rom. **racīmus*, for L. *racēmus* cluster of grapes.

raj (Indian hist.) sovereignty. XVIII. - Hindi *rāj* reign.

raja(h) XVI. prob. through Pg. *raja* - Hindi *rājā* :- Skr. *rā́jan-*, cogn. with L. *rēx*, *rēg-*, OIr. *rī* king.

rake[1] implement consisting of a comb-like cross-bar fitted to a long handle. OE. *raca* m., *racu* fem. = MLG., MDu. *rāke* (Du. *raak*), rel. to Goth. *ufrakjan* stretch out, f. Gmc. base **rak-* :- IE. **roĝ-* **reĝ-* move in a straight line, stretch, repr. also by RIGHT. So vb. XIII. - ON. *raka* scrape, shave, rake; also f. the sb.

rake[2] (naut.) projection of hull at stem and stern beyond the keel line. XVII. f. **rake** vb. (XVII) have a rake, incline from the perpendicular; of unkn. orig. Hence **rakish**[1] (-ISH[1]) having a smart appearance like a fast-sailing ship. XIX (partly assoc. with next).

rake[3] man of dissipated or loose habits. XVII. Clipped form of *rakel* (XVII), var. of arch. **rakehell** (XVI), f. RAKE[1] + HELL. Hence **rakish**[2] (-ISH[1]) XVIII.

rallentando (mus.) direction for reducing the tempo. XIX. - It., prp. of *rallentare* slow down, f. *lento* slow.

rally[1] reassemble, revive XVI; also intr. XVII. - F. *rallier*, f. RE- + *allier* ALLY[2]. Hence sb. XVII.

rally[2] treat with good-humoured ridicule. XVII (in early use also *railly*). - F. *railler* RAIL[4]. Cf. RAILLERY.

ram male sheep; battering-ram OE.; weight of a pile-driving machine XV. OE. *ram(m)*, corr. to (M)LG., (M)Du., OHG *ram* ram (G. *ramme* rammer), perh. rel. to ON. *ram(m)r* strong. Hence vb. XIV, whence **rammer** XV.

ramadan ninth month (30 days' fast) of the Muslim year (supposed orig. to have been a hot month). XVI. - Arab. *ramaḍān*, f. *ramaḍa* be hot.

ramble vb. XVII. prob. - MDu. *rammelen* (of cats, rabbits, etc.) be excited by sexual desire and wander about, frequent. f. *rammen* copulate with, cover, corr. to OHG. *rammalōn* (G. *rammeln*); ult. f. *ram* RAM; see -LE[3]. Hence sb. XVII.

ramekin cheese with breadcrumbs, etc. baked. XVIII. - F. *ramequin*, of Gmc. orig.

ramify form branches, branch out. XVI. - (O)F. *ramifier* - medL. *rāmificāre*, f. L. *rāmus* branch; see -FY. So **ramification** XVII. - F.

ramose branching. XVII. - L. *rāmōsus*, f. *rāmus* branch; see -OSE.

ramp[1] rear or stand on the hind legs (threateningly) XIII; rage violently XIV; (dial.) climb, scramble XVI. - (O)F. *ramper* creep, crawl (a sense rarely repr. in Eng.), climb = It. *rampare*. So **rampant** standing with fore-paws in the air XIV (spec. in her. XV); violent and unrestrained XVII. - (O)F., prp. of *ramper*; see -ANT.

ramp[2] inclined plane. XVIII. - F. *rampe*, f. *ramper* RAMP[1].

rampage behave violently XVIII; push about excitedly XIX. orig. Sc., of unkn. orig.
rampart XVI. - F. *rempart*, †*rampart*, alt. of †*remper*, †*ramper*, f. *remparer* fortify, f. RE- + *emparer* take possession of.
rampion species of bell flower. XVI. f. some var. of the Rom. forms derived from medL. *rapuncium*, *rapontium* (It. *raperonzo*, F. *raiponce*, Sp. *reponcha*).
ramshackle XIX. Later form of **ramshackled** XVII, orig. pp. of †*rans(h)ackle* ransack, f. RANSACK + -LE[3].
ranch hut or house in the country; cattle-breeding establishment. XIX. - Sp. *rancho* mess on board ship, soldiers' quarters, (in S. America) hut for herdsmen, etc.
rancid XVII. - L. *rancidus*, f. **rancēre* (in prp. *rancēns*) be putrid; see -ID[1].
rancour, U.S. **rancor** XIV. - OF. *rancour* (mod. *rancœur*) :- late L. *rancor*, *rancōr-* rankness, (Vulg.) bitter grudge, f. **rancēre* be putrid; see prec., -OUR[2].
rand (dial.) border, margin OE.; (dial.) strip, long slice XIV; strip of leather used in the sole of a boot or shoe XVI. OE. *rand* brink, bank, shield, corr. to OS. *rand* (Du. *rand* edge, ridge), OHG. *rant* (G. *rand*), ON. *rǫnd* edge, rim of a shield.
randan style of rowing (or boat) in which the middle of three rowers pulls a pair of sculls, the others an oar each. XIX. of uncert. orig.
random †impetuosity, great speed or violence XIV; *at (the) r.*, orig. in hawking and the tournament XV; *at r.*, at great speed, (hence) at haphazard, without purpose XVI; †full range of a piece of ordnance, elevation of a gun; adj. XVII. ME. *rand(o)un* - OF. *randon*, rel. to *randir* run impetuously, gallop, of Gmc. orig.
ranee Hindu queen. XVII. - Hindi *rānī* :- Skr. *rā́jñī-*, fem. of *rā́jan-* RAJAH.
range A. †rank, file XIII; row, line, series XVI; B. moving about over an area; area itself XV; extent over which a missile ranges XVI; scope XVII. C. form of fire-grate or cooking apparatus XV. - OF. *range* row, rank, file, f. *ranger* (f. *rang* RANK[1]), whence **range** vb. place in a line, arrange, dispose XIV, take up a position, extend XVI, move over a certain area XVI. Hence **ranger** (arch.) gamekeeper XV; wanderer XVI; (esp. U.S.) pl. body of mounted troops XVIII.
rank[1] row, line; grade of station or dignity. XVI. - OF. *ranc*, var. of *renc* (now *rang*) - Gmc. **χreŋgaz* RING[1].
rank[2] A. †proud, rebellious OE.; †stout and strong XII; †swift, violent XIII; B. †full-grown OE.; vigorous or luxuriant of growth; coarsely luxuriant XIII; grossly rich or fertile; gross, coarse in manner XIV; of offensively strong smell; absolute, downright XVI. OE. *ranc* proud, stout, valiant, showy in dress = (M)LG. *rank* long and thin, ON. *rakkr* erect, f. Gmc. **raŋkaz*.
rankle fester (now only fig.) XIV; fret, chafe (as, or as with, a sore) XVI. - OF. *ra(o)ncler* (var. of *draoncler*), f. *ra(o)ncle* (var. of *draoncle*) ulcer, festering sore - medL. *dranculus*, for L. *dracunculus*, dim. of *dracō* serpent.
ransack †search (a person); search (a place), examine thoroughly XIII; search (a place) with intent to rob, plunder XIV. - ON. *rannsaka* search for stolen goods, f. *rann* house (= OE. *ærn*) + *-saka*, rel. by gradation to *sœkja* SEEK.
ransom procuring the release of a prisoner by a payment, sum so paid. XIII. ME. *rans(o)un* - OF. *ransoun*, *raençon* (mod. *rançon*) :- L. *redemptiō*, *-ōn-* REDEMPTION. So **ransom** vb. XIII. - OF. *ransouner* (mod. *rançonner*).
rant †be uproariously merry; declaim in an extravagant manner. XVI. - Du. †*ranten* talk foolishly, rave. Hence sb. XVII.
ranunculus crowfoot, buttercup. XVI. - L. *rānunculus* little frog, tadpole, medicinal plant (perh. crowfoot), dim. of *rāna* frog.
rap[1] strike or knock smartly. XIV. prob. imit.; cf. Sw. *rappa* beat, drub, and *clap*, *flap*, *slap*, *tap*. So sb. XIV.
rap[2] counterfeit coin current in Ireland XVIII; type of the smallest coin, (hence) least bit XIX. abbrev. of Ir. *ropaire*.
rapacious XVII. f. L. *rapāx*, *rapāc-*, f. *rapere* snatch; see -IOUS. So **rapacity** XVI. - F. or L.
rape[1] any of the six administrative districts of the county of Sussex. XI (*rap*, Domesday Book; taken up by legal and antiquarian writers from XVI). Identical with OE. *rāp* ROPE (the var. *rope* is found occas. XIV), the reference being to the fencing-off of land with a rope.
rape[2] turnip; plant producing oil-seed. XIV. - L. *rāpum*, *rāpa* turnip, obscurely rel. to Gr. *rhápus*, *rháphus* turnip, OSl. *rěpa*, OHG. *ruoba* turnip.
rape[3] take by force XIV; ravish (a woman) XVI. - AN. *raper* - L. *rapere* seize, snatch, take by force. So **rape** sb. †violent seizure, robbery; carrying away of a person by force XIV; violation of a woman XV. - AN. *ra(a)p*, *rape* rape of a woman, f. the vb.
rapid moving with great speed XVII; acting or happening quickly XVIII. - L. *rapidus* lit. carrying along or away, f. *rapere* seize, carry off quickly or violently; see -ID[1]. So **rapidity** XVII. - F. or L.
rapier XVI. prob. - Du. *rapier* or LG. *rappir* (cf. Sc. †*rapper*) - F. *rapière*, orig. *espee rapiere* 'rapier sword', of unkn. orig.
rapine XV. - (O)F. *rapine* or L. *rapīna*, f. *rapere* seize; see -INE[4].
rapparee Irish pikeman or irregular soldier. XVII. - Ir. *rapaire*, pl. *rapairidhe* short pike.
rappee coarse snuff, orig. produced by rasping a piece of tobacco. XVIII. - F. (*tabac*) *râpé*, pp. of *râper* RASP.
rapport †report XVI (rare); relationship, connection XVII. - F., f. *rapporter*, f. RE- + *apporter* bring - L. *apportāre*, f. AP- + *portāre* carry.
rapprochement XIX. - F., f. *rapprocher*, f. RE- + *approcher* APPROACH; see -MENT.
rapscallion XVII. Later form of *rascallion* (XVII), f. RASCAL.
rapt taken and carried up *to heaven*, etc. XIV; carried away by force; carried away *in spirit* XV; transported *with* emotion, plunged *in* thought XVI. - L. *raptus*, pp. of *rapere* seize, rel. to Lith. *aprēpiu* take by force. So **rapture** †carrying off, violent seizure, rape; transport of mind, ecstatic

state; rhapsody XVII. - medL. *raptūra* seizure, ecstasy.

rare[1] †not thick or closely set; few and widely separated; of unusual merit XV; uncommon XVI. - L. *rārus*. So **rarefy** XIV. - (O)F. *raréfier* or medL. *rārificāre*. **rarity** XVI. - F. *rareté*, †*rarité*, or L. *rāritās*.

rare[2] underdone. XVII. later form of *rear*, OE. *hrēr*, of unkn. orig.

rarebit in *Welsh rarebit* (BIT[1]), alt. of *W. rabbit*. XVIII.

raree-show peep-show. XVII. prob. Savoyard's pronunc. of *rare show*.

rascal †rabble; †young or inferior deer of a herd XIV; †one of the rabble, man of low station XV; low or unprincipled fellow XVI. - OF. *rascaille* (mod. *racaille*), prob. f. ONF. **rasque* :- Rom. **rāsica*, f. **rāsicare* scratch, f. *ras-*, pp. stem of L. *rādere* scrape, scratch, shave. As adj. XV. Hence **rascally** (-LY[1]) XVI.

rase †scratch, slit, slash; scrape XIV; level with the ground, RAZE XVI. - (O)F. *raser* shave close :- Rom. **rāsāre*, f. *rās-*; see prec.

rash[1] (dial.) active, brisk XIV; hasty or impetuous in action or behaviour XVI. OE. **ræsć* = (M)Du. *rasch*, OHG. *rasc* (G. *rasch*), ON. *rǫskr* doughty, brave :- Gmc. **raskuz*.

rash[2] superficial eruption of the skin. XVIII. corr. in form to OF. *ra(s)che* skin eruption = It. *raschia* itch, but the late emergence of the word is against direct connection.

rasher slice of bacon or ham (to be) cooked by boiling or frying. XVI. of unkn. orig.

rasp coarse file. XVI. - OF. *raspe* (mod. *râpe*), f. *rasper* scratch, scrape :- Rom. **raspāre* - WGmc. (= OHG.) *raspōn* scrape together. So **rasp** vb. scrape as with a rasp XIV; make a grating noise XIX. In ME. - OF. *rasper*; later f. the sb.

raspberry XVII (*ras-*, *resberry*). f. synon. *rasp* (XVI), shortened form of †*raspis* (XVI), †*raspes*, †*respis*, which was used as coll. pl. or as sg.; of unkn. orig., but identical in form with †*raspis* (XV-XVI) a kind of wine. See BERRY.

rat[1] rodent of the genus *Rattus*. OE. *ræt*, reinforced in late ME. from (O)F. *rat* :- Rom. **rattus*; ult. orig. unkn. In ME. *raton* (mod. dial. *ratton*, *ratten*) was the more frequent word. (- OF. *raton*, f. *rat* with augm. suffix).

rat[2] (mild imprecation) XVII. repr. affected pronunc. of ROT vb.

ratafia cordial flavoured with fruits or their kernels. XVII. - F., prob. of Creole origin and rel. to *tafia* rum.

rataplan drumming sound. XIX. - F., of imit. orig.

rat-a-tat XVII. imit. So **rat-tat** XVIII.

ratchet XVII (*rochet*). - F. *rochet* (in OF.) blunt lance-head, (later) bobbin, spool, ratchet (wheel), corr. to or partly - It. *rocchetto* spool, ratchet, dim. f. Rom. **rokk-*. Later assim. to *ratch* distaff (XVIII), which may depend upon G. *ratsche*.

rate[1] A. †estimated quantity or worth XV; †price XVI; B. quantity in relation to another, value of one thing in respect of that of another XV; fixed relative charge XVI; degree of speed XVII; relative amount of variation XIX; C. †standard, measure XV; class (as of ships) XVII. - OF. - medL. *rata* (evolved from phr. *pro ratā*, short for *pro ratā parte* or *portiōne* according to an estimated or fixed part, proportionally), fem. of *ratus* fixed (see RATIFY). Hence **rate** vb. †fix the amount of, allot XV; estimate, reckon, assess XVI.

rate[2] chide angrily. XIV. Also †*arate*, of which *rate* may be an aphetic form; perh. to be referred to OF. *(a)reter* accuse, blame :- L. *reputāre* REPUTE.

rathe (arch. and dial.) quick, eager OE.; early XIII (in compar.), XV. OE. *hræð*, var. of *hræd* (ME. and dial. *rad*) = OHG. *(h)rad*, ON. *hraðr*, Goth. **raþs* :- Gmc. **χraþaz*, cogn. with Lith. *krečiù*, MIr. *crothaim* I shake. So **rathe** adv. †quickly, soon OE.; early XIV (now arch. and dial.; comp. *rathe-ripe* XVI). OE. *hraðe*, *hræðe* = MLG. *rade*, OHG. *(h)rado*.

rather †more quickly, (dial.) earlier, sooner; *the* more readily, *the* more OE.; more properly; somewhat XVI. OE. *hraðor* (= Goth. *raþizō*), compar. of *hræðe* RATHE adv.; see -ER[3].

ratify XIV. - (O)F. *ratifier* - medL. *ratificāre*, f. L. *ratus* fixed, established, pp. of *rērī* reckon, think; see -FY. So **ratification** XV. - (O)F. - medL.

ratio relation of one quantity to another XVII; †ration XVIII. - L. *ratiō*; see REASON.

ratiocination XVI. - L. *ratiōcinātiō*, *-ōn-*, f. *ratiōcinārī* calculate, deliberate, f. *ratiō* REASON; see -ATION. So **ratiocinate, ratiocinative** XVII.

ration allowance of victuals or provisions. XVIII. In naval and military use - F. - It. *razione* or Sp. *ración* - L. *ratiō*, *-ōn-* reckoning, computation, sum or number (for other senses see REASON).

rational endowed with reason XIV; based on or pert. to reason XVI; (math.); agreeable to reason, reasonable XVII. - L. *ratiōnālis*, f. *ratiō* REASON; see -AL[1]. So **rationale** reasoned exposition; rational basis. XVII. - modL. *ratiōnāle*, sb. use of n. of *ratiōnālis*. Hence **rationalism** XIX, **rationalist** XVII, **rationalize** XIX.

ratlin(e), -ling (naut.) thin line or rope XV; pl. small lines fastened horizontally on the shrouds XVII. Early forms *ratlin*, *raddelyne*, *radelyng*; of unkn. orig.

rattan palm of the genus *Calamus*, stem of this, switch or stick made therefrom. XVII. var. of earlier *rot(t)ang* - Malay *rotan*.

rat-tat(-tat) see RAT-A-TAT.

rattle give out a rapid succession of short sharp sounds XIV; various transf. uses from XVI. prob. - (M)LG., MDu. *ratelen* = MHG. *razzeln* (G. *rasseln*), of imit. orig. Hence sb. rattling sound; instrument for making a rattling noise; plant having a seed-pod that rattles XVI.

ratty pert. to, infested with, rats; miserable, wretched; irritated. XIX. f. RAT[1] + -Y[1].

raucous XVIII. f. L. :- **ravicus*, f. *ravus* hoarse; see -OUS. So **raucity** XVII. - F. or L. *raucitās*.

ravage devastation. XVII. - (O)F., alt., by substitution of -AGE, of *ravine* RAVINE, both being used in the sense 'rush of water'. So vb. XVII. - F. *ravager*.

rave †be mad; (hence) talk wildly. XIV. prob. - ONF. *raver*, of uncert. orig.

ravel (dial.) entangle, become entangled XVI; unravel XVII. poss. - Du. *ravelen* tangle, fray out, unweave.

ravelin (fortif.) outwork of two faces forming a salient angle. XVI. - F. - It. †*travellino*, (now) *rivellino*, of unkn. orig.

raven[1] large black bird with raucous voice. OE. *hræfn* = OS. *-hraban*, MLG., MDu. *rāven* (Du. *raaf*), OHG. (*h*)*raban*, ON. *hrafn* :- Gmc. **χrabnaz*; of imit. orig.

raven[2] †take by force, divide as spoil XV; devour voraciously (also intr.). XVI. - (O)F. *raviner* rush, ravage, (now) hollow out, furrow :- Rom. **rapīnāre*, f. L. *rapīna* RAPINE. So **ravenous** XV. - OF. *ravineux*.

ravin (arch.) rapine; voracity; spoil, prey. XIV. - (O)F. *ravine* :- L. *rapīna* RAPINE.

ravine †violence, violent rush (rare) XV; deep narrow gorge, mountain cleft XIX. - (O)F. *ravine* in mod. sense XVII, (formerly) violent rush, impetuosity, fall (of earth), torrent (of water) :- L. *rapīna* RAPINE, in Rom. (by assoc. with *rapidus* RAPID) impetuous or violent action.

ravish seize and carry off (a person), remove from sight XIII; transport with strong feeling XIV. - *raviss-*, lengthened stem of (O)F. *ravir* :- Rom. **rapīre*, for L. *rapere* seize; see -ISH[2].

raw uncooked OE.; in a natural or unwrought state; crude XIV; inexperienced XVI. OE. *hrēaw* = OS. *hrāo* (MDu. *ra(e)u*, Du. *rauw*), OHG. (*h*)*rāo*, *rō* (G. *roh*), ON. *hrár* :- Gmc. **χrawaz* :- IE. **krowos*, f. a base repr. also by OIr. *crú*, Lith. *kraũjas*, OSl. *krŭvĭ* blood, Gr. *kréas*, Skr. *kravi-* raw flesh, L. *crūdus* raw.

ray[1] line of light XIV (various techn. senses from XVII). - (O)F. *rai* :- L. *radius*; see RADIUS.

ray[2] edible sea-fish allied to the shark. XIV. - (O)F. *raie* :- L. *raia*.

raze †scratch, graze; †scrape *out*, erase; sweep away, efface. XVI. var. sp. of RASE.

razor XIII. ME. *raso(u)r* - OF. *raso(u)r* (superseded by *rasoir* :- Rom. **rāsōrium*), f. *raser* RASE; see -OR[1].

razzia hostile incursion, raid. XIX. - F. - Algerian Arab. *ġāzya*, var. of Arab. *ġazwa*, *ġazāt* military expedition, f. *ġazw* war.

razzle-dazzle riotous jollity. XIX. jingling formation on DAZZLE.

re[1] (mus.) second note of the scale in solmization. XIV. See UT.

re[2] in the matter of, concerning. XVIII. abl. of L. *rēs* thing, affair.

re- repr. L. *re-*, (before a vowel in the classical period) *red-* (e.g. *redimere* REDEEM, *redundāre* REDOUND); pref. restricted to the Italic group, having the general sense of 'back' or 'again', occurring in many Eng. words of L. or Rom. origin (cf. F. *re-*, *ré-*, Sp., Pg. *re-*, It. *ri-*), or of Eng. formations freely modelled on these. From the L. was derived an adj. **recos*, repr. in *reciprocus* RECIPROCAL, and an adv. *retrō* backwards, RETRO-. In combination with *a-* the prefix is disguised in *rally*, *rampart*, and *ransom*, and in the non-naturalized *rallentando*, *rapport*, *rapprochement*. The meanings of the L. prefix, which are all repr. in Eng., are: (1) backwards from a point reached or to the starting-point, e.g. *recēdere* RECEDE, *revocāre* REVOKE; passing sometimes into 'away', e.g. *removēre* REMOVE; (2) back to an earlier state or over to another condition, e.g. *renovāre* RENOVATE, *resūmere* RESUME; (3) back in a place, from going forward, e.g. *residēre* RESIDE, *retinēre* RETAIN; (4) again, in return, (the most frequent use in new formations); (5) in a contrary direction, so that what has been done is annulled or destroyed (= UN-[2]), e.g. *renuntiāre* RENOUNCE, *revēlāre* unveil, REVEAL[1]; (6) in opposition or conflict, e.g. *rebellis* REBEL, *recrīminārī* RECRIMINATE; (7) in response to a stimulus, with intensive force, e.g. *requīrere* REQUIRE, *resolvere* RESOLVE.

Words containing the prefix occur as early as *c.*1200 and become more frequent in XIV; it became an Eng. pref. in XVI, formations on native words being modelled to some extent on foreign comps., as *recall* on L. *revocāre*, *recast* after F. *refondre*. There are double forms with different meanings (with or without hyphen) arising from the coining of new formations from els. identical with those of already existing ones, e.g. *re-cover* (cover again) beside RECOVER.

reach[1] stretch *out*, extend (in various lit. and fig. uses). OE. *rǣcan* (pt. *rǣhte*, *rāhte*) = MLG., (M)Du. *reiken*, (O)HG. *reichen* :- WGmc. **raikjan*, with which Lith. *ráižytis* stretch has been connected. The typical ME. forms of pt. and pp. were *rau(g)ht(e)*; the new *reched* appeared *c.*1400. Hence **reach** sb. continuous stretch, as of a waterway XIII (in place-names); act or extent of reaching XVI.

reach[2] †spit, hawk OE.; make efforts to vomit XVI. OE. *hrǣcan* = ON. *hrækja* spit, f. Gmc. **χraik-*, repr. also by OE. *hrāca*, ON. *hráki* spittle; of imit. orig.

react act in turn or in response to a stimulus XVII; move or tend in a reverse direction XIX. f. RE- + ACT vb. So **reaction** XVII, whence **reactionary** XIX. **reagent** (chem.) substance employed to detect the presence of another by the reaction produced. XVIII.

read †think, suppose, guess; discern the meaning of (chiefly in *read a riddle*, *a dream*); inspect and interpret aloud or silently (signs representing speech); also intr. OE. *rǣdan* = OS. *rādan* (Du. *raden* advise, guess), OHG. *rātan* (G. *raten* guess, read (a riddle), advise), ON. *ráða* advise, plan, rule, explain, read, Goth. *-rēdan* :- Gmc. **rǣðan*, prob. rel. to OIr. *imrádim* I deliberate, consider, OSl. *raditi* take thought, attend to, Skr. *rādh-* accomplish.

The orig. senses of the Gmc. vb. are those of taking or giving counsel, taking charge, controlling; the sense of considering or explaining something secret or mysterious is common to several langs., but that of interpreting written symbols is peculiar to OE., and ON. (perh. through OE. infl.).

Hence **reader** (-ER[1]) one who reads OE.; reading-book XVIII. **reading** (-ING[1]) OE.

ready in a state of preparation *for* something, prompt, quick. XII. ME. *rædi(ȝ)*, *re(a)di*, also *ȝeredi*, *iready*, extended forms (with -Y[1]) of OE. *rǣde*, usu. *ġerǣde* (ME. *irede*) = MLG. (*ge*)*rēde* (Du. *gereed*), OHG. *reiti*, MHG. *gereite*, parallel to

OE. *ġerād* straight, wise, prudent, -conditioned, MLG. *gerēd*, MHG. *gereit* ready, ON. *(g)reiðr* ready, Goth. *garaiþs* arranged; f. Gmc. **raið-* prepare, arrange.

real[1] (orig. leg.) pert. to things (as dist. from persons) XV; actually existing or present; that is truly what its name implies XVI. orig. - AN. *real* = (O)F. *réel*; later - its source, late L. *reālis*, f. *rēs* thing; see -AL[1]. So **reality** XVI. - (O)F. or medL. **realize, realization** XVII. - F. Hence **realism** XIX, **realist** XVII, **really** (-LY[2]) XV.

real[2] small Spanish silver coin. XVII - Sp., sb. use of *real* = F. *royal* ROYAL.

realgar native disulphide of arsenic. XIV. - medL. - Arab. *rahj al-ġār* 'powder of the cave or mine' (*rahj* powder, *al* AL-[2], *ġār* cave).

realm (now rhet. and techn.) kingdom. XIII. ME. *reaume*, later *reume*, *rea(l)me* (XIV) - OF. *reaume*, *realme* (mod. *royaume*) - L. *regimen* REGIMEN; blending with OF. *reiel* ROYAL, etc. produced forms with *-l-*, which finally prevailed in Eng., *realm* being established *c.*1600.

ream 20 quires of paper. XIV. - OF. *raime*, *reyme*, *remme* (mod. *rame*), also *riesme* - Arab. *rizma* bundle, f. *razama* collect into a bundle.

reap cut (grain) for harvest. The present form descends from ME. *re(o)pen*, repr. OE. (i) *reopan*, **riopan*, var. of *ripan* (pt. *ripde*, **ripte*), and (ii) **repan* (pt. pl. *rǣpon*); no certain cogns. are known. (OE. pt. pl. *ripon* implies an inf. **rīpan*, pres. **rīpe*, **rīpð*, repr. by ME. and dial. *ripe*, pt. *rope*.)

rear[1] set up, lift up, raise (lit. and fig.) OE.; bring up, breed XV; intr. rise on the hind feet XIV. OE. *rǣran* = ON. *reisa* (cf. Goth. *urraisjan* awaken) :- Gmc. **raizjan*, causative of **reisan* RISE. Superseded in many senses by the Scand. RAISE.

rear[2] hindmost part. XVI. In earliest use military and naval; prob. extracted from phr. *in the rear-ward* (XV) or simply a shortening of *rearward* or *rearguard*. See next.

rearguard †rear portion of an armed force XV; portion detached from the main force to protect the rear XVII. - OF. *rereguarde*, f. *rer*, *riere* :- L. *retrō* back + *guarde* GUARD. The AN. var. *rerewarde* is repr. by **rearward** XIV; see WARD[1].

reason fact or circumstance serving as ground or motive for action; intellectual power, thinking faculty. XIII. ME. *res(o)un*, *reson*, *reisun* - OF. *reisun*, *res(o)un* (mod. *raison*) :- L. *ratiō*, *-ōn-* reckoning, judgement, understanding, reasoning, method, motive, f. *rat-*, pp. stem of *rērī* think, reckon; see -TION. So **reason** vb. †question, call to account XIV; †hold discourse XV; think connectedly or logically XVI. - OF. *raisoner* (mod. *-onner*). **reasonable** agreeable to reason XIII; †endowed with reason; having sound judgement; not exceeding limits assigned by reason XIV. - (O)F. *raison(n)able*.

Réaumur Name of a thermometer invented by René Antoine de *Réaumur* (1683-1757), French physicist. XVIII.

reave pt., pp. *reft* (arch.) commit robbery; despoil; take forcible possession of. OE. *rēafian* = OS. *rōbon* (Du. *rooven*), OHG. *roubōn* (G. *rauben*), Goth. *-raubōn* :- Gmc. **raubōjan*, f. **raub-* (whence also OE. *rēaf* plunder, equipment, clothing = OS. *rōf*, OHG. *roub*), **reub-* (whence OE. *rēofan* break, tear, ON. *rjúfa* break, violate); the orig. sense is 'break', as in cogn. L. *rumpere*, *rup-*. Hence **reaver**, Sc. **reiver** robber, plunderer. OE. *rēafere* = MDu. *rōvere* (Du. *roover*), OHG. *roubari* (G. *räuber*).

rebate †deduct, subtract; reduce, diminish XV; †dull, blunt XVI. ME. *rabat* - (O)F. *rabattre*, f. RE- + *abattre* ABATE; later alt. by substitution of *re-* for the first syll. Hence sb. deduction. XVII.

rebeck (hist.) three-stringed fiddle. XVI. - F. *rebec*, †*rabec*, unexpl. alt. of OF. *ribebe*, *rubebe* (whence ME. *ribibe*, *ru-*, *ribible*) - Arab. *rabāb* (dial. *rabēb*) one- or two-stringed fiddle.

rebel adj. that refuses obedience or allegiance XIII; sb. one who does this XIV. - (O)F. *rebelle* adj. and sb. - L. *rebellis* adj. and sb., f. RE- + *bellum* war. So **rebel** vb. XIV. - (O)F. *rebeller* - L. *rebellāre*. **rebellion** XIV. - (O)F. *rébellion* - L. *rebelliō*, *-ōn-*. Hence **rebellious** XVI (preceded by †*rebellous* XV). - F. †*rebelleux*.

rebound vb. XIV. - OF. *rebonder*, (also mod.) *rebondir*, f. RE- + *bondir* BOUND[4]. Hence (or - F. *rebond*) **rebound** sb. XVI.

rebuff vb. XVI. - F. †*rebuffer* - It. *ribuffare*, *rabbuffare*, f. *ribuffo*, *rabbuffo*, f. *ri-* RE- + *buffo* gust, puff, of imit. orig. So sb. XVII. - F. †*rebuffe* - It. *ribuffo*.

rebuke †break down, force back; chide severely. XIV. - AN., ONF. *rebuker* = OF. *rebuchier*, f. RE- + *bu(s)chier*, *bukier* beat, strike, prop. cut down wood, f. *busche* (mod. *bûche*) log, prob. of Gmc. orig. Hence sb. XV.

rebus enigmatic representation of a name, word, etc. by pictures suggesting its syllables. XVII. - F. *rébus* - L. *rēbus*, abl. pl. of *rēs* thing.

rebut †revile, reproach XIII; †repel, repulse XIV; check XV; (leg.) repel by counter-proof XIX (intr. XVII). - AN. *rebuter*, OF. *rebo(u)ter*, f. RE- + *boter* BUTT[1]. So **rebutter** (leg.) defendant's answer to plaintiff's surrejoinder. XVI. Hence **rebuttal** (-AL[2]) XIX.

recalcitrant XIX. - F. *récalcitrant* - L. *recalcitrāns*, *-ant-*, prp. of *recalcitrāre* kick out, (later) be refractory, f. RE- + **calcitrum* kick, f. *calx*, *calc-* heel; see -ANT.

recall call back; revoke. XVI. f. RE- + CALL. Hence sb. XVII.

recant XVI. - L. *recantāre* recall, revoke, f. RE- + *cantāre* sing, CHANT. Hence **recantation** XVI.

recapitulate XVI. f. pp. stem of late L. *recapitulāre*, f. RE- + *capitulum* section of a writing, CHAPTER; see -ATE[3]. So **recapitulation** XIV. - (O)F. or late L.

recast cast (metal) again; refashion. XVIII. f. RE- + CAST.

recede retire from a place. XV. - L. *recēdere*, f. RE- + *cēdere* go, CEDE. So **recess** †retirement, withdrawal XVI; (period of) retirement from occupation; retired, receding, or inner part XVII. - L. *recessus*. **recession** retirement. XVII (whence **recessional** (hymn) sung during the retirement of clergy, etc., after a service (XIX)). - L.

receipt A. recipe. B. reception (of money, etc.); money received XIV (written acknowledgement of this XVII); office for the reception of moneys XV (*r. of the Exchequer*). ME. *receit(e)* - AN. (ONF.) *receite* = OF. *reçoite*, var. of *recete* (mod. *recette*) - medL. *recepta*, sb. use of fem. pp. of *recipere* RECEIVE. The sp. with *p* appears in OF. *recepte*, a latinized form of *recete*.

receive take to oneself XIII; accept, take in, admit; be the object of XIV. - OF. *receivre*, var. of *reçoivre* or later (refash.) *recevoir*, ult. :- L. *recipere*; see RECIPIENT. So **receiver** (-ER[2]) XIV. - AN. **receivere, -our* = OF. *recevere*.

recension †enumeration, survey XVII; critical revision of a text, text so revised XIX. - L. *recēnsiō, -ōn-*, f. *recēnsēre* reckon, survey, review, revise, f. RE- + *cēnsēre* assess, appraise; see -ION.

recent XVI. - F. *récent* or L. *recēns, -ent-*.

receptacle XV. - (O)F. *réceptacle* or L. *receptāculum*, f. *receptāre* receive, f. *recept-*, pp. stem of *recipere* RECEIVE.

reception action of receiving XIV (in astron. sense); in gen. sense XV (not freq. till mid-XVII). - (O)F. *réception* or L. *receptiō, -ōn-*, f. *recipere* RECEIVE; see -TION. So **receptive** XVI. - medL.

réchauffé warmed-up dish. XIX. - F., pp. of *réchauffer* warm up again, f. RE- + *échauffer*; see CHAFE, -Y[5].

recherché very choice or rare. XVIII. - F., pp. of *rechercher* search for carefully.

recidivist XIX. - F. *récidiviste*, f. *récidiver* - medL. *recidīvāre*, f. L. *recidīvus*, f. *recidere* fall back, f. RE- + *cadere* fall; see -IVE, -IST.

recipe †(imper.) take XIV; sb. formula for a medical prescription XVI, for a dish in cookery XVIII. - L. *recipe*, imper. sg. of *recipere* RECEIVE.

recipient one who or a thing which receives. XVI. - F. *récipient* - It. *recipiente* or L. *recipiēns, -ent-*, prp. of *recipere* RECEIVE, f. RE- + *capere* take; see -ENT.

reciprocal done in return; inversely related XVI; corresponding to each other; (gram.) reflexive XVII. f. L. *reciprocus* moving backwards and forwards, alternating :- **recoprocos*, f. **recos* + **procos*, f. (respectively) RE- and PRO-[1]; see -AL[1]. So **reciprocate** (-ATE[3]) XVII. f. pp. stem of L. *reciprocāre*. **reciprocation** XVI. - F. or L. **reciprocity** XVIII. - F.

recite XV. - (O)F. *réciter* or L. *recitāre* read out, f. RE- + *citāre* CITE. Hence **recital** (-AL[2]) XVI. So **recitation** XV. - (O)F. *récitation* or L. *recitātiō, -ōn-*. **recitative** adj. and sb. XVII. f. It. *recitativo*; see -ATIVE.

reck take care, heed, concern oneself. OE. shows two types: (i) **rēċan*, pt. *rōhte* (whence ME. *reche, rouhte*, later *rought* till XVII) = OS. *rōkjan*, OHG. *ruohhen*, ON. *rœkja* :- Gmc. **rōkjan*; (ii) *reċċan*, the orig. of which is obscure, paralleled in *reċċelēas* RECKLESS. The present form, which appears XII, is due partly to generalization of the *k* of ME. 3rd sg. pres. ind. *rekþ* (OE. *recð*, which may belong to either **rēċan* or *reċċan*), partly to the infl. of ON. *rœkja*. New pt. and pp. in *-ed* appear XV.

reckless OE. *reċ(ċ)elēas*, corr. to MLG. *rōkelōs*, (M)Du. *roekeloos*, OHG. *ruahhalōs* (G. *ruchlos*); f. base of RECK + -LESS; forms with *-(c)k-* are extant from XII, by assoc. with the vb.

reckon A. †recount, relate OE. (once); enumerate, name serially XII; count, compute XIII; estimate, consider XIV. B. make a calculation, settle accounts with; calculate or design *to* XVI; depend *on* XVII. OE. *ġerecenian* = (M)LG., (M)Du. *rekenen*, OHG. *rehhanōn* (G. *rechnen*) :- WGmc. **(ʒa)rekenōjan*, perh. f. **rekenaz* (OE. *recen*) ready, rapid, straightforward.

reclaim †call (a hawk) back XIII; recall, bring back; reduce to obedience XIV; claim restoration of XVI; bring (land) under cultivation XVIII. - (O)F. *réclamer* - L. *reclāmāre* cry out, exclaim; see RE-, CLAIM. So **reclamation** XVI. - F. or L.

recline †lay down XV; (of a dial) incline from the vertical XVI; rest in a recumbent position XVII. - OF. *recliner* lean, of a dial (as above), and reinforced from its source L. *reclīnāre* bend back, lay aside, recline, f. RE- + *-clīnāre* (cf. LEAN[2]).

recluse sb. person shut up from the world for the purpose of religious contemplation XIII; person of retired life XVIII; adj. XIV. - (O)F. *reclus*, fem. *recluse*, pp. of *reclure* :- L. *reclūdere* (pp. *reclūsus*) shut up, (earlier) open, f. RE- + *claudere* CLOSE.

recognition †(Sc. leg.) resumption of lands by a feudal superior XV; acknowledgement as true or valid XVI; identification of a person or thing XVIII. - L. *recognitio, -ōn-*, f. *recognit-*, pp. stem of *recognoscere* examine, recognize; see RE-, COGNITION. So **recognize** †(Sc. leg.) resume possession of XV; †revise, amend; †acknowledge, admit; treat as valid, approve; know again XVI. Early forms *raccunnis* (Sc.), *recognis(h)*, soon assim. to vbs. in *-ise*, -IZE. - OF. *recon(n)iss-*, pres. stem of *reconnaistre* (mod. *reconnaître*) :- L. *recognoscere*. **recognizance** legal bond or obligation XIV; †recognition; †badge XV. - OF. *recon(u)issance* (mod. *reconnaissance*); cf. COGNIZANCE.

recoil †beat or drive back XIII; retreat, retire XIV; †go or draw back XV; spring back XVI. - (O)F. *reculer* - Rom. **recūlāre*, f. L. RE- + *cūlus* posteriors. Hence sb. XVI (once XIV).

recollect call back to one's mind XVI. var., with distinctive pronunc., of *re-collect* †collect; collect again XVI; summon up (one's spirits, courage, etc.) XVII; f. *recollect-*, pp. stem of L. *recolligere* collect again, f. RE- + *colligere* COLLECT[1]. So **recollection** A. gathering together again XVI; B. concentration of thought; recalling to the memory XVII. - F. or medL.

recommend commend or commit to God; †praise, commend XIV; mention or introduce with approval; make acceptable XVII. - medL. *recommendāre*, f. RE- + *commendāre* COMMEND. So **recommendation** XV.

recompense reward, requite. XV. - (O)F. *récompenser* - late L. *recompensāre*, f. RE- + *compensāre* COMPENSATE. So sb. XV. - F. *récompense*.

reconcile bring again into friendly relations or agreement XIV; make compatible XVI. - (O)F. *réconcilier* or L. *reconciliāre*, f. RE- + *conciliāre* CONCILIATE. So **reconciliation** XIV.

recondite †hidden away; removed from ordinary understanding or knowledge. XVII. - L.

reconditus, pp. of *recondere* put away, hide, f. RE- + *condere* hide.

reconnaissance ascertainment of the position and strength of an enemy. XVIII. - F., f. stem of *reconnaître*, later form of *reconnoître* (:- L. *recognoscere* RECOGNIZE), whence **reconnoitre** make a reconnaissance (of). (XVIII).

record (leg.) fact of being committed to writing as evidence XIII; fact of being preserved as knowledge XIV; (leg.) authentic report of proceedings XV; account of a fact in writing, etc. XVI. - (O)F. *record* remembrance, f. *recorder* bring to remembrance :- L. *recordāre*, usu. *-ārī* think over, be mindful of, f. RE- + *cor, cord-* HEART; whence vb. A. †commit to memory XIV; practise (a song, tune) XV; B. †recall, remember; relate, set down in writing XIV. So **recorder** (1) magistrate holding a court of quarter-sessions, orig. lawyer appointed by the mayor and aldermen (of London) to keep in mind proceedings of the court, etc. XV. - AN. *recordour*, OF. *recordeur*; see -ER². **recorder** (2) wind instrument of the flute kind. XV. f. *record* vb. in the sense 'practise a tune' + -ER¹.

recount relate, tell in detail. XV. - AN., ONF. *reconter*, f. RE- + *conter* COUNT.

recoup †interrupt XV (rare); (leg.) deduct; recompense for loss or outlay XVII. - OF. *recouper* cut back, retrench, interrupt, re-sell, f. RE- + *couper* cut.

recourse †return; †course, movement; resort *to* a person or thing XIV; means resorted to XV. - (O)F. *recours* - L. *recursus*, f. *recurs-*, pp. stem of *recurrere* run or turn back, resort (see RECUR).

recover tr. get or bring back, regain; intr. regain a status. XIV. - AN. *recoverer*, OF. *recovrer* (mod. *recouvrer*), - L. *recuperāre* regain; see RECUPERATE. So **recovery** XIV. - AN. *recoverie*, OF. *reco(u)vree*.

recreant confessing oneself vanquished, (hence) cowardly, craven XIV (also sb.); false, apostate XVII (sb. XVI). - OF. *recreant* adj. and sb. use of prp. of *recroire* yield, surrender :- medL. (*sē*) *recrēdere* surrender (oneself), f. RE- + *crēdere* entrust, believe; see -ANT.

recreate restore to a good or wholesome condition, refresh. XV. f. pp. stem of L. *recreāre*, f. RE- + *creāre* CREATE. So **recreation** †refreshment, nourishment; refreshment by pleasant occupation. XIV. - (O)F. - L. **recreative** XVI.

recriminate retort an accusation, accuse in return. XVII. f. pp. stem of medL. *recrīmināre*, f. L. RE- + *crīminārī* accuse, f. *crīmen, crīmin-* accusation; see -ATE³. So **recrimination** XVII. - F. or medL.

recrudescence XVIII. f. L. *recrūdēscere*, f. RE- + *crūdēscere* become raw; see -ESCENCE. So **recrudescent** XVIII.

recruit †reinforcement (abstr. and concr.) of troops; †pl. reinforcements, (hence) one of the men composing these, newly enlisted soldier. XVII. - F. dial. †*recrute* = F. *recrue*, sb. use of fem. pp. of *recroître* increase again :- L. *recrēscere*, f. RE- + *crēscere* grow. So **recruit** vb. reinforce; replenish; enlist new soldiers; recover health or vigour XVII; enlist (men) XIX. - F. *recruter*.

rectangle XVI. - F. *rectangle* or medL. *rēctangulum*, for earlier *rēctiangulum*, sb. use of n. sg. of **rēctiangulus*, f. L. *rēctus* straight, RIGHT + *angulus* ANGLE². Hence **rectangular** XVII.

rectify put right, remedy XIV; refine by chemical process XV; adjust XVI. - (O)F. *rectifier* - medL. *rēctificāre*, f. L. *rēctus* RIGHT; see -FY. So **rectification** XV - (O)F. or late L.

rectilinear XVII. f. late L. *rēctilīneus*, f. *rēctus* RIGHT + *līnea* LINE¹; see -AR.

rectitude †straightness XV; moral uprightness XVI. - (O)F. *rectitude* or late L. *rēctitūdō*, f. *rēctus* RIGHT; see -TUDE.

recto right-hand page of a book when open, front of a leaf. XIX. - L. *rēctō* on the right side, abl. of *rēctus* RIGHT.

rector †ruler, governor XIV; incumbent of a parish whose tithes are not impropriate; head of a university, etc. XV. - OF. *rectour* (mod. *recteur*) or L. *rēctor, -ōr-*, f. pp. stem of *regere* rule. So **rectory** (-ORY¹) benefice held by a rector XVI; rector's residence XIX. - AN., OF. *rectorie* or medL. *rēctōria*; see -Y³.

rectum XVI. - L. *rēctum*, n. of *rēctus* straight.

recumbent XVII. - L. *recumbēns, -ent-*, prp. of *recumbere* recline, f. RE- + *-cumbere* (cf. INCUMBENT).

recuperate †recover, regain XVI; restore (esp. in health) XVII; (intr.) recover health, etc. XIX. f. pp. stem of L. *recuperāre*, f. RE- + **cup-* (as in *occupāre* OCCUPY). So **recuperation** †recovery XV (rare before XVII); restoration of health XIX. - L.

recur go or come back, return (now in abstr. senses) XV; occur again XVII. - L. *recurrere*, f. RE- + *currere* run. So **recurrence** XVII, **recurrent** XVI.

recusant Roman Catholic (etc.) who refused to attend services of the Church of England. XVI. - L. *recūsāns, -ant-*, prp. of *recūsāre* refuse, f. RE- + *causa* CAUSE; see -ANT.

red OE. *rēad* = OS. *rōd* (Du. *rood*), OHG. *rōt* (G. *rot*), ON. *rauðr*, Goth. *rauþs* :- Gmc. **rauðaz* :- IE. **roudhos*, f. base repr. also by Skr. *rudhirá-*, Gr. *eruthrós*, L. *rūfus, ruber*, OIr. *ruadh*, W. *rhudd*, OSl. *rudŭ*, Lith. *raũdas*. comp. **redbreast, red deer, red herring, red lead.** XV. **redstart** song-bird having a red tail. XVI (OE. *steort* tail). Hence **redden** vb. XVII (-EN⁵), **reddish** XIV (-ISH¹).

red- var. of RE-.

-red repr. OE. *rǣden* condition, which was freely used as a suffix, as in *brōðorrǣden* brotherhood, *frēondrǣden* friendship, *sibrǣden* relationship. Only a few were retained in ME., but there were some new formations, as *felawrede* fellowship, *haterede(n)* HATRED, *kinrede(n)* KINDRED.

redaction preparation for publication. XIX. - F. *rédaction* - late L. *redactiō, -ōn-*, f. *redact-*, pp. stem of *redigere* drive back, collect, reduce, f. RED- + *agere* drive, etc.

redan (fortif.) field-work having two faces forming a salient angle. XVII. - F., var. of *redent* notching as of a saw, f. RE- + *dent* tooth.

reddle red ochre. XVIII. var. of RUDDLE.

rede †rule, govern OE.; †guide, guard, appoint XIII; advise, counsel OE.; interpret XVIII. ME.

form of READ, retained for arch. senses. So **rede** sb. (arch.) counsel; †plan of action; †succour, remedy OE.; tale, story XIV. OE. *rǣd*, corr. to OS. *rād* (Du. *raad*), OHG. *rāt* (G. *rat*), ON. *ráð* :- Gmc. **rǣðaz, -am*, f. base of **rǣðan* READ.

redeem buy back; free (mortgaged property) by payment; free by paying ransom; deliver, spec. from sin XV; make up for, compensate XVI. - F. *rédimer* or L. *redimere*, f. RED- + *emere* buy, orig. take. Hence **redeemer** (-ER[1]) XV. So **redemption** action of freeing or delivering; ransom. XIV. - (O)F. *rédemption* - L. *redemptiō, -ōn-*, f. *redempt-*, pp. stem of *redimere*. **Redemptorist** member of the Congregation of the Most Holy Redeemer. XIX. - F.

red-gum papular eruption. XVI. alt., by assim. to GUM[1], of †*redgown(d)*, †*-gowm* (XV), later form, infl. by RED, of *radegound* (XIV), f. obscure first el. + (dial.) *gound* pus, esp. from the eyes, OE. *gund* = OHG. *gunt* pus, Goth. *gund* carcinoma.

redintegrate restore to completeness or unity. XV. f. pp. stem of L. *redintegrāre*, f. RED- + *integrāre* INTEGRATE. So **redintegration** XV.

redolent †sweet-smelling XIV; smelling *of* or *with* XVII. - OF. *redolent* or L. *redolēns, -ent-*, prp. of *redolēre*, f. RED- + *olēre* emit a smell; see -ENT. So **redolence** XV. - OF.

redouble double in quantity XV; repeat XVI. - F. *redoubler*; see RE-, DOUBLE vb.

redoubt †small work within a fortification; square or polygonal outwork or field-work. XVII. - F. *redoute*, †*ridotte* - It. †*ridotta*, now *ridotto* - medL. *reductus* refuge, retreat, f. pp. stem of *redūcere* draw off, withdraw (see REDUCE). The *b* is due to assoc. with next.

redoubtable XIV. - (O)F. *redoutable*, f. *redouter* fear, dread, f. RE- + *douter* DOUBT; see -ABLE.

redound †overflow; †abound; †flow or go back; †resound XIV; turn or contribute *to* some advantage or disadvantage XV; attach or accrue *to* XVI. - (O)F. *redonder* :- L. *redundāre* (see REDUNDANT).

redress †set upright again; restore, amend, remedy XIV. - (O)F. *redresser*; see RE-, DRESS. So sb. XIV. - AN. *redresse*.

reduce †bring or lead back XIV; bring or restore *to* a condition; bring into subjection, bring down XV; diminish XVI. - L. *redūcere* bring back, restore, replace, f. RE- + *dūcere* lead, bring. So **reduction** XV. - (O)F. or L.

redundant characterized by superfluity or excess. XVII. - L. *redundāns, -ant-*, pp. of *redundāre* overflow, etc., f. RED- + *undāre* (of the sea) be agitated, surge, f. *unda* wave; see -ANT. So **redundance, redundancy** XVII. - L.

reduplicate make double or twofold XVI; (gram.) XIX. f. pp. stem of late L. *reduplicāre*, f. RE- + *duplicāre* DUPLICATE. So **reduplication** doubling XVI; (gram.) repetition of an element of the radical or base of a word XVIII. - late L. *reduplicātiō, -ōn-*.

reed (tall straight stem of) any plant of the genera *Phragmites* and *Arundo*. OE. *hrēod* = OS. *hriod*, OHG. *(h)riot* (Du., G. *riet*) :- WGmc. **χreuda*.

reef[1] (naut.) horizontal strip of a sail that can be taken in. XIV (*riff*). - (M)Du. *reef, rif* - ON. *rif* (RIB) in same sense; cf. next. Hence **reef** vb. reduce (a sail) by taking in a reef. XVII. Hence **reefer** (-ER[1]) reefing-jacket (close-fitting jacket). XIX.

reef[2] ridge of rock at or near the surface of the water XVI; (in gold-mining, orig. Austral.) lode of auriferous quartz XIX. Earlier *riff(e)*, in nautical use - MLG. *ref, rif*, pl. *rēves*, MDu. *rif, ref* - ON. *rif* (RIB) in same sense; cf. prec.

reek smoke OE.; vapour, steam XIV; exhalation, disagreeable smell XVII. OE. *rēc*, **rīec* = OS. *rōk* (Du. *rook*), OHG. *rouh* (G. *rauch*), ON. *reykr* :- Gmc. **raukiz*. From the grade **reuk-* is **reek** vb. smoke (trans. and intr.); emit hot vapour OE.; emit unwholesome vapour, stink XVIII. OE. *rēocan* = (M)Du. *rieken*, OHG. *riohhan* (G. *riechen*), ON. *rjúka*. The normal repr. of the OE. sb. is ME. and dial. *reech*; the *k*-form is due partly to Scand. infl., partly to assoc. with the native verb.

reel winding instrument, orig. for thread or silk OE.; (orig. Sc., f. the vb.) whirling movement, staggering roll; lively dance of Sc. origin XVI. OE. *hrēol*, of which no cogns. are known. Hence **reel** vb. wind on a reel; whirl; stagger, sway XIV; dance a reel XVIII.

reeve[1] (chiefly hist.) in Anglo-Saxon times, high official having local jurisdiction; later, variously applied to local officers. OE. *rēfa*, aphetic var. of OE. *ġerēfa*, earlier *ġirǣfa*, f. *ġe-* Y- + **rōf* in *secġrōf* host of men, *stæfrōf* alphabet = OHG. *ruova, ruoba*, ON. *stafróf*.

reeve[2] pt. and pp. *reeved*, later *rove* (naut.) pass (a rope) through a hole. XVII. perh. - Du. *rēven* reef, with shift of meaning.

refection refreshment, recreation XIV; partaking of food, meal XV. - (O)F. *réfection* - L. *refectiō, -ōn-*, f. pp. stem of *reficere* remake, renew, f. RE- + *facere* make; see -TION. So **refectory** (-ORY[1]) XV. - late L. *refectōrium*.

refer attribute *to* a source or related thing; have relation or allusion *to* XIV; commit *to* an authority, etc. XV. - (O)F. *référer* - L. *referre* carry back, f. RE- + *ferre* BEAR[2]. Hence **referable** XVII, **referee** (-EE[1]) (leg.); **reference** XVI. So **referendum** XIX. gerund or n. gerundive of L. *referre*. **referent** (gram.) XIX. - prp. of L. *referre* (see -ENT).

refine XVI. f. RE- + FINE vb.[2]. Hence **refinement** XVII, **refinery** XVIII.

reflect divert, deflect XV; throw back (beams, etc.), turn one's thoughts *upon* XVII; cast reproach. - OF. *réflecter* or L. *reflectere*, f. RE- + *flectere* bend. So **reflection, reflexion** throwing back of light or heat XIV; animadversion, imputation; fixing of the thoughts XVII. - (O)F. or late L.

reform A. form again XIV; B. †restore; convert into another and a better form XIV; change for the better XV. - OF. *reformer* (mod. *réformer*) or L. *reformāre*; see RE-, FORM vb. In sense A, a new formation since XVI, and now usu. sp. **re-form.** Hence (or - F. *réforme*) sb. XVIII. So **reformation** improvement, radical change for the better XV; (hist.) spec., with *R.* XVI. - (O)F. or L. Hence **reformatory** adj. XVI; sb. institute for the reformation of juvenile offenders XIX.

refract deflect the course of (light, etc.). XVII. f. *refract-*, pp. stem of L. *refringere*, f. RE- + *frangere* BREAK[1]. So **refraction** †breaking open or up XVI (rare); deflection of rays, etc. XVII. - F. or L. **refractory** (-ORY[2]) stubborn, unmanageable XVII; resisting the action of heat XVIII. alt. of †*refractary* (XVI) - L. *refractārius*.

refrain[1] burden of a poem or song (recurring at intervals and so breaking the sequence). XIV. - (O)F. *refrain*, †*refrein*, succeeding to earlier *refrait*, *-eit*, sb. use of pp. of †*refraindre* break, etc. :- Rom. **refrangere*, for L. *refringere*, f. RE- + *frangere* BREAK[1].

refrain[2] †restrain; abstain. XIV. - (O)F. *refréner* - L. *refrēnāre* bridle, f. RE- + *frēnum* bridle.

refresh impart freshness to, restore to a fresh condition. XIV. - OF. *refreschi(e)r*, f. RE- + *fres*, fem. *fresche* FRESH. Hence **refreshment** XIV.

refrigerate cause to become cold. XVI. f. pp. stem of L. *refrīgerāre*, f. RE- + *frīgus*, *frīgor-* cold; see -ATE[3]. So **refrigeration** XV. - L. **refrigerator** cooler XVII; apparatus for maintaining a cold temperature XIX; earlier **refrigeratory** (-ORY[1]) XVII.

reft see REAVE.

refuge shelter from danger or trouble. XIV. - (O)F. - L. *refugium*, f. RE- + *fugere* flee. So **refugee** (-EE[1]) XVII (*refugie* and *-gee*). - F. *refugié*, pp. of (*se*) *refugier* take refuge; the ending was early assim.

refulgent XVI. - prp. of L. *refulgēre*, f. RE- + *fulgēre* shine; see -ENT.

refund †pour back XIV; pay back, repay XVI. - OF. *refonder* or L. *refundere*, f. RE- + *fundere* pour; in later use based on FUND.

refuse †avoid; decline to accept or *to do* a thing; †renounce XIV; decline to grant XVI. - (O)F. *refuser* - Rom. **refūsāre*, prob. alt. of L. *recūsāre* refuse, after *refūtāre* REFUTE. Hence **refusal** (-AL[2]) XV. So **refuse** sb. rejected matter. XV. perh. - OF. *refusé*, pp. of *refuser*.

refute †refuse XVI (rare); prove in error, disprove XVI. - L. *refūtāre* repel, rebut, f. RE- + **fūt-* (of uncert. orig.; cf. CONFUTE). So **refutation** XVI. - L.

regal royal, kingly. XIV. - OF. *regal* or L. *rēgālis*, f. *rēx*, *rēg-* king, f. a base repr. by Gaul. **rīx* (as in *Dumnorīx*, *Vercingetorīx*), (O)Ir. *rí* king, Skr. *rā́jan-* RAJA(H); see -AL[1]. So **regality** XV. - OF. or medL.

regale entertain or feast in a choice manner. XVII. - F. *régaler*, f. *ré-* RE- + OF. *gale* pleasure, joy.

regalia royal powers or privileges XVI; insignia of royalty XVII. - medL. *rēgālia* royal residence, royal rights, n. pl. of *rēgālis* REGAL; see -IA[2].

regard A. †aspect, look XIV; (arch.) look, glance XV; (hist.) official inspection of a forest XVI; B. †repute, esteem XIV; observation, attention XV; thing to be considered; kindly feeling or wish XVI. - (O)F., f. *regarder* look at, etc. (see RE-, GUARD vb.), whence **regard** vb. look at, take notice of XV; heed, take into account, consider XVI; concern, have respect or relation to XVII (prp. *regarding*, passing into prep. XVIII). So **regardant** (leg.) attached to a manor XV; (her.) looking backwards. - AN., (O)F. *regardant*, prp. of the vb.

regatta boat-race held on the Grand Canal, Venice XVII; hence gen. XVIII. - It. (orig. Venetian) †*regatta*, †*rigatta*, *regata*, f. *rigattare* wrangle, contend.

regelate freeze again. XIX. f. RE- + pp. stem of L. *gelāre* freeze.

regenerate cause to be born again or reproduced. XVI. f. pp. stem of L. *regenerāre* (see RE-, GENERATE); based on earlier **regenerate** adj. (-ATE[2]) reborn, formed anew XV; spiritually reborn XVI. So **regeneration** re-creation XIV; spiritual rebirth XV. - (O)F. or L.

regent adj. presiding over disputations in a university XIV; acting as regent of a country XVI; sb. one who rules, has royal authority, etc. XV. - (O)F. *régent* or L. *regēns*, *-ent-* ruling, ruler, governor, prp. of *regere* rule; see -ENT. So **regency** office of a ruler or regent XV; body of persons acting for a sovereign; period during which a regent or regency governs XVIII. - medL. *regentia*.

regicide[1] one who kills a king. XVI. f. L. *rēx*, *rēg-* king + -CIDE[1]. So **regicide**[2] (-CIDE[2]) killing of a king. XVII.

régime †regimen of health; system of government. XVIII. - F. - L. *regimen*, f. *regere* rule. So **regimen** regulation of matters pert. to health XIV; rule, government XV; (gram.) government XVI. - L. **regiment** †rule, government; †control, management; †place under a certain rule XIV; †regimen of health; body of troops forming a unit XVI. - (O)F. *régiment* - late L. *regimentum* rule; see -MENT. Hence **regiment** vb. XVII, **regimental** adj. and sb. pl. (-AL[1]) XVIII.

region †kingdom, realm; tract of country, division of the world XIV; part or division of the air, a city, the body XVI. - (O)F. *région* - L. *regiō*, *-ōn-* direction, line, boundary, quarter, district, province, f. *regere* direct, guide, rule; see -ION. So **regional** (-AL[1]) XVII. - late L.

register[1] A. volume in which particulars are systematically entered XIV; B. slider in an organ XVI; plate for regulating the passage of air, heat, or smoke; adjustment of printing type XVII. ME. *registre*, *-estre* - (O)F. *registre*, †*regestre* or medL. *registrum*, *-estrum*, alt. of *regestum*, sg. of late L. *regesta* list, register, sb. use of n. pl. of pp. of L. *regerere* transcribe, record, f. RE- + *gerere* carry, carry out, execute; the senses under B are due to assoc. with F. *régir* guide, manage - L. *regere* guide, rule. So **register** vb. XIV. - (O)F. *régistrer* or medL. *registrāre*. **registration** XVI. - obs. F. or medL. **registry** registration XVI; place of registration; register XVII. Reduced form of *registery* (XV) - medL. *registerium*. **registrar** one who keeps a register. XVII; superseding in general Eng. use older **registrary** XVI (- medL. *registrārius*), **register**[2] XVI (app. alt. of †*registrer* (XIV) - AN. **registrere* = OF. *registreur*, medL. *registrātor*; see -ER[2]).

Regius designation of professors appointed by the Crown, instituted by Henry VIII. - L., f. *rēx*, *rēg-* king.

reglet †column of a page XVI; (archit.) narrow band separating mouldings, etc.; (typogr.) narrow strip for making white spaces XVII. - (O)F. *réglet*, also *réglette*, dim. of *règle* rule; see -ET; in archit. sense - It. *regoletto*.

regnal XVII. - medL. *regnālis*, f. *rēgnum* REIGN; see -AL[1].

regnant reigning, ruling. XVII. - L. *rēgnāns*, *-ant-*, prp. of *rēgnāre* REIGN; see -ANT.

regrate (hist.) buy up (commodities) to sell again at a profit. XV. - OF. *regrater*, supposed to be f. RE- + *grater* (mod. *gratter*) scratch (of Gmc. orig.). Hence **regrater** (-ER[1]) XIV.

regress return, re-entry. XIV. - L. *regressus*, f. pp. stem of *regredī* go back, f. RE- + *gradī* step, go, rel. to *gradus* step. So **regression** XVI. - L. Hence **regressive** XVII.

regret remember with pain or longing XIV; grieve at XVI. - (O)F. *regreter* bewail (the dead) (mod. *regretter*), with var. †*regrater*; perh. f. RE- + Gmc. **ʒrǣtan* weep, GREET[2]. So **regret** sb. †complaint, lament; sorrow, esp. for something lost. XVI. - (O)F.

regular †subject to a religious rule XIV; conforming to a rule, principle, or standard XVI. ME. *reguler* (later with ending assim. to L.) - OF. *reguler* (mod. *régulier*) - L. *rēgulāris*, f. *rēgula* RULE; see -AR. So **regularize** XVII (once; thereafter not before XIX). **regulate** (-ATE[3]) control, adjust. XVII. f. pp. stem of late L. *rēgulāre*. Hence **regulation, regulator** XVII.

regulus (astron.) bright star in Leo; †metallic antimony, app. so called from its ready combination with gold; metallic part of a mineral XVI; petty king XVII; golden-crested wren XIX. - L., dim. of *rēx*, *rēg-* king.

regurgitate gush back again XVII; cast out again XVIII. f. pp. stem of medL. *regurgitāre*, f. RE- + late L. *gurgitāre* engulf, f. *gurges*, *-git-* whirlpool. So **regurgitation** XVII. - medL.

rehabilitate restore to former status. XVI. f. pp. stem of medL. *rehabilitāre*; see HABILITATE. So **rehabilitation** XVI. - medL.

rehearse recite, relate XIII; practise the performance of XVI. - AN. *rehearser*, OF. *reherc(i)er*, perh. f. RE- + *hercer* harrow. Hence **rehearsal** (-AL[2]) recital XIV; practice *of* a play, etc. XVI.

reify convert mentally into a thing. XIX. f. L. *rēs* thing + -IFY. So **reification** XIX.

reign (arch.) royal rule, sovereignty, (poet.) sway; †kingdom, realm XIII; period of rule XIV. - OF. *reigne*, (also mod.) *règne* kingdom - L. *rēgnum*, rel. to *rēgula* RULE. So vb. XIII. - OF. *reignier* (mod. *régner*) - L. *rēgnāre*.

reimburse XVII. f. RE- + *imburse* (XVI) put into a purse, pay - medL. *imbursāre*, f. IM-[1] + *bursa* PURSE.

rein long narrow strap for guiding a horse. XIII. ME. *rene* - OF. *re(ig)ne*, *raigne*, *rainne*, etc., earlier *resne* (mod. *rêne*) :- Rom. **retina*, f. L. *retinēre* RETAIN. Hence vb. XIV.

reindeer XIV. - ON. *hreindýri*, f. *hreinn* (= OE. *hrān*) reindeer + *dýr* DEER.

reinforce strengthen with additional men XVI; also gen. XVII. alt., by analysis into RE- and *inforce*, ENFORCE, of †*renforce* (XVI) - (O)F. *renforcer*, in mil. use prob. - It. *rinforzare*.

reins (arch.) kidneys, loins. XIV. - (O)F. *reins* :- L. *rēnēs* pl. kidneys.

reinstate re-establish in a position XVI; restore to a former state XVIII. See RE-, INSTATE.

reintegrate, -ation, vars. of REDINTEGRATE, -ATION, after F. or late L. XVI.

reiterate XVI. f. L. *reiterāt-*; see RE-, ITERATE. So **reiteration** XVI. - F. or L.

reiver see REAVER.

reject refuse to have, recognize, etc. XV. f. *reject-*, pp. stem of L. *reicere* throw back, discard, f. RE- + *jacere* throw. Hence sb. †castaway XVI; thing rejected XIX. So **rejection** XVI. - F. or L.

rejoice †enjoy possession of; gladden; †refl. and intr. be joyful. XIV. ME. *reioshe*, *reioische*, *reioyse*, f. *rejoïss-*, lengthened stem of OF. *re(s)joïr*, later *réjouir*, f. RE- + *esjoïr* (*éjouir*), f. *es-* EX-[1] + *joïr* JOY vb.

rejoin[1] reply to a charge or plea XV; say in answer XVII. f. *rejoin-*, stem of (O)F. *rejoindre*; see RE-, JOIN. So **rejoinder** defendant's answer XV; answer to a reply, reply XVI. - AN. **rejoinder*, for (O)F. *rejoindre*, inf. used as sb. (see -ER[5]).

rejoin[2] join again. XVI. - (O)F. (as prec.) or f. RE- + JOIN.

rejuvenate restore to youth. XIX. irreg. f. RE- + L. *juvenis* YOUNG + -ATE[3]. So **rejuvenescence** renewal of youth. XVII. f. late L. *rejuvenēscere*. **rejuvenescent** XVIII.

-rel, -erel ME. suffix of dim. and depreciatory force, repr. OF. *-erel* (mod. *-ereau*), found first in animal names, the earliest of which is *maquerel* (XIII) MACKEREL, followed by DOGGEREL in XIV and in XV by COCKEREL, DOTTEREL, MONGREL, PICKEREL, and later KESTREL, WHIMBREL. Formations of a more general kind are SCOUNDREL, WASTREL.

relapse vb. XVI. f. *relaps-*, pp. stem of L. *relabī*, f. RE- + *labī* slip. Hence (or - F. *relaps*, medL. *relapsus*) sb. XVI.

relate give an account of XVI; (leg.) refer *back* XVI; bring into connection or comparison XVII. f. stem of L. *relātus*, functioning as pp. of *referre* REFER, but formally f. the base of *tollere* raise; see -ATE[3]. So **relation** narration XIV; connection; relative XVI. - (O)F. or L. **relative** adj. having relation *to* XVI; sb. (gram.) XIV; (gen.) XV; kinsman XVII. - (O)F. *relatif*, *-ive* or late L. *relātīvus*.

relax loosen, †lit. and fig. XV; (Sc.) free from legal restraint XVI; make less strict XVII. - L. *relaxāre*, f. RE- + *laxus* LAX. So **relaxation** remission of penalty, etc.; release from ordinary occupations XVI; diminution of firmness or strictness XVII. - L.

relay set of fresh hounds, etc. posted to take up the chase from others XV; set of fresh horses at a stage XVII; relief gang XIX; (stage of) a relay race XX. - OF. *relai* (mod. *relais*), f. *relayer* (f. RE- + *laier*, ult. repr. L. *laxāre*; see LEASE), whence or from the sb. **relay** vb. †let go (fresh hounds) XV; provide with relays XVIII.

release A. †revoke, cancel XIII; †relieve; remit (now leg.); give up, surrender XIV; B. set free XIV. ME. *reles(s)e* - OF. *relesser*, *relaiss(i)er* :- L. *relaxāre* RELAX. So sb. freeing, deliverance XIV; (leg.) conveyance of an estate XV. - OF. *reles*.

relegate send into exile XVI; consign *to* obscurity XVIII; refer for decision XIX. f. pp. stem of L. *relēgāre* send away, refer, f. RE- + *lēgāre* send; see -ATE[3].

relent †melt, dissolve XIV; grow gentle or forgiving XVI. - medL. **relentāre*, f. RE- + L. *lentāre* bend, medL. soften, f. *lentus* flexible.

relevant pertinent *to*. XVI. In earliest use Sc. and prob. of leg. orig.; not in gen. Eng. use before 1800. - medL. *relevāns, -ant-*, prp. of L. *relevāre* raise up, RELIEVE.

reliable XVI (*raliabill*, Sc.). f. RELY + -ABLE. Frequent in gen. use only since *c.* 1850. Hence **reliability** XIX.

reliance XVII. f. RELY + -ANCE. So **reliant** XIX.

relic object remaining as a memorial of a departed saint XIII; (pl.) remains XIV; surviving trace or memory XVI. ME. *relike* - (O)F. *relique*, orig. pl. - L. *reliquiæ* remains, fem. pl. of *reliquus* remaining, f. RE- + base of *linquere* leave behind.

relict †(chiefly Sc.) relic; widow; pl. remains XVI. - L. *relictus*, n. sg. *-um*, n. pl. *-a*, pp. of *relinquere* leave behind, RELINQUISH. In the sense 'widow' (in earliest use Sc.) - OF. *relicte*, late L. *relicta*.

relief[1] A. payment made to an overlord on taking possession XIV; B. alleviation of distress etc. XIV; release from occupation or duty XVI. - AN. *relef*, (O)F. *relief*, f. *relever* (tonic stem *reliev-*) RELIEVE.

relief[2] elevation of (parts of) a design from a plane surface. XVII. - F. - It. *rilievo*, f. *rilevare* raise; cf. next.

relieve assist in trouble or difficulty XIV; ease, mitigate XV; (Sc.) release XVI; (after RELIEF[1]) release from guard or watch XVII; (after RELIEF[2]) bring into relief XVIII. ME. *releve* - (O)F. *relever* :- L. *relevāre* raise again, succour, alleviate, f. RE- + *levāre* raise, f. *levis* LIGHT[2].

religion state of life (as of monks) bound by vows and a rule XII; religious order or rule; system of faith in and worship of a divine power XIII; recognition of a divine being to whom worship is due XVI. - (O)F. *religion* - L. *religiō, -ōn-* obligation (as of an oath), bond between man and the gods, scrupulousness, scruple(s), reverence for the gods; (in late L. from v) religious (monastic) life; of uncert. orig. So **religious** bound by monastic vows; imbued with religion XIII; pert. to religion XVI; sb. as pl. monks, etc. XIII, as sg. XIV. - OF. *religious* (mod. *-ieux*) - L. *religiōsus*. **religiosity** XIV. - L.

relinquish †abandon; desist from XV; resign, surrender XVI. f. *relinquiss-*, lengthened stem of OF. *relinquir* - L. *relinquere*, f. RE- + *linquere* leave; see -ISH[2].

reliquary vessel to contain relics. XVII. - (O)F. *reliquaire*, f. *relique* RELIC; see -ARY.

relish taste, flavour XVI; appetizing taste; liking, zest XVII. Later form of ME. *reles* taste (XIV), corr. formally to OF. *reles*, var. of *relais* remainder, f. *relaisser* leave behind, RELEASE, but the senses of the Eng. word are not recorded in OF. Hence **relish** vb. give a relish to; have a taste for XVI; have a certain taste XVII.

reluctant †struggling, resisting XVII; unwilling XVIII. - L. *reluctāns, -ant-*, prp. of *reluctārī* struggle against, f. RE- + *luctārī* struggle; see -ANT. Hence **reluctance, -ancy** XVII.

rely †gather together, assemble, rally (trans. and intr.) XIV; †rally *to*, trust, adhere, or be devoted *to* XIV; depend trustfully *on* XVI. - OF. *relier* :- L. *religāre* bind closely, f. RE- + *ligāre* bind.

remain be left over; continue to exist XIV; stay in a place XV; continue to be XVI. f. *remain-, remein-*, tonic stem of OF. *remanoir* :- L. *remanēre*, f. RE- + *manēre* remain; or - OF. *remaindre* :- Rom. **remanere*, for L. *remanēre*. So sb. remainder, relic, remaining member or part (now chiefly pl.). XV. Earliest instances Sc.; partly - OF. *remain*, f. *remaindre*; partly immed. f. the vb. **remainder** (leg.) residual interest of an estate XV; what is left over XVI; (math.) XVI. - AN. *remainder* = OF. *remaindre*; sb. use of inf. (see -ER[6]).

remand send back XV, spec. (a prisoner) into custody XVI. - medL. *remandāre* (in late L. send back word, repeat a command), f. RE- + *mandāre* command, send word. Hence sb. XVIII.

remanet remainder XVI; (leg.) cause of which the hearing is postponed XVIII. - L., 'there or it remains', 3rd sg. pres. ind. of *remanēre* REMAIN.

remark †distinguish, point out; take notice of; utter as an observation. XVII. - F. *remarquer*, superseding OF. *remerquier, -merchier*, prob. after It. *rimarcare*; see RE-, MARK vb. So sb. XVII. - F. *remarque*. **remarkable** XVII. - F. *remarquable*.

remedy cure for disease; redress, relief XIII; legal redress; small margin within which coins as minted are allowed to vary from the standard XV. - AN. *remedie* = (O)F. *remède* - L. *remedium* medicine, means of relief, in medL. concession, f. RE- + *med-*, stem of *medērī* heal. So **remedial** XVII. - late L. *remediālis* **remedy** vb. XV. - (O)F. *remédier* or late L. *remediāre*.

remember retain in or recall to the memory, bear in mind; (arch., dial.) remind XIV. - OF. *remembrer* :- late L. *rememorārī* call to mind, f. RE- + *memor* mindful. So **remembrance** calling to mind, recollection. XIII. - OF. **remembrancer** (-ER[1]) official responsible for collection of dues, etc. XV. - AN. *remembrauncer*.

remind †remember, recollect; put in mind *of*. XVII. f. RE- + MIND vb. Hence **reminder** (-ER[1]) XVII (rare before XIX).

reminiscence XVI. - late L. *reminiscentia*, f. *reminiscī* remember, f. RE- + **men-*; see MIND, -ENCE. So **reminiscent** XVIII. Hence by back-formation **reminisce** vb. XIX.

remise coach-house; hired carriage XVII; (fencing) second thrust made when the first has missed; (cards) XIX. - F., f. *remis*, pp. of *remettre* put back.

remiss †diluted, weak, mild; slack, lax, loose. XV. - L. *remissus*, adj. use of pp. of *remittere* slacken, relax, REMIT.

remit A. forgive (sin); abstain from exacting (a penalty) XIV. B. give up, desist from XIV. C. refer for consideration, etc. XIV; put back, XVI; put off XVII; transmit; D. intr. abate XVII. - L. *remittere* send back, slacken, relax, postpone, f. RE- + *mittere* put, send. Hence **remittance** XVIII. So

remission forgiveness XIII; remitting (*of* debt, etc.) XIV; diminution of force XVII. - (O)F. - L.

remnant (small) part remaining over. XIV. contr. of earlier *remenant* (XIII) - OF. *remenant*, sb. use of prp. of *remenoir*, *-manoir* REMAIN; see -ANT.

remonstrate †demonstrate XVI; †point out (a fault, etc.) *to*; †raise an objection *to*; urge strong reasons *against* XVII. f. pp. stem of medL. *remōnstrāre* demonstrate, f. RE- + *mōnstrāre* show; see -ATE³. So **remonstrance** †appeal XV; †demonstration XVI; formal statement of grievances XVII. - F. †*remonstrance* (mod. *remontrance*) or medL. **remonstration** XV. - obs. F. or medL.

remora sucking-fish. XVI. - L. *remora* delay, hindrance, f. RE- + *mora* delay.

remorse XIV. - OF. *remors* (mod. *remords*) - medL. *remorsus*, f. *remors-*, pp. stem of L. *remordēre* vex, torment, f. RE- + *mordere* bite.

remote XV (rare before late XVI). - L. *remōtus*, pp. of *removēre* REMOVE.

remount †set up again; replace on horseback XIV; get on horseback again XVI; supply with fresh horses XVII. In early use - (O)F. *remonter*; later in part a new formation on RE- and MOUNT².

remove move from the place occupied. XIV. ME. *remeve*, *remove* - OF. *remeuv-* and *remov-*, str. and unstr. stems respectively of *removeir* (mod. *remouvoir*) :- L. *removēre*; see RE-, MOVE. Hence **removal** (-AL²) XVI. **remove** sb. removing, removal XVI; promotion at school from one division or class to another, (hence) title of a class or form XVIII.

remunerate XVI. f. pp. stem of L. *remūnerārī* (later *-āre*), f. RE- + *mūnerāre*, *-ārī*, f. *mūnus*, *mūner-* gift, reward; see -ATE³. So **remuneration** XV. - F. or L.

renaissance 'revival of learning' in Europe beginning in Italy in the 14th century. XIX. - F., f. RE- + *naissance* birth (:- L. *nāscentia*, f. *nāscī* be born; or f. *naiss-*, pres. stem of *naître* :- Rom. **nascere*); see -ANCE. So **renascence** rebirth, renewal XVIII; as substitution for *renaissance* XIX. f. **renascent** XVIII (- L. *renāscēns*, *-ent-*, prp. of *renāscī*).

renal XVII. - F. *rénal* - late L. *rēnālis*, f. L. *rēnēs* kidneys; see -AL¹.

rend pt., pp. *rent* tear apart. OE. *rendan* = OFris. *renda*.

render A. †repeat, recite XIV; give in return XV; give *back*; represent, reproduce XVI; B. hand over, give up, surrender XIV; submit (an account, etc.) XV; give, pay XVI; C. bring into a specified state XV; D. melt XIV; give a first coating of plaster XVIII. - (O)F. *rendre* :- Rom. **rendere*, alt. of L. *reddere* give back, give up, recite, represent, imitate, make to be or appear, f. RED- + *dare* give.

rendezvous place for the assembling of troops; place of meeting. XVI. - F. *rendez-vous*, sb. use of *rendez-vous* present or betake yourselves, imper. pl. of *se rendre*, refl. of *rendre* RENDER. Hence as vb. XVII.

rendition surrender XVII; translation, rendering XVII; performance XIX. - F. †*rendition*, f. *rendre* RENDER; see -ITION.

renegade apostate XVI; deserter of a cause, etc. XVII. Anglicization of **renegado** (much used XVI-XVIII) - Sp. - medL. *renegātus*, sb. use of pp. of *renegāre*; see next and -ADE, -ADO.

renegue deny, renounce; refuse XVI; revoke at cards XVII. - medL. *renegāre*, f. RE- + L. *negāre* DENY.

renew XIV. f. RE- + NEW. Hence **renewal** (-AL²) XVII.

rennet curdled milk in a calf's stomach, preparation used in curdling milk for cheese. XV. prob. south-eastern repr. of an OE. **rynet* (f. **run-* RUN) and corr. to (dial.) *runnet* (XV).

renounce XIV. - (O)F. *renoncer* - L. *renuntiāre* announce, proclaim, protest against, f. RE- + *nuntiāre* bring news, report. So **renunciation** XIV. - (O)F. or L.

renovate XVI. f. pp. stem of L. *renovāre*, f. RE- + *novāre* make new, f. *novus* NEW. So **renovation** XV. - F. or L.

renown XIV. - AN. *reno(u)n*, OF. *renon*, *renom*, f. *renomer* make famous, f. RE- + *nomer* name (:- L. *nōmināre* NOMINATE). Hence **renowned** XIV (see -ED¹).

rent¹ †source of income XII; †revenue; †tax; payment made by tenant to landlord XIII. - (O)F. *rente* :- Rom. **rendita*, f. **rendere* RENDER. So vb. †endow XIV; pay rent for XVI. - (O)F. *renter*. **rental** (-AL¹) †rent-roll XIV; amount of rent XVII. - AN. *rental* or AL. *rentāle*.

rent² tear in a piece of stuff. XVI. f. (dial.) *rent* tear, rend (XIV), var. of REND based on pt., pp. *rent*.

rentier one who derives his income from property or investments. XIX. - F., f. *rente* revenue, RENT¹ + *-ier* -ER².

rep¹ textile fabric with corded surface. XIX. - F. *reps*, of unkn. orig.

rep² (1) abbrev. of *representative* XIX; (2) abbrev. of *repertory* (*theatre*, etc.) XX.

repair¹ betake oneself, resort. XIV. - OF. *repair(i)er* (mod. *repairer*, *repérer*) :- late L. *repatriāre* return to one's country; see REPATRIATE. So **repair** sb.¹ (place of) resort. XIV. - OF. *repaire*, *repeire* (mod. *repaire*, *repère*).

repair² †adorn; restore to sound condition. XIV. - (O)F. *réparer* - L. *reparāre*, f. RE- + *parāre* make ready, put in order. Hence **repair** sb.² act of restoring to sound condition, etc. XVI. So **reparable** XVI. - F. **reparation** action of repairing XIV; amends XV. - (O)F. - late L.

repand (nat. hist.) undulating, wavy. XVIII. - L. *repandus* bent backwards, f. RE- + *pandus* bent.

repartee XVII. - (O)F. *repartie*, sb. use of fem. pp. of *repartir* set out again, reply readily, f. RE- + *partir* PART.

repast XIV. - OF. *repast* (mod. *repas*), f. *repaistre* (mod. *repaitre*) feed :- late L. *repascere*, after OF. *past* (:- L. *pastus* fodder, food); see RE-, PASTURE.

repatriate XVII. f. pp. stem of late L. *repatriāre* go back home, in medL. causative, f. RE- + *patria* native land, sb. use of *patrius*, f. *pater* FATHER; see -ATE³. So **repatriation** XVI. - medL.

repay XVI. - OF. *repaier*; see RE-, PAY¹. So **repayment** XIV.

repeal vb. XIV. - AN. *repeler*, for OF. *rapeler*

(mod. *rappeler*), f. RE- + *appeler* APPEAL. So sb. XV. - AN. *repel*.

repeat A. say again XIV; say over, recite; say *after* another XVI; B. return to, undergo again XV; do or perform again XVI. ME. *repete* - (O)F. *répéter* - L. *repetere*, f. RE- + *petere* aim at, seek. Hence sb. †repeated word(s), refrain XV; repetition XVI. So **repetition** XVI. - (O)F. or L. **repetitious** XVII, **repetitive** XIX.

repel XV. - L. *repellere*, f. RE- + *pellere* drive. So **repellent** XVII.

repent refl. and intr. feel contrition XIII; tr. be sorry for XIV. - (O)F. *repentir*, f. RE- + OF. *pentir* :- Rom. **pænitīre*, for L. *pænitēre*; cf. PENITENT. So **repentant** XIII, **-ance** XIV. - (O)F.

repercussion †repulsion, repulse, recoil; reverberation. XVI. - (O)F. or L.; see RE-, PERCUSSION. So **repercussive** (med.) repellent XIV; reverberating XVI.

repertory †index, list; storehouse, repository XVI; (after F. *répertoire*) stock of dramatic pieces XIX. - late L. *repertōrium*, f. *repert-*, pp. stem of L. *reperīre* find; see -ORY[1].

repine feel or show discontent. XVI. f. RE- + PINE[2].

replace restore to a former place XVI; fill the place of XVIII. f. RE- + PLACE vb.

replenish A. (obs. or arch.) fill or stock abundantly XIV; B. fill up again XVII. f. *repleniss-*, lengthened stem of OF. *replenir*, f. RE- + *plenir*, f. *plein* :- L. *plēnus* FULL; see -ISH[2].

replete XIV. - (O)F. *replet*, fem. *-ète*, or L. *replētus*, pp. of *replēre* fill. So **repletion** XIV. - (O)F. or late L.

replevin (writ for) recovery by a person of goods or chattels taken from him. XV. - AN., f. OF. *replevir* recover (whence **replevy** XVI), f. RE- + *plevir* pledge.

replica XIX. - It., f. *replicare* reply.

replication reply, rejoinder. XIV. - OF. *replicacion* - L. *replicātiō*, *-ōn-* folding back, repetition, legal reply, f. pp. stem of *replicāre* unfold, reflect on, reply, f. RE- + *plicāre* fold. So **reply** answer, respond. XIV (whence **reply** sb. XVI). - OF. *replier* turn back, reply (in this sense repl. by *repliquer*) :- L. *replicāre*.

report rumour XIV; account of a matter XV; †musical response, note; resounding noise XVI. - OF., f. *reporter* :- L. *reportāre* carry back, bear away (spec. an account), f. RE- + *portāre* carry. So vb. XIV. - OF. *reporter*. **reporter** (-ER[2]) XIV. - OF. *reporteur*.

repose[1] †replace XV; place (trust, etc.) *in* XVI. f. RE- + POSE[1], after L. *repōnere*.

repose[2] rest, tr. XV, intr. XVI. - (O)F. *reposer*, earlier *repauser* :- late L. *repausāre*, f. RE- + *pausāre* PAUSE. So **repose** sb. rest. XVI. f. the vb. or - (O)F. *repos*.

repository vessel or chamber for storage of things XV; storehouse (fig.) XVII; warehouse, mart XVIII. - F. †*repositoire* or L. *repositorium*, f. *reposit-*, pp. stem of *repōnere* replace, store away; see REPOSE[1], -ORY[1].

repoussé beaten into relief. XIX. - F., pp. of *repousser*, f. RE- + *pousser* PUSH.

reprehend XIV. - L. *reprehendere*, f. RE- + *prehendere* seize. So **reprehensible** XIV. - late L. **reprehension** XIV. - L.

represent †bring into one's presence; bring before the mind; display to the eye; symbolize; XIV; stand in place of XV; speak for, as in parliament XVII. - (O)F. *représenter* or L. *repræsentāre*, f. RE- + *præsentāre* PRESENT. So **representation** †presence, †appearance, likeness XV; presentation to the eye, mind, etc. XVI. - (O)F. or L. **representative** adj. XIV; sb. XVII. - (O)F. or medL.

repress XIV. f. *repress-*, pp. stem of L. *reprimere*; see RE-, PRESS. So **repression** XIV. - late L.

reprieve †send back *to* prison; †postpone; delay the punishment of. XVI. First in pp. *reprived*, unexpl. alt. of earlier *repryed* (*to prison*) - AN., OF. *repris*, pp. of *reprendre*, f. RE- + *prendre* take. Hence sb. XVI.

reprimand XVII. - F. *réprimande*, †*-ende* - Sp. *reprimenda* - L. *reprimenda*, n. pl. of gerundive of *reprimere* REPRESS. So vb. XVII. - F. *réprimander*.

reprisal seizing of property in retaliation or by way of indemnity XV; (esp. pl.) act of retaliation in warfare XVIII. - AN. *reprisaille* - medL. *repræsāliæ*, *-ālia*, contr. of *repræ(h)ēnsāliæ*, *-ia*, f. *repræhēns-*, pp. stem of L. *repræhendere*, f. RE- + *præhendere* take; see -AL[2].

reproach cast up (a thing) *against* a person XV; upbraid XVI. - OF. *reprochier* (mod. *reprocher*) :- Rom. **repropiāre* 'bring back near', f. RE- + *prope* near. So sb. XV. - (O)F. *reproche*.

reprobate rejected by God; of abandoned character; also sb. XVI. - late L. *reprobātus*, pp. of *reprobāre* disapprove, f. RE- + *probāre* approve, PROVE. So vb. disapprove of XV; reject, cast off XVI. f. pp. stem of L. *reprobāre*; see -ATE[3]. **reprobation** XV. - (O)F. or late L.

reproduce create anew XVII; repeat in a copy, etc. XIX. f. RE- + PRODUCE vb. So **reproduction** XVII.

reproof †shame; †insult; censure. XIV. ME. *reprove*, *reprof(e)* - OF. *reprove*, f. *reprover* - late L. *reprobāre* disapprove; cf. PROOF, REPROBATE. So **reprove** †reject; censure; reprehend. XIV. - OF. *reprover* (mod. *réprouver*).

reptile creeping animal XIV (rare before XVII); mean person XVIII. - (O)F. *reptile* or late L. (Vulg.) *reptile*, n. of late L. *reptilis*, f. *rept-*, pp. stem of *repere* creep, crawl; see -ILE. Also adj. XVII. So **reptilian**, f. **reptilia** (zool.) XVII (-IA[2]).

republic †state, common weal; state in which the supreme power resides in the people. XVII. - F. *république* - L. *rēspublica*, f. *rēs* affair, thing + fem. of *publicus* PUBLIC. Hence **republican** †pert. to the commonwealth; pert. to (sb. advocate of) a republic XVII; whence **republicanism** XVII.

repudiate put away (a wife); reject XVI; (orig. U.S.) refuse to acknowledge (a debt, etc.) XIX. f. pp. stem of L. *repudiāre*, f. *repudium* divorce; see -ATE[3]. So **repudiation** XVI. - L.

repugnant contrary or contradictory *to* XIV; distasteful *to* XVIII. - F. *répugnant* or L. *repugnāns*, *-ant-*, prp. of *repugnāre* (whence **repugn** be contrary, oppose XIV), f. RE- + *pugnāre* fight; see -ANT.

repulse driving back; refusal, rejection. XVI. - L. *repulsus, repulsa,* f. pp. stem of *repellere* REPEL. So vb. XVI. **repulsion** †repudiation XV; act of repelling XVI; feeling of being repelled XVIII. - late L. **repulsive** XVI. - (O)F. *répulsif, -ive,* or f. *repulse* vb.

reputation †opinion, estimation; †general estimate; high esteem or credit. XIV. - L. *reputātiō, -ōn-* computation, consideration, f. *reputāre,* f. RE- + *putāre* reckon; see -ATION. So **repute** consider, esteem. XV. - (O)F. *réputer* or L. *reputāre.* Hence **repute** †estimate; reputation (in neutral sense) XVI; (in favourable sense) XVII.

request sb. XIV. - OF. *requeste* :- Rom. **requæsita,* sb. use of fem. pp. of L. *requærere* REQUIRE. So vb. XVI. f. the sb. or - OF. *requester.*

requiem Mass for the departed. XIV. - L. *requiem,* acc. of *requiēs* rest, first word of the introit of the Mass, '*Requiem* æternam dona eis, Domine' Rest eternal grant unto them, O Lord; see RE-, QUIET.

require XIV. ME. *requere, require* - OF. *requer-, requier-,* stem of *requere* (now refash. *requérir*) :- Rom. **requærere,* for L. *requīrere,* f. RE- + *quærere* seek, ask. Assim. to the L. form. So **requisite** adj. XV; sb. XVII. - L. *requisītus,* pp. of *requīrere.* **requisition** sb. XVI. - (O)F. or L.; hence vb. XIX. **requite** XVI. f. RE- + *quite,* var. of QUIT²; hence **requital** (-AL²) XVI.

reredos ornamental screen at the back of an altar; (hist.) back of a fireplace. XIV. - AN. **reredos,* aphetic of OF. *areredos,* f. *arere* behind + *dos* back.

rescind †take away, remove; abrogate, cancel. XVII. - L. *rescindere,* f. RE- + *scindere* cut or tear asunder.

rescript decretal epistle from the Pope in reply to a question; edict, decree. XVI. - L. *rescriptum* imperial decision, sb. use of n. of pp. *rescriptus* of *rescrībere* reply in writing to a petition, etc., f. RE- + *scrībere* write.

rescue vb. XIV. ME. *rescowe, reskewe* - *rescou-, reskeu-,* stem of OF. *rescoure, reskeure* (mod. *recourre*) :- Rom. **reexcutere,* f. RE- + *excutere* shake out, discard, f. EX-¹ + *quatere* shake. Hence sb. XIV.

research intensive searching XVI; investigation directed towards discovery XVII. - OF. *recerche* (now *recherche*). So vb. XVI. - OF. *recercher.* See RE-, SEARCH.

reseda genus of plants including mignonette. XVIII. - L. *resēda,* of uncert. orig. (acc. to Pliny, f. imper. of *resēdāre* assuage, allay, with ref. to the plant's supposed curative powers).

resemble be like; †compare XIV. - OF. *resembler* (mod. *ressembler*), f. RE- + *sembler* seem :- L. *similāre,* f. *similis* like. So **resemblance** XIV. - AN.

resent orig. †refl. feel pain; show strong feeling; trans. †feel deeply or painfully; feel oneself injured by, show displeasure at. XVII. - F. †*resentir,* now *ressentir,* f. RE- + *sentir* feel. So **resentment** XVII. - F. †*resentiment,* now *ress-.*

reserve keep for future use; keep or set apart. XIV. - (O)F. *réserver* - L. *reservāre,* f. RE- + *servāre* keep, save. Hence sb. A. something reserved; (mil., pl. and sg.) force(s) kept in reserve (whence **reservist** XIX) XVII; B. self-restraint XVII. So **reservation** XIV. - (O)F. or late L.

reservoir capacious receptacle for storage, also fig. XVII; reserve supply XVIII. - F. *réservoir,* f. *réserver* RESERVE + *-oir* = -ORY¹.

reside †take up one's abode XV; dwell permanently XVI; be vested or inherent *in* XVII. perh. orig. back-formation from *resident,* but later infl. immed. by F. *résider* and L. *residēre.* So **residence** act or fact of residing XIV; place of residence XVI. - (O)F. or medL. **resident** residing XIV; sb. XV. - (O)F. *résident* or L. *residēns, -ent-,* prp. of *residēre* remain behind, rest, f. RE- + *sedēre* settle, SIT. **residentiary** one bound to official residence XVI; adj. XVII. - medL.

residue XIV. - (O)F. *résidu* - L. *residuum,* sb. use of n. of *residuus* remaining, f. *residēre* remain, RESIDE; see -UOUS. Hence **residual** (-AL¹) XVI. So **residuum** XVII. - L.

resign give up, surrender, abandon XIV; intr. XV. - (O)F. *résigner* - L. *resignāre* unseal, cancel, give up, f. RE- + *signāre* SIGN. So **resignation** XIV. - (O)F. - medL.

resile draw back, shrink, recoil. XVI. - F. †*resilir* or L. *resilīre* leap back, recoil, f. RE- + *salīre* leap. So **resilient** (whence **resilience** XVII) XVII. - L. *resiliēns, -ent-* prp.

resin, rosin adhesive substance secreted by plants. XIV. ME. *recyn, resyn, rosyn, rosine* - L. *resīna* and medL. *rosīna,* of unkn. orig. So **resinous** XVII. - F. - L.

resist XIV. - (O)F. *résister* or L. *resistere,* f. RE- + *sistere* stop, redupl. formation on *stāre* STAND. So **resistance** XV. - F. *résistance.*

resolute †determinate, absolute; of fixed resolve. XV. - L. *resolūtus,* pp. of *resolvere.* So **resolution** †dissolution; resolving into components XIV; decision, determination XVI. - L., f. *resolvere* (f. RE- + *solvere* SOLVE), whence **resolve** †dissolve (trans. and intr.) XIV; †soften, slacken XV; separate *into*; answer; solve; determine; †assure XVI; hence sb. XVI.

resonance XV. - F. †*reson(n)ance* (mod. *résonnance*) - L. *resonantia* echo, f. prp. stem of *resonāre* RESOUND. So **resonant** XVI. - (O)F. *résonnant.*

resort †return, revert XIV; betake oneself, repair or proceed *to* XV. - (O)F. *resortir* (mod. *ressortir*), f. RE- + *sortir* go out, of unkn. orig. So sb. XIV. - (O)F. *ressort.*

resound XIV. ME. *resoune,* f. RE- + *soune* SOUND³ vb.

resource XVII. - F. *ressource,* †*-ourse,* sb. use of fem. pp. of OF. (dial.) *resourdre* rise again, recover :- L. *resurgere.*

respect relation, reference XIV; relationship XV; discriminating or deferential regard XVI. - (O)F. *respect* or L. *respectus,* f. pp. stem of *respicere* look (back) at, regard, consider, f. RE- + *specere* look. So **respect** vb. regard; refer or relate to. XVI. f. *respect-,* pp. stem of L. *respicere,* or its frequent. deriv. *respectāre.* In prp. *respecting* passing into prep. XVIII. Hence **respectable** XVI. So **respective** XVI. - F. or medL.

respire †(rare) come up to breathe XIV; breathe again, recover XV; breathe (trans. and intr.) XVI. - (O)F. *respirer* or L. *respīrāre,* f. RE-

+*spīrāre* breathe; see SPIRIT. So **respiration** XV. - F. or L. Hence **respirator** XVIII.

respite delay or extension of time XIII; temporary cessation of labour, etc. XIV. - OF. *respit* (mod. *répit*) :- L. *respectus* RESPECT. So vb. grant respite to or delay of. XIV. - OF. *respitier* :- L. *respectāre*.

resplendent XV. - L. *resplendēns*, *-ent-*, prp. of *resplendēre*, f. RE- + *splendēre* shine; see -ENT.

respond (liturg.) responsory XIV; response to a versicle XVI. - OF., f. *respondre* (mod. *répondre*) :- Rom. **respondere*, for L. *respondēre* answer to an engagement, f. RE- + *spondēre* make a solemn engagement. So **respond** vb. answer. XVI. - L. *respondēre*. **respondent** one who defends a thesis; (leg.) defendant. XVI. **response** answer, reply XIV; (liturg.) verse corresponding to a versicle XVII (earlier, responsory XV). - OF. *respons* (mod. *répons*) or *response* (mod. *réponse*) or L. *responsum* (pl. *-a*), f. pp. of *respondēre*. **responsible** †corresponding *to* XVI; answerable *to* another *for* something; reliable XVII. - F. †*responsible*. **responsive** responding, corresponding. XVI. - F. *responsif*, *-ive*, or late L. **responsory** (-ORY[1]) (liturg.) anthem to be recited antiphonally after a lesson. XV. - late L. *responsōrium*.

rest[1] A. relief from activity by sleep, intermission of labour, repose of body or mind OE.; repose of death XIV; (mus.) XVI. B. (from the vb.) support for a fire-arm XVI; gen. support XVII. OE. *ræst*, *rest* repose, bed, corr. to OS. *rasta* place of rest, OHG. *rasta* rest, league (G. *rast*), ON. *rǫst*, Goth. *rasta* mile (as a distance after which one rests). So **rest** vb.[1] take or be at rest; remain OE.; give rest to XIII. OE. *ræstan*, *restan* = OHG. *resten*, *rastōn* (G. *rasten*). Hence **restful** XIV, **restless** OE. *restlēas*.

rest[2] †remainder, remnant; †sum remaining over (XV; reserve fund of a bank XIX); remaining part, number, members XVI. - (O)F. *reste*, f. *rester* (whence **rest** vb.[2] remain so-and-so) - L. *restāre*, f. RE- + *stāre* STAND.

rest[3] in medieval armour, contrivance fixed to the cuirass to receive the butt-end of a lance. XIV. Aphetic of ARREST sb.

restaurant XIX. - F., sb. use of prp. of *restaurer* RESTORE; see -ANT. So **restaurateur** XVIII.

restitution action of giving back XIII; restoration to a former state XIV; tendency to resume a previous position XVII. - (O)F. *restitution* or L. *restitūtio*, *-ōn-*, f. *restituere* restore, f. RE- + *statuere* set up, establish; see -TION.

restive †inactive, inert XVI; †obstinate in opinion or action; refusing to move or follow a course, resisting control XVII. Later form (by assim. to -IVE) of †*restif* (XV) - OF. *restif* (mod. *rétif*) :- Rom. **restīvus* 'inclined to remain stationary', f. *restāre* REST vb.[2]

restore give back; build up again; reinstate; renew, re-establish XIII; bring back *to* an earlier condition XIV. - OF. *restorer* (mod. *restaurer*) :- L. *restaurāre*; see RE-, STORE vb. So **restoration** action of restoring; (*R*-) re-establishment of the monarchy in England in 1660. XVII. Later form (assim. to the vb.) of *restauration* (XIV) - (O)F. or late L. **restorative** adj. and sb. XIV. var. of †*restaurative* (XIV) - OF. *restauratif*, *-ive*.

restrain XIV. - OF. *restrei(g)n-*, *-ai(g)n-*, pres. stem of *restreindre*, *restraindre* :- L. *restringere* bind fast, confine, f. RE- + *stringere* draw tight. So **restraint** XV. - (O)F. *restreinte*, f. pp. of *restreindre*.

restrict XVI. f. *restrict-*, pp. stem of L. *restringere* confine; see prec. So **restriction** XV, **restrictive** XIV. - (O)F. or late L.

result arise as a consequence or effect. XV. - medL. fig. use of L. *resultāre* spring back, reverberate, re-echo, f. RE- + *saltāre* leap. Hence sb. (now U.S.) decision, resolution; effect, consequence of action, etc. XVII. So **resultant** †shining by reflection; resulting XVII; sb. †mathematical result XV; composite effect of forces XIX. - prp. of the L. vb.

resume XV. - (O)F. *résumer* or L. *resūmere*, f. RE- + *sūmere* take. So **resumption** XV. - (O)F. or late L. **résumé** XIX. - F., sb. use of pp. of *résumer*.

resurge rise again. XVI. - L. *resurgere*; see RE-, SURGE vb. So **resurgent** (see -ENT) XVIII.

resurrection rising again of Jesus Christ from the dead or of all men at the Last Day. XIII. - (O)F. *résurrection* - late L. *resurrēctiō*, *-ōn-*, f. pp. stem of L. *resurgere*; see prec. and -TION. Hence, by back-formation, **resurrect** vb. XVIII.

resuscitate XVI. f. pp. stem of L. *resuscitāre*, f. RE- + *suscitāre* raise, revive, f. *sus-* SUB- + *citāre* put in motion, excite; see -ATE[3]. So **resuscitation** XVI. - late L.

ret soak (flax, etc.) in water. XV. The E. Angl. forms *ret(t)en* corr. to MDu. *reeten*, (also mod.) *reten*; but the north. forms *ra(y)te* point to an ON. **reyta*; rel. to ROT.

retable reredos, shelf or ledge at the back of an altar. XIX. - F. *rétable*, *retable* - Sp. *retablo* - medL. **retabulum*, for *retrotabulum* (XIII) 'structure at the back of an altar-table', f. L. RETRO- + *tabula* TABLE.

retail the sale of (commodities) in small quantities XIV; attrib. XVII. - AN. **retaille*, spec. use of OF. *retaille* piece cut off, shred, f. *retaillier*, f. RE- + *taillier* cut. This use, which is not in F., is prob. of It. orig. So **retail** vb. sell by retail XIV; recount XVI. Hence **retailer** (-ER[1]) XV.

retain †restrain XIV; keep hold or possession of, keep in one's service; keep in mind XV; keep attached to one XVI. - AN. *retei(g)n-*, repr. tonic stem of OF. *retenir* :- Rom. **retenēre*, for L. *retinēre*, f. RE- + *tenēre* hold. Hence **retainer**[1] (-ER[5]) (authorization of) retaining for oneself XV; fee for retaining a barrister's services XIX. **retainer**[2] (-ER[1]) maintainer, preserver; dependant on a person of rank. XVI. So **retention** XIV. - (O)F. or L. **retentive** XIV. - (O)F. or medL.

retaliate XVII. f. pp. stem of L. *retaliāre*, f. RE- + *tālis* of such a kind; see -ATE[3]. Hence **retaliation** XVI, **retaliatory** (-ORY[2]) XIX.

retard XV. - (O)F. *retarder* :- L. *retardāre*, f. RE- + *tardus* slow. So **retardation** XV. - (O)F. or L.

retch hawk in the throat XVI; make efforts to vomit XIX. var. of REACH[2].

reticence maintenance of silence. XVII (rare

before XIX). - L. *reticentia*, f. *reticēre* keep silence, f. RE- + *tacēre* be silent. So **reticent** XIX. - L. *reticēns, -ent-*.

reticular resembling or constructed like a net. XVI. f. L. *rēticulum* RETICULE; see -AR. So **reticulate** adj. (-ATE[2]) XVII. - L. Hence **reticulate** vb. (-ATE[3]), **reticulated** XVIII.

reticule reticulate structure used in a microscope XVIII; small bag used as a pocket or workbag XIX. - F. *réticule* - L. *rēticulum* network bag, omentum, dim. of *rēte* net; see -CULE.

retina XIV. - medL., perh. f. L. *rēte* net.

retinue †retention in service; company of persons retained in one's service. XIV. - OF. *retenue*, sb. use of fem. pp. of *retenir* RETAIN.

retire draw back, withdraw. XVI. - (O)F. *retirer*, f. RE- + *tirer* draw. Hence **retiral** (-AL[2]) XVII, **retirement** XVI.

retort[1] repay, requite; cast back (a charge, etc.) XVI; reply in kind to XVII. f. *retort-*, pp. stem of L. *retorquēre*, f. RE- + *torquēre* twist. Hence sb. XVI.

retort[2] vessel with a long neck used for distillation. XVII. - F. *retorte* - medL. *retorta*, sb. use of fem. pp. of L. *retorquēre* (see prec.).

retract[1] draw back XV; †restrain, withdraw XVI. f. *retract-*, pp. stem of L. *retrahere*, f. RE- + *trahere* draw.

retract[2] recall, revoke XVI; intr. XVII. - (O)F. *rétracter* or L. *retractāre*, f. RE- + *tractāre*, frequent. of *trahere* draw. So **retractation** (pl.) title of a work of St. Augustine containing further treatment and correction of former works XV; recantation XVI; withdrawal from an engagement XVII. - L. *retractātiō, -ōn-*. **retraction** XIV (rare before XVI). - L. *retractiō, -ōn-*.

retreat (mil.) signal to retire XIV; act of retiring in the face of danger, etc.; withdrawal into privacy; place of seclusion XV. Late ME. *retret* - OF. *retret*, etc., vars. of *retraite*, sb. uses of m. and fem. pps. of *retraire* :- L. *retrahere* RETRACT[1]. So vb. retire XV; †retract, revoke XVI. - OF. *retraitier* - L. *retractāre* RETRACT[2].

retrench †cut short, repress; cut down, reduce; also intr. XVII. - F. †*retrencher*, early form of *retrancher*; see RE-, TRENCH vb. So **retrenchment** XVII. - F. Both words are earlier used in fortif. (XVI) for inner line of defence.

retribution recompense, requital XIV; recompense *for* evil XVI. - ChrL. *retribūtiō, -ōn-*, f. L. *retribuere*, f. RE- + *tribuere* assign; see -TION. Hence **retributive** XVII (rare before XIX).

retrieve †(of dogs) find again (game that has been lost) XV; recover, regain XVI; bring in (killed or wounded game) XIX. ME *retreve* - OF. *retroev-, -euv-*, tonic stem of *retrover* (mod. *retrouver*), f. RE- + *trover* find. Hence **retriever** (-ER[1]) †dog used to set up game again XV; breed of dog adapted for recovering game XIX.

retro- pref. repr. L. *retrō-* adv. ('behind') used in combination as in *retrospicere* (cf. RETROSPECT), *retrogradus* (see next), f. RE- + compar. suffix as in *intrō-* INTRO-; in anat. and path. denoting 'situated behind' the part of the body indicated by the second el., as *retro-ocular, -uterine*.

retrograde (astron., of planets) moving apparently in a direction contrary to the order of the signs XIV; tending or inclined to go backwards XVI. - L. *retrōgradus*, f. RETRO- + *gradus* step. So vb. XVI. - L. *retrōgradī*, later *retrōgradāre*. **retrogradation** XVI. - late L. Hence **retrogression** XVII.

retrospect regard or reference *to* some fact, etc.; survey of the past. XVII. f. *retrōspect-*, pp. stem of L. *retrōspicere* look back. So **retrospection, retrospective** XVII.

retroussé (of the nose) turned up at the end. XIX. - F., pp. of *retrousser*, f. RE- + *trousser* turn up, TRUSS.

return come or go back, lit. and fig. XIV; turn, bring, or send back XV; give back, render XVI. - OF. *retorner, returner* (mod. *retourner*) - Rom. **retornāre*; see RE-, TURN. So sb. XIV. - AN. *retorn, return*.

reunion coming together again. XVII. - F. *réunion*, f. *réunir* reunite. So **reunite** XVI. See RE-, UNION, UNITE.

reveal[1] disclose in a supernatural manner XIV; divulge by discourse, etc. XV; make visible XVI. - (O)F. *révéler* or L. *revēlāre*, f. RE- + *vēlum* VEIL. So **revelation** XIV. - (O)F. or ChrL.

reveal[2] side of an opening or recess at right angles to the face of a work. XVII (*revale*). f. †*revale* lower, bring down - OF. *revaler*, f. RE- + *avaler* lower.

reveille morning signal given to soldiers. XVII (*revelley, revalley*). - F. *réveillez*, imper. pl. of *réveiller* awaken, f. RE- + *veiller* :- L. *vigilāre* keep watch.

revel vb. XIV. - OF. *reveler* (refl.) rebel, rejoice noisily :- L. *rebellāre* REBEL. So sb. XIV.

revenge refl. (XIV), pass. (XV) take vengeance; exact retribution for XV. In earliest use Sc. - OF. *revenger*, var. of *revencher* (mod. *revancher*) :- late L. *revindicāre*, f. RE- + L. *vindicāre* VENGE. Hence sb. XVI.

revenue †yield or profit *of* property; income from possessions XV; (annual) income gen.; department of the civil service dealing with national funds XVII. - (O)F. *revenu*, †*revenue*, m. and fem. pp. of *revenir* :- L. *revenīre* return, f. RE- + *venīre* COME.

reverberate †beat or drive back; re-echo; also intr. XVI. f. pp. stem of L. - *reverberāre*, f. RE- + *verberāre* strike, beat, f. *verbera* rods, scourge. So **reverberation** XIV (rare before XVI). - (O)F. or late L. Hence **reverberatory** (furnace) so constructed that the flame is forced back upon the substance exposed to it. XVII.

revere XVII. - F. *révérer* or L. *reverērī*, f. RE- + *verērī* feel awe of, fear. So **reverence** deep respect XIII; gesture indicative of this; condition of being revered; as a title XIV. - (O)F. *révérence* - L. *reverentia*. So **reverence** vb. XIV. - AN. *reverencer*; cf. modF. *révérencier*. **reverend** worthy of reverence (spec. as an epithet of respect) XV. - (O)F. *révérend* or L. *reverendus*, gerundive of *reverērī*. **reverent** †reverend XIV; deeply respectful XV. In first sense - OF. *reverent* or after medL. *reverentissimus* most reverend (of bishops); in second sense - L. *reverēns, -ent-*. **reverential** XVI. - F. †*reverencial, révérentiel* or medL. **reverentiālis*.

reverie †wild delight, violent or riotous action

XIV; †fanciful idea; abstracted musing XVII. In ME. - OF. *reverie* rejoicing, revelry, wildness, f. *rever* revel, act or speak wildly (mod. *rêver* †talk in delirium, dream), of unkn. orig. In XVII-XVIII (often *resverie*) - later F. *resverie*, now *rêverie*; see -ERY.

reverse opposite, contrary XIV (thereafter not till XVIII); mil. commanding the rear XVIII. - OF. *revers(e)* - L. *reversus, -a*, pp. of *revertere* turn back, etc., f. RE- + *vertere* turn. So sb. A. contrary XIV (thereafter not till XVIII); back of a coin, etc. XVII. B. †back-handed stroke XV; adverse change of fortune XVI. - (O)F. *revers* or †*reverse* - sb. uses of the L. pp. **reverse** vb. (whence **reversal** (-AL²) XV) †bring, send, etc. back; †overthrow; invert, turn the other way. XIV. - OF. *reverser* (now *ren-*) - late L. *reversāre*. **reversion** (leg.) return of an estate; right of succession. XV. - (O)F. or L. **revert** †recover consciousness XIII; return, go back XIV. - OF. *revertir* or L. *revertere*.

revetment (fortif.) retaining wall supporting the face of a rampart. XVIII. - F. *revêtement*, f. *revêtir* (whence **revet** XIX) - late L. *revestīre*, f. RE- + *vestīre* clothe; see -MENT.

review revision; formal inspection XVI; general survey or account XVII. - F. *reveue*, now *revue*, f. *revoir*, f. RE- + *voir* see :- L. *vidēre*. So or hence vb. †inspect again; revise, survey XVI; etc.; after F. *revoir*.

revile XIV. - OF. *reviler*, f. RE- + *vil* VILE.

revise †look *at* or behold again; read over again. XVI. - (O)F. *réviser*, †*reviser* or L. *revīsere*, f. RE- + *vīsere* VISIT, examine. Hence sb. review, revision XVI; revised form of proof-sheet XVII. **revisal** (-AL²) XVII. So **revision** XVII. - (O)F. or late L.

revive XV. - (O)F. *revivre* or late L. *revīvere*, f. RE- + *vīvere* live; the causative meaning, which has developed in Eng., corr. to the uses of F. *raviver*. Hence **revival** (-AL²) XVII; whence **revivalism, -ist** XIX.

revoke †bring back, recall; annul, cancel XIV; (at cards) fail improperly to follow suit XVI. - (O)F. *révoquer* or L. *revocāre*, f. RE- + *vocāre* call. So **revocation** XV.

revolt cast off allegiance XVI; affect with disgust XVIII (prp. adj. *revolting* XIX). - F. (*se*) *révolter* - It. *rivoltare* (refl. *-arsi*) - Rom. **revolvitāre*, intensive of L. *revolvere* REVOLVE. So **revolt** sb. XVI. - F. *révolte* - It. *rivolta*.

revolution moving of a celestial body in an orbit XIV; complete change of affairs or reversal of conditions XV; overthrow of established government XVI. - (O)F. *révolution* or late L. *revolūtiō, -ōn-*, f. pp. stem of *revolvere* REVOLVE; see -TION. Hence **revolutionary, revolutionize** XVIII.

revolve †turn or roll back or round XIV; turn over in the mind, consider XV; cause to travel in an orbit XVII; intr. XVIII. - L. *revolvere*, f. RE- + *volvere* roll, turn. Hence **revolver** (-ER¹) XIX.

revulsion (path.) diminishing a morbid condition in one part by acting on another XVI; drawing away XVII; strong reaction XIX. - F. *révulsion* or L. *revulsiō, -ōn-*, f. *revuls-*, pp. stem of *revellere*, f. RE- + *vellere* pluck, pull.

reward †regard; †assign as a recompense; recompense, requite XIV. - AN., ONF. *rewarder* = OF. *reguarder* REGARD. So **reward** sb. †regard; return, recompense. XIV. - AN., ONF. *reward* = OF. *reguard*.

Rhadamanthine inflexibly severe. XIX. f. L. *Rhadamanthus*, Gr. *Rhadámanthos* one of the judges in the lower world; see -INE¹.

rhapsody epic poem or part of one suitable for recitation at one time; †miscellany, medley XVI; extravagant effusion XVII. - L. *rhapsōdia* - Gr. *rhapsōidiā*, f. *rhapsōidós* rhapsodist, f. *rháptein* stitch + *ōidḗ* song, ODE; see -Y³. Hence **rhapsodic** XVIII, **-ical, -ist, -ize** XVII.

rhatany S. Amer. shrub of genus *Krameria*. XIX. - modL. *rhatania* - Pg. *ratanha*, Sp. *ratania* - Quechua *rataña*.

rhea three-toed ostrich of S. America. XIX. arbitrary use of the myth. female name L. *Rhea*, Gr. *Rhéā*.

Rhenish pert. to the Rhine, chief river of Germany XIV; sb. Rhine wine XVI. ME. *rynis(ch)*, *renys* (assim. XVI to L.) - AN. *reneis*, OF. *rinois*, *rainois* - medL. **Rhēnēnsis*, for L. *Rhenānus*, f. *Rhēnus* Rhine; see -ISH¹.

rheo- comb. form of Gr. *rhéos* stream, current, used in scientific terms with the meaning 'electric current', as **rheometer, rheostat** XIX.

rhesus one of the macaques. XIX. arbitrary use of L. *Rhēsus*, Gr. *Rhêsos*, name of a myth. king of Thrace.

rhetor professor of rhetoric XIV; (professional) orator XVI. ME. *rethor* (later *rhetor*) - late L. *rethor*, var. of L. *rhētor* - Gr. *rhḗtōr*, f. **ϝrā*, f. IE. **wer-* (cf. WORD). So **rhetoric** art of using language for persuasion. XIV. ME. *ret(h)orique* - OF. *rethorique* (mod. *rhétorique*) - L. *rhētorica* (medL. *reth-*) - Gr. *rhētorikḗ*, sb. use of adj. **rhetorical** XV. f. L. *rhētōricus*. **rhetorician** XV. - OF.

rheum watery matter secreted by mucous glands or membranes; mucous discharge, catarrh XIV; (poet.) tears XVI. ME. *reume* - OF. *reume* (mod. *rhume*) - late L. *rheuma* - Gr. *rheûma* flow, stream, bodily humour. So **rheumatic** consisting of watery discharge XIV; suffering from, characterized by this XVI. - OF. *reumatique* (mod. *rhu-*) - L. - Gr. **rheumatism** rheumatic disease XVII. - F. or L. - Gr. **rheumatoid** XIX.

rhino¹ (sl.) money. XVII. Presumably f. RHINOCEROS in some allusive sense now lost.

rhino² abbrev. of RHINOCEROS. XIX.

rhino- comb. form of Gr. *rhī́s*, *rhīnó-* nose, pl. nostrils, in scientific terms (XIX).

rhinoceros XIII. - L. *rhīnocerōs* - Gr. *rhīnókerōs*, f. *rhī́s*, *rhīnó-* nose + *kéras* HORN. So **rhinocerotic** XVIII. - late L.

rhizo- comb. form of Gr. *rhíza* root, in many scientific terms. XIX.

rhizome (bot.) root-like stem. XIX. - Gr. *rhízōma*, f. *rhizoûsthai* take root, f. *rhíza* root.

rhodium¹ rosewood (*Convolvulus*). XVII. modL., n. of *rhodius* rose-like, f. Gr. *rhódon* rose.

rhodium² (chem.) white metal of the platinum group. XIX. f. Gr. *rhódon* rose + -IUM; so called from the rose colour of a solution of salts containing it.

rhododendron XVII. - L. *rhododendron* oleander - Gr. *rhodódendron*, f. *rhódon* rose + *déndron* tree.

rhomb plane figure having the four sides and opposite angles equal. XVI. - F. *rhombe* or L. *rhombus* (whence **rhombus** XVI) - Gr. *rhómbos*. Hence **rhombic** XVII. So **rhomboid** adj. XVII, sb. XVI. - F. or late L. - Gr. **rhomboidal** XVII. - modL.

rhubarb XIV. ME. *rubarbe* - OF. *r(e)ubarbe* (mod. *rhubarbe*) - Rom. **r(h)eubarbum*, shortening of medL. *r(h)eubarbarum*, alt. (by assoc. with Gr. *rhêon* rhubarb) of *rhabarbarum*, foreign 'rha' (late L. *rhā* - Gr. *rhâ*).

rhumb (naut.) †line on a chart indicating the course of a ship moving continuously in one direction; point of the compass XVI; angular distance between two successive points XVII. - F. *rumb*, †*rum*; of uncert. orig.

rhyme XVII. var. sp. of RIME². So vb. XVII; hence **rhymer** (-ER¹) XVII, **rhymester** (-STER) XVIII.

rhythm A. †(piece of) rhymed verse XVI; B. metrical movement or flow as determined by the recurrence of features of the same kind XVI; also transf. and gen. XVII. In A graphic var. of RIME²; in B - L. *rhythmus* or F. *rhythme* - Gr. *rhuthmós*, rel. to *rheîn* flow. So **rhythmic** XVII, **-ical** XVI. - F. or L. - Gr.

riant smiling, gay. XVI. - F., prp. of *rire* laugh; see -ANT.

rib any of the curved bones articulated to the spine OE.; wife, woman (in allusion to Gen. 2: 21) XVI; various transf. and techn. uses from XIV. OE. *rib(b)*, corr. (with variations in gender and decl.) to OS. *ribbi* (Du. *rib(be)*), OHG. *rippi*, *rippa* (G. *rippe*), ON. *rif* :- Gmc. **rebja-*, *-jō*, rel. to OSl. (Russ.) *rebró* rib, side, and prob. further to Gr. *orophḗ* roof, *eréphein* roof over.

ribald †retainer of low class XIII; †rascal, licentious person; offensive or scurrilous person XIV; adj. XVI. ME. *ribaud* - OF. *ribau(l)t*, *-auld*, (also mod.) *ribaud*, f. OF. *riber* pursue licentious pleasures, f. Gmc. base repr. by OHG. *hrība* (MHG. *rībe*) whore, MHG. *rīben* be on heat, copulate. So **ribaldry** XIV. - OF. *ribauderie*.

riband see next.

ribbon narrow woven band of fine material. XIV. ME. *reban*, *riban*, *ryban*, later (with parasitic *d*) *ryband* XV, **riband** XVI (freq. till XIX) - OF. *riban* (still dial.), *reuban*, (also mod.) *ruban*, prob. - Gmc. comp. of *band* BAND².

rice XIII. ME. *rys* - OF. *ris* (mod. *riz*) - It. *riso* :- Rom. **orīzum*, for L. *orȳza* - Gr. *órūza*.

rich †powerful, great; having abundant means OE.; costly, splendid, sumptuous XII; various transf. and fig. uses from XIII. OE. *rīċe* = OS. *rīki*, OHG. *rīchi* (Du. *rijk*, G. *reich*), ON. *ríkr*, Goth. *reiks*; CGmc. - Celt. *rīx* (Ir. *rí*) = L. *rēx* king; reinforced in ME. by (O)F. *riche* orig. powerful, of Gmc. orig. From the same Gmc. stem are OE. *rīċe* = OS. *rīki*, MLG., MDu. *rīke* (Du. *rijk*), OHG. *rīhhi* (G. *reich*), ON. *ríki*, Goth. *reiki* kingdom, royal power, surviving in *bishopric*. So **riches** abundance of means XIII. var. (simulating Eng. pls. in *-es*) of †*richesse*, †*richeise* (XII) - OF. *richeise*, *-esce* (mod. *-esse*); f. *riche* + *-eise*, *-esse* -ESS².

rick¹ stack of hay, etc. OE. *hrēac* = MDu. *rooc*, *roke* (Du. *rook*), ON. *hraukr*, of unkn. orig.

rick² sprain, wrench XVIII; var. of WRICK.

rickets disease marked by softening of the bones. XVII. of unkn. orig.; assoc. by medical writers with Gr. *rhakhitis* RACHITIS, which was adopted as the technical designation. Hence **rickety** (-Y¹) affected with rickets XVII; shaky, tottering XVIII.

ricksha(w) XIX. Abbr. of JINRICKSHA.

ricochet (method of firing characterized by) the skipping of a shot along a surface. XVIII. - F., orig. in phr. *fable du ricochet* endless exchange of question and answer, unending argument; of unkn. orig. Hence vb. XIX.

rictus (techn.) throat, orifice, gape. XVIII. - L. 'open mouth', f. ppl. stem of *ringī* gape.

rid clear (a space); set free *from*, *of* XIII; disencumber *of* XVI. - ON. *ryðja* (pt. *ruddi*, pp. *ruddr*). Hence **riddance** XVI.

riddle¹ puzzling or dark utterance, enigma. OE. *rǣdels*, *rǣdelse* opinion, riddle, corr. to OS. *rādisli*, *rādislo* (Du. *raadsel*), OHG. *rādisle* (G. *rätsel*); f. **rǣdan* READ; see -LE¹. Hence **riddle** vb.¹ speak in riddles; solve a riddle. XVI; whence **riddlemeree** XVIII, fanciful var. of *riddle my rede* or *riddle*.

riddle² coarse-meshed sieve. Late OE. *hriddel*, rel. to synon. *hrīder* and *hrīdrian* sift, of WGmc. extent and based on IE. **krī-* with widespread cogns., as in Gr. *krī́nein* separate, decide, L. *crībrum* sieve, in Gmc. **χrain-* clean, pure (e.g. G. *rein*), etc. Hence **riddle** vb.² †sift XIII; pierce with holes XIX.

ride pt. *rode*, pp. *ridden* sit upon and be carried by a horse, etc.; lie at anchor OE.; trans. (of ON. orig.) XIII. OE. str. vb. *rīdan* = OS. *-rīdan* (Du. *rijden*), OHG. *rītan* (G. *reiten*), ON. *ríða*, rel. to OIr. *riadaim* I travel, Gaul. *rēda* chariot. Hence sb. XVIII. **rider** (-ER¹) †knight XI; one who rides a horse, etc. XIII; (pl.) additional timbers to strengthen the frame of a ship; additional or supplementary clause XVII; corollary XIX. Late OE. *rīdere*.

ridge †back, spine; top, crest; coping of a roof; long stretch of high ground; raised strip of arable land OE.; narrow raised part across a surface XVI. OE. *hryċġ* = OS. *hruggi-* (MDu. *ruc*, Du. *rug*), OHG. *hrucci* (G. *rücken*), ON. *hryggr* :- Gmc. **χruʒjaz*.

ridicule †ridiculous thing, nature, character; making fun *of*. XVII. - F. *ridicule* - L. *rīdiculus*, f. *rīdēre* laugh. So **ridiculous** XVI. f. L. *rīdiculus* or - L. *rīdiculōsus*.

riding any of the three districts of Yorkshire (East, West, and North). XI. In *Est Treding*, *Estreding*, *Nort Treding* (Domesday Book), *Nort riding*, etc. (XII), alt., by change of *tþ* to *t(t)*, of late OE. **þriding*, **þriðing* - ON. *þriðjungr* third part, f. *þriði* THIRD; see -ING³.

rife prevalent, widespread; abundant XII; generally current XIV. Once in late OE. *rȳfe*, for **rīfe*; subsequently *rif*, *riif*, *riue*, in northern, eastern, and west midl. texts; prob. - ON. *rífr* good, acceptable = MLG. *rīve*, MDu. *rīve*, *rijf* abundant.

riff-raff persons of the most disreputable class

xv; worthless stuff xvi. f. phr. †*trif and raf* (xiv) one and all, every bit - OF. *rif et raf*.

rifle[1] despoil; carry off as booty. xiv. - OF. *rif(f)ler* graze, scratch, plunder, of unkn. orig.

rifle[2] spiral groove inside a gun-barrel; (perh. for *rifle* or *rifled gun*) fire-arm having a rifled bore. xviii. f. **rifle** vb. (xvii) form spiral grooves in - F. *rifler* scratch, scrape, plane, of unkn. orig.

rift †rending, splitting xiii; cleft, fissure xiv. of Scand. orig. (cf. Norw., Da. *rift* cleft, chink); rel. to RIVE.

rig[1] fit *out*, esp. with clothes; make ready for sea, supply with tackle xv; provide, fit *up* xvi; fix, adjust xvii. perh. of Scand. orig. (cf. Norw. *rigga* bind or wrap up). Hence sb. arrangement of masts, sails, etc.; outfit (*rig-out*). xix. **rigging** xv; concr. xvi.

rig[2] (dial.) banter, ridicule; trick, prank (phr. *run a rig*). xviii. f. *rig* vb. (xvi) wanton, romp, of unkn. orig.

rigadoon (hist.) lively dance for two persons. xvii. - F. *rigodon, rigaudon*; of uncert. orig.

right †standard or rule of action; that which is equitably or morally just; just treatment; justifiable claim. OE. *riht* = OS., OHG. *reht* (Du., G. *recht*), ON. *réttr*; the sb. corr. to **right** adj. †straight; †upright, righteous; just, correct, proper; real, true; epithet of the hand that is normally the stronger OE.; mentally normal xii; (of an angle) of 90° xiv; correct in opinion, etc. xvi. OE. *riht* = OS., etc., as in the sb., Goth. *raihts* :- Gmc. **reχtaz*, pp. formation with IE. **-to-*; equiv. formations are L. *rēctus*, OIr. *recht* law, W. *rhaith*, Gr. *orektós* upright; f. IE. base **reĝ-* denoting movement in a straight line, extension. So **right** vb. †guide, direct; †set up; set in order, set right, etc. OE. *rihtan*; Gmc. wk. vb. **right** adv. OE. *rihte*. **righten** (-EN[5]) set right xiv (rare before xvi). **rightly** (-LY[2]) OE. *rihtlīċe*. **rightful** (-FUL[1]) OE. *rihtful*.

-right repr. the adj. and the adv. *right*, as in OE. *forðriht(e)* FORTHRIGHT, *upriht(e)* UPRIGHT, after which were formed ME. DOWNRIGHT, OUTRIGHT.

righteous upright, virtuous. OE. *rihtwīs*, f. *riht* sb. or adj. + *wīs* manner, state, condition; see RIGHT, -WISE. The form in *-eous* (xvi) is by assim. to *beauteous, bounteous, plenteous*. So **righteously** (-LY[2]) OE. *rihtwīslīċe*. **righteousness** OE. *rihtwīsnisse*.

rigid not pliant or yielding; strict xvi; precise in method xvii. - F. *rigide* or L. *rigidus*, f. *rigēre* be stiff; see -ID[1]. So **rigour** (-OUR[2]), U.S. **rigor** severity, strictness xiv; severity, as of climate; severe exactitude; sudden chill xvi (now usu. *rigor*). - (O)F. *rigour* (mod. *rigueur*) - L. *rigor, -ōr-*, f. *rigēre*. **rigorous** xiv. - OF. *rigorous* - late L. *rigōrōsus*.

rigmarole rambling or meaningless talk. xviii. alt. of †*ragman roll* list, catalogue (xvi), earlier †*roll of ragman*. *Ragman('s) roll* was used in most of the senses of *rag man*, which was applied orig. (xiii) to (i) a statute of Edward I and articles of inquisition made under this statute, (ii) a game of chance played with a written roll having strings attached to the items of it, which the players drew.

rigveda principal sacred books of the Hindus. xviii. - Skr. *ṛgveda*, f. *arc-* praise + VEDA knowledge.

rile (colloq.) make turbid; disturb in temper, vex. xix. orig. var. of (dial.) *roil* (xvi), of uncert. orig.

rill small stream. xv. of uncert. orig.; cf. LG. *ril(le)*, Du. *ril*.

rim (raised) edge, margin, verge OE.; outer ring of a wheel xiv. OE. *rima* (in *dægrima* break of day, *sǣ(s)rima*, sea-shore, etc.) = ON. *rimi* ridge of land, of which no other cogns. are known.

rime[1] hoar frost. OE. *hrīm* = (M)Du. *rijm*, ON. *hrím*.

rime[2] †metre xii; consonance of terminal elements in words; (rhyming) verse xiii; word that rhymes xvi. - (O)F. - medL. *rithmus, rythmus* (used spec. of accentual verse which was usu. rhymed), for L. *rhythmus* RHYTHM. So **rime** vb. xiii. - (O)F. *rimer*. The sp. *rime* prevailed till xvi, when the tendency to respell on classical models led to the use of *rithme, r(h)ythme*; these were succeeded after 1600 by *rhime*, RHYME.

rind bark of a tree; crust OE.; peel or skin xiv. OE. *rind(e)*, corr. to OS. *rinda*, MDu. *rinde, rende, runde* (Du. *run*), OHG. *rinta* (G. *rinde*); of unkn. orig.

ring[1] circle or circlet of metal, etc.; circular group OE.; various transf. and fig. uses esp. from xiv. OE. *hring* = OS., OHG. *hring* (Du., G. *ring*), ON. *hringr* :- Gmc. **χreŋgaz*. Hence vb. put a ring or circle around; from xv, with corr. formations in the cogn. langs.; cf. OE. *be-, ymbhringan* surround. Comps. **ringdove** wood-pigeon. xvi. prob. after LG. or Du. **ring-finger** third finger. OE. *hringfinger*. **ringleader** xvi. f. phr. *lead the r.* **ringlet** xvi. **ringworm** skin disease marked by circular patches. xv.

ring[2] pt. *rang* (*rung*), pp. *rung* give out a resonant sound OE.; cause (a bell) to do this xii. OE. *hringan*, corr. to ON. *hringja*; orig. wk. (OE. pt. *hringde*, early ME. *ringde*), but strong forms appear in early xiii.

rink †area allotted to a contest xiv; stretch of ice for the game of curling xviii, for skating xix. Only in Sc. use till xix; poss. later form of **renk* - OF. *renc* (mod. *rang*) RANK[1].

rinse xiv. - (O)F. *rincer*, earlier *raincier, reincier*, of unkn. orig.

riot †debauched living, dissipation xiii; †noisy feast, wanton revel; violence, violent disturbance of the peace xiv; (hunting) hound's following the scent of a quarry other than that intended xv (phr. *hunt* or *run riot*; hence fig. use of the latter xvi). - OF. *riote, riot* (mod. *riotte*) debate, quarrel, of unkn. orig. So vb. xiv. - OF. *riot(t)er*. **riotous** (arch.) dissolute, extravagant xiv; turbulent xv. - OF. *riotous, -eus*.

rip[1] tear or pull away vigorously. xv. of unkn. orig.

rip[2] worthless thing, old knacker; dissolute person. xviii. poss. alt. of *rep*, short for *reprobate*.

riparian pert. to the banks of a river. xix. f. L. *rīpārius*, f. *rīpa* bank; see -ARIAN.

ripe ready for reaping or gathering OE.; in various transf. and fig. uses 'matured, mature' from *c.*1200. OE. *rīpe* = OS. *rīpi* (Du. *rijp*), OHG. *rīfi* (G. *reif*). So **ripe** vb. (arch.) become ripe OE.; make ripe XIV. OE. *rīpian* = OS. *rīpon* (Du. *rijpen*), OHG. *rīfēn* (G. *reifen*); superseded gen. by **ripen** (-EN[5]) XVI.

riposte return thrust in fencing XVIII (*risposte*); effective reply XIX. - F. *riposte*, earlier †*risposte* - It. *risposta*, sb. use of fem. pp. of *rispondere* respond.

ripple (of water) present a surface of small waves. XVII. Hence sb. U.S. piece of shallow water in a river where rocks cause obstruction; light ruffling of the surface of water XVIII. of unkn. orig.

rise pt. *rose*, pp. *risen* get *up*, go *up*, ascend; rebel; increase XII; come into existence XIII; (dial., techn.) raise XV. OE. str. vb. *rīsan* = OS., OHG. *rīsan* (Du. *rijzen*, G. *reisen* of the sun), ON. *rísa*, Goth. *-reisan* :- Gmc. str. vb., of which no cogns. are known. Hence sb. XV (rare before late XVI).

risible inclined to laughter XVI; pert. to laughter; laughable XVIII. - late L. *rīsibilis*, f. *rīs-*, pp. stem of *rīdēre* laugh; see -IBLE. So **risibility** XVII. - late L.

risk sb. XVII. - F. *risque* - It. †*risco* (mod. *rischio*), f. *rischiare*, *risicare* run into danger; of unkn. orig. Hence vb. XVII. - F. *risquer*. **risky** XIX (later, partly after F. pp. *risqué*).

rissole XVIII. - F. *rissole*, later form of OF. *ruissole*, dial. var. of *roissole*, *roussole* :- Rom. **russeola*, sb. use of fem. of late L. *russeolus* reddish, f. *russus* red.

rite formal (esp. religious) procedure or act XIV; general use or practice, esp. in religion XV. - (O)F. *rit*, later *rite* or L. *rītus* (religious) usage. So **ritual** (-AL[1]) pert. to rites XVI; sb. (book containing) prescribed order of the performance of rites XVII. - L. *rītuālis*; in sb. use after medL. *rituāle*, sb. use of n. sg. **ritualist** one versed in ritual or who advocates its observance. XVII; hence **ritualism** XIX.

rival sb. XVI. - L. *rīvālis* one who uses the same stream with another, f. *rīvus* stream; see -AL[1]. Hence vb. XVII, **rivalry** XVI.

rive (arch., dial.) tear, rend. XIII. ME. *rive* (pt. *rōf*, pp. *riven*) - ON. *rífa*; of unkn. orig.

river XIII. - AN. *river(e)*, (O)F. *rivière* †river bank, river = It. *riviera* bank (spec. of the Genoese coast as far as Nice, adopted in Eng. use as **Riviera**) :- Rom. **rīpāria*, fem. used sb. of *rīpārius* RIPARIAN. Hence **riverine** (-INE[1]) situated on or pert. to a river (contemp. with **riverain** - F. *riverain*). XIX.

rivet small nail or bolt. XIV. - OF., f. *river* fix, clinch, of unkn. orig. Hence vb. XIV.

rivière necklace of gems. XIX. - F.; see RIVER.

rivulet XVI. alt. of earlier synon. †*riveret* - F. dim. of *rivière* RIVER, perh. after It. *rivoletto*, dim. of *rivolo*, dim. of *rivo* :- L. *rīvus* stream; see -LET.

roach small freshwater fish. XIV. - OF. *roche*, with vars. *roce*, *roque*, of unkn. orig.

road A. †riding; †RAID OE.; B. sheltered water where ships may ride XIV; C. line of communication between places (also *roadway*) XVI; (gen.) way, course. OE. *rād* = MDu. *rēd*, ON. *reið*, rel. to *rīdan* RIDE. Sense C may be generalized from such comps. as OE. *hwēolrād* wheel-track, *strēamrād* course of a stream.

roam wander, rove. XIII. of unkn. orig.

roan[1] (of horses, etc.) having a coat in which the prevailing colour is intermingled with another. XVI. - OF. *roan* (mod. *rouan*), of unkn. orig.

roan[2] soft flexible leather used in bookbinding. XIX. of unkn. orig.

roar utter full deep or hoarse prolonged cry OE.; make a loud noise or din XIV. OE. *rārian*, corr. to MLG. *rāren*, *rēren*, MDu. *reeren*, OHG. *rērēn* (G. *röhren*); WGmc., of imit. orig. Hence sb. XIV.

roast XIII. - OF. *rostir* (mod. *rôtir*) - WGmc. **raustjan* (Du. *roosten*, OHG. *rōsten*, G. *rösten*).

rob deprive (one) of by force; plunder, pillage. XIII. - OF. *rob(b)er* f. Gmc. base **raub-*, repr. also by REAVE. So **robber** (-ER[2]), **robbery** XII. - AN. *rob(b)ere*, *-erie*.

robe XIII. - (O)F. :- Rom. **rauba*, of Gmc. orig. (see prec.), the orig. sense being 'booty', (hence) clothes, regarded as spoil. Hence vb. XIV.

robin small red-breasted bird. XVI. Short for *r. redbreast* (XV), both being Sc. in their earliest use. - OF. *Robin*, familiar var. of the masculine name *Robert* (used XV for 'robin'). In *round r.* (XVIII) the adj. describes the circular unpunctuated list of names on the document; the reference of the sb. is unkn.

robot mechanism doing the work of a man, automaton. XX. - Czech, f. *robota* compulsory service.

robust XVI. - (O)F. *robuste* or L. *rōbustus* oaken, firm and hard, solid, f. *rōbus*, older form of *rōbur* oak, strength. Hence **robustious** XVI.

roc gigantic bird of Eastern legend. XVI. In early use in *roche*, *roque*, *ruc(h)* - Sp. †*rocho*, Pg. *roco*, It. †*roche*, Sp., Pg., It. *ruc* - Arab. *rukẖ*.

rochet linen vestment of the surplice kind worn by bishops, etc.; (dial.) smock frock. XIV. - (O)F. *rochet*, var. of *roquet*, dim. f. Gmc. base found in OE. *rocc*, OS., (M)Du. *rok*, OHG. *roch* (G. *rock*) coat; see -ET.

rock[1] move from side to side on a pivot. Late OE. *roccian*, prob. f. Gmc. **rukk-* move, remove, repr. also by MLG., MDu. *rukken*, *rocken* (Du. *rukken* tug, jerk, snatch), OHG. *rucchan* (G. *rücken* move, push), ON. *rykkja* pull, tug.

rock[2] solid part of the earth's crust, mass of this. XIV. - OF. *ro(c)que*, var. of (O)F. *roche*; of unkn. orig. Hence **rocky** (-Y[1]) XV.

rock[3] (arch., dial.) distaff. XIV. - MLG. *rocken*, MDu. *rocke* (Du. *rok*, *rokken*) or ON. *rokkr* = OHG. *rocco* (G. *rocken*); of unkn. orig.

rocket[1] cruciferous annual, *Eruca sativa*. XVI. - F. *roquette* - It. *rochetta*, var. of *ruchetta*, dim. of *ruca* :- L. *ērūca* caterpillar, plant with downy stems.

rocket[2] cylindrical paper or metal case designed to be projected on ignition of explosive contents. XVII. - (O)F. *roquette* - It. *rocchetto*, dim. of *rocca* ROCK[3]; so called from the cylindrical form. Hence vb. XIX.

rococo †old-fashioned; characterized by conventional shell-and-scroll-work, as of the time of Louis XIV and XV of France. XIX. - F. *rococo*, fanciful alt. of *rocaille* pebble- or shell-work, f. *roc* ROCK[2].

rod straight slender wand XII; stick for measuring with; measure of length and of area XV. Late OE. *rodd*, synon. with Continental forms cited s.v. ROOD, but formally distinct; prob. rel. to ON. *rudda* club.

rodent gnawing, belonging to the Rodentia. XIX. - L. *rōdēns, -ent-*, prp. of *rōdere* gnaw; see -ENT.

rodeo round up of cattle XIX; exhibition of lassooing, etc. XX. - Sp., f. *rodear* go round, based on L. *rotāre* ROTATE.

rodomontade vainglorious or extravagant boast. XVII. - F. *rodomontade*, It. †*rodomontada, -ata*, f. F. *rodomont*, It. *-monte* bragger, boaster, appellative use of *Rodomonte* name (lit. 'roll-mountain') of a boastful Saracen leader in Boiardo's 'Orlando Innamorato' and Ariosto's 'Orlando Furioso'.

roe[1] small species of deer. OE. *rā*, earlier *rāha* = OS., OHG. *rēho* (Du. *ree*, G. *reh*), ON. *rá* :- Gmc. **raiχ-*.

roe[2] milt or spawn of a fish. XV. ME. *row(e)*, *rough, roof* :- **roȝe* - MLG., MDu. *roge* = OHG. *rogo* (MHG. *roge*); ult. orig. unkn.

rogation A. (pl.) litanies used on the Monday, Tuesday, and Wednesday before Ascension Day (*R. Days*) XIV; B. (Rom. hist.) submission by consuls, etc. of a proposed law to the people XV. - L. *rogātiō, -ōn-*, in medL. pl. (in sense A) *Rogātiōnēs*, f. *rogāre* ask; see -ATION.

rogue one of a class of vagrants XVI; unprincipled man; mischievous person XVI; (rendering Sinhalese *horā, sorā* :- Skr. *corá-* thief) savage elephant living apart from the herd XIX. orig. one of the numerous canting words that are recorded from mid-XVI; perh. based on †*roger* begging vagabond pretending to be a poor scholar from Oxford or Cambridge (XVI), prob. f. L. *rogāre* ask, beg + -ER[1]. Hence **roguery, roguish** XVI.

roil see RILE.

roister revel noisily, be uproarious. f. †*roister* swaggerer, reveller XVI. - (O)F. *rustre* ruffian, alt. of *ruste* :- L. *rusticus* RUSTIC.

rôle, role XVII (*rowle, roll*). - F. †*roule*, †*rolle*, *rôle* ROLL[1], orig. the 'roll' containing an actor's part.

roll[1] piece of parchment, etc. made into cylindrical form XIII; such a piece inscribed with formal records, register XIV; quantity of material, mechanical object in cylindrical form, etc. XVI. - OF. *ro(u)lle* (mod. *rôle*) :- L. *rotulus*, var. of *rotula*, dim. of *rota* wheel. Hence **roll-call** XIX.

roll[2] turn or cause to turn over and over as on an axis or in a socket XIV; coil or cause to coil into a mass; make a reverberating noise XVI. - OF. *rol(l)er*, (also mod.) *rouler* :- Rom. **rotulāre*, f. L. *rotulus* ROLL[1]. Hence sb. act of rolling. XVII. **roller**[1] (-ER[1]) cylindrical object, as of wood, metal, etc. XV.

roller[2] bird with brilliant plumage. XVII. - G. *roller*, f. *rollen* - (O)F. *rouler* ROLL[2]; perh. so called from its cry.

rollick romp; esp. in prp. *rollicking* boisterously sportive. XIX. of unkn. orig.

roly-poly †worthless fellow XVII (*rowle powle, rowly powly*); name of various games involving the rolling of a ball XVIII; pudding in which a sheet of paste covered with jam, etc. is rolled on itself XIX. Fanciful formation on ROLL[2]; the second el. may contain POLL[1] (head); the orig. of the first sense is obscure.

rom male gipsy. XIX. - Romany *rom* man, husband - Skr. *ḍoma, ḍomba* minstrel-dancer of low caste. So **Romany** gipsy, gipsy language. XIX. - Romany *Romani*, pl. and fem. of *Romano* adj., f. *Rom*.

Romaic pert. to the vernacular language of modern Greece. XIX. - Gr. *Rhōmaikós*, f. *Rhṓmē* Rome, used spec. of the Eastern Empire.

Roman pert. to (native or inhabitant of) ancient Rome XIII; pert. to (adherent of) the Roman Catholic Church XVI; (typogr.) based on the characteristic form of the ancient Roman inscriptions. ME. *Romein, -ain* - (O)F. *Romain* - L. *Rōmānus*, f. *Rōma* Rome; later assim. in sp. to L.; preceded by OE. *Romane, -an* sb. pl.; see -AN. So **R. Catholic** XVII. Based on the official L. title of the Roman Church, Ecclesia *Romana Catholica* et Apostolica, 'Roman Catholic and Apostolic Church'.

romance tale in verse embodying adventure, esp. of medieval legend XIII; fictitious narrative in prose; (after Sp. and F. *romance*) Spanish historical ballad XVII. ME. *roma(u)nz, -a(u)ns* - OF. *romanz, -ans*, fem. *romance* the vernacular tongue (as dist. from literary L.), work composed in this :- popL. **rōmānice* 'in the Romanic tongue', adv. of L. *Rōmānicus*, f. *Rōmānus* ROMAN; see -IC. So vb. (XIV), XVII. - OF. *romancier*. **romancer** (-ER[2]) (XIV), XVII. - OF. *romancëor, -cier*.

Romance vernacular language of France, later applied to the related tongues. XIV. - OF. *romanz*, fem. adj. *-ance* expressed in the vernacular (see prec.).

Romanesque †(of a language) Romance XVIII; (archit.) pert. to building of Romanized style XIX. - F. *romanesque*, f. *roman* ROMANCE; see -ESQUE.

Romanic Romance, Romance-speaking. XVIII. - L. *Rōmānicus*, f. *Rōmānus* ROMAN; see -IC.

Romanist Roman Catholic. XVI. - G. *Romanist* or modL. *Romanista*. So **Romanize** render Roman or Roman Catholic. XVII. **Romano-** comb. form (see -o-) of L. *Rōmānus* ROMAN XVII.

Romany see ROM.

romaunt (arch.) romance. XVI. - OF. *roma(u)nt*, (later *roman*), deduced (as if an obl. case) from *roma(u)nz* ROMANCE. Hence or - F. *romantique* **romantic** of the nature of or suggestive of romances or their imaginative or extravagant qualities. XVII.

Romish Roman Catholic (chiefly in hostile use). XVI. f. *Rome* (seat of the papal see) + -ISH[1].

romp frolic boisterously. XVIII. perh. alt. of RAMP[1] with modification of sense. So sb. XVIII.

rondeau poem with two rhymes throughout and the opening words used twice as a refrain. XVI (rare before late XVII). - (O)F. *rondeau*, later form of *rondel* (f. *rond* ROUND[1]) whence **rondel** (-EL[2]) XIV.

rondo (mus.) piece in which a return is continually made to the principal subject. XVIII. - It. - F. *rondeau* (see prec.).

Röntgen name of the German scientist W. C. *Röntgen* (1845-1923), applied to certain rays. XIX.

rood A. cross, spec. that on which Jesus Christ suffered (*Holy Rood*); crucifix (as on a rood loft or screen); B. (now local) rod, pole, or perch OE.; superficial measure, 40 square poles. XV. In sense A, OE. *rōd* = OS. *rōda*; in the sense of ROD (only in OE. *seglrōd* sailyard), the Continental forms are OS. *rōda*, MDu. *ro(o)de* (also mod. *roede*), OHG. *ruota* (G. *rute*).

roof upper covering of a building; palate of the mouth. OE. *hrōf* = (M)LG. *rōf*, MDu. *roof* (Du. *roef* cabin, coffin lid), ON. *hróf* boat shed, of which no certain cogns. are known.

rook[1] harsh-voiced crow. OE. *hrōc* = (M)LG. *rōk*, MDu. *roec* (Du. *roek*), OHG. *hruoch*, ON. *hrókr* :- Gmc. **χrōkaz*, prob. of imit. orig. In the sense 'cheat, swindler, sharper', with corr. vb., a gaming sl. use of late XVI. Hence **rookery** XVIII.

rook[2] piece at chess also called castle. XIV. ME. *rok(e)* - OF. *roc(k)*, *rok*, corr. to Sp., Pg. *roque*, It. *rocco*, and various Gmc. forms of the same ult. origin, Arab.-Pers. *rukk*.

room space OE.; †place XIV; chamber in a building XV. OE. *rūm* = OS., OHG., ON., Goth. *rūm* (Du. *ruim*, G. *raum*), sb. use of Gmc. adj. **rūmaz* spacious (OE. *rūm*, etc.). Hence **roomy** (-Y[1]) XVII.

roost perch for fowls. OE. *hrōst* = (M)Du. *roest* and perh. OS. *hrōst* spars of a roof; of unkn. orig. Hence vb. XVI.

root[1] part of a plant below the earth's surface OE.; source, basis XIV; (math., philol.) XVI. Late OE. *rōt* - ON. *rót*; rel. to L. *rādīx*. Hence **root** vb. A. in pp. firmly fixed XIII; B. furnish with roots XIV; C. uproot, eradicate XIV.

root[2] turn over (soil) with the snout. XIV. Later var. of *wroot*, OE. *wrōtan* = (M)LG. *wrōten*, (M)Du. *wroeten*, OHG. *ruozzen*, ON. *róta* (partly the immed. source), rel. to OE. *wrōt*, LG. *wrōte*, G. *rüssel* snout.

rope OE. *rāp* = (M)LG. *rēp*, (M)Du. *reep*, (O)HG. *reif*, ON. *reip*, Goth. *-raip* :- Gmc. **raipaz*.

Roquefort cheese made at *Roquefort*, village in S.W. France. XIX.

roquelaure (hist.) man's cloak reaching to the knee. XVIII. - F., f. name of Antoine-Gaston, duc de *Roquelaure* (1656-1738), marshal of France.

roquet in croquet, hitting another player's ball with one's own. XIX. presumably arbitrary alt. of CROQUET.

rorqual species of whale. XIX. - F. - Norw. *røyrkval* :- ON. *reyðarhvalr*, f. *reyðr* (specific name) + *hvalr* WHALE.

rosaceous resembling the roses. XVIII. - L. *rosāceus*, f. *rosa* ROSE; see -ACEOUS.

rosary base coin current in England in the 13th century XIV; rose-garden XV; set of devotions, spec. that of the B.V.M. ('Our Lady's psalter'), set of beads for its recitation. - L. *rosārium* rose-garden, AL. *rosārius* (coin), sb. uses of n. and m. of adj. f. *rosa* ROSE; see -ARY.

rose plant and flower of the genus *Rosa* OE.; rose-shaped figure XIV. OE. *rōse*, corr. to MDu. *rōse* (Du. *roos*), OHG. *rōsa* (G. *rose*), ON. *rósa*; Gmc. - L. *rosa*, rel. obscurely to synon. Gr. *rhódon*; reinforced in ME. from (O)F. *rose*. Hence **rosy** (-Y[1]) XIV (rare before XVI). So **rosette** XVIII. - (O)F.

rosemary evergreen shrub. XV. alt., by assoc. with ROSE and MARY, of †*rosmarine* (XIV), either immed. - L. *rōs marīnus* 'sea-dew', late L. *rōsmarīnum*, or through (i) OF. *rosmarin* (mod. *romarin*) or (ii) MDu. *rosemarine* (Du. *ros(e)marijn*).

Rosicrucian member of a society reputed to have been founded in 1484 by Christian *Rosenkranz*, the modL. tr. of which, viz. *rosa crucis* or *crux* i.e. 'rose (of the) cross', is the basis of the name. XVII. See -IAN.

rosin see RESIN.

roster list or plan exhibiting an order of rotation. XVIII. - Du. *rooster* (i) grating, gridiron, (ii) table, list (from the appearance of a paper ruled with parallel lines), f. *roosten* ROAST; see -ER[1].

rostrum platform for public speakers in ancient Rome, adorned with beaks of captured ships XVI; beak of a galley XVII; platform, stage, pulpit XVIII. - L. *rōstrum* beak, snout, etc., f. *rōdere* gnaw.

rot undergo decay OE.; trans. XIV; in imprecations XVI. OE. *rotian* = OS. *roton*, MDu. *roten*, (also mod.) *rotten*, OHG. *rōzzēn*, rel. to MLG. *röten*, MHG. *rœzen*; cf. ROTTEN. Hence (or - Scand.) sb. XIII.

rota political club founded in 1659 by J. Harrington, which advocated rotation in the offices of government; rotation, routine; (R.C.Ch.) supreme court for all causes XVII; roster XIX. - L. *rota* wheel. So **rotary** (of motion) circular; operating by rotation. XVIII. - medL. *rotārius*. **rotate** XIX. f. *rotāt-*, pp. stem of L. *rotāre* turn round, revolve. **rotation** XVI. - L.

rote †custom, habit; regular procedure, routine, esp. in *by rote*. XIV. of unkn. orig.

rotten decomposed, putrid XIII; fig. corrupt XIV. - ON. *rotinn*, which has the form of a pp. of the base **raut-* **reut-* **rut-*, repr. by ROT; see -EN[6].

rotund round, rounded XVIII; sonorous XIX. - L. *rotundus*, f. *rotāre* ROTATE. So **rotunda** round-shaped building. XVII. alt. (after L. *rotundus*) of *rotonda* (XVII) - It., sb. use of fem. of *rotondo* round. **rotundity** XVI. - F. or L.

rouble XVI. Earliest forms *rubbel*, *robel*, *ruble*, later *rouble* (after F.). - Russ. *rubl'*.

roué debauchee, rake. XVIII. - F., pp. of *rouer* break on the wheel, f. *roue* wheel :- L. *rota*.

rouge A. *R. Croix* and *R. Dragon*, two pursuivants of the English College of Arms, so called from their badges XV; B. red powder used as a cosmetic XVIII. - (O)F. :- L. *rubeus* red. Hence vb. XVIII.

rough not even or smooth OE.; turbulent, violent XIII; harsh, sharp XIV. OE. *rūh* = MLG., MDu. *rū(ch)* (Du. *ruig*, *ruw*), OHG. *rūh* (G. *rauh*) :- WGmc. **rūχ(w)az*, rel. to Lith. *rùkti* be wrinkled, Skr. *rūkṣá-* rough. Hence **roughen** (-EN[5]) XVI. **roughcast** XVI. f. *cast* †cover by casting mortar on.

roulette XVIII. - F., f. *rouelle*, dim. of *roue* wheel :- L. *rota*; see -ETTE.

round[1] A. of the form of a ball XIII; B. full, complete XIV; C. vigorous, severe XIV; plain, straightforward XVI. ME. *ro(u)nd* - OF. *ro(u)nd-*, inflexional stem of *ro(o)nt*, earlier *rëont* (mod. *rond*) :- Rom. **retundus*, for L. *rotundus* ROTUND. Hence sb. XIV, vb. XIV, adv. XIII; prep., perh. aphetic of AROUND XVII.

round[2] (arch.) whisper. OE. *rūnian*, ME. *ro(u)ne* = OS. *rūnon*, MLG., MDu. *rūnen*, OHG. *rūnēn*; f. OE. *rūn*, ME. *ro(u)n* dark saying, counsel, RUNE; with parasitic *d*.

roundel circle, circular object XIII; rondeau XIV. - OF. *rondel* or *-elle*, f. *rond* ROUND[1]; see -EL[2].

roundelay short song with a refrain. XVI. - (O)F. *rondelet*, dim. of *rondel* RONDEAU, with ending assim. to VIRELAY or LAY[2]; see -ET.

roup disease of poultry. XVI. of unkn. orig.

rouse[1] refl. and intr. (of a hawk) shake the feathers XV; start (game); cause to rise from slumber, etc. XVI. orig. techn. term of hawking and hunting, of unkn. orig.

rouse[2] (arch.) bumper of liquor, carousal. XVII. perh. aphetic of CAROUSE.

rout[1] company, troop; disorderly company XIII; †*the r.*, the common herd XIV; riot, uproar XV; fashionable gathering XVIII. ME. *ro(u)te* - AN. *rute*, OF. *route* :- Rom. **rupta*, sb. use of fem. of pp. of L. *rumpere* break. Cf. next.

rout[2] disorderly retreat. XVI. - F. †*route* (in the sense of *déroute*), prob. - It. *rotta* breakage, discomfiture of an army :- Rom. **rupta* (see prec.). Hence vb. XVI.

route way, course XIII (obs. in ME. in XV; re-adopted XVI); (mil.) order to march, marching orders XVIII. - OF. *rute*, (also mod.) *route* :- Rom. **rupta* (see ROUT[1]).

routine XVII (*rotine*). - F. *routine*, †*rotine*, f. *route* (see prec.).

rove †A. shoot with arrows *at* a selected mark for finding the range XV, B. wander at random XVI. poss. form of (dial.) *rave* stray (XIV), prob. of Scand. orig. (cf. Icel. *ráfa*); sense B perh. due to infl. by ROVER.

rover sea-robber, pirate. XIV. - MLG., MDu. *rōver*, f. *rōven* rob, REAVE.

row[1] number of persons or things set in a line. ME. *raw*, *row* (XIII) points to OE. **rāw*, var. of *rǣw* (ME. *rew*), perh. rel. to MDu. *rīe* (Du. *rij*), MHG. *rīhe* (G. *reihe*).

row[2] use oars OE.; trans. XIV. OE. str. vb. *rōwan* (weak inflexions appear XIII) = MLG. *rōjen* (Du. *roeijen*), MHG. *rüejen* steer, ON. *róa*, f. Gmc. **rō-* steer, belonging to the IE. base **er-* repr. in Gr. *erétēs* rower, L. *rēmus*, OIr. *ráme* oar, Lith. *irti* row, Skr. *aritá* rower.

row[3] violent commotion, noisy dispute. XVIII. of unkn. orig.

rowan mountain ash. XVI (*rountree*). of Scand. orig.; cf. Norw. *rogn*, *raun*, Icel. *reynir*.

rowdy backwoodsman of a rough type; violent disorderly person. XIX (orig. U.S.). of unkn. orig.

rowel spur-wheel. XIV. - OF. *roel(e)* (mod. *rouelle*) :- late L. *rotella*, dim. of *rota* wheel; see -EL[2].

rowlock XVIII. alt., by substitution of ROW[2] for the first syll., of *oarlock*, OE. *ārloc*, f. *ār* OAR + *loc* fastening, LOCK[2].

royal XIV. - OF. *roial* (mod. *royal*) :- L. *rēgālis* REGAL. Hence **royalist** XVII. So **royalty** XIV. - OF. *roialte* (mod. *royauté*).

rub subject a surface to friction with pressure, tr. and intr. XIV. perh. - LG. *rubben*; ult. orig. unkn. Hence **rub** sb. obstacle, produced as if by rubbing a surface (techn., at bowls) XVI; often fig. as in *there's the r.* **rubber**[1] (-ER[1]) rubbing implement XVI; piece of a substance used for this (short for *India(n) rubber*) XVIII.

rub-a-dub XVIII. imit. of drumming sound.

rubber[2] set of (usu.) three games, as of bowls, whist, etc. XVI (the earliest exx. have (*play*) *a rubbers*). of unkn. orig.

rubbish waste or refuse material. XIV. ME. *robous*, *robys*, *-ishe*, *rubbes* - AN. *rubbous*, of uncert. orig.; cf. RUBBLE.

rubble waste fragments of stone, esp. from demolished buildings XIV, pieces of undressed stone XVI. ME. *robyl*, *rubel*, of uncert. orig.; cf. -EL[1], -LE[1], and prec.

rubicund †inclined to redness XVI; of ruddy complexion XVII. - F. *rubicond* or L. *rubicundus*, f. *rubēre* be red.

rubidium element of the alkali-metal group. XIX. f. L. *rubidus*, f. *rub-* of *ruber* RED; in allusion to the two red lines in its spectrum; see -IUM.

rubric A. †red earth, ruddle XV; B. direction (in red) for the conduct of divine service XIV; heading of a division of a book, etc. XV. Rare before XVII, *rubriche*, *-ishe* being the usual form XIV-XVI. - OF. *rubric(h)e*, beside *rubrique*, or its source L. *rubrīca* red earth, title of a law, law itself (written with red ochre), sb. use of adj. f. *ruber* RED.

ruby XIV. - OF. *rubi* (mod. *rubis*) - medL. *rubīnus*, sb. use of adj. f. base of L. *rubeus*, *ruber* RED.

ruche frill of light material. XIX. - F. *ruche* beehive, and (with allusion to the plaits of a straw hive) frill.

ruck[1] heap, stack, pile XIII; multitude, throng XVI; undistinguished crowd XIX. app. of Scand. orig. (cf. Norw. *ruka*).

ruck[2] crease, fold. XVIII (presumably of much earlier occurrence). - ON. (Norw.) *hrukka*.

rucksack XIX. - G. *rucksack*, f. dial. *rucken* (= *rücken* back, RIDGE) + *sack* SACK[1].

ruction (colloq.) disturbance, disorderly action (esp. pl.). XVIII (rare before XIX). of unkn. orig.

rudder †steering oar OE.; steering-gear mounted in a boat or ship XIV. OE. *roðer* = MLG., MDu. *rōder* (Du. *roer*), OHG. *ruodar* (G. *ruder*) :- WGmc. **rōþra-*, rel. to ROW[2].

ruddle red ochre. XVI. f. base of RUDDY; see -LE[1], and cf. contemp. *raddle*.

ruddock (dial.) redbreast, robin. OE. *rudduc*, rel. to RUDDY; see -OCK.

ruddy red, reddish, orig. of the face. Late OE. *rudiġ*, f. base of *rudu* red colour, redness, rel. to RED; see -Y[1].

rude in various transf. and fig. senses of 'rough'. XIV. - (O)F. - L. *rudis* unwrought, crude, uncultivated, orig. techn. term of handicraft, rel. to *rūdus* rubble.

rudiment (pl.) first principles or elements. XVI. - F. *rudiment* or L. *rudīmentum*, f. *rudis* RUDE. Hence **rudimentary** XIX.

rue[1] (arch. exc. as surviving in **rueful** XIII) sorrow, regret OE.; compassion XIII. OE. *hrēow* = MLG., MDu. *rouwe* (Du. *rouw*), OHG. *(h)riuwa* (G. *reue*), rel. to next.

rue[2] affect with contrition or sorrow OE.; affect with pity XII; repent of. OE. str. vb. *hrēowan* = OS. *hreuwan* (Du. *rouwen*), OHG. *(h)riuwan* (G. *reuen*); no certain cogns. are known.

rue[3] shrub of the genus *Ruta*. XIV. - (O)F. :- L. *rūta* - Gr. *rhūtḗ*.

ruff[1] small freshwater fish of the perch family, with prickly scales. XV. prob. sb. use of ROUGH.

ruff[2] †ruffle on a garment; article of neckwear consisting of linen, etc. starched in folds. XVI. poss. sb. use of *ruff*, ROUGH.

ruff[3] †former card-game XVI; kind of trump at cards XVII; (from the vb.) act of trumping XIX. - OF. *ro(u)ffle*, earlier *ronfle*, *romfle* (corr. to It. *ronfa*), poss. alt. of *triomphe* (It. *trionfo*) TRUMP[2]. Hence vb. XVI.

ruff[4] male of the sandpiper, distinguished in the breeding-season by a ruff. XVII. transf. use of RUFF[2].

ruffian XVI; †pander, bawd XVII. - (O)F. *ruf(f)ian* - It. *ruffiano*, f. dial. *rofia* scab, scurf, of Gmc. orig. (cf. OHG. *ruf* scurf).

ruffle[1] spoil the orderly arrangement of XIII; (gen.) disorder, disarrange XVI; disturb the mind or temper of XVII. of unkn. orig. Hence sb. disorderly state XVI; ornamental edging to a garment XVIII.

ruffle[2] (arch.) contend *with*; swagger, hector. XV. of unkn. orig. Hence **ruffler** (-ER[1]) †one of a class of vagabonds; swaggering fellow. XVI.

rufous reddish. XVIII. f. L. *rūfus*, rel. to *ruber* RED; see -OUS.

rug †rough woollen stuff; piece of thick woollen stuff used as a coverlet XVI; floor mat XIX. perh. of Scand. orig. (cf. Norw. dial. *rugga* coverlet, Sw. *rugg* ruffled or coarse hair) and rel. to RAG[1]. So **rugged** (-ED[1]) †shaggy, hirsute XIV; rough, uneven (also fig.) XVI. prob. pp. formation of Scand. orig. on the same base; cf. RAGGED.

Rugby name of a public school at Rugby in Warwickshire, after which one of the two chief games of football is named. XIX. Hence (sl.) **rugger** (-ER[6]) XIX.

rugose wrinkled. XVIII. - L. *rūgōsus*, f. *rūga* wrinkle; see -OSE[1].

ruin (state consequent upon) giving way and falling down XIV (concr. XV); downfall, utter loss XIV. - (O)F. *ruine* - L. *ruīna*, f. *ruere* fall. So vb. XVI. - (O)F. *ruiner* or medL. *ruīnāre*. †**ruinate, ruination** XVI. **ruinous** XIV. - (O)F. or L. *ruīnōsus*.

rule principle of procedure, conduct, etc.; code of religious life XIII; standard of estimation, etc.; graduated strip of wood or metal XIV; *rule of thumb* XVII. ME. *riule*, *reule* - OF. *riule*, *reule*, *ruile* :- Rom. **regula*, for L. *rēgula* straight stick, bar, pattern, rel. to *regere* rule, *rēx*, *rēg-* king. So **rule** vb. govern XIII; mark with lines XV. - OF. *reuler* - late L. *rēgulāre* REGULATE. Hence **ruler** (-ER[1]) XIV.

rum[1] spirit distilled from sugar-cane products. XVII. perh. shortening of slightly earlier *rumbullion*, *rumbustion*, of unkn. orig.

rum[2] (sl.) queer, odd. XVIII. of uncert. orig. Also **rummy**[1] (-Y[1]) XIX.

rumble make a low heavy continuous sound. XIV. prob. - MDu. *rommelen*, *rummelen* (Du. *rommelen*); of imit. orig. Hence sb. XIV.

ruminate meditate (upon); chew the cud. XVI. f. pp. stem of L. *rūminārī*, *-āre*, f. *rūmen*, *rūmin-* throat, gullet, (in mod. scientific use) first stomach of a ruminant; see -ATE[3]. So **ruminant** (animal) that chews the cud. XVII. **rumination** XVI.

rummage †stowage, orig. in a ship's hold; (dial.) commotion XVI; (from the vb.) overhauling search XVIII. - AN. **rumage* (cf. AL. *rumāgium*), aphetic of OF. *arrumage* (mod. *arrimage*), f. †*arrumer*, var. of OF. *arimer*, *aruner*, *ariner*, f. *a-* AD- + *run* ship's hold - (M)Du. *ruim*; see -AGE. *R. sale* is first recorded (XIX) for the sale of unclaimed goods at docks or odds and ends left in a warehouse. Hence vb. †stow in the hold, †set (a ship) in order; search (orig. the hold), also intr. XVI.

rummer (arch.) large drinking-glass. XVII. Of Du. or LG. orig.; cf. Du. *roemer*, LG. *römer*, f. *roemen*, etc. extol, boast.

rummy[1] see RUM[2].

rummy[2] card game. XX (orig. U.S.). of unkn. orig.

rumour †favourable report; general report or hearsay XIV. ME. *rumur*, *rumo(u)r* - OF. *rumur*, *-or* (mod. *-eur*) - L. *rūmor*, *-ōr-*.

rump hindquarters, buttocks XV; small or contemptible remainder XVII. prob. of Scand. orig.; cf. (M)Da. *rumpe*, (M)Sw. *rumpa*, Icel. *rumpr*; corr. forms in (M)Du., (M)LG., and (O)HG. mean the trunk of the body; the orig. sense may be tree-stump.

rumple XVII. f. *rumple* sb. wrinkle, fold (XVI) - (M)Du. *rompel*, f. MDu. *rompe*, MLG. *rumpe* wrinkle, or - MDu., MLG. *rumpelen*, *rompelen*, rel. to OE. **rimpan*, in pp. *ġerumpen* contracted, wrinkled, (M)LG., (M)Du. *rimpel* wrinkle, OHG. *rimpfan* (G. *rümpfen*).

rumpus XVIII. of fanciful formation (?).

run pt. *ran*, pp. *run* go along at quicker than walking pace; (gen.) move forward with speed. OE. str. vb. *rinnan* = OS., OHG. *rinnan*, (MLG., MDu., G. *rinnen*), ON. *rinna*, Goth. *rinnan*; of unkn. orig. The common ME. pres. tense forms *rinne*, *renne*, were prob. due to ON. *rinna*, *renna*. The *-u-* of the mod. pres., current from XVI (*ronne* is earlier), is the result of levelling from older pt. pl. *runnen*, pp. *runne(n)*, *ronnen*. Hence **run** sb. XV (act or spell of running; later in many techn. uses).

runagate †apostate; (arch.) deserter, runaway; vagabond. XVI. alt. of *ren(n)egate* (see RENEGADE), by assoc. with *renne* RUN and *agate* on the way, away (f. A-[1] + *gate*, GAIT).

runcible *r. spoon* kind of fork for pickles curved like a spoon and having three broad prongs (one with a sharp edge). XIX. First used by Edward Lear as a nonsense word in *r. cat*, *r. hat*, *r. spoon*.

runcinate irregularly saw-toothed. XVIII. - modL. *runcinātus*, f. L. *runcina* joiner's plane (formerly taken also to mean a kind of saw); see -ATE[2].

rundale form of joint occupation of land. XVI (Sc. *ryndale, rindaill,* later *rendal, rennal,* anglicized *rundale*). f. *rin,* Sc. var. of RUN + *dale,* north. form of DOLE[1].

rune character of the earliest Germanic alphabet. XVII. Adopted from Danish writers on Northern antiquities, and repr. ON. **rún,* pl. *rúnar, rúnir* secret or hidden lore, runes, magical signs (Sw. *runa,* Da. *rune*) = OE. *rūn* mystery, runic letter, secret consultation, OS., OHG., Goth. *rūna* (cf. ROUND[2]). So **runic** XVII. - modL. *rūnicus.*

rung stick of rounded form used as a rail, etc. OE.; stave of a ladder XIII. OE. *hrung* = MLG. *runge* (Du. *rong*), OHG. *runga,* Goth. *hrugga.*

runnel small stream. XVI. Later form (by assim. to RUN) of *rinel,* OE. *rynel(e), rinnele,* f. *run-, rin-,* base of RUN; see -EL[1].

runt (dial.) old tree-stump XVI; small breed of cattle; uncouth, ill-conditioned, or dwarfish person XVII; stout variety of domestic pigeon; small pig XIX. of unkn. orig.

rupee monetary unit of India. XVII. - Urdu *rūpiyah* :- Skr. *rū́pya-* wrought silver.

rupture breach XV; abdominal hernia XVI; break XVII. - F. *rupture* or L. *ruptūra,* f. pp. stem of *rumpere* break; see REAVE, -URE.

rural XV. - (O)F. *rural* or late L. *rūrālis,* f. *rūs, rūr-* the country; see -AL[1].

Ruritania imaginary kingdom of Central Europe in Anthony Hope's novels *The Prisoner of Zenda* (1894) and *Rupert of Hentzau* (1898); transf. petty state, esp. as a scene of court romance and intrigue XIX. f. L. *rūs, rūr-* country + *-tania,* of *Lusitania,* etc. Hence **Ruritanian** XIX.

ruse †detour, doubling in the track XV; trick, dodge XVII. - (O)F., f. *ruser* drive back; of uncert. orig.

rush[1] marsh or waterside plant. OE. *rysċ(e),* corr. to MLG., MHG. (Du., G.) *rusch.* OE. *rysċ(e),* with the vars. *resċ(e), risċ(e), *rex(e), rix(e),* surviving dial. in *resh, rish, rex, rix,* and corr. to MLG., MDu. *risch,* etc., point to a Gmc. series **rask- *resk- *rusk-,* with poss. further connections in L. *restis,* Skr. *rájju-* rope.

rush[2] †force out of place, move with force or speed; also intr. XIV. - AN. *russher,* var. of OF. *rus(s)er* (see RUSE).

rusk (piece of) bread re-fired so as to be hard and crisp. XVI. - Sp., Pg. *rosca* twist, coil, twisted roll of bread, of unkn. orig.

russet coarse woollen cloth of reddish-brown or other subfusc colour XIII; adj. reddish-brown XIV (hence sb. russet colour XVI; russet apple XVIII). - AN., var. of OF. *ro(u)sset,* dim. f. *rous* (mod. *roux*) :- L. *russus* (rel. to RED); see -ET.

rust brownish coating formed on iron and steel by oxidation. OE. *rūst* = OS., (O)HG. *rost,* (M)Du. *roest,* rel. to RED. Hence vb. XIII. **rusty** (-Y[1]) OE. *rūstiġ.*

rustic pert. to the country XV; sb. countryman, peasant XVI. - L. *rūsticus,* f. *rūs* country. So **rusticate** (-ATE[3]) retire to the country XVII; trans. XVIII. f. pp. stem of L. *rūsticārī* live in the country. **rustication** XVII. - L. **rustic[i]ty** XVI. - F. or L.

rustle give forth a succession of light crisp sounds XIV; (U.S. colloq.) move about vigorously XIX. of imit. orig.

rut[1] sexual excitement of male deer, etc. XV. - (O)F. *rut,* †*ruit* rutting (time), †bellowing (of stags) :- Rom. **rūgitus,* for L. *rugītus,* f. *rugīre* roar, f. **ru-,* of imit. orig.

rut[2] track made in soft ground. XVI (early forms also *ro(o)te, rupt*). prob. - OF. *rote,* early form of ROUTE.

ruth (arch.) pity. XII. f. RUE[2]. Survives in gen. use in **ruthless** XIV.

ruthenium (chem.) metal of the platinum group, discovered 1828, being first observed in platinum ores in the Ural mountains XIX. f. medL. *Ruthenia* Russia; see -IUM.

-ry suffix, reduced form of -ERY used chiefly after an unstressed syll. ending in *d, t, l, n,* or *sh,* and rarely after vocalic els.; exx. of the types are: *heraldry; dentistry; devilry; yeomanry; Englishry; Jewry;* in a few words *-ry* and *-ery* are alternative, e.g. *jewel(le)ry.*

rye OE. *ryġe* = ON. *rugr* :- Gmc. **ruȝiz* (cf. **roȝȝan-, *ruȝȝn-* in OS. *roggo* (Du. *rogge, rog*), OHG. *rokko*); cf. Lith. *rugỹs,* OSl. *rŭžĭ* (Russ. *rozh'*). Hence **rye-grass** A. for earlier *ray-grass* (XVII), grass of the genus *Lolium* (†*ray* darnel XIV, of unkn. orig.); B. wild rye. XVIII.

ryot Indian peasant. XVII (*riat*). - Urdu *raiyat* - Arab. *ra'īya(t)* flock, herd, subjects, f. *ra'ā* graze.

S

-s repr. OE. g. sg. *-es* of many m. and n. sbs., written *'s*, as *boy's*, *horse's*, *lady's*, with extension to certain pls., as *men's*; special cases are its use (1) as a euphem. repr. of *God's* in oaths, as *'sblood* (XVI), *'sdeath* (XVII), *'swounds* (XVI; see ZOUNDS); (2) in the terminal el. *-sman*, the extensive use of which, as in *craftsman*, *kinsman*, *spokesman*, *sportsman*, *tradesman*, is a generalization of the combination found in OE. *stēoresmann* STEERSMAN, *tūnesmann* TOWNSMAN.

Identical with the inflexion of the g. sg. is the *-s* surviving in certain adv. forms, as *always*, *needs*, *nowadays*, *-wards*, *-ways*; the use is exemplified by such OE. advs. as *dæġes* by day, *sōðes* in truth, truly, *þances* voluntarily. There were also OE. advs. compounded with *tō* TO and a genitive, as *tōġeġnes* against, *tōmiddes* amidst, by the side of which were synon. *onġeġn* AGAIN, *onmiddan* AMID; hence there arose in ME. mixed forms such as *aȝeines*, *amiddes*; and *-(e)s* became generalized, as in -WARDS, -WAYS. In *once*, *twice*, *thrice*, *hence*, *thence*, *whence*, *since*, the suffix has been otherwise spelt in order to avoid the suggestion of pronunc. with z which is associated with *-ns*, viz. nz. In AGAINST, AMIDST, AMONGST there is a parasitic *t*.

In the disjunctive prons. *hers*, *ours*, *theirs*, *yours* (ME. *hires*, etc.) the *-s* is presumably analogical after *his*.

Sabaoth in phr. *Lord (God) of S.* in Eng. N.T. (Rom. 9: 29, Jas. 5: 4) and Te Deum. XIV. - L. *Sabaōth* (Vulg.) - Gr. *Sabaṓth* (LXX and N.T.) - Heb. *ṣebāôth*, pl. of *ṣābā* army, host.

Sabbatarian pert. to the observance of the Sabbath (Saturday); sb. observer of the Lord's Day as a Sabbath (7th day of the week). XVII. f. late L. *sabbatārius* Jew, f. *sabbatum*; see next, -ARIAN.

Sabbath seventh day of the week observed by Jews as a day of rest OE.; the Lord's Day, Sunday XVI; midnight meeting of demons and witches XVII. OE. *sabat* - L. *sabbatum* and (O)F. *sabbat*, †*sabat* - Gr. *sábbaton* - Heb. *šabbāth*, f. *šābath* rest. The sp. with *th* and the consequent pronunc. are due to learned assoc. with the Heb. form.

sabbatical pert. to the Sabbath; pert. to the seventh year prescribed by Mosaic law to be observed as a Sabbath XVI; hence of an academical year of absence from duty XIX. f. late L. *sabbaticus* - Gr. *sabbatikós*, f. *sábbaton*; see prec., -ICAL.

sable[1] (fur of) a small carnivore. XV. - OF. *sable* sable fur - medL. *sabelum*; ult. of Balto-Sl. orig. (cf. Lith. *sābalas*, Russ. *sóbol'*).

sable[2] black colour (spec. in her.); black clothing XIV; adj. XV. - OF.; gen. presumed to be identical with prec., but sable fur is brown.

sabot wooden shoe made of a single piece of wood. XVII. - F., of unkn. orig. So **sabotage** sb. XX. - F., f. *saboter* clatter with shoes, execute badly, destroy (tools, etc.).

sabre, U.S. **saber** cavalry sword with curved blade. XVII. - F. *sabre*, unexpl. alt. of *sable* - G. *sabel*, local var. of *säbel*, earlier †*schabel* - Pol. *szabla* or Hung. *szablya*.

sac bag-like cavity. XVIII. - F. *sac* or L. *saccus* SACK[1]. See also SACK[4].

saccharine sugary. XVII. f. medL. *saccharum* SUGAR + -INE[1]. So **saccharin** (also **-ine**) sweet substance obtained from coal tar XIX. - G. Hence **saccharimeter** polariscope for testing sugars. XIX. - F. *saccharimètre*. **saccharometer** hydrometer for testing the amount of sugar. XVIII. f. **saccharo-** comb. form of Gr. *sákkharon* SUGAR.

sacerdotal XIV. - (O)F. *sacerdotal* or L. *sacerdōtālis*, f. *sacerdōs*, *-dōt-* priest :- **sakrodhōts* 'offering sacrifices', f. **sakro-* SACRED (cf. L. *sacra* sacrifices) + **dhō-* make, DO[1]; see -AL[1].

sachet small perfumed bag; dry perfume in packet form. XIX. - (O)F., dim. of *sac* SACK[1]; see -ET.

sack[1] large oblong bag open at one end. OE. *sacc* - L. *saccus* bag, sack, sackcloth (whence (O)F. *sac*, It. *sacco*), corr. to Gr. *sákkos* packing-material, of Sem. orig. Comp. **sackcloth** coarse textile fabric, esp. as a material for penitential garb. XIV. Hence **sack** vb.[1] A. put into a sack XIV; B. dismiss, discharge XIX. In A, partly after medL. *saccāre* or MDu. *sacken*, etc.; in B, f. phr. *give* (a person) *the sack* (XIX), which has analogues in F. *donner son sac à quelqu'un*, (M)Du. *iemand den zak geven*, and in F. vb. *sacquer*.

sack[2] gen. name for a class of white wines from Spain and the Canaries. XVI. orig. (*wyne*) *seck* - F. *vin sec* dry wine (see SEC); perh. orig. applied to dry wines of the sherry class, but later extended to others. The alt. of *seck* to *sack* is unexpl.

sack[3] plundering. XVI. - F. *sac* - It. *sacco*. Hence **sack** vb.[2] plunder XVI.

sack[4], also **sac**, (pseudo-F.) **sacque** loose gown for women XVI; loose-fitting coat XIX. prob. orig. a use of SACK[1], later assoc. with F. *sac*.

sackbut bass trumpet with a slide. XVI. - F. *saquebute*, earlier *-boute*, *-bot(t)e* (XV), recorded earlier in the sense of a hooked lance for pulling a man off his horse, f. *saquer*, var. of OF. *sachier* pull; the second el. is obscure.

sacrament any of certain sacred rites of the Christian Church XII; spec. *the S.*, the Eucharist, Holy Communion XIII; (arch.) sacred or solemn pledge XIV. ME. *sacrement* (also *sacra-*, by assim. to L.) - (O)F. *sacrement* - L. *sacrāmentum* solemn engagement, caution-money deposited in a suit, military oath, (in ChrL.) used to render Gr. *mustḗrion* MYSTERY[1], f. *sacrāre* hallow, consecrate, f. *sacer* SACRED; see -MENT. So **sacramental** adj. XIV; sb. rite analogous to a sacrament XVI. - OF. or late L. **sacramentarian** XVI. f. modL. *sacrāmentārius*, applied to those denying the Real Presence. **sacrarium** sanctuary of a church. XVIII. - eccl. use of L. *sacrārium* place in which sacred objects were kept. **sacred** consecrated, dedicated *to* XIV; dedicated to a religious purpose XV; reverenced as holy, secured against violation XVI. orig. pp. (see -ED¹) of †*sacre* consecrate - (O)F. *sacrer* - L. *sacrāre* consecrate, dedicate to a divinity, f. *sacer, sacr-* consecrated, holy, rel. to *sanctus* sacred (see SAINT). **sacrifice** offering of a slaughtered animal, etc. to a deity; that which is so offered XIII; Jesus Christ's offering of himself XIV; applied to the Eucharist; gen. (so *self-s.*) XVI. - (O)F. - L. *sacrificium*; see -FIC; hence vb. XIII. **sacrificial** XVII. **sacrilege** violation of a sacred person or thing, prop. theft of a sacred object XIII; profanation XIV. - (O)F. *sacrilège* - L. *sacrilegium*, f. *sacrilegus* one who steals sacred things, f. *sacer, sacri-* + *legere* take possession of; hence **sacrilegious** XVI. **sacring** (hist.) consecration of the Eucharist. XIII. f. †*sacre* consecrate + -ING¹; hence **sacring-bell** XIV. **sacrist** one having charge of sacred vessels, etc. XVI. - (O)F. *sacriste*, or medL. *sacrista*. **sacristan** XIV. - medL. *sacristānus*. **sacristy** repository in a church for sacred objects. XVII. - F. *sacristie*, It. *sacrestia* or medL. *sacristia*. **sacro-** used as comb. form (see -O-) of SACRUM in anat. terms. XIX. **sacrosanct** secured by religious sanction. XVII. - L. *sacrōsanctus*, f. *sacrō*, abl. of *sacrum* sacred rite, sb. use of n. of *sacer* + *sanctus* sacred (see SAINT). **sacrum** (anat.) lowest bone of the spine. XVIII. Short for late L. *os sacrum*, tr. Gr. *hieròn ostéon* 'sacred bone'.

sad A. †sated, weary OE.; †steadfast, firm; †grave, serious; sorrowful XIV; deplorably disappointing or bad XVII. B. †solid, dense XIII (cf. *sad-iron*, solid flat-iron); dark-coloured XVI; (of bread, etc.) that has not 'risen' XVII. OE. *sæd* = OS. *sad* (Du. *zat*), OHG. *sat* (G. *satt*), ON. *saðr*, Goth. *saþs* :- Gmc. **saðaz* :- IE. **sətós*, pp. formation (see -ED¹) on a base repr. also by Gr. *áatos* (:- **n̥sətós*) insatiate, L. *sat, satis* enough, *satur* sated, OIr. *sathech* satiated, Lith. *sotùs* satisfying. Hence **sadden** (-EN⁶) (dial.) make solid XVI; make sorrowful XVII.

saddle sb. OE. *sadol, -ul* = MDu. *sadel* (Du. *zadel, zaal*), OHG. *satal, -ul* (G. *sattel*), ON. *sǫðull* :- Gmc. **saðulaz*, perh. ult. to be referred to IE. **sed-* SIT, which is repr. in the parallel formations Goth. *sitls* seat (see SETTLE¹), L. *sella* (:- **sedlā*), Gr. *hellá* seat, OSl. *sedŭlo* saddle. Hence vb. OE. *sadolian*.

Sadducee member of one of the three Jewish sects (the others being Pharisees and Essenes) of the time of Christ. OE. *sad(d)ucēas*, ME. *saduceis, saduce(e)s*, later *Sadduces*, pl.; - late L. *Saddūcæus* - late Gr. *Saddoukaîos*, f. late Heb. *ṣaddūḳī*, prob. f. personal name *ṣaddūḳ, ṣādhôḳ* Zadok (2 Sam. 8: 17 etc.), the high priest of David's time from whom the priesthood of the Captivity and later periods claimed to be descended.

sadism XIX. - F. *sadisme*, f. name of the Count (usu. called Marquis) de *Sade* (1740-1814), infamous for his crimes and the character of his writings; see -ISM. Hence **sadist, sadistic** XIX.

safe¹ free from hurt or damage XIII; free from danger, secure XIV. ME. *sauf, sāf* - (O)F. *sauf* (AN. *saf*) :- L. *salvus* uninjured, entire, healthy, rel. to Gr. *hólos*, Skr. *sárva-*, W. *holl* whole. Comp. **safeguard** XV (*sauf garde*; also *saue warde* XIV). - AN. *salve garde*, (O)F. *sauve garde*.

safe² receptacle for safe keeping. XV. orig. *save*, f. SAVE¹; later assim. to prec.

safety XIII ('salvation'). ME. *sauvete* - (O)F. *sauveté* :- medL. *salvitās, -tāt*, f. *salvus* unharmed. See SAFE¹, -TY².

safflower (dried petals of) the plant *Carthamus tinctorius*. XVI (*samfloure*). - Du. *saffloer* or G. *safflor* - OF. *saffleur* - It. †*saffiore*, of unkn. orig.; infl. by assoc. with *saffron* and *flower*.

saffron (orange-red product of) the plant *Crocus sativus* XIII; autumn crocus XV. ME. *saffran, safron* - (O)F. *safran* - Arab. *za'farān*.

sag subside XV; hang loose XVI; (naut.) drift XVII. Corr. in form to Norw. dial. *sagga* walk slowly and heavily, in sense to MLG. *sacken*, Du. *zakken*, Norw. dial. *sakka* subside, Da. *sakke* lag behind, drop astern; perh. ult. of W.Scand. orig. and adopted in Du., LG. and Eng. first in nautical use. Hence sb. movement to leeward XVI; subsidence XIX.

saga medieval Norse narrative in prose. XVIII. - ON. (Icel.) *saga* SAW².

sagacious †of acute perception, esp. of smell; gifted with mental discernment. XVII. f. L. *sagāx, sagāc-*, f. **sāg-*, repr. also by L. *sāgīre* discern acutely; see SEEK, -IOUS. So **sagacity** XVI. - F. or L.

sage¹ plant of the genus *Salvia*. XIV. ME. *sauge* - (O)F. :- L. *salvia* 'the healing plant', f. *salvus* uninjured (SAFE¹).

sage² wise XIII; sb. man of profound wisdom XIV. - (O)F. :- Gallo-Rom. **sapius*, f. *sapere* be wise (cf. SAPIENT).

saggar in ceramics, protecting case of fire-proof clay. XVIII. perh. a reduction of SAFEGUARD.

Sagittarius zodiacal constellation. XIV. - L. *sagittārius* archer, f. *sagitta* arrow; see -ARY.

sago XVI (*sagu*; later *sagow, sagoe*; in XVIII, after Du., *sago*). - (orig. through Pg.) Malay *sagu*.

sahib title used by natives of India in addressing an Englishman or European. XVII. - Urdu use of Arab. *ṣāḥib* companion, friend, lord, master.

sail piece of canvas, etc. fastened to a mast, etc. to catch the wind OE.; similar arrangement attached to the arms of a windmill XV. OE. *seġ(e)l* = OS. *segel* (Du. *zeil*), OHG. *segal, -il* (G. *segel*), ON. *segl* :- Gmc. **seȝlam*, of unkn. orig. So **sail** vb. OE. *seġl(i)an*. **sailor** XVI. In earliest use *sayler* (see -ER¹); later alt., by assim. to agent-nouns in -OR¹ (e.g. *tailor*), to distinguish the designation of a regular calling from the unspecialized form.

sainfoin herb *Onobrychis viciaefolia*; also lucerne, *Medicago sativa*. XVII. Early forms *saintfoin, St. Foine* - F. †*saintfoin* (mod. *sainfoin*) orig. lucerne - modL. *sanctum fœnum* 'holy hay', alt. of *sānum fœnum* 'wholesome hay', which was based on L. *herba medica* 'healing plant', itself erron. alt. of *herba Mēdica*, Gr. *Mēdikḗ póa* 'Median grass'.

saint holy (prefixed to a name, now regarded as the sb. used attrib.); sb. canonized person; one of the elect of God XIV; person of great holiness XVI. OE. *sanct*, superseded (XII) by *seint(e)*, *sa(i)nt* (before a name with initial cons., *sein*, *sayn*) - OF. *seint*, (also mod.) *saint*, fem. *seinte*, *sainte*, prefixed occas. †*sain* :- L. *sanctus* sacred, holy, prop. pp. of *sancīre* (see SANCTION), used sb. in the Vulg., e.g. Ps. 29: 5. Hence **saintly** (-LY[1]) XVII.

sake[1] †strife, contention (in OE. also, legal suit); †guilt OE.; †charge, ground of accusation XII; surviving in phr. *for the sake of* XIII (prob. modelled on ON.). OE. *sacu* = OS. *saka* (Du. *zaak*), OHG. *sahha* (G. *sache*), ON. *sǫk* :- Gmc. **sakō*, f. **sak-*, repr. also by OE. *sacan* quarrel, claim at law, accuse, OS. *sakan* accuse, OHG. *sahhan* strive, quarrel, rebuke, OE. *sæċ*, Goth. *sakjō* strife; rel. to SEEK.

sake[2] fermented liquor made from rice. XVII (*saque*). - Jap.

saker large falcon, *Falco sacer* XIV (*sacre*, *sagre*); old form of cannon XVI. - (O)F. *sacre* - Arab. *ṣaḳr*; identified with L. *sacer* SACRED.

saki S. Amer. monkey. XVIII. - F., of Tupi orig.

salaam Oriental salutation, ceremonious obeisance accompanying this. XVII. - Arab. *salām* (in full *(as)salām 'alaikum* peace be unto you) = Heb. *šālôm* peace. Hence vb. XVII.

salacious XVII. f. L. *salāx*, *salāc-*, f. base of *salīre* leap; see -IOUS.

salad XV. - (O)F. *salade* - Pr. *salada* :- Rom. **salāta*, sb. use of pp. fem. of **salāre* salt, f. L. *sāl* SALT.

salamander lizard-like animal supposed to live in fire XIV; tailed amphibian; poker used red-hot XVII. - (O)F. *salamandre* - L. *salamandra* - Gr. *salamándrā*.

sal-ammoniac ammonium chloride. XIV (*salarmoniak*). - L. *sal ammōniacus*, medL. *sal armōniacum*; see SALT, AMMONIAC.

salary XIV. - AN. *salarie* = (O)F. *salaire* - L. *salārium* orig. money allowed to Roman soldiers for the purchase of salt, (hence) pay, stipend, sb. use of *salārius*, f. *sāl* SALT; see -ARY.

sale act of selling. Late OE. *sala* - ON., f. base of Gmc. **saljan* SELL. Hence **sal(e)able, salesman** (-S) XVI.

saleratus (U.S.) impure sodium bicarbonate used in baking-powders. XIX. - modL. *sāl āerātus* 'AERATED SALT'.

salicional (mus.) reedy organ stop. XIX. - G., f. L. *salix*, *salic-* willow, SALLOW[1]. Also **salicet** XIX. - G.

salicyl (chem.) diatomic radical of **salicylic** *acid*. XIX. - F. *salicyle*, f. L. *salix*, *salic-* SALLOW[1]; see -YL.

salient leaping (first in her.) XVI; jetting forward, pointing outward XVII; prominent XVIII; sb. salient part or angle XIX. - L. *saliēns*, *-ent-*, prp. of *salīre* leap; see -ENT. *S. point* †the heart as it first appears in an embryo, (hence) first beginning, starting-point (XVII), tr. modL. *punctum saliens*, the source of which is Aristotle's 'Historia Animalium' VI iii.

saline pert. to salt XV; sb. salt lake, etc.; saline purge XIX. - medL. *salīnum*, f. L. *sāl* SALT; see -INE[1].

saliva XVII. - L. *salīva*. So **salivary** XVIII. - L. *salivārius*. **salivate** (-ATE[3]) XVII. f. pp. stem of L. *salīvāre*. **salivation** XVI. - F. or late L.

sallender (now only pl.) dry scab on a horse's hock. XVI (*selander*). of unkn. orig., but with a remarkable formal parallel in MALANDERS.

sallet, salade globular headpiece in medieval armour. XV. - F. *salade* - Pr. *salada*, It. *celata*, or Sp. *celada* - Rom. **cælāta*, sb. use of fem. pp. of L. *cælāre* engrave, f. *cælum* chisel.

sallow[1] willow. OE. (Angl.) *salh* (repr. directly by dial. *saugh*, †*salfe* XIV) :- Gmc. **salχaz*, rel. to OHG. *salaha* and ON. *selja*, and outside Gmc. to L. *salix*, Gr. *helíkē*, OIr. *sail*. The form *sallow* (ME. *salwe*) descends from OE. inflexional *salg-*.

sallow[2] of a sickly or brownish yellow. OE. *salu* dusky, dark = MDu. *salu*, discoloured, dirty, OHG. *salo* dark-coloured, ON. *sǫlr* yellow :- Gmc. **salwa-*.

sally sortie from a besieged place XVI; sudden start or outburst XVII; sprightly remark XVIII. - (O)F. *saillie*, sb. use of fem. pp. of *saillir* issue forth, refash. of OF. *salir* leap :- L. *salīre*. Hence vb. XVI.

Sally Lunn kind of tea-cake. XVIII. Said to be so named after a woman who made and cried them in Bath.

salmagundi dish of chopped meat with condiments. XVII. - F. *salmigondis*, †*-gondin*, of unkn. orig.

salmi ragout of game. XVIII. shortening of F. *salmigondis*; see prec.

salmon large fish of the genus *Salmo*. XIII (*sa(l)moun*). - AN. *sa(u)moun*, (O)F. *saumon* :- L. *salmō*, *salmōn-*, rel. to *salar* trout or young salmon.

salon large reception room. XVIII. - F.; see next.

saloon large apartment for assemblies, etc. XVIII; large cabin or railway carriage; (U.S.) drinking bar XIX. - F. *salon* - It. *salone*, augm. of *sala* - Rom. **sala* hall - Gmc. **salaz*, **saliz*, repr. by OE. *sæl*, OHG. *sal* (G. *saal*) and OE. *sele*, OS. *seli*, OHG. *sali*, *seli*, ON. *salr*; see -OON.

Salopian pert. to Shropshire. XVIII. f. *Salop*, alternative name of Shropshire, evolved from *Salopesberia* (XI) and *Salopescire* (XI), AN. alt. of ME. forms of OE. *Scrobbesbyriġ* Shrewsbury and *Scrobbesbyriġscīr* Shropshire; see -IAN.

salpiglossis herbaceous garden-plant. XIX. modL., irreg. f. Gr. *sálpigx* trumpet + *glôssa* tongue; so named from its trumpet-shaped corolla.

salsify purple goatsbeard, *Tragopogon porrifolius*. XVIII. - F. *salsifis* - It. †*salsefica* (mod. *sassefrica*); of unkn. orig.

salt substance (sodium chloride) prepared as a condiment OE.; (old chem.) solid non-inflammable substance having a taste XIV; (mod. chem.) compound formed by an acid with a basic radical XVIII. OE. *s(e)alt* = OS. *salt* (Du. *zout*), (O)HG. *salz*, ON., Goth. *salt* :- Gmc. **saltam*, sb. use of adj. **saltaz* (see below), extension of IE. **sal-*, repr. by L. *sāl*, *sal-*, Gr. *háls*, OSl. *salĭ*, Latv. *sâls*, OIr. *salann*. So **salt**

adj. OE. *s(e)alt*. **salt** vb. OE. *s(e)altan*. Hence **salty** (-Y[1]) XV.

saltation leaping, dancing. XVII. - L. *saltātiō, -ōn-*, f. *saltāre* dance, frequent. of *salīre* leap; see -ATION. So **saltatory** XVII. - L. *saltātōrius*; hence **saltatorial** XVIII.

saltcellar XV. f. SALT + *saler, sel(l)er* - AN. **saler(e)*, OF. *sal(l)iere* (mod. *salière*), also *salier* saltcellar; Rom, f. L. *sāl* SALT. The sp. was assim. to *cellar*.

saltern (hist.) salt-works. OE. *sealtærn*, f. *sealt* SALT + *ærn* dwelling, building, house.

saltigrade (zool.) spider having legs developed for leaping. XIX. - modL. *Saltigradæ* pl., f. L. *saltus* leap + *gradī* step.

saltimbanco mountebank. XVII. - It., f. *saltare* leap + *in* on + *banco* bench.

saltire (her.) ordinary in the form of a St. Andrew's cross X. XIV. Early forms *sawturoure, sawtire*, later *saltier, -ire* - OF. *saut(e)our, -ouer, sau(l)toir* stirrup cord (perh. forming a deltoid figure when in use), stile with cross-pieces, saltire :- medL. *saltātōrium*, sb. use of n. of *saltātōrius* SALTATORY.

saltpetre potassium nitrate, nitre. XVI. alt., by assim. to SALT, of †*salpetre* (XIV) - (O)F. *salpètre* - medL. *salpetra*, prob. for **sāl petræ* 'salt of rock' (the substance being so named because it occurs as an incrustation on stones).

salubrious XVI. f. L. *salūbris*, f. *salūs* health; see next and -IOUS. So **salubrity** XV. - L.

salutary conducive to wellbeing XV; conducive to health XVII. - (O)F. *salutaire* or L. *salūtāris*, f. *salūs, salūt-* health, welfare, greeting, salutation, rel. to *salvus* SAFE[1]; see -ARY. So **salutation** greeting in words. XIV. - (O)F. *salutation* or L. *salūtātiō, -ōn-*, f. *salūtāre*, whence **salute** greet XIV, (mil. and naval) XVI. **salute** sb. XIV. partly - (O)F. *salut*, partly f. the Eng. vb.

salvage payment to persons who have saved a ship or its cargo; action of saving a ship, etc.; property salved XVII. - (O)F. - medL. *salvāgium*, f. L. *salvāre* SAVE[1]; see -AGE. Hence, by back-formation, **salve** vb.[2] save from loss at sea or by fire. XVIII. **salvor** (-OR[1]), †*salver* XVII.

salvation saving of the soul XIII; preservation, means of this XIV. ME. *sa(u)vacioun, salv-* - OF. *sauvacion, salv-* (mod. *salvation*) - late L. *salvātiō, -ōn-*, f. *salvāre* SAVE[1]; see -ATION.

salve healing ointment. OE. *salf, sealf(e)* = OS. *salba* (Du. *zalf*), OHG. *salba* (G. *salbe*) :- Gmc. **salbō*; cf. Skr. *sarpi-* clarified butter, Gr. *élpos* oil. So **salve** vb.[1] †anoint OE.; heal, remedy XIII; soothe (irritation, an uneasy conscience) XIX (partly by assoc. with †*salve* clear up, explain - L. *salvāre*). OE. *s(e)alfian* = OS. *salbon* (Du. *zalven*), OHG. *salbōn* (G. *salben*), Goth. *salbōn*.

salver XVII. f. F. *salve* tray for presenting objects to the king, or its source Sp. *salva* †foretasting or assaying of food or drink, tray on which assayed food was placed, f. *salvar* SAVE[1], render safe, assay; the ending *-er* is due to assoc. with *platter*.

salvia genus of plants, including sage. XIX. modL. use of L. *salvia*, SAGE[1].

salvo[1] saving clause; dishonest mental reservation XVII; expedient for saving one's reputation or soothing one's conscience, etc. XVIII. - L. *salvō*, abl. of n. of *salvus* uninjured, intact, SAFE[1], occurring as the first word of medL. law phr. such as *salvo jure* (abl. of L. *jūs* right) without prejudice to the right of; cf. SAVE[2].

salvo[2] simultaneous discharge of firearms, esp. as a salute. XVII. repl. earlier (XVI) †*salve* and occas. †*salva*, by substitution of *-o* for *-a*; ult. - It. *salva*.

sal volatile aromatic solution of ammonium carbonate. XVII. - modL. *sāl volātile*; see SALT, VOLATILE.

sambo half-breed, mostly between Negro and Indian. XVIII. - Sp. *zambo* (also in Eng. use XIX), identified with *zambo* bandy-legged; perh. not the same word as *sambo* nickname for a negro (XIX).

Sam Browne officer's belt introduced by General *Sam*uel J. *Browne* (1824-1901). XX.

same not different, identical. XII. - ON. *sami* m., *sama* fem., n. = OHG., Goth. *sama* :- Gmc. adj. **saman-*, f. IE. **som-*, whence also Skr. *samá-* level, equal, same, Gr. *homós*, OIr. *som* same; the vars. **sem-* **sōm-* **səm-* of the base are seen in L. *similis* SIMILAR, SEEM, and SOME.

samite (hist.) rich silk fabric. XIII. - OF. *samit*, ult. - medL. *examitum* - medGr. *hexámiton*, f. Gr. HEXA- + *mítos* thread; the ref. to sixth thread is variously explained.

samlet young salmon. XVII. alt. of earlier *samonet* (XVI; f. SALMON + -ET) by assoc. with -LET.

samovar Russian tea urn. XIX. - Russ. *samovár*, f. *samo-* self- + stem of *varít'* boil.

Samoyed one of a Siberian Mongol people XVII; (also *-ede*) breed of dog XIX. - Russ. *samoéd*, prob. f. Lapp. Norw.

sampan small Chinese boat. XVII. Chinese *san pan*, f. *san* three, *pan* board.

samphire cliff plant. XVI (*samp(i)ere*). - F. (*herbe de*) *Saint Pierre* 'St. Peter's herb'.

sample †illustrative or confirmatory fact, etc.; †example, warning XIII; specimen of material or goods XV. Aphetic - AN. *assample*, var. of OF. *essample* EXAMPLE. Hence vb. XVI.

sampler †example, pattern XIII; beginner's exercise in embroidery done on canvas XVI. Aphetic - OF. *essamplaire*, var. of *essemplaire* EXEMPLAR.

Samson's post (POST[1]) †kind of mousetrap having a triangular pillar XVI; (naut.) strong pillar or stanchion XVIII. prob. with allusion to Judges 16: 29 ('And Samson took hold of the two middle pillars . . .').

sanatorium establishment for the treatment of invalids; room for the sick. XIX. - modL. *sānātōrium*, f. pp. stem of L. *sānāre* heal, f. *sānus* healthy, SANE; see -ATE[3], -ORIUM.

sanbenito (under the Sp. Inquisition) penitent heretic's garment. XVI. - Sp. *sambenito*, f. *San Benito* St. Benedict; so called ironically from its resemblance in shape to the Benedictine scapular.

sanctify †consecrate, hallow XIV; make holy XV. In earliest use *seintifie* - OF. *saintifier*, later influenced by *sanctifier* - ChrL. *sanctificāre*, f. L. *sanctus* holy (see SAINT). So **sanctification**

XVI. - ChrL. *sanctificātiō, -ōn-*. **sanctimonious** †holy, sacred; affecting sanctity. XVII. f. L. *sanctimōnia* sanctity (whence **sanctimony** †sanctity XVI; affected holiness XVII). **sanction** †law, decree XVI; (leg.) penalty exacted to compel obedience; clause of a law prescribing this; motive, etc. involved therein; binding force XVII; influential encouragement XVIII. - F. *sanction* authoritative approval of a law, penalty prescribed in an enactment; (gen.) approval - L. *sanctiō, -ōn-* act of establishing as inviolable under a penalty, clause decreeing a penalty, f. *sanct-*, pp. stem of *sancīre* render inviolable, decree, forbid under penalty, f. var. (with nasal infix) of base of *sacer* SACRED; hence vb. XVIII. **sanctity** holiness XIV; sacredness XVII. partly (in forms *sauntite, saintite*) - OF. *sain(c)tité* (mod. *sainteté*); partly immed. - L. *sanctitās*. **sanctuary** building for religious worship; part of a church immediately surrounding the altar; sacred place giving immunity from arrest; also fig. XIV. - AN. *sanctuarie*, (O)F. *sanctuaire* - L. *sanctuārium*. **sanctum** holy place of the Jewish tabernacle XVI; short for *sanctum sanctorum* in the second sense XIX. - L., n. sg. of *sanctus*. **sanctum sanctorum** Holy of Holies of the Jewish temple XIV; person's private retreat XVIII. - L., n. sg. and n. g. pl. of *sanctus*, tr. (= LXX *tòn hágion tôn hagíōn*) of Heb. *ḳōdeš haḳḳodāšīm* holy of holies. **sanctus** the 'angelic hymn' (see Isa. 6: 3), beginning *Sanctus sanctus sanctus* Holy, holy, holy, which concludes the preface to the Eucharistic canon. XIV. - L.

sand OE. *sand* = OS. *sand*, OHG. *sant* (Du. *zand*, G. *sand*), ON. *sandr* :- Gmc. **sandam, -az*, rel. to Gr. *hámathos*, L. *sabulum* sand. Hence **sandy** (-Y[1]) OE. *sandiġ*.

sandal[1] covering for the sole of the foot XIV; half-shoe for ceremonial wear XV. - L. *sandalium* - Gr. *sandálion*, dim. of *sándalon* wooden shoe, prob. of Asiatic orig.

sandal[2] scented wood of species of *Santalum*. XIV. - medL. *sandalum*; ult. - Skr. *candana-*.

sandarac A. realgar XVI; B. resin of a N.W. Afr. tree; †C. bee-bread XVII. - L. *sandaraca* - Gr. *sandarák(h)ē*, of Asiatic orig.; the connection between the senses is not clear.

sand-blind (arch. and dial.) half-blind, purblind. XV. repr. ult. OE. **samblind*, f. *sam-* half- (shortening of WGmc. **sāmi-* :- IE. **sēmi-* SEMI-) + BLIND; assim. to SAND.

sanders sandalwood. XIV. - OF. †*sandre*, var. of *sandal*, (also mod.) *santal* - medL. *sandalum* SANDAL[2].

sandiver scum rising through glass in a state of fusion. XIV (*saundyuer*). - F. *suint de verre* (XVII), i.e. *suint* exudation from wool, *de* of, *verre* glass; presumably assim. to SAND.

sandwich article of food consisting of two slices of bread with meat, etc. between them. XVIII. f. name of John Montagu, 4th Earl of *Sandwich* (1718-1792), for whom it was said to have been invented so that he might not leave the gaming-table.

sane sound in mind XVII; †healthy in body XVIII. - L. *sānus*. So **sanity** †bodily health XV; mental soundness XVII. - L. *sānitās*.

sang-froid XVIII. - F., 'cold blood'.

sangrail, -greal holy grail. XV. - OF. *saint graal*; see SAINT, GRAIL[2]. The sp. has been infl. by assoc. with OF. *sang real* royal blood.

sanguinary bloody; bloodthirsty. XVII. - L. *sanguinārius*, f. *sanguis, sanguin-* blood; see -ARY. So **sanguine** blood-red XIV; pert. to the physiological complexion in which blood predominates over the other humours; disposed to hopefulness XVI. - (O)F. *sanguin*, fem. *-ine* - L. *sanguineus* (whence **sanguineous** XVI).

sanhedrin, -im highest court and supreme council of the Jews at Jerusalem. XVI. - late Heb. *sanhedrīn* - Gr. *sunédrion* council, f. *sún* together (SYN-) + *hédra* seat (see SIT). The common incorrect form in *-im* seems to be due to the notion that the orig. *-īn* was the Aram. pl. suffix equiv. to Heb. *-īm*.

sanicle umbelliferous plant of the genus *Sanicula*. XV. - OF. - medL. *sanicula, -ulum*, perh. f. L. *sānus* healthy (SANE), with ref. to the plant's reputed healing powers.

sanies XVI. - L. *saniēs*.

sanitary pert. to health or to sanitation. XIX. - F. *sanitaire*, f. L. *sānitās* health, f. *sānus* healthy (SANE); see -ARY. Hence (irreg.) **sanitation** XIX.

sanity see SANE.

sans (arch., chiefly after Sh. 'As You Like It' II vii 166) without. XIII. ME. *san(s), saun(z)* - OF. *san(z)*, (also mod.) *sans*, earlier *sen(s)* :- Rom. **sene*, for L. *sine*.

sansculotte in the French Revolution, a republican of the poorer classes in Paris. XVIII. - F., f. *sans* without + *culotte* knee-breeches; usu. taken to mean lit. 'one who wears trousers (*pantalon*), not knee-breeches'.

sanserif printing type without serifs. XIX. prob. f. SANS + SERIF.

Santa Claus imaginary person who brings presents for children on Christmas Eve. XVIII (*St. A Claus*), XIX (*Santiclaus*). orig. U.S. - Du. dial. *Sante Klaas* (Du. *Sint Klaas*), i.e. *sant, sint* SAINT, *Klaas*, abbrev. of *Nicolaas* Nicholas (patron of children).

sap[1] vital juice of plants OE.; sapwood, alburnum XV. OE. *sæp*, corr. to (M)LG., (M)Du. *sap*, OHG. *saf* (G. *saft*), prob. repr. Gmc. **sap(p)am*, and rel. to ON. *safi*; cf. L. *sapa* must boiled until it is thick. Hence **sapling** young tree XV; young person XVI.

sap[2] †undermining a defence; construction of covered trenches to approach a besieged place XVI; trench so constructed XVII. Early forms *zappe, sappe* - It. *zappa* and the derived F. †*sappe*, †*zappe* (now *sape*) spade, spadework. Hence **sap** vb. dig a sap XVI; undermine XVII; weaken insidiously (assoc. with SAP[1], as if 'drain the sap from') XVIII. - F. *saper*, †*sapper* - It. *zappare*.

sap[3] (colloq.) simpleton XIX. Short for *sapskull* (XVIII) 'skull of sapwood'.

sapajou S. Amer. monkey. XVII. - F., said to be a Cayenne word.

sapan, sappan dye-wood obtained from the genus *Cæsalpinia*. XVI. - Du. *sapan* - Malay *sĕpang*.

sapid savoury, palatable; having a taste. XVII. -

L. *sapidus*, f. *sapere* have a taste; see next and -ID[1].

sapient (now usu. iron.) wise. XV. - OF. *sapient* or L. *sapiēns*, *-ent-*, prp. of *sapere* Have a taste, be sensible or wise, rel. to OS. *afsebbian* perceive, notice, OHG. *intseffen* notice, taste, OE. *sefa* mind, understanding, OS. *sebo*, ON. *sefi*; see -ENT. So **sapience** XIV. - OF. - L. *sapientia*. **sapiential** †pert. to wisdom XV; pert. to the 'wisdom' books of the Bible XVI. - F. *sapiential* or ChrL. *sapientiālis*.

sapodilla (fruit of) an evergreen tropical Amer. tree. XVII. - Sp. *zapotillo*, dim. of *zapote* - Nahuatl *tzápotl*.

saponaceous soapy. XVIII. f. modL. *sāpōnāceus*, f. L. *sāpō*, *-ōn-* SOAP; see -ACEOUS.

sapor taste. XV. - L. *sapor*, f. *sapere* have a taste; see SAPIENT.

Sapphic pert. to Sappho or metres used by her; also sb. pl. verses in Sapphic metre. XVI. - F. *saphique*, †*sapphique* - L. *Sapphicus* - Gr. *Sapphikós*, f. *Sapphṓ*, name of the poetess (c. 600 B.C.) of Lesbos, Greece; see -IC.

sapphire XIII. ME. *saphir*, *safir* - OF. *safir* (mod. *saphir*) - L. *sapphīrus*, also *sapp(h)ir* - Gr. *sáppheiros* (prob.) lapis lazuli, prob. of Sem. orig.

sapro- comb. form of Gr. *saprós* putrid, rel. to *sḗpein* rot (see SEPTIC) used in some techn. terms, the earliest of which is **saprophagous** living on decomposing matter XIX.

saraband (music for) a slow and stately Spanish dance. XVII. - F. *sarabande* - Sp., It. *zarabanda*, of unkn. orig.

Saracen name of nomadic peoples of the Syro-Arabian desert, (hence) Arab, Moslem; †pagan, infidel. XIII. - OF. *Sar(r)azin*, *-cin* (mod. *Sarrasin*) late L. *Saracēnus* - late Gr. *Sarakēnós*, perh. f. Arab. *šarḳī* eastern, f. *šarḳ* sunrise, east.

sarcasm cutting expression or remark, sarcastic language. XVI (in L. form), XVII. - F. *sarcasme* or late L. *sarcasmos* - late Gr. *sarkasmós*, f. *sarkázein* tear flesh, gnash the teeth, speak bitterly, f. *sárx*, *sark-* flesh. So **sarcastic** XVII. - F. *sarcastique*.

sarcenet see SARSENET.

sarco- comb. form of Gr. *sárx*, *sark-* flesh. **sarcoma** †fleshy excrescence XVII; kind of tumour XIX. - modL. *sarcōma* - Gr. *sárkōma*, f. *sarkoûn* become fleshy; see -OMA.

sarcophagus stone reputed by the ancient Greeks to consume corpses and hence used for coffins XVII; stone coffin XVIII. - L. - Gr. *sarkophágos*, sb. use of adj. f. *sárx*, *sark-* flesh + *-phágos* -eating, -PHAGOUS.

sard variety of cornelian. XIV. - F. *sarde* or L. *sarda* SARDIUS.

sardelle fish resembling the sardine. XVI. - It. *sardella*, dim. of *sarda* :- L. - Gr. *sárdē*.

sardine[1] precious stone of Rev. 4: 3. XIV. - late L. *sardinus* - Gr. *sárdinos*, var. reading for *sárdios* SARDIUS.

sardine[2] small fish of the herring family. XV (*-eyne*). - (O)F. *sardine*, corr. to It. *sardina* - L. *sardīna*; cf. late Gr. *sardḗnē*, *-ínē*, *sardinos*, and L. *sarda*, Gr. *sárdā*; prob. connected with the name of the island Sardinia.

sardius precious stone, sard. XIV. - late L. - Gr. *sárdios*, prob. f. *Sardṓ* Sardinia.

sardonic (of laughter) marked by bitterness or scorn. XVII. - F. *sardonique*, alt. of †*sardonien*, f. L. *sardonius* - late Gr. *Sardónios* Sardinian, which was substituted for *sardánios* as an epithet for scornful laughter, from the notion that the word orig. referred to the effects of eating a Sardinian plant said to produce facial convulsions resembling horrible laughter; see -IC.

sardonyx variety of onyx. XIV. - L. - Gr. *sardónux*, presumably f. *sárdios* SARDIUS + *ónux* ONYX.

sargasso seaweed found floating in the Gulf Stream and esp. in the *S. Sea* (bounded by the Azores, the Canaries, and the Cape Verde islands). XVI. - Pg. *sargaço*, of unkn. orig.

sari, saree XVIII (*saurry*). - Hindi *sāṛhī*, *sāṛī*.

sark (dial.) shirt, chemise. XIII. ME. (north.) *serk* - ON. *serkr* :- Gmc. **sarkiz*, f. base repr. also by OE. *serċe*, *syrċ(e)*. Hence **sark** vb. clothe with a sark; (in building) cover (a roof) with planks. XV.

sarmentose (bot.) producing slender prostrate branches or runners. XVIII. - L. *sarmentōsus*, f. *sarmentum* (chiefly pl.) twigs lopped off, brushwood, f. *sarpere* prune, lop; see -MENT, -OSE[1]. So **sarmentous** XVIII.

sarong Malay garment wrapped round the waist. XIX. - Malay, (prop.) sheath, quiver.

sarsaparilla (dried roots of) tropical Amer. smilax. XVI. - Sp. *zarzaparrilla*, f. *zarza* bramble.

sarsen large boulder. XVII. Earlier in *Saracen's* and *Sarsdon stones*, *Sarsdens*, and supposed to be identical with SARACEN.

sarsenet, sarcenet soft fine silk material. XV. - AN. *sarzinett*, perh. dim. of *sarzin* SARACEN; see -ET.

sartorial XIX. f. L. *sartor* tailor, f. pp. stem of *sarcīre* patch, botch; see -IAL.

sash[1] †turban XVI; scarf worn round the body XVII. orig. *shash* - Arab. *šāš* muslin, turban.

sash[2] window-frame fitted with glass. XVII. First in pl. *shashes*, var. of *chasses*, used as pl. of *chassis* - OF. *chassis* (mod. *châssis*) frame, framework (CHASSIS).

sasine (Sc. law) giving possession of feudal property. XVII. var. of SEISIN, after law-L. *sasina*.

sassaby large S. Afr. antelope. XIX. - Tswana *tsessébe*, *-ábi*.

sassafras small tree native to N. America. XVI. - Sp. *sasafrás* or Pg. *sassafraz*, of unkn. orig.

Sassenach XVIII. - Gael. *Sasunnoch* = Ir. *Sasanach*, f. *Sasan-* - L. *Saxonēs* Saxons.

Satan the Devil. OE. - late L. *Satān* (Vulg.) - Gr. *Satân* - Heb. *śāṭān* adversary, plotter, f. *śāṭan* oppose, plot against. Hence **satanic** XVII, **satanical, Satanism, -ist** XVI.

satchel small bag. XIV. - OF. *sachel* :- L. *saccellus*, dim. of *saccus* SACK[1]; see -EL[2].

sate satisfy to the full. XVII. prob. alt. of dial. *sade* (OE. *sadian*, rel. to *sæd* satiated, SAD), by assoc. with SATIATE.

sateen cotton or woollen stuff with satiny surface. XIX. alt. of SATIN; see -EEN[1].

satellite A. attendant on an important person XVI (rare before XVIII); B. heavenly body revolving round a planet XVII. - (O)F. *satellite* or L. *satelles, satellit-*.

satiate †satisfy XVI; surfeit, glut XVII. f. pp. stem of L. *satiāre*, f. *satis* enough (see SAD), after †*satiate* pp. (XV) - L. *satiātus*; see -ATE[2,3]. So **satiety** XVI (*sacietie*). - (O)F. *sacieté* (mod. *satiété*) - L. *satietās, -tāt-*.

satin XIV. - (O)F. - Arab. *zaitūnī*, pert. to the city Tseutung (Tsinkiang) in China.

satire poetical (or prose) work in which vices or follies are ridiculed. XVI. - (O)F. *satire* or L. *satira*, later form of *satura* (in earliest use) verse composition treating of a variety of subjects, spec. application of the sense 'medley'. So **satiric(al)** XVI. - F. or late L. **satirize** XVII. - F. *satiriser*. Hence **satirist** XVI.

satisfaction performance by a penitent of acts enjoined by his confessor XIII; payment in full of a debt, etc.; atonement made by Jesus Christ for sin; action of gratifying to the full XIV; release from uncertainty XVI. - (O)F. - L. *satisfactiō, -ōn-*, f. pp. stem of *satisfacere* (whence, through OF. *satisfier*, **satisfy** XV), f. *satis* enough (cf. SAD); see -FACTION, -FY.

satrap governor of a province in ancient Persia. XIV. - (O)F. *satrape* or L. *satrapa, satrapēs* - Gr. *satrápēs*, also *exatrápēs*, of Iranian orig.; cf. OPers. *χšaçapāvan-* satrap, f. *χšaça-* (:- **χšaθra-*) Kingdom + *pā-* protect. So **satrapy** (-Y[3]) XVII.

saturate †satisfy, satiate XVI; cause to combine with the utmost quantity of another substance XVII; soak thoroughly XVIII. f. pp. stem of L. *saturāre*, f. *satur* full, satiated; see SAD, -ATE[3]. So **saturation** XVI. - late L.

Saturday seventh day of the week. OE. *Sætern(es)dæġ, Sæterdæġ*, corr. to MLG. *sater(s)dach*, MDu. *saterdach* (Du. *zaterdag*), tr. of L. *Sāturnī diēs* day of (the planet) Saturn.

Saturn Italic god of agriculture OE.; (astron.) one of the primary planets XIV (in OE. *Sæternes steorra*); †(alch.) lead. - L. *Sāturnus*, poss. of Etruscan orig. So **Saturnalia** festival of Saturn marked by unrestrained revelry XVI (transf. XVIII). - L., sb. use of n. pl. of *Sāturnālis*; see -AL[1]. **Saturnian** ancient Roman metre. XVI. **saturnine** (-INE[1]) born under Saturn, (hence) of cold and gloomy temperament. XV. - F. *saturnin* - medL. **sāturnīnus*.

satyr woodland god or demon, half man half beast, of lustful propensities. XIV. - (O)F. *satyre* or L. *satyrus* - Gr. *sáturos*. So **satyric** epithet of the Gr. drama in which the chorus were habited as satyrs. XVII. - L. - Gr.

sauce liquid preparation taken as a relish with articles of food XIV; piquant addition XVI; (prob. from *saucy*) †impudent person XVI; impudence XIX. - (O)F. *sauce* :- Rom. **salsa*, sb. use of fem. of L. *salsus* salted. Hence **sauce** vb. season XV; †belabour, rebuke XVI; address impertinently XIX. **saucy** (-Y[1]) †savoury; insolent towards superiors XVI; (of a ship or boat) †rashly venturous XVI, smart XIX.

saucer †receptacle for condiments at a meal XIV; shallow circular dish XVII; esp. one to support a cup XVIII. - OF. *saussier(e)* (mod. *saucière*) sauce-boat, f. *sauce* SAUCE.

sauerkraut XVII (*sower crawt*). - G., f. *sauer* SOUR + *kraut* vegetable, cabbage.

saunter †muse XV; †wander aimlessly XVII; walk leisurely, stroll XVIII. of uncert. orig.

saurian pert. to reptiles of the order Sauria (crocodiles and large extinct lizard-like animals). XV. f. modL. *Sauria*, f. Gr. *saúrā, saûros* lizard; see -IAN.

sausage XV. ME. *sausige* - ONF. *saussiche* (var. of OF. *salsice*, mod. *saucisse*) :- medL. *salsīcia*, n. pl. of *salsīcius*, f. *salsus* salted (see SALT).

sauté fried in a pan, being tossed from time to time. XIX. - F., pp. of *sauter* leap :- L. *saltāre*, used trans. in causative sense.

sauterne(s) wine of the district of *Sauternes*, near Bordeaux, France. XVIII.

savage that is in a state of nature XIII; of wild or unrestrained behaviour XV; uncivilized XVI; furiously angry XIX; sb. XVI. ME. *sa(u)vage* - (O)F. *sauvage* (AN. also *savage*) :- Rom. **salvāticus*, for L. *silvāticus* woodland-, wild, f. *silva* wood, forest; see -AGE. Hence **savagery** XVI.

savanna(h) treeless plain, esp. of tropical America. XVI (*zavanna*; hardly naturalized before late XVII). - Sp. †*çavána* (mod. *sabana*), of Taino orig.

savant man of learning. XVIII. - F., sb. use of orig. prp. of *savoir* know :- Rom. **sapēre*, for L. *sapere*.

save[1] make or keep safe XIII; preserve from damnation; reserve, lay aside XIV; avoid or enable to avoid XVII. ME. *sauve, sa(l)ve* - AN. *sa(u)ver*, OF. *salver*, (also mod.) *sauver* :- late L. *salvāre* save, f. L. *salvus* SAFE[1].

save[2] (arch.) with the exception of XIII. ME. *sauf* and *sauve* - OF. *sauf* (m.) and *sauve* (fem.), orig. varying with the gender of the accompanying sb. (now invariable, *sauf*) :- L. *salvō* and *salvā*, abl. sg. of m. or n. and fem. of *salvus* SAFE[1], as used in absolute constructions such as *salvo jure, salva innocentia* without violation of right, of innocence, (hence) without injury or prejudice to, with reserve of. The later exclusive use of the form *save* is prob. due to the identification of the word with the imper. of SAVE[1].

saveloy XIX. alt. of F. †*cervelat*, (also mod.) *-as* - It. *cervellata*, f. *cervello* brains; cf. -ATE[2].

savin(e) kind of juniper. XIV. - OF. *savine* (repl. by latinized *sabine*) :- L. (*herba*) *Sabīna* 'Sabine (plant)'.

saving (arch.) except, save. XIV. prob. f. SAVE[2].

saviour, U.S. **savior** one who saves, spec. the Redeemer. XIII. ME. *sauve(o)ur* - OF. *sauvëour* (mod. *sauveur*) :- ChrL. *salvātor, -tōr-*, f. *salvāre* SAVE[1].

savory herb of the genus *Satureia*. XIV. ME. *saverey*, perh. repr. OE. *sæðerie* - L. *satureia* fem. sg. and n. pl.

savour, U.S. **savor** taste; †smell, aroma. XIII. - OF. *savour* (mod. *saveur*) :- L. *sapor, sapōr-* taste, occas. smell, f. *sapere* taste; see SAPIENT, -OUR[2]. So **savour** vb. have a taste XIII; relish, like XIV. - (O)F. *savourer* :- late L. *sapōrāre*.

savoury pleasant to the taste XIII; appetizing XIV; fragrant (now chiefly in *unsavoury*) XVI;

stimulating to the palate (also sb.) XVII. ME. *savure*, later *savori* - OF. *savouré* sapid, fragrant, f. *savour* (see prec.) + *-é* -ATE²; the ending was assim. to -Y¹.

savoy *S. cole, cabbage* XVI; *S. biscuit* XVIII. - F. *Savoie*, name of a region of S.E. France.

savvy know. XVIII. Negro and Pidgin Eng., repr. the first word of Sp. *sabe usted* you know (*saber* :- Rom. **sapēre*, for L. *sapere* know; see SAPIENT). Hence sb. practical sense, nous XVIII.

saw¹ cutting tool with teeth. OE. **sagu* (in obl. cases *sage*), also *saga* = MLG., MDu. *sage* (Du. *zaag*), OHG. *saga*, ON. *sǫg* :- Gmc. **saʒō*, **saʒan-*; cf. OHG. *sega* (G. *säge*), MDu. *seghe*; rel. to OE. *seax* knife, OS., OHG. *sahs* :- **saχsam*, f. IE. **sok-* **sek-* cut. Hence **saw** vb. XIII (pp. *isahet*); orig. with wk. conj., but str. forms appear XV (occas. pt. *suwe*, *sew*, pp. *sawen*, mod. *sawn*).

saw² †saying OE.; maxim, proverb XIII. OE. *sagu* = MLG., MDu. *sage*, OHG. *saga* (G. *sage*), ON. *saga* :- Gmc. **saʒō*, **saʒōn*, f. base of **saʒjan* SAY¹.

sawder (colloq.) *soft s.* blarney, flattery. XIX. fig. use of var. of SOLDER.

sawney (colloq.) nickname for a Scotchman; simpleton. XVII. Sc. var. of *Sandy* (XV), pet form of the proper name *Alexander*; see -Y⁶. The connection of the two senses is doubtful.

sawyer one who saws timber. XIV. ME. *sawier*, alt. of †*sawer* (f. SAW¹ vb. + -ER¹), with assim. of the ending to F. *-ier* -ER².

Saxe derived from Saxony, as *S. china*. XIX. - F. *Saxe* - G. *Sachsen* Saxony.

saxhorn brass musical instrument. XIX. f. name of Charles Joseph *Sax* (1791-1865) + HORN. So **saxophone,** invented about 1840 by his son Antoine Joseph, known as Adolphe; see -O-.

saxifrage plant of the genus *Saxifraga*. XV. - (O)F. *saxifrage* or late L. *saxifraga*, f. *saxum* rock + *frag-*, base of *frangere* break. The name was prob. given because many species are found growing among stones and in the clefts of rocks.

Saxon one of a Germanic people, of which one portion took part in the Anglo-Saxon invasions of Britain, while the other, the Old Saxons, remained in Germany. XIII. - (O)F. *Saxon* - L. *Saxō, -ōn-* - WGmc. **Saxan-* (OE. pl. *Seaxan*, *Seaxe*, OHG. pl. *Sahso*, G. *Sachse*), perh. f. **saχsam* knife (see SAW¹), as the name of the characteristic weapon of the people.

saxophone see SAXHORN.

say¹ pt. and pp. *said*. OE. *seċġan* = OS. *seggian* (Du. *zeggen*), OHG. *sagēn* (G. *sagen*), ON. *segja* :- Gmc. **saʒjan* and **saʒǣjan*; the IE. base **soq-* **seq-* is repr. also by OSl. *sočiti*, Lith. *sakýti*, OL. (imper.) *insece*, *inquam* (:- **insquam*) I say, Gr. (imper.) *énnepe*, OW. *hepp* says, OIr. *aithesc* answer.

OE. inf. *seċġan*, 1 pres. ind. *seċġe*, pl. *seċġað*, etc., are repr. normally by ME. *segge(n)*, etc. These began to be repl. in XII and were finally ousted by forms derived from OE. *sæġ-*, *seġ-*, of 2 (and 3) pres. ind., viz. *sæġ(e)st*, *seġ(e)st* (*sæġ(e)ð*, *seġ(e)ð*), pt. *sæġde* said, pp. *sæġd*. Hence sb. XVI.

say² (hist.) serge-like cloth. XIII. - (O)F. *saie* :- L. *saga*, coll. pl. (used as sg.) of *sagum* coarse woollen blanket, military cloak, cloth covering.

scab A. †skin disease XIII; cutaneous disease in beasts; crust formed over a wound XIV; B. low scurvy fellow XVI; non-unionist XIX. - ON. **skabbr* (OSw. *skabber*, Sw. *skabb*, (O)Da. *skab*) = OE. *sċeabb* (see SHABBY). The application to persons may have been due partly to MDu. *schabbe* slut, scold. Hence **scabby** (-Y¹) XVI.

scabbard sheath of sword, etc. XIII. ME. *sca(u)berc*, later *scaberge*, *scaubert*, *scaubard*, aphetic - AN. **escauberc*, pl. *escaubers*, *-erz*, *-erge*, prob. - comp. of OHG. *scala* shell (see SCALE¹) or *scār*, *scāra* scissors, occas. sword + **berʒ-* protect.

scabious plant of the genus *Scabiosa* (formerly of repute for the cure of skin diseases). XIV. - medL. *scabiōsa*, fem. of *scabiōsus*, f. L. *scabiēs* roughness, itch, f. *scabere* scratch, scrape; see SHAVE, -IOUS.

scabrous rough with minute points XVII; fig. harsh XVI. - f. L. *scaber*, *scabr-*, f. *scab-*; see prec., -OUS.

scaffold raised platform or stage XIV; (for the execution of criminals) XVI. ME. *scaffot*, *scaffald* - AN. **scaffaut*, OF. *(e)schaffaut*, mod. *échafaud*, earlier *escadafaut* :- Rom. **excatafalcum*, f. EX-¹ + **catafalcum*; see CATAFALQUE. Hence **scaffolding** XIV.

scald¹ burn with hot liquor; (dial.) burn. XIII. ME. *sc(h)alde*, aphetic - AN., ONF. *escalder*, OF. *eschalder* (mod. *échauder*) :- L. *excaldāre* wash in hot water, f. EX-¹ + L. *cal(i)dus* hot, rel. to *calēre* be warm. Hence sb. XVII.

scald² see SKALD.

scale¹ †drinking-bowl XIII; pan of a balance XIV; sg. and pl. weighing instrument XV. - ON. *skál* bowl, pl. weighing-scales = OHG. *scāla* (G. *schale*) :- Gmc. **skǣlō*, rel. to **skalō*, whence OE. *sċealu* shell, husk, drinking-cup, weighing scale, OS. *skala* cup (Du. *schaal*), OHG. *scala* shell, husk (G. *schale*). Hence vb. weigh XVII.

scale² thin horny plate on the skin of animals XIV; lamina of skin, etc. XV; (after F. *écaille*) metal plate worn as an epaulette XIX. Aphetic - OF. *escale* (mod. *écale* husk, chip of stone) - Gmc. **skalō* (see SCALE¹), rel. to **skaljō*, whence Rom. (medL.) *scalia* (OF. *escaille*, mod. *écaille* fish-scale, oyster-shell). Hence **scale** vb. remove scales from. XV. **scaly** (-Y¹) XVI.

scale³ A. †ladder XV; B. (mus.) series of graduated sounds XVI; C. set of graduations for measuring distances XIV (rare before XVI); graduated instrument; D. relative dimension, standard of measurement XVII. - L. *scāla* usu. pl. steps, staircase, (sg., late) ladder, f. base of *scandere* climb.

scale⁴ climb, mount. XIV. - OF. *escaler* or medL. *scālāre*, f. L. *scāla* SCALE³.

scalene (of a triangle) having three unequal sides. XVIII. - late L. *scalēnus* - Gr. *skalēnós* uneven, unequal, scalene, rel. to *skoliós* oblique, crooked, *skélos* leg, L. *scelus* wickedness, crime, OE. *sċeolh* wry, oblique.

scallion shallot, onion. XIV. - AN. *scal(o)un* = OF. *escalo(i)gne* :- Rom. **escalōnia*, for L. *Ascalōnia* shallot, f. *Ascalō* (Gr. *Askálōn*) Ascalon, a port in S. Palestine.

scallop, scollop kind of shellfish; shell of

this, esp. as a pilgrim's badge XIV; formation resembling the edge of a scallop-shell XVII. Aphetic - OF. *escalope*, app. of Gmc. orig.

scallywag (sl.) disreputable fellow. XIX (orig. U.S.). of unkn. orig.

scalp (dial.) top of the head, skull XIII; integument of this XVII. north. ME. *scalp*, prob. of Scand. orig., but the Eng. senses are not found in any Scand. or other Gmc. lang.; cf. ON. *skálpr* sheath (Da. dial. *skalp* shell, husk), MLG. *schulpe*, MDu. *schelpe* (Du. *schelp*) shell. Hence vb. remove the scalp of. XVII.

scalpel small light knife for surgical operations. XVIII. - F. *scalpel* or L. *scalpellum*, *-us*, dim. of *scalper*, *scalprum*, cutting tool, chisel, knife, f. base of *scalpere* scratch, carve; see -EL².

scammony gum-resin obtained from *Convolvulus scammonia*. XV. - OF. *escamonie*, *scamonee* (mod. *scammonée*) or L. *scammōnea*, *-ia* (also *-eum*, *-ium*) - Gr. *skammōniā*, *-ṓnion*.

scamp¹ idle about mischievously XVI; commit highway robbery XVIII. prob. - MDu. *schampen* slip away, decamp - OF. *esc(h)amper* :- Rom. **excampāre*, f. EX-¹ + *campus* field (see CAMP). Hence **scamp** sb. †highway robber or robbery XVIII; ne'er-do-well, waster XIX.

scamp² do negligently or hurriedly. XIX. perh. identical with prec., but allied in sense to SKIMP.

scamper †decamp; run nimbly. XVII. prob. frequent. f. SCAMP¹ + -ER⁴.

scan analyse the metre of XIV; †criticize, test; examine or consider closely; †interpret; †discern XVI; look at searchingly XVIII. - L. *scandere* (pp. *scansus*) climb, (late) 'measure' (verses), with allusion to raising and lowering the foot to mark rhythm; cf. next. The var. †*scand* was presumably the earlier, though not so shown by the evidence, and was apprehended as pp., from which an inf. *scan* was deduced. So **scansion** XVII.

scandal discredit to religion caused by a religious person; occasion of unbelief, stumbling-block; damage to reputation; grossly discreditable thing; defamatory speech. XVI. - F. *scandale* - ChrL. *scandalum* (Vulg.) cause of offence - Hellenistic Gr. *skándalon* snare for an enemy, cause of moral stumbling, orig. trap, rel. to Skr. *skándati* jumps, L. *scandere* climb. So **scandalize**¹ †make public scandal of XV; †be an occasion of stumbling to; slander; disgrace XVI; horrify by impropriety XVII. - (O)F. *scandaliser* or ChrL. *scandalizāre* - ecclGr. *skandalizein*. **scandalous** XVI. - F. or medL.

scandalize² (naut.) reduce the area of (a sail). XIX. alt. of †*scantelize* shorten (XVII), f. †*scantle* (f. SCANT) + -IZE.

scansorial pert. to climbing, that climbs. XIX. f. L. *scansōrius*, f. *scans-*, pp. stem of *scandere* climb; see -ORIAL.

scant stinted in measure; †parsimonious XIV; limited in extent or amount XVI. - ON. *skamt*, n. of *skammr* short, brief. Superseded largely by **scanty** (-Y¹) XVI.

scantling measured size; small or scanty amount; †pattern XVI; small piece of wood, etc. XVII. alt., by assoc. with -LING¹, of †*scantlon* gauge (XIII), dimension (XIV), sample (XV), aphetic - OF. *escantillon* (mod. *échantillon* sample), alt. of *eschandillon*, f. medL. **scandalium*, *-ilium*, f. L. *scandere* climb.

scape¹, **'scape** vb. and sb. (obs. or arch.) Aphetic of ESCAPE. XIII. Hence (from the vb.) **scapegoat** (XVI), intended to render the supposed literal meaning of Heb. *azāzel* (Lev. 16: 8, 10, 26) 'the goote on which the lotte fell to scape' (so Vulg. *caper emissarius*); the correct interpretation is prob. 'goat for Azazel' (a demon of the desert). **scapegrace** incorrigible scamp ('one who escapes the grace of God') XIX.

scape² (bot.) long flower-stalk rising from the root. XVII. - L. *scāpus*, Gr. *skâpos*, rel. to Gr. *skêptron* SCEPTRE.

scaphoid boat-shaped. XVIII. - modL. *scaphoīdēs* - Gr. *skaphoeidḗs*, f. *skáphos* boat; see -OID.

scapular monastic garment covering the shoulders. XV. - late L. *scapulāre*, f. late L. *scapula* shoulder (anat. in Eng. use XVI), earlier pl. *-æ*; see -AR. So **scapulary** XIII (*scapelori*). - AN. **scapelorie*, var. of OF. *eschapeloyre* (XII) - medL. *scapelōrium*, *scapularium*; assim. to -ARY.

scar¹ †rock, crag XIV; precipice XVII; sunken rock XVIII. ME. *skerre*, *scarre*, - ON. *sker* low reef, SKERRY.

scar² trace of a healed wound. XIV. Aphetic - OF. *esc(h)arre*, *eschare* - late L. *eschara* scab - Gr. *eskhárā* hearth, brazier, scab. Hence vb. XVI.

scarab beetle XVI; gem cut in the form of a beetle XIX. - L. *scarabæus*; cf. Gr. *kárabos* stag beetle.

scaramouch stock character of Italian farce, cowardly or foolish boaster constantly cudgelled by Harlequin; rascal, scamp. XVII. Early forms *Scaramuzza*, *-moucha*, *-muchio* - It. *Scaramuccia*, joc. use of *scaramuccia* SKIRMISH; hence F. *Scaramouche*, source of the present form.

scarce †scanty XIII; †niggardly; deficient in quantity or number XIV. - AN., ONF. *scars*, aphetic of *escars*, OF. *eschars* (mod. *échars*) (of coin) below standard value, (of wind) slight :- Rom. **excarpsus* plucked out, pp. of **excarpere*, for L. *excerpere* select out, EXCERPT. Hence **scarcely** (-LY²) †scantily, sparingly; only just, not quite. XIII. **scarcity** XIII. - ONF. *escarceté*, OF. *eschar-* (mod. *écharseté*).

scare terrify. XII. ME. *skerre*, later *skere*, *ska(y)re* (XV), *scar(r)e* (XVI) - ON. *skirra* frighten, (also) avoid, prevent, refl. shrink from (cf. Norw. *skjerra*, Sw. dial. *skjarra* scare), f. *skjarr* shy, timid. Hence **scarecrow** XVI.

scarf¹ joint for connecting two timbers into a continuous piece. XIV. orig. naut.; prob. - OF. **escarf* (mod. *écart*), f. **escarver* (mod. *écarver*), perh. f. an ON. base repr. by Sw. *skarf*, Norw. *skarv* piece to lengthen a board or a garment, joint or seam effecting this; the ult. orig. remains obscure. Hence vb. XVII.

scarf² broad band of stuff as an article of clothing XVI; (her.) XVII. prob. alt. (by assoc. with prec.) of *scarp*, which is recorded from XVI in the heraldic sense of a diminutive bend sinister. - ONF. *escarpe* = OF. *escherpe* (mod. *écharpe*); prob. identical with OF. *escreppe* SCRIP¹. comp. **scarfskin** outer layer of the skin. XVII.

scarify make incisions or scratches in. XV. - (O)F. *scarifier* - late L. *scarīficāre*, alt. of L. *scarīfāre* - Gr. *skarīphâsthai* scratch an outline, sketch lightly, f. *skárīphos* pencil, stilus; see -IFY. So **scarification** XIV (rare before XVI). - (O)F. or late L.

scarious dry and shrivelled. XIX. - F. *scarieux* or modL. *scariōsus*.

scarlatina scarlet fever. XIX. - modL. - It. *scarlattina*, fem. of *scarlattino*, dim. of *scarlatto* SCARLET.

scarlet sb. †rich cloth, of various colours, freq. bright-red XIII; bright vivid red colour XV; adj. XIV. Aphetic - OF. *escarlate* fem. (mod. *écarlate*); of unkn. orig.

scarp (fortif.) steep bank or wall XVI; steep slope XIX. - It. *scarpa*. Hence vb. XIX.

scarus parrot-fish. XVII. - L. - Gr. *skáros*.

scathe (arch., dial.) injury, damage. XIII. - ON. *skaði* = OE. *sċeaða* malefactor, (rarely) injury, OS. *skaðo* malefactor, OHG. *skado* (G. *schade*) injury, harm :- Gmc. **skaþan-*, f. **skaþ-*, whence also Goth. *skaþis* harm, *skaþjan* injure. So vb. injure XII; wither, sear XIX. - ON. *skaða* = OE. *sċeaðian*, OS. *scaðon*, OHG. *skadōn* (Du., G. *schaden*) :- Gmc. **skaþōjan*. The sb. survives in gen. literary use in the comp. **scatheless** (XII, - ON. *skaðlauss*), the vb. in **scathing** (-ING[2]) (poet.) blasting, searing XVIII; fig. as of invective XIX; **unscathed** (-ED[1]) uninjured XIV (orig. Sc.).

scatology XIX. f. Gr. *skôr*, *skato-* dung + -(O)LOGY.

scatter †squander, dissipate; disperse in many directions. XIII (*skatere*). prob. var. of SHATTER under Scand. influence.

scaup-duck duck of the genus *Aythya*. XVII. f. *scaup* bank providing a bed for shellfish, Sc. var. of *scalp* (XVI) bare piece of rock above water, perh. transf. use of SCALP.

scaur (Sc.) precipitous bank, cliff. XIX. var. of SCAR[1].

scavage (hist.) toll formerly levied in London on merchant strangers. XV. - AN. *scawage* = ONF. *escauwage*, f. *escauwer* inspect - Flem. *scauwen* = OE. *sċēawian* see (SHOW).

scavenger †officer who took 'scavage' and (later) kept the streets clean; person employed to clean streets XVI. alt. of *scavager* - AN. *scawager*, f. *scawage*; see prec. and -ER[1]. Hence by back-formation **scavenge** vb. XVII.

scazon (pros.) choliamb. XVII. - L. *scazōn* - Gr. *skázōn*, sb. use of m. prp. of *skázein* limp, halt.

scenario outline of the plot of a play. XIX. - It., f. *scena* SCENE; anglicized as †*scenary* XVII.

scend see SEND[2].

scene apparatus for setting forth the action of a play; division of an act of a play; place of an action; †stage performance XVI; †stage of a theatre; view of an action, place, etc.; episode, situation in real life XVII; stormy encounter XVIII. - L. *scēna*, *scæna* stage, scene - Gr. *skēnḗ* tent, stage, scene, rel. to *skiā́* shadow. So **scenery** †dramatic action; decoration of a theatre stage; aggregate of features in a landscape. XVIII. alt. of †*scenary* (see SCENARIO) by assim. of the ending to -ERY. **scenic** XVII. - L. *scēnicus* - Gr. *skēnikós*. **scenical** XV.

scent track (animals) by the smell; †exhale an odour XIV; (from the sb.) perfume XVII. ME. *sent(e)* - (O)F. *sentir* feel, perceive, smell :- L. *sentīre* feel, perceive. Hence **scent** sb. odour of beast or man as a means of pursuit XIV; sense of smell; distinctive odour XV. The unexpl. sp. *scent* appears XVII.

sceptic, U.S. **skeptic** one who doubts. XVI. - F. *sceptique* or L. *scepticus*, in sb. pl. *scepticī* followers of the Greek philosopher Pyrrho of Elis - Gr. *skeptikós*, sb. pl. *skeptikoí*, f. *sképtesthai* look about, consider, observe. The pronunc. has been infl. by Gr. Hence **sceptical, scepticism** XVII.

sceptre, U.S. **scepter** rod or wand as a symbol of regal or imperial authority. XIII. ME. *ceptre*, *septre* (with later assim. to L. and Gr.) - OF. *ceptre*, (also mod.) *sceptre* - L. *scēptrum* - Gr. *skêptron*, f. *skḗptein* prop.

schedule †ticket, label XIV; †explanatory slip accompanying a document XV; appendix to an act of parliament; classified statement or list XVI. ME. *cedule*, *sedule* - (O)F. *cédule* - late L. *scedula* small slip of paper, dim. of *sceda*, also *scheda* leaf of papyrus; see -ULE.

scheme †figure of rhetoric XVI; †diagram; analytical or tabular statement; plan, design XVII. - L. *schēma* - Gr. *schêma* form, figure. Hence vb. XVIII. So **schematic** XVIII. - modL. *schēmaticus*, f. *schēma-*, *schēmat-*. **schematism** XVII.

scherzando (mus.) playfully. XIX. - It., gerund of *scherzare* play, sport, f. *scherzo* sport, jest, (mus.) lively movement - (M)HG. *scherz*.

schism breach of the unity of the visible Church XIV; offence of promoting this XV; sect so formed XVI. ME. *s(c)isme* - OF. *s(c)isme* (mod. *schisme*) - ecclL. *schisma* - Gr. *skhísma* rent, cleft, in N.T. division in the Church, f. base of *skhízein* split, cleave. The sp. was assim. XVI to the L. form. So **schismatic** XIV (sb.) - (O)F. - ecclL. - ecclGr. **schismatical** XVI.

schist (geol.) fissile crystalline rock. XVIII. - F. *schiste* - L. *schistos* - Gr. *skhistós*, pp. adj. f. base of *skhízein* split. Hence **schistose** XVIII.

schizo- comb. form irreg. repr. Gr. *skhízein* split. **schizophrenia** (path.) 'split mind', condition characterized by cleavage of mental functions. XX (Gr. *phrḗn* mind; see -IA[1]); hence **schizophrenic** adj. and sb. XX.

schnap(p)s spirit resembling Hollands gin. XIX. - G. *schnap(p)s* dram of drink, liquor (esp. gin) - LG., Du. *snaps* gulp, mouthful, f. *snappen* seize, snatch (see SNAP).

schnauzer German breed of house dog. XIX. - G., f. *schnauze* snout.

schnorkel see SNORKEL.

scholar pupil in a school; one devoted to learning, learned person XIV; student receiving emolument from a school, etc. XVI. ME. *scoler*, aphetic - OF. *escol(i)er* (mod. *écolier*) - late L. *scholāris*, f. L. *schola* SCHOOL; see -AR. Hence **scholarly** (-LY[1]) XVII, **scholarship** XVI.

scholastic pert. to the schoolmen XVI; pert. to education in schools XVII; characteristic of 'the schools', pedantic XVIII; sb. schoolman XVII. - L. *scholasticus* - Gr. *skholastikós* studious, learned, sb. scholar, f. *skholázein* be at leisure, devote one's leisure to learning, f. *skholḗ* leisure; see SCHOOL[1], -IC. So **scholastical** XVI (in all senses earlier). Hence **scholasticism** XVIII.

scholium, pl. **-ia** explanatory note, comment. XVI. - modL. - Gr. *skhólion*, f. *skholḗ* learned discussion (see SCHOOL[1]). So **scholiast** commentator. XVI. - late Gr. *skholiastḗs*.

school[1] place or establishment for instruction; body of teachers of a subject in a university. OE. *scōl*, *scolu*, corr. to MLG., MDu. *schōle* (Du. *school*), OHG. *scuola* (G. *schule*); Gmc. - medL. *scōla*, for L. *schola* - Gr. *skholḗ* leisure, employment of leisure in disputation, lecture, (later) school; reinforced in ME. by aphetic - OF. *escole* (mod. *école*) - Rom. **scola*. Hence vb. XVI. **schoolman** (cf. OE. *scōlmann* learner) in medieval universities, one who treated of logic, metaphysics, and theology. XVI.

school[2] shoal of fish, etc. XIV. - MLG., MDu. *schōle* (Du. *school*) troop, multitude, spec. 'school' of whales = OS. *scola*, OE. *scolu* troop.

schooner small sea-going fore-and-aft-rigged vessel. XVIII (*skooner*, *scooner*). of uncert. orig.

schorl (min.) (black) tourmaline. XVIII. - G. *schörl*, of unkn. orig.

schottische dance resembling the polka. XIX. - G. (*der*) *schottische* (*tanz*) the SCOTTISH dance.

sciagraphy projection of shadows, delineation of light and shade. XVI (*sciographie*). - F. *scia-*, *sciographie* - L. *scia-*, *sciographia* - Gr. *skiā-*, *skiographiā*, f. *skiā́* shadow; see -GRAPHY.

sciatic pert. to or affecting the hip. XVI. - (O)F. *sciatique* - late L. *sciaticus*, alt. of *ischiaticus*, for L. *ischiadicus* (after *-aticus* -ATIC) - Gr. *iskhiadikós*, f. *iskhíon* hip-joint, pl. *iskhía* haunches, hams. So **sciatica** XV (*cyetica*, *sytyca*). - late L.

science knowledge, esp. of a technical kind. XIV. - OF. - L. *scientia*, f. *scient-*, prp. stem of *scīre* know; see -ENCE. So **scientific** concerned with science or the sciences XVI; (of proof, etc.) demonstrative XVII; pert. to science XVIII. - (O)F. *scientifique* or late L. *scientificus*. Hence **scientist** XIX.

scilicet, abbrev. **scil.**, **sc.** that is to say, to wit. XIV. - L., contr. of *scīre licet* 'it is permitted to know'.

scilla liliaceous plant of the genus *Scilla*. XIX. - L. - Gr. *skilla*.

scimitar short curved one-edged sword. XVI. Introduced in various forms (*cimiterie*, *cemitere*, *cymitare*, *scimitar*) repr. F. *cimeterre*, *cimiterre*, It. *scimitarra*, †*cimitara*, Sp., Pg. *cimitarra*, Pers. *şimşīr*.

scintilla minute particle. XVII. - L., spark. So **scintillate** sparkle. XVII. f. pp. stem of L. *scintillāre*; see -ATE[3]. **scintillation** XVII. - L.

sciolist smatterer. XVII. f. late L. *sciolus*, dim. f. *scius* knowing, f. base of L. *scīre* know; see SCIENCE, -IST.

scion shoot, slip, graft XIV; heir, descendant XIX. ME. *sioun* - OF. *ciun*, *cion*, *sion* (mod. *scion*), perh. alt. of *chion* (of Gmc. orig.).

scirrhous pert. to a scirrhus. XVI. - F. *scirrheux* (now *squirreux*) - modL. *scirrhōsus*, f. *scīrrhus* (used in Eng. since XVII) hard tumour - Gr. *skírros*, *skiros* hard (substance); see -OUS.

scission cutting, division. XV (rare before XVIII). - (O)F. *scission* or late L. *scissiō*, *-ōn-*, f. pp. stem of *scindere* cut, cleave; see -ION.

scissors XIV. ME. *sisoures* - (O)F. *cisoires* (now only 'large shears', the sense 'scissors' being appropriated to *ciseaux*, pl. of †*cisel* CHISEL), repr. medL. **cīsōria*, pl. of late L. *cīsōrium*, f. *-cīs-*, *-cīdere*, var. in comps. of L. *cæs-*, *cædere* cut. The sp. with *sc-* (XVI) is due to assoc. with L. *scindere* cut (see prec.).

sciurine pert. to squirrels. XIX. f. L. *sciūrus* - Gr. *skíouros*, f. *skiā́* shadow + *ourā́* tail; see -INE[1].

sclero- comb. form of Gr. *sklērós* hard. XIX. So **sclerosis** morbid hardening. XIV. - medL. *sclērōsis* - Gr. *sklḗrōsis*, f. *sklēroûn* harden; see -OSIS. **sclerotic** XVI.

scoff[1] contemptuous ridicule; also vb. XIV. perh. of Scand. orig.; cf. early modDa. *skof*, *skuf* jest, mockery, *skuffe* jest, mock.

scoff[2] (sl. and dial.) eat voraciously; seize, plunder. XIX. orig. var. of synon. (dial.) *scaff* (XVIII), rel. to contemp. *scaff* food; later assoc. with S. Afr. *scoff* food, meal - Afrikaans (Du.) *schoft* (prop.) quarter of a day, (hence) any of the four meals of the day.

scold ribald or abusive person (esp. a woman). XIII. prob. - ON. *skáld* poet, SKALD, in comps. also with dyslogistic implication (e.g. *skáldskapr*, prop. poetry, which has in the Icel. lawbooks the spec. sense of libel in verse), hence (perh. by a spec. Eng. development), libellous, scurrilous, or ribald person. Hence **scold** vb. †quarrel noisily, (later) be vehement or persistent in reproof or faultfinding (to). XIV.

scollop see SCALLOP.

sconce[1] lantern or screened candlestick carried by a handle XIV; bracket-candlestick XV. Aphetic - OF. *esconse* (i) hiding-place, (ii) lantern; or - medL. *sconsa*, aphetic of *absconsa*, sb. use of fem. pp. of L. *abscondere* hide.

sconce[2] (arch. sl.) head. XVI. perh. joc. use of prec.

sconce[3] (fortif.) small fort or earthwork. XVI. - Du. *schans*, †*schantze* brushwood, screen of brushwood for soldiers, earthwork of gabions - (M)HG. *schanze*, of unkn. orig.

sconce[4] (Univ. sl.) fine in a tankard of ale, etc., e.g. for breach of discipline or convention. XVII. perh. a joc. ref. to SCONCE[2]. Hence sb. XVII.

scone round cake of wheat or barley meal baked on a griddle, quadrant-shaped section of this. XVI (*scon*). orig. Sc., perh. shortening of MLG. *schonbrot*, MDu. *schoonbrot* 'fine bread'.

scoop utensil for baling or ladling XIV; kind of shovel XV. - MLG., MDu. *schōpe* (Du. *schoep*) vessel for baling, bucket of a water-wheel = MHG. *schuofe* (G. †*schufe*) :- WGmc. **skōpō(n)*, f. **skōp-* var. of **skap-*, whence **skappjan* draw water (repr. by OS. *skeppian*, Du. *scheppen*, OHG. *scephan*, G. *schöpfen*); cf. SHAPE. Hence **scoop** vb. †ladle or bale out XIV; remove (as) with a scoop XVII. Also in mod. use, orig. U.S., to take up in large quantities; cut out (a rival newspaper editor, etc.) XIX (whence sb. exclusive piece of news).

scoot go suddenly and swiftly. XVIII (naut.). The orig. form is *scout*, which became obs. in early

XIX; the present form seems to have been imported later from the U.S.; of unkn. orig.

scope object aimed at; room for exercise, free course; range of activity XVI; length of cable at which a ship rides XVII. - It. *scopo* aim, purpose - Gr. *skopós* mark for shooting at, f. **skop-* as in *skopeîn* observe, aim at.

-scope terminal el. repr. L. *-scopium* - Gr. *-skópion* (as in *hōroscopium* - *hōroskópion* casting of nativities), f. *skopeîn* observe (see prec.); extended in medL. use in *microscopium* MICROSCOPE and *tēlescopium* TELESCOPE, on the model of which have been formed terms denoting scientific instruments for enabling the eye or the ear to make observations, e.g. *laryngoscope*, *stethoscope*. The corr. adjs. end in **-scopic,** with advs. in **-scopically** (-LY[2]) and nouns of action in **-scopy** (-Y[3]).

scorbutic pert. to scurvy. XVII. - medL. *scorbūticus*, f. *scorbūtus* scurvy, perh. for **scorbūcus* - MLG. *schorbūk*, Du. *scheurbuik*, f. MLG., MDu. *schoren* (Du. *scheuren*) break, lacerate + *būk* (*buik*) belly.

scorch heat so as to dry up. XV. of uncert. orig.

score A. set of twenty (prob. orig. as marked on a tally) XI; B. notch, mark, stroke; account of times kept on a tally or board XIV; amount of a bill or reckoning XVI; account, reason XVII; record of points in a game XVIII; C. written or printed piece of concerted music XVIII. Late OE. **scoru*, pl. *scora*, *-e* - ON. *skor* notch, tally, twenty :- Gmc. **skurō*, f. **skur-* **sker-* cut, SHEAR. So **score** vb. XIV. partly - ON. *skora*; partly f. the sb.

scoria slag, clinkers. XVII. - L. *scōria* dross - Gr. *skōriā*, f. *skôr* dung.

scorn †behave contemptuously XII; †deride, (now) hold in disdain XIII. Aphetic - OF. *escharnir*, *eschernir* :- Rom. **escarnīre*, **eskernīre* - Gmc. **skarnjan*, **skernjan*, f. base of OS. *skern*, etc., jest, mockery. So sb. XII. - OF. *escarn*. In sb. and vb. forms with *-a-* and *-o-* are equally early; the orig. of the latter is obscure.

scorpion arachnid whose sting causes intense pain XIII; (after 1 Kings 12: 11) knotted or armed cord XIV. - (O)F. :- L. *scorpiō*, *-ōn-*, extension of *scorpius* - Gr. *skorpíos*.

scorzonera plant of the genus so named. XVII. - It., f. *scorzone* poisonous snake (:- Rom. **scurtiōne*, alt. of medL. *curtiō*, *-ōn-*), for whose venom the plant may have been an antidote.

scot payment, contribution; *scot and lot*, taxes levied by a municipal corporation in proportionate shares upon its members. XIII. In ME. partly - ON. *skot* (= OE. *sċot* SHOT), partly aphetic - OF. *escot* (mod. *écot*), of Gmc. orig.; in later use to some extent an antiquarian revival of the OE. form. Hence **scot-free** exempt from the payment of scot, fine, etc.; exempt from injury or punishment. XVI.

Scot (hist.) one of a Gaelic-speaking people first known in Ireland, and later settled in north Britain (Scotland) OE.; native of Scotland XIV. OE. **Scot*, only in pl. *Scottas* - late L. *Scottus*; ult. orig. unkn. So **Scotch** XVI, **Scots** XIV (*Scottis*), reduced vars. of **Scottish** (-ISH[1]) XIII (repl. OE. *Scyttisc*). **Scotchman** XVI, **Scotsman** XIV (*Scottis man*).

scotch[1] make an incision in XV; (from Theobald's emendation of *scorch* in Sh. 'Macbeth' III iv 13) injure or obstruct so as to render harmless for a time XVIII. of unkn. orig. Hence sb. incision XV; so in HOPSCOTCH.

scotch[2] block, etc. placed under a circular object to prevent slipping. XVII. occas. *skatch*, which may indicate identity with *scatch* (XVI) stilt - OF. *escache*.

scoundrel XVI. of unkn. orig. See -REL.

scour[1] rid, clear (an area) XIII; purge XIV; cleanse by hard rubbing; clear out, get rid of XV; rake with gunshot XVI. prob. - MLG., MDu. *schūren* - OF. *escurer* (mod. *écurer* clean, scour) :- late L. *excūrāre* (medL. (*e*)*scūrāre*), f. L. EX-[1] + *cūrāre* take care of, medL. clean, f. *cūra* CURE.

scour[2] move *about* rapidly; pass rapidly over XIV. of unkn. orig.

scourge whip XIII; instrument of divine chastisement XIV; cause of calamity XVI. Aphetic - OF. *escurge*, *escorge*, f. *escorgier* vb. whip :- Rom. **excorrigiāre*, f. EX-[1] + *corrigia* thong, whip. So vb. XIII. - OF. *escorgier*.

scout[1] spy, reconnoitre. XIV. Aphetic - OF. *escouter* (mod. *écouter*) listen, alt. of *ascolter* :- Rom. **ascultāre*, for L. *auscultāre*. So **scout** sb. one sent ahead to reconnoitre. XVI. - OF. *escoute*; earlier in †*scout-watch* sentinel, spy (XIV), unless this is a comp. of the vb.

scout[2] flat-bottomed boat. XV. - MDu. *schūte* (Du. *schuit*), adopted earlier as *schoute* (XIV); rel. to ON. *skúta* light fast vessel.

scout[3] †mock, deride XVII; reject with scorn XVIII. prob. of Scand. orig. (cf. ON. *skúta*, *skúti* a taunt); if so, the word must have been in colloq. use long before it is recorded.

scout[4] (at Oxford) college servant. XVIII. of unkn. orig.

scow large flat-bottomed square-ended lighter. XVIII. - Du. *schouw*, earlier *schouwe*, *schoude* = LG. *schalde*, rel. to OS. *skaldan* push (a boat) from the shore.

scowl vb. XIV. prob. of Scand. orig. (cf. Da. *skule* cast down one's eyes, give a sidelong look); perh. ult. rel. to late OE. *sċūlēġede* squint-eyed (varying with *sċȳlēġede*). Hence sb. XVI.

scrabble make marks at random, scrawl; scratch about XVI; scramble XVII. - MDu. *schrabbelen*, frequent. of *schrabben* scratch, scrape.

scrag[1] lean person or animal XVI; lean end of a neck of mutton XVII; neck XIX. perh. alt. of †*crag(ge)* XV–XVIII. Hence vb. hang by the neck, throttle. XVIII. **scraggy** (-Y[1]) lean. XVII.

scrag[2] (dial.) stump of a tree, rough projection. XVI. Parallel to dial. *scrog* stunted bush, pl. brushwood (XIV), *shrag* rag (XIV), twig (XVI), *shrog* bush, pl. underwood (XV). Implied in ME. **scraggy** (-Y[1]) rough, rugged, ragged. XIII.

scramble make one's way by clambering, etc.; struggle *with* others for something. XVI. of symbolic form.

scrannel (dial.) lean, thin. XVII (Milton 'Lycidas' 124 *s. pipes*, from which subsequent users of the word have inferred the meaning 'harsh, unmelodious'). Obscurely rel. to synon. dial. *scrank*, Sc. *scranky*, *scranny*; all prob. ult. of Scand. orig. (cf. Norw. *skran* shrivelled, *skrank* lean large-boned figure).

scrap[1] pl. remains of food XIV; fragmentary portion XVI. - ON. *skrap* scraps, trifles, f. base of *skrapa* SCRAPE. Hence **scrappy** (-Y[1]) XIX.

scrap[2] †villainous plot XVII; struggle, tussle XIX. perh. f. SCRAPE.

scrape remove an outer layer from XIV; rake *together* with effort; draw harshly or noisily over a surface XVI. - ON. *skrapa* or (M)Du. *schrapen* = OE. *sċrapian* scratch, rel. to Du., LG. *schrappen*, MHG. *schrapfen*, *schrepfen*; for other prob. cogns. cf. SHARP.

scratch wound the surface of the skin with the nails, etc. XV; rub lightly with the nails or claws XVI; make linear abrasions on XVII. prob. blending of synon. (dial.) *scrat* (XIII) and †*cratch* (XIII); the orig. of these forms is obscure, but cf. MLG., MDu. *kratsen*, OHG. *krazzōn* (G. *kratzen*), OSw. *kratta* scratch. Hence **scratch** sb. result of scratching XVI; mark indicating starting-point XVIII; adj. hastily done, collected, etc. XIX.

Scratch (dial.) usu. *Old S.*, the Devil. XVIII. alt. of (dial.) *scrat* (XV) hermaphrodite - ON. *skrat(t)i* wizard, goblin, monster, rel. to OHG. *scrato* (G. *schrat*) satyr, sprite.

scrawl write in a sprawling untidy manner. XVII. perh. transf. use of (dial.) *scrawl* sprawl, crawl (XIV), prob. blending of CRAWL and SPRAWL. Hence sb. XVII.

scream vb. XIII. Either aberrant repr. of late OE. **sċrǣman*, ME. *shreame* (XIII) or - the rel. MDu. **schreemen*. Hence sb. XVI.

scree mass of detritus on a mountainside. XVIII. prob. back-formation from *screes*, for **screethes* pl. - ON. *skriða* landslip, rel. to *skríða* slide, glide (= OE. *scrīðan*).

screech XVI. alt. (with expressive lengthening of vowel) of †*scritch* (*scriche* XIII), f. imit. base repr. in OE. *sċriċċettan*; cf. (dial.) *screak* (XV), *scrike* (XIV), of Scand. origin (cf. ON. *skrǽkja*). So *screech-owl* (XVI), earlier †*scritch-owl*.

screed (dial.) fragment severed, torn strip XIV; long roll or list, lengthy discourse XVIII; levelled strip of plaster XIX. prob. var. repr. of OE. *sċrēade* SHRED.

screen contrivance to ward off heat, wind, light, etc.; partition in a building XV; (fig.) XVI; sifting apparatus XVI. Aphetic - ONF. *escren*, var. of *escran* (mod. *écran*), of Gmc. orig. (cf. OHG. *skrank* bar, barrier, fence). Hence vb. shelter, shield XV; sift XVII.

screw A. mechanical contrivance of which the operative part is a spiral groove or ridge XV; worm or boring part of a gimlet XVI; (fig.) XVII. B. (from the vb.) act of screwing XVIII; object screwed or twisted up XIX. C. (sl. senses of obscure development) unsound horse; wages, salary XIX. In A - OF. *escroue* fem. (mod. *écrou* m.) either (i) - WGmc. **scrūva* (MHG. *schrūbe* (G. *schraube*), corr. to MDu. *schrūve*), or (ii) :- (the source of the Gmc. forms) L. *scrōfa* sow, medL. female screw. Hence **screw** vb. XVII. **screwed** (sl.) intoxicated. XIX; also (earlier) *screwy*.

scribble write carelessly or hastily. XV. - medL. *scrībillāre* (cf. rare L. *conscrībillāre*), dim. formed on L. *scrībere* write (see next); see -LE[3].

scribe doctor of the Jewish law XIV; secretary, clerk; copyist, transcriber XVI. - L. *scrība* official or public writer, f. *scrībere* trace characters, write, f. IE. base **skreibh-* scratch, incise, repr. also in Gr. *skarīphâsthai* scratch. So vb. (in carpentry) mark or score (wood, etc.), shape the edge of. XVII; of obscure development; varying with *scrive*; perh. orig. for *describe*, †*descrive*.

scrimmage, scrummage †skirmish XV; noisy contention, confused struggle XVIII (spec. in rugby football XIX; cf. SCRUM). alt. of †*scrimish*, var. of SKIRMISH, with assim. of the ending to -AGE.

scrimp scanty. XVIII. In early use Sc.; of unkn. orig.; for possible cogns. see SHRIMP, and cf. SKIMP. So **scrimp** vb. scant, skimp. XVIII.

scrimshaw (sl.) handicrafts practised by sailors on long voyages. XIX. of unkn. orig.

scrip[1] wallet, satchel. XIII. Aphetic - OF. *escrep(p)e* purse, bag for alms, var. of *escherpe* (mod. *écharpe*) or - ON. *skreppa*, which may itself be - OF.; ult. Gmc. **skerpā* (latinized as *scerpa* equipment).

scrip[2] (orig.) receipt for the portion of a loan subscribed, (now) share certificate. XVIII. abbrev. of *subscription* (*receipt*).

script piece of writing XIV (examinee's written papers XIX); (kind of) handwriting XIX. Aphetic - OF. *escript*, for *escrit* (now *écrit*) :- L. *scrīptum*, sb. use of n. pp. of *scrībere* write (see SCRIBE). So **scriptorium** writing-room. XVIII. - medL. **scripture** Holy Writ, the Bible XIII; (arch.) inscription XIV. - L. *scrīptūra*; see -URE. **scriptural** (-AL[1]) XVII. - late L.

scrivener professional scribe XIV; notary XV. f. ME. *scrivein* (XIII), aphetic - OF. *escrivein* (mod. *écrivain*) :- Rom. **scribano*, f. L. *scrība* SCRIBE; see -AN, -ER[1].

scrofula disease characterized by degeneration of the lymphatic glands. XIV. In early use pl. after late L. *scrōfulæ*, dim. f. L. *scrōfa* breeding-sow (supposed to be subject to the disease); in sg. form XVIII. Hence **scrofulous** XVII.

scroll roll of paper or parchment; writing, list, roll; inscribed paper XV; scroll-like ornament XVII. ME. *scrowle*, alt., after *rowle*, ROLL[1], of *scrow* (XIII), aphetic - AN. *escrowe*, OF. *escroe* strip, esp. of parchment - Gmc. **skrauða* SHRED.

scrotum XVI. - L. *scrōtum*; cf. *scrautum* skin sheath for arrows.

scrounge (sl.) acquire illicitly. XX. var. of dial. *scrunge* steal.

scrub[1] rub hard. XIV. ME. *scrobbe*, beside *shrubbe*, prob. - MLG., MDu. *schrobben*, *schrubben*.

scrub[2] low stunted tree XVI (doubtfully XIV); dwarf cattle; mean little fellow XVI. var. of SHRUB.

scruff nape of the neck. XVIII. orig. alt. of *scuff*, *scuft* (XVIII), of which there is a synon. var. *cuff* (XVIII); perh. based ult. on ON. *skoft* (= OHG *scuft*, Goth. *skuft*) hair of the head.

scrum XIX. Shortening of *scrummage*, SCRIMMAGE.

scrumptious (orig. U.S. colloq.) first rate, 'grand'; (also formerly) fastidious, 'particular'. XIX. of unkn. orig.
scrunch (colloq.) XIX. Expressive alt. of CRUNCH.
scruple A. small unit of weight or measurement; B. thought or doubt troubling the conscience. XVI. - F. *scrupule* or L. *scrūpulus, -ulum* in above senses, dim. of *scrūpus* rough or sharp pebble, anxiety. Hence or so **scruple** vb. XVII. f. the sb. or - F. So **scrupulous** XV, **scrupulosity** XVI. - F. or L.
scrutator one who examines closely. XVI. - L. *scrūtātor*, f. *scrūtārī* search, examine, f. *scrūta* trash, rubbish, the orig. application being to the rummaging of rag-pickers or the searching of persons; see -ATOR. So **scrutiny** (-Y[4]) formal taking of votes XV; close investigation XVII; official examination of votes XVIII. - L. *scrūtinium*. Hence **scrutineer, scrutinize** XVII.
scry (dial.) descry; act as a crystal-gazer. XVI (revived XIX). Aphetic of DESCRY.
scud move briskly, now esp. of objects driven by the wind. XVI. poss. alt. of SCUT, as if to race like a hare.
scuffle struggle confusedly together. XVI. prob. f. Scand. base (cf. Sw. *skuff, skuffa* push) to be referred to Gmc. **skuf-* SHOVE.
sculduddery, skul- (Sc.) fornication XVIII; obscenity XIX. of unkn. orig.
sculduggery, skul- (U.S.) tricky doings. XIX. of unkn. orig.
scull kind of oar. XIV. of unkn. orig. Hence vb. XVII.
scullery (hist.) department of a household concerned with kitchen utensils XV; room attached to a kitchen XVIII. - AN. *squillerie*, for OF. *escuelerie*, f. *escuelier* maker or seller of dishes, f. *escuele* :- Rom. **scūtella* (by assoc. with L. *scūtum* shield), for L. *scutella* salver, dim. of *scutra* wooden dish; see -ERY.
scullion (arch.) servant who performed menial offices in the kitchen. XV. of unkn. orig.
sculpin any of several spiny fishes. XVII. perh. alt. of *scorpene* - L. *scorpæna* - Gr. *skórpaina*, presumably f. *skorpíos* SCORPION.
sculpture art of carving in hard material, products of this. XIV (rare before XVII). - L. *sculptūra*, f. pp. stem of *sculpere*, var. of *scalpere* scratch, carve; see -URE. So **sculptor** XVII. - L.; see -OR[1]. Hence **sculpt, sculptural** (-AL[1]) XIX, **sculpture** vb. XVII.
scum †foam, froth XIII; film of floating matter on liquid XV; fig. XVI. - MLG., MDu. *schūm* (Du. *schuim*) = OHG. *scūm* (G. *schaum*) :- Gmc. **skūma-*, f. IE. **skū-* cover. Hence vb. †skim XIV; †scour the surface of XV; throw up as scum XVII.
scumble spread colour over a picture to soften hard lines, etc. XVIII. poss. f. SCUM vb. + -LE[3].
scuncheon (archit.) bevelled inner edge. XV. Aphetic - OF. *escoinson* (mod. *écoinçon*), f. *es-* EX-[1] + *coin* corner.
scupper[1] opening in a ship's side on a level with the deck. XV. perh. - AN. aphetic deriv. of OF. *escopir* (mod. *écopir*) :- Rom. **skuppīre* spit, of imit. orig.
scupper[2] (mil. sl.) surprise and massacre; (pass.) be done for. XIX. of unkn. orig.
scuppernong variety of muscadine. XIX. name of a river and lake in N. Carolina, U.S.A.
scurf Late OE., prob. alt. of *sċeorf* by the influence of ON. **skurfr*, implicit in *skurfóttr* scurfy, f. base allied to that of OE. *sċeorfan* gnaw, *sċeorfian* cut into shreds. Hence **scurfy** (-Y[1]) XVII (isolated ex. XV).
scurrilous coarsely opprobrious or jocular. XVI. f. synon. †*scurrile* (XVI) - F. *scurrile* or L. *scurrīlis*, f. *scurra* buffoon; see -OUS, -ILE. So **scurrility** XVI.
scurry go rapidly or hurriedly. XIX. Second el. of HURRY-SCURRY used independently.
scurvy characterized by scurf. XVI. f. SCURF; see -Y[1]. Hence **scurvy** sb., partly ellipt. for †*s. disease* XVI, the spec. application being determined by assoc. with the like-sounding F. *scorbut*, LG. *schorbūk* (see SCORBUTIC).
scut †hare XV; short erect tail of rabbit, etc. XVI. rel. to †*scut* adj. short, sb. short garment, vb. cut short, dock; of unkn. orig.
scutage (hist.) tax levied on knights' fees, esp. in lieu of military service. XV. - medL. *scūtāgium*, f. L. *scūtum* shield; see -AGE.
scutch dress (fibre) by beating. XVIII. - OF. **escoucher*, dial. var. of *escousser* :- Rom. **excussāre*, f. pp. stem *excuss-* of L. *excutere*, f. EX-[1] + *quatere* shake.
scutcheon XVI. Aphetic var. of AN. *escuchon* ESCUTCHEON.
scuttle[1] †dish, trencher (OE.), XV; (dial.) corn-basket, grain-shovel XIV; wide-mouthed basket XV; bowl-like vessel for coal XIX. Late OE. *sċutel* does not seem to have survived; ME. *scutel* is - ON. *skutill*, corr. to OS. *skutala* = MLG. *schötele*, MDu. *schotele* (Du. *schotel*), OHG. *scuzzila* (G. *schüssel*); all - L. *scutula* or *scutella*, rel. to *scutra* dish, platter.
scuttle[2] opening in a ship's deck XV; trap-door XVIII. perh. - F. †*escoutille* (mod. *écoutille*) hatchway - Sp. *escotilla*, dim. of *escota* cutting out of cloth, f. *escotar* cut out, f. L. EX-[1] + Gmc. **skaut-* SHEET. Hence **scuttle** vb. cut a hole in sides, bottom, or deck of (a ship). XVII.
scuttle[3] run with quick hurried steps. XV. Parallel with synon. (dial.) *scuddle* XVII, frequent. of SCUD; see -LE[3].
scutum (nat. hist.) shield-shaped part or segment. XIX. techn. use of L. *scūtum* oblong shield.
scythe long-handled long-bladed instrument for mowing. OE. *sīðe*, earlier **siġði* (written *sigdi*) = MLG. *segede, sigde* (LG. *seged, seid, sichte*), ON. *sigðr* :- Gmc. **seȝiþō*, f. **seȝ-* :- IE. **sek-* cut (see SECTION).
'sdeath see -S.
se- prefix occurring in derivs. from Latin, repr. *sē* (also *sēd*) prep. and adv. without, apart, as in SECEDE, SECLUDE, SECRET, SECRETE, SEDUCE, SEPARATE.
sea OE. *sǣ* = OS. *sēo, sēu* (Du. *zee*), OHG. *sē(o)*, (G. *see*), ON. *sǽr*, Goth. *saiws* :- Gmc. **saiwiz*, of unkn. orig. Comp. **sea-coal** (XIII) mineral coal (as dist. from charcoal) is in orig. prob. coal derived from the sea.
seal[1] aquatic mammal. OE. *sēol-*, inflexional

form of *seolh* = MLG. *sēl*, MDu. *seel*, *zēle*, OHG. *selah*, ON. *selr* :- Gmc. **selχaz*, of unkn. orig.

seal[2] (piece of wax for impressing) a device used in attesting a document. XIII. - AN. *seal*, OF. *seel* (mod. *sceau*) :- L. *sigillum* small picture, statuette, seal, dim. of *signum* SIGN. So **seal** vb. XIII. - OF. *seeler* (mod. *sceller*).

seam junction made by sewing; line made by two abutting edges. OE. *sēam* = MDu. *sōm* (Du. *zoom*), OHG. *soum* (G. *saum*), ON. *saumr* - Gmc. **saumaz*, f. **sau-* **su-* SEW. Hence **seam** vb. XVI, **seamstress, sempstress** XVII.

seaman OE. *sǣmann*, with Gmc. parallels.

séance session of a body of persons, spec. spiritualists' meeting. XIX. - F., f. OF. *seoir* :- L. *sedēre* SIT; see -ANCE.

sear[1] become withered OE.; cause to wither XV; burn, char XVI. OE. *sēarian* = OHG. *sōrēn* :- Gmc. **saurōjan*, f. **sauraz* SERE.

sear[2] portion of a gun-lock that engages with the notches of the tumbler. XVI. prob. - OF. *serre* grasp, lock, bolt, (now) foot of a bird of prey, f. *serrer* grasp, hold fast :- Rom. **serrāre*, for late L. *serāre* bar, bolt, f. *sera* bar for a door.

search examine thoroughly; look for; also intr. XIV. - AN. *sercher*, OF. *cerchier* (mod. *chercher*) :- late L. *circāre* go round, f. L. *circus* CIRCLE. So **search** sb. XIV. - AN. *serche*, OF. *cerche* (†*cherche*), if not f. the vb.

season (appropriate) time or period XIII; period of the year (spring, summer, autumn, winter); time of breeding, etc. XIV. ME. *seson*, *-(o)un* - OF. *seson* (mod. *saison*) :- L. *satiō*, *-ōn-* sowing, in Rom. time of sowing, seed-time, f. IE. **sə-*, as in L. *satus* sown (cf. SOW[2]). So **season** vb. render more palatable by the addition of a spice, salt, etc. XIV; bring to maturity XVI. - OF. *saisonner* (repl. by mod. *assaisonner*). Hence **seasonable, seasonably** XIV, **seasonal** XIX. **seasoning** †impregnation; savoury addition to a dish. XVI. The sense-development in the vb., as shown in Rom. dialects, is presumed to have been: 'sow', 'cultivate at a favourable time', 'ripen, mature', 'cook well', 'add flavouring to'.

seat †sitting XII; place or thing to sit on XIII; place of residence. - ON. *sǽti* = OE. *ġesete*, MDu. *gesaete* (Du. *gezeet*), OHG. *gasāzi* (G. *gesäss*) :- Gmc. **ȝasǣtjam*, f. **sǣt-* **set-* SIT. Hence vb. XVI.

sebaceous greasy, oily. XVIII. f. L. *sēbāceus*, f. *sēbum* tallow, rel. to SOAP; see -ACEOUS.

sebesten plum-like fruit of the genus *Cordia*. XIV. - medL. *sebestēn* - Arab. *sibistān* - Pers. *sapistān*.

sec (of wines) dry. XIX. - F. :- L. *siccus*.

secant in full *s. line*. XVI. - F. *sécant* adj., *sécante* sb. - modL. use of L. *secāns*, *-ant-*, prp. of *secāre* cut; see SECTION, -ANT.

secateurs XIX. - pl. of F. *sécateur*, irreg. f. L. *secāre* cut (see SECTION) + *-ateur* -ATOR.

secede withdraw *from* an association. XVIII. - L. *sēcēdere*, f. SE- + *cēdere* go, CEDE. So **secession** XVII. - F. or L.

seclude shut off or away. XV. - L. *sēclūdere*, f. SE- + *claudere* shut; see CLOSE. So **seclusion** XVII. - medL.

second[1] coming next after the first XIII; next in rank or succession (e.g. *s. lieutenant*) XIV; from XVI in various techn. (mainly ellipt.) uses as sb. - (O)F. *second*, fem. *-onde* - L. *secundus* following, favourable, second, f. base of *sequī* follow. So **second** sb. $\frac{1}{60}$ of a minute. XIV. - (O)F. *seconde* - medL. *secunda*, sb. use of fem. of *secundus*, *secunda minuta* 'second minute' being the result of the second operation of sexagesimal division. **secondary** belonging to the second class or order XIV; also sb. XV. - L. *secundārius*; hence **secondarily** XV.

second[2] support, back up. XVI. - F. *seconder* - L. *secundāre* favour, further, f. *secundus* (see prec.).

second[3] (mil., etc.) transfer (an officer) temporarily to other duties. XIX. f. F. phr. *en second* in the second rank (said of officers). Hence **secondment** XIX.

seconde (fencing) the second of the eight parries. XVIII. - F., sb. use of fem. of *second* SECOND[1].

secrecy XVI. repl. †*secretie* (XV), f. *secre* or SECRET + -TY[2] or -Y[3].

secret adj. and sb. XIV (also *secre(e)* - OF. *secré*). - (O)F. - L. *sēcrētus* (n. *sēcrētum* used sb.), pp. of *sēcernere*, f. SE- + *cernere* separate, distinguish, secrete, (pp. sifted).

secretary †confidant XIV; one employed to conduct correspondence, keep records, etc. XV; minister at the head of a department of state XVI. - late L. *sēcrētārius* confidential officer, sb. use of adj. f. *sēcrētus* SECRET; see -ARY. So **secretariat** office of secretary. XIX. - F. *secrétariat*; see -ATE[1].

secretaire writing-bureau. XIX. - F. *secrétaire* secretary, with transf. meaning prob. suggested by ESCRITOIRE, *secretoire* (XVII-XIX).

secrete[1] produce by secretion. XVIII. f. *sēcrēt-*, pp. stem of L. *sēcernere* separate (see SECRET), partly as a back-formation on **secretion** (XVII) - F. *sécrétion* or med. use of L. *sēcrētiō*, *-ōn-*. So **secretory** (-ORY[2]) XVII.

secrete[2] hide out of sight. XVIII. alt., after L. *sēcrētus* SECRET, of *secret* vb. (XVI), f. the adj.

secretive XIX. Back-formation from *secretiveness* (also XIX), name in phrenology of a propensity, modelled on F. *secrétivité*, f. *secret* SECRET; see -IVE.

sect †class (of persons); †religious order; †sex; religious following; philosophical school XIV; religious denomination XVI; school of opinion XVII. - (O)F. *secte* or L. *secta* following (used as cogn. obj. in *sectam sequi* follow a certain course of conduct), party faction, school of philosophy, f. older pp. stem *sect-* of *sequī* follow. So **sectary** member of a sect. XVI. - medL. *sectārius*. Hence **sectarian** adj. and sb. XVII; whence **sectarianism** XIX.

section cutting; subdivision of a written or printed work or document; part cut off XVI; drawing of an object as if cut through XVII. - F. *section* or L. *sectiō*, *-ōn-*, f. *sect-*, pp. stem of *secāre* cut, f. IE. **sek-*.

sector plane figure contained by two radii and the arc of a curve intercepted by them; instrument invented by Thomas Hood for the mechanical solution of mathematical problems (orig. containing a graduated arc) XVI. - late L. techn. use of L. *sector* (agent-noun of *secāre* cut); see prec. and -OR[1].

secular A. pert. to the world, worldly XIII; not sacred, profane XV; non-religious XVI; B. occurring once in an age XVI; living or lasting for an age or for ages XVII; sb. secular cleric XIII. In A - OF. *seculer* (mod. *séculier*) - L. *sæculāris*, f. *sæculum* generation, age, in ChrL. the World (esp. opp. to the Church); in B immed. - L. *sæculāris*; see -AR. So **secularity** XVII. - (O)F. or medL.

secure (arch.) feeling no care; safe, certain. XVI. - L. *sēcūrus*, f. SE- + *cūra* care (see CURE); cf. SURE. Hence **secure** vb. make secure XVI; make sure of, get hold of XVIII. So **security** XV. - (O)F. *sécurité* or L. *sēcūritās*.

sedan closed vehicle for one person carried by means of two poles. XVII. poss. based on a dial. var. of a Rom. deriv. of L. *sella* SADDLE.

sedate adj. XVII. - L. *sēdātus*, pp. of *sēdāre* settle, assuage, calm, f. **sēd*- **sed*-, as in *sedēre* SIT; see -ATE². So **sedation** XVI. - F. or L. **sedative** adj. XV; sb. XVIII. - (O)F. or medL.

sedentary remaining in one place XVI; pert. to or involving a sitting posture XVII. - F. *sédentaire* or L. *sedentārius*, f. *sedent*-, prp. stem of *sedēre* SIT; see -ENT, -ARY.

sederunt (Sc.) sitting of an assembly. XVII. sb. use of L. *sēdērunt* '(there) sat' (viz. the following persons, i.e. at a meeting), 3rd pl. pt. indic. of *sedēre* SIT.

sedge coarse grassy plant. OE. *secġ* :- Gmc. **saʒja*-, f. **saʒ*- **seʒ*- :- IE. **sek*- cut, repr. by L. *secāre*.

sedilia (n. pl.) series of (three) seats in the sanctuary of a church; rarely sg. **sedile** XVIII. - L. *sedīlia*, pl. of *sedīle*, f. *sedēre* SIT; see -ILE, -IA².

sediment XVI. - F. *sédiment* or L. *sedimentum* settling, f. *sedēre* SIT, settle; see -MENT.

sedition †violent party strife XIV; †revolt, mutiny XVI; behaviour inciting to rebellion XIX. - (O)F. *sédition* or L. *sēditiō*, *-ōn*-, f. *sēd*- SE- + *itiō* going, f. *it*-, pp. stem of *īre* go. So **seditious** XV. - (O)F. or L.

seduce divert from allegiance or service XV; induce (a woman) to surrender her chastity; lead astray XVI. In earliest use *sedu(i)se* - (O)F. *seduis*-, inflexional stem of *séduire*; later assim. to L. *sēdūcere*, f. SE- + *dūcere* lead. So **seduction** XVI. - F. or L.

sedulous diligent or persistent in application. XVI. f. L. *sēdulus* eager, zealous, f. *sēdulō* zealously, carefully, for *sē dolō* 'without guile', (hence) with zeal; see SE-, -OUS.

sedum (bot.) genus the British species of which are known as stonecrop. XV (*cedum*). - L.

see¹ pt. *saw*, pp. *seen* perceive with the eyes. OE. str. vb. *sēon* = OS., OHG. *sehan* (Du. *zien*, G. *sehen*), ON. *sjá*, Goth. *saihwan* :- Gmc. **seχwan* - IE. **seq*-, by some identified with the base of L. *sequī* follow, the etym. sense being 'follow with the eyes'.

see² seat, spec. bishop's seat or throne XIII; episcopal office or authority XIV. - AN. *se(d)*, OF. *sie(d)* :- Rom. **sedem*, alt. (after L. *sedēre*) of *sēdem* (nom. *-es*) seat, f. **sēd*- **sed*- SIT.

seed that which is or is to be sown; †offspring OE.; †semen XIII. OE. *sǣd*, Ang. *sēd*, corr. to OS. *sād* (Du. *zaad*), OHG. *sāt* (G. *saat*), ON. *sáð*, Goth. *-sēþs* :- Gmc. **sǣðiz*, **sǣðam*, f. **sǣ*- SOW². Hence **seed** vb. XIV (intr.). **seedling** XVII. **seedy** full of seed XVI; (sl.) shabby (from the appearance of a plant that has run to seed) XVIII; unwell XIX. Hence **seedlip** basket for seed. OE. *sǣdlēap*; f. *lēap* basket.

seek pt., pp. *sought* (arch.) try to find or obtain; also intr. OE. *sēċan*, earlier *sœ̄ċan* = OS. *sōkian* (Du. *zoeken*), OHG. *suohhan* (G. *suchen*), ON. *sœkja*, Goth. *sōkjan* :- Gmc. **sōkjan*, f. base **sōk*- :- IE. **sāg*- **sag*-, repr. also by L. *sāgīre* perceive by scent, Gr. *hēgeisthai* lead, OIr. *saigin* I seek, approach.

seel stitch up the eyes of (a hawk, etc.), also transf. XV. Later form of †*sile* (XIV) - OF. *ciller*, *siller* or medL. *ciliāre*, f. L. *cilium* eyelid.

seem †befit, BESEEM XII; appear to be XIII. - ON. *sœma* honour (MSw. befit), f. *sœmr* fitting, seemly, f. **sōm*-, whence also OE. *sōm* reconciliation, *sēman* settle, reconcile, rel. to **sam*- SAME. So **seemly** XIII. ME. *semeliche* - ON. *sœmiligr*.

seep ooze; percolate. XVIII. perh. dial. development of OE. *sipian*, rel. to MLG. *sīpen*, MHG. *sīfen*, presumably = OE. *sīpian*, surviving in dial. *sipe*, of unkn. orig.

seer one who sees visions of divine things XIV; one who sees XV; magician, crystal-gazer XVII. f. SEE¹ + -ER¹.

seersucker XVIII. - Pers. *šīr o šakkar* 'milk and sugar', striped linen garment.

see-saw redupl. formation based on SAW¹ (as if orig. sung by sawyers), and used in rhythmical jingles, *see saw sacke a downe* (*sacaradown*), *see saw sack a day*, *see saw Margery Daw* XVII; game at which children sitting on each end of a pivoted plank move each other up and down XVIII; plank so used XIX. Hence as vb. XVIII.

seethe †boil OE.; soak, steep XVI; be inwardly agitated XVII. OE. str. vb. *sēoðan* = OS. **sioðan*, OHG. *siodan* (Du. *zieden*, G. *sieden*), ON. *sjóða*, f. Gmc. **seuþ*- **sauþ*- **suð*-, repr. also by ON. *sauðr* sheep ('boiled flesh'), Goth. *sauþs* sacrifice, and OE. *sēað* pit, cistern, pond.

segment sb. XVI. - L. *segmentum*, f. *sec*-, stem of *secāre* cut; see -MENT. Hence vb. XIX.

segregate XVI. f. pp. stem of L. *sēgregāre*, f. SE- + *grex*, *greg*- flock; based on *segregate* pp. (XV); see -ATE³. So **segregation** XVI. - late L.

seguidilla Spanish dance of $\frac{3}{4}$ or $\frac{3}{8}$ time. XVIII. - Sp., f. *seguida* following, sequence, f. *seguir* :- Rom. **sequere*, for L. *sequī* follow.

seidlitz *s. powder* (XIX), named after †*S. salt* and *water* (XVIII), because of its aperient properties; name of a village in Bohemia where there is a spring impregnated with magnesium sulphate and carbonic acid.

seigneur French feudal lord XVI; in Canada, one of the landed gentry XVIII. - (O)F. :- L. *senior*, *-ōr*- SENIOR. So **seigniory** (-Y³) †lordship XIII; feudal lordship XV. Hence **seigniorial** XIX (earlier **seigneurial** XVII).

seine large fishing-net. OE. *segne* = OS., OHG. *segina* :- WGmc. **sagina* - L. *sagēna* (whence OF. *saïne*, mod. *seine*) - Gr. *sagḗnē*; reinforced in ME. from OF.

seisin (chiefly leg.) possession. ME. *se(i)sin(e)* -

AN. *sesine*, OF. *seisine*, (also mod.) *saisine*, f. *seisir* SEIZE; see -INE[4].

seismic XIX. f. Gr. *seismós* earthquake, f. *seíein* shake; see -IC. So **seismo-**, comb. form.

seize A. put in (feudal) possession (of); B. take possession or hold of XIII; †C. arrive at XVI; D. (naut.) lash together with cord, etc. XVII; (of surfaces) unite XIX. - OF. *seisir*, (also mod.) *saisir* :- Gallo-Rom., Frankish L. *sacīre*, of Gmc. orig. Hence **seizure** XV.

selachian (pert. to) a shark or allied fishes. XIX. f. modL. *Selachē* (- Gr. *selákhē*, pl. of *sélakhos* shark) or *Selachiī*; see -IAN.

selah Heb. *selāh*, occurring often at the end of a verse in the Psalter and in Habbakuk 3, supposed to be a musical or liturgical direction, perh. indicating a pause.

seldom OE. *seldan* (with late var. *seldum*), corr. to MLG., MDu. *selden* (Du. *zelden*), OHG. *seltan* (G. *selten*), ON. *sjaldan*, f. Gmc. *selda-, repr. also in OE. *seldlić*, *sellić* strange, wonderful, Goth. *sildaleiks* wonderful.

select specially chosen, picked. XVI. - L. *sēlectus*, pp. of *sēligere* choose out, f. SE- + *legere* collect, choose. So vb. pick out. XVI. f. pp. stem of the L. vb. **selection** XVII. - L. Hence **selective** XVII.

selenite sulphate of lime or gypsum (identity of the mineral so named by ancient writers is dubious). XVI. - L. *selēnītēs* (also *-ītis*) - Gr. *selēnítēs*, f. *selḗnē* moon, so called because supposed to wax and wane with the moon. So **selenium** (chem.) rare non-metallic element. XIX. - modL., f. Gr. *selḗnē*; so named because of its similarity in properties to *tellurium* (f. L. *tellus* earth), with ref. to the moon's relation to the earth as a satellite.

self A. (arch.) in apposition with a sb. or pron., e.g. *he self*, superseded by emphatic prons., as *himself*, *ourselves* OE.; B. adj. †*the* same, *the* very OE.; (of a colour) the same throughout XVII; C. sb. (pl. *selves*) individual or particular person XIII; (chiefly philos.) *the* ego XVII. OE. *self* str., *selfa* wk. = OS. *self*, *selƀo*, OHG. *selb*, *selbo* (Du. *zelv*, *-zelve*, *-zelfde*, G. *selb-*, *selbe*), ON. (only str.) *sjálfr*, Goth. (only wk.) *silba* :- Gmc. *selƀa-, *selƀan-, of unkn. orig. Hence **selfhood, selfish** XVII; **selfsame** *the* very same XV.

Seljuk epithet of certain Turkish dynasties. XIX. Turk. *Selçuk* name of the reputed ancestor of these. So **Seljukian** XVII.

sell pt., pp. *sold* †give up; dispose of for money. OE. *sellan* = OS. *sellian*, OHG. *sellen*, ON. *selja* give up, sell, Goth. *saljan* offer sacrifice.

sellender var. of SALLENDER.

seltzer effervescent mineral water obtained near Nieder Selters in Germany; also a similar artificial one. XVIII. alt. of G. *Selterser* (with g. pl. ending), f. *Selters*.

selvage, selvedge edge of a piece of woven material finished so as to prevent unravelling. XV. f. SELF + EDGE, after early mod. Du. *selfegghe* (now *zelfegge*), LG. *sülfegge*.

semantic †relating to signs of the weather XVII (rare); pert. to meaning XIX; sb. pl. science of the meanings of words XX. - F. *sémantique* - Gr. *sēmantikós* significant, f. *sēmaínein* show, signify, f. *sêma* sign; see -IC. So **semasiology** XIX. - G. *semasiologie*, f. Gr. *sēmasiā* signification. Hence **sematology** doctrine of signs in relation to knowledge XIX; semasiology XIX.

semaphore signalling apparatus. XIX. - F. *sémaphore*, irreg. f. Gr. *sêma* sign, signal + *-phoros* -PHORE. So **semaphoric** XIX.

semblance †act of appearing XIII; appearance, likeness XIV; outward seeming *of* XVI. - (O)F., f. *sembler* :- L. *similāre*, *simulāre*, see SIMULATE, -ANCE.

semée (her.) covered with many small spots or figures. XVI. - F., pp. fem. of *semer* :- L. *sēmināre* SOW.

semeio- comb. form of Gr. *sēmeîon* sign, f. *sêma* signal. **semeiology** sign language XVII; branch of medicine concerned with symptoms XIX. **semeiotic** XVII, **-ical** XVI relating to symptoms. - Gr. *sēmeiōtikós*.

semen seed of male animals. (XIV) XVIII. - L. *sēmen*, f. base of *serere* sow[2].

semester academic half-year. XIX. - G. - L. *sēmestris*, f. *sē-*, comb. form of *sex* SIX + *mēnsis* MONTH.

semi- comb. form repr. L. *sēmi-* (partly through F., It., etc. *semi-*) 'half', (less strictly) 'partly', 'partially', equiv. in meaning to DEMI- and HEMI-, but in much more extensive use. L. *sēmi-* corr. to Gr. *hēmi-*, Skr. *sāmi*, and OS. *sām-*, OHG. *sāmi-*, OE. *sām-* (as in *sambærned* half-burnt, *samcwic* 'half-alive', half-dead). Exx. are **semibreve** XVI, **semicircle** XVI (L. *sēmicirculus*), **-circular** XV (late L. *-circulāris*), **semicolon** XVII, **semiquaver** XVI, **semitone** XVII (cf. late L. *sēmitonium*), **semivowel** XVI (L. *sēmivocālis*).

seminar group of students meeting for systematic instruction XIX. - G. - L. *sēminārium* (see next).

seminary †seed-plot XV; place of production, cultivation, or education XVI. - L. *sēminārium*, sb. use of n. of *sēminārius*, f. *sēmen*, *sēmin-* seed; see -ARY. Hence **seminarist** one trained in a seminary. XVI.

semio-, etc. see SEMEIO-.

Semite Hebrew, Arab, Assyrian, or Aramaean, regarded as a descendant of Shem (Gen. 10). XIX. - modL. *Sēmīta*, f. (Vulg.) *Sēm* - Gr. *Sḗm* Shem; see -ITE. So **Semitic** XIX.

semolina hard grains left after bolting of flour. XVIII. alt. of It. *semolino*, dim. of *semola* bran, based on L. *simila* flour.

sempiternal everlasting. XV. - (O)F. *sempiternel* - lateL. *sempiternālis*, f. L. *sempiternus*, f. *semper* always, for ever + *æviternus ETERNAL.

sempstress see SEAM.

senarius (pros.) iambic trimeter. XVI. - L. *sēnārius*, sb. use of adj., f. *sēnī* six each, f. *sex* SIX.

senate XIII. - (O)F. *sénat* - L. *senātus*, f. *senex*, *sen-* old (man); see SENIOR, -ATE[1]. So **senator** (-OR[1]) XIII. - (O)F. *sénateur* - L. *senātor*, *-ōrem*.

send[1] pt., pp. *sent* cause or direct to go. OE. *sendan* = OS. *sendian* (Du. *zenden*), OHG. *sendan* (G. *senden*), ON. *senda*, Goth. *sandjan* :- Gmc. *sandjan, f. *sand- (whence OE. *sand* message, messenger) :- *sanþ-, causative of *senþ-, repr. by OE., OS. *sīð*, OHG. *sind*, *sint*, ON. *sinn*, Goth. *sinþs* journey. Comp. **send-off** XIX (orig. U.S.).

send[2] (naut., of a ship) fall with head or stern

deep in the trough of the sea. XVII. Often written (')*scend*, as if aphetic of DESCEND, which may in fact be the source.

sendal thin rich silk material. XIII. - OF. *cendal, sendal*, obscurely derived from Gr. *sindṓn*.

seneschal official in a great household administering justice, etc. XIV; governor XV. - OF. *seneschal* (mod. *sénéchal*) :- medL. *seni-, siniscalcus* - Gmc. **siniskalkaz*, f. **seni-* old (cf. SENIOR) + **skalkaz* servant (OE. *sċealc*, etc., Goth. *skalks*).

senhor XVIII. Pg. analogue of SEÑOR; fem. **senhora** (dim. **senhorita**).

senile pert. to old age. XVII. - F. *sénile* or L. *senīlis*, f. *sen-* of *senex* old; see next and -ILE.

senior person superior by reason of age or station XIV; adj. older, elder XV; that ranks higher XVI. - L. *senior*, compar. of *senex* old, rel. to Gr. *hénos* (in *hénē* last day of the moon), Goth. *sineigs* old, *sinista* elder. So **seniority** XV. - medL.

senna (leaflets of) the cassia plant. XVI. - modL. *sen(n)a* - Arab. *sanā'*.

sennet set of notes on a trumpet, etc., to announce ceremonial entrances and exits. XVI. perh. var. of SIGNET.

sennight (arch.) week. OE. *seofon nihte* seven nights, ME. *seouenih(e)*, later *senny3t* (XV); see SEVEN, NIGHT, and cf. FORTNIGHT.

sennit var. of SINNET.

señor Sp. title of respect for a man. XVII. - Sp. :- L. *senior, -ōr-* SENIOR; fem. **señora** (XVI) (dim. **señorita**).

sensation operation of any of the senses, physical feeling XVII; condition of excited feeling XVIII. - medL. *sensatiō, -ōn-*, f. L. *sēnsus* SENSE; see -ATION. Hence **sensational** XIX.

sense meaning, signification XIV; faculty of perception or sensation; actual perception or feeling XVI. - L. *sēnsus* faculty of feeling, sensibility, mode of feeling, thought, meaning, f. *sēns-*, pp. stem of *sentīre* feel. Hence **sense** vb. perceive (in several techn. uses). XVI. **sensuous** XVII (-UOUS). So **sensible** perceptible by the senses XIV; cognizant, conscious XV; having good sense XVI. - (O)F. or L. **sensitive** having sensation. XIV. - (O)F. or medL. **sensorium** seat of sensation in the brain. XVII. - late L. **sensual** (-AL[1]) XV. - late L.

sentence †meaning, sense XIII; †way of thinking; opinion, judgement, or decision pronounced; †apophthegm, maxim XIV; †passage of a writing; grammatically complete expression of a thought XV. - (O)F. - L. *sententia* mental feeling, opinion, judgement, f. *sentīre* feel; see -ENCE. So vb. XIV. - (O)F. *sentencier*. **sententious** †full of meaning XV; aphoristic XVI. - L. *sententiōsus*. **sentient** capable of feeling. XVII.

sentiment †feeling, sensation; mental attitude, opinion; mental feeling, emotion XVII; refined and tender feeling XVIII. - (O)F., refash. of OF. *sentement* - medL. *sentīmentum*, f. L. *sentīre* feel; see -MENT. Hence **sentimental** (-AL[1]) XVIII.

sentinel sentry; †duty of a sentry; †military watch-tower XVI; †(in full *private s.*) private soldier XVIII. - F. *sentinelle* - It. *sentinella*, of unkn. orig. Hence vb. XVI.

sentry †sentinel; armed member of the fighting forces set to keep guard. XVII. perh. shortening of †*centrinell, -onel* (XVI), vars. of SENTINEL, with assim. to -RY. comp. **sentry-go**, †orig. phr. consisting of *sentry* sb. (used vocatively) and imper. of GO; (hence) patrol or duties of a s. XIX.

sepal (bot.) division of the calyx. XIX. - modL. *sepalum*; formed (1790) by N. J. de Necker, perh. f. SEPARATE + PETAL.

separate vb. XV. f. pp. stem of L. *sēparāre*, f. SE- + *parāre* make ready, PREPARE; partly after †*separate* pp. (XV); see -ATE[3]. So **separation** XV. - (O)F. - L. **separatist** one who advocates (ecclesiastical) separation. XVII. f. *separate* adj., which was used contemp. as sb. in the same sense.

sepia A. cuttlefish XVI; B. rich brown pigment prepared from its inky secretion XIX. - L. *sēpia* - Gr. *sēpíā*. In B prob. immed. - It. *seppia*.

sepoy †(rare) horseman XVII; Indian native soldier under European discipline XVIII. - (prob. through Pg. *sipae*) Urdu - Pers. *sipāhī* horseman, soldier, f. *sipāh* army.

seps very venomous serpent XVI; skink of the genus *Chalcides* XIX. - L. *sēps* - Gr. *sḗps*, cf. base of *sḗpein* rot.

sepsis putrefaction. XIX. - modL. - Gr. *sêpsis*, f. *sḗpein* rot, putrefy. So **septic** XVII. - L. - Gr. *sēptikós*.

sept (Irish) clan. XVI. poss. alt. of *sect* (also so used XVI); cf. AL. *septus* (XVI), and medL. *septa*, repr. OF. *sette* sect, It. *setta*.

September ninth month of the year, formerly seventh month of the year beginning in March. XI. - L. *September* or (in ME.) F. *septembre*, earlier †*setembre*, f. *septem* SEVEN.

septenarius (pros.) line of 7 feet or stresses. XIX. - L., f. *septēnī*, distributive of *septem* SEVEN. So **septenary** sb. XVI, adj. XVII. **septennial** XVII; see BIENNIAL. **septentrional** northern. XIV. - L. *septentriōnālis*, f. *septentriōnēs* 'seven plough-oxen' (*triō* plough-ox), i.e. the seven stars of the Great Bear; see -AL[1]. **septet(te)** (mus.) composition for seven voices or instruments. XIX. - G. *septet*; see -ET, -ETTE.

septi- comb. form of L. *septem* SEVEN. **septillion** XVII. - F.; see BILLION. **septuagenarian** 70 years old XVIII; also sb. - L. *septuagēnārius*, f. distrib. *septuagēnī*, f. *septuāgintā* seventy; see -ARIAN. So **septuagenary** XVII. **Septuagesima** third Sunday before Lent; †the seventy days beginning with this. XIV. - L. fem. of *septuāgēsimus*, ordinal of *septuāgintā*. **Septuagint** †the 'seventy translators' of the Old Testament into Greek XVI; the translation traditionally attributed to them XVII. - L. *septuāgintā*.

septum (anat., bot., zool.) dividing wall or partition. XVIII. - L. *sēptum, sæptum*, f. *sēpīre, sæpīre* enclose, f. *sēpes, sæpes* hedge.

sepulchre XII. ME. *sepulcre* - (O)F. *sépulcre* - L. *sepulcrum*, erron. *-chrum*, f. stem of *sepultus*, pp. of *sepelīre* bury. So **sepulchral** XVII. - F. or L.; see -AL[1]. **sepulture** (arch.) burial. XIII. - (O)F. *sépulture* - L. *sepultūra*.

sequacious given to following another (slavishly). XVII. f. L. *sequāx, sequāci-*, f. *sequī* follow, f. IE. base repr. also by Gr. *hépomai*, Ir. *sechur*

I follow; see -IOUS. So **sequel** †train of followers, following XV; what follows as a result XV; ensuing course of affairs, narrative, etc. XVI. - (O)F. *séquelle* or L. *sequēla* (*-ella*), f. *sequī*. **sequela**, pl. **-ae** morbid affection resulting from a disease. XVIII. - L. **sequence** (liturg.) piece of rhythmical prose or accentual metre following the epistle at Mass XIV; order of succession, run of cards XVI. - late L. *sequentia*, f. *sequēns*, *-ent-* (whence **sequent** following XVI), prp. of *sequī*.

sequester set aside, remove XIV; confiscate XVI. - (O)F. *séquestrer* or late L. *sequestrāre*, f. *sequester* depositary of a thing in dispute, lit. 'one standing apart', f. **sequos*, *secus* apart, otherwise. So **sequestrate** XVI. f. pp. stem of L. *sequestrāre*. **sequestration** XIV. - (O)F. or late L.

sequin Italian gold coin XVII; small spangle for the ornamentation of dresses XIX. - F. - It. *zecchino*, f. *zecca* the mint - Arab. *sikka* die for coining.

sequoia (tree of a) genus of large American conifers. XIX. - modL., f. *Sequoiah*, name of a Cherokee Indian who invented a syllabary for his native language.

serac tower of ice on a glacier. XIX. - Swiss F., orig. name of a compact white cheese, prob. deriv. of L. *serum* whey.

seraglio harem; Turkish palace. XVI. - It. *serraglio* - Turk. - Pers. *sarāi* palace.

serai CARAVANSERAI; Turkish palace. XVII. - Turk. - Pers. *sarāi* lodging, residence, palace.

seraph one of the seraphim. XVII. Back-formation from SERAPHIM, *-in*. So **seraphic** pert. to the seraphim; ecstatic in worship or devotion. XVII. - medL. *seraphicus*. **seraphical** XVI.

seraphim the living creatures with six wings of Isaiah 6, in early Christian interpretation taken to be a class of angels. OE., ME. *seraphin*, later *seraphim* (XVI) - biblical L. *seraphim*, *-in* (= Gr. *seraphím*, *-pheím*) - Heb. *sᵉrāphīm*, pl. of *sārāph*.

sere (arch.) dry, withered. OE. *sēar* = MLG. *sōr* (LG. *soor*, Du. *zoor*) :- Gmc. **sauraz* :- IE. **sousós*, repr. also by Gr. *aûos*, (Attic) *haûos*, and rel. to L. *sūdus* dry.

serenade music performed at night in the open air, esp. by a lover. XVII. - F. *sérénade* - It. *serenata*, f. *sereno* SERENE, in sense infl. by *sera* evening; see -ADE. Hence vb. XVII.

serendipity faculty of making happy discoveries by accident. XVIII. Coined by Horace Walpole from the title of the fairy-tale 'The Three Princes of Serendip', the heroes of which were always making such discoveries; see -ITY.

serene (of weather, etc.) clear and calm; honorific epithet of a prince XVI; (of persons) calm, untroubled XVII. In both the early senses first in Sc. - L. *serēnus* clear, fair, calm (whence It. *sereno*). So **serenity** XV (first in Sc. as a title of honour). - (O)F. or L.

serf †slave XV; person in servitude 'attached to the soil' XVII. - (O)F. :- L. *servus* slave.

serge woollen fabric. XIV. ME. *sarge*, later *serge* (XVI) - OF. *sarge*, later *serge* :- Rom. **sārica*, for L. *sērica*, fem. of *sēricus* - Gr. *sērikós* of SILK.

sergeant, serjeant †servant XII; †common soldier; †tenant by military service below a knight; officer charged with the arrest of offenders, etc. (now in *s. at arms*); (after law L. *serviens ad lēgem* serjeant-at-law) XIII; officer of the Corporation of London XV; military non-commissioned officer XVI. - OF. *sergent*, *serjant* (mod. *sergent*) :- L. *servientem* (see -ANT), prp. of *servīre* SERVE (cf. SERVANT). The form with *j* has become appropriated to leg. use.

sericulture cultivation of silk. XIX. Shortened - F. *sériciculture*, f. late L. *sēricum* silk, n. of *sēricus*; see SERGE, CULTURE.

series XVII. - L. *seriēs* row, chain, series, f. *serere* join, connect. So **serial** XIX (first of the publication of a literary work). - modL. *seriālis*; see -AL¹. **seriatim** XVII. - medL.

serif (typogr.) fine cross-stroke at top or bottom of a letter. XIX. perh. - Du. *schreef* dash, line.

seringa XVIII. - F. - L. SYRINGA.

serious of grave or solemn disposition XV; requiring earnest thought XVI. - (O)F. *sérieux* or late L. *sēriōsus*, f. *sērius* (used only of things in classical times), perh. rel. to the Gmc. base repr. by OE. *swǣr*, *swār*, OHG. *swār* (G. *schwer*) heavy; see -IOUS. **serio-** used as comb. form (see -O-), as in **serio-comic** (XVIII).

sermon XII. ME. *serm(o)un* - AN. *sermun*, (O)F. *sermon* :- L. *sermō*, *-ōn-* talk, discourse.

sero- used as comb. form (see -O-) of SERUM. XIX.

serous pert. to serum. XVI. - F. *séreux* or medL. *serōsus*, f. SERUM.

serpent scaly limbless reptile, snake XIV; wind instrument of wood shaped with three U-shaped turns XVIII. - (O)F. *serpent* :- L. *serpēns*, *-ent-*, sb. use of prp. of *serpere* creep, cogn. with Gr. *hérpein*, Skr. *sárpati*; see -ENT. So **serpentine** XIV. - (O)F. - late L.; see -INE¹.

serpigo creeping skin disease. XIV. - medL., f. *serpere* crawl. So **serpiginous** XVII. - modL.

serpula marine annelid which inhabits a tortuous calcareous tube. XVIII. - modL. use of late L. *serpula*, dim. f. L. *serpere* (see SERPENT).

serrate notched like a saw. XVII. - L. *serrātus*, f. *serra* saw; see -ATE². So **serrated** (-ED¹) XVIII.

serried in close order. XVII. Either (i) f. (arch.) *serry* press *close together* in the ranks (XVI), prob. f. (O)F. *serré*, pp. of *serrer* :- Rom. **serrāre* press close, alt. of L. (in comps.) *serāre*, f. *sera* lock, bolt; or (ii) sp. of †*serred* (disyll.), pp. of †*serr* (XVI) - (O)F. *serrer*; see -ED¹.

serum watery animal fluid. XVII. - L. *serum* whey, watery fluid.

serval †lynx; bush cat. XVIII. - modL., F. *serval* - Pg. (*lobo*) *cerval* 'deer-like (wolf)', f. *cervo* :- L. *cervus* deer; see -AL¹.

servant personal or domestic attendant XIII; one under obligation to work for (and obey) another XIV. - OF. *servant* m. and fem. (now only fem. *-ante*), sb. use of prp. of *servir* SERVE; see -ANT and cf. SERGEANT.

serve be a servant (to). XIII; many deriv. uses from the same date. - (O)F. *servir* or L. *servīre*, f. L. *servus* slave. So **service**¹ condition or work of a servant. XII (*serfise*, *seruise*). - OF. *servise*, (also mod.) *service*, or - L. *servītium* slavery. **serviceable** XIV. - OF. **serviette** table napkin. XV. In earliest use only Sc. (*seruiot*, *-iat*, later *seruit*), since *c*.1800 re-adopted in gen. Eng. use with F. sp. - (O)F. *serviette* towel, napkin, f. *servir*; see -ETTE. **servile** pert. to a slave or to laborious or mechanical work XIV; of slavish character XVII. - L. *servīlis*. **servitor** †(man)servant XIV; †one who serves in war XVI; former class of exhibitioner at Oxford university XVII. - OF. *servitor* (mod. *serviteur*) - late L. *servītor*. **servitude** slavery XV; (Sc. leg.) subjection or subservience of property XVI. - (O)F. - L. *servitūdō*. **servo-** XIX, in **servo-motor** - F. *servomoteur* auxiliary motor (see -O-).

service² tree of the genus *Sorbus* XVI (*sarves, servyse*). orig. pl. of †*serve*, OE. *syrfe* :- Gmc. **surbjōn* - popL. **sorbea*, f. L. *sorbus* service tree.

sesame E. Indian plant, *Sesamum indicum*. XV (in early use hardly naturalized and appearing in various forms). - L. *sēsamum, sīsamum, sēsama, -ima* - Gr. *sḗsamon, sēsámē*. Since late XVIII the currency of *sesame* is due to translations of 'The Arabian Nights' from F. (*sésame*) and the trisyll. pronunc. to Gr. *sēsámē*.

sesqui- prefix denoting one and a half. - L. :- **sēmisque* a half in addition (see SEMI-); in musical terms, e.g. **sesquialtera** (denoting the proportion 1½:1) XVI; in other terms, e.g. **sesquipedalian** a foot and a half long XVII; in chem. terms, denoting a proportion of 3 to 2 between constituents of compounds XIX.

sess var. of CESS (in Ir. use). XVI.

sessile (path.) adhering close to the surface; (nat. hist.) immediately attached to the base XVIII; sedentary XIX. - L. *sessilis*, f. *sess-*, pp. stem of *sedēre* SIT; see -ILE.

session sitting together for conference, spec. judicial sitting XIV; continuous series of meetings XVI; act of sitting, occupation of a seat XVII. - (O)F. *session* or L. *sessiō, -ōn-*, f. *sess-*, pp. stem of *sedēre* SIT; see -ION.

sesterce ancient Roman coin, orig. equiv. to 2½ asses. XVI. - L. *sestertius* that is two and a half, f. *sēmis* half + *tertius* third; see SEMI-. So **sestertium** 1000 sesterces. XVI. - L.

sestet (mus.) composition for six voices or instruments; last six lines of a sonnet. XIX. - It. *sestetto*, f. *sesto* sixth; see -ET.

sestina poem of six six-line stanzas. XIX. - It. *sestina*, f. *sesto* sixth; see prec.

set¹ pt., pp. *set* cause to sit; (hence) place, put, with many spec. applications lit. and fig. OE.; †subside OE. (late); (of a luminary) go down, sink below the horizon XIII (prob. after ON. refl. *setjask*). OE. *settan* = OS. *settian* (Du. *zetten*), OHG. *sezzan* (G. *setzen*), ON. *setja*, Goth. *satjan* :- Gmc. **satjan*, causative of **setjan* SIT.

set² A. setting of a luminary XIV; B. in various applications of the senses 'act of setting', 'manner or position in which a thing is set', 'something that is set' from XV. Mainly f. SET¹; but sense A may be in part due to ON. *-setr, -seta* (as in *sólarsetr, -seta* sunset).

set³ number or group of persons XIV; number or collection of things XVI. orig., in sense 'sect' - OF. *sette* :- L. *secta* SECT, but in later developments infl. by SET¹ and apprehended as 'number set together' (cf. SET²); the application to things may be partly due to MLG. *gesette* set or suite of things.

seton thread, etc. drawn through a fold of the skin to maintain an issue XIV; the issue itself XVI. - medL. *sētō, -ōn-*, app. f. L. *sētā* bristle, in medL. also silk.

settee¹ (hist.) vessel with lateen sails used in the Mediterranean. XVI (*settea*, later *sattee, satia, settee*). - It. *saettia*, held to be f. *saetta* arrow :- L. *sagitta*.

settee² seat to hold two or more persons. XVIII. of uncert. orig.

setter dog of a breed trained to mark the position of hunted game. XVI. f. SET¹ + -ER¹.

setterwort species of hellebore. XVI. prob. - MLG. *siterwort*, the first el. of which is of unkn. origin; see WORT¹.

settle¹ †seat OE.; long wooden bench with a high back XVI. OE. *setl*, corr. to MLG., MDu. *setel*, OHG. *sezzal* (G. *sessel*), Goth. *sitls* :- Gmc. **setlaz*, **setlam*, rel. to L. *sella* saddle :- **sedlā*, f. **sed-* SIT; see -LE¹.

settle² place in a certain position OE.; come to rest after movement or agitation XIII; sink down XIV; render stable, establish XIV; fix, determine, make an agreement XVI. OE. *setl(i)an* place (rare; implied also in *setlung* sitting-down, setting of the sun), f. *setl* SETTLE¹.

setwall (root of) the plant *Valeriana officinalis*. XIII. ME. *zedewal, zeduale, cetewale* - AN. *zedewale*, OF. *citoual* - medL. **zedoāle*, var. of *zedoārium* ZEDOARY.

seven OE. *seofon* = OS. *sibun* (Du. *zeven*), OHG. *sibun* (G. *sieben*), ON. *sjau*, Goth. *sibun* :- Gmc. **sebun* :- IE. **septḿ*, repr. by Skr. *saptá*, Gr. *heptá*, L. *septem*, OSl. *sedmĭ*, Lith. *septynì*, OIr. *secht*. So **seventeen** OE. *seofontīene*. **seventh** XIV. New formation, directly f. SEVEN + TH², repl. (i) OE. (Angl.) *seofunda*, ME. *sevende* = OS. *sivondo*, OHG. *sibunto* (G. *siebente*), ON. *sjaundi* :- Gmc. **sebundan-*, (ii) OE. *seofoða*, ME. *seveþe*, repl. in ME. by *sevenþe* = OS. *sivoðo* :- Gmc. **sebunþo-*. **seventy** OE. (*hund*)*seofontiġ* = OS. *sivuntig*, OHG. *sibunzug*, ON. *sjautigr*; see -TY¹.

sever XIV. - AN. *severer*, OF. *sevrer* (now, wean) :- Rom. **sēperāre*, for L. *sēparāre* SEPARATE. So **several** existing apart; pert. to an individual; also sb. XV. - AN. *several* (whence medL. *severālis*) - medL. *sēparālis*, f. L. *sēpār* separate; see -AL¹. **severance** XV. - AN. *severance*, OF. *sevrance*.

severe extremely strict XVI; extremely grievous, exacting, or painful XVII. - (O)F. *sévère* or L. *sevērus*. So **severity** XVI. - (O)F. or L.

severy (archit.) compartment of a roof or scaffolding. XIV (revived XIX). - AN. **civorie*, OF. *civoire* ciborium.

Sèvres Name of a town in France, near Paris, designating a costly porcelain. XVIII (*Sev(r)e*).

sew pt. *sewed*, pp. *sewn, sewed* join together with thread, etc. OE. *si(o)wan* = OHG. *siuwen*, ON. *sýja*, Goth. *siujan* :- Gmc. **siwjan*, f. IE. **siw-* **sju-*, repr. also by L. *suere*, Gr. *-súein*.

sewer¹ artificial channel for draining. XV. - AN. *sever(e)*, ONF. *se(u)wiere* channel to carry off overflow from a fishpond :- Rom. **exaquāria*, f.

**exaquāre* (f. L. EX-[1] + *aqua* water), whence OF. *essever* drain off.

sewer[2] (hist.) attendant who arranged a meal and tasted the dishes. XIV. Aphetic - AN. *asseour*, f. (O)F. *asseoir* place a seat for :- L. *assidēre*, f. AS- + *sedēre* SIT.

sewin kind of salmon trout. XVI. of unkn. orig.

sex males or females collectively XIV (rare before XVI); condition in respect of being male or female XVI. - (O)F. *sexe* or L. *sexus* m., rel. to synon. *secus* n. So **sexual** XVII. - late L.; see -AL[1].

sex- comb. form of L. *sex* SIX, as in techn. terms, e.g. (zool.) *sexdigital*, (chem.) *sexvalent*. **sexagenarian** XVIII. **sexagenary** pert. to 60 XVI; aged 60 XVII. **Sexagesima** XVI (earlier †*-ime* XIV) second Sunday before Lent (cf. SEPTUAGESIMA). **sexagesimal** (-AL[1]) (math.) pert. to or based on 60 XVII. **sexcentenary** of 600 XVIII; of a period of 600 years XIX. **sexennial** see BIENNIAL. **sext** (eccl.) the third of the day hours of the Church, so called because orig. allocated to the sixth hour of the day (midday). XV. - L. *sexta*, sb. use of fem. of *sextus* SIXTH.

sextant (astron.) instrument resembling a quadrant having a graduated arc equal to $\frac{1}{6}$ of a circle. XVII. - modL. use of L. *sextāns, -ant-* sixth part (of an as, etc.), f. *sextus* SIXTH. **sextet(te)** XIX. alt. of SESTET after L. *sex* SIX. **sextile** (astrol.) pert. to the aspect of two heavenly bodies which are 60° or $\frac{1}{6}$ of the zodiac distant. XVI. - L. *sextīlis*, f. *sextus* SIXTH. **sextillion** see BILLION. †**sextodecimo** size of a book in which the leaf is $\frac{1}{16}$ of the sheet, †decimosexto; sixteenmo. XVII. **sextuple** sixfold. XVII.

sexton sacristan, (later) guardian of a church fabric and churchyard, bell-ringer and grave-digger. XIV. ME. *segerstane, secristeyn, sekesteyn, sexteyn*, (from XVI) *sexton* - AN., OF. *segerstein, secrestein* - medL. *sacristānus* SACRISTAN.

sforzando (mus.) direction for emphasis. XIX. - It., gerund of *sforzare* use force.

sh excl. to enjoin silence, also written *'sh* as if an abbrev. of HUSH, of which it is the common int. equiv. XIX.

shabby dingy and faded; contemptibly ungenerous. XVII. Parallel to †*shabbed* (OE. *sċeabbede*), as *scabby* to *scabbed*; f. *shab* scab (OE.), low fellow (XVII), OE. *sċeabb* = ON. **skabbr* SCAB; see -Y[1].

shabrack saddle-cloth. XIX. - G. *schabracke*, F. *schabraque*; ult. - Turk. *çaprak*.

shack (N. Amer.) XIX. of uncert. orig.

shackle sb. fetter OE.; transf. uses from XIV. OE. *sċ(e)acul*, corr. to LG. *schäkel* link of a chain, hobble, Du. *schakel*, ON. *skǫkull* wagon-pole, f. Gmc. **skak-*; see -LE[1]. Hence vb. XV.

shad fish of the genus *Alosa*. Late OE. *sċeadd*, of unkn. orig.

shaddock fruit of *Citrus grandis*. XVII. f. name of Captain *Shaddock*, who introduced it into Barbados.

shade shadow; protection from glare or heat OE.; concr., as in *lampshade, sunshade* XVII; disembodied spirit (pl. *the shades* Hades); degree of colour; slight degree XVIII. OE. *sċ(e)adu* fem. (obl. cases repr. by SHADOW), and obl. cases *sċeade, sċeadu*, etc. of *sċead* n.

shadow comparative darkness; image cast by a body intercepting light; shelter from light and heat. XII. ME. *sceadewe, shadewe*, repr. obl. forms, *sċead(u)we*, of OE. *sċeadu* SHADE, corr. to OS. *skado* (Du. *schaduw*), OHG. *scato* (G. *schatte*, later *schatten*), Goth. *skadus* :- Gmc. **skaðwaz, *skaðwō*; cf. Gr. *skótos* darkness, OIr. *scāth* shadow. So vb. OE. *sċeadwian* = OS. *skadowan, skadoian* (Du. *schaduwen*), OHG. *scatewen*, Goth. *-skadwjan*. Hence **shadowy** (-Y[1]) XIV.

shaft[1] rod of spear, etc. OE.; long straight part of an object XIV; long bar or rod in a vehicle or machine XVII. OE. *sċæft, sċeaft* = OS. *skaft*, OHG. *scaft* (Du., G. *schaft*), ON. *skaft* :- Gmc. **skaft-* perh. to be referred to IE. **skāp-, *skābh-* support, as in L. *scāpus* shaft, stem, shank, Gr. (Doric) *skâpton* staff.

shaft[2] long well-like excavation giving access to a mine XV. - MLG. *schacht*, prob. spec. application of SHAFT[1].

shag[1] rough hair or wool OE.; cloth having a velvet nap XVI; fine-shredded tobacco (in full *s. tobacco*, i.e. a use of the adj.) XVIII. Late OE. *sċeacga*, rel. to ON. *skegg* beard (:- **skaȝjam*), OE. *sċeaga* coppice, SHAW. Hence XVI. †**shagged.** Late OE. *sċeacgede* (-ED[2]); superseded by **shaggy** (-Y[1]) XVI. Not evidenced between OE. and late XVI.

shag[2] cormorant. XVI. perh. a use of SHAG[1] (sb. or adj.), with ref. to the bird's shaggy crest.

shagreen untanned leather. XVII. var. sp. of *chagrin* - F. - Turk. *sağrı* rump, skin of this.

shah king of Persia. XVI (*shaw, shaugh*). - Pers. *šāh*, shortening of OPers. *χšāyaθiya-*.

shake pt. *shook*, pp. *shaken* †go, move; vibrate, cause to vibrate. OE. str. vb. *sċ(e)acan* = OS. *skakan*, ON. *skaka* :- Gmc. **skakan*. Hence **shaky** (-Y[1]) XVIII.

shako military cap. XIX. - F. *schako* - Hung. *csákó* peak, peaked cap - G. *zacken* point, spike.

shale XVIII. prob. - G. *schale* (not used in this sense, but cf. *schalstein* laminated limestone, *schalgebirge* mountain system of thin strata) = OE. *sċ(e)alu* SCALE[1]. So **shaly** (-Y[1]) XVII.

shall pt. *should*. Gmc. preterite-pres. vb., with a new wk. pt. (cf. CAN[2], etc.) orig. meaning †I owe, (hence) †I ought, must, am to, passing thence into a tense-sign of the future and a mark of contingency. OE. *sċeal* = OS. *skal* (Du. *zal*), OHG. *scal* (G. *soll*), ON., Goth. *skal*; Gmc. (**skel-*) **skal- *skul-*, repr. also by OE. *ġesċola*, OS., OHG. *skolo*, Goth. *skula* debtor, OE. *sċyld*, OS. *skuld*, OHG. *sculd, sculda* (G. *schuld*) debt, guilt.

shalloon woollen fabric. XVII. - (O)F. *chalon*, f. name of *Châlons*-sur-Marne, France.

shallop sloop; dinghy. XVI. - F. *chaloupe* - Du. *sloep* SLOOP.

shallot small onion, *Allium ascalonicum*. XVII. Aphetic of †*eschalot* - F. *eschalotte* (now *échalotte*), alt. of OF. *esc(h)aloigne* SCALLION.

shallow not deep. XV. Obscurely rel. to synon. OE. *sċeald*, ME. *schald*; see SHOAL[1].

sham sb. †trick, fraud XVII; spurious imitation XVIII; adj. false, counterfeit XVII; vb. †defraud, hoax; †attempt to pass *off*; counterfeit, assume appearance of XVII. of uncert. orig.; poss. north. dial. var. of SHAME.

shaman priest among N. Asiatic tribes. XVII. - G. *schamane*, Russ. *shamán*.

shamble walk with an ungainly gait. XVII (late). f. *shamble* adj. ungainly, shambling (early XVII), perh. orig. in *s. legs*, which may have orig. meant 'legs straddling like those of the trestles of a meat table' (see next); see -LE[3].

shambles (dial.). meat-market (orig. *flesh s.*) XV; slaughter-house XVI. orig. pl. of *shamble* table or stall for the sale of meat (XIV), spec. use of OE. *sć(e)amul* stool, table = OS. *-skamel*, OHG. *-scamil* footstool; WGmc. - L. *scamellum*, dim. of *scamnum* bench.

shame feeling of disgrace; state of disgrace, circumstance causing this OE.; modest feeling XIV. OE. *sć(e)amu* = OS., OHG. *skama* (Du. *schaam-* in comps., G. *scham*), ON. *skǫmm* :- Gmc. **skamō*; on the same base are formed OE. *scand*, OHG. *scanda* (G. *schande*), Goth. *skanda* disgrace. So **shame** vb. OE. *sć(e)amian* intr. and impers. **shamefaced** modest, bashful. XVI. alt., by assim. to FACE, *-faced*, of (arch.) *shamefast*, OE. *sć(e)amfæst* (FAST[1]; *-fæst* is a common suffix of OE. adjs. equiv. to *-ful*, *-ous*). **shameful, -less** OE. *sć(e)amful*, *-lēas*.

shammy XVIII. repr. pronunc. of CHAMOIS.

shampoo massage (as now in a Turkish bath) XVIII; wash and rub (the scalp) XIX. - Hind. *cā̃po*, imper. of *cā̃pnā*.

shamrock XVI. - Ir. *seamróg*, dim. of *seamar* clover.

shandy(gaff) mixture of beer and ginger-beer or lemonade. XIX. of unkn. orig.

shanghai (naut. sl., orig. U.S.) render insensible and ship on board a vessel wanting hands (perh. orig. one destined for Shanghai). XIX. f. *Shanghai*, name of a Chinese seaport.

shank shin-bone, tibia OE., stem, shaft XVI. OE. *sćeanca* = LG. *schanke*, Flem. *schank* :- WGmc. **skaŋkan*, rel. to MLG. *schenke*, Du. *schenk* leg bone (:- **skaŋkiz*), LG., (M)HG. *schenkel* (:- **skaŋkilaz*); the base corr. formally to that of ON. *skakkr* (:- **skaŋkaz*) wry, distorted, lame, and Gr. *skázein* limp. Phrs. *Shanks's mare, pony* for 'the legs as a means of transport' are orig. Sc. (XVIII), the pl. of the common noun being joc. turned into a surname.

shanty[1] roughly built cabin or hut. XIX (first in N. Amer. use). perh. - Canadian F. *chantier*.

shanty[2] sailor's song. XIX. app. corruption of F. *chantez*, imper. of *chanter* sing.

shape external or visible form; †sexual organs OE.; guise XVI; form or kind of structure XVII. orig. OE. *ġesćeap* creation, creature, form, pudendum, decree, destiny, corr. to OS. *giskapu* pl. creatures, decrees, ON. *skap* condition, pl. fate; f. Gmc. **skap-* base of the vb. So **shape** vb. †create; fashion, form. Early ME. new formation on the pp., repl. orig. OE. **sć(i)eppan*, corr. to OS. **giskeppian*, Goth. *gaskapjan*; f. Gmc. **skap-* create, fashion; first established as a wk. vb. XVI; the OE. pp. survives chiefly in *misshapen*. **shapeless** XIII. **shapely** †fit, suitable; well-shaped. XIV (see -LY[1]).

shard, sherd (dial.) gap; fragment of broken earthenware. OE. *sćeard*, corr. to MLG. *skart* crack, chink, MDu. *scarde*, *schart* flaw, fragment (Du. *schaard*), (M)HG. *scharte*, ON. *skarð* notch, gap, sb. uses of the adj. repr. by OE. *sćeard*, OS. *skard*, OHG. *-scart*, ON. *skarðr* :- Gmc. **skarðaz* cut, notched, diminished, pp. formation on **skar-* **sker-* SHEAR.

share[1] cutting blade of a plough. OE. *sćær*, *sćear*, corr. to MLG. *schar(e)*, OHG. *scar(o)*, *scare* (G. *schar*); WGmc. deriv. of Gmc. **skar-* **sker-* SHEAR.

share[2] allotted portion XIV; portion of a property owned by a number in common XVI. The earliest exx. are in AN. and AL. documents; repr. spec. development of OE. *sćearu* lit. 'cutting, division', recorded only in senses 'tonsure', 'fork of the body', and in comps.; corr. to OS. *skara* feudal service, troop, MLG. *schare* troop, share, OHG. *scara* troop, share of forced labour (Du. *schaar*, G. *schar* troop, multitude), ON. *skari* :- Gmc. deriv. of **skar-* **sker-* cut, divide, SHEAR. Hence **share** vb. XVI.

shark large voracious seafish XVI; rapacious or extortionate person XVIII. of unkn. orig.

sharp having a keen edge or point; keen, acute; severe, harsh; pungent OE.; shrill XIV; (mus.) XVI; sb. uses date from XIV. OE. *sć(e)arp* = OS. *skarp* (Du. *scherp*), OHG. *skarf*, *scarpf* (G. *scharf*), ON. *skarpr* :- Gmc. **skarpaz*; cf. OE. *sćearpe* scarification, *sćearpian* scarify, OHG. *scurfen* (G. *schürfen* scratch), and SCRAPE. Hence **sharpen** XV. superseding (dial.) *sharp*, OE. **sćierpan*, *sćerpan*; see -EN[5]. **sharper** cheat, swindler. XVII. See -ER[1]; cf. *sharp* vb. swindle (XVII). **sharply** (-LY[2]), **sharpness** OE.

shatter (dial.) scatter, disperse XII; break in pieces XV. orig. and relation to SCATTER uncert., there being no evidence for either word before XII.

shave scrape, pare away OE.; remove with a razor XIII. OE. str. vb. *sć(e)afan* = OS. *skaban*, OHG. *scaban* (Du. *schaven*, G. *schaben*), ON. *skafa*, Goth. *skaban* : Gmc. **skaban*. The vb. became wk. XIV, with the literary survival str. pp. *shaven*. Hence **shaveling** (-LING[1]) tonsured ecclesiastic. XVI. **shaver** (-ER[1]) one who shaves XV; †plunderer, swindler; (hence colloq.) fellow, chap, wag XVI.

shaw (dial.) thicket, copse. OE. *sćeaga*, corr. to NFris. *skage* farthest edge of cultivated land, ON. *skagi* promontory, rel. to OE. *sćeacga* (see SHAG[1]).

shawl Oriental oblong article of dress made in Kashmir from the hair of a goat of Tibet XVII; in the West, outer covering for the shoulders (and head) XVIII. Earliest forms *(s)chal*, *scial*, *shaul*; ult. - Urdu, etc. - Pers. *šāl*, prob. f. *Shāliāt*, a town in India.

shawm (hist.) medieval wind instrument. XIV. ME. *schallemele*, pl. *chalm(e)yes*, *schalmes*, later (sg.) *schalmuś*, *shawme* (XVI). - (i) OF. *chalemel* (mod. *chalumeau*) :- Rom. **calamellus*, dim. of L. *calamus* reed - Gr. *kálamos*; (ii) OF. (unexpl.) *chalemie*; (iii) OF. *chalemeaus*, pl. of *chalemel*.

shay chaise. XVIII (also *chay*). Back-formation from CHAISE, misapprehended as pl.

she 3rd sg. fem. nom. pers. pron. This form repr. east midl. ME. *scæ* (XII), *sȝe*, *sse*, *sche* (XIII), parallel with which there were ME. *scho*, *sho* and ȝho, ȝhe. All types appear to be developments of the OE. fem. pers. pron. hēo, acc. hīe.

sheaf OE. sċēaf = OS. skōf (Du. schoof), OHG. scoub sheaf, bundle or wisp of straw (G. schaub), ON. skauf fox's brush :- Gmc. *skaubaz (-am), f. *skaub- *skeub- *skub- (see SHOVE).

shear pt. sheared, †shore, pp. sheared, shorn. OE. str. vb. sċ(i)eran = OS. -skeran (Du. scheren), OHG. sceran (G. scheren), ON. skera :- Gmc. *skeran. Hence **shearling** (-LING¹) sheep that has been shorn once. XIV. **shearwater** bird of the genus Puffinus. XVII. **shears** pl. (rarely sg.) scissors, now only of a large kind. OE. (i) sċērero pl., (ii) sċēara, pl. of sċēar fem., corr. to MLG. schēre, MDu. scāre, scēre (Du. schaer), OHG. skār, pl. skāri (G. schere), ON. skǣri n. pl.

sheat-fish freshwater fish Silurus glanis. XVI. Earlier sheath-fish, prob. f. SHEATH + FISH.

sheath OE. sċæð, sċeað = OS. skēðia (Du. scheede, schee), OHG. sceida (G. scheide), ON. skeiðir pl. scabbard :- Gmc. *skaiþiz, *skaiþjō, prob. f. *skaiþ- divide (see SHED¹).

sheave pulley. XIV. repr. OE. *sċife, rel. to OS. skība, (M)LG, MDu. schīve (Du. schijf), OHG. scība (G. scheibe), f. base meaning variously disc, wheel, pulley, pane of glass, slice of bread.

shebeen illicit public house XVIII. - Anglo-Ir. síbín, séibín, f. séibe liquid measure, mug.

shed¹ pt., pp. shed †separate, divide OE.; (dial.) spill, let fall, pour, send forth as an emanation XII; give forth, diffuse XIV; cast off XVI. OE. str. vb. sċ(e)ādan, corr. to OS. skēdan, OHG. sceidan (Du., G. scheiden), Goth. skaidan :- Gmc. *skaiðan, *skaiþan. Beside orig. OE. sċ(e)ādan, repr. by early ME. shode, a var. with falling diphthong sċēadan arose, from which the present shed descends. The OE. vb. retained its str. conjugation in WS., but is found only wk. in Nhb.; str. forms persisted to some extent in ME., but wk. forms finally prevailed.

shed² †separation OE. (dial.) parting of the hair XIV; ridge of ground dividing valleys (cf. WATERSHED) XVI; spacing between the threads of the warp XVIII. OE. (ġe)sċēad, alt. of (ġe)sċēad f. base of SHED¹.

shed³ slight structure for shelter. XV (shadde). prob. specialized use of shad(de), shed(de), by-forms of SHADE.

sheen (poet.) beautiful, bright, resplendent. OE. (Angl.) sċēne, (WS.) sċiene = OS., OHG. skōni (Du. schoon, G. schön), Goth. skauns :- Gmc. *skauniz, *skaunjaz, f. *skau- behold (see SHOW). Hence sb. brightness. XVII. Apprehended as abstr. noun of SHINE; whence **sheeny** (-Y¹) XVII.

Sheeny (sl.) Jew. XIX. of unkn. orig.

sheep OE. (Angl.) sċēp, (WS.) sċǣp, sċēap = OS. skāp (Du. schaap), OHG. scāf (G. schaf) :- WGmc. *skǣpa, of which no cogns. are known. Hence **sheepish** (-ISH¹) XII.

sheer¹ †bright, shining; (of fabrics) thin, fine; unmixed, unqualified XVI; rising perpendicularly without a break XVIII. prob. alt. of (dial.) shire clear, pure, mere, thin, weak, OE. sċīr = OS. skīr(i), ON. skírr, Goth. skeirs :- Gmc. *skīraz, *skīrjaz, f. *skī- SHINE.

sheer² (of a ship) turn aside. XVII. perh. - (M)LG., (M)HG. scheren; identical with SHEAR.

sheer³ (naut.) curve of a ship. XVII. prob. f. SHEAR.

sheer hulk hulk of a disused ship fitted with hoisting shears. XVIII. f. sheers (identical with SHEARS) device for raising masts, etc., the form of which suggests a pair of shears + HULK.

sheet¹ broad piece of linen (etc.) covering OE. (as an article of bedding XIII); piece of paper or parchment for writing or printing on; broad expanse XVI. OE. (Angl.) sċēte, (WS.) sċiete, f. Gmc. *skaut- *skeut- *skut- (see SHOOT), one meaning of which is 'project'. The unmutated stem is repr. by OE. sċēat corner, region, lap, bosom, skirt, cloth = MLG. schōt, (M)Du. schoot lap, sail-rope, OHG. scōz (G. schoss) skirt, lappet, lap, ON. skaut corner, quarter, skirt, bosom, sail-rope, Goth. skauts hem of garment, and the forms s.v. SHEET².

sheet² rope attached to lower (leeward) corner of a sail. XIV. repr. OE. sċēata lower corner of a sail, but used for sċēatline (see LINE²) = MLG. schōtlīne (cf. ON. skautreip), prob. after ON. skaut or MLG., MDu. schōte, both in this sense. OE. sċēata corr. to (M)LG. schōte, OHG. scoza skirt, ON. skauti kerchief; cf. SHEET¹.

sheet-anchor largest of ship's anchors. XV (shute anker), XVII (sheet a.). The earliest forms point to deriv. from †shoot sheet of a sail (XV to XVII) - (M)LG. schōte, (M)Du. schoot (see SHEET¹,²); the connection in sense is not obvious.

sheikh XVI. ult. - Arab. šaiḳ (prop.) old man, f. šāḳa grow old.

shekel Semitic unit of weight, chief silver coin of the Hebrews. XVI. - Heb. šeḳel, f. šāḳal weigh.

shekinah manifestation of the Divine Majesty 'between the cherubims' (Exod. 25: 22, etc.). XVII. - late Heb. šᵉkhīnāh, f. šākhan rest, dwell.

sheldrake bird of the genus Tadorna. XIV. prob. f. (dial.) sheld particoloured, pied, rel. to MDu. schillede variegated, f. schillen diversify (modDu. verschillen differ) + DRAKE².

shelf¹ horizontal slab of wood, etc. to hold objects XIV; ledge or terrace of land XIX (shelfy adj. XVIII). - (M)LG. schelf shelf, set of shelves; rel. to OE. sċylfe partition, compartment, sċylf rugged rock, crag, pinnacle. Hence **shelve** vb. †project like a shelf; provide with shelves. XVI.

shelf² sandbank in the sea or a river. XVI. prob. alt., by assoc. with prec., of synon. †shelp (XV), repr. OE. sċylp, of unkn. orig.

shell hard outer covering of an animal, fruit, etc.; scale or scale-like object OE.; hollow or concave object XVI; exterior cover or case (spec. one containing powder and shot) XVII. OE. (Angl.) sċell, (WS.) sċiell = (M)LG., MDu. schelle, schille, Du. schel, schil pod, rind, scale, shell, ON. skel sea-shell, Goth. skalja tile :- Gmc. *skaljō, f. *skal- (cf. SCALE¹,²). Hence vb. XVI.

shellac lac melted into thin plate for use as varnish. XVIII. f. SHELL sb. + LAC.

Shelta cryptic language of Irish tinkers, gipsies, etc., known also among them as sheldrū, shelter. XIX. of unkn. orig.

shelter sb. XVI. of uncert. orig. Hence vb. XVI.

shelve †tilt XVI; slope gradually XVII. perh. back-formation from shelvy having sandbanks (XVI), f. SHELF² + -Y¹.

shemozzle (sl.) muddle, quarrel, mêlée. XIX. Also *shlemozzle*; of Yiddish orig., and based on late Heb. *šellō'mazzāl*, i.e. *šel* of, *lō'* not, *mazzāl* planet, planetary influence, luck.

shepherd sb. Late OE. *scēaphierde*; see SHEEP, HERD[2]. Hence vb. XVIII, **shepherdess** XIV.

Sheraton name of Thomas *Sheraton* (1751–1806), furniture-maker and designer, applied to his products. XIX.

sherbet Oriental drink XVII; preparation in powder form for making an effervescing drink XIX. - Turk. *şerbet*, Pers. *šarbat* - Arab. *šarāb*, f. *šariba* vb. drink.

sherd see SHARD.

sherif, shereef descendant of Muhammad through his daughter Fatima; sovereign ruler of certain states. XVI. - Arab. *šarīf* noble, glorious, f. *šarufa* be exalted.

sheriff representative of the royal authority in a shire or county. OE. *scīrġerēfa*, f. *scīr* SHIRE + *ġerēfa* REEVE. Hence **sheriffalty** XVI; see SHRIEVALTY.

sherry still white wine of a type orig. made near Xerez (now Jerez), a town in Andalusia, Spain. XVI. alt. of *sherris* (XVI), apprehended as a pl. or derived from *sherris sack* (see SACK[3]), i.e. *Sherries*, repr. old pronunc. of *Xerez*.

shew see SHOW.

shewbread twelve loaves placed every Sabbath 'before the Lord' in the Jewish temple. XVI. f. *shew*, var. of SHOW vb. + BREAD, after G. *schaubrot*, repr. Heb. *leḥem pānim* 'bread of presence'.

shibboleth Heb. word used by Jephthah as a test word to distinguish the fleeing Ephraimites, who could not pronounce *sh*, from his own men, the Gileadites (Judges 12: 4-6) XIV; (gen.) word used as a test for detecting foreigners; catchword adopted by a party XVII. - Heb. *šibbōleth* stream.

shiel (Sc. and north. dial.) shed, shanty, hut. XIII. ME. *shāle*, *shēle*, of unkn. orig. Hence **shieling** piece of pasture for cattle; rough hut. XVI. See -ING[1].

shield article of defensive armour; (fig.) protection. OE. *sc(i)eld* = OS., OHG. *scild* (Du., G. *schild*), ON. *skjǫldr*, Goth. *skildus* - Gmc. **skelduz*, prob. orig. 'board' and so f. base **skel*- divide, separate (cf. SCALE[1]). Hence vb. OE. *sċeldan*, *sċildan*.

shift A. †arrange OE.; B. change XIII; C. alter the position of XIV. OE. *sċiftan* = MLG. *schiften*, *schichten*, MHG. *schihten* (G. *schichten*), ON. *skipta* divide, separate, change, f. base **skip*- as in ON. *skipa* arrange, assign. Hence **shift** sb. A. expedient, contrivance, evasion; B. †change; (spec.) of clothing; (esp.) woman's chemise XVI; C. change of position, removal XVIII. Hence **shifty** (-Y[1]) XVI.

Shiite member of the Shiah sect of Muslims. XVIII. f. *Shiah* (XVII) - Arab. *šī'a* sect, f. *šā'a* follow; see -ITE.

shikar hunting, sport. XVII. - Urdu - Pers. *šikār*.

shillelagh Irish cudgel. XVIII. f. name of a barony and village in County Wicklow, Ireland, known for its oaks.

shilling OE. *sċilling* = OS., OHG. *skilling* ((M)Du. *schelling*, G. *schilling*), ON. *skillingr*, Goth. *skilliggs* :- Gmc. **skilliŋgaz*, of unkn. orig.

shilly-shally phr. *stand* or *go shill I*, *shall I* vacillate, be irresolute XVII; adj. vacillating; sb. vacillation XVIII. f. *shall I*, with variation of vowel.

shimmer Late OE. *sċymrian*, **sċimerian* = (M)LG., (M)Du. *schēmeren* be shaded or shadowy, glimmer, glitter, G. *schimmern*, iterative (see -ER[4]) f. Gmc. **skim*-, extension of **skī*- SHINE[1]. Obs. in XVII; revived by Scott XIX. Hence sb. XIX.

shin OE. *sċinu* = (M)LG., MDu. *schēne* (Du. *scheen*), OHG. *scina*, shin, needle (G. *schiene* thin plate); the basic meaning is prob. 'thin or narrow piece'.

shindy shinty; spree; commotion. XIX. unexpl. alt. of **shinty** (i) game resembling hockey (XVIII), (ii) row, commotion (XIX), later var. of *shinny* (XVII), an earlier name of the game. *Shinny* and *shinty* appear to be derived from cries used in the game, *shin ye*, *shin you*, and *shin t'ye*; of unkn. orig.

shine[1] pt., pp. *shone*. OE. str. vb. *sċīnan* = OS. *skīnan*, OHG. *scīnan* (Du. *schijnen*, G. *scheinen*), ON. *skína*, Goth. *skeinan* :- Gmc. **skīnan*, f. **skī*-; cf. SHEER[1], SHIMMER. Hence **shine** sb. XVI; whence (unless f. the vb.) **shiny** (-Y[1]) XVI.

shine[2] (dial.) convivial party; (colloq.) row, disturbance. XIX. perh. uses of prec. sb., but the senses are like those of SHINDY.

shingle[1] piece of wood used as a house tile. XII. ME. *scincle*, *scingle*, *singel*, repr., with unexpl. modification, L. *scindula*, later form of *scandula* after Gr. *skhídax*, *skhindalmós*. Hence vb. roof with shingles XVI; (orig. U.S.) cut (the hair) so as to produce the effect of overlapping tiles XIX.

shingle[2] (beach covered with) small roundish stones. XVI. of obscure orig. and history.

shingles eruptive disease often extending round the middle of the body. XIV. Late ME. *schingles*, *cingules*, *sengles* - medL. use of L. *cingulus*, var. of *cingulum* girdle.

Shinto native religion of Japan. XVIII. - Jap. *shintō* - Chinese *shin tao* way of the gods.

shinty see SHINDY.

ship sb. OE. *sċip* = OS. *skip* (Du. *schip*), OHG. *skif* (G. *schiff*), ON., Goth *skip* :- Gmc. **skipam*, of unkn. orig. So **ship** vb. late OE. *sċipian*. Hence **shipman** (arch.) seaman, sailor. OE. *sċipman*. **shipment** XIX. **shipmoney** (hist.) impost for providing ships for the navy. XVII. **shipper** (-ER[1]) †seaman OE.; one who ships goods XVIII. **ship-shape** trim, orderly. XVIII. alt. of †*ship shapen* (XVII) 'arranged in ship fashion', i.e. SHIP sb., and pp. of SHAPE. **shipwreck** what is cast up from a wreck XI; destruction or loss of a ship XV.

-ship suffix denoting state or condition: (1) added to adjs. and pps.; of the numerous OE. exx., only HARDSHIP and WORSHIP survive; (2) added to sbs. to denote the state or condition of being what is expressed by the sb., the qualities or character associated with, the power implied by, and spec. the position or dignity designated by the sb., as in OE. *frēondsċipe* FRIENDSHIP, *hlāfordsċipe* LORDSHIP, similarly in *authorship*, *craftsmanship, fellowship, horsemanship, kingship, stewardship.* In early mod. Eng. it is added to a sb. to denote a state of life relating to what is denoted by the sb.; *courtship* (XVI) is the chief instance. TOWNSHIP is the one survival of a group of OE. sbs. with coll. sense.

shire †official charge; †district under a governor, bishop's see, etc.; administrative district later called *county* OE. (hence terminal element in names of counties XII). OE. *sċīr* = OHG. *sċīra* care, official charge; of uncert. orig.

shirk †practise fraud or trickery; (dial.) slink, sneak away XVII; evade (duty, etc.) XVIII. rel. to †*shirk* sponger, perh. - G. *schurke* scoundrel.

shirt OE. *sċyrte*, corr. formally to (M)LG. *schört(e), schorte*, MDu. *schorte* (Du. *schort*), G. *schürze* apron, ON. *skyrta* shirt; based on Gmc. **skurt-* SHORT. Hence **shirty** (sl.) out of temper XIX; f. phr. *get* (a person's) *shirt (out)*, cause him to lose his temper; see -Y[1].

shit vb. XVII. Superseding (dial.) *shite*, OE. *sċītan* = MLG. *schīten* (Du. *schijten*), OHG. *skīzan* (G. *scheissen*), ON. *skíta*; f. Gmc. **skīt- *skit-*. Short *i* was generalized from the pp. **shitten** (-EN[6]). Hence sb. XVI.

shiver[1] fragment, chip. XIII. Early ME. *scifre, scivre*, corr. to OHG. *scivaro* splinter (G. *schiefer* slate, for *schieferstein*), f. Gmc. **skīf-* split. So vb. XII (in †*to-shiver*). Cf. MDu. *scheveren*, MHG. *schiveren* (G. *schiefern*).

shiver[2] tremble as with cold or fear. XIII. Early ME. *chivere*, superseded by *shiver* XV, prob. by assoc. with *shake* (cf. *chivere and schake* XIV); perh. orig. referring to chattering of the teeth (cf. *chevere with the chin* XV) and so an alt. by substitution of -ER[4] of ME. *chavele, chefle* wag the jaws, chatter, and *chevele, chivele* shiver (XIV), f. OE. *ċeafl* jaw, JOWL.

shoal[1] shallow. XVI. alt. of late ME. *scho(o)ld*, Sc. *schald* (XIV), repr. OE. *sċ(e)ald* (only in local names) :- **skaldaz*, rel. to SHALLOW. Hence **shoal** sb. shallow place, sandbank XVI; succeeding to late ME. *schald, sholde*, earlier *shelde*.

shoal[2] large number of fish, etc., swimming together. late XVI. prob. - MLG., MDu. *schōle* (adopted earlier as SCHOOL[2]).

shock[1] pile of sheaves of grain. XIV, but implied earlier in AL. *socca* (XII), *scoka* (XIII), either repr. OE. **sċ(e)oc* or - (M)LG., (M)Du. *schok* shock of corn, group of 60 units, in OS. *skok* = MHG. *schoc(h)* heap, also (as in G. *schock*) sixty; of unkn. orig. Hence vb. XIV.

shock[2] encounter of armed forces XVI; violent concussion XVII; sudden and disturbing impression on body or mind XVIII. In early use also †*cho(c)k*, †*choque* - F. *choc*, f. (O)F. *choquer* (whence **shock** vb. XVI), of unkn. orig. Hence **shocking** (-ING[2]) XVIII.

shock[3] thick mass (of hair). XIX. prob. for *shock head*, in which *shock* is adj. (XVII) rough and thick, based on †*shock*, †*shock-dog* poodle (XVII), presumably var. of †*shough* (XVI), of unkn. orig.

shoddy woollen yarn obtained by tearing up refuse rags; cloth made of this, which does not show its origin. XIX. of unkn. orig. Hence as adj. counterfeit and trashy. XIX.

shoe outer covering for the foot OE.; horseshoe XIV; various transf. senses from XV. OE. *sċō(h)* = OS. *skōh* (Du. *schoen*), OHG. *scuoh* (G. *schuh*), ON. *skór*, Goth. *skōhs* :- Gmc. **skōχaz* or **skōχwaz*, with no known cogns. Hence **shoe** vb. pt., pp. *shod*. OE. *sċōg(e)an*.

shogun hereditary commander-in-chief of the Japanese army. XVII. - Jap. *shōgun*, for *sei-i-tai shōgun* 'barbarian-subduing great general' (*shōgun* repr. Chinese *chiang chün* 'lead army').

shoo repr. excl. used to drive away birds, etc. XV (*schowe, ssou*). Hence vb. XVII.

shoot pt., pp. *shot* go swiftly and suddenly; send forth (spec. missiles); wound or kill with a shot. OE. str. vb. *sċēotan* = OS. *skietan* (Du. *schieten*), OHG. *sciozzan* (G. *schiessen*), ON. *skjóta* :- Gmc. **skeutan*, f. **skeut- *skaut- *skut-*. Hence sb. act of shooting XVI; sloping channel or conduit (cf. SHUTE) XIX.

shop building where goods are sold XIII (in AL. *schopa* XI); building set apart for work XV. Aphetic - AN., OF. *eschoppe* (mod. *échoppe*) lean-to booth, cobbler's stall - MLG. *schoppe*, corr. to OE. *sċ(e)oppa*, OHG. *scopf* porch (G. *schopf*).

shore[1] land bordering on a piece of water. XIV. - MLG., MDu. *schōre*, perh. f. the base of SHEAR.

shore[2] oblique support for the side of a building. XV. - MLG., MDu. *schōre* (Du. *schoor*) prop, stay. So vb. prop *up*. XIV. - (M)LG., (M)Du. *schōren*.

short opp. long OE.; not reaching a certain standard XIV; friable, brittle XV. OE. *sċeort* = OHG. *scurz* :- Gmc. **skurtaz*. Hence **shortage** (orig. U.S.) XIX. **shortcoming** XVII. f. phr. *come s.* **shorten** (-EN[5]) XVI. **shorthand** XVII.

shot act of shooting; that which is shot; payment, share (cf. SCOT). OE. *sċ(e)ot, ġesċ(e)ot* = OS. *-skot*, MLG. *(ge)scot*, OHG. *giscoz* (G. *(ge)schoss*), ON. *skot* :- Gmc. **skutaz, *ʒaskut*, f. **skut- *skeut-* SHOOT.

shotten pp. of SHOOT, used of a fish that has spawned XV (*s. herring* fig. XVI). See -EN[6].

shoulder sb. OE. *sċuldor*, corr. to MLG. *schuldere*, (M)Du. *schouder*, OHG. *sculter(r)a* (G. *schulter*) :- WGmc. **skuldr-*, of unkn. orig. Hence vb. push with the shoulder(s) XIII; support with the shoulder(s) XVI.

shout loud cry; vb. utter this. XIV. ME. *schoute*, poss. repr. a deriv. of **skūt- *skut- *skeut-* send forth forcibly, SHOOT.

shove pt., pp. *shoved* thrust, push. OE. str. vb. *sċūfan* = MLG., MDu. *schūven* (Du. *schuiven*), OHG. *sciuban* (G. *schieben*), Goth. *-skiuban* :- Gmc. **skeuban, *skaub-, *skub-*; cf. ON. *skúfa* wk. The str. pt. and pp. began to be repl. by wk. forms in XIV.

shovel sb. OE. *sċofl*, corr. to (M)LG. *schuffel*, MDu. *schof(f)el* (Du. *schoffel*) shovel, hoe; with rel. forms showing a long vowel, as in OHG. *scūvala* (G. *schaufel*); f. Gmc. **skŭf- skūb-* SHOVE; see -EL[1]. Hence vb. XV.

show, shew pt. *showed*, pp. *shown* †look at, examine OE.; cause to be seen, point out, exhibit; make known, explain XII; be seen, appear XIII. OE. *sċēawian* = OS. *skcwon* (Du. *schouwen*), OHG. *scouwōn* (G. *schauen*) :- WGmc. wk. vb. **skauwōjan*, f. **skau-* see, look :- IE. **skou-*, repr. in Gr. *thuoskó(ϝ)os* priest, lit.

'one who attends to sacrifices', a form without initial *s-* being repr. by Skr. *kaví-* sage, poet, Gr. *keeîn* observe, L. *cavēre* beware. The reversal of meaning from 'see' to 'cause to be seen' is unexpl. The str. pp. *shown* is attested XII; the wk. *showed, shewed* continued till XIX. The sp. *shew, shewn*, repr. orig. a falling diphthong (*scēaw-*), as against *show*, which repr. a rising diphthong (*sceāw-*), is now of limited currency. Hence **show** sb. XIII; whence **showy** (-Y[1]) XVIII.

shower fall of rain OE.; copious fall (of missiles OE.; of tears, etc. XIV); †conflict, attack, pang XIII. OE. *scūr* = OS. *skūr*, MDu. *schuur* (Du. *schoer*), OHG. *scūr* (G. *schauer*):- WGmc. **skūra* m., beside **skūrō* fem. (ON. *skúr* shower of rain, of missiles, Goth. *skūra* storm). Hence vb. XVI.

shrapnel shell that bursts scattering bullets. XIX (*S. shell*). f. name of General Henry *Shrapnel* (1761-1842), who invented this shell during the Peninsular War.

shred fragment cut or broken off OE.; fragment of textile material, also fig. XIV. OE. **scrēad* (pl. *scrēada*), *scrēade*, corr. to OS. *skrōd*, MLG. *schrōt, schrāt*, cut off piece, OHG. *scrōt* (G. *schrot*); f. WGmc. **skraud-* **skreud-* **skrūd-* cut. So **shred** vb. †pare, trim OE.; cut into small strips or slices XIV. OE. *scrēadian*.

shrew[1] mammal of the genus *Sorex*, formerly held to be venomous. OE. *scrēawa, scrǣwa*, rel. to OHG. *scrawaz* dwarf, MHG. *schrawaz* devil, Icel. *skrǫggr* old man, Norw. *skrugg* dwarf. Comp. **shrewmouse** XVI.

shrew[2] †malignant man XIII; person (now, woman) given to railing XIV. perh. transf. use of prec., but poss. spec. application of a word meaning 'ill-disposed being'. Hence **shrewish** †wicked XIV; ill-natured, given to scolding XVI.

shrewd (dial.) wicked XIV; †hurtful, dangerous, grievous, serious; (arch.) severe, hard XV; †cunning, artful, (eulogistically) astute, sagacious XVI. ME. *schrewed(e)*, f. SHREW[2] + -ED[2]; but some of the senses suggest that the formation is a pp. (-ED[1]) of **shrew**[3] vb. curse.

shriek vb. XVI. Also †*shreak*, †*shreik*; parallel to (dial.) *screak* (XV) - ON. *skrækja*; other *shr-* forms are (dial.) *shrike* (XII) and *shritch* (XIII), repr. the base of OE. *scriccettan*. Hence sb. XVI.

shrievalty office of a sheriff. XVI. f. *shrieve* (XV-XIX), SHERIFF + *-alty*, repr. OF. *-alté* (mod. *-auté*), as in *mayoralty*.

shrift (†penance imposed after) auricular confession. OE. *scrift*, corr. to (M)Du. *schrift*, OHG. *scrift* (G. *schrift*), ON. *skript, skrift*, f. SHRIVE; see -T[1]. The meanings 'penance', 'confession' are confined to Eng. and Scand. and appear to have arisen from a sense of 'prescribed penalty'; the other langs. have only the senses immed. connected with writing.

shrike XVI. of obscure orig.; corr. formations are OE. *scrīc* thrush, MLG. *schrīk* corncrake, rel. to vbs. cited under SHRIEK.

shrill XIV. Contemp. with ME. *shrille* vb.: superseding (dial.) *shille* adj. and vb., OE. **sciell, scyl*, and **sciellan, scyllan*; cf. LG. *schrell*, G. *schrill*, rel. to OE. *scralletan*, Du. *schrallen*.

shrimp small crustacean; puny person. XIV. Obscurely rel. to MLG. *schrempen* contract, wrinkle, *schrimpen* wrinkle the nose, *schrumpen* wrinkle, fold, MHG. *schrimpfen* contract, ON. *skreppa* slip away, and SCRIMP.

shrine †box, chest; repository for a saint's relics OE.; casket for a dead body, tomb XIV; temple, church XVII. OE. *scrīn* = MLG. *schrīn*, MDu. *schrīne* (Du. *schrijn*), OHG. *scrīni* (G. *schrein*), ON. *skrín*; Gmc. - L. *scrīnium* case or chest for books or papers.

shrink pt. *shrank*, pp. *shrunk, shrunken* †wither, cower, huddle OE.; become reduced in size or extent XIII; retreat, recoil XIV; trans. XIV. OE. str. vb. *scrincan*, corr. to Sw. *skrynka* wrinkle, Norw. *skrekka, skrøkka*. *Shrunk*, reduced form of *shrunken* pp., is now differentiated from the latter by being applied to the condition of being contracted by immersion or lowering of temperature.

shrive pt. †*shrove*, pp. *shriven* hear the confession of OE.; pass. (OE.), refl. and intr. (XIII) make one's confession. OE. str. vb. *scrīfan* assign, devise, impose as a sentence or penance, regard, care for = OS. *skrīban*, OHG. *scrīban* write, paint, describe, prescribe (Du. *schrijven*, G. *schreiben* write, spell); WGmc. (cf. ON. *skrifa* wk.) - L. *scrībere* write.

shrivel XVI. poss. of ON. orig. (cf. Sw. dial. *skryvla* wrinkle).

shroud A. †garment OE.; winding-sheet; veil, screen XVI; B. †place of shelter XIV; (pl.) crypt, vault XVI; C. (pl.) ship's ropes leading from a mast-head XV. OE. *scrūd*, corr. to ON. *skrúð* and *skrúði* fittings, gear, ornaments, apparel, furniture, textile fabric, f. Gmc. **skrūð-* **skreuð-* cut. Hence **shroud** vb. †clothe; cover, screen XIII.

Shrovetide the three days preceding Ash Wednesday. XV. Abnormally f. pt. stem *shrōv-* of SHRIVE + TIDE sb. So *Shrove Tuesday* (XV). The reference is to the practice of going to confession before Lent.

shrub[1] woody plant smaller than a tree. OE. *scrybb* (evidenced once), **scrubb* prob. 'shrubbery, underwood'; cf. NFris. *skrobb* broom, brushwood, WFlem. *schrobbe* climbing wild pea or vetch, Norw. *skrubba* dwarf cornel, Da. dial. *skrub* brushwood. Cf. SCRUB[2]. Hence **shrubbery** XVIII.

shrub[2] drink prepared from acid fruit, etc. XVIII. - Arab. *šarāb* sb. drink, f. *šariba* vb. drink.

shrug shiver, shudder XIV; raise (the shoulders) in disdain, etc. XV. of unkn. orig.

shuck (dial., U.S.) husk XVII; valueless thing (pl. used as int.) XIX. of unkn. orig.

shudder vb. XIII. ME. *shod(d)er* - MLG. *schōderen*, MDu. *schūderen*, frequent. (see -ER[4]) f. Gmc. **skūd-* shake, repr. in OS. *skuddian*, (M)LG. *schudden*, OHG. *scutten*, *scutisōn*. Hence sb. XVII.

shuffle Evidenced in the latter half of XVI in a series of senses expressive of pushing along, putting together, into, or off in a disorderly or evasive manner, and the like. - or cogn. w. LG. *schuffeln*, based on Gmc. **skuf-*; see SHOVE, -LE[3].

shun †abhor OE.; avoid, eschew XII. OE. *scunian* (chiefly in *ā-*, *onscunian*). of unkn. orig.

shunt †swerve, shy, shrink away XIII; (dial.) shove XVIII; move (a railway train) from one line to another XIX. ME. *schunte*, perh. a deriv. of SHUN.

shut pt., pp. *shut* †fasten (a bolt), (a door, etc.) with a bolt; move (a door, etc.) so as to close an aperture XIII. OE. *sċyttan* (more freq. in the comp. *forsċyttan*) = (M)LG, (M)Du. *schutten* shut up, obstruct :- WGmc. **skuttjan*, f. Gmc. **skut-* **skeut-* SHOOT. Hence **shutter** XVII. Short for †*window-shutter* (XVII); see -ER[1].

shute channel for conveying water to a lower level XVIII; steep channel down which stuff is shot XIX. Partly var. of SHOOT sb., partly var. sp. of CHUTE.

shuttle weaver's instrument for shooting the thread of the weft backwards and forwards. XIV. repr. OE. *sċytel* dart, arrow, corr. to ON. *skutill* harpoon, bolt :- Gmc. **scutilaz*, f. **skut-* SHOOT; see -LE[1].

shy[1] †easily frightened OE.; timidly averse to meeting anything XVI; unwilling to commit oneself XVII. OE. *sċēoh* = OHG. **scīoh*, MHG. *schiech* :- Gmc. **skeuχ(w)az*, whence also OHG. *sciuhen* (G. *scheuen* shun, *scheuchen* scare). Hence vb. XVII.

shy[2] throw (a missile). XVIII. of uncert. orig.

shyster (U.S. sl.) tricky lawyer, unscrupulous business man, etc. XIX. of uncert. orig.; see -STER.

si (mus.) seventh note of the scale in solmization. XVIII. - F. - It. *si*; see UT.

sialagogue medicine that produces saliva. XVIII. - F. - modL. *sialagōgus*, f. Gr. *síalon* saliva + *agōgós* leading, drawing forth, f. *ágein* lead.

siamang large ape with long black hair. XIX. - Malay.

sib related by blood. OE. *sib(b)* = MDu. *sib(b)e*, OHG. *sippi*, ON. pl. fem. *sifjar*, Goth. *-sibjis*, of unkn. orig.

sibilant XVII. - L. *sībilāns, -ant-*, prp. of *sībilāre* hiss, whistle, f. *sībilus* whistling sound, of imit. orig.; see -ANT. So **sibilation** XVII. - late L.

Sibyl woman possessing powers of divination. XIII. - OF. *Sibile* (mod. *Sibylle*) or medL. *Sibilla*, L. *Sibylla, Sibulla* - Gr. *Síbulla*. So **Sibylline** XVI. - L.; see -INE[1].

sic - L. *sīc* so, thus.

sick ill, ailing OE.; out of condition XIV; weary *of* XVI; inclined to vomit, vomiting XVII. OE. *sēoc* = OS. *siok* (Du. *ziek*), OHG. *sioh* (G. *siech*), ON. *sjúkr*, Goth. *siuks* :- Gmc. **seukaz*, of unkn. orig. Hence **sicken** (-EN[5]) XII. **sickly** adj. (-LY[1]) XIV; whence **sick** vb. XVII.

sickle OE. *sicol, sicel* = MLG., MDu. *sekele, sikele* (Du. *zikkel*), OHG. *sichila* (G. *sichel*) - var. **sicila* of L. *secula*, f. *secāre* cut.

side long surface, opp. to top, bottom, or end; place or aspect with reference to a centre; lateral slope, shore, etc. OE.; situation with respect to an opinion XIII. OE. *sīde* = OS. *sīde* (Du. *zij(de)*), OHG. *sīta* (G. *seite*), ON. *síða* :- Gmc. **sīðō*, prob. f. **sīðaz* adj. long, deep (OE. *sīd*, MDu. *sīde, zide*, ON. *síðr*), and rel. further to OE. *sīð* late, etc. (see SINCE). Hence **side** vb. XV. **sidelong** sideways, obliquely; also adj. XVI. alt. of *sideling* (XIV); see -LING[2], -LONG. **sidesman** XVII. alt. of †*sideman* (XVI-XVII), 'a man who stands at the side of a churchwarden'. **sideways** from one side, laterally, obliquely. XVI. **siding** taking sides XVII; concr. piece of something at the side XVIII; see -ING[1]. **sidle** move obliquely, edge along XVII; back-formation from *sideling, sidelong*, after vbs. in -LE[3].

sideral pert. to the stars. XVI. - L. *sīderālis*, f. *sīdus, sīder-* constellation, star. So **sidereal** XVII. f. L. *sīdereus*; see -AL[1].

siderite †loadstone XVI; various min. uses from XVIII. In early use - F. *sidérite* or L. *sidērītēs, -ītis* - Gr. *sidērī́tēs, -îtis*, f. *sídēros* iron; in later use f. Gr. *sídēros*; see -ITE.

siege XIII. ME. *sege* - OF. *sege* (mod. *siège*), f. *assegier* (mod. *assiéger*) BESIEGE.

sienna (ferruginous earth used as) a reddish-brown pigment. XVIII. Earlier *terra-sienna*, for It. *terra di Sienna* 'earth of Sien(n)a', a town in Tuscany.

sierra mountain range in Spain, etc. XVII. - Sp. :- L. *serra* saw.

siesta XVII. - Sp. :- L. *sexta* (sc. *hōra*) SIXTH hour of the day.

sieve sb. OE. *sife* = MLG., MDu. *seve* (Du. *zeef*), OHG. *sib, sip* (G. *sieb*) :- WGmc. **siƀi*.

sift OE. *siftan* = MLG., MDu. *siften, sichten* (Du. *ziften*); f. WGmc. **siƀ-* (see prec.).

sigh vb. First in ME. pt. *siȝide, syhid, sighed*, gerund *syȝing, sighing* (XIII), based on the stem of *sihte, siȝte*, wk. pt. of †*siche* :- OE. *sīcan* (orig. str.); of unkn. orig. Hence sb. XIV.

sight thing seen, spectacle OE.; eyesight, vision; show, display, (hence) lot XIV; device to guide the eye XVI. OE. *sihð*, more usu. *ġesihð, ġesiht* (see Y-), corr. to OS. *gisiht*, MLG. *sichte*, MDu. *sicht* (Du. *zicht*), OHG., MHG. *(ge)sicht* (G. *gesicht*) sight, vision, face, appearance; WGmc. deriv. of **seχ(w)-* SEE[1]; see -T[1]. Hence **sightly** †visible; pleasing to the sight. XVI. See -LY[1]; now more freq. in UNSIGHTLY.

sigla characters used as abbreviations. XVIII. - late L. *sigla*, perh. for *singula*, n. pl. of *singulus* SINGLE.

sign gesture to convey a meaning; mark having a meaning, token XIII; division of the zodiac XIV; device for a shop or inn XV. - (O)F. *signe* - L. *signum* mark, token. So vb. mark with a sign XIV; affix one's mark or name (to) XV. - (O)F. *signer* - L. *signāre*. **signal**[1] sign or token (*of*); sign agreed upon XVI. - (O)F., alt. of earlier *seignal* :- Rom. (medL.) *signāle*, sb. use of n. of late L. *signālis*; see -AL[1]. Hence **signal** vb. XIX, **signalize** XVII. **signal**[2] striking, remarkable. XVII. - F. *signalé*, earlier †*segnalé* - It. *segnalato*, pp. of *segnalare* make illustrious, f. *segnale* = OF. *seignal* (see above). **signatory** †used in sealing XVII; (forming) one of those whose signatures are attached XIX. - L. *signātōrius*; see -ORY[2]. **signature** XVI. - F. *signature* (- It. *segnatura*) or medL. *signātura*, f. pp. stem of L. *signāre*. **signet** small seal. XIV. - (O)F. *signet* or medL. *signētum*, dim. of *signe, signum* SIGN. **significance** meaning XV; importance XVIII. - OF. *significance* or L. *significantia*, f. prp. of *significāre*; see -ANCE. So **significant** XVI. *significāns, -ant-*. - L. **signification** XIII. - (O)F. - L. **signify** XIII. - (O)F. *signifier* - L. *significāre*.

signor sir, Mr.; man of distinction or authority.

XVI. - It., clipped form of *signore* :- L. *senior, seniōr-* SENIOR. So **signora** title of respect corr. to *madam, Mrs.* XVII.

Sikh XVIII. - Hindi, rel. to Skr. *śikṣate* learns.

silage ensilage. XIX. Alt. of ENSILAGE, after SILO.

silence abstinence from speech XIII; absence of sound XIV. - (O)F. - L. *silentium*, f. *silēns, -ent-*, prp. of *silēre* be silent; see -ENCE. So **silent** XVI. - L. prp.

silhouette portrait or picture in solid black. XIX. From F. phr. *à la silhouette*, f. name of Étienne de *Silhouette* (1709-67), controller-general in 1759; divergent reasons are given for the application.

silica silicon dioxide. XIX. f. L. *silex, silic-* flint. So **siliceous** pert. to flint or silica. XVII. f. L. *siliceus*. **silicium** XIX, repl. by **silicon** XIX. Hence **silicate** (-ATE[1]) XIX.

siliqua (bot.) pod of seeds of the mustard family. XVIII. - L. *siliqua* pod. So **siliquose, siliquous** XVII.

silk OE. *sioloc, seol(e)c*, for *siluc, corr. to ON. *silki* and OSl. *šelkŭ* (Russ. *shelk*), Lith. *šilkaĩ* - L. **sericum*, for *sēricum*, n. of *sēricus*, f. *sēres* - Gr. *Sêres*, oriental people from whom silk was first obtained and passed through Slavonic countries into the Baltic trade. Hence **silken** (-EN[3]) OE. *seol(o)cen*. **silkworm** OE. *seolcwyrm*. **silky** (-Y[1]) XVII.

sill beam forming the foundation of a wall OE.; lower horizontal part of a window opening XV; threshold XVI. OE. *syll(e)* = MLG. *sul(le)*, MDu. *sulle*, rel. to MLG., MDu. *sille*, ON. *svill, syll*, and MHG. *swelle*, OHG. *swelli, swella* (G. *schwelle* threshold), Goth. *gasuljan* found, establish, *sulja* sole.

sillabub, syllabub dish of milk curdled with wine, etc. XVI. The earliest exx. show *sol-, sul-, sel-, sil-*; also dial. *sillibouk*; of unkn. orig.

silly (dial.) deserving of pity XV; †weakly; †simple, ignorant; feeble-minded, foolish XVI. Later form of *seely* (orig.) happy, blessed :- OE. **sǣliġ* (as in *unsǣliġ* unhappy, *sǣliġlīċe*, adv.) and *ġesǣliġ*, corr. to OS., OHG. *sālig* (Du. *zalig*, G. *selig*) :- WGmc. **sǣliʒa*, f. **sǣli* luck, happiness (OE. *sǣl*), sb. f. Gmc. base repr. also by ON. *sǣll* happy, Goth. *sēls* good, and abstr. sb. OE. *sǣlð*.

silo pit or underground chamber for storing grain, etc. XIX. - Sp. :- L. *sirus* - Gr. *sirós* pit to keep corn in.

silt XV. of uncert. orig.; perh. - a Scand. word repr. by Norw., Da. *sylt*, Norw. and Sw. dial. *sylta* salt marsh, sea beach, corr. to OLF. *sulta* (LG. *sulte, sülte*; Du. *zult*), OHG. *sulza* (G. *sülze*) salt marsh, salt pan, brine, f. Gmc. **sult-* **salt-* SALT.

silvan see SYLVAN.

silver OE. *siolfor, seolfor* = OS. *silubar, silobar*, (Du. *zilver*), OHG. *sil(a)bar, silbir* (G. *silber*), ON. *silfr*, Goth. *silubr*; Gmc. **silubr-*, rel. indeterminately to various Balto-Sl. forms, perh. all ult. of Oriental orig.

simian ape-like. XVII. f. L. *sīmia* ape, perh. f. *sīmus* - Gr. *sīmós* snub-nosed, flat-nosed; see -IAN.

similar †homogeneous; like, alike. XVII (†*similary* XVI). - F. *similaire* or medL. *similāris*, f. L. *similis*, based on IE. **sem-* **som-* (cf. SAME); see -AR, -ARY. Hence or - F. **similarity** XVII. So **similitude** XIV. - (O)F. or L.

simmer XVII. Later form of (dial.) †*simper* (XV), perh. of imit. orig.; see -ER[4].

simnel bread made of fine flour. XIII. - OF. *simenel*, ult. f. L. *simila, similāgō*, or Gr. *semídālis* fine flour.

simony XIII. - (O)F. *simonie* - late L. *simōnia*, f. name of *Simon* Magus in allusion to his offer of money to the Apostles Peter and John for the gift of conferring the Holy Ghost (Acts 8: 18, 19); see -Y[3]. So **simoniac** XIV (sb.; adj. XVII). - (O)F. *simoniaque* or medL. *simoniacus*. **simoniacal** (-AL[1]) XVI.

simoom hot suffocating sand-wind. XVIII. - Arab. *samūm*, f. *samma* vb. poison.

simper XVI. Similar forms with rel. meanings in Scand. langs., MDu., and G. may be the immed. source or point to a Gmc. imit. orig. with the suffix -ER[4].

simple A. free from duplicity; free from pride XIII; B. of humble condition; ordinary, homely XIII; deficient in knowledge XIV; silly XVII; C. with nothing added XIV; not complex XV; D. sb. pl. persons of humble status; unlettered people XIV; sg. (gram.) simplex; (arch.) uncompounded substance, herb for use as such XVI. - (O)F. - L. *simplus*, corr. to Gr. *haplóos*, f. IE. **sm-* **sem-* **som-* (cf. SAME) + **pl-*, as in *duplus* DOUBLE, *triplus* TRIPLE, etc. Hence **simply** XIII. So **simplex** consisting of a single part XVI; sb. (gram.) uncompounded word XIX. - L., with second el. as in *duplex, multiplex, -plic-* (see PLY[1]). **simplicity** XIV. - (O)F. or L., f. *simplex, -plic-*. **simplify** XVII. - F. - medL. **simplification** XVII.

simpleton XVII. f. SIMPLE + -TON.

simulate XVII. - pp. stem of L. *simulāre*, f. *similis* SIMILAR; see -ATE[3]. So **simulation** XIV. - OF. or L.

simultaneous XVII. f. L. *simul* at the same time, prob. after *instantaneous* or *momentaneous*; see SAME, -EOUS.

sin transgression of the divine law. OE. *syn(n)* wrongdoing, offence, (also) enmity; :- **sunjō*, rel. to OS. *sundea*, OHG. *sunt(e)a, sund(e)a* (G. *sünde*), ON. *synd*. So **sin** vb. OE. *syngian* (:- **sunniʒōjan*), ME. *sun(i)gen, singen*, repl. by *sinne*, based on the sb.

sinapism mustard plaster. XVII. - F. *sinapisme* or late L. *sināpismus* - Gr. *sināpismós* use of a mustard plaster (*sinā́pisma*), f. *sínāpi* mustard; see -ISM.

since adv. †thereupon; from then till now; ago, before now XV; prep. from (a certain time) till now XVI; conj. from the time that; seeing that XV. ME. *syn(ne)s*, either (i) reduced form of †*sithenes* (XIV), f. †*sithen*, OE. *siððan*, f. *sīð* after, or (ii) directly f. (dial.) *sin* (XIV), syncopated form of †*sithen* + -S.

sincere XVI. - L. *sincērus*. So **sincerity** XVI.

sinciput (anat.) front part of the skull. XVI. - L. *sinciput*, for **senciput*, f. *sēmi-* half, SEMI- + *caput* HEAD.

sine (math.) one of the three trigonometrical functions. XVI. - med. use of L. *sinus* bend, fold of toga, bosom, used to translate Arab. *jaib* bosom in this sense.

sinecure benefice without cure of souls; position with emolument but without duties XVII. - L. (*beneficium*) *sine cūra* (*sine* without, *cūra* care).

sinew tendon OE.; mainstay, chief support (*sinews of war* money, after L. *nervi belli pecunia*, Cicero) XVI. OE. *sin(e)we, sionwe*, etc., obl. forms of *sinu, seonu* = (M)LG., MDu., MHG. *sene* (Du. *zeen*, G. *sehne*), ON. *sin* :- Gmc. **senawō*.

sing pt. *sang* (also *sung* XVI-XIX), pp. *sung* utter with musical inflexions of the voice. OE. str. vb. *singan* = OS., OHG. *singan* (Du. *zingen*, G. *singen*), ON. *syngva*, Goth. *siggwan* :- Gmc. **seŋʒwan*, rel. to Gr. *omphḗ* voice. comp. **singsong** jingling verse XVII; informal concert XVIII; formed on the model of DING-DONG (XVI).

singe OE. *senċġan, sænċġan* (usu. *besenċġan*) = OS. *bisengian* (Du. *zengen*), (M)HG. *sengen* :- WGmc. **saŋgjan*, f. **saŋg-* **seŋg-* **suŋg-*, repr. also by Du. *sengel* spark, MHG. *senge* dryness, etc.

single unaccompanied; unmarried; individual; not double XIV; separate XV; one (*one* or *a*) only XVI. ME. *sengle* - OF. *sengle, single* :- L. *singulus* f. *sim-* as in SIMPLE. Hence **single** vb. separate, pick out. XVI. **singlet** (-ET) unlined under-garment for the trunk. XVIII. **singleton** (-TON) a single card of a suit in the hand. XIX. **singly** (-LY[2]) XIII.

singular †alone, solitary; one only; (gram.); †separate, single, personal; †special, particular; not customary, peculiar XVII. ME. *singuler* - OF. *singuler* (mod. *singulier*) - L. *singulāris*, f. *singulus* SINGLE; see -ER[2]. The form in *-er* was not finally displaced by the latinized *-ar* till XVII. So **singularity** XIV. - (O)F. - late L.

sinister A. marked by †ill-will, †suspicion, dishonesty XV; unlucky, unfavourable XVI; B. situated on, or directed to, the left side (spec. her.) XV. - (O)F. *sinistre* or L. *sinister* left.

sink pt. *sank*, pp. *sunk, sunken* be submerged; drop to a lower level OE.; trans. (repl. ME. *senchen*, OE. *senċan*) XIII. OE. str. vb. *sincan* = OS., OHG. *sinkan* (Du. *zinken*, G. *sinken*), ON. *sǫkkva*, Goth. *sigqan*; of unkn. orig. Hence **sink** sb. †pit for the receipt of water, conduit XV; basin, etc. of stone, etc. having an escape pipe for water XVI (also fig.).

Sinn Fein Irish movement formed in 1905 by Arthur Griffith. - Ir., 'we ourselves'.

sinnet, sennit (naut.) cordage made by pleating several strands of yarn, etc. XVII. of unkn. orig.

Sino- comb. form of Gr. *Sínai*, L. *Sinæ* the Chinese; in **Sinologue** one versed in Chinese civilization, etc. (XIX) modelled on F. or G. comps.

sinter incrustation formed by precipitation from mineral waters. XVIII. - G. *sinter* CINDER.

sinuous marked by turns or bends. XVI. - L. *sinuōsus* or F. *sinueux*; see next and -OUS.

sinus (path.) abscess, etc. XVI; (bot., anat.) cavity, depression XVII. - L. *sinus* semicircular fold, bosom, bay.

-sion repr. F. *-sion*, L. *-siō, -ōn-*, f. *s* of pps. and supines + -ION.

sip imbibe liquid in small quantities XIV; tr. XVII. prob. symbolic modification of SUP[1], to express less vigorous action; but cf. LG. *sippen*, which, if early enough, might be the immed. source. Hence sb. XVII.

siphon, syphon bent tube for drawing off liquid by atmospheric pressure. XVII. - F. *siphon* or L. *sīphō, -ōn-* - Gr. *síphōn* pipe, tube.

sippet small piece of bread to be dipped in liquid. XVI. Intended as a dim. of SOP; see -ET.

sir title prefixed to the name of a knight or male superior, or used vocatively XIII; as a gen. term of respect XIV. ME. *sir, ser, sur*, unstr. vars. of SIRE.

sirdar military chief, as in India and Egypt. XVII. - Urdu, f. Pers. *sar* head + *dār* possessor.

sire †as a prefixed title or a vocative; †master, sovereign; (arch.) father XIII; male parent of a quadruped XVI. - (O)F. :- **sieire* :- Rom. **seior*, for L. *senior* SENIOR.

siren (classical myth.) fabulous female monster having an enchanting voice XIV; dangerously attractive person XVI; instrument for producing musical tones XIX. In some early texts (i) *sereyn, -ayn*, (ii) *sirene* - OF. (i) *sereine, -aine*, (ii) *sirène* - late L. *Sīrēna*, fem. form of L. *Sīrēn* (to which the Eng. word was finally assim.) - Gr. *Seirḗn*, pl. *Seirênes*.

sirkar †court, palace of native prince XVII; native agent, etc.; province, state XVIII. - Urdu - Pers. *sarkār*, f. *sar* head + *kār* agent, doer.

sirloin upper part of a loin of beef. XVI (*surloyn, serlyn*). - OF. **surloigne*, var. of med. and modF. *surlonge*, f. *sur* over, above (see SUR-) + *longe* LOIN. The final prevalence of the sp. with *sir-* (from XVII) may have been due to the fiction that the joint was knighted by an English king.

sirocco oppressively hot and blighting wind blowing from the north coast of Africa. XVII. - F. *sirocco*, earlier †*siroc(h)* - It. *scirocco* - Arab. *šarūḳ*, var. of *šarḳ* east (wind), f. *šaraḳa* (the sun) rose.

sirrah condescending or contemptuous term of address to men and boys. XVI. Early forms *syrra, sirah*, also *serray, sirry, surry*, later (XIX) **siree**, prob. alt. of late ME. disyll. pronunc. of SIRE.

sirvente (pros.) form of poem used by the troubadours. XIX. - F. - Pr. *sirventes*, the final *s* of which was misapprehended as the pl. ending; of unkn. orig.

sisal (fibre of) species of Agave, etc. XIX. f. name of a port in Yucatan, Mexico.

siskin songbird allied to the goldfinch. XVI. - MDu. *sīseken*, early Flem. *sijsken* (Du. *sijsje*), dim. based on MLG. *sīsek*, MHG. *zīse(c)* (G. *zeisig*), of Sl. orig.; see -KIN.

sister daughter of the same parent(s) as another person. XIII. - ON. *systir*; superseding native forms (*suster, soster*) repr. cogn. OE. *sweoster, swuster* = OS. *swestar*, MLG., MDu. *suster* (Du. *zuster*), OHG. *swester* (G. *schwester*), Goth. *swistar* :- Gmc. **swestr* :- IE. **swesr-*, **swesŏr*, repr. in L. *soror* sister, Gr. *éor* daughter, niece, etc. Hence **sisterhood** XIV, **sisterly** XVI; see -HOOD, -LY[1].

sistrum jingling instrument or rattle used by ancient Egyptians. XIV. - L. - Gr. *seistron*, f. *seíein* shake.

Sisyphean useless and ineffective like the toil of the legendary Sisyphus in Hades. XVII. f. L. *Sīsypheius* - Gr. *Sīsúpheios*, f. *Sísuphos*; see -EAN.

sit pt., pp. *sat* be seated, seat oneself, †be situated OE.; †fit, suit XIII. OE. str. vb. *sittan* = OS. *sittian* (Du. *zitten*), OHG. *sizzan* (G. *sitzen*), ON. *sitja* :- Gmc. **sitjan* (cf. Goth. *sitan*), f. **set-* :- IE. **sed-* **sod-* **sd-*, repr. also by Skr. *sídati*, Gr. *hézomai*, Lat. *sedēre*, etc.

site †place occupied XIV; ground on which a building, etc. is set up XV; situation of a place or building XVI. - AN. *site* or L. *situs* local position, perh. f. *sit-*, pp. stem of *sinere* leave, allow to remain. Hence vb. XVI.

sith (arch., dial.) since. OE. *siððа*, ME. *siþþe*, *siþ(e)*, clipped form of *siððan* (see SINCE).

situate situated. XVI. - late L. *situātus*, f. L. *situs* SITE; see -ATE². Hence **situate** vb. (-ATE³), **situated** XVI. So **situation** XV. - (O)F. or medL.

six OE. *siex*, *syx*, *se(o)x* = OS., OHG. *sehs* (Du. *zes*, G. *sechs*), ON. *sex*, Goth. *saihs* :- Gmc. **seks*, varying in IE. with **sweks*, and repr. by L. *sex*, Gr. *héx*, OIr. *sē*, W. *chwech*, etc. So **sixth** (-TH²) new formation repl. *sixt(e)*, OE. *siexta* = OS., OHG. *sehsto*, ON. *setti*, Goth. *saihsta*. **sixteen** OE. *siextīene*. **sixteenth** (-TH²). repl. OE. *syxtēoða*. **sixty** (-TY¹), **sixtieth** (-ETH). OE. *siextiġ*, *siextiġoða*.

size¹ A. (dial.) assize(s); †ordinance for payment of tax, etc. XIII; †fixed standard of food, etc. XIV; B. magnitude XIV. - OF. *sise*, *size*, aphetic of *assise* ASSIZE, or aphetic var. of Eng. word. So **size** vb.¹ XIV; hence **siz(e)able** fairly large. XVII. Hence **sizar** at the Univ. of Cambridge, an undergraduate receiving a fixed allowance of food, etc. XVI.

size² glutinous substance used to produce a ground for gilding, etc., or to mix with colours. XV. perh. identical with SIZE¹, but the history is obscure. Hence **size** vb.² XVII.

sizzle burn with a hissing sound. XVII. imit.; see -LE³.

sjambok whip made of hide. XIX. - Afrikaans - Malay *sambok* - Urdu *chābuk*.

skald poet of ancient Scandinavia. XVIII. - ON. *skald*, of unkn. orig. Hence **skaldic** XVIII.

skat three-handed card game. XIX. - G. - It. *scarto* cards laid aside, f. *scartare* discard.

skate¹ fish of the genus *Raja*. XIV. - ON. *skata*.

skate² device fixed on the sole of a boot for gliding over ice. XVII. orig. in pl. *scates*, occas. *scatses* - Du. *schaats* (pl. *schaatsen*), in MDu. *schaetse* - (with unexpl. development of sense) ONF. *escace*, OF. *eschasse* (mod. *échasse*) stilt. The *-s* of the Du. word was apprehended as a pl. ending. Hence vb. XVII.

skedaddle retreat hastily; (gen.) run away, clear out. XIX. of unkn. orig.

skein XV. Aphetic - OF. *escaigne* (mod. *écagne*), of unkn. orig.

skeleton XVI. - Gr. *skeletón*, sb. use of n. of *skeletós* dried up, f. *skéllein* dry up.

skene knife or dagger of the Irish kerns and Scottish highlanders. XVI. - Ir. and Sc. Gael. *sgian* (g. *sceine*, *scine*).

skep specific quantity of grain, etc. XI; basket, hamper XIII; beehive XV. Late OE. *sceppe* - ON. *skeppa* basket, bushel, rel. to synon. OS. *skepil*, MLG., (M)Du. *schepel*, OHG. *sceffil* (G. *scheffel*).

skerry rugged insulated sea rock. XVII. Orkney dial., f. ON. *sker*.

sketch rough drawing; brief account or description. XVII. - Du. *schets* or G. *skizze* - It. *schizzo*, f. *schizzare* make a sketch :- Rom. **schediāre*, f. L. *schedius* - Gr. *skhédios* done extempore. Hence vb. XVII.

skew †escape XIV; move sideways or obliquely XV; look sideways XVI. Aphetic - ONF. *eskiu(w)er*, *eskuer*, var. of OF. *eschuer* ESCHEW. So adj. oblique, slanting. XVII. f. the vb. or ASKEW. Also **skew-whiff** adj. and adv. XVIII.

skewbald irregularly marked with white and brown or red. XVII. f. synon. †*skued* (XV), of uncert. orig., perh. f. OF. *escu* (mod. *écu*) shield :- L. *scūtum*; modelled on PIEBALD.

skewer long wooden or metal pin. XVII. var. of dial. *skiver* (XVII), of unkn. orig.

ski sb. XIX. - Norw. :- ON. *skíð* billet of cleft wood, snow-shoe = OE. *scīd*. Hence vb. XIX.

skiagram radiograph. XIX. f. Gr. *skiá* shadow + -GRAM. So **skiagraphy** XIX; cf. SCIAGRAPHY.

skid supporting timber XVII; wooden fender; wheel-locking device XVIII. of unkn. orig., but in form and sense resembling ON. *skíð* (see SKI). Hence **skid** vb. lock (a wheel) with a skid XVII; (of a wheel) be dragged along by having a skid applied; slip sideways XIX.

skiff small sea-going ship XVI; sculling- or racing-boat XVIII. - F. *esquif* - It. *schifo* - Lombardic **skif* = OHG. *schif* SHIP.

skill †reason; †what is reasonable XII; †cause; practical knowledge with ability XIII. - ON. *skil* distinction, discernment, knowledge, pleading, rel. to *skila* give reason for, expound, decide, *skilja* divide, distinguish, decide, etc., and MLG. *schēle*, (M)Du. *geschil*, *verschil* difference, MLG., MDu. *schillen*, *schēlen* differ, make a difference. Hence **skilled** (-ED²) XVI.

skillet saucepan, stew-pan. XV (*skelet*). of unkn. orig.; see -ET.

skilly thin gruel, soup, etc. XIX. Shortening of *skilligalee* (XIX), of unkn. orig.

skim clear (a liquid) of surface matter XV; move or act lightly over XVI. Back-formation f. *skimmer* vessel for skimming liquids (XIV), †*skemour*, †*skymour* (later with assim. of ending to -ER¹) - OF. *escumeure* (mod. *écumoire*), f. *escumer*, f. *escume* SCUM.

skimp (adj.) scanty XVII; (vb.) scrimp XIX. of unkn. orig.

skin hide of an animal stripped off XI; derma, epidermis; outer coat or covering XIV. Late OE. *scin(n)* - ON. *skinn* :- **skinþ-*, rel. to MLG. *schinden* (Du. *schinden*) flay, peel, OHG. *scindan* (G. *schinden*). Hence vb. cover with or strip of skin. XV. **skinner** (-ER¹) one who deals with skins. XIV.

skink small lizard. XVI. - F. †*scinc* (now *scinque*) or L. *scincus* - Gr. *skígkos*.

skip¹ leap lightly off the ground XIII; pass from

one thing to another omitting what intervenes XIV. prob. of Scand. orig., but the synon. MSw. *skuppa, skoppa* does not formally agree.

skip[2] footman, manservant; spec. college servant at Trinity College, Dublin. XVII. Short for †*skip-kennel* (XVII) lit. gutter-jumper.

skip[3] Shortening of SKIPPER (captain of a team). XIX.

skipper master of a small ship. XIV. - MLG., MDu. *schipper*, f. *schip* SHIP; see -ER[1].

skippet (hist.) cylindrical wooden box to contain a seal. XIV. of unkn. orig.

skirl cry out shrilly XIV; (of the bagpipes) XVII. prob. of Scand. orig.; early forms *scrille, skrille*, corr. to Norw. dial. *skrylla*; ult. imit. Hence sb. XVI.

skirmish irregular engagement between small bodies of fighters. XIV. Late ME. (i) *skarmuch*, aphetic - OF. *escar(a)muche* - It. *scaramuccia*, of unkn. orig.; superseded by (ii) *skarmich, skyrmish*, which were based on OF. *eskermiss-, eskirmiss-* (whence **skirmish** vb. XIV) lengthened stem of *eskermir, eskirmir* - Frankish **skirmjan* = OHG. *skirmen* (G. *schirmen*) defend. See -ISH[2].

skirr (poet., arch.) move rapidly XVI; pass rapidly over XVII. of unkn. orig.

skirret water-parsnip. XIV. ME. *skirwhit(e)*, perh. f. †*skire* clear, bright (- ON. *skírr* SHEER[1]) + WHITE.

skirt part of a dress or robe from the waist down XIII; flap of a saddle, etc. XIV; border, edge XV. - ON. *skyrta* shirt = OE. *sċyrte* SHIRT. Hence vb. be on the border of. XVII.

skit vain or wanton woman XVI; satirical remark, parody XVIII. vb. move lightly and rapidly XVII; make satirical hits XVIII. **skittish** excessively lively XV; disposed to shy, frolicsome XVI; fickle, coy XVII. perh. all ult. based on ON. **skyt-*, mutation of **skut- *skeut-* SHOOT.

skittle (pl.) game of ninepins. XVII. of unkn. orig.

skiver thin kind of leather split from a sheepskin. XIX. f. *skive* split - ON. *skífa*.

skivvy XIX. of unkn. orig.

skua predatory gull. XVII. - modL. *skua* - Faroese *skúgvur* = ON. *skúfr*, of unkn. orig.

skulk XIII. of Scand. orig. (cf. Norw. *skulka* lurk, lie watching, Sw. *skolka*, Da. *skulke* shirk, play truant).

skull XIII. ME. *scolle, schulle*, of unkn. orig. comp. **skull-cap** XVII.

skunk N.Amer. animal of the weasel kind, noted for emitting an offensive smell XVII; contemptible person XIX. of Algonquian orig.

sky †cloud; *the* vault of heaven, *the* firmament. XIII. - ON. *ský* cloud (:- **skiuja*), rel. to OE. *sċēo*, OS. *skio* (:- **skeuw-*) and OE. *sċuwa*, OHG. *scuwo*, ON. *skuggi* shade, shadow, Goth. *skuggwa* mirror (:- **skuwwan-*). Comp. **skylark** XVII.

Skye name of the largest island of the Inner Hebrides used attrib. as in *S. terrier*, a small breed of dog. XIX.

slab[1] flat, broad, and thick piece. XIII. of unkn. orig.

slab[2] (dial.) marshy place, slush. XVII. So adj. viscid XVII. prob. of Scand. orig. (cf. ODa. *slab* mud, Icel., Norw., Sw. *slabb* wet filth).

slack[1] indolent, careless, remiss OE.; loose XIII; dull, inactive XIV. OE. *slæc* = OS., (M)Du. *slak*, OHG. *slach*, ON. *slakr* :- Gmc. **slakaz*, rel. to L. *laxus* LAX. Hence **slack** vb. (cf. OE. *slacian* relax efforts), **slacken** (-EN[5]) XVI.

slack[2] small or refuse coal. XV. ME. *sleck*, prob. of LG. or Du. orig. (cf. LG. *slakk*, Du. *slak*).

slade valley, dell; forest glade. OE. *slæd* = OS. *slada*, LG. *slade*, Icel. *slǫðr*, Da., Norw. *slad(e)*. The present form descends from OE. obl. cases.

slag refuse matter from smelting. XVI. - MLG. *slagge*, perh. f. *slagen* strike, SLAY[1], with ref. to fragments resulting from hammering.

slake A. †relax one's efforts OE.; abate, moderate XIII; B. †loosen, slacken XII; mitigate, appease, allay XIII; disintegrate (lime) with water XVII. OE. *slacian*, f. *slæc* SLACK[1]; corr. to (M)Du. *slaken* relax, diminish.

slam[1] (at cards) †ruff and honours; winning all the tricks in a game. XVII. perh. shortening of †*slampant, -am, -aine*, in phr. *give* (one) *the slampant* trick, hoodwink.

slam[2] (dial.) beat XVII; shut with a noise XVIII. prob. of Scand. orig. (cf. ON. *slam(b)ra*).

slander †be a stumbling-block to XIII; †disgrace; defame XIV. ME. *sclaundre*, aphetic - AN. *esclaundre*, OF. *esclandre*, alt. of *escandle* SCANDAL. So vb. XIII. - OF. *esclandrer*. **slanderous** †disgraceful, scandalous; characterized by slander or calumny. XV. - OF. *esclandreux*.

slang (orig., but now differentiated from) †cant, jargon XVIII; colloquial language of an undignified kind XIX. In its earliest appearance a cant term variously applied, with gen. implication of irregular or lawless activity variously specialized; of uncert. orig. Hence **slang** vb. †exhibit at a fair XVIII; rail, or rail at, abusively (as in *slanging match*) XIX.

slant slope, as of ground XVII; inclination, obliquity XIX. f. earlier adv. (XV, *slonte*), aphetic of ASLANT, and vb. (XVI, *sklaunt*), obscurely rel. to dial. *slent* sb. and vb., which are presumably of Scand. orig.

slap smart blow as with the open hand. XVII. - LG. *slapp*, of imit. orig. So vb. and adv. XVII. In comb. with vbs. *slap-bang* XVIII, *slap-dash* XVII.

slash cut with a sweeping blow XIV (rare before XVI); cut slits in (a garment); assail severely XVII. perh. aphetic - OF. **esclaschier*, var. of *esclachier* break.

slat (dial.) slate XIV; long narrow slip of wood or metal XVIII. Aphetic - OF. *esclat* (mod. *éclat*) splinter, piece broken off, f. *esclater* split, splinter, shatter.

slate[1] (tablet of) variety of stone that splits readily into plates. XIV (*sclate, sklatestane*). - OF. *esclate*, fem. corr. to m. *esclat* SLAT.

slate[2] (sl.) 'knock the hat over someone's eyes'; thrash; assail with abuse. XIX. app. f. prec.

slattern XVII. prob. alt. of corr. adj. (dial.) *slattering*, prp. of *slatter* spill or splash awkwardly, slop, frequent. (see -ER[4]) of *slat* dash, perh. of Scand. orig. (cf. ON. *sletta* slap).

slaughter killing of cattle, etc. for food, killing of a person XIII; carnage, massacre XIV. - ON.

*slahtr, slátr, f. *slaχ- SLAY¹; repl. ME. slaʒt, repr. OE. *slæht, *sleaht. Hence vb., esp. of massacring people and killing cattle XVI.

Slav XIV (*Sclave*). In earliest use - medL. *Sclavus*, corr. to medGr. *Sklábos*; later, after medL. *Slavus*, F., G. *Slave*. So **Slavonian** XVI, **Slavonic** XVII. f. medL. *S(c)lavōnia*.

slave XIII. ME. *sclave*, aphetic - (O)F. *esclave*, prop. fem. of *esclaf* - medL. *sclavus*, *-va*, identical with the ethnic name *Sclavus* SLAV, the Slavonic races having been reduced to a servile state by conquest. Hence **slavery** XVI. **slavey** †male servant or attendant; female domestic servant. XIX; see -Y⁶. **slavish** XVI.

slaver allow saliva to fall. XIV (also sb.). prob. of symbolic orig. (cf. SLOBBER); see -ER⁴.

slay¹ pt. *slew*, pp. *slain* (rhet.) †strike; kill. OE. str. vb. *slēan* = OS., OHG. *slahan* (Du. *slagen*, G. *schlagen*), ON. *slá*, Goth. *slahan*; the Gmc. base **slaχ*- **slaʒ*- **slōʒ*- strike has no recognizable cogns. The present form of the inf. and pres. stem appeared XIV and is derived from the pp., finally superseding *slea*, *slee* (ME. *slēn*).

slay², sley instrument for beating up the weft. OE. *slege* = OS. *slegi*; f. base of prec.

sled sledge, sleigh. XIV. - MLG. *sledde*, corr. to MHG. *slitte* (G. *schlitten*), and rel. to MLG., MDu. *slēde*, (Du. *slede*, *slee*), OHG. *slito*, ON. *sleði*, f. **slid*- **slīd*- SLIDE.

sledge¹ large heavy hammer. OE. *slecg* = (M)Du. *slegge*, ON. *sleggja* :- Gmc. **slaʒj*-, f. **slaχ*- strike (see SLAY¹).

sledge² carriage mounted on runners. XVII. - MDu. *sleedse* (Du. dial. *sleeds*), rel. to *slēde* SLED.

sleek having a perfectly smooth surface. XVI. var. of SLICK (XIV), ME. *slike*, prob. repr. OE. **slice*, rel. to **slician* (as in *nigsliced* 'newly polished', glossy) and Icel. *slikja* be or make smooth.

sleep unconscious state in which the physical powers are suspended. OE. (Angl.) *slēp*, (WS.) *slǣp* = OS. *slāp* (Du. *slaap*), OHG. *slāf* (G. *schlaf*), Goth. *slēps* :- Gmc. **slǣpaz*, rel. to corr. vb. **slǣpan*, whence OE. *slǣpan* (mod. **sleep**), OS. *slāpan*, etc., and by gradation, to **slap*-, whence LG., Du. *slap* inert, sluggish, G. *schlaff* slack, lax. Hence **sleeper** one who sleeps XIII; stout horizontal timber XVII; apartment for sleeping (orig. U.S.) XIX.

sleet falling snow partially thawed. XIII. repr. OE. **slēte* :- **slautjan*-, rel. to MLG. *slōten* pl. hail, MHG. *slōze*, *slōz* (G. *schlosse*) hail(stone).

sleeve OE. (Angl.) *slēfe*, (WS.) *slīefe*, and *slīef*, *slȳf*, corr. to EFris. *slēwe*, NFris. *slēv*, *slīv* sleeve, and ult. rel. to MDu. *sloove*, *sloof* covering.

sleigh XVIII. orig. N. Amer. - Du. *slee* (see SLED).

sleight †craft, cunning XIII; dexterity, adroitness. XIV (surviving gen. in phr. *s. of hand*). ME. *sleʒþ* - ON. *slǽgð*, f. *slǽgr* SLY.

slender not stout or fleshy XIV; slight XV. of unkn. orig.

sleuth †track, trail XII; (short for *sleuth-hound* XIV) bloodhound, (hence) detective XIX. - ON. *slóð* track, trail.

slew turn or swing *round* XVIII (*slue*). orig. naut.; of unkn. orig. Hence **slewed** (sl.) intoxicated. XIX.

slice †shiver, splinter; applied to various flat utensils XIV; thin, flat piece XV. ME. *s(c)lice*, aphetic - OF. *esclice* (mod. *éclisse*) small piece of wood, etc. f. *esclicier* splinter, shatter (whence **slice** vb. XV), of Gmc. orig. (rel. to SLIT).

slick sleek XIV; smooth-spoken, plausible XVI; adroit, smart XIX; hence adv. (orig. U.S.) XIX. See SLEEK.

slide pt. and pp. *slid*. OE. str. vb. *slīdan* = LG. *slīden*, MHG. *slīten*, rel. to OE. *slidor* slippery, *slid(e)rian* SLITHER. Hence sb. XVI.

slight (dial.) smooth, sleek XIII; slender, slim; of light texture XIV; small in amount XVI. ME. (orig. north.) *sleght*, *slyʒt* - ON. **slehtr*, *sléttr* level, smooth, soft = OS. *sliht*, MLG., MDu. *slecht*, *slicht* simple, defective (Du. *slecht* bad), OHG. *sleht* level, MHG. *sleht* (G. *schlecht* bad, *schlicht* (after the vb.) smooth, plain, simple), Goth. *slaihts* level :- Gmc. **sleχtaz* (repr. in OE. only by *eorðslihtes* adv. even with the ground). So **slight** vb. †smooth, level. XIII. - ON. **slehta*, *slétta*, f. *sléttr*; in (obs.) sense 'level to the ground, raze' XVII - Du. *slechten*, LG. *slichten*; in sense 'treat with disdain' XVI f. the adj. in the sense 'of little account'. Hence sb. XVII.

slim slender, gracefully thin; slight, poor; (orig. dial.; since XIX from Afrikaans) cunning, wily. XVII. - LG., Du. *slim*, repr. MLG. *slim(m)*, MDu. *slim(p)* slanting, cross, bad = MHG. *slimp* (*-b*) slanting, G. *schlimm* grievous, awkward, bad :- Gmc. **slimbaz*.

slime soft sticky mud OE.; viscous fluid XIII. OE. *slīm* = MLG., MDu., MHG. *slīm* (Du. *slijm*, G. *schleim* phlegm, slime, mucus), ON. *slím* :- Gmc. **slīm*-, rel. to Balto-Sl. words meaning 'saliva', 'mucus', and L. *līmus* mud, slime, Gr. *límnē* marsh. Hence **slimy** (-Y¹) XIV.

sling¹ strap for hurling missiles. XIII. prob. of LG. or Du. orig. (cf. MLG. *slinge*, corr. to OHG. *slinga*). See foll.

sling² device for securing or grasping bulky objects XIV; strap, band, loop for suspension XVIII. The immed. source is doubtful; poss. identical with prec. (the senses of LG. *slinge*, G. *schlinge* noose, snare, arm-sling, to some extent correspond). Hence vb. XVI.

sling³ pt., pp. *slung* throw, cast with or as with a sling. XIII. prob. - ON. str. vb. *slyngva*; cf. OHG. *slingan* (G. *schlingen* wind, twist).

sling⁴ Amer. drink with a basis of spirit; juice of the sugar-cane. XIX. of unkn. orig.

slink pt., pp. *slunk* move stealthily XIV; drop (young) prematurely or abortively XVII. repr. OE. *slincan* creep, crawl, corr. to (M)LG. *slinken* subside.

slip¹ semi-liquid mass OE.; curdled milk (now U.S.) XV; semi-liquid cementing material XVII. OE. *slipa*, *slyppe* slime (so *slipig* slimy); cf. Norw. *slip(a)* slime on fish, and SLOP².

slip² pass lightly, quickly, or quietly XIII; slide, lose foothold or grasp, err XIV; cause to slide, get loose from; let go XVI. prob. - MLG., Du. *slippen* = MHG. *slipfen* (cf. SLIPPERY). Hence **slip** sb. artificial slope XV; leash for a dog; act of slipping or sliding (cf. *landslip* XVII); error XVI; garment readily slipped on XVII.

slip³ small shoot of a plant XV; young person;

long and narrow strip XVI. prob. - MLG., MDu. *slippe* (Du. *slip*) cut, slit, strip.

slipper XV. cf. (dial.) *slip-shoe* (XVI); presumably f. SLIP[3].

slippery XVI. First recorded from Coverdale's tr. of the Bible (Ps. 35: 6); prob. modelled on Luther's *schlipfferig*, MHG. *slipferig*, f. *slipfern*, extension of *slipfen*, f. Gmc. **slip-* as repr. in OE. *slipor* (dial. *slipper*) slippery, morally unstable; see -Y[1].

slipshod wearing slippers or very loose shoes XVI; untidy, slovenly XVII. f. SLIP[3] + *shod*, pp. of SHOE vb., after *slip-shoe* (XVI) slipper.

slipslop sloppy mess of food XVII; blundering use of words XVIII. redupl. f. SLOP[2].

slit pt., pp. *slit* cut into, cut open. XIII. ME. *slitte*, in pp. *islit*, repr. OE. **slittan*, rel. to *slītan* = OS. *slītan* (Du. *slijten*), OHG. *slīzan* (G. *schleissen*), ON. *slíta*, f. Gmc. base having no known cogns. Hence **slit** sb. XIII; cf. OE. *ġeslit* rending, biting, *slite* tear, rent.

slither XIII. alt. of ME. *slidere* (dial. *slidder*), OE. *sliderian* = MLG., MDu. *slid(d)eren*, G. dial. *schlittern*, frequent. (see -ER[4]) f. weak grade of SLIDE.

sliver XIV. Obscure formation on the base of (dial.) *slive* (XIV), OE. **slīfan* (in pt. *tōslāf* split up). Hence vb. XVII.

slobber behave (e.g. feed) in a slovenly fashion. XV. Earlier in ME. *byslober*, *beslobber* (cf. *slobber* mud, slime XIV), and corr. to Du. *slobberen*, with parallel formations in (dial.) *slabber*, *slubber* (XVI), Du. *slabberen*, MLG., MDu. *slubberen*; of imit. or symbolic orig.

sloe (fruit of) the blackthorn. OE. *slā(h)* = MLG., MDu. *slē*, *sleuuwe* (LG. *slē*, *slī*, Du. *slee*), OHG. *slēha*, *slēwa* (G. *schlehe*) :- Gmc. **slaiχwōn*.

slog A. hit hard; B. plod. XIX. In sense A parallel to synon. dial. *slug*; of unkn. orig.

slogan war-cry, battle-cry XVI (first in Sc. use: *slog(g)orne*, etc.); party cry or watchword XVIII. - Gael. *sluaghghairm*, f. *sluagh* host + *gairm* shout, cry.

sloid see SLOYD.

sloop XVII (*slup*). - Du. *sloep*, †*sloepe*; of unkn. orig.

slop[1] †bag; (dial.) loose tunic or gown XIV; (pl.) wide breeches XV; ready-made garments XVII. OE. *-slop*, in *oferslop* surplice, corr. to MDu. *(over)slop*, ON. *(yfir)sloppr*, f. Gmc. **slup-*; rel. to **slūp-* in OE. *slūpan*, MLG. *slūpan*, OHG. *sliofan* (G. *schliefen*), Goth. *sliupan* glide.

slop[2] (dial.) muddy place, slush XIV; liquid food (esp. pl.) XVII; refuse liquid XIX. prob. repr. OE. **sloppe* as in *cūsloppe*, var. of *cūslyppe* COWSLIP; cf. SLIP[1]. Hence **sloppy** (-Y[1]) XVIII.

slop[3] (sl.) policeman. XIX. alt. of *ecilop*, back-slang for POLICE.

slope[1] †adv. in an oblique direction or position XV. Aphetic of *aslope* (of uncert. orig.). Hence as vb. intr. take an oblique direction XVI, tr. (spec. mil.) bring into a slanting position XVII; and as sb. XVII.

slope[2] (sl.) make *off*, decamp. XIX. orig. U.S.; perh. spec. use of prec. vb.

slosh XIX. var. of SLUSH.

slot[1] (dial.) hollow of the breast bone XIV; elongated narrow depression in wood, etc. XVI. - OF. *esclot* (in first sense), of unkn. orig.

slot[2] animal's track XVI; deer's foot XIX. - OF. *esclot* horse's hoof-print, prob. - ON. *slóð* track.

sloth inactivity, sluggishness XII; S. Amer. arboreal mammal of sluggish habits XVII. ME. *slawþe*, *slowþe*, f. *slāw*, *slōw*, SLOW + -TH[1]; repl. OE. *slǣwð*, ME. *sleuþ(e)*.

slouch ungainly fellow XVI; (for *slouch(ed) hat*) hat with flopping brim XVIII; (from the vb.) stooping ungainly carriage XVIII. Hence **slouching** prp. adj. XVII (see -ING[2]), whence **slouch** vb. XVIII. Of unkn. orig.

slough[1] soft muddy piece of ground. OE. *slōh*, *slō(g)*, of unkn. orig.

slough[2] outer skin shed by a reptile. XIII. ME. *sloh*, *sloȝ*, poss. rel. to LG. *sluwe*, *slu* husk, peel, shell. Hence vb. be shed as skin XVIII; cast off XIX.

sloven †knave, rascal XV; †idle fellow XVI; careless or negligent person. perh. based on Flem. *sloef* dirty, squalid, Du. *slof* negligent.

slow OE. *slāw* = OS. *slēu*, (M)Du. *slee(uw)*, OHG. *slēo*, ON. *slǽr* :- Gmc. **slǣwaz* :- IE. **slēwos*, of unkn. orig. Hence **slow** vb. XVI.

slow-worm small lizard, *Anguis fragilis*. OE. *slāwyrm*; the first el., which has been assim. to SLOW, is of uncert. orig.

sloyd, sloid system of manual instruction adopted from Sweden. XIX. - Sw. *slöjd* :- ON. *slǿgð* SLEIGHT.

sludge mire, ooze XVII; matter mixed with water or slime XVIII. See SLUSH.

slug[1] sluggard XV; †slow-sailing vessel XVI; slow-moving shell-less land-snail XVIII. Based on a stem *slug-*, repr. also by **slug** vb. be slow or inert (XV) and earlier by, e.g., †*sluggy* sluggish (XIII); prob. of Scand. orig. (cf. Sw. dial. *slogga* be sluggish, Norw. dial. *slugg* large heavy body). So **sluggish** (-ISH[1]), **sluggard** (-ARD) XIV, **slugabed** XVI.

slug[2] irregularly shaped bullet XVII; (typogr.) metal bar, line of type XIX. perh. identical with prec.

sluice structure for regulating flow of water in a river, etc. XIV (*scluse*). - OF. *escluse* (mod. *écluse*) :- Gallo-Rom. **exclūsa*, sb. use of fem. pp. of L. *exclūdere* EXCLUDE. Hence vb. XVI.

slum A. †room; B. (orig. *back s.*) dirty or squalid back street, etc.; C. †gammon, blarney, gipsy jargon; all early XIX. of unkn. (cant) orig. Hence vb. visit slums; **slummy** (-Y[1]). XIX.

slumber vb. XIII. ME. *slūmere*, f. *slūme*, OE. *slūma* or vb. *slūmen* (XIII), corr. to MDu., MLG. *slūmen*, MLG. *slummen*, G. †*schlummen*, with parallel formations in MLG., MDu. *slūmeren* (Du. *sluimeren*), MHG. *slummeren*, G. *schlummern*. Hence sb. XIV.

slump fall or sink *into* a bog, etc. XVII; transf. and fig. XIX. of symbolic orig. Hence sb. XIX.

slur A. (dial.) fluid mud XV (*sloor*, *slore*); gliding movement XVI; sliding mechanism XVIII; B. deliberate slight XVII; (mus.) mark indicating a smooth connected passage XIX. Hence **slur** vb. A. (dial.) stain, sully; disparage XVII; B. slide XVI; (mus.) XVIII. of uncert. orig.; partly corr. forms are (M)Du. *sloor* sluttish woman, LG. *slurren* shuffle, (M)LG. *slūren*, MDu. *sloren*, Du. *sleuren* drag, trail.

slush melting snow or ice XVII; liquid mud XVIII. contemp. with synon. SLUDGE, *slutch*, with which it forms a series of expressive words parallel to ME. *sloche*, *sliche* (XIV), *sleech* (XVI), and SLOSH, to which the closest foreign parallels are Da. †*slus* sleet, mud, Norw. *slusk* sloppy ground or weather.

slut dirty slovenly woman XIV (implied in *sluttish*); loose woman, hussy XV. of unkn. orig.

sly (dial.) skilled, clever XII; dyslogistic connotations appear very early. ME. *sleh*, *sley*, *sli(ȝ)* - ON. *slœgr* clever, cunning, etym. 'able to strike', f. *slóg-*, pt. stem of *slá* strike (see SLAY[1]).

slype covered way from one part of a cathedral, etc. to another. XIX. perh. a use of *slipe* long narrow piece (as of ground XVI-XVII), varying with SLIP; of unkn. orig.

smack[1] taste, flavour OE.; (fig.) trace, tinge, 'touch' XVI. OE. *smæc* = MLG., MDu. *smak* (Du. *smaak*), OHG. *gismac* (G. *geschmack*). Hence vb. taste XIV, savour *of* XVI.

smack[2] separate the lips with a sharp noise XVI; crack (a whip) XVII; strike sharply with a flat surface XIX. - MLG., MDu. *smacken* (LG., Du. *smakken*); cf. OE. *ġesmacian* pat, caress, G. *schmatzen* eat or kiss noisily; of imit. orig. So sb. XVI.

smack[3] light single-masted sailing-vessel. XVII. - LG., Du. *smacke* (mod. *smak*); of unkn. orig.

small (dial.) slender, thin; †narrow; of limited size or extent; of fine texture OE.; of low strength or power XII. OE. *smæl* = OS. (Du.), OHG. *smal* (G. *schmal*), ON. *smalr*, Goth. *smals* :- Gmc. **smalaz* (:- IE. **smol-*). Comp. **smallpox** XVI (*small pokkes*).

smallage variety of celery or parsley. XIII. ME. *smal ache*, i.e. SMALL, †*ache* celery, parsley, etc. - (O)F. :- L. *apium*.

smalt glass coloured deep-blue by oxide of cobalt XVI; deep-blue colour XIX. - F. - It. *smalto* - Gmc. **smalt* (OHG. *smalz*, G. *schmalz*), rel. to SMELT[2].

smarm (dial.) smear, bedaub XIX; plaster *down*; behave fulsomely XX. Also *smalm*; of unkn. orig. Hence **smarmy** (-Y[1]) XX.

smart be acutely painful OE.; feel sharp pain, suffer severely *for* XII. OE. **smeortan* (in *fyrsmeortende* fiery, painful, *smeortung* itching) = MDu. *smerten*, (also mod.) *smarten*, OHG. *smerzan* (G. *schmerzen*), based on WGmc. **smert-* **smart-* **smurt-*. So **smart** adj. †biting, stinging XI; causing acute pain XII; brisk, vigorous XII. Late OE. *smeart*. **smart** sb. XII.

smash vb. XVIII. prob. imit. Hence sb. XVIII.

smatter †smirch, defile XIV; †prate, chatter XV; have a superficial knowledge *of* XVI. of unkn. orig.

smear †anoint; cover thickly (as) with some greasy matter. OE. *smierwan*, corr. to MLG. *smeren*, OHG. *smirwen* (G. *schmieren*), ON. *smyrva*, *smyrja* :- Gmc. **smerwjan*. So sb. †fat, grease, ointment OE.; in later senses f. the vb. OE. *smeoru*.

smegma (physiol.) sebaceous secretion. XIX. - L. - Gr. *smêgma*, f. base of *smḗkhein* rub, cleanse.

smell pt., pp. *smelled*, *smelt* A. perceive by the sense of which the nose is the organ; B. have an odour. XII. ME. *smelle*, also *smülle*, *smille*, pointing to OE. **smiellan*, **smyllan*, of which no cogns. are known. Hence sb. XII; superseding *stink* and *stench* in the neutral application of sense B.

smelt[1] small fish of the genus *Osmerus*. OE. *smelt*, *smylt*, obscurely rel. to similar Continental names for species of fish; cf. SMOLT.

smelt[2] fuse (ore) to obtain the metal. XV (implied in *smelter*). - MLG., MDu. *smelten* = OHG. *smelzan* (G. *schmelzen*), f. **smelt-*, var. of the base of MELT.

smew saw-billed duck, *Mergus albellus*. XVII. Obscurely rel. to synon. (dial.) *smee* (XVII), and *smeath* (XVII), Du. *smient*, LG. *smēnt* widgeon, G. *schmi-*, *schmü-*, *schmeiente* wild duck (*ente* duck).

smilax climbing shrub. XVII. - L. *smīlax* - Gr. *smīlax* bindweed.

smile vb. XIII. perh. of Scand. orig. (cf. Sw. *smila*, Da. *smile*; a parallel form is OHG. **smīlan*); f. the base repr. by forms cited s.v. SMIRK. Hence sb. XVI.

smirch defile, sully. XV. of unkn. orig.

smirk smile, (later) esp. in a silly manner. OE. *sme(a)rcian*, f. **smar-* **smer-* (**smīr-*), repr. by OE. *smerian* laugh at, *bismer*, *bismerian* scorn, OHG. *smierōn* (G. †*schmieren*) smile; rel. to Skr. *smera-* smiling, *smáyate* smiles, OSl. *smijati sę*, Gr. *meidân* laugh.

smite pt. *smote*, pp. *smitten*, (arch. or joc.) *smit* administer a blow to XII; in various applications lit. and fig., now chiefly arch. or joc. OE. str. vb. *smītan* smear, pollute = OS. *bismītan*, MLG., MDu. *smīten* (Du. *smijten*), OHG. *smīzan* smear, (G. *schmeissen* throw, fling), Goth. *-smeitan* :- Gmc. **smītan*.

smith one who works in iron, etc. OE. *smið* = MDu. *smit*, (also mod.) *smid*, OHG. *smid* (G. *schmied*), ON. *smiðr* :- Gmc. **smiþaz*; orig. prob. craftsman, f. IE. **smei-*, repr. by Gr. *smī́lē* chisel, *sminúē* mattock. So **smith** vb. OE. *smiðian* = OS., OHG. *smithōn*, ON. *smiða*, Goth. *gasmiþōn*. **smithy** XIII. - ON. *smiðja*, corr. to OE. *smiððe*.

smithereens (colloq., dial.) small fragments. XIX. f. (dial.) *smithers* (XIX), of unkn. orig. Cf. Ir. *smidirín*.

smock (dial.) shift, chemise OE.; loose coarse-linen overall garment XIX. OE. *smoc* = OHG. *smoccho*, ON. *smokkr* (perh. from Eng.); rel. to MHG. *gesmuc* (G. *schmuck* ornament); parallel to forms based on **smūȝ-*, e.g. OE. *smūgan* creep, MHG. *smiegen*, ON. *smjúga* creep into, put on a garment.

smoke sb. OE. *smoca*, f. wk. grade of the base repr. by MLG. *smōk*, MDu. *smoock* (Du. *smook*), MHG. *smouch* (G. *schmauch*) and OE. *smēoc*, *smī(e)ċ*, *smēċ*, and vbs. *smēocan*, MDu. *smieken*, (M)LG., (M)Du. *smōken*. So vb. OE. *smocian*.

smolt young salmon between a parr and a grilse. XIV (in earliest use Sc.). of unkn. orig.; cf. SMELT[1].

smooth having a surface free from irregularities OE.; pleasant, affable XIV; bland, plausible XV. Late OE. *smōð* (rare, the usual form being *smēðe*, ME. *smethe*, dial. *smeeth*); of unkn. orig. Hence **smooth** vb. XV; superseding ME. *smethe* (dial. *smeeth*), OE. *smēð(i)an*.

smother (often with *smoke*) dense or stifling smoke. XII. Early ME. *smorðer*, later *smoþer*; f. base of OE. *smorian* (dial. *smore*) suffocate, corr. to (M)Du., (M)LG. *smoren* (whence G. *schmoren*), of unkn. orig. Hence vb. (early ME. *smorðren*).

smoulder †smother, suffocate XIV; burn and smoke without flame XVI. rel. obscurely to LG. *smöln*, MDu. *smōlen* (Du. *smeulen* smoulder).

smudge XV. of unkn. orig., but parallel to synon. *smutch* sb. (XVI), vb. (XVII), *smooch* vb. (XVII). Hence sb. XVIII.

smug neat, smooth, sleek XVI; self-complacent XIX. of unkn. orig.; cf. †*smudge* adj. smart, vb. deck out (XVI), LG. *smuck* pretty, G. *schmuck* ornament.

smuggle XVII (also *smuckle*). - LG. *smuggeln*, *smukkeln*, Du. *smokkelen*; of unkn. orig.

smut blacken, smudge XVI; affect (grain) with smut XVII. Parallel formations with *sm..t* are OE. *smitt* smear, *smittian* pollute, *smītan* SMITE, ME. *ismotted*, *besmotered* stained (XIV), and also LG. *smutt*, MHG. *smuz*, *smutzen* (G. *schmutz*, *schmutzen*). So sb., fungous disease of plants marked by blackness; black or sooty mark; indecent language XVII. Hence **smutty** (of grain) XVI; dirty, blackened, obscene XVII.

snack (dial.) bite (esp. of a dog) XV; share, portion; drop of liquor XVII; morsel of food, light repast, 'bite' XVIII. - MDu. *snac(k)* in the first sense, rel. to *snacken*, var. of *snappen* SNAP; perh. orig. imit.

snaffle form of bridle-bit. XVI. prob. of LG. or Du. orig.; cf. (M)LG., (M)Du. *snavel* beak, mouth, corr. to OHG. *snabul* (G. *schnabel*); see -LE[1].

snag short stump projecting from a tree; sharp projection XVI; (orig. U.S.) trunk or branch in a river, etc. interfering with navigation; hence gen. obstacle XIX. prob. of Scand. orig. (cf. ON. *snaghyrndr* sharp-pointed (axe), Norw. dial. *snag(e)* sharp point, spike).

snail OE. *snæġ(e)l*, *sneġ(e)l* = OS. *snegil*, MLG. *sneil*, OHG. *snegil* (LG. *snagel*), ON. *snigill*, f. Gmc. **snaȝ-* **sneȝ-*; cf. -LE[1].

snake OE. *snaca* = MLG. *snake*, ON. *snákr*, *snókr*; rel. to OHG. *snahhan* crawl, and further to Ir. *snaighim* I crawl.

snap sb. quick or sudden bite XV; catch, effort, sound XVII; vb. bite quickly or suddenly, seize with sudden action XVI; break clean; make a cracking sound XVII. prob. - (M)LG., (M)Du. *snappen* seize; but partly imit. Comp. **snapdragon** A. antirrhinum XVI; B. Christmas game of snatching raisins from burning brandy XVIII.

snare trap consisting of a string with a running noose. Late OE. *sneara* - ON. *snara* = OS. *snari* (Du. *snaar*) string, OHG. *snarahha* snare. As applied to the strings of gut or hide stretched across the lower head of a side-drum prob. - MDu. or MLG. *snare*. Hence **snare** vb. XIV. So synon. **snarl**[1] XIV; see -LE[1].

snark imaginary animal invented by 'Lewis Carroll' (C. L. Dodgson) in 'The Hunting of the Snark', 1876.

snarl[2] make an angry sound with showing of the teeth. XVI. f. synon. †*snar* (XVI) - (M)LG. *snarren* = MHG. *snarren* (G. *schnarren*); see -LE[3].

snatch make a sudden snap at or seizure of. XIII. Obscurely rel. to SNACK. Hence **snatch** sb. †catch, hasp; †trap, snare XIV; hasty catch, sudden grab; short period; snack; small amount XVI.

sneak go stealthily, creep furtively. XVI. Obscurely rel. to early ME. *snike*, OE. *snīcan* creep, crawl, ON. *sníkja*.

sneer †snort XVI; smile contemptuously XVII. of unkn. orig. Hence sb. XVIII.

sneeze sb. and vb. Appears first (XV) in the form *snese* as a substitute in printed texts for an original *fnese* (from OE. *fnēsan*), which had become obs. XV.

snick cut, snip XVIII; (in cricket) XIX. Deduced from †*snick-a-snee*, †*snick or snee*, (alt. of) †*stick or snee* fight with knives (XVII) - Du. *steken* thrust, STICK, and *snee*, dial. var. of *snij(d)en* cut.

sniff vb. XIV. of imit. orig. Hence sb. XVIII.

snigger vb. XVIII. var. of *snicker* (XVII), of imit. orig.; see -ER[4]. Hence sb. XIX.

snip †snap, snatch; cut (up or off). XVI. - LG., Du. *snippen*, of imit. orig. Hence (or - LG. or Du. forms) **snip** sb. XVI.

snipe bird of the genus *Gallinago*. XIV. prob. of Scand. orig. (cf. Icel. *mýrisnipa*, Norw. *myr-*, *strandsnipa*).

snivel run at the nose XIV; be in a tearful state XVII. repr. OE. **snyflan*, implied in *snyflung* mucus of the nose, f. synon. *snofl*; cf. -LE[3]. Hence sb. XV.

snob (dial.) shoemaker, cobbler; †(Cambridge Univ.) townsman XVIII; †one with no claim to gentility XIX; one who vulgarly admires those of superior rank. of unkn. orig. Hence **snobbery, snobbish** XIX.

snoek (S. Afr.) large edible sea-fish. XIX. - Du. (cf. SNOOK).

snood hair-band. OE. *snōd*; of unkn. orig.

snook[1] sergeant-fish. XVII. - Du. *snoek* = (M)LG. *snōk*, prob. rel. to SNACK.

snook[2] derisive gesture with thumb to nose (phr. *cock a s.*). XIX (*snooks*). of unkn. orig.

snooker XIX. of unkn. orig.

snoop XIX. - Du. *snoepen* to eat (on the sly).

snooze vb. XVIII. Cant word of unkn. orig.

snore (dial.) snort; make harsh noises in sleep through mouth and nose. XIV. f. imit. base **snor-*; cf. (M)LG., (M)Du. *snorken*, and SNORT.

snorkel, schnorkel underwater breathing device, esp. on a submarine. XX. - G. *schnorchel*.

snort †snore; make an explosive noise by driving the breath through the nostrils. XIV. ult. of imit. orig.; cf. SNORE.

snot (dial.) snuff of a candle XIV; mucus of the nose XV. prob. - (M)LG., MDu. *snotte*, Du. *snot*, corr. to OE. *ġesnot*, MHG. *snuz*, f. Gmc. **snŭt-* (cf. next). Hence **snotty** (-Y[1]) XVI.

snout †elephant's trunk; nose, muzzle. XIII. ME. *snūte* - MLG., MDu. *snūt(e)* (Du. *snuit*); ult. f. Gmc. **snūt-*, whence also late OE. *snȳtan* clear the nose = (M)LG. *snûten*, OHG. *snûzen* (G. *schneuzen* snuff a candle, blow the nose), ON. *snýta*.

snow[1] frozen vapour of the air falling in flakes. OE. *snāw* = OS., OHG. *snēo* (Du. *sneeuw*, G. *schnee*), ON. *snǽr*, Goth. *snaiws* :- Gmc. **snaiwaz*, cogn. with Balto-Sl. forms, Ir. *snigid* it snows, Av. *snaēžaiti*; cf. L. *nix*, *niv-*, etc. Hence **snow** vb. XIII; repl. ME. *snewe*, OE. *snīwan* (G. *schneien*) :- WGmc. **sniȝwan*. Comps. and derivs. **snowball** XIV, **snowdrop** XVII, **snowflake** XVIII, **snow-shoe** XVII, **snow-white** OE. *snāwhwīt*, **snowy** OE. *snāwig*.

snow[2] small sailing-vessel. XVII. - Du. *sna(a)uw* or LG. *snau*; of unkn. orig.

snub rebuke or reprove sharply XIV; check, stop (obs. exc. naut.) XVI; (dial.) shorten XVIII. - ON. *snubba* (cf. Norw. and Sw. dial. *snubba*, Da. *snubbe* cut short, make stumpy); of unkn. orig. Hence adj. short and turned up, in **snub-nose** and **-nosed** adj. XVIII.

snuff[1] portion of candle-wick partly consumed. XIV. of unkn. orig. Hence **snuff** vb. remove the snuff from XV; extinguish XVII (sl. intr. with *out*, die XIX).

snuff[2] powdered tobacco for inhaling through the nostrils. XVII. - Du. *snuf*, prob. short for *snuftabak*, f. MDu. *snuffen* snuffle, whence Eng. *snuff* (XVI) inhale through the nostrils.

snuffle †sniff *at* in contempt; smell *at*; speak or draw air through the nose. XVI. prob. - LG., Du. *snuffelen*, f. imit. base **snuf-*, repr. also by SNUFF[2]; see -LE[3] and cf. SNIVEL.

snug (of a ship) trim, secure against bad weather XVI; in ease or comfort XVII. First in naut. use and prob. of LG. or Du. orig. (cf. LG. *snögger* slim, smart, Du. †*snuggher*, †*snoggher* (mod. *snugger*) clever, smart). Hence (see -LE[3]) **snuggle** lie snug or close. XVII.

so in such a manner; in that way, to that extent. OE. *swa*, lengthened *swā*, corr. to OS. *sō* (Du. *zo*), OHG. *sō*, *suo* (G. *so*), ON. *svá*, Goth. *swa* (also *swē*), rel. to OL. *suad* so, Oscan *svai*, *svae* if, *swā* and, Gr. *hōs* (:- **s*ϝ*ōs*) as.

-so adv. attached to *wh-* prons. and advs., and *how*, e.g. ME. *hwa so* whoso, *hwer so* whereso (reduced forms of OE. *swā hwā swā*, *swā hwǣr swā*, etc.), repl. gen. by *-ever* (*whoever*, *wherever*) and -SOEVER.

soak steep (trans. and intr.) OE.; permeate thoroughly XIV; percolate XV. OE. *socian*, corr. to WFlem. *soken*, *zoken*, rel. to OE. *soc* sucking at the breast, f. **suk-*, wk. grade of OE. *sūcan* SUCK.

soap sb. OE. *sāpe* = (M)LG. *sēpe*, MDu. *seepe* (Du. *zeep*), OHG. *seipha* (G. *seife*) :- WGmc. **saipō*. Hence vb. XVI.

soar XIV. Aphetic - (O)F. *essorer* (used refl.) :- Rom. **exaurāre*, f. L. EX-[1] + *aura* air in motion.

sob vb. XII. perh. of LG. or Du. orig. (cf. WFris. *sobje*, Du. dial. *sabben* suck).

sober temperate in food or drink; not drunk or drunken; grave, serious, sedate; subdued in tone XVI; restrained in thought, etc. XVII. - (O)F. *sobre* - L. *sōbrius*. So **sobriety** XV. - (O)F. or L.

sobriquet, soubriquet XVII. - F. *sobriquet*, earlier *soubriquet* (XV); identical with *soubriquet* (XIV) tap under the chin.

socage (hist.) tenure by service other than knight-service. XIV. - AN. *socage*, f. *soc* SOKE; see -AGE.

soccer see -ER[6].

sociable XVI. - F. *sociable* or L. *sociābilis*, f. *sociāre* unite, ASSOCIATE; see -ABLE. So **sociability** XV. **social** (-AL[1]) †allied, occurring between allies; marked by mutual intercourse XVI; pert. to human society XVIII. - (O)F. *social* or L. *sociālis* allied, companionable, sociable. So **socialism** XIX. - F. *socialisme*. **socialist** XIX. **society** A. (living in) association XVI; aggregate of persons living together XVII; B. collection of persons forming a community XVI. - (O)F. *société* - L. *societās*, *-tāt-*; see -TY[2]. **sociology** XIX. - F. *sociologie*.

Socinian (pert. to) a member of a heretical sect denying the divinity of Jesus Christ. XVII. - modL. *Sociniānus*, f. *Socinus*, latinization of *Soz(z)ini*, surname of two It. theologians of XVI.

sock[1] †light shoe OE.; half-hose XIV; shoe worn by comic actors on the Greek and Roman stage XVI. OE. *socc*, corr. to MLG., MDu. *socke* (Du. *sok*), OHG. *soch* (G. *socke*), ON. *sokkr*; Gmc. - L. *soccus* - Gr. *súkkhos*, *sukkhás*.

sock[2] (sl.) blow, beating; also vb. XVII. of unkn. orig.

socket †lance- or spear-head of the form of a ploughshare XIII; cavity to receive an object fitting into it XV. - AN. *soket*, dim. of (O)F. *soc* ploughshare; see -ET.

socle plain block or plinth serving as a pedestal. XVIII. - F. - It. *zoccolo* prop. wooden shoe, repr. L. *socculus*, dim. of *soccus* SOCK[1].

sod[1] piece of grass-grown earth. XV. - (M)LG., MDu. *sode* (Du. *zode*); of unkn. orig.

sod[2] gross term of abuse for a male person; also in milder use. XIX. sl. shortening of SODOMITE.

soda sodium carbonate. XVI. - medL., perh. back-formation f. *sodānum* glasswort, based on Arab. *ṣudā'* headache (for which the plant, containing soda, was used as a remedy), f. *ṣada'a* split. Hence **sodium** (chem.) metal forming the base of soda. XIX.

sodality religious guild for mutual help, etc. XVI. - F. or L., f. *sodālis* member of a brotherhood or corporation; see -ITY.

sodden †boiled XIII; †dull, stupid, expressionless XVI; saturated with moisture XIX. pp. of SEETHE.

sodomy XIII. - medL. *sodomia*, f. *Sodoma* the city of Sodom in Palestine the wickedness and destruction of which are recorded in Gen. 18-19. So **sodomite** one who commits sodomy XIV; inhabitant of Sodom XV. - (O)F. - late L. *Sodomīta*; see -ITE.

soever poet. **soe'er** SO + EVER used with generalizing or emphatic force. XVI. hence as a var. of *-ever*, as in *whosoever*, *wheresoever*.

sofa in the East, dais furnished with cushions and carpets XVII; long stuffed couch XVIII. ult. - Arab. *ṣuffa*, through F. *sofa*, etc.

soffit (arch.) under surface or ceiling of an architrave, etc. XVII. Earliest forms *soffita*, *-ito*, later *sof(f)ite, soffit* - F. *soffite* or It. *soffito, -ita* :- **suffictus, -icta*, for L. *suffixus* (see SUFFIX).

soft A. agreeable OE.; B. gentle, mild XII; C. impressionable, compliant XIII (silly, simple XVII); presenting a yielding surface. Late OE. *sōfte*, repl. earlier mutated *sēfte* = OS. *sāfti*, OHG. *semfti* :- WGmc. **samfti*; the un-mutated form, due to influence from the adv. (OE. *sōfte*, etc.), is paralleled in MLG. *sachte, safte*, LG. *sacht*, MDu. *sachte, safte* (Du. *zacht*), (M)HG. *sanft*. Hence **soften** (-EN[5]) XIV.

soggy (dial., U.S.) swampy. XVIII. f. dial. *sog* marsh + -Y[1].

soh var. of SOL[2].

soi-disant self-styled XVIII; pretended XIX. - F., *soi* oneself, *disant*, prp. of *dire* say.

soil[1] (piece of) ground or earth, land, country; ground as cultivated. XIV. - AN. *soil* land, perh. repr. L. *solium* seat, *solum* (F. *sol*) ground.

soil[2] †muddy place; stretch of water as refuge for a hunted animal XV; stain, pollution XVI; filth, ordure XVII. - OF. **soille, souille* (mod. *souille* muddy place), f. *souiller* SOIL[3].

soil[3] A. defile, pollute XIII; sully, tarnish XVI; B. take to water or marshy ground XV. - OF. *soill(i)er, suill(i)er* (mod. *souiller*) :- Rom. **suculāre*, f. L. *suculus, -ula*, dim. of *sūs* SOW[1].

soil[4] (dial.) feed (cattle) with green fodder, orig. for purgation. XVII. perh. a use of SOIL[3].

soirée XIX. - F., f. *soir* evening :- L. *sērum* late hour, n. of *sērus* late.

sojourn reside, stay. XIII. - OF. *so(r)jorner* (mod. *séjourner*) :- Rom. **subdiurnāre* 'spend the day', f. L. SUB- + late L. *diurnum* day. So **sojourn** sb. XIII. - AN. *su(r)jurn*, OF. *sojor*, etc. (mod. *séjour*).

soke right of local jurisdiction; area of this. XIV. - medL. *sōca* - OE. *sōcn* attack, resort, right of prosecution or jurisdiction, administrative district = ON. *sókn*, Goth. *sōkns* search, inquiry :- Gmc. **sōkniz*, f. **sōk-* (see SEEK).

sol[1] sun; (alch.) gold XIV; (her.) or XVII. - L. *sōl* SUN.

sol[2] (mus.) fifth note of the scale in solmization. XIV. See UT. Hence **solfa** set of syllables (do, re, mi, etc.) sung to the notes of the major scale XVI; as vb., repl. †*solf(e)* (XIV) - (O)F. *solfier*. So **solfeggio** exercise in which the solfa is employed. XVIII. - It. **solmization** XVIII. - F., f. *solmiser*, f. *sol* SOL[2] + *mi* MI. See -IZE, -ATION.

solace consolation or means of it; †delight, amusement. XIII. - OF. *solas, -atz* (mod. dial. *soulas*) :- L. *sōlātium*, f. *sōlārī* relieve, console. So **solace** vb. XIII. - OF. *solacier*.

solan gannet. XV. In earliest use Sc.; obscurely f. ON. *súla* gannet.

solander box made in the form of a book to contain botanical specimens, etc. XVIII. f. name of D. C. *Solander*, Sw. botanist (1736–82).

solar XV. - L. *sōlāris*, f. *sōl* SUN; see -AR. So **solarium** sundial; apartment or area exposed to the sun. XIX; see -IUM.

solder sb. XIV (*soudur*). - (O)F. *soudure*, f. *souder*, †*solder* :- L. *solidāre* fasten together, f. *solidus* SOLID. Hence vb. XV.

soldier XIII (*sauder, souder, souldeour*, etc.). - OF. *soud(i)er, saudier, so(l)dier*, f. *sou(l)de* pay :- L. *solidus* gold coin of imperial times, sb. use of *solidus* SOLID; see -IER[2].

sole[1] under-surface of the foot XIV; bottom of a boot or shoe; †foundation; sill XV; lower part, bottom XVII. - OF. :- popL. **sola* (whence OE. **solu* or **sola*, once in pl. *solen*), for L. *solea* sandal, sill, f. *solum* bottom, pavement, sole of the foot.

sole[2] flatfish of genus *Solea*. XIV. - (O)F. - Pr. *sola* :- Rom. **sola* for L. *solea*, identical with prec.; so named because of its shape.

sole[3] single, unmarried XIV; alone, solitary XV; one and only; exclusive XVI. ME. *soul(e)* - OF. *soul(e)* (mod. *seul(e)*) :- L. *sōlus*, fem. *sōla* alone, sole.

solecism violation of good grammar or good manners; impropriety. XVI. - F. *solécisme* or L. *solœcismus* - Gr. *soloikismós*, f. *sóloikos* using incorrect syntax, etc., said by ancient writers to refer to the corruption of the Attic dialect by Athenian colonists at *Soloi* in Cilicia; see -ISM.

solemn accompanied with ceremony; grave, serious. XIV. ME. *solem(p)ne* - OF. *solem(p)ne* (superseded by *solennel*) - L. *sollem(p)nis, -ennis*, celebrated ceremonially and at a fixed date, festive, customary, f. *sollus* whole, entire. So **solemnity** XIII. - OF. *solem(p)nité* (mod. *solennité*) - L. *sollem(p)nitās*. **solemnize** XIV. - OF. *solemniser* - medL. **solemnization** XV.

solen razor-fish. XVII. - L. *sōlēn* - Gr. *sōlḗn* channel, pipe, shellfish.

solfa, solfeggio see SOL[2].

solfatara volcanic vent exhaling sulphurous vapour. XVIII. f. name of a volcano near Naples, Italy, f. *solfo* SULPHUR.

solicit A. †disturb, trouble XV; †entreat, petition, incite XVI; B. †manage, attend to (affairs) XV; †urge, plead; sue for; also intr. XVI. - (O)F. *solliciter* - L. *sollicitāre* agitate, harass, entice, (medL.) look after, f. *sollicitus* agitated, f. *sollus* whole, entire + *citus* put in motion, pp. of *ciēre*. So **solicitation** †management, transaction XV; entreaty XVI. - (O)F. - L. **solicitor** †instigator, †manager, agent, deputy XV; agent in a court of law XVI. - (O)F. *solliciteur*. **solicitous** anxious, careful. XVI. f. L. *sollicitus*. **solicitude** XV. - (O)F. - L.

solid free from empty spaces XIV; of three dimensions XV; of dense consistency; firm and substantial XVI. - (O)F. *solide* or L. *solidus*, rel. to *salvus* SAFE, *sollus* whole. Also sb. XV. So **solidarity** XIX. - F. *solidarité*. **solidity** XVI.

solifidian (theol.) one who holds that faith alone is sufficient for justification. XVI. f. L. *sōli-*, comb. form of *sōlus* SOLE[3] + *fides* FAITH; see -IAN.

soliloquy XVII. - late L. *sōliloquium*, f. *sōlus* SOLE[3] + *loquī* speak. Hence **soliloquize** XVIII.

soliped animal with uncloven hoof. XVII. - F. *solipède* or modL. *soliped, -pēs*, for L. *solidipēs*, f. *solidus* SOLID + *pēs* FOOT.

solipsism (philos.) theory that the self is the only object of knowledge. XIX. f. L. *sōlus* SOLE[3] + *ipse* self- + -ISM.

solitary XIV. - L. *sōlitārius*, f. *sōlitās* solitariness, f. *sōlus* SOLE[3]; see -ITY, -ARY. So **solitaire** recluse; precious stone set by itself; game to be played by one person; loose necktie. XVIII.

- (O)F. **solitude** XIV (not frequent before XVII). - (O)F. or L.

solmization see SOL[2].

solo (mus.) part to be sung or played by one performer alone. XVII. - It. *solo* :- L. *sōlus* SOLE[2]. Hence **soloist** XIX.

solstice XIII. - (O)F. - L. *sōlstitium*, f. *sōl* SOL[1] + *stit-*, var. of *stat-* (as in STATION).

soluble †free from constipation XIV; capable of being melted or dissolved XV; solvable XVIII. - (O)F. - late L. *solūbilis*, f. *solvere* loosen, SOLVE; see -BLE. So **solution** solving, explanation, dissolving XIV; breach XVI.

solve †loosen, unbind XV; explain, clear up; clear off (a debt) XVI. - L. *solvere* unfasten, free, pay, for **seluere*, f. **se* SE- + *luere* pay. So **solvent** able to pay; dissolving (also sb.) XVII. - prp. of L. *solvere*.

somatic pert. to the body. XVIII. - Gr. *sōmatikós*, f. *sôma*, *sōmat-* body; see -IC. So **somato-**, comb. form of Gr. *sôma*.

sombre marked by gloom XVIII; dark in colour XIX. - (O)F., adj. use of OF. sb., based on Rom. *subombrāre*, f. L. SUB- + *umbra* shade, shadow.

sombrero †Oriental umbrella XVI; broad-brimmed hat XVIII. - Sp., f. *sombra* shade = OF. *sombre* (see prec.).

some †a certain; one or other; a certain amount or number of; also as sb. or pron. OE. *sum* = OS., OHG. *sum*, ON. *sumr*, Goth. *sums* :- Gmc. **sumaz* :- IE. **sm̥os*, the base of which is repr. also by Gr. *hamôs* somehow, Skr. *samá-*, Av. *hama-* some, every. Cf. SAME. Comps. **somebody, -one** XIV, **somehow** XVIII, **something** OE., **sometime** XIII, **-times** XVI, **somewhat, -where** XII.

-some[1] suffix repr. OE. *-sum*, rel. by gradation to OS., OHG. *-sam* (Du. *-zaam*, G. *-sam*), ON. *-samr*, Goth. **-sams*, added to sbs., adjs., and vbs., to form adjs. denoting a quality, condition, temperament, etc. Of the OE. formations *winsome* remains in literary use, *longsome*, *lovesome* are arch. or dial.; many others are of ME. age, as *cumbersome*, *fulsome*, *handsome*, *wholesome*; later are *quarrelsome*, *tiresome*. In *buxom* and *lissom* the suffix is disguised.

-some[2] repr. OE. *sum* SOME, used after g. pl. of a numeral, as *fiftēna sum* (being) one of (a company of) fifteen, surviving in descriptions of games or contests in which persons of the number designated take part, as *twosome*, *threesome*, *foursome*.

somersault sb. XVI. - OF. *sombresau(l)t*, alt. of *sobresault* (mod. *soubresaut*) - Pr. **sobresaut*, f. *sobre* (:- L. *suprā*) above + *saut* (:- L. *saltus*) leap. Hence vb. XIX.

somnambulism XVIII. f. L. *somnus* sleep + *ambulāre* walk + -ISM. So **somnambulist, somnambulation** XVIII.

somni- comb. form of L. *somnus* sleep, as in **somniferous** XVII.

somnolent inclining to sleep XV; inclined to sleep XVI. - F. *somnolent* or L. *somnolentus*, f. *somnus* sleep. So **somnolence** XIV.

son OE. *sunu* = OS., OHG. *sunu* (Du. *zoon*, G. *sohn*), ON. *sunr*, *sonr*, Goth. *sunus* :- Gmc. **sunuz*, rel. more immed. to Balto-Sl. and Indo-Iran. forms (OSl. *synŭ*, Skr. *sūnú-*), and remotely to OIr. *suth* (:- **sutu*) offspring, Gr. *huiús*, *huiós* (:- **sujus*) son.

sonant (phon.) voiced. XIX. - L. *sonāns*, *-ant-*, prp. of *sonāre* sound.

sonata (mus.) †piece of instrumental music; now, one for one or two instruments, normally consisting of three or four movements. XVII. - It. *sonata*, fem. pp. of *sonare* sound.

song OE. *sang* (*song*) = OS. *sang* (Du. *zang*). OHG. *sanc* (G. *sang*), ON. *sǫngr*, Goth. *saggws* :- Gmc. **saŋʒwaz*, f. **saŋʒw-* **seŋʒw-* SING. Hence **songster** singer. OE. *sangestre*; whence **songstress** (XVIII; see -ESS[1]).

sonorous XVII. f. L. *sonōrus*, f. *sonor*, *sonōr-* sound; see -OUS.

sonnet (pros.) †short poem; poem of fourteen 10-syllable lines with a particular rhyme-pattern. XVI (*sonet*). - F. *sonnet* or its source It. *sonetto*, dim. of *suono* sound; see -ET. Hence **sonneteer** XVII. Partly - It. *sonettiere*.

sonsy lucky, fortunate XVI; buxom, comely and pleasant XVIII. orig. Sc., Ir. and north. dial.; f. (dial.) *sonse* (XIV) abundance, prosperity - Ir., Gael. *sonas* good fortune, f. *sona* fortunate, happy; see -Y[1].

soon OE. *sōna* = OS. *sāno*, *sān(a)*, OHG. *sān(o)* :- WGmc. **sǣnō*.

soot OE. *sōt* = MLG. *sōt* (G. dial. *sott*), MDu. *soet*, *zoet*, ON. *sót* :- Gmc. **sōtam* 'that which settles', f. IE. **sōd-* **sēd-* SIT. Hence **sooty** (-Y[1]) XIII.

sooth (arch. as in *in (good) s.*) truth. OE. *sōð* = OS. *sōð*, f. corr. adj. OE. *sōð* = OS. *sōð*, ON. *sannr*, *saðr* :- Gmc. **sanþaz* :- IE. **sontos*, rel. to Goth. **sunjis* true (in fem. *sunja*) :- IE. **sn̥tyós*; cf. Skr. *satyá-*. Hence **soothfast** truthful, faithful. OE. *sōðfæst*. **soothsayer** †one who speaks the truth; one who claims to foretell the future XIV.

soothe †prove to be true OE.; †declare to be true XVI; †confirm, encourage; †please or flatter by assent; †gloss over; calm, mollify XVII; allay, assuage XVIII. OE. (*ġe*)*sōðian*, f. *sōð* SOOTH.

sop piece of bread, etc. dipped in liquid OE.; milksop XVII. Late OE. *sopp*, corr. to MLG. *soppe*, OHG. *sopfa* bread and milk, prob. f. wk. grade of the base of OE. *sūpan* SUP[1]. So **sop** vb. dip in liquid OE. *soppian* (thereafter not till XVI, f. the sb.); drench, soak XVII; become wet XIX. **sopping** XIX. **soppy** †full of sops XVII; (colloq.) foolishly sentimental XIX.

sophism specious but fallacious argument. XIV. ME. *sophime*, *-eme* - OF. *sophime* (also mod. *sophisme* after L. and Gr., to which the Eng. form was later assim.) - L. *sophisma* - Gr. *sóphisma* clever device, trick, argument, f. *sophízesthai* devise, f. *sophós* wise, clever; see -ISM. So **sophist** XVI. - L. *sophistēs* - Gr. **sophister** sophist. XIV. **sophistic** XVI, **-ical** XV. **sophisticate** (-ATE[3]) †adulterate XIV; corrupt, falsify, as by debasing admixture XVII. **sophistication** XIV. - OF. or medL. **sophistry** XIV. - OF. *sophistrie* (mod. *-erie*) or medL. *sophistria*.

sophomore (at universities, now U.S.) student in his second year. XVII. Earlier *sophumer* (-ER[1]), beside prp. *sophuming*, f. *sophum*, obs. var. of SOPHISM.

soporiferous producing sleep. XVI. f. L. *sopōrifer*, f. *sopor*, *-ōr-* sleep; see -IFEROUS. So **soporific** (-FIC). XVII.

soprano XVIII. - It., f. *sopra* above.

sorb (fruit of) the service tree XVI; rowan XVIII. - F. *sorbe* or L. *sorbus* service tree, *sorbum* service berry.

sorbet XVI. - F. - It. *sorbetto* - Turk. *şerbet* SHERBET.

sorcerer XVI. Extension, with -ER[1], of late ME. *sorser* - (O)F. *sorcier* :- Rom. **sortiārius*, f. *sors*, *sort-* lot (see SORT); see -ER[2]. So **sorceress** (-ESS[1]) XIV. - AN. *sorceresse*. **sorcery** XIII. - OF. *sorcerie*.

sordid foul, dirty (lit. and fig.) XVI; characterized by mean or ignoble motives XVII. - F. *sordide* or L. *sordidus*, f. *sordēre* be dirty; see -ID[1].

sore †bodily suffering, disease; place where the skin is broken or inflamed; †grief, trouble. OE. *sār* = OS., OHG. *sēr* (Du. *zeer*, G. †*sehr*), ON. *sár*, Goth. *sair* :- Gmc. **sairam*. So adj. (arch.) painful, grievous; painful, aching, (now) with skin inflamed, etc. OE.; pained, distressed XIII. OE. *sār* = OS., OHG. *sēr* (Du. *zeer*, G. *sehr*), ON. *sárr* :- Gmc. **sairaz*. adv. (arch., dial.) painfully, grievously. OE. *sāre* = OS., OHG. *sēro* (Du. *zeer*, G. *sehr* greatly, very). **sorely** (-LY[2]). OE. *sārlīċe*.

sorghum Indian millet XVI; Chinese sugar cane; genus of grasses XIX. modL. - It. *sorgo*, perh. :- Rom. **syricum* (cf. medL. *sur(i)cum*) Syrian.

sorites (logic) chain syllogism, in which the conclusion is formed of the first subject and the last predicate. XVI. - L. *sōrītēs* - Gr. *sōrítēs*, f. *sōrós* heap.

sorner (Sc.) sponger. XV. f. *sorn* vb., f. *sorren* (XIII, *sorthyn*) service of vassals in Scotland and Ireland consisting of giving hospitality to the superior or his men - Ir. †*sorthan* free quarters.

sororicide[1] one who kills his or her sister. XVII. f. *soror* SISTER + -CIDE[1]. So **sororicide**[2] (-CIDE[2]) the killing of one's sister XVIII.

sorrel[1] (leaves of) plant of the genus *Rumex*, having a sour taste. XIV. - OF. *sorele*, *surele* (mod. dial. *surelle*), f. *sur* sour - Gmc. **sūraz*; see SOUR, -EL[2].

sorrel[2] (horse) of bright chestnut colour. XV. - OF. *sorel* adj., f. *sor* yellowish, of Gmc. orig.; see -EL[2].

sorrow mental pain or distress. OE. *sorh*, *sorg* = OS. *sor(a)ga* (Du. *zorg*), OHG. *s(w)orga* (G. *sorge*), ON. *sorg*, Goth. *saurga*; Gmc. sb. of unkn. orig., with corr. vb. OE. *sorgian*, etc. Hence **sorrowful.** OE. *sorhful*.

sorry pained at heart OE.; worthless, poor XIII. OE. *sāriġ* = OS., OHG. *sērag* :- WGmc. **sairaʒ-*, *-iʒ-*, f. Gmc. **sairam* SORE sb.; see -Y[1].

sort kind, species XIV; (arch.) manner, way XVI. - (O)F. *sorte* :- Rom. **sorta*, alt. of L. *sors*, *sort-* voting tablet, lot, fortune, condition (AL. sort, kind). So **sort** vb. †allot; arrange, assort XIV; (arch.) agree or associate *with* XVI. - OF. *sortir* or L. *sortīrī*; later f. the sb. or aphetic of ASSORT.

sortie †knot of ribbon XVII; sally by a besieged garrison XVIII. - F. *sortie* a going out.

sortilege casting of lots. XIV. - (O)F. *sortilège* - medL. *sortilegium*, f. *sortilegus* diviner, f. *sors*, *sort-* lot + *legere* choose.

sostenuto (mus.) in a sustained manner. XVIII. - It., pp. of *sostenere* SUSTAIN.

sot †fool OE.; habitual drunkard XVI. Late OE. *sott* - medL. *sottus*, of unkn. orig.; reinforced from (O)F. *sot*.

sotto voce in a subdued voice. XVIII. - It., i.e. *sotto* under, *voce* voice.

sou French coin. XIX. - F., sg. form deduced from *sous*, †*soux*, pl. of OF. *sout* :- (sb. use of) L. *solidus* SOLID.

soubrette lady's maid, maidservant (in a play or opera). XVIII. - F. - modPr. *soubreto*, fem. of *soubret* coy.

soubriquet see SOBRIQUET.

souchong fine variety of black tea. XVIII. - Chinese *hsiao chung* small sort.

soufflé light dish made by mixing materials with white of egg. XIX. - F. *soufflé*, pp. of *souffler* :- L. *sufflāre*, f. SUB- + *flāre* BLOW[1].

sough rushing or murmuring sound. XIV. ME. *swo(u)gh*, *swow*, f. *swoghe*, OE. *swōgan* make such a sound, rel. to OE. *swēgan* sound, Goth. *-swōgjan*.

soul †life; spiritual or emotional part of man; disembodied spirit of a man OE.; vital principle XIV; essential part *of* XVI. OE. *sāwol*, *sāw(e)l* = Goth. *saiwala*, corr. to OS. *sēola* (Du. *ziel*), OHG. *sē(u)la* (G. *seele*); Gmc. **saiwalō*, corr. formally to Gr. *aiólos* quick-moving, easily moved.

sound[1] †swimming; †sea, water OE.; swimming-bladder of fish XIV; (from Scand.) narrow channel of water XV. OE. *sund* = ON. *sund* swimming, strait :- Gmc. **sundam*, f. **sum-* **swem-* SWIM.

sound[2] unhurt, uninjured XII; healthy XIII; based on fact or good grounds XV; solid, ample XVI. ME. *sund*, aphetic of *isund*, OE. *ġesund* = OS. *gisund* (Du. *gezond*), OHG. *gisunt* (G. *gesund*) :- WGmc. **ʒasundaz*. Hence adv. fast *asleep* XIV.

sound[3] that which is or may be heard. XIII. ME. *sun*, *so(u)n* - AN. *s(o)un*, (O)F. *son* :- L. *sonus*. So **sound** vb. cause to make a sound XIII; emit a sound XIV. ME. *sune*, *so(u)ne* - AN. *suner*, OF. *soner* (mod. *sonner*) :- L. *sonāre*. The form with *-d* appears XV, and is established XVI.

sound[4] †penetrate XIV; intr. and trans. ascertain the depth of water XV; measure or examine as by sounding XVI. - (O)F. *sonder* use the sounding-lead :- Rom. **subundāre*, f. L. SUB- + *unda* wave. So **sound** sb. †act of sounding XVI; (surg.) instrument for probing XVIII.

soup XVII. - (O)F. *soupe* (i) sop, (ii) broth poured on slices of bread :- late L. *suppa*, f. **suppāre* soak, of Gmc. orig. Cf. SOP.

soupçon slight trace (of). XVIII. - F., repr. OF. *sou(s)peçon* :- late L. *suspectiō*, *-ōn-*, for L. *suspiciō* SUSPICION.

sour of tart or acid taste OE.; bitter, extremely distasteful XII; morose, peevish XIII. OE. *sūr* = OS., OHG. *sūr* (Du. *zuur*, G. *sauer*), ON. *súrr* :- Gmc. **sūraz*. Hence **sour** vb. XIV. **sourness** OE. *sūrnes*.

source A. †rising on the wing; B. fountain-head of a stream; place of origin. XIV. ME. *sours(e)* -

OF. *so(u)rs* m., *sourse*, (also mod.) *source* fem., sb. uses of m. and fem. pp. of *sourdre* rise, spring :- L. *surgere* rise, SURGE[2].

souse steep (meat, etc.) in pickle XIV; plunge in water XV; drench, soak XVI. f. (dial.) *souse* (XIV) pickled meat - OF. *sous, souz* - OS. *sultia*, OHG. *sulza* (G. *sülze*) brine, f. Gmc. **sult-* **salt-* SALT.

soutache narrow flat braid. XIX. - F. - Hung. *sujtás*.

soutane XIX. - F. - It. *sottana*, f. *sotto* under.

souter (Sc. and north.) shoemaker, cobbler. OE. *sūtere*, corr. to OHG. *sūtāri*, ON. *sútari* - L. *sūtor* shoemaker, f. *suere* SEW, stitch; see -TOR, -ER[1].

south adv., adj. OE.; sb. XIII. OE. *sūð* = OS. *sūth* (LG. *sud*), OHG. *sunt*, ON. (with *r*-suffix) *suðr* (:- **sunþr*). So **southerly** (-LY[1]) XVI. **southern.** OE. *sūðerne*. Also comp. **southeast, -west, southward(s)** OE.

souvenir XVIII. - F. 'memory', 'keepsake', sb. use of *souvenir* :- L. *subvenīre* come to the mind, f. SUB- + *venīre* COME.

sovereign (supreme) ruler XIII; English gold coin of 20 shillings value XVI. ME. *soverein* - OF. *so(u)verain, -ein* (mod. *souverain*) :- Rom. **superānus*, f. *super* above. Also adj. supreme, paramount. XIV. So **sovereignty** (-TY[2]) XIV. - OF. *so(u)vereinete* (mod. *souveraineté*).

soviet XX. - Russ. *sovét* council.

sow[1] female swine OE.; structure to cover a besieging force XIII; (prob. after Du.) oblong mass of metal XVI. OE. *sugu* = OS. *suga*, MLG., MDu. *soge* (Du. *zeug*), rel. to OE., OHG. *sū* (G. *sau*), ON. *sýr*; f. IE. base **sû-*, repr. also by L. *sūs* pig, Gr. *hûs*, etc.; cf. SWINE.

sow[2] pt. *sowed*, pp. *sown* scatter or plant seed so that it may grow. OE. str. vb. *sāwan*, corr. to OS. *sāian* (Du. *zaaien*), OHG. *sāwen, sā(h)en* (G. *säen*), ON. *sá*, Goth. *saian*; Gmc. **sǣjan*, repr. IE. base **sē(i)-*, as in L. pt. *sēvī* (of *serere*), and in SEED.

soy sauce prepared from the soya bean. XVII. (prob. through Du. *soya*) - Jap. *shōyu* (dial. *sōyu*). So **soya** XVII. - Du.

spa medicinal spring or well XVII; locality possessing this XVIII. f. name *Spa* of a watering-place in Belgium noted for its curative mineral springs.

space extent of time or distance. XIII. Aphetic - (O)F. *espace* - L. *spatium* (in medL. also *spacium*). So **space** vb. place in respect of distance or extent. XVI. - (O)F. *espacer*, or f. the sb. **spacious** XIV. - L. *spatiōsus* or OF. *spacios* (mod. *-ieux*).

spade[1] tool for digging, etc. OE. *spadu, spada* = OS. *spado* (Du. *spade, spa*), a word of the LG. area; rel. to Gr. *spáthē* blade, paddle, etc.

spade[2] (pl.) suit of playing cards with black spade-shaped marks. XVI. - It. *spade*, pl. of *spada* - L. *spatha* - Gr. *spáthē* (see prec.).

spadille ace of spades in ombre and quadrille. XVIII. - F. - Sp. *espadilla*, dim. of *espada* sword.

spadix (bot.) inflorescence consisting of a thick fleshy spike. XVIII. - L. *spādīx* - Gr. *spádīx* palm-branch.

spae (north. and Sc.) prophesy. XIII. - ON. *spá*, of unkn. orig.

spaghetti XIX. - It., pl. of dim. of *spago* string, of unkn. orig.

spall chip, splinter. XV. var. of contemp. *spale*, of unkn. orig.

spalpeen labourer, farm-hand XVIII; scamp, rascal XIX. - Ir. *spailpín*, of unkn. orig.

spam name of a variety of tinned meat. XX. **P.**; f. initial and final letters of *sp*iced h*am*.

span[1] distance from tip of thumb to extended tip of little finger OE.; small piece or space XIV; short space of time XVI; space between supports of an arch, etc. XVIII. OE. *span(n)* = MLG. *spen(ne)*, (M)Du. *spanne*, OHG. *spanna* (G. *spanne*), ON. *spǫnn*; in ME. prob. also - OF. *espan(n)e, espan* (mod. *empan*), of Gmc. orig. Hence vb. †seize XIV; measure with outstretched hand XVI; form an arch over XVII. perh. partly - MLG. *spannen*; not continuous with rel. OE. *spannan*. So **spanner** †tool for winding up the wheel lock of a firearm XVII; instrument for turning a nut, etc. XVIII. - G. *spanner*; see -ER[1].

span[2] harness, yoke (e.g. to a vehicle) XVI; (naut.) fix, attach XVIII. - (M)Du. or (M)LG. *spannen* = OE. *spannan*, OHG. *spannan* (G. *spannen*).

spandrel (archit.) space between either shoulder of an arch and the surrounding rectangular framework. XV. perh. f. AN. *spaund(e)re*, poss. f. *espaundre* EXPAND; see -EL[2].

spangle thin piece of glittering metal for ornament XV; small sparkling particle XVI. dim. (see -LE[1]) f. synon. †*spange* (XV) - MDu. *spange* (Du. *spang*) or rel. ON. *spǫng, spang-* clasp, brooch :- Gmc. **spangō*.

Spaniard XIV. ME. *Spaynard*, aphetic - OF. *Espaignart, Espaniard*, f. *Espaigne* (mod. *Espagne*), whence Eng. **Spain** (XIII); corr. to Sp. *España* :- late L. *Spānia* for earlier *Hispānia, Ispānia*; see -ARD. Prob. infl. by MDu. *Spaensch* (Du. *Spaansch*). So **Spanish** pert. to Spain XIII (*Spainisce*); the language of Spain XV.

spaniel XIV (*spaynel*). Aphetic - OF. *espaigneul* (mod. *épagneul*) :- Rom. **spāniōlūs*, for *Hispāniōlus* Spanish, f. *Hispānia* Spain, see prec.

spank[1] slap with the open hand. XVIII. perh. imit. of the sound.

spank[2] (dial.) travel with vigour and speed. XIX. Presumably back-formation from **spanker** (-ER[1]) †gold coin XVIII; fine large thing; fast horse XIX; or **spanking** (-ING[2]) very large or fine XVII; fast-moving XVIII; of unkn. orig.

spar[1] (dial.) rafter of a roof XIII; (orig. and esp. naut.) pole or length of timber XIV. - ON. *sperra* or aphetic - OF. *esparre* (mod. *épare, épar*) or :- its Gmc. source, repr. by MLG., MDu. *sparre* (Du. *spar*), OHG. *sparro* (G. *sparren*), ON. *sparri*.

spar[2] †strike out with the feet or a weapon OE.; engage in or practise boxing XVIII. OE. *sperran, spyrran, *spierran*, corr. to ON. *sperrask* kick out; of unkn. orig.

spar[3] gen. term for certain crystalline minerals. XVI. - MLG. *spar*, rel. to OE. *spæren* of plaster or mortar, *spærstān* gypsum.

sparable small headless wedge-shaped iron nail. XVII. alt. of *sparrow-bill* (XVII), so named from the shape; see SPARROW, BILL[2].

spare leave unharmed, abstain from destroying, injuring, using OE.; part with, do without, keep in reserve XIII; avoid incurring XIV. OE. *sparian* = OS. *sparon*, OHG. *sparōn* (Du., G. *sparen*), ON. *spara* :- Gmc. **sparōjan*. So adj. XIV. Cf. OE. *spær* sparing, frugal.

spark A. small particle of fire OE.; vital principle XIV; B. woman of beauty or wit XVI; elegant young man XVII; beau, lover XVIII. OE. *spærca*, *spearca* = (M)LG., MDu. *sparke*, of unkn. orig. The identity of group B of the senses is doubtful. Hence vb. XIII. **sparkle** vb. XII (see -LE[3]), sb. XIV.

sparling (north.) smelt, *Osmerus eperlanus*. XIV. Aphetic - OF. *esperlinge* (mod. *éperlan*), of Gmc. orig. (cf. MLG., MDu. *spirlinc*, G. *spierling*).

sparrow OE. *spearwa* = OHG. *sparo*, MHG. *sparwe*, ON. *spǫrr*, Goth. *sparwa* :- Gmc. **sparwan-*, **sparwaz*.

sparrowhawk XV. repl. arch. or dial. *sparhawk*, f. OE. *spearhafoc* (= ON. *sparr-haukr*), f. stem of *spearwa* SPARROW + *hafoc* HAWK[1].

sparse widely spaced or distributed. XVIII. - L. *sparsus*, pp. of *spargere* scatter.

Spartan native of Sparta XV; adj. XVI. - L. *Spartānus*, f. *Sparta* (Gr. *Spartā*, *-ē*); see -AN.

spasm sudden or violent muscular contraction. XIV. - (O)F. *spasme* or L. *spasmus*, *spasma* - Gr. *spasmós*, *spásma*, f. *spân* draw, pull. So **spasmodic** marked by spasms or twitches XVII; intermittent XIX. - modL. *spasmōdicus*, f. Gr. *spasmṓdēs*. **spastic** marked by spasmodic symptoms. XVIII. - L. *spasticus* - Gr. *spastikós*.

spat[1] spawn of shellfish. XVII. - AN. *spat*, of unkn. orig.

spat[2] short gaiter worn over the instep. XIX. Shortening of *spatterdash* (XVII) long gaiter or legging for protection from splashing, f. SPATTER + DASH.

spatchcock (orig. in Ir. use) fowl prepared by being summarily split open and grilled. XVIII. of unkn. orig.; cf. *spitchcock* (XVI) eel cut into short pieces, dressed, and cooked.

spate flood or rising in a river. XV (orig. north. and Sc.). of unkn. orig.

spathe (bot.) large sheathing leaf enveloping inflorescence. XVIII. - L. *spatha* - Gr. *spáthē* (see SPADE[1]).

spatial XIX. f. L. *spatium* SPACE + -AL[1].

spatter XVI. frequent. f. imit. base repr. also in LG., Du. *spatten* burst, spout, WFlem. *spatteren*; see -ER[4].

spatula flat elongated implement, XVI. - L., var. of *spathula*, dim. of *spatha* SPATHE.

spavin hard bony tumour in a horse's leg. XV. ME. *spaveyne*, aphetic - OF. *espavin*, var. of *esparvain* (mod. *éparvin*), of uncert. orig.

spawn cast spawn XIV-XV; engender XVI. Aphetic - AN. *espaundre* shed roe, var. of OF. *espandre* (mod. *épandre*) shed, spill, pour out :- L. *expandere* EXPAND. Hence **spawn** sb. eggs of fishes, etc. XV.

spay remove the ovaries from (a female). XV. Aphetic - AN. *espeier*, OF. *espeer*, f. *espee* (mod. *épée*) sword :- L. *spatha* (see SPADE[1]).

speak pt. *spoke*, pp. *spoken* utter words. Late OE. str. vb. *specan* (corr. to MDu. *speken*, OHG. *spehhen*); superseding parallel OE. *sprecan*, which did not survive beyond XII = OS. *sprekan* (Du. *spreken*), OHG. *sprehhan* (G. *sprechen*). Hence **speaker** (of the House of Commons) XIV; see -ER[1].

spear sb. OE. *spere* = OS., OHG. *sper* (Du., G. *speer*), ON. (pl.) *spjǫr*. Hence vb. XVIII.

spec colloq. abbrev. of SPECULATION. XVII (orig. U.S.).

special exceeding what is usual or common XIII; having a particular purpose XIV. Aphetic - OF. *especial* ESPECIAL or - L. *speciālis*, f. *speciēs* SPECIES; see -AL[1]. Hence **specially** XIII, **specialist** XIX. So **speciality** XV. - OF. *especialité*. **specialize** XVII. - F. *spécialiser*. **specialty** XIV. - OF. *(e)specialté*.

species outward form (surviving spec. theol. of the elements in the Eucharist); kind (gen. and spec.). XVI. - L. (sg. and pl.) *speciēs*, f. *spec-* of *specere* look, behold. So **specie** phr. *in s.*, in kind; in the real form XVI; in actual coin XVII; hence sb. coined money XVII; abl. sg. of *speciēs*. **specific** XVII. - late L. *specificus*. **specification** XVII. - medL. **specify** XIII. - OF. or medL. *specificāre*. **specimen** †experiment; †pattern; typical example. XVII. - L. *specimen*. **specious** †fair to look upon XIV; attractive or plausible but lacking in genuineness XVII. - L. *speciōsus*.

speck small spot. OE. *specca*, repr. otherwise only in **speckle** sb. XV. - MDu. *spekkel* (Du. *spikkel*); see -LE[1]. Also vb. XVI. Hence **speckled** (-ED[2]) XIV.

specs colloq. abbrev. of *spectacles* (see next). XIX.

spectacle prepared display, object exhibited; (now usu. pl.) device for assisting defective eyesight. XIV. - (O)F. - L. *spectāculum* public show, spectators in a theatre, f. *spectāre*, frequent. f. *specere* look at. So **spectator** onlooker. XVI. - F. or L. **spectre,** U.S. **specter** XVII. - F. *spectre* or L. *spectrum* (whence also **spectrum** spectre; coloured band into which a beam of light is decomposed. XVII; comb. form **spectro-**, as in **spectroscope**). **speculate** (-ATE[3]) †observe, consider XVI; engage in thought XVII; engage in buying and selling for gain XVIII. f. pp. stem of L. *speculārī* spy out, watch, f. *specula* lookout, watch-tower. **speculation, speculative** XIV. - (O)F. or late L. **speculum** surgical instrument for examining XVI; mirror, reflector XVII. - L.

speech act of speaking. OE. (Angl.) *spēċ*, (WS.) *spǣċ*, rel. to *specan* SPEAK; repl. earlier *sprǣċ* = OS. *sprāka* (Du. *spraak*), OHG. *sprāhha* (G. *sprache*), WGmc. sb. f. **sprǣk-* **sprek-* SPEAK. Hence **speechify** make a speech or speeches (usu. with derogatory force) XVIII.

speed †success (surviving in phr. *wish good s.*); quickness. OE. *spēd*, earlier *spœ̄d* = OS. *spōd*, OHG. *spuot*; f. Gmc. **spōan* (OE. *spōwan*, OHG. *spuo(e)n̥* prosper, succeed). Hence **speed** vb. OE. *spēdan*, usu. *ġespēdan* = OS. *spōdian* (Du. *spoeden*), OHG. *spuoten*.

spell[1] †discourse OE.; formula of incantation, first in *night-s.* XIV. OE. *spel(l)* = OS., OHG. *spel*, ON. *spjall*, Goth. *spill* recital, tale :- Gmc. **spellam*; of unkn. orig. Comp. **spellbound** enchanted XVIII; hence **spellbind** vb., whence (U.S.) **spellbinder** XX.

spell[2] pt., pp. *spelled*, (usu.) *spelt* read *out* as if letter by letter XIII; name or set down the letters of XV; make out, decipher XVI. Aphetic - OF. *espel(l)er* (mod. *épeler*), *espelir*, for older **espeldre*, *espeaudre*, of Gmc. orig. (cf. prec.).

spell[3] relieve (another) at work XVI. Later form of †*spele* take the place of, OE. *spelian*, rel. to *spala* substitute, of unkn. orig. Hence **spell** sb. †relief gang XVI; turn of work taken in relief of another XVII; continuous course of time XVIII.

spelt species of grain, *Triticum spelta*. Rare before XVI; in late OE., ME., and modEng. due to independent adoptions from the Continent of OS. *spelta*, MLG., MDu. *spelte* (Du. *spelt*) = OHG. *spelza*, *spelta* (G. *spelz*).

spelter zinc XVII; zinc alloy XIX. corr. to OF. *espeautre*, MDu. *speauter* (Du. *spiauter*), LG. *spialter*; rel. to PEWTER.

spence (arch.) buttery, pantry XIV; (Sc.) parlour XVIII. Aphetic - OF. *despense* (mod. *dépense*) :- sb. use of fem. pp. of L. *dispendere* DISPENSE. So †*spencer* steward, butler (surviving as a surname) - AN. *espenser*, for OF. *despenser*.

spencer †kind of wig XVIII; short double-breasted overcoat XVIII; form of life-belt XIX. f. family name *Spencer*; in the several senses respectively after Charles *Spencer*, third Earl of Sunderland (1674-1722), George John *Spencer*, second Earl *Spencer* (1758-1834), Knight *Spencer* (fl. 1803).

spend pt., pp. *spent* give or pay out OE.; use, use up XIII. Partly (i) OE. *spendan*, corr. to MLG., MDu. *spenden*, OHG. *spentōn* (G. *spenden*), ON. *spenna* - L. *expendere* EXPEND; partly (ii) aphetic of *dispend* - OF. *despendre* :- L. *dispendere* distribute, DISPENSE. Comp. **spendthrift** XVII; *thrift* being taken in the sense 'substance', 'wealth'.

sperm XIV. - late L. *sperma* - Gr. *spérma*, *-at-*, f. base of *speírein* sow. Comb. form **spermato-** XIX. So **spermatic** XVI. - late L. - Gr.

spermaceti fatty substance obtained from the sperm whale. XV. - medL. *spermacētī* (so named from an erron. notion of the nature of the substance), f. *sperma* SPERM + *cētī*, g. of *cētus* - Gr. *kêtos* whale; attrib. in *s. whale* (XVII), shortened to *sperm whale* (XIX).

spew vomit. (i) OE. str. vb. *spīwan* = OS., OHG. *spīwan* (G. *speien*), ON. *spýja*, Goth. *speiwan*; (ii) OE. wk. vb. *spēowan*, *spīowan*, corr. to L. *spuere*, Gr. *ptúein*; of imit. orig.

sphagnum (bot.) genus of mosses. XVIII. f. Gr. *sphágnos*.

sphenoid (anat.) irregularly-shaped bone at the base of the skull wedged in between other bones. XVIII. - Gr. *sphēnoeidḗs*, f. *sphḗn* wedge; see -OID.

sphere globular body or figure; globe conceived as appropriate to a particular planet, hence (one's or its) province or domain XVII. ME. *sper(e)* - OF. *espere*, later (with assim. to L.) *sphère* - late L. *sphēra*, earlier *sphæra* - Gr. *sphaîra* ball, globe. So **spheric, spherical** XVI. - late L. *sphē-*, *sphæricus* - Gr. *sphairikós*. **spheroid** XVII.

sphincter (anat.) muscular ring normally closing an orifice. XVI. - late L. - Gr. *sphigktḗr* band, contractile muscle, f. *sphíggein* bind tight.

sphinx (Gr. myth.) hybrid monster which propounded a riddle; figure of creature having a human head and breast with a lion's body; inscrutable being. XVI. - L. - Gr. *Sphígx*, presumably f. *sphíggein* (see prec.).

sphragistic (as pl.; see -ICS) scientific study of seals or signet rings; adj. pert. to these XIX. - F. *sphragistique* - Gr. *sphrāgistikós*, f. *sphrāgís* seal.

spicate (bot.) having a spike-like inflorescence. XVII. - L. *spīcātus*, pp. of *spīcāre* furnish with spikes, f. *spīca* SPIKE[2]; see -ATE[2].

spice aromatic vegetable substance used for its pungency or fragrance. XIII. Aphetic - OF. *espice* (mod. *épice*) :- L. *speciēs* appearance, specific kind, SPECIES, (late) pl. wares, merchandise. So **spice** vb. XIV, **spicery** XIII. Hence **spicy** (-Y[1]) XVI.

spick and span brand new XVII (*speck and span*); trim, spruce XIX. Shortening of (dial.) *spick and span new* (XVI), extension of (dial.) *span-new* (XIII) - ON. *spánnýr* 'new like a freshly shaved chip', f. *spánn* chip + *nýr* NEW; the el. *spick* is prob. due to synon. Du. *spikspelldernieuw*, *-splinternieuw* 'spike-splinter-new'.

spider OE. *spīðra* :- **spinþran-*, f. *spinnan* SPIN.

spiel (U.S.) talk, speech. XIX. - G. *spiel* play.

spiffing (dial., sl.) first-rate, smart. XIX. of unkn. orig.

spignel (aromatic root of) *Meum athamanticum*. XVI. perh. contr. of obscure ME. †*spigurnel* (XIV-XV) - medL. *spigurnella*.

spigot XIV. of uncert. orig.

spike[1] sharp-pointed piece of metal, large nail. XIII. ME. *spyk* (also *spiknail*), of uncert. orig. (perh. - (M)LG., MDu. *spīker* (Du. *spijker*)); rel. to SPOKE. Hence **spike** vb. XVII.

spike[2] A. ear of corn XIV (rare before XVII); inflorescence of sessile flowers on a long axis XVI; B. lavender XVI. - L. *spīca*, *-us*, *-um*.

spikenard XIV. - medL. *spīca nardī* (see SPIKE[2], NARD), or more immed. - OF. *spicanard(e)* or MLG. *spīkenard*, MDu. *spīkenaerde* (Du. *spijknardus*).

spill[1] pt., pp. *spilt*, *spilled* †put to death, destroy, waste OE.; shed (blood) XII; allow or cause (liquid) to fall or pour XIV (hence intr. XVII). OE. *spillan* = (M)LG., (M)Du. *spillen*, rel. to OE. *spildan* destroy = OS. *spildian*, OHG. *spilden*, ON. *spilla* (:- **spilþjan*), of unkn. orig. Hence **spilth** (-TH[1]) XVII.

spill[2] splinter or slip of wood, etc. XIII; thin slip of wood, etc. for lighting XIX. of uncert. orig.

spin pt. *span*, *spun*, pp. *spun* draw and form into thread OE.; form (a thread) XIII; shoot, gush XIV; revolve XVII. OE. str. vb. *spinnan* = (M)Du. *spinnen*, OHG., Goth. *spinnan* (G. *spinnen*), ON. *spinna*.

spinach XVI (*spinache*, *-age*). prob. - MDu. *spinaetse*, *spinag(i)e* (Du. *spinazie*) - OF. *espinache*, *-age* (mod. *épinard*) - Sp. *espinaca* - medL. *spinac(h)ia*, *-ium*, of uncert. orig.

spinal pert. to the SPINE. XVI - late L. *spīnālis*; see -AL[1].

spindle slender rod serving to twist and wind thread in spinning OE.; rod serving as an axis XIV. OE. *spinel*, corr. to OS. *spinnila*, (M)Du.

spindel, OHG. *spin(n)ila*, *-ala* (G. *spindel*), f. **spin-* SPIN; see -LE[1].

spindrift continuous driving of spray. XVI. orig. Sc. var. of *spoondrift* (actually recorded later, XVIII), f. †*spoon* run before the wind or sea + DRIFT.

spine backbone XIV (rare before XVII); thorn or thorn-like process XV. Aphetic - OF. *epine* (mod. *épine*), or - its source L. *spīna* thorn, prickle, backbone.

spinel gem resembling the ruby. XVI. - F. *spinelle* - It. *spinella*, dim. of *spina* spine.

spinet XVII. Aphetic - F. †*espinette* (mod. *épinette*) - It. *spinetta*.

spinifex coarse grass of the Australian deserts, having spiny leaves. XIX. - modL. *spīnifex*, f. *spīna* SPINE + *-fex* maker, f. base of *facere* make.

spinnaker (naut.) three-cornered sail carried by racing yachts. XIX. Said to be a fanciful formation on *spinks*, mispronunciation of *Sphinx*, name of the first yacht that commonly carried the sail.

spinney XVI. Aphetic - OF. *espinei* (mod. *épinaie*) :- Rom. **spīnēta*, coll. form of L. *spīnētum*, f. *spīna* thorn, SPINE.

spinster woman (rarely, man) engaged in spinning XIV; appended to names of women to denote occupation, later (from XVII) legal designation of one still unmarried. f. SPIN vb. + -STER.

spiraea genus of rosaceous plants. XVII. - L. *spīræa* - Gr. *speiraía*, f. *speîra* SPIRE[2].

spiral coiled as round a cylinder or cone. XVI. - F. *spiral* or medL. *spīrālis*, *spīra* SPIRE[2]; see -AL[1].

spirant (philol.) XIX. - L. *spīrāns*, *-ant-*, prp. of *spīrāre* breathe; see -ANT.

spire[1] †stalk, stem OE.; (dial.) reeds XIII; shoot, sprout XIV; tapering portion of a steeple XVI (earlier *sphere* XV). OE. *spīr* = MLG., MDu. *spier*, *spīr*, MHG. *spīr* (G. *spier* tip of blade of grass).

spire[2] coil, spiral. XVI. - F. - L. *spīra* - Gr. *speîra* coil, winding.

spirit A. breath of life; B. vital principle; C. incorporeal being XIII; immaterial element of a human being; D. vital power XIV; E. †any of four substances so named of the alchemists XIV; liquid of the nature of an essence XVII. - AN., aphetic of *espirit*, OF. *esperit*, (also mod.) *esprit* - L. *spīritus* breathing, breath, air, life, soul, pride, courage, (in Chr. use) incorporeal being, f. *spīrāre* breathe. Hence **spirit** vb. (arch.) enliven, inspirit XVI; carry *away* mysteriously XVII. **spirited** (-ED[2]) XVI. **spiritism** XIX. So **spiritual** pert. to the spirit XIV; ecclesiastical XIV. ME. *spirituel* (later latinized) - (O)F. *spirituel* - L. *spīrituālis*; see -AL[1]. **spirituality** XV. - (O)F. or late L. **spiritualism** XIX. **spirituous** †spirited XVI; ardent, alcoholic XVII. - F. *spiritueux* or f. L. *spīritus*.

spirometer instrument for measuring breathing-power. XIX. f. L. *spīrāre* breathe; see -OMETER.

spirt †short space XVI; slight spell of wind XVIII; brief spell of activity XIX. of unkn. orig.; cf. SPURT[1].

spit[1] pointed rod on which meat is stuck for roasting OE.; sword; small tongue of land XVII. OE. *spitu* = MLG., MDu. *spit*, *spet* (Du. *spit*), OHG. *spiz* (G. *spiess*) :- Gmc. **spituz*.

spit[2] pt., pp. *spat* eject saliva. late Nhb. OE. *(ġe)spittan* = G. dial. *spützen*, f. imit. base **spit-*, of which there are other expressive vars. repr. by OE. *spātlian*, *spǣt(l)an*, *spǣtl*, *spātl*, *spāld* saliva, MHG. *spiutzen*, ON. *spýta*; see SPITTLE.

spit[3] spade's depth of earth. XVI. - (M)LG., (M)Du. *spit*, rel. to OE. *spittan* (dial. *spit*) dig with a spade, and hence prob. ult. to SPIT[1].

spitchcock method of preparing an eel by cutting it up and frying it. XVI. of unkn. orig.; cf. SPATCHCOCK.

spite †outrage, insult XIII; strong ill-will XIV; *in s. of* notwithstanding. Aphetic - OF. *despit* DESPITE. So **spite** vb. †regard with contempt XIV; treat maliciously XVI. Aphetic - OF. *despiter* - L. *dēspectāre*.

spittle XV. alt., by assoc. with SPIT[2], of (dial.) *spattle*, OE. *spātl*, *spādl*, *spāld* (ME. *spold*), corr. to MLG. *spēdel*, f. Gmc. **spāt-*, repr. also by OE. *spǣtl*, *spǣtan* spit. Hence **spittoon** XIX (orig. U.S.).

spitz Pomeranian dog, having a very pointed muzzle. XIX. - G. *spitz*, also *spitzhund*, spec. use of *spitz* pointed.

splanchnic pert. to the viscera. XVII. - modL. *splanchnicus* - Gr. *splagkhnikós*, f. *splágkhnon*, usu. pl. *-a* inward parts; see -IC.

splash dash water, etc. upon, also with *water*, etc., as obj., and intr. XVIII. Expressive alt. of *plash*, prob. of imit. orig.

splay †unfold (a banner) XIV; spread out XV. Aphetic of DISPLAY. Hence sb. (archit.) work deviating from a right angle; adj., as in *splayfoot(ed)*. XVI.

spleen gland in the abdomen anciently held to be the seat of (i) melancholy, (ii) mirth XIII; used of various emotions and states of mind XVI. Aphetic - OF. *esplen* - L. *splēn* - Gr. *splḗn*. Comp. **spleenwort** XVI; after L. *splēnium*, *asplēnon* - Gr. So **splenetic** XVI. - late L. *splēnēticus*. **splenic** XVII. - L. - Gr.

splendid XVII. - F. *splendide* or L. *splendidus*, f. *splendēre* be bright or shining. So **splendent** XV. - L. prp. **splendiferous** XV (now joc.). - medL. *splendiferus*, for late L. *splendōrifer*.

splendour, U.S. **splendor** great brightness XV; magnificent display, brilliant distinction XVII. - (O)F. *splendeur* or L. *splendor*; see -OUR.

splice join (ropes) by interweaving the strands XVI; join (two pieces of timber) by overlapping the ends XVII; (sl.) join in marriage XVIII. prob. - MDu. *splissen*.

splint plate of overlapping metal in medieval armour XIII; slender or thin slip of wood, etc.; (dial.) splinter XIV; (in farriery) tumour developing into a bony excrescence XVI; laminated coal XVIII. - MLG. *splente*, *splinte*, MDu. *splinte* (Du. *splint*); rel. to next.

splinter sb. XIV. - (M)Du. *splinter*, rel. to prec. Hence vb. XVI.

split break up (a ship) on a rock, etc.; cleave, rend longitudinally. XVI. In earliest use naut. - (M)Du. *splitten*, obscurely rel. to *spletten* and to MDu., MLG. *splīten*, MHG. *splīzen* (G. *spleissen*); of unkn. orig.

splodge XIX. expressive alt. of next.
splotch XVII. prob. of symbolic orig.
splurge (U.S.) ostentatious display. XIX. of symbolic orig.
splutter (dial.) noise, fuss; violent and confused utterance XVII; loud sputter or splashing XIX. alt. of SPUTTER.
spode china ware manufactured by Josiah *Spode* (1754-1827). XIX.
spoil goods captured from an enemy XIII; (esp. pl.) arms or armour so captured, (also gen.) XVI; refuse material XIX. Aphetic - OF. *espoille*, f. *espoillier* :- L. *spoliāre*, f. *spolium*, pl. *-ia* skin stripped from an animal, booty. So **spoil** vb. A. strip, despoil XIII; B. damage, ruin XVI; C. deteriorate XVII; *be spoiling for* (orig. U.S.) desire eagerly XIX. - OF. *espoillier*, or aphetic of DESPOIL.
spoke one of the staves of a wheel OE. *spāca* = OS. *spēca* (Du. *speek*), OHG. *speihha* (G. *speiche*) :- WGmc. **spaikan-*, f. **spaik- *speik-* SPIKE[1].
spokesman †interpreter; one who speaks on behalf of another XVI; †speaker of an assembly; public speaker XVII. irreg. f. *spoke*, pt. of SPEAK + *-sman* (see -S).
spoliation XIV. - L. *spoliātiō*, *-ōn-*, f. *spoliāre* SPOIL; see -ATION.
spondee (pros.) metrical foot of two long syllables. XIV. - (O)F. *spondée* or L. *spondēus* - Gr. *spondeîos* sb. use of adj. f. *spondḗ* libation, the spondee being a foot characteristic of melodies accompanying libations. So **spondaic** XVIII. - F. *spondaïque* or late L. *spondaicus*, alt. of *spondīacus* - Gr. *spondeiakós*.
spondulicks (sl.) money. XIX (orig. U.S.). of unkn. orig.
sponge sb. OE. *sponge*, corr. to OS. *spunsia* (Du. *spons*) - L. *spongia* - Gr. *spoggiá*, f. *spóggos*, *sphóggos*; reinforced in ME. from OF. Hence vb. XIV.
sponsion solemn or formal engagement. XVII. L. *sponsiō*, *-ōn-*, f. pp. stem of *spondēre* promise solemnly, rel. to Gr. *spéndein* pour a libation, promise; see -SION. So **sponsor** godfather, godmother; one who gives surety. XVII. - L.
sponson (naut.) extension beyond the ordinary line or bulk of a vessel. XIX. Formerly also *sponsing*, *sponcing*; of unkn. orig.
spontaneous XVII. f. late L. *spontāneus*, f. L. (*suā*) *sponte* of (one's) own accord.
spontoon (hist.) kind of halberd. XVIII. - F. †*sponton* (mod. *esponton*) - It. *spuntone*, f. *spuntare* blunt.
spoof (card) game of a hoaxing character; (gen.) hoax, humbug. XIX. Invented by Arthur Roberts (1852-1933), Eng. comedian.
spook (colloq.) spectre, ghost. XIX. - Du. *spook* = (M)LG. *spōk*; of unkn. orig.
spool XIV. Aphetic - OF. *espole* (mod. *époule*), or - its source MLG. *spōle* = MDu. *spoele* (Du. *spoel*), OHG. *spuolo*, *-a* (G. *spule*); WGmc., of unkn. orig.
spoon A. †chip, splinter OE.; B. shallow oval bowl with a long handle XIV. OE. *spōn* = MLG. *spān*, MDu. *spaen*, OHG. *spān* (G. *span* shaving), ON. *spónn*, *spánn*. The Scand. sense (B) prevailed in this word. Comp. **spoonbill** bird of the family Plataleidae. Hence **spoony** foolish person, silly XVIII; *spoon* was similarly applied contemp. to person making love sentimentally, whence a corr. use of **spoon** vb. (XIX).
spoonerism accidental transposition of initial sounds or syllables of words associated in a context. XIX. f. name of the Rev. W. A. *Spooner* (1844-1930), who was said to have been addicted to this; see -ISM.
spoor track, trail. XIX. - Afrikaans *spoor*, repr. MDu. *spo(o)r* = OE., OHG., ON. *spor* (G. *spur*); rel. to SPUR.
sporadic XVII. - medL. *sporadicus* - Gr. *sporadikós*, f. *sporás*, *-ad-* scattered, dispersed, f. base of *sporá* sowing, seed, whence modL. *spora*, used spec. bot., minute reproductive body in flowerless plants, anglicized **spore** XIX. See -IC.
sporran XIX. - Gael. *sporan* = Ir. *sparán* purse, MIr. *sboran*, W. *ysbur* - L. *bursa* PURSE.
sport pleasant pastime, diversion XV; object of diversion XVII; pl. series of athletic contests XVI. So **sport** vb. †(refl.) amuse oneself XIV; (intr.) XV; display XVIII. Aphetic of DISPORT sb. and vb. Hence **sportive** XVI, **sportsman** (see -S) XVIII.
spot moral stain XII; small roundish mark XIII; small piece or particle; small plot or area XIV. perh. - MDu. *spotte*, LG. *spot*, corr. to ON. *spotti* small piece, bit, obscurely rel. to OE. *splott* spot, plot of land (cf. *ġesplottod* spotted, and rare ME. *splotti* adj.). Hence **spot** vb. XV. **spotted** (-ED[2]) XIII, **spotty** (-Y[1]) XIV.
spouse XII. Early ME. *spūs(e)* - OF. *sp(o)us* m., *sp(o)use* fem., aphetic var. of *espous(e)* (mod. *époux*, *épouse*) :- L. *spōnsus* bridegroom, *spōnsa* bride, sb. uses of m. and fem. pp. of *spondēre* betroth.
spout pipe for discharge of water, etc. XIV; discharge of water, waterspout XVI. corr. to Flem. *spuyte*, Du. *spuit*, but prob. immed. f. **spout** vb. (XIV) - MDu. *spouten* (Du. *spuiten*), f. imit. base **spūt-*, repr. also in ON. *spýta* spit.
sprain vb. and sb. XVII. of uncert. orig.
spraints excrement of the otter. XV. - OF. *espraintes* (mod. *épreintes*), sb. use of fem. pp. of *espraindre* squeeze out.
sprat XVI. Later var. of †*sprot*, OE. *sprot* = MLG., (M)Du. *sprot*, of unkn. orig.
sprawl (dial.) kick convulsively; spread one's limbs awkwardly. OE. *spreawlian*; of symbolic orig.
spray[1] †small twigs, fine brushwood XIII (earlier in place-names); slender shoot or twig XIV. of unkn. orig.
spray[2] water in the form of a fine shower XVII; jet of vapour XIX. orig. *spry*, immed. source unkn.; formally corr. to MDu. vb. *spra(e)yen* = MHG. *spræjen*, *spræwen*. Hence vb. XIX.
spread pt., pp. *spread* stretch so as to display, send out in various directions XII; overlap *with*; be extended, become diffused XIII. OE. **sprǣdan* (in comps. *ā-*, *ġe-*, *ofer-*, *tōsprǣdan*, and *sprǣdung* diffusion) = OS. *tōspreidan*, MLG., MDu. *sprēden* (Du. *sprei(d)en*), OHG. *spreitan* (G. *spreiten*) :- WGmc. **spraidjan*, causative of **sprīdan*, repr. by OHG. *sprītan* be extended.
spree (colloq.) boisterous frolic. XIX. of unkn. orig.

sprig[1] small slender nail. XIV. of unkn. orig.
sprig[2] shoot, twig. XV. of unkn. orig.
sprightly XVI. f. *spright* (XVI), var. of SPRITE + -LY[1].
spring[1] A. place of rising, as of a stream OE.; B. action or time of rising or beginning XIII; †C. young growth XIII; D. first season of the year XVI (earlier †*springing time* XIV, *spring time* XV, etc.); E. rising of the sea to its extreme height XIV (*s. tide* XVI); F. elastic contrivance XV. OE. *spring*, *spryng*, f. Gmc **spreŋʒ-*, **spruŋʒ-* (see next); in sense E perh. of LG. or Du. orig.
spring[2] pt. *sprang*, pp. *sprung* bound, leap (*up*, etc.); issue *forth*; grow OE.; originate XII; cause (a bird) to rise XVI. OE. *springan* = OS., OHG. *springan* (Du., G. *springen*), ON. *springa* :- Gmc. **spreŋʒan*, f. base rel. to **spruŋʒ-*, repr. in prec. and (O)HG. *sprung*, (M)Du. *sprong*.
springbok XVIII. - Afrikaans, f. Du. *springen* SPRING[2] + *bok* goat, antelope (see BUCK).
springe snare to catch small game, esp. birds. XIII. repr. OE. **sprenċġ* :- **sprangjan*, f. base of SPRING[2].
sprinkle scatter in drops XIV; bedew, bespatter XV; cover with specks of colour XVIII. perh. - (M)Du. *sprenkelen*; see -LE[3].
sprint †dart, spring XVI; run, etc. fast for a short distance XIX. - ON. **sprinta* (Sw. *spritta*); ult. orig. unkn.
sprit pole OE., (naut.) boom or pole crossing a sail diagonally XIV. OE. *sprēot* = (M)Du., (M)LG. *spr(i)et*, f. Gmc. **spreut- sprūt-*; cf. SPROUT.
sprite spirit, elf, fairy. XIII. ME. *spryte*, also *spreit*, *sprete*, alt. with lengthened vowel of *sprit*, contr. of SPIRIT.
sprocket triangular piece of timber XVI; projection on the rim of a wheel engaging with the links of a chain XVIII. of unkn. orig.
sprout shoot forth, spring up. XII. ME. *sprūten*, OE. **sprūtan* (in pp. *āsproten*), OS. *sprūton* = MLG. *sprūten*, (M)Du. *spruiten*, MHG. *spriezen* (G. *spriessen*) :- WGmc. **sprūtan*, f. **sprūt-*, as also in OE. *sprӯtan*, *spryttan*, OHG. *spriozan*. Hence, or - MLG., MDu. *sprūte* (Du. *spruit*), **sprout** sb. XIII.
spruce †brisk, lively; trim, neat. XVI. poss. from a particular collocation of *Spruce* = *Pruce* Prussia, e.g. *Spruce leather* (*jerkin*). Hence vb. XVI.
spruit small watercourse in S. Africa. XIX. - Du. (see SPROUT).
spry active, brisk. XVIII. of unkn. orig.
spud †short or poor knife or dagger XV; spade-like implement for digging or weeding XVII; stumpy person or thing XVII; potato XIX. of unkn. orig.
spume foam, froth. XIV. - OF. *(e)spume* or L. *spūma*, gen. connected with *pūmex* PUMICE, OE. *fām* FOAM.
spunk spark; touchwood XVI; fungus growing on trees XVII; (Sc.) match XVIII; spirit, mettle. of unkn. orig.
spur device attached to a rider's heel for pricking on his mount. OE. *spora*, *spura* = OS. *sporo* (Du. *spoor*), OHG. *sporo* (G. *sporn*), ON. *spori* :- Gmc. **spuran-*, based on IE. **sper-* strike with the foot; cf. SPURN, SPOOR. Hence vb. XIII.
spurge plant of the genus *Euphorbia*, species of which have been used as purgatives. Aphetic - OF. *espurge* (mod. *épurge*), f. *espurgier* purge :- L. *expurgāre*; see EX-[1], PURGE.
spurious illegitimate XVI; not genuine XVII. f. L. *spurius* illegitimate, false.
spurn strike with the foot (†intr. and trans.); reject with contempt. OE. str. vb. *spurnan*, corr. to OS. *spurnan*, OHG. *spornōn*, *spurnan*, ON. **spurna*; cogn. with L. *spernere* scorn.
spurr(e)y plant of the genus *Spergula*. XVI. - Du. *spurrie*, earlier *sporie*, *speurie*, obscurely based on med. L. *spergula*.
spurt[1] short period, brief unsustained effort. XVI. var. of contemp. SPIRT.
spurt[2] issue in a sudden forcible jet. XVI. var. of contemp. *spirt*, of unkn. orig. Hence sb. XVIII.
sputter spit out in small particles XVI; utter hastily or confusedly XVII. - Du. *sputteren*, of imit. orig.; cf. SPLUTTER.
sputum XVII. - L. *spūtum*, sb. use of n. pp. of *spuere* spit.
spy one who watches secretly. XIII. Aphetic - OF. *espie*, f. *espier* ESPY (whence **spy** vb. act as a spy; catch sight of XIII) - Gmc. **speχ-*, as in MLG. *spēen*, MDu. *spien* (Du. *spieden*), OHG. *spehōn* (G. *spähen*), ON. *speja*, *spæja*, repr. IE. **spek-* (L. *specere* look).
squab young bird; squat person; couch, soft cushion. XVII. of uncert. orig. Also adj. squat. XVII.
squabble vb. and sb. XVII. prob. of imit. orig.
squad XVII. Aphetic (after next) - F. *escouade*, †*esquade* (XVI), var. of *escadre* - Sp. *escuadra*, It. *squadra*, corr. to F. *équerre* SQUARE.
squadron †body of soldiers in square formation; military and naval unit. XVI. - It. *squadrone*, f. *squadra* SQUARE; cf. -OON.
squails ninepins. XIX. of unkn. orig.
squalid repulsively foul. XVI. - L. *squālidus*, f. *squālēre* be dry, rough, dirty; see -ID[1]. So **squalor** (-OR[2]) XVII.
squall cry out violently. XVII. prob. alt. of SQUEAL by assoc. with BAWL. Hence perh. sb. sudden and violent gust of wind (and rain). XVIII.
squaloid shark-like. XIX. f. L. *squalus* sea-fish, used in zool. for the shark; see -OID.
squamose scaly. XVII. - L. *squāmōsus*, f. *squāma* scale; see -OSE[1]. So **squamous** XVI. - F. or L.
squander (dial.) scatter, disperse; spend prodigally. XVI. of unkn. orig.
square A. implement for determining a right angle XIII; B. rectangular figure with four equal sides XIV; rectangular area XVII. Earliest form *squire* (XIII-XVII) chiefly in sense A, later *square* (XV), aphetic - OF. *esquere*, *esquare* (mod. *équerre*) :- Rom. **exquadra*, f. **exquadrāre*, f. L. EX-[1] + *quadra* square (see QUADRANT). So **square** adj. XIV. - OF. *esquarré*, pp. of *esquarrer* (whence **square** vb. XIV).
squarrose having scales, etc. standing out at right angles. XVIII. - L. *squarrōsus* scurfy, scabby; see -OSE[1].
squarson (joc.) parish priest who is also squire. XIX. f. SQU(IRE) and (P)ARSON.
squash[1] crush to a flat mess or pulp. XVI.

Aphetic - OF. *esquasser* :- Rom. **exquassāre*; see EX-[1], QUASH.

squash[2] kind of gourd. XVII. of Algonquian orig.

squat A. (dial.) crush, flatten XIII; B. refl. and intr. sit in a crouching attitude XV. - OF. *esquatir*, *-ter*, f. *es-* EX-[1] + *quatir* press down, crouch, hide :- Rom. **coactīre*, f. L. *coāctus*, pp. of *cōgere* drive or force together, f. co- + *agere* drive.

squaw N. Amer. Indian woman or wife. XVII. of Algonquian orig.

squawk vb. and sb. XIX. of imit. orig.

squeak vb. XIV. of imit. orig. Hence sb. XVII.

squeal vb. XIII. of imit. orig. Hence sb. XVIII.

squeamish affected with nausea XV; distant, prudish, fastidious XVI. alt., by substitution of -ISH[1] for -OUS, of ME. *squaymes*, *squeymous*, earlier *scoymus*, *squoymous*, aphetic - AN. *escoymos*, of unkn. orig.

squeegee implement fitted with rubber for removing moisture from a surface. XIX. Arbitrarily f. *squeege* (XVIII), expressive alt. of SQUEEZE; see -EE[2].

squeeze vb. XVI. var. of earlier †*squise*, †*squize* (XVI); ult. orig. unkn. Hence sb. XVII.

squelch crush down (something soft). XVII. of imit. orig.

squib kind of firework; smart hit, lampoon. XVI. prob. imit.

squid XVII. of unkn. orig.

squiffy (sl.) slightly drunk. XIX. of unkn. orig.

squiggle make wavy or writhing movements. XIX. of symbolic orig.

squill (root of) the sea-onion. XIV. - L. *squilla*, var. of *scilla* - Gr. *skílla*.

squinch (archit.) †stone cut for a scuncheon XV; support constructed across an angle XIX. Shortening of SCUNCHEON.

squint adv. †(looking) obliquely with the eyes differently directed XIV (in *squyntloker*); adj. (as in *s. eye*, *-eyed*), vb. XVI. Hence **squint** sb. strabismus XVII; hagioscope XIX. Aphetic of ASQUINT.

squire young man in attendance on a knight XIII; one who attends on a lady XVI; country gentleman XVII. Aphetic - OF. *esquier* ESQUIRE. Hence **squirearchy** class of squires. XVIII; after *hierarchy*. **squireen** petty squire XIX.

squirm XVII. of symbolic orig.

squirrel XIV. Aphetic - AN. *esquirel*, OF. *esquireul*, *escureul* (mod. *écureuil*) :- Rom. **scūriōlus*, dim. of **scūrius*, for L. *sciūrus* - Gr. *skíouros*.

squirt vb. XIV. Earlier *swirt*; of imit. orig. Hence sb. XV.

squish (dial.) squeeze, squash. XVII. of imit. orig. Hence sb. XIX.

squit (dial., sl.) insignificant or contemptible person. XIX. prob. rel. to (dial.) *squit* squirt.

squitch alt. of QUITCH. XVIII.

stab vb. XIV. of unkn. orig.; cf. synon. (dial.) *stob* (XVI). Hence sb. XV.

stable[1] building for the housing of horses and †cattle. XIII. Aphetic - OF. *estable* stable, pigsty, etc. (mod. *étable* cowhouse) :- L. *stabulum*, Rom. **stabula* (pl. used as fem. sg.) stall, enclosure for animals, lit. 'standing-place', f. base of L. *stāre* STAND. Hence, or - OF. *establer* - L. *stabulāre*, **stable** vb. XIV.

stable[2] able to remain erect, not liable to fail or vary, steadfast. XIII. - AN. *stable*, OF. *estable* (mod. *stable*) :- L. *stabilis*, *-em* firm as a foundation or support, standing firm, secure, steadfast, f. base of *stāre* STAND; see -BLE. So **stability** XV. ME. *stablete* - OF. *(e)stableté* - L. *stabilitās*. **stabilize** XIX. - F. *stabiliser*. **stablish** (-ISH[2]) XIII. Earlier var. of ESTABLISH.

staccato (mus.) with abrupt breaks between successive notes. XVIII. - It. *staccato*, pp. of *staccare*, aphetic of *distaccare* DETACH.

stack pile, heap XIII; cluster of chimneys XVII. - ON. *stakkr* haystack :- Gmc. **stakkaz*. Hence **stack** vb. pile up XIV; (U.S.) pack (cards) fraudulently XIX.

stacte fragrant spice of the ancients. XIV. - L. - Gr. *staktḗ*, sb. use of fem. of *staktós* distilling in drops, f. **stag-*, base of *stázein* flow, drip.

staddle †foundation OE.; young tree left standing XVI; lower part of a rick, etc.; platform on which a rick stands XVIII. OE. *staðol* base, support, tree trunk, fixed position = OS. *staðal* standing, OHG. *stadal* barn (G. dial. *stadel*), ON. *stǫðull* milking-place :- Gmc. **staþlaz*, f. **sta-* STAND.

stad(t)holder †governor of a fortress XVI; in the Netherlands, viceroy of a province, etc. XVII. - Du. *stadhouder*, f. *stad* place (STEAD) + *houder*, agent-noun of *houden* HOLD[1].

stadium ancient Greek and Roman measure of length XVI; course for foot-racing; stage of a process XVII. - L. - Gr. *stádion*, earlier *spádion* racecourse, f. *spân* draw.

staff pl. **staves** (now chiefly literary exc. in senses in which STAVE is now the usual sg.), *staffs* (the only form in C). A. stick, pole, rod OE. (later in many spec. uses); B. †letter OE.; †line of verse XV; †stanza XVI; (mus.) set of horizontal lines for the placing of notes XVII; C. body of officers or persons employed XVIII. OE. *stæf* = OS. (Du.) *staf*, OHG. *stap* (G. *stab*), ON. *stafr* :- Gmc. **stabaz*. C is of Continental orig.; cf. Du. *staf*, G. *stab*, the use being prob. developed from the sense wand of office, 'baton'. Hence **staff** vb. provide with a staff of officers, etc. XIX.

staffage accessories of a picture. XIX. - G. *staffage*, pseudo-F. formation on G. *staffieren* fit out, garnish; see -AGE.

stag male of the (red) deer XII; (north.) young horse XIV; (dial.) full-grown castrated animal XVII; male of birds; (sl.) informer XVIII. OE. **stacga*, **stagga*, of unkn. orig.; perh. orig. 'male animal in its prime' (cf. ON. *staggr*, *staggi* male bird).

stage A. storey, floor XIII; B. †station, position XIII; † C. raised floor, platform XIV (in a theatre XVI); D. division of a journey or process; short for *s. coach* XVII. Aphetic - OF. *estage* dwelling, stay, situation (mod. *étage* storey) :- Rom. **staticum* standing-place, position, f. L. *stāre* STAND; cf. -AGE. Sense D perh. arose from a supposed connection with STADIUM. So or hence **stager** *old s.*, one qualified by long experience. XVI. perh. - OF. *estagier* inhabitant, resident.

stagger move involuntarily from side to side;

cause to reel or totter. XVI; alt. of (dial.) *stacker* (XIII) - ON. *stakra*, frequent. of *staka* push, stagger. Hence sb. spec. pl. as name of a disease XVI.

stagnant (of liquid) †that is at rest in a vessel; not moving. XVII. - L. *stagnāns*, *-ant-*, prp. of *stagnāre* (hence **stagnate** XVII), f. *stagnum* pool; see -ANT, -ATE[3]. Hence **stagnation** XVII.

staid †fixed, permanent; settled in character; of sober or steady demeanour. XVI (*stayed*). adj. use of pp. of STAY vb.

stain A. change the colour of, †deprive of colour; sully, blemish; spot or blotch with dirt, etc. XIV; B. impart its colour to, tinge; †ornament with colour XV; colour (fabric, etc.) with pigment XVII, (glass) XVIII. Aphetic of *distain* - OF. *desteign-*, pres. stem of *desteindre*. The development of sense B is obscure. Hence **stain** sb. XVI; dye, pigment XVIII.

stair flight of steps OE.; coll. pl. XIV; any one of these XVI. OE. *stǣġer* = (M)LG., (M)Du. *steiger* scaffolding, quay, f. Gmc. **staiʒ-* **stiʒ-* climb (cf. STY[1]). For *staircase* (XVII) see CASE[2].

staithe (dial., esp. north.) landing-stage, wharf. XIV (*stath*). - ON. **staþwō*, *stǫð*, rel. to OE. *stæð* = OS. *stað*, OHG. *stad*, Goth. *staþa* (d. sg.) bank, shore :- Gmc. **staþaz*, **-am*, f. **sta-* STAND.

stake[1] stout stick or post. OE. *staca*, corr. to (M)LG., MDu. *stake* (Du. *staak*); f. **stak-* **stek-* (see STICK[1]). Hence **stake** vb. XIV; cf. OE. *stacung* impaling.

stake[2] sb. that which is placed at hazard; vb. wager, hazard. XVI. of unkn. orig.

stalactite icicle-like deposit of carbonate of lime pendent from a cave-roof. XVII. - modL. *stalactītēs*, f. Gr. *stalaktós* dropping, dripping, f. *stalak-*, base of *stalássein* drip, let drip; see -ITE. So **stalagmite** similar deposit rising from the floor of a cave. XVIII. - modL. *stalagmītēs*, f. Gr. *stálagma*, *stalagmós*.

stale[1] †(of liquor) that has stood long enough to clear, (hence) old and strong XIII; that has lost its freshness XVI. prob. - AN., OF. **estale* (mod. *étale*, naut. of stationary water), f. *estaler* come to a stand, STALL[2].

stale[2] urinate, esp. of horses. XV. perh. - OF. *estaler* take up a position (see next), in spec. sense.

stalemate (in chess) position in which the player has no allowable move open to him, but is not in check. XVIII. f. synon. †*stale* (XV-XVII), prob. - AN. *estale* position, f. *estaler* be placed, STALL[2]; see MATE[2].

stalk[1] slender stem of plant or flower. XIV. prob. dim. of ME. *stale*, OE. *stalu* side of a ladder, stave, rel. to OE. *stela* stalk, support; cf. WFlem. *stalke(n)*, Norw. dial. *stalk*.

stalk[2] †walk stealthily OE.; pursue game by method of stealthy approach XIV (trans. XIX); walk with stiff measured steps XVI. Late OE. **stealcian* (repr. in *bistealcian* and vbl. sb. *stealcung*) : **stalkōjan*, frequent. f. **stal-*, **stel-* STEAL. Hence **stalking-horse** XVI.

stall[1] †place, position; division in stable or shed OE.; each of a row of seats in a choir; board in front of a shop for the sale of goods, booth, stand XIV; sheath for the finger, etc. XV (*finger-stall*). OE. *steall* = (M)Du., OHG. *stal* (G. *stall*), ON. *stallr* pedestal, stall for a horse :- Gmc. **stallaz*, prob. :- **staðlaz*, f. **sta-* STAND. In ME. partly - OF. *estal* (mod. *étal*) place, stall in church, etc., of Gmc. orig.

stall[2] A. †have one's abode; B. †install; C. put (an animal) in a stall XIV; †assign, fix; D. come or bring to a stand XV. of mixed orig.; partly (i) - OF. *estaler* stop, sit in choir, f. *estal* (see STALL[1]), (ii) f. STALL[1], and (iii) aphetic of INSTALL.

stallion XIV. ME. *staloun* - AN. var. of OF. *estalon* (mod. *étalon*) - Rom. deriv. (cf. -OON) of Gmc. **stall-* STALL[1] (stallions for breeding being kept in the stable); the orig. of the form *-ion* (*stalyone* XV) is unkn.

stalwart XIV. Sc. var. of *stalward*, *stalworth*; OE. *stǣlwierðe* (ME. *stalworþe*, *-worde*, *-warde*), f. *stǣl* place; see -WORTHY.

stamen †warp, thread; (bot.) male or fertilizing organ of a plant. XVII. - L. *stāmen* warp, thread of warp, stamen, corr. to Gr. *stḗmōn* warp, *stêma* part of a plant.

stamina †native elements or rudiments of a thing XVII; †congenital vital capacities XVIII; vigour of bodily constitution; intellectual or moral robustness XIX. - L. *stāmina*, pl. of *stāmen*; see prec. The senses arise partly from the orig. L. sense 'warp of cloth', partly from the application of L. *stāmina* to the threads spun by the Fates.

stammer speak with halting articulation OE; (dial.) stagger XIV. Late OE. *stamerian* = OS. *stamaron*, (M)LG., (M)Du. *stameren* :- WGmc. **stamrōjan*, f. **stamra-* (repr. by OE. *stamor* stammering), f. **stam-*, repr. by OE. *stam(m)*, OHG. *stammēr*, ON. *stamr*, Goth. *stamms* stammering, etc.; cf. -ER[4].

stamp A. †bray, pound XII; B. bring down the foot heavily XIV; C. strike an impression on something XVI. prob. OE. **stampian* = (M)LG., (M)Du. *stampen*, OHG. *stampfōn* pound (G. *stampfen* stamp with the foot, pound, crush), ON. *stappa* :- Gmc. **stampōjan*, f. **stampaz*, *-ōn* pestle, mortar, prob. f. nasalized var. of **stap-* tread, STEP; reinforced or infl. in sense in ME. by (O)F. *estamper* stamp, of Gmc. orig. Hence, or - F. *estampe*, **stamp** sb. stamping instrument XV; stamped or impressed mark XVI; kind, character; act of stamping as with the foot.

stampede (orig. U.S.) sudden rush and flight, orig. of panic-stricken cattle. XIX. - spec. Mex. use of Sp. *estampida* crash, uproar :- sb. use of fem. pp. of Rom. **stampīre* - Gmc. **stamp-* STAMP.

stance XVI. - F. *stance* †stay, stanza - It. *stanza* station, stopping-place (see STANZA).

stanch[1], **staunch**[1] stop the flow of; arrest the progress of, allay; †quench, extinguish. XIV. - OF. *estanchier* (mod. *étancher*) :- Rom. **stancāre*, f. **stancus* dried up, weary, of unkn. orig. For the rel. adj. see STAUNCH[2].

stanchion upright bar or stay. XV. - AN. *stanchon* - OF. *estanchon*, *estanson*, f. *estance* prop, support :- Rom. **stantia* (cf. STANZA).

stand pt., pp. *stood* A. assume or maintain an erect position on the feet; be upright on a base; be set or placed OE.; B. confront, face XIV; cause to stand, set upright XIX. OE. str. vb. *standan* = OS. *standan* (Du. pt. *stond*), OHG. *stantan* (G.

pt. *stand*), ON. *standa*, Goth. *standan* :- Gmc. **standan*, formed, with suffix *-*nd*- (:- IE. *-*nt*-) in the pres. stem and *-*þ*-, *-*ð*- (:- IE. *-*t*-) in the perfect stem, on the base **sta*- **stō*- :- IE. **st(h)ə*- **st(h)ā*- stand, cause to stand, repr. in L. *stāre*, Gr. *histánai*, OSl. *stati*, Skr. *sthā*-. In some Gmc. langs. the pres. stem has a shorter form (by infl. of *gān*, *gēn* GO), e.g. OS. *stān* (Du. *staan*), OHG. *stān*, *stēn* (G. *stehen*). Hence sb. †delay OE. (late Nhb.); place of standing, position XIII; act of standing, stop, halt XVI; appliance to stand on XVII. Comps. **standpoint** (physical or mental) point of view. XIX. f. STAND vb. + POINT sb., after G. *standpunkt* (XVIII). **standstill** XVIII. f. phr. *stand still* (STILL[1]).

standard A. military or naval ensign XII; B. (gen.) erect or upright object; stump of tree left standing XIII (first in place-names); C. exemplar of measure or weight; level or degree of quality or achievement XV. Aphetic of AN. *estaundart*, OF. *estendart* (mod. *étendard*), f. *estendre* EXTEND; see -ARD. The group of meanings under B is mainly by assoc. with STAND. Hence **standardize** XIX.

standish (arch.) stand for writing materials. XV. of unkn. orig.; presumably based on STAND.

stanhope applied to (i) a light open two-seated vehicle first made for the Hon. and Rev. Fitzroy *Stanhope* (1787-1864), and (ii) a lens and a printing press invented by Charles, third Earl *Stanhope* (1753-1816). XIX.

staniel kestrel. OE. *stān(e)ġella* 'stone-yeller', f. *stān* STONE + **ġella*, f. *ġellan* YELL.

stannary *the Stannaries*, the districts comprising the tin mines and smelting works of Cornwall and Devon. XV. - medL. *stannāria* n. pl., f. late L. *stannum* tin, properly *stagnum* alloy of silver and tin; see -ARY.

stannic containing tin. XVIII. f. late L. *stannum*; see prec., -IC.

stanza XVI (*stanze*, *-o*, *-a*). - It. *stanza* standing, stopping-place, dwelling, room, strophe :- Rom. **stantia*, f. L. *stāns*, *stant*-, prp. of *stāre* STAND. Hence **stanzaic** XIX.

staple[1] †post, pillar OE.; short U-shaped metal rod or bar XIII. OE. *stapol*, corr. to MLG., (M)Du. *stapel* pillar, steeple, emporium, OHG. *staffal* foundation, ON. *stǫpull* pillar, steeple :- Gmc. **stapulaz*; see -LE[1].

staple[2] place in which merchants have trading privileges; principal market or commercial centre XV; principal article of commerce or industry XVII; chief object of employment, etc. XIX. - OF. *estaple* emporium, mart (mod. *étape* halting-place) - (M)LG., (M)Du. *stapel* (see prec.). Hence **staple** adj. having the chief place in production or use. XVII.

staple[3] fibre of wool, etc. as determining the quality. XV. perh. f. †*staple* vb. inspect and sort at a staple (see prec.).

star luminous celestial body OE., image or figure of one of them XIV. OE. *steorra* = OS. *sterro* (Du. *ster*, *star*), OHG. *sterro* :- WGmc. **sterran*- (cf. OHG. *sterno* (G. *stern*), ON. *stjarna*, Goth. *stairnō*); f. IE. **ster*- **stēr*-, repr by L. *stēlla* (:- **sterlā*), Gr. *astḗr* (*aster*-), *ástron*. Hence **starry** (-Y[1]) XIV. **star-gazer** XVI; see GAZE.

starboard OE. *stēorbord*, f. *stēor* guidance, steering paddle, rudder (see STEER[2]) + *bord* BOARD. The ref. is to the steering by means of a paddle worked over the right side of the vessel.

starch †stiffen, compose (the features); stiffen (linen, etc.) with starch XV. repr. OE. **sterċan* make rigid (cf. *sterċedferhð* of fixed or resolute mind) = OS. *sterkian* (Du. *sterken*), OHG. *sterken* (G. *stärken*) strengthen :- WGmc. **starkjan*, f. Gmc. **starkaz* STARK. Hence **starch** sb. XV.

stare gaze fixedly OE.; (of hair) stand on end XVI. OE. *starian* = MLG. *staren*, OHG. *starēn*, ON. *stara*, f. Gmc. **star*- **ster*- be rigid, repr. also by MDu. *star* rigidity of the eyes, Du. *staren*, G. *starren* be rigid, OE. *stær(e)blind* quite blind.

stark †hard, unyielding; †violent, severe OE.; (arch.) strong, stout XIII; (dial.) rigid, stiff; sheer, absolute XIV; naked XVIII. OE. *stearc* = OS., (O)HG. *stark*, (M)Du. *sterk*, ON. *sterkr* :- Gmc. **starkaz*, the weak grade of the base being repr. by OHG. *gistorchanēn* grow rigid, Goth. *gastaurknan* dry up, ON. *styrkr* strong, strength. In *s. blind* (XV) and *s. dead* (XIV) used adv. for 'quite', from the sense 'rigid'; similarly *s. naked* (XVI), for earlier (dial.) *start naked* (XIII) *steort naket*, f. †*start* (OE. *steort*) tail, as if orig. 'naked even to the tail'.

starling Late OE. *stærlinc*, f. *stær* starling, corr. to MLG. *star*, OHG. *star* m., *stara* fem. (G. *sta(h)r*), ON. *stari* :- Gmc. **staraz*, *-ōn*, *-an*-, rel. to L. *sturnus*; see -LING[1].

start A. †leap, jump (OE); move with a sudden or violent impulse; issue swiftly XIII; make a sudden involuntary movement; break away XVI; set out for a race XVII; set out on a journey; B. cause to move in such ways XIV. ME. *sterte*, *starte*, *stürte*, repr. OE. **stiertan* or **steortian*, **steartian*, **styrtan* (perh. seen in late Nhb. prp. *sturtende*), f. Gmc. **stert*- **start*- **sturt*-, repr. also by (M)LG. *störten*, (M)Du. *storten*, OHG. *sturzen* (G. *stürzen*) overthrow, pour out, rush, fall headlong.

startle †kick, struggle OE. (only); (dial.) rush XIII; †start with surprise, etc.; cause to start XVI. OE. *steartlian*, f. **start*-; see prec. and -LE[3].

starve †die OE.; die of hunger; cause to die of hunger, cold, etc. XVI. OE. str. vb. *steorfan* = OS. *sterban* (Du. *sterven*), OHG. *sterban* (G. *sterben*) :- WGmc. **sterban*, perh. orig. 'be rigid' and thus rel. to ON. *stjarfi* tetanus, *stirfinn* obstinate, *starf* effort; outside Gmc., cf. OIr. *ussarb* (:- **ud-sterbhā*) death; extension of the base **ster*- be rigid (cf. STARE). The orig. str. forms of the pt. became obs. XV, of the pp. XVI. Hence **starvation** XVIII.

stasis (path.) stoppage of the fluids of the body. XVIII. - Gr. *stásis*, f. **sta*- STAND.

-stat repr. Gr. *-státes*, *-statós*, f. **sta*- STAND; first in HELIOSTAT (XVIII), intended to mean an instrument for causing the sun to appear stationary.

state A. condition XIII; B. †status, (high) rank XIII; solemn pomp; C. estate of the realm XIV; D. commonwealth; body politic, territory belonging thereto XVI; E. (partly from the vb.) statement XVII (spec. mil., report of forces XIX). Partly aphetic of ESTATE, partly direct - L. *status* manner of standing, condition, f. base of *stāre* STAND. Hence **state** vb. †place XVI; set out in due form, declare in words XVI. **stately** (-LY[1]) befitting or indicating high estate. XIV. **statement** XVIII. **statesman** (see -S) man concerned with affairs of state. XVI.

stater ancient weight and coin. XIV. - late L. *statēr* - Gr. *statḗr*, f. **sta-*, base of *histánai* STAND used in the sense 'weigh'.

static †pert. to weighing or weight XVII; pert. to forces in equilibrium or bodies at rest XVII; pert. to a fixed condition XIX. - Gr. *statikós* pert. to weighing, f. **sta-* (see prec.). Hence **statical** XVI. So †**static** sb. XVI, later altered to **statics** XVII. - Gr. *statikḗ* science of weighing, fem. of *statikós*.

station in spec. or occas. use (e.g., to render the L. word), place assigned or prescribed for some (religious) observance XIV; †act of a play XVI; act of standing (now techn.); standing-place, position; stopping-place (of a conveyance). - (O)F. - L. *statiō*, *-ōn-*, f. **stā-* STAND. Hence, or - F. *stationner*, **station** vb. XVIII. **stationary** XV. - L. *statiōnārius*. **stationer** (-ER[2]) †(hist.) bookseller, †publisher XVI; tradesman who sells writing materials (at one time part of the stock-in-trade of a bookseller) XVII. - medL. *statiōnārius* tradesman having a regular 'station' or shop (i.e., not itinerant), whence **stationery** articles sold by a stationer, writing materials. XVIII.

statist †politician, statesman XVI; statistician XIX. perh. - F. *statiste* or It. *statista*, f. *stato* - L. *status* (see STATE). Similarly **statistic** XVIII, **statistical** †political XVII; pert. to **statistics** (see -IC, -ICAL), first applied to the political science concerned with the facts of a state or community XVIII; all derived immed. from G. *statistisch* adj., *statistik* sb.; whence **statistician** XIX.

statue XIV. - (O)F. - L. *statua*, f. pp. *stat-* of *stāre* STAND. So **statuary** maker of statues; art of making them. XVI. - sb. uses of L. *statuārius*, *-āria*. **statuette** XIX. - F. Hence **statuesque** XIX.

stature XIII. - (O)F. - L. *statūra*, f. pp. *stat-* of *stāre* STAND. So **status** †height, acme XVII; legal standing XVIII. - L. **status quo** XIX. Based on L. phr. *in statu quo ante*, *prius*, or *nunc* . . . in the STATE in which (things were) before, (or are) now.

statute XIII. - (O)F. *statut* - late L. *statūtum* decree, decision, law, sb. use of n. pp. of *statuere* set up, establish, decree, f. *status* (see STATE). Hence **statutable** prescribed or allowed by statute, of statutory quality, etc. XVII. **statutory** (-ORY[2]) †enacting; pert. to statutes. XVIII.

staunch[2], **stanch[2]** watertight; strong, firm XV; (of a sporting dog) reliable XVI; standing firm XVII. - OF. *estanche*, fem. of *estanc*, used as m. XIV (mod. *étanche*); see STANCH[1].

stave stick or lath of wood XIV; verse, stanza XVII; set of lines to carry musical notation XVIII. Back-formation from *staves*, pl. of STAFF. Hence **stave** vb. break up (a cask) into staves XVI; break a hole in (a boat, etc.), make a hole *in*; drive *off* with a staff or stave; keep or ward *off* XVII.

stavesacre plant *Delphinium staphisagria*. XIV (*stafisage*, *staphisagre*). - L. *staphisagria* - Gr. *staphis agriā* 'wild raisin', i.e. *staphis* raisin, *agriā*, fem. of *ágrios* wild.

stay[1] (naut.) large mast-rope. OE. *stæġ*, corr. to MLG. *stach*, Du., ON. *stag* :- Gmc. **staȝa-*.

stay[2] support, prop, lit. and fig. XVI; pl. stiffened underbodice XVII. Partly - OF. *estaye* (mod. *étai*), partly f. **stay** vb. support, sustain (XVI) - OF. *estayer* (mod. *étayer*), of Gmc. origin (cf. prec.).

stay[3] cease moving, remain; cause to cease, stop, check XV. prob. - pres. stem (AN.) *estai-*, *estei-* of OF. *ester* :- L. *stāre* STAND.

stead place, in various applications lit. and fig. (surviving in *in one's s.*, and INSTEAD) OE.; site for a building (surviving in *farmstead*, *homestead*) XIII; †framework of a bed (surviving in *bedstead*) XV; advantage, profit (surviving in phr. *stand in good s.*) XIII. OE. *stede*, corr. to OS. *stad*, *stedi* (MLG. *stad*, *stede* place, town), MDu. *stat*, *stede* (Du. *stad* town, *ste(d)e* place), OHG. *stat* (MHG. *stat*, *stete*, G. *statt* place, adv. prep. instead (of), *stadt* town), ON. *staðr*, Goth. *staþs* place :- Gmc. **staðiz* :- IE. **st(h)ətis*, f. **st(h)ə-* **st(h)ā-* STAND. The sense 'advantage' may be due to assoc. with MLG. *stade* opportunity, help. Hence **steadfast** OE. *stedefæst* (FAST[1]). **steady** (-Y[1]) †fixed, immovable; firm in position or movement; regular in operation or force XVI; not easily perturbed or disturbed XVII; whence **steady** vb. XVI.

steak XV. - ON. *steik*, rel. to *steikja* roast on a spit, *stikna* be roasted.

steal pt. *stole*, pp. *stolen* take dishonestly OE. (in various uses with immaterial object from XIII); come or go secretly XII (prob. after ON. *stelask* refl.). OE. str. vb. *stelan* = OS., OHG. *stelan* (Du. *stelen*, G. *stehlen*), ON. *stela*, Goth. *stilan*, f. Gmc. **stel-* **stæl-* **stul-*, of unkn. orig. Hence **stealth** (-TH[1]) †theft; furtive or underhand action (surviving in *by s.*) XIII. OE. **stǣlð*, repr. in ME. by *stalþ* and *-stelþ*. Whence **stealthy** (-Y[1]) XVII.

steam vapour, fume OE.; vapour into which water is converted by heat XV. OE. *stēam* = Du. *stoom* :- Gmc. **staumaz*. So **steam** vb. OE. *stēman*, *stȳman*.

stearin (chem.) glyceride formed by combination of stearic acid and glycerine. XIX. - F. *stéarine*, f. Gr. *stéar* tallow, suet; see -IN. So **stearic** (-IC) derived from or containing stearin. XIX. **steatite** massive variety of talc, soapstone. XVIII. - L. *steatītis*, *-ītēs* - Gr. **steatîtis*, *-ítēs* resembling tallow; see -ITE.

steato- used as comb. form of Gr. *stéar*, *steat-* tallow, as in **steatopyga** protuberance of the buttocks (Gr. *pūgḗ* rump). XIX.

steed in OE. stallion; in ME. and early mod. Eng. high-mettled horse, from XVI poet. and rhet. for 'horse'. OE. *stēda*, f. base of Gmc. **stōðō* STUD[2].

steel sb. OE. (Angl.) **stēle*, (WS). **stīele*, *stȳle* = OS. *stehli* :- WGmc. **staχlja*, f. Gmc. **staχla-*, repr. by MLG. *stāl*, MDu. *stael* (Du. *staal*), OHG. *stahal* (G. *stahl*), prob. rel. to STAY[1]. Hence **steel** vb. edge, etc., with steel OE. (first in pp. *steeled*); (fig.) XVI. **steely** (-Y[1]) XVI. Comp. **steelyard** (YARD[2]) balance consisting of a lever with unequal arms, moving on a fulcrum. XVII.

steenbok S. Afr. antelope. XVIII. - Du., f. *steen* STONE + *bok* BUCK. Cf. STEINBOCK.

steenkirk, steinkirk neckcloth with long lace ends. XVII. - F. (*cravate à la*) *Steinkerke*, named from the French victory at Steenkerke, Belgium, in 1692.

steep[1] †high, towering; †(of eyes) prominent, glaring OE.; precipitous XII. OE. *stēap* = OFris. *stāp* :- WGmc. **staupa*, f. **staup-* **stūp-* (see STOOP[1]).

steep[2] soak in liquid XIV; in various transf. and fig. uses from late XVI. repr. formally OE. **stēpan*, **stīepan* = Sw. *stöpa*, Da. *støbe*, Norw. *støypa* steep (seeds, barley for malting) :- Gmc. **staupjan*, f. **staup-* (see STOUP).

steeple tall tower OE.; spire XV. OE. *stēpel*, WS. **stiepel*, *stȳpel*, f. **staup-* STEEP[1]; see -LE[1]. Hence **steeplechase** XVIII, orig. race having a church steeple in view as goal.

steer[1] young (esp. castrated) ox. OE. *stēor* = MLG. *stēr*, OHG. *stior* (Du., G. *stier*), ON. *stjórr*, Goth. *stiur* :- Gmc. **steuraz*.

steer[2] guide the course of. OE. *stīeran* = MLG. *stūren*, (M)Du. *stūren*, *stieren*, OHG. *stiuren* (G. *steuern*), ON. *stýra*, Goth. *stiurjan* settle :- Gmc. **steurjan*, f. **steurō*, whence OE. *stēor* steering, etc. So **steersman** OE. *stēoresman*, f. g. of *stēor* (see -S), beside *stēorman*.

steeve[1] compress and stow in a ship's hold. XV. - F. *estiver* :- L. *stīpāre* press, pack. Cf. STEVEDORE.

steeve[2] (naut.) incline upwards. XVII. of unkn. orig.

steinbock Alpine ibex. XVII. - G., f. *stein* STONE + *bock* BUCK. Cf. STEENBOK.

steinkirk see STEENKIRK.

stele sculptured upright slab. XIX. - Gr. *stḗlē*. So **stela** XVIII - L. - Gr.

stellar XVI. - late L. *stellāris*, f. L. *stella* STAR; see -AR. So **stellate** (-ATE[2]) †studded with stars XVI; star-shaped XVII. - L. *stellātus*. **stellify** place (a person) 'among the stars', deify. XIV. - OF. - medL.

stem[1] main body of the portion of a tree or other plant above ground OE.; stock of a family XVI; upright stroke, etc. XVII; cylindrical or tubular support XIX. OE. *stemn*, *stefn*, corr. to LG., Du. *steven* :- Gmc. **stamniz*, of which a parallel and synon. formation **stamnaz* is repr. by (M)LG., (M)Du., OHG. *stam* (G. *stamm*), also by OS., ON. *stamn*, recorded only in the naut. sense (see next); f. **sta-* STAND. Hence **stem** vb. †rise erect XVI; remove the stalk from XVIII; (orig. U.S.) derive *from* XX.

stem[2] †timber at either end of a vessel OE.; upright at the bow of a vessel XVI. OE. *stemn*, *stefn*, spec. use of STEM[1].

stem[3] †intr. stop, delay XIII; trans. stop, check, dam up XV. - ON. *stemma* = (O)HG. *stemmen* :- Gmc. **stamjan*, f. **stam-* check (cf. STAMMER).

stem[4] head in a certain direction XIV; †ram (a vessel) with the stem XV; make headway against XVI. f. STEM[2].

stench †odour, smell; spec. foul smell. OE. *stenċ*, corr. to OS. *stanc*, OHG. *stanch* (Du., G. *stank*); f. **staŋkw-* **steŋkw-* STINK.

stencil †ornament with bright colours XIV; (from the sb.) produce with a stencil plate XVIII. ME. *stansel*, *stencel* - OF. *estanceler*, *estenceler*, f. *estencele* (mod. *étincelle*) :- Rom. **stincilla*, for L. *scintilla* spark. Hence **stencil** sb. perforated plate for producing a pattern. XVIII.

Sten gun XX. f. initials of the inventors' surnames, Shepherd and Turpin + *-en*, as in *Bren* gun.

stenography writing in shorthand. XVII. f. Gr. *stenós* narrow + -GRAPHY.

stentorian loud like the voice of Stentor, a Greek warrior in the Trojan war ('Iliad' v 785). XVII. f. *Stentor* + -IAN, after late L. *stentoreus*, Gr. *stentóreios*.

step pt., pp. *stepped* lift the foot and set it down; proceed on foot OE.; fix (a mast, etc.) in its step XVIII. OE. str. vb. *steppan*, *stæppan* = OS. **steppian*, (M)LG., (M)Du. *steppen*, OHG. *stapfōn*, *stepfen* (G. *stapfen*), wk. forms are found from the end of XIII, and became universal by XVI. So **step** sb. OE. *stepe*, *stæpe* :- **stapiz*. No certain cogns. are known.

step- el. prefixed to terms of relationship to designate a degree of affinity resulting from the remarriage of a widowed parent. OE. *stēop-* (as in *stēopċild* step-child, *-fæder* -father, *-mōder* -mother, *-sunu* -son), corr. to OS. *stiof-*, (M)Du. *stief-*, MLG. *stēf-*, OHG. *stiof-* (G. *stief*), ON. *stjúp-*; the prim. sense is indicated by its relation to OE. *āstīeped* bereaved, OHG. *stiufen* bereave, and the meaning 'orphan' of OE. *stēopbearn*, *-ċild*. Later formations are *stepbrother*, *-sister* (XV), *stepdame* (XIV).

stephanotis (bot.) genus of tropical plants. XIX. - Gr. *stephanōtís* (fem.) fit for a crown or wreath, f. *stéphanos* crown.

steppe vast plain in S.E. Europe and Siberia. XVII. - Russ. *step'*.

-ster suffix repr. OE. *-istre*, *-estre*, corr. to MLG. *-(e)ster*, (M)Du. *ster* :- WGmc. **-strjōn*, added to vbs. and sbs.; primarily applied to females, but in OE. also to males. Survivals from OE. are *seamster* (*sempster*), *songster*, *tapster*; in ME. appear *brewster*, *huckster*, *maltster*, *spinster*. From XVI *-ster* has been used for comps. having derogatory force, as in *daubster*, *rhymester*, *trickster*; *gangster* is a modern (U.S.) coinage (XIX). A few formations on adjs. date from XVI; as *youngster* (on which was modelled *oldster*). Feminine formations made with the addition of -ESS[1] are *huckstress*, *sempstress*, *songstress*.

stercoraceous pert. to dung. XVIII. f. L. *stercus*, *stercor-* dung + -ACEOUS.

stere cubic metre. XVIII. - F. *stère* - Gr. *stereós* solid.

stereo- comb. form of Gr. *stereós* solid, as in **stereography** XVII, **-phonic** XX, **-scope, -scopic** XIX, **-type** XVIII.

sterile unproductive, barren. XVI. - (O)F. *stérile* or L. *sterilis*, f. IE. **ster-*, repr. also by Skr. *starī-*, Gr. *steîra* barren cow, Goth. *stairō* fem. barren; see -ILE. Hence or - (O)F. *stériliser* **sterilize** XVII. So **sterility** XV. - (O)F. or L.

sterlet small sturgeon. XVI (*sterledey*). - Russ. *stérlyad'*.

sterling English silver penny of Norman and later dynasties XIII; (genuine) English money XVI; adj. in *pound s.* etc. (for earlier *pound of s—s* of English money) applied to lawful or standard money XV; of standard or excellent quality XVII. Recorded earlier in OF. *esterlin* (XI or XII), medL. *sterlingus, libræ sterilensium* 'pounds of sterlings' (XII); plausibly referred to late OE. **steorling*, f. *steorra* STAR + -LING[1], some of the early Norman pennies bearing a small star.

stern[1] severe, rigorous OE.; expressing displeasure or austerity XIV. OE. **stierne* (implied in *stiernlīce* adv.), late WS. *styrne* :- **sternjaz*, prob. f. **ster-* **star-* be rigid (cf. STARE).

stern[2] hinder part of a ship XIII; †steering gear of a ship XIV; tail, buttocks XVI. prob. - ON. *stjórn* steering, f. base of *stýra* STEER; but the existence of OFris. *stiārne, stiōrne* stern, rudder, may indicate that there was a corr. form in OE.

sternum (anat.) breast-bone. XVII (earlier †*sternon*). - Gr. *stérnon* chest, breast.

sternutation (act of) sneezing. XVI. - L. *sternūtātiō, -ōn-*, f. *sternūtāre*, frequent. of *sternuere* sneeze, rel. to Gr. *ptárnusthai*; of imit. orig.

stertorous pert. to snoring. XIX. f. L. *stertere* snore.

stet direction to the printer to restore deleted matter. XIX. 3rd pers. sg. pres. subj. of L. *stāre* STAND; 'let (it) stand'.

stethoscope XIX. - F. *stéthoscope*, f. Gr. *stêthos* chest; see -SCOPE.

stetson man's slouch hat with wide brim. XX. f. the name of J. B. *Stetson*, Amer. hat-maker (d. 1906).

stevedore XVIII (orig. U.S.). - Sp. *estivador*, f. *estivar* stow a cargo :- L. *stīpāre* press, pack. Cf. STEEVE[1].

stew[1] A. †stove, heated room; †(arch.) brothel XIV; B. (from STEW[3]) preparation of meat stewed XVIII; (sl.) state of anxiety XIX. ME. *stuwe, st(e)we* - OF. *estuve* (mod. *étuve*), rel. to *estuver* STEW[3].

stew[2] pond or tank for fish. XIV. - OF. *estui* place of confinement, fish-pond (mod. *étui*), f. *estoier* shut up, reserve :- Rom. **studiāre* care for, f. L. *studium* STUDY.

stew[3] bathe in a hot bath XIV; boil slowly in a closed vessel XV (intr. for pass. XVI); confine or be confined closely XVI. - OF. *estuver* (mod. *étuver*) :- Rom. **extūpāre*, **extūfāre*, prob. f. EX-[1] + **tūfus* - Gr. *tûphos* smoke, steam.

steward officer of a (royal) household OE.; high administrative officer XIV; ship's officer who keeps stores, etc.; (Sc. hist.) magistrate administering crown lands XV. OE. *stiġweard, stīweard*, f. *stiġ* (prob.) house, hall (cf. *stiġwita* householder, and STY[2]) + *weard* WARD[1].

stich line, verse. - Gr. *stíkhos* row, line (of objects), line of writing, verse, rel. to *steikhein* advance, proceed, f. IE. **stigh-* (see STY[1]). So **stichic** XIX. - Gr. *stikhikós*. comb. form **sticho-** as in **stichometry** measurement of a manuscript by lines of a certain length. XVIII. - late Gr. *stikhometriā*. **stichomythia** dialogue in alternate lines of verse. XIX. - Gr. *stikhomūthiā*, f. *mûthos* speech, talk, MYTH.

stick[1] rod, staff, or slender piece of wood OE., object in long slender form XV. OE. *sticca* stick, peg, spoon = MDu. *stecke* (Du. *stek* slip, cutting), OHG. *stecko* (G. *stecken* stick, staff) :- WGmc. **stikkan-*, syn. vars. of which w. single **-k-* are repr. by OHG. *stehho*, ON. *stika* stick, yardstick; f. Gmc. **stik-* **stek-* pierce, prick (see next).

stick[2] pt., pp. *stuck* pierce, thrust; remain fixed OE.; cause to adhere XIII. OE. *stician* = OHG. *stehhan* prick, stab, with parallel forms in (M)LG., (M)Du. *stikken*, OHG. *sticchen, sticken* (G. *sticken* embroider); f. Gmc. **stik-* **stek-* pierce, be sharp :- IE. **stig-*, **steig-*, repr. by Gr. *stízein* prick, L. *instīgāre* spur on. Hence **sticky** (-Y[1]) XVIII.

stickle †act as umpire; †settle (a dispute, etc.); †strive persistently XVI; contend *for* XVII; make difficulties XIX. alt. of †*stightle*, †*stiȝtil* arrange, control (XIII), bestir oneself, strive (XIV), frequent. (see -LE[3]) of †*stight*, OE. *stiht(i)an* arrange, corr. to ON. *stétta* (:- **stihtan*) support, help. Hence **stickler** (-ER[1]) (dial.) moderator, umpire, †active partisan XVI; one who is insistent *for* XVII.

stickleback small spiny-finned fish. XV. f. OE. *sticels* sting, goad, thorn = OHG. *stihhil* goad, ON. *stikill* point of a horn, rel. to *sticol* steep, rough, f. Gmc. **stik-* **stek-* STICK[1] + BACK[1].

stiff not flexible, rigid, OE.; (dial.) stalwart; (of wind) strong, steady XIII; steep so as to be difficult XVIII. OE. *stīf*, corr. to MLG., MDu. *stīf* (Du. *stijf*), ON. *stífr* :- Gmc. **stīfaz*; rel. to L. *stīpāre* press, pack, *stīpes* stake, Lith. *stiprùs* strong. Hence **stiffen** (-EN[5]) XVI.

stifle[1] joint at the junction of the hind leg and the body in a horse, etc. XIV. of unkn. orig.

stifle[2] cause to choke, suffocate, esp. kill by suffocation. XIV (*stuf(f)le*). of uncert. orig.; see -LE[3].

stigma (arch.) mark branded XVI; mark of disgrace, (pl. *stigmata*) mark(s) corresponding to those on the body of the crucified Christ XVIII. - L. - Gr. *stígma, -mat-* mark made by a pointed instrument, brand, f. **stig-*, as in *stízein* prick; see STICK[2]. So **stigmatize** †brand XVI; set a brand upon XVII. - F. *stigmatiser* or medL. - Gr. *stigmatízein*.

stile[1] barrier of steps or rails allowing passage through a fence. OE. *stiġel*, corr. to OHG. *stigilla* (MHG. *stiegel, stigele*), f. Gmc. **stīȝ-* climb (see STY[1]).

stile[2] vertical bar of a wooden framework. XVII. prob. - Du. *stijl* pillar, prop, doorpost.

stiletto short dagger. XVII. - It., dim. of *stilo* dagger; see -ET.

still[1] not moving; (dial.) silent; free from commotion. OE. *stille* = OS., OHG. *stilli* (Du. *stil*, G. *still*) :- WGmc. **stillja*. **still life** XVII; after Du. *stilleven*; presumably applied orig. to representation of living things in a state of rest. So **still** vb. quiet, calm. OE. *stillan* = OS. *(gi)stillian* trans., *stillon* intr., OHG. *stillen* trans., *stillēn* intr., ON. *stilla*. **still** adv. without change of position OE.; †quietly; †without change or cessation, always XIII; until then or now XVI; in or to a further degree; (as sentence adv.) even then, notwithstanding XVII. OE. *stille* = OS., OHG. *stillo* (Du. *stil*, G. *stille*) :- WGmc. **stillō*. **stilly** (-Y[1]) †secret XIII; (poet.) quiet XVIII. prob. f. the adv. OE. *stillīce* (see -LY[2]).

still[2] apparatus for distillation. XVI. f. †*still* vb. (XIII), aphetic of DISTIL.

stilt (dial.) crutch XIV; †handle of a plough XIV; each of a pair of poles with brackets raising a walker's feet above the ground XV; post or pile on which a building is raised XVII. ME. *stilte*, corr. immed. to LG., Flem. *stilte*, Norw. *stilta* :- Gmc. **stiltjōn*; rel. to MLG., MDu. *stelte* (Du. *stelt*), OHG. *stelza* (G. *stelze*) :- **steltōn*, and Sw. *stylta*, Da. *stylte* :- **stultjōn*. Hence **stilt** vb. elevate artificially XVII (pp. *stilted* in the sense 'artificially or affectedly elevated' XIX).

Stilton rich cheese made in Leicestershire, so called from having been orig. sold to travellers at a coaching inn in *Stilton*, Cambridgeshire. XVIII.

stimulant adj. and sb. XVIII. XIX. - prp. of L. *stimulāre*, f. *stimulus* goad, spur, incentive. So **stimulate** (-ATE[3]). XVI. f. the pp. stem of L. *stimulāre*.

stimy var. of STYMIE.

sting pt., pp. *stung* †pierce with a sharp instrument; wound with a sharp-pointed organ. OE. str. vb. *stingan* = ON. *stinga*, f. Gmc. **steŋʒ*- **staŋʒ*- (whence ON. *stanga* pierce). So sb. act of stinging OE.; stinging organ XIV. OE. *sting*, *styng*.

stingo strong ale or beer. XVII. f. STING (with ref. to the sharp taste) + -O.

stingy niggardly XVII; (dial.) ill-tempered XVIII. perh. based on a (dial.) var. *stinge* of STING; see -Y[1].

stink pt. *stank*, pp. *stunk* emit a smell; smell offensively. OE. *stincan* = (M)LG., (M)Du. *stinken*, OHG. *stinchan* (G. *stinken*) :- WGmc. **stiŋkwan*. Cf. STENCH.

stint A. (arch. or dial.) cease XII; cause to cease XIII; B. limit XVI. OE. *styntan* (once), more fully repr. in comps. *āstyntan*, *ætstyntan*, *forstyntan* blunt, dull; corr. to ON. **stynta* (OSw. *stynta*, OIcel. *stytta*) shorten, the source of some Eng. uses :- Gmc. **stuntjan*, f. **stunt*- (see STUNT[1]). Hence **stint** sb. †cessation, limitation XIII; amount allotted or fixed XV.

stipe (bot.) footstalk. XVIII. - F. - L. *stīpes* log, post, tree trunk. So **stipes** XVIII. - L.

stipend †soldier's pay; salary XV (*stipendy*, *stipende*). - OF. *stipende*, *stipendie* - L. *stīpendium*, for **stipipendium*, f. *stips*, *stip*- money payment, wages, alms + *pendere* weigh, pay. So **stipendiary** adj. and sb. XVI. - L. *stīpendiārius*.

stipple paint or engrave in dots. XVIII. - Du. *stippelen*, frequent. of *stippen* prick, speckle, f. *stip* point; see -LE[3]. So or hence **stipple** sb. †(pl.) dots used in shading, etc. XVII; method of using such dots XIX.

stipulate make a contract; specify or require as a condition XVII; make a demand for XVIII. f. pp. stem of L. *stipulāri*, of uncert. orig.; see -ATE[3]. So **stipulation** XVI. - L.

stir set in motion, agitate, excite; also intr. OE. *styrian*, corr. to OS. *farsturian* subvert (MLG. *vorsturen*), MHG. *stürn* stir, poke, MSw. *styr(i)a*, Norw. *styrja* make a disturbance :- Gmc. **sturjan*.

stirk young bullock or heifer. OE. *stirc*, *styr(i)c*, Kentish *stiorc* (with doubtful vowel-quantity), perh. f. *stēor* STEER[1] + *-oc*, *-uc* -OCK.

stirrup OE. *stigrāp* = OS. *stigerēp*, MDu. *steegereep*, OHG. *stegareif*, ON. *stigreip*; f. Gmc. **stiʒ*- climb (see STY[1]) + **raipaz* ROPE.

stitch †prick, puncture OE. (only); sharp sudden local pain; (from the vb.) movement of a needle and thread XIII; portion of thread left as a result of this XIV. OE. *stiċe* = OS. *stiki* prick, stab, OHG. *stih* (G. *stich*) prick, sting, stitch, Goth. *stiks* point :- Gmc. **stikiz*, f. **stik*- STICK[2]. Hence **stitch** vb. †stab with pain; fasten with stitches XIII. Hence **stitchwort** plant reputed to cure the stitch in the side. XIII.

stithy anvil XIII; forge, smithy XVII. ME. *steþi*, *stiþi* - ON. *steði* :- **staðjan*-, f. Gmc. **sta*- STAND. The form is due to assoc. with SMITHY.

stiver small coin of the Low Countries XVI; (colloq.) typical coin of low value XVII. - Du. *stuiver*, in MLG. *stüver*.

stoat European ermine in its brown summer coat. XV. of unkn. orig.

stock A. trunk, stem OE.; B. supporting structure; frame of timber for punishment XIV; C. hollow receptacle XIV; D. massive portion of an instrument XIV (of a gun XVI); E. line of descent XIV; F. part of hose (*upper* and *nether*; cf. STOCKING) XV; G. fund, store (as of money) XV; quantity XVII; H. object of contemptuous treatment XVI; I. stiff neckcloth XVII. OE. *stoc(c)* = OS., (M)Du. *stok* (G. *stock* stick), ON. *stokkr* trunk, block, log :- Gmc. **stukkaz*, rel. to **stukkjam* piece, repr. by OE. *styċċe*, OS., OHG. *stucki* (Du. *stuk*, G. *stück*), ON. *stykki*; of unkn. orig. Used adj. 'kept in stock' XVII. Hence **stock** vb. in various senses, †'put in the stocks' being the earliest (XIV), 'supply with a stock of' the latest (XVII) in appearance. Comp. **stock-dove** wild pigeon. XIV; perh. so called from its breeding in hollow tree-trunks. **stockfish** cod, etc. split open and dried. XIII. - (M)Du., (M)LG. *stokvisch*, variously expl. **stockgillyflower** plant of the genus *Matthiola*. XVI; so called from its woody stem; abbrev. **stock** XVII. **stockstill** motionless. XV.

stockade XVII. - F. †*estocade*, alt. of †*estacade* - Sp. *estacada*, f. *estaca* - Rom. - Gmc. **stak*- STAKE; see -ADE.

stockinet(te) XIX. prob. alt., simulating a dim. in -ET, -ETTE, of earlier *stocking-net*.

stocking XVI. of obscure formation with -ING[1], repl. †*nether-stock* (see STOCK).

stodge fill quite full. XVII. of symbolic orig. Hence sb. and **stodgy** (-Y[1]) XIX.

stoep (S. Afr.) raised verandah. XIX. - Du. *stoep*, rel. to Gmc. **stap*- STEP. Cf. STOOP[2].

Stoic pert. to the school of philosophers founded by Zeno (*c*.300 B.C.); also sb. XVI. - L. *stōicus* - Gr. *stōikós*, f. *stoá* the Porch in which Zeno taught at Athens. Also **Stoical** (-AL[1]) XV.

stoker XVII. - Du. *stoker*, f. *stoken* feed (a furnace), MDu., MLG. *stoken* push, poke, f. **stok*-, rel. to **stek*- thrust, prick, STICK[2]; see -ER[1]. Hence by back-formation **stoke** vb. XVII (*stoking-hole*).

stole (arch.) long robe; (eccl.) vestment consisting of a narrow strip of stuff worn over and hanging from the shoulders. OE. *stole* fem., *stol*

n. - L. *stola* - Gr. *stolḗ* equipment, clothing, garment, f. **stol-* **stel-* place, array, lead, send.

stolid XVI (rare before XIX). - F. †*stolide* or L. *stolidus*, poss. rel. to *stultus* foolish; see -ID[1]. So **stolidity** XVI.

stolon (bot.) prostrate branch that takes root at the tip. XVIII. - L. *stolō, -ōn-* shoot, sucker.

stoma (anat., bot.) small opening. XVII. - Gr. *stóma* mouth.

stomach internal pouch or cavity of the body in which food is digested; abdomen, †chest; appetite *for* XIV; †seat of emotion; †temper, disposition XVI; †courage, pride, anger. ME. *stomak* - OF. *stomaque*, (also mod.) *estomac* - L. *stomachus* - Gr. *stómakhos* throat, gullet, mouth of an organ, as of the stomach, (later) stomach, f. *stóma* mouth. So **stomach** vb. †take offence; †offend, incite XVI; put up with, brook XVII. orig. - F. *s'estomaquer* (refl.) be offended, L. *stomachārī* be resentful, be angry with. **stomachic** XVII. - F. or late L. - Gr.

stomacher †man's waistcoat XV; part of woman's dress covering the chest XVI. prob. aphetic - OF. *estomachier*, f. *estomac* STOMACH; see -ER[2].

stone piece of rock or hard mineral substance OE.; measure of weight (14 lb.) XIV. OE. *stān* = OS. *stēn* (Du. *steen*), (O)HG. *stein*, ON. *steinn*, Goth. *stains* :- Gmc. **stainaz*, rel. to OSl. *stěna* wall, Gr. *stíā*, *stíon* pebble. Comps. **stonechat** XVIII; the clash of pebbles is supposed imit. of the bird's alarm cry. **stonecrop** OE. *stāncrop* (the second el. is not identified). **stonewall** vb. (f. *stone wall* wall of stone as presenting an obstacle) offer resistance or obstruction XIX. Hence **stone** vb. XII. **stony** (-Y[1]) OE. *stāniġ*.

stooge (sl.) one who cooperates or deputizes in a subservient fashion. XX (orig. U.S.). of unkn. orig.

stook shock of corn. XV. ME. *stouk*, corr. to or - MLG. *stūke*, formally = MLG. *stūke*, OHG. *stūhha* sleeve.

stool A. wooden seat for one person OE.; B. base, support, stand XIV; C. seat enclosing a chamber utensil XV; evacuation of the bowels XVI; D. (figure of) a bird secured to a stool or perch, serving as a decoy XIX. OE. *stōl* = OS. *stōl* (Du. *stoel*), OHG. *stuol* (G. *stuhl*), ON. *stóll*, Goth. *stōls* throne :- Gmc. **stōlaz*, f. **stō-* **stā-* STAND + -LE[1], the basic sense being 'stand', 'station'; cf. OSl. *stolŭ* throne, seat, Gr. *stḗlē* pillar.

stoop[1] bow or bend down, incline from the vertical; condescend. XVI. OE. *stūpian* = MDu. *stūpen*, ON. *stúpa*, f. Gmc. **stūp-*, rel. to **steup-* STEEP[1].

stoop[2] (U.S., Canada) uncovered platform before the entrance of a house. XVIII. - Du. STOEP.

stop A. fill up, close, plug; B. bring to a stand or halt XIV; C. come to a stand XVI. OE. **stoppian* in *forstoppian* plug (the ear), corr. to G. *verstopfen*, MLG. *stoppen*, OHG. *stopfōn* (G. *stopfen*); see STUFF. Hence **stoppage** XV. **stopper** XV; in the sense 'plug, cork' (XVI) repl. *stopple* (XIV).

storax fragrant gum resin. XIV. - L. - Gr. *stórax*, var. of *stúrax* STYRAX.

store necessaries for future use (now pl.); †live stock XIII; storage, reserve XIV; sufficient supply, stock laid up XV; animal kept for fattening; warehouse XVII; large shop XVIII. ME. *stor*, aphetic of †*astor* - OF. *estor*, f. *estorer* (whence **store** vb. XIII) :- L. *instaurāre* renew, repair, RESTORE. Hence **storage** action and place of storing. XVII.

storey, story[2] any of the parts one above another of which a building consists XIV; tier of columns XV. Aphetic - AL. *(h)istoria*, spec. use of L. *historia* HISTORY, STORY[1]; perh. orig. tier of painted windows. Hence **storeyed, storied**[2] having storeys. XVII.

storied[1] decorated with scenes from history or legend XV; recorded in history XVIII. f. STORY[1] + -ED[1].

storied[2] see STOREYED.

stork tall white wading bird. OE. *storc* = OS. (Du.) *stork*, OHG. *stor(a)h* (G. *storch*), ON. *storkr* :- Gmc. **sturkaz*, prob. f. **sturk-* **sterk-* (see STARK), the name being supposed to refer to the bird's rigid habit.

storm violent disturbance of the atmosphere, fig. of affairs OE.; paroxysm, violent access XVI; (from the vb.) assault of troops on a place XVII. OE. = OS. (Du.) *storm*, (O)HG. *sturm*, ON. *stormr* :- Gmc. **sturmaz*, prob. f. **stur-*, repr. also by STIR. Hence **storm** vb. be tempestuous XV; (of persons) rage XVI; make an assault (on) XVII. **stormy** (-Y[1]) late OE.

story[1] †historical relation or anecdote, historical writing XIII; recital of events XIV; narrative designed for entertainment, tale XIV; account XVII. Aphetic - AN. *estorie* (OF. *estoire*, mod. *histoire*) - L. *historia* HISTORY.

story[2] see STOREY.

stoup (Sc.) pail, bucket XIV; drinking-vessel XV; holy-water vessel against or in a church wall XVIII. - ON. *staup* = OE. *stēap*, MLG. *stōp*, (M)Du. *stoop*, OHG. *stouf* :- Gmc. **staupaz*, *-am*, rel. to OE. *stoppa*, OS. *stoppo* pail :- WGmc. **stoppan-*, f. *stup-*. Cf. STEEP[2].

stout[1] †proud, fierce, brave; strong in body or build XIV; corpulent XIX. - AN., OF. (N.E. dial.) *stout*, for *estout* :- WGmc. **stult-* (MLG. *stolt*, MDu., Du. *stout*, (O)HG. *stolz* proud), perh. rel. to **stelt-* (see STILT).

stout[2] strong beer XVII. prob. ellipt. for *s. ale* or *s. beer* (STOUT[1]), the adj. being current XVII-XIX as applied to drink having a good body.

stove †heated chamber or building XV; closed box containing burning fuel XVII; fire grate XVIII. - MLG., MDu. *stove* (Du. *stoof* footwarmer) = OHG. *stuba* (G. *stube* living-room), rel. to OE. *stofa* bathroom.

stow †place XIV; put away to be stored XV; place (cargo) in a ship XVI. Aphetic of BESTOW; naut. sense perh. infl. by Du. *stouwen*. Hence **stowage** XIV. Comp. **stowaway** person who hides in a ship. XIX; f. phr. *s.* (oneself) *away*.

strabismus (med.) squinting. XVII. modL. - Gr. *strabismós*, f. *strabízein* squint, f. *strabós* twisted, squinting.

straddle spread the legs wide apart XVI; bestride XIX. frequent. f. **strād* **strīd* STRIDE; cf. contemp. and synon. *striddle*, back-formation from *striddling(s)* astride (XV), f. **strid-*, wk. var. of STRIDE; see -LE[3].

Stradivarius (colloq. abbrev. **Strad**) latinization of the name of Antonio *Stradivari* of Cremona (1649-1737) applied to violins made by him and his relatives.

strafe punish, damage, attack fiercely. **XX**. f. G. phr. *Gott strafe England* God chastise England, current in Germany *c*.1914. Hence sb. fierce assault.

straggle vb. XIV. perh. alt. of **strackle*, f. (dial.) *strake* move, go, f. **strak-* base of STRETCH; see -LE[3].

straight not curved or bent XIV; not oblique; honest XVI (obs. in XVII, revived in XIX); in proper order XIX; adv. XIV (*s. away*, *s. off* XVII). ME. *strezt*, *strazt* (as pp. adj. extended at full length), pp. of *strecche* STRETCH. Hence **straight** vb. †(Sc.) stretch XIV; make straight XVI; superseded by **straighten** (-EN[5]) XVII. **straightforward** acting in a direct manner. XIX. f. phr. *s. forward* in a direct path onwards. **straightway** †by a direct course XV; immediately XVI.

strain[1] †gain, treasure OE.; †generation, offspring XII; †pedigree, ancestry, XIII; race, stock XIV; breed, inherited character XVII. OE. **strēon* (Nhb. *strīon*), aphetic of *ġestrēon* = OS., OHG. *gistriuni*, rel. to OE. *(ġe)strēonan*, *(ġe)strīenan* gain, get, beget = OHG. *(gi)striunen*, f. Gmc. **streu-* pile up, rel. to L. *struēs* pile, heap, *struere* build.

strain[2] A. draw tight, stretch XIII; force the sense or application of; force to extreme effort XV; B. bind or compress tightly (obs. or arch. except in *s. to one's bosom*, etc.); C. press through a filtering medium XIV; D. refl. and intr. exert oneself XIV (in *s. at* make a difficulty of 'swallowing' or accepting XVI, misunderstanding of *s. at a gnat* in Matt. 23: 24, which means 'strain the liquor if they find a gnat in it'). ME. *strayne*, *streyne*, aphetic - OF. *estrei(g)n-*, stem of *estreindre* (mod. *étreindre*) :- L. *stringere* draw tight, bind tightly. Hence or - AF. **estreignour* **strainer** (-ER[1]) filter, sieve. XIV.

strain[3] section of a piece of music; melody, tune; passage of song or poetry XVI; †stream of impassioned language; tone, tenor, drift XVII. f. STRAIN[2] used in the senses 'lift up (the voice) in song', 'utter in song, sing', which are of doubtful orig.

strait (arch., dial.) tight, narrow; strict, rigorous; limited in extent XIII; sb. narrow place, (now only) narrow waterway XIV; (now only pl.) straitened circumstances, difficulty, fix XVI; adv. tightly, etc. XII, surviving in gen. use only in *strait-laced* †narrow in scope, mind, etc., excessively rigid (XVI), orig. tightly-laced (XV). ME. *streit*, aphetic - OF. *estreit* tight, close, narrow, sb. narrow place, strait of the sea, distress :- L. *strictus* STRICT. The forms show confusion with *strezt* STRAIGHT at an early date. Hence **straiten** (-EN[5]) XVI, surviving mainly in pp. (*straitened circumstances*, etc. XVIII).

strake strip of iron; stripe of colour; ray of light XIV; line of planking in the side of a vessel, breadth of a plank XV. prob. f. **strak-*, base of OE. *streċċan* STRETCH; largely coincident in form and meaning with *streak* from XVI.

stramonium (bot.) plant of the genus *Datura*. XVII. - modL. *stram(m)onium*, poss. alt. of Tatar *turman* medicine for horses.

strand[1] (arch., dial.) land bordering the sea or other water. OE. *strand* = MLG. *strant*, *-nd-*, ON. *strǫnd*; of unkn. orig. Hence **strand** vb. force on to a shore. XVII.

strand[2] one of the strings twisted together forming a rope or cord. XV (*strond*). of unkn. orig.

strange †foreign, alien; belonging to another place; unfamiliar, unknown. XIII. Aphetic - OF. *estrange* (mod. *étrange*) :- L. *extrāneus* EXTRANEOUS, f. *ext(e)r-* (see EXTRA-). So **stranger** (arch.) foreigner; guest, visitor; unknown person XIV; newcomer XV. Aphetic - OF. *estrangier* (mod. *étranger*) :- Rom. **extrāneārius*, f. L. *extrāneus*; see -ER[2].

strangle XIII. Aphetic - OF. *estrangler* (mod. *étrangler*) - L. *strangulāre* - Gr. *straggalân*, rel. to *straggálē* halter. So **strangulation** XVI. - L.

strangury (path.) slow and painful urination. XIV. - L. *strangūria* - Gr. *straggouriā*, f. *strágx*, *stragg-* drop squeezed out + *oûron* URINE.

strap leather band XVI; strop in naut. use XVII; razor strop XVIII. var. of STROP. Hence **strap** vb. XVIII. **strapping** (-ING[2]) †vigorous, lusty; sturdily built. XVII. **strapper** (-ER[1]) strapping person. XVII.

strappado torture in which the victim was hoisted by a rope and dropped with a jerk. XVI. - F. *(e)strapade* - It. *strappata*, f. *strappare* drag, snatch - OF. *estraper*, var. of *estreper*, *esterper* :- L. *extirpāre* EXTIRPATE; see -ADO.

strass paste for artificial gems. XIX. - G. *strass*, F. *stras*; f. the name of the inventor, Joseph *Strasser*.

stratagem artifice to surprise an enemy XV; device, trick XVI. - F. *stratagème* - L. *stratēgēma* - Gr. *stratḗgēma*, f. *stratēgein* be a general, f. *stratēgós* commander-in-chief, f. *stratós* army + *-ăg-* lead (see ACT). So **strategic** XIX. - F. *stratégique* - Gr. *stratēgikós*. **strategy** XVII. - F. *stratégie* - Gr. *stratēgiā*.

strath (Sc.) wide valley or tract of low-lying land. XVI. - Gael. *srath* = Ir. *srath(a)*, W. *ystrad* dale.

stratify XVII. - F. *stratifier* - modL. *strātificāre*, f. L. *strātum*. So **stratification** XVII. - medL. **stratigraphic** pert. to **stratigraphy** geological study concerned with the strata of the earth's crust. XIX. **stratosphere** stratum of the atmosphere above the troposphere. XX. f. *-sphere* of ATMOSPHERE. **stratum** pl. *strata* XVI. - modL. use of L. *strātum* 'something laid down', sb. use of n. pp. of *sternere* lay or throw down. **stratus** (meteor.) form of cloud having the appearance of a broad sheet of uniform thickness. XIX. Comb. form **strato-**, as in *strato-cirrus*, *-cumulus*.

straw[1] (coll. sg.) stems or stalks of cereals OE.; single stem XII. OE. *strēaw* = OS., OHG. *strō* (Du. *stroo*, G. *stroh*), ON. *strá* :- Gmc. **strāwam*, rel. to STREW. Comp. **strawberry** OE. *strēa(w)beriġe*, *strēow-*; the reason for the name is unkn.

straw[2] (arch.) scatter XII; cover with something scattered XIII. Differentiated repr. of OE. *streawian*, var. of *stre(o)wian* STREW.

stray domestic animal that is found wandering. XIII. - AN. *strey*, aphetic of *astrey* used as sb. So **stray** vb. escape from confinement, wander, roam. XIV. Aphetic - AN., OF. *estraier* (see ASTRAY). Hence (from the sb.) **stray** adj. that has escaped from control and goes free. XVII.

streak †mark, stroke OE.; thin line of different colour or substance from the rest XVI; stratum of coal or ore XVII; strip of land or water XVIII. OE. *strica* stroke of the pen, mark, line of motion, orbit, corr. to MLG., MDu. *strēke* (Du. *streek*), (O)HG. *strich*, Goth. *striks*, f. **strik-* (see STRIKE). Hence **streak** vb. †strike out XV; mark with streaks XVI.

stream course of water, etc.; fig. continuous flow. OE. *strēam* = OS *strōm* (Du. *stroom*), OHG. *stroum* (G. *strom*), ON. *straumr* :- Gmc. **straumaz* :- IE. **sroumos*, f. **srou-* **sreu-* **srû-* flow, repr. also by Gr. *rheîn* flow, *rheûma* stream, OIr. *sruaim*, Skr. *srávati* flows. Hence **stream** vb. XIII; whence **streamer** (-ER[1]) flag floating in the air. XIII.

street paved road, highway; road in a town or village. OE. *strǣt* = OS. *strāta* (Du. *straat*), OHG. *strāȝ(ȝ)a* (G. *strasse*); WGmc. - late L. *strāta*, sb. use of fem. pp. of *sternere* throw or lay down.

strength OE. *strengðu* = OHG. *strengida* :- Gmc. **straŋȝiþō*; see STRONG, -TH[1]. Hence **strengthen** (-EN[6]) XIII.

strenuous vigorous; (now esp.) ardently energetic. XVI. f. L. *strēnuus* brisk, active, valiant.

strepto- comb. form of Gr. *streptós* twisted, pp. adj. of *stréphein* turn, twist, in scientific terms. XIX. **streptococcus** bacteria in which the cocci are arranged in chains. XIX.

stress †hardship, affliction; †force, pressure XIV; physical strain; legal distraint XV; overpowering adverse force XVI; emphasis, spec. of utterance XVIII. Aphetic of DISTRESS or, in part, of OF. *estrece*, *-esse* narrowness, straitness, oppression :- Rom. **strictia*, f. L. *strictus* STRAIT, STRICT. So **stress** vb. †constrain, restrain XIV; †distress; overstrain XVI; lay stress on XIX. In earliest use aphetic - OF. *estrecier* :- Rom. **strictiāre*. Later senses are f. the sb.

stretch lay at full length; extend OE.; tighten, lengthen, widen by force XIV. OE. *streććan* = MLG., MDu. *strecken* (Du. *strekken*), OHG. *strecchan* (G. *strecken*) :- WGmc. **strakkjan*, of uncert. orig. Hence **stretch** sb. extension XVI; extent of time or space XVII.

stretto (mus.) in quicker time. XVII. - It. :- L. *strictus* STRICT.

strew pt. *strewed*, pp. *strewed*, *strewn* scatter, sprinkle. OE. *stre(o)wian*, corr. to OS. *strōian* (Du. *strooien*), OHG. *strewen* (G. *streuen*), ON. *strá*, Goth. **straujan* (in pt. *strawida*). Differentiated vars. are STRAW[2] and **strow** (XIV-XVII).

stria (archit.) fillet between flutes of columns, etc. XVI; small groove, narrow stripe XVII. - L. *stria* furrow, grooving. Hence **striate** (-ATE[2]), **-ated** (-ED[1]) XVII.

stricken arch. pp. of STRIKE: *s. in years*, †*age*, advanced in age XIV (sense 'go' of *strike*); (arch.) wounded in the chase; struck with a blow XVI; *s. field*, pitched battle XVII (sense 'fight (a battle)' of *strike*); afflicted with disease, overwhelmed with grief XVII.

strickle rod for levelling contents of a heaped measure OE.; tool for sharpening a scythe XVII. OE. *stricel*, f. **strik-* STRIKE; cf. -LE[1].

strict †tight, close; restricted in space, narrow; (techn.) straight and stiff; in various non-physical senses close, intricate; rigorous, exact. XVI. - L. *strictus*, pp. of *stringere* draw tight.

stricture A. (path.) morbid narrowing XIV (rare before XVII); †binding, tight closure; B. †touch, slight trace; incidental comment; (now) adverse criticism XVII. - L. *strictūra*, f. *strict-*, pp. stem of *stringere*, repr. two orig. different words, (A) touch, stroke, fig. blame, rel. to STRIKE, (B) draw tight, rel. to STRANGLE, STRING.

stride pt. *strode*, *strided*, pp. *stridden* †straddle OE.; walk with long steps XII. OE. str. vb. *strīdan* = (M)LG. *strīden* set the legs wide apart; formally corr. to a set of str. and wk. vbs. meaning 'strive, quarrel', viz. (M)LG., (M)Du. *strīden*, OHG. *strītan* (G. *streiten*), and OS. *strīdian*, ON. *stríða*, with rel. sbs. Hence sb. XIII.

strident making a harsh noise. XVII (not current before XIX). - L. *strīdēns*, *-ent-*, prp. of *strīdēre* creak; see -ENT.

strife XIII. Aphetic - OF. *estrif*, rel. to *estriver* STRIVE, of unkn. orig.

strigil instrument for scraping the skin. XVI. - L. *strigilis*, f. **strig-*, base of *stringere* touch lightly.

strigose (nat. hist.) covered with stiff hairs. XVIII. - modL. *strigōsus*, f. L. *striga* furrow, in modL. row of stiff hairs; see -OSE[1].

strike pt., pp. *struck* (see also STRICKEN) A. move, go (now with restriction); B. (obs. or dial.) stroke, smooth OE.; C. lower (a sail, etc.); D. deal a blow XIII; impinge (upon) XIV; E. settle, arrange XVI (partly from phr. *s. hands* XV, partly from L. *fœdus ferire* strike a treaty); F. refuse to work (perh. f. *s. tools*) XVIII. OE. str. vb. *strīcan* = MLG. *strīken*, (M)Du. *strijken*, OHG. *strīhhan* (G. *streichen*); WGmc. deriv. of **strīk-* **straik-* :- IE. **strig-* **streig-* **stroig-*. Hence **strike** sb. from XIII in various techn. applications.

string[1] line, cord OE.; number of things strung together XV. OE. *streng* = MLG. *strenge*, MDu. *strenc*, *stranc*, OHG. *stranc*, ON. *strengr* :- Gmc. **straŋȝiz* (see STRONG). Hence **string**[2] pt., pp. *strung* fit (a bow) with its string XVI (isolated ex. of pp. *ystrenged* XIV); make tense XVI; bind (as) with string XVII. f. prec. **stringed** (-ED[2]) having a string or strings. First in OE. *tȳnstrenged* ten-stringed (Psalm 91: 4). **stringy** (-Y[1]) XVII.

stringent †astringent, styptic; †compelling assent XVII; rigorously binding XIX. - L. *stringent-*, prp. stem of *stringere* bind; see -ENT. Hence **stringency** XIX.

stringhalt disease contracting a horse's hind legs. XVI. Obscurely f. STRING[1] + HALT[1].

strip[1] narrow piece (as of textile material). XV. - or cogn. w. (M)LG. *strippe* strap, thong, prob. rel. to STRIPE[2].

strip[2] unclothe, denude; doff, tear or peel off. XIII. ME. *stripe*, *strepe*, *strupe*, pointing to an OE. **strȳpan*, **strīepan* (as in *bestrīepan* plunder, strip), corr. to (M)Du. *stroopen*, OHG., MHG. *stroufen* (G. *streifen*) :- Gmc. **straupjan*.

stripe[1] (arch.) stroke with a staff, scourge, etc. XV. of unkn. orig.

stripe[2] narrow portion of a surface, esp. of different colour or texture XVII; narrow strip of cloth, etc., e.g. chevron of soldier's uniform XIX. perh. back-formation on pp. *striped* (XV or XVI) marked with narrow bands, poss. of LG. or Du. orig.; cf. MLG., MDu. *strīpe* = MHG. *strīfe* (G. *streifen*).

stripling XIII. f. STRIP[1] + -LING[1], 'one who is slender as a strip'.

strive pt. *strove*, pp. *striven* †be at variance, quarrel; contend or struggle *against*. XIII. ME. *strīven*, aphetic - OF. *estriver*, rel. to *estrif* STRIFE.

strobilus fir-cone XVIII; formation resembling this XIX. - late L. - Gr. *stróbīlos* anything twisted.

stroke[1] rub softly with the hand or an implement. OE. *strācian* = MLG., MDu. *strēken* (Du. *streeken*), OHG. *streihhōn* (G. *streichen*), f. Gmc. **straik*- **strīk*- STRIKE.

stroke[2] act of striking XIII; striking of a clock XV; linear mark XVI; (earlier *s. of God's hands* XVI) seizure by disease XVII. ME. *strōk* :- OE. **strāc* :- Gmc. **straikaz*, f. **straik*- **strīk*- STRIKE.

stroll applied in early XVII, as a cant word (with *stroller*), first to itinerant vagrant persons, later used of aimless or leisurely walking; prob. - G. *strolchen*, (dial.) *strollen* wander as a vagrant (*strolch* vagabond), of unkn. orig.

stroma (anat., etc.) framework of an organ or cell (as of connective tissue). XIX. - modL. use of late L. *strōma* mattress - Gr. *strôma*.

strong OE. *strong*, *strang* = OS., Fris. *strang*, MDu. *stranc*, ON. *strangr* :- Gmc. **straŋʒaz*, f. a base of which the mutated form is repr. in OE. (rare) *strenge* severe, MLG., MDu. *strenge* (Du. *streng*), OS. *strang*, OHG. *strengi* (G. *streng*), and for which see further STRING[1]. Comp. **stronghold** fortified place. XV. Hence **strongly** (-LY[2]) OE. *stronglīċe*.

strontia monoxide of strontium. XIX. f. **strontian** (XVIII) a former name for strontia and strontium, prop. for native strontium carbonate; f. name of a parish in Argyllshire, where are the lead mines in which the mineral was discovered. Hence **strontium** (XIX). See -IA[1], -IUM.

strop (naut.) band of rope, etc. XIV; strip of leather, etc., for sharpening a razor XVIII. - (M)LG., (M)Du. *strop* = OE. *strop*, OHG. *strupf* (cf. MHG., G. *strüpfe* fem.); WGmc. - L. *struppus*, *stroppus*.

strophe (pros.) series of lines forming a system. XVII. - Gr. *strophḗ* verse unit, lit. 'turning', f. **stroph*- (as also in *stróphos* cord, string), **streph*- (as in *stréphein* turn). Hence **strophic** XIX.

strow see STREW.

structure †erection, construction XV; manner of this; edifice, fabric XVII. - (O)F. *structure* or L. *structūra*, f. *struct*-, pp. stem of *struere* build; see -URE. Hence **structural** (-AL[1]) XIX.

struggle contend in close grapple XIV; get with difficulty *out of*, etc. XVII. frequent. (see -LE[3]) f. base of obscure orig. (prob. symbolic).

strum XVIII. of imit. orig.

struma (path.) scrofula XVI; scrofulous swelling, goitre XVII; (bot.) swelling at base of petiole XIX. - L. *strūma* scrofulous tumour.

strumous XVI. - L. *strūmōsus*, f. prec. + -OUS.

strumpet harlot, prostitute. XIV. of unkn. orig.

strung pp. of STRING[2]: †fitted with strings; threaded on a string XVII; in a state of tension XIX.

strut[1] bar to resist pressure in a framework. XVI. prob. f. next.

strut[2] †bulge, swell; †protrude stiffly, stand out XIV; †flaunt, swagger; walk upright with stiff step XVI. unexpl. alt. of ME. *stroute*, repr. formally OE. *strūtian* ?be rigid, but a short vowel is seen in (M)HG. *strotzen* and in the Scand. langs.

struthious pert. to an ostrich. XVIII. f. L. *strūthiō* - Gr. *strouthíon*, f. *stroûthos* sparrow, ostrich; see -OUS.

strychnine poisonous vegetable alkaloid. XIX. - F., f. modL. use of L. *strychnos* - Gr. *strúkhnos*, -*on* kind of nightshade; see -INE[5].

stub stump. OE. *stub(b)* = MLG., MDu. *stubbe*, ON. *stubbr*, *stubbi* :- Gmc. **stubbaz*, **stubban*-; OE. had also *styb* (:- **stubbjaz*), which coalesced with the other form; rel. to MLG. *stūve*, ON. *stúfr*, Gr. *stúpos* stump, stock.

stubble stump(s) of grain-stalks left in the ground. XIII. - AN. *stuble*, OF. *estuble* (mod. dial. *éteu(b)le*) :- L. *stup(u)la*, for earlier *stipula* straw.

stubborn pertinacious in refusing compliance XIV; difficult to treat or manage XVI. ME. *stibourne*, later *stoburn(e)*, *stuborn*; of unkn. orig.

stucco plaster for covering walls, etc. XVI - It. - Gmc. word repr. by OHG. *stukki* fragment, piece, (also) crust.

stud[1] A. †post, prop (later as in a building) OE., B. knob, boss, or nail head XV; adjustable button XVI. OE. *studu* = MHG. *stud*, ON. *stoð*, rel. to G. *stützen* prop, support.

stud[2] establishment for breeding of horses OE.; horses bred by or belonging to one person XVII. OE. *stōd*, corr. to MLG. *stōt*, OHG. *stuot* (G. *stute* mare), ON. *stóð* :- Gmc. **stōðam*, **stōðō*, f. **stō*- STAND.

studding-sail, stunsail sail set on an extension of the yard-arm. XVI (*stoytene sale*). perh. f. MLG., MDu. *stōtinge*, noun of action of *stōten* thrust (Du. *stooten*).

student XV. - L. *studēns*, -*ent*-, prp. of *studēre* be eager or diligent, study.

studio sculptor's or painter's workroom (XIX). - It. - L. *studium* STUDY.

studious XIV. - L. *studiōsus*, f. *studium* STUDY.

study †perplexity; serious application of mind, mental effort in learning XIII; room for study, †seat of learning XIV; state of reverie (obs. exc. in *brown s.*). Aphetic - OF. *estudie* (mod. *étude*) - L. *studium* zeal, affection, painstaking application. So vb. †deliberate, consider XIII; apply oneself to study XIV. Aphetic - OF. *estudier* (mod. *étudier*) - medL. *studiāre* (f. L. *studium*), for L. *studēre* be zealous, apply oneself, study.

stuff †equipment, stock; material. XIV. ME.

stof(fe), stuff(e) - OF. *estoffe* (mod. *étoffe*), perh. f. *estoffer* (*étoffer*) vb. - Gmc. **stopfōn* (G. *stopfen*) - late L. *stuppāre* plug, STOP up (implied in *stuppator* caulker), f. *stuppa* tow, oakum. So **stuff** vb. †furnish XIV; line, fill (out) XV. - OF. *estoffer*. Hence **stuffy** (-Y[1]) †full of substance XVI; (of air) close XIX.

stultify (leg.) prove of unsound mind XVIII; reduce to absurdity XIX. - late L. *stultificāre*, f. L. *stultus* foolish; see -IFY.

stum unfermented must. XVII. - Du., sb. use of *stom* dumb.

stumble XIV. - ON. **stumla* (Norw., Sw. dial. *stumla*, Da. dial. *stumle*), parallel to synon. *stumra*, f. Gmc. **stum- *stam-* (see STAMMER).

stump[1] part remaining of maimed limb, broken-off end XIV; portion of tree left in the ground after felling; part of a broken tooth left in the gum XV; stub, fag end XVI; short pillar XVII; (in cricket) XVIII. - MLG. *stump(e)*, (M)Du. *stomp* = OHG., G. *stumpf*, sb. uses of corr. adjs.; of uncert. orig.

stump[2] blunt instrument used for rubbing down hard lines. XVIII. prob. - F. *estompe* - Du. *stomp*, with support from prec.

stun XIII. Aphetic of †*astune*, †*astone* (XIII) - AN. **astoner*, **astuner*, *estuner*, OF. *estoner* (mod. *étonner*) :- Gallo-Rom. **extonāre*, for L. *attonāre* stun, stupefy, f. AT- + *tonāre* THUNDER. Hence **stunning** (-ING[2]) (colloq.) first-rate, 'topping'. XIX.

stunt[1] †irritate, provoke XVI; †nonplus; check the growth of (esp. in pp.) XVII. f. *stunt* adj. †foolish (OE.), †short (XV), stubborn (XVI) = MHG. *stunz*, ON. *stuttr* (:- **stuntr*) short :- Gmc. **stuntaz*.

stunt[2] athletic event or feat, (gen.) enterprise, performance. XIX (orig. U.S.). of unkn. orig.

stupe[1] piece of steeped tow, etc. for fomenting a wound. XIV. - L. *stuppa* tow - Gr. *stúppē*.

stupe[2] (colloq., dial.) shortening of STUPID (sb.). XVIII.

stupefy †stun with amazement XVI; make stupid or torpid XVII. - F. *stupéfier* - L. *stupefacere*, f. *stupēre* be amazed or stunned; see STUPID, -FY. So **stupefaction** XVI. - F. - medL.

stupendous XVII. f. L. *stupendus*, gerundive of *stupēre*.

stupid wanting in mental perception XVI; †stunned with surprise, grief, etc. XVII. - F. *stupide* or L. *stupidus*, f. *stupēre* be stunned or benumbed, f. base **stup-* strike, thrust; see -ID[1]. So **stupidity, stupor** (-OR[2]) XVII.

sturdy †fierce, violent; rough, harsh XIII; stalwart, strong XIV; sb. stupefying brain disease in cattle XVI. Aphetic - OF. *est(o)urdi* stunned, reckless, violent (mod. *étourdi* thoughtless), pp. of *estourdir* stun, daze.

sturgeon XIII. - AN. *sturgeon*, (O)F. *estourgeon* :- Rom. **sturiōne* - Gmc. **sturjan-*, whence OE. *styrġa*, etc.

stutter vb. XVI. f. late ME. *stutten* (dial. *stut*) + -ER[4]; cf. (M)LG. *stötern*, Du. *stotteren*, G. *stottern*. The stem (Gmc. **stut-*, **staut-*) is repr. also in ME. *stotaye* falter, totter, MLG. *stōten*, OHG. *stōȝan* (G. *stossen*) strike against.

sty[1], **stye** inflamed swelling on the edge of an eyelid. XVII. Deduced from dial. *styany* (XV), prop. eye affected with a sty (apprehended as *sty-on-eye*), f. synon. *styan* (:- OE. *stīġend*, lit. 'riser', prp. used sb. of *stīġan* rise, ascend, climb) + EYE. OE. str. vb. *stīġan* corr. to OS., OHG. *stīgan* (Du. *stijgen*, G. *steigen*), ON. *stíga*, Goth. *steigan* :- Gmc. **stīȝan*, f. **stīȝ- *staiȝ-* :- IE. **steigh-*, **stoigh-*, *stĭgh-* advance, go, rise, repr. by Gr. *steikhein*.

sty[2] enclosed place for swine. XIII. repr. OE. **stī* (as in *stīfearh* 'sty-pig'), perh. identical with *stiġ* hall, corr. to ON. **stí* (in *svínstí* swine-sty); :- Gmc. **stijam*, of which a parallel formation **stijōn* is repr. by MLG. *stege*, MDu. *swijnstije*, ON. *stía* pen, fold.

Stygian pert. to the river Styx (river of Hell); infernal. XVI. f. L. *Stygius* - Gr. *Stúgios*, f. *Stúx*, *Stug-*, rel. to *stugein* hate; see -IAN.

style stylus; †written work XIII; proper name or title; manner of expression or discourse XIV; manner, fashion XV (of art or architecture XVIII); mode of expressing dates XVI. - (O)F. - L. *stilus*. The sp. with *y* is due to erron. assoc. with Gr. *stûlos* column. Hence **stylish** (-ISH[1]) XVIII, **stylist, -istic** XIX.

stylet pointed instrument (e.g. surgical probe) or natural process. XVII. - F. - It. *stiletto* (see STILETTO).

stylite ascetic living on a pillar. XVII. - eccl. Gr. *stūlítēs*, f. *stûlos* pillar; see -ITE.

stylobate (archit.) basement supporting a row of columns. XVII. Earlier **stylobata** - L. - Gr. *stulobátēs*, f. *stûlos* pillar + *-batēs*, f. base of *bainein* walk.

stylus writing instrument XVIII; gnomon of a sundial XVIII. - erron. sp. of L. *stilus*; see STYLE.

stymie, stimy (in golf) opponent's ball lying in the way of the player's. XIX. of unkn. orig. Hence vb. XIX (esp. fig.).

styptic having contracting properties. XIV. - L. *stypticus* - Gr. *stuptikós*, f. *stúphein* contract; see -IC.

styrax STORAX. XIV. - L. - Gr. *stúrax*.

suasion XIV. - OF. *suasion* or L. *suāsiō*, *-ōn-*, f. *suās-*, pp. stem of *suādēre* urge, PERSUADE; see -ION.

suave pleasing, agreeable XVI; blandly polite XIX. - F. *suave* or L. *suāvis* SWEET, agreeable. So **suavity** †sweetness XV; pleasurableness XVI; bland urbanity XIX. - (O)F. or L.

sub[1] L. prep. under, underneath, beneath, at the bottom of (cf. next), corr. to Gr. *hupó*; the first word of various L. phrs. current from XVII, as *sub judice* 'under a judge', being the subject of judicial inquiry, *sub rosa* 'under the rose', secretly (of unkn. orig.), *sub voce* under the word (so-and-so in a list), abbrev. *s.v.*

sub[2] short for, e.g., SUBORDINATE XVII; SUBALTERN XVIII; SUBSTITUTE, SUBSCRIPTION, SUBSIST (*money*) XIX.

sub- pref. repr. L. *sub-*, the prep. SUB[1] under, close to, up to, towards, used in comps. The full form is retained before vowels and *b, d, l, n, s, t*; the *b* is assimilated to *c, f, g, p*, and often to *m* and *r*. A by-form *subs-* was normally reduced to *sus-* in comps. with initial *c, p, t*. As a living prefix it is used with words of any orig.

It is used with the foll. senses: (1) under, underneath, below, at the bottom (of), as *subaqueous*, *subterranean*; (2) subordinate, subsidiary, secondary, esp. in titles, as *subdeacon*; (3) (math.) expressing a ratio the inverse of that of the radical element, as in *submultiple*, *subtriple*; (4) next below or after, near or close (to), as in *subsequent*, *suburb*; (5) incomplete(ly), imperfect(ly), partial(ly), as in *subcylindrical*, *subtriangular*; (6) secretly, covertly, as in *suborn*; (7) from below, up, (hence) away, as in *succour*, *suspicion*; (8) in place of another, as in *substitute*; (9) in addition, as in *subjoin*.

subaltern of inferior status XVI; sb., esp. subaltern officer in the army XVII. - late L. *subalternus*. Earlier *subalternate* XV; see SUB-, ALTERNATE.

subaudition mentally supplying or 'understanding'. XVIII. - late L. *subaudītiō, -ōn-*, f. L. *subaudīre* supply mentally, f. SUB- + *audīre* hear; see AUDITION.

subconscious XIX. see SUB- 5.

subdeacon XIV. - ecclL. *subdiaconus*, also *subdiacon* - ecclGr. *hupodiákonos*; see SUB-, DEACON.

subdivide XV. - late L. *subdīvīdere*. So **subdivision** XVI. - late L. See SUB-, DIVIDE.

subdue conquer XIV; bring into subjection XVI. ME. *sodewe*, *sudewe*, later *subdewe* - AN. **soduer*, **su(b)duer* = OF. *so(u)duire*, *suduire* deceive, seduce - L. *subdūcere* withdraw, evacuate (f. SUB- + *dūcere* lead, bring), with sense derived from †*subdit* subject - L. *subditus*, pp. of *subdere* bring under, subdue, f. SUB- + *-dere* put (cf. ADD).

suberose (bot.) cork-like. XIX. f. L. *sūber* cork; see -OSE[1].

subfusc of dusky or sombre hue. XVIII. - L. *subfuscus*, var. of *suffuscus*, f. SUB- + *fuscus* dark.

subjacent underlying. XVII. - L. *subjacens, -ent-*, prp. of *subjacēre*; see SUB-, ADJACENT.

subject A. one who is under the dominion of a sovereign, etc. XIV; B. (philos.) †substance XIV; matter operated upon XVI; (gram.) XVII; thinking agent XVIII. ME. *soget*, *sug(i)et*, later *subiect* (XVI) - OF. *suget*, *soget*, *subg(i)et* (mod. *sujet*) - L. *subjectus* m., *subjectum* n. pp. of *subicere*, f. SUB- + *jacere* throw, cast. So **subject** adj. that is under the rule of a power XIV; exposed or liable *to* XIV. - OF. - L. **subject** vb. make subject. XIV. - (O)F. *subjecter* or L. *subjectāre*, frequent. f. *sub(j)icere*, *subject-*. **subjection** XIV. - (O)F. or L. **subjective** †pert. to one who is subject XV; pert. to the subject in which attributes inhere XVII; pert. to the thinking subject XVIII. - L.

subjoin XVI. - F. † *subjoindre* - L. *subjungere*, f. SUB- + *jungere* JOIN.

subjugate XV. f. pp. stem of late L. *subjugāre*, f. SUB- + L. *jugum* YOKE; see -ATE[3]. So **subjugation** XVII. - late L.

subjunctive (gram.) XVI. - F. *subjonctif* or L. *subjunctīvus*, f. pp. stem of *subjungere* SUBJOIN; see -IVE.

sublapsarian (theol.) XVII. See SUB-, LAPSE, -ARIAN.

sublimate †raise to a high state XVI; act upon so as to produce a refined product XVII. Preceded by pp. *sublimate* (XV), f. pp. stem of L. *sublīmāre*, f. *sublīmis*; see below, -ATE[2,3]. So **sublimate** (-ATE[1]) sb. XVII. **sublime** adj. lofty, exalted, in earliest use (XVI) of language or style, later in physical senses. - L. *sublīmis*, *-us*, f. SUB + an el. variously identified with *līmen* threshold and *līmus* oblique. **sublime** vb. †sublimate XIV; raise to a higher state XVI. - (O)F. *sublimer* or L. *sublīmāre*. **sublimation** XIV. - (O)F. or L. **subliminal** (psych.) applied to states supposed to exist but not strong enough to be recognized. XIX. f. SUB- + L. *līmen*, *līmin-* threshold + -AL[1].

sublunary existing or situated beneath the moon. XVI. f. late L. *sublūnāris*, f. SUB- + *lūna* moon (cf. LUNAR); see -ARY.

submarine adj. XVII. See SUB-, MARINE.

submerge XVII. - L. *submergere*; see SUB-, MERGE. So **submersion** XVI. - late L.

submit (refl. and intr.) place oneself under control; so trans. XIV. - L. *submittere*. So **submission** XV. - OF. or L. **submissive** XVI. f. *submiss-*, pp. stem of L. *submittere*.

subordinate adj. XV. - medL. *subordinātus*, pp. of *subordināre* (whence **subordinate** vb. XVI, **subordination** XVII); see SUB-, ORDAIN, ORDINATION, -ATE[2,3].

suborn procure by underhand or unlawful means. XVI. - L. *subornāre*, f. SUB- + *ornāre* equip. So **subornation** XVI. - medL.

subpoena (leg.) writ issued by a court commanding the appearance of a person. XV. - L. *sub pœnā* under a penalty, being the first words of the writ; see SUB, PAIN.

subreption (eccl. leg.) misrepresentation of the truth. XVII. - L. *subreptiō, -ōn-*, f. *subripere*, f. SUB- + *repere* creep; see -TION.

subscribe write (one's name) on XV; intr. w. *to* XVI; promise over one's signature to pay XVII. - L. *subscrībere*, f. SUB- + *scrībere* write. So **subscript** sb. †signature XVIII; adj. written underneath XIX. - L. *subscriptus*, pp. of *subscrībere*. **subscription** signature at end of a document XV; declaration of assent XVI; contribution to a fund of money XVII. - L.

subsequent XV. - (O)F. *subséquent* or L. *subsequēns*, *-ent-*, prp. of *subsequī*, f. SUB- + *sequī* follow.

subservient serving as an instrument or means. XVII. - L. *subserviēns*, *-ent-*, prp. of *subservīre* (whence **subserve** XVII); see SUB-, SERVE.

subside XVII. - L. *subsīdere*, f. SUB- + *sīdere* settle, sink. So **subsidence** †sediment; sinking or settling to the bottom XVII. - L. *subsīdentia*.

subsidy †help, aid; pecuniary aid granted by parliament, etc. XIV. - AN. *subsidie* = (O)F. *subside* - L. *subsidium* reserve of troops, support, assistance, rel. formally to (rare) *subsidēre*, f. SUB- + *sedēre* sit. So **subsidiary** auxiliary XVI. - L. *subsidiārius*. Hence **subsidize** XVIII.

subsist exist as substance or entity XVI; provide for XVII; support oneself *on*. - L. *subsistere* stand still or firm, f. SUB- + *sistere* STAND. So **subsistence** substantial existence XV; provision of support for animal life XVII; *s. money*, money paid on account of wages, etc. XVII; shortened to *subsist money* XIX. - late L.

subsoil XVIII. f. SUB- + SOIL[1].

substance essence XIII; a being XIV; (philos.) that which underlies phenomena; material, matter; means, wealth. - (O)F. - L. *substantia* being, essence, material property, f. *substāre*, f. SUB- + *stāre* STAND. So **substantial** XIV. - (O)F. *substantiel* or ChrL. *substantiālis*; see -AL[1]. **substantially** (-LY[2]) XIV. **substantiate** give substance to. XVII. f. pp. stem of medL. *substantiāre*; see -ATE[3]. **substantive** self-existent XV; (gram.) denoting a substance XVI; having substance XIX; sb. for *noun s.* (late L. *nomen substantivum*) XIV. - (O)F. *substantif, -ive* or late L. *substantīvus*.

substitute †appoint as deputy or delegate; put one in place of another. XVI. f. pp. stem of L. *substituere*, f. SUB- + *statuere* (see STATUTE). So sb. XIV. - L. *substitūtus*, pp. of *substituere*. **substitution** XIV. - late L.

substratum XVII. - pp. of L. *substernere*; see SUB-, STRATUM.

subsume †bring under, subjoin; state a minor premiss XVI; bring (one idea) *under* another XIX. - medL. *subsūmere*, f. SUB- + *sūmere* take.

subtend (geom.) extend under, be opposite to. XVI. - L. *subtendere*; see SUB-, TEND[2].

subter- prefix repr. L. *subter* adv. and prep. below, underneath, in the sense 'secretly' in **subterfuge** XVI. - F. or - late L. *subterfugium*, f. L. *subterfugere* escape secretly.

subterranean XVII. f. L. *subterrāneus*, f. SUB- + *terra* earth; see -AN, -EAN.

subtle of thin or fine consistency; marked by acumen or fine discrimination. XIV. ME. *sutil, sotil* - OF. *sutil, so(u)til* - L. *subtīlis*, prob. for **subtexlis*, **subtēlis*, f. **sub texlā*, **sub tēlā* (passing) under the warp (weaver's term). So **subtlety** (-TY[2]) XIV. - OF. *s(o)utilté* :- L. *subtilitātem*. Hence **subtly** XIV. The var. **subtil(e)** (- OF. *subtil*, latinized form of *sutil*) arose in late ME. and remained till modern times along with **subtil(i)ty** in arch. or affected use.

subtract †withdraw; deduct. XVI. f. *subtract-*, pp. stem of L. *subtrahere*, f. SUB- + *trahere* draw. So **subtraction** †withdrawal XIV; taking of one quantity *from* another XV. - late L. *subtractiō, -ōn-*.

subulate (nat. hist.) awl-shaped; slender and tapering. XVIII. f. L. *sūbula* awl; see -ATE[1].

suburb XIV. - (O)F. *suburbe* or L. *suburbium*, f. SUB- + *urbs* city. So **suburban** XVII. - L. *suburbānus*. Hence **suburbia** XIX.

subvention †subsidy levied by the state XV; †provision of support XVI; grant of money in aid XIX. - (O)F. - late L. *subventiō, -ōn-*, f. *subvenīre* come to the help of, f. SUB- + *venīre* COME; see -TION.

subvert overturn, overthrow. XIV. - OF. *subvertir* or L. *subvertere*, f. SUB- + *vertere* turn. So **subversion** XIV. - (O)F. or late L.

subway underground passage or tunnel. XIX. f. SUB- + WAY.

succedaneum substitute. XVII. - n. of L. *succēdāneus*, f. *succēdere* come close after; see next.

succeed come next after another XIV; follow in the course of events XV (trans. XVI); have a certain issue (now always fortunate) XV; attain a desired end XVI. ME. *succede* - (O)F. *succéder* or L. *succēdere* go under or up, come close after, go near, go on well, f. SUB- + *cēdere* go. So **success** †issue, result; †fortune (good or bad); prosperous achievement XVI. - L. *successus*, f. pp. stem of *succēdere*. Hence **successful** XVI. So **succession** XIV. - (O)F. *succession* or L. *successiō, -ōn-*. **successive** XV. - medL. **successor** XIII. - OF. *successour* (mod. *-eur*) - L. *successor, -ōr-*.

succentor †one who takes up the chant after the precentor; precentor's deputy. XVII. - late L. *succentor*, f. L. *succinere* sing the accompaniment to, f. SUB- + *canere* sing; see -OR[1].

succinct †pp. girded, girt XV; adj. brief and concise XVI. - L. *succinctus*, pp. of *succingere*, f. SUB- + *cingere* gird.

succory chicory plant. XVI. alt. of *cicoree, sichorie*, early forms of CHICORY, after MLG. *suckerie*, MDu. *sūkerie* (Du. *suikerei*).

succotash N. Amer. Indian dish of green maize and beans. XVIII. of Algonquian orig.

succour help, aid. XIII. ME. *sucurs, soc(o)urs* - OF. *sucurs, socours* (mod. *secours*) :- medL. *succursus*, f. *succurs-*, pp. stem of L. *succurrere*, f. SUB- + *currere* run. The final *s* was early (XIII) apprehended as the pl. suffix and a new sg. (*socour*) came into existence. So **succour** vb. XIII. - OF. *socorre* (:- L. *succurrere*) and *suc(c)urir* (mod. *secourir*).

succubus demon in female form having intercourse with men XVI; strumpet XVII. - medL. *succubus*, m. form with fem. meaning; corr. to late L. *succuba*, f. SUB- + *cub-* lie down (see INCUBUS).

succulent juicy. XVII. - L. *succulentus* (*sūcu-*), f. *succus* (*sūcus*) juice; see -ULENT.

succumb †bring down, overwhelm XV; †(Sc.) fail in a cause XVI; sink under pressure XVII. - (O)F. *succomber* or L. *succumbere*, f. SUB- + *-cumbere* lie (see INCUMBENT).

such of the kind described or implied. OE. *swilċ, swelċ, swylċ*, ME. *swich, swech, swuch*, mod. dial. *sich, sech*; cogn. Gmc. forms a· e OS. *sulīk*, OHG. *sulīh, solīh* (Du. *zulk*, G. *solch*), ON. *slíkr*, Goth. *swaleiks*; f. Gmc. **swa*, **swe* SO + **līk-* body, form (see LIKE[2]). Hence **suchlike** (LIKE[1]) XV.

suck draw liquid with the mouth OE.; in various fig. uses from XIV. OE. str. vb. *sūcan* (becoming weak from XIV), corr. to L. *sūgere*, (O)Ir. *súgim*, f. IE. **sug-*, of which a parallel imit. base **suk-* is repr. by OE. *sūgan*, OS., MLG., MDu. *sūgen* (Du. *zuigen*), OHG. *sūgan* (G. *saugen*), ON. *súga*. Hence **suck** sb. XII. **sucker** young mammal before it is weaned XIV; shoot of a plant XVI; sucking organ, part, etc. XVII.

suckle XV. perh. back-formation f. **suckling** infant at the breast XV, young animal that is suckled XVI, f. SUCK + -LING[1].

suction XVII. - late L. *sūctiō, -ōn-*, f. *sūct-*, pp. stem of *sūgere* SUCK; see -TION.

sudarium napkin for wiping the face. XVII. - L. *sūdārium*, f. *sūdor* SWEAT.

sudd floating vegetation obstructing the White Nile. XIX. - Arab. *sudd* obstruction.

sudden XIII. ME. *sode(i)n, -ain* - AN. *sodein, sudein*, (O)F. *soudain* :- late L. *subitānus*, for L.

subitāneus, f. *subitus* sudden, pp. of *subīre* go stealthily, f. SUB- + *īre* go.

sudorific promoting sweat. XVII. - modL. *sūdōrificus*, f. *sūdor* SWEAT; see -FIC.

suds †dregs, filth; †flood-water, fen-water; (frothy mass of) soapy water (†barber's lather). XVI. of uncert. orig.; cf. MLG., MDu. *sudde*, MDu. *sudse* marsh, bog. The base is prob. Gmc. **suð*-, wk. grade of SEETHE.

sue †follow XIII; prosecute (an action), follow up, make a legal claim to (now *sue for*); apply for the grant of (a writ); institute legal proceedings (against) XIV. - AN. *suer*, *siwer*, *sure*, *suir(e)*, f. pres. stem *si(e)u*-, *seu*- of OF. *sivre* (mod. *suivre*) :- Rom. **sequere*, for L. *sequī* follow.

suède XIX. First in *suède gloves*, tr. F. *gants de Suède*, i.e. gloves of Sweden.

suet XIV. - AN. **suet*, **sewet*, f. *su(e)*, *seu*, OF. *seu*, *si(e)u*, *sif* (mod. *suif*) :- L. *sēbum* tallow, suet, grease.

suffer undergo, endure; tolerate, allow. XIII. ME. *suffre*, *so(e)ffre* - AN. *suffrir*, *soeffrir*, *-er*, OF. *sof(f)rir* (mod. *souffrir*) :- Rom. **sufferīre*, for L. *sufferre*, f. *suf*- SUB- + *ferre* BEAR². So **sufferance** (arch.) suffering, long-suffering; sanction, permission, toleration (now only in phr. *on s.* and in legal use). XIII. - AN., OF. *suffraunce*, *soffrance* (mod. *souffrance* suffering) :- L. *sufferentia*.

suffice XIV. f. OF. *suffis*-, pres. stem of *suffire* :- L. *sufficere*, f. *suf*- SUB- + *facere* DO¹. So **sufficient** XIV. - OF. *sufficient* or L. *sufficiēns*, *-ent*-, prp. of *sufficere*. **sufficiency** XV. - late L.

suffix element attached to the end of a word XVIII; (math.) inferior index XIX. - *suffīxum*, n. pp. of L. *suffīgere*, f. *suf*- SUB- + *fīgere* FIX. So **suffix** vb. subjoin XVII; add as a suffix XVIII. Partly f. L. *suffīxus*, partly f. the sb.

suffocate XVI. f. pp. stem of L. *suffocāre*, f. *suf*- SUB- + *faucēs* throat; see -ATE³.

suffragan bishop considered in relation to his metropolitan, by whom he may be summoned to give his suffrage; subsidiary bishop in the Church of England. - AN., OF. *suffragan*, medL. *suffragāneus*, f. L. *suffragium* SUFFRAGE; see -AN.

suffrage pl. (intercessory) prayers XIV; vote XVI. - L. *suffrāgium*, partly through F. *suffrage*; of uncert. orig.

suffuse overspread as with fluid, colour, etc. XVI. f. *suffūs*-, pp. stem of L. *suffundere*, f. *suf*- SUB- + *fundere* pour. So **suffusion** XIV. - L.

Sufi one of a Muslim sect. XVII. - Arab. *ṣūfī*, f. *ṣūf* wool (with ref. to their garments).

sugar sweet crystalline substance obtained from fruit juices XIII (*suker*); (old chem.) compound resembling sugar in form or taste XVII; (mod. chem.) soluble more or less sweet carbohydrate XIX. ME. *suker*, *sucre*, *sugre*, *suger* (*sugar* from XVI) - OF. *çukre*, *sukere* (mod. *sucre*) - It. *zucchero*, prob. - medL. *succarum* - Arab. *sukkar*. So **sugar-candy** sugar clarified and crystallized. XIV. - OF. *sucre candi* - Arab. *sukkar ḳandī*. **sugar-cane** XVI, **-loaf** XV. Hence vb. XV, **sugary** (-Y¹) XVI.

suggest XVI. f. *suggest*-, pp. stem of L. *suggerere*, f. *sug*- SUB- + *gerere* bear, carry, bring. So **suggestion** XIV. - (O)F. - L. Hence **suggestive** XVII.

suicide¹ one who takes his own life. XVIII. - modL. *suīcīda*, f. L. *suī* of oneself; see -CIDE¹. So **suicide**² taking one's own life. XVII; see -CIDE². Hence **suicidal** (-AL¹) XVIII.

suint grease in the wool of sheep. XVIII. - F. *suint*, earlier †*suing*, f. *suer* sweat.

suit A. (hist.) attendance at court XIII; B. †pursuit XIV; legal process XV; C. †train, suite XIII; D. †livery, garb XIII; E. set, series XV. ME. *siute*, *siwte*, *s(e)ute* - AN. *siute*, OF. *si(e)ute* (mod. *suite*) :- Gallo-Rom. **sequita*, sb. use of fem. pp. of **sequere* follow, SUE. Hence **suit** vb. †sue, pursue XV; provide with apparel; be agreeable or convenient to XVI. Whence **suitable** †matching, to match; †agreeing, accordant XVI; fitting, appropriate XVII.

suite A. train of attendants XVII; B. succession, series XVIII; C. set of rooms XVIII, of furniture XIX. - F. *suite*; see SUIT. Sense C is of English development.

suitor †frequenter XIII; †adherent XIV; (arch.) petitioner XVI; wooer. - AN. *seutor*, *suitour*, *sut(i)er*, *-or* - L. *secūtor*, *-ōr*- follower, f. *sequī*, *secūt*- follow, after *suite* SUIT.

sulcate grooved. XVIII. - L. *sulcātus*, pp. of *sulcāre* plough, f. *sulcus* groove, furrow (which has been used in Eng. in spec. senses since XVII).

sulk indulge in ill-humour. XVIII. perh. back-formation from somewhat earlier **sulky** adj., used also as sb. for a carriage seated for one person. *Sulky* was perh. an extension with -Y¹ of an adj. †*sulke* (XVII) hard to dispose of, slow in going off.

sullen marked by gloomy ill-humour; of gloomy condition or aspect. XVI. Later form of †*solein*, †*-eyne* sole, solitary, morose (XIV) - AN. **solein*, **solain*, f. *sol* SOLE³, after OF. *soltain*, *soutain* :- late L. *sōlitaneus*, f. L. *sōlus*.

sully pollute, †intr. for pass. XVI. perh. - F. *souiller*; see SOIL³.

sulphur, U.S. **sulfur** greenish-yellow non-metallic element; brimstone. XIV. ME. *soufre*, *solfre*, *sulph(e)re* - AN. *sulf(e)re*, (O)F. *soufre* :- L. *sulfur*, *-phur*. Comb. form **sulpho-**, before a vowel **sulph-**. So **sulphate/sulphite** salt of sulphuric/sulphurous acid. XVIII. - F. *sulphat/sulphite*. **sulphureous** pert. to sulphur XVI; †hellish, satanic XVII. f. L. *sulphureus*. **sulphuretted** combined chemically with sulphur. XIX. f. *sulphuret* - modL. *sulphuretum*; see -URET. **sulphuric** *s. acid* XVIII. - F. *sulfurique*. Hence **sulphide** compound of sulphur with another element. XIX. **sulphurous, sulphury** (-Y¹) XVI. See -Y¹.

sultan Muslim sovereign XVI; despot, tyrant XVII; sweet-scented annual, *Centaurea moschata* and *C. suaveolens*. - F. *sultan* or medL. *sultānus* - Arab. *sulṭān* power, dominion, ruler, king. So **sultana** sultan's wife XVI; mistress, concubine XVIII; purple gallinule XIX; (*s. raisin*) small seedless raisin. - It., fem. of *sultano* sultan. Hence **sultanate** (-ATE¹) XIX.

sultry oppressively hot and moist. XVI. f. †*sulter* be sweltering hot (XVI), prob. for **swulter*, rel. to SWELTER; see -Y¹.

sum quantity *of money*; total amount XIII; summary, epitome XIV; quantity resulting from the addition of quantities XV. ME. *summe, somme* - OF. *summe*, (also mod.) *somme* :- L. *summa*, sb. use of fem. of *summus* :- **supmus*, superl. f. stem of *super, superus* (see SUPERIOR). So **sum** vb. XIII. - (O)F. *sommer* or late L. *summāre*. **summation** XVIII. f. late L. *summāre*.

sumac(h) preparation of dried leaves of plants of the genus *Rhus* XIV; plant of this genus XVI. - (O)F. *sumac* or medL. *sumac(h)* - Arab. *summāḳ*.

summary comprising the chief points or substance XV; done without delay, (leg.) carried out without certain formalities XVIII (the adv. **summarily** (-LY²) is XVI). - medL. *summārius* (in classL. only in n. sb.), f. *summa* SUM; see -ARY. As sb. XVI. - L. *summārium*. Hence **summarize** XIX.

summer¹ second and warmest season of the year. OE. *sumor*, corr. to OS., OHG. *sumar* (Du. *zomer*, G. *sommer*), MLG. *sommer*, ON. *sumar*; rel. to Skr. *sámā* half-year, year, OIr. *sam, samrad*, W. *ham, haf* summer.

summer² †packhorse; (archit.) horizontal bearing-beam. XIV. - AN. *sumer, somer*, OF. *somier* (mod. *sommier*) - Rom. **saumārius*, for late L. *sagmārius*, f. *sagma* pack-saddle - Gr. *ságma*.

summit XV. - OF. *som(m)ete*, also *somet, sumet* (mod. *sommet*), f. *som, sum* :- L. *summum*, n. sg. of *summus* (see SUM); the sp. with *-it* (from XVII) is due to assim. to †*summity* summit (XIV-XVIII) - (O)F. *sommité* - late L. *summitās* (see -ITY).

summons sb. XIII. ME. *somouns* - OF. *somonce, sumunse* (mod. *semonce*) :- Gallo-Rom. **summonsa*, for L. *summonita*, fem. pp. (used sb.) of *summonēre*.

summum bonum XVI. - L., i.e. *summum* n. sg. of *summus* highest, *bonum* n. sg. of *bonus* good used sb.

sump †marsh XV; (dial.) dirty pool; pit for collecting water XVII. - (M)LG., MDu. *sump*, or in mining use - G. *sumpf*, rel. to SWAMP.

sumpter †driver of a pack-horse XIV; pack-horse XVI. - OF. *som(m)etier* :- Rom. **saumatārius*, f. late L. *sagma, sagmat-* pack-saddle (see SUMMER²).

sumptuary pert. to expenditure. XVI. - L. *sumptuārius*, f. *sumptus* expenditure, expense, f. *sūmere, sumpt-* consume, spend; see -ARY. So **sumptuous** made at great cost XV; †spending largely XVI. - (O)F. *somptueux* - L. *sumptuōsus*.

sun OE. *sunne* (fem.) = OS., OHG., ON. (poet.) *sunna* (Du. *zon*, G. *sonne*), Goth. *sunnō*, beside OE. *sunna* (m.), OHG., OS. *sunno* :- Gmc. **sunnōn, -an-*; f. IE. **su-* with *n*-formative, beside **sāu-* with *l*-formative in Homeric Gr. *ēélios* :- **sāwelijos* (Attic *hḗlios*), L. *sōl*, ON. *sól*, Goth. *sauil*, W. *haul*. Hence vb. XVI; **sunny** (-Y¹) XIII. Comps. **sunbeam** OE. *sunn(e)bēam*. **sunburn** sb. XVII; f. the vb. (XVI), back-formation from *sunburning* (XVI), *sunburnt* (*sunne ybrent* XIV). **sundew** plant of the genus *Drosera*. XVI. tr. Du. *son-, sundauw* = G. *sonnentau*, tr. L. *rōs sōlis*. **sundial** XVI. **sundown** setting of the sun XVII. perh. shortening of †*sunne gate downe* (XV), †*sun go downe* (XVI). **sunflower** †heliotrope; plant of the genus *Helianthus*, with showy golden-rayed flowers. XVI. tr. modL. *flōs sōlis* XVI. **sunrise** XV. perh. evolved, through syntactical ambiguity, from a clause such as *before the sun rise* (pres. subjunctive of the vb.); cf. ME. *sonne rist* (XIII). **sunset** OE. (late Nhb.) *sunset*; perh. partly from a clause like *ere the sun set*. **sunshade** parasol. XIX. **sunstroke** XIX. For earlier *stroke of the sun*, tr. F. *coup de soleil*. **sun-up** (U.S.) sunrise XIX. After *sun-down*.

sundae portion of ice cream served with syrup, etc. XX (orig. U.S.). perh. alt. of next.

Sunday OE. *sunnandæġ* (Nhb. *sunnadæġ*) = OS. *sunnondag*, OHG. *sunnuntag* (Du. *zondag*, G. *sonntag*), ON. *sunnudagr*; Gmc. tr. of L. *diēs sōlis*.

sunder phr. *in s.*, asunder, apart XIII. alt. of ASUNDER (OE. *onsundran, -um*) by substitution of IN¹ for ON, partly after ON. *í sundr*. So **sunder** vb. separate, part. Late OE. *sundrian* (beside *syndrian*), for earlier *āsundrian*, and *ġe-, on-, tōsundrian*, corr. to OHG. *sunt(a)rōn, sund(e)rōn* (G. *sondern*), ON. *sundra*, f. Gmc. adv. ('separately') repr. by OE. *sundor*, OS. *sundar* (MLG. *sunder*; Du. *zonder* prep.), OHG. *suntar* (MHG. *sunder*; G. *sonder*, with var. *sondern* but), ON. *sundr*, Goth. *sundrō*; f. IE. **su-*, repr. also by Skr. *sanitúr* besides, Gr. *háteros* (Attic *héteros*) one of two, and (without *t*-suffix) L. *sine* without. So **sundry** OE. *syndriġ* separate, special, private, corr. to MLG. *sunder(i)ch*, OHG. *sunt(a)rīc*; see -Y¹. **sundries** XIX.

sunn E. Indian shrub, cultivated for its fibre. XVIII. - Hind. *san* - Skr. *śaṇá-* hemp.

Sunni orthodox Muslim, who accepts the *Sunna* (body of tradition) as of equal authority with the Koran. XVII. - Arab. *sunnī* lawful, f. *sunna* form, way, course, rule.

sup¹ take liquid into the mouth in small quantities. OE. str. vb. *sūpan* = MLG. *sūpen*, OHG. *sūfan* (Du. *zuipen*, G. *saufen* drink, booze), ON. *súpa*. Hence sb. XVI.

sup² take supper. XIII. - OF. *super, soper* (mod. *souper*), f. Gmc. **sup-* (see SOP, SUP¹, and cf. SOUP).

sup- see SUB-.

super short for SUPERFICIAL, SUPERFINE, SUPERINTENDENT, SUPERNUMERARY. XIX.

super- prefix repr. L. *super-*, being the adv. and prep. *super* above, on the top of, beyond, besides, rel. to SUB-.

The chief meanings are: (1) over, above, at the top (of), in adv., prep., or adj. force, as *superaltar* (XIV), *-celestial* (XVI), *superstructure* (XVII); (2) higher in rank, quality, or degree, as *superessential* (XVI), *supermundane* (XVII), *supersensual* (XVII); (3) in or to the highest or a very high degree, (hence) in excess, as *superabound, -abundant, -fine* (XV); (4) expressing addition, as *superadd* (XV), *super-tax* (XX). Cf. SUPRA-, SUR-².

superable XVII. - L. *superābilis*, f. *superāre* overcome, f. SUPER-; see -ABLE.

superannuated disqualified or impaired by age. XVII. f. medL. *superannuātus*, alt. of *superannātus*, f. SUPER- + *annus* year, with assim. to *annuus* ANNUAL; see -ATE², -ED¹. So **superannuation** XVII.

superb XVI. - (O)F. *superbe* or L. *superbus* proud, superior, distinguished, f. *super* above (SUPER-).

supercargo (naut.) officer who superintends the cargo. XVII. alt., by substitution of SUPER-, of *supracargo* (XVII-XIX) - Sp. *sobrecargo*.

supercilious XVI. - L. *superciliōsus*, f. L. *supercilium* eyebrow, f. SUPER- + *cilium* (lower) eyelid.

supererogation performance of good works beyond what is required. XVI. - late L. *supererogātiō, -ōn-*, f. L. *supererogāre*, f. SUPER- + *erōgāre* pay out, f. E- + *rogāre* ask. So **supererogatory** (-ORY²) XVI. - scholL. *supererogātōrius*.

superficies surface. XVI. - L., f. SUPER- + *faciēs* FACE. So **superficial** †(math.) compounded of two prime factors XIV; pert. to the surface XV; concerned only with the surface XVI. - late L. *superficiālis*.

superfine †extremely subtle XV; over-refined XVI; extremely fine XVII. - medL. **superfīnus* (implied in *superfīnitās*), f. L. SUPER + medL. *fīnus* FINE².

superfluous XV. f. L. *superfluus*, f. SUPER- + *fluere* FLOW; see -OUS. So **superfluity** XIV. - (O)F. - late L.

superhuman XVII. - late L. *superhūmānus*; see SUPER-, HUMAN.

superintend XVII. - ecclL. *superintendere*; see SUPER-, INTEND. So **superintendent** official having chief charge or oversight; in earliest use applied to Christian ministers in some church polities, as repr. Gr. *episkopos* 'overseer' (see BISHOP). XVI. - ecclL. *superintendēns, -ent-*.

superior situated higher XIV; of higher degree or status XV; *s. to* (†*s. than*) XVI; sb. XV. - OF. *superiour* (mod. *supérieur*) - L. *superior, -ōr-*, compar. of *superus* that is above, f. *super*; see SUPER-, -IOR. So **superiority** XVI. - (O)F. or medL.

superlative (gram.) XIV; surpassing all others XV. - (O)F. *superlatif, -ive* - late L. *superlātīvus*, f. *superlātus* (used as pp. of *superferre*), f. SUPER- + *lāt-*, pp. stem of *tollere* take away; see -IVE.

superman ideal superior type of man. XX (G. B. Shaw). tr. of G. *übermensch*, as used in 'Zarathustra', by F. W. Nietzsche, G. philosopher (1844-1900), f. *über* OVER + *mensch* human being.

supernaculum (drink) to the last drop. XVI (*super nag-*). modL., tr. G. *auf den nagel* (*trinken*) on to the nail.

supernal existing in the heavens. XV. - OF. *supernal* or medL. *supernālis*, f. L. *supernus*, f. *super* above.

supernatural XVI. - medL. *supernātūrālis*, f. L. SUPER + *nātūra* NATURE. So **supernaturally** XV.

supernumerary XVII. - late L. *supernumerārius*, f. *super numerum*; see SUPER-, NUMBER, -ARY.

superpose place above or upon. XIX. - F. *superposer*, after L. *superpōnere* (see SUPER-, POSE¹). So **superposition** (geom.) XVII; (gen.) XIX. - F. or late L.

superscribe inscribe on the top or surface of. - L. *superscrībere*, f. SUPER- + *scrībere* write. So **superscription** XIV. - late L.

supersede †postpone XV; †desist or refrain from; †render superfluous or void XVI; take the place of something set aside XVII. In early use often *-cede*. - OF. *supercéder*, later *-séder* - L. *supersedēre* (in medL. often *-cēdere*) set above, be superior to, refrain from, omit, f. SUPER- + *sedēre* SIT. **supersession** setting aside of a rule, etc. XVIII; substitution of a person in the place of one removed XIX. - F. or medL.

superstition XV. - (O)F. *superstition* or L. *superstitiō, -ōn-*, f. *superstāre* stand on or over, f. SUPER- + *stāre* STAND; see -TION. So **superstitious** XIV. - (O)F. *superstitieux* or L. *superstitiōsus*.

supersubstantial spiritual (in *s. bread*, i.e. of the Eucharist), transcending all substance. XVI. - ecclL. (Vulg.) *supersubstantiālis*, tr. Gr. *epioúsios* Matt. 6: 11 in the Lord's Prayer, which is usu. taken to mean '(bread) pert. to the coming day'; see SUPER-, SUBSTANTIAL.

supervene XVII. - L. *supervenīre*, f. SUPER- + *venīre* COME.

supervise †survey XVI; have the oversight of XVII. f. *supervīs-*, pp. stem of medL. *supervidēre*, f. L. SUPER- + *vidēre* see. So **supervision** XVII. - medL.

supination action of turning the hand or fore limb so that the back of it is downward or backward. XVII. - L. *supīnātiō, -ōn-*, f. *supīnāre*, f. *supīnus* SUPINE; see -ATION.

supine adj. lying on one's back XV; mentally or morally inert XVII. - L. *supīnus*, f. **sup-*, repr. in L. *super* above, *superus* higher, SUPERIOR; see -INE¹. So **supine** sb. form of verbal noun ending in *-tum, -tū, -sum, -sū*. XVI. - n. sg. of *supīnus* used sb.; this usage is unexpl.

supper XIII. ME. *super(e), soper(e)*, later *so(u)pper, sopper, supper* - OF. *soper, super* (mod. *souper*), sb. use of *soper* SUP²; see -ER⁴.

supplant dispossess another, esp. treacherously XIII (implied in *supplanter*); †trip up XIV; bring down, bring low; †uproot XVI. - (O)F. *supplanter* or L. *supplantāre* overthrow, f. SUB- + *planta* sole of the foot, PLANT.

supple †soft, yielding XIII; pliant, flexible XIV; compliant XIV. ME. *souple* - (O)F. :- Rom. **supples*, f. L. *supplex, -plic-* submissive, suppliant, lit. bending under, f. SUB- + **plic-* bend (see PLY¹).

supplement XIV. - L. *supplēmentum*, f. *supplēre* SUPPLY; see -MENT.

suppliant XV. - F., prp. of *supplier* - L. *supplicāre* SUPPLICATE; see -ANT. Also as adj. XVI.

supplicate beg humbly XV; at Oxford University, present a formal petition for a degree XVII. f. pp. stem of L. *supplicāre*, f. SUB- + †**plic-* bend (see PLY¹); see -ATE³. So **supplicant** sb. and adj. XVI. - L. prp. of *supplicāre*. **supplication** XIV. - (O)F. - L.

supply †help, succour, complete, supplement; make up for, compensate; fill (another's place) XIV; †fulfil, discharge (office or function) XV; furnish, provide XVI; take the place of (now only as a minister's substitute) XVII. ME. (in earliest use mainly Sc.) *sup(p)le, sowple*, later *supplie* - OF.

so(u)pleer, later *supplier* (mod. *suppléer*) - L. *supplēre* fill up, make good, complete, f. SUB- + *-plēre* fill. Hence **supply** sb. XV (in early use mainly Sc.).

support endure, tolerate XIV; strengthen the position of; furnish sustenance for XV; keep from failing XVI. - (O)F. *supporter* - L. *supportāre*, f. SUB- + *portāre* carry. Hence, or partly - F., **support** sb. XIV.

suppose †believe, think, guess; assume as a hypothesis XIV; infer hypothetically, incline to think XVII. - (O)F. *sup(p)oser*, f. SUB- + *poser* POSE[1], as a vb. corr. to **supposition** †something held to be true as the basis of argument XV; assumption of this hypothetical inference or belief XVI. - (O)F. *supposition* or medL. *suppositiō, -ōn-* (in older L. recorded only in senses 'placing under' and 'substitution'); cf. POSITION. So **supposititious** deceitfully substituted. XVII. f. L. *supposititius, -icius*, f. pp. stem of *suppōnere*. **suppository** XIV. - medL. *suppositōrium*.

suppress put down by force or authority XIV; subdue (feelings, etc.) XVI; keep secret. f. *suppress-*, pp. stem of L. *supprimere*, f. SUB- + *premere* PRESS. So **suppression** XVI - L. **suppressive** XVIII.

suppurate †cause to form pus XVI; secrete pus XVII. f. pp. stem of L. *suppūrāre*, f. SUB- + *pūs* PUS; see -ATE[3]. So **suppuration** XVI. - L.

supra- prefix repr. L. *suprā* adv. and prep., above, beyond, in addition (to), before the time of, in comps. parallel to those of *super-*, but with a different distribution; used in many techn. terms, esp. anat. and zool. (opp. INFRA-, SUB-). **supralapsarian** pert. to the view that God's election of some was antecedent to the Fall of Man XVII.

supreme A. (poet.) loftiest, topmost; B. highest in authority or rank; of the highest quality or degree. XVI. - L. *suprēmus*, f. *suprā*; see prec. and cf. EXTREME. Hence **supremacy** XVI.

sur-[1] var. of SUB-.

sur-[2] - (O)F. *sur-*, earlier *sor-*, *sour(e)-* :- L. *super*, used in various senses of SUPER-.

sura section of the Koran. XVII. - Arab. *sūra*.

surah soft twilled silk fabric. XIX. repr. F. pronunc. of SURAT.

sural pert. to the calf of the leg. XVII. f. L. *sūra* calf; see -AL[1].

surat designating cotton goods orig. made in *Surat*, a town and district in India. XVII.

surcease (arch.) cessation, suspension. XVI. f. *surcease* vb. (arch.) leave off, cease, desist (XV), f. OF. *sursis*, fem. *-sise* (cf. AN. *sursise* omission), pp. of *surseoir* refrain, delay, suspend :- L. *supersedēre* SUPERSEDE; early assim. in sp. to CEASE.

surcharge excessive or exorbitant charge. XVII. f. the vb. (XV) - OF. *surcharger*. See SUR-[2], CHARGE.

surcingle girth for a horse, etc. XIV. - OF. *so(u)rcengle*, f. *sor-* SUR-[2] + *cengle* (mod. *sangle*) :- L. *cingula*, f. *cingere* gird.

surcoat XIV. - OF. *s(o)urcot*; see SUR-[2], COAT.

surd (math.) irrational XVI; (phon.) voiceless XVIII. - L. *surdus* deaf, mute, silent, (of sound) dull, indistinct. The sense in math. arises from the use of L. *surdus* to render Gr. *álogos* (Euclid, book X, definition 10) speechless, irrational, absurd.

sure †safe, secure XIV-XVII; trustworthy, steadfast XIV; subjectively certain XIV; objectively certain XV. - OF. *sur(e)* (mod. *sûr*) :- L. *sēcūrus* SECURE. So **surety** †safety, security, certainty; bond entered into for the performance of an undertaking XIV; person undertaking this, bail XV. - OF. *surte* (mod. *sûreté*) :- L. *sēcūritās, -tāt-* SECURITY; see -TY[2]. Whence **suretyship** XVI.

surf swell of the sea breaking on the shore XVII; mass of foamy water on a shore XVIII. In early use sometimes in phr. *surf of the sea*; continuing in sense and chronology †*suff (of the sea)* XVI-XVII, and perh. an alt. of the latter.

surface XVII. - F., f. SUR-[2] + *face* FACE.

surfeit excess, superfluity XIII; excessive indulgence esp. in eating or drinking XIV; morbid condition arising from this XVI; nausea, satiety XVII. - OF. *sur-*, *sorfe(i)t* :- Rom. **superfactum*, sb. use of pp. of **superficere*, f. L. SUPER- + *facere* do, act. Hence **surfeit** vb. XIV.

surge[1] †fountain, source XV; rolling swell of the sea XVI; (naut.) slipping back of a rope wound round a capstan XVIII. In the earliest exx. of the first sense tr. OF. *sourgeon* (mod. *surgeon*) and prob. - its base *sourge-*, pres. stem of *sourdre* (see next).

surge[2] †toss or ride on the waves; †rise, spring; swell or heave, as a large wave XVI; (naut.) slip back, as a rope, etc. XVII. f. OF. *sourge-*, pres. stem of *sourdre* :- L. *surgere* rise, beside *surrigere*, f. SUB- + *regere* RULE; or - OF. *sorgir* (mod. *surgir*) - L. *surgere*.

surgeon one who heals by manual operation XIV; medical officer in the forces XVI. ME. *surg(i)en* - AN. *surgien*, contr. of OF. *serurgien, cir-* (mod. *chirurgien*) - Rom. **chirurgiānus*, f. L. *chīrurgia* surgery - Gr. *kheirourgíā*, f. *kheír* hand + *erg-* WORK. So **surgery** surgeon's art XIV; medical practitioner's consulting room XIX. - OF. *surgerie*, contr. of *sirurgerie*. Hence **surgical** XVIII.

surly †lordly, majestic; †masterful, imperious, haughty XVI; churlishly ill-humoured XVII. alt. of †*sirly* (XIV-XVII), f. SIR + -LY[1].

surmise †charge *upon*, allege against XV; †devise, suppose XVI; infer conjecturally XVII. f. AN., OF. *surmis(e)*, pp. of *surmettre* - late L. *supermittere* (in medL. accuse), f. SUPER- + *mittere* put. So **surmise** sb. †allegation XV; conjecture XVI.

surmount XIV. - (O)F. *surmonter*; see SUR-[2], MOUNT[2].

surmullet red mullet. XVII. - F. *surmulet*, OF. *sor* (mod. *saur*) red (of unkn. orig.) + *mulet* MULLET.

surname †name or epithet added to a person's name(s), derived from his birthplace or from some quality or achievement; person's family name XIV. Partial tr. of †*surnoun* (XIV) - AN. *surnoun*, (O)F. *surnom*, f. SUR-[2] + *noun* NAME (cf. NOUN). Hence vb. XVI.

surpass XVI. - F. *surpasser*, f. SUR-[2] + *passer* PASS.

surplice XIII. - AN. *surplis*, OF. *sourpelis* (mod.

surplis) - medL. *superpellicium*, *-eum*, sb. use of n. of adj. f. SUPER- + *pellicia* fur garment; so called because orig. put on over furred garments worn in church.

surplus XIV. - AN. *surplus*, OF. *so(u)rplus* (mod. *surplus*) - medL. *superplūs*, f. SUPER- + *plūs* more. So **surplusage** XV. - medL. *surplūsāgium*.

surprise (mil.) sudden attack or capture XV (phr. *take by s.*); something unexpectedly sudden XVI; feeling caused by this XVII. - (O)F., sb. use of fem. pp. of *surprendre*. So **surprise** vb. †overcome *with* desire, etc. XV; assail suddenly, take unawares XVI; affect with surprise XVII. prob. first in pp. f. (O)F. *surpris(e)*, pp. of *surprendre* :- medL. *superprehendere*, f. L. SUPER- + *præhendere* seize.

surrealism XX. - F. *surréalisme*; see SUR-[2], REALISM. So **surrealist, surrealistic** XX.

surrebutter (leg.) plaintiff's reply to a defendant's rebutter. XVII. f. SUR-[2] + REBUTTER, after **surrejoinder** (XVI), plaintiff's reply to defendant's rejoinder.

surrender (leg.) giving up of an estate or tenancy; giving up of oneself. XV. - AN. *surrender*, OF. inf. *surrendre* used as sb. (see -ER[6]), whence **surrender** vb. XV; see SUR-[2], RENDER.

surreptitious obtained by fraudulent misrepresentation XV; obtained by stealth XVII. f. L. *surreptītius*, *-īcius*, f. *surrept-*, pp. stem of *surripere* seize secretly, (Vulg.) make false suggestions, f. SUB- + *rapere* seize; see -ITIOUS.

surrogate deputy, spec. of a judge, bishop. XVII. - L. *surrogātus*, var. of *subrogātus*, pp. of *subrogāre* put in another's place, f. SUB- + *rogāre* ask, ask for or propose the appointment of.

surround †A. overflow XV; B. encompass, go round XVII. - AN. *sur(o)under*, OF. *s(o)uronder* overflow, abound, dominate :- late L. *superundāre* overflow (fig.), f. SUPER- + *undāre* rise in waves, f. *unda* wave.

surtax XIX. - F. *surtaxe*; see SUR-, TAX.

surtout greatcoat. XVII. - F., f. *sur* above (cf. SUR-) + *tout* everything.

surveillance XIX. - F., f. *surveiller*, f. SUR-[2] + *veiller* watch (:- L. *vigilāre*); see -ANCE.

survey oversee, supervise XV; determine the conditions of (a tract of ground); †inspect XVI; take a wide view of. - AN. *survei(e)r*, OF. *so(u)rveeir* (pres. stem *survey-*) :- medL. *supervidēre*, f. L. SUPER- + *vidēre* see. Hence sb. XVI. So **surveyor** (-OR[1]) XV. - AN., OF. *sur-*, *sorve(i)our*.

survive remain alive, live on XV; outlive XVI. - AN. *survivre*, OF. *sourvivre* (mod. *sur-*) - L. *supervīvere*, f. SUPER- + *vīvere* live. Hence **survival** (-AL[2]), **survivor** (-OR[1]) XVI.

susceptible capable of undergoing or being affected (by) XVII; subject to impression XVIII. - late L. *susceptibilis*, f. *suscept-*, pp. stem of *suscipere*, f. SUB- + *capere* take.

suslik species of ground squirrel. XVIII. - Russ. *súslik*.

suspect under suspicion; †having suspicion XIV; sb. suspected person XVI; disused in the adj. after *c.*1700, and in the sb. after *c.*1600 until revived in XIX after the F. use of the word for 'one suspected of hostility or indifference to the Revolution'. - (O)F. *suspect* or L. *suspectus*, pp. of *suspicere* look up (to), admire, suspect, f. SUB- + *specere* look; on the pp. stem of this L. vb. was formed **suspect** vb. XV.

suspend A. hold up, put off XIII; B. hang (up) XV. - (O)F. *suspendre* or L. *suspendere*, f. SUB- + *pendēre* hang. Hence **suspender** (-ER[1]) †one who suspends XVI; (orig. U.S.) that by which something is suspended XIX. So **suspense** XV. - AN., OF. *suspens(e)* abeyance, delay, repr. medL. sb. uses of n. and fem. of pp. of L. *suspendere*. **suspension** XVI. - (O)F. or L.

suspicion action of suspecting. XIV. - AN. *suspeciun*, var. of OF. *sospeçon* (mod. *soupçon*) :- medL. *suspectiō*, *-ōn-*; see SUSPECT.

suspire (arch.) sigh (*for*). XV. - L. *suspīrāre*, f. SUB- + *spīrāre* breathe.

sustain †support, uphold the course of, keep in being XIII; endure without failing; bear the weight of XIV. ME. *sos-*, *susteine* - AN. *sustein-*, OF. *so(u)stein-*, tonic stem of *so(u)stenir* (mod. *soutenir*) - L. *sustinēre*, f. SUB- + *tenēre* hold, keep. So **sustenance** means of subsistence XIII; act of sustaining XIV. - AN. *sustenaunce*, OF. *so(u)stenance* (mod. *soutenance*). **sustentation** XIV. - (O)F. or L.

susurration whispering. XIV. - late L. *susurrātiō*, *-ōn-*, f. L. *susurrāre*, f. *susurrus* whisper (of imit. orig.); see -ATION.

sutler army follower selling provisions to soldiers. XVI. - Du. †*soeteler* (mod. *zoetelaar*), MLG. *suteler*, *sudeler*, f. †*soetelen* befoul, perform mean duties, follow a low trade.

suttee Hindu widow who immolated herself with her husband's body XVIII; such immolation XIX. - Hind. :- Skr. *satī* faithful wife, f. *sat* good, wise, lit. being, prp. of *ásti* is (see BE).

suture sewing, stitching; (anat., bot.) junction. XVI. - F. *suture* or L. *sūtūra*, f. *sūt-*, pp. stem of *suere* SEW; see -URE.

suzerain feudal overlord. XIX. - F., prob. f. *sus* above, up (:- L. *sūsum*), after *souverain* SOVEREIGN.

svelte XIX. - F. *svelte* - It. *svelto* :- popL. **exvellitus*, pp. of **exvellere*, f. L. EX-[1] + *vellere* pluck.

swab mop XVI; absorbent mass of fabric for cleansing XVIII. f. Gmc. base meaning 'sway about', 'splash in water', as in (M)LG. *swabben* splash, sway, Norw. *svabba* splash, wade, LG. *swabber* (G. *schwabber*) mop, swab, Du. *zwabberen* mop. So **swab** vb. (dial.) sway about XV; mop *up* XVIII. **swabber** (-ER[1]) member of a crew that swabs decks. XVI.

swaddle bind (an infant) in lengths of bandage. XV. f. SWATHE[2] + -LE[3]. The earliest record of the formation is in *swaðelbond* swaddling-clothes XIII. Hence **swaddling-band(s)** XIV, **-clothes** XVI.

swag (dial.) swaying movement XVII; ornamental wreath or festoon XVIII; thief's booty XIX. of obscure orig.; cf. Norw. *swagga* sway. So **swag** vb. (dial.) move or cause to move unsteadily XVI; sink down XVII.

swage tool for bending cold metal. XIX. - F. *suage*, earlier *souage*, of unkn. orig.

swagger behave overbearingly as if among inferiors. XVI. Presumably f. SWAG + -ER[4].

swain †young man attending on a knight; man of low degree XII; †male servant XIII; †man, youth; farm hand, shepherd, rustic XVI; (country) lover. - ON. *sveinn* boy, servant, attendant = OE. *swān* swineherd, MLG. *swēn*, OHG. *swein* :- Gmc. **swainaz*.

swallow[1] bird of the genus *Hirundo*. OE. *swealwe* = OS. *swala* (Du. *zwaluw*), OHG. *swal(a)wa* (G. *schwalbe*), ON. *svala* :- Gmc. **swalwōn*.

swallow[2] take into the stomach through the mouth and gullet; also transf. and fig. OE. str. vb. *swelgan* = OS. *farswelgan* (Du. *swelgen*), OHG. *swel(a)han* (G. *schwelgen*), ON. *svelga* :- Gmc. **swelʒan*, f. **swelʒ-* **swalʒ-* **swulʒ-*, repr. also by OE. *ġeswelg* gulf, abyss, OHG. *swelgo* glutton, ON. *svelgr* whirlpool, devourer. Weak forms of pt. and pp. appeared XIV.

swami Hindu idol XVIII; Hindu religious teacher XX. - Hindi *svāmī* master, lord, prince (used as a respectful address) :- Skr. *svāmín-*.

swamp low-lying wet ground XVII; (local) depression in land XVIII. Identical in form with (dial.) *swamp* sunk (XIV), the notion of 'depression, subsidence' being perh. the connecting link. Hence vb. (orig. pass.) XVII.

swan OE. *swan* = OS. *suan*, OHG. *swan* (G. *schwan*), ON. *svanr* :- Gmc. **swanaz*; perh. based on IE. **swon-* **swen-*, repr. by Skr. *svaná-* noise, L. *sonere*, *sonāre* SOUND[3]. Comp. **swan-upping** taking up swans to mark them for ownership. XVI. *upping* f. *up* vb. drive up and catch swans; see -ING[1].

swank (sl.) behave ostentatiously. XIX. of uncert. orig.

swap, swop †strike, hit; †move quickly; †strike hands on a bargain XIV; †strike (a bargain) XVI; exchange *for*. prob. imit. of a smart resounding blow. Hence **swap, swop** sb. XIV.

sward †skin of the body; (dial.) rind of pork OE.; upper layer of the earth (esp. *greensward*; cf. MLG. *grönswarde*) XV. OE. *sweard*, corr. to MLG., MDu. *swarde* hairy skin, MHG. *swarte* (G. *schwarte* bacon rind, crust), ON. *svǫrðr* skin (of the head), walrus hide, greensward; of unkn. orig. The OE. word, if it survived, was reinforced in ME. by the Scand. and LG. forms.

swarm[1] body of bees in a compact mass. OE. *swearm* = OS., MLG. *swarm*, OHG. *swar(a)m* (G. *schwarm*), ON. *svarmr* :- Gmc. **swarmaz*. Hence **swarm** vb. gather in a swarm or dense crowd. XIV. Cf., with mutation, OE. *swirman*, **swierman* = MLG., MDu. *swermen*, MHG. *swärmen* (G. *schwärmen*).

swarm[2] climb *up* a pole, etc. XVI. of unkn. orig.

swart (arch., dial.) of dark colour. OE. *sweart* = OS. *swart* (Du. *zwart*), OHG. *swarz* (G. *schwarz*), ON. *svartr*, Goth. *swarts* :- Gmc. **swartaz*.

swarthy of dark hue, blackish. XVI. unexpl. alt. of †*swarty*, extension of *swart* with -Y[1].

swash[1] dash violently, make a noise as of clashing swords XVI. of imit. orig. Comp. **swashbuckler** swaggerer XVI; lit. one who makes a blustering noise by striking his own or his opponent's shield with his sword.

swash[2] (in turning, etc.) inclined obliquely to the axis of the work; (typogr.) having flourished strokes to fill gaps. XVII. of unkn. orig.

swastika the symbol 卐. XIX. - Skr. *svastika-*, f. *svasti-* well-being, fortune, luck.

swat (dial.) squat XVII; hit smartly XVIII. dial. var. of SQUAT.

swath, swathe[1] †track, trace OE.; width of grass, etc. cut, measure of grass land; now of grass, etc. reaped XIV. OE. *swæð* and *swaðu*, corr. to MLG. *swat*, *swāde* (Du. *zwad*, *zwade*), MHG. *swade* (G. *schwade*).

swathe[2] wrapping of linen, etc. Late OE. **swæð*, only in d. pl. *swaðum*; rel. to **swathe** vb. late OE. *swaðian*.

sway †bias; rule, dominion XVI. So vb. move or swing to one side and the other XVI. corr. formally to Du. *zwaaien* swing, wave, walk totteringly, LG. *swājen* move to and fro as with the wind; but preceded by late ME. *sweigh*, *sweye*, applied to sweeping or swinging motion, the vocalism of which corr. to that of ON. *sveigja* bend, (intr.) give way; the history is obscure.

swear pt. *swore*, pp. *sworn* A. take a solemn oath, intr. and trans. OE. B. bind by an oath OE. C. use profane language XV. OE. str. (rarely wk.) vb. *swerian* = OS. *swerian* (Du. *zweren*), OHG. *swer(i)an* (G. *schwören*), ON. *sverja* :- Gmc. **swarjan* (cf. Goth. *swaran*), f. **swar-*, repr. also by ON. *svar*, *svara* answer (sb. and vb.), OE. *andswaru* ANSWER. Comp. **swear-word** XIX (orig. U.S.).

sweat emit sweat, intr. and trans.; work hard. OE. *swǣtan* = MLG., MDu. *swēten* (Du. *zweeten*), OHG. *sweizzan* roast (G. *schweissen* fuse, weld) :- Gmc. **swaitjan*, f. **swaitaz* sb., whence OE. *swāt*, OS. *swēt* (Du. *zweet*), OHG. *sweiz* (G. *schweiss*); IE. base **swoid-* **swid-*, whence also L. *sūdor*, Skr. *svéda-*, Gr. *hidrṓs*, W. *chwŷs*.

sweat sb. †life-blood (so OE. *swāt*); hard work XIII; moisture excreted through the pores XIV; colloq. (orig. Sc. and U.S.) state of impatience or anxiety XVIII. Superseded ME. *swote* (OE. *swāt*). **sweater** (-ER[1]) one who sweats XVI; vest of wool to protect from cold XIX.

Swede native of Sweden XVII; (for earlier *Swedish turnip*) large variety of turnip (introduced into Scotland from Sweden XVIII) XIX. - MLG., MDu. *Swēde* (Du. *Zweed*), prob. - ON. *Svíþjóð* 'people of the Swedes', Sweden, f. *Svíar* Swedes + *þjóð* people.

sweep pt., pp. *swept* A. remove with or as with a broom or brush; clear (a surface) in this way XIII; B. intr. move with a strong or swift even motion XIV. ME. *swēpe*, repl. ME. *swōpe* (OE. *swāpan*), either by extension of the vowel *ē* of the pt. (OE. *swēop*), or by development *ĭ* to *ē* in OE. **swipian* (pt. *swipode*) scourge, or ON. intr. *svipa*. Hence **sweep** sb. in many uses covered by the definitions 'act of sweeping' (from XVI) and 'apparatus for sweeping' (from XV); in the sense 'chimney-sweeper' (XIX) preceded by *chimney-sweep* and †*sweep-chimney* (both XVII). Comp. **sweepstake** †one who takes the whole of the stakes in a game XV; †total removal XVI; (prize won in) a contest in which the stakes are contributed by the competitors XVIII.

sweet pleasing to the senses or the mind; dearly

loved or prized; kindly, gracious. OE. *swēte* – OS. *swōti* (Du. *zoot*), OHG. *s(w)uozi* (G. *süss*), ON. *sœtr* :- Gmc. *swōtja-, *swōti- (cf. Goth. *suts*), f. *swōt- :- IE. *swād-, repr. by Skr. *svādú-*, Gr. *hēdús*, L. *suāvis* (:- *swadwis). Comps. **sweetbread** pancreas. XVI; perh. OE. *brǣd* flesh = OS. *brādo* ham, calf of leg, etc.; but the reason for the name is unkn. **sweetheart** XIII. **sweetmeat** †sweet cake, etc.; sugarplum, lollipop XV; cf. OE. *swēt-*, *swōtmettas* dainties. **sweet william** species of pink. XVI. Hence **sweet** sb. XIII. **sweeten** (-EN[5]) XVI. **sweetie** (-IE) sweetmeat XVIII; sweet one XIX. **sweeting** (-ING[3]) sweetheart XIII; sweet variety of apple XVI. **sweetly** (-LY[2]), **sweetness** OE.

swell pt. *swelled*, pp. *swollen*, *swelled*. OE. str. vb. *swellan* = OS. **swellan* (Du. *zwellen*), OHG. *swellan* (G. *schwellen*), ON. *svella* :- Gmc. **swellan*; no cogns. outside Gmc. are known. So or hence **swell** sb. †morbid swelling XIII; condition of being swollen, protuberance XVII; heaving of the sea.

swelter be oppressed with heat XV; be oppressive with heat XVI. f. base of (dial.) *swelt* be overcome as with heat (XIV), OE. *sweltan* die, perish; see -ER[4].

swerve turn aside, deviate in movement. XIV. repr. formally OE. str. vb. *sweorfan* file, scour.

swift moving far in a short time, taking place at high speed. OE., f. base of *swīfan* move in a course, sweep = ON. *svífa*. Hence **swift** sb. (dial.) applied to various swiftly-moving reptiles XVI; bird of the family Apodidae XVII.

swig (dial.) drink, liquor (applied dial. to special drinks) XVI; deep draught XVII. Hence vb. XVII. of unkn. orig.

swill wash or rinse out OE.; drink greedily or to excess XVI; flow freely XVII. OE. *swillan*, *swilian*, of which no certain cogns. are known. Hence **swill** sb. liquid food XVI; copious drinking, liquor XVII.

swim pt. *swam*, pp. *swum*. OE. str. vb. *swimman* = OS., OHG. *swimman* (Du. *zwemmen*, G. *schwimmen*), ON. *svim(m)a* :- Gmc. **swimman*, f. **swimm-* **swamm-* **swumm-*. Hence sb. XVI.

swindle vb. XVIII. back-formation f. **swindler** - G. *schwindler* giddy-minded person, extravagant projector, cheat, f. (M)HG. *schwindeln*, OHG. *suintilōn*, frequent. (cf. -LE[3]) of *swintan* (= OE., OS. *swindan*) waste away, languish, lose consciousness; see -ER[1]. Hence sb. XIX.

swine OE. *swīn* = OS., OHG. *swīn* (Du. *swijn*, G. *schwein*), ON. *svín*, Goth. *swein* :- Gmc. **swīnam*, sb. use of n. of adj. (cf. L. *suīnus*, OSl. *svinŭ* pert. to swine, and see -INE[1]), f. IE. **sū-*, **suw-*, repr. by L. *sūs*, etc. (see SOW[1]). Comp. **swineherd** (HERD[2]) late OE. *swȳnhyrde*.

swing pt., pp. *swung* †A. scourge, flog OE.; †B. move impetuously OE.; C. flourish, brandish (a weapon, etc.) XIV; D. move backwards and forwards XVI. OE. str. vb. *swingan* = (M)LG. *swingen*, OHG. *swingan* (G. *schwingen* brandish, shake, etc.).

swinge beat, flog. XVI. Later form of ME. *swenge* smite, dash, OE. *swenġan* shake, shatter. Hence **swingeing** (-ING[2]) very forcible or large, immense. XVI.

swingle wooden instrument for beating hemp, etc. XIV. - MDu. *swinghel*, corr. formally to OE. *swingel*, *swingle* stroke with a rod; see SWING, -LE[1].

swipe drink hastily and copiously; strike *at*. XIX. perh. local var. of SWEEP. Hence sb. heavy blow. XIX.

swipes beer, esp. weak beer. XVIII. perh. f. prec.

swirl whirlpool XV; twist, whirling motion XVIII. orig. Sc., perh. of LG. or Du. orig. (cf. Du. *zwirrelen* whirl) and frequent. formation (cf. -LE[3]) on the imit. base seen in MLG. *swirren*, G. *schwirren*, Da. *svirre* whirl.

swish make a sound as of an object moving forcibly through air or water. XVIII. of imit. orig. So int. and sb. XIX.

switch slender tapering riding-whip XVI; thin flexible shoot XVII; mechanical device for altering direction XVIII; long bunch or coil of hair XIX. In early use also *swits*, *switz*; prob. - LG. word repr. by *swutsche*, var. of *swukse* long thin stick. Comp. **switchback** form of railway used on steep slopes, in which the train or car can be 'switched back' (BACK adv.) or reversed. XIX.

swither hesitate, vacillate. XVI (orig. Sc.). of unkn. orig.

swivel fastening device on which the object fastened turns freely. XIV. f. wk. grade of OE. *swīfan* (see SWIFT) + -EL[1].

swizzle intoxicating drink. XIX. of unkn. orig.

swoon fall into a fainting-fit. XIII. perh. back-formation from ME. gerund *swoȝning*, *swo(u)ning*, f *iswoȝen*, *iswowen*, OE. *ġeswōgen* overcome, dead, pp. of **swōgan*, as in *ā-*, *oferswōgan* suffocate, choke (with weeds), of unkn. orig. So **swoon** sb., orig. in phr. *i(n) swowne*, etc. (XIII).

swoop †sweep along as with trailing garments XVI; †pounce upon XVII; come down suddenly *upon* XVIII. perh. dial. development of ME. *swōpe*, OE. *swāpan* SWEEP.

swoosh imit. of the sound made by rushing air or water. XIX.

swop var. of SWAP.

sword OE. *sw(e)ord*, *swyrd* = OS. *swerd*, OHG. *swert* (G. *schwert*), ON. *sverð* :- Gmc. **swerðam*, of uncert. orig.

swot (sl.) vb. and sb. study at school or college. XIX. dial. var. of SWEAT.

sy- assim. form of SYN- before *s* + consonant, *z*.

-sy terminal el. of uncert. orig.; in hypocoristic and trivial use, e.g. *tricksy* (XVI), *flimsy* (XVIII), *tipsy* (XVI), *tootsy* (XIX).

sybarite XVI. - L. *Sybarīta* - Gr. *Subarítēs*, f. *Súbaris*, ancient Greek city of S. Italy, noted for its effeminacy and luxury; see -ITE.

sycamine black mulberry. XVI. - L. *sȳcamīnus* - Gr. *sūkámīnon*, f. Heb. *šiḳmāh* sycamore, with assim. to Gr. *sûkon* fig.

sycamore, sycomore species of fig-tree XIV; species of maple XVI. - OF. *sic(h)amor* (mod. *sycomore*) - L. *sȳcomorus* - Gr. *sūkómoros*, f. *sûkon* fig + *móron* mulberry.

sycophant one of a class of informers in ancient Greece; mean flatterer, toady. XVI. - F. *sycophante* or L. *sȳcophanta* - Gr. *sūkophántēs*, f. *sûkon* fig + **phan-*, base of *phaínein* show; the reason for the name is uncert.

sycosis ulcer or eruption resembling a fig. XVI. - modL. *sȳcōsis* - Gr. *sûkōsis*, f. *sûkon* fig; see -OSIS.

syenite (min.) crystalline rock allied to granite. XVIII. - F. *syénite*, G. *syenit* - L. *syēnītēs*, f. *Syēnē*, Gr. *Suḗnē* town of Upper Egypt (now *Aswan*); see -ITE.

syl- assim. form of SYN- before *l*.

syllable XIV. - AN. *sillable*, alt. of OF. *sillabe* (mod. *syllabe*) - L. *syllaba* - Gr. *sullabḗ*, f. *sullambánein* take, put, or bring together, f. SYL- + *lambánein* take. So **syllabary** set or table of syllables. XVI. - n. sg. of late L. *syllabārius*. **syllabic** XVII. - medL. *syllabicus* - Gr. *sullabikós*. **syllabication** XVII. - medL. **syllabification** XIX. - medL. **syllabize** divide into syllables. XVII. - medL. - Gr.

syllabub see SILLABUB.

syllabus pl. **-bi, -buses** concise statement or table of heads of a discourse, etc. XVII. - modL. *syllabus*, originating in a misprint in early editions of *syllabos* for *sittýbas*, in Cicero's Letters to Atticus (IV iv), acc. pl. of *sittyba* - Gr. *sittúbā* title-slip or label.

syllepsis (gram.) figure by which one word or form is made to refer to two or more in the same sentence while strictly applying to only one. XVI. - late L. *syllēpsis* - Gr. *súllēpsis*, f. SYL- + *lēpsis* taking, f. *lēb- lāb- lab-*, base of *lambánein* take.

syllogism argument expressed in the form of two propositions called the premisses and a third called the conclusion. XIV. ME. *silogisme*, occas. *silogime* - OF. *sil(l)ogisme*, earlier *silogime* (mod. *syllogisme*) or L. *syllogismus* - Gr. *sullogismós*, f. *sullogízesthai*, intensive of *logízesthai* reckon, compute, conclude, f. *lógos* discourse, consideration, account; see SYL-, -ISM. So **syllogistic** XVII. - L. *syllogisticus* - Gr. *sullogistikós*. **syllogize** XV. - OF. *sil(l)ogiser* - late L. *syllogizāre* - Gr. *sullogízesthai*.

sylph one of a race of beings supposed to inhabit the air. XVII. - modL. pl. *sylphes* and *sylphi*, G. pl. *sylphen*, of uncert. orig.

sylvan, silvan sb. inhabitant of the woods; adj. pert. to a wood or woods, wooded. XVI. - F. *sylvain*, †*silvain*, or L. *silvānus*, *syl-* (only as the name of a god), f. *silva* wood; see -AN.

sym- assim. form of SYN- before *m, b, p*.

symbol summary of Christian belief, creed XV; something that represents something else XVI; written character XVII. - ChrL. *symbolum* - Gr. *súmbolon* mark, token, watchword, f. SYM- + **bol-*, as in *bolḗ*, *bólos* a throw, rel. to *bállein* throw. So **symbolic(al)** XVII. - F. *symbolique* or late L. *symbolicus* - Gr. *sumbolikós*. **symbolize** †agree, harmonize; have similar qualities (techn. term of early physics) XVI; be a symbol of XVII.

symmetry †mutual relation of parts, proportion; due or just proportion. XVI. - F. †*symmetrie* (mod. *symétrie*) or L. *symmetria* - Gr. *summetriā*, f. *súmmetros* commensurable, proportionable, symmetrical, f. SYM- + *métron* measure; see -Y³. Hence **symmetrical** XVIII.

sympathy affinity; agreement; conformity of feelings or temperament. XVI. - L. *sympathīa* - Gr. *sumpátheia*, f. *sumpathḗs* having a fellow-feeling, f. SYM- + **path-* base of *páthos* feeling, PATHOS; see -Y³. So **sympathetic** XVII. - Gr. *sumpathētikós*. **sympathize** be affected like another XVI; have a fellow-feeling XVII. - F. *sympathiser*.

symphony †used vaguely for musical instruments XIII; †harmony XV; (mus.) passage for instruments XVII (spec. XVIII). - (O)F. †*sim-*, *symphonie* - L. *symphōnia* instrumental harmony, voices in concert, (Vulg.) musical instrument - Gr. *sumphōníā*, f. *súmphōnos* harmonious, f. SYM- + *phōnḗ* sound; see -Y³.

symphysis (anat.) union of two bones. XVI. - Gr. *súmphusis*, esp. of bones, f. SYM- + *phúsis* growth.

symposium drinking party, convivial meeting for conversation, etc.; meeting for discussion. XVIII. - L. *symposium* - Gr. *sumpósion*, f. *sumpótēs* fellow-drinker, f. SYM- + **pot-* (cf. POTION). Earlier (XVI) the latinized title of one of Plato's dialogues. So **symposiac** convivial; †sb. symposium. XVII. - L. - Gr.

symptom XVI. Earlier in late L. form *symptōma* - Gr. *súmptōma* chance, accident, mischance, f. *sumpíptein* fall upon, happen to, f. SYM- + *píptein* fall. So **symptomatic** XVII. - F. or late L.

syn- latinized form of Gr. *sun-*, comb. form of *sún* prep. together, similarly, alike; assim. before *l* to *syl-*, before *b, p, m* to *sym-*, before simple *s* to *sys-*, before *s* + consonant and *z* to *sy-*.

synaeresis contraction of two vowels. XVI. - late L. *synæresis* - Gr. *sunaíresis*, f. SYN- + *haireîn* take.

synagogue congregation of Jews for worship XII; building for Jewish worship XIII. ME. *sinagoge* - OF. *sinagoge* (mod. *synagogue*) - late L. *synagōga* - Gr. *sunagōgḗ* meeting, assembly, in LXX. synagogue, f. *sunágein* bring together, assemble, f. SYN- + *ágein* lead, bring (cf. ACT).

synchronic XIX. f. late L. *synchronus* - Gr. *súgkhronos*, f. SYN- + *khrónos* time. So **synchronism** XVI. - Gr.; whence **synchronize** XVII. **synchronous** XVII. f. late L. *synchronus*.

syncopation (gram.) contraction of a word by elision of one or more syllables XVI; (mus.) beginning a note on a normally unaccented part of the bar and continuing it into the normally accented part XVI. - medL. *syncopātiō*, *-ōn-*, f. late L. *syncopāre*, f. *syncopē*; see next, -ATION.

syncope (path.) failure of the heart's action; grammatical syncopation. XVI (XV †*syncopis*). - late L. *syncopē* - Gr. *sugkopḗ*, f. SYN- + *kop-* strike, cut off.

syncretism union of opposite tenets, etc. XVII; (philol.) merging of cases XX. - Gr. *sugkrētismós*, f. *sugkrētízein*.

syndic civil magistrate in some countries of Europe; one deputed to represent a corporation. XVII. - (O)F. *syndic*, †*-ique* delegate, chief magistrate of Geneva - late L. *syndicus* delegate of a corporation - Gr. *súndikos* defendant's advocate, f. SYN- + **dik*, base of *díkē* judgement, *deiknusthai* show; see -IC. So **syndicalism** industrial unionism. XX. - F. *syndicalisme*, f. *syndical*, as in *chambre syndicale* trade union.

syndicate †office of a syndic; body of syndics XVII; combination of financiers or other promoters of enterprise XIX. - F. *syndicat* - medL. *syndicātus*; see -ATE[1].

syndrome (path.) concurrence of symptoms XVI; †concurrence, concourse XVII. - Gr. *sundromḗ*, f. SYN- + **drom*-, *drameîn* run.

syne (Sc. and north.) immediately afterwards, thereupon; later; since then XIV; before now, ago XV (esp. in *lang syne* long ago, made familiar by Burns's 'Auld Lang Syne'). Contracted form of ME. *sithen* SINCE.

synecdoche - L. *synecdochē* - Gr. *sunekdokhḗ*, f. *sunekdékhesthai*, f. SYN- + *ekdékhesthai* take up.

synizesis (gram., pros.) coalescence of two adjacent vowels without forming a recognized diphthong. XIX. - late L. *synizēsis* - Gr. *sunízēsis*, f. *sunizánein* sink down, f. SYN- + *hizánein* sit.

synod XIV. - late L. *synodus* - Gr. *súnodos* meeting, f. SYN- + *hodós* way, travel. So **synodal** XV. - late L.; see -AL[1].

synonym XVI. In early use first in pl. in L. form (*-a*) or anglicized (*-es*, *-aes*), later in sg. *-ymum*, *-ymon*, *-ime*, *-yme*. XV. - L. *synōnymum* - Gr. *sunṓnumon*, sb. use of n. sg. of *sunṓnumos*, f. SYN- + *ónuma* NAME. So **synonymous** XVII. **synonymy** (-Y[3]) XVII. - late L. - Gr.

synopsis XVII. - late L. - Gr. *súnopsis*, f. SYN- + *ópsis* view. So **synoptic** XVIII, **-ical** XVII; see OPTIC.

synovia fluid of the joints in the body. XVII. - modL. *synovia*, *sinovia*, an invention, perh. arbitrary, of Paracelsus (d. 1541). Hence **synovial** (-AL[1]) XVIII, **sinovitis** XIX.

syntax †orderly arrangement of parts; (gram.) arrangement of words in their appropriate forms and order. XVII. - F. *syntaxe* or late L. *syntaxis* (adopted in Eng. XVI) - Gr. *súntaxis*, f. *suntássein*, f. SYN- + *tássein* arrange. So **syntactic** XIX, **-tactical** XVI.

synthesis proceeding from cause to effect XVII; formation of a compound by combining its elements XVIII. - L. - Gr. *súnthesis*, f. *suntithénai*, f. SYN- + *tithénai* place, put. Hence **synthesize** XIX (beside **synthetize** XIX, - Gr. *sunthetízesthai*). So **synthetic, -etical** XVII. - F. or Gr.

syphilis XVIII. - modL. *Syphilis* title of a poem, in full 'Syphilis sive Morbus Gallicus' (syphilis or the French disease), 1530, by Girolamo Fracastoro, physician, astronomer, and poet, of Verona; the poem is the story of a shepherd *Syphilus*, represented as the first sufferer. Hence **syphilitic** XVIII.

syphon, syren see SIPHON, SIREN.

syringa shrub of the genus *Philadelphus*. XVII. - modL. *syringa*, f. Gr. *sûrigx*, *surigg*- pipe; first applied to the mock orange from its stems being used for pipe stems, later to the lilac.

syringe sb. XV. - late L. *syringa*, f. L. *syrinx* (see next).

syrinx Pan-pipe; narrow rock-cut channels or tunnels XVII; organ of voice in birds XIX. - L. - Gr. *sûrigx* pipe, tube, channel.

syrup, U.S. **sirup** thick sweet liquid. - (O)F. *sirop* or medL. *siropus*, *sirupus*, ult. from Arab. *šarāb* beverage, drink. Hence **syrupy** (-Y[1]) XVIII.

systaltic pert. to contraction. XVII. - late L. *systalticus* - Gr. *sustaltikós*, f. SY- + *staltós*, f. *stéllein*, *stal*- place.

system XVII. - F. *système* or its source late L. *systēma* - Gr. *sústēma* organized whole, f. SY- + **sta*- STAND. So **systematic** XVII. - F. - late L. **systematize** XVIII. - F. *systématiser*. **systemic** (physiol., path.) XIX. irreg. formation used for differentiation of meaning from *systematic*.

systole (physiol.) regular contraction of the heart and arteries. XVI. - late L. *systolē* - Gr. *sustolḗ*, f. SY- + **stol*- **stel*- place, after *sustéllein* contract.

syzygy (astron.) †conjunction, (now) conjunction and opposition of two celestial bodies XVII; applied to various unions or combinations XIX. - late L. *sȳzygia* - Gr. *suzugiā* yoke, pair, conjunction, f. *súzugos* yoked, paired, f. SY- + **zug*- YOKE.

T

T in phr. *to a T* exactly, to a nicety. XVII. perh. for earlier *to a* TITTLE.

-t[1] suffix of abstr. sbs. derived from vbs., repr. IE. *-t-* in **-tis, *-tus*, which is preserved as Gmc. *-t* after guttural, labial, and sibilant cons., e.g. *draught, drift, thirst*.

-t[2] repl. (by dissim.) -TH[1] after spirant cons., e.g. *drought, height, theft*.

-t[3] var. of -ED[1], as in *blest, burnt, dreamt*.

ta infantile and joc. colloq. substitute for THANKS. XVIII.

tab short broad strip, etc. XVII; depending or projecting piece on a dress XIX; label; (U.S) reckoning, check. of unkn. orig.

tabard loose upper garment with short sleeves or none. XIII. - OF. *tabart*; of unkn. orig.

tabaret fabric of alternate stripes of material. XIX. f. TABBY. So **tabinet** XVIII.

tabasco pungent sauce made from capsicum. XVII (*tauasco*). Name of a river and state of Mexico.

tabby silk taffeta, orig. striped XVII; short for *t. cat* (XVII), cat having a striped coat XVIII; (colloq.) elderly maiden lady. - (O)F. *tabis*, †*atabis* - Arab. *'attābī* name of a quarter of Baghdad in which the stuff was manufactured.

tabernacle tent containing the Ark of the Covenant; canopied structure XIII; tent (gen.), dwelling-place (esp. temporary) XIV; place of worship (not a church) XVII. - (O)F. *tabernacle* or L. *tabernāculum* tent, booth, dim. of *taberna* TAVERN.

tabes slow emaciation. XVII. - L. *tābēs*.

tablature (mus.) notation, spec. for the lute, flute, etc. XVI. - F. - medL. *tabulātūra*, f. late L. *tabulāre*, f. L. *tabula* TABLE; see -URE.

table A. slab, tablet (now mainly techn.) XII; †(pl.) backgammon XIII; †board on which chess, etc. are played XV; (pl.) leaves of a backgammon board (phr. *turn the tables* reverse the situation XVII); B. raised board at which one sits XIII; C. arrangement of numbers, words, etc. XIV. - (O)F. - L. *tabula* plank, tablet, list. Hence **table** vb. XV.

tableau picture, graphic description XVII; dramatic grouping of persons, etc. XIX. - F. *tableau*, OF. *tablel*, dim. of *table* (see prec.).

table d'hôte XVII. - F., 'host's table'; see TABLE, HOST[2].

tablet slab for an inscription or carving XIV; slab or panel for a painting XVI; sheet or leaf or (pl.) a set of them for writing on XVII; flat cake, lozenge XVI. - OF. *tablete* (mod. *tablette*); Rom. dim. of L. *tabula* TABLE; see -ET.

tabloid trade-mark term for medicinal tablets XIX; used attrib., transf., applied to written or printed matter in condensed form. alt. of TABLET (see -OID).

taboo, tabu consecrated or restricted to a special use; prohibited, inviolable. XVIII. - Tongan *tabu*.

tabo(u)r (hist.) (small) drum. XIII. - OF. *tabour* (mod. *tambour*); ult. of Pers. orig.

tabouret low stool, so called from its shape. XVII. - F. *tabouret*, dim. of *tabour*; see prec., -ET.

tabular of the form of a tablet or slab XVII; pert. to a schematic table XVIII. - L. *tabulāris*, f. *tabula* TABLE; see -AR. So **tabulate** XVII. f. pp. stem of late L. *tabulāre*; see -ATE[3].

tacamahac aromatic resin of Mexico and S. America. XVI. - Sp. †*tacamahaca* (now *tacamaca*), of Nahuatl orig.

tachometer instrument for measuring speed. XIX. f. Gr. *tákhos* speed + METER.

tachy- comb. form of Gr. *takhús* swift, as in **tachygraphy** XVII, **tachygraphic** XVIII, **tachymeter** XIX.

tacit XVII. - L. *tacitus*, prop. pp. of *tacēre* be silent. So **taciturn** XVIII. - F. *taciturne* or L. *taciturnus*. **taciturnity** XV. - (O)F. or L.

tack[1] A. fastening, as a clasp, sharp-pointed nail, etc. XIV. B. (naut.) rope, wire, etc. to secure sails XV. Parallel to later *tach(e)*, the two forms presumably repr. OF. vars. **taque*, (dial.) *tache*. So **tack** vb. A. †attach XIV; fasten loosely or temporarily XV; B. (naut.; from sense B of the sb.) shift the tacks in going about XVI.

tack[2] food-stuff, as in *hard t.* ship's biscuit. XIX. of unkn. orig.

tackle apparatus, gear, rigging. XIII. prob. - (M)LG. *takel*, f. *taken* = MDu. *tacken* lay hold of; see -LE[1]. Hence **tackle** vb. furnish with tackle XIV; harness XVIII; grip, grapple with XIX.

tacky slightly sticky. XVIII. f. TACK[1] (presumably in the gen. sense of holding or fastening together) + -Y[1].

tact A. †sense of touch XVII; B. faculty of mental perception XVIII; C. sense of propriety, faculty of doing the right thing at the right time XVIII. - (O)F. *tact* or L. *tactus* touch, f. **tag-*, base of *tangere* touch. In sense C immed. after F. *tact*.

tactics XVII. repr. modL. *tactica* - Gr. *tà taktiká*, n. pl. of *taktikós*, f. *taktós* ordered, arranged, f. base of *tássein* set in order. So **tactical** XVI. f. Gr. *taktikós*. Hence **tactician** XVIII.

tactile XVII. - L. *tactilis*, f. *tact-*, pp. stem of *tangere* touch; see -ILE.

tadpole XV (*taddepol*). f. *tadde* TOAD + *pol* POLL, as if 'a toad that is all head'.

taenia, tenia band, fillet XVI; tapeworm XVIII. - L. - Gr. *tainiā*.

taffeta XIV. - OF. *taffetas* or medL. *taffata*, ult. - Pers. *tāfta*, sb. use of pp. of *tāftan* shine.

taffrail aftermost part of the poop-rail of a ship. XIX. alt. of *taff(e)rel* †(carved) panel XVII; upper part of the flat portion of a ship's stern XVIII. - Du. *tafereel* panel, picture, for **tafeleel*, dim. of *tafel* TABLE; the final syll. is assim. to RAIL[2].

tafia rum-like liquor obtained from molasses. XVIII. of uncert. orig.

tag[1] small pendent piece, orig. on a garment XIV (implied in *tagged*); ornamental pendant XVI; point of metal, etc. at the end of a lace; something appended to a piece of writing, etc., brief quotation XVIII. of unkn. orig. Hence **tag** vb. XVI mark with a tag.

tag[2] children's game, otherwise called **tig.** XVIII. of unkn. orig.

tail[1] posterior extremity of an animal OE.; in various transf. senses from XIII. OE. *tæġ(e)l* = MLG. *tagel* twisted whip, rope's end, OHG. *zagal*, ON. *tagl* tail, Goth. *tagl* hair of the head, of the camel :- Gmc. **tazlaz*. Hence **tail** vb. in many (esp.) specialized senses from XVI.

tail[2] (leg.) limitation of a freehold estate or fee to a person. XIV. - (O)F. *taille* division, partition or assessment of a subsidy, tax, f. *taillier* cut, fix the precise form of limit. So **tail** adj. XV. - AN. *tailé*, OF. *taillié*, pp. of *taillier*.

tailor XIII. ME. *taillour*, *taylo(u)r* - AN. *taillour*, (O)F. *tailleur* cutter :- Rom. **tāliātor*, *-ōr-*, f. *tāliāre* cut :- **tal(l)iāre*, f. L. *tālea* rod, twig, cutting; see -OR[1].

taint A. †attaint XIV; B. tint, dye XVI; stain, blemish XVII. Partly aphetic of ATTAINT; partly - OF. *teint*, *taint* :- L. *tinctus* and *teinte* :- medL. *tincta*, sb. uses of pp. of *tingere* TINGE. So **taint** vb. †convict XIV; †hit, strike XVI; †tinge, dye XV; affect perniciously XVI.

take pt. *took*, pp. *taken* seize (also in earliest use, touch), capture. XII. Late OE. str. vb. *tacan* - ON. *taka* = MDu. *tāken*, rel. by gradation to Goth. *tekan* touch; of uncert. orig. OE. *oftacan* may point to the native currency of *tacan*.

talbot kind of hound formerly used for hunting, (her.) figure of this as borne in the arms of the ancient Talbot family. XV (as the proper name of a dog XIV). prob. generalized from the family name.

talc species of translucent or shining minerals, e.g. mica. XVI. - F. *talc* or medL. *talcum* (whence **talcum** XVI) - Arab. *ṭalḳ* - Pers. *talk*.

tale A. †talk, discourse OE.; what is told, story, narrative XI; B. reckoning, number XII. OE. *talu* = OS. *tala* (Du. *taal* speech), OHG. *zala* (G. *zahl* number), ON. *tala* talk, tale, number :- Gmc. **talō*, f. **tal-*, as in **taljan* TELL. Sense B was prob. from ON.

talent A. †inclination, disposition XIII; B. ancient weight and money of account XIV; C. mental endowment or aptitude XV. - OF. *talent* will, desire :- L. *talentum* in Rom. sense of 'inclination of mind' - Gr. *tálanton* balance, weight, sum of money. Sense C is from the use of the word in the parable of the talents, Matt. 25: 14-30.

tales writ for summoning jurors; list of persons so summoned. XVI. - L. *tālēs* pl. of *tālis* such in phr. *tales de circumstantibus* such persons from those standing about.

talion retaliation. XV. - (O)F. - L. *tāliō*, *-ōn-*, f. *tālis* such; see -ION. So **lex talionis** principle of exacting compensation, 'eye for eye, tooth for tooth'. XVI. - L., *lex* law + g. sg. of *tāliō*.

talisman XVII. - F., Sp. *talisman*, It. *talismano*; ult. (prob. via Arab. or Pers.) - late Gr. *télesma* (whence Arab. *ṭilsam*) completion, performance, religious rite, consecrated object, f. *telein*, complete, perform (a rite), consecrate, f. *télos* end, result.

talk vb. XIII. ME. *talk(i)en*, f. the base **tal-* of TALE, TELL. Hence **talk** sb., **talkative** XV.

tall †seemly, decent, comely; †doughty, valiant XIV (phr. †*t. of his hands* dexterous, formidable in arms XVI); high of stature, lofty XVI. repr. OE. *ġetæl* swift, prompt = OS. *gital*, OHG. *gizal* quick. Comp. **tallboy** tall-stemmed glass XVII; tall chest or bookcase mounted on a high stand XVIII.

tallage tax, levy, orig. one levied by Norman kings. XIII. - OF. *taillage*, f. *taillier* cut, determine the form of, limit :- Rom. **talliāre*.

tallith garment worn by Jews at prayer. XVII. - Rabbinic Heb. *ṭallith*, f. *ṭālal* cover.

tallow harder kinds of fat used for candles, soap, etc. XIV. ME. *talȝ*, *talow* - MLG. *talg*, *talch*, of unkn. orig.

tally rod of wood marked with notches recording payments XV; reckoning, score XVI; counterpart XVII. - AN. *tallie* = AL. *tal(l)ia*, for L. *tālea* cutting, rod, stick. So **tally** vb. †score, mark down XV; agree, accord XVIII.

tally-ho huntman's view-halloo. XVIII. Cf. F. *taïaut* (XVII), †*taho*, †*theau* (XVI).

Talmud body of Jewish law (Mishnah) and commentary on this (Gemara). XVI. - late Heb. *talmûdh* instruction, f. *lāmadh* instruct.

talon XIV. - (O)F. *talon* heel :- Rom. **tālō*, *-ōn-*, f. *tālus* ankle-bone.

talus[1] (fortif.) sloping side of an earthwork XVII; (geol.) sloping mass of detritus XIX. - (O)F., of unkn. orig.

talus[2] (anat.) ankle, astragalus. XVIII. - L.

tamarind fruit of the tree *Tamarindus indica*. XVI. - medL. *tamarindus* - Arab. *tamr hindī* date of India.

tamarisk plant of the genus *Tamarix*. XV. - late L. *tamariscus*, var. of earlier *tamarix*.

tambour drum XV (adopted afresh XVIII); circular frame on which material is stretched XVIII; (archit., etc.). - F., var. of *tabour* TABOR. So **tambourine** †(in uncert. sense) XVI; musical instrument made of a hoop with parchment stretched over one side and cymbals at the edge XVIII. - F. *tambourin*, dim. of *tambour*.

tame adj. OE. *tam* = (M)LG., (M)Du. *tam*, OHG. *zam* (G. *zahm*), ON. *tamr* :- Gmc. **tamaz*, f. IE. **dom-*, repr. also by L. *domāre*, Gr. *damân* tame, subdue. Hence **tame** vb. XIV; superseding ME. *teme*, OE. *temian*.

tammy see next.

Tam o' Shanter round Scotch cap. XIX. f. name of the hero of Burns's poem so entitled (1790). Abbrev. **tammy** XIX.

tamp to stop with clay, etc.; to ram down hard. XIX. Back-formation from TAMPION.

tamper †work in or temper clay XVI; †scheme, plot; deal improperly, meddle *with* XVII. In all senses the earlier form is TEMPER.

tampion †bung XV; †wad for a gun; stopper for the muzzle of a gun XVII; plug for the top of an organ-pipe XIX. - F. *tampon* (whence **tampon** XIX), var. of *tapon*, of Gmc. orig.

tan convert (skin) into leather by steeping in an infusion of astringent bark OE.; make brown by the sun XVI; colloq. (orig. *tan* a person's *hide*) thrash XVII. late OE. **tannian*, in pp. *ġetanned* and agent-noun *tannere* (see -ER¹), prob. - medL. *tannāre*; reinforced in ME. from OF. vb. *tan(n)er*. Hence sb. crushed bark of oak, etc. for tanning XVII; brown or tawny colour XIX. **tanner** OE. *tannere* (or later - OF. *tanere*). **tannery** XV.

tanager bird of the family Thraupidae. XIX. alt. of Tupi *tangara* (current in Eng. use XVII-XIX).

tandem two-wheeled vehicle drawn by two horses harnessed one in front of the other; the horses themselves; bicycle, etc., with seats one behind another. XIX. orig. sl. punning use of L. *tandem* at length (of time).

tang¹ A. (dial.) serpent's tongue, insect's sting XIV; point or spike, spec. of a metal tool XV; B. penetrating taste XV; slight smack XVI. of Scand. orig. (cf. ON. *tangi*, Da. *tange* point, spit).

tang² sharp ringing note. XVII. perh. imit.

tang³ large coarse seaweed. XVIII. of Scand. orig. (Norw., Da. *tang*, Icel. *þang*).

tangent (geom.) adj. touching at a point XVI; sb. XVI. - L. *tangēns, -ent-*, prp. of *tangere* touch. See -ENT. Hence **tangential** XVII.

tangerine applied to a small variety of orange obtained from *Tangier* (*Tanger*), seaport of Morocco. XIX. orig. adj. in *T. orange*; see -INE¹.

tangible touchable XVI; discernible by touch XVII; realizable, palpable XVIII. - F. *tangible* or late L. *tangibilis*, f. *tangere* touch; see -IBLE.

tangle¹ †involve (a person) in embarrassment XIV; ENTANGLE XVI. ME. *tangil, -el*, var. of *tagil*; of uncert. orig. Hence sb. XVII.

tangle² gen. term for the larger seaweeds. XVI (earliest Sc.). prob. - Norw. *tongul*, Faroese *tangul*, repr. ON. *þǫngull*.

tango XX. - Amer. Sp. (locally, dance and music for this, and instrument of the tambourine kind).

tangram Chinese geometrical puzzle. XIX. of unkn. orig.

tank¹ in India, reservoir or water for irrigation, etc.; artificial receptacle for liquids in large quantities. XVII. - Indian vernacular word such as Gujarati *ṭā̃kū*, Marathi *ṭā̃kē*. Hence **tanker** vessel for conveying oil. XX.

tank² armoured military vehicle. XX. So named for reasons of secrecy.

tankard †large tub XIV; drinking-vessel (esp. one-handled) XV. of unkn. orig.

tannin astringent having the property of converting hide into leather. XIX. - F. *tanin*, f. *tan* TAN + *-in* -IN. So **tannic** XIX. - F. *tannique*.

tanrec, tenrec insectivorous mammal allied to the hedgehog. XVIII. - F. *tanrec* - Malagasy *t(r)àndraka*.

tansy herbaceous plant. XV. - OF. *tanesie* (mod. *tanaisie*), of unkn. orig.

tantalize XVI. f. L. *Tantalus* (Gr. *Tántalos*), name of a mythical king of Phrygia condemned to stand in Tartarus up to his chin in water which receded as he stooped to drink.

tantalum (min.) a rare metal. XIX. f. *Tantalus* (see rec.), partly with allusion to its non-absorbent quality.

tantalus genus of storks; spirit stand containing decanters locked up but visible. XIX. - L. *Tantalus* (see TANTALIZE).

tantamount XVII. f. †*tantamount* sb. equivalent, vb. amount to as much - It. *tanto montare*, i.e. *tanto* as much (:- L. *tantum*), *montare* amount.

tantivy †adv. at full gallop; sb. rapid gallop XVII; post-Restoration high churchman or Tory (from a caricature of such clergymen mounted on the Church of England and 'riding tantivy' to Rome). perh. intended to repr. the sound of horses galloping.

tantrum XVIII. of unkn. orig.

tap¹ device for drawing liquid from a vessel. OE. *tæppa* = MLG., MDu. *tappe* (Du. *tap*), OHG. *zapho*, MHG. *zapfe* (G. *zapfen*), ON. *tappi* :- Gmc. **tappan-*. Hence **tap** vb. fit with a tap OE.; draw (liquor) with a tap XV. Late OE. *tappian*.

tap² strike lightly. XIII (*teppe*). Either - (O)F. *taper* or independent imit. formation.

tape OE. *tæppa* or *tæppe*, repr. obscurely by ME. *tāpe*; of unkn. orig.

taper wax candle OE.; long wick coated with wax for use as a spill XIX. OE. *tapor, -er, -ur* - (with dissim. of *p . . p* to *t . . p*) L. *papyrus*. Hence **taper** adj. becoming continuously narrower in one direction XV; whence **taper** vb. XVI.

tapestry XV. alt. of †*tapisery*, †*tapecery* (XV) - (O)F. *tapisserie*, f. *tapissier* tapestry-worker, or *tapisser* cover with carpet, f. *tapis* carpet, cloth :- Rom. **tappētium*, for late L. *tapētium* - Gr. *tapḗtion*, dim. of *tápēs, -ēt-* tapestry.

tapioca prepared flour of the cassava. XVIII (*tipioca*). - Tupi-Guarani *tipioca*, f. *tipi* residue, dregs + *ok, og* squeeze out.

tapir swine-like animal of tropical America. XVIII. - Tupi *tapira*.

tapis phr. *on the t.* (XVII), partial tr. F. *sur le t.* 'on the table-cloth', under discussion; see TAPESTRY.

tapster †woman who draws liquor OE.; man who does this XVI (? XV). OE. *tæppestre*, orig. fem. of *tæppere*, agent-noun of *tappian* TAP¹; see -STER.

tar¹ dark thick liquid distilled from wood or coal. OE. *te(o)ru*, corr. to MLG. *ter(e)* (LG. *teer*), MDu. *tar, ter(re)*, ON. *tjara* :- Gmc. **terw-*, gen. held to be f. **trew-* TREE, the primary application having been to the black oily liquid produced by trees such as pines. Hence **tarry** (-Y¹) XVI.

tar² (colloq.) sailor. XVII (also *Jack Tar* XVIII). Short for TARPAULIN.

tarantass 4-wheeled Russian travelling carriage. XIX. - Russ. *tarantás*.

tarantella rapid whirling S. Italian dance. XVIII. - It., dim. formation on *Taranto* name of a town in Apulia, Italy (the ancient *Tarentum*). The dance was popularly supposed to be a remedy for **tarantism** hysterical malady characterized by an impulse to dance (XVII), f. *Taranto*; the malady itself was pop. attributed to the bite of the tarantula.

tarantula large wolf-spider of S. Europe XVI;

applied to other spiders XVIII. - medL. - It. *tarantola*, f. *Taranto* (see prec.), where it is commonly found.

taraxacum (drug prepared from) dandelion. XVIII. - medL. - Arab. *ṭar(a)ḵšaḳūḳ* - Pers. *talḳ chakūk* 'bitter herb'.

tarboosh Muslim cap. XVIII. - Egyptian Arab. *ṭarbūš*.

tardigrade slow paced XVII; (zool.) belonging to the family comprising the sloths XVIII. - F. *tardigrade* or L. *tardigradus*, f. *tardus* slow + *-gradus* stepping, walking; see next, -GRADE.

tardy slow XV; late, behindhand XVII. ME. *tardif*, *-ive* - (O)F *tardif*, *-ive* :- Rom. **tardīvus*, f. *tardus* slow; see -IVE, -Y[1].

tare[1] (seed of) vetch; in versions of the Bible (Matt. 13: 25) rendering L. *zīzania*, Gr. *zīzánia* injurious weed among corn, darnel, cockle. XIV. of unkn. orig.

tare[2] weight of the wrapping, receptacle, or conveyance containing goods. XV. - F. *tare* waste in goods, deficiency, tare - medL. *tara* - Arab. *ṭarḥa* what is thrown away, f. *ṭaraḥa* reject.

targe (arch.) shield. XIII. - (O)F. *targe*, of Gmc. orig. (cf. OE. *targa*, *targe*, ON. *targa* shield, OHG. *zarga*, (M)HG. *zarge* edging, border).

target (hist.) light round shield XIV; object marked with concentric circles to be used as a butt XVIII. dim. of TARGE (see -ET).

targum Aramaic translation or paraphrase of portions of the O.T. XVI. - Aram. *targūm* interpretation, f. *targēm* interpret.

tariff †arithmetical table; schedule or system of the rates of customs, item of this XVI; gen. classified list of charges XVIII. - F. *tarif* - It. *tariffa* - Turk. *tarife* - Arab. *ta'rīf*, f. *'arrafa* notify, make known.

tarlatan kind of thin muslin. XVIII (*tarn-*). - F. *tarlatane*, alt. of *tarnatane*.

tarmac (XX) registered trademark of a kind of *tar* MACADAM (XIX).

tarn small mountain lake. XIV. ME. *terne*, *tarne* - ON. **tarnu* (*tjǫrn*, Sw. dial. *t(j)ärn*, Norw. *tjörn*).

tarnation damnable, -bly. XVIII. var. of *darnation*, euph. var. of DAMNATION.

tarnish XVI. - F. *terniss-*, extended stem (see -ISH[2]) of *ternir*, of unkn. orig.

taro tropical food plant. XVIII. native Polynesian name.

tarot one of a set of playing-cards. XVI. - F. - It. *tarocco* (pl. *-chi*), of unkn. orig.

tarpaulin (sheet of) tarred canvas XVII (*-ing*); nickname for a sailor XVII (also †*tarpaulian*; cf. TAR[2]). Presumed to be f. TAR[1] + PALL[1] + -ING[1].

tarpon large game-fish. XVII. - Du. *tarpoen*, of unkn. orig.

tarragon XVI. Given first as repr. medL. *tragonia* and *tarchon*, the latter of which goes back to medGr. *tarkhṓn*, which may be an Arab. deformation of Gr. *drákōn*.

tarry †defer, retard; delay, linger XIV. In earliest use identical in form with ME. *tary* vex, harass, repr. OE. **tærġan*, *terġan*, and OF. *tarier* provoke, excite, of unkn. orig.; but the sense is against identity.

tarsia mosaic inlaid wood. XVII. - It. *tarsia*, of unkn. orig.

tarsus (anat.) posterior parts of the foot. XVII. - Gr. *tarsós* flat of the foot.

tart[1] piece of pastry (now open) with fruit or jam filling. XIV. - OF. *tarte*, of unkn. orig.

tart[2] †painful OE.; sharp to the taste XIV; sharp or biting in tone XVII. OE. *teart*, of unkn. orig.

tartan (orig. Sc.) woollen cloth woven in stripes crossing at right angles. XVI. perh. - OF. *tertaine*, var. of *tiretaine* cloth half wool, half linen or cotton, of unkn. orig.

tartar deposit of acid potassium tartrate adhering to the sides of wine casks. XIV. - medL. *tartarum* - medGr. *tártaron*, or unkn. orig. Hence (or - F.) **tartaric** XVIII.

tartrate (chem.) salt of tartaric acid. XVIII. - F., f. *tartre* TARTAR; see -ATE[2].

task XIII. - ONF. *tasque*, var. of OF. *tasche* (mod. *tâche*) - medL. *tasca*, alt. of *taxa*, f. L. *taxāre* TAX.

tass cup, small goblet. XV. - (O)F. *tasse* - Arab. *ṭass(a)* basin - Pers. *tast*.

tassel †clasp, fibula XIII; pendent ornament consisting of a knob with fringe attached XIV. - OF. *tas(s)el*, of unkn. orig.

taste †examine by touch, try, test; experience or try the flavour of XIII; have a particular flavour XVI. - OF. *taster* (mod. *tâter*) touch, feel, try, taste :- Rom. **tastāre*, supposed to be blend of L. *tangere* touch and *gustāre* taste. So **taste** sb. - OF. *tast*, f. the vb. Hence **tasty** (-Y[1]) pleasant to taste. XVI (in *untasty*).

tat (in phr. *tit for tat*) see TIT[3].

tatter (chiefly pl.) irregularly torn piece. First recorded in *tatarwagges* (*c.* 1400), but implied in earlier *tattered* orig. †clothed in slashed garments, *tatering* slashing of garments (XIV). - ON. **taturr* (Icel. *töturr*, Norw. dial. *totra*), pl. *tǫtrar* rags, rel. to OE. *tættec* rag, and prob. further to OHG. *zæter* rag.

tatterdemalion ragged fellow. XVII. f. TATTER or *tattered* (see prec.) + an obscure el.

tatting kind of knotted lace work. XIX. of unkn. orig.

tattle †falter, stammer XV; talk idly or without reticence XVI. - MFlem. *tatelen* (parallel to MFlem., MDu., MLG. *tateren*), of imit. orig.; see -LE[3].

tattoo[1] signal by beat of drum, etc., for soldiers to return to quarters XVII; military entertainment based on an elaboration of this XVIII. orig. *tap-too*, *-tow* - Du. *taptoe*, f. *tap* TAP[1] + *toe*, for *doe toe* 'do to', shut; the primary application seems to have been to a signal for the turning off of the taps of barrels of drink.

tattoo[2] designs on the skin made by puncturing it and inserting pigments. XVIII (*tattow*). of Polynesian orig. Hence vb. XVIII.

taunt †in phr. *taunt pour* (or *for*) *taunt* tit for tat in reply; †smart rejoinder, witty jibe; scornful reproach or challenge XVI. orig. - F. phr. *tant pour tant* 'so much for so much', like for like (L. *tantum*, n. of *tantus* so great). Hence **taunt** vb. †answer back; reproach scornfully. XVI.

tauromachy bullfighting, bullfight. XIX. - Gr. *tauromakhiā*, f. *taûros* bull + *mákhē* fighting; see -Y[3].

taut †tense, distended XIV; tightly drawn XVII. For earlier *taught*, alt. of *tought*, ME. *touht*, *toȝt*, prob. identical with the common var. *tought* of TOUGH, with the sense influenced by assoc. with *toȝ-*, pp. stem of *tee*, OE. *tēon* draw, pull.

tautology XVI. - late L. *tautologia* - Gr. *tautologiā*, f. *tautológos* repeating what has been said (whence **tautologous** XVIII), f. *tautó* the same + *-logos* saying; see -LOGY.

tavern XIII. - (O)F. *taverne* :- L. *taberna*.

taw[1] prepare or dress (raw material), spec. in the conversion of skins into leather. OE. *tawian*, rel. to MLG., MDu. *touwen*, OHG. *zouwen*, Goth. *taujan* :- Gmc. **tawōjan*, **tawjan* do, make, prepare.

taw[2] large choice or fancy marble. XVIII. of unkn. orig.

tawdry †short for *t. lace*; cheap and pretentious finery; hence adj. of the nature of this. XVII. orig. in *Seynt Audries lace*, *tawdrie lace* (XVI) 'lace' or necktie such as was sold at St. Audrey's fair in remembrance of St. Audrey, i.e. Etheldrida, or Æðelðryð (daughter of Anna, king of East Anglia, and patron saint of Ely), who died of a tumour in the throat which she regarded as a just retribution for her youthful fondness for splendid necklaces.

tawny XIV. - AN. *tauné*, OF. *tané* dark like tan, f. *tan* TAN. Cf. -Y[5].

taws(e) (chiefly Sc.) whip for a spinning top; leather thong used for chastisement. XVI. pl. of *taw* tawed leather, thong, f. TAW[1].

tax determine the amount of (a fine, etc.) XIII; impose a tax on XIV; censure, take to task XVI. - (O)F. *taxer* - L. *taxāre*. Hence sb. compulsory contribution. XIV. So **taxation** XIV. - (O)F. - L.

taxi short (XX) for *taxi-cab*, which is for *taximeter cab* cab fitted with a **taximeter** (XIX) automatic contrivance to indicate distance traversed and fare due; - F. *taximètre*, f. *taxe* tariff + *-mètre* -METER. Hence **taxi** vb. travel by taxi; (of aircraft). XX.

taxidermy XIX. f. Gr. *táxis* arrangement + *dérma* skin; see -Y[3]. Hence **taxidermist** XIX.

taxonomy scientific classification. XIX. - F. *taxonomie*, irreg. f. Gr. *táxis* arrangement; see -NOMY.

tazza shallow ornamental bowl. XIX. - It. **tazza** = (O)F. *tasse* TASS.

T.B. XX. abbrev. of *tubercle bacillus*, colloq. of *tuberculosis*.

te, ti seventh note of the scale in solmization. XIX. alt. of SI.

tea XVII (early forms also *tay*, *tey*). prob. immed. - Du. *thee* - Chinese (Amoy) *t'e*, in Mandarin dial. *ch'a*, whence earlier *cha(a)*, *chia* (XVI).

teach pt., pp. *taught* †show; show by way of information or instruction. OE. *tǣċan* :- **taikjan*, rel. to *tācen* TOKEN.

teak (wood of) large E. Indian tree. XVII. - Pg. *teca* - Malayalam *tēkka*.

teal small freshwater duck. XIV. rel. to MLG. *tēlink*, MDu. *tēling*, *teiling* (D. *teling*); ult. imit. of its call.

team A. †child-bearing, †offspring, (dial.) family, brood OE.; B. set of draught animals OE.; number of persons in concerted action XVI; †C. (leg.) vouching to warranty OE.; D. (dial., after ON. *taumr*) chain for yoking draught animals XIV. OE. *tēam* = OS. *tōm*, OHG. *zoum* (G. *zaum*), ON. *taumr* bridle, rein :- Gmc. **taumaz*, prob. for **tauȝmaz*, f. **tauχ-* draw, rel. to L. *dūcere*. Hence **teamster** XVIII (orig. U.S.).

teapoy three-legged stand. XIX. - Hindi *tīn*, in comb. *tir* three + Pers. *pāy* foot.

tear[1] drop of fluid shed by the eye. OE. *tēar* = OHG. *zah(h)ar* (G. *zähre*, orig. pl.), ON. *tár*, Goth. *tagr* :- IE. **dakru-*, repr. also by Gr. *dákru*, *dákrūma* (whence OL. *dacruma*, L. *lacruma*, *-ima*), W. *deigr*, Ir. *dér*.

tear[2] pt. *tore*, pp. *torn* pull asunder by force. OE. str. vb. *teran* = OS. *terian*, MLG., (M)Du. *teren*, OHG. *zeran* (G. *zehren*) destroy, consume, Goth. *distairan*; the IE. base **der-* is repr. by Gr. *dérein* flay, Skr. *dṛṇā́ti* bursts, tears.

tease A. separate the fibres of (wool, etc.) OE.; B. irritate by persistent action XVII. OE. *tǣsan* = (M)LG., MDu. *tēzen* (Du. *teezen*), OHG. *zeisan* (G. dial. *zeisen*) :- WGmc. **taisjan* (**taisan*).

teasel, teazle plant of the genus *Dipsacus*; the prickly flower heads of which are used for teasing cloth. OE. *tǣs(e)l* = OHG. *zeisala* (MHG. *zeisel*), f. base of **taisan* TEASE; see -EL[1], -LE[1].

teat nipple of breast or udder. XIII. ME. *tete* - OF. *tete* (later and mod. *tette*), prob. of Gmc. origin (see TIT[1], which it repl. in the standard lang.).

tec (sl.) short for DETECTIVE. XIX.

technic, technical pert. to art or an art. XVII. - L. *technicus* - Gr. *tekhnikós*, f. *tékhnē* art, craft; see -IC, -ICAL. So **technique** XIX. - F., sb. use of adj. **technology** scientific study of the arts; technical terminology. XVII. - Gr. *tekhnologíā*; whence **technological** XVII.

tectonic pert. to building or construction. XVII. - late L. *tectonicus* - Gr. *tektonikós*, f. *téktōn*, *-ton-* carpenter.

ted (dial.) spread out for drying, scatter. XV. - ON. *teðja*, rel. to *tad* dung, *toddi* small piece, OHG. (G. dial) *zetten* spread.

teddy pet-form (see -Y[6]) of *Edward*, *Edmund*, *Theodore*; **teddy bear** stuffed figure of a bear, with ref. to Theodore Roosevelt, president of U.S.A. 1901-9. **teddy boy**, with ref. to Edward VII of England (1901-10), the style of costume of whose reign is imitated by the boys so named.

Te Deum opening words of the canticle beginning *Te Deum laudamus* 'Thee God we praise', recited at matins in the Western Church. XIV.

tedious XV. - OF. *tedieus* or late L. *tædiōsus*, f. L. *tædium* (whence **tedium** XVII) weariness, disgust; see -IOUS.

tee[1] letter T or T-shaped object. XV.

tee[2] starting-place at golf. XVIII. Clipped form of earlier †*teaz* (XVII), of unkn. orig.

tee[3] mark on the ice at curling. XVIII. of unkn. orig. (perh. identical with TEE[1]).

tee-hee see TEHEE.

teem †bring forth OE.; be prolific, abound *with* XVI. OE. (Angl.) *tēman*, (WS.) *tīeman* :- **taumjan*, f. Gmc. **taumaz* TEAM.

-teen OE. *-*tīene*, -*tēne*, -*tȳne* = OS. -*tein*, OHG. -*zehan*, Goth. -*taihun* (Du. -*tien*, G. -*zehn*), inflected form of TEN added to cardinals from three to nine. Based on these are the ordinals in **-teenth** (-TH²) ME. -*tenþe*, alt. (by assim. to TEN) of -*teþe*, OE. -*teo(go)ða*, corr. to OHG. -*zehanto* (Du. -*tiende*, G. -*zehnte*), ON. -*tándi*. Hence **teen-age, -ager** XX.

teeny expressive alt. of TINY. XIX.

teethe cut teeth. XV. f. *teeth*, pl. of TOOTH.

teetotal pert. to total abstinence. XIX. Said to have been first used by one Richard Turner, of Preston, Lancashire, about September 1833, in a speech advocating total abstinence from intoxicating liquors, in preference to abstinence from ardent spirits only. Perh. based on *teetotally* wholly, entirely (XIX; U.S.), a strengthened form of *totally* (quasi *T-totally*).

teetotum top with four sides lettered to decide the spinner's luck. XVIII. orig. *T totum*, formed by prefixing to L. *tōtum* all, the whole, its initial T, which stood on one of the four sides, the other letters A, D, N, standing for L. *aufer*, *depone*, *nihil*.

teg sheep (formerly ewe) in its second year. XVI. ME. **tegge*, **tagge* in place-names repr. OE. **tegga*, **tagga*, parallel to OSw. *takka*, Sw. *tacka* ewe.

tegument covering, envelope. XV. - L. *tegumentum*, f. *tegere* cover; see -MENT.

tehee repr. light (derisive) laughter. XIV.

telaesthesia perception at a distance. XIX. f. Gr. *tēle* TELE- + *aisthēsis* perception; see -IA¹.

tele-, before a vowel prop. *tel-*, but more often in the full form; pref. repr. Gr. *tēle-*, comb. form of *tēle* afar, far off (rel. to *télos* end). Comp.: **telegraph** †semaphore, signalling apparatus XVIII; apparatus for conveying a message to a distance by electricity XIX. - F. *télégraphe*. Hence **telegram** XIX, **telegraphy, telegraphic** XVIII. **telepathy** communication from mind to mind without aid of the senses. XIX (Gr. -*patheiā* feeling, perception). **telephone** XIX (see -PHONE); hence **telephonic, telephonist** XIX. **teleprinter** XX. **telescope** XVII. - It. *telescopio* or modL. *telescopium* (see -SCOPE); hence vb. (orig. U.S. XIX) cause to move into another object or collapse like the sliding parts of a telescope; **telescopic** XVIII. **television** XX. **Telex** XX. f. *tele*printer + *ex*change.

teleo-, before a vowel **tele-**, repr. *teleo-*, comb. form of Gr. *téle(i)os* perfect, complete, f. *télos* end, as in **teleology** doctrine of final causes. XVIII. - modL. *teleologia*.

tell pt., pp. *told* A. mention in order, narrate OE.; B. make known, declare; inform; relate OE.; (arch., exc. in *all told*, *untold wealth*, *tell one's beads*), mention numerically, count OE.; be of account (e.g. in *telling* ppl. adj.) XVII. OE. *tellan* = OS. *tellian*, (M)LG., (M)Du. *tellen*, OHG. *zellen* (G. *zählen* reckon, count), ON. *telja* :- Gmc. **taljan*, f. **talō* TALE. Hence **teller** one who relates XIII; one who keeps tally XV; one selected to count votes XVII.

tellurium (min.) one of the rarer elements. XVIII. f. L. *tellūs*, *tellūr-* earth + -IUM.

telpher travelling unit in a system of **telpherage**, transport effected automatically by electricity. XIX. contr. form of **telephore*, f. TELE- + Gr. -*phoros* bearing.

telson (zool.) last segment of some crustaceans, etc. XIX. - Gr. *télson* limit.

temerarious unreasonably bold or venturous. XVI. f. L. *temerārius* fortuitous, rash, f. *temere* blindly, rashly, orig. instr. abl. of **temus*, **temer-* darkness; see -ARIOUS. So **temerity** XV. - L.

temper †due mixture of elements XIV; chiefly in various senses of *temperament* and *temperature* from XV; mental balance XVII; frame of mind; (outburst of) ill humour XIX. f. **temper** vb. †mingle, blend; restrain, †regulate OE.; impart due hardness, etc. to (steel) XIV. OE. *temprian* (= OS. *temperon*) - L. *temperāre* mingle, restrain oneself, perh. orig. combine in due proportion, and rel. to *tempus*, *temper-* time, due season. So **tempera** painting in distemper. XIX. - It. in phr. *pingere a tempera*, f. *temperare* - L. **temperament** †due mixture of elements XV; combination of the four cardinal humours XVII; natural disposition XIX. - L. *temperāmentum*. **temperance** self-restraint XIV; spec. in food and drink XVI. - AN. *temperaunce* - L. *temperantia*. **temperate** moderate XIV; of the zones between the torrid and frigid XVI. - L. *temperātus*, pp. of *temperāre*; see -ATE². **temperature** †mixture; †temperament XVI; state with regard to heat and cold XVII. - F. or L.

tempest XIII. - OF. *tempeste* (mod. *tempête*) and *tempest* :- Rom. **tempesta* and **tempestum*, for L. *tempestās* season, weather, storm, f. *tempus* time, season. So **tempestuous** XVI. - late L. *tempestuōsus*.

templar A. member of an order of knights orig. occupying a building on or near the site of the Temple of Solomon at Jerusalem XIII; B. barrister of the Inner or the Middle Temple, London XVI. - AN. *templer*, (O)F. *templier* - medL. *templārius* or *templāris*, f. *templum* TEMPLE¹; see -AR.

template see TEMPLET.

temple¹ sacred edifice. OE. *temp(e)l* (reinforced in ME. by (O)F. *temple*) :- L. *templum* space marked out by an augur for taking observations, broad open space, consecrated space, sanctuary; of uncert. orig.

temple² flat part of the head between forehead and either ear. XIV. - OF. *temple* (mod. *tempe*) :- Rom. **tempula*, alt. of L. *tempora*, pl. of *tempus*.

temple³ weaver's stretcher. XV. - F., ult. identical with TEMPLE².

templet plate of timber XVII; pattern XIX. prob. f. TEMPLE³ + -ET; now usu. **template** (by assoc. with PLATE).

tempo (mus.) relative speed or rate of movement. XVIII. - It. :- L. *tempus* time.

temporal¹ †temporary; pert. to human life, wordly; secular XIV; (gram., pros.) relating to time or tense XVII. - (O)F. *temporel* or L. *temporālis*, f. *tempus*, *tempor-* time; see -AL¹. So **temporality** †temporal things XIV; material possessions XV. - late L. *temporālitās*. **temporary** XVI. - L. *temporārius*. **temporize** XVI. - F. *temporiser* pass one's time, wait one's time

- medL. *temporizāre*. Hence **temporalty** (-TY[2]) temporal things; laity. XIV.

temporal[2] pert. to the temples. XVI. - late L. *temporālis*, f. *tempora*; see TEMPLE[2], -AL[1].

tempt test, try (surviving in *tempt God, fate, fortune, the sea*, etc.); try to attract, entice. XIII. - OF. *tempter*, learned form beside *tenter* :- L. *temptāre* feel, try the strength of, test. So **temptation** XIII. - OF. - L.

ten OE. (Angl.) *tēn(e)*, (WS.) *tīen(e)* = OS. *tehan* (Du. *tien*), OHG. *zehan* (G. *zehn*), ON. *tíu*, Goth. *taihun* :- Gmc. _*teχan_, beside _*teχun_ :- IE. _*deḱm̥_, whence also L. *decem*, Gr. *déka*, OSl. *desętĭ*, Skr. *dáśa*. So **tenth** ME. *tenþe* (XII), alt., by assim. to TEN, of *tethe*, OE. *teogoða* (see -TH[2]).

tenable XVI. - (O)F., f. *tenir* hold; see -ABLE.

tenace at whist, combination of next above and next below the opponents' highest card. XVII. - F. - Sp. *tenaza* lit. pincers, tongs :- L. *tenācia*, f. *tenāx* (see next).

tenacious XVI. f. L. *tenāx, tenāc-*, f. *tenēre* hold; see next and -IOUS. So **tenacity** XVI. - (O)F. or L. *tenācitās*.

tenant XIV. - (O)F., sb. use of prp. of *tenir* hold - (with change of conj.) L. *tenēre*, rel. to *tendere* stretch, TEND[2]; see -ANT. Hence **tenantry** XIV.

tench freshwater fish. XIV. - OF. *tenche* (mod. *tanche*) :- late L. *tinca*.

tend[1] orig. in various senses of *attend* and *intend* XIV; now only in gen. use, take care of, be in charge of, look after XV. Aphetic of ATTEND and †*entend*, INTEND. Hence **tender**[3] †attendant, ministrant XV; boat attending a larger one XVII; car attached to a locomotive XIX; one who has charge of a bar, etc. XIX. Partly f. *attender* (XV), partly immed. f. TEND[1] + -ER[1].

tend[2] have a disposition *to* or *towards*. XIV. - (O)F. *tendre* :- L. *tendere* stretch, extend, aim (at).

tendency XVII. - medL. *tendentia*, f. L. *tendēns, -ent-*, prp. of *tendere* stretch, etc. (see prec.); see -ENCY. Hence **tendential** (XIX), **tendentious** (XX) having a (purposed) tendency.

tender[1] easily broken or injured XIII; having delicacy of feeling; susceptible to moral or spiritual influences XVI. - (O)F. *tendre* :- L. *tener* tender, delicate.

tender[2] offer for acceptance. XVI. - (O)F. *tendre* :- L. *tendere* stretch, hold forth (cf. TEND[2]). Hence sb. XVI.

tendon XVI. - F. *tendon* or medL. *tendō, -ōn-*, f. L. *tendere* stretch, tr. Gr. *ténōn* sinew, sb. use of aorist ppl. of *teínein* stretch.

tendril slender thread-like appendage of a plant. XVI. prob. alt., after F. dim. †*tendrillon*, of †*tendron* young shoot, (pl.) cartilages of the ribs (XIV) - (O)F. *tendron* tender part or shoot, cartilage :- Rom. _*tenerūmen_ shoots, f. L. *tener* TENDER[1].

tenebrae Holy Week devotion (matins and lauds) at which candles lighted at the beginning are successively put out. XVII. - L. (pl.) darkness.

tenement †tenure; holding XIV; dwelling-place XV. - OF. *tenement* (mod. *tènement*) - medL. *tenementum*, f. L. *tenēre* hold; see -MENT.

tenet XVII. - L. *tenet* (he) holds, 3rd pres. sg. of *tenēre* hold.

tenné (her.) tawny. XVI. - obs. F. *tenné*, var. of *tanné* TAWNY.

tennis ball game played with rackets in a walled court XIV; short for *lawn t.*, XIX. ME. *tenetz, tene(y)s, tenyse*, usu. taken to be - (O)F. *tenez*, imper. of *tenir* hold, take, presumably the server's call to his opponent.

tenon XV. - F., f. *tenir* hold.

tenor A. general sense of a discourse, etc. XIII; continuous progress XIV; †quality, condition XVI; B. (mus.) voice or part between alto and bass XIV. ME. *ten(o)ur* - AN. *tenur*, OF. *tenour* (mod. *teneur* course, import) - L. *tenor, -ōr-* continuous course, substance, import of a law, etc., f. *tenēre* hold; see -OR[2]. Sense B. was in OF. *tenor* (mod. *ténor*) - It. *tenore* and medL. *tenor*; the sense ('holding or continuous part') is due to the allotting of the melody to that part.

tenrec see TANREC.

tense[1] †time; (gram.) form of a verb indicating time. XIV. - OF. *tens* (mod. *temps*) :- L. *tempus* time.

tense[2] drawn tight XVII; highly strung XIX. - L. *tensus*, pp. of *tendere* stretch, TEND[2]. So **tensile** ductile XVII; pert. to tension XIX. - medL. **tension** XVI. - F. or L. Hence **tensor** (-OR[1]) (anat.) muscle that tightens some part XVIII; (math.) in quaternions XIX.

tent[1] portable shelter of canvas, etc. XIII. - (O)F. *tente* :- Rom. _*tenta_ n. pl. used as fem. of _*tentum_, for L. *tentōrium* tent, f. *tent-*, pp. stem of *tendere* stretch, TEND[2], based on the use of phr. *pelles tendere* stretch out skins, in the sense 'pitch tents'. Hence **tent** vb., **tented** (see -ED[1,2]) XVII.

tent[2] †probe; roll of material for searching a wound XIV. - (O)F. *tente*, f. *tenter* :- L. *temptāre* feel, try, TEMPT.

tent[3] deep-red Spanish wine. XVI (*tynt*). - Sp. *tinto* dark-coloured :- L. *tinctus*, pp. of *tingere*, dye, TINGE.

tentacle XVIII. f. L. *tentāre*, var. of *temptāre* feel, try, TEMPT; see -CLE.

tentative XVII (*tentatively* XVI). - medL. *tentātīvus*, f. pp. stem of L. *tentāre*; see prec. and -ATIVE.

tenter wooden frame on which cloth is stretched. XIV. - AN. _*tentur_ - medL. *tentōrium*, f. pp. stem *tent-* of L. *tendere* stretch, TEND[2]. Comb. **tenterhook** (XV) hook fixed on a tenter, in gen. use now only in fig. phr. *on tenterhooks* (XVI).

tenth see TEN.

tenuis (phon.) voiceless stop. XVII. - L. *tenuis* thin.

tenuity thinness, meagreness. XVI. - L. *tenuitās*, f. *tenuis* thin; see -ITY. So **tenuous** XVI; see -OUS.

tenure holding of a tenement, condition under which it is held. XV. - OF. *tenure*, f. *tenir* hold; see TENANT, -URE.

teocalli place of worship of the ancient Mexicans. XVII. - Nahuatl, f. *teotl* god + *calli* house.

tepee wigwam. XIX. of Siouan orig.

tepid XIV. - L. *tepidus*, f. *tepēre* be warm; see -ID[1].

ter- - L. *ter* thrice, used occas. in comp. XVII; spec. in chem. (XIX), now superseded by TRI-.

teratology account of marvels XVII; (biol.) study of abnormalities XIX. f. Gr. *téras, terato-* marvel, prodigy + -LOGY.

terce var. of TIERCE, usual in the name of the canonical hour. XIV (*terse*).

tercel, tiercel male hawk. XIV. - OF. *tercel* - Rom. **tertiōlus*, f. *tertius* THIRD; perh. so named because it was believed that the third egg of a clutch produced a male bird.

tercet (pros.) set of three lines rhyming together. XVI. - F. - It. *terzetto*, f. *terzo* (:- L. *tertius* THIRD) + *-etto* -ET.

terebinth tree *Pistacia terebinthus*, the source of turpentine. XIV. - OF. *t(h)erebinte* (mod. *térébinthe*) or its source L. *terebinthus* - Gr. *terébinthos*.

teredo boring mollusc, esp. ship-worm. XVII. - L. *terēdō* - Gr. *terēdṓn*, f. base **ter-* of *teírein* rub hard, wear away, bore.

terete smooth and round (spec. in nat. hist.) XVII. - L. *teres, teret-*.

tergiversation desertion of a cause, etc.; contradictory behaviour. XVI. - L. *tergiversatiō, -ōn-*, f. *tergiversārī* (whence **tergiversate** XVII), f. *tergum* back + *vers-*, pp. stem of *vertere* turn.

term limit in time, period XIII; (pl.) limiting conditions XIV; form in which a matter or subject is expressed, expression. - (O)F. *terme* :- L. *terminus* limit, boundary. So **terminal** pert. to a boundary XV; situated at or forming the end XIX; sb. terminal element XIX. - L.; see -AL[1]. **terminate** †determine XVI; bring to an end XVII. f. pp. stem of L. *termināre*; see -ATE[3]. **termination** †determination; end XV; (gram.) ending XVI. - (O)F. or L. **terminology** system of terms. XIX. - G. *terminologie*. **terminus** pl. *-i* finishing point XVII; end of a line of railway XIX. - L.

termagant (*T-*) deity attributed to Muslims, etc., represented in mystery plays as an overbearing character XIII; violent domineering person (esp. woman) XVI. Earlier form *tervagaunt*, later *term-* (XIV) - OF. *Tervagan(t)* - It. *Trivigante, -vag-*, expl. as f. L. TRI- + *vagāns, -ant-*, prp. of *vagārī* wander and so designating the moon wandering under the names of Selene (Luna), Artemis (Diana), and Persephone (Proserpina), in heaven, earth, and hell respectively.

termite XVIII. - late L. *termes, termit-* woodworm, alt. of *tarmes* woodworm (perh. by assim. to *terere* rub).

termor one who holds property for a term of years. XIV. - AN. *termer*, f. *terme* TERM; see -ER[2].

tern sea-bird of the genus *Sterna*. XVIII. of uncert. orig.

ternary threefold, triple. XIV. - L. *ternārius*, f. *ternī* three at a time, three by three, f. *ter* thrice; see -ARY. So **ternate** (-ATE[2]) XVIII.

terpene (chem.) hydrocarbon found in essential oils. XIX. f. *terp* in *terpentine*, obs. form of TURPENTINE + -ENE.

Terpsichorean pert. to dancing. XIX. f. Gr. *Terpsikhórē* muse of dancing and of the dramatic chorus, f. *térpein* delight + *khorós* dance, CHORUS; see -EAN.

terra - L., It. 'earth', as in **terracotta** unglazed pottery. XVIII. - It. 'baked earth' (*cotta* :- L. *cocta*, fem. pp. of *coquere* COOK); **t. firma** †mainland; dry land. XVII. - L., 'firm land' (fem. of *firmus* FIRM); **t. incognita** unexplored territory. XVII. - L., 'unknown land'. **terrae filius** person of obscure parentage XVI; (Univ. of Oxford) formerly orator privileged to make humorous comments at a public act XVII. - L., 'son of the earth'.

terrace †gallery, balcony; raised level walk. XVI. - OF. *terrace*, (also mod.) *-asse* †rubble, platform :- Rom. **terrāceus, -ācea*, f. L. *terra* earth; see -ACEOUS.

terrain XVIII. - F. - pop. L. **terrānum*, var. of L. *terrēnum* TERRENE.

terramare ammoniacal earth found in the valley of the Po, Italy. XIX. - F. - It. dial. *terramara*, for *terra marna*, i.e. *terra* earth + *marna* MARL.

terrapin XVII. of Algonquian orig.

terraqueous composed of, living in, land and water, chiefly in *t. globe*. XVII. f. medL. *terraqueus*, f. *terra* earth + *aqua* water.

terrene earthly. XIV. - AN. - L. *terrēnus*, f. *terra* earth.

terreplein (fortif.) sloping bank behind a wall or rampart XVI; level base for a battery XVII. - F. *terre-plein* - It. *terrapieno*, f. *terrapienare* 'fill with earth', f. *terra* (:- L. *terra* earth) + *pieno* (:- L. *plēnus*) FULL.

terrestrial earthly, mundane XV; pert. to the earth XVI. f. L. *terrestris*, f. *terra* earth; see -IAL.

terret circular ring as part of horse-harness, etc. XV. ME. *tyret*, var. of *toret* - OF. *to(u)ret*, dim. of *tour* circuit, circumference, TOUR; see -ET.

terrible exciting terror XV; very violent, severe, or bad, excessive. XVI. - (O)F. - L. *terribilis*, f. *terrēre* frighten; see -BLE.

terrier[1] register of landed property. XV. - OF. *terrier*, sb. use of adj. :- medL. *terrārius*, f. L. *terra* land.

terrier[2] small breed of dog. So called from its pursuing the quarry into its earth. XV. - early modF. *terrier* - medL. *terrārius*; cf. prec.

terrific causing terror. XVII. - L. *terrificus*, f. *terrēre*, frighten; see -FIC. So **terrify** XVI. - L. *terrificāre*.

terrine see TUREEN.

territory XV. - L. *territōrium*, f. *terra* land. So **territorial** XVIII. - late L.

terror XIV. - OF. *terrour* (mod. *terreur*) :- L. *terror, -ōr-*. So **terrorism, -ist** XVIII. - F. *terrorisme, -iste*.

terry loop raised in pile-weaving left uncut. XVIII. of unkn. orig.

tersanctus (liturg.) SANCTUS. XIX. See TER-.

terse †smoothed, polished, neat; polite, refined XVII; neatly concise XVIII. - L. *tersus*, pp. of *tergēre* wipe.

tertian (of a fever) of which the paroxysms occur every third (i.e. alternate) day; also sb. XIV. - L. *tertiānus*, f. *tertius* THIRD; see -IAN. So **tertiary** pert. to (a member of) the third series, order, etc. XVI. - L. *tertiārius*. **tertium quid** (old chem.) third substance distinct from its two components. XVIII. - late L., n. of *tertius* + *quid*, n. of *quis* somebody.

terza rima It. form of verse rhyming *aba, bcb, cdc*, of the 'Divina Commedia' of Dante. XIX. - It., fem. of *terzo* third, *rima* rhyme.

tessellated formed with a mosaic pattern. XVII. f. L. *tessellātus* (or the derived It. *tessellato*), f. *tessella*, dim. of *tessera*; see next, -ATE[2], -ED[1].

tessera small quadrilateral tablet, esp. as used in mosaic; (hist.) square tablet on which watchword, etc., was written; hence (gen.) symbol, token. XVII. - L. - Gr. *téssera*, n. of *tésseres*, Ionic var. of *téssares* FOUR.

test A. cupel used in treating gold and silver alloys or ore XIV (rare before XVI); B. trial, examination XVI. - OF. *test* pot (mod. *têt* cupel) :- L. *testū, testum*, by-form of *testa* tile, in B mainly f. the vb. Hence **test** vb. XVII (first in pp.).

testaceous (zool.) having a shell; shell-like. XVII. f. L. *testāceus*, f. *testa* tile, earthen pot, shell; see -ACEOUS.

testament †covenant between God and man; each of the two divisions of the Holy Scripture or Bible XIII; will disposing of property and appointing an executor XIV. - L. *testāmentum*, f. *testārī* bear witness, make a will, f. *testis* witness; see MENT. So **testamentary** XV. - L. **testator** XV. - AN. *testatour* - L. *testātor*.

tester canopy over a bed. XIV. - medL. *testerium, testrum, testura* f. Rom. **testa* head (L. *testa* tile).

testicle XV. - L. *testiculus*, dim. of *testis* witness (the organ being evidence of virility). So **testicular** XVII.

testify XIV. - L. *testificāre, -ārī*, f. *testis* witness; see -FY.

testimony XIV. - L. *testimonium*, f. *testis* witness; see -MONY. So **testimonial** adj. & sb. XV. - (O)F. or late L.; see -AL[1].

testis (anat.) TESTICLE. XVII. - L.

testudo screen for the protection of armed forces. XVII. L. *testūdo* lit. 'tortoise', f. *testa* tile, pot, shell.

testy †headstrong, impetuous XIV; prone to be easily irritated XVI. ME. *testif* - AN., f. OF. *teste* (mod. *tête*) head :- L. *testa* tile, pot, shell, (Rom.) head; see -IVE.

tetanus spasm and rigidity of the muscles. XVI (in late ME. anglicized *tetane*). - L. - Gr. *tétanos*, f. base of *teínein* stretch.

tetchy XVI. prob. f. *tecche*, var. of *tache* spot, blemish, fault - OF. *teche*, (also mod.) *tache*; see -Y[1].

tête-à-tête XVII. - F., 'head to head'.

tether sb. XIV. - ON. *tjóðr*, corr. to MLG., MDu. *tūder, tudder* (Du. *tuier*), repr. Gmc. **teuðr-*, f. **teu-* fasten. Hence vb. XV.

tetra-, before a vowel *tetr-*, repr. Gr. *tetra-*, comb. form of *téttares, téttara* four, as in **tetrachord** XVII. **tetragon** four-angle figure. XVII. - Gr.; whence **tetragonal** (-AL[1]) XVI. **tetragrammaton** Heb. word written JHVH JEHOVAH. XIV. - Gr., f. *grámma, -at-* letter. **tetrahedron** four-sided figure. XVI. - late Gr. **tetralogy** series of four related dramas. XVII. - Gr. *tetralogiā*. **tetrameter** (pros.) element of four measures. XVII. - late L. *tetrametrus* - Gr. *tetrámetros*. **tetrastich** strophe of four lines. XVI. - L. *tetrastichon* - Gr. *tetrástikhon*. **tetrasyllable** XVI. - Gr. *tetrasúllabos*.

tetrad group of four. XVII. - Gr. *tetrás, tetrad-*, f. *téttares* four; see -AD.

tetrarch ruler of one of four divisions of a country, subordinate ruler. XIV. - late L. *tetrarcha*, classL. *-ēs* - Gr. *tetrárkhēs*, f. TETRA- + *-arkhēs* ruling. So **tetrarchy** XV.

tetter pustular eruption of the skin. OE. *teter*, cogn. with Skr. *dadrú-* skin disease, f. *dṛṇâti* bursts; cf. OHG. *zittaroh*.

Teuton member of a people of unknown race reckoned among the peoples of Germania. XVIII. - L. *Teutonī, Teutones* (pl.), f. IE. base meaning 'people', 'country', 'land'. So **Teutonic** pert. to this people, later identified with *Germanic*. XVII. - F. *teutonique* - L. *Teutonicus*. Comb. form **Teut(o)-** XIX.

text wording of a passage; short passage used as a motto, subject of discourse, etc. XIV; theme XVII. ME. *text(e), tixt(e)* - ONF. *tixte*, (also modF.) *texte* - L. *textus* tissue, style of literary work, in medL. the Gospel, written character, f. pp. stem of *texere* weave.

textile adj. and sb. woven (fabric). XVII. - F. *textile* or L. *textilis*, f. pp. stem of *texere* weave.

textual †well-read in texts; pert. to the or a text, esp. of the Scriptures. XIV. - (O)F. *textuel*, f. *texte* TEXT.

texture †weaving XV; character of a textile fabric, also fig. XVII. - L. *textūra*, f. *text-*, pp. stem of *texere* weave.

-th[1] suffix denoting action or process, formed on vb.-stems (1) in words such as *bath, birth, death*, of Gmc. age, (2) in others of later emergence, as *growth, spilth*; (3) in OE. words of quality or condition, in *-ðu, -ðo* (:- Gmc. *-iþō*), based on adjs., as *breadth, filth, health, mirth, truth*.

-th[2] suffix or ordinal numbers from *fourth* upwards, repr. OE. *-(o)ða, -(o)ðe*; with the tens (*twenty*, etc.) the ending is *-eth* (OE. *-oða, -oðe*).

thalamus (anat.) part of the brain at which a nerve originates; receptacle of a flower. XVIII. - L. - Gr. *thálamos* inner chamber.

thalassic pert. to the sea or inland seas. XIX. - F. *thalassique*, f. Gr. *thálassa* sea; see -IC.

thaler German silver coin. XVIII. - G. *t(h)aler* DOLLAR.

thallium (chem.) metallic element. XIX. f. L. *thallus* green shoot - Gr. *thallós*; see -IUM. So named from the green line distinguishing its spectrum.

than conjunctive particle used after comparatives, *other*, and *else*. OE. *þanne, þonne, þænne*, orig. identical with the adv. THEN, from which it was not finally differentiated in form until *c.*1700.

thane †(military) servant or attendant; (hist.) in A.-S. times, one who held lands by military service OE.; (Sc. hist.) man holding lands of the King XV. OE. *þeġ(e)n* = OS. *thegan* man, OHG. *degan* boy, servant, warrior, hero (G. *degen* warrior), ON. *þegn* freeman, liegeman :- Gmc. **þeʒnaz* :- IE. **teknós* (cf. Gr. *téknon* child), f. a base **tek-* repr. also by Gr. *tíktein* (:- **titk-*) bring forth. The sp. *thane* is derived from Sc. usage of XV-XVI.

thank †thought; †kindly thought, favour, gratitude; expression of gratitude (now only pl. *thanks*). OE. *þanc* = OS. *thank*, MDu., OHG. *danc* (Du., G. *dank*), Goth. *þagks* :- Gmc. **þaŋkaz*, f. **þaŋk-*, **þeŋk-* (see THINK). So **thank** vb. OE. *þancian*. Comps. **thankoffering, thanksgiving** XVI. Hence **thankful** showing gratitude; †deserving gratitude. OE. *þancfull*. **thankless** ungrateful; that brings no thanks. XVI. phr. **thank you** XV for *I thank you*.

that[1] dem. pron. (orig. n. of THE). OE. *þæt*, corr. to OS. *that*, (M)Du. *dat*, OHG. *daz* (G. *das*), ON. *þat*, Goth. *þata* (with suffix) :- IE. **tod*, repr. also by Skr. *tát*, Gr. *tó*, L. *-tud* in *istud*, OSl. *to*. As adj. XII, with pl. THOSE; as adv. XV.

that[2] rel. pron. equiv. to *who* and *which*, in OE. a generalized use of the n. of THE (cf. prec.), repl. OE. and ME. indeclinable *þe*.

that[3] conj.; in uses developed from those of THAT[1] and THAT[2]; the development is Gmc., with differentiation of sp. (*dass*) in modG., and affix in Goth. *þatei*.

thatch roof (a building), esp. with straw. XIV, repr. OE. *þeċċan* = OS. *thekkian* (Du. *dekken*), OHG. *decchan* (G. *decken*), ON. *þekja* :- Gmc. **þakjan*, f. **þakam* (OE. *þæċ* = MDu. *dac*, Du. *dak*, (O)HG. *dach* roof, ON. *þak* roof, thatch), f. **þak-* :- IE. **tog-* **teg-* cover, repr. also by L. *tegere*. Hence **thatch** sb. XIV.

thaumaturge wonder-worker. XVIII (*-urg*). - medL. *thaumaturgus* - Gr. *thaumatourgós*, f. *thaûma*, *thaumat-* wonder + *-ergos* working; later assim. to F. *thaumaturge*.

thaw reduce to a liquid state OE.; intr. XIV. OE. *þawian* = MLG. *dōien*, Du. *dooien*, OHG. *douwen* :- WGmc. **þawōjan* (cf. ON. *þeyja* :- **þaujan*), of unkn. orig. Hence sb. XV.

the[1] dem. adj. (definite article). Late OE. *þē*, ME. *þe*, at first nom. m., but ult. superseding all cases of OE. m. *sē*, fem. *sēo*, *sīo*, n. *þæt*, corr. to OS. *se*, *thē*, *thie*, *thiu*, *that* (Du. *de*, *dat*), OHG. *der*, *diu*, *daz* (G. *der*, *die*, *das*), ON. *sá*, *sú*, *þat*, Goth. *sa*, *sō*, *þata* (with suffix). The orig. Gmc. **sa*, **sō*, **þat* = Gr. *ho*, *hē* (dial. *há*), *tó* (:-**tod*), Skr. *sá*, *sā́*, *tát*.

the[2] (preceding an adj. or adv. in the compar. or superl. degree, e.g. *the more fools they*, *the more the merrier*, *the less said*, *the sooner mended*) by that amount; by how much . . . by so much. repr. OE. *þē*, varying with *þȳ*, *þon*, instr. of THE[1], THAT[1] (e.g. *þȳ māra* the greater, *þȳ mā* the more).

the-, var. of THEO- before a vowel, as in **theandric, theanthropic** pert. to God and man, divine and human, **thearchy** rule of God. All XVII.

theatre, U.S. **theater** in antiquity, open-air structure for plays and spectacles XIV; playhouse XVI. - OF. *t(h)eatre* (mod. *théâtre*) or L. *theātrum* - Gr. *théātron* 'place for viewing', f. *theâsthai* behold. So **theatrical** XVI; sb. pl. XVII. f. late L. *theātricus* - Gr. *theātrikós*.

theca receptacle, cell, case. XVII. - L. *thēca* - Gr. *thḗkē* case, cover.

thee acc. and d. of THOU. OE. (i) acc. *þec*, later *þē* = OS. *thic*, *thī*, OHG. *dih* (G. *dich*), ON. *þik*, Goth. *þuk* :- Gmc. **þeke*, f. IE. **te* (repr. by L. *tē*, Gr. *sé*); (ii) d. *þē* = OS. *thī*, (O)HG. *dir*, ON. *þér*, Goth. *þus* :- Gmc. **þez*. Hence vb. XVII.

theft OE. (WS.) *þīefð*, *þȳfð*, *þȳft*, non-WS. *þēofð*, *þēoft* = ON. *þýfð*, *þýft* :- Gmc. **þiūbiþō*, f. *þeuƀaz* THIEF; see -T[2].

thegn var. of THANE.

their of them. XII. - ON. *þeir(r)a* (= OE. *þāra*), g. pl. of *sá*, *sú*, *þat* THE[1], THAT[1], used also as g. pl. of the 3rd pers. pron. Cf. THEM, THEY. Hence **theirs** XIII; see -S.

theism belief in one God, esp. as creator and supreme ruler. XVII. f. Gr. *theós* god. So **theist** XVII, **theistic** XVIII, **-istical** XVII.

them d. and acc. of THEY. XII. - ON. *þeim* (= OE. *þǣm*), d. pl. of *sá*, *sú*, *þat* THE[1], THAT[1], used also as d. pl. of the 3rd pers. pron. Cf. THEIR, THEY.

theme subject of a discourse XIII; exercise, essay XVI; inflexional base or stem. ME. *teme* - OF. **teme* (*tesme*) - L. *thēma* (to which it was soon conformed in sp.) - Gr. *théma* proposition, f. **the-* base of *tithénai* place (see DO[1]). So **thematic** XVIII. - Gr. *thematikós*.

then at that time, in that case, that being the case. ME. *þenne*, *þann(e)*, OE. *þænne*, *þanne*, *þonne* = OS. *than(na)*, OHG. *danne*, *denne* (G. *dann*), f. dem. base Gmc. **þa-* (see THAT[1], THE[1]).

thence XIII. ME. *þannes*, *þen(ne)s*, f. *þanne*, *þenne* thence, OE. *þanon(e)* = OS., OHG. *danana*, *danān* (Du. *dan*, G. *dannen*) :- WGmc. **þanana*.

theo- comb. form of Gr. *theós* god. See THE-.

theodicy vindication of the divine attributes. XVIII. - F. *théodicée*, title of a work by Leibniz (1710), f. Gr. *theós* God + *díkē* justice; the ending is assim. to -Y[3].

theodolite portable surveying instrument for measuring (orig. horizontal) angles. XVII. Earlier (XVI) in modL. form *theodelitus*; of unkn. orig.

theogony generation or genealogy of the gods. XVII. - Gr. *theogoniā*, f. *theós* god + *gon-* **gen-*; see GENESIS, -Y[3].

theology XIV. - (O)F. *théologie* - L. *theologia* - Gr. *theologiā*, f. *theológos* one who treats of the gods, f. *theós* god; see -LOGY. So **theologian** XV. - (O)F. *théologien*. **theological** XVI. - medL.

theorbo kind of lute. XVII. - It. *tiorba*, of unkn. orig.

theorem general proposition demonstrable by argument. XVI. - F. *théorème* or late L. *theōrēma* - Gr. *theṓrēma* speculation, theory, proposition to be proved, f. *theōrein* look at, f. *theōrós* spectator (see THEORY). So **theoretic(al)** †speculative, contemplative; pert. to theory. XVII. - late L. *theōrēticus* - Gr. *theōrētikós*. Hence **theoretician** XIX.

theory mental conception, scheme of thought. XVI. - late L. *theōria* - Gr. *theōríā* contemplation, speculation, sight, f. *theōrós* spectator, f. *thea-* base of *theâsthai* look upon, contemplate. So **theorize** XVII. - medL. *theōrizāre*. Hence **theorist** XVI.

theosophy system of philosophical speculation basing the knowledge of nature on that of the divine nature. XVII. - medL. *theosophia* - late Gr. *theosophiā*, f. *theós* god + *sophós* wise; see -Y[3].

Hence **theosophist,** earlier **theosopher, -sophic(al)** XVII.

therapeutic (pl., formerly sg.) art of healing XVI. - F. *thérapeutique* or late L. *therapeutica* - Gr. *therapeutikḗ*, sb. f. *therapeutḗs* attendant, f. *therapeúein* administer to, treat medically, f. *théraps, therap-* attendant; see -IC. So **therapeutic** adj. XVII. - Gr. *therapeutikós*. **therapy** medical treatment. XIX. - Gr. *therapeíā*; see -Y[3].

there A. in, at, or to that place. B. used to indicate existence or occurrence. OE. *þǣr, þēr* = OS. *thār* (Du. *daar*), OHG. *dār* (G. *da*); cogn. with ON., Goth. *þar*; f. dem. base Gmc. **þa-* (see THE[1], THAT[1]) + adv. suffix *-r*, as in *here, where*. The comps. *thereabout, -after, -at, -in, -of, -on, -out, -to, -with* are of OE. date.

theriac (arch.) antidote. XVI. - L. *thēriaca, -cē* - Gr. *thēriakḗ*; see TREACLE.

therio-, before a vowel **theri-,** repr. Gr. *thērion*, dim. of *thḗr* wild beast.

thermal pert. to hot springs XVIII; pert. to heat XIX. - F. *thermal*, f. Gr. *thérmē* heat; see -AL[1].

thermite mixture of finely powdered aluminium and oxide of iron, etc. producing on combustion very great heat. XIX. - G. *thermit*, f. Gr. *thérmē* heat; see -ITE.

thermo- repr. comb. form of Gr. *thérmē* heat, *thermós* hot, in many scientific terms.

thermometer XVII. - F. *thermomètre* or f. Gr. *thérmē* heat; see -METER.

thesaurus treasury, spec. of knowledge. XIX. - L. *thēsaurus* TREASURE - Gr. *thēsaurós*.

these pl. of THIS. ME. *þēse* (XIII), developed from *þīse*, f. *þis* THIS + pl. suffix *-e*; superseded *þās, þōs*, THOSE, which became the pl. of THAT[1].

thesis pl. **theses** A. proposition, theme XVI; (theme of) a dissertation XVII. B. (pros.) unaccented or unstressed element XIV; accented or stressed element XIX; - late L. *thesis* - Gr. *thésis* placing, setting, f. **the-* base of *tithénai* place (see DO[1]).

Thespian pert. to *Thespis*, traditional father of Gr. tragedy; tragic, dramatic. XVII; sb. tragedian XIX. See -IAN.

theurgy magic of the Egyptian Platonists XVI; divine agency in human affairs XIX. - late L. *theūrgia* - Gr. *theourgíā*, f. *theós* god + *-ergos* working; see -Y[3].

thew †custom, habit OE.; †(good) quality, virtue XIII; (pl.) bodily powers, physical endowments XVI. OE. *þēaw* usage, conduct = OS. *thau*, OHG. *thau, dau* discipline, of unkn. orig.

they pl. of HE[1], SHE, IT. XII. - ON. *þeir* (= OE. *þā*), pl. of *sá, sú, þat* THE[1], THAT[1], used also as pl. of the 3rd pers. pron. Cf. THEIR, THEM.

thick OE. *þicce* = OS. *thikki*, (Du. *dik*), OHG. *dicchi* (G. *dick*), ON. *þykkr* :- Gmc. **þeku-*, *þekwia-*, of unkn. orig. Hence **thicken** (-EN[5]) XV, **thickness** OE.

thicket OE. *þiccet*, f. *þicce* THICK.

thief OE. *þīof, þēof* = OS. *thiof* (Du. *dief*), OHG. *diob* (G. *dieb*), ON. *þjófr*, Goth. *þiufs*; Gmc. word of which no further cogns. are known.

thigh OE. (Angl.) *þēh*, (WS.) *þēoh, þīoh* = OLF. *thio* (Du. *dij*), OHG. *dioh*, ON. *þjó* :- Gmc. **þeuχam*, f. IE. **teuk-* **tauk-* **tuk-*, whence Lith. *táukas*, OSl. *tukŭ* fat, OIr. *tón* posteriors (:- **tukná*).

thill shaft of a cart, etc. XIV. of uncert. orig.; cf. OE. *þille* board, planking.

thimble †finger-stall OE. (only); finger-cap used in sewing XV. OE. *þȳmel*, f. *þūma* THUMB; see -LE[1].

thin OE. *þynne* = OS. *thunni* (Du. *dun*), OHG. *dunni* (G. *dünn*), ON. *þunnr* :- Gmc. **þunnuz* (:- **þunw-*), based on IE. **tn̥*, zero-grade of **ten-* **ton-* draw out, stretch (repr. also in Lat. *tenuis* thin, etc.).

thine of or pert. to THEE. OE. *þīn* = OS. *thīn* (Du. *dijn*), OHG. *dīn* (G. *dein*), ON. *þinn*, Goth. *þeins* :- Gmc. **þīnaz* :- IE. **t(w)einos*, f. **tū* THOU.

thing A. †(deliberative or judicial) assembly; †legal process or charge OE. (only); affair, business; deed, act OE.; that which is said XIII; B. that which exists, being OE. (inanimate object XVII). OE. *þing* = OS. *thing*, OHG. *ding, dinc*, assembly for deliberation and/or business, ON. *þing* :- Gmc. **þinȝam*. Hence, with meaningless additions, †*thingum* (XVII), *thingumbob, thingummy* (XVIII) *thingamajig, thingumabob* (XIX).

think pt., pp. *thought*. OE. *þenċan* = OS. *thenkian*, OHG. *denken* (G. *denken*), ON. *þekkja*, Goth. *þagkjan*; factitive formation on OE. *þynċan* seem, perh. orig. meaning 'cause to appear to oneself'.

thio-, before a vowel *thi-*, repr. comb. form of Gr. *theîon* sulphur. XIX.

third ordinal of the numeral three OE.; sb. third part XIV; musical interval XVI. OE. (late Nhb.) *þird(d)a, -e*, var. of *þridda* = OS. *thriddio* (Du. *derde*), OHG. *dritto* (G. *dritte*), ON. *þriði*, Goth. *þridja* :- Gmc. **þriðjaz* :- IE. **tritjós* (cf. Skr. *tr̥tī́ya-*, Gr. *tritos*, L. *tertius*, OSl. *tretij*, W. *trydydd*), f. stem of THREE. Hence **thirdly** (-LY[2]) XVI. **third-rate** XVII. **thirteen** OE. *þrēotīene* = OS. *thriutein* (Du. *dertien*), OHG. *drīzehan* (G. *dreizehn*), ON. *þrettán*. **thirteenth** OE. *þrēo-, þrīetēoða*, ME. *þrittеþe, þreottenþe* (XII), *þrittenþe* (XIV), *þirttenth* (XV), *thirteenth* (XVI); see -TH[2].

thirty OE. *þrītiġ* = OS. *thrītig* (Du. *dertig*), OHG. *drizzug* (G. *dreissig*), ON. *þrírtegr*, Goth. (acc.) *þrins tiguns*; see -TY[2]. **thirtieth** OE. *þrītigoða, þritteogoða*.

thirst sb. OE. *þurst* = OS *thurst* (Du. *dorst*), (O)HG. *durst* :- WGmc. **þurstu* (cf. ON. *þorsti*, Goth. *þaurstei*); f. **þurs-* :- IE. **tr̥s-* **tors-*, repr. also by L. *torrēre* dry, parch, Skr. *tŕ̥ṣyati* thirsts, OIr. *tart*. So **thirst** vb. OE. *þyrstan* (till late ME. also impers.).

this pl. THESE. dem. pron. and adj. The form *this* in generalized use dates from *c.*1200; it is identical with the OE. n. nom. and acc. and the stem of most of the inflected forms. OE. *þes* m., *þēos* fem., *þis* n., corr. to OS. **these, thius, thit*, OHG. *dese(r), desiu, diz*, ON. *þessi, þetta*; WGmc. and ON. formation on **þa-* (see THE[1], THAT[1]). As adv. equiv. to *thus* in various uses (XIV; now esp. in *this much, this far*, and the like), perh. from OE. instr. *þȳs, þīs*, or acc. sg. n. *þis*.

thistle OE. *þistel* = OS. *thīstil*, OHG. *distil(a)* (Du., G. *distel*), LG. *diestel, distel*, ON. *þistill* :- Gmc. **þīstilaz, -ilō*, of unkn. orig.

thither OE. *þider*, alt. by assim. to *hider* HITHER

of earlier *þæder*, corr. to ON. *þaðra* there, thither, f. dem. base **þa-* of THAT[1], THE[1] + suffix denoting 'towards' as in L. *intrā* within, *extrā* outside, Skr. *tátra* there, then.

thole[1] peg, pin, spec. in the gunwale of a boat. OE. *þol(l)* = MLG., MDu. *dolle* (Du. *dol*), ON. *þollr* (fir-)tree, peg, referred to Gmc. **þul-*, IE. **tul-* (cf. Gr. *túlos* peg). The want of evidence between OE. and XV prob. indicates loss of the OE. word and its supersession by the ON.

thole[2] (arch., dial.) suffer. OE. *þolian* = OS. *tholon, tholian*, OHG. *dolōn, dolēn*, ON. *þola*, Goth. *þulan*; f. Gmc. **þul-*, repr. weak grade of IE. **tol- *tel- *tḷ-* raise, remove, as in Gr. *tlênai* endure, bear, L. *tollere* raise, *tulī* (pt.) bore.

Thomist follower of *Thomas* Aquinas (*c.*1225-74), scholastic philosopher and theologian. XVI. - medL. *Thōmista*, f. L. *Thomas*; see -IST. Hence **Thomism** XVIII.

thong OE. *þwang, þwong* (*þong* XIII) = MLG. *dwank* constraint, OHG. *dwang* rein (MHG. *dwanc, twanc*, G. *zwang*), f. Gmc. **þwaŋg-*.

thorax (anat.) part of the body between the neck and the abdomen. XVI. - L. *thōrāx* - Gr. *thṓrāx, -āk-* breastplate, breast, chest. So **thoracic** XVII. - medL. - Gr.

thorium (chem.) dark-grey metallic element. XIX. f. *Thor* Norse god + -IUM.

thorn sharp-pointed process on a plant; thorn-bearing plant. OE. *þorn* = OS. *thorn* (Du. *doorn*), (O)HG. *dorn*, ON. *þorn*, Goth. *þaurnus* :- Gmc. *þurnuz* :- IE. **tr̥nus*, f. **tr̥n- tern-*, repr. also by OIr. *tráinín* small stalk of grass, OSl. *trŭnŭ* thorn, Skr. *tṛ́ṇa-* grass-stalk, Gr. *térnax* cactus prickle. Hence **thorny** (-Y[1]) OE. *þornig*.

thorough obs. or arch. as adv. and prep. in senses of *through*; in gen. use as adj. (application of the adv.) fully executed, affecting every part XIII. Disyllabic development, *þuruh*, of OE. *þurh* THROUGH, paralleled in OS. *thuru(h)*, OHG. *duruh*. Comps. **thoroughbass** (mus.) bass part extending through a composition. XVII. **thoroughbred** XVIII; **thoroughfare** XV; **thoroughgoing** XIX.

thorp (arch., hist.) hamlet, village. OE. *þrop*, occas. (prob. from ON.) *þorp* = OS. *thorp* (Du. *dorp*), (O)HG. *dorf* village, ON. *þorp* hamlet, farmstead, Goth. *þaurp* field, land, estate :- Gmc. **þurpam*, of uncert. orig.

those pl. of THAT[1]. OE. *þās*, ME. (south.) *þōs*, pl. of THIS; from XIV, first in north. and later in midl. and south. speech, pl. of dem. pron. and adj. *that*.

thou 2nd sg. pers pron. OE. *þû* = OS. *thû* (LG. *du*), OHG. *dû* (G. *du*), ON. *þú*, Goth. *þu* :- Gmc. repr. of IE. **tû*, whence also L., Av. *tū*, OIr., Gr. (Doric) *tú*, OSl. *ty*, Lith. *tù*, W. *ti*, Skr. *tvám*.

though adv. for all that; conj. notwithstanding that. XII. ME. *þoh* - ON. **þōh, þó*, earlier **þauh* = OE. *þēah* (whence ME. *þe(i)h, þeigh*, and *þa(u)h, þauȝ*), OS. *thoh*, OHG. *doh* (Du., G. *doch*), Goth. *þauh* or, yet; Gmc. advb. formation on base **þa-* of THE[1], THAT[1] + the particle repr. by L. *-que*, Gr. *té*, Skr. *ca* and.

thought action or act of thinking; †anxiety, solicitude XIII; very small amount XVI. repr. OE. *þōht* and the more freq. *ġeþōht* = OS. *githāht* (Du. *gedachte*), OHG. *gidāht* :- Gmc. **ȝaþaŋxt-*, f. **þaŋkjan* THINK.

thousand OE. *þūsend* = OS. *thūsundig* (Du. *duizend*), OHG. *thū-, dusunt* (G. *tausend*), ON. *þúsund*, Goth. *þūsundi* :- Gmc. **þusundi*; cogn. with Lith. *túkstantis*, OSl. *tysęšta*.

thrall villein, serf, slave, OE *þræl* - ON. *þræll*, perh. :- **þraχilaz*, f. Gmc. **þraχ- *þreχ-* run. Hence **thrall** vb. (arch.) bring into bondage, ENTHRALL. XIII. **thraldom** XII.

thrash A. thresh (corn, etc.) XVI; B. chastise by beating XVII; C. (naut.) beat (one's way) XIX; D. lash out, plunge XIX. metathetic alt. of an early form repr. by OE *þærsċan*, parallel with *þersċan* THRESH, which is now the prevalent form in sense A.

thrasonical given to boasting. XVI. f. L. *thrasō, -ōn-* - Gr. *Thrásōn* name of the braggart soldier in Terence's 'Eunuchus', f. *thrasús* bold, resolute.

thread cord composed of spun fibres of flax, etc. OE.; length of yarn forming a constituent of a woven fabric XII; transf. and fig. XIV. OE. *þrǣd* = OS. *þrād* (Du. *draad*), OHG. *drāt* (G. *draht*), ON. *þráðr* :- Gmc. **þrǣðuz*, f. **þrǣ-* twist. Hence **thread** vb. XIV. **threadbare** leaving bare the thread of warp and woof. XIV; fig. XV.

threat †throng, troop; †oppression, affliction OE.; denunciation of evil to come (?OE.) XI. OE. *þrēat* m., cogn. with ON. *þraut* fem. struggle, labour, f. Gmc. **þraut- *þreut- *þrut-*, base of OE. *þrēatian* (see below), *þrēotan* trouble, Du. *verdrieten*, weary, OHG. *irdrioȝan* vex (G. *verdriessen*) Goth. *usþriutan* trouble. So vb. (arch. or dial.) OE. *þrēatian*, superseded by **threaten** (-EN[5]) †press, urge OE.; utter threats against XIII; be ominous (of) XVII. OE. *þrēatnian*.

three OE. *þrī(e)* m., *þrīo, þrēo* f., n. = OS. *thria, threa, thriu* (Du. *drie*), OHG. *drī, drīo, driu* (G. *drei*), ON. *þrír, þriár, þriú*, Goth. **þreis, þrija* :- Gmc. **þrijiz* :- IE. **trejes*, whence also L. *trēs*, Gr. *treîs*, Skr. *tráya-*, etc.

threnody lament for the dead, dirge. XVII. - Gr. *thrēnōidiā*, f. *thrênos* funeral lament + *ōidḗ* ODE; see -Y[3].

thresh separate the grain from (corn) by beating, etc. ME. *threshen* (XII), continuing metathetic alt. of OE. str. vb. *þersċan* = MLG., MDu. *derschen* (LG., Du. *dorschen*), OHG. *dreskan* (G. *dreschen*), ON. *þreskja*, Goth. *þriskan*, f. Gmc. **þersk-* :- IE. **tersk-*, repr. in Balto-Sl. by words denoting 'crackle', 'crash', 'rattle'. Hence **thresher** (-ER[1]) person or machine that threshes XIV; shark so named from the upper division of its tail with which it lashes an enemy XVII.

threshold sill of a doorway, entrance to a building. OE. *þersċold, þresċold* = ON. *þresk(j)ǫldr* (cf. OHG. *driscūfli*); the first el. is OE. *þersċan* THRESH, in the sense 'tread, trample', the second el. is unexpl.

thrice XII. ME. *þriȝes, þries*, f. synon. *þrie* :- OE. *þrīga*, var. of *þrīwa* = OS. *thrī(uu)o*, f. **þri-* THREE + advb. *-a*; see -S.

thrift †thriving condition XIII; †prosperity, success; †gains, savings XIV; industry; economical management; plant of the genus *Armeria* XVI.

- ON. *þrift*, f. *þrífask* THRIVE; see -T[1]. Hence **thrifty** (-Y[1]) thriving; †worshipful, respectable XIV; careful of expenditure XVI.

thrill A. †pierce (lit. and fig.) XIII; B. affect, be affected, with a wave of emotion XVI; C. †hurl (a piercing weapon) XVII; D. quiver XVIII. Metathetic var. of (dial.) *thirl*, OE. *þȳrlian*, f. *þȳr(e)l* perforation, hole, aperture :- **þyrhil*, **þurhil*, f. *þurh* THROUGH + -EL[1]. The rise of senses C and D is not clearly accounted for. Hence sb. XVII.

thrips minute insect infecting plants. XVIII. - L. - Gr. *thrips*, pl. *thrîpes* wood-worm.

thrive pt. *throve*, pp. *thriven*; also pt., pp. *thrived* †grow, increase XII; prosper XIII. - ON. *þrífask*, refl. of *þrífa* lay hold of suddenly, grasp.

throat OE. *þrote*, *þrotu* = OHG. *drozza* (MHG. *drozze*), f. Gmc. **þrut-* **þrūt-* (repr. also by ON. *þroti* swelling, OE. *þrūtian*, ON. *þrútna* swell). Hence **throaty** (-Y[1]) XVII.

throb (of the heart) beat strongly XIV; (gen.) pulsate XIX. Presumably of imit. orig. Hence sb. XVI.

throe †spasm, paroxysm XII; agony of death XIII; violent convulsion or struggle XVII. ME. *þrowe*, north. *þrawe* (Sc. *thraw*), also 'time', 'occasion' - OE. *þrāg*, of unkn. orig.

thrombosis (path.) coagulation of the blood. XVIII. - Gr. *thrómbōsis* curdling, f. *thromboûsthai* become curdled or clotted, f. *thrómbos*, lump, clot, whence **thrombus** XVII; see -OSIS.

throne seat of state, of a deity XIII; third (from Col. 1: 16) order of angels XIV. ME. *trone*, (assim. early to the L. form) *throne* - OF. *trone* (mod. *trône*) - L. *thronus* - Gr. *thrónos* elevated seat. Hence **throne** vb. (arch.) ENTHRONE XIV; be enthroned XVII.

throng A. crowd XIII; B. crowding, crowded condition XIV. In sense A - ON. *þrǫng*, corr. to OE. *ġeþrang*, MLG., MHG. *gedrang* (G. *drang* crowd, pressure); in sense B. f. **throng** vb. †press, crush; push one's way XIV; form a crowd, crowd round, press upon XVI; fill *with* a crowd XVII. The vb. is prob. orig. f. (dial.) *throng* adj. pressed close together (XIV) - ON. *þrǫngr* narrow, close, crowded, rel. to OE. *þringan* press, crowd, throng.

throstle thrush. OE. *þrostle* = OS. *throsla*, OHG. *drōscala* (G. *drossel*), f. Gmc. **þrau(d)st-*, *-sk-*, rel. to L. *turdus*, etc. Cf. THRUSH[1].

throttle compress the throat of, so as to suffocate. XIV. ME. *throtel*, *-il*, perh. f. THROAT + -LE[3]. So later sb. throat (XVI), which has the form of dim. of THROAT, like synon. G. *drossel*.

through prep. from end to end or from side to side of; by the agency or means of; adv. from end to end. OE. *þurh* = OS. *thurh*, *thuru*, (M)Du. *door*, OHG. *duruh*, *-ih* (G. *durch*) :- WGmc. **þurχ*, of which a var. **þerh* is repr. by OE. (late Nhb.) *þerch*, *þærch*, Goth. *þairh* through, OHG. *derh* perforated; cf. further OE. *þȳrel* hole; the IE. base **tr-* is seen in OIr. *tre*, *tri*, L. *trans* across. The metathetic forms (*þruh*, etc.) appear *c.*1300. Comp. **throughout** adv. right through OE.; prep. XI. OE. *þurhūt*.

throw pt. *threw*, pp. *thrown* twist (now only dial. or in techn. sense of preparing and twisting raw silk into thread XV); from XIII in various uses of *cast*. OE. str. vb. *þrāwan* = OS. *thrāian* (Du. *draaien*), OHG. *drā(j)en*, *drāwen* (G. *drehen*); WGmc., based on IE. **ter-*, repr. by L. *terere* rub, Gr. *teírein* wear out. Hence sb. XVI.

thrum[1] end of a warp-thread left unwoven, short piece of waste thread. XIV. repr. OE. *þrum* in *(under)tungeþrum* ligament of the tongue = MDu. *drom*, *drum* (Du. *dreum* thrum), OHG., MHG. *drum* end-piece, remnant (G. *trumm*), f. Gmc. **þrum-* **þram-*; the IE. base **tṛm-* is repr. also by L. *terminus*, Gr. *térma* end.

thrum[2] play on a stringed instrument XVI; strum upon XVII; recite in singsong fashion; drum (*on*) XVIII. of imit. orig.

thrush[1] bird of the family Turdidae. OE. *þrysċe* (:- **þruskjōn*), rel. to synon. OE. *þrǣsċe*, **þrēasċe* = OHG. *drōsca* (:- **þrauskōn*). Cf. THROSTLE.

thrush[2] A. disease (esp. of infants) marked by white specks in the mouth XVII; B. in the horse, inflammation of the frog of the hoof XVIII. of unkn. orig.

thrust vb. XII. - ON. *þrýsta*. Hence sb. XVI.

thud †(Sc.) come with a blast of gust XVI. produce a dull heavy sound XVIII. prob. identical with OE. *þyddan*, ME. *thüdde* thrust, push (:- **þudjan*), rel. to OE. *þoddettan* push, beat (:- **þudatjan*) and *þoden*, ME. *þode*, early mod. *thode* violent wind. Hence **thud** sb. blast, gust XVI; heavy blow XVIII; dull heavy sound XIX.

thug (*Thug*) professional robber and murderer in India, (hence) cut-throat, ruffian. XIX. - Hindi, Marathi *ṭhag* cheat, swindler. So **thuggee** system practised by the thugs. XIX. - Hindi *ṭhagī*.

thuja now the more usual form of THUYA. XVIII.

thumb sb. OE. *þūma* = OS. *thūma*, MLG., MDu. *dūme* (Du. *duim*), OHG. *dūmo* (G. *daumen*) :- WGmc. **þūman-*; repr. IE. **tum-*, one of several extensions of **tu-* swell. Hence vb. XVI.

thump strike or beat heavily. XVI. So as sb. XVI. of imit. orig.

thunder sb. OE. *þunor* = OS. *thunar* (Du. *donder*), OHG. *donar* (G. *donner*), ON. *þórr* :- Gmc. **þunra*, f. IE. **tn̥-* **ton-*, as in L. *tonāre* thunder. So vb. OE. *þunrian*. In *thunderbolt* (XV), *thunderstroke* (XVI) the reference is to the supposed destructive power of thunder as the accompaniment of lightning.

thurible censer. XV (*turrible*, *thoryble*). - (O)F. *thurible* or L. *t(h)ūribulum*, f. *t(h)ūs*, *t(h)ūr-* incense - Gr. *thúos* sacrifice, offering, incense. So **thurifer** one who carries a thurible. XIX. - ecclL. (cf. -IFEROUS).

Thursday OE. *þur(e)sdæġ*, for *þunresdæġ*, f. g. of *þunor* THUNDER; partly assoc. with ON. *þórsdagr*; rendering late L. *Jovis dies* Jupiter's day.

thus OE. *þus* = OS. *thus*, (M)Du. *dus*, of unkn. orig. Hence **thusness** (joc.) XIX.

thuya one of a genus of conifers. XVIII. irreg. repr. of Gr. *thúia*, var. of *thúā*. See THUJA.

thwack beat or strike as with a stick. XVI. of imit. orig. Hence sb. XVI.

thwart[1] (arch.) adv. and prep. athwart XII (first in *þwert ut* thoroughly); adj. obstinate, perverse XIII. ME. *þwert* - ON. *þvert*, orig. n. of *þverr* transverse, cross = OE. *þwe(o)rh* crooked, cross, perverse, OHG. *dwerh*, G. *zwerch*, Goth.

þwairhs cross, angry :- Gmc. **þwerχwaz*, f. IE. **twerk-* **twork-*, as in L. *torquēre* twist. Hence **thwart** vb. †oppose XIII; †extend from side to side of XV; †place crosswise XVI; foil, frustrate.

thwart² rower's bench. XVIII. var. (presumably after THWART¹) of *thought*, which is evidenced from XIV as a var. of earlier dial. *thoft*, OE. *þofte* = MDu. *dofte*, *dochte* (Du. *doft*), OHG. *dofta*, ON. *þopta* :- Gmc. **tuftō*; the history is obscure.

thy clipped form of THINE (ME. *þi* XII).

thylacine Tasmanian wolf (a carnivorous marsupial). XIX. - F., f. Gr. *thúlakos* pouch; see -INE¹.

thyme XIV. - (O)F. *thym* - L. *thymum* - Gr. *thúmon*, f. *thúein* burn sacrifice.

thyro- used as comb. form of next. XIX.

thyroid (anat.) *t. cartilage* Adam's apple; *t. gland*, *t. body* one of the 'ductless glands'. XVIII. - F. †*thyroïde* or modL. *thyroidēs* - Gr. *thuroidḗs*, erron. for *thureoeidḗs*, f. *thureós* stone put against a door, oblong, shield (as door-shaped), f. *thúrā* DOOR; see -OID.

thyrsus pl. **thyrsi** (Gr. and Rom. antiq.) staff or spear tipped with a pine-cone ornament; (bot.) form of inflorescence. XVIII. - L. - Gr. *thúrsos* stalk of a plant.

thyself emph. and refl. vars. of THOU and THEE. ME. *þi sülf*, *þi self* (XIII), repl. *þē self* (OE. to XIV), i.e. THEE and SELF; cf. MYSELF.

ti see TE.

tiara conical cap of ancient Persians XVI; pope's triple crown XVII; lady's ornamental headband XVIII. - L. *tiāra* - Gr. *tiára*, *tiárās*, partly through It. *tiara*.

tibia larger of the two bones of the lower leg. XVIII. - L. *tībia* shin-bone, flute. So **tibial** (-AL¹) XVI. - L.

tice (dial.) Aphetic of †*attice*, *-ise*, ENTICE, but earlier than these forms and prob. immed. - OF. *atisier*. Hence sb. yorker (in cricket).

tick¹ kind of mite. OE. **ticca* or **tica* (recorded once as *ticia* VIII), ME. *tyke*, *teke*, later *ticke* (XVI), corr., with variation of vowel and cons., to MLG., MDu. *tēke* (Du. *teek*), OHG. *zēcho* (G. *zecke*), f. WGmc. **tīk-* **tikk-*; the ME. forms may be partly due to MLG. or MDu.

tick² (dial.) touch or tap lightly, esp. toy, dally XIII; make short quick beats XVIII; mark with a dash, etc. XIX. prob. imit. So sb. slight touch XV; quick dry sound XVII; small dot or dash XIX. The parallel LG. *tikk* touch, instant, Du. *tik* pat, touch, *tikken* pat, tick, OHG. *zekōn* pluck, etc., may point to a WGmc. base, or the various forms may be independent expressive formations.

tick³ case or cover of a mattress or pillow, (hence) material of this. XV (*tikke*, *tēke*, *tȳke*). corr. to and prob. immed. - MLG., MDu. *tēke* and MDu. *tīke* (Du. *tijk*), rel. to OHG. *ziahha*, *ziecha* (G. *zieche* bed-tick, pillow-case); WGmc. - L. *thēca* - Gr. *thḗkē* case, f. IE. **dhē-* place (see DO¹).

tick⁴ in phr. (*go*, *run*, *play*) *on tick* on credit, on trust XVII. Short for TICKET.

ticket (short) written notice, label; †voucher, warrant, promise to pay XVI; slip bearing evidence of the holder's title to something XVII; (U.S.) list of candidates for election XVIII; *the t.*, the correct thing XIX. Aphetic - F. †*étiquet*, OF. *estiquet(te)*, f. *estiquier*, *estequier* fix, stick, var. of *estichier*, *estechier* - MDu. *steken*; see -ET. Hence vb. XVII.

tickle †be thrilled XIV; excite agreeably; touch, stroke, or poke so as to excite XV. prob. frequent. of TICK²; see -LE³.

ticktack expressive of duplicated or alternating ticking sound. XVI. So **tick-tick** XVIII, **tick-tock** (of the ticking of a clock) XIX.

tidal XIX. f. TIDE¹ B + -AL¹.

tiddlywink A. (sl.) beershop; B. (pl.) game played with (1) dominoes, (2) counters. XIX. of unkn. orig.

tide¹ A. †portion of time, season, age; †hour; (arch.) point of time, due time; definite time of day or of the year (surviving in *eventide*, *noontide*, *springtide*); church anniversary or festival (arch. except as in *Eastertide*, *Shrovetide*, *Whitsuntide*) OE.; B. swelling of the sea or its alternate rising and falling XIV. OE. *tīd* = OS. *tīd* (Du. *tijd*), OHG. *zīt* (G. *zeit*), ON. *tíð* :- Gmc. **tīdiz*, f. **tī-* :- IE. **dī-* **dā(i)-* divide, cut up, repr. by Gr. *daiesthai* divide, distribute, Skr. *dā́ti*, *dyā́ti* cuts, harvests, shares. In B prob. after MLG. *(ge)tīde*, *tīe*, MDu. *ghetīde* (Du. *(ge)tij*), a special development of the sense 'fixed time'. So **tide** vb. (arch.) happen, befall. OE. *tīdan*, earlier *ġetīdan*, f. the sb.

tide² flow or carry along like the tide XVI; get *over*, surmount XVII. f. TIDE¹ B.

tidings (pl.; formerly also sg.) piece of news. Late OE. *tīdung*, prob., with assim. to -ING¹, anglicization of ON. *tíðendi*, *-indi* events, news, f. *tíðr* adj. happening, occurring.

tidy in good condition, of good appearance XIII; timely, seasonable (presumably the orig. sense); excellent, worthy XIV; of neat habits or appearance XVIII; pretty good, pretty big XIX; sb. object for keeping persons or things neat XIX. ME. *tīdi*, f. *tīd* time, TIDE¹ + -Y¹. Hence vb. XIX.

tie that with which anything is fastened OE.; fig bond, connection XVI; equality between competitors XVII. OE. *tē(a)g* = ON. *taug* rope :- Gmc. **tauʒō*, f. **tauχ-* draw. So **tie** vb. make fast. OE. *tīgan*, late form of WS. **tīeġan*, Angl. **tēgan* (ME. *tēȝen*) :- Gmc. **tauʒjan* (cf. ON. *teygja* draw).

tier row, rank of seats, shelves, etc. XVI. - (O)F. *tire* sequence, rank, order, f. *tirer* draw, draw out :- Rom. **tīrāre*, of unkn. orig.

tierce †third part XV; third hour of the day (9 a.m.); canonical office said at this hour (TERCE) XIV; wine measure or cask XVI; third of the parries in fencing; sequence of three playing cards XVII; (mus.) note two octaves and a major third above a fundamental note XVII; (her.) division of a shield into three equal parts XIX. - (O)F. *t(i)erce* :- L. *tertia*, sb. use of fem. of *tertius* THIRD.

tiff †slight fit of temper; slight quarrel. XVIII. of unkn. orig.

tiffany kind of thin transparent silk. XVII. perh. punning use (quasi transparency) of *tiffany* - OF. *tifanie* :- ecclL. *theophania* - Gr. *theopháneia*, *-phánia* Epiphany, f. *theós* god + *phan-* appear.

tiffin in India, etc., a light midday meal. XVIII. For *tiffing*, gerund of (sl. or dial.) *tiff* drink, sip (XVIII).

tiger XIII. ME. *tygre* - (O)F. *tigre* - L. *tigris* - Gr. *tígris*. Hence **tigress** (-ESS[1]) XVII.

tight †dense XIV; of close construction so as to exclude air, etc.; firmly fixed; taut; (dial.) capable, vigorous XVI; (dial.) neat, trim XVII; close-fitting XVIII; (sl.) close-fisted; drunk XIX. prob. alt. of *thight* - ON. **þehtr*, *þéttr* watertight, of close texture = OE. *-þiht* firm, solid, MLG., MDu. *dicht* :- **þiŋχtaz*, f. **þiŋχ-* grow, repr. by OE. *(ġe)þēon*, OHG. *gidīhan* (G. *gedeihen* grow, thrive), Goth. *(ga)þeihan*. As sb. pl. for *tight breeches*, *trousers* XIX. Hence **tighten** (-EN[6]) XVIII.

tilde sign ~ placed over *n* in Spanish to indicate the palatalized sound. XIX. - Sp. - L. *titulus* TITLE.

tile thin slab of burnt clay for roofing, paving, etc. OE. *tiġele* (*tiġule*), corr. to OS. *tiegla* (Du. *tegel*), OHG. *ziagal(a)* (G. *ziegel*), ON. *tigl* - L. *tēgula*, f. IE. **tĕg-* cover.

till[1] labour upon, cultivate. OE. *tilian* strive after, attempt, obtain, treat, (late) cultivate = OS. *tilian*, *tilon* obtain (Du. *telen* produce, raise, cultivate), OHG. *zilōn*, *zilēn* (G. *zielen* aim, strive), Goth. *gatilōn* :- Gmc. **tilōjan*, **tilējan*, f. **tilam* aim, goal (see next). Hence **tillage** XV.

till[2] prep. (Sc. and north.) to OE.; up to the time of XIV; conj. to the time that XII. OE. (Nhb.) *til* prep. = ON. *til*; prob. from adv. use of Gmc. sb. **tilam*, repr. by OE. *till* fixed point, station, MLG. *til*, *tel* aim, point of time, OHG. *zil* (G. *ziel* end, goal), ON. *aldrtili* 'end of life', death, Goth. *til* opportunity. In ME. (and later) use due to adoption of the ON. word.

till[3] †small box, etc. contained within a larger one XV; box or drawer for holding cash in a shop XVII. of unkn. orig.

tiller beam or stock of a crossbow XV; bar or beam attached to the rudder-head XVII. ME. *tiler*, *telor* - AN. *telier* weaver's beam :- medL. *tēlārium*, f. L. *tēla* web.

tilt[1] †throw down or over; †fall over XIV; move unsteadily up and down; cause to lean or slant XVI. ME. *tilte*, *tylte* may repr. OE. **tyltan*, **tieltan* :- **taltjan*, f. **taltaz* (OE. *tealt* unsteady). Hence **tilt** sb. inclination. XVI.

tilt[2] covering of coarse cloth, esp. awning over a cart or boat XV; in Labrador, etc. fisherman's or woodcutter's hut XIX. var. of *tild*, *teld* (= (O)HG. *zelt*), perh. influenced by TENT[1].

tilt[3] barrier separating combatants in an exercise in which the participants ride against each other with lances; the combat itself. XVI. of unkn. orig.

tilth tillage, husbandry; †harvest OE.; tilled land XIV. Late OE. *tilð(e)*, f. *tilian* TILL[1]; see -TH[1].

timbal (arch.) kettledrum. XVII. - F. *timbale*, alt. of †*tamballe* - (with assim. to *tambour* drum) Sp. *atabal* - Arab. *aṭ-ṭabl* drum (*aṭ-* is AL-[2]).

timbale membrane resembling a drumhead in certain insects; dish of meat, etc. cooked in a crust, so called from its shape. XIX. - F. (see prec.).

timber †building, edifice; †building material, (later) wood for building; growing trees OE.; wooden object, spec. beam XIV. OE. *timber* = OS. *timbar*, OHG. *zimbar* (G. *zimmer* room), ON. *timbr* :- Gmc. **timram* :- IE. **demrom*, f. **dĕm-* **dōm-* **dm̥-* build.

timbre XIX. (O)F. *timbre* (orig.) timbrel, bell, (whence) sound as of a bell :- Rom. **timbano* - medGr. *tímbanon*, Gr. *túmpanon* TYMPANUM.

timbrel tambourine-like instrument of percussion. XVI (*timberal*). perh. dim. of synon. †*timbre* (XIII) - OF. *timbre*; see prec. and -EL[2].

time limited stretch of continued existence; period or point in the course of this OE.; indefinite continuous duration XIV. OE. *tīma* = ON. *tími* time, good time, prosperity :- Gmc. **tīman-*, f. **tī-* stretch, extend. Cf. TIDE[1]. Hence **time** vb. †befall XIII; fix, note, etc. the time of XIV. **timely** well-timed, †early. XII. Modelled on *timely* adv., OE. *tīmlīċe*; see -LY[1,2]. **timeous** (chiefly Sc.) timely. XV. **timepiece** XVIII.

timid XVI. - F. *timide* or L. *timidus*, f. *timēre* fear; see -ID[1].

timocracy polity with a property qualification for its ruling class XVI; polity in which love of honour is the dominant motive with the rulers XVII. - (O)F. *timocratie* - medL. *tīmocratia* - Gr. *tīmokratíā*, f. *tīmḗ* honour, value + *kratíā* -CRACY.

timorous XV. - (O)F. *temoros*, *-eus* (mod. *timoreux*) - medL. *timorōsus*, f. L. *timor* fear; see -OUS.

tin white highly malleable metal. OE. *tin* = (M)LG., (M)Du. *tin*, OHG. *zin* (G. *zinn*), ON. *tin* :- Gmc. **tinam*, of unkn. orig.

tinamou S. Amer. bird. XVIII. - F. - Galibi *tinamu*.

tincture †dye, pigment XIV; hue, colour (spec. in her.) XV; †imparted quality, tinge; †(alch.) supposed spiritual principle XVI; †essential principle of a substance; solution of a medicinal principle XVII. - L. *tinctūra* dyeing, f. *tinct-*, pp. stem of *tingere* dye, TINGE; see -URE.

tindal native petty officer of Lascars; foreman of a gang. XVII. - Hind. *tanḍel* - Malayalam *tanṭal*, Telugu *tanḍelu*.

tinder dry material that readily takes fire from a spark. OE. *tynder*, *tyndre*, corr. (with variation in suffix and gender) to (M)LG. *tunder* (Du. *tonder*), OHG. *zuntara* (G. *zunder*), ON. *tundr*, f. Gmc. **tund-* **tend-* **tand-*, whence OE. causative *-tendan*, dial. *tind* kindle, ignite, Goth. *tandjan*.

tine sharp projecting point, spec. of an antler. OE. *tind* = MLG. *tind*, OHG. *zint*, ON. *tindr*, rel. to synon. MLG. *tinne*, OHG. *zinna*.

tinea ringworm. XVII. - L. *tinea* gnawing worm, moth, worm in the body.

ting sound (a small bell, etc.) XV; emit a high singing note XVI. of imit. orig.

tinge impart a slight change of colour to. XV. - L. *tingere* dip in liquid, moisten.

tingle be affected with a ringing or thrilling sensation. XIV. app. modification of TINKLE.

tinker mender of pots, kettles, etc. XIII; (dial.) gipsy, itinerant trader, etc. XVI. of uncert. orig.

tinkle (of the ears) ring, tingle XIV; give forth short sharp ringing sounds XIV. app. f. †*tink* chink (vb.) (XIV), of imit. orig.; see -LE[3].

tinnitus (path.) ringing in the ears. XIX. - L. *tinnītus*, f. *tinnīre* ring, tinkle, of imit. orig.

tinsel †attrib. embellished with gold or silver

thread; sb. fabric so embellished; thin plates, strips, etc. of shining metal used for ornament XVI; fig. showy but valueless stuff XVII. First in *tinsell(e) saten*, prob. repr. AN. **satin estincelé* (hence, by ellipsis, used sb.); (O)F. *estincelé*, f. *estincele* (mod. *étincelle* spark), repr. popL. **stincilla*, f. L. SCINTILLA.

tint (slight or delicate) hue. XVIII. alt. (perh. by assim. to It. *tinto*) of †*tinct* (XVII) - L. *tinctus* dyeing, f. pp. stem of *tingere* dye, TINGE. Hence vb. XVIII.

tintinnabulum small tinkling bell. XVI. - L., f. *tintinnāre*, redupl. f. *tinnīre* ring, tinkle. Hence **tintinnabulation** XIX.

tiny XVI. In the earliest exx. always preceded by *little*; extension with -Y[1] of synon. †*tine* (XIV), of unkn. orig.

-tion ME. *-cio(u)n*, repr. (O)F. *-tion*, earlier *-cion*, *-ciun*, repr. L. *-tiō*, *-ōn-*, comp. suffix f. *-t-* of a pp. stem + *-iō*, *-ōn-* -ION; orig. expressing the state of being what the pp. imports, e.g. *complētiō* COMPLETION, thence transferred to the action or process involved, and so acquiring a concr. or quasi-concr. notion, as in *dictiō* DICTION, *nātiō* birth, NATION, *orātiō* mode of speaking, ORATION. So **-tious** repr. L. *-tiōsus*, forming adjs. rel. to sbs. in *-tion*, as *ambition/ambitious*, *nutrition/nutritious*.

tip[1] fine or slender extremity XV; vb. (first in pp.) furnish with a tip XIV. - ON. *typpi* sb., *typpa* vb., f. Gmc. **tupp-* TOP[1]; prob. reinforced by (M)LG., (M)Du. *tip*.

tip[2] tap or touch lightly. XIII (in fig. use; thereafter not till XVI); give, hand, pass XVII; give a gratuity to XVIII. perh. orig. identical with TIP[1], as if 'touch the point of', or 'touch as with a point'. Hence **tip** sb. gratuity XVIII; friendly hint XIX; whence **tipster** XIX.

tip[3] (dial.) overturn, be overturned XIV; incline, tilt; empty out by tilting XVII. of uncert. orig.

tipcat game in which a 'cat' (short piece of wood tapered at both ends XVII) is struck with a stick. XIX. f. TIP[2] + CAT.

tippet (hist.) long narrow piece of cloth as part of a dress XIV; garment covering the shoulders XV; (eccl.) clergyman's scarf XVI. perh. - AN. deriv. of TIP[1] (see -ET).

tippler †retailer of drink, tapster XIV; (from the vb.) habitual drinker XVI. of unkn. orig. Hence **tipple** vb. †retail drink XV; drink habitually XVI.

tipstaff †staff with a tip carried by some officials; such an official, bailiff, etc. XVI. Alt. of *tipt* (*tipped*) *staff*; see TIP[1].

tipsy slightly drunk. XVI. f. TIP[3] + -SY.

tiptoe (pl.) the tips of the toes. XIV; adv. XVI. f. TIP[1] + TOE.

tiptop sb. highest point; adj. very highest. XVIII. redupl. of TOP[1], prob. with assoc. of TIP[1].

tirade volley of words; section of verse on a single theme. XIX - F. - It. *tirata* volley, f. *tirare* :- Rom. **tīrāre* draw, of unkn. orig.; see -ADE.

tire[1] †fail, give out; become exhausted; exhaust, weary. OE. *tēorian*, freq. in comps. *ātēorian*, *ġetēorian*, of unkn. orig. Hence **tiresome** XVI.

tire[2] †get ready, equip; †attire XIV; dress (the hair or head) XVI. Aphetic of ATTIRE. Hence (arch.) *tiring house* XVI, *-room* XVII, dressing-room of a theatre.

tire[3] see TYRE.

tiro, tyro beginner, novice. XVII. In earliest use pl. *tyrones* (with occas. sg. †*tyron*) - L. *tīrō*, pl. *tīrōnes*, in medL. also *tȳrō*, *-ōnēs*, young soldier, recruit, beginner.

tissue (arch.) rich cloth, esp. interwoven with gold or silver; †band of rich stuff XIV; woven fabric XVI; (fig.) fabric, network XVIII; animal or vegetable substance XIX. - OF. *tissu*, sb. use of pp. of *tistre* weave :- L. *texere* weave.

tit[1] (dial. and vulgar) TEAT. OE. *tit*, corr. to (M)LG. *titte*, Du. *tit*, (M)HG. *zitze*. Hence **titty** (-Y[6]) XVIII.

tit[2] (dial.) small horse, (later) nag; (dial.) girl, young woman XVI; short for *titmouse* XVIII. Occurs much earlier in comps. TITMOUSE (XIV) and *titling* †small kind of stockfish (XIV), (dial.) hedge-sparrow, etc. (XVI), prob. of Scand. orig. (cf. Icel. *titlingr* sparrow, Norw. dial. *titling* small size of dried stockfish).

tit[3] in phr. *tit for tat* (cf. synon. †*tip for tap*) XVI. of symbolic orig.

Titan the sun-god XV; (pl.) family of giants, born of Uranus and Gaea, (sg.) ancestor of these XVII; (gen.) giant XIX. - L. *Tītan*, *-ān-*, elder brother of Kronos - Gr. *Tītā́n*, pl. *Tītânes*. Hence **titanic** XVII.

titanium (chem.) metallic element. XVIII. f. Gr. *Tītā́n* TITAN, after *uranium*; see -IUM.

titbit delicate or toothsome morsel XVII; interesting item XVIII. Earliest form *tyd bit*, i.e. *tid*, dial. word equiv. to *nice*, + BIT[2].

tithe adj. (arch.) tenth OE.; sb. tenth part of annual produce paid to the Church XII; tenth part XVI. OE. *tēoða*, contr. of *teogoða*, ME. *tiȝ(e)þe*, *tīþe*; see TENTH. Hence **tithe** vb. OE. *tēoðian*, *teogoðian* grant a tithe of. So **tithing** (-ING[1]) church tithe; company orig. of ten householders in the system of frankpledge. OE. (Angl.) *tīġeðing*; (WS.) *tēoðung*.

titillate tickle. XVII. f. pp. stem of L. *tītillāre*; see -ATE[3]. So **titillation** (pleasurable) excitation XV; tickling XVII. - (O)F. or L.

titivate XIX. Earlier *tid(d)ivate*, perh. f. TIDY after *cultivate*.

title †inscription or legend; ground of right or claim XIII; name of a book, etc., descriptive appellation XIV; (eccl.) certificate of presentation to a benefice, etc.; legal right to possession XV. - OF. *title* (mod. *titre*) - L. *titulus* placard, inscription, title.

titmouse small bird of the genus *Parus*. XIV. ME. *titmōse*, f. TIT[2] + *mōse*, OE. *māse* = MLG., MDu. *mēse* (Du. *mees*), OHG. *meisa* (G. *meise*) :- WGmc. **maisōn* (cf. ON. *meisingr*). Alt. XVI by assoc. with MOUSE.

titrate (chem.) ascertain the amount of a constituent in, by volumetric analysis. XIX. f. F. *titrer*, f. *titre* TITLE, qualification, fineness of gold or silver, (chem.) proportioning of the fixed quantity of a reagent used in analysis; see -ATE[3].

titter laugh in a suppressed manner. XVII. of imit. orig.

tittle point or dot over or under a letter XIV; smallest part or amount XV; *to a t.* with minute exactness XVII. ME. *titel*, *-il* - L. *titulus* TITLE, in medieval sense of 'little stroke', 'accent'.

tittle-tattle idle talk or chatter. XVI. redupl. formation on TATTLE or combination of this with (dial.) *tittle* (XIV).

titty see TIT[1].

titubate stagger, totter. XVI. f. pp. stem of L. *titubāre*; see -ATE[3]. So **titubation** XVII. - L.

titular pert. to, serving as, or existing only in title. XVIII. - F. *titulaire* or f. L. *titulus* TITLE; see -AR.

tmesis (gram.) separation of the elements of a word by interposing another. XVI. - Gr. *tmêsis* cutting.

T.N.T. initials of the els. of *t*ri*n*itro*t*oluene. XX.

to prep. expressing motion or direction towards an object, addition, or the notion of the dative; with inf. meaning 'for the purpose or with the object of' (doing something), hence serving without meaning as a sign of the inf.; adv. (with full stress) surviving as in *to and fro*, *shut to*, and the like, and in TOO. OE. *tō* adv. and prep. (mainly with dat.) = OS. *tō* (Du. *toe* adv.), OHG. *zō*, *zuo* (G. *zu*) :- WGmc. **tō*, alongside OE. (ME.) *te* = OS. *te*, *ti* (Du. *te*), OHG. *ze*, *zi*, *za* :- WGmc. **ta*. The IE. base **dŏ*, *dĕ* is repr. also by L. *endo*, *indu* (poet.) in, *dōnec* until, Gr. *oikonde* homewards, OSl. *do* to, till.

toad OE. *tāda*, *tādde* (in place-names), shortening of *tādi(ġ)e*, early ME. also *tadde* (XII); of unkn. orig. Comp. **toadstool** XV (*tode stole*; earlier *tad(e) stole* XIV).

toady servile parasite. XIX. Based on *toad-eater* charlatan's attendant who ate toads (held to be poisonous) XVII, fawning flatterer, humble friend or dependant XVIII; see -Y[6]. Hence vb. XIX.

toast[1] parch XIV; brown (bread, etc.) by exposure to heat XIV. - OF. *toster* roast, grill :- Rom. **tostāre*, f. *tost-*, pp. stem of L. *torrēre* parch. Hence sb. toasted bread. XV.

toast[2] orig. favourite lady whose health is drunk to. XVII. Said to have been so named as being supposed to flavour the bumper like a spiced toast (TOAST[1]) in drink.

tobacco XVI (*tabac(c)o*). - Sp., Pg. *tabaco*, of uncert. orig. Hence **tobacconist** †tobacco-smoker XVI; seller of tobacco XVII.

toboggan sb. XIX. - Canadian F. *tabaganne*, of Algonquian orig. Hence vb. XIX.

Toby familiar form of the name *Tobias* used as the name of (1) a jug or mug in the form of a stout old man with a three-cornered hat, (2) a trained dog in the Punch-and-Judy show. XIX.

toccata (mus.) piece for keyboard instruments intended to exhibit touch and technique. XVIII. - It., sb. use of fem. pp. of *toccare* TOUCH.

tocher (Sc. and north. dial.) dowry. XV (*toquhyr*). - Ir., OGael. *tochar* (modGael. *tochradh*) assigned portion, f. (OIr.) *tochuirim* I put to, assign, f. *cuirim* I put.

tocsin alarm signal given by a bell. XVI (*tocksaine*). - F. *tocsin*, OF. *touquesain*, *toquassen* - Pr. *tocasenh*, f. *tocar* strike + *senh* bell.

tod[1] (dial.) fox. XII. of unkn. orig.

tod[2] weight used for wool XV; bushy mass (esp. of ivy) XVI. prob. of LG. or Du. orig. (cf. LG. *todde* bundle, pack).

today on this very day OE.; in these days XIII; sb. this day XVI; this present time XIX. OE. *tōdæġ*, f. *tō* TO + *dæġ* DAY.

toddle †toy *with*; walk with short unsteady steps. XVI. of unkn. orig.

toddy sap obtained from species of palm XVII; beverage made with whisky and hot water and sugar XVIII. Earlier also *tarrie*, *terry*. - Hind. *tāṛī*, f. *tāṛ* palm tree :- Skr. *tāla-* palmyra.

to-do activity, bustle, fuss. XVII. Evolved from such phr. as *with much* or *more to do*, in which *much* and *more* were orig. sbs. but were later apprehended as adjs. with *to-do* as a sb.

toe sb. OE. *tā* = MLG. *tē*, (M)Du. *tee*, OHG. *zēha* (G. *zeh(e)*), ON. *tá* :- Gmc. **taiχ(w)ōn*, of unkn. orig. Hence **toe** vb. furnish with a toe XVII; touch, etc., with the toe XIX.

toff (sl.) stylish or smart person. XIX. The occas. var. *toft* may point to an alt. of TUFT as applied to noblemen and gentlemen-commoners at the university of Oxford.

toffee XIX. alt. of earlier north. *taffy*; of unkn. orig.

toft site of a house. Late OE. *toft* - ON. *topt*.

tog (sl.) †outer coat XVIII; (pl.) clothes XIX. prob. shortening of cant *tog(e)mans* cloak, loose coat (XVI-XVII), f. F. *toge* or L. *toga* (see next) + *-man(s)*, as in *darkman(s)* night, etc.

toga XVI. - L., rel. to *tegere* cover. Hence **togaed** (-ED[2]) XIX; earlier †*toged* (XVII). Based on L. *togātus*.

together into one company OE.; in one company or body XIII. ME. *togedere*, repl. *togadere*, OE. *tōgædere* = MDu. *tegadere* (Du. *-er*); f. **tō* TO + **gad-*, as in OE. *gæd* fellowship, *ġegada* associate; cf. GATHER.

toggle (orig., naut.) device, e.g. a pin, to hold a thing in place. XVIII. of unkn. orig.

toil[1] †verbal dispute, strife, turmoil XIII; (from the vb.) severe labour XVI. - AN. *toil* = OF. *tooil*, *touil*, *tueil* bloody mêlée, trouble, confusion, f. *tooillier* (see below). So **toil** vb. †contend in a lawsuit, dispute; labour arduously. XIV. - AN. *toiler* dispute, wrangle = OF. *tooillier* (mod. *touiller* mix, stir up) :- L. *tudiculāre* stir about, f. *tudicula* machine for bruising olives, f. **tud-*, base of *tundere* beat, crush.

toil[2] (sg. and pl.) net(s) set to enclose game. XVI. - OF. *toile*, *teile* (mod. *toile* cloth, linen, web) :- L. *tēla* :- **texlā*, f. **tex-* weave.

toilet †cloth wrapper XVI; cloth cover for a dressing table, furniture of this, the table itself; dressing XVII; (lady's) dress XIX. - F. *toilette*, dim. of *toile* cloth, etc.; see prec., -ET.

tokay rich sweet wine made near *Tokaj* in Hungary. XVIII. - F. *vin de Tokay*, G. *Tokayerwein*, tr. Hung. *tokaji bor* (*bor* wine).

token sign, symbol, signal OE.; stamped piece of metal XVI; quantity of press work XVII. OE. *tāc(e)n* = OS. *tēcan* (Du. *teeken*), OHG. *zeihhan* (G. *zeichen*), ON. *teikn* :- Gmc. **taiknam* (cf. Goth. *taikns* :- **taikniz*), rel. to **taikjan* show, TEACH. So **token** vb. OE. *tācnian* = MLG. *tēkenen*, OHG. *zeihhanen*, *-ōn* (G. *zeichnen*), Goth. *taiknjan*.

tolbooth †custom-house XIV; town hall, guildhall; town prison (orig. cells under the town hall) XV. f. TOLL[1] + BOOTH.

Toledo (arch.) *T.* (*blade, sword*), one made at Toledo in Spain, long famous for finely tempered swordblades. XVI.

tolerable bearable, endurable XV; †allowable; passable, moderate XVI. - (O)F. *tolérable* - L. *tolerābilis*, f. *tolerāre* bear, endure; see -ABLE. So **tolerance** †endurance XV; disposition to be indulgent. XVIII. - (O)F. *tolérance* - L. *tolerantia*. **tolerant** XVIII. - F. *tolérant*, prp. of *tolérer*. **tolerate** †endure; allow to exist XVI. - pp. stem of L. *tolerāre*; see -ATE[3]. **toleration** †endurance; †permission; forbearance XVI; allowance of the exercise of religion XVII. - F. - L.

toll[1] payment for a privilege OE.; charge for a right of passage XV. OE. *toll* = OHG. *zol* (G. *zoll*), ON. *tollr* m., with by-forms OE. *toln* (†*tolne* XI-XV), OS. *tolna* fem. - medL. *tolōneum*, alt. of late L. *telōneum* - Gr. *telṓnion* toll-house, f. *telṓnēs* collector of taxes, f. *télos* toll, tax.

toll[2] (of a bell or the ringer) give forth a sound from a bell repeated at regular intervals. XV. perh. spec. use of *toll* pull, usu. fig. entice, OE. **tollian*, rel. to *fortyllan* seduce.

tolu balsam obtained from the *tolu tree* (*Myroxylon balsamum*). XVII. Name of a town in Columbia, S. America. Hence **toluol** (chem.) earlier term for **toluene**, obtained from tolu balsam. XIX.

Tom familiar abbrev. of the pers. name *Thomas*, used (i) as the name of certain large bells (XVII), and long guns (XIX, *Long Tom*); (ii) in designations originating in quasi-proper names as **tom-fool** †half-witted man (XVI), buffoon (XVII), stupid person (XVIII); hence **tomfoolery** (XIX); **tom-noddy** puffin (XVIII), foolish person (XIX); (iii) as the colloq. designation of a male cat, originating in 'The Life and Adventures of a Cat' (1760) in which the hero, a male cat, is called *Tom the Cat*. Hence dim. **Tommy** (-Y[6]) spec. short for *Tommy Atkins* familiar form of *Thomas Atkins*, name of a typical private soldier in the British army arising out of its use in specimen forms of description in official regulations from 1815. Also **tomboy** †bold boy or woman; wild romping girl XVI; **tomtit** TITMOUSE (XVIII).

tomahawk XVII. of Algonquian orig.

tomato XVII (*tomate*). - F. or Sp., Pg. *tomate* - Nahuatl *tomatl*; *tomato*, *tomata*, and *tomatum* were pseudo-Sp. and L. modifications (XVIII).

tomb XIII. ME. *t(o)umbe* - AN. *tumbe*, (O)F. *tombe* :- late L. *tumba* - Gr. *túmbos* mound, tomb.

tombac alloy of copper and zinc. XVII. - F. - Malay *tĕmbaga* copper.

tombola XIX. - F. for It., f. *tombolare* turn a somersault, tumble.

tomboy see TOM.

tome †volume of a literary work; (large or heavy) book XVI. - F. - L. *tomus* - Gr. *tómos* slice, piece, roll of papyrus, volume.

-tome[1] terminal el. repr. Gr. *-tómon*, n. of *-tómos* -cutting, forming names of surgical instruments used in separations expressed by the corr. words in -TOMY.

-tome[2] terminal el. repr. Gr. *tomḗ* cutting, section, segment.

tomentose closely covered with down. XVII. f. L. *tōmentum* stuffing for cushions; see -OSE[1].

Tommy see TOM.

tomorrow adv. XIII; sb. XIV. ME. *to mor(e)we*, earlier *to morwen* (mod. dial. *to morn*), OE. *tō morġenne*, i.e. *tō* TO + d. of *morġen* MORN, MORROW.

tom-tom XVII. - Hind. *tam tam*.

-tomy terminal el. repr. Gr. *-tomiā*, often through L. *-tomia*, F. *-tomie*, forming abstract sbs. from adjs. in *-tómos* cutting.

ton[1] unit used in measuring the carrying capacity of a ship, orig. space occupied by a tun of wine XIV; measure of capacity for solid commodities XV; 20 cwt. Identical in origin with TUN, of which it is a differentiated var. established in these senses since late XVII.

ton[2] the vogue, the mode. XVIII. - F. :- L. *tonus* TONE.

-ton terminal el. of many town names, repr. unstressed development of OE. *tūn* TOWN, and consequently in many surnames, e.g. *Longton*, *Somerton*, whence extended to form designations of persons and things, as *simpleton*, *singleton*.

tondo circular painting. XIX. - It. *tondo* round, circle, aphetic of *rotondo* round.

tone musical sound or note XIV; larger interval between notes in the diatonic scale XVII; pitch, modulation of voice, etc.; degree of tension; style of thought, etc. prevailing state of conduct, etc.; any of the nine plainsong tunes XVIII; word or syllable accent; quality of colour XIX. repr. various adoptions of (O)F. *ton* or its source L. *tonus* tension, sound, tone - Gr. *tónos*. So **tonal** XVIII. - medL. *tonālis*; see -AL[1]. **tonality** XIX.

tonga two-wheeled vehicle used in India. XIX. - Hindi *tāṅgā*.

tongs OE. *tang(e)*, corr. to OS. *tanga* (Du. *tang*), OHG. *zanga* (G. *zange*), ON. *tǫng* :- Gmc. **taŋg-* :- IE. **dank̂-* bite, repr. also by Gr. *dáknein* bite, Skr. *dáśati* bites.

tongue muscular organ in the mouth; speech, language OE.; tongue-like object XIV. OE. *tunge* = OS. *tunga* (Du. *tong*), OHG. *zunga* (G. *zunge*), ON. *tunga*, Goth. *tuggō* :- Gmc. **tuŋʒōn*, rel. to L. *lingua* - **dingua*.

tonic pert. to tension XVII; increasing or restoring the tone of the body XVIII; (mus.) pert. to the keynote; pert. to tone in speech XIX; sb. tonic medicine XVIII; keynote XIX. - F. *tonique* or Gr. *tonikós*, f. *tónos* TONE.

to-night on the night following this day OE.; on this present night XIII; †(dial.) last night XIII; sb. this night, the night following this day XIII. OE. *tōniht*, f. *tō* TO + *niht* NIGHT.

tonka *t. bean*, seed of S. Amer. tree of the genus *Dipteryx*. XVIII. - local name in Guyana.

tonnage duty levied on wine imported in tuns XV; †charge for the hire of a ship at so much per ton of her burden XVI; charge per ton of freight XVII; shipping in relation to carrying capacity; carrying capacity of a ship expressed in tons of 100 cubic feet XVIII. - OF. *tonnage*, f. *tonne* TUN; later assoc. directly with TON[1]; see -AGE.

tonneau rear body of a motor car. XX. - F., spec. application of *tonneau* cask (OF. *tonnel*), dim. of *tonne* TUN.

tonsil (usu. pl) gland at either side of the back of the mouth. XVII. - F. *tonsilles* or L. *tonsillæ* pl.

tonsorial pert. to a barber. XIX. f. L. *tonsōrius*, f. *tonsor* barber, f. *tons-*; see next and -IAL.

tonsure shaving of the head. XIV. - (O)F. *tonsure* or L. *tonsūra*, f. *tons-*, pp. stem of *tondēre* shear, clip; see -URE.

tontine a financial system. XVIII. - F., f. name of Lorenzo *Tonti*, Neapolitan banker who initiated the scheme in France *c.*1653.

too in addition, besides, moreover; †exceedingly; in excess, excessively. Str. form of TO adv., so sp. since XVI.

tool OE. *tōl* = ON. *tól* (n. pl.) :- Gmc. **tōwlam*, f. **tōw-* **taw-*, whence OE. *tawian* prepare; see -EL[1], TAW[1].

toot sound a horn. XVI. prob. - (M)LG. *tūten*, unless a parallel imit. formation. Hence **tootle** (-LE[3]) XIX.

tooth pl. **teeth.** OE. *tōð* = OS. (Du.) *tand*, OHG. *zan* (G. *zahn*), ON. *tǫnn* :- Gmc. **tanþ-*, beside Goth. *tunþus*; IE. **dont-* **dent-* **dṇt-* is repr. by Skr. *dán, dánt-*, Gr. *odṓn, odónt-*, L. *dēns, dent-*, OIr. *dét*, W. *dant*, Lith. *dantìs*; prp. formation on **ed-* EAT, the literal meaning being 'the eater or chewer'.

tootsy XIX. Playful alt. of FOOT + -SY.

top[1] (dial.) tuft (of hair; etc.), crest; highest point or part OE.; upper part or covering (platform at head of mast XV (†*top-castle* XIV-XVI), uppermost part of a high boot XVII); first or foremost part XV. Late OE. *topp* = (M)Du. *top* crest, summit, tip, (O)HG. *zopf* plait, tress, ON. *toppr* top, tuft :- Gmc. **toppaz*. Hence **top** vb. deprive of the top XIV; put a top on; overtop XVI. **topper** (-ER[1]) exceptionally good person or thing XVIII; top-hat, tall hat XIX. comp. **topgallant** top at head of topmast (XV), so called as having a superior position and making a brave show.

top[2] circular toy having a point on which it is made to spin. Late OE. *top* (once); further evidence is not freq. until after 1400; the orig. is unkn.

topaz precious stone. XIII. ME. *topace* - OF, *topace*, (also mod.) *topaze* - L. *topaz(i)us, -ion* - Gr. *tópazos, -ázion*.

tope[1] small species of shark. XVII. of unkn. orig.

tope[2] clump or plantation of trees. XVII. - Telugu *tōpu*, Tamil *tōppu*.

tope[3] dome or tumulus to contain relics, etc. XIX. - Hind. *tōp* :- Skr. *stūpa-*.

tope[4] drink (heavily). XVII. perh. alt. of synon. †*top* XVI (of unkn. orig.) by assoc. with †*tope* (XVII) int. used as a pledging formula in drinking - F. *tôpe*.

topee, topi Indian name for the European hat, esp. sun helmet. XIX. - Hindi *ṭopī* hat.

tophus soft porous stone, esp. deposited by calcareous springs XVI; (path.) gouty deposit XVII. - L. *tōphus*.

topiary pert. to the trimming of shrubs into ornamental or fantastic shapes. XVI. - F. *topiaire* - L. *topiārius*, f. *topia* fancy or landscape gardening - Gr. *tópia*, pl. of *tópion*, dim. of *tópos* place; see -ARY. Hence sb. XX.

topic †adj. pert. to or of the nature of a COMMONPLACE; sb. (pl.) name of Aristotle's treatise *Tà topiká* (lit. matters concerning commonplaces) XVI; †consideration, argument, head XVII; subject of a discourse, theme XVIII. - Gr. *topikós* f. *tópos* place; see -IC. So **topical** local; †pert. to general maxims XVI; pert. to subjects or current affairs XIX.

topo- comb. form of Gr. *tópos* place, locality. **topography** description of the features of a locality. XV. - late L. *topographia* - Gr. *topographíā*. So **topographer, -graphic** XVII, **-graphical** XVI. **toponymy** place-names of a region. XIX. f. Gr. *ónoma, ónuma* NAME; see -Y[3].

topple (dial.) tumble about; fall through being top-heavy. XVI. f. TOP[1] vb. + -LE[3].

topsy-turvy XVI. Earliest records have *topsy tervy* or *tyrvy*, but the somewhat later forms *topset, topside*, may point to the origin in pp. *set* or sb. *side*; for the second el. connection with †*tirve* (turn) has been suggested; for the suffix see -Y[1].

toque small cap or bonnet. XVI. - F., of unkn. orig.

tor high rock, pile of rocks (esp. in local names). OE. *torr*, of Celt. orig. (cf. OW. *twrr* bulge, belly, Gael. *tòrr* bulging hill).

-tor repr. L. terminal el. f. *-t-* of pps. + -OR[1], as in *actor, inventor*.

Torah Mosaic law, Pentateuch. XVI. - Heb. *tôrāh* direction, instruction, doctrine, law.

torch XIII. - (O)F. *torche* :- Rom. **torca*, for L. *torqua*, f. *torquēre* twist; the primary meaning is taken to have been 'something twisted, as tow'.

toreador XVII. - Sp. *toreador*, f. *torear* fight (bulls) in the ring, f. *toro* bull :- L. *taurus* bull. So **torero** XVIII.

toreutic pert. to working in metal or ivory. XIX. - Gr. *toreutikós*, f. *toreúein* work in relief; see -IC.

torii decorative gateway of a Shinto temple. XIX. - Jap.

torment †torture with the rack, etc.; state of severe suffering; †violent storm XIII. OF. *torment*, (also mod.) *tourment* :- L. *tormentum* (:- **torquementum*) engine for throwing missiles, cord, instrument of torture, f. *torquēre* twist. So **torment** vb. XIII. - (O)F. *tourmenter*. **tormentor** XIII. - OF. *tormentëor*; see -OR[1].

tormentil yellow-flowered herb. XV. - (O)F. *tormentille* - medL. *tormentilla*, of unkn. orig.

tornado †violent thunderstorm of the tropical Atlantic XVI; rotatory storm of Africa, etc. XVII (*ternado*). perh. orig. alt. - Sp. *tronada* thunderstorm (f. *tronar* thunder), later assim. to *tornar* TURN; see -ADO.

torpedo (zool.) electric ray XVI; case charged with gunpowder to explode under water, self-propelled submarine missile XIX. - L. *torpēdō*, f. *torpēre* be stiff or numb.

torpid benumbed, lacking animation or vigour. XVII. - L. *torpidus*, f. *torpēre* be sluggish; see -ID[1]. So **torpor** XVII. - L.; see -OR[2].

torque necklace, twisted band. XIX. - F. - L. *torquēs*, f. *torquēre* twist.

torrefy roast. XVII. - F. *torréfier* - L. *torrefacere*, f. *torrēre* scorch; see -FY.

torrent XVII. - F. - It. *torrente* - L. *torrēns*, *-ent-*, sb. use of prp. (scorching, (of streams) boiling, roaring, rushing) of *torrēre* scorch; see -ENT. Hence **torrential** XIX.

torrid scorched, scorching hot. XVI. - F. *torride* or L. *torridus*, f. *torrēre* scorch; see -ID[1].

torsion †griping XV; twisting, twist XVI. - (O)F. - late L. *torsiō*, *-ōn-*, by-form of *tortiō*, f. *tort-*, pp. stem of *torquēre* twist.

torso XVIII. - It. *torso* stalk, stump, trunk of a statue :- L. *thyrsus* stalk; see THYRSUS.

tort †injury, wrong XIV (rare before XVI); (leg.) breach of a duty XVI. - OF. :- medL. *tortum*, sb. use of n. of L. *tortus*, pp. of *torquēre* twist, wring.

torticollis (path.) wry-neck. XIX. f. L. *tortus* (see prec.) + *collum* neck.

tortilla in Mexico, thin round cake of maize flour. XVII. - Sp., dim. of *torta* round cake :- late L. (Vulg.) *tōrta*.

tortoise XV. The earliest exx. show a variety of forms reflecting medL. *tortūca*, (O)F. *tortue*, and (occas.) Sp. *tortuga*; the present form (of obscure orig.) appears in XVI.

tortuous XV. - OF. *tortuous* (mod. *tortueux*) - L. *tortuōsus*, f. *tortus* twisting, f. *tort-*, pp. stem of *torquēre* twist; see -UOUS.

torture sb. XVI. - (O)F. *torture* or late L. *tortūra* twisting, writhing, torment, f. *tort-*; see prec., -URE. Hence vb. XVI.

torus pl. **tori** (archit.) large convex moulding XVI. - L. *torus* swelling, round moulding.

Tory (hist.) from *c*.1645 one of the dispossessed Irish who became outlaws, rapparee; in 1679–80 applied to anti-exclusioners; from 1689, member of one of the two great political parties of Great Britain. Presumably - Ir. **tóraighe* pursuer, implied in *tóraigheachd* pursuit, f. *tóir* pursue.

tosh (sl.) rubbish, nonsense. XIX. of unkn. orig.

toss throw or pitch about (in earliest use freq. of the sea). XVI. of unkn. orig.

tot[1] (colloq.) very small child XVIII; small drinking vessel, dram of drink XIX. of unkn. orig.

tot[2] (colloq.) sum *up*. XVIII. f. *tot*, abbrev. of TOTAL.

total pert. to or comprising the whole. XIV. - (O)F. - scholL. *tōtālis*, f. *tōtum* the whole, sb. use of n. of *tōtus* entire, whole. So **totality** XVI. - scholL. *tōtālitās*. Hence **totally** (-LY[2]) XVI. **totalize** XIX, whence **totalizator** apparatus for registering the total of operations, spec. the number of tickets sold to betters on a horse race (XIX).

totem among Amer. Indians, hereditary badge of a tribe or group. XVIII. of Algonquian orig.

tother (dial.) *the t.* the other. XIII. ME. *þe toþer*, for *þet oþer*, orig. n. of OE. *se ōðer* the other, the second; see THE[1], THAT[1], OTHER.

totter †swing XII; rock to and fro on its base XIV; move with unsteady steps XVII. ME. *toter* swing - MDu. *tourteren* swing, corr. to OE. *tealtrian* totter, stagger.

toucan XVI. - Tupi *tucana*, Guarani *tucā*, *tucā*.

touch vb. XIII. ME. *toche*, *t(o)uche* - OF. *tochier*, *tuchier* (mod. *toucher*) :- Rom. **toccāre* make a sound like *toc*, of imit. orig. Much used in comps., spec. with ref. to ready ignition (prob. from OF. *toucher* set fire), as in **touch-hole**, **touchwood** XVI; also **touchstone** stone to test gold and silver alloys (XVI), based on OF. *touchepierre*. Hence **touchy** easily moved to take offence; †easily ignited; risky. XVII. perh. partly an alt. of TETCHY; see -Y[1].

touching prep. concerning, relating to. XIV. - (O)F. *touchant*, prp. of *touch(i)er* touch.

tough of strongly cohesive substance OE.; severe,violent XIII; capable of great endurance XIV; difficult to solve XVII. OE. *tōh* = OHG. *zāh*, MLG. *tā* :- Gmc. **taŋχuz*.

toupee (artificial) lock of hair. XVIII. - F. *toupet* tuft of hair esp. over the forehead, f. OF. *to(u)p*, of Gmc. orig.; see TOP[1], -ET. Superseded by **toupet** XVIII.

tour *one's* turn, spell of duty XIV; †circular movement XV; travelling round, circuitous journey XVII. - (O)F. *tour*, earlier *tor* :- L. *tornus* lathe (see TURN). Hence **tour** vb. make a tour (of). XVIII. **tourist** XVIII, **tourism** XIX.

tourmaline brittle pyro-electric mineral orig. from Ceylon. XVIII. - F., ult. f. Sinhalese *toramalli* cornelian.

tournament medieval tilting match. XIII. ME. *turne-*, *tornement* - AN. vars. of OF. *tur-*, *torneiement*, f. *torneier*; see next, -MENT.

tourney tournament. XIII. - OF. *tornei* (mod. *tournoi*), f. *torneier* (whence vb. XIII) :- Rom. **tornidiāre*, f. L. *tornus* TURN.

tourniquet XVII. - F., taken to be alt. of OF. *tournicle*, var. of *t(o)unicle* coat of mail, by assoc. with *tourner* TURN.

tousle pull about roughly, dishevel. XV. frequent. f. (dial.) *touse*, ME. *t(o)use* in *totuse* (XIII), *betouse* (XIV), repr. OE. **tūsian* = LG. *tūsen* pull or shake about, OHG. *zirzūsōn*, *erzūsen* tear to pieces, clear of undergrowth (G. *zausen*), rel. to L. *dūmus*, earlier *dusmus* bushes, brambles, Ir. *doss* bush; see -LE[3].

tout †peep, peer XIV; (sl.) watch, spy on XVII; solicit custom or votes importunately XVIII. ME. *tūte* :- OE. **tūtian*, f. **tūt-* project, stick out, repr. by OE. *tȳtan* (once) peep out, become visible, MLG. *tūte* horn, funnel (LG. *tūt(e)* spout), MDu. *tūte* nipple (Du. *tuit* spout, nozzle), ON. *túta* teat-like prominence. Hence **tout** sb. †thieves' scout XVIII; touter for custom, etc. XIX.

tow[1] fibre of flax, etc. XIV. - MLG. *touw* :- OS. *tou* = ON. *tó* wool, tow, rel. to OE. *tow-* in *towcræft* spinning, etc.

tow[2] †drag OE.; draw (a vessel) on the water by a rope XIV. OE. *togian* = MLG. *togen*, OHG. *zogōn*, ON. *toga* :- Gmc. **toȝōjan*, f. **toȝ-* **tuȝ-* (cf. TEAM). So **towage** charge for towing a vessel XVI; action of towing XVII. orig. - AN. *towage*, AL. *towagium*, f. ME. *towe*, *toȝe* tow.

toward adj. †coming, future, impending OE.; †promising, disposed to learn, docile XIII; favourable, propitious XIX. OE. *tōweard* = OS. *tōward*, *-werd*, OHG. *zuowart*, *-wert* 'directed forwards', f. Gmc. **tō* TO + **warð-* -WARD. Hence prep. in the direction of. OE. *tōweard*, n. of the adj. **towards** in same sense. OE. *tōweardes*; see -WARDS.

towel XIII. ME. *towaile*, *towelle*, *touel* - OF.

toail(l)e (mod. *touaille*) :- Gmc. **þwaχljō* (OHG. *dwahila*, G. dial. *zwehle* napkin), f. **þwaχan* wash (OE. *þwēan*, etc.); see -EL[1].

tower sb. XII. ME. *tūr*, later *tour*, *towr* - AN., OF. *tur*, *tor* (mod. *tour*) :- L. *turris*, *turr-* - Gr. *túrris*, *túrsis*, *túrsos*. Hence **tower** vb. rise to a great height; soar like a hawk. XVI.

town †enclosure, garden, yard; (now Sc.) building(s) on a piece of enclosed land, farmstead; (dial.) cluster of buildings or houses OE.; inhabited place having an independent administration XII; inhabitants of a town XIV; (U.S.) division for local or state government XIX. OE. *tūn* = OS. *tūn* (Du. *tuin* garden), OHG. *zūn* (G. *zaun*) fence, hedge, ON. *tún* :- Gmc. **tūnaz*, **tūnam*, rel. to Celt. **dūn-* in place names (e.g. *Augustodunum* Autun), OIr. *dūn*, W. *din* fort, castle, camp, fortified place. Comps. and derivs. **town-clerk** XIV. **townee,** U.S. **towny** one of the townspeople XIX. **township** OE. *tūnscipe*. **townsman** †villager, villein OE.; man of a town XV. OE. *tūnesman*.

toxic poisonous XVII; due to poisoning XIX. - medL. *toxicus*, f. L. *toxicum* poison - Gr. *toxikón* (*phármakon*) (poison) by smearing arrows, n. of *toxikós*, f. *tóxa* pl. (bow and) arrows, f. *tóxon* bow; see -IC. Hence **toxin** poison produced by a microbe. XIX.

toxophilite devotee of archery. XVIII. f. *Toxophilus*, title of a book (1545) by Roger Ascham, intended to mean 'lover of the bow', f. Gr. *tóxon* bow + *-philos* -PHIL; see -ITE. Hence **toxophily** (-Y[3]) XIX.

toy A. †amorous play XIV; †sportive or fantastic action, antic, trick XV; B. trifling object; thing to play with XVI. of unkn. orig.

trace[1] †path, course XIII; †series of footprints, track XIV; vestige, mark XVII. - (O)F., f. corr. vb. OF. *tracier* (mod. *tracer*) :- Rom. **tractiāre*, f. L. *tractus* TRACT[3]. So **trace** vb. A. proceed in a line or track; B. make marks on a plan, etc. XIV. - OF. Hence **tracery** †place for tracing XV; intersecting rib-work in a Gothic window XVII.

trace[2] pair of ropes, etc. attached to the collar of a draught animal XIV; each of these XV. ME. *trais*, first as coll. pl., later as sg. - OF. *trais*, pl. of *trait* draught, harness-strap :- L. *tractus* draught, f. pp. stem of *trahere* draw.

trachea (anat.) tube extending from the larynx to the bronchi. XVI (earlier in *trache arteria* or *arterie* XV). - medL. *trāchēa*, for late L. *trāchīa* - Gr. *trākheîa*, fem. of *trākhús* rough.

trachyte gritty volcanic rock. XIX. - F., f. Gr. *trākhús* rough or *trākhútēs* roughness.

track mark left by the passage of something XV; line of travel or motion XVI; path laid down XIX. - (O)F. *trac*, perh. - MDu., LG. *tre(c)k* drawing, draught, pull. Hence, or - F. *traquer*, **track** vb. XVI.

tract[1] tractate, (later) short pamphlet. XV. poss. shortening of L. *tractātus* TRACTATE. Hence **tractarian** writer of tracts (spec. of contributors to the 'Tracts for the Times' 1833-41 published at Oxford). XIX.

tract[2] (liturg.) item replacing the Alleluia in the Mass from Septuagesima to Easter Eve. XIV. - medL. *tractus*, spec. use of L. *tractus* (see next).

tract[3] act of drawing or something drawn in various uses identical with those of TRACE[1] and TRACK (rare before XVI), now chiefly 'stretch or extent of territory' (so in L.). - L. *tractus*, f. pp. stem of *trahere* draw.

tractable XVI. - L. *tractābilis*, f. *tractāre* TREAT; see -ABLE.

tractate XV. - L. *tractātus*, f. *tractāre* TREAT; see -ATE[1].

traction drawing, draught XVII; drawing of vehicles or loads along a road (hence *t. engine*) XIX. - F. *traction* or medL. *tractiō*, *-ōn-*, f. pp. stem of *trahere* draw; see -ION. So **tractor** (-OR[1]) (med.) device to be drawn or rubbed over the skin XVII; instrument for pulling XIX; traction engine XX.

trade †course, way, track XIV; regular practice of a business or profession XVI; buying and selling in this. - MLG. *trade* track (OS. *trada* = OHG. *trata*), rel. to TREAD. **trade wind** orig. any wind that blows in a constant direction. XVII. f. phr. †*blow trade* blow in a regular or habitual course.

tradition that which is handed down as belief or practice XIV; delivery, transmission XVI. - (O)F. *tradicion*, (also mod.) *-tion*, or L. *trāditiō*, *-ōn-*, f. *trādere* hand over, deliver, f. TRANS- + *dāre* give; see -ITION. Hence **traditional** (-AL[1]) XVII.

traduce †transport; †translate; †transmit; propagate; speak evil of (falsely). XVI. - L. *trādūcere*, f. *trāns* TRANS- + *dūcere* lead.

traffic transportation of goods for purposes of trade XVI; passing to and fro of people, etc. XIX. - F. *traf(f)ique* (mod. *trafic*); ult. orig. unkn.

tragacanth medicinal gum from plants of the genus *Astragalus*. XVI. - F. *tragacante* or L. *tragacantha* - Gr. *tragákantha* goat's-thorn, f. *trágos* he-goat + *ákantha* thorn.

tragedy dramatic piece (†earlier, tale) having a disastrous ending XIV; calamitous event XVI. - (O)F. *tragédie* - L. *tragœdia* - Gr. *tragōidíā*, usu. taken to be f. *trágos* goat + *ōidḗ* ODE. So **tragedian** tragic poet XIV; tragic actor XVI. - OF. *tragediane*, F. *tragédien*. **tragic** XVI. - F. *tragique* - L. *tragicus* - Gr. *tragikós*, f. *trágos*, but assoc. with *tragōidíā*. **tragical** XV. f. L. *tragicus*; see -AL[1]. **tragicomedy** XVI. - F. *tragicomédie* or It. *tragicommedia* - late L. *tragicōmœdia*, for *tragicocōmœdia*.

tragopan pheasant of the genus *Tragopan*, having fleshy horns. XIX. - L. - Gr. *tragópān*, f. *trágos* goat + *Pā́n* Pan.

trail intr. hang down and drag along; trans. drag or draw along. XIV. prob. of mixed orig. - OF. *traillier* or MLG., MFlem. *treilen* haul (a boat), which point to Rom. or popL. **trāgulāre* (to which OE. *trægelian* 'carpere' conforms), f. L. *trāgula* drag-net, etc.

train tarrying, delay XIV; thing that drags or trails (first of the trailing part of a garment) XV; sequence or series; number of carriages, etc. coupled together XIX. - (O)F. *train* m., *traine* fem., f. OF. (orig.) *trahiner*, *traïner*, (mod. *traîner*) :- Rom. **traginūre*, f. **tragere* for L. *trahere* draw; the OF. vb. is the orig. source of

train vb. †draw, allure, etc. XV; instruct and discipline XVI.
train-oil oil obtained by boiling from whale blubber, etc. XVI. repl. earlier *train, trane* (XV) - (M)LG. *trān*, MDu. *traen* (Du. *traan*) = G. *tran*, rel. to *träne* tear, drop.
traipse *see* TRAPES.
trait †stroke XVI; feature, characteristic XVIII. - F. :- L. *tractus* drawing, draught (see TRACT[2]).
traitor XIII. - OF. *trait(o)ur* :- L. *trāditor, -ōr-*, agent-noun f. *trādere* deliver, betray, f. TRANS- + *dāre*, give; see -TOR.
trajectory XVII. - medL. *trājectōrius*, f. *trāject-*, pp. stem of *trāicere*, f. TRANS- + *jacere* throw; see -ORY[1].
tram[1] A. †contrivance, lit. and fig. XIV; B. loosely twisted silk thread used for weft XVII. In A. - (O)F. *trame* woof, cunning device, machination :- L. *trāma* woof; in B. a new adoption from modF.
tram[2] (Sc.) shaft of a barrow or cart XVI; (coalmining, north.) frame or skeleton truck for carrying coal-baskets XVI; line or track or wood, stone, or iron, road laid with such lines, (short for *tram-car*) passenger car running on tramlines XIX. (in AL. *trama* XIV) - MLG., MDu. *trame* balk, beam, rung of a ladder, of unkn. orig.; the sense-development in Eng. is obscure.
trammel fishing-net having three layers of netting XIV; hobble for a horse XVI; thing that hinders free action XVII. - (O)F. *tramail* (mod. *trémail*) - medL. *tramaculum*, var. of *tre-, trimaculum*, perh. f. L. TRI- + *macula* mesh. Hence **trammel** vb. in several techn. uses XVI; (fig.) hinder the action of XVIII.
tramontane lying beyond the mountain (spec. the Alps) from Italy. XVI. f. It. *tramontana* north wind, pole star, *tramontani* dwellers beyond the mountains - L. *trānsmontānus*, f. TRANS- + *mōns, mont-* MOUNT[1].
tramp stamp, tread heavily XIV; walk steadily XVI. prob. of LG. or Du. orig.; cf. MLG. *trampen*.
trample †tramp, stamp XIV; tread *upon* XVI. f. TRAMP + -LE[3].
trance †extreme dread or doubt; suspension of consciousness, hypnotic state XIV. - OF. *transe* (mod. *trance*), f. *transir* depart, be benumbed - L. *transīre* pass over (see TRANSIENT).
tranquil XVII. - F. *tranquille* or L. *tranquillus*.
trans- comb. form of L. prep. *trāns* across, beyond, over, corr. to Umbrian *tra(ha)f, tra(ha)* with cogns. in Skr., Celt., and Gmc. (see THROUGH). In several L. vbs. and their derivs. the prefix was reduced to *trā* before a cons., e.g. *trādere* (see TRADITION), *trāicere* (see TRAJECTORY); *ss* resulting from composition with an initial *s* is simplified, as in *transcribe*.
transact †do business, treat XVI; carry through, manage XVII. f. *transact-*, pp. stem of L. *transigere* drive through, accomplish, f. TRANS- + *agere* drive, do. So **transaction** †adjustment of a dispute XV; action of transacting, matter transacted XVII. - late L.
transcend pass (a limit) or the limits of XIV; rise above, surpass XV; †go beyond, climb over XVI. - OF. *transcendre* or L. *tran(s)scendere* climb over, surmount, f. TRANS- + *scandere* climb. So **transcendence, -ency** XVII. - late L. *transcendentia*. **transcendent** XVI, **transcendental** XVIII.
transcribe make a copy of XVI; transliterate XVII. - L. *transcrībere*, f. TRANS- + *scrībere* write. So **transcript** XIII. ME. *transcrit* - (O)F., later (XV) assim. to L. *transcriptum*, sb. use of n. pp. of *transcrībere*. **transcription** XVI. - F. or late L.
transect cut across. XVII. f. TRANS- + *sect-*, pp. stem of L. *secāre* cut.
transept transverse part of a cruciform church, either arm of this. XVI. - modL. *transeptum* 'cross division'; see TRANS-, SEPTUM.
transfer convey from place to place XIV; make over by legal process XVI; convey (a design) from one surface to another XIX. - L. *transferre* (or F. *transférer*), f. TRANS- + *ferre* BEAR[2]. Hence **transfer** sb., **transference** XVII.
transfigure XIII. - (O)F. *transfigurer* or L. *transfigūrāre*, f. TRANS- + *figūra* FIGURE. So **transfiguration** XIV (first in ref. to the change in the appearance of Jesus Christ as narrated in Matt. 17: 2, Mark 9: 2-3).
transfix impale upon a sharp point XVI; fig. XVII. f. *transfix-*, pp. stem of *transfigere*; see TRANS-, FIX.
transform XIV. - (O)F. *transformer* or L. *transformāre*; see TRANS-, FORM. So **transformation** XV. - (O)F. or late L.
transfuse pour from one place to another. XV. - *transfūs-*, pp. stem of L. *transfundere*; see TRANS-, FUSE[2].
transgress go beyond the bounds prescribed by law, etc. XVI. - *transgress-*, pp. stem of L. *transgredī*; see TRANS-, DIGRESS. So **transgression** XV. - (O)F. - L.
tranship. XVIII. f. TRANS- + SHIP vb.
transient XVII. - L. *transiēns, transeunt-*, prp. of *transīre* pass over, f. TRANS- + *īre* go. So **transit** XV. - L. *transitus*. **transition** XVI. - (O)F. or L. **transitive** (gram.) taking a direct object; passing into another condition. XVI. - late L. *transitīvus*. **transitory** XIV. - AN. *transitorie*, (O)F. *transitoire* - ChrL. *transitōrius*; see -ORY[2].
transire warrant permitting the passage of merchandise. XVI. - L. *transīre* pass over, f. TRANS- + *īre* go.
translate A. remove from one place to another; B. turn from one language into another. XIII. prob. first in pp. *translate* - L. *translātus*, functioning as pp. of *transferre* TRANSFER; but perh. reinforced by OF. *translater*, medL. *translātāre*. So **translation, translator** XIV. - OF. or L.
transliterate replace (letters of one language) by those of another for the same sounds. XIX. f. TRANS- + L. *littera* LETTER + -ATE[3]. So **transliteration** XIX.
translucent †shining through XVI; transparent XVII. - L. *translūcēns, -ent-*, prp. of *translūcēre*; see TRANS-, LUCID.
transmarine that is beyond the sea. XVI. - L. *transmarīnus*; see TRANS-, MARINE.
transmigration †removal of the Jews into captivity at Babylon XIII; passage from one place to another XIV; passage of the soul at death into another body, metempsychosis XVI. - late L.

transmigrātiō, -ōn- change of country, f. *transmigrāre*, whence **transmigrate** XVII (pp. XV); see TRANS-, MIGRATE, -ATION.

transmit send across a space XIV; pass on by communication XVII; cause to pass through a medium. - L. *transmittere*. So **transmission** XVI. - L. *transmissiō, -ōn-*; see TRANS-, MISSION.

transmogrify (colloq.) transform, esp. into a strange shape. XVII. of unkn. orig.; see -IFY.

transmutation †change of condition XIV; conversion into something else; (alch.) XV; (biol.) XVII. - (O)F. *transmutation* or late L. *transmūtātiō, -ōn-*, f. L. *transmūtāre* (whence **transmute** vb. XV); see TRANS-, MUTATION.

transom cross-beam, esp. spanning an opening. XIV. ME. *traversayn, transyn, -ing* - (O)F. *traversin* in same sense, f. *traverse* TRAVERSE.

transparent that can be seen through XV; (fig.) XVI. - (O)F. *transparent* - medL. *transpārēns, -ent-*, f. L. TRANS- + *pārēre* APPEAR. So **transparency** XVI.

transpire emit as vapour XVI; pass out as vapour XVII; come to be known, leak out XVIII; (hence, by misapprehension, first U.S.) happen XIX. - F. *transpirer* or medL. *transpīrāre*, f. L. TRANS- + *spīrāre* breathe.

transplant XV. - late L. *transplantāre*; see TRANS-, PLANT.

transpontine that is across the bridge, spec. any of the London bridges, i.e. south of the Thames, and so pert. to the drama of Surrey-side theatres in XIX. XIX. f. TRANS- + L. *pōns, pont-* bridge + -INE[1].

transport convey from place to place XIV; carry away with emotion XVI. - OF. *transporter* or L. *transportāre*, f. TRANS- + *portāre* carry. Hence or - (O)F. *transport* conveyance from one place to another or means of this XV; state of being 'carried out of oneself' XVII. Hence **transportation** conveyance XVI; penal removal XVII.

transpose †change into something else XIV; change the position or order of XVI. - (O)F. *transposer*, f. *trans-* TRANS- + *poser* POSE. So **transposition** XVI. - F. or late L.

trans-ship see TRANSHIP.

transubstantiation change of substance XIV; spec. of the Eucharistic bread and wine XVI. - medL. *tran(s)substantiātiō, -ōn-*, f. *tran(s)substantiāre*, whence **transubstantiate** XVI (as pp. XV); see -ATE[2,3], -ATION. Hence **consubstantiation** controversialist's term to designate the Lutheran doctrine of the Eucharistic presence in, with, and under the substantially unaltered bread and wine. XVI. See CON-.

transverse XVII. - L. *transversus*, pp. of *transvertere* turn across; see TRANS-, VERSE. So **transversal** (-AL[1]) XV. - medL.

trap[1] contrivance for catching animals OE.; movable covering as of an opening in a floor XIV; means of confining and releasing objects XVI; (perh. for *rattle trap*) small carriage on springs XIX. OE. *træppe* (in *coltetræppe* Christ's thorn), *treppe*, corr. in form and sense to MDu. *trappe*, medL. *trappa*, OF. *trape* (mod. *trappe*), but the mutual relations are obscure. So **trap** vb. OE. *betreppan*. **trapper** (-ER[1]) XVIII.

trap[2] (min.) igneous rock. XVIII. - Sw. *trapp*, f. *trappa* stair; so named from the stair-like appearance.

trapes, traipse (colloq., dial.) walk in slovenly or aimless fashion. XVI. of unkn. orig. Hence sb. sloven XVII; tiresome walk XIX.

trapeze gymnastic apparatus consisting of a crossbar supported by two ropes. XIX. - F. *trapèze* - late L. *trapezium* (see next).

trapezium (geom.) irregular quadrilateral XVI; quadrilateral having only one pair of opposite sides parallel XVII. - late L. - Gr. *trapézion*, f. *trápeza* table, for **tetra-peza*, f. TETRA- + IE. **ped-* FOOT. So **trapezoid** quadrilateral no two sides of which are parallel. XVIII. - modL. *trapezoidēs* - late Gr. *trapezoeidḗs*.

trapping (chiefly pl.) covering spread over harness XIV; (in wider use) external ornaments XVI. f. base of synon. †*trappo(u)r* (XIII) - AN. **trapour*, var. of OF. *drapure*, f. *drap* cloth; with substitution of -ING[1].

Trappist monk of a Cistercian community established in 1664 by De Rancé, abbot of La *Trappe*, Normandy. XIX. - F. *Trappiste*, f. *La Trappe*; see -IST.

traps (colloq.) personal effects, belongings. XIX. of uncert. orig.; perh. contr. of TRAPPINGS.

trash broken twigs, etc.; worthless stuff. XVI. of unkn. orig.

traumatic caused by a wound. XVII. - late L. *traumaticus* - Gr. *traumatikós*, f. *traûma, traumat-* wound (whence **trauma** XVIII); see -IC.

travail (arch.) labour, toil; labour of childbirth. XIII. - (O)F. *travail* painful effort, trouble, work f. (O)F. *travailler* (whence obs. or arch. **travail** vb. XIII) :- Rom. **trepāliāre*, f. medL. *trepālium* instrument of torture, presumably f. L. *trēs, tria* THREE + *pālus* stake. The etymol. meaning of the vb. was 'put to torture', whence, through the refl. use ('put oneself to pain') the sense 'toil, labour', which survives in F., whereas the Eng. vb. ult. became restricted to the sense 'journey', with the sp. **travel** (XIV). Hence **traveller** (-ER[1]) XIV; *traveller's joy* kind of clematis which adorns the wayside XVI. **travelogue** talk or lecture about travel. XX. irreg., with *-logue* of *monologue, dialogue*.

traverse run, move, or pass across or through; act against or in opposition to. XIV. - (O)F. *traverser* :- late L. *trāversāre, transversāre*, f. *transversus* TRANSVERSE. So **traverse** sb. something that crosses (lit. and fig.). XIV. - OF. *travers* and *traverse*, partly f. the vb., partly repr. sb. uses of n. and f. pp.

travertin(e) concretionary limestone deposited from water. XVIII. - It. *travertino*, for earlier †*tivertino* :- L. *tīburtinus*, adj. of *Tībur* (now *Tivoli*) in ancient Latium; see -INE[1].

travesty XVII. freq. in XVII in *Virgil travesti(e)*, adoption of the title of Scarron's 'Le Virgile travesty en vers burlesques' (1648); - F. *travesti*, pp. of *travestir* - It. *travestire*, f. *tra-* (:- L. TRANS-) + *vestire* clothe.

trawl fish with a drag-net XVII; use a seine-net to catch fish XIX. prob. - MDu. *traghelen* drag, rel. to *traghel* drag-net, perh. - L. *trāgula* dragnet, obscurely f. *trahere* draw. Hence **trawl** sb. XVIII, short for *trawl-net* (XVII). **trawler** (-ER[1]) one who fishes with a trawl-net XVI; vessel using trawl-nets XIX.

tray shallow open vessel, now a flat board with raised rim. OE. **trēġ, *trīeġ*, recorded only late as *trīġ* = OSw. *trø* corn-measure :- Gmc. **traujam*, f. **trau-*, **treu-* wood (see TREE).

treachery XIII. - (O)F. *trecherie*, (also mod.) *tricherie*, f. *tricher* cheat; see TRICK, -ERY. So **treacherous** XIV. - OF. *trecherous*.

treacle †salve regarded as an antidote to venomous bites, etc. XIV; †in names of plants of reputed medicinal value XV; †sovereign remedy XVI; uncrystallized syrup produced in refining sugar XVII. ME. *triacle* - OF. :- L. *thēriaca* - Gr. *thēriakḗ*, sb. use of fem. of adj. f. *thērion* wild beast, venomous animal, dim. of *thḗr* wild beast.

tread pt. *trod*, pp. *trodden* step or walk upon; intr. with *on, upon* OE.; thresh by trampling XIV. OE. str. vb. *tredan* = OS. *tredan* (Du. *treden*), OHG. *tretan* (G. *treten*) :- WGmc. **tredan*; cf. wk. grade Gmc. **truð-* repr. by ON. *troða*, Goth. *trudan*. Hence **tread** sb. XIII. Comps. **treadmill** XIX, **treadwheel** XVI.

treadle †step, stair OE.; lever worked with the foot XV. OE. *tredul*, f. *tredan*; see prec. and -LE[1].

treason betrayal of trust XIII; violation by a subject of his allegiance XIV. ME. *treison, tresoun* - AN. *treisoun, tres(o)un*, OF. *traison* (mod. *trahison*) :- L. *trāditiō, -ōn-*, f. *trādere* deliver up, BETRAY, f. TRANS- + *dāre* give. Hence **treasonable** perfidious XIV (chiefly Sc. till XVII).

treasure wealth, riches; valued thing. XII. ME. *tresor* - (O)F. *trésor* :- Rom. **tresaurus*, unexpl. alt. of L. *thēsaurus* (see THESAURUS). Hence **treasure** vb. XIV (rare before XVII). So **treasurer** (-ER[2]) XIII. - AN. *tresorer*, (O)F. (mod.) *trésorier*. **treasure trove** treasure found hidden of unknown ownership. XVI (also *trovey*). - AN. *tresor trové*, i.e. *tresor* TREASURE, *trové*, pp. of *trover* (F. *trouver*) find. **treasury** XIII. - OF. *tresorie*, for *tresorerie*; see -Y[3].

treat deal *with* XIII; trans. XIV. ME. *trete* - AN. *treter*, OF. *tretier, traitier* (mod. *traiter*) :- L. *tractāre* drag, handle, manage, investigate, discuss, negotiate, f. pp. stem of *trahere* draw. So **treat** sb. †agreement, treaty XIV; entertainment XVII. **treatise** book or writing in which a subject is treated. XIV. - AN. *tretis*, OF. **traitiz*. Hence **treatment** XVI.

treaty †literary treatment, discussion XIV; discussion of terms; covenant, contract XV. ME. *trete(e)* - AN. *treté*, (O)F. *traité* :- L. *tractātus* TRACTATE; see -Y[5].

treble threefold, triple XIV; sb. quantity 3 times as great as another XV; (mus.) highest or upper part in a harmonized composition, soprano XIV. - OF. - L. *triplus* TRIPLE. The development of the mus. use is obscure.

tree perennial plant having a woody stem and of considerable height and size; piece of wood (as in *axle t., cross t., swingle t., saddle t., boot t.*, and *treenail*) OE.; pedigree XIII. OE. *trēo(w)* = OS. *trio, treo* (MDu. *-tere*), ON. *tré*, Goth. *triu* :- Gmc. **trewam*, f. zero-grade of IE. **deru- *doru- *dru-*, repr. by Skr. *dắru, dru-* tree, Gr. *dóru*, pl. *doûra* wood, spear, Lith. *dervà* pinewood, OIr. *daur*, W. *derwen* oak. Hence **tre(e)nail** cylindrical pin of hard wood used in fastening timbers together. XIII.

trefa, trifa meat not slaughtered according to Jewish law. XIX. - Heb. *ṭ'rēphāh* flesh of an animal torn, as by a wild beast, f. *ṭāraph* tear, rend.

trefoil plant of the genus *Trifolium*, having triple leaves. XIV. ME. *treyfoyle, trifolie* - AN. *trifoil* - L. *trifolium*, f. TRI- + *folium* leaf, FOIL[2].

trek (S. Afr.) make a journey by ox wagon, (hence) travel. Also sb. XIX. - Afrikaans - (M)Du. *trekken* draw, pull, travel.

trellis grating used as a support or screen. XIV. ME. *trelis* - OF. *trelis, -ice* :- Rom. **trilīcius, -ia*, f. L. *trilīx, -līc-*, f. TRI- + *līcium* thread of a warp.

tremble XIV. - (O)F. *trembler* :- Rom. **tremulāre*, rel. to L. *tremulus* TREMULOUS.

tremendous terrific, dreadful XVII; immense XIX. f. L. *tremendus*, gerundive of *tremere* tremble, tremble at, rel. to TREMOR; see -OUS.

tremolando (mus.) with tremulous effect. XIX. - It., prp. of *tremolare* tremble. So **tremolo** XIX.

tremor †terror XIV; involuntary shaking of the body; tremulous movement, as of the earth XVII. - OF. *tremour* and (later) L. *tremor*, rel. to *tremere*, Gr. *trémein* tremble. So **tremulous** XVII. f. L. *tremulus*.

trenail see TREE.

trench †track cut through a forest XIV; long narrow excavation XV. - OF. *trenche* cutting, cut, ditch, slice, f. *trenchier* (mod. *trancher*) cut (whence **trench** vb. XV) :- Rom. **trincāre* - L. *truncāre*.

trenchant cutting (lit. and fig.). XIV. - OF. *trenchant* (mod. *tranchant*), prp. of *trancher*; see prec., -ANT.

trencher †cutting instrument; board on which food was served XIV (hence *t.-man* feeder, eater XVI); (also *t.-cap*) academic cap thought to resemble a square platter XVIII. - AN. *trenchour*, OF. *trencheoir*, f. *trenchier* cut; see TRENCH, -ER[2], -OR[1].

trend †revolve, roll OE.; take a specified direction XVI. OE. *trendan*, f. Gmc. **trend- *trand- *trund-*, repr. also by OE. *trinda* round lump, ball, *ātrendlian* roll away; cf. TRUNDLE. Hence **trend** sb. the way something turns away, general direction. XVIII.

trental set of thirty requiem masses. XIV. - OF. *trentel* and medL. *trentālis*, f. popL. **trenta*, for L. *trīginta* thirty.

trepan (surg.) saw for cutting out pieces of bone. XIV. - medL. *trepanum* - Gr. *trúpanon* borer, f. *trupân* pierce, bore. So vb. and **trepanation** XIV. - (O)F. *trépaner, trépanation*.

trepidation tremulous agitation, flurry; vibration, tremor. XVII. - L. *trepidātiō, -ōn-*, f. *trepidāre*, f. *trepidus* alarmed, agitated; see -ATION.

trespass transgression XIII; actionable wrong or offence XIV. - OF. *trespas* (mod. *trépas*), f. vb. *trespasser* (whence **trespass** vb. XIV) - medL. *transpassāre*; see TRANS-, PASS[2].

tress plait or long lock of hair. XIII. - (O)F. *tresse*, †*tresce*, of unkn. orig.

-tress comp. suffix formed by the addition of -ESS[1] to sbs. in *-ter, -tor*, as *actor/actress, hunter/huntress*.

tressure †headdress XIV; (her.) diminutive orle XV; (numismatics) circular enclosure XVIII. ME. *tressour* - OF. :- L. **triciātōrium*; later *tressure* - OF. *tress(e)ure*. See TRESS, -URE.

trestle XIV. - OF. *trestel* (mod. *tréteau*) :- Rom. **transtellum*, dim. of L. *transtrum* beam; see -EL².

tret allowance of 4 lb. in 104 lb., after deduction of tare. XV. poss. - AN., OF. *tret*, var. of *trait* draught, but the sense-development is obscure.

trews close-fitting trousers. XVI (Sc.). - Ir. *trius*, Gael. *triubhas* (sg.).

trey three at cards, etc. XIV. - OF. *trei(s)* (mod. *trois*) :- L. *trēs* THREE.

tri- repr. (partly through F.) L. and Gr. *tri-*, comb. form of L. *trēs*, Gr. *treîs* THREE.

triad set of three. XVI. - F. *triade* or late L. *trias*, *-ad-* - Gr. *triás*, *-ad-*, f. TRI-; see -AD.

trial act of trying, fact of being tried. XVI. - AF. *trial*, also *triel*, f. *trier* TRY; see -AL².

triangle three-sided figure. XIV. - (O)F. *triangle* or L. *triangulum*, sb. use of n. of *triangulus* three-cornered, f. TRI- + *angulus* ANGLE². So **triangular** XVI. - late L.; see -AR.

trias three, triad XVII; (geol., after G. *trias*) series of strata between the Jurassic and Permian, so called because divisible into three groups XIX. - late L. - Gr. *triás* TRIAD. Hence **triassic** XIX.

tribe community claiming a common ancestor, spec. each of the 12 divisions of Israel XIII; political division of the ancient Roman people XVI; race of people; class or set of persons; group in the classification of animals, etc. XVII. First in pl. †*tribuz*, †*tribus* - (O)F. *tribus*, pl. of *tribu*, or L. *tribūs*, pl. of *tribus*, whence immed. *tribe* (XIV). Hence **tribal** (-AL¹) XVII, **tribesman** (-S) XVIII.

triblet cylindrical rod for forging nuts, etc. XVII. - F. *triboulet*, of unkn. orig.

tribrach (pros.) foot of 3 short syllables. XVI. - L. *tribrachys* - Gr. *tríbrakhus*, f. TRI- + *brakhús* short.

tribulation XIII. - (O)F. - ecclL. *trībulātiō*, *-ōn-*, f. L. *trībulāre* press, oppress, afflict, f. *trībulum* threshing-sledge, f. **trī-*, var. of **ter(e)-* rub.

tribune¹ officer in the administration of ancient Rome. XIV. - L. *tribūnus*, prob. orig. sb. use of adj. f. *tribus* TRIBE. So **tribunal** dais, raised throne, judgement seat; court of justice XVI; place of judgement, judicial authority XVII. - (O)F. *tribunal* or L. *tribūnal(e)*.

tribune² saloon in the Galleria degli Uffizi in Florence, Italy XVII; apse of a basilica XVIII; dais, rostrum, bishop's throne. - F. - It. *tribuna* - medL. *tribūna*, for L. *tribūnal*.

tribute tax paid to a superior XIV; transf. and fig. XVI. - L. *tribūtum*, sb. use of n. of *tribūtus*, pp. of *tribuere* assign, allot, grant, prop. to divide among the tribes, f. *tribus* TRIBE. So **tributary** adj. paying tribute XIV; paid in tribute XVI; subsidiary, auxiliary XVII; sb. one who pays tribute XIV; tributary stream XIX. - L. *tribūtārius*.

trice phr. †*at a t.*, *in a t.* in an instant, instantly. XV. f. *trice* vb. pull, haul - MDu. *trīsen* (Du. *trijsen* hoist) = MLG. *trīssen*, rel. to MDu. *trīse*, etc. windlass, pulley, of unkn. orig.

-trice suffix of fem. agent-nouns, F. repr. of -TRIX.

triceps having three heads or (of a muscle) points of origin. XVI. - L. *triceps*, f. TRI- + *-ceps*, adj. comb. form corr. to *caput* HEAD.

trichinosis disease due to trichinae (parasitic worms) in the alimentary canal. XIX. f. modL. *trichina*, f. Gr. *tríkhinos* of hair, f. *thríx*, *trikh-* hair; see -INE², -OSIS.

tricho-, before a vowel **trich-**, repr. comb. form *trikho-* of Gr. *thríx* hair.

trichotomy threefold division. XVII. f. Gr. *tríkha* in three, triply, after DICHOTOMY.

trick A. crafty or mean device XV; dexterous artifice XVI; B. (bad or unpleasant) habit XVI; C. (her.) sketch of a coat of arms XVI; D. cards played and won in a round XVI. - OF. *trique*, dial. var. of *triche*, f. *trichier* (mod. *tricher*) deceive, cheat. Hence (presumably) **trick** vb. A. cheat; B. attire, deck; C. sketch, draw in outline. XVI. **trickery** XVIII. **tricksy** (-SY) smart, spruce XVI; playful, whimsical; ticklish XIX. **tricky** (-Y¹) deceitful XVIII; difficult to handle XIX.

trickle flow in successive drops. Forms with variation of vowel and cons. have been current since XIV, viz. *trygle*, *tri(n)kle*, *trekel*, *tri(n)gle*. of imit. orig.; see -LE³. Hence sb. XVI.

triclinium couch on three sides of a dining table. XVII. - L. *triclīnium* - Gr. *triklínion*, dim. of *triklīnos* dining room with three couches, f. TRI- + *klī́nē* couch.

tricolour, -color three-coloured, esp. of the red, white, and blue French national flag. XVIII. - F. *tricolore* - late L. *tricolor*, *-ōr-*, f. TRI- + *color* COLOUR.

tricorne three-horned (creature, hat). XVIII. - F. *tricorne* or L. *tricornis*, f. TRI- + *cornū* HORN.

tricycle XIX. f. TRI- + CYCLE.

trident three-pronged instrument. XVI. - L. *tridēns*, *-dent-*, f. TRI- + *dēns* TOOTH.

Tridentine pert. to the city of Trent (Trento) in N. Italy and the Council of the Roman Catholic Church held there 1545–63. XVI. - medL. *Tridentīnus*, f. *Tridentum* Trent; see -INE¹.

triennial lasting three years; recurring every three years. XVII. f. late L. *triennis* of three years, *triennium* period of three years, f. TRI- + *annus* year; see ANNUAL, -AL¹.

trifid divided into three. XVIII. - L. *trifidus*, f. TRI- + *fid-*, base of *findere* split.

trifle †false or idle tale XIII; matter of little value; trinket, knick-knack XIV; slight piece, small sum XVI; light confection. ME. *truf(f)le* - OF., by-form of *truf(f)e* deceit, gibe, of unkn. orig. Hence **trifle** vb. XIV (earlier †*bitrufle* cheat, delude XIII).

triforium (archit.) gallery in the wall over the arches at the sides of nave and choir. - AL. (XII; taken up by antiquaries XVIII); of unkn. orig.

trigger movable catch or lever. XVII (*tricker*). - Du. *trekker*, f. *trekken* pull; see -ER¹.

triglyph (archit.) in the Doric order, block with three vertical grooves. XVI. - L. *triglyphus* - Gr. *tríglyphos*, f. TRI- + *gluphḗ* carving.

trigonometry branch of mathematics dealing with the measurements of triangles. XVII. - modL. *trigōnometria*, f. Gr. *trigōnon* triangle; see TRI-, -GON, -METRY.

trilby man's soft felt hat; (pl.) bare feet. XIX. Name of the heroine of the novel 'Trilby' (1893), by George du Maurier, as applied to a kind of hat used in the dramatized version, and to the heroine's use of bare feet.

trill tremulous utterance of a note XVII; vibration of tongue, etc. in pronouncing a consonant XIX. - It. *trillo*, †*triglio*. So **trill** vb. XVII. - It. *trillare*.

trillion third power of a million (in France and U.S.A., a thousand billions). XVII. - F. *trillion* or It. *trilione*, formed like BILLION on *million* with substitution of TRI-.

trilobite member of a group of extinct arthropodous animals having a three-lobed body. XIX. - modL. *trilobītes*; see TRI-, LOBE, -ITE.

trilogy XIX. - Gr. *trilogíā*; see TRI-, -LOGY.

trim well equipped, esp. neatly made. XVI. Earliest in the adv. *trimly*; rel. to **trim** vb., which became widely applied in the first half of XVI, but is of obscure orig., since, though formally it could repr. OE. *trymian*, *trymman* strengthen, confirm (f. *trum* firm, strong), there is no certain connecting evidence between OE. and 1500. Hence **trim** sb. trim condition (often of a ship), proper array or equipment. XVI. **trimmer** (-ER[1]) one who trims. XVI (spec. in statecraft, between opposing parties XVII).

trimeter (pros.) verse of three measures. XVI. - L. *trimetrus* - Gr. *trímetros*, f. TRI- + *métron* measure.

trine triple XIV; (astrol.) pert. to the aspect of two heavenly bodies that are a third part of the zodiac distant from each other XV; fig. benign. - OF. *trin*, fem. *trine* :- L. *trīnus*, *-a* threefold, f. *trēs*, *tria* THREE.

trinity (*T-*) being of God in three Persons XIII; (*t-*) set of three. - (O)F. *trinité* :- L. *trīnitās*, *-tāt-*, triad, trio, f. *trīnus* TRINE; see -ITY. So **trinitarian** XVI. The earliest uses are †(1) holding unorthodox opinions about the Trinity, (2) belonging to the order of the Holy Trinity XVII; since XVIII the sense 'relating to the Trinity, holding the doctrine of the Trinity' has been established. f. modL. *trīnitārius*.

trinket †small article belonging to an outfit; small ornament or decoration. XVI. of unkn. orig.

trinomial (math., etc.) consisting of three terms. XVIII. f. TRI- + *-nomial* of BINOMIAL.

trio composition for three voices or instruments. XVIII. - It. (partly through F.), f. L. *trēs*, *tria* THREE.

triolet (pros.) stanza of 8 lines in which the 1st line is repeated as the 4th and 7th and the 2nd as the 8th. XVII. - F., f. *trio*; see prec., -LET.

trip A. tread or step lightly XIV; B. cause to stumble by striking the foot (feet) from under the body; make a false step XV; C. (naut.) †tack XVII; raise (an anchor) clear from the bottom XVIII. - OF. *treper*, *trip(p)er* - MDu. *trippen* skip, hop, rel. to OE. *treppan* tread, trample. Hence sb. A. act of tripping XV; B. light movement with the feet XVI; short journey XVII. **tripper** (-ER[1]) one who trips XIV; excursionist XIX.

tripartite XIV. - L. *tripartītus*, f. TRI- + pp. of *partīrī* divide, PART.

tripe stomach of an ox, etc. used for food. XIII. - (O)F. *tripe*, It. *trippa*, of unkn. orig.

triphthong combination of three vowels in one syllable. XVI. - F. *triphtongue*, f. TRI-, after DIPHTHONG.

triple adj. XVI; sb. XV. - (O)F. *triple* or L. *triplus* - Gr. *triploûs*, f. TRI- + *pl-* (see FOLD[2]), for L. *triplex* (whence **triplex** XVII). So **triplicate** adj. XV; sb. XVIII. - L. *triplicātus*, pp. of *triplicāre*, f. *triplex*, *-ic-*. **triplicity** threefold condition; division into three groups of the signs of the Zodiac. XIV. - late L. *triplicitās*. Hence **triplet** set of three, as of lines of verse (XVII), notes of music (XIX); one of three at a birth (XVIII).

tripod three-legged vessel or support (spec. stool). XVII. - L. *tripūs*, *-pod-* - Gr. *trípous*, *-pod-*, f. TRI- + *poús* FOOT.

tripos †tripod XVI; at Cambridge Univ., formerly, bachelor of arts appointed to dispute humorously at Commencement (so called from the tripod on which he sat), (hence) set of verses written for this, (later) list of candidates qualified for honours in mathematics printed on the back of the paper containing the verses, (subsequently) final honours examination for the bachelor's degree, first in mathematics, later in other subjects XVII. Unexpl. alt. of L. *tripūs* TRIPOD.

triptych tablet or card folded in three XVIII; picture or carving hinged in three divisions XIX. f. TRI-, after DIPTYCH.

triquetrous three-cornered. XVII. f. L. *triquetrus*; see -OUS.

trireme ancient galley with three banks of oars. XVII. - (O)F. *trirème* or L. *trirēmis*, f. TRI- + *rēmus* oar.

Trisagion (liturg.) Eucharistic hymn beginning with a threefold invocation of God ('Holy, Holy, Holy') XVII. - Gr. *triságion*, n. of *triságios*, f. *trís* thrice + *hágios* holy.

trisect XVII. f. TRI- + *sect-*, pp. stem of L. *secāre* cut.

triste dismal, gloomy. XVIII. - F. - L. *tristis*. Anglicized *trist* (now obs.) from XV.

tritagonist third actor in a Gr. tragedy. XIX. - Gr. *tritagōnistḗs*, f. *trítos* THIRD + *agōnistḗs* actor.

trite worn out by use. XVI. - L. *trītus*, pp. of *terere* rub.

Triton (Gr. and Rom. myth.) sea-god, son of Poseidon and Amphitrite XVI; (*t-*) genus of marine gasteropods XVIII. - L. *Trītōn* - Gr. *Trī́tōn*.

triturate pulverize. XVII. f. pp. stem. of late L. *trītūrāre* thresh corn, f. L. *trītūra* rubbing, threshing, f. *trīt-*, pp. stem of *terere* rub; see -URE, -ATE[3].

triumph (Rom. hist.) solemn entry of a victorious general into Rome; victorious achievement XIV. - OF. *triumphe* (mod. *triomphe*) - L. *triumphus*, earlier *triumpus*, prob. - Gr. *thríambos* hymn to Bacchus. So vb. XVI. **triumphal** (-AL[1]), **triumphant** (-ANT) XV. - (O)F. or L.

triumvir (Rom. hist.) one of a board of three magistrates. XVI. - L., sg. deduced from pl. *triumvirī*, back-formation from *trium virōrum*, g. pl. of *trēs virī* three men. So **triumvirate** (-ATE[1]) XVI. - L. *trium virātus*.

triune (of the Godhead) three in one. XVII. f. TRI- + L. *ūnus* ONE. So **triunity** XVII.

trivet stand or support for a pot, etc., orig. three-footed. XV. ME. *trevet*, repr. OE. *trefet* (once) - L. *tripēs, -ped-*, f. TRI- + *pēs* FOOT.

trivial pert. to the trivium of medieval learning XV; †such as may be met with anywhere XVI; of small account; (nat. hist.) specific XVIII, popular XIX. - L. *triviālis*, f. next; see -AL[1].

trivium in the Middle Ages, the lower division of the seven liberal arts (grammar, rhetoric, logic), the upper four (**quadrivium**; see QUADRI-) being arithmetic, geometry, astronomy, and music. XIX. - medL. use of L. *trivium* place where three roads meet, f. TRI- + *via* way.

-trix suffix of L. fem. agent-nouns corr. to m. -TOR, as *adjūtrix, imperātrīx, venātrīx*, fems. of *adjūtor* helper, *imperātor* commander, *venātor* hunter; such sbs. were adopted from XV from L. of various periods, as *administratrix, executrix, testatrix*; (geom.) applied to certain straight lines or curves, as *directrix*.

troche flat round tablet or lozenge. XVI. Early in pl. *trochies, trotches*, alt. of *trocis(ce), -iske* (XIV-XVIII) - F. *trochisque* - late L. *trochiscus* - Gr. *trokhískos* small wheel or globe, pill, lozenge, dim. of *trokhós* wheel.

trochee (pros.) foot consisting of a long followed by a short syllable (— ᴗ). XVI. - L. *trochæus* - Gr. *trokhaios* running, tripping, f. *trókhos* running, course, rel. to *trékhein* run. So **trochaic** XVI. - L. *trochaicus* - Gr. *trokhaikós*.

trochilus small Egyptian bird said to have picked crocodile's teeth. XVI. - L., - Gr. *trokhílos*, f. var. stem of *trékhein* run.

troglodyte cave-dweller (chiefly prehistoric). XVI. - L. *trōglodyta* - G. *trōglodútēs*, corrupt form of *trōgodútēs*, after *trṓglē* hole.

troika Russ. vehicle drawn by three horses abreast. XIX. - Russ. *tróĭka*, f. *tróe* THREE.

Trojan pert. to, native of, ancient Troy; roisterer, good fellow; brave fellow. XVII. repl. earlier *Troian* (XIV), *Troyan* (XV) - L. *Trōiānus*, f. *Trōia* Troy; see -AN. OE. had *Troiānisc*.

troll[1] †A. move about or to and fro XIV; B. roll, bowl XV; C. sing in full round voice XVI; D. angle with a running line XVII. of unkn. orig.; cf. F. *trôler* (†*troller*) wander casually, (M)HG. *trollen* stroll, toddle.

troll[2] (Scand. myth.) one of a supernatural race of giants, dwarfs, or imps. XIX. (preceded by a Sc. ex. of XVII). - ON., Sw. *troll*; of unkn. orig.

trolley XIX. Presumably f. TROLL[1]; cf. dial. *troll* (XVII).

trollop XVII. of unkn. orig.; cf. TRULL.

trombone XVIII. - F. *trombone* (earlier †*trombon*) or its source It. *trombone*, augm. of *tromba* TRUMP[1]; cf. -OON.

tronometer instrument for measuring earth-tremors. XIX. f. Gr. *trómos* trembling + -METER.

troop body of soldiers, (pl.) armed forces; number of persons collected together XVI; signal on a drum for assembling troops XVII. - F. *troupe*, poss. back-formation from *troupeau* flock, herd, dim. f. medL. *troppus* herd of mares, prob. of Gmc. orig. Hence **troop** vb. gather in a troop XVI; *t. the colour* beat the drum for the reception of the colour at the mounting of the guard XVII. **trooper** (-ER[1]) cavalry soldier. XVII.

tropaeolum S. Amer. genus of herbs. XVIII. - modL., f. L. *tropæum* TROPHY; so called from the resemblance of the leaf to a shield and of the flower to a helmet.

trope (rhet.) use of a word or phrase in a sense not proper to it, figure of speech XVI; (liturg.) phrase introduced into the text for musical embellishment XIX. - L. *tropus* figure of speech - Gr. *trópos* turn, rel. to *trépein* vb. turn. So **troper** book of tropes. OE. *tropere* - medL. *troperium*, var. of *tropārium*.

trophic pert. to nutrition. XIX. - Gr. *trophikós*, f. *trophḗ* nourishment.

tropho- comb. form of Gr. *trophḗ* nourishment.

trophy erection serving as a memorial of victory in war; prize, booty; monument, memorial. XVI. - F. *trophée* - L. *trophæum*, earlier *tropæum* - Gr. *trópaion*, sb. use of n. of *tropaîos*, f. *tropḗ* turning, putting to flight, defeat, rel. to *trépein* turn.

tropic †each of the two solstitial points XIV; each of the two circles of the celestial sphere touching the ecliptic at the solstitial points XVI; either boundary of the torrid zone; pl. region between these XIX; adj. tropical XVI. - late L. *tropicus* - Gr. *tropikós* (1) pert. to the 'turning' of the sun at the solstice, (2) fig., f. *tropḗ* turning; see prec., -IC. So **tropical** pert. to a tropic XVI (of the torrid zone XVII); metaphorical XVI.

trot gait of a quadruped between walking and running. XIII. - (O)F., f. *troter* (mod. *trotter*), whence **trot** vb. XIV; Rom. **trottāre*, of Gmc. orig.; cf. OHG. *trottōn* (G. *trotten*), intensive f. base of *tretan* step, walk, TREAD. Hence **trotter** (-ER[1]) trotting horse XIV; (pl.) feet of a quadruped, esp. used for food (?XIV) XVI.

troth (arch.) plighted word XV; good faith, loyalty XVI; †truth. Later form of ME. *trouth(e)*, *trowth(e)*, var. with stress-shifting and assim. to TROW of *treowþ* TRUTH.

troubadour Provençal lyric poet. XVIII. - F. - Pr. *trobador* = OF. *trovere*, obl. *troveor* TROUVÈRE, f. Pr. *trobar*, OF. *trover* (mod. *trouver*) compose, (later) invent, find.

trouble mental distress XIII; public disturbance XIV; pains, exertion; *in* or *into tr.* liable to punishment, etc. XVII. - OF. *truble, t(o)urble* (mod. *trouble*), f. *tourbler*, etc. (mod. *troubler*), whence **trouble** vb. XIII. :- Rom. **turbulāre*, f. **turbulus*, for L. *turbidus* TURBID. So **troublous** XV. - OF. *troubleus*. Hence **troublesome** †full of trouble; giving trouble. XVI.

trough oblong open vessel, esp. to contain liquid OE.; channel, pipe XIV; hollow, valley XVI; *t. of the sea* hollow on the surface between waves XVII. OE. *trog* = OS. *trog*, OHG. *troc* (Du., G. *trog*), ON. *trog* :- Gmc. **truʒaz* :- IE. **drukós*, f. **dru-* wood, TREE.

trounce †afflict, harass; thrash, belabour XVI; censure severely XVIII. of unkn. orig.

troupe company of players, dancers, etc. XIX. - F.; see TROOP.

trousers †trews; loose-fitting garment for the

loins and legs XVII. Extension, after DRAWERS, of (arch.) *trouse* (XVI) - Ir., Gael. *triubhas* TREWS.

trousseau bride's outfit of clothes, etc. XIX. - F., dim. of *trousse* TRUSS.

trout Late OE. *truht* - late L. *tructa*.

trouvère one of a school of epic poets of N. France. XVIII (*trouveur*). - F., and OF. *trovere*, obl. *troveor* = Pr. *trobador* TROUBADOUR.

trove short for TREASURE TROVE.

trover (leg.) act of finding and keeping possession of a property. XVI. - AN. sb. use of OF. *trover* (mod. *trouver* find); see -ER[6].

trow (arch., esp. in *I trow*) believe, suppose. of mixed orig.; (1) OE. *trēow(i)an*, f. *trēow* faith, etc.; (2) OE. *truwian*, f. *truwa* faith, etc.

trowel XIV. ME. *truel*, *trowel* - OF. *truele* (mod. *truelle*) - medL. *truella*, alt. of L. *trulla* ladle, scoop, f. *trua* skimmer, spoon.

troy system of weights used for precious stones and metals. XIV. orig. in phrs. *marc. de troye*, *pound of troye*; said to be taken from a weight used at the fair of *Troyes*, in France.

truant †sturdy beggar, idle rogue XIII; pupil absent from school without leave XV; adj. XVI. - OF. *truant* (mod. *truand*) :- Gallo-Rom. **trūgant-*, prob. of Celt. orig. (cf. W. *truan*, Gael. *truaghan* wretched).

truce XIII. ME. *trew(e)s*, *trues* (repl. OE. pl. *trēowa*, used as sg.), pl. of *tru(w)e*, OE. *trēow*, corr. to OS. *treuwa* (Du. *trouw*), OHG. *triuwa* (G. *treue*), Goth. *triggva* covenant; rel. to Gr. *droós* firm, OIr. *derb*, W. *drūd* strong; cf. TRUE, TRUST.

trucial pert. to a truce (1835) regulating the relations of Arab sheikhs to each other and to the British Government. XIX. f. TRUCE + -IAL.

truck[1] give in exchange XIII; barter away XVII; pay otherwise than in money XIX. ME. *trukie*, later *trukke* - AN. **truquer*, OF. **troquer* (reflected in medL. *trocāre*), of unkn. orig. Hence sb. (cf. AN. *truke* XIV) barter XVI; dealings, traffic XVII; payment in kind, goods supplied instead of wages XVIII.

truck[2] small solid wooden wheel or block XVII; wheeled vehicle for heavy weights XVIII. poss. shortening of next.

truckle pulley, sheave; small roller or wheel under a bed, etc. XV; (short for *t.-bed* XV) low bed running on castors, usu. pushed under a high bed when not in use XVII. ME. *trocle*, *trokel*, *trookyll* - AN. *trocle* - L. *trochlea* - Gr. *trokhil(e)iā* sheaf of a pulley. Hence vb. †occupy a truckle-bed XV; yield obsequiously *to* XVII.

truculent XVI. - L. *truculentus*, f. *trux*, *truc-* fierce, savage; see -ULENT.

trudge †be off, depart; walk laboriously XVI. Early forms also †*tredge*, (dial.) *tridge*; of unkn. orig.

trudgen swimming stroke familiarized by one John *Trudgen* about 1865. XIX.

true steadfast; trustworthy OE.; consistent with fact XIII; real, genuine XIV. OE. *ġetrīewe*, *trēowe*, later *trȳwe* (ME. *trewe*, *tru(we)*) = OS. *triuwi* (Du. *getrouw*), OHG. *gitriuwi* (G. *treu*), ON. *tryggr*, Goth. *triggws*, f. the Gmc. sb. repr. by TRUCE. The sp. *true* dates from XV.

truffle XVI. prob. - Du. *truffel*, †*truffele* - F. *truffle* (now *truffe*), perh. to be referred ult. to popL. **tūfera*, for L. *tūbera*, pl. of *tūber* TUBER.

truism XVIII. f. TRUE + -ISM.

trull (arch.) drab, trollop; †girl, wench. XVI. of unkn. orig.; cf. TROLLOP.

truly adv. of TRUE, OE. *trēowliċe*; see -LY[2].

trump[1] (arch.) trumpet. XIII. ME. *trompe* - (O)F., of Gmc. orig. (cf. OHG. *trumpa*, *trumba*, ON. *trumba*, prob. of imit. orig.). So **trump** vb. XIII - (O)F. *tromper*.

trump[2] card of a suit that ranks above all others XVI; first-rate fellow XIX. alt. of TRIUMPH, also used in this sense and for an obs. card-game. Hence **trump** vb. put a trump on (a trick); †get in the way XVI; †bring *up* or forward XVII; get *up* unscrupulously.

trumpery †fraud, trickery XV; trash, rubbish XVI; adj. paltry, trashy XVI. - (O)F. *tromperie*, f. *tromper* deceive, of unkn. orig.; see -ERY.

trumpet sb. XIII. - (O)F. *trompette*, dim. of *trompe* TRUMP[1]; see -ET. Hence, or - (O)F. *trompeter*, *-eur*, **trumpet** vb. XVI, **trumpeter** XV.

truncated XV. - f. L. *truncātus*, f. *truncus* TRUNK; see -ATE[2], -ED[1]. So **truncation** XVI. - late L.

truncheon †piece broken off; †fragment or shaft of a spear XIII; short thick staff; staff as symbol of authority XVI. - OF. *tronchon* (mod. *tronçon*), repr. Rom. **trunciō*, *-ōn-*, f. L. *truncus* TRUNK.

trundle small wheel, roller, or revolving disc. XVI. So vb. roll, bowl. XVI. Earlier in *trundle-tail* curly-tailed dog (XV) and *trundle-bed* truckle-bed (XVI). The late appearance of this form as compared with *trendle* (OE. *trendel* circular or spherical object) and *trindle* (early ME. *trindel* wheel) involves difficulty in connecting it with OE. words containing *u* or its mutation *y*, as in *trundulnis* circuit, *sintrundel*, *-tryndel* round, *healftryndel* hemisphere; for the basic forms cf. TREND; see -LE[1].

trunk A. main stem of a tree XV; B. human or animal body XV; C. chest, box XV; D. (assoc. partly with TRUMP[1]) †pipe, tube; elephant's proboscis XVI; E. †pl. trunk-hose XVI; short breeches XIX. ME. *tron(c)k* - (O)F. *tronc* :- L. *truncus*. comp. **trunk-hose** (hist.) full bag-like breeches. XVII.

trunnion each of a pair of gudgeons on a cannon XVII; each of a pair of similar supports XVIII. - (O)F. *trognon*, of unkn. orig.

truss bundle, pack XIII; (naut.) tackle or fitting for a yard; (surg.) supporting appliance XVI. - OF. *trusse*, *torse* (mod. *trousse*), perh. f. OF. *trusser* (mod. *trousser*), whence **truss** vb. XIII; of unkn. orig.

trust confidence XIII; reliability, fidelity XV; thing or person committed to one XVII; (short for *t. company*) body of traders controlling a business XIX. So vb. have confidence (in). XIII. of obscure history; early ME. forms of sb., adj., and vb. are *trust(e)* (beside *trūst(e)*, *trist(e)*, *trest(e)*), corr. to a possible OE. **tryst*, **trystan*, and *trost(e)* (presumably - ON. *traust* help, support, confidence, *traustr* firm, strong, confident; parallel forms are MLG., MDu. *trost* (Du. *troost*), (O)HG. *trōst* consolation, Goth. *trausti* covenant), the formation being ult. that of an abstr. noun on the base **tru-* of TRUE, TROW. Hence **trusty** (-Y[1]) XIII, **trustee** (-EE[1]) XVII.

truth quality of being true, †faith, loyalty OE.; something that is true XIV. OE. *trīewð, trēowð* corr. to OHG. *triuwida*, ON. (pl.) *trygðir* plighted faith, f. *-trīewe, trēowe* TRUE; see -TH[1]. Hence **truthful** (of statements, etc.) XVI; (of persons) XVIII; (of ideas, artistic or literary presentation, etc.) XIX.

try A. examine and determine, esp. judicially XIII; †B. separate XIV; C. test; attempt XIV; D. (naut.) lie to XVI (hence **trysail** XVIII). - OF. *trier* sift, pick out, of unkn. orig.

trypanosome genus of protozoa, species of which are parasitic in the blood. XIX. f. Gr. *trúpanon* borer + *sôma* body.

trypsin chief digestive enzyme of the pancreatic juice. XIX. perh. for **tripsin*, f. Gr. *tripsis* rubbing, f. *tríbein* rub; so named because first obtained by rubbing down the pancreas with glycerin; see -IN.

tryst mutual appointment to meet. XIV (chiefly Sc. before XIX). spec. use of †*trist*, at first prob. extension of the sense 'appointed station in hunting', var. of †*tristre* - OF. *trist(r)e*.

tsar see CZAR.

tsetse Afr. fly of genus *Glossina*. XIX. - Tswana.

tuatara large lizard having a dorsal row of spines. XIX. - Maori, f. *tua* on the back + *tara* spine.

tub open wooden vessel of staves and hoops XIV; (orig. *bathing tub*) XVI; heavily-built boat XVII; (joc.) pulpit (hence †*tubman*, †*tubpreacher*, *tub-thumper*). prob. of LG. or Du. orig. (cf. MLG., MDu. *tubbe*).

tuba XIX. - It. - L. *tuba* war trumpet.

tube XVII. - F. *tube* or L. *tubus*, rel. to *tuba* (see prec.).

tuber thickened portion of the underground stem of a plant. XVII. - L. *tūber* hump, swelling. So **tubercle** small rounded projection XVI; (path.) swelling or nodule XVII. - L. *tūberculum*, dim. of *tūber*. **tubercular, tuberculous** XVIII. **tuberculosis** disease characterized by the formation of tubercles (tubercle-bacilli). XIX.

tuberose[1] plant *Polianthes tuberosa*, having a tuberous root. XVII. - L. fem. of *tūberōsus* (see next).

tuberose[2] tuberous. XVIII - F. *tubéreux* or L. *tūberōsus*; see -OSE[1]. So **tuberosity** XVI. **tuberous** of the form or nature of a tuber. XVII; see -OUS.

tubi- comb. form of L. *tubus* TUBE.

tubule small tubular structure. XVII. - L. *tubulus*, dim. of *tubus* TUBE. So **tubular** XVII.

tuck fold or pleat of drapery XIV; gathering of ends XVII; hearty meal XIX (hence *tuck-shop* pastry-cook's shop). f. **tuck** vb. pull or gather up; put up or away XIV; consume (food) XVIII (also intr. *tuck in* XIX) - MLG., MDu. *tucken* (= OHG. *zucchen*, G. *zucken* twitch, snatch), f. Gmc. base **teuχ-* (see TUG).

tucker piece of lace, etc. worn at the neck. XVII. f. TUCK, -ER[1].

tucket flourish on a trumpet. XVI. f. †*tuck* beat the drum, sound on a trumpet. XIV. - ONF. *toquer* = OF. *tochier* TOUCH; see -ET.

-tude suffix repr. F. *-tude*, L. *-tūdō, -tūdin-*, forming abstr. nouns on adjs., as *altitude, fortitude, gratitude, latitude, multitude*, derived from L. either directly or through F.

Tudor Welsh surname *Tewdwr* as that of the line of English sovereigns from Henry VII to Elizabeth I, descended from Owen Tudor, who married the widow of Henry V. XVIII.

Tuesday OE. *Tīwesdæġ* = OHG. *zīestag*, ON. *tý(r)sdagr*; f. g. of *Tīw* (= OHG. *Zīo*, ON. *Týr*), name of a Gmc. god identified with Mars :- Gmc. **Tīwaz*, cogn. with L. *deus*.

tufa (geol.) porous stone. XVIII. - †It. *tufa*, local var. of *tufo* - late L. *tōfus, tōphus*. So **tuff** XVI. - F. *tuf(f)e, tuf* - It. *tufo*.

tuffet tuft or tussock. XVI. prob. alt. of next by substitution of -ET.

tuft bunch as of hairs XIV (also *toft*); clump XVI; tassel on a cap, e.g. as worn by a titled undergraduate XVII. presumably - OF. *tof(f)e* (mod. *touffe*), of unkn. orig., with parasitic *t*.

tug vb. XIII (*togge*). f. weak grade of Gmc. **teuχ-* (repr. by OE. *tēon*, OHG. *ziohan*, G. *ziehen*) draw, pull :- IE. **deuk-* (repr. by L. *dūcere* lead). Hence **tug** sb. (chiefly pl.) chains, traces, studs, to maintain attachment, connection, etc. XIII; act of pulling, or struggling XVI; (dial.) timber waggon XVIII; small powerful vessel for towing XIX.

tuition †guardianship, tutelage XV; instruction of a pupil. XVI. - (O)F. - L. *tuitiō, -ōn-* protection, f. *tuērī* look after; see -ITION.

tulip XVII (earlier in forms *tulip(p)a, -ipan(t)* XVI) - modL. *tulipa*, F. †*tulipan, tulipe* - Turk. *tul(i)band* (now *tülbend*) TURBAN (the expanded flower was thought to resemble a turban).

tulle fine silk bobbin-net. XIX. - F., named from Tulle, in France, where it was first made.

tumble †dance with posturing; fall helplessly XIII; cause to fall XIV. - MLG. *tummelen* = OHG. *tumalōn* (G. *tummeln*), frequent. (see -LE[3]) f. base of OHG. *tūmōn* (MHG. *tūmen*), *tūmalōn* (G. *taumeln*); cf. OE. *tumbian* dance, MHG. *tumben*, ON. *tumba* tumble. Hence **tumbler** †acrobat XIV; lurcher XVI; variety of domestic pigeon XVII; footless goblet (made so as not to stand upright) XVII.

tumbrel, -il instrument of punishment XIV; tip-cart, dung-cart XV. - OF. *tomb-, tumberel* (mod. *tombereau*), f. *tomber* fall; see -EL[2].

tumid swollen. XVI. - L. *tumidus*, f. *tumēre* swell; see -ID[1]. So **tumour,** U.S. **tumor** †act of swelling, swollen condition; swollen part. XVI. - L. *tumor, -ōr-*; see -OUR[2], -OR[1].

tummy XIX. alt. (partly euph.) of STOMACH; see -Y[6].

tumult commotion of a multitude XV; (gen.) disturbance XVI. - (O)F. *tumulte* or L. *tumultus*. So **tumultuary** XVI. - L. *tumultuārius* (of troops) raised hastily. **tumultuous** XVI. - (O)F. or L.

tumulus pl. **-li** sepulchral mound. XVII. - L., rel. to *tumēre* swell.

tun large cask OE.; †tub, vat, etc. XIII; measure of wine, etc. equiv. to 4 hogsheads XV. OE. *tunne*, corr. to MLG., MDu. *tunne, tonne* (Du. *ton*),

OHG. *tunna* (G. *tonne*), late ON. *tunna* - medL. *tunna*, prob. of Gaul. orig.

tundra vast level treeless region of Russia. XIX. - Russ. *túndra*, of Lappish orig.

tune †sound, tone; air, melody XIV; proper intonation or pitch XV. ME. *tune*, *tewne*, unexpl. var. of TONE.

tungsten (min.) †calcium tungstate; heavy steel-grey metal. XVIII. - Sw., f. *tung* heavy + *sten* stone.

tunic body garment or coat of various kinds; (nat. hist.) sheath, integument. XVII. - F. *tunique* or L. *tunica*. So **tunicle** †small tunic XIV; dalmatic XV. - OF. *tunicle* (alt. of *tunique*) or L. *tunicula*, dim. of *tunica*; see -CLE.

tunnel †tubular net for catching birds XV; †shaft, flue XVI; subterranean passage XVIII. - OF. *tonel* (mod. *tonneau* tun, cask), f. *tonne* TUN; see -EL².

tunny large edible sea-fish. XVI. - (O)F. *thon* - Pr. *ton* :- L. *thunnus* - Gr. *thúnnos*; the ending *-y* is unexpl.

tup male sheep, ram. XIV. Chiefly north. and Sc. (in earliest use *to(u)pe*); of unkn. orig.

tupelo N. Amer. tree of the genus *Nyssa*. XVIII. of Creek orig.

turban Eastern headdress of Muslim origin. XVI. Three main types are repr. by *tolibant*, *tulipan*, *turban(t)* - F. †*tolliban*, †*tulban*, †*turbant* (mod. *turban*), It. †*tolipano*, *-ante*, Sp., Pg., It. *turbante* - Turk. *tülbend* - Pers. *dulband*.

turbary turf-land XIV; right to cut turf XVI. - AN. *turberie*, OF. *tourberie*, f. *tourbe* turf; see -ARY.

turbid thick with suspended matter; also fig. XVII. - L. *turbidus*, f. *turba* disturbance, crowd, beside *turbō* whirlwind, reel, whirl, spinning-top, perh. - Gr. *túrbē* confusion, disorder; see -ID¹. So **turbinal** (XVI), **turbinate** (XVII) top-shaped. f. L. *turben*, *-bin-*, var. of *turbō*; see -AL¹, -ATE².

turbine XIX. - F., - L. *turbō*, *-bin-* (see prec.). Comb. form **turbo-** XIX.

turbit small variety of domestic pigeon. XVII. prob. f. L. *turbō* top, from its shape.

turbot large flat-fish. XIII. - OF. - OSw. *törnbut*, f. *törn* thorn + *but* BUTT².

turbulent disorderly, unruly. XVI. - L. *turbulentus*, f. *turbāre* disturb, agitate, f. *turba* disturbance; see TURBID, -ULENT.

turd (piece of) excrement. OE. *tord* = MDu. *tort*, *torde* :- Gmc. **turdam* :- IE. **dr̥tom*, pp. formation on **dr̥-* **der-* TEAR².

tureen deep table vessel with a lid. XVIII (*terrene*, **terrine**). - F. *terrine* large circular flat-bottomed earthenware dish, sb. use of fem. of OF. *terrin* earthen :- Rom. **terrinus*, f. L. *terra* earth; see -INE¹.

turf sod of grass; greensward OE.; slab of peat XIII. OE. *turf*, corr., with variation of gender and declension, to OS. (Du.) *turf*, OHG. *zurba*, *zurf*, ON. *torf(a)*; Gmc. f. **turb-* :- IE. **dr̥bh-*, the base of Skr. *darbhá-* tuft of grass.

turgid swollen, distended XVII; of inflated style XVIII. - L. *turgidus*, f. *turgēre* swell; see -ID¹. So **turgescence** XVII, **-escent** XVIII.

turkey †guinea-fowl; large gallinaceous bird of Amer. orig. (genus *Meleagris*) XVI. The name of the country, first applied to the Afr. bird prob. because it was orig. brought from New Guinea by the Portuguese through Turkish dominions.

turmeric (powder made from) the root-stock of the East Indian plant, used in curry powder, etc. XVI. Early forms also *tarmaret*, *tormarith*, which appear to be - F. *terre mérite*, modL. *terra merita*, of unkn. orig.; the ending shows assim. to -IC.

turmoil †agitate, distress; †live or move in agitation; (dial.) toil, drudge. XVI. of unkn. orig. Hence **turmoil** sb. XVI.

turn vb. of extensive sense-development the basic notions of which are rotation and deviation from a course. OE. *tyrnan*, *turnian* - L. *tornāre*, f. *tornus* lathe - Gr. *tórnos* lathe, circular movement, taken to be cogn. with L. *terere* rub; prob. reinforced in ME. from OF. *turner*, *torner* (mod. *tourner*) :- L. *tornāre*. Comp. **turncoat** XVI. **turnkey** one who has charge of keys. XVII. **turn-out** action or manner of turning out. XVII. **turn-over** person or thing that is turned over or transferred XVII; tart of which one half is turned over the other XVIII; amount of business done, etc. XIX. **turnpike** spiked barrier XV; barrier for collection of toll XVII. **turnscrew** screwdriver. XIX. **turnspit** dog or person kept to turn a roasting spit. XVI. **turnstile** XVII. **turn-table** XIX. **turn-up** part of a garment that is turned up XVII; card turned up XIX. Hence **turn** sb. XIII (or - AN. *t(o)urn*). **turner** one who fashions objects of wood, etc. on a lathe. XIV. - OF. *tornere*, *-eor* - late L. *tornātor*, *-ōr-*. **turning-point** point marked by change of procedure. XIX.

turnip XVI (*turnep(e)*). The first el. is unexpl.; the second is *neep*, OE. *nǣp* - L. *nāpus* turnip.

turnsole violet blue or purple colouring matter XIV; plant yielding this, the flowers of which face the sun XVI. - (O)F. *tournesole* - Pr. *tournasol*, f. L. *tornāre* TURN + *sōl* sun.

turpentine orig. resin of the terebinth tree, (now) any oleo-resin from a conifer. XIV. - OF. *ter(e)bentine* - L. *ter(e)benthina*, f. *terebinthus* TEREBINTH; see -INE¹.

turpeth cathartic drug. XIV. earlier *turbit(h)* - medL. *turbit(h)um*, *turpetum* - Pers., Arab. *turbid*, *-bed*.

turpitude XV. - F. *turpitude* or L. *turpitūdō*, f. *turpis* base, disgraceful; see -TUDE.

turps (colloq.) XIX. f. first syll. of TURPENTINE, with coll. use of the pl. ending *-s*.

turquoise precious stone, of sky-blue to apple-green colour. XIV. ME. *turkeis*, later *turkes*, *turques* (XV), *turkoise*, *turquoise* (XVI) - OF. *turqueise*, later *-oise*, for *pierre turqueise* 'Turkish stone'; so called from being first known in Turkestan or conveyed through Turkish dominions.

turret XIV (*t(o)uret*). - OF. *to(u)rete*, dim. of *t(o)ur*, *tor* TOWER; see -ET.

turtle¹ dove of the genus *Streptopelia*. OE. *turtla* m., *turtle* fem. = OHG. *turtulo* m., *-ula* fem., also *turtulatūba* (G. *turteltaube*) = MLG. *torteldūve* (so **turtledove** XIII); in OE. and ME. also *turtur*, in ME. *turture* partly - OF. *turtre* (mod. *tourtre*) or ON. *turturi*; all - L. *turtur*, of imit. orig.

turtle[2] marine tortoise. XVII. perh. alt. of F. *tortue* TORTOISE. Phr. *turn t.* (orig. †*the t.*) capsize (XIX), with allusion to turning turtles over so as to incapacitate and capture them.

tusk long pointed tooth. XIII. Metathetic alt. of OE. *tux* (var. of *tusċ*) = OFris. *tusk*, *tosk*.

tussive pert. to a cough. XIX. f. L. *tussis* cough + -IVE.

tussle †pull or push roughly XV; struggle vigorously XVII. perh. f. (dial.) *touse* (whence TOUSLE); see -LE[3].

tussock tuft of hair XVI; tuft or matted growth of grass, etc. XVII. contemp. with synon. (dial.) *tusk* (of unkn. orig.), of which it is prob. an alt. form with assim. to -OCK.

tussore coarse brown silk. XVII (*tessar*, *-ur*). - Urdu - Hindi *tasar* shuttle :- Skr. *tásara-*.

tutelage guardianship as of a ward. XVII. f. L. *tūtēla* keeping, f. pp. stem of *tuērī* watch, look after; see -AGE. So **tutelary** XVII. - L. *tūtēlārius*.

tutenag alloy of copper, zinc, and nickel. XVII (also *too-*, *-aga*, *-agal*). - Marathi *tuttināg*, said to be f. Skr. *tuttha-* copper sulphate + *nāga* tin, lead.

tutor †guardian XIV; one employed as an instructor, esp. of youth; supervisor of an undergraduate XVII. - ME. *tutour* - AN., OF. *tutour* (mod. *tuteur*) or L. *tūtor*, agent-noun (see -TOR) f. *tuērī* look at or after, protect.

tutsan name of various plants to which healing properties are attributed. XV. - AN. †*tutsaine*, F. *toute-saine*, f. *toute* fem. of *tout* all, *saine* fem. of *sain* wholesome.

tutti (mus.) direction that all performers are to take part. XVIII. - It., pl. of *tutto* :- L. *tōtus* (see TOTAL).

tutty crude oxide of zinc. XIV (*tutie*). - OF. *tutie* - medL. *tutia* - Arab. *tūtiyā*.

tu whit tu whoo imit. of the call of an owl. XVI.

tuxedo (U.S.) dinner-jacket. XIX. f. name of a fashionable country club at *Tuxedo* Park, near New York.

tuyere nozzle conveying blast. XVIII. - F. *tuyère*, f. *tuyau* pipe.

twaddle sb. XVIII (also *twiddle-twaddle*). alt. of *twattle* (XVII) and †*twittle-twattle* (XVI); the corr. vb. (dial. *twattle*) is earlier (XVI) and varied formerly with †*twittle*, itself alt. of *tittle* (see TITTLE-TATTLE); *w* of the alt. forms is unexpl.

twain (arch.) two. OE. *tweġen*, corr. to OS. *twēne*, OHG. *zwēne* (G. arch. *zween*), nom. and acc. m. of the numeral of which fem. and n. are repr. by TWO.

twang sound produced by plucking string of bow, harp, etc. XVI; vocal sound modified by passage through the nose XVII; individual or local pronunciation. of imit. orig.

twayblade orchid of the genus *Listera*, etc., having two broad leaves. XVI. tr. medL. *bifolium*; f. *tway*, clipped form of TWAIN + BLADE.

tweak vb. XVII. prob. alt. of (dial.) *twick*, OE. *twiccian* = OHG. *zwicchan*, rel. to TWITCH. Hence sb. XVII.

tweed XIX. Trade name originating in a misreading of *tweel* or *tweeled*, Sc. forms of TWILL, TWILLED, assisted by assoc. with the river *Tweed*.

tweedle make a succession of sounds on a fiddle, etc. XVII. imit. of the sounds, combined playfully in *tweedledum and tweedledee* to indicate two rival musicians (XVIII).

tween aphetic of †*atween* or BETWEEN XIV. Hence **tweeny** (-Y[6]) between-maid (one assisting two others) XIX.

tweet sb. and vb. XIX. of imit. orig.

tweezers XVII. alt., by assoc. with *pincers*, etc., of †*tweezes*, pl. of †*tweeze* case of small instruments, aphetic of †*etweeze*, repr. pl. of ÉTUI.

twelve OE. *twelf*, inflected *twelfe* = OS. *twelif*, *twilif* (MDu. *twalef*, Du. *twaalf*), OHG. *zwelif* (G. *zwölf*), ON. *tólf*, Goth. *twalif* (*-lib*); Gmc., prob. f. **twa-* TWO + **lif-* as in ELEVEN. So **twelfth** OE. *twelfta* = MDu. *twalefde* (Du. *twaalfde*), OHG. *zwelifto* (G. *zwölfte*), ON. *tólfti*, f. *twelf*, etc. (see -TH[2]); the new formation with *-the* substituted for *-te* appeared XIV and became general from XVI.

twenty OE. *twentiġ* = OS. *twēntig*, OHG. *zweinzug* (G. *zwanzig*); the first el. is obscure; cf. ON. *tuttugu*, Goth. *twai tigjus*; see -TY[1]. Hence **twentieth** (-TH[2]) OE. *twentigoða*.

twi- prefix meaning 'two', 'twice', OE. *twi-*, *twy-* (= OHG. *zwi-*, ON. *tví-*; rel. to TWO). Of the 45 or so OE. comps. none survived exc. (arch.) *twifold*, (dial.) *twibill* two-edged axe, mattock, *twi-* being gen. repl. by *two-*, as *twofold* (ME. *twafald* XII, OE. *twifeald*), *two-headed* (OE. *twihēafdode*).

twice on two occasions XII; two times as much (as) XIV. ME. *twiġes*, f. *twiġe*, earlier *twiġ(e)a* = OS. *tuuīo* (f. **twi-*; cf. prec.) + *-es*, -s.

twiddle †trifle XVI; turn about esp. with the fingers XVII. prob. of symbolic orig.; cf. *twirl*, *fiddle*.

twig[1] minor shoot of a tree or shrub. OE. (late Nhb.) *twigge*, obscurely rel. to *twiġ*, *twī*, corr. to ODa. *tvige* fork and (with long vowel) MLG. *twīch*, Du. *twijg*, OHG. *zwīg* (G. *zweig*); all based on Gmc. **twi-* (cf. TWI-).

twig[2] (sl.) look at, perceive XVIII; understand XIX. of unkn. orig.

twilight XV (cf. †*twilighting* XIV). f. TWI- (in uncert. sense) + LIGHT[1].

twill woven fabric having parallel ridges. XIV. orig. north. and Sc. reduction of †*twilly*, ME. †*twyle*, OE. *twili* = OHG. *zwilīh* (G. *zwillich*); semi-tr. of L. *bilīx*, *-līc-* two-threaded, f. BI- + base of *līcium* thrum, thread.

twin twofold, double OE.; in *t. brother*, etc. XVI; forming a pair; sb. pl. two born at a birth OE. Late OE. *twinn*, earlier *ġetwinn* adj. and sb., corr. to ON. *tvinnr*, *tvennr* twofold, double :- Gmc. **twisnaz* :- IE. **dwisno-*; cf. TWI-.

twine thread of two or more strands. OE. *twīn*, *twiġin* linen = Du. *twijn* twine, twist, f. Gmc. **twi-* TWI-. Hence vb. XIII.

twinge (dial.) pinch, squeeze OE.; (arch.) cause sharp pain to XVII. OE. *twenġan* = MLG. *twengen*, OHG. *zwengen*, f. Gmc. **twaŋg-*, repr. by MHG. *zwange* tongs, *zwangen* pinch, OHG. *zwangōn*. Hence **twinge** sb. †pinch XVI; sharp wringing pain XVII.

twink †wink, blink XIV; (arch.) twinkle XVII.

corr. to MHG. *zwinken* (cf. G. *zwinkern* blink, wink, twinkle).

twinkle emit tremulous radiance OE.; wink XIII (obs. exc. in *twinkling of an eye* XIV). OE. *twinclian*, f. base repr. by TWINK; see -LE[3].

twirl spin rapidly XVI; twiddle (the thumbs) XVIII. prob. alt., by assoc. with *whirl*, of †*tirl* (XVI), metathetic var. of TRILL.

twist †A. divided object or part (band of a hinge, twig, junction of two parts in the body) XIV; B. cord or threads intertwined XVI (of tobacco XVIII); C. act of twisting, turning on an axis, or spinning XVI. of complicated history; partly dependent on OE. *twist*, in comps. denoting a hinged or branched object, viz. *candeltwist* snuffers, *mæst twist* mast rope, stay, *yltwist* bird-trap, and in place-names prob. denoting 'fork'; presumably f. the base **twis-*, identical with that of TWIN. So **twist** vb. †divide into branches; wring, wrench XIV; combine, unite (threads) XV. of mixed orig. (partly f. the sb.).

twit find fault with, taunt. XVI. In earliest use *twite, twight*, aphetic of †*atwite*, OE. *ætwītan* reproach with, f. *æt-* from, away (denoting opposition) + *wītan* blame, corr. to OS. *wītan*, OHG. *wīȝan*, ON. *víta* punish, Goth. *-weitan*, rel. to OE. *wīte* punishment.

twitch pull or jerk sharply. First in *totwicche* (XII–XIV) pull apart, corr. to LG. *twikken*, OHG. *gizwickan* (G. *zwicken*), f. Gmc. **twik-*, repr. also by OE. *twiccian* (dial. *twick*) pluck.

twite species of linnet. XVI. imit. of the bird's call.

twitter utter light tremulous notes, as a bird. XIV. of imit. orig.; see -ER[4].

twizzle (dial., colloq.) twirl, twiddle. XIX. alt. of TWIDDLE or dial. *twistle* (XVIII), f. TWIST; see -LE[3].

two OE. *twā* fem., *twā, tū* n. (cf. TWAIN) = OS. *twā, twē* (Du. *twee*), OHG. *zwā, zwei* (G. *zwei*), ON. *tvær, tvau*, Goth. *twōs, twa*; cogn. with Skr. *dvá*, Gr. *dúo*, L. *duo*, Lith. *dù*, OSl. *dŭva*, OIr. *dau, dō*, W. *dau*; IE. **d(u)wō(u)* with various modifications. Comp. **twofold** consisting of two combined. XII. ME. *twafald*, repl *twifald*, OE. *twyfeald* (see TWI-).

-ty[1] final syll. of the tens. OE. *-tiġ* = OS. (Du.) *-tig*, OHG. *-zug* (G. *-zig*) (ON. *tigr* and Goth. *tigus* are separate words, not suffixes, e.g. *tveir tigir, twai tigjus* twenty); rel. to TEN.

-ty[2] suffix denoting state or condition; early ME. *-teð, -te(e)*, later *-tie* - (O)F. *-té* (AN. *-tet, -ted, -teth*) :- L. *-tās, -tāt-*.

tycoon foreigners' title for the shogun of Japan XIX; (fig., sl.) business magnate XX. - Jap. *taikun*.

tyke dog, esp. cur, mongrel; ill-conditioned fellow XIV; in full *Yorkshire t.* Yorkshireman XVII. - ON. *tík* bitch.

tympan †tympanum OE.; (typogr.) in a printing press, frame for equalizing pressure XVI. OE. *timpana* and ME. *timpan* (in renderings of biblical passages) - L. *tympanum* TYMPANUM, reinforced by (O)F. *tympan*.

tympanites (path.) distension of the abdomen by gas. XIV. - late L. - Gr. *tumpanítēs*, f. *túmpanon* TYMPANUM.

tympanum drum, tambourine, etc.; ear-drum. XVII. - L. - Gr. *túmpanon* drum, f. nasalized var. of base of *túptein* strike.

Tynwald annual convention in the Isle of Man. XV. - ON. **þingwall-*, stem of *þingvǫllr*, f. *þing* assembly + *vǫllr* field, level ground.

type emblem XV; mark, stamp XVI; characteristic or representative form XVII; block carrying a letter or figure used in printing XVIII. - F. *type* or L. *typus* - Gr. *túpos* blow, impression, image, figure, f. base of *túptein* strike, beat. Comp. **typewriter** (-ER[1]) XIX (whence **type** vb., **typist** XIX). So **typic** typical. XVII. - F. *typique* - late L. *typicus* - Gr. *tupikós*. **typical** XVII. - medL. *typicālis*. **typography** XVII. - F. *typographie* or modL. *typographia*. **typographical** XVI. - modL. **typographer** XVII. - F. *typographe* or modL. *typographus*. Hence **typify** XVII.

-type repr. F. *-type*, L. *-typus*, Gr. *-túpos*, f. *túptein* (see prec.).

typhlitis (path.) inflammation of the caecum (blind gut). XIX. f. Gr. *tuphlón* caecum, n. of *tuphlós* blind; see -ITIS.

typhoon cyclonic storm in the China seas. XVI. - Chinese *tai fung*, dial. vars. of *ta* big, *fēng* wind. Earlier †*tuffoon* (XVII), identified in form with †*touffon* (XVI), †*tuffon* (XVII) violent storm in India - Pg. *tufão* - Hind. (- Arab.) *ṭūfān* hurricane, tornado, beside which there was a contemp. †*typhon* (XVI) - L. *tȳphōn* - Gr. *tūphôn*, rel. to *tûphein* (see next).

typhus infectious fever. XVIII. - modL. *tȳphus* - Gr. *tûphos* smoke, vapour, stupor, f. *túphein* smoke. Hence **typhoid** resembling typhus; applied spec. to a fever marked by intestinal inflammation and formerly supposed to be a variety of typhus. XVIII. f. TYPHUS + -OID.

tyranno- comb. form of Gr. *túrannos* TYRANT, as in **tyrannosaurus** (XX).

tyrant absolute ruler; despotic ruler. XIII. - OF. *tyrant, tiran* (mod. *tyran*) - L. *tyrannus* - Gr. *túrannos*. (OF. *tyrant* is analogical after forms in -ANT.) So or hence **tyrannic** XV. - (O)F. **tyrannical** XVI. **tyrannous** XV. **tyranny** XIV. - (O)F. *tyrannie* - late L. *tyrannia* - Gr. *turanníā*. **tyrannize** XV. - (O)F. *tyranniser*.

tyre, (now U.S.) **tire**[3] †curved plating for the rim of a wheel XV; rim of metal forming a continuous hoop XVIII; cushion of rubber for the same purpose XIX. perh. a use of TIRE[2].

Tyrian pert. to Tyre, ancient Phoenician city on the Mediterranean, spec. of a purple or crimson dye obtained from molluscs. XVI. f. L. *Tyrius*, f. *Tyrus* Tyre; see -IAN.

tyro see TIRO.

tzar see CZAR.

tzigane Hungarian gipsy. XIX. - F. *tzigane* (with *tz* of G. origin) - Hung. *cigány*.

U

ubication location. xvii. - medL. *ubicātiō, -ōn-* (cf. Sp. *ubicación*, Pg. *ubicação*), f. *ubicāre* (cf. Sp. *ubicarse* be in a determinate place), f. L. *ubī* where = Umbrian *pufe*, Oscan *puf* :- **quubī* (cf. L. *alicubī* elsewhere, *necubī* nowhere), f. base of *quī* WHO, with loc. ending; see -ATION.

ubiety condition in respect of place. xvii. - medL. *ubietās*, f. L. *ubī* where. So **ubiquity** quality of being everywhere at the same time. xvi. f. L. *ubīque* everywhere, f. *ubī* + generalizing *-que* (whence **ubiquitous** xix).

U-boat xx. - G. *U-boot*, for *unterseeboot* 'undersea boat'.

udal of lands held by an old pre-feudal form of freehold tenure. xvi (*outhell, uthall, udall*). Orkney and Shetland form of ON. *óðal* ODAL.

udder OE. *ūder* = OS. *ūder*, MLG., MDu. *ūder* (Du. *ui(j)er*), OHG. *ūter* (G. *euter*) :- WGmc. **ūdr-*; cf. OS. *ieder*, MLG. *jeder, jüdder*, ON. (with unexpl. cons.-change) *jú(g)r* :- **euðer*; IE. **ūdhr-* is repr. by L. *ūber*, Gr. *oûthar*, Skr. *ū́dhar-*.

udometer rain-gauge. xix. - F. *udomètre*, irreg. f. L. *ūdus* damp; see -METER.

ugly †frightful, horrible, terrible; morally offensive xiii; physically offensive, repulsive to the eye xiv; causing offence or disquiet xvii; hazardous, dangerous; cross, ill-tempered. - ON. *uggligr* to be feared, f. *ugga* fear; see -LY[1].

uhlan cavalryman, lancer in Continental armies. xviii. - F. *uhlan*, G. *u(h)lan* - Pol. *(h)ulan* - Turk. *oğlan* youth, servant.

Uitlander in S. Africa, foreigner, alien. xix. - Afrikaans, f. Du. *uit* OUT + *land* LAND; see -ER[1].

ukase decree, orig. of Russian emperor. xviii. - Russ. *ukáz*, f. *ukazát'* show, order, decree.

ukulele xix. of Hawaiian orig.

-ular repr. L. *-ulāris* (sometimes through F. *-ulaire*), f. *-ulus, -ula, -ulum* -ULE + *-āris* -AR, as in L. *populāris* POPULAR, *rēgulāris* REGULAR, *sæculāris* SECULAR. Some adjs. function as if connected directly to the bases of derivs. in *-ule*, as *granular*, apprehended as f. *grain*.

ulcer xiv. - (O)F. *ulcère* or - L. *ulcus, ulcer-*, rel. to Gr. *hélkos* wound, sore. So **ulcerate** (-ATE[2]) xv, **ulceration** xiv, **ulcerous** xvi. - L.

-ule suffix repr. F. *-ule* - L. *-ulus, -ula, -ulum*, as in *capsula* CAPSULE, *globulus* GLOBULE, *grānulum* GRANULE. Some words in *-ule* that were temporarily current, e.g. †*scrupule*, gave way finally to earlier forms in -LE[1]; others, e.g. †*formule*, to the orig. L. form. The corr. adjs. end in -ULAR, -ULOSE, -ULOUS.

ulema body of Muslim doctors in the law xvii; one of these xix. - Arab. *'ulamā'* pl. of *'ālim* learned, f. *'alima* know.

-ulent repr. L. *-ulentus*, used to form adjs. usu. with the sense of 'abounding in, full of', as *corpulentus* CORPULENT, *opulentus* OPULENT, *truculentus* TRUCULENT.

ullage amount by which a cask or bottle falls short of being full. xv (*oylage, ulage*). - AN. *ulliage* = OF. *ouillage, œillage*, f. (O)F. *ouiller, eullier, œiller* fill up (a barrel) :- Gallo-Rom. **oculāre*, f. L. *oculus* EYE, used in the sense of bung-hole; see -AGE.

ulna (anat.) larger inner bone of the forearm. xvi. - L. *ulna* forearm, ELL. Hence **ulnar** xviii.

-ulose adj. suffix repr. L. *-ulōsus*, compounded of *-ulus* -ULE and *-ōsus* -OSE[1] and f. sbs. in *-ulus, -ula, -ulum*.

-ulous adj. suffix repr. L. *-ulōsus* -ULOSE and *-ulus*; to the former belong, e.g., *fabulous, meticulous, populous*, to the latter, e.g., *credulous, garrulous, sedulous*. In a few instances L. adjs. of both types exist, as *querulus, querulōsus* QUERULOUS, *rīdiculus, rīdiculōsus* RIDICULOUS.

ulster (*U-*) king-of-arms for Ireland xvi; long loose overcoat of rough cloth introduced by J. G. McGee & Co. of Belfast, capital of Ulster xix. Name of the most northerly province of Ireland, the earlier form of which was *Ulvester* - ON. *Ulfastir*, also *Ulaztir, Ulaðstir*, f. Ir. *Ulaidh* men of Ulster; the el. *-ster* is perh. to be referred to (O)Ir. *tír* land = L. *terra*.

ulterior beyond what is immediate or present xvii; locally more remote xviii. - L. *ulterior* further, more distant, compar. of **ulter*. So **ultimate** (of an end, stage, etc.) last, final. xvii - medL. *ultimātus*, pp. of late L. *ultimāre* come to an end, f. L. *ultimus*, superl. of **ulter*; see -ATE[2]. **ultimatum** final terms final point, extreme limit. xviii. sb. use of n. of late L. *ultimātus*. **ultimo** †on the last day xvi; of the last month xvii. abl. of L. *ultimus*.

ultra- prefix repr. L. *ultrā* beyond, rel. to ULTERIOR, etc.; in mod. use (from early xix) a living prefix (1) prepositionally, surpassing the limits of (the specified concept), as *ultra-human*; (2) adverbially, marked by an extreme degree of the quality denoted by the adj. qualified; (3) spec. in *ultra-violet* applied to the rays beyond the violet end of the visible spectrum; (4) denoting instruments recording very minute measurements, as *ultramicroscope*.

ultramarine A. applied to a blue pigment obtained orig. from lapis lazuli xvi; B. situated beyond the sea xvii. In A. - medL. *ultramarīnus* (see ULTRA-, MARINE); in B. - It. †*oltramarino* (mod. *oltre-*) in *azzurro oltramarino* 'azure from overseas', the substance being of foreign origin; later assim. to medL.

ultramontane (one) representing the R.C.Ch. beyond (i.e. north of) the Alps and so not favouring extreme views of papal authority xvi; (orig. from the French point of view) pert. to the R.C.Ch. beyond (i.e. south of) the Alps, (and hence) the Italian party favouring such views xviii. - medL. *ultrāmontānus*; see ULTRA-, MOUNT[1], -ANE[1].

ululate howl. xvii. f. pp. stem of L. *ululāre*, of

imit. orig.; see -ATE[2]. So **ululation** XVI. - obs. F. or late L.

umbel (bot.) inflorescence in which the flowers are borne upon nearly equal pedicels springing from a common centre. XVI. - F. †*umbelle* (mod. *ombelle*) or L. *umbella* sunshade, dim. of *umbra* shadow; see UMBRA. So **umbellifer** XVIII, **umbelliferous** XVII.

umber kind of brown earth used as a pigment. XVI. - F. *ombre* or It. *ombra*, either identical with the words derived from L. *umbra* shadow, darkness; or from L. *Umbra*, fem. of *Umber* belonging to the ancient province of *Umbria*, Italy.

umbilical pert. to the navel. XVI. - medL. *umbilīcālis*, f. L. *umbilīcus*, f. base of UMBO; see -AL[1].

umbles XV. var. of NUMBLES; in attrib. use *umble-pie* (XVII); cf. HUMBLE-PIE.

umbo boss of a shield; round or conical projection. XVIII. - L. *umbō* (see NAVEL).

umbra phantom, ghost XVI; uninvited guest accompanying an invited one; (astron.) shadow XVII. - L. *umbra* shadow, shade, phantom, etc.

umbrage †shade, shadow XV; shade of trees, (hence) foliage XVI; †shadowy appearance, semblance XVII; †suspicion, inkling, pretext; displeasure, resentment. - OF. *umbrage*, (also mod.) *ombrage* :- Rom. **umbrāticum*, sb. use of n. of L. *umbrāticus* pert. to retirement or seclusion, f. *umbra* shadow, shade, retirement. Hence **umbrageous** shady XVI; suspicious, jealous XVII. - (O)F. *ombrageux*.

umbrella XVII (also *-ello*). - It. *ombrella, -o*, dim. of *ombra* :- L. *umbra* (shadow, shade), after *umbella* (see UMBEL).

umlaut (philol.) change in the sound of a vowel due to partial assimilation to an adjacent sound. XIX. - G., f. *um-* about + *laut* sound.

umpire one who decides between disputants or arbitrators. XV. ME. *owmpere, umpere*, arising from misdivision of *a noumpere*, as *an oumpere*; †*noumpere* (XIV-XV) - OF. *no(u)mper*, f. *no(u)n-* NON- + *per* PEER, i.e. a third man called in to decide between two. Hence as vb. XVI.

umpty signaller's sl. for 'dash' used in reading morse code messages; by assoc. with numerals in -TY[1] used for an indefinite fairly large number; whence **umpteen**, after numerals in -TEEN. XX.

un-[1] OE. *un-* = OS. (LG.), (O)HG., Goth. *un-*, (M)Du. *on-*, ON. *ú-, ó-*, corr. to OIr. *in-, an-*, L. *in-* IN-[3], Gr. *an-, a-* A-[4], AN-[2], Skr. *an-, a-* :- IE. **n̥-*, gradation-var. of **ne* not. This prefix, expressing negation or contradiction, has been most frequently used with ppls. and adjs., but there has been restriction with short simple adjs. (e.g. *unbold, unglad, unstrong*), there being usu. available simple forms with opposite positive meanings; *unclean, uneven, unmild, untrue, unwise*, etc. are of OE. date, while *unable, undue, uneasy, unjust, unsafe* are notable exx. of comps. with adjs. of alien origin. On the other hand derivs. from adjs. in *-able, -al, -ant, -ar, -ary, -ent, -ful, -ible, -ic(al), -ish, -ive, -ous, -y* are very numerous. Formations with ppls. appear freely from OE. times onwards. There are several comps. in common use of which the simplex is now obs. or rare, as *unfailing, unfeeling, ungainly, unruly, unspeakable, unwieldy*. Participles with pendent particles are freely used, e.g. *uncalled-for, unreferred-to, unthought-of*.

There are many parallel formations with IN-[3], esp. in the earlier periods, e.g. *inconstant, immeasurable, insatiable*, beside *unconstant, unmeasurable, unsatiable*.

un-[2] prefix expressing reversal or deprivation. OE. *un-, on-, an-* = OS. *ant-* (Du. *ont-*), OHG. *ant-, int-* (G. *ent-*), orig. identical with *and-* in OE. *andswaru* ANSWER, *andlong* ALONG. Most of the OE. formations have a simple vb. as their base, as *unbindan* unbind, *undōn* UNDO, *unġeocian* unyoke, and denote reversal of the action; the few denoting removal or deposition were increased later, as *unfasten, unfix, unlace, unsettle, unstitch*, as also those denoting freedom or release, as *unbosom, uncage, unearth, unhouse, unsheathe*; from late XVI comps. denoting deprivation of a quality or status appear, as *unchurch, unking, unman*.

The redundant use of the prefix is rare, the chief ex. being *unloose*.

Both *un-*[1] and *un-*[2] may be repr. in such a pp. form as *unsaddled*, which may mean 'not saddled or having a saddle' or 'removed from or deprived of a saddle'.

unable not able XIV; weak, feeble XVI (in later use Sc.). f. UN-[1] + ABLE.

unaneled not having received extreme unction. XVII. f. UN-[1] + pp. of †*anele* (XIV), f. *an-* + †*ele* anoint (f. OE. *ele* OIL); see -ED[1].

unanimous XVII. f. L. *ūnanimus*, f. *ūnus* ONE + *animus* mind; see -OUS. So **unanimity** XV. - (O)F. or L.

unanswerable †discrepant; not admitting of an answer; not responsible *for*. XVII (UN-[1]). So **unanswerably** XVI. **unarm** XIV, **unarmed** XIII (UN-[1,2]). **unawares** without being aware; without warning. XVI. alt. of *unwares* (XII), var. of *unware* (XII), adv. f. OE. *unwær* = ON. *úvarr*; see UN-[1], AWARE, -S. So **unaware** adv. XVI; adj. XVIII.

unbeknown in adv. phr. *u. to* without the knowledge of. XVII (UN-[1]). Hence, with *-st* (f. -S with parasitic *t*), **unbeknownst** XIX.

unbend relax XIII; straighten XVII; free oneself from restraint XVIII (UN-[2]). **unbending** unyielding, inflexible XVII; remaining erect XVIII (UN-[1]). **unbosom** disclose. XVI (UN-[2]). **unbound** OE. *unbunden*; see UN-[1]. **unbounded** XVI (UN-[1]). **unbridled** XIV (UN-[1]). **unbroken** XIII (UN-[1]). **unburden** XVI (UN-[2]).

uncanny †A. malicious XVI; B. (dial.) careless, unreliable XVII; C. not safe to deal with XVIII; D. of a mysterious or weird nature XIX. f. UN-[1] + CANNY; sense D. is of Eng. development.

unchancy (chiefly Sc.) ill-fated XVI; dangerous, unsafe XVIII. See UN-[1]. **unchurch** exclude from membership of a church. XVII (UN-[2]).

uncial A. pert. to an inch or an ounce XVII; B. (palaeogr.) after late L. *unciales litteræ*, having the large rounded forms characteristic of early Gr. and L. manuscripts XVIII. - L. *unciālis*, f. *uncia* INCH[1], OUNCE[1]; see -AL[1]. In sense B the orig. application is obscure.

unciform hook-shaped. XVIII. f. L. *uncus* hook;

see -FORM. So **uncinate** hooked. XVIII. - L. *uncīnātus*, f. *uncīnus*, f. *uncus*; see -INE[1], -ATE[2].

uncle XIII. - AN. *uncle*, (O)F. *oncle* :- late L. *aunculus* uncle, for earlier *avunculus* maternal uncle, dim. (see next) of **awon-*, var. of the base of L. *avus* grandfather (:- **awos*).

-uncle suffix repr. OF. *-uncle*, and its source, L. *-unculus*, *-uncula*, a comp. form with *-ulus*, *-ula*, -ULE, on *-unc-* (as in *homunciō* little man).

unco (Sc.) adj. strange, unusual XV; remarkable, great XVIII; adv. extremely XVIII. Clipped form of UNCOUTH.

unconscionable not conscientious; not reasonable, unreasonably great, etc. XVI (UN-[1]). **unconscious** XVIII (UN-[1]). **uncouple** release (dogs) from the leash XIV; disconnect XVI. See UN-[2].

uncouth †unknown; †unfamiliar; (dial.) unusual OE.; †unfrequented XVI; uncomely, awkward. OE. *uncūð* = MDu. *oncont* (Du. *onkond*), OHG. *unkund*, ON. *úkunnr*, Goth. *unkunþs*; Gmc., f. UN-[1] + pp. of **kunnan* know (see CAN[1]).

uncover XIII (UN-[2]).

unction A. anointing as a rite or symbol XIV; B. (after 1 John 2: 20) spiritual influence XIV; spiritual feeling XVII; C. lubrication, ointment XVI. - L. *unctiō*, *-ōn-*, f. *unct-*, pp. stem of *ung(u)ere*; see UNGUENT, -TION. So **unctuous** greasy, oily XIV; fat, rich XV. - medL. *unctuōsus*.

undaunted †untamed XV; †(Sc.) unrestrained XVI; not discouraged XVI. See UN-[1].

under adv. and prep. OE. *under* = OS. *undar* (Du. *onder*), OHG. *untar* (G. *unter*), ON. *undir*, Goth. *undar* :- Gmc. **unðer* :- IE. **n̥dher-* and **n̥ter-*, compar. formations.

under-[1] repr. OE. *under-*, comb. form of UNDER adv. and prep. = OS. *undar-*, etc. (see prec.) denoting (1) lower or inferior position or locality, status or rank; (2) defect, or insufficiency.

under-[2] pref. originating in the coalescence of UNDER prep. with a following sb., the resulting comp. forming an adj. or adv., e.g. *underfoot* (XII); UNDERGROUND, UNDERHAND; *undersea* (XVII).

undergo pt. *-went*, pp. *-gone* †undermine OE.; †pass under XIII; endure, submit to; experience XVI. Late OE. *undergān* (with Gmc. cogns.); see UNDER-[1], GO.

undergraduate XVII (shortened to **undergrad** XIX). See UNDER-[2]. Hence irreg. **undergraduette** XX.

underground adv. XVI; adj. XVII. See UNDER-[2].

underhand adv. and adj. secret(ly), covert(ly). XVI. See UNDER-[2].

underhung having the lower jaw projecting beyond the upper. XVII. f. UNDER + *hung*, pp. of HANG.

underlay place beneath, support. OE. *underleċġan* = (M)Du. *onderleggen*, etc.; see UNDER-[1], LAY[1].

underlie †be subject to; submit to OE.; subtend XVI; form a basis to XIX. OE. *underliċġan* = (M)Du. *onderliggen*, etc. See UNDER-[1], LIE[1].

underling XII. f. UNDER (in the sense 'in a state of subjection') + -LING[1].

undermine mine beneath XIV; overthrow by underhand means XV. f. UNDER + MINE[2].

underneath prep. beneath, below; adv. down below. OE. *underneoðan*, f. UNDER + *neoðan* (see BENEATH).

understand grasp or know the meaning (or the fact) of OE.; recognize as present or implied XVI. OE. *understandan*, see UNDER-[1]; cf. MLG. *understān* understand, step under, MDu. *onderstaen* (Du. *-staan*), MHG. *understān*, *-stēn* (G. *unterstehen*), and with another prefix, OE. *forstandan*, OS. *farstandan*, OHG. *firstantan*, MHG. *verstān*, *-stēn* (G. *verstehen*), MDu. *verstaen* (Du. *-staan*). Hence **understanding** XI.

understrapper underling, subordinate. XVIII. f. UNDER-[1] + (prob.) *strapper* in dial. sense of 'labourer' or 'one who grooms a horse' (cf. STRAP).

undertake †entrap XII; †accept, receive XIII; take in hand, take in charge; †commit oneself XIV; become surety *for* XVI. f. UNDER-[1] + TAKE. Hence **undertaker** †helper; one who undertakes a task XIV; contractor, now only for *funeral-undertaker* XVII. **undertaking** †energy, enterprise; pledge, promise XIV; action, etc., undertaken XV.

undertone low or subdued tone; undercurrent of feeling, etc. XIX. f. UNDER-[1] + TONE.

underwrite write underneath XIV (in pp.); †subscribe (a document) XVI; spec. (a policy of insurance) XVII (hence **underwriter** XVII). f. UNDER-[1]; tr. L. *subscrībere* SUBSCRIBE.

undies (colloq.) pl. women's undergarments. XX. f. *under-* in *underclothes*, *underwear*, etc.; see -IES (and cf. -Y[6]).

undine water-nymph. XIX. - modL. *undina*, *undena*, f. *unda* wave; see -INE[1].

undo A. unfasten; B. annul, make of no effect; bring to nought, destroy, ruin OE.; † C. expound XIII. OE. *undōn* = (M)Du. *ontdoen*, OHG. *intuon*; see UN-[2], DO[1]. Hence **undone** ruined, destroyed XIV.

undoubted XV (UN-[1]). Hence **undoubtedly** XV.

undress[1] partial or informal dress. XVII. UN-[1] + DRESS sb. So **undressed** not dressed, trimmed, clothed XV.

undress[2] divest of clothes. XVI (UN-[2]).

undue not owing; improper, unseasonable XIV; excessive XVII. f. UN-[1] + DUE. So **unduly** XIV.

undulate move in or as in waves. XVII. f. L. *unda* wave (cf. L. *undulātus* waved, f. late L. *undula*, dim. of *unda*); see -ULE, -ATE[3]. So **undulation** XVII, **undulatory** XVIII.

undying XIII (*undeiand*). See UN-[1].

unearth exhume XV; expel (an animal) from its earth XVII; (fig.) bring to light XIX. f. UN-[2] + EARTH sb. **uneasy** XIII (UN-[1]). **uneath** (arch.) with difficulty; hardly, scarcely. OE. *unēaðe*, f. UN-[1] + *ēaðe* easily. **unemployment** XIX (UN-[1]). **unending** XVII (UN-[1]). **unequal** XVI (UN-[1]). **uneven** OF. *unefen*; see UN-[1], EVEN[2]. **unfailing** XIV (UN-[1]). **unfasten** XIII (UN-[2]). **unfeeling** OE. *unfēlende*; f. UN-[1] + prp. of FEEL vb. **unfit** XVI (UN-[1]). **unfitting** XVI (UN-[1]). **unfix** XVI (UN-[2]). **unfold** open the folds of; disclose. OE. *unfealdan*; see UN-[2], FOLD[2]. **unfrequented** XVI (UN-[1]). **unfrock** XVII (UN-[2]). **ungainly** XVII. f. UN-[1] + (dial.) *gainly*, after *ungain* (dial.) not straight; inconvenient

(xv) - ON. *úgegn*, f. *ú-* UN-[1] + *gegn* straight; see -LY[1].

ungodly XVI (UN-[1]).

unguent ointment, salve. XV. - L. *unguentum*, f. *unguere* anoint, rel. to Skr. *anákti* anoints, OIr. *imb*. W. *ymenyn*, OHG. *ancho* butter.

ungulate hoof-shaped, hoofed. XIX. - lateL. *ungulātus*, f. *ungula* claw, hoof, f. *unguis* NAIL; see -ULE, -ATE[2].

unhand take the hand(s) off. XVII. f. UN-[2] + HAND sb.

unhappy †causing misfortune XIII; unfortunate, ill-fated, (later) wretched in mind, marked by misfortune XIV. f. †*unhap* misfortune, mishap (XIII) - ON. *úhapp*, f. *ú-* UN-[1] + *happ* HAP sb.; see -Y[1].

unhinge XVII (UN-[2]). **unhorse** XIV (UN-[2]). **unhouse** XIV (UN-[2]).

uni- repr. L. *ūni-*, comb. form of *ūnus* ONE, a single (repr. by only a few words during the classical period); freely used in XIX in techn. terms.

Uniat, -ate (pert. to) a member of an Orthodox Eastern church in communion with the R.C.Ch. XIX. - Russ. *uniát*, f. *úniya* - L. *ūniō* UNION.

unicameral consisting of one CHAMBER. XIX. UNI- + CAMERA + -AL[1].

unicorn fabulous one-horned equine beast XIII; carriage drawn by three horses arranged one and two XVIII. - (O)F. *unicorne* - L. *unicornis* one-horned, (Vulg.) unicorn, f. UNI- + *cornū* HORN.

uniform of one or the same form XVI; sb. distinctive uniform dress XVIII. - (O)F. *uniforme* or L. *ūniformis*, f. UNI- + *forma* FORM. So **uniformity** XV. - (O)F. or late L.

unify XVI. - (O)F. *unifier* or late L. *ūnificāre*; see UNI-, -FY. So **unification** XIX.

unilateral XIX. f. UNI- + LATERAL.

union act or fact of uniting or being united XV; body of units joined together XVII; textile fabric composed of two or more materials XIX. - (O)F. *union* or ecclL. *ūniō, -ōn-* the number one, unity, f. *ūnus* ONE; see -ION. *U. flag*, national flag introduced to symbolize the union of the crowns of England and Scotland XVII; *u. jack*, orig. small union flag flown as a jack (see JACK[3]) XVII.

unique XVII. - F. *unique*, †*unic* m. - L. *ūnicus* one and only, alone of its kind, f. *ūnus* ONE; see -IC.

unison (mus.) identity of pitch XVI; exact agreement XVII. - (O)F. *unison* (mod. *unisson*) or late L. *ūnisonus* of the same sound, f. UNI- + *sonus* SOUND[3].

unit (math.) indivisible whole regarded as the base of number XVI; single individual XVII; quantity serving as a standard of measurement XVIII. f. L. *ūnus* ONE, prob. after *digit*.

unitarian one who affirms the unipersonality of the Godhead. XVII. f. modL. *ūnitārius*, f. L. *ūnitās* UNITY; see -ARIAN.

unite trans. make one XV; intr. form one (*with*) XVII. f. *ūnīt-*, pp. stem of L. *ūnīre* join together, f. *ūnus* ONE. So **unity** fact or condition of being one XIII; †unit XV; the number one XVI. - (O)F. *unité* - L. *ūnitās*.

universal comprehending the whole XIV; pert. to the universe; of the Church Catholic, forming a whole XV; widely learned or accomplished XVI; (logic) pert. to the whole of a class or genus; also sb. XVI. - OF. *universal* (mod. *-el*) or L. *ūniversālis*, f. *ūniversus*; see next and -AL[1]. So **universality** XIV (once, thereafter not till XVI). - (O)F. or late L. Hence **universally** XIV. **universalism** XIX, **-ist** XVII.

universe A. †*in u.* (L. *in universum*) universally XIV; B. the whole of created things XVI; the world XVII. - (O)F. *univers* or L. *ūniversum* the whole world, sb. use of n. of *ūniversus* all taken together, lit. 'turned into one', f. UNI- + *versus*, pp. of *vertere* turn.

university body of teachers and scholars engaged in the higher branches of learning in a certain place. XIV. - (O)F. *université* - L. *ūniversitās* the whole, the whole number (of), the universe, (in later juridical lang.) society, corporation, f. *ūniversus*; see UNIVERSE, -ITY.

unkempt XV. var. of *unkem(be)d*, f. UN-[1] + pp. of *kemb*, OE. *cemban* comb.

unless (*not*) on a less condition *than* XIV; except it be that, if . . . not XV; prep. except, but XVI. ME. phr. *o(n) lesse*, also *in lesse* (followed by *than*), modelled on (O)F. *à moins que*; with assim. of the first syll. to UN-[1].

unlettered XIV (UN-[1]). **unlicked** not licked into shape. XVI (UN-[1]).

unlike not like, different XII. The early distribution of the word in north. and eastern areas suggests orig. accommodation of ON. *úlíkr*, *úglíkr* = OE. *ungelīc* (ME. *uniliche*), MLG. *unlīk* (Du. *onlijk*), OHG. *ungilīh* (G. *ungleich*); Gmc., see UN-[1], LIKE[1]. So **unlikely** XIV.

unloose relax; release XIV; unfasten XVI. f. UN-[2], LOOSE; cf. OE. *onlīesan*, ME. *unlese*. **unlucky** XVI (UN-[1]). **unmake** XV (UN-[2]). **unman** deprive of manly qualities. XVI (UN-[2]). **unmask** XVI (UN-[2]).

unmentionable not to be mentioned XIX; sb. pl. trousers XIX (orig. U.S.). See UN-[1].

unmitigated XVI (UN-[1]). **unmixed** XVI (UN-[1]). **unmuzzle** (UN-[2]), **unmuzzled** (UN-[1]) XVI. **unnail** XV (UN-[2]). **unnatural** XV (UN-[1]). **unnerved** XVII (UN-[2]). **unpaid** XIV (UN-[1]). **unparalleled** XVI (UN-[1]).

unready not ready or prepared XIII; not prompt XVI. f. UN-[1] + READY. From XVI used as a form of †*unredy* (XIV), f. *unrede* (see -Y[1]), OE. *unrǣd* lack of counsel or wisdom (OE. *rǣd* counsel), traditional epithet from XIII of king Ethelred II, originating in the jingling collocation *Æthelred Unred* 'Noble Counsel, Evil Counsel'.

unreal XVII (UN-[1]). **unreality** XVIII (UN-[1]). **unreason** †injustice XIV; inability to act reasonably XIX. See UN-[1]. **unreasonable** XIV (UN-[1]).

unreliable XIX (UN-[1]).

unruly undisciplined, disorderly. XIV. f. UN-[1] + †*truly* orderly (XIV), f. RULE + -Y[1].

unsaid OE. *unsǣd*, with Gmc. cogns.; see UN-[1]. **unsay** (OE., once), XV (UN-[2]). **unseat** XVI (UN-[2]). **unseemly** XIII (UN-[1]). **unseen** XII (UN-[1]). **unsettle** XVI (UN-[2]). **unsex** XVII (UN-[2]). **unship** XV (UN-[2]). **unsightly** XV (UN-[1]).

unspeakable A. that cannot be expressed in words XIV; B. indescribably bad XIX. See UN-[1].

unsteady XVI (UN-¹).

unstrung having the string(s) relaxed XVI; unnerved XVII (UN-²).

unsung not sung XV; not celebrated in song XVII (UN-¹).

unsymmetrical XVIII (UN-¹). **unsystematic** XVIII (UN-¹).

untidy †untimely, unseemly XIII; not in good order XIV. See UN-¹.

untie OE. *untīġan*; see UN-².

until adv. and conj. XIII. f. ON. **und* (retained in *un(d)z*, for **und es* 'till that', and corr. to OE., OFris., OS. *und*) + TILL².

untiring not growing weary. XIX. f. UN-¹ + prp. of TIRE¹ (intr.).

unto to (in all uses exc. as marking an inf.); (arch.) until. XIII. f. (Scand.) *un-* of UNTIL + (native) TO.

untold †not reckoned OE.; immense, vast XIV; not recounted. OE. *unteald*; see UN-¹.

untouchable that cannot or may not be touched XVI; sb. non-caste Hindu XX. See UN-¹.

untoward †disinclined; intractable; †awkward, ungainly; unlucky XVI; unpropitious XVII. f. UN-¹ + TOWARD adj. Earlier in *untowardly* adj., *untowardness* XV.

untrodden not trodden on, untraversed. (XIII), XVI. See UN-¹.

untrue unfaithful OE.; false XIV; wrong. OE. *untrēowe* (with Gmc. cogns.); see UN-¹.

untruth †unfaithfulness OE.; falsehood XV. See UN-¹. Hence **untruthful** XIV.

untutored XVI (UN-¹). **unused** XIII (UN-¹). **unusual** XVI (UN-¹).

unutterable above or beyond description. XVI (UN-¹).

unwashed XIV (UN-¹). Earlier †*unwashen* (OE. *unwæscen*).

unwell XV (before late XVIII mostly north., Sc., Anglo-Ir.). See UN-¹.

unwept XVI (UN-¹).

unwieldy †impotent, feeble XIV; awkward in movement XVI; difficult to handle. f. UN-¹ + †*wieldy*, extended form with -Y¹ of †*wield*, OE. (*ġe*)*wielde* vigorous, active :- Gmc. *(*ʒa-*)*walðja-*, f. **walð-*, base of WIELD.

unwilling OE. *unwillende*; newly formed in XVI. See UN-¹.

unwise OE. *unwīs* (with Gmc. cogns.); see UN-¹.

unwitting not knowing or aware, OE. *unwitende* (rare after 1600 till XIX); see UN-¹, -ING². Hence **unwittingly** XIV.

unworthy worthless; not worthy, undeserving XIII; unmerited XIV; not befitting (one). See UN-¹.

-uous suffix repr. L. *-uōsus* or deriv. OF. *-uous* (mod. *-ueux*), f. *u*-stems + *-ōsus* -OSE¹, -OUS, as in †*monstruous*, *sinuous*, *sumptuous*; or f. L. *u*-stems + -OUS, as in *arduous*, *conspicuous*, *incongruous*, *promiscuous*, *strenuous*. So **-uity**, **-uosity**.

up to or at an elevated position. repr. two OE. words (i) *up(p)* (said primarily of motion) = OS. *up* (Du. *op*), ON. *upp*, (ii) *uppe* (said primarily of position) = OS. *uppa*, ON. *uppi*; rel. to OHG. *ūf* (G. *auf*). The use of *up* adv. to express complete consumption was prob. adopted from Scand. (e.g. ON. *drekka upp* drink up). By ellipsis of preps., such as *against*, *along*, etc., a new prep. was developed to form collocations like *upstairs* (XVI).

up- pref. repr. OE. *up(p)-*, corr. to (M)Du. *op-*, OS., (M)LG. *up-*, OHG. *ūf-* (G. *auf-*), ON. *upp-*.

upas Javanese tree yielding a poisonous sap. XIX. - Malay *ūpas* poison, in *pōhun* or *pūhun ūpas* poison-tree. Earlier (XVIII) of a tree fabled to have existed in Java, having poisonous properties such that it destroyed life for many miles around.

upbraid †adduce as a fault OE.; find fault with, carp at XIII; censure, reprove soundly. Late OE. *upbrēdan*, perh. after ON. **uppbregða*, f. *upp* UP + *bregða* BRAID.

upbringing XVI. Gerund of †*upbring* (XIII), with Gmc. cogns.

upheaval (geol.) raising by volcanic action; hence freq. fig. XIX. f. *upheave* (XIII; spec. in geol. XIX), f. UP- + HEAVE; see -AL².

uphill ascent XVI; adj. †high, elevated XVII; going upwards, arduous; adv. XVII. f. UP prep. + HILL.

uphold XIII. f. UP- + HOLD¹; with Gmc. cogns.

upholsterer XVII. Extended form with -ER¹ of †*upholster* (XV) dealer in or repairer of small or secondhand articles, f. prec. + -STER. Hence **upholster** vb. XIX, **upholstery** XVII.

upkeep maintenance in good condition. XIX. f. phr. *keep up* maintain (XVI).

upland (arch.) land lying away from the sea; high ground XVI; also adj., repl. earlier *uplandish* (XIV; cf. OE. *uplendisċ* rustic). f. UP, used adj., raised, elevated + LAND sb.

upmost uppermost, highest. XVI. f. UP + -MOST.

upon XII. f. UP + ON, after ON. *upp á*.

upper higher, top. XIV (not common before XV). f. UP + -ER³. Hence sb. XIX, **uppermost** XV.

uppish from XVII in various sl. uses implying elevation or elation. f. UP + -ISH¹.

upright erect, perpendicular OE.; †lying on the back OE. (late); of unbending rectitude XVI; sb. †vertical face; architectural elevation XVII; upright part or member. OE. *upriht*, corr. to (M)Du. *oprecht*, OHG. *ūfreht* (G. *aufrecht*), ON. *uppréttr*; see UP-, RIGHT.

uproar A. †insurrection, tumult; B. outcry, noise of tumult. XVI. - Du. *oproer* (MDu. *uproer*), MLG. *uprōr*, f. *op* UP- + *roer*, *rōr* = OS. *hrōra*, OHG. *ruora* (G. *ruhr*) motion; in B influenced by ROAR. Hence **uproarious** XIX.

ups-a-daisy, upsidaisy encouraging excl. on lifting a child from the ground. XIX. vars. of *up-a-daisy* (XVIII; *-dazy*); see UP, and for the ending cf. LACKADAISICAL. XIX.

upset †A. set up, raise, erect XIV (in pp.); (Sc.) make good XVI. B. overthrow, overturn; throw into disorder XIX. f. UP + SET¹.

upshot †final shot in an archery match, fig. parting shot; †mark aimed at; †end, conclusion; *in the u.* at last, (hence) result, issue. XVI. f. UP- + SHOT.

upside down XVI. Alt. of (dial.) *upsidown* (XV), var. of †*upsedown*, †*up sadown*, for earlier †*up so down* (XIV), orig. meaning 'so as to be upset or overturned'. The form of this phr. is difficult to account for.

upsides even or quits *with*. XVIII (orig. Sc.). f. UP, SIDE sb., -S.

upstairs see UP.

upstart (one) newly or suddenly risen in position. XVI. equiv. to contemp. †*start-up*, f. *start*, pp. of START[2] + adv. UP; cf. *upstart* vb. (now rare) start up (XIV).

uptake capacity for understanding. XIX. f. *uptake* vb. XVIII (Sc.) understand, f. UP + TAKE.

upward OE. *upweard*, corr. to MLG. *upwart*, MDu. *opwaert* (Du. *opwaart*), MHG. *ūfwert*; see UP, -WARD. So **upwards** OE. *upweardes*.

ur- primitive, original, earliest. repr. G. pref. as in *ursprache* primitive language.

uraemia (path.) presence in the blood of urinary constituents. XIX. f. Gr. *oûron* urine + *haîma* blood.

uraeus representation of the sacred asp or serpent on the headdress of ancient Egyptian deities and kings. XIX. - Gr. *ouraîos*, of Egyptian orig.

uranism homosexuality. XIX. - G. *uranismus*, f. Gr. *ouránios* heavenly, taken to mean 'spiritual', f. *ouranós* heaven; see -ISM.

uranium (chem.) metallic element. XVIII. f. URANUS + -IUM.

urano- comb. form of Gr. *ouranós* sky, heaven(s), roof of the mouth; e.g. **uranography** (XVII), **uranometry** (XVIII).

Uranus planet situated between Saturn and Neptune. XIX. - L. *Ūranus* - Gr. *Ouranós* husband of Gaea (Earth) and father of Cronos (Saturn).

urban XVII (rare before XIX). - L. *urbānus*, f. *urbs*, *urb-* city; see -AN.

urbane †urban XVI; having the manners or culture characteristic of town life XVII; civil, polite. - (O)F. *urbain*, *aine* or L. *urbānus*, *-āna*; see prec. So **urbanity** refined civility; †polished wit; city or town life. XVI. - (O)F. or L.

urceolate pitcher-shaped. XVIII. f. L. *urceolus*, dim. of *urceus* pitcher; see -ATE[2].

urchin hedgehog XIII; (dial.) deformed person XVI; mischievous youngster; little fellow, brat. ME. *urchon*, beside *yrichon* (XIII), *hirchon*, *irchoun* - ONF. *herichon*, **ir(e)chon*, **urchon*, vars. of OF. *heriçon* (mod. *hérisson*) :- Rom. **hēriciō*, *-ōn-*, f. L. *hērīcius*, late form of *ērīcius* hedgehog.

-ure suffix repr. (O)F. *-ure* - L. *-ūra*, denoting primarily action or process or the result of this, (hence) office or rank, collective body or organization; usu. affixed to pps., but in L. *figūra* FIGURE being exceptionally attached to a pres. vb.-stem. Various other F. endings have been assim. to this in Eng. adoptions, as in *leisure*, *manure*, *pleasure*, *tenure*, *treasure*.

urea constituent of urine. XIX. f. F. *urée*, f. Gr. *oûron* urine or *ourein* urinate.

-uret (chem.) suffix now gen. repl. by -IDE. - modL. *-urētum* (also *-orētum*), proposed XVIII by F. chemists.

ureter (anat.) urinary duct. XVI. - F. *uretère* or Gr. *ourētḗr*, f. *ourein* make water, f. *oûron* urine. So **urethra** tube which discharges urine from the bladder. XVII. - late L. *ūrēthra* - Gr. *ourḗthrā*.

urge demand or entreat insistently; press or drive forward. XVI. - L. *urgēre* press, drive, compel. So **urgent** XV. - (O)F. - prp. of L. *urgēre*. Hence **urgency** XVI.

-uria final el. in L. form repr. Gr. *-ouriā*, f. *oûron* urine (see -IA[1]) in terms of path. denoting morbid conditions of the urine, e.g. *albuminuria*, *haematuria*.

uric pert. to urine. XVIII. - F. *urique*, f. Gr. *oûron* urine; see -IC.

-urient suffix repr. L. *-ūriēns*, *-ent-*, prp. ending of L. desiderative vbs. in *-ūrīre*.

urinal †glass vessel to hold urine for inspection XIII; †vessel for chemical solution XIV; chamber-pot XV; place provided for passing urine XIX. - (O)F. - late L. *ūrīnal*, sb. use of n. of late *ūrīnālis* urinary, f. *ūrīna* URINE; see -AL[1].

urine XIV. - (O)F. - L. *ūrīna*. So **urinary** XVI. - medL. **ūrīnārius*. **urinate** make water. XVI. f. pp. stem of medL. *ūrīnāre* (in classL. dive); see -ATE[3].

urn vessel in which to preserve the ashes of the dead XIV; vessel for holding voting-tablets or the like XVI; oviform pot or pitcher XVII (*tea urn* XVIII). - L. *urna* :- **urcnā*, rel. to *urceus* pitcher.

urning male homosexual. XIX. - G., f. (*Venus*) *Urania*, taken to mean 'heavenly love' and applied to homosexuality as being 'spiritual'; cf. URANISM.

uro-[1] comb. form of Gr. *oûron* urine, as in *urology* (XVIII).

uro-[2] comb. form of Gr. *ourā́* tail.

ursine pert. to or like a bear. XVI. - L. *ursīnus*, f. *ursus* bear; see -INE[1].

urticate sting like a nettle. XIX. f. pp. stem of medL. *urtīcāre*, f. L. *urtīca* nettle (whence **urticaria** XVIII); see -ATE[3]. So **urtication** XVII. - medL.

urus AUROCHS. XVII. - L. *ūrus* - Gmc. **ūrus* (OE. *ūr*, etc.).

us d. and acc. of WE. OE. *ūs* = OS. *ūs*, (M)Du. *ons*, (O)HG. *uns*, ON. *oss*, Goth. *uns* :- Gmc. **uns* :- IE. **n̥s*, reduced grade of **nes* (Skr. *nas*).

usage habitual use, custom, or conduct. XIII. - (O)F., f. L. *ūsus* USE; see -AGE. So **usance** †usage XIV; period allowed for the payment of a bill of exchange XVII. - OF. :- Rom. **ūsantia*, f. **ūsāre* (see next). **user** (leg.) continual use or enjoyment. XIX. Evolved from †*abuser*, *non-user* (XVII); see -ER[5].

use act or manner of using, fact of being used. XIII. ME. *us* - (O)F. *us* :- L. *ūsus* use, usage, f. *ūs-*, pp. stem of *ūtī* vb. use. Hence **useful, useless** XVI. So **use** observe (a custom, rite, etc.), follow as a custom XIII; engage in, employ, deal with XIV; habituate, accustom (*be used to* XV); intr. be accustomed (now only in pt.). - (O)F. *user* †employ (now *user de*), consume, wear out :- Rom. **ūsāre*, f. L. pp. stem *ūs-*.

usher officer having charge of the door of a hall, etc. XIV; officer whose ceremonial duty it is to precede a person of rank XVI; (fig.) precursor; assistant master in a school. - AN. *usser* = OF. *u(i)ssier*, (mod. *huissier*) :- medL. *ūstiārius*, for L. *ōstiārius* door-keeper, f. *ōstium* door, f. *ōs* mouth; see -ER[2]. Hence vb. XVI.

usquebaugh WHISKY[1]. XVI. - Ir. and Sc. Gael. *uisge beatha* 'water of life', i.e. *uisge* WATER, *beatha* life.

usual XIV. - OF. *usual*, (also mod.) *usuel*, or late L. *ūsuālis*, f. *ūsus* USE; see -AL[1]. Hence **usually** (-LY[2]) XV.

usucapion (leg.) acquisition of ownership by long use. XVII. - F. *usucapion* or L. *ūsūcapiō*, *-ōn-*, f. *ūsūcapere*, f. *ūsū*, abl. of *ūsus* USE + *capere* take, seize. So **usucaption** XVII. - OF. or medL.

usufruct right of temporary possession or use. XVII. - medL. *ūsūfrūctus*, for L. *ūsusfrūctus*, more fully *ūsus et frūctus* use and enjoyment; see USE, FRUIT.

usurp XIV. - (O)F. *usurper* - L. *ūsūrpāre*, seize for use, prob. for **ūsūripāre*, f. *ūsū*, abl. of *ūsus* USE + *rapere* seize. So **usurpation** XIV. - (O)F. or L.

usury lending money at interest XIV; (arch.) interest on money lent XV. - AN. **usurie* = (O)F. *usure* or medL. *ūsūria*, f. L. *ūsūra*, f. *ūsus* USE; see -Y[3]. Hence **usurious** XVII. So **usurer** XIII. - AN. *usurer*, OF. *usureor*, (also mod.) *usurier*; see -ER[2].

ut (mus.) first note of Guido Aretino's hexachords, and of the octave in modern solmization (cf. DOH). - (O)F. *ut*; the lowest of the series *ut*, *re*, *mi*, *fa*, *sol*, *la*, *si*, said to be taken from the office hymn for St. John Baptist's day: *Ut* queant laxis *re*sonare fibris / *Mi*ra gestorum *fa*muli tuorum / *Sol*ve polluti *la*bii reatum, / *S*ancte *I*ohannes. See GAMUT.

utensil †(coll. sg.) domestic vessels or implements XIV; domestic implement, etc. XV; sacred vessel XVII. - OF. *utensile* (mod. *ustensile*) - medL. *ūtēnsile*, sb. use of n. of L. *ūtēnsilis* fit for use, useful (n. pl. *ūtēnsilia* implements, materials), f. *ūtī* USE.

uterus (anat.) womb. XVII. - L. *uterus* belly, womb, obscurely rel. to Skr. *udára-*, Gr. *hóderos*. So **uterine** having the same mother XV; pert. to the uterus XVII. - late L. *uterīnus*.

utility usefulness XIV; useful thing or feature XV. - (O)F. *utilité* - L. *ūtilitās*, f. *ūtilis* useful, f. *ūtī* USE; see -ILE, -ITY. Hence **utilitarian** XVIII. So **utilize** make useful, convert to use. XIX. - F. *utiliser* - It. *utilizzare*. **utilization** XIX. - F.

utmost outermost OE.; of the highest degree XIV; †latest, last XV; also sb. †furthest part OE.; extreme degree or limit XV. OE. *ūt(e)mest*, f. *ūt(e)* + *-mest*; see OUT adv., -MOST.

utopia name of Sir Thomas More's imaginary republic XVI; place or condition of ideally perfect government XVII. - modL. *ūtopia* 'no-place', f. Gr. *ou* not + *tópos* place; see -IA[1]. So **Utopian** XVI.

utricle small sac or bladder. XVIII. - F. *utricle* or L. *ūtriculus*, dim. of *ūter* leather bottle; see -CLE.

utter[1] outward, outer OE.; extreme, total XV. OE. *ūter(r)a*, *ūttra*, compar. formation (see -ER[3]) on *ūt* OUT, corr. to MDu. *ūtere* (Du. *uiter-*), OHG. *ūzaro* (G. *äusser*). Hence **utterly** (-LY[2]) †plainly, straight out XIII; absolutely, completely XIV. **uttermost** outermost; utmost. XIV.

utter[2] give out audibly, speak, pronounce; †reveal; †put on the market, sell; give currency to (coin, etc.). XIV. - MDu. *ūteren* (Du. *uiteren*) drive away, speak, show, make known, MLG. *ūtern* turn out, sell, speak, demonstrate, with assim. to UTTER[1]. Hence **utterance**[1] †disposal by sale; speaking, speech. XV.

utterance[2] extremity of force, esp. in phr. (now arch.) *to the u.* to the utmost limit. XIII. - (with assim. to UTTER[1]) (O)F. *outrance*, †*oultrance*, f. *ou(l)trer* go beyond bounds :- Rom. **ultrāre*, f. L. *ultrā* beyond; see -ANCE.

uvula fleshy part of the soft palate. XIV. - late L. *ūvula*, dim. of L. *ūva* grape; see -ULE.

uxorious excessively devoted to one's wife. XVI. f. L. *uxōrius*, f. *uxor* wife; see -IOUS.

V

vacant not held or occupied XIII; devoid of contents XIV; free from occupation XVI; expressionless, inane XVIII. In early use - (O)F.; not freq. before late XVI, the word appears to have been taken in afresh from L. *vacāns, -ant-*, prp. of *vacāre* be empty or unoccupied, with arch. var. *vocāre*, see VOID, -ANT. So **vacancy** XVI.

vacate make void or vacant XVII; withdraw from XVIII. f. pp. stem of L. *vacāre*; see prec., -ATE[3]. **vacation** release from occupation XIV; period of formal suspension of activity XV. - (O)F. or L.; abbrev. **vac** XVIII.

vaccine in *v. disease* cowpox, *v. matter* or *virus v., v. inoculation* vaccination. XVIII. - L. *vaccīnus*, as used in modL. *variolæ vaccinæ* cowpox, *virus vaccinus* virus of cowpox used in vaccination, f. *vacca* cow; see -INE[1]. Also **vaccine** sb. vaccine matter. XIX. - F. Hence **vaccinate** (-ATE[3]) XIX, **vaccination** XVIII.

vacillate swing or sway unsteadily XVI; waver XVII. f. pp. stem of L. *vacillāre* sway, totter; see -ATE[3]. So **vacillation** XV. - L.

vacuity emptiness; empty space; vacancy of mind. XVI. - (O)F. *vacuité* or L. *vacuitās*, f. *vacuus* empty (whence **vacuous** XVII), f. *vacāre* be VACANT. So **vacuum** emptiness, empty space XVI. sb. use of n. sg. of *vacuus*.

vade-mecum handy book of reference. XVII. - F. - modL. *vade-mecum*, sb. use of L. *vāde mēcum* go with me, i.e. imper. of *vādere* go and *mēcum* (*mē* me, *cum* with).

vagabond wandering without settled habitation XV; sb. itinerant beggar XV; idle good-for-nothing XVII. - (O)F. *vagabond* or L. *vagābundus*, f. *vagārī* wander, f. *vagus* wandering.

vagary †roaming, ramble; †wandering in speech; †frolic, prank XVI; capricious or eccentric act XVII; fantastic notion XVIII. - L. *vagārī* wander (see prec.).

vagina canal connecting vulva with uterus XVII; sheath, theca XVIII. - L. *vāgīna* sheath, scabbard.

vagrant (person) wandering from place to place and maintaining himself by begging, etc. XV. ME. *vagaraunt* - AN. *vagarant, -aunt(e)*, app. f. L. *vagārī* wander + -ANT.

vague XVI. - F. - L. *vagus* wandering, inconstant, uncertain.

vail[1] †benefit, profit XV; (arch.) casual profit or emolument XV; pl. gratuities, perquisites XVI. f. †*vail* vb. avail, profit (XIII) - OF. *vail-*, tonic stem of *valoir* be of value - L. *valēre* be strong, powerful, of value.

vail[2] (arch.) lower XIV; doff XV. Aphetic of †*avail*, †*avale* descend, lower - (O)F. *avaler* lower, swallow.

vain worthless, futile XIII; †senseless, silly XIV; having an inordinate opinion of oneself XVII. - (O)F. *vain*, fem. *vaine* :- L. *vānus, -a* empty, without substance, rel. to *vacuus* VACANT. The phr. *in vain* reflects (O)F. *en vain*. Comps. **vainglory** XIII (after (O)F. *vaine gloire*, L. *vāna glōria*), **vainglorious** XV (after OF. *vaneglorieus*, medL. *vānaglōriōsus*).

vair fur from a squirrel with grey back and white belly XIII; (her.) fur having spaces tinctured alternately XVI. - (O)F. :- L. *varius* particoloured.

valance drapery attached lengthwise and hanging down. XV. perh. - AN. **valance*, f. *valer* lower, aphetic of (O)F. *avaler* (see -ANCE); or from the pl. of the prp. used sb.

vale[1] valley. XIII. ME. *vaal, va(i)le* - (O)F. *val* :- L. *vallēs, vallis*.

vale[2] farewell. XVI. - L. *valē*, imper. of *valēre* be strong or well.

valediction XVII. f. L. *valedīcere*, i.e. *valē dīcere* say farewell; see prec. and DICTION. So **valedictory** XVI.

Valenciennes kind of lace named from *Valenciennes*, a town of northern France celebrated for lace-manufacture. XVIII.

valency (chem.) capacity of an atom to combine with other atoms. XIX. - late L. *valentia* power, competence, f. *valēre* be powerful; see -ENCY.

valentine person chosen or drawn by lot on St. Valentine's day (14 February) as one's sweetheart for the coming year XV; folded paper with the name of a person to be drawn as a valentine XVI; card, etc., sent to a person of the opposite sex on St. Valentine's day XIX. f. (O)F. *Valentin* - L. *Valentīnus* name of two Italian saints whose festival falls on 14 February.

valerian herb of the genus *Valeriana*. XIV. - (O)F. *valériane* - medL. *valeriana*.

valet gentleman's manservant. XVI. - (O)F. *valet*, also †*vaslet*, †*varlet* :- Rom. **vassellittus*, dim. of **vassus* (see VASSAL).

valetudinary not in robust health, constantly concerned with one's ailments XVI; sb. XVIII. - L. *valētūdinārius*, in ill health, f. *valētūdō, -din-* state of health, f. *valēre* be strong or well; see -TUDE, -ARY. Hence **valetudinarian** adj. and sb. XVIII.

valiant †stalwart; courageous, bold. XIV. ME. *vailaunt, valiaunt* - AN. *valiaunt*, OF. *vail(l)ant* (mod. *vaillant*) :- Rom. **valiente*, for *valēns, -ent-*, prp. of L. *valēre* be strong; see -ANT.

valid adequate in law XVI; well founded and applicable XVII. - F. *valide* or L. *validus* strong, powerful, effective, f. *valēre* be strong, etc.; see -ID[1]. So **validity** XVI. - F. or late L.

valise XVII. - F. - It. *valigia*, of unkn. orig.

valley XIII. - AN. *valey*, OF. *valée* (mod. *vallée*) :- Rom. **vallāta*, f. L. *vallis, -ēs*; see -Y[6].

vallum rampart of earth, etc. XVII. - L., coll. f. *vallus* stake, palisade.

valonia acorns of certain species of oak. XVIII. -

It. *vallonia* - modGr. *balánia, belánia*, pl. of *baláni, beláni* (Gr. *bálanos*) acorn.

valour A. †value, worth XIV; B. (after *valorous*) courage in conflict, prowess XVI. - OF. *valour* (mod. *valeur* value) :- late L. *valor, -ōr-*, f. *valēre* be strong; see -OUR². So **valorous** valiant, courageous. XV. - OF. *valerous* (mod. *valeureux*) or medL. *valōrōsus*.

valse waltz. XVIII. - F. - G. *walzer* WALTZ.

value adequate equivalent; material or monetary worth; †worth, worthiness; relative status or estimate XIV; amount represented by a symbol XVI. - OF., fem. pp. formation from *valoir* be worth :- L. *valēre* be strong, be worth. Hence **value** vb. estimate the value of XV; consider of value XVI; whence **valuable, valuation** XVI.

valve either of the leaves of a folding door XIV; one of the halves of a hinged shell XVII; (anat.) membranous fold; device resembling a flap, lid, etc. - L. *valva* leaf of a door. So **valvular** XVIII. f. *valvula*, dim. of L. *valva*.

vambrace defensive armour for the arm. XIV. ME. *vaun(t)bras* - AN. *vauntbras*, aphetic of OF. *avantbras*, f. *avant* before + *bras* arm.

vamo(o)se to make off, decamp. XIX (orig. U.S.). - Sp. *vamos* let us go :- L. *vādāmus* 1st pers. pl. pres. subj. of *vādere* go.

vamp¹ part of hose covering the foot and ankle XIII; part of a boot or shoe covering the front of the foot XVII. - AN. **vaumpé*, aphetic of OF. *avantpié* (mod. *avantpied*), f. *avant* before + *pie(d)* foot. Hence **vamp** vb. provide with a vamp, patch XVI; produce as by patching XVII; extemporize (an accompaniment, etc.) XVIII.

vamp² (sl.) woman who employs her sexual attraction unscrupulously. XX. Shortening of next.

vampire preternatural malignant being, supposed to suck blood; person who preys upon others; kind of bat supposed to suck blood. XVIII. - F. *vampire* or G. *vampir* - identical form in Sl. langs., in which there are vars. such as Russ. *upýr'*, Pol. *upiór*.

vamplate plate on a lance serving as a guard for the hand. XIV. - AN. *vauntplate*, f. *vaunt-*, aphetic of (O)F. *avant-* before + *plate* PLATE.

van¹ winnowing basket or shovel XV; shovel used in testing ore, etc. XVII; (poet.) wing; sail of a windmill XIX. south. and western var. of FAN¹, prob. reinforced by (O)F. *van* or L. *vannus*.

van² short for VANGUARD. XVII.

van³ covered vehicle for conveying goods. XIX. Shortening of CARAVAN.

vanadium metallic element. XIX. - modL. *vanadium*, f. ON. *Vanadís* name of the Scand. goddess Freyja; see -IUM.

Vandal member of a Gmc. tribe which invaded Western Europe in the fourth and fifth centuries A.D., and in 455 sacked Rome XVI; (*v*-) destroyer of beautiful or venerable things XVII. - L. *Vandalus* - Gmc. **Wandal-, -il-, -ul-* (repr. by OE. *Wendlas* pl., etc.). Hence **vandalism, -ize** XVIII.

Vandyke portrait by Vandyke; lace or linen collar in the style of those depicted in his portraits XVIII; deep-cut point on a garment, etc. XIX. Name of Sir Anthony *Vandyke* (anglicized form of *Van Dyck*), Flemish painter 1599-1641. Hence as vb. provide with deep-cut points or zigzag ornament. XVIII.

vane plate of metal rotating on a spindle to show the direction of the wind XV; sail of a windmill XVI; sight of a surveying instrument; web of a feather XVIII. south. and western var. of †*fane* (1) flag, banner, (2) weather-cock, OE. *fana* = OS., OHG. *fano* (G. *fahne*), Goth. *fana* cloth :- Gmc. **fanan-*, rel. to L. *pannus* piece of cloth.

vang (naut.) rope for steadying the gaffs of a sail. XVIII. - Du. *vang* in *vanglijn* painter.

vanguard foremost division of an army. XV. Earlier *vandgard*, var. of †*vantgard*, aphetic of †*avantgard* (XV) - (O)F. *avant-garde*, †*avangarde*, f. *avant* before + *garde* GUARD.

vanilla (pod of) climbing orchid of the genus *Vanilla* XVII; aromatic substance obtained therefrom XVIII. - Sp. *vainilla*, dim. of *vaina* sheath :- L. *vāgīna* VAGINA.

vanish XIV. Aphetic - *e(s)vaniss-*, lengthened stem (see -ISH²) of OF. *e(s)vanir* :- Rom. **exvānīre*, for L. *ēvānēscere*, f. *ē-* EX-¹ + *vānus* empty.

vanity vain or worthless thing XIII; quality of being vain XIV. - (O)F. *vanité* :- L. *vānitās, -tāt-*, f. *vānus* VAIN; see -ITY.

vanquish XIV. Early forms *vencus* (Sc. *vincus*), *venquis(she)*, the *ven-* forms being superseded by *van-* in XVI, by assoc. with late OF. *vain-*, and the ending assim. to -ISH² in XV; f. pp. *vencus* and pt. *venquis* of OF. *veintre, vaintre* (mod. *vaincre*) :- L. *vincere* conquer.

vantage †advantage, profit XIII; position of superiority XV; †additional amount XVI; (in lawn tennis) XIX. - AN. *vantage*, aphetic of OF. *avantage* ADVANTAGE.

vapid flat, insipid (of beverages) XVII; (of talk, etc.) XVIII. - L. *vapidus*, rel. to *vappa* flat or sour wine, and perh. further to *vapor* VAPOUR; see -ID¹.

vapour steam, steamy exhalation XIV; (pl.) exhalations arising in the human body XV; (arch.) morbid condition resulting from these XVII. - (O)F. *vapeur*, †*-our* or L. *vapor, -ōr-* steam, heat; see -OUR². So **vaporous** XVI. f. late L. *vapōrus* or - late L. *vapōrōsus*.

varec(h) seaweed XVII; carbonate of soda obtained from it XIX. - F. *varec(h)*, OF. *warec*, *vrec* - ON. **wrek* WRECK.

variable liable to vary. XIV. - (O)F. - L. *variābilis*, f. *variāre* VARY; see -ABLE. Hence **variability** XVIII. So **variance** variation, difference XIV; discrepancy; dissension XV (*at v.* XVI). - OF. - L. *variantia*. **variant** †inconstant, not uniform; diverse, differing (*from*) XIV; sb. XIX. - (O)F. **variation** †difference, divergence XIV; fact or instance of varying XVI. - (O)F. or L.

varicose (of a vein) affected with a varix. XVIII. - L. *varicōsus*, f. *varix, -ic-* dilated vein (whence **varix** XIV); see -OSE¹.

variegate XVII. f. pp. stem of L. *variēgāre*, f. L. *varius* VARIOUS; see -ATE³. So **variegation** XVII.

variola (med.) smallpox. XVIII. - late L. *variola* pustule, pock, f. L. *varius* speckled, variegated, VARIOUS.

variorum edition of a work containing the observations of various commentators. XVIII. g.

pl. m. of L. *varius* VARIOUS in phr. *editio cum notis variorum* 'edition with the notes of various (editors)'.

various †variable, changeable XVI; varied, variegated XVII; (with pl.) differing from one another. f. L. *varius*; see -IOUS. So **variety** XVI. - (O)F. or L.

varlet attendant, e.g. on a knight XV; knave, rascal XVI. - OF. *varlet*, var. of *vaslet*, *vadlet* VALET.

varmint (dial.) vermin XVI; troublesome or mischievous creature XVIII. var. of *varmin* VERMIN, with parasitic *t*.

varnish solution of resinous matter used for providing a hard shiny coat XIV; fig. XVI. ME. *vernisch* - (O)F. *vernis* :- medL. *veronix*, *-nic-* fragrant resin, sandarac, or - medGr. *berenī́kē*, prob. appellative use of the town-name *Berenice* (in Cyrenaica). So **varnish** vb. XIV. - OF. *verniss(i)er*, *-ic(i)er*.

varsity XIX (earlier †*versity* XVII). colloq. clipped form of UNIVERSITY.

varsovienne dance resembling Polish national dances. XIX. - F., fem. of *varsovien*, f. *Varsovie* Warsaw.

vary intr. and tr. XIV. - (O)F. *varier* or L. *variāre*, f. *varius* VARIOUS. Hence **varied** diverse XVI; variegated XVIII; see -ED[1].

vascular pert. to tubular vessels. XVII. f. L. *vāsculum*, dim. of *vās* vessel; see next and -AR.

vase ornamental vessel of circular section. XVII. - F. - L. *vās*, *vāsum* vessel, utensil. A comb. form **vaso-** is used in physiol. and path. terms relating to vascular parts XIX.

vaseline a petroleum jelly used in ointments, etc. XIX. **P.**; irreg. f. G. *wasser* WATER + Gr. *élaion* OIL + -INE[5].

vassal tenant in fee XIV; transf. and fig. XV. - (O)F. :- medL. *vassallus* man-servant, retainer, of Celt. orig.; the simplex *vassus* corr. to OGaul. *-vassus* in personal names, e.g. *Dagovassus*, W. *gwas*, Ir. *foss* servant. So **vassalage** XIV. - OF. *vassalage* (mod. *vasselage*).

vast XVI. - L. *vastus* waste, uncultivated, immense, pp. formation on a base **wās-*, repr. also by L. *vānus* VAIN, Ir. *fás* empty, and WGmc. **wōst-* (OE. *wēste* uninhabited, desolate; etc.).

vat cask or tun for liquid. XIII. south. and western var. of *fat*, OE. *fæt* = OS. *fat* (Du. *vat*), OHG. *faz* (G. *fass*), ON. *fat* :- Gmc. **fatam* vessel, cask, rel. to MLG. *vaten*, OHG. *fazzōn* (G. *fassen*) hold, contain, seize.

Vatican palace of the Pope on the Vatican Hill in Rome. XVI. - F. *Vatican* or L. *Vāticānus* (sc. *collis* hill, *mōns* mountain); see -AN.

vaticinate predict. XVII. f. pp. stem of L. *vāticinārī*, f. *vātēs* seer, prophet, poet, rel. to Ir. *fáith* poet, W. *gwawd* song of praise, and Gmc. **wōð-* (whence OE. *wōd* mad, *wōð* song, etc.); see -ATE[3]. So **vaticination** XVII. - L.

vaudeville light popular song XVIII; light stage performance with songs XIX. - F. *vaudeville* †typical song or play, theatrical piece with rhymes, alt. of *vaudevire*, f. *Vau de Vire* 'valley of Vire', name of a region of Calvados, Normandy, the songs of which had a vogue in XV.

vault[1] arched roof or ceiling XIV; burial chamber XVI. ME. *voute*, *vaute* - OF. *voute*, *vaute* (mod. *voûte*) :- Rom. **vol(vi)ta*, pp. fem. (for *volūta*) of L. *volvere* turn. So **vault** vb. XIV. - OF. *vouter* (mod. *voûter*). The sp. with *l* appeared XV (after later OF. usage).

vault[2] †leap on to (a horse) XVI; leap with the support of the hand XVII. - OF. *vo(u)lter* turn (a horse), gambol, leap :- Rom. **voltāre*, **volūtāre* or **volvitāre*, frequent. f. L. *volvere* roll; assim. to prec.

vaunt boast. XIV. - AN. *vaunter*, (O)F. *vanter* :- late L. *vānitāre*, later *vantāre*, f. *vānus* VAIN; partly aphetic of earlier †*avaunt* (- OF. *avanter*).

vaunt-courier one of an advance guard; forerunner. XVI. Aphetic of *avant-courier* - F. *avant-courrier*, f. *avant* before, *courrier* COURIER.

vavasour feudal tenant immediately below a baron. XIII. - OF. *vavas(s)our* (mod. *vavasseur*) - medL. *vavassor*, of uncert. orig.

veal XIV. - AN. *ve(e)l* = OF. nom. *veiaus*, obl. *veel* (mod. *veau*) :- L. *vitellus*, dim. of *vitulus* calf.

vector †(astron.) for *radius v.* variable line drawn to a curve from a fixed point XVIII; (math.) quantity having direction as well as magnitude XIX. - L. *vector* carrier, traveller, rider, f. *vect-*, pp. stem of *vehere* carry; see -TOR.

Veda any of the four ancient sacred books of the Hindus. XVIII. - Skr. *veda* knowledge, sacred knowledge, sacred book, f. **wid-* know (see WIT[2]). Hence **Vedic** pert. to the Vedas; sb. the language of these, an early form of Sanskrit. XIX. - F. *védique* or G. *vedisch*.

vedette mounted sentry in advance of outposts. XVII. - F. *vedette* scout, sentinel - It. *vedetta*, alt. (after *vedere* see) of south. It. *veletta*, f. Sp. *vela* sb. watch, f. *velar* vb. watch :- L. *vigilāre*; see -ETTE.

veer[1] †run *out* (a line) XV; allow to drift further off XVI; pay out (a cable) XVII. - (M)Du. *vieren* let out, slacken.

veer[2] change course or direction (spec. clockwise) of wind. XVI. - (O)F. *virer* :- Rom. **vīrāre*, perh. alt. of L. *gȳrāre* GYRATE, by assoc. with a verb beginning with *v*, e.g. *vertere* turn or *vibrāre* shake.

vegetable adj. †having the life characteristic of a plant XIV; pert. to plants XVI; sb. plant XVI; plant cultivated for food XVIII. - (O)F. *végétable* or late L. *vegetābilis* animating, vivifying, f. L. *vegetāre* animate, enliven, f. *vegetus* active, f. *vegēre* enliven; see -ABLE. So **vegetal** XV. - medL. **vegetālis* (whence F. *végétal*, etc.); see -AL[1]. **vegetarian** XIX. irreg. f. *vegetable*. **vegetate** grow or develop after the manner of a vegetable XVII; live the life of a vegetable, i.e. a dull monotonous existence XVIII. f. pp. stem of L. *vegetāre*; see -ATE[3]. **vegetation** growth as of plants XVI; concr. XVII. - L. **vegetative** pert. to growth. XIV. - (O)F. *végétatif*, *-ive* or medL. *vegetātīvus*.

vehement intense, severe; very forcible. XV. - (O)F. *véhément* or L. *vehemēns*, *-ent-* impetuous, violent, perh. for **vēmēns* 'deprived of mind', alt. by assoc. with *vehere* carry. So **vehemence** XVI. - F. - L.

vehicle medium of application or transmission (first in medical use); means of conveyance or transport. XVII. - F. *véhicule* or L. *vehiculum*, f. *vehere* carry; see WAY, -CLE. So **vehicular** XVII. - late L.

vehmgericht (hist.) secret tribunal active in Westphalia from XII to XVI. XIX. - G. *vehmgericht* (now *fe(h)mgericht*), f. *vehm* (of unkn. orig.) + *gericht* court, tribunal.

veil article of attire covering head or face; piece of cloth used as a hanging XIII; fig. XIV. - AN. *veile* and *veil* = OF. *voile* and *voil* (mod. *voile* m. veil, fem. sail) :- L. *vēla* pl. sails and *vēlum* sg. sail, curtain, veil.

vein A. tubular vessel in which blood is conveyed through the animal body XIII (of a leaf XVI); B. †small channel through which water flows XIII; line of deposit of mineral or earthy matter XIV; C. strain of some quality; characteristic style; personal disposition; mood XVI. - (O)F. *veine* :- L. *vēna*. Hence **veiny** (-Y[1]) XVI.

velar A. (archit.) resembling a sail XVIII; B. pert. to the velum XIX. - L. *vēlāris*, f. *vēlum* curtain; see VELUM, -AR.

veld, veldt (S. Afr.) unenclosed country. XIX. - Afrikaans *veld*, earlier *veldt* :- Du. *veld* FIELD.

velitation skirmish. XVII. - L. *vēlitātiō, -ōn-*, f. *vēlitāre*, f. *vēlitēs*, pl. of *vēles* light-armed soldier; see -ATION.

velleity low degree of volition. XVII. - medL. *velleitās*, f. L. *velle* to wish; see -ITY.

vellum fine parchment prepared from calfskin. XV (*velim*). - (O)F. *vélin*, f. *veel* VEAL + *-in* -INE[1].

velocipede (hist.) light vehicle propelled by pushing it along with the toes; early form of pedal bicycle XIX. - F. *vélocipède*, f. L. *vēlox* (see next) + *pēs, ped-* FOOT.

velocity swiftness of motion XVI; rapidity of operation XVII. - (O)F. *vélocité* or L. *vēlōcitās*, f. *vēlox* swift, rapid; see -ITY.

velour hatter's plush pad XVIII; fabric with velvety pile XIX. - F. *velours*, alt. of OF. *velous* :- L. *villōsus* hairy, f. *villus* growth of hair.

velum (anat.) soft palate XVIII; (zool., bot.) membranous structure XIX. - modL. use (in full *v. palati, v. pendulum* veil of the palate, pendulous veil) of L. *vēlum* (see VEIL).

velvet fabric of silk having a dense smooth pile XIV; soft downy skin of a deer's horn XV. - OF. *veluotte*, f. *velu* velvety - medL. *villūtus*, f. L. *villus* growth of hair. Hence **velveteen** XVIII.

venal exposed for sale; capable of being bought over XVII; mercenary XVIII. - L. *vēnālis*, f. *vēnum* (also *vēnō, vēnuī*), obl. cases of **vēnus* that is for sale; rel. to Gr. *ônos* purchase price, Skr. *vasná-* price; see -AL[1].

venatic pert. to hunting. XVII. - L. *vēnāticus*, f. pp. stem of *vēnārī* hunt; see -ATIC.

vend sell; give utterance to. XVII. - (O)F. *vendre* or L. *vēndere*, f. *vēnum* (see VENAL) + *dare* give. So **vender, vendor** XVI. - AN. *vendo(u)r* (modF. *vendeur*); see -ER[1], -OR[1]. **vendible** saleable. XIV. - L. Hence **vendee** XVI.

vendace small freshwater fish. XVIII. - OF. *vendese, -oise* (mod. *vandoise*) - Gaul. **vindēsia*, f. **vindos* white (cf. OIr. *find*, W. *gwynn* white).

vendetta blood-feud. XIX. - It. :- L. *vindicta* vengeance.

vendue (U.S. and W. Indies) public sale, auction. XVII. - Du. *vendu*, †*vendue* - (O)F. (now dial.) *vendue* sale, f. *vendre* VEND.

veneer cover with a thin coating of finer wood. XVII. Recorded first in the gerund *faneering*, later *fineering, veneering* - G. *furni(e)rung, fourni(e)rung*, vbl. sb. of *furniren* - (O)F. *fournir* FURNISH. So **veneer** sb. XVIII.

venerable XV. - (O)F. *vénérable* or L. *venerābilis*, f. *venerārī*; see -ABLE. So **venerate** XVII. f. pp. stem of L. *venerārī*, f. *venus, vener-* love; see -ATE[3]. **veneration** XV - (O)F. or L.

venereal pert. to sexual desire or intercourse XV; (of disease) communicated by sexual intercourse XVII. f. L. *venereus*, f. *venus, vener-* love.

venery[1] sport of hunting; †animals hunted. XIV. - (O)F. *vénerie*, f. *vener* :- Rom. **vēnāre*, for L. *vēnārī* hunt; see -ERY.

venery[2] indulgence of sexual desire. XV. - medL. *veneria*, f. L. *venus, vener-* love; see -ERY.

venesection phlebotomy. XVII. - medL. *vēnæ sectiō* 'cutting of a vein'; see VEIN, SECTION.

vengeance act of avenging oneself or another. XIII. - (O)F., f. *venger* (whence arch. **venge** XIII) :- L. *vindicāre* VINDICATE; see -ANCE. Hence **vengeful** XVI. f. *venge*.

venial (theol., of sin) not mortal XIII; that may be excused XVI. - OF. *venial* (mod. *véniel*) - late L. *veniālis*, f. *venia* forgiveness, indulgence, f. base of *venus* love; see -IAL.

venire XVII. Short for **venire facias** (XV) writ requiring a sheriff to summon a jury; L. *venīre* COME, *faciās* you are to cause, 2nd pers. sg. pres. subj. of *facere* DO[1], make.

venison flesh of an animal killed in the chase XIII; (arch.) beast of the chase XIV. ME. *veneso(u)n, venisoun* - OF. *veneso(u)n, -ison* (mod. *venaison*) :- L. *vēnātiō, -ōn-* hunting, game, f. *vēnārī* hunt; see -ATION.

Venite invitatory psalm at matins. XIII. - L. *venīte*, imper. pl. of *venīre* COME; first word of Ps. 95, beginning 'Venite, exultemus Domino' O come, let us sing unto the Lord.

venom poison, lit. and fig. XIII. ME. *venim* - OF. *venim*, (also mod.) *vénin* :- Rom. **venīmen*, alt. of L. *venēnum* potion, drug, poison. So **venomous** †pernicious XIII; poisonous XIV. - (O)F. *venimeux*.

venose veined. XVII. - L. *vēnōsus*, f. *vēna* VEIN; see -OSE[1]. So **venous** (-OUS) pert. to a vein or veins XVII; contained in the veins XVIII.

vent[1] †provide with an outlet for gas, etc. XIV; †discharge (fluid) XVI; give free course to, utter; intr. †(of animals) scent, (of otters, etc.) rise to the surface to breathe. prob. aphetic of †*avent* (XIV) - OF. *aventer*, var. of *esventer* (mod. *éventer*) create wind, expose to the air, divulge, scent :- Rom. **exventāre*, f. L. EX-[1] + *ventum* WIND[1]. Hence (partly after F. †*esvent, évent*) **vent** sb. A. †discharge, utterance; issue, outlet XVI; means of outlet, opportunity of escape XVII; B. anus; aperture, outlet XVI; way out XVII.

vent[2] opening or slit in a garment. XV. var. of (dial.) *fent* (XV) - (O)F. *fente* slit :- Rom. **findita* (repl. L. *fissa*), sb. use of fem. pp. of L. *findere* cleave, split.

ventiduct passage serving to introduce cool or fresh air. XVII. f. L. *ventus* WIND[1] + *ductus* DUCT.

ventil valve controlling wind supply in an organ. XIX. - G. - It. *ventile* - medL. *ventile* sluice.

ventilate †blow away XV (once); investigate freely, sift by discussion XVI; give free utterance to XVII; †winnow; †increase (flame), set (air) in motion; blow upon; supply with fresh air XVIII. f. pp. stem of L. *ventilāre* brandish, fan, winnow, agitate, in late L. discuss, air a subject, f. *ventus* WIND[1]; see -ATE[3]. So **ventilation** †motion in the air XV; †fanning, blowing XVI; free course of the air XVII; aeration; admission of fresh air; free discussion. - (O)F. or L. Hence **ventilator** XVIII.

ventricle (anat.) any of the cavities of the heart, brain, etc. XIV. - L. *ventriculus*, dim. of *venter* belly; see -CLE.

ventriloquy XVI. f. L. *venter*, *ventr-* belly + *loquī* speak; see -Y[4]. So **ventriloquism** XVIII, **ventriloquist** XVII.

venture chance XV (chiefly, after 1500, in phr. *at a v.* at random, by chance); chancy or speculative enterprise XVI. Aphetic of *aventure* ADVENTURE, partly through apprehending *a-* as the indef. art. So vb. XV. Aphetic of *aventure* ADVENTURE vb. Hence **venturer** (-ER[1]), **venturous** (-OUS) XVI, **venturesome** (-SOME[1]) XVII.

venue A. †assault, attack XIV; thrust, esp. in fencing XVI; fencing bout; B. †arrival XIV (rare); (leg.) place where an action is laid or to which a jury is summoned XVI; place of meeting, locality XIX. - (O)F., sb. use of pp. fem. of *venir* :- L. *venīre* COME.

Venus A. ancient Roman goddess of beauty and love OE.; beautiful woman XVI; †venery; B. (astron.) second planet in distance from the sun XIII; †(alch.) copper XIV; (her.) green XVI; (member of) genus of bivalve molluscs XVIII. - L. *Venus* goddess of the ancient Romans = *venus*, *vener-* love.

veracious observant of the truth XVII; conforming to the truth XVIII. f. L. *vērāx*, *vērāc-*, f. *vērus* true; see VERY, -IOUS. So **veracity** XVII. - F. or medL.

veranda(h) XVIII. - Hindi *varandā* - Pg. *varanda*, †Sp. *baranda* railing, balustrade, balcony, of unkn. orig.

veratrine poisonous alkaloid obtained from sabadilla, etc. XIX. - F. *vératrine*, f. L. *vērātrum* hellebore; see -INE[5].

verb XIV. - (O)F. *verbe* or L. *verbum* word. So **verbal** dealing with words XV; consisting of words, oral XVI; pert. to a verb; concerned with words only XVII. - (O)F. *verbal* or late L. *verbālis*; see -AL[1]. **verbatim** word by word. XV. - medL. **verbiage** excessive accumulation of words XVIII; wording XIX. - F., f. †*verbeier* chatter. **verbose** XVII. - L. *verbōsus*. **verbosity** XVI. - L.

verbena (Rom. antiq., usu. pl. *verbenae*) certain leaves or twigs used in sacred rites; vervain. XVI. - L.

verb(um) sap. XIX. Shortening of L. *verbum sapienti* (*sat est*) (used in Eng. from XVII) a word (is enough) for a wise person.

verdant XVI. of obscure orig.; perh. - OF. *verdeant*, prp. of *verdoier* (mod. *-oyer*) :- L. **viridiāre*, f. *viridis* green.

verd-antique variety of green serpentine marble. XVIII. - F. †*verd antique* (now *vert a.*) antique green.

verderer royal forester. XVI. - AN. *verderer*, extended form of *verder* = (O)F. *verdier* :- Rom. **viridārius*, f. L. *viridis* green; see -ER[2].

verdict decision of a jury. XIII. ME. *verdit* - AN. *verdit* = OF. *veir-*, *voirdit*, f. *veir*, *voir* :- L. *vērum* true + *dit* :- L. *dictum* saying, speech, sb. use of n. pp. of *dīcere* say. The sp. with *ct* became current XVI.

verdigris green rust of copper. XIV. ME. *verdegres*, *vertegres* - OF. *vertegrez*, earlier *vert de Grece* (mod. *vert-de-gris*) 'green of Greece'. The reason for the name is unkn.

verditer pigment made by adding chalk to a solution of nitrate of copper. XVI. - OF. *verd* (mod. *vert*) *de terre* 'green of earth'.

verdure fresh green colour; green herbage XIV; †rich tapestry ornamented with vegetation XVI; †freshness; †taste, savour, odour. - (O)F., f. †*verd* green; see -URE.

verge[1] †penis XIV; rod or wand of office XV; *within the v.* within the area subject to the Lord High Steward (with ref. to his rod of office); extreme edge, margin, bank, border; space within a boundary, scope XVII. - (O)F. :- L. *virga* rod. Hence **verge** vb. †border, edge XVII; border (*up*)*on*, esp. fig. XVIII.

verge[2] †descend towards the horizon; move in a certain direction, incline, tend. XVII. - L. *vergere* bend, incline.

verger official bearing a rod before a church or university dignitary. XV. - AN. **verger* (cf. late L. *virgārius*), f. *verge* VERGE[1]; see -ER[2].

verify prove to be true XIV; ascertain the correctness of XVI. - (O)F. *vérifier* - medL. *vērificāre*, f. *vērus* true; see VERY, -FY. So **verification** XIV. - (O)F. or medL.

verily in truth XIII; in versions of the Bible, rendering late L. (Vulg.) *amēn*, Gr. *amḗn* AMEN XIV. ME. *verr(a)ily*, *verreli*, f. VERY + -LY[2].

verisimilar XVII. f. L. *vērīsimilis*, *vērī similis* 'like the truth', i.e. g. sg. of *vērus* true, *similis* like. So **verisimilitude** XVII. - L. See VERY, SIMILAR.

verity truth XIV; true statement or opinion XVI. ME. *verite* - (O)F. *verité*, repl. OF. *verté* :- L. *vēritās*, *-tāt-*, f. *vērus* true; see VERY, -ITY. So **veritable** †true; genuine, real XV; (after modF.) that is really so XIX. - (O)F. *véritable*; out of use by *c.*1650, re-adopted *c.*1830.

verjuice acid juice of unripe fruit. XIV. - OF. *vertjus*, (also mod.) *verjus*, i.e. *vert jus* 'green juice'.

vermeil (arch.) vermilion; adj. XV; sb. XVI; (from modF.) silver gilt, gilt bronze XIX. - (O)F. :- L. *vermiculus* little worm, grub (used in Vulg. Ex. 35: 25 for *coccum* scarlet), dim. of *vermis* WORM.

vermi-, comb. form of L. *vermis* WORM, as in **vermicide** (-CIDE[1]) XIX, **vermifuge** adj. XVII, sb. XVIII, **vermivorous** XVIII.

vermicelli pasta prepared in long slender hard

threads. XVII. - It., pl. of *vermicello*, dim. of *verme* :- L. *vermis* WORM.

vermicular †peristaltic XVII; pert. to a worm or worms, vermiform XVIII. - medL. *vermiculāris*, f. L. *vermiculus*, dim. of *vermis* WORM; see -CULE, -AR. So **vermiculation** being infested with worms; tortuous boring, as of a worm. XVII. - L., f. *vermiculārī* be worm-eaten.

vermilion cinnabar or red mercuric sulphide XIII; colour of this, bright red XIV. ME. *vermelyon* - OF. *vermeillon*, f. *vermeil* VERMEIL.

vermin animals of a noxious or offensive kind. XIII. - OF. *vermin*, (also mod.) *vermine* :- Rom. **vermīnum, -īna*, f. L. *vermis, -min-* WORM; see -INE[1]. So **verminous** XVII. - F. or L.

vermouth white wine flavoured with wormwood, etc. XIX. - F. *vermout* - G. *wermut* (see WORMWOOD), with assim. to the early G. sp. *wermuth*.

vernacular pert. to the native language. XVII. f. L. *vernāculus* domestic, native, indigenous, f. *verna* home-born slave; see -AR. Also sb. XVIII.

vernal pert. to the spring. XVI. - L. *vernālis*, f. *vernus* of the spring, f. *vēr* spring; see -AL[1]. So **vernation** (bot.) arrangement of leaves or fronds in the bud. XVIII. - modL., f. L. *vernāre* bloom.

vernicle cloth with which, according to legend, a woman wiped the face of Jesus Christ on the way to Calvary and on which his features were impressed; representation of this. XIV. - OF., alt. of *vernique*, (also mod.) *véronique* - medL. *veronica*, which has been supposed to be a perversion of **vēra īcōn* 'true image' and was subsequently taken as the name of the woman herself. Also **veronica**[2] XVII.

vernier movable scale for taking minute measurements. XVIII. - F., f. name of Paul *Vernier* (1580-1637), F. mathematician, who described it in 'Quadrant nouveau de mathématiques' (1631).

veronal sedative drug. XX. - G., f. *Verona*, name of an It. town; see -AL[1].

veronica[1] plant of the genus *Veronica*. XVI. Obscure use of the name *Veronica*.

veronica[2] see VERNICLE.

verrucose full of warty excrescences. XVII. - L. *verrūcōsus*, f. *verrūca* (whence **verruca** XVI), ult. rel. to WART; see -OSE[1].

versatile changeable, inconstant; marked by many-sidedness of talent. XVII. - F. *versatile* or L. *versātilis*, f. *versāt-*, pp. stem of *versāre*, frequent. of *vertere* turn; see -ILE.

verse metrical line; versicle OE.; section of a psalm or canticle XII (now: one of the small sections into which a chapter of the Bible is divided XVI); metrical composition XIII; stanza XIV. OE. *fers*, corr. to MLG., OHG. (Du., G.), ON. *vers* - L. *versus* turn of the plough, furrow, row, line of writing, verse, f. *vers-*, pp. stem of *vertere* turn; reinforced or repl. in ME. by adoption of (O)F. *vers*.

versed[1] (math.) in *v. sine* (XVI). tr. modL. *sinus versus*, i.e. L. *sinus* sine, *versus* turned, pp. of *vertere* turn; see -ED[1].

versed[2] experienced or skilled in. XVII. - F. *versé* or its source L. *versātus*, pp. of *versārī* stay, be situated, be occupied or engaged, pass. of *versāre*, frequent. of *vertere* turn; see -ED[1].

versicle (liturg.) short sentence or phrase recited antiphonally with a response XIV; little verse XV. - (O)F. *versicule* or L. *versiculus*, dim. of *versus* VERSE; see -CLE.

versicoloured of changing colour. XVIII. f. L. *versicolor*, f. *versus*, pp. of *vertere* turn + *color* COLOUR; see -ED[2].

versify write in verse. XIV. - (O)F. *versifier* - L. *versificāre*; see VERSE, -IFY. So **versification** XVII. - L. **versifier** XIV. - AN. *versifiur*, OF. *-fiour, -fieur*.

version rendering from one language into another XVI; particular form of a statement, document, etc. XVIII. - (O)F. - medL. *versiō, -ōn-*, f. *vers-*, pp. stem of *vertere* turn; see -SION.

verso back of the leaf of a book, being the side presented to the eye when the leaf has been turned over. XIX. - L. *versō* 'being turned', abl. sing. of pp. of *vertere* turn.

verst Russ. measure of length (⅔ of an Eng. mile). XVI. - Russ. *verstá*, partly through G. *werst* and F. *verste*.

versus (leg.) against. XV. - medL. (XIII) use of L. *versus* towards, in the sense of *adversus* against.

vert green vegetation in a wood XV; (her.) green XVI. - (O)F. *vert* :- L. *viridis, virid-* green, rel. to *virēre* be green; see -ID[1].

vertebra, pl. **-ae** joint of the spinal column. XVII. - L. *vertebra*, f. *vertere* turn; prop. pivot of bone. So **vertebrate** (-ATE[2]) XIX. - L.

vertex (geom.) point opposite the base XVI; zenith XVII; top, summit. - L. *vertex, vertic-* whirl, vortex, crown of the head, highest point, f. *vertere* turn. So **vertical** pert. to the zenith XVI; perpendicular, at right angles to the axis, etc. XVIII. - F. or late L.; see -AL[1].

vertigo XVI. - L. *vertīgō, -gin-*. So **vertiginous** XVII. - L. *vertīginōsus*.

vertu see VIRTU.

vervain herbaceous plant of the genus *Verbena*. XIV. - (O)F. *verveine* - L. *verbēna* VERBENA.

verve †special vein or bent in writing XVII; spirit, dash, go XIX. - (O)F. *verve* †form of expression, †empty chatter, †whim, vigour - L. *verba*, pl. of *verbum* WORD.

very adj. true XIII; exact, precise, actual XIV; sheer; mere XVI; adv. †truly, really XIV; highly, extremely XV. ME. *verray* - OF. *ver(r)ai* (mod. *vrai*) :- Rom. **vērāius*, obscurely f. L. *vērus* true :- IE. **wēros*, whence also OS., OHG. *wār* (Du. *waar*, G. *wahr*), OIr. *fīr*, W. *gwīr*. The termination was assim. to -Y[1].

Very (light) XX. f. name of the inventor, E. W. *Very*.

vesica bladder; †copper vessel used in distilling XVII; *v. piscis* 'fish bladder', painted oval figure used as an aureole XIX. - L. *vēsīca, vessīca, vensīca* bladder, blister. So **vesical** pert. to the urinary bladder. XVIII. - late L. **vesicate** blister. XVII. f. pp. stem of late L. *vēsīcāre*; see -ATE[3]. **vesication** XVI. **vesicle** small sac or cyst XVI; small elevation of the cuticle containing fluid XVIII. - F. *vésicule* or L. *vēsīcula*.

vesper A. evening star, Hesperus XIV; evening

XVII; B. pl. †public disputations held on the eve of the commencement of a bachelor of arts XVI; pl. sixth of the canonical hours, evensong XVII. A. - L. *vesper* evening star, evening = Gr. *hésperos*; B. - OF. *vespres* (mod. *vêpres*) - ecclL. *vesperās*, acc. pl. of L. *vespera* evening, eventide = Gr. *hespérā*.

vessel †(coll. sg.) domestic utensils; article designed to serve as a receptacle; in and after biblical use, human body or person; boat or ship. XIII. - (i) AN. *vessel* = OF. *vaissel* (mod. *vaisseau* vessel, vase, ship) :- late L. *vascellum* small vase, dim. of *vās* vessel; (ii) AN. *vessele* = (O)F. *vaisselle* pots and pans, plate :- Rom. **vascella*, pl. of L. *vascellum* used as coll. sg. fem.

vest[1] (hist.) loose outer garment; †vestment; sleeveless garment worn by men beneath the coat XVII; undergarment for the upper part of the body worn next to the skin XIX. - F. *veste* - It. *veste* garment :- L. *vestis* clothing, attire, garment, f. IE. **wes-* (see WEAR[1]). So **vestiary** pert. to dress. XVII. - L. *vestiārius*. **vestment** garment, article of clothing XIII; spec. in eccl. use XIV. ME. *vesti-*, *vestement* - OF. *vesti-*, *vestement* (mod. *vêtement*) - L. *vestīmentum*. **vestry** room in a church in which clerics robe, and vestments, etc., are kept XIV; assembly of parishioners XVI. - AN. **vest(e)rie*, alt. of (O)F. *vestiaire*, †*vestiarie*, by assoc. with *-erie* -ERY. **vesture** (article of) apparel XIV; (leg.) what grows upon the land, except trees XV. - OF. *vesture* (mod. *vêture*) - medL. *vestūra*, for late L. *vestītūra*.

vest[2] A. settle (a person) in the possession of something or (a thing) in the possession of some one, invest XV; B. clothe XVI. In both uses first in pp. *vested* (-ED[1]) - OF. *vestu*, pp. of *vestir* (mod. *vêtir*) clothe, †invest :- L. *vestīre* clothe, in medL. put in possession, as by investing a person with the insignia of an office, f. *vestis* attire (see prec.).

Vesta (Rom. myth.) goddess of the household XIV; one of the minor planets XIX; kind of wax or wood match. - L., corr. to Gr. *Hestiā*, personification of *hestiā* hearth, house, household. So **Vestal**, *v. virgin* one of the priestesses having charge of the sacred fire in the temple of Vesta in ancient Rome XV; pert. to, chaste as, a priestess of Vesta XVI; sb. vestal virgin, chaste woman. - L. *vestālis*; see -AL[1].

vestibule entrance hall or court XVII; (anat., zool.) XVIII. - F. *vestibule* or L. *vestibulum*.

vestige trace of something lost or gone XVII; slight trace XVIII. - F. - L. *vestīgium* sole of the foot, footprint, trace.

vet colloq. shortening of VETERINARY *surgeon* or of its equiv. *veterinarian* sb. XIX. Hence as vb. subject to (professional) examination. XIX.

vetch (fruit of a) plant of the genus *Vicia*. XIV. ME. *fecche*, *ficche* and *vecche* - AN., ONF. *veche* = OF. *vece* (mod. *vesce*) :- L. *vicia*. Hence **vetchling** plant of the genus *Lathyrus*. XVI; see -LING[1].

veteran experienced soldier XVI; adj. XVII. - F. *vétéran* or L. *veterānus*, f. *vetus*, *veter-* old; see -AN.

veterinary pert. to the treatment of cattle and domestic animals. XVIII. - L. *veterīnārius*, f. *veterīnus* pert. to cattle (*veterīnæ* fem. pl., *veterīna* n. pl. cattle), perh. f. *vetus*, *veter-* old (see prec.), as if the orig. ref. was to animals past work; see -INE[1], -ARY. So **veterinarian** XVII.

veto prohibition designed to prevent a proposed act XVII; act of a competent person or body of preventing legislation XVIII. - L. *vetō* I forbid (1st pers. sg. pres. ind. of *vetere*). Hence vb. XVIII.

vex trouble, afflict, annoy. XV. - (O)F. *vexer* - L. *vexāre* shake, agitate, disturb. So **vexation** XV. - (O)F. - L.; whence **vexatious** XVI.

vexillum banner; (bot.) large external petal of a papilionaceous flower. XVIII. - L. *vexillum* banner, f. base of *vehere* carry.

via[1] (astron.) *Via Lactea* the Milky Way XVII; *via media* intermediate course XIX. - L. *via* way, road; see WAY.

via[2] by way of. XVIII. - L. *viā*, abl. of *via* VIA[1].

viable capable of living or existing. XIX. - F., f. *vie* life (:- L. *vīta*); see -ABLE. So **viability** XIX.

viaduct XIX. f. L. *via* VIA[1], after *aqueduct*.

vial XIV. ME. *viole*, alt. of *fiole* PHIAL.

viand article or kind of food, orig. and esp. pl. XIV. - (O)F. *viande* †food, (now) meat :- Rom. **vī(v)anda* fem. sb., alt. of L. *vīvenda* gerundive of *vīvere* live.

viaticum Holy Communion as administered to the dying; necessaries for a journey. XVI. - L. *viāticum* travelling money, provisions for a journey, sb. use of n. of *viāticus*, f. *via* VIA[1]; see -ATIC.

vibrant †agitated, energetic XVI; vibrating XVII. - prp. of L. *vibrāre*, move rapidly to and fro, shake, be agitated; see -ANT. So **vibrate** swing to and fro. XVII. f. pp. stem of L. *vibrāre*; see -ATE[3]. **vibration** XVII. - L. **vibratory** (-ORY[2]) XVIII.

vibrio (zool.) bacterioid organism having a vibratory motion. XIX. f. L. *vibrāre* VIBRATE.

viburnum shrub of the genus *Viburnum*, e.g. guelder rose. XVIII. - L., 'wayfaring-tree'.

vicar representative of God on earth XIII; the Pope as Vicar of Christ XIV; person acting in a parish for the parson or rector, (later) incumbent of a parish of which the tithe is impropriated or appropriated; bishop's deputy. - AN. *vikere*, *vicare*, (O)F. *vicaire* (now) assistant curate, deputy - L. *vicārius* substitute, deputy, f. *vicis* (g.). etc., change, alteration, time, turn; see VICE[4], -AR. So **vicariate** (-ATE[1]) XVII. - medL. **vicarious** taking the place of another. XVII. f. L. *vicārius*. Hence **vicarage** XV.

vice[1] corruption of morals, wicked practice XIII; fault, defect XIV. - (O)F. - L. *vitium* physical or other defect, fault, vice.

vice[2] †winding staircase XIV; †screw XV; tool with two jaws opening and closing by means of a screw XVI. - (O)F. *vis* :- L. *vītis* vine, vine stem, prop. tendril, plant with tendrils, rel. to *viēre* twine.

vice[3] orig. sb. use of the prefix VICE- in the sense 'deputy'; in more recent use, the second el. is usu. implied or expressed in the context.

vice[4] in place of. XVIII. - L., abl. of **vix*, extant only in obl. forms *vicis*, *vicem*, *vice*, *vicēs*, *vicibus*.

vice- repr. L. *vice* in place of (see prec.), which, prop. construed with a genitive, was prefixed immed. to a nominative in late L., e.g. *vice-*

quæstor, and so used widely in medL. The oldest Eng. exx., of which *vice-chancellor* (XV) is the earliest, show the prefix in the OF. forms *vi(s)-*, which were later repl. by the L. form, except in *viscount*.

vicennial (Sc. law) extending to 20 years. XVIII. f. late L. *vīcennium*, f. *vīcies* 20 times.

viceroy XVI. - F. *viceroy*, †*visroy* (mod. *viceroi*), f. *vice-* VICE- + *roi* king. So **viceroyalty** XVIII. - F. *viceroyauté*.

vicesimal XVII. - L. *vīcēsimus* twentieth, f. *vīcēnī* twenty each + -AL[1].

vice versa XVII. - L. 'the position being reversed'; *vice*, abl. of **vix* (see VICE[4]), and abl. sg. fem. of *versus*, pp. of *vertere* turn.

vicinage neighbourhood. XIV. - OF. *visenage* (mod. *voisinage*) - Rom. **vīcīnāticum*, f. L. *vīcīnus* neighbouring, neighbour, prop. of the same quarter or village, f. *vīcus* cluster of dwellings, street, quarter of a town, village, corr. to Goth. *weiks* and rel. to Gr. (*ϝoîkos*, Skr. *veśá-* house; see -AGE. So **vicinity** XVI. - L. *vīcīnitās*.

vicious A. pert to vice XIV; addicted to vice XIV; (of horses, etc.) inclined to be savage XVIII; B. (leg.) made void XIV; impaired by fault or defect XVI. - OF. *vicious* (mod. *vicieux*) - L. *vitiōsus*, f. *vitium* VICE[1]; see -IOUS.

vicissitude mutation, mutability XVI; change in human affairs XVII. - (O)F. *vicissitude* or L. *vicissitūdō*, f. *vicissim* by turns, f. *vic-* turn; see VICE[4], -TUDE.

victim living creature offered in sacrifice XV; one who suffers death or severe treatment XVII. - L. *victima*, perh. rel. to Goth. *weihan*, etc. consecrate. Hence **victimize** XIX.

victor XIV. - AN. *victo(u)r* or L. *victor*, f. *vict-*, pp. stem of *vincere* conquer; see -OR[1].

Victoria XIX. Name of the Queen of Great Britain (1837-1901) given to various objects: a gigantic water-lily, a luscious red plum, a light four-wheeled carriage. Hence **Victorian** XIX. **victorine** lady's fur tippet. XIX.

victory state or fact of having conquered XIV; Rom. goddess of victory XVI. - AN. *victorie* = (O)F. *victoire* - L. *victōria*, f. *victor* VICTOR; see -Y[3]. So **victorious** XIV - AN. *victorious* = (O)F. *victorieux* - L.

victual (coll. sg. and pl.) provisions for food, articles of food. XIV. ME. *vitaile(s)* - OF. *vitaille*, later (and mod.) *victuaille* :- late L. *vīctūālia* n. pl. of *vīctūālis*, f. L. *vīctus* livelihood, f. base of *vīvere* live; see -AL[1]. The sp. has been assim. to L. So vb. XIV. - OF. *vitaillier*, *vi(c)tuaillier*. **victualler** XIV. - OF. *vitaill(i)er*, *-our*; see -ER[2].

vicuna S. Amer. animal allied to the llama XVII; vicuna cloth XIX. - Sp. *vicuña* (Pg. *vicunha*) - Quechua.

vide see, refer to. XVI. - L. *vidē*, imper. sg. of *vidēre* see (see WIT[2]).

videlicet that is to say, namely. XV. - L. *vidēlicet*, f. *vidē-*, stem of *vidēre* see + *licet* it is permissible; see WIT[2], LICENCE.

vidimus (leg.) copy of a document bearing an attestation that it is authentic. XV. - L. *vīdimus* we have seen, 1st pers. pl. perf. of *vidēre* see (see WIT[2]).

vie make a challenge XV; enter into rivalry *with* XVII. prob. aphetic of late ME. *avie*, *envie* - OF. *envier* outbid :- L. *invītāre* INVITE, in Rom. challenge, make a bid.

vielle hurdy-gurdy. XVIII. - F. *vielle*, OF. *viele*; see VIOL.

view A. †formal inspection XV; exercise of the faculty of sight; sight, look, vision XVI; B. mental vision XV; conception, opinion XVI; survey XVII; aim, intention. - AN. *vewe*, *vieue*, OF. *veue* (mod. *vue*), ppl. sb. from *veoir* (mod. *voir*) to see, f. L. *vidēre*; see WIT[2]. Hence (or aphetic of †*aview* - F. *avuer*, †*aveuer*, f. *à* AD- + *vue*) vb. XVI.

vigesimal pert. to 20. XVII. f. L. *vīgēsimus*, var. of *vīcēsimus* VICESIMAL.

vigil eve of a church festival XIII; watch XVII. - (O)F. *vigile* - L. *vigilia* watch, watchfulness, f. *vigil* awake, alert, rel. to *vigēre* be vigorous or lively. So **vigilant** XV. - L. *vigilāns*, *-ant-*, prp. of *vigilāre* keep awake.

vigneron wine-grower. XV. - (O)F., f. *vigne* VINE.

vignette ornamental design on a blank space in a book XVIII; photograph of head (and shoulders) XIX. - (O)F., dim. of *vigne* VINE; see -ETTE.

vigour, U.S. **vigor** active strength or force XIV; legal force XV; energetic action XVII. - OF. *vigour* (mod. *vigueur*) - L. *vigor*, *-ōr-* liveliness, activity, f. *vigēre* be lively, flourish; see -OUR[2]. So **vigorous** XIV (not in gen. use before XVII). - OF. *vigorous* (mod. *vigoureux*) - medL. *vigōrōsus*.

viking XIX (first in Icel. form *vikingr* or vars. of this, *vikinger*, *-ir*). - ON. (Icel.) *víkingr*, commonly held to be f. *vík* creek, inlet + *-ingr* -ING[3], as if 'frequenter of inlets of the sea'; but the existence of the word in OE. as early as VIII (in *wīcingsċeaða*) and in OFris. (*wī(t)sing*) suggests that it may have originated in that linguistic area (f. OE. *wīc*, OFris. *wīk*, in the sense 'camp').

vile of low or base quality or character. XIII. - (O)F. *vil* m., fem. *vile* :- L. *vīlis* of low value or price, common, base. So **vilify** †debase in value XV (freq. in XVII); depreciate in language XVI. - late L. *vīlificāre*. **vilipend** treat contemptuously XV; represent as contemptible XVI. - (O)F. *vilipender* or L. *vīlipendere*, f. *vīlis* + *pendere* consider.

villa country residence, orig. one with farm buildings, etc. XVII; residence in the suburbs of a town or in a residential district XVIII. Partly - L. *vīlla* country house, farm; partly - It. *villa* :- L. *vīlla*. So **village** - (O)F. :- coll. deriv. of L. *vīlla*.

villain base fellow, (later) depraved scoundrel, (hist.; often sp. VILLEIN by mod. historians) feudal serf, peasant cultivator in subjection to a lord XIV. ME. *vilein*, *vilain* - OF. *vilein*, *vilain* (mod. *vilain*) :- Rom. **vīllānus*, f. L. *vīlla*; see prec., -AN. So **villainy** XIII. - (O)F. *vilenie*. Hence **villainous** XIV.

villanelle †rustic song or tune XVI; pastoral or lyric poem in stanza form with two rhymes throughout XIX. - F. - It. *villanella*, fem. of *villanello* rural, rustic, f. *villano* peasant = (O)F. *vilain* VILLAIN.

villeggiatura residence in the country. XVIII. - It., f. *villeggiare* to stay in the country, f. *villa* VILLA.

villein (hist.) see VILLAIN. So **villeinage** XIV. - AN., OF. *vilenage*, medL. *villenagium*.

villous covered with numerous thick-set stout hairlike projections. XIV - L. *villōsus* (whence also **villose** XVIII), f. *villus* growth of hair; see -OUS, -OSE[1].

vim (orig. U.S.) force, energy, 'go'. XIX. usu. supposed to be - L. *vim*, acc. of *vīs* strength, energy; but poss. a symbolic formation.

vimineous made of or producing flexible twigs. XVII. f. L. *vīmineus*, f. *vīmen*, *-min-* osier; see -EOUS.

vinaceous wine-coloured. XVII. f. L. *vīnāceus*, f. *vīnum* WINE; see -ACEOUS.

vinaigrette A. small two-wheeled carriage formerly used in France (said to be so called from resembling vinegar-sellers' carts) XVII; B. smelling-bottle XIX. - F., f. *vinaigre* VINEGAR; see -ETTE.

vincible that may be overcome (spec. in theol. *v. ignorance*). XVI. - L. *vincibilis*, f. *vincere* overcome; see -IBLE.

vinculum bond, tie XVII; (math.) straight line drawn over two or more terms XVIII. - L., f. *vincīre* bind; cf. -ULE.

vindicate †set free XVI; †avenge XVII; clear from censure, justify; defend the claims of. f. pp. stem of L. *vindicāre* (also *vendicāre*) claim, set free, punish, avenge, f. *vindex*, *-dic-* claimant, protector, deliverer, avenger; see -ATE[3]. So **vindication** †avenging XV; defence against censure, etc. XVII. - OF. or L. **vindictive** revengeful. XVII. f. L. *vindicta* vengeance.

vine XIII. - OF. *vine*, (also mod.) *vigne* :- L. *vīnea* vineyard, vine, sb. use of fem. of *vīneus* pert. to wine, f. *vīnum* WINE.

vinegar liquid formed by the acetous fermentation of wine. XIII. ME. *vinegre*, later *vineger* (XV-XVII), *vinegar* (from XVI) - OF. *vyn egre* (mod. *vinaigre*), repr. Rom. **vīnum acrum* (for L. *acre*) 'sour wine'; see WINE, EAGER.

vineyard XIV. f. VINE + YARD[1]; superseding ME. *winyard*, OE. *wīngeard*.

vingt(-et)-un game of cards in which the object is to make the number 21. XVIII. - F., 'twenty (and) one'.

vinous pert. to wine. XVII. - L. *vīnōsus*, f. *vīnum* WINE; see -OUS. So **vinosity** XVII. - late L.

vintage crop of a vineyard XV (since XVIII spec. with ref. to the age or year of a wine); grape harvest XVI. alt., by assoc. with †*vinter*, VINTNER, of late ME. *vyndage*, *vendage* - (O)F. *vendange* :- L. *vindēmia*, f. *vīnum* WINE + *dēmere* take away, f. DE- + *emere* buy.

vintner wine merchant. XV. - AL. *vintenārius*, var. of *vini-*, *vin(e)tārius* - AN. *viniter*, *vineter*, OF. *vinetier* - medL. *vīnātārius*, *-ētārius*, f. L. *vīnētum* vineyard, f. *vīnum* WINE; see -ER[2].

viol XV (*vyell*). - OF. *viel(l)e* (mod. *vielle* viol, hurdy-gurdy), alt. of *viole* - Pr. *viola*, *viula*, prob. rel. to FIDDLE; the present form (- F. *viole*) dates from XVI. So **viol da gamba** XVIII (earlier *gambo* XVI-XVII). - It. *viola da gamba* 'leg-viol', i.e. the instrument when played being placed between the legs.

viola[1] †violet XV; single-coloured pansy XIX. - L. *viola* violet. So **violaceous** XVII. f. L. *violāceus* violet-coloured.

viola[2] alto or tenor violin. XVIII. - Sp., It., prob. - Pr. *viola*; see VIOL.

violate infringe, transgress; ravish, rape; desecrate, profane XV; disturb violently XVII. f. pp. stem of L. *violāre*, f. *vīs*, *vi-* force, corr. to Gr. *ϝís*; see -ATE[3]. So **violation** XV. - (O)F. or L. **violence** exercise of force. XIII. - (O)F. - L. *violentia*, f. *violēns*, *-ent-*, beside *violentus*, whence (O)F. *violent*, the source of Eng. **violent** (XIV).

violet A. plant of the genus *Viola*; B. dress of purplish-blue, the colour itself XIV. - (O)F. *violette*, †*-ete* in both senses and (O)F. *violet* in the second sense, dims. of *viole* - L. *viola* VIOLA[1].

violin XVI. - It. *violino*, f. *viola* VIOLA[2]. Hence **violinist** XVII.

violoncello XVIII. - It., dim. of *violone* double-bass viol; abbrev. CELLO.

viper XVI. - (O)F. *vipère* or L. *vīpera* serpent :- **vīvipera*, f. *vīvus* alive + *parere* bring forth. So **viperine** XVI. - L. *vīperīnus*. Hence **viperous** XVI.

virago †name given by Adam to Eve, after the use in Vulg. Gen. 2: 23 ('Hæc vocabitur virago, quoniam de viro sumpta est') OE.; man-like or heroic woman, female warrior (as in L.) XIV; bold or violent woman. - L. *virāgō*, obscurely f. *vir* man.

virelay short-lined poem on two rhymes. XIV. - (O)F. *virelai*, alt. of †*vireli* (perh. orig. a refrain) after *lai* LAY[2].

virement application of resources intended for one end to the purposes of another. XX. - F., f. *virer* turn (cf. VEER[2]) + -MENT.

vireo small Amer. bird. XIX. - L.

virescent greenish. XIX. f. L. *virēscēns*, *-ent-*, prp. of *virescere* become green, f. *virēre* be green; see -ENT, -ESCENT.

virgate early land-measure. XVII. - medL. *virgāta*, f. L. *virga* rod, VERGE[1]; see -ATE[1].

virgin unmarried or chaste woman or girl XIII; adj. XVI. - AN., OF. *virgine*, *-ene* (mod. *vierge*) - L. *virgō*, *-gin-*. So **virginal** XV. - (O)F. or L. (see -AL[1]); as sb. (sg. and pl.) applied to a musical instrument (XVI), perh. so called because it was intended for young ladies. **virginity** XIII. - (O)F. *virginité* - L. *virginitās*.

Virgo constellation lying between Leo and Libra; sixth sign of the zodiac. XIV. - L., 'virgin'.

virgule sloping or vertical line used in medieval MSS. as a mark of punctuation. XIX. - F. *virgule* comma - L. *virgula*, dim. of *virga* rod.

virid green. XVI. - L. *viridis*, f. *virēre* be green; see -ID[1]. So **viridity** XV.

virile pert. to or characteristic of a man. XV. - (O)F. *viril* or L. *virīlis*, f. *vir* man = OE., OS., OHG. *wer*, OIr. *fer*, W. *gŵr* :- IE. **wiros*, beside **wīros*, whence Skr. *vīrá-*; see -ILE. So **virility** XVI. - (O)F.

virtu, vertu taste for works of art. XVIII. - It. *virtù* (see next) used in this sense.

virtue †power, influence; efficacy, conformity to moral principles; excellence XIII; (arch.) high merit or accomplishment XIV; †valour. - (O)F. *vertu* = It. *virtù* :- L. *virtūs*, *-tūt-* valour, worth, merit, moral perfection, f. *vir* man (see VIRILE). So **virtual** †effective XIV; that is so in essence or effect XVII (whence **virtually** XV). - medL. *virtuālis*; see -AL[1]. **virtuoso** XVII. - It. - late L. *virtuōsus* (whence, through (O)F. *vertueux*, **virtuous** †valiant XIII; righteous XIV).

virus venom XVI; (path.) poison of a disease XVIII. - L. *vīrus*, rel. to OIr. *fí* poison, Gr. *īós* venom, rust, Skr. *viṣá-*. So **virulent** XIV. - L. *vīrulentus* poisonous.

visa certificate of examination on a passport. XIX. - F. - mod. use of L. *vīsa* 'things seen', n. pl. of pp. of *vidēre* see (see WIT[2]).

visage XIII. - (O)F., f. OF. *vis* :- L. *vīsus* sight, appearance, in Rom. face, f. pp. base of *vidēre* see; see WIT[2], -AGE.

vis-à-vis either of two persons facing each other; carriage for two sitting face-to-face. XVIII. - (O)F., 'face to face'; OF. *vis* face (see prec.), *à* to (:- L. *ad*).

viscacha S. Amer. rodent. XVII. - Sp. - Quechua *(h)uiscacha*.

viscera XVII. - L., pl. of *vīscus* VISCUS.

viscid glutinous, sticky. XVII. - late L. *viscidus*, f. L. *viscum* mistletoe, birdlime; see -ID[1]. So **viscous** XIV. - AN. *viscous* or late L. *viscōsus*. **viscosity** XV. - (O)F. or medL.

viscount (hist.) deputy of a count or earl, (high) sheriff XIV; member of the fourth order of the British peerage XV. AN. *viscounte* (OF. *vi(s)conte*, *viconte*, mod. *vicomte*) - medL. *vicecomes*, *-comit-* (see VICE-, COUNT[2]).

viscus soft internal organ of the body. XVIII. - L.

visible XIV. - (O)F. *visible* or L. *vīsibilis*, f. *vīs-*, pp. stem of *vidēre* see; see WIT[2], -IBLE. So **visibility** XVI. - F. or late L.

vision something that appears to be seen otherwise than by ordinary sight XIII; seeing something not present to the eye XIV; bodily sight XV. - (O)F. - L. *vīsiō*, *-ōn-* sight, thing seen, f. *vīs-*, pp. stem of *vidēre* see; see WIT[2], -ION. Hence **visionary** adj. XVII; sb. XVIII.

visit (of God) come to, in order to comfort or benefit; go to persons in sickness, etc. to comfort them; †make trial of XIII; deal severely with, assail, afflict XIV; punish, requite; go to see in a friendly way (attend as a physician XVI); go to in order to inspect, for worship, etc. - (O)F. *visiter* - L. *vīsitāre* go to see, frequent. of *vīsāre* view, see to, visit, f. *vīs-*, pp. stem of *vidēre* see (see prec.). The earlier uses are based on those of L. *visitare* in Vulg. So **visit** sb. XVII. - F. *visite*, or immed. f. the vb. **visitant** XVI. - F. or L. **visitation** XIV. - (O)F. - late L. **visitatorial** XVII. f. *vīsitāt-*, ppl. stem of L. *vīsitāre*. **visitor** XIV. - AN. *visitour*, (O)F. *visiteur*.

visor, vizor part of a helmet covering the face; mask. XIV. ME. *viser* - AN. *viser* = (O)F. *visière*, f. OF. *vis* face; see VISAGE, -OR[2].

vista view, prospect; opening in a wood, etc. affording a view; fig. XVII. - It.

visual proceeding from the eye XV; pert. to sight or vision XVII; pert. to the object of sight XVIII. - late L. *vīsuālis*, f. *vīsus* sight, f. *vīs-*; see VISION, -AL[1]. Hence **visualize** XIX.

vital pert. to life XIV; sustaining or essential to life XV; endowed with life XVI; life-giving; essential or indispensable to the existence of something XVII. - (O)F. - L. *vītālis*, f. *vīta* life :- **vīvita*, f. *vīvus* living; see -AL[1]. So sb. pl. **vitals** XVII. - L. *vītālia* n. pl. used sb. **vitality** vital force, principle of life XVI; active force, vigour XIX. - L. Hence **vitalize** XVII.

vitamin XX (*vitamine*). - G. *vitamine*, f. L. *vīta* life (cf. prec.) + *amine* AMINE. So named because it was first believed that an amino-acid was present, the sp. being later modified in order to avoid the suggestion.

vitellus (biol.) yolk of egg. XVIII. - L.

vitiate render faulty or corrupt XVI; render of no effect XVII. f. pp. stem of L. *vitiāre* (after †*vitiate* pp. XV), f. *vitium* VICE[1]; see -ATE[2,3]. So **vitiation** XVII. - L.

vitreous of or resembling glass. XVII. f. L. *vitreus* of glass, glassy, clear, transparent, f. *vitrum* glass; see -EOUS. So **vitrify** XVI. - F. *vitrifier* or medL. **vitrificāre*.

vitriol sulphate of iron, copper, etc. XIV; *oil of v.* concentrated sulphuric acid XVI; caustic speech, feeling, etc. XVIII. - (O)F. *vitriol* or medL. *vitriolum*, f. L. *vitrum* glass; so named on account of the glassy appearance of vitriol salts. So **vitriolic** XVII.

vitta - L. 'band', 'fillet', 'chaplet'; used in various deriv. techn. senses from XVII.

vituperate blame in strong language. XVI. f. pp. stem of L. *vituperāre*, f. *vitu-*, for *viti-*, stem of *vitium* VICE[1]; see -ATE[3]. So **vituperation** XV. - OF. or L.

viva[1] cry of 'long live...!', cheer, hurrah. XVII. - It., 3rd sg. pres. subj. of *vivere* :- L. *vīvere* live. So **vivat** XVII. - F. or L. (3rd sg. pres. subj. of *vīvere*).

viva[2] XIX. (colloq.) short for **viva voce** (XIX) oral examination, 'with living voice', abl. of fem. of L. *vīvus* living + *vōx* VOICE.

vivacious full of liveliness or animation. XVII. f. L. *vīvāx*, *-āc-* conscious or tenacious of life, lively, vigorous, f. *vīvus* alive; see VIVID, -ACIOUS. So **vivacity** XV. - (O)F. - L.

vivarium enclosed place for keeping live animals, esp. fish. XVI. - L. 'warren, fishpond', sb. use of *vīvārius*, f. *vīvus* alive; see -ARY.

vivid XVII. - L. *vīvidus*, f. *vīvere* be living, *vīvus* alive, lively, corr. to Skr. *jīvati*, *jīvá-*, rel. to Gr. *bíos* life, and QUICK; see -ID[1].

viviparous bringing forth young in a live state. XVII. f. L. *vīviparus*, f. *vīvus* alive + *-parus* bring forth; see -OUS.

vivisection XVIII. f. *vīvi-*, comb. form of L. *vīvus* alive + SECTION, after *dissection*.

vixen XV. ME. *fixene fox* 'vixen of the fox'; not recorded in OE., which had *fyxe* and adj. *fyxen*, but there is a parallel sb. in late OHG. *fuhsin* (G. *füchsin*); see FOX, -EN[3].

viz. = VIDELICET. XVI. repr. medL. *viȝ*, in which *ȝ* is the normal symbol for the termination *-et*.

vizard mask. XVI. alt. of *visar* (XV-XVI), *vizar* (XVI-XVII), vars. of VISOR; see -ARD.

vizier in Muslim countries, high official, viceroy, etc. XVI. Early forms *vezir*, *vizir* - F. *visir*, *vizir* or Sp. *visir* - Turk. *vezir* - Arab. *wazīr*. Hence **vizierate** dignity of a vizier. XVII.

vizor see VISOR.

vocable word. XVI. - F. *vocable* or L. *vocābulum*, f. *vocāre* call; see -BLE. So **vocabulary** list of words with their meanings attached XVI; range of words in a written language, etc. XVIII. - medL. *vocābulārius*, *-ārium*; see -ARY.

vocal pert. to or uttered or formed by the voice. XIV (rare before XVI). - L. *vōcālis* uttering voice, f. *vōx*, *vōc-* VOICE; see -AL[1]. Hence **vocalism** exercise of the voice; (philol.) system of vowels. XIX. **vocalist** †speaker XVII (rare); vocal musician XIX.

vocation XV. - (O)F. *vocation* or L. *vocātiō*, *-ōn-*, f. *vocāre* call. So **vocative** (gram.) XV. - (O)F. *vocatif* or L. *vocātīvus*.

vociferate XVII. f. pp. stem of L. *vōciferārī*, f. *vōx*, *vōc-* VOICE + *fer-*, stem of *ferre* BEAR[2]; see ATE[3]. So **vociferation** XIV. - (O)F. or L. **vociferous** XVII; see -IFEROUS.

vodka XIX. - Russ. *vódka*, dim. of *vodá* WATER.

voe (Orkney and Shetland dial.) bay, inlet. XVII. Norw. *vaag*, ON., Icel. *vágr* = OE. *wǣg* wave.

vogue †*the v.* foremost place in estimation, greatest currency XVI; popular esteem XVII; course of success; prevailing fashion. - F. - It. *voga* rowing, fashion, f. *vogare* row, be going well, presumably of Gmc. orig. and f. the base repr. by (M)HG. *wogen* wave, float, be borne by the waves.

voice sound(s) produced by the organs of utterance XIII; expressed will or choice, vote XIV; vocal capacity, as for singing XVII. - AN. *voiz*, *voice*, OF. *vois*, *voiz* (also mod. *voix*) :- L. *vōx*, *vōc-*. Hence **voice** vb. speak of, state XV; give utterance to XVII; endow with voice XVIII.

void not occupied, empty XIII; ineffective, useless XIV; having no legal force XV; sb. empty space XVII. - OF. *voide*, dial. var. of *vuide* (mod. *vide*) fem., superseding *vuit* m. :- Rom. **vocitus* pp. formation on **voc-*, repr. also in L. *vocīvus*, with parallel **vac-* of *vacāre* (see VACANT).

volatile evaporating rapidly; lively. XVII. - (O)F. *volatil* or L. *volātilis*, f. pp. stem of *volāre* fly; see -ILE.

volcano XVII. - It. - L. *Volcānus*, *Vulcānus* Rom. god of fire. So **volcanic** XVIII. - F. *volcanique*.

vole[1] winning of all the tricks in certain card games. XVII. - F., f. *voler* :- L. *volāre* fly.

vole[2] mouse-like animal (short-tailed field mouse, water-rat, etc.). XIX. orig. *vole-mouse* - Norw. **vollmus* (cf. Icel. *vollarmús*), f. *voll* field (ON. *vǫllr*) + *mus* MOUSE.

volitant flitting. XIX. - prp. of L. *volitāre*, frequent. of *volāre* fly; see -ANT.

volition willing, resolving. XVII. - F. *volition* or medL. *volitiō*, *-ōn-*, f. *volō* I wish, WILL[2]; see -ITION.

volley simultaneous discharge of firearms or flight of missiles; utterance of many words, etc.; phr. *at the v.* of a ball in its flight, etc., (fig.) without consideration, at random XVI; return stroke at a ball before it has touched the ground XIX. - (O)F. *volée* :- Rom. **volāta* flight, sb. use of pp. fem. of L. *volāre* fly; see -Y[3]. Hence vb. XVI.

volplane aeronautical glide. XX. - F. *vol plané*, i.e. *vol* flight (f. *voler* fly), *plané*, pp. of *planer* hover.

volt unit of electromotive force. XIX. Named after Alessandro *Volta* (1745-1827), It. physician and chemist, whence also **voltaic** XIX.

volt(e) †*volta*, *lavolta*, a kind of dance XVI; sudden movement to avoid a thrust in fencing XVII. - F. *volte* - It. *volta*, sb. use of fem. pp. of *volgere* to turn :- L. *volvere*.

volte-face XIX. - F. - It. *voltafaccia* 'turn-face', f. *voltare* turn :- Rom. **volvitāre*, frequent. of *volvere* roll + *faccia* face.

voluble †variable; †rotatory; rapid and fluent (of speech). XVI. - F. *voluble* or L. *volūbilis*, f. *volū-*; see next, -BLE. So **volubility** XVI. - F. or L.

volume (hist.) roll of parchment, etc. forming a book; tome XIV; size, bulk (†of a book) XVI, (of other things) XVII; (poet.) coil, convolution XVII. ME. *volym*, *volum(e)* - OF. *volum*, (also mod.) *volume* - L. *volūmen* roll of writing, book, coil, f. *volū-*, var. of base **wolw-* of *volvere* roll = Gr. *eilúein*, f. IE. **wel-* **wol-* turn. So **voluminous** XVII. - late L. *volūminōsus*.

voluntary adj. XIV; sb. piece of music selected by an organist to be played e.g. while a congregation departs XVIII. - (partly after (O)F. *volontaire*, †*voluntaire*) L. *voluntārius*, f. *voluntās* will, for **voluntitās*, f. prp. form of the same type as *eunt-* going (f. *volō* I WILL[2]) + *-tās* -TY[2]; see -ARY. So **volunteer** one who voluntarily offers his services, orig. mil. XVII. - F. *volontaire* - L. *voluntārius*; the suffix was assim. to -IER[2] and (later) -EER. Hence **volunteering** XVII; whence by back-formation **volunteer** vb. XVIII.

voluptuous pert. to sensual pleasure. XIV. - (O)F. *voluptueux* or L. *voluptuōsus*, f. *voluptās* pleasure, f. *volup* agreeably, f. **wol-* **wel-* WILL[2]; see -UOUS. So **voluptuary** XVII. - L. *voluptuārius*.

volute spiral conformation. XVII. - F. *volute* or L. *volūta*, pp. of *volvere* roll.

volva (bot.) membrane covering fungi. XVIII. - L., f. *volvere* roll, wrap.

vomer (anat., etc.) applied to various bones. XVIII. - L., 'ploughshare'.

vomit sb. XIV. - OF. *vomite* or L. *vomitus*, f. *vomere* vomit, rel. to Skr. *vámiti*, Gr. *emein*. So **vomit** vb. spew. XIV. f. *vomit-*, pp. stem of L. *vomere* or - L. frequent. *vomitāre*.

voodoo use of or belief in sorcery, etc. current among W. Indies and U.S. Negroes and creoles. XIX. - Dahomey *vodu*.

voracious greedy for food. XVII. f. L. *vorāx*, *-āc-*, f. *vorāre* DEVOUR; see -IOUS. So **voracity** XVI. - (O)F. or L.

-vorous terminal el. forming adjs., f. L. *-vorus* devouring, eating (see DEVOUR, -OUS), as in *carnivorous*, *herbivorous*, *omnivorous*.

vortex supposed rotation of the cosmic matter XVII; violent eddy XVIII; (fig.). - L. *vortex* eddy, whirlpool, whirlwind, var. of *vertex* VERTEX.

vorticism principles of a school of painting originating in 1913 among some members of 'the London Group'. XX. f. L. *vortex*, *-ic-* VORTEX, taken in the sense of the artist's conception of relations in the universe; see -ISM.

votary one bound by vow to a religious life or devoted to a pursuit, etc. XVI. f. *vōt-*, pp. stem of

L. *vovēre* vow + -ARY. Hence **votaress** (-ESS[1]) XVI, **votarist** XVII.

vote sb. XVI (in earliest use Sc.). - L. *vōtum* vow, wish, sb. use of n. pp. of *vovēre* vow, desire. So vb. give a vote (for); †vow, †devote. XVI (in earliest use Sc.). f. *vōt-*, pp. stem of L. *vovēre*. So **votive** XVI. - L. *vōtīvus*.

vouch cite as witness XIV; guarantee the truth of XVI; be surety or witness *for* XVII. - OF. *vo(u)cher* summon, invoke, claim, obscurely repr. L. *vocāre* call. So **voucher** summoning of a person into court to prove a title XVI; piece of evidence, esp. written XVII. - AN. sb. use of OF. inf. *voucher*; see -ER[5]. **vouchsafe** confer, bestow, esp. in condescension; show a gracious willingness XIV. orig. as two words, f. VOUCH warrant + SAFE, adj. in predic. use.

voussoir (archit.) one of the stones forming part of an arch or a vault. XVIII. - F. :- popL. *volsōrium*, f. **vols-*, pp. stem of *volvere* roll.

vow[1] solemn promise, esp. of a religious nature. XIII. - AN. *vou*, *vu(u)*, OF. *vo(u)* (mod. *vœu*) :- L. *vōtum* VOTE. So **vow** vb. make a vow. XIII. - (O)F. *vouer*.

vow[2] affirm, asseverate. XIV. Aphetic of AVOW.

vowel XIV. - OF. *vouel*, var. of *voiel* (superseded by later OF. *voielle*, mod. *voyelle*) :- L. *vōcālem (sonum)* or *vōcāle (signum)* 'VOCAL sound or sign' (the L. sb. *vōcālis* is fem.).

vox in *v. angelica*, *v. humana* ('angelic, human voice'), organ stops imitative of vocal sounds. XVIII. - L. *vōx*, *vōc-* VOICE, f. base widely repr. in IE.

voyage journey (spec. by water). XIII. ME. *ve(i)age*, *v(a)iage* - AN. *voiage*, OF. *ve(i)age*, *vayage* (mod. *voyage*) :- L. *viāticum* money or provisions for a journey, in late L. journey. So **voyage** vb., **voyager** XV. - (O)F.

vraic seaweed found in the Channel Islands. XVII. - F. dial. *vraic*, var. of *vrec*, *vrac* - MLG., Du. *wrak* WRACK[2]; cf. VAREC.

vulcanite †pyroxene; preparation of india-rubber and sulphur hardened by heat. XIX. f. *Vulcan* (L. *Vulcānus*), name of the ancient Rom. god of fire + -ITE. So **vulcanize** (-IZE) treat (india-rubber) with sulphur to render it more durable. XIX.

vulgar adj. that is in common or ordinary use XIV (rare before XVI); ordinary, common, commonplace XVI; lacking in refinement XVII; sb. †*the* vernacular XV; †(chiefly pl.) common or vulgar person XVI. - L. *vulgāris*, f. *vulgus*, *volgus* the common people; see -AR. So **vulgarity** †common people XVI; †common use, quality, etc. XVII; vulgar character XVIII. - late L. **vulgarize** †be vulgar XVII; make vulgar XVIII. **Vulgate** in common use as a version of the Bible (spec. the Latin of St. Jerome completed in about 405 A.D.) XVII; sb. the Vulgate Bible XVIII; received text of the Bible; (*v-*) ordinary reading in a text XIX. - late L. *vulgātus*, pp. of L. *vulgāre* make public or common, f. *vulgus*; see -ATE[2]. Hence **vulgarism** †ordinary expression XVII (rare); vulgar expression, quality, etc. XVIII. **vulgarize** †be vulgar XVII; make vulgar XVIII.

vulnerable that may be wounded XVII; open to attack XVII (of a place XVIII). - late L. *vulnerābilis* wounding, f. *vulnerāre* wound, f. *vulnus*, *vulner-* wound. So **vulnerary** used for healing wounds XVI; also sb. XVII. - L. *vulnerārius*.

vulpine fox-like. XVII. - L. *vulpīnus*, f. *vulpēs*, *volpēs* fox; see -INE[1].

vulture XIV. - AN. *vultur*, OF. *voltour* (mod. *vautour*) :- L. *vulturius*, f. *vultur*, *voltur*. So **vulturine** XVII. - L.

vulva (anat.) external genitals of the female. XVI. - L. *vulva*, *volva* womb, matrix.

W

wabble see WOBBLE.

wacke (geol.) sandstone-like rock. XIX. - G. *wacke* (OHG. *wacko* pebble).

wad †wadding; (dial.) bundle of hay, etc. XVI; tightly-rolled bundle XVIII. In form and early meaning corr. to AL. *wadda* wadding; obscurely rel. to Du. *watten*, F. *ouate*, It. *ovatta* padding, cotton-wool. Hence **wad** vb. put a wad in (a gun, etc.) XVI; lay up in bundles XVII. **wadding** (-ING[1]) material for wads. XVII.

waddle vb. XVII. perh. frequent. of WADE; see -LE[3]. Hence sb. XVII.

wade †go OE.; walk through water or any liquid XIII. OE. str. vb. *wadan* = MDu., MLG. *waden* (Du. *waden*), OHG. *watan* (G. *waten*), ON. *vaða* :- Gmc. **waðan* go, go through; f. IE. **wădh-*, repr. by L. *vādere* go.

wadi ravine or gully turned into a watercourse in the rainy season. XIX. - Arab. *wādī*.

wafer very light thin crisp cake XIV; thin disc of unleavened bread used at the Eucharist XVI; disc used for sealing, etc. XVII. - AN. *wafre*, var. of ONF. *waufre*, (O)F. *gaufre* (see GOFFER).

waffle (U.S.) batter-cake. XIX. - Du. *wafel*, early *waefel* = MLG. *wāfel*.

waft †convoy; convey safely by water XVI; †pass or propel through the air XVII; carry through the air or through space XVIII. Back-formation from †*wafter* armed vessel used as a convoy (XV *wa(u)ghter*) - LG., Du. *wachter* guard, f. *wachten* guard.

wag[1] tr. †stir, move XIII; sway from side to side XIV; intr. †brandish, wave XIII; move to and fro XIV. ME. *waggen*, iterative formation on OE. *wagian* totter, sway), ME. *waȝe*, *waw(e)* = MLG., MDu. *wagen*, OHG. *wagōn*, ON. *vaga*. So **waggle** XV; see -LE[3] and cf. (M)LG., Du. *waggelen* stagger, totter, which may be the immed. source.

wag[2] mischievous boy, youth, chap; habitual joker. XVI. prob. shortening of †*waghalter* (vars. †*wagstring*, †*wagwith*) one who is likely to swing in the hangman's noose, gallows-bird XVI; see prec., HALTER. Hence **waggery, waggish** XVI.

wage †a pledge or security; †a challenge or engagement to fight; payment for service rendered; fig., reward, recompense XIV; †payment for use or possession of property XV. - AF., ONF. *wage* = OF. *guage*, (also mod.) *gage* - Gmc. **waðjam*; see GAGE[1]. So **wage** vb. A. †deposit or give as a pledge or security, esp. for the fulfilment of (something promised) XIV; †agree to forfeit in some contingency XV; †(exc. hist.) pledge oneself to judicial combat XVI; B. †engage or employ for wages, hire; †pay wages to XIV; C. carry on (war, a contest) XV. - AF., ONF. *wagier*, *wa(i)gier* = OF. *guagier* (mod. *gager*).

waggon, wagon strong four-wheeled vehicle for transport; †carriage, car, chariot XVI; covered vehicle for conveyance by road XVII; truck, van running on a mining roadway or (later) railway line. Early forms *wagan*, *wag(h)en* - Du. *wagen*, †*waghen* WAIN. So **wag(g)oner** XVI. - Du. *wagenaar*, †*waghenaer*. Hence **wag(g)onette** four-wheeled (open) carriage. XIX.

wagtail small bird of the genus *Motacilla*. XVI. f. WAG[1] + TAIL[1], with ref. to the continual characteristic wagging of its tail.

waif piece of property found ownerless XIV; person without home or friends, unowned child XVIII. - AN. *waif*, *weif*, var. of ONF. *gaif*, fem. *gaive*, prob. of Scand. orig. (cf. ON. *veif* something wavering or flapping, rel. to *veifa* wave).

wail vb. XIV. - ON. **weila*, f. *vei* int. = OE. *wā* WOE; the recorded ON. vb. is *vǽla*, f. *vǽ* int. Hence sb. XIV.

wain large open vehicle for heavy loads; (astron.) used of the Great Bear. OE. *wæġ(e)n*, *wǣn* waggon = OLF. *-wagan*, (M)LG., Du. *wagen*, OHG. *wagan* (G. *wagen*), ON. *vagn* cart, barrow :- Gmc. **waȝnaz* or **weȝnaz* :- IE. **woĝhnos* or **weĝhnos* (whence OIr. *fén* waggon), f. **woĝh-* **weĝh-* carry (cf. WAY), whence Gr. *ókhos* (:- **woĝhos*) chariot, OSl. *vozŭ*, Skr. *vā́hana-* chariot, ship.

wainscot superior oak boarding imported from the Continent XIV; panelling of wood XVI. - MLG. *wagenschot*, presumably f. *wagen* WAGGON + *schot* (?) boarding planking.

waist middle section of the body XIV; middle part of a ship XV; narrowest or slenderest part XVII. ME. *wa(a)st*, later *waste*, *waist*; perh. repr. OE. **wæst*, for **weahst*, corr. to ON. **wahstur* (Icel. *vöxtr*), Goth. *wahstus* growth, size, f. Gmc. **waχs-* grow, WAX[2]. Comp. **waistcoat** XVI.

wait A. †watch as an enemy or spy XII; †await XIV; remain, stay; defer action XVII; B. serve at table XVI. - ONF. *waitier*, var. of OF. *guaitier* (mod. *guetter* watch for) - Gmc. **waχtan* (OHG. *wahtēn*, MHG. *wahten*, f. **wak-* WAKE[2]). So **wait** sb. †watch; †watchman; as in phr. *lie in wait*, etc. XV; pl. town musicians XIII (street singers at Christmastide XVIII). Partly - ONF. **wait*, *wet*; partly f. the Eng. vb.

waiter †watcher, watchman XIV; †attendant, servitor XV; man who waits on guests XVII; (for *waiting salver*, in which *waiting* is gerund) small tray XVIII. f. WAIT + -ER[1]. Hence **waitress** (-ESS[1]) †handmaid XVI (rare); woman or girl who waits at table XIX.

waive †outlaw XIII; relinquish, abandon XIV, (esp. a right) XV; refrain from enforcing (a rule), or from persisting in or entering upon (an action) XVII. - AN. *weyver*, var. of OF. *gaiver*, *guesver* make a 'waif' of, abandon, f. *gaif* WAIF. So **waiver** (leg.) dispensing with a requirement. XVII. - AN. (law F.) *weyver*, sb. use of inf.; see -ER[5].

wake[1] watching, watch, vigil OE. (spec. beside a

dead body; hence, observances incidental to this XV); vigil of a church festival, esp. as an occasion of merrymaking XIII. OE. **wacu* (only in *niht-wacu* night-watch), corr. to MLG., MDu. *wake* (Du. *waak*), OHG. *wahha* (G. *wache*) watch, wakefulness, ON. *vaka* watch, vigil, eve; rel. to WAKE[3]. In the last sense prob. - ON. *vaka*.

wake[2] track left on the water's surface by a moving vessel. XVI. prob. - MLG. - ON. **vaku* (*vǫk*), *vaka* hole or opening in ice, perh. orig. one made for itself by a vessel.

wake[3] A. remain awake OE.; become awake; B. rouse from sleep XIII. (i) OE. str. vb. **wacan* (repr. by *onwacan*, *āwacan* AWAKE), only in pt. *wōc*, corr. to ON. **vaka* (repr. by pp. *vakinn* awake); (ii) OE. wk. vb. *wacian* = OS. *wakon*, OHG. *wahhēn*, *-ōn* (G. *wachen*), ON. *vaka*, Goth. *wakan* :- Gmc. **wakǣjan*, **wakōjan*, f. **wak-* (see also WATCH) :- IE. **woĝ- *weĝ-* be lively or active. Sense B, which is expressed in OE. by *weċċan* (:- **wakjan*), depends partly on ON. *vaka* (intr. and tr.). Hence **wakeful** XVI.

waken become awake; rouse from sleep. XII. - ON. *vakna* wake up = OE. *wæcnan*, also *wæcnian* (recorded only in the sense 'rise, spring, be derived'), Goth. *gawaknan* (prp. only), f. Gmc. **wak-*; see prec., -EN[5].

wake-robin lords-and-ladies, cuckoo-pint. XVI. of unkn. orig.

Waldensian pert. to the *Waldenses* adherents of a religious sect which originated through the preaching of Peter *Waldo* of Lyons, France, *c.*1170. XVII. See -IAN.

wale weal on the flesh OE.; horizontal timber round the top of the sides of a boat XIV; raised line in a fabric XVI; ridge of a horse's collar XVIII. Late OE. *walu* ridge of land, etc., weal = LG. *wāle* weal, ON. *vala* knuckle.

wale-knot see WALL-KNOT.

Waler horse imported from Australia, esp. New South Wales. XIX. f. *Wales* + -ER[1].

walk[1] intr. †roll, toss; †move about, journey, go OE.; travel on foot, (tr.) traverse on foot XIII; lead at a walk XV. OE. str. vb. *wealcan*, corr. to (M)LG., (M)Du. *walken* full, work (felt), cudgel, OHG. **walchen*, in pps. *ge-*, *forwalchen* felted, matted (MHG. *walken* knead, full, cudgel), ON. *valka* drag about, torment, refl. wallow; f. Gmc. **walk-*, of unkn. orig. Hence **walk** sb. XIV. Cf. next.

walk[2] full (cloth). XV. - (M)LG., (M)Du. *walken* (see prec.); perh. partly from the agent-noun **walker** (-ER[1]) OE. *wealcere*, (M)LG., (M)Du. *walker*, OHG. *walkāri* (G. *walker*); ult. identical with WALK[1].

wall rampart; defensive structure enclosing a town, etc.; lateral or vertical division of a building. OE. (Angl.) *wall*, (WS.) *weall*, corr. to OS., (M)LG., (M)Du. *wal* - L. *vallum* rampart, orig. palisading, f. *vallus* stake. Comp. **wallflower** plant of the genus *Cheiranthus*, which grows wild on old walls, etc. XVI. Hence **wall** vb. XIII (OE. had *ġeweallod* walled).

wallaby XIX. - Austral. aboriginal word.

wallah in words of native Indian languages adopted by European residents, e.g. *howdah-w.* elephant accustomed to carrying a howdah, *punkah-w.*, hence, by extension, in *competition-w.* XVIII. - Hindi *-wālā*, terminal el. expressing relation forming adjs. and sbs., apprehended by Europeans as a sb. meaning 'man', 'fellow'.

wallet bag for provisions for a journey, pilgrim's scrip, pedlar's pack XIV; (orig. U.S.) pocket-book to hold papers XIX. prob. - AN. **walet*, perh. f. **wall-* roll (see WELL[1,2]); see -ET.

wall-eyed having eyes of an excessively light colour or showing divergence of some kind. XIV (*wawilezed*, *waugleeghed*). - ON. *vagleygr*, f. **vagl* (Icel. *vagl* film over the eye, Sw. *vagel* sty in the eye) + *-eygr* -eyed, f. *auga* EYE; see -ED[2]. Hence by back-formation **wall eye** XVI.

wall-knot, wale-knot knot made on the end of a rope by unlaying and intertwining the strands. XVIII. rel. obscurely to Norw., Sw. *valknut*, Da. *valknude* double knot, secure knot, G. *waldknoten* (assim. to *wald* wood, forest), in hunting parlance, double knot.

Walloon one of a people of Gaulish origin speaking a dialect of French and inhabiting south-eastern Belgium XVI; their language XVII. - F. *wallon* - medL. *Wallō*, *-ōn-*, f. Gmc. **walχaz* foreign. Cf. WELSH, -OON.

wallop †gallop XIV; †bubbling motion XVI; violent noisy movement; beat of the heart, resounding blow XVIII. So vb. †gallop XIV; boil, bubble XVI; make violent noisy movements XVIII; beat soundly XIX. - ONF. *walop*, var. of (O)F. *galop*, and its source *waloper*, *galoper* GALLOP.

wallow roll about or from side to side OE.; be plunged *in* degraded living XIII. OE. (Angl.) *walwian*, (WS.) *wealwian* :- WGmc. **walwōjan*, rel. to *wielwan* tr. roll = Goth. *-walwjan*; f. Gmc. **walw- *welw-* :- IE. **wolw- *welw-*, whence Gr. *elustheis* rolled, wrapped, L. *volvere* roll.

walnut Late OE. *walh-hnutu* (once), corr. to MLG. *wallnut*, MDu. *walnote* (Du. *walnoot*), ON. *walhnot*; Gmc. formation on **walχaz* foreign and **χnut-* NUT.

walrus XVII. prob. - Du. *walrus*, *-ros*, f. the els. of such forms as OE. *hors(c)hwæl*, ON. *hrosshvalr* ('horse-whale'), but the mutual relations are obscure.

waltz sb. and vb. XVIII. - G. *walzer* the dance, f. *walzen* roll, revolve, dance the waltz, f. Gmc. **walt-*, extension of **wal-* roll.

wampum beads threaded on strings used by N. Amer. Indians as currency, etc. XVII. Shortening of somewhat earlier *wampumpeag* (which was falsely analysed as *wampum* + *peag*), of Algonquian orig.

wan †dusky, dark; livid, leaden-hued OE.; pallid, unusually pale XIII. OE. *wan(n)*, of unkn. orig.

wand (dial.) straight, slender stick XII; slender stem, sapling XIII; rod or staff of office XV; magic rod. - ON. **wandur* (*vǫndr*) = Goth. *wandus*, prob. f. Gmc. **wand- *wind-* turn, WEND, the basic notion being that of flexibility.

wander move aimlessly about OE.; deviate without purpose *from* XV. OE. *wandrian* = MLG., MDu. *wanderen* :- WGmc. **wandrōjan*, f. **wand- *wend-* WEND; see -ER[4].

wane grow less, decrease, spec. of the periodical decrease of the visible illuminated portion of the moon. OE. *wanian* lessen (intr. and tr.) = OS. *wanon*, OHG. *wanōn, wanēn*, ON. *vana*, Goth. **wanan* :- Gmc. **wanōjan, *wanǣjan*, f. **wana-* lacking. So **wane** sb. †want, lack OE.; amount by which a plank falls short of the squared shape XVII. OE. *wana*. Hence **waney** (of timber) XVII; see -Y[1].

wangle accomplish or obtain by irregular or insidious means. XIX. First recorded as printers' sl., 'arrange or fake to one's own satisfaction'; of unkn. orig. Hence sb. XX.

wanion (arch.) phr. *with (in) a w.* with a vengeance. XVI (revived XIX). alt. of †*waniand* (XIV) in phr. †*in the w.*, prob. with ellipsis of *mone* moon, repr. OE. *on waniġendum mōnan* at the time of the waning moon, i.e. in an unlucky hour; see WANE.

want condition or fact of being deficient XIII; lack of the necessaries of life XIV; requirement XVI. Earlier (XII) used as predicative adj. 'lacking', 'wanting' - ON. **want, vant*, n. of *vanr* lacking, missing. So **want** vb. is lacking; be without XII. - ON. **wanta, vanta* impers. vb.

wanton †undisciplined XIII; lascivious, lewd XIV; †sportive, capricious; †insolent XVI; (poet.) luxurious; reckless of justice or pity. ME. *wantowen, wantoun*, f. *wan-*, prefix equiv. to UN-[1], MIS-[1], OE. *wan-* = OS., OHG. *wan(a)-* (Du. *wan-*, G. *wahn-*), ON. *van-*, orig. identical with adj. †*wane* (see WANE) + *towen, toȝen*, OE. *togen*, pp. of *tēon* discipline, train.

wapentake subdivision of some shires (in which the Danish element of the population was large), corr. to a hundred. Late OE. *wǣpen(ġe)tæc* - ON. *vápnatak*, f. *vápna*, g. pl. of *vápn* WEAPON + *tak* act of taking, f. *taka* TAKE. The evolution of the Eng. sense from that of the ON. word, 'vote or consent expressed by waving or brandishing weapons', can only be conjectured.

wapiti N. Amer. elk. XIX. of Algonquian orig.

war sb. XII (*werre, wyrre*). - AN., ONF. *werre*, var. of (O)F. *guerre*, of Gmc. orig., f. base repr. by OHG. *werra* confusion, discord, strife, OS., OHG. *werran* bring into confusion (G. *wirren* confuse, perplex). Hence **war** vb., partly after AN. *werreier* (in F. *guerroyer*) XII. Comp. **warfare** (FARE[1]) XV.

warble †tune, melody XIV, later (infl. by the vb.) act of warbling. Late ME. *werble* - ONF., var. of OF. **guerble* - Frankish **hwirbilōn* whirl, trill; cf. OHG. *wirbil* whirlwind, and see WHIRL. So **warble** vb. XIV. - ONF. *werbler*, OF. *guerbl(oi)er*.

ward[1] A. watching, guarding, custody OE.; charge of a prisoner XIII; B. administrative division of a city, etc. XIV (in AL. *warda* XIII); C. separate room or division of a prison, hospital, etc. XVI; D. pl. notches or projections in a key or lock to prevent opening XV. OE. *weard* = MLG. *warde*, OHG. *warta* watch (G. *warte* watchtower) :- WGmc. **wardō* (whence ONF. *warde*, with the repr. of which the native word coalesced = (O)F. *garde* GUARD), f. **ward-, extension of* **war-* be on guard, watch (see WARE[2]).

ward[2] guard, defend OE.; parry, fend off XVI. OE. *weardian* = OS. *wardon*, OHG. *wartēn* (G. *warten* nurse, look after), ON. *varða* :- Gmc. **warðōjan, *warðǣjan*, f. **warðō* WARD[1]; reinforced in ME. by ONF. *warder*, var. of (O)F. *garder* GUARD vb.

-ward suffix denoting direction, orig. (and so only in OE.) appended to local advs. (e.g. *hāmweard* homeward); a second stage is repr. by *to heavenward*, etc., followed by forms lacking the prep. (e.g. *earthward, Godward*). OE. *-weard* = OS. *-ward*, OHG. *-wart*, f. Gmc. *-*warð*, var. of **werþ-* :- IE. **wert-* turn (cf. L. *vertere*).

warden †guardian; in various designations of office involving control or governorship. XIII. - AN., ONF. *wardein*, var. of OF. *g(u)arden* GUARDIAN.

warder[1] soldier set to guard an entrance XIV; gaoler XIX. - AN. *wardere, wardour*, f. OF. *warder*; see WARD[2], -ER[2].

warder[2] (arch.) staff, truncheon XV. Reduced form of †*warderer* (XIV), perh. orig. joc. use of †*warderere* look out behind - AN. **ware derere*, i.e. *ware* var. of (O)F. *gare* (- Gmc. **war-* WARE[2]) + *derere* (modF. *derrière*) behind.

wardrobe †room in which wearing apparel was kept XIV (movable closed cupboard for this XVIII); department of a great household charged with the keeping of this XV; person's stock of this. - ONF. *warderobe*, var. of (O)F. *garderobe*, f. *garder* keep, GUARD, WARD[2] + *robe* garment, ROBE.

-wards OE. *-weardes*, corr. to OS., MLG. *-wardes* (Du. *-waarts*), OHG. *-wartes*, f. Gmc. **warða-*; g. sg. n. formation gen. identical in sense with -WARD.

ware[1] articles of merchandise or manufacture (in comps. *earthenware, hardware*). OE. *waru* = MLG., MDu. *ware* (Du. *warr*), ON. *vara* :- Gmc. **warō*, perh. orig. 'object of care' and f. **war-* (see next). Comp. **warehouse** XIV; hence vb. XVIII.

ware[2] (arch.) †aware; careful in avoiding (surviving in BEWARE). OE. *wær*, also *ġewær* = OS. *war*, (also OHG.) *giwor*, Goth. **wars* :- Gmc. **(ga)waraz*, f. **war-* **wer-* observe, take care.

ware[3] †intr. take care; trans. beware of. OE. *warian* = OS. *waron*, OHG. *biwarōn* beware, ON. *vara*; in ME. coalescing with ONF. *warer* (mod. *garer*), of Gmc. orig.

warlock †traitor, scoundrel; †the Devil; savage or monstrous creature OE.; sorcerer, wizard XIV. OE. *wǣrloga* (= OS. *wārlogo*), f. OE. *wǣr* covenant = OHG. *wāra* truth, ON. *várar* pl., solemn promise, vow + **loȝ-*, wk. grade of the base of *lēoġan* LIE[2]. ME. *warlow(e)* (repr. OE. *wǣrloga*) was superseded by the Sc. var. *warlo(c)k* (XVI).

warm moderately hot OE.; †comfortable, securely established XIV; ardent, eager; cordial, tender XV; lively, heated, excited XVI; comfortably off. OE. *wearm* = OS. (Du.) *warm*, OHG. *war(a)m* (G. *warm*), ON. *varmr* :- Gmc. **warmaz*. So **warm** vb. (i) OE. **wierman, werman, wirman* tr. = OS. *wermian* (Du. *warmen*), OHG. *wermen* (G. *wärmen*), ON. *verma*, Goth. *warmjan* :- Gmc. **warmjan*; (ii) OE. *wearmian* intr. = OHG. *war(a)mēn* (early modG. *warmen*) :- Gmc. **warmǣjan*. **warmth** XII. OE. **wiermðu, *wærmðu* = MLG. *wermede* (Du.

warmte), MHG. *wermede* (G. †*wärmte*) :- WGmc. **warmiþō*; see -TH[1].

warn put on one's guard, give a caution to OE.; inform, notify XIII. OE. *war(e)nian, wearnian* = MLG. *warnen*, OHG. *warnōn, warnēn* (G. *warnen*) :- WGmc. **waranōjan, -ǣjan*, f. **war*- be cautious (see WARE[2]).

warp A. †cast, throw OE.; (after ON. *orðum verpa*) †utter XIII; B. (after ON. *orpinn* pp. warped) tr. and intr. bend, twist aside XIV (fig. distort XVI); C. weave, twine XIII; D. tow XVI. OE. str. vb. *weorpan* = OS. *werpan* (Du. *werpen*), OHG. *werfan* (G. *werfen*), ON. *verpa*, Goth. *wairpan*; no certain cogns. outside Gmc. So **warp** sb. threads extended lengthwise in the loom OE.; rope, hawser XIII. OE. *wearp*; some later senses are from the vb.

warrant A. †protector, defence; authoritative witness; authorization XIII; B. document conveying authority or security XV; justifying reason XVI. - ONF. *warant*, var. of OF. *guarant*, *-and* (mod. *garant*) - Frankish **werēnd* (= OHG. *werēnt*, f. *giwerēn* (G. *gewähren*) be surety for, guarantee). So **warrant** vb. †keep safe XIII; guarantee the security of XVI. - ONF. *warantir*, *warandir*, vars. of OF. *g(u)arantir, -andir*. **warranty** (-Y[3]) legal covenant. XIV. - AN. *warantie*, var. of *garantie* GUARANTEE.

warren piece of land preserved for breeding game, esp. for the breeding of rabbits XIV; fig. XVII. - AN., ONF. *warenne*, var. of (O)F. *garenne* game-park, now esp. rabbit warren - Gaul. **varrenna* area marked off by palisading, f. **varros* post (cf. Ir. *farr* pillar, post). So **warrener** (-ER[2]) officer having charge of a warren. XIV. - AN. *warener*, ONF. *warrennier*, (O)F. *garennier*.

warrigal dingo; wild Austral. aboriginal. XIX. Austral. aboriginal word.

warrior XIII. ME. *werre(y)our* - ONF. *werreieor*, *werrieur*, var. of OF. *guerreieor* (mod. *guerroyeur*), f. *werreier, guerreier* vb., Rom. deriv. of **werra* WAR; see -OR[1].

wart round dry tough excrescence on the skin. OE. *wearte* = OS. *warta* (Du. *wrat*), OHG. *warza* (G. *warze*), ON. *varta* :- Gmc. **wartōn*.

wary XVI. Extension of WARE[2] by the addition of -Y[1].

was see BE.

wash cleanse with or as with water OE. (also refl. and intr. XII); of the sea, etc., flow over or past XIII; remove with or as with water XV. OE. str. vb. *wæsċan, wasċan, waxan* = OS. *wascan* (Du. *wassen*), OHG. *wascan* (G. *waschen*), ON. (wk.) *vaska* :- Gmc. **waskan* :- **watskan*, f. **wat*- WATER. Traces of wk. conjugation appear XIV, but str. forms prevailed till XVI. Hence **wash** sb. (not continuous with OE. *wasċ*, *ġewæsċ*) in various senses from XIV. Comp. **wash-leather** XVII; earlier †*washen leather* (*wesshyn leddyr* XV), †*washed leather* (XVII) suggest that the orig. ref. was to the washing which was a part of the manufacture.

washer[1] one who washes. XV. See prec., -ER[1]. Comp. **washerwoman** XVII, earlier (now U.S.) *washwoman* XVI.

washer[2] perforated disc to prevent friction or looseness of parts. XIV (*whasher*). of unkn. orig.

wasp OE. *wæsp, wæps, wæfs*, corr. to OS. *wepsia*, *wespa, wasp*, OHG. *wafsa, wefsa* (G. *wespe*), MLG. *wepse, wespe, wispe* :- WGmc. **wabis*-, **waps*- :- IE. **wobhes*-, **wops*-, whence OSl. (Russ.) *osa*, Lith. *vapsvà*, OBret. *guohi*, Corn. *guhien*, L. *vespa* (:- **wopsā*), usu. taken to be f. **webh- wobh*- WEAVE[1], with ref. to the weblike construction of the insect's nest. Hence **waspish** XVI.

wassail salutation used when presenting drink to a guest or drinking his health XIII (*wæs hæil*, *wassayl, -ail*; after XIV only hist. and dial.); liquor for drinking healths; carousal XVII. - ON. *ves heill* 'be in good health' (see HALE[1]).

waste A. desert land XII; B. action of wasting XIII; C. waste matter XV. - ONF. *wast(e)*, var. of OF. *guast(e), gast(e)*, partly repr. L. *vāstum*, n. of *vāstus* waste, desert, partly f. *waster* vb. So **waste** adj. uncultivated, barren XIII; superfluous, refuse XV. - ONF. *wast*, var. of *g(u)ast* :- Rom. **wasto*, repr. (with infl. from Frankish **wōsti*) L. *vāstus*. **waste** vb. devastate, consume by loss, decay, etc. XIII; consume or expend uselessly XIV. - ONF. *waster*, var. of *g(u)aster* :- Rom. **wastāre*, for L. *vāstare*. Hence **wasteful** causing devastation XIV; extravagant XV. **waster** (-ER[1]) XIV.

wastrel (in Cornwall) tract of waste land XVI; article rejected as unserviceable XVIII; unhealthy animal XIX; good-for-nothing person, waster. f. WASTE vb. + -REL.

watch †be awake OE.; be on the alert or look-out XIII; keep in view XIV. OE. **wæċċan* (in Nhb. *wæċċa*, WS. prp. *wæċċende*), doublet of *wacian* WAKE[2]. So **watch** sb. A. †vigil; action of watching XIV; (naut.) period of watching XVI; one set to watch; B. †alarm-clock XV; small spring-driven time-piece for the pocket XVI. OE. *wæċċe*, f. stem of **wæċċan*; in some later uses directly f. the vb. Hence **watchful** XVI. Comps. **watchman**, **watchword** XIV.

water transparent liquid forming the material of seas, lakes, and rivers OE.; (prob. after Arab. *mā'* water, lustre, splendour) transparency and lustre of a gem (whence in popular phr. *of the first w.*) XVII. OE. *wæter* = OS. *watar* (Du. *water*), OHG. *wazzar* (G. *wasser*) :- WGmc. **watar* (ON. *vatn*, Goth. *watō*, g. *watins*, show a var. with *n*-formative), f. Gmc. **wat*- :- IE. **wod*-, repr. by OSl. (Russ.) *voda*; the var. **wēd*- is repr. by WET, the var. **ud*- (sometimes with nasal infix) by L. *unda* (cf. UNDULATE), Gr. *húdōr*, g. *húdatos* (:- *udṇtos*), *hudro*- HYDRO-, Skr. *udán*. So **water** vb. tr. OE.; intr. XIV. OE. *(ġe)wæterian*, corr. to MLG. *wateren, weteren* (Du. *wateren*), MHG. *wezzern* (G. *wässern*). **watery** OE. *wæteriġ* = MLG. *waterich*, etc.; see -Y[1]. Comps. **waterfall** XIV (cf. OE. *wætergefeall*). **watershed** line separating waters flowing into different river basins XIX. See SHED[2].

waterlog render unmanageable by flooding with water. XVIII. perh. orig. with sense 'make like a LOG[1]'.

water-souchy fish boiled and served in its liquor. XVIII. - Du. *waterzootje*, f. *water* WATER + *zootje, zoodje* boiling (of fish).

watt (physics) unit of activity or power. XIX. f.

name of James *Watt* (1736-1819), inventor of the modern steam engine and a pioneer in the science of energy.

wattle[1] (pl. and coll. sg.) stakes intertwined with twigs or branches used as fencing, etc. OE. *watul*, of uncert. orig. Hence vb. XIV.

wattle[2] fleshy lobe pendent from the head or neck of poultry, etc. XVI. of unkn. orig.

wave[1] move to and fro, shake or sway as with the wind. The word in the above senses as at present used is not clearly evident before XVI; not certainly continuous with OE. *wafian* (recorded twice) make a movement to and fro with the hands, corr. to MHG. *waben* wave, undulate, f. Gmc. **wab-*, repr. also by ON. *vafi* doubt, uncertainty, and WAVER.

wave[2] movement in an extent of water by which a portion of it rises above the general level. XVI. alt., by assoc. with WAVE[1], of ME. †*wawe*, earlier *waʒe*, rel. to OE. *wagian*, ME. *wawe*, sway to and fro, wave (cf. WAG[1]). Hence **wavy** (-Y[1]) XVI.

waver †wander, rove; fluctuate, vacillate; †sway. XIV. - ON. *vafra* move unsteadily, flicker = MHG. *waberen* (G. *wabern*) move about, frequent. f. Gmc. **wab-*; cf. WAVE[1], -ER[4].

wavey snow-goose. XVIII. var. of **wawa**, of Algonquian orig.

wax[1] substance produced by bees to make the honeycomb; beeswax melted down, etc. (as used for sealing, superseded by a compound of lac, etc.). OE. *wæx*, *weax* = OS., OHG. *wahs* (Du. *was*, G. *wachs*), ON. *vax* :- Gmc. **waχsam*, cogn. with OSl. *voskŭ*; ult. f. IE. **weg-* weave. Hence **wax** vb., **waxen** (-EN[3]) XIV; repl. OE. *wexen*, **wiexen*. **waxwork** modelling in wax. XVII.

wax[2] grow OE.; become XII. OE. str. vb. *weaxan* = OS., OHG. *wahsan* (Du. *wassen*, G. *wachsen*), ON. *vaxa*, Goth. *wahsjan* (with *-ja-* in pres. stem) :- Gmc. str. vb. f. **waχs-* :- IE. **woks-*, **aweks-*, **auks-*, **uks-* repr. by Gr. *aéxein*, *aúxein*, *auxánein* increase, Skr. *úkṣati* grows, L. *augēre* increase.

wax[3] (sl.) fit of anger. XIX. perh. evolved from a usage such as *wax wroth* (WAX[2]).

way road, path; course of travel, life, or action, distance travelled. OE. *weġ* = OS., OHG. (Du., G.) *weg*, ON. *vegr*, Goth. *wigs* :- Gmc. **weʒaz*, f. **weʒ-* move, journey, carry :- IE. **weĝh-*, repr. also by L. *vehere* carry. So phr. *under way* (naut.) having begun to move through the water. XVIII. - Du. *onderweg*; whence perh. sense 'rate of progress, velocity' XVIII.

-way terminal el. orig. joined in a phr. with an adj. surviving in a few comps., as *anyway*, *halfway*, *midway*, *noway*, *someway*, *straightway*, the earliest being *alway* (OE. acc. *ealne weġ*); most of these have parallel and synon. forms in -WAYS.

wayfare (arch.) travelling. XIV. f. WAY + FARE, after *wayfaring*, OE. *weġfarende*. Hence **wayfarer** (-ER[1]) traveller by road. XV. **wayfaring-tree** *Viburnum lantana*, growing wild in hedges. XVI.

waylay lie in wait for. XVI. f. WAY + LAY[1], after MLG., MDu. *wegelāgen*.

wayleave permission to convey supplies, apparatus, etc. over land, etc. XV. f. WAY + LEAVE[1].

-ways repr. *weġes*, g. sg. of OE. *weġ* WAY, as in *ōðres weġes* (XII), dial. *otherways* by another route, *alles weis* always, *nanes weis* (XIII) noways.

wayside side of a road or path. XIV. See WAY, SIDE.

wayward disposed to be self-willed XIV; capriciously wilful XVI. Aphetic of *awayward* (XIV), f. AWAY + -WARD; the sense development was prob. infl. by the notion of the word being f. WAY, as if 'bent on going one's own way'.

wayzgoose entertainment given to printers orig. at Bartholomew-tide (24 August), when working by candle-light began; later, annual feast held in summer. Earlier *waygoose* (XVII), of uncert. orig.

we 1st pl. pers. pron. OE. *wē*, corr. to OS. *wī*, *wē* (Du. *wij*), (O)HG. *wir*, ON. *vér*, *vǽr*, Goth. *weis*. These forms repr. more than one Gmc. type; Goth. *weis* repr. Gmc. **wīz* :- **weis*, extension (with pl. *-s*) of **wei*, repr. also by Skr. *vayám*; other forms may repr. **wīz*. For the obl. cases see OUR, US.

weak not strong, feeble XIII; †pliant, flexible XIV. - ON. **weikr*, *veikr* = OE. *wāc* weak, slothful, pliant, insignificant, mean (ME. *wōke*), OS. *wēk* (Du. *week*), OHG. *weih* (G. *weich* soft) :- Gmc. **waikwaz*, f. **waikw-* **wikw-* yield, give way. Hence **weaken** (-EN[5]) XIV, **weakling** (-LING[1]) XVI, **weakly** (-LY[1]) XVI, (-LY[2]) XIV, **weakness** (-NESS) XIII.

weal[1] †wealth, riches; welfare OE.; the public good XV. OE. *wela* = OS. *welo* :- WGmc. **welan-*, f. **wel-*; see WELL[2].

weal[2] var. of WALE infl. by WHEAL.

weald the tract of country, formerly wooded, lying between the North and the South Downs. OE. (WS.) *weald*, (Angl.) *wald* WOLD. Hence **wealden** (pert. to) a formation of cretaceous deposits extensively developed in the weald. XIX; the use of the suffix -EN[3] is arbitrary.

wealth A. †well-being XIII; welfare of a community XIV; B. worldly goods, riches XIII. ME. *welþe*, f. WELL[2] or WEAL[1], after *health*; see -TH[1]. Hence **wealthy** (-Y[1]) XIV.

wean accustom to the loss of its mother's milk. OE. *wenian* accustom, (rare) wean (usu. *ā-*, sometimes *ġewenian*) = OS. *wennian* (Du. *wennen*), OHG. *giwennen* (G. *-wöhnen*), ON. *venja* :- Gmc. **wanjan*, f. **wanaz* accustomed (ON. *vanr*), f. **wan-* **wun-* (see WONT[1]).

weapon OE. *wǣpn* = OS. *wāpan* (Du. *wapen*), OHG. *wāf(f)an* (G. *waffe*), ON. *vápn*, Goth. **wēpn* :- Gmc. **wǣpnam*, of unkn. orig.

wear[1] pt. *wore*, pp. *worn* A. be dressed in OE.; B. waste, decay XIII; C. last out in use XVI. OE. wk. vb. *werian* = OS. *werian*, OHG. *werien*, ON. *verja*, Goth. *wasjan* clothe :- Gmc. **wazjan*, f. **was-* **wes-* :- IE. **wos-* **wes-*, repr. also by L. *vestis* clothing, Gr. *hennúnai* (:- **wesnu-*) clothe, Skr. *váste* wears. The change of conjugation from wk. to str., due to assoc. with *bear*, *swear*, *tear*, is shown in XIV but is hardly established before XVI; anticipated in late OE. *forworen* worn away, wasted. Hence **wear** sb. action of wearing XV; what is worn XVI (now current esp. in comps., *footwear*, *knitwear*).

wear[2] pt., pp. *wore* (naut.) come round on the other tack by turning stern to windward. XVII. Early forms *weare, wayer, warre, werr*; of unkn. orig.

weary adj. OE. *wērig, wǣrig*, corr. to OS. *sīðwōrig* weary (with journey), OHG. *wuarag* drunk :- WGmc. *wōriʒa,*-aʒa, f. *wōr-, repr. also by OE. *wōrian* wander, go astray, ON. *órar* pl. fits of madness, *œrr* mad, insane (:- *wōrja); cf. Gr. *hōrākiân* faint. Hence **weary** vb. OE. *wēr(i)ġian, ġewēriġian*.

weasand (dial.) gullet OE.; windpipe XIV; throat XV. OE. *wāsend*, corr. to OS. *wāsend(i)*, OHG. *weisant, -ont, -unt* (early modG. *waise(n)*); a WGmc. word having the appearance of a prp. formation.

weasel OE. *we(o)sule, wesle* = MLG. *wesel, wezel*, OHG. *wisula* (G. *wiesel*) :- WGmc. *wisulōn, of unkn. orig.

weather condition of the atmosphere with respect to heat or cold, calm or storm, etc. OE.; (with adverse implication) XII; direction of wind (perh. - ON.) XIV. OE. *weder* = OS. *wedar* (Du. *weer*), OHG. *wetar* (G. *wetter*), ON. *veðr* :- Gmc. *weðram :- either IE. *wedhrom (OSl. *vedro* good weather) or IE. *wetróm (Lith. *vétra* storm, OSl. *vĕtrŭ* wind); prob. f. *wē- WIND[1]. Comp. **weathercock** vane in the form of a cock. XIII. Hence **weather** vb. tr. and intr. in various uses concerning exposure to wind and weather XV; earlier in **weathering** XII.

weave[1] pt. *wove*, pp. *woven* fabricate by interlacing yarns. OE. str. vb. *wefan* = (M)LG., (M)Du. *weven*, OHG. *weban* (G. *weben*), ON. *vefa* :- Gmc. *weban, f. *web- *wab- :- IE. *webh- *wobh- *ubh-, repr. also by Gr. *huphḗ, húphos* web, Skr. *ūrṇavā́bhi-* spider, lit. 'wool-weaver'.

weave[2] move repeatedly from side to side, pursue a devious course XVI; (pugilism) creep close into one's opponent XIX. prob. continuation of ME. †*weve* (XIII) move from place to place, wave, brandish, var. of †*waive* - ON. *veifa*, corr. to (M)Du. *weiven*, OHG. *-weiben* :- Gmc. *waibjan, rel. ult. to L. *vibrāre* VIBRATE.

web woven fabric OE.; cobweb; tissue, membrane XIII. OE. *web(b)*, corr. to OS. *webbi* (MDu. *webbe*, Du. *web*), OHG. *wappi, weppi*, ON. *vefr* :- Gmc. *wabjam, -az, f. *wab- WEAVE[1].

weber unit of magnetic flux. XIX. f. name of Wilhelm *Weber* (1804-91), G. physicist.

wed marry, tr. OE., pass. XII, intr. XIII. OE. *weddian* covenant, marry, bind in wedlock = MLG. *wedden*, OHG. *wettōn* (G. *wetten*) pledge, wager, ON. *veðja* pledge, Goth. *gawadjōn* espouse :- Gmc. *waðjōjan, f. *waðjam pledge (OE. *wedd*, OS. *weddi*, Du. *wedde*, OHG. *wetti*, G. *wette*, ON. *veð*, Goth. *wadi*), rel. to L. *vas, vad-* surety. Hence **wedding** (-ING[1]) late OE. *weddung*.

wedge piece of wood, etc. thick at one end and tapering to a thin edge at the other; †ingot OE.; other special senses from XVI. OE. *weċġ* = OS. *weggi* (Du. *wegge* wedge-shaped cake), OHG. *weggi, wecki*, ON. *veggr* :- Gmc. *waʒjaz.

Wedgwood designating a kind of pottery; name of inventor, Josiah *Wedgwood* (1730-95), and his successors at Etruria, Staffordshire. XVIII.

wedlock †marriage vow OE.; union of man and woman as husband and wife. XIII. late OE. *wedlāc*, f. *wed* pledge, WED + *-lāc* -LOCK.

Wednesday XIII. corr. to OFris. *wēnsdei*, app. repr. a form with mutation (*wōðinaz) repl. OE. *wōdnesdæġ* = OFris. *wōnsdei*, MLG. *wōdensdach* (Du. *woensdag*), ON. *óðinsdagr* 'day of Odin', tr. late L. *Mercurii diēs* 'day of the planet Mercury'. OE. *Wōden* = OS. *Wōden*, OHG. *Wuotan*, ON. *Óðin* is referred to the Gmc. base *wōð- be excited or inspired.

wee sb. orig. chiefly in *a little wee*, †a small thing or quantity; a short time XIII; adj. extremely small, tiny XV. north. ME. *we(i)*, repr. OE. (Angl.) *wēġ(e)*, (WS.) *wǣġ(e)* weight, rel. to *weġan* WEIGH; the use appears to have originated in such a phr. as *a little wee thing* 'a small amount of a thing', similar to *a bit thing* 'a bit of a thing'. The adj. use has been current in southern Eng. since *c.*1600.

weed[1] small plant, esp. one that cumbers the ground. OE. *wēod* = OS. *wiod*, rel. to OHG. *wiota* fern; of unkn. orig. Hence **weed** vb. clear of weeds. OE. *wēodian*. **weedy** (-Y[1]) XV.

weed[2] garment OE.; now chiefly pl. deep mourning apparel, spec. of widows XVI. ME. *wēde*, repr. two OE. formations: (i) *wǣd* = OS. *wād*, OHG. *wāt*, ON. *váð, vóð* :- Gmc. *wǣðiz; (ii) OE. *(ġe)wǣde* = OS. *(gi)wādi* (Du. *gewaad*), OHG. *giwāti* :- Gmc. *gawǣðjam.

week OE. *wice, wicu* = OS. *-wika* (Du. *week*), OHG. *wehha, wohha* (G. *woche*), ON. *vika*, Goth. *wikō* order :- Gmc. *wikōn, prob. orig. 'succession, series', usu. referred to *wīk- bend, turn, change, repr. also by OE. *wīce*, OS., OHG. *wehsal* (G. *wechsel*), ON. *-víxl* change.

ween (arch.) think, suppose, expect. OE. *wēnan* = OS. *wānian* (Du. *wanen* fancy, imagine), OHG. *wān(n)ēn* (G. *wähnen* suppose wrongly), ON. *vǽna*, Goth. *wēnjan* hope :- Gmc. *wǣnjan, f. *wǣniz opinion, expectation, hope (OE. *wēn*, etc.).

weeny (colloq., dial.) very small. XVIII. f. WEE; cf. TINY, TEENY.

weep pt., pp. *wept* shed tears. OE. str. vb. *wēpan*, corr. to OS. *wōpian* bewail, OHG. *wuofan* (also *wuoffen* wk.), ON. *œpa* (wk.) scream, shout, Goth. *wōpjan* (wk.); f. Gmc. *wōp- (repr. also by OE. *wōp* weeping, etc.); without cogns., prob. of imit. orig. Weak inflexions appeared XIII and became prevalent XIV. Hence **weeper** (-ER[1]) mourner XIV; badge of mourning XVIII.

weever fish of the genus *Trachinus*, having venomous spines. XVII. perh. orig. *wiver* - transf. use of OF. *wivre* serpent, dragon, var. of *guivre* :- L. *vīpera* VIPER.

weevil beetle the larva of which is destructive to grain, etc. XV. ME. *wevyl*, prob. - MLG. *wevel* = OE. *wifel* beetle, OS. *goldwivil* glowworm, OHG. *wibil, wipil* beetle, chafer, ON. *vifill (in *tordýfill* dung-beetle) :- Gmc. *webilaz. Continuity with OE. *wifel* is not shown, and the word may be due to commercial relations with the Low Countries.

weft threads that extend from side to side of a web. OE. *weft(a)*, corr. to ON. *veptr, vipta* weft,

MHG. *wift* fine thread :- Gmc. **weftan-*, *-az*, *-iz*, f. **web-* WEAVE[1].

weigh A. bear, carry, lift (spec. raise an anchor XIV); B. balance in the scales; C. have heaviness or weight. OE. str. vb. *wegan* = OS. *wegan* (Du. *wegen*) weigh, OHG. *wegan* move, shake, weigh (in G. *bewegen* move), ON. *vega* lift, weigh, Goth. **wigan* in pp. *gawigans* shaken :- Gmc. **wezan*, f. **wez-* **waz-* **wǣz-* :- IE. **weĝh-* **woĝh-* **wēĝh-* (see WAY). So **weight** measurement or amount determined by weighing. The OE. form was *wiht*, more usu. *ġewiht*, corr. to MDu. *wicht*, *ghewichte* (Du. *(ge)wicht*), MHG. *gewichte* (G. *gewicht*), ON. *vétt*, *vǽtt* :- Gmc. *-weχtiz* and **gaweχtjam*, f. **wez-*; see -T[1]. This form was directly repr. by ME. *wi(g)ht*, *wiʒt*, which was superseded by *weght*, *wei(g)ht*, *weʒt* - ON. **weht*, *vétt*; the prevalence of this form was assisted by WEIGH. Hence **weighty** (-Y[1]) XV.

weir river-dam; enclosure for taking fish. OE. *wer*, corr. to OS. *werr*, MLG., MHG. *wer(e)* (LG. *wēr(e)*, G. *wehr*), f. OE. *werian* defend = OS. *werian*, OHG. *werian* (G. *wehren*), ON. *verja*, Goth. *warjan*.

weird (arch.) fate, lot, destiny, as in phr. *dree one's w.*, suffer one's fate. OE. *wyrd* = OS. *wurd*, OHG. *wurt*, ON. *urðr*, f. wk. grade of Gmc. **werþ-* **warþ-* *wurþ-* become (see WORTH[2]). So adj. controlling the destinies of men XIV; unaccountably mysterious, uncanny, odd XIX. First in *w. sister*, one of (i) the Fates, (ii) the witches in Shakespeare's 'Macbeth', the later currency and adj. use being derived from its occurrence in the story of Macbeth.

Welch var. of WELSH.

welcome used as voc. to express pleasure at a person's coming; hence in predicative and later (XVI) attrib. use. ME. *welcume* (XII), f. WELL[2] and *come* pp. as a rendering of (O)F. *bienvenu* (f. *bien* well, *venu* come) or ON. *velkominn* (i.e. 'well-come'); in part repl. OE. *wilcuma*, f. WILL[1] + *cuma* comer, agent-noun of *cuman* COME. So vb. greet with 'welcome'. Late OE. *wellcumian*, early ME. *welcume(n)*, repl. OE. *wilcumian*.

weld[1] plant yielding yellow dye; the dye itself. XIV. ME. *welde*, also *wolde*, repr. OE. **wealde*, **walde* = (M)LG. †*walde*, †*wolde*, *waude*, MDu. *woude* (Du. *wouw*), poss. rel. to WOLD.

weld[2] intr. be joined by heating and hammering XVI; trans. join in this way XVII. var. of WELL[2], from XV in this sense; the *-d* appears to have come from the pt. and pp.

welfare good fortune, well-being. XIV. f. phr. ME. *wel fare* (see WELL[3], FARE[1]), prob. after ON. *velferð*.

welkin †cloud OE.; (arch.) sky, firmament XII. OE. *weolcen*, *wolc(e)n*, corr. to OS. *wolkan* (Du. *wolk*), OHG. *wolkan* (G. *wolke*).

well[1] spring of water, pit dug to obtain a supply of spring water OE.; various transf. senses from XVII. OE. (Angl.) *wella*, *wælla*, **well(e)*, (WS.) **wiella*, late *will(a)*, *wyll(a)*, *wylle*, corr. to OHG. *wella* (G. *welle*) wave, ON. *vella* boiling heat, ebullition, f. Gmc. **wall-*; see WELL[2].

well[2] †boil, melt OE.; rise *up* to the eyes XIV; (dial.) weld XV. OE. str. vb. *weallan* = OS. *wallan*, OHG. *wallan* (G. *wallen* boil, swarm) :- WGmc. **wallan*; cf. prec.

well[3] in a good manner, to a good extent, fully. OE. *wel(l)* = OS. (Du.) *wel*, ON. *vel*; also with adv. suffix (and vowel-variation) OS. *wela*, *wala*, *wola*, OHG. *wela*, *wola* (G. *wohl*), Goth. *waila*; prob. f. IE. *wel-* *wol-* WILL[2]. As adj. †happy, fortunate XIII; prosperous (now only in *well to do*, *well off*) XIV; in sound health XVI; orig. developed from the adv. in impers. uses, e.g. *wel is þe*. Comp. **well-wisher** XVI.

welladay excl. of lamentation. XVI. alt., by substitution of *day* or *aday* as used in *wo worth the day* and *lackaday*, of **wellaway**, ME. *weleaway*, earlier *welawei*, *wailawai*, OE. *weġ lā weġ*, var. of *wā lā wā*, f. *wā* WOE, *lā* LO, infl. by ON. *vei* WOE and WELL[3].

wellington short for *w. boot*, *coat*, etc., named after Arthur, first duke of *Wellington* (1769-1852). XIX. So **wellingtonia** sequoia. XIX.

well off favourably or fortunately situated. XVIII. f. phr. *come* (etc.) *well off* be prosperously circumstanced in the event; see WELL[3], OFF.

welsh swindle out of money laid as a bet. XIX. Hence **welsher** (-ER[1]) XIX. of unkn. orig.

Welsh pert. to the native British population as opp. to the Anglo-Saxons, (hence) pert. to Wales. OE. (Angl.) *Wēlisċ*, *Wǣlisċ*, (WS.) *Wīlisċ*, *Wȳlisċ*, **Wīelisċ*, corr. to OHG. *wal(a)hisc*, *walesc* (G. *wälsch*, *welsch*) Roman, Italian, French, Du. *waalsch* Walloon, ON. *valskr* Gaulish, French; f. OE. *W(e)alh*, corr. to OHG. *Wal(a)h*, ON. **Valr*, pl. *Valir* :- Gmc. **walχaz* foreign (Celtic or Roman) - L. *Volcæ* (pl.) name of a Celtic people, of unkn. orig.

Welsh rabbit dish of toasted cheese. XVIII. See prec., RABBIT. Alt. without justification to *Welsh rarebit* XVIII.

welt in shoemaking, strip of leather placed between the edge of the sole and the upper XV; border, hem XVI; ridge, raised stripe. of unkn. orig.

welter roll about (in various ways). XIII. - MLG., MDu. *welteren* = MHG. *welzern*, frequent. f. **welt-* **walt-* roll, be unsteady, repr. also by OE. **wealt* (in *unwealt* steady), *-wæltan*, **wieltan*, *wyltan*, OHG. *walzan*, *welzen* (G. *wälzen*, WALTZ), ON. **welta* intr. (str.) and tr. (wk.), Goth. *waltjan*. Hence **welter** sb. turmoil XVI, rolling of the sea; heavy-weight horseman or pugilist XIX (whence *w. weight*).

wen morbid lump on the body; (in mod. use) sebaceous tumour under the skin. OE. *wen(n)*, *wæn(n)* = Du. *wen*, prob. rel. to MLG. *wene*, LG. *wehne*, *wähne* tumour, wart; of unkn. orig.

wench young woman, girl XIII; (arch.) wanton woman XIV; maidservant. ME. *wenche*, clipped form of *wenchel*, OE. *wenċel* :- **waŋkil-*, perh. rel. to OE. *wancol* unsteady, inconstant, f. **waŋk-* waver, falter, repr. by OHG. *wankōn*.

wend turn (tr. and intr. in many senses), go. OE. *wendan* = OS. *wendian*, OHG. *wentan* (Du., G. *wenden*), ON. *venda*, Goth. (Gmc.) *wandjan*, causative of **windan* WIND[3]. From *c.*1500 the new formation *wended* has prevailed for pt. and pp. in the tr. senses, and *went*, regularly evolved from OE. *wende, ġewend*, has repl. the older pts. belonging to GO.

Wensleydale name of a district of the North Riding of Yorkshire designating a long-woolled breed of sheep and a variety of blue-mould cheese. XIX.

went see WEND.

wept pt. of WEEP.

were see BE.

werewolf, werwolf person transformed or capable of transforming himself into a wolf. Late OE. *werewulf* (once) = LG. *werwulf*, (M)Du. *weerwolf*, MHG. *werwolf* (G. *we(h)rwolf*). The first el. is doubtful, but it has been identified with OE. *wer* (= L. *vir*) man.

wergeld, -gild (hist.) price set upon a man according to rank. OE. *werġeld*, WS. *-ġild*, f. *wer* man (= L. *vir*) + *ġield* YIELD. The OE. forms were taken up by antiquaries in XVII.

werwolf see WEREWOLF.

Wesleyan XVIII. pert. to John *Wesley* (1703-1791), originator of Methodism; see -AN.

west in or to the quarter of the horizon where the sun sets. OE. *west* = OS., OHG. (Du., G.) *west*, ON. *vestr* :- Gmc. **westaz*, f. IE. **wes-*, repr. also in Gr. *hésperos*, L. *vesper*. Hence **west** sb. XII, adj. XIV (anticipated by OE. comps. such as *westdǣl* west part, *westwind*). **westerly** adj. XVI; adv. XVII; see -LY[1,2]. **western** late OE. *westerne*. **westward** XIII, **-wards** XVI. OE. *westweard*, *-weardes*; see -WARD, -WARDS.

wet adj. From XIV. repr. pp. of the vb. *wet*, repl. *wēt* (mod. dial. *weet*) in standard Eng., from OE. (WS.) *wǣt*, (Angl.) *wēt* = ON. *vátr*, based on the lengthened stem of WATER. So sb. and vb., with shortening of vowel of OE. *ẇǣt*, *wǣtan*, ME. *weet(e)*.

wether male sheep, ram. OE. *weðer* = OS. *withar* (Du. *weer*), OHG. *widar* (G. *widder*), ON. *veðr* ram, Goth. *wiþrus* lamb :- Gmc. **weþruz*, of uncert. orig.

wey standard of dry-goods weight. OE. *wǣġ(e)* balance, weight = OS., OHG. *wāga* (Du. *waag*, G. *wage*), ON. *vág* :- Gmc. **wǣȝō*, *-ōn*, f. **wǣȝ-* **weȝ-* WEIGH.

whack vigorous resounding blow. XVIII. First recorded in Sc.; of imit. orig. (perh. alt. of THWACK). So vb. XVIII.

whale OE. *hwæl* = OHG. *wal* (in modG. *walfisch*), ON. *hvalr*, rel. to OHG. *walira*, (M)HG. *wels* (:- **χwalis*) sheath-fish. The present form reflects obl. cases of OE. *hwæl*. Comp. **whalebone** elastic bony substance of the upper jaw of whales XVII.

whangee cane made from bamboo-like plants. XIX. f. Chinese *huang* bamboo sprouts too old for eating.

wharf structure built along the water's edge. Late OE. *hwearf*, *w(e)arf* (earlier in poet. comp. *merehwearf* seashore), corr. to MLG. *warf*, *werf* mole, dam, wharf; f. Gmc. **χwerƀ-*, **χwarƀ-* repr. also by a series of vbs. having the meanings turn, change, wander, go.

wharfinger owner or keeper of a wharf. XVI. app. alt. of **wharfager* (-ER[1]), f. **wharfage** provision of, charge for use of, a wharf (XV).

what n. of interrog. pron. OE.; interrog. adj. XII (from OE. use of *hwæt* with partitive g.); as relative XII; as indefinite (*somewhat*) XIII. OE. *hwæt* = OS. *huat* (Du. *wat*), OHG. *(h)waȝ* (G. *was*), ON. *hvat*, Goth. *hwa* :- Gmc. **χwat* :- IE. **qod* (cf. L. *quod*), n. of **qos* WHO. In phrasal comps. **what d'ye call it** XVI. **what not** anything whatever XVI; article of furniture for holding odds and ends XIX. **what's-his-name** XVII. Hence **whatever** XIV, **whatso** (arch.) XII, **whatsoever** XIII.

wheal XIX. var. of WALE due to assoc. with †*wheal* suppurate, OE. *hwelian*, rel. to **hwele*, ME. *whele* pustule, and OE. *hwylca*, arch. or dial. *whelk*.

wheat OE. *hwǣte* = OS. *hwēti* (Du. *weit*), OHG. *weiz(z)i* (G. *weizen*), ON. *hveiti*, Goth. *hwaiteis* :- Gmc. **χwaitjaz*, f. var. of **χwīt-* WHITE. Hence **wheaten** (-EN[2]) OE. *hwǣten*.

wheatear small bird. XVI. of uncert. orig., but the dial. syns. *whiteass*, *white rump*, *white-tail* suggest that †*wheatears* (XVII) is for **whiteeres* 'white ARSE'; the present form being inferred as a sg. of *wheatears*, in which the first syll. had been assim. to WHEAT.

wheedle entice or persuade by cajolery XVII. perh. - G. *wedeln* fawn (upon), cringe or crouch (to), f. *wedel* tail, fan (OHG. *wedil*).

wheel sb. OE. *hwēol*, *hweogol*, *hweowol* = (M)LG. *wēl*, (M)Du. *wiel*, ON. *hjól*, *hvél* :- Gmc. **χwe(ȝ)ula*, **χweχula* :- IE. **qeqlo-*, repr. by Skr. *cakrá-* wheel, Gr. *kúklos* CYCLE (rel. to Gr. *pólos* axis). Hence **wheel** vb. intr. XIII, tr. XIV. **wheeler** (-ER[1]) wheelwright XV. **wheel-wright** XIII.

wheeze breathe hard with a whistling sound. XV. prob. - ON. *hvǽsa* hiss; or imit.

whelk mollusc of the genus *Buccinum*. OE. *weoloc*, *wioloc*, of unkn. orig.

whelm †capsize XIII; (dial.) turn upside down XIV; (arch.) engulf, OVERWHELM XV. repr. OE. **hwielman*, **hwelman*, parallel to OE. *hwylfan*, **hwielfan* = OS. *bihwelƀian* cover over, OHG. *welben* (G. *wölben*) vault, ON. *hvelfa*, f. Gmc. **χwalƀ-*, whence also OE. *hwealf* sb. arch, adj. vaulted.

whelp young of the dog and other animals. OE. *hwelp* = OS. *hwelp* (Du. *welp*), OHG. *hwelf*, (also mod.) *welf*, ON. *hvelpr*; a Gmc. word of which no cogns. are known. Hence **whelp** vb. bring forth young. XII.

when at what time?. OE. *hwenne*, *hwænne*, beside *hwanne*, *hwonne* when (interrog. and rel.), corr. to OS. *hwan(na)* when, at some time, when, MDu. *wen*, *wan*, OHG. *wenne*, *wanne* (G. *wenn* if, *wann* when), Goth. *hwan* when, how :- Gmc., adv. deriv. of the interrog. base **χwa-* WHO, WHAT; as THEN, THAN of the dem. **þa-* THE[1], THAT[1]. So **whence** from what place. XIII. ME. *whannes*, *whennes*, f. *whanne*, *whenne*, OE. *hwanon(e)*, = OS. *hwanan(a)*, OHG. *(h)wanana*, *(h)wanān*; cf. HENCE, THENCE. Hence **whensoever** XIV.

where in what place?. OE. *hwǣr*, beside *hwār* and *hwāra*, corr. to OS. *hwār* (Du. *waar*), OHG. *(h)wār*, *wā* (G. *wo*), ON. *hvar*, Goth. *hwar*; Gmc. derivs. of **χwa-* WHO, WHAT (cf. HERE, THERE). The earliest comps. with preps. are **whereat**, **whereby**, **wherein** (XIII), **whereof** (XII), **wherethrough**, **whereupon** (XIII), **where-**

with (XII); later are **whereunto** (XV), **wherewithal** (XVI). So **wherefor** for what purpose or cause XII; for which XIII; (now **-fore**) on what account; sb. cause, reason XVI.

wherry light rowing-boat for transport XV; barge XVI. of unkn. orig.

whet sharpen (also fig.). OE. *hwettan* = (M)LG., (M)Du. *wetten*, OHG. *wezzan* (G. *wetzen*), ON. *hvetja* :- Gmc. **χwatjan*, f. **χwattaz* sharp (OE. *hwæt* quick, active, brave, OS. *hwat* keen, bold, OHG. *(h)waz* sharp, rough, severe, ON. *hvatr* bold, vigorous). Comp. **whetstone** OE. *hwetstān*.

whether pron. and adj. which of the two; conj. introducing a question expressing choice between alternatives. OE. *hweðer*, beside *hwæðer*, corr. to OS. *hweðar*, OHG. *(h)wedar* (G. *weder* neither), ON. *hvaðarr*, Goth. *hwaþar* :- Gmc. **χwa-*, **χweþaraz*, f. **χwa-*, **χwe-*, WHO + compar. suffix as in OTHER.

whew excl. of astonishment, dismay, etc. XVI. prob. intended to repr. a whistling sound.

whey watery part of milk remaining after the curd is separated. OE. *hwæġ*, *hweġ* = MDu. *wey* (Du. *wei*) :- **χwaja-*, rel. by gradation to MLG. *huy*, *hoie*, Du. *hui* :- **χwuja-*.

which †of what kind?; †what?; what one? OE.; as rel. adj. and pron. XII. OE. *hwilċ* = OS. *(h)wilik*, MLG., MDu. *wilk*, ON. *hvílíkr*, corr. with a different grade to OE. *hwelċ* = MDu. *wel(i)c*, *walc*, OHG. *hwelīh*, Goth. *hvileiks*; Gmc. formation on **χwa-* **χwe-* (see WHO) and **līka-* body, form; cf. EACH, SUCH. Hence **whichever** XIV, **whichsoever** XV.

whidah, whydah name of a town (now Ouidah) in Dahomey, W. Africa, applied spec. to animals found in this locality; *w. bird* (XVIII), alt. of *widow-bird*, which is based on L. generic name *Vidua* 'widow' (so called from the mainly black plumage and long train of tail feathers of the male).

whiff A. slight puff or gust; inhalation of tobacco-smoke XVI; wave or waft of odour XVII; puffing or whistling sound XVIII; B. flag hoisted as a signal XVII; C. light outrigger XIX. of imit. orig. Hence vb. XVI.

Whig (*w-*) †yokel; adherent of the Presbyterian cause in Scotland (esp. one of the rebellious covenanters who marched on Edinburgh in 1648); exclusioner (opposing succession of James, duke of York) XVII; from 1689, one of the two great political parties in England. prob. shortening of Sc. *whiggamaire*, *-mer*, *wiggomer* (used in the second sense, the expedition being called 'the whiggamore raid'), f. *whig* drive + *mere* MARE.

while time (now chiefly in phr. *a good*, *great* (etc.) *while*, *a while* for a certain or some time, *between whiles* at intervals of time); as conj. (XII), shortening of ME. *þe while þat*, in OE. *þā hwīle þe* during the time that. OE. *hwīl* = OS. *hwīl(a)* time (Du. *wijl*), OHG. *(h)wīla* point or period of time (G. *weile*), ON. *(h)víla* bed, Goth. *hweila* time :- Gmc. **χwīlō*. So **whilom** †at times OE.; (arch.) at some time past XII. OE. *hwīlum* (d. pl. of *hwīl*). **whilst** alt., with parasitic *t* (as in *amidst*, *amongst*), of †*whiles*, formed with adv. -s on the sb. and used finally (XIII) as conj. like *while*.

whim A. †pun, play on words; †fanciful creation; odd fancy XVII; machine for raising ore, etc. from a mine XVIII. of unkn. orig. Synonyms are (1) **whims(e)y** XVII, whence **whimsical** XVII, and (2) **whim-wham** XVI, redupl. formation with vowel-variation.

whimbrel curlew. XVI (*whympernell*). f. (dial.) *whimp* (XVI) or WHIMPER, on account of the bird's cry.

whimper utter a feeble broken cry. XVI. Extension of (dial.) *whimp* (XVI), of imit. orig.; see -ER[4]. Hence sb. XVII.

whin furze, gorse. XI. prob. of Scand. orig.; cf. Sw. *hven*, ODa. *hvine*, *hvinegræs*, *-strå*, Norw. *hvine*, applied to certain grasses. First recorded in place-names of Scandinavianized areas. Hence **whinchat** bird allied to the stonechat. XVII.

whine utter a low somewhat shrill protracted sound OE.; complain querulously XVI. OE. *hwīnan* (once, of an arrow). An immed. cogn. is ON. *hvína* whiz, whistle in the air; a wk. grade of the imit. base is repr. by ON. *hvinr* whizzing, late OE. *hwinsian* (whence dial. *whinge* whine) = OHG. *win(i)sōn* (whence G. *winseln*).

whinny neigh. XVI. of imit. orig.

whip move briskly XIII; strike with a whip XIV; overlay with cord, thread, etc. XV. ME. *(h)wippen*, prob. - (M)LG., (M)Du. *wippen* swing, vacillate, leap (= MHG. *wipfen* dance), f. Gmc. **wip-* move quickly. So **whip** sb. instrument of flagellation XIV; †brisk movement XVI.

whipper-snapper sprightly but insignificant young person. XVII. orig. a canting term for a 'rough'; perh. f. **whip-snapper*, cf. *whipster* (XVI) 'cracker of whips', lively, violent, or mischievous person, insignificant fellow.

whippet †lively young woman XVI; small breed of dog XVII. prob. f. †*whippet* vb. move briskly (XVI), i.e. *whip it*.

whip-poor-will Amer. nightjar. XVIII. imit. of the bird's note.

whirl move in a circle XIII; revolve or cause to revolve XIV; move or cause to move swiftly; hurl XV. - ON. *hvirfla* turn about, rel. to *hvirfill* circle, ring, summit = (M)LG., (M)Du. *wervel* †whirlpool, †spindle, vertebra, OHG. *wirbil* whirlwind (G. *wirbel*) :- Gmc. **χwerƀilaz*.

whirlpool XV. f. WHIRL + POOL.

whirlwind XIV. prob. - ON. *hvirfilvindr* (see WHIRL, WIND[1]).

whir(r) †fling, hurl; move swiftly with a vibratory sound. XIV. prob. first of Scand. orig. (cf. Da. *hvirre*, Norw. *kvirra*, Sw. dial. *hvirra*); reinforced later by being imit.

whish int., vb. XVI. imit. of the sound made by something rushing through air or over water. Hence sb. XIX.

whisk sb. (XIV) and vb. (XV) denoting light rapid sweeping motion. orig. *wisk*, *wysk* (*quhisk* XV) and first in Sc. texts; - Scand. stem repr. by ON. *visk* wisp, Sw. *viska* besom, wisp, *viska* whisk (off), sponge, Norw. *visk* wisp, corr. to (M)Du. *wisch* wisp, LG. *wisk* quick movement, OHG. *wisc* (G. *wisch*) wisp of hay, *wisken* (*wischen*) wipe, †move briskly, f. symbolic Gmc. base **wisk-*. Hence **whisker** (-ER[1]) †fan, †switch, (dial.) feather brush XV; hair on the face, †moustache XVI.

whisky[1] spirit distilled from malted barley, etc. XVIII. Shortening of *whiskybae*, var. of USQUEBAUGH.

whisky[2] light carriage. XVIII. f. WHISK + -Y[1], so named from its swift motion.

whisper vb. OE. *hwisprian* = early Flem. *wispeeren*, f. Gmc. imit. base **χwis-*, whence also synon. MLG., MDu. *wispelen*, OHG. *(h)wispalōn* (G. *wispeln*), ON. *hvískra, hvísla*. Hence sb. XVI.

whist[1] excl. to call for silence. XIV. of imit. orig. Hence as adj. silent, hushed XV; as vb. become or †make silent XVI.

whist[2] card-game. XVII. alt. (perh. by assoc. with prec.) of earlier *whisk* (XVII), perh. f. WHISK vb. from the action of whisking away the tricks.

whistle sb. tubular wind instrument OE.; throat XIV; act of whistling XV. OE. *(h)wistle*, of imit. orig. So vb. OE. *(h)wistlian*; cf. WHISPER.

whit (arch.) very small or the least portion or amount. XV. Early mod. *w(h)yt, whit(t)*, prob. alt. of WIGHT, as in *any wight, no wight*.

white adj. OE. *hwīt* = OS. *hwīt*, OHG. *(h)wīʒ* (G. *weiss*), ON. *hvítr*, Goth. *hweits* :- Gmc. **χwītaz* (cf. with short vowel (M)Du., (M)LG. *wit*); f. IE. **k̂wit-, *k̂wid-*, found also in Skr. and Balto-Sl. words denoting brightness or light. Comps. **whitebait** small fry of fish XVIII; **white friar** Carmelite XV; **white-livered** cowardly (having, acc. to popular belief, a liver lacking bile or choler) XVI; **whitesmith** worker in metal XIV; **whitethorn** hawthorn XIII; **whitethroat** warbler XVII; **whitewash** plaster with a white composition XVI; hence sb. XVII. Hence **white** vb. †become or make white OE.; whitewash XII. **whiten** (-EN[5]) XIII.

whither to what or which place. OE. *hwider*, f. Gmc. **χwi-* (see WHICH); for the suffix cf. HITHER, THITHER. Hence †**whitherso** OE., **whithersoever** XIII.

whiting[1] fish of the genus *Merlangus*. XV. - (M)Du. *wijting*; see WHITE, -ING[3], and cf. ON. *hvítingr* white whale, late OE. *hwītling* (perh.) whiting.

whiting[2] †whitewashing; finely powdered chalk as used for this XV. f. WHITE vb. + -ING[1].

whitleather leather dressed with alum instead of being tanned. XIV. f. WHITE, LEATHER.

whitlow inflammatory sore on finger or thumb. XV. perh. orig. *whitflaw* (XIV), *-flow* (XV), i.e. WHITE + FLAW[1] breach, fissure (but cf. Du. *fijt*, LG. *fīt*); the alt. to *whitlow* is unexpl.

Whit Sunday, Whitsunday seventh Sunday after Easter Day, Pentecost. Late OE. *Hwīta Sunnandæġ* 'White Sunday', so named prob. from the ancient custom of wearing white robes by the newly baptized at the Feast of Pentecost. The shortening of the vowel of the first syll. obscured the composition of the word, so that it has been differently divided (whence *Whitsun eve* and *week* (XIII) beside *Whit Monday* (XVI), etc.). Hence **Whitsuntide** Whitsunday and the days immediately following. XIII.

whittle cut thin slices from XVI; fig. XVIII. f. (dial.) *whittle* large knife (XV), var. of *thwittle*, f. *thwite* (OE. *þwītan* shave off).

whiz(z) make, or move with, a sound as of a body rushing through the air. XVI. of imit. orig.

who what or which person?; used as relative pron. from XIII. ME. *hwo* (XII-XIII), *who* (from XIII), *hoo* (XIII-XV), repr. OE. *hwā*, corr. to OS. *hwē, hwie* (Du. *wie*), OHG. *(h)wer* (G. *wer*), OSw. *ho*, ODa. *hwa* (Da. *hvo*), Goth. *hwas* :- Gmc. **χwaz *χwez* :- IE. **qos *qes* (cf. Skr. *ká-*), parallel to **qi* (cf. L. *quis*); cf. L. *quī* who. Hence **whoso** XII, **whosoever** XIII, **whosomever** XV.

whoa call to a horse to stop. XIX. var. of *who* (XV), var. of HO; preceded by †*whoa ho* call from a distance XVII.

whole in good or sound condition; not divided into parts OE.; sb. *the* complete amount XIV; a combination of parts XVII. OE. *(ġe)hāl* = OS. *hēl* (Du. *(ge)heel*), (O)HG. *heil*, ON. *heill*, Goth. *(ga)hails* :- Gmc. **(ga)χailaz* :- IE. **kailos* (repr. also in Balto-Sl.). **wholesale** first in phr. *by w.*, †*by the w.* XV. **wholesome** conducive to well-being XII. prob. OE. **hālsum*, with Gmc. parallels. **wholly** to the full or complete extent, in full. OE. **hāllīċe*; see -LY[2].

whom acc. and d. of WHO. OE. *hwām*, late var. of *hwǣm*, d. of *hwā* WHO, *hwæt* WHAT; in its later uses *whom* combined the functions of OE. *hwone, hwane*, acc. sg. of *hwā*, and those of *hwǣm*. Hence **whomever** XIV, **whomso** XII, **whomsoever** XV.

whoop shout, hollo XIV. of imit. orig. So sb. XVI. Hence **whoopee** excl. accompanying riotous enjoyment. XIX (orig. U.S.). **whooper** whistling swan XVII. **whooping-cough,** cough accompanied by a sound like 'whoop'. XVIII.

whoosh imit. of a sibilant sound as of something rushing through the air. XIX.

whop cast or pull violently XIV; strike heavily XVI. var. of *wap* (XIV), of imit. orig. Hence **whopper** (-ER[1]) uncommonly large one XVIII. **whopping** (-ING[2]) that is a whopper. XVII.

whore Late OE. *hōre*, corr. to (M)LG. *hore*, MDu. *hoere* (Du. *hoer*), OHG. *huora* (G. *hure*), ON. *hóra* :- Gmc. **χōrōn*, f. base repr. also by ON. *hórr*, Goth. *hōrs* adulterer; the IE. base **kār-* appears in L. *cārus*, OIr. *cara* friend. So **whoredom** XII. prob. - ON. *hórdómr*. Hence **whore** vb. XVI. Comps. **whoremaster, whoremonger** XVI. **whoreson** bastard, term of abuse XIII.

whorl small fly-wheel or pulley in a spinning machine XV; ring of leaves, etc. round a stem XVI. Earliest forms *wharwyl, whorwhil*; prob. vars. of *wherwille*, WHIRL.

whortleberry bilberry. XVI. s.w. dial. var. of *hurtleberry*, of unkn. orig.

whose g. of *who* and *what*. Early ME. *hwās, hwōs* (XII-XIII), alt., by assim. to *hwā, hwō* WHO, of *hwas, hwes*, OE. *hwæs* g. of m. *hwā* and n. *hwæt* WHAT (in interrog. use only). Hence **whosesoever** XVII.

why for what reason or purpose? OE.; int. as a note of surprise or calling attention XVI. OE. *hwī, hwȳ*, instr. case of *hwæt* WHAT, corr. to OS. *hwī*, ON. *hví*.

wick[1] bundle of fibre by which a flame is kept

supplied with fat. OE. *wēoc* (in *candelwēoc*), *wēoce*, corr. to MDu. *wiecke* (Du. *wiek*), MLG. *wēke*, OHG. *wiohha* (G. *wieche*), of unkn. orig.

wick[2] †dwelling; (dial.) town, hamlet OE.; farm XI. OE. *wīc* = OS. *wīc* (Du. *wijk* quarter, district, ward), OHG. *wīh* (G. in *weichbild* municipal area), Goth. *weihs*; prob. Gmc. - L. *vīcus* row of houses, quarter of a town, street, village, cogn. with Gr. *oîkos* house.

wicked XIII. f. (dial.) *wick*, adj. use of OE. *wiċċa* wizard, the fem. of which is *wiċċe* WITCH. For the unusual formation cf. WRETCHED.

wicker pliant twig or rod. XIV. of Scand. orig. (cf. Sw. *viker*, Da. *viger* willow), f. base of Sw. *vika* bend (cf. OE. *wīcan* give way, collapse, and WEAK).

wicket small door or gate XIII; (in cricket) XVIII. - AN., ONF. *wiket* = (O)F. *guichet*, of uncert. orig.

widdershins var. of WITHERSHINS.

wide of great extent (esp. horizontally), (in limited use) from side to side. OE. *wīd* = OS. *wīd* (Du. *wijd*), OHG. *wīt* (G. *weit*), ON. *víðr* :- Gmc. **wīdaz*, of uncert. orig. So **wide** adv. OE. *wīde*. Hence **widen** (-EN[5]) XVII. Comps. **wideawake** fully awake with eyes open; said to be applied joc. to a kind of soft felt hat because of its having no 'nap'. XIX. **widespread** XVIII.

widgeon, wigeon wild duck. XVI. perh. f. imit. base **wi-*, after PIGEON[1].

widow sb. OE. *widewe*, *wuduwe* = OS. *widowa* (Du. *weduwe*, *weeuw*), OHG. *wituwa* (G. *witwe*), Goth. *widuwō*, adj. formation of IE. range, **widhewo-*, repr. by Skr. *vidhávā* widow, Gr. *ē(ϝ)íthe(ϝ)os* unmarried man, L. *viduus* bereft, void, widowed (fem. *vidua* widow), OSl. *vŭdova*, OIr. *fedb*, W. *gweddw* widow; poss. f. **widh-* as in L. *dīvidere* DIVIDE. So **widower** (-ER[1]) XIV; substituted as an unequivocal form for †*widow* (OE. masc. *widewa*). Hence **widow** vb. XV, **widowed** (-ED[1]) XVI, **widowhood** OE. *widewanhād*.

width XVII. f. first syll. of *wīdness* (the normal form from OE. *wīdnes* wideness, f. *wīd* WIDE + *-nes* -NESS) + -TH[1].

wield †rule, direct, command; handle with skill or effect. ME. *wēlde(n)*, repr. (1) OE. str. vb. *wealdan* = OS. *waldan*, OHG. *waltan* (G. *walten*), ON. *valda*, Goth. *waldan*, and (2) OE. wk. vb. *wieldan*, f. mutated form of Gmc. **walð-*, cogn. with Balto-Sl. forms denoting rule and power, and prob. ult. with **wal-* of L. *valēre* be strong. Hence **wieldy** (-Y[1]) †capable of easy movement XIV; (now chiefly as back-formation from UNWIELDY) manageable, handy XVI.

wife woman (surviving in *fishwife*, *old wives' tale*); woman joined to a man by marriage OE.; mistress of a household (surviving in *goodwife*, *housewife*) XIV. OE. *wīf* = OS. *wīf* (Du. *wijf*), OHG. *wīp* (G. *weib* woman), ON. *víf*; of unkn. orig.

wig XVII. Shortening of PERIWIG.

wigeon see WIDGEON.

wiggle move to and fro irregularly. XIII. - (M)Du., (M)LG. *wiggelen*, frequent. (see -LE[3]) of **wig-*, repr. by LG. *wiggen*.

wight †living creature OE.; (arch.) being XII. OE. *wiht*, corr. (with variation of gender and meaning) to OS. *wiht* thing, (pl.) demons (MLG. *wicht* thing, creature, demon, (M)Du. *wicht* little child), OHG. *wiht* creature, thing (G. *wicht* being, infant), ON. *vǽttr*, *véttr*, *vítr* creature, thing, Goth. *waiht* n. (in *ni* ... *waiht* nothing); further connections uncert.

wigwam N. Amer. Indian cabin, tent, or hut. XVII. of Algonquian orig.

wild living in a state of nature; uninhabited, waste; uncontrolled. OE. *wilde* = OS., OHG. *wildi* (Du., G. *wild*), ON. *villr*, Goth. *wilþeis* :- Gmc. **wilþijaz*, prob. rel. to W. *gwyllt*, Ir. *geilt* wild.

wildebeest gnu. XIX. - Afrikaans (now *wildebees*, pl. *wildebeeste*), f. Du. *wild* WILD + *beest* BEAST.

wilderness uncultivated tract of land. XIII. perh. OE. **wild(d)ēornes*, f. *wild(d)ēor* wild beast (cf. (M)Du., G. *wildernis*); see WILD, DEER, -NESS.

wile crafty or deceitful trick. XII. poss. - ON. **wihl-* (*vél*) craft, artifice, rel. to *véla* defraud. Hence **wily** (-Y[1]) XIII.

will[1] desire, act or power of willing OE.; testamentary document XIV. OE. *willa* = OS. *willio* (Du. *wil*), OHG. *will(i)o* (G. *wille*), ON. *vili*, *vilja-*, Goth. *wilja* :- Gmc. **wiljan-*, f. **wel-* be pleasing (cf. next). Hence **wilful** self-willed XII; †willing, wishful XIV; earlier in adv. (late OE. *wilfullīċe*).

will[2] pt. *would* expressing desire, wish, intention, or determination; in combination with SHALL forming a future tense. OE. **willan*, *wyllan* (pt. *wolde*) = OS. *willian* (Du. *willen*), ON. *vilja*, Goth. *wiljan* :- Gmc. **wel(l)jan*, parallel with Gmc. **wal(l)jan*, repr. by OHG. *wellen* (G. *wollen*), ON. *velja*, Goth. *waljan*; based on IE. **wol-* **wel-* (cf. L. *velle*, *volō*, *voluī*, and see WILL[1], WELL[2]).

will[3] pt., pp. *willed* wish or desire (to); determine by the will. OE. *willian* = OHG. *willōn* (G. *willen*), f. WILL[1].

willet N. Amer. bird of the snipe family whose cry is expressed by *pill-will-willet*. XIX.

willies *the w.* spell of nervousness. XIX (orig. U.S.). of unkn. orig.

willing vbl. sb. desire, inclination OE.; voluntary choice XIV. OE. *willung*; see -ING[1]. So **willing** (-ING[2]) ppl. adj. XIII.

will o' the wisp phosphorescent light on marshy ground. XVII. The earliest form is *Will with the* or *a wisp*, i.e. *Will* (pet form of *William*) and WISP in the sense 'bundle of hay, etc., for use as a torch'.

willow plant of the genus *Salix*. OE. *weliġ* = OS. *wilgia* (Du. *wilg*), (M)LG. *wilge*.

willy-nilly whether one likes it or not. XVII. Later sp. of *wil I nil I* (XVI) 'I am willing, I am unwilling'; based on WILL[2] and its neg. (OE. *nyllan*, f. *ne* (see NO[3]) + *willan*).

wilt[1] become limp. XVII. of uncert. orig.

wilt[2] 2nd pers. sg. pres. ind. of WILL[2].

Wilton kind of carpet made at *Wilton* in Wiltshire. XVIII.

wimple woman's garment enveloping head, chin, sides of the face and neck (now worn by nuns). XIII. Late OE. *wimpel* = (M)LG., (M)Du.

wimpel, OHG. *wimpal* veil, bonnet (G. *wimpel* streamer, pennon), ON. *vimpill*.

win pt., pp. *won* †work; †vanquish OE.; gain XII; be victorious (also tr.) XIII. OE. str. vb. *(ġe)winnan* = OS. *winnan* suffer, win, MLG., MDu. *winnen* till, obtain, OHG. *winnan* rage, contend, *gewinnan* gain by labour (G. *gewinnen* earn, gain), ON. *vinna* labour, gain, Goth. *(ga)winnan* suffer; Gmc. vb. of uncertain relations. So **win** sb. †A. conflict, strife OE.; †gain, wealth XII; B. victory XIX; gains. In A. OE. *(ġe)win(n)*, ME. *(i)win*; in B f. the vb.

wince (dial.) kick restlessly XIII; make an involuntary shrinking movement XVIII. - AN. **wencir*, var. of OF. *guenchir* turn aside, avoid - Gmc. **weŋkjan* (OHG. *wenken*, OS. *wenkian*).

wincey durable cloth having a linen warp and a woollen weft. XIX. orig. Sc., app. alt. of *woolsey* in LINSEY-WOOLSEY.

winch reel, roller OE.; hoisting or hauling apparatus XVI. Late OE. *winċe* :- Gmc. **wiŋkjo-*, f. IE. **weŋg-* WINK.

Winchester A. name of a city in Hampshire, used as a designation of certain measures XVI; B. name of Oliver F. *Winchester* (1810-80), an American manufacturer, designating a type of breech-loading rifle XIX.

wind[1] air in motion. OE. *wind* = OS. *wind*, OHG. *wint* (Du., G. *wind*), ON. *vindr*, Goth. *winds* :- Gmc. **windaz*, based on IE. prp. **went-* (whence L. *ventus* wind, W. *gwynt*), with parallel forms on **wē-* in OSl. *vějati* blow, OIr. *feth* air, Gr. *áēsi* (:- **aϝēsi*) blows, Skr. *vā́ti* blows. Comp. **windfall** something blown down by the wind XV; unexpected acquisition XVI.

wind[2] pt., pp. *wound* †move in a certain direction OE.; move in a circular path XIII; pass (a thing) round something else XIV; set (a mechanism) in order XVII. OE. str. vb. *windan* = OS. *windan*, OHG. *wintan* (Du., G. *winden*), ON. *vinda*, Goth. **windan* :- Gmc. **windan*, rel. to **wand-* in WEND.

wind[3] A. get the wind of XV; deprive of breath XIX; B. sound a horn, etc. by blowing into it XVI. f. WIND[1].

windlass XIV. Presumably obscure alt. of †*windas* - AN. *windas* = OF. *guindas* - ON. *vindáss*, f. *vinda* WIND[2] + *áss* pole.

windlestraw (dial.) withered stalk. OE. *windelstrēaw*, f. *windel* basket, f. *windan* WIND[2] (see -LE[1]) + *strēaw* STRAW[1].

window XIII. ME. *windoȝe* - ON. *vindauga*, f. *vindr* WIND[1] + *auga* EYE.

Windsor town in Berkshire, place of residence of British Royal Family (*W. Castle*), designation of the family (*House of W.*); used attrib. in *W. chair* (XVIII), *soap*, *uniform* (XIX) (worn by the Royal Family).

wine OE. *wīn* = OS., OHG. *wīn* (Du. *wijn*, G. *wein*), ON. *vín*, Goth. *wein* :- Gmc. **wīnam* - L. *vīnum*, rel. to Gr. (ϝ)*oînos* wine. Comps. **winebibber, winepress, winevat** XVI.

wing organ of flight XII; lateral part or appendage XIII; protection, care; division (right or left) of a force XIV; side scene in a theatre XVIII. First in pl. *wenge(n)*, *-es* - ON. *vængir*, pl. of *vængr* wing of a bird, aisle. Hence **wing** vb. use the wings XVII; wound in the wing XIX. **winged** (-ED[2]) XIV.

wink †close the eyes; †give a significant glance OE.; blink XIII; 'shut the eyes' to (const. *at*) XV; close one eye momentarily in a flippant manner XIX. OE. *wincian* = OS. *wincan* (MLG., MDu. *winken*), rel. to OHG. *winchan* (G. *winken*) move sideways, stagger, nod, f. Gmc. **wiŋk-* **waŋk-* move sideways or from side to side.

winkle XVI. Shortening of PERIWINKLE[2].

winnow free (grain) from chaff, separate (chaff) from grain. OE. *windwian*, f. *wind* WIND[1]; rel. to OHG. *wintōn*, ON. *vinza* winnow, Goth. *diswinþjan* scatter like chaff.

winsome †pleasant OE. to XIII; of attractive appearance or disposition XVII. OE. *wynsum* (= OS. *wunsam*, OHG. *wunnisam*), f. *wyn(n)* joy, pleasure = OS. *wunnia*, OHG. *wunnia*, *wunna* (G. *wonne*), f. Gmc. **wun-*, repr. also in WISH, WONT[1]; see -SOME[1].

winter OE. *winter* = OS., OHG. *wintar* (Du., G. *winter*), ON. *vetr*, Goth. *wintrus* :- Gmc. **wintrus*, prob. f. nasalized var. of IE. base **wed-* **wod-* be wet (see WATER, WET). Hence **winter** vb. spend the winter. XIV. **winterly** (-LY[1]), **wintry** (-Y[1]). OE. *winterlić*, *wintriġ*, with cogns. in OHG., etc.; present currency is due to new formations in XVI.

wipe rub gently with a cloth, etc. OE.; fig. uses from XIII. OE. *wīpian*, corr. formally to OHG. *wīfan* wind round, Goth. *weipan* crown, and rel. further to OHG. *waif* bandage, ON. *veipr* head-covering, Goth. *waips* wreath. Hence **wipe** sb. slashing blow or remark XVI; act of wiping XVII; (sl.) handkerchief XVIII.

wire (piece or length of) metal in the form of a slender rod OE.; network of this XVI. OE. *wīr*, corr. to MLG. *wīre* (LG. *wīr*), ON. **vírr* in *víra virki* filigree work, rel. to OHG. *wiara* (ornament of) finest gold; prob. f. base **wi-* of L. *viēre* plait, weave (cf. WITHE). Hence **wireless** XIX. **wire-puller** one who exerts underhand influence. XIX (orig. U.S.). **wireworm** larva of click-beetles. XVIII. **wiry** (-Y[1]) XVI.

wisdom quality of being wise; †knowledge, learning. OE. *wīsdōm* = OS. *wīsdōm*, OHG. *wīstuom* (G. *weistum* legal sentence, precedent), ON. *vísdómr*; see WISE[2], -DOM.

wise[1] (arch.) manner, fashion. OE. *wīse* (rarely *wīs*) mode, condition, thing, cause, corr. to OS. *wīsa* (Du. *wijze*), OHG. *wīs(a)* manner, custom (G. *weise*), ON. **vīs* in *ǫðruvís* otherwise :- Gmc. **wīsōn*, **wīsō*, f. **wit-* WIT[2].

wise[2] having sound judgement; †learned OE.; informed XII. OE. *wīs* = OS., OHG. *wīs(i)* (Du. *wijs*, G. *weise*), ON. *víss*, Goth. *-weis* :- Gmc. **wīsaz* :- **wittos*, f. IE. **weid-* WIT[2] + ppl. suffix **-tos*.

-wise suffix descending from OE. *wīse* WISE[1] as used in various adv. expressions meaning 'in such-and-such a manner, way, or respect' and containing an adj. or an attrib. sb. with or without a governing prep., e.g. OE. *(on) ōðre wīsan* in another fashion, OTHERWISE, *on sċipwīsan* after the manner of a ship.

wiseacre pretender to wisdom. XVI. - (with unexpl. assim. to *acre*) MDu. *wijsseggher* soothsayer, prob. - (with assim. to *segghen* say) OHG.

wīssago, alt., by assoc. with *wīs* WISE² and *sagen* SAY¹, of *wīʒago* = OE. *wītega* prophet, f. **wit-* WIT².

wish have a desire (for). OE. *wȳsċan* = MLG. *wünschen*, MDu. *wonscen*, *wunscen*, OHG. *wunsken* (G. *wünschen*), ON. *œskja* :- Gmc. **wunskjan*, f. *wunska-*, *-ō* (OE. *wūsċ*, MDu. *wunsc*, *wonsc*, OHG. *wunsc* (G. *wunsch*), ON. *ósk* wish), f. **wun-* **wen-* **wan-*; cf. Skr. *vāñchati* wishes. Hence **wish** sb. XIV. **wishful** †desirable, †longing XVI; desirous XVIII; coloured by what one desires for the future XX.

wishy-washy weak and insipid. XVIII. redupl. formation on *washy* (XVII), with vowel alternation; so **wish-wash** washy drink or talk XVIII.

wisp handful, bunch, twisted band (of hay, etc.). XIV. corr. forms are only in WFris., but cf. synon. vars. s.v. WHISK.

wistaria, -eria climbing plant. XIX. f. name of Casper *Wistar* or *Wister* (1761-1818), Amer. anatomist; see -IA¹.

wistful †closely attentive; yearningly eager, mournfully expectant. XVII. perh. f. †*wistly* intently (XV), var. of †*whishtly* silently (cf. WHIST¹) + -FUL¹, and assoc. with WISHFUL.

wit¹ A. †mind, understanding, sense OE.; B. right mind, good judgement, (pl.) senses XII; C. (power of) giving pleasure by combining or contrasting ideas XVI. D. †wise man XVI; witty man XVII. OE. (*ġe*)*wit*(*t*), corr. to OS. *wit* (Du. *weet*), OHG. *wizzi* (G. *witz*), ON. *vit*, Goth. *unwiti* ignorance, f. **wit-* (see next).

wit² know; surviving in phr. *to wit* that is to say, namely, viz., short for *that is to wit*. OE. preterite-present vb. *witan* = OS. *witan* (Du. *weten*), OHG. *wizzan* (G. *wissen*), ON. *vita*, Goth. *witan*, f. Gmc. **wait-* **wīt* :- IE. **woid-* **weid-* **wid-*, whence Skr. *véda* knows, Gr. *oída*, L. *vidēre* see, OSl. *viděti* see, *věděti* know.

witch OE. *wiċċe*, fem. corr. to *wiċċa* male magician, sorcerer, wizard, rel. to *wiċċian* practise magic arts, corr. to (M)LG. *wikken*, *wicken*; of unkn. orig. Hence **witchcraft** OE. *wiċċecræft*.

witch elm, hazel see WYCH-ELM, WYCH HAZEL.

with †A. denoting opposition OE. B. denoting accompaniment or addition (esp. repl. OE., ME. *mid*). C. denoting instrumentality, causation, agency XII. OE. *wið* = OS. *wið*, prob. shortening of Gmc. prep. repr. by OE. *wiðer* = OS. *withar* (Du. *we*(*d*)*er*), OHG. *widar* (G. *wieder* adv. again, *wider* prep. against), ON. *viðr*, Goth. *wiþra*; f. IE. **wi-* denoting separation or division + compar. suffix **-tero-* (cf. Skr. *vitarám* further).

with- repr. OE. *wið-*, prep. WITH used as a prefix to vbs. (and derived sbs.) in the senses (1) away, back, (2) against, as in WITHDRAW, WITHHOLD, WITHSTAND.

withal adv. (arch.) along with the rest, as well XII; with it or them XIII; prep. with. f. WITH + ALL sb.

withdraw take back or away. XIII. see WITH-. Hence *withdrawing-room* room to withdraw into XVI; see -ING¹ and DRAWING-ROOM. **withdrawal** (-AL²) XIX.

withe (dial.) band or tie made of a flexible twig OE.; †halter XIII; metal band or hoop XVII. OE. *wiððe* = MDu. *wisse* (Du. *wis*), OHG. *wit*(*hi*), *wid*(*i*), Goth. *kunawida* bonds, ON. *við*, *viðja* :- Gmc. **wiþōn*, **wiþi*; f. IE. base **weit-* **wit-*, of IE. range (rel. to L. **wi-* as in L. *viēre* plait, WIRE).

wither become dried up and shrivelled XIV; tr. XVI. The earliest forms are *wydder*, *widder*, the present sp. dating from XVI. gen. assumed to be a use of WEATHER vb., ult. differentiated for certain senses.

withers (sb. pl.) highest part of a horse's back. XVI. Shortening of †*widersomes*, *-sones*, f. *wider-*, *wither-* (see WITH) + (perh.) var. of SINEW; the force of the first el. is obscure.

withershins A. (Sc.) the wrong way; B. in a direction contrary to the apparent course of the sun. XVI. - MLG. *weddersin*(*ne*)*s* - MHG. *widersinnes*, f. *wider-* against = OE. *wiðer* (see WITH) + g. of *sin*(*d*), *sint* = OE. *sīð* journey, course (cf. SEND¹); in sense B. with vars. *-sones*, *-sonnis*, by assoc. with SUN.

withhold hold or keep back. XII. f. WITH- + HOLD¹.

within adv. on the inner side OE.; prep. in the interior of, in the limits of XII. Late OE. *wiðinnan*, f. *wið* WITH + *innan*, ME. *inne* IN¹.

without adv. outside; prep. on the outside of OE.; not accompanied by, not having XII. Late OE. *wiðūtan*, f. *wið* WITH + *ūtan*, ME. *ute*(*n*) OUT.

withstand pt., pp. *withstood* stand or maintain one's position against. OE. *wiðstandan* = OFris. *withstonda*, ON. *viðstanda*; see WITH-, STAND.

withy willow. OE. *wīðiġ* (cf. OHG. *wīda* (G. *weide*), ON. *víðir* willow), for the connections of which see WITHE.

witness †knowledge, wisdom; attestation of a fact, etc., testimony. OE. (*ġe*)*witnes* (ME. *iwitnesse*), f. WIT¹ + -NESS; cf. OHG. *giwiznessi*, MDu. *wetenisse*, ON. *vitni*, *vitnis-*. Hence **witness** vb. bear witness to XIII; be a witness of XVI.

witticism XVII. f. WITTY, irreg. after CRITICISM.

wittingly XIV (*witandly*). f. *witting*, prp. of WIT² + -LY².

wittol (arch.) acquiescent cuckold. XV. ME. *wetewold*, perh. formed on *cokewold* CUCKOLD by substituting *wete* WIT² for the first syll.

witty †wise OE.; †clever, ingenious XIV; cleverly amusing XVI. OE. (*ġe*)*wittiġ* = OS. *wittig*, OHG. *wizzīg*, ON. *vitugr*; cf. WIT¹ + -Y¹.

wive take a wife OE.; take as a wife. OE. (*ġe*)*wīfian* = MLG., MDu. *wīven*; f. WIFE.

wivern see WYVERN.

wizard †philosopher, sage XV; man skilled in occult arts XVI. Earliest forms *wis*(*e*)*ard*, *wissard*; f. ME. *wīs* WISE² + -ARD. Hence **wizardry** XVI.

wizened shrivelled, shrunken. XVI (rare before XVIII). In early use Sc.; pp. of *wizen*, repr. OE. *wisnian* dry up, wither, corr. to OHG. *wesanēn*, ON. *visna*, f. Gmc. **wis-* with widespread IE. cogns., as L. *viēscere*, W. *gwyw*, OIr. *feugud*.

woad blue dye-stuff obtained from the plant *Isatis tinctoria*. OE. *wād* = MLG., MDu. *wēt*, (also mod.) *weede*, OHG. *weit* (G. *waid*) :- WGmc. **waida-*.

wobble, wabble move erratically from side to side. XVII. prob. f. base of WAVER; see -LE³. Hence **wobbly** (-LY¹) XIX.

wodge (sl.) lumpy protuberant object. XX. Expressive alt. of WEDGE.

woe A. int. and adv. as excl. of distress or grief (with dative) OE.; B. sb. (arch.) misery, misfortune XII; C. adj. grieved, wretched XII. OE. *wā* (also *wǣ*), corr. to OS., MLG. *wē*, (M)Du. *wee*, OHG. *wē* (G. *weh*), ON. *vei*, *vǽ*, Goth. *wai*; cf. Gr. *oâ*, L. *væ*, W. *gwae*. Hence **woeful** XIII.

woe-begone †oppressed with misfortune or grief XIV; (of looks, etc.) revealing a state of distress or sorrow XIX. Evolved from constructions such as ME. *me is wo begon* woe has beset me (†*bego* beset as an affecting influence), which gives place to *I am wo begon*.

wold †forest, wooded upland OE.; hill, down XIII; piece of open country, (later) upland, moorland. OE. (Angl.) *wald*, (WS.) *weald* = OS., OHG. *wald* (Du. *woud*, G. *wald*) forest, ON. *vǫllr* untilled field, plain :- Gmc. **walþus*, perh. cogn. with WILD.

wolf pl. **wolves** OE. *wulf* = OS. *wulf*, OHG. *wolf* (Du., G. *wolf*), ON. *ulfr*, Goth. *wulfs* :- Gmc. **wulfaz* :- IE. **wḷqos*, repr. also by L. *lupus*, Gr. *lúkos*, OSl. *vlŭkŭ*, Lith. *vil̃kas*, Skr. *vṛ́ka-*. Hence **wolfish** (-ISH[1]) XVI (†*wolvish* XV).

wolfram (min.) tungstate of iron and manganese. XVIII. - G., perh. f. *wolf* WOLF + *rahm* cream or MHG. *rām* soot.

wolverine, -ene XVI (*-ing*). Obscurely f. *wolv-*, inflexional stem of WOLF.

woman pl. **women** OE. *wīfman(n)* m., later fem., f. *wīf* woman + *man(n)* MAN; a formation peculiar to Eng. (not in the oldest OE. records). Assim. of *-fm-* to *-mm-* is evident in late OE. sp., and rounding of *wim-* to *wum-*, *wom-* in XIII. Hence **womanish** (-ISH[1]) XIV, **womankind** XIV, **womanly** (-LY[1]) XIII. **womanize** emasculate XVI; consort XIX.

womb †belly; uterus. OE. *wamb*, *womb* = MLG., MDu. *wamme* (Du. *wam*), OHG. *wamba*, *wampa* (G. *wamme*), ON. *vǫmb*, Goth. *wamba*; Gmc., of unkn. orig.

wombat burrowing marsupial. XVIII. Austral. aboriginal word.

wonder astonishing or marvellous thing OE.; perplexed astonishment XIII. OE. *wundor* = OS. *wundar* (Du. *wonder*), OHG. *wuntar* (G. *wunder*), ON. *undr*; of unkn. orig. So **wonder** vb. OE. *wundrian* = OS. *wundron*, etc.

wont[1] accustomed, used. OE. *ġewunod*, pp. of (*ġe*)*wunian* dwell, continue, be accustomed or used = OS. *wunon*, *wonon* (Du. *wonen*), OHG. *wonēn* (G. *wohnen*) be accustomed, remain, dwell, ON. *una* be content in a place, enjoy, Goth. **wunan* :- Gmc. **wunōjan*, **wunǣjan*, f. **wun-* **wen-* **wan-* (see WISH).

wont[2] custom, habit. XIV (rare before XVI). of doubtful orig.; perh. due to a conflation of *it is my wone* (OE. *ġewuna* custom) and *I am wont* (see prec.).

won't (colloq.) will not. XVII. contr. of *wonnot*, assim. of *wol not* WILL[2] not.

wonted accustomed, customary. XV. of doubtful orig.; f. either WONT[1] or WONT[2] + -ED[1] or -ED[2].

woo sue in love (intr.) XI; (tr., also fig.) XIII. Late OE. *wōgian*, whence *wōgere* **wooer** (-ER[1]); of unkn. orig.

wood †A. tree. B. collection of trees growing together; substance of which trees consist. OE. *wudu*, later form of *wi(o)du* = OHG. *witu*, ON. *viðr* :- Gmc. **widuz*, rel. to OIr. *fid* tree, wood, Gael. *fiodh*, W. *gwŷdd* trees. Comps. **woodbine, -bind** any of various climbing plants, e.g. honeysuckle, ivy, convolvulus. OE. *wudubinde*, f. base of *bindan* BIND. **woodchuck** N. Amer. marmot. XVII. alt., by assoc. with *wood*, of the Algonquian name. **woodcock** OE. *wuducocc*. **woodpecker** XVI. **woodruff** plant of the genus *Asperula*. OE. *wudurofe* (the second el. is of unkn. orig.). Hence **wooden** (-EN[3]) XVI. **woodsy** (U.S.) sylvan. XIX. f. pl. *woods* of WOOD; see -Y[1]. **woody** †wooded XIV; ligneous XVI; see -Y[1].

woof[1] threads crossing the web at right angles to the warp OE.; woven fabric XVII. OE. *ōwef*, alt. of *ōwebb* (see WEB) after *wefan* WEAVE; ME. *oof* became *woof* partly by assoc. in the phr. *warp and (w)oof*.

woof[2] imit. of a dog's low gruff bark. XIX.

wool OE. *wull* = MLG., MDu., *wulle*, *wolle* (Du. *wol*), OHG. *wolla* (G. *wolle*), ON. *ull*, Goth. *wulla* :- Gmc. **wullō* :- IE. **wḷnā*, whence Skr. *ū́rnā*, OSl. *vlŭna*, L. *lāna*, beside *vellus* (:- **welnos*) fleece.

woozy (sl.) fuddled; muzzy XIX. of uncert. orig.

Wop mid- or south-European (esp. It.) immigrant in the U.S.A. XX. of unkn. orig.

word (coll. pl. and sg.) things or something said; report, tidings; divine communication; vocable. OE. *word* = OS. *word* (Du. *woord*), (O)HG. *wort*, ON. *orð*, Goth. *waurd* :- Gmc. **wordam* :- IE. **wṛdho-* **werdh-*, which is held to be based on **wer-*, repr. by Gr. (ϝ)*ereō̂* I shall say, L. *verbum* word, Skr. *vratá-* command, law, vow, Lith. *var̃das* name. Hence **wordy** OE. *wordiġ*; see -Y[1].

work something done, what one does; manufactured article (esp. with qualification, as *fire-*, *frame-*, *wax-*). OE. *we(o)rc*, *worc*, *wurc* = OS. *werk*, OHG. *werah*, *werc* (Du., G. *werk*), ON. *verk* :- Gmc. **werkam* :- IE. **werĝom*, whence also Gr. (ϝ)*érgon*. So **work** vb. OE. *wyrċan* (pt. *worhte*, pp. *ġeworht*; see WROUGHT) :- **wurkj-*; repr. directly by ME. *wirch(e)*, *wyrch(e)*, but infl. at an early date by the sb. and the various ON. vbs. (*virkja*, *verk(j)a*, *yrkja*), *-k-* prevailing in XV. For parallel forms cf. OS. *wirkian*, OHG. *wirchen* (G. *wirken*), ON. *verkja*, *virkja* feel pain (cf. Goth. *waurkjan*). Comps. **workaday** XII. (*werkedai*), of uncert. formation **workday** XV. **workhouse** †workshop OE.; poor-law institution XVII. **workman** OE. *weorcman(n)*.

world human existence or a period of it; *the* earth, *the* universe; *the* human race, human society. OE. *weorold*, *wor(o)ld* = OS. *werold* (Du. *wereld*), OHG. *weralt* (G. *welt*), ON. *verǫld*; Gmc., f. **weraz* man (OE., OS., OHG. *wer*, cogn. with L. *vir*) + **alð-* age (cf. OLD), the etym. meaning being, therefore, 'age' or 'life of man'. Hence **worldling** (-LING[1]) XVI. **worldly** OE. *woruldliċ*; see -LY[1].

worm (arch.) serpent, dragon; †reptile; creeping limbless invertebrate; endoparasitic helminth; larva of insect, maggot OE.; spiral tool, etc. XVI. OE. *wyrm*, later *wurm*, corr. to OS., (O)HG. *wurm* (Du. *worm*), ON. *ormr* serpent,

Goth. *waurms* :- Gmc. **wurmiz* and **wurmaz*, rel. to L. *vermis* worm, Gr. *rhómos*, *rhómox* woodworm, Lith. *vařmas* insect, midge. Hence vb. hunt worms; get rid of, make one's way, etc. by subtle means XVI. Comps. **worm-eaten** XIV, **worm-hole** XVI.

wormwood plant of the genus *Artemisia*, proverbial for its bitter taste. XV. alt., by assim. of the second syll. to WOOD, of late ME. *wormod*, OE. *wormōd*, corr. to MLG. *wormōde*, OHG. *wormuota*, alt. by assim. to WORM (because used as a remedy for worms in the body) of OE. *wermōd* = OS. *wer(i)moda*, OHG. *wer(i)muota* (G. *wermut*); of unkn. orig.

worrit worry. XIX. dial. var. of next.

worry †strangle OE.; †choke XIII; seize by the throat with the teeth XIV; harass, assail XVI; afflict mentally XIX; intr. for refl. OE. *wyrgan* = MLG., MDu. *worgen* (Du. *wurgen*), OHG. *wurgan* (G. *würgen*) :- WGmc. **wurȝjan*.

worse OE. adj. *wiersa*, *wyrsa* = OS. *wirsa*, OHG. *wirsiro*, ON. *verri* (:- **wersi*), Goth. *wairsiza* :- Gmc. **wersizan-*, f. **wers-*, found also in OS., OHG. *werran* (G. *verwirren* entangle, confound; cf. WAR); see -ER[3]. So **worse** adv. OE. *wiers* = OS., OHG. *wirs*, ON. *verr*, Goth. *wairs*. Hence **worsen** (-EN[5]) make worse XIII; become worse XVIII.

worship (arch.) good name, credit, dignity, importance; respect shown OE.; veneration of a power held divine XIII. OE. *weorðsċipe*, *wurð-*, *wyrð-*, f. *weorð* WORTH[2] + *-sċipe* -SHIP. Hence **worship** vb. XII. ME. *worþshipie*. **worshipful** XIII; as an honorific title XIV.

worst adj. and adv. OE. *wierresta*, *wyrresta* = OS. *wirsista*, OHG. *-isto*, ON. *verstr*; see -EST. Hence **worst** vb. †impair, damage; overcome, defeat. XVII.

worsted (woollen fabric made of) closely twisted yarn. XIII (*wrstede*). f. *Worstead*, name of a parish in Norfolk.

wort[1] herb, vegetable OE.; cabbage XIV. OE. *wyrt* root, plant = OS. *wurt*, (O)HG. *wurz*, ON. *urt*, Goth. *waurts*; cf. ROOT[1].

wort[2] infusion of grain for the making of beer. OE. *wyrt* = OS. *wurtja* spicery, (M)HG. *würze*.

worth[1] money value (e.g. *pennyworth*) OE.; relative value in character XIV; (high) personal merit XVI. OE. *w(e)orð*, *wurð* = OS. *werð*, OHG. *werd* (G. *wert*), ON. *verð*, Goth. *wairþ*; sb. use of next. Hence **worthless** XVI.

worth[2] of the value of a specified amount OE.; having a value of (so much) XII; possessed of XV. OE. *w(e)orð*, *wurð* = OS. *werð*, MDu. *w(a)ert* (Du. *waard*), OHG. *werd* (G. *wert*), ON. *verðr*, Goth. *wairþs*; Gmc., of uncert. orig.

worth[3] (arch.) come to be, become. OE. str. vb. *weorðan*, *wurðan* = OS. *werðan* (Du. *worden*), OHG. *werdan* (G. *werden*), ON. *verða*, Goth. *wairþan* :- Gmc. **werþan*, f. IE. **wert*, whence L. *vertere*, OSl. *vrĭtěti* turn, Skr. *vártate* turns, passes on, takes place.

worthy (arch.) having worth or value; of sufficient worth XIII; sb. XIV. ME. *wurþi*, *worþi*, f. WORTH[1] + -Y[1]; superseding OE. *wurðe*, *weorðe*, *wierðe* and *weorð* WORTH[2].

-worthy the adj. WORTHY used from XIII (e.g. in *deathworthy*) as a second el. of comps., repl. *-wurthe*, repr. OE. *-wyrðe*, *-wierðe*, f. *weorð* WORTH[2].

wot (arch.) know. XIII. repr. 1st and 3rd sg. (OE. *wāt*) of WIT[2], carried over into other parts.

would see WILL[2].

wound bodily hurt, external injury; also fig. OE. *wund* = OS. *wunda* (Du. *wond*), OHG. *wunta* (G. *wunde*), ON. *und*; Gmc., of uncert. orig. So **wound** vb. OE. *wundian*. Comp. **woundwort** pop. name of various plants reputed to heal wounds. XVI.

wove var. of *woven*, pp. of WEAVE XVIII; from early XIX in techn. use of paper.

wow excl. of aversion, surprise, or admiration. XVI (orig. Sc.). Hence sb. (U.S. sl.) something sensational. XX.

wrack[1] (arch.) retributive punishment, vengeance OE.; damage XV. OE. *wræc*, f. var. of base of *wrecan* WREAK.

wrack[2] (dial.) wreck, wreckage XIV; marine vegetation XVI. - MDu. *wrak*, corr. to OE. *wræc* WRACK[1].

wraith XVI (orig. Sc.). of unkn. orig.

wrangle dispute angrily or noisily. XIV (not common before XVI). prob. of LG. or Du. orig.; cf. LG., G. dial. *wrangeln*. See -LE[3]. Hence **wrangler** (-ER[1]) disputant XVI; spec. one placed in the first class in the mathematical tripos at Cambridge university XVIII.

wrap cover or enfold in clothing or the like XIV; in various transf. and fig. uses from late XIV. of unkn. orig.

wrasse fish of the family Labridae. XVII. - Corn. *wrach*, var. of *gwrach* = W. *gwrach* wrasse, old woman.

wrath OE. *wrǣððu* (whence ME. *wraþþe*, *wreþþe*; *wrath* from XIV), f. *wrāð* WROTH; see -TH[1].

wreak †drive away, expel, give vent to (anger, etc.); avenge, revenge OE.; take (vengeance) *on* XV. OE. str. vb. *wrecan* = OS. *wrekan* (Du. *wreken*), OHG. *rehhan* (G. *rächen*), ON. *reka*, Goth. *wrikan* persecute :- Gmc. **wrekan*, f. **wrek-* (cf. **wrak-* s.v. WRETCH) :- IE. **wreg-*, prob. cogn. with L. *urgēre* subject to pressure, drive, URGE, Gr. *eírgein* shut up.

wreath A. twisted band or coil OE.; bank or drift of snow XVIII; B. chaplet or garland of flowers, leaves, etc. XVI. OE. *wriða*, f. reduced var. of the base of WRITHE. So **wreathe** twist, coil. XVI. perh. back-formation f. *wreathen* (XIV) arranged in coils or curves, ME. *wrēthen*, OE. *wriðen*, pp. of *wrīðan* WRITHE.

wreck what is cast ashore by the sea; ruined or disabled ship XIII; disabling of a vessel XV. - AN. *wrec* - ON. **wrek*, f. **wrekan* drive (see WREAK). Hence **wreck** vb. make a wreck of. XV (cf. AL. *wrecāre* XII). **wreckage** wrecking; remains of a wrecked vessel. XIX.

wren OE. *wrenna*, *wrænna*, obscurely rel. to OHG. *wrend(il)o*, Icel. *rindill*.

wrench turn, twist (intr. OE.; tr. XIII). Late OE. *wrenċan* = OHG. *renchen* (G. *renken*), of unkn. orig.

wrest turn, twist OE.; pull or pluck away XIII; strain the meaning of, deflect the course of XVI.

OE. *wrǣstan* = ON. **wreista* (ONorw., Icel. *reista*) :- Gmc. **wraistjan*; cf. WRIST.

wrestle OE. **wrǣstlian* (implied in late OE. *wrǣstlung*), corr. to MLG. *worstelen, wrostelen*, (M)Du. *worstelen*; cf. OE. *wraxlian*.

wretch †exile; miserable being; despicable person OE.; †niggard, miser XIV. OE. *wrećća* = OS. *wrekkio* (applied to the Magi), OHG. *(w)recch(e)o* exile, adventurer, knight errant (G. *recke* warrior, hero) :- WGmc. **wrakjan-*, f. **wrak-* (see WREAK).

wretched marked by distress or misery XII; contemptible XIII. f. WRETCH + -ED[2]; for the unusual formation cf. WICKED.

wrick sprain, strain. XIX (earlier **rick**[2] XVIII). of uncert. orig.

wriggle vb. XV. - (M)LG. (= Du.) *wriggelen*, frequent. of *wriggen*; see -LE[3], and cf. WIGGLE. Hence sb. XVII.

wright artificer, handicraftsman (esp. one who works in wood), surviving mainly in *cartwright, playwright, shipwright, wainwright, wheelwright*. OE. *wryhta*, metathetic var. of *wyrhta* = OS. *wurhtio*, OHG. *wurhto* :- WGmc. **wurhtjan-*, f. **wurk-* WORK.

wring pt., pp. *wrung* squeeze, twist, wrench, wrest (lit. and fig.). OE. str. vb. *wringan* = OS. *-wringan* (MLG., Du. *wringen*); WGmc., f. base **wreŋȝ-*, rel. to **wraŋȝ-* WRONG.

wrinkle †winding; fold XV. OE. *ġewrinclod* winding (of a ditch), ppl. formation with no recorded infin.; the earliest subsequent members of the group are *wrinkling, wrinklingly* (XIV). of unkn. orig. So **wrinkle** vb. undergo contraction into small folds. XVI.

wrist OE., corr. to (M)LG. *wrist*, (M)HG. *rist* wrist, instep, withers, ON. *rist* instep :- Gmc. **wristiz*, prob. f. **wrið-*, f. wk. grade of the stem of WRITHE. Comp. **wristband** part of a sleeve that covers the wrist. XVI. Hence **wristlet** XIX.

writ writing spec. legal document. OE. *writ* = OHG. *riz* stroke, written character, ON. *rit* writing, writ, letter, Goth. *writs* pen-stroke, f. **writ-* **wrīt-* WRITE.

write pt. *wrote*, pp. *written*. OE. str. vb. *wrītan* engrave, draw, depict, write = OS. *wrītan* cut, write, OHG. *rīzan* tear, draw (G. *reissen* †sketch, tear, drag), ON. *ríta* score, write :- Gmc. **wrītan*, of unkn. orig.

writhe twist, e.g. the body (tr. and intr.). OE. str. vb. *wrīðan* = OHG. *rīdan*, ON. *ríða*.

wrong (perh.) †crooked, twisted OE.; deviating from equity or the right XIII; incorrect, erroneous XIV. Late OE. *wrang, wrong* - ON. **wrangr, rangr* awry, unjust = MLG. *wrangh* sour, tart, MDu. *wrangh* bitter, hostile (Du. *wrang* acid), rel. to WRING. Hence **wrong** adv. XIII; sb. that which is wrong, unjust, or immoral XI; vb. XIV. **wrongful, wrongly** (-LY[2]) XIV.

wroth (arch.) angered, wrathful. OE. *wrāð* = OS. *wrēð* (Du. *wreed* cruel), OHG. *reid*, ON. *reiðr*, f. Gmc. **wraiþ-* **wrīþ-* WRITHE. Rare XVI-XIX exc. in or after biblical use, its revival being begun by early-XIX poets.

wrought fashioned or formed, esp. by labour or art XIV; manufactured; decorated, elaborated XV; (of metals) shaped by hammering, etc. XVI. ME. *wroȝt*, metathetic var. of *worȝt, worht*, pp. of WORK.

wry twisted, distorted (lit. and fig.) XVI. f. (dial.) *wry* vb., OE. *wrīġian* strive, go forward, tend, in ME. deviate, swerve, contort. Comp. **wryneck** bird of the genus *Jynx*, distinguished by a habit of writhing head and neck XVI.

wyandotte breed of domestic fowl. XIX. f. name of a tribe of N. Amer. Indians.

wych-elm, witch-elm witch hazel. XVII (*weech elm*). Earlier *witchen elm* (XVI); f. *wych, witch*, OE. *wić(e)* (prob. f. Gmc. **wik-* bend; see WEAK) + ELM.

wych hazel, witch hazel applied to various trees with pliant branches XVI. See prec., HAZEL.

Wykehamist past or present member of Winchester College. XVIII. f. name of William of *Wykeham* bishop of Winchester and founder of the college (1382); see -IST.

wyvern, †wivern (her.) winged two-footed dragon. XVII. alt. of †*wyver* (XIII) - OF. *wivre*, (also mod.) *guivre* :- L. *vīpera* VIPER.

X

xanth(o)- comb. form of Gr. *xanthós* yellow, used in many techn. terms. XIX.

xebec small three-masted Mediterranean vessel. XVIII. alt., after Sp. †*xabeque* (now *jabeque*), of *chebec* - F. - It. *sciabecco* - Arab. *šabbāk*.

xeno- repr. comb. form of Gr. *xénos* guest, stranger, foreign, strange, used in techn. terms. XIX. **xenophobia** morbid dislike or dread of foreigners. XX.

xenon (chem.) heavy inert gaseous element. XIX. - Gr., n. of *xénos* (see prec.).

xero- comb. form of Gr. *xērós* dry, used in techn. terms. XIX.

xiphoid sword-shaped. XVIII. - Gr. *xiphoeidēs*, f. *xiphos* sword; see -OID.

X-rays form of radiation discovered by W. C. Röntgen (1895). XIX. tr. G. *x-strahlen*.

xylo- comb. form of Gr. *xúlon* wood, used in techn. terms XIX. **xylonite** celluloid. XIX; earlier form *xyloinite*, irreg. f. *xyloidin*, afterwards assim. to Gr. *xúlon*. **xylophone** musical intrument consisting of flat wooden bars. XIX.

xystus pl. **-i** portico, colonnade. XVII. - L. - Gr. *xustós*, *xustón*.

Y

y- prefix repr. OE. *ġe-* = OS. *gi-*, *ge-*, *i-*, MLG., MDu. *g(h)e-* (LG., Du. *ge-*), OHG. *ga-*, *ka-*, *gi-*, *ki-* (G. *ge-*) Goth. *ga-* :- Gmc. **ʒa-*. The parallelism of form and meaning of such words as L. *commūnis* and Goth. *gamains*, OE. *ġemǣne* COMMON has suggested the identity of Gmc. **ʒa-* and L. COM-. This prefix is disguised in form or its force is obliterated in AFFORD, AWARE, EACH, EITHER, ENOUGH, EVERYWHERE, HANDICRAFT, HANDIWORK, NEITHER. From mid-XVI archaizing poets created new formations, e.g. *ychain'd*, *yshrilled*. The orig. physical meaning 'with', 'together', yielded the notion of associations, and hence of appropriateness and collectivity, the final stage being the notion of completeness, a special application being the use of the prefix in pps., regular in OE. and continuing in south. ME. till XV. The OE. form *ġe-* was succeeded in ME. by *ʒe-*, *i(e)-*, *y-*, the last of which is regular in Spenser and his imitators, as in YCLAD, YCLEPT.

-y[1] suffix of adjs. denoting 'having the character of . .', 'inclined to . .', 'full or consisting of . .'. OE. *-iġ*, earlier *-eġ*, *-ǣġ*, in early ME. *-i*, later *-ie*, *-ye*, finally *-y*. Some adjs. of OE. date have ceased to show their etym. relations, as *empty*, *dizzy*, *merry*. For the addition of *-y* to produce a more adjectival appearance see, e.g., *chilly*, *murky*, *wary*. In the foll. the orig. is different, but the suffix is assoc. with this: *faulty*, *hardy*, *jolly*, *risky*, *sturdy*, *tardy*. Recent derivs. (since *c.*1800) have been very numerous, and have tended to be joc., undignified, or trivial, as *balmy*, *batty*, *bossy*, *cushy*, *doggy*, *dotty*, *hors(e)y*, *oniony*, *sexy*, *shirty*. The suffix is added less frequently to vbs., as in *drowsy*, *slippy*, *sticky*.

-y[2] suffix orig. of wk. vbs. of the second class, of OE. inf. *-ian* = OS. *-on*, OHG. *-ōn* (Du., G. *-en*), Goth. *-ōn* :- Gmc. **-ōjan*. By XIII it was restricted to south. and western areas.

-y[3] suffix repr. ultimately, partly through (O)F. *-ie*, Rom. **-ía*, L. *-ĭa* -IA[1].

-y[4] repr., partly through AN. *-ie*, L. *-ium* as appended to verbal bases, as in *colloquy*, *perjury*, *obloquy*, *remedy*, *subsidy*.

-y[5] suffix repr. AN., OF. *-e*, *-ee* (modF. *-é*, *-ée*) :- L. *-ātu-*, *-āta* (see -ATE[1,2]); in sbs. = -ATE[1] as in (1) *county*, *pasty*, *treaty*, (2) *army*, *entry*, *livery*; in adjs. = -ATE[2], as in *easy*, *puny*, *tawny*.

-y[6] also *-ie*, (in some special cases) *-ey*, as *Charley* (beside *Charlie*), *jockey*, *slavey*; originating in hypocoristic Sc. formations, and forming pet names and familiar dims., as well as transf. uses such as applications to implements; miscellaneous exx. are *daddy*, *dandy*, *jemmy*, *johnny*, *kiddy*, *namby-pamby*, *nanny*, *teddy*, *Tommy*. Addition to a curtailed form of a disyllable or polysyllable is exemplified by *baccy*, *cabby*, *hubby*, *nighty*, *tummy*. For applications of the pl. see -IES.

yacht XVI. - early modDu. *jaght(e)*, now *jacht*, short for *jaghtschip* (ship for chasing), f. *jaght* hunting, chase, f. *jagen* hunt, chase; see -T[3]. Hence **yachting** (-ING[1]), **yachtsman** XIX.

yahoo name invented by Swift ('Gulliver's Travels', 1726) for a brute in human form.

yak bovine animal of Tibet. XIX. - Tibetan *γyag*.

Yale lock form of lock invented by Linus *Yale* (1821-68), a locksmith of New England; **P.** XIX.

yam (tuberous root of) species of *Dioscorea*. XVII (earlier in Eng. writings in various alien forms, e.g. *inany*, *nname*, *igname*). - Pg. *inhame* or Sp. †*iñame* (mod. *ñame*); ult. orig. unkn.

yank (colloq.) pull suddenly and vigorously; also sb. XIX. of unkn. orig.

Yank short for YANKEE. XVIII.

Yankee native of New England (hence of the U.S.A.). XVIII. None of the proposed etyms. is convincing; most plausibly on formal grounds, spec. application of *Yankee*, *Yank(e)y* (XVII-XVIII) as a surname or nickname, perh. based on Du. *Jan* John and intended as a dim. form (= *Jantje*).

yaourt semi-solid curd-like food prepared from milk. XIX. - Turk. *yoğurt*.

yap bark sharply. XVII. of imit. orig.

yapock S. Amer. water-opossum. XIX. f. name of a N. Brazilian river (*Oyapok*, *Oiapoque*).

yapp book-binding with projecting limp leather cover. XIX. Name of a London bookseller to whose order the binding was first made.

yarborough hand containing no card above a nine. XIX. Said to be named after an Earl of *Yarborough* who bet 1000 to 1 against its occurrence.

yard[1] enclosed space attached to a building OE.; enclosure in which animals are kept or some work is done XIII. OE. *ġeard* fence, enclosure, courtyard, dwelling, region, corr., with variation of declension, to OS. *gardo* (Du. *gaard*), OHG. *gart(o)* (G. *garten* garden), ON. *garðr*, Goth. *gards* house, *garda* enclosure, stall :- Gmc. **ʒarðaz* **ʒarðan-* rel. to OSl. *gradŭ* city, garden (Russ. *górod* town).

yard[2] †rod, staff; (naut.) spar to which a square sail is bent; †measuring-rod; †rood (of land) OE.; measure of 3 feet XIV. OE. *ġerd*, (WS.) **ġierd*, *ġird*, *ġyrd* = OS. *gerdia* switch (Du. *gard* twig, rod), OHG. *gart(e)a*, *gerta* (G. *gerte*) :- WGmc. **ʒazdjō*, f. Gmc. **ʒazdaz* (see GADFLY).

yare ready OE.; (of a ship) easily manageable XIV. OE. *ġearu* = OS., OHG. *garo* (Du. *gaar* done, dressed, clever, G. *gar* ready, prepared, adv. quite), ON. *gǫrr*, *gǫrv-* ready-made, prompt, skilled :- Gmc. **ʒarwu-*.

yarn spun fibre of cotton, silk, etc. OE. *ġearn* = MDu. *gaern* (Du. *garen*), (O)HG., ON. *garn*, prob. f. base repr. also by **ʒarnō* in ON. *gǫrn*, pl. *garnar* guts, and **ʒarnjo-* in OE. *micġern*, OS. *midgarni*, OHG. *mittigarni* entrail fat, suet, and rel. outside Gmc. to Lith. *žárna* intestine, L. *haruspex* one who divines from inspection of entrails, Gr. *khordḗ* intestine, guts. The sense 'story, tale' (XIX) is from naut. sl. phr. *spin a yarn*.

yarrow plant of the genus *Achillea*. OE. *ġearwe*, corr. to MDu. *garwe, gherwe* (Du. *gerwe*), OHG. *gar(a)wa*; WGmc., of unkn. orig.

yashmak Muslim woman's veil. XIX. - Turk. *yaşmak*, Arab. *yašmaķ*.

yataghan sword of Muslim countries. XIX. - Turk. *yatağan*.

yaw (orig. naut.) deviate in the course. XVI. of unkn. orig.

yawl ship's boat; small sailing-boat or fishing-boat. XVII (*ya(u)le, yall*). - (M)LG. *jolle* or Du. *jol*; ult. orig. unkn.

yawn open the mouth wide (now only from fatigue, etc.); lie wide open. XVI. spec. symbolic alt. of ME. *ʒone*, which with *ʒene* repr. OE. *ġeonian*, var. of *ġinian* = OHG. *ginōn, -ēn*, MDu. *ghenen*, rel. to synon. OE. *gānian*, OHG. *geinōn* and OE. *ġīnan*, OS. *gīnan*, ON. *gína*; all *n*-formations on Gmc. **ʒai- *ʒī-* :- IE. **ĝhoi- *ĝhei- *ĝhi-* repr. by L. *hiāre, hīscere* gape, yawn, OSl. *zijati*, Lith. *žióti*.

yaws contagious skin-disease of tropical countries. XVI. of unkn. orig.

yclad (arch.) clothed. See Y-, CLAD.

yclept (arch.) called (so-and-so). OE. *ġecleopod*, pp. of *cleopian, clipian* call; see Y-, -T[3].

ye[1] (arch. and joc., dial.) nom. pl. of 2nd pers. pron. OE. *ġē* = OS. *gi, ge* (Du. *gij*), OHG. *ir* (G. *ihr*), ON. *ér* (:- **jēr*).

ye[2] late writing of *þe* THE[1].

yea affirmative adv. (now dial. and arch.) OE. *ġē*, (WS.) *gēa*, corr. to OS., OHG. *jā* (Du., G. *ja*), ON. *já*, Goth. *ja, jai*; ult. Gmc. **ja, *je*.

yean (arch., dial.) of a ewe, bring forth. XIV. repr. OE. **ġeēanian*, f. *ġe-* Y- + *ēanian* = WFris. *eandje*, Du. dial. *oonen* :- Gmc. **aunōjan*, f. **aun-* :- IE. **agʷn-*, whence also L. *agnus*, Gr. *amnós* lamb.

year period of the earth's revolution round the sun; 12 months; pl. age OE.; pl. period, times XIII. OE. (Angl.) *ġēr*, (WS.) *ġēar* = OS. *jār, gēr* (Du. *jaar*), OHG. *jār* (G. *jahr*), ON. *ár*, Goth. *jēr* :- Gmc. **jǣram*, f. IE. base **jēr- *jōr-*, repr. also by Gr. *hôros* year.

yearn OE. *ġiernan* = OS. *ġernean, ġirnean*, ON. *girna*, Goth. *gairnjan* :- Gmc. **ʒernjan*, f. **ʒernaz* (OE. *ġeorn* eager, OS., OHG. *gern* (G. *gern* willingly), ON. *gjarn*, Goth. *seinagairns* selfish), f. **ʒer-*, repr. also by OHG. *gerōn* (G. *begehren*) desire, ON. *gerr* greedy.

yeast frothy substance produced by fermentation of malt, etc. OE. (Angl.) **ġest*, WS. **giest* (late *ġist*), corr. to MLG. *gest* dregs, dirt, MDu. *ghist, ghest* (Du. *gist, gest* yeast), MHG. *jist, jest, gist, gest* (G. *gischt*) yeast, froth, ON. *jǫstr*; IE. **jes-* is repr. also by Skr. *yásyati*, Gr. *zeîn* boil, W. *iās* seething.

yell utter a loud strident cry. OE. str. vb. (Angl.) *ġellan*, (WS.) *ġiellan* = MLG., MDu. *ghellen* (Du. *gillen*), OHG. *gellan* (G. *gellen*), ON. *gjalla*, f. Gmc. **ʒel- *ʒal-*, whence also OE., OHG. *galan*, ON. *gala* sing, cry out. Wk. inflexions begin XIV.

yellow of the colour of gold, etc. OE.; †jealous XVII; in phr. *y. press* sensational XIX. OE. *ġeolu* = OS. *gelo*, (M)LG. *geel*, MDu. *gel(e)u, geel* (Du. *geel*), OHG. *gelo* (G. *gelb*) :- WGmc. **gelwa* :- IE. **ghelwo-*, rel. to L. *helvus*, Gr. *khlóos*, Lith. *želvas*. Hence sb. XIV.

yellowhammer species of bunting having bright yellow plumage. XVI. The second el. is of uncert. orig.

yelp A. †boast OE.; †cry aloud XV; B. utter a cry characteristic of dogs, etc. XVI (the corr. sense of the sb. is earlier in Sc.). OE. str. vb. *ġ(i)elpan, ġilpan* = MHG. *gel(p)fen*, f. imit. base otherwise repr. in OS. *galpon* (LG. *galpen*), ME. *ʒolpe*.

yen Jap. monetary unit. XIX. - Jap. - Chin. *yüan* round, round thing, dollar.

yeoman pl. **yeomen** attendant below the rank of 'sergeant' XIV; freeholder below the rank of a gentleman, (hence) man of good standing XV. ME. *ʒoman, ʒuman, ʒeman, ʒiman*, prob. reduced forms of *ʒong-, ʒung-, ʒeng-, ʒingman*, i.e. *youngman*, which was similarly used in ME.

yes OE. *ġēse, ġīse, ġӯse*, prob. for **gīese*, f. **ġīa sīe* 'yea, may it be (so)'.

yester- of or pert. to the day before today. OE. *ġeostran, ġiestran* = OHG. *gestaron, gesterēn*, MHG. *gester(n)* (G. *gestern*), MLG. *ghist(e)ren* (Du. *gisteren*); in comps. **yesterday** OE. *ġeostran, ġystran dæġ* (cf. Goth. (once) *gistradagis* tomorrow). **yestereve** XVII, **-even** XV, **-morn** XVIII, **-morning** XVII. **yesternight** (arch.) OE. *ġystran niht*. **yesteryear** last year. XIX.

yet (arch.) in addition, further, moreover, still; till now. OE. *ġīet(a)* = OFris. *iēta, ēta, īta*, of unkn. orig.

yeti XX. Native Sherpa (Tibetan) name of the Abominable Snowman, a subhuman animal supposed to leave tracks in the snow of the Himalayas.

yew OE. *īw, ēow*, corr. with cons.-alternation and variation in gender to OE. *ī(o)h, ēoh*, OS. *īh*, MLG., MDu. *ī(e)we, uwe*, OHG. *īwu, īwi, īwa, īhu, īga* (G. *eibe*), ON. *ýr* :- Gmc. **īχwaz, *īʒwaz, *īχwō, *īʒwō*, with parallel forms in Celt. and Balto-Sl.

Yiddish language of Jews in Europe and America, orig. a G. dial. XIX. - G. *jüdisch* Jewish, f. *Jude* Jew + *-isch* -ISH[1].

yield pay, repay (mainly obs.) OE.; give forth, produce XI; give way, surrender XIII. OE. str. vb. (Angl.) *ġeldan*, (WS.) *-ġieldan* = OS. *geldan* (Du. *geldan*), OHG. *geltan* (G. *gelten*), ON. *gjalda*, Goth. *-gildan* :- Gmc. **ʒelðan* pay, requite, further cogns. of which are doubtful.

-yl terminal el. of chem. terms - F. - Gr. *húlē* wood, matter, substance.

ylang-ylang tree (*Cananga odorata*) of Malaysia, etc. XIX. of Tagalog orig.

yodel sing with mixture of falsetto like Swiss and Tyrolese mountain-dwellers. XIX. - G. *jodeln* (prop.) utter the syll. *jo*.

yoga union with the universal spirit. XIX. - Hind. :- Skr. *yóga-* union. So **yogi** Indian ascetic who practises this. XVII. - Hind. :- Skr. *yogi-*.

yog(h)urt var. of YAOURT. XIX.

yoicks fox-hunting cry. XVIII. contemp. with *yoaks* and *hoicks* (also *hoick, hoik* XVII), which appears to be a var. of earlier *hike* (XVI).

yoke contrivance for coupling draught animals

by the neck; pair of animals so coupled; fig. subjection, suppression. OE. *ġeoc* = OS. *juc* (Du. *juk*), OHG. *joh* (G. *joch*), ON. *ok*, Goth. *juk* :- Gmc. **jukam* :- IE. **jugom* (L. *jugum*, Gr. *zugón*, W. *iau*, OSl. *igo*, Skr. *yugá-*, f. **jug-* **jeug-* **joug-*, repr. also by L. *jungere* JOIN, Gr. *zeugnúnai*, etc.). So **yoke** vb. OE. *ġeocian*.

yokel illiterate rustic, country bumpkin. XIX. Identical in form with dial. *yokel* green woodpecker, yellowhammer, of which it may be a fig. application.

yolk[1] yellow of an egg. OE. *ġeol(o)ca*, f. *ġeolu* YELLOW.

yolk[2] greasy substance of sheep's skin glands. XVII. repr. OE. **eowoca*, in the adj. *eowociġ*; see -Y[1].

yon (arch., dial.) yonder. adj. (OE., once), pron. (XIII). OE. *ġeon*, corr., with variation of vowels, to MLG. *gene*, MDu. *ghens*, OHG. *jenēr* (G. *jener* that one), Goth. *jains* that; there is a parallel series of forms without cons. initial, viz. OHG. *enēr*, ON. *enn*, *inn* (definite article), cogn. with Gr. *énioi* some, OSl. *onŭ* that, Skr. *ana-* this one. So **yond** (dial.) yonder (adv. used adj.). OE. *ġeond*, corr. to MLG. *gent(en)*, *jint*, LG. *gunt(en)*, Du. *ginds*, Goth. *jaind* thither. **yonder** (now lit., arch., or dial.) over there XIII; adj. XIV. ME. *ȝonder* (beside *ȝender*), corr. to OS. *gendra* (adj.), MDu. *ghinder*, *gunder* (Du. *ginder*), Goth. *jaindre*.

yore (arch.) †a long time ago, †formerly OE.; †for a long time past XIII; *of y.*, formerly, of old XIV. OE. *ġeāra*, *ġeāre*, *ġeāro*, adv. formations of obscure orig.

yorker (in cricket) ball that pitches inside the crease. XIX. prob. f. *York*, capital of Yorkshire, as being introduced by Yorkshire players; see -ER[1].

you orig. acc. and d. pl. of the 2nd pers. pron.; began to be used XV for nom. YE[1] and somewhat earlier (XIV) as a substitute for *thee* and *thou* in respectful address to a superior; also from late XVI as an indef. pron., 'one', 'anyone'. OE. *īow*, *ēow* = OS. *iu* (Du. *u*), OHG. d. *iu*, *eu*, acc. *īuwih*, *iuch* (G. *euch*) :- WGmc. **iwwiz*, paralleled by **izwiz* in ON. *yðr*, Goth. *izwis*. The stem **jū* is repr. by Skr. *yūyám*, Gr. *úmme*, Lith. *jūs* you.

young OE. *ġ(e)ong*, *ġung*, later *iung* = OS. *jung* (Du. *jong*), OHG. *junc* (G. *jung*), ON. *ungr*, Goth. *juggs* :- Gmc. **juŋȝaz*, contr. of *juwuŋȝaz* :- IE. **juwn̥kós*, repr. by Skr. *yuvaśá-* youthful, L. *juvencus* young bull, W. *ieuanc*, OIr. *ōac*, *ōc* young, extension of **juwen-*, **jūn-*, repr. directly by Skr. *yúvan-*, L. *juvenis* young. Hence **youngling** young person. OE. *ġeongling* = OS. *jungling*, OHG. *jungaling*, ON. *ynglingr*; see -LING[1]. **youngster** young person. XVI; see -STER.

your of or belonging to you. (i) OE. *ēower*, usu. in partitive sense, g. of *ġē* YE, corr. to OS. *iuwar*, OHG. *iuwēr* (G. *euer*); cf. ON. *yðr*, Goth. *izwara*; (ii) OE. *ēower* m. and n., *ēowru* fem., poss. adj. corr. to OHG. *iuwar* (G. *euer*); cf. ON. *yð(v)arr*, Goth. *izwar*. Hence **yours** poss. pron. (repl. †*your*). XIII; see -S. **yourself** XIV, **-selves** XVI.

youth fact or state of being young; young people OE.; young person XIII. OE. *ġeoguð* = OS. *juguð* (Du. *jeugd*), OHG. *jugund* (G. *jugend*) :- WGmc. **juȝunþ-*, alt. of **juwunþ-* (cf. L. *juventa*, *-tus*, Goth. *junda*), f. **juwuŋ-* YOUNG; see -TH[1]. Hence **youthful** XVI.

yowl (dial.) cry loudly with pain; caterwaul, howl. XIII. of imit. orig.

yo-yo XX. of unkn. orig.

yttrium (chem.) metallic element. XIX. f. *yttria* kind of earth, f. name of *Ytterby*, Sweden, whence also **ytterbium** (min.) element occurring in gadolinite.

yucca (in Central and S. America) cassava XVI; N. Amer. plant of the genus *Yucca* XVII. of Carib orig.

Yule Christmas. OE. *ġēol*, earlier *ġeo(h)ol*, *ġeh(h)ol*, also *ġēola* Christmas Day, (pl.) Christmastide, corr. to ON. *jól* pl. heathen feast lasting twelve days, (later) Christmas; rel. to OE. (Angl.) *ġiuli* December and January = ON. *ýlir* month beginning on the second day of the week falling within November 10–17, Goth. *jiuleis* in *fruma jiuleis* November; ult. orig. unkn.

Z

zaffre impure cobalt oxide. XVII. - It. *zaffera* or its source (O)F. *safre*.
zag second el. of ZIGZAG used to denote a change of direction in a zigzag course. XVIII (*zig here, zag there*).
zany comic performer attending on a clown, etc. and imitating him XVI; †attendant, hanger-on XVII; †mimic, buffoon; simpleton, idiot XVIII. - F. *zani* or its source It. *zani, zanni* servant acting as clown in the commedia dell'arte, orig. Venetian and Lombardic form of *Gianni* = *Giovanni* John.
Zarathustrian see ZOROASTRIAN.
zariba fenced camp in the Sudan, etc. XIX. - Arab. *zarība* enclosure for cattle, f. *zarb* sheepfold.
zeal (in biblical language) fervour XIV; †ardent love, fervent longing XV; intense ardour in a pursuit XVI. ME. *zele* - late L. *zēlus* - Gr. *zêlos*. So **zealot** member of an ancient Jewish sect XVI; zealous person XVII. - late L. *zēlōtēs* - Gr. *zēlōtḗs*. **zealous** XVI. - medL. *zēlōsus*.
zebra XVI. - It. or Pg., of Congolese orig.
zebu humped species of ox. XVIII. - F. *zébu*; of unkn. orig.
zedoary (root of) species of *Curcuma*. XV. - medL. *zedoārium* - Arab. *zadwār*.
Zeitgeist XIX. - G., f. *zeit* time + *geist* spirit; see TIDE[1], GHOST.
zemindar (Indian hist.) collector of revenue from land held by a number of cultivators. XVII (*gem-, jem-*). - Hind. - Pers. *zamīndār*, f. *zamīn* earth + *dār* holder.
zenana E. Indian harem. XVIII. - Hind. (- Pers.) *zenāna*, f. *zan* woman.
zenith point of the sky directly overhead, †point of the horizon at which a heavenly body rises XIV; highest point or state XVII. ME. *cenyth, senith, cinit* - OF. *cenit* (mod. *zénith*) or medL. *cenit*, obscurely - Arab. *samt* in *samt ar-ra's* 'path over the head' (*samt* way, *al* the, AL-[2], *ra's* head).
zeolite (min.) generic name of a group of minerals consisting of hydrous silicates, characterized by swelling up and fusing under the blowpipe. XVIII. - Sw., G., etc. *zeolit*, f. Gr. *zeîn* boil + *líthos* -LITE.
zephyr west wind XVI (earlier in L. form); mild gentle wind XVII; light article of clothing XVIII. - F. *zéphyr* or L. *zephyrus* - Gr. *zéphuros*.
Zeppelin rigid dirigible airship as built by the German Count Ferdinand von *Zeppelin*. XIX.
zero cipher, 0 XVII; point marked 0 on a scale, temperature denoted by this XVIII; nought, nothing XIX. - F. *zéro* or its source It. *zero* - OSp. *zero* (mod. *cero*) - Arab. *ṣifr* CIPHER.
zest †orange or lemon peel used for flavouring XVII; something that imparts a relish XVIII; keen relish, gusto. - F. *zeste*, †*zest*, *zec* orange or lemon peel, of unkn. orig.
zetetic pert. to, adherent of, the ancient Greek sceptic school of philosophy; investigator, investigation. XVII. - Gr. *zētētikós*, f. *zēteîn* seek; see -IC.
zeugma (rhet.) figure by which a single word or phrase is made improperly to apply to two or more words or phrases XIX (earlier in wider use XVI). - L. - Gr. *zeûgma* yoking, f. *zeugnúnai* vb. rel. to *zugón* YOKE.
zibet var. of CIVET. XVI. - medL. *zibethum*.
zig see ZAG.
zigzag sb. and adj. XVIII (*ziczac*). - F. *zigzag*, †*ziczac* - G. *zickzack*, of symbolic formation. Hence **zigzag** vb., **zigzagged** XVIII.
zinc hard bluish-white metal. XVII. - G., of unkn. orig. Comb. form **zinco-** as in **zincography**.
Zingaro gipsy. XVI. - It., alt. of †*zingano* = Gr. *Athígganoi*, an oriental people.
zinnia plant of the genus *Zinnia*. XVIII. - modL., f. name of J. G. *Zinn*, German botanist; see -IA[1].
Zion, Sion one of the hills of Jerusalem on which the city of David was built; (hence) house of God, the Christian Church, place of worship. OE. *Sion* - ecclL. *Siōn*, Gr. *Seṓn*, *Seiṓn* - Heb. *ṣīyôn*.
zip slight sharp sound accompanying a movement, etc. XIX. of imit. orig. Comp. **zip fastener** XX.
zircon (min.) native silicate of the metallic element zirconium. XVIII. - G. *zirkon*.
zither XIX. - G. *zither* (OHG. *cithara, zitera*) CITHER. Also **zithern** XIX; after CITHERN.
zodiac belt of the celestial sphere within which the apparent motions of celestial bodies take place, divided into 12 'signs' named after the 12 constellations. XIV. - (O)F. *zodiaque* - L. *zōdiacus* - Gr. *zōidiakós*, f. *zṓidion* sculptured figure (of an animal), sign of the zodiac, dim. of *zôion* animal, f. *zōós* living; see -AC. So **zodiacal** XVI. - F.
zoetrope optical toy converting a series of pictures into the semblance of continuous motion. XIX. irreg. f. Gr. *zōḗ* life + *-tropos* turning.
zoic showing traces of life, containing organic remains. XIX. - Gr. *zōïkós*, f. *zôion* animal; see -IC. Taken as if f. Gr. *zōḗ* life.
zollverein union of states of the German Empire for the maintenance of uniform custom dues. XIX. - G., f. *zoll* tax, TOLL[1] + *verein* union.
zone each of the 5 belts into which the earth's surface is divided XV; climatic region XVI; girdle, ring; stripe of colour, etc. XVIII. - (O)F. *zone* or L. *zōna* girdle - Gr. *zṓnē*.
zoo XIX. Shortening of *Zoological Gardens*.
zoo- repr. Gr. *zōio-*, comb. form of *zôion* animal.
zooid animal-like creature. XIX. f. Gr. *zôion*.
zoology science which treats of animals (first applied to that part of medical science which treats of remedies obtainable from animals). XVII. - modL. *zōologia*, modGr. *zōiologia*, f. Gr. *zôion* animal; see ZODIAC, -LOGY. Hence **zoological** XIX, **-logist** XVII.

zoom make a continuous low-pitched hum XIX; (of aircraft) rise abruptly from level flight XX. of imit. orig.

zoophyte †plant (such as the sensitive plant) having some qualities of animals; gen. term for organisms regarded as intermediate between animals and plants. XVII. - F. or modL. *zōophyton* - Gr. *zōióphuton*, f. *zôion* animal + *phúesthai* grow (cf. BE).

zoril Afr. animal allied to the skunks. XVIII (*zorille*). - F. *zorille* - Sp. *zorrilla*, *-illo*, dim. of *zorro* fox.

Zoroastrian (XVIII), **Zarathustrian** (XIX) pert. to (adherent of) the religious system of *Zoroaster*, *Zarathustra* (Av. *Zarathustra*, Gr. *Zōroástrēs*), Persian founder of the religion in the 6th cent. B.C.; see -IAN.

zouave one of a body of light infantry in the French army. XIX. - F. *zouave* - *Zwāwa* name of an Algerian tribe, from which the force was first recruited.

zounds (arch.) euph. abbr. of (*by*) *God's wounds*. XVI (*zownes*, *zoones*).

zucchetto ecclesiastic's skull-cap. XIX. Incorrect but usual form for It. *zucchetta* small gourd, cap, dim. of *zucca* gourd, head.

zwieback rusk. XIX. - G., tr. It. *biscotto* 'twice-baked' (see BISCUIT).

Zwinglian pert. to (a follower of) Ulrich *Zwingli* (1484-1531), Swiss religious reformer. XVI. See -IAN.

zygo- repr. comb. form of Gr. *zugón* YOKE.

zygoma (anat.) bony arch on each side of the skull. XVII. - Gr. *zúgōma*, f. *zugón* YOKE.

zymo-, before a vowel **zym-**, comb. form of Gr. *zûmē* leaven, in techn. terms (gen.) fermentation XIX. So **zymosis** XIX. - Gr. *zū́mōsis*. **zymotic** XIX. - Gr. *zūmōtikós* causing fermentation.

zymurgy practice of fermentation. XIX. f. Gr. *zûmē* leaven + *-urgy* (rel. to WORK) as in *metallurgy*.

OXFORD

PAST MASTERS

General Editor: Keith Thomas

SHAKESPEARE

Germaine Greer

'At the core of a coherent social structure as he viewed it lay marriage, which for Shakespeare is no mere comic convention but a crucial and complex ideal. He rejected the stereotype of the passive, sexless, unresponsive female and its inevitable concommitant, the misogynist conviction that all women were whores at heart. Instead he created a series of female characters who were both passionate and pure, who gave their hearts spontaneously into the keeping of the men they loved and remained true to the bargain in the face of tremendous odds.'

Germaine Greer's short book on Shakespeare brings a completely new eye to a subject about whom more has been written than on any other English figure. She is especially concerned with discovering why Shakespeare 'was and is a popular artist', who remains a central figure in English cultural life four centuries after his death.

'eminently trenchant and sensible . . . a genuine exploration in its own right' John Bayley, *Listener*

'the clearest and simplest explanation of Shakespeare's thought I have yet read' Auberon Waugh, *Daily Mail*

PHILOSOPHY IN OXFORD PAPERBACKS

THE GREAT PHILOSOPHERS

Bryan Magee

Beginning with the death of Socrates in 399, and following the story through the centuries to recent figures such as Bertrand Russell and Wittgenstein, Bryan Magee and fifteen contemporary writers and philosophers provide an accessible and exciting introduction to Western philosophy and its greatest thinkers.

Bryan Magee in conversation with:

A. J. Ayer
Michael Ayers
Miles Burnyeat
Frederick Copleston
Hubert Dreyfus
Anthony Kenny
Sidney Morgenbesser
Martha Nussbaum
John Passmore
Anthony Quinton
John Searle
Peter Singer
J. P. Stern
Geoffrey Warnock
Bernard Williams

'Magee is to be congratulated . . . anyone who sees the programmes or reads the book will be left in no danger of believing philosophical thinking is unpractical and uninteresting.' Ronald Hayman, *Times Educational Supplement*

'one of the liveliest, fast-paced introductions to philosophy, ancient and modern that one could wish for' *Universe*

THE OXFORD AUTHORS

General Editor: Frank Kermode

THE OXFORD AUTHORS is a series of authoritative editions of major English writers. Aimed at both students and general readers, each volume contains a generous selection of the best writings—poetry, prose, and letters—to give the essence of a writer's work and thinking. All the texts are complemented by essential notes, an introduction, chronology, and suggestions for further reading.

Matthew Arnold
William Blake
Lord Byron
John Clare
Samuel Taylor Coleridge
John Donne
John Dryden
Ralph Waldo Emerson
Thomas Hardy
George Herbert and Henry Vaughan
Gerard Manley Hopkins
Samuel Johnson
Ben Jonson
John Keats
Andrew Marvell
John Milton
Alexander Pope
Sir Philip Sidney
Oscar Wilde
William Wordsworth

OXFORD POETS

Winner of the 1989 Whitbread Prize for Poetry

SHIBBOLETH

Michael Donaghy

This is Michael Donaghy's first full-length collection. His work has a wit and grace reminiscent of the metaphysical poets, and his subjects range widely, responding in unexpected ways to his curiosity and inventiveness. Among the varied pieces collected here are a number of love poems remarkable for their blend of tenderness and irony; a terse 'news item'; playful 'translations' of a mythical Welsh poet; and an 'interview' with Marcel Duchamp.

As the American critic Alfred Corn says:

'Michael Donaghy's poems have the fine-tuned precision of a ten-speed bike, the wit of a streetwise don, a polyphonic inventiveness . . . Poems so original, wry, and philosophical as these are hard to come by. Don't think of passing them up.'

OXFORD BOOKS

THE OXFORD BOOK OF ENGLISH GHOST STORIES

Chosen by Michael Cox and R. A. Gilbert

This anthology includes some of the best and most frightening ghost stories ever written, including M. R. James's 'Oh Whistle, and I'll Come to You, My Lad', 'The Monkey's Paw' by W. W. Jacobs, and H. G. Wells's 'The Red Room'. The important contribution of women writers to the genre is represented by stories such as Amelia Edwards's 'The Phantom Coach', Edith Wharton's 'Mr Jones', and Elizabeth Bowen's 'Hand in Glove'.

As the editors stress in their informative introduction, a good ghost story, though it may raise many profound questions about life and death, entertains as much as it unsettles us, and the best writers are careful to satisfy what Virginia Woolf called 'the strange human craving for the pleasure of feeling afraid'. This anthology, the first to present the full range of classic English ghost fiction, similarly combines a serious literary purpose with the plain intention of arousing pleasing fear at the doings of the dead.

'an excellent cross-section of familiar and unfamiliar stories and guaranteed to delight' *New Statesman*

OXFORD REFERENCE

THE CONCISE OXFORD COMPANION TO ENGLISH LITERATURE

Edited by Margaret Drabble and Jenny Stringer

Based on the immensely popular fifth edition of the *Oxford Companion to English Literature* this is an indispensable, compact guide to the central matter of English literature.

There are more than 5,000 entries on the lives and works of authors, poets, playwrights, essayists, philosophers, and historians; plot summaries of novels and plays; literary movements; fictional characters; legends; theatres; periodicals; and much more.

The book's sharpened focus on the English literature of the British Isles makes it especially convenient to use, but there is still generous coverage of the literature of other countries and of other disciplines which have influenced or been influenced by English literature.

From reviews of *The Oxford Companion to English Literature*:

'a book which one turns to with constant pleasure . . . a book with much style and little prejudice' Iain Gilchrist, *TLS*

'it is quite difficult to imagine, in this genre, a more useful publication' Frank Kermode, *London Review of Books*

'incarnates a living sense of tradition . . . sensitive not to fashion merely but to the spirit of the age' Christopher Ricks, *Sunday Times*

Oxford Reference

The Oxford Reference series offers authoritative and up-to-date reference books in paperback across a wide range of topics.

Abbreviations
Art and Artists
Ballet
Biology
Botany
Business
Card Games
Chemistry
Christian Church
Classical Literature
Computing
Dates
Earth Sciences
Ecology
English Christian Names
English Etymology
English Language
English Literature
English Place-Names
Eponyms
Finance
Fly-Fishing
Fowler's Modern English Usage
Geography
Irish Mythology
King's English
Law
Literary Guide to Great Britain and Ireland
Literary Terms
Mathematics
Medical Dictionary
Modern Quotations
Modern Slang
Music
Nursing
Opera
Oxford English
Physics
Popes
Popular Music
Proverbs
Quotations
Sailing Terms
Saints
Science
Ships and the Sea
Sociology
Spelling
Superstitions
Theatre
Twentieth-Century Art
Twentieth-Century History
Twentieth-Century World Biography
Weather Facts
Word Games
World Mythology
Writer's Dictionary
Zoology